ENCYCLOPEDIA OF THEOLOGY

The Concise *Sacramentum Mundi*

ENCYCLOPEDIA OF THEOLOGY

The Concise

Sacramentum Mundi

Edited by Karl Rahner

Published in India by ST PAULS, Mumbai, by arrangement with:
Continuum International Publishing Group Inc.
15 East 26th Street, Suite 1703, New York, NY 10010, USA
Burns & Oates, The Tower Building, 11 York Road, London SE 1, 7NX, U.K.

First published in 1975 by Burns & Oates

Executive Editor: J. Cumming

ISBN 81-7109-697-2

ISBN 0-86012-006-6

Printed and bound in India by Rekha Printers Pvt. Ltd.,
New Delhi-110 020 and Published by ST PAULS,
Post Box No. 9814, 23rd Road, TPS III, Bandra, MUMBAI-400 050, India.
2004

FOREWORD

In a time of fast, pluralistic change in all areas of human theory and practice, when a believing Christian has to face the rest of the world with a proficiently thought-out, well-founded and wholly open understanding of his faith, the publishers decided to draw on all their resources to make available to students and the general public a basic encyclopedia of Christian theology for the modern age.

The existing manuals, such as the great *Lexikon für Theologie und Kirche* and the six-volume *Sacramentum Mundi*, are heavy and expensive works, which take up much space and are often beyond a student's or pastor's, let alone an interested layman's, means. It was thought best, therefore, to compress as much as possible of the major post-conciliar reference works into one handy volume, dispensing with material of interest only to the scholar, and providing new articles in certain important areas. Of course this book is not intended to replace the longer works, which are indispensable for those with the appropriate linguistic proficiency and other resources.

We decided to discard all articles on subjects purely or largely of interest to those specializing in the individual disciplines, and to give pride of place to more inclusive and humanly relevant entries which not only offer a contemporary reader theologically essential information but speak to present-day secular and human questions of universal importance – the framework within which theology has nowadays to unfold and take effect. The fundamental theological questions are not presented here in exclusively theological terms; this tendency is appropriate to the essence of Christian faith, which is first and foremost the practical realization of a saving mystery intended for all men. Nevertheless, by its very nature a theological work cannot wholly dispense with a special terminology. This work is offered to its readers in the hope that it will serve the proclamation of faith and show the relevance of dogmatic theology to actual human life, without relaxing the standards proper to theology at any time. The reader should remember that the chief aim is that of the earlier *Sacramentum Mundi*: to formulate present-day developments in our understanding of the Christian faith, drawing on modern investigations of the key-themes of the theological disciplines, in the hope that they will thus be fruitful for personal reflection in faith and in practice. This book, therefore, has a strongly marked orientation to the future, and is marked by its openness to the other Christian Churches, the non-Christian religions, and the world in general.

Karl Rahner

PREFATORY NOTE

This volume contains revised versions of the major articles on theology, biblical science and related topics from *Sacramentum Mundi*, together with a large number of articles from the major German works *Lexikon für Theologie und Kirche* and *Theologisches Taschenlexikon*, and entirely new articles on topics of major importance written for the occasion by Professor Rahner and others. While every attempt has been made to present the work of Professor Rahner and his associates in comprehensible English and to allow a much wider audience of those interested in theology access to his thought, the requirements of the discipline have not been neglected in the interests of a reductive even if superficially attractive paraphrase.

In order to accommodate as much material as possible in this book and to make it – for its size – a theological reference-work of unrivalled scope, the bibliographies found in the larger works have been dispensed with. Many of the references in such lists of books and articles are to works in languages and places that the average interested reader or even student has no real chance of acquiring, or visiting. It would be pretentious to reproduce them in a work of this kind, which is intended for ready consultation on the desk or reference-shelf, and can even serve as a one-volume theological library.

New articles not originally written in English have been translated for this volume by John Griffiths, Francis McDonagh, and David Smith. In a work of this kind certain inconsistencies are inevitable; the publishers would be grateful for any pertinent comments and corrections so that all possible defects can be remedied in future editions.

John Cumming
Executive Editor

LIST OF ARTICLES

LIST OF ARTICLES

LIST OF ARTICLES

ABBREVIATIONS

The following list does not include biblical and other well-known abbreviations.

AAS	*Acta Apostolicae Sedis* (1909ff.)
ACW	J. Quasten and J. C. Plumpe, *Ancient Christian Writers* (1946ff.)
Billerbeck	(H. L. Strack and) P. Billerbeck, *Kommentar zum Neuen Testament aus Talmud und Midrasch*, I–IV (1922–28; reprint, 1956), V: rabbinical index, ed. by J. Jeremias and K. Adolph (1956)
CBQ	*Catholic Biblical Quarterly* (1939ff.)
Chalkedon	A. Grillmeier and H. Bacht, eds., *Das Konzil von Chalkedon, Geschichte und Gegenwart*, 3 vols. (1951–54; 2nd enlarged ed., 1962)
CIC	*Codex Iuris Canonici*
CIO	*Codex Iuris Canonici Orientalis* (Unless stated otherwise, the references are to the law relating to persons.)
Collectio Lacensis	*Collectio Lacensis: Acta et Decreta Sacrorum Conciliorum Recentiorum*, ed. by the Jesuits of Maria Laach, 7 vols. (1870–90)
CSEL	*Corpus Scriptorum Ecclesiasticorum Latinorum* (1866ff.)
D	H. Denzinger, *Enchiridion Symbolorum, Definitionum et Declarationum de Rebus Fidei et Morum* (31st ed., 1957); see also *DS*
DB	F. Vigouroux, ed., *Dictionnaire de la Bible*, 5 vols. (1895–1912)
DBS	L. Pirot, ed., *Dictionnaire de la Bible, Supplément*, continued by A. Robert (1928ff.)
DS	H. Denzinger and A. Schönmetzer, *Enchiridion Symbolorum, Definitionum et Declarationum de Rebus Fidei et Morum* (33rd ed., 1965); see also *D*
DSAM	M. Viller, ed., *Dictionnaire de Spiritualité ascétique et mystique. Doctrine et Histoire* (1932ff.)
DTC	A. Vacant and E. Mangenot, eds., *Dictionnaire de théologie catholique*, continued by É. Amann, I–XV, *Table analytique* and *Tables générales*, XVIff. (1903ff.)
Enchiridion Biblicum	*Enchiridion Biblicum. Documenta Ecclesiastica Sacram Scripturam Spectantia* (3rd ed., 1956)
ETL	*Ephemerides Theologicae Lovanienses* (1924ff.)
GCS	*Die griechischen christlichen Schriftsteller der ersten drei Jahrhunderte* (1897ff.)
Hennecke-Schneemelcher-Wilson	E. Hennecke, W. Schneemelcher and R. McL. Wilson, eds., *New Testament Apocrypha*, 2 vols. (1963–65)
HERE	J. Hastings, ed., *Encyclopedia of Religion and Ethics*, 12 vols.+index (1908–26; 2nd rev. ed., 1925–40)
JBL	*Journal of Biblical Literature* (1881ff.)
JTS	*Journal of Theological Studies* (1899ff.)
LTK	J. Höfer and K. Rahner, eds., *Lexikon für Theologie und Kirche*, 10 vols.+index (2nd rev. ed., 1957–67)

Mansi	J. D. Mansi, *Sacrorum Conciliorum Nova et Amplissima Collectio*, 31 vols. (1757–98); reprint and continuation ed. by L. Petit and J. B. Martin, 60 vols. (1899–1927)
NRT	*Nouvelle Revue Théologique* (1879ff.)
NTS	*New Testament Studies* (1954ff.)
PG	J.-P. Migne, ed., *Patrologia Graeca*, 161 vols. (1857ff.)
PL	J.-P. Migne, ed., *Patrologia Latina*, 217 vols.+4 index vols. (1844ff.)
Pritchard	J. B. Pritchard, ed., *Ancient Near Eastern Texts relating to the Old Testament* (1950; 2nd revised and enlarged ed., 1955)
RGG	K. Galling, ed., *Die Religion in Geschichte und Gegenwart*, 6 vols.+index (3rd rev. ed., 1957–65)
RHE	*Revue d'histoire ecclésiastique* (1900ff.)
RHPR	*Revue d'histoire et de philosophie religieuse* (1921ff.)
RSPT	*Revue des sciences philosophiques et théologiques* (1907ff.)
RSR	*Recherches de science religieuse* (1910ff.)
RSV	Revised Standard Version of the Bible
TS	*Theological Studies* (1940ff.)
TWNT	G. Kittel, ed., *Theologisches Wörterbuch zum Neuen Testament*, continued by G. Friedrich (1933ff.); E. T.: *Theological Dictionary of the New Testament* (1964ff.)
ZAW	*Zeitschrift für die alttestamentliche Wissenschaft* (1881ff.)
ZKT	*Zeitschrift für Katholische Theologie* (1877ff.)

A

AFTERLIFE

Belief in survival after death seems to go very far back into prehistory. Funeral rites of the late paleolithic age (deposits of arms and food, red ochre) leave little doubt as to the existence of a conception of the "living corpse", such as is to be found amongst many primitive peoples, as well as in the popular mind in advanced cultures possessing a more elaborate form of eschatology. The special value attached to the cranium implies perhaps the localization in the head of the faculties essential to life and their being related to the heavenly vault. The discovery of decorated rhombs in a Magdalenian stratum suggests that the complex of ideas about initiation and the cult of ancestors connected with it for many primitives have a very distant prehistoric origin. The tomb as a dwelling place, where the dead man pursued a life similar in every point to that of the living, seems vouched for as far back as the megalithic age and in any case at Uruk I (Mesopotamia). Generally speaking, the notions of the primitives about the afterlife are connected on the one hand with their notions of action at a distance between living beings (animism, presence of the absent, haunting) and on the other with belief in the fundamental unity of all the members of the same consanguineous group. The primitives usually distinguish a number of "souls", for example, a soul which is distinct and detachable from the immanent vital principle. Their ideas about survival depend on this. The deceased excited both fear and affection, which again augments the complexity of these ideas. The positive aspect of the survival of ancestors is often bound up with a cult of fertility, the exchange between the realms of life and death being conceived on the model of the seasonal changes in nature.

Certain figures with a special relationship to the collective life of the group (chieftains, warriors, women in childbirth), who remain present to the memory as especially mourned or feared, survive as individuals. The "eponymous hero" is the object of a funeral cult in which the clan is awakened to a consciousness of values which guarantee its own survival. There is perhaps some analogy between the making of a hero or the apotheosis of a "cultural hero" and the "rites of passage", with which the funeral rites present obvious similarities. In certain cases the trials that the soul is thought to undergo on the way to its place of rest have the character of initiation ordeals. The purpose of the sacraments conferred in some Gnostic sects is to furnish the soul with the passport to be used in the course of its heavenly journey. The special destiny reserved to the "cultural heroes", like Osiris, was sometimes extended to many others. "Ozirization", for instance, was first the privilege of the Pharaoh alone. In Egypt, the archaic ideas about the multiplicity of souls and survival in the tomb attracted other conceptions belonging to higher cultures (as, for instance, immortality through solidarity with the cosmo-biological cycle, the "paradise of Osiris", "solar" immortality), but without any real fusion taking place. Belief in a sanction after death appears as far back as the fifth dynasty and was later expressed in the "negative confession" (denial of guilt) and the "weighing of the heart", employed as magic in the Book of the Dead.

At the heart of the mystery religions are to be found rites which have as their purpose the integration of the believer into the life-giving rhythm of the cosmos. As the formulas were secret, it is difficult to get a clear idea of the eschatological ideas they embodied, but there is no doubt that dating from a certain period the initiate of Eleusis hoped for a privileged destiny in the life to come. The nature of this survival did not in ancient times depend on moral dispositions. But Orphism and Pythagoreanism made the purity of the soul an essential condition for its beatitude, and in this came close to the Indian ideas on the transmigrating soul. An anthropology of dualist tendencies often implies the undergoing in the beyond of cathartic trials which are recommended to the living under the form of ascetic precepts. As there is never a great distance between dualism and monism, the universal cosmic movement was seen as destined in the end to restore all things, and souls in particular, to the unity of their beginning. After a period of rest the journey of the souls is continued in another cosmic period. Into the systematic structure which such speculations all contribute to build up are harmoniously integrated all the archaic concepts of the "living corpse", the places of delights or punishments (Orphic Katabases taken over by Christian writers, the hell and storeyed paradises of Buddhism) and the ethereal body which the soul assumes. The journey of the soul in the beyond generally corresponds very closely to the ascetical itinerary proposed by the salvation religions to the believer eager to attain to perfect freedom – for example, *jivan-mukta*, the higher heavens of Buddhism corresponding to the four higher meditations and the "stations" of the soul in Origen and in Gnosticism – according to the internal logic of a cathartic vision of salvation.

Theosophy and spiritualism integrate all the traditional views of the afterlife into a vast and comprehensive system. The framework of the system is usually provided by an anthropology and cosmology of neo-Platonic or Gnostic type. Despite the wholesale integration of exotic elements, the essentials are ear-marked by Western preoccupations, in particular the concern to give an experimental basis and scientific appearance to ideas detached from their original religious context and now dangled as a bait to satisfy a real religious need debased into idle curiosity.

Humbert Cornélis

AGNOSTICISM

While general scepticism doubts on principle the possibility of true knowledge, agnosticism is a particular form of scepticism which declares that there can be no knowledge of anything beyond the reach of the senses and hence denies the existence of metaphysics as a science, and in particular the knowability of God. The word was introduced by T. H. Huxley

(1825–1895) to distinguish his position from metaphysics (that of the "Gnostics").

In the strict sense, the representatives of all forms of positivism, pragmatism and materialism are agnostics. Against these, the great traditional philosophies maintain that there is certain knowledge of truth beyond the empirical, and this is also maintained by the general conviction of the Christian faith, the teaching of Scripture (Wis 13; Rom 1:20) and the magisterium of the Catholic Church, which declare that God can be known by man's natural reason (*DS* 2853, 3004, 3026, 3475, 3538, 3892). This position is supported by philosophical reasons which demand and justify a rejection of agnosticism. It is also supported by faith's knoweldge of the nature and powers of man, with its sense of responsibility to the claim of revelation. This claim is seen as binding on all men and hence as something which can be urged on them, even on unbelievers, who must therefore have a preliminary understanding of it, without which the claim could not be perceived at all and men could not be placed before the decision of accepting or rejecting it.

To uphold the dignity of this decision (and thereby the dignity of him from whom the decision is demanded), Catholic theology also rejects the more nuanced forms of agnosticism which do not deny all knowledge beyond the empirical, but still refuse to concede a rational knowledge of God which is objectively valid, can be theoretically articulated and justified and so is (in principle) communicable to all. This is the position of Kant's critical idealism, and also of the metaphysics of N. Hartmann in its concept of the "transintelligible". The influence of Kant has been decisive on many modern philosophies of religion, which understand the act of religious knowledge onesidedly as a "decision" and a "leap", so unheralded that no justification of it can be given, nor can it be explained in any rational way. The element of knowledge in the religious act is referred to a special faculty not reducible to any other, a "feeling" and experience which are described in various ways, but which do not include intellect, argument and justification but are expressly opposed to them. This is the position generally held in modern Protestant philosophy and theology of religion, which mostly starts from a critical *a priori* in philosophy, as does modernism. In dialectical theology, however, the main motive for agnosticism is a supernaturalist understanding of man and of the claim of revelation, which is not to be falsified and "emptied" by human achievement. But this effort to go beyond the visible to procure a place for faith is a destructive stunting of the person as much as absolute agnosticism. For to restrict knowledge in this way is to eliminate the possibility of responsible decision. And when natural reason's quest for meaning is answered in the negative, it is hindered from reaching that openness into which alone revelation can give an audible answer.

The ultimate questions about being and meaning can also be given an affirmative answer which is as effective as the negative in stopping up the openness of the finite spirit for the historical word of the divine self-communication. It finds expression in the various forms of rationalism, and above all in an absolute idealism, which refuses on principle to admit that any thing is unknowable, because in the last resort it does not acknowledge any reality which transcends consciousness. In face of such pretensions, as indeed against the modern idea of knowledge in general, which sees it as a rule as technical efficiency and a conquest of power, the claims of agnosticism appear to be relatively just. Just as the possibility of natural knowledge of God is indispensable for the Christian faith, so too the religious character of this knowledge is essential to it. God is only known as God when he is known as the incomprehensible and is acknowledged in his incomprehensibility (Rom 11:33; 1 Tim 6:16; *D* 254, 428, 1782). This incomprehensibility is not merely *de facto* and provisional, as if man only did not yet know God but could grasp him by progressive efforts. It is essential and permanent. And as such, it does not stem so to speak from man, from individual, social and historical limitations, which would forbid him all correct knowledge, but from the nature of God himself who is the absolute mystery. Mystery is not the remainder of knowledge yet to be acquired, but the unfathomable principle of all knowledge and intelligibility: tradition speaks of the light that makes things visible but which can itself be "seen" only as the invisible and must not be confused with what is illuminated. Hence according to Christian teaching even the vision of God is not something perspicuous, but the disclosure and sight of the very mystery which is adored. If this holds good of the highest form of knowledge, then insight is gained into the structure of metaphysical and personal knowledge in general in contrast to scientific understanding. The Catholic defence of rational knowledge of God is misunderstood when it is taken to this sort of understanding, for instance if analogy is seen as a process of technical "extrapolation". On the contrary, it exists only to serve the mystery, which can only bestow itself as itself, and can only shine in its incomprehensibility when all that is comprehensible – yet still uncomprehended – is removed from it, and when it is itself known *as* the impenetrable and overwhelming: overwhelming not as sense-sapping chaos – the senseless is not a mystery – but as meaning embraced in its incomprehensibility.

Jörg Splett

ANGELS

I. Problem and History of Angelology

A. Problem of Angelology

The doctrine of the angels, even where it inalienably belongs (when placed in its correct context) to the content of the Christian message, meets with special difficulties at the present time. People nowadays in fact, though without justification, do not like to be told to look beyond the range of elementary immediate experience. Furthermore, even in their knowledge of what concerns salvation, they see no reason to be interested in the possible existence of angels, with whom even pious but rational people of today have, after all, nothing to do. Finally, as a matter of religious history, the angels appear relatively late in the Old Testament as a sort of incursion from outside, while in the New Testament, if one omits marginal religious phenomena which need very careful handling, the angels (demons) rather appear when worship of them is rejected or when the Christian is reminded of his superiority to all cosmic "principalities and powers". Now both these points would retain a concrete religious meaning even if no good or bad individual beings called angels existed. Even from these simple remarks a few hermeneutical principles of angelology can be drawn and these have their kerygmatic importance.

1. Despite the character of the numerous good or evil angels as personal substances (*D* 2318), we cannot and do not need to think of them anthropomorphically, as spatio-temporal forms – a collection of immaterial sprites which like the "spirits" at spiritualist séances are active in the material, human world at will, or else solely as a consequence of special divine commissions, but without any really intrinsic permanent and essential relation to the world. But the angels can be

regarded as incorporeal (which is not the same thing as lacking any relation to the one material cosmos), yet as "principalities and powers" essentially belonging to the world, i.e., the totality of the evolutionary spiritual and material creation; in other words as conscious (and therefore free and personal), created, finite principles of the structure of various parts of the cosmic order. As such they are at least in principle *not* inaccessible to natural empirical knowledge (which latter is not identical with scientific, quantitative experiment), and so they are not in themselves directly and necessarily a matter of revelation. Wherever in nature and history instances of order, structure and meaningful patterns emerge which – at least conjecturally and when envisaged without preconceptions – do not appear to be purely mechanical, material compositions "from below" nor to be planned and produced freely by men, and when such meaningful patterns in nature and history exhibit even for us at least traces of non-human intelligence and dynamism, it is meaningful to regard these as grounded on and guided by such "principles". For it is methodologically false always immediately to regard such complex, large-scale configurations in nature (cf. Rev 16:5 etc.) and history ("angels of the nations": Dan 10:13,20f.) as direct expressions of the divine mind, particularly since the antagonism of such large-scale units at least *in history* indubitably points in the first place rather to antagonistic cosmic "principalities and powers".

Such a conception presupposes that the activity of angels in nature and history as principles in this sense is not perceived only at particular moments of the individual history of salvation and perdition of men, but that their operation is thought of in principle as naturally antecedent to their and our free decision, even though the latter has a part in shaping their operation. This does not exclude a function of the angels as guardian angels. For every spiritual being (and consequently the angels too) has a supernatural vocation and therefore each in its own way has or had a history of salvation or perdition, and so even through its natural function itself, each spiritual being is of importance for every other. But we need not use this line of thought to develop and systematize further the doctrine of the angel guardians. This view of the angels also makes it clear why they cannot be an object of scientific, quantitative experimental knowledge, for the latter always has to move *within* such structures both objectively and subjectively. And if the angels' natural relation to and operation in the world has its ground in principle in their essence and not in any personal decision of theirs, it is also clear that through them as principles of partial structures of cosmic order the certainty and exactitude of the natural sciences is not called in question. Conversely, however, every other kind of experience of the angels (see above) is not thereby excluded either. Anthropomorphic representations, dubious systematizations, inappropriate applications, particular forms assumed in the history of religions and open to doubt, and purely symbolic use, are not peremptory objections against the validity of the fundamental experience of such principalities and powers in nature and history, and in the history of salvation and perdition. At the present time when people are only too ready to think it reasonable to suppose that because of the tremendous size of the cosmos there must be intelligent living beings outside the earth, men should not reject angels outright as unthinkable, provided that they are not regarded as mythological furnishings of a religious heaven, but primarily as "principalities and powers" of the cosmos.

2. If this is presupposed, it is clear on what basis and to what degree an

angelology has a place in a religious doctrine of revelation. Revelation does not really introduce into the realm of human existence a reality (the angels) which otherwise would not be there, but interprets a reality in relation to God and his saving action in man, because that reality is already there. This is what happens with all other realities of man's range of experience which require elucidation in the light of faith and whose relation to man (and of man to them) have to be "redeemed". Consequently the angelology of revelation has the same function as revelation has for the rest of the created world of man's environment. It confirms his experience, preserves him from idolatry and from mistaking the numinous character of the world for God himself. At the point where, and because, the world is spiritual and personal revelation divides it (progressively) into two radically opposed realms and incorporates them into the one event with which everything in human existence is concerned, the coming of God in Christ into his creation. In this way angelology appears for the theology of man as a doctrine about the non-human world-setting, whether personal or material, of redemptive history which is a factor in theological anthropology. That is so whatever the context in which from a didactic or technical point of view it may be appropriate to deal with it. It makes man recognize a section of the world of persons of which he is a member for the decision of faith and prevents him from diminishing its dimensions – he realizes that he stands in a more comprehensive community of salvation and perdition than that of mankind alone.

From this position in theological anthropology angelology receives its importance, its measure and an intrinsic *a priori* principle which may be used for our enquiry here and to systematize the meagre data of Scripture. On this basis, for example, the nature of the angels, without detriment to their difference as incorporeal spirits from man, could most radically be determined; it could be shown that they belong to the world by the very ground of their being, that they stand in a natural unity of reality and history with man, have a supernatural history of salvation with him which has its first design and ultimate goal (comprising the angels too) in Christ. As, however, theological anthropology and Christology are intrinsically connected, the nature of angelology is also determined by this more comprehensive context. If the possibility of the creation (although it could have been realized alone) and the actual creation as it in fact is, are grounded in the possible or actual free decision of God to express himself absolutely in the self-emptying of his Word, who by his self-utterance becomes man, then angelology too can only ultimately be understood as an inner element of Christology. The angels by nature form the society of persons surrounding the Word of the Father uttered and self-emptied, a Word uttered and heard in person. Their difference from man would have to be conceived as a variant (even if a "specific" one) of the one (generic) nature common to angels and man, and which attains its highest grace-given fulfilment in the Word of God. This would provide the basis for the treatment of such traditional themes as "the grace of angels as grace from Christ", "Christ as the head of the angels", "the radical unity of the world and of redemptive history with angels and men in their reciprocal relations of subordination and superiority", "the change which occurred in the role of the angels in sacred history". Angelology draws its ultimate measure and basis from Christology.

B. History of Angelology

1. Christian angelology has a prehistory; this fact is of fundamental impor-

tance for understanding its nature. It may be the case that even in the oldest strata of the Old Testament belief in angels is to be found. But it is scanty and is only developed in later books (Job, Zechariah, Daniel, Tobit). It nowhere appears as the result of an event in the historical revelation of God's Word, in the same way, for example, as the Covenant. The angels are taken for granted; they are simply there, as in all the religions of the world surrounding the Bible, and are simply known to exist. In this way, their relation to God, created character, clear division into good and bad, etc., could be calmly taken as a matter for subsequent theological reflection in Scripture. That would be inexplicable if their existence and nature were themselves the direct object of a revelation by God's Word. Recourse has been had to the contention that doctrine about the angels belongs to the data of "primitive revelation". But even if this were conceded, we should have to ask how such a primitive revelation endured so long in the way it did, continuing to develop in a way that was essentially similar both outside and inside the history of revelation proper. A real answer to such a question would probably show that a tradition of this kind always has been and continues to be handed down because it can always originate anew. Why in fact should there be no experience (of a kind that does not intrinsically involve divine revelation) of non-human personal powers which are not God himself?

The prehistory of the treatise on the angels shows that the original source of the actual content of angelology was not divine revelation as such. Consequently angelology must bear this constantly in mind. Where revelation proper, especially in the NT, does occur in regard to the angels through reference to the word of the prophets and other primary bearers of revelation, or to inspired Scripture, it nevertheless has an essential function of selection and guarantee. "Archaic" angelology of alien origin prior to revelation was purified or kept free of elements incompatible with the real content of revelation (the unicity and truly absolute character of the God of the Covenant and of Christ as a person and mediator of salvation). The residue was confirmed as human experience legitimately handed down, preserving such knowledge for men as an important factor in their religious life which might otherwise be lost. That is shown by various features: lack of systematization, intermittent appearance of angels, general mention as an expression of other more comprehensive and religiously important truths (God's universal dominion, precariousness of the human situation, etc.), lack of interest in the precise number and hierarchy of the angels, in their sex or names, use of certain traditional non-revealed ideas without precise reflection on their meaning (angels as psychopompoi, their white garments, their dwelling-places), and in general the carefree spontaneity with which angels are introduced (e.g., appearance with the four animals of the Apocalypse, etc.).

2. The later history of the doctrine need not be gone into here (see below under II). We need only bring out what is important for the theoretical inquiry. The official doctrine of the Church codifies the actual content of what Scripture teaches about the angels, exercising reserve and restricting it to what is really religiously important "for us and our salvation", leaving all speculative questions for theological treatment. All that is taught as really a matter of dogma is the existence of a spiritual creation consisting of angels (Lateran IV: *D* 428; Vatican I: *D* 1783); this is meant to express the belief that apart from the unique Creator there exist only his creatures, so that in this way the angels too belong to a freely chosen, supernatural history of salva-

tion and perdition (*D* 1001–5). In opposition to Jewish apocalyptic and Hellenistic ideas about angels, the Fathers of the Church insist from the first on the creatureliness of the angels, who are not to be thought of as sharing in the creation of the world, as in various Gnostic systems. A systematic treatise on the angels comes into existence: Pseudo-Dionysius wrote the first systematic treatise about 500 and in the West Gregory the Great, following Augustine, devoted considerable attention to the angels; both were of fundamental importance for medieval angelology.

The treatise on the angels was constructed by exploiting scriptural texts in probably too uniform a way without precise regard for their exact literary character, the *Sitz im Leben* or social setting in which they were composed and the actual intention of what they say (e.g., a number of individual names became a corresponding number of different choirs of angels). At the same time data of importance for the theology of salvation were to some extent neglected. The natural unity of the earthly and angelic world was not made really clear and explicit, although it is presupposed by the unity of redemptive history. Moreover, the treatise sometimes employed for its construction debatable ideas drawn from philosophical systems without sufficient express verification of their source and their right to a place in a theology of salvation. The pure "spirituality" of the angels was taught in the 6th century and was then made the absolute starting point of angelology in such a way that theologically the unity of angels and men in the one saving history of the *incarnate* Word and the natural conditions of that unity remained relatively obscure (the question whether all angels can be "sent"; when the angels were created, etc.). Consequently, the subordination of angelology to Christology (an explicit theme with Paul) does not receive its due theological weight. Even today there are textbooks of dogmatics – Schmaus is an exception – in which angelology is conceived quite non-Christologically. It was not, however, completely lacking when (as with Suarez in contrast to Aquinas and Scotus) the grace of the angels was viewed as the grace of Christ.

In the Middle Ages the angel became to a large extent the locus for metaphysical elaboration of the idea of a finite non-material intellectual being, a *forma subsistens, substantia separata* (in the wake of Arab philosophy). Such speculation, however useful and theologically stimulating it may have been, led to often quite considerable conceptual difficulties; *formae separatae* of this kind become almost like the monads of Leibniz and do not easily fit the theological data. Similarly the problem of the nature of the angels as "higher" than that of man was affirmed in a way that took for granted too readily and indiscriminately neo-Platonic conceptions of scales and degrees. For it must not be overlooked that the intellectual nature of man cannot so easily be characterized as inferior to that of the angels. That nature possesses absolute transcendence which in the beatific vision is brought to (unmerited) fulfilment and (at least, for example, in Christ) to an even more perfect fulfilment than in the angels. Why should it be an index of inferiority in every respect if a nature reaches further down into greater material depths, if it possesses the possibility of rising equally high? If reference is made to Ps 8:6 and Heb 2:7, then we must not overlook 1 Cor 6:8 and the Pauline teaching about the superiority of the incarnate Christ to the angels and that of Christians to the Law which was mediated by angels (cf. also Eph 3:10; 1 Tim 3:16; 1 Pet 1:12). Naturally the authentic Christian element always returned to the charge, and the hierarchical stages leading up to the transcendent God (regarded neo-Platonically as supreme and aloof instead of as truly transcendent and therefore immediately close to all) were constantly ignored. Much in systematic angelology is merely transposition (justified on the whole, but sometimes carried out too simply) of the data of theological anthropology to the angels on the ground that they too are intellectual beings and called to the same goal of the vision of God.

A theological anthropology is in a certain sense for us the whole of theology, because it is self-possession through self-knowledge by the personal subject who asks the theological questions, and also because of the incarnation and grace. Yet without regard for this special position, the treatise on the angels is simply made the first section of the treatise on the creation, following the discussion of creation in general, and is usually placed before a section on man (cf., for example, Peter Lombard, *Sententiarum libri quatuor*, II, d. 1–11; Aquinas, *Summa Theologica*, I, qq. 50–64, and qq. 106–14, etc.). This purely accumulative structure does not make very clear the function of angelology in a human doctrine of salvation. Though in the post-Tridentine period the history of dogma began (with Petau) to include angelology, there has been hardly any explicit reflection on angelology from the point of view of disciplined theological investigation.

II. Doctrine of Angels

A. Introduction

The great danger at the present time is that affirmations about angels in the teaching of the Christian faith will be rejected as a mythology which is no longer credible, and so succumb to demythologization. In all particular statements about the angels it must, therefore, be kept clear that such assertions are meant as elements of a theological anthropology and Christology. In other words, it is the insertion of the angels into such a context which is actually affirmed while the "angels in themselves" remain a presupposition. Man's situation as a created being in regard to salvation and perdition, even prior to his own decision, has a dimension in depth which extends beyond his scientific and empirical experience. This is already partly qualified as good and evil by created freedom in history. But even in regard to the situation in which his life is placed when it is understood in this way, man is enabled and redeemed by the grace of God, so that he is free for a direct relation to God. He received his lot from God, not in the last resort through the cosmic "principalities and powers" of the purely created order. That is ultimately what Christian teaching regarding the angels reveals to man.

It might therefore be said, paradoxically, that this doctrine would have something to teach men even if no angels existed. However great, manifold and powerful man may think the created framework of his existence and destiny, however much he may think that this is already partly determined by higher freedom and guilt, he nevertheless remains in direct relation with God. God himself acts in him; his action is not wholly through intermediaries. Ultimately in grace by self-communication God is man's destiny and definitive life. On that basis it is also possible to make intelligible the hermeneutical situation regarding the biblical statements about angels (and demons). The existence of angels cannot be disputed in view of the conciliar declarations (*D* 428, 1783). Consequently it will be firmly maintained that the existence of angels and demons is *affirmed* in Scripture and not merely assumed as a hypothesis which we could drop today. This will be maintained without detriment to a more precise interpretation of particular statements in Scripture about angels and demons which make use of mythological, historically conditioned representational material which must not simply be included in the content of the statements. But even for Scripture, the really anthropological and Christian point of all these statements must always be carefully noted (cf., e.g., Jn 12:31; 16:11; Rom 8-38; 1 Cor 2:8; 8:5f.; 15:24; Eph 2:2; 6:12; Col 2:8–23). Existing as they do, the good angels are simply fellow servants of God with us (cf. Rev 22:9), and from the dominion of the evil angels we are set free.

The following must also be noted. If we consider on the one hand that the world as a whole and consequently the mutual relations of its components have a real history, are dynamic and not static, and on the other hand that the angels (good and bad) by their very nature, which means, in free personal activity, are integral parts of this world, then it must be reckoned with from the start that man's relation to the good and evil angelic powers will have a real history (within the history of salvation and perdition). It is, therefore, not always the same and so, for example, the angels may have had a greater role as mediators for good or ill before Christ than they have now (cf. Gal 3:19). Some loss of interest in them need not, therefore, be without justification. Even if all dimensions of human reality always remain important for salvation and consequently also the principalities and powers assigned to these dimensions as their entelechy, as it were, so that in fact many "lords" and "elements" remain in the world (cf. Gal 4:1–6; 1 Cor 8:5f.; 15:24; Eph; Col), we ourselves in a historical process of salvation become gradually more and more "grown up" (cf. Gal 4:1–4) in relation to them, and this can be regarded as being the case in regard to the good angelic powers. – As regards the "time" when the angels were created, revelation teaches nothing (not even by the *simul* of *D* 428, 1783). Yet in view of the cosmic function of the angels, it is quite meaningful to think with scholastic tradition of a simultaneous creation of the angels and the material world.

The angels are represented in Scripture as very numerous (cf., e.g., Mt 26:53; Heb 12:22; Rev 5:11). It is difficult to decide how far that is an affirmation or only a metaphor for their power. Consequently, what follows is to be read on these suppositions and in this context.

B. The Teaching of Scripture

Old Testament. The Old Testament belief is rooted, as far as the history of religions is concerned, in vestiges of the ancient Canaanite popular belief, in alien gods who have faded into servants of Jahweh, in Babylonian and late Iranian ideas.

The most important and thoroughly attested angelic figure is the Angel of Yahweh *mal'āk IHWH* sent by God with a mission. Particularly in popular belief in earlier times, he was regarded as a helpful, benevolent messenger (2 Sam 14; 2 Kg 19:35; Exod 14:19, etc.), and in Israelite theology as the organ of Yahweh's special relation by grace with Israel. In Gen 16:7; 21:17ff., etc., he is even identified with Yahweh himself, and it is clear that the angel was inserted by a later editor in order to safeguard Yahweh's transcendence.

There were also other heavenly beings, regarded in ancient Israel as belonging to the heavenly court. These were what Jacob saw on the heavenly ladder. They are called b[e]nē ha-'elohīm, "sons of God" or divine beings; they appear in warlike guise but play only a secondary role in belief and worship.

The post-exilic belief in angels is elaborated into a real angelology (Job, Daniel). The angels receive names, become the guardians of countries, the heavenly court becomes immeasurably vast, they rank as explanatory mediators (*angelus interpres* in Zechariah and Ezekiel). The priestly code avoids (with polemic intent?) any statement about angels. In Job, mention is made of the limits of their holiness; before God they are not without blemish (4:18; 5:15ff.). In the strict belief in creation, Yahweh was absolute Lord of history, and this left relatively little room for belief in angels and demons. After Daniel, Hellenistic rationalism was influential and was represented chiefly by the Sadducees (cf. Philo, Josephus), among whom belief in angels was regarded as a specifically Essene matter, and angelic appearances were termed by them φαντάσματα. On the other hand, ideas about angels had wide scope in apocalyptic and in Jewish popular piety. The Essenes, Qumran and the rabbis took them over, to some extent with dualist interpretations, in contrast to the growing rationalism, but with a strict regard for the transcendence of God. Men were assisted by special angels as guardians, companions and intercessors.

New Testament. The OT view of angels was taken over by the NT in a rather more matter of fact way. As an expression of the dawn of the reign of God, they accompany Jesus in the Temptation, in Gethsemani, at the Resurrection, etc. At the Annunciation and the birth of Jesus, the Angel of Yahweh appears. A large share in the eschatological judgment is attributed to the angels (Lk 12:8; 2 Thess 1:7, etc.; cf. Rev). A specifically angelological interest is not found; in fact Christ's superiority to the angels is emphasized, particularly at Mk 13:32; Gal 1:8; 3:19; Heb 1:4; 2:2, etc. Colossians (1:16; 2:18) seems to be directed against Gnostic doctrines about the angels.

As well as the idea of guardian angels taken over from Judaism, mention is frequently found of "powers", "authorities", "thrones", "dominions", "rulers", but it is not possible to establish precise differences between them. Some angels have demonic attributes and are in league with Satan (1 Cor 15:24; Eph 2:2). Actual angels of the devil (e.g., Mt 25:41 etc.) or fallen angels (Jude 6; 2 Pet 2:4) are also mentioned. Most copious mention of angels – comparable with Jewish speculation – is made in Revelation. They convey God's judgments and commands, and even plagues, to the world, and surround the heavenly throne of almighty God. On occasion they are viewed as cosmic powers. Those of the demonic kind have been overcome by Christ in his death and resurrection. But they are still an active threat to the faithful, and will be still more so at the end of time.

C. Systematic Theology

1. As regards their essence, the angels are to be thought of as spiritual, personal "principalities and powers" (*creaturae personales:* "Humani generis", *D* 2318). This is what is always implied in the official doctrinal pronouncements of the Church; cf., e.g., *D* 228a, 248; *DS* 991, *D* 428; 530; 1673; 1783; and also all the statements of the magisterium about the devil (e.g., *D* 427, 428) and his influence on sinners (*D* 711ff.; 788; 793; 894). If at the same time it is presupposed that the angels are "incorporeal" in contrast to man (cf. *D* 428; 1783), this does not decide the more precise question of their relation to the material world. The Thomistic speculation regarding the metaphysical essence of angels (*DS* 3607; 3611) is an opinion which one is free to hold or not. At all events their relation to the world, which is both material and spiritual, must be thought of in such a way that they are really understood to be "principalities and powers" of the cosmos in virtue of their very nature and do not merely intrevene in the world by arbitrary decision contrary to their real nature, and in certain cases out of sheer malice.

Further speculation in scholastic theology about their spiritual nature was based on neo-Platonic philosophical theories about non-material pure spirit and is not theologically binding. The same probably applies (despite Ps 8:6) to the natural superiority of the angelic nature to man. All such theses, when they claim theological validity, go beyond the basis of all dogmatic angelology and the limits it sets to our knowledge of the angels. Similarly the classification of the angels, which like everything created are rightly to be thought of as different in nature from one another, into definite "choirs" and "hierarchies" is arbitrary and has no real foundation in Scripture.

2. Angels exist, but are merely creatures. The profession of faith of Lateran IV and the teaching on creation of Vatican I affirm the creation of spiritual beings, angels, in addition to men (*D* 430; 1783; cf. also *D* 2318, and statements of the creeds about *invisibilia* created by the one God). It cannot be said that the conciliar statements only mean that if there are such personal spiritual principalities and powers, they like everything else are creatures of the one, absolute God, though this, the ultimate import of the affirmation, is what is finally decisive. At all events the affirmation of their created character places from the start all spiritual, personal cosmic powers, and therefore their power and even their wickedness, within the circle of realities which are absolutely subject to a good and holy God and which are good by their origin. They must never be over-estimated as quasi-divine contrary principles on a level with God and against him (cf. *DS* 286; 325; *D* 237; 428; 574a, etc.). This used to happen only too often in popular preaching, tacitly and unconsciously, of course. There is little likelihood today that corporeality, marriage, carnal pleasures, etc. will be described as the work of the devil.

But what was meant by that and is rejected by the Church (cf. *D* 237–244, etc.) is in another guise still a temptation for man even today. He attributes an absolute character, as something purely and simply evil, to the occasions and aspects of his own guilt (e.g., technology, society, etc.), in order morally to exonerate himself in this way.

3. The angels, like man, have a supernatural goal of grace in the direct beatific vision of God (*D* 1001; 1003–5; 1009; *DS* 2800; *D* 2290). This conception follows from the uniformity of the divine treatment of the spiritual creation. By this, if God grants in grace his self-communication to any, then it is to all such spiritual, personal creatures. It also follows from the idea of Scripture and tradition that the good angels with God in heaven are his "court" (*D* 228a; *DS* 991; *D* 530). They therefore also enjoy the beatific vision. They have decided freely for or against this goal (cf. *DS* 286; 325; *D* 211; 427; 428f.). No declaration is contained in the official teaching of the Church regarding the chronological moment of this decision. We must not attribute to it that kind of extended temporality which belongs to man in his history in time. We have to think of it as single and total and as one which from the beginning contributed to determining man's situation in the history of salvation and is manifested in the latter.

4. This final decision of the angels for God as their goal or away from him does not involve any definitive predetermination of man's history of salvation or perdition (*D* 428; 907), but it is a factor in the situation in which men freely work out their salvation or freely fail to attain it. This also applies to the good angels, so that in regard to them (just as in regard to the saints, who have attained beatitude), a certain veneration (*cultus*) is possible and permitted (*DS* 3320; 3325; *D* 302; Vatican II, Dogmatic Constitution on the Church, ch. VII, art. 50). The liturgy and pious

tradition consequently acknowledge guardian angels (Mt 18:10; *Catechismus Romanus*, IV, 9, 4), i.e., give concrete expression to the connection between men and angels in the one history of salvation of the one world by linking particular angels with particular human beings. No objection can be raised to this, provided it is not pictured too anthropomorphically or even childishly.

5. From the kerygmatic point of view there is no necessity at the present time to place truths concerning the angels particularly in the foreground of preaching and instruction. Yet there are occasions on which the preacher cannot avoid this theme. In the first place he must provide readers of the Bible with guidance for understanding biblical statements about the angels, so that they can read with faith (without false demythologization) and yet critically, i.e., with due regard for the historically conditioned perspectives and the literary genre of such statements. Secondly, he has to answer questions about demons and the devil, and for this a correct grasp of angelology is required. Angelology makes it clear that the evil "principalities and powers" are a condition of the supra-human and relatively universal character of evil in the world and must not be trivialized into abstract ideas, but at the same time that these supra-human and relatively personal principles of wickedness must not be exaggerated in a Gnostic or Manichean way (as often happens in unenlightened popular piety) into powers opposed to the good God who are almost his equals in might. They are not God's rivals, but his creatures. And as with man, even evil freely chosen in a definitive state is the purely relative corruption of a natural, permanent being who has a positive function in the world; for something absolutely evil would be self-contradictory.

Karl Rahner

ANTHROPOMORPHISM

I. Philosophical

To think of God with human form and qualities (anthropomorphism) appears at first sight merely as an instance of the general structure of knowledge, which is to assimilate the thing known to the knower ("quidquid recipitur ad modum recipientis recipitur"), with all the attendant risks and benefits. The advantage is that man draws closer to God, whom he knows not just as a vague and unattainable being or perhaps as the silence or demonic strangeness of theriomorphism, but as one who speaks and can be spoken to, who cares about man and gives sense to his life. The danger is this closeness itself, which may lose sight of the majesty and inaccessibility of the holiness of God. But Xenophanes' criticism of the Homeric pantheon, that oxen would have gods in the form of oxen, misses the real point. From the philosophical point of view, it must be pointed out that while man, and man alone, cannot shake himself loose from imagery even in his knowledge of God, since he is a bodily spirit, still, as a spiritual body, he is conscious of this limitation and thus transcends it without being able to abolish it. In a fully developed theological anthropology, however, man appears as *the* manifestation and revelation of God – as that which God becomes when he expresses himself in a medium other than himself. "God – in what is other than himself" constitutes the dialectical relationship within which anthropomorphism, properly understood, has its validity and must be examined for its limitations. In this sense anthropomorphism reflects the theomorphic nature of man. It does not try to explain God in the light of man, as Feuerbach tried to do when transforming theology into anthropology, but rather reduces man to the mystery of God – which thereby appears all the more clearly in its own proper character, since it is not merely apprehended as the negative contrast to man. The mystery of the incarnation is the supreme justification of anthropomorphism.

Jörg Splett

II. Biblical

Human attributes are often ascribed to Yahweh in the OT. He has hands, feet, eyes, lips, mouth, tongue, face, head, heart and inward parts, and is represented as a man (Exod 15:3; 22:19; Is 30:27; Ezek 1:26); he retains human traits even in prophetic visions (Is 6:1; Dan 7:9). This way of thinking of God is also characterized by the frequency with which human reactions are attributed to God: he laughs (Ps 2:4), is angry and whistles (Is 5:25f.), sleeps (Ps 44:25), awakes (Ps 78:65), walks about (Gen 3:8) and has regrets (Gen 6:6). Even the incomprehensibility of God is given anthropomorphic expression, in so far as God's decisions are presented as purely arbitrary (Gen 12:13; 20:2; 27:33, etc.) – a process which reveals, however, as for instance in the book of Job, the intrinsic limitations of anthropomorphism. Thus Yahweh is never clearly and completely portrayed; there are only partial descriptions of him. Along with these anthropomorphisms, we find a portrayal of God as the inaccessible and transcendent (Gen 18:27; Exod 3:5; Deut 3:24; Is 28:29, etc.). Its climax is the prohibition of images in the decalogue (Exod 20:4; 20:22; Deut 4:12, 15–18), which is a radical restriction of all attempts to give material expression to knowledge of God, except in word and name, a restriction necessary in view of the constant pressure towards materialization from the nature gods of the surrounding nations. The prophets have no misgivings about anthropomorphisms (Is 30:27ff.), which they use to express the immediacy of their experience of God, but they are as emphatic about the infinite transcendence of God as are the early accounts of meeting God in the Pentateuch (Is 31:3; Hos 11:7). In the priestly writings, a type of thought constrained by taboos appears: God is accessible only in worship and by means of angels. In post-exilic times, the notion of God begins to be more abstract. The LXX in particular renders concrete images by means of abstract terms (Is 4:24; Exod 15:3; Ps 8-6, etc.). This is compensated for by a parallel growth of avidity for miracles in popular piety, with a highly imaginative belief in angels and spirits.

Anthropomorphic representations of God also survive in the NT (Rom 1:18ff.; 5:12; 1 Cor 1:17, 25; Heb 3:15; 6:17; 10:31). We are also told, however, that we do not see God like a man, but as though in a mirror (1 Cor 13:2), that he does not dwell in temples built by man (Acts 17:24) but in inaccessible light (1 Tim 6:16), and that God is spirit (Jn 4:24). The full vision of God is granted only at the end (1 Cor 13:9; 2 Thess 1:7). But the portrayal of God is still possible, on an entirely new basis: Jesus Christ is the image of God (2 Cor 4:4), the likeness of the invisible God, who took on the form of man (Phil 2:7). The once distant God has come close to us (Eph 2:18). Anthropomorphisms in the OT were justified by man's being made in the image of God, in the NT by the revelation of God in Jesus Christ. But along with anthropomorphisms, we find that the supreme transcendence of God is emphasized, and in many cases this is to be taken as a deliberate reaction against anthropomorphisms. This tendency gradually prevailed and the notion of God became more abstract, which, somewhat like the abandonment of mythological assertions, prepared the way for dogmatic propositions in post-biblical times. From the point of view of hermeneutics, anthropomorphism may be interpreted as an expression of the inadequacy of human language when speaking of God, but also as an expression of a lively faith in a personal God.

Werner Post

ANTICHRIST

No single and consistent portrayal of the eschatological figure of "Antichrist" is to be found in Scripture and tradition. It varies alike in the manner in which it is presented and in the characteristics ascribed to it and in the significance attached to it. In the course of the Church's history the idea has been so much bandied about in ecclesiastical controversies both between hostile sects and between warring factions within the Church itself; under the impulse of hatred or fear it has so often been identified with the ideas, systems or personages of particular epochs that as a result ". . . today the concept of Antichrist is no longer real and effective" (Tüchle). However welcome this conclusion may be from the aspect of rising above the level of heresy hunting, the question must still be put whether the idea of Antichrist in its eschatological and parenetic aspect does not still possess a vital and urgent relevance.

In contemporary theology this question is answered in the affirmative: "This teaching gives Christians a permanent right not merely to wage war upon anti-Christian powers and ideas in the abstract, but to recognize and to flee from men and powers in the concrete as its representatives" (Rahner). "Among the traditions concerning the last days, the doctrine of Antichrist has a special pastoral function to fulfil. It serves to arm the believing community to do battle with the compact forces of darkness, in the form in which they encounter them in their own age" (Frör).

It is necessary, however, to beware of presenting the idea of Antichrist as a "doctrine". Such a presentation could hardly be made without bringing the scriptural references into a forced harmony by suppressing the variations and straining the meanings of the more obscure statements. Such a procedure would rather obscure than bring to light the idea of a coming Antichrist in its enduring value for the Christian community. When we consider the reasons for the obscurity of the Antichrist idea, we realize that these lie in the constant necessity for readjusting the eschatological understanding of the present and the future. For this there is no "blueprint" but only the general guidance given by faith. We must not attempt to achieve a composite picture of Antichrist from the various forms in which the idea appears in the Bible, and then look eagerly for it in the world about us. Each element of biblical tradition has its own distinctive mode of expression, and it is the intention underlying each of these that must rather be explored. Thus we may hope to depict an Antichrist which will indicate how Christian life today may be orientated.

New Testament. The expression "Antichrist" appears in the Bible only in 1 and 2 Jn. The advent of an opponent of Christ is presupposed as part of the eschatological expectation of the early Christian community (this idea probably developed under the influence of Old Testament and late Jewish conceptions, as well as of the preaching of Jesus). But the author regards Antichrist, or alternatively the Antichrists in the plural, as already come in the teachers of heresy of his own time. Hence he concludes that it is "the final hour" (1 Jn 2:28). He gives no Antichrist doctrine, but applies the traditional expectation of Antichrist (which was clearly open to such an interpretation) to the situation of his Church, threatened as it is by heretical teachers. The traditional expectation is interpreted in such a way that it serves the interests of exhortation, the eschatological equipment of the community (cf. 2 Jn 8).

The early Church's expectation of Antichrist as attested in 1 and 2 Jn is elsewhere discernible only in 2 Thess 2:3ff.; Rev 13:1ff.; 19:19ff., and in these passages it appears in a markedly different form. (Mk 13:14 par.; Jn 5:43; 2 Cor 6:15 are not instances of it.) a) In 2 Thess the belief in the coming of Antichrist, filled out with pre-existing apocalyptic material, is used to curb the fever of eschatological excitement in the Thessalonians ("The day of the Lord has come", 2:2). The "man of lawlessness . . . the son of perdition" (2:3) must first come. He who is now still being restrained must appear openly (2:6f.) but then be annihilated by the Christ of the parousia "with the breath of his mouth" (2:8). The constant state of preparedness in which the community stands (cf. 1 Thess 5:2) must not be weakened by the expectation of Antichrist (about which they have already been told, cf. 2 Thess 2:5), but misguided enthusiasm must be guarded against. The expectation of Antichrist is here invoked as an argument against this, and in a parenetic sense which runs counter to the manner in which it is used in 1 and 2 Jn. b) In Revelation characteristic traits both of the Anti-Messiah and of the Pseudo-Messiah are combined in the image of the "beast from the sea" (13:1ff.). The description of the first beast points to an idolatrous power (*Imperium Romanum?*) which persecutes Christians (13:7). It is declared that the representative of this (emperor worship?) will be destroyed in the "lake of fire" (19:21). In the framework of Revelation the parenetic application of the ancient motifs (above all those found in Daniel) is already verifiable in the long introduction consisting of the letters to the seven churches (Rev 2–3). Here again no "blueprint" is given for the final age. Ever since the coming of Christ into history the "Antichrist alert" has been constantly in force, and ever since then the combined strength of the powers hostile to God as already depicted in the Old Testament and later Judaism (cf. Ezek 38f.; Dan 2:20–45; 7:7f.; Ps 2; 4 *Esdr* 11f.; *Apoc Bar* (*Syr*) 36; 39, 5–8, etc.) have been, as they continue to be, directed against *him* (Rev 12:1ff.) and *his* community (Rev 12:17), in a form which is expected to grow in intensity as the end draws near.

Rudolf Pesch

APOCALYPTIC

A. General Notions

In the Greek of the Septuagint and of the New Testament the verb ἀποκαλύπτω (Hebrew *gālāh*, Aramaic *g^elā'*) means "to reveal", and the noun ἀποκάλυψις means "revelation". Apocalyptic is the form taken by the literature of revelation in Judaism from the 2nd century B.C. on. By its very success, it had a marked influence on the literary expression of revelation in the NT, and it retained a considerable place in early Christianity, while it suffered a decline in rabbinical Judaism.

The revelation furnished by this literature bears on all the mysteries which are inaccessible to man's natural knowledge (to "flesh and blood", Mt 16:17): God alone can give knowledge of them through his Spirit and his Wisdom (Dan 2:19, 28; 5:11–14; 1 Cor 2:10–11). Several regions may be distinguished. a) The mysteries of God, of the heavenly world where he resides, of the angelic hosts who surround him, of the armies of demons who fight against him. From this point of view, apocalyptic provides a literary expression for mysticism, Jewish and Christian (cf. 2 Cor 12:1–4; *Ascension of Isaiah*, 8–11; *Apocalypse of Abraham*, 15–20), and for angelology and demonology, which in apocalyptic is closely linked with the history of salvation (*Ethiopian Enoch*, 1–6; Rev 12). b) The mysteries of the origins of the world and of the government of creation by the Wisdom of God. This theme gives rise to the cosmological passages in certain books, which describe the world of earth and the infernal abysses (*Eth. Enoch*, 17–19; 22–26) or the functioning of the stars on which the calendar is based (*Eth. Enoch*, 72–82). c) The mysteries of the divine plan which governs the course of history: here apocalyptic takes over from both the theological reflection of the ancient writers of sacred history and the eschatology of the prophets. d) The mystery of the destiny of the individual (Wis 2:22): here the texts reflect both collective eschatology (c) and the descriptions of heaven (a) and hell (b). Apocalyptic covers therefore a very wide field. This is why, apart from the works which are directly concerned with it, it also influenced works in other fields as soon as they took up matters with which apocalyptic was concerned.

B. Origin and Development of the Literary Form

The evolution of prophetic literature. After 586 B.C. prophetic literature undergoes notable changes. a) It had always contained an element of mysticism: symbolic visions describing the supernatural world (1 Kg 22:12–22; Amos 9:1–4; Is 6). In Ezekiel this literary form is given pride of place (Ezek 1), to depict the judgment of God on Jerusalem (Ezek 9–10) as well as the final resurrection of Israel (Ezek 37:1–14) and the glory of the new Jerusalem (Ezek 40–48). The message of Zechariah is presented systematically as a series of visions in which an angel acts as interpreter. This type of structure is to some extent conventional, and the convention became a constant element in apocalyptic writing. b) The horizon of the prophetic message was always a "latter time" (Is 9:1 [8:23]), the "latter days" (Is 2:2) which was to include the judgment of all sinners and the salvation of the remnant of the just. The judgment evoked spontaneously the thought of a cosmic cataclysm (Jer 4:23–26), and salvation that of the garden of paradise (Hos 2:20–24; Is 11:6–9). History thus came to a close in a final act which was still part of it and brought it to its fulfilment. But after the exile, the portrayal of the close of history came to stand more and more on its own, in a series of anonymous texts which sought to sustain Jewish hopes by "eschatological" promises (Is 4:4–5; 24–27; 30:19–26; 34–35; 59:15–20; 63:1–6; 65:1–25; 66:5–16; Ezek 38–39; Joel 3–4; Zech 12:1–13:6; 14). It is an abuse of terminology to call these texts apocalypses. But it is true that a number of essentially apocalyptic themes are accentuated strongly: the final judgment executed by God himself, the opposition of the Two Cities (Is 24ff.); the inauguration of the reign of God in which the Davidic Messiah seems to play no part; the entrance of the just into a world transformed, the "new heavens and the new earth" (Is 65:17).

The psychological climate. It is quite easy to discern the psychological situation in which this literary evolution took place. It is the feverish expectation which characterizes the times of crisis which the post-exilic community lived through. The disappointment which follows the return of the first exiles, between 515 and 440, the political upheavals of the 4th century with their inevitable repercussions on Judaism, arouse feelings of eschatological anguish (cf. Ps 44; 74; 79), which are brought to a climax by the bloody conflict with the totalitarian pagan empire of Antiochus Epiphanes (170–164 B.C.). Neither the legalism bequeathed by Ezra to the Jewish theocracy nor the reflective wisdom of the rising schools of sages are enough to satisfy this passionate expectation. And "there is no longer any prophet" to sustain the people's courage (Ps 74:9; 1 Macc 4:46), for prophecy as practised of old is now decried (Zech 13:2–6). But the Scriptures are searched in the hope of learning when and how "the end" will come (Dan 9:1–2). This is the climate in which the eschatological message is given a new form of expression, that of a supernatural wisdom coming from meditation of the Scriptures and revealing the divine secrets to the sorely-tried believers. At the height of the Maccabean crisis, apocalyptic produces its first masterpieces, with Daniel (especially Dan 2; 4–5; 7–12) and the most ancient portions of Enoch (*The Book of Dreams*, 83–90; *The Apocalypse of Weeks*, 93; 91:12–17).

Foreign influences. At every stage of history, the sacred writings succeeded in assimilating elements borrowed from neighbouring cultures to propound its own message. Ezekiel clearly has recourse to Mesopotamian symbolism (Ezek 1). The angelology and demonology of Tobit makes use of Iranian elements (Tob 3:8; 12:14). And apocalyptic was born in an environment where an Iranian and Babylonian syncretism encountered Hellenistic civilization. Judaism found itself at the meeting-place of many cultures and turned them to its advantage. This is clearly proved by the undeniable contacts of the Enoch legend with Mesopotamian traditions and by the references in Daniel to the Babylonian techniques of interpreting dreams (Dan 2; 4; 7) and presages (Dan 5). The oriental diaspora must have played an important part here. But the Judaism of Palestine itself was certainly open to influences from surrounding Hellenism, even while it was struggling to save its religious originality. In apocalyptic, the influence of Iranian eschatology is a possibility which must be reckoned with; the influence of Hellenism is restricted to marginal elements. Whatever their contribution, apocalyptic was born of the effort to oppose the authentic revelation contained in the Scriptures, bestowed on Israel by the prophets, to the pagan literature of revelation which was powerless to know the divine secrets (Dan 2:28; 5:7–17). To forge for itself means of expression, it drew without scruple on a set of widely used symbols which stemmed from the ancient mythologies of Greece and the Orient. Thus traces of the mythical combat between Marduk and Tiamat can still be seen in Dan 7 and Apoc 12.

C. The Standard Features of Apocalyptic Writing

In spite of the wide variety of forms, which correspond to the diversity of the subjects treated, certain general characteristics recur, in varying degrees, nearly everywhere.

Pseudonymity. The classical prophets related their own personal visions. The complements added to their books after the exile were guarded by the veil of anonymity. But the writers of apocalypse had recourse to borrowed names, chosen from among the heroes of ancient times: Enoch, Abraham, Isaiah or some other prophet, Baruch, Ezra, Daniel and so on. So too non-canonical Christian writings were to invoke the authority of Peter, Paul, John and so on. The conventional spokesmen chosen by the authors always appear as the typical prophet – who becomes the typical apostle in the NT – whom God charges to transmit his message to men. The message envisages of course the contemporaries of the author, but it is given an esoteric appearance, not because it is reserved for a small circle of initiates, but because it is presented as something reserved for future times. In the NT, however, prophecy passes over directly to the apocalyptic style without having recourse to pseudonymity (so Mk 13 and par.; 1 Thess 4:15–17; 1 Cor

15:24–28, 52–53; Revelation of St. John).

The prophetic view of history. The apocalyptic writers were mainly concerned with the working out of God's plan in history in the perspective of the last judgment and a transhistorical eschatology. By letting an ancient seer speak for them, they take their stand in the distant past, thus gaining a vantage point from which they can survey at a glance considerable periods of history (e.g., Dan 7–8; 10–12). When their view of human history is compared to the theology of the prophets and the writers of sacred history, some notable differences emerge.

a) It underlines further, in a one-sided manner, the divine causality which is the sovereign master of events. These take place inevitably, as the realization of the divine plan inscribed on the "heavenly tablets". The existence of a divine judgment proves indeed that men are really free, but their liberty is exercised within the limits assigned to it by God. As a result past history appears to be a merely mechanical process, which guarantees in its own way the certainty of its eschatological consummation. This climax is always felt psychologically as imminent: once history has reached the crest formed by events contemporary to the author, divine judgment and the salvation of the just follow at once (Dan 7:23–27; 11:21–12:3).

b) Even more than in the classical prophets, history is a battle-field where God, his angels and his people are opposed to all the demonic forces of whom sinners and the pagan nations are the tools on this earth. This spiritual dualism results in two worlds being opposed to one another: the present world, which is delivered over to the power of evil and so is doomed to the wrath of God and the final catastrophe; the world to come, in which a transfigured universe will rejoin the heavenly realities and the just receive the reward for their sufferings. Thus the eschatology of the prophets undergoes a radical transformation, and the problem of individual retribution is solved on a new plane (Dan 12:1–3; Wis 4:20–5:23).

c) *The symbolic language.* The literary expression of the message is a tissue of symbols. The ancient Scriptures are exploited systematically and the images they use are often combined in unexpected ways. The Revelation of St. John offers good examples of this. The conventional presentation of doctrine in the form of dreams and visions often involves symbolic descriptions of the supernatural world, and even earthly realities are hidden behind masks: in Dan 7 as in Rev, the pagan empires appear as beasts. To create this world of imagery which they conjure up, the writers draw freely on the odds and ends of oriental literature. Landscapes, plants, animals, precious stones, and stars are endowed with peculiar meanings which allow the author's thought to be rendered in code-language. The symbolism of numbers is not omitted. These enigmatic pictures may have been clear for his contemporaries, but it is sometimes difficult for us to find the key. On the whole, nothing is more artificial than the apocalyptic style when it is employed without due measure, but its intriguing symbols lend it an undeniable poetic force.

D. The Extent of Apocalyptic

Old Testament and Judaism. This form of literature, which was evolved among the Hassideans during the Maccabean crisis, enjoyed great popularity about the beginning of the Christian era. The Essenes employed the style, and the caves of Qumran have yielded manuscripts of Enoch and Jubilees, and of other works hitherto unknown. It does not seem that the Pharisees objected to it at first: the Syrian Baruch and 4 Esdras seem to derive from Pharisee circles. Later on, many apocalyptic works of Essene or other origin were proscribed, though texts dealing with Jewish mysticism were spared (*Hebrew Enoch*). The surviving apocalypses were preserved by Christian scribes, translated into various languages.

The New Testament and ancient Christianity. In the New Testament the eschatological perspective has been perceptibly modified. The new world has been already inaugurated in Jesus Christ and in the Church. The Son of Man has appeared in history and awaits the moment of the Parousia to return again. The kingdom of God has begun and the new Jerusalem is present in the Church. It is not surprising therefore that the Christian revelation should be essentially an apocalypse (Mt 16:17; Gal 1:16; Rev). But a last revelation was still hoped for, in which the heavenly realities would descend upon earth (1 Jn 3:3; Col 3:4; Rev, etc.). The apocryphal NT contains several apocalypses which describe this event. The literary form is still found in the *Pastor of Hermas*, and it is perpetuated by the writings of visionaries in all ages, as well as in such works as the *Divine Comedy* of Dante.

Pierre Grelot

APOLOGETICS

A. Theological Situation

Apologetics, in a general and fundamental way, is a permanent feature of all Christian theology. The effort to answer for the faith is as old as Christian theology as such and is inspired by the testimony contained in the Bible itself (see B). As a result of the new cultural and political situation of the Enlightenment, where Christianity and religion in general were no longer identified, and Christianity ceased to be an interest of all society as such, apologetics was developed as an independent discipline at the beginning of the 19th century. The lead was taken among Catholics by the Tübingen school of S. Drey, among Protestants by the school of Schleiermacher. It is now more or less identified with the theological themes and enquiries which are grouped under the name of fundamental theology.

1. The readiness to give an account of the faith which is voiced in apologetics is a readiness to accept responsibility, that is, a readiness to share the questioning and problems of the world in which it lives. This readiness is not a sort of afterthought, a purely apologetical concession, when the Christian faith is fully established. It is part of its very essence (see below, B, 2).

When the believer gives an account of his faith to the world around him, he himself penetrates more deeply into the realities of faith. He is only "hearer of the word" in a theological sense when he listens at the same time to the objections and difficulties of the social and historical situation of which he himself forms part.

2. Though it may be necessary to treat apologetics as a separate subject for technical reasons, it may never be pursued in isolation so that it loses its constant reference to the basic character of all theology, which is to "give answer". The history of apologetics shows that two typical dangers arise here. One is that apologetics ceases to see itself as a theological discipline, in spite of the fact that when it comes into contact with the non-theological and non-Christian mind, the full force of the Christian faith must be mobilized, its intellectual appeal, its power to form and transform the mind. The other danger is that apologetics may adopt the typical features of a purely apologetic attitude and policy, such as conclusions reached with a haste which savours of ideology, formalism in argument, loss of the sense of the permanent danger to which faith itself is exposed, insensibility to the nuances and intrinsic variations of the social and historical situation, the inclination to be on the defensive in a negative way which surrenders

to the very mentality to which it is opposed, incomprehension of the historically valid elements of the opposing positions, and the temptation to treat as permanently relevant the set of questions raised by a given situation.

B. Biblical Motivations

There are two themes above all in the NT message which determine the basic task of apologetical theology.

1. There is the theme of the universal nature of the gospel and the mission. In the NT, the horizon within which faith explicates itself is universal. The wall of partition between Jews and gentiles is broken down, the veil of the temple is torn asunder, and the synagogue becomes the Church among the nations and for the nations. The passage of the frontiers is obligatory. Such a faith necessarily entails an attitude to the universalism of Hellenistic philosophy and a conscious detachment from a setting now recognized as unduly restricted. The language of the Palestinian homeland is abandoned and the danger of sectarian isolation averted. Facing a Hellenistic system where all were on principle citizens of the world, the "apologetic" attitude, of which there are already traces in the NT, begins to develop, not primarily to build up defensive barriers but to remove obstacles and give the missionary impulse free rein.

2. The second theme is the readiness of the faith to give an account of itself. The Christian faith is thereby distinguished from all religious ideologies which by means of intolerance and the arbitrary apotheosis of a particular viewpoint strive to impose themselves universally. The universal conquest which Christianity aims at cannot be attained by any power except that of love and truth. It must give a responsible account of the faith to all who ask to know the grounds of its hope (1 Pet 3:15). This calls for complete mental integrity and unmasks the "blind faith", which refuses to reflect and see clearly, as a lower and defective form. Christian theology must be the account (*logos*) of a faith which knows it must answer for its hope or for the universal divine promise which that hope accepts. Hence it cannot but strive to explain itself in the terms relevant to its given historical situation. Nonetheless, the intrinsic limits of this apologetical effort to communicate the Christian faith must not be blurred or disregarded. Apologetics is not adaptation or accommodation. And it is not an effort to embody the faith in a ready-made thought-form, no matter how purely formal or generalized, of any type whatever – cosmological and metaphysical, transcendental, existential or personalist. In its account of the faith, apologetics is the critic and emancipator who strives to break through all the thought-forms of this faith, by constantly fixing his gaze on the foolishness of the cross and resurrection of Jesus Christ (which Bonhoeffer calls the *Gegenlogos* – the anti-logos, the reason the other way round). It is a truth which cannot be guaranteed like a pure idea, but only in a (historical) action orientated to its eschatological promises.

C. The Changing Forms of Modern Apologetics

By the very nature of apologetics, which is a critical, responsible re-affirmation of the understanding of faith in face of a given situation, it cannot itself determine what questions it must ask. It cannot set itself its problems, in the light of its own history, or it will exhaust itself fruitlessly in the reproduction of problems of the past. Its themes and tasks change more than in any other theological discipline.

1. *The changing audience*. Apologetics first addressed itself in its defence of its hope to the pagan world of the Roman Empire, whose intellectual representatives were Hellenistic philosophy and the political principles of

Rome. In the Middle Ages, Islam in particular was envisaged, as by Aquinas in his *Summa contra Gentiles*. After the Reformation, it was primarily non-Catholic Christians, and after the Enlightenment, the critics of religion who based themselves on philosophical, scientific or socio-political grounds. In any case the audience envisaged was the outsider from the point of view of Church theology, the unbeliever or the heterodox. Hence apologetics mainly took the form of an apologia *ad extra*. Today apologetics is more and more an apologia *ad intra*, the account of the believer's hope given to the believer himself. The menaces to which faith is exposed by its very nature are being expressed more and more in terms which go beyond the situation of the individual to take in the world: the separation of religion and society; the isolation of believers as in a diaspora; the untoward intellectual and spiritual demands made of believers by the inevitably pluralistic milieu in which the experience of faith has to prove its worth. The days of simple faith, when at least society and its traditions posed no question, are drawing to a close. The faith of the individual is challenged by his milieu as well as by his own sinful failings and no level of life in the Church is exempt. Hence the clear and responsible account of the possibility of faith is not just a secondary development, a sort of theoretical superstructure for the educated faithful of an arsenal of arguments in ideological controversy with non-believers. It is becoming more and more an intrinsic element of the individual believer's situation and a condition of possibility for his own belief. Hence the apologia *ad intra* must also be envisaged in preaching, which must not reserve discussion of difficulties against the faith to the encounter with "outsiders". The sermon which envisages unbelievers is by no means out of place in the Church itself.

2. *The changing method*. We confine ourselves here to the most important changes in method which have ensued since apologetics became an independent discipline. It has taken the form, above all in the 19th century, of a rational and historical enquiry which sought to "defend" the Christian faith or demonstrate the grounds of its credibility by philosophical and historical arguments. Prescinding for the moment (but see below, 2c) from the basic question which was little discussed in classical apologetics, as to how the use of philosophy and history is based on the notion of faith itself, that is, how apologetics can be a legitimate *theological* discipline, we shall illustrate the changing methods of apologetics from its three classical elements – the philosophical, the historical and the strictly apologetical.

a) *The philosophical element*. A change has come about in the presuppositions of the rational argument, which considered philosophy as the "purely rational" and unprejudiced theory of reality and hence the ideal basis for a demonstration of the credibility of faith. Since the Enlightenment, the relationship of theory and practice, of truth and social reality has been re-considered, and since Kant "the end of metaphysics" is at least an unavoidable subject of discussion. Philosophy, which in apologetics was practically identical with the medieval Aristotelian tradition of the West, has ceased to be homogeneous and has become a pluralism which the individual thinker cannot bring fully into focus in his search for *the* one philosophy. Philosophy itself threatens to become a sort of irrationalism, not the result of lack of reflection, but of lack of conclusiveness in all reflection. At any rate, there is now no such thing as a standard philosophy to which apologetics can appeal without more ado. Apologetics must provide its own philosophy. And this it understands more and more not as a pre-existing system which it can simply "apply", but as the hermeneutic, maieutic and critical reflection which is demanded by each new situation of apologetics. On the hermeneutic element, see further 2b below. As regards the maieutic and critical elements, it may be said that philosophy functions not as a material but as a "formal" system. It is the relentless questioning of all assumptions, a fertile negativity which robs the conventionally "obvious" of its self-assurance. It is a struggle against the surreptitious efforts of all particular thought-forms or sciences to erect themselves into absolutes and trespass beyond the categories, and a protest against the anonymous dictatorship of the purely factual. It is a perpetual summons to a critical aloofness which can understand itself – to use a phrase of Hegel's – as "its own times summed up as a question". It is partial only to what offers ever greater scope to human existence, which can never be reduced to the merely factual. And thus it manifests, if only negatively, that concrete "openness" of human thought and action in its historical changes which faith must constantly create, if it is to proclaim its hope responsibly.

b) *The historical element*. To the problems posed since the Enlightenment by the historical criticism of the foundations of the Christian faith theology sought an answer in historical apologetics, which appealed in turn to historical science to establish the historicity of the events attested in the Bible. But meanwhile the starting-point of historical apologetics has changed. First, the self-understanding of faith embraces more and more clearly its own immanent historicity. This makes inevitable the discussion of the basic hermeneutical question of the relationship between faith and history, as adumbrated by Lessing, Hegel and Kierkegaard. Then, the notion of historical science itself has been modified by the hermeneutical question as to the nature and conditions of historical understanding in general, and by allowance being made for the various forms in which historical reality may appear and be expressed. This was discussed in the theological sphere since Schleiermacher, in that of the history of thought by such writers as P. Yorck von Wartenburg, W. Dilthey and M. Heidegger (see Gadamer, *Truth and Method*). Further, the most recent research on the Bible (such as form-criticism and history of redaction) has shown the special nature of the biblical assertions and the many levels on which they are made. They can appear for instance as attestations of the faith which are orientated to the kerygma and moulded by theological reflection. Hermeneutical reflection on the form of historical understanding appropriate in this case is obviously necessary. Finally, against the background of the technological reasoning dominant today, knowledge of a reality which happened only once and cannot be reproduced is in danger of becoming less and less decisive and more and more a matter of taste. The upshot of it all is that historical apologetics must be more subtle and critical in its approach. Two tasks are particularly urgent. One is the development of the category "future" for the understanding of history, in contrast to a too one-sided attention to history as something in the past. This will enable historical apologetics to escape certain dilemmas of the hermeneutical question, and also to display a dimension of history to which a technical civilization seems particularly responsive. The other task is the examination of the relevance and validity of the hermeneutical reflection on time, which threatens to turn a faith conscious of its historical foundations into a new type of irrationalism. Here the relationship between theological reflection and religious institution appears in a new, "post-critical" form.

c) *The apologetical element as such.*

APOLOGETICS

Here the change is characterized by the fact that the process of apologetics is no longer a marginal effort which takes place in the non-theological approach to faith. It is a basic effort of theological responsibility in which the "spirit", the full intelligibility of Christian faith itself, and its immanent power to form and transform the mind are mobilized for the task. The theological answer has the following fundamental traits. First, it excludes all ideological features. It may and need make no pretensions to a knowledge and an answer of which it is not itself in possession. It may and need not expose itself to the charge of being a modern mythology by claiming to have too many answers and too few questions. While it need not fall into the other extreme, the barren cult of questioning everything, the theological answer cannot consist of a discussion which will dispose of all challenges and problems, as if man could become fully perspicuous to himself with the help of a well-formulated religion, and thus be spared the questionableness of his existence and the hazards of the future. The theological answer must be determined by the permanent menace which is indissolubly linked to the faith itself. It must be guided by the conviction that the question of unbelief is first and foremost a question put by the believer to himself. Then, apologetics must be built up on a critical sense of solidarity with the menaced values of man. This does not mean that the theological answer is abandoned and reduced to purely humanist terms. This could well be branded as the typical danger to which an aging religion is exposed. It tries surreptitiously to attain, by purely humanistic thinking, the universality and validity which is denied it in terms of its historical mission. But solidarity with all that is human is vital to the intelligibility and persuasiveness of a theological answer which confronts the radical threat to the humanity of man with the proclamation of a universal salvation, a salvation implying brotherly responsibility "for the least of these", a salvation in the light of which all is false which only appears true to the individual in isolation. It is especially important today that the theological answer should have this orientation, because unbelief does not now take primarily the form of a vision of life and the world which is planned contrary to God, but of the offer of a positive possibility of existence, of a humanity fully achieved without God. An articulate and militant atheism is not the focus of this unbelief, but its presupposition. We are in an age which is to some extent "post-atheist" and strives to understand itself as "humanistic", without intermediate stages.

It follows further that the theological answer must now expound above all the social implications of the Christian faith and promise. Modern criticism of religion, which has been there in germ since the Enlightenment, appears above all as criticism of ideologies. It tries to expose Christianity as a function or the champion of a given system of social and political rule. And then, the claim of the Christian message must not be reduced to the private interests of the individual or restricted to ideals. Here it is important to explain the purifying force of Christian hope in the evolution of society. Finally, the theological account of the faith in apologetics is becoming more and more of a "dialogue". This does not mean uncritical adaptation, cursory compromise and the levelling down of the Christian message to a symbolical paraphrase of the spirit of the times. It is an effort to stimulate the fruitful conflict which goes on within our pluralistic society and its common strivings. And one motive of this effort is the recognition of "how weighty are the questions which atheism raises" (Vatican II, Pastoral Constitution on the Church in the Modern World, article 21).

Johannes-Baptist Metz

APOSTLE

Methodological note. The apostolic office will be considered here not only in its origin but also in regard to its permanent presence in the course of the Church's development. The historical consideration must proceed from an attempt to understand the original nature of the apostolic office, and must take into account the intentions of Jesus in instituting the office, as well as the significance which it has for the constitution of the Church. One can trace with some certainty the constitutive significance which the apostolic office had for the early Church both from the exercise of the office as recorded in the NT, which is the founding document of the early Church, as well as from the place which that office assumed in the course of the history of the Church. But the intention which Jesus had with regard to the apostles can only be deduced from a comparison of the parallel texts forming the record of the words and deeds of Jesus. In trying to determine the exact meaning of the concept "apostle" in the NT it is difficult to decide when the actions of the apostles are to be ascribed to their office or to their purely personal capacity. The office is not limited to the institutional and its function is therefore difficult to fix. Besides this, the different stages through which the concept of the apostle and the apostolic office evolved are all dove-tailed and overlapped in the various writings of the NT.

New Testament. 1. The NT term ἀπόστολος derives from the *šālîaḥ* of late Judaism. The idea embodied by the Hebrew word is already attested by the time of Jesus (Jn 13:16), though the term itself is only verified in the 2nd century A.D. It is related to the Semitic law of delegation and means the authoritative representation of an individual or a group in juridical or religious matters. The dignity and respect shown to a representative depend entirely upon the authority of the sender. The LXX translates *šālûaḥ* by ἀπόστολος (1 Kg 14:6 – the prophet as a messenger of God).

2. The concept of apostle in the older Pauline letters, as the earliest NT record of the title, is especially significant because it precedes all controversy about the nature of the apostolic office. In 1 Thess 2:7 Paul refers to himself together with Silvanus and Timothy as apostles of Christ. This clearly shows that the office of apostle did not necessarily depend upon the fact of one's having seen the Lord. The apostolic charge did not have to be a charge imposed directly by the risen Lord; it could also be delegated indirectly. The encounter with the risen Lord was important for Paul because he thereby became a direct witness of the resurrection of Jesus (1 Cor 15:8). Similarly, we may deduce from 1 Cor 15:6 (the appearance of the risen Lord to the five hundred brethren) that according to the earliest Pauline letters, a meeting with the risen Lord is not the sole requisite for the office of apostle. Later, however, the early Church came more and more to consider the witness of the resurrection next to the call to apostleship as a criterion for the title of apostle.

What is essential for the concept of apostle in the older letters of Paul is that the apostle proclaims the gospel as one so delegated by Christ. The apostles are responsible to God alone. Since God speaks through them, the Spirit of Christ is present in the community. The salvation or damnation of men depends upon their acceptance or rejection of the apostolic message (2 Cor 2:15f.). The charge of proclamation as imposed by Christ (cf. Gal 2:7ff.) is the basis of the apostolic office of the original apostles who remained in Jerusalem, as well as of the travelling missionaries, Paul and his companions.

3. The synthesis of the Pauline con-

ception with that of the evangelists (to be treated later in another connection) is to be found in the description of the apostolic office in the Acts. According to Acts 1:2f. and 1:21, three things characterize the apostle. a) The apostle must have been a disciple of Jesus. b) Only a reliable witness of the ministry, passion and resurrection of Jesus can be an apostle and his testimony must rest upon the actual fact of having "seen" the risen Lord and of having received the Holy Spirit. (Acts 14:14 appears to be evidence of an older tradition, since along with Barnabas Paul is also called an apostle, though he was not a witness of the public ministry of Jesus.) c) But the decisive criterion for apostleship is the fact of having been sent by Christ to proclaim the gospel (Acts 1:8; 10:42). This criterion is indispensable, universal, and final. According to Acts, therefore, only the Twelve and Paul can be called apostles in the strict sense of the word.

4. How does the intention of Jesus in sending forth his apostles correspond to the concept of Acts which was decisive for the further interpretation of the apostolic office? That Jesus called men to follow after him (Mk 1:16–20), and the Twelve in a special way (Mk 3:14: "and he appointed twelve"), cannot be open to doubt. The word ἀπόστολος, however, seems to have been transposed by the synoptics back into the time of the public ministry of Jesus. Nevertheless it is certain that Jesus at least occasionally charged his disciples to proclaim the kingdom of God in word and signs (1 Cor 9:14; cf. Mt 10:10; Lk 10:7; Lk 9:1f.). This mission which was only temporary during the public ministry of Jesus became, after the resurrection of Christ, an office through the gift of the Spirit (Mt 28:18ff.). The apostles share in the power of Jesus to bring salvation and doom, according to Lk 10:16, "He who hears you hears me, and he who rejects you rejects me, and he who rejects me rejects him who sent me" – words which already have a Johannine ring.

Theology. Even at the time of the apostles, the Church saw in the apostolic office one of its essential marks (Eph 2:20; Rev 21:14), though the self-designation of the Church as apostolic in the Creed dates from the 4th century (*D* 14, 11). That the Church is apostolic guarantees its truth as opposed to all the other Christian communities. The apostolicity of the Church not only involves claims with respect to the authenticity and extent of revelation, treated of in fundamental theology (*D* 783, 1836, 2021), but it also has ecclesiological consequences with respect to the unity and the visible nature of the Church. The Church's understanding of the juridicial and institutional character of the apostolic office cannot, it is true, be substantiated by Jn 21:15–18 alone – the thrice repeated mandate given to Peter before witnesses. Its character as office is rather witnessed to by tradition and is seen to be a necessary consequence of the basic incarnational structure of the Church. The author of the fourth gospel had the clearest insight into a theology of the apostolate which follows from the very mystery of the Incarnation, and gave it the fullest development (although in Jn the term ἀπόστολος appears but once, in 13:16).

The Incarnation embodies a comprehensive revelation which is addressed to all men. With the incarnation of the Word, the pre-existent Logos subjected himself to the conditions of human life. But to comply with the universality of his mission, Jesus had to make use of human emissaries. As the Incarnation meant God's rendering himself visible on the fixed categories of the spatial and the temporal, the Twelve together with Paul were made mediators and witnesses of revelation in a concrete and as it were hierarchical order after Christ. They share in the authority of

Christ (Jn 20:21; cf. 17:18), which in turn derives from the authority of the Father (Jn 12:44). For John, the essential elements of the apostolate are the following.

a) Unity with Jesus assures for the disciples the intimate love of the Father (Jn 1:12f.; 16:27). b) Union with Christ is guaranteed through the gift of the Spirit. The Spirit enlightens the disciples so that their teaching is true (Jn 14:16f.; 16:14). c) Election passes into mission: Christ made his disciples his representatives, his ἀπόστολοι. In their hands he places the fullness of authority which he received from the Father (Jn 14:27; 15:15; 17:2, 14, 18, 22, 26), the mission which has its source in the Father. It is therefore understandable that the world treats the envoys in the same manner as it treated the Son (Jn 15:19f.).

Through the inseparable unity with Christ, there is in his Church a) the message of the apostles which is the word of Christ, which is in turn the fathomless wisdom of the Father (Jn 21:15); b) the apostles are trustworthy witnesses of Christ – revelation is indeed an act of the grace of God which can only be responded to with faith; c) the apostles are representatives of Christ whose messianic powers as shepherd, priest and teacher are bestowed upon them. (Similarly, the number twelve which was stressed by the synoptics is an indication that Jesus claims for his apostles the position of emissaries of the Messiah.) This transmission of power was a real one so that the saving activity of Christ should have a visible continuation, and at the same time it represents a vicarious exercise of authority so that the unity of the mission might not be endangered, the mission which was reserved solely to the one mediator between God and man. Thus, because the transmission of the office was a real one, the office of apostle represents the invisible presence of Christ in his Church. The bond between the Church founded upon the apostles and the ἐκκλησία is so close that the Scriptures sometimes ascribe the founding of the Church to Christ (1 Cor 10:4) and sometimes to the apostles (Mt 16:18; Eph 2:20). The apostolic founding of the Church continues for all time, inasmuch as the apostolic preaching remains active in the Church through the Scriptures. This lasting confrontation of the Church with the apostles as those empowered with the authority of Christ does not only occur over and over again with each new confrontation with the Scriptures, but it is also guaranteed in an abiding way through the episcopate as the institution which derives from the apostolic office – as the ultimate logic of the Incarnation. Thus, along with the handing on of the word, the transmission of the sacraments is assured. And so 1 Clem expands the Johannine conception in the following manner: "The Father sent his Son, the Son lives on in his apostles, and the apostles bestowed the teaching office upon their successors the bishops."

Antonio Javierre

APOSTOLIC CHURCH

I. Primitive Community

Concept and date. The terms "Apostolic Church", "Primitive Community" and "Primitive Christianity" designate, not very precisely, the Palestinian Christianity of the first decades of the Church. The notion is based on the existence of the NT canon, seen as a mirror of the primitive community, on the important role which the apostles played for a definitely limited period in NT revelation, and also on romantic notions of the ideal and normative character of the first Christian community – drawing on the presentation given in Acts. The *terminus a quo* depends on how one answers the question of when and how Jesus founded a Church. Thus R. Bultmann and H. Braun make the beginnings of the primitive community coincide with the dawn of faith in the resurrection, while H. Schürmann stresses the objective and personal continuity with the pre-Easter group of disciples, especially Peter. As regards the *terminus ad quem*, A. Vögtle suggests the end of the apostolic generation, the growing sense of the delay of the parousia, the cessation of charisms and religious enthusiasm, and the appearance of heresies and persecutions. Protestant writers like W. G. Kümmel suggest the time when the Church became an institution within which salvation was to be sought, while H. Conzelmann thinks of the time when the Church began to be conscious of having a past which could be designated as "apostolic" – this period then being obviously "post-apostolic". This would have brought with it a temporal dimension of the Church and a changed notion of tradition.

But since the concept of "apostle" varies widely in the NT (in John it is only used by Jesus), the notion of "apostolic" is also somewhat artificial. Since according to Conzelmann the transition from primitive Christianity had already been made when the Church started to reflect on its past, only a few writings of the NT would belong to primitive Christianity. Kümmel too finds that the transition has been made where the parousia is no longer seen as imminent, as in the Pastoral Letters and 2 Peter. On the question of the significance of the primitive period, Kümmel affirms that it is "a historical norm, to be traced by critical reflection". But the whole notion of norm becomes questionable if one remembers how restricted was the field of unity in Church life and theology, and that the contrasts have already appeared which were to remain operative in the Church of later times. It is only the systematic presentation of Lk which imparts the notion of a norm, as an interpretation of the first days of the community. Hence when the question of "primitive Christianity" is analysed, the answers depend partly on the previous decision with regard to the notion of the Church in general, and partly on the assumption that there were in fact such historical entities as a single primitive community and Christianity.

Historical treatment. An approach may be made to determine the period in which the primitive community flourished by using the NT to see what theological aspects were prior to others. Thus the Pastoral Letters presuppose Paul, as does 1 Peter. But this way of determining what is primitive Christianity leads only to the definition of basic types of theology (synoptic, Johannine, Pauline, Letter to the Hebrews), none of which can be deduced from the others; a uniform basic kerygma can be provided for them only by a process of abstraction, as the contrast between Paul and John in particular shows. And one must agree with Wilckens, against Geiselmann, that such a kerygma cannot be deduced from the missionary discourses of Acts, since these are Lucan compositions. Hence from the point of view of the history of theology, primitive Christianity should be defined as the sum total of a number of different theological principles, all equally primordial, used to interpret the coming of Jesus. Another approach to primitive Christianity may be made through the historical events and early Christian forms of fellowship which can be deduced from the NT. According to Galatians, 1 Corinthians and Acts, the decisive elements were the conflicts between Jews, Jewish Christians and gentile Christians, and also the beginnings of the mission to the gentiles. .

The beginnings of the primitive com-

munity. The origin of the primitive community presupposes the pre-Easter calling of the disciples, the call of Peter, John and James being beyond all critical doubt. According to the ancient tradition of 1 Corinthians 15, which also appears in John and Luke, Peter was also granted the first and decisive apparition of the risen Lord. The apparition to the Twelve is presented as a parallel to this. It must be maintained, against Bultmann, that visions as such cannot have been generative of the community. It is also certain that there was now a fact of decisive importance for salvation, which, once it was formulated as a confession of faith, needed to be embodied in tradition. Hence its acceptance in faith was also a factor in the constitution of the community. Phenomenologically, the common recourse to the fact of the resurrection of Jesus was the initial factor in the formation of a post-Easter community. And here the affirmation that it was Jesus who rose again presupposes that there were men who already knew who Jesus was and could also recognize that the resurrection was the fulfilment and confirmation of his eschatological claim. In a fellowship with a structure of this nature, the witnesses of an apparition of the Lord were necessarily the first and chief members. Hence later writings also presuppose (Jn, Heb) that the leaders of the community were those who had seen the risen Lord. (The five hundred brethren of 1 Cor 15 form an exception.) The apparition to Peter remained throughout the norm. The first believers in the resurrection were undoubtedly centred on Jerusalem – in spite of the indication of Galilee in Mk 16 and the general tendency of transposing the apparitions to Jerusalem. In addition, "pneumatic" events were clearly very numerous after Easter, and gave a special stamp to the primitive community. Luke sums up these events in the sending of the Spirit on the Twelve together. No doubt, after Pentecost, the regular channel for the reception of the Spirit by Christians was the imposition of the hands of the apostles, which followed baptism, but the descent of the Spirit could also be direct (Acts 10:44). According to Luke, the preaching of the Twelve also began after Pentecost. It seems that the Twelve went in pairs to preach to the Jews, using a style which may have resembled that of the Baptist and Jesus (Mark). Luke's placing the Twelve permanently in Jerusalem need not be taken too literally, since Paul did not meet them when he visited Jerusalem and according to Luke's own presentation, in Acts, there is another group, the Elders, who have charge of the community. According to Gal 1 and 2, Cephas and James represented Jerusalem, and he met no other apostles. Fourteen years later James, Cephas and John are the "pillars" of the Church in Jerusalem. The order of the names may indicate some change of function, but it is certainly clear from Acts 21:18 that in later times James "the brother of the Lord" was the sole head of the Jewish-Christian community at Jerusalem. (He was put to death in A.D. 62 according to Josephus, *Antiquities*, XX, 200.) He was probably the head of the group of Elders mentioned by Luke. Acts as far as 2:41 practically confines its attention to the Twelve, but Acts 2:42–47 gives a brief sketch of the life of the community. The community of goods (2:44) is described in terms of the Hellenistic ideal of friendship, adding lustre to the sunny beginnings of the Church as depicted by Luke.

It is no doubt historically accurate that the eschatology preached by Jesus and the faith in the resurrection of Christ which characterized the community caused no breach with Judaism. Nor did the titles of "the holy one, the elect, the just", which were probably applied to Jesus very early. These titles, like the institution of the Twelve, show that the community applied to itself the notion of the "Remnant". Nonetheless, the rites of baptism and the Eucharist were already paving the way for a breach with Judaism. There is a clearer picture of conditions in Acts 6, according to which there were two relatively independent groups at an early stage, the Hellenists (Jews speaking only Greek) and the Hebrews (Palestinian Jewish Christians). The conflict signalled by Luke apropos of the relief of widows explains only their function of "deacons". But they must also have been independent missionaries ("evangelists"). Wilckens suggests that for linguistic reasons they could have had no access to the pre-Easter traditions about Jesus – a view not confirmed by the third volume of the *Discoveries in the Judaean Desert* which depicts Palestine as largely bilingual, if not trilingual (Aramaic, Greek and Latin). The question at issue between the two groups was probably the one which brought about Stephen's death at the hands of the Jews: the relation of the Hellenists to the temple and the law. In their concept of the law, these Hellenists may have been essentially at one with the liberal circles of the Jews of the diaspora. And as regards the temple, their attitude was probably determined not only by Hellenistic criticism of external religion but also by the saying which played so important a role in the trial of Jesus – the prophecy of the destruction and re-building of the temple in three days (Mt 26:62; 27:40; cited only here by Luke, Acts 6:14). This was interpreted as an attack on the temple, and therefore provoked sharp nationalistic reactions. The stoning of Stephen made the Hellenists still more critical of Jewish tradition. They fled (Acts 8:4) and founded the community of Antioch (11:19ff.). Obviously, these were the events which occasioned the actual breach with Judaism on the part of the community. They also opened up the way for a mission to the gentiles without the preaching of circumcision.

The gentile mission, the law and circumcision. The breach with Judaism could not have merely been the consequence of the conviction that the resurrection of the crucified Jesus was the beginning of the end of the world. There must also have been differences in actual religious practice. The mission to the gentiles, with no obligation of circumcision, began at Antioch, before Paul came on the scene. No definite answer can be given to the question of how these Jewish-Christian Hellenists arrived at the notion of a gentile mission. It may be taken as certain that Jesus himself saw his mission as a task confined to Israel. And the Jewish notion of an eschatological pilgrimage of the nations (Mt 8:11f. par.) is specifically distinct from that of an active mission to the gentiles. The notion of a gentile mission without circumcision probably presupposes the following principles: a) The coming judgment is universal, affecting all men. b) The omission of circumcision signifies that under this judgment Jews and gentiles are on the same plane. Possibly the importance of baptism as the rite of initiation had made circumcision meaningless. c) The omission of circumcision means that the division of mankind into just and unjust, common in late Judaism, was regarded as in principle independent of Israel – since it depended only on moral factors. d) Omission of circumcision presupposes the definitive breach between this group and Judaism. And in fact it was also in Antioch, according to Acts 11:26, that the new name of Χριστιανοί was given to the group. Henceforward the fellowship between the baptized is stronger than the link with Judaism. e) The tendency already present in Hellenistic Judaism to eliminate national idiosyncrasies, was thus combined with the eschatology of Jesus (so too the attitude to the temple combined elements from Hellenism and from the preaching of Jesus); the missionary impulse itself was inspired by the example of Jesus.

But the new type of mission underlined the contrast with the Jewish Christians of Jerusalem. F. C. Baur regarded the ensuing opposition between a Pauline freedom from the law and a Petrine adherence to the traditions of Judaism as constitutive for Christianity. E. Reuss, however, rightly distinguished between Jewish Christians of the strict and of the moderate observance. But apart from the law and "doctrine", there were also differences in the type of communities which developed. The "Council of Jerusalem" was to clear up the question of the law. In Acts it appears as an answer given to Paul and Barnabas by the Twelve and the Elders, while Paul presents it as an agreement between Paul and Barnabas on the one hand, and James, Peter and John on the other. But in both versions the gentiles are granted freedom from the law. Nonetheless, the link with Jerusalem, and the bond between the Church and Israel, are considered so essential by Paul (see Romans) that he lays an increasing stress on the collections there agreed upon for the community in Jerusalem (Gal 2:10; 2 Cor 8; 9; Rom 15:20f.). Thus the collection gives expression to the fact that the link with the historical existence of Jesus among the Jewish people was maintained.

The "apostolic decree" (Acts 15:20, 29; 21:15), which Paul makes no mention of, can hardly have been an immediate fruit of the Council. It is much more likely to have been the result of the conflict at Antioch (Conzelmann). For it is, in fact, a decree envisaging cases left unsolved by the Council of Jerusalem, the very type of case which was the occasion of the conflict at Antioch – the question of Jewish and gentile Christians eating together. The agreement reached at the Council, permitting gentile missions without circumcision, could only be applied directly in purely Jewish-Christian or purely gentile Christian communities. It raised problems in mixed communities, since the Jewish Christians always went in fear of incurring ritual impurity. The decree imposed on gentile Christians the minimum of ritual purity, just enough to enable meals to be taken together. But the decision in favour of a gentile mission without circumcision was not universally accepted among the Jewish Christians of Jerusalem. There was an uncompromising minority which reacted first by trying to introduce circumcision for gentile Christians (which occasioned the disturbances in the Pauline mission of which Galatians gives some idea), and then by schism (possibly the kernel of the later Ebionites). At the beginning of the revolt against the Romans, the Jewish Christians left Jerusalem for Pella (Eusebius, *Hist. eccles.*, III, 5, 2). But the influence of Jewish traditions remained particularly strong in the Syrian missions, which was important for Matthew. A few decades later, the Great Church was composed almost exclusively of gentile Christians. Thus before the end of the 1st century, the basic theology and ecclesiology of the Hellenistic group in the disciples of Jesus at Jerusalem had prevailed, being enriched and differentiated in many ways during the process.

Klaus Berger

II. Apostolic Church

1. Apostolic Church means the Church of apostolic times and thus covers the period up to about A.D. 70. The apostolic Church is known to us above all through the writings of the NT which either, like the gospels, present its tradition about Jesus Christ, or, like Acts and the epistles, describe its way of life. But a number of ancient non-canonical texts, such as the *Didache*, the *Epistles* of Clement and Barnabas,

contain liturgical, exegetical and disciplinary elements which date back to early Christianity. The NT gives us the picture of official Christianity, but, as Baur has shown (in *Rechtgläubigkeit und Ketzerei*), early Christianity included various marginal currents of thought. We must add that geographically the NT describes only the expansion of the Church in the Graeco-Roman world of the Mediterranean. But there was also an Aramean mission in Transjordania, Syria and Osroenes of which only traces have come down to us through traditions which were difficult to check, such as those concerning Thomas's mission to Edessa.

This early period presents a number of definite characteristics. The first is the pre-eminent place occupied by the apostles. They were witnesses to the faith and founders of the community. But we see that they also chose others to collaborate with them in their twofold function, such as James at Jerusalem and Titus and Timothy in Asia Minor and Crete. Another characteristic of early Christianity was the place occupied in it by charismatic gifts, of which Pauline letters in particular have much to say. Though the simultaneous existence of ecclesiastical office and of charisms is certain, it is often difficult to decide to which category certain figures, described variously as teachers, prophets and apostles, belonged. A further characteristic was the normative role of the oral tradition passed on by the apostles. The writings of the NT were only just beginning to be compiled during this period. Scripture meant the OT and the instruction given by the "teachers" was for the most part a Christological exegesis of the OT in the manner of the Jewish Rabbis (Gerhardsson, *Memory and Manuscript*). Many examples of this type of exegesis have been preserved in the *Testimonia*. Finally, the whole period was dominated by the conflict between Jewish and gentile Christians, as appears from the Acts of the Apostles and the letters of St. Paul. Such a conflict implies great differences between the communities.

2. The primitive community has always appeared in Christian history as a point of reference with regard to a certain number of problems. But in most cases the idealistic image of the community is a creation of theology bearing little relation to reality. Here we can distinguish a number of questions.

a) The primitive community was very soon put forward as a model of charity and poverty, the embodiment of evangelical perfection. This is the picture portrayed in the Acts of the Apostles. Luke describes the union of hearts and the sharing of possessions in a way which is possibly inspired by the Essene ideal with perhaps a suggestion of Platonist influence (Cerfaux). This nostalgia for the primitive state inspired many spiritual renewals in the Church. This was so in the case of St. Basil, St. Francis of Assisi, the evangelism of the Reformers and also the apostolic vision of St. Ignatius. But it seems that the early community was split by serious divisions which first came to the surface in the controversy over the widows and then when the problem of the observance of the Mosaic law had to be faced.

b) A certain number of writers (Harnack, Loisy) contrast early Christianity with what they call *Frühkatholizismus*, early Catholicism. For them early Christianity had the following characteristics. It was essentially charismatic, guided by the Holy Spirit and completely free. The existence of a hierarchical authority was a secondary phenomenon due to the requirements of organization. Early Christianity was dominated by the expectation of the imminent return of Christ and it was only secondarily that the Church sought an anchorage on this earth, which entailed a compromise with the world.

This version of early Christianity is accurate in certain respects, but completely disregards the primitive character of the hierarchical structure established by Christ during his life on earth and also the existence of different currents of thought in early Christianity.

c) The importance of the primitive community is also exaggerated in the *formgeschichtliche Schule*. For Dibelius and Bultmann, the writings of the NT are the expression of the faith of the primitive community. They tell us very little of the historical Christ. For Oscar Cullmann the apostolic times have a privileged character which is normative in relation to post-apostolic Christianity. Here again the early community appears as highly idealized. Studies of 1st century Rabbinism (Gerhardsson, Le Déaut) have shown that the tradition of Christ's own teaching was of great importance in the NT and that the part played by the community was less than has been suggested. Moreover, the writings of the NT are not so much the expression of the faith of the community as of the faith of the apostles and their successors. The creative genius of the communities found its expression rather in an abundant apocryphal literature. Hence it is not the primitive which is the criterion, but the apostolic. And the criterion of apostolicity is continued in the apostolic succession. As such primitive Christianity has no privileged character. It simply represents a form of expression of Christianity which is characterized by its Semitic structure.

Jean Daniélou

APOSTOLIC FATHERS

Definition. By Apostolic Fathers is meant a group of post-canonical (and non-canonical) early Christian authors, whose number has been differently determined according to inconsistent criteria, and which has recently been reduced with a view to "saving and clarifying the concept" (J. A. Fischer). The decisive feature is direct contact with the apostles, or just an evident nearness to them according to the time and content of their preaching. The reason for the fluidity of the concept of "Apostolic Fathers" lies in the difficulty of applying this principle. In any case the distinctive point is that they were men of the apostolic age, whose writings were disregarded when the canon of the NT was being formed, even though some of them achieved, occasionally and regionally, canonical prestige. Their delimitation in contrast to the Apocrypha of the same time and to related literature is based on their nearness to the apostolic preaching as attested by the NT.

Writings. Under these conditions the following writings, among those which are normally designated as Apostolic Fathers, are to be included in any case under this name: the (first) letter of *Clement* of Rome, the seven letters of *Ignatius* of Antioch, as well as the letter (or the two letters) of *Polycarp* of Smyrna to the Philippians. Whether the apologetical fragment of *Quadratus* is added (Fischer) or not, makes little difference to the corpus of the Apostolic Fathers. If one applies a strict historical standard, then we have only these writings to deal with. In the case of other documents, which are also commonly reckoned among the Apostolic Fathers, the following points are to be considered: the *Didache* is too uncertain in age and authorship to be accounted as belonging to early times. The *Letter of Barnabas* as well as the *Second Letter of Clement* must be considered as pseudonymous; in their content they do not display any particularly close connection to apostolic times. The early form of the traditions of presbyters from Asia Minor, used by Irenaeus, is too uncertain to justify an early dating in apostolic times. According to Eusebius (*Hist. Eccl.*, III,

39, 2), Papias does not reckon himself in the first generation. The anonymous *Letter to Diognetus* is to be dated most likely about A.D. 200 (H. I. Marrou) and, in line with its intention and content, must be reckoned among the Apologists. For the *Shepherd of Hermas* one must reckon with more than one author (St. Giet); its content shows a considerable departure from the original apostolic kerygma. And finally, the *Martyrdoms of Ignatius and Polycarp* were reckoned among the Apostolic Fathers merely because of the heroes whom they celebrated; objectively and chronologically, however, they do not belong to them.

But even with the group which then remains (*1 Clement*, *Ignatius*, *Polycarp*, *Quadratus Fragment*) the idea of the Apostolic Fathers, seen purely historically, is not entirely without problems; it encompasses an inconsistent body of writings and these writings show, in terms of their contents, various degrees of approximity to the apostolic preaching. It may well be that for these authors the designation as Apostolic Fathers is valid in a historical sense, since the fact that they go back to the apostles cannot be reasonably doubted; but none of these writings is ultimately a repetition of the apostolic New Testament message.

Apart from the literary uniformity of the short list (the form of a letter) they have the following characteristics in common. The concept and collective name Apostolic Fathers is not, particularly if it is to be taken in the larger sense, useful as a *genus literarium* or chronological classification, but as a grouping in the history of theology. It encompasses – over and beyond all differences – the written documents of the post-apostolic era "between" the NT and the Apologists, i.e., of a stage in Christian self-understanding which stands on the threshold of the transition from the first generation to the later age of the Church. We have, of course, to reckon with the fact that part of the Apostolic Fathers is not later than some canonical writings of the NT. And there are traces in later NT writings of the same transition to an age in which one is conscious of being at one remove from the source. On the other hand, some writings, which do not belong to the apostolic age, testify to a situation in the history of faith which is basically the same. The grouping of these writings can, therefore, be separated from strict questions of form, authorship and dating, so that there would be no objection to a more comprehensive concept of the Apostolic Fathers. Thereby the consequence would merely be drawn from the fact that it concerns a category in the history of theology. The content of the writings of the limited group, as well as their comparison with documents of a few decades later, which are now generally distinguished from them, places the value of this narrow grouping in doubt as far as an "epochal" classification is concerned. One cannot speak of their more obvious apostolicity in all points, and so deduce a characteristic which might bind them closer to one another than to writings of a slightly later date. Here the possible association of some authors with the apostles carries less weight. The specific connection with the apostolic age, which is what one wants to emphasize by the concept of Apostolic Fathers, is not dependent upon the decade in which a work was composed. Here too, thought which is of the one temper and impact cannot be exactly delimited chronologically. Early Christian pseudepigraphy is instructive on this point.

This concept of Apostolic Fathers might comprise the diverse testimony of this early age, which is no longer the age of origin, but not yet the age of the Apologists – in a distant and formal analogy to the NT canon with its rich diversity. Writings such as the *Didache*, *Barnabas*, or the *Shepherd of Hermas* could well find a place under this concept because it would stand for the post-canonical and non-canonical early Church literature *in toto*.

Characteristics and thought. The few surviving writings from this epoch of the early Church are the remains of a much more copious literature. No independent form of expression was aimed at in this early stage "between the time of revelation and the time of tradition" (Quasten). The authors rather sought to demonstrate their continuity with the apostolic writings by using the epistolary form. This is so clear that possible influences of secular literature may be disregarded. They are for use in the Church, in the form of a written sermon and, beyond this simple role, can claim no literary value. The interests of this age are concentrated on the fixation, proclamation and handing-on of the preaching as attested by the apostolic age. The method of direct address and disregard of art-forms and erudition is continued. An exclusively Christian circle of readers is addressed. This explains the fluidity of the boundary between the primordial and later tradition, between immediate interests and permanent claims. The development of a special Christian language, despite many borrowings, takes on clearer contours. An explicit confrontation with the surrounding world is prepared for by the struggle with heresies and the rejection of all syncretisms with the paganism which has been discarded. The keynote is the consciousness of the redemption which has occurred and which is attainable, as well as the anxiety about final loss of salvation through apostasy. The questions of the permanent and institutional raise their claims.

The contrasts with the age of origin are unmistakable, and characterize the Apostolic Fathers as representatives of a period of transition in the early Church. It faced an extended period of time, which was to be mastered in the light of the origin. A wholesale characterization is only possible with reserves, because it necessarily distorts the diversity of the testimony and cannot be just to the individuality of the writings. Some more general elements may, however, be mentioned as common characteristics.

Of fundamental importance is the vivid expectation of the parousia; however, it is not the eschatological understanding of time and history as found in the original apostolical kerygma, but becomes more and more the otherworldly and futuristic eschatology of the Church existing permanently in the world. Christian behaviour is considered in view of detailed prescriptions, sometimes based on non-Christian models. Next to a hope in the future, the Christian faith, understanding itself biblically, gains in importance in its retrospective, preservative element as knowledge of the truth, being confronted with heresies and lacking a circumscribed tradition. In a varied Christology a repetition of biblical terminology goes hand in hand with the rudiments of an independent set of notions. Redemption is attained in the future sacramentally (or through martyrdom) and above all by reason of moral effort. In consequence of an imprecise concept of the Spirit trinitarian ideas are correspondingly fluid. The constitution of the Church and its structure of ministries are delineated with increasing clarity. The explosive spread of the Christian message in these decades clearly goes hand in hand with a swift consolidation of the structural forms of the Church and its liturgy. The process is by no means uniform and leaves many directions open for the following age.

In comparison with the first generation it is characteristic of the Christian situation of this epoch that the separation of the Church from Judaism is completed and the question of the law as posed in the NT no longer presents a relevant problem. The Bible of the early Church was, as it had always been, the OT. Christ speaks in it and through it, the Gospel is its fulfilment. Despite the use of some of the writings of the later canon of the NT by the Apostolic Fathers one can only say that they had collections of various extent. There is no question of the existence of a NT biblical canon. After the oral message of Christ comes the OT (in a thoroughgoing christological interpretation) as the only norm; it is "Scripture".

In numerous elements of their theological as well as practical and pastoral remarks the Apostolic Fathers share the intensity of earnest faith, of joy and hope, to which the NT testifies for the apostolic age; in others, however, they express themselves differently. Their relationship to the apostolic preaching cannot aptly be described as simply an unfolding development, or as decadence. The Apostolic Fathers represent the age immediately after the beginning, which still participates in the origin, does not, however, know properly a Christian past, and yet already has to endure the circumstances of the later generation and feel all its difficulties. It is the epoch of orientation within the Church in the changed situation of a relaxing tension and an incalculable duration. The understanding of faith, as testified to in these documents, remains the practically orientated theology of the ecclesiastical communities, along with the projects and systems of the theologians, as in the subsequent generations.

Norbert Brox

APOSTOLIC SUCCESSION

1. *The present issue.* The notion of Apostolic Succession presents the office of the Church (hierarchical ministry) as the authority which succeeds the office of the apostles. It is constituted through sacramental admission into ecclesiastical office by means of the visible sign of the laying on of hands. According to the prevalent view, the sacramental laying on of hands is the primary prerequisite for the legitimacy of the office-holder as administrator of (most of) the sacraments. In the era of the undisputed Catholic understanding of the office, the conviction of this connection between the administration of sacraments and a sacramentally ordained office-holder was rather taken for granted than demonstrated. It was all the more evident because even the OT and the antique religions obviously had priests. The Protestant questioning of such a chain of succession as bearer of the most important priestly functions in the Church, or the express denial of it, was felt to be an attack on the hierarchical structure of the Church. Hence the emphasis on the demonstration that the authority of Christ himself had willed this office, and that the apostles had obediently handed it over to the Church in order to preserve for all times this hierarchical structure willed by Christ. If this train of thought appears altogether too simple to the Christian of today, it is not because the authority of Christ does not suffice for him. Rather, he has recognized the Church as an institution of Christ in the sense that Christ's directives essentially concerned the mode in which he himself, as the real content of the life of the Church, could and should be "handed on" in word, sacrament and pastoral guidance. In other words, the question involved here is that of demonstrating, in the office with its succession, the structure which manifests its ministry as a *traditio Christi* in accordance with the nature of the Church. That is, the succession in office must be examined as to how and why it is the organ of the *traditio Christi* in his Church.

2. *Apostolic Succession and preaching.* The significance of the transmission of the office is seen in the Pastoral Letters,

especially in connection with the ministry of preaching. If we view the emphasis on the commission to teach as the most important characteristic appertaining to "the bishop" (1 Tim 3:2; Tit 1:9), according to the basic intention of the Pastoral Letters (as expressed, for example, in connection with the office, 2 Tim 1:6, 13f.; 2:2), it follows that it is the function of the bishop to preserve the congregation on the foundation on which it was built. The foundation is the apostolic preaching of Christ. Even though Christ is the only content of this preaching, the apostolic form of its mediation also plays a role, according to the manifold witness of the NT. The apostles had fellowship with, and received their commission from, the risen Jesus whom "God has made . . . Lord and Christ" (Acts 2:36). It is from this authority that their mission derives. It also bestows authority on the envoys, but for a very specific "ministry": namely, to mediate further fellowship with the living *Kyrios* and thus open the Church for all times to all men. In this way the conviction that Christ is the only foundation (1 Cor 3:11) is inextricably linked with the other, that the Church is built on the foundation of the apostles (Eph 2:20; Acts 21:14; cf. also Mt 16:18). The apostles do not replace the only foundation, but their *communio* with Christ, the foundation, is itself in turn fundamental for the Church.

3. *Constitutive function in the Church.* If the meaning of the apostolate is in harmony from the start with a theology of the Church which sees it as the house of God founded on the *mysterium paschale* (the Jesus made Christ and *Kyrios*), then the scanty theology of the ecclesiastical office in the NT fits into this picture of the Church founded by Christ: the office has a function of building up the Church, and this function is a gift of the Lord who imparts the *Pneuma* (Eph 4:11f.). Acts 6:1–4 explains the first transmission of the office by the necessity of easing the burden of the apostles. The transmission of the office authorizes the execution of functions hitherto performed by the apostles. The burdens of the apostles are eased, however, in order to enable them to fulfil their pastoral function all the more clearly. The organization of missions, as reported in the Acts of the Apostles, takes for granted the establishment of official ministries of leadership (Acts 20:17, 28). This is also affirmed by direct testimonies from the sphere of the Pauline mission (1 Cor 12:28; Phil 1:1; 1 Thess 5:12; Eph 4:11). Paul knows that this constitution may also be taken for granted in the Church of Rome (Rom 12:7). Though we know practically nothing about the concrete manner of the exercise of this ministry, some of the Pauline letters show how much Paul himself remained the responsible leader of his churches. Accordingly, in addition to the original motive behind the transmission of office (easing the apostles' burdens), the motive behind succession becomes evident only with the departure of the apostles (Acts 20:28). It is in this perspective that the above-mentioned Pastoral Letters should be viewed. The successors in office do not, however, simply assume the function of apostolic ministry. Nor can they do so, if the fellowship of eye-witnesses with the risen Lord is its foundation. But the office has the active function of preserving the Church on this decisive apostolic foundation. In its turn, it is so indispensable because it alone leads to communion with the living Lord.

4. "To preserve on the apostolic foundation" is a thoroughly conservative activity. Nonetheless it requires the creative principle of the Church, which manifests itself at every point in history: the *Pneuma* (1 Tim 5:14; 2 Tim 1:6). The preaching of the conservative office-holder is not a mechanical repetition of apostolic formulae – which would require no charism – but, in

response to each given situation, a proclamation of the Lord whom the apostles preached (2 Tim 2:1ff.; 4:1ff.), communicating himself by means of the faith preached and accepted by the Church, and so re-presenting his primary mystery. The preaching office preserves the Church on its paschal foundation, by constantly re-interpreting the gospel. In this sense the office-bearer is the successor of the apostles. The situation of "succession" distinguishes him from those who have been apostles, but also supplies the cohesion, because it is precisely the apostolic foundation which the succession presents. Within the living house of God the foundation is also preserved through a dynamic and active force. The dynamic pneumatic gift of the office always hands on to the Church the one and the same Christ. "Thus it is seen that 'apostolic tradition' and 'apostolic succession' mutually define each other. The succession is the form of tradition, and tradition is the content of succession." (Joseph Ratzinger.)

5. This truth was recognized in all its significance in the 2nd century confrontation with Gnosticism. It was this which first led to a conscious and articulate understanding of what had already been practised in the Church as *Successio Apostolica* and which could be used as a proof in the opposition to Gnosticism. The secret traditions which the Gnostics alleged could be confronted by the authentic apostolic tradition of the Churches, whose list of bishops could be traced back with certainty to an apostolic founder. As early as Papias, the ascertainable line of the bearers of tradition acts as a criterion for the authenticity of the preaching. During his journey from the East to Rome, Hegesippus was interested in the tradition of the Churches which, on the basis of their bishops' lists, could be verified as apostolic. In Irenaeus we find the fully developed principle of Apostolic Succession (*Adversus omnes Haereses*, 3, 3, 1, and *passim*). Similar ideas are to be found in the African Church in Tertullian, who employs the expression *Ordo Episcoporum* for the line of succession (*Adversus Marcionem*, 4, 5, 2).

In the anti-Gnostic argument the main role is played not by the tradition of an apostolic community as an individual witness, but by the common tradition of the apostolic Churches. Underlying this was the conviction which we also find in the NT itself: the Church is not a sum total of individual Churches, but, transcending them all, it is the fellowship by which all Churches are formed into one Church. Hence that we can speak of *the* Church as a concrete reality with one faith and one fellowship of life and prayer is also due to the functions of the office. The structure of the office is in keeping with this truth: it is itself constituted collegially. The practice and theological statements of the primitive Church show that this truth was taken for granted as an obvious presupposition; hence it was not formulated directly. (Cf. the procedure of Irenaeus and others when determining the tradition.) It is in the Second Vatican Council's Constitution on the Church (art. 21) that we first find an express statement. But the statement of the Constitution is based on the ancient facts: the office, in its very inception in the college of the Twelve, was founded as τάξις (*1 Clem*), as *ordo*, as brotherhood of a plurality of office-holders. The special position of Peter (Mt 16:18ff.) does not weaken the collegiate character of the office. It is only the other aspect of the institution of the office, namely that in the Church the office exists only as indivisible unity. And precisely this aspect is based on the fact that Peter is one of the Twelve to begin with. The collegial office does not proceed from him; rather, he amalgamates it into an effective unity. The indivisible unity is, of course, also a characteristic of the entire Church itself; yet the office does not impose itself as a super-Church over the community, but rather stands in the service of this one indivisible *communio* of the Church with its Lord. It thus becomes a ministry for the building up and edifying of the Church.

6. In ancient times this fact was mirrored most clearly in the rite of episcopal consecration, as depicted in the Egyptian Church Order. This type of rite was already in use in most parts of the Church and was definitively prescribed by the Council of Nicaea (with the stipulation that there must be at least three consecrators). In accordance with its sacramental character, the succession admits the recipient to the one common office. It is because the bishop is admitted to the college, the *Ordo Episcoporum*, that he can be bishop, pillar, of his local Church.

7. The priests, who help the bishop, *participate* in his ministry; they themselves are incorporated, collegially around the bishop, into the one office, and, in turn, themselves stand in the line of the ministries attested by the NT, which aided the apostles.

8. The firm incorporation of the office-holder into the one common office does not jeopardize his position in the individual community, but rather establishes it. What he represents in the Church, the link of the individual Church with the Church, he also effects, by bringing into his local Church the life of the whole Church – Christ as he is really present in the preaching and the sacraments. The individual Church is Church insofar as it participates in the whole Christ, in *the* Church. This – and not the general adoption of a conception of priesthood in terms of the history of religion – also explains the position of each consecrated minister in the sacramental life of the community which he presides over and administers. In this function he is not reduced to the impersonality of a sacred sign. He brings into his *ordo* his entire human individuality as a building stone. But he does so not only by virtue of his ancestral line of predecessors taken individually; rather, he can do so only "una cum famulo tuo, Papa nostro . . . et omnibus orthodoxis" (=bishops).

It is in this fact that the familiar theological distinction between *successio materialis* and *successio formalis* is rooted.

Although ordination makes the office-holder a member of the one office fraternally administered (*successio materialis*), the ordained, as a servant who builds, stands in the succession only insofar as he is member of the Church, insofar as in him the *communio* with all bishops united with the Pope (and thus with all Churches in the one Church) is realized (*successio formalis*). This is the same as saying that the college of bishops is a body which succeeds the college of apostles (Constitution on the Church, ch. iii) and that the individual bishop is a successor of the apostles insofar as he belongs to the college. Hence the affiliation of the schismatic bishop to the college would be analogous to the affiliation of the schismatic Christian to the Church.

At the same time it becomes clear that the jurisdiction of the individual bishop ensues from his membership of the college, and that it must also be subject, according to circumstances, to certain limitations imposed by his membership, because he can never build up his Church alone on his own behalf. But it also becomes clear that in a theology of succession conceived in terms of the college, both the spheres of Church office – priestly worship, and authoritative preaching as pastor – spring from a Church office which is one in its source.

9. Thus, in the correct understanding of succession, two theological lines converge, which are attested very early. *1 Clem* places the ministry of ecclesiastical office in the context of the com-

mission: the Father sends Jesus, Jesus sends the apostles, the apostles pass on the commission further (ch. 44). Ignatius, on the contrary, sees the bishop in a sacramental-representative way as steward of God or Christ. Both lines disclose their meaning only when one takes into account the fraternal institution of the office: the line of commission shows the authorship of salvation from above. But the ecclesiastical envoy is not, at any time, the authoritative representative of God, as he might seem in a paternalistic conception of society. He is himself a brotherly participant in the office, and so represents and brings into his Church the brotherly fellowship which builds up the whole Church. Even the apostles first had fellowship with Christ; it was only then that they were sent. However, their commission concerned only this fellowship with Christ, which they were to pass on in such a way that the Church's fellowship with Christ was not to be less than that of the envoys. And it is only by experiencing fellowship with Christ in the reception of Christ's envoys that the Church can ever have fellowship with Christ.

Wilhelm Breuning

ARISTOTELIANISM

I. The Philosophy of Aristotle

A. Aristotle's Place in Philosophy

The life and work of Aristotle are usually distinguished into three periods: the first or Athenian, when Aristotle was still entirely under the influence of Plato; the intermediate period in Asia Minor; and the second Athenian period, when Aristotle opposed Platonism by his own "Peripatetic" philosophy. The decisive impulse to the study of Aristotle's development was given by Werner Jaeger's famous *Aristoteles*. The significance of Aristotle in the history of philosophy is generally ascribed to two achievements:

1. The transformation of the speculative idealism of Plato into a speculative realism. Like his teacher Plato, Aristotle holds that the supra-individual, universal and spiritual which transcends particulars of time and space is on a higher plane of being and value than the sensible, which is characterized by spatio-temporal material individuality. But in spite of this superiority of being and value, the spiritual is only real when it has entered beings as a principle and is sustained by beings which along with this spiritual principle have another non-spiritual constitutive principle; or when it is living spirit which is its own principle of being as an immaterial entity; so God who is the object of his own thought is actual pure spirit as pure thought (νόησις νοήσεως). The spiritual is not *eo ipso* real as being, form, exemplary form and structure, norm and value as in Plato. All these are only real either in beings which contain them or in a life which actuates them or as life really as such.

2. The second decisive characteristic is generally taken to be the transition from the oneness of philosophy to a multiplicity of philosophical disciplines. Aristotle gave separate treatment to movement in general (physics), vital movement on the human and infra-human level (psychology and philosophy of biological life), pure thought (the Organon, logic), art (the *Poetics*) and social life (Politics and Ethics). The factor common to all these "second" philosophies is that they combine Aristotle's empirical observations – an enormous collection for his day – with speculative principles of order on a comprehensive scale: act and potency, substance and accident and the various modes of causality: formal cause, material cause, efficient cause and final cause, and also the basic modes of movement itself, etc. Prior to all these comes a type of knowledge

sought and striven after by Aristotle (ἐπιστήμη ζητουμένη) which calls for a new justification, the "first philosophy" (πρώτη φιλοσοφία). It implies that the question of beings in so far as they "are", in so far as they are considered simply as being (the question of ὂν ᾗ ὄν, later to be known as ontology) is one with the question of the supreme and divine, the one self-sufficient being (θεῖον, from which the word theology derives). Here ontology is intrinsically linked with theology in as much as it is only the relationship to the divine (as the οὐσία, strictly speaking) which determines the degree and value of being in all other beings. Hence it is only through theology that the ontological question can be pursued to its close. This combination of the ontological and theological question was given the title of "metaphysics" soon after Aristotle. Thus Aristotle may be termed the founder of metaphysics as the primary, fundamental and supreme discipline.

B. The Structure of Aristotle's Philosophy

It is through the question of movement that the first philosophy is linked with the second philosophies (later to be known as the philosophical disciplines, but in Aristotle still identical with the various branches of science, which had not yet been fully distinguished from philosophy). Aristotle's empirical starting-point is always change, movement, the imperfect which moves towards fulfilment (or at any rate to another state of being) – processes not self-explanatory for which the explanation must be sought. Hence the intention of Aristotle is to go from beings as they are met with in the state of movements to the permanent principles and elements (ἀρχαί) underlying the restless movement which is not its own sufficient reason. This effort of speculative thought seeks to refer all becoming to an intelligible being which is the only possible beginning and end because of its being self-contained. This being which is the beginning and end of all movement is ultimately the divine movement of which circular motion is the image. The divine self-contemplation is the absolute mover of all things, since it is the one mode of being which reposes and is rounded off in itself, does not need to go out of itself and pass over into anything else, and is striven after in all movement (ὡς ἐρωμένον, "as that which is striven after"). This self-sufficiency and self-containment is also the true prototype of all that can be understood as "fulfilment" or "happiness".

Thus Aristotle's philosophy does not allow for a God who is really superior or transcendent to the world; hence there is in it no creator of the world. The world is eternal, and in its perpetual movement tends towards the centre of its movement which as such is the divine, blessed and self-sufficient life and movement of the spirit. This spirit (νοῦς) is also co-active in the vital movement of man (ψυχή). But while my soul is my own, proper only to me as the determinative principle ("form") of my movement as far as it is self-engendered, the spirit remains, even in me, the one, divine, supra-individual mind which is no one's own but is owner of all things. It is the loftiest thing in man, and hence supreme happiness and supreme fulfilment are to be found in "theoria", the spirit's own vision, the contemplation of the philosopher, in which all particularity is merged and disappears and the individual life becomes unimportant in the supra-individual life of the philosopher. It is a type of life at which few can succeed. If it is to be successful, it needs the basis of a well-ordered society within which contemplation can be pursued without the distractions and hindrances of material cares. Hence the notion of happiness as the "theoria" or contemplation of the spirit which does not belong to us but to which we belong must be completed by the doctrine of the accessible happiness of individual life and self-realization. Hand in hand with metaphysics go ethics and politics, along with contemplation there is the practical and productive life (*praxis* and *poiesis*). The practical life is individual life orientated to the actualization of all its innate potentialities.

Thus, besides the distinction between first and second philosophies, and the distinctions taken over from Plato between logic, physics and ethics, theories of thought, nature and life, there came a further division into contemplation, practical life and productive life. The practical life is involved with the individual material things in time and space and in this situation uses the powers of the soul as it investigates, weighs, takes counsel and decision, to attain in manifold wise to what the spiritual vision achieves directly as a unity: the vital movement of a life which is completely self-sufficient. But if *praxis* is to be a successful realization of life, it must produce the objects of common endeavour which together make this life possible and protect and further it. This productive work and the heritage of intelligence exercised on it are called *poiesis*, its scientific synthesis "poetics", as the doctrine of the art and skill (τέχνη) which are at the service of the practical life as the realization of the individual existence of man.

Having thus described the characteristic structures of Aristotle's philosophy, we can do no more here than enumerate briefly the chief headings of its contents. Aristotle bases formal logic on the doctrine of the proposition and inference, and sets forth basic concepts and rules of the syllogism which have undergone no essential development except in our own day. Their validity is founded on the indissoluble intrinsic relationship between thought and being, so that the categories, for instance, are both formal basic modes of thought (the concept in its basic forms) and basic structures of being (the fundamental types under which beings are classified).

We have already spoken of the principles of metaphysics, which deals with beings as beings and hence also is concerned with that which supremely is. Movement is understood as act and potency and hence points to the unmoved source from which it originates, in the light of which the gradation of beings in the analogy of being is to be understood. This order, as the totality of movement in space and time beneath the incorruptible substances of the heavenly world is chiefly considered in *Physics*. In ascending degrees, it goes from lifeless things to living things, in which the soul produces substantial unity as the "first act" and unique essential form, vegetative in plants, sensible in animals – and so on to man in whom the supreme element is the immortal spirit. The spirit enters as it were from without (θύραθεν), as an event which happens to the soul, and alone enables it to exercise the properly human activities of generalized knowledge and free decision in its permanent relationship of acceptance ("passivity") by which it is bound to the world.

In keeping with this complex nature of man, ethics provides the frame of reference for his values, the virtues being the mean between faulty extremes. Politics likewise describes the right order in the State as the well-calculated mean (monarchy, aristocracy and democracy as opposed to tyranny, oligarchy and ochlocracy). There is no transcendent norm in the ethics of Aristotle, its place being taken by the insight of the prudent man and by the judgment built up by tradition in the healthy community. Man, after all, as λόγον ἔχων, that is, having not only reason but the faculty of discourse, is essentially a social being (ζῶον πολιτικόν). Hence a social phenomenon also takes place when man and nature are interpreted in the process of *poiesis* (τέχνη) of which the theory is given in *Rhetoric* and in the fragmentary *Poetics*. Even the life of contemplation, lived apart from the community, has a social task: to keep man open to the all-encompassing good which is the supreme end of man.

Max Müller

II. Historical Influence

In antiquity. In the philosophy of antiquity the differences between Plato and Aristotle made themselves felt in the formation of opposing schools. But the general attitude was so eclectic that it is hard to define exactly the influence of Aristotle. His logic was very generally adopted and developed, particularly by the Stoa, with regard to the logic of propositions. The real successor to Aristotle was the Peripatetic school, which continued to exist down to the 3rd century A.D. Its last great figure was Themistius, at Constantinople. In contrast to the mysticism and other-worldliness of Platonism, the school was strongly marked by the spirit of empirical research, beginning with Theophrastus, the first leader of the school, and continuing with the great scientists of the following centuries (Aristarchus of Samos, Ptolemy, Galen). A decisive factor in the spread of Aristotelianism was the publication of the works of Aristotle by Andronicus of Rhodes (about 50 B.C.), who was also the first commentator of Aristotle. The work of commenting reached its most intense level with Alexander of Aphrodisias in A.D. 200. Then, with neo-Platonism, the differences between the schools became almost completely blurred; but study of Aristotle continued. The neo-Platonist Porphyrius is the author of one of the most important text-books of early Scholasticism, the Εἰσαγωγή to Aristotle's treatment of the categories.

In the Middle Ages. Though in the patristic age the influence of Aristotle was less felt than that of neo-Platonism and the Stoa, it gained greater importance in later times. Boethius, basing himself on various forerunners, especially Marius Victorinus, tranmitted the logic of Aristotle to the Middle Ages, as the instrument (ὄργανον) of philosophy and theology – which at the start were mostly not treated as distinct subjects. The only philosophical discipline generally taught was logic, as one of the seven liberal arts. Through it the influence of Aristotle came to be of increasing importance, as may be seen from the abandonment of (Platonic) realism in favour of a more moderate view (Abelard). The *Organon*, however, as then known, contained only the Περὶ ἑρμηνείας and the *Categories* with the introduction by Porphyrius. Boethius's other translations had been lost. But then in the 12th century the two *Analytics*, the *Topics* and the *Sophistics* were re-discovered and became the *logica nova*, in contrast to the *logica vetus*.

At the same time, translations of the *Metaphysics* and the works on natural philosophy appeared. With this Aristotle begins to influence the philosophy and theology of Scholasticism to a greater extent. His indirect influence had been felt hitherto through Syria and the Jewish-Arab philosophers. After the conquest of Syria, the Abbassides had set Syrian scholars to work on translating Greek treatises on medicine, mathematics and philosophy into Arabic. The result was the combination of neo-Platonic and Aristotelian thought which is characteristic of the doctrines of Alfarabi and Avicenna (Ibn Sina). The most professedly Aristotelian is Averroes (Ibn Rashid), whom St. Thomas calls "the Commentator" as he calls Aristotle "the Philosopher". This Arab philosophy is responsible for the essential traits of the Jewish philosophy of Avicebron or Avencebrol (Solomon ibn Gebirol) and Moses Maimonides (Maimuni). The homeland of this philosophy, like that of Averroes, was Spain, and here, especially at Toledo, a translating centre was set up which, along with Arab and Jewish writings, translated the works of Aristotle himself from Arabic into Latin, partly via Spanish. The translators include Raymond of Toledo, Dominic Gundissalinus, John the Spaniard, Gerard of Cremona, Michael Scotus, Hermann the German.

Inspired by the work at Toledo, scholars at Oxford like Robert Grosseteste took over the task. Robert went back to the original Greek text, especially for his first translation of the *Nicomachean Ethics*. The third centre of translation was Italy, including Sicily, where it was done on the original texts, the work beginning in the middle of the 12th century with Henricus Aristippus and Eugene of Palermo, and being completed in the 13th. Among others (like Bartholomew of Messina) William of Moerbeke is of particular importance, who worked above all for St. Thomas Aquinas, improving previous translations and producing some of his own.

However, the adoption of the Aristotelian philosophy did not come about without friction and opposition. This was less marked with regard to his writings on logic, to which Tertullian, St. Gregory of Nyssa and St. Jerome, and later St. Peter Damian and Walter of St. Victor had raised objections. It was his writings on metaphysics and natural philosophy above all which were obscure enough in part to seem to contradict the Christian faith. Thus in 1210 the provincial council of Paris forbade under pain of excommunication the public use and the private reading of Aristotle's writings on natural philosophy and the commentaries on them. Warnings against his philosophy were issued to the University of Paris by Pope Gregory IX, and to Dominican theologians by the constitutions of their order. In 1231 the same Pope extended the prohibition of Aristotle to Toulouse, but declared that he was prepared to have the works on metaphysics and natural philosophy submitted to investigation. We do not know the result of this step: the commission heard, among others, William of Auxerre and Simon de Alteis. At any rate, the universities paid little heed to the prohibition (at Paris, Roger Bacon, of the school of Grosseteste, was one of the first to ignore it), and it resulted in the faculty of arts' attaining a higher status than that of a preparatory course.

One of the upholders of Aristotelianism, Siger of Brabant, became the centre of the Averroist controversy, since Averroes, where Siger claimed to find the true doctrine of Aristotle, maintained the necessity and eternity of the world and denied the existence of free will and personal immortality (the *intellectus agens*, the immortal active intellect, being supposed to be a single entity in all men). In 1270 and 1277 Archbishop Tempier condemned philosophical and theological theses which were upheld by St. Thomas in his moderate form of Aristotelianism as well as by Siger. The condemnation affected St. Thomas chiefly in so far as he divided theology from philosophy, contrary to the Augustinian view, and defined metaphysics as an independent science (based on *ens qua ens*, on *esse*). Even the Dominican Archbishop of Canterbury, Robert Kilwardby, officially rejected several propositions of Aquinas. But the prohibition fell into oblivion; in the same 13th century, St. Thomas was declared Doctor ordinis by a general chapter of the Dominicans, and the study of all the works of Aristotle was demanded by the papal legates for the licence in the faculty of arts.

Though the Aristotelians – including no doubt even Siger – did not teach the doctrine of the double truth, still, the debates between the various schools (Thomists, Scotists, Gandavists [Henry of Ghent], Augustinians [Aegidius of Rome], etc.) led to theology being so sharply divided from philosophy that the controversy proved baneful for both subjects. Philosophers turned from metaphysics to logic and mathematics and natural philosophy, while theology lost its ontological basis. Its metaphysical roots were replaced by "positive" determinations (of God's will in Scotus and especially in Occam) and by the dialectical method, which, while developing more and more along the lines of natural philosophy, was thought to provide the links between propositions of theology. There was a similar development – inspired above all by the debate with Platonism and the Alexandrist Aristotelianism (the school of Alexander of Aphrodisias) – in the doctrine of creation and of the *intellectus agens* of Averroistic Aristotelianism. Its protagonist P. Pomponazzi was condemned in 1513 at the Fifth Lateran Council (*D* 1440; cf. 738). Its doctrine of the State was notably affected by the development (cf. the *Defensor Pacis* of Marsiglio of Padua).

In modern times. After the anti-dialectical movement about 1400, which aimed at a true and reverent theology (especially John Gerson), and the basically anti-Scholastic propaganda of the humanists came the Reformation with its hostile attitude to all philosophy. The response was the revival of Scholasticism in Spain and Italy in the 16th century (Francis de Vitoria, Melchior Cano, Thomas Cajetan, Francis Silvestris de Ferrara). The influence of Suárez affected even the philosophy of the schools in Protestantism. In the 17th century Aristotelianism loses its force: the Enlightenment, Kant and German idealism hardly know Aristotle at all. Hegel pays some attention to him, but what divides them is greater than what unites them. The neo-Scholasticism of the 19th and 20th centuries took up the threads again, both in historical studies (H. Denifle, C. Baeumker, F. Ehrle, M. Grabmann) and in philosophical systems (the Louvain school, Cardinal Mercier). See also the works of E. Gilson, A. D. Sertillanges, F. van Steenberghen, A. C. Pegis, A. Marc, M.-D. Chenu, C. Fabro. The magisterium of the Church, from *Aeterni Patris* (Leo XIII, 1879) to *Humani Generis* (Pius XII, 1950) emphasized the value of Aristotelian-Scholastic philosophy. J. Maréchal brought it into the dialogue with German idealism; his intention was followed out by P. Rousselot and others, and in Germany – in relationship above all to M. Heidegger – by M. Müller, K. Rahner, G. Siewerth, B. Welte and others. But the Thomism represented here is not simply an Aristotelianism, which is indeed also true of the Aristotelianism of the Middle Ages, which can now be seen to have been essentially much more differentiated than it was thought to be, before the finds and researches of recent years. Even where Aristotle is principally followed, in contrast to other traditions of thought, the Aristotelian philosophy has been essentially marked and moulded by neo-Platonic, Arab and Jewish thought, and not least by Christian thought and experience. One result of modern research is precisely a clearer insight into the difference between Aristotle and Aristotelianism.

Jörg Splett

ASCENSION OF CHRIST

The account of the ascension of Christ (Acts 1:1–14) constitutes part of the Lucan kerygma of the exaltation of the Lord. For this reason it must be viewed in the context of the NT theology of exaltation as a whole. In Matthew and Paul resurrection and exaltation constitute a unity. The raising of Jesus from the dead by the Father is at the same time his installation in regal authority as the Lord to whom all power is given in heaven and on earth (Mt 28:18). The Johannine theology depicts the Crucifixion as already an exaltation (3:14; 8:28; 12:32f.). Thereby it reveals a mysterious two-fold significance in the cross, in that it is not only the cross but the royal throne of Christ as well, from which he exercises his cosmic power and draws mankind to himself. The contradiction between the essential hiddenness inherent in all these presentations of Christ's exaltation on the one hand, and the Lucan description of it as a visible ascension into heaven on the other is apparent rather than real. For in Matthew, Paul and John too the exaltation is depicted as an event which took place before witnesses in the apparitions of the risen Christ.

Thus it is not wholly confined to the realm of the "other-worldly" and the suprahistorical. On the contrary, it also has a solid basis in history, even though in its inward reality it exceeds the limits of that history and so must remain hidden from the unbeliever. For this exaltation takes place in the dimension of a concrete encounter with the Lord after he has passed through death. It is this aspect of verifiability by witnesses that is brought out in the Lucan account of the Ascension. It is based upon the greater length of time ("forty days") during which encounters with the risen Christ took place. The whole context in which this account is embedded is pervaded by the idea of witness, and it is in the light of this idea that it is to be understood (G. Lohfink).

It also follows that it would be a misunderstanding of the Ascension if some sort of temporary absence of Christ from the world were to be inferred from it. The "sitting on the right hand of the Father" of which Scripture speaks (e.g., Acts 2:33; 5:31; 7:55; Rom 8:34; Eph 1:20; Col 3:1, etc.) signifies rather the human Jesus' participation in the kingly power of God, and so precisely his authoritative presence in the world and among those whom he has made his own (cf. Mt 28:20). On this basis the Johannine theology finds it possible to combine the Resurrection with the return of Christ (e.g., 14:18ff.). With the resurrection of the Lord, in virtue of which he is henceforward and forever in the midst of his own, the parousia has already begun. Hence we must understand that the Lucan account of the Ascension is directed against a fever of false eschatological excitement, and – without denying the reality of eschatology (Acts 1:11) – lays the emphasis on the "present tense" of the time of the Church with its two factors: the gift of the Holy Spirit, through whom the Lord is already present here and now, and the task of bearing witness which the Christian takes up in response to his experience of the Spirit, placing himself at the service of the kingship of Christ.

It could also be said that although the reality of the exaltation of the Lord remains hidden in the age of history through which the world is passing, it still makes itself felt in history by the witness of the faithful who spread his message (Jn 15:26f.: ". . . he will bear witness to me; and you also are witnesses . . ."). This implies that exaltation and mission are closely connected. The mission is the form in which the world-embracing kingship of Christ expresses itself in the intermediate period during which he exercises his lordship through the humble medium of the word.

The idea of witness, then, is used to express the fact that the exaltation of Jesus is already beginning to be revealed, while at the same time including the further idea that this exaltation must of its nature be veiled from the eyes of the world. This Luke expresses by the image of the cloud (Acts 1:9) familiar from the OT theology of the temple, while John includes it in his presentation by the device of fusing the theology of the cross with that of the exaltation both in their existential significance and in their significance for the theology of history. The Christological hymn of Phil 2:5–11 has the same tendency. Here Christ is presented in the "emptying" of himself on the cross as the counterpart of that divinization of self which was the hybris of the first Adam. Moreover, by opposing the exaltation of the humble Christ to the downfall of hybris this hymn makes it clear to man that the way to "divinization" lies not through the self-sufficiency of hybris, but through participation in the humiliation of Christ's cross. Thereby this cross becomes paradoxically a sign of the exaltation of the Lord in this world. Hence the apostle boasts precisely of his weakness, for in this he experiences most of all the victory of God's strength (2 Cor 12:9f.).

From what has been said it will also be clear that the message of the Ascension as presented in the NT is, so far as its central statements are concerned, completely independent of the so-called "three-storeyed mythical" picture of the world, and hence cannot be "dismissed" along with it (against Bultmann). On the contrary, it opens up a new and positive understanding of the reality called "heaven", which is totally independent of any theories concerning the structure of the world. What the "Ascension" tells us about heaven is that it is the dimension of divine and human fellowship which is based upon the resurrection and exaltation of Jesus. Henceforth it designates the "place" (in the strictly ontological sense) in which man can live eternal life. Thus the Christian is aware that even in the present time his true life is hidden in "heaven" (Col 3:3) because, by believing in Christ, he has entered into the dimension of God and so, already in the here and now, into his own future.

Joseph Ratzinger

ATHEISM

A. In Philosophy

1. *Concept and incidence.* Philosophically speaking, atheism means denial of the existence of God or of any (and not merely of a rational) possibility of knowing God (theoretical atheism). In those who hold this theoretical atheism, it may be tolerant (and even deeply concerned), if it has no missionary aims; it is "militant" when it regards itself as a doctrine to be propagated for the happiness of mankind and combats every religion as a harmful aberration. We speak of the practical atheism (indifferentism) of a mode of life in which theoretical recognition of God's existence has no perceptible consequences. To decide precisely what constitutes atheism depends on just what conception of God is assumed. All systems of materialism and materialistic monism are certainly atheistic (early Greek atomists, post-Socratic Cynics, Epicureanism, certain philosophers of the Renaissance such as Campanella; the naturalism of the Enlightenment in France: Voltaire, Holbach, Lamettrie; German positivism and monism of the 19th century: Vogt, Büchner, Moleschott, Haeckel; left-wing Hegelianism: Feuerbach, Marx; popular 19th century socialism; dialectical materialism and bolshevism; the State-encouraged militant atheism of the godless movement in the Communist States); unqualified positivism, sensualism and pragmatism; all forms of philosophy for which atheism is a postulate, that is to say, theories such as those (deriving from Nietzsche) of A. Camus or the existentialism of J.-P. Sartre, or the ethics of N. Hartmann, which seek positively to prove that God cannot or ought not exist. Whether

every form of pantheism (especially in German idealism) is to be classified as atheism depends on how far it succeeds in not simply identifying man and the world with the absolute.

Polytheism will have to be characterized as atheism to the extent to which it makes the act of genuine religion directed to the absolute ground of the world difficult or, in an extreme case, impossible. (Conversely, the polytheism of antiquity persecuted as atheist the monotheism of some philosophers and of Christianity because it rejected the gods of the State; and again the Fathers of the Church sought to detect a hidden atheism behind heresies.) In the perspective of the history of ideas, atheism as a philosophical system has always appeared at moments of crisis and transition from one intellectual, cultural and social epoch to another. That shows that it is a crisis phenomenon, the projection of a question disguised as an answer, not the answer of an age that has attained assured certainty. In every transition to a new epoch of man's experience of himself, some particular experience of his own limitation appears to be overcome; this obscures man's recognition of his radically finite character and produces the impression that there is no place for a genuinely infinite and absolute reality. Further, the new grasp of the problems posed by modes of representation and terms once thought adequate to express the knowledge of God, now suggests that to speak about God would be to apply such concepts to a non-existing "object". Or at least the impression is given that no meaningful assertions may be made about it.

2. *Its possibility*. That theoretical athesim is possible is shown by actual experience in the history of religion and philosophy. How this fact is to be theologically interpreted will be considered later. Even from the purely philosophical point of view, atheism is not simply one of the many differences of opinion between men about the existence or demonstrability of some particular being. For if atheism really understands itself and comprehends what is meant by God, it denies that the whole question of being, and of the personal subject as such who is propounding that question, can or may be raised at all. But such a question arises anew as a condition of its very denial. To the extent, therefore, that atheism understands its own nature, it suppresses itself. Nevertheless it is possible, because man is a being who by misconceiving his own nature and through his own real fault, can be in contradiction with himself.

3. A *philosophical criticism of atheism* will first have to show, by a transcendental method, that, epistemologically (critically) and metaphysically, absolute scepticism or a positivist, pragmatist or "criticist" restriction of human knowledge to the realm of immediate experience is self-destructive, and that therefore the very possibility of metaphysics is always affirmed by its implicit existence in man's necessary knowledge. Then on that basis, in a rightly conceived proof of God's existence, God's existence and nature would both have to be made explicit together. The absolutely unique character of this knowledge (as a knowledge by analogy of the mystery of God's incomprehensibility) would have to be brought out, and on that basis the possibility of atheism would have to be completed by an interpretation in sociological and cultural terms of the milieu in which atheism appears as a mass phenomenon, by an explanation in terms of depth psychology of the "defence mechanism" which lies at the root of doubt and the "impossibility" of accepting the transcendent (atheism as a "flight" from God). A philosophical critique of atheism would also have to include a critique of theism whether popular or philosophical as it exists in fact. For atheism essentially lives on the miscon-

ceived ideas of God from which theism in its actual historical forms inevitably suffers. The criticism of atheism would finally have to be linked to a sort of maieutic of the religious act because in the long run theoretical knowledge of God only lives when it is taken up into the yes of consent to God given by the whole person, and a whole life.

B. In Theology

1. *The teaching of the Church.* Materialist atheism is characterized as shameful (*D* 1802). Atheism as a denial of the one true God, Creator and Lord of all things visible and invisible (*D* 1801), and as pantheism in various forms (*D* 1803–5; cf. 31, 1701), is anathematized. The anathema is necessarily only a recent one. That God can be known with certainty by the natural light of reason is actually defined (*D* 1785, 1806; on the demonstrability of God's existence: *D* 2145, 2317, 2320). At the same time, however, it is emphasized that he is inexpressibly raised above everything that exists apart from him or that thought can conceive (*D* 428, 432, 1782). The teaching of modernist agnosticism is described as "atheism" in the encyclical *Pascendi* (*D* 2073, 2109). The doctrine that theism is the product of social conditions or only affirmed on the basis of social conviction is, objectively speaking, also rejected by the Church's condemnation of Traditionalism (*D* 1649–52, 1622, 1627). That does not of course deny the essential importance of tradition and society for the individual's knowledge of God.

The Church first dealt really seriously with atheism as a new, world-wide mass-phenomenon at the Second Vatican Council. It was considered rather incidentally in the Dogmatic Constitution on the Church, art. 16, in the following terms: "Nor does divine Providence deny the help necessary for salvation to those who, without blame on their part, have not yet arrived at an explicit knowledge of God, but who strive to live a good life, thanks to his grace." "Inculpable" atheism (in the domain of clearly articulated knowledge, *expressa agnitio*) is obviously considered as a real possibility, which does not exclude salvation. Two questions remain unanswered here. One is whether in the existential, spontaneous act of existence there can be an inculpable no to the theism which is necessarily implied in this act. The other is whether such explicit atheism can remain inculpable in an individual, on the level of conscious reflection, throughout his whole life. The answer to the first question must be in the negative. As regards the second, in view of our present-day experience of atheism, we must be more cautious in saying either yes or no than most theologians have been hitherto when they denied the possibility of inculpable theoretical atheism being maintained for a long period.

But the most important text (a pastoral rather than a doctrinal one) is in art. 19–21 of ch. 1 of the Constitution on the Church in the Modern World. It first gives the various forms and causes of atheism, then the modern forms of theoretical atheism, and concludes with the attitude of the Church to atheism. The urgency of the present-day problem is recognized. Then come a number of concessions. Atheism is at times merely the rejection of a god who does not really exist. It is often the reaction to the atrophy of a genuine religious experience, or to the theodicy problem – the evil of the world. Its causes can be social. It is often a wrong interpretation of a legitimate sense of freedom and autonomy in modern man, or of his will to emancipate himself from economic and social bonds in order to mould his life "creatively". Or it may be the erection of human values into absolutes. The possibility of atheism as sin is recognized, but with great reserve, briefly, and without going deeply into this particular problem. Christians are said to share the guilt of atheism in so far as it is a critical reaction against defective forms of theism in theory and in life. The Council stresses the fact that theism is not a self-alienation of man but the answer to a question which in the long run and at decisive moments man cannot evade. The task of moulding the future by action within the world loses none of its meaning through theism and the Christian eschatological hope, which are, on the contrary, the real source of its nobility and dynamism. Here the Council speaks of an *intima ac vitalis coniunctio* between man and God, of an *inquietudo religiosa*, and of the *quaestio insoluta subobscure percepta* which is none other than man himself. The perspective is that of a more existential and comprehensive relation to God which is already there when man poses the question of God in intellectual reflection. But these initiatives of Vatican II remain at the stage of preliminary efforts.

2. *Scripture*. In general in Scripture (as in the whole Semitic world) God's existence is assumed or affirmed as a matter of course. The folly of the man who says there is no God (Ps 10:4; 14:1; 53:2) refers to the denial of his government of the world as providence and judge. Interest, development, conflict and confession of faith in the Old and New Testaments all in this respect concerned monotheism, so that the most fundamental article of faith proclaimed the activity of the living God of the Covenant, and the Father of Jesus, experienced in the history of salvation (Dt 4:35; 6:4; Mk 12:29, 32; Jn 17:3; Rom 3:30, etc.). In this connection the doctrine of creation is important, as is the doctrine of the angels, and the interpretation of the gods as really demons. Both these show that men knew of profound realms of existence lying beyond experience, but that even in comparison with these God is totally different and incomparable (1 Cor 8:5). That testifies to awareness of God's radical transcendence. This should be taken into account when the scriptural doctrine of the possibility of knowing God by natural reason (Wis 13; Rom 1:20) is to be more precisely expounded. The doctrine of the creation of the whole reality of the universe and the principle, already clearly perceptible in Aquinas, that the world is to be explained as far as possible by "second causes", anticipate, fundamentally, the modern conception of the universe as in itself susceptible of investigation and control. But that is how there arises the temptation of modern times, to contrive to "explain" the world without God. The biblical removal of "magic" from the world, by the doctrine of creation (leaving in it, however, created "numinous" aspects, which was, however, often overlooked), is necessary for true, reverent theism. But it involves as its inevitable counterpart the danger of atheism to a degree unknown in antiquity.

At all events in Scripture man does not simply have God "also" as one of his possible objects of thought. Men, as "God's offspring", are created expressly that "they should seek God" (Acts 17:27ff.). Consequently the atheists (cf. Eph 2:12) are not to be excused, for their refusal to know and give recognition to God is the profound folly, which takes itself for wisdom, of really knowing God and yet not acknowledging him, and of exchanging the known God for something else (Rom 1:21ff., 25, 28) in a culpable "suppressing" of the truth (Rom 1:18). Scripture therefore knows no atheism of a purely neutral kind, which would be merely incidental (or at least does not reflect on any such atheism). It only recognizes an atheism which lies somewhere (impossible to locate in the individual case) between pious inarticulate veneration of the "unknown God" (Acts 17:22 in the light of Eph 2:12) and the guilty ignorance of the God whom in actual fact one knows in the "suppressed" accomplishment of one's own human nature (Rom 1).

3. *Traditional theology* chiefly deals with the question of the possibility of atheism. The basic view of the Fathers of the Church was that the knowledge of God is easy, almost inescapable and in that sense "innate". In view of the (relatively easy: Wis 13:9) possibility of knowing God and the "inexcusable" character of "foolish" atheism (Wis; Rom 1), Catholic theologians generally hold the doctrine that an atheism which is inculpable and negative (i.e., reaching no judgment on the question of God) is in itself (i.e., in normal human conditions) not possible over a certain length of time for the individual human being. Positive atheism (i.e., which positively asserts God's non-existence or unknowableness) is conceded to be a possible fact and also a lasting condition (and is lamented as a militant mass-phenomenon which has only appeared very recently: Pius XI in *AAS* 24 [1932], pp. 180ff., 29 [1937], p. 76), but is declared to be culpable. But this teaching admits of many shades and in fact has been given them. L. Billot stressed the social and cultural dependence of individuals on their milieu and consequently considered it conceivable that many "grown-ups" do not reach the adult stage in regard to the question of God. Conversely, M. Blondel and H. de Lubac put so much stress on the radical orientation towards God as the essence of man, that at bottom there cannot be any atheists, but only those who simply think they do not believe in God. In view of the mass-phenomenon of modern atheism and the teaching of Vatican II, the latter view will probably be more widely adopted in future, with the necessary developments and modifications.

As against the first of these opinions, it will have to be stressed that in view of God's universal salvific will it is not theologically possible to assume that so many human beings will remain inculpably, and despite their having lived their lives, excluded from their vocation. As against the second opinion, it has to be said that empirical atheism cannot after all, according to Scripture, be an ultimately harmless misinterpretation of a hidden theism. Alexander VIII condemned (*D* 1290) as a theological error the proposition that there could be a sin which was only an offence against human nature and not against God. We may then say that a fundamental moral decision, even when not recognized as an attitude towards God, nonetheless involves such an attitude, at least implicitly. On the one hand we must hold fast to this connection between theism and ethics. On the other hand we see more clearly today (in agreement once again with Aquinas) that the dependence of the individual (beyond his free and personally responsible decision) on the opinion of the society of which he is a member, is greater than was previously realized. The right to distinguish between men as a whole and in general and a particular individual, in regard to the knowledge of God, is certainly guaranteed by Vatican I. (See *Collectio Lacensis*, VII, 236, 150, 520.)

4. *Systematic treatment*. a) Generally speaking theology will have to refer in the first place to man's absolute transcendence. (This is to be understood from the start as his openness to the "living" God freely acting, so that "natural" knowledge of God does not draw up a closed theological system which would represent an *a priori* law imposed on the revealed word of God.) This transcendence which, as the condition of the very possibility of all intellectual knowledge and free action, implicitly refers to God and tacitly but truly makes that reference in every act of cognition and of freedom, can be present as obediently accepted or as

denied; or it may be present as merely implicit and not thought about, or it may be taken as the theme of reflection and consequently it may name God as the term to which it tends, and which does in fact correspond to it.

From this it follows (by way of systematic elucidation of the data of Scripture and tradition) that there cannot be a serene atheism which is in harmony with itself, for even atheism draws life from an implicit theism; there can be a nominal theism which despite its conceptual talk about God either does not yet genuinely accomplish in personal freedom the true nature of the transcendent orientation towards God or else fundamentally denies it atheistically, i.e., godlessly; there can be an atheism which merely thinks it is one, because in a tacit way transcendence is obediently accepted but there is no success in making it expressly and explicitly clear enough to the person concerned; there can be a total (but as a consequence, necessarily culpable) atheism in which transcendence is denied in a proud closing of the self, and precisely this is consciously made into atheism expressly and deliberately. Which of these possible forms of atheism is present in the individual and in what combination they are present in any age, is ultimately the secret of God who alone can judge. As, however, by the nature of man and the nature of Christianity (in which the Absolute himself in an "incarnational" way has entered the empirical world and its categories) transcendence is only fully realized and accepted when it finds explicit expression in "religious acts" addressed to God named and invoked, an atheism which explicitly doubts or denies (whatever its basis) is the most terrible thing in the world, a revelation of the folly and guilt of mankind and a sign of the growing eschatological distinction of men's lot because of God.

b) In particular the impossibility of a serene atheism can be shown in the domain of moral experience. Whenever an absolute moral obligation is affirmed, an implicit affirmation of God is present, even when the individual concerned does not succeed in giving it objective expression in a conceptually explicit theism. For absolute affirmation here and now in the concrete of an absolute obligation and consequently of the existence of an objective foundation for it, is an affirmation of God, even if not an explicit one. And when the moral law is not seen and willed as an absolute obligation, either explicitly or in the concrete accomplishment of moral action, there can be no question of complete presence of morality as such (even if this is contradistinguished from its foundation in God as law-giver); conduct would remain on the plane of the instinctive, conventional, utilitarian, etc. There can of course be an atheist ethics, to the extent that there are values, and the norms that derive from them, which are distinct from God (the personal nature of man and all that corresponds to it) and which can be perceived and affirmed without explicit knowledge of God. To that extent ethics and its norms constitute a natural domain of reality which like other domains of created reality possesses its relative independence and is directly accessible to cognition, so that agreement can be reached about it, at least in principle, even with atheists. But the absolute validity of all these values (their obligatory character because absolute) has its foundation in man's transcendence. It is only grasped as absolute to the extent that man grasps it and implicitly affirms it in affirming the absolute being and value which is implied in the open acceptance of his own transcendence. (It can be left entirely an open question whether that affirmation is explicit or only implicit.)

To the extent, therefore, that morality includes this absolute affirmation in its very concept, it is not merely one domain of reality among others, on which human *a posteriori* knowledge and behaviour are intent. It possesses in the absolute claim of moral duty an incomparable dignity which other domains do not. And this special dignity cannot simply be thought of as only indirectly grounded in God in the same way as all other realities have their "ultimate" ground in God. In the absolute obligation there is found precisely in the moral domain an active transcendent relation to God, so that in this respect an atheistic ethics complete in itself, even subjectively, and as a consequence atheism, are not possible. Certainly someone can think he is an atheist whereas in truth he affirms God by the absoluteness with which he bows to the claim of morality, provided he is really doing so, which does not follow from the mere fact that in civil life he is a "respectable man". He also knows it in the depth of his conscience, even though in the actual conceptual apparatus of the ideas he consciously holds he wrongly interprets what in actual fact he is doing.

c) In the effort to overcome atheism, Christians must realize – in the present and future situation of mankind – that they will meet all the factors which dogmatic theology sees in sin in general. Its roots are permanent. There is a sense in which it is potent even in the justified. It is not merely ineradicable in the world but its power will be eschatologically intensified as history proceeds. There is a difference between objective and merely subjective sin. Man cannot finally judge whether a given phenomenon involves subjective guilt or not. All this must now be applied to the theology of atheism, because it is the form of sin which marks the present age most clearly and powerfully, and which will no doubt continue to make itself felt in history. Just as the Church has faced and still faces serenely the phenomenon of sin – which is at least objective, but often *merely* objective – and believes throughout this inescapable experience that grace will triumph in the individual and in mankind, it must learn to maintain the same attitude in face of atheism.

Rational proofs of the existence of God remain valid and important, but they can now only be effective if they are combined with an apt initiation into the religious experience of the transcendence which is intrinsic to the concrete moral life in general, to the acceptance of active responsibility for the future, and above all to a really personal and genuine love of others. As we address ourselves to the atheist, culpable or inculpable (a distinction whose concrete application always escapes us), we must try to show him where he encounters God in his actual existence – even though he does not call this ultimate end and source of his moral freedom and love "God", shrinks from "objectivating" it, and often (wrongly) feels that intellectual and institutional religion is in contradiction with this inexpressible mystery of his existence. We can now no longer suppose that "God" means what it should mean to everyone, and that the only question is whether this God really exists. We must be extremely careful that all religious discourse makes the incomprehensibility of God, his holy mystery, definitely real and vital. Otherwise "God", as we call him, will not remain the true God, and the God whom we profess may be rejected by an atheism which considers itself purer and more "pious" than everyday theism.

The "struggle" against the mass-phenomenon of atheism must begin by taking it seriously, learning to know it, giving their due weight to its causes and values, and must not shrink from admitting publicly that theism was often misused as "opium for the people". There must be genuine dialogue with atheists, with all that true dialogue presupposes and entails. And hence we must be ready to co-operate with atheists in shaping our common world. The "struggle" cannot be confined to the doctrinal level. It is carried on above all in the testimony of life, in the individual Christian and in the whole Church, by means of constant self-criticism, self-purgation and reform, by means of a religious life demonstrably free from superstition and false security. Christians must let their light shine in true justice, love and unity, and by being a living testimony that one can accept the darkness of existence in faith and hope, as the dawn of the infinite meaning of existence, which is none other than the absolute God who communicates himself (cf. Vatican II, Pastoral Constitution on the Church in the Modern World, art. 21).

Karl Rahner

AUGUSTINIANISM

A. The Augustinian Tradition

Aurelius Augustinus (354–430) is one of the most remarkable figures in the history of the Western Church and in the development of Christian thought. He is one of those personalities whose influence upon antiquity, the Middle Ages, and modern times has been equally great and constant. It is to Augustine that men have gone again and again for insight into the question of their own self-understanding, so much so that in the course of the centuries an "Augustinian" dialogue has developed within which varying interpretations of the master and his work have been proposed, to which corresponded a varying interpretation of each period of history. It is this changing dialogue which may be referred to as a whole under the name "Augustinianism". The works of Augustine are, with those of Thomas Aquinas, the basis and determining influence in the acceptance and application of classical metaphysics within the Judaeo-Christian tradition. This application, nevertheless, was accomplished in different ways at the hands of both men, and thus ever since the 13th century Augustine's influence had largely been determined by its relation to Thomism. Augustinianism refers in a narrower sense to certain philosophical and theological theses which are based upon actual or purported works of Augustine.

B. Life and Work of Augustine

Along with some biographical data, we shall give here in outline the main aspects of Augustine's thought, which may help to provide a consistent explanation of his historical influence. The course of his great spiritual Odyssey, so uniquely chronicled in the famous *Confessions*, led him from the Christian faith in which his mother Monica had reared him through a period of aimless passions brought on by the reading of Cicero's *Hortensius* (now lost), to the religion of Mani (Manicheism). Though he remained a Manichean for eleven years, he finally abandoned Manicheism in his disillusioned search for truth, to lapse then into a phase of fundamental scepticism. Through the study of neo-Platonism and his acquaintance with Ambrose of Milan he drew ever closer to Christianity, until finally, at the climax of a long and intense inward crisis, he decided – under the influence of his reading of the Letter to the Romans – to accept the Christian faith and to lead a monastic life. Being baptized at the hands of Ambrose, he then retired from his position as teacher of rhetoric and returned to Africa, settling in Hippo. Most of his works were composed in Hippo, of which he was elected bishop in 396. His *Confessions* inform us in detail of the development of his way of life, and an accurate list of his own works is to be found in his *Retractions*. Other works of his which should be mentioned are the *Soliloquia*, *De Libero*

Arbitrio, De Vera Religione, De Trinitate, Enarrationes in Psalm I–XXXII (the title was given by Erasmus), and the *De Civitate Dei*.

Augustine never received a systematic scholarly education but was essentially a self-taught man; and it is this which gives to his thought a genuinely independent cast and to his language a spontaneous vitality. His works were produced not out of scholarly interest alone but as a result of his involvement in the discussions and disputes of his day. In the question of grace, for example, he develops his theses with reference to Pelagianism, and in the teaching upon the sacraments it was the Donatist dispute which stimulated and determined his writings on that subject. His philosophical and theological principles were conceived in the course of his encounter with the neo-Platonists. As his thought was thus constantly pursued in the course of his varied dialogue with travelling companions, friends, and opponents, and also under the influence of his progressive dialogue with his God, Augustine never produced a self-contained system. His thought and writing were determined by and correspond to the concerns of a given situation. Nevertheless, the history of his dialogues is the history of his truly fundamental search for truth. It is this constant questioning, ever stimulated by his original experience of truth, of God, which is the source of his life and thought. It is from such experience that he derived the insight that man need not fly to that which is without, but only to return to that which is within: "in you yourself does the truth dwell". It is more intimate than one is to oneself. In the consciousness of this most intimate relation of the understanding of the self and of truth he is led to say (addressing God): "When I recognize myself, I recognize You!"

Point of departure for Augustine's thought. Such experiences of God, of truth in his sense, led Augustine to develop his ideas on illumination. Here he proposes that that which makes man what he is, is primarily his relation to truth; in all knowledge "truth" is also known as the indispensable light of consciousness; and in every activity its goodness is willed, as the necessary life of all freedom. Truth, in the form of illumination and the source of vitality, is not something which is possessed by man, like a fixed attribute or condition of reason. For Augustine it is rather an event – the confrontation of man with God. Truth is thus in one way the constant illumination of man by God, to which man, however, does not always actually respond in his free decisions (because of his original sinfulness); and in another way it is those individual instances of illumination in which the glory of God, both judging and forgiving, is experienced as salvation. God is present to a man as the *mysterium tremendum ac fascinosum*, and is experienced in both the dread and the happiness of man's heart, the *acies mentis*. Man experiences himself as one addressed in an I-Thou dialogue with his divine partner. In Aristotelian metaphysics the absolute ground, the being of beings, is part of the universe, immanent to the spirit or to the world, where it is the permanent principle of order: the κόσμος νοητός is not "other-worldly" in relation to the κόσμος αἰσθητός. In Platonism there is at least a presentiment of a living God who is the "wholly other" but who nonetheless draws nigh to man as person to person. But Augustine clearly recognized that man is constituted as such by the call of God. Illumination is a dialogue in which the transcendence and the historicity of man are realized at the same moment. The history of transcendence and of freedom are the two dimensions which Augustine had to add to Greek thought, while making their immanence radical. Such a penetrating grasp of the relationship between transcendence and history, conceived of as dialogue and event, seems not to have been attained even by Thomas Aquinas. For Augustine the relationship was perfected in God's becoming man while man became man.

Having thus briefly sketched the permanent principle and framework of the life and thought of Augustine, we may at least catalogue the specific teaching and positions which Augustine adopted in the course of his work. These positions cannot here be presented as they proceeded from the original context of Augustine's thought, but will simply be treated in the terminology by which they were developed and handed down in the course of dogmatic theology even though such language does not always correspond fully to the original purposes of Augustine.

Main teachings. a) Augustine applied his speculative abilities most intensively to the teaching on the Trinity. He developed the conception of the divine persons as subsistent relations, proceeding from a consideration of the nature (*essentia*) of God, and not from the Father as origin – in contrast to the approach of the Greek Fathers. Augustine explains the generation of the Son and the procession of the Holy Spirit from the Father and from the Son as being analogous to processes of mental life, such as the act of speaking and that which is spoken. The possibility of a self-revelation of God *ad extra* is attributed to the three divine persons in the *same* way, which is to propound, according to sense if not in actual words, the appropriation-theory.

b) In his works on grace and predestination, composed before his consecration as bishop, Augustine interpreted the relationship set up by revelation between the free personal God and man as one to which man's activity made an essential contribution. Later he was to restrict all salutary value to the activity of grace alone, asserting that the will of man is itself totally impotent unless assisted by God. Goodness and badness, belief and unbelief, salvation or reprobation – all is made to depend so much on the divine will that those who are saved by a sovereign and inscrutable act of God attain to blessedness independently of meritorious deeds; while the rest, because of the "passivity" of God, are eternally lost. There is no wrong done to them as no one has any claim upon salvation after the Fall and original sin. Thus, Augustine recognizes a predestination to blessedness according to which God grants to the elect even the gift of perseverance, and also a predestination – not *ad peccatum* – but *ad sempiternum interitum* (*Tract. in Jo.*, 48, 46). He thereby limited the salvific will of God. According to Augustine, the absolute justice of God must be upheld even when it is impossible to explain how it is that he is just.

c) In Christology Augustine anticipates the teaching of Ephesus (431) and Chalcedon (451), according to which there are two natures (*substantiae*) in Christ. He is God and man but only one person – the Logos, the second divine person. Augustine's soteriology, which is not consistent, is determined by his conviction that through the sin of Adam the devil obtained the right to tempt man to his undoing. But this right was then abolished through the death of Christ. The devil was caught in the "trap" of the cross. Attacking Christ as though he had a claim upon him, which in fact he did not have, he forfeited his right and thus man can be delivered from the snares of the devil.

d) In his ecclesiology Augustine sees those who have received Christ's grace and redemption as forming the *one* community of the Church. He accepts the principle *salus extra eccelsiam non est*; and the Church is to be recognized through its unity, holiness, and apostolicity. In its totality it forms the body of Christ. In this sense there is an invisible Church as well as the visible one. Hence, outward membership is no guarantee of salvation, and conversely, those who are not members of the visible Church through no fault of their own, may in fact be among its invisible members.

e) In antiquity, history was sometimes conceived of after the pattern of physics, where nature eternally repeated its cycles. But Augustine saw man and his history as constituted by the confrontation with and the relation to the God who is transcendent to history. Human history begins with the "illumination" and is to end with the perfect revelation of God. The meaning of history is the revelation of God and union with him. Human history is thus the story of the acceptance or the rejection of God in Jesus Christ, the history of salvation or damnation. Only those events are meaningful by which God enters into the affairs of the world; the history of iniquity will remain impenetrable and will only be revealed in its full meaning at the end of time. The majority of men belong to the *civitas terrena*, the *civitas diaboli*. The *civitas Dei* is the community of the elect and the redeemed. But no concrete community or institution in history can be identified with either of these titles. The Church and the State, for example, are *civitates permixtae*, and the Church itself is only the prefiguration of the *civitas Dei* to be fully revealed at the end of time.

C. AUGUSTINE'S INFLUENCE

The general approach and the main tenets of Augustine's thought reveal the themes which inspired "Augustinianism": the relation between habitual and actual illumination, the contrast between nature and grace, metaphysical order and salvific events, empirical knowledge of the world and experience of God in dialogue, and finally the relation between reason and revelation, philosophy and theology in general. But those who took over his rich and comprehensive thought had not the same penetrating insight, and soon after his death many themes were taken out of their context and treated in isolation. The darker side of Augustine also remained influential: the dualism of his esteem and scorn for the body, his love for man and also a certain contempt for him – a dualism which was finally projected upon God (as the notion of predestination shows). These gloomier aspects are to be understood in the light of his whole development, and have only a relative value in the light of his personality as a whole. But their effects may be seen in many of the ascetical, pastoral and even philosophical and theological trends which invoke Augustine most zealously.

Patristic period and the Middle Ages. Even within the lifetime of Augustine disputes arose with regard to his teaching on grace, between Semi-Pelagians and "Predestinarians". The Pelagianizers advocated synergistic ideas, while the latter stressed Augustine's view of the depravity of human nature and the essential role of grace in the freedom to do good. The Augustinian notion of the absolute efficacy of grace (*gratia irresistibilis*) was reinforced, and joined to the doctrine of the non-universal salvific will of God. The image of the God working in the background given by the champions of predestination who invoked Augustine, seemed sinister to their contemporaries. Such a "terrifying concept of God" (Altaner) was bound to lead to dispute and demanded clarification. At the Council of Orange in 529 the official decision was in favour of a "moderate Augustinianism". Against the Semi-Pelagians the Council defended the necessity of grace for the initial movement towards salvation, that is, for the first conversion of the will towards God and the *initium fidei* and hence the necessity of grace for the healing of human nature as such (*D* 176f.; 186). The conception of the limited saving will of God was abandoned, though the predestination tendency was again to appear three centuries later in the teaching of Gottschalk of Orbais (d. *c.* 867) in a very pronounced form. In the name of Augustine, whom he called *maximus post apostolos Ecclesiarum instructor* and upon whose Anti-Pelagian positions he especially based himself, Gottschalk proposed with great vigour and stubbornness the thesis of total predestination: to blessedness as well as to damnation. At the two Synods of Quiercy (849 and 853), convened to deal with this problem, Gottschalk and his teaching were severely condemned. Finally, at the Synods of Savonnier (859) and Toncy (860), the moderate Augustinianism was again reaffirmed and was to remain the basic tendency in Scholasticism and in theology in general.

Early Scholasticism. Similarly, in the debates of early Scholasticism, the opposing parties based themselves upon Augustine: from Anselm of Canterbury (d. 1109) to Abelard (d. 1142), from Peter Damian (d. 1072) to Bernard of Clairvaux (d. 1153). For Anselm, Hugo of St. Victor (d. 1141), and Peter Lombard (d. 1160), Augustine was the authority most frequently quoted. Through the *Sentences* of Peter Lombard, which was the basis for many commentaries in succeeding periods and which finally came to be used as a general textbook, many quotations from Augustine became a classical heritage. Through this tradition Augustine's teaching on the Trinity and his stress on the primacy of love over knowledge (the *bonum* before the *verum*) were especially influential and together created an attitude in which the life of faith could give rise to a theocentric union of theology and philosophy.

Classical period of Scholasticism. This period was ushered in by the discovery of the work of Aristotle, as handed down by the Arabian philosophers and their Latin translators. In a remarkably short period this teaching was so widely adopted that from that time on, along with the hitherto undisputed authority of Augustine, there was a new master finally quoted by Aquinas simply as "the Philosopher". Aristotelian philosophy had the effect of disjoining philosophy from revelation, at least in principle, and of creating a separate discipline. It thus stimulated the development of a logically conceptualist method within theology. It was inevitable that this revolution should lead to conflicts. And for the first time the followers of Augustine, faced with the adoption of Aristotle by the Thomists, had to consider themselves simply as "Augustinians". They sought to protect theology from being appropriated by merely natural knowledge. The Aristotelian analysis of abstraction which Thomas took up and further developed in the sense of the transcendence of the human spirit for infinite being, seemed to the Augustinianists to lose sight completely of the old concept of illumination. They felt in general that the value of the world for theology was too strongly stressed. A climax in the dispute of Augustinianism with Aristotelianism, in the form of the Averroism of Siger of Brabant (d. 1282) and also in the adaptations of Albertus Magnus (d. 1280) and Thomas Aquinas (d. 1274), was the condemnation of several Aristotelian-Thomistic theses by the Bishop of Paris, Stephan Tempier, in 1277. This restricted the influence of the new school (which, however, by no means excluded Augustinian thought, Augustine being one of the authorities most frequently quoted by Thomas), and Augustinianism had scored a victory. But a profound rethinking of it could not be long delayed. The Augustinianists tried gradually to combine the theory of illumination and of abstraction, the latter being allowed validity with regard to the understanding of worldly experience. Augustine's doctrine of the "seminal forms" (*rationes seminales*) which God implanted within matter as intrinsic principles at the beginning of time, was the starting-point of the discussion, together with the concept of the "plurality of forms" whereby the spiritual soul was considered to be the last but not the only essential form of the human body. These are the classical doctrines, as it were, of Augustinianism, in opposition to the Thomistic doctrine of abstraction. Its main proponents at this time were Bonaventure (d. 1274), John Peckham (d. 1294) and William de la Mare (d. 1298).

Late Scholasticism. In this period it was the Augustinian Hermits who preserved the legacy of their master. Giles of Rome (Aegidius Romanus, d. 1316) founded the school of the "Early Augustinians". He achieved a far-reaching reconciliation between the Augustinian and Thomistic positions, though in the process many important interests of Augustinianism were lost sight of. Nevertheless, it was these monks, standing apart from the disputes between the schools of Thomas and Scotus, who occupied themselves with the works of Augustine and who together with the tradition of the Dominican and Franciscan Orders formed the link between Augustine and modern times.

There was a growing interest in the Middle Ages in thoughts developed in the *De Civitate Dei* with regard to the relations between Church and State. But the *civitas caelestis* (which Augustine had understood eschatologically) came to be more and more identified with the institution of the Church, as was the *civitas terrena* with the temporal State. According to this interpretation, the Church was to represent the *civitas caelestis* in political matters and also to be the last judge of the secular state. This "political Augustinianism" was of great historical importance. It gave rise, after the collapse of the Roman Empire, to the notion of an empire universal enough to absorb all individual kingdoms. Through the theocratic ideas of Charlemagne, this finally issued in the medieval notion of the Holy Roman Empire, which was regarded as the manifestation of the *corpus Christi*. The unique authority of Augustine was used in the ideological opposition between papacy and empire. In the course of this struggle between crown and tiara for the *plenitudo potestatis*, the Decretalists of the 13th and 14th centuries, who regarded the Augustinian writings as a source for canonic papal law, used Augustine just as much as did William of Occam when championing the national State and opposing absolute curial power. So too later, when the reform of the papacy was being urged on all sides, both parties appealed to Augustine, the Conciliarists as well as those who claimed that reform was a matter for the central authorities of the Curia. Although Augustine's thought was treated in this debate in a distorted ideological way, the constant invocation of his authority assured him of great influence in the development of social and political theory.

Modern times. Augustine was of great importance to the Reformers (which started a new Augustinian tradition, that of Protestantism), and the Council of Trent was strongly influenced by the medieval Augustinian tradition. The controversy about the Augustinian doctrine of grace broke out once more in France with Baianism, Jansenism and Quesnel, extreme positions being defended both as regards the goodness and the depravity of human nature. Henry Noris formed a school of Later Augustinianism, in opposition to the Jansenists. The interpretation of Augustine's teaching on grace put forward by this group was finally held to be as valid as that of Thomas and Molina, which gives freedom greater play. The dispute concerning grace which had already arisen in the life-time of Augustine, and which was always resolved in favour of a moderate form of Augustinianism, was thus cleared up as regards the extreme positions, though the question itself has remained basically undecided and open to the present day. It was at this time that the first scholarly editions of the works of Augustine were published and thus for the first time the question of the "real" Augustine arose. This is the main question in the present discussion of Augustine and it is channelling studies into a critical analysis of the history of Augustinian tradition.

The basic Augustinian positions were taken up as the fundamental philosophical questions by German idealism, and considered in terms of its revolutionary transcendental approach. Great speculative energy was applied, for instance, to the great themes of the relationship between (or the primacy of) the theoretical and/or practical reason, faith and knowledge, life and concepts. The great insights of Augustine into the relation between self-understanding and the understanding of revelation, between transcendence and history, are here both confirmed to a great extent and more thoroughly systematized and enunciated. Similarly, in the life-philosophy and in existentialism Augustinian insights are found, e.g., with regard to the significance of concrete life as opposed to all merely abstract conceptuality, and the "historical" understanding of self and of being, as opposed to merely static and generalized concepts of essences and orders. The analysis of existence employed in this type of thought, oriented primarily upon phenomena, has heightened the sense of personal decision and responsibility and also brought more to the fore the misery and perils of personal existence as such. Present-day theology, influenced as it has been by German idealism and by existentialism, has a new regard for Augustine, as it evaluates its transcendental and existential elements in its pursuit of its dialogue with God.

Eberhard Simons

AUTHORITY

A. Modern Man and Authority

Men are ambivalent towards authority today. They are credulous when experts speak and avid for commanding personalities who they hope have the secret of prosperity. They are buoyed up by the past achievements of specialists and recognize that a process of collectivization is at work which needs first-class guidance. They are sometimes ready to accord disproportionate value to the pronouncements of specialists even outside their own spheres. But men are also distrustful of authority, feeling there a vague threat to their personal life. They know of the abuses of authority and are uncomfortable under its totalitarian trends.

Nonetheless, the continual extension of authority is inevitable in this age of technology, with its new powers of control and need of co-ordinated effort. The sciences, from biology to sociology, make it so easy to manipulate public and private life that at times the exercise of freedom is drastically curtailed. Even the Churches can mould opinion massively, right down to the realm of conscience. The growing complexity of modern culture and the greater interdependence of its members also demand greater efforts at co-ordination. It is becoming more and more difficult for the individual to survey the whole of society and its structures and hence he is more and more dependent on the authority which mediates to him the achievements of the age – and also suffers more from the incompetence of authority. Men also feel that the authorities themselves are unsure of the future. The profound "crisis of authority" is therefore understandable.

An antidote is sought in the conferring of greater responsibility on the individual and a general "democratization". In the Church, it is emphasized that the layman has "come of age". In education, the relationship of teacher and student is being revised in terms of partnership, and the role of authority is being reconsidered. This is the general background to the problem of authority today.

B. Definition

1. The word authority is from the Latin *auctoritas*, from *auctor* (cause, sponsor, promoter, surety), from *augere* (to increase [transitive and intransitive], to enrich). It is hardly accidental that the term comes from Roman culture, with its sober rule of law. *Auctoritas* was the legal term for a surety in a transaction, responsibility for a minor, the weight of an opinion. It then came to mean the respect, dignity and importance of the person concerned. Later, the Senate had an institutional "authority", which had to be heard – though this authority did not exercise the power of governing. Nowadays "authority" is attributed to persons with special abilities and prestige or with an official function in society. The former may be called subjective or personal, the latter objective or official.

2. Personal authority comes from the recognition of someone's superiority in a given sphere. It exists in so far as it is respected. For this a personal moral decision is needed.

3. Official authority is the authority which a person has, not by reason of his personal superiority, but by reason of a function conferred on him or at least respected by society. It is desirable that the wielder of such authority should also have personal authority, but since it is based essentially on its role in the good of society, its range and nature must be determined by its function, and not by the bearer's qualities. An office sanctioned by society and hence legitimate, can impose obligations and so be "authoritative" even when the office-holder is inadequate and unworthy. But the exercise of such authority is confined to his function in society – within which he can claim recognition.

4. It is only in a derivative sense (going back to personal or official authority) that we can speak of "something", like a book, an institution, a code of laws or a symbol, having authority. Their claims are founded on the "subject's" personal relationship to the authorities which they embody in some way. If such "authorities" are honoured, it is the persons behind them that are honoured. At times, as for instance in American culture, the symbols are more respected than the wielders of authority. This is probably due to a fear of an exaggerated cult of personalities.

C. The Nature of Authority

Authority is therefore the subjective or objective superiority of certain persons, by which they are entitled to make demands on others. It is formally an exigent superiority. It appears as valuable in itself for the authority's fellow-men. It is ontologically valuable in so far as it shares in the fullness of God's being and can thus impart its own fullness to those under it, and so help them to greater fulfilment. Authority comes from God and has a right to exist only in so far as it possesses and mediates perfection which it does by its transparency to the divine demand on man, that he should be perfect as our heavenly Father is perfect.

Authority can only exist with respect to intellectual beings. Man's freedom and reason are addressed by authority. It appeals to the free assent of the person. For its task is to further the fulfilment of man by demanding personal involvement from him. Hence authority must be fully integrated into the freedom of the subject's decision.

Thus authority must be distinguished from power and coercion. Power is the ability to exercise one's own freedom without the previous consent of the other and so alter the conditions of his decisions. Coercion or force further implies that one's will is imposed on another contrary to his will. Knowledge, for instance, confers authority where one can reckon on a hearing by reason of one's knowledge. Knowledge confers power in so far as it makes it possible to intervene in another's situation without his consent and create a mentality which prevents him from treating a problem in the usual way or in the way he originally intended. Hence authority begins where it is freely recognized and ends where it becomes power. And it is obviously typical of authority that it addresses itself to freedom. Authority is exercised on children only in so far as they are free, reasoning agents, and cannot be exercised over beasts or the insane. And real authority does not compel, but persuades. It appeals to the moral element of man, and can be exercised only in so far as subjects are capable of moral actions. But since imperfect man is only capable to a limited extent of moral actions, it may at times be right and necessary to influence others by power and coercion. But this is precisely not an authoritative procedure. To have authority is not just the same as to rule, lead, educate or exercise power. There is a certain polarity here. Rule should strive to become ruling authority and so on. But on this sinful earth this identification will never be total, and all the elements must be continually employed to complete each other.

Hence official authority, with its rights, privileges and power, does not summon the individual directly to free action. What it demands first is the recognition of the justification or necessity of the group in question, and then the recognition of the authority serving this organization. For the immediate foundation of official authority is the priority of society over its individual members. It follows that authority is a function of society and not vice versa, that it is limited by the needs of society which define its claims. To belong freely to a certain organization or necessarily to a society means that one freely acknowledges authority or at least necessarily respects it. But real authority exists for the subjects only in so far as they accept willingly the necessary social order. The anarchist rejects all official authority because he rejects social directives for his freedom. It remains true that official authority summons man to freedom, in its own ways.

It follows that authority is always in the service of others and their freedom. Its object is always to help men to attain their personal values and their full manhood. It embodies the claim of an end to which it and its subjects are ordained. This end is human, and therefore personal fulfilment. And it is this which gives authority its dignity and validity. The authority of reason, for instance, represents the claims of truth, which we strive after for its own sake. It serves truth by trying to establish and explain it. Parental authority represents the claims of human maturity – of the adult who is of himself adequate to his various tasks. This is the end and object of education, and parental authority serves it by helping the child to free itself from the slavery of instinct, ignorance and helplessness in order to reach mature independence.

Human nature calls for such authority because man is not only a person but a free creature of undefined possibilities who must become a "personality" in his historical development. Basically both a social being and an individual, he is further ordained to find his fulfilment in dependence on others –

through mutually complementary functions of rule and obedience in society. Here it is well to remember that authority can sin and make mistakes. It does not always lead automatically to fulfilment, as is too readily assumed in classical interpretations of authority.

Like everything human, the measure of excellence in authority is its ordination to God, and its success in ordaining its subjects to God. Because of the relative autonomy of the earthly, this orientation to God must conform to the intrinsic laws of the various limited fields where authority is exercised. To exaggerate the transcendence of authority would lead to a pseudo-consecration of it and impede its proper functioning in the world. But neglect of the relationship to God would lead to a total absolutism and the arbitrary manipulation of subjects, since earthly authorities would proudly treat contingent values as absolutes. How in the concrete authority is to be ordained to God cannot be determined *a priori*, since we can only see *a posteriori* how it contributes to man's fulfilment and hence represents the will of God. This is because its tasks change as potentialities change. And the constant change of potentiality is determined by the history and historicity of freely developing man.

Two functions of authority may be deduced from its role in helping man to his fulfilment.

1. Authority functions as a substitute (improperly) in a tutelary role. This is exercised when it helps those who are non-adult in any respect to reach their goal – a goal of which they would have been frustrated through lack of the autonomy which would have made the intervention of authority superfluous. As long as children, for instance, cannot be responsible for their own destiny, their parents must guide it – to educate them to independence and thus prevent disaster. Or again, where men cannot assure their basic rights to health, work or education, the State may enforce fitting laws, e.g., compulsory schooling, social security for the sick and aged, prevention of alcoholism, etc. Otherwise those under authority could themselves make their autonomous development impossible. Such authority seeks to persuade, though it can take compulsory powers in the interests of those entrusted to it.

It should be the effort of such "vicarious" authority to make itself superfluous, since only thus can it attain its real goal. Hence educators, the State, and all other authorities must grant as much freedom as possible and develop the spirit of independence, while using compulsion where necessary, but even here leaving as much scope as possible to freedom. We call vicarious authority in this sense "improper", since its task is to eliminate itself and it works by methods of compulsion – though force is used only to make force avoidable. But in many cases the imperfection of man and the necessity of the goal in view will mean that coercive authority can never fully eliminate itself. In one respect or another we all need care of a paternal or maternal kind, and hence of an authoritative nature.

2. But authority also has a permanent function which must be considered its essential task. It always has the task of regulating and organizing, when its goal demands the co-ordination of the persons affected by it. This is perhaps clearest in the State's task with regard to "objective culture", which we understand as the totality of the citizens' individual contributions, as co-ordinated by the State for the common good. The diversity of individual functions must not be a source of division. They must be distributed and directed towards the necessary ends. A unity of action must be realized, and the objective culture must further the subjective culture of the individuals. Hence order is the formal element of society, that is, the many are properly directed to the

one end. Society is a unity of order, and, as Aquinas says, the chief task of authority in society is the preservation of order.

The need for authoritative order grows with the diversity of elements of which a society is composed. A highly cultured society is less homogeneous than a primitive one. To regulate and order all its elements to one end demands a much more complex organization. All progress makes the preservation of order more difficult, and demands a more complicated structure of the measures and institutions which we call society. Hence the essential task of social authority is not based on the inadequacies of its members, but corresponds to social progress.

Hence the members of society whose initiatives and self-fulfilment promote objective culture are not in opposition to social life, but rather enrich it. If personal initiatives are suppressed rather than favoured by the State, diversification, that is, the source of a rich and fruitful life, is also suppressed (L. Janssens).

The greater the evolution of a society, the more necessary authority becomes. The maturer an objective culture is, the more freely can the individual develop. And the more fully personal initiative is given play, the stronger the objective culture will be. Hence freedom and authority, when rightly used, are not opposed but complementary. They involve one another, because both serve man by reverencing the person and personal values, and hence ultimately God.

D. Conclusions

Each personal value must be served by authority in the appropriate way. Hence the one formal concept of authority has various analogous applications. Parental authority, which is concerned with the family unit and the education of children, has another scope than that of the teacher, who takes on tasks which the parents cannot execute. State authority is different from that of the Church, the former aiming at the temporal good of all, the latter serving a supernatural end. The task of any particular authority can only be determined when general notion and concrete end are compared. The more concretely the goal can be envisaged (*a posteriori*), the more exact the authoritative measures can be. Hence the tasks of Church or State should properly be discussed in connection with the doctrine on the Church and so on.

The analogous character of the various forms of authority can hardly be stressed strongly enough. It results in very varied forms of the exercise of authority, in keeping with the varied ends. If this had been borne in mind throughout Church history, the Church could not have borrowed so many of its outward forms and so much of its self-understanding from the State (cf. Y. Congar). The application of *societas perfecta* to the Church and to the State should also be considered in this connection. Discussion of the specific tasks of the various forms of authority is proceeding, but not with the same speed in each case.

A second point to note is that authority must not only respect freedom, it must promote it, avoiding authoritarian measures which would degrade it to mere power or coercion. Power does not promote freedom, and coercion ends it. Authoritarian procedures generally reflect pride and arrogance, or an inferiority complex. True authority is aware of its limitations and tries the method of persuasion, respecting the personal dignity and the fundamental equality of those it addresses. It therefore also seeks to temper the social inequalities which may arise in the various order of those under authority.

The service which authority gives to men consists in the exercise of authority, as it fulfils its task of educating, sanctifying, organizing and so on. The danger is always that the authority will not be exercised. For it must contribute to the individual's personal development inwardly and essentially as well as outwardly and accidentally. The *laissez faire* policy of classical liberalism, and the naturalism of the Enlightenment, with nature doing everything well, overlooked the real freedom of man – which has to integrate the laws of nature into his personality, by autonomous decisions which are not always basically correct. Authority comes in here, with its pressures and its appeal to reason and freedom. Not to give due authoritative directives would be to hinder or waste the potentialities of the subjects. Since authority is equally responsible to the values it represents and to the men it seeks to persuade, the golden rule is *fortiter in re et suaviter in modo*. Success depends on the degree of synthesis between these values and these subjects. The reason for neglect of authoritative functions is generally a selfish disregard of others' needs or a feeling of inadequacy in the wielder of authority. Moral theology has put a great deal of emphasis on the proper obedience of subordinates. But the ethics of authority and command have been to a great extent neglected (cf. A. Müller). A full study should include the findings of modern management experts (cf. H. Hartmann). The way authority is exercised as a service depends, of course, on the service to be done, since the love which serves takes many forms. The function of authority as service is stressed particularly in the NT. Lk 22:24–27, for instance, tells the master to be like a servant, and Jn 13:1–17 makes the washing of the feet by the Lord an example for the disciples.

The authority which comes from God and is ordained to God will always try to preserve equilibrium among its contrasting elements by making its relationship to God as clear as possible, thus putting its pre-eminence and dignity in the proper light. It will therefore strive ultimately not for loyalty towards itself, but towards our absolute origin and end. In a democracy, for instance, the absolute supremacy of the will of the people would in certain cases be the supremacy of the wilfulness of the people. The people can determine who are to wield political authority, but the authority of the leaders does not come from the people but from God ("designation theory"), to whom the official rulers are therefore ultimately responsible. It is in this sense that the Syllabus of Pius IX opposed certain positivistic views and condemned the proposition that "authority is nothing but the sum-total of numbers and of material forces" (*D* 1760). This is also true of other forms of authority, *mutatis mutandis*. An earthly authority which does not point beyond itself becomes demonic and will show itself as arbitrary naked power.

The response to authority will be faith, obedience, reverence and so on, corresponding to the type of authority in question. But the ambivalence of earthly authority and its intrinsic connection with historical change makes it always necessary for authority to rely on dialogue with those entrusted to it. Otherwise it will miss its goal, which is to serve men and the absolute authority of God – which last it can never represent except in an analogous way.

Waldemar Molinski

B

BAPTISM

I. Sacrament of Baptism

It is difficult for us today to feel the resonant joy in the opening words of Tertullian's *De Baptismo*: "Felix sacramentum aquae nostrae" – the bliss of the oath of allegiance taken in the sacramental water. For the early Christians baptism was the conscious and blessed beginning of the Christian life, a new birth and a re-birth in the image of Christ, accomplished by bathing in water while a few words were uttered. With all the simplicity of a divine act, in contrast to the pomp of the initiation rites in pagan religions, "the washing of water with the word" (Eph 5:26) brought about something incredibly magnificent, the life of eternity (cf. Tertullian, *op. cit.*, 1–2).

Nonetheless, the content of our belief is the same. For the Christian of today baptism is still the entrance to all the sacraments, the gate to Christian life and hence to the eternal life which is its ultimate, eschatological consequence. Baptism blots out original sin and all personal sins, makes the Christian sharer of the divine nature through sanctifying grace, gives the adoption of sons, calls him and entitles him to the reception of the other sacraments and to share actively in the priestly adoration of the Church. These are abstract formulae which contain vital truths. We must try to penetrate their riches once more, in the light of the original sources of revelation.

A. New Testament and Liturgy

How the apostolic preaching interpreted "washing of water with the word (of life)" is plain to see in the NT.

Words of the Lord. It is intimately bound up with the injunction of the risen Christ: "Go therefore and make disciples of all nations, baptizing them in the name of the Father and of the Son and of the Holy Spirit, teaching them to observe all that I have commanded you" (Mt 28:19f.). These words certainly record the will of the glorified Christ to institute the sacrament of baptism, though the trinitarian formula may be an echo of apostolic practice. The inner meaning of baptism is intimated by the mysterious images our Lord uses in his conversation with Nicodemus (Jn 3:1–10). These, of course, are fully intelligible only to one who has experienced Christian baptism. At any rate the reception of baptism is regarded from the beginning as the foundation of all discipleship and Christian life (Acts 2:37–41 and *passim*). After the descent of the Holy Spirit at the first Pentecost, the apostles looked upon baptism as a rite already hallowed by tradition and administered it as such. Attempts to show that baptism was borrowed from the religions of the Hellenistic world have been fruitless, but the practice is certainly foreshadowed in the OT.

Earlier analogies. The OT frequently mentions practices analogous to baptism (which took the form of washings; among other texts see Exod 40:12; Lev 8:6; 13:6; 14:4–9; 16:4, 24; Ezek 36:25). In the time of Christ such "baptisms", that is, washings, were much in use (Mk 7:2–4); Jewish sects like the Essenes made much of them (Josephus, *Jewish War*, 2, 117–61) and they were a special feature of Qumran (*1 QS*, 6, 16f.; 3, 4–9). It is easier to understand the "baptism of John" against this background, though he contributed important new features: as an emissary of God he baptized *others* to call them in repentance, in preparation for a nobler baptism to come. Jesus' disciples baptized during his lifetime in an obviously similar manner (Jn 4:1–3).

Apostolic practice. But after the glorification of the Lord the apostles administered the traditional rite in a new way and with a new import; they now baptized in the name of Jesus, that is, in accordance with the gospel in the name of Jesus, assigning men to him, invoking his name over the candidate. Finally (a further development), they baptized in the name of the Father, Son, and Holy Spirit. (The continuity of usage emerges in Acts 18:25–26 and 19:2–6, where the transition to the new form is indicated.) The washing with water and the word is the climax of a whole process: penance and faith are perfected in baptism. With this procedure, because it intimately unites one with Christ, come salvation, the remission of sins, and the gifts of the Holy Spirit. Christ is the light which shines in baptism; he is the life that it bestows, the truth that the baptized person confesses and to which he pledges his loyalty, the source whence flow the rivers of living water, the water and the blood from the open wound in his side. They wash away all the guilt of a man's sins.

Deeper insights. These relatively sparse data from the synoptics, from Acts, and not least from the fourth gospel – when full justice is done to the intentions underlying its composition – are admirably expounded in other books of the NT especially in St. Paul, 1 John, and 1 Peter. These books work out a theology of the washing of water with the word, as a unique personal and sacramental act that confers "being-in-Christ", which is the sum of Christian existence. For "you were buried with him in baptism, in which you were also raised with him through faith in the working of God, who raised him from the dead" (Col 2:12). Fruitful controversy in recent years has again brought these results to the fore. Passing over minor obscurities and differences of interpretation, this article will simply be concerned with what was arrived at in common as part of the faith. The essential thing, then, is that by baptism, when we were dead through our trespasses and sins, God who is rich in mercy, out of the great love with which he loved us, made us alive together with Christ, and raised us up with him, and made us sit with him in the heavenly places in Christ Jesus (Eph 2:1, 4–6). For all its noble simplicity, the rite of initiation through the washing of water with the word – so that we may gain salvation by the forgiveness of sins and the gift of the Holy Spirit – conveys several truths. First of all, baptism is the culmination of a man's personal encounter with God in Christ, of his personal response to the appeal of God's word. "So those who received his word were baptized" (Acts 2:41). In order to be baptized one must obey the word, listen to it: "Repent" (Acts 2:38), and respond to the good news Jesus brings: "Yes, I believe that Jesus Christ is the Son of God." (Acts 8:37, the Western reading.) Baptism bodies forth the faith which is the fundamental way of our living in Christ; without faith it would be a lifeless outward show. But it is more than a "symbolic" expression of active faith; the washing by water in the word is real access to Christ and his redemption; it is "being baptized into his death", it is dying with him and rising with him, truly sharing his sufferings, so that becoming like him in his death we may attain the resurrection from the dead (see Phil 3:10f.).

Another important aspect of baptism is that of purification. Washing of water with the word cleanses the Church (Eph 5:26); as this pure water sprinkles the body it cleanses our hearts from an evil conscience (see Heb 10:22). Sharing in Christ's death, being purified in the sacred waters that flow forth from him, brings about fellowship with the living Christ, a new life; one is a new creation, born again, enjoying even now a share in his resurrection that will be perfected in the eschatological future when the Lord returns. All this is reality, but the Christian's faith must apprehend and affirm its fullness in advance, ponder the consequences and accept them in the serious constancy of a truly Christian life. "So (after all that has been said about this reality) you also must consider yourselves dead to sin and alive to God in Christ Jesus." (Rom 6:11.) Baptism, then, must produce the whole breadth and depth of a life rooted and grounded in Christ (Eph 3:16–19). In Rom 6:12–14 the apostle forcefully points out the practical ethical consequences of baptism. What is demanded of the baptized is nothing less than a thoroughgoing conversion. Baptism has given them a completely new being and they must walk – shape their lives – accordingly. The ancient Church took this passage from the "indicative" to the "imperative" in baptism very seriously: "it is impossible to restore again to repentance those who have once been enlightened (in baptism), who have tasted the heavenly gift, and have become partakers of the Holy Spirit, and have tasted the goodness of the word of God and the powers of the age to come, if they then commit apostasy" (Heb 6:4–6). We cannot here examine the problem of penance after baptism; but Heb 6:4–6 shows what weight was then attached to the obligations imposed by baptism.

The baptismal liturgy. The evolution of the baptismal liturgy now reveals the riches of that simple but mighty action. We are able to trace it thanks to Justin's *Apology* (I, 61), Tertullian's treatise on baptism, and in particular Hippolytus's *Apostolic Tradition* (*c.* A.D. 200). First comes a lengthy catechetical preparation of the candidates; next an immediate preparation of fasting, prayer, and solemn promises; then the solemnity of baptism itself. Baptism proper is an actual bath in flowing water. The candidate is thrice immersed, and each time one of the divine names is pronounced (*epiclesis*). Finally come the anointings and the imposition of hands. The new Christian is now admitted to the common worship of the faithful, to the kiss of peace, and to the Eucharist.

These basic lines were kept unchanged subsequently. The ritual added a confession of faith, the renunciation of Satan and the baptismal promises. The central act of baptizing and the ceremonies that follow were re-moulded. The catechumenate included a series of scrutinies. After a certain amount of fluctuation this liturgy then settled into the form we now have in the Roman Ritual.

The basic structure. The basic structure of baptism remains quite visible even when its liturgy has fully evolved: faith and penance as personal acts of the adult candidate; the sacramental power of ablution in the name of God; immersion, that is, insertion into the death of

Christ so that our sins being forgiven, we may live a new life in Christ, the earnest and the beginning of eternal life, symbolized by the white garment, the burning candle, the admonition, "Preserve thy baptism". These things remind us that when the Lord returns we must go to meet him with our lamps alight.

All this imagery is fraught with meaning for the adult candidate. The baptism of adults is presupposed throughout the NT and the early Christian period.

Infant baptism. As yet we find no references to the baptism of young children. But this is no proof, of course, that the practice was unknown. Infant baptism developed naturally out of the entirely different circumstances in which Christianity found itself when society had become Christian. It was thought fitting to receive children into the fellowship of Christ and the Church. But no special rite of infant baptism was ever devised. In the early days the baptism of children was something almost "incidental", a sort of appendage to the baptism of adults, which was always the main concern; the catechumenate did not include children. But child baptism became the normal practice from about the 4th or 5th century onwards. The existing rite was slightly modified for the purpose, the various stages coalescing in a continuous ceremony. But basically nothing changed, so that even today through the intermediary of their godparents infants are treated at their baptism as if they were adults: they renounce Satan, confess the faith, and state that they wish to be baptized.

Present practice. Though its outward form may not be altogether appropriate, the present baptismal liturgy of the Latin Church proclaims clearly enough what baptism has been ever since its origin in the NT, namely a sacred action, a washing of water (though now confined to pouring water over the head) with the word, a sharing in the death, burial, and resurrection of Christ, purification by water hallowed in the power of God's name, the remission of all sin, the communication of life, a new birth, adoption as a child of God – but all this ratified by the personal faith, resolution, and obedience of the candidate who undertakes to embody these things in his own life.

In baptism, then, the Church possesses something that is alive and operative. We depend on it; it is the beginning of everything, the source of all our obligations; by uniting us with Christ's death and resurrection it enables us to hope for the great eschatological fulfilment in the future.

B. Baptism in Theological Thought

The early period. It is the riches bestowed in baptism that first engages attention. Descent into the water washes away our old mortality (sin), ascent from the water is the passage from death to life (*Pseudo-Barnabas*; *Shepherd of Hermas*). Thus baptism is a bath that washes away sin, the free remission of the penalties of sin and illumination on the way of salvation. It perfects and seals us, transports us over the frontier of death into the life of Christ (St. Clement).

Origen. As occasion arises, Origen fits these truths into his own profound view of the history of salvation, which was to be so widely influential. Baptism sums up all the OT types and prefigurations which are fulfilled in Christ. As usual Origen upholds the primacy of the interior spiritual order over the outward and visible. Thus ecclesiastical baptism has its true place between the OT (with John the Baptist), and the new heaven and new earth of the end of time. The OT merely hinted at things to come; it will culminate in eschatological baptism "with the Holy Spirit and with fire" (Mt 3:11). The link between the two is the Church's baptism, the fulfilment of the antecedent sign, yet itself a sign of the consummation that is to come, drawing all its force from Christ. Origen does not lose sight of the meaning or absolute necessity of baptism. He simply wishes to insist that the outward form of baptism derives its meaning from the spiritual realities, that Christian baptism fulfils the ancient types, gives us the grace of Christ, and thus bears us onward to the final stage of baptism, the final resurrection from the dead. Origen further stresses that the person being baptized must seek practical understanding of what baptism signifies. Baptism is renunciation, conversion, penance. It completes sacramentally the ascetical death of the catechumen; but "if anyone comes to the washing of water (continuing) in sin, then his sins are not remitted" (21st homily on Luke).

Controversy on heretical baptism. These thoughts, however, remain fragmentary. Practical necessities drew attention to the truth that baptism cannot be repeated. Controversy arose about baptism conferred by schismatics and especially heretics. When a member of such a sect was reconciled, the African and some Eastern Churches rebaptized, whereas the Churches of Rome and Alexandria recognized his "heretical baptism" as valid and merely received him into communion with a solemn laying on of hands. This difference in practice led to open conflict between Cyprian and Pope Stephen I. Both agreed that baptism could not be repeated; the question was whether heretics had validly baptized. Eventually the Roman view prevailed. By defending a primacy of the official and sacramental element, independent of the personal holiness of the minister, even if he belongs to a body that is not the true Church, Rome vindicated the primacy of God's power, which is decisively exercised in baptism regardless of human limitations.

St. Augustine. This principle underlies the theology of baptism which St. Augustine worked out against the heretics of his own time. Augustine reaffirms that since Christ, the author and possessor of baptism, is its real minister, the sacrament is valid even when administered by a heretic; he too confers the Church's baptism, the baptism of Christ, "which is always holy of its own nature and therefore does not belong to those who separate themselves but to that (communion) from which they separate" (*De baptismo*, I, 12, 19). Later, notably during his struggle with the Pelagians and his preoccupation with the problems of infant baptism, he laid even more stress on the objective aspect of the sacrament. Unless a man be in sacramental communication with Christ's redemptive act (fundamentally through baptism, and then through the Eucharist), "he cannot reach the kingdom of God, nor gain salvation and eternal life" (*De peccatorum meritis et remissione et de baptismo parvulorum*, I, 24, 34). On the other hand – and this is the real heritage that comes down to us from the Donatist controversy – Augustine never ceased to inveigh against a mechanical conception of the sacraments. Without faith there can be no sacrament at all. Every sacrament embodies a personal act of faith, at least on the part of the Church: it is a sacrament of this faith, a holy sign of belief in Christ and his salvation; furthermore, though valid of itself, without love it remains barren. Such considerations finally brought it home to Christians that baptism, conferred in the proper form, in the power of Christ who is its real minister, is and remains valid (not, of course, because of any "magic" power in the rite but because of the sustaining faith which gives access to Christ), but that its fruitfulness depends on the dispositions of the recipient, his faith and love. Here are the foundations for the later doctrine, familiar to us today, that baptism imprints an indelible character on the soul.

The mature doctrine. The theology of baptism reached maturity in the 4th and 5th centuries, the classical patristic age. The various strands of NT and early patristic theology are harmoniously interwoven, and an impressive summary of the great mystery of baptism is now found in the baptismal catechesis of the bishops: baptism is that sacred action whereby Christ's redemption, his death, and his resurrection are given to us here and now, initiating us into Christian life by a concrete, tangible, symbolic confession of the faith, so that we may be made conformable to the crucified and risen Lord. What once happened to Christ now happens to us in baptism, so that we may be reborn to a new life; and the Holy Spirit, sent by the risen Lord who sits at the right hand of the Father, fills and consecrates the water, so that this sensible element may wash us immaculate and clothe us in splendour.

The Fathers from Tertullian on call this "washing of water with the word" a *sacramentum* or *mysterium* (μυστήριον), a term they also use for other sacred acts. By the 3rd or 4th century at the latest the word had permanently acquired this technical sense. Baptism is sacrament, an initiation that involves swearing fidelity in the service of Christ (like the oath of allegiance, the sacramentum of the Roman soldier). But since *sacramentum* also took on the fuller force of μυστήριον, it was a sacred act which communicated symbolically what it represented, and moulded the believer to its likeness. As image of the death and resurrection of Christ, the mystery made the believer participate in the Passover of Christ from death to life.

Parallel to this very Pauline theology of baptism into the death of Christ, another conception looms even larger – the impregnation of the baptismal water with the sanctifying power of Christ's spirit. Baptism produces its wonderful effects by the might of the crucified and risen Lord. Invoked during this solemn ceremony – which becomes more and more elaborate as time goes on – he fills the water with the power of his Holy Spirit and fructifies it, so that it may beget new life in the Church: "... may a heavenly offspring, conceived in holiness and re-born into a new creation, come forth from the stainless womb of this divine font" (Roman Missal: rite for the blessing of baptismal water on Holy Saturday).

Scholastic synthesis. This patristic doctrine was then preserved and made more systematic. Thus the schoolmen saw baptism as a holy sign – *sacramentum fidei*, a sacrament of faith which acknowledges and lays hold on Christ and the whole work of our redemption – a sign composed of an element (matter) and certain words (form), which represents our sanctification in a threefold manner: in its cause (which belongs to the historical past but is still efficacious today), the passion of Christ; in the formal being of its grace (which exists in the present but has its archetype in Christ); and in its eschatological fulfilment (which is yet to come and will perfectly conform us to the image of Christ). But at the same time, in the hands of the real author of all salvation, Christ himself, this sign is the instrumental cause of the sanctification it signifies. Christ remains master of his gifts and chooses on occasion to save a soul without the intermediary of the sacraments – as when an unbaptized martyr turns to him in death, or a catechumen dies in the faith but is baptized only in desire.

This analysis of the nature of baptism is followed by an exhaustive treatment of all that relates to the administration, the minister, the recipient, and the effects of the sacrament; its place in the general structure of the seven sacraments of the NT is described.

Much attention is paid to the indelible character which baptism imprints on the soul. It is thought to be because of this character that baptism cannot be repeated. Baptism administered with the right intention is always valid, even when it remains fruitless for want of the proper dispositions in the (adult) baptized. (Such a case does, of course, presuppose a minimum of faith and goodwill, without which no salvation at all can be bestowed.) Validity without fruitfulness is explained by the sacramental character, a mysterious, impersonal, objective gift of grace, a mark of dignity and distinction which foreshadows greater things to come and occupies a middle ground between the outward, merely symbolic sacramental act (the *sacramentum*) and the ultimate inner being of the life of grace (the *res*), as a kind of basic conformation to Christ. St. Thomas ingeniously and suggestively argues – though not all theologians today accept his view – that the character is "a certain power in respect of hierarchical (cultic) acts, that is, dispensing and receiving the sacraments and other things proper to the faithful" (*In Sent.*, IV, d. 4, 1.1 sol.).

The Reformers and Trent. Exaggerating as they did the importance of the word and of fiducial faith, the 16th century Reformers theoretically repudiated the Catholic idea of the sacraments, but in fact shrank from fully implementing the revolutionary logic of their own principle. At any rate (with the exception of the Baptists) they were content to continue baptism, especially infant baptism, as a means of grace in the strict sense of the word. The Council of Trent defended the traditional doctrine as it had developed in the course of the history of dogma: efficacious Christian baptism takes precedence over that of John the Baptist; the washing of water (with the word) must be something physical; rightly administered in accordance with the intention of the Church, baptism is always valid; it is not a mere sign of faith but takes effect *ex opere operato*, that is, by the power of God that is at work in the sacrament (not by the will or sanctity of men); infant baptism too is valid by the same operation of God's power; any repetition of baptism is void; the stress here laid on the power of the sacrament in no way diminishes the necessity for the adult candidate for baptism to approach it in the proper frame of mind; baptism is necessary for salvation; baptismal grace may be lost through serious sin (Sess. 7, Canons on the Sacrament of Baptism, 1–14, *D* 857–70).

C. Modern Theology

These Tridentine decrees are merely designed to set down and secure the traditional faith concerning baptism. Within their framework all of us must try to grasp the positive truth in full measure; it will not do simply to repeat anathemas. Such, however, was the tendency of theologians in the ensuing age; understandably enough, the remarkable achievements of Trent had the effect in practice of narrowing a little their field of vision. But today the situation is quite different. Not only the exigencies of ecumenical dialogue but, even more important, the new vitality that is stirring thanks to liturgical reform and deeper study of God's word, impel us to recast our theology of baptism in an ampler mould, taking full account of Scripture, liturgical experience, and the storehouse of patristic and scholastic theology.

Liturgical renewal. The renewal of the liturgy has given us a keener sense of baptism. We have a deeper understanding of the sacrament itself, a sacred action full of inner meaning that should be plainly expressed in a becoming ceremony. A certain sacramental minimalism, therefore, which paid too little attention to the concrete symbolism of baptism, is now in retreat. We realize that the solemn administration of baptism is essentially linked with the celebration of Easter Eve: baptism is a paschal sacrament, the sacrament of a person's "passover" – *transitus paschalis* – from death to life, from sin and the old man to the resurrection and the new man in Christ. Precisely because we have this new awareness of the reality of the sacrament, we long for a clear and convincing expression of this reality.

Desire for reform. The suggested reforms which have also been discussed at the Second Vatican Council mainly concern the ritual for infant baptism, which in practice means the majority of all baptisms. To pretend that the infant is a responsible partner is forcing matters. Our keener sense of authenticity demands that the child be treated as such, and regarded as a "partner" only within his limitations. We must state what really happens: here is a human being on whom God is pleased to bestow salvation in Christ through the intermediary of the Church, giving the Church, the parents, and the sponsors the duty of bringing him to the point where he can freely affirm the saving grace he has been vouchsafed and thenceforward preserve it for himself. Otherwise no changes of any importance would need to be made in the rite of infant baptism.

A more urgent matter is the reform of the ritual for adult baptism, no rarity nowadays even outside missionary countries. We seem to be faced with the following choice: in order to give the adult convert a genuine and active part in his own baptism, we must either prune the present unbalanced set of ceremonies (much of them a mere anachronism preserved by force of habit, since they are a condensation of the catechumenate which ceased to exist long ago) by discarding all that is antiquated, or else revive the catechumenate in a form adapted to modern conditions. There is much to be said for the latter idea, which would mean that a certain interval would once more elapse between the preparation and the baptism. What is now done all at once might be allotted to three separate occasions, at intervals to be decided in each case. The first stage, *ad catechumenum faciendum* (opening of the catechumenate), would set forth the partnership between the candidate and the Church; the second would be mainly "exorcist" in character; the third stage would be the actual sacrament: abjuration (with anointing) – confession of faith – the act of baptism – concluding ceremonies.

Problems of infant baptism. Important as adult baptism is at the present time, we must not forget that infant baptism exists in its own right and has its own claims to our appreciation. The problems it raises have much exercised Protestant theologians in the past few years. For anyone who takes seriously the original Protestant principles that we have mentioned, infant baptism presents all but insuperable difficulties. But the fact that all Churches, including the Reformed, accept infant baptism in practice shows that they take a realistic view of baptism and see it as something objective.

Sacramental realism. It is precisely Protestant exegetes, Church historians, and experts in comparative religion, who now acknowledge the realism of the ancient Christian sacramental idea. At first, to be sure, they felt that this realist conception smacked of magic; and even today the fear that a sacrament may be confused with magical signs (when there is in fact no such confusion) sometimes makes it difficult for these theologians to form a balanced judgment. But they often emphasize "that St. Paul ascribes an 'action réelle mystique' to baptism, which makes of the sinner a man freed from sin, who is bound in a mysterious way with the death and resurrection of Christ" (Neunheuser, following M.-J. Lagrange).

Such an insight opens the door to a

new defence of infant baptism, but has, of course, a much broader significance – it allows of a new approach to the traditional doctrine, in terms of the immediate action of God's word. Catholic theologians must now stress the following points;

a) The event of baptism is a sacred mystery; it is a sacrament that communicates grace, but it is no less a highly personal act on the part of the adult convert. As a mystery, baptism is an act of initiation – an introduction to truly Christian life – whereby the redemptive death of Christ which happened but once in history is cultically made present in the shape of a visible rite (in this case the symbolic immersion which remains recognizable even in its present abbreviated form, and the invocation of the Blessed Trinity). The person baptized can die with and like Christ, and rise again with him to the new life that is being-in-Christ-Jesus, in the hope of one day attaining the full glory of the resurrection.

b) But if we consider the outward sign as an ablution – the dominant aspect at present – then baptism is seen to be the cleansing of sinful man in the precious blood of the Lamb of God, by the water that flowed from the open side of the Crucified. The baptismal water is the instrument Christ uses to effect this redemptive purification: filled with the power of the Holy Ghost, on the invocation of God's name, it purges of all sin and awakens one to the new life of those "born again of water and the Holy Spirit" (Jn 3:5). The door to the kingdom of God is opened in baptism. As fellowship with Christ in his crucifixion, death, and risen life, or as instrument in the hands of the Redeemer to cleanse and give grace and life, baptism remains a sovereign act of God's omnipotence, applying Christ's redemption to the sinner out of mercy and prevenient love, without any merit on our part, and demanding thenceforward a life of obedience to God.

c) Nothing at all in this sacramental action savours of magic. Magic, indeed, is fatal to all true religion. If the action which proceeds from faith and is achieved in baptism is unfailingly efficacious, that is simply evidence of the power of God, who of his own free grace has willed this way of salvation appropriate to the basic event which is the incarnation of the Logos, appropriate as well, therefore, to the double structure of man. Baptism proclaims the utter sufficiency of the redemption which Christ wrought once for all in history and which takes effect now in the sacrament.

The obligations of baptism. Baptism imposes obligations in keeping with the spiritual nature of man. It gives the child all it can bear: to be a child of God, freed from the burden of original sin, of the wrath of God. But by this very fact he has the duty when he reaches the estate of a responsible person, of freely confessing the reality of his baptism by faith and love and shaping his life accordingly, in the hope of preserving that grace till he can enjoy its consummation in eternity. Otherwise baptism would fail to achieve its real and ultimate effect. But baptism addresses the adult convert directly. Unless he approaches the sacrament in the dispositions that become a responsible person, yields the assent of his faith, resolutely turns his back on sin, and freely commits himself to Christ crucified and risen, the baptism remains barren, even though it be correctly administered and even though it truly gives the convert that first contact with Christ which marks him forever as Christ's possession, so that whatever his present deficiencies he can at any time turn repentant to the Lord and giver of true life. Baptism is living fellowship with Christ, the inauguration of that New Testament life which is inwardness, spontaneous obedience to God in the power of Christ's Holy Spirit, the mature freedom of the sons of God (e.g., Heb 8:8–13 and 10:15–17 in the light of Jer 31:31–34).

Baptism may be conferred only when a person believes with all his heart (Acts 8:37), freely desires this sacrament, is ready to be "baptized into Christ's death" (Rom 6), ready to preserve his baptism, to remain a true disciple by obeying the commandments, so that when the Lord comes to the wedding feast of the Lamb at the end of time he may hasten forth to meet him, lamp still alight, with all the saints, entering by grace into the kingdom of heaven.

As the primal sacrament, then, baptism is in a special sense both the sacrament of faith in Christ and the embodiment of that faith. This is why, should circumstances make baptism impossible, faith alone can impart fellowship with Christ and redemption, through what is called baptism of desire. Baptism does not thereby become superfluous. One who truly believes in the Lord is prepared to do his bidding without reserve, and therefore wishes, so far as in him lies, to receive baptism. He is not saved without the desire (at least the implicit desire) of baptism; and once justified in this way, he must still receive the sacrament, for it aggregates him to the Church's visible communion, thus entitling him to take part in all its sacramental and liturgical life in Christ.

D. The Foundation of All Christian Life

When we reflect on this plenitude we perceive that baptism is indeed "the blessed sacrament of our washing in water", the foundation of a high-minded life, life in Christ Jesus; for "our commonwealth (even now) is in heaven, and from it we await a Saviour, the Lord Jesus Christ, who will change our lowly body to be like his glorious body" (Phil 3:20–21). For the "little while" remaining until then, baptism demands that being dead to sin, we live in Christ our Lord. Moreover, it requires of us a life of active worship befitting the man of the New Testament and the dignity of that royal priesthood whose character we received in baptism. We must be prepared to join in celebrating the eucharistic mystery, calling to mind what the Lord did, giving thanks to God the Father through Christ, offering the Father that adoration in spirit and in truth which he expects (Jn 4:23–24).

But this is by no means all. We must abide in the love to which and in which Christ has called us, bear one another's burdens and so fulfil the law of Christ. Strong in the fellowship with Christ that baptism gives us, we can and must discharge what is known today as "the responsibility of Christians to the world": by playing our proper part on earth we shall also bear witness to Christ in the midst of the world, hoping for the final revelation of his glory till God is everything to every one (1 Cor 15:28).

Burkhard Neunheuser

II. Baptism of Desire

Historical sketch. The Fathers of the Church, interpreting the message of the Scriptures, taught that there was no salvation outside the baptism and faith of the Church. During the Middle Ages theologians began to reflect systematically on the ways in which grace is accessible to men outside of the visible boundaries of the Church. It was generally taught that while the sacraments are the normal means of grace, the perfect disposition to receive them, created by faith and charity, would already communicate justification. Since such a disposition was ordained towards the sacrament by a *desiderium sacramenti*, the justification prior to the reception of the sacrament was regarded as a kind of anticipation of sacramental grace. In regard to baptism this doctrine was commonly taught. It was adopted by the Council of Trent (*D* 797).

The medieval theologians reflected on the kind of disposition necessary to receive the effects of baptism. A widely held position, taught by St. Thomas, was that prior to the coming of Christ it was sufficient to believe in God and his merciful providence in regard to men. Such a belief was regarded as implicit faith in the Christ who was to come. However, according to St. Thomas, after the coming of Christ the explicit acknowledgment of the Christian message is required. This, at least, was his view when discussing the general plan of God's redemptive action.

It was generally assumed in the Middle Ages that the world as a whole had been evangelized; the infidels were regarded as living in comparatively small numbers on the edges of civilization. After the discoveries of America and the Far East, however, the question of human salvation was asked with a new urgency. Many theologians taught that the peoples across the seas who had never heard the message of Jesus were in the same state as men before the coming of Christ in the flesh: their faith in a God who regarded the universe with mercy and justice was an implicit acknowledgment of the Christian gospel and therefore counted for them as the baptism of desire. Speculating on how God acted in men beyond the reach of the gospel, these theologians were convinced of two things: that Christ was the one and unique mediator of salvation and that the grace of Christ touched the heart of every single man in an invitation to which he must respond.

This general understanding of baptism of desire received its most formal ecclesiastical expression in the Boston Letter, sent by the Holy See to Cardinal Cushing in 1949, explaining the meaning of the dogmatic statement "No salvation outside the Church". According to this letter, it is Catholic doctrine that under certain circumstances, which are specified, an implicit desire to belong to the Church is sufficient for salvation, as long as this desire is inspired by a supernatural faith and alive with the love of God, in other words as long as this desire is the work of God himself in the heart of man.

Vatican II speaks of the universal salvific will of God in connection with membership of the Church: "Finally, those who have not yet received the gospel are related in various ways to the People of God. In the first place there is the people to whom the covenants and the promises were given and from whom Christ was born according to the flesh (cf. Rom 9:4–5) . . . But the plan of salvation also includes those who acknowledge the Creator. In the first place among these there are the Moslems, who, professing to hold the faith of Abraham, along with us adore the one and merciful God, who on the last day will judge mankind. Nor is God himself far distant from those who in shadows and images seek the unknown God, for it is he who gives to all men life and breath and every other gift (cf. Acts 17:25–28), and who as Saviour wills that all men be saved (cf. 1 Tim 2:4). For those also can attain to everlasting salvation who through no fault of their own do not know the gospel of Christ or his Church, yet sincerely seek God and, moved by grace, strive by their deeds to do his will as it is known to them through the dictates of conscience." (Dogmatic Constitution on the Church, art. 16; see also art. 9.) For those, however, who have recognized the necessity of the Church for salvation, baptism is indispensable as the "door" to the Church and hence to salvation (*ibid.*, art. 14; Decree on the Church's Missionary Activity, art. 7).

Theology. In our own day when we realize more than ever before that the biblical people of the Old and New Testaments is a small minority in the totality of the human family, the need to reflect on the destiny of the majority of mankind is still more urgent than in the age of the great discoveries. Does the gratuitous election of God's own people imply that his saving action outside of this people is rare or exceptional? May we not suppose that the God who has revealed his universal will to save in Christ, is working for the salvation of men within the Church where his action is acknowledged, as well as outside the Church where his action is not as such acknowledged? Many contemporary Catholic theologians believe that God's irrevocable election of mankind in the Incarnation, the once-for-allness of Christ's sacrifice and the completeness of his victory imply that, with Jesus, mankind as a whole has entered a new situation, that is, has acquired an objective orientation, based not on its own nature but on the free divine choice, to be reconciled with God.

Under the notion of "baptism of desire", then, we may include the vast action of God to save and sanctify men outside the visible boundaries of the Church. While this baptism, as distinct from the baptism of water, does not introduce men into a believing community in which they are fed by an intimate communion with their God (and hence remains a weak initiation into a reality which is fully present only in the Church), one may seriously wonder whether baptism of desire is not the way of salvation for the great majority of men in this world, chosen to be saved.

If baptism of desire is the way of salvation for the vast majority of men chosen by God, we must attempt to describe the necessary predisposition of the mind for this with some psychological plausibility. What happens in the hearts of men beyond the reach of the gospel who submit to God's saving action? Since Christ is the only mediator, we believe that the mystery of salvation in non-Christians must be in basic continuity with the salvation of Christians through faith, hope and charity.

We believe that holiness is always the work of Christ. Because we are by nature divided, torn between two opposing tendencies in us, the decision making the selfless triumph over the selfish tendency in us is God's merciful doing in us. Wherever a man finds in himself the freedom to renounce his self-centredness and give way to a selfless concern for another, what happens to him may be described as a dying unto himself and a rising to a new life, liberated – at least on one level – from the connatural ambiguity of his own striving. Since such a victory is the work of grace, we may justly describe what happens to such a person as a share in the death and resurrection of Jesus, in other words as a kind of baptism. In some way, however tentative and faint, the image of Jesus has been imprinted on that person.

Yet the victory over the death of self-centredness is not in any way experienced as a moral achievement of which one may be proud. It is not a work on account of which such a person feels justified before God (if he believes in him) or entitled to the gratitude of men. On the contrary, the person capable of being engaged in selfless action regards himself as the recipient of gifts, of gifts which do not really belong to him, which transcend him, which he wants to share with others, and for which he wants no credit or reward. This person has accepted himself, *in an act of faith*, as one who has been enriched, undeservedly endowed with seeing and loving, as one who no longer belongs to himself but is turned to others in a gesture of sharing. It is from such an act of faith and not from an ambitious will to be virtuous that selfless action proceeds. In this faith the person finds the freedom to forget himself, to abandon the fear of others, and to transcend the insecurity of his lone existence.

Such a person – and who will say that he has never met one? – knows that this consciousness of being undeservedly rich will only last if he is willing to turn away again and again from the self-centredness still existing in him and its symptoms of which he becomes ever more sensitive. At the same time he will experience himself as one who is loved: forgiven, secure, ready for action. He will feel at one and the same time unworthy and reconciled. If you ask him how this transformation has come to him, he will say, "I did not do it myself."

If this is a valid description of baptism and faith as they are available to men to whom the gospel is either inaccessible or meaningless, then it must also express an experiential dimension of the Christian faith as lived in the Church. This is the theological context of studies, such as the controversial *Honest to God* by the Anglican bishop Robinson, which try to express the Good News of salvation in terms taken from contemporary thought and experience. It is a great mystery that the divine truth revealed to the Church, which is altogether unique, shows itself to the Christian reflecting on it in faith as truly universal.

Gregory Baum

BEATIFIC VISION

1. In theological language "beatific vision" usually means perfect salvation in its entirety, though verbally it particularly stresses the intellectual component in the single whole which constitutes salvation. This is the full and definitive experience of the direct self-communication of God himself to the individual human being when by free grace God's will has become absolute and attained its full realization. Since this absolute will (efficacious grace of perfect salvation in predestination) attains the individual precisely as a member of redeemed humanity in Christ and because of Christ, the term also implies in the concrete, if not formally, the unity of the redeemed and perfected in the perfect Kingdom of God, "heaven", as the communion of the blessed with the glorified Lord and his humanity, and with one another – the perfect accomplishment of the "communion of saints". As the definitive, irrevocable completion of God's action on man and on human freedom (which freely wills what is final), the beatific vision is "eternal life". The difference of "time" (to the extent that it can and has to be conceived) between the perfect fulfilment of the one human being in his spiritual and personal dimension and his perfect accomplishment in his corporeal dimension, is ultimately of little account. Scripture in fact always refers to the total fulfilment of man and simply envisages it from different aspects. This is why Scripture sometimes speaks of the "resurrection of the flesh" (1 Cor 15), which means total fulfilment, another time of "being with Christ" (Phil 2:23) and seeing God "face to face" (1 Cor 13:12). Consequently the perfect fulfilment of man's bodily nature must quite simply be included in the actual concept of the "beatific vision". Theologically in fact it is an open question whether the vision of God does not actually receive an increment through man's bodily transfiguration, i.e., is in fact partly constituted by the latter. All this in no way calls in doubt the truth that with Benedict XIV (*D* 530) we must firmly hold that the direct vision of God ensues "at once" (*D* 530; 693; 696) in those who are free from sin and the consequences of sin (temporal punishment for sin).

2. The beatific vision is totally gratuitous (*D* 475), because it is God's

free personal self-communication and the culmination of supernatural grace, i.e., grace which is not owed to any spiritual creature even prior to its eventual sinfulness and unworthiness. It is the miracle of God's love which on the part of those to whom it is addressed can never constitute a claim in justice or equity, or a mere consequence of their nature which the Creator of that nature could not reasonably refuse to it as its exercise and fulfilment (cf. also 1 Tim 6:16; Jn 1:16; 6:41; Mt 11:27; 1 Cor 2:11, none of thich could be true if the beatific vision were the natural fulfilment of the human mind). The beatific vision is indeed the most perfect conceivable actuation of a spiritual creature inasmuch as the latter is open absolutely without limits to being, truth and value. But this unlimited transcendent capacity of man still has meaning and purpose even if it is not fulfilled by God's self-communication. For it serves to constitute meaningful, spiritual, interpersonal life in a freedom and history oriented towards a definitive possession of such life, none of which is possible without such transcendence. Consequently God's perfect self-communication even to a spiritual creature as such (as "nature") is free grace, yet can be the perfect and ultimately the only absolute fulfilment of the spiritual creature. To say that the beatific vision is purely gratuitous is not to deny that in the *de facto* order of reality the spiritual creature is freely willed by God *because* God willed to communicate himself freely. Hence nature is, because grace was to be. In every creature endowed with freedom there is, therefore, an indelible orientation towards the beatific vision of God (a "supernatural existential") by which the highest "claim" of the spiritual creature and the ultimate meaning and the goal of the drama of its history is precisely the beatific vision.

3. a) As regards the ultimate essence of the beatific vision in the strictest sense, we must start from the position that the specific nature of created mind is spiritual knowledge and love which determine one another in radical unity, just as the transcendentals *verum* and *bonum* are inseparable though not identical attributes of being and of beings as such, and just as there are two and neither more nor less than two necessary "processions" in God, the Word of truth and the power of love. And this knowledge and love exist in intercommunication between persons. It must also be noted that "salvation" in its definitive sense means the perfect fulfilment of the spiritual person as such and as a whole, and therefore principally concerns his specific essence which distinguishes him from beings below the level of spirit. We must also consider that if this perfect fulfilment of man consists of God's gracious *self*-communication, then from the start the very concept of such a fulfilment cannot leave out of account the fact that this God is necessarily the Trinitarian God, that the Trinity of the economy of redemption is the immanent Trinity, that this is confirmed by the whole christological and pneumatological structure of redemptive history, the perfect fulfilment of which is the beatific vision. The doctrine of the beatific vision must, therefore, from the start make its Trinitarian aspect clear. When reference is made to a "sharing in the divine nature", it must not be overlooked that this participation is necessarily triune and is given for there to be a direct relation between God and the spiritual person of the creature. It is, therefore, implied that there is a direct relation of the creature to God precisely as Father, Son and Spirit.

b) However, it is of course true that by the nature of things the beatific vision can best be described on its intellectual side. For the knowledge of the personal spirit when put into words most easily describes spirit in terms of knowledge itself. Consequently it is described in Scripture as knowledge of God as he is, face to face, without mirror or image, as vision in contrast to hope (1 Jn 3:2; 1 Cor 13:12; cf. Mt 5:8; 18:10; 2 Cor 5:7). The parallel drawn between this knowledge and being known by God (1 Cor 13:12) emphasizes the personal character of the mutual loving reception and self-communication as compared with purely objectivating cognition. Benedict XII (*D* 530) accordingly describes the beatific vision as *visio intuitiva et facialis* of God's essence. The specific feature of this is that no object other than God conveys this knowledge. The divine essence itself shows itself directly, clearly and openly (*D* 530; cf. also *D* 693), in contradistinction to analogous knowledge of God which is mediated by the knowledge of finite beings different from God. To this, theological speculation rightly adds that what specifies really and ontologically the cognitive power of the creature and by which this must be actuated for direct knowledge of God, must be God himself as he is. God himself fulfils in a quasi-formal way the necessary function of a *species impressa* for cognition. If in addition a *created* real, ontological specification of the mind is required (the *lumen gloriae* as perfecting the *habitus* of faith – *D* 475), the relation of this to God's quasi-formal self-communication for the beatific vision must be described in a similar way to the relation between "created" and "uncreated" grace. The beatific vision does not of course annul God's incomprehensibility (*D* 428; 1782). It is rather the direct experience and loving affirmation of God as incomprehensible. His mystery is not merely the limit of finite cognition, but its ultimate positive ground and final goal, the beatitude of which consists in the ecstatic raising and merging of cognition, without suppressing it, into the bliss of love. In God, as the origin and goal of all reality that is not God, all other reality is known and loved, in the manner and measure in which it concerns us (cf. Aquinas, *Summa Theologica*, III, q. 10, a. 2).

Karl Rahner

BEING

I. Being and Beings

1. *The state of the question.* Philosophy has revolved about the notion of being since the beginning. And here a fundamental distinction stands out, that between beings and being. Every thing and every man is a being, as that which is; but being is the ground by which all beings are or a being is. For this distinction Heidegger chose the term of the "onto-logical difference", since it distinguishes being from each being (ὄν), as its ground (λόγος). In infra-human beings, this difference remains latent. It is only known as such in man, where being displays itself as different from beings. This gives man, in contrast to the non-intelligent infra-human, understanding both of beings and of being. He understands beings by referring them to being; but he understands being by understanding beings with reference to being and in the light of being. Thus being provides man first with understanding of the being which he himself is, and then of all other beings. The understanding thus circumscribed characterizes the whole life and action of man, all of whose activities are illuminated by being. When such understanding becomes fully conscious and methodical, man enters upon philosophy. More precisely, philosophy is implicitly present in the experience of the ontological difference; philosophy begins explicitly with the express recognition of this difference, which is therefore its foundation and its whole life, and finds in philosophy its full development.

Here various emphases are possible, by reason of the connection between beings and being. There is a consideration of beings by virtue of being where being itself and the difference between it and beings only come into play as the obscure and unarticulated background. Nonetheless, reflection based on beings can also be brought to bear explicitly on being and on its difference from beings. According to Heidegger, the philosophy of the West has persistently taken up the former and thus bogged down in "oblivion of being", while it was only the thinking that began with him that came to formulate explicitly the oblivion of being and hence began to take being itself into its perspective. Gilson comes to a similar conclusion, though making an important exception for Thomas Aquinas, who already investigated being explicitly. The problems here outlined throw some light on the main stages in which being disclosed itself to the thought of the West.

2. *History of the philosophy of being*. In Heraclitus, being at once displays and conceals itself in the Logos, in which, as the conflicting harmony of opposites all things are based and unified (frs. 50 and 51). Though men have a constant and most intimate perception of the Logos or being, they turn away from it, and hence though present they are absent and all beings are alien to them (frs. 1, 34, 72). For Parmenides, being appears in sharpest contrast to non-being. Only the way of being is passable, while that of non-being cannot be divined (fr. 2). Being alone is, while beings in their becoming and their multiplicity cannot be truly said to be (frs. 7, 8). Hence being is imperishable and unchangeable; as the one all it is at once all things (*ibid.*). As regards man, his thinking is most intimately identical with being (fr. 3).

According to Plato, the multiplicity of things which is subject to becoming have indeed being, but not in the full sense. They participate in the forms, which alone are truly beings (*Phaedrus*, 247 c), eternal, imperishable, unchangeable, and fully what they are (*Symposium*, 210e–211d). The supreme form is the Good, which alone is being in its absolute perfection, and is even perhaps beyond being (*Republic*, 509b). Man is most intimately akin to being in the guise of the forms, and above all to the form of the Good. He attains the forms by anamnesis or dialectics (*Republic*, 510b–511d). Aristotle also regards earthly things as real beings, through which he penetrates to the "first philosophy", in which beings are considered as beings (*Metaphysics*, IV, 1; 1003a, 21–26). It is also the task of this science to investigate the divine as the highest type of all beings. It is the eternal, unmoved or unchangeable, and separated from all that is visible, to some extent therefore transcendent (*Metaphysics*, VI, 1; 1026a, 10–30). Nonetheless, Aristotle does not designate God as being itself, because he understands being as substance and hence attaches it too closely to earthly beings (*Metaphysics*, VII, 1: 1028b, 2–4). In neo-Platonism, as represented by Proclus, the first emanation from the ultimate ground is being, which mediates between the ultimate and the multiplicity of things. The ultimate ground, as the One, is above being, since this is at once one and many, finite and infinite.

In the Middle Ages, Thomas Aquinas was inspired by ancient philosophy and the revealed mystery of creation to consider being more explicitly than had ever been done previously. Though he does not make being so expressly central in his work as Heidegger, he penetrated further into its ultimate depths. According to Aquinas, being is not merely the opposite of nothing(ness), or the actual. It is the infinite fullness of all perfection or of all that exists and can exist (*Summa Theologica*, I, q. 4, a. 1 ad 3; q. 4, a. 2). The real things which we encounter are beings since they have being or have share in being according to the measure of their nature (*ibid.*, I, q. 3, a. 4; q. 75, a. 5 ad 4). By the fact that they merely have share ("part-take") in being, finite beings point on to infinite subsisting being, where the philosophical approach to God is opened up (*ibid.*, I, q. 4, a. 2). God is being itself, or being according to its inmost self, which is therefore identical with the ultimate ground (*ibid.*, I, q. 3, a. 4; q. 75, a. 5 ad 4). Thus the question of being and the question of God are intrinsically connected and belong to the same science (*In Metaphysica*, Prooem.), which can be investigated by man because his spirit is intrinsically orientated to being (*Summa Theologica*, I, q. 5, a. 3; *De Ver.*, q. 1, a. 1).

Thinking did not succeed in remaining on this level. In Cajetan and John of St. Thomas, for instance, the place of being is taken by existence, which is actuality as contrasted with possibility. This perspective continued to be dominant as time went on, through the influence of Suárez, though he himself at times reflects Aquinas's view of being. Thus he speaks of the whole fullness of being which God contains as subsisting being and in which finite beings participate (*Disp. Metaph.*, XXIX, sect. 3, n. 19; XXX, sect. 4, n. 3). The development here initiated gradually transferred the primacy of being to essence, with a corresponding mode of thinking, while the essence was more and more at the mercy of subjectivity. This gave rise to modern rationalism, and to empiricism as its opposite pole. Oblivion of being grew more and more widespread.

The situation did not change fundamentally with the great synthesis of Kant, of which the influence is still at work today. The theoretical reason at any rate did not attain to being, in as much as the thing in itself remained inaccessible to it. It is restricted to the essences under the guise of the categories, among which being was ranged by a total misunderstanding of it. The categories are *a priori* forms of consciousness, which knows objects as phenomena by means of the categories (*Critique of Pure Reason*, B 166). The practical reason opens up that which is-in-itself, but only in faith, and this means that we come to the three realities or beings corresponding to the postulates, without passing through being. Among the German idealists we may mention Hegel, who undoubtedly returns to the thing in itself and so to being, but reduces being to spirit and considers it as posited by spirit. The spirit is ultimately the absolute spirit, in which the human spirit is absorbed as a dialectical moment of it. The spirit comes to (full consciousness of) itself, just as being does, namely in becoming. Hence being is only fully itself as becoming, which combines with nothingness to build it up. Since becoming also falls under the categories in its development, being disappears not only in becoming but in the essences (cf. especially Hegel's *Logic*). Just as here being is sacrificed to becoming on the plane of the infinite, so too in Nietzsche on the plane of the finite. Nietzsche sees "the supreme achievement of thought" in "stamping the character of being upon becoming" (*The Will to Power*, no. 617). This comes from the eternal return of the Same, a process in which "the closest possible approximation of a world of becoming with that of being" takes place (*ibid.*). In the "cycle of absolutely identical series" (*ibid.*, no. 1066) the will to power develops, which is "the innermost essence of being" (*ibid.*, no. 693). Thus being is submerged in becoming as the will to power, whereby it is also put on a lower plane than value, for every thing is in so far as it has value, that is, contains the necessary "conditions for sustaining and intensifying" (*ibid.*, no.

715) the "growth in power" (*ibid.*, no. 14).

At the same time the return to being became more and more definite. Schelling in his later works sought to go beyond Hegel, and completed reason by freedom and essence by existence or being. Kierkegaard's struggle for "a fully human existence" took him in the same direction, though on different principles. The all-important thing was "to find himself", which inevitably meant that he was "implanted in the divine". The free act of man's will raises him to realized existence and hence to his authentic being, through which he at once adheres to God or is founded on absolute being. Here the way to being is opened up once more, though the quest for being remains involved in the quest for (Christian) man. This is also more or less true of Jaspers and Marcel.

Heidegger's is the supreme effort to place being at the centre of thought, since he unreservedly gives being precedence over man. For existing ontology or metaphysics, which considered beings in the light of being, he substitutes fundamental ontology, which considers being itself as the foundation of beings and the difference between it and beings. Thought is claimed by being and for being (*Humanismus*, p. 5); hence man is not there as a subject for himself, but as "there-ness" or existence is the historical "there" of being, and as "eksistence" is both a standing out into being and a standing within being (*ibid.*, pp. 20f., 25, 35f.). Man and being, though distinct, are indissolubly one, "since human nature itself contains the relationship" to being (*Seinsfrage*, p. 27), while "being is released into the act of attention" (*ibid.*, p. 30). By reason of this correlativity, thought stops at the historical communications of being, though openness for the supra-historical being of God is not excluded (*Humanismus*, pp. 35ff.).

At the same time, oblivion of being continues. Neo-Kantianism with its theory of sciences does not escape it. Husserl's phenomenology, developed as a description of essence, also excludes the question of being; furthermore, the essences are constituted by the transcendental subject. A universal ontology only appears marginally and late. So too N. Hartmann surmounted idealism, but only to reach beings, while being strictly speaking remains outside his vision. "Analytical philosophy" – logical positivism or linguistic analysis – misses being entirely by its positivist logic which retains of being only the copula, as a function of thought. All philosophical content is, of course, rejected, since to ignore being is to lose the kernel of philosophy and consequently philosophy itself.

3. *Systematic view*. The historical survey has brought us to the situation in which thought finds itself today with regard to being; it must also be the starting-point for an explicitation of the content of being which will do justice to the points of view put forward above.

a) *The claim of being*. Being is disclosed to us in the action of man, who never ceases to understand being in his contacts with beings in the world. In contrast to the beasts, he has beings as such before him, instead of merely feeling their impact dully and stupidly; but this involves, as condition of its possibility, that being discloses itself to him. This, therefore, is the intellectual horizon which reveals beings according to the being proper to them; and there also being discloses itself as the ground of beings. Thus man is not merely referred to beings. He is, above all, claimed by being, and thus distinguished from all mere things. Nonetheless, he can lose himself in the beings which occupy the foreground of his world. If so, being, which at first forms only the background, eludes his grasp, by being dissolved very often into mere appearances. But the more man gives himself to being, the more imperiously does he experience the unconditional precedence of being over all beings. In the same proportion, being dawns on him in the limitless fullness and significance from which his destiny most profoundly depends. Thus the communication of being bestows on man freedom in face of being; he is called to make the decision through which alone he can truly find being. He wins or loses himself accordingly, having to preserve himself in his history and historicity by taking the risks which they never cease to impose upon him.

b) *Being and world.* More precisely, man finds himself confronted by two types of beings in the world, things and persons, which are distinguished by their different relationship to being. Things participate in being according to their essence, and strive towards the fullness of being accordingly. But they cannot distinguish being from its crystallization in essence, and hence their actuation does not break through to being itself and ultimately explicitate the essence. Hence things remain blanks for themselves and for other things. Consequently, they are of themselves silent partners for man, who can only make them speak in so far as he makes them participate in his own openness to being. In persons, man encounters beings like himself, that is, other men; through their essence they participate in being in such a way that in their actuation they at once distinguish being from essence and so attain to being itself. In other words, the person is capable of complete reflection on himself (*reditio completa*), by virtue of which he can reduce the outermost externals of things to the most intimate inwardness of being itself. Hence the person, in the course of explicitating his essence, strives not merely implicitly but explicitly to the limitless fullness of being. At the same time, he is disclosed to himself, a process expressed in the self-consciousness in which he says "I" and in his free disposal of himself. And since all beings are rooted in being, the person is likewise opened up to all others. Consequently, with regard to other persons, he is a partner who responds, bringing about thereby the "I-You" encounter dialogue.

Clearly, there is an essential connection between person and being. In things, being is alienated from itself, while in the person it is at home or has possession of itself. Consequently, things appear as diminished beings, over which persons tower as full beings. Being is most intrinsically personal; that is why it appears in its own self only as person. Heidegger's switch from beings to being is completed by the switch from things to persons, which by all appearances is now being made and will be decisive for the future of philosophy.

c) *Being and reflection.* Being, as the non-explicitated background, is attained by the reflection which goes hand in hand with our encounter with beings. Reflection, in its experience of objects, experiences being as that which transcends objects. Then reflection looking back on our action places this being in the foreground and explicitates it according to its kind. Here the supra-conceptual being revealed in the beings grasped in concepts must be provided with an adequate set of conceptual expressions. The instrument is the analogous concept, in which agreement and difference are indissolubly mingled, and which can therefore grasp being in the light of beings, without the distortion which would place it among beings.

How then does being appear in this process of explicitation? Heidegger's explanations revolve around the historical communications of being, and hence its finite and historical, that is, its relative form. Its further depths are not indeed ignored, but they are not included in the investigation. Nonetheless, it is precisely these depths which are the enabling grounds for our human action and the transcendental explanation of these grounds leads to absolute and hence infinite and supra-historical being. This may be demonstrated with regard to three fundamental types of action, the contemplative, practical and artistic (*theoria, praxis, poiesis*), that is, the absolute validity of knowledge, the absolute obligation of the moral imperative and the absolute radiance of the beautiful form.

d) *Being and the judgment.* Let us take the claim of the judgment to absolute validity. The characteristic element of the judgment is the affirmation of identity, in which the "is" usually links a predicate with a subject and hence appears as the copula. This logical element of the copula is as far as logical positivism or linguistic analysis goes; such analytical philosophy gives all its attention to the affirmation of beings and has no room for the different language of being. But in fact the logical function of the copula already signals its onto-logical significance; for the judgment is essentially an affirmation that beings are or that being is characteristic of beings, the predicate marking the way in which being belongs to beings. But every "is" that is uttered tends towards absolute validity, and this presupposes that we know what absolute validity means and can distinguish it from non-absolute or relative validity. But whereas relative validity holds good only for certain aspects or limited regions, validity conceived as absolute leaves all such restrictions behind, since it is simply there and hence is true for all minds. Consequently, the "is-so" which is the expression of absolute validity has the same extension, and so the being contained in it is all-comprehensive or displays itself as absolute. Beings are therefore revealed in the judgment according to their grounds in absolute being and their participation in it. In other words, finite historical beings are seen to be made possible by infinite supra-historical being. It is only through the dawning of this being that man's action is possible and hence man himself.

e) *Being and divine being.* We encounter absolute being as it meets us in its historical communications, but it is always distinct from these. Thus subsistent or self-sufficient being, infinitely transcendent and immanent with regard to all beings, announces itself as profoundest mystery and thus lays open the philosophical way to God. Absolute being, as found by man in himself and in all beings, is at first indeterminate; but its progressive determination elaborates its intrinsic relationship to subsistent being and hence leads on to subsistent being itself.

Johannes Lotz

BIBLE

I. Introduction

A. Exegesis

1. *Old Testament*

a) *Name and contents of the Old Testament.* The collection of books which Jesus, the primitive community and the subapostolic generation regarded as sacred Scripture is known to Christians as the Old Testament, in the form later determined by the fixing of the canon. The term "Old Testament", by which it is distinguished from the New and honoured as the attestation of the first divine plan of salvation, ordained by God in earlier times (cf. Heb 9:15), occurs first in St. Paul. He speaks in 2 Cor 3:14 of the "reading" of the documents of "the Old Testament". The old Latin translation of the text gave currency to the word testament which stresses the gratuitous nature of the covenant established by God, even more than the term διαθήκη. With the "New Testament" as its counterpart, it became the general term for the writings which after 1 Macc 12:9 (τὰ βίβλια) were known as "the Bible".

According to the Jewish view, the OT comprises three groups of writings, designated as the law (*Torah*), that is, the Pentateuch ascribed to Moses, the prophets (*Nebiim*), divided into the earlier (Jos, Jdg, 1 and 2 Sam, 1 and 2 Kg) and later prophets (Is, Jer, Ezek, the twelve [minor] prophets), and the writings (*Ketubim*), Pss, Job, Prov, Song of Solomon, Eccles, Lam, Est, Ruth, Dan, Ezra, Neh, 1 and 2 Chr. The placing of the so-called historical books, Jos – 2 Kg, among the prophetic writings is justifiable, since they recount the deeds and sayings of such prophets as Samuel, Nathan, Gad, Ahijah of Siloh, Elijah and Elisha, and are not mere annals, but history interpreted by the word of God and seen in faith. The Church took over with the books of the Hebrew Bible also the additions of the Greek version, the Septuagint, in keeping with the broader view of the canon prevalent in Alexandria. These are the deuterocanonical writings: Tob, Jud, 1 and 2 Macc, Wis, Ecclus and Baruch. By calling it the Old Testament, the Church put it beside the New and accepted it along with it as the word of God. The term Old Testament can only be used by those who accept this theological evaluation and relationship. The term Old Testament is necessarily a Christian one.

b) *The origin of the Old Testament.* The OT contains the writings of the people of Israel, which knew itself called to hear the word of God and to observe his commands. The whole literature of the people of Yahweh has not been preserved, and not all its documents have been incorporated into the OT. It is the record of what was recognized as the word and self-attestation of Yahweh, and as human response – all, in fact, that appeared essential and important for faith in the sight of God. This alone tells us that the growth of the collection had a long history, that it included uncertainties as regards the inclusion of certain parts such as the Song of Solomon, and that it did not come to an end before NT times. Israel was convinced that the impulse and command to write down events (Exod 17:14), divine directives (Exod 34:27) and words (Is 30:8; Jer 30:2; 36) came from Yahweh. What was written down was to be a living and inspiring "witness for the time to come" (Is 30:8). It was to be the Lord's way of addressing those for whom it was written (Jer 36:2).

The commandments of the law may have been the first writings produced among the people of Yahweh, as seems to be indicated by the texts which say that Moses caused the law to be written down (Exod 24:4; Deut 31:24). The covenant by which the tribes were linked together and to Yahweh needed to be expressed in fixed terms. But the Decalogue (Exod 20; Deut 5), the Book of the Covenant (Exod 20:22–23:33), the Law of Deuteronomy (Deut 12–26) and the Law of Holiness (Lev 17–26), in their present form, which contains many changes and additions, is from a later time, about the 9th to the 6th century B.C. The great deeds of Yahweh, as experienced by the tribes of Israel, were recounted at the great liturgical feasts. At Gilgal the conquest of the land was given special mention (Jos 4–6), at Shechem, the covenant (Jos 24), on Tabor the victory of Taanach (Jg 5), and at Siloh probably all the ancient traditions of the covenant. At sanctuaries like Bethel and Hebron the traditions about the patriarchs and the divine promises to them were kept alive.

Under Solomon, however, interest began to grow in writing down the past of the people of Yahweh. The story of the succession to the throne of David recounted how the God of Israel had granted the great king a worthy successor (2 Sam 9–1 Kg 2). This work inspired the Yahwist to write the first account of the history of salvation, in which he used the story of human origins and of the patriarchs as a prelude to the traditions of the exodus, the desert wanderings, Sinai and the entry into Canaan, which had perhaps already been combined into a basic narrative.

Then the second half of the 8th century was of importance for the writing down of traditional material. Not long after the work of the Elohist, the prophets Amos, Hosea and Isaiah, and especially their disciples, began to commit prophetic words to writing. When the northern kingdom was conquered and reduced to an Assyrian province, its corpus of tradition was transferred to Judah, where King Hezekiah had paid attention to the collection of traditional material. It was probably there that the Yahwist and Elohist were combined into what has been called the Jehovist work. This possibly took the historical presentation down to the fall of the northern kingdom or the end of the 8th century, which would mean that the basic elements of Jos – 2 Kg 17 were then committed to writing. Other matter, including in particular laws, went to make up the book of Deuteronomy, which also contained material pertaining to Jerusalem. In its basic form, it was found in the temple in 621.

The exile was a fruitful period from the literary point of view. Shortly before the destruction of Jerusalem (587), Jeremiah dictated to Baruch the scroll which was to be the basis of the book of Jeremiah. Ezekiel, at Babylon, wrote down his visions and sayings in a sort of diary. The message of Deutero-Isaiah (Is 40–55) was written down by his disciples before the end of the exile. The Deuteronomic writings (Deut–2 Kg), which had been worked over at various stages, were perhaps brought to a conclusion in Palestine about 550. But above all, it was the age of the collection, redaction, elaboration and re-working of the prophetic writings. This activity was continued after the exile, by the Levitical priests who had been deprived of their office when the "high places", the sanctuaries outside Jerusalem, were abolished in the reform of Josiah, and also no doubt by the non-Zadokite priests of Jerusalem. These former priests became "doctors of the law". In the 5th century, the "Priestly Writings" were still being composed and elaborated in Babylon, on the basis of older material. But Ezra, returning to Jerusalem from the Persian diaspora, could already bring with him the Pentateuch as the whole law. In the lands of exile, as in the homeland (Lam), psalms were collected and composed.

After the restoration (539–22) there was much literary activity in the religious community of Jerusalem. Work on the prophetic books continued. The collection of sayings known as Trito-Isaiah (Is 56–66) was formed. The writings of Zechariah were drafted (Zech 1–6), added to (7–8) and completed by two short prophetic books (9–11; 12–14). Malachi and Joel were written, and Haggai edited. Sayings of older prophets were expanded into books (Obad, Mic, Nah, Hab, Zeph) into which cultic chants were inserted (e.g., Is 33f.; Hab 3). About 350, the Jerusalem community used Sam and Kg, old traditions and documents, the memoirs of Ezra and of Nehemiah to compose the "Chronicler's" historical work (1 and 2 Chr; Ezr; Neh). The authors of Job and Eccles posed their critical questions. Edifying stories were written, some in the diaspora, at times in the style of the novel (Tob, Ruth, Est, Judith, Bar, Jon). The prophetic vision of the future developed in the direction of apocalyptic (Zech, Joel, Ezek 38f., apocalypse of Isaiah, Is 24–27).

A new impulse to literary activity was given in the time of the Maccabees. As early as 190, the tension between Judaism and Hellenism had given rise to Ecclesiasticus, of which the motto was that the law was the true wisdom. Later, at Alexandria, about 100 B.C., the author of the Book of Wisdom sought a solution in a different direction: the faith and traditions of Israel also merit the title of "Wisdom". The apocalyptic vision was in full flower at the beginning of the religious persecution (Dan 7–12). Sufferings, struggles and victories are portrayed, with edifying embroidery, in 1 and 2 Macc. The other works of the Chasidim and the groups which stemmed from them remained outside the canon (the "apocrypha"). The formation of the canon, with the rejection of many books, was the end of the development of the OT.

c) *Spiritual trends and theological principles*. The growth of the OT was not as consistent in all its manifold developments as the final redaction would suggest. The tribes and clans which migrated across the Jordan into central Palestine brought with them the experience of a special salvific intervention of Yahweh at the exodus and on the way to the land of Canaan. From the beginning they found themselves sharply opposed to the peoples of Canaan and their gods, and therefore formulated the theological statements of the separate and unique position of the people of Yahweh, of the covenant and of God's promises, claims and saving guidance. This theological trend is clear in the Elohist. It appears in Hosea along with the exodus tradition and the proclamation of God's love of his people. In Deuteronomy it takes the form of emphasis on the election of Israel, on the graciousness of the covenant and the obligations of the covenant. Jeremiah, influenced by Hosea and the language and mentality of Deuteronomy, is also tributary to this northern Israelite theology, since he is preoccupied by Israel's relationship to God in the desert period and by the thought of a new covenant. The verdict of Deuteronomy on the causes of the great catastrophe is formed by the fundamental notions of this theology.

The fundamental assertions of Israel's faith had been also cherished by Jerusalem and Judah. They came to them from the same covenant of the tribes, but were given a different emphasis. The southerners, installed in the great kingdom of David, which offered them and their neighbours spacious living-room in the land of Canaan, God's gift to his people, envisaged salvation for all the nations. Influences from the spiritual currents at work in their environment were adopted and exploited. Their religious perspective included Yahweh's work of creation, his kingship, and the place of his presence. This mentality inspired the narratives of the coming of David to power and of the succession to his throne, and also of the adventures of the ark (1 Sam 4–6; 2 Sam 6), which with 2 Sam 24 forms the foundation story of the sanctuary at Jerusalem. The Yahwist's presentation of the ancient traditions was guided by the thought of the salvation of the nations, the blessed gift of the land and the divine guidance mirrored in the story of David. The theology of creation was the occasion of his story of the origins. Isaiah, the prophet from Jerusalem, was chiefly interested in the Sion theology – which was carried on by Deutero-Isaiah and Trito-Isaiah – and in the Anointed of Yahweh. Deutero-Isaiah constructed his theology in the light of the notion of creation. Ezekiel planned for the New Jerusalem (40–48).

These two basic trends are not unconnected. Isaiah remembers the events of the exodus (the framework of the promises in Deutero-Isaiah) and the laws of the covenant (Is 5), as does Micah (2f.). Jeremiah does not pass over in silence the hope of an anointed of the Lord who will rule in justice (23:1–6), while Ezekiel takes up the theme of the new covenant (36:26ff.). In both prophets the theme of the land given by Yahweh, announced long before by the Yahwist in the story of the patriarchs, plays a great part. The law of the central sanctuary, which confines sacrifices to the one place chosen by Yahweh (Deut 12 in particular), shows the interest of Deuteronomy in Jerusalem, in its final redaction.

After the fall of the northern kingdom, the northern Israelite theology was incorporated into that of Jerusalem and Judah. From then on, and especially after the exile, the latter theology was predominant, as may be seen from the Chronicler's work, which is centred on the temple and its founders, David and Solomon, and which excludes northern Israel from sacred history after the beginning of the divided monarchy. The books of the OT were given their final form in Jerusalem, so that only some typical features of the theology of northern Israel can be distinguished. It is hardly possible now to say how far such theology was under sapiential and priestly influences.

A tradition of sapiential teaching was built up in Jerusalem under Solomon. It absorbed the practical wisdom and nature-lore of the neighbouring countries, especially Egypt and Canaan, in its effort to shape daily life successfully in dealings with men and things and to develop personal qualities. First directed to the formation of state officials, and then made available to all, the study of wisdom covered a field which was regulated neither by cultic encounters nor by the express command of Yahweh. Wisdom was concerned with mastering the world and life. Precepts for social life were developed from its rules of personal conduct. Even the perspectives, content and formulation of the doctrine of creation were determined by the study of wisdom. It also influenced the other sets of concepts and traditions.

In particular, the mentality of the priestly school and its theology had close contacts with the sapiential, as may be seen from its statements on the order of creation and the nature of man (Gen 1; Ps 8; 104). But the priest's task included knowledge, enforcement and explanation of the divine commands as well as the charge of public worship and the temple. The wise man had to give counsel, the prophet had to announce the work of God, but the priest had to give Torah, that is, directives. He was entrusted with care of the ritual precepts and also, especially after the fall of the kingdom of Judah, with the law. The holiness of God, of the place of worship and of divine service performed in ritual purity were his main interests, the expiation of sins and the assuring of salvation his great work.

These characteristic ideas and efforts coloured the traditions which arose or were preserved in the holy place. They are fully voiced in the "Priestly Writings", which proclaimed in their history of salvation and "Law of Holiness" that Yahweh would restore to a pure and holy people the land which he had promised the fathers in his eternal covenant. Circumcision and the sabbath, observance of the law and the true worship of God were the preconditions of God's dwelling with his people and of the salvation promised in the covenant. The unalterable order of creation was to be a motive for confidence in the equally steadfast promises of God.

The priestly theology was strong at Jerusalem. Since the building of the temple its influence was great, and after the exile it was all-powerful. Drawing on Canaanite tradition, which had revered here at his immovably fixed site a supreme God as creator and hence as Lord of heaven and earth, it developed a theology of the holy place which was moulded by faith in Yahweh: Sion was chosen by Yahweh as the place of his presence, the dwelling-place of his name, where the people of God and the kingship of God would have a focus.

This perspective dominates the work

of the Deuteronomists and the Chronicler. But the royal ideology worked out in Judah was also subordinated to this theology of Sion. The descendant of David is the anointed of Yahweh, chosen and installed by Yahweh as steward and mediator of blessings at the site of God's kingship. Ritual and courtly language were no doubt borrowed from Egypt, partly through pre-Israelite Jerusalem, but subordinated to faith in Yahweh (Ps 2; 110). The king is the adoptive son of Yahweh and receives his coronation titles from him (cf. Is 9:5); Yahweh proclaims him as king, makes him sit at his right hand and bestows on him the sceptre. He is placed by God in the special realm ot sanctity established by the covenant with David. To establish the claims or the house of David and its special position in the eyes of Yahweh, use was made of the promise uttered by Nathan (2 Sam 7), which was the prophetic deduction from David's triumph. It became the source of all messianic expectations, such as were intoned by Isaiah, grew stronger at the end of the monarchy (Ezek 34) and then applied texts from the royal ideology, especially from the psalms, to the ruler and saviour of the future.

The two fundamental perspectives, the sapiential and the priestly thought, the theology of the holy city and palace were all enriched by views from levitical and prophetic circles. Mutual influences were not lacking. This is evident throughout the whole of the OT writings. The reader can only have access to their essential statements and purposes if he bears in mind the important theological trends in Israel.

d) *Old Testament theology*. The theology of the Pentateuch is to be found in the thought of the four sources, the Yahwist, Elohist, Deuteronomist and Priestly Writings. The combination of these documents resulted in a work which is practically all narrative matter as far as Exod 19 and then mainly laws and precepts, so that the covenant on Sinai is the turning-point, the climax and the centre of all, even on the most mechanical reckoning. The narrative comprises the time between creation and the conquest of Palestine, all of which is seen in the light of God's will and action as history of salvation, which, however, through human sin and refusal often becomes a history of calamity. Nonetheless, Yahweh's will to save prevails. It is presented in five themes which make up Israel's experience of salvation – the patriarchs, the exodus, the desert wanderings, the covenant, the conquest of Palestine – which are summed up in a sort of confession of faith, Deut 26:5–9. The history of salvation also comprises the story of the first men, which is prefixed to the other five themes. In the covenant Yahweh promises salvation and manifests his will, hence Israel is given the law. It is a gift of God which is the key to the covenant relationship and hence to God's presence (Deut 4:7f.) and to life (Deut 30:15–19), the sign of election (Deut 7). Hence the events of the desert and the voice of "Moses" summon Israel to observe this law faithfully. Only by doing so can it have life and continue to be the people of God, gaining the salvation of the call anew each day.

The prophets who wrote down their preaching understood themselves as mediators of the word of Yahweh, which they proclaimed in his name as messengers – "Thus says the Lord". This word is of irresistible force (Jer 23:29) and accomplishes what it signifies. It is the instrument of the Lord by which he achieves what he has decreed (Is 55:11). The prophet speaks by Yahweh's command, and indeed as his mouth (Jer 15:19). He pronounces menaces which bring down God's judgment on men's actions. This message of judgment is addressed to the people of the Lord and its rulers. Israel is thereby warned that the word of judgment will bring punishment with it, if Israel continues to reject the will of Yahweh. The message of salvation is also conditional. No doubt the Lord does not make his gifts dependent on human achievement. But their continuance and their growth to a new plenitude are linked to the demonstration of the will to serve Yahweh. When speaking of salvation the prophets concentrate in particular on the great promises: the call as God's people, the land, the anointed of Yahweh and the covenant. Since Yahweh is Lord of the whole earth, the other nations also come under his judgment. This can be salvation for Israel. Its enemies having become adversaries of Yahweh, their punishment means deliverance for the people of Yahweh. But the nations are not excluded from the promise of salvation. The words of the prophets are a message addressed to men in their historical situation at a given time, not an abstract timeless doctrine. Immediate and actual, it comes warning, judging, punishing, guiding and restoring those to whom the envoy of God is sent. The events of the day are interpreted as a summons of Yahweh to his people.

The prophets describe the attitude which God demands by means of these events and point to the elements of guilt and punishment in them. Amos, for instance, sees in droughts and failures of crops Yahweh's answer to the fertility cult offered to Baal, and a new effort to bring the people to acknowledge. Yahweh as the giver of all that brings life (4:6–9). According to Isaiah, the Syro-Ephraimite war is a test of faith (7:9) and Sennacherib's attack a warning to trust only in Yahweh (30:15). The triumphant advance of Nebuchadnezzar shows Jeremiah that God has made him master of the world and hence that Israel must submit to him (Jer 27). Ezekiel affirms that Jerusalem must be destroyed, and explains why. The conquering march of Cyrus allows Deutero-Isaiah to see in him the anointed of the Lord (Is 45:1). The topical element in the prophets' words does not diminish their valid and permanent truth, but brings it out in the form of examples: just as Yahweh acts here and now in judgment and salvation, so too he will always act. He is always Lord of history, his will always prevails and events are shaped by him to form a summons to men.

The prophets were not innovators in the sense of trying to place Israel's life and faith on a new basis. They were concerned with enforcing the ancient law of God, especially the social demands of the covenant: "He has showed you, O man, what is good; and what does the Lord require of you but to do justice, and to love kindness, and to walk humbly with your God?" (Mic 6:8) They were sharp in their condemnation of a worship which sought to assure salvation through outward observances and even through magic. They demanded a worship of God which would be the expression of inward obedience (Amos 5:21ff.; Is 1:11–17; Jer 7; Hos 6:6). They argued from Israel's past to denounce a false faith in election (Amos 3:1f.; 9:7) and to restore Israel to the purity of its origins (Hos 2; Jer 2–4).

But the prophets did not confine themselves to the here and now. Their faith and their perspectives were wide open to the future, since they knew that they were sent to announce what Yahweh would do in the light of his faithfulness to the covenant and the conduct of his people. The words of the prophets, condemning or promising good, are necessarily related to the future: and "the Lord God does nothing, without revealing his secret to his servants the prophets" (Amos 3:7). They look into the future and include it in their words. They proclaim the coming of God to judgment (and salvation), whose Day will be darkness and disaster for all his enemies (Amos 5:20). Their view of the future leads them to expect God's intervention. The present is to be judged in the light of that future, and the shape of the future is determined by the present.

But each prophet has his own theological perspective. Hosea thinks chiefly of Yahweh's love for Israel, Amos of his action on the nations, Isaiah of the sovereign rule of the holy One of Israel, exercised from Sion. Jeremiah thinks of Yahweh's care for the misguided and apostate people of the covenant, Ezekiel of his care for the individual exposed to tribulation in the divine judgment of the exile. For Deutero-Isaiah, the creator God, the Lord of history, is the one God and redeemer. Habakkuk thinks of his justice, Trito-Isaiah and Malachi of his proper worship, while Haggai and Zechariah concentrate on the establishment of his kingdom. What they all have at heart is that man should have a true and genuine relationship to God. Amos demands that Israel should seek Yahweh, Hosea calls for knowledge and love of God, Isaiah for faith and confidence, Jeremiah for whole-hearted conversion, Ezekiel for responsible obedience to the will of God. All proclaim the almighty, transcendent, personal, morally exigent and freely gracious God, whom Israel had encountered at each stage of its history.

The verdict of the Deuteronomical writers on the history of Israel is based on the main ideas of Deuteronomy, with which they began. But they then also see it in the light of the exile. Israel is the people of Yahweh, through the covenant which he has bestowed on them: they must serve him alone and keep the law. Obedience brings blessing and life, disobedience malediction and ruin. The misery of the exile was their own fault. It had to come, because in spite of frequent warnings and punishments the people (especially its kings) had not been obedient, that is, had fallen away from Yahweh, worshipped other gods, failed to abolish the "high places" or persisted in the sin of Jeroboam (the image of Yahweh as a bull at Bethel). Nonetheless, as the favours bestowed on Jehoiachin show (2 Kg 25:27ff.), he can begin anew with Israel if he wills. But true conversion to God must be presupposed (1 Kg 8:47f.).

The writings of the Chronicler treat the post-exilic community of Jerusalem, which has to serve God in holiness and in ritual purity at and around the temple, as the realization of God's kingship on earth and the goal of history. The psalms were really chanted, it was thought, as David had desired, as hymns of praise, extolling God's help, the grace of his covenant and his gifts of salvation.

The older parts of the Wisdom literature (Prov 10:1–22:16; 25–29) give rules for living based on experience, which presuppose an order of creation according to which the action determines the result. The words of exhortation include religious and ethical motivation, which later becomes predominant. The innocent sufferer Job criticizes the schema of cause and effect. Yahweh, the cause of all, is completely free, bound to no world-order, incalculable in his actions but still true to his justice and kindness. Hence Job flies to Yahweh, his seeming enemy, as to his saviour. The Ecclesiast, himself a Wisdom teacher, flatly denies the Wisdom principle, that a law can be recognized in events and exploited for the successful shaping of life. There is nothing to be done but to be modest and temperate, to fear God and take his good gifts gratefully. But when Wisdom was identified with the faith and law of Israel, Yahweh spoke through it. It became teacher of men (Prov 1–9), mediator of revelation (Ecclus 24), moulder of history (Ecclus 44–50; Wis 10) and agent of creation (Prov 8; 3:19; Wis 7:22).

Various theological interests made use of the edifying tale, partly coloured by sapiential teaching. Jonah proclaimed God's salvific will for the pagans, Ruth his providence at work among David's ancestors, choosing its beneficiaries in response to human loyalty. Esther praises the divine retribution meted out to the enemies of God's people, Judith his mighty intervention through the hands of a weak woman. Tobit holds up the example of a God-fearing life in a pagan country (cf. Dan 1–6).

Towards the end of the OT era, the ever-widening prophetic view of the future (eschatology in the broad sense) became apocalyptic (Dan 7–12). Apocalyptic puts a radical break between this evil world dominated by forces hostile to God and the future blessed world to be brought about by God as his kingdom. The goal is a new heaven and a new earth (Is 66:22), after the universal judgment and the resurrection of the dead.

e) *The unity of the OT.* This survey of the growth and contents of the OT has shown that its theological trends and statements are very diverse. The various statements, at times seemingly opposed to one another, are linked by the profession of faith: Yahweh is our God, we are his people. For all the writers and all the books, Yahweh is the God who has turned to man, willing to save and about to judge. His people remain the one same Israel. The future belongs to God's kingship. The OT is open to this fulfilment. Here the NT begins. It sees and esteems the whole of the OT as the promise of the lordship of God, fulfilled and to be fulfilled in Jesus Christ.

f) *History of interpretation.* The use of the OT in the NT, every translation, all application of it in instruction and liturgy is interpretation. Interpretation began in the OT itself with the redaction of the prophetical books and continued in Jewish circles in the *Targums*, the *Midrashim* and the *Mishnah*. In patristic as in medieval times allegorical and typological interpretation was predominant, mainly under the influence of the NT, to the detriment of the literal sense. Four senses of Scripture were distinguished in the Middle Ages. (on which see *Biblical Exegesis*, I, III). A new approach was opened up by historical criticism, which began effectively with R. Simon and his work on the Pentateuch. Literary criticism, which reached its high-point with J. Wellhausen, was followed by form-criticism, comparative religion (Gunkel, H. Gressmann), and then the history of traditions and of redactions (M. Noth, G. von Rad). The aim is to find the real statement of each book and each section. More recently, stylistic criteria have been developed with a view to grasping the literary production as a whole in its true import.

g) *Present-day methods.* Modern exegesis is based on historical criticism in its various branches as mentioned above, with of course the textual criticism which has always been basic. The latter strives to reach the original text as far as possible and produces critical editions of the text. Literary criticism strives to decipher the possibly multiple stages in the composition of a work, to determine their origins, authors and sources, and to assign them their various dates. This makes it possible to hear the voices of the individuals through whom God announced the biblical message and to distinguish their words. Form-criticism takes seriously the affirmation that "God spoke of old in many and various ways to our fathers" (Heb 1:1). It enquires into the literary genres employed (proverb, song, psalm, prophetic oracle, treaty, charter, list, letter, law, tale, midrash, etc.), their *Sitz im Leben* or site in real life and their mode of assertion. It thus traces the content and the message aimed at in the individual items. It recognizes that genres were adopted which, from the point of view of form-criticism, must be designated as saga and legend. Israel was able to make use of them to depict the origins of humanity and pre-history in the light of its faith, and to express the holiness and divine power attached to certain persons or places.

The history of redaction aims at showing the motives at work in the juxtaposition of the individual items, while the history of traditions investigates the principles at work in the combination of pre-existing matter. Cultic history investigates the forces and tendencies which sprang from the religious life and worship of the people of Yahweh. The history of religions is invoked for comparison with the religions of the surrounding nations, in order to demarcate what is special to the OT. All these methods are used in harmony by Christian exegesis in the theological exposition which strives to make the OT message, in and by virtue of the whole divine message of both Testaments, audible to the people of God of today.

Joseph Schreiner

2. *New Testament*

a) *The name.* The expression "New Testament" is used to designate a group of twenty-seven canonical writings, the products of the Christian communities of the 1st and 2nd centuries, which were brought together to form a collection in two parts (gospels and letters). The expression "New Testament" was first used in Jer 31:31 (which is quoted in Heb 8:8) and is to be found in the NT in the Pauline-Lucan tradition of the Last Supper, in Jesus' words over the cup (1 Cor 11:35; Lk 22:20), and in 2 Cor 3:6; Heb 9:15; 12:24. The complementary expression παλαιὰ διαθήκη is first found in Paul (2 Cor 3:14). In every case the καινὴ διαθήκη stands for the order of redemption inaugurated by the death of Jesus in contrast to the order deriving from Moses. Thus διαθήκη in the NT is used much in the same sense as the Hebrew *b^e^rīt* (in the theological sense: the covenant established by God). While διαθήκη in Hellenism was only occasionally used in the sense of "arrangement" (Aristophanes, Dinarchus) and mostly meant "testament", in the LXX and NT it acquired the broader meaning of *b^e^rīt* (except in Gal 3:15, 17), that is, "order of salvation". The rendering "new testament" (first used by Tertullian) narrows the meaning of διαθήκη once more to "final disposition" (which is also the meaning of the word in the title of apocryphal writings such as the *Test. XII* and the *Testament of Our Lord Jesus Christ*. The expression "New Testament", as the title of a book, is really a shortened form of the genitive – meaning the writings "of the New Testament". Thus, *c.* 180 Melito of Sardes drew up a list of books τῆς παλαιᾶς διαθήκης; *c.* 192 we find the expression ὁ τῆς τοῦ εὐαγγελίου καινῆς διαθήκης λόγος, while Tertullian speaks of "totum instrumentum utriusque testamenti". The way was thus open to call the books themselves the "New Testament". But Eusebius *(Hist. Eccl.*, V, 16, 3) still speaks of the "gospel of the new covenant". It was therefore customary at that time to speak of the writings of the New Covenant when one contrasted them with those of the OT and claimed for them at least an equal standing.

Jesus and the authors of the NT understood by the expression ἡ γραφή only the OT. The NT writings, however, are not primarily an interpretative canon of the OT but the transmission of the eschatological message of salvation, which could not have been derived from the OT but was made known only in the messianic age which began with Jesus. Jesus and the post-resurrection community already felt themselves outside the OT, the imperfect product of a past age of salvation, which the new stage of the history of salvation had left behind. The OT only became a problem when the now "unfaithful" Jews appealed to their scriptures against the Church. Thus began the struggle for the secondary legitimation of the message of Christ before the Jews, which made it necessary for Christians to interpret the whole of the OT in a positive and consistently Christian way. It began with the assertion that the suffering and resurrection of Jesus were "according to the Scriptures". From this positive assertion there soon followed the negative one, that the Jews did not understand the Scriptures, an accusation which then proceeded to a discussion of individual passages. As early as the reflective citations of Mt, the prophetic and Deuteronomic schema of "promise-fulfilment" was applied, and in Mt 5:17 it was invoked for Jesus' interpretation of the Law. Whereas the life and teaching of Jesus were originally considered against the horizon of the apocalyptic tradition, as the fulfilment of the sacred history of the Jewish people, they then became more and more the exegetical principle for the interpretation of the OT. But the promise-fulfilment schema was soon largely abandoned for the allegorical method (*Letter of Barnabas*). The proof from Scripture basically had only a secondary and anti-Jewish function, whereas the NT writings primarily derived their validity from the eschatological authority of the Lord or the "apostles". In 2 Clem we have the first instance of a NT citation referred to as "scripture".

b) *The different types of writings*. The different literary genres in the NT depend to a certain extent on the theological purposes of the writings in question. The genre "gospel" was created by Mark, for a collection of traditions concerning the earthly life of Jesus which were viewed in the light of a post-resurrection theology. With the help of biographical data, the whole of the theological outlook of a community was moulded into a description of Jesus' preaching. With the addition of the infancy narratives this draft was considerably expanded by Mt and Lk and became an early sort of "Life of our Lord". Whereas Mk grafts his whole theological conception on to the period before Easter, Mt distinguishes between the time of Jesus in Israel before his death and the sending out of the Twelve to the gentiles after Easter (Mt 28). With this the gospel-form was decisively changed; it now contained post-Easter meetings with Jesus and his words on those occasions. This trend is carried still further by Lk. The history of Jesus is followed by the history of the gospel among Jews and gentiles in Acts. The two volumes of Lk's work are an expression of the theological notion of the time of Jesus as the "middle of time". In Jn, as in Mk, the post-Easter period has been fully incorporated into the pre-Easter, the theological work appearing much more clearly, however, than in Mk. The addition of the "prologue" was a decided innovation in the gospel genre.

While each of the gospels preserves the form of historical narration, the theology expressed in the second part of the NT, the letters, is largely independent in content of such historical reports. Because of the different nature of this theology it seems highly unlikely that Paul could have written a gospel, or even that he would have wanted to. Paul's theology, entirely and exclusively centred upon the risen Lord, is expressed in community-letters (e.g., Gal), didactic epistles (Rom), open letters (Col), and private letters (Phm). These distinctions can be applied to other NT letters: Heb can be considered as an epistle; Eph, 1 and 2 Pet and Jude are "open letters"; 1 Jn etc. are like sermons; and the pastoral letters are similar in form to the community-letters. A special genre from late Judaism is found in the Book of Revelation. The degree of literary independence in the writers varies. In the four gospels one must presume the existence of written sources (Mk for Mt and Lk; Q for Mt and Lk; the so-called *semeia-source* for Jn). In Rev and the Pastoral Letters the material from other sources is much more extensive (liturgical hymns in 1 Tim 3:16; Rev 12) than in the letters of Paul (1 Cor 15:3f.; 11:23ff.). The problem of pseudepigraphy must be dealt with on its merits for each individual work. One must always reckon with the possibility that writings were handed on under the names of apostles which merely came from where the traditional influence of the apostle in question was at work (cf. the non-canonical gospels of Peter, James and Thomas).

c) *Methods of research.* These begin with textual criticism, which has the task of comparing manuscripts and establishing the main families in the tradition of a text (an "original text" can hardly be hoped for). It must determine the value of various readings and possibly offer conjectural emendations. Literary criticism examines a text (or a whole book) for its literary unity. Negative criteria include grammatical, stylistic or conceptual harshness, unnecessary repetitions (e.g., in Mk 2:27 "and he said to them" which is repeated after v. 25, although Jesus had not been interrupted) and doublets. Thus the text is broken down into the basic elements of its literary composition and its technique laid bare. After literary criticism there follows the establishment of the "smallest unities", i.e., certain phrases which can be shown to be fixed formulas by comparison with other texts (a concordance is used for this). The next step is to determine the various literary forms (e.g., controversies, didactic passages, hymns, etc.).

Form criticism is the comparison of a form as it appears in various texts. The *Sitz im Leben* or actual setting of a form varies according to where it is used. Thus the original setting of the controversy was Jesus' opposition to the Pharisees, but its later context was the general anti-Jewish polemic of the early community. Not enough attention is paid as a rule to the distinction between the literary form or unit and the literary genre, the latter being difficult to define. The history of the genre should be noted as well as the history of the form. The genre contains as a rule more than one literary form, and has a more definite sociological function. Hence its content is also easier to determine. The gospel is a genre linked to a biographical type of presentation and is not confined by its nature to doctrinal exposition. Its *Sitz im Leben* is the communal liturgy. An examination of Lk on the basis of the history of genres shows that it approximates to biographies of the profane type. Forms foreign to the literature in question must not be adduced. Saga and legend, for instance, occur in completely different cultural milieux and are unsuitable as classifications of biblical forms. And form-criticism is not concerned with the historicity of the material, but only with literary techniques. To throw light on the material, the history of concepts and motifs may be used, along with comparative religion and history of traditions. History of traditions must be applied to the text itself, to bring to light, with the help of the history of redaction, the various stages in the development of a text and their theologies. History of redaction tries to see how a tradition is affected by the theological "system" of the author. Hence the object of historical criticism is to determine the theology of the individual author.

d) *The problem of theological unity.* The various theologies of the NT can be divided into three basic types: the Pauline (between *c.* A.D. 35 and 60), the synoptic (70–90), and the Johannine (*c.* 100). The Letter to the Hebrews represents a theology of its own. The starting-point in each system is the death and resurrection of Jesus. While

Mk uses the life of Jesus to reflect his interpretation of the death and resurrection – a procedure developed most unmistakably in Jn – the epistles and Rev do not. Paul appeals to sayings of Jesus only in three places, and in Jas 5:12 what appears as a saying of Jesus in Mt 5:33ff. appears as a precept of the author. Paul teaches by the authority of his apostolate (for which of course he can also invoke the risen Lord), while the synoptics feel bound to attribute all teaching to Jesus himself. What is common above all to these three theologies is the conviction that the community of salvation possesses the Spirit. It is this which is decisively and demonstrably new in the condition in which the post-Easter community finds itself. It is the link between the receding past (Jesus' life, death, and resurrection) and the still unseen future. This conception of the Spirit, however, as salvation, is combined with different viewpoints regarding the manner of the presence or the futurity of the imminent kingdom of God. Whereas in Jesus' preaching of the coming kingdom the central salvific event is in the future, after the resurrection salvation was considered as already definitively granted in the person of Jesus. Jesus, indeed, already saw in his own possession of the Spirit the beginning of the kingdom, and this is also the pre-Easter origin of Christology. The danger threatening post-Easter theology was to lose sight of the eschatological perspective by making the resurrection of Jesus too exclusively the centre of history. The Gnostics succumbed to this danger.

Against such groups Paul stresses that salvation is linked both to the historical existence and death of Jesus, and to the judgment which is yet to come. Mk solves the problem by depicting the Spirit as already poured out upon Jesus and manifest in the activity of the Twelve, but not to be given to all until the end. The justification of such a long intermediary period preceding the end became one of the more pressing problems facing post-Marcan theology, the problem of what is called the delay of the parousia. In Lk and Jn the time of the Church is presented in a positive way as a planned and necessary time of salvation. According to Jn this is the time of the Paraclete through whom alone the full revelation of Jesus is uttered. But even in Paul the presence of the Spirit in the community was not distinct from the presence of the risen Lord. Thus the problem of the intermediary period and of the function of the community was solved independently of the kingdom of God: with respect to the kingdom of God the community is characterized not only by the fact that its universality is as yet unfulfilled, but also by the fact that in it the return of the Lord has already occurred in the possession of the Spirit. The varieties of theologies in the NT are based not only on different views of the coming end, but also on the different views of the person of Jesus and consequently of the role of the community.

These Christologies are expressed in a series of titles, each of which comprises only one aspect and which are hard to define on account of the obscurity of their origins. The pre-Easter titles are: rabbi, teacher, prophet, son of David, king of the Jews; the title "Son of man" is found on the lips of Jesus himself (only in the third person). The title most important subsequently was "Son of God". Other names are: servant of God, Messias, Kyrios, Christos, redeemer, the holy and just one, lamb of God, and high-priest. The titles which the community applied to itself either indicated its pre-Easter relationship to Jesus as teacher, such as μαθηταί (disciples), or placed the community on the level of the Israel of the OT, e.g., "the saints" (Paul, Acts), the "little ones", also the poor, the elect, the called, χριστιανοί, *ecclesia*, brethren, people of God, household and friends of God, strangers, Nazareans and Galileans. It is striking that the plural titles with a personal character (saints, etc.) predominate over the singular collective titles (*ecclesia*, people). The death of Jesus in particular is given different interpretations. The Synoptics are hardly aware of the significance of Jesus' death for the salvation of Christians; only the formula "for many" in Mk 10:45; 14:24 seems to indicate the vicarious function of his death. The predominant interpretation is that of the suffering just man. In Jn terms descriptive of suffering are avoided, and the death of Jesus is presented only as exaltation and the departure requisite for the sending of the Spirit. It was Paul above all who saw the death of Jesus as the decisive condition of possibility of salvation: through his death Jesus took upon himself the burden of sin which man had borne since Adam and the malediction which fell upon all. Here too the death itself has a merely negative function, the removal of malediction and sin; the positive gift of salvation is seen by Paul also as the possession of the Spirit through the presence of the risen Lord. In this view the sphere of the *sarx* is eliminated only by that of the *pneuma*.

In contrast to the Pauline theology, the basic idea of Hebrews is that Jesus' death on the cross was a high-priestly act, through which he could win the blood with which he could purify the heavenly sanctuary. Rev also considers the blood of Jesus to be the most important element of the death, for through it Christians were cleansed and their accuser conquered; it also saw the exaltation as a victory. Next to these dogmatic differences of the authors there is also another aspect which should be considered. The NT writings are witnesses of the history of early Christianity as a whole as well as theological products of the individual authors. The development therefore is not only dogmatic but concerns the constitution, liturgy and ethics of the communities. These differences in the NT interpretation of the salvation brought by Jesus need not be a difficulty for dogmatic theologians, who will see there the temporal variations of a revelation in Jesus Christ which must necessarily remain many-sided until the final revelation in glory. Accordingly, ecclesiastical tradition has the task of unifying these theologies to some extent, to prepare in a way for the unity of the final revelation. This procedure of tradition does indeed run counter to the direction of exegesis, since the latter by determining the peculiarities of each of the theologies shows that the unity in question, though valid, is only provisional, in relation to the *eschaton*. But the two efforts are complementary, since the Church must constantly look back to its beginnings as it longs for the end.

e) *History of interpretation*. To use any piece of writing is at once to give it an interpretation; the NT writings were first used in the liturgy, which interpreted them chiefly by combining them with other texts. A similar type of interpretation is represented by the fact that they were combined to form the canon, since this meant that they were considered to be of apostolic origin, free from heresy (Gnosticism), acceptable by the Catholic Church (Muratorian Canon), and substantially uniform in content. This interpretation of the NT was then adopted by systematic theology in particular, which sometimes included even the OT in this perspective. A special type of interpretation is represented by the textual history of the NT, since the text itself was altered to introduce interpretations of varying degrees of importance. This is a wide field, as the texts include 72 papyri, 242 majuscules, 2570 minuscules, and 1909 lectionaries.

Another type of exegesis takes the form of translations, paraphrases, glosses, scholions, commentaries, postils, and catenae. A strictly scientific examination of the text, to see what the author meant and not how the reader could use it, was first introduced, for all practical purposes, by Richard Simon (1693). His lead was subsequently followed mainly by Protestants, especially J. S. Semler and J. D. Michaelis. The beginning of the 19th century was dominated by "critique of tendencies" of F. C. Baur, Tübingen, and the "mythical" explanations of D. F. Strauss. The most important Protestant exegetical trends of the 20th century are the "thoroughgoing (*konsequente*) eschatology" (J. Weiss, A. Schweitzer), the school of history of religions (Bousset), form-criticism (Dibelius, Bultmann) and the return to theological interpretation in the programme of demythologizing put forward by R. Bultmann. The acme of Catholic exegesis was the Humanist period of the 16th century; the pioneer work of R. Simon, and other efforts in the time of the Enlightenment were not followed up.

A revival of Catholic exegesis set in at the beginning of the 20th century, chiefly stimulated by J.-M. Lagrange. Important achievements may be signalled in textual criticism, translation and archaeology. The critical reading of the text was encouraged in particular by the encyclical "Divino afflante Spiritu" of Pius XII in 1943 and by the Constitution on Revelation of Vatican II.

Klaus Berger

B. Theology

1. *The theological basis of a theology of holy Scripture.* a) It must not be forgotten in the first place that for us Christians today this fundamental basis can and must be a specifically Christian one. Only then can the OT be seen as a part of our sacred Scripture. For us the situation is just the opposite to what it was in NT times, when the significance for salvation of the events concerning Christ had to be demonstrated from the OT scriptures, for it was their validity which was taken for granted. This historically conditioned starting-point is unavoidable and should not be blurred (Vatican II, for example, in *Dei Verbum*, art. 2 [cf. art. 7] takes its starting-point for the concept of revelation the revelation in Jesus Christ and not revelation in general which it only begins to discuss in art. 3). Consequently we must first seek a theological basis for the theology of the NT. For our purpose here we must assume that the questions of the relation of faith to the rational and historical demonstration of its legitimacy, and of dogmatic to fundamental theology, have already been answered. We are dealing with a strictly theological question, not really with one that belongs to fundamental theology.

b) The theological conception of Scripture (in regard to its inspiration, canon, inerrancy, its relation to tradition, its normative character for the Church and the Church's profession of faith and theology) has its sole root in the faith under two of its aspects. On the one hand – and this becomes historically clear for the first time in the Christ-event – God mercifully communicates himself by turning in his grace to mankind throughout its whole history of salvation, of which he is the origin and goal. On the other hand, this history and God's self-communication shows itself to be victorious by attaining its irreversible manifestation and final form in Jesus Christ crucified and risen. And the now irreversible historical manifestation of God's grace-giving will involves the abiding existence of the community of those who believe in Jesus Christ. This is the Church, which in its faith and worship always remains related to the eschatological saving event itself, which is Jesus Christ, and therefore to its own history. It can only remain true to its own nature if it understands itself to be the Church of the apostolic age, however ready it has to be to accept its own changes in the course of history. For it is only through the apostolic Church and its testimony to the faith that the Church attains Jesus Christ.

c) The normative presence of the Church of the apostolic age in the later Church primarily occurs through tradition (as life and teaching), in the legitimate authoritative mission of the ministry. The preaching which produces faith by the power of the Spirit, and the formal authority conferred by the mission condition one another. But precisely this perpetual recourse, in tradition, to the first age of the Church requires the Church to be able to distinguish between its own attestation of the activity and teaching of the apostolic Church and the content of its testimony: the activity and faith of the primitive Church. For that reference has to serve as a critical standard of the Church's activity and teaching. That need is met if written testimony of a normative kind concerning the activity and belief of the primitive Church is available. The importance of authoritative tradition is not diminished by it. For the interpretation of the written testimony has to be given existentially in a way binding on faith by the living magisterium of the Church (which preserves the historical link with the primitive Church and so with Jesus Christ). And above all, this reality which serves as a critical standard has itself to be transmitted by tradition, both as regards its nature (inspiration) and extent (canon). The written testimony is therefore not something which stands quite outside tradition and its authoritative representatives (magisterium). It is an element of, and in, tradition itself. Only the abidingly victorious power of the Spirit ultimately guarantees that a unity and distinction of that kind will remain effective, in other words, that the normative function of Scripture will endure. Belief and hope that this power will prevail and preserve that unity and distinction is involved in faith in God's eschatological victory in Jesus Christ. There can therefore only be sacred Scripture in an authoritative tradition. But the latter "posits" Scripture for itself as its own criterion, i.e., as an element intrinsic to it but distinct from it, needed for tradition itself to exist.

d) We can therefore provisionally say that holy Scripture is the verbal, written objectivation of the apostolic Church in its activity and confession of faith, as an element and intrinsic norm of the tradition in which the Church of later times attests the eschatological saving event itself, which is Jesus Christ. If the "beginning" of the Church is envisaged not just as its first phase in time but as laying the permanent foundation for its continued existence, that beginning must be permanently present. It must remain present in the Church's historical dimension (though not only in this) in the explicit profession of faith (even when this faith is given conceptual formulation), in the norm of faith binding on all, in the possibility of a humanly verifiable recourse to this enduring normative beginning of the Last Days. Consequently there exists a pure and therefore absolutely normative objective expression of the permanence of that beginning, a *norma non normata*. This is what we call Scripture.

2. *Inspiration of Scripture*. From what has been said it is clear that the origin of Scripture is not to be imagined as dictation from God received by the sacred writers in a purely passive way. They are truly authors (*Dei Verbum*, art. 11), each writing his own work under the "inspiration of the Holy Spirit" (*ibid.*). But while it is their own work, in each particular case it also attests the faith of the community to which the writer belongs. And that community knows that it is a valid member of the one Church. Conse-

quently these writings in their unity and multiplicity attest the faith of the apostolic Church, which was to be the permanently valid norm of the faith of the Church in following ages. These writings are "inspired", because willed by God in formal predefinition as a permanent norm of that kind. For God in Jesus Christ willed the Church to be permanent and apostolic, the latter understood in its two aspects as norm and as normative, as apostolic Church and as later Church. The Church recognizes these writings to be in conformity with its own kerygma and is conscious that it is permanently bound to them because they are writings of the Church which is the norm. It does not thereby constitute their inspiration, but recognizes it, without needing any special and detailed revelations in order to do so. Such revelations are improbable in view of the historically merely "occasional" character of some of these writings and the late date of some in relation to the apostles themselves.

3. *The canon and its formation.* The theologically decisive statement about the canon and the Church's recognition of it has already been made. The canon as a dogmatic question, and the problem it raises in the history of dogma, hinges on the problem of how it could be recognized. How can the revelation of the canon appear historically probable? In particular, how is it compatible with the fact that the formation of the canon was long and hesitant? A revelation must in fact be involved, for the truth of the canon cannot be regarded as *fides ecclesiastica* as opposed to *fides divina*. In the first place the idea of the apostolic Church (the Church of the first generation, of the period when revelation was still taking place, down "to the death of the last apostle") must not be taken too narrowly. Otherwise difficulties will arise over the rather late date of composition of some NT writings. But there is no need to interpret it too narrowly if we regard the first generation not on the merely biological plane but in intellectual history. A reality of that kind cannot be fixed *a priori* by a precisely ascertainable measure of years and days. On the other hand, the formation (i.e., recognition) of the canon in the post-apostolic period had a long history, although no new revelation was then possible. But if it were necessary to regard revelation concerning the canon as the direct communication of particular propositions about the various writings, then a new revelation in the post-apostolic period would have been needed, because of the slow and hesitant formation of the canon. The question therefore is whether it is possible to conceive an original revelation of the canon in the apostolic period which was so implicit that its explication took time and passed through various fluctuations (the development of dogma). Can the nature of Scripture be conceived as being essentially willed by God as an element of the primitive Church which was to be normative for all time, an element forming part of the divinely established constitution of that Church in its character as norm of the future? If so, its inspiration would be radically revealed *in* the revelation of the comprehensive reality of the normative primitive Church. This would then be the explicit element from which the later Church was able gradually to recognize the limits of the canon without a new revelation.

4. "*Sufficiency*" *of Scripture.* On the basis of the relation between Scripture and tradition which we have briefly outlined, it is also possible to give some answer to the question of the "sufficiency" of Scripture and so arrive at a Catholic answer to the Protestant principle of *sola scriptura*. In the first place it is obvious that the Church's kerygma of the apostolic period preceded Scripture. That authoritative Church kerygma, which was proclaimed with

perpetual reference to previous preaching, did not cease when Scripture came into existence. Consequently that kerygma is "tradition"; and hence tradition is not purely and simply a reference back to Scripture as such (*Dei Verbum*, arts. 7 and 8). This tradition also transmits Scripture as inspired, and as having such and such an extent (canon). Tradition therefore attests the character and range of Scripture and to that extent Scripture is not self-sufficient. At least to that degree too it is clear "that the Church does not derive from holy Scripture alone the certainty it possesses about all that has been revealed" (*ibid.*, art. 9). In the concrete therefore it can only be a question of whether the aposolic tradition in fact originally contained not only the attestation of the nature and extent of Scripture but some particular propositions which are not found in any way in Scripture, and which were transmitted as binding in faith by purely "oral tradition". If that is so, revelation (over and above the testimony of tradition to Scripture) comes to us in two "streams" which in content are partly distinct and which are often misleadingly called "sources". To the question framed in these terms the Council of Trent gives no plain answer (*D* 783). At any rate the interpretation of its text is disputed to this day. Vatican II strictly avoided adopting any position on the question. In seeking an objective solution it has to be noted first that an obscure and largely unsolved problem arises about the development of dogma. How exactly are we to conceive the explication of what was implicit in the original revelation?

Only on the assumption that an answer has been found to this question is it possible to attempt to determine *a posteriori* whether or not some particular dogma at the present day which cannot be found explicitly in Scripture may nevertheless be contained there implicitly. Conversely it is possible to say that it is unlikely that something which was defined later as a dogma of the Church should have existed as an explicit proposition in the apostolic age without also being present in Scripture, and that we could prove this historically. Yet this would have to be the case if the appeal to an apostolic tradition materially different from Scripture were to have any meaning and not remain a purely dogmatic postulate. Appeal to a materially distinct apostolic tradition, therefore, solves no concrete problems of the history and development of dogma. In that direction at least, nothing stands in the way of an assertion of the material sufficiency of Scripture, within the limits stated. What is not explicitly or in some way contained in Scripture cannot be historically proved to have been part of the original apostolic kerygma. The definition of a proposition by the magisterium guarantees of course the fact that it is so contained (at least implicitly) but does not dispense the theologian from raising the question how this presence there is to be conceived. It is no easier to find an answer to this question by appealing to oral tradition than to the implications of Scripture.

5. *The Old Testament in the canon of the Church.* The old covenant was part of the context of the Christ-event and was willed by God precisely as such. The primitive Church understood and held fast to the old covenant as its own legitimate pre-history. Consequently the OT scriptures, as an element of that covenant, were willed by God and inspired. While this is true, it must be remembered that in the old covenant there was no authoritative, infallible court of appeal able to determine the canon. It was impossible for there to be one, for such a thing is an eschatological reality and could exist only in and after Christ. Before Christ, therefore, the holy scriptures of the OT were still in process of coming into existence as

scriptures in the absolute NT sense (in contradistinction to the vague sense of sacred writings such as is used in comparative religion). This will be clear if we realize that the setting up of Scripture as a definitive *norma normans* plainly marked off from other writings necessarily demands the setting up of a subject who recognizes it for what it is. The OT is only Scripture in the *full* sense to the extent that the new covenant is already present in a hidden way in the old – already there but still hidden (*Dei Verbum*, art. 16). Consequently the writings of the old covenant only "*acquire* and display their full signification in the New Testament" (*ibid.*).

It is important to realize this because it is the basis of the principle of interpreting the OT in the light of Christ (cf. arts. 14–16). Of course that does not mean that the experience of the sacred history of redemption and of the relation between God and man as reflected in the OT is only important for men in the new covenant by its specifically Christological implications. The OT books not only "illuminate and interpret" the Christ-event (art. 16) but are in themselves of permanent validity, despite "much that is imperfect and ephemeral" (art. 15) in them because of the phase of sacred history to which they belong, which is no longer ours. There is an OT theology of the OT scriptures and a NT theology of these writings, just as there is a unity, a difference and a relation between the two covenants. Conversely, it must also be remembered, however, that in the new covenant Jesus Christ himself is what is revealed. Furthermore, in his eschatologically victorious Spirit he turns men's hearts to faith and causes this victory to be made manifest in the Church. Consequently, NT revelation essentially goes beyond the letter of something written. From this point of view, therefore, Scripture is more essential to the old covenant than it is to the new. The NT does not simply continue the scriptures of the old covenant in the same line.

6. *Inerrancy of Scripture*. The inerrancy of Scripture follows from its divine inspiration and authorship and its function as *norma non normata* in the Church and for its infallible magisterium. The latter is not superior to Scripture but serves it (*Dei Verbum*, art. 10). This inerrancy is a dogma of faith, as far as the authentic revealed doctrine of Scripture is concerned (*D* 706f., 1787, 1809, 1950, 2180). But this statement does not answer the more precise question that inerrancy raises. In this respect the best starting-point will be the declaration of the Dogmatic Constitution *Dei Verbum*, art. 11: "It is to be professed that the books of Scripture teach certainly, faithfully and without error the truth that God for our salvation willed to be recorded in the sacred Scriptures." (Cf. on this the references quoted by the Council, *D* 783, *Enchiridion Biblicum*, 121, 124, 126–7, 539.) That statement is certainly not positively intended to bear a restrictive sense and to teach that only truths regarding salvation, in contradistinction to secular truths, are meant. But neither is such a meaning clearly excluded, for it is not clear that the references appended are to be regarded as a binding interpretation of the text. The distinction between salutary truth and secular statements – the latter assumed to be made as absolute affirmations in Scripture – was chiefly current at the time of Modernism, and was rejected in this connection from Leo XIII to Pius XII.

In practice the distinction perhaps leads to a superfluous, unreal dilemma. If it is made, the answer (at least according to Leo XIII and Pius XII) must be that even secular statements of that kind in Scripture cannot be false. But in fact the real question is whether, if the rules of biblical hermeneutics (cf. *Dei Verbum*, arts. 12, 19; *D* 2294; *Enchiridion Biblicum*, 557–62; instruction of the Biblical Commission, "Sancta Mater Ecclesia", *AAS* 56 [1964], p. 715) are applied precisely and strictly, Scripture really contains any purely secular affirmations the correctness of which the sacred writer intends absolutely to guarantee in the sense of a modern historical (and scientific) concept of truth, and the accuracy of which creates a problem for us. If we can deny that this question arises, then the statement of *Dei Verbum*, art. 11, can be taken as affirming only the inerrancy of truths of salvation in Scripture, without thereby coming into real conflict with papal declarations from Leo XIII to Pius XII. In scriptural statements, whether theological or secular in content, we must be slow to assume that there is an error in a proposition which is really affirmed as binding. This can be avoided if note is taken of the following.

a) The *genus litterarium* (*D* 1980, 2302, 2329). What are the precise limits of what the text is intended to affirm, in other words, what is really meant and asserted by the statement? b) The unavoidable blurring of outline which characterizes all human speech and therefore even every true statement. This cannot be described as error. This is evident, e.g., in reports from two sources. c) We must carefully distinguish between mode and content of statement, between what is meant and the pattern of notions which is used but not affirmed (the perspective in which a statement is made and conceptual schemata which are assumed but not subjected to judgment), between personal statement and mere report of current opinions and mere appearances (implicit quotations: *D* 1979, 2090, 2188). d) It must be remembered that an absence of knowledge which is apparent in the mode of statement is not itself a denial of what is not known. Nor does the impossibility of harmonizing two statements on the plane of representative schemata of itself mean that it is impossible for the two statements nevertheless to agree in content. The fact that a statement is made within a certain limited perspective does not mean that it is erroneous.

The dogmatic theologian starts from Scripture's origin as the normative attestation of revelation and formulates the thesis of the inerrancy of Scripture *in globo* on that basis. The exegete starts from the individual writings, their statements and their immediate meaning. He then inquires critically into the correctness of the various statements. In this way there arises a tension, impossible to resolve in every particular case, between the postulates of the dogmatic theologian and the findings of the exegete. This is so particularly because the former determines the meaning of a particular statement on the basis of his general principle, whereas the second determines the meaning and limits of the general principle on the basis of an exegesis of the particular statement. If the dogmatic theologian is clear about his method and its limitations, he cannot forbid the exegete to qualify as inaccurate, in the light of modern demands for truth, certain sentences which are taken by themselves and do not concern any salutary truth. That does not contradict what is really meant by the Church's doctrine of the inerrancy of Scripture. There are such statements in Scripture, and a judgment of that kind cannot be avoided in exegesis, where the individual statement in itself has to be examined as regards its meaning and correctness and not only in regard to what it means in relation to the whole of Scripture and the ultimate *genera litteraria*.

7. *Theologies in the New Testament.* The Church is composed of historically unique, free persons, and their uniqueness (which cannot be reduced to being a mere instance of the universal term "man") shows itself even in their faith. In all ages the Church has been a unity

of Churches differing in time, place, culture and theology. This also applies to the Church of the apostolic period. By the very nature of the Church, then, these features must also appear in the NT writings since these are an expression of the Church of that age, and they do not simply contain the simple statement of the original revelation-event. They also embody theological reflection on it. Consequently by the very nature of the Church and of Scripture there must be a variety of theologies in the NT itself. That means that it contains what in the later history of the Church were called "schools of theology". Now the real nature of these schools does not of course reside in the points where they contradict one another and where one of them at most can be right. It consists in the difference of their general perspectives, of the concepts they employ, etc., things which need not necessarily be in flat contradiction, yet which cannot simply be replaced by a higher synthesis.

It is the exegete's right and function to perceive and work out such a plurality of theologies in the NT. Before a biblical theology is possible, he must expound the biblical theologies. From the dogmatic point of view the ultimate unity of these theologies is ensured and guaranteed by the Church's awareness of its faith, which determines the canon and understands Scripture as a unity therein. But that does not mean that the biblical theologian can overlook the plurality of theologies in the NT, nor that he (or the dogmatic theologian) has the task of completely replacing that plurality by raising it into a single higher system. For various reasons, that is impossible, though such a "reduction to unity" is a goal which theology seeks to approach asymptomatically. What the exegete may not do is to assert that in canonical Scripture statements are to be found which contradict one another even when each is correctly interpreted (with due regard for the analogy of faith: *Dei Verbum*, art. 12), so that one or other must be accepted and the other rejected. It is of course possible to conceive of a "canon within the canon" (as a norm which would permit of a certain critical, i.e., more precise interpretation) in the sense in which the Decree on Ecumenism, art. 11, speaks of "basic Christian belief". But a canon of that kind cannot be set up as a norm in opposition to Scripture, to individual elements or to theologies within it, as for example against what has been termed "early Catholicism" in later writings of the NT.

8. *Scripture (biblical theology) and dogmatics*. a) All tradition is always a unity of divine and human tradition which it is not possible absolutely to separate by reflection. Every stage of the development of dogma and of the history of theology confirms this. Any theological thought examining and appealing to one or other of these particular traditions therefore requires a criterion of what precisely in each can be regarded as *traditio divina* and what can only be held to be *traditio humana*. Especially when clarification is sought about some proposition which may perhaps be definable as a truth of faith, but which had not previously been expressly handed down as such, as well as in other previously controverted questions which are to be elucidated by the magisterium, tradition as it in fact stands does not of itself provide this discrimination. In Scripture, on the other hand, such a mixture of divine and human tradition is not found. It is, if we may use the expression, pure *traditio divina*. And so it can serve as one criterion at least for this distinction within the rest of tradition.

This does not of course mean that such a process of clarificatory discrimination does not require a long time. The application of that criterion is not a mechanical or even a purely logical operation. It is itself history. And Scripture, like all human truth, bears the stamp of history and has an intrinsically temporal character. It employs an already existing terminology which need not necessarily be simply and in every respect the best. It envisages the truth, which it attests, from various points of view and within mental perspectives which are not the only possible ones. Its statements may in many respects be historically conditioned. Scripture expresses a truth which will have a further history, the history of dogma, in fact. But, unlike any other possible or actual literature of the apostolic age, Scripture is a pure expression of divine truth in a human embodiment. In Scripture, knowledge of divine truth has indeed a starting-point which is both divine and human. But it has no starting-point from which a definite human element would have to be eliminated if we were not to miss the truth from the start. That of course can be so when we are dealing with "unpurified" tradition. Consequently, for theology, Scripture is a reality which has to be interpreted in the spirit and under the guidance and guarantee of the Church and its magisterium. Yet such interpretation is not really a criticism of Scripture but of its reader. Even the magisterium which interprets Scripture under the assistance of the Spirit, does not thereby place itself above Scripture but under it (cf. *Dei Verbum*, art. 10); it knows that Scripture brought into existence by the Spirit and read by the Church with the assistance of the Spirit conveys its true meaning. In that way Scripture remains the *norma non normata* of theology and the Church.

b) This is the basis on which the relation of biblical to dogmatic theology should be viewed. Dogmatic theology cannot avoid engaging in biblical theology. For dogmatic theology is a systematic, deliberate attention to God's revelation in Jesus Christ. It is not merely a theology of conclusions drawn from the principles of faith assumed as premisses, as medieval theology theoretically conceived itself to be, though its real practice was quite different. Consequently dogmatic theology must listen most attentively to revelation where the most direct and ultimate source of Christian revelation is to be found, namely in Scripture. Of course dogmatic theology always reads Scripture under the guidance of the magisterium, because it reads Scripture in the Church, and therefore instructed by the Church's present proclamation of the faith.

It follows that theology always reads Scripture with a knowledge which is not simply to be found in that precise form in Scripture. The theologian has always to study his theology on the basis of the Church's present awareness of its faith. And there has been a genuine development of dogma. Nevertheless theology has not simply the task of expounding the present teaching of the faith by the Church's magisterium and of showing it to be justified from Scripture by finding *dicta probantia* for it there. Its own function as dogmatic theology in regard to Scripture goes beyond this process, which is unfortunately too often almost the only one. In the first place, the existing Church itself is always reading Scripture, reading it to the faithful and ordering it to be read. It is, therefore, not the case that *only* what is taught in the Church by councils, encyclicals, catechisms, etc. belongs to the actual teaching of the Church's magisterium. Scripture itself is also what is actually officially proclaimed at all times in the Church. If then the present teaching of the Church is assigned to the dogmatic theologian as the immediate object of his reflection, by that very fact Scripture itself it assigned to him as the immediate object of his endeavours as a dogmatic theologian. Scripture is therefore not merely a *fons remotus*, i.e., the ultimate source to which the dogmatic theologian traces back the Church's teaching. It is his direct concern, because he cannot really totally separate Scripture as a distinct reality and source from the Church's present teaching.

Furthermore, theological concern with God's revelation in the actual teaching of the Church's magisterium, and in the mind of the Church of one's own time, inevitably leads back to Scripture. That is so even where that teaching is not the actual reading of Scripture in the Church of the present. The full understanding of present doctrine demands a perpetual return to the source from which, on its own admission, this doctrine is derived. There has to be a return to the doctrine which the Church's teaching itself is intended to expound and actualize here and now. In other words, there has to be recourse to Scripture (cf. on this *Optatam totius*, art. 16). Biblical theology is therefore an intrinsic element in dogmatic theology itself. And it is so not merely as one element side by side with other elements of "historical theology". It is an absolutely pre-eminent and unique part of dogmatic theology itself. This does not mean of course that biblical theology should not for various reasons establish itself as an independent branch of study within theology as a whole. That is quite appropriate, even on practical grounds. In practice it is only in the rarest cases that the dogmatic theologian himself can be a professionally qualified exegete, as he would have to be if he were to try to do his biblical theology for himself. The pre-eminent position which belongs to biblical theology within dogmatics, in comparison with its other concerns (patristic theology, medieval scholasticism, modern scholastic theology) is therefore better provided for, if biblical theology is not pursued solely as part of dogmatics. Perhaps in the course of the reform of ecclesiastical studies, a separate specialist department will be formed in which biblical theology will be pursued neither as a mere prolongation of ordinary exegesis nor as a mere element in dogmatic theology, but as a separate branch of study which will represent the correct intermediary between exegesis and dogmatic theology.

9. *Scripture, spiritual life and pastoral work*. a) As regards "holy Scripture in the life of the Church", we may simply refer here for the sake of brevity to Vatican II, *Dei Verbum*, chapter vi (arts. 21–25). To this should be added what is said in arts. 7, 24, 51, 56, 92 of the Constitution on the Liturgy, in *Optatam totius*, art. 16, in the Decree on Ecumenism, art. 21, and in *Presbyterium ordinis*, art. 13. Nothing needs to be added here to these urgent admonitions that Scripture should be read by all Christians, that they should live by it, that it should be made the living principle of theology, given its right place in the liturgy and employed as the starting-point of ecumenical theology.

b) These conciliar admonitions are now probably the most imperative prescription for the life and work of the Catholic Church, because Scripture still to a large extent does not occupy its rightful place in the Church. There is, however, also the danger of a false biblicism which also has to be avoided. The scriptural homily must be cultivated more than it usually is. But it would be a mistake to neglect sermons devoted to a particular subject. Christians have the right and need to receive instruction on many questions connected with their present situation which can only be given in very general terms, if at all, in a biblical homily. The mental world of the present time is so remote in the history of ideas from the world of the Scriptures that the average Christian of today cannot usually find his own way from Scripture to the circumstances in which his own life is set. Often the preacher himself will have to find this way. He will have to preach in a way which proclaims the gospel as it has already been actualized in the Church's present consciousness of its faith.

Karl Rahner

II. Versions

A. General

1. *Historical survey*. Translation of the Bible began in the OT period, in the 3rd century B.C., when Hebrew had been replaced by Aramaic as the usual language of popular intercourse. Since the religious and national consciousness of the Jews was centred on their sacred Scriptures, it was vitally necessary to have these in the language of daily life. The first versions were the Aramaic Targums (at first only oral paraphrases), following the readings of the Hebrew in the synagogues. A more consistent effort was the Greek translation made in the diaspora for the benefit of Hellenistic Jews (the Septuagint). This was the Bible of the young Christian Church, and other Jewish translations (Aquila, Symmachus, Theodotion) were produced in reaction to the use of the Septuagint by Christians. Latin translations appeared from about A.D. 200 on, the Old Latin being a translation of the Septuagint while the Vulgate of St. Jerome was translated from the original Hebrew.

The NT was also translated at an early date, though at first the original Greek could be understood throughout almost the whole of the Roman empire. But before the end of the 2nd century, a harmony of the gospels appeared in Syriac in the *Diatessaron* of Tatian, while other Syriac translations followed (Old Syriac, 2nd or 3rd century, Peshitta, etc., 5th to 7th century). Other translations include Coptic (3rd to 6th century), Gothic (4th century), Armenian (4th or 5th century), Georgian (5th century) and Ethiopic (6th century). Thus there was no question of the NT being the reserve of the educated or the priestly class, nor was it kept behind the barriers of a purely religious or liturgical language. Nonetheless, the development of the various vernaculars always left the original translations – the received or authentic Church books – in a remote and somewhat artificial position. The Old Church Slavonic, for instance, soon became as unintelligible to the Slavs as Latin to the West.

Till the beginnings of modern times, in spite of many complete or partial translations into English, French, German and other languages, the message of the Bible was mediated to the people through the preaching of the Church. The advent of vernacular translations – which of course could only become "popular" with the invention of printing and the spread of literacy – was both a tendentious effort to eliminate the mediatory function of the Church in general as well as the positive desire to have the word of God in a language "understood of the people". The connection between vernacular translation and immediate access to the word of God was to some extent accidental, and kerygmatic and liturgical motives also played their part. Nonetheless, on the whole translation was a symptom of the trend towards individualistic emancipation which marked the coming of modern times. Thus the great watershed in Germany was marked by Martin Luther's translation – a work enhanced by the warmth, vigour and general accuracy of the language. So too the French of Jacobus Faber (Lefèvre d'Etaples) in 1528 was not wholly inspired by orthodox motives. It cannot be said, however, that the Italian of Nicola Malermi (1471), the Spanish Bible of Valencia (by Boniface Ferrer in 1478), the Dutch Bible of Delft (1477) and of Cologne (1478) were in any sense polemical. But the English versions from Tyndale and

Coverdale on (1525 to 1535) were "reforming" works, copiously buttressed by tendentious notes, which had their Catholic counterparts in the Reims NT of 1582 and the Douai OT of 1609.

2. *Texts.* As the Renaissance developed a sense for textual criticism (of which earlier times were not unaware, as the 13th century *Biblia Parisiensis* and the numerous subsequent *correctoria* of the Vulgate show) and provided better tools, demands for more accurate texts and versions grew. The Protestant NT suffered for centuries from the influence of the Greek *Textus Receptus*, supposedly more "original" than the Latin Vulgate, but actually based on a few late manuscripts only, of the Byzantine or conflational type. A glance, for instance, at the version of the Lord's Prayer in Lk 11 in the Authorized Version shows that the English Catholic version, in spite of being based on the Vulgate, has here, as in many other places, a superior text from the scientific point of view (since St. Jerome had followed some of the best of the most ancient Greek manuscripts). More modern translations such as the English Revised Version of 1881–85, and the innumerable translations into other modern languages have always sought the best Hebrew and Greek texts available, with the result that no more than nuances remain as a rule between the various translations. Thus the (American) Revised Standard Version (NT 1946, OT 1952) could be published in a Catholic edition in 1966, and a "common version" in 1973, with little difficulty and negligible textual changes. The "authenticity" of the Vulgate as decreed by the Council of Trent (*D* 1506) referred to the choice among Latin texts, and to its authority in matters of faith and morals, especially in public debates. Its authenticity was not "critical" but "juridical" (cf. the encyclical *Divino Afflante*, *D* 2292). Hence the closer attention in modern times to the original texts is a break not with dogmatic but at most with scholarly tradition in the Catholic Church.

3. *Problems.* In so far as Christianity is a "religion of the book", difficulties necessarily arise from the double effort required in reading the Bible. First, it must always be read in the light of the particular historical occasions or practices for the sake of which the various elements were incorporated in the course of centuries, that is, with an eye to the *Sitz im Leben* throughout. But secondly, it has to be read and translated in such a way that it can form the basis of the living faith of the Church in each day and age. This tension can perhaps be best exemplified from the original Greek of the NT itself, which was basically a rendering of a Semitic world of thought. It should be obvious that the NT writers on the whole were more intent on the first way of reading – the preservation of the original thought-forms and expressions – than in "popularizing" in the everyday language of the readers. No doubt everyone could read Greek. But the Greek of the NT, in spite of its being Koine, the common Greek of Hellenistic times, was still strongly "Semitizing", often merely transliterating, so to speak, a religious idiom (e.g., that of the Septuagint or of rabbinical Judaism) unfamiliar and enigmatic to the Greek world. On a minor and comparatively indifferent level, we can see the contrast between the NT and the ordinary Greek by comparing the first paragraph of Luke's gospel with the remainder. The prologue is in normal literary Greek, but the gospel proper begins with an "It came to pass" which sets the key-note for a persistently Semitizing or Septuagint style. On a more challenging level, there are such phrases as the "kingdom of heaven", or even "kingdom of God", especially in the introduction to parables ("the kingdom of God is like . . .") which are

simple reminders of how much translation – in the second sense of the word, mentioned above – the NT itself required of its first readers. Modern readers in general are so habituated to biblical expressions that they fail to realize how far they would have been from ordinary language. But Origen felt compelled to apologize to his Greek readers for the simple "man of iniquity", which was actually uncouth in Greek.

The language of religion and liturgy always tends to be "hieratic" and static out of a certain sense of awe before a "sacred" text, and by reason of its intrinsically "traditional" nature – inevitable above all in Christianity, because it is a historical religion, where the "horizontal" component can never be ignored. This brings with it a certain tension between the language of religion and of life. This is not always happily resolved by stressing the "horizontal" component, as when "biblical" terms are retained to the exclusion of, say, "scholastic" terms in theology and preaching. When, for instance, certain schools try to confine language about the after-life to such terms as "being made conformable to Christ", they are taking a biblical term but stripping it of the field of reference and connotations which it had in the minds of the original writers and readers. Whatever be the hermeneutical justification of such a procedure, the problem of translation strictly speaking is hardly solved. The history of Bible translations mostly represents an effort to make a unique, remote and unrepeatable past live again in the language of different ages.

The Jewish paraphrases in the Targums were a laudable hermeneutic effort, though scientifically unsatisfactory because of the freedom with which the original text was handled, and because of the uncritical importation of the theological preoccupations of each era into the sprawling paraphrase. The Septuagint, much closer verbally to the original, reveals at once the immense difficulties of Bible translations. It deliberately adapted itself to the thought-forms of "middle-brow" Hellenistic philosophy, avoiding for instance anthropomorphisms where this could be easily done, and substituting Kyrios, as being readily understood by Greeks, for the divine name Yahweh. Thus the effort to find Greek equivalents for Hebrew thought often led to the substitution of vaguely analogous expressions. But the Targums and the Septuagint are simply basic instances of the problem of translation, which becomes more acute when it is done into Asian or African languages with their own peculiar heritages of symbolism and connotations.

Modern translations are generally based on the principle that paraphrases should be relegated to footnotes, while the text should render the original as literally as possible (within the true idiom of the language in question at a given date). E. Dhorme says in his introduction to the French OT in the *Bibliothèque de la Pléiade* that the first concern of the translator must be faithfulness not only to the thought but to the expression of the original. This principle has the advantage of a certain "objectivity", which many find desirable for the wrong reasons, such as that of "verbal inspiration". This type of translation throws much of the burden on the reader – as did, however, the NT writers themselves – and sometimes retains an aura of "sacred language" remote from ordinary life. It is sometimes criticized for reducing the Bible to the status of historical documents of the past. This objection means simply that such translations do not make the Bible "live", in the sense of addressing directly the reader of the day. On the other hand, since Christianity is a "historical" religion, the constant reminder that it is rooted in past times and places and thought-forms can only be stimulating and salutary. The objective method may encourage a certain fundamentalism or biblicism, but it can never be superseded.

It has been said that such translations as that of Luther or the Authorized Version succeeded in making the language of their day an adequate and popular vehicle of biblical thought. But this is only partly true, because Luther was to some extent crystallizing and standardizing the modern German language – almost creating as he went, though moulding popular speech. So too the Authorized Version rather imposed than reflected a language. The great competitors of the "objective" translation, such as the versions in "modern English", are of quite a different calibre. They deliberately substitute conventional modern phraseology for biblical expressions and even images, basing themselves sometimes on the mistaken principle that the NT was written in the popular speech of the day, but more fundamentally and correctly on the "kerygmatic" or directly communicative character of the NT message.

Such modernizing translations have been immensely popular, which is, however, a testimony to the wide interest in the Bible rather than to the technical achievements of the translators. This is clear from the success of the Knox version, written in a supposedly "timeless" English, which is, however, a highly questionable concept – saved only by the constant brilliance of the execution. The technical difficulty of the "living" translations is to produce a text which is suitable for liturgical, scientific and private reading. And then, above all, translators are working in a medium – modern popular speech – which is so fluid that the relevance to "life in the concrete" is speedily lost. Further, modern widely-spoken languages are so diversified in idiom that classes and professions tend to have almost specialist languages of their own. The effect of this multiplicity of idioms is that "foreign" idioms are assimilated by a process of emptying them of their distinctive content and blurring their contours. It is sometimes said that modern popular speech is "degenerate", but such judgments are often based on sophisticated "literary" standards. What is true is that popular speech tends to smooth out all awkwardness and to reduce all language to a uniform vapidity. A simple instance may be seen in the use of the word "dedicated" in the New English Bible to translate "holy" or "saints". Such is the attraction of the mass-media and handy jargon that people are now familiar with the notion of "dedicated" – but as applied to actors, writers, explorers or even jockeys. The sense intended by the translators is buried among the modern connotations, with their tendency to level out the sublime and the trenchant – all the more so, since modern language, being the reflection of a mostly "secularized" world, has practically eliminated such concepts as "holiness" from its world of ideas.

There are no rules to be laid down for translation, since it must always be a vital struggle with language, which has a life and history of its own. Translators of the Bible can only be warned against the archaic if they tend to be "objective", against the paltry and inadequate if they seek to modernize. But translations which pretend to smooth away all difficulties and dispense from study do a disservice to the message and to the (underestimated) reader. Ancient translations like the Targums and the Septuagint performed a hermeneutical task as well. The other ancient translations left their readers with the same problems which the NT writers posed. Modernizing translations, in their search for the clear and topical, have often tended to rob language of its history – to present the Bible as if it had been written for the first time in the present day. The fault does not lie with the effort, which is laudable, but with the lack of appreciation of the "historical" character of the writings and the wish to simplify what should be a challenging and rewarding study. As an ancient Eastern book, the Bible can only be read – in literal or periphrastic translation – in the context of historical scholarship. And as the book of revelation, and therefore permanently relevant, the translation can only be "living" when to the efforts of scholarship is added the correct orientation to the historical present moment. But this is no doubt rather the task of the preaching Church, which can never wholly surrender its books even to the scholar-poet, where such masters of language are available. The simplest fundamental statement of the NT, "Jesus is Lord" (which would probably appear in an equivalent form in all cultured languages) needs a further translation, both intellectually and kerygmatically – to render the sense and convey the summons – which is ultimately the function of the authorized preachers of the gospel. Thus the permanent problem of translation can only be solved from day to day as the books are returned by scholars to the preaching Church, and the studious reader.

III. Biblical Hermeneutics

Hermeneutics (ἑρμηνευτική sc. τέχνη, the art of interpretation) is to be distinguished from exegesis, which is the actual process of interpretation. In the technical sense, biblical hermeneutics is the investigation and determination of the rules and principles which guide the interpretation of Scripture. It is the theory or method of scriptural interpretation.

1. *History*. The effort to work out hermeneutical principles was begun in the ancient Church by Origen.

It received new impulses from the Reformation, the rationalism of the Enlightenment and the progress of modern science and historical research. A new approach was opened up by Schleiermacher, who defined hermeneutics as the art of understanding. Then, in the present century, as existential philosophy pointed out how deeply the hermeneutical question was rooted in human life itself, R. Bultmann took it up in a much more radical way than had hitherto been attempted. Catholic hermeneutics received strong impulses from the great biblical encyclicals of Leo XIII, Benedict XV and especially Pius XII (1943: *Divino Afflante*), which opened up perspectives which were only fully exploited by the most recent exegesis. The widespread tendency to restrict the principles of interpretation given by *Divino Afflante* to the OT was countered in 1964 by the "Instruction on the Historical Truth of the Gospels" published by the Pontifical Biblical Commission, as also, in general, by the Dogmatic Constitution of Vatican II on Divine Revelation (*Dei Verbum*). Ch. 2 of the Constitution proposed a very significant re-assessment of the truth of Scripture. "The books of Scripture must be acknowledged as teaching firmly, faithfully, and without error that truth which God wanted put into the sacred writings for the sake of our salvation" (art. 11). In the next article the most important hermeneutical principles are discussed at length. The Constitution should inspire Catholics to new efforts, especially as it emphasizes that scientific research prepares and helps the Church to form its mature judgment (art. 12). This verdict on the relationship of exegesis and magisterium acknowledges implicitly that it is of fundamental importance to work out a hermeneutics which will do full justice to Scripture.

2. *Possibility and necessity of biblical hermeneutics*. The fact that Scripture can and must be interpreted implies biblical hermeneutics. According to *Dei Verbum*, God has spoken through men in Scripture in a human way, and these

men, under the influence of inspiration, still functioned as real authors (*veri auctores*, art. 11; earlier official documents had merely called them – cautiously – *auctores instrumentales*). It follows that the writings in the two Testaments are products of human language in the full sense of the term. It was through human language that God said what he wished to say, and hence the meaning intended by God is that which is given in human words. Since Scripture is truly human utterance, since the words of Scripture are uttered by men undergoing the historical process, its thought and language are necessarily linked with the date, place and mentality of the authors. This quality of Scripture, that it is human words, brings with it, as for all the products of human language, the possibility of following its thought, since its expression in language is not intrinsically obscure, being aimed at communication, intelligibility. It also brings with it the task, that is, the necessity of interpretation.

3. *General hermeneutical approaches.* Among the ordinary tools of hermeneutics is the reconstruction of the original text as far as this is possible (textual criticism). Then there is the study of biblical languages and concepts, in general and with attention to linguistic and stylistic peculiarities in given periods, authors or works. Studies must also include archaeology, topography, ethnography, comparative religion and in general the developing cultures and history of the surrounding nations, with reference to the two Testaments and to the individual books. Another task is to find out all that is possible about the author of a given work, his background, state of life and culture, the situation which his work envisages.

4. *Basic hermeneutical principles.* The fundamentals are determined by the double claim of the Bible, to be word of God and word of man. Since the word of God is met with in the Bible as human speech, we must first enunciate the principles which are valid even when we prescind from the claim of Scripture to be the word of God, and then the principles which result from this claim.

a) *General principles.* "Since God speaks in sacred Scripture through men in human fashion, the interpreter of sacred Scripture, in order to see clearly what God wanted to communicate to us, should carefully investigate what meaning the sacred writers really intended, and what God wanted to manifest by means of their words." This statement of the Constitution on Revelation (art. 12) recognizes the assertion which the sacred writer intended to make as the real and literal sense (which does not necessarily coincide with the superficial meaning of the words). It lays down as the fundamental and general principle of biblical hermeneutics the precise investigation of the intention of the text in each case. To find out the intention of the assertion three main instruments are to be used. The first is the consideration of the fact that the mode of expression is determined by the thought and language of the general environment. Here, for instance, the peculiarities of Semitic, Hellenistic and Judaeo-Hellenistic thought and expression must be taken into account. Then there is the investigation of the *genus literarium*. The Council explains here that "truth is proposed and expressed in a variety of ways, depending on whether a text is history of one kind or another (*in textibus vario modo historicis*), or whether its form is that of prophecy, poetry or some other type of speech" (art. 12). This leaves open the number of literary forms that have been or may be determined, and also notes the variability of the concept of "history". Finally, there is the investigation of the milieu in which and for which the writer composed his work. Over and above these three approaches, we must note the procedure known as the "hermeneutical circle". This means that a general picture is built up from the clearer and more easily intelligible statements, and this result is used in turn to throw light on what is uncertain and difficult. This process may be used with regard to individual writings, groups of writings and for the Bible as a whole.

b) *Theological principles*. In the light of the Church's teaching that the writings of the Old and New Testaments are the "word of God" by virtue of inspiration, the normative testimony to the divine revelation which was brought to its completion in and by Jesus, three principles of hermeneutics are ordinarily accepted. They are also mentioned expressly in the Constitution *Dei Verbum*, art. 12. The first is the living tradition of the Church universal. The second is the reading of Scripture as a unified whole. The third is the analogy of faith. The validity of the living tradition of the universal Church as a rule of interpretation is at once established by the fact that all the books of the NT were produced within the Church in the service of its actual preaching. Further, the definitive fixing of the canon of the Old and New Testaments, as a *norma non normanda*, is also a function of this living Church, in which, as the NT asserts, the glorified Christ is at work through the Holy Spirit as the agent of the self-disclosure of God. However, the positive heuristic contribution of the living tradition of the Church universal is not to be overestimated or overtaxed. The "unity of Scripture" means that an individual text or work may be explained by the whole biblical context. This is primarily a matter of comparing parallel texts, especially in later books. The "analogy of faith" means that a text is explained by means of the inner harmony of the whole revelation proposed by the Church. When these two means are invoked in interpretation, care must be taken with regard to individual texts that forced comparisons are not made, apart from the legitimate use of the proximate or remote context. To avoid mistakes in this matter, attention must also be paid to the stage of revelation to which a particular text belongs (see *Enchiridion Biblicum*, 109).

Scripture is the message of the God of the covenant, the testimony to his will to save and sanctify as revealed definitively in Christ. And understanding and decision go hand in hand in the historicity of human existence. It follows that interpretation can only reach its real goal when the greatest possible mastery of historical method is accompanied by a basically existential and personal attitude on the part of the exegete. He must be ready to be a "disciple" as well as a "historian" (L. Bakker), seeing the works and words of God attested in Scripture as having "historical" significance, as an event which impinges on himself, bringing promise and fulfilment, grace and judgment. It is only when the exegete confronts Scripture in this "connaturality" of mind that the supreme demands of biblical hermeneutics can be met.

5. *A consistent hermeneutical principle.* The debate on demythologizing has brought into the forefront of discussion the meaning of "faith" in the Bible, especially the NT, as well as the concomitant question of "pre-comprehension" (that is, of the philosophical framework within which the Bible is read). As is now generally recognized, there is no such thing as an absolutely unprejudiced interrogation of historical texts. Even the present-day exponent starts from a concrete historical situation and brings with him his own instinctive and acquired pre-comprehension, philosophical or theological. His subjectivity is of a certain order, and this it is which inspires his interrogation of the sources and his effort

to gain a comprehensive understanding of the phenomena attested in the Bible. If by pre-comprehension (or prejudice) we mean some general or particular "sketch-plan" which the exegete brings with him, certain previously settled opinions or judgments, then he must be ready to have them called in question, tested or corrected by the texts, in so far as these provide surer or at least better justified solutions. But apart from such cases, it must be admitted, as is maintained in particular by R. Bultmann, "that every interpretation is inspired by some pre-comprehension of the matter in question", that is, by "the previous vital relationship to the matter" treated in the text, a relationship which alone makes understanding of it possible (*Glauben und Verstehen*, II). Bultmann is also right in saying that the pre-comprehension necessary for the understanding of Scripture is implicit in the quest for God which is the mainspring of all human life, and which can take on various forms, such as the question of happiness, of the meaning of the world and history, of deliverance from death, of security amid the vicissitudes of destiny, of the purpose and object of each individual life. Finally, he is also correct in saying that it is a legitimate hermeneutical question to ask what is the understanding of human existence and its fulfilment which is expressed in the NT's message about Christ, that is, that Scripture is to be interpreted existentially.

That men should acknowledge and lay hold of revelation as the fulfilment through grace of their deepest yearnings, would undoubtedly be in keeping with the supreme goal of scriptural interpretation as propounded above. Misgivings only arise with the hermeneutical demand that this "mythologically" couched message about Christ can only be appropriately interrogated in terms of an understanding of reality and of self possible to modern man, whose understanding of existence is supposed to be currently determined by the natural sciences. Nevertheless, we still await the solution of the problem posed by the varying explicitations of the Christian revelation adduced in the NT, which are far from being co-ordinated into a system. Can a hermeneutical principle be found which will enable us to grasp the exact import of the various biblical assertions, conditioned as they are by the notions and modes of expression current in their times, and also by the pastoral exigencies of their situation? One of the happy results of the recent discussion has been to bring out the hermeneutical value of the exact meaning of divine revelation, action and speaking, that is, how the self-communication of God can take place and has in fact taken place.

6. *The hermeneutical problem of the Old Testament.* Two elements have contributed to enliven the discussion here. One was the general desire to evaluate the theological relevance of a historical criticism which was accepted in principle as a method of exegesis. The other was the hermeneutical postulate put forward by R. Bultmann, that the OT history of the Jews was prophecy precisely "in its inner contradiction, in its failure". The main question is the relationship of the Old and New Testaments, the legitimacy of a Christian pre-comprehension in the hermeneutics of the OT. If we prescind from the extreme position which reduces both Testaments to the one level, there are two main tendencies among Protestants. One emphasizes the difference between the Testaments and hence affirms that the OT is to be read on its own terms, without any appeal to the gospel for the justification of its self-understanding. It is thus that it is a force which impinges on our existence and which must be integrated into our understanding of the gospel (so P. Baumgärtel). The other view is based on the notion of the unity of the biblical testi-

mony. The action of the OT has a "prefigurative" significance, which allows of a "typological" explanation, applied with moderation and with many different nuances (cf. G. von Rad; W. Eichrodt; J. Barr). The hermeneutical justification varies from text to text, and sometimes the procedure is understood as not coming under strict hermeneutical rules.

Modern Catholic exegesis also seems to find the conflict between "historical" and "Christian" interpretation "the most exciting hermeneutical problem of the Old Testament" (N. Lohfink). There is general agreement that both are necessary. "We have to give a historical interpretation, because intellectual honesty demands that we investigate the original meaning. We have to give a Christian interpretation, because the Bible speaks to us as the word of God." (N. Lohfink). The most common attempt to reach a synthesis makes use of the *sensus plenior*, by virtue of which the literal sense also contains a fullness of meaning intended by God which goes beyond that which was recognized and willed by the sacred writer, or which was at best only vaguely guessed at by him. The full sense is defended, for instance, by D. de Ambrogi, R. E. Brown, P. Benoît, P. Grelot, and rejected by such authors as R. Bierberg, G. Courtade, J. Schmid and B. Vawter. Even where the existence of the full sense is admitted on principle, the great problem remains as to what justifiable and practical hermeneutical criteria can be used to extract the full sense from any particular text. There is also the difficulty that the ancient methods of exegesis used by the NT writers and their explanation of individual texts, sometimes as mere illustrations, sometimes as prophetical proofs of the Christian message, are often in conflict with the obvious demands of historical exegesis. And it is impossible to show that the OT quotations or scriptural proofs in the NT in general are in harmony with the literal sense of the OT texts, as established by historical scholarship. It is true that there are many quotations where "the meaning intended by the OT writer, or at least by God, is already in line with the *sensus plenior* of the words in the Christian sense" (J. Schmid, But there are many cases where the NT writer attributes to OT texts a different meaning from that intended by the OT writers, and sometimes even the opposite meaning. In such cases there is no direct link with the literal sense. Efforts have been made to reach a synthesis of historical and Christian interpretation which will exclude arbitrary judgments. B. H. Gross, for instance, speaks of "correspondence on a higher plane as the structural principle of biblical promise and fulfilment". N. Lohfink calls for a Christian interpretation which makes use of the complete history of tradition, including the interpretation given by the NT. In any case, once it has been emphasized that the coming of revelation and the scriptural attestation are intrinsically ordained to Christ, the genuinely historical character of revelation in general and of that which began in Jesus in particular must be borne in mind. And we must avoid the untenable notion that the person, way and work of the eschatological redeemer can be seen as the simple, straightforward execution of a programme outlined in the OT, or at least to be deduced from its data or a combination of them. The question of a valid and consistent principle of interpretation for the Old and New Testaments, and for the canon as a whole, still needs further investigation.

Anton Vögtle

IV. Scripture Reading

In the tradition of the New Testament as of the Old, Scripture reading made an important contribution to the knowledge and vitality of faith. In the Synagogue and in the Christian community, the written word had such high esteem because the writings of the OT, the gospels, and later the letters of the apostles, were understood to be the "Word of God". Scripture reading was therefore a religious act. This is clearest when Scripture is read as part of divine worship. The theology of Scripture reading affirms that when Scripture is thus read, it is not merely retailed and relayed. The reading renders God's action actually present, so that God here and now addresses his people. God himself speaks when his representative reads from Scripture. This understanding of the liturgy was taken over from Israel by the primitive Church, where the Kyrios, powerful in the Spirit, is present when the gospels or the letters of the apostles are read out. Hence it is ancient tradition that the Church's preaching at divine service should be on themes from the liturgical Scripture readings. And in this it is less a question of the re-telling of an event than of bringing out its importance for concrete decisions here and now.

Liturgical Scripture reading is regulated by the order of appointed passages, and the real purpose of this is to allow the kerygmatically important sections and themes of holy Scripture to be heard. The old Roman order of lessons applied this principle, despite the *lectio continua*, by having a cycle of three or four years. In a one year cycle and with only two readings in the "Liturgy of the Word" at Mass, it is impossible to do justice even to the NT. Attempts are at present being made to supplement the present one year cycle of the Roman liturgy by an additional three year scheme, so creating a four year cycle. As the Sunday reading is the only one for many of the faithful, such an enrichment of the material would be welcome from a pastoral point of view.

A derivative of the scriptural readings in the Mass are the lessons in the Divine Office. Readings from the Old and New Testaments have had a place in it, with the psalms and prayers, since the 4th century. The close connection between gospel and exposition is shown by the fact that patristic homilies now form part of the Breviary lessons. Private reading of Scripture in addition to liturgical, corresponds to the importance of the Word of God for the whole life of the Christian in the world. This private reading shares the religious character of Bible reading generally; here too the living Kyrios speaks through the words of holy Scripture. If that is understood, private Scripture reading can advance beyond acquiring information about biblical narratives to a grasp of biblical history, that is, God's action in regard to his people. To the liturgical Scripture reading there corresponds the homily, and to private there corresponds meditation. Neither mental prayer nor theological study can do without the reading of Scripture. For either to bear fruit, however, a minimum of knowledge of exegetical principles is needed, and these differ according to the literary genre of the various books of the Old and New Testaments.

Ingo Hermann

BIBLICAL EXEGESIS

I. Historical Survey

1. *Old Testament and Judaism.* The interpretation of the Bible begins in the OT when later authors, such as the prophets and certain psalms, give a theological interpretation of the history of Israel handed down in the older writings (see Ezek 38:7; Dan 9; Ecclus 44ff., and especially the re-moulding of the matter of the Books of Samuel by Chronicles, and the midrash on the ancient history of Israel in Wis 10ff.). There was particular need to interpret the Torah in the post-exilic period

because of its importance as the foundation of the whole religious and social life of the community. Ezra is regarded as its first exponent (Ezra 7:10; Neh 8:8). Later the task was taken over by the Pharisee "doctors of the law" who endeavoured to draw from the Torah new laws adapted to the constantly changing conditions of life. The mention of the "school" in Ecclus 51:23 indicates that this institution goes back at least to Sirach's time. The legal interpretations of the older rabbis, the Tannaites, at first transmitted by word of mouth only, were written down towards the end of the 2nd century A.D. in systematic order in the Mishnah in the form of commentaries on Exodus – Deuteronomy in the oldest midrashim. The Amoraites for their part took as their task the interpretation of the Mishnah, and the result of their work is contained in the Talmud. We find similar interpretation of the OT to meet contemporary needs in the Qumran sect.

In the 10th century A.D., after a long period of sterility, Saadia opened the way to a new study of the OT and was a pioneer of Jewish linguistic studies. He found no followers in the East, but a new centre of intensive biblical and linguistic study sprang up in Spain. The Jewish scholars of the Middle Ages produced a large number of scriptural commentaries and grammatical and lexicographical works which also influenced Christian biblical scholarship. It was in accord with their strong attachment to tradition that Jewish scholars only hesitantly adopted the critical methods of modern Christian biblical research (Moses Mendelssohn, 1786). Interpretation of Scripture is also found in the Targums, the Aramaic translations of the OT which first became necessary for liturgical use when Hebrew was replaced in common speech by Aramaic. The Targums, however, are to a large extent paraphrases, free renderings of the Hebrew text.

Comparable to them is the LXX, the Greek translation of the OT made when most Jews in Egypt knew only Greek. The LXX, however, as well as a translation is also an interpretation of the original, its transposition into Greek thought. This is even truer of the exegetical writings of Philo of Alexandria, loyal in principle to the Jewish faith in the Bible, but at the same time influenced by the philosophy of Plato and the Stoa. He wanted to show that the Bible and Greek philosophy could be perfectly well harmonized and that Greek wisdom is contained in the Torah. By the allegorical method which he took over from the Greek interpretation of Homer, Philo also exercised a lasting influence on Christian exegesis from the Alexandrians onwards. The Latin Fathers of the Church then transmitted this legacy to the exegesis of the Latin Middle Ages.

2. *Primitive Christian community*. The earliest Christian community took over from Judaism the OT as holy Scripture and applied it by an eschatological and Christological interpretation to Christ's redemptive work and to the Church as the true Israel. The influence of the exegetical method of Palestinian Judaism is particularly evident in the rabbinically educated Paul.

3. *Patristic period*. The oldest Christian exegesis after the NT period is characterized by controversy with Judaism (Letter of Barnabas; Justin), and with Gnosticism. The starting-point for all later exegesis was provided by the Alexandrian school (Clement, Origen), as compared with which the earlier writer, Hippolytus of Rome, was of slight importance. The Alexandrian Origen was the most important exegete of the ancient Church, both by the range of his writings, which chiefly consist of biblical commentaries of various kinds, and by the influence of his allegorical method on the whole subsequent patristic age and at least indirectly on the Antiochene school.

For him it is not the facts of sacred history which are important but the supra-historical truth which is revealed in Scripture. Side by side with the Alexandrian school, and in conscious oposition to it, was the Antiochene school founded by Lucian of Antioch (d. 312); its most important members were Diodore of Tarsus, Theodoret of Cyrrhos and especially Theodore of Mopsuestia, the "blessed exegete" of the Nestorians; with these must be numbered the great homiletic writer John Chrysostom. The great Cappadocians, in particular Gregory of Nyssa, were under Origen's influence. The Antiocheans resolutely rejected allegory and emphasized the typological meaning of Scripture, viewing biblical revelation in the perspective of the sacred history of redemption. The 6th century produced the only two commentaries on the Revelation of John, which after Dionysius of Alexandria never attained undisputed recognition among the Greeks; they were by the Severian Oecumenius and his orthodox opponent Andrew of Caesarea. In general, however, in the 6th century the age of independent biblical exegesis in the Greek Church was at an end. Its place was taken by the catenae which, renouncing original work, assembled fragments from the standard exegetes into continuous commentaries. And after the 2nd Trullan Synod (692) declared the interpretations given by the Fathers to be binding, we find no more independent works with the exception of a commentary on Paul by the Patriarch Photius (9th century), for even the commentaries of Euthymius Zigabenus and Theophylact (11th and 12th centuries) are simply free excerpts from John Chrysostom and other ancient exegetes.

The first *Latin* exegete known to us is the commentator on the Apocalypse, Victorinus of Pettau (d. 314). In the Latin Church too the allegorical method became predominant. Ambrose, and in his earliest years Jerome, as well as Augustine, adopted it and under Augustine's influence Gregory the Great at the end of the patristic period (d. 604). Lasting influence was also exercised by Tyconius the Donatist, highly esteemed by Augustine, through his commentary on the Apocalypse, and through his *Liber Regularum*, in the spirit of which Augustine composed a handbook of hermeneutics in his *De doctrina christiana*. The Antiochene method of exegesis is represented by the important commentary on Paul by an unknown author, the so-called Ambrosiaster, and that of Pelagius and his disciple Julian of Eclanum. Isidore of Seville was only a compilator.

4. *The Latin Middle Ages*. The scriptural exegesis of the early Middle Ages was entirely designed for practical purposes, preaching and liturgy. The oldest commentaries were catena-like compilations of patristic texts, chiefly from Ambrose, Jerome, Augustine and Gregory the Great, which also means that the allegorical interpretation prevailed, as suited the practical purpose of these works. The first author of commentaries of that kind was the Venerable Bede (d. 735), whose reputation endured for centuries. With Alcuin and Theodulf of Orleans we see the first attempts to reduce the considerable textual confusion of the Vulgate manuscripts to some uniformity. Similar to Bede's commentaries were those of Rabanus Maurus, while those of Paschasius Radbertus, Christian of Stablo and especially of John Scotus Eriugena and Remigius of Auxerre (all 9th century) already attempted greater independence. In the 11th century the schools of Laon (Anselm) and Utrecht (Lambert) became centres of biblical study. In the "gloss" produced by Anselm and his collaborators the form given in preceding centuries to the exegetical tradition came to a provisional conclusion. Partly between the

lines of the biblical text (*glossa interlinearis*), partly in the margin (*glossa marginalis*), short comments were added from the works of the Fathers or other ancient exegetes. For the books most frequently commented, the Psalter and Paul, Anselm's work was improved by later editors, in particular by Peter Lombard, and in this form became the standard "handbook" for all the later Middle Ages.

Of importance for the growth of medieval theology was the production of *Quaestiones*, the more detailed treatment of particularly important single texts. Robert of Melun (d. 1167) then took the decisive step of separating the *Quaestiones* from the Gloss, and so dogmatic theology freed itself from the sacred text and became a separate branch of study. But even in the golden age of Scholasticism in the 13th century, the Gloss was retained as a basis for treating biblical matters in lectures and disputations. Important theologians of the 13th century who made significant contributions to scriptural exegesis were Bonaventure, Albert the Great and especially Thomas Aquinas. In the same period also, Alcuin's and Theodulf's efforts to provide a uniform biblical text were resumed in correctories and concordances, in particular by Hugh of St. Cher. The latter was also the first to use the term "postilla" for the continuous commentary on the biblical text. The most important work of this kind is considered to be the Postilla of Nicolas of Lyra (d. 1349). With Lorenzo Valla and G. Manetti, classical scholars begin to occupy themselves with the Bible and its text, and this heralds a new period of biblical study.

5. *From Renaissance humanism to the present day*. The Catholic exegesis of this epoch may be divided into three periods, the last of which is not yet closed: a) a flourishing period from 1500 to about 1650, characterized by the great number of Catholic biblical scholars, particularly Spaniards and Italians, and the abundance of their works: b) the period from 1650 to about the end of the 19th century, in which biblical scholarship declined in comparison with other branches of study; c) recent times.

With Renaissance humanism, a new age in the intellectual history of Europe began and brought with it a shift of interest in the Bible and a change of exegetical method. There was an awakening interest in history, especially that of Greco-Roman antiquity and its literature. This involved both a turning away from the philosophical speculation of Scholasticism and the abandoning of allegorizing, though the latter only took place gradually. Interest began to be directed to questions of the kind now treated in general introductions to scriptural study, and to the auxiliary sciences (biblical geography, biblical archaeology, ancient history). It began to be recognized how important for the correct understanding of the biblical text is the study of ancient languages, which previously had been so seriously neglected. The uncertainty of the current text of the Vulgate had, of course, been recognized in the Middle Ages, without its being possible effectively to remedy the fault. Now the invention of printing created a new possibility of establishing and distributing without difficulty a uniform text of the Bible. Then came the Reformation which declared the Bible to be the sole source of faith and so attributed pre-eminent importance to it. Catholic biblical scholarship could not remain unaffected. It is true that controversy with the Protestant view of the Bible was inevitably detrimental to its Catholic interpretation; for on both sides men looked to the Bible primarily for *dicta probantia* for dogmatic theology, apologetics and polemics. In this respect the commentaries of G. Seripando are typical. Moreover, a long time was needed for the new knowledge and methods to find general recognition.

Many commentators were still as intent as ever on supplying materials for homilectics and ascetics (e.g., Salmeron, Cornelius a Lapide). The decree of the Council of Trent regarding the Bible declared the Vulgate to be the official text of the Latin Church and so gave textual criticism a powerful impetus. Though the humanists primarily cultivated the study of the Greek and Latin languages, people now began to recognize more clearly the importance of Hebrew, especially under the influence of the Jew Elias Levita. Eminent for their knowledge of Hebrew were Lefèvre d'Étaples (Vatablus) in France, Johannes Reuchlin in Germany, Santes Pagnino and Giles of Viterbo (the pupil of Elias Levita) in Italy. At this time the Collegium Trilingue was founded at the University of Louvain. Luther separated himself from the Middle Ages by abandoning the multiple sense of Scripture; he distinguished only between the spiritual, i.e., Christological sense and the literal sense. Of theological importance was his classification of the books of the Bible according to their religious value and according to the degree to which they "concern Christ". Calvin and especially Zwingli were strongly influenced by humanism. On the Catholic side the first representatives of a new kind of biblical exegesis were Cardinal Cajetan in Italy, Erasmus of Rotterdam in Germany, and J. Lefèvre d'Étaples in France. Of these Cajetan in particular, by his astonishingly modern principles, with which he placed himself in contrast not only to Scholasticism but even to the Fathers, roused a storm of opposition. In order effectively to meet the Protestants, he held, the Bible must be expounded in its original text instead of the Vulgate and, instead of penetrating its mystical sense, we must ask what its words really say. Erasmus too wished to liberate exegesis from Scholasticism but thought that the allegorical sense must be retained, at least in the OT. As opposed to the exaggerated dogmatism of many representatives of Protestant orthodoxy, who, like M. Flaccus, regarded as inspired not only every word of the Bible, but even the vowels of the Massoretic Hebrew text, Catholics such as S. Masius, B. Pererius, J. Bonfrère and J. Morinus adopted a detached attitude to the Massoretic text. Among the numerous commentators of that age the two Spaniards J. Maldonatus and F. de Ribera and the Dutchman W. Estius stand preeminent.

That flourishing period was followed by an even longer period in which Catholic theology turned in the main to other fields and achieved little in biblical scholarship, especially as far as progress in method is concerned. Its closed, self-contained character, which was in sharp contrast to the multiplicity of trends and schools of Protestant exegesis at that time, was not due solely to dogma, but to a traditionalism averse to new thought. As a consequence, it had no better and more effective method to oppose to the hypotheses of English Deists, French Encyclopaedists and Protestant Rationalists of the 17th and 18th centuries. The 18th century counts a few useful achievements in the domain of biblical archaeology and textual criticism (the work on the *Vetus Latina* by the Maurist P. Sabatier). The outstanding figure of this period was the French Oratorian Richard Simon (d. 1712), who was far in advance of his time and as a consequence was opposed and persecuted from all sides, but who was the real creator of the critical historical method. The fact that his principles, universally rejected by his contemporaries, were first adopted by the rationalist J. S. Semler, definitely made them suspect and robbed them for a long time of their effect, to the detriment of Catholic biblical research.

In the meantime Protestant biblical study produced not only a large number of commentaries, among them the important works of H. Grotius and J. J. Wettstein, but also valuable philological aids (John Lightfoot, Ch. Schöttgen), as well as the gigantic collection of variants in the text of the NT by John Mill (d. 1707). With Semler (d. 1791) there began in Protestant research the emancipation of scriptural study from dogmatic theology. Since then the conflict between Rationalism and Supernaturalism has dominated Protestant research down to the present day, though in method the conservative tendency has gradually come closer and closer to the rationalist. Just as in the 19th century Pentateuchal criticism and the history of OT religion, discussion of which had been brought by J. Wellhausen to a certain provisional culmination, was to the fore, so too work on the NT was dominated by literary criticism of the synoptic gospels and in conjunction with this, research on the life of Jesus. A major influence was that of F. C. Baur, who was inspired by Hegel's philosophy of history to try to depict the NT as a reflection of the conflict between the original Jewish Christianity and Pauline gentile Christianity moving away from the Law in the direction of the Catholic Church. A lasting inheritance from the controversy for and against the "Tendency-critique of Tübingen" was the recognition that the various NT writings must be understood on the basis of their historical situations. The investigation of the history of the text of the NT was pursued almost exclusively by Protestant scholars (Tischendorf, Tregelles, Westcott and Hort), and the *textus receptus*, previously regarded as almost inviolable, was shown to be in the main the latest stage of the text.

Towards the end of the 19th century a strong influence was exercised by the students of history of religions, H. Gunkel for the OT, W. Bousset, W. Heitmüller, R. Reitzenstein and others for the NT; their programme was to provide a genetic explanation of OT religion, and that of Judaism and the NT, from their earliest roots, which they considered were to be found in the syncretism of the surrounding world. From the controversy about this school and its methods, present-day scientific Catholic exegesis has retained the principle that biblical religion cannot be understood at any stage without study of the religious currents present in the environment; but this does not necessarily reduce that religion to a syncretist formation. Interest in history of religions was superseded by form-criticism and history of traditions, methods opened up for the OT by H. Gunkel, for the NT by K. L. Schmidt, M. Dibelius, R. Bultmann and others. In the NT this chiefly concerned the synoptic gospels. This led to the conclusion that the gospels have their basis in the original Christian kerygma and are therefore testimonies to the original Christian belief in Christ; this also involves the question how far we can know the historical Jesus through this picture of Christ. This is the question which chiefly occupies NT research at the present time and not only Protestant scholarship. As contributions to NT research of special importance and world-wide influence, we must mention the commentary on the NT from the Talmud and Midrash of the Lutheran pastor P. Billerbeck, and the theological dictionary of the NT founded by G. Kittel (both in German; the latter in course of translation).

Even in the 19th century Catholic exegesis was chiefly determined by defence against Rationalism and therefore by apologetics, and was extremely tied to tradition. It was only at the end of the 19th century that an advance set in in Germany, France and Belgium which can really be called the beginning of a new age. The foundation of the École Biblique in Jerusalem by M.-J. Lagrange (1890) was epoch-making in the first place for the advance in geographical and archaeological research on the soil of Palestine itself, but above all because Lagrange resolutely declared himself in favour of the historico-critical method which, he urged, was objectively required and which alone was capable of debating seriously the results of Protestant research and of recognizing what was of value in them. The organ of the École Biblique was the *Revue Biblique* (1892 onwards), to which after 1900 were added the *Études Bibliques*. Lagrange's discourse at the international Catholic Congress in Fribourg in 1899 and his book *La méthode historique* (1903) precipitated, however, a long dispute between the *école large* and a strictly traditionalist trend (L. Méchineau, J. Brucker, A. Delattre, L. Fonck) on the compatibility of the historico-critical method with the Catholic conception of inspiration. On the same lines as Lagrange there were F. Prat in France, A. van Hoonacker in Belgium (Louvain) and in Germany the *Biblische Zeitschrift* (1903ff.), edited by J. Goettsberger and J. Sickenberger, as well as N. Peters, K. Holzhey, A. Schulz and others. The debate was still going on when the movement suffered a set-back through the reaction against Modernism, of which the exegete A. Loisy was one of the protagonists, for the progressive trend was suspected of a Modernist attitude.

The Pontifical Biblical Commission founded in 1902 by Leo XIII issued from 1906 onwards a number of decrees on controverted questions. The Pontifical Biblical Institute founded in 1909 by Pius X was intended to ensure the formation of future professors of biblical sciences according to the mind of the Church. Of the three papal encyclicals concerning biblical research (*Providentissimus Deus* of Leo XIII, 1893, *Spiritus Paraclitus* of Benedict XV, 1920, *Divino Afflante Spiritu* of Pius XII, 1943), the last-named, the "liberation encyclical", which explicitly declared the historical-critical method to be appropriate and necessary, opened the road for modern Catholic biblical scholarship and so gave it a powerful impetus. The restrictions under which it suffered even in the first decades of the 20th century and which forced it to excessively cautious formulas or to take refuge in "safe" questions, if it did not wish to be completely silent, are now removed, at least in principle, though attacks from the conservative side have not yet been ended. It is now possible to deal more simply with important matters like the Pentateuch, the synoptic problem, form-criticism and history of traditions. So too as regards the methods, problems and results of Protestant scholarship, its attitude has more and more "changed from critical rejection to respectful discussion" (W. Michaelis, *RGG*, I, col. 1084) and in many fields collaboration between Catholic and Protestant exegetes has been started.

If it is possible at the present time to note with good reason that Catholic biblical scholarship displays a new vitality, it is simply because it now enjoys a freedom of movement which it did not before, and can now investigate the manifold problems of the Bible and especially the revelation it contains, in their historical development, instead of merely providing *dicta probantia* for dogmatic theology. In this way and only in this way, in constant fruitful discussion with Protestant biblical scholarship, can it penetrate more and more deeply the thoughts of the Bible. Only when it is allowed to do this does it fulfil its real task as a theological science and only then will its results endure.

Joseph Schmid

II. NT Exegesis

Gospel Criticism

The respect due to books that are divinely inspired in no way deprives men of the right, even the duty, they have to subject these books to the scrutiny of textual, literary, and historical criticism.

1. *Textual criticism.* The gospels have come down to us in over 12,000 manuscript copies dating from before the invention of printing, some containing the complete text and others portions of it, either in the original language or in ancient translations. So close is the agreement among all these codices, and between them and the innumerable quotations from the gospels found in ancient Christian writers, that we may conclude that the original text has reached us in an excellent state of preservation. Textual criticism has substantially accomplished its task.

2. *Literary criticism.* The gospels are inspired books; they were born of a mysterious collaboration between certain human writers and God, the principal author, who really used the literary activity of those writers as his instrument; and therefore literary criticism is interested in knowing, for example, who the human authors were, when, where, in what language, and for whom they wrote, to what extent their books depend on each other, what literary influences they were exposed to, what genres they adopted.

It was contended at one time that the sources of the gospels must be looked for in profane literature outside the biblical world, but that view is now completely outdated. Modern scholars agree that the literary features of the gospels mainly derive from the books of the OT, or rabbinical writers, or earlier Hebrew literature apart from Scripture. These influences make themselves felt particularly in the oral catechesis that existed before the gospels were committed to writing and on which, no doubt, the authors of the synoptics heavily drew.

3. *Historical criticism.* The basic problem, however, where the gospels are concerned, is that of historical criticism. How accurate, historically speaking, is the portrait of Christ given us by the evangelists, who after all reflect the faith of the Christian community in the first century? May not the figure of the historical Jesus have been idealized by the belief of the evangelists, or of the authors of the primitive catechesis?

For Christians, of course, the inerrancy of the books God has inspired, and therefore of the gospels, is a revealed dogma. Inerrancy, however, must not be confused with historicity. Everything the Bible says is free of error but not everything it says is historical. Inerrancy admits of no degrees, but historicity does. However, the range and degree of the gospels' objective historicity depend on the purpose the authors had in mind, a purpose that is to be gathered from, and understood in the context of, the literary genre they chose to employ. What historical criticism must do is ascertain how far the authors meant the gospels they wrote to be objectively historical.

Here we must recollect that there were at least two stages in the formation of the gospels: their written composition by the evangelists, and the earlier oral catechesis which provided the evangelists with their material.

Actually the evangelists did very little, though perhaps not quite so little as students of the history of forms maintain. Most of their source material had already become stereotyped by use in oral catechesis and they respected these established forms. Suffice it to recall what Papias says about Mark: "Mark, the interpreter of Peter, carefully wrote down the things he remembered. But not in the order in which the Lord had said and done them. He had not heard the Lord, nor followed him, but later – as I have said – he was with Peter, who preached the gospel according to the needs of his hearers, not designing to relate the words and deeds of the Lord in chronological order. Mark made no mistake in recording certain things as he remembered them. His idea was to omit nothing of what he had heard, much less falsify anything." (Eusebius, *Hist. eccl.*, III, 39.) The historical purpose of the synoptics was to make an exact record of the Christian catechesis, or to some extent of the testimony "of those who from the beginning were eye-witnesses and ministers of the word" (Lk 1:2). Accordingly their accounts reveal a substratum of thoroughly Semitic language dating from the period before Christianity had spread through the Hellenistic world. Moreover, the social life, the religious customs, the cast of thought underlying the whole, are all anterior to the vast changes brought about in Palestine by the disaster of A.D. 70. Compared with the Pauline literature, the catechesis set down in the gospels is decidedly archaic; it portrays Jesus in surroundings still remote from the ecclesiastical organization and systematic doctrine that are already far advanced in the letters of the apostle. All this is proof that the evangelists soberly and conscientiously recorded the earlier oral catechesis as they knew it, and rules out the hypothesis that the figure of Jesus was over-idealized either in the gospels themselves or in the period just before their composition. Throughout, it is the archaic catechesis that dominates, not the influences of the contemporary world. The concerns of the moment would have suggested quite a different approach.

So much can be taken as agreed. But our problem is not thereby resolved, it is only shifted a stage farther back: what historical objectivity had the original form of oral catechesis? Its authors, being much closer to the events concerned, eye-witnesses indeed, were in a position to know their subject and while they lived it was, to say the least, improbable that idealization would get out of hand.

Nevertheless we have good reason to be wary of crediting those witnesses with historical objectivity in the modern sense. Assuredly the catechesis is based on historical fact: it bears the stamp of truth. Yet what carries conviction is the substance of the facts related and not the details, much less their exact situation in space and time. Papias pointed out, in the text quoted above, that "Peter preached the gospel according to the needs of his hearers, not designing to relate the words and deeds of the Lord in chronological order"; and doubtless this was also true of the original Aramaic catechesis, of which St. Peter must have been a principal author and which must have formed the basis of his preaching at Rome. The deeds and sayings he cited in support of his doctrine were necessarily authentic; but for the practical reason mentioned, details need not have been so. It was only logical that his material should have been systematized for the purposes of preaching, with the result that the acts of Christ may on occasion have been taken out of their precise historical context.

Nor is this all. Given the Palestinian background of the primitive catechesis and its scrupulous fidelity to the Aramaic original, even after Christianity had spread through the Hellenistic world, we must conclude that those who composed or edited it expressed themselves in Semitic literary genres – deriving particularly from the books of the OT – whose historical objectivity, in the modern sense, is more than dubious. Consider, for example, the fondness of the OT for "exteriorizing", "materializing", dramatizing, interior signs or revelations from God, and one will see why modern authors who are perfectly orthodox question the *strict* objective historicity of certain passages in the gospels, like the temptation of

Christ or the angelic apparitions in Luke's Gospel of the Infancy. To deny that these things ever happened at all would be jumping to conclusions. But to take the texts literally without regard to the type of writing they represent – the Midrashic influence is obvious – would be "to make the mistake of applying to them the norms of a literary genre with which they have no connection", as the Pontifical Biblical Commission said of the first eleven chapters of Genesis (Letter to Cardinal Suhard, 16 Jan. 1948).

Historical criticism, then, not only may but must be applied to the gospels, and its conclusions will be sound if the aim in view is neither to dismiss everything supernatural nor to attempt to prove the strict objective historicity of the whole text.

It has the noblest of tasks: to seek out the real historical intention of the evangelists, which is the intention God had when he inspired them; to show what truth it is those writers meant to teach whose books can contain only truth; to translate in terms of our modern conception of history the picture of the historical Christ which the gospels painted according to the literary conventions of their day.

In the course of this unavoidable duty exegetes may on occasion hazard opinions that later meet with the disapproval of the Church's magisterium. These are new and difficult matters. But fear of making a mistake must not deter them from throwing themselves whole-heartedly into this work. Pastors of souls will prudently refrain from making use, in preaching, of purely tentative opinions, but should keep abreast of these and give them due consideration so long as the magisterium has not rejected them, requiring no more of anyone than the Church requires of all.

And in any case "as to the efforts of these zealous workers in the vineyard of the Lord, let all the other sons of the Church judge them not only with all fairness but also with the utmost charity, shunning that imprudent attitude which leads people to think that anything new, simply because it is new, must be attacked or held suspect" (Pius XII, *Divino Afflante Spiritu*).

Salvador Muñoz Iglesias

III. Spiritual Exegesis

Writers of the first Christian centuries were familiar with a literal exegesis and a critical exegesis which hardly differed in aim from our present exegesis; only they did not have the benefit of our tools and improved methods. Origen, the pioneer of Christian allegory, became with his *Hexapla* the first great critical exegete and a great literal exegete whom St. Jerome often simply copied. Neither these two men nor their successors saw any such conflict between the different methods as certain moderns do. But here we shall only consider the kind of interpretation which was peculiar to the Fathers and which was used throughout the Middle Ages: spiritual exegesis.

Because of the many influences it has undergone, spiritual exegesis is a complicated subject. One can see why certain historians of our day have tried to distinguish what is properly Christian and what is the result of extraneous cultural influences more or less compatible with Christianity. Unfortunately, the distinction between "typology" and "allegory" which has been contrived to that end seems to us a dubious one. Apart from the fact that neither the ancient and medieval exegetes nor the magisterium of the Church ever betrayed the least awareness of this distinction and the value judgments that it involves, it seems to us to rest on too systematic and limited an idea of Christian time. Christian time, unlike the recurrent cycles of some Greek thinkers, has the horizontal dimension of a unilinear, progressive, irreversible evolution, marked by the event of the Incarnation and culminating in the second coming of Christ. The partisans of the distinction identify as "typological" such interpretations as fit into this scheme, considering them the only really Christian exegesis. But Christian time also has a vertical dimension, its reference to a higher, supernatural world, which the theory we are discussing uses to identify an allegory as of non-Christian origin. But the NT does not admit of such an exclusion, which moreover would ignore the sacramentality of time in the Church's eyes: the Christian already possesses supernatural, eschatological realities, "in a mirror dimly", while hoping for the full possession of them. Besides, man's attempt to know God – through his intelligence, his life and his love – always has to work on the two levels: God can only be represented anthropomorphically, even in the loftiest theological concepts and the best of our approaches; and yet one realizes that God is infinitely beyond all that. Unless one is content to pass a superficial judgment or to consider nothing more than literary genres, it is impossible to isolate a "typological" dimension and an "allegorical" dimension in a given exegesis: the two co-exist in fact, and rightly so, because they are inseparable.

A. Grounds for Spiritual Exegesis

It is the example of Scripture, more particularly the NT, which forms the main justification for spiritual exegesis. The OT paves the way by frequently using symbolic language, by attributing bodily members or human passions to God, and especially by its constant rethinking and further spiritualization, in the prophetic and sapiential books, of the great events in Israel's history, above all the exodus. In many passages of historical value in both Testaments the modern exegete discovers a didactic purpose beneath the narrative which is the sacred author's motive for writing: thus the miracles and other facts related by St. John illustrate the spiritual themes of the fourth gospel. Today this didactic purpose will be recognized as an essential part of the literal sense, which *Divino afflante Spiritu* defines as what the sacred author intended to say. But the early Fathers used different terms: for them the "corporal" or literal sense covered only the material narrative, parable, or metaphor, whereas the symbolic meaning, whether intended by the author or not, formed the spiritual sense.

The OT, however, could only prepare for Christian exegesis, which only came into being through the event of the Incarnation. Spiritual exegesis substantially identical with that of the Fathers is found in the gospels and the apostolic writings, where certain facts of the old covenant are shown to foreshadow realities of the new. In the synoptics, for example, the temple symbolizes Christ's body (Mt 26:61), the three days Jonah spent in the belly of a whale represent the time in which Jesus' body lay in the tomb (Mt 12:40), and Jonah's preaching to the Ninevites represents the preaching of the gospel to the Gentiles (Mt 12:41). In St. John's Gospel the brazen serpent prefigures Christ on the cross (Jn 3:14), and manna the Bread of Life (Jn 6:49–50). The Letter to the Hebrews considers the high priest an image of Christ's priesthood and sacrifice. Everywhere in the NT the Church is the New Israel and the Christian "the spiritual Jew" (Rom 2:29).

But the exegesis which the Fathers most often appeal to is St. Paul's, especially 1 Cor 10:1–11 and Gal 4:21–31. According to the former text the cloud and the passage through the Red Sea prefigure baptism; manna and water from the rock, the Eucharist; and the rock itself, Christ. These events are "types" for us. Indeed "these things happened to them (the men of the OT) as a warning, but they were written down for our instruction, upon whom the end of the ages has come". The second text makes the two wives of Abraham symbols of the two covenants, for "this is an allegory"; that is to say, underneath the obvious sense there lies a deeper meaning. But the symbolic interpretation does not prejudice the historicity of the account for Paul any more than it does for the Fathers.

Two other texts help the early theologians to work out the theory of their exegesis: 2 Cor 3:6–16, setting forth the antagonism between the letter, all that the Jews apprehend, and the spirit which Christ reveals; and Heb 10:1 with its distinction: "The law has but a shadow of the good things to come instead of the true form of these realities ..." Origen and St. Ambrose understand this text to mean that the eschatological good things of the OT are the figure, the hope, the foretaste, but that the NT gives us their true form here below, a real though imperfect possession of them "in a mirror, dimly". Hence will emerge the doctrine of the fourfold sense.

It may be said that all this justifies a spiritual exegesis of the Old Testament but not of the New. The NT applies to each Christian the events of Jesus' life: I must be personally identified with them if I would share in his redemption. One could cite all the NT texts which speak of imitating or "following" Christ, but the opening of the Christological hymn in Phil 2:5–11 will suffice: "Have this mind among yourselves, which you have in Christ Jesus" when he humbled himself and became obedient unto death; or Rom 6:35, which says that baptism conforms one to the death and resurrection of Christ. So there is a spiritual exegesis of the NT which draws from the facts of Christ's life the lessons the contain for each Christan – either the good things to come that we hope for or the life we are to lead through the "time of the Church" in the veiled possession of eschatological realities and the expectation of them.

Scripture, therefore, attests and supports the kind of interpretation we are examining, which reflects truths of a theological order. Revelation is not primarily a book, the Bible, but a Person, Christ: the Word, God speaking to men, becomes flesh to translate that divine word into a human person, into the gestures, deeds, and speech of man. The NT is revelation because it gives us this witness; the OT can be revelation only if it does the same. On the one hand the early Fathers consider the Second Person, as well as the Third, to be the author of all Scripture: to their mind the theophanies of the old covenant are the direct work of the Son, the only mediator, and not of the Father; again, God's word sent to the prophets is Christ, for God has no other word. Scripture and the Word are not two different words but one, for the Word speaks in Scripture. Thus the Bible is as it were an incarnation of the Word in the letter, which prepares and proclaims the one Incarnation, and the whole OT must be looked on as a prophecy of Christ. But this is possible only "when Jesus reads it to his Church" (Origen) as he did to the disciples at Emmaus, showing them that the Bible speaks of himself.

Must we then, like the exegetes of antiquity, seek this kind of meaning in every detail, at the risk of interpretations that are strained or arbitrary? The Fathers had an oversimplified idea of inspiration. They thought of it as dictation and neglected the part of the human author, who expresses himself in a human way even if the Spirit gives his writing a transcendent meaning. Thus they felt that it was beneath God's dignity to dictate an idle word: mysteries must be hidden in every jot and tittle. Nevertheless behind this exaggeration there lies a truth which must not be overlooked. Unless they have a spiritual sense, what are the ordinances and ceremonies of the Law to me, since Christ has abolished the letter of them? What are the historical narratives to me if those past events have no present meaning? The approach of the Fathers is spiritual and pastoral; they are not historians or archaeologists. All those things "were written down for our instruction, upon whom the end of the ages has come" (1 Cor 10:11a). And so those ordinances and chronicles have a meaning which Christ discloses.

For spiritual exegesis is only comprehensible against a background of prayer and contemplation. Through the Bible God speaks to the Christian, provided that his soul can grasp the Lord's interior word. Origen considers that the charism of the exegete is the same as that of the sacred author: a man will not understand Daniel unless he have within him the Spirit that spoke to Daniel. No doubt spiritual exegesis must be rooted in literal exegesis with all its research – critical, grammatical, historical, geographical, and even scientific. Origen and St. Jerome use all their learning to this end. But the voice which God makes the soul hear, even in connection with a text, is tied to no words and no objective sense of words. When a preacher fills out his sermons with the lights he has received at prayer, he is not laying down his interpretations as unquestionable truths unless he has found them in the NT. His chief aim is to provide "food for meditation", to show his hearers the Christian mystery, its implications for the life of the individual Christian, the eschatological good things in store for us which in a measure we already possess. As St. Ignatius would have the director of the *Spiritual Exercises* do, he tries to raise the hearer's mind to God and give him a start at prayer: if the soul, once in contact with God, feels him leading it, it must surrender to his leading.

Moderns as a rule think all this is arbitrary. The writer attaches his own ideas to a text of Scripture instead of setting himself to listen to God's Word. The early Fathers would have resented this charge. In most cases it is unfair, whatever the distance one sometimes finds between the literal sense and the elucidations which the exegete draws from it. These modern critics show that their understanding of the notion of tradition is not all it might be. Jesus did not dictate the writings of the NT. The apostles bore his message in themselves, delivered to them by his word and the example of his life, but they would not have been able to itemize it all in a set of propositions. They were promised the Holy Spirit, who in the course of the Church's history would gradually unfold that message fully. Now a part of considerable historical importance in this progressive explicitation of the faith was played by patristic exegesis, which is in good measure the source of theology. For if the bond between the letter and its interpretation sometimes seems arbitrary, the interpretation is linked with tradition by a bond that is not arbitrary. The exegete has drawn on the instinct of faith which is his as a member of the Church. Spiritual exegesis and its status cannot be properly appreciated without a sound idea of tradition, which antedates and in a sense embraces the writings of the NT, giving one the mind with which to understand them in Christian fashion and the OT with them.

In order to understand spiritual exegesis it is particularly necessary to distinguish its purpose from the purpose of literal exegesis. The latter tries to establish what the sacred author meant to say; the former relates his message to that of Christ.

B. History of Spiritual Exegesis

1. A variety of influences have affected Christian exegesis, complicating a relatively simply pattern. First there are the Jewish interpretations apart from the OT: rabbinical, apocalyptic and

those which have come to light in the Qumran scrolls. They influenced the NT itself, notably St. Paul, the 2nd century Fathers, and through them their successors. The Greeks were also acquainted with an allegorical exegesis which discovered various philosophical meanings, according to the school concerned, in the myths of Homer and Hesiod; working on the assumption that their interpretation must be worthy of the deity (θεοπρεπές, an idea that Christian exegetes adopted), they tried to dispose of by exegesis the many shocking passages in those poems, in reply to the criticisms voiced by Xenophanes of Colophon and by Plato. Many of their methods, like onomastics or symbolic arithmetic, were taken up by Christian writers, who also found them in the Bible and in Jewish writing. Besides the example of his philosophic myths, Plato furnished patristic exegesis with a framework for its symbolism: the two planes, that of the "forms", which alone are perfectly existent and intelligible, and that of sensible things, which have only a participated existence and intelligibility, become the plane of mystery, that is, of supernatural and eschatological values summed up in Christ, and of symbol, embracing sensible things and the letter of Scripture, the shadow and image of the supernatural. This world-view particularly influenced the Alexandrians. Then we must consider Hellenizing Judaism, the first blend of Jewish and Greek exegesis, which affected the NT in the Letter to the Hebrews. Its chief representative, after Aristobolus of Paneas and the Letter of Aristeas, was Philo, who sees the history and institutions of Israel as symbols of the wise man's interior life, under the influence of Posidonius and the Middle Stoa, an amalgam of Stoicism and Platonism. Certain Philonic exegeses, with no mention of Christ, are found in the Alexandrian school. And finally let us not forget that symbolism was a trait common to all the Eastern civilizations of which Alexandria was the meeting-place.

2. The exegesis of the 2nd-century Fathers is more restrained than that of later times, for it is much influenced by Jewish sources, including Hellenistic Judaism and the Epistle of Barnabas. We find it in Melito, St. Justin, St. Irenaeus, and in the 3rd century in Hippolytus. With his contempt for the OT Marcion rejects all interpretations of this sort, which might redeem it, and the work of the Alexandrians is partly inspired by their polemics against him. By showing figures of Christ in the history of Israel they affirm the unity of the two Testaments – the main purpose of spiritual exegesis – and the value of the Old. Though various Gnostic sects share Marcion's contempt for the old Scriptures, allegorical interpretation is nevertheless part of their method: Heracleon, the disciple of Valentinus, uses it to find the substance of his doctrine in St. John's Gospel.

After his teacher Clement, Origen is the great theorist of spiritual exegesis, which he brings to full flower. He explains it by his theory of the three senses of Scripture – corporal (historical), psychical (moral), and spiritual (mystical), which correspond to the three elements of his anthropology, body, soul, and spirit. This trichotomy comes from St. Paul (1 Thess 5:23, among other texts), not from Plato as is often asserted. Plato's "concupiscence", "noble passion" and "intellect" play a different role. In fact, as we shall see, the theory of the three senses does not really account for Origen's method, on which the theory is imposed from without; it is not intrinsic to it.

Opponents of this type of exegesis were by no means lacking in the Great Church at the time. We are given glimpses of them through the homilies of Origen. Confused by the depth and occasional over-subtlety of his explanations, these literalists are said to adhere to "Jewish fables", that is, the literal sense of the OT stripped of all reference to Christ: they are akin to the Anthropomorphists, who take scriptural anthropomorphisms literally, to the Millenarians or Chiliasts, who understand future beatitude in a bodily sense. Though they often murmur against their preacher, they do not seem to form an organized opposition. The only name that can be mentioned, after the death of Origen, is that of the Egyptian bishop Nepos, a Millenarian who repudiated Origen's exegesis of the promise made to God's people. Against Nepos Dionysius the Great defends the interpretations of his master in his book "On the Promises".

3. In the 4th century disciples of Origen, in exegesis, abound: at Alexandria there are Didymus and St. Cyril; in Palestine Eusebius; in Cappadocia St. Gregory of Nyssa; there is also the leader of the Origenists, Evagrius of Pontus. Though St. Basil does not allegorize the first chapters of Genesis, he still takes an interest in Origen's method of exegesis (witness the *Philocalia* which he compiles together with his friend St. Gregory of Nazianzus) and sometimes follows it. Epiphanius, the first to criticize Origenism, lists allegorism among his complaints but is not above using it on occasion for his own purposes.

But opposition to the "School of Alexandria" hardened, led by the "School of Antioch". Founded in the late 3rd or early 4th century by the martyr Lucian of Antioch, teacher of Arius, it produced a series of great exegetes who forcefully attacked the Alexandrian interpretations. After Eustathius of Antioch and Diodorus of Tarsus its leading theorist was Theodore of Mopsuestia. But other representatives of the Antiochene trend – Isidore of Pelusium, St. John Chrysostom, Theodore of Cyrrhus – baulked at Theodore's radicalism and steered a middle course between the two schools.

The friction between Alexandria and Antioch has often been called a misunderstanding rather than a conflict. If the two most characteristic theologians of each school are compared, they prove to agree on the basic issues, concern for the literal sense and belief that the OT contains a more hidden sense revealed by Christ. But the temperaments are worlds apart. Aristotle rules Antioch with his positivism, his logic, and his rationalism: it is prepared to recognize only those types of Christ which are quite plainly such. Theodore drastically cuts down their number. In prophecy what Antioch mainly sees is prediction and its miraculous character, which can be useful in apologetics. It accepts indirect prophecies couched in hyperbolic terms that are not borne out by any speedy fulfilment, but requires the prophet to be at least dimly aware of the discrepancy. Having the spiritual sense squarely based on the literal sense in this way is what the Antiochenes call θεωρία, contrasting it with Alexandrian ἀλληγορία which they hold is not so based. Alexandria continued loyal to the mystical orientation of the Platonic type. The prophet is not so much the herald of the future as the interpreter of all things in relation to God, and of biblical history in relation to Christ. Alexandrian exegesis also starts with the letter but rises above it with more ease, tending to transfigure everything in the OT, to see everything as symbolic of the eschatological blessings revealed by Christ. If the Antiochenes often give a sounder interpretation of a particular text, the Alexandrians have a profounder grasp of what Scripture means as a whole. M. Wiles has compared the commentaries of Theodore and Origen on the fourth gospel and finds that only Origen fathoms the mind of the Evangelist, while Theodore remains at the surface.

4. In the 4th century the Alexandrian exegesis of Origen's followers was adopted on behalf of the West by

Ambrose and Hilary, Jerome and Rufinus. The Antiochene reaction seems hardly to have affected the Latins, except for the Pelagian, Julian of Eclanum. A new classification of the senses of Scripture, "the four senses", which the celebrated couplet of the Dominican Augustine of Dacia was to popularize in the 13th century ("Littera gesta docet, quid credas allegoria, moralis quid agas, quo tendas anagogia"), holds its ground side by side with "the three senses", throughout the Middle Ages. It first occurs, apparently, in Cassian, but it chimes in far better with Origen's practice than that of the three senses. Besides the literal it distinguishes the allegorical sense, which affirms Christ as the centre of history (note that in the present contrast seen between "typology" and "allegory" this allegorical sense belongs to the latter); the tropological or moral sense, which guides a Christian's conduct between the two comings of Christ; and the anagogical sense, which gives a foretaste of heaven. In fact tropological and anagogical meanings are mere corollaries of the allegorical. The main difference between the two formulae is that in the formula of the three senses the moral sense precedes the spiritual, thus seeming to prescind from the coming of Christ, as in the "Philonic" exegeses of the Alexandrians, whereas in the formula of the four senses the moral sense follows from the spiritual.

Most of the great Western writers of late antiquity and the early Middle Ages persevere with Alexandrian exegesis: among many others St. Augustine, St. Gregory the Great, the Venerable Bede, and St. Bernard. Until the upheaval of the 12th century, theology remained much as it was in the Fathers. It is a science in which all sciences meet, and exegesis, often spiritual exegesis, is its foundation. Or rather exegesis makes possible that progressive penetration of the data of the faith whereby tradition evolves. The lessons drawn from it are many: dogmatic and speculative theology, moral and ascetical theology, mystical theology, pastoral theology. In many of these writers, as in their predecessors, attachment to spiritual exegesis follows a careful and laborious study of history and the literal sense of Scripture. At times, like the Fathers before them, they indulge in fantasies which the moderns find distasteful.

With the advent of Scholasticism, the rise of Aristotelian dialectic, and the division of theology into various branches, spiritual exegesis gradually loses its importance. But St. Bonaventure assiduously cultivates it and St. Thomas sets forth the traditional doctrine of the four senses.

At the Renaissance Erasmus is always sympathetic towards this sort of interpretation, characterizing as it does the work of his favourite authors, the ancient Fathers. But the rationalism of modern times could hardly pass fair judgment on it. First many Protestants and then many Catholics dismissed it as an absurdity, an insult to the letter and to history, not adverting to the profound Christian vision of the world to which it gives utterance. Only very recent historians, pre-eminent among them Père de Lubac, have rehabilitated patristic exegesis.

5. A knowledge and understanding of spiritual exegesis as offered by these historians is indispensable to the historian of ancient and medieval theology and to the historian of art, for it dominates many works of the period; it is indispensable to the exegete, for the work of scientific modern exegesis would be of little us to the Christian if it did not help him find spiritual nourishment in Scripture. But is spiritual exegesis merely an element in the culture of the past, of interest to none but specialists? One must be able to read the Fathers without too much exasperation if the spiritual riches they

contain (now available to the reader in modern languages) are not to be lost on one. And how, without an understanding of spiritual exegesis, is one to take a real part in the liturgy of the Church, which abounds with it? How, for example, can one read the psalms of vengeance which the Church has retained in the breviary, not as museum pieces but as food for a cleric's prayer? Without this exegesis they would clash with the gospel. To meditate on Scripture is to practise such exegesis. No doubt the bare literal sense of the OT is itself of value; but if one sees in it no foreshadowing of Christ, then one reads it as a Jew, not as a Christian. Again, how can one meditate on the life of Jesus as on events that have no meaning for us in our heart of hearts? What we say of prayer applies equally to preaching. Of course we cannot take such liberties as the ancients did and we must keep spiritual exegesis pruned down to its essentials. But no one can preach as a Christian on the two Testaments without making use of spiritual exegesis. The dogmatic truths it evokes are of such weight for the spiritual life and even for preaching that one may wonder whether we do not often practise it unaware.

Henri Crouzel

BIBLICAL HISTORIOGRAPHY

The historian E. Meyer remarked that "an independent historical literature in the true sense only appeared with the Israelites and the Greeks". It is generally agreed that history, as understood in our culture, originated at two points very distant in space and time, in 5th-century Greece with Herodotus and Thucydides, and, five centuries or more earlier, with the first redactor of Genesis whose work can be identified, the anonymous author called the "Yahwist" and the other author who recounted the story of the succession from David to Solomon (2 Sam 9–20; 1 Kg 1–2). These are the first two examples of historical narratives which embrace a certain length of time and group a number of diverse events, of which they bring out the special features and show the continuity. They connect the facts by a deliberate and objective appeal to the manifold and complex factors which constitute human history: the play of natural elements, passions, characters and social customs, along with the plan and will of God who directs all from within by his creative action.

These two histories, the story of the establishment of a people on earth, the story of the establishment of a dynasty on a throne, can, on a more modest scale and a field more restricted in general, be compared favourably for firmness of design, truth of analyses and depth of insight either with the immense fresco in which Herodotus confronts the fabulous world of the Orient with the brand-new world of Greece, or with the political study in which Thucydides lays bare the causes of the Peloponnesian War and the intrinsic connections of its events.

Though the Israelite histories are clearly superior to those of their neighbours, this does not mean that the originality of Israel does not allow of natural links and analogies with the culture of the ancient East.

1. *History in the ancient East.* The effort to record and fix the memory of past events plays no little part in the culture of the ancient East. This interest in preserving a record of the past is shown in royal inscriptions in palaces and temples, in the annals registered by scribes and preserved in archives, in chronicles of reigns and chronological tables. Till about 2000 B.C., this interest is predominantly practical, concerned with administrative needs. From 2000 B.C. on the first historical syntheses appear, consecrated to re-creating the past. Their object is to legitimate

existing authority by showing its continuity with that of the past. Thus lists of kings and lists of royal cities were drawn up. They are sometimes taken back beyond historical times and the deluge, to the days when the gods reigned on earth.

These syntheses show history as a series of crests and troughs: it is a vision of a succession of conquests and ruins, of advances and collapses, of periods of prosperity and of catastrophes. The explanation of these cycles is religious. They depend on the changing favours of the gods, and this in turn is generally explained by their reaction to the piety or irreligion of the sovereign.

The historical value of these documents is far from negligible. Under serious critical inspection, they furnish modern historians with a large number of solid data. It would have been impossible to write the history of Egypt without them, and so too the history of Sumer and Accad, of Assyria and the Hittites. Nonetheless, these documents never constitute the history of a reign, a people or a city. The histories of Egypt or of Babylon are the creation of modern historical science.

These historical records are in fact little more than enumerations, without real unity, intrinsic continuity or human depth. They do not recount the march of events, they do not describe their special features. They simply list the memorable feats of kings, their great warlike deeds, their hunting exploits, their political conquests, their administrative and architectural achievements, their munificence towards the sanctuaries. At times, however, they take another tone, when trying to justify the claims of a conqueror or a usurper, and then they enumerate the series of faults and crimes which have brought down the anger of the gods.

The fact that the king appears everywhere as the sole protagonist of the action is not simply to be attributed to a sense of mission. It can also testify to authentic piety towards the gods. Triumphal inscriptions are often carved in front of gods' statues to show that they are meant to be read by the gods. Still, this way of concentrating all the action in the person of the king, of reducing all the other personages to the role of defeated adversaries or admiring witnesses, to the elimination of all human conflict, all personal attitudes, all encounter between the actors, all risk of defeat, only retains the most superficial aspect of events and leaves them without coherent links and real intelligibility. Hence they can be interchanged without difficulty: it was, for instance, the common practice of Ramses II in Egypt to efface the name of the sovereign who had had an inscription engraved and insert his own name instead. Only some Hittite inscriptions of about 1300 B.C., especially those of Mursilis II and Hattusilis III, evoke the adventures of a royal succession, the diplomatic manoeuvres and the strategic calculations of these princes in such a way as to form, in spite of their primitive style and awkward narrative, the first attempts at true history in the eastern world.

Similar principles and structures seem to have dominated the history-writing of the Persian and Seleucid empires. The constant effort is to legitimate the reigning monarch by showing that the sovereigns had never acted like conquerors or usurpers, but as the legitimate heirs, charged by the divinity to rid the earth of an unworthy master. Every change of dynasty claims to be based on the bonds of kinship, real or fictive, with the preceding dynasty. The official history of the Achaemenids sees the Persian empire as the third (and final) empire of the world, the definitive successor of the Medes and the Assyrians. After Alexander, the official view maintained by the Seleucids substitutes a system of four empires for the previous three. The apocalypse of Daniel (Dan 2:37–45) makes use of this system against the Seleucids, by announcing the coming of a fifth empire, that of the God of heaven (2:44; cf. 4:31; 7:14) which will be inaugurated by the Son of Man.

2. *The origins of history in Israel.* In contrast to these compositions, at once monumental and bloodless, the literature of Israel presents, from the 9th century onwards, typical examples of real works of history, solidly historical enough to form to the present day, even among critical historians, the framework of the history of Israel.

The soundness of these histories does not come principally from the exceptional quality of their documentation. The records were drawn up and transmitted in Israel more or less as in the courts and administrations of its neighbours. The author of the books of Samuel probably used archives, and these were necessarily affected by political currents. The redactors of Genesis collected traditions about the patriarchs coming from the distant past, which could not have escaped being coloured by intervening events. Modern historians are struck by the archaic atmosphere preserved in these memories, which is a good sign of their authenticity. Biblical inspiration, however, does not render the tradition any the less human, or any the less subject to the hazards of human transmission.

The factor that seems to have been decisive in the origins of historical writing in Israel was the following: the first compilations do not come from the courts and chancelleries, like the annals of the eastern kings, which were usually composed for the glory of the sovereign. They are based on memories which crystallized round well-known personages, and were gathered and repeated orally by storytellers. This explains the fact that in Israel the historical genre is popular in origin, anonymous and therefore ancient, existing long before the royal court and administration. It also explains why Israelite history adopts so readily and preserves so long the form of biographical narrative, a set of tales grouped round a venerable figure like a patriarch, Moses, Samuel, David, Elijah and Elisha. It explains the lively and dramatic movement of the narrative.

But this factor alone does not explain the origins of Israelite history or the forms it took in the Bible. Its origins are religious. History is the history of the deeds of God. The originality of this history manifests the unique nature of this God.

The royal annals and chronicles outside Israel are also religious: they proclaim the power of guardian and avenging deities. But this power is exercised in a series of reactions, sometimes beneficent, sometimes fearsome, to be explained either by the natural bent of the deity or by the way it has been treated by men. These reactions are sometimes capricious, but again, they may be well-adjusted and serious. But along with superhuman power and insight, along with a cosmic immensity, they always manifest something defective and dependent: these gods react. In the last resort, they are almost puppets. They cannot create. They cannot really initiate an enterprise or bring it to a close. The perpetual ups and downs of history are the reflection of their primordial impotence: nothing is settled finally, either in advance or subsequently.

There is no real difference between present history and the mythic history of the beginnings, between the history of men and that of the gods. There is no real history. The same drama is played out throughout the ages, only the personages change.

It is different in Israel. The histories are determined by a definite goal, a single event fixed from the start. The history of David's successors originates in the prophecy of Nathan (2 Sam 7).

The history of the settlement in Canaan is based on the promise to Abraham. The historical narratives of the Bible are all the story of a word of God, promise or threat, which has just been fulfilled. This principle is universal, and works at all dimensions, at that of an isolated episode like the victory of Deborah and Barak over Sisera (Jg 4), or at that of a biography like David's, or finally at that of a whole period of the people's existence, from the time it leaves Egypt till it is established in Palestine, or from David's arrival at Jerusalem till the departure of the last of his successors into captivity. This is real history because there is unity of design, and because this design, though formed and realized by God, is still carried out in the real world, through the play of natural forces, human passions and contrivances, and indeed of chance encounters, in a succession of episodes which unquestionably form part of human history. This history is our history and we see ourselves reflected there: but it is at the same time and indeed primarily the history of him who guides it and brings it to its goal, the sacred history of the true God.

At the basis of this authentically historical view of things lies the fundamental religious experience of Israel, that of the covenant. The most ancient historical accounts in the Bible, the professions of faith at Jos 24:2–13 or Deut 26:5–9, are liturgical confessions, incorporated into sacred gestures, pronounced in sacred places, founded on the decisive act of God, the covenant. But this act is essentially historical, not only because it was accomplished at a given place and date, being linked to the historical figure of Moses, but because it is itself the culminating point of a previous history, that of the election, and the starting-point of a further stage of history, the definitive establishment of Israel in the promised land. The experience of the covenant is not only the experience of a fact that was to remain without parallel; it is also the experience of a directed movement which has a beginning, a continued existence and a perfect achievement in time and in the general existence of the world. There is history, because there is an experience destined to be perceived and understood, to be recounted and fixed for ever, and because this experience is a decisive event in the evolution of the world. Something happened which the Bible was composed to express.

3. *From the history of the covenant to the history of the world.* Historical from its beginnings, the experience of the covenant led naturally to the great historical compilations of the Bible. It is almost impossible to reconstruct the stages of this process. It was certainly gradual, and it probably consisted of grouping and combining along a continuous thread memories and traditions which were originally independent, attached to individual groups and scattered shrines. There is no doubt a certain amount of artificiality in the continuous narrative which the hexateuch now offers. The artificial element is particularly noticeable in the book of Judges, but it is not confined to it. Throughout it all, the narrative remains fundamentally historical and interprets the real process which gave birth to the people of Israel and established it in its land.

But the history of Israel is wider than Israel, and goes beyond it in all directions. It goes back not only to the history of Abraham but to the origin of the world. The procedure seems to resemble what went on in Sumer, where the annalists were led to prolong the lists of reigns and royal cities back beyond the deluge, to the times when the gods reigned on earth. But in reality, the motives at work were completely different. In Sumer it was a matter of legitimating the ruling authority by showing that it went back without interruption to the primordial rulers. The histories of Israel, those of the Yahwist or those which told of the succession to David, also aimed at legitimating either the throne of Solomon or the possession of Palestine by Israel. But this legitimacy does not rest on the primordial order of things, on something which is in the end only the recognition of a divine value in the destiny of empires. On the contrary, it rests on an initial fact without anterior explanation and without precedent, on a purely divine initiative which intervened to shatter the normal course of events: the historical fact of the divine election. History up to Abraham was not for Genesis a course of events which led up naturally to Abraham, making what happened to Abraham a repetition of the primordial mythic event. On the contrary, history is built up round Abraham, and it makes the world the framework and the setting in which God raised up Abraham. This framework has the same human and historical consistency as the call of Israel and the covenant.

The description of the world and man presented in the first eleven chapters of Genesis does not offer any historical data which the historian can really make use of. It is not based on documents miraculously preserved, or even on privileged traditions. It puts before us an artificial picture, composed on the model of images furnished by oriental myths. But this picture is no longer mythic. It does not describe an unreal world, half human and half divine. It depicts the real framework of a true history, and this framework is the mankind of history.

4. *The prophets and the history of the world.* Situated in the real history of humanity, the history of Israel also rejoins it at its end. This encounter was envisaged from the time of the first promise to Abraham, a promise destined to embrace "all the families of the earth" (Gen 12:3). The encounter is proclaimed by the prophets as a certain historical event of the future. The culmination of the history of Israel is also to be that of the history of the peoples. The prophets are constantly preoccupied with history, which interests them from two points of view, different and complementary. On the one hand, they are very well informed of the past history of their people, very attentive to the religious traditions concerning the patriarchs, the exodus from Egypt and the conquest of Palestine. They consider these facts as fundamental. On the other hand, they are very alert to the events of their own day and strive hard to clarify their immediate significance for Israel. But this double direction of their attention is not based on the conviction that the lessons of the past are bound to furnish them with the interpretation of the present, as if the present action of God was simply the prolongation of what he had done in the past. On the contrary, there is often a profound breach of continuity between God's past actions and his present decisions: "Remember not the former things . . . Behold, I am doing a new thing" (Is 43:18f.). The past will not return again: it has been abolished both by the sins of Israel and by the inventive power of God. But there remains an absolute certainty with regard to the past, an unshakeable conviction with regard to its meaningful historicity: and this is the faith of the prophets. Once it is certain that God never ceases to govern the destiny of Israel, he must be present throughout all its history: and it is in the actual events of the present day that he pursues his purpose and brings it to its goal. The historicity of the original experience of Israel makes the prophets attentive to the religious meaning of each historic moment. They are certain that God will not abandon the work which he has undertaken. They feel themselves gripped by God and constrained to live out their lives under his hand (Jer 15:17). So they know that the history of their

people cannot slip from his grasp and that the decisive event, the reign of God over the world, must surely come, in a way of which they can have only very remote conceptions.

5. *The history of Jesus Christ.* The story of Jesus Christ is completely in line with the writing and interpretation of history as done by the chroniclers and prophets of the OT. But it claims at the same time to make a completely fresh start, which both leaves behind and uniquely fulfils the previous history of the people. It is akin to the royal annals of the ancient Orient and to Israelite histories in its intention of legitimating the actual authority. From the very start, the object of the preaching of the gospel is to show how God gave to Jesus his due sovereignty over all flesh, accrediting him by signs during his life, delivering him from death and giving him possession of the Holy Spirit (Acts 2:29–36 and parr.). It is a question of giving the meaning of a series of historical events. But in this case the sequence of events, crowded though it is, is a matter of a few years, and its historical attestation does not rest on more or less ancient memories, on more or less tendentious archives, but on the testimony of disciples who know that they are bound to tell the truth, both out of fidelity to their Lord, and by reason of watchful adversaries always ready to pounce upon error. Of course, we must also remind ourselves that the writers of the gospels did not start from the concept of history which we have today, as produced in the 19th century. Their history writing is determined by the kerygma. The hearer of the message is presented with the historical processes as they are brought to life in faith in the "Pneumatic" Christ living on in his Church. The plane of the purely historical is left behind. The tendency to overcome and eliminate myth which is characteristic of all biblical history is brought to its highest degree in the history of Jesus Christ. The legitimation of Christ is based on the series of events which make up his existence, and this in turn gives meaning and consistency to all the history of Israel and to its prophecies.

The history of Jesus Christ is likewise a perfect example of human history. No other shows so clearly the forces at work in history, the conflict of passions, the import of decisions, the responsibilities of man in face of his destiny. And no other reveals more unmistakably that the history of men, precisely where it is most self-assured and most deliberately willed, remains entirely in the hands of God and accomplishes his design.

Jacques Guillet

BIBLICAL THEOLOGY

More complicated methods, the scope of the material and the difficulty of the problems make biblical theology as a relatively autonomous discipline alongside dogmatic theology necessary merely for the sake of academic organization. This practical and technical division does not, however, solve the fundamental problem of the relation between the two disciplines. It would be perfectly possible for biblical theology to be practised as dogmatic theology once was (though with a wider range and some use of the methods and results of modern exegesis): to collect "proof texts" from Scripture and make them into backing for a system of dogmatic statements which did not derive – in the first instance, at least – from biblical theology itself, but were prior to its work. Nor, conversely, could dogmatic theology ever simply hand over all work on Scripture (the systematic and sympathetic examination of its statements) to another discipline ("biblical theology") and simply take over its finished results. Dogmatic theology has questions of its own to put to Scripture, and it cannot take for granted *a priori* that those are the questions an independent biblical theology would ask, since in that case biblical theology would have to be a reproduction of the whole of dogmatic theology, with all its questions, perspectives, norms and aims.

It does not, however, follow from all this that biblical theology is no more than a purely technical subdivision of the all-embracing science of "dogmatic theology" (including a theologically formulated moral theology) and is as such governed only by the norms of a dogmatic theology homogeneous in structure in all its parts. It is true that if dogmatic theology is defined – broadly and comprehensively – as the systematic and precise effort to obtain the fullest possible understanding of the revealing word of Christ in his Church with all the means available, then biblical theology must be only one part of dogmatic theology in this sense. Yet even this "part" of general dogmatics derives a character and status of its own from its subject-matter which make it more than just a part of general dogmatics. The reason for this is the special, unique character of holy Scripture. This is not to say that wherever exegesis and biblical theology are not practised as strictly separate disciplines theology exists only as a series of non-binding theologoumena; that is, that dogmatic theology (in the sense of the systematic exposition of the propositions of the faith, as opposed to theological opinions) is in the strictest sense identical with biblical theology (as Protestant theology must fundamentally say). In the Catholic view, (general) dogmatic theology depends on the guidance of the magisterium and on "tradition" as one of its sources (however the relationship of the latter to Scripture is to be described). Hence it must deal with a history of dogmas (not just of theology) and development of dogma which contain types of statement which demand faith but are not in any simple way directly identical with the statements of Scripture. Yet Scripture is not merely one source from which dogmatic theology draws knowledge; one existing alongside others of equal status, from all of which dogmatic theology must draw the same material in the same way, according to rules and attitudes of its own established in advance of its use of this source. Of course, like the rest of dogmatic theology, biblical theology is bound to understand Scripture in the Church, under the "immediate" norm of the current proclamation of the faith by the official teaching Church which was endowed with authority by Christ in the Holy Spirit (in this connection we shall leave aside the question of the possibility and scope of a more or less pre-dogmatic, "fundamental" biblical theology). Even this current authoritative proclamation of the Church's faith, however, takes place in a context of permanent, necessary and continually new reference back to the specificity of the origin and beginning of this proclamation, which is permanent, guaranteed by God as "pure" and distinguishable from the later development of the Church's teaching.

This specificity, with the three characteristics mentioned, exists in Scripture and only in Scripture. "Tradition", whether or not it has any contents apart from Scripture and the definition of the canon, in its objective composition can offer no guarantee of purity from merely human additions. When a reference to tradition is made, tradition must be examined about the very things it handed down in the past in unexplicit and unclear form as the substance of divine revelation. This means that the distinction between *traditio divina* and *traditio humana* in a reference back to tradition is in fact the work of the magisterium, which makes the reference; consequently it affords no basis for a distinction between the norm and what is governed by the norm; this paradox constantly recurs in problems concerning the concept of tradition and its distinction from the magisterium. Nonetheless, within these limits, in spite of the existence of a *traditio divino-apostolica*, Scripture is a pre-eminent and unique source and norm for the current proclamation of the Church's faith, and therefore for the dogmatic theology which is guided by that proclamation and assists in preparing it (cf. *D* 1942). Although the guarantee of the correct interpretation of, and proper respect for, Scripture as source and norm by the magisterium is vested in the Church by the promise of the help of the Spirit given to the Church (and not to individuals independently of the Church), Scripture, and Scripture alone, is still our originally pure source (*quoad nos* and not just *in se*) and *norma non normanda* for the Church's knowledge of the faith and its dogmatic theology. When (general) dogmatic theology listens to God's revealing word in and with the authoritative Church (to be strictly accurate, the hierarchical Church must also do this), a process takes place which occurs in no other circumstances. This gives biblical theology the special character setting it apart from all other functions of dogmatic theology. Here, and here only, dogmatic theology is directed and not director, listener and not judge, as it really is in its other ("historical" and "speculative") functions. From this it follows, on purely theoretical grounds, that if, on the pattern of the accepted (and in itself quite possible and defensible) pattern of scholastic dogmatics, the only enquiry into Scripture was directed to finding "proof texts" for the statements and views of dogmatics, that would not constitute biblical theology. It is rather the task of biblical theology to exercise a critical function with regard to this scholastic dogmatics and the current proclamation of the faith at any time, even though neither of these derives from biblical theology. The pure beginning of the kerygma of faith (which remains present in Scripture), though a beginning, is always something permanently greater and more comprehensive, which continually makes development possible and pervades it. For this process to happen at all in dogmatic theology and in the specialized branch of biblical theology, there has to be a biblical theology in a fundamental sense (in the sense in which it has always existed to the necessary degree in the Church). This will be a part of (general) dogmatic theology, but at the same time the guiding element of dogmatic theology. The Church insists on the need for a continual return to the "sources" in general on the part of "speculative" theology (i.e. on the part of a theology which attempts to win an all-encompassing understanding of revelation from the totality of all data, intellectual possibilities and lines of enquiry), and this applies in a special way to biblical theology. As experience shows, without a continually new return to the beginning which is never exhausted and therefore constantly presents itself to us as new, all theology becomes sterile: "Sacrorum fontium studio sacrae disciplinae semper iuvenescunt" (Pius XII: *D* 2314).

Karl Rahner

BIRTH CONTROL

1. *Systematic theological considerations.*

a) Today the deliberate regulation and even the limitation of births is in many instances a serious moral duty for parents, for otherwise serious harm is done to marriage and the family and the greater social order.

b) Sexual intercourse has a moral value beyond and independent of procreation when it is the chaste expression of the total dedication of love.

The problem of the morality of the regulation of births can thus be precisely formulated in the question: in what circumstances can the sexual union be the expression of love even when fertility is excluded? The usual answer is: when it is sought as dedication and when there is no intervention to deprive it of its intrinsic ordination to fertility (unless intervention is necessary for the health of the person in question). Intervention would be an effort to take back the total gift of self and its intrinsic dynamism. The act would be a self-contradiction and hence nugatory. The practice of rhythm is considered acceptable because it does not interfere with the biological act and remains ordained to the established order of things. But it should be remembered that the history of married love does not simply run parallel to the biological cycle of the woman. Hence intercourse can be very suitable at the very moment when it does not suit the calendar (Beirnaert). If intervention occurs for the sake of health, it makes further giving of self possible. It has thus a simultaneous double effect and is therefore justified. Consequently the use of contraceptive methods is always allowable when, along with their contraceptive effect, they have at the same time a medical purpose and when this purpose, which justifies the intervention, is intended.

Recently, the main discussion centred on the circumstances in which such curative effects can be ascribed to medicaments that hinder ovulation. The particular point was how far regulation of the cycle is medically desirable. The main cases envisaged were the first months after childbirth, the menopause, and irregular cycles. Obviously, only medical indications can decide when medical measures are to be taken. Nevertheless, one may say that as a consequence of medical progress, indirect assistance can be given in a number of cases in which regulation of births is particularly urgent, though application, from the traditional viewpoint of moral theology, was formerly hard to justify. The principle of the double effect has been given wider application by the authors who allow contraceptive methods not only where both contraception and protection of health actually coincide, but also where the contraceptive effect is directly intended as a means to a greater end (or the interests of the subject). This is the case, for example, when sterilization is allowed, because on medical grounds there is no possibility of childbearing, though there is the possibility of conception, which, however, in this case has lost its intrinsic finality. A still larger view allows temporary contraceptives to overcome psychosomatic anomalies. This is meant, with the help of therapy, to bring the patient to the stage of accepting normally a possible conception.

A growing number of moral theologians go even further. They suggest that the final criterion for judging the lawfulness of contraceptives should be still more generally and formally the good of the family and the marriage and indeed the good of mankind, according to the good or bad effects of prevention of births. They arrive at this view on the basis of the conviction that contraception in itself is neither morally good nor evil, and that the moral value of concrete actions is to be judged by whether or not they serve the moral developments of human dignity in the free and responsible person, that is, whether they serve or hinder the total fulfilment of man or only a certain dimension of his being. This cannot be determined from the objective end of the action as such, but only from the end which it is given by man in regard to man as such. If one accepts these principles, contraception would always be permitted when it promotes love between married couples and other persons indirectly concerned, and when a new conception could not be responsibly allowed in the concrete situation of those concerned. The question, how far certain contraceptives correspond to the dignity of the sexual union, depends upon how the method employed, with its psycho-physiological effects, can be integrated within the ever-changing relationships which constitute the good of the persons involved. Whether such an integration is possible in a given case is to be determined by the relevant sciences such as medicine, eugenics, psychology, sociology, etc., and, where these are insufficient, by the prudent judgment of those concerned. In this view, the lawfulness of a given means cannot be determined *a priori*, but only *a posteriori* and in the concrete. *A priori* one could only determine in a formal way (as in a model case) under what circumstances the use of contraceptives would be justified; the actual process would depend upon the concrete situation and must be determined with the help of the pertinent sciences and by the exercise of prudent judgment. A number of the authors who think along these lines proceed, nevertheless, from the *a priori* assumption that the dignity of intercourse demands the integrity of the act itself, and only permit contraceptives which leave the actual act unchanged. These are the authors who gave the first and strongest impulse to the personalist approach to birth regulation (L. Janssens, van der Marck).

2. *Pastoral theology*. Pastoral theology, according to various needs, must alert consciences to the possible duty of family planning as part of the divine charge laid upon man, of shaping his destiny and not simply submitting to nature but controlling it to create human culture even in the realms of procreation. It must further explain that the integration of sexuality into self-command is a slow struggle including setbacks, and depends on many factors outside the moral sphere. Its dynamism must be inspired by a view of marriage which sees it as a sacred state in which both partners strive for perfection. Offences against this ideal, departures from the way leading to it, defects in its realization, must be judged according to the extent to which that ideal is known and willed. If the married couple makes this basic attitude their own, they can simply act according to Augustine's principle, *ama et fac quod vis* – "love and do what you will". Their decisions will be guided more and more by the optimum, and less by the defective element possibly included in a given realization of the act.

Offences against this more or less clear and unprejudiced ideal must be judged according to the extent to which they depart from the basic attitude. When forming consciences, pastors may confidently take the married couple's own verdict as the basis of their own. Those who are conscious of no serious sin should be encouraged to partake of the sacraments and from that living source to receive new strength and hope in their effort at perfection.

Waldemar Molinski

BISHOP

I. New Testament

The Christian episcopate is a blend of two different systems: episcopal order and presbyteral order, these in turn being based on two different conceptions of apostleship, two different ways of being Jesus' representative. In the synoptics the apostle is one of a college, not tied to one place, but working solely within Israel as a representative of the earthly Jesus. The Twelve preach as Jesus does. This Jewish-Christian, collegiate apostolate continues in the council of presbyters which we find in the local Christian community at the period of Luke's gospel (transposed into Acts), in James, 1 Peter, Titus, 1 Timothy, and Revelation.

Contrasted with it we have the Pauline concept of apostleship, which 2 Cor 8:23 shows must have prevailed in other gentile churches as well. Here the risen Lord is represented by a single apostle, later by a single *episkopos*. There is no presbyter. Whereas the pre-NT *episkopos* was a secular official with limited duties, in the NT he is generally associated with deacons (Phil 1:1; 1 Tim 3:2, 8; cf. *Didache*, 15, 1) and much is made of the connection between *episkopos* and "shepherd" of the flock, intimated in the Septuagint: see 1 Pet 2:25; 5:2, 4; Acts 20:28; cf. Num 27:16. We may gather from 1 Pet 2:15, where ἐπισκοπή is used in the non-technical sense of "visitation", that office is primarily a matter of juridical supervision, whereas the parallel shepherding of the flock positively leads them to salvation (cf. Ecclus 18:13); so that the two functions of the episcopal office are conveyed by combining the two terms.

Our oldest text is Phil 1:1, according to which there are still several bishops in the local community, presumably the heads of largish families who also have supervisory duties in the Church (cf. Tit 1:6ff.; 1 Tim 3:4–5). On the other hand, we are already on the road to the monarchical episcopate with Timothy's mission as Paul's representative (Phil 2:19). As the apostles disappeared, representatives of this kind gathered the episcopal duties into the hands of one individual. Thus the local character and the duties of the episcopal office derive from the "collective" episcopate, whereas its monarchical character derives from the apostolic office. If we compare the theological concept of the apostle in 2 Cor with 1 Pet, we shall perceive the theological relevance of the monarchical element. According to 2 Cor there can be only one apostle for the community, because he alone represents and communicates with the one Lord Jesus Christ in a communion of suffering and labour in the domain (κανών) that is his responsibility. 1 Pet shows how the idea of the highest local authority as an image of Christ also colours the concept of the *episkopos*: Christ is the *episkopos* of the community (2:25) and its supreme shepherd (5:4); the rulers of the community are presbyters (5:1), but their work too is ἐπίσκοπος, parallel to Christ's "shepherding" the flock. So the presbyters' episcopal work parallels that of Christ the *episkopos*. Here the presbyters represent the glorified Lord, and he is pictured in their image. Several presbyters exercise the function of the supreme shepherd. In this way 1 Pet combines the idea of an *episkopos* with presbyteral order. The monarchical episcopate arises from the image of Christ the one *episkopos*, blended with the Pauline idea of one apostle in each community. Thus the germ of the monarchical episcopate is found in the Hellenistic area which St. Paul evangelized, in the mission of Timothy, in 1 Pet and the pastoral letters. On the other hand, by way of contrast with the synagogue, the Law, and traditional Jewish thought, Paul had no trace of presbyteral order in his communities. True, that order soon penetrated the Pauline churches: by the time Acts was written the churches in Lycaonia and Pisidia had elders, like Corinth when *1 Clem* was written. (Here the Hellenistic term *episkopoi* is used.)

Acts and the Pastoral Letters show us the blending of Hellenistic episcopal order with Jewish presbyteral order. In Acts 20 the presbyters (v. 17) are called *episkopoi* (v. 28). Possession of the Holy Spirit is the decisive criterion of their vocation and authority. We may not suppose from Acts 1:20 that the episcopate is equivalent to the apostolate, since ἐπισκοπή in this text is taken from Ps 108:8. Acts 6:3 uses ἐπισκέπτεσθαι for the institution of the seven deacons. So the language of Acts shows that the word was still taken in the general sense of ruling the community and could therefore be applied to a presbyteral system as well.

Tit 1:6–9 and 1 Tim 3:1–13 belong to the same literary genre as Acts 20:18–38 (the ideal *episkopos*). According to 1 Tim 3:1 ἐπισκοπή is a permanent office which one may aspire to. The qualities necessary in the candidate are described, not the duties of the office: probity, good management of his own family, an aptitude for preaching, modesty. We have a basically presbyteral system crowned by episcopal order: in 1 Tim 5:17 the καλῶς προεστῶτες are obviously the *episkopoi* worthy of double honour. They represent the development which underlies the pre-eminence of the episcopate.

According to Tit 1:5–9 Titus is to appoint elders in Crete (which Paul himself had done: see Acts 14:23), but in v. 7 they are also called *episkopoi*. 1 Tim 3:2 and Tit 1:7, however, already speak of the *episkopos* – "a bishop" (RSV) – in the singular. Even supposing that this is a merely generic singular, the duties which Timothy and Titus had with regard to several communities soon pass to the individual *episkopos*.

Klaus Berger

II. Church History

The episcopate is among those structural elements in the Church which go back to Christ. Nevertheless its precise shape and function were left to be worked out by the Church in the course of time. From the point of view of emphasis we can distinguish three major periods in that process, of which the earlier periods point to the problems of the later and vice versa.

1. *Material and formal development of the episcopal office (1st to 9th century)*. At first both forms of Church government found in the NT exist side by side. *1 Clement* still recognizes the collegiate system, with presbyteral *episkopoi* whom "other eminent men" (44:3) appoint after the death of the apostles. Other successors of the apostles are itinerant missionaries (*Didache:* ἀπόστολοι). We have the transition to the monarchical episcopate towards the end of the 1st century, when a single superintendent or *episkopos* takes over in each local church. About the year 110 the letters of St. Ignatius of Antioch, with their theology of the episcopate, show us the fully developed monarchical episcopate. It is the bishop, the representative of Christ and image of the Father, who makes celebration of the Eucharist lawful, thereby guaranteeing unity in the local church; and he ensures the catholicity of that church because of his (necessary) union with the bishops of the Church universal (*Letter to the Smyrneans*, 8, 2). The *Didascalia Apostolorum* provides the canonical elaboration of this model.

By the middle of the 2nd century Ignatius's Christocentric theology of the episcopate yields to the more general notion that the bishop is a successor of the apostles. This doctrine finds classic expression in the anti-Gnostic arguments of St. Irenaeus of Lyons. The bishop is the living witness to tradition because his ancestry in office (recorded in the lists of bishops given by Irenaeus, Epiphanius and Eusebius) goes back to the apostles (*Adv. haer.*, III, 2, 1; later in Tertullian, *De praescr.*, 20, 2–4; St. Augustine, *De civitate Dei*, 18, 50). This rather juridical view is complemented by theological elements: the bishop is full of the Holy Spirit (Hippolytus). Now the episcopate is seen as linked with the historical Jesus by the Apostolic Succession and with the glorified Christ by consecration (holy orders). This twofold bond with Christ guarantees the Church's faith: παράδοσις κατὰ διαδοχήν.

As early as Ignatius we find the threefold division of office (bishop, priest, deacon). Priests and deacons are closely connected with the bishop, but the layman too plays an important part as the bishop's helper, especially in preaching (Origen, St. Cyprian, St. John Chrysostom). Laymen are likewise essentially involved in electing the bishop (St. Leo the Great, *Ep.*, 16, 10: "Qui praefuturus est omnibus, ab omnibus eligatur"), though once elected he is not the delegate of the people but *Dei episcopus*. When the Fathers work out a lofty ideal of the episcopate (St. Gregory the Great), exempting the bishop from all accountability to men because of his commission from God but at the same time binding him to perfection, they do not always escape the temptation of making the legitimacy of office depend on personal holiness (Origen, for example). A bishop's duties, according to the Fathers, include preaching the gospel (in catechesis and missions), conducting worship (where he has certain prerogatives, especially that of ordaining priests), exercising discipline (excommunicating and reconciling), and legislative and executive functions. These duties are regarded as essentially a matter of service, a charism for building up the Church (St. Augustine, *Sermo*, 46, 2: "Christiani propter nos, praepositi propter vos").

On theological foundations laid by St. Ignatius and St. Cyprian an effective ecclesiology of the *communio* is reared, especially from the fourth century onward, which dwells upon the individual bishop's responsibility for the whole Church (several bishops at a consecration, the sending of the *eulogia* [blessed bread] and the *fermentum* [consecrated hosts], bishops' encyclicals; above all, synods and councils). Under the later empire it leads to a firmer concentration (and centralization) of dioceses into units on a higher level (provinces; patriarchates). The Roman See acts as the guardian of Church unity in this process, guiding it, by the exercise of its jurisdiction, for the good of the whole Church.

2. *Relations with State, papacy, and priesthood (10th to 15th century)*. Because of the various cultures in that region, several patriarchates grow up in the East. The position of the bishop (as established in the first centuries) is not challenged here; the only real controversy concerns the place of the patriarchates in the complex of the Churches. But in the West, a social and cultural unity, the Roman See remains the only centre to claim special authority over the whole Church as the See of Peter. This claim, together with political and theological developments, brings the episcopate into three magnetic fields:

a) *The State*. From the Constantinian age onwards, in accordance with the unity of the State as conceived of in antiquity, the bishops are assimilated into the hierarchy of secular dignitaries. Very soon the rulers of the empire and of the successor States claim the right to appoint bishops, a right acknowledged in 921 by Pope John X (no bishop to be consecrated *absque jussione regis*). More and more the episcopate becomes a fixed part of the feudal system; as princes of the empire the bishops are pillars of the medieval State. Their consequent involvement in the narrow selfish interests of temporal rulers (lay investiture) meant a secularization of the episcopate which was very dangerous for the Church.

b) *The papacy*. In this respect the struggle of the 11th century reforming Popes to separate the two powers, Church and State, was primarily a struggle to safeguard episcopal autonomy. But it was not long before the tension between Pope and bishops inherent in the Church's structure led to a struggle for supremacy between the two hierarchical powers, which notably enhanced the might of the papacy. Thanks mainly to the theological influence of the mendicant orders (St. Thomas Aquinas, Thomas of York,

St. Bonaventure) an unduly papalist theory grew up which made the Bishop of Rome a universal bishop, concluding that the Church as one society must be subject to a single jurisdiction ("unus grex sub uno pastore"). Now the bishops figured as papal officials (Bernold of Constance, *Apol.*, 23, in *PL*, 148, 783). By way of reaction another school (Henry of Ghent, Godfrey de Fontaine, Jean de Pouilly) harked back to the ecclesiology of *communio* in the early Church and sought to make the bishops preponderant in ecclesiastical government. Owing to the weakness of the papacy during the 14th century this episcopalianism placed the bishops in a dominant position which was translated into terms of canon law in the 15th century by Conciliarism (Constance, Basle) and into terms of constitutional law by Gallicanism (Pragmatic Sanction of Bourges). But under both these headings fall a wide variety of views, ranging from repudiation of the Church's structure to justifiable defence of that same structure against papal encroachment. And apart from these controversies we find the beginnings of a collegiate interpretation of the episcopate quite consistent with the papal primacy (Ivo of Chartres, Gratian).

c) *The priesthood.* Following St. Jerome and Ambrosiaster, medieval theologians concentrated the powers of order on the *corpus Christi eucharisticum*. Since priests possess such powers no less than bishops do, practically all the Schoolmen (except William of Auxerre, Durandus, Duns Scotus, and Gabriel Biel) denied the episcopate a separate sacramental dignity, so that there seemed to be little difference between bishop and priest. The "parochialism" which some deduced from this view (parish priests are an institution of divine right) was countered by the theologians of the mendicant orders, who explained the bishop's juridical authority as a power to organize the Church (St. Thomas).

3. *Explanation of the nature of the episcopate (16th to 20th century).* The Reformation of the 16th century attempted to resolve these conflicts over the episcopate, whose representatives had become a source of scandal owing to their worldly manner of life, by casting aside the office itself or treating it as a purely human expedient in the Church. The episcopal structure, variously interpreted, is preserved in the Lutheran Churches of Scandinavia, the Reformed Church of Hungary, among the Moravian Brethren and American Methodists, since 1918 in many territorial Lutheran Churches of Germany, and in the Church of South India. The Churches of the Anglican Communion regard the historic episcopate as part of the Church's *plenum esse*.

Catholic theologians, drawing on patristic tradition, are now working out a new and largely pastoral conception of the episcopate. The Council of Trent clearly distinguished the episcopate from the priesthood (*D* 967) but without specifying how it is related to the primacy, so that much discussion ensued as to whether bishops receive their jurisdiction directly from God or through the Pope. Bishops were exhorted to care for their flocks in an apostolic spirit (duty of residence). 16th century writers inspired by the Council (Contarini, Giberti, Bartholomew of the Martyrs, L. Abelly) described the ideal bishop as a likeness of the Good Shepherd, a likeness that became flesh and blood in such men as St. Charles Borromeo, St. Francis de Sales, St. Robert Bellarmine, Fénelon and Bossuet. While the papal system grew towards its climax in the tight centralization of the 19th century (concordats, struggle over nunciatures, Joseph de Maistre), and a new episcopal particularism arose in the form of Febronianism, the collapse of the Catholic bishops' power through secularization led men to ponder the spiritual function and autonomy of the bishops under the primacy (J. A. Möhler). Defining the Pope's universal episcopate, Vatican I condemned extreme episcopalianism (*D* 1831), but at the same time rejected extreme papalism by stressing the inherent rights of the bishops (*D* 1828; cf. *DS* 3112–3117). Because the Council was prematurely broken off, there was no time to work out a more thorough theology of the episcopate, a task which remained for Vatican II.

The ground having been prepared by historical and systematic studies of the main issues involved (Bertrams, Botte, Colson, Congar, Dejaive, Küng, Lécuyer, Karl Rahner, Ratzinger), this Council dwelt particularly on the sacramental character of episcopal consecration, the derivation of all episcopal powers from *ordo*, the collegiality of the episcopate under the primacy, the importance of local Churches, and their communion with the Church universal. In the changed conditions of today, when the centrifugal tendencies of earlier episcopalianism are no longer to be feared, the Council wished to do justice to the plurality of cultures by strengthening the Church's peripheral structures in a spirit of true Catholicity. But the heritage of history demands that we further explore certain problems, particularly the practical relations between the primacy and the episcopate (the function of episcopal synods), the bishops' power of jurisdiction, the relations between bishops and priests, and the exercise of collegiality (episcopal conferences).

Wolfgang Beinert

III. Theology

1. *Successors of the apostles.* The institution of the episcopate is to be understood only in relation to the institution of the apostles by Christ. Examination of the texts in the NT permits one to make the following observations:

a) The apostles are called to the *service* of the whole Church, a *diakonia* which finds its most perfect exemplar in Christ, who came not to be served but to serve (Mk 10:42–45; Mt 20:25–28).

b) According to Mt 28:19–20, their mission is to teach all men, to sanctify them by the sacraments, and to bring the faithful to obey the commands of the Lord.

c) In order to accomplish this mission, the apostles receive a special gift of the Holy Spirit (Jn 20:21–23; Acts 1:8; 2:2–5).

d) Each of the apostles receives this mission and this grace in union with the other apostles. Together they form a whole, a well-defined body to which the NT often applies the expression: *The Twelve* (Mk 3:14–16, etc.). It is to this group, reduced to eleven by the defection of Judas, that Matthias is admitted, to become *with them* a witness of the Resurrection (Acts 1:26).

e) To this group, the unity of which is so manifest, one can apply the title "college", provided that one does not take it to mean that all the members of it are equal. Peter occupies a special place and is endowed with a higher authority which no one contests, founded as it is on the words of Christ himself (Mt 16:16ff.; Lk 22:31ff.).

But the office of the apostles was not to cease with them. We know from Acts and the epistles that they chose helpers in their tasks of preaching and governing the communities (Phil 2:25; Col 4:11). These helpers shared the apostles' authority: "The Holy Spirit has made you guardians, to feed the church of the Lord." (Acts 20:28.) The faithful are to recognize them as their rulers (cf. Heb. 13:7, 13, 24). It is not always possible to distinguish between "elders" (Acts 11:30; 14:23 and *passim*) and "bishops" (Phil 1:1; Acts 20:28, etc.). The fellow-workers of the apostles are warned not to try to lord it over the faithful (1 Pet 5:3). Their office, like that of the apostles, is a ministry, a service for the good of the community.

According to Clement of Rome, the apostles "having received a perfect foreknowledge, appointed the above-mentioned bishops and deacons, and afterwards they made a law according to which other tried men were to succeed to their ministry after their own death" (*1 Clem*, 44). The expression "successors of the apostles" was a common way of designating bishops from the time of St. Irenaeus; cf. First Vatican Council, *D* 3061.

The third chapter of Vatican II's Dogmatic Constitution on the Church bases the connection between the apostles and the bishops on Scripture. The existence of the episcopate is explained by the character of the gospel message: ". . . since the gospel which was to be handed down by them (the apostles) is for all time the source of all life in the Church. For this reason the apostles took care to appoint successors in this hierarchically structured society." (Art. 20.) More precisely, the Council affirms that the college of the apostles with and under Peter corresponds to the college of bishops with and under the Roman Pontiff, the holder of the Petrine office. "Just as by the Lord's will, St. Peter and the other apostles constituted one apostolic college, so in a similar way (*pari ratione*) the Roman Pontiff as the successor of Peter, and the bishops as the successors of the apostles are joined together." (Art. 22.)

2. *Sacramentality of the episcopate*. To aid them in their task, the apostles received a special gift of the Holy Spirit. Hence from the beginning, in appointing collaborators, they used a liturgical rite consisting of prayer and the imposition of hands, signifying the gift of a special grace in view of the task to be fulfilled. A similar rite was used for the appointment of the first deacons (Acts 6:6), and of the presbyters in the course of the journeys of St. Paul (Acts 14:28). In the case of Timothy (1 Tim 4:4; 2 Tim 1:6), the imposition of hands conferred a special spiritual gift, that of "power, love and self-control", like that which St. Paul himself was conscious of having received (2 Tim 1:7, 11).

Christian tradition has understood episcopal consecration to be the continuation of this rite. It is a sacramental rite, composed of external signs and liturgical words, which confers a grace. An attentive study of liturgical documents, beginning with those of the greatest antiquity, reveals that the Church has always considered this rite to be a sacrament which confers the fullness of the priesthood and bestows a grace enabling the bishop to carry out his own special duties. Doubt could arise on this point only when theology, instead of beginning with the bishop, began with the priest in order to ask what the episcopate could add to his dignity. But episcopal consecration is not something added to one who has previously been ordained a priest. When conferred on one simply baptized, it at once bestows the fullness of priestly power, enrolling him in the ranks of the supreme pastors of the Church. Before receiving this sacramental rite, a layman can already have authority over other Christians, even over the faithful as a whole. Such would be the case of a layman who is elected Pope. From the time of entering upon office he would enjoy jurisdiction (i.e., every Christian would owe him obedience) as well as personal infallibility (i.e., God would not allow him to affirm an error if he decided to make a definition *ex cathedra*). But even in this case such a possibility is linked to consecration. A layman called to the episcopate must not only have himself consecrated, but any authority he may have depends on his intention of receiving the sacrament. In the Apostolic Constitution *Sacramentum ordinis* of 1947 (*D* 2301) it is assumed that episcopal consecration is a sacrament and not just a sacramental, though this is not formally decided.

Episcopal consecration, therefore, confers a grace which is ordained to the service of the faithful. Liturgical and patristic documents refer to it as the office of pastor, witness, and high priest. By virtue of it the bishops, in carrying out their duties, become the official representatives, the vicars, of the one high priest Jesus Christ. And as, according to the Council of Trent (*D* 964), the sacrament of orders confers a character, the episcopate marks him who receives it with an indelible spiritual sign for the exercise of the *magisterium*, of the priesthood, and of authority in the Church in such a manner that, by means of the bishops, the glorified Christ continues visibly to teach, to sanctify, and to govern his flock. Vatican II developed further the theology of Trent. Christ himself is present and active in the bishops. "In the bishops . . . our Lord Jesus Christ the supreme High Priest is present in the midst of those who believe." (Dogmatic Constitution on the Church, art. 21.) The authority and dignity of the office is conferred by the sacrament of episcopal consecration. "This sacred Synod teaches that by episcopal consecration is conferred the fullness of the sacrament of orders." (*Ibid.*) Thus the bishops are entrusted with "the apex of the sacred ministry" (*ibid.*), that of the ministerial or hierarchical priesthood, which presupposes the common priesthood of all the faithful (art. 10).

3. *Ordo Episcoporum*. Just as Peter and the other apostles constitute a community, an established group or body, so the successor of Peter forms with the other bishops an episcopal body (*ordo episcoporum*) which offers many signs of the unity and solidarity which reign among its members. The terms employed, *ordo* (Tertullian), *corpus* (Cyprian), *collegium* (Cyprian, Optatus of Milevis), ought not, however, to lead one to imagine – what the word *collegium* can mean in certain cases – an established group in which all are equal and in which the only authority is that which results from the agreement of all its members (or at least the majority). In the body or college formed by the bishops there is one supreme authority – that of the Bishop of Rome, the Pope, whose prerogatives have been defined by Vatican I. Without him the body of bishops would lose its unity and its stability.

Episcopal consecration manifests and brings about the adoption of a new member into the episcopal college. The most ancient prayers (Apostolic Tradition, *Canones Hippolyti*, Apostolic Constitutions) ask for the new bishop the power of the Spirit, which Christ had given to his apostles. These prayers ask for him the grace necessary to guide the Church of God. Here it is not merely authority over a particular region of the Church (for some bishops have no diocese) but "ad regendam ecclesiam tuam et plebem universam" (*Sacramentarium Leonianum*). In other words, he is to take a certain part in the government of the universal Church: the sacred rite incorporates him into the episcopal order (Roman Pontifical). An extremely ancient tradition requires all the bishops present, or at least three of them, to impose their hands on the newly elected bishop. It is not merely that a bishop consecrates a successor: the consecration of a new member is the concern of the entire episcopal body, represented by several members.

The doctrine of the *ordo episcoporum* has been re-formulated to some extent by Vatican II, inasmuch as it lays stress on the collegiality which we have mentioned above. The college is not just the sum of its members. It is something prior to the individuals, and as such, goes back to the will of the Lord in instituting it. The individual must be incorporated into the college if he is to become a bishop. "Hence, one is constituted a member of the episcopal body by virtue of sacramental consecration and by hierarchical communion with the head and members of the body." (Dogmatic Constitution on the Church, art. 22.) In this college, the members are united to their head, the Roman Pontiff, and to the other members of the hierarchy. The structure of the Church has therefore two aspects. One is that the bishops of the whole world remain "linked with one another and with the Bishop of Rome by the bonds of unity, charity, and peace" (*ibid.*). The other is that the monarchical principle is combined with the synodal. "The Roman Pontiff, as the successor of Peter, is the perpetual and visible source and foundation of the unity of the bishops and of the multitude of the faithful. The individual bishop, however, is the visible principle and foundation of unity in his particular church, fashioned after the model of the universal Church. In and from such individual churches there comes into being the one and only Catholic Church." (Art. 23.)

4. *Duties and powers.* As with the apostles, one may readily distinguish three forms of episcopal service or ministry: doctrinal, priestly (administration of sacraments), and pastoral.

a) *The teaching office.* The first duty of the apostles was to teach all nations (Mt 28:19). That mission of teaching all men has passed to the successors of the apostles, and they have received that inheritance in common according to the expression used by Pope Celestine to the Council of Ephesus in 431. Therefore, from the very fact of his incorporation into the episcopal body, each bishop is responsible for the preaching of the gospel, not only to the faithful of his diocese, but to all mankind. Each of the faithful is obliged to participate in the diffusion of the word of God, but the mission of the bishops remains a very special one. Consecration confers a "special charism of truth" (Irenaeus, *Adv. Haer.*, IV, 26, 2), an illumination and force often compared with that which the apostles received at Pentecost. Hence in the bishops as a body, the assistance of the Spirit makes this *magisterium* infallible. The individual bishop is not infallible, but the episcopal body is. Here the collective or collegial character of the episcopate appears. Infallibility belongs to the body of bishops with and under the Bishop of Rome. It is guaranteed to the teaching body united with its head, and in a special way to the latter as leader of this body and centre of the unity of the Church. This infallibility is one of the concrete forms taken by that of the Church itself (First Vatican Council, *D* 1839). When the Pope defines alone a question of faith, the whole fellowship of the bishops which speaks through him, is included.

But it would be wrong to reduce the episcopal magisterium to infallibility, which is a negative notion. The power of the Spirit helps positively to preach the truths of faith so that they correspond to each new situation of the faithful. The bishops are responsible for the study of the word of God, and must be vigilant to exclude all error. "Keep watch, you have received a Pneuma which does not sleep." (Ignatius, *Ad Polycarp.*, I, 3.)

b) *The priestly office.* By his consecration, the bishop receives the fullness of the priesthood. The whole people of God is priestly and royal through baptism, but the one high priest, Jesus Christ, consecrates in a special manner to his service those whom he has chosen for the episcopate, in order that they may be the visible representatives of his sovereign priesthood (cf. Cyprian, *Epistolae*, 63, 14). Because it is especially by the sacraments that the priestly action of Jesus extends to us, the bishops are the principal ministers of the sacraments. If, in this ministry, they provide themselves with helpers who participate in their priesthood, the entire sacramental order still remains under their authority and dependent upon them. There is no legitimate Eucharist, says Ignatius of Antioch, save that "which is celebrated under the presidency of the bishop or of him whom the bishop shall have charged with it" (*Smyrn.*, 8, 1). Likewise St. Thomas teaches, "It pertains to the bishop to give simple priests what is necessary for the fulfilment of their proper function. That is why the blessing of the holy chrism, of the oil of catechumens, of altars, of churches, of vestments, and of sacred vessels . . . is reserved to the bishop as head of the whole *ordo ecclesiae*." (*Summa Theologica*, III, q.82, a. 1, ad 4.) Besides, the bishop is the ordinary minister of certain sacraments: such is the case with confirmation and holy orders.

If we prescind from the restrictions in canon law (*CIC*, can. 337), which do not affect the validity but the lawfulness, the power conferred by consecration on the bishop is not restricted to one diocese. It is universal. This means that through consecration each bishop receives a clearly-defined power over the whole Church, for the unity and growth of the mystical body, through the sacraments.

c) *The pastoral office*. Episcopal consecration confers a charism which enables the bishop to govern the people of God. Like the power to consecrate, the pastoral office is for the whole Church. However, for reasons of order and convenience (of which the head of the body of bishops is the judge) the exercise of the individual bishop's power can be (and is) limited. It can only be exercised (with corresponding jurisdiction) over a limited portion of the Church. Yet the bishops remain jointly responsible for the general good of the Church, whose unity and progress in charity they ought to promote, not only by obeying their head, but also by active co-operation with the Pope and with each other. The more fully the local Church is the Church of God, the more fully does it embody the whole Church. This solidarity of pastoral rule is particularly evident when all the bishops are united in Council under the presidency of the successor of Peter. They form with their head, the successor of Peter, the supreme and sovereign authority. Hence as representatives and interpreters of the law of Christ, the law of love, the bishops merit the title which Augustine gave the bishop: "Servant of the servants of God" (*Ep.*, 217; *PL*, XXXIII, col. 978).

On the authority conferred by consecration, Vatican II teaches that the one sacramental power is divided into three offices. The first to be named is the office of preaching the gospel. "Among the principal duties of bishops, the preaching of the gospel occupies an eminent place." (Dogmatic Constitution on the Church, art. 25.) Then comes the office of mediating salvation through the sacraments. The bishop is the "steward of the grace of the supreme, priesthood", especially in the Eucharist, which he himself offers or causes to be offered (art. 26). "Through the sacraments, the regular and fruitful distribution of which they direct by their authority, they sanctify the faithful." (*Ibid.*) Thirdly, the bishop is pastor of his Church, governing the local Church entrusted to him as "vicar" and "ambassador" of Christ (art. 27). The word "entrusted" points to the fact that the sacramental-ontological office, which is to be distinguished from the canonical-juridical aspect, cannot be exercised without an act of the Roman Pontiff, however this takes place (N.B. to the *Nota praevia* on ch. 3 of the Constitution on the Church).

Joseph Lécuyer

IV. Canon Law

1. *Meaning of episcopate*. The episcopate is that ministry established in the Church of Jesus Christ which bestows a share in the Church's office of teaching, sanctifying, and governing. Those called to

it are successors of the apostles and consequently exercise their ministry as vicars and envoys of Christ, individually as the head, bishop, of a particular Church, as a collegiate body of several bishops serving a group of particular Churches, and as the collegiate body of all the bishops, united in serving the Church universal. The ministry carries with it a sacred authority which arises from episcopal consecration and becomes an exercisable power through canonical mission from the competent ecclesiastical superior. Catholic tradition regards the bishop as the shepherd of his flock, sometimes expressed in the image of the spiritual marriage. The essential relationship is noted as early as Ignatius of Antioch: "Wherever the bishop appears let the congregation be present; just as wherever Jesus Christ is, there is the Catholic Church." (*Letter to the Smyrnaeans*, 8, 2.) The bishop presides over a component Church which in its own field represents the whole Church – is part of a whole in the sense that the whole works through the part. This presiding ministry is the episcopal office in the juridical sense.

In the *CIC* the term episcopate is always used in this restricted sense (can. 108, § 3; 332, § 1; 333, 334, § 2; 629, § 1; 2398). The Pope's office of supreme jurisdiction and this episcopal office which is subordinated to it, are the two offices of divine institution. They have been supplemented by other ranks by virtue of ecclesiastical institution (can. 108, § 3). Here we have the framework of the Church's constitution so far as the *CIC* is concerned (lib. II, tit. VII and VIII). In canonical parlance the episcopate also means all the bishops or a body of bishops, for example the bishops of a country, but the collegiate aspect of the episcopate is not brought out. Attributive adjectives are generally used to indicate the whole episcopate: thus *universus episcopatus* in the motu proprio *Arduum sane munus* of 19 March 1904, calling on all bishops to collaborate in codifying the canon law, and *totus catholicus episcopatus*, which the episcopal synod created by Pope Paul VI (motu proprio *Apostolica Sollicitudo*, 15 Sept. 1965, no. 1, b) is now to represent. Though this document avoids making any reference to the principle of collegiality, in the light of the doctrine on the episcopal college set forth by Vatican II the word episcopate doubtless includes the collegiate element of the bishops' ministry.

2. *Nature and purpose of the episcopate.* All members of the new people of God share in the mission of the Church. When treating of laymen the Council repeatedly declares that all members share, each in his own way, in the threefold office of Christ and the Church – the office of teaching, sanctification, and governing – and carry out the mission of the whole Christian people in the Church and the world (Vatican II, *De Ecclesia*, art. 31; see *De Ap. Laic.*, art. 2). Without prejudice to this share that all have in the Church's mission, there is a diversity of ministry, for Christ instituted an authority in his Church which does not fall to every member of the Church, but only to those who are called in tangible, juridical form to govern God's people in the name of the Lord. Ecclesiastical authority exists only in order to serve; it is part of the Church's nature, the foundation of its hierarchical structure, of which the Church as a sacramental sign is the theological setting. As a visible society rooted in Christ and ordained to him, the Church is the sign of salvation, raised up for all men by the Lord, "a kind of sacrament or sign of intimate union with God, and of the unity of all mankind" (Vatican II, *De Ecclesia*, art. 1). Because the divine element proper to the Church shows through its human element and becomes tangible in it, and because the Lord, the invisible Head of the Church, is visibly represented in it by men, the Church is a sign of salvation, something analogous to the mys-

tery of God's Son made flesh, as Vatican II teaches (*De Ecclesia*, art. 8). Without a visible head the Church cannot visibly represent the body of the Lord. And therefore the Lord appointed the twelve apostles, making them, as the word indicates, his representatives in the juridical sense, and set Peter at their head. Peter's successor is the Pope, and the successors of the apostles are the bishops, who are called to represent the Lord in collegiate union with the Pope – he too is a bishop – and in subordination to him. "He who hears them hears Christ, while he who rejects them, rejects Christ and Him who sent Christ." (Lk 10:16 and Vatican II, *De Ecclesia*, art. 20.) The image of the mystical body shows us that the Church is structurally one as head and members are: the invisible Lord is represented for the universal Church by the Pope, and for each particular Church by a bishop.

In this connection the Council observes: "The Roman Pontiff, as the successor of Peter, is the perpetual and visible source and foundation of the unity of the bishops and of the multitude of the faithful. The individual bishop, however, is the visible principle and foundation of unity in his particular church, fashioned after the model of the universal Church. In and from such individual churches there comes into being the one and only Catholic Church. For this reason each individual bishop represents his own church, but all of them together in union with the Pope represent the entire Church joined in the bond of peace, love, and unity." (Vatican II, *De Ecclesia*, art. 23.) This text occurs at the point of transition in the Council's thought from the doctrine of the episcopal college to the doctrine of the bishop as ruler of a local Church and enables us to grasp the inward coherence of the bishop's two roles, the personal and the collegiate. At the head of the whole Church and of each particular Church respectively, we have a personal ruler, and all the heads of the particular Churches, in union with the Pope, represent the universal Church. It is not simply a matter of parts joining to form a whole; at the same time, though we are not expressly told so here, the whole Church is present in the particular Church, and through his hierarchical communion with head and members of the episcopal college each bishop represents the universal Church, present in his particular Church, for the flock that is entrusted to him. Accordingly the bishops have a twofold representative function. They represent the universal Church consisting of many particular Churches, and the particular Churches in which the universal Church is present. In the one case the parts must be integrated into the unity of the whole, while in the other the particular Church must be capable of that integration. There is a reciprocal connection between the personal and collegiate elements, each as it were becoming operative in the other; it would be wrong to play off one element against the other.

3. *Gradations in the episcopal ministry.* Besides the ministry of sanctification, episcopal consecration bestows the ministries of teaching and governing, which by their nature can only be exercised in hierarchical communion with the head and members of the episcopal college (Vatican II, *De Ecclesia*, art. 21). Though all bishops have this same sacramental power, there are nevertheless many gradations within the episcopal ministry which cannot be accounted for in terms of order but only in terms of office. Pope, patriarch, metropolitan, and diocesan bishop are all in the same episcopal orders, but in respect of office they form a hierarchical pyramid for the sake of the unity of God's people. Apart from the office of the Pope and that of the episcopal college, which concretely exist in the Church by divine institution, so that the Church can neither bring them into being nor do away with them, all other

episcopal offices, relating as they do to particular societies in the Church, need to be fixed by the appropriate ecclesiastical authority. Law or custom must establish particular forms of episcopal office and then concretely set up a given office. In these two respects the gradations of the episcopal ministry flow from the Church's power to organize itself, but the content of the concrete ministries that are to be exercised remains of divine right because the episcopate is of divine institution.

The major gradations are the following:

a) The office of diocesan bishop, of prime importance among the episcopal ministries because the organization into episcopal Churches is an essential part of the Church's constitution. The diocesan bishop presides over part of the people of God (diocese) in such a way that he possesses, as a successor of the apostles, all ordinary, proper, and immediate authority necessary for discharging his pastoral duties (Vatican II, Decree on the Bishops' Pastoral Office in the Church, art. 8a). To the flock allotted him he represents the invisible Lord; and working with his priests he so binds the individual faithful into union with Christ and for Christ that "the one, holy, catholic, and apostolic Church of Christ is truly present and operative" in this particular Church (*ibid.*, art. 11). His proper power of jurisdiction extends to legislation, judgment, and administration. So widely may the duties of a diocesan bishop vary, according to the size of his diocese, that without any change in his juridical position one bishop may find himself doing some of the work of a parish priest and another bishop some of the work of a metropolitan.

b) The office of metropolitan, who as an archbishop presides over an ecclesiastical province and has a certain superiority over the diocesan bishops of that province (called his suffragans) – much less in the Latin Church than used to be the case. The metropolitan cannot legislate, but has the right to convoke and preside over provincial synods (*CIC*, can. 284). As to administration he has certain supervisory and supplementary rights (*CIC*, can. 274, nn. 1–5). He is the ordinary court of appeal at common law from judgments pronounced by his suffragans (*CIC*, can. 274, n. 8, 1594, § 1), but for his own part must allow appeals to the court of one of his suffragan bishops (*CIC*, can. 1594, § 2). A metropolitan wears the pallium in token of his metropolitan power and his communion with the Pope. The Eastern Churches in communion with Rome distinguish between a metropolitan within a patriarchate and one outside. The former is immediately subject to the patriarch, the latter immediately to the Pope. Both were given the right by the First Council of Nicaea (can. 4) to consecrate and enthrone the bishops of their province (*CIO*, can. 319, n. 1, 320 § 1, n. 4). Where metropolitan organization has not yet been restored, the duties of the metropolitan fall to the patriarch (*CIO*, can. 242). Vatican II directed that the boundaries of the ecclesiastical provinces be duly reconsidered and the rights and privileges of metropolitans set down in appropriate new rules (Decree on the Bishops' Pastoral Office, art. 40). In future all dioceses and similar local Churches will be assigned to an ecclesiastical province; and so dioceses now directly subject to the Apostolic See are to form a new ecclesiastical province or to be joined with a neighbouring province and placed under the metropolitan jurisdiction of the archbishop (*ibid.*). Obviously there is an effort to enhance the dignity of the metropolitan office.

c) The office of patriarch, which has remained intact in the Eastern Churches united with Rome, is absorbed by the papal primacy in the Latin Church, whose patriarch is the Bishop of Rome. The new Oriental Canon Law of persons, codified by Pius XII's motu proprio *Clerici Sanctitati*, 2 June 1957, devotes nearly 100 canons to the patriarch (can. 216–314). In the East the patriarch is the hierarchical head of his patriarchate, that is, a group of episcopal Churches of the same rite. "Father and head" of his patriarchate, the patriarch has ordinary jurisdiction over all the bishops (including metropolitans), clergy, and people of his territory or rite; but besides the link with the supreme pastor of the Church, the patriarch's jurisdiction must often be exercised conjointly with synodal bodies (patriarchal synods and standing synods). The patriarchal territories of various rites overlap, so that several patriarchs have (a basically territorial) jurisdiction over the same area, but each only in respect of members of his own rite. Outside the patriarchate Eastern patriarchs still have jurisdiction over the faithful of their rite insofar as this is expressly affirmed by the common law or local canons (*CIO*, can. 216). Patriarchs are elected by the bishops of the patriarchate assembled in the electoral synod. Papal confirmation is required only if the patriarch-elect is not yet a bishop. A bishop who is elected patriarch takes office by accepting his election; he is then proclaimed patriarch by the electoral synod and enthroned, but must inform the Pope that the election has taken place and ask for the pallium in token of communion with the Pope, before either calling a patriarchal synod or holding episcopal elections or ordinations (*CIO*, can. 221ff.).

Vatican II speaks with high esteem of certain ancient patriarchal Churches, which have engendered "daughter" Churches in the faith (*De Ecclesia*, art. 23), and rules that the rights and privileges of patriarchs shall be restored in accordance with the ancient traditions of each Church and the decrees of the ecumenical councils, as they stood when East and West were still united, though a certain adjustment to present-day conditions is in order (*De Eccles. Orient.*, art. 9). Since the patriarchate is the traditional form of ecclesiastical polity in the Eastern Churches, the Council wishes that new patriarchates be set up where necessary. This is the business of the ecumenical synod or of the Pope (*De Eccles. Orient.*, art. 11). The constitution of the Church provides that the supreme jurisdiction of the Pope and all higher episcopal office, like that of patriarchs or metropolitans, shall be connected with a particular see: that is, Pope, patriarch, and metropolitan also rule a particular diocese, just as any other diocesan bishop does. This feature of the Church's constitution, which has hardly any parallel in secular society, draws attention to the collegiate aspect of the episcopate and at the same time to the inner bond between episcopal orders and episcopal office. Only in the case of the titular (arch-)bishop, who is consecrated for an abandoned see but receives no power of jurisdiction over his fictitious Church, do order and office not go together. He bears the personal character of a bishop but has no episcopal office. The forerunner of the titular bishop was the bishop who had been driven from his homeland, whose right to his lost see it was important to uphold. Titular bishops are employed in many ways: as auxiliaries to a diocesan bishop, as coadjutors with the right of succession, as interim rulers of a diocese (apostolic administrators), as heads of a local Church which is not yet ready to become a diocese (usually as episcopal vicars-general and, in mission territories, vicars or prefects apostolic), and above all in the upper ranks of the Roman Curia.

4. *Collegiate aspect of the episcopate.* The collegiate aspect of the episcopate is no novelty in the ecclesiastical constitution. It is found at lower levels no less than at the level of the Church universal, and to the eye of a historian comes into play mainly in non-ecu-

menical synods. Many of these, it must be observed, have exerted an influence far beyond their own sphere, affecting the general juridical evolution of the Church quite as much as the decrees of ecumenical councils have done. We must also note that the principle of collegiality is better seen in its purity below ecumenical level, because the fact that these collegiate organs do not have the Pope at their head decisively affects the formation of policy.

At the ecumenical level. With its doctrine of the episcopal college Vatican II settled the question, left open by Vatican I, of the relationship between Pope and bishops. According to this doctrine the bishops form a college which succeeds the apostolic college in the office of teaching and governing, and has the Pope, the successor of Peter, for its head (*De Ecclesia*, arts. 19–22). Just as the apostolic college represented the unity of the twelve tribes of Israel (Mt 19:28), so the bishops united with the Pope represent the unity of the new people of God. Here the word college must not be taken to mean a body of men equal in rank, with a head who is but *primus inter pares* and who derives his authority from the college; rather it means a permanent body whose structure and authority derive from revelation. It is a unique sort of college, whose composition and work are largely determined by its head. "One is constituted a member of the episcopal body by virtue of sacramental consecration and by hierarchical communion with the head and members of the body." (*De Ecclesia*, art. 22.) Consecration as a bishop imprints an indelible character. Hierarchical communion is a thing that is given and may be withdrawn from one who proves unworthy of it. The two elements, that which cannot be forfeited and that which can, are equally necessary for reception into the college; the latter elements shows us at once that membership of the college ceases when hierarchical communion is lost. In order to become and remain a member of the bishops' college it is absolutely necessary to be received into communion by the Pope, whereas communion with the members of the college depends on communion with its head and plays no separate part in making one a member.

This fact would seem to be contradicted by the statement that bishops receive the newly elect into membership by episcopal consecration (*ibid.*, art. 21); but the statement simply means that only a bishop can consecrate a bishop and leaves open the disputed question of whether a priest can validly ordain a priest in certain circumstances. In its character as a juridical person the episcopal college always exists and is always active as the body responsible for the whole Church, even though there are certain limits to its juridical activities. It possesses "supreme authority" over the whole Church (*ibid.*, art. 22), but must scrupulously respect its own hierarchical structure in wielding that power. It solemnly exercises its supreme power at an ecumenical council, and possibly outside a council as well if the Pope calls on the bishops throughout the world to act in concert, or at least sanctions or freely accepts a concerted act by the bishops dispersed throughout the world. Whether the supreme power of the college be used in the one way or the other, the Pope's consent is not added to the collegiate act as from outside but forms a constituent element of that act. In practice the exercise of the supreme power of the college is restricted to an ecumenical council, and therefore it would have been well to give such councils a more flexible form, so that ecumenical councils could be held at frequent intervals, attended by a representative body. Vatican II could not bring itself to do this. Meantime, by creating the Synod of Bishops, although its technical functions are purely advisory, Paul VI has provided an organ through which the representatives of the episcopate – some *ex officio* and some elected – and also the representatives of the religious communities, can have a voice in weighty matters of Church government. The Synod of Bishops is a flexible affair. Basically, as a general assembly, it is something like what an ecumenical council of representative composition would be. As an extraordinary assembly it can be called on at practically any time, and as a special assembly it has a very wide field of operation.

By putting forward the doctrine of the episcopal college Vatican II has in no way retreated from what Vatican I defined as to the Pope's primacy of jurisdiction. In practice it only says about the episcopal college what has long been held about an ecumenical council (*CIC*, can. 229, § 1). There is a difference from the law we have known in that an ecumenical council only comes into being when the bishops assemble, whereas the episcopal college is always there. Thus we have two organs of supreme power, the Pope and the college of bishops, but the distinction between them is not an adequate one, since the Pope is the head of the college. A recent doctrine affirms that there is only one organ, the episcopal college, which wields power in two different ways: through the head alone and through a collegiate act. But one can object that the episcopal college is confined to "teaching authority and pastoral rule" (*De Ecclesia*, art. 22) and that only a physical person is able to represent the Church's invisible Lord in every respect.

At the sub-ecumenical level. As a rule, particular Churches are not integrated directly into the unity of the Church universal but through certain larger ecclesiastical entities, among which the Eastern patriarchates with their special autonomy, and lately in the West the episcopal conferences, play the leading part. Vatican II points out that episcopal conferences can help in the most various and fruitful ways to make the collegiate outlook a concrete reality of our time (*De Ecclesia*, art. 23). Besides fostering the collegiate outlook, of course, they must also bring into effective play that collegiality which, below ecumenical level, is normally active in synodal affairs. Synods of their nature involve the assembling of their members in a given place. The members of a synod, once they are assembled and while they remain so, form a college which takes common counsel and reaches common decisions. The acts of a synod, in the sphere of its own competence, are collegiate acts in the strict sense of the word; and the same is true of an episcopal conference when as a hierarchical authority it takes decisions within its own appointed sphere that juridically bind the dioceses within the territory of the conference. One advantage the bishops' conference has over sub-ecumenical synods is that it is not tied to particular forms: thus it can more readily and more effectively foster and co-ordinate Church work over a largish area (*regio ecclesiastica*). In the Latin Church it assumes the function of the Eastern patriarchal synod, differing from it chiefly in that it is conducted by an elected president instead of by a patriarch.

Klaus Mörsdorf

BODY

1. *The phenomenon.* The body is the most immediate and proximate object of our experience. It is always with us, inseparable from us, the means whereby alone, along the "ways" of its senses, we attain the world in its manifold aspects and dimensions. But before this, and concurrently, the body is not merely an object with which man is confronted, it is something which he himself *is*: the pleasure and the pain of the body are his own pain and pleasure. The world too is not just opposed to the body as

the space outside it: it is rather its and hence our "extension", and is only there insofar as it is seen, heard, and so on – down to the atmosphere which is our breath. Therefore, just as there is a distinction between the self and the body, as between the body and the world (man is not simply body [alone]) so too there is such a unity that we must affirm: man is really and truly *corporeal* in all his dimensions.

It is only through this actual bodily quality that the spiritual nature really comes to be: in the work and the action (instead of the mere potentiality of thought and will) where alone it has actuality and efficacity and concrete expression. But it is likewise this bodily nature which sets limits to the self-realization of man: outwardly, it limits him in space and time; inwardly, it prevents him expressing himself fully, as every thinker, lover and artist has experienced. It cannot but offer resistance to the will, it must absorb energies in the effort to speak which should really be devoted to the actual statement, and thus it clouds the purity of all assertion.

This dialectical situation affects every happening of everyday life, but is most apparent in the supreme events of eros and death. At these pre-eminent moments too the temptation to which man is exposed by this tension is displayed most clearly. It is the temptation, first of all, to give up the effort of unification and to live on two different planes, which would therefore cease to be human and so to be themselves. It is, secondly, the temptation to restrict oneself to any one of the two regions, either a corporeal existence hostile to the spirit, or a spiritual existence filled with hatred of the body – an effort which always destroys the object of its choice and is soon followed by a revulsion which leads to the other extreme. Finally, it is the temptation to try to set up an undialectical unity, either that of a bodily entity simply accepted by the soul ("the soul is just an element of the body"), or that of a spiritual entity accepting the body without discernment ("mens sana in corpore sano"). The truth is that the fluid dialectical relationship of unity and opposition between body and soul can neither be transcended nor dissolved. And no completely satisfactory solution has been found for it in the whole history of thought.

2. *The history of the problem*. The dualism of body and soul is a tenet of Orphism and the Pythagoreans in Greek philosophy (in contrast to the delight in the body displayed by Homer, who uses σῶμα only for a corpse and considers the after-life as a shadowy existence, which Achilles would gladly exchange for the hardships of a drayman). The body is the garment, ship, prison and tomb of the soul ("σῶμα—σῆμα"), which is hindered and thwarted by the body, where it is in exile, banished "from above", and from which it frees itself by detachment and philosophical effort and finally by death (through a series of re-births, metempsychosis). So above all – as in Indian thought – Plato. Aristotle opposes to this purely accidental body-soul relationship the substantial concept of hylemorphism, in which the soul is essentially the form of the body and constitutes with it the one concrete subsistent. But no explanation is offered for the relationship between (immortal) spirit-soul and (mortal) body-soul and hence the primordial unity of man remains obscure.

The Semitic thinking of the Bible contributes a completely different perspective to this tradition. The OT has no special word for the body. The whole man is "flesh" (*bāšār*), but also soul (*nefeš*, i.e., life). And in death the whole man loses his life (in Sheol, there is no thought of God, nor does God think of it, Ps 88). A stronger distinction between body and soul appears only in late Judaism, under the influence of Hellenism. The real survival of the soul is taught, and the doctrine of the resurrection of the flesh is developed from some hints in the later books of the OT.

The doctrine of body and soul in the NT is especially noteworthy in St. Paul. It would be wrong to interpret him dualistically (in a Hellenistic or Gnostic way), even though his assertions are not completely clear and cannot be fully harmonized. The σάρξ (flesh) constitutes the nature of sinful, doomed man after Adam (e.g., Rom 8:12f.). But it is not simply identical with σῶμα, even though the fleshly condition is most clearly embodied and active in the body (Rom 6:6; 7:23; Col 3:5), which is the visibility of man himself (1 Cor 5:3; 7:15f., see 1). Hence the redemption which St. Paul preaches and hopes for is not liberation from the σῶμα but its transformation into a "pneumatic" body (1 Cor 15:36ff.), into the likeness of the resplendent body of Christ (Phil 3:21).

When the two streams of tradition meet in the Fathers and in Christian philosophy, however, the more highly developed Greek line of thought, in its Platonic form, is preponderant at first, especially in the conflict with Gnosticism. The Aristotelian concept only penetrates the scholastic discussion gradually from Arab tradition and is finally given its Christian form in the teaching of St. Thomas Aquinas. His explanation is that the soul is the "unica forma corporis", which is not therefore contrasted with an already existing ("informed") body which would be a partial component of the whole along with it; the soul manifests and effectuates itself in the purely potential medium of "materia prima". The (permanent) duality of body and soul is not to be understood as a merely ontic fact, but as an ontological actualization; the body is wholly the body of the soul, while the soul is essentially embodied (and yet immortal – with a permanent relationship to the body and matter).

Later, this ontological view of the way soul and body "participate" in each other recedes into the background, and the relationship is considered more ontically, so that it is seen from either a monist or a dualist point of view. The dualism of modern times was founded by Descartes, who separated soul and body as *res extensa* and *res cogitans*, which were supposed to preside over the central organ of the pineal gland in a sort of mutual causality. But even in Descartes it is really God, and fully and expressly so in the occasionalism of N. Malebranche and in Leibniz, who closes the unbridgeable gulf between the two fields, either by a constant intervention or by the basic institution of the *harmonia praestabilita*. Later, as in modern vitalism, the doctrine of mutual causality found supporters again (H. Lotze, E. Becher), though the difficulties of this theory could not be satisfactorily answered.

Monism is represented by Spinoza, who regards body and soul as merely two modes of existence of the same thing; so too the psycho-physical parallelism of G. T. Fechner, who understands the body-soul relationship as the convex and concave sides of a single spherical surface. And while spiritualism takes the body to be merely the appearance of the soul, which alone is real and true (G. Berkeley, W. Wundt), materialistic monism maintains on the contrary that everything mental and spiritual is a bodily (and glandular) function (C. Vogt, J. Moleschott, L. Büchner).

In the light of psychology as well as of biology, man is now seen again more explicitly as a unity of soul and body, which does not allow of a clear division between the two components, though the presence of both is recognized; psychotherapy and psychosomatic medicine above all try to meet the demands of this more primordial view.

3. *Philosophical and theological explanation.* The magisterium of the Church has defined the unity of man (primarily in view of Christological controversy),

having recourse when doing so to the philosophical position of hylemorphism, though without giving a decision on the system or any precise form of its exposition (*D* 481, 1914). As phenomenological considerations show, man is as a whole and essentially a bodily entity. He *has* a body and at the same time he *is* his body in a true sense. He can never distinguish himself adequately from his body; on the contrary, he is the particular man he is precisely on account of his body (individuation). So too the upsurge of his enthusiasm in work and love does not lift him above and out of his body, nor is death simply the separation of body and soul. In each case the one, whole man is wholly involved and challenged, and summoned precisely to accept and take over his spirit-body, which, in keeping with what has been said, calls for a submissive as well as an active Yes, and a submissive as well as an active No to the body. In his body, man is opened out to his environment and the exterior world, becomes accessible, attackable (Sartre, *La Nausée*) and vulnerable; his body disturbs and hinders his development. But it is in the body and its activity that man shows himself and sees himself: there the "invisible soul" becomes visible (art of self-expression). In the body, man "knows" man (Gen 4:1 – sexuality), and man comes to be by means of this fully human event (generation). In the body he is bound up with and allied to the sub-human – he is "dust" (needs, instinct); but in the body (as in itself something spiritual, and not merely because his spirit is in it) he is also higher than the sub-human ("visage", "look", "posture", speech). The body is man's "primordial activity" (G. Siewerth), the "symbolic reality" of man (K. Rahner), his "medium of being" (B. Welte), in which he lives and "is there" and is present – precisely insofar as it is not the body itself which is intended (e.g., pleasure, the voice) but the essence and its reality (love, the song). The traditional clear-cut pattern is replaced by a multi-dimensional one, in which the person "expounds" itself. And the isolated individualistic view of the body is merged into the dimensions of society, history and historicity, to which it essentially belongs, and in which alone the tension of openness and hiddenness can make the person a "countenance" and a reality.

This unity in duality which can never be fully perspicuous and amenable to philosophical thought is seen at the height of its tension when theology considers the bodily nature of man. The guiding principle of a theology of the body is given in the expression of Tertullian: "caro salutis est cardo" (*De carnis resurrectione*, 8). God, the Logos, becomes "flesh" and true man and redeems the human race by his obedience unto death, in the body. And hence the order of grace which he set up has also an "incarnational" structure. If it seems at first only to affect the soul, this is precisely a symptom of the untoward condition resulting from the loss of the grace of bodily and spiritual integrity in the state of original justice. Thus though sin is manifested precisely in the body (see St. Paul, above), the body is still already sanctified here and now, and is the temple of the Holy Spirit; it is called to the work of co-redemption (1 Cor 6:15; Col 1:24; 1 Cor 6:19) and above all to the glory of the resurrection, in which the very spatio-corporal reality here achieved – and not just a reward for it – will be transformed and be man's definitive state and his eternity. Since this eternity is characterized as conformity to the body of Christ (1 Cor 15:49) and fellowship with it (2 Cor 5:8), it implies that the humanity and the bodily nature of Christ (and hence of man in general) play a role of permanent and indispensable importance. And since finally man's body implies his openness to personal confrontation with others, makes him present to them and constitutes him in an essential relation to his environment, the same will be true in a perfect way, with all obscurity and ambiguity abolished, of the heavenly body: fellowship is of its essence. Hence the ascension of Christ, "the first-fruit of those that slept" (1 Cor 15:20), demands the corporal fulfilment of his brothers, indeed, it calls for and implies "even now" at least a partial realization of this extension of his own definitive state, "in due order" (1 Cor 15:23) (Mt 27:52f.; Eph 4:8–10; the Assumption of the Blessed Virgin). This final, definitive stage is already proclaimed visibly on earth in the sacramental reality and practice of the Church, the "body of Christ" (1 Cor 12:27; Eph 1:23), and in its worship. And we can also begin to understand on the same principle that the fulfilment of the body is not confined to the body. Just as its glorification is not merely an addition appended to the redemption of the soul, but the fulfilment and completion of the soul, so too its fulfilment extends into the world and transforms the whole cosmos along with it (Rom 8:19–23; Rev 21), as the completion of the incarnation in the pneumatic unity where all differences are preserved but where God is "all in all" (1 Cor 15:28).

Jörg Splett

C

CALVINISM

A. Calvinism and Calvin

Calvinism is the name given to that form of Protestantism which had its origin, either directly or indirectly, in the reforming activity of John Calvin (1509–1564). The name itself was introduced by the Lutherans against Calvin's wish. Calvinism took root in the French and Swiss humanism of the early 16th century and, accordingly, it cannot be considered merely as a variant of Lutheranism, though it is true that "the basic teaching of Luther is also that of Calvin" (E. Troeltsch). The influence of Bucer, Melanchthon and Bullinger upon Calvin effected further modifications of Calvinism. Calvin's "conversion" (between 1530 and 1533) was occasioned by his readings of Scripture, chiefly the OT. He read it as the word of God spoken to him personally, and he considered it to be the one source and norm of the Christian faith. This principle that Scripture is not only the one source but also the one norm whereby the faithful can attain to certitude with regard to the content of revelation without the need of an infallible ecclesiastical interpretation, is a basic tenet of the whole Reformation. In this sense, Calvinism always understands itself to be a Church reformed by the word of God and to be corrected by each of the faithful according to the Scriptures. The intention of founding a new Church was as far from Calvin's mind as it was from Luther's. The purpose of Calvin was to affirm the transcendence of revelation in which man could share through grace alone. This basic intention does not contradict Catholic teaching. The criticism that he directed against the Roman Catholic Church, however, was not limited to the elimination of abuses, but aimed at a radical recasting of the whole structure and function of the Church. The reason for this drastic criticism lay in Calvin's repudiation of a mediation of salvation where the Church, by virtue of the Holy Spirit animating it, is a supernatural instrument.

To avoid the danger of presenting as Calvinist teaching something that would not be applicable to every form and stage of its development, we limit outselves in B) to Calvin's teaching, and then in C) to a brief description of the development in the later and variant forms of Calvinism.

B. Calvin's Teaching and Reforms

Calvin's main work, the *Institutio Religionis Christianae*, underwent a series of editions from 1536 to 1560 in which the author further elaborated this handbook of biblical theology and completed his synthesis of Christian teaching. Its final form was the Latin edition of 1559, divided into four books (the French translation followed in 1560). The following references will be to the edition of 1559, indicated by *Inst.* followed by book and chapter number. Calvin presents an orthodox interpretation of the teaching on the Trinity (*Inst.*, I, 13) and makes it clear that there is no basis for the charge that his teaching is Arian in tendency. His Christology (*ibid.*, II, 12–17) is likewise orthodox, though an occasional tendency toward Nestorianism is unmistakable. The role of the Holy Spirit is stressed: his activity in the creation and the conservation of the cosmos, his general providence with regard to man, and his special activity in the individual believer and in the Church (*Corpus Reformatorum*, 36, 349). The significance of the humanity of Christ suffers a corresponding diminution. Calvin's doctrine and later Calvinism are strongly theocentric. Calvin is always preoccupied by the sovereignty of God, his absolute freedom, his omnipotence with a tendency to making him the sole agent, his providence and (only as a consequence of that) the double predestination of man, his election and damnation. That man can remain human and that he can accomplish anything in the realms of art and science, is only to be attributed to the intervention of God through the Holy Spirit, through whom he sustains will and understanding as human functions and even produces relatively good and noble deeds. Yet this remains, as it were, between brackets, the brackets of sin (*Inst.*, II, 1, 7–12). It is the same with what is relatively good in the social order: human laws, the capacity for rule, and indeed for accomplishment in any sort of vocation. All is the gift of the general activity of the Holy Spirit through which the profound corruption of man is confined within certain bounds (*ibid.*, IV, 202). This pessimism is the consequence of Calvin's doctrine of the total corruption of human nature.

Like Luther, Calvin is convinced that man, since the fall of Adam, is born with a nature vitiated at its root. Man is not a sinner because he commits sins, but he commits sins because he is essentially a sinner. Luther and Calvin rightly consider that in the actual order of salvation all man's acts must be at least implicitly performed out of love of God, the supernatural end, and that man is impotent to do this by reason of original sin (Luther: cf. *Confessio Augustana*, art. 2; Calvin: *Inst.*, II, 1, 8–9), but in this they limit unwarrantably the action of the grace of Christ. They do not see that Christ's universally active grace makes an initial ordination towards God, as the supernatural end, possible even in unregenerated man (contrast *Summa Theologica*, II, II, q. 83, art. 16; I, II, 112, art. 2).

1. *The activity of the Holy Spirit in the individual believer*. The "special activity" of the Holy Spirit, for Calvin, is accomplished primarily in the individual believer (in the form of a strictly individual *testimonium Spiritus Sancti*) and only secondarily in comparison in the Church as a whole.

This testimony of the Holy Spirit is an assurance both of the divine truth of sacred Scripture and of the promise of God for the individual in question. The outward testimony of the Spirit in the Scriptures concerning the unshakable fidelity of God to his promises is confirmed by the inner testimony in the heart and from this proceeds the certitude of eternal salvation (*Inst.*, I, 9, 3). Calvin gradually came to consider, more properly, that this *testimonium Spiritus Sancti* is only one aspect of the special activity of the Holy Spirit in applying to the individual the salvation won by Christ (*ibid.*, III, 1, 3–4).

This application takes place in justification and sanctification. Calvin, like Luther, teaches that justification comes through faith alone. Not only can man in no way prepare himself by his own strength for justification (which is also

Catholic teaching), but in justification itself his grace-inspired Yes to the revelation of faith does not make him co-active with God's saving act. It is the same in all further sanctification, which Calvin stresses more than Luther. The Holy Spirit remains the sole supernatural agent. He accomplishes everything alone (though he also makes use of certain instruments) and asks for obedience freely proffered. This means also the "absolute sovereignty" of the Holy Spirit. He not only needs no mediation in applying the salvation achieved by Christ, but he can also withhold his activity when men use correctly the means given and prescribed by Christ, so that some of those who rely on the sacraments do not escape their (well-merited) damnation (*ibid.*, III, 2, 11; III, 24, 8). The spiritual life of Calvinists is largely determined by the notion of the activity of the Holy Spirit which has been briefly sketched. Together with the consciousness of the radical depravity of man, one finds a steadfast trust in the promises of God, and from this there issues not infrequently a vigorous life of virtue, inspired by thankfulness for salvation received and obedience to the Lord of the covenant. It is this which gives Calvinist piety its sturdy character. The word of God is not only the good news of salvation, but also *law*. "God is the Lord; I am the servant." This rigour in theology and piety is, nevertheless, tempered by what may be called an almost mystical trait (though mysticism is abhorred by Calvinism as a confusion of the divine with the human). It has found beautiful expression in the *Heidelberg Catechism* (question 1): "That I belong, body and soul, both in life and in death, not to myself but to my true saviour Jesus Christ", this is "my one consolation." Fellowship with Christ is, therefore, a feature of Calvinist piety (*Inst.*, III, 1, 1; III, 11, 10).

2. *The Christology and ecclesiology of Calvin.* Almost from the beginning, Calvin had to fight on two fronts: against the Roman Catholic Church, and against the "Libertinists" who rejected fundamental articles of faith, sometimes even the doctrine of the Trinity, and claimed to be led individually by the Spirit, while maintaining very tenuous links with Scripture.

In opposition to the Roman Catholic Church, Calvin based on his Christology his repudiation of the papacy and the Church as a supernaturally effective medium of salvation. For him Christ is the Son of God who had become a man to reconcile the predestined to God. As mediator, he then sent the Holy Spirit after his ascension, to apply fully to the predestined alone the fruits of his work. Calvin thought that the glorified body of Christ remained subject to the spatial limits of this old aeon (*ibid.*, IV, 17, 12). That is why he stressed that the glorified body of Christ remains locally in heaven, and the Church, visible and invisible, of sinful men, is confined to earth. It is only the "power of the Holy Spirit" that bridges this gap, which will endure till the last day. This "power of the Holy Spirit" does not effect an ontological relation to the glorified Lord, who would thereby be present and active in his Church, as Catholic teaching asserts. For Calvin, the power of the Spirit brings about a link with the power of the glorified body of Christ, whereby Christ exercises his lordship over the Church (*ibid.*, II, 15, 3; 75). It is then understandable that Calvin, in his teaching on the Eucharist, explains the presence of Christ in terms of his power and not of his glorified body as such (*ibid.*, IV, 17, 26). Calvin's vigorous affirmations on fellowship with Christ must always be understood within these bounds. Thus the activity of the Holy Spirit extends to the realization of salvation, to the detriment of the Incarnation and consequently of the place of the Church. But if Christ is not present with his glorified body in the Eucharist, and, analogously, in the

Church, the Church would not be inwardly sanctified through the sacred humanity and hence cannot effectively co-operate in salvation by its own God-given activity. But this does not prevent Calvin from calling the Church "the mother of the faithful" (*ibid.*, IV, 1, 4), and by this he refers not merely to the invisible (the *universus electorum numerus*) but also to the visible Church. However, the Church is only "mother" insofar as the Holy Spirit exercises in her that activity which is exclusively his own.

But Calvin is equally opposed to the "Libertinists" who tried to separate radically the work of the Spirit from the function of the Church. This cannot be, he says, for divine providence has established an extrinsic link between them. In this way, the activity of the Holy Spirit is bound first to the word of Scripture, then to the word preached by the Church (*ibid.*, IV, 1, 4), and finally also to the sacraments. Hence, Calvin can also say: where the Gospel is preached in its purity and the sacraments rightly administered, the Holy Spirit is active and there the true Church of Christ is to be found (there is, as has been indicated, a discrepancy between this and the absolute "sovereignty" of the Holy Spirit). To these two characteristics, already cited by the *Confession of Augsburg*, Calvin frequently added "proper Church discipline". He was convinced that Church discipline should be dictated not only by historical circumstances and freely adopted measures, but primarily by biblical directives. He maintained the same with regard to liturgical forms. Consequently, he attempted, from the few basic characteristics given in Scripture, to develop a Church order (his *ordinances ecclésiastiques*), and a liturgy reformed according to the word of God ("la forme de prières et chants ecclésiastiques"). Thus Calvin gave to his Church not only its own creed, but also a very characteristic Church order. He based this order on the general priesthood of all the faithful. Then he found in Scripture that for the proper structure of the community four functions were indicated: that of ministers, doctors, elders, and deacons. All the faithful are priests through the "spirit of sonship" in which they are all reborn. The offices are based only upon the "charismata" of the Holy Spirit which are necessary for the right ordering of the Church, but which do not establish a special priesthood.

And so the aristocratic Calvin was able to build up a "democratically" structured, visible Church by the practical application of the doctrine of the general priesthood. There are a number of levels. Each community is a Church in the full sense, led by a "consistory" formed from the ministers and elders (these "elders" were to guard especially the purity of teaching and Church discipline within the community – whence later the name "Presbyterian Church"). It is the task of doctors to explain the Scriptures and so to preserve the authentic teaching among the faithful. The deacons should fulfil the function of service in the Church and manifest it to those without. The communities together form the national or regional Church (usually there is also an intermediary level in the "presbytery", *classis*). The national Church is governed by a synod or general assembly composed of pastors (ministers) and elders. Calvin recognizes, however, not only the national Church, but also the universality of the visible Church; and hence he constantly strove for the union of all Christians (in practice, only of Protestants). He still strove to discover this unity in the divisions of Christianity.

Calvin's emphasis upon outward structure does not indicate a lack of consideration for the inner bonds of the living organism. He repeatedly stresses that all the gifts of those in official positions as well as of the ordinary faithful are given for the building up of the "body of Christ" (*Inst.*, IV, 3, 2). But in this regard it must be added that this building up of the body of Christ, and growth in fellowship with Christ, takes place "in the power of his Spirit and not in the substance of his body" (*Corpus Reformatorum*, 79, 768). The Church, as the *corpus Christi mysticum*, has no ontological bond with the personal, glorified body of Christ and consequently has no "pneumatic" reality of its own. And so also the leaders of the Church cannot interpret Scripture infallibly, though the charisms of the officials give a certain authority to the Church's preaching. The "presumption" is in favour of the interpretation of the Church, until the contrary becomes clear to the individual from the Scriptures themselves. Councils, such as were held in earlier times, still have a special authority for Calvin, though not an infallible one. He can find nothing good to say of the Pope, who is only an "unsightly hump on the back" which disfigures the symmetry of the body of the Church (*ibid.*, 202), or, in a word, the Antichrist (*ibid.*, 29, 624). One valuable and practical application of the general priesthood is the stress on professional activity as service and praise of God.

C. The Development of Calvinism

This vigorous ecclesiastical structure with its emphasis on the lay element has given proof of its quality in the course of history, though history has also shown its defects. Along with the confession of faith worked out by Calvin (*Confessio Gallicana*), it was ratified in 1559 at the First National Synod of France and introduced, with some variations, in all Presbyterian Churches. Since *c.* 1550 Calvinism spread swiftly, particularly in many European countries. The international academy founded in 1559 by Calvin in Geneva had no little part to play in that development. After Calvin's agreement with Bullinger, the successor to Zwingli (in the *Consensus Tigurinus* of 1549, the "Zurich Agreement"), Calvinism swiftly spread in Switzerland. At the same time it took root in France, where it has maintained itself to the present day in spite of many persecutions and religious wars. It then established itself in the Netherlands, which in the 17th century was the intellectual centre of Calvinism (cf. the Dordrecht Synod 1618/19). It came to England under Edward VI, 1547–53, where under Cromwell (1649–59) the Calvinist Puritans came to power, though later they migrated in great part, under pressure, to Holland and North America. In Scotland John Knox introduced Calvinism in the second half of the 16th century with lasting success. In Germany Calvinism only took permanent root in a few provinces (the Palatinate, 1563: the Heidelberg Catechism). In Hungary it developed into a strong "Reformed Hungarian Church" and in Poland it took hold swiftly but was then almost fully repelled by the Counter-Reformation. In the United States and in Canada, Calvinism developed strongly and combined into the large "Presbyterian Churches" and also the smaller Free Churches of the same type (usually "fundamentalist" in their creeds). Besides this, the Presbyterians (called the Reformed in Continental Europe, and numbering altogether *c.* 45 million) have been very active in various mission areas where they founded Presbyterian Churches (which have now become independent). Since 1875 most Presbyterians have united in the "Presbyterian World Alliance".

In order to understand the worldwide impact of Calvinism, it is necessary to take account of the large groups which branched out and separated from the body of the Anglican Church in the course of history and adopted Calvinist teaching and Church organization in various forms. In chronological order, after the "Puritans", the first to be mentioned are the Congregationalists, who broke with the Anglican Church in the 17th century and then applied Calvin's notion of the community in its most extreme form: every local Church is a Church in the full sense and hence they are an association of fully independent local Churches (today Congregationalists number *c.* 5 million). In the 18th century the Methodists, under the leadership of John Wesley, broke away from the Anglican Church under pietistic and Calvinistic influence, and took up a more or less pure form (varying according to countries) of Calvinist teaching and Church organization (they number today *c.* 40 million). Also in the 17th century, the Baptists who had left the Anglican Church came more and more under the influence of Calvinism; their Church organization is that of Congregationalism (today they are *c.* 55 million). All these groups are especially well represented in the United States and in the former mission countries.

It is understandable that in the present strong ecumenical movement among Calvinists, most efforts at union concern Presbyterians and the groups just mentioned. But Anglicans are also envisaged.

In Calvinistic doctrine developments have taken place parallel to general currents of thought in Europe and America, and these trends still continue in the various Churches. In the 17th century, the successors of the Reformers developed an orthodox theology which was often scholastic in type. It often lost itself in over-subtle disputes with Lutherans about the Real Presence in the Eucharist and led in general to a narrowing of theology and a desiccation of the spiritual life.

The pietist reaction followed in the 18th century, though spirituality remained orientated to action and averse to mysticism, true to the character given it by Calvin. Calvinistic trends in Anglican pietism found expression in the ethical activities of Methodism. As elsewhere, pietism brought with it into Calvinism an anti-intellectual and anti-orthodox trend which led on occasion to schisms. The rationalism of the 18th and 19th centuries often wrought havoc in theology and spirituality. Christ was reduced to a moral exemplar. The Holy Spirit was understood not as a person but as "divine force" and replaced more and more by human reason. The Lutheran Schleiermacher likewise had a marked influence on Calvinist theology in the 19th century, with his immanentist and anthropocentric theology, which was clearly opposed to Calvin's. Similarly, his relativizing of the concept of Church ("each Church is a unique creation of the Christian spirit") was taken over by the Calvinist theology of his time. Already in the 19th century there set in, more as a reaction to extreme rationalism, a pietistic yet orthodox *réveil* (starting from Geneva). Rationalism was finally overcome only after the end of the First World War, with the rise of "dialectical theology", especially that of Karl Barth. It defended in an extreme way, especially at the beginning, the transcendence of revelation ("God, the wholly Other"), and succeeded in reintroducing the orthodox teaching on the Trinity and Christology in practically all Calvinist Churches. At the same time, Calvinists in general became more conscious of the Church, and this, along with the re-vitalized orthodoxy created in large part the possibility of dialogue with the Catholic Church. On the Catholic side, it is becoming clear that the picture of Calvin was often distorted in polemics. Similarly, among many Calvinists, there is a new awareness of the nature of the papacy and of the Church as a whole, especially since Vatican II has shown that many of Calvin's objections were groundless. But the fundamental opposition unfortunately remains.

Johannes Witte

CANON OF SCRIPTURE

1. *Significance and problem.* Vatican II has called attention in various documents to the greater esteem for Scripture which has characterized theology for some years, and which should also mark Christian life. Not only are the Council texts themselves highly biblical in their language, but in ch. 2 of the Constitution on Revelation, where sacred tradition is discussed (art. 8), the apostolic preaching, "which is expressed in a special way in the inspired books (of sacred Scripture)", is explicitly accorded priority. This should not be lost sight of, even though the statement of the preliminary draft on the sufficiency of Scripture in contrast to oral tradition was not adopted into the constitution. All those whose office it is to serve the word must deepen their knowledge of sacred Scripture by diligent reading and thorough study (art. 25), since "theology rests on the written word of God . . . the sacred Scriptures contain the word of God . . . and so the study of the sacred page is, as it were, the soul of sacred theology" (art. 24). Further, the Decree on Ecumenism pays special attention to the sacred books of Scripture as "precious instruments in the hands of God", especially in the dialogue, "for obtaining that unity which the Saviour holds out to all men" (art. 21). "Like the Christian religion itself, all the preaching of the Church must be nourished and ruled by sacred Scripture." (Constitution on Revelation, art. 21.)

Hence in spite of the formal equality between Scripture and tradition which appears in the decisions of the Council, the material priority which is in fact accorded to Scripture should not be overlooked. Yet in view of the Council's alertness to change, manifested, for instance, in the fact that the historical character of the gospels is understood in terms of the development of tradition, the manner in which inspiration (Constitution on Revelation, art. 11) and the canon are treated of is surprisingly traditional, the actual criterion of the canonicity of Scripture being left undefined. It is indeed stated (art. 8) that through the Church's tradition the full canon of sacred books is known. The "Church's tradition" here implies, however, that the recognition of the canonical status of the books of Scripture was arrived at progressively and presupposed a series of preliminary stages in the history of dogma, above all during the first four centuries of the Christian era. This is a factor of the highest importance in the process by which the Church determined its own definitive form. Historically inexplicable, it must be ascribed to the mysterious guidance of the divine Spirit in the Church. Its importance has, however, been emphasized more by the non-Catholic than the Catholic theologians of our time. These latter, at least since the Council of Trent (*D* 783ff.), have regarded the discussion of the canon as closed. However, one decisive exception to this has recently appeared: Whereas Trent (*D* 783) and Vatican I (*D* 1787) require *all* the books of the Old and New Testaments to be recognized and honoured with equal devotion and reverence, Vatican II refers *expressis verbis* to differences between them, notably to a priority of the gospels (Constitution on Revelation, art. 18). This means that the discussion of whether some books take precedence over others in the canon is reopened. The same question regarded from the aspect of fundamental theology or hermeneutics might be expressed as "is there a canon within the canon?" From the outset it is hardly possible to doubt where the answer to such a question would lie: in the priority of the gospels. This in turn throws new light upon the question of what kind of authority is implied when we call the Scriptures canonical.

The difficulty of the question of canonicity lies in the historical disparity between the fundamentally inspired nature of the OT and NT writings on the one hand, a factor which is presupposed by their canonical status, and the progressive circumscribing of the (NT) canon on the other, a process which continued until the 4th century. The explicitation of an authoritative revelation, which must have been already implicitly present in the apostolic age, is therefore completed at a far later stage. Indeed the hagiographers themselves were generally unaware of the fact that their writings were inspired and that their significance extended far beyond the particular occasions for which they were composed. The earliest stages in the history of the Christian Church make this clear.

From the outset a different meaning was ascribed to the word κανών from that which it bore in non-biblical Greek, namely "series", "list" or "chronological table". As used in Christian circles it acquired the fundamental meaning of "rule of right conduct", "reliable standard", "norm" of behaviour or of teaching. Thus Gal 6:16 speaks of the rule of true Christianity as opposed to the standards of the old world. And *1 Clem*, 7, 2 refers clearly to the norms contained in tradition as the guiding rule for Christian preaching and ethics. In the first three centuries of the Christian era the canon designates the *regula fidei*, all therefore that was already in existence as the guiding rule of truth and as the norm of faith prior to the biblical writings. In the second place (since Nicaea, 325) the canon meant the decisions of synods, and finally, from the 4th century onwards, it meant the list of biblical books which are to be used in the Church. This double meaning of the canon as guiding rule and as list or series in which the books of the Bible are enumerated has set the terms for the discussion of the canon by historians of theology to the present day. Hence, ever since the scholastic definition of the doctrine of inspiration, the canon of Scripture – as distinct from ecclesiastical law – has come to be understood more and more simply as "list" or "inventory" of the books of the Bible.

2. *History of the canon*. In spite of the legal prescription directing that the books of the OT canon were to be preserved unaltered in the temple (Deut 31:26), at the time when these books were adopted by the Christian Church the limits of that canon were still far from being finally determined. The first group of OT writings, the Pentateuch, had undergone substantial additions in the shape of Deuteronomy in the 7th century and the priestly source at the beginning of the 4th century. With the writing of the Books of Chronicles, and the translation of the Septuagint (*c.* 350), the five books of the Pentateuch had acquired the force of law. At a later date the Sadducees and Samaritans actually held that these books alone constituted sacred Scripture.

The second group of OT writings, namely the books of the prophets, is already recognized as a distinct collection *c.* 190 B.C. (Ecclus 48:22–49:12). The threefold division of the OT canon as attested in Lk 24:44 presupposes the existence of the third group, the *Writings* or *hagiographa*. It should be noticed that with the exception of the psalms these were not intended to be read publicly in the course of liturgical ceremonies. To a large extent these *Writings* owe their inclusion in the canon to the supposition that they derive from Solomon or Jeremiah, or that they originally belonged to one or other of the key festivals of the temple. The theory of canonicity upheld by the Pharisees is explained for the first time by Flavius Josephus *c.* A.D. 95. According to him (cf. *Contr. Apion*, I, 8) the distinctive characteristics of this theory were as follows: divine inspiration, the holiness of their content, the idea that the books were twenty-two in number, the unalterable nature of the text, and the supposition that the books were composed between the time of Moses and that of Artaxerxes I (d. 424), whose death, according to Josephus, marked the close of the period of the prophets. The theory of the canon put forward in *4 Esdras*, 14, 8–48, is based on the supposition that in 557 Ezra, guided by the Holy Spirit, dictated within the space of forty days the writings of the OT which had been destroyed. Thereby, with the help of a direct intervention of God (verbal inspiration) the canon of 24 books was completed in the shortest possible time. This theory of the canon, later adopted by the Jewish Synod of Jamnia (Jabneh) *c.* A.D. 100, also provides the basis for the Christian notion. In spite of this it was precisely in the early Christian period that the writings of later Judaism, which had been rejected as apocryphal, had considerable influence. The Alexandrine canon was wider, and included certain additional books or parts of books which were known as deuterocanonical. Through the Septuagint it became the basis of the Vulgate. Hence this Alexandrine canon was declared binding for the OT both at the Council of Florence (*D* 706) and again at Trent. It comprises twenty-one historical books, seventeen prophetic books and seven wisdom books. Of these forty-five documents Catholic theologians designate eight as deuterocanonical (= apocrypha for Protestants), while the apocalyptic writings of later Judaism are designated as apocryphal (= Protestant pseudepigrapha).

For the community of the faithful of NT times these same books of the OT were at first considered to be the only books of sacred Scripture. Jesus had come to fulfil the promises contained in them (Lk 4:15ff.; 24:44ff.), and the community had no intention of challenging their canonical authority (Mt 5:17f.) or of replacing them with canonical writings of its own (cf. 2 Pet 1:20f.). The expectation of a return of Christ in the near future at first ruled out any notion of a new canon of Scripture corresponding to the new covenant. The occasional writings of the apostles and their disciples rather sought to show that the salvific event of Christ was "according to the Scriptures" of the OT. And in the light of the same event, they sought to interpret the OT books in such a way as to show that fulfilment of the law had come (2 Cor 3:6, 15ff.). But with the delay of the parousia, it was only a matter of time till such "comments" took on an independent value. "The idea of setting new canonical books alongside those handed down by ancient tradition is wholly out of place in the apostolic age. The abundance of living canonical authorities, a multitude of prophets, charismatics and teachers, made any further additions to sacred Scripture . . . completely superfluous. The need to create a canon belongs to less privileged times." (A. Jülicher and F. Fascher.)

While continuing to accept the authority of the OT canon, the early Christians regard Jesus Christ the Saviour as the ultimate and supreme authority. In virtue of the fact that he is the divine son of the God of the OT and that his saving work has its origin in the eternal decree of Yahweh's own will to bestow salvation on mankind, his own person becomes the canon and the norm of interpretation for the OT writings (Jn 14:10, 24; 10:30). Christ's deed of salvation, as expressed in the kerygma of the death and resurrection of Jesus Christ, is itself this norm; but the early Christian community also hands down individual sayings from the preaching of Jesus while still on earth, for he, as the exalted Kyrios, is at once the subject of the early apostolic tradition (Col 2:6), its origin (1 Cor 11:23), and in the abiding work of the Holy Spirit (2 Cor 3:17ff.) its author and guarantor (cf. Jn 14:26; 16:13). After his resurrection the Lord transmits to his apostles (Jn 17:18; 20:21; 2 Pet 3:2) the authoritative power of his own word and deed of salvation. Since the fate of the disciples is the same as that of their Lord, and since their word is accepted or rejected as that of their Lord (Lk 10:16; Jn 15:20), their claim to announce God's salvific will is also the same. Thus they constitute the third element in the unfolding of revelation as set forth in *2 Clem*, 14, 2: OT – Jesus Christ – apostolic preaching (cf. also *Ign. Magn.*, 7, 1; *Polyc.*, 6, 3). The idea of the NT canon as a list or collection of writings constituting an authoritative rule of faith develops independently of this principle of canonicity based on christological or apostolic origin. As the primary preachers of the Christian message and the eye-witnesses of Jesus' life and resurrection died out, their writings, which had often been composed for particular occasions, and sayings from their sermons which had been handed down by word of mouth acquired increasing authority for Christians of the second generation onwards. Thus 2 Pet 3:15f. already refers to a collection of the Pauline letters, and Polycarp seems already to know of nine of the canonical letters of Paul. The gospels, which were composed in the second half of the 1st century, were initially written for the inhabitants of particular regions, but as early as *c.* 130 in the reign of Hadrian they were assembled into a single collection (A. von Harnack), and Justin (*1 Apol.*, 6, 6f.) recommends them to be used in the liturgy alongside the OT prophets. The fact that they were four in number did, however, constitute a problem from the outset. Hence *c.* A.D. 170 Tatian composed a harmony of the gospels, the Diatessaron, corresponding to the one Pauline εὐαγγέλῐον, taking the four gospels as the basis. Finally, Irenaeus explained the four forms of the one gospel by the significance of the number four in the vision of Ezekiel (Ezek 1:10; Rev 4:7; *Adv. Haer.*, III, 18, 8; Tertullian, *Adv. Marc.*, IV, 2; Clement of Alexandria, *Strom.*, III, 13, 93; I, 21, 136). The third group of NT writings, the Catholic letters, the Acts of the Apostles, Revelation and Hebrews, first acquired canonical authority in the second half of the 2nd century. Even then the degree of authority attached to individual writings varied considerably.

The excommunication of Marcion for his Gnostic and anti-Jewish ideas, which took place at Rome about the middle of the 2nd century, provided a decisive stimulus for the formation of the Church's canon. Marcion rejected the entire OT on the ground that it portayed a vengeful God. He admitted only ten Pauline letters, as well as a version of Luke's gospel which had been purged of its OT citations and also of the infancy narrative. This Marcionite canon represents a first attempt to provide a substitute for the OT. To guard against the Marcionite heresy the Church provided a prologue to all four of the gospels to show that they were authentic and, in addition to the ten Pauline letters of the Marcionite canon, pronounced the pastoral letters, Acts of the Apostles and Revelation to be canonical. An official expression of this measure is found towards the end of the 2nd century in the Muratorian fragment, which enumerates twenty-two NT writings: the four gospels, Acts, thirteen Pauline letters, three Catholic letters, Revelation and the Apocalpyse of Peter, this last not being universally recognized. Thus about 200 the formation of the canon in the Western Church was completed with the exception of Hebrews, which was declared not to be of Pauline provenance, and with some uncertainty still remaining as to the number of the Catholic letters. In the Greek Church Hebrews was recognized, but not Revelation, which was only able to gain a place in the canon gradually from the 6th century onwards. Here too the number of the

Catholic letters remained in dispute. In 367, Athanasius (*Festal Letter* 39) designated the twenty-seven books of the NT in addition to the books of the OT, as together comprising a firmly established canon. ("Let no one add anything to these or take anything away from them"; cf. Rev 22:18.) At the anti-Arian synods in the middle of the 4th century the Eastern and Western canons were brought into closer agreement. In the second chapter of the *Decree of Gelasius*, going back to the Synod of Rome of 382, the canon of the twenty-seven writings of the NT was defined, and this was confirmed at the latest in 405 by a letter of Pope Innocent I as well as by the African synods of Hippo Regius (393) and Carthage (297, 419).

After the 5th century no new decrees on the canon are found. Nevertheless the canonical validity and rank of individual NT writings were constantly discussed in connection with the question of their authorship, except during the brief interval of Pietism in the 18th and 19th centuries. In 1546 Trent defined the canon of the Old and New Testaments once and for all, joining its decree to that of Florence and also maintaining the idea of canonicity upheld in the 4th century. Nevertheless it did not decide the question of the authenticity of individual NT writings. Theologians are unanimous in holding that the Council only defined that the books enumerated belonged to the canon. It had no intention of giving an authoritative decision on the historical problems concerning the authors of these books or the authenticity of disputed sections in them. Authenticity and canonicity are notions which must be kept clearly apart.

In so-called "liberal theology" and in the methods of historical criticism of the 20th century the question of the "necessity and limit of the NT canon" (W. G. Kümmel) becomes once more a crucial problem of Protestant theology, which turns upon the unity of the canon of the Bible and the Reformation principle of *sola scriptura*. Thereby a discussion has recently been revived on how Scripture can provide a basis for mutual understanding between the Churches on the principle of Christian theology.

3. *A theological solution of the problem.* We are here concerned with the question of how the biblical writings, especially those of the NT, came increasingly to be regarded as authoritative norms. The history of the canon makes it clear that the theory of inspiration, as developed in later Judaism, and then in the history of dogma, has little light to throw upon this unless inspiration is taken in the widest possible sense, as the sum of all those criteria which led the Church of the first four centuries to define and evaluate its written sources. This is not to say that canonicity is the result of purely historical circumstances. The writings of the NT were used for liturgical reading and hence undoubtedly became the basis of a living experience of faith. Moreover, being in the broader sense of apostolic origin, they were a radiation of that authoritative revelation which was in principle deemed to be closed with the death of the last apostle. Prior to the point at which the canon was closed these writings had entered into the history of the Church. In the course of that history they had proved to be a norm which stimulated, sustained and tested critically the faith of the Church.

In spite of this it would be inadequate to describe the formation of the canon purely as a process of human history or as an official measure or measures taken by the Church. We should rather accept the judgment of faith and acknowledge with it that the canon is a special gift of God to the Church, and that in its efficacy we can see the special working of the Holy Spirit which was promised to the Church (W. Joest, K. Aland). This might be described as inspiration in the broader sense, but perhaps it should more correctly be called canonicity.

Strathmann speaks of "the creeping sickness of Protestant theology, and so of the Protestant Church; the obscurity of its relationship to the letters patent of its origins, that is, to the canon of the Bible". Perhaps this creeping sickness could be arrested if Protestant exegesis could bring itself to accept this criterion, which goes beyond the methods of historical criticism, and if it could add it to the Lutheran "Urgemus Christum contra scripturam" (*Weimarer Ausgabe*, XXXIX, I, 47). Protestants would have to bring themselves to suppose a decision which partook of the nature of revelation, part of the history of salvation and hence not amenable to historical criticism – a decision which was to bind the whole Church of the future.

As expounded in Catholic theology the principle of canonicity is decisively affected not only by the doctrine of inspiration but by the idea of the Church. For although Augustine (*Contra Epistolam Manichaei*, 5, 6) held that sacred Scripture was to be believed because it belonged to the Church, today a distinction which does not belong merely to the history of dogma is drawn between the initial composition of the canonical writings (inspiration) and the subsequent recognition of them as canonical by the Church (the definition of the canon). For with regard to their original formation Scripture and the Church are on the same level and cannot, in the last analysis, provide a mutual basis for each other. To suggest this would be to fall into the circle of "Church – canon – Church". Hence what is treated in the history of the canon is the subsequent recognition of original revelation. It is all the more important to notice this since when the Church distinguished the canonical writings both from Gnostic and other heretical writings and also from the writings of the early Fathers, it can have been no part of its intention to set later tradition side by side with this canon as of equal value with it. Thus too today the Church must regard itself as in a pre-eminent manner tied to the canon. Qualitatively speaking, this canon is what it brought forth from within itself in the period of its origin. Quantitatively speaking, it consists of those books which it subsequently set apart as sacred from all other writings. The canon of Scripture is the real *norma non normata* of the Church for all time. Implicitly revealed in the apostolic age, it was explicitly defined and delimited in the decrees produced by the Church under the guidance of the Holy Spirit in the first four centuries of its existence.

Paul Neuenzeit

CATECHESIS

A. Historical Review

The noun "catechesis" (κατήχησις) does not occur in the NT; only the verbal form (κατηχεῖν) is to be found there, though not in the technical sense it was later to acquire, being taken rather by the NT authors in the current sense of "recount" or "give *viva voce* instruction". (This is a transferred sense, derived from the physical which was to "echo" or "resound".) It is so used in Acts 21:21, 24: "they [the Jews] have been told [concerning Paul]".

In other contexts the word κατηχεῖν takes on a religious colouring. The reason for this is that the object to which it applies is itself something religious. This is so, for example, when it is a question of the Jews being instructed in the Law (Rom 2:17–21), the Christian in the inspired word (Gal 6:6; 1 Cor 14:19), or in the way of the Lord (Acts 18:25), or yet again in the events of his life (Lk 1:4).

The NT has nothing to say about the *forms* of this teaching. The choice of the word merely emphasizes that it is oral and that it is the handing on of what has been received. The NT itself is a catechesis. The specifically Christian teaching which it contains is designated by a variety of words (ὁδός. διδαχή, παράδοσις, λόγος: way, doctrine, tradition, word). Certain passages suggest different kinds of teaching. Thus Heb 6:1 distinguishes elementary teaching from that reserved for the proficient, and gives the content of the first instruction about Christ: conversion, faith, resurrection from the dead, eternal sanctions, baptism. In the same way the NT accords special treatment to the "kerygma", the unfolding of the Good News to the heathen for the first time (Lk 24:47, Acts 10:42).

In the course of the 2nd and 3rd centuries the vocabulary of our subject became more exact and gradually took on a technical meaning. Derivatives appeared, such as κατηχίζειν, "Catechizare", "Catechisatio", neither standard Greek nor classical Latin.

Hippolytus makes use of the word "catechesis" in its precise sense of teaching given to someone preparing for baptism, in other words to a catechumen, as the candidate came to be termed. (*Traditio Apostolica*, 17; cf. *Constitutiones Apostolicae*, VIII.)

As the catechumenate developed, the word "catechesis" and its derivatives took on specific meanings. These were the instructions given in the framework of the catechumenate, this being either preparatory to baptism – baptismal catechesis – or subsequent to it – the mystagogical catechesis of the neophytes. The great catechetical works of the 3rd and 4th centuries illustrate this latter kind abundantly, those of Tertullian, St. Ambrose, St. Cyril of Jerusalem, St. John Chrysostom, Theodore of Mopsuestia, St. Augustine.

From the beginning the catechesis preserved its character of oral teaching. The catechumenate took on fixed forms: instruction for the *rudes*, *competentes*, or *illuminati* as the case may be. The content was at once doctrinal – centred on the Creed – and moral – a study of the Two Ways, i.e., of Life and Death and the Decalogue. The context in which this whole teaching was situated was the liturgy.

Catechesis and catechumenate are so intimately linked that the disappearance of one means the disappearance of the other. The term "catechesis" vanished with the catechumenate in the 8th and 9th centuries. With it there passed away a primordial form of Christian teaching.

Other forms succeeded it, with a new terminology. The Middle Ages spoke of "catechismus", "catechizare", "catechizatus" (cf. St. Thomas, *Summa Theologica*, III, 71, 1), meaning the elementary teaching given by parents or sponsors to the baptized child. The message of the faith is thus passed on inside the Christian community, the liturgy and the accompanying preaching playing a decisive role.

Later ages re-discovered the need for some institution specifically designed for basic instruction in the faith. The pupils, however, were no longer adult converts but baptized children and adults only exceptionally. Consequently, the term "catechesis" was not revived, and the institution which emerged instead was called "Catechism", the name being then applied to the book, which was the prime source of that form of teaching.

In 1529 Luther published his own "Catechism". Among the Reformers, as in the Catholic Church, catechisms multiplied. Prominent examples were those of Canisius (1556), Bellarmine (1598), and the *Catechismus Romanus* of the Council of Trent (1566).

These pioneers were intent on the living word of God and a Christocentric approach. "The important thing is that pastors should never forget that the whole science of Christian living – or rather as our Lord says, eternal life itself – consists in this, that they know him, the one true God, and Jesus Christ whom he has sent." So runs the preface to the Catechism of the Council of Trent.

In the course of the three centuries which followed, however, the trend of the catechisms was away from the living word of God. Catechism as an institution, no less than the study of the catechism-book, proved inadequate to maintain the living word in the Christian community.

That is why the word "catechesis" has been rehabilitated these latter years. The change of vocabulary indicates that the teaching of the faith cannot be reduced to the provision of a "catechism class" for children. There is also the catechesis of adolescents, youths and adults. Neither is the passing on of the faith a simple memorizing of the catechism. Both in its content and in its form, the catechesis should present the word of God as a living thing. The whole contemporary effort in catechetics is an attempt to restore its due place to the *catechesis* in the life of the Church.

B. Present-Day Problems

1. *Uses of the word "catechesis"*. The word "catechesis" is now used habitually in two senses.

In the restricted sense catechesis means "the passing on of the deposit of faith to the new members acquired by the Church" (J. Daniélou). This is the technical, historical sense of the word. As in the early centuries of Christianity, it denotes the elementary teaching given to the convert with a view to baptism. Catechesis in this sense differs from the antecedent evangelization and the proclamation of the "kerygma"; it differs also from subsequent higher forms of teaching designed for the baptized – preaching, Church discipline, etc. In this sense we speak of catechesis with reference to an adult catechumen. Similarly, the term is used of the first rudimentary teaching given to baptized children.

In a wider sense, the word "catechesis" is co-extensive with the teaching of the faith, from the first announcement of the kerygma to the higher forms of "scientific" theology. This definition underlines the unity between the various stages: the initial hearing of the Good News, or the preparation for baptism, and the more advanced teaching designed to nourish the Christian life. Hence some writers designate the instruction before conversion as "pre-catechesis". This word, in the context of an adult catechumenate, brings out the point of this time of preparation, namely to provide for a fitting reception of the gospel message. It is not unlike "evangelization", which, however, rather indicates the nature of the preaching.

Both usages serve to clarify each other. The narrower sense emphasizes the formal aspect of the catechesis. It is by analysing the elements of this primary teaching of the faith that we are enabled to determine the content and modes of the catechesis as such, i.e., those things that are necessary for every baptized person. The wider sense, on the other hand, ensures that attention is paid, under pain of imprecision and error, to the time-sequence involved, especially in the case of evangelization and religious instruction. In this larger sense the word "catechesis" may apply legitimately to every form of religious teaching subsequent to evangelization and conversion.

2. *Towards a definition.* Catechesis can be defined in terms of its origin. Seen thus, it is simply the transmission of the word of God, which is the source of the catechesis in two ways.

To begin with, the word of God determines the *content* of the catechesis, which must present the word of God in a well-balanced way. Accordingly, the mystery of Jesus Christ must be central, i.e., his saving death and resurrection, and the whole history of salvation as referred to him. The content of the catechesis is not therefore in the first place a system of ideas or a set of precepts; it is the proclamation of events in which God revealed himself and continues to reveal himself today. In the faith of the Church and its members these events become present once more and hence the catechesis has various stages: Bible history, the world of the liturgy, and finally doctrinal syntheses.

The word of God also determines the *form* of the catechesis. It is "revelation", "good news". It is the present echo of what was accomplished "once upon a time". Consequently, it must preserve the dynamic and joyful character which was intrinsic to the original message of salvation.

From another standpoint, we could define catechesis in terms of the word itself. The word of God is addressed to someone, who is called to accept it. Hence catechesis is the education of the baptized in the faith. Its ultimate aim is that the whole man should experience conversion and salvation through the word of God. The word penetrates man's heart – in the biblical sense – as well as his mind, and thus transforms him, giving him a new understanding of himself and the world, giving him a new place and attitude in society, making him live as he is and as he must be in the kingdom of God, in the fellowship of the people of God. Hence the various forms of catechesis, trying to embrace all the conditions of human life, age, milieu and culture, striving to make man once more at one with himself. The catechesis helps the individual and society to recognize and accept the signs and promises of salvation and to make the *one* word of God the dominant factor in all dimensions of life.

When all aspects are taken into account, catechesis must be defined as "the proclamation of the word of God in view of the education of man to faith". This avoids the danger of immanentism, which might sacrifice the character and originality of the gospel to a wrongly-conceived adaptation. And it avoids the danger of a wrongly-conceived transcendence, which ignores the real conditions under which God reveals himself. But the catechesis must be the privileged place for the encounter of the initiative of God's revelation and man's response in faith. All the efforts of Church preaching aim at this encounter. Biblical events, liturgical signs, dogmatic formulas, the testimony of sanctity – all are revelation made concrete. They are answers to the great questions of man. Thus the catechesis is centred on the relationship between God and man, as it is actualized in the redemptive incarnation.

3. *Catechesis and theology*. Reflection on the revelation received by the Church gives rise to the sacred sciences. Theology, exegesis, biblical theology and liturgy are the sources of the catechesis, which finds in them the content of its message and the criteria which are a guarantee of its soundness and precision.

Still, catechesis is different from theology or exegesis or liturgy. "Applied" catechesis makes use of the data supplied by these sciences, but refers them to their source and their end, namely the word of God and the faith of man respectively. And the manner in which catechesis uses the materials of theological sciences differs from the method which constitutes the latter as sciences. Catechesis presupposes these sciences, but it is not instruction in them. It goes beyond the technical aspects to embrace the living man and the active initiative of God as he turns to man. The theological sciences provide catechesis with its matter and the norms for judging its methods. But it is in itself the living word of God addressed to the man of today.

4. *Catechesis and the human sciences.* In the last hundred years the sciences of the human spirit have made undreamt-of progress. An anthropology

has been worked out which is the indispensable prerequisite for catechesis, and it cannot do without the findings of psychology, sociology and pedagogics, though it must avoid superficial adaptations. This means in fact that these sciences help insofar as they are related to an understanding of man which can be orientated to the end of man. This is the real task of a "Christian anthropology". It has to explain what present-day man is in the light of revelation, and how he can do justice to his revelation. And to do this it must take tradition and Scripture into account as well as modern science. It asks how present-day man can accept the word of God, and hence enquires into his understanding of the world and of himself. Here the human sciences can further a catechesis which takes account of the various ages and mentalities of cultural and national groups – always mindful of putting the actual individual into contact with the living God.

C. Implementation of the Catechesis

1. *The degrees of Christian catechesis.* Père Liégé makes the following distinctions:

a) *Catechesis of initiation or fundamental catechesis.* This is the catechumen's first contact with the teaching of the faith during his preparation for baptism. The same term could be applied to the teaching a baptized child receives when preparing for first confession and Communion. It conveys the message of salvation in its entirety, though in an elementary manner, with special attention to a proper balance of the various factors involved – doctrine, liturgy, life. On the quality of this first-stage catechesis all subsequent development depends.

b) *Permanent catechesis.* The essentials acquired during the initiation period grow and develop in the course of life. The function of "permanent catechesis" is to draw out the implications of the gospel in the various situations of life, as far as is possible and practical. Preaching aside, this can assume a variety of forms, courses for adolescents or adults, study-circles, conferences and so forth.

c) *Perfective catechesis* (also called Sapiential) is directed to those whom a special mission or vocation impels to a deeper penetration of their faith. It can mean "wisdom" in the theological sense, mysticism or contemplation.

2. *Catechesis and catechism.* Catechism for the young remains a privileged instrument of the catechesis as a whole. It makes use of suitable pedagogical devices, always with an eye on the goal of catechesis, that is, to make the child receptive to the word of God. Its originality, as compared with other forms of teaching, consists in that. It is with that in mind, too, that any "manual of Catechism" is to be judged. A privileged instrument of the catechesis unquestionably, it is nevertheless not the sole one. One could conceivably make use instead of other methods, Scripture classes with suitably detailed commentaries and the like.

3. *Catechesis and the pastoral ministry.* The word of God is propagated not only through the medium of catechetical institutions, but also in a more diffuse way by means of the whole life of the Church itself. The child is taught the faith in the family circle. The adolescent and the grown-up encounter the gospel in educational or apostolic groups, in community life – here the liturgy comes in – as well as by way of the different mass-media, press, radio and so on. These unlimited possibilities in the means of communication are from one point of view a great advantage, but some additional unifying force is called for. This is the work of God's grace in the mystery of each one's faith, but it will display itself in the various forms of the Church's activity. There will be a unity of goal, which keeps the mystery of Easter at the heart of faith

and life; a unity of language, which will ease the difficulties of those who find it hard to connect the older, more analytic form of catechesis with the newer and more living forms. The task of those who have the care of souls is to show the convergence between the various kinds of language used in the Church.

This of course is only another way of saying that the catechesis and the pastoral ministry constantly interact on each other.

4. *Catechetical studies.* Reflection on the teaching of the faith and its place in the Church is the specific object of "catechetics". Catechetical studies have of late seen a renewal, in the light of the comparable developments in the theological and biblical areas, not to mention the advances in anthropology and scientific method. The Munich School must take much of the credit for this. If one were to draw up an ideal syllabus of catechetical studies, it would include: a) The theology of the word of God, its place in the Church, the instruments it uses, the laws of its transmission (formal catechesis); its content (material catechesis) in general or under individual aspects such as biblical or liturgical catechesis. b) Man as a believer, that is to say, Christian anthropology, which would have to face the problem as to how the various natural sciences, psychology, sociology, etc., could be integrated and pressed into the service of the catechesis. c) Catechesis proper, the act by which the word of God is conveyed to man either in a general way or with an eye to actual conditions of age, milieu, or special circumstances. The former could be called general, the latter special catechetical pedagogy. d) Finally the connection between the catechesis itself and other forms of Church apostolate should be studied, in particular the mutual relations between catechetical activities and the various forms of the ministry.

Jacques Audinet

CELIBACY

Celibacy here means not simply the fact of not being married, though such a state can be of theological and pastoral relevance when it serves to promote certain ends. Celibacy is here understood as the unmarried state chosen in the light of the Christian faith, and in particular as one of the duties of the state in life of the clergy of the Latin Church, by which they are forbidden to marry and obliged to live in total continence.

A. History

1. The biblical foundations for celibacy are taken to be the saying of the Lord about not marrying ("becoming a eunuch") for the sake of the kingdom of heaven (Mt 19:10ff.); also the saying about leaving one's wife for the sake of Jesus and the gospel (Mk 10:29) or for the sake of the reign of God (Lk 18:29); and also the saying which affirms that in the resurrection there will be no marriage (Mt 22:30; Mk 12:25). Paul wished all men to be in the same state as himself (1 Cor 7:7). The unmarried is devoted to the things of the Lord, while the attention of the married is divided (1 Cor 7:32f.). These texts, however, do not link celibacy directly to the priestly ministry. In early Christianity, they were rather connected with baptism and looked on as counsels which many in fact followed. Support for this tendency was found in such biblical parables as Mt 9:15; 22:1–14; Mk 2:19; Lk 5:34; 12:35ff.; 14:15–24; Jn 3:29. Celibacy as a duty of the priestly state was introduced only gradually. It derived from the high value attached to virginity (cf. 2 Cor 11:2; Eph 5:25ff., 30ff.; Acts 21:9), the perspective of the final consummation (Rev 14:3f.; 19:7ff.; 21:2, 9) and the way of life of ascetics and monks with their recourse to the OT laws of purity. The evolution of the law of celibacy was greatly influenced by the precept laid down in the Pastoral Letters, that bishops, priests

and deacons should be "husband of only one wife" (1 Tim 3:2, 12; Tit 1:6f.), though the precise meaning of the principle was debated.

2. Laws dealing with celibacy are found as early as the beginning of the 4th century. Inspired by the desire for total dedication and also to some extent under the influence of dualistic Gnostic tendencies of a Manichaean type, many priests felt bound to discontinue marriage relationships after their ordination. In the Eastern Churches celibacy prevailed only for those who were equipped with the fullness of the priesthood, the bishops, and was given force of law in the 7th century by the Emperor Justinian and the second Trullan Synod. But in the West the decrees of the Synod of Elvira were widely imposed by Pope Siricius (*DS* 118f.; 185). An effort to prescribe celibacy as a universal Church law was made at the First Council of Nicaea (325), but did not meet with success. Leo I and Gregory I extended the law to include sub-deacons. Since what was forbidden was not so much marriage as the continuation of married life, promises of continence were often demanded of candidates for the priesthood (and their wives) between the 5th and 7th centuries. From the 6th century on, separation of the spouses was also demanded. The constant necessity of synodal intervention in this matter shows how much practical difficulty was involved. A historical factor in the promotion of celibacy in the Middle Ages was the problem which had already exercised minds in the 5th and 6th centuries – the effort to prevent the alienation of Church property, which might otherwise pass into the possession of the priest's family. This gave rise in the 12th century to the statutory declaration of the nullity of the marriage of those in major orders. In spite of sharp controversy at the time of the Reformation, the Council of Trent re-affirmed the principle that clerics in major orders were incapable of contracting matrimony (*DS* 1809). In the form already laid down by the Council of Nicaea "by virtue of ancient tradition" – that there should be no marriage after the reception of a major order – the magisterium held fast to this law, as though it were an apostolic regulation, even in Vatican II and the documents which have appeared since then.

3. According to the law in force in the Latin Church, as laid down by the *CIC*, clerics in minor orders lose their clerical status by contracting matrimony (can. 132, § 2). Clerics in major orders are forbidden to marry. They are obliged in a special way to preserve chastity. A sin against chastity is a sacrilege (can. 132, § 1) and if it involves an external breach of the law (can. 2195) incurs sanctions (can. 2325). All attempts to contract matrimony are null and void (can. 1072) and to presume to enter even upon a civil form of marriage involves irregularity (can. 985, § 3), loss of ecclesiastical office (can. 188, § 5) and excommunication (can. 2388). The laws concerning absolution from excommunication (can. 2252; Decree of the Sacred Penitentiary of 18 April 1936 and 14 May 1937), dispensation from the impediment to marriage for deacons and sub-deacons in danger of death (can. 1043), laicization with release from the obligation of celibacy (can. 214, 1993–8) have been eased and complemented by various acts of "grace and favour" on the part of the Holy See and above all by the documents of Vatican II (*Lumen Gentium*, art. 29; *Presbyterorum Ordinis*, art. 16), the motu proprio *Sacrum Diaconatus Ordinem* (nos. 4, 11–13, 16) and the encyclical *Sacerdotalis Caelibatus* (nos. 42, 84f., 87f.). Thus pleas of lack of freedom and proper qualification which were formerly (can. 214) not provided for may now be put forward in cases of ordination, and dispensation from all obligations may be obtained on other grounds as well. Married men, with

the consent of their vives, may now be ordained deacons, if – according to the conditions laid down in 1 Tim 3:10ff. – they have been married for some years and are over thirty-five years of age. But those who have been ordained deacons while unmarried may no longer contract matrimony. That married men should become priests (cf. can. 132, § 3; 987, § 2) is foreseen only in the case of ministers of other Churches or Christian communities who desire unity with the Catholic Church and wish to exercise their sacred ministry.

B. The Doctrine of the Magisterium

1. A characteristic of the doctrine of the magisterium on celibacy is that it sees itself bound by the canonical prescriptions while taking an intermediate position between these and theological reflection on them. There is also the point that the law of celibacy has not lacked opponents in the Church. The constantly recurring trend away from celibacy which has been manifested throughout the centuries has influenced the magisterium in the choice and presentation of the themes concerning celibacy, according to the various types of attack made upon it and the various reasons which they invoked. Hence the documents of the magisterium have often taken the form of apologetics, polemics or exhortation. Celibacy is mostly discussed from the point of view of chastity and placed on the same level as virginity.

2. Though the Council of Trent emphasized very strongly the dignity of sacramental matrimony, it condemned those who maintained that "the married state is preferable to that of virginity or celibacy and that it is not better and more blessed to continue in the state of virginity or celibacy than to enter on the state of matrimony" (*DS* 1810). This verdict, however, which considers the various states of life, does not deny that many married persons can be closer to God than those obliged to celibacy. In the encyclical *Sacra Virginitas*, which also dealt with celibacy, Pius XII rejected the opinion that "only marriage guarantees a natural development of the human person" and that the sacrament "sanctifies married life to such a degree that it becomes a more effective means of union with God than virginity itself" (*DS* 3911f.). This way of putting things, which is a variation on the Council of Trent, is an indirect invitation to work out the manifold relationships between marriage and celibacy, which may be evaluated from more than one standpoint.

3. A new field is opened up in the development of the doctrine by Vatican II, in as much as the dogmatic constitution *Lumen Gentium* does not restrict the undivided heart to such Christians as remain unmarried (art. 42). The call to supreme holiness, such as that of "your Father who is in heaven" (Mt 5:48) is understood as directed to all Christian believers and not merely to those who remain unmarried for religious reasons (art. 40). Nonetheless, the conciliar decree *Optatam Totius*, on priestly formation, demands that candidates for the priesthood should clearly recognize the precedence of virginity consecrated to Christ over marriage (art. 10). According to *Lumen Gentium*, the holiness of the Church is advanced by the observation of the many counsels which our Lord proposed to his disciples in the gospel. A pre-eminent place is held by the precious gift of divine grace which the Father gives to some, so that they may *more easily* devote themselves whole-heartedly to God in the state of virginity or celibacy. Thus celibacy is a sign of love and an impulse towards it (art. 42). Practically the same terms are used in the decrees *Optatam Totius* (art. 10) and *Perfectae Caritatis* (art. 12) to re-affirm for priests and for religious the law of celibacy "for the sake of the kingdom of heaven". According to *Presbyterorum*

Ordinis, art. 16, celibacy is not demanded by the nature of the priesthood, but is appropriate for many reasons and is founded on the mystery of Christ and his mission. Hence the law of celibacy in the Latin Church is re-affirmed for those who have been marked out for the priesthood. This formulation, which in comparison with earlier ones is reserved, allows for married deacons.

4. The encyclical *Sacerdotalis Caelibatus* develops the notion of celibacy with reference to Christ, the Church and the consummation of all things, stressing anthropological viewpoints with an emphasis hitherto unknown in documents of the supreme magisterium. While rejecting all changes in the law of celibacy and adhering unmistakably to the legislation of the Latin Church, the encyclical still raises the question of whether this "difficult law" should not be left to the free choice of the individual (art. 3) and whether candidates should not be admitted who feel the call to the priesthood but not to celibacy (art. 7). When choosing the Twelve, Jesus did not demand celibacy (art. 5). The charism of priestly ministry is distinct from that of celibacy, the law of celibacy is historically conditioned (arts. 14, 17) and the way of life of the Eastern Churches is likewise the work of the Spirit (art. 38). Nonetheless, the encyclical expects that insight into a priestly ministry wholly united to Christ will throw ever greater light on the bond between the priesthood and celibacy (art. 25). Marriage and the family are not the only possibilities of total maturity (art. 56). Bishops must extend their tender care in particular towards those of their brothers who suffer under the burden of celibacy or have come to grief thereby (arts. 87, 91–94).

C. The Present Situation

1. Celibacy is at present a subject of discussion inside and outside the Church. The substance and the actual framing of the arguments may be gathered from the encyclical *Sacerdotalis Caelibatus*, which is attentive to present-day questions without actually answering them, preferring to present copious doctrinal matter from various theological approaches. The encyclical also adopts traditional themes which Vatican II passed over or at least tried to present more moderately: thus for instance the encyclical speaks of *castitas perfecta* (nos. 6f., 13) and suggests a mystical identification of the priest with Christ, giving the priest a specially exalted place which almost makes him an exceptional type (nos. 13, 24f., 31f., 56). Was it perhaps the intention of the encyclical to show that religious and Christian truth is always too great to be fully grasped by any given age? It calls, in any case, for careful study of unresolved problems and provides valuable impulses for such study, which include the recognition of important historical facts and of new pastoral methods.

2. Objective theological discussion, neither aggressive nor defensive but simply bent on the truth, has become difficult at the present day. Two fronts have been formed even within the Church, and the extreme wings either treat the subject as taboo or consider celibacy as disposed of. But no party can register real gains at the cost of objectiveness. Honest expression of opinion is desirable, but lyrical panegyrics and one-sidedly negative criticism merely arouse opposition which obscures the essential values of celibacy. Comprehension is still far from being magnanimous, as may be seen from the un-Christian attitude towards married converts to Catholicism. And those who point to the milder rule of the Eastern Churches as regards celibacy often forget that it can demand considerable sacrifices, especially from priests who are widowers.

3. On theological grounds, the present problems concerning celibacy arise from a new understanding of marriage

and of the priestly ministry. In the past marriage was at times considered as something just permissible. But the pastoral constitution *Gaudium et Spes* affirms that it is a union which our Lord has dignified, healed, perfected and exalted by special gifts of his grace and love (art. 49); that he himself dwells with the spouses, who by the help of his Spirit attain their own perfection, sanctify each other and glorify God together (art. 48). Priests, who are so often looked upon as a sort of higher beings, are said in the decree *Presbyterorum Ordinis* to remain disciples of our Lord along with the other faithful, in spite of their lofty and necessary office. Along with all those who were re-born in the fountain of baptism, they remain brothers among brothers, members of the one and the same body of Christ, the building up of which is entrusted to all. Under these circumstances the traditional conventional arguments for celibacy no longer seem conclusive. Where they are still used, they meet with justifiable objections from those who welcome the ideas put forward by the Council. Then, on social grounds, problems arise from the fact that today in practically all walks of life marriage is left to the private judgment of the individuals. The contrast in the ecclesiastical law of celibacy appears to be a relic of former ages. The problem has become more acute with the emphasis on marriage as a partnership, the social equality of women, the new appreciation of the body, and the positive value attributed to sexual relationship in the self-realization, development and maturity of all men, and not merely of that of married people. New answers are called for to meet the demands of the times. On the other hand, no reasonable judgment can be passed on celibacy as a special form of Christian life, except by those who have the Christian faith.

D. Pastoral Tasks

1. Pastoral considerations are urgent. Celibacy is a gift of grace. Whether it is given to few or to many is outside human control. But if, as is the case today, it becomes a problem for debate within the Church, pastoral theology must try to determine the obstacles to its realization in the life of faith. Has the divine seed of celibacy been choked by the weeds of too purely human motivations? Or has the wheat also been plucked up in the effort to remove the weeds? One of the inspirations of priestly celibacy was the example of the apostolic Church, where many of the faithful experienced the overwhelming surge of the grace of the kingdom of God so strongly that they simply "could" not marry, but "had" to remain completely free for the building up of the community for the sake of the Lord. Is this still really true of the official ministers of the Church who are celibate today?

2. To be effective in the ministry of salvation, celibacy must be lived simply and spontaneously. It is this sense of the normal which needs to be renewed about celibacy. It grows, no one knows how, in stillness (cf. Mk 4:27), being one of the *magnalia Dei* and not one of man's achievements. All the noisy and excited discussion of celibacy will prove to be harmful. And the persistence of talk about the impurity of the body and sexual activity on the one hand, and of "perfect" chastity on the other, not only gives rise to misunderstandings today but is regarded as arrogant and as telling against celibacy. It is best to take a very sober view of celibacy. To remain unmarried for the sake of important tasks which claim one's whole attention can be seen to be rational even in terms of purely human experience, and can be recognized as a way of personal self-realization which is naturally possible. Hence the saying of our Lord that it can be good to remain unmarried for the sake of the kingdom of God can be made quite intelligible to the faithful. There is no need to deny that continence

is a source of power which has constantly proved itself to be creative. But the point is secondary, and indeed irrelevant, as regards celibacy for the sake of the kingdom of God. Nonetheless, it does not follow at once from the fact that the priest is unmarried that he is fully at the disposition of the reign of God. But celibacy remains appropriate for the priest, because it is a typical way of achieving full freedom for the kingdom and because those who serve in the priestly ministry should in fact be wholly at the disposition of the kingdom. It remains true, however, that there are married people who show themselves to be wholly responsive and open to the demands of Christ and of the kingship of God.

3. According to the ecclesiastical magisterium, the law of celibacy now in force must remain a strict condition for the priestly ministry. Hence (apart from special exceptions) it regards as suitable for the priesthood only those to whom God has granted the gift of celibacy, along with the other signs of vocation (*Sacerdotalis Caelibatus*, nos. 14f., 62). In spite of this rule, pastoral considerations must include the fact that the canonical precept does not only strengthen the charism of celibacy (no. 62). It may also obscure its effectiveness, since there is a tension between law and charism. The law being what it is, celibacy is often merely endured as a necessary condition of the priesthood, and then it loses the convincing quality of sign which it should have as the expression of a really existential inability to marry for the sake of Christ and his kingdom. Has not this charism also come to light once more within the Protestant Churches without any law which imposes it? But there is another side to the problem, which makes it possible to understand celibacy as a law. The biblical term χωρεῖν need not be translated as "grasp" or "understand", which gives for Mt 19:11 the translation, "Not all men understand this, but only those to whom it is given ... He who is able to understand this, let him understand it." The term can also mean "receive", "make room for", "adopt", "achieve", "dare". And something of universally human appeal is thereby expressed: "Not all can do this. But if you can summon up the strength, then dare it!" Hence celibacy is probably not one of the charisms which is either there or not, but one of those which may also be striven for, according to the counsel of the Apostle Paul (1 Cor 12:31). This is important to note for the preaching of celibacy.

4. In the formation of priests and in their further development, many of the supports of celibacy which were hitherto relied on will fall away, having proved themselves unreal or erroneous. They must no longer be appealed to. In their place theologically valid arguments must be used, and new aids which correspond to present realities. The celibacy of the contemplative monk and that of the priest engaged directly in the ministry of salvation will develop differently. But both will need not only a personally responsible decision with the will to persevere, but also an effective maturity and growth which corresponds to each phase of age and development. Since the sexuality of the celibate should not remain an isolated element, and since integration is only possible in a genuine relationship between the sexes, appropriate means for such integration must be sought for and provided. Just as celibacy has undergone different developments in various nations (some spiritualizing it, others accepting it simply as law or institution), so too it can have various degrees of realization in the life of individual priests. Here it may range from a loving loneliness with Christ to a highly individual type of friendship with the other sex. Now that women have been recognized as fully qualified lay people in their own right in the Church, dialogue and pastoral co-operation between

priests and women can no longer be evaded, but must be boldly undertaken and brought to perfection. A brotherly relationship between the priests and a well-ordered *vita communis* will be a safeguard in such matters. But celibacy is never merely a precept to be fulfilled. It must also remain a cherished goal.

5. Meanwhile new pastoral tasks are taking shape. When the motives of a vocation are being examined to see whether a candidate is fitted or not for priestly celibacy, the encyclical *Sacerdotalis Caelibatus* lays it down that the services of a doctor or psychologist must be availed of (nos. 63ff.). For the formation of character and for the counselling of priests undergoing mental or moral strain or finding themselves in difficulties with their vocation, the help of a suitable team of professionals will also be necessary. Apart from private circles which voluntarily assist, there are organizations for this purpose in France and other countries. It will be especially important to maintain contact with all who have left the priestly ministry and are more or less happily married. They must be kept at work in the Church in an appropriate way, where they are willing to undertake such tasks. This should be done even at the cost of financial sacrifices. Against the background of the new possibilities, those who contemplate the present crisis of celibacy in the light of faith will be able to welcome it as a work of purification and grace in the service of the kingdom of God.

Leonhard M. Weber

CHARISM

In the earliest period there was no sign of hostility between ecclesiastical authority and charisms, either in the language of the New Testament or in practice. As well as being the "holy Church" through its truth, foundation by Christ, the sacraments and the salvation which is present in it (the *communio sanctorum* in the objective sense), the Church is also, as the eschatological community of the victorious grace of God, holy throughout because of the actual faith and love of God in its members. As such it compels faith and is a reason for faith in its outward appearance, by which it must bear witness to its nature (*D* 1794). This, however, is only possible with the help of charisms. Even the sacraments can only sanctify through the action of God's extra-sacramental grace (*D* 789f, 819), and even those justified by the sacraments need extra-sacramental grace, sometimes in an exceptional degree (*D* 132). The charismatic dimension is therefore as necessary and permanent a part of the life of the Church as are offices and sacraments. Charisms were not given simply to help the Church in its beginnings, but it is of the nature of charisms as an essential feature of the Church that they should appear in constantly new forms and therefore constantly have to be rediscovered (in contrast to ministries and their transmission). This characteristic of charisms is also the explicit teaching of the Church (*D* 2288; Pius XII, *Mystici Corporis* [AAS 35 (1943) 200f]; Vat. II, *De Ecclesia* 11, 12, 4, 34f., 40f., 48f.); and by it the action of the Spirit can be recognized outside the Catholic Church (*De Eccl.* 15; *De Oec.* 3). Such charisms may equally be regarded as an assistance to ministries in the Church, without which they cannot be properly performed, as a promise to the ministries for which their holders have a duty to remain ready, and (when already present) as a sign of suitability for a ministry.

The actual fulfilment of the promise of indestructibility made to the Church and its ministries is due in part to the charisms continually given to it. But non-institutional charisms are essential alongside "official" charisms, since the holy Church which witnesses to the eschatological victory of God's grace by its visible presence in the world is not composed of its ministers only, but is the "holy people of God". Charisms may be present in all Christians, and are present in germ in all who are justified and are therefore members of the body of Christ each with his own function. The only distinction between charisms and the Christian virtues may be (as in the modern terminology of the Church, cf. *Mystici Corporis*: 1 c) that charisms give additional prominence to the social, public, witnessing and missionary character which always accompanies Christian virtues in the Church, though in varying degrees. It follows from the connection of charisms and virtues that in addition to the great charismatic gifts and "enthusiastic" movements which have continually appeared, and must continually appear, in the Church, heroic loyalty in bearing with daily life, perseverance in unfavourable cultural situations and similar achievements may be charismatic in the full sense. If charisms are part of the essence of the Church, the authorities must not merely tolerate, but critically encourage them (1 Thess. 5.19f.), and must make sure that the impulses of the Spirit need not act on office-holders alone, but that something can also "go out from the (holy) people". They must have the courage to allow new and hitherto unknown forms of charism to emerge, and must encourage and correct the institutional embodiments which even charisms need for their full development, and give them a place in the life of the Church as a whole.

After the apostolic period distinctions were gradually introduced into the earlier naïve unity of ministry and charismatic gifts. Virginity, asceticism and martyrdom were considered as charisms. Nevertheless by the third century a slackening of the charismatic movement can be felt; "baptismal enthusiasm", still familiar to Cyprian, had become rare by the time of Origen. Not long afterwards, many free charisms were incorporated in "ministries" such as that of "exorcist". Montanism was the first serious crisis for the unity between ministry and charisms. Ministry rightly prevailed, but from that time open and unprejudiced assessment of charismatic phenomena became rarer. Nevertheless, monasticism felt itself from the beginning to be the heir of the charismatic movement in the primitive Church. In keeping with this, the earliest form of hagiography is one in which the saint appears not simply as a moral hero, but as basically a charismatic wonder-worker, although in the theology of this monasticism the isolated mysticism of individualistic union with God to some extent pushed the prophetic and charismatic sense of a mission for the building up of the Church into the background. An internal (and external) history of the later Church too cannot be written without an assessment of the charismatic dimension in it. The founding of religious orders in the Middle Ages often resulted from an original mystical experience of a call. There is also a history of holy women with prophetical and mystical missions to the Church. Also within this category are "enthusiastic" but still ecclesial movements, the various "movements of the interior life", the movements which started at the sites of visions or places of pilgrimage, the influence exercised in the Church by visions and private revelations, and the explicitly charismatic figures among saints and preachers. All these charismatic manifestations within the Church must be seen against the background of a heterodox charismatic movement. The history of the theology of the charismatic movement in the Church and in the service of the Church is still to be written. It has not yet been written because the theology has remained relatively undeveloped. The medieval theology of charisms cannot be regarded as fully developed except in limited areas. Ignatius of Loyola constructed a logic of the existential recognition of

God's charismatic impulses, but it has not yet been properly assimilated. Together with, and going beyond this charismatic dimension, there is in the Church a movement of the Spirit which continually enables it, "in virtue of its miraculous generation, its outstanding holiness and inexhaustible fruitfulness in all goodness, in its catholic unity and unconquerable perseverance", to bear witness to itself as the continually new creation of the Spirit (*D* 1794).

Karl Rahner

CHARITY

Love of Neighbour

1. *Concept and problems.* The love which is open to and interested in those close to us is universally recognized as a noble form of moral action. But the question arises as to who are our "neighbours" and how far should charity towards them go. The spontaneous answer of natural ethics is to distinguish between love of those nearest and dearest to us and readiness to help those outside this circle. Men feel bound to love others in proportion to their "social proximity". In the Greek city-state this attitude was deliberately extended to take in the commonwealth of free citizens as a sort of enlarged family, which meant a certain exclusion of those outside the city. The OT also contains an ethics of special charity towards fellow-believers. But since love of the neighbour is based on the fatherhood of God, and since the God of Israel is the God of all men, this love is ready in principle to regard all men as neighbours. But since Israel considered itself a chosen people in a special way, with a special relationship to the fatherhood of God, there was a feeling of a special obligation of love towards the members of the chosen people, which led to a strong tendency to exclude foreigners, especially in late Judaism. Nonetheless, the duty of love went beyond the community to take in foreigners, because they were also creatures of God and descendants of the fathers of the race of man, Adam and Noah (Exod 22:20; 23:9; Deut 14:29, etc.; Lev 19:33f.; 19:10; 23:22; Num 9:14; 15:14ff.; 35:15; see the concordances under the word "stranger"). But while in some cases late Judaism linked love of God and of the neighbour the main foundation of Jewish ethics was justice.

A different type of love of the neighbour is found in the mystery religions. Entry into an esoteric community made men neighbours. These communities arose from the wish to find closer fellowship, and hence sometimes developed a hostile attitude to those outside the group. But the political unification of the Hellenistic world brought with it, especially in Stoic philosophy, a cosmopolitan ethics, so that Epictetus, for instance, could regard all men as brothers since they all had their origin in God. Thus the one basic attitude of love of the neighbour embraced all men. In the Enlightenment, universal brotherhood and the resulting duty of equal love for all was based on the oneness of nature in all men. The habit of making distinctions was to be overcome, as an irrational atavism. This unrealistic ethics of universal love was abandoned by Marxism in favour of love of one's own class. Those who love the proletariat must be enemies of the capitalists. The division is due to the historical process of the self-alienation of man, which can only be eliminated in the classless society. Dialogical existence-philosophy stresses the I-Thou relationship and communication in contast to generalizing thought-forms and hence does more justice to the primordially personal and historical in each man. The neighbour is he with whom we are confronted in each unique and incalculable situation. Jaspers, for instance, holds that love is directed to the individual as he appears in his uniqueness. One is not urged to help him by virtue of general ethical principles and duties, but because in the encounter with him, the situation forms a decisive challenge for our destiny. Here love comes to the aid of the neighbour as the situation demands and without conditions. There is no objective absolute ethical duty, but only the summons to personal communication with this unique individual, of which the nature and limits can never be fully fathomed.

In all these ethics, the love of the neighbour is limited by love of self, in the sense of the "golden rule" (Mt 7:12; Lk 6:31), that one should love one's neighbour as oneself. Or again, society is given priority over the individual in the sense of an absolute precedence; or finally, no attempt is made to assess objectively the measure of love of the neighbour. The Christian notion of charity, however, is based on the union of love of God and love of the neighbour. They are linked significantly by Jesus in the "great commandment" Mk 12:28–31 parr.). Then love of the neighbour appears more precisely as the one norm according to which man will be judged (Mt 25:34–46). No bounds are set to loving the neighbour as oneself: the highest form of love is love of enemies (Mt 5:43ff.; Lk 6:27ff.) and giving one's life for one's friends (Jn 15:13). Thus love is the sum-total of the law (Mk 12:31; cf. 3:1–7; Mt 5:23f.; 9:13). Its motive and its model is the all-embracing love of God (Lk 6:36) and the service rendered by Jesus himself (Mk 10:44f.; Lk 22:26; Jn 13:14f.). In Paul, love of the neighbour is the fulfilment of the whole law (Rom 13:8–10; Gal 5:14), and the perfection of Christian life (Col 3:1). Love of God and of the neighbour are seen as unity (1 Cor 13). In James, love is seen as the royal commandment (Jas 2:8). According to John, love of the neighbour is a new commandment (Jn 13:34; 1 Jn 2:8), motivated by the love with which God first loved men (Jn 3:16; 16:27; 1 Jn 4:11), and by the love with which the Son chose the disciples (Jn 15:9f., 12).

2. *The theology of love of the neighbour.* Love of the neighbour determines the basic structure of the moral act, inasmuch as we cannot turn to God without turning to our neighbour. We can only be with God insofar as we are with our fellowmen. It is only through love of the neighbour that we can find fulfilment in the love of God. Our relationship to transcendence can only come about through our concrete, historical relationship to our fellowmen. The "transcendental depth" of man in the encounter with the "other" always points beyond itself, at least implicitly, to God and at the same time back to him who loves also, since it is only in such encounters that he really possesses his own identity. For it is only when man is materially and implicitly in face of being, while formally and consciously in face of objectivated reality, that he can be consciously and truly himself. So too, man can only see himself distinct, as person, from the objective reality of the world when at least materially and implicitly he refers himself to God as the personal being as such, and to his fellowmen formally and explicitly. Hence the explicit and formal reference to God is only possible insofar as there is ordination towards man. This is the kernel of truth in the position of the modern non-Catholic theologians who maintain that God is only a "mode of being fellowman". The more we welcome our fellowmen in their uniqueness and their openness to God, the more we surrender ourselves to God without reserve. This openness need not be conscious and explicit, but it is at least materially there. Hence every act of neighbourly charity is materially an act of the love of God. If this love of God is made explicit, it is formally an act of the love of God. Hence our neighbour is every man potentially, and actually every man who meets us in his subjective uniqueness and in the mea-

sure in which he does so. He may be someone sought out by me, or one who irrupts unasked into my personal existence. That we can attain through love of the neighbour a fulfilment which surpasses all human understanding, and that we are called to an unconditional love of others, are truths which can only be lived in faith.

Faith reveals the call of all men to sonship of God in the Son, according to God's universal salvific will. It follows that every moral act is in principle ordained through grace to salvation. Justification makes all the justified brothers of one another in Christ by grace (Mk 3:31–35; Jn 14:21; 15:14f.), so that they can love one another in a supernatural way. Only those justified in Christ are brothers in the strict sense. The others are "those outside" (1 Thess. 4:10–12; cf. 1 Cor 5:12, 13; Col 4:5). Accordingly, the attitudes prescribed in the Pauline letters for conduct towards those outside are sometimes outgoing (Rom 13:8; 1 Thess 3:12; 5:15; Tit 3:2; also 1 Cor 9:19; 1 Tim 2:1; Rom 13:1; Tit 3:1; Phil 2:15; Rom 12:17; 2 Cor 8:21; 1 Thess 4:12; 5:22; Rom 15:2; 1 Tim 4:12), sometimes deliberately restrictive (Col 4:5; cf. 2 Cor 6:15; Eph 4:28; 1 Thess 4:11–12; Eph 5:6–7; 2 Cor 6:17). But the demarcation of the Christian fellowship is not aimed at producing an esoteric coterie. It is in the service of the whole, as is particularly clear from Rom 5:12–21. Since Jesus died for all men and since all are therefore called to this supernatural brotherhood, the supernatural love of the neighbour must embrace all men, and in the concrete those who are in need, spiritually or materially (Lk 10:30–37; Mt 25:31–46), especially as the justified are called for the non-elect. For there is a mystery of substitution which was instituted in Christ and which forms the basis of all election, and according to the will of God it continues from Christ on in an economy of salvation which is a series of substitutions. This is in fact the structural law of the history of salvation itself.

Election is always ultimately election on behalf of others. This is true of individuals as of the Church, and hence election is none other than the missionary mandate. This means that Christianity recognizes the existence of various spheres of neighbourly charity, while confining the name of "brother" to fellow-believers. But there is no desire of exclusivity for its own sake. The ultimate meaning of the demarcation is simply to perform the due service for all men. Love of the neighbour is most fully expressed in substitutional or vicarious suffering along with the Lord, in the martyrdom of total dedication in love of the neighbour, since ultimately a parousia of God in Christ takes place in him. Where there is genuine love of the neighbour, the totality of Christianity is presence in substance and in germ, and needs only to be explicitly unfolded.

Waldemar Molinski

CHRISTIANITY

I. The Essence of Christianity

A. Preliminary Observations on Method

1. The question of what Christianity "really" is in "essence", is not one which arises only when doubt is thrown on the unique character of Christianity, its absolute claim. Since the beginning of modern times the question has of course been raised in that way in ever more insistent and explicit terms. As a consequence, the question has been misconstrued. Contrary to the nature of a unique concrete historical personal event based on God's historical act of self-communication, the inquiry has been taken to concern a criterion which is applicable by the individual from "outside", and which would entitle him to distinguish between essentials and

merely incidental historical accessories. In fact, however, the question was always present, and indeed belongs to the very nature of Christianity, because Christianity does not regard itself as something simply to be taken for granted. It has its historical development from one starting-point, only gradually reaches individuals, and it always solicits their individual, free and yet rational decision of faith. In doing this it has first to say what it is and why it demands faith. Its view of itself is, therefore, an intrinsic element of Christianity. The reality which is aware of itself in this way regards itself as not comprised within any pre-existing system of spiritual co-ordinates which would permit it adequately to be described and critically evaluated.

2. Nevertheless, according to the Catholic conception of faith, it is possible to speak of Christianity in two ways, both legitimate. The authentically Christian conception can be stated (i.e., the dogmatic teaching of the Roman Catholic Church about itself and about Christianity generally). And it is possible to say what, at least in principle, can be perceived of Christianity "from outside", i.e., by those who do not yet believe (but who are necessarily always placed in the light of the grace of potential belief). There is, therefore, a dogmatic account of the Church and one that belongs to fundamental theology (apologetics), and the latter includes the relevant religious phenomenology and general historical and sociological considerations. In the Catholic view of the relations between faith and reason and of the rational possibility of recognizing the fact of revelation, such an account "from outside" need not necessarily fail to correspond to Christianity, even though the innermost nature of the latter can only be grasped in the light of faith from the message of faith itself and in the obedience of faith.

3. It is legitimate not simply to identify Christianity and the Catholic Church. This is shown by Catholic doctrine, which recognizes certain non-Catholics as Christians (*CIC*, can. 1325, § 2), regards grace and justification to be possible even outside actual membership of the Church (baptism of desire), teaches the validity of (correctly administered) sacraments outside the Church and acknowledges a sacred Scripture which in itself is the Word of God and does not only become the Word of God when actually (and rightly) preached. An account of Christianity need not, therefore, simply coincide with an account of the Church. Yet, theologically speaking, Christianity is not the sum of empirically observable Christians and their opinions. Even a correct external point of view in apologetics does not permit such a detached summary treatment of all as on an equal footing. The saving act of God in Christ which founded Christianity is present, with the full embodiment (in principle) which it implies, in the one Catholic Church. Consequently an account of Christianity must ultimately find its completion in an account of the one actual Church. And this of course will conceive the Church as constituting the sole salvation of all in such a way that the salvation of all who live outside the Church and yet by the Church, is regarded as possible.

4. A critical account of the actual realization of the nature of Christianity and of its history is, in the Catholic view, quite legitimate and indeed necessary, despite Christianity's claims to possess absolute character. But it is ultimately a function of the Church itself, not of a critic standing "outside" it. For Catholicism holds a rational justification of faith to be possible, in the sense of a demonstration of the credibility of revelation and the obligation to believe, in ways and within limits which cannot be gone into further here. Ultimately it regards Christianity as a reality which integrates everything into itself, includ-

ing therefore all intellectual activities. It therefore claims that the critical function belongs to its own nature, that is, the function of discriminating between the nature of what ought to be and what in fact externally is the case.

5. It is not to be expected that there is a formula, an abstract essential definition so expressive of the nature of Christianity that everything essential can be deduced from it in such a way that what cannot be so deduced is thereby to be eliminated as a mere historical accessory. For what is concrete and historical necessarily possesses intrinsic pre-eminence over human reflection about it in the philosophy of religion and in theology, and reflection can never entirely exhaust it. This applies to Christianity which was founded by God's saving action and rests on the real person of Jesus Christ and which conceives itself to be the total integration of all reality (God – salvation – world-history) into its own reality, though in various degrees.

6. An attempt at a relatively brief statement of the nature of Christianity is of some practical importance for the proclamation of the faith. Short syntheses of this kind are necessary for preaching Christianity to non-Christians and have always existed, starting with the Apostles' Creed, but those handed down by tradition are not of a kind to be easily assimilable in the intellectual and cultural situation of the present day. If an almost hazardous attempt is risked here to formulate a brief synthesis, it obivously can only have "Western" (European and American) civilization in mind. For other cultures a different standpoint would have to be chosen, because the rationalized technical one-world civilization has not yet produced such a unified concept of man for this to be yet capable of providing a possible universal basis, and a universal public, for a statement about the nature of Christianity.

B. History of Definitions of Christianity

1. There is such a history, of course, which coincides with the history of Christianity itself and its dogmatic theology (cf. A, 1), but it is only possible to speak of such a history in a special sense since the beginning of "modern times", from the moment when as a result of the influence of Christianity itself on the history of ideas, man consciously directed his attention to himself in his radical subjectivity. Then Christianity ceased to be simply the sum-total of the religious environment as it in fact existed, with the demands it made. The question had to be raised of its one essential nature in relation to man's own subjectivity. This question, which was and could only be formulated explicitly and consciously in modern times, has probably not yet been sufficiently understood by orthodox Christianity and even less worked out. Catholic dogmatic theology does not raise the question. Yet there "must" be heresies (in the biblical sense of "must", in which in the actual history of salvation what ought not to be becomes, beyond men's plans, a positive means for realizing God's intentions). And heresies, which never draw their vitality from mere negation, may in fact contain in a more explicit way, and earlier, much that is Christian but which in Catholic Christianity remains latent, more unarticulated, less conscious. Moreover, to the extent that heresies derive from Christianity itself, they belong to its own "image". Consequently we have to include in the distinct new history constituted in this way those interpretations of Christianity with which that history chiefly began, and in which a comprehensive normative definition permitting a positive evaluation was attempted. This was done on a basis which on principle lay outside Christian faith (which is an unconditional readiness to hear the historical revelation of the Word), but

there was no intention on that account to reject Christianity outright.

2. It is possible to speak of such a history, one which in fact was influenced by heresy, from the 18th century Enlightenment onwards, though signs of it appeared in post-Tridentine scholastic theology, particularly in the *analysis fidei* and cognate themes. The non-Christian criterion and starting-point, from which the nature of Christianity was to be determined and evaluated and by which its historical manifestation was to be subjected to critical discrimination, has since that time either been human nature (either as "universally valid" or as existentially unique), or the phenomenon of religion in general as such, and the latter can ultimately be reduced to the former starting-point. At first, then, all kinds of attempts were made to interpret the essence of Christianity as the perfect representative of "natural religion" or of religion as such. In this respect it is quite immaterial in principle that with the Enlightenment it was thought possible to trace the outlines of this natural religion by pure reason, independently of "truths of fact" and of any encounter with Christianity, as the universal element which, attained by reason, can then be found in all religions, even if in differing degrees of purity, whereas with the Romantic movement and German Idealism, it was detected in the historical phenomenon of Christianity itself. In this case the "mediation" imposed by Christianity on the individual is a mere historical contingency in relation to a universal nature (of man, of religion, of the relation to the Absolute), which with equal justification can make use of other intermediaries. Similarly, the "illustrative material" may from the start be the totality of religions presented by the history and psychology of religions, among which Christianity is inserted (W. Dilthey, E. Troeltsch, G. Mensching, etc.). Finally, it makes no difference in that respect whether on the basis of an autonomously ascertained "nature", the historical manifestation of Christianity in dogma and theology, in ecclesiastical and sociological form, is given positive evaluation as the unimportant though inevitable husk of what is really in question (something chiefly inward and individual), or whether the attempt is made to disentangle the "pure essence" from its previous concrete embodiments (as in Modernism). According to the way man himself and the nature of religion in general are understood (but always as ultimately independent of the historical factual contingency of a free act of revelation by God), the nature of Christianity is differently understood: as pious inwardness (Pietism), freedom of the moral conscience before God, contemplation of the "universe" (in a special sense of the religious act as "feeling" or as "intellectual intuition"), as a sentiment of absolute dependence, as the numinous value feeling for the holy, and so on. If the "nature" of man is posited as absolutely unique and incommensurable, ever in radical solitude, freedom and responsibility, then his religion can only consist in the obedient and therefore liberating acceptance of that existence, and Christianity will have to be the "religion" in which, in contrast to the illusions of mythologically objectivating statements, man is summoned to have the courage to assume his existence in that way. And this initial position will again become the criterion, applicable only by the individual himself, of what is really meant by Christianity, that is to say, of what it must conceive itself to be. Once the ground of the authentic theology of revelation is abandoned in one of these ways, it is no longer of particular Christian or theological importance which fundamental philosophical views are preferred as the basis for the inquiry into the nature of Christianity. They may involve, for example, the question of what in principle is the relation of the

universal and the historical, and whether a permanently valid, regulative essence of the kind postulated is possible at all, and whether it is knowable, or whether anything of that kind is to be denied from the start out of historicist and relativist scepticism. It may be urged that only a knowledge of historical phenomena can be admitted, the subjective conditions of which remain entirely closed to rational justification.

3. From a really Christian standpoint such analyses are questionable for two reasons. The first is that the really concrete religion, which is still universal because founded by God, can only be known and judged by itself. There is no external standpoint from which such a judgment is possible, though there is an access from outside which does not destroy the non-derivative character of faith. But in the second place it is possible that in such an attempt to interpret Christianity from outside, the interpreter may unwittingly and unintentionally, but in fact, be judging from a standpoint which is not really external to Christianity at all. The inner life of the person who is putting forward the interpretation and evaluation itself bears the stamp of grace, of the interior light of faith and of an unconsciously Christian conception of life. Consequently he may give objective expression to more of Christianity than the standpoint explicitly adopted would of itself permit. And Christianity's own understanding of itself may find in this apparently non-Christian interpretation of its nature more that is genuinely Christian than at first sight might be expected in view of the objectively incorrect or inadequate starting-point.

C. Christianity in Relation to Other Religions

What are in question here are actual features observable from outside which make it possible to compare Christianity with other religions. The common elements which can be perceived in such a comparison only prove that Christianity can be the universal religion without losing its historical character. Precisely such a comparison, however, reveals decisive differences between Christianity and other religions, such as the successful synthesis of elements otherwise divergent, the actual convergence of tendencies of themselves historically independent into a genuine unity; a pure exemplification of the nature of religion in contrast to other religions which are always in fact in decay and which can never critically dissociate themselves on principle by an official authority from their inner decadence, though some noble individual representatives may seek reform. It is at least relatively the best actual concrete religion. This observation can be made by means of objective verifiable standards, partly *a priori*, partly derived from comparative religion and from the phenomenology of religion. Once made, it presents the possibility and the obligation of an absolute affirmation of Christianity, as soon as it is realized on the one hand that in the concrete it is only possible to live, religiously speaking, in absolute affirmation, and on the other hand that among all religions only Christianity has the courage seriously to make an absolute claim and not one that is simply justified by pointing to the universal element found in the particular religion in question.

1. Christianity regards itself as the universal religion of mankind. Not every religion and religious community does this, and therefore it is not to be taken as a matter of course. Although it spread from one particular point in history, and regards itself not as having always existed but as deriving its existence from that point, and although it has a pre-history which it acknowledges and appropriates, nevertheless it ascribed to itself from the start a universal mission. It does not view itself as a relative, particular manifestation of religion, side by side with which other

concrete forms of expression of religion are to be found, differing from region to region, culturally, ethnically or in some other mere matter of degree. It holds that it is the only valid relation of man to God, because founded by God himself for all. In contrast, other religions are to be regarded only as previous stages in sacred history, produced by God's action in historical revelation but now superseded. They were "precursors" or independent, human and of themselves empty adumbrations of the true religion, or apostasy from the possibility of that relation with God which God intends and offers by his saving action, or as effects as yet imperfectly developed, or already curtailed by men, of God's salvific will operative, because of Christ, in all men everywhere, and impelling towards tangible revelation. Christianity therefore regards absolutely every human being of whatever race and culture as called to receive its message, gifts and promises, as a "potential Christian", however much it is aware even apart from sin, the realization of this possibility demands time and conditions which are not equally present everywhere (*anima naturaliter christiana*). Christianity has never even in fact (and to a Christian this appears providential) belonged to a single closed homogeneous civilization. It arose on the frontier between East and West, so that its roots penetrate directly into almost all the earlier higher civilizations. In the course of history it has in fact become a world religion, even more patently than all other religions, which have scarcely extended beyond the civilization of their origin. Eastern Buddhism is no parallel, partly because of the ethical atheism, and partly because of the radical difference of the religious forms in which it has appeared. Moreover, Christianity spread in the course of that European history which produced the modern planetary unification of the whole of mankind into a single history. But since that unifying force did not operate without Christianity, which in fact was actively at work through missionary enterprises and did not simply spread over the globe through the spread of Western civilization, Christianity alone among religions really did make itself a world religion in fact. It is universal in time and space.

2. Christianity is a higher religion. Though it traces its presuppositions and pre-history, even as divinely effected sacred history, to the very beginnings of mankind (as appears from its notion of primitive revelation, of the universal grace of Christ and from its Old Testament), and deliberately holds fast to what belongs to ancient tradition and to what is fundamental in humanity, it is nevertheless a higher religion which includes elements which are only possible on a higher level of civilization. It therefore comprises the entire intrinsic range of human possibilities as the material in which to embody the religious factor. Consequently in regard to the future also it has a universal perspective and is in no danger of being dismissed at some point as belonging to a superseded stage of civilization.

3. Christianity is a historical, revealed religion. It is of course true that it includes valid statements about God, the world and man which in themselves and in principle are attainable by reason at any point of history. Nevertheless Christianity conceives itself essentially as a historical, revealed religion. It shares this claim of course with Judaism and Islam, so that this aspect too belongs to its "external" phenomenology, but in such a way that the three claims are not simply juxtaposed without relation; it is therefore simply a question which of the three religions can rightly claim to possess the one revelation occurrence in its entirety and without adulteration. Christianity as a historically revealed religion means that the reality which it brings, the truth it proclaims, are in the world because at quite precisely located

points of space and time the action of revelation by the living God distinct from the world occurred freely and grace-given in the prophets and in Christ. It occurred "within" the world, therefore, and not merely by means of it. It therefore demands a retrospective link between human beings who inevitably exist in history and not in the abstract, and those distinctive points, by means of Church and tradition, anamnesis and succession, so that men may fully accomplish their union with God. But this corresponds precisely to man's nature which in decisive matters has always to exist in a historical mode, for he will always have an ancestry. The claim of Christianity to be such a historical revealed religion is incompatible with a syncretist account of its origins, which in actual fact breaks down at least at the underivative immediacy of the person of Jesus and his claims. We have already pointed out the positive importance for fundamental theology of this claim to be God's historical revelation and moreover the absolute and eschatological one. Since this revelation occurrence as a factual event is not only the object of faith but also a reason for faith, which presents itself as credible to the mind of a person willing to believe, this is also a feature which belongs to the marks of Christianity which can be observed "from outside". But according to Catholic doctrine what is most central and ultimate in this revelation occurrence, despite its historical concentration in one point of space and time, can reach every human being in grace and faith, because of God's universal salvific will. Moreover, the actual concrete elements of Christianity in sacrament and word (when both are understood correctly in a Christian way) can and are intended to be the most direct and most actual encounter with God in the life of each individual. Consequently the historical character of revealed religion does not involve an anthropomorphic restriction of the God who really rules everywhere and in everything, for the very concreteness of this rule, penetrating by its universality every dimension of man, can, and wills to, comprise man's concrete historical nature. It would be an anthropomorphism to think of God as having exclusively one sole relation to a single potentiality of man (his abstract mind, his "inwardness", etc.) as "absolute", to the exclusion of others.

4. Christianity knows itself to be a dogmatic religion. Though the reality which Christianity brings is God's action in man, and transcends all definitive, exhaustive comprehension, for it is God's self-communication to what is not God, nevertheless precisely this incomprehensibility is expressed in words, and can be so stated, for all understanding of man himself is based precisely on his transcendent dynamic ordination towards the holy mystery of God. Since this statement takes place in human terms which already have a long history behind them, it is effected only in analogy, imperfectly, as a provisional stage towards the direct vision of God. For all that, it is absolute truth, because the statement is true and not false, its truth is guaranteed by the God who speaks, and it brings with it over and above the analogous conceptual statement the very reality which it signifies: the self-communication in grace of God forgiving and divinizing his creatures. And this truth has remained unchanged in the authentic Christianity of the Church despite and throughout historical change. This is itself a fact which is empirically verifiable and yet significant for the rational basis of faith. The development of dogma displays beyond human design and control an intrinsic pattern and a convergence of the various lines of development and trends which was not intended by men and manifests the operation of a transcendent power. Christianity therefore possesses a formulated doctrine as well as a teaching authority in the Church's hierarchical

leaders and this distinguishes it from religions which do not aim at doing more than producing a numinous experience by means of their rites, and from religious and philosophical interpretations of human life (and from Christian sects), which in sceptical resignation falsely hold that the Absolute impinges on human existence and disposes over a human being's whole actual concrete reality when it is simply "honoured" in mute remoteness and awe of its ineffability. Views of that kind reduce the religion of man in his whole nature to an ethereal "otherworldliness".

5. The Christian religion views itself as eschatological, that is to say, Christianity takes history and man's historical character and its own with profound seriousness. Nevertheless it considers itself to be absolute. This involves three things:

a) Despite its own origin in history, it is not a phase of a process leading to the future history of religion within the world in the course of which it may be superseded by another religion. The legitimate future of religion is its own future, because it is the last, irreplaceable and definitive religion for this world-epoch, which is itself judged and limited. That is also so because in principle it has room within it for all genuine religious creativity and for the possible dispensation of grace by the one God outside Christianity. For it is only finding itself when, through adaptation, it integrates into its abiding nature the intellectual and religious experience of mankind.

b) It regards itself as provisional and conditional, to the extent that, as the "pilgrim" Church, it is dynamically directed towards that end in which the revelation of the glory of God will definitively conclude time and history and therefore the Church as well.

c) Christianity inevitably reduces what surrounds it, i.e., the world, history, civilization and progress, to merely relative importance, for as a permanent "thorn in the flesh" to the world, it opposes any attribution of absolute value to any power of this passing world. It leaves all these things their real validity and does not merely tolerate them, for they all belong to the divinely created world, whereas Christianity is God's eternity in time and is therefore not called either absolutely to affirm the world or to negate it, but to "wait" and "hope" until God is manifest and the final yield of the transitory world is harvested. Precisely as eschatological, supernatural, revealed religion, Christianity leaves earthly realities their relative independence and is not of itself (unlike other religions) confronted with the dilemma either of administering and controlling everything or of abdicating even as a religion. The historical process of the progressive emancipation of an independent secular civilization is therefore in principle an effect of Christianity itself, not the beginning of its death, even though the realization of that independence often, but wrongly, took place at the expense of the enduring historical presence of Christianity in the world.

6. Christianity is integral (not integralist) religion. Produced by the Creator of all earthly realities, Christianity has a doctrine and a summons valid for all domains of human life, but does not on that account seek to deprive man of his own responsibility and historical nature in the perspectives which open out onto an unknown world future. It speaks equally to person and to society and with equal independence of each. Because Christianity is salvation for the individual before God in grace and personal decision, it can never be merely a cultural arrangement in the public life of society. Yet because God in his Word addresses himself to all in a historically tangible form, Christianity by the will of its founder is only wholly present in the one visible Church. This represents the full historical and tangible reality of

God's saving act in Christ for all ages and peoples. Constituted as a society, organized in offices and functions, it extends to all times and places in uninterrupted historical continuity, the Apostolic succession, the self-manifestation of God's saving action to men in its sacraments and doctrinal teaching. Comprehending all dimensions of man, Christianity is a rational religion, i.e., it can never wish to impose itself by excluding from its religious activity rational and critical self-reflection, in order to achieve immunity from such reflection (contrast fideism and modernism).

D. Dogmatic Self-Expression of Christianity "from Within"

With the proviso already made (A, 5), Christianity may be defined as the occurrence of God's free communication of himself to what is created and distinct (and in itself remote) from himself, revealing itself as such and effecting its own acceptance on the part of man. This occurrence has in Jesus Christ its ultimate ground, its highest realization and its unsurpassable historical manifestation. From the human side it may be regarded as the event in which man by faith in Christ accepts the sacred mystery, called God, as absolutely and intimately present and freely pardoning him, whereas humanly speaking that mystery entirely rules his existence as the remote ground and judge of being and spiritual consciousness.

1. In Christianity as a historical revealed religion, the infinite, personal, holy God acts in man and with man. He is utterly distinct from the world and from man as their Creator who posits what he freely creates from nothing as other than himself, in such a way that *a priori* and in every respect it is relative to and oriented towards him as the infinite mystery, but cannot determine purely by itself what its precise relation to God will be, but must remain open for God to dispose of it.

2. By grace God has freely admitted the world created by him, and in particular spiritual creatures, to a share in his own divine life. He is, therefore, not only the efficient cause of the world creating things other than himself, but freely, in grace, he communicates himself in his own being, and so reveals and manifests his own glory and innermost life (in the Trinity of persons) as the grace-given goal of spiritual creatures, angels and men. As a consequence, the ultimate meaning and goal of man in the concrete is transferred to the infinite mystery both absolute in kind and at the same time radically close and intimate. Every earthly self-development of man and every such "evolution" is surpassed and at the same time opened out towards its infinite fulfilment. Because what is involved is a true communication of God to the world, it is plain that the structure of the relation of God to his created world based on this supernatural communication is God's inner reality itself. The unoriginated who communicates himself ("Father"), the uttered "Word", who enduringly possesses the plenitude of his source ("Son"), and the loving affirmation of the unity of originating source with uttered Word in the enduring presence of the divine plenitude in the term of the procession ("Holy Spirit") form the Trinity of Persons of the one God in himself.

3. God's free and grace-given orientation of man towards his own communication of himself, which everywhere and always determines man's nature and through him, the world (the supernatural existential), is the transcendental ground and the enduring dynamism of the individual and collective history of salvation and revelation. Just as the nature of man, although the ground permanently presupposed by history, finds its accomplishment *in* history itself (and the latter is not merely

an incidental which leaves the nature itself untouched), and is given to man himself as a task *in* history, so too with the supernatural existential. That existential is never a datum for man apart from a historical concrete form (of a changing and growing kind), and these concrete forms – worship, human speech, miracles, etc. – constitute the sacred history of salvation and revelation only to the extent that they are accomplished and are understood expressly or implicitly in virtue of that *a priori* supernatural existential.

4. The history of the free acceptance or rejection by man of God's self-communication takes place in every human life which attains the exercise of its freedom. It is *per se* possible at all times and in all the changing historical situations of man. Where that history of grace by God's will and attestation becomes a *datum* consciously known, with a tangible social form, an accredited, formulated doctrine and institutional embodiment, which themselves become factors in the situation of that general history of grace, we have the history of revelation and salvation in the narrower sense. These historical, objective expressions (in doctrine, worship, religious institutions) of the supernatural existential are found tacitly and implicitly throughout the individual and collective course of history (particularly in its moral aspect), and explicitly in all religions. But they are present inextricably combined with what is purely natural to man, with erroneous conceptions of man and with morally reprehensible behaviour. Everywhere and always, however, by virtue of God's universal salvific will, the historical situation of man is such that it can enable him to work out in faith his supernatural existential, providing he does not culpably shut himself to God's transcendental self-communication.

5. To distinguish and discern history of salvation from history of perdition, history of revelation from history of religious decadence, is ultimately only possible with Christ as criterion. In that perspective, the immediate and very brief pre-history which Jesus and the apostles recognized in the "Old Testament" as legitimately their own, acquires in a special degree the character of history of revelation and salvation. It was so objectively, because it was monotheism, which interpreted its own course as a history of salvation and perdition in living partnership with God, was oriented towards the coming of the historical manifestation of *universal* salvation in the Messiah and in fact did prepare the coming of the Word of God in the flesh. It can be evaluated with discernment by the help of the Christian Scriptures if these are read in the light of Christ.

6. a) God wills to be man's fulfilment directly himself, not merely through something created. His self-communication as offered is called grace; as accepted, justification; and the actual acceptance in the concrete, faith, hope, love. It exhibits man as *capax infiniti*, as absolutely open (both ontologically and existentially), to the holy mystery which is the ground of all and itself incomprehensible and which we call God. That mystery is then in itself not only the aloof horizon and unfathomable ground of knowledge and freedom and their predicamental objects, but gives itself in its very self to the spiritual creatures.

b) This receptivity to God's own self-communication has its absolute culmination in what we call the hypostatic union, though this does not mean that we are able, even supposing the possibility of grace is known, to perceive with certainty for ourselves the possibility of this kind of divine self-giving previous to its actual occurrence. But at least it lies in the hypothetical "extension" of grace in its own line: as the actuation of the potentiality of a creature by a supervening act inserted in it, as the rendering possible of the possession of God and of the acceptance of God, by God himself as the quasi-formal principle of that very act itself. If grace is an interior, supernatural determinant of man's personal life, it provides an immanent principle for forming some idea of the Incarnation. This then appears from within, as it were, as the qualitatively unique culmination of God's self-communication. In it God's offer of himself, and its acceptance by man in virtue of this offer itself, absolutely coincide, are realized in the most radical way and at the same time are historically manifested. Consequently it is the culmination of God's communication of himself to the world, and the foundation of the whole of his self-communication and its historical manifestation, as the goal is the cause of the movement towards it.

c) Christianity acknowledges this unique perfection of divine self-communication to the creature to have occurred in Jesus Christ. It recognizes this, because man in grace is open to the expectation of that culmination, and is oriented towards it; because Jesus credibly testified to himself as exemplifying it, if by nothing else than by his awareness that he was the absolute, unsurpassable bringer of salvation, an awareness which implies that of the Incarnation; because he showed himself as the beginning of definitive salvation by the Resurrection; because in actual historical effect he met with such belief in his reality and mission that faith cannot justly be rejected as an illusion by someone who is judging on real historical grounds, i.e., who is not in the grip of a quite unhistorical rationalism.

d) This God-man by his existence, his human acceptance of it in the death of the Cross and by the divine and perfect acceptance of that acceptance (the Resurrection), is the guarantor, the ultimate purpose, the historical manifestation and the revelation, of God's salvific will in regard to the world, divinizing and forgiving; he is the mediator absolutely. When man recognizes Jesus (by explicit faith), or implicitly (by accepting in faith his own life from God's free disposition which in fact has its purpose in Christ), as the man whose existence is that of God living as man with us, and in whose life, fate, death and victory over death, God himself has shared our existence and so accepted it and given it validity, man knows that his own reality is revealed to him, interpreted and given ultimate validity.

7. The history of grace and salvation not only means the communication of God to the world and its spiritual creatures and the revelation of that communication, but an ever more radical experience of what its recipient is, not only the recipient of God's freely bestowed communication of himself (grace as supernatural gift), but one who by his own sin is positively unworthy of the gift. He is the sinner who himself produces alienation from God in condemnation, affirms it as definitive, and in this attitude wills death as the earthly manifestation of his sin. In the unconditionally radical quality of his salvific will, God in view of Christ has both permitted the mystery of sin as the creature's refusal, irretrievable by the creature itself, and at the same time encompassed it in his mercy in Christ and repaired it. Of himself man would be lost, if God – of himself without repentance, and absolute – in the sharing in the death of the sinner by the sinless Mediator obedient to the death of the Cross, did not offer his grace as forgiveness of guilt and in it the actual free acceptance of the offer.

8. Christ willed the foundation of a visible, socially organized embodiment of the fellowship of those who are redeemed in Christ and share in the divine life and who publicly profess themselves to be such. This is the Church. With an organic structure, led by its hierarchy, it is the definitive eschatological manifestation of God's grace, "without repentance", and preserves Christ's truth in this infallible proclamation of the faith,

transmits his grace efficaciously in visible and tangible form in the sacraments. It continues the worship of its founder in the sacrifice of the Mass, in which he is present in holy anamnesis, binding the Church into unity, with the power of his redemptive act and in the anticipation of the fulfilment. It rules its members through its precepts, instructions and the charismata bestowed by the Spirit along the way of salvation. The Church is the mystical body of Christ.

9. Christianity views every individual human being as a corporeal spirit of absolute dignity who, in intellectual knowledge and free choice, in his one life on earth within Christ's domain, makes an irrevocable decision for or against God (explicitly known as such or unnamed but implied), and so involves his salvation or final loss. The content of this action that constitutes his life is supplied and regulated by the three theological virtues of faith, hope and charity, which also include the fulfilment of the natural moral law and the positive commandments of God which are implied in the foundation of the Church, its authority and sacraments.

10. The Church and with it the world in its history, in individuals and as a unity, is on pilgrimage towards God's final revelation. In this, God's self-communication, which in a hidden way is the ground of the creation and of history, will be made manifest. God, no longer mediated by human signs that conceal him, will give himself to his creatures unveiled and face to face, and God, himself all in all, will have what is created and other than himself, spirit and world, in bliss with himself.

E. On the History of Christianity

1. *Principles.* a) As a historical revealed religion, Christianity is not only historical, but is aware of its own history and historical character. This knowledge belongs to its nature, in anamnesis directed towards its beginning and in expectation looking forward to its end, which is to be the complete revelation of the beginning, the second coming of Christ. It is therefore itself essentially a theology of history, possessing a theology of its own history and preserving in the history of the Church its own past as the permanently binding basis of its present.

b) As a consequence the fundamental aspects of its own historical view of itself are themselves data of revelation. The historical Word of God intrinsically includes the concrete perspectives which interpret the history of the hearing it obtains, and the provision of its own understanding is itself a historical process. The history of revelation known in this way, and Church history, are therefore not homogeneous portions of the universal history of religions, but a theological branch of study indispensable to the Church's actual understanding of itself. The Church is Christianity in its entirety, historically existing, on pilgrimage in faith, and presents a lasting and perpetually changing enigma in its own concrete form and that of its historical situation determined by the mutual relation of what ought to be (deriving from God), and what, through human guilt, is merely what "must" be. Precisely on account of this historical character and despite the fact, essential to its nature, that its gaze is turned towards the ultimate fulfilment, the Church in principle cannot derive any practical temporal prognosis regarding its future from its historical self-awareness. On the contrary, the interpretation, in faith and hope, of its situation at any moment in terms of God's victory (which cannot be deduced from the situation in question), is an essential feature of the Church and its historical situation, which the Church masters through its genuine faith that God alone is the master of history.

c) The following factors present fundamental aspects of the history of Christianity. That history is ultimately the history of the word of God, which creates for itself and for its own history, both in advance and subsequently, the appropriate environment in nature and world history; with the Christ-event the eschatological phase of this whole history has even now begun (cf. C, 5); in it God intervenes repeatedly as ever present and forgiving, despite what "must" be in human contradiction and failure, because the Church is both the invincible Church, even in its historical concrete form, because it is the sign of the victory of God's grace over man's obstinacy, as well as the Church of sinners, which cannot but involve miscalculation and failure. The Church is necessarily in distress. Where it is not, it is not as it should be. This is so because despite and transcending its sinfulness, it must always share in the life of the Logos, the life of Jesus, which the Church continues to live. The Church in its history as a whole clearly bears the mark, for any person who regards it with the free assent of the grace of faith, of its having been effected by God's saving action (*D* 1794). Nevertheless, within that history the individual and his action taken in themselves are ambiguous, and only the further history of the Church will reveal to some degree, and the "day of Christ" plainly, whether the individual was a positive factor in the whole history under God's guidance or a factor in man's resistance in spite of which God remains victorious.

2. *Aspects and divisions of this history.* There can, of course, be no question here of presenting this history itself; at most a few indications of its content can be given and a division into phases for which some theological basis can be provided.

a) This history is a history of what is "subjective" and enduring. Christianity is not merely a phenomenon belonging to external history and civilization, so that a description of the development and structure of its spatio-temporal and factual objective expressions would itself be a statement about Christianity itself. Christianity by its very nature is the interior life of the human being endowed with grace from God with God as his end, though indeed this interior life provides for the believer, in its manifestations, an unambiguous motive for faith, and hence for theological Church history. For that reason the history of dogma, for example, belongs to this history, for it is the history of faith interpreted in faith, and is therefore a summons and a binding criterion of life in faith. The same is true of the lives of the saints, of the history of charismata and miracles in the Church. This is the appropriate place for the "history of souls", of the complete redemption of Christian persons, each of them unique, to the extent that such history is possible by reason of the faith of the Church (in canonizations); it is the perpetual story of conversion, martyrdom, the evangelical counsels, of service to the poor, perseverance in resisting the idolatry of the world, and so on. That history takes precedence of the other kind which can describe on a natural basis the development of the social organization and cultural achievements of the Church, its relation to the State, to civilization and to the community of nations. Though accounts of sources and history of development are of no avail in the former, the more important kind of history, the perpetually renewed contemplation in every age of the fact that God was present. is in the most eminent Christian sense historiography, for the apparently identical in this case is a free historical act of the God whose gifts are without repentance for the Church.

b) Christianity as the historical and yet universal religion of all nations is only fully itself when it is in actual fact the universal Church, i.e., when it has a tangible and historical reality among all nations and civilizations. Because it starts from a point located historically in time and space, the entire first phase of the achievement of this world-wide mode forms its first great period. The second period, the concrete form of which is not yet clear, that of global Christianity in a globally united (not necessarily peacefully reconciled) history of humanity, is only now beginning. The first period is usually and rightly taken (even from the theological point of view) as falling into the following phases: i) the foundation of the Church (age of the generation of the apostles; the primitive Church); ii) the assimilation of the cultural and political environment of that Church, an environment which also constituted the pre-history of the future West (i.e., the Church in the world of Graeco-Roman civilization in its first hostile encounter – until Constantine – and then in positive relationship with the Empire, the Constantinian era); iii) preparation of a world-wide mission by the Church through the formation of the West as the cause of the one unified history of mankind as it has now become (Church of the Middle Ages); iv) transition from what was in fact the regional Church of the West to the world-wide Church (from the beginning of "modern times" down to the present day).

This assimilation (by content and by regions) of the surrounding world in which and for which the Church has to develop its own proper mission is, however, also a period of growing detachment in which Christianity becomes more and more conscious of its "ontological difference" from its environment, though of course it always knew of it. Ultimately it is Christianity which separates itself in order to be able genuinely to take its environment for granted as fully developed; it is not really forced out of the world by the latter's growth. In this reverse movement, perhaps two great phases can be distinguished, first the Church of the Empire which, viewed theologically, extends from Constantine at least to the Investiture Dispute, a period in which the Church, viewed from outside, though remaining an independent entity, lived as it were in the bosom of political society, and second, the phase of polar opposition between a consciously Christian *imperium* and a *sacerdotium* which, relative to the narrow field involved, was very strongly committed in the secular sphere. This phase ended to all intents and purposes with the French Revolution, but its influence has still been operative down to the present day both in the Catholic Church and among Protestants. It is not easy to say what the new period whose arrival we can foresee will look like. The whole of this first period falls from another point of view into two phases. In both it is again a question of the achievement of full consciousness of the nature of Christianity in the immanence of subjectivity (cf. B, 1, 2). There was first the phase of conceptual development and articulation of the faith in its objective reality (patristic and medieval theology and piety); and second the phase of subjective reflection since the beginning of modern times, the Renaissance and classical humanism and the Reformation (separate rational apologetics; formation of a critical historical self-awareness in biblical criticism and history of dogma; *analysis fidei*; discovery of what is Christian outside Christianity as a social organization; inquiry into the essence of Christianity, etc.). This second phase seems still to have unaccomplished tasks ahead. As the rhythm of history cannot be synchronic in all its dimensions, the variety of these divisions is not surprising. They can, however, be co-ordinated without difficulty. This beginning of the history of Christianity (which came on the scene quite late, at the end of an almost inconceivably long and almost static history of mankind, perhaps extending over a million years), must nevertheless be the attainment of full self-awareness of the history of salvation of mankind as a whole, for this also belongs to the nature of what is both a historical and yet the universal religion. Consequently the pre-history of Christianity must comprise all history back to its very origins, even if this for technical reasons is omitted in practice in the writing of Church history. Since the history of Christianity is the history of the dialogue between God and man, it has its own centre and real beginning (as opposed to its pre-history) in the absolute and enduring intimacy of the dialogue between God and humanity in Jesus Christ, in whom word and answer of that dialogue are one person. On the other hand, since the dialogue takes place, as human dialogue, by affirmation and denial, it always involves the other partner outside (mankind called by God) and the refusal and failure within (Christians themselves). In this connection it is to be noted that the Church's own genuine theological and historical conception of itself as the society which must understand itself on the basis of the promised future, must be formed on the basis of that future. Theological Church history must look into the future in order to be able correctly to perceive the past. Otherwise it inevitably becomes simply a part of the general history of the world and of religions.

Karl Rahner

II. Absoluteness of Christianity

A. Notion and Problem

The notion of the absoluteness of Christianity derives from the philosophy of German Idealism, not from theology itself. From the outset, therefore, theology must beware lest an inappropriate attitude should be thrust upon it from without. Christianity is based on a historical revelation and therefore implies history and historicity, which cannot simply be disposed of by speculating about the Absolute. On the other hand the attempt of Ernst Troeltsch to establish the absolute character of Christianity by proofs drawn from comparative religion was doomed from the start. All that could be shown in such a way was that the world's religions converge to some extent upon Christianity; and that approach, by reducing Christianity to the level of historical phenomena – that is, to the relative – necessarily emptied Christianity's absolute claim of all real content. Dialectical theology (Karl Barth), therefore, chose a third approach. God in his otherness was so remote from history that Christianity, far from fulfilling human religion and culture, judged and abrogated both.

Catholic theologians as a rule take the absoluteness of Christianity to mean that Christianity is not only *de facto* the noblest of all living religions but is God's one ultimate self-disclosure, completely valid for all men in whatever age they may be living, essentially definitive, never to be superseded. A great many modern people consider this claim not only insufferably offensive but inconsistent with the known facts of comparative religion as well as with the fundamental historicity of all things human. It strikes them as unloving and intolerant, as a rupture of communication and a source of fanaticism. Moreover, it seems plainly contradicted by the sinfulness of Christian history. Finally, it seems to belittle all human efforts at progress and to make any theology of earthly things impossible. A purely apologetical or dogmatic response to these objections serves little purpose; what we must do is to consider with more care than before what we really mean, and then point out that the absolute claim is not advanced on behalf of a particular religious body but on behalf of the gospel of grace; its necessity for all men is what we affirm.

B. Theological Argument

If we are to see clearly in this matter we must remember that the absolute claim of Christianity is a strictly theological proposition, which consequently cannot be established by evidence drawn from either comparative religion or the philosophy of religion. Neither, of course, can faith simply contradict facts that have been verified by human reason. Instead, faith recognizes such facts, but interprets them anew in its own light.

What the absolute claim of Christianity means in theological terms is that Christianity is an eschatological religion. The kerygma of Scripture declares as much when it says that with Christ's coming the fullness of time has come (Mk 1:15; Gal 4:4; Eph 1:16, and *passim*); Christianity must be something absolute because we believe that Jesus is the Χριστός (Messiah), the Lord, the Son of God, the only Mediator between God and men (1 Tim 2:5). He fulfils the promises of salvation made to the people of the Old Covenant and to all mankind (Gen 3:15; 8:21f.; 9:1f.; 12:3; 2 Cor 1:19f.). By hypostatically assuming a concrete human nature, God has uttered himself, and communicated himself to his creation, once for all in a way that can never be superseded, and this act of God's is also the one supreme and incalculable fulfilment of man. For it is not a neutral openness that fulfils our nature but only free adherence to the absolute mystery of human existence. Thus the event of Christ and faith in him, far from doing violence to man, perfect him at every level.

The absolute character of Christianity means an absolute acceptance and affirmation of man and the world because in Christ God has absolutely and irrevocably assumed a concrete human nature, yet in such a way as to preserve its native character intact and unalloyed (*D* 302). The absoluteness of Christianity is less a claim than the "good news" that the world is not ultimately hollow and worthless, or absurd and insane, because God has accepted it, because he cherishes it with the absolute love of which only God is capable (Jn 3:16).

C. Evolution of the Claim

If we consider the eschatological character of Christianity, we shall find that it offers six insights into our problem:

1. Fullness and fulfilment, in theology, are dialectical notions. On the one hand fulfilment realizes and seals a promise. In this sense Christianity is less an exclusive than an inclusive religion; instead of repudiating other religions and other efforts to discover truth it embraces them, and therefore its very nature disposes it to dialogue with the religions of the world and with philosophy. On the other hand Christ the fulfilment of the law is also its end (Rom 10:4); he fulfils the law by annulling it (Eph 2:15; Col 2:14); because fulfilment here is the wonderful doing of God, it is something creatively and incalculably new. Thus Christianity must always seem a paradox in this world; it can never renounce its character of "scandal". It must both affirm and negate, fulfil the religions and culture of mankind and sit in judgment on them.

2. In the biblical view, the fullness of time comes about in the concrete where the proclamation of it summons it forth, makes it present and bestows it. Word and sacrament make the unique event an event for all times. Only when a concrete individual, or religion, or culture, hears Christianity preached – which is essentially more than an audible phenomenon –, when the absolute claim is perceived as such and not misunderstood (as colonialism, for example, or cultural imperialism, or camouflage for vested interests, or as a historical curiosity), only then will the fullness of time have come upon that man, or religion, or culture. Accordingly it is clear that in fact a great many people even today are still living in a pre-Christian era.

3. Eschatological fulfilment hovers between what has already happened

and what is yet to come. Our present situation as Christians is governed by a conflict between saving history and secular history, the Church and the world, nature and grace, creation and the covenant, the law and the gospel. Only at the end will "God be everything to everyone" (1 Cor 15:28). The absolute claim of Christianity, therefore, is not a claim advanced on behalf of Christendom and the Church. The Church too has its eschatological judgment to undergo (Mt 19:28). A certain *intégrisme* that would do away with this dualism, in effect denying the relative autonomy of the world and its structures, clashes with this situation of the Church in history, where it can never be *ecclesia gloriae*. Error, indeed, has not the same objective rights as truth; but given the continuance in history of this aeon, the time of error persists until the eschatological harvest (Mt 13:30). Thus Christianity's absolute claim, rightly understood, is not only quite consistent with freedom of conscience and religion but forbids the use of any kind of coercion in the service of the gospel.

4. For our sake Jesus Christ assumed our concrete human nature – subject as it is to the consequences of sin – even unto death on the cross, thus redeeming it once for all. Christ's vicarious obedience drew together in his person the unique and the universal. Being a Christian is imitating this representative obedience, sharing in it. What really shows the absolute character of Christianity, then, is this representation in faith, hope, and love that unites the particular with the universal. The Church's mission, which is rooted in the absolute claim of Christianity, is not so much to save the individual – who in principle can be saved outside its visible communion – as to represent and proclaim the love of God, to give testimony to hope, and so to be a sign among the nations (*D* 3014). What Christianity affirms, with its absolute claim, is not its dominion but its vicarious service of all mankind.

5. The eschatological character and absolute claim of Christianity, however, do not make genuine historicity impossible for the Church; quite the contrary. As has been observed, if Christianity is something absolute, the Church is not. Like the individual Christian, the Church too must grow until it attains the full measure of Christ (Eph 4:13; Col 2:2). For the Church as it actually exists, the fullness of Christ is always both a gift and a goal. It has yet to be guided by the Spirit of Christ to all truth (Jn 14:26; 16:13). The gospel is not perfectible, but the Church's love and its understanding of the faith are. That is why a genuine development of theology and of dogma can exist. The historicity of the Church is also evident from the fact that in this aeon its grasp of faith and dogma always remains "imperfect" (1 Cor 13:9) and that it always remains a sinful Church on pilgrimage.

6. For the same reasons Christianity as an eschatological and absolute religion does not deny but rather affirms the theological significance of human progress. True though it be that the last day is known to the Father alone (Mk 13:32), we need not think of it as bursting upon us like a *deus ex machina*. God's revelation is always uttered in human language and through human organs. Consequently, it is theologically possible to suppose that just as the whole Graeco-Roman culture of Christ's day (what Karl Jaspers calls the pivotal period) was a *praeparatio evangelica*, so the powerful modern trend towards the amalgamation of mankind in the fields of technology, economics, and science may be paving the way, under God, for a response of all the human race to the increasingly actual universality of the Christian religion which technical advances will have made possible. Not that we are preaching a foolish optimism and naively assume all secular progress

to be the equivalent of religious progress. Secular progress, we must realize, makes it possible for mankind to react to the gospel either with a collective Yes or a collective No. When we say, then, that Christianity is an absolute religion, we mean that grace has been absolutely promised to all, and that it demands of all an absolute decision.

Walter Kasper

CHURCH

I. History of Ecclesiology

A. From the Fathers to the Middle Ages

The Fathers and the theologians of the Middle Ages never composed a treatise on the Church. This is a consequence of the nature of both revelation and of dogmatic development. Prior to its appearance as a subject of teaching, the reality of the Church is presupposed in the proclamation of the gospel and cannot be separated from the whole dogmatic structure of which it forms the existential foundation. Because of this, the experience of the Church regenerated by the Spirit (given as a gift of the Father by the risen Son) conditions the whole of Christian reflection. The Church is built upon the "foundation of the apostles and prophets" (with a special role for Peter) and gathers together in Christ all his disciples. It must be understood in the light of the whole of revelation, and especially of the life and work of Christ which are once more called to mind by the Holy Spirit who makes of the community of believers the dwelling-place of a completely new existence and the sign of the accomplishment of God's plan for the world.

As early as the time of the Apologists, the Church was presented to the world as the proclamation and the presence of the salvation brought by Jesus Christ. In it the new life in the Spirit is imparted, and the apostolic faith is preserved in its memory. As the effective sign of the resurrection of Christ, the Church sees its relationship with God as the principle of salvation through the sending of his Son and as the goal of salvation through the gift of the Spirit. Its position in relation to the Jews and pagans was clarified by its proclamation that in the Spirit it had the power of interpreting the Scriptures in a Christological sense and could communicate the Spirit to all men. The whole of Catholic dogma takes its rise from reflection on the salvation communicated by the Spirit in the Church. To defend its own mystery the Church explicitated its faith: ecclesiology is thus a presupposition of formal Christology and the theology of the Trinity. Starting from the experience of the Church's life, patristic theology paid close attention to the history of salvation as based on the dynamic presence of the Word through the signs of his humanity, and recognized the movement of the economy of salvation which proceeds from the Father through Christ to the Church. The Church sprang from the preaching of the Word, which is achieved in the sacraments, especially the Eucharist and, as the primordial Sacrament of *divinisatio*, was seen as fellowship of those called to Wisdom in the Spirit whilst awaiting the manifestation of glory. The Church came into view, like the Incarnation and Pentecost, as the unfolding of the paschal mystery. It was seen to be constituted by the sacraments (points of contact with the death and resurrection of Christ and conductors of the power of the Spirit), and because of this it empowered the human race to pass from its fragmentary existence into the unity of Jesus Christ in God. Since it was the human race itself insofar as it must eventually come to Christ and be vivified by his Spirit, the Church was no stranger to the life of the world. It is the human race existing in Christ and already saved in hope.

For the Fathers the whole of Scripture spoke of Christ and the Church: they saw it through the imagery of the Bible (people, body, temple, house, spouse, flock, vineyard, kingdom, field, and net) and the typological interpretation of the OT. Because they were conscious of the eternal and eschatological reality of salvation already present and active in the local Churches, the Fathers insisted upon: a) the Holy Spirit and the Eucharist; b) the spiritual maternity of the whole Church through faith, love, prayer, penance and witness; c) charity, peace and concord between the local Churches; d) the collegiality of the episcopate; e) the Pope as the guardian of the charity of the universal Church. Several important ecclesiological ideas emerge: apostolicity and the apostolic succession (Irenaeus); the episcopate (Cyprian); catholicity, the validity of sacramental acts independently of the personal holiness of the minister, the sacramental character (Augustine), etc. And again as early as the 3rd to the 5th centuries the Popes asserted their role as bishop of the Church and their prerogatives of magisterium and jurisdiction (cf. Leo the Great, d. 461).

The theologians of the Middle Ages remained faithful to the vision of the Fathers which was centred on the history of salvation and the Eucharist. St. Thomas treats of the Church within the mystery of Christ. The Church is participation in the mystery of the Trinity, bringing about in us the image of God through the Incarnation and the Resurrection, in the Spirit. Using the theory of the instrumental causality of the humanity of Christ, St. Thomas developed a theology of Christ as Head and of the Church as Body of Christ. In this way ecclesiology was always envisaged in a theological and christological perspective against the background of Easter and the eschaton. Though the primary conception of the Church in the minds of the theologians of the Middle Ages was that of a spiritual society of communion with God in Christ, vivified by the Spirit, a *congregatio fidelium*, they did not ignore the visible institution, the actual shape taken by this spiritual society, its sacraments and its ministry. But various indications, such as the formation of the treatises on the sacraments and the priesthood show that the need was felt for a more exact analysis of the channels of grace. This whole patristic and theological conception signified for ecclesiology the primacy of the Spirit and of the ontology of grace. The Church proceeds from the eternal plan of the Father, from the mission of the Son and of the Holy Spirit and is meant for the whole of the human race.

B. The Formation of the Treatise on the Church

Because the Church was for them salvation itself and because the universal Church appeared to them as a communion of local Churches, the Fathers placed comparatively little emphasis on its structure as a universal body. This was certainly not ignored: the Second Council of Nicaea (787) declared that an ecumenical council could not be assembled without the consent of the Pope and evidence from the East leaves no doubt as to the impossibility of legislating in ecclesiastical matters without the agreement of the Pope.

But the Gregorian reform, which was bound up with the critical struggle for freedom between the Church and the world, and also with the breach with the East, brought out the fact that the universal Church is divinely endowed with a supreme ecumenical authority. The Church depends immediately not only on charity, but on the authority and sacred power of the Church of Rome. It is united to the successors of St. Peter and its first rule is to be "unius sententiae cum Apostolico" (John VIII to his legates – Mansi, XVII, p. 469).

The Church of Rome represents in a way the whole Church. It is the *ecclesia universalis, ecclesia mater, fons, origo, cardo, fundamentum*, and the Pope is the *vicarius Christi*. Here we have dogmatic teaching on the constitution of the Church as a society under the monarchical rule of the successor of Peter and founded on the *soliditas* of the *princeps apostolorum*. The first treatises on the Church, which were entitled *De Ecclesia Catholica Romana, De Primatu Romanae Ecclesiae*, bear witness to this.

Favoured by the canon law which was worked out to serve the papal authority and so promote the liberation of the Church from lay control and its independence in regard to the secular power, even that of the Emperor, there emerged, at least in germ, the conception of the Church as a *societas perfecta:* this meant that the unity of the Church was now conceived as being like that of a city or a kingdom, and in this way juridical and sociological categories were introduced into ecclesiological thought. Its main principles having originated in the ideas which dominated the Gregorian reform, the treatise on the Church gradually took shape under the pressure of two series of events which directly affected one another: a) the struggle between the Church and the political powers (starting with Philip the Fair and reaching its climax in the 19th and 20th centuries) forcing the Church to define itself as a free agent; b) the critical questionings of the whole charter of the Church and of the way in which man is related to God. The spiritualistic and dualistic heresies of the 12th century, those of the Waldenses, the Albigenses and the Poor Men of Lyons attacked the Church for its worldly interests and political power, and questioned the mediation of the Church in the most radical fashion. (The theme of the Pope as Antichrist dates from the 12th century; the rejection of the hierarchical priesthood by the Waldenses was given its most extreme form at the Reformation and then later in rationalism.)

In his *Adversus Catharos et Valdenses*, Moneta of Cremona was the first to show the impossibility of discussing the Church while abstracting from the concrete forms of its existence on this earth. The study of the actual economy of divine grace was the beginning of a development which with Canisius and Bellarmine was to lead to the inclusion in the definition of the Church of its Roman character. The treatises on the sacraments and the priesthood had already taken shape by the 12th century, but it was the rise of Gallicanism (the struggle between Philip the Fair and Boniface VIII, and then between John XXII and the protégés of Philip the Bavarian) which led to the writing of the first treatises on the Church, which were really treatises about the *potestas papalis*, the authority and rights of the Church: the *De Regimine Christiano* of James of Viterbo (1301–1302), called "the oldest treatise on the Church"; the *De Ecclesiastica Potestate* of Giles of Rome; the *De Potestate Regia et Papali* of John of Paris and finally the *De Potestate Papae* directed against the claims of the lower clergy.

The denial of the absolute character of the ecclesiastical and social fabric of Christianity by the extreme spiritualistic teaching of Huss and Wycliffe, based on a distorted interpretation of the Augustinian themes of the *ecclesia praedestinatorum, electorum* or *sanctorum* and of grace, attenuated the necessity of belonging to the visible and historical body of the Church and showed the need for a better analysis of what ecclesiastical life meant for membership of the Body of Christ. The development of conciliarist ideas, interpreting the definition of the Church as a *congregatio fidelium* from the viewpoint of individualistic and representative theories about the Church, prompted John of Turrecramata (*Summa de Ecclesia*, 1436) and John of Ragusa to compose their great works. These were the first *systematic* treatises on the Church, with a pronounced emphasis on the notions of kingdom and power. The year 1440 was a sort of solstice (M. Ourliac), a turning point in the history of ecclesiological thought.

The Reformers questioned the whole system of ecclesial mediation (the primacy of the Pope, the powers of bishops and priests, the authority of tradition, the magisterium, the priesthood and the sacraments). This led theologians to concentrate in the definition of the Church on its juridical and visible reality and to give less prominence to the reality of grace. With Bellarmine the juridical power of the Pope enters into the definition of the Church, as does the magisterium into that of tradition. But there is no longer any mention of the relation of the Eucharist to the Church. Jansenism led to a further accentuation of the power and rights of the Roman Pontiff; Febronianism and secularism necessitated the development of the idea of the Church as a perfect society fully equipped with rights and resources, with a hierarchy and powers of jurisdiction, legislation and administration. Liberal Protestantism and Modernism obliged the theologians to insist on Christ's foundation of a visible "society", hierarchically organized and juridically instituted.

Of the notion of the mystical body there remained above all the external and socially organized aspect of the Church. Compared with the patristic and medieval tradition this was a theologically impoverished treatise, for *De Ecclesia* had become for all practical purposes an appendix to the commentary on the *Summa Theologica*, II, IIae, q. 1, a. 10, that is, to the question of the magisterium. The pneumatological aspects, the life of the faithful, the Eucharist and the communion between the local Churches were passed over practically in silence.

C. Theological Progress

In the 19th century, after the upheavals of the 18th century and the French Revolution, along with a movement for renewal which was centred on authority and which was to lead to the First Vatican Council, there developed a movement for the restoration of ecclesiology through a return to the patristic and medieval sources. It originated with the Tübingen school (Sailer, Drey, Möhler, Kuhn) which brought out once again the notion of the Body of Christ animated by the Spirit, in the perspective of a "kingdom of God" theology. The Church was not primarily a visible and hierarchical society endowed with a magisterium, but an organic fellowship with Christ. In spite of the influence of Romanticism, their ideas of "the people" and "organic life", the Church in all its fullness, became once more the object of theology. Through the efforts of Passaglia, who was much influenced by these ideas, and of his disciples, Franzelin and Schrader, the theology of the mystical body found new vigour. It was introduced into the first schema of *De Ecclesia* at Vatican I, but to most of the Fathers it appeared too romantic a notion. Following Franzelin, M. J. Scheeben developed a theology whose inspiration was basically sacramental, and which sought to bring together the aspects of authority and of the organic and vital. The result of these efforts was that the theology of the mystical body was taken up by the encyclical of Leo XIII, *Satis Cognitum*, which depicted the Church from the viewpoint of the saving action of God and Christ. It was to come to full flower in the theological renewal of post-war years. The Church appeared as essentially the *congregatio fidelium*, the Body of Christ, completely permeated by the divine life which issues from the Trinity.

The encyclical *Mystici Corporis*, which saw in the Church – with Christ as its Head, constituting it in existence, sustaining and ruling it – a social, visible and living reality whose ultimate principle of action is the Holy Spirit, gave the stamp of official approval to this fundamental rediscovery of the vision of the Church. From then on theological studies developed in complementary directions: the Church as sacrament, the Church as fellowship, the Church as mystery. And this development of ecclesiology took place under the combined influence of the biblical and liturgical revivals, the ecumenical movement, lay action, the mission, a new understanding of development (J. H. Newman) and of the historical nature of the Church. All this led to the restoration of the notion of the "People of God", the realization of the dynamic nature of missionary activity, eschatological tension, a new understanding of the community as a fellowship, collegiality, etc. Through the work of contemporary theologians a synthesis of ecclesiological thought is being formed, which is totally centred on the mystery of Christ and totally open to the world. Vatican II came to crown this great ecclesiological renewal and to re-establish the links with the broad stream of patristic and theological tradition. The time is now ripe for the construction of a harmonious synthesis of ecclesiological thought.

Marie-Joseph le Guillou

II. Ecclesiology

A. The Teaching of the Church

If in the future Vatican II will stand as a synthesis of the teaching of the magisterium on the Church, three important documents should not be forgotten: *Pastor Aeternus* of Vatican I; *Satis Cognitum* (Leo XIII); *Mystici Corporis* (Pius XII). Formerly the declarations of the magisterium dealt only with particular points. An explanation of the teaching of the Church on "outside the Church no salvation" was given by the Holy Office in 1949 (*DS* 3869–80). The primacy of the Pope was asserted at the Councils of Lyons (*D* 466) and Florence (*D* 694), and Vatican I confirmed his universal jurisdiction and doctrinal infallibility. The ecclesiological heresies which over-spiritualized the Church were rejected at Constance (*D* 627ff.); conciliarism was condemned (*D* 740) and the hierarchical structure of the Church vindicated (*D* 666) at the Council of Trent. In papal documents from the time of Pius IX and Leo XIII to the present day we find a detailed examination of the relations of the Church with the State, culture, etc.

B. The Place of Ecclesiology

Under the guidance of the magisterium and in particular of the teaching of Vatican II, the development of ecclesiology today is marked by a return to the sources: Scripture, patristics, liturgy, tradition and the life of the Church (consciousness of the pastoral situation, the sense of mission, relations with the world). Ecclesiology endeavours to combine the different elements which go to make up the mystery of the Church in a living unity whose intelligibility stems from the mystery of God as he has revealed himself. In this way it brings out very clearly the relation of the mysteries between themselves, as was recommended by the First Vatican Council.

As a specifically theological treatise standing in its own right, ecclesiology, being essentially dependent on trinitarian theology, Christology, Mariology and anthropology, appears as a synthesis of the other treatises. But this was not always so. For a very long time ecclesiology had no special place: it was often developed as a mere appendix to Christology or in one or other of the treatises because of its connections with them. Above all it became the object of fundamental theology and apologetics.

Fundamental theology considers the

Church as the foundation and necessary condition of theology and of the disciplines which depend upon it, and it analyses its significance as *ministra obiecti*, as the permanent mediator of revelation and the subject of faith (the connection between faith and the Church appears clearly in the sacrament of baptism). It shows the credibility of the Church in its role of transmitting revelation by an analysis of the different forms this transmission takes (mediation, ministry, witness, mission), so as to prove the continuity of the Catholic Church with the Church of the early centuries. This involves a detailed examination of the relation between revelation, Scripture and the Church to show in what sense the Church is the normative interpreter of revelation. Fundamental theology also studies the foundation of the Church by Jesus Christ and its identification with the Roman Church, concentrating on the Church as an institution, and characteristics which are externally verifiable and intelligible. Finally, it treats of the Church as a sign recognizable from the outside by every man. The *admirabilis propagatio*, the *eximia sanctitas*, the *inexhausta in omnibus bonis fecunditas* are, according to Vatican I, the irrefutable signs of the mission of the Church and motives of credibility in regard to the Church itself and the revelation it transmits. Taking into account its objective validity, which in principle always remains the same, this type of apologetic must be adapted to the needs of the contemporary mind.

Strictly theological ecclesiology always presupposes a theology of revelation and of the word of God, and its starting point must always be the growing consciousness that the Church, in faith, has of itself (Vatican II: discourse of John XXIII at the opening of the first session; discourse of Paul VI at the opening of the second session; *Ecclesiam Suam*). Besides the development and the actual historical forms of the Church, this consciousness also necessarily includes the facts of revelation.

C. The Theology of the Church

The Church is first of all a concrete and tangible reality whose meaning is revealed only to the eyes of faith. "The mystery of the Church is not just an object of theological knowledge, it must be a reality lived by the faithful soul, who has, as it were, a connatural experience of it, even before he has a clear idea of it." (*Ecclesiam Suam*.)

The word of God helps us to understand the Church through a multiplicity of concepts and images. After a period which concentrated too much on concepts, Vatican II restored the biblical imagery through which the mystery of the Church was first revealed: body, spouse, temple, city, vineyard, house, flock; all these words, as Y. Congar has remarked, express collective realities whose gradual realization – in which all are concerned, but some with a special position and responsibility – is part of a great design.

We shall now see what concepts and images should form the basis for a treatise on the Church by a critical analysis of each.

1. *The Church as mystery and sacrament of salvation*. In Eph 3:4 the Church is seen as the "mystery of Christ", because in it is realized the eternal plan of the Father, inaugurating on the cross the union of humanity, Jews and Gentiles, in the Church, and leading it to the consummation where "God will be everything to everyone" (1 Cor 15:28). The word "mystery" comes from Jewish apocalyptic (Dan 2:18f.), and now means the act whereby God manifests his love in the wisdom incarnate of Jesus Christ, to bring mankind to glory. It is the word of God as the fullness of revelation and it is the accomplishment of the "secret" hidden for ages in God (Col 1:16; Eph 3:3–9; 1 Cor 2:6–10). Hence the mystery implies that the saving incarnation takes effect in the

Church through the preaching of the word and through the sacraments, thus leading it to the glory of heaven. The redemption of Christ calls the Church into being (Eph 2:13–16; 5:25ff.; Col 1:20–22) and there achieves its fulfilment, as all mankind is assembled in the Church.

Hence ecclesiology is to be conceived in terms of the mission of the Son and the Holy Spirit (*Lumen Gentium*, art. 14; *Ad Gentes*, arts. 2–5). The idea of the Church as sacrament takes on its full meaning within the trinitarian perspective in which God's plan is revealed: "The Church is in Christ the sacrament or sacramental sign of intimate union with God and of unity for the whole human race." (*Lumen Gentium*, art. 1.) Or even more explicitly, in a line of thought which stresses the place of the Resurrection and the Holy Spirit in the constitution of the Church: "Lifted up from the earth, Christ draws all men to himself (cf. Jn 12:32); risen from the dead, he has sent his life-giving Spirit upon the disciples; through the Spirit he has established his body, which is the Church, as *the universal sacrament of salvation*; sitting at the right hand of the Father, he is at work in the world without ceasing, to bring men to the Church, to join them more closely to himself through her." (*Ibid.*, art. 48; see also *Ad Gentes*, arts. 2–5; *Gaudium et Spes*, art. 45; Constitution on the Liturgy.)

As the dwelling place of the Christian sacraments or the "sacrament of sacraments" (τελετῶν τελετή, Pseudo-Dionysius, *Hier. Ec.*, III; see *PG* III, 424c), the Church is the sacrament of Jesus Christ, just as Jesus Christ himself in his humanity is the sacrament of God, according to the words of Augustine: "Non est enim aliud Dei mysterium, nisi Christus" (*PL*, XXXVIII, 845). So to define the Church as sacrament is to see it in the context of the mystery which binds it closely to Christ and to return to the fundamental, generic meaning of the word sacrament. It is to place it in the line of the economy of salvation, understanding it in terms of the sacrament *par excellence*, which is the humanity of Christ, and as the subject of all the sacraments. The Church is thus the assembly in which, through the action of the Holy Spirit, the past, Jesus Christ in his Passover of salvation, becomes present in view of the eschatological future of the world (cf. Constitution on the Liturgy). Called to "reveal to the world the mystery of the Lord" (*Lumen Gentium*, art. 8), the Church is word and sign for the whole world (*ibid.*, art. 17). Because its vocation is to place the world in the presence of the mystery of Christ in the Spirit, all its structures are completely subordinated to the mystery of Christ. The visible and social structure of the Church is thus only the sign and means of the action of Jesus Christ in the Spirit. As the great theologians of the Middle Ages used to say (St. Thomas, *Summa Theologica*, I, IIae, q. 106, a. 1), what principally constitutes the Church is the Holy Spirit in men's hearts, all the rest (hierarchy, papacy, Eucharist, sacraments) are in the service of this inner transformation.

Such statements do not mean that the social institution of the Church is indifferent. They merely underline that an understanding of the true nature of the Church as a sign presupposes that it is seen in all its spiritual dimensions. In itself and by itself it has no consistency, but draws all its substance from its relationship to Christ, in whom, through whom and for whom it is a sign. It is completely relative to the spiritual reality which it signifies; namely, the whole Christ, head and members, in the Holy Spirit and growing in grace. It stands for ever in dependence on the free saving act of Jesus Christ and thus, in the Spirit, the Church is the place of the theophanic manifestation of the Lord. It is only truly a sign when it allows the Holy

Spirit to centre it upon Christ and not upon itself.

As mystery and sacrament the Church is always to be seen as proceeding from its source, which is the Trinity. It appears in the divine thought which establishes it in Jesus Christ and it descends from God's presence to become the "messianic" people of God (*Lumen Gentium*, art. 9). It is sent to the scattered, imperfect and potential people of God, the human race called to the salvation already purchased by the blood of Jesus Christ and even now permeated by the action of grace. As the bearer of the gift made to the world by God in Jesus Christ, the Church thus draws the principle of its universal dynamism from the Trinity.

This mystical and sacramental vision of the Church (that of the Fathers and the theologians of the Middle Ages) indicates that all theological thinking about the Church must be based on this communion with the mystery of the Trinity as well as on a real understanding of the history of salvation.

2. *The Church as the fullness of Christ and of fellowship*. The sacramental conception of the Church could, in fact, present a danger if one was tempted to separate in the Church the sign from the reality which is signified. To think of the Church as purely a sign and cause would be to forget that it is already the reality that it serves and signifies. The true notion of the Church as mystery or sacrament necessarily implies – as shown by our insistence above on its spiritual truth in the Spirit – the notion of the fullness of Christ and of fellowship.

The Church derives its intelligibility from its end which is the entry of all men into "the fullness of God" (Eph 3:19).

In dependence on Christ in whom is given the fullness of revelation and of God's communication to the human race (Col 2:9), the Church is the fullness of Christ. It is "the fullness of Him who fills all in all" (Eph 1:23), because in it is revealed and realized the mystery of God's own life, giving men fellowship in his charity. This idea of fullness has an essentially eschatological value and is connected with the theme of the spouse sharing the life of her husband. In this way the Church is defined as an extension to the human race of the life of the Trinity through the mystery of the Incarnation, or again, as fellowship in the Holy Spirit (the patristic tradition; St. Thomas; *Lumen Gentium*, art. 8). As a consequence of the communication of the Holy Spirit, the Church is thus defined by its relation to the communion between the persons of the Trinity, the source and exemplar of ecclesial communion (*ibid.*, art. 4).

This eschatological fellowship realized through the Spirit gathering the Church into unity through the diffusion of charity, a fellowship in life, love and truth (*ibid.*, art. 9) is brought to fruition here below through a sacramental communion. The NT describes the Church in terms of fellowship (Acts 2:42) which is at the same time an agreement of minds in the faith, a sharing in the Eucharist and the same prayer, fellowship with the hierarchy (1 Jn 1:4; Gal 2:9) and the service and care of the poor (2 Cor 9:13).

So the Church can be described as the fellowship in the Spirit which is manifested sacramentally. It is the temple of the Spirit, an organic whole constituted by spiritual bonds (faith, hope, charity) and the bonds of visible structures (profession of faith, the sacramental economy, the pastoral ministry) and which is continually developing and moving towards its eschatological completion.

3. *The Church as the Body of Christ.* In St. Paul the idea of the Body of Christ can be understood only through the notions of *mystery*, *fullness* and *sacrament*.

The Fathers of Vatican I were afraid of using the idea of the Body of Christ because they saw in it the danger of a metaphorical expression which was too vague and imprecise. The German bishops reacted in a similar way in 1940. But the Fathers of Vatican II finally gave it an important place in association with other biblical images. The idea of the Body of Christ had been developed at length by the encyclicals *Satis Cognitum* and above all *Mystici Corporis*.

In St. Paul the notion of the "Body of Christ" means the actual being of the Lord, the personal body of the dead and risen Christ, the beginning of a new creation.

Thus when St. Paul applies the expression of Body of Christ to the Church, he means the one body which gathers together within it, in the Spirit, the whole assembly of believers by means of the sacraments, and principally the Eucharist. So it is God himself who calls the faithful together in Christ, and it is he who unites them in one body through the Holy Spirit. And that is why the unity binding them together, whilst dwelling within them, does not derive from them, being of the divine order. It is based essentially on the unity of the Body of the Lord who died and rose again.

The Church is thus the Body of Christ, because once brought into existence through the fellowship of the faith professed in baptism – *congregatio fidelium* – it is perfected through communion in the same eucharistic bread which puts Christians in contact with the risen body of the Saviour, drawing those who believe in him into his own body. Ecclesial unity then is something spiritual and real and quite unique (involving even the bodies of the faithful), and clearly showing the connection between the Eucharist and the Church.

The eschatological reality of the Church is thus brought out through this incorporation into Christ who exercises absolute authority over his Body and who, in the Spirit, is the vital principle of the organic union of the whole body. The Church now appears as a visible body made up of men in whom are manifested all the different graces given by the one Spirit who animates and governs the Church. In the texts of the Council which speak about the Church, the role of the Spirit is rightly stressed: "When he provides his brethren with his own Spirit, after assembling them from all the nations, he is making them, as it were, his own body in a mystical fashion." (*Lumen Gentium*, arts. 7, 48; *Orientalium Ecclesiarium*, art. 2.) For it was at Pentecost that the Church was born: "The apostles were thus the seeds of the new Israel, and, at the same time, the origin of the sacred hierarchy." (*Ad Gentes*, art. 5.) So the foundation of the Church as fellowship and sacrament is the Holy Spirit, which presupposes an analysis of the relations between ministries and charismatic gifts and between institution and event.

The building up of the Church in time by means of the ministries and charismatic gifts established by Christ tends towards perfect spiritual unity in the eschatological Christ (Eph 4:11–16). Through the will of Christ, its head, and through his permanent action within it, the Church, which is both fellowship with Christ and an institution of salvation, bears within itself all that it needs to complete its construction.

The ministry entrusted to the Church as a gift to be used is also an essential part of its make-up, because the ministry is charged with the preaching of the gospel and celebrating the Eucharist which together build up and develop the Body of Christ. The Church is conceived in the same line as the sacramental mission of Christ, as part of a whole conception which affirms that the whole work of the Church is a continuation of that of Christ.

This means that a sound ecclesiology involves a study of the relations between the Church as a whole and the hierarchy, between the primacy and episcopal collegiality, as well as a study of the theology of the episcopal ministry, the relation between prophecy and authority and of the exercise of authority in the Church, etc.

4. *The Church as the people of God.* Because they involve the unfolding of God's plan of salvation, the notions that we have examined so far are bound up with that of the people of God. The Church must certainly be seen from the point of view of the mystery of God, but the historical process which brought it into existence must also be given its due weight. The Church is the people of God established by the Spirit as the Body of Christ.

The notion of the people of God originally expressed the national and religious unity of Israel (cf. Exod 6:6b), and the covenant that God established with it (cf. Lev 26:9–12). It was used in the NT to give vivid expression to the eschatological consciousness of the Church. It thus brings out the *continuity* of the Church with the people of the old covenant and, even more, it stresses with the liturgy that the Church is a growing community, involved in history and affected by the weakness of its members which always stands in need of the mercy of God. But this notion has the serious drawback that it expresses only those characteristics which are common to the peoples of the old and new covenants. It gives no direct intimation of the overwhelming change brought about by Christ (eternal life in the fellowship of the Father and the Holy Spirit). It can be an excellent description of the Church, and because of its involvement in history and real life can even act as a safeguard against a too abstract treatment of the notion of the mystical body. But to become a definition of the Church, it needs to be completed by the notion of the Body of Christ.

The Church (Ἐκκλησία, the Septuagint translation of the word *qahal*) understood itself originally in terms of the people of God. The ancient people of God was an assembly established by the summons of the divine word which gathered it together, taught it and created the covenant sealed in the offering of sacrifice (cf. the proclamation of the law on Sinai, Exod 19ff.; the promulgation of Deuteronomy, 2 Kgs 23; the return from the exile, Neh 8–10).

This call placed the people of God under a system of election which was worked out through a gradual process of segregation: the escape from Egypt, the separation from the tribes of Canaan, the formation of a faithful "remnant" (Amos 5:15; Is 4:2–3 and 11–16; Jer 23:3 Ezek 9:8 and 11:13), and the final reduction to the one faithful servant who is charged with bringing about the final gathering of all the nations.

The Church was foreshadowed in the twelve gathered around the suffering servant, the tiny elected remnant destined to spread out over the whole world. It was then born on the cross and at Pentecost as the people of God of the new and eternal covenant. From then on it is constituted by the preaching of the gospel, by baptism and the response of faith, and is established in unity through fellowship with the dead and risen Christ (1 Cor 10:16, 17; Col 3:11; Gal 3, 28), as it awaits his return.

The newly-born Church was thus conscious of living in continuity with Israel, whose history was interpreted in the light of the central event of the coming, death and resurrection of Christ Jesus. According to Eph 2, henceforward the Gentiles share, in Jesus Christ, in the grace and the good news promised to Israel (cf. also Acts 15:8; 15:24). The phrase used in 1 Peter: "You (the believers) . . . are God's own people" (1 Pet 2:9) – a translation of the "*'am segulah*" describing Israel in its historical and spiritual relationship with God – expresses the mystery of the Church's belonging to the God of Israel because of its "election" in, through and for Jesus Christ. The faith expressed through baptism and the Eucharist is the conclusive mark of belonging to this people authenticated by the seal of the Spirit.

So it is in Christ, "over God's house as a Son" (Heb. 3:6; 1:2), the first-born embodying the complete loyalty of God to his people, that the unique people of God, from now on to be the bearer and witness of salvation, is brought into existence. The theology of the Church as the people of God finds its true basis only in Christology. This people in virtue of its re-creation in Christ is a free people. "The condition of this people is the dignity and freedom of God's sons, whose hearts are like a temple, the dwelling place of the Holy Spirit" (*Lumen Gentium*, art. 9), and so it must live in a spirit of freedom (2 Cor 3:17), as a witness to eschatological hope. This is a point on which the great tradition of the Fathers and Scholasticism, and in particular St. Thomas (*Summa Theologica*, I, IIae, 106a), especially insisted.

So the notion of the people of God by itself is not capable of expressing the whole reality of the Church. Under the new dispensation the people of God has a Christological and pneumatological connotation which can only be expressed through the notion of fellowship in the mystery and the Body of Christ. M. Schmaus writes: "The Church is the people of God of the New Testament, established by Jesus Christ, hierarchically constituted, serving to promote the reign of God and the salvation of men, and this people exists as the mystical body of Christ" (*Katholische Dogmatik*, III/1, p. 48).

5. *The Church as a society*. This idea of people, as the whole ancient tradition saw (cf. St. Thomas, *Com. in Hebr*., ch. viii, no. 3), immediately suggests that of society and kingdom. But we must say a few words about the limitations of the application of the notion of society to the Church.

Since the 16th century at least, treatises on the Church, which were principally composed as answers to attacks on the concept of the Church's structure as a social body, made great use of the philosophical concept of society as "a stable union of human beings with a view to attaining an end by action pursued in common". It affirms that the Church is a perfect society, i.e., self-sufficient and independent; unequal, i.e., organized hierarchically, and supernatural, by reason of its efficient and final causes. "The Catholic Church instituted by Jesus Christ is a visible society, composed of men who have received baptism and who, united amongst themselves by the profession of the same faith and the bonds of mutual communion, strive for the same supernatural end, under the authority of the Roman Pontiff and the bishops in communion with him." (Catechism of Cardinal Gasparri.)

This concept has had the advantage of bringing out to a certain extent the *sui iuris* character of the Church in relation to other societies: a new community, independent of every human factor of race, culture and power, affirming also the true and proper subsistence of temporal society.

But because of a one-sided development which led to the underestimation of almost all the expressions used to describe the Church in the Bible (except those of kingdom and mystical body, which, however, were understood from a predominantly sociological point of view), the notion of society obscured to some extent the specifically Christian character of the common good, authority, obedience, of the relations between communities and their heads and between the Church and temporal society, and also led to a neglect of the importance of the personal element as well as of the anthropological values contained within the Christian community. It also led to a static conception of the Church as a fully-formed juridical institution, standing outside time, and resulted in the practical disappearance of the whole dynamic vision of the Church as the instrument of a plan of universal and cosmic dimensions.

However, the new appreciation of the whole range of biblical expression does not mean the complete elimination of the concept of society, which is to be found on many occasions in *Lumen Gentium*. The Church, the presence of the mystery, appears then under the form of a social body. It is concrete society raised up to the divine level. The full analogical value should be restored to the idea of society, so that all the different ecclesiological themes presented above can be brought harmoniously together. The people of God, the body of Christ and the temple of the Holy Spirit will then be seen as the society (or fellowship) of Christian grace: a truly supernatural and Christ-engendered society, not only in its purpose, but also in its very make-up. A community of men, visibly structured and gathered together, it has an inner principle of fellowship of a supernatural and divine character which makes it the body of Christ. In its complex nature it comprises its sociological aspects, now essentially supernaturalized.

6. *The Church and the kingdom.* The heavenly Church will be still an actual society living in glory, but the make-up of the Church here below is marked by the tension between the Church and the kingdom, by reason of its sacramental structure. The NT shows the connection existing between the Church and the kingdom, but does not authorize a complete identification. The Church will become the perfect divine community of the kingdom only after the proving and sifting time of the judgment. Vatican II sees in the Church the seed and the beginning of the kingdom (*Lumen Gentium*, arts. 3, 5, 9). In the past theologians have sometimes stressed the distance between the Church and the kingdom, and at other times brought out their continuity. This can be easily understood if it is true that the Church is already in substance the kingdom of God, but in a state of pilgrimage in the obscurity of faith. The Church is in a sense the *eschaton* already present and realized, appearing now in what are the last days (Mk 1:14; Acts 2:17; 1 Pet 1:20); it is the anticipated but only partial realization of the kingdom. The benefits of the kingdom (the inheritance) which are the fruits of the Spirit, knowledge and glory, are possessed by the Church individually and collectively, in an imperfect manner (1 Cor 13:2), in "mystery", but really and truly.

But if the kingdom denotes consummation and fullness, there is even now in the Church a clear and growing sense of the distance which still separates it from that glorious consummation and which explains the growing tension which must dominate it in its yearning for the return of the Saviour. This midway situation, standing between what is come and what is yet to come, has a profound effect on the whole nature of the Church and explains a great number of its characteristics, in particular its crucified state. The Church is the realm of the king who is the suffering servant. Just like its Lord, it must suffer to enter into its glory (cf. Lk 24:26). That is why the Church is here below a pilgrim Church (2 Cor 8:6, etc.; cf. 1 Pet 2:11, "aliens and exiles"; the superscription of the letter of Polycarp to the Philippians: "The Church which is on pilgrimage", etc.).

The tension between the kingdom and the Church which, we repeat, results from the sacramental structure of the Church, can also be understood as a consequence of the divine action which involves the whole process of salvation – summons, justification, glorification – and whose final goal is the glory to be revealed (Rom 8:18–30).

All the images and concepts which

depict the Church are thus seen to be mutually complementary. They must all be interpreted in the light of the mystery of God whose purpose is to establish men in the fellowship of his Son. One of the fruits of the constitution *Lumen Gentium* has been a deeper theological understanding of the Church. Now, in the light of revelation, the Church is recognized as a society of fellowship with God, the sacrament of salvation, the people of God established as the body of Christ and the temple of the Holy Spirit.

D. The Catholic Church and the Other Communions

The sacramental structure of the Church is also the foundation of ecumenism as well as of mission, of the relations between the Church and the world and of renewal of the Church.

In fact all Christians owe their Christianity to the mediation of the ecclesiastical structure of their own community, or at least to that of baptism. Baptism, with its act of faith, is the primary element of the visible unity which still remains between Christians and is the basis for their search for a more visible unity. Between Christians (not only on the individual but also on the community level), there thus exists an elementary visibility which is at once an imperative, a motive for hope and the seed of ultimate unity, since it is a common sharing in the death and resurrection, the sacrifice and victory of Christ, a common indwelling by the Spirit, a common divine sonship. It all calls to be expanded and developed into the fullness of eucharistic Church unity. And so the relations of Christians between themselves is to be defined as a sacramental fellowship, which is admittedly imperfect, but nonetheless real, while the common desire of all Christians for the full manifestation of this sign of Christ, which is the Church, is the heart of ecumenism.

But then arises the problem of the relations of the Catholic Church with the other communions. In the first chapter of *Lumen Gentium*, after having clearly asserted the unity of the hierarchically organized Church with the mystical body of Christ, the Council goes on: "This Church (the one Church of Christ), founded and organized in this world as a society, subsists in the Catholic Church (*subsistit in*) . . . although outside its framework there are found many elements of holiness and truth, and they give an impetus to universal unity, inasmuch as they are gifts which belong to Christ's Church." (Art. 8.) It would be a false interpretation of the expression *subsistit in* to read into it some sort of ecclesial Platonism, as if the Church had a kind of super-self which pre-exists its tangible manifestation, and as if this manifestation was never adequate to its original archetype. Certainly the Church is never fully itself, and of its very nature there is in it a movement towards its full realization that we must accept and will, so that we can work for its fulfilment. But the starting point for any true conception of the Church is of necessity the risen Christ himself in the historical growth of his Body. There is no place for a kind of universal essence of the Church, of which the real world contains only vestiges or drafts, even if one goes on to say that there is one particular and privileged place, namely the Catholic Church, where this mystery, although never completely realized, really does "subsist".

In the text quoted above, the Roman Catholic Church expresses essentially the belief it has of being the realization as a society (and of being the only one to do so completely) of the form of visible communion that God desires for his Church. But we should notice the difference between the text above, as eventually promulgated, and what appeared in the preliminary draft: "that is why rightly (*iure*) only the Catholic Church is called (the) Church". The expression used in the definitive text has the advantage of suggesting that there is a relation between the Catholic Church and non-Roman Christians not only as individuals, but by reason of the different Christian groups and communities through which these Christians receive faith and are sanctified. *Lumen Gentium*, art. 15 (to be taken with *Unitatis Redintegratio*, art. 3) goes into further detail: the spiritual blessings which constitute the Church of Christ are not present only in the Roman Catholic Church as it is defined through its structure. In different degrees they are also present in other Christian communities which thus partly share in the reality of the mystery of the Church. This recognition includes the assertion of the ecclesial character of these communities. The name of Church, in the proper sense of individual Church, that is to say, as realizing the mystery of the Church, even if only imperfectly and incompletely in a particular place, will, however, be given to them only by reason of the presence in them of the essential hierarchical structures (a ministry of priesthood understood in the same way as, and in continuity with, the ministry of priesthood exercised by the apostles). So there is a distinction to be made between Churches and ecclesial communities by reason of the presence or absence of an espiscopal priesthood.

However, *Unitatis Redintegratio* makes it clear that the whole power of the blessings present in the other Churches flows from the fullness of grace and truth entrusted to the Catholic Church (art. 3), and that the separated brethren – whether we are talking of them as individuals or of their communities and Churches – do not enjoy that unity which Jesus Christ wished to bestow upon all whom he has regenerated and vivified to form a single body with a view to a new life (*ibid.*).

At the same time that it defines its relation to other communions the Catholic Church becomes more and more conscious of the distance there is between the demands that Christ makes upon its life and the actual reality of the empirical communities (art. 4). From this comes its consciousness of the need for renewal. One could also say that the Roman Catholic Church judges itself and other Christian communities and Churches in relation to the eschatological reality that its own sacramental structure reveals and signifies, but which always transcends the Church as it actually exists now in the world and passes judgment upon it.

E. The Church and the Mission

The sacramental structure of the Church is also the foundation of the mission of the Church. The first two words of the constitution *Lumen Gentium* (taken from Is 49:6; cf. Lk 2:32 and Acts 13:47) present the Church as entrusted with a mission of salvation for the world by reason of its sacramental nature. This vivid realization that the Church has of its own unique character is the basis for the absolute necessity of missionary activity (*Lumen Gentium*, art. 17; *Ad Gentes*, art. 2). "Sent by God to the Gentiles to be 'the universal sacrament of salvation', the Church . . . strives with all its might to preach the gospel to all men" (*ibid.*, art. 1). Thus "of its nature, the Church, during the time of its earthly pilgrimage, is a missionary Church because it derives its origin from the mission of the Son and from the mission of the Holy Spirit according to the design of God the Father" (*ibid.*, art. 2). At the same time the nature of missionary activity is defined as being completely directed to the fullness of the *eschaton*. "Missionary activity is nothing less than the manifestation of God's plan, its presence and realization in the world and its history, in which God guides the whole history of salvation to its appointed end by means of the mission" (*ibid.*, art. 9). So the Church is a wholly missionary

Church, for if a commandment, in the true sense of the word, was given to the apostles and after them to their successors, then the whole Church must co-operate in carrying it out (see *Ad Gentes*, art. 5, *Lumen Gentium*, art. 17).

The mission of the Church, which involves the recognition of the sacramental nature of the ministry as seen in *Lumen Gentium*, art. 3, is the foundation of the missions properly so called. The eschatological vision dominating all missionary activity regulates the relations of the Church with others in respect of what they are. The Church strongly asserts that accepting the faith presupposes complete religious freedom. Preparing thus for a new style of relations between the Church, Christian communities and secular States, the Church shows itself in favour of genuine interconfessional dialogue as a function of the mission of the Church. But general statements are not enough. The Church proclaims not only its connections with Israel (connections based on divine revelation itself), but also with the other religions. It recognizes all the spiritual, moral and sociocultural values of other religions (*Nostra Aetate*, art. 2) and affirms strongly that a convert from one of these religions to Christianity does not betray the religious and cultural genius of his own people. Like the whole of ancient tradition, the Church sees there "a preparation for the gospel" (*Ad Gentes*, art. 8). This is not the recognition of an economy of salvation parallel to Christ, for the Council solemnly declares that it is in Christ alone, who is made present for us in his body which is the Church, that men are called to find the fullness of religious life: all authentic religious experience tends towards the fundamental structure willed by God: its Catholic ecclesial form (*Nostra Aetate*, art. 2). The human race, which in its entirety is ordained to salvation in Christ, is therefore no stranger to the Church, but is bound close to it by many different bonds (*Lumen Gentium*, arts. 14–15).

F. The Church and the World

Relations between the Church and the world are also ultimately based on the sacramental character of the Church. "All the good that the people of God, during the time of its earthly pilgrimage, can bring to the human family derives from this fact that the Church is 'the universal sacrament of salvation'" (*Lumen Gentium*, art. 48), at the same time both showing forth and actualizing the mystery of God's love for man. Through becoming more conscious of itself in its missionary function, the Church has realized that it must proclaim salvation to a human race which is real, personal, social and historical reality reborn in every generation, and to a world which is in process of being completely transformed – and also that it has much to learn from mankind.

Henceforward a new solidarity of the Church in regard to the world is proclaimed in the name of the freedom and dignity of man: "The Church is both the sign and the safeguard of the transcendent character of the human person." (*Gaudium et Spes*, art. 76.) The people of God must thus appear to the world as the eschatological and seminal realization of the urgent desire for unity, peace, justice, liberty and love which dominates all mankind (*Lumen Gentium*, art. 9).

This means that the Church is obliged to take seriously the problems of mankind throughout history, its objections and refusals (atheism). This does not prevent the Church from exercising its function of prophetic judgment or condemnation with regard to certain tendencies which jeopardize man's full development.

G. The Deficiencies of the Church and Reform

The eschatological and sacramental structure of the Church enables us to see in proper perspective the historical nature of a Church now conscious of its own deficiencies: "Although the Church, through the power of the Holy Spirit, has never ceased to be in the world the sign of salvation, it knows only too well that during the course of its long history, amongst its members, both clerical and lay, there have not been lacking those who showed themselves unfaithful to the Spirit of God." (*Gaudium et Spes*, art. 44.) This text takes up a similar statement in the decree *Unitatis Redintegratio* (art. 4). So we see that the very foundation of the ceaseless reform of the Church is the sacramental structure of the Church: in it there is a continuous struggle to be faithful to the Spirit. "The Church, in the course of its earthly pilgrimage, is called by Christ to this continual reform of which it always stands in need as a human and earthly institution." (*Ibid.*, art. 6.)

Recognition of the deficiencies of the Church throughout the course of history stands out very clearly. In the Declaration on Religious Freedom, for instance, mention is made of the unchristian attitudes which have marked the behaviour of Catholics at different times in history (*Dignitatis humanae*, art. 12). *Gaudium et Spes* declares: "In the rise of atheism believers also can have a not inconsiderable part, insofar as through negligence in their own education in the faith, through fallacious presentations of doctrine and also through the short-comings of their religious, moral and social life one might say that they distort the true appearance of God and of religion rather more than they reveal it." (Art. 19; cf. also arts. 21; 36; 43.) And again the common declaration of Paul VI and Patriarch Athenagoras about the excommunications of 1054 (7 December 1965) ratifies solemnly, so to speak, this confession of the historical deficiencies of the Church.

So the Church, which includes sinners within its fold, has need of incessant renewal and purification (cf. *Lumen Gentium*, art. 8; taken up in *Gaudium et Spes*, art. 44, and in *Unitatis Redintegratio*, art. 6), and through its encounter with the world it discovers the full implications of our redemption in Jesus Christ. It learns from human history, which enables it to appreciate better the riches of its faith.

By recognizing its weaknesses the Church, the effective sign of the encounter with God which transforms mankind and of the new creation of all in Christ, knows that it must imitate more closely the self-emptying of Christ who became poor. The foundation of the Church's poverty is also to be sought in its sacramental nature which refers it entirely to Christ in the Spirit.

With this renewed desire to be faithful to Christ and the resolution to be of service to the world, the Church is exploring its own mystery. In the light of events which impose new demands upon the Christian life and call for a more profound understanding of the word of God under pressure of the trials of history, the Church discovers the unsuspected depths of the mystery and contemplates in the light of faith with a growing love the wonderful guidance of God, seeking to conform it to his own death and resurrection.

H. Outside the Church No Salvation

The Church is for the world the universal and efficacious sign of salvation. No one can be saved apart from the efficacy of this sign.

It is, however, important to add that its invisible action infinitely surpasses its visible effectiveness. As the sacrament of salvation, the Church brings about invisibly what it signifies visibly: universal salvation. This means that the axiom, "Outside the Church no salvation", must be interpreted in the light of the sacramental nature of the Church.

In the course of history the magisterium has put forward two series of apparently contradictory statements: the necessity of belonging to the Church for salvation and the condemnation of those who maintain that grace confines its action to the visible boundaries of the Church.

a) The formula of St. Cyprian, "extra ecclesiam nulla salus", is to be found in a profession of faith imposed upon the Waldenses by Innocent III (*DS* 792, 802) and its clearest statement is in the Bull *Unam Sanctam* of Boniface VIII (*DS* 875).

b) But there have also been constant statements that the action of grace is not restricted to the visible boundaries of the Church alone (cf. *DS* 1305, 2429, 2304; and above all 3860, 3872).

A reconciliation between these two contradictory positions was effected through the use of the idea of "error in good faith". Pius IX was the first to refer to invincible error in explaining the axiom "outside the Church no salvation" (*Singulari quadam*). In the same line it is interesting to consult one of the chapters of the schema *De Ecclesia* of Vatican I where it was proposed to define "outside the Church no salvation" as a dogma of faith. But the most important text is the letter of the Holy Office to the Archbishop of Boston (*DS* 3869–80). It recalls first of all that "incorporation through baptism into the Body of Christ, which is the Church, is a very strict commandment of Jesus Christ" (*DS* 3867). "The Saviour has not only ordained that all men and all people should enter into the Church, but he has also established that there is a means of salvation without which no one can enter into the kingdom of heavenly glory." (*DS* 3868.) But the necessity of the Church as a means of salvation is explained more fully: there is no question of a necessity of means, that is to say, of an intrinsic necessity bound up with the nature of things, which, as absolutely indispensable, have to be really and effectively employed. Such would be the necessity of the interior disposition of faith and love of God for salvation. The necessity of the Church is that of a precept. It corresponds to a positive institution, and the effect to which such a means is ordered can be obtained even where the means itself cannot be effectively employed. "For someone to obtain eternal salvation, it is not always required that he be in fact incorporated into the Church as a member, but it is at least required that he be united to it by desire or wish." (*DS* 3870.)

There is clear progress in this document beyond the preparatory project of Vatican I, which still spoke of a necessity of means. Vatican II confirms this by alluding to the document of the Holy Office: "Those also can attain to everlasting salvation who through no fault of their own do not know the gospel of Christ or his Church, yet sincerely seek God and, moved by grace, strive by their deeds to do his will as it is known to them through the dictates of conscience." (*Lumen Gentium*, art. 16.) In short, to be saved, every man, at least by an act of implicit faith and theological desire for salvation, must become a son of the Church. The axiom "Outside the Church no salvation" is only a way of expressing the ecclesiological truth: the Church is the sacrament of salvation.

Marie-Joseph le Guillou

III. Constitution of the Church

1. If one wishes to speak in terms of sacred law of a "constitution" of the Catholic Church on the grounds that it is a *societas perfecta*, then the actual details of such a constitution have already been dealt with in other articles. The Church is, among other things, a social reality, a juridically constituted society, the highest governing body of which is the universal episcopate which

has as its head the Roman Pontiff with his primatial authority. Here the Pope is not merely a representative commissioned by the college of bishops and the executor of the collegiate will. He is their head in the sense that he always acts as their head, just as of course he only is Pope and only acts as such as the head of the Church, not as an entity separate from and in contrast to the Church. But he acts with an authority which is given him as his own by Christ and which embraces every individual bishop and the entire Church with truly sovereign power (*potestas iurisdictionis plena et universalis*). As regards the function of individuals in the Church, there is a distinction *iuris divini* between clergy (hierarchy) and laity. The clergy itself is graded in respect of the sacramentally conferred *potestas ordinis* as well as the *potestas iurisdictionis*. There are bishops, priests and deacons; there is clergy with actual jurisdiction or without it, although its ontological basis is conferred in the sacrament of holy orders itself. There exist two fundamental powers (*potestas ordinis, potestas iurisdictionis*) which are neither unrelated nor simply identical. The Church is divided territorially into dioceses, but these must not be regarded as merely administrative districts (of the papal primatial authority). They are themselves truly "the Church", governed by the bishop in the name of Christ, not of the Pope. They are *sui iuris*, with their own traditions and an independent function in the Church as a whole. Corresponding to its social nature, the Church has a sacred law which in part belongs to its immutable essence, in part is created by the Church itself, as in canon law. By this law other institutions, offices, regions, etc. are set up in the Church which belong to its concrete nature, to its actual historical condition and partly to its constitution, as far as the norms of their existence and function are concerned. To this extent, therefore, the "constitution" of the Church has in fact been dealt with under these other headings.

All that remains, therefore, is a fundamental theological reflection on the constitution of the Church. The question is a topical one because there is a general demand nowadays that larger societies of longer duration should be juridically organized. A State today must live by the "rule of law", have a juridical organization and therefore a written constitution which can be legally invoked even against the authorities of the State (separation of powers, supreme court, etc.). In our democratic age, therefore, a similar question also arises for the Church, for the Church also sees itself as a "perfect society" and Catholic ecclesiology does not hesitate to use the analogy between Church and State, despite the radical differences between them.

2. The first striking fact is that in the Catholic Church there is no actual *written* constitution (of divine or human right). There are statements in the doctrine of faith, even defined ones, regarding the Church, but they are not gathered into a single corpus in a written constitution. Even now that for the first time in the *Lumen Gentium* of Vatican II there is a sort of summary of Catholic ecclesiology (though without any new definitions), this is not a constitution. Most of what it says does not involve juridical norms, but consists almost entirely of the statements of revelation. Consequently, it passes over the *ius humanum* which after all belongs to the Church's concrete structure and therefore offers in regard to the concrete condition of the Church practically only the basic rights, the ultimate constitutional norms, an extensive constitutional preamble. Similarly, the code of canon law is not a written constitution, although it contains numerous juridical constitutional norms. It corresponds rather to the civil, criminal and administrative law of a modern State. There is the further point that, whereas in the

modern State the constitution has a higher validity and dignity than the rest of the law, it is not possible in the Church to distinguish divinely established constitutional elements from other juridical norms which are also divinely established, or between humanly established constitutional elements and other norms of humanly established canon law as regards their formal aspects – validity, mutability, authority to change them, etc.

3. Considering the liking of the *Roman* Church for law, this is a surprising fact. Its explanation is not ultimately that juridical development has not yet for historical reasons advanced so far and that the mentality of the Church delays this development (just as, for example, in England there is not really a written constitution). The deepest reason lies in the nature of the Church itself. The legal element in the Church cannot be distinguished from the rest of what it is in other respects and what it does precisely as Church, in the way this can be done in secular society and in the State. Ultimately this derives from the religious character of the Church on the one hand and from its sacramental and eschatological character on the other. The *ius divinum* which forms the basis of its constitution is religious, revealed truth. To this, however, there belongs (even in respect to the *ius divinum*) not only what has been formulated by explicit reflection at a certain point of time but also, and equally essentially, what has (temporarily or permanently) only been grasped and lived implicitly, what is still only unfolding historically in the Church's consciousness of its faith. This alone shows that a written constitution, with its restrictions and definitions, excluding the unwritten as legally invalid, would be of doubtful value to the Church, even though to a certain extent there is something analogous in the constitution of the State – the living criticism of the written constitution through the unwritten meta-juridical basic rights of man, etc. Furthermore, it is not possible wholly to distinguish in the Church between the *forum internum* and the *forum externum*, for example in the sacrament of penance. The very fact that in ecclesiology and canon law recourse must be had to the paraxodical concept of *forum internum* shows the strange combination which prevails in the Church between what can be comprised in legal terms and what as an individual religious saving even cannot wholly be given juridical form. All the sacraments involve the union of an institutional element (as the social, and therefore juridically regulated, efficacious sign of grace) and grace itself, which can never be controlled but always remains at the sole disposition of God, since, for instance, efficacious grace is needed for the disposition for fruitful reception of a sacrament. The entire guarantee of the indestructibility of the institutional (and only as such is it really ecclesiastically institutional) and every "guarantee" of its producing its genuine effect (infallible teaching, fruitful administration of the sacraments, permanent apostolic succession, etc.) resides in the power of the Spirit, not in the social and legal element as such, and its victory has always to be believed and hoped for anew.

We can therefore only speak of the constitution of the Church if and where it is something more than what is merely juridical in the social domain as such, just as a sacrament is only an effective and fruitful sacrament if it is more than a sacrament (in the sense of a sign with juridical efficacy of a social kind), namely, grace. The Spirit of the Church does not belong to the constitution, but without it this constitution would cease to be itself. To the extent that the Spirit itself belongs to the essence of the Church, just as "uncreated grace" belongs to the justified person, there is in the Church itself a critical principle, a dynamism directed towards the further development of its constitution and a perpetually renewed criticism of the concrete application of this "constitution" which always lags behind the task it imposes. To the extent that the Church knows itself to be a pilgrim, still making its way towards the kingdom of God, its constitution with office and sacrament is something that the Church itself regards as part of the pattern of this "aeon" in which the Church still shares. It is something that the Church knows to be not only historically conditioned by the age (as everyone knows a secular constitution to be): it is that whose end it prays for in its impatient eschatological longing (cf. *Lumen Gentium*, art. 48).

The absence of a really closed, rounded, self-sufficient written constitution of the Church is an expression of the fact that it does not live by the letter, but by the Spirit, that the Church is not law but gospel, however much the letter is the embodiment of the Spirit, of order, of freedom from the arbitrary and the mark of the historical Incarnation.

4. On the other hand this "written" and "unwritten" constitution of the Church is not a mere human, everyday necessity, imperative just because human beings happen to want social organization even in their religious needs and this is not possible without order and regulation. Of course man's social character is an essential factor, and as confirmed and consecrated by the Incarnation is the ultimate reason why there is such a thing as a constitution even in the Church. But the consequence following from this, namely the constitution of the Church by the will of the Father and of Christ made flesh and history, is an element in the Church itself precisely as such. Faith is always the faith of a community confessing its faith under authoritative decision; in virtue of what it is, grace takes concrete form in sacraments "necessary for salvation" (*D* 847, etc.). Salvation takes place in history, in the covenant, in the Church, whose visible social constitution belongs to the occurrence of grace itself, without being identical with it.

5. The "constitution" of the Church in the concrete can still develop further even today, even if the whole of changing canon law cannot be counted as part of its constitution. Some things which even at the present time are clearly in process of historical change can be reckoned as belonging to the concrete constitution of the Church (*iuris humani*): the division between the Eastern and the Latin parts of the Church and their mutual relations, the coexistence of an Eastern and a Latin canon law; the renewed tendency in the Latin Church to form large regional Churches (of a new type however), corresponding to the old patriarchates of the East; the tendency towards a clearer institutional form of the rights and duties of the laity in the Church, and to a clearer institutional form of the collaboration between Pope and the college of bishops (the "Synod of Bishops"); the duty of internationalizing the Roman Curia; a better determination of the relation between the episcopate of a country and the papal nuncio; the revival of the synodal principle within the individual dioceses; the statutory definition of episcopal conferences; the enhancement of the function and importance of auxiliary bishops and coadjutors where these are needed; the possibility of bishops with supra-diocesan functions; the speedy establishment of a native episcopate in the Churches of the missionary countries as local Churches with their own character and equal rights. These and similar matters after all belong to some extent to the domain of constitutional law and show that this constitution is involved in historical change. Because, however, there is no definite written constitution in the Church, this change does not mean "revolution", "change of constitu-

tion", or "constitutional legislation" which would have to be enacted in the Church in a different way from other ecclesiastical laws, *iuris humani*.

Karl Rahner

IV. Universality of the Church

1. This article should be regarded as supplementary to the articles *Church* II (Ecclesiology) and *Church and World*. To some extent it stands midway between them. Its theme is a topical one, for it is only at the present time that the Church has manifestly and in historical fact become approximately a world-wide Church, as was clearly shown by Vatican II. Quite considerable consequences follow from this fact for the Church's action.

2. In a first, purely dogmatic and always valid sense, the Church can be called world-wide or universal because it is intended for all men whether or not they belong or will belong to the Church (since Pentecost) in the sense of full membership of the Church in its existence as a social institution. This sense of universality (Church as universal *potentia et destinatione*) implies two facts. In the first place the Church is for *all* men the *sacramentum salutis*, whether they belong actually and fully to the visible unity of the Church or not. In other words, the grace of God in Christ, without which absolutely no one finds supernatural salvation in God's triune life, has its historical and eschatological manifestation (even for the unbaptized) in the Church. Secondly, no human being can in principle be exempted from the obligation of belonging to the visible unity of the Church. This second point follows immediately from the necessity of the Church and of baptism for salvation. We had, however, to formulate this second sense of the universal necessity of the Church for salvation in this way, because theologically it is no longer possible, at any rate at the present time, to affirm that all men receive by the saving providence of God such an actual possibility of recognizing the Church as necessary for salvation and of entering it that they can only miss this opportunity by their own fault. If, however, many individual human beings inculpably until their death fail to belong in an actual visible way to the Church, it is impossible to say that in regard to *every* single human being God has a will which *directly* imposes an *actual* obligation upon this human being of visible membership of the Church. Otherwise God would have to give him such a possibility of fulfilling this will that he could only fail to do so by his own fault. Consequently the necessity of the Church for salvation and the obligation of Church membership (over and above the Church as *sacramentum salutis omnium*) can only be formulated as we have done. No one can justifiably affirm *a priori* that visible membership of the Church does not enter into the question as a concrete possibility for him personally and therefore as an actual duty, and cannot be *the* chance of salvation by which in fact his salvation is decided.

3. The Church today, however, can and must be called universal or world-wide in a narrower historical and real sense. The Church today has become world-wide in its actual empirical reality, a Church for the whole world. This of course does not mean that all men are Christians (baptized persons) and Catholics. Nor does it mean that the Church, at least today, is so actually present, as the call of God's grace, that this summons can go unheeded through personal guilt alone. Nor does it mean that the Church is already so well-established in all nations and civilizations that it has already ceased to be a missionary Church anywhere in the sense of Vatican II's Decree on the Church's Missionary Activity (cf. art. 19). It cannot in fact even be disputed that there are still regions in the world in which the Catholic Church (which

means more than "Christianity") is in practice not yet present at all, e.g., certain parts of Asia. At all events the Church in large parts of Asia (China, Siberia, etc.), in the domain of Islam and in many parts of Africa, is still a mission Church. In other words, the community of the faithful is not yet rooted in the social life of that country and not yet adapted to its civilization, the number of priests, religious and laity is still very small, organization is still on a very modest scale, there is no native bishop and so it is not yet possible to say that missionary activity has to a certain extent come to an end. Yet it is already possible to speak of a world-wide Church at the present time. What could still not be said even 150 years ago can be said today. The Church is almost everywhere present in some way. At least if we leave out of account the very large area under the domination of militant Communism, the Church possesses local Churches or missions throughout the world. Its doctrine and existence are among the things which are known to public opinion and with which people reckon. Its highest governing body includes representatives from all the important nations, racial groups, etc. Furthermore – and this is perhaps the decisive factor, although primarily determined by profane history – the peoples and their histories which were formerly almost totally separated by historical no man's land, have now grown together into an actual family of nations and a single world history, largely as a result of European colonialism since the 16th century. This process is of course still going on and its consequences are becoming more marked.

At the present time, therefore, every particular history of a nation, a civilization, a continent, has become an empirically contributory factor in every other (as Vatican II's Pastoral Constitution on the Church in the Modern World frequently emphasizes). It follows immediately that the major higher religions, even though they originated at a particular place in history which continues to be the root of their life and influence, have become a contributory factor in the history of the world generally, even if their physical presence (constituted by their institutions and greater numbers of their adherents) is in certain places very slight or even absent. That, however, also holds good of Christianity because of the relatively large number of its adherents and because it is the religion of the civilization from which the unification of the one world-history of today proceeded. It therefore also applies to the largest Church of Christendom. It must be noted that the unification of world-history did not just in fact contribute to the actual universality of the Church. It is true that European expansion and the world-wide mission have interacted since the 16th century, though sometimes to the detriment of the mission because it roused the suspicion that it was a piece of European imperialism. There is a more fundamental connection. The European, rational attitude to the world which aims at its active transformation, and European technology, were the condition and foundations of the European expansion which created world-history. Now these sprang from a radically Christian attitude to the world, for which the world has no numinous character but instead is a created reality, the environment and the material for man's self-realization. This is so despite the deformations of rationalism and technocracy, and despite even the profanation of the world under practical or militant atheism.

4. Universality involves consequences for the Church itself and its action, only a few of which can be indicated here. In a world-wide Church contained within the unity of a single world-history, the mutual importance, duties and interdependence of all the regional Churches are greater. When old regional

Churches found young Churches in non-Christian countries, the destiny of the latter reacts upon the mother Churches themselves. This in fact increases the missionary obligation, because it has now become even empirically a part of the duty of self-preservation of the ancient Churches themselves, whose own fate is partly determined by that of Christianity throughout the world. In this situation of a universal world-history in which all nations are simultaneously becoming independent, the Church has clearly to manifest its character as a world-Church to all the nations, which have equal rights in it. This is done by creating as rapidly as possible a native clergy and episcopate, the incorporation of all civilizations and national mentalities on an equal basis into the Church's life, the removal of the earlier European features from the missions, internationalization of the Roman Curia, the "naturalization" of the liturgy, whereby it will have to be a world-liturgy varying in form, not a Latin liturgy (in fact almost that of the city of Rome). As a world-Church in a unified world-history the Church will have more clearly to show itself acting as a single whole, not only in the action of the Pope as highest guarantor and representative of the visible unity of the Church, but also through the universal episcopate as highest collegiate presiding body of the universal Church; by the distribution of priests throughout the whole world out of wider concern than the sectional interest of a regional Church; by ecclesiastical "help for underdeveloped countries" – the missions and South America; by each bishop's (and even each Christian's) coming to take a share of practical responsibility for the Church as a whole in all its parts, though not for its government. Over and above national concordats, etc., the world-Church will have to discover and develop a relation of dialogue and collaboration with other institutions which represent in a social form the unity of the human family and its history – UNO, UNESCO, the World Council of Churches, etc.

5. The unification of mankind is a *process*, which is not yet at an end. For that reason alone, apart from properly and directly theological grounds, the one world-wide Church is still in process of realization, and forms part of the responsibility of all Christians.

Karl Rahner

CHURCH AND STATE

Because Church and State essentially differ, the relationship between them is always a dialectical one. Though with different ends in view, each claims the allegiance of the same person. The State's business is to defend and promote the natural goods of its citizens on earth, whereas the Church is called upon to continue the redemptive work of its founder on earth and lead men by word and sacrament to their eternal salvation. Church and State being composed of the same members, the relations between them must be regulated in accordance with historical evolution and the concrete situation at a given time. All attempts to fix the relations between Church and State in the abstract are foredoomed, because they ignore the historicity of both Church and State. In the West the many forms of relationship between Church and State over the centuries reflect varying political situations but even more the ideas men had of Church and State from time to time.

A. In the New Testament

While the NT contains no doctrine or explicit statement on the concrete relationship between Church and State, it does have something to say about the State. It teaches that the Christian is not excused from obeying civil authority and it sets forth the meaning and measure of that obedience. The biblical view of the Christian's position vis-à-vis civil authority – as found in the logion on paying taxes (Mk 12:13–17 and parr.), in Rom 13:1ff.; 1 Pet 2:13; 1 Tim 2:2; Tit 3:1; but also in Rev 13:1ff. – must be compared with what natural theology and natural law tell us of Church and State, before the Catholic Church can find a basis for its relations with the State. The variety of statements on the civil power which are encountered in the NT (compare Rom 13:1ff. with Rev 13:1ff.) shows us the dialectical position of the Christian and the Church vis-à-vis secular rulers; at the same time it shows that the attitude of the Church towards the State must be governed not only by the possible abuse of the State's authority (with which the Church always has to reckon) but also by the dignity of the State, which the Church recognizes as a power different from and completely independent of itself. At the same time the NT constantly reminds the Church that its normal lot in this world is not tranquillity and peace but persecution (see Mt 10:17f.; Rev 13:1ff.), persecution meaning not only attacks on the Church but the temptation, in an over-friendly State, for the Church to try to do its work through the State and in the State's interest. Two NT themes govern the relationship between Church and State: on the one hand the affirmation of civil authority because it comes from God, and on the other the rejection of the State's claim to complete dominion. The State is not the supreme and ultimate value; being an element of order in this aeon, it is finite and provisional (see Phil 3:20) and its business differs from the business of the Church.

Any identification of the State with the Church (even *de facto*) is repugnant to the nature of Church and State alike. But this does not mean that the two exist side by side without any sort of connection between them. Each is an enterprise of God in the world and each has its service to render man, which can best be done through peaceful co-operation with the other, each retaining its own nature, independence, and inviolable sphere of competence. A sound scriptural idea of the Christian's position vis-à-vis the State cannot have us ignore the institutions and affairs of this world; rather it will move us to play a responsible and serviceable part in both; for where the NT speaks of civil authorities it calls on the Christian to obey them and pray for them, whether they be Christian or not. Indeed the religion of the ruler presents no problem at all to the NT: we must remember that Rom 13:1f. was written while Nero governed the Roman Empire. Nevertheless, Scripture takes a more personal view than the abstract, institutional one which is deduced from natural theology and natural law. Foreshortening the biblical view has had the most harmful effect on relations between Church and State over the centuries; and it is also foreshortening the biblical view to interpret certain texts (that on paying taxes, for example, Mk 12:13–17 and parr., or Rom 13:1f. in particular) as enunciations of natural law, so that their meaning for redemptive history, eschatology, and concrete life is lost from sight. The deliberations and pronouncements of Vatican II have clearly shown that today the question of the relations between Church and State is deeply embedded in the broader question of the Church's relations with the world at large. Vatican II certainly seems to mark a break with the past, when the question of the Church's relations with the world and human society was often reduced to the question of Church and State. (Leo XIII's encyclicals on civil society still reflect that view.)

But once we are clear that the relationship between Church and State is only one element, though a very important one, in the total problem of "the Church and the world", then the purely juridical approach to the problem of Church and State is seen to be quite inadequate. Not as though it were irrelevant to inquire what the legitimate relationship between Church and State may be (trying to work out, for instance, how far they are independent and how they should co-operate), or as though we would ignore those matters in favour of a purely sociological approach. We only wish to fit them into a wider context which future juridical arrangements will also have to take into account.

B. Autonomy of Church and State

The modern Catholic view of the autonomy of Church and State undoubtedly reflects a notion of the State which has only developed in modern times, and also a new self-consciousness of the Church, as totally different from the State, which the Church has acquired by meditating on its nature as the "mystical body", the "people of God", the "primordial sacrament" (all of which it is, of course, as the institutional, hierarchical, official Church) and its mission of ministering to human society. True, since later antiquity the Church has stressed its independence of the State, but the principle has been interpreted and applied in a great variety of ways. Since the competence of the Church derives from the authority of God, not that of the State, and the competence of the State likewise derives from the authority of God, not that of the Church, the State is independent in its own temporal, political domain, in pursuing its natural end, which is the defence and promotion of its citizens' temporal well-being; and the Church is independent in performing its supernatural tasks (teaching faith and morals, celebrating the liturgy, preaching the word, administering the sacraments, in all that concerns the structure and administration of the Church). The many attempts that the State has made in the past and in our own day to control the inner or outer order of the Church (various kinds of State Church, Gallicanism, Febronianism, Josephinism) are inconsistent with this independence; but so are the claims of the Church (mainly in the Middle Ages) to supremacy over the State and the attempt to enforce them when the Church was able (papal institution and deposition of princes and attempts to subject the State to canon law).

Following the doctrine of the "two swords", which Pope Gelasius I propounded against Byzantium, medieval theories of Church and State sometimes went to extremes (like the hierocratic doctrine of the *potestas ecclesiae directa in temporalibus*). But in evaluating them we must remember that the historical background and the philosophico-theological idea of a single Christendom – *ecclesia universalis* – embracing crown and clergy, the spiritual and the temporal power, in one metaphysical sweep, meant that Church and State were closely interwoven. Given the idea that the society which pursues the nobler end is the nobler society, men compared the two powers to gold and lead or sun and moon. (Unlike the State, the Church works for our supernatural, eternal good and so its end is the higher. We find the Fathers themselves, St. Gregory of Nazianzus, for instance, and St. John Chrysostom, comparing Church and State to soul and body or heaven and earth.) This meant that the Church was regarded as essentially superior to the State. In the investiture controversy Gregory VII fought not only for the freedom of the Church (*libertas ecclesiae*) but also for its supremacy within the total *Corpus Christianum* which embraced both Church and State; and his attitude develops logically, by way of Innocent III and Innocent IV, to Boniface VIII and the bull *Unam Sanctam* (18 November 1302). This bull presents the Pope as the source of both powers, though it recognizes that Church and State differ in their general nature. The hierocratic theory itself affirmed the autonomous jurisdiction of the State and the Pope's duty to pass on the temporal sword. Papal intervention in temporal affairs was considered legitimate only *ratione peccati*, that is, if the salvation of souls were at stake. But since the Pope was sole judge of whether a given case involved the salvation of souls, the formula *ratione peccati* could in fact be used to justify any political move on the Pope's part.

St. Thomas Aquinas considered the State an institution of natural law, and, therefore, part of the natural order, whereas the Church belonged to the supernatural order of revelation and grace. His doctrine combined scriptural and Augustinian thought with Aristotle and stressed the origin of both powers in God: "Both powers derive from God, the spiritual and the temporal. Temporal authority, therefore, is subject to the spiritual insofar as God has subordinated it, namely in matters concerning the salvation of souls; so in these matters a man must obey the spiritual power rather than the temporal." (*II Sent*. d. 44, q. 2, a. 3 and 4.) In accordance with the Aristotelian teleology of his thought, St. Thomas affirms the superiority of the spiritual power, but not without qualification: "Civil authority is subject to ecclesiastical authority only where the exigencies of our supernatural end – eternal life – are involved; in its own sphere the civil power enjoys ample independence." (M. Grabmann.) In St. Thomas we already have a sharper distinction of the ends of Church and State which Bellarmine accentuates and which produces the doctrine of the Church's indirect power *in temporalibus*.

On Thomistic foundations Leo XIII constructed a doctrine of Church and State which has prevailed down to the present time. Leo also proceeds on the assumption that the State, being an institution of natural right, comes directly from God. "Like civil society, the civil power has its source in nature and therefore in God himself. Whence it follows that civil authority as such is from God alone." (*Immortale Dei*, 1 November 1885.) Church and State are autonomous societies, each with its own native right; each is a *societas perfecta*, each sovereign in its own sphere. "God has divided the care of the human race between two powers, the ecclesiastical and the civil. One is in charge of divine concerns, the other of human concerns. Each is supreme in its own sphere, each is confined within certain limits which follow from its nature and proximate goal." (*Ibid.*) And *Sapientiae Christianae* (10 January 1890) says: "Since Church and State each has its own authority, neither of the two societies is subject to the other in the ordering and conduct of its own affairs – within the limits, of course, that each is assigned by its proximate goal." Just as the Church acknowledges the independence of the State in all purely civil matters, so the State must also acknowledge the sovereignty of the Church in its own sphere: "Whatever, therefore, in human affairs is in any way sacred, whatever concerns the salvation of souls or the worship of God, either by its own nature or by reason of the end to which it is referred – all this is subject to the authority and judgment of the Church. On the other hand civil and political matters are quite rightly subject to the authority of the State." (*Immortale Dei.*) It is still disputed whether Leo XIII teaches a *potestas indirecta* or only a *potestas directiva*. His utterances certainly advance no explicit claim to jurisdiction; but since he does not discuss what power, if any, the Church can have over temporal things (much less over the State) and what means it can use to give its principles effect in the world, his teaching will not tell us the nature of the Church's power *in temporalibus*.

On the other hand it is increasingly recognized today that the independence of Church and State ultimately depends on the nature and origin of each one's authority; these also determine the means which Church and State may use in pursuance of their various ends. The spiritual nature and the spiritual authority entrusted to it determine the nature and scope of the Church's work in the world.

C. Co-operation between Church and State

Though Church and State pursue two different ends, they are composed of the same members. The same individuals are expected to satisfy the requirements of both powers, and so those requirements must be attuned as far as possible. This is particularly necessary in "mixed matters", which concern Church law under one aspect and State law under another (for instance, marriage, education, schools, appointments to ecclesiastical office [insofar as they may affect the State], establishing Church holidays, Sunday work, the legal position of Church property, and the like). If there is to be lasting agreement on such matters, which the Church has traditionally preferred to settle by concordat, each side must be prepared to meet the other half-way and accept a solution that takes account of all citizens, not only of the Church's members. As the champion of personal freedom the Church must take care that no agreement it makes with the State shall prejudice the rights of third parties who are not Catholics. In such arrangements the Church seeks first of all recognition and contractual guarantees of its independence. Its chief requirement is always that the State allow it to carry out its mission without hindrance, that the citizens of the State shall be free to discharge their supernatural duties, and that the State's demands within its own sphere shall not conflict with the natural moral law or the revealed law of God.

Here most Catholic canonists and moral theologians warn us not to conclude, from the sovereignty of the two powers, that their respective goals and purposes are equal in rank; because, they say, the Church firmly maintains that its supernatural end is higher than the purely natural end of the State (and therefore it must take precedence over the State). This point has relevance for the individual in a concrete case of conflict; but it is quite irrelevant to the legitimate relations of Church and State nowadays when the State, indifferent to all Churches and religions, would reject any such argument simply on the grounds of civil liberty, so that in case of conflict between itself and the State it would be futile for the Church to argue the subordination of ends.

Even in the case of an individual, the theoretical superiority of the Church will not mean that its law must always be obeyed in preference to the law of the State if the two happen to conflict. For the principle that the Church's law takes precedence rests on the assumption that a man is faced with a choice between supernatural duty (represented by the Church) and natural, earthly duty (represented by the State). If the case is otherwise, then the principle cannot apply. The fact that the Syllabus condemned the proposition (no. 42), "In conflictu legum utriusque potestatis ius civile praevalet", does not mean that the Church claims precedence for its law over the law of the State in every case; it means that the law of the State does not take precedence in every case. If the civil law conflicts with the natural moral law or God's revealed law, then it is equally wrong to impose or to obey such a law (see the relevant passages in the encyclicals *Diuturnum Illud* and *Sapientiae Christianae*). In every age the Church proclaims with St. Peter: "We must obey God rather than men" (Acts 5:29; see also Acts 4:19),

The right and duty which the Church has to declare with binding authority what is contained in divine revelation and to condemn such doctrines and practices as offend against revelation, extends to the civil and political sphere, which is subject to God's commandments like every other sphere of human life. The State is no less bound to obey God than the Church is. But this right of the Church implies no coercive power over the State. The history of theory about Church and State reflects the many forms which actual relations between them have taken down the ages. Yves Congar rightly warns against overlooking this variety: "Let us not turn the law and arrangements of one period into an absolute, but recognize that the three successive theories of the *potestas directa*, *indirecta*, and *directiva* reflect a historical evolution which is normal but irreversible." Decisions that the Church makes in virtue of its *potestas spiritualis directa* are not acts of civil jurisdiction. At the same time it would be an error to regard them as mere exhortations that oblige no one; they are commands which bind members of the Church in conscience, and the Church can demand that they be strictly obeyed (for example, forbidding Catholics to be members of a given political party under pain of excommunication).

D. Separation of Church and State

New thinking about the relationship between the two powers also affects our ideas about the separation of Church and State. The complete separation championed by liberals and socialists was meant to deprive the Church of all influence in public life. The demand was used as a weapon in a struggle to destroy the Church completely, and as such the Church could not and cannot accept it. This is the sense in which we must interpret the many condemnations by 19th- and 20th-century Popes (see especially Gregory XVI against Lamennais, encyclical *Mirari Vos*, 15 August 1832; Pius IX, *Syllabus of Errors*, 8 December 1864; Leo XIII, encyclicals *Immortale Dei*, 1 November 1885, and *Libertas Praestantissimum*, 28 June 1888; Pius X against the French law separating Church and State, encyclicals *Vehementer Nos*, 11 February 1906, *Gravissimo Officii*, 10 August 1906, *Une fois encore*, 6 January 1907, and the similar Portuguese law, *Iamdudum*, 24 May 1911; Benedict XV, encyclical *Ad Beatissimi*, 1 November 1914; Pius XII various addresses after 1945).

If the separation of Church and State is designed to treat the Church as though it were non-existent or a mere private concern of individual citizens, who are even denied the right to organize as a religious body (as happened in France in 1905), then the modern State is not simply affirming its neutrality towards all religions, it is attacking the very existence of religion. But a constitutional separation of the two powers which recognizes the public existence of the Church or at least allows it to work unhampered, is another matter. Thus separation in the U.S.A., for example, has benefited the Church, allowing it to flourish in the public sphere free of any State tutelage. In the libertarian democracies today the old idea of separation is increasingly yielding to the idea of partnership between Church and State, and it is not felt to be a major concern whether this new partnership is secured by a concordat or results from the State's acceptance of a plurality of social forces. A constitutional separation of the two powers which does not interfere with the Church's free growth in social life but guarantees it the area of freedom necessary for carrying out its saving mission can do justice to the nature of Church and State alike. A. Hartmann pertinently observes that for the State to bear its own limited competence in mind does not make it a laicized State. The *État laïque* is not an *État laïcisé*, and confining the State to its proper domain must not be confused with separating State from Church as many 19th-century liberals and socialists wished to do.

So it is inconsistent with the modern view of both powers to maintain traditional rights which the State has had to supervise the Church. These are historical relics from the days of established Churches and are incompatible with the autonomy of the Church. Any future agreement between Church and State must take account of altered circumstances. The problem of the separation of Church and State has entered a new phase, as is clear from the lively discussion of John Courtney Murray's ideas on the subject, and we must ask whether the term "separation", with its many historical overtones, is a suitable term to use at all of the relationship existing between Church and State in the libertarian democracies. More distance between Church and State does not mean that the Church renounces any attempt to influence public life; rather, "being henceforth wholly independent of the State, the Church can and must take that much closer an interest in the world and the State" (R. Smend).

E. The Church and the Secularized State

The altered conception which modern democracy has of itself has made it possible for the Church to establish a positive relationship with the "neutral" State (neutral towards all religions and philosophies). On the one hand the Church has to give up a number of privileges in the civil order; it can no longer identify its own work wholly or in part with the work of the State and it acknowledges the State's autonomy in secular affairs. On the other hand the State leaves the Church entirely free to carry out its saving mission in the world, part of which is to preach the truth that is necessary to human dignity rightly understood. Of course before one can approve of the secular State one must realize that religious liberty is a civil right of the individual even according to the Church's doctrine, and that the Church, certain as it is of objective truth, does not merely tolerate the erroneous conscience of the individual but acknowledges it as responsible decision. Only on this basis can the Church not merely tolerate the State's neutrality towards all religions and philosophies but affirm it as consistent with the natural moral order. Vatican II decided in favour of religious liberty thus understood, with its Declaration on Religious Freedom.

The drawing apart of Church and State in democracy means at once an opportunity and a responsibility for the Church. When the State recognizes a plurality of social forces, which often assert a group interest to the prejudice of the national interest, it is the more difficult for the State to ensure the common good; especially since the parties, being dependent on votes, are always tempted to court organized interests. Here the Church is as it were the conscience of the public; it is its business to awaken and fortify in the State and society a sense of their duty to the common good. It is the business of the Church, the guardian of the moral order, to keep that order present to the minds of men, both those who command and those who obey. Even in a pluralistic world the Church can exercise its native right and work for a fair consideration of its interests, so that its adherents may freely cultivate their convictions in contrast to other views within the State.

By using its due freedom to awaken the conscience of all men, proclaiming that they must always observe justice and love in their doings, it makes its contribution to the State and society. This is the real "social mission" of the Church, so much talked of and so much misunderstood. Thus the Church consciously influences the temporal sphere but not in order to rule, to impose its own commands, but to serve, to make known to men that they are subject to God's law individually and as society. True, the Church regards itself as the accredited organ of God's commands, but does not on that account claim that the State is in any way subordinate to it, even in moral or spiritual matters; for the secular State is free to decide which moral values it wishes to make the foundation of the civil order. In the eyes of the Church, moral principles are objective truths; but in the eyes of the State they are subjective value-judgments – except for human rights which exist antecedent to the State. So long as the State is a libertarian democracy the Church has an opportunity to make objective truth prevail in the realm of politics through its faithful. This method of redemptive work necessarily means a further shift from the institutional to the personal approach.

The Pastoral Constitution of Vatican II on the Church in the Modern World confirms the fact that the Church, without succumbing to "progressivism", is moving towards a new view of the world and of its relations with the State; it is prepared to admit that the bond between the State and man is willed by God, at the same time differentiating this bond from man's inalienable status as a son of God and his saving bond with the Church of Jesus Christ. The constitution deliberately places the modern idea of Church and State in the context of the pluralist society and distinguishes what Christians do as citizens, individually or in groups, guided by their own Christian conscience, from activities which they carry on in the name of the Church and in union with their pastors (art. 76, 1). It stresses the point that the Church has no wish whatever to encroach on the business of civil society and is not committed to any political system (art. 76, 2). Henceforth, therefore, there can be no question of identifying the work of the Church with that of the State or at least confounding the two. The activity which the Christian as a citizen chooses to engage in, following his own judgment and inspired by his faith, is differentiated from his activity as a member of the Church, under its authority. The constitution expressly acknowledges the independence of Church and State alike, but points out that both serve the personal and social vocation of man (art. 76, 3). Above all it is the Church's duty to continue fostering justice and love among the nations. A comparison of this declaration with Leo XIII's doctrine of Church and State as the "two powers" will throw into sharp relief the change there has been, from the idea of domination to that of service.

Breaking with the traditional view that the State is to help the Church carry out is mission, the Council concludes: "But it [the Church] does not lodge its hopes in privileges conferred by civil authority. Indeed, it stands ready to renounce the exercise of certain legitimately acquired rights if it becomes clear that their use raises doubts about the sincerity of its witness or that new conditions of life call for some other arrangements." (Art. 76, 5.)

The willingness of the Church to give up outdated privileges and duly acquired rights proves that it accepts the implications of being different from the State as it follows Christ in this world. It now turns to its spiritual mission, which enables and constrains it to undertake a dialogue with the world. This means that the Church in the whole of its life has become an intellectual and spiritual partner indispensable for the State precisely because it is neutral towards all religions and psychologies. It is citizens making their own personal decisions according to their Christian conscience who represent Christian values in the State and ensure the presence of Christ's Church in the secular State. Instead of confronting the State as a kind of outside power, almost another nation, the Church now works and lives its life in the same society which produces the

State, though it does not identify itself with society and the State. Co-operation between Church and State is seen in a new light. Now the question is not so much defining each one's rights and sphere of competence as practical adaptation in their joint responsibility for man; for Church and State are both entrusted with the welfare of man, though in two entirely different ways, according to the nature and operation of each. Wherever the Church awakens and sensitizes conscience, wherever it proclaims the gospel and teaches Christian moral principles, wherever it spreads justice and love, it is accomplishing its true mission. Of temporal powers it expects freedom to work without let or hindrance, freedom vis-à-vis the State and other social forces as well.

F. The Present Situation

There are now roughly three types of relationship between Church and State in the West and in the other countries with a Christian background. Certain countries still preserve the old forms of an established Church; most countries have made a separation between Church and State, some enforcing a strict break (with complete religious freedom) and others co-operating with the Church in various ways; and the Communist countries have a separation designed to exclude the Church altogether from public life. This general classification, however, does not tell us how far religious freedom – freedom of conscience for the individual and freedom of worship and witness for religious bodies – is allowed in the libertarian democracies (even those which maintain a traditional established Church). The practice varies widely and is often of quite recent introduction. On the other hand totalitarian States in the East thwart the practice of religion so far as possible, even when religious freedom is guaranteed in the constitution. Many States regulate their relations with the Churches not only by relevant constitutional provisions but also by concordats and other agreements reached with the religious bodies.

1. *Established Churches.* Originally, the special feature of an established Church was that it relegated to an inferior legal status such citizens as did not belong to it. But today all States which retain an established Church not only allow religious freedom but give all citizens full equality before the law. Only here and there are specially representative State offices reserved to members of the State Church: thus the Sovereign and Lord Chancellor in England, the King and Minister for Worship in Sweden, the King in Denmark, and the Head of State in Spain must belong to the established Church. Even as to purely religious matters, the State shares in the government of modern established Churches. In the United Kingdom only the Church of England (Anglican) and the Church of Scotland (Presbyterian) are still established. The Sovereign is head of the Church of England but not of other Churches of the Anglican Communion.

The British Parliament, where certain bishops are members of the Upper House as Lords Spiritual, maintains in many ways its right to determine the doctrine and liturgy of the Church of England. In Norway and Sweden the Sovereign is also head of the established Lutheran Church. The "Danish National Church" really has no head. Lutheranism is still the official religion of Iceland and Finland. The Finnish President nominates bishops of the Lutheran Church and the Orthodox Church as well. Both these Churches are financially supported by the State and their synodal decrees must be confirmed by Parliament. The only other country which has an established Orthodox Church is Greece. The position in Switzerland is exceptional in a number of respects. Some cantons (Zurich, Waadt) have a Calvinist established Church or, having separated Church and State, only recognize the Calvinist Church as existing at law (Basle Town, Appenzell-Ausserrhoden). Some recognize only the Catholic Church in the same way (Ticino, Valais). Most cantons recognize both Churches, either as the established Churches of the canton or, where Church and State have been separated (Neuchâtel, Geneva), as the only Churches with a legal existence there.

Elsewhere in Europe Catholicism is the State religion only in Italy and Spain. The Lateran Treaty of 1929 established the Church in Italy and was confirmed by the republican constitution (1946), which, however, also guarantees freedom of religion and organization to non-Catholics, reserving their relationship to the State to special agreements. Until recently, non-Catholics in Spain were subject to real disabilities. Now, as a result of the Council's Declaration on Religious Freedom, a law of 1967 has given them a large measure of freedom, as individuals and as religious bodies.

In Latin America the Catholic Church is the State Church of Argentina, Bolivia, Colombia, Costa Rica, the Dominican Republic, Haiti, and Paraguay. Nevertheless religious freedom is guaranteed by the constitution, although a few years ago the Colombian government took measures against Protestants. Costa Rica and Bolivia still retain the right to nominate bishops which was enjoyed by the Spanish crown; Argentina surrendered the right in 1966 (responding to the desire expressed by the Council in its Decree on the Bishops' Pastoral Office in the Church, art. 20).

2. *Separation of Church and State in the West.* All other States in the West which have a Christian background provide in their constitutions for separation of Church and State and religious freedom. Even where the separation was brought about by secularist, anti-clerical forces, relations have improved. In France, for example, despite the hostile legislation of 1905 and 1914, there was a *rapprochement* of Church and State after the First World War. In 1921 diplomatic relations were resumed with the Vatican and it was agreed to hold consultations before bishops were appointed (though so far there has been no concordat). Thus the Church is free to expand. Close co-operation has grown up between Church and State in West Germany, on the basis of relevant articles from the Weimar Constitution which are now embodied in the fundamental law of 1949, together with the concordats still in force (those of constituent States of the Federal Republic and the concordat made with Germany in 1933). Legislation envisages the Churches' engaging in public activities, especially social work and relief, and provides them with substantial sums.

In Austria too, religious bodies may be recognized by the State as legal corporations. The ecclesiastical reorganization provided for by the concordat of 1933 has been carried out and ill-feeling about State subsidies to the Churches and religious instruction in State schools has been allayed. The Belgian constitution of 1831, much admired in the last century for the freedom it secured the Church, exempts all recognized religions from State control. But the State pays the salaries of the clergy – Catholic, Protestant and Jewish. In Luxemburg the position is similar. The Netherlands also allows religious bodies to carry on social and political activity without interference from the State; here an extensive school system and broadcasting stations of their own are very useful to them. In the Republic of Ireland the constitution provides for religious liberty and the separation of Church and State, and forbids the State to subsidize any religion. It recognizes that the Catholic religion, for which there is no concordat, is that of the great majority, but also protects the Protestant Churches and Jewish congregations. The constitution of 1933 still separates Church and State in Portugal and the concordat of 1940 accepts that position. Though the Catholic Church is recognized as a corporate body, the State is free to extend the same recognition to other religious bodies; they can, however, worship and organize without such recognition. Portugal still claims and uses the right of patronage in the mission areas of its overseas provinces.

The two powers are completely separate in the U.S.A. There the Supreme Court has ruled that the First Amendment forbids providing a religion with any local or national subsidy, and therefore that no religious instruction can be given in "public" schools. At the same time the separation ensures the widest religious freedom. Churches are free, for instance, to set up schools and even universities – an opportunity of which the Catholic Church has made full use, so that today it has a complete system of independent schools. A similar freedom exists in the Philippines, whose constitution is modelled on the American one. In Canada the separation is not so sharp; Church schools can obtain a degree of State assistance. Even the radical separation in Mexico (constitution of 1917), which was meant to annihilate the influence of the Catholic Church, has been ineffective to that end, despite the persecutions from 1923 to 1928. Today religious liberty prevails, and the anti-Catholic legislation is tending to become a dead letter. Other Latin American countries have various forms of separation. In 1964, even before Argentina, Venezuela gave up the right to nominate bishops, an agreement to that effect being made with the Holy See.

3. *Separation of Church and State in Communist countries.* Modelled on the constitution of the U.S.S.R., the system of separation in Communist countries demands "separation of the State from the Church and of the Church from the schools", so as to deprive religion of influence, especially over the young. Constitutional texts may proclaim freedom of conscience and worship but the State does much to paralyze the Churches while offering atheist propaganda every facility, for atheism is considered scientific and therefore worthy of State patronage. The concrete situation varies a great deal from country to country. In Poland and East Germany pastoral work can be carried on, though often amid difficulties. While the Church in Czechoslovakia, strictly supervised by the State, is left with very little scope for its life and work, conditions in Yugoslavia and in Hungary have improved recently.

Paul Mikat

CHURCH AND WORLD

1. *Introduction.* The Church's reflection and teaching on the mutual relation of world and Church have to some extent entered on a new stage with Vatican II. The Church has always been concerned with the theme. Scripture itself raises the question of the significance of secular authority and of the obligation and limit of Christians' obedience to it. The patristic period, the Middle Ages and modern times all dealt in theory and in actual practice, which often involved bitter conflicts, with the relation between Sacerdotium and Imperium, the question of the relation between Church and State, the Church's freedom in face of the State, the relative autonomy of the State in face of the Church, the right of the Church to a particular kind of influence on the action of the State, the question of the separation of Church and State, the task of the State in regard to the true religion and the Church. But if we leave aside the perpetually recurring question of the relation between revelation (dogma, magisterium) and secular science and learning (which of course is also an essential por-

tion of the "world"), almost the only question formerly raised was that of Church and State, the latter regarded in terms of authority. Today it is a question of the relation between the Church and the *world*. And the "world" is envisaged as it is experienced at the present time – as a history of humanity as a single whole, and as a world which is not simply an antecedent datum, a situation of interest solely in the perspective of salvation. It is a world planned and produced by man himself and it therefore concerns man even in its own empirically observable importance. This new way of raising the question was plainly seen at Vatican II. The Church deliberately set itself this question. It had been prepared for in the Church's dispute with 19th century Liberalism and with Marxism (chiefly, however, in the economic domain). Marxism was really the first to work out a genuine theory of a world to be constructed by man himself in order to escape his own "self-alienation". Vatican II explicitly took up this comprehensive set of themes in the Pastoral Constitution on the Church in the Modern World. And other texts dealt with other aspects of the same themes. For the Church lives in a divided Christendom, a world of many non-Christian higher religions, a pluralist society in which the State with its authority has a quite different function from its task in an ideologically homogeneous society, or in one which became so after short periods of transition and conflict. Consequently we are certainly justified in understanding the Council's declarations on ecumenism, the non-Christian religions and religious freedom as symptomatic and as a partial answer to the frankly stated general question of the relation between the Church and the historical and changing world of the present day.

2. Before anything more precise can be said on this relation, the two concepts must be briefly explained.

a) For theology "the world" in the first place signifies in a neutral sense the whole of creation as a unity (in origin, destiny, goal, general structures, interdependence of part on part). It either includes man, or is distinguished from him as his environment, the stage set by God for the history of his salvation. In this sense world has the same meaning as "heaven and earth", and is a revelation of God, exists for his glory; it is good, meaningful and beautiful, the freely and lovingly created recipient of God's self-communication (Jn 3:16f.; *D* 428, 1805). It does not separate man from God but mediates between God and man, as is shown above all in the Incarnation. Through guilt in the realm of the angels and by the initial guilt of man in original sin and by his subsequent calamitous history, this world and especially that of man is also deeply affected, even in the material realm, so that it is hostile to God and in conflict with its own ultimate structures and characteristics. The world in this sense (biblically "this" cosmos, "this" aeon) signifies the totality of "principalities and powers" hostile to God, i.e., everything in the world which prompts to new guilt and is the tangible embodiment of this guilt. In this sense the Christian must not be "of the world" (Jn 18:36 and *passim*), even if he must be "in" the world (Jn 17:11). Yet even as this sinful world it is nevertheless loved by God. It is in need of redemption but also capable of it, enveloped by God's grace despite its guilt and in its guilt, and its history will end in the kingdom of God. Consequently, despite its opposition to God it constitutes a task for the Christian, who by the power of grace is to uphold its true order, discern the possibilities of its development, while critically distinguishing the forces present in it and patiently bearing its burden and darkness which will never cease until the end.

This world has a history which has

entered on its eschatological stage through the incarnation, cross and resurrection of the eternal Word of God. The outcome of this history in its entirety is already decided by Christ in the depths of reality, even though that outcome is still hidden and is only grasped by faith. Hence the world or aeon "to come" is already present and operative in the present world. It is clear from this that while Christianity recognizes a certain dualism between God and world in redemptive history, a dualism which is already in process of dissolution, it does not acknowledge any radical and insuperable dualism. No such dualism should therefore secretly colour the practical life of Christians.

The various aspects of this theological, many-sided concept of the world can never be wholly separated from one another in practice, and this is what makes the whole problem so difficult. Two things must therefore be borne in mind. The three meanings of the term "world" (the good created world, the sinful world of perdition, the redeemed world orientated supernaturally by grace, which is the situation in which salvation is worked out) are not three simply disparate uses of a single term. They are linked by the fact that this world (as the world of man) is a history which is still in progress. Because the world is history and not merely an unchanging stage on which history unfolds, it has a beginning, presuppositions and a goal towards which it moves in the decisions open to men. This is the world as creation and as partner of God's supernatural self-communication in grace. Because it is a history, the outcome of which remains hidden within it because it is still unfolding, it is possible for this world to form a unity in multiplicity, which we can never fully distinguish. It comprises both personal decision in relation to God, and the external factors which make this possible and fulfil it, yet which also have their own intra-mundane significance. It is a unity in difference of saving action and guilt. This world is not only a history (because changing). It has now become a history which can be planned, actively manipulated and guided by men, even in its empirical space-time reality, and not merely in its transcendent meaning in God's sight for salvation and perdition, in a way which was not possible earlier to any considerable extent.

b) The meaning of the term "Church" need not of course be developed at length here. Only what is of particular importance for the questions which occupy us need be emphasized. The Church is not identical with the kingdom of God. It is the sacrament of the kingdom of God in the eschatological phase of sacred history which began with Christ, the phase which brings about the kingdom of God. As long as history lasts, the Church will not be identical with the kingdom of God, for the latter is only definitively present when history ends with the coming of Christ and the last judgment. Yet the kingdom of God is not simply something due to come later, which later will replace the world, its history and the outcome of its history. The kingdom of God itself is coming to be in the history of the world (not only in that of the Church) wherever obedience to God occurs in grace as the acceptance of God's self-communication. And this does not take place solely in the Church as the socially constituted, historically visible society of the redeemed. It does not take place solely in a secret inwardness of conscience, in meta-historical religious subjectivity, but in the concrete fulfilment of an earthly task, of active love of others, even of collective love of others.

It is of course true that this history remains ambiguous in its empirically observable external expressions, and that the "occurrence" of grace is just as hidden as the material character of its acceptance. The thesis of the kingdom of God as "the world" is fundamentally implied by the Catholic doctrine that grace and justification are in fact to be found outside the visible unity of the Church, so that Church history and the history of salvation are therefore not identical. It follows from Catholic teaching on the inseparable unity of material and formal morality, which demands definite, material, meaningful activities in this world, and cannot be reduced to a purely religious or formally "believing" frame of mind. It also follows from the unity of love of God and the neighbour. For this kingdom of God in the world, which of course can never simply be identified with any particular objective secular phenomenon, the Church is a part, because of course the Church itself is in the world and in its members makes world history (cf. *D* 1783). Above all, however, the Church is precisely its special fundamental sacrament, i.e., the eschatological and efficacious manifestation (sign) in redemptive history that in the unity, activity, fraternity, etc. of the *world*, the kingdom of God is at hand. Even here, therefore, as in the various individual sacraments, sign and thing signified can never be separated or identified (cf. Vatican II, *Lumen Gentium*, art. 9).

3. This relation between Church and world has a history. The relation is not and must not always be the same. It is historically changing because the world as an individual and collective history of freedom and also the Church in its official ministry and above all in its members is subject to faults and even succumbs to guilt. This can distort and falsely determine the relation between the two realities through one's trespassing on the domain of the other, through neglect or misinterpretation of the function which each in its own way can and should perform for the other. But this relation is subject to change even prior to such guilt in the course of history, simply because both parts are historical, i.e., changing realities. Their mutual relationship itself changes as a consequence. There is not only a secular history of the world, in its knowledge, culture, self-emancipation from the domination of nature, in its increasingly complex social structures, its whole conception of itself, its attitude to its past and to its open future. The Church itself is only slowly led into the fullness of the truth which it already possesses, in a historical process under the guidance of the Spirit, and this history of the Church's truth as the standard of its action also alters its relation to the world in all its domains. For example, the Church only slowly learns fully to appreciate the freedom of the individual and of human groups, or to value the unity and multiplicity of the many Churches which the one Church comprises and also their basis in natural and secular history (cf. Vatican II: Decrees on Eastern Catholic Churches and on Ecumenism). The Church only slowly came to acknowledge the relative autonomy of secular sciences and the potential variety of the social, political and economic organization of human groups (decline of mistrust of democracy or of certain forms of socialization, etc.). The Church is slowly attaining a more unconstrained, comprehensive and personal appreciation of human sexuality.

And despite the secular occasions of such growth and change in theory and practice, this alteration in the Church is ultimately regulated by the standard of the Church's own spirit and its own ancient truth. It is not merely a case of enforced adaptation to a historical situation which the Church is powerless to alter. Changes in the Church and in the world mutually interact. The change in the Western mind in modern times ultimately sprang from the spirit of Christianity itself, even though it often rightly or wrongly turned against the actual existing Church and forced it slowly to learn what it really always knew. That change led from a Greek cosmocentrism to anthropocentrism, meant destroying the numinous character of the world and making it the material of human activity. Other aspects were its rationality and technology, conscious reflection on its own historical character with a consequent critical relation to the past and openness to a novel future, and the reduction of human tradition to a merely relative value.

Because the relation between Church and world is really history and has a history, it always has to be determined anew in the concrete, although all its fundamental structures remain. Similarly it retains the unforeseeable and incalculable character of history. It cannot simply be deduced in its entirety from eternal principles capable of concretely determining it once and for all. It is also an original decision of the human beings in the Church and in the world acting in history. It is therefore always a struggle. It is not a matter for doctrinal tribunals alone, but for the Church's pastoral office *and* for the charismatic representatives of a freely adopted attitude towards the world in the dialectical, changing union of flight from the world and affirmation of the world, the relation between which cannot in the concrete be laid down once and for all. Precisely because this history is history, it is difficult to reduce it to a formula, and this cannot be done without express reserves. Yet we might perhaps say that it is the history of the Church's growing self-discovery and of the increasing emancipation of the world into its own secular nature by the Church. The Church comes to know itself more and more as "not of this world" and at the same time as the sacrament of the absolute future of the world, which is not produced by the world by its own power but is given to it by God, as a supra-mundane grace, thus relativizing in theory and practice any conception which the world forms of itself, in other words, opens it out to the absolute future.

4. Two fundamental ways of misconceiving the relation between Church and world can definitely be noted. World in the comprehensive sense which, as we have seen, it now bears, was not a theme of explicit reflection in earlier ages of the Church and consequently these two fundamental heresies concerning this relationship were scarcely constituted consciously and explicitly. As latent but operative, however, they play a part everywhere in history. We may call the one heresy "integrism", the other, for want of a better, current term, "esotericism".

a) Integrism regards the world as mere material for the action and self-manifestation of the Church, and wants to integrate the world into the Church. Even if it is conceded that there are "two swords" in the world, the secular sword is regarded as conferred by the Church to be employed in the service of the Church and its higher purposes. Even a doctrine of the *potestas indirecta* of the Church *ratione peccati* over secular realities can be misconstrued in an integrist way. It is sufficient to start from the false but widespread tacit assumption that the moral principles of human action which are defended by the official Church and applied by its pastoral ministry to men's action are of such a kind that (at least in principle) in each case a concrete prescription can be deduced from them for the particular action in question. Then all earthly action in the history of the world is nothing but the putting into practice of the principles taught, expounded and applied by the Church. The activity of the world in State, history and social life is then simply a realization of the Church's principles, and in fact an embodiment of the Church itself. The world would be the *corpus christianum* and nothing else.

If the Church at some point was not interested in a particular form of the world (and left "worldly business" to the "princes"), this, on the view we are describing, could only be a consequence of the factual impossibility of the Church's permeating the world. It was not an emancipation by the Church of the world into its secular nature. Or else its origin was that such secular action was regarded as without importance for salvation simply because it cannot be fully determined by the explicit principles of the Church and so, as *adiaphora*, could not be performed by man himself before God with the passion of moral and historical decision. But this tacit assumption of integrism is false. It is not possible wholly to derive from the principles of natural law and the gospel the human action which ought to be done *here and now*, although of course all action must respect those principles. Nor when such action is more than the carrying into effect of those principles and of the official instructions of the Church, does it cease to be morally important from the point of view of God and in relation to him as goal. It still concerns salvation and has to be performed with the absolute earnestness of moral responsibility. It can even be the subject of charismatic inspiration from on high, and, while remaining secular, a factor in the coming of the kingdom of God.

Integrism also overlooks the Catholic doctrine of man's intrinsic pluralism which he can never overcome. Man always finds himself exposed to a multiplicity of experiences (sources of knowledge) and impulses, which are not directly interrelated, and in addition, to a situation of "concupiscence". The will to integrate and synthesize this human plurality is of course justified and is a duty. It can include the will to form a sum of all knowledge in a humane and Christian philosophical view of the world; to action which springs from love of God; to a positive relation between Church and State; to Christian inspiration of culture. But integrism falsely believes that this synthesis can fully succeed, that the secular and the Christian can be wholly interrelated. Above all, it holds that this synthesis can be produced by the official Church precisely because it is the Church, that this total synthesis can be not merely the asymptotic goal of history in the kingdom of God beyond history, but can become an event in history itself.

Integrism is therefore the false opinion that everything has to be given an ecclesiastical stamp because everything of importance for salvation belongs to the official Church, at least in principle, and all that is non-ecclesiastical is merely indifferent secular business which has no serious significance for man as such as a unity and therefore for his salvation and the kingdom of God. What is radically false about this position becomes particularly clear (and dangerous) at a moment when the world is moving from a static condition and a theoretical way of looking at things to one which can be altered and manipulated by man and man's action. For then it becomes palpably evident that the actively created future is no longer wholly to be deduced from eternal principles but, as something really new and the outcome of active decision, stands under the summons of God and the responsibility of man in a way which is not the purely official, ecclesiastical way. As a consequence the Christian himself and above all the layman in his secular task is more than a recipient of orders from the Church's ministry. Yet even where he is not in receipt of them, he does not cease to act as a Christian in responsible historical decision. Action regulated by the Church and Christian action which is genuinely human do not coincide.

b) We might give the name "esotericism" to a false attitude towards the world of the factual Church or of the Christian, in which what is secular is regarded as a matter of indifference for Christianity, for a life directed towards salvation and therefore towards God's absolute future. Here a Christian considers flight from the world as the only genuinely Christian attitude, and therefore regards affirmation of the world, its values, enjoyment, achievement and success as in principle suspect from a Christian point of view, unless it is already directly and explicitly inspired and commanded by a "supernatural", "religious" intention. He cannot see it as merely inevitably interwoven with a world that is also a sinful one.

The sources and varieties of such esotericism are many. It may be based on a latent dualism which simply identifies the empirical aspect of the world with its sinfulness, so that remoteness from the world (its civilization, sexuality, self-development) is identified with detachment from sin and regarded undialectically as identical with greater closeness to God. Esotericism may think itself well-founded because of the NT attitude of the Sermon on the Mount, the recommendation of sexual abstinence, indifference to social conditions, imminent expectation of the end of the world, etc. On that basis it may consider that all Christian life has in this NT attitude not only an ever necessary warning and correction but its total expression, and all that has to be done is simply to maintain and reproduce this.

Such esotericism can in certain circumstances be extended into the doctrine of the invisible Church of the predestined known only to God. It can be based on the view that what is genuinely moral and valid in God's sight is absolutely meta-historical, beyond any concrete material determinable action; that it is purely a disposition, inwardness (faith, a "commitment" which remains purely formal in character); that there is no Christian ethics with positive Christian content; that the "secular" is totally inaccessible to a Christian attitude, remaining indifferent to this or even simply and solely sinful in all its shapes and forms; that it stands only under the law, not under the gospel which redeems and sanctifies the world itself. A Catholic variety of such esotericism may hold, for example, that life according to the evangelical counsels in the religious orders is of itself the sole or self-evidently the higher realization of the Christian spirit from which the many are dispensed only because of their weakness. Integrism and esotericism can form a strange combination in the tendency, e.g., in the Irish monastic Church, to make the world a monastery. The Calvinist conception of the theocracy of the Christian community with its Church discipline has a certain element of such a combination about it.

The decisive feature of esotericism is that the secular is abandoned to itself, as an indifferent or sinful residue in an explicitly religious life which as far as possible is carried on as exclusively as possible in the small circle of religious esoterics. It is not regarded as constituting in itself a positive task for the Christian as such.

5. The true relation of the Christian and the Church to the world lies in the mean between these two extremes. This mean should not be regarded as a facile compromise which is imposed by circumstances and which simply has to be because the world as a matter of unfortunate fact will never allow itself to be wholly integrated into the ecclesiastical and religious domain and because even the exclusively pious person cannot avoid serving the secular necessities of life. It is a question of a mean which, as we shall have to explain, lies above the two extremes as a radical unity, combining on its own basis both the unity and the difference of what is explicitly Christian and ecclesiastical on the one hand, and the world and secular ction on the other. Furthermore, the true relation between Church and world has to be determined in one way when it is a question of the relation of the official Church – the magisterium and pastoral

office, the "official" action of the Church engaging the responsibility of the socially constituted Church – to the world, and in another when it is a question of the relation to the world of Christians, especially the laity, for all of them also are, of course, the Church.

The relation to the world of the Christians who form the Church is not identical in all, for each has his own vocation and function in the Body of Christ, and this can and should shape his relation to the world in very different ways, extending, for example, from what is to a certain extent the flight from the world of the contemplative monk to the apparently wholly secular involvement of an ambitious statesman eager to make history. And these manifold aspects of the Church (official Church, Church as people of God) have themselves, as has already been noted, a history which changes them, and so, for example, all these aspects, despite their differences, can have a common "period style". Nowadays, for instance, the contemplative monk will be more explicitly conscious of his apostolic function than formerly, and this will contribute to determine his style of life.

a) For the official Church and its relation to the world at the present time it will be decisive to renounce all integrism even merely in practice. As a concrete, juridically constituted society, it cannot of course renounce having institutionalized relations with the world and its groupings, States, other Churches, etc. and their organizations. Nor should it renounce this in the genuine freedom of a pluralist society. Where it is really possible and useful, concordats, for example, can be concluded, even though the time for regulating relationships between Church and world by such methods is perhaps coming to an end. The Church can have diplomatic representatives, can work for State recognition of its own schools system and itself maintain an educational system if and where a good one is really possible. In this way, it inevitably and quite rightly has a certain social power, even if this is lessening rather than increasing with the growing diaspora status of the Church throughout the world. This in fact is changing the Church even in formerly "Christian nations" from a national Church to a Church of professed believers.

But the official Church has to take care not to turn unconsciously these institutional contacts with the world, and its own social power, into a means of exerting pressure in order to attain its legitimate aims, i.e., the effective proclamation of the gospel and the Christianization of as many human beings as possible. For to do so would mean that the Church was having recourse to something other than men's free, unforced obedience in a faith which has perpetually to be exercised anew. And in this respect, at least in practice and as far as public life is concerned, the difference between baptized and unbaptized on which in former times great stress was laid, is now of little account. Even where it could, the Church may no longer use secular means of coercion, e.g., economic sanctions, against its baptized members who act in an un-Christian way. In its whole attitude it must make it quite clear that the Church is and wills to be nothing but the socially constituted community of those who freely believe in Christ, joined with him and with one another in their love of him; that it is not the religious institution of a State or of a secular society as such. It must radically respect the freedom of conscience and religion of individuals and groups because of its own nature, not simply because in certain circumstances it cannot do otherwise. Precisely as such a free society of those who personally believe, it will no longer give the impression of being a traditional institution, almost a piece of folk-lore, a set of religious trimmings to life for those who were baptized as children of Catholic parents and for that reason have to keep up religious custom. On the other hand the Church can then much more readily be a missionary Church, addressing all, seriously seeking to win serious adults to baptism even in "Christian countries", making room in the Church for "modern" men with their own attitudes to life and their personalities already formed.

The official Church will also have to realize clearly that nowadays in a dynamic, extremely complex world with an extreme man-made abundance of goods, plans and possibilities, it is no longer possible for the Church to give directly concrete prescriptions regarding detailed economic organization, the actual direction of culture, the allocation of revenue for under-developed countries, space travel, regulation of the growth of population, armaments or disarmament, etc., even if it were in principle able to do so. The Church will proclaim the general principles of the dignity of man, freedom, justice and love, and will certainly not be of the opinion that such proclamation is useless or unimportant, or that it is merely an ideological veneer on a brutal existence which pursues its course by quite different laws. The Church can certainly have the courage in certain circumstances like John XXIII, or Paul VI before the United Nations, to come forward as representative spokesman of a Christian feeling for history or a Christian decision, even when the latter is "charismatic" rather than purely and simply a deduction from Christian principles, provided the distinction between the two is not obscured. But the Church must also really make clear the difference between Christian principles and the concrete decision which cannot be deduced from them alone, so that the limits of the possibilities open to the official Church (free of integrist claims) are plain. This problem becomes particularly acute when a statesman who is a Christian must take decisions for the pluralist society itself of which he is the representative.

If the distinction in question is made clear, it is then possible really to fight against the misconception which is still very prevalent among Christians, that the Christian can be assured of the morality of his action, and of its accordance with God's will, by the mere fact that it does not come into clear conflict with the material content of the Church's norms. Then it will also be clear that Christian action as such is possible and obligatory even in the secular domain, even where it is not "ecclesiastical", and that secular action objectively appropriate to the historical moment and situation is Christian action of importance for salvation without ceasing to be secular in character, provided it is performed as obligatory in the way indicated and on the basis of an ultimately Christian attitude. This liberating modesty of the official Church in encouraging what is really Christian outside the ecclesiastical sphere, is not a restriction imposed from outside on the Church's power and influence but flows from the Christian conception of the world itself, as will have to be shown even more clearly in a moment.

b) Christians, and therefore the Church as the people of God, stand in a relation to the world which is partly different from that of the official Church. It is in the last resort based on the fact that, as is shown most clearly and in the highest way in the incarnation of the divine Logos, the acceptance of the world by God – that is, grace, the really "Christian" feature – does not involve a destructive, annihilating absorption of the world (as recipient of God's self-communication) into God and the disappearance of the world. It means the setting free of the world into independence, intrinsic significance and autonomy. Closeness to God and the world's own intrinsic reality are not inversely but directly proportionate.

Two things which have already been referred to briefly are to be noted in this respect. This acceptance of the world has its own (redemptive) history. Consequently the emancipation of the world into its own secular nature through its acceptance on the part of God can become fuller and clearer, and this has happened in the course of Christian history. This growth of the world's secular character continues to be a Christian phenomenon even where, viewed superficially, it takes place by purely secular means (progress of rational science, technology, the higher stages of human social organization and life) and although it has often taken place under protest from Christians. The emancipation of the world into its growing independence by its acceptance on the part of God, in fact, however, also establishes the world at the same time in a "concupiscent" condition, yet it is not possible for this aspect of the world's secular nature to be grasped as inevitable. Ultimately it is the free disposition of divine love which willed to be triumphant in futility and death.

This means that the liberating acceptance of the world by God is not simply a transparent fact in its secular nature. The secularity is also the veil concealing the acceptance, which is only accessible to faith and hope. For us the world's plurality is not integrated empirically and tangibly into the movement of all reality towards God under the creative and merciful will of God. Man always finds himself from the start exposed to a plurality of factors in his life, of unsynthesized experiences, of contradictory impulses, in short, the secular world. And these cannot be adequately integrated by him from one ultimate point, that of the love of God. And this world in its development does not simply move in an evolutionary way towards its integration into the love of God, into his epiphany in the world and into the kingdom of God. It moves towards this goal through collapse, futility, the zero of death. This "concupiscent" situation of the world which contributes to its secular nature, is from a Christian point of view (in a way which is never wholly explicable by man within his history) both the manifestation of the "sin of the world" and the mediation and manifestation of the redemptive sharing in Christ's lot, for the salvation of the world and the attainment of its absolute future which is God himself.

For the Christian, therefore, the world is not the "esoterically" indifferent which lies outside his heavenly calling. In its permanent and even increasingly secular character something Christian occurs, even if the latter as such must have an empirical manifestation of a historical and social kind limited and distinct in scope within the world, i.e., an ecclesiastically Christian form. However, for this very reason the secular world as such in its direct secular empirical character (before faith and hope) is not for the Christian the Christian element itself, in such a way that nothing further would be needed except a candid, historically responsible identification with the world experienced in this way alone. Rather its own peculiar dimension of depth, inserted into it by the grace of God, and its ultimate dynamism must be experienced and accepted, for it is in these that it is open towards a direct relation to God. This experience and acceptance, which are significant for salvation, can, of course, where inculpably they have no longer any predicamental and social objective expression – that is, no ecclesiastical element – take place in responsible administration, endurance and obediently trusting acceptance of this world subject to death, in accordance with the judgment of a good conscience. Consequently in certain circumstances this can occur inculpably in purely secular conditions, and may even be done by someone who in the sphere of conceptual reflection is an atheist.

This world must furthermore (contrary to all integrism) be accepted as having been accepted by God in Christ precisely in its concupiscent secular nature and therefore as enduring and growing in this form.

The Christian understands this concupiscent secularity from the point of view of the meaning of the saving Cross. He is, therefore, far from thinking that the world is only Christian (and nothing but Christian) where he has mastered it by a successfully religious interpretation and integration and an ecclesiastical one. Therefore, despite his serene endeavour to integrate life into what has explicitly religious motives, he can also calmly be secular, and have earthly wishes and goals and enjoy the empirical world without religious mediation. He may spontaneously understand this as the way in which he obediently submits to God's transcendent decrees, especially if he is also ready to accept the frustration of the world, and death, obediently and with hope against hope. The earthly task and the "heavenly" vocation therefore are different, but this does not destroy their unity (contrary to esotericism) and they form a unity without being identical (as against integrism). This also means that their relation cannot be clearly determined in the concrete. The Church, being on the one hand the people of God and on the other the sacrament of the salvation of the *world*, can and must manifest this relation only in itself as a whole. Individuals in the Church have each a different call and task in this respect. Consequently there are rightly and necessarily found in the Church asceticism, flight from the world, the life of the evangelical counsels as imitation of the Crucified and as inchoative advance towards that renunciation of the world which is demanded of everyone in death, and the life of the religious orders. All this flight from the world is not merely a well-tried method of combating sin and its threat, but is the sign in the Church for the Church and the world that the world is the world of God, of grace, of hope in the absolute future of God, which God himself bestows and which is not simply identical with the autonomous development of the world. Legitimate flight from the world is an exercise of faith and hope in the divinely bestowed fulfilment of the world and consequently a sign of that courage of faith which can serenely allow the world to be world, i.e., finite, and does not need to place a strain on the world it cannot bear by divinizing it. Such a flight from the world would, however, become un-Christian if it were to posit itself as absolute, overlook its intermediate function of service in the Church, regard itself as the sole truly radical Christian element, viewing itself as the coming of grace.

Grace after all is ultimately given to the growing world (even though it has to pass through death), as the grace of the living risen Lord. Christian flight from the world cannot therefore in principle, not merely in practice, intend to be complete. It is always a partial factor, even if a very emphatic one, in a Christian life which with thanksgiving also takes the earth seriously, and can enjoy it while acknowledging that God has given himself to the earth so that it may be free and independent and that this gift is the ultimate content of the world's significance. From that point of view alone, not as a concession to human weakness, it is meaningful that there should, for example, exist in the Church more strict and less strict religious orders. And for the same ultimate reason there is in the same Church a ministry to the world, responsibility for the world, real though Christian acceptance of the secular nature of the world, a positive will for its development in all the domains which through man exist in it.

This Christian ministry to the world does not begin only when a worldly task is undertaken from explicitly Christian motives or when the secular is incorporated into Christian theology. It is contained within the secular itself because this itself is opened out towards God by the grace of God. But this must not only be taught theoretically for the life of Christians in the world. It must also be lived in practice. This can of course in certain circumstances take place in an "anonymously" Christian life. And for the same reason there also belong to the life of the Christian, together with joy in the world and secular activity, readiness for death with Christ, the spirit of the Sermon on the Mount, of the evangelical counsels; the practice of readiness for renunciation, for scepticism in regard to any identification with the world which would make an absolute of the world and idolize it, i.e., identify it ultimately with God.

How, in the individual, flight from the world and activity in the world must be united is a matter for the individual, of his vocation and spiritual experience. Only if the Church in multifarious ways and at the service of different vocations is both detached from the world and critical of it and at the same time belongs to the world, is it the sacrament of the salvation of that world which itself has to exist and grow. Provided that the spirit of detachment from the world, of criticism of the world, of penance, contemplation and renunciation (even to a heroic degree in individuals) remains alive in the Church, there need be no mistrust of the present course of the Church in seeking dialogue with the world, in announcing the unity of love of God and the neighbour, in taking up arms on behalf of the social development of society, freedom, racial equality, fraternity, etc. In a world which has itself changed from a static one to a world of man which has still to be created, tasks and modes of Christian existence accrue to the Christian and the Church which simply did not exist earlier but which now must be accepted and mastered by the Church in a *new* spirit and a positive will to affirm the world. Not everything which in this way exists in the Church in contrast to earlier times can be suspected of being a concession to the spirit of the evil world, as worldliness in the bad sense.

6. Particular problems and maxims regarding the relation between Church and world.

a) The world of today has become a single world and its unity is increasing. For the Church this does not simply mean that it is, as it always was, juridically a "perfect society" and that as a *single* community of believers it has to act as a unity in doctrine, liturgy and constitution. It does not simply mean that the Church's world mission receives a new urgency in the situation of universal interdependence of men beyond the range of local groups (nations, states), because now even the fate of Christianity in a "Christian country" is beginning to be dependent on its fate throughout the world, even among the "non-Christian peoples". The new situation also means that the whole Church as such has duties in respect of the shaping and further development of the one world in its unity. The speech of Paul VI before the United Nations is a symbol of this, and the Pastoral Constitution of Vatican II to a certain extent provides a basic programme for it. In spite of the justifiable emphasis on the special character and independence of particular, regional Churches by Vatican II (Decree on the Eastern Churches; bishops' conferences with greater powers; national liturgies, etc.), the Church as a whole must be in a position to act in regard to the world as a unity, and needs new and appropriate organs and institutions (charitable organization by the Church as a whole, the various new secretariats, help to underdeveloped countries by the Church as a whole, contacts with UNO, UNESCO, etc.).

b) If the Church necessarily has to be everywhere in the unified world of today and is so, though with very different degrees of intensity, and if the Church is always "the sign which is contradicted", then quite apart from any other reasons, the Church will necessarily everywhere, though of course in varying degrees, be a diaspora-Church in a pluralist world. And in practice it will remain so, despite its fundamental claim on all men, in accordance with which it has to undertake an active mission within and without, actively aiming at success. This also means that the Church must have the courage to make the transition from a national Church to a community Church of those who personally believe by their own decision. That is, it may in the concrete lay *more* weight on having communities which, though numerically small in comparison with the total surrounding population, are composed of those who believe seriously and personally and live in a Christian way, rather than on reaching and maintaining "everyone" in traditional Church-membership. This also means that the Church may organize its pastoral strategy and tactics accordingly.

In this way the Church will naturally become a Church of open dialogue with the world, both within and without. Even within itself, for such a community Church, despite its abidingly hierarchical constitution, will be a Church the existence of which is based on the laity as personal believers, and less on the institutional element or on the clergy as the traditional supports and recipients of its social prestige. A laity of that kind, however, by its very nature is the world (in the legitimate sense) in the Church. That laity's culture, mentality, aspirations, etc. (even to the extent that they find expression in the Church) are no longer created solely by the Church as an institution (as was almost entirely the case in earlier times). They are brought into the Church by the laity as part of the already existing world, and also by the clergy themselves as men of our time. In that way there is and must be a dialogue within the Church between Church and world. Outwardly there will be a similar dialogue because a community Church in the diaspora, which also has to be a missionary one, may not and cannot shut itself off in itself in a sectarian way. It must engage openly in dialogue with the world, its civilization, endeavours and creations. For it cannot and may not want to live solely on such culture as it produces within its own circle ("Christian literature", "Christian art"). It cannot have a ghetto-mentality in which people think they can live in social and cultural autarchy. To be able to give, the Church must receive.

c) The forces of the present time (and also of the future) are those without which the realization of the universality of the Church is not conceivable. Precisely for that reason – leaving deeper ones out of account – the Church has the duty of meeting the age as it is openly and with trust, however radically the Church criticizes world-civilization in detail. The Church as Church can neither fall into a reactionary resistance to the approaching future nor into an eschatologism which instead of sober waiting for the Lord would mean a flight forwards impelled by what in fact would be an ideology of this world. Because the Church is the Church, it has to recognize the Cross promised by Christ's coming in the very fact that we have to endure the sober harshness of an unromantic, planned technical world with all the burdens which such a situation brings upon itself and Christianity. No doubt when Christianity finds willing minds and hearts it changes not merely men's dispositions but also their conditions. But the Church cannot think on that account that it can exist, especially in the way incumbent on it today, only if the very elements of the situation which cannot seriously be expected to disappear were other than they are – a mass-society, a secular civilization, the relative lack of distinctive character in the Christianity of the present time, the diaspora situation, etc.

Consequently the smallest victory in this situation and against it is more important than anything else achieved in other situations which still exist but are in process of disappearance, or any success obtained in transitory counter-attempts to restore the past in contradiction to the decisive fundamental trend of history. Wherever a victory is won in the new situation of the unified secular world history, it is a victory for the whole world, and consequently for those non-European non-Christian peoples who to an increasing extent are entering upon this same situation. The Church, therefore, must abandon in its actual attitude to life and not merely in its abstract theory, the medieval ideal of a very direct and universal control of all human realities. Anyone who is a Christian and really intends to be one will of course do all human things differently from non-Christians, or from most of them. But this different manner of doing them will seem to the tolerant non-Christian simply to be one possible conception of human existence and activity side by side with others. And the Christian himself will never be able to say with absolute certainty in regard to his shaping of terrestrial reality, to which he knows himself in duty bound here and now as an individual and as a Christian, that precisely the shape he gives it is the Christian one as such. Even he will not know whether a possibility may not be tested for the first time by the non-Christians around him, which himself will later recognize as possible for him too as a Christian.

d) If despite its enduring ministry to the world and despite its teaching and pastoral office, the Church recognizes in this way that in all its members it commits itself less directly than in former times as regards the concrete shaping of social reality as a whole, this is not a flight into the realm of the utopian or the comfortable and safe, nor into the sacristy. It must be regarded as a more attentive reflection and concentration on its own authentic nature. For the Church is not a world-organization ("moral rearmament") for a better world – on earth. It is the community of believers in that eternal life in God, into which history is raised and transcended. Only in the measure in which the Church is the "kingdom not of this world" does it in the long run hold the promise that it is the blessing of eternity for time.

Karl Rahner

CHURCH HISTORY

A. Subject-Matter

The subject-matter of Church history is the Church's past. As a historical religion of revelation, Christianity originates in the historical person and saving work of Jesus Christ, the God-man. It not only has this local and temporal origin; its historical existence as this original Christianity is also continued in the Church. Its historicity is essential to its existence; it not merely *has* a history, it also *is* historical in its entire self-realization, for it is in and with history that it realizes itself. From this it follows that in order to experience and realize this essential element in its being it must turn its attention to history. Church history as a scientific theological discipline reminds Christianity of its origin and past as the permanently binding basis of its existence.

1. The *character*, and therefore the task and method, of Church history is determined by the view taken of the Church and by the function assigned to it within the history of the world and the history of salvation. In the Christian revelation attested in the NT, the nature

of the Church is not expressed in timeless abstract concepts but in metaphors (analogies). The Church is presented as the people of God, the bride of Christ, flock, family, communion of saints, the new Israel. This variety of metaphors and aspects permits a multi-dimensional view. Since for the most part these analogies are employed dynamically rather than statically, stressing the building of the house, the cultivation of the field, and the feeding of the flock, rather than the house itself, etc., they allow for the possibility of historical developments and changes in the Church's understanding of itself with the passage of time.

The profoundest theological interpretation of the Church is the concept of the "body of Christ", formulated by Paul. The Church is Christ's body (Col 1:24), the organism in which the believers as the members constitute a living unity with Christ the head (1 Cor 12:12ff.; Rom 12:4f.); Paul can even call the Church simply "Christ", because on the Damascus road Christ revealed himself to Paul as the one whom he had been persecuting in persecuting the Church ("Saul, why do you persecute *me*?", Acts 9:4). Paul defines the Church unequivocally as "the mystery of Christ" (Eph 3:4) and sees in it the fulfilment of God's eternal plan of salvation for the whole of mankind. The Church continues and brings to fruition among men the saving work of Christ who "reconciled" God and man "in one body through the cross" (Eph 2:16). It is the exalted pneuma-filled Christ who is at work in the Church. His Spirit, the Holy Spirit himself, is its life-principle by whom it is furnished with heavenly powers (Eph 4:4; 1 Cor 12:3ff., 13).

It is significant that when men sought to understand and describe the Church's life and growth, each of these metaphors, and especially that of the "body of Christ", could become historically influential. Augustine defined the Church as the continuing life of Christ, as the *totus Christus*, comprising both head and members. But this notion was most fully developed by J. A. Möhler, who spoke of the continued incarnation of Christ in his Church: "The Church is the Son of God continuing to manifest himself among men in human form, constantly renewing and ever rejuvenating himself, the permanent incarnation of the same Son of God." He regarded the history of the Church as the unfolding of "the principle of light and life imparted to and shared with mankind by Christ in order to reconcile it with God and to make it capable of glorifying him".

While the central mystery of Christianity (the incarnation and the Pauline view of the Church as the continued life of Christ) is rightly taken here as the starting point for the presentation of Church history, it must also be remembered that the metaphor would be distorted were Christ simply to be identified with the Church without qualification. He is its head; it is his body. We should be in danger of "ecclesiological monophysitism" (H. Fries) if we were to obliterate the distinction between Christ and the Church as his body and ignore the distance (not separation) between them. The function and even the existence of the body and its members are not identical with those of its head. Christ is the Lord of the Church; the Church is his bride, the mother who brings forth believers. When we speak of Christ's becoming the body, this must be understood in the sense of a spiritual generation by which believing, hoping, loving and obedient children are born to him in the Church. It is not only Christ's incarnation but also his appointment to suffering, death and resurrection which determine the life and function of the members of his body (*theologia crucis*). Paul exhorts the faithful not just to accept the life, suffering and death of Christ as objective historical facts but also to realize them subjectively after him in order in this way to participate in his grace.

As the community of believers, the Church exhibits a great variety of offices and gifts (1 Cor 12) and also possesses a structure deriving from Christ. This too must be clearly distinguished (though not separated) from the community of persons.

To this divine structure of the Church belongs what was given it by God through Christ for its journey and for the realization of the divine economy of salvation in humanity: the preaching of the word, the sacraments, the missionary task and the fundamental hierarchical order. This structure is unchangeable and partakes of God's perfection and holiness. In word, sacrament, and ministry the *Christus praesens* imparts his invisible grace directly in the Church through the Holy Spirit. God's saving activity is by its very nature structurally supra-historical. But since it is essentially related to men and becomes visible in the Church, it enters history. As the visible form of invisible grace, the Church is the "primordial sacrament" (O. Semmelroth). We describe as sacramental every supernatural saving reality which finds historical expression in our life under some visible sign. The Church is essentially both a divine structure and a visible sign, both a mystery of grace which acts invisibly and also historical human life.

This divine structure is not rigid and immobile but adapted to men, with a genuine evolution and development in history which in no way diminishes its constant and unchanging identity of substance. Itself a *mysterium fidei*, it shares the uniqueness of the divine process of revelation which moves forward under the formative impulse of the Holy Spirit. Just as in the OT God's speech and action find expression in forms and saving events which are embedded in the theological notions of the time and are accommodated to contemporary forms of experience, so too in the NT.

Salvation is a historical event. The Church, having its origin in the fact of Christ – in his incarnation, sacrificial death, and resurrection – stands in direct continuity with the OT history of salvation. With the foundation of the Church by the Holy Spirit at Pentecost, this history entered upon its final phase, the "time of the Church", which lasts until the parousia. As the "pilgrim people of God", journeying in the time between Christ's incarnation and return, the Church watches for the coming of God's kingdom in which salvation is to be achieved and manifested.

In its consummation, the salvation of mankind is an ultimate eschatological mystery of faith, transcending history. As such it is not a moment of history, though it involves the resurrection of the body. Yet salvation is already taking place concretely in history in those to whom God offers his grace. It is within history that God carries out his plan to save mankind, to lead them to salvation; and he does this "in such a way that his intervention on man's behalf is recognizably divine. God's saving activity is history because it is revealed and it is revealed in becoming history" (H. Schillebeeckx).

Thus the very concept of the Church again and again directs us back to history. When we turn to the Church's outward form, the historical element comes even more palpably into view. Church history in fact only comes to be by the interaction and co-operation of the divine and human factors throughout the ages.

The special character of revelation and respect for the Church's incarnational principle require the Church to be embodied in the humanity to which salvation is to be proclaimed and in which Christ is to be born anew. For the Church this adaptation does not involve any relativizing of its divine structure; it means, rather, a progressive self-realization in the direction of its eschatological goal. In this process the Church continually allows fresh aspects of its being to emerge in the course of time and in its confrontation with different peoples and cultures; in its developing doctrine, in its worship, in its preaching and pastoral care, in its constitution and administration. The aid of the Holy Spirit preserves it from fundamental error and guarantees at all times its substantial truth and holiness. This does not, however, exclude the possibility of distortions in the human aspects. Revelation and grace do not work by compulsion but presuppose genuine human partnership. As the meeting point between God and man, the Church stands in the field of tension between divine holiness and human frailty. It is the stage on which the dramatic struggle for the salvation or perdition of mankind is being waged.

On its human side, Church history gives no occasion for pride and boasting; it is on the contrary a depressing story of continual failure and miserable weakness. The moral deficiencies of individuals can operate even in the highest offices and institutions (e.g., Alexander VI). In its first stages, the history of doctrine (development of dogma) seems to be a tangle of conflicting views right up to the very point when by the aid of the Holy Spirit heresy is finally fended off and it is possible for the Church to frame and promulgate a valid formulation of dogma. Yet however true it is that this history is indeed the story of the search for truth and of progress in the victory of the truths of faith, it is also true that it inevitably obscures other aspects of the same truth. In other and less important areas of the Church's life, history corrects the erroneous temporary developments. "One of the finest and most impressive aspects of the history of the Church is the fact that the Church, despite the appalling developments and the many sicknesses through which it has passed, has nevertheless remained true to its nature, infallible at its core and unerringly unchangeable." (J. Lortz.)

Grace alone has saved the Church from being overwhelmed by the human element. In fact its history is in this respect a signal demonstration of the grace which is made perfect in weakness (2 Cor 12:9). It is "holy" Church not only in virtue of the indwelling holiness of God but because in every age it also accomplishes holy things in its members and produces "saints". In the figures of its great saints, the Church demonstrates its salutary force in a pre-eminent way. Though it is never an exclusive "Church of saints" for a few choice souls and always remains a redemptive institution for all who need salvation and are called by God, it is nevertheless in its saints that it continually finds its finest expression as "holy" Church. As long as the Church remains on earth there must and will also always be saints in it. "In the saints Christ himself strides through history and causes something of the light of his own earthly life to shine in our midst." (K. Rahner.)

Human weakness and sinfulness in the Church continually distort the image of Christ in it. Personal guilt, erroneous temporary developments, various failures and deformities obscure its form. Its dealings with the world and its own rapid development bring dangers to which it is not always equal. Instead of forming itself in genuine conformity to Christ and, in the Spirit of Christ, re-shaping this form in the world and in history, adapting itself to men and cultures, i.e., informing them with the image of Christ, the Church becomes "worldly" and by its conformity to the world becomes unfaithful to its destiny. Whenever the *forma Christi* is distorted in the Church, reform is necessary, a return to conformity to Christ. Christ's image and commission always constitute the centre and focus of its existence. In this sense, reform is of the Church's essence: *ecclesia semper reformanda*.

The call for reform always acquires special urgency whenever wide areas and whole states within the Church become unfaithful to their calling and serious disorders take root in the Church's institutions. Superficial observers usually begin then to talk of decline and fundamental apostasy from Christ, calling for a return to primitive Christian conditions and believing that the purity of the ideal can be restored by copying the forms of primitive Christianity. Such sectarians and heretics lack a genuine feeling for history and in demanding an anachronistic restoration of former conditions are seeking something not merely inherently impossible but also contradictory to the very nature of the Church. The Church which God wills should remain open to all men, to all times and cultures, cannot identify itself with any period or culture, not even with the primitive Church. True reform means recalling Christ as the Church's original form and fulfilling his saving commission, given from the outset and binding on every generation. Certainly we may learn from the primitive Church how genuine conformity to Christ is lived out. But the contemporary expression of this ideal continues to be a task set to each generation afresh. The form of Christ shines out in the saints. They therefore have more justification than anyone else for calling for reform and carrying it out. Reform is a task for saints.

Even the emergence of schisms and heresies seems to be a part of the authentic reality of the Church (1 Cor 11:19) and it would be wrong to misinterpret the moral quality of the conduct of the heretic, springing as this often did from a zealous search for the truth. "No one can establish a heresy unless he has an ardent heart and natural gifts created by the divine Artist", declared Jerome. "Do not imagine, brethren, that heresies can possibly arise from petty minds. Only great men have produced heresies", said Augustine (*In Ps.* 124). Yet both these issue warnings against heresy. Paul regarded heresy as a fearful threat to salvation not just for the individual but still more for the Church, which the devil seeks by heresy to divert from the truth and from its eschatological goal. Augustine calls heresy the Church's excreta ("quo partim digessit ecclesia, tamquam stercora", *Sermo* V). In order to assure the salvation of its children the Church must conquer heresy.

No less dangerous is the narrow-minded truncation of the faith by rigorous encratistic sectarianism such as Montanism, Tertullianism, Jansenism, Integralism. Nothing harms the Church more than anything which makes it narrow.

2. *The function of Church history as a scientific discipline* is already implicit in the concept of the Church. Church history must investigate closely what historically took on various forms; it must test this history for its essential content and measure it against its normative origin. The account of the origin and growth of the Church shows its connection and essential identity with the community founded by Jesus Christ and also serves to sharpen the Church's conscience and to stimulate a true understanding of its history and a better understanding of its own being. The nature of the Church is not grasped by systematic theology alone; it appears only against the background of its total history; only at the end of time, at the parousia, will it be fully revealed.

B. Task and Method

The task and method of Church history are likewise determined by the concept and nature of the Church. Since the Church historian is dealing with a subject-matter which is both visible and invisible, both historical and an object of faith, his thinking about history must be at once factual and theological. It must proceed *a posteriori* by first establishing the historical facts, investigating their contexts and connections and analysing their significance. At the same time, it must proceed on the *a priori* theological assumption that what has taken place in the historically verifiable facts is the revelation of God's saving activity.

As a historical science, Church history continues to depend on the strict scientific investigation of the facts. The demonstration of facts and dates is a primary requisite and, for a historical religion, an indispensable presupposition. Since "the Church itself is not an idea but a fact" (H. Jedin), its history cannot be dissolved into a history of ideas or philosophy. It is "a science of the facts; it is tied to the facts; it respects the facts; it seeks to inculcate reverence for the facts" (H. Jedin). The facts and dates constitute the scaffolding; if these are not known and assured, each further step in the direction of connected argument and theological and philosophical evaluation would be insecure. Nothing is gained by unfounded speculations; they do not advance knowledge. The historian must always start from the sources and treat the facts with respect even when they lead to apparent difficulties with the faith. To clarify the facts he employs all the tools and methods of the secular historian. Only the objective presentation based on the facts ("pragmatic" presentation) does justice to the honour and holiness of the Church. *Ne audeat historia falsa dicere, ne audeat vera non dicere* (Leo XIII). Exaggeration, touching-up, falsification of the facts – these would be a poor apologia for the Church. The only important question is the question of truth.

A purely positivistic historical presentation, limited to the accumulation and listing of facts and dates, cannot, of course, do justice to historical realities of any kind, least of all to a spiritual reality such as the Church. The aim of the Church historian's research must be to see beyond the facts, to grasp the abiding in the changing and temporary, and to press forward to the essence of the Church. It is the synthesis which brings the history alive. The past is connected up and interpreted from certain standpoints in the mind of the historian. Being a mystery of faith, the Church can in the last resort only be understood by faith. Thus even the interpretation of facts, the assessment of religious and intellectual movements and personalities, and the entire inner life of the Church is only accessible to faith. The non-believing historian cannot grasp or present the phenomenon of the Church in its profundity. In his interpretation of the facts and in his arrangement of them into the total picture, the believing historian will take faith and dogma into account, so that real contradictions cannot arise.

Church history is a science of faith; as such it is a part of theology. It not only adopts the theological concept of the Church, but also puts its own historical and theological questions to its subject-matter, the Church, and tries to answer them from theological standpoints. It is not satisfied with an analytical description of the form taken by the Church at different periods, among different peoples and cultures; it probes deeper, questions the theological presuppositions and tries to interpret events in the light of revelation.

It has been deplored that "we have never yet had a genuine theology of history or of the Church's historicity" (K. Rahner), although there have been a number of praiseworthy approaches and attempts in this direction. A convincing theology of history would have to begin by explaining, within the framework of dogmatic ecclesiology, "how and why the Church lives historically, changes, must present in ever new forms one and the same Christianity in truth, law and religious life, in order to present the fullness of Christ throughout the totality of all its times" (K. Rahner).

Church history can only be understood as a whole as a theology of history. It is a part of the history of salvation. Imbued with the conviction that the Holy Spirit is the "soul" of the Church, guiding and impelling it to fulfil its task of continuing among men through the centuries Christ's saving work, the Church historian in his capacity as theologian becomes an "interpreter of the activity of the Holy Spirit on earth" (J. Spoerl); indeed, his discipline has been called "an auxiliary science serving the knowledge of God". Yet he never forgets that unlike the systematic theologian he must always start from the facts of human life, from the sober and sobering realities of history. His business is not "dogmatic" historical research in the sense of trying to prove from history the doctrinal theses and ideas of the systematic theologian. He avoids all new style "pragmatism", which scours Church history for illustrations and documents to furnish historical proof of the Church's invisible divine character. He proceeds always from the outward to the inward, from below upwards. He sees the stains and frailties of the pilgrim Church as it follows its Lord along his *via dolorosa*. "Church history is *theologia crucis*" (H. Jedin). In this way Church history tries to assist the Church to understand itself better.

C. Historiography

The changing form and self-understanding of the Church is reflected in the way Church history is written. The distinctive Christian view of history first appears in the NT. Its consistent interpretation of universal history in terms of the history of salvation involved a breach with certain ancient views of history as an unending recurrence, and the replacement of the cyclical view by the linear teleological view according to which history is a development under divine providence from creation to Christ's incarnation and from the incarnation to the final judgment. The incarnation of the Logos in the "fullness of time" is both the centre of universal history and the beginning of a new epoch, the "time of the Church" which lasts until the parousia.

The more unreservedly the early Church knew itself committed to the unique reality of the event of Christ and to the gospel, the more care it felt obliged to take to ensure the unalloyed preservation of what the apostles as eye-witnesses entrusted to it. The "apostolic tradition" became the kernel of belief; to guarantee and establish this tradition the formation of the canon was undertaken (2nd century). The drawing up of episcopal lists in the apostolic communities and the stress on apostolic succession (Hegesippus, Irenaeus, Tertullian) bear witness to this early Christian awareness of history.

The universal and theological aspects of history were also stressed very early. The chronographers (Theophilus of Antioch, d. after 180; Hippolytus of Rome, d. 235; Sextus Julius Africanus, d. after 240; Eusebius of Caesarea, d. 339) sought to set Christianity in its universal context and in this way to demonstrate its antiquity and priority. Eusebius, "the father of Church history", was the first to synchronize Christian chronology with world history and the history of the Caesars. He already discerned an essential historico-theological connection between the *Imperium Romanum* and the emergence and expansion of Christianity. To Eusebius, not only the OT but also the whole of ancient history seemed to be a preparation for Christ. This positive evaluation provided him with the basis of his later "theology of the Empire", developed in his *Vita Constantini*.

The great value of Eusebius's *Church History* (down to 324) as a source, now generally acknowledged, soon prompted the Greek writers Socrates (d. *c.* 450), Sozomenus (d. after 450) and Theodoret of Cyrrhus (d. after 450) to expand and continue it. They in turn were translated into Latin by Rufinus of Aquileia (403) and Epiphanius (6th century), while Cassiodorus (*c.* 490–583) worked them together into a *Historia Tripartita*. It was in this form that they became known in the West and served the whole medieval period as the principal handbook of Church history. The Chronicles were also continued (Jerome, Sulpicius Severus, Prosper of Aquitaine, Cassiodorus, Isidore of Seville) and frequently imitated in the Middle Ages.

The greatest influence on the understanding of history was that of Augustine (354–430) with his *De Civitate Dei* (413–26). Augustine also left his mark on the Christian view of the State. Deliberately abandoning the Eastern notion of religio-political unity, for which Eusebius provided a basis by his "theology of the Empire", he conceived the relationship between Church and State in dualistic terms. In this respect as in many others he was the teacher of the West. It was a misunderstanding of Augustine when later rulers like Charlemagne, the German Emperors and the French kings used him as an authority for a new "theology of the Empire" in the West.

When in 525 Dionysius Exiguus (*c.* 470–550) transposed the dates of Roman history (reckoned from the foundation of the city of Rome) into a new reckoning from the birth of Christ, he introduced into chronology the "Christian era". He placed Christ's birth 4 or 5 years too late, assigning it to 754 A.U.C. instead of to 749 A.U.C. which would have been the correct date. He thereby introduced an error which has not yet been corrected.

Ancient Christian historians divided the course of history according to one or other of three theologico-historical schemes: a) The *six world-ages*, analogous to the six days of creation, each world-day being equivalent to 1000 years (in accordance with Ps. 90:4; 2 Pet 3:8). The seventh day, the universal sabbath, would bring the "millennium" of divine peace and rest under the rule of Christ (Rev 20:1–6). This "Milleniarism", an interpretation of history which constantly recurred, took on various forms in Cerinthus, Papias, Justin, Irenaeus, Julius Africanus, Tertullian and Hippolytus; in the medieval theologians, the Venerable Bede, Wilfred Strabo, Rupert of Deutz, Richard of St. Victor and many others down to Joachim of Flora (d. 1202) and the Franciscan "Spirituals" of the 14th century. Once this view had been rejected by Thomas Aquinas on theological grounds, it was not long before it was condemned by the Church and, in one precise form, branded as heresy. Right down to modern times it has continued as an "enthusiastic" hope among the sects (Anabaptists, Moravian Brethren, Adventists, Mormons, Jehovah's Witnesses). b) The *four world-empires* (Assyrian-Babylonian, Persian, Macedonian [Alexander the Great], and Roman, an interpretation of Dan 2:36ff.; 7:3ff.); the fourth of these empires, the Roman, now Christianized, would last, it was thought, to the end of the world, which is why men clung to it so tenaciously even in the Middle Ages. c) The *threefold scheme* of Augustine: *ante legem, sub lege, post legem*. In the Middle Ages this was varied (Otto of Freising: *ante gratiam, tempore gratiae, post praesentem vitam*) and interpreted in a trinitarian sense (Joachim of Flora).

In the Middle Ages history was seen as the history of salvation. There is a remarkable change in the picture of the

Church. In the early Middle Ages the universal idea was completely eclipsed. The chief interest then was in describing the Christian history of one's own people or of the monastery or diocese. Hagiography occupied much space. It is impossible to speak of this as genuine Church history, for the concept of the Church is absent. Instead, the chronicler or annalist offers us simply Christian historiography, linked to the history of salvation at most by a brief prologue. This was a continuation of the concept of history held by the post-Constantinian imperial Church. In the Carolingian and subsequent period the symbiosis of the secular (or temporal) and the "spiritual" found expression in the casual replacement of the word *mundus* by the word *ecclesia*. Charlemagne called himself *caput ecclesiae*; Church and State merge into one. This notion of unity is echoed in the early medieval chronicles.

It was only with the monastic reform of the 11th century that awareness of the Church as such was quickened. The signs of deterioration in that period (wealth, secularization, feudalism) were opposed by the ideals of the *ecclesia primitiva*, the *imitatio Christi* and the *vita apostolica*. A new self-understanding began to emerge in the Church (Odericus Vitalis, John of Salisbury). The threefold scheme was applied to the history of salvation and interpreted in a trinitarian sense. Rupert of Deutz (d. 1129) distinguished three periods: creation (God the Father), redemption (God the Son), and sanctification (God the Spirit). Joachim of Flora collected triple typological sequences from the OT and the NT (law, grace, love; science, wisdom, full knowledge; slavery, service, freedom; etc.) and from these deduced that succeeding the era of the Father in the OT and the era of the Son in the NT the era of the Holy Spirit in love and freedom would now soon follow. He prophesied that in the year 1260 the present Petrine hierarchical Church would be replaced by the new "Johannine" Church of the Spirit.

The medieval world chronicles quarried from Eusebius and Jerome and for the most part simply revised these writers for purposes of edification (Regino of Prüm, Hermann the Lame, Sigebert of Gembloux). Otto of Freising, the most important historical thinker of the Middle Ages, was the first to link up with Augustine. The annals, unlike the more individualistic chronicles, are completely anonymous and utilitarian. The papal chronicles represented a special class, providing in the *Liber Pontificalis* a pattern for the chronicling of successive "lives". Imperial, diocesan and monastic annals, and lives of saints and bishops multiplied.

From about 1300 on, a slow but steady breakdown in the medieval consciousness of the Church becomes apparent. The struggle between Papacy and Empire, Boniface VIII and Philip the Fair, the Avignon Papacy (1309–78) and finally the great Western Schism (1378–1417) shook men's confidence. Joachim of Flora's criticism of the hierarchical Church, taken further by the Franciscan "Spirituals", favoured the theory of decline, which regarded the post-Constantinian Church as increasingly a victim of decline, and needing to be replaced by the pure, ideal, invisible "Spirit Church" (*ecclesia spiritualis*).

A vigorous theological reflection on the Church began. In strong opposition to the Papal Church, Marsilius of Padua (d. 1343) and William of Occam (d. 1349) developed a new democratic concept of the Church, placing the Council, as representative of the Christian people, above the Pope. A serious ecclesiastical constitutional crisis was precipitated by the conciliarism of the Councils of Constance (1414–18) and Basle (1431–37). Papalism (Jacob of Vitry, Aegidius Romanus, Alvar Pelayo, Augustinus Triumphus) which since Gregory VII had been developed in an increasingly one-sided way by the canonists, was forced into an impasse by the Great Schism. The doctrine of the Church had become the sole concern of the canonists, and this legalism on the eve of the Reformation was to have far-reaching consequences.

By opening up the sources the humanists both extended the knowledge of history and at the same time promoted a critical approach, e.g., to the Donation of Constantine (Nicholas of Cusa, Lorenzo Vally). The new editions of the Fathers (Erasmus of Rotterdam) threw fresh light on the NT and primitive Church. The call for reform which continued throughout the entire 15th century became a call to return to the *ecclesia primitiva*. Luther and the Protestants gave it explosive force.

The Reformation challenged everything which the medieval Church had constructed, and called for a return to the ancient Church. It sought "witnesses of the truth" in primitive times to support its reforms. Matthias Flaccius (1520–75) in his *Catalogus Testium Veritatis* (1556) and in his *Historia Ecclesiastica* ("Magdeburg Centuries", 1559–74) tried to prove from the sources that Lutheranism alone, and not the Papal Church, was in agreement with the ancient Church in doctrine and discipline. In opposition to him Caesar Baronius (1538–1607) produced in Rome (1588–1607) his historical work *Annales Ecclesiastici* (12 vols., down to 1198) which was also quarried wholly from the sources. His work was continued by Abraham Bzovius (d. 1637) down to Pius V; Odorico Rinaldi (d. 1671) and Jacob Laderchi (d. 1738) corrected and expanded it. A new interest in Church history developed.

Melanchthon had in 1520 introduced the study of Church history as part of his reform of the University of Wittenberg, and it became a compulsory subject in 1583 at Frankfurt-am-Oder and soon afterwards at Helmstedt as an independent discipline. Protestant criticism stimulated an intensive study of the sources on the Catholic side, and this led to the development of critical historical methods in the analysis of sources and progress in auxiliary disciplines (chronology, diplomatics, palaeography). For the first time Church history now became a "science". The Bollandists (Jan Bolland, d. 1665, Gottfried Henschen, d. 1681, Daniel Papebroch, d. 1714, and other Jesuits) published the monumental *Acta Sanctorum* from 1643 onwards. The Maurists (Benedictines of St. Maur in France) provided critical editions of the Fathers. Jean Mabillon accomplished astonishing feats (science of documents and editions, the *Acta Sanctorum OSB* and the *Annales OSB*) as did Edmond Martene de Sainte-Marthe (*Gallia Christiana*, 1656), F. Ughelli (*Italia Sacra*, 1644–62), L. Wadding (*Annales Ordinis Minorum*, 1625–54), J. Quétif and J. Echard (*Scriptores Ord. Praedicatorum*, 1719–21), L. A. Muratori (*Rerum Italicarum Scriptores*, 1723–51), E. Florez (*España Sagrada*, 1747–75), D. Farlati (*Illyricum Sacrum*, 1751ff.), M. Gerbert of St. Blaise (*Germania Sacra*, 1764ff.). So too the great conciliar collections, the *Collectio Regia* (37 vols., 1644ff.), that of J. Hardouin (12 vols., 1714/15) and of G. D. Mansi (31 vols., 1759–98), and the narrative histories of Louis Sebastien le Nain de Tillemont, Alexander Natalis and C. Fleury, are all monumental achievements. In his *Discours sur l'histoire universelle* (1681) J. B. Bossuet tried to provide once more a total survey of history from the standpoint of the history of salvation.

Meanwhile the Enlightenment, with its fundamental rejection of theological principles, brought about a complete secularization of Church history. Church history now became in Catholic countries an official subject in the universities (Curriculum of Maria Theresa, 1752); but the Emperor Joseph II described it as the task of Church history (Instruction, 1775) to "discuss" the morality of historical events. His concern was that the relationship between Church and State should be presented as far as possible in accordance with his own view. For this reason the "Dark Middle Ages" were to be ignored as far as possible.

Opposition to the pragmatism of the Enlightenment came from the Catholic Renewal of the 19th century, from Ultramontanism in Italy (M. Cappellari, later Gregory XVI) and Traditionalism in France (J. de Maistre, Lamennais). Neo-Scholasticism was also an influence for renewal both by reason of its origin and because of its fundamental impulse. Its lack of interest in history derived from its philosophical approach. But the real renewal of the Catholic spirit in Church history originated with J. A. Möhler (1796–1838) and the Tübingen School.

The burgeoning of historical sciences in the 19th century had a stimulating influence on Church history. The critical researches of I. Döllinger (1799–1890), C. J. Hefele (1809–93), F. X. Funk and many others elevated Church history in Germany to a high scientific rank. The monumental works, the *Monumenta Germaniae Historica* (from 1819), the *Corpus Scriptorum Eccl. Lat.* (from 1866) and *Die griechischen christlichen Schriftsteller der ersten drei Jahrhunderte* (from 1893) enriched the basic source material. The opening of the Vatican archives by Leo XIII (1884) gave fresh impetus to research. In addition to the newly founded National Historical Institutes in Rome, H. Denifle, F. Ehrle, and Ludwig von Pastor (d. 1928), author of the *History of the Popes*, did outstanding work. The French register of Popes, P. F. Kehr's work on papal documents, the edition of the diplomatic reports and the *Concilium Tridentinum* of the Görres Society are major achievements both in content and form. All periods profited from this upsurge: the early period (archaeological research into the catacombs, by de Rossi, J. Wilpert; history of the early Church, by L. Duchesne, P. Batiffol, Fr. J. Dölger, and the *Reallexikon für Antike und Christentum*; patrology, by A. von Harnack, O. Bardenhewer); the Middle Ages (by A. Hauck and others); history of the Reformation (*Corpus Reformatorum* and the Weimar edition of Luther, *Corpus Catholicorum* and countless studies and accounts – J. Lortz, A. Herte, K. Holl). In France, H. Bremond's *Histoire littéraire du sentiment religieux en France* (12 vols., 1916–36) laid the foundations for the history of spirituality.

Increasing specialization brought greater independence to certain individual disciplines within Church history (hagiography, iconography, liturgics, history of missions, history of dogma, religious anthropology). Numerous specialist journals provided information about the mass of new publications resulting from this research, especially valuable being the Louvain *Revue d'histoire ecclésiastique* (from 1900).

Since the Second World War a new theological emphasis is evident in Church history, turning away from 19th century positivism and towards a theologico-historical and ecclesiological orientation. K. and H. Rahner, H. U. von Balthasar, Y. Congar, H. Lubac, J. Daniélou and others have posed afresh the question of the Church's historicity from the standpoint of its nature and are seeking to develop a new theology of its history. A Church which experiences and progressively realizes itself in its history cannot regard its past as an inert possession. Accordingly, the uniform concern of recent full-scale accounts of Church history is to go beyond the mere presentation of historical facts and to seek to understand the events in terms of the history of ideas and to interpret them theologically: J. Lortz (*Geschichte der Kirche in ideengeschichtlicher Betrachtung*, 21st ed., 2 vols.,

1962), H. Jedin and J. Dolan (eds., *Handbook of Church History*, 1965ff.), R. Aubert, D. Knowles and L. J. Rogier, eds., *Christian Centuries*, 5 vols. (1964ff.), the recent volumes of Fliche and Martin, *Histoire de l'Église*, 24 vols. (1935ff.), and K. Bihlmeier and H. Tüchle, *Church History* (15th ed., 1956). This more profound approach to Church history enriches ecclesiology just as it was ecclesiology which first stimulated this new approach.

D. Periodization and Survey

To facilitate a survey of the whole, it is reasonable and necessary to arrange the material into epochs. This often seems quite impossible, however, since every principle of division proves inadequate. The continuous flow of history recognizes no pauses. When changes take place they never involve the whole but only certain partial areas. But because the total history is a confluence of many single forces and various streams, it can nevertheless still be useful to isolate particular aspects which have helped in important respects to shape the total picture.

Down to the 17th century the schema of the history of salvation seemed to be adequate. It was the Protestant historian Christoph Cellarius (1634–1707) in Halle who introduced the division into epochs: ancient, medieval, modern. 15th and 16th century humanists and Protestants had coined the term "Middle Ages" in a pejorative sense because they saw there nothing but a decline in language and religion and wished for that reason to link up again with classical "antiquity", with its pure Latin speech and undefiled Christianity. The 18th century Enlightenment thought even less of the "dark" Middle Ages, the period from about 500 to 1500. The intrinsic value of this period was only rediscovered by Romanticism and the burgeoning science of history in the 19th century which filled it with positive content by intensive research into documents and sources. J. A. Möhler applied the threefold scheme to Catholic Church history, and since then it has dominated historical writing as a whole although doubts about its objective adequacy are everywhere in evidence. Today in an age of ecumenical thinking, the threefold division, designed mainly to fit the European West, seems doubly inadequate.

Yet it is difficult to replace it. Philosophical interpretations of history (Hegel, Marx, historicism and metaphysical relativism, existentialism) are excluded as alien to the nature of the Church, and the same applies to the purely politico-geographical view of Halecki (Mediterranean, European, Atlantic periods) and to the theories of civilization-cycles (Spengler and Toynbee). But even from the nature of the Church itself no particular division into periods imposes itself, since the biblical revelation nowhere informs us by what stages and in what forms the divine plan of salvation is to be realized; the gracious inner working of the Holy Spirit certainly cannot be measured and defined, even though recognizable by its outward effects.

Thus the only remaining possibility is to seek a theologically practicable division into periods in the context of the "Church and the world", more precisely within the actual way in which the Church has carried out its divine task in the world. We could perhaps start from the expansion of Christianity (history of missions) and distinguish two main periods: a) the period of its growth from Jerusalem over the entire Graeco-Roman world (antiquity) to the Western Church (Middle Ages), and from the (*de facto*) regional Church of the West to the world Church (modern period down to the present day) and b) the period of universal Christianity in an age of universal human history only just beginning (K. Rahner). But this solution would mean adhering to the old threefold division for the early period, and this should surely be corrected. H. Jedin's proposal of four periods is therefore preferable: a) the Church within Graeco-Roman civilization (1st–7th century); b) the Church as the dominant factor of the Western community of Christian nations (about 700–1300); c) the disintegration of the Christian unity of the West and the transition to the world-mission (1300–1750); d) the Church in the industrialization period (19th and 20th centuries). For a true understanding of the third period (1300–1750) it is important to insist that the period from 1300 to 1500 is no longer "medieval" while that from 1500 to 1750 is not yet "modern". This third period has a pronounced transitional character and is marked by a new self-awareness in the Church and by a struggle for reform.

Whenever an era comes to an end, the Church is summoned to detach itself from the previous environment in which it has made itself at home, and to open itself to new peoples and cultures. For the sake of its divine commission it must not identify itself with any civilization but must "accommodate" itself to the new order in order to assimilate it to itself, i.e., in order to make possible Christ's incorporation into it. Such transitions, which usually take place only to the accompaniment of great upheavals, have always greatly altered the Church's appearance: for example, the change from Judaic to Gentile Christianity (Apostolic Council of Jerusalem), from Graeco-Roman to Western Germanic civilization (between 400 and 700), from the unified religio-political culture of the Middle Ages to the disintegration of the unity of Church and Empire (about 1300), and from the great radical change introduced by revolution and secularization down to the present day (1800–1975). It is clear that once again today an era is ending and a new beginning heralded.

First period: the Church in the world of Graeco-Roman civilization (1st–7th century). The first section, from the time of the Church's foundation at the first Pentecost down to Constantine the Great, is particularly important as the foundation period of the Church. The period of the primitive Church and of the apostles (apostolic age), i.e., the first and second generations of Christians, saw the emergence of the NT writings. As authentic interpreters of the mind of Jesus, the twelve apostles, eye-witnesses of the Word and themselves bearers of Christ's revelation, created "the Church", under the guidance of the Holy Spirit, as a reality which is an integral part of the Christian fact. In the doctrine, worship, order and discipline of the primitive Church the "apostolic tradition" was laid down, to which Christianity in all ages has known itself to be bound as a matter of life and death. It is on this that the normative significance of the first period rests, a significance which has again and again demonstrated itself in the call for reform and for a return to the *ecclesia primitiva* and the *vita apostolica*.

Judaism and the mother Church of Jerusalem greatly influenced the form taken by the life of the early Christian communities. But Christianity was not to enter upon its course through history as a sect of the Jewish religious community, but as an independent universal religion. At the Apostolic Council (*c.* 50) it detached itself from Judaism and soon invaded the world of Graeco-Roman civilization. The "Apostolic Fathers", themselves still pupils of the apostles, and the early Christian "Apologists" developed further the life of the Church and entered into discussion with the intellectual world around them. They unhesitatingly made use of the language and concepts of Hellenism. At the end of the 2nd century the Alexandrian school of theology came into being as a voluntary missionary enterprise on the part of educated Christians (Pantaenus, *c.* 180; Clement of Alexandria; Origen). About 260 Lucian founded another school of theology, the Antiochene. Greek philosophy, Hellenistic culture and Christian doctrine entered into alliance. From this alliance developed the remarkable Greek patristic writings of the 4th and 5th centuries, upon whose massive theological labour the first "ecumenical" councils depended.

The lofty spirituality and richness of thought of revelation, its genuine historicity and the part played by the human factor in its development are sufficient explanation of the frequent emergence of erroneous views and overt heresies in Christianity. Christian heresy and schism began already in the 1st century: Judaizers, Ebionites, Nazarenes, Elkesites and Cerinthus were contemporary with the apostles. The main threat in the 2nd century was Gnosticism. Because the Christian "Gnostics" were fond of appealing to their private revelations, the Church found itself compelled to establish the canon of Scripture as the sole norm of faith and to develop the Church's teaching office. Bishops standing in the "apostolic succession" were seen as guarantors of the pure apostolic tradition. From the latter half of the 2nd century the bishops met together in synods in order to present a common defence of the true faith against Gnosticism, Montanism, Marcionism and other heresies (Donatism, Manicheism). The more widespread heresy became, the more representative the synods. Local synods were soon replaced by provincial ones. The Church's sense of universality was reinforced; despite persecution and danger, great councils assembled from the middle of the 3rd century on, in the metropolis Rome, in Carthage, Alexandria, Antioch and Caesarea in Asia (later councils of the Patriarchates), and when, following the conversion of Constantine, Arianism and Donatism threatened the entire empire (=*oekumene*), the Christian Emperor summoned the first ecumenical imperial council to Nicaea (325). At such councils, the Church acted as a universal community. Heretical opposition also forced it to grapple more closely with the treasure of revelation; the history of the discovery and unfolding of the truth of faith, the development of dogma, is inseparably connected with the continual invasion of heresies and the accompanying discernment of spirits in the Church.

Once Christianity became a historical factor (beginning of the 2nd century) Christians were persecuted in the Roman Empire. This persecution was in three phases. The last and severest of them, under Diocletian, ended in the victory of Christianity with Constantine the Great (306–37). His "conversion" (312/13) gave the Church freedom and brought it to a turning-point. Subsequently the Church was integrated with the State as an "established" religion. This gave rise to many problems and remained an important factor for almost fifteen hundred years of Western history. But it was not long before joy at the "Christianization" of the State was mingled with laments at the secularization of the Church. Many Christians, bishops, priests and laity, failed to maintain the detachment from the world obligatory on all Christians.

It was then that God raised up in the Church the monastic movement, not as a "protest" but as a clearly visible sign of Christian perfection. If in the days of persecution the martyr's death was the supreme form of Christian discipleship, its place was now taken by the supreme spiritual sacrifice, martyrdom according to the spirit. The original Christian *pneuma* was united with an asceticism penetrated by mysticism to form a perfect imitation of the suffering and dying Redeemer (*theologia crucis*) and thus gave expression to an essential aspect of Christian living. The religious dynamism of monasticism saved the Church from becoming mere outward show in the Constantinian era, and also gave it fresh impulses. All the great bishops and theologians of the 4th century were closely connected with monasticism. The strong missionary impetus, the remarkable development of pastoral care, the effort to Christianize the Roman State, and above all the theological work of the great councils of the 4th to the 7th century are inconceivable without monasticism.

In the struggle against Arianism, Subordinationism and Monarchianism, Athanasius and the "three great Cappadocians" – Basil, Gregory of Nazianzus, and Gregory of Nyssa – elaborated the theological doctrine of the Trinity (2nd general council, Constantinople I, 381). In conflict with Monophysitism, Nestorianism and Monothelitism, the theology of the Greek Fathers clarified Christology (Councils of Ephesus, 431, Chalcedon, 451, Constantinople II, 553, Constantinople III, 680/81). All these councils took place in the Greek East.

But Latin patristic theology too attained great heights in Augustine (354–430). It turned more to soteriological problems, to the doctrines of justification and grace. Pelagianism provided a special stimulus here. The West was then caught up in the vortex of the great Germanic invasions (from about the beginning of the 5th century). In the 7th century, the onslaught of the Arabs dealt the Mediterranean world its death blow. For the Church, which had so closely identified itself with this civilization, it was far from certain that it would survive its overthrow and open itself to the newly emerging Germanic Western world.

Second period: the Church as the dominant factor of the Western community of Christian nations (c. 700–1300). The Arianization of the Germans made access to them impossible for a long period. Only with the Catholic baptism of Clovis, king of the Franks (*c.* 496), did new possibilities arise, though little use was made of them by Rome. Pope Gregory the Great (590–604) finally seized the opportunity when in 596 he inaugurated the Anglo-Saxon mission. The work of Boniface (d. 754), the alliance between Pepin and the papacy (751–54), and the imperial coronation of Charlemagne (Christmas 800) were further steps leading to the establishment of the Western Christian community of nations.

Antiquity, Germanic culture and Christianity were welded into one and the Church itself took on a new form. The "Germanization" of Christianity had far-reaching effects on every aspect of the Church's life.

A profound grasp of the Christian ethos and a naïve openness to the world produced in time a genuine organic union of Church and State and, in the early medieval German and French kingdoms, an impressive unified religio-political culture. With the feudalization of the imperial Church and a theocratic concept of the ruler, the boundaries between Church and State disappeared completely. The Emperor took the place of a papacy which had lapsed into insignificance in the *saeculum obscurum* (10th and 11th centuries). The papacy, renewed by the Gregorian Reform, had to win back the Church's freedom, threatened chiefly by lay investiture, in the course of the Investiture Controversy (Gregory VII, 1073–85; Henry IV, 1056–1106; journey to Canossa, 1077; Concordat of Worms, 1122).

Although in the ensuing struggles for power between the *imperium* and the *sacerdotium* it was ostensibly the restoration of a proper balance between the two powers which was the issue (political dualism of the West), in reality it was a struggle for supremacy. Under Innocent III (1198–1216) the papacy was undisputed leader of the Christian West. But when the Hohenstaufen empire collapsed (1286) the dominant position of the papacy was not long maintained. About 1300 it was subordinated to the national power of Philip the Fair of France.

The renewal which began at Cluny in the 10th century had by the 11th and 12th centuries embraced the entire Western Church. New monastic orders appeared: Camaldolenses (Romuald, d. 1027), Carthusians (Bruno, d. 1101), Cistercians (Robert of Molesme, d. 1111; Bernard of Clairvaux, d. 1153) and the Orders of Chivalry (Johannites, 1099, Templars, 1118, Teutonic Knights, 1189/90). Clergy reform was carried through by the Canons Regular movement (Augustinians, Premonstratensians or White Canons, Norbert of Xanten, d. 1134). The laity formed Bible groups and the Poverty Movement. The Crusades generated tremendous religious energy; they strengthened the consciousness of solidarity in the Western community, widened the European horizon, and assisted the advance of knowledge through the encounter with Byzantine and Islamic culture. The amazing development of Western philosophy and theology in Scholasticism would be inconceivable without this encounter with the Orient.

Critical minds had since the middle of the 11th century ceased to be satisfied with the early medieval scriptural theology of the monastic schools. Independent schools came into being and sought new ways in their theology (Anselm of Canterbury, d. 1109, *theologia scholastica*). When *c.* 1200 several such schools in Paris united to form a single corporation, the *universitas magistrorum*, the first university, came into existence. Not long after followed Bologna, Padua, Naples, Montpellier, Oxford, Cambridge, Salamanca and Valencia. Germany had to wait until the 14th century for the universities of Prague (1348), Vienna (1365), Heidelberg (1386) and Cologne (1388).

There were new heresies too: Berengarius of Tours (d. 1088), Tanchelm (d. 1115), Arnold of Brescia (d. 1155), Catharists and Waldensians. When to purely spiritual weapons in the struggle against heresy the Inquisition was added, special processes of law were introduced (Innocent III) and torture was used to secure proof; one of the most lamentable chapters in Church history began. Later the Inquisition was used in the service of an insane hunt for witches. But Francis of Assisi (d. 1226) and Dominic (d. 1221) showed that there was another way of combating heresy. The mendicant orders, the Franciscans and Dominicans, were a more persuasive influence by their ideal of voluntary poverty and by their preaching than were weapons and courts. Their pastoral concern and preaching ministry led to a deep interest in theology. Their greatest theologians, the Dominicans Albertus Magnus (d. 1280), Thomas Aquinas (d. 1274) and Master Eckhart (d. 1328), and the Franciscans Alexander of Hales (d. 1245), Bonaventure (d. 1274) and Duns Scotus (d. 1308) were the most brilliant masters of Scholasticism.

The papacy meanwhile, renewed and consolidated by the reform of Gregory VII, rose to the pinnacle of its authority. The proclamation of supreme jurisdiction in the *Dictatus Papae* (1075) and the systematic development of the Roman Curia into the central organ of Church government gave Innocent III (1198–1216) a unique position of authority and leadership among all the Western nations. This found expression in the new Western general councils (Lateran: 1123, 1139, 1179, 1215; Lyons I, 1245; Lyons II, 1274) and was undergirded by the Church's canonists.

Unfortunately, the Christian East was absent from these councils. The growing division had led in this period to ever increasing estrangement (iconoclast controversy, *filioque* clause, problem of the two Emperors, question of primacy) and finally to the Eastern Schism (1054). The Crusades, especially the senseless fourth Crusade and the establishment of the Latin Empire in Constantinople (1204–61), widened the gulf still more with the result that no union ever materialized again.

Third period: the disintegration of Western Christian unity and the transition to world mission (1300–1750). The unified civilization of the West rested on the two universally recognized authorities, Empire and Papacy. Only together, in an "elliptical" tension, could they fulfil their task. The disintegration of European political unity brought in its train that of the Church. When Boniface VIII (1294–1303) asserted his papal authority over the French national state (Bull *Unam Sanctam*, 1302), he was humiliatingly arrested by Philip the Fair at Anagni (Sept. 1303). The decline of the papal power showed itself in the period following this, in the Avignon Exile (1309–78) and the great Western Schism (1378–1417).

This third period is chiefly characterized by the dissolution of the unified order created by the previous period. The process began in the 14th century, continued in the 15th, and reached its ecclesiastical climax in the great division of the Church in the 16th century. The process was only arrested in the 18th century.

In France, England and Spain, the trend towards national states was at first accompanied by a marked trend towards national Churches. In Germany the growing strength of the territorial princedoms already foreshadowed the territorial Churches which would prove so significant for the Reformation of the 16th century. The social order was disturbed by the conflict between princes and nobility, patricians and guilds, a conflict arising from economic changes (transition from an agrarian to a financial economy, early capitalism). The feudal Church was involved in both. Tensions between territorial Church authorities on the one hand, and the nobility and cities on the other, largely prepared the way for the decline of the faith in the 16th century. The fiscal policies of the papacy alienated people from the Church. But still more important was the loss of intellectual unity. The traditional Thomist-Scotist philosophy (*via antiqua*) was superseded by the new Occamist-nominalist philosophy (*via moderna*). Moreover, humanism provided a new cultural ideal.

In the Great Schism it was ultimately the Church itself which became problematical. As Pope and anti-Popes excommunicated one another, no one knew which of the three was the legitimate one and on which side the true Church was to be found. At the councils (Pisa, 1409; Constance, 1414/15; Basle–Ferrara–Florence, 1431–42) conciliarism provoked the most serious constitutional crisis of the hierarchical Church. Even though it proved possible to avert the catastrophe once again, disquiet nevertheless remained as regards the papacy. The Renaissance Popes soon found fresh burdens adding to their anxiety. *Reformatio in capite et membris* was the most pressing concern of the 15th century. Since the papacy declined this task, reformation came from below.

Considered as a historical process, the 16th century Reformation is an extremely complex event in which almost all the aspirations of the age meet – religious, intellectual, political, and social. As an ecclesiastical process it was a major turning-point which decisively shaped all subsequent developments. With the breach in the Church's unity, even the common basis of faith was shaken. The unified Christian consciousness of the West was fragmented into denominational thinking. Luther (1483–1546), Zwingli (1484–1531) and Calvin (1509–64) created their own Church bodies; these came into vigorous conflict with the papal Church and with one another. The era of the wars of religion began (16th and 17th centuries).

It took the Church far too long to rediscover the way to renewal and self-realization. But once the foundations of faith and discipline had been re-affirmed at the Council of Trent (1545–63) the inner reform of the Church could begin and the progress of Protestantism checked through the Catholic Reform and Counter-Reformation. This work of reconstruction is one of the most astonishing phenomena of Church history. True reform is always the work of saints. The reform of the papacy only became convincing when a saintly Pope appeared in the person of Pius V (1566–72). There were now many saints in all walks of life. The "century of saints" dawned. In these saints the purified "holy" Church found and understood itself once more.

New orders, especially the Jesuits and Capuchins, led the reform. A disabling apathy gave way to a new Catholic vitality which found fresh expression in the art, piety, and theology of the Baroque age (1550–1750). Theological study was stimulated by Protestantism and encouraged by the work of the Council of Trent. Baroque scholasticism dispelled much of the obscurity of pre-Reformation theology. Spanish and Italian theologians distinguished themselves (Bellarmine, Soto, Suárez, Cano and others – mostly Jesuits and Dominicans) and later, French theologians. The main themes treated were the Trinity, Christology and grace. The intellectual movement started by the Jesuit Suárez (1548–1617) influenced every branch of theology (dogmatics, moral theology, canon law) and philosophy. It was his declared aim to penetrate the latter with Christianity. Suarezianism was also fruitful religiously. The Spanish mystics (Teresa of Ávila and John of the Cross) helped forward the deepening of religious life in the Church, influencing France especially. In France P. de Bérulle established a distinctive priestly spirituality which left its mark on the French clergy of the 17th century.

But the dangers also persisted. In the controversy with Calvinism, Michael de Bay of Louvain (1513–89) sought to develop a modern theology closely related to life, but produced instead a doctrine of original sin and grace which was based on a misunderstanding of Augustine and which had to be condemned by the Church. Baianism had fateful consequences through his Louvain pupil Cornelius Jansen (d. 1638) who adopted his ideas and introduced them into Catholic theology and piety. Jansenism's rigoristic doctrine of grace and sacramental practice dealt heavy blows to the French Church in the 17th and 18th centuries.

The other main currents which affected the Church between 1600 and 1800 were also French: Gallicanism, State Absolutism, and Episcopalism. These ideas were transplanted to Germany in the form of the "Febronianism" of Johann Nikolaus von Hontheim, auxiliary bishop of Trier, in the period when the union of Church and State, under the Emperor Joseph II (1780–90), reached its zenith in Austria. The Western mind became increasingly alienated from religion and the Church and intellectual secularization progressed rapidly in the 18th century under the stimulus of the Enlightenment. By the end of the century the papacy had finally lost the leadership of Europe.

One ray of light in this period was the world mission which began with the discovery of new territories by the Spanish and Portuguese in the early years of the 15th century. It reached its climax in the 16th and 17th centuries but was also to meet with discouraging setbacks in the 18th century. The missionary work, which in any case suffered because of Spanish and Portuguese colonialism, was also hindered by internal disagreements in the Church over missionary methods. The controversy on the Chinese (1645–92, 1704) and Malabar rites brought the promising Jesuit missions in China and India to an end.

Fourth period: the world Church in the industrial age (19th and 20th centuries).

The French Revolution (1789) represents the great watershed. The renewal was prepared by the Enlightenment, which brought the Church a long-needed modification of traditional forms and of intellectual rigidity. It was introduced by the great secularization (1803), which liberated the Church from the old feudalism and, while depriving it of its earthly sovereignty, at the same time gave it the "grace of destitution". It proceeded to the accompaniment of a continuous controversy with the new forces of national Churches and movements. Liberalism, Socialism, Communism and Materialism were hostile. Permeated by an immense faith in progress, modern society turned more and more away from the Church and from positive Christianity. This movement involved especially the upper classes and the industrial workers. Yet in all European countries there was a discernible renewal of religious and Church life, and a strengthening of the papacy.

Reconstruction involved a twofold process: on the one hand the material re-ordering of the Church's organization and legal relationships with the civil authorities by means of concordats concluded between the Holy See and the individual countries, and on the other hand the inner renewal of the religious life of the Church. In Germany, the Romantic Movement was an important spiritual factor for the revival of religion in general and for the new respect for Catholicism in particular. Catholic "revival groups" came into existence (J. M. Sailer, Princess Gallitzin, K. M. Hofbauer, Bishop Zirkel) as well as new theological schools. G. Hermes (d. 1831) in Bonn employed the concepts of Kant and of Fichte in an effort to vanquish the rationalism of the Enlightenment in a positive way; his system was condemned by the Church in 1835 as semi-rationalistic. Similar efforts were made by A. Günther (d. 1863) and J. Frohschammer (d. 1893). The Tübingen School (Drey, Hirscher, Möhler) was influential; it too linked itself to the spirit of the age (Romanticism, German Idealism) but combined it with the tradition of the Church. The common concern of all these was to combat prevailing religious scepticism by a new apologia of religion. Reaction against the Enlightenment led in France to a rigid traditionalism distrustful of human reason in religious matters and denying it any capacity to know God; all order, whether intellectual, ethical, social or political, has its basis and support in revelation and tradition alone (Fideism, Integralism, Supernaturalism); the Church and the papacy are in all such matters the primary authorities (Ultramontanism, de Maistre, de Lamennais, Veuillot).

Supported by ideas of this kind and upheld by the affection of the Catholic people, the papacy became increasingly important for religion and the Church, while it was at the same time vigorously attacked. In 1854 Pius IX proclaimed *ex cathedra* the dogma of the Immaculate Conception; in his *Syllabus* of 1864 he declared war on *Liberalism* as a philosophy of life and on other opinions; at the First Vatican Council (1869/70) he secured the dogmatic definition of the primacy and infallibility of the Pope. At the same time he encountered stiff opposition (Risorgimento, Old Catholicism), was deprived of the Papal States (Sept. 1870) and suffered the loss of political power. Nevertheless the moral prestige of the papacy was on the whole enhanced and under Leo XIII (1878–1903) actually reached great heights.

The 19th century was a time of dramatic struggles. Within the Church the scene in the latter half of the century was dominated by the struggle between the so-called German theology and neo-Scholasticism; this came to a head in the First Vatican Council and ended in the victory of neo-Thomism (Leo XIII in various encyclicals). The encounter with the non-Catholic

Churches, favourably influenced by pietism at the beginning of the century, developed on both sides into an aggressive denominationalism; liberal Protestant theology constantly called for an answer. The positive encounter introduced by J. A. Möhler's famous book *Symbolism*, which presented a comparison between the dogmatic positions of Catholics and Protestants on the basis of their confessional statements (1832), unfortunately degenerated on both sides by the end of the century into increasingly bitter polemics until finally the alliance of militant Protestantism, Liberalism, and Bismarck's *raison d'état* set in motion the momentous *Kulturkampf* against the Catholic Church in Germany. Nor did the experience of Catholicism with modern industrialism bring much encouragement. Certainly the considerable pastoral efforts to remedy the condition of the workers and the contributions of charitable works to this end represent a glorious chapter and testify, along with the upsurge of the religious orders, to the Church's inner vitality. But the social question itself was recognized as such too late (Leo XIII, 1891). The mass of industrial workers were outside the Church and adopted socialism both as a political party and as a philosophy of life. In the political sphere too, difficulties arose in almost every country.

These experiences produced a certain anxiety and narrowness of view in the Catholic camp. Pius X (1903–14), honoured within the Church as a reforming Pope, conducted a stern fight against Modernism. Ecclesiastical integralism soon began to suspect heresy in anyone who sought an accommodation with modern culture and science. The retreat into the ghetto eliminated Catholicism as a cultural force in public life.

The turning point came with the First World War. The experience of war and revolution summoned Catholics too back to a greater sense of responsibility for the world. At the same time a new awareness of the Church became evident. "The Church awakens in men's souls", wrote R. Guardini in 1922. The liturgical movement, lay action, the encounter between the Churches, the *una sancta* and the ecumenical movement stressed the fellowship of Christians. The juridical picture of the Church determined by the Counter-Reformation (Bellarmine) gave way to a new conception of the *corpus Christi mysticum*. Pius XII summed up this concept in the encyclical *Mystici Corporis* of 29 June 1943: the Church really is the body of Christ, not just in a spiritual, moral or metaphorical sense but as a visible, social, all-embracing hierarchically-ordered corporation. The joint responsibility of the laity in the Church's life was seen in a fresh light. In connection with the liturgical renewal, a new encounter with holy Scripture took place. Theological science, preaching, and Church life came together in the biblical movement. The life of the religious orders also flourished and in conjunction with the new theology and spirituality of the laity brought about the great "secular institutes".

The dialogue (and co-operation) between the Churches developed into a genuine conversation. Instead of denominational quarrels there emerged tolerance, mutual respect and co-operation, particularly during the period of persecution under the Third Reich. The Churches saw their own mistakes and shortcomings and recognized that the desired reunion in faith had to be preceded by profound reflection upon the essentials. This was the thought which made John XXIII convoke a council: The Second Vatican Council (1962–65) was to lay the foundations for the renewal of the Catholic Church with a view to the reunion of divided Christendom. Union was no longer thought of as an unconditional return but prepared for as a real integration. With this intention the Secretariat for the Promotion of Christian Unity was established in 1960 under Cardinal Bea in Rome. The Catholic *oekumene* in alliance with the non-Catholic ecumenical movement was to make the 20th century the "century of the reunited Church". The meeting between Pope Paul VI and the Ecumenical Patriarch Athenagoras in Jerusalem (Jan. 1964), the surrender of the papal tiara, and the conciliar Decree on Ecumenism, all underline the sincere desire of the Catholic Church for reunion.

The Church's openness both internally and externally is the characteristic of our time. John XXIII broke with the centralism of the Curia and re-emphasized the joint collegial responsibility of the bishops in the leadership of the whole Church. The adaptation of the Church to present-day needs (*aggiornamento*) demanded consideration of the Church in the modern world. The Catholic world mission, which had long been coloured by colonialism and Europeanism and had therefore been unable to strike roots in the indigenous cultures, was given its first native bishops in 1926. Pius XII furnished the mission countries with their own hierarchies. But it was John XXIII who first emphasized the Church's duty to go to meet the peoples and not to uproot them from their cultures; the world Church was not European but universal and the continued incarnation of Christ in the Church was not restricted to the Western nations alone but intended for all who come to believe in him. The conversation with the other major religions (Buddhism, Hinduism, Islam) which Paul VI officially endorsed by his journey to India (Eucharistic World Congress, Bombay, 1964) also stands under the sign of this new openness. This visit was intended not as a missionary journey but as a simple pilgrimage. The Pope's large charitable donation to the Hindu people was intended, in his own words, as "the first concrete expression of the brotherly dialogue which the Church desires to enter into with the whole world".

Is one era ending today and a new era dawning? There are many signs pointing in this direction. The global extension of the Church and its worldwide encounter with all nations and cultures made possible by modern means of communication, the process whereby world civilization is being rearranged and standardized, the new picture of the world presented by science and research, and finally the inner secularization of man and growing unbelief, all confront the Church today with new tasks. The need of the hour is not identification with and rigid insistence on what now exists, but rather openness to what is to come. There can, of course, be no progress without constant reference to what is essential. The Church is still bound to maintain the *traditio apostolica* as a matter of life and death.

August Franzen

COMMANDMENTS OF THE CHURCH

1. *Notion*. In the wider sense one understands under the term "Commandments of the Church" all the general precepts of the Church's pastoral office which define in the concrete the divine law in view of the salvation of the faithful (canon law). They must be distinguished from the instructions which may be imparted by the ecclesiastical superiors to particular members of the faithful. Taken in the strict sense, however, the commandments of the Church grew up in the Middle Ages, in association with confessional practice, out of obligatory ecclesiastical custom. Under the influence of the *Summa Confessionalis* of Antony of Florence (1389–1459) the teaching on the commandments acquired a clearer form. Since 1444 five commandments can be verified, and the

decrees of the Council of Trent on the administration of the sacrament of penance have led to the stronger emphasis subsequently laid on them. In a typical formulation the catechism of Cardinal Gasparri, for example, describes them as those commandments "which are of very great significance for the general spiritual life of the faithful". In their present most widespread form they are derived from the catechism of Peter Canisius (1555): i) observance of particular feastdays: ii) reverent attendance at Mass on Sundays and holy days of obligation; iii) observance of obligatory days of fasting and abstinence; iv) annual confession; v) reception of Holy Communion at Eastertide.

To this catalogue of the commandments of the Church others have been added, such as the duty of supporting the Church, which was adduced under the influence of Bellarmine, or the observance of "forbidden times" regarding marriage and dancing. In many countries the duty of sending children to Catholic schools is counted as one of the Church's commandments, and the censorship of books and the rejection of cremation have also functioned as precepts of the Church. No matter how they have been summed up, the Church has not taken over any of the lists as official. Thus one does not find any special list of the commandments of the Church in the *Catechismus Romanus*.

In the popular conception, the commandments of the Church are a means used by the hierarchy to lead the individual in a fatherly manner to a minimal fulfilment of his religious duties and in this way to safeguard the common good of the Church. Here it is assumed that commandments of the Church are necessary and effective in order to attain the aims envisaged by such means.

2. *Difficulties*. Pastoral practice shows that commandments have in fact contributed in great measure towards sustaining and giving concrete expression to the common life of the Church. It also shows, however, that the interpretation of them as privileged instruments in the moral guidance of the individual believer, and the over-emphasis of obedience lead to a dangerous legalistic morality, which restricts the effort of many too one-sidedly to loyalty to the law and misleads them to equate the observance of the commandments with a life according to Christian morality, or to adhere to them to the detriment of higher values.

Moral handbooks, intended originally as practical guides for confessors, by their undue emphasis on the commandments of the Church, by their methods and their casuistry, have greatly hindered the development of personal responsibility and proper judgment of the situation in moral action. The most obvious abuses of this legalism are gradually being rectified, but it still persists subconsciously in moral thought and attitudes.

The deeper reason for this legalism is no doubt to be found in a false need of religious security. This attachment to the law shuns the responsibility of personal decision and evades God's call in the ever-changing situation of the moral act. As soon as one begins to think legalistically the tendency arises to construct as far as possible a cast-iron system of external laws. Then, out of consideration for real life, enforced by pastoral needs, this tightly-woven legal system is again loosened by an extensive system of dispensation and casuistic interpretations. Thus the impression is established that one need only know sufficient about the matter to be released from following the law or that one need only have oneself dispensed. Then the initial rigorism of the legalistic approach easily switches to laxism. Many of the faithful, then, especially those who are aiming at moral maturity, feel that many commandments of the Church are out of date, arbitrary and superfluous. The severe sanctions which are sometimes attached to them are regarded as paternalistic leading-strings. Further, the duty of obedience with regard to the precepts is often unduly emphasized without corresponding explanation of their meaning. Here one proceeds from the erroneous concept that the human legislator, as God's representative, is able to bind morally – something which God alone can do. The consequence is that obedience for its own sake is juridically overestimated.

3. *Meaning*. Hence arises the question of the meaning and obligatory character of the commandments of the Church. We must start from the premise that all general laws imposed from outside have as their immediate object the safeguarding of the common good, and only serve indirectly the perfection of the individual. The individual is affected only insofar as his rights and duties towards the community and his neighbour are defined. The commandments of the Church, like ecclesiastical law in general, have therefore as their immediate object the preservation of public order in the Church. This must take place of course in view of the end and object of the Church, which is the sacramental re-presentation of Christ and his work in this world as sign and means of salvation for mankind. Therefore, all commandments of the Church are meaningful which promote the common good of the Church under this aspect. Insofar as they are necessary to this end they can be legitimately urged and if need be upheld by appropriate ecclesiastical penalties. Conversely, in conformity with the principle of subsidiarity nothing should be prescribed which is not necessary for the common good of the Church. In adhering to this fundamental principle, no resistance is offered to the free working of the Holy Spirit, room is left for a corresponding initiative in the individual, and ecclesiastical office can perform its allotted task in the service of the Church under the guidance of the Spirit. The question of what is needed for the common spiritual welfare is not always kept clearly enough in mind. Thus, for example, we lack a theory about the extent to which impediments to marriage are possible.

What is necessary for the common good of the Church cannot be laid down *a priori* once and for all, but is dependent on changing ecclesiastical situations and must be worked out *a posteriori*. However, since laws should always have as much permanence as possible for the sake of sureness, it follows that the commandments should be drafted as widely as possible but also with the necessary precision, as they would not otherwise be able to fulfil their purpose. A system of dispensations is always necessary to a certain extent on account of the imperfection of human legislation, but it should be reduced to a minimum. Otherwise there is uncertainty with regard to the law and the danger arises of a paternalist tutelage of the faithful.

4. *Their binding character*. The common good of the Church calls for common and co-ordinated action. The faithful should fulfil the commandments in an obedience which strives to perceive their significance for the welfare of the Church. In this way the faithful will contribute to the building up and preservation of the body of Christ not only by their obedience but also by their exercise of the corresponding virtue. Insofar as the commandments serve this end they transmit the divine law and thus far are morally binding. The binding character of the Church's commandments is, therefore, to be measured according to their function with regard to the common good, and the legislator can only demand obedience insofar as the common good demands it. This means that the legislator in his law does not bring about the will of God as his delegate but manifests the divine will in the exercise of his office.

It is well to bear in mind here that on account of the subjective incertitude of the individual with regard to what is necessary for the common good, the legislator must create through his law the unity of judgment necessary for the common action. The faithful must therefore obey him insofar as a law is necessary for the common good and its observance is required. If a law is unnecessary, then it is unjust; if the observance of a law in a particular case is absurd, then the obligation lapses. If the observance of the spirit and not of the letter of the law is apposite, then one must act according to the virtue of epikeia. In order to have a balanced attitude towards the commandments of the Church, as loyal as it is responsible, the faithful must be equally prepared for obedience to the ecclesiastical legislator and for the service of the common good of the Church which is demanded in the circumstances.

In view of the above, we can now deal with the classical controversy as to whether the ecclesiastical legislator can demand an internal act or merely external acts and the internal act only indirectly. We may say that internal acts necessary for the common good of the Church can also be demanded, for, in contrast to the State, these acts are essential to the ends of the Church. The thesis that the commandments are fulfilled by positing the required external act fails to recognize the spiritual character of canon law. So too the view that a violation of the Church's commandments may be under certain circumstances only an offence against obedience. Rather, if there is any offence at all, it is always also an offence against the virtues demanded by the commandment.

5. *Pastoral requirements.* From such a view of the commandments of the Church it follows that in practice the faithful should always have the significance of the respective precepts explained to them as clearly as possible. It is also fitting that the commandments of the Church and their actual topical relevance be discussed in open dialogue within the Church and that the faithful be duly offered the opportunity of bringing their influence to bear in the shaping of the commandments of the Church to meet the needs of the times. This will always promote a rational observance of the commandments, because in the ecclesiastical sphere, much more than in the secular, it is important that the line of conduct demanded be followed from an internal conviction. For here the salvation of man is at stake which fundamentally demands personal compliance with God's call.

Furthermore, ecclesiastical legislation must not aim at sustaining and assuring as extensively as possible the spiritual life of the faithful. Such a "socialization" of the spiritual life would be opposed to the free working of the Holy Spirit and detrimental to the personal initiative of the faithful. The commandments of the Church must attempt, then, to promote equally the common good of the Church and the possibility of free spiritual development. The present commandments of the Church do not always do justice to the need of developing personal responsibility in keeping with our times. The Pope has therefore set up a commission for the reform of canon law and several changes have already been made, e.g., in respect of fasting and the censorship of books. However, the tension between the common and individual good will never be finally harmonized even in the sphere of spiritual legislation. Rather, in the end, the individual must bridge this gap by his *sentire cum ecclesia* and interpret the commandments by applying an enlightened epikeia, in keeping with God's will, which is manifested interiorly and which alone imposes an absolute obligation.

Pastoral education should therefore be more concerned with enabling the faithful to observe the precepts in a meaningful way. For this it is necessary that the predominant religious individualism be abandoned in favour of a strong Church consciousness. This will also serve to explain the necessity of appropriate commandments and strengthen the authority of the Church.

Waldemar Molinski

COMMUNION OF SAINTS

1. The article of faith asserting the communion of saints is first found in the Western creed at the end of the 5th century in the form given by Nicetas of Remesiana. From the 5th century onwards it is found in the Gallic variations (Faustus of Riez, Caesarius of Arles; *DS* 26,27) and later in all the Western forms. Nicetas used the word *sanctorum* as the genetive form of the neuter *sancta*, i.e., a share in the sacred things of the Church, in keeping with the Augustinian concept of the *communio sacramentorum* (*Sermo*, 214, 11). The phrase κοινωνία τῶν ἁγίων was, however, used much earlier in the East, though not as part of the creed; it was used there also in the sense of participation in the blessings of salvation, including therefore the personal element of fellowship. κοινωνία as such is not a share in things or effects but a personal community relationship whose quality is determined by the ἅγια. Although this community of salvation encompasses the entire Church, heavenly and earthly, it was only gradually that the term was expressly used to denote communion between the heavenly and the earthly Church and its members. The insertion of the phrase into the creed was probably meant to emphasize the nature of the Church as a fellowship (*communio*) of persons constituted and determined as such by the blessings of salvation. The limitation of the phrase in modern times to indicate the possibility of a salutary exchange of blessings between the individual members within the *communio* should again be broadened by a re-stressing of the fact that the *communio* represents the *res* of the *sacramentum* which is the Church itself.

2. This *res* of the primordial sacrament, the Church, must be first presented in biblical terms. The theological meaning of the NT fellowship (κοινωνία) is especially developed in the theology of Paul and John. It is significant for the history of religion that the OT does not speak of fellowship with God – in spite of the great stress which it places upon the personal element in the covenant given by God and in spite of the recognition that Israel owes its existence as a people to its covenant with Yahweh. Though Greek philosophy spoke of a fellowship or participation of man in the realm of the "ideas" or with the divine, Paul and John were able to proclaim the unique reality of the mystery of Christ with the help of existing concepts (1 Cor 1:9, etc.; 1 Jn 1:3, etc.)

Our fellowship with Christ presupposes that God has given us his Son as our companion. Fellowship comes about by the Son's participating in our nature (Heb 2:14–17; also Rom 5:8–10; 8:3, 32ff.; Jn 1:14). In this way the fellowship of the Son with us stands in the direct line of sacred history which had its beginning in the first covenant; thus it also includes the OT whose true goal was only to be revealed in Christ: that God wills to be "for us" just as he is "for himself". God's "being-for-us" in Christ is the great liberation. It constitutes the new beginning of salvation within the history of human iniquity, in that it makes human history the sphere of fraternal unity with the Son. Man's nostalgia for the secure and promising unity of a fresh start is consoled, since this yearning is more than satisfied by the brotherliness of the second Adam. For his brotherliness is characterized by the fact that he is the beloved Son. That salvation which is "in Christ" leads in its realization to an existence "with Christ", the realization of the κοινωνία. It is already communion with the body given for our sakes and the blood shed for us (1 Cor 10:16ff.); it leads to full conformity with Christ at the resurrection (Rom 8:21). But it is communion with the body and blood of Christ which first constitutes the Church as a fellowship. Here one sees most clearly the intimate relation between the concept of fellowship with Christ and the designation of the Church as the "body of Christ".

3. Fellowship with Christ is thus the basis for the "two communities" which are implicit in Christian fellowship: fellowship with Christ is also fellowship with the Father. It is true that Paul does not speak explicitly of fellowship with the Father, but the thought is implied in his conception of Christian fellowship as participation in the form of the Son. The thought is explicit in 1 Jn 1:3. Fellowship with Christ is also the basis of the fellowship of the justified, which is not merely the sum total of all individual relationships to Christ.

4. Nevertheless, these two aspects of the Christian fellowship are rooted in the one mystery of Christ which, because of the trinitarian mystery of God and the inclusion of mankind within it, is "many-sided". This unity must be considered in relation to the divine reality which has revealed itself as Spirit and which in the NT is expressly related to the fellowship (2 Cor 13:13). A developed scriptural doctrine of the Holy Spirit must show that "communion with the Holy Spirit" is communion with Christ and with the Father, because the Holy Spirit is himself this communion. The fellowship between the Father and Son is a divine reality, as is the Father and the Son. As their fellowship it is distinct from them and thus constitutes in the one divine nature the relationship between Father and Son. But as the immanent intercommunication between the Father and the Son, he is nevertheless the same Spirit who as the *Pneuma* from the glorified body of Jesus (Jn 7:37–39) is also the intercommunication of the Church with its Lord. As such the Spirit is also the intercommunication between all members of Christ who are living in grace. Through this trinitarian structure of the divine being, which is in itself fellowship, the doctrine of the communion of saints may be distinguished – in spite of its considering that fellowship with the Father is communicated "through Christ" and "in the Spirit" – from the notion of a participation in the divine on a lower level of emanations, as is found in neo-Platonism.

5. Since intercommunication between Christ and his own is treated of in soteriology, the traditional doctrine of the communion of saints is mostly restricted to the intercommunication between the other members of Christ as it is made manifest in the mystery of salvation, Here it must be noted that the Holy Spirit can bestow his gift of fellowship in such a way that a creaturely and historical crystallization of it is not only not excluded, but quite possible. Just as through the Holy Spirit it was possible for the Son to live his Sonship in a human being, so too the Church is given access to participation in that Sonship. And this is its human realization in the people of Christ. This human manifestation reveals the sacramental character of the communion of saints. The fullness of the *Sacramentum Christi* continues to present and communicate itself through the action of the Spirit, and the Church is led deeper and deeper into the *res* of this *sacramentum*, according to the salvific will of God. The more profoundly it is rooted in Christ, the stronger grows the unity of the communion of saints. At the same time, the fellowship thus constituted by Christ bears the individual along the way to Christ. The signs of Christ's salvation which have been en-

trusted to the Church, which signify and effect salvation infallibly through the power of Christ, find expression in a Church which as a totality can only pray for the coming of the Spirit (the Epiclesis).

The salutary effect of the activity of the members on behalf of each other is explained by the fact that when the Church prays for its members, or the individual for the Church and for other individuals, this intercession takes place in the medium constituted by the Spirit in the communion of saints. When the Spirit takes up the cry of the Bride, and makes it resound before the Father along with the voice of Christ, Christ is not thereby lessened: "he is glorified in his own" (cf. Jn 17:10). If this supplication takes the form of enterprising and active service, this work of love is also inspired by the Spirit, who gives it the deep conformity to Christ which is proper to such action on behalf of others. Above all, the Spirit brings about in the members of Christ that steadfast conquest of suffering which wrought our salvation in the sacrifice of Christ. The whole Church is to be drawn to share this dedication, and thus the obedient dedication of the one is meaningful for all, because there too the Son is glorified. Nonetheless, Christ's position remains unique, because it is only he, as the man glorified who is also the Son, who sends the Spirit. The fruitfulness of the members for each other is rooted in the same Spirit, but they do not send him, they only receive him. This has been expressed technically by the magisterium, in terms that lack somewhat in expressiveness, by saying that only Christ merits for us *de condigno*, while we may merit for each other *de congruo*.

6. The form of "inter-aid" so far described envisaged the communion of saints more particularly in its state of pilgrimage. But the *status perfectionis*, the consummation, does not interrupt communications. Nothing new accrues to these members, but their having been made perfect is of particular importance, as being not merely an example but also a gift to the people on pilgrimage. The pilgrim is always in danger of feeling constricted and oppressed by his anxiety for his salvation. When the Spirit gives him the perfected angels and saints as brothers in every way close to him, he reveals himself as the love who gives the one Christ, the life of all, ever more fully as the fellowship grows wider.

7. Finally, there is also the loving care of the pilgrims for the members who must still suffer to attain their consummation. This care does not lead them to bargain with God for what is still wanting to the perfection of the suffering. The pilgrims are only impelled by the conviction that in the Spirit their supplications help those who still suffer on the way to salvation, since even in purgatory "no man is an island". There are no fully isolated individuals even there.

Wilhelm Breuning

CONFIRMATION

A. Methodology

Most studies of confirmation are unconvincing because the problems are envisaged in too narrow a perspective. Since the beginning of the Middle Ages the Scholastics sought, by an analysis of the fruits proper to this sacrament, to define its special nature, in contrast to baptism, or even the Eucharist, on account of Ps 103:3, "panis cor hominis *confirmat*". This method was based on "axioms" of a rather meagre sacramental theology. The sacraments were considered too exclusively as "instruments of grace", and not sufficiently as "mysteries of salvation in the Church". There was too much effort to differentiate the so-called "sacramental graces", with too little attention to the primordial source of all grace, sacramental or otherwise. But once one considers all grace as necessarily implied in the saving presence of the Trinity, as the reality of salvation coming from the Father, in the image of the Son and by the power of the perfecting Spirit, the proper efficacy of the sacraments in general, and of confirmation in particular, is seen to be inseparable from this loving activity of the three divine persons – insofar as it is visibly attested and sacramentally effected in the liturgical prayer of the Church, i.e., in the celebration of the mystery of salvation.

Further, a theology of confirmation must include the fact that confirmation, with baptism and the Eucharist, is one of the three sacraments of Christian initiation, which make up together the fullness of Christian life, by the consecration and mission which they confer. Hence the three sacraments, since they communicate the saving action of the Father in the Son through their Spirit, must necessarily be considered in their organic unity.

Finally, the NT and liturgical and theological tradition reveal a notable accord, too often neglected in technical discussion, with regard to the central fact that confirmation bestows on us above all the "gift of the Holy Spirit". This must guide our reflection above all else, but in the framework of a sacramental, ecclesial and trinitarian theology much broader than before.

B. Data of Revelation

1. *Scripture*. It will not be enough, therefore, to study confirmation on the basis of the few texts of Acts which probably attest the existence of a still very rudimentary rite in apostolic times: prayer, imposition of hands and gift of the Holy Spirit, sometimes manifested by the charismatic character which it took on in the primitive Church (Acts 8:12–17; 19:1–7; Heb 6:2 is less certain). A biblical theology of confirmation must also envisage the salvific action of the Spirit as messianic gift (the OT doctrine), given by the risen Saviour (Jn 19:30), offered to the nascent Church as a body (Acts 2:1–47), to the nations universally (Acts 10; 11; 18 – the Pentecost of the gentiles) and individually to each of the faithful (e.g., Acts 1:7–8, the general theme of Acts). We must go back with Scripture to the mystery of the incarnation as mission from the Father and prototype of our new life. It was in and by the power of the Spirit (cf. esp. Lk) that Christ was conceived by Mary, and consecrated prophet and Messiah when baptized by John. It was through the same Spirit that he preached, worked miracles, prayed and died (Heb 9:14). Finally, reflection on the rich data of the Bible (that is, theology stemming from the "economy" or dispensation) allows us to recognize the true nature of the Spirit and hence to understand better what the NT means when it says so often that the Spirit has been "given" us, that he is the great gift of the risen Lord.

Clearly, in the NT, the proper activity of the Spirit is to sustain the whole of Christian life from the birth of faith in the heart. I. de la Potterie has shown, after an ancient tradition, that the "anointing of the Christian" (2 Cor 1:21–22; cf. Eph 1:13) or the "chrism" (1 Jn 2:20, 27) was not ritual but spiritual, like the anointing of the prophets in the OT and the prophetic anointing of Christ (Lk 4:18; Acts 4:27; 10:38; Heb 1:9). Paul links it with the seal of baptism, while John sees its influence in the whole development of Christian life through the faith which precedes (1 Jn 5:6), accompanies (Jn 19:34–35) and follows (Jn 3:5) baptism. "This divine anointing signifies the action of God in arousing faith in the hearts of those who listen to the word of truth." This faith is "confirmed" by the Spirit. Incidentally, we may note that the notion of *gratia ad robur* is not wholly foreign to apostolic and sub-apostolic tradition, though it is not attributed exclusively to the Spirit (1 Cor 1:6–8; 2 Cor 1:21–22; Col 2:7; Phil 1:7; 1 Clem, 1, 2; Ignatius, *Magn.*, 13, 1; Polycarp, *Phil*, 1, 2). We must be reborn by the water of baptism, but we must also be born again through the Spirit, that is through faith in the word (Jn 3;5; 19:35; 1 Jn 5:6–8). This doctrine corresponds to the synoptic doctrine of the necessity of faith for salvation.

The Spirit is also the source of our charity (Rom 3:5; 1 Cor 13). He inspires our prayer (Rom 8:16; Gal 4:6). He is the source of the charisms (1 Cor 12:4–12), through which he "builds up" the Church (1 Cor 14:4, 12, 26) and consecrates it as the temple of God (1 Cor 3:16; Eph 2:22) in the "communion" (Eph 4:3; Phil 2:1). He is truly the soul of all Christian existence (Gal 5:25; 6:9; Rom 8:9, 13; Eph 4:30). Through faith he is already present at baptism (1 Cor 6:11; 2 Cor 1:22; Tit 3:5) and in the Eucharist (1 Cor 12:13), a tradition retained by the ancient Church in the practice of the epiclesis.

This doctrine of wide and varied perspectives allows the NT to distinguish baptism from confirmation. Baptism is linked only with salvation, the remission of sins, the new creation, entrance into the Church ("circumcision") and above all with belonging to Christ (εἰς τὸ ὄνομα). Confirmation is concerned only with the "gift of the Spirit" defined above all by the experience of the first Pentecost. But it would be wrong to make of them totally separate entities. For the primitive Church they form together one rite of initiation (Acts 10:44–48). Theologically they both derive from the initial mystery of the baptism of Christ in the Jordan (Jn 1:19–34). In any case, especially in Paul, Christian life is indissolubly one in Christ and in the Spirit.

2. *Liturgy*. a) *Confirmation as an integral part of the rite of initiation*. During the first eleven centuries, confirmation, along with baptism, is part of the solemn rite of initiation celebrated at the Easter and the Whit vigils. It is sometimes hard, and possibly incorrect, to allot to one sacrament or the other a given rite, such as the second anointing. The main rites of confirmation are the imposition of hands, with the epiclesis, the anointing and the sign of the cross on the forehead (an allusion to the "Tau" of Ezek 9:4).

The *Apostolic Tradition* of Hippolytus of Rome proves the importance of the imposition of hands in the Roman (and perhaps the Alexandrian) Church in the 3rd century. In the East, the imposition of hands is replaced about this time by the anointing with consecrated oil, the perfumed μύρον, except in Egypt. This also happened in northern Italy, Gaul and Ireland. The imposition of hands is rarely mentioned for Africa and Spain. When the Roman liturgy came into widespread use in Europe, in the era of the "sacramentaries" and the "ordines", Frankish influence seems to have been responsible in some places for the replacement of the imposition of hands by the anointing. In the 11th century, however, a temporary restoration of the ancient rite can be noted, in the form of the laying on of hands over a group or on each individual. The origin of the rite of anointing at confirmation is unknown, but no doubt the biblical texts cited above had something to do with it. The peoples of Europe perhaps found the laying on of hands less meaningful a symbol. In this context it should be noted that the anointing before baptism in the ancient Syrian Church, so close to Palestine, was not an exorcism. It seems to have been regarded as a consecration of the faith of the catechumen by the Spirit.

b) *Confirmation as a separate rite*. Towards the 11th century, confirmation takes on a liturgy of its own, especially in the West, where the bishop remains the ordinary minister. The multiplication of parishes makes it harder to link confirmation with baptism, especially in the case of children. Meanwhile, the anointing of the forehead with chrism is merged into one ritual gesture with the sign of the cross, sometimes combined with the laying on of hands (so in Alcuin, *D* 419, 450). In an effort to unify the liturgy, Innocent VIII in 1485 ordered the use of the Pontifical of Durandus of Mende (1293–95) which was already widespread. After the 1497 edition of this Pontifical the imposition of hands disappears completely, the Council of Florence having ratified the omission (*D* 697), as did the Tridentine reform. The rite of the "alapa", probably of Germanic origin, became general in the West. The imposition of hands at the anointing was re-introduced by Benedict XIV in 1752, in the appendix of his Pontifical. Leo XIII and the *editio typica* of the Pontifical of 1925 give the rite very clearly: "per manus impositionem cum unctione chrismatis in fronte" (cf. *CIC*, can. 780). The laying on of hands now seems to be considered as the principal rite (*AAS* 27 [1935], p. 16). Vatican II ordered the rite of confirmation to be revised so as to bring out its character of Christian initiation, and allowed its conferring during Mass (Constitution on the Sacred Liturgy, art. 71).

The dogmatic import of the liturgy is to be sought above all in the prayers, which according to St. Thomas and the whole medieval tradition are expressions of the faith of the Church. The ancient liturgy indicated the meaning of confirmation chiefly in the epiclesis. Is 11:2 is quoted from the earliest times. The East has preserved a formula of consecration from the 4th century: Σφραγίς δωρέας Πνεύματος Ἁγίου. Ἀμήν. Similar consecratory formulae were used for a time in the West. The one we now use came in about the 10th century: "Signo te signo crucis (the ancient *consignatio*) et confirmo te chrismate salutis in nomine Patris et Filii et Spiritus Sancti. Amen." Various prayers some of them very ancient, expound the biblical doctrine of the gift of the Spirit.

3. *Doctrinal tradition.* We should not wish to maintain with G. Dix and L. Bouyer that Scholasticism was not in continuity with patristic theology, but it is undeniable that the theology of confirmation presents very different characteristics between one epoch and the other. There are various reasons for this. The Fathers generally give their doctrine during the great catechetical instructions in preparation for the Easter vigil, of which they spontaneously respect the liturgical unity. Their intentions are pastoral and devotional. The central truth that confirmation gives us the Spirit is enough for them, all the more so because their theology of the Trinity brings out more clearly the proprieties of the divine persons. The biblical texts which mention χρῖσμα or σφραγίς are used to elaborate by means of fertile allegories a wide-ranging doctrine of the presence and activity of the Spirit in the soul.

The early Scholastics seem to be at a loss when they find themselves confronted with confirmation as a separate sacrament. Their whole theology is an effort to define the sacramental grace proper to confirmation, in contrast to baptism and the Eucharist. The success of the pseudo-Melchiades tended to underline too strongly a secondary aspect of the ancient tradition, the famous *gratia ad robur*. But sometimes theologians resigned themselves to the simple *augmentum gratiae*. These are the two aspects, unfortunately, which were retained by Peter Lombard, the "Master of the Sentences" in his *IV Sent.*, d. 7.

But it would be incorrect and unjust to reduce scholastic theology to these meagre findings. The more spiritual tradition of the "fullness of the Spirit" (Is 11:2), preserved in any case in the liturgy, never ceased to be influential. The doctrine of the "character" allowed the great Scholastics to develop the ecclesial and cultic aspects of confirmation. The great patristic themes of the royal priesthood (1 Pet 2:5) and of the analogy between the anointing of Christ or the descent of the Spirit at Pentecost, and the anointing of the faithful at confirmation, too frequently omitted in technical theology, come constantly to the fore. This is particularly true of the last fifty years, sometimes, however, because of subsidiary preoccupations, such as Catholic Action or the emancipation of the laity.

4. *The magisterium.* a) *General doctrine.* The magisterium confirmed the theological teaching at the Council of Florence in the Decree for the Armenians (*D* 695, 697, a résumé of the *De Fide et Sacramentis* of St. Thomas) and at the Council of Trent (*D* 844, 852, 871ff.). This is the doctrine summarized in *CIC*, can. 780–800. Confirmation is one of the seven sacraments (*D* 52d, 98, 419, 424, 465, 669, 697, 871) and like baptism and orders imparts a sacramental character (*D* 695, 852, 960, 996).

b) *The minister.* In the East, the priest has been the ordinary minister since the 4th century, but the consecration of the μύρον was always reserved to the bishop, preferably to a patriarch. In the West, between the 4th and 8th centuries, delegation to a priest is envisaged in case of necessity or by special decree (Mansi, IV, 1002; IX, 856). The Roman Church always considered the bishop as the ordinary minister, and imposed this regulation first in the suburbicarian dioceses (Innocent I, *D* 98; Gregory I, *PL*, LXXVII, 677 and 696; Gelasius I, *PL*, LIX, 51), and then throughout the West, where the *False Decretals* also influenced events. The practice became so common, under the influence of the *Decretum* of Gratian and of Peter Lombard, that the question soon arose of the necessity of papal delegation if confirmation by a priest was to be licit or even valid. The bishop's privilege, confirmed by the Council of Florence (*D* 573, 697), was maintained by the Popes from the 13th century (apropos of the missions in Asia) till Pius XII, when the parish priest was delegated to confirm when there was danger of death (*AAS* 38 [1946], pp. 349–58).

After Trent, theologians even asked whether confirmation by a priest in the East was valid. It was thought to be invalid, especially in countries where papal delegation was not supposed to exist (*D* 1459, n. 2), as in the case of the "Greeks" of Italy (*D* 1086, n. 1; 1458). Benedict XIV recognized the validity of confirmation in the other Oriental jurisdictions "ob tacitum privilegium a Sede Apostolica illis concessum" (*De Syn. Disquis.*, VII, 9). This opinion then became common among theologians (cf. the preliminaries of Vatican I, Mansi, IV, 1115–27, 1162–65) and was ratified by Vatican II (Decree on Ecumenism, art. 16; Decree on Eastern Catholic Churches, art. 13). Vatican II gives priests of the Latin rite the privilege of confirming Christians of Oriental rites according to the norms of canon law (*ibid.*, art. 14; *CIC*, can. 782, par. 4; *S. C. pro Eccl. Orient.*, decree of 1 May 1948).

c) *The subject of confirmation* is any baptized Christian in the state of grace (*CIC*, can. 786). The most controversial pastoral question is the age of confirmation. There is no universal practice. In the East, baptism, confirmation and the Eucharist are given to the infant, the unity and structure of the rite of initiation being respected. In Spain, Portugal and their former colonies, confirmation is given a few years after baptism. It was sometimes postponed till the age of fifteen in the Middle Ages (*D* 437), and after the Council of Trent the usual age was from seven to eleven years. In some European countries, after the French Revolution, it was delayed till twelve, and then, after Pius X's decree in 1910 on first Communion about the age of seven, was combined with the so-called "solemn Communion". Rome made discreet efforts through various instructions of the Congregations to re-establish the ancient sequence of initiation, and put confirmation about the age of seven (*CIC*, can. 788).

The whole question is simply a pastoral one. It is important, no doubt, to restore the old order of initiation, and above all, to make the Eucharist the climax of initiation, with the people of God united around their Lord. But it is equally certain that there are grave pastoral reasons in some countries for confirming children only when they are about to become adults. Vatican II wisely refused to impose a uniform rule on all.

d) *The sacramental sign.* In the anointing, the Western Church uses chrism, made of olive oil and balsam (*D* 419, 450, 697, 872, 1458), while the Eastern mixes the μύρον sometimes with as many as forty aromatic substances. The chrism is consecrated only by the bishop (*D* 93*, 98, 450, 571, 697, 1088). We have already discussed the evolution of the rites of the imposition of hands (*D* 424, 1963) and of anointing (*D* 419, 450, 465, 697), as also of the sacramental words, in the East and in the West.

e) *The character and the special grace.* The magisterium has never stated the precise doctrine of the character. As regards the grace, the magisterium followed the fluctuations of the theologians. The Holy Spirit is given in confirmation (*D* 98, 450), which is a new Pentecost (*D* 697) and perfects baptism (*D* 52d, 695). In the Middle Ages, the magisterium stressed more strongly the increase of grace, and the grace of fortitude (*D* 419, 695) to confess the faith (*D* 697). We may conclude that the magisterium leaves plenty of latitude to theologians as regards the theoretical interpretation of the essence of the sacrament.

C. Theology

1. *Fundamental positions.* We have already stated the fundamental aspects. Confirmation is the "gift of the Spirit" and hence a new Pentecost. As sacrament of consecration in Christian initiation it perfects baptism and is the normal preparation for the full ecclesial communion in the Eucharist. The theology of confirmation must justify and explain these three constitutive elements.

The Spirit revealed himself at Pentecost, when the Church was constituted in its primordial state, and hence as the model for future ages. In the Pentecostal experience, the Spirit made known the nature of his mission of salvation, as "promise of the Father" and "gift of Christ" crucified and risen from the dead; implicitly, the intra-trinitarian propriety of his person was revealed. A divine person cannot be revealed in his salvific mission without manifesting in a certain way his proper identity in the mystery of the Trinity. When he reveals himself in his work, in the function which he exercises "for us", he cannot but give a glimpse of what he is "in himself" and "for himself". Formerly, theologians may have spoken with too much assurance of what the divine persons are "in themselves", but today we are inclined to yield to the temptation of considering only their function "for us". The two aspects necessarily exist in a dialectical relationship which must not be lost sight of.

In the apostolic Church, the Spirit is not allotted a work which is exclusively proper to himself. He consummates the work of the Father in Christ. What is this achievement? Primarily, it is to take us *out of ourselves* in the act of bearing witness, which is one of the aspects preserved most clearly in the theological tradition. Such testimony is more than the techniques of the apostolate, of government or organization. It comprises the whole range of mysterious influences (consolation, peace, persuasion, love, etc.), which flow out from the human person in its own authenticity and its profound solidarity with others. These personal relationships are purified, intensified and entirely transformed (in the dialectic of the natural and the supernatural) through the force of the Spirit who unites us all in his "communion". But the dimension of "for others" is dialectically inseparable from that of our being "in ourselves". Hence the Spirit also leads us *into ourselves*, perfecting our participation in the existence of the Son and so directing us to the Father, the transcendent and immanent source of divine life and salvation. For through grace, to be "in ourselves" and "for ourselves" becomes being "in God", the interior source which nourishes perpetually the mystery of our person and its communion with others. In a word, the grace of the Spirit is a constantly growing "interiorization", and an "exteriorization" in testimony and in prophecy, two aspects in which are realized our participation in the existence of Christ and our encounter with the Father.

This is how baptism is completed by confirmation. Baptism unites us to Christ, communicating to us the fundamental grace of being "servants in the Servant and adoptive sons in the Son". Confirmation gives full reality to this act of salvation, in the dialectic of mystical union and testimony. In the history of salvation, baptism applies to us the death and resurrection of the Lord, while confirmation communicates the grace of Pentecost. Basically, the necessity of confirmation is that of the descent of the Holy Spirit with regard to the salvific act of Christ. In other words, the relationship between baptism and confirmation stems from the relationship between the resurrection and Pentecost in the history of salvation. Thus the two sacraments are truly mysteries and divine acts of salvation, manifested and realized sacramentally in the Church and applied to a given person, who is thereby taken into the community of the people of God. Hence too these sacraments may be termed "constitutive", since the consecration and the mission which they confer constitute men as members of the community of salvation established by Christ and his Spirit.

The doctrine of the sacramental character comes in here. There are various theological explanations of it. The Thomist notion of the *ordinatio ad cultum* remains valid. Theologians have overlooked the fact that the character (*sacramentum et res*) had originally a visible aspect, being in the nature of a "sign". The ontological structures of the character have perhaps been exaggerated. We prefer to restore to the sacramental character its ancient aspect of sign. Existentially, the sacramental character is based on the divine fidelity, which is the basic reason for the sacrament's not being repeated; this fidelity is also manifested visibly and attested by the Church in the sacramental act. The character exists on three levels of growing interiority: a complex of rights and duties in the visible Church; a particular mission, participating in the priesthood of Christ, in the sacerdotal Church (the notion of worship); a consecration to God in the spiritual Church. These three aspects are united to one another and ultimately to the sacramental grace by the dialectic of symbol and its realization (*sacramentum et res*).

Hence above all, confirmation gives us the full rights of membership in the Church. This juridical status signifies and brings about a real mission which is a participation of the priesthood of Christ (the royal priesthood of the faithful). This mission signifies and brings about a consecration (the anointing by the Spirit). The consecration signifies and brings about our sanctification through the grace of the Spirit. This aspect above all makes it disastrous to separate totally confirmation from baptism. The two make up together the totality of our Christian initiation in the unity of being "in Christ" and "in the Spirit" in the one salvation wrought by the Father.

2. *Comparison with standard opinions.* This truth has been retained by the theological tradition, though often in a too narrow and materialistic formulation. In the wider context of a sound theology of the "gift of the Spirit" we can understand better how confirmation can "increase" the grace of baptism and give us a *gratia ad robur in protestatione fidei*. Some theologians define confirmation as the sacrament of Christian maturity, which is acceptable, provided the term is not taken unwittingly in a biological or psychological sense, but in the dogmatic sense of Christian fullness in the Spirit. In the same order of ideas we can see the importance of confirmation for the spiritual emancipation of the laity, since it completes the consecration of the baptized within the royal priesthood of the faithful. It is just as important for priests and bishops, who remain fundamentally "of the faithful". Orders is not a constitutive sacrament like baptism and confirmation. But it confers on certain of the faithful, hence within the people of God, a consecration and a *functional* mission to exercise prophetic authority and be ministers of sanctification. A priest is not "constituted" in an order superior to that of the faithful, but he is ordained for the service of Christ and the community.

Piet Fransen

CONSCIENCE

1. *General description.* The word conscience (the "inwit" of Chaucer and Joyce) derives from *conscientia*, as does this from συνείδησις. While it is used in many senses, both in popular and scientific language, it denotes, in its specifically moral usage (French: *conscience morale*), a series of related phenomena of the soul, the kernel of which is an impressive basic experience reaching deep into personal consciousness. Long familiar, especially in the form of the so-called bad conscience, it has been apprehended and expressed in a variety of ways, and provides an appropriate starting point for a system of empirical, inductive ethics. Because of the present great lack of clarity in the use of the word a scientific description more properly starts, not from the linguistic usage, but from daily experience of conscience.

a) A careful analysis shows that in conscience man has a direct experience in the depths of his personality of the moral quality of a concrete personal decision or act as a call of duty on him, through his awareness of its significance for the ultimate fulfilment of his personal being. "The depths of his personality" means the nucleus, the centre of his integral, personal life, whose powers are first experienced as a unity before the various acts of soul and spirit come to be differentiated. Conscience is distinguished from moral knowledge (consciousness of value) on which it constantly draws and for which it provides the most vital content, by its immediate reference to one's own concrete action. Simplicity of experience – *simplex intuitus* in the scholastic psychology of knowledge – does not connote primitiveness but the intuition of a genuine and most delicate reality of the spirit, namely the moral value of one's own decision. An experience is made, not so much of norms capable of formulation, but of the immediate attraction of value or its opposite, of a richness and fullness encouraging and drawing one on towards what is good or of constriction and threat from evil and its harmful consequences. The basis is a capability in man for the moral, including the ultimate capability of decision about one's personal being. A certain parallel to conscience as a primary disposition may be found in the human power of language, in view of its elemental qualities, its integral and intuitive, at once mental and emotional receptivity for meaning, the general character of its laws of development and formation, and its essentially purposive nature.

b) Conscience is not correctly explained by the assumption of innate moral ideas. Neither does Kant's explanation as a transcendental faculty suffice. Inadequate also are theories which find an explanation of the origin, development and activity of conscience in extra-moral factors, naturalistic and evolutionary doctrines according to which conscience is a development from experiences of its usefulness in the history of the person or the species, of the individual or of society. F. Nietzsche, under the influence of biological evolutionism, regards the bad conscience as a product of human civilization. According to him it reveals a decadent, psychopathological development of man whose thwarted instincts have turned in on themselves. Very widely accepted is the explanation stemming from the depth psychology of S. Freud according to which an imperfectly developed form of conscience (Super Ego) is a product of the unconscious activity of the underlying instinctive reality. Existential philosophy accepts a formal concept of conscience which is not really moral, and which contains substantially the call to existential realization.

c) The primary intellectual and emotional receptivity for moral values, including the ordination to the good, which is present in the structure of conscience, can, through faulty training, not indeed be made false in itself, but weakened to the point of being practically ineffective. This incapability of being falsified, rooted as it is in the ultimate reality of personal existence and of consciousness, ensures the ethical dependability and authority of conscience and points as well to their limitation. The total lack of conscientious response (moral insanity), apart from cases of severe mental deficiency, can be caused by the psychopathic lack of that emotional function which is essential for conscience, even though intelligence remains intact. The development of conscience comes about under the influence of all the morally significant impressions drawn from the human environment, together with one's own life-experience. Beginning with the adoption of external patterns and norms of conduct and the acceptance of moral attitudes and values from others (authoritarian, legal conscience), it progresses to the point where an independent position is adopted as a response to one's appreciation of the claim of moral values (personal conscience). Defects in the normal psychological development frequently result in inhibitions or interferences with the development and functioning of conscience (fixation, regression to earlier stages of development, unhealthy guilt feelings, transference of guilt, compulsion of conscience or scruples).

d) The training of conscience, the aim of which is the fully developed conscience functioning in terms of autonomy (independence), intensity (depth, immediacy, vitality of experience) and extent of moral knowledge at one's command, is only partly the result of moral instruction and incomparably more the result of the encouragement of genuine activity of conscience implemented throughout the entire field of personal experience. Its aim is the fullest possible exercise of conscientious decision, and therefore the opportunity of adopting a personal point of view must not be taken away. Decisions of conscience are necessarily incomplete and partial because of the limiting circumstances of the individual, the time and environment. As a result they can be one-sided and are subject to prejudice and error. Critical examination and continuing formation of conscience are indispensable. As with every genuine appreciation of value, an attitude of reverence and love is an essential precondition both for the development and for the activity of conscience. To be aimed at is the sensitively alert conscience, dependable in every question of moral significance, reacting quickly and weighing accurately all the factors involved (opposite: the slow, dull, lax conscience).

e) In individual judgments of conscience a distinction is to be made between true and false propositions (*conscientia recta – falsa, vera – erronea*, or *error conscientiae*) according to whether the particular judgment agrees with the objective norm or not. The judgment which precedes action (*conscientia antecedens*) includes a warning, restraining from evil or urging to what is good; the latter, as the response to the claim of the good which is never capable of full realization, is a true function of conscience. The judgment of conscience following an action (*conscientia consequens*) is either the bad conscience (condemning and punishing) or the good conscience. This is not, as a mere correlative to bad conscience, a judgment on the goodness of one's own action, but the experience of overcoming an evil which is somehow felt as impending or threatening.

2. *Theology of conscience*. a) *Biblical*. The OT describes experiences of conscience without using the word itself. (The word first occurs, and then only in isolated instances, in the Wisdom books.) Instead it uses "heart" or "reins" or other such images. Conscience is always related to God as the hearing of his word, the acceptance of his will, consciousness of one's own position, one's own responsibility before God, of the divine judgment. In the NT conscience has a central significance (the inward moral attitude). With συνείδησις, a word taken from contemporary popular philosophy and not always given the same meaning, St. Paul indicates the essential functions of conscience in Christian life, without, however, developing a systematic teaching on conscience. The Christian knows himself to be confronted with the demands and judgments of God, which makes him conscious of the commandments and the grace of God (2 Cor 1:12), and is the guiding line for a life lived in the sight of God (Acts 24:16; Rom 13:5; 1 Cor 10:25f.; 1 Tim 1:5, 19), whether as a pure conscience (2 Tim 1:3; Heb 13:18; 1 Pet 2:19), or as a bad conscience (1 Tim 4:2; Tit 1:15; Heb 10:2, 22). As good conscience it makes him free and independent of the judgments of others (Acts 23:1; 1 Cor 10:29; 2 Cor 1:12; 1 Pet 3:16). As a human power it can give no certainty about God's judgment (1 Cor 4:4). It transmits the commandment even outside revelation as a law given by nature (Rom 2:15). Linked to human knowledge, it is subject to deception but remains a moral norm of the individual in this case (1 Cor 8:7f.; 10:25ff.; Rom 14). In the Christian it is active in the Holy Spirit (Rom 9:1), through the power of Christ's resurrection (1 Pet 3:21), cannot be purified and perfected through sacrifice but only through Christ's blood, in the power of the eternal Spirit (Heb 9:9, 14). Conscience is also an organ of the religious life to which the apostolic revelation of truth is made (2 Cor 4:2) and which preserves the mysteries of faith in their purity (1 Tim 3:9). It can in fact take on the meaning of the theologically deeper and more precise Pauline term πίστιζ (Rom 14:23).

b) *History of the doctrine*. The rich foundations in NT for a theological teaching on conscience were not followed up by the Church Fathers. We find numerous single statements and opinions, especially in Tertullian, Origen, Chrysostom, and more details in Augustine, who describes especially the religious functions of conscience. In the Middle Ages, as well as a remarkable practical religious teaching on conscience (Bernard of Clairvaux, Petrus Cellensis, Gerson, etc.), there gradually developed from the 12th century on in relation to a text of St. Jerome (*Commentary on Ezek*, ch. 6), a systematic theological teaching on conscience on the basis of the two terms *synteresis* (*synderesis*) and *conscientia*. In general *synteresis* was taken as the natural nucleus of the conscience remaining essentially intact even after the fall of man, as the *a priori* intellectual and volitive basis of all activity of conscience. Bonaventure attributes the affective processes in conscience to the *synteresis*, the more intellectual functions both habitual and actual to the *conscientia*. Thomas Aquinas calls the *synteresis* the permanent natural *habitus* of the primary moral principles, *conscientia* the actual judgment of conscience arrived at by way of conclusion. The full recognition of conscience as the valid norm for the individual made much difficulty for the extremely objectively orientated medieval theology. St. Thomas Aquinas was the first to overcome this difficulty in principle and his success had its effect on succeeding generations. The reformers sought a meaning of conscience in line with their theological anthropology and their teaching on justification. In modern times our theological understanding of conscience had to be secured against a secularized notion of conscience with its tendency to absolute moral autonomy.

c) *Modern problems relating to conscience*. Theology must develop the traditional teaching into an understanding which is in the full sense Christian and theological as well as personal, taking cognizance of the insights of psychology and depth psychology, of sociology and ethnology. An intensive study of the teaching of the Bible is essential, as well as a thorough appreciation of the role of conscience in the entire Christian life, especially in its significance for the spiritual life and for the circumstances of the individual Christian. Conscience itself cannot be taken as being equivalent to moral evaluation or moral knowledge. Primarily and directly it applies to the claim on the human ego in a concrete situation of decision as being what is of ultimately radical significance for the person as such. In connection with this there also arises of itself in most cases a new or deeper insight into objective moral value precisely in its relation to the particular circumstances of the individual person and the unique situation of decision. As the faculty for ultimate personal commitment, the conscience of the Christian responds on the basis of the faith to the personal demands made by God's work and word in revelation, having an immediate experience of their significance for personal salvation. Conscience has here become the conscience of the believer. Theology must reject all attempts to restrict the understanding of conscience to the sphere of the moral, even though this can in fact set the limits for the experience of conscience by the unbeliever. The conscience of the Christian will fulfil its function only when every dawning value is deeply experienced as a gracious approach of the divine perfection and every situation of decision as "the fullness of time", as a gift and a call of God, as a possibility of Christian loyalty in the presence of the divine "Thou".

3. *Conscience as moral norm*. Conscience brings to mind the objective moral norm in its relation to the concrete decision to be made in the present situation. Since the role of conscience is thus an intermediary one, it does not set the moral norms itself in an autonomous sense. This is true even though this receptivity of conscience can by no means be regarded as merely passive, and no matter how creatively active in personal reverence and love conscience is in discovering with delicate sensitivity the good that is to be done together

with its most minute circumstances, and no matter how much it brings to bear the entire extent of personal knowledge and experience of life in moral matters. It interiorizes, in fact ("autonomizes"), the objective norms. The relation of the objective norms to conscience cannot be understood as the meeting of two competing values. The objective "law" is the will and order of God in his creation and this is made known in the conscience of man who carries on his life within this creation and its plan of salvation. For moral orientation in a situation where a concrete decision is called for, conscience cannot be dispensed with or bypassed. Its place cannot be taken either by moral knowledge or opinion or by direction from another. The judgment of conscience is the ultimate definitive norm for the individual decision (*regula proxima moralitatis*), but it does not thereby become a general norm for people faced with similar decisions. The moral value of an action is measured exclusively according to the judgment of conscience arrived at after due consideration of all the circumstances.

The judgment of conscience retains its normative value in the case where there is a genuine error of conscience (*error invincibilis*), that is, where in an individual case something that is done in accordance with the dictate of conscience is at variance with the objective norm. As the final subjective norm for moral action the judgment of conscience must be definite and unambiguous so that a well-grounded uncertainty is excluded (*certitudo moralis*). Where certainty cannot be attained there arise doubts of conscience (*dubium practicum conscientiae*, also *error vincibilis*). The actual (practical) doubt of conscience is not a moral defect, but rather a necessary stage especially in cases where a decision is difficult. It can occur over the entire range of moral life in the form of a lack of clarity in respect of moral norms (*dubium iuris*) or their application in a particular situation (*dubium facti*); also in the case of several competing moral claims. Higher experiences of the spiritual life move often at the margin of the certain conscience. The most difficult situation is the conflict of conscience: the conjunction of conflicting obligations, even in the most extreme form, where, in consequence of a life permeated in all its relationships and circumstances with evil, conscience can show no possibility of action that does not entail sin (*conscientia perplexa*). The causes of the individual's doubts of conscience are, apart from the natural limitation of knowledge, ignorance in moral matters and lack of certainty in moral judgment. To act with positive practical doubts of conscience implies indifference to the danger of sin (Rom 14:23). The objectively safest way must be chosen when the attainment of an end is absolutely demanded (e.g., the validity of administration of the sacraments).

Generally speaking, practical certainty in the judgment of conscience must be striven for: a) through clarification of the moral position by personal reflection or with the help of the advice of another (*certitudo directa*); b) when this is impossible, a morally justifiable decision must be arrived at from moral considerations of a general nature (*certitudo indirecta sive reflexa*); c) finally, the Christian must have as his general moral attitude the desire to discover what is good and commit himself to it with all his personal moral power (risk in the positive sense), so as purely out of love of God and loyalty to him to make his way through the darkness which cannot be enlightened. Historically, the attempt to arrive reflexively, with the help of rationally enunciated general principles, at the best possible solution to the most difficult problems arising from doubts of conscience, led to the construction of the so-called moral systems. For the overcoming of doubts of conscience there is need above all of prudence.

Rudolf Hofmann

CONTRITION

1. *Concept.* Contrition is an element or aspect in that process of individual salvation which is usually called *metanoia*, conversion (in the sense of change of heart and life), repentance, justification. It can therefore only be correctly understood and judged in that larger context. Since it is a rejection of sin, it presupposes a theologically correct understanding of sin and guilt.

2. *The teaching of the Church.* The Council of Trent describes contrition as "sorrow of heart and detestation for sin committed, with the resolution not to sin again" (*D* 897, 915). The Church's doctrine declares that for anyone who has personally sinned, such contrition has always been necessary as a condition of obtaining forgiveness of the guilt, that it must be linked with trust in the divine mercy, cannot simply consist of a good resolution and beginning of a new life but (in principle) must include the explicit, voluntary rejection of previous life. The same Tridentine doctrine distinguishes between *contritio caritate perfecta* and *contritio imperfecta* = *attritio*, according to whether the explicit motive of rejection of the sin committed is the genuine theological virtue of love of God or some other moral motive which, while less than the motive of love, is nevertheless a moral one (the intrinsic evil of sin, sin as cause of the loss of salvation, etc.) and is chosen under the influence of God's grace and unambiguously excludes the will to sin (*D* 898). (Mere fear of punishment as a physical evil is therefore not "imperfect contrition", or *attritio*; it would be that "gallows remorse" which Luther rightly rejected, but which he wrongly took to be the Catholic idea of *attritio*.) Perfect contrition (which presupposes at least the implicit will to receive the sacrament of penance) justifies immediately, even before the actual reception of baptism or penance. Imperfect contrition only justifies when linked with reception of the sacrament (*ibid.*). Such voluntary contrition (*D* 915) is not (as the Council understood the Reformers to suppose) an attempt at human self-justification by man's own power, which would indeed make man a sinner. It is a gift of grace by which man entrusts himself to the merciful God (*D* 915, 799, 798). The Church's magisterium forbade (*D* 1146) the partisans of "contrition" and of "attrition" to apply theological notes of censure to one another.

3. *Theological reflection.* a) *Anthropological presuppositions.* Important in the first place for theological understanding of contrition is the general anthropological realization that man as a free spiritual person with a history in time has a cognitive and volitive relation to himself, in regard to his past, present and future and their inextricable interrelations. Consequently man cannot and may not simply leave his past behind him with indifference as something which is no longer real; it still exists as an element of his present, which he himself has brought about in personal freedom, and since he has a relation to himself, he has a relation to his past, and by his present deliberate attitude he gives it its possibly quite different meaning in relation to his future. The degree of explicitness of these interrelationships differs very considerably from individual to individual, and according to age and situation in life. But it follows from what has been said that man cannot in principle reject forthwith a deliberate attitude towards his past as an element in his relation to himself "now". Consequently, "formal" contrition is meaningful and of itself necessary, but in certain circumstances merely virtual contrition can

suffice. By this man turns to God with faith, hope and love, without explicit advertence to his past, for even in this case an implicit attitude to the past is involved in this fundamental decision regarding a human life.

b) *On the phenomenology of contrition.* The repudiation of a past free action which is accomplished by contrition (*dolor et detestatio*) must be very carefully interpreted for it to be intelligible to people today. In the first place it has nothing to do with a psychological, emotional shock (melancholy, depression) which may often, though not necessarily, follow from the bad action for psychological and physiological or social reasons (loss of prestige, fear of social penalties, exhaustion, conflict in the psychic mechanisms involved, etc.). It is more a question of the rejection freely made by the spiritual person of the moral worthlessness of the past action and of the attitude which gave rise to it as its concrete expression. This rejection does not mean flight from and repression of the past, but is the appropriate way for a spiritual subject to face his past, acknowledge it and assume responsibility for it. Nor does this rejection involve any mere fiction or unreal hypothesis ("I wish I had acted differently then"). It has an actual reality as its object: the present disposition of the subject in his fundamental decision and attitude, to the extent that this is partly constituted by the past action. The repudiation does not contest the theoretically and practically undeniable fact that even the evil action in the past was directed to something "good" and has often produced very considerable good (e.g., in human maturity, etc.) which in some cases cannot be left out of account at all in the life of the doer of the action. In this way there arises psychologically an apparently almost insoluble problem, when an event has to be repudiated which, because of its good consequences, can scarcely be left out of account in the person's life. In this case, unconditional turning to the merciful God in love will be a better method of contrition than analytic reflection on the past.

c) *Contrition as a response.* Contrition derives from God's initiative and must therefore realize that it is a response. It is of course based in essence and in its actual occurrence on the grace of God, like every moral act which is to be of any significance for salvation. It does not therefore bring about God's saving will, which has its definitive historical manifestation in Christ. It is a response of acceptance of that will and is aware that the free acceptance is itself the work of God's saving will. Contrition therefore "causes" justification only by receiving it from God as a pure gift. All the "merit" of contrition, however this is conceived according to different stages of contrition, ultimately derives from a first efficacious grace of God which is preceded by absolutely *no* human merit and work. Whatever is said of such merit (whether thought of as *meritum de condigno* or as *meritum de congruo*), it ultimately simply means, therefore, that God himself effects in our freedom what is "worthy" of him. It is only necessary to avoid the misconception that the activity of our freedom comes less from God than what we undergo passively and automatically.

d) *The formal object of contrition.* The movement of contrite repudiation of one's own past can take various forms because, corresponding to the multiplicity of different aspects of reality willed in their variety by God, there are a multiplicity of moral values which, if affirmed, can form the direct positive intent of contrition and so provide grounds for rejection of what is opposed to them. Yet for all that it must not be overlooked that the multiple world of values which makes it possible for there to be a variety of motives for contrition, forms a unity in which each particular motive points to the whole and is open to it, and that all motives and the response to them are only perfected in God and his love. *Per se* one would even have to distinguish between the intrinsically specifying formal object of an act and the external motive for the positing of the act (though the two can coincide). The formal object of contrition as such, which does not need to be envisaged in a very explicitly conscious way, is always fundamentally the contradiction between sin and the holy God or, positively, God's claim on men because of his holiness. The motives (of a moral kind) which prompt one to posit this act with this formal object can be very multifarious. They can even be "inferior" to the formal object of the act which they "prompt", or can even extend to the formal object of the love of God which in this way becomes the motive of perfect contrition. In what follows, however, we leave out of account this more precise distinction.

e) *Attritionism and contritionism.* On this basis it is possible to understand the attrition-contrition controversy. Attritionism is the doctrine that *attritio* (imperfect contrition, from a motive which is morally good but from the religious point of view inferior to that of unselfish, theological love of God) is sufficient for the sacrament of penance. The term first appeared in the 12th century, and at first meant an inadequate endeavour, insufficient for justification even in the sacrament, to have *contritio* as the repentance which justifies. Later *attritio* was used to mean a genuine repentance prompted by serious moral motives (chiefly fear of divine justice) but not yet based on love. This was opposed by Luther as "gallows remorse" because he identified *timor serviliter servilis* (mere fear of punishment as a purely physical evil) and the *timor simpliciter servilis* (real renunciation of *guilt* out of fear of punishment). Before the Council of Trent, the discussion centred on whether the power of the sacrament itself changed this *attritio* into *contritio* (repentance based on love). Trent recognized *attritio* as a morally good preparation for the sacrament (*D* 898). After Trent, controversy continued on whether *attritio* is sufficient as proximate preparation or disposition for the sacrament or whether in addition an explicit act at least of initial love (which again was variously interpreted) is required (cf. *D* 798). If an at least initial unselfish love of God (*amor benevolentiae* as opposed to *amor concupiscentiae*) is regarded as a proximate disposition necessary even for the sacrament of penance, even if that love is of a kind which is not sufficient for justification without the sacrament, we have contritionism in the form which was current particularly in the 17th and 18th centuries. The controversy between attritionism and contritionism in this form was never decided by the Church (*D* 1146).

On closer examination this controversy is pointless, both in theory and as regards pastoral theology. For where there is no unambiguous renunciation of sin for religious motives, there is no *attritio*. And such renunciation necessarily includes the will to fulfil God's commandments and consequently, before all else, the commandment to love God with one's whole heart. But how would such a will to love God be distinguished practically and in the concrete from love of God? Real attrition and contrition may therefore in the concrete be different in the explicitness with which various motives appear in the foreground of reflective conceptual consciousness, but not in the unanalysed global motivation of the fundamental decision of a human life. The dispute is therefore based on a false reification of the motives on both sides, and on the presupposition that only what is explicitly known as a motive is effectively one. In reality, however, the ultimate fundamental freedom of man cannot remain at all neutral, provisional and indefinite. The God loved in man's fundamental decision is either the true God or an idol of sin. If, therefore, the fatal line is crossed with genuine morality and religion away from sin towards God, there is no danger that God is not yet loved, even if a development *in time* can be assumed to be involved. Furthermore, a distinction would have to be drawn between the proximate disposition for the reception of the sacrament (*sacramentum*) and the proximate disposition for the reception of the grace of the sacrament (*res sacramenti*). Then the doctrine of attritionism could be applied to the reception of the grace of the sacrament. For it is quite meaningful to assume with Aquinas that the reception of justifying grace (the "infusion of the theological virtue of charity") by an adult can only take place in the act of free acceptance of precisely this gift as such, in other words, in the act of charity. Consequently, in any case the *attritus* becomes *contritus* at least in the sacrament. Where someone has really turned away from sin and towards God, this is a conception which does not present any psychological difficulty, unless the view is held that a motive is only present if it is present in an explicitly conceptual form.

Karl Rahner

CONVERSION

A. Theology

1. *Methodology.* a) The content of the theologically important and indeed central concept of conversion will be presented here from the point of view of dogmatic theology, but that of biblical theology will also be taken into account.

b) It is difficult to distinguish the concept precisely from related theological concepts: faith (as *fides qua*) and consequently hope and love, contrition, metanoia, justification (as an event), redemption. Reference must therefore be made to these terms. In accordance with the corporeal-spiritual, historical and social nature of man, conversion has always, though in very varying degrees, a liturgical and social aspect in all religions, including Christianity (rites of initiation, baptism, penitential liturgy, revivalist meetings, etc.). This can be the embodiment and social side of conversion, but if it is not performed with genuine personal conviction, it constitutes a deformation of conversion and of religion generally. This aspect cannot, however, be dealt with further here.

c) The biblical terms שׁוּב, ἐπι-, ἀποστρέφειν, μετάνοια and others are specifically religious terms which denote more than an intellectual change of opinion (as in Greek). They concern the whole human being in his fundamental relation to God, not merely a change of moral judgment and attitude in regard to a particular object (and commandment).

2. *Conversion as fundamental decision.* From the point of view of the formal nature of freedom, conversion is the religiously and morally good fundamental decision in regard to God, a basic choice intended to commit the whole of life to God inasmuch as this takes place with some definite, if only relatively higher, degree of reflection and consequently can be located at a more or less definite point in a lifetime. For the freedom which finds realization in one individual life as a whole is not a mere sum of moral or immoral free actions, simply following one another in time. It involves one act of freedom as fundamental decision. Nevertheless, this fundamental decision is not wholly accessible to analytical reflection. It cannot, therefore, be fixed with certainty by such reflection at a quite definite moment in the course of life. This must always be borne in mind in the theological interpretation of conversion.

3. *Conversion as response to God's call.* From the biblical and dogmatic point of view, man's free turning to God has always to be seen as a response, made possible by God's grace, to a call from God. And he himself in the summons gives what he asks. This call of God is both Jesus Christ himself, as the presence of the Kingdom of God in person, with the demands this involves, and his Spirit which, as God's self-communication, offers freedom and forgiveness to overcome the narrow limits and sinfulness of man. It also comprises the actual situation of the person to whom the call is addressed. This is the precise particular embodiment of the call of Christ and the Spirit.

4. *The content of the call*, which cannot be separated from its utterance, is a summons, imposing an obligation and making obedience to it possible, to receive God, who communicates himself, liberates man from enslaving "idols" (principalities and powers), and makes it possible to have courage to hope for final liberation and freedom in the direct possession of God as our absolute future. The call therefore summons us from mere finitude (since grace is participation in the divine life itself) and from sinfulness, in which man in mistrust and despair makes an idol of himself and of certain dimensions of his own existence in the fundamental decision of his life (since grace is forgiveness). The call is not simply a command to fulfil particular moral obligations, to "amend one's life".

The content of the call can, of course, also be described the other way round. Where a man is detached from self ("denies himself"), loves his neighbour unselfishly, trustingly accepts his existence in its incomprehensibility and ultimate unmanageableness as incomprehensibly meaningful, without claiming to determine this ultimate meaning himself or to have it under his control; where he succeeds in renouncing the idols of his mortal fear and hunger for life, there the Kingdom of God, God himself (as the ultimate ground of such acts) is accepted and known, even if this occurs quite unreflectingly. In this way the conversion remains implicit and "anonymous" and in certain circumstances Christ is not expressly known (though attained in his "Spirit") as the concrete historical expression of God's definitive self-utterance to man. Ultimately the intention is the same, whether Jesus calls for conversion (*metanoia*) to the *basileia* of God present here and now in himself and confronting the whole man with its radical demands, whether Paul calls us to faith in God who justifies without works through the Cross of Christ, or John admonishes us to pass from the darkness to light in faith in the Son who has appeared in the flesh. All continue the preaching of penance by the prophets of the OT and give it a radical character through the faith that in Jesus crucified and risen the call of God, which makes conversion possible, is definitively present and invincibly established, but precisely for that reason imposes the gravest obligation.

5. *The "today" of conversion.* Conversion itself is experienced as the gift of God's grace (as preparation) and as radical, fundamental decision which concerns a human life in its entirety, even when it is realized in a particular concrete decision in everyday life. It is faith as concrete concern about the call, which in each instance uniquely concerns a particular individual, and as the obedient reception of its "content". Conversion is hope as trusting oneself to the unexpected, uncharted way into the open and incalculable future in which God comes (which is predestination). It is a turning from one's past life (freely performed yet experienced as a gift), ending the repression by which the past was detained in sin. It is love for the neighbour, because only in conjunction with this can God really be loved, and without that love no one

really knows with genuine personal knowledge who God is. It means standing firm and grasping the unique situation which is only found at this particular moment "today", not soothing oneself with the idea that it will come again, that the chance of salvation is "always" available. It is the sober realization that every conversion is only a beginning and that the rest of daily fidelity, the conversion which can only be carried out in a whole lifetime, has still to come.

6. *Conversion in non-Christian religions* (and even the secular analogies in psycho-therapeutic practice) has to be judged by the same general criteria as are used to interpret theologically non-Christian religions and perhaps even "implicit Christianity".

B. Pastoral Aspects

1. In ordinary Catholic pastoral practice the occurrence of conversion as a central event in the history of an individual's salvation is very often masked. The reasons are easy to see. Baptism, which was *the* event of conversion in the early Church with its baptismal devotion, is in most cases administered to infants. Confirmation also for the most part does not in practice figure as the ritual expression of a conversion. The same applies to our practice of First Communions in early childhood. Furthermore, our pastoral practice treats as the normal case a Christianity lived in a relatively homogeneous Christian society, where the ultimate Christian attitudes and decisions are taken as a matter of course (even if it is questionable whether this is really the case). Practice in the confessional, frequent confession and preaching on morals, which deals chiefly with the particular demands of Christian daily life, also tend to a perpetually repeated rectification and improvement of Christian everyday life on its average level rather than to a fundamental, unique "new birth".

2. Pastoral practice and theology, however, ought not to overlook the phenomenon of conversion as a decisive function of pastoral care of the individual. Not only because freedom in the sense of man's unique, historical self-realization intended to be final in regard to God, implies a fundamental decision (*option fondamentale*), but also because a decision of this kind ought to be carried out as consciously and explicitly as possible, since reflection and history are constitutive of man's very essence. From this point of view, conversion is not so much or always a turning away from definite particular sins of the past, as a resolute, radical and radically conscious, personal and in each instance unique adoption of Christian life. And in this, freedom, decision as absolutely final, and grace are really experienced (cf., e.g., Gal 3:5). Furthermore, in a society which in philosophical outlook is extremely heterogeneous and anti-Christian, Christianity in the individual, deprived of support from the milieu, cannot survive in the long run without a conversion of this kind, i.e., personal fundamental choice of faith and Christian life.

3. Pastoral theology and practice should therefore cultivate more the art of spiritual initiation into this kind of personal experience of conversion. Not that a genuine conversion can simply be produced at will by psycho-technical methods. But as clear and conscious as possible an accomplishment of the fundamental Christian decision can be considerably furthered by really wise and skilled spiritual guidance on the part of an individual pastor (as the preambles of faith demand). In an age of atheism which declares it cannot discern any meaning in the question of God even as a question, or discover any religious experience whatsoever, this spiritual initiation into conversion has not primarily a moral decision as its immediate goal, but the bringing about and voluntary acceptance of a

fundamental religious experience of the inescapable orientation of man towards the mystery which we call God.

Catholic pastoral practice was and is mistrustful of any deliberate production of conversion phenomena ("methodism", "revivalist campaigns"), and with good reason (regard for "objectivity", fear of pseudo-mysticism, fanaticism, will to preserve the ecclesiastical character and sobriety of Christian everyday life, etc.). Nevertheless, there have also been in existence for a long time in Catholic pastoral practice all kinds of ways of methodically promoting conversion, adapted to the general human and cultural level of Christians, e.g., popular missions, retreats, days of recollection, novitiates, etc. All such pastoral methods directed towards conversion ought, however, to be examined to see whether they are precise enough and correctly adapted to the dispositions of men today which make possible for them a genuine religious experience and conversion. Catholic pastoral practice should realize its own particular dangers and obviate them by a determined effort to provide genuine spiritual guidance towards really personal conversion. The dangers are those of the merely liturgical and sacramental, of legalism, of the practice of comfortable church-going and mere conventionalism, of conforming to the average level in the Church.

4. Since the fundamental decision has perpetually to be maintained or renewed in quite novel situations, the fundamental phases of life constitute so many situations and specific forms of conversion. Puberty, marriage, entry into a profession, beginning of old age, etc. ought to be regarded as situations offering the opportunity for conversion, and pastoral practice ought to know how its spiritual initiation into religious experience and conversion must be specially adapted to fit these situations.

5. From the very nature of freedom, the fundamental decision of which has to be concretely realized and maintained in the multiplicity of particular voluntary choices in daily life, and because of the connection between conversion and the limits of human life, its individual differences and phases of growth, it is understandable that a Christian life may run its course like a slow uninterrupted process of maturation, without very clearly marked breaks (though these are never wholly lacking). On the other hand it may appear as a dramatic event with one or more apparently almost revolutionary conversions which can be dated with considerable precision (as, e.g., with Paul, Augustine, Luther, Ignatius Loyola, Pascal, Kierkegaard, etc.). But even a sudden conversion can be the result of long but imperceptible development.

C. Conversion from Another Christian Community to the Catholic Church

1. Special problems arise on the "conversion" of a Lutheran or Orthodox Christian to the Catholic Church. What is in question here is not solely (or not even necessarily in all cases) an interior change in the ultimate fundamental attitude concerning the whole of life. It is a change in the ecclesiastical situation of the convert. On the one hand it is conceivable, for example, that in such a case a "saint" may be converted, and then only the external ecclesiastical status would be altered. It is possible for someone merely to change his denominational membership without special inward change of heart, although this is really needed, and to become a Catholic, even for reasons which have no religious significance at all. The normal case, however, will be one in which conversion to the Catholic Church also involves something in the nature of an inward religious conversion.

2. "It is clear that the preparation and

reception of those individuals who desire full ecclesiastical communion is in essence different from ecumenical work; the two, however, are not incompatible, for both derive from God's wonderful design." (Vatican II, Decree on Ecumenism, art. 4.) In practice this conciliar declaration means that the ecumenical work of Catholics as such must take care not to aim at individual conversions to the Catholic Church, for this would bring that work into disrepute and make it impossible. On the other hand, even in the age of ecumenism such individual conversion is legitimate and indeed a duty, the necessary conditions being presupposed. The same applies, therefore, to the endeavours of Catholics and of the Catholic clergy to promote such individual conversions. At all events, however, in case of actual conflict in practice, ecumenical work must take precedence in importance and urgency over individual conversion.

3. The following principles might perhaps be indicated as important in the endeavour to promote individual conversions.

a) If such work is not to degenerate into a false proselytism, the pastoral missionary work at the present day in the countries which are called Christian but are largely de-Christianized ought to be concerned with the re-Christianization of contemporary atheists, of people who belong to no denomination and of the unbaptized, rather than with promoting individual conversions of the kind mentioned. Winning the former to the Catholic Church then represents simply the final stage of a conversion in the genuine religious sense of the term.

b) In view of the limited pastoral resources in personnel of the Catholic Church, non-Catholic Christians are not in practice suitable "subjects" for the work of conversion, even if this gave promise of success, if they are pursuing a Christian life in the genuine Christian spirit in their own Church and if they would not be much changed or advanced in the central and essential concern of Christianity, which they are of course in a position to live in accordance with their concrete religious possibilities and needs. Consequently, for them a denominational conversion could scarcely mean in practice a conversion in the real sense. It is different with those who denominationally belong to a non-Catholic Church or community but do not practise and religiously speaking are homeless.

c) Anyone who wishes to become a Catholic on genuinely religious grounds may not be turned away but must be afforded most attentive pastoral care.

d) If ecumenical or personal grounds suggest it, the interval of time between recognition of the Catholic Church as the true Church of Jesus Christ and official conversion to it need not be restricted to a very short period.

4. The pastoral care of converts involves more than instruction in Catholic dogmatics and moral theology. As far as may be, it ought to aim, in preparing for the act of entering the Catholic Church, at making this a conversion in the full religious sense of the word. This presupposes a good knowledge of non-Catholic theology and an understanding of ecumenical work. It must endeavour to counter rather than to strengthen a purely negative attitude of protest in the convert against his former ecclesiastical community. It must encourage the convert not to lose any element of his positive Christian heritage by his move, and assist him to cope in faith and patience with the often very imperfect life of the Catholic parish. The pastoral care of converts cannot, therefore, simply be regarded as ended by their conversion.

Karl Rahner

COUNCIL

I. Theology

1. *Concept.* Councils or Synods are assemblies (σύνοδοι, *concilia*) of representatives of the universal Church or local Churches for mutual consultations and for reaching decisions on Church affairs. A distinction must be drawn between Ecumenical Councils representing the universal Church and the various kinds of particular councils (general, patriarchal, plenary, primatial, imperial and provincial synods).

2. *Historical sketch.* The forms taken even by the Ecumenical Councils have been of diverse kinds. According to existing canon law, no Ecumenical Council can take place unless it be convened by the Pope. The rights of the Pope also include the chairmanship (either in person or through his delegates) of the Council, the fixing of subjects for discussion and the rules of procedure, the location, adjournment and dissolution of a Council, and the confirmation of the decisions reached (*CIC*, can. 222; cf. can. 227). All cardinals, patriarchs, archbishops and bishops, abbots and prelates with an area of jurisdiction of their own, the abbot primate, the superiors of religious congregations and the superiors-general of exempt orders, and also the titular bishops have the right to vote, provided nothing to the contrary had been laid down in the terms of convocation. The theologians and canonists summoned to the Council possess only an advisory vote (can. 223; on representation and premature departure cf. can. 224–5). Council Fathers can also propose questions for treatment at their own initiative, but such proposals are subject to the approval of the president (can. 226). The Ecumenical Council possesses the highest jurisdiction over the universal Church; appeal from the Pope to the Council is excluded; in the event of the death of the Pope the Council is suspended (can. 228–9).

These stipulations codify, in all essential points, the procedure followed at Trent and at the First Vatican Council. Among them there is hardly a point which was not disregarded at one or many or perhaps even at most of the Ecumenical Councils. In particular, it is historically untenable that the "Ecumenical Councils" of the first century were generally convened, presided over and confirmed by the Pope. What all these questions primarily involve are stipulations of canon law, insofar as the constitution bestowed on the Church by the gospel is not embodied in them.

The Petrine office must be effectively represented at an Ecumenical Council, since it is of the essence of the constitution of the Church, of which the Council must be representative. However, this representation was verified in very different ways at the Councils, sometimes merely through subsequent approbation. And it cannot be denied that conflicts have occurred in the past between Church and Pope, or that they may occur in future – as in the possible case of a heretial or schismatical Pope and his "deposition".

Direct representation of the laity at the Councils (and not merely indirect, through the clergy) is not only dogmatically possible, but also desirable from the theological viewpoint of the universal priesthood. The laity's direct knowledge of and responsibility for the world also make it desirable; under some circumstances it is absolutely necessary. On the other hand, a Council directed against the authorities of the Church would conflict with the order of the Church and, in particular, with the nature of the Ecumenical Council, which is intended as a representation of the universal Church, for such representation is not possible without the bishops.

Considerable differences are to be found in every respect between the provincial Councils of the 2nd and 3rd centuries (out of which the Ecumenical Councils developed), the eight ancient Ecumenical Councils of the Byzantine East convened by the Emperor, the papal General Synods of the Latin Middle Ages, the late medieval reform Councils of Christendom, the purely ecclesiastical Tridentine Council of Catholic reform and Counter-Reformation, and the First Vatican Council which was dominated by the Pope.

3. *Theological meaning*: The Church itself is the comprehensive "assembly" (=ἐκκλησία, from καλέω), called together by God himself; it is a "concilium" (con-kal-ium, from *concalare*, i.e., to call together; Greek: καλέω) of those who believe. Thus in a deep theological sense the Church itself can be called an "Ecumenical Council of divine convocation". The universal Church, as a fellowship of the faithful, has a conciliar, synodal (collegial) structure throughout; this is true of the local (parish), particular (diocese), provincial and universal Church.

In this perspective the Ecumenical Council in the usual sense (i.e., Ecumenical Council of human convocation) can be described as a comprehensive representation (not merely in the sense of delegation, but as portrayal and as realization) of the Ecumenical Council of divine convocation (of the universal Church), very suitable for consultations and reaching decisions, ordering and shaping the universal Church, but not essential. (The Church is also assembled in a true and very intense manner in liturgical worship, especially at Mass.) The first Christian account of Church Councils expresses this meaning of the Council: "Aguntur praeterea per Graecias illa certis in locis concilia ex universis ecclesiis, per quae et altiora quaeque in commune tractantur, et ipsa repraesentatio totius nominis Christiani magna veneratione celebratur." (Tertullian, *De Paenitentia*, 13, 6–7; *Corpus Christianorum*, II, 1272.)

The idea of representation – whatever form it took – has always been fundamental to an understanding of the Ecumenical Council. The Ecumenical Council is or ought to be an authentic representation of the *ecclesia una* (in concord and moral unanimity of the decisions), *sancta* (the external framework, basic attitude and conciliar decisions should be determined by the gospel), *catholica* (the obligation of individual Churches to recognize the Council), *apostolica* (the apostolic spirit, the apostolic witness and – serving these – the apostolic office are decisive for the Council). Insofar as the Holy Spirit operates in the Church according to the promise of Jesus, he also operates in the special event of its representation, in the Ecumenical Council of human convocation. Therefore, the Ecumenical Council can claim a special, binding authority, even if its decrees and definitions are imperfect, fragmentary human words (cf. 1 Cor. 13:9–12). Its documents – the doctrinal decrees should be distinguished from the disciplinary ones – only possess the binding character which the Council concerned itself bestows on them. Every Council and every conciliar decree should be understood historically and interpreted in its historical context.

Hans Küng

II. History

A distinction is still usual today between assemblies which represent the universal Church by virtue of their composition (Ecumenical Council) or which gather together bishops of a number of ecclesiastical provinces (plenary council) or of a single province (provincial council) and, on the other hand, the diocesan synod. The terms σύνοδος and *concilium* were originally equivalent; there was as yet no hierarchy of different kinds of assembly. Today, 21 assemblies are reckoned as Ecumenical Councils. The authoritative list of these Ecumenical Councils only began to take firm shape in the 16th century. The inclusion of a General Council in this category is settled neither by the application of criteria derived from canon law nor by a synod's view of its own status. The diversity of forms of Church assembly has an independent history just as has the (sometimes retrospective) inclusion of a particular synod in one or other category. Every assembly represents a conscious intention to guide the Church: it follows, therefore, that the history of Councils mirrors changes in the Church's constitution. This factor clearly marks out the middle of the 11th century as undoubtedly the great turning point, for, after the Gregorian reform, the unqualified authority of conciliar decisions was established by papal jurisdiction. The authoritative formulation of the Christian faith and the standardization of Church practice are the constant concerns of conciliar action.

A. Christian Antiquity and Early Middle Ages

1. *Pre-Nicene Councils.* No direct line can be traced from the Council of Jerusalem, A.D. 50, to the Church's synodal practice. The initial stages of synodal activity appear only from the middle of the 2nd century onwards. Like the sacred ministries, the synod grew from the meeting of the local congregation for worship. From 175 onwards a growing awareness of the apostolic succession of the episcopate as well as the wider significance of local controversies led to meetings of bishops from several communities. Prior to 325, of course, participation was less on the basis of the imperial provincial system than of the relationship to the mother Church and the geographical distribution of Christian communities. Towards the end of the 2nd century, Italy and Asia Minor had already developed a lively synodal activity; the Church of Gaul did so only sporadically in the 4th century. The first to make the transition from occasional assemblies for specific purposes to regular synods was the African Church in the 3rd century; the last, the Gallo-Frankish Church in the 6th century. Controversy over the date of Easter led at the end of the 2nd century to the first exchange of opinions between groups of synods. Synodal decisions in the 3rd century were communicated to other Churches with a view to securing common policy in the question of the *lapsi* and of Novatianism or to obtaining other Churches' recognition of disciplinary decisions. This rudimentary form of Church universalism nevertheless failed to reconcile differences; African synods in 255 and 256, under Cyprian, dealing with the validity of baptism conferred by heretics, appealed to previous synodal decisions and sided with the Antiochene synod against the Roman view. The authoritarian attitude of Bishop Stephen of Rome did not silence opposition.

While the universal aspect here took the form of an exchange of views between particular groups of councils, with the West taking a leading part, a new form appeared in the Antiochene synods of 252, 264 and 268. In these synods the Western Churches played no part or only a minor one. The Novatian question and the heresy of Paul of Samosata, then occupying the attention of the Christian East, led to a meeting of all the Churches from the Black Sea to Egypt. This was a new grouping. The condemnation of Paul of Samosata was the first to be communicated to the entire οἰκουμένη; according to Alexander of Alexandria (320) it was effected by a synod and the sentence of bishops from all places. This same group of councils, embracing almost the entire Christian East, was destined (at the instigation of Constantine) to arrange at Antioch in 324 for the Council of Nicaea, and to provide the majority of the participants. It represented a step on the way to the expression of ecumenicity in the form of a single assembly of bishops. The form taken by this assembly at Antioch later proved to be the prototype of the first Ecumenical Council.

2. *The Ecumenical Councils of antiquity.* The unity of the now Christian Roman Empire following Constantine's victory over Licinius made it possible for the Emperor in the year 325 to summon, open and lead the Council of Nicaea. This was the first of the eight Ecumenical Councils of Christian antiquity, as reckoned by the present-day canon. Representation of all the Churches of both East and West was intended to give visible expression to the unity of the Church as the spiritual basis of a unified empire. In Constantine's view, the security of the empire and the unity of the Church were inseparably linked. This idea was decisive in the completion of the preliminaries. It was strengthened at Nicaea itself by the final agreement about the date of Easter, the reorganization of the Church's districts to correspond to the imperial provincial system and the transformation of regional into provincial councils. The status of the Emperor in the Council made the assembly of bishops of all the Churches into a kind of imperial council, an imperial institution, and accordingly the Council's decisions were given imperial endorsement and its disciplinary measures were supervised by the civil magistrates.

But adoption by the empire was not itself enough to constitute the ecumenicity of the Councils of antiquity. Not every Council summoned as ecumenical by the Emperor (e.g., Sardica 342/43, Rimini 359, Ephesus 449) proved to be such, for unanimity was not always attainable. Not even the high number of participants was decisive. In 431 it was thought sufficient to invite to an Ecumenical Council at Ephesus only the most important sees, along with a few of their suffragans. Even at Chalcedon – with 500 bishops participating, the largest of the ancient Councils – not all the sees were represented. Above all, the West invariably attended only in the persons of a few representatives. The First Council of Constantinople (381), not intended as ecumenical, united only the Eastern bishops, yet was subsequently recognized as ecumenical by the Council of Chalcedon (451) and by Pope Hormisdas (519). What constituted the ecumenicity of a Council, therefore, was convocation by the Emperor, the eventual agreement of the participating bishops, their awareness that in virtue of their office their assembly represented the Church, and the subsequent acceptance by the whole Church. The conviction that a Council had, as the embodiment of the whole Church and by agreement after free discussion, affirmed the Church's faith and the apostolic tradition, is what established the authority of the Council's decision; it was regarded as an expression of the divine will, unalterable and binding on all Churches.

The structure of conciliar organization did not change in the course of the first seven Ecumenical Councils. The decisions were made by the assembled bishops while the Emperor was responsible for the legal form in which these decisions were expressed. But the balance shifted. The legates of the Bishop of Rome frequently brought with them the view of a Roman synod which already anticipated the matter to be discussed; because the decision reached in Rome represented in essence the view of the Western Church, the papal legates to a General Council acquired incontestable weight. At Ephesus in 431, Cyril of Alexandria and the legates of Pope Celestine worked so closely together that the Fathers of Chalcedon could say in 451 that these two bishops had taken the leadership. Pope Leo I claimed the leadership of the Council at Chalcedon through his legates; all the discussions were dominated by his authority and he determined its decision by his appeal to the succession of Peter. Yet at Chalcedon it was the Emperor Marcian's version of the Creed which was accepted; and the Emperor himself was acclaimed by the Council as the "new Constantine, the new Paul, the new David". Pope Gregory II still admitted Leo III to be Emperor and priest, though he pointed out to this iconoclastic ruler that the title "priest" had only been given to rulers who had summoned Councils with the full accord of the priests in order that the true faith might be defined, whereas Leo had defied the decisions of the Fathers and usurped priestly functions.

The mutual relationship of the two powers was interpreted to mean that the Emperor acted in lawful succession to Constantine as "bishop appointed by God for the external affairs of the Church". The incapacity of the imperial commissioners at the Synod of Ephesus in 449, which turned that stormy assembly into a "Robber Synod", underlined the need for a strong controlling hand. But the apostolicity of the Roman See, which came increasingly to the fore in the 5th century, secured for the Pope an undisputed leadership and authority in doctrinal matters. This tended logically to the recognition of a primacy of jurisdiction. This evolution of full spiritual authority, which as yet went no further than an explicit approval of decisions taken only in the absence of the papal legates, was opposed to the conciliar position of the Byzantine ruler which was incapable of further development, and which was gradually replaced by the Eastern Church's concept of a supreme authority vested in the pentarchy of the five patriarchal sees. Hence, following the confusion over the Patriarch Photius, it remained uncertain whether the Fourth Council of Constantinople (869/70) should, as the Western Church believed, count as the eighth Ecumenical Council or whether the Council of 879/80, also held in Constantinople, should be so regarded, as the Eastern Church desired.

It was in virtue of their doctrinal decisions that the Ecumenical Councils enjoyed clearest precedence over the regional synods. The First Council of Nicaea condemned Arianism and formulated the Creed; the First Council of Constantinople dealt with Arians, semi-Arians, and Sabellians; the Council of Ephesus (431) condemned Nestorianism, that of Chalcedon Monophysitism, and both defined the hypostatic union. The Second Council of Constantinople (553) rejected the Three Chapters of the Nestorians; the next Council in Constantinople (*Trullanum* 680/81) condemned Monothelitism, and the Second Council of Nicaea (787) asserted the legality of the veneration of images. Yet a legally binding hierarchy of Councils had still not established itself. The first four Ecumenical Councils already formed a separate group when Gregory the Great compared them with the four gospels (or Isidore of Seville with the four rivers of Paradise); he accepted the Second Council of Constantinople as ecumenical on the ground that it was in accord with the "four most holy synods". This fourfold group was henceforth regarded as a standard for all other conciliar decisions because it had formulated the fundamental Trinitarian and Christological faith. It was only in the 9th century, however, that Ecumenical Councils were distinguished as such from regional synods, and not finally until the 10th century; in the opinion of theologians they served as a standard for the local synod and were themselves related to the fourfold group, within which the First Council of Nicaea enjoyed special eminence. The pre-eminence of this group is referred to as late as 1080 by Gregory VII, with of course the important qualification that the decisions of these Councils had been recognized by his predecessors.

3. *The General Synods of the German Empire*. The type of synod representa-

tive of all the Churches of a Germanic national territory derives from three roots. The Germanic peoples brought with them the idea of a national council, partly from the Christian East and partly from their traditional modes of government; Western Romance territories had only the provincial council or, where partition into provinces was still inoperative, met in regional councils like that of Arles. The Arian kings required councils to be held on the national scale, but held personally aloof. The Visigoth kings only brought their habitual influence to bear after their conversion to Catholicism, while the Merovingians did so as soon as they had consolidated their rule. The first national synods took place more or less at the same time, the Visigoth synod at Agde and the synod at Arles in 506. In 517, the Burgundian synod at Epaon united, for legal reasons, the Church provinces of Lyons and Vienne. The Frankish synod at Orleans in 511 was a definite example of this new type of synod in the Western Church.

The Visigoth synods at Toledo did not all have the character of a national council. Of the eighteen synods held there, long described as national councils, seven have to be excluded as provinical; only the third (589), the fourth (633), the fifth (636), the sixth (638), the seventh (646), the eighth (653), the twelfth (681), the thirteenth (683), the fifteenth (688), the sixteenth (693) and the seventeenth (694) were national councils. After the conversion of Recared, the indigenous Romance population was integrated into the Visigothic state on the grounds of national unity, by way of the episcopate, at the Third Council of Toledo (Toletanum). Chiefly influenced by Isidore of Seville, the Fifth Council of Toledo perfected the national type of council. In questions of faith and in national affairs the general council alone was competent. The Visigothic Church regarded itself as part of the whole Church but the synod claimed the right to examine all doctrinal decisions taken outside the kingdom. There was a second session with the nobles present to treat of national affairs. Like the Byzantine Emperor, the king had the right to summon the synod; by the reading aloud of the *tomus regius* he determined its agenda, and his approval was enough to give its decisions force of civil law. The national council was regarded as representative of Church and State; along with the king, it was the supreme authority in civil and religious matters, laying down and approving laws and supervising their execution. The ecclesiastical and civil affairs of the provinces were regulated in a similar way by the two powers in the provincial councils. When in the years 653–81 the Visigoth monarchy assumed the characteristics of the Byzantine ruler and the Archbishop of Toledo tried to secure patriarchal status, the general council forfeited part of its functions. Instead of exercising normative control over Church and secular power and deciding the legal force of the oath of allegiance which had to be sworn to the chosen king, it became an instrument in the hands of the king for enforcing his will legally.

Provincial and diocesan synods were of little importance in the Frankish kingdom; really important decisions were taken at the national councils, which were largely dependent on the king. The ruler exercised little pressure on the diocesan synods while in the case of provincial synods he claimed only supervisory rights. But from the outset the right to summon the national council and to determine its meeting-place belonged to the king; the choice of the bishops to be invited was also reserved to him; they had to attend in obedience to the royal command and were not allowed to send representatives instead. For these reasons alone, the Frankish national councils had a quasi-civil and parliamentary character. The participants were resident bishops, abbots and clergy. The last mentioned had only advisory functions; from the 9th century onwards the abbots participated in the voting with, in fact, a position equivalent to that of the bishops. Matters discussed were not so much doctrinal as legal and pastoral questions, and more rarely, cases of discipline. The authority of synodal decisions was rooted in the early medieval feeling for law; men wished neither to formulate new doctrines nor to promulgate new law but to re-discover the good old ways. Hence discussion was strongly influenced by authoritative personalities.

In the history of the evolution of national councils a distinction must be made between the Merovingian and Carolingian periods. The Merovingian kings either attended the national council in person or else sent their representatives. They took no part, however, in the formal decisions, claiming only to decide how much civil authority they would lend to Church law. The *canones* thus ratified were binding on the bishops and royal officers. The ecclesiastical council of the Merovingian period became under the Carolingians a court session which externally was like an assembly of the nobility. The king and the council co-operated in making ecclesiastical laws; only when matters affecting both the spiritual and temporal spheres were being discussed were secular leaders brought in as among the Visigoths. To this corresponded the existence of ecclesiastical, secular, and mixed capitularies. The sole lawgiver was the king; the bishops acted only by his mandate. In this phase the national council appeared as a section of a national parliament which ordinarily met in two separate groups under the king.

Again, like the national synod of the Visigoths, Charlemagne believed himself able to approve or reject the decisions of foreign councils; he refused to recognize the Council of Nicaea of 787 as ecumenical, and in 794, concious of his quasi-imperial status at the Frankfurt national council, caused the rejection of Adoptionism in formal agreement with Pope Hadrian I, and even of the veneration of images, in a mistaken interpretation of the text of the Nicene synod. The *Concilium Germanicum* of 743 made regular national councils part of the national constitution. The disintegration of the Frankish kingdom in the 9th century did not alter this regulation; but it could not prevent the atrophy of the council's structure. In the new divisions, the unity of parliament and council was maintained, but only the rulers of the Western kingdom clung to their exclusive right to give decisions force of law; this, however, slipped from their grasp with the rapid disintegration of their power.

The imperial Church of the Saxon-Salic period was in the main governed according to traditional regulations; its synodal decisions, insofar as they were not disciplinary, were therefore of little importance. At this period there was no formal difference from previous synodal law. Synod and Reichstag continued to meet at the same time, though they were not so closely interlocked; the ruler continued to attend as *Vicarius Christi* and "teacher of bishops", and he influenced decisions though legally he only determined their civil validity. It was not the weakening of the Council which determined development, but the integration of the Papacy into the imperial Church by the *Pactum Ottonianum* (962), which joined together the national council and the long standing Roman patriarchal or provincial synod, where in future the important decisions would be made.

B. Late Middle Ages and Modern Period

1. *The papal General Councils of the late Middle Ages.* The temporary union of the old Roman synods with the national council paved the way for the transformation of the former into universal

papal General Councils. Under Nicholas I and his successors papal legates constantly attended regional synods and the Pope's immense influence gradually took the form of concrete governmental action even at the conciliar level. The Reform Papacy succeeded to the Emperor at the councils and extended its power of leadership far beyond the limits of the previous period, since now convocation, agenda, and formulation of decisions could be all the more exclusively determined by the Pope; the *Dictatus Papae* of Gregory VII in 1075 declared that no Council might be called universal, even in retrospect, without the Pope's approval. The number of episcopal participants constantly increased, the themes were enlarged to include concerns of the universal Church, and the choice of meeting-place, always conditioned by political considerations, was no longer automatically confined to the city of Rome. The reform Councils of Leo IX at Pavia and Reims (1049), the Roman Synod of 1059 (papal election decree), the Roman Lenten Council of Gregory VII in 1075 (Church Reform) and the Councils of Urban II in Piacenza and Clermont in 1095 (Crusade and Peace of God) were decisive steps leading consistently to the Ecumenical Lateran Councils of 1123 (settlement of the Investiture Controversy), 1139 (schism of Anacletus II), and 1179 (peace with Barbarossa).

It may have been because of the gradual evolution of the Roman provincial synod into a General Council that an ecumenical character was only very tardily attributed to the first meetings of this type of council. The Fourth Lateran Council of the year 1215, which in accord with the wish of Innocent III was by its careful preparations linked again with the great Councils of antiquity, was, along with the Second Council of Lyons (1274) and the Council of Vienne (1311), the only medieval one to be recognized as ecumenical from the very beginning; this Council and the earlier Third Lateran Council dealt with the Catharist heresy. Even the First Council of Lyons (1245), described by Innocent IV himself as ecumenical, was only later included in the list of such Councils.

The universal authority of these Councils was no longer immanent in their structural origin but was established beforehand, in the view of the canonists, by the papal primacy; material ecumenicity lost in importance. The Popes still wished to know that their decisions had the support of the Council Fathers. At the demand of the assembled bishops and laity, Paschal II in 1112 had to withdraw the treaty of Ponto Mammolo negotiated with the Emperor Henry V; the Lateran Council of 1116 declared the Emperor excommunicated, though the Pope declined to promulgate the ban. The First Lateran Council was summoned to confirm the Concordat of Worms secured by Calixtus II. Lucius III regarded the alteration of a decree issued by one General Council as admissible only by the decision of another. At the Fourth Lateran Council, the Archbishops of Braga and Narbonne opposed any discussion of the primatial status of Toledo on the ground that they had not been called together for that purpose. Even Gregory VII exercised his power to promulgate law at a Council in the traditional way; yet he it was who, in 1075, was the first to declare that the Pope could promulgate laws for the whole Church without a Council, depose or absolve bishops and alter the Church's jurisdictional boundaries. The papal claim gradually made the Pope independent of the Council. In a short period of time Gregory VII promulgated no less than five general laws without a Council. In 1215 Innocent III had the essential work of a Council carried out by a small group of participants gathered together on his own authority. And Gregory X enforced the decisions of the Second Council of

Lyons in his own amended form. The provincial councils, whose legitimation depended on the papacy, were in the same period transformed into purely administrative courts.

Change in the composition of the Council corresponded with this development. It was already customary in the Ottonian period for bishops, abbots and lay princes from an area not restricted to the city of Rome to participate. The custom was adopted and, along with a comprehensive agenda, soon extended to all countries of Western Christendom. The First Lateran Council of 1123 was the first to display a *de facto* representation of the Latin Church. The universal diaspora attained systematic representation in 1215. Representatives of the cathedral chapters were added in 1274; at the same time, with the custom of inviting an abbot from each bishopric, the beginnings of a principle of selection emerge which logically pointed towards representation of all orders. The Council of Vienne, under strong pressure by the King of France, Philip the Fair, in the end brought together only a limited number of bishops whose invitation had first to be ratified by the King. As early as the 11th century laymen already had the right to participate in the discussion of matters affecting their interests. Their participation became increasingly a matter of course the more the Council tried to bring together all ranks. Influenced by this development, the Council of Vienne was already a Council of bishops and deputies. From 1215 onwards the College of Cardinals created a special position for itself among these groups; as a small advisory group to the Pope, it often substituted the formula *de consilio fratrum nostrorum* for the older and more comprehensive formula *sacro approbante concilio*.

2. *The Council as representative of all ranks in the Church*. From the Middle Ages onwards, the Church appeared as a predominantly juridical institution, while ecclesiology modelled itself on political society. Radical papalistic canonists regarded the papacy as concentrating the whole Church in its functions, with a fullness of authority subject to no control. The liturgical-sacramental concept of the *corpus mysticum* was obscured in favour of the sociological-realist aspect of the Church and hardened into a *regnum ecclesiasticum, principatus ecclesiasticus, apostolicus, papalis*. Analogously to Christ as the head of his own mystical body, the Pope came to be regarded as the head of the mystical body of the Church. In the Avignon Exile this theory was translated into action in the form of a centralizing absolutism. Then the election of a Pope and anti-Pope in 1378, the background to which made any settlement of the dispute impossible, at once brought to light the limits of papal efficiency and permitted a second, hitherto little observed, range of ideas to come to the fore. This new conception, though it also started from the corporative idea, instead of concentrating the community in its apex to the exclusion of the legitimate claims of its members, regarded the apex as a delegation of the authority of the total community, from time to time renewed by an election which involved the endorsement of each act of government. This range of ideas which began to appear in the 13th century in tentative and sporadic fashion, began to harden after 1378 into a theory which is given the general title of Conciliarism.

Only in the early 15th century was agreement reached that the Council was the basis for the restoration of the Church's unity, though in this context the basis of the Council needed a different structure from its late medieval one. At the Council of Pisa (1409) cardinals of both obediences declared the two Popes to be heretical by reason of their personal inflexibility in questions of Church unity, and therefore deposed. They elected a new Pope; and the Church was now split into three obediences. The Council of Pisa regarded itself as a General Council, but its decisions were rendered obsolete by the Council of Constance, 1414–18 (itself only subsequently recognized as ecumenical), when it decided to annul all three papal titles and in 1417 elected a new Pope of uncontested legality, Martin V. The Councils of Pisa and Constance were also attended by delegates from the universities and almost all the princes. Pisa was dominated by the cardinals; in Constance the Emperor appeared as *advocatus ecclesiae*, in effect for the last time. But the awareness of representing all members of the Church and so of authorizing its own decisions was first fully expressed at the Council of Constance. The division of the Council into nations, a move directed against control of the Council by the Curia, and already foreshadowed at Vienne, was now applied even to the voting procedure with all participants having equal voice.

The *Haec Sancta* decree of the Council of Constance is still disputed today because, provoked by the flight of John XXIII, it subordinated the papacy to the will of the Church represented in a Council, and, in the later decree *Frequens*, obliged it to pursue a programme of reform dictated by the Council. Regarded by many while it was still being drafted simply as a way out of a particular emergency, it was later held by Conciliarists as sanctioning their theory of the Church which regarded the Pope as, in principle, subordinate to a universal Council. This question was constantly debated throughout the entire 15th century. In pursuance of the programme of regular Reform Councils, laid down at Constance, Eugene IV in 1431 summoned a General Council to Basle, but a general weariness of Councils soon caused it to disband. Appealing to the decree *Haec Sancta*, a section of the Council continued to meet and gradually established itself as a supreme legal and administrative court of the Church; attended by hardly any bishops and increasingly by professors and procurators, this assembly set about taking over the long term direction of the Church in the style of a modern parliament. But by their election of the anti-Pope Felix V in 1439, the Basle Conciliarists discredited themselves. When Eugene was negotiating with the Greeks about Church union in 1437 at his Council at Ferrara (transferred to Florence in 1439) – this Council is reckoned today along with Basle as the seventeenth Ecumenical Council – most of the Christian powers remained neutral, partly from uncertainty, partly because of a latent Conciliarist attitude. Only when the French king abandoned his neutrality in 1449 and Felix accordingly resigned, did the Council, which had been transferred from Basle to Lausanne in 1443, break up without any decision.

The Conciliarist theory was still not completely overthrown, for in the thought of the time Council and Church reform continued to be closely connected. The papacy saw in this connection of ideas a constant threat to its supremacy, the more so because the Council was actually misused in this way as a political weapon. Louis XII of France actually arranged a *conciliabulum* directed against Julius II which met at Pisa in 1511 and renewed the decrees of the Council of Constance. The Fifth Lateran Council (1512–17), which consciously ranked itself with the papal General Councils, had no difficulty in suppressing this attempt to revive Conciliarism.

3. *The Ecumenical Councils of the modern period.* With certain modifications, the nineteenth Ecumenical Council, at Trent, maintained the structure of the papal General Councils of the Middle Ages and fixed the pattern of succeeding Councils. Called for by the German Protestants, who were still thinking in terms of the type of Council so recently rejected, the Council of

Trent by its very success led to a strengthening of papal authority. The idea of a representation of the whole Church was rejected; with its relatively small number of participants and its permanent majority of Italian bishops, the ecumenicity of the Council depended once again on the papal convocation, the support of the participants and the papal confirmation of its decisions. Invitations were sent only to bishops, generals of orders and representatives of monastic congregations, all of whom voted as individuals, and to the secular powers, whose delegates, however, had no voting right; the direction of the Council was entrusted from now on to papal legates.

The course of the Council of Trent falls into two main periods: the so-called Imperial Epoch (1545–52) was directed to dealing with the Lutheran Reformation in an enforced co-operation with an absent Emperor; at the request of the French king, the second Epoch (1562/63) was devoted rather to Calvinism. Summoned in 1536 by Paul III under pressure from Charles V, and adjourned without opening, after the naming of Mantua and Vicenza as meeting-places, it was only after the Peace of Crépy that the Council was able to meet, in Trent. In 1547–51, because of typhus, it was transferred to Bologna and was suspended until 1562 because of the rebellion of the German princes. If we take into account the immediate consequences of the Council, for example the acceptance of its decisions in various countries, a process which lasted in part into the 17th century, it begins to take on the dimensions of an epoch even in terms of duration. In significance it rivals the First Council of Nicaea.

Hoping for union with the forces of reform which had already broken away, the Council from the outset tackled simultaneously the two main tasks of affirming traditional doctrine and of bringing about a comprehensive reform of the Church. Since the majority of the Council Fathers lacked a clear concept of the Church, the Council did not succeed in producing an exhaustive and systematic presentation of doctrine but was content with particular measures of reform and doctrinal clarification, with a view to closing the gaps which had arisen in the existing system under the impact of Protestant thought. But the few German Protestants who were present for a short time (1551–52), and then the Peace of Augsburg (1555), made it clear that differences were irreconcilable. The word "Catholic" came to be used more and more, instead of "Christian", now that Christendom was divided.

In retrospect the Council of Trent proved to be the starting point for a renewed Church within a changed environment. Men came to terms both institutionally and spiritually with the division of Christendom. Against this background, the implementation of the Council's decisions was not a process of adaptation to the previous Church tradition; tradition was integrated into the *corpus* of the decrees, which now was regarded as adequate, complete and final, in contrast to the view of many of the Council Fathers. Pius IV established a Congregation for the authoritative interpretation of the decrees; Pius V published an official edition to guide their execution, and Gregory XIII entrusted the supervision of the implementation of the decrees to the nuncios. Respect for the Council's decisions, thus raised to a unique status, shaped the so-called Tridentine system, down into the 17th century; this system in turn determined the new characteristics of Church administration. The vertical hierarchical aspect was superimposed upon the character of the Church as a fellowship; it displaced the collegial function of the cardinals and of the episcopate, this being taken over by curial Congregations and by the supervisory functions of the nuncios. This was one of the main reasons why the Church had to wait more than 300 years for the next General Council.

The First Vatican Council (1869/70) was convoked to put an end to the spiritual confusion of the 19th century, which affected even Christians, by clarifying the Catholic faith and the Catholic view of the Church. The *Syllabus* had been the first step. The only constitutions to be promulgated were the *Dei Filius*, dealing with the relation between faith and knowledge, and *Pastor Aeternus*, dealing with the extent of papal jurisdiction and doctrinal infallibility. The Council ended prematurely with the occupation of the Papal States by Piedmontese troops as a result of the Franco-Prussian War; decrees in preparation on the Church and pastoral questions never reached the voting stage. The definition of the Pope's primacy and infallibility, intended as part of a comprehensive definition of the Church, thus remained a torso. The primacy question presented the greater difficulty in view of the inherent rights of the diocesan bishops. But widespread alarm was aroused by "infallibility" even before the Council opened. Yet this definition did not have the unhappy consequences which had been feared. While excluding existing Gallican ideas, it also set limits to extreme ultramontane views; in substance it did not go beyond the traditional doctrinal teaching of the 13th and 16th centuries. The declaration of the universal jurisdiction of the Pope, on the other hand, was fraught with far greater consequences in the intensification of curial centralization.

In its formal structure the Second Vatican Council (1962–65) differed neither from the First Vatican Council nor from the Council of Trent. Summoned by John XXIII, directed by a special commission, its decisions solemnly ratified by the personal presence of the Pope at the close of each session, it, too, assembled bishops, superiors-general of exempt orders, and prelates with their own special sphere of jurisdiction, all having an individual vote. But unlike the First Vatican Council which was in large measure an assembly of the bishops of the entire world, the composition of the Second Vatican Council was no longer exclusively European in character. Another difference at the last Council was the presence once more of lay people, invited as observers (not as *oratores* of the Christian powers as at Trent). And this time the non-Catholic Christian Churches and alliances accepted the invitation to send observers.

The careful preparation (a further contrast with the Council of Trent) together with the collaboration between the preparatory commission and the appropriate central authorities of the Curia gave rise to an impression that the Fathers of the Second Vatican Council were to be allowed simply to give formal approval to previously prepared schemata. But a sense of collegial responsibility and independent initiative already established itself in the episcopate in the first plenary session, and this soon led to the formation of new groupings linking up with the system of episcopal conferences already in existence for over a century in some places such as Belgium and Germany and extending it, rather than the quite insignificant provincial synods, on the horizontal plane, with its own authority and a limited power of legislation. The representation of the non-Catholic Churches ensured that the themes were always discussed in the context of the hope for future reunion. Decisive was the declaration of John XXIII that the task of the Council was not to repeat traditional theology nor to condemn errors but rather to examine abiding doctrine and to interpret it in contemporary terms. The division of a Council's tasks into dogma and discipline which had existed since the earliest Councils was thus overcome by a deeper fundamental pastoral concern, and the defensive post-Tridentine attitude was abandoned. The consequences of this approach cannot yet be foreseen.

Odilio Engels

COVENANT

1. *Before the biblical revelation.* The pagans of the ancient East know nothing of a covenant which binds the divinity to man. But they know that there are relations between man and his god. Not only is the divinity witness and guarantor of pacts between men, it also intervenes in the life of man; it hears prayers and supplications; it can heal and give long years of life; it has certain wishes, not always clear, and is irritated with those who transgress them and they fall thereby into misery. It has its favourites and its elect, often predestined long beforehand, and it grants them power and descendants. It adopts them, because men, like gods, can be its children. It sustains their life, guides them by revealing itself in dreams or otherwise, saves them from danger and preserves them from illness. The religious paganism of Babylon, Egypt, and Syria culminates in an ill-defined kinship where the god, brother, mother, or father, penetrates human life but does not really raise it to his own level. As the Gilgamesh epic tells us, "When the gods created mankind they gave it death for its portion but kept immortality for themselves." Yet the hero of the epic, the son of a goddess, was two-thirds divine. For paganism the union of God and man does not go beyond sharing in dominion over the earth and the divinized forces of nature.

2. *The patriarchs.* While the gods of pagan kings and believers disappear from history one after the other, the God of Abraham remains a living God. And from being the God of one man, he becomes the God of a clan, a nation, a Church. But in the beginning, the patriarchs' manner of honouring their God differs little from the way in which their contemporaries honour theirs. He makes them repeated promises (Gen 12:1; 13:15; 15:1, etc.) and at the same time gives them his directives (Gen 26:2; 46:3, etc.). The true God binds himself closely to Abraham, just as according to the belief of the times the *ilu* (god) Gilgamesh made himself the associate (*tappu*) of Enkidu, a man, and received offerings of association from him. In the same way, at Ugarit in the 13th century B.C. the god Ansukka receives such offerings from a certain Takhulu. But the treaties of "alliance" concluded by Abraham (Gen 21:27, 32) and Isaac (Gen 26:28), and so on down to David (2 Sam 5:3), are rather treaties between men with the divinity as witness, treaties of vassalage of which we have numerous examples outside the Bible.

3. *Moses and the covenant.* The covenant between God and his people of which Moses is to be the intermediary goes beyond the association between God and the patriarchs, though the biblical redactor again uses the word *b^erīt*, as he did when speaking of Abraham in Gen 15:18. The Mosaic covenant is preserved for us in two conflated traditions, one of which puts it at Sinai (Exod 19:1, 2, 18; 34:2), the other at Horeb (Exod 17:6; 33:6; cf. Exod 3:12b). The resulting narrative is complex. Without entering into detail, we note that the covenant of Sinai is presented above all as a sacred meal in the presence of God (Exod 24:1f., 9f.), and that it is sanctioned by a decree of the Lord (Exod 34:10–28) in which, like the kings of the time, he regulates the worship, the sacrifices, and the annual feasts at which the people comes into his presence, "to the house of Yahweh" (v. 26).

In the other narrative, the covenant is presented rather as a contrast based on the Decalogue (Exod 20:1–17). Moses repeats these "words" to the people and they pledge themselves solemnly to carry them out, after a rite performed in front of twelve *stelae* representing the twelve tribes, in which the blood of victims is poured on the altar and sprinkled on the people. It seems probable that this rite was renewed at the sanctuary of Gilgal where twelve *stelae* were set up (Jos 4:20). In both traditions it is Moses who writes down the order of God which is the condition for the blessing given to his people. The covenant with Israel is not simply an alliance based on the bonds of blood, as between kindred; it is a conditional alliance in which the people is bound to respect the demands made upon it in the moral and religious order.

4. *From Joshua to David.* Joshua is the heir of Moses and it is this Ephraimite who makes Israel master of the mountains this side of Jordan. His activity culminates at Shechem in the temple of the "God of the covenant (*b^erît*)". A solemn covenant is made in which his followers, as well as other peoples for whom fidelity will be more difficult (Jos 24:19, 25), pledge themselves to the Lord who must be served. A great stone is set up as a witness (Jos 24:26) near the oak of the sanctuary (cf. Jg 9:6). This is the stone, apparently, on which Joshua inscribed the text called the "curses of Shechem" ("stones", plural: Jos 8:32), in accordance with the prescription of Moses in Deut 27:4ff. Henceforth the promises made to the patriarchs, the "words" of Horeb-Sinai and the blessings of the twelve tribes (Deut 23, which is to be attached to Gilgal), are accompanied by curses. Shechem is the meeting-place of the so-called "amphictyony" of the tribes of Israel, where they renew their covenant every year and where each tribe provides for the upkeep of the central shrine for one month.

The life of Israel during the period of the Judges is marked by infidelities, chastisement, appeals to the Lord, and the re-grouping of the people around the warrior God enthroned on the ark of the covenant who delivers his people. The danger was even greater in the time of Samuel when the transition was made, not without opposition, from the amphictyony to the monarchy, from the judge to the anointed king. The danger came from the Philistines. The function of the monarch in the ancient East was to protect the people and give it prosperity in the name of the national god. First Saul and then David were chosen as *nāgîd*, shepherds of the people of God. But the institution of kingship was only indirectly dependent on the covenant. Later texts speak above all of the covenant made by God with David (Ps 89:4).

5. *The covenant under the monarchy.* For the theology of the covenant, the establishment of the monarchy is of central importance. David installs the ark of the covenant in his palace, and it will then be placed in the most sacred part of the national temple built by his son. A difficult verse (2 Sam 23:5) in which the "house of David" is mentioned already affirms that God "has made with me an everlasting covenant". The monarchy introduces a note of perpetuity, or rather stability, into the covenant, and the permanence is manifested by the dynastic national sanctuary which attracts the festive pilgrimages of the nation. It is true that the northern tribes, Israel, abandon the dynasty after the death of Solomon. But the ark of the covenant, along with the tables of the law, make it always possible for the faithful to find the true God, as Isaiah says (Is 8:14–18). The ark of the covenant is confided to a priesthood (2 Sam 8:17) which under Solomon is restricted to Zadok and his sons (1 Kg 2:35). It is perhaps to this priestly group that we owe the preservation of the national traditions which are found in the synthesis which critics call the Yahwist document (J) of the Pentateuch. As in 1 Sam 7, it insists more on the promises and the blessings than on the covenant,

but the demands of God are indicated in the law for the Pasch (Exod 13) and in the code of Exod 34:17–27.

6. *The prophets.* It fell to the prophets, at the decline of the monarchy, to develop all the latent virtualities of the Mosaic covenant. But a crisis began which was to lead to the revelation of a "new covenant" after the rupture of the old. They are not mutually exclusive, because the same God is author of both. Nevertheless, a profound change ensues in the structure of the Israel of God.

The crisis makes itself felt first of all in the northern kingdom, which was more exposed to the disturbing influences of the international trends of the day. The continuity of the dynasties was constantly interrupted, and as early as the Aramaean wars of the 9th century the prophets appear, like Elijah and Elisha, as the religious guides of the people, taking the place of an incompetent monarchy. They appeal to the traditions of the past. Elijah makes a pilgrimage to Horeb, and a new synthesis of the national traditions is probably made, inspired by the prophetic outlook – the Elohist document (E) of pentateuchal criticism. It goes back beyond the monarchy and the conquest to base itself on the Mosaic tradition of which the levitical clergy is the depositary, especially the clergy of Dan, who are the descendants of Moses, and perhaps the clergy of Bethel. But the latter, descendants of Aaron through Phinehas (Jg 20:26–28), were more contaminated.

The covenant is an unequal contract, conceived on the lines of a treaty of vassalage, where the people binds itself by oath to carry out the stipulations of Yahweh its God. This solemn undertaking was preceded by a history in which God, the sovereign protector, the "shield of Abraham" (Gen 15:1), protected the patriarchs and their descendants against all the powers with whom the Israelites were tempted to enter into alliances. But the Yahweh of Horeb alone is God, and it is he who gives the people its good things (Hos 2), and not the Baals to whom Israel "prostitutes" itself like a wife unfaithful to her husband. Israel has been unfaithful from the beginning (Hos 11) but the covenant allows of repentance and penance (Exod 33:5–6), just as Jacob's family purified itself before going to Bethel, by "putting away the foreign gods" (Gen 35:2–5).

The ancient curses of Shechem are transformed into a punishment, which Yahweh finds hard to inflict, as is revealed in the heart-rending cries of Hosea and Isaiah (ch. 1). He "roars from Zion" (Amos 1:2), irritated by its injustices and transgressions. As the true king of Israel, the God of Micah upbraids the princes of the house of Jacob who ought to have "known justice" but prove to be enemies of goodness and lovers of evil (Mic 3:1). Yahweh is so much the Lord of Israel that according to Ezekiel he went so far as to give statutes that were not good and ordinances by which they could not have life (20:25), having them kill their first-born and allowing wicked foreign customs to come in. Instead of letting the people perish by its sins, God is so faithful to the covenant that he takes responsibility for their misery and makes of it a chastisement to lead the people to repentance and penance.

But the evil is so profound, Jerusalem is a city so deeply "rusted", that the rust can no longer be removed (Ezek 24:6), and the prophets say clearly that the covenant has been broken off. Amos had already seen Yahweh standing upon the altar and destroying the sanctuary (Amos 9:1). Instead of this cultic image, Hosea speaks of the divorce between Yahweh and Israel. The Israelites can accuse their mother, "for she is not my wife and I am not her husband", says Yahweh (Hos 2:2 [4]). Micah sees the mountain of the temple transformed into a wooded height (Mic 3:12). Jeremiah is the most explicit. Taking up once more the image of divorce used in Hosea, he recalls the law of Deut 24:1–4 to affirm that a new marriage should be impossible (Jer 3:1): the nation has changed gods (Jer 2:11). "The house of Israel and the house of Judah have broken my covenant which I made with their fathers. (Jer 11:10.)

At the beginning of his ministry Jeremiah still thinks that there is room for repentance and return to God (Jer 3:6–18; 18:8), but later it seems to him more and more impossible (Jer 13:33), as God withdraws from him the right to intercede (Jer 14:11). A *new covenant* will be needed (Jer 31:31–34). Ezekiel takes the same attitude (Ezek 16: 59–63). The covenant has been broken (v. 59), but God will remember it (*zaqar*, very important for the theology of the "memorial" of the covenant) and "raise up" (*heqim*) an eternal covenant (v. 60) in which Sodom and Samaria will share, "but not on account of the covenant with you" (v. 62).

Finally, for Deutero-Isaiah as for Jeremiah (Jer 30:17), Israel is a forsaken wife (Is 54:1, 6), but God redeems her; his love is unshakeable and from now on he has "a covenant of peace (*shālōm*, fullness)" for his bride which is likewise unshakeable (Is 54:10). This eternal covenant is founded on God's "steadfast love for David" (Is 54:3) in which the nations will share (v. 4), the only condition being that men turn towards Yahweh the God of Israel (v. 7) and abandon their evil ways.

7. *Towards the new covenant.* The prophets have thus orientated the theology of the covenant towards new horizons and a new foundation. It is less a pact than a gracious act of God. It is based rather on God's promise than on Israel's dedication. Though it maintains the just demands laid down in the Decalogue of Moses, it will be founded on the favour accorded to David. For Ezekiel the good shepherd will be no ordinary king but a new David "raised up" by God, to "make a covenant of peace" (Ezek 34:23–25).

Deuteronomy, which is so close to Jeremiah, had already voiced this new way of thinking. The covenant undoubtedly remains a pact in the nature of a treaty of alliance, with stipulations, undertakings, blessings, and curses. But above all it is a free act of God (Deut 7:7ff.), founded on the promises made to the patriarchs. Its implementation supposes love above all (Deut 6:4ff.), the memory of God's great deeds (Deut 6:12), and fidelity. The king is a brother who draws inspiration continually from the law (17:14–20), and Moses is rather a prophet than a law-giver (18:15). As for Jeremiah, fidelity is essentially a personal question for each man before God (24:16), rather than a collective loyalty to the covenant on the part of the nation. Hence circumcision of the heart is demanded rather than that of the flesh (Deut 10:16). But the object of this covenant is a life with God among brothers, in which strangers too will share, even the Egyptians (23:9).

The "priestly" texts of the Pentateuch deepen and enlarge this notion of the covenant under the influence of Ezekiel. The texts no longer speak of "concluding" a covenant, but of "giving" or "establishing" it, and "covenants" appear in the plural (Gen 6:18; 9:11; 17:7, 19; Exod 6:4). St. Paul reminds his readers that the OT contained covenants (Rom 9:4). Each of them comprises a gift, a demand, and a sign. God "establishes" the covenant of Noah for all humanity. God continues to sustain life in spite of cosmic catastrophes, but only for those who do not shed blood; and the sign is a cosmic one: the rainbow in stormy weather. The second covenant is the covenant with Abraham, an eternal covenant under which God grants progeny. It calls for integrity (*tāmīm*) of conduct before God, and its sign is bodily circumcision (Gen 17:1ff.). The third covenant is that of Moses on Sinai (Exod 19:5 – this is however disputed, cf. Lev 26:45), given in memory of the covenant with the patriarchs (Exod 6:4ff.). It makes of Israel a kingdom of priests and a holy nation by reason of the calling of Aaron and the institution of the priesthood and the sanctuary. By the covenant of Noah the covenant was broadened to take in all nations; by that of Aaron, the covenant was given a greater depth of holiness and consecration: it is the covenant of salt (Num 18:19) and therefore incorruptible. Since it is a gift and a unilateral action on the part of God, though it still requires a personal response from the individual who lives under it, it could well be translated by διαθήκη in the Alexandrine version.

This divine διαθήκη, which is a testamentary disposition of one's goods in favour of an heir, or the deposition of the written document in a shrine, appears in the book of Daniel as the holy covenant which many are to forsake under persecution (Dan 11; cf. 9:4). In Ecclus the word is used to translate not only *b^e^rît* but *ḥoq* (law, decree), a word which covers the whole will of God for man, especially the date of his death (Ecclus 14:12, 17; 6:22), though it still means also the eternal covenant, the law of life (17:11, 12), the divine commandments (41:19; 46:20; 45:5). Aaron is the beneficiary of the eternal covenant (45:15) of peace (v. 17), while David receives a royal covenant (*ḥoq mamleket*, 47:11) from God. Ecclus also speaks of covenants in the plural, but there is only one "book of the covenant", the law promulgated by Moses (Ecclus 24:23). This law is identified with Wisdom, which shared in the creative action of the Most High and took root in the people where the divine glory dwells (Ecclus 24:11). It is a liturgical Wisdom, which officiates in the holy tabernacle (v. 10) and is the giver of food and life (v. 19), being the earthly paradise restored which is watered by the life-giving stream of Ezek 47, which also flowed from the temple.

8. *The covenant of the New Testament.* The NT speaks comparatively rarely of διαθήκη, 35 times in all, of which 17 are in the Letter to the Hebrews. In the writings of Qumran the term is very frequent, and the "new testament" is mentioned not only in the *Damascus Document* but almost certainly in the commentary (*pesher*) on Habakkuk. *The Rule of the Congregation* (*1 QSa*) of the "men of the covenant" includes regulations for meals, to which only those who have undergone two years of probation are admitted (*Rule of the Community* [*1 QS*], 6, 20–21) and from which one can be excluded for certain faults.

The word covenant does not appear at all in the Johannine literature, except in one quotation from the OT in the Apocalypse. It is the Letter to the Hebrews, with its interest in liturgy, which speaks of it most frequently. Jesus of Nazareth is the mediator of the new covenant (Heb 9:15) and he is the surety (ἔγγυος 7:22) of a covenant better than the former one made with the fathers. "By the blood of the eternal covenant" the Lord Jesus has become the great shepherd of the sheep (13:20). By his death which has redeemed the transgressions of the first covenant, he has given the promised eternal inheritance to those who are called (9:15–16): the allusion to the death of the testator in v. 17 is unmistakable. By his own blood, not by the blood of goats, he enters with our humanity into the eternal sanctuary not made with hands (9:11f.) and purifies our conscience from dead works so that we may worship the living God. This covenant had been promised by God, and the letter quotes Jer 31:31 (8:8), while at the same time it recalls the blood of the covenant of Sinai (9:20). To sanctify the people by his own blood, Jesus suffered "outside the gate" (13:12), and the faithful must go forth from the camp (v. 13) to offer the sacrifice of praise (v. 15), because they have an altar (θυσιαστήριον) "from which those who serve the tent have no right to eat" (v. 10).

The Pauline letters likewise contrast the two testaments or covenants (Gal 4:24). The true διαθήκη is the firm arrangement in which God's promises were embodied (Eph 2:12) and which the gift of the law could not annul (Gal 3:15, 17). It is nonetheless a "new covenant" of which Paul and the apostles are the ministers (2 Cor 3:6). Christ has lifted the veil which hid the face of Moses and which prevented the "old covenant's" being understood (2 Cor 3:14). This was only a covenant of circumcision (Acts 7:8).

Having read the Letter to the Hebrews we are not surprised to find that the great instrument of the establishment of the new covenant was the Lord's Supper: "This cup is the new covenant in my blood. Do this as my memorial." (1 Cor 11:25) This translation, proposed by J. Jeremias, is the one which is most in keeping with the ritual texts of the OT which we have seen above. The Lucan narrative of the Last Supper, like that of Paul, likewise mentions the "memorial" (Lk 22:19) and the "new covenant". Matthew (26:28) and Mark (24:24) also speak of the "blood of the covenant" in a formula which like that of Paul and Luke recalls the sacrifice of Exod 24:8, but what is said to be "new" is the wine, the fruit of the vine, drunk by Christ with the apostles in the kingdom of God which has been established. As in John (Jn 6:54f.), the "eucharistic" meal (Mk 12:22 and par.) is the meal where Christ "raises up" his followers to eternal life in the last days or the last times (Heb 1:2), once the kingdom has been established by his death in the shedding of his blood, and by his resurrection. The sign of Daniel is given from this moment on (ἀπ' ἄρτι, Mt 26:64; ἀπὸ τοῦ νῦν, Lk 22:70), and the transition from the old to the new covenant has taken place before "this generation" (Mk 13:30; Mt 24:34; Lk 21:32) has passed away.

Henri Cazelles

CREATION

I. Theology

A. Meaning of the Term

The term "creation" expresses the way in which the world and everything pertaining to the world have their origin, ground and final goal in God. It can mean, actively, the creative action of God, and passively, the totality of the world.

The concept was expressed in various languages by terms taken from various realms. The Greek Bible preferred κτίζειν which originally meant "to make habitable" and then "to found" (a colony, a city). The corresponding Latin word is *condere*, but the Latin Church preferred *creare*, the strict meaning of which was "to beget". This is the word which was taken over by the Romance languages and then in English, while the Germanic languages used *Schöpfung*, probably akin to the English "shape". None of these words was derived from a pre-Christian religious usage. Hebrew, however, had a word which was reserved for the divine action. Along with more general terms for making or forming, the word בָּרָא (Ezek, etc.) was used from prophetic times on, to designate God's action on the world, on Israel and in the establishment of eschatological salvation. This consistent usage is characteristic of the biblical doctrine of creation.

B. The Old Testament

1. The Semitic peoples honoured the gods of nature, and myths embodying natural processes were the basis of their speaking of the gods. "The loneliness of Israel in the company of the religions of the world" stems from the fact that it

learned to know God not from nature but from history. Israel first knew God as the saviour of the nation; belief in creation grew out of the experience of God's saving deeds.

Belief in creation did not form part of the original kernel of the religion of Israel. The older confession of faith includes the saving actions of God in history but not his creating the world (Deut 26:5–10). Some few ancient texts may reflect belief in creation but it only becomes an explicit theme in the late monarchical period. Belief in creation was an extension of faith in Yahweh as the God of the covenant, of history and of the promises.

The process was probably as follows. The God of Israel gradually revealed himself as Lord of all mankind, and hence the story of the patriarchs was prefaced by the genealogies and the story of paradise, which gave a link between Abraham and all men. Then Yahweh also appeared as Lord of the forces of nature, using them as weapons in the liberation of Israel.

Faith in the God of the covenant begins to take in the whole world. This is the mental climate in which the affirmations and hymns about creation arose (cf. especially Deutero-Is, Jer, Ps). The doctrine of creation serves to confirm God's loyalty to his covenant(Jer 31:35–37) or to illustrate God's sovereign power in the history of salvation (Jer 27:5). God throws all the mighty forces of the world into his work of salvation. Hence creation and deliverance are hymned and praised in one breath as the marvellous works of God (Is 42:5f.; 45:24–28; Ps 74:13–17; 89:10 to 15, etc.). Creation, like the deliverance from Egypt, testifies to the power, the goodness and the fidelity of God.

2. Belief in creation was then given its classical form in the first chapter of Genesis (1:1–2:4a), which serves as an all-embracing prologue to the history of salvation. Creation is not regarded as a timeless revelation which takes place in the orderly course of nature, but a historical and salvific work of God which launches history. It is now generally recognized that Gen 1 does not intend to provide a description of the coming to be of the world. Once this is understood, the doctrine of the passage may be more clearly seen:

a) *The whole world owes its being entirely to the free, sovereign action of God.* God speaks, and creates by his word. This theme, which occurs here and there in other religions, is strongly stressed in Gen 1, and recurs constantly throughout Scripture. The world, like Israel, subsists by virtue of God's word in his covenant. It is not a divine emanation, the natural result of a necessary process of theogony. It exists in so far as God addresses it.

b) *The world is "good"*. The ancient cosmogonies have, as a rule, a markedly dualistic character. Our world, with its mingling of good and evil, comes from an encounter, a conflict, between a good principle of order and light, and an independent principle of disorder and evil. Even Gen 1 uses images taken from such notions, but de-mythized. All things implicitly obey the effortless command of God; they simply correspond to the divine will.

And since from the start Israel knows God as its loving Lord, it is fundamentally impossible for its faith to see the world as a hostile power. Hence the OT view of the world has a tranquillity, a warmth and clarity which we seek in vain outside the Bible. But faith in creation is no ground for naive optimism. Like the covenant, the creative word can become judgment.

c) *The world exists for the sake of man.* Man is the real object of God's love, as the making of the covenant showed at once. He is the true partner in the covenant of creation, the viceregent of God and his image. In obedience to God he is to subject the world to himself. Man must not bow to the mysterious forces of nature. He must, on the contrary, make them serve him. With this, the world loses fundamentally all divine status, though it can be recognized as a sign and a word given to man by God.

Creation itself is regarded as a sort of covenant given to man by God. The very existence of the world is to some degree a salvific work, since it is the theatre of the power and fidelity of God, who entered upon a covenant with Israel and the human race (e.g., Jer 33:20–25; Ps 89; 119:89–91; cf. 1 Pet 4:19).

Efforts have constantly been made to discover *creatio ex nihilo* (as it is formulated in 2 Macc 7:28) in Gen 1. The question is an anachronism, because it supposes that creation is envisaged from the *terminus a quo*, whereas the ancient creation texts are concerned only with the *terminus ad quem*. But the world is explained as containing nothing that does not depend on God's action; all goes back to him.

3. There is a further analogy between creation and covenant inasmuch as creation is also considered as a force dominating history. In the Bible the world is not a stable cosmic order which was set up by creation once and for all. It is "much less a being than a happening". Creation is, therefore, a promise ordained to a fulfilment. It is entirely caught up in the relationship between God and man, of which eventful history salvation is the goal. Hence the one word ברא can indicate the original creation, God's actions in history and his final salvific intervention. In Deutero-Is above all creation and redemption appear almost as one and the same act of God's dramatic initiative. God's creative action is not simply a thing of the past, it takes place here and now and is yet to come.

Though Gen 1 makes creation the beginning of all things, belief in creation is not reduced to a mere protology. Creation is an act of the present instant, and remains true to itself till the hour of eschatological salvation. The association of creation, conception and resurrection in 2 Macc 7:22–29 is characteristic (cf. Rom 4:17). Creation is not a sort of neutral setting for the drama of salvation. It is part of the *magnalia dei* and a salvific act, since it founds and sustains the whole history of salvation.

This is a truth of which primitive Christianity and the ancient liturgy were still aware. Thanksgiving for creation was given a fixed place in the solemn prayers of the Eucharist.

4. *Wisdom*. Along with this history-centred view which was inspired by the very kernel of faith in Yahweh, a more cosmological attitude also developed, probably under the influence of Egyptian and Hellenistic "wisdom". The world becomes a spectacle (Job 36:25f.), and the object of human research (Wis 7:17–20). It evokes astonishment and humility (e.g., Job 28:38–39) and hymns of praise (Ps 8; 19; 24; 33; 93; 96; 104; 148; Ecclus 42; Dan 3:52ff.; Pss 24 and 104 may be pre-exilic). Here creation holds the centre of the stage and becomes the absolute foundation of faith. It almost becomes proof of the existence of God (Wis 13:1–9).

Here creation and salvation are not linked by means of history but through wisdom. Wisdom, which is considered almost as a subsistent entity (Prov 8:22–31; Ecclus 1:1–10; 24:1–34; Wis 7:22–8:1; 9:9–18) is the first work of creation, the instrument which God used to make heaven and earth. In the book of Wisdom, it is described as the master craftsman (Wis 7:21; 8:6). As the divine plan for the world, it is "poured out" upon creation (Ecclus 1:9) so that the world is irradiated by a glory which points back to God. To know and follow this wisdom is salvation, since it is God's will for man and is identified with the law (Ecclus 24:1–34; Bar 4:1). To follow after wisdom is to partake of life, since God's creative will is directed to life (Wis 1:13f.; 2:23).

This opens up the way for an important development, because creation is inscribed throughout the whole realm of profane nature. But it is not without its dangers. As long as the cosmological contemplation still concentrated its faith on the living and loving God of the Fathers, it constituted an enrichment. But where faith in creation loses sight of the history of salvation, the image of the creator can pale into that of a neutral, almost indeterminate being.

C. The New Testament

1. The *synoptic preaching* provides very few allusions to the doctrine of creation. The present salvation is in the foreground, and creation is only evoked as a background on a few occasions (Lk 11:50; Mk 13:19; Mt 25:34; apropos of marriage, Mt 19:4–8; Mk 10:6–9).

But in the *prayer* of the community creation is chanted as one of the *magnalia Dei* (Acts 4:24; cf. Rev 4:11; 10:6; 14:7). Liturgical influence is also suggested by the formula which speaks of all things coming from God and moving towards him (1 Cor 8:6; cf. Rom 11:36; Eph 4:6; Heb 2:10), though here the orientation to God is predicated particularly of the community, which is the new creation.

In the preaching addressed to pagans, however, creation has its place (Acts 14:15–17; 17:24–28. It should be noted, however, how strongly the immediate significance of creation is stressed, as a force pervading history.

2. The New Testament is very conscious of the *power of evil*. In Paul and John the word cosmos can even indicate a reality hostile to God. It is true, of course, that this dualism is a moral one, and not strictly ontological. But it runs counter to the permanent and fundamental optimism of faith in creation, and greatly weakens the existential import of this faith as the inspiration of a joyous Yes to the world. The fulfilment of creation in Christ displays most vividly the inadequacy and brittleness of the old creation.

3. The *Christocentric character of creation* can only be discussed here insofar as it forms a new element in the doctrine of creation. It is at once apparent when Christ is designated as the new Adam, when the existence of the faithful and the Church is considered as a new creation, and when baptism is seen as a rebirth in which the events of the Exodus and of creation are renewed. Christ is the man who is God's image (2 Cor 4:4; Col 1:15), in whom the ancient word of creation has been fully verified. There is an allusion to the role of Christ in creation when the words "through Jesus Christ" are added to the "from God" of 1 Cor 8:6. But Christ was first recognized as Lord of salvation, and only then as Lord of creation; the development is the same as in the OT.

Col 1:15–17, Heb 1:2ff., 10–12, and Jn 1:1–18 then proceed in their different ways to identify creative wisdom and the word of the creator with the man Jesus Christ. These texts were the foundation of the doctrine of the pre-existence and the two natures of Christ. It should be noted, however, that they are also affirmations about the historical figure of the man Jesus Christ. The tendency to eliminate history, which is found in the description of the creative role of Wisdom, is now radically avoided. In the man Jesus Christ, God's creative word is fully uttered, and his plan of creation definitively accomplished in his saving acts. Jesus is truly the creature willed by God in creation.

Here the ultimate truth of the ancient theological proposition, that man is the goal of creation, is displayed to the full. Here it can also be seen that creation is obedience, partnership in a covenant. This mystery also affirms the unthinkable proximity of the creature to the creator: the Son who is in the bosom of the Father is a man. Creation is orientated to this intimacy.

Creation is history, because it makes man and his whole world responsible to the creative will of God and thus involves all creation in the drama of refusal and forgiveness (Rom 8:19–21). All things are from God, and look for his Lordship, when he will be all in all (1 Cor 15:28).

D. History of the Dogma

The dogma of creation had no very chequered history. Faith in creation had its place in the liturgy. The oldest creeds confess the *Pater omnipotens*, with *omnipotens* designating not abstract omnipotence but God's sovereign rule, and *Pater* probably expressing his role as first cause and creator.

From the 4th century on, this confession is enlarged by the words *factorem caeli et terrae* etc. But *creatio ex nihilo* was emphasized as early as the middle of the 2nd century, as in the confession of faith in Hermas (*Mand.*, 1, 1; *Vis.*, 1:6), which is often cited. It was done polemically against Gnostic dualism, and in apologetics to counter the philosophical view that matter was eternal. In the anti-Arian struggle, creation from nothing was often contrasted with the generation of the Son by the Father in unity of being.

The opposition to dualism and to the eternal matter of Greek philosophy soon made cosmology and protology the chief interests in the Church's doctrine of creation, an attitude which has persisted down to recent times. The view of Irenaeus, centred on the history of salvation, found little echo. The documents of the Church are directed against the dualism or the Priscillianists (*DS* 191, 199, 285f.) or of the Catharists (*ibid.*, 800) or against the pantheistic tendencies of 19th-century idealism (*ibid.*, 3001f.; 3021–5). This polemic against philosophical error gave rise to a one-sided philosophical view on the part of the Church.

The reflections of Augustine, however, on the nature of time were important. They maintained on principle the unity of creation and conservation and thus avoided a purely protological concept. The contribution of Scholasticism was a strong emphasis on causality, which was corrected and enriched among the great Scholastics by the notion of participation. But the influence of such principles on current preaching remained restricted, so that to a great extent a purely protological approach prevailed, with emphasis on efficient causality.

This was a very naive type of faith in creation and proved unequal to the challenge of science. For theology, creation as the action of God became further and further removed from the chain of natural causes, and was restricted to the beginning of the world which was being placed further and further back, or restricted to a few exceptional cases in the history of evolution. A reaction set in only in recent years (Teilhard de Chardin).

E. Systematic View

Since creation implies a comprehensive action of God on the world and a total relationship of the world to God, it transcends all categories of thought. It is easier to say what it is not than what it is. It is easy to criticize standard definitions, but to indicate lines of thought which give a positive approach to its meaning is a task which is never mastered fully. Let us therefore first examine what it is not.

1. Creation is not an answer to the question of the origin of the world and of evolution, as posed by science. Science talks of causes in intra-mundane categories, and to reduce creation to such categories would be to misinterpret it and ignore its character as a divine act. Creation can never be met or grasped in terms of experience.

2. The doctrine of creation is not a proof of the existence of God nor a theodicy. It is based on a knowledge of the living God which is communicated only by the history of salvation. It is true that one can argue from the contingence of the world to its origin from

absolute being, but it is questionable whether this origin can be recognized as creation (Vatican I, *DS* 3026). Theodicy is actually made more difficult by the doctrine of creation, since it makes the question of evil still more acute.

3. Certain metaphysical systems, like pantheism, emanationism and dualism cannot be reconciled with the doctrine of creation. But this does not make it the equivalent of a metaphysics. If it were, it would lose its link with faith in the redemption and thereby its essential character. The last word of creation is uttered in the God-man; but that the creator was so interested and involved in his creation will probably never be deduced by metaphysics.

We are now in a position to turn to the positive aspects.

1. The following general presuppositions are to be made:

Personal categories are the most suitable to express creation. It is the action of the personal God and the person is the most characteristic of his creations, so that "the full dimensions of the creature can only be seen in the personal creature". Hence the concept of authorship or responsibility is better than that of causality (cf. Hengstenberg).

Creation embraces the whole reality of the world; not just its beginning but its whole existence, including its consummation; and not just its static being, but its dynamism and activity.

2. In the standard description, the formula *productio rei* is defective, because it concentrates attention exclusively on the beginning and is impersonal in character. *Ex nihilo* is easily misunderstood, as if a "nothingness" preceded it. *Secundum totam substantiam* could suggest that only the static substance, but not the activity and perfectioning, was the result of creation.

3. Creation means that everything without exception is God's action and God's beneficent action towards man.

a) God is the author of all. He is this as the personal Saviour-God who has revealed himself as pure love and initiative. This means that creation is a spontaneous act which can have no other source or cause but the initiative of love. The definition of Vatican I concerning God's freedom means positively (*DS* 3002, 3025) that all reality originates in the pure initiative of God's love. This love does not presuppose its object, but brings about its lovableness.

b) The object of creation is everything, without exception, in all its dimensions.

"Without exception": this is the positive meaning of *ex nihilo*. The whole of reality comes from God's action and is comprised by it.

"In all dimensions": in the unity of beginning, development and fulfilment, including not only the material creation but man, and man not only as nature and a datum imposed on man himself, but as person and freedom, who realizes himself and freely affirms, fetches in and perfects himself and his world around him. In contrast to frequently held opinions, it is probably necessary to emphasize that man is created precisely in his free act.

The creative act of God does not eliminate the action proper to the creature, it brings it about. "God empowers the creature to found itself on itself". Though the doctrine of creation was always aware of this (cf. the *concursus*), it was always exposed to the danger of slipping into a sort of deism, according to which God created the power to act, while the activity itself stemmed only from the creature. Such a misunderstanding becomes all the more pernicious when science has shown the world as a closed system of natural energy which constructs itself in a natural process. For it would then appear that the creative activity of God was being excluded more and more by the intrinsic activity of the world, and that the creature was in competition with the creator (cf. Vatican II, *Gaudium et Spes*, art. 34).

The resistance of the faithful to the theory of evolution stems to a great extent from this misunderstanding of creation.

It must be clearly understood that God creates a "world coming into being" (Schoonenberg), which is bringing itself about and is precisely a creature by doing so. This means, however, that the creative act of God is not to be considered as an extrinsic condition of or a supplement to the intrinsic activity of the creature, but as its inmost core. Even in my activity God is more intimate to me than my inmost self. The creator is not "a cause within the category of causes besides others in the world but the living and transcendent ground of the world's own movement" (K. Rahner, "Bemerkungen zum Begriff der Offenbarung", *Interpretation der Welt* [1965], p. 715).

c) Creation is God's beneficent action towards man. "To believe in creation is to see Someone behind all things . . . to see the world as a gift".

The "motive" of God's creative act is described by Vatican I in the words, "ad manifestandam perfectionem suam per bona, quae creaturis impertitur" (*DS* 3002), of which the official explanation was, "ut bonitatem suam creaturis impertiret (*Collectio Lacensis*, VII, pp. 85f., 110). Creation is pure generosity, the act of loving and giving.

Hence the goal of creation is man, as person and as community. Only man can receive love as love. Everything exists in relation to man, who in the course of history gathers the cosmos to himself, takes in himself gradually in his freedom and so responds to the creative word with all the strength of his own being and of the world.

The fullness of human existence is identical with the glory of God. The more man realizes himself, and the world in himself, the brighter the glory of the creator radiates from him. And insofar as man, as such a perfected freedom, himself thanks God, he gives glory to God. "Gloria Dei vivens homo; vita autem hominis visio Dei." (Irenaeus, *Adv. Haer.*, IV, 20, 7; *PG*, VII, col. 1037.) Thus Jesus the Lord is the goal of all creation, the final Yes of God to his work and the full Yes of man to God (cf. 2 Cor 1:20).

F. Conclusion

Creation is to be considered as the free act of God whereby he gives the world and man entirely to man, as a gift of his goodness and as a task to be carried on to a fulfilment in which man responds to this word of his creator with the fullness of his own being and of his world. Creation means that man is revealed as one addressed by God in such a way that the whole of reality comes to him as a word of God, summoning and inviting him to an equally total response.

Pieter Smulders

II. Protology

1. *The concept.* Protology is a term formed on the analogy of eschatology to designate the dogmatic doctrine on the creation of the world and man, paradise and the fall, hence the doctrine of the origins. In the ordinary textbooks of dogmatic theology the subject is generally treated under "De Deo Creante", "De Deo Elevante", "De Peccato Originali". These seemingly disparate themes form a real unity. For protology describes in terms of dogma one half of the permanent proprieties and existentials of each individual human being, that is, the permanent and unavoidable pre-conditions, established by God or by man himself (in his origins), for the exercise of man's free decision for or against God. The other "half" of his situations is described in the dogmatic treatise on soteriology. The two together make up theological anthropology, since the total "essence" of man is only really disclosed in the history of his fall and salvation which

takes it beyond an implicit preliminary self-understanding. There is a more than material connection between the themes of protology, because the beginning is a permanent determination of man, and hence like eschatology can only be grasped in a retrospective aetiology in the light of each changing historical situation. And hence the progress of the history of salvation is the progress of protology in the progressive development of its starting-point.

Since it is only in Jesus Christ and his Pneuma that man knows explicitly and through official revelation that he can be, and has been throughout his history, the subject of an absolute self-communication of God (which can be surpassed only by the beatific vision), it is only since Jesus Christ that a full protology is possible and hence also intelligible in its formal nature. This also explains, for instance, why a doctrine of the "first things" including the supernatural elevation of man and original sin was only possible in the NT. The general doctrine of creation (on the beginning of the world) can undoubtedly be taken as an element of protology, because it is not ultimately an account of what once happened without reference to man, but the doctrine of the immediate, but nonetheless ancient creatureliness of the world as the environment of man – a world which itself only attains its true being in the Spirit.

2. *Present-day problems.* a) There is need of a clearer demonstration of the *a priori* and *de facto* inner unity of protology. This would affect the treatment of the actual components and complete its themes, which are not fully envisaged in the dogmatic treatises which now correspond to protology. Once we ask what are the universal and permanent proprieties of man which are theologically accessible and existentially relevant, we are provided with a set of themes which are only partially treated in the manuals of scholastic theology. The matter of protology would then include, for instance, the historicity of man, the unity of mankind and its history (which is more than mere biological monogenism) and the sexual nature of man (which should not be left to moral theology). Even the theology of Gen 1–11 contains more matter than is treated explicitly in the theology of the schools.

b) Formal or transcendental theological protology, which presupposes such matters as the doctrine of creation and the original state of man, needs to be more explicitly developed. The general horizon within which the questions of material protology are put must be interrogated as to its constitution and its proper history. In such formal protology light would be thrown on the correspondence between protology and eschatology as well as their real difference, which is not simply obvious (as is supposed in theories of "return to paradise", and the like).

c) The permanent, justifiable, dialectical but not contradictory opposition to a profane protology "evolving from below" must be demonstrated. Such protology, including natural history, evolution and hominization, age of the world and of mankind, characteristics of primitive man, etc., is not and cannot be protology strictly speaking. It would have to be shown that the protology sketched in the light of Christian eschatology, as already given in Jesus Christ, is concerned with a beginning which is "withdrawn" from our grasp, and which therefore cannot on principle be attained in secular sciences of the origin of the world and man, while still not contradicting them. The adoption of the doctrine of creation into dogmatic anthropology does not exclude but rather provides for a correct understanding of an evolutionist cosmology and some understanding at least of man as situated within such an evolution of the world, of which the goal is man.

Adolf Darlap

originality of the beginning man can deny it (cf. Job 3) or use its hiddenness to ignore or misinterpret it. Or again, he can accept it as the divine disposition more and more fully as it is revealed to him in the course of his history and thereby attain the precise fulfilment assigned to him. Hence the beginning matters for the end, as the end for the beginning.

c) *The beginning as origin of the maturely valid.* The authentic and primordially posited beginning gives rise to a truly temporal sequence, but by virtue of its being itself directly posited by God is not a moment of a time really antecedent to it. Hence the goal of the movement which it launches is not the end as termination but as fulfilment of this temporal sequence, where the harvest of the time run is preserved as valid and definitive. Hence what corresponds to the authentic (intrinsic) givenness of the beginning is not the end as a terminal stage within continuing time, but the fulfilment which absorbs a time which may be thought of as continuing. The beginning is truly a potentiality. Of itself it enters the time in which alone its fulfilment can be brought to maturity. It thus exposes itself to the incalculable sway of God over these open possibilities in time, and the end, though the safeguarding, fulfilment and revelation of the beginning is not just the implementation of the law of the beginning by which man was launched. The beginning rather lives by virtue of the movement towards the fulfilment whose achievement is accomplished by God. For he alone is both beginning and end at once, and hence as transcendent unity both separates and combines beginning and end in the finite, and communicates himself in grace to the finite being as this transcendent unity of beginning and end.

4. The end is the whither of the beginning as its goal. And then it is the fully-formed existence of that which was posited with the beginning as that which had to mature in order to be; or it is the limit which defines the totality of the existence. This end may be realized in various ways which are analogous to one another, according to various potentialities in question.

a) Whether the material world has an authentic end which may be discerned by inspection of it, that is, whether it is orientated to a permanent goal of perfection which will absorb its temporality on a higher plane beyond which any essentially new phase is inconceivable, or whether it merely continues to go through new phases of what is fundamentally the same thing, is a question which we need not try to decide. So too it remains an open question, philosophically and theologically, whether simple inspection of the world can show that it had a beginning. (It is unthinkable that the material world should tend to nothingness; its possibility of non-being by virtue of its createdness remains a purely transcendental threat.) But the question is not ultimately important, because there is no such thing as a material world *qua* purely material, which could be interrogated in the concrete as to its intrinsic destiny. Theologically we are compelled to affirm that there is a history of nature, and hence an end and object of nature simply because it has been posited by God as the precondition and setting of the history of the spiritual creature which ends up in the free self-communication of God to the spiritual creature (as the history of salvation). Hence at least the *de facto* end of the history of nature will preserve all the natural elements which can enter into the fulfilment of the created spirit.

b) The end of the biological as such is the re-establishment of the beginning. As a spatio-temporal element demarcated within nature as a whole, the biological rests on the purely material and physical which it integrates into itself. It is exposed to being a mere undifferentiated moment of the "history" of all nature. Hence each individual biological element can have an end which is terminal. But this does not exclude the fact that the end of the biological as such is the regaining of the beginning, its self-propagation. At this level one can begin to see to some extent that the end is not the cessation of what hitherto was and now is simply no more, but the taking over and the attainment of potentialities which were given with the beginning merely by virtue of its transcendent cause and are achieved in time as an inheritance.

c) The end of the spiritual personal being, in keeping with his ontological nature, that is, one which knows itself and takes conscious possession of itself, in keeping with its beginning, is the freely activated acceptance of the authentic beginning. The proper concept of end in theology is the end which is achieved in the history of freedom before God and orientated to God. This end is neither the negation of being nor an ultimately arbitrary caesura in a time which had indeed a beginning but now runs on indefinitely. It is a real fulfilment of time which ends temporality because it ends up in the absolute validity of freedom, the definitiveness of decision. Maturing freedom is always achieved in the decision between possibilities opening on the future, and hence in view of the totality of free possibilities, that is, in view of and by virtue of the end. The various types of end distinguished above in relation to the ontological degrees of beings are so many possible modes (though obviously not equally true) in which man can understand the end. Since man is irresistibly drawn towards his end – though the mode of approach may be falsified by efforts to resist the insistent end – and since his present existence is engaged on a sketch-plan of his future, even if timorously, the end is present as what is to come, displaying itself as a task, a summons and an imperative. Thus the end permeates and determines every instant of existence and constitutes its uniqueness. Insofar as this still outstanding but present end is the end of a finite being, it is never absolutely within its power but is determinant in its veiled and sovereign impact. But insofar as the being in question opens out towards its end and appropriates it as truly its own, the end is at the same time something produced by it. The incalculable (diastatic) unity of impinging end from without and maturing end from within is the mystery which always enshrouds the clearness of the present.

5. Since men are essentially historical beings, their self-understanding and notion of salvation in each individual actual existence must involve an aetiological retrospect of a truly temporal past and the prospect and sketch-plan of a truly temporal future, embracing the life of each and of all mankind. Hence this basic reference cannot be whittled down to the atomized actualism of a demythologization or a simply existential interpretation. And the historical "descendence" (in tradition) may not be truncated in favour of a one-sided "transcendence" towards the future, in the Marxist utopian fashion, just as the imperative of the future may not be suppressed by the conservative effort to restore an unchanged past.

6. Man must learn from the future and from his end, which are part components of his present, how to understand his actual existence. But where existence is directed to a supernatural goal, and hence determined by revelation strictly so called, this revelation – which speaks of man's present constitution in the order of salvation – must also speak of his future as still outstanding and as having arrived, while it speaks of his end. Hence this utterance must be couched in terms of a realized (actualist) eschatology and of a genuine "later on", a tension of now and later, and be embodied at once as the now and the end in an actual event which is

temporal – and can therefore only express the now by the future and the genuine future only by the present. This is the hermeneutical principle which must be applied to all eschatological assertions. Where they are not "realized", they are understood one-sidedly, and when the realization blocks the perspective of the temporal future, the realization is false.

Adolf Darlap

IV. Doctrine of Creation

1. *The doctrine of creation in the whole of dogmatic theology.* In this section, we have to consider the relationship between this doctrine and the other themes dealt with in dogmatic theology. No attempt will be made to answer two questions of secondary importance. The first of these is concerned with whether this relationship is merely a kind of perichoresis of two (or more) themes which remain distinct and have to be dealt with in different treatises because it is impossible to say everything at once. The second less important question is whether these are two (or more) aspects of the one indivisible theme.

a) If the formal basic structures of the history of salvation have to be elaborated within the framework of a formal and fundamental theology as the science which precedes the "special" dogmatic theology. The doctrine of creation has, after all, to consider not only and primarily the beginning of the reality created by and different from God as a temporal element, but also and above all the created state as a lasting basic relationship between man and God. Seen in this light, the doctrine of creation is the first element to be considered in formal and fundamental theology.

b) This basic theme of the doctrine of creation and its relationship with formal and fundamental theology is revealed even more clearly in its relationship with the dogmatic doctrine of God (*De Deo uno et trino*) that has been known since the patristic period (theology as distinct from "economy"). The doctrine of God presupposes a doctrine of creation. This does not mean, however, that it is not mainly concerned with God in himself and that it should not form the first section of "special" dogmatic theology. It is, after all, important to remember that in a "natural" doctrine of God, understood metaphysically, God is never an "object" alongside other objects that can be reached. He is rather the transcendental sphere and ground of all possible experience of the world. In the dogmatic doctrine of God, God is not discussed as the one who says something about himself that is a matter of indifference to us. On the contrary, the absolute "in itself" of God described in the doctrine is what God himself communicates to us in his personal and absolute disclosure of himself (the "absolute" and the "economic" doctrine of the Trinity being the same). Moreover, seen in the light of the theology of revelation, God discloses himself personally and absolutely (he is absolutely independent of the world and raised above it) in our experience of his free dealings within the history of our salvation with us (in revelation, the covenant, his appeal to our free decision). In other words, he discloses himself in the formal structures of the "creatural state" or "creatureliness". Who and what God is is expressed by calling ourselves his creatures.

c) The doctrine of creation has therefore not to consider an object which is placed alongside the object of the doctrine of grace and of the supernatural order as something quite different from it. It is, on the contrary, concerned with the formal relationship between the world and God, including the (necessary) distinction between nature and grace. What is expressed by the creatural state (difference from God, a state of being founded in the freedom of God, justification) is given in the most intensive possible way in the reality of God's communication of himself in grace. The doctrine of creation is not simply a doctrine of the origin of nature in the world and in man. Nature, as created, should always be seen as accompanied by a supernatural existential and as a *potentia oboedientia* ("obediential potency") for grace as God's communication of himself. Its created state can, moreover, be characterized not as a state of *natura pura*, but rather as a precondition for God's free action of self-communication becoming "exterior". The doctrine of creation is therefore presupposed by the doctrine of the covenant. God's creation is an aspect of his power to give himself freely in grace and in the incarnation to the other aspect of himself. He is able to create because he can give himself freely in love. Because he is able to express himself, his word can also express the other aspect of himself and in fact says (as the subject) the other aspect as the one addressed by a possible (but always free) self-expression. From this point of departure, it is possible for a doctrine of creation to embrace the entire meaning of the biblical doctrine of creation in the divine Logos, without diluting this so that it becomes a merely accidental appropriation and without obscuring such magisterial texts as *D* 432, 704 and 2290.

d) Firstly, subjective creatureliness is the primary and radical mode of the creatural state (of which the created state of what is purely present is no more than a deficient mode). Secondly (as is apparent irrevocably and definitively in Christology), man should not be seen, as he was in the (Greek) cosmocentric view, simply as a part of the world. He is, on the contrary, a subject with an environment conditioning his subjectivity. As a subject, moreover, man is what is intended in creation as the condition of God's communication of himself to the world. Insofar as these two presuppositions apply to the doctrine of creation, the latter can be regarded as the formal aspect of a theological anthropology. As such, the doctrine of creation can achieve its purpose only if it always directs its attention towards man as the essence of creatureliness coming to consciousness. As we have already indicated (see *Angels*), theological angelology is not an independent part of a doctrine of creation (because "there are also" angels). It is rather an aspect of a Christocentric anthropology, in which the numinous character of man's environment is both recognized and submitted to man's immediate relationship in grace with God in Christ.

e) It should therefore also be apparent that a doctrine of creation should, in making the creatural state concrete, be aware that the world in which the creatural state is fulfilled must be Christocentric. In other words, it must be orientated towards Christology. If this Christology is not, moreover, to seem mythological and therefore incredible, but is rather to be authentic, then Christ should not be presented as the incarnate God in a world which is in itself already present, complete and intelligible, without reference to the appearance of Christ. At the same time, creation (precisely as nature) must also be understood, in the doctrine of creation, as being orientated towards God's communication of himself which reaches its climax and becomes final and definitive in the hypostatic union.

f) Creation must also be seen, in the doctrine of creation, as constituting history; the creatural state must be seen as the basis of historicity and finally creation must be considered as constituting the possibility of the history of salvation. Viewed in this light, the doctrine of creation is a formal aspect of a doctrine of the history of salvation and therefore also the doctrine of condition governing the possibility of an eschatological completion. Insofar as both spirit and matter are included in salvation history and both have the same beginning and the same end, it is important to clarify, in the doctrine of creation, not the difference between them, but their unity of origin and aim. Matter has to be understood as the condition governing the possibility of the creaturely spirit. (This, of course, includes the doctrine that the angels form part of the world.) If, on the other hand, creation (nature) is seen as conditioning a history that does not take place *in* the world, but is rather a history *of* the world, then creation will be understood as freely initiating a continuous process of creation in a state of becoming (the preservation of the world and God's collaboration). It will, in other words, make it continuously possible for the finite aspect of the created world to transcend itself again and again in an upward movement, thus enabling creation to reach an increasingly high level of development.

We cannot outline in detail here a fully systematized doctrine. As a whole, the general theme is the state of man (and of his world), insofar as this forms the context of and conditions his freedom and his guilt (original sin) as well as his share in shaping history. Since it conditions the history of man's salvation in the concrete, the theme dealt with in *De Deo elevante* can therefore be treated in the doctrine of creation as part of a doctrine of creation in the concrete (bearing in mind the distinction between nature and grace). This is above all because the real interpenetration of creation and the covenant is expressed in it, even though the impenitence of sinful man in God's covenant does not have any real place in the doctrine of creation. The (mysterious) Christocentricism of the world does, however, belong to the doctrine of creation. Bearing in mind these presuppositions and with explicit reference both to the traditional themes dealt with in the doctrine of creation and to what has already been said under I above, we will summarize a few of the themes that are all too easily overlooked in the scholastic treatises on this doctrine.

a) *The gnoseology of the doctrine of creation.* An explicit exposition of man's way of knowing the creatural state is required in the doctrine of creation. A simple division into natural knowledge (as a possible knowledge, but one which is in fact not attained outside the revelation of the Old and New Testaments) and revealed knowledge is not sufficient. The interpenetration and relationship of reciprocal conditioning (in accordance with a correct understanding of the philosophy of Christianity) of these two ways of knowing are worth special consideration. The existential need to return to the origin and the beginning for man as a pre-condition of being able to hear the revelation concerning creation, the transcendental experience of creatureliness (free subject confronted with the free mystery that is not at man's disposal) also merits our attention. In this context, we have to try to think more precisely about the revelation concerning the "beginning". In other words, we have to decide whether revelation ought to be thought of in itself either as a direct and separate revelation of the word or whether it should be interpreted as an inner aspect of man's experience of the history of his salvation, in which God has dealings with him in word and deed in a genuinely historical relationship. Another aspect of the gnoseology of this doctrine is the theological doctrine of knowledge (hermeneutics) concerning the interpretation of statements about creation in Scripture. In this context too, we are bound to consider the created and developing world as God's disclosure and forgiveness, which are also aspects of the history of salvation.

b) *The formal and fundamental doctrine*

of creation. What is meant by this has already been indicated under 1 (a) above. Bearing in mind the present state of existential ontology, and its teaching about time, the historical reality of man, freedom and so on, it is obvious that these themes have not been given enough attention in the doctrine of creation in its customary form. It is also clear that they have not been sufficiently subjected to theological scrutiny and examined in the light of the Christian revelation. The doctrine of creation is still far too dependent on an armoury of philosophical terms and concepts derived from cosmocentric Greek thought and an ontology of what is merely objectively present. Time, for instance, is seen too one-sidedly as purely physical time and not as a bringing about in time of freedom. The world is regarded as a purely static stage on which the history of salvation is enacted and therefore as something that is bound to share in the result of that history. If *De Deo elevante* really forms part of the doctrine of creation and man is, in the supralapsarian sense, a historical being, then the formal structures of his relationship to the history of salvation must also belong to the doctrine of creation.

c) *The concept of the one "world"*. The unity of the world (consisting of spirit and matter) has to be worked out (incorporating the angels) in greater detail in the doctrine of creation. This has to be done so that the reality of the unity of cosmological and personal history and the completion of history (that is, transcendentally and therefore dispelling in advance any suspicion of mythology) will be understood.

d) *The lasting relationship between God the creator and the created world.* Various aspects of this question are the preservation of the world and God's collaboration as making the transcendence of every stage of the history of the world possible; the unity of this preservation and "providence"; the unity and the difference of historicity and the history of salvation (in accordance with the history of nature and grace, which also has a history).

e) *The supralapsarian Christocentricism of the world* as created in the Logos of God and (without ceasing to be "material") transcending itself and becoming the unity of God and the world in the God-man (theology of history).

f) *The special anthropological doctrine of creation*. For this special aspect of the doctrine, see man.

D

DEATH

1. *Introduction.* It cannot be said that the theology of death usually receives in scholastic theology the attention which the theme deserves. People think they know from everyday experience what death is, and quickly turn to the question of what comes after death, as though the theology of death only began there. Yet death necessarily also contains within itself all the mysteries of man. As the Constitution *Gaudium et Spes* of Vatican II notes, it is the point where man in the most radical way becomes a question for himself, a question which God himself must answer. Furthermore, Christianity is the religion which regards the death of a certain man as the most fundamental event of the history of salvation and of world history. Finally, death is not something which happens to a man alongside much else. Death is the event in which the very man himself becomes his definitive self. It is therefore certainly and eminently a topic for theology.

Death is an occurrence which concerns a man as a whole. Now man is a unity of nature and person, i.e., a being who, on the one hand, even prior to personal free decision is constituted in existence in a certain way which has its determinate laws and consequently necessary development, and, on the other hand, disposes of himself freely, so that he is finally what he freely wills to consider himself to be. Death is therefore at once a natural and a personal occurrence. If biology does not really know why all life, and in particular man, dies, then the reason for death which is given by faith – the moral catastrophe of mankind (Rom 5) – is the only reason propounded for the undeniable universality of death among men. And this theological reason also furnishes the certainty that even throughout the future the inevitability of death will be one of the necessary forces dominating human reality, and that death can never be abolished.

2. *Magisterium and Scripture.* Before attempting a definition of death, it will be well to mention the pronouncements of the magisterium expressly concerning death. Death is a consequence of original sin (*D* 101, 109a, 175, *DS* 413, *D* 788f.). This does not of course mean that if there were no original or personal sin man would have continued in perpetuity his biological life in time, or that before "Adam" there was no death in the animal kingdom. Even without sin man would have ended his biological, historical life in space and time, and would have entered into his definitive condition before God by means of a free act engaging his whole life. Death as we know

it now, as part of man's constitution subject to concupiscence, in darkness, weakness and obscurity regarding its actual nature (see below 3), is a consequence of sin. This does not mean that we can necessarily be successful in distinguishing between death as personal fulfilment of life and death as a manifestation of sin. Consequently all men in original sin are subject to the law of death (*D* 789). Even those who according to 1 Cor 15:51 will be found alive at Christ's second coming, must attain eternal life by a radical "change" which in substance is the same as death. With death man's individual history finally ends (cf. Lk 16:26; Jn 9:4; 2 Cor 5:10; Gal 6:10). The doctrine of apocatastasis has always been rejected by the Church (*D* 211; cf. *D* 778, 530, 693). At Vatican I a definition was projected regarding the impossibility of justification after death (*Coll. Lac.*, VII, 567). In this way any doctrine of transmigration of souls is rejected as incompatible with the conception of the uniqueness and decisive dignity of human history and the nature of freedom as definitive decision.

3. *Definition of death.* a) Christian tradition gives a provisional description of death in the phrase "separation of body and soul". This implies that the spiritual principle of life in man, his "soul", assumes in death a different relation to what we are accustomed to call the "body". But it does not say much more than this. Consequently the phrase is not a definition of death adequate to metaphysical or theological requirements. For it is absolutely silent about the characteristic feature of death, that it is a human event concerning man as a whole and as a spiritual person, an event which concerns his very essence: his definitive free, personal self-realization. This must certainly not be conceived as occurring "with" or "after" death, but as an intrinsic factor of death itself. Whilst plants and animals "perish", only man "dies" in the proper sense.

The above-mentioned description of death is also inadequate because the concept of separation remains obscure and leaves room for some very important distinctions. For since the soul is united to the body, it clearly must also have some relationship to that whole of which the body is a part, that is, to the totality which constitutes the unity of the material universe. This material unity of the world is neither a merely conceptual sum of individual things nor the mere unity of an external interaction of individual things on one another. As the soul by its substantial union with the body as its essential form also has a relationship to this radical unity of the universe, the separation of body and soul in death does not mean the absolute cessation of this relation to the world so that the soul (as people like to think in a neo-Platonic way) becomes absolutely a-cosmic, and other-worldly. It is much truer to say that the termination of its relation to the body, by which it maintains and forms the latter's structure and delimits it from the whole of the world, means a deeper and more comprehensive openness in which this comprehensive relation to the universe is more fully realized. In death the human soul enters into a much closer and more intimate relationship to that ground of the unity of the universe which is hard to conceive yet is very real, and in which all things in the world communicate through their mutual influence upon each other. And this is possible precisely because the soul is no longer bound to an individual bodily structure.

This conception also follows from the scholastic doctrine that the substantial act of the soul as *forma corporis* (*D* 481) is not really distinct from it, and therefore could only absolutely cease if the soul itself were to cease to exist, and were not immortal, as philosophy shows and the Church's dogma affirms. A substantial relation to matter of this kind, identical with the soul itself and not one of its "accidents", can change but cannot simply cease. It must also be taken into consideration that even before death the spiritual soul through its embodiment is already in principle open to the whole world and is therefore never a closed monad without windows but is always in communication with the whole of the world. Such a comprehensive relation to the world means that the soul, by surrendering its limited bodily structure in death, becomes open towards the universe and a co-determining factor of the universe precisely in the latter's character as the ground of the personal life of other incarnate spiritual beings. Indications of this are, for example, certain parapsychological phenomena, the Church's doctrine of purgatory, of the intercession of the saints, etc. Purgatory, for instance, would mean that the soul, even after surrendering its bodily structure and through that surrender, experiences in its freely posited self-determination more clearly and acutely its own harmony or disharmony with the objectively right order of the world and, conversely, itself contributes to determining the latter.

b) Another definition of death states that death is neither the end of man's existence nor a mere transition from one form of reality to another having something essentially in common with it, namely indefinite temporal sequence; death is the beginning of eternity, if indeed and so far as we may use the term "beginning" at all in regard to this eternity. The totality of created reality, the world, grows in and through incarnate spiritual persons, and the world is in a certain sense their body. Their death slowly brings the universe to its own final stage. Yet this immanent maturing of the world towards its consummation, like that of the individual human being, is at the same time, in a mysterious dialectical unity, a rupture, an ending from without, by an unpredictable intervention of God through his coming in judgment, of which "no one knows the day or the hour" (Mk 13:31). Man's death is, therefore, an occurrence passively undergone, which man as a person faces powerlessly as coming from outside. But it is also and essentially personal self-fulfilment, "one's own death", an act which a man interiorly performs; death itself (rightly understood) is the act, not simply an attitude the human being adopts towards death but which remains extrinsic to it.

Death, therefore, as the end of the man as a spiritual person, is an active consummation from within brought about by the person himself, a maturing self-realization which embodies the result of what a man has made of himself during life, the achievement of total personal self-possession, a real effectuation of self, the fullness of freely produced personal reality. At the same time the death of man in his unity but as the end of his biological life is simultaneously, and in a way which affects the whole man, an irruption from without, a destruction, so that a man's own death from within through the act of the person is at the same time an event of the most radical spoliation of man, highest activity and greatest passivity in one. And in view of man's substantial unity it is not possible simply to divide these two sides of the one death between soul and body, for this would dissolve the very essence of human death.

c) Because of this ambiguous duality, death is essentially obscure, i.e., it is not possible, humanly speaking, to say with certainty in the concrete case whether the full term of life reached in death is not in fact the emptiness and futility of the individual in question as a person, which till then was concealed, or whether the apparent emptiness in death is only the outward aspect of a true plenitude, the liberation of the person's true essence. Because of this obscurity, death can be the punishment and expression of sin, the culmination of sin, mortal sin in the proper sense, or the culmination of the whole act of a man's life in which he surrenders himself in faith to the incomprehensible mystery of God, which has its most radical manifestation in man's dispossession by death. In this definition of death there is no question of asserting that this essence is realized precisely at the chronological instant of medical "extinction". Death in this view is an event which is ultimately identical with the one history of man's freedom in its totality, which creates man's definitive condition, inasmuch as this event is completed "at" (rather than "by") the end, which is marked by extinction in the medical sense.

4. *Christ's death.* Since Jesus Christ became man of the fallen race of Adam and assumed "the flesh of sin" (Rom 8:3), he entered human life in a situation in which it reaches its fulfilment only by passing through death in its ambiguous, obscure form. Consequently he took death upon himself inasmuch as in the existing order of things it is an expression and manifestation of the fallen state of creation in both angels and man. He did not simply offer a certain satisfaction for sin. He enacted and suffered death itself, which is the expression, manifestation and revelation of sin in the world, He did this in absolute liberty as the act and the revelation of that divine grace which divinized the life of his humanity and by reason of his divine person of necessity belonged to him. In that way, however, death became something absolutely different from what it would be in a human being who did not possess in his own right the life of grace and perfect freedom secure from any weakness of concupiscence. It is precisely by its darkness that the death of Christ becomes the expression and embodiment of his loving obedience, the free transference of his entire created existence to God. What was the manifestation of sin becomes, without its darkness being lifted, the manifestation of an assent to the will of the Father which is the negation of sin. By Christ's death his spiritual reality, which he possessed from the beginning and actuated in a life which was brought to consummation by his death, becomes open to the whole world and is inserted into this whole world in its ground as a permanent determination of a real ontological kind. (Cf. on this feature of human death in its realization by Christ, the biblical affirmation regarding Christ's descent into hell.)

The world as a whole and as the scene of personal human actions has, therefore, become different from what it would have been if Christ had not died. Possibilities of a real ontological nature have been opened up for the personal action of all other men which would not have existed without the death of our Lord. By that death his human reality and the grace which was definitively ratified by the real concrete human freedom precisely of his death, became a determining feature of the whole cosmos. To the innermost reality of the world there belongs what we call Jesus Christ in his life and death, what was poured out over the cosmos at the moment when the vessel of his body was shattered in death, and Christ actually became, even in his humanity, what he had always been by his dignity, the heart of the universe, the innermost centre of all created reality.

5. *Dying.* Knowledge, even if mostly an implicit knowledge, of the inevitability of death, though not of its when and where, intrinsically determines the whole of life. In this knowledge death is always already present in human life and only by this does life assume its full gravity, through the necessity of its activities, the uniqueness of its opportunities and the irrevocability of its decisions. Just as personal failure before the absolute claim experienced in conscience is the most poignant, so death is the most tangible expression of man's finitude. But precisely in the explicitly

conscious presentiment of death in natural mortal anguish it is apparent that life itself points limitlessly beyond death. For in mortal anguish death does not appear (as in the mere fear of death) only as a possibly painful single event at the end of life, but rather as an event of such a kind that in face of it man is freed from his attachment to all that is individual and he is confronted with the truth, namely, that in death the fundamental decision which a man has made in regard to God, the world and himself, and which dominates his whole life, receives its definitive character (Jn 9:4; Lk 16:26; 2 Cor 5:10; *D* 457, 464, 493a, 530f., 693). Man hopes that at the same time it means fulfilment, yet he remains uncertain whether this is achieved. The will of man maturing from within to the totality and finality of his attitude to life is always alienated by the dispersion of bodily existence and is robbed of its power of disposing of all in a coherent whole. He therefore cannot bring to open, unambiguous certainty the totality of a definitively composed personal life which he strives for. Consequently the act of human life remains essentially impenetrable in face of death, threatened from without, and in death finally comes to its sharpest contradiction, the simultaneity of highest will and extreme weakness, a lot which is actively achieved and passively suffered, plenitude and emptiness.

This fundamentally obscure and ambiguous situation of death is the consequence of original sin which affects all men and becomes in them a natural expression of the fall of man in Adam from his grace-given immortality (cf. Rom 5:12; *D* 101, 175, 793), the clear fulfilment of an earthly existence transfigured by communion with God. According to whether a man wills autonomously to understand and master this death, due to original sin and beyond his clear power of control, which he accomplishes as a personal action throughout his life, or whether he holds himself open in death with unconditional readiness in faith for the incomprehensible God, his death will become either a personal repetition and confirmation of the sinful emancipation of the first human being and so the culmination of sin, definitive mortal sin, or it will be the personal repetition and appropriation of Christ's obedient death (Phil 2:8) by which Christ inserted his divine life into the world itself. In this way it becomes the culmination of man's salutary activity. Conformation to the death of Christ, anticipated throughout life in faith and sacraments, is now personally accomplished and becomes a final blessed "dying in the Lord" (Rev 14:13), in which the experience of the end becomes the dawn of perfect fulfilment.

Karl Rahner

DEMONOLOGY

For the history of demonology as a theological treatise, see *Angels*. The experience of evil "principalities and powers" (of a personal kind) in the world, which is not in itself primarily a real revelation (cf. Aquinas, *ST*, q. 115, a. 5: *experimento enim scitur multa per daemones fieri*, "by experience, we know that a great deal is done by demons"), forms part of the critical context of the real revelation of the living God in Christ and his power to redeem man. It is therefore in the light of this revelation of Christ that the experience of demons is meaningful in the Christian sense and can be critically defined and limited. The history of demonology subsequent to the New Testament can be considered under four main headings.

1. It is in the first place a history which includes elements of often presumed experience or knowledge of demons which are not in themselves illegitimate, but are in many ways superfluous and have the effect of ob-

scuring the real revelation. Among these elements are, for example, patristic and medieval theories about the so-called subtle bodies of demons, demonic knowledge or power, demonic possession, witches, magic and divination.

2. It is a history of a Christian attempt to correct natural demonology in the light of revelation and to guard against an absolute dualism and similar tendencies to stress the existence of demons by means of spiritualism, superstition and witchcraft.

3. It is a history of theologoumena which have been unable to go beyond this stage of development because there is no strictly theological point of departure for this further development. These theologoumena include teachings about the "nature" of these principalities and powers, the reason for their fall, the relationship between the many demons and the one devil, the way in which demons tempt man, the "abode" of the demons, their situation at the Last Judgment, the question of the relationship between individual man and the tempter, compared with the individual guardian angel, and so on.

4. It is a history of the ascetic doctrine of demonic temptations and the distinguishing of the "spirits".

The official teaching of the Church is confined to what is strictly necessary (and to what is possible): that is, to the existence of finite, created powers of a personal kind which are, because of their own fault, evil, and have been rejected, and which cannot be restored to a state of perfection (apocatastasis). The Church teaches, in other words, the existence in the world of evil which is not absolute and which cannot be identified with human evil. A clearly articulated pattern, we may conclude, never emerged in the post-biblical history of demonology. From the early scholastic period onwards, it formed part of dogmatic theology and almost always appeared in treatises on creation, occupying a position before the anthropological aspect of creation and thus often disrupting the original theological connection between anthropology and Christology. As for the place of demonology in "external" systematic theology, this can still remain in a treatise on creation, on condition that this treatise is regarded not as a mere collection of facts about the world presented formally on the basis of revelation, but as theological teaching about the world of man in the presence of God in Christ. Its "inner" place, on the other hand, and its real theological theme are derived from the real point of departure of demonology as a whole. In other words, teaching about the devil and the demons has its place in Christology and Christian anthropology insofar as man experiences in these sciences the liberating message of God's power to overcome his own human situation, which is revealed to him as lost, beyond his own ability to deal with, and capable of being overcome only in Christ. In this sense, demonology is an expression of the personal basis of our guilt and mortality which is not within our power to control or reach by any human action in history. It is also an expression of the fact that, as a human situation, evil in the world has a certain depth which is not simply attributable to man and the history which is subject to his autonomous control, but is something that can only be overcome by God's eschatological act in Christ in fulfilment of his promise. Even though this is hardly ever expressed as a theme in demonological teaching as a whole, this is, in relation to us and our salvation, the essential subject-matter of demonology. The rest is no more than conjecture or at the most an application of general theological principles which may be correct, but which are incapable in themselves of reaching the specific element in this sphere.

Karl Rahner

DEMYTHOLOGIZATION

I. General

1. *The problem.* Bultmann was not the first to affirm the existence of myths in the NT. It was he, however, who centred the theological and exegetical problem on the question of the necessity of a demythologization. And it is because of what he sought to do that the problem of demythologization occupies many theologians and exegetes at the present time.

The idea of the necessity of demythologization is already found several times in Bultmann's early works. It was in 1941, however, that he gave it systematic exposition under the title *New Testament and Mythology*. This lecture-manifesto was to have considerable repercussions. The discussions that it provoked are not yet over. The problem of demythologization still remains extremely topical.

Bultmann's fundamental idea was that of the abyss which separates the world in which the NT was conceived and expressed, from our own. The world-view to which the NT is tributary is mythical, whereas the one to which we refer explicitly or implicitly is scientific. According to Bultmann we are to regard as mythical the mode of representation in which what is not of this world, the divine, appears as though it were of this world, as human, the beyond as something here below; a mode of representation according to which, for example, God's transcendence is thought of as spatial remoteness, and in virtue of which ritual worship is viewed as an action transmitting by material means forces which are not material. Modern thought, on the contrary, inevitably conditioned by science, is characterized by the principle of immanence, according to which the reason for phenomena cannot be sought except in the phenomena themselves, without any possibility of a gap in their succession.

It appears evident to Bultmann that the NT world-view was a mythical picture. He describes that universe as a three-tiered structure (heaven, earth, hell) whose parts communicate with each other, man's earth being the scene of supra- or infra-terrestrial influences rather than shaped by the decisions and work of those who live on it. It is a mythical history of the world that presents it as now in the power of Satan, sin and death, rushing towards its imminent end in a universal catastrophe, after passing through extraordinary "tribulations" which will only be ended by the coming of the celestial Judge bringing salvation or condemnation. According to Bultmann there corresponded to this mythical world-picture a mythical representation of the saving event "which forms the proper content of the New Testament message": the sending down to earth of the pre-existent Son of God who effects by his death the expiation of sins, rises from the dead, is raised to heaven at the right hand of God . . .; and this saving work is rendered present to men in an equally mythical manner in the sacraments.

Demythologization must, therefore, Bultmann maintains, be radical. It cannot consist merely in eliminating certain elements and retaining others, but must reach to the very heart of the NT message. That, in fact, is where it is most urgently imperative, since it is the very kernel of the NT to which we must penetrate in order to draw sustenance from it.

Moreover, the necessity of demythologization does not derive for Bultmann solely from the need of adapting the NT message to the modern mind. "It is rather a matter", he writes, "of enquiring whether the message is purely and simply mythical or whether the very attempt to understand it and its specific intention, does not lead to the elimination of myth." The NT in fact aims at doing something quite different from transmitting to us a mythical picture of the world which it shares with other documents of its period. It does not aim at communicating a world-view but a living word of salvation, a word, therefore, which must be really heard in order effectively to transform human existence.

Thus the idea of demythologization represents for Bultmann only the negative aspect of an enterprise which is intended to be essentially positive and strives for maximum fidelity to the NT itself. This positive aspect finds its chief expression in his programme of existential interpretation. Is it possible, however, to accept a problem of demythologization stated in these terms? This question must now be examined.

2. *Unacceptable aspects of Bultmann's idea of demythologization.* For several reasons we cannot accept the problems of demythologization as Bultmann formulates it. In the first place it is based on distorting over-simplifications. There are over-simplifications in the way in which allegedly mythical data of the NT are expounded. In the book that Karl Barth devoted to him, Barth inquires what interest there can be in listing in a "caricatural" way, as Bultmann does, all those elements, in reality of very different kinds, which he simply lumps together in the category of myth. Does the NT doctrine of the sacraments, for example, belong to the same kind of thought and raise the same problems as the three-tiered picture of the world? And is it so astonishing to find transcendence expressed by reference to space? Do we, who can no longer re-enter the mythical universe, succeed in removing all traces of spatiality from our thought? Does not our picture of the world become strangely mythical again when we speak of the "sublimity" or "loftiness" of a thought or a life or a testimony?

Consequently the radical opposition which Bultmann establishes, or claims to observe, between the world-view of the first Christian generations and our own, is quite evidently due to an over-simplification with pernicious consequences. It was in the same sort of way that Lévy-Bruhl and his school believed they could establish a fundamental difference between what they called the "pre-logical" mentality of primitive peoples and the logical mentality of civilized societies. At all events it seems difficult to admit a real discontinuity between the mode of thought and way of seeing things of the apostolic generations and our own mode of thought and of looking at the world today. The technology of two thousand years ago was certainly very different from the kind that dominates our lives in the 20th century. Nevertheless the first tools foreshadowed our technology. The fishermen of Tiberias and the temple tradesmen had more than a merely mythical relation to the world. Conversely the relations which link modern men to that same world are not solely of a scientific and technical kind. It is sufficient to recall the world of art or poetry. Depth psychology also shows the enduring function of myths, and ethnologists are continually coming to a better realization of their deep significance. From this point of view Bultmann displays a narrow rationalism which is largely out of date today.

He does indeed speak of the symbolic power of myths. Their meaning, he points out, is not so much to give a "picture of the world" as to express "the way man understands himself within his world". But he attributes to mythical representations only a very general meaning. And consequently the NT data which he regards as "mythical" hold no other meaning for him than to indicate the "importance" of the subject of which the text speaks: the Christian event. The break noted between the world of the NT and ours is paralleled by an equally deep disjunction between the (non-mythical) sense of the biblical data and the (mythical) mode of expression in which those data are presented.

But would it not be legitimate to ask whether the principle of these various divisions is not to be found in the denominational position of the man who formulated the project of demythologization? Was the abyss which Bultmann thinks he observes between the world of the NT and our own not created in the first place by a movement which itself consisted in breaking with the historical reality of the Church and the continuity of its tradition? And is it not that "abstraction" from the world and history which we meet once again in the hiatus asserted to exist between the concrete images and their meaning, between alleged myths and a kerygma which ends up by having no content?

The weakness in Bultmann's manner of stating the problem of demythologization ultimately derives from the fact that he does not extend his criticism to the initial situation from which his inquiry starts and on the basis of which he draws his conclusions. No doubt he rejects any idea of making modern man the measure of all things. Yet it is certainly on the basis of modern man, or more exactly of his rationalist illusions, that he defines and criticizes the allegedly mythical world of thought inhabited by the men of the NT. He has not in fact profited by the criticism of "modernity" which Nietzsche in particular undertook and which a whole current of contemporary philosophy continues to carry further. From this point of view, Bultmann has not profited from the teaching of Heidegger, on whom in other respects he so deliberately draws. For Heidegger it is characteristic of modern times to see the "world" in terms of its own epoch. It would therefore involve from the very start a radical misunderstanding of myth to speak of a "mythical picture" of the world. At the very least it would mean contemplating the myth from outside and, in fact, turning the very narrow point of view of modern man into the absolute norm.

3. *Demythologization and Catholic theology*. Catholic exegesis is in principle immunized against this danger by the duty it acknowledges of fitting into the movement of a tradition extending from apostolic times to the present day. That is why it will never entirely recognize its own problem in Bultmann's demythologization problem. But that does not mean that the question is of no concern to Catholic exegesis.

Although the problem of demythologization is in part linked to the denominational position of the man who has drawn a whole programme from it, certain aspects of the problem cannot fail to concern Catholic theology too. The latter can share Bultmann's preoccupation to the extent that this consists simply in seeking out and expressing as adequately as possible and in the most effective way the data of faith contained in Scripture. From this point of view one could say that all theology embodies what is authentic in Bultmann's project.

The term demythologization is not appropriate, however, to describe this enterprise. It may well suggest that the NT presents us with myths in the proper sense, whereas the NT formally rejects them (cf. 1 Tim 1:4; 4:7; 2 Tim 4:4 . . .) and claims to bear witness to a real history. This essential link with history, maintained not only by NT but also by OT revelation, explains why it has been possible to describe that revelation as a veritable process of demythologization (so, for example, G. von Rad, *Old Testament Theology*). What at most can be found in the biblical writings are terms and images, originally connected with myths, but which are employed as part of a whole context where quite evidently they bear an entirely new meaning. Consequently, to equate the hermeneutical problem with a problem of demythologization would reduce it to a relatively superficial undertaking. The search for and elucidation of the meaning of Scripture, ceaselessly pursued for generations, represent a very much profounder and more exacting task.

Does this mean that the problem raised by Bultmann corresponds to no special difficulty and that the modern times to which he refers have brought no new obstacle to our understanding of the Bible in faith, not only in regard to the OT but also to the NT? It would certainly be vain to claim that the critical sense has not considerably developed in the last two thousand years or that the relation of men of the 20th century to the Bible is still spontaneously the same as that of the Fathers of the Church or of medieval theologians. The modernist crisis at the beginning of the present century, for example, shows that a certain tension can develop between the traditional affirmations of faith and the task that is proper to criticism. At the present time, too, attention has been drawn to the difficulties which are met with in harmonizing perfectly developments in dogma and exegetical research. That means that an often difficult effort is needed to harmonize our modern critical demands with an understanding of the faith which will be identical with that of the apostolic and indeed of all Christian generations.

René Marlé

II. Existential Interpretation

1. *Nature.* The idea of existential interpretation corresponds to the positive aspect of Bultmann's hermeneutical project, just as demythologization expresses its negative side, "Myth", he explains, "does not call for a cosmological interpretation, but an anthropological or rather an existential one . . . In the mythology of the New Testament, it is not the objective content of the representations in itself that must be studied, but the understanding of human existence which these representations express." To extract this "understanding of human existence" implied in all that the biblical texts present to us, and to show what vital significance for man's life the different statements of Scripture can, and in fact are intended to, have, are the aims of existential interpretation.

2. *Its necessity.* It must not be thought that the project of existential interpretation only springs from interest in man and from a regard for intelligibility leading to the elimination of everything which exceeds man's measure. The principle of existential interpretation does not belong to one of those types of rationalism which are unwilling to recognize any reality except what the human understanding can grasp. In fact that principle, prior to expressing a human need, finds its justification and in a certain way its necessity, in God himself. Reference to human existence is, in fact, a condition of an authentic religious language. One cannot speak seriously of God without speaking of the relationship to him, for there is no standpoint at which one would be external to God, ultimately. God is "the reality which determines our existence . . . Hence, if one wishes to speak of God one must obviously speak of oneself". (*Glauben und Verstehen*, vol. I, pp. 28f.)

3. *A committed and responsible interpretation.* "To speak of oneself" does not, however, mean to talk of one's experiences or inner states, as if we regarded these as direct manifestations of God's action in us. It is not a matter of speaking "about" our existence, but of speaking "out of" it, with it as starting-point. There is this strange truth about our existence, which also applies to that of God: we can speak about neither of them in strictly proper terms, and neither is at our disposal. "Two features alone" of this thought-defying existence "are clear; firstly, that we have the care and responsibility of it: *tua res agitur*; secondly, that it is

devoid of all security and we cannot provide it with any, for in order to do so we should have to stand outside it, we should have to be God." In other words, the reference to existence in no way aims at linking us to the familiar universe of our experience or ideas, but very much rather to project us into the heart of the most ineluctable and hopeless of situations and hence to challenge us. It is the condition of all authentic religious language, because there is no authentic religious language which is not concerned with the decision of faith.

4. *Method.* Though it is impossible to speak "about" existence, the latter is not to be assimilated to something irrational which understanding cannot grasp at all. On the contrary, existence is never without an "understanding of existence", just as our ideas and utterances express in a very general way a certain concrete existential attitude or manner of approach. It is in this relation between existence and understanding, which makes them in some respects co-extensive, that the legitimacy of existential interpretation can be founded. But that relation may be more or less immediate and more or less evident. That is why it is necessary to employ a practical method aimed at bringing fully to light the significance for existence of NT assertions which concern it only indirectly and which may even at first sight appear quite alien to it.

Existence, in fact, may be expressed directly in certain very simple words: I love you, I hate you, I forgive you . . . More often it finds expression by seeming to speak of what is other than itself. The aim of existential interpretation is then to show how it is existence which is really speaking and, by showing this, to display the true goal of existence.

To achieve this, this interpretation uses a particular technique drawn from a particular philosophy which, under the name of "existential analysis", lays bare the general structures of human existence and so supplies "the concepts thanks to which it is possible adequately to speak of human existence".

Existential interpretation aims at remaining on this formal plane, indicating the general significance for existence that the text to be interpreted may possess, but leaving to man's freedom the practical recognition of the validity of that significance. It remains on the plane of structures, and that is why it is called existential in the universal sense (existenz*ial*), aiming solely at opening out the possibility of an authentic and personal decision, which will then be called existential in the concrete sense (existenzi*ell*).

5. *Criticism.* It is theologically legitimate to seek for a principle of existential interpretation which will retain faith in its original dimension, that of a summons to man. Only such a reduction of faith can appeal to each man in his authentic situation in each age. The words of Scripture are "Spirit and life", and hence it can be useful to use certain methods of analysis and indeed a language elaborated by philosophy.

The limits, and therefore the dangers, of existential interpretation are determined by the idea of existence which is taken as the starting-point. Obviously it is only acceptable if the existence in question, and the understanding we can achieve of it, can be radically called in question and be opened up to new horizons. K. Barth reproached Bultmann for wanting to confine biblical revelation within a carapace of existentialist philosophy. Without attempting to go into the grave question of the relations of philosophy and theology, of man's quest for God and the answer which revelation provides, we must be content to note that the existence to which Bultmann refers (since he is the chief advocate of existential interpretation), is of a very formal type, in which the body, work, "natural" relations with the world and with one's fellow-men play practically no part. Within the framework of that existence several features or fundamental components of revelation are not given their full importance: in particular everything concerned with the objective chronological facts of history, or the intimate, disinterested and potentially contemplative knowledge of the mystery of God. An existential interpretation undoubtedly makes God's claim and promises stand out clearly, and this helps us to understand how God's action on us in Christ is *propter nos et propter nostram salutem*. But such an interpretation also provides an articulate though always analogous statement about God's revelation and his work of salvation.

It is not possible to say *a priori* what might be achieved by an exegesis and a theology inspired by the endeavour to make contact with existence, yet freed from the limitations imposed on Bultmann by the philosophy and anthropology which explicitly or implicitly he takes as his frame of reference.

René Marlé

DESPAIR

1. Despair as a *sin* consists in the relinquishing of present or possible hope. It is, therefore, the voluntary rejection of a consciously recognized dependence of man upon his fellowmen and upon God, as well as of the corresponding duty of seeking perfection and salvation in harmony with them. The motives for despair can be various; it may be, for example, moral sloth (accidie, acedia) which shrinks from the effort of following Christ and which prefers earthly blessings to union with men or God; or it may be a lack of confidence which fears the responsibility of links with others or refuses to surrender to the known will of God. Fear of God may hold acts of despair in check, but only the virtue of hope can truly overcome despair itself.

2. To be able to despair in the *moral sense*, a man must have recognized his duty of placing his hope in God and his neighbour, and he must at the same time be in the position to reject that love which is asked of him if it should appear as of no value to him for any reason. This means that a man is by nature bound to God and his neighbours, and that he may also freely reject this bond by treating it as of less than absolute value.

Hence, sinful despair is only possible in those who at least are capable of the personal relationships which enable them to perceive and to accept the love of another. This presupposes a sufficient experience of love bestowed on them. Only those are capable of despair in the full sense, however, who have not only withheld their own response, but also consciously choose to do so. For in spite of the recognition of their own nothingness, they arrogantly choose to live for themselves alone and arbitrarily refuse to place their hope in love.

3. Such an attitude is glorified in contemporary literature and in various forms of nihilism which, after rejecting the faith, has despaired of reason also. Indeed, one may speak of a renaissance of despair. This can be expressed in euthanasia, suicide, pseudo-heroics in the face of death, as well as in the flight towards hedonism. From the religious viewpoint, every attempt to attain justification through works is seen as an expression of disguised despair. For this reason it is accepted that the task of the law within the divine plan is either to drive us to despair or to bring us to the point of placing our hope entirely in Christ. Despair, like those limitations of our freedom which spring from sin in general, cannot be adequately grasped in psychological terms. Every sin is in its root a form of despair, which consists of a rebellion against our recognized duty of being dependent in our self-fulfilment. It is a rejection which can be made good again only by means of repentance and forgiveness. Ultimately every resistance to offered grace

is an act of despair. It is for this reason that scholastic theology always related despair to the sin against the Holy Spirit.

4. Accordingly, one cannot speak of despair in the moral sense when proffered love cannot be recognized as such, or when one does not possess sufficient will-power to respond to it and to open himself trustingly to others and to God. This incapacity is often pathological, and in such a case one must seek to enlist the aid of psychiatry and psychotherapy. There are doubtless many forms of melancholy and scruples which are due to mental illness, as well as other disturbances caused by delusions and fantasies or other emotional stresses which induce feelings of despair and block either partially or completely the capacity to form relationships and which may eventually lead to suicide. In contra-distinction to this there is another type of despair which is based upon a metaphysical incapacity resulting from the underdevelopment of the perceptive capacity and freedom, so that the naturally negative response to hardship cannot be neutralized. For this reason one cannot call the hopeless attitude of "moral outlaws" despair in the moral sense; it results from a man's inability to see in God and other men anything else but enemies who wish him evil. A man can be driven to such a state if he is unworthily treated and never has the chance of experiencing the joy of another's love, or if he is unable to recognize the blessing and providence of God in the incomprehensible and bitter experiences of his fate.

Waldemar Molinski

THE DEVIL

1. *Methodological considerations.* a) By "the devil" we are to understand, in a sense to be defined, the "highest" of the evil spirits. It is clear that the background for a theologically correct idea of the devil will have to presuppose and include all that has been said in the article on *Angels*. Explicit reference must be made to it.

b) Firstly, the devil (leaving out of account for the moment the question of his exact relation to the other demons) is not to be regarded as a mere mythological personification of evil in the world; the existence of the devil cannot be denied. Secondly, the devil, like the other evil spirits, cannot be regarded, as in absolute dualism, as an independent counterpart to God. He is a finite creature whose evil remains comprised within the scope of the power, freedom and goodness of the holy God. We must therefore apply to the devil whatever theology has to say about evil, sin, its permission by God in a positive divine intention, about the negative character of evil, the impossibility of an evil substance, about concrete, finite good as the goal even of evil freedom, etc. Thirdly, the teaching of Scripture and revelation about the devil (as about evil spirits in general) appears rather to be a natural presupposition of human experience which is incorporated, critically corrected, into the doctrine of the victory of the grace of God in Christ and of the liberation of man from all "principalities and powers".

c) Once it is clear that the doctrine of angels, demons and the devil is the conscious conceptual interpretation of natural experience of a variety of supernatural principalities and powers (and not derived directly from the word of revelation properly so called), the findings of comparative religion become intelligible. Such a doctrine can be, and is, widespread. Interpreted and criticized, it penetrates revealed religion slowly from outside. It does not necessarily at first distinguish clearly between good and bad principalities and powers. It may overestimate such powers in a polytheistic way or again it may reduce the great powers of polytheism to the mere rank of angels or demons under the one God. Reflection on a certain hierarchical order among these principalities and powers may be more or less advanced, and such hierarchical arrangement can underestimate the natural heterogeneity of the spiritual personal world prior to man and the inner contradiction of the "realm" of evil, or it may in the concrete identify the evil spirits with the one devil, or employ the term devil as a summary formula for the evil principalities and powers. Remarks of this kind apply to some extent to the Old and New Testaments.

d) All this shows that the doctrine of the devil has really a very simple content which has nothing to do with mythology in the proper sense. The calamitous situation which man recognizes as his own, presupposed by the message of redemption and at the same time overcome by God's grace, is not one that is constituted solely by human freedom. A created freedom contributes to its constitution, one which is supra-human and antecedent to the history of human freedom. The opposition to God which appears as prior to man in man's calamitous situation, is itself manifold. "Evil" even in itself is disunited, and in that way constitutes man's situation. But this intrinsic disunity of evil itself which is at once one of the factors of its power and of its powerlessness, is not such that it could destroy the unity of the world, of its history (even in evil) or the "unity" of the calamitous situation in its opposition to God. Evil is still something like one kingdom, one rule. That is what is meant when we speak of a highest among the evil spirits, the devil. And this shows that we can only speak in a very vague sense of "pattern" in the disunity of evil in the world and consequently of a chief among the evil spirits. This is so, if for no other reason (though it is not the only one) than that the hierarchy among the good angels is very difficult to determine, because of course each of those angels is a radically unique being.

2. *Scripture*. a) The Septuagint translated the Hebrew *sātān* (adversary) by διάβολος. This word then passed into the various European languages. The names διάβολος and Satan at first bear various very wide meanings, then become narrower and coalesce in the demonology of later Judaism. The devil is then the prince of the angels who with his adherents fell away from God and was thrust out of heaven.

b) The NT assumes the general Jewish teaching about evil spirits and the devil. New designations of the devil are: the evil one (Mt 13:19, etc.), the enemy (cf. Lk 10:19), the ruler of this world (Jn 12:31, etc.), the god of this aeon (2 Cor 4:4), murderer from the beginning and father of lies (Jn 8:44). A new feature is the opposition between Christ and the devil. The devil's enmity with God reaches its historical culmination in Jesus' passion (Lk 22:3, 31; Jn 13:27; 1 Cor 2:8) but also its final defeat (1 Cor 2:8; Jn 12:31; Acts 12:7ff.), just as the exorcisms of devils were the prelude to the victorious coming of God's reign in the person of Jesus. This opposition continues in the history of the Church until the devil is finally cast into hell (Rev 20:8, 10).

3. *Dogmatic theology*. a) Most of what has been said by the magisterium about the devil is to be found in connection with doctrinal pronouncements about evil spirits and has the same content (their creation as good, their own sin and eternal reprobation: *D* 427ff., 211; *DS* 286, 325); a certain power over sinful man and his death is ascribed to the devil (*D* 428, 788, 793, 894) and his power is taken from him by Christ's redemption (*DS* 291, *D* 711f., 894). But the Church's doctrine guards against exaggeration of the influence of the devil's temptations on the sins of man (*D* 383, *DS* 2192, *D* 1261–73, 1923). The devil (*diabolus*) is often

tacitly assumed to be a sort of chief of the evil spirits. Vatican II is very reserved about statements concerning the devil, but they are not avoided altogether. We are freed by the Son of God from the devil's domination (Constitution on the Sacred Liturgy, art. 6; Decree on the Church's Missionary Activity, art. 3 and 9). "The evil one" led men astray into sin but his power was broken by Christ's death and resurrection (Pastoral Constitution on the Church in the Modern World, art. 13; cf. art. 2).

b) Speculative theology will take into consideration that the multitude of principalities and powers, by the very fact of their creation as part of the unity of the world, cannot be without a certain hierarchical order and gradation (cf. Mk 3:24). This order is not destroyed even by their guilt, because there cannot be an absolutely powerful sin which totally destroys specific nature and unity. This provides the basis for the idea of a leader of the evil spirits (Mk 3:22), called the devil, as the representative of all the principalities and powers. But it is not possible to attempt to individualize the devil as distinct from the rest of the evil spirits (cf., e.g., *D* 242 and 243). Particularly in regard to the devil as head of the demons, Christian piety must avoid the picture of Antichrist as a counterpart to God in history on an equal footing with him. The devil is a creature who must retain a created essence which is good and which he must employ according to its nature even to be capable of evil ("natura eius opificium Dei est": *DS* 286, *D* 237f., 242, 457).

4. *Kerygmatic treatment of the devil.* a) There is no reason to put the doctrine of the devil in the forefront of the hierarchy of truths when preaching the faith today, as was to some extent done in earlier times (e.g., by Luther). Not because there is no enduring statement of faith concerning the devil, but because what it means for the actual practice of Christian life can be said, as far as its decisive content is concerned, even without explicit teaching about the devil. And at the very least, because access to this doctrine is relatively difficult for people today. Nor is the devil mentioned in the great creeds. Consequently we must very definitely avoid drawing on the traditional arsenal of popular pictures of the devil (distinct classes of demons with special functions, proper names for some devils, etc.). Probably the exorcisms at baptism, etc., will have to be more soberly expressed in the new liturgy. In defending genuine dogmatic teaching about the devil, appeal to spiritualistic phenomena or to phenomena of possession are generally ineffective, for both meet with scepticism from men accustomed to the scrupulous empiricism of the natural sciences.

b) When an explanation and defence of the Church's teaching about the devil is required, e.g., in expounding the NT, liturgical texts, etc., people today must first have their attention drawn to the sinister suprahuman power of evil in history. This has its ground in the doctrine of the "principalities and powers", and this prevents its being glossed over and reduced to triviality. It need not be overlooked or contested that in such an argument it is not, and need not be, possible to draw a perfectly clear distinction between what is purely conceptual projection based on the experience of evil in history, and what is actually specifically affirmed about these substantial, created and personal principalities and powers, provided that such an intrinsic content of the affirmation is not denied in principle. It can also be helpful for the understanding of this teaching to point out that such principalities and powers, in accordance with their nature, which remains good, always retain a constant positive function (*actus naturalis*) for the world. It is not possible to object to this doctrine by asking why God does not remove the waste-products of the personal history of spirit completely from his creation. The free and eschatological refusal to open the natural activity of their essence into the mystery of God's free self-communication in grace does not destroy that natural activity as a permanently valid factor in the world.

Karl Rahner

DIALECTICAL THEOLOGY

Dialectical theology is the name given to a movement of thought which appeared within Protestant theology after the First World War and which at that time held the place in theologico-philosophical debates which the problems of demythologization and existential interpretation have occupied since the Second World War. Its chief protagonists were K. Barth, E. Thurneysen, E. Brunner, F. Gogarten and R. Bultmann.

1. *The beginnings of dialectical theology.* The common viewpoint of these theologians was presented to the public in the course of the same year. Between 1921 and 1922 Gogarten published *The Religious Decision*, Brunner, *Experience, Knowledge and Faith*, Thurneysen, *Dostoievsky*, and Barth, the second edition of his commentary on the Letter to the Romans, which Bultmann received favourably. During the autumn of 1922, Barth, Gogarten and Thurneysen founded the journal *Zwischen den Zeiten*, with G. Merz as editor. This was intended to be the organ for their work together, and Brunner and Bultmann soon began to contribute articles to it. It was in the same year that an observer gave to the newly-founded circle the name of "dialectical theology".

But unity was soon seen to be unstable. Dialectical theology was the first form of a theology of the word of God which was to appear in many different guises. What characterized the movement at the start was the reaction of its first supporters against the traditional liberal theology. Disturbed by the needs of the pastoral ministry and by the spiritual crisis caused by the war, they sought a new basis in the writings of Blumhardt, Kutter, Kierkegaard, Overbeck, Dostoievsky, etc. They held that traditional Protestant theology, centred as it was on religion and piety and studying their manifestations in human psychology and history, was really only speaking about man, whilst all the time it believed that it was speaking about God. They went on to affirm the transcendence of God in relation to all human knowledge and every human work, including religion; the sovereignty of the divine revelation in Jesus Christ, the authority of the Bible. They affirmed that sinful man, even when he believes, always stands before God with empty hands. And so they came back once more to the thought of the Reformers without returning to ancient Protestant orthodoxy.

The second edition of Barth's commentary on the Letter to the Romans is generally considered as the most vigorous and radical expression of "dialectical theology". So we must look at it first and then go on to define the rest in relation to it.

2. *Barth's dialectic.* Dialectic is produced by negation. In Barth's *Epistle to the Romans* this appears under the name of *critical negation*. It means the negation or denial that God himself pronounces upon man in the death and resurrection of Christ. And so it appears that there is a relationship with God only to the extent that God dialectically suppresses man. It is through judging us that God gives us grace; it is in the "no" of his anger that we hear the "yes" of his mercy. All human existence, religion included, stands in subjection to the divine "no". The true God, who can never be regarded as an object, is the origin of the *krisis* of every "objective" thing, the judge, the negation of this world.

This critical negation creates *distance*. A "line of death" separates God from man and time from eternity: what Kierkegaard called an infinite qualitative difference. God cannot be discovered either in experience or in any historical entity. In Jesus Christ he is revealed precisely as the "Wholly Other", as the unknown God. The Calvinist notion of the *maiestas Dei* here informs what Barth takes from R. Otto or from the religious philosophy of neo-Kantian inspiration. Even in the most exalted communion between God and man, God remains God and man nothing but dust and ashes. Their encounter takes place only in the miracle and paradox of faith.

But the cross of Christ throws a bridge over the distance between God and man, by the very act of setting it up. "Critical negation" has a *dialectical* character; which means that it includes in itself an assertion and its reversal, which tend to ultimate unity. As the *unknown* God, God is *known* in Jesus. "Insofar as he is the non-being of things, he is their true being." "Judgment is not annihilation; by it all things are established." This characteristic appears to the full in the dialectic between Adam and Christ, which constitutes both our justification and our resurrection. "The dualism of Adam and Christ, between the old and the new, is not metaphysical but dialectic. The dualism exists only insofar as it dissolves itself. It is a dualism of movement . . . (For) the *krisis* of death and resurrection, the *krisis* of faith, is the change of the divine 'no' to the divine 'yes'. There is no subsequent reverse movement."

Yet this turning or transition does not take place in human psychology and human history. It is the *actus purus* of an incomprehensible event in God. Just as the resurrection of Jesus is not a historical event alongside the other events of his life and death, so the new life that it introduces into my being is not an event alongside the other events of my own existence. The new man that I am is not what I am. "It is only by faith that I am what I am (not!)." "We can only believe and may believe that we believe." This faith is essentially hope, an awaiting for an eternal future. Insofar as it is man's act, it is pure "empty space", just like the life of Jesus itself. The non-historical character of the relationship between God and man (i.e., the notion that it is not worked out within the bounds of human history) is most clearly expressed in this celebrated declaration: "In the resurrection the new world of the Holy Spirit touches the old world of the flesh, but touches it as a tangent touches a circle, that is, without touching it. And precisely because it does not touch it, it touches it as a frontier, as a *new* world." The history of salvation unfolds on the frontier of time and eternity, in "the eternal moment".

As human endeavours, religion and the Church stand in the shadow of sin and death; for us the ethical problem is a mortal sickness. Religion, the Church and moral action are of value only as sign, witness, parable and reference, "an allusion to the revelation itself which is always far beyond all historical reality".

The situation of theology is the same. The theologian must speak about God; but as a man he cannot do so. All his talking will be only "witness rendered to the truth of God". To that end, he must follow by preference the dialectical way, which contains and unites within itself both the dogmatic and critical ways, by keeping his gaze fixed on their common presupposition, the living and ineffable truth which stands at the centre and which gives their meaning to both affirmation and negation. This centre, namely the fact that God has become man, can be neither apprehended nor contemplated and so cannot be directly expressed. All that remains is to relate the statement and the negation *to one another*, to illuminate the "yes" by the "no" and the "no" by the "yes", without ever stopping for more than a moment at the "yes" or on the "no". The dialectician must not forget that his speaking rests on "the presupposition of this original living truth, which is to be found there at the centre".

In 1927 in his preliminary sketch of *Church Dogmatics* Barth again explains, and in practically the same sense, that dogmatic thought is dialectic thought, i.e., a thought expressed in contradictories, moving endlessly from affirmation to negation, with no conclusive statement. But he purposely replaces the theme of critical negation by a definite assertion of the faithfulness of God. No longer does he say that God is the Wholly Other, nor that faith is empty space. He tries to introduce revelation into history. The *Church Dogmatics* was to emphasize this feature even more. It also gives great prominence to the "yes" that God says in Jesus Christ and no longer puts forward the idea that theology must be dialectics.

3. *The dialectic of Gogarten, Bultmann and Brunner*. The thought of Gogarten, Bultmann and perhaps to a lesser degree that of Brunner from about 1921 to 1924 was remarkably close to Barth in the role given to negation. "The idea of God", said Gogarten, "signifies the absolute *krisis* of everything human, and that means of all and every religion." Bultmann wrote: "God signifies the complete suppression of man, his repudiation, his being called into question and his judgment." And Brunner: "It is only in the *krisis* where man comes to an end, that grace can intervene as grace." All of them held that revelation and faith transcend historical knowledge and religious experience, that God is revealed in Jesus Christ as the Wholly Other, that he pronounces an essential "no" which accompanies an original and final "yes", that justified man remains a sinner and can only believe in the divine pardon. For them, however, the radical opposition of time and eternity does not separate two worlds, as with Barth. It divides the world which is our world. Dialectic or *krisis* is not as in the *Epistle to the Romans*, the *actus purus* of an incomprehensible event in God. The moment in which it takes place is not an eternal moment beyond all time, but the unique and specific moment when the Word of God made flesh encounters the human decision of faith. But it must be said that this difference is hardly perceptible; especially as Barth affirms that divine revelation is the reply to the question of human existence.

But after 1926, when the others made room for the decision of faith by integrating into their theology, as a necessary presupposition, the understanding that man has of himself, it was quite clear that they conceived dialectical theology in a way quite different from Barth.

For Gogarten, the reason for which all speaking about God is dialectical is that we have no knowledge of God that is not at the same time and first of all knowledge of ourselves. It is not our relation to God, but our existence which is dialectical. The duality of the creator and the creature does away with the possibility of dialectic relationship, because it prohibits all unity and all relative exchange between the two terminal elements. There is only a dialectic of the creature, a dialectic within history, insofar as my present decision takes away and take up my perishable past and thus confers upon it an imperishable character. Gogarten then explains that the constitutive element of history is faith in creation, the content of this faith being the encounter with the individual *thou* and the response to the call of one's neighbour. His later work sought to base relations between the individual and society on the *I-thou* relationship and here his analysis leans heavily upon the work of F. Ebner and M. Buber.

Bultmann likewise declared that theology cannot speak of God without at the same time speaking of man, and that consequently in its statements it presupposes a particular conception of man. This "pre-comprehension" he takes over from Heidegger after 1928: man's being is "historical", that is, its lot is at every moment at stake in the actual situations of life and moves through decisions in which man chooses himself as his *own possibility*. The expression "dialectical theology" actually means insight into the historical nature of man and of human speech in relation to God. The proposition: "God is merciful to me", is dialectical, not in the sense that it must be completed and made more precise by the correlative mention of God's anger with the sinner (which is also accurate), but insofar as it is historical, insofar as it expresses the irruption of the grace of God.

For Brunner, the knowledge of man through himself, to which the unbeliever can come, and which as such is taken up into theological anthropology, constitutes the point of insertion of revelation in human reason. Wholly a sinner, but without ceasing to be the image of God, in the formal sense, man is a contradiction. That is why the divine summons is both an attack upon and the fulfilment of man. That is also why theology must be dialectical. The word "dialectical" can be paraphrased as: "reflecting contradiction". Because the word of God encounters man in contradiction, it stands itself "in contradiction"; its message is of the God who is man, wisdom which is foolishness, freedom which is the service of God, etc. And so it is most properly expressed through paradox.

4. *The parting of the ways.* Thus in spite of their differences, Brunner, Bultmann and Gogarten all agree that the dialectical character of theology is based on human existence, and not on the event of revelation which is the denial or rejection of it. Barth accuses them of accepting a second sovereign court of appeal besides the word of God (*Zwischen den Zeiten*, 11 [1933], pp. 297–314). He continued to maintain that human existence can only be contemplated in the light of the word of God. He deliberately excludes everything in his earlier writings which might suggest that theology was based on a philosophical analysis of existence (see his *Church Dogmatics*, vols. I/1 and VII). He no longer holds that divine revelation is the answer to the question of human existence.

When Gogarten joined the "German Christians" in 1933, Barth announced that he was to cease collaborating with *Zwischen den Zeiten*, and the editor stopped publication. The following year Barth emphatically rejected the "natural theology" which Brunner was developing. From then on each member of the group went his own way. And the vital influence behind their thought is no longer principally that "critical negation" which had first united them. Barth continued to develop his positive interests in his *Church Dogmatics* which has now reached the doctrine of the atonement (vol. IV/3, second part). Bultmann's theological programme of demythologizing and existential interpretation is pursued by Bultmann himself, E. Fuchs, G. Ebeling and others.

Henri Bouillard

DIALECTICS

The origin of the term "dialectic" (διαλέγεσθαι, "to discuss", i.e., the for and against, thoroughly, by means of dialogue) points to the sphere of reasoning (λόγος, Spirit), but can have many shades of meaning. We here examine (1) the early history of the term, (2) its main usage, as seen in Hegel, (3) the correctives to be applied to Hegel, with the resulting perspective of (4) a dialectic of freedom and (5) its theological significance.

1. *Early history of the term.* The history of the philosophical concepts begins with Heraclitus's question: "How is that which differs from itself at agreement? Harmony is the tension of opposites, as in the bow and the lyre" (Fragment 51). This unity in tension is the basic law of the spirit, which it displays in all the polarity of worldly reality: day and night, life and death, war and peace, good and evil. The paradoxes of Zeno invoke against the phenomenon of movement the absolute logical contrast of being and non-being, as does Parmenides. This is the prototype of a dialectic of pure negation. In the opposite direction, the Sophists exploit the trivial contradictions of immediate experience against the universal validity of ethical norms. The spiritual and universal is defended by Socrates in the Platonic dialogues, where he uses the "dialectic" method of refuting mere opinions which are too readily acccepted. In Plato (*Republic*, VI, 511), "dialectic" is the faculty of attaining the forms in themselves, through the opposites in which they are mediated. The later dialogues define the intrinsic connections of such basic concepts as being and nothingness, the one and the many, the self and the other. Aristotle uses "dialectic" for the argument from probabilities. But he also uses it for the probing and explicitating process of investigating opposites (1004b, 25; 1078b, 25ff.), and in his notion of act and potency laid down the basis of a "dialectic of reality" which corresponds to the movement of the empirical world itself. For the Stoics, dialectic was part of logic, and meant the art of putting arguments and refuting objections. The neo-Platonists regarded it as the contemplation of the process of becoming in the world.

In the later tradition (scholasticism, mysticism, Nicholas of Cusa), the dialectical thought-forms of (neo-) Platonism and Aristotelianism continued to be stressed, rather than the meaning of the term in logic. Dialectical thought was given new dimensions in the Christian faith in the incarnation and Trinity. In Kant, the word took on once more a pejorative sense. Dialectic is the logic of the (inevitable) phenomenal, by which reason is carried away if it leaves the solid ground of experience and is thus trapped in the antinomies of reason. In Fichte, and above all in the systematic analysis of Hegel, dialectic is *the* logic of being, the inward Logos which pervades all reality.

2. *Hegel.* In the *Enzyklopädie*, nos. 79–82, Hegel describes the dialectical movement of thought according to the following three moments: a) the abstract or intellectual moment which distinguishes clearly-defined concepts; b) the negative rational moment in which these concepts pass over into their opposites; c) the positive rational moment which comprises "the unity of the determinations in their opposition" (*ibid.*, 82). He does not speak of thesis, antithesis and synthesis, but of the universal and immediate "in itself" which becomes "for itself", exteriorizes, expounds, particularizes itself in its elements as it posits its contrary. This mediation leads to that which is "in and for itself" which comprises in one the self and the other as the fully formed individuality and the new "mediated immediacy". The dialectical movement takes up the initial position into the (preliminary) end position, where it is preserved on a new plane though taken away. The antithetical force of the negation, when applied to itself leads to synthesis with the original. (The simple negation shows the progressive and revolutionary trend of dialectic, while the double negation displays its conservative and reactionary character.) The effect is the process itself. "The truth is the whole."

Dialectic is the way in which the Spirit comes to consciousness of itself, extrapolating itself by positing its opposite to find itself. Its self-externalization as the world is its entrance into its own depth and fullness – an "immanent outgoing". The process by which the Spirit explicitates itself is the law of becoming and being in the universe, from immediate, general being as the starting-point of the logical movement, to the absolute Spirit which knows itself in all, as the completion of the whole system. It takes in the various degrees of material nature, organic life, human spirit, law, State, history, art and religion, including the mysteries of the Christian faith: all is "taken up" in the concrete universality of the all-embracing Spirit. The dynamism which launches and sustains all is the discrepancy between the final goal and the emergent realities, whose very inadequacy forces them to strain onwards till the Spirit has worked itself out in and through all and so become utterly itself in the all of knowing, the "circle of circles" of its dialectical spirals.

3. *Criticism of Hegel.* The Marxist criticism of the Hegelian dialectic took the form of demanding its complete reversal, from top (the Spirit-idea) to bottom (material production): the determinant element is matter. The dialectical cycle which tends towards the universal self-identity of the Spirit by its reconciliation with the existent must be broken by a constant revolutionary negation based on the irreconcilable non-identity of the material (cf. T. W. Adorno, *Negative Dialektik* [1966]). Kierkegaard, in his *Philosophical Fragments*, protested against the Hegelian dialectic as a "Gnostic" bracketing of God and the world, and opposed to it the uniqueness of the free person, the moments of decision, the scandal of the historically unaccountable, the leap of faith. "Dialectical theology" insisted on the sharpest possible contradiction between God and the world; any mediation would be the work of Antichrist. The "dialogical" approach worked out since 1920 by such authors as F. Ebner and M. Buber tries to open up systematic *a priori* thinking for the relationships of interpersonal experience.

4. *The dialectic of freedom.* The dialectic of Hegel leaves no loop-holes for attack from outside; and it is not easy to distinguish between dialectic as a valid method and an erroneous system. But the Hegelian dialectic of knowledge can be adopted – transposed and re-cast – into an open dialectic of freedom (which we can do no more than indicate here). What is, in fact, the necessary presupposition of the dialectical movement? It is not matter – which is in any case only the penultimate stage as an opposite – but the reality of the free will, the real opposite of the Spirit's knowing. This in fact is what was recognized by Hegel when he placed the *decision* to arrive at true knowledge at the outset. The freedom of the subjectivity is the condition of possibility of true objectivity. Since freedom determines the self-consciousness of the Spirit as it comes to know, it is never fully absorbed by it. Its immediacy is not lost in the process of mediation, of which it is the permanent and all-pervading foundation. This makes it impossible to reduce the "other" to a mere moment in the self-apprehension of the subject, as the totality of the Spirit embraces both. It is the specific law and function of the will to achieve "in" the object the identity of the Spirit as subject and object. Hence the ultimate must necessarily be the affirmation of the other qua other.

In contrast to the necessary essences and all-embracing unity of a purely cognitive system, we have the finite which is permanently valid in its diversity and multiplicity, the individual which is permanently significant, a historicity which is free and not summed up already, the hope of the new and the hopeful act in creative fellowship. In the space thrown open by a dialectic of freedom, the constructive elements in Hegel's thought retain their real force: the intensity of experience, the relentless effort to close in on the concrete, the resolution of over-rigid schemes of thought, the reconciliation of ostensible opposites, the manifestation of the spiritual structure of all beings – compare the scholastic transcendental, "omne ens est intelligibile" – and the meaningful contradiction ot the contradictoriness of things. The free reality of the human spirit which dialectic supposes experiences itself, in its truth-obscuring fragility, as posited by a primordial freedom. It is welcomed and wooed to its own selfhood.

5. *Theological significance.* We may now consider the theological significance of an open dialectic. The structural law is provided by the metaphysics of creation: "The closer a being is to God . . . the greater is its natural tendency to self-realization" (Thomas Aquinas, *De veritate*, 22, 4). The degree in which true selfhood is realized is the co-efficient of the constitutive transcendental relation to God, who gives and sustains being creatively, and it is also the co-efficient of free mastery of self. Dependence and freedom are here not in inverse proportion, but are dialectical equivalents of each other. The creative freedom of God makes men free. The supreme liberating inauguration of human being in its essential fulfilment takes place in the personal union of the Logos-God with human nature in Jesus Christ. Its effective expression is also in the fellowship, the *one* earthly and eternal community of the "Christus totus caput et membra" (Augustine) in the Spirit of the unity of the Father and Son – called grace (*ad intra*) and Church (*ad extra*). Here too, in the expansion beyond space and time of the fundamental union of God and man in Christ, "grace presupposes nature" – in the literal ontological sense of "positing it beforehand" – "and fulfils it". In the creative, incarnational, grace-giving and Church-founding event of the union, which makes man freer and freer, we can see manifested and active the "immanent" Trinity of Father, Son and Spirit, which is the primordial instance of personal relation and mutual constitution in the spirit, and hence of dialectic.

At the same time, the original event of Christ, with the liberating installation of man in the Spirit-fellowship of the *Christus totus*, provides the universe for all the further dialectical traits, which now, with a certain inevitability, make up Christian faith and life: the relationships of presupposition as between faith and knowledge (and on a higher, more systematic degree of reflection, between philosophy and theology); history and revelation; human *religio* and the gospel of the apostles of Jesus; letter and spirit; sacramental gesture and word; love of God and love of the neighbour. All of which is given unfathomable depth by the relation of opposition between human sin and divine redemption (cf. Rom 5:20f.), in the cross of Jesus Christ: the utterly real and not merely "speculative" Good Friday.

Walter Kern

DISPOSITION

1. A being which is changing, which acquires new determinations, states and attributes, requires certain conditions either intrinsically in itself or in its external circumstances, if it is to be able to receive the new determinations, etc. These conditions are called a disposition for the new determination, to which the disposition stands in the relation of potency to act (in the widest sense of the term). This relation may be found in all orders of reality, so that there are physical, juridical and moral dispositions. The relationship of condition, between disposition and "act", may derive from the nature of the two realities, e.g., mathematical knowledge as condition of the solution of a prob-

lem of calculation. Or it may be the result of legal enactment, e.g., a certain age for episcopal consecration. The disposition may "demand" the "act" (e.g., economic production requires remuneration) or not (e.g., canonical age is required for ordination but gives no right to it). A disposition may always be present or may be produced specially. To bring it about may be a duty or may be left to a person's discretion. In certain circumstances it may be brought about by the act for which it is to be the disposition, or by another cause. The lack of a disposition or the impossibility of producing it may entail the absence of the act or the impossibility of achieving it. It must not be overlooked, however, that God as omnipotent cause standing outside the system of finite, temporal things, can always produce a disposition if he absolutely wills the act for which the disposition is meant to prepare. For example, God can produce the repentance which is the disposition for forgiveness of personal sin. Consequently, the doctrine of the necessity of a disposition for a particular grace (justification) does not involve any diminution of the sovereignty and power of the grace of God.

2. The doctrine of disposition has an important field of application in the Catholic theology of grace and justification. If a human being who is fully capable of using his reason and freedom is to obtain justification (sanctifying grace), certain free acts intrinsically ordained to salvation (*actus salutares*, acts of faith, hope and contrition) are absolutely necessary (*D* 797ff., 814, 817, 819, 898), by the very nature of the case – the freedom of the person and justification itself. The first antecedent grace which in the very first instance makes possible such salutary and disposing acts (supernaturally elevating grace) and which in fact effects these acts in their very freedom (efficacious grace), is independent of any moral disposition on the part of man. God can bestow it even on the sinner who has no merit to show for it. There is no "natural moral merit" as disposition for saving grace as Pelagianism held (*D* 811, 813). The first salutary movement of man towards God, which is then a disposition for man's further advance in salvation, occurs without any disposition morally effected by man as its condition. It occurs by the free initiative of God's grace, in which God gives grace on account of his universal salvific will. Consequently, the whole process of salvation remains until its perfect fulfilment (and despite all merits) based on this initial disposition which God alone has produced by his grace without prior religious or moral conditions on the part of man. Where, however, such a salutary act is freely posited through God's grace, its "degree" (i.e., its actual personal and potential depth and resoluteness) is a disposition for further salutary activity and as such the "measure" of the grace (e.g., grace of justification) bestowed for this further salutary activity (*D* 799).

3. The concept of disposition is also used in the field of sacramental theology. An adult must prepare himself for the reception of a sacrament and for the grace of the sacrament, for despite their character of *opus operatum* the sacraments are not causes which operate magically (*D* 799, 849, 819, 898). In other words, the adult must not have merely the intention of receiving the sacrament, but for the fruitful reception of the sacraments he also requires a certain disposition, faith, hope and at least an inchoative love (as in contrition). This disposition which is ultimately dependent on the efficacious, freely bestowed grace of God, but which is freely brought about, is the measure, but not the cause, of the grace given by the sacrament as instrumental cause (*D* 799). Yet it must be noted that the sacrament itself as a religious event and by the grace offered in it, can

deepen this disposition or even produce it where it does not exist, so that in this way the grace offered in the sacrament finds in the disposition the measure of its acceptance.

It is an urgent task of sacramental theology and of preaching on the sacraments to bring out even more clearly the unity of the objective action of God in man by grace in the sacrament and the subjective salutary action of man occurring in grace (which is precisely the "disposition"). We must not be content casuistically to determine the minimum disposition for the various sacraments and so encourage the prejudice that the sacrament does the rest, or does so if received with the maximum frequency (Eucharist, sacrament of penance). It is meaningless to increase the frequency with which a sacrament is received if there is no growth in the personal moral participation by the individual in the accomplishment of the sacrament, i.e., in his disposition. In the case of sacraments which can be validly received without being fruitful (sacraments which confer a sacramental character: *D* 852; and matrimony: *D* 2238), the disposition can be supplied or personally deepened after the reception of the sacrament and so the effect of the sacrament can be obtained or deepened. It is important to realize this, particularly on account of the practice of infant baptism. Pastoral endeavour ought to promote the rekindling of sacramental grace on a higher level (baptism, priestly ordination: 1 Tim 4:14; 2 Tim 1:6; matrimony) by deepening the personal attitude to a sacrament already received but lasting in its effects. This may be done by preaching, devotion, meditation (renewal of baptismal vows, e.g., at the Easter Vigil, retreats for married couples, the celebration of sacerdotal jubilees, etc.). This is no make-believe but true growth in sacramental grace.

Karl Rahner

DOGMA

I. Theological Meaning of Dogma

A. Dogma in Christianity

1. For an understanding of dogma and its necessity in terms of a philosophical anthropology, it is to be noted that there is a transcendental necessity for man as mind and spirit (and consequently for every human society) to affirm certain truths absolutely. And this in principle has to be done through their conceptual formulation (though in certain circumstances this may be of a merely pre-scientific kind), at least in logic, formal ontology and ethics. This necessity can only be contested and denied self-destructively. Consequently man's existence is essentially a "dogmatic" one. It can be shown that since man must act he must to some extent necessarily affirm some contingent facts as unconditionally valid. In view of this, historical revelation and the acceptance of propositions to be affirmed absolutely cannot be repugnant to man's nature. The absolute character of the claim and obligation of dogma is addressed precisely to man's freedom; dogma expresses a truth which can be rightly heard and attained only in the free decision of faith (*D* 798, 1791, 1814). And freedom as knowledge in action achieves its own true nature only in absolute commitment. Dogma and freedom are, therefore, actually complementary terms. Precisely because the Church proclaims dogma (and not in spite of doing so), it must appeal to and respect this freedom (*D* 1875; *CIC*, can. 752, § 1; Vatican II: Declaration on Religious Freedom).

2. The actual nature of dogma is not, however, deduced solely from the abstract idea of divine communication of truth and its obligatory character, but from revelation in the concrete. For a) revelation is the saving event, in which God communicates himself to the free, spiritual person and does so in such a

way that the immediate recipient of the communication is the community, the Church, which is constituted precisely by this. And b) this self-communication by God has reached its definitive, eschatological stage. For by God's definitive and unsurpassable saving action in the incarnate Word, revelation is concluded (because it now directly opens out on the vision of God), and God's definitive word is present (even if embodied only in the enigma of human speech). Consequently, dogma now exists in the full sense of the absolute and supreme claim by which ultimate salvation and perdition is decided. Hence dogma is not merely a statement "about" something, but one in which, because it is an "exhibitive" word with a "sacramental" nature, what it states actually occurs and is posited by its existence: God's self-communication in grace which is also the grace of its absolute acceptance (faith). In the proclamation and the hearing of dogma in faith, therefore, what is affirmed is itself present.

3. Dogma has an ecclesial, social character. For the revelation which is the ground of dogma is addressed and entrusted to the Church, and is so in the unity of its three elements, as word, as event and as the revealed and communicated reality of God himself. The Church is both hearer and preacher of God's revelation. The latter does not cease to be God's word because it is spoken by the Church. Consequently, dogma is not only the unifying pattern of a common act of hearing but also the unifying pattern of God's word being addressed to all. And since this word remains the ever-new event of God's gracious self-communication in the history of the Church, and therefore always has to be spoken afresh, there has to be dogmatic adaptation and development of dogma (and not merely of theology) and history of dogma. Since in the proclamation of dogma the one, identical and definitive revelation of God in Christ takes place which has taken place once and for all (ἐφάπαξ), dogma is the *form* of the abiding validity of the tradition of the deposit of faith in the Church which itself remains always the same. Dogma helps to constitute the unity of faith and makes it visible. Consequently, when it is determined and proclaimed, there always occurs not only a manifestation of the reality to which it refers, but also a terminological determination of common linguistic usage. The definition of a dogma often consists just as much in fixing the common mode of expression as in distinguishing between true and false propositions.

4. To the extent that dogma is God's absolute self-communication in the form of human truth to the Church and through the Church, it is integrated into the religious act. For this act has a complex but unified structure, deriving from the very essence of man, comprising and actualizing all his powers in its circumincession; it therefore itself is "life". Dogma as believed is in itself "life" and, provided it is rightly affirmed and personally assimilated, stands in no need of any subsequent defence in respect of its value for life. In itself it is a source and standard of authentic piety.

5. Since God's word is announced in human terms, dogma is in vital contact with the whole mental life of man. It employs in principle not only the common terms of every day but, like Scripture itself, can use the terminology of human learning and science if the needs of a particular intellectual situation require it. Usually in doing so it critically modifies them and to some extent brings them nearer to everyday usage. Such a use does not, however, sanction a scientific or philosophical system itself. Everyday language and that of science and learning are not after all essentially different. Conversely, knowledge of dogma provides a spur to building up a Christian philosophy, such as may be used in apologetics.

B. Nature of Dogma
Dogma in the sense in which the term is used nowadays in the Church and in theology (a usage which only became definite and universal in the 18th century) is a proposition which is the object of *fides divina et catholica*, in other words, one which the Church explicitly propounds as revealed by God (*D* 1792; *CIC*, can. 1323, §§ 1, 2), in such a way that its denial is condemned by the Church as heresy and anathematized (*CIC*, can. 1325, § 2; 2314, § 1). It may be so propounded either by the ordinary and universal magisterium or by a papal or conciliar definition. The decisive characteristics of dogma (divine origin, truth, the obligation to believe it, immutability, incarnational structure as a genuine union of divine and human unmixed and undivided, etc.) are therefore dealt with under more general headings such as revelation, faith, theology, the ecclesiastical magisterium. The declaration that a proposition expresses a dogma is also the highest theological qualification.

Two elements are therefore required formally to constitute a dogma. a) A proposition must be set forth by the Church explicitly and definitively as a revealed truth (formal element). This does not necessarily require an express definition. b) This proposition must belong to divine, public and official Christian revelation (in contrast to private revelation). Consequently, it must be contained in the word of God addressed to us in Scripture and/or tradition (material element).

The declaration of Vatican I on the object of *fides divina et catholica* (*D* 1792) makes this the unambiguous and generally accepted definition of dogma. A few questions regarding more detailed interpretation remain open, however, and are controverted in theology. These are chiefly the following.

a) The question how exactly dogma taught by the ordinary magisterium can be distinguished from the rest of its teaching which is not, or not yet, presented explicitly and with absolute finality engaging the whole authority of the Church's magisterium, as revealed by God. On this matter the admonition of *CIC*, can. 1323, § 3, must be noted, but at the same time it must be remembered that in the concrete the practice of Christian faith can never relate solely to actual formal dogmas. The latter are only possessed in a personal way appropriate to the nature of the Church if they are assimilated in connection with other knowledge, convictions and attitudes. Consequently, the importance of drawing an exact distinction between the two must not be exaggerated, and in fact is not possible with absolute precision (cf. *D* 1684, 1722, 1880, 2007f., 2113, 2313).

b) The question how we are to think of dogma as being contained in divine revelation. It is indubitable that much is taught by the Church today as dogma (and therefore as contained in revelation) which was not always taught as such or even consciously recognized as such. Consequently, the essential condition of forming part of revelation can doubtless be satisfied by one truth being contained in another truth. The question is, therefore, what "implication" (on the first use of this term in the language of the magisterium cf. *D* 2314) is necessary and sufficient for it to be possible to regard a proposition derived from primary revelation as still constituting a communication from God attested by God himself, and believed on this ground because of his authority (formal, or merely virtual implication; virtual implication which requires for its explication a material premiss not derived from revelation, or explication purely within considerations themselves revealed; a kind of implication different from that of formal logic; subjective or purely objective implication). No unanimity of view has been reached by theologians in these questions. Post-Tridentine theology was for the most part inclined to regard as potential dogma only those propositions which can be explicated from the original deposit of faith by a rigorously formal logical procedure without the use of "natural" premisses. At the present time, however, in view of the actual facts of the development of dogma there seems to be an increase in the number of theologians who also identify as potential dogma propositions which explicitly formulate what was "virtually" implicit. These theologians endeavour in various ways to explain, by various interpretations of this virtuality, why propositions of this kind can also be considered as communicated by God himself and as directly guaranteed by him.

c) The question whether dogma and defined proposition are identical or not, i.e., whether in addition to dogma there can be other defined truths of the Church, guaranteed with absolute authority by the Church, and if so, which (dogmatic facts; truths of a purely "ecclesiastical faith", which is not an act of faith in the word of God as such but which is directly based simply on the [divinely appointed] authority of the Church as such [Catholic truths]).

C. Division of Dogmas

1. *According to content and scope*. General (fundamental truths of Christianity) and special (particular) dogmas (fundamental articles, articles of faith, *regula fidei*). Although of course the formally equal value of all dogmas as guaranteed by God and definitively held by the Church must be emphasized, a division of this kind is justified. For according to the reality signified, dogmas have objectively different importance for salvation (cf. Vatican II, Decree on Ecumenism, art. 11). For this reason canon law, for example, does not qualify every heretical denial of a dogma as total apostasy from Christianity (can. 1325, § 2). The strictest measure regarding fundamental dogmas is applied when a distinction is drawn between dogmas necessary or not necessary for salvation. This is determined by whether they must be believed explicitly for salvation to be possible – either because they are a necessary means or prescribed as necessary (*necessitas medii – necessitas praecepti*) – or whether a *fides implicita* in them is sufficient. Since God's revelation, the teaching authority of the Church and divine faith refer to "theoretical" and to "practical" affirmations, these various types of proposition can all be dogmas.

2. *According to their relation to reason.* Dogmas pure and simple (only knowable through revelation: mysteries in the strictest sense), and mixed dogmas (the contents of which can also be known by natural reason). Even on the supposition that truths which really are wholly accessible and intelligible to reason can also be believed by a person who knows them, mixed dogmas still differ from the truths of reason materially identical with them. For when they are attained and believed on the basis of the whole of revelation and saving faith, they present their content under a supernatural formal object, in a context and with the aspect of pure dogmas quite inaccessible to the apparently identical affirmation of reason. On the other hand, such dogmas are an expression of the fact that God's revelation really concerns the actual world of man himself. They show that articles of faith are not *a priori* propositions relating to some particular function of man, but involve the whole reality of man.

3. *According to the way they are propounded by the Church:* formal and (simply) material dogmas, according to whether the formal element in dogma (cf. B 1a) is already present or not.

D. Modernist Conception of Dogma

Negatively, the concept of dogma in Modernism was characterized by a) the rejection of an authentically supernatural reality and consequently of a mystery which can only be known through a personal self-disclosure on the part of God. "Dogma" expresses man's experience of himself in his religious indigence and only in that way something of the "divine". Another feature was b) the rejection of the genuine possibility of intellectual statement of the reality to which dogma refers, a statement which would belong to the constitution of religious experience itself. For Modernism, the conceptual, intellectual proposition which constitutes dogma is not merely "inadequate" to the reality signified, nor is it an "analogical" statement, which orientates and directs man into mystery utterly beyond his scope. For Modernism, dogma is secondary and derivative as compared with religious experience, which can possess the reality signified, in total independence of conceptual expression in dogma. Viewed positively, dogma, according to Modernism, is a derivative expression of religious experience, unavoidably necessary for the religious community, but always subject to revision or even to change into its contrary, and religious experience itself is given an immanentist interpretation (cf. *D* 2020ff., 2026, 2031, 2059, 2079ff., 2309–12).

Karl Rahner

II. Development of Dogma

A. Revelation and Dogma

1. "In many and various ways God spoke of old to our fathers by the prophets; but in these last days he has spoken to us by a Son." (Heb 1:1f.) These words indicate the progressive character of God's revelation which culminated in Christ. In him the final and definitive stage of that history has been enacted: in Christ God has spoken his final and unsurpassable word to men. What went before Christ (the OT law) was a preparation, a training for the revelation that is embodied in him, for the faith we must have in him (Gal 3:23ff.). "For all the prophets and the law prophesied until John" (Mt 11:13); but Jesus is the fullness of revelation; he says of himself, "All things have been delivered to me by my Father, and no one knows the Son except the Father, and no one knows the Father except the Son and anyone to whom the Son chooses to reveal him." (Mt 11:27.) Jesus revealed to the apostles all that he had "heard from the Father" (Jn 15:15). But this text, which must be interpreted in the light of other texts, only means that Jesus has revealed all that is necessary to salvation. After the Ascension, therefore, the supreme work of the Holy Spirit is to recall Christ's words to the apostles' minds (Jn 14:25). Now Christ was revelation in his own being, not merely by his preaching but also by his life, death and resurrection, because all this manifests the mystery of God's salvation to us. Man's response to God speaking is faith, the acceptance of a message (or testimony) from God (Jn 3:11f., 32–36). A purely human interpretation of the life, death and resurrection of Jesus would be only human speculation, not the word of God, and as such, unacceptable to faith. But the apostles are authentic and privileged witnesses and interpreters of Jesus' own revelation. Thus St. Paul says of his gospel (the interpretation of the Lord's life, death and resurrection): "I did not receive it from man, nor was I taught it, but it came through a revelation of Jesus Christ." (Gal 1:12; cf. 1:16f.) Probably Jn 16:12–15 refers to such inspired interpretation of Jesus' spoken message. Such interpretative additions are limited by their object, since they are always confined to the mystery of Christ, the new messianic order of salvation; cf. Lk 18:30. They complete the preaching of Jesus (i.e., give it its fullness by teaching "all the truth", those many things which according to Jn 16:12 Jesus still had to

say), which is why Jesus declares that the Spirit "will take what is mine".

2. This process of authentic interpretation of the message of Jesus, through inspired meditation on the saving acts of the Lord, and hence not restricted to human insight but aided by revelation, is restricted in time to the age of the apostles and of the primitive apostolic Church. In any case we must sharply distinguish between the foundation period of the Church (apostolic age) and its subsequent history. This the Church has done by condemning the proposition: "Revelation, constituting the object of Catholic faith, was not completed with the apostles" (*D* 2021; cf. also 783, which presupposes this doctrine by linking "the purity of the gospel", which the Church must preserve, with that foundation period). No doubt it was with the same idea in mind that the apostles themselves looked on their message as a deposit that must be faithfully preserved (1 Tim 6:20; 2 Tim 1:13f.), without any alteration or addition (Gal 1:8f., where St. Paul repudiates "any gospel contrary to [παρ' ὅ, outside] that which we preached to you"). This deposit is a "paradosis" (2 Thess 2:15; 3:6): transmitted by the apostles, who received it from the Lord (cf. 1 Cor 11:23), it must be handed down from age to age because the gospel must be preached until the end of time (Mt 28:20). The first sub-apostolic generation is well aware of the dividing line. The Apostolic Fathers consider themselves different from the apostles (for example, the *First Letter of St. Clement*, 42; St. Ignatius of Antioch, *Letter to the Romans*, 4, 3) and base what they say on apostolic doctrine (*1 Clem*, 42, 1f.), a deposit received from the apostles (St. Polycarp, *Letter to the Philippians*, 7, 2) to which nothing may be added and from which nothing may be taken away (*Didache*, 4, 13; *Barnabas*, 19, 11). The sub-apostolic Church holds that its first duty is to preserve the deposit of revelation.

As an absolute guarantee of that mission, the Church and its supreme shepherd the Pope have been promised "the Holy Spirit, not so that by revelation they might make known new doctrine, but so that by the assistance of the Spirit they might preserve inviolate and faithfully expound the revelation handed down by the apostles, that is, the deposit of faith" (*D* 1836, with reference to the successors of St. Peter; but they are endowed with the same infallibility as the Church and for the same purpose; cf. *D* 1839). Notwithstanding the faithful preservation of the deposit, certain truths contained in it may on occasion recede into the background. Perhaps, indeed, such a thing is inevitable. Considering the wealth of content in Christianity and the limitations of man who is called on to live that religion, it is never possible for all Christian truths to occupy the foreground of interest and attention at the same time. But neither can the Church ever repudiate or lose a revealed truth, or allow the central truths of the gospel to become obscured (*D* 1501; cf. also 1445).

B. Problem of Development of Dogma

1. On the other hand the Church's duty is not simply to preserve the deposit of revelation but also to interpret it, authoritatively setting forth its content (*D* 1800, 1836). It must preach its message in every age and to every nation, which obviously involves more than the mere repetition of set words. The constant effort which the Church must make to convey its message in intelligible terms leads to a growing understanding of that message. Furthermore, since the gospel is chiefly concerned not with obvious truths but with mysteries that do not carry conviction of themselves, a Christian who accepts the gospel by faith, relying on the authority of God who attests it, is induced as it were automatically to make

an effort to grasp the objective content of his religion (cf. St. Thomas, *De Veritate*, q. 14, a. 1, 6). Now this effort is the deepest sense of theology as the understanding of faith and the noblest function it has, though understanding is limited by the mystery of God. Further, as St. Thomas says (II, II, q. 2, a. 3, ad 2), when we make this effort, the grace by which we make an act of faith (the light of faith) gives us a connatural knowledge of the thing that is believed. This connaturality in the act of faith is always a new kind of adhesion to the object of faith (*De Veritate*, q. 14, a. 8, c.); but it may also, by a sort of instinct, give one a better understanding of that object. This process goes on both in individual Christians and in the Church as the holy people of God, as a supernatural *sensus fidei*. In the latter, it is the infallibility, since this efficacious grace means that "the faithful as a whole, who have received the anointing of the Spirit (cf. 1 Jn 2:22, 27) . . . cannot err in faith" (Vatican II, Constitution on the Church, art. 12). It is by this operation of grace that Christ brings about in his mystical body "the growth that is from God" (Col 2:19), "until we all attain to the unity of the faith and of the knowledge of the Son of God, to mature manhood, to the measure of the stature of the fullness of Christ . . ., from whom the whole body, joined and knit together by every joint with which it is supplied, when each part is working properly, makes bodily growth and upbuilds itself in love" (Eph 4:13 and 16).

2. This growth in our understanding of the gospel becomes dogmatic development in the strict sense when the fuller insight that has been reached is infallibly proclaimed by the Church's magisterium to be a truth contained in the deposit of revelation, that is, a dogma (cf. *D* 1792). The solemn promulgation is the climax of the process, which now enters the express understanding of the official Church. The historical fact of development is undeniable, however it is to be explained, since certain dogmas cannot be found as truths of faith before a given moment in history (the truth concerned may have been known before but the Church did not teach that it was revealed), or the truth as such was not yet known at least in its present form.

3. If revelation is a deposit that has been complete since the end of the apostolic age, then the new dogmas must have been objectively contained in the deposit from the start. For only what has been really "said" by God (in his revelation and in the interpretative words accompanying the history of salvation – which is always more than can be communicated as propositions through the medium of Church preaching) can be the object of faith. Whether this includes conclusions deduced from the data of revelation with the help of non-revealed premisses, is a matter of controversy. And the mode in which a later dogma is objectively implicit in the original revelation, and subjectively explicated has not yet been adequately explained theologically. Hence there is no uniform Catholic view of how the climax of a development is contained from the start in the deposit of faith, that is, of what are the objective limits of the development of dogma. It may be said in general, however, that a clear distinction must be made between the development of dogma and the apostolic task of making the truths of faith one's own in a process of intellectual elaboration. Now that no new public revelation could be looked for, such a process would seem to be a human creation, not a message from above which the Christian could believe as God's word. The goal of dogmatic development must be a truth which can be the object of divinely-revealed faith, and it would seem that the only possible object of divine faith is what God has actually said, taken in the same extension as is the human word (an extension sometimes wider than the implicit content

that is discoverable by purely logical analysis), and not what can be deduced from God's word. It will not do to argue that God knows what deductions can be drawn from his word: that fact does not make such deductions a part of his word. When God is pleased to use human words, what he says must be understood according to the rules governing human language.

On the other hand, the Church's definition of a dogma is purely declaratory: the truth defined must be God's word beforehand, and nothing the Church may do can make it so. At any rate it is important to stress the fact that while the term of the development of dogma must be objectively contained in the deposit and must remain demonstrably of a piece with it, still, as the word of God, the new dogma may well evolve otherwise than by logical analysis of the gospel. By virtue of the connatural knowledge of faith, certain goals of dogmatic development may be attained by a procedure insufficient to generate logical certainty and using only arguments of congruity. Once the dogma has evolved, the task theology has of showing its homogeneity with the deposit will sometimes be a difficult and delicate one. The theologian is not always helped in his search by any guidance from the magisterium, which on occasion simply defines that a truth is revealed without giving any indication of where it is revealed.

4. Now in saying that the growth of dogma is rooted in understanding of the deposit, we have suggested the forces behind that growth (cf. Vatican II, Constitution on Divine Revelation, art. 8). The Church's infallible magisterium takes the final step, bringing the process to a close and sanctioning it, presenting a truth to Catholics as a dogma to be believed (cf. *ibid.*; also *D* 1792). It is within the framework of this concern to answer the questions men ask that the role of heresy in the development of a number of dogmas needs to be considered.

Theological reflection is a second factor in development. It has undoubtedly a vital function in the Church and stems from the psychological need of clarifying the truths of faith. Theological reflection, insofar as it is the *intellectus fidei*, and not mere deduction in the Aristotelian sense of a (theological) science, is obviously a factor of the development of dogma in the strict sense. Only such efforts to understand the faith can give rise to "truths of faith" which were included in the original deposit. Such reflection is stimulated by the same factors as work on the magisterium, though very often the work of understanding better proceeds to a certain extent independently of outside forces, when the very obscurity of an element in the deposit invites reflection.

A third factor is the consciousness of faith or the instinct of faith (*sensus fidei*) in the faithful as a whole, founded on the grace-given connaturality of this sense with the objects of faith (Vatican II, Constitution on the Church, art. 12). The living faith which guarantees knowledge by connaturality works above all in the realm of Christian spirituality and life. This explains the preponderant role of the *sensus fidei* in the development of the Marian dogmas, according to many theologians (Dillenschneider). Meanwhile, the distinction between the Church teaching and the Church learning was generally understood to signify that the latter was a passive partner. But there is no such thing as passivity under the action of grace. A proper understanding of the role of the faithful in the development of dogma throws light on a profound saying of Paulinus of Nola: "Let us seek the word of God in all things. Let us hang on the lips of the faithful, since the Holy Spirit inspires them all." (*Ep.*, 23, 36.)

5. This list of factors which influence the development of doctrine in one way or another shows that the history of dogma and the lines along which development proceeds are fully contin-

gent. Had historical conditions been different, other themes would have emerged. But the contingency of the lines of development does not mean that the results arrived at are contingent. All that comes under an infallible declaration of the Church, which is the last stage of the development of dogma, is absolutely irreformable (*D* 1800, 2145). Nonetheless, this infallible answer to a previous question can open up avenues to new questions. The ensuing answers will form new stages in dogmatic progress which will gradually explicitate further what is already acquired. The immutability of definitions does not impede further development (*D* 1800). This also shows that though dogma is necessarily expressed in a given language making use of the concepts of a given culture, the multiplicity of potentialities means contingency of growth but not deficiency in the results. Infallibility excludes the use of inappropriate terms (and has always done so). If, therefore, certain terms have not only been used by general councils but explicitly ratified by them, we are not free to depart from such terms (*D* 2311).

Candido Pozo

III. History of Dogma

A. As a Theological Discipline

History of dogma as a theological discipline and an integral part of dogmatic theology itself, is the methodical, systematic investigation and exposition of the history of the various individual dogmas and of the whole Christian understanding of faith, studying the mutual relations of its various constituents and its relation to the themes and epochs of the history of ideas. In contrast to the history of revelation, the history of dogma begins with the close of revelation in Jesus Christ and of the apostolic preaching. Yet even in Scripture it discovers its subject-matter in paradigm, because in Scripture itself "theology" is already found (even though it is theology guaranteed by inspiration), which may be distinguished from the original revelation-event. Consequently there is already development of dogma there.

Since dogma does not consist only of explicit definitions of the extraordinary magisterium, the distinction, possible in principle, between the history of dogma and the history of theology cannot always be clearly effected. As a result, the history of theology is mostly written as part of the history of dogma. At the basis of the history of dogma lies the fact of the development of dogma and at the basis of this the intrinsically temporal, historical character of man, and therefore of his knowledge of truth. For dogma is God's truth heard, believed and formulated in human historically conditioned terms by man in this world. Moreover, dogma is a living function of the Church, which in an essentially historical and socially articulated process has to accept, make explicit and proclaim the truth bestowed and guaranteed by God himself, in ways appropriate to the ever-changing intellectual perspective of the world around it. The method of the history of dogma is a *theologically* historical one. It is not merely a part of the general history of civilization and religion, but a theological discipline, and therefore regulated by faith. At the same time, however, it is genuine critical history using the method proper to such history. The unity of the two methods is possible because it is already present in the inquirer and in the subject-matter of the history of dogma: genuine *history* under *grace*. The history of dogma inquires into the meaning and scope of dogmatic propositions (and therefore cannot wholly be separated from dogmatic theology), but does so in order to determine and understand the history of these propositions; it is therefore not dogmatics pure and simple. It also comprises the greater part of the history of heresies, because the meaning of dogmatic definitions is often clearest when they are confronted with their contradictories.

History of dogma establishes the meaning and scope of the various dogmatic propositions, compares them with one another, traces the development of the formulas employed, discloses the forces at work in their development (objective, personal, cultural, social, etc.), endeavours to grasp the dynamic trend of that development towards the future and so to prepare future dogmatic theology. It does not seek only what remains the same in the same faith under its changing forms (the apologetical aspect of the history of dogma), but also the differences and sequence of these changing forms themselves. It does so, not only because it is only in this way that the meaning and justification of the later statement of the faith (perhaps formulated in an actual definition) is made clear, but also because only in this way is the fullness of the Church's awareness of its faith manifested. For the history of dogma does not advance only in linear fashion from the less explicit and less determinate towards a more explicit formulation incapable of any further improvement. In principle the history of the understanding of the faith is always incomplete and open towards the future. The past ("tradition") always remains as source and critical measure of what comes later and is never fully replaced by later formulation in such a way as to be rendered superfluous for dogmatic theology itself. It follows that genuine history of dogma can only be pursued in living contact with a dogmatic theology which exposes itself to questions set by the actual preaching of the gospel today and tomorrow.

B. As Subject-Matter of Historical Research

1. *Preliminary hermeneutical considerations.* It is impossible of course to recount in detail here the history of all the statements of faith in dogmatic theology. Even a brief survey, if it is not to confine itself to the purely external facts of a few of the most important dogmas, depends on whether some fundamental features and structures of this history can be indicated. This in turn depends on whether despite the incalculable freedom of this history on the part of God and of man, it is possible to find an objective guiding principle for its formal division into epochs which would make it possible to analyse it in a theologically appropriate manner. On account of the close relation between Church history (assuming that this is understood and analysed in a truly theological way) and history of dogma (as a decisive factor in the former), it is to be expected from the start that the structural principle sought must be identical with, or a specification of, the principle of a theologically interpreted Church history. This refers us to what was said about this structural principle of Church history in the article on Christianity, which must be considered again here in regard to the specific features of the history of dogma. It becomes clear that for the purpose of the analysis, methodical arrangement and characterization of the history of dogma, it is possible to make use of the encounter and dialogue between the understanding of the faith formed within the Church and the world situation which confronts and makes demands upon that understanding. This does not mean that the determination of the structure of the history of dogma is given over to a random element alien in character to the nature of dogma and its history. For on the one hand the history of dogma itself develops as a history of the faith which is aware that it is called responsibly to answer for its hope (cf. 1 Pet 3:15) and the promise accepted therein. And on the other hand a theological interpretation of the "secular" intellectual situation and its history

would show that this itself is disposed by God in relation to the growing attainment of full self-awareness in the understanding of the faith. And since its coming, Christianity has contributed to determine that situation even in the apparently secular domain. Consequently Christianity encounters itself in that situation, often in something Christian which the Church has not yet explicitly realized. The actual history of dogma took place, therefore, not in the style of a purely logical continuity of statement and explanation, but in the perpetual interaction of sacred and secular history, history of faith and of thought, which cannot wholly be displayed in theoretical form. Of course, to a history of dogma composed on this basis, further subsidiary divisions would have to be added for its more precise articulation: in regard to organization (what institutions actively promote the historical growth of dogma and theology?), history of style (interaction of history of dogma and literary history), individual history (the uniquely great thinkers of original creative power), social history (theology in its dependence on a particular social and economic situation), Church history (interaction of history of theology and other aspects of Church history), etc. All these in turn are mutually interdependent. It is impossible here, however, to go into such patterns of arrangement and division.

2. On the basis of these hermeneutical considerations the following can be said about the phases and course of the history of dogma.

a) Just as Christianity only reached its full development as the universal religion of all nations when it found tangible historical realization among all nations and civilizations through the intermediary of the unity they had historically achieved in a "world civilization", so too the Church's dogma. It too only attains its own full development when as a message of salvation in the course of history it encounters, in a dialogue involving both partners, the whole mind of the world in the epoch of world civilization, and by this dialogue contributes to determine the further course of history and shares in it, in a manner which cannot be foreseen today. In this perspective, the history of dogma has two great epochs, that of the process of the attainment of this full development and that of global dialogue with the entire unified (which does not mean peacefully reconciled) mind of humanity. The first fundamental period is only now slowly coming to an end, the second only just beginning (cf. Vatican II, Decree on the Church's Missionary Activity). From this point of view, the whole previous history of dogma was "local", the dialogue of faith with Judaism in the time of Christ, Hellenism in Roman antiquity and the Occident later. All this contributed to make the Church a competent partner in the dialogue which divine revelation was to continue with the world as a whole. The great task of earlier times was to show, in the actual process of dogmatic development which the Lord of history and not men's deliberate thinking engineered, that the message of Christianity is not tied to any particular stage or region of man's self-understanding. This meant that the understanding of the faith had to be detached from the mental horizons of Judaism and Hellenism, to become, as it ought to be, a dialogue with the "world".

In the latter process, the Church has to take cognizance, in an ever-increasing measure, of three truths. The first is that it is permanently confronted with a permanently distinct secular partner, which demands a growing acceptance of the "worldliness" of the world, of its relative autonomy, of its basic inability to be fully "consecrated", of the powerful forward drive of its dynamism, the resulting distance between Christianity and any given, stable order of social and political economy, etc. The second truth is that the Church really has a message for the life and history of this partner. This means a growing knowledge in faith of Christian anthropology with its bearings on the secular sphere, where it insists on the free personal subjectivity of man, greater theological insight into the nature and foundations of natural law, into the need for the "humanization" of man individually, into the possibilities and ethical bounds of man's self-manipulation, the rejection of an esoteric indifference to a sinful world to be abandoned to its corruption, etc. The third truth is that the Church must uphold against the world all that is most truly its own and not of the world. This is the story of the defence and interpretation of its supernatural message about God and his gracious self-communication against efforts to reduce it to a human ideology, the story of the "discernment of the Christian spirit", of a theology of the endless task of detachment from the world, which justifies the action of the Church. These are the three truths which had to become more and more clear and explicit – in many concrete forms, no doubt, which cannot be fully embodied in a system – in the former period. It is on this basis that the faith of the Church can now take up in earnest the dialogue which is now beginning with a unified and independent world.

b) To some extent, therefore, this first great period of the history of dogma (and of theology) permits of further analysis. Measured by the usual themes and divisions of the traditional history of dogma, this analysis may apparently not be very sharply defined and profound, but it should be remembered that the importance for personal salvation of later formulations of dogma as compared with earlier, and therefore of the history of dogma in this respect, should certainly not be exaggerated. In this case, too, what is more important is the enduring element in the Church. Consequently, the structural analysis can only really be based on the notion of the encounter with successive epochs in the history of civilization. This principle, however, rightly makes some of the changes and advances in the history of dogma appear less significant than they seem in a history of dogma written on purely positivist lines. The first great period of the history of dogma can perhaps be divided theologically into phases as follows, to give a general sense of the movement of ideas which took place in it.

(i) The history of dogma in the *primitive Church*, which for the most part took place in Scripture itself. Here the early Church's new sense of faith was expressed spontaneously and directly with the means available in the world of the OT (and only marginally with those of Hellenism). Precisely by doing so, it went beyond the mental perspectives of that world. What was radically new (the universality of the gospel of the absolute mediator of salvation in death and resurrection) was envisaged on the basis of the divinely ordained OT (theology of the fulfilment of Scripture), and so had to preserve continuity with (Rom 9–11; opposition to Marcion), and distinction from, its prehistory (the Pauline theology of freedom from the Law; polemics against the Jews; theology of separation of the Church from the Synagogue, cf. Letter of Barnabas).

(ii) The theology of the first contacts with *Hellenistic civilization*. In the 2nd and 3rd centuries the universalism of the message of the Christian faith, disengaged from the particularity of its origins, met for the first time a mental perspective of a certain universality – a philosophy and (to a certain extent) a world-empire. For the boundaries of the Church coincided in practice with those of the Roman empire. On the other hand, within those frontiers there was a "pluralism" of East and West etc., which later took on in fact tragic dimensions: schism, cessation of dialogue between Eastern and Western theology. This first encounter, still under the cross of persecution, produced, as was to be expected, a first general response which, as a comprehensive outline (details of which therefore were to be worked out later), was to serve as a permanent model. The response to secular universalism (Hellenistic Gnosticism as the catchment of Eastern and Western conceptions of man, a "system" with religious application) inevitably developed in two directions and phases. On the one hand there was the defensive self-affirmation of revelation from above against its absorption in human Gnosis; the conquest of Gnosticism by the theology of saving *history* together with the first theology of tradition and the formation of the Canon (Irenaeus). On the other hand there was in a positive sense the first attempt at a systematization of the Christian faith with Hellenistic instruments, with all the dangers this involved, as Origenism shows. The negative and positive dialogue with the real world led to the beginnings of a theology of martyrdom and asceticism (virginity: Methodius), and also, in opposition to an esoteric conception of the Church in Montanism and Novatianism, a theology of a soberly realistic but affirmative relation to a truly redeemable world (where "canon law" had a place).

(iii) The third period extends *from the turning-point under Constantine to the beginning of "modern times"*, comprising, that is, the theology of the "imperial Church" of antiquity and that of the medieval West. This is ultimately a single period because despite the change in ethnic substratum the same mental perspectives dominated (Platonism and Aristotelianism as a cosmocentric philosophy). Both in Roman and medieval times Christianity was involved in the same task, that of assimilating a civilization already to some extent formed by Christianity, even in its distinctive rational, secular and dynamic character and which was (because of this providential fact) to be the active agent of the creation of the intellectual unity of the world in the second great period.

Significance for the theology of the imperial Church. This meant a theology of the radical distinction between God and world in opposition to the latent panentheism of Arianism, the elaboration of an orthodox theology of the Trinity in which the Logos and Pneuma, the principles of the economy of redemption, are not derivatives of the true God but are the absolute God himself. The Trinity continues to be seen as "economic" and for just that reason, as immanent. In this way there was also preserved, both as a matter of course and in opposition to Manichaeism, at least the outlines of a theology of a good created world established in its own reality by God. The temporal, historical character of man, of salvation and of faith itself was firmly maintained in principle against an (ultimately Gnostic) closed system of the world, by maintaining the doctrine of the "resurrection of the flesh" and rejecting that of apocatastasis. Protology and eschatology, however, scarcely advanced theologically beyond the statements of Scripture.

There was a theology of the radical acceptance of this world distinct from God, through the elaboration of orthodox Christology balanced between separation (Nestorianism) and confusion (Monophysitism, Monotheletism). In Christology the Christian conception of the general relation between God and the world finds expression during this period: the closest proximity of the world to God is also its most complete liberation to be itself.

Other matters remain unsettled or an open question for the West, or else are only found discussed in a rudimentary way; the true relation between Church and world (the State) is still (despite

Gelasius) to a large extent obscured by an imperial theology of the sacred state (in Byzantium), and this was only really shaken for the first time in the investiture controversy. Augustine developed for the first time a universal theology of history, but in such a way that the danger of an identification of "Christian" State and God's Kingdom (represented by the Church but not identical with it) was not yet banished; in Augustine (in particular by his doctrine of free grace for the individual in his personal life of salvation which is not simply an aspect of the cosmic and "incarnational" process of divinization), the first outline of an existence-centred orientation is found. But this is linked with a questionable pessimism as regards salvation after original sin. In his opposition to Donatism he upholds an institutional conception of the Church, but his appeal to the secular arm against Donatism linked Church and State in a questionable way that was to have grave consequences.

Significance for medieval theology in the West. In the same fundamental perspective "progress" in the history of dogma can broadly be characterized as follows.

At first there was a fairly complete systematization of Christian dogma with the help of an Aristotelianism of Platonic and Augustinian stamp (cf. the theological *Summas*). This meant an approach to dogma in a cosmocentric and not in a "transcendental" or personal, existential, anthropocentric or really historical perspective. But it also meant, at least in principle, the emancipation of a secular philosophy relatively independent of faith and theology. By way of the doctrines of the independence of secondary causes (Aquinas) and of the supernatural character of grace, it led for the first time to a recognition of the independence of the secular world and at the same time represented a unity of world and Christianity, though one conditioned by the age.

There was a clearer distinction between the Church and the world. An initial theological analysis of the social constitution of the Church showed its independence of the State (even a "Christian" State). The relation between collegiality and primacy was not yet worked out, as Conciliarism shows. There was still a tendency to incorporate the secular order directly and completely into that of salvation and its mediation by the Church. Hence the notion of the *corpus christianorum* and the *sacrum imperium*.

(iv) The theology of the *transition from a culturally and intellectually restricted milieu into the situation of the world Church*. Wherever this era of transition to modern times is considered to have begun, as early as Aquinas or in the later Middle Ages, at the Reformation, the Enlightenment or the French Revolution, at all events its end has come, broadly speaking. This is reflected even in the Church. Vatican II's dialogue was with the world as a whole, with non-Christian religions and with "atheism", in "religious freedom". That era of transition constituted the period of immediate preparation (more or less well exploited) of the Church and especially of its theology for the present "pluralistic" world which is being rationalized and humanized by technology. That preparation involved the ecclesial and theological mastering of the pluralist situation within Christianity itself by elaborating distinctive doctrines in the face of the Reformation (in controversial theology), and by entering into positive discussion with non-Catholic Christians (in "ecumenical theology"). The "emancipation" of the world continued, as progress was made in the doctrine of natural law, in the theory of society (*ius gentium*) and a distinctively Catholic but flexible social doctrine. There was optimism about salvation, in contrast to Jansenism, and the rudiments of a positive theology of non-Christian religions. The Church recognized its distinction from other social structures of secular society and its autonomy and capacity for independent action (Vatican I and II). The Church proclaimed more clearly the essentials of Christianity against the theology of the Enlightenment and Modernism. It disengaged itself from a particular mental perspective determined in advance by the conditions of a particular epoch and place by the admission of historical criticism into exegesis and theology and the advent of the history of dogma and of biblical criticism. There was a growing familiarity with a limited pluralism of philosophical systems through recognition of an Eastern theology and through growing acceptance of the anthropocentric transcendental philosophy of modern times and of a philosophy of the temporal, historical nature of man, as possible instruments of orthodox theology. There developed a theology of freedom and of personal conscience in a pluralist civil society. The conflict between natural science (theory of evolution) and theology was gradually eliminated. Post-Tridentine Scholasticism of the Baroque period was itself a phenomenon of transition. As in the Middle Ages, the attempt was made with considerable success to construct a vast system which would integrate into itself the whole secular view of the world. At the same time, however, theological understanding slowly began to respond to the new situation that was approaching. Examples of this were the first attempts at historical theology, the independent pursuit of philosophy, the development of international law, of the psychology of faith, of freedom under grace.

C. Relevance to Pastoral Activity

1. The pastor today must have some knowledge of the history of dogma. Only in this way can he announce the Word of God with the inner flexibility which is necessary today precisely in order to preserve true orthodoxy. If he is to have the courage to open out new perspectives and to change relative emphases, he must know how rich in variety of perspectives and emphases the history of the Church's preaching and theology has been. He must have learnt from the history of dogma that serious questions and profound difficulties regarding faith can often only be dealt with slowly. In this way he will be ready in his own situation to practise patience and hope in faith. Through his studies in the history of dogma he should have learnt to go beyond monotonous repetition of dry catechism statements and to draw on the wealth of tradition as a whole.

2. The pastor should realize that he plays his part in the advance of the history of dogma. Preaching the faith is not merely repetition of a simplified theology, but an anticipation of theology. Its living vigour, its problems and solutions carry the history of dogma onwards. And it is precisely that dynamic movement towards the future of preaching which ought to give life and energy to the pastor and which gives the question of the past the gravity and significance without which the history of dogma would degenerate into mere erudition.

Karl Rahner

IV. Dogmatics

1. *General description.* Dogmatics is the science of the Church's dogma, i.e., systematic reflection undertaken on methodological principles appropriate to dogma and aiming at as comprehensive a grasp of it as possible. This involves reflection on everything necessary or helpful, in method or content, for the understanding of dogma. As in every branch of knowledge, reflection on its own history is an integral part of dogmatics. Its first and proper object is Christian revelation (from the formal point of view: fundamental and formal theology; from the material point of view: "special" dogmatic theology).

This also includes those dogmas which concern the Christian accomplishment of man's salvation in nature and grace and which therefore have a directly moral significance.

Since dogmatics is a part and indeed the central part of Catholic theology, it is a science of *faith*, i.e., it is pursued by the believer in the light of faith. For all its scientific reflection, therefore, it is a "committed" knowledge of the saving self-manifestation of the triune God in Christ and in the Church as his Body. And because revelation and dogma primarily exist as the faith of the Church, dogmatic theology from the start is an ecclesiastical science. It is of course always pursued by individuals, but its starting point is always the Church's kerygma, as heard, believed and announced by all the faithful and the Church's ministry. And it returns to the Church's understanding of its faith as source of an understanding of the faith which develops and is perpetually renewed. Kerygma (and its derivative, dogma) is of course always a summons calling for men's actual submission to the mystery of God. But it has a content, for it is the proclamation of the historical saving deeds of God (and of the ultimate, "eternal" structures implied in them: dogma as concerned with "essences"). Dogmatic theology, therefore, also has a historical and "metaphysical" content. In many respects it remains a historically-conditioned discipline (depending on historical presuppositions of the prevailing world-view etc.). Yet the historical situation which is properly its own is that of the definitiveness of historical revelation in Christ. This does not diminish the divinely-created and grace-endowed reality of the world or nullify analogical statements about it ("affirmative" theology); but through this revelation, direct and permanent access to the enduring, "silent", adorable mystery of God in himself is available, really, and not merely ideologically or in mystical contemplation ("negative" theology as an intrinsic constituent of truly Christian theology, and one which must permeate the whole). Through this historical "eschatological" situation which is proper to it, dogmatic theology always transcends the historical limitations which in other respects affect it.

2. *Distinction from other theological disciplines.* a) *From moral theology.* By the themes which constitute its content, moral theology remains intrinsically a part of dogmatic theology. For God's self-communication in grace and faith is a theme of dogmatic theology precisely because this self-communication of God himself (as the very substance of revelation as such) is the principle of man's action in regard to salvation. Now moral theology rightly understood concerns precisely this kind of human activity. It is only on practical grounds, therefore, that (since the Baroque period of Scholasticism) it has – quite rightly – been established as a separate discipline. This was done in particular because in this section of dogmatic theology many auxiliary sciences have to be called upon which do not concern the other sections of dogmatic theology. But even with the present-day division of these branches of study for technical reasons, dogmatic theology does not relinquish themes of "moral theology" (*De peccato; De gratia*; *De virtutibus infusis*, etc.), and in Vatican II's Decree on Priestly Formation, moral theology is strictly charged not to neglect its authentic dogmatic origin and purpose.

b) *From exegesis and biblical theology.* Scripture is, of course, always the *norma non normata* of all theology, because it permanently opens out for us genuine access to God's definitive self-disclosure in Jesus Christ. But biblical theology as such (and the exegesis which it presupposes) cannot itself be dogmatic theology or take its place. This is so even if it is assumed that biblical theology, being an ecclesiastical science, must be carried on within the Church's understanding of its faith and not merely as part of the scientific study of religion. Precisely because it is to be a critical (and therefore distinct) standard and a perpetually fresh source of dogmatic theology (*D* 2314), biblical theology must not seek to take over the task of demonstrating and critically testing the legitimacy of its own exegesis in the history of the Church's teaching, throughout the history of the development of the Church's dogma. Nor should it attempt to effect the "actualization" of the message of Scripture in order to renew the kerygma of the Church in the encounter of the Church's understanding of the faith with whatever is the predominant secular conception of man. This quite apart from the question of the relation in which non-scriptural tradition, in the "material" sense, stands to the content of Scripture (cf. on this the cautious formulas of Vatican II in the Constitution on Divine Revelation, according to which at least the extent of the Canon and the inspired character of the absolute norm of faith *cannot* be derived from Scripture alone, so that Scripture itself requires a "dogmatic" foundation supplied by the understanding of the faith by the Church and its tradition). Precisely these tasks which cannot be fulfilled by a biblical theology as such are those of dogmatic theology. This distinction between the two in no way settles of course the loftier question (which is omitted here) whether at least biblical theology (as opposed to purely textual exegesis) is nevertheless not actually, in a profounder and more exact theological methodology, an essential constituent of dogmatic theology itself. The latter after all has to listen to Scripture itself (the *themata biblica*: Vatican II, Decree on Priestly Formation, art. 16) and not merely supply *dicta probantia* from Scripture for its own theses.

c) *From fundamental theology*. From its nature as the demonstration of the credibility of the actual occurrence, i.e., existence, of Christian revelation, fundamental theology is certainly distinct from dogmatic theology, which is systematic reflection on the content of faith. Yet two things must not be overlooked. Fundamental theology is a theology of Christian *faith*, not metaphysics and philosophy of religion. Furthermore, at the present day in particular, a purely abstract, formal demonstration of the credibility of the existence of revelation would seem to be insufficient. Nowadays each of the various mysteries of faith requires an initiation into its credibility and the possibility of its actual concrete assimilation by the individual. Only such initiation in its totality, therefore, would represent an adequate demonstration of the credibility of revelation. Whether such a task should be carried out to a large extent by special dogmatic theology alone (dogmatic theology cannot renounce the task entirely) or whether fundamental theology itself is to assume the task, is a secondary question, of a more technical and pedagogical kind, which cannot be settled here. In the latter case fundamental theology would certainly be considerably extended, and in a certain way would have to keep before it the whole of dogmatics and interpret its fundamental affirmations in relation to the "credibility" (concrete assimilability) and so perhaps discover the true nature of that *cursus introductorius* which the Vatican II plan of studies calls for without precisely determining in what, from the methodological point of view, it consists.

d) *From other theological disciplines*. All other historical and regulative theological sciences can be summed up and distinguished from dogmatic theology by the fact that though theological disciplines, they relate to history and the (desirable) action of the Church insofar as this is not determined solely by its enduring nature, i.e., by dogmatic ecclesiology. These sciences include, therefore, Church history with the history of liturgy, history of law, history of ecclesiastical literature (patrology and the history of theological literature, history of theology); practical theology (i.e., canon law, pastoral theology with catechetics, liturgical studies, homiletics). These disciplines study the Church as it appears in the human contingencies of history and in the action flowing from the authority for free decision granted to the Church together with the norms of such action: the Church as the (divinely effected) response of men to God's word.

3. *Methodology of dogmatic theology*. An important instruction is given in the Decree of Vatican II on Priestly Formation (art. 16). Dogmatic theology must be *positive* theology, i.e., it must begin with the "biblical themes" and the history of the continued proclamation of the biblical message of salvation by the Church in preaching, authoritative doctrinal pronouncements, history of dogma and history of theology. But then it also has to be "speculative" and systematic, i.e., it has to serve a really personal assimilation of the truth as heard historically. That, however, demands a confrontation of the revealed truth heard with the totality of the hearer's (transcendental and historically-conditioned) conception of himself and of the world. Of course the two phases of theological work in dogmatics, the historical and the speculative, cannot simply follow one another chronologically, for they mutually condition and involve one another. It is noteworthy that the decree of Vatican II is clearly departing from the too exclusively analytic dogmatics of later Scholasticism and neo-Scholasticism, in which the "positive sources" were consulted too one-sidedly simply in support of certain traditionally prescribed theses. Historical revelation should obviously be listened to receptively and serenely, even for what is not already current in the explicit consciousness of theology. Living dogmatic theology is also always a "philosophical' work, for any particular conception of man and the world is expressed principally in the prevailing philosophy of the age, while dogmatic theology speaks in human terms (just as revelation itself does). Now these human terms require perpetually to be called in question anew, both in the light of revelation itself and of human experience (transcendental and historical).

This does not mean that dogmatic theology presupposes a complete philosophical conception of man which has come into existence absolutely independently. On the contrary, obedient hearing of revelation alters the historical situation of philosophy and therefore philosophy itself. In fact it is quite conceivable that dogmatic theology in the future may integrate philosophy into itself even more fully, because it is the more comprehensive and more radically concrete and vital study, and nothing really philosophical can remain entirely a matter of indifference to it. Only theology itself can consider the method of its listening, because this is determined by its own proper object (the historically personal self-manifestation of the absolute God to the free consent of faith and love, not to mere *theoria*). Hence from the critical point of view of theology itself its object comprises metaphysics (as statement of the hearer's self-comprehension) and also hermeneutics, for dogmatic theology is also fundamental and formal theology, though it cannot be reduced to hermeneutics. Theory of historicity and historical experience on the one hand and history and its concrete experience on the other are never purely and simply identical. And salvation consists in encounter with historical reality itself, not merely in the acceptance of formal historicity.

4. *Inner structure of (special) dogmatic theology*. The fundamental difficulty of an intrinsically appropriate arrangement (articulation) of dogmatic theology lies

in the fact that its object is at once "essential" and "existential". The revelation of God which finds expression in it is not primarily a doctrinal communication of truths in propositional form comprehensible in themselves independently of the moment of time of their communication. That moment is not merely extrinsic to them. Revelation and its history is at one and the same time salvation and history of salvation. "Revelation" as God's *action* among men, which, it is true, has an intrinsically constitutive gnoseological factor, can therefore only be received in historical experience which remains alive and is correctly heard as anamnesis and as "prognosis" (hopeful statement about the future as the accomplishment of what is experienced). Consequently, dogmatic theology must be an account of sacred history. It must be a historical science not only in the handling of its "sources" but also in regard to its object. It can therefore never simply be concerned with "theological conclusions", simply taking its highest "premisses" for granted. At the same time, however, dogmatic theology is necessarily a study of essences and to that extent systematic: the history recounted has a unity and a coherent structure which have to be taken into consideration, and which need to be examined in a general, formal and fundamental theology. The basis of that history is always the permanently identical reality which has a history and which has to be grasped theologically: God's one turning in grace to the world. In it the immutable essence of God appears. And that history has entered the eschatological phase in which the historically contingent and the essential, in their historically conditioned and changing mutual relationship, have converged definitively and indissolubly (and only as a consequence of this is it possible really to distinguish them). That history has therefore reached the phase in which the Church pursues theology according to its content and also its form.

On the basis of the unity and difference of the historically existential and essential aspects of all dogmatic theology, it is understandable that there cannot be a compulsory and universally received structure and consequent articulation of the various dogmatic tractates. It is only possible to explain the chief kinds of emphasis of possible dogmatic theologies. At one extreme there is a dogmatics which is almost purely and simply an account of redemptive history. At the other there are those which are either almost purely systems of theological conclusions, assuming the history with its content as a prior datum, or else consider practically nothing but the formal structures of that history and their incorporation in a formal theology of the enduring structures of the history of redemption and revelation or in a hermeneutics of the manner of their incorporation. A "pure" type of dogmatic theology would contradict the inner plurality of its object and claim presumptuously to grasp adequately the unity of this object.

Karl Rahner

DUALISM

A. Notion

In general, dualism, in contrast to monism, is used to describe the view which reduces reality to two equally primordial and mutually opposed principles. The various forms of dualism are determined by the ontological natures of these principles and by the manner of their opposition. Since the total reality can neither be simply two realities which have nothing at all to do with each other, and it cannot be simply one reality, the question of how the historical forms of dualism are to be understood involves the basic question of the origin of, or the ultimate relationships and distinctions between, all reality. A readiness to condemn out of hand the historical forms of dualism could lead one to miss the real problem, just as much as if one refused to investigate the nature of the unity of reality. Dualism cannot be avoided by taking refuge in the (false) alternative of simple unity, but only by clarifying the relationship between duality and unity.

Purely speculative theorizing on the problem cannot provide a solution. The actual duality-in-unity of existence cannot be realized and resolved except in the duality-in-unity of the dialogue which is lived out in the love between the "I" and "You". But since man has renounced this love by original sin, and hence has falsified his relationship to himself as well as to God, existence, both in the individual and in society, must always be experienced as to some extent dualistic. This existential dualism, affecting man to his very core because it is a dualism of personal relationships and of the will, is the most radical of all forms of dualism. Man can ultimately prescind from all other forms of theoretical or practical dualism, but not from the dualism of man himself in his deliberate self-contradiction as sinner. This contradiction in man's will which he is impotent to obviate strikes home all the more violently because it is also projected on to God, and so is reaffirmed as a quasi-metaphysical dualism – as a contradiction between what is and what ought to be.

In face of this distress which plagues all human existence throughout its history, all facile speculative attempts at reconciliation remain unconvincing. Hence for instance, throughout the history of religions various types of dualism sought to express themselves directly in more or less mythical forms. But this effort to provide man with symbols of salvation for the understanding of his destiny remained unintelligible to abstract conceptual thought. The direct interpretation of life offered by such religions has a justifiable tendency to choose contradictory images, of which the intrinsic mutual relevance generally has to be divined. But the experience of existence given in Christian faith also knows the pain of being torn by conflicting imperatives. This contradiction, since it cannot be attributed to God's antagonism, is felt all the more sharply as a flaw in all experience within this world. And so far from being always resolved at once by faith, it rather becomes more acute. Indeed, it is only in the initial experience of salvation that it can be fully revealed. This existentially dualistic situation, tragic because combining salvation and doom, cannot be resolved by any theoretical reflections. The believer can only hold out under it, in a hope inspired by the initial experience of salvation, till the unimaginable mode of salvation is realized definitively in actual truth. Nonetheless, it is always the Jewish-Christian religion which counteracts the hardening of the various forms of existential dualism into the finality of metaphysical determinism, to which the contradiction in the will so readily resigns itself.

B. The Morphology and Theory of Dualism

1. *History of philosophy*. Western philosophy begins with the question of the *one* "material element" which persists throughout all change and is the principle of all things. Abandoning the mythical explanation of reality, this quest for the elements or the one basic element – the ἀρχή – of the cosmos erects into a "principle" the unity experienced in the multiplicity of reality and so induces a mentality which henceforth urges the thinker to look for the ultimate grounds of reality. Since it is never a search for one isolated ultimate principle, but for the unity-in-duality of this principles with its own reality which it has itself produced, the history of the quest for the origin of all reality is also the history of various types

of monism and dualism which combat or complement each other.

Though the first exponents of natural philosophy among the Greeks tried to reduce the cosmos to one primordial element – Thales, for instance, to water, Anaximenes to air and Anaximander to "the unbounded" (ἄπειρον) – the question of the connection of all reality in the one ἀρχή suggested in each case was not explicitly raised. But Heraclitus and Parmenides posed more clearly the problem of the ultimate opposites and their compatibility (immutability and movement, imperishability and finiteness, truth and appearance). Inspired by the traditional (Eleatic) understanding of being, and also by the thinking of Socrates, a fundamental metaphysical dualism crystallized in the philosophy of Plato, with the opposition of the "forms", the authentic eternal being, and the appearances of this being, which make up nature as it comes to be and passes away. This duality between eidetic, authentic being and the non-being (μὴ ὄν) of transitory appearances cannot be an absolute dualism in the mind of Plato, since the form of all forms, the good, is ultimately the source of all beings. For Aristotle, the form exists essentially only as the form of concrete substance, combining with the "matter" informed by it to make up the concrete sensible thing. But though it is true that Aristotle's hylemorphism constitutes a fundamental advance on Plato, it is scarcely possible to bring together in a unified relationship the basic elements of his philosophy – matter and form, act and potency, immortal νοῦς ποιητικός and mortal νοῦς παθητικός, unmoved mover and moving world, supralunar and sublunar cosmos.

When Greek philosophy was adopted by Christianity, the Fathers and the scholastics opposed all forms of radical or metaphysical dualism, in the light of their faith in the one God and creator – Augustine, for instance, basing himself on Plato and the distinction between sensible and suprasensible being, as more sharply delineated by Plotinus; Thomas Aquinas interpreting the νοῦς of Aristotle as transcendence orientated to the God beyond the world, who is the origin and principle of all reality. On the whole, Greek philosophy, in spite of its initial quest of the one ἀρχή, displays a tendency towards a dualistic conception, while the following age of patristic and scholastic thinking was inspired by faith in the oneness of God – reinforced in the Middle Ages by the notion of the hierarchy of being – and strove to eliminate all metaphysical dualism. But here too the *prima principia* were not systematically thought out in view of their intrinsic and mutual relationships; such systematizing only flourished in modern times.

Nicholas of Cusa was mainly preoccupied by the problem of the union of the ultimate opposites, not merely in his speculative thought, but as a dominant element of his whole life. The themes of the *coincidentia oppositorum* which he developed were later to engage the attention of German idealism, under the headings of "identity" and "difference". Modern pre-Kantian philosophy is characterized by the more radical way in which it poses the problem of the ultimate opposites, which it approaches in the light of the Cartesian dualism of *res cogitans* and *res extensa* and the "pre-established harmony" of Leibniz.

Kant brought the whole of his speculative effort to bear on the problem thus posed, endeavouring to grapple with dualisms which his own empiricism and rationalism made even more pointed, and seeking either to reduce them to a synthesis in the unity of a critical philosophy or to reject them entirely. Nonetheless, it may be said that Kant is still haunted by a dualism which affects the two sources of knowledge, sense perception and intellect, and appears in the distinction between the thing in itself and its sensible phenomenon, between moral duty and inclination and between practical and theoretical reason in general.

Fichte attacked the problems left by Kant with an energy and a drive for systematization of unique intensity. He reduced all reality to three principles, each intelligible in the light of the others, all being modes of manifestation of the one primordial origin, which, however, is not itself a principle and is only known as a limit or in the positing of a limit. Fichte's thought was always dominated by the question of the ultimate difference between, or the twofold unity comprising, the Absolute (God) and absolute appearance (creation). The basic theme in Hegel and Schelling is also "identity and difference".

While Fichte left open the questions posed by the contradictions of history, which he held could not be solved by speculative theory, Hegel, though taking these contradictions equally seriously, tries to see them as ultimately resolved in the absolute "idea" or God, as the "identity of all identity and non-identity". Under the influence of German idealism, especially that of the Kantian type, Schopenhauer attributes the cleavage throughout nature to the blindness of will, and since for him the world is only will and representation, his main interest is to rid himself from the will itself which is the source of all contradiction. This he tries to do through art, *ascesis* and inward mortification, understood in Buddhistic terms.

The trend of positivist and materialist philosophy since Hegel was to pay little attention to systematic principles of thought. Dualistic themes like matter and consciousness, body and soul, reason and instinct, the contrast between sciences of the mind and of nature were treated on a rather naive level. Nietzsche's declaration of war on Christian morality and indeed on all Christian and idealistic thought stemmed from his conviction that these doctrines of salvation really promoted dissociation, and was carried on with a passionate longing for the undivided life which by creating its own transcendence ultimately makes itself its own God and can thus abandon all dualistic types of self-expression. Heidegger's approach was to show that the miserable state of man was due to the erection of the subject-object dualism into an absolute, and that this dualism itself sprang from the predominance of conceptual thought. With the effort to surmount this by means of essential thinking, that is, thought directed to the relation between subject and object as such, and to the whence of this relationship, "being", understood as a transcendent communication, Heidegger finally tries seriously to abandon all thinking in terms of systems, to try to say simply how the event of existence comes about as the there-ness of being.

2. *History of religions*. In the cosmological dualism of the cosmos-centred thought of China, the whole life of the universe is set in motion and sustained by Yin and Yang, the opposition of the male and female. The religion of Zarathustra, in the form, that is, of Iranian Mazdaism, understands the history of the world as the struggle between the equal and opposite forces of good and evil. In the Samkhyra philosophy of India, which must be regarded as a soteriological dualism, salvation comes through the separation of soul and body. In Plato's anthropological dualism the body also appears as the prison of the soul (*Gorgias*, 493a). Gnosis also seeks liberation from the body to enable man to ascend to the heavenly world of light.

In the apocalyptic of late Judaism an eschatological dualism gradually develops, which regards the history of the world as an aeon of misfortune, death and sin, at the mercy of wicked demons till the other aeon dawns which is full of goodness and blessing: "The Most High has not made one aeon but two" (*4 Esdr*, 7, 50). The conflict between chthonian and uranian gods, represented, for instance, in Greece by the struggle between Zeus and the Titans, among the Germans between the earthly Vanas and the heavenly Aesir, can be termed a numinous dualism, which is intensified when the godhead itself has two visages, as in many Indian religions – for instance, Varuna and Indra. These religious dualisms rarely see themselves as such, since they do not reach the stage of conscious and articulate reflections. They are a way of reacting directly to destiny, in an effort to use such images to attain self-understanding and mastery of life.

3. *Biblical theology*. Faith in the one Lord who is creator and lord of creation's history rules out of course on principle any absolute form of dualism in the OT. Nonetheless, it leaves room for Israel to display its strength of mind in its refusal to attempt facile reconciliations of the unfathomable contrast between sin and forgiveness, misery and salvation. This uncompromising realism persists into the NT, where the new experience of salvation is still expressed antithetically, especially by Paul and John. The dialectical movement of Paul's thought, faced with the enormous task of at once combining and separating Judaism and Christianity, can find expression only in the form of antithesis: the law and the promises, works and faith, flesh and spirit or the old and new man, the inner and the outer man. The Gospel of John is dominated by the experience of the opposition between light and darkness, grace and law, life and death, truth and the lie, spirit and flesh.

4. *Dogmatic theology*. It was first necessary to refute Marcion, who appealed to Paul to set up a contrast between the God of might of the OT and the God of mercy in the NT, proposing therefore a dualism between the Old and New Testaments. At the same time Gnostic and Manichean dualism, appealing to the Gospel of John, had to be rejected. When the great dogmatic themes of God and the world, grace and freedom, faith and knowledge came to be enunciated, the forms of expression chosen were those of a modified or restricted dualism which maintained the oppositions and refused to adopt the short-sighted solutions of monism. Hence the rejection of pantheism, predestination and (absolute) Pelagianism as well as of fideism and rationalism. The basic (soteriological) problem, the surmounting of the existential dualism of the "mystery of iniquity" by the "mystery of salvation", is left open for an eschatological solution. Nonetheless, it is the task of present-day theology to attempt an explicit reconciliation of the dualism between Church and world, word and sacrament, office and charism and so on. In general, dogmatic theology must reflect more purposefully on itself and its history, for its self-understanding and justification, since only a dogmatic theology of this self-searching type can perform the heavy task of studying theology as a consistent whole and thus avoid the dualism which threatens to separate dogmatic theology from exegesis.

Eberhard Simons

E

EARLY CHURCH

The early period is of particular importance in Church history, as is seen not only from the long debate on the subject but above all from the intrinsic structures of the early Church, which grew out of its unique situation and problems. It is also a historical unity, clearly distinct from the following Constantinian period.

A. The Demarcation

The early Church covers the period from about A.D. 30 till its recognition as a religion of the empire under Constantine the Great (306–37). Though the Church only became "established" in course of time, basically under Theodosius I (380), the decisive change came at the beginning of the 4th century, with the change in the State's attitude to religion, as evinced by the Edict of Toleration under Galerius (311) or the Peace of Milan, between Constantine and Licinius (313). It would be wrong, however, to over-emphasize the new externals of the Church at the expense of historical continuity. Still, this turning-point shows how closely the Church is linked with world history, even for the demarcation of its chronological stages.

The three hundred years of the early Church can be divided according to internal factors.

1. The apostolic and sub-apostolic age is basic for the whole history of the Church. When this, the "primitive Church", is regarded as the age of the giving of revelation, it is primarily the concern of NT history. But without prejudice to the unique importance of the ἀποστολικοὶ χρόνοι (Eusebius, *Hist. eccles.*, III, 31, 6), when revelation was committed to writing, the notion of primitive Church may well be extended to take in the following period, up to Irenaeus of Lyons (*c.* 180), when the mind of the Church was formed as regards the extent of the apostolic testimony to Christ – the period of the formation of the canon. This extension of the notion is also justified by the fact that it was in these years that the "église naissante" (P. Batiffol) developed its characteristic structures – the personal and oral transmission of tradition and the formation of creeds in the struggle against heresy. Though the origin and development of such forms pose many problems, on the whole the period is characterized by its determination to take on ecclesiastical form.

2. In the following period, *c.* 180–313, these structures already determine essentially the image of the Church, which claims a universal mission in the Roman empire. It has rightly been

termed the period of the Great Church, in view of its numerical growth, its constitutional development and its intense theological activity. The 3rd century prepared the ground for the development which ensued in the following ages. In spite of intense persecutions on the part of the State, the Church presents itself to a crisis-racked empire as a ferment of unification. It makes Greek and Hellenistic culture its own in a resolute and flexible process of adaptation. The history of the Great Church is that of a growing openness to the world of the empire, where a unity of Church and State is achieved once more when the religious policy of Constantine begins to aim at an imperial Church. Thus the history of the Church from the death of Jesus to its recognition by the State displays a consistent trend, which allows us, and even forces us, to see it as a well-marked whole.

B. Phases of Development

The aptness of the divisions outlined above still leaves room for problems with regard to the individual phases. On the whole, schematic verdicts take the finer points of research into account. But there is often disagreement on details, due in part to the special (dogmatic) implications of this period.

1. *The primitive Church.* This period is naturally the most debated, since the characteristic structures of the Church were determined by its origin. NT research is decisive in our verdict on the genesis of the Church, which based itself from the start on faith in Jesus of Nazareth as Christ and Lord. Conscious of fulfilling Jesus' will (the acts whereby he founded a Church), the believing community came together and proclaimed him, from Pentecost on, as the promised Messiah. But this faith, the response to the word of the hidden Messiah and the exalted Lord, did not merely launch the Church, it remained constitutive of the people of God all through its history.

a) The first concrete manifestation of the ἐκκλησία is the primitive community of Jerusalem, its faith and theology nourished by the traditions of Israel but also influenced by special trends among the Jews. Parallels are drawn in particular between the Qumran community and the primitive Church, though the independence of the latter, in the central fact of faith in Christ, remains unquestionable. But Jewish Christianity went on to develop in various ways by no means free from tension. And its theology and Church order were still strong influences in the early Church after the catastrophes which befell Jerusalm in A.D. 70 and 135. Following in the footsteps of Jewish missionaries, Judaeo-Christians spread the gospel outside Palestine, especially eastwards. This activity, which soon gave rise to heterodox trends, was reflected for centuries in the Christian writings "adversus Judaeos".

b) We must not underestimate Jewish Christianity, but the turning-point in Church history was the mission to the gentile Hellenistic world, initiated by Peter (Acts 10:48) and carried on vigorously by Paul. The emancipation from the Law asserted in this type of preaching was ratified at the Council of the Apostles (49 or 50), which meant an official break with Judaism. Freed from the restrictions of the Law, the Church threw itself open to Hellenistic culture with its far-reaching effects on language (Bible, liturgy), thought-forms (theology, dogma) and sociological structure (the State). The subsequent interchange left its mark on the Church both in its imposing universality and in the limitations thus placed upon it. The new orientation did not affect the legitimacy of the Jewish-Christian branch, but it led in practice to the general acceptance of the structure of gentile Christianity – a process conditioned by historical factors and for that very reason of supreme interest.

c) The missionary urge of the primitive Church was obviously not inhibited by apocalyptic expectations of an imminent parousia. The structure of the communities also assures us that believers were prepared for an "intermediate period" from the start and hence could absorb the delay of the parousia without too much shock. New problems were posed thereby, but their importance also came from their being symptoms of Christian existence in history. This perspective explains the increasing emphasis on pastoral and paraenetical elements, which is apparent as early as the pastoral letters and makes itself strongly felt in the Apostolic Fathers. Obviously, there was a certain relaxation of Christian effort which led to the Christian message of salvation being presented as a code of morals. And ecclesiastical regulations did not simply result from disappointment about the parousia, but from the desire to fortify the Church during the "intermediate period" (Acts 20:18–35). As early as apostolic times, the constitutional organization of the Church set in, on the basis of the office of the apostles, which went back to the institution of Christ. Existing models suggested themselves, especially the organization of Judaism under "elders", which was adopted by the primitive Church. Out of this collegiate structure the monarchical episcopate crystallized. It soon became the dominant office in the Church, as the precedence of the charisms gradually disappeared.

Under pressure of circumstances, even greater emphasis was laid on Church office in post-apostolic times. In the struggle with the advance of heresy, the revelation received from the apostles was linked more strongly with the bearers of office. In particular, the timeless myths of Gnosticism in all its forms were opposed by a history-centred tradition and the succession of the ancient episcopal sees, especially of Rome (Irenaeus). Thus, to preserve the purity of the gospel, the primitive Church adopted a constitution in which local and universal Church formed a closely-knit but thoroughly pluralistic unity, a κοινωνία which the celebration of the Eucharist fostered and voiced.

To designate this process as "Proto-Catholicism" (*Frühkatholizismus*) is to assume a norm for primitive Christianity which can scarcely be justified historically, but must be arrived at by an interpretation aiming at the heart of the gospel. The transition from a purely biblical and charismatic Christianity to the institutional Church of history is already reflected in, for instance, Acts. That the initial stages of "Proto-Catholicism" are already evident in the NT supports the (Catholic) conviction that the early Church was essentially identical with the Church of the beginning.

d) The theology of the primitive Church is characterized by the effort to formulate the faith in terms of NT vocabulary, using suitable thought-forms of Hebrew or Hellenistic origin. The needs of preaching, liturgy and apologetics gave the process a doctrinal orientation. Judaism had to be shown that Jesus of Nazareth was the fulfilment of OT *testimonia*; the heathen world demanded a new approach, quite apart from the discussion of polytheism, which is clearly depicted in the works of the early apologists. The adoption of Hellenistic categories was not without danger, but was on the whole a missionary necessity. It was the only way in which the Christian message could find an echo in the world of paganism.

e) The Christian Churches and hence the primitive Church suffered from being a minority, and had to be content with a subordinate role, in numbers and social status, among the many religions of the Roman empire. Nonetheless, the constant intercourse between the local Churches shows that they had the sense of an all-embracing unity. Though holding itself aloof from the world, the primitive Church was ready to come to terms with the State, recognizing precisely its earthly authority (Rom 13). Persecution in this period was rather the result of a ground-swell, manifested in local upheavals in the nature of pogroms. The loyal addresses of the apologists to the emperors heralded the fundamental conflict between Church and State.

2. *The Great Church of early Christianity*. The epoch of the Great Church began about the end of the 2nd century. In spite of oppressive measures Christianity became firmly established numerically and structurally and so paved the way for the Church of the empire.

a) The growing importance of Christianity is best shown by the systematic character of the persecutions. Previously sporadic, they are now organized by the State on a broad scale to further its policy of the restoration of paganism. Under Decius (249–51) and Diocletian (285–305) they reached their height. There were heroic examples of fortitude, but also constant displays of mediocrity, which forced bishops like Cyprian to pose once more the ancient problem of Christian sin, in this case apostasy, when the persecution had passed.

b) The general response to the Christian message justifies the appellation of Great Church in this period. According to prudent estimates, at the beginning of the 4th century Christians numbered some seven million in a total population of fifty million in the Roman empire, that is, about fifteen per cent, very unequally distributed. The geographical expansion can be traced very definitely. In the West, the missions penetrated Gaul, Spain and the marginal zones of Germany and Britain, and Christianity was equally widespread in the East (Edessa). But here racial characteristics and the fluidity of the imperial *limes* were already engendering special forms of Church life. In spite of the considerable growth of the Great Church, throughout all classes of the population, the majority were still pagan under Constantine, even in their reactions to the crises through which they were passing.

c) Pastoral measures had to be taken in the Church to cater for the influx of Christians in great numbers. The institution of the catechumenate ensured the formation of believers and provided the religious and spiritual instruction which was so imperative in face of the pagan world. The sacramental rites and in particular the celebration of the Eucharist were adapted to meet the new situation; thus, for instance, the spirituality of the times was profoundly marked by the theology of baptism, as also by that of martyrdom. Within the Church order, there developed a multiplicity of ministries under the bishop, to assure a well-regulated pastoral care. The territorial divisions mostly followed the existing organization of the empire. At the same time, bishoprics began to be organized into higher (patriarchal) unities, whose hierarchical heads demonstrated the limits of the Roman claim within the college of bishops. Theological reflection on the primacy, which began in this age (Cyprian), is characterized by a clear consciousness of the rights of the bishops.

d) The development of theology in this period was of major importance in the history of the Church. In spite of much resistance, the original conflict between the cross and Greek culture (*paideia*) was smoothed out; desire for well-defined concepts and debate with or polemics against Hellenism (especially neo-Platonism) made it necessary to reflect more and more on revelation. At Alexandria, Clement (d. before 215) and Origen (d. 254) sought to reinterpret and systematize the faith, using well-known principles of interpretation (typology, allegory) and philosophical categories to present revelation for the first time in a scientific form. Origen also made serious efforts to produce a critical text of Scripture as the basis of his studies (the hexapla). It must be admitted, however, that exegesis was at times inadequate to its task, as may be seen from its reserves as regards the message of the cross, which was presented in a theology of symbols which was undoubtedly profound but nonetheless made the character of scandal less apparent. It was, no doubt, a concession to the mentality of the times.

The major themes of the future were already intoned by the theologians of the Great Church. Following Irenaeus of Lyons (d. about 202), the Alexandrians emphasized the continuity of the redemption in Christ with the whole history of salvation, and hence necessarily made Christ central in their thought. As the Oikonomia (dispensation, redemption) became the object of theological reflection, the question at once arose as to the agents of this one salvific action. The problems posed by Monarchianism, with its effort to reconcile the godhead of Christ and monotheism, gave rise to subtle speculation (Logos Christology, subordinationism) which opened the way to Arianism. Another point worth noting here is the tension between biblical language and the philosophical concepts which were put forward as the sole means of advance in theological thought. Against the Gnostic doctrine of self-redemption the Church found itself compelled to stress salvation by grace. Here too the Fathers strove to preserve the links in the history of salvation (the fall of man, the mission of the Spirit) while guiding future theological language by careful distinction (e.g., between *imago* and *similitudo*, *natura* and *gratia*). Delicacy of expression and profundity of symbolism characterize their efforts to describe the mystery of the Church; the individual Christian was clearly seen as a member of the Church (e.g., in the discipline of penance).

e) The keen sense of belonging to the Church did not, however, prevent Christians from recognizing how much they differed. This diversity was soon to express itself linguistically as well as in the organizational independence of the chief Churches. The redistribution of the Roman empire into a tetrarchy under Diocletian was a deliberate effort to tip the balance in favour of the East, and the effect of this administrative measure on the Church was to set independent developments on foot which were based on differences of temperament and culture. Diversity within the Church found its most marked expression in the variety of liturgies which evolved in each main regional Church. But the essential unity did not suffer from such diversification.

Thus situation and task clearly distinguish the Great Church from the primitive Church, on whose traditions it is wholly based, though developing themes of its own, as is proved notably by the rise of a Christian art.

C. The Significance of the Early Christian Church

The early Church was always held in high esteem, because it was supposed to embody Christianity in its purest form. It was undoubtedly a high point in Church history, though its normative character has been exaggerated and oversimplified, especially in more critical views, which were influenced by the theory of a steady "deterioration". Jerome was lauding this era for its martyrs, contrasting the depravation of the Church in his own day (*Vita Malchi*, 1). The revivalist movements of the Middle Ages likewise conjured up the ideal of the *ecclesia primitiva*, against which they measured their own Church. For the Reformation also the early Church was the norm, insofar as it was precisely in this period that the truth of the gospel maintained its uncompromising claims. As classicism turned once more to antiquity, the early Church gained a new measure of esteem, as the canon of "noble simplicity and tranquil grandeur" was applied to it. Even in modern Church history the postulate of the pure and unadulterated Church of the beginning is still put forward, especially in the discussion of the "turning-point" under Constantine.

In this schematic view, the early Church is undoubtedly idealized, in a way which cannot survive historical analysis, highly as the age may be esteemed. The view is influenced by the notion of natural evolution, and looks for a renewal of the Church in a return to the "youthful freshness" of its early days. Though such notions do not correspond to facts or to the nature of the historical process, we must still ask whether the early Church has a normative character and what these norms may be.

In principle, it must be affirmed that the Church, even as a supernatural entity, is essentially involved in history and hence must undergo evolution: it has a beginning which determines in a certain way the whole future. Since the acts of Jesus as founder of the Church aim at the permanence of the believing community in history, the "Twelve", as immediate witnesses of the word and transmitters of the office, have a central function. Hence too "the sub-apostolic period of proximity to the sources remains dogmatically relevant and historically definable, singular and valuable in a way that can neither be repeated nor surpassed" (K. Rahner). The unique status of the apostolic age is guaranteed by the canon of inspired Scripture; and the age of the primitive Church, the time of the formation of the canon, preserves the full gospel, marking the boundaries against apocryphal writings and heterodoxy.

Along with this fundamental and essential value, the early Church has a special role even from the point of view of history. Even taking into account the obvious defects, we must affirm that the first centuries represent a high point. The active responsibility for the gospel and life according to the gospel in a hostile environment remain exemplary. Hence when due consideration is paid to each historical "hour" (*kairos*), the development of Christianity may be judged in the light of the early Church.

Peter Stockmeier

EASTERN CHURCHES

A. Notion

In the term Eastern Churches, the geographical reference derives from the world-view of antiquity, and means the Eastern part of the Roman empire. Like the sun, the gospel comes from the East, from Palestine. "You shall be my witnesses in Jerusalem, and in all Judaea and Samaria, and to the end of the earth." (Acts 1:8.) The first Churches were founded in Jerusalem and from there Churches were founded in Samaria, Antioch, Cyprus, Asia Minor, Greece, Crete, Syria, Persia, Egypt, Armenia, Ethiopia, Georgia, India and later in the Slavonic lands. Of great importance for the division into East and West was the division of the Roman empire after the death of Emperor Theodosius I (395). The boundary ran between Italy and Greece. Accordingly, we understand by the Eastern Churches those Churches which originated in the Eastern empire and those which were dependent on them. Within this Eastern Church a hierarchical structure was soon formed, within the empire in the form of patriarchates and outside of it (in Persia, Armenia and Georgia) in the form of catholicates. As the seat of the Emperor, Constantinople tried to assert its primacy among the Eastern patriarchates (Alexandria, Antioch, and later Jerusalem) since the 4th century.

B. Unity and Diversity

Christ sent the apostles to teach, baptize and make disciples of all peoples (Mt

28:19–21). This threefold commission is the basis of the essential unity of the gospel in both East and West: in doctrine, in sacrifice and sacraments, and in the essential structure of the Church as founded upon Peter and the apostles and transmitted through their successors. It is also the basis of diversity a) in the way in which the truths of faith were presented (the Synoptics, John, Paul; the Greek, Latin, and Syriac Fathers), b) in the many Eastern and Western liturgies, in sacrifice, sacrament and blessings, and c) in the legal and administrative structure. Such variety, naturally arising from the differences of peoples and cultures, could only become a hindrance to unity after separation from the universal Church and its magisterium. Differences in doctrine only harm unity when they depart from revealed truth or deny a dogma.

Differences are also legitimate in rites whether rites are understood as the customs used in the celebration of the Eucharist, the administration of the sacraments, fasting, etc., or in a broader (juridical) sense as the customs, laws, and discipline of a local Church, inluding rites in the narrower sense (cf. *CIC*, can. 98). Since various Eastern Churches (Catholic and non-Catholic) use the same liturgical rite, while representatives of the same people belong to different rites, a distinction must be made between the various Eastern liturgical rites and the various Eastern Churches or communities.

C. Schisms and Reunions

Of decisive importance for the Eastern Churches were the three great divisions brought about by Nestorianism, Monophysitism and the controversies between Old and New Rome, i.e., between Rome and Byzantium (Constantinople). Hence the turning-points were the ecumenical councils of Ephesus (431) and Chalcedon (451) and the year 1054, to which the definitive break between East and West is usually dated. To the history of the divisions there corresponds the history of the attempts at reunion by Rome and unions that were actually effected through the centuries. The union with the Maronites (1181) was a lasting one. The reunions brought about by the Councils of Lyons (1274) and Florence (1438/39–45) with the Greeks and other Orientals did not last. The major reunions of recent times are those of Brest-Litovsk (1595) with the Ruthenians (Ukrainians and White Russians) and of Alba-Julia (1697) with the Rumanian Siebenbürgers. There have been smaller groups of Uniat Albanians since the latter half of the 15th century in Southern Italy, of Uniat Serbians in Croatia since the end of the 16th century, and later also Uniat groups among the Bulgarians and the Greeks. Greater success in the Near East attended the efforts of the Latin religious orders under the protection of the Western powers, especially France. Approximately every fourth Christian there is Catholic. But even here there was a series of divisions and reunions. The unions with the Chaldeans, Syrians, Melchites, Armenians and Copts are important. In India, the Portuguese brought about a measure of union with the Christians of Malabar (Diamper, 1599). Since 1930 many other Malabar Christians have accepted the union (the Malankarese).

D. Rites and Churches

There are five Eastern rites: the Alexandrian (among Copts and Ethiopians), the Antiochene (among West Syrians, Maronites and Malankarese), the Chaldean (among the Syro-Chaldeans and Malabarites), the Armenian, and the Byzantine which has the most numerous branches (among the Greeks, Melchites, Bulgarians, Russians and Serbians, Ruthenians, Ukrainians, Russian Old Believers, Rumanians, Georgians, Albanians, Hungarians, Japanese, Chinese, Africans in Uganda, in Italy in the monastery of Grottaferrata near Rome, and among the Italo-Albanians). The Eastern rites are distinguished by venerable antiquity, the pomp and splendour of their ceremonies and their deep piety.

The term "Eastern Church" is often used, but it is inexact. In fact, the local Eastern Churches or Eastern communities do not form a unity. They comprise five more or less united groups: the Nestorians, the Monophysites, the Orthodox, the Catholic Uniats and the Protestants. Of the once very numerous group of Nestorians who in the Middle Ages penetrated as far as India, China and Mongolia, there are now only about 70,000, mainly in Irak, and 5,000 in India. The Monophysites are considerably stronger (some fourteen million all told), opponents of the definitions of Chalcedon and for this reason more recently called the "non-Chalcedonian Orthodox". They include the Copts and Ethiopians, the West Syrians (mainly in India) and Armenians. The strongest of all the Eastern groups is the Orthodox. They include the ancient patriarchates of Constantinople, Alexandria, Antioch and Jerusalem (all together about two million). Numerically the strongest Orthodox Churches, however, are those in Greece (8 million) and in the Communist countries (as far as one is able to tell): in Russia, Rumania, Yugoslavia, and Bulgaria (all together perhaps 80 million). The number of *émigré* Russian Orthodox in the four different communities of the Moscow patriarchate, the Paris hierarchy, and two hierarchies in the U.S.A. may be around one million. In general, each Eastern rite includes a Catholic group. The Maronites, Italo-Albanians, Slovaks and Malabar Christians are all Catholic, while the Georgians, Esthonians, Latvians, Finns, Japanese and Chinese have no Catholic counterparts. There are also Eastern Christians in various countries who have gone over to Protestantism (the Mar Thoma Christians in India; the Nestorians who went over to Presbyterianism in the U.S.A.; the Ukrainians who became Congregationalists in Canada). There are Protestant missions in the Near East.

There are numerous patriarchates in the Churches separated from Rome; besides those already mentioned, the Coptic and the Ethiopian (since 1959), those of the Monophysites of Antioch (Jacobites; the Jacobites of India have a catholicate) and of the Nestorians; there are two catholicates and two patriarchates of the Armenians; one catholicate of the Orthodox Georgians; the patriarchates among the Orthodox in Russia, Serbia, Rumania and Bulgaria are more recent. The Orthodox Church of Greece is autocephalous (with the Archbishop of Athen at the head), as are those of Cyprus, Albania, Poland and Czechoslovakia. For the Catholics of the Eastern Churches there are six patriarchates (the Coptic, Syrian, Maronite, Melchite, Armenian and Chaldean) and one *Archiepiscopus maior* with patriarchal rights among the Ukrainians. There are metropolitans for the Catholic Ethiopian Church (1), the Malankarese (1) and the Malabar Christians (2), the Catholic Rumanians (1) and the Ukrainians (3). The remaining Catholics of the Eastern Church are directly under the Apostolic See (with the exception of the two groups in Yugoslavia and Hungary which are subject to a Latin bishop).

E. The Orthodox

The Churches of the Byzantine rite are given many different names: the "Orthodox Church of the East", the "Orthodox Church", or simply the "Eastern Church". It is also known as the "Church of the Seven Ecumenical Councils", or, after its main representatives, the "Byzantine-Slavonic" or the "Greek-Slavonic Church". This great Church of the East, which today is spread over the whole world, represents, like the Monophysite, no strict unity, but is made up of a number of separate national Churches grouped according to patriarchates and later as autocephalous Churches, i.e., local or national Churches each of which has its own head and is autonomous. Some of the autonomous Orthodox Churches are very much at variance with each other (for example, the Russian émigré Church first at Karlowitz, later at Munich and New York, in its relation to the Moscow patriarchate; and the Russian Old Believers in their relation to the chief Russian Church).

F. Byzantine and Slav Theology

The inner development of doctrine is historically closely connected with the external divisions of the Eastern Churches. The history of Eastern piety, asceticism, and mysticism is very instructive. After the patristic age, which is usually considered as closing with John Damascene (d. *c.* 749), that is to say, after the time of the Trinitarian and Christological controversies (especially those of Arianism, Nestorianism, Monophysitism and Monotheletism), and after the time of the first seven ecumenical councils (from the first to the second Council of Nicaea, 325–787), the conversion of the Slavs began in the 9th century. In the same century the temporary schism under the Patriarch Photius heralded the separation between Christians of East and West which has obtained since the middle of the 11th century. Further, the history of the Christian East cannot be understood without reference to the Arab, Mongol, and Turkish domination and the Crusades undertaken against Islam. In the middle of this period occurred the unfortunate conquest of Byzantium by the Crusaders (1204) and the setting up of the Latin Empire there (1204–61). The conquest of Constantinople by the Turks (1453), which put an end to the Orthodox Byzantine Empire, affected even more deeply the history of Orthodoxy. It was only in the 19th century that the Balkan countries ceased to be under Turkish rule. As the separation of the Orthodox East from Rome had marked effects on doctrine, one can date the beginning of Orthodox theological history as about the middle of the 11th century.

The history of Byzantine theology, however, as a continuation of Greek patristic theology, began much earlier. Its main periods may be characterized as follows: the period of the iconoclast disputes, 730–850; the period from Photius to Cerularius, 850–1050, i.e., the beginning of the controversy on the procession of the Holy Spirit; the period from Cerularius to the Latin Empire in Byzantium, 1050–1200; the period between the conquest of Constantinople by the Crusaders and the Hesychasm of Gregory Palamas, 1200–1330; the period from Palamas to the conquest of Constantinople by the Turks, 1330–1453. The centre of Orthodoxy then shifted from Constantinople to Kiev and then to Moscow and St. Petersburg. Greece and the Balkan countries are still recovering from the time of Turkish domination.

The history of Slavonic Orthodox theology may be divided into the following periods: from its beginning in Bulgaria (9th–10th century) and the Kingdom of Kiev (10th–11th century) to the rejection of the Union of Florence; the period after the Reformation; the great period of the Kiev School (end of the 17th and beginning of the 18th century); the beginning of the great Russian Schism, that of the Raskolnians (at approximately the same time); the replacement of the patriarchates by the Holy Synod under Peter the Great (1721); from the anti-Protestant Reform in Russia (1836) until the Communist Revolution of 1917, or from the origin of Slavophile theology to 1917; and lastly, the recent period since the Revolution of 1917 which saw the reinstitution of the patriarchates for the Russian Church through the Pan-

Russian Council of 1917/18, but which also brought oppression and persecution. Many theologians fled and founded centres of Orthodox theology in other countries, the most notable of which are the Orthodox Theological Institute of St. Sergius in Paris and the Orthodox Seminary of St. Vladimir in New York.

Byzantine theology felt the influence of philosophy from the beginning, especially that of Plato, Aristotle and Plotinus, though different schools, as in the West, can hardly be distinguished. The influence of Western Scholasticism can be traced only from the 14th century on. Catholic influence predominated in the post-Tridentine Orthodox theology, even within the Kiev school; but Protestant influence was strong in the school of Theophanes Prokopovič who assisted Peter the Great in his reform of the Church. Since the reform carried out by the chief procurator of the Holy Russian Synod, Protasov, in the year 1836, Catholic influence has predominated in the official Russian theology, but Protestant influence in the theology of Alexius Chomjakov. Byzantine theology reached its last heights in Gregory Palamas, whose synthetic power showed itself not so much in the teaching on the nature and energies of God as in Mariology. The last important Byzantine and also Palamite theologian was George Scholarius, whose aim was to synthesize Byzantine and Scholastic theology.

In the 16th and 17th centuries the Orthodox sought to protect themselves from the influence of Protestant ideas by making use of teaching borrowed from Catholicism and the Scholastics. This is clear (i) from the three answers of the Patriarch of Constantinople, Jeremias II, to the Protestant theologians of Tübingen (1576; 1579; 1581); (ii) from the condemnation by Patriarch Cyril Contarenus of the confession of faith of the Patriarch of Constantinople, Cyril Lucar (d. 1638), which had been influenced by Calvinism, and (iii) especially from the fact that the Synod of Jassy (1642) confirmed the confession of faith of Peter Mogila, and the Synod of Jerusalem that of the Patriarch of Jerusalem, Dositheus. The *Confessio* of Dositheus has recently been regarded as the apex of a doctrinal *rapprochement* between Orthodoxy and Catholicism. The well-known Orthodox theologian Gabriel Severus (1541 to 1616) also based himself in his disputes upon Catholic teaching. In the theological school of Kiev since the end of the 17th century, even the scholastic method penetrated. In this school, founded in 1631 by Peter Mogila (1596–1646), philosophy was introduced as a discipline in 1685 and theology in 1690; in 1701 it became a theological academy. While in the first centuries following the conversion of the Slavs in Bulgaria, Serbia, and in the Kiev and later in the Moscovite Kingdoms, theological writings, such as there were, showed Greek influence – in Moscovia still apparent under Maximos the Greek (Maksim Grek, d. 1556) who is called the "first illuminator of the Russians" – the Kiev Academy later became so important in its own right that it attracted not only Ruthenians, i.e., Ukrainians and White Russians, but also Moscovites, Greeks, Rumanians and Serbs. There the authority of Aquinas was unchallenged. His *Summa* was mostly known through the commentaries of the Jesuits Gregory of Valencia, Suárez, Hurtado, Arriaga, and De Lugo.

Theologians also frequently appealed to other Catholic authors, especially Bellarmine, on whom the famous work of Stephan Javorsky against Protestantism, *Kamen Very* (*Cornerstone of the Faith*) depends. Javorsky (1658–1722) had studied in Kiev and with the Jesuits, and in 1700 was named Patriarchal Administrator by Peter the Great. The publication of his main work met with great difficulties. His teaching on justification, merit and good works, the form of the Eucharist, purgatory and the canon of Scripture was that of Catholic theology. The Kiev school taught the same doctrines, with the inclusion of the Immaculate Conception of Mary, but it did so in terms of the Byzantine-Slavonic tradition and liturgy rather than by appealing to Catholic theology.

Opposition to the *Cornerstone* of Javorsky was led by Theophan Prokopovič (1681–1736), the counsellor of Peter the Great who after the death of the Emperor became Archbishop of Novgorod. He introduced a theology with Protestant leanings into the Moscow Kingdom. Born in Kiev, Prokopovič became a Catholic in his youth, joined the Order of St. Basil, and studied in Rome. Upon his return, however, he again espoused the faith of his parents, taught at the Kiev Academy and was appointed rector. In 1716 he was called to Petersburg by Peter the Great. His writings influenced Russian handbooks of dogmatics from *c.* 1759, and he is considered the founder of systematic theology in Russia. He was the first there to separate dogmatic from moral theology, while also attempting to synthesize the various treatises of theology. His dogmatic teaching was completed only later by Samuel Mislavsky (1782); Prokopovič himself only wrote a tractate on the gratuitous justification of the sinner by Christ, which was strongly influenced by Luther. Even earlier than Prokopovič, however, Lutheran elements had penetrated the writings of some of the Greek theologians (e.g., the Catechism of Zacharias Gerganos and the confession of faith of Metrophanes Kritopulos). But in the Byzantine sphere nothing is seen of the Protestantism which showed itself in the writing of Prokopovič, as regards Scripture as the sole rule of faith, the canon of the OT, ecclesiology, and justification. The last representative of the theology of Prokopovič was the famous Metropolitan of Moscow, Philaret Drozdov (1782–1867), as can be seen from the first editions of his catechism.

A change came in the year 1836 with Count Protasov, who had been educated for 15 years in Jesuit schools and was somewhat partial towards the Latins. It was through him that the confessions of faith of Peter Mogila and Dositheus as well as the work of Stephan Javorsky again became influential. He promoted the study of the Fathers and introduced patrology into the theological curriculum. A number of textbooks of dogmatic theology were produced in Russian, which were in use until the Revolution of 1917 and are still read today by the students of theology in the Russian Patriarchate. Philaret was forced to revise his catechism, much against his will. The third edition appeared in 1839 and was frequently reprinted since then. Protosov sought to have his reform measures carried out by imperial decrees, but in this he was not entirely successful.

Along the lines of Prokopovič's theology, there now arose the increasingly influential school of Slavophile philosophy and theology. It was influenced by the German idealism (especially of Schelling and Hegel) which it sought to combat, but was also inspired by the ancient oriental patristic and ascetical tradition. Its first philosophical leader was Ivan Kirejevsky (1806–56), while its theological head was his friend Alexis S. Khomyakov (1804–60). Vladimir Soloviev, the most important Russian philosopher and lay-theologian (1853–1900), also began as a Slavophile, but then came to differ from them more and more on central theological issues. In 1896, he privately accepted the Catholic creed. Khomyakov, who influenced most Russian Orthodox theologians greatly in the sphere of ecclesiology, was a moving force in the new independent Russian theology. He was followed by several representatives of the official theology (including E.

Akvilonov and P. Svetlov) but especially by the better-known of the Russian theologians abroad (L. Karsavin – who, however, died as a Catholic – V. Zenkovsky, S. Bulgakov, G. Florovsky, and the internationally known philosopher N. Berdyaev). Karsavin, Bulgakov, and Berdyaev were also under the influence of Soloviev who was at the origin of Russian Sophia theology. The main representatives of the latter were P. Florensky and S. Bulgakov, and the movement also attracted L. Karsavin, S. and E. Trubeckoy and V. Ivanov.

Much may be learned of modern trends from the acts of the First Congress for Orthodox Theology (Athens, November to December 1936); the controversy between Moscow and Constantinople over the primacy within Orthodoxy; the efforts of the Orthodox to attain inner and outward unity (as on the occasion of the Pan-Orthodox conferences in Rhodes, 1961, 1963 and 1964, and Belgrade, 1966); the attempts to clarify the relations of the Orthodox Churches to the ecumenical movement and to the World Council of Churches, to Vatican II and to the Catholic Church.

G. Doctrinal Bonds and Conflicts between East and West

The history of the Eastern Churches and their relations to the Catholic Church is closely connected with the dogmatic and liturgical disputes which led to the separation or which arose in the centuries following it. It must first be stressed that between Catholic and Orthodox teaching – and also, more or less, that of the other Eastern Churches – there are large areas of agreement. This is also true of the liturgy and the sacraments, as well as the spiritual life. All Eastern theologians – with few exceptions – look for revealed truth not only in sacred Scripture, but also oral tradition. Most of them oppose the principle of "Scripture alone" and adhere to the principle of "Scripture in the Church". They consider Scripture and tradition to be linked to each other and to form a unity. There are differences of opinion as to the extent of oral tradition: some limit it to the explanation of Scripture, while others rather stress a tradition independent of Scripture. All Eastern theologians hold the books of Scripture to be inspired. The Orthodox agree with Catholic tradition in their canon of the books of the NT; but in the canon of the OT, with regard to the so-called deuterocanonical books, the Russians, Rumanians and Serbians have differed to some extent since the 17th century while the Greeks have wavered. The Greeks consider the Septuagint as the only authentic translation of the OT.

The sources of tradition for the Orthodox are above all the ancient professions of faith: in the first place the Nicene-Constantinopolitan Creed, and then the so-called Athanasian Creed in its Greek translation. To these are added the decisions of the first seven ecumenical councils (sometimes an eighth is added: the Synod of 879–80 under Photius), together with the decrees of the Trullan Synod complementing the two Councils of Constantinople (553 and 680–81). Basic also to Orthodox teaching are the writings of the Fathers, of whom Athanasius, the three Cappadocians, Chrysostomus, the Pseudo-Areopagite, and Maximus the Confessor are given places of honour. Less often, John Damascene is quoted, and of the Latin Fathers only the Popes Leo I and Gregory I – the reason being ignorance of the Latin tongue, as for the Latins it was a lack of Greek. It was only in the Byzantium of the 14th century and then later in the Kiev school that the Latin Fathers were quoted with more frequency. In the post-Reformation period, the touchstone of orthodoxy were the "Confessions of Faith", whose authority remained very great for about two centuries. In the following period these came under criticism, especially the Confessions of Mogila and Dositheus, for their too great dependence upon Catholic teaching.

There are, no doubt, differences of mentality between the Orthodox East and the Catholic West; but there is also much in common. These differences should neither be exaggerated, nor glossed over where they affect the faith. Photius's primary objection against the Latins was the teaching on the *filioque*. It is impossible to prove, as V. Lossky maintains, that all the differences between East and West in the spiritual life go back to the doctrine of the procession of the Holy Spirit, i.e., from the Father alone, or from Father and Son. In general, there is agreement in both East and West that the main source of dissension lies in the recognition or denial of the Roman primacy. Besides the *filioque* and its addition to the creed, Photius names as points of controversy (in his letter to the Archbishops of the East in 867, in his *Mystagogy of the Holy Spirit* and elsewhere) the primacy of the Bishop of Rome, the Latin custom of fasting on Saturday, the use of milk, cheese, etc., in the first week of Lent, priestly celibacy, and the exclusive power of bishops to dispense the sacrament of confirmation. In the 11th century, at the time of the final separation, this list of Latin errors was notably enlarged. Michael Cerularius enumerates twenty-two such errors, especially the use of unleavened bread at the celebration of the Eucharist. Many of these complaints do not concern the faith at all, but only discipline (e.g., the shaving of the beard, marriage of priests, wearing of rings by the Latin bishops, etc.), as Archbishop Theophylactus of Bulgaria then pointed out.

From the 12th to the 15th century the number of complaints against the Latins rose to over sixty. Then came the controversy about the fire of purgatory and the form of the Eucharist. The Council of Florence (*D* 691–4) settled five controversial questions: (i) the Holy Spirit proceeds "from the Father and the Son" and likewise "from the Father through the Son"; (ii) the addition of the *filioque*, to the creed is justified; (iii) the Eucharist may be celebrated with either leavened or unleavened bread according to the custom of East or West; (iv) between heaven and hell there are purifying punishments for the souls of penitent sinners; (v) the Roman Bishop, as the successor to Peter, possesses a universal primacy in the Church. Maximus the Greek (d. 1556) recognized only three "great heresies" of the Latins: the *filioque*, unleavened bread and the fire of purgatory.

Of the greatest importance today in the dialogue between Catholics and Orthodox, as well as the other Eastern Churches separated from Rome, are the following: the primacy and infallibility of the Pope and in connection with this, the hierarchical structure of the Church; the *filioque* and its addition to the creed; the unknowability of the essence of God; the juridical conception of redemption; the eucharistic epiclesis as the form of consecration; the Immaculate Conception of the Mother of God and her Assumption into heaven; the last things. Yet it must be stressed that while on each of these points the great majority of the Orthodox depart from Catholic teaching, there have always been, among Eastern theologians, very great differences of opinion, for or against Catholic teaching. Since the separation the number of doctrinal differences has grown. In the beginning the differences were concerned with individual dogmatic and liturgical questions, but since the separation from the Catholic Church and the denial of its magisterium as a binding norm of faith, the differences have become more profound and have had effects later in fundamental theology and even in philosophy. Revealed truth has further unfolded itself inside as well as outside the Catholic Church and it was interpreted in different, often opposing ways.

H. Some Points of Doctrine

One task of the present-day ecumenism is to distinguish merely ritual or non-essential differences from the essential ones and to limit controversy to the essential. Even at the time of Photius and Cerularius, and indeed before the completion of the schism, the real underlying reason for the separation was the differing types of hierarchical structure. Hence, we must first discuss the Eastern conception of Church structure, and then, more briefly, the problem of the knowledge of God, modern Sophia theology, Christology and soteriology, the Mother of God and her privileges, and finally the sacraments and the last things. This will throw light on what is the characteristic in the Orthodox approach to theology, especially in modern times, and the way theology, patristics, and liturgical piety are united.

1. *The Church.* Like the local Church (bishop, priests, and people), the universal Church has been hierarchically organized from antiquity. The local Churches were not merely juxtaposed. They were organically united and interwoven. There was fellowship and interconnection, and even mutual dependence, just as one part of an organism is dependent on the others. The individual local Churches were dependent upon the assembly or the council of the regional Church and ultimately upon the universal Church whose head, according to Catholic teaching, is the successor of Peter. In the first centuries the government of the universal Church by the Bishop of Rome was restricted to a minimum, as the Church only gradually developed fully its hierarchical organization, and communication in the modern sense was not possible. Much was necessarily left to the local and regional Churches to decide. This situation gave rise in the very first centuries to the patriarchates, which were to be so important for the Christian East, and which stood, as it were, between the primacy and the episcopacy. The precedence of old Rome as the see of the successor of Peter was acknowledged in the Byzantine East before the temporary and then the final separation, although of course some were ready to question the primacy, first in practice and then on theoretical grounds. This was done, at least virtually, by the drawing up of can. 3 of Constantinople and can. 28 of Chalcedon. That the hierarchy instituted by Christ possesses the supreme authority in the Church has till modern times never been doubted in the Christian East.

Before and after the separation there were two theories especially which were put forward with regard to the supreme authority in the Church: that of the pentarchy and that of the ecumenical councils. To these there must be added in modern times the theory of the *Sobornost* and eucharistic ecclesiology. Between all these theories there is a historical and theological connection. The theory of the pentarchy attributes the highest jurisdiction to the Patriarchs of Rome, Constantinople, Alexandria, Antioch, and Jerusalem. Three forms of this theory may be distinguished. The first was put forward by the defenders of the cult of images, especially by Theodore of Studiou (759–826) and Patriarch Nicephorus of Constantinople (d. 829). Theodore speaks of the "five-pinnacled body of the Church"; he asserts that the true councils are those accepted by all five patriarchs. The power given to Peter (Mt 16:19) belongs in the concrete to the successors of the apostles and the five patriarchs. On the other hand, he recognizes the Roman primacy. According to Nicephorus, the patriarchs together with the Bishop of Rome represent the whole Church in its ordinary jurisdiction.

A second form of the pentarchy was formulated in opposition to the primacy of Rome and was systematically developed by the Byzantine canonist Theodor Balsmon towards the end of the 12th century. He traces the origin of the Eastern patriarchates to the apostles or to the second ecumenical council, but of the Roman patriarchate to the Emperor Constantine. He thinks that the patriarchs are the visible head of the Church representing the invisible Christ; they have power over all the Churches, just as the five senses serve to govern the body; all the patriarchs have equal power. Another form of the pentarchy excludes Old Rome as apostate. Such a "tetrarchy", i.e., a diminished pentarchy, was put forward by Maximus the Greek. As the theory of the pentarchy is based upon the patriarchates which were not directly instituted by divine right, it includes a relative element. Hence the number of the patriarchs among Orthodox and Uniats has grown in the course of the centuries; among the Orthodox especially in modern times, because of their principle that every country or people can and should have its own independent Church government. The last-mentioned form of the pentarchy went hand in hand with the development of polemics against the Roman primacy: it is not of divine institution but is based only upon ecclesiastical law; the episcopal office of Peter was passed on to his successor but not his primacy; the Pope has fallen into heresy; Christ is the one invisible head of the Church; the primacy is based on the False Decretals (of "Isidore"); Rome has turned the primacy of love into a primacy of jurisdiction.

2. *Authority in the Church*. The supreme authority of the patriarchs, which developed from custom, was given juridical force by the ecumenical councils. The patriarchs and bishops, however, make their decisions about the concerns of the entire Church only at ecumenical assemblies. The ecumenical council remained the organ of supreme authority for the Eastern theologians, even when they denied the universal primacy of the Pope. There were, however, seven ecumenical councils up to the separation of the Churches in the 11th century, which were recognized both in the East and in the West. (In the Catholic West the eighth is considered to be the Council which condemned Photius in 869–70; while in the East the eighth is sometimes considered to be the Photian Council of 879–80.) The Eastern theologians termed the Orthodox Church "the Church of the seven ecumenical councils". In more recent times, however, the Archpriest Sergius Bulgakov objected strongly to the opinion that in the living Church of Christ there could only be seven ecumenical councils, as new problems continually arise and demand a common solution. For Orthodox theology this is the greatest problem: how is the lack of an ecumenical council in the East for more than a thousand years to be explained or justified? Efforts have hence been made in the past years, by means of preparatory pan-Orthodox conventions, to prepare for a new ecumenical council. In the Catholic Church, the series of ecumenical councils was continued from antiquity, through the general councils of the Middle Ages up to Vatican II.

For Orthodox theology, the reunion councils have a special importance among the Catholic ecumenical councils: that of Lyons (1274) and that of Ferrara-Florence (1438/9 to 1445), especially the latter. For at these councils, under the leadership of the Byzantine Emperor and the Patriarch of Constantinople, the whole Orthodox world was represented. It was, according to the traditional Eastern as well as Western concept, properly convoked and ecumenical. The union, however, lasted only a short time and was then completely abandoned again. Orthodox theologians attempt to justify this delayed rejection of the council by putting Florence on a level with the "Robber Synod" of 449, asserting that the bishops who accepted the union with

Rome were apostates, whereas the entire people under divine inspiration unanimously rejected the false union.

There are indications of a similar explanation as early as the history of the Council of Florence written by Silvester Syropulos, but it was first clearly formulated by the Russian lay-theologian Khomyakov, whose explanation has grown in popularity among the Orthodox. Khomyakov thought he could substantiate his opinion by the letter of the Eastern patriarchs of 1848 with its negative answer to Pope Pius IX who had invited them to union with Rome. According to Khomyakov, the conciliar decrees must be either accepted or rejected by the whole Church community, for there had been heretical councils in which Emperor, bishops, patriarchs and Pope had accepted false teaching. Infallible faith could not depend upon a hierarchical order but is preserved by the people of the Church as a whole. The gift of faith must be clearly distinguished from the tasks of the hierarchy (i.e., sacramental and disciplinary authority). Infallibility in the Church does not rest on individuals, but on the entire Church united in love and holiness. To divorce true faith and true knowledge from the mutual love of all the faithful would be the error of rationalism, with which he reproaches the Christian West. The Church is unity, freedom, and love. Khomyakov sees Catholicism as unity without freedom and Protestantism as freedom without unity, whereas Orthodoxy is the synthesis of unity and freedom in love (one is reminded of the Hegelian thesis-antithesis-synthesis).

The followers of Khomyakov give this conception of the Church the Russian name of "sobornost", as Khomyakov took the word "Catholic" in the creed (in Slavonic "sobornyj", from the root "sobirati", i.e., gather) not in the extensive, but in the intensive sense: it is not the physical diffusion of the Church, but the free and perfect unity and unanimity of all the faithful. Even earlier than Khomyakov, Russian theology knew of a doctrine similar to that of the Gallican Richer and the Synod of Pistoia, according to which the bearer of infallibility is the entirety of all the faithful, while the bishops in council act as their delegates. The theology of Khomyakov was under ecclesiastical censure in Tsarist Russia until the beginning of the present century. E. Akvilonov (1894) tried to introduce Khomyakov's ecclesiology into official ecclesiology, and was followed by well-known Russian theologians, priests (P. Svetlov, P. Florensky, S. Bulgakov, G. Florovsky, V. Zenkovsky, G. Grabbe) as well as laymen (N. Berdyaev, L. Karsavin – who, however, died a Catholic – and N. Arseniev). These are mostly Russian *émigrés*. To these must be added the well-known Bulgarian theologian, the Archpriest S. Zankov. Among the Greeks the ideas of Khomyakov are still largely unknown. Still, in recent times Balanos, Bratsiotis and especially Alivisatos have favoured them, while Greek theologians such as Dyovuniotis and Trempelas have been critical.

The original neo-Russian ecclesiology is largely influenced by Khomyakov and Soloviev, as is especially clear in the understanding of the Church which one finds in N. Berdyaev and S. Bulgakov. For both, the Church is the mystical body of Christ, a divine-human organism ("Bogočelověčestvo"), the transfigured divine world. Soloviev sharply criticized Khomyakov's conception of the Church: it represented the Church in its idealized image of unanimity, which did not correspond to fact among the disunited Orthodox Churches. Moreover, the Russian Church since 1917 was divided into a plurality of hierarchies. In view, no doubt, of these difficulties, the Archpriest N. Afanasiev, professor at the Orthodox Theological Institute of St.

Sergius in Paris, recently attempted to place the Orthodox ecclesiology on a new foundation, or rather, to return again to the original conception of the primitive Church. He distinguishes between *universal* and *eucharistic* ecclesiology.

In universal ecclesiology, the Church is considered as an organism whose parts are the local Churches. The fullness of Church life is to be found only in the entire Church; the local Churches are only subordinate parts of the whole. Such a conception is foreign to the writings of the NT, especially those of Paul, and to the early Church. Yet this false conception took the place of the original ecclesiology since the 3rd century, in the East as well as in the West, in the West especially in the form of the Roman primacy. The jurisdiction of the Roman pontiff over the whole Church would reduce the dioceses to the status of parishes.

According to Afanasiev, the principles of eucharistic ecclesiology, on the contrary, are based on 1 Cor 10:16–17 and 12:27, where Paul speaks of the body of Christ and his members, of those who share one eucharistic bread and who, though many, form one body. The source and the fullness of Church life is to be found in the eucharistic assembly of the local Church. Ignatius the martyr describes how the bishop together with the priests and people celebrates the Eucharist; and each local Church is for him the Catholic Church, autonomous and on an equal level with the other local Churches to which it has a living relationship and whose teaching and decrees it freely accepts. No doubt Rome exercised a primacy even in Christian antiquity, but it was not a juridical primacy; it was one of prestige, service and love. There is no real subordination of one local Church to another. The primitive Church had no juridical structure. Power, jurisdiction, law – these are categories borrowed from the Roman Empire and from the civil State. Here we note that Afanasiev, who tries to exclude every form of law from the Church, was originally a professor of canon law. The truth lies surely in between: true ecclesiology must be eucharistic as well as universal, and in the Church there is both love and law.

3. *The nature of God.* In the Eastern theological tradition the absolute transcendence of God is stressed: God dwells in inaccessible light (1 Tim 6:16). The Fathers of the 4th century inculcated this doctrine in the struggle against Eunomius. On the other hand, the Eastern ascetical tradition taught that God can be experienced in a mystically immanent way. Gregory Palamas, Archbishop of Thessalonica (1296–1359), attempted to harmonize these conflicting doctrines: one must distinguish in God between the absolutely unknowable essence and the knowable perceptible attributes, the energies or the activity of God. Among the divine energies, which are eternal and uncreated, grace and the "light of Tabor" which was seen by the three chosen disciples and by the mystically gifted ascetics, have a special place. There is a real distinction in God between his nature and his energies, between his nature and the three divine persons. The energies are not immanent but the outward revelations or processions of the divine nature. About the middle of the 14th century this teaching was first condemned in Byzantium, but in 1351 accepted at a council and prescribed and remained dominant in the Greco-Russian Church for nearly two centuries. Then it fell into oblivion. In recent years the Russian theologians above all, especially Florovsky and Meyendorff, have tried to prove that the Palamite teaching was the genuine Eastern tradition. The year 1959 was celebrated in Thessalonica as the Palamas-Jubilee. A new edition of his works is now appearing.

4. *Sophia.* The new Russian Wisdom-teaching, Sophiology or Sophia theology, was developed from the teaching of Soloviev especially by Florensky and Bulgakov. It is as it were the link between theology and *oikonomia* and it ponders the foundation of the world, its beauty and its splendour in God. It enquires especially how man, the microcosm, how humanity in its totality, and above all how the human nature of the God-man is founded in God; how the incarnation of God and the divinization or transfiguration of the world is possible. In the Sophia theology, Plato's theory of ideas lives on. To substantiate the theory the wisdom texts of the Old and New Testaments are used, among others, as well as the writings of the Fathers, the Eastern liturgy and iconography. Soloviev, Florensky, and Bulgakov see in the winged angel of the Sophia-icon of Novgorod not a representation of Christ, but one single great being, the ideal humanity. Accordingly, divine wisdom appears not as the person of Christ (cf. 1 Cor 1:24), to whom the Hagia Sophia in Constantinople is dedicated, but as the one divine nature of all three persons considered primarily in the person of the Word and the Spirit, insofar as the creation is founded in the nature of God and is his image. At the same time, however, wisdom is depicted as the ideal creation itself, either as its prototype or as the transfigured, divinized creation. Wisdom then appears to be identical with God and distinct from him; as one with the creation and yet distinct from it, or intermediate between God and creation. For this reason the followers of the Sophia theology are accused of introducing, like the Gnostics of old, an intermediate being, indeed a fourth hypostasis in God, or of confusing the world with God in a pantheistic way. In the ensuing controversy, the teaching of Bulgakov was condemned as erroneous by the Moscow and Karlowitz hierarchy. Nonetheless, the Sophia theology conveys a great universal insight which contains much truth.

5. *Christology.* In recent times the Orthodox theologians have attempted to develop further the dogma of Chalcedon, especially Bulgakov with his Sophia theology, Soloviev with his concept of the God-man and Vladimir Lossky with his patristic studies. The problem of the divine self-consciousness of Christ was also discussed in connection with Protestant theology of the 19th century, even before the controversy about the "I" of the God-man in Catholic theology. New Russian theology returns again and again to the motif of the self-emptying of Christ, with new attempts to explain Phil 2:5-11. As Bulgakov identifies person, consciousness, and "I" in Christ, he attributes only one consciousness to the God-man and teaches, like Apollinaris of Laodicea in antiquity, that the Logos, the Word, took the place of the human soul in Christ.

6. *Soteriology.* Russian Orthodox soteriology developed in an independent direction about the beginning of the 20th century, primarily under the influence of Metropolitan Philaret of Moscow, Khomyakov and Dostoievsky. Representatives of this new soteriology are Světlov, later Patriarch Sergius of Moscow (d. 1944), Metropolitan Antonius (1917/18, candidate for patriarch; d. 1936), Tarejev, Nesmelov, and S. Bulgakov. Concepts of Catholic theology such as the satisfaction or merit of Christ sound suspect to these theologians and remind them of Roman or medieval penal law, or of debits and credits or bank transactions. The struggle against the juridical elements of such concepts led some of these theologians to deny the objective aspect of redemption through Christ, the result of the life, suffering, death and resurrection of Christ as already at hand before its application to the redeemed, and to allow only the subjectively conscious aspects of redemption, such as the merciful love

of Christ, his compassion for sinners, his example and the acceptance of his influence by repentant sinners. Tarejev stresses the redeeming value of the temptations of Christ; Nesmelov the soteriological meaning of his resurrection. Like Philaret, Svetlov and Bulgakov attempt to reconcile love and justice. Philaret propounds the mystery of redemption on three levels; in the eternal loving plan of the triune God, in the historical life and death of the Redeemer, and in the history of the Church for each Christian.

7. *Mary*. Since the patristic age there has always been theological speculation concerning Mary in the East, especially in homilies on the feasts of the Lord and the feasts of the Nativity of Mary, her Presentation in the Temple, the Annunciation and the Assumption. The authors of theological textbooks treat of her in Christology. Only recently have monographs on Mary appeared: among the Russians, e.g., S. Bulgakov, *The Burning Bush* (1927), and among the Greeks, J. O. Kalogerou, *Mary the Ever Virgin Mother of God According to Orthodox Belief* (1957). At the centre of Orthodox Mariology stands the virginal motherhood of Mary; stress is laid on the sublimity and holiness of Mary, her share in the redemption, her place as mediatrix. This Mariology flourished strongly among Byzantine theologians in the 14th century, as it did again in our days among the Russian Sophia theologians, especially Florensky and Bulgakov. The Byzantine theologians see Mary together with her Son in the centre of the cosmos, as the recapitulation and goal of world-history (cf. Eph 1:10). For the Sophia theologians Mary is the embodiment of the Wisdom, the heart of the Church and the centre of creation. Most Orthodox theologians today deny the Immaculate Conception of Mary. Many consider the Assumption of the Mother of God into heaven only as a pious opinion and not a revealed truth.

8. *The sacraments*. In the sacramental theology the separation of East and West has meant divergent development in more than one respect. Among the controversial subjects were the sacramental character, the validity of sacraments dispensed outside of the one Church (especially baptism if not by triple immersion), the repetition of confirmation, the penance or satisfaction in the sacrament of penance, the indissolubility of sacramental marriage. The largest place, however, was taken by the controversies concerning the Eucharist: leavened or unleavened bread; the necessity of the epiclesis for the consecration of the elements; communion of children under the age of reason; and communion under both species. The only really dogmatic question concerns the necessity of the epiclesis. An explicit Orthodox sacramental theology only arose in the post-Reformation period, leaning heavily on Trent. Efforts to discard Catholic (as well as Protestant) influences and to reflect on the genuine Eastern tradition brought many differences to light and gave rise to new controversies, especially on the question of sacraments in general: the nature of grace, its action in the sacraments; the repetition or non-repetition of certain sacraments; the author and the number of the sacraments; their validity and efficacy outside of the Church. The Orthodox in great part reject a too juridical conception of the sacraments.

9. *The last things*. The ordinary doctrine of the Orthodox (as of Catholics) is: after death there can no longer be any atonement or merit; the general resurrection is yet to come; at the last judgment the good will be definitely separated from the evil; rewards will differ according to merit; the renewal of the world will follow the judgment; prayer for the dead is justified. Other than this there is no fixed teaching among the Orthodox on this subject. The controversy on the fire of purga-

tory, ever since 1231/32 and especially at the Council of Ferrara-Florence, centred on whether the sufferings of purgatory are caused by fire and whether the lot of the deceased will be decided before the last day. Some Orthodox theologians deny that there are any torments in purgatory and assert that God forgives the souls of the deceased in view of the prayers of the Church. The Council of Florence defined the existence but not the fire of purgatory. In the following period, many Greeks and Slavs held fast to the teaching on an intermediate state, while others vigorously repudiated it. The teaching of the credal books is not consistent, so that many authors still waver.

The doctrine of the intermediate state is also testified to by the Byzantine liturgy. Besides this, the conviction is widespread among Orthodox theologians that it is only at the last judgment that the good and the evil will receive full reward or punishment in body and soul, as was taught already by Photius in the 9th and Theophylactus in the 11th and 12th centuries, and by Mark of Ephesus at the Council of Florence. Other Byzantine theologians, however, taught an immediate recompense for the souls of the good who have been purified, and for the unrepentant wicked, as was later defined at Florence.

After the council the doctrine of the delay of the recompense spread more among the Greeks, while the Slavs, especially the representatives of the Kiev school, held the Catholic position. Orthodox as well as Catholics agree that the resurrection of the body brings with it a fuller bliss for the good and a greater torment for the wicked. In the catechism of Philaret of Moscow, the good are granted only the vision of Christ immediately after death, the vision of God after the last judgment. Hence many recent Slav theologians differ with regard to the final recompense immediately after death. Some are convinced, on the basis of a homily of John Damascene which found its way into the Byzantine liturgy, that with death the lot of the unrepentant sinner is not irreparably decided. This belief was nourished by the rite of a last anointing of the dead, originating in the 13th century, which included prayers that the soul of the deceased might be freed from hell. While the Greeks found the doctrine of purgatory suspect because it seemed to reflect the error of Origen on the apocatastasis, various Russian authors, such as N. Berdyaev and S. Bulgakov, uphold the teaching of Origen and deny the eternity of and objective hell.

1. The Catholic Church and the Eastern Churches

The Catholic Church has always considered itself to be the one Church of Christ and hence has continually worked for reunion after each schism, the Holy See being particularly active. This is evident from the long history of the attempts at union and their partial success. But the attitude of the Catholic Church towards the Christian East has not always been the same; it has changed in keeping with the times. There have been alternating periods of great understanding and also deep estrangement. Undoubtedly, sympathy and concern for the separated Eastern Churches received a decided impulse from Pope John XXIII, and from the Council convoked by him, a feature of which was the new ecumenical movement in the Catholic Church. Yet this did not happen all of a sudden, but was prepared by a series of papal letters and measures undertaken by Pius IX, Leo XIII, Benedict XV, and especially Pius XI. A movement interested in the Eastern Churches has long existed in Germany, France, and elsewhere. Pius XI made the Benedictine monastery of Amay-sur-Meuse in Belgium, later Chevetogne, a centre of the movement. Benedict XV founded the Pontifical

Oriental Institute in Rome, which was then greatly helped by Pius XI, whose encyclical *Rerum Orientalium* of 8 September 1928 recommended study of the Eastern Churches and especially their theology. Scholarly and informative periodicals have been published for years by the Benedictines, Augustinians, Assumptionists, Dominicans, Jesuits, and other orders to further the knowledge of the Christian East.

Vatican II not only promulgated a special Decree on the Eastern Catholic Churches, but also included in this decree (art. 24–29) and in the Decree on Ecumenism (in Part I of the third chapter: art. 13–18) a special reference to the Eastern Churches separated from Rome. These decrees express great esteem for the institutions, liturgy, and traditions of the Eastern Churches. The first decree speaks of the local Eastern Churches, of the preservation of their spiritual heritage, of the venerable institution of the patriarchate (all Catholic Eastern patriarchs are equal in dignity; their rights and privileges are stressed); it speaks also of the sacramental discipline, the celebration of feasts, of contact and inter-communion with the separated Eastern Churches (the practice with regard to *communicatio in sacris* is modified; cf. the Decree on Ecumenism, art. 8). In the second decree the elements which unite East and West are stressed.

Bernhard Schultze

ECCLESIASTICAL LAW

I. Concept and System

A. Definition and Division

1. *Definition.* Ecclesiastical law, or canon law, is the entirety of the norms of the law laid down by God and by the Church, which regulate the constitution and life of the Church of Jesus Christ united under the Pope as its one visible head. The laws of the State which regulate Church affairs, which apply where the Church is "established" in the State, are civil and not ecclesiastical law. Law which arises from agreement between Church and State, especially through concordats, is both ecclesiastical and civil law.

2. *Division.* Ecclesiastical law is distinguished according to its origin either as divine or as human law. Divine law is either positive divine law as expressed in revelation, or natural law based on the order of creation. Human law (purely ecclesiastical law) is either the result of legislation or of custom.

Divine law is unchangeable. But the following considerations should not be overlooked in this regard. For a certain institution to qualify as an expression of divine law it is not necessary that it be found explicitly as such in the pages of sacred Scripture; it is enough if it is unanimously considered by the ecclesiastical magisterium to belong to the inalienable nature of the Church and has some sort of basis in sacred Scripture. No greater demands can be made upon legal institutions in this regard than are made with respect to dogmatic assertions. Also, it is necessary to be mindful of the intrinsic law of development in the Church. Like the development which characterizes organic life, the course of Church history has been marked by the stirrings of new tendencies and new developments under the guidance of the Holy Spirit which have given rise to offices and institutions which in their fully developed form are considerably different from those of primitive Christianity and the early Church. As the instrument of God, the Church has an essential share in the creation of these institutions. With regard to those juridical forms which the Church considers to be essential to its being, the process is an irreversible one.

The purely ecclesiastical portions of Church law are changeable. Human law always has one relation, and often a twofold one, to divine law, insofar as the juridical authority legitimately functions in virtue of divine law, and insofar as formal ecclesiastical law largely codifies what is materially divine law.

B. The Foundations of Law

The justification for the existence of law in the Church is in the very nature of the redemptive work of God. The bringer of revelation is the God-man Jesus Christ; redemption is achieved in the historical actions centred on his person. Historicity cannot be divorced from society, and society cannot exist without law. The redemptive work of God and the means he chose for its realization contain the presuppositions and the basis for a juridical order.

1. *Preaching*. Revelation is the saving activity of God in Jesus Christ. The answer to revelation and to the offer of salvation which it contains is faith, which is essentially also obedience (Rom 1:5). Insofar as the content of revelation is intelligible, it represents a doctrine which is imposed by God upon all men. The teaching of Jesus must be retained unfalsified and conscientiously observed (Mt 28:20; Jn 17:6–8). The Christian message is the proclamation not only of the words of Jesus, but also of his life, his works and his suffering. Redemption is unthinkable without the underlying historical events of the death, burial and resurrection of Jesus. Saving faith encompasses all these actions (Rom 10:9). To substantiate the factual nature of the resurrection of Jesus, Paul offers the proof of witnesses (1 Cor 15:5–8). These historical events are an essential part of the gospel; to abandon them is to destroy Christianity (1 Cor 15:2). Since God willed to effect the salvation of mankind through the unique and unrepeatable history of Jesus Christ, his will includes the obligation of proclaiming historical facts; these facts are the norm of the contents and of the form of the preaching. The relation of preaching to these concrete historical facts and the duty of handing on this tradition unchanged are of a juridical nature.

The juridical character of the Church's preaching is also based on the fact that it is done in the name of Christ and by his mandate. In order to be able to proclaim the resurrection of Jesus, it is not enough to be an eye-witness of his apparitions; it is also necessary to be commissioned by the risen Christ and to be empowered by the Holy Spirit (Acts 10:42; 1:8). To become a witness of Christ one must possess both an inner charismatic element, the power of the Spirit, and an outward juridical element, the authorized mission.

2. *Confession of faith*. The preaching of the salvation bestowed through Christ must correspond in content and form to the message of the witnesses of the events themselves, namely that of the apostles. The Christian communities persevere "in the teaching of the apostles" (Acts 2:42). For the preaching of the decisive events of salvation the missionaries used fixed concepts and expressions (Acts 4:10; 8:12; 9:20). Paul showed himself to be in conscious agreement with the preaching of the entire Church, not only in the general sense of what he preached but also in the very expressions and formulas he used (1 Cor 15:11, 14). Thus, preaching necessarily involves a fixed confession of faith.

Similarly, the sacramental activity of the Church cannot dispense with its efficacious performative and significant words and with fixed formulations of the faith. The Christian is dedicated to Jesus Christ in baptism; the meaning of the baptismal event makes the profession of faith in Jesus Christ and the acknowledgment of acceptance by Jesus Christ indispensable. The neophyte must acknowledge that Jesus is the Lord (Rom 10:9; Eph 4:5) and the minister baptizes in the name of the Lord Jesus (Acts 8:16; 19:5; 1 Cor 1:13). With these the necessary formulas of the baptismal creeds come about. This is also true of the trinitarian creeds (cf. Tertullian, *De Spectaculis*, 4; *Constitutiones Apostolicae*, VII, 41), and baptismal formulas (Mt 28:19; *Didache*, 7, 1–3; Justin, *Apologia*, 1, 61, 3; Tertullian, *Adversus Praxean*, 26; *Constitutiones Apostolicae*, VII, 43). Christian community worship, like the worship of the Jewish people, always embodied remembrance and praise of the great deeds of God in history. The unique, historical, and fixed character of this proof of the providence and faithfulness of God requires an established formulation. Formulas of faith, therefore, have had a place in the worship of the Christian community from the very beginning (1 Cor 12:3; cf. 2 Cor 1:20) both in the liturgy (1 Cor 16:22) and in the preaching of the word (Tit 1:9; 1 Thess 4:14ff.; 1 Cor 15:1ff.; Heb 1:1ff.; 1 Jn 1:1ff.; Acts 1:4ff.; *2 Clem*, 1, 1). They are the normative basis of both liturgy and preaching. The ordinand is required to make a profession of faith (1 Tim 6:12) and is bound to adhere to this profession (2 Tim 2:2). Thus from the beginning, there was a dogmatic tradition in the primitive Church. The formulations of the faith used by the apostles and their followers have an authoritative character; they comprise the norms of Christian teaching, and to them the following generations of Christians are bound.

3. *Tradition.* Primitive Christianity was conscious of being chosen and saved through the historically unique activity of God in Jesus Christ. It belongs to the very foundation of the Church's existence to hold fast in faith to this event and to attest and hand on the confession of faith in it. Paul bids the Corinthians to preserve the tradition which he passed on to them (1 Cor 11:2, 16). If God has covenanted himself to mankind in a binding way, mankind has the duty of accepting, attesting and transmitting faithfully the truth thus received. Each generation must hand on unchanged to the next that which it has received from the previous one (1 Cor 11:23; 15:3; 2 Tim 2:2). When the witnesses of the event of Christ transmit their experiences and their faith, they found the tradition. The obligation to hold to that which is handed on and the duty to transmit it further loyally, are, in the ecclesiastical community, of a juridical nature. Inasmuch as the recipients are bound to hand on that which they have received, they are subject to a juridical bond.

The tradition-principle is related to the hierarchical principle of Church order by the concept of succession. The direct lineage of a tradition is the guarantee of its correctness, of the soundness of teaching (2 Tim 1:13f.). The handing on of the truth is the presupposition of the authority of the teachers. Their authority is based on the fact that the teachers form a link in the chain of tradition, and that the transmitter is closer to the origin of the traditional doctrine than the recipient. The necessity of forming a link in the chain of witnesses or teachers is of a juridical nature. The methods of active tradition and the criteria of objective tradition are likewise juridically determined.

4. *Dogma.* Those to whom the divine revelation or the doctrinal tradition of the Church is entrusted must preserve it (1 Tim 6:20); and that active preservation expresses itself in doctrinal declarations and definitions.

The revelation of a truth by God and the founding of an institutional Church implies at once, according to God's intention, the declaration of this truth officially, authentically and in a binding way by the Church. The Church has the task of formulating the faith in clear concepts, insofar as it can be comprised in true propositions, and of binding its members to the profession of such formulations. At the same time it has the right and the duty to give binding interpretations of the official declaration of the faith, to determine when teaching departs from this, and to decide finally and imperatively disputed questions. Both the authoritative declaration of the truths of faith and the authoritative decision on doctrinal questions have normative value and are of a juridical nature.

The most important expression of the ecclesiastical magisterium is the infallible definition, which is the explicit and irreformable declaration of a proposition as revealed truth. Dogma is a truth of revelation in the form of an ecclesiastical law, a law of faith. To the obligation of accepting divine revelation, there is added the obligation by virtue of ecclesiastical law.

5. *Worship*. Jesus commissioned and empowered the apostles to baptize, to celebrate the Eucharist and to forgive sins in the sacrament of penance. Only those who are commissioned and empowered can validly (or lawfully) perform these liturgical actions. In the execution of their commission and in the exercise of their authority the ministers are bound to the will of Christ; they can and must only perform these actions in the manner which the Lord has determined. When they duly carry out the commands of Christ, God works infallibly with them and through them. The imparting of grace is linked to a fixed order determined by divine law.

This bond is especially clear in the celebration of the Eucharist. At the Last Supper, Jesus charged the apostles to continue to celebrate the meal in the future, after his death and return to the Father; he bade them do it in that form which he himself had used (Lk 22:19; 1 Cor 11:24f.). Jesus instituted the essence and the form of the celebration. Only when the disciples do what Jesus himself did is the memorial of Jesus and his sacrificial death proclaimed, i.e., only then is the death of Jesus made present in its saving power. The Christian communities recognized that they were bound by the command to celebrate the Lord's Supper and to celebrate it in the manner instituted by Jesus himself. Only if the celebration of the Eucharist is carried out by authorized members of the Church, with the elements and words which the Lord himself used, is the command of Jesus fulfilled and the full content of the celebration guaranteed. But where the reality and the validity of a liturgical event is bound to delegated faculties and the observance of certain norms, law comes into force.

The duty to observe the command of Jesus and to hold to the form which he himself used are juridical elements, from which as the Church became clearer about the meaning of Jesus' command and of the eucharistic celebration, other norms followed, especially the injunction of worthiness. Paul saw clearly that the nature of the commemoration of the death of the Lord implied necessary consequences for behaviour of the community and of the individual. The Eucharist stands in closest relation to the last meal of Jesus. When the community eats "this bread" and drinks of the cup, it "proclaims the death of the Lord" (1 Cor 11:26), it celebrates the memory of the death of Jesus. At the same time, the Eucharist brings us into communion with the glorified Christ. "The cup of blessing which we bless, is it not a participation in the blood of Christ? The bread which we break, is it not a participation in the body of Christ?" (1 Cor 10:16.) From the knowledge that the community joins itself to the living Lord in the celebration of the Eucharist and particularly in the partaking of the food and drink, there follows the demand for worthiness on the part of the participants. Whoever takes part in the sacred meal "unworthily" makes himself "guilty of profaning the body and blood of the Lord" (1 Cor 11:27) because he does not distinguish the body of the Lord from ordinary food. Starting from the requirement of worthiness in the participants, the Church made explicit the individual elements of the requisite conditions and made them obligatory.

In a similar way the other sacraments also clearly show their intrinsic relationship to law. In the sacrament of baptism the pouring of water and the invocation of the name of Jesus brings the candidate into the fellowship of Christ's disciples (Mt 28:19; 1 Cor 12:13; Eph 5:26; Tit 3:5). The process as such is necessary for the attainment of salvation through union with Christ. Without this Christian initiation which is accomplished in baptism, the reception of the other sacraments is not possible; baptism is the prerequisite by divine right. For the efficacy of baptism, both elements of the process, contact with water and the pronouncing of the words, are indispensable. Their determination and association are elements of an institution of divine right.

In the sacrament of Orders the gift of grace is mediated by the outward juridical act of the imposition of hands (1 Tim 4:14; 2 Tim 1:6). The power thus bestowed distinguishes clerics from laymen; it either confers the office or disposes a subject for the reception of such and is thereby the basis of the juridical organizational structure of the Church.

6. *Office*. It belongs to the nature of Christianity that the divine both appears and veils itself in human form. In Christ, God has really and actively entered into history, though veiled in the form of Jesus of Nazareth, who as a child lay in a manger (Lk 2:12, 16) and was known as the son of Joseph (Lk 3:23), and as a man died hanging upon a cross (Mk 15:24f., 37). The manner in which the divine and the human are thus conjoined so that the human serves the divine, though it at the same time conceals it, runs through the whole of the redemptive work of God. It also characterizes the organization and the activity of the Church. The Church is the organ and the instrument of the kingdom of God. It is of divine origin and contains divine treasures; it is vivified and sustained by divine power. But it is also a society of men and is subject to the historical and sociological conditions of such society, which include authority and order. The special nature of authority and order in the Church is that they are determined in their essential features by the founder of the Church himself. Jesus handed on to the apostles the mission which the Father had given to him (Mk 3:13–19); the disciples preach in his name and by his mandate (Lk 10:16). Because sent by Jesus, they can give a message which demands response, and take binding decisions.

In certain regards Jesus delegated the power which he had received from the Father to the apostles (Jn 13:20; 20:21). This delegation took place in their vocation and mission by Jesus (Mk 3:14 par.; Mt 28:19; Acts 9:27; Gal 1:15f.). A mandate given by a historical act is of a formal and therefore a juridical nature; a formal action in the past is the basis of the apostolic status and gives it a juridical character.

Jesus established in the Church a power of binding and of loosing (Mt 18:18). He thereby conferred upon the Church the power to impose obligations and to absolve from obligations, i.e., in the first place to make and abrogate laws. The exercise of the power of binding and loosing is assured of divine ratification.

The two essential elements of the constitution of the Church, the primacy and the episcopacy, go back to Jesus. From the manner of their institution or bestowal, we can conclude to their nature. The formally juridical nature of the conferring of Christ's authority is very clear in the special case of Peter. The pastoral mandate announced by Christ (Mt 16:18f.) was given to the head of the apostles before witnesses and was repeated three times

(Jn 21:15–18). This public commission by Jesus is the warrant of that mission; authority rests upon a formal act of conferring. The use of a juridical formula indicates that it is the conferring of an office. An office is a stable set of rights and duties which is conferred upon someone by the competent authority and gives to the official actions of that person an objectively binding power; it is an institution which is essential and proper to law.

The Church therefore recognized from the start the existence of ecclesiastical offices. The apostles knew that they had certain powers and duties. They proclaimed the word of God and called for obedience to it (Gal 4:14; 1 Thess 2:13; 2 Cor 5:20); they celebrated the liturgy and performed baptisms (Acts 2:41; 1 Cor 1:14), the Eucharist (Acts 20:7–11), the imposition of hands (Acts 6:6; 8:15–17; 1 Tim 4:14; 5:22; 2 Tim 1:16); they founded and ruled Churches (Acts 8:14f.; 15:2; Rom 15:15; 1 Cor 11:34; 2 Cor 10:13–16; 13:10; 2 Thess 3:4) and they exercised disciplinary and judicial functions in the Church (1 Cor 5:3–5; 1 Tim 1:20). Because of their mission, the apostles could claim the obedience of the community (Rom 15:18; 1 Cor 14:37; 2 Cor 10:18; 13:13).

These offices in the Church did not cease with the death of the apostles; they handed on their ordinary power to proclaim the word, to dispense the sacraments and to rule the Church, to other men chosen as their representatives and successors (1 Tim 4:14; 2 Tim 1:6). Those whom the apostles appointed were considered to be appointed by the Holy Spirit (Acts 20:28). The apostles acted, therefore, by the mandate of God and with his approbation. The directives which they issued for the handing on of their transferable powers have the character of divine law. "The line already drawn in *1 Clem*, 42, 4 – God-Christ-apostle-bishop – is thus not a shift in the direction of the juridical, but reflects the data of the NT." (H. Bacht, *LTK*, I, col. 738.) Thus, the hierarchical structure and the juridical nature of the Catholic Church are shown to be of divine law. To speak of the Church as juridical simply means that the Church "is bound in its outward form to a historical, and basically closed revelation and that in the essential characteristics of this outward form, as contained in Church law, it cannot be changed" (H. Barion, "Katholische Kirche", *RGG*, III, col. 1505). As our knowledge of divine law is bound up with the development of dogma as a part of revelation, growth and progress is possible in the recognition of the elements of Church organization which are of divine right, and consequently in the elaboration of the basic order of the Church.

C. Special Nature and Task of Church Law

Church law is law in an analogous sense, i.e., it is both similar and dissimilar to civil law. It is similar in that it agrees fundamentally with civil law in its nature and goal; but it is dissimilar in that it is the order of a supernatural community instituted by God.

1. *Special nature*. Church law is a spiritual law: its basic elements were determined by Christ himself. Ecclesiastical legislators are directly or indirectly authorized by revelation. Matters regulated by canon law stand in more or less close relationship to the life of grace in the mystical body of Christ.

a) *Mediation of salvation*. Church law, by its attempt to harmonize the interests of individuals and of the community, seeks to bring about peace, justice, certainty, and freedom in the Church. By preserving order, it does its part in making the Church a suitable instrument of the mysterious divine activity within it. Thus, the ultimate purpose of this order is to lead the individual to his eternal goal. Because Church law is not separable from the

Church and because the visible and hierarchically ordered Church is necessary for salvation, canon law has a function in the mediation of that grace. This is true both for divine and for human law, though in different degrees and in different ways. It remains true that salvation is a free grace of God, even though the observance of law is indispensable in the attainment of salvation.

b) *Inward and outward spheres.* One characteristic feature of Church law which is of special significance is its distinction between the inward and the outward spheres (*forum externum* and *internum*). As with all forms of juridical order, Church law begins with the external. But it does not remain with the externals: it strives to give insight and awaken a free personal response. Outward and inward concerns should normally correspond. What is of decisive importance in the last analysis, however, is the inward attitude. Thus, in the case of conflict, the inward intention has precedence over the declared will. An example of such a case is the marriage consent (can. 1081, § 1; 1086). Of course the inward intention can only be relevant in law, if it can somehow be demonstrated. This is true, for example, of the *poenitentiae signa* in the question of the granting of Church burial (can. 1240, § 1) and of the repentance required for the lifting of excommunication (can. 2242, § 3). The evidence of the activity of grace in the inward sphere can mitigate in an individual case the necessary universality of the law and can take account of individual persons and circumstances. In the inward sacramental sphere, in the sacrament of penance, Church law penetrates to depths beyond the reach of civil law.

c) *Aequitas canonica.* Canonical equity consists of a higher justice, which, in its concern for the spiritual good of the whole or of an individual, may in certain cases mitigate the strictness of the law (as is most often the case) or (rarely) intensify it. The subordination of law to equity is an attempt to allow moral values to predominate over the letter of the law, and thus to realize the ideal of justice in the juridical sphere. Canon law distinguishes between *aequitas scripta* and *non scripta*, according to whether the law itself prescribes a procedure according to equity, or whether an action guided by equity is only possible by virtue of general legal principles. Equity obliges and justifies one in taking cognizance of the local, temporal, and personal circumstances of a given case. It is a dynamic principle of Church law.

d) *Particular legislation.* The *CIC* is fundamentally adapted to particular legislation, i.e., laws that are made for a certain locality or a personally defined legal group. Differences in particular laws, insofar as they are based on a necessary and legitimate adaptation of principles to special circumstances and relationships, are fully justified. The Church can and must express its Catholic nature also in its legal order. It should be observed, nevertheless, that countries and continents, and therefore also the different types of communities within the Church, are coming more and more into contact as a result of improved means of communication. For this reason, the justification for particular legislation, at least of that which represents a modification of general laws, must be constantly reviewed by the competent ecclesiastical legislators. The faithful all too easily take offence at the differences in the ecclesiastical law in neighbouring countries, when they cannot see that the differences are due to varying situations or to political situations.

e) *Continuity.* Church law is the order of a spiritual community with a history of almost two thousand years. The goal remains the same, though the means may vary, within relatively narrow bounds, however, as the essential means of salvation are intrinsic to the Church.

Because of this, even purely ecclesiastical law reveals a marked continuity. Furthermore, to educate the members of the Church to respect for the law and to avoid uncertainties, a certain permanence of juridical institutions is indispensable. Changes and especially inconsistencies following rapidly upon each other in the same legal sphere undermine confidence in the lawgiver and also the obedience of the subjects. Likewise, individualistic anticipations of an awaited or desired change disrupt the unity of observance. Those entrusted with the implementation of Church law easily lose sight of the entire state of legislation. The result may be defective or unworkable changes in law. Changes in law thus demand great circumspection and profound historical studies. This conservative trait of canon law, which is also an intrinsic trait of law in general, does not imply an easy-going dependence upon tradition or a blindness to necessary changes; it implies rather the preservation of the valid, the rejection of unjustifiable experiments, the quest for permanent norms, an effort to preserve continuity and creativeness while maintaining sound tradition.

2. *Tasks.* a) *The preservation of order.* The activity of the Holy Spirit in the Church does not exclude the need for law in the maintenance of right order; it is the basis of that need. Those who are appointed as shepherds of the Church by the Holy Spirit (Acts 20:28) are under the guidance of that Spirit when they make and implement laws, a guidance which in certain acts of doctrinal legislation can even preserve from error and equip with infallibility. God himself, according to revelation, sustains the human endeavour to maintain good order. In reference to the gift of prophecy, Paul writes "... God is not the God of confusion but of peace" (1 Cor 14:33).

The Church laws apply to the faithful, to those who have become bearers of the Spirit through baptism and confirmation (Rom 8:9). The Spirit of God, who dwells within them, enables them to recognize the precepts and prohibitions of the law as the way of the Spirit and fulfil the demands of the law from inner conviction. Observance of the law is the fruit of redemption and of the gift of the Holy Spirit. Nevertheless, the Spirit also bestows the gift of the proper use of freedom under the law. The law of the Church does not enslave the faithful but helps them to become more and more Christian in daily life. It is a part of that imperative of the realization of salvation which in Christianity is inseparably bound to the indicative of the presence of salvation (O. Kuss).

b) *Protective function.* Church law has an essentially protective function: it has in the first place the task of guarding the purity of doctrine by fidelity to tradition. A typical expression of this function is that all teaching in the name of the Church has as its unvarying prerequisite the *missio canonica.* The task of protecting the purity of teaching is carried out also by other prescriptions of doctrinal legislation, such as the rules governing censorship and the making of professions of faith. The servants of the Church must present in their teaching not opinions but truths of faith.

The most fully worked out part of the *CIC* and the most important in pastoral work is the section on marriage laws. Its basic purpose is to preserve the sacredness of marriage and its indissolubility. The ideal is the marriage between partners of the same faith who are blessed with children.

Church law must also have a developed penal law, providing for ecclesiastical penalties and courts. Sanctions express the will to live and the desire for justice. A community which leaves unpunished those who offend against its own ideals gives the appearance of having but a low estimation of the good things it offers; it invites violation of its laws and imperils its own existence.

In its system of penalties the Church shows its fidelity to the truths of revelation and the seriousness of its mission in the world. Insofar as the holiness of the Church is the moral task of its members, it is also served by the Church's penal legislation. Justice demands that the public law-breaker be recognized as such and that compensation be made for his misdeeds in the form of a restriction of his rights. One who discredits the community to which he belongs deserves that the community in some way withdraw itself from him. Just as observance of the law is deserving of praise, so too its violation is deserving of censure. In view of the different possible violations and the degrees of responsibility involved, a graduated penal system is required to deal with them justly. Starting from the traditional penalty of excommunication, the Church has developed an organized system of penalties. The Church does not forget, however, that its mission sets a limit to punishments, and that it cannot presume to anticipate the eschatological judgment of God.

D. Binding Power and Limits of Law

1. *Binding power.* The human law promulgated by the holders of ecclesiastical office of divine institution, or by their delegates, claims obedience for two reasons. In the first place their power to command derives directly or indirectly from Jesus; they stand, in a sense, in the place of God. In the second place, the common good of the Church requires the rule of law in ecclesiastical life, even in matters that appear to be of secondary importance. Just law opposes caprice and ensures due uniformity of action. How far uniformity should extend is a matter of opinion; but not its basic necessity.

Purely ecclesiastical law restricts as a rule its demands upon the faithful to a minimum. It is to mistake the meaning and the goal of the law to think that he who fulfils that law has done enough, that he has thus "fulfilled all justice". The demands of God can in individual cases reach further than the laws of the Church. The law determines what is under normal conditions indispensable for the common good and for the salvation of the individual; it fixes the lower limit. It cannot and will not set a limit upwards. It is left to the enlightened Christian conscience of the individual to determine what God requires from him here and now over and above the codified law.

Between law and love there is no real opposition; the rule of law is rather the expression of the maternal love of the Church. The most elementary and minimal effort of love must be to create order and justice, stability and freedom. This is precisely what the law seeks to realize. Love must therefore normally first fulfil the law and give to each one his due before it seeks to do something more. Conflicts between the common and the individual good are inevitable. The ensuing hardships must either be borne for the sake of the common good or may be removed or lessened by dispensation and privilege, two legal processes which exemplify the principle of the equity at law. By dispensation we mean here the removal of the obligatory character of a law in a concrete case; by privilege the institution of an exceptional rule in favour of individual need. Both measures, however, are to be used with discretion and restraint, for every deviation from the rule tends to lessen the validity of the norm, not in itself but in the eyes of those subject to the law.

Ecclesiastical law does not deprive the faithful of responsibility for their actions, but rather heightens it. It is true that the course of our personal actions is irrevocably determined by divine law, and similarly in the sphere of purely ecclesiastical legislation one is normally to presume that the law is to be followed both in its particulars and according to its letter. Nevertheless, the Christian must always take account of the circumstances of his actions; he must remember that the law represents only a minimum demand which he must complete in a spirit which accepts law not as an alien power but as an expression of his personal will. The observance of the law will not be seen as his own achievement but as the fruit of the Spirit. For Paul the new creation in Christ (2 Cor 5:17; cf. Eph 2:10, 15; 4:24; Col 3:10) is the "canon", i.e., the guideline, the rule for the behaviour of the Christian (Gal 6:15f.). Responsibility may cause the Christian to go beyond the law and do more than it commands. But it may also permit, suggest or even require that the law be disregarded. Justification for such freedom with regard to purely ecclesiastical law is: grave fear, necessity, and grave disadvantages as recognized by law (can. 2205, § 2). Another justification would be the elimination of the end envisaged by the law (cf. can. 21).

A decision against the law demands great discretion and high moral seriousness. *Epikeia* (equity, "sweet reasonableness") is a moral virtue; it measures the grounds for excusation against the weight of the law, i.e., its importance for the community and the individual. One's own relationship to the law, and especially the duty of avoiding scandal, must also be considered. The legislator denies the validity of the excuses given above when disregard of the law would lead to contempt of the faith or of Church authority or to harm to souls (can. 2205, § 3). The way of true Christian obedience lies between the extremes of a false legalism and libertinism. The Christian must guard himself from the twofold error of believing either that he himself can attain salvation by his observance of the law or that the observance of the law is indifferent to salvation.

2. *Limits*. The law of the Church is necessary for the realization of salvation; it is the necessary condition for its mediation. Nevertheless, it is not itself the saving event or the reality of salvation. Rather, canon law is inwardly and essentially directed to a meta-canonical sphere: it has its significance and its necessity for salvation not in itself but in its transcendence towards the meta-canonical sphere (G. Söhngen).

In the framework of ecclesiastical life, canon law has a comprehensive task insofar as juridical order is always necessary; but of itself it is incapable of making an essential contribution to the life of the Church. Law does not create life but protects and maintains a life which is already present. Great expectations attached to changes in the law are usually disappointed. Too much cannot be asked of the law. On the other hand, spiritually gifted personalities have also made use of law to prepare the way for their ideas. The great reform movements in Church history have always had repercussions upon Church law. The reformers were aware that ideas need a juridical embodiment if they are to endure and be efficacious. Spiritual renewal intends, and indeed must intend, to shape the practice of ecclesiastical life and hence also ecclesiastical law. Thus, such movements as the Carolingian, Gregorian, and Tridentine Reforms have also proved to be sources of new legislative activity. They gave to the collection and systematization of canon law powerful and enduring impulses. Renewal in the Church and highpoints of juridical development generally go hand in hand. Not a few of the most eminent Popes were also capable canonists.

E. Sources

1. *Up to the CIC*. The most important source for the law in force up to Pentecost 1918 is the *Corpus Iuris Canonici*. It is composed of the *Decretum* of Gratian, the Decretals of Gregory IX (*Liber Extra*), of Boniface VIII (*Liber Sextus*), of Clement V (*Clementinae Constitu-*

tiones) and the two collections of *Extravagantes* (*Extravagantes Ioannis XXII, Extravagantes Communes*). The *Corpus Iuris Canonici* is not a code but rather a group of various collections and law books. It embraces a period of about 400 years.

The development of ecclesiastical law did not stop with the completion of the *Corpus*. The Council of Trent and the legislation of the Popes of modern times, such as Benedict XIV and Pius IX, produced much new material which was scattered in diverse sources frequently difficult of access. General need was felt for a codification, i.e., a unified, authentic summary of the current common law.

2. *The CIC*. The main source of the present law is the *Codex Iuris Canonici*. Pope Pius X began the work of codification; the new code was promulgated on 27 May 1917 and came into force on 19 May 1918. The *CIC* first appeared as Pars II of vol. 9 (1917) of the *Acta Apostolicae Sedis*. Editions of the *CIC* were published with and without references to sources. Appended to the text are various important documents. The index published with it was the work of Pietro Gasparri; Gasparri and I. Serédi published in the years 1923–39 the *Codicis Iuris Canonici Fontes*, in nine volumes. The authentic interpretations of the *Pontificia Commissio ad Codicis canones authentice interpretandos* have been collected by I. Bruno up to 1950 (1935, 1950).

The *CIC* is intended as a law book for that part of the Church which uses Latin as the language of its official worship, though it also has limited application to the communities of the Eastern rite. For the latter a separate book of law is being compiled. In spite of its many borrowings from the law of the Latin Church, justice is being done to the special characteristics of the Oriental rites.

3. *Subsequent development*. Since the *CIC* came into force, law has been steadily developing and in many respects, due to the legislative activity of the Popes and the Roman Congregations, it has gone beyond the *CIC*. One could mention here the extensive legal activity of Pius XII which broke new ground in several areas. Of special significance is the constitution concerning the election of the Pope, *Vacantis Apostolicae Sedis*, of 8 December 1945. Similarly John XXIII issued new prescriptions, e.g., concerning the administration of suburbicarian sees, the episcopal dignity, the right of option for cardinals, and supplements to the constitution on papal elections.

John XXIII announced a revision of the *CIC* on 25 January 1959, and appointed a commission for that purpose. The revision has many tasks to cope with. To bring the code abreast of the development of the last 50 years will demand many additions and changes. A greater systematization and unification of legal language is necessary; the declarations, trends and goals of Vatican II must be translated into law, as far as is possible and necessary. The Council itself laid down a sort of programme for legislation, outlining its principles, especially in its Constitution and Decrees on the Liturgy, Instruments of Social Communication, the Church, Eastern Catholic Churches, Ecumenism, Bishops' Pastoral Office, Religious Life, Priestly Formation, and the Apostolate of the Laity. Under the impulse issuing from Vatican II, Paul VI promulgated new laws, such as those concerning the powers of the bishops, and the institution of a synod of bishops. Partly in imitation of the conciliar decrees or in their implementation, Congregations of the Roman Curia have been active in legislating. The Congregation for the Doctrine of the Faith issued instructions on cremation and mixed marriages, and the SC Rit. instructions on the implementation of the Constitution on the Liturgy. Similarly particular law has been considerably increased in consequence of Vatican II and the legislation which followed it.

New treaties have been concluded between the Church and various States, such as the concordat with Spain, with the Dominican Republic and with Venezuela, the *modus vivendi* with Tunisia, and the treaty with Austria.

F. THE SCIENCE OF CANON LAW

1. *Definition.* The science of canon law is the systematic study and presentation of the law of the Church in itself and in its historical development.

2. *Method.* Canonists employ three methods: a) the historical method which traces the development of law in connection with the entire inward and outward development of the Church; b) the dogmatic method whose task it is to show which juridical norms are binding law, to explain them and their application; c) the philosophical method which attempts to explain the relation of the individual laws to all the rest and to the legal principles themselves, and also to show the agreement between the laws and the nature and goal of the Church, thus building up a system of canon law. It is also the task of the canonist to exercise responsible criticism with regard to the laws based upon human institution, by pointing out mistaken developments and encouraging reform.

The mixture of the juristic method of formal text-interpretation in canon law with the method of logical deduction from general principles and from the theological sources of Scripture and tradition in moral theology, gaining ground ever since the 16th century, has for a long time given way to the analytical movement back to the sources.

3. *History.* Church law is as old as the Church, yet for the first eleven centuries it received no special systematic treatment; it was taught in the schools as a part of theology. The earliest method which we find in canonistic literature is almost exclusively that of a simple collection of legislative documents. In Italy in the 11th century there was a renewed interest in antiquity and especially in Roman law. The schools of jurisprudence in Bologna ushered in a period of high development of Roman law under the influence of the scholastic method which was then gaining ground.

Inspired by this example and hoping to remedy the many contradictions in Church law which had resulted from the uncritical collection of old and new, general and particular, spiritual and temporal law, the Camaldolese monk Gratian, teacher of theology in the monastery of SS. Felix and Nabor in Bologna, made a new collection of Church law, the *Concordia discordantium canonum*, later called the *Decretum Gratiani*, probably between 1100 and 1120. His work is really a textbook in which the commentary is woven into the text itself. Gratian had the gift of arranging existing material clearly; he was able to elaborate the guiding principles of the canons, to bring out contradictions and to find, in the spirit of canon law, the right solution for actual or apparent antinomies. He was the first to teach canon law as an independent discipline. This was the beginning of the science of canon law which was soon to be zealously studied at the new universities.

Canonistic science schooled itself in the work of composing glosses, commentaries, and summaries of the law books promulgated by the Popes, all of which were gathered together along with private collections into the *Corpus Iuris Canonici*. It was, however, also – thanks to important figures such as Popes Alexander III, Innocent III, and Innocent IV who themselves went through that schooling – in a certain sense the co-creator of canon law itself. The technically perfected and flexible *Ius Canonicum* was enforced as the common law of the whole Church, having world-wide significance next to the

Ius Civile and forming with it up to modern times the *Ius Utrumque*.

In the period of the classical canonists, the period of the Glossators (between Gratian and Johannes Andreae, d. 1348), the system of canon law was so soundly developed that it remained determinative in the following centuries and even for present-day law. The two main divisions of study concerned the *Decretum* of Gratian, and the collections of Decretals.

In the period of the post-classical canonists, the epoch of the post-Glossators (*c.* 1350–1550), the traditional teaching was further handed on; the literature was predominantly practical.

In the period of the neo-classical canonists (*c.* 1550 to the 19th century), alongside the older and more exegetical method, a new systematic method was employed which maintained the traditional study of the original sources, but which arranged that material in a single comprehensive work. The authors of the great commentaries of this period are still today identified to some extent with the *auctores probati*.

In the 19th century there was a variety of systematic presentations of canon law, some of which are especially deserving of attention. The history of canon law made great progress.

Ever since the *CIC* came into force the systems based on the Decretals and the *Decretum* of Gratian have been definitively superseded. The method of interpretation of *CIC* was for the first time officially determined by two instructions from the Sacred Congregation of Studies dealing with teaching and examinations in view of academic degrees. The text of the *CIC* is to be studied according to the analytical exegetical method; independent synthetic presentation is excluded. The Constitution *Deus Scientiarum Dominus* of 24 May 1931 requires the application of the historical and philosophical method as well as the exegetical one for an appropriate understanding of canon law. Commentaries generally keep within the limits of practical exegesis. Not a few of them, however, try to penetrate deeper into the basic principles of law and to grasp the inner relation between the norms.

The promulgation of the *CIC* gave a great impetus to the study of canon law. The number of text-books has risen notably; a variety of monographs on the history of Church law and on dogmatic aspects of law have appeared; new periodicals devoted to canon law have been launched. In France a dictionary of canon law is almost complete.

The history of canon law has received special attention. The jubilee of Gratian in 1952 gave a lively impulse to historical research. In France a new history of the Law and the institutions of the Western Church is in process of publication. In Washington in 1955, the canonist S. Kuttner founded the Institute of Research and Study of Medieval Canon Law, for the purpose of collecting and examining all the material relating to canon law in the Middle Ages. The immediate goal of this work is a survey of the present state of studies in this field and the critical edition of the works of the "Decretists" and "Decretalists", as well as a new edition of the *Decretum Gratiani* on the basis of broader source-material and modern literary criticism.

4. *Place of Church law in science.* Canonistic science, in keeping with its subject matter, stands between theology and jurisprudence. It is closely linked to theology because it derives its principles from various theological disciplines and presupposes them, e.g., dogmatics – the very basis of canonical science is the Church in its dogmatic conception and in its dogmatic juridical order; and secondly, as *theologia practica*, it completes the system of theological science. From jurisprudence canonistic science took over its formal method. And there was a far-reaching reciprocal influence between the matter of civil and canon

law and between ecclesiastical and civil jurisprudence. In a word: "canonistic science is a theological discipline using the method of jurisprudence" (K. Mörsdorf).

5. *Auxiliary disciplines.* Among the auxiliary disciplines which canonistic science needs for the expounding and explanation of its principles we must distinguish between those of theology and jurisprudence. Theological auxiliaries are exegesis, which points out the elements of divine law; dogmatics, which with its dogmas is the foundation of ecclesiastical law; moral theology, which expounds the moral law as basis of ecclesiastical law; pastoral theology, which indicates how ecclesiastical law can best be implemented for the salvation of souls; and Church history and the history of liturgy, which include the description of the development of canonical institutions. The auxiliary disciplines of jurisprudence are: the study of natural law, which provides the basic concepts; Jewish law, insofar as the OT was in many respects the model for ecclesiastical institutions; Roman law, insofar as the Church often modelled itself on it, erected civil into ecclesiastical law (*leges canonizatae*) and used Roman law as a subsidiary; Germanic law, because canon law adopted various Germanic principles and institutions; constitutional and administrative law, where the Church has an established relationship to the State, and its law – as in Germany – is recognized as an element of public law; international law, insofar as State and Church meet in concordats, etc.; and finally economics, since the principles elaborated hold good to a great extent for the administration of ecclesiastical property.

G. Revision of Canon Law

The Synod of Bishops which met for the first time on 29 September 1967, in Rome, laid down the following principles for the revision of canon law, and once approved of by the Pope, they will be normative for the work of the commission in question. The special nature of ecclesiastical law as the means of ordering a spiritual society is to be taken into account. The external forum is to be both kept apart from and coordinated with the internal. The pastoral intention is to be primary. The principle of subsidiarity is to be maintained. Personal rights are to be assured. Penal laws need to be simplified. The new law governing judicial procedures must aim at speeding up the processes of law. The division of the *CIC* is to be more strictly systematic. The spirit of love, moderation and equity is to predominate throughout. No decision has yet been taken about the three possible structures of the new code of law: a) a single codex for the whole Church, b) separate codes for the Western and Eastern Churches, or c) a basic law for the whole Church, to be completed by codes for the various Churches.

Georg May

ECCLESIASTICAL OFFICE

It is not seldom that one finds, in the explanation of the nature of the Church, that office and charism are set one against the other. Those in official positions can interpret their task in so rigid a fashion as to take up a more or less uncomprehending attitude with regard to charisms. Likewise, it is not seldom that charismatics are tempted to see in the officials of the Church their born enemies. It has occasionally been put forward on principle that a Church characterized or dominated by offices contradicts the spiritual and charismatic nature of the community of Christ, just as on the other hand a juridically oriented ecclesiology has been too prone to eliminate the charismatic element in its description of the Church. According to Scripture, however, the Church rests "upon the foundation of the apostles *and* the prophets" (Eph 2:20). And we are undoubtedly justified in interpreting the "apostles" as the beginning of that which is later expressed in the Church as office, and the "prophets" as one expression of that charismatic influence from above which together with the office determines the reality of the Church.

The following discussion will be concerned with 1) how office and charism are two essential characteristics of the Church; 2) how their relation to each other must be interpreted as an intrinsic connection; and 3) how there is between them, nevertheless, an essential polarity and tension.

1. To show how office and charism both belong to the life of the Church, it must first be shown how the Church must be both institutional and spiritual, and then it must be shown how office and charism embody these two elements.

a) The Church of the present lives at the intersection of two lines or planes, both of which must be taken seriously in any description of the Church. One line, horizontal, is the historical origin of the Church from the apostles, and hence from Christ its founder. One must understand this "apostolic succession" not only as the sacramental transmission of the spiritual office but as the apostolicity of the Church in general. The Church is not only apostolic because its faith and life correspond to the teaching of apostolic times, but also because they come from them in an unbroken historical line. This horizontal historical line of the institutional existence of the Church is sacramentally founded. In the sacrament of baptism the Church is continuously enlarged throughout the course of history. And in the sacrament of order the office of the apostle is perpetuated for each new generation. This movement of the institutional Church along the horizontal line through the course of history must be understood as a coordinate of another line, the vertical or charismatic, for it is at the junction of these two that the actual place and condition of the Church are to be found. The activity of the glorified Lord through his Holy Spirit comes from above to the institution as it makes its way through history, fills it charismatically and really makes it the Church.

b) Office and charism have their place in the Church not only because they both come from Christ – that is, from his historical institution of the office and from his activity from on high in charisms – but also because both of them possess an intrinsic relation to one another. But it is a relation that does not exclude a certain tension. It is based upon the different way in which both represent the same thing; it is a fruitful and necessary complementary interaction. That which is common to both, though in different ways, is the presence of Christ in his Church.

(i) The meaning of the spiritual office is the visible and personal representation of Christ in the social sphere of the Church. Though the spiritual presence of the glorified Lord is, through the Holy Spirit, objectively more real than any physical presence could have been, it has less perceptible reality in the experience of men whose salvation depends upon that presence. This is the reason why Christ instituted the spiritual office within the Church as a visible reality with a social stamp. This is the meaning which St. Paul noted when he said "So we are ambassadors for Christ" (2 Cor 5:20). When the spiritual office is exercised in the service of the word and sacramental worship in the community, the encounter of the glorified Christ with the present Church which occurs in the vertical and charismatic dimension is, so to speak, transferred to the horizontal and social plane. This does not exclude or replace the charismatic element but gives it bodily form and sacramental guarantee.

(ii) The institutional representation of Christ through the spiritual office is entirely in the service of the charismatic presence of the glorified Lord. Charism must be taken in its largest sense here and not be too hastily restricted to those extraordinary manifestations of the Spirit of God within the Church. By charism is meant the whole sphere or God's self-communication in grace to the Church and to its members. In this sense it includes personal salutary graces – the sanctifying activity of God in the actions of men and the indwelling of God in the state of justification – as well as those special gifts and extraordinary actions of the Spirit of God which are bestowed upon individuals or groups for the good of the community.

2. The fact that office in the Church is conferred through a sacrament is already an indication of the connection between office and charism. The continuation of the Church and its offices in the course of its apostolic succession through history is thus seen to be an abiding and sacramental embodiment of the promise of the Lord, that he would send his Spirit from above to permeate the activity of the office. The relation of office and charism can be expressed in a threefold manner.

a) The function of the office is first of all to effect in the faithful the disposition for the reception of the grace of the Holy Spirit. The official teaching and exhortation move the faithful to open their hearts to the grace of God, and in this sense to his charismatic activity. The activity of the office can even be charismatic in type, insofar as it not merely exerts its authority but adds to it the "prophetic" force and urgency of a charism bestowed by the Spirit of God. Of itself, however, this effect of the office upon the disposition of the believer stands only in an indirect relation to the charismatic life within the Church.

b) But the work of the office in disposing the hearts of the faithful is also itself charismatic in a much deeper sense. The activity of the office in the Church is a sacramental embodiment of the divine activity of grace from above. Where the office of the Church, in virtue of the authority given it, announces the word of God and celebrates the sacramental worship, a sign and an assurance is given of the working of the glorified Lord.

c) But it is not only the activity of the office which is charismatic. The office itself in the Church is charismatic in nature. Its activity is the pledge of the self-communication of the Lord in grace and charisms, and the spiritual office itself is the representation of the most charismatic of all realities, Christ, who is present in the Church through his Holy Spirit. "In the bishops and the priests who stand at their side, the Lord Jesus Christ, the high-priest, is present in the midst of the faithful", as Vatican II says (*Lumen Gentium*, art. 21).

3. The close relationship and connection between office and charism (the latter in the strict sense) is often experienced as painful tension. Both poles, however, must strive to maintain each other in their purity in the life of the Church.

a) The office, as an institutional element, belongs to the sphere of the world. There is, therefore, a danger that it will take on the form of the world and allow itself to use the rules and instruments of the world, to make an absolute of what should merely serve. Such rigidity and worldliness in the office is then opposed by the charismatic, in the form of the sudden irruption of the Spirit into the life of the Church, with special calls to individuals or communities. Such charismatic supplements or corrections to the endangered office may themselves take on permanent form. Certain charisms in the primitive Church had almost the function of an office in the life of the community (e.g., 2 Cor 8:23; Phil 2:25; Rom 16:1). And in the state of life inspired by the evangelical counsels, charismatic vocations themselves became in fact an institution. In such charismatic activity the glorified Lord asserts himself again and again as the real Lord of the Church.

b) On the other hand, since primitive Christian times, the office has had the charge of watching over the charisms (cf. 1 Cor 1:10ff.; 14:37f.). It must protect the genuine charism against pseudo-charisms and unhealthy phenomena, and maintain the community in the good order which the charisms themselves are meant to serve (1 Cor 14:33). This charge may induce in the holder of the office an anti-charismatic attitude which unduly heightens the tension. But the genuine charism, being of divine force, will also overcome such exaggerations on the part of the office. The office-holder must always remember the warning of the Apostle: "Do not quench the Spirit; do not despise prophesying" (1 Thess 5:19f.).

Otto Semmelroth

ECCLESIASTICAL PENALTIES

Everybody is aware, however vaguely, that the Church sometimes inflicts penalties on its members; they may, for example, be excommunicated or deprived of Christian burial or, if clerics, they may be suspended from the exercise of their functions.

1. *Principles.* It may be objected that such repressive measures contradict the principle of the "holy liberty of the children of God". Nobody, however, will dispute the need for discipline within the Church. The Church's mission is to guide the faithful along the way that leads to salvation. To fulfil this mission it tells its members what they ought to believe and how they ought to behave; it imposes a discipline of faith and morals, a religious discipline. Is it not the living presence of Jesus Christ in their midst? The Church's discipline does not aim at annihilating the will of its members or paralysing their initiative; its purpose is to guide their footsteps so that each may be fully aware of the spiritual import of his or her action. The liberty of the faithful will then have an object, an orientation. The message of Jesus Christ is a message of love; the Church's discipline reflects the claims that love has upon its members, upon all mankind.

The faithful, moreover, form a community – the mystical body of Christ; all its members are mutually dependent, jointly and severally responsible. Discipline ensures concord within the community, guarantees to each his place and his rights, and entrusts to each his appropriate task. Liberty is, indeed, the intelligent acceptance of solidarity and responsibilities.

Ecclesiastical penalties are only one aspect – and not the most important one – of this discipline. They penalize infractions of what is prescribed or forbidden by the Church by virtue of its disciplinary power. Like all penalties in all organized communities, they have a threefold object – punishment of the offender, protection of the common good, and reformation of the transgressor. "Religion in spirit and in truth" does not imply the absence of organization, of discipline and of sanctions. It is rather a refusal to degrade organization, discipline and sanctions into a pernickety legalism, a refusal to distort their proper meaning. It implies intense and unremitting effort to maintain organization, discipline and sanctions in the service of their supernatural end, which is the salvation of mankind united in one living community. In order to safeguard this essential liberty which nobody has the right to renounce and which nobody can be deprived of, it is necessary and sufficient that the sanctions shall not be supplemented by physical restraint, such as the prevention of persons from leaving the Church, should they wish to do so.

That condition, as it will presently appear, is fulfilled in the Church of today.

The *basis* of ecclesiastical penalties was laid down by Jesus Christ himself (Mt 18:15–18). From the beginning ot the Church's history, in fact, we find that penalties are in force. St. Paul does not hesitate to inflict severe punishment on members of his communities who are guilty of some offence (1 Cor 5:5; 2 Cor 2:6; 1 Tim 1:20). As time went on, the Church's penal system developed. For a long time grievous penalties were visited on heretics. We cannot but deplore the excesses of the Inquisition in the Middle Ages. Fortunately those days are over.

2. *Characteristics.* All this does not mean that the Code of Canon Law (1918) which now governs the Latin Church has wiped out all traces of the past. Certain provisions in force today bear the impress of history. They sometimes envisage customs and juridical concepts now out-dated and institutions that have little life left in them. Occasionally, also, they prescribe cumbersome dealings with the Roman Curia.

This, however, is not by any means the dominant note of the system. Canon 2214 of the Code renews the warning of the Council of Trent to the bishops: "They (the bishops) will remember that they are pastors and not executioners, and must govern their subjects not in any domineering spirit but lovingly as children and brethren; frequently, indeed, benevolence is more efficacious than harshness as a means of correction, exhortation may be more effective than threats, and charity than authority. And so they will temper rigour with mildness, justice with mercy, and severity with tenderness." The Church never rests until it has brought the strayed sheep back into the fold, and it knows it will succeed in doing so through trust, patience and love. This mildness is displayed in various features of the Church's penal system; there is, for example, solicitude for the reformation of the offender, concern that his reputation should be spared, willingness to adapt punitive measures to individual cases, on the principle that it is not the difference of the offences that matters most, but the difference of the offenders. These factors make the system extremely flexible; the law places great confidence in the judge and also in the transgressor. Another result of this is that the Church's penal law, even in its most ancient manifestations, occasionally figures as a forerunner of contemporary secular legislation, which may have just discovered what the Church has practised for many centuries past.

3. *Infractions.* Ecclesiastical penalties are attached to two broad categories of infractions. In the first place there are the *delicta fori mixti*, misdemeanours punishable by both ecclesiastical and the civil authorities. Accordingly, the Church punishes infractions that constitute particularly serious and prevalent deviations from moral principles – for example, suicide, abortion and duelling.

In the second category are misdemeanours which involve only specifically ecclesiastical laws, and may injure the spiritual and religious interests for whose protection the Church is responsible. Their gravity is, therefore, measured by religious criterions. This category is today more numerous than "mixed" misdemeanours. It is not possible to enumerate them all here. The principal are, in descending order of gravity: profanation of the Holy Species, violence to the person of the Sovereign Pontiff, direct violation of the seal of sacramental confession, apostasy, heresy, impeding the exercise of ecclesiastical jurisdiction, adherence to freemasonry, violation of the enclosure of nuns, participation in the activities of a non-Catholic sect, manufacture of false relics, etc.

The above list gives an idea of the Church's preoccupations and of the dangers it wanted to guard against at the time the list was drawn up. It would be all the better, no doubt, for a little retouching. Duelling is not now among Catholics the scourge it used to be; neither is the manufacture or sale of false relics. In the present ecumenical climate it is easy to imagine that certain cases of "participation in the activities of a non-Catholic sect" would not be punished as severely as formerly – in particular as regards the exchange of matrimonial consent in the presence of a non-Catholic minister of religion. On the other hand, there is a multiplication of purely civil marriages following upon civil divorce, even among those who say they are, and would like to be considered, "good Catholics"; these are not subject to any penalty. This extension of civil divorce is a relatively recent sociological problem.

4. *Penalties.* The memory of the medieval Inquisition was evoked in an earlier paragraph. Its judges undoubtedly handed over parties guilty of the crime of heresy to the "secular arm", but, in doing so, they were well aware that they were sending those parties to the stake. In those days the Church was not entirely averse to punishments of a temporal order. Since then, however, ecclesiastical penalties have more and more taken the form of deprivation of the spiritual benefits dispensed by the Church, and so the essential liberty of the faith has been safeguarded.

There are two categories of ecclesiastical penalties, differentiated in accordance with the main object the Church has in mind. "Censures" or "medicinal penalties" envisage first and foremost the reformation of the guilty party, while "vindictive penalties" are primarily aimed at punishing the delinquent. (To be absolutely complete, the category of "penances" should be added; these provide for the "satisfaction" or reparation accepted by a contrite offender.) Vindictive penalties are usually of fixed duration, while censures have to be removed by a special "absolution", distinct from the sacramental absolution that the offender is entitled to when he has amended. Certain penalties are sometimes vindictive and sometimes medicinal, according to the manner of their imposition. Excommunication, which is the gravest penalty of all and the most frequent, is always medicinal, a fact which stresses the importance attached by the Church to the reformation of the offender. Certain sanctions, moreover, are not always penalties in the precise sense of the term; this is so, in particular, with the deprivation of Christian burial generally enforced in the case of public sinners (concubines and the like), unless they have shown evident signs of penitence. Some penalties are proper to clerics; these include deposition, privation of the right to wear ecclesiastical dress, degradation, and more recently "suspension", which entails privation of the right to exercise certain functions specified in the sentence or prescribed by law – for example, celebrating Mass and hearing confessions. A penalty known as "exclusion from legitimate ecclesiastical acts" notably entails in practice, for lay offenders, privation of the right of sponsorship at baptism and confirmation; it is either supplementary to other penalties or is the principal penalty for certain infractions, such as "suspicion of heresy". "Interdict" is a penalty very closely related to excommunication, which will now be considered.

5. *Excommunication.* From Scripture we learn that excommunication was already in use among the Jews in our Lord's time; anyone who acknowledged Jesus to be the Messiah was expelled from the synagogue (Jn 9:22). The texts of St. Paul quoted in a previous section undoubtedly relate to the first Christian excommunications; the offender is cut off from the Christian

community to compel him to mend his ways. This penalty took more definite shape in the centuries that followed. It now operates to separate the delinquent not from the Church, to which he is definitively attached by baptism, but from the communion of the faithful. That is to say, he is deprived of a number of rights, notably, in the case of lay persons, of the right to assist at divine offices (but not of the right to be present at sermons or instruction). He is debarred from *lawful* reception of the sacraments. (If he nevertheless receives a sacrament he will receive it validly but *unlawfully*.) He cannot participate in the fruits of indulgences or of the suffrages and public prayers of the Church. (But excommunicates may be prayed for privately and Masses may be offered for them privately.) To all these is added the penalty of "exclusion from legitimate ecclesiastical acts", already described. It is this separation from the communion of the faithful that makes excommunication a very grave penalty indeed. It is never final, for, as we have already seen, it is a "medicinal" penalty. The Church never despairs of the conversion of sinners.

Excommunication is the penalty inflicted on the greatest number of misdemeanours particularly those listed above, from the profanation of the Holy Species to the fabrication and sale of false relics.

Excommunication, therefore, is a penalty attached to infractions of unequal gravity, but it is graduated according to the gravity of the offence.

First, however, we must distinguish between the various classes of excommunicates, that is to say, between the *tolerati*, the *notorii* and the *vitandi*. The *tolerati* are those guilty of "secret" delinquencies (committed in private and not likely to be made public), for which no "declaratory" judicial sentence has been added to the penalty of excommunication already attached to the misdemeanour by the specific law concerned. (More will be said of this later on.) The declaratory sentence is pronounced only in the case of particularly serious offences. Excommunicates have no right to assist at the divine offices, but they need not be excluded absolutely. *Notorii* ("notorious" excommunicates) are those who have been guilty of a public and manifest misdemeanour or have been the object of a declaratory sentence; these must be excluded from active, but not passive assistance at the offices, and must be deprived of Christian burial unless evident signs of repentance are forthcoming. Lastly, the *vitandi* must be excluded even from passive assistance at the offices, and the faithful must not communicate with them (hence the designation *vitandi*, i.e., to be avoided), except for a reasonable cause, such as family relationship or professional services. An excommunicate is declared *vitandus* only by a special, express and public decision of the Holy See; such a decision is very rarely given and only in cases of exceptional gravity. The *vitandi* today are very few in number.

A second graduated "scale" also regulates the application of excommunication penalties. Excommunication, as we have seen, is a medicinal penalty, and the offender has a right to absolution when he amends. Now absolution is given by different authorities, varying with the gravity of the offence. Every confessor can absolve minor misdemeanours, major ones have to be absolved by the bishop or the Holy See. Furthermore, when absolution is to be given by the Holy See, certain cases are reserved "very specially", "specially" or "simply". For example, absolution is "very specially reserved" in cases of profanation of the Holy Species and of explicit violation of the seal of confession; it is "specially reserved" in cases of apostasy and heresy. Absolution is reserved to the bishop in abortion cases. These various reservations impress upon the faithful the gravity of the relevant offences. It should be noted that, in case of urgency, and especially if there is danger of death, any priest can absolve from all censures, with the proviso that where the censures are of the most severe class, the penitent is obliged to have recourse to the Holy See afterwards. Certain confessors, too, can absolve from certain reserved censures.

6. *Procedure*. As regards the manner in which the penalties are inflicted, there is a distinction between penalties *latae sententiae* (that is, where the penalty follows automatically by law) and penalties *ferendae sententiae* (where the penalty is imposed by judicial sentence). The latter are subject to the prevailing procedure governing the trial, which takes place before a judge. The former are a special type; a penalty *latae sententiae* is incurred automatically upon infraction of the law; if proceedings are subsequently instituted in such a case, they will not give rise to a "condemnatory" sentence, since the penalty has already been incurred; the sentence will be merely "declaratory". (Sentences of this kind have been referred to in an earlier section.) Excommunication is most frequently a penalty *latae sententiae*. Today, in fact, penalties *ferendae sententiae* are rarely imposed on lay members of the Church.

The automatic infliction of the penalty *latae sententiae* would seem to have the deplorable effect of depriving the offender of the opportunity to defend himself; in fact, this is not so, because the penalty is incurred only if the offender is aware, at least in a general way, that the act he sets out to commit is punished by the Church, if the actual offence is grave in itself, and if its gravity is adverted to by the offender at the time. It is not possible, then, to draw down upon oneself, quite inadvertently, a penalty of this kind, particularly so serious a penalty as excommunication. This procedure, also, has the advantage of compelling the attention of the faithful to the gravity of certain faults; it safeguards the reputation of the offenders insofar as declaratory sentences are only pronounced in the gravest cases; and it obviates overburdening of tribunals.

As regards the penalties *ferendae sententiae*, the procedure is in accordance with the customary rules. The accused has the right to the assistance of an advocate and to information as to the precise nature of the charge, etc. He can bring an appeal from the tribunal of first instance (diocesan tribunal) to the appeal judge (metropolitan tribunal) or the supreme tribunal of the Sacred Roman Rota or the Apostolic Signature. In the course of the action, the proceedings can be stopped by the judge who can simply pronounce a "judicial reprimand". When the time comes for sentence to be pronounced, the penalty is sometimes discretionary, and, in the case of a first offence, a suspended sentence is possible. Sometimes the law leaves to the judge the choice of an "appropriate penalty"; sometimes it allows him to increase the penalty normally incurred "if exceptionally aggravating circumstances require it". And after sentence has been passed, remission of the penalty is still possible. The flexibility of the system is obvious, and so is the care taken to adapt the penalty to the individual delinquent.

An administrative procedure, involving appearance before the bishop, can be substituted for the normal judicial procedure; this is more expeditious and more discreet, but it is prohibited in the most serious cases, because the guarantees offered to the accused are less than those available in the judicial procedure.

This diversity of rules occasionally proves somewhat burdensome; some of them, indeed, rarely have a chance to operate. A lightening of the legal load is certainly desirable in order to make it comply with modern conditions. The faithful, too, have grown more lukewarm, more passive, and less actively irreverent than formerly – a sign of the times. But the rules, as they stand, testify to the Church's solicitude for those who are entrusted to its care.

Louis de Naurois

ECONOMIC ETHICS

The ethics of economics is part of social ethics, dealing with the law and order of economics according to moral principles. Ethics and economics are in themselves independent realms with laws of their own in each case. But in any given culture the two orders are closely inter-connected. Economic thinking, the style of an economy, will be the reflection of a given culture and style of life. Hence natural law among Christians is applied in economics mostly in the form of a supplementary code (Thomas Aquinas), that is, as a deduction from the changing circumstances of the development of society.

The notions of work and property are fundamental in the ethics of economics. Their contents are constantly changing.

1. *Historical survey*. Historians of religion are now convinced that primitive man followed clear ethical notions in his economic action. His thought, which was dominated by magico-religious categories, saw higher aids to his weak life in work, hunting, robbery, barter and trade. Property and ownership were felt to be sacred (for himself personally, for his family or community). He saw a relationship between sacrifice and barter; magic and handicrafts were both signs of human "superiority" (G. van de Leeuw), money had a magical origin. Work, however, was part of his very life, for which he had no distinct term or concept (Fourastié).

The agricultural communities which were flourishing over seven thousand years ago had as a rule no doubts about the right of property. Like work it was "part of the substance of life in the world, ethically legitimate and economically excellent" (A. Gehlen). Respect for property, the desire for stability and the readiness to subordinate private to public interests gave rise to the order of law as culture progressed. In the higher cultures of the Greeks and Romans work, except farming, was considered contemptible and hence was the business of foreign settlers (*metoikoi*) and slaves. This was possibly why no technology developed in the modern sense, in spite of high scientific achievements.

In the Christian lands of the West, Roman law, with Germanic modifications, continued in force, but was given new stresses. When Thomas Aquinas said: "Private property is legitimate, but must be used for the common good", he was describing the right to property as an assurance of freedom which brought with it an obligation towards the community (property as a "social pledge"). Work had been respected from primitive Christian times as obedience to the divine order of creation and a means of doing penance. Benedict of Nursia gave it a spiritual value (*ora et labora*) which made it one of the main factors in the shaping of the medieval world.

Thus the agricultural and feudal society, including ownership of land, was based till well into modern times on the notion of "the legally and ethically admissible" (H. Mittels) and hence ruled by the "natural law". All social structures were rooted, so to speak, on the natural bed-rock. Loyalty on one side meant care and protection on the other. Furthermore, handicrafts, trade and city life in general accepted the notion of an income in keeping with one's state in life. All classes had certain rights and duties by birth, and traditional rights could be defended by revolt if necessary. The difference between rich and poor was regarded (within certain bounds) as the result of the divine order of things. (The system included grave injustices which were felt to be such.)

Hence it was only with industrialization, capitalism and its counterpart, socialism, that the great questions now posed by economic ethics were framed. Industrialization is now often described as the "passing of a second great threshold of culture" in human history (A. Gehlen, H. Freyer), comparable to the transition in the neolithic age to life in settlements. The second great change was of course preceded by gradual developments, such as the secularization of thinking and despotism or absolutism; on the economic level, by physiocracy, commerce, manufacture and banking. These preludes to the great ages of capitalism had their own proper economic ethics. The citizens were to prosper by being formed into a working society. This meant, for instance, a fierce struggle against poverty, begging and idleness. Penitentiaries, workhouses and orphanages were used as training-schools in disciplined work, which helped to create a working class which already resembled a proletariate. The industrial revolution itself (mechanization of spinning and weaving, the steam-engine, the whole manufacturing system) was supported by the principles of "liberalism" which claimed that in view of changed economic conditions "the profits of private enterprise were justified as a service to the community" (J. Messner).

The successors of the classical economists held that equilibrium could only be achieved in a trading economy by the incentive of private profit, which ultimately at least would bring about the harmonization of all interests. Ethics had no place in such economic theory. Its place was taken by the economic law of free competition, which left capitalist enterprise with an easy conscience. The upshot was the reduction of the working classes to the state of a proletariate, living in conditions of misery which were to endure for a hundred years (starvation wages, recurrent waves of unemployment, child labour, widespread in England as late as 1875).

Industrialism also fully reorganized the actual work in the factories by the division of labour, first as between the workers and then between men and machines. Work was regarded as a "commodity", and very often became a soulless repetition of operations (the conveyor belts of the twenties). Factories and business became a "skilful combination of partial human beings" (W. Sombart). The costs of this ethicless economy were paid a million times over in human dignity. Even the most inhuman hardships were not eliminated for many long years.

The development of industrialization was undoubtedly necessary and inevitable. In barely two hundred years it enabled world population to triple. Standards of living were raised in an undreamt-of way, and its means of communication (travel and news media) were responsible for the present unity of the human race. But it may certainly be assumed that had the human losses, especially those of the classical period of capitalism, been avoided by a just ethics of economics, the progress of industrialization might have been delayed, but would not have been prevented. For modern technology was and is used by the economic system, but is almost independent of it. On the other hand, it is one of the pillars of industry when combined with appropriate economic thinking.

The "social question" provoked by classical capitalism brought mighty forces into play, above all the trade unions and the socialist parties. In addition, voices were raised strictly in defence of social justice or economic ethics, in the Churches or among social scientists. These efforts and the social policies of various States were the real cause of the development of a modern theory of economic ethics. Like the so-called "sciences of relationships", psychology, sociology, political economy and anthropology (previously only in embryo in philosophy and theology), it was a product of the industrialized society of modern times. It may be affirmed that present-day Christian social teaching is based to a great extent on economic ethics and was developed also in opposition to an individualistic and utilitarian view of the world. This throws an enormous responsibility on Christian economic ethics.

The great target of Marxist socialism was liberal capitalism, whose enormities it pilloried fiercely and mercilessly. K. Marx protested passionately against the exploitation of men by the ruling classes, and the "self-alienation" which it brought with it. His doctrine was not aimed, however, at the reform of the class structure, but at its destruction by world revolution. Only the triumph of the revolution and the rule of the proletariate can enable man to find himself once more. This alone will enable him to live well in a being which is of itself well. Marx was fully convinced of the omnipotence of the technological and scientific man, who was to form a society which could not but dominate history and nature and hence redeem itself. His historical materialism and ethical determinism contain no economic ethics strictly speaking. His doctrine is rather a millenarist philosophy of history.

The ethical values presupposed in Marxism were soon recognized by the "revisionists". Hence modern communistic socialism often displays trends towards an ethics of economics and culture. They differ chiefly from the Christian view by regarding human society more or less as a "utilitarian institution without intrinsic bonds" (J. Schaschling).

2. *Present trends in economic ethics.* Modern economic ethics finds it desirable that there should be not merely a wide and equitable distribution of income but also the possibility of acquiring property (housing, savings, part ownership of the means of production). Social security and welfare should not be extended to the point that the will to self-help is lamed. Political economy must aim at a sound balance between a stable currency and full employment, since inflation is at least as harmful as a certain amount of unemployment.

Since freedom is a primary principle of social order, it should also have as much play as possible in economics, e.g., in the choice of calling and place of work, in the spending of income and the encouragement of free enterprise. Property should be restricted only in so far as this is absolutely demanded by the common good (hence, no nationalization merely as an electoral programme).

The two main principles of Catholic social doctrine, solidarism and the principle of subsidiarity, also hold good for economics. Hence on principle the State should not interfere with the initiatives and independence of economic life, and all forms of *dirigisme* are to be avoided, even in the developing countries which are only passing through the critical initial stage of building up capital.

Nonetheless, the needs of the emerging countries are the great social question of today for the Western countries. The income per head in the U.S.A., Canada, Australia and the countries of Central and North-Western Europe is between 500 and 1500 dollars a year. In the whole of South-Eastern Asia and in the majority of African and South American countries it is about or less than 100 dollars. Thirty per cent of the population of the world controls eighty per cent of its riches, while seventy per cent has to do with the remaining twenty per cent. This appalling inequality demands to be evened out, in the name of a genuine economic ethics, by generous aid for development.

Max Pietsch

ECUMENISM

A. Catholic Ecumenism

1. What has to be said under this heading is in substance a repetition of what was said in the Vatican II Decrees on Ecumenism and on the Eastern Catholic Churches. For details, reference may be made to these decrees generally, and in particular to chapter ii of the Decree on Ecumenism. The very fact that the possibility of dialogue and co-operation exists shows the profound change that has occurred in the Catholic Church's relation to other Christian Churches and ecclesial communities. The Catholic Church of course is conscious of itself, now as always, as the Church in which the one Church of Christ subsists, and in its own understanding of its own nature (as a part of its faith in the whole of the revelation of God in Jesus Christ), it cannot simply concede the same character to the other Churches. Nevertheless, it does not now regard these Churches and ecclesial communities primarily as something which ought not to exist, which has to be abolished as soon as possible by the repentance and conversion of individuals, as heresy and schism to be anathematized. It now regards them primarily as partners in a dialogue and a collaboration between Christians who have more in common than separates them and possess a common task in regard to the "world".

2. The foundation of this dialogue is the realization of what is really common to all or is accepted as a task by all. This includes the common faith in God and Jesus Christ as our only Lord and Saviour; the mutual recognition (as a Christian and human duty) of one another's good will; unconditional respect for one another's religious freedom; the common baptism and common incorporation in Christ; the existence of other sacraments in these Churches; the conviction that grace and justification are found among non-Catholic Christians also; the recognition that the non-Catholic Churches as such have in fact a positive saving function for non-Catholic Christians and that these Churches preserve and live out a valuable Christian inheritance which need not necessarily be found in every respect equally clearly in the Catholic Church as it actually exists in fact; the conviction that the Churches are therefore not separated from one another in every respect, that they are not only "separated brethren"; awareness of *common* responsibility for the division of Christendom, blame for which cannot be attributed simply and solely to present-day Christians, so that we cannot regard the others as formal heretics; recognition that the actual appearance presented by one's own Church is always in need of penance and reform, and obscures the testimony it bears to its origin in Christ's will to found it; acknowledgment of Christian life in other Churches, even to the point of martyrdom, life which also contributes to the building up of the Catholic Church; and finally the common concern of all for the unity of the Church.

3. A dialogue which is something different from polemics or a direct and onesided attempt at conversion, presupposes that *both* parties assume that they have something to learn from the other and endeavour to learn it. The Catholic can make this assumption. For even though he is convinced that the Church of Christ subsists in the Roman Catholic Church, this does not exclude the possibility and the will to receive and learn from others as well. Nor does this capacity to receive consist solely in the fact that dialogue can provide better information about the attitude, doctrine and Christian life of the non-Catholic partner and the latter's difficulties in regard to the Catholic Church, in other words, knowledge which to a considerable extent is not sufficiently found among Catholics, even among theologians. There is also

a capacity to receive because the non-Catholic Christian and his Churches possess a wealth of Christian life and of other developments of the one identical Christianity, of theology, of charismatical impulses, of experience of Christian action in regard to the "world", etc., which need not necessarily be present with the same intensity and clarity in the Catholic Church. Ecumenical discussions of the kind envisaged also have the character of dialogue to the extent that they are not directly concerned with individual conversions to the Catholic Church, though this, if the necessary conditions are presupposed, is a legitimate aim, but one which must be carefully distinguished from ecumenical discussion. They also have the character of dialogue because even from the standpoint of a Catholic conception of the Church the unity striven for must not simply be thought of as a "return". For the Church of the future which is aimed at, even in its character as Roman Catholic, must also contain the significant Christian past and the treasures of other Churches. In a certain sense, therefore, it will be a different Church from the present Catholic Church in the historically-conditioned form it will bear in that age. Discussion is therefore to that extent a dialogue in relation to an open future. Christians nowadays cannot live side by side in indifference to one another as though their separation were an unalterable fact. A truly Catholic conception of the Church (the Catholic Church as the Church of all) would in fact be unfaithful to itself if it were to take the divisions of Christendom simply as a fact about which nothing can be done. Such infidelity to itself does not happen in theory but does happen very often in practice. Dialogue is necessary and is possible as an open dialogue; this need not forbid any of the partners from pursuing it on their own assumptions.

4. As its object this dialogue has everything which can serve the unity of Christians in belief, Church, Christian life and responsible action for the world. It would therefore extend to mutual information about life and doctrine; improved understanding of one another's theology; the endeavour by each to translate their own theology into the language of the other; the endeavour to overcome real differences in doctrine; agreement for common action (cf. No. 5 below).

5. Dialogue can lead to concrete results and real collaboration even before its ultimate goal is reached. There still exist mutual intolerance and un-Christian forms of competition in the everyday social world, which could readily and broad-mindedly be abandoned. Questions of mixed marriages and denominational schools (and their relations and collaboration) await attention and might be solved in a better way than they have been so far. Concrete organized collaboration in theology would be possible. More translations of the Bible could be made in common, as encouraged by Paul VI. Unfair exploitation of conversions for propaganda purposes by either side could be tactfully avoided. Agreements should be concluded as to how even now the scandal of a divided Christendom might be avoided in the missions and how, despite the right in principle to pursue missionary activity everywhere, a right which for the Catholic Church is an inalienable one, a friendly, and in view of the shortage of missionaries, realistic division of missionary work or of missionary territories, might be arrived at. Elements actually common to all, in liturgy, hymns and religious customs, could be encouraged. Prior mutual consultation could avoid the creation of new obstacles to unity in doctrine and practice, unless these derived from the conscientious belief of each. Everything possible which from the point of view of dogmatic and moral theology is *communicatio in sacris* should not only be

tolerated but encouraged cautiously and tactfully, but without undogmatic "irenism". Not everything is possible, of course, but a good deal is, to a different extent it is true in regard to the various Churches. Services can be held in common for prayer and the liturgy of the word without celebration of the Eucharist, and their content need not necessarily only consist of prayer for the reunion of Christendom. With the Eastern Orthodox Churches even a considerable sacramental *communicatio in sacris* is possible, as is expressly stated by the decree of Vatican II on Eastern Catholic Churches (arts. 26ff.). There is a wide field of collaboration available in the duty of all Christians to shape the secular world in a more humane and therefore more Christian way in the social, cultural, economic, political and welfare spheres. In very many respects the Churches acting in common could be the conscience of secular society. In common they could intervene, even in brave contradiction to egotistical people in their own ranks, in favour of peace, the abolition of racial discrimination, social justice, the eradication of nationalist prejudices, protection of the poor and weak. For all these purposes common institutions could be set up by common action.

B. Ecumenical Theology

1. *State of the question.* The notion of "ecumenical theology" has been in use now for over twenty years in the theological discussion of the various Christian Churches. With the new sense of the contradiction prevailing between profession of faith in the one Church of Jesus Christ and the actual divisions in this Church, the notion of "ecumenical" theology has become the touchstone of sincerity in the theology of all denominations and in all their theological disciplines, and a criterion for the alertness of theological thought in general. For the one gospel of Jesus Christ, which must be preached in dialogue with the world of today – the gospel not merely of conformity with the world, but of the cross and resurrection, that is, of discontinuity with the world in the matter of salvation (since Christ and not the world is our redemption and salvation) – knows nothing of the non-evangelical scandal of this gospel's being preached by divided Churches. On the contrary, it presupposes the unity of the Church in faith and love, something that is not merely of secondary relevance to the credibility of the gospel, but is meant to be a sign through which the world may believe. In this perspective, the divisions between the Churches are a scandal running counter to the words of Scripture, and one which all Churches are bound to try to remove. This can only be done if the Churches carry on a comprehensive dialogue with one another in which all questions of their self-understanding and their understanding of the world and the faith can be voiced and treated. There has always been confrontation and debate between the Churches. Hence the dialogue demanded today can be regarded as a continuation or counterpart of the past.

2. *Earlier forms.* The real counterpart of ecumenical theology in the past was the comprehensive polemics carried on by the Churches. The polemical mentality was due to the conviction on both sides that each alone had a monopoly of the truth, while the other was living in error. The salvation of the opponent was in peril, because of the errors of which he was victim. Since this could not be a matter of indifference, every effort had to be made to detach him from his heresy and lead him back to the true Church. The claim to be the true Church was maintained by the Protestant denominations as well as by Catholics. The conviction of being in sole possession of the truth was formulated in doctrinal articles and propositions. The truths in question were put through a process of fragmentation

and isolation in which too little attention was paid to the theological context of each proposition. Controversy, carried on with a religious intensity which regarded all opponents as dangerous heretics, was concerned with defending one's own truth and refuting the adversary point by point. Secondary matters were often treated as essentials, while essentials were often overlooked, so that misunderstandings were bound to arise by the nature of things. It was taken for granted, without critical investigation, that one's own way of thinking was correct, so that one's own theses never came up for discussion and the controversialists never seem to have tried to see things except from their own point of view. This could only lead to a hardening of positions on both sides, to narrow and one-sided views.

But along with controversy, there was always a certain amount of irenism. There were theologians who strove passionately for reconciliation and peace between the Churches and presented concrete programmes for reunion. There are several larger groups which could be named, which can be ranged – though only loosely, no doubt – under the heading of "irenism". There were, for instance, the efforts at union inspired directly or indirectly by Erasmus of Rotterdam. The theologians in question kept mainly before their eyes the picture of the primitive Church, and gave a large place to the distinction between fundamental and non-fundamental truths of faith (Melanchthon, Bucer, Gropper, Witzel, Cassander, Capito, de Dominis, Calixt and Leibniz). But it must be admitted that in doing so they underestimated the historical importance of dogmatic decisions in the teaching and practice of the Churches. This is clear from Erasmus's proposition that the dogmatic claims of the various Churches should be reduced in such a way as to bring about unity.

Among the irenical theologians we must also include the mystical "spiritualists" (such as Franck, Schwenkenfeld, Weigel and Böhme) who thought that a radical spiritualization of the notion of the Church had made room for all denominations and so restored unity. The groups which they formed were early heralds of pietism, though pietism is not a direct prolongation of the thought of the mystical spiritualists. Zinzendorf regarded the confessional Churches as modes and expressions of the one true Church of Christ. Hence all denominations had their legitimate place in his Herrnhuter Brotherhood. This was his way of keeping open, on principle, a link with all Churches, without denying the reality of the Churches. In spite of certain differences, the "Branch Theory" of Anglicanism has certain affinities with Zinzendorf's "Theory of Modes". The Branch Theory held that all Churches – or at least all Churches with apostolic succession of their bishops – were branches of the one Church of Christ.

While irenical theology always had some solution to offer to the question of the unity of the Church, credal theology (comparative "symbolism", from *symbolé*, creed) went other ways. It was concerned with the understanding, presentation, comparison and estimation of the doctrine of the various Churches. Two procedures may be distinguished here. A purely comparative method concentrated exclusively on study of doctrines, sometimes inspired ultimately only by historical interests. But there was also a "normative" credal theology, which based itself on its own Church to work out criteria for judging the doctrines of other Churches (as in J. Möhler's *Symbolik*, E. T.: *Symbolism*).

Credal theology has had a successor in the study of denominations, which is concerned with a comprehensive description of the doctrine and life of other Churches. A purely historical and descriptive type, such as that of K. Algermissen may be contrasted with the dogmatic and normative studies of E. Wolf and K. Barth.

Finally, there is the controversial theology which is concerned with the theological discussion of matters which divide the Churches. Where it presents itself as a basic form of inter-confessional encounter (R. Kösters), the question arises as to whether it does not isolate differences too sharply. When they are seen in the light of the greater whole of what is believed, confessed and thought by all Churches – the primary object of study – the ecumenical goal of overcoming them can be better and more promisingly expounded than when deliberate attention is paid to all that divides. Hence it must be admitted that while controversial theology is an important part of ecumenical theology, its value must not be overestimated.

3. *The theological meaning of "ecumenical"*. Five different meanings have been given to the word "ecumenical" in the course of Church history. All of them have even today fundamental significance for theology and its special role in the preaching of the Church. Ecumenical means (i) belonging to or representing the whole (inhabited) world (originally applied to the Roman Empire – belonging to or representing the the Empire); (ii) belonging to the Church universal or representing it; (iii) possessing universal validity in the Church (the ancient Councils); (iv) having to do with relationships between several Churches or Christians of various denominations (the sense which the word took on in the modern ecumenical movement); (v) implying knowledge of Christian unity and the desire to attain it (the ecumenical movement). When these five senses of the word are applied to the nature of theology and the goal it serves, the following points arise.

a) Theology must remain conscious of the fact that the revelation of God in Jesus Christ and its proclamation by the Church is directed to all men. This universal aspect obliges theology not to confuse the findings of Western theology with the revelation in Jesus Christ. Thus the way is open for other regions of culture to articulate their understanding of revelation in their own concepts and their own languages. The way is open to a real pluralism in theology.

b) Such a plurality of theologies would be sustained by the one Church and would be established in the certain knowledge that theology is always a function of the Church and has its living roots there. The plurality of theology was for long the clearest sign of the multiplicity of the Churches, and the bounds of theology coincided with the bounds of the Churches. But the true task of theology is to assimilate comprehensively the revelation which came in Jesus Christ. If it is to do this properly when confronted with the questions of a highly differentiated modern world, there must be a plurality of several theologies within the one Church, but not a plurality of theologies of several Churches.

c) In this connection the question of the norm arises, and of the significance of the traditions of the Churches. The questions arise in connection with the normative element in the term ecumenical when used of the validity of ancient Church Councils and creeds. Here the point to be made is the following: in view of the questions put by the modern world and the situation of the present day, the real meaning of Scripture (the gospel, Christ) must be propounded in such a way that it can be heard and grasped. In this process of interpretation, the supreme norm and hence the norm of all other norms is Scripture, of which the inmost centre and central content is Christ and his work of salvation. It is in the light of this central message and only with reference to it that the traditions of the various Churches and even their common tradition are to be interpreted. The dogmatic tradition of the Churches, interpreted in this way and in no other way, but amenable in fact to such interpretation, must be integrated into the new exposition of the truth of the gospel for our own days.

d) The process of re-interpreting the message of the gospel for our own day, into which the tradition of the Churches are integrated, because interpreted in the light of their inmost core, in view of Christ, can only succeed if the Churches are engaged in a comprehensive dialogue with one another. They must allow themselves to be determined exclusively by the word of God and the questions of the present time.

e) This dialogue about the heart of the matter and the effort to solve outstanding questions in the light of the common faith will also help to solve the ecclesiological question of Church unity. Hence an ecumenical theology understood in this sense will not be exclusively concerned with the question of the unity of the Church. It will rather consider itself as a way to unity in the most comprehensive possible sense.

4. *Conclusions*. It follows that ecumenical theology in the sense outlined above is not a new special discipline along with other theological disciplines. It is rather a structural element and a dimension of all theology in all its disciplines. It is impelled by the question of the divisions in faith and their possible elimination. It does not simply accept division as a fact which it tries to explain by a theology of history. It sees division as a challenge to overcome divisions, "so that the world may believe". Then, ecumenical theology is a theology of fellowship, a theology which has discovered that what is common is proportionally much greater than the differences and divergencies, these being only properly known and estimated in the perspective of the common faith. Thus new possibilities of encounter and openness are created. This new openness makes ecumenical theology a theology of mutual understanding, which is not merely concerned with understanding others, but also strives vigorously to propound its own faith and its own understanding of the faith in such a way that they can be understood by others, in spite of different presuppositions, in the framework of their theology. Further, ecumenical theology is a theology of the sources and the origins. It is concerned with Scripture and its relevant preaching today. Finally, ecumenical theology is a theology of dialogue and is therefore aware of the fact that God is constantly engaged in dialogue with man and that we are addressing in every man the eternal You of God. A God who does not speak is a dead God, and a Church which remains aloof from dialogue testifies only to the death of God, because what it preaches – the word of God, which demands to be heard and answered – would no longer be a living word. This reminds all the Churches that only dialogue among the Churches, carried on in, with and under the word of God, the common dialogue of the Churches with the world of today can really help them to accomplish the true task of the Church in accordance with the gospel.

Heinrich Beck

EDUCATION

Education, though always implying a personal (an I-You rather than an I-It) relationship, has two main acceptations, each of which is stressed variously. 1: Education as socialization: as the systematic imparting of information; as instruction in eloquence and the tenets or main lines of a culture or sub-culture; as training (according to supposed or assessed abilities) in the skills needed to support or survive in (an advanced technological) society; as rehearsal in the formularies and rituals characteristic of a national, religious or other élite, or a lower class; as general education (*eruditio*). 2: Education as evolution: as the discovery and development of a unique personal identity (*educatio*). *Eruditio* and *educatio* have been variously interpreted throughout the history of Christianity, and have been thought of as complementary or as opposed. The chief end of the two processes (or the single process in its two aspects) has been viewed as conformity to the will of God: whether revealed unmistakably for all time, or revealed in the course of history and therefore in social behaviour.

The right kind of personal development has too often been construed as the role appropriate to members of the Church in a specific society, in the sense of conformity to that society's goals; and less often as helping in the interested discovery of diverse ways of life in a pluralistic society, and of right modes of response to them.

The more prophetic among those charged with education in and for the Church have seen the appropriate social role as one emancipating men from the bonds of this world or a social system as it is at this or that time; and have stimulated a desire for improvement of, and opposition to any imitation of, a coercive society or relationship. Some Christian educators, however, have insisted on the acceptance of one (linguistic) relational form as uniquely valid for all human time.

Christianity, therefore, has tended to adopt and re-emphasize (in the light of liberation through Christ) concepts of education known in classical antiquity and retained or modified in secular forms until the present day.

Since the eighteenth-century Enlightenment, however, one emphasis in the secular sphere has been on self-development and a critical consciousness (following, say, Rousseau); and another on social development and egalitarianism (following, say, Condorcet). Accordingly, man is conceived of as a product of society (=necessity, when education is *social* and ethical), and/or of his own self (=freedom, when education is *individual* and ethical).

Recently the emphasis on ethical education in freedom has been stronger in the Church. Since Vatican II, there has been a greater insistence on religious education in the sense of *educatio*: a lifelong personal growth in a community of selfless care and spiritual strength through solidarity and conviction, offering not just knowledge to be checked against experience but openness, values and (it is hoped) the experience of their goodness (*life*), as against violence, coercion, hatred, overdependence, authoritarianism, and mental as well as physical imprisonment (*death*).

Contemporary and some traditional Christian concepts of education have therefore stressed the importance of discussing, deciding, transmitting, and again discussing *values*: those things worth doing, and those things which ought to be done because they are worth doing. The educator has been seen not as embodying an authority to transmit immutable categories, but as offering in dialogue a variety of means which a child or an adult can adapt to *make* his own life. The stress has been on showing this one how, or urging that one to learn directly from (sense) experience, to act (with a purpose), to be free, and to create or recreate (himself). Education is then support in, as well as the actual process of, learning to be oneself; a call *and* a response to a call to emerge from the darkness of self alone into the light of self known through the world and others, and for others; but it is also the certain expectation, despite everything, of individual and social harmony: "That perfection of the intellect, which is the result of education, and its *beau ideal*, to be imparted to individuals in their respective measures, is the clear, calm, accurate vision and comprehension of all things, as far as the finite mind can embrace them, each in its place, and with its own characteristics upon it . . . it has almost the beauty and harmony of heavenly contemplation, so intimate it is with the eternal order of things and the music of the spheres" (Newman).

In educational terms, Christianity has offered not only a community of faith but a unique community of scholarship which in its best instances has favoured the discussion and teaching of religion, and the investigation of the historical forms and suasions governing the Church's oral and written traditions; its many-layered language and rituals; the memory and recreation of joys and ideals; celebration and aspirations; sympathy and understanding; compassion and brotherhood; and fruitful doubt as well as assurance on the way to the full liberation of men in this world.

New views of religious education are to be expected in the light of the foregoing; they are influenced by the continuing study of human psycho-social development, the revised understanding of basic human needs at different stages of the life-cycle, and the notion of phases in language acquisition, in logical competence and in moral subtlety. This learning from the sciences affects the various modes of child and adult learning in and through the Church: the languages of worship, of Christian statement about God and the world, of the study of the Bible, and of moral judgment; and the ways in which those languages or codes are affected by, and affect, the norms of a society, its prejudices and its insights. Psychological and medical discoveries are incorporated in care or instruction deemed "religious", and in models for problem-solving in such major situations of human choice as marriage, work, child-bearing and child-rearing, death; in collaboration and in creation.

Religious education, like education "pure and simple", means helping men to find out what it is to be human, to adapt to their particular situation of being human, and to offer the first elements of changing that situation for the real benefit of self and others. The "conscientization", or making aware, of the underprivileged (*informed* literacy), and their education to a proficient understanding of the reasons for their repression but also their potential creativity in a changing world (Paulo Freire), has proved one of the most inspiring aspects of the theology of liberation of the 1960s–70s. The critique of institutionalization has even included a call for "deschooling" of society: "School is the advertising agency which makes you believe that you need the society as it is" (Ivan Illich). Such interpretations of the school system as the central myth-making ritual of an industrial society which is wasteful (and ultimately destructive) of limited resources for replenishment of nature-for-man stand in the long tradition of Christian *educatio*. They accord with the notion that religion (and therefore religious education) should motivate but not inculcate individual and social morality; the notion that it should prompt a man responsibly to interrogate his society and his Church for practical, loving answers as well as reflective percipience in response to questions about the nature, purpose and destiny of man – this particular man as he is in his dealings with these particular men, in this particular space and time.

J. Cumming

EMPIRICISM

Empiricism is generally taken to be a philosophical attitude based on epistemological preliminaries, which takes experience (internal and external) alone as the foundation of true knowledge and of science.

Even when the name of empiricism is reserved for the Enlightenment of the 17th and 18th centuries in England, especially for the work of J. Locke (1632–1704) and D. Hume (1711–76), we need to consider it in the context of the history of thought and of the spirit, if empiricism is to be properly characterized. Not every recourse to empirical facts is at once empiricism; yet the tension between the experimental and the ideal pervades the whole of the history of philosophy. Great attention was already paid in antiquity, especially by Aristotle, to experience or sensible perception of beings; and in the course of the Middle Ages in Europe, sensible knowledge, duly tested, became more and more a court of appeal to check the verdicts of metaphysics and the theology of revelation (so, for instance, in nominalism, the school of Chartres, and in such figures as St. Thomas Aquinas, St. Albert the Great, Roger Bacon, William of Occam and so on; Frederick II could make bold to say: "fides enim certa non provenit ex auditu" [*De arte venandi*, c. 1]). But it was only in modern philosophy, strongly influenced by the rapid growth of the knowledge of nature, that reflection on experiment and experience became a systematic programme. Noteworthy here are Francis Bacon's *Novum Organon Scientiarum* (1620), Locke's *Essay concerning Human Understanding* (1690) and the critical writings of Hume.

Whether a thoroughgoing empiricism ever existed, however, is a question which must be left to future special studies. Locke and above all Berkeley cannot be regarded as representatives of empiricism. Hume comes closest to it. Many motives enter into the basically "empiricist" attitude of Condillac, Diderot, Voltaire, J. St. Mill. This is also true of the so-called *Empiriokritizismus* of E. Mach and R. Venarius. Similar tendencies are to be found in sensism, positivism and materialism: Kant's effort at synthesis in his "transcendental philosophy" did not succeed in overcoming the empiricist climate of modern times and its scientism.

Many ideological currents of the present day display basically empiricist trends: so atheism of a scientific stamp, mechanicist and to some extent dialectic materialism, the exaggerated respect paid to psychology and sociology, especially the sociology of knowledge. The same is true of the rationalist technological approach in general. In the various schools of modern logistics and linguistic analysis the norm of all (philosophically valid) knowledge is taken to be the possibility of verifying a statement on the basis of data furnished only empirically.

The permanent objection against a professed empiricism is that it fails to reflect sufficiently on the conditions of experience. In spite of this necessary correction on the philosophical level, it would be foolish to reject completely the aims and mentality of empiricism. In a "hominization of the world" of Christian intent, the beings of the world must be considered in such a way that their possibilities can be experimentally explored. For the elimination of a divinized or "numinous" world, by reason of the biblical faith in the Creator, has as its logical consequence the "desacralizing" of the world, and hence necessarily implies the fundamental possibility of science and technology in the modern sense. To this extent, the Christian understanding of the world inevitably calls for the application of the empirical method, and so preserves the element of truth in empiricism, without accepting its naive theories of knowledge.

Heinz Robert Schlette

ENLIGHTENMENT

The Enlightenment denotes the most revolutionary of all movements which the Occident has undergone in the course of its history. It has not yet been sufficiently investigated, but it may be admitted that it affected various countries, Churches and generations in different degrees. The historian Troeltsch has characterized it as the beginning of the really modern period of European culture, in contrast to the ecclesiastical and theological culture which had been hitherto predominant.

The Enlightenment originated in the Netherlands and in England in the mid-17th century. Varying considerably in intensity and influence during its expansion throughout almost all of Europe and the Anglo-Saxon and Spanish-American areas of the New World, it reached its high-water mark in French rationalism and materialism (Voltaire, Helvetius, Holbach) and found political expression in the French Revolution. Its richest philosophical and political results (enlightened despotism) were achieved in German territories (Leibniz, Wolff, Thomasius, Lessing, Kant, Frederick the Great, Joseph II). In Southern and Eastern Europe its impact was less widespread and less profound. The 19th century saw the crisis and decay of the Enlightenment (popular rationalism, pseudo-culture) but also a partial success and revival (especially among the working classes). It is represented today in all areas of life by modern scientific rationalism (in particular in materialism, positivism, and communism) and its end is not yet in sight.

The Enlightenment sees itself and presents itself as a goal, a criticism, a function, rather than as an attainment (the state of being enlightened). Lacking any rigid system, indeed self-contradictory to the point of complete amorphousness, yet constantly critical of ignorance, culpable infantilism, intolerance and laziness, it influenced every area of life and culture by its striving for mathematical abstraction, rational clarity (*saeculum mathematicum*), order and progress. Basic aspects of the Enlightenment are its confidence in reason and scientism, an optimistic view of the world and man, a predominantly and almost pharisaically critical stance ("the real century of criticism" – Kant). From knowledge of the regularity of the natural order and faith in the organizability of human life was derived an enthusiastic belief in progress which banished baroque pessimism and the theory of "decline", rejected the Christian understanding, and strove for a utopian perfectionism as the objective for both the individual and society, encouraging thus the eudaemonism of the age.

For the historian of thought, the Enlightenment is a specific form of modern subjectivism and individualism for which nominalism and humanism paved the way. It adopted their passion for enquiry, their critical stance and laicized culture. It gained stimulus from the intellectualism of baroque scholasticism, and was encouraged by pietism and by the effects of the wars of religion, by the hardening of the social and economic order into absolutism, and finally by the enlarging of man's view of the world (e.g., the discarding of the biblical chronology, discovery of new regions of the world and of new cultures) and the growing importance of the natural sciences and mechanized industry (Newton and Laplace). Nature became the philosopher's book (Galileo); the laws of nature assumed a metaphysical validity; the observance of the laws brings happiness and virtue (C. Wolff); mathematics and natural science, regarded as absolute sciences, become the indispensable bases of philosophical thought (Kant).

Supported at first by the nobility and then increasingly, from about 1740, by the prosperous and educated middle classes, and strengthened by a sense of solidarity among writers, the Enlightenment broke up the aristocratic court society and introduced the bourgeois century. Its social aims often coincided with those of the middle classes, though at the widest extent of its expansion its influence reached beyond them, which was one reason for the emergence of the working classes in the 19th century. The impact of the Enlightenment remained weakest among the peasant class. Freemasonry, semi-religious in character and purely bourgeois in origin, played an important role in disseminating the Enlightenment, as did other secret societies in due course (Illuminati, Rosicrucians, etc.), though the "conspiracy theory" is untenable.

Man and man's fulfilment are the primary concern of Enlightenment thought. The concern is, if not exclusively, at least more centrally than hitherto, with education, *cultura animi*, humanity, civilization. For this purpose supernatural revelation and grace seemed hardly necessary. The Enlightenment's passion for education sought to advance the moral and social welfare both of the individual and of society by the more intensive cultivation of the mind. Relieved of the burden of original sin and anxiety about existence, the anthropocentrism of the Enlightenment strove for the *regnum hominis* (instead of the *regnum Dei*), for equality and for excellence (the élite consciousness) simultaneously, patronizing the "common herd" and aiming at the perfect happiness of mankind (the welfare state of enlightened absolutism). The rejection of the supernatural and the progress of secularization (the latter difficult to pinpoint) varied from country to country and in its effects on the Churches in each period. But we can see unmistakably the tendency to rationalize religion (Kant, *Religion within the Limits of Pure Reason*, 1793), to humanize it as ethical deism, to reduce the confessions to a common denominator of "natural religion", and to dissolve theology into a philosophy of history. Yet despite a growing religious indifference and a hostility to revelation and Church within the Enlightenment, it would be inadequate to stress anti-supernaturalism and irreligion as its main features. The fact that it was tied to the maintenance of a bourgeois Christian and enlightened absolutist order kept 18th-century deism, pantheism, militant atheism and hatred of the Church within bounds. It was only the popular Enlightenment of the 19th century which alienated from the Church the *petit-bourgeois* and working-class masses. It was chiefly in Protestant countries that a distinctive Enlightenment Christianity spread, with its characteristic retreat from dogmas, sacraments and ceremonies, its faith in providence, its obligation to "virtue", its tendency to reconcile Christianity, science and culture; but it happened in Catholic countries too. The Church often came to be regarded in the Enlightenment merely as an institution concerned with morals and education, simply as an auxiliary to the enlightened welfare state. To an anti-curialism and anti-clericalism often merely intensified by the Enlightenment (hostility to the monastic orders, hatred of the Jesuits) were added violent attacks on dogmas and sacraments.

The distinctively Catholic Enlightenment (still insufficiently investigated and everywhere complex) brought about a renewal of Church life as early as the 18th century, particularly in the Catholic states of Germany. Without this renewal – taking the form of advances in positive historical and exegetical methods, improvements in the education, discipline and morality of the clergy, the struggle against superstition and credulity, the decrease in the number of festivals and processions, reform of the liturgy, catechesis and pastoral work, the furtherance of popular education and charitable works – the 19th-century restoration (e.g., Clemens Wenceslaus of Saxony, Max Franz of Austria, Franz Ludwig of Erthal) would have been impossible. The Catholic Enlightenment, marked by efforts to establish contact with the development of culture and science which were generally little influenced by Catholicism, and by a longing for tolerance and the reunion of the Church, was not untainted by destructive and heterodox features (rejection of the revelation-based authority of God and the Church, impoverishment of worship, devaluation of contemplation; e.g., E. Schneider, Blau, Eybel, Isenbiehl). The Enlightenment had relatively little influence on Febronianism, which stemmed from late medieval episcopalism, and the traditional demands and grievances of the State Churches. Its connection with the Jansenist movement of opposition and reform within the Church is complex and defies easy summary. The Enlightenment had a lasting influence on the State Churches of later absolutism by its acceptance, reshaping and systematization of the pre-Reformation and Counter-Reformation Church establishment in the Catholic states, with its *iura maiestatica circa sacra*. It considered all aspects of the Church's life to be under State control as a religious society under the jurisdiction of the State. The interventions of Josephinism in Church life, which were partly justified by the need for reform (dissolution of monasteries, amortization laws, parish organization, diocesan controls, etc.) sufficiently illustrate the special problems of the Catholic Enlightenment. They resulted from the interaction and tension between the Enlightenment, efforts at reform, ecclesiastical conservatism and religious decline. Attacked as it was from all sides, the 18th-century Church Enlightenment was incapable of bringing about a thoroughgoing renewal; the times were unpropitious and its own position was difficult. Yet in many respects its reforms and not a few of its exponents (e.g., J. M. Sailer, E. Klüpfel, G. Zirkel) paved the way for the Church renewal of the 19th century.

Heribert Raab

ENTELECHY

The term entelechy was first introduced into philosophy by Aristotle who used it in several different but related senses. We shall understand by it an intrinsic tendency within a physical body, by virtue of which it is orientated towards some goal, e.g., the perfection of the individual concerned or of the species to which it belongs. The principle of entelechy is sometimes known as the principle of finality or teleology.

The question whether there is intrinsic finality in the physical world has been much disputed. Aristotle and most of the medieval philosophers held that all physical bodies, whether living or inorganic, have entelechy; this view has also been supported by later scholastic philosophers. Elsewhere, however, the theory that inorganic bodies have intrinsic finality has been generally rejected, chiefly as a result of the growth of physical science which can find no use for final causes within its own domain. In the biological realm there has been less unanimity. Mechanists have regarded living organisms simply as complicated machines subject to the same laws as inorganic matter; some would extend this conclusion also to man. Vitalists, on the other hand, postulate that the organism has a special vital principle which distinguishes it essentially from a machine and renders it capable of genuinely teleological action. At the present time most biologists hold, at least as a working hypothesis, that all vital activity is reducible to the laws of physics and chemistry. Catholic doctrine denies that human acts can be wholly determined by physical law but is not directly concerned with non-human vital activity. In this realm, recent advances in biochemistry make the possibility of complete physico-chemical explanation seem less remote than was formerly the case and this is true also of many aspects of man's vital processes. It is becoming doubtful, therefore, whether one can make a sharp distinction between organic processes which are teleological, and inorganic which are not. Either entelechy is to be found at all levels of being or its existence can be called in question at any level except, perhaps, man. The first of these alternatives has been strongly urged by Teilhard de Chardin. He held that the whole physical world is intrinsically orientated towards the fulfilment of a single divine plan. Thus inorganic matter tends, of its nature, towards the production of living organisms; simple organisms tend to evolve towards the human level; man tends towards an ever closer hyper-personal social unity with his fellow-men. This tendency, elevated to the supernatural order by virtue of the Incarnation, will be finally perfected by the union of man with God in the mystical body of Christ. Teilhard's views have been criticized in some respects but it seems probable that any satisfactory solution of the problem of finality must be along some such lines as these.

John Russell

ENTHUSIASM

1. *Its meaning.* The original Greek word means rapture, being inspired or possessed by a god. Used disparagingly in the 17th century of the religious attitude of the Puritans and in the 18th of that of the Methodists, the English word now has the general sense of passionate eagerness in any pursuit.

2. *Its nature.* Enthusiasm is not something a man "has", but something which he is plunged in. To be enthusiastic means that one's life is caught up in something which, however, is also within man and impelling him on. The other basic trait of enthusiasm is an active outgoing: man is "beside himself", carried away and driven forward by the spirit which intoxicates him. Three co-ordinates ensue. First, the spirit which impels the enthusiast in his primary and indeed unique and unconditional source and impulse. Then there is an equally comprehensive aim: all is grist to the enthusiast's mill, he knows no bounds, shrinks from no enterprise, lays claim to all means of expression, transcends all limits. Finally, the human ego, caught midway between the source and the goal of enthusiasm, is "beside itself", averted from itself, yet by the very fact at one with itself. When enthusiasm blossoms from it, the ego itself achieves a new, more vivid originality: receptive now to all things, it takes possession of all things and of its own being. Enthusiasm takes a person out of himself, to make him one with all things and thereby with himself.

3. *Contrast with ordinary feelings.* Even in his ordinary consciousness, man is secretly "enthusiastic". His spontaneous reaction is not: I see things this way or that, but: This is the way things are! He is instinctively outgoing, intent on the world, and in this very attitude he affirms the truth: Yes, things are truly so, even apart from me, unconditionally. He only appears as a personal being insofar as the truth dawns with him, in its pristine originality – which is the import of his affirmation. But in ordinary consciousness, the primordial guidance of truth is obscured by the strain of man's anxieties, questioning, assertions and efforts to dominate. Here it is possible that man is not securely at one with the truth. He always gives out what he says as true, and his vital impulse always comes from a "spirit", from the inexorable tendency to interpret the truth and the world. But that it is the spirit of truth is not predetermined. His essence is revealed in enthusiasm as unity with the unconditioned, but his existence is not fully in harmony with his essence. It is not clear that he should exist at all, and it cannot be taken for granted that his existence attains the level of his

essence and is "fulfilled". Hence enthusiasm is as essential as it is unusual. It can neither be "produced" nor "preserved".

4. *Criteria of enthusiasm*. Enthusiasm is genuine if its moving spirit is really absolute and universal, is the spirit of truth, and if the ardent ego is simply the instrument of that spirit. Man, being predisposed to exaggerated enthusiasms, is tempted to arrogate to himself the spirit that can only be received as a gift. An unspiritual, counterfeit enthusiasm may intoxicate individuals, even whole societies, serving merely to unleash the ego, to assert and intensify it. Such false enthusiasm is fanaticism. The spirit of truth allows all things to be what they are, its enthusiasm is the other face of its tranquillity and composure: it has one passionate desire – that the absolute shall remain absolute, the relative merely relative.

5. *Theological significance*. There is only one instance of the enthusiasm which corresponds to man's nature and sets up a tension with his existence. It is that which transcends nature and is based on the divine revelation which came in Jesus. Being human means, paradoxically, becoming something more than human: being open to and at one with the absolute source which wells up secretly with each human person and from which each person springs. The mystery of Jesus – Godhead and manhood united in a single person without separation and without confusion – brings about this fulfilment of humanity in a sublime degree, at the same time revealing perfect man as God first conceived of him in grace. Humanity, therefore, finds its fulfilment, human enthusiasm its "redemption", in membership of Christ through the Holy Spirit. The enthusiasm of primitive Christianity thus appears as an initial stage of the Church's being, which, however, in this present age of the world must necessarily be combined with everyday feelings. The cross is the simultaneous presence of enthusiasm and ordinary feelings, the permanent mediator between them and the proof of their authenticity.

Klaus Hemmerle

EPISCOPALISM

"Episcopalism" is often used to designate the doctrine and organization of the Episcopalian Churches of the Reformation. It is the ordinary English and American usage, adopted by the *Enciclopedia Cattolica*, V, 447, and by the short article *Episcopalismo* in the *Enciclopedia Universal*, XX, 321. But Ettore Rota, in the article *Reforme* (*Età delle*) in the *Enciclopedia Italiana*, uses the word in a very different sense, a sense which is also that of H. Raab in the article "Episkopalismus" in *LTK*, III, 1959, cols. 948–50. To avoid confusion, we use the term Episcopalism in the latter sense, now to be described.

In general terms, Episcopalism is essentially that doctrine according to which supreme power in the Church is vested in the collectivity of the bishops, whether they be dispersed throughout the world or, above all, united in Council, and not in the Pope alone (assisted by the Roman Curia). However, in the course of time this current of thought has taken very diverse forms, some of which are unacceptable.

1. *Doctrinal bases*. The doctrinal bases of Episcopalism are to be found in the most ancient documents of the life of the Church and in the NT itself. Christ founded the apostolic college, of which the bishops are the successors; it is on this foundation that the Church is built (Eph 2:20; Rev 21:14). Peter is not outside this college; he is one of the Twelve and their leader: this is why he receives special promises and particular powers, and this as a personal privilege, at least in the sense that he did not receive them from the other apostles but from Christ himself who designated him as the stone or rock on which the Church

is built. The authority of the apostolic college is not opposed, therefore, to that of Peter but is rather strengthened and guaranteed by this latter, which gives it its centre of cohesion and direction. The writings of the Apostolic Fathers acquaint us with the exercise of the authority of the bishops, successors of the apostles: the bishop is never isolated, any more than he is strictly limited to the territory which has been given him. He must concern himself with the common good of the whole Church and this responsibility finds expression in many bonds of communion with the other bishops. The theorists of Episcopalism have cited many texts of St. Ignatius of Antioch, of St. Cyprian, of St. Augustine, etc., in this sense.

2. *History*. Despite the action of the reforming Popes of the 11th century, and the unanimous recognition of the supreme and universal power of the Sovereign Pontiff, the Middle Ages preserved a number of currents of Episcopalism: in fact no one succeeded in elaborating a coherent synthesis in which the respective powers of Pope and bishops were harmoniously reconciled. The Avignon papacy, the Western Schism, the conflicts with Philip the Fair and Louis of Bavaria favoured the development of the theory of the superiority of Council over Pope. The need of a reform in head and members by a return to the ancient law of the Church and to its primitive purity was felt vividly. The Councils of Pisa, of Constance and of Basle, the Concordats of Constance (1418) and of the Princes (1447), the Pragmatic Sanction of Bourges (1438), etc., were little by little forming the dossier which the partisans of Episcopalism would invoke, such as John of Paris, Marsilius of Padua, William of Occam, Gerson, d'Ailly, etc.

It was above all Gallicanism which was responsible for the spread of Episcopalist ideas. Without really calling pontifical primacy in question the Gallican theologians, against the very excesses of the Ultramontanists, insist on the episcopacy of divine right and sometimes affirm the superiority of Council over Pope and the subordination of the latter to the ecclesiastical canons. The opinions are manifold, ranging from the very moderate opinions of Almain, Tournély, Peter of Marca, and Bossuet, to the frankly heterodox position of Richer.

In Germany it was above all after the Council of Trent and the Peace of Westphalia that the Episcopalist currents manifested themselves. The Council, while strengthening the position of the Pope, had also affirmed the divine origin of the episcopate, though without specifying the exact relations between the papacy, the episcopate and the Council; in this context J. K. Barthel and his disciples G. Zallwein, P. A. Schmidt and Martin Gerbert must be mentioned. Febronius is the most extreme representative in the 18th century. In the 19th century the Germans discover, beyond that sociological aspect so dear to the Ultramontanists (J. de Maistre, Rohrbacher, Guéranger, etc.) the sacramental aspect of the Church, a community of life with Christ and the Holy Spirit, especially by means of the sacraments; they affirm, as Bossuet had already done, that the analogy with human societies cannot be the point of departure of a manifestation of the nature of the Church, and that a formulation in terms of authority cannot suffice. This leads to a rediscovery of the mystery of the episcopate and of its unity: J. A. Möhler was the principal architect of this renewal.

The eve of the First Vatican Council saw a new awakening of Episcopalism, represented especially by Mgr. Maret and Mgr. Darboy. The Council confirmed in fact a number of their ideas: the divine origin of the episcopate, limits to papal infallibility, and the ordinary and immediate jurisdiction of the bishops who are true pastors.

Vatican II gave new expression to the orthodox element in Episcopalism, and thereby excluded its heterodox forms by declaring that the office of the apostles is transmitted by divine right to the college of the bishops, to which the individual bishops are subordinated: "It devolves on the bishops to admit newly elected members into the episcopal body by means of the sacrament of orders" (*Lumen Gentium*, art. 21). The structure of this college follows the will of its founder, Christ our Lord. Its centre and head is the Roman Pontiff, who exercises the office of Peter. In this way the Church combines both the synodal principle and that of a personal primacy. This structure is most clearly visible in the unity of the (collegial) subject of supreme doctrinal and jurisdictional authority in the Church. This authority is exercised either by the college of bishops or by the Pope alone but functioning *as* head of the college, even in a non-collegiate act.

Joseph Lécuyer

ESCHATOLOGY

This article will not deal with the Last Things in general or in detail. What is intended is a fundamental reflection on the nature of the theological treatise on eschatology. The question is not merely of theoretical and learned interest but has its importance for the proclamation of the Christian message itself. In a world which is now in movement, which is programming its own future, even if only for this world, a great eschatological aspiration is certainly bound up with (though not really derived from) secular goals and hopes of that kind. This undoubtedly makes the proclamation of the Christian hope for the future more difficult than it used to be. Furthermore, precisely in this part of theology the general problem of demythologization recurs in an urgent form. Finally, the preaching of the Last Things presents its own problems. In the course of history this proclamation itself has been strangely concentrated on the individual and this in itself calls for criticism. A cosmic eschatology involving the whole of history has become very colourless and insignificant as compared with a doctrine of the individual immortality of spiritual souls and of their individual destiny. Yet it is quite possible that this *way* of proclamation – valid though its actual content may be – was in fact determined by the conditions of a particular age. It is therefore possible to ask whether that age is not now coming to an end and a new one slowly emerging, one which by its own dynamic orientation towards the future will have a more direct relation to the cosmic eschatology of Christianity which concerns the whole history of humanity.

1. *On the history of this branch of theology*. The history of the revelation of the Last Things down to and including the whole NT, is long and rich, but the history of eschatology is meagre in comparison with that of other sections of dogmatic theology, at least within the limits of ecclesiastical orthodoxy or in contact with this. Since a systematic treatment of the whole of dogmatic theology came into existence, the treatise on eschatology has been placed at its very end. This arrangement can be justified by reference to the creeds and to some extent by the nature of the Last Things. Yet one must at least know what one can hope for before morals can be dealt with as a part of dogmatic theology. And it must not be forgotten, as often does happen, that in substance and even expressly (*D* 16, 86) the creeds directly profess the "expectation" of what is to come. In other words, they are directly concerned with something present. It is this which must provide the fundamental structure of the whole for the real understanding of what is to come. Conversely, the fundamental structure of our present life can only be

understood on the basis of its reaching out towards the future. The treatise on eschatology at the end of dogmatic theology has scarcely had any real history until now. The very unselfconscious course of the very early transition from imminent to remote expectation of the parousia, the slow and imperceptible surmounting of millenarianism and of the doctrine of a real apocatastasis (as a thesis, not simply as a hope open to man), the rejection of a salvation of its nature not open to all in Gnosticism, the refusal of a doctrine of eschatological phases which abolished the absolute, universal and truly eschatological significance of Christ in Montanism and Joachim of Flora, the defence of the grace-given character of beatitude against heretical mysticism (*D* 475), Baianism (*D* 1002–7), German Idealism (*D* 1808) and A. Rosmini (*D* 1928ff.), the locating of the essence of beatitude in the vision of God, are all particular questions of eschatology which have a history, as are the questions of purgatory, the nature of the beatific vision, the nature of the "fire" of hell, etc.

All these are events in the history of this branch of theology, but do not constitute occurrences of such a kind as to give that history a clear structure and historical articulation, or the content of the treatise on eschatology a systematic self-sufficient form. The only clear and important break which we observe in the history of the treatise so far is Benedict XII's definition that the direct vision of God in the case of the just who are fully purified, and the punishment of hell for those dying in mortal sin, begin even "before" the general judgment (*D* 530f., *Benedictus Deus*). This does not of course establish a balance on the plane of systematic speculative theology between the universal, cosmic, ecclesiological eschata occurring at the end of time in the "flesh", and the individual, existential eschata occurring in each particular case now in the spirit. Yet, since the universal and ancient eschatology remains, it establishes once and for all the inescapability of a genuine and enduring dialectic between these two aspects of fulfilment. Eschatology can never sacrifice one to the other. Eschatology has therefore become bipolar, and will so remain and cannot "de-mythologize" fulfilment into the multiplicity of individual eschata. Yet it has to speak of the eschata of individuals and would not do this if it were to speak solely of the end of all. For the rest, as a simple comparison with the history of other branches of theology shows, eschatology has not advanced in theological reflection beyond a relatively superficial arrangement of the statements of Scripture. A gnoseology is lacking and a hermeneutic specially adapted to eschatological statements. The absence of a properly elaborated theology of history and temporality in general and of saving history in particular makes itself felt unfavourably in eschatology as it does elsewhere. The relation between protology and eschatology remains unexamined; that between Christian eschatology and secular utopianism has scarcely yet been considered. The theology of the eschatological attitude of the Christian in his own present life is abandoned to the literature of piety alone. The fundamental terms of eschatology (beginning, ending, fulfilment, orientation of the course of history, time [as a specifically human "occurrence"], future, axiological and teleological presence of what is to come, modes of presence, death, eternity as fulfilling and confirming time as well as suppressing it by raising it to a higher level [as opposed to "continued duration"], judgment, place of beatitude, etc.) are still far from having received the necessary and possible analysis and explicit treatment in a philosophical ontology of human reality, which in the perspective of the present-day view of the world would really facilitate the acceptance in faith of the eschatological message and permit its philosophical synthesis with the conception of existence which modern men hold in other respects.

The treatise on eschatology is still very much at the beginning of its history. What is most concerned with history has had no history in Christian theology. Christian eschatology must come to realize its own nature by thinking out its own implications more thoroughly than it has done so far. This is called for by the situation created by the modern scientific picture of a world in process of becoming; by the unleashing of the will to prospective, planned and rationalized transformation of the whole human condition by man as a being who makes himself and his environment; by the possibility of extending the living space of humanity beyond the earth; by the modern militant political world-heresies of secular utopianism, etc. Then it will be possible, for example, to develop the original Christian fundamental conception of the Last Things and to conceive the origin of the "domain" of salvation as resulting from the time of salvation much more clearly than this was possible with the conceptual apparatus of previous eschatology which regarded saving history as unfolding in an already present, spatial domain, static and fixed by nature (the immutable empyrean, etc.). This new phase of the history or eschatology has so far been initiated chiefly among non-Catholics. Liberal Protestant theology (W. M. L. de Wette, J. Weiss, A. Schweitzer, M. Werner) interpreted Christianity and its theology as the history of the parousia which failed to occur. In R. Bultmann's demythologization an attempt is made to existentialize the eschata in the individual instance of each particular believer (similarly C. H. Dodd: realized eschatology). In orthodox Protestant theology either a one-sided eschatologism is pursued or the whole of theology is essentially reconstructed on the basis of a radical rejection of the Calvinist doctrine of predestination.

2. *Themes for an eschatology.* In what follows an attempt is made to indicate in outline the themes of a doctrine of eschatology as it ought to be (and which has for the most part not yet been worked out in the text-books). But an inventory of themes is intended rather than a statement of the systematic arrangement which a treatise of that kind would have.

a) The correct single basic principle for the problem and conception of eschatology would have to be worked out. Eschatology is not an advance report of events taking place "later". That is the basic intention of false apocalyptic as opposed to genuine prophecy. Eschatology is a forward look which is necessary to man for his spiritual decision in freedom, and it is made from the standpoint of his situation in saving history as this is determined by the Christ-event. This situation is the aetiological ground of the cognition. The gaze is directed towards the definitive fulfilment of precisely this human situation which is already an eschatological one. And it is intended to make possible a man's own enlightened decision in relation to what is obscure and open. The aim is that the Christian in that decision may accept his present as a factor in the realization of the possibility established by God in the beginning (*transcendent* return to the "Garden of Eden") and as a future which is already present and definitive in a hidden way. For that future presents itself as salvation now, precisely if it is accepted as God's action, incalculable in its when and how, because determined by God alone. And in that way the stumbling-block presented by the contradiction which still exists between the redemption already present in Christ and the world's sin, the divisions of the nations, the discrepancy between nature and man, desire, death, is endured in patience and hope as a sharing in the Cross of Christ. In other words, eschatology concerns redeemed man as he now is. With him as basis it knows what is to come as something blissfully incomprehensible which is to be accepted in freedom (and therefore in danger of being lost). What is to come (understood in this way) can be evoked in imagery but not described here and now in a report, and it is announced to man because he can only endure his present if he knows he is in movement towards his future, which is the incomprehensible God in his own very life.

b) It would be necessary to create a hermeneutics (theological gnoseology) of eschatological statements. If the above-mentioned basic principle of eschatology is clearly worked out and coherently maintained, definite fundamental norms follow from it concerning the meaning, scope and limits of eschatological statements both in Scripture and in dogmatic theology. These hermeneutical norms also have a basis in Scripture. They are grounded in the fundamental theological teaching of Scripture (unity and uniqueness of history, God's incomprehensibility, unity of spirit and matter in man and his history, salvation as the fulfilment of man as a unity and a whole, etc.). But Scripture also indicates that a real distinction is to be drawn between representation or image on the one hand and reality signified on the other. Scripture freely employs a multiplicity of representative models irreducible to any system – the end as a world conflagration, as a judgment assembling all together, as a triumphant going out of the saints to meet Christ, etc. Consequently a false "apocalyptic" conception of eschatology is excluded as well as its demythologizing and absolute existentializing. The latter forgets that man lives in a genuinely temporal condition which is directed towards what has really still to come, and in a world which is not simply abstract personal existence but must attain salvation in all its dimensions, even that of the secular temporal process. It must be made clear in theology and preaching that in basic principle what is said about heaven and what is said about hell are not on the same plane. The Church eschatologically proclaims as a *fact* already realized in Jesus and the saints that saving history (in its totality) ends victoriously as the triumph of the grace of God. It only proclaims as a serious *possibility* that the freedom of each individual may operate to his eternal ruin. The theology of hell and the necessary prophetic commination in the Church require, in order to be Christian, always to be kept open in character, since they are statements about our possibilities as they are now, and which cannot at present be superseded. This is in contrast to esoteric knowledge about an apocatastasis and also to anticipatory knowledge of damnation as having already occurred, despite the fact that God's judgment is unknown to us. These principles of hermeneutics can permit an essentially more accurate (even if never plainer) distinction than is usually made between content and mode of expression in the eschatological statements of Scripture and tradition. It is only necessary repeatedly to remind oneself of what has just been said in section 2a. Then it is at once clear that the content of the statements comprises everything which (but no more than) can be understood as fulfilment and definitive condition of that Christian human reality which revelation states to be present here and now. All else is figurative representation of this fulfilment of Christian existence. Because, for example, Christian life as redeemed concerns all dimensions of human existence, the resurrection of the flesh is a dogma of faith, yet we cannot on that account form any precise idea of the glorified body. Because there is a single saving history of mankind as such, its fulfilment cannot be reduced to that of the various individuals. Yet it is not possible to co-ordinate precisely and in detail the cosmic and individual eschatology or precisely to distinguish them. Because the history of the freedom of individuals, each of whom is unique, is not a mere factor in history as a whole, it is necessary to speak of individual fulfilment (the vision of God), and this history of individual freedom must be held quite open, despite the certainty of the blessed outcome as a whole. Yet it is not possible on that account clearly to mark the occurrence of general and of individual salvation on a common time-scale. This distinction between content of statement and adaptable mode of representation applies above all to the history of the end of the world (before the Last Judgment) and the signs of its coming. The application of these principles to the question of the fate of infants dying without baptism would have to be examined.

c) The actual universal propositions contained in eschatology which precede its various material propositions would likewise form part of a properly elaborated eschatology and would include: the intrinsically limited character of time and its historical configuration from genuine beginning to a genuine irreplaceable end; the uniqueness of each part of sacred history; death, and the "change" effected as an event by God, as a necessary mode of genuine fulfilment of time (since the Fall); the fact that the end has already come with the incarnation, death and resurrection of the Logos made flesh; the presence of this end as constituting the fact of the victorious mercy and self-communication of God (in contradistinction to a double outcome, on an equal footing which would be specified by man's freedom alone); the special character of the time now still unfolding "after" Christ; the persistent character of this period as a conflict (with Antichrist), which necessarily becomes more intense as the end approaches; the question of the convergence of the natural and supernatural finality of man and cosmos (the factors of a "natural" eschatology which involves more than merely the "immortality of the soul"), etc. It is only on this basis that the particular themes usually dealt with in eschatology become really intelligible, because in these the whole inevitably recurs under some particular aspect. Among these particular themes room must be found for a number of things which the theology of the schools scarcely notices, for example the final removal of the cosmic powers of the Law, of death, etc.; the enduring significance of Christ's humanity for beatitude; the positive meaning of the inequality of the glory of heaven; the vision of God as the abiding mystery (the positive meaning of the permanent incomprehensibility of God); the relation between the heaven of the redeemed and the reprobate world of the demons; the positive significance of the persistence of evil and the nature of the latter; the metaphysical essence of the glorified body; the one "Kingdom of God" formed of angels and men; the true nature of the "intermediate state" (between death and general judgment) which must not be regarded as purely "spiritual".

d) Special attention has to be given to the dialectic which necessarily prevails between the statements regarding individual and universal eschata as a consequence of man's Christian being and fulfilment, which comprise all his dimensions. Precisely this dialectic displays the difference between content and mode of representation in eschatological statements. If that dialectic is not taken into account, these statements take on a mythological flavour and consequently are no longer very convincing in the proclamation of the faith. For of course these statements cannot be harmonized, as usually happens, simply and solely by dividing them among different realities which are then treated separately (beatitude of the "soul" – resurrection of the "body"). Nor can it be done by ignoring individual eschatology in favour of universal (simply denying an intermediate state, impossible as it is, of course, to describe this state), or by eliminating universal eschatology in favour of individual as being merely the sum of the latter. For man in body and soul is united into one reality which forms the ontological basis of the dialectical and irreducible unity in duality of the mutually related statements which always concern the totality of his being.

e) Eschatology must always be seen in connection with the other branches of theology, for it concerns what forms the content of other treatises, but in fulfilment. Consequently between eschatology and these other treatises there is a relation of mutual inclusion and they throw light on one another. That is true not only of protology and the states of man, of the theology of history in general, of the theology of grace (grace as possessed "in hope"), but above all of Christology, soteriology (the definitive acceptance of the world in Christ), ecclesiology (the Church of the last days, willing to be abolished yet raised to a higher plane, into the *basileia* of God; the Church of those awaiting the second coming of Christ in contradistinction to the Synagogue and to religious organizations which regard themselves as timeless), and the doctrine of the sacraments (as *signa prognostica* of definitive salvation).

f) To eschatology there necessarily also belongs the dogmatic (not merely edifying) treatment of the eschatological attitude of the Church and of the individual Christian, and the Christian criticism and redemption of the secular utopias and of the eschatologies of other religions, to the extent that this is not already done by soteriology.

Karl Rahner

ESSENCE

1. The noun "essence" comes from the verb "esse", "to be", and was formed as if from the present participle, like "be-ing". In German the word for essence, *Wesen*, is both verb and noun. As verb it means to occur, happen, prevail. For Heidegger, for example, the *Wesen der Wahrheit* (essence of truth) goes beyond the "usual concept of *Wesen* (essence)" (*Vom Wesen der Wahrheit*, 3rd ed., 1954, p. 27), and is identical with the *Walten des Geheimnisses* (dominance of mystery) (*ibid.*, p. 24). Behind this stands the *Wahrheit des Wesens* (the truth of essence), where *Wesen*, essence, is being thought of as "be-ing" (*ibid.*, p. 27). This, however, meets us as the "destiny of being" or the unparalleled "event" (*Identität und Differenz*, 1957, p. 72), which unites "man and being in their essential connection" (*ibid.*, p. 31). Because here *Wesen*, essence, always means happening, it is identical with the historicity of being (its undergoing a destiny), or with the ontological history of being, in which the particular factual history of an individual existent has its ground.

2. As a noun, essence has developed from two main points of view. a) In the first place we observe in every existing thing in the world of our experience that it perpetually changes and that it maintains its identity. The individual existent perpetually changes as regards its various appearances, as can be seen, for example, in the growth of living things (eggs, grub, chrysalis, cockchafer); it remains the same as regards its inner core which continually unfolds in various external manifestations yet persists in them, as the example of the cockchafer shows. On this basis, essence means what necessarily belongs to a thing and most intimately constitutes it, determining its particular character both statically and dynamically; without its essence a thing would not be what it is. Furthermore, it is possible to

speak of the essence even of individual beings, for example the essence of a particular human being, as his own special qualities which characterize him and distinguish him from all others, which manifest themselves in all his behaviour and in which he remains true to himself. In philosophy, we mean by essence the persistent structure in which many individuals agree or resemble one another and in virtue of which they are bearers of the same specific qualities or are of the same kind; this can easily be seen in the case of man. The data just recalled provide the basis for the general concept of essence which by abstraction transcends the particular features which distinguish individuals and retains only the traits or structures in which individuals agree or coincide. The content of the essence obtained in this way is said to be general or universal because it is realized in all the individuals and therefore can be predicated of each individual without in itself designating any individual in particular. The essence is often said to be timeless and changeless; this is true in the sense that its identity persists in the flux of time. At the same time, however, the essence of a thing is the ground of the possibility, and often of the actual realization, of the thing's changing in this or that way, or of its appropriate alterations unfolding in the course of time, as is the case with living things. Nor does the essence exclude, but rather includes, the possibility of one thing's becoming another and so of passing from the domain of one essence to that of another, which is what happens when food is digested, for example. Above all, the essence of man is not rigid and immobile but is precisely the ground of his intrinsically temporal and historical character; in that way the one essence of man is differentiated into many historical forms which persist during an epoch (e.g., men of Graeco-Roman antiquity) or a civilization (e.g., men of the Far East). Finally, man's essence or specific nature demands that it finds fulfilment in authentic personal self-realization; in other words, essence in the case of man always implies personal existence inasmuch as, in virtue of his essence and under the continual changing summons of being, he realizes himself and actually makes himself by his free acts the person he ultimately is. Consequently, with man it has always to be asked not only what he is but also who he is.

b) The second point of view from which essence is used as a noun has also to be explained on two levels. Each existent in the world of our experience prompts two questions. Because things are in a state of becoming and passing away, the question arises as to whether anything is; because things are distinct from one another in kind, they prompt the question of what something is.

(i) The answer to the first question is given by existence or "there-ness", to the second by "what-ness" or quiddity, which is also often called essence or nature. We should prefer to reserve the latter terms for use on the plane of the second set of problems which will be presented in a moment. There-ness and what-ness refer to the concrete finite being in two different respects; these can be completely separated in thought from one another because in the what-ness actual existence is not comprised and there-ness does not imply this particular what-ness. Since both are found in the individual existent, they are themselves subject to individuation; consequently here it is a question of the particular or individual what-ness, this man Peter, for example, viewed in regard to what he is as opposed to the fact that he exists.

(ii) The second plane of problems moves on from the two aspects which characterize already constituted finite beings as a whole, to the two structural factors or principles, the union of which is needed for the constitution of finite beings as a whole. Because the two principles are not aspects of the whole but partial elements of the whole, they are really distinct from one another; here the real distinction is ontological, not one of empirical fact, i.e., the distinction is one between the intrinsic grounds (λόγοι) of a being, not between this being and that as wholes. In precise terms the principles represent the (ontological) essence or quidditative entity (*essentia*) and existence; moreover, the individual existent shares according to the measure of its finite essence in the *per se* unlimited plenitude of being. The essence is necessarily distinct from being because it does not exhaust the plenitude of being. Essence and being stand to one another as potency to act; and in this connection the essence is singular or individual, like the "what-ness" referred to above. The two dualities of being-there and being-so and of essence and being correspond to some degree to one another, but do not coincide completely because they belong to different planes, as has been explained.

Surveying the various uses of essence as a noun, we observe that "what-ness" is primarily contrasted with appearance, essence primarily with being. Above essence and the being which is related to it as its principle, and hence limited, is being itself which comprises both as their single ground. In its whole limitless plenitude it is real as subsistent being, which we call God. As his infinite essence totally exhausts the plenitude of being, it coincides absolutely with the latter. Consequently, since the finite essence, as a way of sharing in being, has its total ground in being, it can only be understood on the basis of being and orientated to it. It follows that metaphysics is most intimately concerned not with the essence or "being-ness" of beings (Heidegger), but with being, and cannot be limited to the philosophy of essences as in Rationalism, but is necessarily a philosophy of being. Historically speaking, Plato located essence, as the universal or eternal changeless Form, in a place above the heavens and so separated it from individual earthly things. The latter indeed are related to the Forms or what truly is (ὀντῶς ὄν) as to their exemplary and final cause, but do not have an intrinsic essence as their own ground. Consequently, despite his theory of participation (μέθεξις), imitation (μίμησις), fellowship (κοινωνία), Plato could never clearly explain their relation to the Forms. In contrast to this, Aristotle found the essence in the individual thing and particularly as concentrated in the essential form (μορφή) actuating matter (ὕλη). The universal concept of an essence is obtained by abstraction from things. Since for Aristotle the immanent essence is not rooted in the transcendent archetypal Form, some of his followers have been inclined to hold conceptualist views. Inspired by neo-Platonism, Augustine returned to the archetypal Forms, locating them in the primordial creative mind as God's guiding patterns; yet Augustine too does not do justice to the essence intrinsic to things and for that reason the Forms are known less from things than through direct illumination. Thomas Aquinas accomplished a synthesis of Augustine and Aristotle; in virtue of their essential form, earthly beings are stamped with the likeness of the eternal archetypes in the divine mind and thereby things share in the infinite plenitude of subsisting being. Correspondingly man is able to discern their essence in things themselves (*intus legere*) and to grasp this essence in universal concepts obtained by abstraction, which likewise reflect the eternal Forms. Man is only in a position to do this because his active intellect (*intellectus agens*) involves a permanent irradiation of divine light (*Summa Theologica*, I, q. 84, a. 5).

This great tradition was broken by late medieval conceptualism, according to which the universal essence is entirely absorbed by the individual existent and the latter, therefore, provides no basis for an act of abstraction that would penetrate to the essence; consequently the concept of the essence is simply a mental construct which we produce for its practical utility. Influenced by this, rationalism and empiricism took opposite roads which Kant brought together again. According to Kant, the essence intrinsic to the thing in itself is inaccessible to us; the essential structures which we grasp belong solely to the thing as phenomenon and derive from the *a priori* forms of the transcendental subject. In German Idealism Hegel taught that the human mind penetrates to the essence of things, but only inasmuch as it is dialectically one with the absolute mind. At the same time Hegel equated the order of being with that of essence and consequently the primordial reality appears as the absolute idea; in it all all other essence are taken up and away, as its finite moments, in the movements of dialectics.

This predominantly essentialist philosophy is offensive to a mode of thought centred on man as capable of personal existence and which, at least as regards man, either denies or minimizes essence as a prior and enduring datum. Such an essence is regarded as incompatible with the freedom and the temporal, historical character of personal self-realization or with the constantly renewed happening of the self-sending of being; according to J.-P. Sartre, personal existence posits its own essence or nature, so that it always is what it makes itself to be. The phenomenology developed by Husserl defined philosophy as the investigation of essences; essence manifests itself in the intuition of essences or ideation (eidetic reduction) when actual existence is prescinded from; essence then appears as the noema related to noesis and as ultimately constituted by the transcendental consciousness. On the basis of his critical realism, N. Hartmann recognized an at least empirical essence of things, which he discerned in realities and analysed as categorical structures. Positivism and neo-Positivism, on the other hand, restrict themselves solely to phenomena and volatilize essence into the regular and empirically observable connections between phenomena.

Joh.-Baptist Lotz

ETHICS

1. *Notion and history*. History of philosophy and philosophy are inseparable, and for ethics history is essential in another sense also. Philosophy, as a deliberate study, takes place within man's history. But it is not the interest of all men. All need a more or less explicit view of the world, but this need not be philosophical. It may be a religious orientation. But men at all times, whether they give themselves to philosophy or not, have to live, that is, they have to give their lives a meaning. Hence they must plan beforehand and then implement their plans, they must choose between possibilities, do this and omit that, take decisions and form habits, adopt attitudes, make use of things, shape their own lives. In this sense man always has an impiicit philosophy, but it is precisely this philosophy which always has an ethical dimension, since it is itself determined by an *option fondamentale* of an ethical nature. And this appears most readily (though perhaps only in a rudimentary way), not in the form of theoretical propositions, but as maxims for action – what man is or is not to do, good or evil. Hence man is inevitably a moral being in the original sense of the word – as will be demonstrated more fully in the following. He is responsible for his life, that is, he has to take charge of it and answer for it.

Man is engaged in "creating" himself in the whole course of his life, like mankind throughout its history. This individual and social, but always historical notion is the primary basis of "morality". It means morals in action, not yet based on θεωρία but on πρᾶξις, on self-realization through bringing about reality.

We are concerned, then, first of all, with this moral reality, this realization of a "sketch-plan" for life. But men do not live and act at random. They follow certain patterns. These are first adopted spontaneously and only later become recognized ideals. In general they stem from models and attitudes adopted as historical cultural factors. This is the second sense of the word "moral" here. It means not only the mere "sketch-plan" as the directive for life, but the shaping of one's life in accordance with certain moral directives, that is, certain *mores*, customs. These *mores* are not yet moral philosophy or ethics, which comes later, if at all, and appears as comprehensive reflection on the moral behaviour of men, not as a moral lived out in action. Hence there are three meanings for the word "moral", the first of which was hitherto left outside explicit consideration, in spite of its unique importance. Consciously or unconsciously, moral philosophy always built on the data of an existing moral (in the second sense).

The relationship between moral philosophy and moral life explains the importance of the history of morals. The concept of morals must be extended to take in instinctive reaction to and philosophical reflection on morals. A history of moral philosophy as such, that is, of doctrines and opinions expressed on morality, would be a pure history of ideas, completely cut off from the soil on which these ideas were nourished. The history of *mores* alone, however, would be merely a positivist compilation of material facts.

The history of morals in the full sense has yet to be written. It would take in both the most important findings of social and cultural anthropology and of general history, and also the state of philosophical (and pre-philosophical) reflection. This would demonstrate its understanding of the moral consciousness of a given historical situation. The writing of such a history would be a laborious, but not a difficult task. The ethics of Aristotle, for instance, the first systematic moral philosophy, is almost exclusively reflection on the ethical consciousness of the Greeks. The four cardinal virtues of the *Nicomachean Ethics* represent the virtues striven for and practised in the course of Greek history. Aristotle's effort to provide as it were a handbook of Greek ethics is one last effort to preserve an ethics of fellowship in the City-State. Its failure signalled a new age of political figures who looked farther afield and wielded greater powers, but which was also an age in which Stoicism and Epicureanism offered two different ways by which philosophy could withdraw into the sphere of private, inward reflection and evade the effort to set up a genuine political ethics.

From the point of view considered here, Christianity brought with it a fundamental renewal of morals. Life was given through faith a new meaning which has been hitherto insufficiently noted by moral philosophy. Modern ethics became a mere imitation of the classical, Graeco-Roman ethics and lost touch with the reality of its own times. This unhealthy situation, in which a new set of morals was given no philosophical "translation", lasted till Kant. Kant replaced an ethics based on human nature and aiming at the good and at happiness, by a moral of pure duty, too formal to do justice to the material content of the act. Fichte, however, saw this formalism as a "material formality" – of life, love. Hegel, the Aristotle of his times, since he outlined a philosophical and ethical "Encyclopaedia", considered the ethics of Kant as a mere "moment" of his own ethics. The Kantian "morality" is abstract, out of touch with reality, lofty indeed but completely restricted to the individual and ineffective. It is taken up and away into the "ethical", the objective and supra-individual sphere of the State. Here Hegel anticipated a question which is urgent today, that of a social ethics with its own intrinsic justification and not put forward merely as a corollary to or mere expansion of a general individualistic moral philosophy. The two systems which have had the most lasting effects on the contemporary mind in general are those of Marxism and existentialism. Both derive from Hegel. Marx took over from him the supra-individual, social approach to the function of ethics, while rejecting his idealism. Kierkegaard's approach, however, was personalist, anti-idealist and existential. One of the great tasks of our times is to make a synthesis of the personal and the social, as has already been attempted by the representatives of a humanistic socialism. See the works of such socialist existentialists as Sartre (e.g., *Critique de la raison dialectique* [1960]) and certain contemporary Christian thinkers.

2. *Morality as an anthropological and social structure*. That man has to shape his life means negatively that it does not come to him ready-made. In contrast to the animal's imprisonment in its environment, where its responses are definitely determined by the combination of stimulus and psycho-biological constitution, man is free in his world and capable of various determinations. The stimuli are used by him, through his intellect, with which he derives or elicits possibilities from them, as sketch-plans for his actions. The possibilities may be many, and hence a choice must be made between the various sketch-plans envisaged. Hence human freedom is not bound by a fixed schema of stimulus and response, but can choose between various real possibilities. This process of choice and decision is not of course one single event. It must be constantly repeated. All truly human acts (the *actus humani* of the Scholastics) are decided upon in this way, and life is composed of such acts. The chosen possibility is realized, not only in my environment, the world, but – what is essential here – in myself. It is integrated into my own reality. Hence all human action must be considered moral action. Man is responsible for his actions because he plans his life freely and executes his plans freely, though with a paradoxical sort of freedom, since, as Ortega y Gasset says, he is "necessarily free". This morality of freedom is expressed in the "sketch-plan", the progressive shaping of actual life. Morality gives a man a "second nature", as Aristotle says, that is, a new reality, the ethos, the moral character or moral personality.

But human action is not determined merely by a set of perpetually new choices between proffered possibilities. The situations which man encounters may be each special and unrepeatable in its own way, but they show nonetheless similarities and point to the past in which other men in similar situations have taken similar decisions. The basis of a civilization or a culture is in fact the comprehensive repertoire of vital responses given at a special epoch. These responses have become consciously articulate and form models and patterns of behaviour. If we consider, not the single act, but human life in its fullness, we have to admit that we confine ourselves for the most part to a choice between various modes of existence and patterns of life – states, professions, avocations – which are offered by the society in which we live.

Thus human behaviour is determined by individual responsibility, by social conditioning and historical cultural traditions. This creates a dependence which is both negative and positive. Some "possibilities" have to be given up as unrealistic, others are multiplied in a way which would have been impossible without these social and traditional conditions. The genuine and not merely ostensible possibilities offered by society vary very widely. Given patterns of behaviour and custom bring about in a society, in spite of the rights of all men, considerable differences and tensions. Groups and classes are repressed or discriminated against. Individuals who do not conform are not always the solely guilty ones.

3. *The indicative and the imperative moment in ethics.* Man is necessarily free, and *has* to shape his life as an individual and as a member of society. It seems, however, that he can shirk this necessity of being free, this perpetual duty of choice, when he finds it tiresome. Hence men readily bow to tyrannies, if conditions are made comfortable enough for them, because there is a certain relief in placing the responsibility for choice on others. To do what "is done", to conform to the general consensus, to direct one's life by the customs and prescriptions of convention, makes things undoubtedly simpler. But it is an illusion to think that man could thus unburden himself of all responsibility, since the initial expression of freedom which leads to complete renunciation of independence is itself an act of decision. And even when an individual renounces completely his political and social freedom – though he thereby strives to destroy what is really human in him – a remnant of personal responsibility survives.

This allows us to distinguish in morality as a principle of structure and order (without going outside this frame of reference) an indicative and an imperative moment, the latter being implicit in the former. What ought to be is already comprised in what is. If man, as we have seen, must plan and anticipate what he desires to be, this is because he is a being which must realize itself at a distance from itself, in the tension between being and ought, in the difference between what it is and what it will be. The imperative of bridging this distance is called duty, the failing in this duty is called guilt. It should be noted, however, that this is not a separation of two realms as in Kant, the ontological and the deontological. The two realms are at one, in a unity in which a distinction is made simply for the sake of clarity. The notion of the "tension of being and ought" is prior to its ethical significance and is the foundation of it. A whole world of anthropological fundamentals – sketch-plan of existence, vocation, the general teleological purpose of existence, moral consciousness, conscience, sense of duty, and, on another plane, phenomena such as discontent, concupiscence, sense of inadequacy and self-pity – all are manifestations of this paradoxical nature of human being.

The imperative moment can be considered from two points of view, either purely formally and structurally, as has just been done, or materially, by considering the concrete content of the imperative. In the latter case, morality is taken as a concept full of content, of which we shall now speak.

4. *Moral formalism and the meta-ethical content of moralaity.* Hitherto we have spoken exclusively of the conditions by which human action and human freedom are determined. We have not yet discussed what man has to do to be good and not evil. Since Kant, the question of the content has been answered by a formalism according to which morality is measured by *how* something is done, not by *what* is done. The answer is sought in the form and not in the matter, in the structure and not in the content of action. In actual fact, the Kantian and the existentialist formalism conceals more or less effectively a material morality, based in Kant on Protestant principles and in atheism on the notion of emancipation from the supposed tyranny of God, in Marxism on the notion of the emanci-

pation of the exploited classes (see, for instance, Sartre).

It is instructive to compare the supposedly "ethical" formalism of Kant and Sartre. Both derive from historical conditions which are very important from the point of view of religious criticism. In the time of Kant, for the first time in the history of the West, Deism had gained great influence, though restricted to a minority. In the time of Sartre an (anti-theistic) atheism had gained ground for the first time. Atheism and Deism had been hitherto marginal phenomena. It was only after the Enlightenment that they became attitudes which determined action. In both cases the religious element – in reverse – provided the content of morality. Apart from antiquity, the various ways in which Christianity manifested itself have always provided the content for Western morality.

It would be wrong to try to understand the content of a morality uniquely in the light of its religious origins. The secularization of life which had already begun in the Middle Ages and made rapid strides from the Renaissance on, and especially through the Enlightenment, produced a morality which was completely orientated to the world (though even here religious roots have been discerned). Many of its demands, such as the right to work, security in the world, exploitation of natural resources, just distribution of goods, are nonetheless justified. Whether orientated to religion or to social life in general, the prescriptions of a morality are formed, not by philosophical or religious reflection, but by experience, in history. But if the contents of morality are meta-ethical, how can they be adopted by ethics or moral philosophy, if this is not to lose its true character and independence? This brings up the problem of the relationship between ethics and history and between ethics and religion.

Since ethics strives to be a philosophy, it cannot invoke religion but must derive its principles from reason alone. Reason can help to articulate the reality of evil in the world, the contingence of man, the dramatic character of life and the "mysterious" and "absurd" character of death. But these and similar phenomena also show the philosophical inadequacy of ethics and "open" it to religion.

It should be noted that the problem is not restricted to subordinating the philosophical realm of ethics to the meta-philosophical realm of religion. The problem is that ethics, as regards its material, is inadequate in its own realm. The content of a morality is based at least in part on religion. If ethics consists in philosophical reflection on a morality whose content is already furnished by religion, it always comes too late, so to speak. Hence it is not a matter of ethics retracing its steps half-way, till it reaches the point where it finds itself faced with the necessity of opening up to religion. The problem lies deeper. As regards its content, ethics always and necessarily points beyond itself to religion.

As regards the relation of ethics to history and historicity, it must also be remembered that the content of a morality is not given once and for all. Its concrete expression is always a function of history. The conventional ethics here calls upon the notion of natural law. But today ethics is far from being able to offer a systematic and harmonious doctrine of the natural law.

What is the solution of the difficulty that ethics is unable to determine philosophically and master reflectively the content of a morality? If we are working towards a strictly philosophical ethics, there is only one possible solution: to renounce a descriptive set of categories which will be universally valid, and to treat ethics as in this sense a formal or structural science. We have already seen that formalism in ethics is impossible. But the rejection of moral formalism must be carefully distinguished from the possibility – and indeed the philosophical necessity – of an ethical formalism considered as the only possible general schema of the transcendental content of the good. For philosophical reflection can only attain to formal principles, while concrete assertions as to material content can only be made on the basis of experience.

What are the main questions put in this formal or structural ethics? They have already been indicated. With regard to the moral content, ethics has to show: a) its necessity, b) its meta-ethical character; c) its logical possibility – this last being the main problem of Kant and the Anglo-Saxon ethics of the present day.

Finally, we must note the clear difference between the material object of a morality or ethos and the formal object of an ethics or moral philosophy. The aspect which the latter envisages is not just the repetition on a systematic level of the spontaneous experiences of the former. Its effort is to restrict itself to a purely structural consideration of morality. This formalism, this limitation, is the price it must pay if it is to remain philosophy.

Nonetheless, as has already been indicated (and as is particularly stressed in the works of M. Scheler), this formalism is not entirely formal. It is the giving of structure to a content. God, the ultimate ground of all ethos, the nature of man (as spirit, as freedom in eternal life) and the consequent basic demands of ethics are knowable. They allow of, and indeed demand, an ethics which will be not merely formal but also, in a certain sense, though a very open one, allow of material formulation (as concrete duties). By the nature of rational thought, the positive content will be formulated rather negatively than positively – as universally valid prohibitions – which is relevant to situation ethics. But some positive approaches, such as the "golden rule", are not merely formal, because they aim at keeping man open for his transcendence towards God and hence for the absolute value of the person of his fellows.

A further concrete step has to be taken by ethics in each historical epoch. It has to go beyond the transcendental experience of the good to articulate it in the form appropriate to the epoch, and thus formulate valid positive norms of good order.

The ultimate individual concrete formulation, which is, however, decisive, cannot, in the nature of things, be achieved on general principles. The traditional effort in this direction made use of casuistry and epikeia. But the crystallization can only be aimed at in reflection upon the structure and preconditions of a "logic of existential knowledge", and in a programme of the practical and theoretical formation of conscience. Ethics can never give the concrete individual directive.

The traditional utterances of the magisterium, on the moral necessity for revelation if the natural moral law is to be known, appear now in a new light, since not only general "principles" but above all concrete "imperatives" have to be addressed to each age and each individual. (See on this K. Rahner, *The Dynamic Element in the Church* [1964].) But still the possibility of a philosophical ethics must be maintained (*D* 1650, 1670, 1785, 1806, 2317, 2320). Ethics remains philosophy but in the sense which philosophy seems to be taking on today, that of anthropology.

José Luis L. Aranguren

EUCHARIST

I. Theological

A. Concept

Eucharist is the designation for the sacramental meal of the Church celebrated according to the example and the instructions of Jesus, a designation appearing as early as the 1st century and predominating ever since. The word expresses fundamental insights into the nature of the action. The term, which derives from the "thanksgiving" of Jesus at the Last Supper (Lk 22:19; 1 Cor 11:24; Mk 14:23; Mt 26:27) means, as does the root verb εὐ-χαριστ-εῖν, the "proper conduct of one who is the object of a gift", and not only (as in profane Greek) the attitude of thankfulness, but also its outward evidence. This Christian meaning goes back to the Hebrew notion of "blessing" as the praise of God which recalls his *magnalia*. Thanks always presupposes a gracious gift which is in fact only real through the thanksgiving, where alone the gift is effective and present. In the case of the Church's sacramental meal, it is the salvific reality placed therein by Christ, which is Christ himself with his being and work. This reality is acknowledged with praise in the words of a grace at meals uttered over and into the gifts of food. It is thereby actualized and objectified in them and made operative in the words and in the elements of the meal. And so the prayer and also the elements consecrated by it early received the name "Eucharist". Thus we arrive at the following definition: the Eucharist is the actualizing of the salvific reality "Jesus", through the words of thanksgiving uttered over the bread and wine.

B. Institution of the Eucharist by the Historical Jesus

The Church celebrates the Eucharist by virtue of the authority and the commission expressly given to it by Jesus. The institution of the supper by the historical Jesus is decisive for all eucharistic practice and dogma. This conviction is today disputed. A radical circle in Protestant theology denies the institution of the sacrament by Jesus in the way it is presented in the NT and in the liturgy and traces it back to the early Church's understanding of itself and of its sacred meal. The historical fact from the life of the Lord in connection with the Eucharist is simply his fellowship at table with his disciples and sinners, which he understood as an anticipation of the eschatological community. After the death of Jesus his followers continued the "breaking of the bread" together and continued to experience it as an eschatological anticipation, animated by the belief that the glorified Lord was there invisibly in their midst. In the fellowship of the meal the community interpreted itself as the "body of Christ", the "new divine covenant (*diatheke*) in virtue of the blood (the bloody death) of Christ", and gave expression to this self-consciousness in the explanatory words over the bread and wine. It was only the spirituality of the Hellenistic community which linked the presence of Christ materially to the elements of the meal, as may be seen from Mk. The real presence of Jesus in the consecrated elements as thus conceived, is, therefore, only a Hellenistic interpretation which is today no longer possible. The actual last supper of Jesus is, according to this same interpretation, a simple, dogmatically irrelevant farewell meal, which in the NT, however, is described and understood by Mk in the terms of the real presence as the institution of Jesus. This, however, projects back into the life of Jesus, in Christological terms, the meal which was experienced eschatologically by the primitive community. In view of this thesis, which illustrates the tendency to deprive Jesus of messianic character and to demythologize the NT, the institution of the Church's supper by the historical Jesus appears today to be of particular importance.

In support of this – if one prefers not to stress the impossibility of inventing the Eucharist – is the antiquity and origin of the tradition. Its earliest witness, Paul, expressly traces his account (1 Cor 11:23ff.) back to a received tradition, one that ultimately derived from Jesus. This claim is strengthened by characteristics that are typical of Jesus' manner of speech (especially in the so-called eschatological perspective: Lk 22:16–18; Mk 14:25). In the Aramaic turns of speech within all the accounts, their Semitic origin is recognizable, and their date and form can be traced back to the forties. But if this is so, there is scarcely room or time for any gradual spread of a Christologizing activity by the Hellenistic community. A further pointer to the historical Jesus is the fact that both of the extant strands of the tradition, that of Paul–Luke, and that of Mark–Matthew, differ according to formulation and theology but agree in their understanding of the essential meaning of the supper. The difference of the formulations can be traced to the transmitters of tradition; the agreement as to its meaning, however, must be traced to Jesus as the source of the tradition. Finally, there is the added weight of the fact that it is precisely not the excision of the supper from the life of Jesus, but its presence there, and the light thrown on it by Jesus' life as a whole which disclose the true character of the sacrament and which make a consistent explanation possible.

Jesus accomplished the decisive purpose of his life, his task as Messiah, in carrying out the mission of the Servant of God of Deutero-Isaiah, who as God's majestic envoy proclaims and inaugurates a new phase in salvation, and who as martyr takes upon himself expiatory sufferings for the sins of the many. This programme already inspired Jesus at his reception of the "baptism of repentance for the remission of sins" from John (Mk 1:4). Taking on alien guilt meant taking on also the necessity of death. As his life went on, Jesus thought more frequently of his death and spoke more frequently of it to his disciples – a death which was in any case a real danger from the Jewish authorities. It was for Jesus not something that merely happened to him, but a conscious and willed deed to which he assented as a necessity in the history of salvation, and on which he freely decided (Lk 12:50). His total readiness for the death which was the mission of the Servant of the Lord is also expressed in the logion of the ransom (Mk 10:45), and the prophecies of the passion (Mk 8:31; 9:31; 10:32ff.). These are at their core genuine prophecies of Jesus but in their NT form represent interpretative elaborations of the early Church based on its knowledge of the actual course of the passion. Jesus maintained his obedient yes to vicarious expiation through all outward and inward afflictions, even in the dread of death, torments, and abandonment by God. His death is total dedication and the deepest fulfilment of his being. Besides his death, Jesus also foretold his resurrection – the *Ebed Jahweh* also experiences as the reward for his expiatory death, according to Is 52:13 and 53:10ff., a triumphant rehabilitation and elevation to cultic dignity. In Jesus' prophecies of resurrection we hear the victorious certainty that his death, which he took upon himself purely out of desire for atonement and in eager obedience to the will of the Father, would find recognition before God. This death is the offering of martyrdom. Unlike the cultic sacrifices, there is no separate gift which stands for the offerer and symbolizes his dedication to God. Here the offerer himself functions as gift in his own person and accomplishes the sacrificial dedication by the real shedding of his blood. Jesus must have been sure that God would accept his sacrifice, his body, and hence that God would fill it with new life. Thus the death of Jesus brings with it the resurrection as an inner consequence, as an essential part of it, regardless of the difference in time between the two events. For the fourth evangelist, accordingly, the lifting up of Jesus on the cross already means his being lifted up in glory (Jn 3:14; 8:28; 12:32ff.).

In this readiness for death and in the certain conviction that the sacrifice of his life would be accepted by God and lead to a new order of salvation, Jesus celebrated his last supper and established it as his testament. He summed up in it his whole messianic being and work, gave them concentrated expression in a visible and even edible blessing, and bequeathed them as a sacrament. Hence the supper must not only be explained in the light of the entire life of Jesus, it *is* this entirety in symbolic compression. Its meaning is already partly indicated by its character as a farewell meal (Lk 22:15ff.; Mk 14:25) such as late Jewish Apocalyptic ascribes to the dying patriarchs. There the departing man of God reveals his approaching death, and gives his special blessing into which he puts the whole fruit of his God-filled life. Then, the last celebration of Jesus, according to the synoptics, is the paschal meal, while according to Jn 18:28 it takes place before the official paschal date. At any rate, its date is near to that of the Pasch, it is influenced by the ritual (the explanation of the foods and the sequence bread-meal-cup), and is permeated by the spiritual atmosphere of the Jewish feast as a cultic memorial of the saving deed of Jahweh. The NT, however, nowhere interprets the Eucharist in the light of the Pasch. A key for the understanding of the supper is given to us by the biblical idea of the prophetic sign (*ôt*) or the prophetic action. This phenomenon is meant not merely as a truth in symbolic dress or the pictorial orientation toward some coming event. It is already the initial realization of a divine decree. An event ordained by God is not merely registered and told of in words, it is brought about and initially realized. The action does not merely represent it symbolically, it anticipates and crystallizes its reality. The prophetic sign is the *signum efficax* of a divine action. Jesus situates his supper within the framework of this specific sphere of divine causality: a) he announces in words the salvific sacrifice of his death; b) he represents it symbolically and makes it present by distributing the food and drink as his body and blood, whereby he c) makes of these elements his person bodily offered up.

a) All the accounts situate the action in the perspective of his death. The primitive apostolic form of the account which is recognizable from Paul and Luke already does this by indicating the time (night of the offering) and by the adjectival phrase at the end of the words over the bread, which is indispensable for the understanding of the action: "given for the many" (ὑπὲρ πολλῶν) instead of ὑμῶν is the original form, reconstructed from Mk 14:24. In a clear allusion to Is 53:12, Jesus' death appears here as the martyr's sacrifice of his person (for σῶμα see below, c), who is the Suffering Servant of God. The same notion is conjured up by the second logion: "this cup is the new *diatheke* in my blood". The predicate "the new *diatheke*" takes up the *Ebed Jahweh* title from Is 42:6 and 49:8, characterizing Jesus as founder of a covenant. He fulfils this task, however, "in his blood", i.e., by shedding his blood, The biblical term "blood" has the connotation of "shed", as the addition "shed for the many" in Mk 14:24 indicates, i.e., instead of, and for the sake of the whole of mankind. This too is dependent on Is 53:10. The core of the variant Marcan logion over the cup – "this is my covenant-blood" – also conjures up Jesus' violent death, though under a somewhat different aspect. This formula derives from Ex 24:8 and characterizes the content of the cup primarily as the cultic sacrificial element "blood", which is separated from the flesh, then also the death of Jesus as the separation of flesh and blood after the manner of a cultic sacrifice. Thus in all the accounts the death of Jesus is the determinant factor in the Last Supper.

b) The sacrificial death thus announced in words by Jesus was also the object of a symbolic action. He actualized the offering of his person to the Father for men by consecrating bread and wine as his own person and by giving them to be eaten by men. His taking and lifting up of the elements, their blessing and consecration as the body and blood of Jesus, means their transfer to God and displays Jesus' dedication to the Father. When Jesus then gives the food and drink as his body and blood, and gives it to be eaten and drunk by men, he portrays visibly the martyr's death which is the dedication of his inmost life for men, but also its recovery in the resurrection. Moreover, not only the proffering, but the proffering as food and drink reveal how his death, indeed his whole human existence, is for (ὑπέρ) men, in their stead and for their sake. Just as it is the nature of food and drink to be wholly and entirely for men, and just as they give up their own being, to belong to men and to become part of men and thereby build up men's life, so too Jesus is there for men (by the very fact of his incarnation) and belongs to men. So too he gives up his life so that they may live to God. Finally, however, the proffered elements of the meal are not merely an outward means of representing his sacrificial offering on the cross. They are identical with the one and the same sacrificial gift of the cross, this man Jesus. And hence, too, the inner identity of both actions and the actual presence of the bloody offering of himself on the cross is established and finally assured in the unbloody offering of himself in the meal.

c) For by the divine power of his determinative words Jesus changes bread and wine into his own sacrificed person. The term "body" means in the mouth of Jesus, as a rendering of the Semitic expression behind it, not only a part of man, as though his body were distinguished from his blood or soul, but the whole man in his bodily existence. Likewise, the "blood" for the Semites represents the life-substance (Dt 12:23; Lev 17:11, 14), and stands for the living being with blood coursing through its veins, especially when it suffers a violent death (Gen 4:10; 2 Macc 8:3; Mt 27:4, 25; Acts 5:28, etc.). It indicates, then, the person in the act of shedding his blood. The adjectival addition to the words over the bread and the cup (Lk 22:19 and Mk 14:24), as also the early apostolic description of the cup as "the new *diatheke*", define the person of Jesus more precisely as the saviour who is the Servant of God. The essential identity of the consecrated elements with the person of Jesus, or (in the traditional language of the schools) the (somatic) real presence of Jesus in the elements of the supper, cannot, however, be based solely on the ἐστίν of the determinative words, as this also has in many biblical phrases a merely metaphorical meaning. It is indicated, however, in the sentence-structure of the blessing which differs from purely metaphorical statements. In the words of consecration we have, in contrast to metaphors, a subject which is of itself colourless and indeterminate, but which is defined by a very concrete predicate. The real presence of Jesus can be better explained from the character of the supper as a prophetic sign in which action and word effect through divine power what they represent. It is supported by the act of distribution which underlines the nature ascribed to the gifts, and also by the fact that they are partaken of. Exegetically, this is ultimately assured by the normative interpretation of the supper in the NT in terms of the real presence, especially in Paul and John. Hence, the bodily person of Jesus is present in the supper, not however in the static manner of being of a thing, but as the Servant of God who in his sacrificial death effects the salvation of us all and more precisely as the sacrificial offering of the Servant who delivers himself up on the cross. The real presence of the person is there to actualize the presence of the sacrificial deed and is united with this in an organic whole. The Eucharist becomes, then, the abiding presence in the meal of the sacrificially constituted salvific event "Jesus", in whom person and work form an inseparable unity.

The inaugurative command τοῦτο ποιεῖτε εἰς τὴν ἐμὴν ἀνάμνησιν gives the Church the power to do what Jesus did. By this command, the re-enactments must be formally similar to the initial supper celebrated by Jesus. It gives them the divinely-effective power of Jesus' supper, and emphasizes and assures their identity of substance with the first supper and with each other. For it characterizes them as the *anamnesis* of Jesus. *Anamnesis* in the biblical sense means not only the subjective representation of something in the consciousness and as an act of the remembering mind. It is also the objective effectiveness and presence of one reality in another, especially the effectiveness and presence of the salvific actions of God, in the liturgical worship. Even in the OT, the liturgy is the privileged medium in which the covenant attains actuality.

The meaning of the logion may perhaps be paraphrased as follows: do this (what I have done) in order to bring about my presence, to make really present the salvation wrought in me.

Besides the narratives of the institution, the NT itself explains Jesus' act in a way which is fundamental and normative for all exegesis and dogmatic theology. Paul affirms the bodily real presence of Jesus when he teaches that the bread which is broken and the cup which is blessed is a sharing (κοινωνία) in the body and blood of Jesus (1 Cor 10:16); when he concludes to the unity of all Christians as one single body (of Christ) from their partaking of the one bread (1 Cor 10:17); and when he points to the unworthy reception of the body of Jesus as explanation of certain judgments of God (1 Cor 11:27–31). Insofar as he places the Lord's Supper in relation to Jewish and heathen sacrificial meals (1 Cor 10:18–22), he presents it as a sacrificial action. A sacrificial meal presupposes and brings with it the killing of the victim. John does not give an account of the institution, but he gives a detailed proclamation of the Eucharist in the great promissory discourse of 6:26–63, which is conceived throughout in the perspective of the sacrament. Its theme is the true bread of heaven. The spiritual reality of this bread – its heavenly origin and its power to mediate life – is there in the historical man Jesus (Jn 6:26–51 b), but the physical reality, as food in the literal sense, is there in his "flesh" (σάρξ) which is intended for the life of the world and which one must really eat ("chew"), just as one must also drink his blood as real drink (6:51 c–58). Such partaking, however, presupposes the sacrifice. The surprising term σάρξ, even in connection with "blood", is not a sacrificial element distinct from the blood, but the whole concrete man Jesus, as 1:14 and the personal pronoun (he who partakes of "me") in 6:57 show. In the Eucharist, the descent of Jesus from the heavenly world, his incarnation for the purpose of the sacrificial offering, remain present (6:57f.). But the ascension of Jesus is also effective there (6:62), since the ascension alone makes the sending of the Spirit possible (7:38; 16:7) and hence also our sacramental meal (6:63). For the element which really mediates life there is not the flesh as such but the accompanying Spirit, by which the Godhead in Jesus is meant (cf. 1 Cor 15:45). For John too the Eucharist remains the presence, in the liturgical meal, of the economy of salvation which is "Jesus".

C. The Liturgical Form of the Eucharist in the Church

The essentials of the Lord's Supper were unalterably prescribed for the Church by Jesus, the consecration of the bread and wine to be his body and blood and their distribution to be eaten and drunk. This decisive core was given a liturgical framework which underwent a development. The oldest community celebrated the sacrament (as did Jesus at the institution) in connection with a fraternal repast and in the order which Jesus observed: bread – repast – cup (cf. the indication: "after the meal", 1 Cor 11:25; Lk 22:20). But very soon the sacramentally significant actions with the bread and wine were brought together and placed at the end of the meal, a process reflected in the accounts of the institution in Mk and Mt and also in *Didache*, 10, 1. In the further course of the development, the actual sacramental action was separated from the repast and combined with the morning liturgy of the word. Thus arose the classical form of the Eucharist which is still in use today, the "Mass" which is discernible in Justin's time, *c.* 160 (*Apologia*, I, 67). This liturgical form is an expression of the conviction that the sacrament should only be celebrated in the fullness of faith, which is nourished by the word of God. The Lord's Supper was celebrated at first (preferably) on the Lord's day, the Sunday (Acts 20:7; *Didache*, 14, 1; Justin, *Apologia*, I, 67), and in the 4th century also on Wednesday and Friday, and later daily (first attested by Augustine). The most obvious as well as the most fundamental characteristic of the celebration was that it was a meal. This stood out even more clearly when the participants brought with them, and provided for, the gifts which made up the meal. The Church expresses the meaning of their action in words, in the prayers said at the Lord's Supper. Very early the Church understood their action as *eucharistia*, as the grateful acknowledgment and acceptance of the salvation wrought by Christ, here symbolically made concrete and actual. The great prayer of the canon called down this salvation upon the gifts and asked that it should enter into them. Here the Eastern liturgies in particular dwell upon the whole salvific work of Christ, some more fully, like the liturgy of Hippolytus, the Clementine, the liturgy of St. James and the liturgy of St. Basil in Egypt, others in a short summary form (liturgy of the Apostles and of St. John Chrysostom). In the West, from the 4th century onwards, the Church year took on the form of a historical sequence of events, the redemption was divided up into individual themes and the particular mystery of each feast day was especially honoured in the "preface". The great prayer of thanksgiving culminates in the account of the institution. This places the death of Jesus in the middle of the action and consecrates the elements as the sacrificial gifts of Jesus. Hence, according to the Fathers, *eucharistia* means in effect the same thing as *anamnesis* and both terms signify an essential characteristic of the sacrament. Under this aspect it is the symbolic anamnesis by which the sacrifice of Jesus Christ is made present. Yet the manner in which this re-presentation is achieved does not consist in the liturgical words alone, but also in the action of the Church, namely, in its offering, and this points to a second basic characteristic of the Eucharist. From the beginning, appealing to Mal 1:11f., the Church asserts that in the Eucharist it also sacrifices. It sees in its spiritual thanksgiving which refers all things back to God, and also in the provision and offering of the material elements which make possible the celebration of the sacrament, a sacrifice offered by Christians. But this action of the Church was not intended as the establishment of an independent sacrifice beside that of Christ. On principle and from the start, it was done only to render visible and to appropriate the sacrifice of Christ. For a liturgical offering of gifts, in which the Church also offers itself, is well able to represent the sacrificial act of Jesus. The offering of the gifts is essentially an anamnesis of this, as the liturgy itself affirms as it reflects on the narrative of institution: *unde et memores passionis et resurrectionis . . . offerimus de tuis donis.*

In the framework of the *Eucharistia*, and by virtue of the *Eucharistia*, of which the essential centre is the narrative of institution, the presence of the body and blood of Jesus also comes about, by the consecration and change of the gifts of food. Hence the Eastern liturgies continue the reflection "unde et memores" with the epiclesis for the consecration (change) of the gifts. In explaining the epiclesis we should note that in this whole section the Church is reflecting on its previous action and bringing its character explicitly to mind. Thus the epiclesis, even in the form of a petition, is not what first brings about the consecration. It simply tries to give expression to the consecratory power and purpose of the whole action, especially to the *Eucharistia* which is concentrated in the narrative of institution. The food-offering thus accomplished has its due and necessary conclusion in the sacrificial meal. The nature of the essential sign (the meal) demands that no Mass should be without a communion, at least that of the priest who also represents the people. Up to the 12th century the faithful, even in the Latin Church, communicated under both species. Since then, for practical reasons, the practice of Communion under one species has prevailed. It had always been in use for small children, the sick, and in general for all who received Communion at home. The dogmatic justification for it – rather than the real reason for introducing it – was the doctrine then worked out about concomitance. This means that along with (*per concomitantiam*) the body (blood) which is present by virtue of transubstantiation, the blood (body), soul and divinity of Jesus are also present. A new era began with Vatican II, when it allowed Communion under both species in certain cases, concelebration and the use of the vernacular, and indeed by its reflection on the essential characteristics of the Eucharist.

D. Official Pronouncements

The Church expresses its understanding of the Eucharist most deeply and most comprehensively in the liturgy, which is an important expression of the ordinary magisterium. The extraordinary magisterium has done justice to this perspective in our own day in Vatican II's Constitution on the Liturgy (cf. previously Pius XII, *Mediator Dei*). Earlier Councils, when rejecting distortions and heretical errors, made infallible pronouncements (which, however, also admit of development) upon certain central aspects of the sacrament; as at the 4th Lateran Council, and at Constance and Trent (sess. XIII, XXI, XXII). The Councils for unity, Lyon II (1275) and Florence, formulated the scholastic understanding of the faith for the Eastern Churches. In the early Middle Ages, the symbolism so strongly underlined by Augustine was exaggerated, and the real presence of Christ was reduced to a merely symbolic and spiritual one, in reaction against a too crudely physical view. This was done in a mild and restrained form in the first Eucharistic controversy, by Ratramnus (opposed by Paschasius Radbertus) but in an extreme and heretical form in the second, by Berengarius of Tours (opposed in particular by Durandus of Troarn, Lanfranc and Guitmund of Aversa). After several local synods had pronounced on the matter, the fourth Lateran finally defined the identity of the consecrated gifts with the historical body and blood of Christ, by virtue of transubstantiation, the change of the being of the natural elements into the being of the body and blood of Christ (*D* 430, *DS* 802). This teaching was reaffirmed and made more precise by the Council of Constance against Wycliffe (*D* 581ff., *DS* 1151ff., *D*626f., *DS* 1198f.) and Huss (*D* 666f., *DS* 1256f.), by the Council of Trent against the Reformers, among whom Zwingli and Calvin denied the real presence while Luther admitted only consubstantiation. In the Eucharist the body and the blood of Jesus is contained not only after the manner of a sign or in its efficacy, but truly, really and substantially by virtue of transubstantiation; only the species of bread and wine remain. Under each form (as already in *D* 626, *DS* 1199), and indeed in each part of them there is the whole Christ, not only for the duration of the partaking but also present and worthy of adoration previous to this and after it. The whole Christ is really partaken of (*D* 883–90, *DS* 1651–8), and in the Latin Church is legitimately received by the faithful under one species only (*D* 934ff., *DS* 1731ff.). Against all the Reformers, the dogmatic teaching of Trent (sess. XXII) is that the Mass is not merely a sacrifice of praise and thanksgiving and not merely a commemoration of the offering of the cross, but a real and proper sacrifice in which the priest offers the body and blood of Christ. It is an expiatory sacrifice for the living and the dead, though it is no affront to or encroachment upon the sacrifice of the cross (*D* 948–62, *DS* 1751–5). It is the representation of that of the cross, its memorial and application, as was explained though not formally defined (*D* 938, *DS* 1740). Christ remains the same victim and the same priest as on the cross, though now acting through the priest; only the manner of offering is different (*D* 940, *DS* 1743). This implies the identity of the sacrificial action then and now, which is explicitly affirmed in the *Catechismus Romanus*, II, 4, 74. According to Pius XII (*Mediator Dei*, *D* 2300, *DS* 3848), the separate presentation of the body and blood of Christ in the consecration represents their separation in death.

The sacrament is effected only by the consecrated priest (Lat. IV: *D* 430, *DS* 802), independent of his personal holiness (Constance: *D* 584, *DS* 1154), essentially in the consecration (Pius XII, *D* 2300, *DS* 3852; Vatican II, Constitution on the Church, arts. 10, 28). Pius XII and especially Vatican II stress the active co-operation of the faithful in the offering of the Eucharist. They offer not merely through the priest but along with him (*D* 2300, *DS* 3852; Vatican II, Constitution on the Liturgy, art. 48), give thanks and receive Holy Communion (Vatican II, Constitution on the Church, arts. 10 and 11). In view of certain modern trends which might fail to do justice to the nature of the Eucharist, Paul VI, in his encyclical *Mysterium Fidei* of 3 September 1965 (*AAS* 57 [1965], pp. 753–74), inculcated once more the real presence (of the body and blood of Christ) by virtue of transubstantiation, calling for the retention of the traditional Church terminology in this matter. He also reaffirmed the continuation of the presence of Christ in the Eucharist after Mass and the rightfulness of adoration by Christians, and also of private Masses. A mere "transignification or transfinalization", by which bread and wine receive a new significance as signs of the self-dedication of Jesus in the Eucharist, are not enough to explain the Eucharist. On the contrary, the new significance and purpose of the sign comes from the fact that it contains, by virtue of transubstantiation, a new ontic reality.

E. Theological Explanations

Theology, which is obliged to seek a deeper *intellectus fidei*, must develop in a systematic way a comprehensive and well-balanced understanding of the

Eucharist in all its aspects – one that preserves the richness of its content, grasps its essential structure, explains its many aspects and arranges them properly in the structure of the whole. As the most intimate and most intensive confrontation of the glorified Christ with the Christian still on his pilgrimage, it cannot be adequately treated of in objective and static categories but must also be interpreted in personal and dynamic ones, though mere symbolism and functionalism must be avoided. In it man is confronted by the glorified Lord not in his proper (glorified) form but in another, a symbolic form, which he assumes as the outward expression of his own self, both revealing and veiling himself, in the sacramental symbol of a meal. In this meal the glorified Lord makes present for us and effectively applies to us here and now the self-sacrifice of his own life by which he accomplished the salvation of all once for all. That he presents his sacrifice in the manner of a meal is not a purely arbitrary decree; it rests, rather, upon a certain intrinsic analogy between the two. The connection between them was prefigured in the history of salvation in the OT food-offerings, of which the Roman canon mentions those of Abel, Abraham, and Melchisedech, and in the bloody sacrifice of animals which were concluded by a sacrificial meal. The relation is factually based on the fitness of food to express the self-surrender of an offerer, the giving of himself for others, and his fellowship with them. The meal also receives a directly sacrificial character through the offering of its elements to God – as was practised already in Judaism and by Jesus. Thus the bloody sacrifice of Jesus is fittingly represented as a food sacrifice and as a sacrificial meal, as an offering and a distribution of the elements of a meal. The active character of the Eucharist as a coming of Christ to us is also indicated in the fact that its "presence" suggests not only a passive or static nearness in space, but also Christ's "presenting" himself to us and proffering his saving action to us (compare the relevant verb *praesentare* in the Latin and Romance languages).

The "pneumatic" Christ is present in the celebration of the Eucharist as the *minister principalis*, as the high-priest who offers himself, and as the giver of the feast who gives himself as food. We could define this presence as the "principal actual presence of the person of Christ" (as the sacrificial *subject*). It is mediated and visibly represented by the salvific reality of the Church, which is the earthly mode of the manifestation of the heavenly high-priesthood of Christ, whose "Body" is the fundamental sacrament of redemption. To this Church he bequeathed his bloody sacrifice as an unbloody sacrificial rite (cf. Trent, *D* 938, *DS* 1740). The local community is representative of the whole Church. However, if the sacrifice of the faithful is to be really identical with the sacrifice of Christ, the participants must have a cultic bond with the high-priesthood of Christ. They must really participate in it. This is the "sacramental character" which is conferred in varying degrees of intensity by baptism, confirmation, and orders. It indicates membership of the Church and thereby enables one to participate in worship. The character conferred by priestly ordination justifies the full actualization of the sacrifice of Christ. "Through the ministry of the priest" Christ now offers his sacrifice (*D* 940, *DS* 1743), just as the priest officiates *in persona Christi* (*D* 698, *DS* 1321; Vatican II, Constitution on the Church, art. 28) and *in virtute Christi*. The character given in baptism and (in a stronger measure) in confirmation enables Christians to be co-offerers at the sacrifice, thanksgiving, and Communion. According to Vatican II (Constitution on the Liturgy, art. 48), the faithful also offer the unblemished sacrifice not only through the priest, but together with him, and thereby offer it themselves (*ibid.*, Constitution on the Church, arts. 10, 11). The celebrating community not only receives the fruits of redemption in the form of a meal, it also actively concurs in and follows out the very deed of redemption, it ratifies for itself after the event the sacrifice of Jesus accomplished previously and without its assistance. The community acknowledges it as something done not only for its good but also in its stead, and appropriates, makes visible and fruitful, this sacrifice of Christ through the symbol of the meal, by offering, consecrating and receiving the elements. The community thereby adds nothing to the value of the work of Christ. Its merit consists in laying hold of the merit of Christ as the only way of salvation. Its real sacrifice is not an attempt at self-salvation nor a repetition of the sacrifice of the cross, but rather its visible representation and appropriation here and now. The Church in this way realizes its nature most deeply in the Eucharist.

But if the faithful are to re-enact the one sacrifice of Jesus Christ, not only must their being receive its essential stamp from the person of Christ as the Saviour (in the sacramental meal), but their activity must receive that stamp from the salvific deed of Christ. This results from the fact that the faithful celebrate the Eucharist principally as the *anamnesis* of the work of redemption. *Anamnesis* here means not only the subjective presence in the consciousness of the participants, but the objective presence, in actual reality, in the acts and words of worship. Further, *anamnesis* is not merely a given part of the Mass, but an essential and basic trait which dominates it from the beginning to the end, and is then expressly formulated and reflected upon in various places (especially in the "unde et memores"). As *anamnesis*, the Eucharist is the actual presence of the sacrificial deed of Jesus which begins with the incarnation and reaches its culmination on the cross, in the death and the exaltation of Jesus. It is signalled in the Offertory which is modelled on the basic act of worship and in which the Church co-offers its own self, it is invoked upon and into the elements in the words of thanksgiving, the essential being the account of the institution, the constitutive *forma sacramenti*. The priest narrates the institution over the elements, in the words of Jesus himself. Thus officiating *in persona Christi*, he alone appears as fully representative of Jesus and only through his words, supported by the power of Christ, does the sacrificial gift of the Church become identical with the sacrificial gift which Jesus himself is as man. Thus too the sacrificial action of the Church shows itself to be one with the sacrificial action of Jesus. The double consecration, whether understood as Jesus' complete and sovereign disposition of his body and blood, or, according to Mk 14:24, as the separation of both vital elements, at any rate symbolizes and actualizes the death of Jesus by effecting the presence of Jesus as victim, as σῶμα διδόμενον and αἷμα ἐχυννόμενον. The actual presence of the sacrificial deed of Jesus objectifies itself in the (somatic) real presence of his person as the victim (sacrificial *object*) and is rooted in it. The real presence, however, comes about within the horizon of and as a moment of the sacrificial event.

This fact, which is significant for the basic structure of the Eucharist, may also be seen from the following considerations. Acceptance by God is essential to a sacrifice; a real sacrifice is a sacrifice accepted by God. God accepts the sacrifice of the Church because it is the sacrifice of Christ made present. Just as he accepted Jesus' sacrifice on the cross and, as a sign of this, gave his body new life in the resurrection, so too he accepts the sacrifice of the Church which is identical with that of Jesus and fills it with Jesus' life, transforms it into the bodily person of Jesus. The consecration concerns the "substance", which in this context means the meta-empirical, proper, ultimate essential being of the natural sensible elements of bread and wine. This is transformed and translated into the being of the bodily person of Jesus. The outward appearance (species, sight) of the food, however, remains, and signifies the bodily presence of Christ and its final purpose, namely partaking of it. For food is to be consumed. The consecration is thus the preparation for the sacrificial meal in which the sacrificial action is brought to completion. The sacrificial gift, however, stands for the giver and its acceptance by God means in principle the acceptance also of the giver, which (in this order of salvation) is the self-communication of God to the person. In the communion, man enters into closest union with the sacrificial offering of Christ and through it is united with the Father. The somatic real presence of Jesus makes possible the deepest confrontation of Christ with Christians and the Communion, the final end in any case of the symbolic meal, the indispensable act at least of the priest, completes it as an essential, not merely an integrating part (so Pius XII, *DS* 3854) of the sacrifice of the Eucharist. The basic structure, accordingly, is the presence of the sacrificial act of Jesus in a manner through which we can assimilate it and appropriate it, in a sacrificial meal.

If we inquire after the inner reasons whereby a past event can become actually present again, we must first consider the nature of the acting subject. As the actions of the eternal person of the Logos, the saving deeds of Jesus have a perennial quality and are always simultaneous with passing finite time. Besides this, they are also somehow taken up into the glorified humanity of Jesus which, according to St. Thomas (*Summa Theologica*, III, 62, 5; 64, 3), remains the efficacious *instrumentum coniunctum* of the exalted Lord. Those past salvific actions, being taken up into the divine person as also into the human nature of Jesus, can now assume a new spatio-temporal presence – in and through a "symbolic reality". This is an entity in which another being enters and reveals itself, is and acts. The real essence of the symbol as symbol is not its own physical reality, but the manifestation and presentation of the primary reality which is symbolized in it. In virtue of his *potestas auctoritatis*, Jesus so incorporated the supper into his sacrificial act that the sacrificial act is accomplished in and finds its visible expression in the supper.

In the setting and as an element of the presentation and application of the sacrificial act of Jesus comes now the somatically real presence of Jesus as victim. The whole Christ is truly, really and substantially present under both species and in each of their parts, beyond the duration of the Mass, so long as the species, the empirical realities of bread and wine as food remain. The presence of Christ in this manner is worthy of adoration, an adoration that should not, however, lose sight of the connection with the sacrifice of Jesus. The Scholastics, who did not use the terms *corpus* and *sanguis* in the comprehensive biblical sense of a bodily person but rather in the limited sense of the physically separate elements of body and blood, established the totality of the presence of Jesus with the help of the idea of concomitance (the blood belongs to the body, the soul to both of them, and the Godhead to the humanity of Jesus). Communion under one species results from practical considerations and is dogmatically defensible, though it corresponds less to the ideal liturgical form of Communion. The effecting of the somatically real presence of Jesus has been expressed in dogma since Lateran IV and Trent by the concept (which belongs rather to popularized philosophy) or transubstantiation (change of substance). What is the object of the dogma and what is infallibly expressed by this term, however, is not a given notion of substance and the expression for it as is found in natural philosophy such as that of Aristotle, but only the truth of faith that to the actual somatic real presence of Jesus under the species, there corresponds an ontic situation in which the meta-empirical being of the consecrated elements (that which makes them what they now are) is no longer their previous being as the natural elements bread and wine, but the being of the body and blood of Christ – that the natural being which they have had up to now, has been made over and is changed. How this change is to be explained in terms of natural philosophy depends on philosophical presuppositions which are not defined, i.e., how one is to understand concretely the concept of physical substance and how the empirical appearance of bread and wine is to be understood in relation to it. Explanatory attempts in this direction are but *theologumena* which have their own worth and rights, but which are not those of dogma.

In view of what has been said, the Eucharist appears (in general) as the sacramental presence and application of the event universally decisive for salvation, the sacrifice "Jesus", in the Church's sacrificial meal which he himself instituted. It is the greatest gift of the Lord, the initial transfiguration of worldly things, the inclusion even of the body in the glory of salvation, the bond of the most intimate unity of man with God and of men with each other, through Christ. It is an essential principle of the spatial and temporal catholicity of the Church and its most profound reality.

Johannes Betz

II. Liturgical

The Mass is the celebration of the Eucharist in the various forms prescribed by the Church. These forms enshrine and explicitate something considered in tradition as the command of the Lord: the utterance in thanksgiving of the sacramental words over bread and wine, and the eating and drinking of the consecrated gifts.

A. Various Names for the Mass

The various *names* for the Mass which have been used from the beginning give us an idea of how these forms developed. In the primitive Church, Mass was called the "Lord's Supper" (1 Cor 11:20) or the "breaking of bread" (Acts 2:42, 46; 20:7), since it continued the Last Supper and the act Christ instituted there in bread and wine. Before long we also find the term εὐχαριστία, which is taken from the biblical account of the institution (1 Cor 11:24; Lk 22:19) and stresses the element of prayer. By the end of the 1st century εὐχαριστία was the usual expression and was soon applied to sacramental gifts resulting from the celebration. But the early Latins already began to call the Mass a sacrifice: for St. Cyprian and St. Augustine it is *sacrificium*, for Aetheria and St. Ambrose *oblatio*, like προσφορά among the Greeks. Similarly the Syrians speak of *kurobho* or *korbono*: Mass is the gift, with which one "approaches" the divine majesty. Other names stress the fact that Mass is a celebration for which the community assembles; it is called σύναξις, *collecta*; *processio* too was used in this sense (Aetheria). The term λειτουργία, which finally prevailed among the Greeks, has the same signification: Mass is the work or service that is performed on behalf of the people or with the people. When we encounter terms like *officium*, (divine) service, High Mass, it is plain to see that set forms are involved. But other names current in the early Church, though they indicate the kernel of the Mass, leave us none the wiser as to its general structure – *dominicum*, "the Lord's" celebration, in the acts of the martyrs, or simply "the holy thing" in the Semitic languages (Arabic *kuddas*; cf. Hebrew *kadosch*). Much the same can be said of *missa*, Mass, which came into use in the 5th century and has been practically the only term in the West ever since (though the old "offering" prevailed in the Celtic Church; cf. the modern Irish "aifreann"). Originally *missa* (=missio =dimissio) meant dismissal. In ecclesiastical usage it meant the closing act of a celebration, which usually involved a blessing. Either the blessing or the celebration itself might be called *missa*. In the end the word was applied only to the eucharistic celebration, to emphasize the blessing for human life which it contained.

B. Early Structure of the Mass

We can only gather from certain hints how Mass was said in the early Church. At first it was associated with a meal, a supper (δεῖπνον, *coena*), since by custom supper was the principal meal of the day in the West. In such a setting Mass was instituted, as St. Paul plainly tells us in 1 Cor 11. No doubt the bread was consecrated at the beginning of the meal, in accordance with the Jewish custom of breaking bread: the father of the family started the meal by breaking the bread and distributing it with a blessing to those at table. Only "after supper" (1 Cor 11:25) was the chalice consecrated, when it was the Jewish custom to pour the third cup of wine and say a solemn prayer of thanksgiving. Between these two acts the meal took its course along the formal lines such as we know from the later *agape* (one spoke, for example, only when addressed by the person at the head of the table), and which were usual at that period (cf. the Qumran texts).

The two sacramental acts must very soon have been brought together, with the result that the Eucharist could be held either before or after the meal, or even separated from it altogether. Analysis of the forms of Mass known to us has shown that the primitive Mass must have comprised seven parts: the taking of bread, a prayer of thanksgiving, Fraction, Communion; taking of the chalice, a prayer of thanksgiving, and Communion. When the two acts were brought together, the seven parts were reduced to four: the taking of bread and the chalice (Offertory), the prayer of thanksgiving, Fraction, and Communion. Dom Gregory Dix, the Anglican liturgical scholar, thinks that a change of such magnitude, universally accepted without demur, can only have been introduced in a place that enjoyed great authority by the end of the 1st century: the Rome of Peter and Paul.

During the 2nd and 3rd centuries the outlines of the eucharistic service become clearly visible. The meal has disappeared. The prayer of thanksgiving is now the chief feature of the rite. Bread and wine are brought out; the prayer of thanksgiving said over them is ratified by the people's Amen; then all present receive Communion. This is the picture of the Mass that we find in Justin Martyr about the year 150. He gives us two descriptions of the Eucharist, one as celebrated after a baptism and one on a Sunday. A text put forward as a model by Hippolytus of Rome about 215 tallies perfectly with Justin and is so instructive that it deserves to be quoted *verbatim*. When the gifts have been brought to the bishop, he stretches out his hands over them and begins: "The Lord be with you." The people answer: "And with thy spirit." "Lift up your hearts." "We lift them up unto the Lord." "Let us give thanks to our Lord." "It is meet and right so to do." The bishop then continues: "We give thee thanks, O God, through thy beloved servant Jesus Christ, whom thou didst send to us in these last days to be our deliverance and our Redeemer and to make known thy counsel. He is thy inseparable Word: through him thou didst make all things and sawest that they were good. Thou didst send him from heaven into the bosom of the Virgin. In her bosom he became flesh and was revealed as thy Son, born of the Holy Ghost and the Virgin. Accomplishing thy will and winning for thee a holy people, he stretched forth his hands in torments to deliver those from torment who should believe in him. And when he was being delivered up to suffer according to his own will, so as to conquer death, to burst the bonds of Satan, to trample underfoot the nether world, to enlighten the just, to set up a landmark, and to proclaim the resurrection, he took bread and giving thanks to thee he said: 'Take, eat, this is my body which is broken for you..' Likewise the cup, saying: 'This is my blood which is poured out for you. When you do this you do it in remembrance of me.' Mindful, therefore, of his death and resurrection, we offer thee the bread and the cup; giving thee thanks, that thou mayest find us worthy to stand before thee and serve thee. And we beseech thee to send down the Holy Ghost upon the offering of holy Church. Gathering them together in unity, mayest thou grant all the saints who partake of it the fullness of the Holy Ghost, strengthening their faith in the truth, that we may praise and bless thee through thy servant Jesus Christ, through whom be all honour and glory unto thee, the Father and the Son with the Holy Ghost, in thy holy Church both now and forevermore." "Amen."

Though details of the service were left to the discretion of the celebrant, especially the phrasing of the prayers, the whole Christian world must have celebrated the Eucharist in much this form until well into the 4th century.

Here the question arises which has been widely debated for the last twenty or thirty years: what is the basic and permanent structure of the Mass that existed from the beginning, that remained intact through all the subsequent changes, and that must come clearly to the fore in any reform of the Mass we may embark on now? Scripture seems to describe nothing more than a meal, a company about a table with bread and wine that is blessed and distributed. The sacrificial character of the proceeding, central as it is, in no way obtrudes. Yet by Justin's time the celebration has become a gathering for prayer. Bread and wine are still there on the table but those present are not a dinner-party, they have come together to worship God. All later forms of the Eucharist are dominated by the prayer of thanksgiving and the offering of the gifts that logically precedes it. So plainly does the opening *Gratias agamus* refer to this offering that the Mass of the East Syrian rite transforms it into: "Let the sacrifice be offered up to God the Lord of the universe." It would seem best, then, to stress the mention of thanksgiving (εὐχαριστήσας), even in the biblical account of the institution, bearing in mind that a gesture of oblation was certainly made with the cup, and probably with the bread as well: it was the custom for the father to raise the cup a handsbreadth above the table, that is, to offer it. Thus the prayer of thanksgiving said over the gifts emerges as the basic structure.

The Eucharist was celebrated every Sunday (but on few other occasions), attended by the whole Christian community of the neighbourhood, early in the morning (now that it was separated from the meal) before work; Sunday was an ordinary workday for the public.

For the Sunday Justin mentions another element which served as an introduction: "the memoirs of the apostles or the writings of the prophets" were read, then there was a sermon by the president of the assembly, and a prayer for general needs concluded the introduction. This means that part of the traditional service of the synagogue must have continued in use as an independent rite among Jewish Christians, since it was first incorporated into Sunday Mass and then, in the 4th century, became a feature of every Mass. The underlying thought was plainly that hearing the sacred word would best prepare Christians for the sacred action. There are also various indications that the Offertory procession began as early as the 3rd century. Giving the faithful the special role of presenting the material gifts of bread and wine for the Eucharist seems to have been a conscious reaction against Gnosis, which despised material creation and taught that it was evil.

C. Evolution since the Fourth Century

With the peace of the Church, the form in which the Eucharist was celebrated began to vary considerably from one country or culture to another, branching out into the various liturgies which are discussed in the article "Liturgy". Here we shall consider how the elements of the original eucharistic rite became diversified in different places. What we shall call the fore-Mass so as to emphasize the unity of the whole proceeding (it is also known as the Mass of the Catechumens, in contrast to the Mass of the Faithful, the Sacrifice), consists principally of readings, and even in St. Augustine's day still began with these. But very early all liturgies developed an introduction to the readings. The *Canones Basilii* (6th century) indicate that the introduction is not yet part of the Mass proper: they say that as long as people are still coming into church "psalms should be read". But this reading, in the Mass of Byzantium and the East Syrian rite, became a formal office composed of three psalms, which has a certain parallel in the Egyptian liturgies with their three *orationes*. Throughout the East these introductory prayers are themselves preceded at every Mass by a solemn incensation, a consecration of the altar and church – sometimes of the congregation too –, as a rule amid prayers and hymns. Nor is this all. The incensation is preceded in the Byzantine rite, for example, by the πρόθεσις, a preparation of the bread and wine under the figure of "the slaughter of the Lamb", with many prayers and scriptural quotations, following another series of prayers and rites that accompany the vesting of the celebrant and the washing of his hands. They serve to prepare him for Mass, and to venerate the sacred icons. Only after all these preliminaries comes the ceremonial procession in which the book of the gospels is solemnly borne to the sanctuary, to the accompaniment of the Trisagion, or some other hymn, so that the readings may begin.

The Roman introduction to the readings, on the other hand, is only a short procession, even at Solemn High Mass where it includes incensation of the altar. Basically the ceremony is the same as that observed when a bishop or other prelate enters a church outside of Mass, as for a visitation: the procession is accompanied by singing, in this case the Introit; upon arrival at the altar there is a moment of silent prayer; then a collect (prayer) concludes the ceremony.

Readings from Scripture, the word of God, form the core of the fore-Mass in every liturgy. Hence it is often simply called "the liturgy of the word"; the faithful should be nourished at the table of the word before they are nourished at the sacramental table. Accordingly the ancient Church read the various books of the Bible one after the other and expounded them in homilies, except that as the liturgical year developed, particular texts were assigned to each feast or season: in Lent there were the books of Moses, in Holy Week Job, after Easter Acts, in Advent the prophets. From the Dark Ages onward it was the universal practice to appoint readings for the entire year, in such a way that a portion of the gospels was read at every Mass, preceded by at least one reading from some book of the Bible apart from the gospels. This practice follows the tradition of the synagogue, where each Sabbath there was one reading from the law and one from the prophets. Indeed the Jewish tradition is carried on intact by the Syrian liturgies, which have one reading each from the law and the prophets before the Epistle and Gospel. The Egyptian liturgies too have four readings, but all from the NT: one from St. Paul, one from the Catholic Epistles, one from Acts, and one from the Gospels. Probably the idea behind the Egyptian practice was that readings from the NT were more appropriate to the sacrifice of the NT. The present Roman rite takes this idea into account to the extent that on Sunday the Gospel is always preceded by a reading from the NT; indeed (except on Whitsunday) it is always from an apostolic letter, so that this reading is simply called "the Epistle".

It is only fitting that the congregation should respond, in prayer or song, to what is read to them in the liturgy; and in fact all rites contain such a response. Significantly, every rite has the Alleluia between the second and the last reading – the Gospel – plainly the people's part in a psalm, or the remnant of it. Here again we have a very ancient common tradition based on the service of the synagogue.

In all liturgies, as we might expect, a good deal of solemnity attends the reading of the Gospel: there are candles and incense: the reader is a person of special rank, stands in a prominent place, sings, kisses the book; the congregation stands. Before the Gospel, in the Egyptian liturgies, the book is borne three times round the altar. After the first few centuries and down to our own times we find little mention of the sermon which explains to the people what has been read. All liturgies have the people respond in unison with the Creed, but in most non-Roman rites this happens later in the Mass, just before the eucharistic prayer.

It is an ancient rule that the liturgy of the word should close with prayer. All liturgies have, or once had, a litany at this point for all the necessities of the Christian people. Originally it began, for instance, with a prayer for the catechumens, who were then dismissed; then came the "prayer of the faithful" strictly speaking for the ecclesiastical and civil authorities, the peace of Church and of State, and all temporal and spiritual necessities.

Bread and wine must be set in readiness for the sacrifice of the Mass. It seemed fitting that this action too should be made a ceremony, not only because the people's share in the sacrifice of Christ could be suitably expressed by material gifts from their hands, but also because the East early saw in these gifts a presage of the great King's coming. The former idea led to the Offertory procession of the faithful, which was customary practically everywhere by the end of ancient times and in the Roman rite survived another thousand years. The latter idea blossomed richly in the East (if we except the East Syrian rite). Before Mass begins the bread and wine are prepared on a kind of credence table. Where the faithful shared in this ceremony, they had to present their gifts beforehand at the specified place. In the Byzantine rite the gifts are brought in a procession called the "Great Entry" (so called in contrast to the "Little Entry" mentioned above), preceded by acolytes with candles, while ancient hymns sing of the invisible hosts of angels. The procession makes its way through the body of the church to the altar, where the gifts are set down, veiled, and incensed to the accompaniment of certain prayers. There is usually another preparatory rite, consisting of a symbolic ablution, and all Eastern liturgies have the kiss of peace, stylized in one form or another, which sometimes includes the people.

Now follows the Eucharist, in every rite and with little variation. We might say that the tone is set by the summons in the opening dialogue: "Let us give thanks to (εὐχαριστήσωμεν, hold the Eucharist in honour of) the Lord." The eucharistic prayer, the "Canon", begins. The thanksgiving is also praise and adoration, and in this sense rises to a climax, in every existing rite, at the Sanctus, which every liturgy too would have the people join in the singing. The Byzantine and Syrian tradition normally puts before the Sanctus a simple invocation to all the powers of heaven and earth and the angelic choirs to praise God, waiting until after the Sanctus to give him thanks for the mighty deeds of redemptive history and their fulfilment in Christ. Then follows the account of the Last Supper. The Egyptian and Latin tradition begins the eucharistic prayer with thanksgiving and a panegyrical exposition of the reasons why we must praise God. After the Sanctus (originally) there is a quick transition to the sacramental action: either "Heaven and earth are full of thy glory, and do thou also fill these gifts with thy blessing" (Egyptian liturgies and, substantially, many old Gallican formularies), or – thanksgiving merging into offering – "Wherefore, O merciful Father, we beseech thee to accept these gifts" (*Te igitur*).

The account of the institution, originally transmitted in pre-biblical formulations, has been reverently supplemented and varies in detail from rite to rite; but today it always closely resembles one of the biblical accounts. While the Roman liturgy has hitherto stressed the holiness of this inner sanctuary, this deepest of mysteries, by saying the whole Canon in an undertone, the Eastern rites convey the same idea by loudly proclaiming the sacramental words. Hereupon the people as often as not cry Amen, or make a formal confession such as that in the Ethiopian Mass: "We proclaim thy death, thy holy resurrection; we believe in thy ascension, we praise thee . . ."

The admonition "Do this in remembrance of me" is followed in all liturgies by the anamnesis: We remember, we do this to commemorate thee. The liturgy can be content with a brief indication of this "memory" here, since the eucharistic (thanksgiving) prayer had to develop it more fully ("thank" and "think" are etymologically akin). The anamnesis now regularly develops instead the description of the sacred act: "we offer". It is remarkable that without any special mention of Christ's sacrifice, all liturgies speak simply of the sacrifice of the Church that is based upon Christ's, asking that God will graciously accept it. The sacrifice of Christ is not in need of acceptance; but the sacrifice of the Church and above all this particular sacrifice is linked to conditions for it to be pleasing.

The close of the eucharistic prayer now introduces the Communion, whereby the faithful partake of the offering – in other words, there is a sacrificial meal – begging God that the communicants may be filled with blessing and grace. Then the eucharistic prayer ends, as it did in the days of Hippolytus, with a solemn doxology.

This straightforward train of thought was early broken up by interpolations. First we have the petitions, spoken by the priest himself at the heart of the sanctuary so as to stress their urgency. From the 4th century onward we find them in every liturgy (except the old Gallican, where they occur only before the beginning of the Canon). They are inserted after the Consecration (Syrian and Byzantine liturgies), or before the Sanctus (in Egypt), or before and after the Consecration (Roman rite). The second interpolation is the *epiclesis* or solemn invocation of the Holy Ghost, which the Oriental rites developed, in the same period, out of the prayer for a fruitful Communion that we have mentioned.

What has been the history of the Communion itself? If not the most ancient, the Our Father is at any rate the most usual element in the preparation for Communion. It was placed here on account of the petition for bread, and also on account of the petition for the forgiveness of sins. In the East, as early as the 4th century, the celebrant said a preparatory prayer of his own and gave the communicants a preparatory blessing (which soon became a blessing of the congregation), crying "Holy things to the holy!" The fraction of the species of bread, coming immediately before or immediately after the ceremony aforesaid, has generally been embroidered with prayers as well. Hardly anywhere has the venerable rite kept its original significance of the distribution of Communion.

First the celebrant and the clergy communicate, then the people, normally to the accompaniment of a hymn. In early times the thirty-third psalm was a favourite for this occasion. After Communion the priest usually says a prayer of gratitude for the heavenly gift. The prayer is especially poignant in the East Syrian rite.

Then the ceremony usually ends rapidly with a valedictory blessing of the faithful (which some Oriental rites elaborate). Purification of the sacred vessels and disposal of any remaining particles commonly takes place after the liturgy proper.

D. Special Features of the Roman Mass

We have Hippolytus's description of Mass (see above) as it was celebrated when Greek was still used in the Church of Rome. The change-over to Latin must have occurred during the 3rd century. It appears that the Canon which we still use comprised the following elements about the year 370: Preface, *Te igitur*, *Quam oblationem*, the account of the institution with the three prayers that follow, and the final doxology. The text of the present Canon, which was settled by the year 600, and other texts, are preserved to us in manuscripts of the 7th and 8th centuries, mainly the work of Frankish scriptoria. The prayers of the priest survive in the sacramentaries, of which there are three: the Leonine (5th to 6th century), the somewhat later Gelasian, and the Gregorian (compiled by St. Gregory the Great, who died in 604). A special feature of the priestly prayers outside the Canon – an opening Collect, a Secret said over the elements after the Offertory, and a Post-Communion – is that they vary according to the liturgical season (as does the Preface of the Canon), even in the Gallican Mass. In addition both older sacramentaries generally have one or two *orationes* after the readings and before the Secret. Even in the most ancient sources the readings are normally restricted to an Epistle and a Gospel. The celebrant enters (Introit) to the accompaniment of alternating chants – apparently also edited by St. Gregory – which are preserved in the Antiphonary (the "Proprium"). Antiphons are also sung between the two readings (Gradual and Alleluia), and accompany the procession at the Offertory and the Communion. The people continued to answer the exhortations and prayers of the priest and to join in the Sanctus, which concludes the Preface in the West as well as the East from the 5th century onward. *Kyrie*, *Gloria*, and *Agnus Dei* were also for the people to sing, or for the clerics in choir (not, that is, for the *schola cantorum* who sang the antiphons): they form the "Ordinary" among the chants of the Mass. This form of the Mass, which took shape during the 6th or 7th century, has continued in use down to the present day. The elaborations which began in the Carolingian period left the basic structure untouched, merely filling in gaps.

The first part of the Mass, designed as a ceremonious entrance culminating in the Collect, was now preceded by the prayers at the foot of the altar, of which the kernel is the *Confiteor*. Originally the priest did no more than fall prostrate and wordless before the altar. The *Kyrie* too, vestige of an older litany that has been confined since the 8th century to nine invocations of Christ, should be regarded as the people's preparation for the priestly prayers, like the *Gloria* that is added on feast days.

A special feature of the liturgy of the word is that since about the year 1000 the different rank of the two readings has been made visible by the position assigned to each: if we look at the church from where the *cathedra* used to be and the crucifix now is, the Epistle is read on the left-hand side, the Gospel on the right. Hence the familiar terms Epistle side and Gospel side. Until the restoration of the *oratio communis* by the Second Vatican Council, all that survived of the closing prayer was the one word *Oremus*, for the Secret that is structurally part of it had become a prayer over the offerings. Until the dawn of modern times the Offertory procession of the faithful was basic to the Roman Mass (originally they brought the bread and wine to the altar, later it was money; in the end the procession was only held on a few special feasts). The silent prayers which are still said during the arrangement of the gifts on the altar are a 9th-century contribution from Northern Europe.

As early as the 6th century the principle that the Preface – first part of the eucharistic prayer – should be different for each Mass was grievously breached: henceforth only the great solemnities had special Prefaces, forms of thanksgiving which illustrated redemptive history. Frankish misinterpretation of the name (*praefatio* was taken to mean "introduction" to the Canon instead of delivery in a ringing voice = *praedicatio*) led to further depreciation of the Preface. Petitions interpolated into the Canon proper had already greatly modified its character as a prayer of offering (intercession for various persons, prolonged during an invocation of the Saints, the *Communicantes*; prayers for various necessities, which St. Gregory cut down to essentials in the *Hanc igitur* we still say today). Now the Carolingian liturgists, wishing to present the Canon as a sanctuary that the priest alone could enter, had it said inaudibly. To compensate in a way for this, the elevation of the host and chalice after the consecration was introduced in the 13th century, in keeping with the adoration of the sacrament then becoming more intensely cultivated. But it is only at the final phrase of the doxology which closes the Canon that the priest resumes contact with the people.

Apart from the general outlines given above (the Our Father and the Post-Communion) and the silent prayers of the priest also interpolated here, practically only fragmentary rites survive in the Communion of the Roman Mass: the fraction of the Host, of which the *Agnus Dei* is part, the mingling of the sacred species, and the call to the Kiss of Peace (now transferred to this position) in the *Pax Domini*. The fact that the Communion of the faithful is not meant to be an exception (it figures only as such in the ordinances of Pius V) and that it should take place at this point, was obscured for centuries, until the days of Pius X and the liturgical movement. Mass ends almost abruptly with the words of dismissal, *Ite missa est*. The late Middle Ages added a substitute for the prayer at the blessing that was once said here (it survives in the *Oratio super populum*) and the prologue to St. John's Gospel.

E. The People's Part in Mass

Pastoral concern lies behind all the developments now going on in the liturgical field. As is obvious from the whole tradition of antiquity and from the actual form of every rite in existence, the Mass was conceived of from the first as a communal service. It assumes that the faithful are present (in whatever strength) and take part: answering the salutation of the priest, making known their assent by acclamations, saying certain of the prayers, singing certain of the chants. The Oriental rites, where they have not been affected by Latin influences, bear striking witness to the communal character of Mass: there is no such thing in the East as a private Mass, and in some rites every Mass is sung. Here too the litany is designed for the people to share: at various points it is prayed by the deacon (by the priest if need be), alternating with the people, in the vernacular.

Parts of the Roman Mass, too, show that the people are meant to share in it: the series of unvarying chants that we call the Ordinary of the Mass – Kyrie, Gloria, Credo, Sanctus, and Agnus Dei. Originally recited by the people, these texts were early allotted to the clergy in choir ("chorale"), and on the rise of polyphony were generally taken over by church choirs, with the result that the people were condemned to silence. Keeping the Mass entirely in Latin had the same effect. At the same time we must bear in mind that Gregorian chant and church music reached their apogee in the post-Tridentine period, notably enhancing the dignity and splendour of Catholic worship.

Despite its communal character, however, the Roman Mass has also been said privately by individual priests since about the 6th century, chiefly in the form of a votive Mass for the necessities of the faithful (who are not necessarily present). Here the impetratory aspect of the Mass has, as it were, been isolated. After some hesitation it was decided that there must always be a server at a votive Mass. This form of Mass (*missa lecta*) in turn gave rise to another development. In recent centuries the desire to give the faithful an active part in the Mass once more led, especially outside the Latin countries, to the introduction of vernacular hymns, often meant to be a substitute for the Ordinary of the Mass. From the latter part of the 19th century, however, the idea steadily gained ground that only Latin hymns are appropriate at a Sung Mass. Perforce the liturgical movement based its efforts on the Low Mass (*missa lecta*) which grew out of the private Mass and imposed no such restrictions. The Dialogue Mass, calling as it does for a reader and someone to lead in prayer, went far towards restoring the Mass to the people.

From what has been said one will gather that so far we have done little more than lurch from one makeshift to the next. It will be for the reform initiated by the Second Vatican Council to devise a congregational Mass that is both correct in its form and meaningful to the men of our time.

Josef Andreas Jungmann

EVANGELICAL COUNSELS

When only the canonical meaning of the term was envisaged, the state of the "counsels" as embraced by religious (can. 487) tended to monopolize any treatment of the evangelical counsels. As a consequence, "seculars", who live in the world, seemed deliberately to choose the opposite, namely the state of the "precepts", and the counsels of Christ would have been of little interest for them. But can we say that the religious themselves still recognize the "counsels", as a higher way containing no element of compulsion, in three vows reduced to the absolute minimum binding under obligation? Before discussing the three counsels and the state of life of the counsels, we shall explore the meaning of the evangelical counsels in the Bible and their pastoral implications for all the faithful – as now placed beyond doubt by Vatican II's Constitution on the Church (*Lumen Gentium*, art. 39).

1. *The biblical revelation of the evangelical counsels*. In the Bible the good life always calls for a generosity which goes beyond the exact observance of a code of obligations. Hence, in the divine "law", the ideal of a "whole-hearted" and free service, revealed in its fullness in Jesus, emerges – an ideal to which only the name of "counsel" does justice ("proprio quodam modo", *Lumen Gentium*, art. 39). This view, with its two aspects of the *spirit* and the *object* of the counsel, follows from the twofold revealed nature of the moral life: it is always in relation to God, and God shows himself as love calling for love in reply. In fact, from the very beginning, the good life presupposes the presence of the Lord: "Walk before me and be blameless" (Gen 17:1), an idea which was to attain its *sensus plenior* in the NT, namely, that the value of every good action is constituted by an implicit movement of love which God bestows upon us and which makes the Trinity dwell within us (1 Cor 13; Jn 14:15–23; Eph 5:2; Rom 13:10). Hence the Lord's presence which appears in the "law" and in every good act becomes clearer and clearer and is inseparable from the biblical revelation (*Lumen Gentium*, art. 42). In the OT God already freely grants his people a covenant, in an intimate, personal love, soon to be described as the love between husband and wife, with God demanding in reply a love freely given, a moral commitment, far surpassing the measure of what is strictly due: "You shall love the Lord your God with all your heart" (Deut 6:5). The Israelite is to imitate God: "You shall be holy, for I the Lord your God am holy" (Lev 19:2). The Christian responds to "the goodness . . . and the love" of Jesus (Tit 3:4), he follows the Son. God's friendship invites and woos, but does not compel. It is a summons to love in the sense of a "law" (*iugum meum*, Mt 11:29) whose essence is the effort after the better, the "counsel" (Deut 6:4–13; Jn 14:21–24; Phil 1:10). "One gives orders to one's subjects, but counsel to one's friends" (Ambrose, *De Viduis*, 12: PL, XVI, 256). From this we see the pastoral significance of the evangelical counsels. Christ, his image and his love must be made to shine through the "law" (*Lex Christi*, Gal 6:2); and in the law the summons to what is better must needs be discovered and serious obligations (for there is no question of forgetting them) must be given their true meaning as "a necessary love". The burdensome beginnings are overcome by regarding the divine benevolence as the source of all expression of the divine will. The counsel is essentially optional: God's merciful love wishes to bring us beyond the point of safety-first calculations. But a counsel does not imply rigorism. A baptized person esteems all the counsels, but freely chooses those which concern his providential situation (St. Francis de Sales, *Treatise on the Love of God*, 8, 9; cf. *Lumen Gentium*, art. 42). Little by little the spirit of a childlike faithfulness, bringing abundant peace, and growing ever more free ("freedom from slavery", St. Augustine), predominates over the weight of obligations, grave or light, which are, however, never ignored or questioned: "Perfect love casts out fear" (1 Jn 4:18). There is no denial of the fact that Christian perfection "pertains to the precepts" (St. Thomas, *De Perfectione Vitae*, 14), that is, to the two limitless precepts of charity. But the counsel shows "in a special way" (*Lumen Gentium*, art. 42) how they are made realities and given their full symbolism.

Thus, in the "well-beloved Son" (Mt 17:5), we are invited to an attitude of supernatural generosity and giving, which corresponds to what we are rediscovering nowadays in the human sphere of work and economics.

2. *The "Sequere me" and the three counsels.* a) During the first three centuries, Christians were simply taught to follow Christ (which does not mean that the ideal was always realized). Morality was summed up in the simple principle: *Christus sola lex*: the only law is Christ. The good news of Jesus was preached (cf. Acts 5:42), which meant that Christianity was presented in terms of the counsels. It was known from the first that the counsels were free (Acts 5:4; virginity and marriage, 1 Cor 7:25), but *all* were taught the ideal of the eucharistic community, essentially a fraternal unity in *Agape* (Acts 4:32): the *koinonia*, or "sharing of goods" (Acts 2:42–44; Heb 13:16), soon to be called the *vita apostolica*. This was not communism without private property (Acts 5:7), but a practical readiness to share one's goods. All goods come from the common Father. "No one must be in need"; that was the rule (Acts 4:34). There was a community chest (see "κοινωνία", no. 3, in *TWNT*; cf. Rom 15:27; 2 Cor 8:13). In the 4th century a sect known as the "Apostolics" was reproached with making a precept of a counsel. The same *sequela Christi* which was preached to all was the basis of a voluntary and closer *koinonia* among some Christians, expressed in virginity (Acts 4:32; Justin, *Apologia*, 10, 16; 1 Cor 7:10) and the distribution of all one's goods. This manifold *koinonia* was seen as a decisive criterion of faith (Justin, Irenaeus, Tertullian; cf. R. Carpentier, *Vie Apostolique*, pp. 44–54). Thus the one Church of the first three centuries held consistently to the teaching of the counsels. Christian marriage was also penetrated by the spirit which inspired the state of virginity.

b) Within this one community, rapidly growing groups were formed in the 4th century. Historically, the hermit, the "Christian of the desert", simply continued the *vita apostolica* (as the whole Church saw) when it had become too arduous for the community, involved as a whole in earthly tasks (L. Bouyer, *La Vie de S. Antoine* [1950], pp. 53, 175 and *passim*). Monasticism simply aimed at living to the full the *vita apostolica*: Obedience (to the spiritual father) stemmed automatically from the example of the twelve disciples. This separation poses no doctrinal problems. The call to the desert was charismatic, a substitute for martyrdom, and did not represent an innovation but was profoundly Christian and ecclesial. "Breathe out Christ", said St. Anthony. A phenomenon which can be fully explained by the life and realities of the Christian Church of the time, should not be explained by Jewish fellowships or pagan mysticism (cf. Bouyer, *op. cit.*, p. 51). The problem of jurisdiction does not enter into this article, but the Church always extended its protection to the groups which sought to live out more profoundly the life of the counsels. In the 12th century the triad of poverty, chastity and obedience was established, which gave definitive shape to this signal realization of the *sequela Christi* (*Lumen Gentium*, art. 43; *Perfectae Caritatis*, art. 2).

c) The neglect of the counsel, and especially of the *koinonia*, in general preaching is explained by a shift of emphasis (the demand for a minimum of good will, for the confession of sins, the call to make sure of salvation). The separation of those who followed the counsels from the rest of the faithful also helps to explain it. Ultimately, however, this separation should stimulate all to a greater perfection of love (cf. *Lumen Gentium*, arts. 12, 13, 44, 46; *Perfectae Caritatis*, art. 24).

3. *The ecclesiastic fellowship of the three evangelical counsels.* a) The faith of Pentecost (Acts 1:6) established the people of the promises, characterized as a religious and social entity (κοινωνία).

As a new human race where love is the supreme law, it differs radically from the juridical society which men need to regulate their intercourse. This distinction, which explains the seemingly strange contrast between justice and love, alone discloses the true nature of the social imperative of the gospel. This explains the need of a public juridical organization of the counsels (as in the religious orders) where the Church displays itself, to itself and to the world, as a fellowship of love and hence of the glory of God and salvation of human society. This centuries-long experience was assured by the bishops, and then by the Popes, by means of "exemption" (*Lumen Gentium*, art. 45), which does not mean a restriction of local authority, but assures it of the social character of the life of the counsels. The other ecclesiastical institutions based on the counsels are to be viewed in the same way (Secular Institutes).

b) When rightly understood, the legal character of these institutions does not present a difficulty. Certainly the counsels, as a commitment to love, exclude all legalism. But the juridical structure of the Mystical Body is demanded by the love of Christ itself. The social order of the gospel, the kingdom of God, must take shape. Its programme of comprehensive unity must be embodied in tangible law, in organizations with their own rules (*Lumen Gentium*, art. 45).

c) Justice would not be done to the state of the evangelical counsels if their legal obligations were explained without regard for the notion and essence of the counsel. This is true of all Christian morals. The only evangelical counsel is Christ, who is loved and followed for himself alone. The threefold vow, understood as perfect adoration, in the sense of the counsel, consecrates the whole existence and not just three obligations reduced to their minimum (*Lumen Gentium*, art. 44). The vow is only the presupposition for the definitive adoption of the spirit of the counsel: it aims at the "freedom" which goes beyond the law (St. Paul), "triumphant joy" (St. Augustine), the connaturality of virtue (St. Thomas Aquinas).

Summary. Because he is tempted to transgress the divine law, man feels himself under "obligation". He must learn to act more and more through a love which loves God more than self: "Walk in love" (Eph 5:2). Only Christ can make him capable of doing this. He draws him to himself and gives the grace. This demands a pastoral ministry which recognizes duties and precepts, but which tries more and more to set men free of temptation and aims at the generous fulfilment of the counsels. The ecclesiastical state of the evangelical counsels lived out in signal fashion gives permanent testimony to the love inspired by grace which is realized in fraternal fellowship. The pastoral ministry must be fully alive to this testimony, in order to communicate it to the world (*Lumen Gentium*, arts. 44, 46; *Perfectae Caritatis*, art. 24).

René Carpentier

EVIL

1. *The problem*. Evil counts as one of the most distressing questions in theology. It cannot be thought of in itself; it is evil solely as opposed to the good. Being holy, God is also good, and is so of himself, not through participation in a good outside or prior to himself or greater than he. He is the principle and pure source of good, good absolutely as such. Consequently it is impossible for him to be the author of evil; he cannot will evil, and no shadow of evil falls on him. But in that case, how can anything be or happen which is opposed to God and his goodness? To the good belongs the power of good, without which it would not be wholly good. God, therefore, is only absolutely good

if his goodness is also absolutely powerful, if he is omnipotently good. If on the other hand God is truly God, the fact of evil, which is contrary to God, points both away from God and back to God. Evil cannot be due to God but he must be responsible for what is responsible for evil. In view of God, evil is evil, but in view of evil, how is God God? A "justification" of God in regard to evil does not exhaust, and in fact does not really touch, the theological question of evil. A clarification of the ground of the possibility of evil is theologically necessary to the extent that it is necessary to think in a way that does justice to God's holiness. The realization of God's holiness in our thought belongs to the coming of his reign, because it prepares the way for it. That is what theology is concerned with. Consequently the question of the ground of the possibility of evil is completed and replaced by the question of the location, overcoming and "end" of evil in God's reign, in his salvific will for man and the world revealed and accomplished in Jesus Christ.

2. *History of the problem.* Pessimism disguises the problem of evil and badness, by denying all meaning to reality: but if it is absurd and meaningless, it is not even open to question. Schopenhauer, who considered the world as the result of blind instinctive will, is the great representative of pessimism. Rationalism and pantheism solve the problem by an optimistic view of the universe. Spinoza, for instance, recognizes nothing as evil, since all finite things are logically necessary modifications of the one divine substance. Hegel, who gives a dynamic version of Spinoza's view, interprets world history as the dialectical self-explicitation of the absolute spirit and holds that evil is what ought not to remain, but not what ought not to be.

Dualistic systems, from Parseeism, Gnosis and Manichaeism to J. Böhme and the later Schelling, take good and evil (or the grounds of their possibility) as two primordial principles, either as two divine beings in conflict or as tension and division in the one godhead.

The biblical doctrine of creation affirms that the holy, omnipotent God is the author of light and darkness, the Lord of grace and obduracy (or predestination). The free, culpable disobedience of man disturbs the harmony of the original state of things, but man is tempted beforehand by an evil power whose origin is obscure. Nonetheless, it is under the power and judgment of God.

In the process of combining revealed truths with Greek and especially Platonic thought, Origen and Augustine developed the principle which was to become the common heritage of Scholasticism. Evil is not something positive, but negative. It is the lack or deprivation of perfection which should really be present in a free spiritual being. This lack is due to a culpable distortion which the free finite spirit brings about in itself. Origen transposes this cause further back, and regards this world as the place of punishment of souls who sinned in their pre-existence. But he also supposes a general apocatastasis, possibly through the general conflagration, hell, in which the world is consumed. Augustine sees sin as Scripture does and teaches the possibility, and indeed the reality, of the hardening of the wicked decision into absolute definitiveness. His central thinking on evil is less concerned with the philosophical negation of its positive existence than with the doctrine of predestination which was rejected by Catholic theology and only came to the fore again in the Reformation. But even if evil is conceded no being of its own but is referred to God only indirectly through the guilt of man, this is not a positive explanation of its meaning. Harmonizing efforts, based for instance on the aesthetic demands of an order of things which must contain "everything", fail to recognize the absolute contradiction and incompatibility of evil, the absoluteness of man's demand for total explanation, and the full claim of the good and holy as such. This permanent tension between the absurdity of evil and the meaningfulness which the world still affirms of itself – a tension which theology does not resolve, but merely recognizes and endures – makes the problem of evil a mystery.

3. *The phenomenon.* a) *Antithesis to the good.* The immediately striking feature of evil is its antithesis to good. Without good, evil is inconceivable, but good does not in the same way require evil in order to be good. Evil exists in virtue of the good, not vice versa. Yet mere denial of good, absence of good, deficiency, a lesser degree of participation in the good, do not amount to the really direct contradiction of the good which makes evil evil. Evil is "more" than simply what is morally bad, the application of the concept of evil, what is not good, to the domain of moral will. As distinguished from what is bad or inferior, evil means the positing of the contradiction of the good, deliberate denial of the good. Evil is a less extensive concept than bad, but more fundamental. In evil the negation of the good becomes conscious of itself; evil is never merely in fact evil, but is always evil "as" evil, i.e., conscious of the good which it actively contests. An "innocent" evil would not be evil. Consequently, "evil" is predicated of the will or, indirectly, of the mode of being of some existent possessed by a certain direction of the will; the relation to good grasped as such is the essence of the will and of its freedom. Mere weakness of will, therefore, does not reach the core of evil; it is nevertheless evil to the extent that the weak will is identical with its weakness and so makes this weakness an inner and therefore free relation to the good.

b) *Self-contradiction.* Evil is in this way not only antithetical to good, but as such it is in contradiction to itself. On the one hand it is "positive": it is posited, accomplished, affirmed, and this gives it its particular appearance of hard, resistant reality. Yet what is posited, accomplished and affirmed is negative: the refusal of the good, its absence – hence the intrinsic "emptiness" of evil. The refusal of the good, accomplished in this way, discloses a further intrinsic contradiction – the contradiction between good and good within its negation posited by the will. The evil will – and this constitutes its evil – contests the good recognized as such and at the same time claims that what it posits in this contestation is good. It cannot do otherwise. Whatever the will wills, it affirms by that very fact to be good. "Good" after all means: Yes, that is how it should be! And "to will" means to affirm and to posit how, according to the person willing, something should be. Even someone who wants to be evil merely for the sake of being evil thinks it good to revolt, in other words, to be evil. And someone who merely allows himself unwillingly to be overcome by evil wills to have peace and quiet at last; he is tired of resistance and considers what appears to be peace with evil, and therefore indirectly the accomplishment of the evil itself, as preferable and therefore as good.

In this way evil is a conflict of good with good in the will. Something present to the will as good, as something that ought to be, is cancelled by the will and in its place something else is posited as good and as what should be. The formula of the good will is: Because this is good, I will this. That of the evil will is: This is good because I will it. But what is truly good? What makes it genuine? All that is, is permitted to be, admitted to being, is to be in virtue of the primary will. Being itself means what should be; being and good are in that way identical (as transcendentals). Here "being" is not thought of as merely "being there", as bare contingent fact, but as what is affirmed and conceded wherever an existent occurs, the "gift" which properly speaking is in every being, by its existing, that which is always intended by the being of beings, that for which they exist. Good as such is, therefore, the plentitude which comprises and transcends all beings, the one source which confers everything, fulfils everything and so is in harmony with itself.

But the finite will itself is set in being by this unconditional source; it too is something that is willed to be. By its being set in being, something is admitted into being which for its part can affirm itself, actively collaborate with the productive movement of causing being, and accomplish it as its own; something to which it is granted, as it makes its decisions and shapes its own being and that of others, to be the origin of its assent to and agreement with the unconditioned origin. Consequently the activity of a finite will necessarily involves a duality. It is its own operative source, the centre from which its own being is decided and with it, in consenting and formative activity, everything else, the world as a whole.

But the finite will is only a second cause, only a derivative centre; before it decides itself and everything it must first put itself in harmony with the primordial source which antecedently has determined the finite will and all things. It must, therefore, for its own part accept as good what has already been determined and granted as good in its regard. For the finite will, good consists in the agreement of its own consent to good with the unconditional fiat of God, in consenting obedience. This obedience is not, however, a mere copy, but an active interpretation of the divine will in the world, causing it to come about and to be given shape and form. This agreement is affirmed in each act of the will. By willing, it not only proclaims: For my part this shall be so, but: It truly should be so. For, as will, it is concerned that something should be as it wills it to be; as will it always strives towards being, which has only in part been given and assigned to it, and affirms its accord with its own condition. The affirmation of that accord is nevertheless not itself its own guarantee; there is an intrinsic possibility of discord, and this is the possibility of evil.

c) *Discord within the good.* By bringing something about, the finite will in each case brings something into being, something which should be, in other words, good. Evil therefore cannot have being as its content. What, then, is the content of evil? The evil will denies the good, cancels some good, destroys, deforms or distorts a good content. At the same time it affirms and posits something, some content, therefore, as good. In fact the evil will always wills something good, if only its power of willing which as such is of course good. Even self-destruction posits as good the power by which it can be achieved, the very energy which is good in origin. The evil in evil is, therefore, not something, but the disunity of good with itself, the discord within the good in the will. All that is, to the extent that it is, is good; but it is good in relation to the absolute good and is only good in itself in dependence on that absolute good. It is only in agreement with itself by being in agreement with the whole and so with the unconditional. It is good which sets everything harmoniously in order, and that order is always prior to the moment of finite decision and yet must always be heard anew and brought to new realization by that decision. Evil is the discord of a being with itself and so with the absolute; it is the discord of its will with itself and with the absolute, and ultimately with what it wills, which is not willed by the absolute primordial source in the way the evil affirms it to be.

4. *Evil in the world.* The intrinsic dependence of evil on good excludes a "dualistic" interpretation of the world, as in Manichaeism: the equally primary character of good and evil as two existing principles or at least as constitutive principles operative within the individual being. "Evil" is not something independent, existing in itself, but only in an existing and therefore fundamentally good will. And since it springs from within the will, from its own self-willing, it is not a power above the individual but is located in the individual will itself. As, however, by the very nature of the will, which is always related to the whole, evil brings this whole into disharmony through the person who wills badly, evil has a radiating power capable of bringing into disharmony the world itself and of seductively determining other wills. Through this cosmic power of disharmony and temptation and through the concord of a number of wills in ill-will, evil does attain a secondary, if only apparent, yet effective "independence".

5. *Ground of the possibility of evil.* The question arises all the more urgently: How is evil possible, when only what the omnipotence of the good God is capable of, is possible? The analysis of evil itself indicates the answer. If finite will exists, by nature it is "the same" as good as such: self-transcendence consenting to all being and consequently unity with itself. But because it is finite will, it is not of necessity what it is and its existence stands in the tension of being posterior to its essence. In fulfilling itself, i.e., its essence, it must of itself accomplish what even without it already is. What is most its own, its essence, is "other" than itself, and it must realize this other as its own, i.e., of itself. Therefore it necessarily accomplishes what it accomplishes as good, but what it accomplishes as good, it always accomplishes of itself and so not of necessity. Ontologically this involves the possibility of a divergence in activity, of disharmony and so of evil. This only occurs through the finite will which is called upon of itself to cancel out its posteriority to the divine will, in order not of itself, but from God, to be "like God", one with him and at the same time quite other than he. God's decision to cause his image, his "nature", to exist in a created likeness, involves the "risk" of the deformation of this likeness. The being of finite mind is the ground of the possibility of evil.

6. *The overcoming of evil.* If evil is the disharmony of the world with itself and with God in the autocratic self-distortion of finite will, the death of Jesus and his resurrection are the overcoming of evil by the free decree of the omnipotent determinative origin. When Jesus became "obedient unto death", he accomplished the act of radical agreement with the will of the Father and so judged and rejected evil, and by this he lovingly assumed the sin and guilt of the world and was "conformed" to it in its likeness on the Cross. Jesus' solidarity with sinful mankind is at the same time the solidarity of the Son's loving obedience to the Father. This new harmony between God and world was revealed and confirmed as the birth of the new man and as the beginning of the new creation by the Easter resurrection. The death and resurrection of Jesus are offered to man as good news to change his evil autocratic self-will by consent in faith, hope and love to God's work in Jesus. The overcoming of evil occurs as the love of God giving his Son as reconciliation, and as the love of the Son which in the one gesture of self-giving embraces both the Father and the sinner, and so links both anew. The Spirit of the Son produces the same love in the redeemed; it overcomes the conflict in the finite will between having to determine itself yet having to allow itself to be determined: love wills as its own, "of itself" what the beloved wills;

it is an unbroken, direct union of man with God and his authoritative creative will, with man himself, and with the world produced in being by the loving will of God.

Klaus Hemmerle

EVOLUTION

I. Anthropological

A. Evolution

By evolution or phylogenetic development the biologist understands that long drawn-out and mighty process which has led, with the passage of the geological epochs, to ever newer and different organic forms, while at the same time guarding the continuity of the stream of life from one generation to the next. Evolution therefore connotes a change or transformation of organic forms with the passage of time. The problem of the origin of life or of the first cell forms a separate question which will be treated separately (see *Life* I). Granted that evolution can be proved, then the properties of the organism will include an inborn power of self-organization and growth which conditions all the stages in the development of an individual from the appearance and maturation of the ovum right up to the highly complex adult form. It includes over and above this individual development an immanent power of evolving into more and more complexly organized forms over the millions of years since the first appearance of life.

In order to justify this concept, the biologist calls on three fundamental facts: a) Living matter arises only from living matter. b) Closely related organisms are essentially similar in their fundamental characteristics (homology). c) Inheritable alterations in plants and animals (mutations) may occur both in the genetic determiners (genotype) and in their outward, visible expression (phenotype). In addition several indirect, so-called suasive proofs drawn from morphology, embryology, physiology, geography and dating techniques, closely inter-connected and completing one another, form a strong argument, supported as they are by the fossil record. Organic forms make their first abrupt appearance in the Cambrian period (which began about 600 million years ago). An abundance of varied and highly organized invertebrate forms appeared which cannot be derived from previously existing forms since practically no fossil remains have been found in the Precambrian. An indescribable richness of fossil organisms has been recovered from all the succeeding geological deposits. These throw light on the vast power of variation possessed by living material which has undergone, on an unimaginable scale, a process in time involving rise and fall, variation and change and self-development.

The evolution of living things revealed by the fossil record appears to be *a periodic process*. Whole groups suddently enter an "explosive" phase (sometimes after a varying preparatory period) in which their basic plan of construction splits with highly accelerated evolutionary velocity into numerous types of organization. An example of this would be the mammals which have developed, since the early Tertiary, into no less than twenty-five orders and 206 families, well documented in the fossil record. The potentiality latent in the basic plan to develop into different functional forms (e.g., carnivore, herbivore, insectivore; or runner, jumper, climber, burrower, swimming or flying forms) is realized. During the succeeding, much longer period all that takes place is that a vast number of genera and species are differentiated out. A quiet, gradual development through small evolutionary steps occurs in the direction of increasing specialization and frequently, also, of increasing size of the whole body or of individual organs. Towards the end of this phyletic development a shrinkage or even an extinction of the various lines that have been formed takes place in most cases. At many of the transitions from one geological period to another, radical changes in flora and fauna may be superimposed independently on these radiational and explosive phases, with a different temporal pattern for each animal group. At these junctures large sections of world-wide groups of land and sea animals belonging to the most varied lines may disappear; others may decrease to a few relict forms, while others survive the transition without disturbance and still others appear for the first time or begin their explosive phase of expansion. Phyletic development thus unfolds, not in a regular, uniform fashion, but with different evolutionary patterns, velocities and possibilities in each group of organisms.

The evolution of living things seems to be a *discontinuous process*; not in the sense that the continuity of the life stream has been interrupted, but rather in the sense that the higher systematic groups make an abrupt appearance in the fossil record. The twenty-five mammalian orders already referred to arise abruptly in the early Tertiary without a trace of their origins; they arise out of a "vacuum of origin". It is true that as one traces the organizational types back towards their ancestral forms, they seem to converge more and more; but in no case is either a true convergence or a transitional form known. This phenomenon of the absence of true transitional forms in the fossil record is universal, i.e., it has been established without exception for all the major animal and plant groups (e.g., within the reptiles, the Mesozoic and early Tertiary mammals, the flowering plants, etc.). Attempts to explain it have been very varied.

A further characteristic of the evolution of living things is its *directional progression*, not, it is true, in the strictly rectilinear sense, but within a definite margin of variation which is characteristic of all living things. The series leading from the small *Eohippus* of the early Tertiary up to the modern horse *Equus* is well known (Eohippus – Orohippus – Epihippus – Mesohippus – Miohippus – Parahippus – Meryhippus – Plichippus – Equus). In this evolutionary series a continuous change, parallel with an increase in size, occurs from browsers with low-crowned teeth of simple pattern to grazers with high-crowned teeth with complex pattern; from four-toed feet with pads to one-toed feet with hooves and springing mechanism; from a reptile-like brain to one with large frontal lobes that are covered with a complex pattern of furrows and mask the other parts. Trends like these almost always appear to follow the same direction in whole "bundles" of independent lines developing parallel to one another. They may, however (e.g., in the changes in lobe outline and shell sculpturing in the Ammonites), repeat the same process several times in periods which are separated from one another in time (iterations). Sometimes they may lead to exaggerated body size or to over-developed organs, to so-called "over-specializations". Since phylogenetic evolution has proved to be irreversible (i.e., not reverting to earlier forms), the evolutionary amplitude or potentiality for developing new patterns is progressively narrowed by specialization, so that eventually new morphological patterns and structures can no longer be formed – or be formed only by devious routes. It is unknown whether an aging of a group, leading eventually to degeneration and extinction, is responsible for these directional processes

A further character of organic evolution is that it is a *constructive process*. Organic structures are formed, conserved, combined and integrated, further developed or broken down again.

This formation of structures occurred not merely in a single or in a few parallel lines, but in numerous lines of the most varied organization and of every systematic rank. They thus created that vast richness of varied forms appearing in the plant and animal kingdom both today and in former epochs. Thus through a repeated self-development and diversification of the lines of descent leading to more novel and varied expressions, a diversification of the organic world took place along every imaginable pathway, almost exhausting all the possible organic patterns. The "natural system" of plant and animal classification makes it clear that an order reigns within this motley pattern. Because of this order, this graded variety or hierarchical structure, not only are groups of organisms of higher and lower ranks (advanced and primitive) distinguishable, but also smaller units may be included within larger ones, e.g., species are united into genera, genera into families, families into orders, etc. This testifies to the fact that a diversification and perfecting took place not only *within* any given structural pattern but also *beyond* any particular level of organization towards higher levels, e.g., from the level of the jawless fishes (Agnatha), through that of fish with jointed jaws (Placoderma), the true fishes, the amphibians, the reptiles up to the level of the warm-blooded birds and mammals.

This highly significant phenomenon of a "biologial ascent" (Anagenesis) is, however, not universal among organic groups. Among the vertebrates it is characterized by increasing differentiation and integration, by an increasing independence from the environment and by individual autonomy. This latter is shown above all by the organization of the nervous system, especially of the brain, and by an intensification of animal interiorization and a higher development of the psychic and conscious elements. The "biological ascent" of an organism reaches a higher point the more its wholeness and autonomy, i.e., its individuality, is realized. The highest point is occupied by man; because of his self-consciousness, i.e., because of his spirituality and freedom, he is not merely an individual but also a person. The causality responsible for these processes has not been explained. So also with the phenomena we have mentioned: the radiation and extinction of groups of organisms, the onset of "explosive" phases and periods of calm advance, the major changes in flora and fauna, the "vacuum of origins" from which the major groups arise, directional evolution in parallel lines, the hierarchically ordered variety and the "biological ascent" – all pose problems and unanswered questions.

No examples of macromutations nor of an accumulation of smaller mutations under the influence of selection and isolation exist among present-day organisms. If they existed, they would give some insight into the causal processes leading to evolutionary transformations or to the creation of plans of organization or of highly complex organs and systems of organs (synorganizations) and of other amazingly "lucky discoveries" of the evolutionary process. The extension or extrapolation of experimental results, especially of genetics (restricted in practice to the intraspecific sphere) to the enormous changes studied in cases of trans-specific evolution, is no more than a working hypothesis. So also is the idea of a deep-reaching, sudden change in the genetic make-up. The large number of hypotheses in existence, their frequent contradictory character and their rapid rate of modification witness to the inadequacy of all causal explanations offered to date; they are no more than attempts towards answering a vast open question. The "family-tree" representation of plants and animals proposed again and again offer no definitive result, only a temporary picture; i.e., they serve to portray the established or presumed historical relationships between groups of organisms as seen by the present state of scientific opinion; they may be altered at any time by new finds or by new facts. Thus the classical "family tree" of organisms in which the uniform "trunk" is supposed to grow upwards higher and higher in the centre, giving off ascending "side-branches", has undergone fundamental alteration. Now it loses itself in a series of parallel main branches which, it seems, are quite distinct structurally from one another even in the oldest fossiliferous strata of the Cambrian and Ordovician. From this point on they exhibit an independent evolution within the framework of their own amazingly conservative basic structure. The classes of fishes, amphibians and reptiles in vogue up to now are seen to be merely grades of organization through which the individually more or less independent stocks passed (polyphyletically). However, even the modern picture of the "family tree" of organisms makes it quite clear that the history of organisms is characterized by an evolution.

It may now be seen that the concept of *biological* evolution is justified. It allows a vast quantity of various facts to be viewed as a whole and leaves them open to a unified explanation. However, its extension to and use in the essentially different world of human affairs with its historical, cultural, political, ethical and religious phenomena make too heavy demands on the evolutionary idea and transgress the bonds of the competency of biology. Using an explanatory principle drawn from purely biological evolution and its regularity in the wider context of human affairs effaces the ontologically graded structure of reality with its distinction of levels of being.

Paul Overhage

II. Theological

A. Evolution

1. *The unity of the world of mind and matter.* Philosophical and theological reflection proceeds on the assumption that the fact of evolution is established by natural science. With the resources of theology or philosophy this can neither be proved nor rejected as impossible.

a) Since according to Christian philosophy and theology every created being, because finite, is in a state of becoming and changing and is part of the unity of the world which is directed towards a single goal of full accomplishment, the concept of evolution can be employed to describe, in a general and comprehensive way, what characterizes all the reality, distinct from God, which lies within the horizon of our experience. That concept would then of course have to be differentiated as variously and as analogously as the notion of becoming. As compared with the latter, however, it has the advantage of bringing out more clearly the directional progression of change.

b) In this "evolutionary" world of becoming there are, however, essential differences between the various beings and therefore their evolution is itself intrinsically heterogeneous. Natural history, the history of mind or spirit, of the person, of human societies, of salvation, all display essentially different kinds of "evolution". It would be a philosophically and theologically false evolutionism to claim that the categories of biological evolution can be transferred in precisely the same sense to the "evolution" of man as such, to history in the proper sense, and to claim that this history can be adequately interpreted and explained on the basis of such categories. Any evolutionism would be unacceptable from the philosophical and theological standpoints, and would have to be rejected as objectively heretical, which affirmed, not within the limits set by scientific method but in an apodictic statement extrapolated so as to refer to the whole of reality, that there are no essential differences within the empirical world. This would imply that man himself is entirely a "product" of the pre-human world, that he does not result from a creative act of God which is terminatively special. It would deny that man is essentially distinguished from all other things that exist in the empirical world around him by a direct relation to God in his spirituality and freedom, because it would imply that what he is and signifies amounts to nothing but a momentary existence in the physical, biological sphere. It would deny that there is any change of an evolutionary kind which requires for its possibility the dynamism of transcendent causality operative in the world. The philosophical and theological proof of the falsehood of evolutionism understood in this way will be outlined partly in what follows and partly in the articles *Man* I–III and *Soul*.

c) The irreducibility of sub-human living things to what is purely material, in the sense of b), may well be a legitimate, well-founded thesis of natural philosophy, and it will be freely assumed in what follows. But the affirmation of an ontological difference in essence between the purely physical world and the biosphere is not, strictly speaking, a theological affirmation.

d) Provided this is clearly and unmistakably presupposed, it is legitimate to speak, though with due caution, of the evolution of the one world. Matter and finite spirit are intrinsically related to one another, even though the relationship is different in each case and differs with each degree of being. They both spring from the creative act of the one God; matter has no meaning except in a world of personal spirit; at least in man it is a necessary condition of mental activity and the scene of personal history and co-being; each in its own way, matter and mind have a single goal in the one plenitude of God's kingdom. The angels too do *not* have to be thought of as beings which by their very nature stand in no relation to the world of matter, even if they have no "body". The "history" of matter must therefore be the "history" of making mind possible, and finds in the incarnation of the Logos and the transfiguration of the universe in the resurrection of the flesh (the two are connected) its own culmination in the perfect fulfilment of the created spirit in God, in the beatific vision and end of man.

e) The unity of the world in spirit and matter, envisaged as the unity of a history, can be thought of as an "evolution", i.e., as development from within towards what is essentially higher, provided "becoming" (in the full sense of the word) is conceived as a being's "self-transcendence". It is possible to do this, for what we call God's conservation and *concursus* in regard to the existence and operation of a finite being must not be regarded as an occasional intervention of God from without, but is an enduring and most intimate intrinsic condition of the being and activity of the creature. It activates the very becoming of beings and can therefore make the immanent or transitive effect of becoming contain more "actuality" (even of a substantial and essential kind) than the finite agent itself possesses. And God's transcendent causality enables the creature *itself* actively to *effect* this supplement and not merely passively to receive it. Such a concept of self-transcendence naturally does not imply that from anything at all anything whatsoever can come. In cases where something essentially new comes into existence from and through something lower (for example, a being which is spiritual as well as biological from a mere living creature) the divine impulsion to such self-transcendence fully realizes the strict concept of "creation".

f) On these assumptions the one world (which from the start is a material world but equally from the start is under the cosmic dynamism of those created spiritual "principalities and powers" which we are accustomed to call "angels") can be thought of as moving from its material beginning towards its spiritual and personal fulfilment, in an evolution under the dynamism of its divine ground which confers self-transcendence and orientation. At all events the great stages of its history need not be thought of as a series of supplements added from outside to its original constitution.

2. *The intrinsic unity of the biosphere.* a) If there is evolution, and if it is possible (for this has not been demonstrated) to assume an ultimately monophyletic evolution, at least as a working hypothesis in biology, then the temporal unity of the biosphere is implied. This supposition may be risked here as a hypothesis because there is such a thing as evolution in general, because hominisation presupposes as its condition a leap to a higher plane (self-transcendence), which is not less than what would have to be postulated in the hypothesis of a monophyletic evolution; and because the metaphysical economy-principle demands that, if possible, a new initiative by God within the one changing world should not be postulated unnecessarily. It follows then that if a monophyletic evolution is assumed, the whole world of living things appears as a real unity linked together in time, and based on, and incorporated in, the temporal unity of matter which itself is one.

b) Such a view, as well as other considerations, leads to the question of the ontological unity of the biosphere. In the first place the ontological unity of the *material* world must not be overlooked. In ontology, what the Scholastics called *materia prima* is not a reality multiple in itself and of itself, occurring many times as an "intrinsic" element in the many things of experience. It is the one, real, substantial principle of the spatio-temporal dispersion of what is materially multiple, the ontological principle of what is partly observed and partly presupposed as the single fundamental field or domain of all concrete phenomena and of physics. The biosphere of course also shares in this ontological unity of space-time. It is comprised within the material world's single space-time manifold, which is its ground, not the subsequent outcome of mutual causal influence. The question whether above and beyond this the temporal unity of the biosphere as such points to a spatial unity of a quasi-substantial kind, leads to the further question whether in this sphere the substantial formal principle (the ground of the spatio-temporal configuration of a living thing) must be thought of both specifically and individually as plural, as "multiplied", or not (the human spiritual person being always excluded). Everyday experience and traditional natural philosophy always answered the question in the first sense. As many really distinct substantial forms were directly assumed to be present as distinct "individuals" of different living "species" were observed.

But this everyday experience is not conclusive. On closer examination the limits of biological individuals very often become vague. (Cf. the phenomenon of the "runners" at first connected with the mother-plant and then separated from it; the fluid transition between various plants and animals which appear to be one; the germ-cell inside and outside the parent organism, etc.) Living forms which present what are apparently very great differences in space and time can ontologically have the same morphological principle, so that enormous differences of external form can derive from the material substratum and chance patterns of circumstance without change of substantial form (caterpillar – chrysalis – butterfly).

A true physical "continuum" (beyond the unity of the physical "field") is not necessary as material for a substantial formal principle of living beings. What for us is a plurality of living things visibly manifested by spatial discontinuity, is therefore no proof of an ontological plurality of living things in respect of their formal principle. The same holds good of the antagonism among living forms, for this is also found within living beings which everyone regards as one and the same. The biosphere would perhaps therefore be more correctly, because more simply, envisaged, if we were to think of it as perpetually based on *one* substantial formal principle. This latter would have a tremendous potentiality of ways of manifesting itself in space and time and would realize these possibilities in space and time in accordance with the conditions of physical matter actually present, even though these conditions themselves receive direction from that formal principle. This picture on the one hand would match the development of physics, which reduces (or seeks to reduce) the plurality of "specifically" different natural substances to the space-time variation of one and the same matter. It would also bring out more clearly the formal ontological difference between biosphere and the "noosphere" of personal minds. Only in the latter would there be individuals simply and substantially distinct from one another; individuals that are no longer the increasingly complex modifications in space and time of the fundamentally one and evolving biosphere.

3. *Theological and ontological problems regarding the causes of evolution.* a) (i) The question of the "mechanics" of evolution is a scientific question. It concerns the "genetic" conditions, inner and external, of a material kind (modification of genes, etc.), under which something biologically "new" arises. In principle they are physically producible conditions susceptible of explanation in terms of function. And natural science by its very method can restrict its attention to that question.

(ii) Because of the unity yet essential intrinsic differentiation of the world, only a certain number of formal structures can and must be named as characterizing this one evolution: a tendency towards a growing complexity of the various individual beings, towards greater "interiority", towards greater specialization combined with greater openness towards the whole of reality, orientation and irreversibility of evolution. On that basis man, together with other beings possessing self-consciousness, freedom and dynamic transcendent orientation towards God, appears as the goal of cosmic evolution. Since he is material and since his materiality is a factor in the material unity of the whole universe as "field" and since he can manipulate himself physically and morally, in this world and in relation to the "other world", it is quite legitimate to affirm that the world becomes aware of itself in man and attains a direct conscious encounter with its ground, God.

(iii) The free gift of God's grace, God's communication of himself, was incorporated in the world from the beginning (for the angels possessed it from the beginning, and man as the goal of the world was intended by God from the start as man divinized); consequently, world evolution really, and not merely in the divine "ideas", moves under the dynamism that is directed towards the "kingdom of God". The history of nature and the world becomes the history of salvation and revelation when man is reached, for man, aware of his supernatural teleology, historically objectivates that orientation. Its "omega point" is in fact Christ, in whom created matter, finite spirit and the divine Logos, in whom all things subsist, are united in one person and this unity is manifested in history.

b) (i) The metaphysical question of

what actually happens in evolution from the ontological point of view, i.e., with regard to the totality of operative causes, must first of all be analysed in such a way that it is clear that the answer will differ according to the differing ontological relation of the "new" that has come about, to the mundane cause (antecedent) that preceded it. If the new is substantially new or even something essentially higher, i.e., if numerically an additional substantial principle appears or even a being which by its very character cannot in principle be understood as a purely space-time modification of the data already present in its antecedent, but has an irreducibly higher ontological position in relation to the very nature of being as such (even though this does not preclude a cosmic causal derivation), then the question must on principle be framed differently from when what is "new" can be understood as a different but physically producible space-time pattern of data already present. In the first sense the question arises with theological and philosophical certainty only in regard to the "evolution" of man and with some philosophical certainty in regard to the transition from the purely material to the biosphere. Within the biosphere itself the question does not necessarily have to be raised in that way. Yet it soon becomes clear (cf. below) that from the ontological point of view this correct and enduring distinction in objective reality and in mode of stating the question is not so important, theologically speaking, as it might at first seem, provided that in general the coming into existence of something new is correctly understood.

(ii) Intramundane becoming as self-transcendence: If and where something really "new" comes about and yet derives from a cause within the world (and supposing that mere occasionalism is rejected on philosophical and above all on theological grounds), its cause "goes beyond" itself; it posits more "reality" than itself is and possesses. According to the metaphysical principle of causality, this self-transcendence, which must at this point still be thought of in a quite general way, is only possible in virtue of the dynamism of the absolute Being which is at the same time what is most intimate to the mundane cause and yet absolutely distinct from the causally operative finite being. The absolute Being constitutes active beings (by conservation and *concursus*) not merely as something static, but in their active self-transcendence whereby they both accomplish their own nature and posit what is "new". The "new", being more than the agent, is at once the effect posited by the mundane cause and by the transcendent causality of the absolute Being. In the mind's transcendent experience, the dialectic of this relationship is directly present: the absolute Being, as asymptotic goal of the movement of mind or spirit is always what is "beyond"; it posits the finite spirit as separate and absolutely other than itself and yet at the same time it is what is most intimate to it, the basis of the ontological movement of becoming in the finite spirit. The latter moves in virtue of that Being's opening itself to it, and does not merely strive towards a horizon which in the last resort would simply be an "object" pursued in virtue of the intrinsic capacity of the knowing subject itself. Since in this transcendental experience the ontology of a being is an immediate datum, there is found there as an actual ontological occurrence a self-transcendence towards what is more, in virtue of the absolute Being. Self-transcendence can therefore be shown here to be a valid metaphysical concept.

(iii) If the ontological concept of active self-transcendence is once metaphysically established, the idea of evolution and its compatibility with divine causality no longer offers any insuperable difficulties from the ontological

substantial unity. If this is kept in mind, "creation of the soul" can only mean that the whole man is directly created by God in the sense that as a corporeal spiritual person he essentially differs from the brutes and consequently is not simply and solely the product of the "biosphere", and is not merely on its level. In that case, evolution of the body can only mean that the whole man takes his origin from the world around him. The two statements made simultaneously about the same man are conceivable because the concepts of becoming and causal dependence do not exclude but rather (usually) include a "qualitative leap". The latter is possible as something posited by a creature through the divine dynamism which supports from within its active becoming.

2. *The teaching of the Church.* a) According to the Church's teaching, it would be heretical to declare that man as a spiritual person is in that respect a product of infra-human reality according to its own natural laws. For the First Vatican Council defined (*D* 1802) that there is a difference of nature between matter and spirit; and man, at least "as regards his soul", is directly created by God (*D* 170, 533, 738, 1185, 1910, 2327; according to Pius XII: "animas enim a Deo immediate creari catholica fides nos retinere iubet").

b) Nevertheless the Church's magisterium, provisionally at least, does not reject the scientific thesis that man, as far as his body is concerned, stands in historical connection with the animal kingdom; the question may be freely discussed (Pius XII in an address in 1941 [*D* 2285] and in *Humani Generis* [*D* 2327]), but this freedom does not extend to the question of monogenism (*D* 2327).

c) There are no further official ecclesiastical pronouncements on the compatibility of the two affirmations. We must be careful not to think that the question is fully solved merely by applying the first proposition to the soul, the second to the body. The spiritual soul which results from one direct creative act of God of necessity also signifies a transforming specification of the bodily component, even if this creative act occurs in living matter. And so the doctrine can and must be maintained that Scripture speaks of a *peculiaris creatio hominis*, as the decree of the Biblical Commission in 1909 (*D* 2123) teaches.

3. *The teaching of Scripture.* God's revelation in Scripture envisages man always and everywhere as one corporeal and spiritual being. And in contrast to everything else met with in the earthly world of human experience, man in his bodily reality is the spiritual and moral partner of God, spoken to by God. In this reality, which is in unique contrast to all else, man is represented as originating in a special creative initiative of God aimed directly at man and producing the image and likeness of God which until then had not existed. It is certainly not possible to deny that so much at least is contained and asserted in the first three chapters of Genesis. And since tradition has always drawn the doctrine from the Genesis account of the creation of man, it is binding on us (cf. *D* 2123). On the other hand it must be said that the Genesis account is not intended to be an eye-witness report of exactly what took place. In other words, what is involved is a statement (probably a historical aetiology), which expresses what it really means in popular terms by the use of vivid imagery. We are not only permitted, but commanded, to take this *genus litterarium* into account, for the Church not merely tolerates such a view but itself teaches it (*D* 2302, 2329).

If this is admitted in principle, however, it follows that Scripture in Genesis 1–3 contains nothing beyond what has been said which, in respect of our present problem, could with certainty be affirmed to belong to the content asserted and not to the mode of presentation. The formation of man from the dust of the earth can and must be taken as a way of expressing the fact of creation. If this *genus litterarium* is taken into account, no argument against transformism can be drawn from Eve's formation from "Adam's rib". It cannot be proved that this image expresses more than a relation of congruity between the first human being and the second, and the unity of both (a view held as early as Cajetan, and at the present time by H. Lesêtre, W. Schmidt, J. Chaine, H. Junker, J. de Fraine, etc.), even if reference is made to *D* 2123. For if the "formatio primae mulieris ex primo homine" which is there defended as historical is soberly interpreted in the light of *D* 3202, all that is asserted is that in this narrative too we have to acknowledge the affirmation of a historical event; it is not thereby denied that any figurative element is to be found in it. And so on the basis of Scripture too we must affirm what the Church's magisterium declares on the present question.

4. *Tradition.* a) It must be admitted that before the 19th century the general interpretation of the Genesis account (leaving aside evanescent suggestions of a more subtle conception) was that God created man's corporeal nature from non-living matter. Yet Christian tradition was aware from the beginning that in the accounts of the world's first origins more than in other passages of Scripture, figurative modes of expression are to be reckoned with. Our present-day question did not arise. It is true, of course, that revelation and tradition, objectively speaking, can answer a question which was only explicitly propounded at a later date, yet in the present case it must be said that tradition does not contain an explicit or formally implicit rejection of a bodily link between man and the animal kingdom. And this is because what tradition certainly intended to affirm with the absolute character of a statement of the faith, namely the special position, and therefore special creation, of man, is still just as true today on the assumption of moderate transformism. But it cannot be shown that this absolute character of a statement of the faith must also be attributed to the modality under which earlier tradition imagined the event in question to have taken place, but without being able either expressly to distinguish that mode from the actual content affirmed or expressly to include it in it. Such absence of a distinction, however, is not necessarily an implicit denial of the possibility of the distinction, if it was not possible, in view of earlier historical conditions, to raise the question of the possibility of such a distinction.

b) The first explicit ecclesiastical pronouncement of an official kind was made at the local synod of Cologne in 1860 (*Collectio Lacensis*, V, col. 292). Here even the moderate theory of descent was rejected. In 1871 the Catholic St. G. Mivart proposed a moderate transformism ("Mivartism"). In 1895, M. D. Leroy, O.P., had to retract the view he had expressed on moderate transformism ("L'évolution restrainte aux espèces organiques"; cf. *Civiltà Cattolica*, XVII, 5 [1899], pp. 48f.). In 1899, P. Zahn for the same reason had to withdraw from commerce his book *Dogma and Evolution* at the command of the Holy Office (*ibid.*, pp. 34–39). No objection was raised to later works defending moderate transformism by Teilhard de Chardin, F. Rüschkamp, P.-M. Périer, E. C. Messenger and others. Nevertheless even until quite recently such moderate transformism was rejected by the great majority of theologians as contrary to Scripture and open to theological objection. In the 19th century it was still regarded as heretical, for example by G. Perrone, C. Mazella, B. Jungmann, J. Katschthaler. Since Pius XII allowed free discussion, the number of Catholics who positively support transformism has considerably increased (C. Colombo, P. Leonardi, J. Marcozzi, P. Denis, J. Carles, B. Meléndez, J. Kälin, F. Elliott, etc.). Yet even now there are theologians who reject transformism even in its most cautious form, because they do not think it scientifically proved and because theological reasons still seem to them to militate against it, even though usually now they do not risk assigning any theological note of censure. So, for example, E. Ruffini, J. Rabeneck, I. F. Sagüès, Ch. Boyer, M. Daffara, C. Baisi. This development of doctrine has not yet been the subject of more detailed theological reflection. At all events it shows that the Church is always learning and that appeal to the unanimous agreement of theologians is an argument that must be handled cautiously.

5. *Systematic treatment of the problem.* If we assume that the doctrine of hominisation through evolution is correct (positively to decide this is not in itself a matter for theology), the following can be said.

a) God supports most intimately, from within, the creature as a mutable being in its becoming, in its movement of self-development and self-transcendence. Becoming ultimately means active rising beyond self, in which God so moves the mover that it receives its own self-movement (and not merely a movement passively undergone) from God (as ground) and as directed towards him (as asymptotic goal). Any other conception of becoming leads in the last resort to occasionalism or to change without cause. What we call matter (and especially when it is already animate and sensitive) has an intrinsic affinity to consciousness, immanence, spirit, because it originates by creation from God the absolute personal spirit, and is the potential intrinsic substantial co-principle of a personal created spirit (man).

b) Since the one universe (even in its material reality) has a single goal, its salvation, transfiguration and accomplishment in the kingdom of God, it is directed and impelled by God from the start towards that goal: the full accomplishment of created spirit, which integrates matter into its final perfection.

c) Consequently the becoming of the material world can certainly be regarded as orientated from within by God, in dynamic self-transcendence towards man, in whom the world achieves immanence, subjectivity, freedom, history and personal fulfilment. Hominisation designates that occurrence in nature in which the universe finds itself in man and is consciously confronted with its origin and goal.

d) When man is in question (whether from the phylogenetic or ontogenetic point of view), God's rendering possible a self-transcendence of the cosmic causal antecedent in the direction of man denotes the same thing as what theology calls immediate creation (*D* 2327). God's transcendental causality in making such self-transcendence possible must be characterized on the basis of its term. If therefore something substantially new arises which *in se subsistit* (i.e., despite its function as the principle of a space-time configuration, always exceeds this function, precisely as spirit), then the divine enablement which is directed precisely to that term, is "creation" and it is "direct". For from God as source something is constituted which involves a new independent being. The example of human procreation (human ontogeny) shows that in such an account the concept of *immediata creatio* can be used. For the language customarily employed by the magisterium applies this expression to the coming into existence of the whole human being (although the matter involved already existed), yet without any intention of denying that the parents are the cause of the human being in question. That God makes possible a mundane causal efficacy does not, therefore, exclude the concept of direct creation, provided that something substantially new and really independent comes into existence and that the divine causality (as is the case as a matter of course) directly terminates in it. In the case of phylogeny that is even more patently so, because the mundane causal antecedent is then specifically inferior to man.

Karl Rahner

EXISTENCE

I. Concept of Existence

A. Introduction

The word "existence" has become one of the signs of the times in modern thinking, having also given its name to one of the predominant trends of philosophy.

It should, however, be noted that even in existentialism the term is understood so differently by such figures as Heidegger, Jaspers, Sartre and Marcel that what they have in common is hard to define briefly, in spite of the general accord of their interests. It may, however, be affirmed that in this philosophy existence means the actuality of human existence. Thus it is not the same as the scholastic *existentia*, which, as opposed to *essentia*, was the actuality of any essence, not just that of man. But even in Scholasticism the concept had varied. In Thomism, for instance, it crystallized another whole concept of reality than in Suarezianism. Thus the history of the concept from its first appearance in Marius Victorinus (d. *c.* 362) to the present day must be envisaged. It can be shown that the variations in meaning are not accidental, but correspond to the changes in metaphysical self-understanding. But it would be wrong to confine such an analysis to the periods in which the term undergoes such changes, since the thing itself, self-understanding as understanding of existence, was always there. For a full history of the interpretation of existence, all epochs would have to be examined, even where the self-understanding effective in all action and thinking was not expressly articulated. It would cover all the fundamental aspects of life – myth, religion, art, law, politics, philosophy, technology – and would coincide with the determination of the spirit of each age. All that can be attempted here is to show briefly that human consciousness does not always interpret itself in the same way. Its variations give rise to epochs in the history of the spirit which have a quality of their own in each case, which can easily be lost sight of by the readiness with which one's own type of self-understanding is taken for granted. Though it cannot be directly grasped, the spirit of an age, embracing the main aspects mentioned above, is clearly seen in its relation to history and its trend, and in the resulting philosophy of the times.

B. The Different Epochs

1. The Greeks are the founders of Western history as well as philosophy. Nonetheless, the main interest of the Greeks was in nature and its ultimate, permanent causes. Philosophy at its highest was only interested in the permanent substratum of all beings which underlies all changes. History, as that which comes to be and passes away, was not knowable and ultimately not worth knowing. Even a thinker as open-minded and comprehensive as Plato thought of his ideal State as isolated from its neighbours and even from its own past. It was so detached from time that once founded it would remain always the same. Aristotle was interested in contemporary politics and gathered much historical material, but for his self-understanding, strictly speaking, only the cyclic and permanent was valid – reason with its eternal laws. Implicit or explicit, even in the great

historian Thucydides, was the basic conviction that nature, including the nature of man, would never change. The self-understanding of the Greeks was drawn up basically on the pattern of nature. The concrete course of events had at most the significance of a paradigm from which the nature of things could be deduced. But there was little notion of possible development and real change, and hence little interest in the future and in history in general. The Roman mind differed only in emphasis, the duration and extent of the Roman empire giving a somewhat different perspective. In common with the Greeks they had a great sense of the permanent, either as the eternal form of all reality or the inevitable necessity of facts. Plato even reached the concept of love and the good as the reality which could provide deliverance from the prison of history. But the perspective of a great future in which history was to attain its fulfilment was unknown to antiquity.

2. The self-understanding of Israel was very different. Israel had little interest in science, art and culture, and little scope for them; but it was supremely alert to the human. If we compare Deutero-Isaiah and Herodotus, who were almost contemporaries, the difference between Greek and Jewish self-understanding stands out vividly. But the mind of Israel was not formed by theoretical knowledge and research. Its self-understanding came from repeated reflection on its own history. It learned from its memories and reflection that it was a people with one God who was very close to his own, demanding from his people loyalty and faith in his promises. This is a completely new dimension of self-understanding. Reality is not the cyclic repetition of nature, but the creation of God. But faith in creation is faith in the promises, the promises of a future made possible by loyalty to God (covenant). The ground of all historical reality, both as its beginning and its end, is a person. This stress on the personal element, including the notion of decision and freedom in history, was unique.

3. Thus existence was no longer determined by fate, as among the Greeks, where even the world of the gods was so determined and thus underlined the rule of fate. Israel's experience was taken up by Christianity, especially in the preaching of Paul and John, where self-understanding was fully conscious of the reality of freedom as a creative, though not identifiable power. This untrammelled grasp of freedom, by virtue of which alone could the reality of guilt and sin be accepted, was not the result of a natural process. It was based on confidence in the God of Israel who became man in Jesus of Nazareth and through him offered salvation to all men. Faith in the Incarnation made the early Christians take man as seriously as God, and reinforced the dialectic and dynamism of the OT, as the event of cross and resurrection shows. This brought about a self-understanding which did not fear death, because it had experienced the creative force whose power and fullness it expressed by the word Pneuma. In spite of the intenser confrontation with sin and death, the Christian mind, characterized profoundly by faith, hope and love, had the courage to believe that all history and the whole cosmos, now that God had entered in, was to attain an ultimate salvation. This self-understanding which reconciles and unites nature and history, sin and redemption, man and God, is unique both as the expression of man's actual experience and as the adumbration of a future salvation.

4. Reflection on these basic experiences gave rise, in the Fathers, and especially Augustine, to a self-understanding which took in all history for the first time. It was this sense of man as a whole, and of his whole history as

a salvific process which determined the nature of the Middle Ages and of modern times down to the present day, in spite of many deviations and much secularization. In the Middle Ages this heritage was transformed in the course of reflection on classical antiquity. The history of salvation, with its primordial sense of freedom, was comprised in an order of creation where heaven and earth, past and future, had a remarkably finished look and where even the notion of God as part of the comprehensive hierarchical order, static and permanent, led to legalism and nominalism. The understanding of self tended to approximate to the understanding of things. The modern age tried to counteract this tendency. The Renaissance and Reformation looked back once more to antiquity and primitive Christianity, initiating a new discussion beween the biblical experience of salvation and the classical notion of culture. Then the elimination of the cosmology of Aristotle and Ptolemy threw man once more back on himself, but at the same time opened up the way to a self-understanding in a cosmic framework. The epochs of Humanism, Baroque, Enlightenment, Romanticism, Classicism and so on followed. The two possibilities of self-understanding offered by the history of the West were made more radical and total, but at the same time relativized. The resulting mentality, in all its practical, intellectual and technical endeavours, is more and more conscious of its historical evolution and setting. It thus aims at a social, scientific and technological control which will assure it absolutely of the future.

C. Philosophical Articulation

Once the two sources of Western self-understanding, Greek and Jewish, had come together, as outlined above, and developed and changed, a change in philosophical theory also ensued. The classical and medieval metaphysics is essentially different from the type of thinking which began with the transcendental philosophy of Kant. This was continued in the systematic philosophy, of the dialogue or dialectical type, of Fichte and Hegel, according to the two basic forms of Western metaphysics. Finally, after Kierkegaard, came the phenomenology of Husserl and the existential or ontological thinking of Heidegger, and also the dialectical materialism of Marx. Both of these deliberately gave up all systematic philosophizing, to help man to an authentic self-understanding. The question of beings *qua* beings had been put by the classical metaphysics, on the basis of Plato's analysis of the difference between becoming and the true being of the form (between ὂν γιγνόμενον and ὄντως ὄν), which became a metaphysical discipline in the hands of Aristotle and was re-stated by Thomas Aquinas. This basic question tries to see beings not from any particular aspect, their usefulness or acceptability, for instance, but from the aspect which it is as itself – namely as a being. This "ontological" question does not separate beings from their essence, which is to be themselves, i.e., beings. But the "cause" which identifies each being with itself, that is, makes it be itself being, must be a supreme totality in which are contained all differentiation and demarcation – and that is being. Hence the basic trait of this metaphysics is to ask after the ground and origin of beings in being. This mediation, for Aristotle and for Thomas, is accomplished by the "active intellect" (νοῦς ποιητικός, *intellectus agens*). Nonetheless, this metaphysics fails to note that the origin of beings in being is not to be thought of as a sort of cosmogony, on the analogy of a natural ontogenesis, but is once more essentially mediated in the consciousness of man. This relationship to the consciousness which was not entirely neglected in classical metaphysics, became fundamental and systematic with Kant and led to the new "transcendental" approach. Here for the first time the principle that all understanding of reality is self-understanding was clearly envisaged. The principle that infinite being was the ground of all beings, the absolute truth and goodness, which had been *per se nota*, intrinsically evident, to classical metaphysics, was now called in question. Kant could find no way of justifying the possibility of ontological knowledge, which he therefore held was beyond the limit of human possibilities. Being became consciousness, essence became category and beings objects. Man, deprived of contact with metaphysical reality of an absolute and universal nature, was thrown back on himself and so knew himself in another way, that is, as subject for objects.

If classical metaphysics had lost sight of its true nature in the myth, so to speak, of ontogenesis, this transcendental changeover (not a denial but a transformation of metaphysics) reminded it that all understanding of reality is likewise self-understanding. Nonetheless, there still remained, even though on a higher level, a fundamental process of objectivation: being becomes the consciousness of the subject with regard to the object. Self-understanding is not complete and authentic.

Fichte eliminated the alienation by envisaging for the first time the personal relationship as the interplay of subject and object, in which the subjective consciousness of Kant now became a mediating element. This medial consciousness is seen as the light and life (truth) of the whole personal realm. It makes the Kantian object mediate between persons and so appear in itself. In contrast to classical metaphysics there has been a mediation, but the meaning of being becomes nonetheless once more infinite, absolute, life and light. And beings cease to be mere objects for subjects and are transformed into independent media. Self-understanding becomes once more complete or absolute, but in a radical interplay of immanence and transcendence. And more clearly than ever before, the question of being or light is posed, in the distinction between the light and the source of light (God). Fichte's philosophy of absolute freedom became in Hegel the philosophy of the absolute spirit. For Fichte, self-understanding is absolute mediation in freedom and hence also in history. It is just as absolute a mediation of the spirit in Hegel, but now necessary, in a necessary process of history. It seemed impossible to go beyond the the stage of total reflection on self attained in German idealism. Nonetheless, in spite of the inclusion of history and historicity, this philosophy reflected self-understanding merely as a system. A new question was adumbrated by Kierkegaard and Marx and then posed expressly by phenomenology: the meaning of existence prior to any mediating system – a meaning not to be attained by way of mere reflection. The question had not been unknown to Fichte and Hegel, and especially to Schelling. But a new effort was made to clarify it by means of the so-called phenomenological analysis, applied to the region of immediate experience of the proper nature of being and not to any proprieties arrived at by deduction.

Heidegger's thought in particular strives to grasp being as the ground which, though the force behind all attempts at systematization, is itself unattainable through reflection. His effort is therefore to describe the experience in pre- or non-philosophic terms. Self-understanding is the medium in which "being" makes itself known as event. The historical or existentialist experience of this event cannot be demonstrated, but only expounded or interpreted (hermeneutics). This "being" has itself a history, which determines the changing self-understanding of man in each different epoch. "Being" impinges on each epoch as a different sense of human existence.

As regards the Christian self-understanding, the question now arises as to whether there is not something similar going on, inasmuch as the self-disclosure of the Logos varies from epoch to epoch. It seems true at any rate to say that antiquity understood itself in terms of nature and cosmology, and that the Middle Ages still remained tributary to a sort of ontogenesis. But the transcendental changeover of modern times brought with it a more anthropological self-understanding, totally systematized in German idealism. It was transformed from system to experience in the turn to existentialism, though even here, as must be noted, full justice is not done to self-understanding as historical *and* social. The reason is that this self-understanding basically views history in the light of its origins rather than as something heading for its destiny. Hence if an outline of philosophy is to be drawn up on the basis of the true Christian experience and the self-understanding which it implies, it must be primarily a transcendental philosophy of freedom which is at once ontological and "dialogue-centred", thus preserving the heritage of tradition. It cannot be bounded within a formal system. Since it takes seriously the non *a priori* nature of the historical experience as a matter of freedom and of dialogue, it must try for a hermeneutics which will be a "phenomenology" of the Incarnation. This means that history is to be made visible as also the history of God (history of salvation). It is only on this basis that the future can be grasped and moulded – in hope – in all its technical, scientific and social manifestations. This will make possible a self-understanding both inspired by revelation and orientated to a future history which moves towards it own absolutness.

Eberhard Simons

II. "The Existential"

A. Philosophical

The term "existential" or "existentials" was introduced by M. Heidegger in his *Sein und Zeit* (1927; E. T.: *Being and Time* [1962]). Since then, it has been used in many different senses, in Protestant theology, for instance, by Bultmann, Fuchs and Ebeling, in their existential interpretation of the NT, in Catholic theology by K. Rahner, with his concept of the "supernatural existential". Heidegger himself did not make use of the term in his later work. But in his *Being and Time* he gave a precise account of the meaning of "existential": "The question (of the ontological structure of existence) aims at displaying what constitutes existence. We give the name of existentiality to the interconnection of these structures" (*Sein und Zeit*, p. 12; cf. E. T., p. 12). "Because the (ontological characteristics of beings) are determined by existentiality, we call these characteristics existentials. They must be sharply distinguished from what we call categories, which are the determinations of beings insofar as they are not related to existence." (*Ibid.*, p. 44; cf. E. T., p. 44.) "The question of existence can only be clarified by existing. The self-understanding which leads to this we call existentiell . . . The interconnection of the structures (which constitute existence) we call existentiality. Their analysis is in the nature of an existential understanding, not an existentiell one." (*Ibid.*, p. 12; cf. E. T., p. 12.)

In contrast, therefore, to the categories, which are regarded as determinations (ontological) of beings within the world, the existentials are the determinations (ontological) of man in his understanding of himself as "existence". Thus Heidegger, having recourse to the origins of Western metaphysics, which had fallen into philosophical oblivion, posed once more the problem of the difference between "being there" and "being something", "is-ness" and "what-ness", *existentia* and *essentia*. The problem was traditional in metaphysics, but remained unanswered as long as the real question of the meaning of being was not put. In working out his "analytics of existence", which adumbrate the meaning of being, and begin thereby to throw light on the meaning of the "categories" of beings, Heidegger defines the "existentiell" as that which directly affects the concrete existence of man – imminent death, for instance. This is distinguished from the "existential", which determines the ontological structure of existence – the character, for instance, of being doomed to death (the being-for-death) which permeates all elements of existence. In Western metaphysics, the understanding of being was based solely on beings as objects in the world – this because of the fated "oblivion of being". Existence and essence were attributed, analogically according to degree, to all beings. It was an attribution (κατηγορεῖν) which veiled the primary nature of truth in being, which is that of event, to concentrate on the thought and representation of the "subject". This metaphysics was re-traced when appropriated by the modern notion of existence, which, however, was enriched with theological content since Schelling and Kierkegaard, though more and more restricted to subjectivity in its terms of reference. Hence the modern notion of existence, being in the strictest sense of the term the *out*-come, i.e., the departure *from* the various interpretations of being which had dominated in the course of history – ἰδέα, ἐνέργεια, *substantia*, *actualitas*, *subiectum* – had to be primarily existential. It had to be achieved in the light of the forgotten ontology of the primal relationship between being and man grasping being, since man as the "thereness" of being is the only possible foundation of any metaphysics of essence-existence. In this way the priority of essence over existence or of existence over essence was no longer determinative for the existence or "being there" of man – Heidegger thus differing from J.-P. Sartre and K. Jaspers and other existentialists, and from the traditional ontology of the West in general. And human existence, as grasp of being, was contrasted with all categorized "beings", whether conceived of as immanent or transcendent, since it was "ek-sistence", that is, the finite human being "standing out" into the fated yet freely-happening openness and security of being (which bring about this outgoing).

Thus the existentials – such as "being thrown there", "being in the world", "being exposed", "being with", "happening to be thus somewhere", understanding, purpose, sketch-plan, care, anxiety, being-for-death, "historicity" – cannot be deduced from a supreme principle of thought, like a systematic table of categories. The existentials could only be markers along the way of a historically engendered and hence always incomplete and non-terminable understanding of being. Hence a categorized interpretation of beings and of man, in the light of the specifically Western notion of being, is to some limited extent legitimate, and indeed necessary, say in the construction of a general or regional ontology. But there can be no exclusion on principle of a different type of experience of being and its past or future articulation by humanity.

As the Western metaphysics of being and its implications are more and more fully appropriated, its "absoluteness" – hitherto conceived of metaphysically – can no longer be the final valid exclusion and hence relativization of another understanding of being. It can only be the existentially minded self-emancipation (always newly available and imperative in history) of the fixed categorical thinking of a culture or epoch or system, under the challenge of the total human experience of being yet to come as a necessary existentiell which must be freely accepted. And, of course, the ever increasing weight of the past to be assimilated is an intrinsic element of the onset of the future. Hence Heidegger's assertion, that "existential analytics is rooted in the existentiell" (*op cit.*, p. 13; cf. E. T.) is decisive. The future of philosophy must be thought of in terms of man's being claimed in the process of history by being which is always still more in the future and hence absolute. And the self-understanding of theology must be that it is uttered to one and all, in the historical word of revelation, and yet that it is still not (eschatologically) uttered to the end. Hence theological critique of the concepts of an objectivating thinking derived from a philosophy or science will be the ceaseless task of propounding and proclaiming the mystery of God as it calls forth the primordial (existential) understanding of man and his primordial (existentiell) freedom.

Franz Karl Mayr

B. Theological

1. *In general.* The ontological and not merely factual superiority of man to things which, according to Christian faith and its doctrine of man, characterizes him, justifies in principle an inquiry into his existentials. It provides good reason for refusing to make the mistake of classifying them from the start among the categories which are supposed to apply to every finite being but which in fact are derived from material things.

2. *Supernatural existential.* The term existential can also be used in a special way in theology. There can be no doubt about the following truths, though their further theological interpretation can be left open. Even prior to justification by sanctifying grace, whether this is conferred sacramentally or outside the sacraments, man already stands under the universal, infralapsarian salvific will of God which comprises within its scope original sin and personal sin. Man is redeemed, and is permanently the object of God's saving care and offer of grace. He is under an absolute obligation to attain his supernatural goal. This situation, "objective justification" in contradistinction to its subjective application by sanctification, is all-inclusive and inescapably prior to man's free action, which it determines. It does not exist solely in the thoughts and intentions of God, but is an existential determination of man himself. As an objective consequence of God's universal salvific will, it of course supervenes through grace upon man's essence as "nature", but in the real order is never lacking to it. This alone explains why, even if he rejects grace, or in perdition, a man can never be ontologically and personally indifferent to his supernatural destiny. Until recently the Catholic theology of the schools had generally held, despite occasional protests such as those of Ripalda and Vásquez, that a real offer of supernatural grace for a salutary act only occurs when a human being encounters the explicit preaching of the gospel, or when revelation as a historical tradition is present in some other way, e.g., transmitted from "primitive revelation", or in the OT. Now Vatican II considers that there is a possibility of salvation for (inculpable) atheists and polytheists (*Gaudium et Spes*, art. 22; *Lumen Gentium*, art. 16; *Ad Gentes*, art. 7), though they also need real faith, and hence the grace of faith (*Ad Gentes*, art. 7). Hence there can be no serious doubt that all men permanently stand under the offer of grace really operative in them. This permanent and ever-present offer is always accepted in their moral activity, unless they shut themselves to it by their own moral guilt. Through the supernatural formal object which is involved in grace itself, the primary feature of revelation, and therefore the possibility of faith, is already present. That man is really affected by the per-

manent offer of grace is not something which happens only now and again. It is a permanent and inescapable human situation. This state of affairs can be briefly labelled "supernatural existential", to prevent its being overlooked. It means that man as he really exists is always and ineluctably more than mere "nature" in the theological sense. The precise relation of the supernatural existential to nature, to original sin (*simul iustus et peccator*), freedom, and justification requires more detailed investigation.

Karl Rahner

F

FAITH

I. Way to Faith

1. *Theological presuppositions.* a) As a result of God's universal salvific will and the offer of the supernatural grace of faith as an abiding feature of man's mode of existence as a person, every human being, even previous to the explicit preaching of the Christian message, is always potentially a believer and already in possession, in the grace that is prior to his freedom, of what he is to believe (i.e., freely accept): God's direct self-communication in Christ. It is quite possible, in fact, that the person whom the preacher of the faith encounters is already justified (because he was obedient to the dictates of his conscience, to the extent this had made itself heard), and therefore already believes, in the theological sense, even if what he explicitly believes is very little. In both respects, therefore, faith may always be assumed to be present. Bringing someone to the faith will mean the endeavour to develop this already existing faith into its full Christological and ecclesiastical, explicit, social, consciously professed form. This endeavour can and should link up with all the elements of faith already present. It must therefore show that the Church's Christian faith is the historically and socially complete form of what the person to be converted already "believes". Consequently, the starting-point which is always present (the condition which may be assumed) never consists merely in a human being's "natural reason". This in fact is already historically determined and bears the stamp of the human being's actual situation and of his personal experience. Furthermore, it is already supernaturally "elevated" and orientated towards the explicit, conscious knowledge of faith.

b) Conversion to faith is always a process with many stages, and these need not necessarily follow the same course in every individual. Nor can it be presumed that if the whole explicit content of the faith is presented in an objectively sufficient way, it can only be due to personal (subjective) guilt in every individual case, whatever the particular situation and limits of time, if in fact all these stages in the genesis of faith are not accomplished. The messenger of the gospel can therefore rightly ask himself what stage in a gradual history of faith has been reached by the collective or individual *kairos*. He can then try to lead as far as that point, i.e., to indicate the ways of access and for the rest patiently leave God to bring about a situation where further progress will be possible. Otherwise he would perhaps waste too much human and ecclesiastical effort.

c) An approach to faith presupposes that a human being who is to be led to faith already has a starting-point, and that from it and from the very nature of that starting-point, there exists a transition to the further reality of faith in whole or in part. The first point has already been dealt with above, section (a). The second implies that the realities and truths of faith are really interconnected, and that there is therefore a connection also between what is always a prior datum and what has to be believed anew and expressly. Faith is never awakened by someone having something communicated to him purely from outside, addressed solely to his naked understanding as such (as, for example, the statement that the chemical formula of water is H_2O). To lead to faith (or rather, to its further, explicit stage) is always to assist understanding of what has already been experienced in the depth of human reality as grace (i.e., as in absolutely direct relation to God). The connection between what has already been experienced (in faith or, it may be, in incredulity), and what has to be accepted anew in explicit faith need not and cannot of course always be of the kind that links conclusions to premisses in logical inference. There are connections of meaningful correspondence. And for this kind of connection it is sometimes quite sufficient to show that to some particular question there is only one answer in the concrete and historically speaking, even if several answers are theoretically conceivable. The intrinsic homogeneity of the whole of dogma in relation to one ultimate primordial question experienced by man elevated by grace would need to be worked out much more clearly in dogmatic theology (and then in the instruction of converts) than is the case nowadays when positive theology predominates. Then the multiplicity of propositions formulated for belief would give a much clearer impression of being something people could make something of, rather than of a mere exercise of formal obedience to propositions which God has of course revealed, but without which it would be quite possible to imagine even the fully explicit accomplishment of salvation. A full understanding of what is meant here is therefore only possible on the basis of a unity of fundamental and dogmatic theology in which – without materially curtailing the Church's teaching, as Modernism did – the whole "system" of doctrines of faith would appear as the one complete answer to the inescapable primordial question of human existence regarding the relation between the absolute mystery (called God) which forms its ground, and that existence itself. The answer would then be that this sacred mystery forms the ground of human existence in the absolute, merciful intimacy of radical self-communication, that this self-communication found its irrevocable historical manifestation in Jesus, that around him there is a community (called the Church), deriving from him and given its structure by him, of those who believe in the self-communication of God in him and who explicitly profess this in historical and social form, and who, believing and hoping, await the revelation of this self-communication at the end of history (of the individual and of the world).

2. *Ways of approach to faith.* a) The primary approach to faith is a man's direct confrontation with himself in his whole nature as free and responsible and thereby with the incomprehensible ground of this human reality, called God. For many people this, of course, is "taken for granted", but must be perpetually re-awakened and accomplished if faith is to be elicited in a really radical way, breaking the crusts of custom formed by its institutionalized formulations. The person who is to act as stimulus to awaken and confront

someone with this way of approach must nowadays be able to perceive and bring to full awareness the comprehensive question set to man by the transcendence of his commitment. He must be able to show that man cannot evade himself as an all-embracing question; that he still affirms the question's existence even when he declares he will leave it as unanswerable; that total commitment cannot be evaded, that the sceptical judgment on man as conditioned and determined is itself an experience of freedom, an act involving freedom, that God is not an object among other objects of experience which under certain circumstances one may fail to discover, but is necessarily affirmed in the accomplishment of man's intellectual and moral activity, even if he is explicitly denied, or not named, or is met with under quite different conceptual modes of expression. This can provide the basis for inquiring whether a man would not really be interpreting his own concrete experience more accurately, at least in its highest moments and as it finds typical objective historical expression in the highest events of religious history, if he were to take it to be the experience of a supreme, most radical, saving and forgiving presence of the mystery of God communicating himself absolutely. Courage to trust in the possibility of the highest fulfilment of meaning, readiness to believe, is needed. And the experience can be the hidden ground of apparent despair at the groundlessness and experienced absurdity of human reality in "Nihilism".

Such experience of grace, for that is precisely what it is, can in fact occur in the most varied forms from individual to individual. The spiritual guide in encouraging explicit faith will have to observe what actual form the experience takes in the particular catechumens he is dealing with. It may, for example, be indescribable joy, unconditional personal love, unconditional obedience to conscience, the experience of loving union with the universe, the experience of the irretrievable vulnerability of one's own human existence beyond one's own control, and so on. On the same basis he would then have to explain what is really meant by God, grace and even by God's "Trinity". At such a point the *perichoresis*, the *circumincessio*, of fundamental and dogmatic theology is apparent. Fundamental theology can never be purely formal, in the sense of furnishing solely a proof of the "fact" of revelation in abstraction from any content of that revelation, while dogmatic theology always appeals to grace-given divinization and what this involves: the light of faith and the experience of grace, which actually comprise the reality conceptually represented in the truths of revelation.

b) On the basis of such faith in God as incomprehensible and intimately present, it would have to be shown that corresponding to man's historicity, in all the dimensions of his existence, including the religious, his transcendental divinization necessarily expresses itself historically, is manifested as an historical and explicitly formulated human datum. This would have to lead to an understanding of the history of revelation, of the history of redemption, individual and collective, and of the vital necessity of religion not in the sense of non-historical reflection on the individual's own "religious need" (which in such a non-historical form is only apparently possible), but in the form of trust in, and insertion into, a historically concrete religion with a social organization. Consequently, the question can only be *which* is the actual historical and social form of religion to which a man must trust himself in order to practise his personal religion in a truly human way, i.e., in actual history and in society. This would be the starting-point from which to interpret people's present-day knowledge of the multiplicity of religions and their history, so as genuinely to overcome the danger of relativism arising from that knowledge. (Frank admission that the history of salvation, of revelation and of faith takes place everywhere in history and society by reason of the universal salvific and grace-giving will of God; concept of a "legitimate" religion outside the history of the Old and New Testament revelation; combination of culpable degradation of religion with grace-given and revelational elements in the non-Christian religions; eschatological surmounting of the plurality of legitimate religions, including that of the OT, by the absolute coming of salvation in Jesus Christ, etc.; these are the keys to such interpretation.)

c) The approach to a confession of faith in Jesus Christ would have to be sought in a "transcendental Christology", i.e., from the "idea" – even if, historically, this can only appear with Christianity itself – of an absolute, historical mediator of salvation in whom God's self-communication to his creation in grace finds its highest and irrevocable historical manifestation. It would have to be shown that the very concept of such an absolute mediator of salvation involves the authentic doctrine of the hypostatic union in its correct, i.e., non-Monophysite, meaning. That doctrine must be presented very precisely, so as to avoid any appearance of mythology, which would be quite unacceptable nowadays. Christ must be shown as a true man with a created consciousness and an active human centre of freedom. In other words, he must appear as the very question which man *is*, and which the hypostatic union "answers" ontologically (and not by a merely factual link of an objective, substantial kind), and which that answer actually validates and posits (*ipsa assumptione creatur*, as Augustine noted). Of course it will then have to be shown also that that "transcendental Christology" is actually realized in Jesus Christ, so that the sacred history of redemption has already entered its eschatological phase. For this again, appeal will be made to the idea (quite familiar from ordinary life), that in order to fulfil his nature, man everywhere has to enter into concrete historical relationships which he can never justify with full theoretical certainty. It must also be noted that in fact nowhere else in history apart from faith in Jesus Christ has even the claim been made to realize the highest transcendental idea of human fulfilment such as is found in the God-man. That has its importance; there is a legitimate question which, though it may have many conceivable answers, has in fact only received one. It has positively to be shown that where a *saving* reality is concerned, the circle linking historical reality (miracles, Jesus' resurrection) as ground of faith, with faith as the sole mode of knowledge of, and testimony to, such a reality, is legitimate. This is the only antidote to present-day scepticism in regard to extraordinary "historical" events. It has to be emphasized that even on a very cautious "historical" interpretation of the gospels (as evidences of faith in Christ and only in that way as reports on Jesus' life-history), Jesus' claim to be the absolute mediator of salvation is sufficiently established – and that includes what is really meant by metaphysical sonship of God.

d) If there is once courage for the act of faith in Jesus as the historically eschatological manifestation of God's absolute self-communication, the next step, grasping the significance of the Church, will no longer be too difficult. If it is seen that the Church was not merely founded from outside by a purely juridical enactment, but is the abiding presence of the eschatological Christ-event, then the existence and meaning of many of the Church's characteristics (e.g., doctrinal infallibility, the *opus operatum* of the sacraments), become much more intelligible. It must also be indicated that among

Christian denominations (prescinding from the Orthodox), only the Roman Catholic Church has the courage unambiguously to claim to be, in constitution and doctrine, representative of Christ historically and as a Church. Protestantism does not have this courage. It can only regard itself as constituting conditional and human forms of organization of individual Christians. Furthermore, the Roman Catholic Church is the "old" Church, with the most tangible historical links of every kind with the early Church. Consequently there is at least a presumption that it is the Church of Christ, and this could only be annulled if it were plainly proved that it has unmistakably fallen from the gospel of Christ and laid an obligation on its members accordingly. But that cannot be done. Such an approach to an understanding of the Church as the necessary historical presence of the interior divinization of mankind by grace, of the Church as "fundamental sacrament", facilitates access to ecclesiology for men of the present day. They can take the Church seriously without identifying it with what it exists to serve.

Karl Rahner

II. Faith

1. *Dimensions of faith.* God has revealed himself to man in his Son made man (Heb 1:1; Jn 1:14–18; Mt 11:25–27); revelation is the mystery of God who draws near to man in the human word of his eternal Word. Man's response to God revealing himself in Christ is called faith; faith, therefore, is as supernatural as revelation itself, and together they constitute the mystery of God's encounter with man in Christ. In this encounter it is God who makes the first move; his inward call enables man to receive the divine word. Man freely decides to submit to the absolute claim of divine revelation. Faith is indissolubly both a gift of God and a human act, both grace and freedom. Faith is a compact act of many different aspects. No doubt these may be analysed, but they form an organic whole and are therefore unintelligible unless studied in their organic interrelation. Modern exegetes are agreed that faith includes knowledge of a saving event, confidence in the word of God, man's humble submission and personal self-surrender to God, fellowship in life with Christ, and a desire for perfect union with him beyond the grave: faith is man's comprehensive "Yes" to God revealing himself as man's saviour in Christ. The magisterium of the Church teaches that the act of faith is a complete surrender of man to God, one which includes acceptance of revealed doctrine, voluntary submission to grace, and trust in God's promises (*D* 798, 1789, 1791; Vatican II, Constitution on Revelation, art. 5). Theologians, recognizing the complexity and intrinsic unity of the act of faith, distinguish in it the following basic dimensions: faith as knowledge of revealed truth (believing in God who reveals himself in Christ: "*fides quae creditur*"); faith as trusting obedience to God and as a personal encounter with him: "*fides qua creditur*" (believing God, the formal structure of faith): in this sense faith is the disposition for justification and ordination to final salvation in the beatific vision, that is, to participation in the life of the glorious Christ (the salvific and eschatological dimension of faith). Thus Christ is the centre, the foundation and the final goal of faith (the Christocentric and Christological aspect of faith).

2. *Faith as knowledge.* Trust in God's promises and obedience to his commandments are the most obvious features of faith in the OT, but it usually implies knowledge of God's salvific intervention in history, whether this has already happened or is yet to come (Gen 15:2–6; 16:11; Exod 4:1–9, 28–31). The whole history of Israel

revealed the God of the covenant as the only saviour, with the result that monotheism became the fundamental dogma of Judaism: "I, I am the Lord, and besides me there is no saviour" (Is 43:10–12). The "knowledge of God" which the prophets preached involved professing faith in the one God (Hos 2:20; 4:1; 5:4; 13:4; Is 45:5, 22; Jer 24:7; Ezek 6:7, 10, 13; 7:27; Joel 2:27; Deut 4:39; 7:9) in certain fixed formulae (Deut 6:20–24; 26:5–9; Jos 24:2–13; Ps 78; 106; 135; 136).

The event of Jesus' death and resurrection caused the aspect of "knowledge" in Christian faith to be particularly stressed. The great profession of faith of the primitive Church was: "Jesus has risen: God has made him Lord and Saviour, according to the prophets" (Acts 2:44; 4:4; 8:13; 11:21; 13:48; 17:2). To believe, according to St. Paul, is to accept the resurrection of Christ and its meaning for salvation as a reality (Rom 10:9, 10; 1 Cor 1:1–19; Phil 3:10–11; 1 Thess 4:14). Faith and its message correspond to each other as the statement and its content: the term πίστις (faith) is used to mean the actual content of the apostolic preaching (Rom 10:8; Gal 1:23; 3:2, 5; Eph 4:5; Acts 6:7; 13:8, 12). By faith one attains to "knowledge of the truth", because the gospel is "the word of truth" (2 Cor 6:7; Col 1:5; Eph 1:13; Gal 1:6–9; 1 Tim 2:4; 4:3; 2 Tim 3:7).

In the Johannine writings "faith" and "knowledge" have the one object, the divine Sonship of Jesus (Jn 8:24, 28; 14:12, 20; 17:21, 23), and each implies the other (Jn 4:42; 6:69; 8:31, 32; 10:38; 17:8; 1 Jn 4:16). To believe is to recognize Jesus as him whom the Father has sent (Jn 17:3), to accept the truth of the testimony he gives of himself (Jn 3:11–13, 31–36; 8:14, 18, 24, 30–32, 40–46), to confess that he is the Son of God (Jn 11:27; 20:31; 1 Jn 4:2, 3, 15), to profess his "doctrine" and to persevere in it (Jn 7:16, 17; 2 Jn 7–11). To be a Christian (Acts 11:26; 26:28) is to accept the truth of the mystery of Christ (the death and resurrection of the Son of God) and its meaning for salvation (Acts 16:31; 26:23; Phil 2:5–11; Gal 4:4; Rom 1:3–5; Jn 1:1–18; 20:31; 1 Jn 5:20).

From the very beginning the Church has expressed its faith in special formulae (1 Thess 1:10; 4:14; 1 Cor 1–8; 12:3; Rom 1:4; 10:9; Phil 2:5–11; Acts 8:37; 1 Jn 2:23; 4:2, 15; 2 Jn 7). Profession of faith in Christ and the Trinity was of basic importance in the baptismal liturgy; in order to belong to the Church, the community of salvation, one had to believe in the mystery of Christ in which man shares through baptism and faith indissolubly united.

It is not difficult to see why the act of faith includes acceptance of the content of revelation as true. Man can only be saved by participation in the saving event of Christ (Acts 4:2; Rom 1:16; 3:22–28; 6:1–9; 10:9, 10; Jn 3:14, 16 36; 20:31); but it is impossible to share in this event without believing in its reality. The cognitive character of faith is an expression of the reality of the mystery of Christ; one cannot be maintained without the other. "If Christ has not been raised, your faith is futile" (1 Cor 15:14, 17); which means that faith apprehends the death and resurrection of Christ as real. Faith lives by the reality of its object, which is God's saving intervention in Christ. But for this reality the act of faith would have no content; it would be reduced to a purely subjective act. If the event of Christ is not real in itself, neither can it be real for me and it would be impossible to live it as a reality (Gal 2:20; Rom 4:24, 25; 2 Cor 5:15).

God has definitively revealed himself in the ineffable religious experience of Christ. The man Jesus was conscious of being the Son of God. But this ineffable experience (the repercussion, in Jesus' human consciousness, of the mystery of the Incarnation) could only be conveyed to men through human signs, symbols, metaphors, concepts and words. The message of Christ conceptualized and objectified the non-conceptual experience in which God manifested himself to Christ as his Father. In the incarnate Word the human word was used to give utterance to God's ineffable self-communication to his Son, the man Jesus. So too the divine person of Christ, the Father's eternal Word, reveals himself to men in human words.

That the human word can be made an expression of the divine Word corresponds to the possibility of man's body-soul nature being personally assumed by the Son of God. This potentiality is identical with the basic structure of the finite spirit which is radically open to the Absolute within the limitless horizon of being; and hence this limitless openness, the proper character of which is displayed in the absolute affirmation of the judgment, could be taken into personal union by the uncreated Word of God. Man's spiritual nature, as openness to being and as conscious self-possession, constitutes the basic potentiality (*potentia obedientialis*) for the Incarnation, grace, revelation, and faith. This concept of man, which any attempt to explain God's supernatural self-communication to man and man's personal encounter with God must logically presuppose, implies the doctrine of the analogy of being.

If God's revelation in Christ is validly expressed in human language, acceptance of this revelation by faith must involve an assent of the intellect: only by this means will it be possible to apprehend the message of Christ and in it the actual reality of God revealing himself. Doctrinal propositions objectify the mystery of Christ, but through the doctrinal message faith attains the revealed reality.

The intellectual nature of faith is inseparable from its ecclesial character. Unity of faith is essential to the Church (Eph 4:5), which would not be the community of believers without their common participation in the same reality of faith; such common participation is impossible without the sociological transmission of revelation, which must be expressed in definite concepts if it is to be preached. Thus the ecclesial kerygma, as the bond of union in the Church, must be accepted as true in the faith of Christians. The Church would not be visible as the community of believers if the act of faith did not include an intellectual assent.

3. *Faith as Christocentric.* At the heart of faith we find Christ, the Son of God made man and the saviour of the world. OT revelation coincides with the history of salvation of the chosen people and is ordained to the universal salvation to be revealed in Christ; NT revelation, especially in the Pauline and Johannine writings (Col 1:15–20, 26–28; Eph 1:10; 3:9–11; Gal 4:4–6; 2 Cor 5:18–20; 1 Tim 2:3–7; Jn 1:1–18; 3:16–17; 17:3; 20:31; 1 Jn 4:9–10; 5:11, etc.), presents Christ as the centre and principle of creation and the supernatural order of salvation. Patristic theology, both Greek and Latin, was aware of the historical development of revelation and its culmination in Christ; the liturgy shows Christ unifying the history of salvation in himself as its last end.

In the mystery of the Son of God made man the personal, immanent mystery of God – the Trinity – and the mystery of the Church – which is humanity called in Christ to a divinizing union with the divine persons – have also been revealed. Faith is theocentric and ecclesial because it is Christocentric. All revelation is summed up in these three fundamental mysteries implicit in the incarnation of the Word, who reveals the Father, sends the Spirit, and saves mankind. Whatever its actual content may be, every act of faith is ultimately ordered to the mystery of Christ.

Thus the religious value of faith in its intellectual aspect is clear. Because the act of faith includes an intellectual assent, the believer attains the actual reality of the saving event which is Christ, and is able to share in it; the personal appropriation of salvation takes place in the inward conviction that God has saved us in Christ. This assent requires that man submit the autonomy of his reason to the transcendence of divine grace and aim at the mystery of the divine life itself, in which he has already begun to share through the Word of God.

4. *Believing God.* The mystery of God who saves us through Christ can only be known insofar as God discloses his divine consciousness to man by giving testimony to himself. "Believing God" formally constitutes faith: this term, which frequently occurs in the OT and is also found in the NT (Gen 15:6; Ex 14:31; Num 14:11; 20:12; Deut 1:32, etc.; Acts 16:34; 27:25; Rom 4:3; Jn 5:24), means the attitude of one who assents to and relies on God's word and promises: believing God, man entrusts himself to him. NT faith looks at what God has done in Christ but also what God will do through him at the end of time, and therefore it is united with hope (Eph 3:12; Rom 5:1; 6:8; 1 Thess 1:3; 4:14; Heb 11:1–40). The fourth gospel uses the expression "to believe Christ" (πιστεύειν with the dative: Jn 4:21; 5:38, 46; 6:30; 8:31, 45; 10:37; 14:11), that is, to accept the witness which the Son of God bears to himself, in which the Father too gives testimony of himself (Jn 8:14, 18; 12:49, 50; 14:10, 24). Faith rests on the human word of the Word of God, so that its ultimate guarantee is the veracity of God himself (Jn 3:32–34; 8:26; 1 Jn 5:10): it is theological to the extent to which it is Christological.

To believe is, formally, to know reality through the knowledge which another person has of it and which he communicates by his testimony; between faith and reality there intervenes the person of the witness, who communicates his knowledge so that the believer may share in it and thereby attain to the reality itself. Testimony is essentially the communication of knowledge and the communication of consciousness (the witness's consciousness of his own veracity); faith is essentially sharing the knowledge and consciousness of another person.

Divine revelation is formally the communication of God's self-knowledge and self-consciousness so that man may rely on God's infallibility as the final guarantee of truth; in revelation, the veracity of God is engaged, that is, he commits and communicates himself in his word. This communication is absolutely supernatural, because no intellectual creature as such can have any claim to God's infallibility as the formal basis of his assent.

When he believes God, man knows revealed truth through the infallible knowledge God has of himself and consequently shares in the divine consciousness; faith is a divinizing, supernatural participation in the very life of God (Thomas Aquinas, *De Ver.*, q. 14, a. 8; *In Boet.*, *De Trin.*, q. 2, a. 2; *Summa Theologica*, I-II, q. 62, a. 1 ad 1; q. 110, a. 4; II-II, q. 1, a. 1; q. 17, a. 6).

Revelation and faith are supernatural by reason of their formal structure. Revelation is formally the personal self-communication of God to man through his word; faith is formally the personal self-dedication of man to God who addresses him. Believing God, man relies on the divine veracity and by that very fact puts his trust in the God of truth; faith essentially entails confidence in the divine testimony, that is, a confident surrender of man to God who reveals himself to man and thus saves him. Like the Incarnation, revelation is in itself a saving event. By the very fact of speaking to man God draws near to him as his saviour, and man experiences this nearness of God, present in the divine word, as his own salvation. Revelation and faith essentially involve a mutual gift on the part of God and man. God communicates himself, and man, by his acceptance, gives himself to God. It is a personal encounter: God offers man his friendship by disclosing the secret of his divine consciousness, and man enters God's intimacy. Faith is fellowship of life shared by man with God. This personal encounter and fellowship of life between man and the self-revealing God takes place in Christ. By faith Christ dwells in the heart of man (Eph 3:17) and man lives by Christ's own life (Gal 2:20; 3:26; Rom 6:4–10; Jn 10:14, 26–28; 17:20–23; 1 Jn 2:23–24; 4:7, 15, 16; 5:1, 20).

5. *Faith as a gift of God.* It is only by the grace of God that man can believe God (Eph 2:8–9; Jn 6:44, 65). The prophets describe what God does to the believer as creating a "new heart", as infusing a "new spirit", that is, as a spiritual transformation in man's inmost thoughts, feelings, and purposes (Jer 24:7; Ezek 36:26–28; Is 54:13). This idea of the interior transformation wrought by grace is further developed in the NT. According to St. Paul, conversion to Christianity radically renews man's interior structure in relation to God. The Spirit (πνεῦμα) inwardly enlightens the heart of the believer with a new knowledge and filial love of God (Eph 4:17–19; Col 1:21; 3:9, 10; 2 Cor 4:4–6; Gal 4:8; 9; Acts 16:14). Only when moved by the Spirit can man accept the mystery of Christ; and if the Christian grows in the knowledge of that mystery, this is also due to the vivifying presence of the Spirit (1 Cor 1:23; 2:10–16; 12:3; Eph 1:15–19; 3:14–19; Gal 2:20). According to Jn 6:44–46 and Mt 11:25–27, the preaching and miracles of Christ do not of themselves enable a man to believe in him. God must also draw the man to himself by an interior revelation. One of the central statements of John is that the "knowledge" of God and Christ that faith involves is a special effect of the presence of grace within man. To "know" and confess Christ one must be "born of God" and "abide" in him, that is, remain in fellowship of life with him (1 Jn 2:3, 5; 3:6, 9; 4:6–8, 15, 16; 5:1). Faith stems from a supernatural faculty of "knowledge". This is plainly stated in 1 Jn 5:20: "... the Son of God ... has given us understanding (διάνοια), to know him who is true (God)." The word διάνοια has always been rendered as faculty of knowledge (J. Alfaro in *Verbum Domini* 39 [1961], p. 90).

We must therefore conclude that according to the NT God himself creates the interior dispositions in man which are necessary if he is to be related to him by faith. The Fathers, particularly from St. Augustine on, envisaged the work of grace in the act of faith as an inward illumination. This concept was embodied in certain documents of the Church's magisterium (*D* 134, 141, 180, 181, 1791; Vatican II, *Lumen Gentium*, art. 12; *Dei Verbum*, art. 5). Under the influence of this Augustinian doctrine the theologians of the 13th century (notably St. Thomas, cf. J. Alfaro, "Supernaturalitas") worked out the first systematic explanation of the supernatural character of faith. God inwardly draws man towards an immediate union with himself, by giving him a new dynamism ordered to the beatific vision, thus enabling him to accept the transcendent credibility of the divine word – that is, to rely on God's word as being of itself absolutely worthy of credence. Grace raises man's spiritual powers above the limitless horizon of being and orders them to a supernatural end, to God in himself.

Occam's extrinsicism, on the other hand, developed a conception of grace entirely opposed to that of the previous century; grace, a created entity infused into man by God, does not affect the natural orientation of man's spiritual powers and their acts. The natural powers of man can accept divine revelation with an assent identical with the act of supernatural faith. From the 14th century down to our own day these antithetical opinions have continued to divide Catholic theologians. Owing, however, to closer study of the NT and the Fathers and keener appreciation of the transcendence of the formal motive of faith and of the vivifying effect of interior grace, there is a marked tendency among contemporary theologians towards the Thomist conception of supernatural faith.

By faith man knows God and his mysteries through the knowledge God has of himself. This sort of knowledge essentially surpasses man's natural powers which can only reach God by rising from the creature to the Creator (Wis 13:1–9; Rom 1:20; *D* 1785). Consequently, man cannot believe God unless his spiritual powers are intrinsically raised to a higher plane by the supernatural light of faith (*lumen fidei*), just as he cannot see God unless he is intrinsically elevated by the *lumen gloriae*. Hence the act of divine faith, in its formal structure, is a supercreaturely participation in the life of of God and therefore it essentially involves a transformation of man that divinizes him. The finite intellect cannot base itself on the divine veracity (that is, on the consciousness of God) unless God inwardly draws it to himself. God must mysteriously become present in the depths of man if man is to come into real contact with the word of God, which is God himself. If one reflects that to believe God is to rise above one's own reason and base one's life on the divine word, it will be obvious that this is impossible without a personal invitation from God to enter into confident fellowship with him.

Grace raises man to a participation in the very life of God. This implies the elevation of man as a spirit, as a being capable of conscious self-possession. This dynamic elevation gives one's supernatural acts their specific character as consciously tending towards God in himself (which orientation is experienced in the consciousness in the strict sense, that is, in the non-objectivated self-possession of the person, in its acts). Through grace man experiences himself in the very depths of his consciousness as a being called to intimate fellowship with God.

The believer already possesses "eternal life", which tends to its eschatological fullness in direct union with God in Christ (Jn 3:16, 36; 4:14; 17:3; 1 Jn 3:2, 15; Rom 8:23; 1 Cor 13:10–13). This supernatural orientation inevitably makes itself felt in the mental life of man as the new experience of being attracted by God himself. If grace did not act upon man insofar as he sets up a relationship to God, it would remain wholly extrinsic to man's religious life, something there by mere juxtaposition, not a force that brings about an interior transformation. Consequently it must be admitted that grace elevates the spiritual dynamism of man to relate it to God himself. Man is thereby enabled to enter upon a personal relationship with God in faith.

The inward illumination of grace has no objective content. It simply enables man to accept the content of revelation (presented to him from without in the preaching of the Church) as the word of God (2 Thess 2:13). Grace operates as a non-conceptual attraction to God in himself, which is prior to the free act, and thus God becomes mysteriously present in man's depths as God, that is, as personal transcendence. God reveals and communicates himself to man by no other intermediary than this attraction to himself, and man knows God non-conceptually through the experience of the actual ordination to God. As man becomes conscious of this ordination or dynamism, he thereby becomes non-conceptually conscious of the goal of this dynamism, God.

There is no vision, no direct experience of God, only the experience of the tendency towards God in himself, in which God is attained non-conceptually. God is not directly present in himself, but in the created dynamism orientated towards himself.

The existence of this supernatural ordination to God in himself is not known through introspection but through theological reflection. The experience of this invitation to divine intimacy cannot normally be an object of reflection in such a way that man can discover there God in himself as the goal of this invitation. The psychological repercussions of grace in man are too obscure, as a rule, to offer certainty of one's vocation to faith; the external signs of revelation are the normal basis of this certainty. Interior enlightenment by grace prefigures the act of faith, implying as it does an obscure, preconceptual presence of God (communicated, and manifested as salvation, by his attraction to himself), and hence ordering man's spiritual powers to a personal encounter with the transcendent You, first in the mystery of faith and finally face to face in eschatological salvation (1 Cor 12:10–13; 2 Cor 5:7; 1 Jn 3:1–3). Hence the operation of grace dynamically anticipates the character of the act of faith itself, disposing the depths of man's being to accept divine revelation freely, and thus to express the mystery of God's salvation in Christ in conceptual terms. The preconceptual and the conceptual are both essential to the act of faith, each requiring the other. Without the non-conceptual divine presence in the supernatural attraction towards God, man would be unable to give his unqualified assent to God's word in reliance on its transcendent credibility; if the content of divine revelation were not affirmed in conceptual terms, man could not reach God his saviour by a genuinely human act.

6. *Faith as a fundamental human choice.* By faith man freely submits to God's salvific love. For the OT, unbelief is rebellion and faith is obedience to God's word (Num 14:9, 11; Deut 9:23; Pss 78; 105; Is 2:2–24; 25:6–8; Jer 16:19). For St. Paul, faith is obedience to the gospel, that is, man's willing submission to the salvific economy that God has established in Christ (Rom 1:5; 10:16; 15:18; 16:26; 2 Cor 9:13; 2 Thess 1:8–10). According to St. John, faith is rooted in the very heart of human liberty, when man sacrifices his own glory, sincerely seeks the truth, and listens in loving docility to the inward voice of God (Jn 5:44; 8:43–47; 10:26, 27; 15:22–24); faith is coming to Christ, following him, accepting his witness to himself – in a word, a radical and total decision for the person and mission of Christ the Son of God (Jn 3:32–36; 5:38, 43; 6:35, 37, 65, 68; 7:37–38; 8:12–24; 10:4, 5, 27, 37; 12:37, 48).

The freedom of faith (*D* 797, 798, 1786, 1791; Vatican II, *Dignitatis Humanae*, art. 10) corresponds to the supreme gratuitousness of revelation and salvation. God's word confronts man with the mystery of Christ, which cannot extort the assent of reason because it transcends reason. On the other hand, the demands of Christianity (its absolute character, the imitation of Christ based on the law of love and the cross, the eschatological orientation of Christian existence) demand of man the most radical decision of his freedom. Christ demands faith in himself that shall be an irrevocable decision (Lk 11:23; 8:22; Mk 9:43–47; Mt 5:1–48). Faith is not so much an act or a series of acts as a basic and total attitude of the person, giving life a new, definitive direction. It comes from depths of human freedom, where man has received the interior invitation of grace to enter the intimacy of God; it embraces his whole being – intellect, will, all that he does (submission to the mystery, the love, and the law of Christ).

By accepting doctrine, faith accepts the revealed reality itself, the person of Christ with its claim on total dedication in love and obedience. Faith is at once an assent of the intellect and a consent of the will, which finds its true fulfilment in action.

Faith is born of desire for eternal life and is thus inseparable from hope, without which no one can wish to be saved. In its formal structure ("believing God"), faith implies trust in the divine witness and submission to the absolute authority of his word. It is a defined doctrine of the Church's magisterium that the loss of God's friendship through sin does not necessarily extinguish faith: man may be a believer and a sinner at one and the same time (*D* 808, 838, 1791, 1814). But it does not follow that faith can exist without a longing for charity; faith is not possible without the desire for salvation, which begins when the sinner is reconciled with God and is fulfilled in perfect friendship with God in glory. Even in its most imperfect form faith is ordained to friendship with God, and only reaches its perfection (even *as* faith) when charity has made it a living faith. Absence of charity deals a mortal wound to the life of faith itself. The believing sinner is torn by a radical inward antinomy: his faith is a constant call to reconciliation with God, while his sinful state draws him towards apostasy from faith. This contradiction tends to resolve itself, either by a return to God's friendship or by a total separation from God in unbelief.

The element of freedom is essential in the act of faith, for the activity of the intellect is subordinated to the will. Thus its assent is a prolongation of the free movement of the will towards the God of revelation. Since intellect and will are rooted in the person, who is actuated in them, in the last analysis it is man who by his free assent lays hold on revelation and salvation. It is the business of the will to unify man, whom God calls upon to decide freely what his own eternal destiny shall be, either accepting salvation as the gift of God's love or imprisoning himself in his own sufficiency. Faith sinks its roots in the very depths of human freedom, that is, in the fundamental and permanent choice by which man opens himself to, or rebels against, the Absolute as grace; here the ultimate meaning of human existence is decided.

7. *The certainty of faith.* God's word demands man's unqualified assent (Acts 2:36; Rom 4:19–21; Gal 1:9; Lk 1:18–20; Heb 10:22; 11:1). It is not possible to believe God as God, subject to certain limitations. The Church's professions of faith breathe an absolute certainty (*D* 40, 428, 706, 1789, 2145) which is based on the infallibility of God's witness (*D* 1789, 2145) and springs from the interior work of grace (*D* 1797). Thus the *absolute* certainty of faith is supernatural. It stems from the supernatural character of its foundation (divine revelation) and its principle (divine grace), which correspond to one another. Faith is infallible because it shares supernaturally in the infallibility of God; its absolute certainty excludes actual doubt, but not the psychological possibility of doubt or denial. The certainty of faith is entirely different from the certainty proper to philosophic or scientific knowledge; it is a special kind of certainty, based neither on the obvious truth of (essentially mysterious) revelation nor on any obvious rational proof of the *fact* of revelation (otherwise faith would not be free). Paradoxically, faith is absolutely certain and essentially obscure. The believer does not accept divine revelation, because he sees the truth of the mystery, or knows from rational evidence that God has spoken, but because under the guarantee of the external signs of divine revelation and the impulse of grace within him, he freely decides to rely on the word of God, who of himself is absolutely worthy of credence.

The assent of faith is both absolutely

certain and free. Hence all theologians conclude that this assent cannot result from a process of reasoning; for in such a case it would either follow from evident premisses, and so be fully certain but not free, or it would not stem from the evidence of the premisses, and so would be free but not absolutely certain. True, this does not altogether explain the *absolute* certainty of faith. The question still remains: if this certainty is not the result of evidence, then where does it come from? It is not enough to recall the influence that the will has over the intellect. The will can move the intellect to assent, but cannot of itself produce an unqualified intellectual assent (which in the natural order only evidence can do). The absolute certainty of faith can only be explained by the inward illumination of grace, which enables man to rise above his natural mode of knowledge and rely on the transcendent credibility of God's word.

8. *Faith and salvation.* The role of faith in salvation is fundamental (*D* 801). By faith man recognizes the reality and the absolute gratuitousness of God's initiative in saving sinful humanity through Christ (Rom 10:9; 3:22–30; 4:16; Gal 2:16; 8:22, 24; Eph 2: 8–10). Man can only be saved by sharing in the mystery of Christ's death and resurrection, which means that he must first of all affirm the reality of this mystery (1 Cor 15:12–16) and freely accept the economy of salvation that God has established and revealed in his Son (Rom 10:16; 2 Cor 9:13; 2 Thess 1:8). Thus faith is man's basic response to God revealing himself as man's saviour. It is an attitude which accepts salvation as sheer grace, renouncing all pride in one's own works (Rom 3:22, 24, 27; 4:2, 20; 1 Cor 1:29; 4:7; Gal 2:16). Man's response to the absolute gratuitousness of God's saving intervention is faith. Hence faith confesses the grace of God. To believe is to consent to be saved by God; it is to accept God as the pure gift of himself, as grace. Faith revolves about God's inscrutable, absolutely gratuitous design to save us in Christ (Eph 1:3–14; 2:5–10; 2 Thess 2:13; 2 Tim 1:9); but it is fulfilled in deeds (which express its vitality) and is perfect, proximately disposes to justification, only when joined with charity (Gal 5:6; 6:15).

From God's universal salvific will (Mk 10:45; 14:24; Rom 5:12–20; 1 Cor 15:20–22; 1 Tim 2:1–6; 4:10; Jn 1:29; 3:14–17; 1 Jn 2:2) and the absolute necessity of faith for salvation (Heb 11:6; Jn 3:16–21; *D* 801) it follows that God calls upon every human being to make the fundamental choice of faith, that is, to decide freely the meaning of his existence by accepting or rejecting grace. Theologians today are agreed (and are confirmed in their view by Vatican II, *Lumen Gentium*, arts. 2, 13, 16) that all men receive an interior invitation from the grace of God. But there remains the problem of how an act of faith is possible for men who through no fault of their own are unaware of the content or even the fact of revelation. Attempts to solve this problem have been numerous, but unconvincing. There is, however, a promising trend in contemporary theology towards a new solution based on a profounder sense of the illuminating function of grace as self-communication and manifestation of God, in non-conceptual terms, in his drawing men supernaturally to himself. The proper effect of grace in man is an interior invitation to familiar fellowship with the Absolute. Through this invitation (not objectified conceptually but experienced in the ordination to God in himself) man experiences himself in his non-objectified consciousness as called to a free and loving acceptance of the Absolute, who gives himself as sheer grace. Man's free response (acceptance or rejection), preformed in the experience of this ineffable call, is radically a decision of faith, in that it either welcomes or repels God communicating and supernaturally manifesting himself in the obscurity of his non-conceptual presence. Since this decision does not grasp divine revelation in conceptual terms, it does not have the full quality of an assent of faith. In this sense it is essentially deficient as an act of faith. But it is a decision which in the manner of a vital act includes an embryonic and not merely virtual faith. It is rooted in the inexpressible depths of human freedom (whose choice may transcend the conceptual knowledge which conditions its exercise), but merely has not yet attained the corresponding expression in categories. It is a faith which is lived but is not (yet) conceptually grasped, because its full development is hindered by circumstances outside the human will. In such a decision, man's life and choice go beyond his objective conscious knowledge. If he could tell himself in conceptual terms the real meaning of his free response, conditioned and preformed by his experience of the attraction of the Absolute, then he would realize that he has (or has not) believed God. This decision implies the *fides qua creditur*, but not the *fides quae creditur*.

This solution does not seek in any way to minimize the conceptual aspect of faith, which is absolutely necessary for man to grasp the content of divine revelation; an act of faith which is properly such will contain both elements, conceptual and non-conceptual. The basic gospel message (God as salvation of men) expresses in conceptual terms the very reality which man apprehends non-conceptually in his experience of grace. Thus without a corresponding knowledge of the objective content of revelation, the decision of faith lacks the appropriate human expression; only the Gospel enables man to understand himself, that is, to understand the meaning of his decision and of his whole life. By the decision that he makes in the supernatural existential situation (in response to the experiential call of the transcendent You to a personal encounter with himself) man opens himself or closes himself to grace, that is, God giving himself and revealing himself in the gift. Such a decision, in its existential aspect, is equivalent to the decision of faith.

9. *The eschatological nature of faith.* The conception of life and fundamental attitude of the Christian are essentially eschatological. Faith looks beyond the world and death in eager expectation of eternal life in the encounter with the risen Christ (1 Cor 1:7–8; 1 Thess 1:10; Rom 8:23–25; Phil 3:20; Tit 2:13; 2 Cor 5:1–10; Phil 1:19–26). The believer already shares in the saving mystery of Christ, yet not fully as he will at the end of time, when the Lord will impart to men and even the material world the glory of his resurrection (1 Cor 13:10–13; 2 Cor 5:6–10; Phil 1:21–23; 3:20–21; 1 Thess 4:17; Rom 8:19–23; Heb 11; Jn 3:36; 17:3, 24; 1 Jn 3:2). Faith is eschatological because it is Christocentric. Because faith is centred on the mystery of Christ, which will only be fully revealed at his second coming, it is dynamically ordered to the perfect union of man with Christ in glory and in him with the Father and the Holy Spirit. In the obscurity of the divine word the believer already knows the personal mystery of God (Incarnation, Trinity) whom it will one day be his eschatological fulfilment to see face to face.

By its formal structure ("believing God") faith already tends towards the vision of God. Through revelation God discloses the mystery of his divine consciousness to man; through faith man enters God's intimacy and begins to share in his divine life. This intimate personal encounter between God and man, which revelation and faith entail, seeks its own fullness in a perfect union. Grace, being God's drawing man to himself, directs the act of faith towards the vision of God. True, the assent of faith, expressed as it is in human concepts, is necessarily bound up with a mediate knowledge of God by analogy and in this respect does not transcend the horizon of being. But its tendency does transcend that horizon, being ordered to God in himself, who makes himself present non-conceptually but without any intermediary other than the experiential attraction he has for himself. The final goal of the supernatural dynamism of faith is immediate union with God. Since the act of faith expresses the totality of man as soul and body (assent to the content of revelation inevitably involves concepts, images, and the like) and eschatological salvation will fully glorify man as man (resurrection of the body), man tends through faith to a perfect union with Christ in glory, and thereby to the vision of God and his personal mystery, the direct revelation of the Father, the Son, and the Holy Spirit. Just as Christ is the centre and foundation of faith, so he is also its last end; man believes God in Christ so as to reach the vision of God in Christ (J. Alfaro in *Gregorianum* 39 [1958], pp. 222–70; in *Catholica* 16 [1962], pp. 20–39).

Christian existence runs its course within history and time; but God's supernatural call gives that existence a new direction destined to transcend time by participation in God's eternity in direct union with the glorified Christ. Through faith man experiences and possesses himself in a new dimension; his consciousness of being present to himself is now set within the *a priori* horizon of ordination for eternity. The believer, in time, is on pilgrimage towards eternity, that is, is on the way to meet the Lord.

Juan Alfaro

III. Motive of Faith

1. *God reveals himself in Christ.* According to the OT to believe God is to rely (הֶאֱמִין = hiphil of אָמַן = to be firm) on his word (Gen 15:1–6; Exod 4:15, 28–30; 14:31; Is 43:1, 10; Jn 3:1–5). St. Paul adopts this concept when saying that faith accepts the Gospel as the word of God (2 Thess 2:13). While Heb 1:1 declares that God has spoken to us in his Son, the fourth gospel outlines a theology of God's testimony (μαρτυρία) through Christ as the foundation of faith: Christ reveals God because he is the Son of God made man; the personal mystery of God is known only to the Son, who alone sees the Father; the human testimony of Jesus is the testimony of the very Son of God and that of the Father as well; consequently to believe Christ is to believe God, trusting in God's own veracity (Jn 1:14–18; 3:11–13, 31–33; 6:46; 8:12–55; 12:44–50; 14:6–11, 24; Mt 11:27; 1 Jn 5:10). Thus the christological nature of faith is a consequence of the Incarnation: the divine person who is the Word speaks to men with human words. Since faith rests ultimately on the person of the witness, when man believes Christ he enters into a relation with the person of the Son of God himself. The formal foundation of faith is Christ, that is, God himself as revealing himself in Christ.

The object of faith is the mystery of God who in Christ calls men to participation in his divine life. This mystery exceeds the native powers of the human intellect – it can only be known by men through the divine testimony. This doctrine, familiar to the Fathers, has been confirmed by the Church's magisterium: the motive of faith is the authority of God's word, his truthfulness and infallibility (*D* 1789, 1811, 2145; Vatican II, *Dei Verbum*, arts. 2, 4).

The signs of divine revelation (miracles and the like), as known solely by the light of reason, are not the motive of faith. Since the assent of faith is absolutely certain and free, it cannot spring from a process of reasoning. Hence it cannot be formally based on the motives of credibility which are the point of departure for a rational proof that a divine revelation exists (*D* 1799, 1813). Faith presupposes the signs of credibility but they are not the formal motive of faith; they are a condition of faith, not its cause.

The teaching authority of the Church's hierarchy is the infallible and obligatory norm of faith, but not its formal motive. The Church, the community of believers, is entrusted with divine revelation, which it proclaims in its preaching and witness. It is the primordial sacrament of the glorified Christ, living by his Spirit, the channel through which men draw the supernatural life of faith; yet it is not strictly the motive of our faith. This can only be Christ, because he alone is the Son of God made man, the personal revealer of God.

2. *The motive of faith as the object of faith.* The fourth gospel represents Christ's testimony as testimony to himself. Christ is always both revealer and revealed, the revealer manifesting himself as such; he demands that one believe his testimony to himself, and he testifies that his testimony is worthy of credence. This absolute demand that one believe what he says of himself, and for the simple reason that he says it, springs from Christ's consciousness that he is the Son of God, and is the exercise of this Sonship. Faith is accepting Christ's testimony to himself, at once believing him and believing in him – believing that he is the Son of God the revealer, and believing him as God's Son and as the revealer (Jn 5:16–18, 38, 40, 43; 6:29–30; 7:25–31; 8:14–20, 25, 28, 30–31, 45; 10:24–39; 11:25–27; 14:2, 10, 11). This is to say that the motive of faith is also its object; the act of faith includes above all its own formal motive; by one and the same act a man believes what God has revealed in Christ and also believes that God has revealed himself in Christ.

Since the 13th century this has been the view of all theologians who recognized the decisive role played by the inward illumination of grace in the act of faith: when interior grace draws a man towards God, he enters confidently into contact with personal and transcendent truth; by a single act he believes God revealing himself and believes that God does reveal himself. The essence and expression of the act of faith is: God has spoken, God has revealed himself, in Christ.

St. Thomas insists that the person must be primary in the act of faith: a person's word is believed. He holds that the formal aspect of faith consists of the fact that God is believed (*Summa Theologica*, II–II, q. 11, a. 1; q. 2, a. 2; etc.). In the act of faith man enters into a personal relationship with the God who speaks to him. This is the kernel of faith, which is therefore essentially religious. When submitting to the divine word and confiding himself to it, man gives himself to God, who communicates himself to him and reveals himself and draws him to himself by an inward illumination. The human response includes the affirmation of the existence of divine revelation (even though the believer is not always conscious of this).

Faith does not merely accept the Gospel, but accepts it as God's word (2 Thess 2:13). The content of revelation deserves credence because God himself attests it, and since the divine testimony includes the reason of its credibility, it is credible in itself. This is the sovereign, transcendent and immediate character of the divine word: God cannot speak otherwise than as God and therefore his word necessarily affirms its own credibility and demands belief of itself. (If Christ had not declared his self-witness to be absolutely valid, he would not have revealed himself as the Son of God.) It would be as absurd to try to base the credibility of God's word on something outside that word, as to seek the source of God's being in something other than that being itself – God is believed as God only if he is believed on the sole authority of his own word. Faith achieves its fulfilment when it declares (giving voice to man's total response): *God has spoken*. The theological opinion which holds that the act of faith merely affirms the content of revelation (the view of those theologians who deny the illuminating function of grace), deprives the act of faith of its formal aspect (that which makes faith faith, believing God), the personal relationship of the believer to the God who speaks to him.

Thus the first thing which the act of faith lays hold on (*primum credibile*) is the actual existence of divine revelation, the fact that God has spoken in Christ. This priority is not one of time (an act of faith necessarily affirms some definite truth contained in revelation) but one of credibility; the primary object of faith is God the author of revelation, because of the supernatural attraction by which God draws men to himself. Man is able to accept the divine word as supremely credible of itself because God communicates himself and discloses himself non-conceptually in the interior call, being himself present in the supernatural tendency towards him. The inward illumination of grace enables man to rise above his natural mode of knowledge and enter into relationship with the transcendent Thou. Through God's non-conceptual presence (not a direct intuition of God but a new contact with God through the sole intermediary of the vital tendency towards him) man is inwardly addressed by divine revelation, and enabled to grasp it in its transcendent character. The ultimate motive of faith, then, is the divine testimony, which man is able to grasp thanks to an interior illumination from God. The structure proper to faith and also the special character of the knowledge which it imparts are here apparent. Faith, like the beatific vision, gives man a share in the knowledge which God has of himself in the divine life; hence the supernatural and mysterious character of faith and vision.

Even though human reason cannot comprehend the intrinsic credibility of God's word (any more than it can comprehend the aseity of God's being), the act of faith still remains a free human act, one therefore that reason can reflect upon. Man must be able to explain to himself his attitude of faith by justifying the free decision of his faith at the bar of his own reason. The act of faith is not unreasonable, because it presupposes the signs of credibility and their rational comprehension – the preambles of faith.

Juan Alfaro

IV. Preambles of Faith

1. This expression refers to an aspect of the theological problem of "reason and faith", which is ultimately the problem of "nature and grace". It is God who of his good pleasure reveals himself and creates in man an ability to receive the divine word; but it is man who freely believes and enters into vital contact with the God of revelation. What is necessary for man to satisfy himself that his free decision to believe God is not an arbitrary choice? How can each of us justify his personal faith at the bar of his own reason? In its formal motive, which is the authority of God himself, faith transcends reason; but faith as a *free choice* must be subject to a man's control, and he can do no less than ask himself the reason for his own decisions: no one may use his freedom in disregard of his intelligence.

From the time of its first appearance in 13th-century Scholasticism, the term "preambles of faith" (*praeambula fidei*, *antecedens fidem*, etc.) has had two meanings. Principally it means a number of metaphysical truths (the existence of a personal God who is the Lord of the world and of man; the intellectual nature of man as openness to the Absolute, his ability to know truth, and his freedom; the validity of the underlying principles of being and the moral law; etc.) which reason can establish and which revelation presupposes – not precisely in the sense that these natural truths must precede faith by a priority of time but in the sense that if they were denied the falsehood of revealed doctrines would logically follow, and that without them the mysteries of faith would lack internal credibility. The business of the preambles of faith is not to prove the fact of divine revelation but to make intelligible the content of revealed doctrine in which they are themselves implicit. But for the ideas and knowledge which make up the preambles of faith, man could attain no understanding at all of revealed mysteries (*D* 1650, 1670, 2305, 2320). Though demonstrable by natural reason, there is nothing to prevent the preambles of faith having been revealed by God and forming in themselves an object of faith (*D* 1785, 1786, 1807, 2305). Since the 17th century some of these metaphysical truths have been held to be necessary assumptions in apologetics (*D* 1799).

2. The term preambles of faith, or some synonym, has also been applied since the Middle Ages to the fact of revelation insofar as that fact can be known by reason through external motives of credibility such as miracles. Both Old and New Testament accept the evidence of the signs whereby God attests his revelation (Exod 4:2, 5–16; 14:5–31; 19:9; Mk 2:10–11; Mt 11:2–6; Jn 2:11, 23; 3:2; 5:36; 10:25, 37; 11:45–47; 15:22–23; 20:30–31). It is defined by the First Vatican Council that the divine origin of Christianity can be proved from such signs (*D* 1813, 1812, 1794, 2305). That definition confirmed a theological conclusion (nothing is said in Scripture of any natural knowledge of the signs of revelation) which was admitted by all Catholic theologians: that *if the free decision to believe God is to be consistent with the rational nature of man, it must be possible to prove the fact of revelation by means of external signs of credibility.*

God's revelation demands of man an unqualified, irrevocable "yes" which gives his whole life a permanent orientation: human freedom is at its most intense in the attitude of faith. Man may not take or abide by so grave a decision without being certain that it is his duty to accept the Christian message as the word of God ("practical judgment of credibility"). Therefore he must be able to determine whether or not his duty to believe is an illusion, something purely subjective: for this he must have criteria at his disposal which guarantee his knowledge of this obligation. Grace may well act within a man in such a way as to prove its own divine origin beyond any doubt; God can call one to the faith through the interior sign of an extraordinary religious experience (in defining the validity of external signs the Vatican Council did not deny the value of interior signs, which Catholic theologians have always admitted: *D* 1812). But experience has shown that in the case of most believers the interior action of grace is not sufficiently clear to establish the certainty of the obligation to believe; as a rule, it is impossible to transform personal religious experience into an unquestionable sign that God is inviting one to believe. Unless we wish to admit that the decision of faith is blind, we must hold that the external motives of credibility offer sound enough evidence of our duty to believe (*D* 1790; apologetics shows the validity of these signs, which are appropriate to the nature of revelation as embodied in an ecclesiastical society. Christ and the Church are the supreme sign of divine revelation). Knowledge of the signs of credibility precedes the act of faith (since the certainty of the obligations of faith is founded on them): this knowledge is a rational inference (a passing from the sign to the thing signified), and therefore an act of the intellect ("speculative judgment of credibility" – *the signs prove that revelation exists*). The act of faith presupposes a conviction that one must believe, and this in turn presupposes that one is able, by some means or other, to uphold the duty of faith at the bar of one's own reason – a thing not normally possible without rational knowledge of the fact of revelation. In actual practice, this rational knowledge is seldom formulated as such, but will usually be implied in a person's concrete realization of his duty to believe, insofar as that realization is produced by the influence of the signs.

3. The signs, and his rational knowledge of them, give man control not of the intrinsic credibility of the divine word but of his *own knowledge* of the duty to believe and of his *own free decision* to believe, which otherwise would be blind. The signs and reason take one only as far as the practical judgment of credibility, not onto the sacred ground of the act of faith itself, which arises solely from the testimony of God interiorized by the divine impulse, and from human freedom. To introduce any rational element into the actual assent of faith would be to destroy its absolute certainty, since full rational evidence of the fact of revelation is not (as a rule) to be gained from the signs of credibility. The possibility of rational knowledge of the signs of revelation is merely a condition of the uprightness of the free decision which man takes to believe God. It is not necessary to suppose that in fact rational knowledge of the signs is the work of human reason alone; God offers man the supernatural light of grace along with the signs of credibility (*D* 1789, 2305). The signs that God has spoken are not presented to man simply as objective data but as proof of a divine intervention in the world that gives human life a new meaning: in these signs God draws near to man and summons him. Before this summons human liberty, and therefore also divine grace, comes into play. In the concrete, realization that one has a duty to believe derives from a rational factor (knowledge of the signs) and a suprarational factor (supernatural light), organically fused in one summons that is both outward and inward. Reason enables us to perceive the divine signs; but grace makes us see in them a personal call to faith (St. Thomas, *Summa Theologica*, II-II, q. 1, a. 5 ad 1). The inward light of grace transforms our rational knowledge of the signs into a realization that "*God is calling me to believe in him*": the "practical judgment of credibility" involves an element that is personal, unutterable, incommunicable, the resonance in our consciousness of the divine call. Inwardly drawing man to itself, Personal Truth gives him a knowledge *per connaturalitatem* in which he vitally experiences an invitation to rise above creatures and trust in the transcendent credibility of God's word.

Juan Alfaro

FAITH AND HISTORY

A. The Problem

The unity and difference in which faith and history combine have been thrown open as a problem only by the modern forms of thought which have made their explicit articulation possible. But the tension between faith and history in a general and fundamental sense is a basic characteristic of Christian existence in general and is therefore as old as Christianity itself. Indeed, in and through Jesus Christ it points back to the history of faith and salvation in the OT.

With the modern opening up of the historical dimension of existence, to some extent in the wake of Christianity, a transcendental horizon of consciousness has been disclosed which makes the Christian event discernible in the phenomenal character which is proper to it.

Theologically speaking, man, as an individual and as a society, must be described as the historical coming of the free, supernatural, absolute self-communication of God which is eschatologically present and manifest in Jesus through his incarnation and resurrection. Faith is historically mediated in Jesus and is itself the free, historical grace-inspired acceptance in confidence of the sovereign disposition of existence in this event. From all this it is apparent that faith is inextricably linked with history. And since man is always freely accepting or rejecting transcendence and reality as a whole, and thereby himself, in a decision which he can never fully analyse (since reflection is afterthought, an effort to illumine and explicitate the living act) it follows that the *a priori* condition of faith, readiness to believe and its actuation, already are constitutive structures of human existence. But this is not the autonomous achievement of the subject; it is a matter of a common interpersonal act, in union at once with the self-realization of other historical freedoms (in society and in language) and with the active acceptance of the freely-bestowed grace which makes the act possible. Thus faith, in the broad sense of readiness to believe, is essentially historical in a threefold sense: it stems from the history of the "I", of the other and of the bestowal of grace. This must be the starting-point for the discussion of the problems which are posed by the concrete relation to history which is intrinsic to the Christian faith.

B. Modern Perspectives

The problem felt most keenly by modern thought was that faith in the theological understanding of the term was based on the definite historical reality, on historical testimony and not on metaphysical truth. The question, therefore, was how the freedom and originality of the act of faith and its supposedly universal validity could be maintained in view of this basis.

Does this not imply a direct and inexplicable transition from the dimension of the historical to that of the absolute assent of faith (cf. G. E. Lessing)? How is the gap between the contingence of a historical truth and the absoluteness of the act of faith to be filled? It cannot be within the power of historical thinking to close the gap, since a "qualitative" decision cannot be attained by "quantitative" means (Kierkegaard). It would also be contrary to faith to consider it as the prolongation of historical knowledge. Lessing sought to bridge the gap between the historical and the absolute by a "leap". Kierkegaard tried to express this leap in positive terms by describing it as "decision", since on the plane of the "objective" the synthesis between history and faith could only be a paradox. "Subjectivity" was the only possible meeting-point of the two. If paradoxical decision alone is able to mediate between faith and history, existence itself is then a paradox.

Lessing's schema for the interpretation of the relationship between faith and history supposes that the historical element is a random one, lying outside all that is essential to the self-understanding of man. And the schema for relating faith to history is that of the subject and the object. But this approach fails to recognize that history and the historicity of the self and its relation to the world are constitutive elements of the existence of man. But if man in his faith and his freedom is a historical being and essentially so, as regards his understanding of being, world and self, it follows that the relationship of faith and history must be mediated by this interpersonal historicity of man.

If what is at stake for man in his relationship to history is his own very self, this relationship is such as to found and permeate his existence. Then, since historical relationship implies at once historical understanding, the latter is not a subsequent extrinsic addition to man's act of faith. If existence itself is the medium in which faith and history are mediated, and if faith is an act of historical existence, it follows that with this mediation a plane has been attained on which alone the identity and difference of faith and history can be consciously discerned.

C. Faith and Historicity

The relationship of man to history by which he understands and interprets it has a primordial and permanent character, inasmuch as man is always history's target prior to all his questioning of history. Hence understanding of history is always self-understanding: as man is to history, so is he to himself. Understanding of and relationship to history form a primordial unity with self-understanding and selfhood, and this unity is a unity of encounter to such a degree that it is valid in both directions. But the relationship to history is prior to all historical "factual" interests, that is, it is of an ontological character. It is only if the relationship of man to history is so primordial that it is the key to his self-understanding that man is referred once more in his search for himself to the *a posteriori* of history which cannot be logically deduced.

But then history, in spite of its *a posteriori* character, has also the *a priori* character of the existentially significant. This means that what is essential for man can also be historical and that the historical can likewise be essential. Hence the function of the historical understanding arising from the confrontation with history is not to allow man to dispose of himself, but to make man totally responsive, with regard to a possibility of selfhood which is a primordial question of man.

Hence historical understanding always has the formal structure of the act of faith. For man has always lived his historical existence and assimilated it before he reflects consciously upon it. But this reflection is not confined to generalities. It is concrete, that is, performed in a way which involves objectifiable elements of a definable "material" nature and hence "history" in the sense of records of the past.

Hence (contrary to Bultmann, at least as generally understood) the explicitation in terms of the records of the past is of the essence of historical understanding and hence of the self-understanding of faith. History is misunderstood both where it is watered down to a merely objectivated record of past facts and where it is made to lose its historical reality, existentialized or ideated.

It is only when history and the record of the past are envisaged in their unity of structure that this concrete character of historicity and history is safeguarded. It is only then that faith can give an account of its foundation. Hence man's being referred to history is not a special case in the sphere of the religious self-understanding of man. It is not simply a *de facto* condition arising *a posteriori* out of the traditional understanding of faith. It is antecedently and fundamentally clear that it must be so, by virtue of the openness of man (in his metaphysical *a priori* condition) to the factual realm which founds his existence. It follows that faith's being history-centred, as regards the historical free act, is only the supreme instance of this basic condition of human existence, in which man always finds himself as a dialogal-historical reality.

D. The Self-Justification of Christian Faith

Thus Christian faith is always within the framework of the articulate history-centredness of "faith" in general. But it is not a mere instance, not even merely the supreme instance of such historicity. It also sees itself as at once the judgment upon history and the incalculable fulfilment which surpasses history's trend. Hence it cannot be content to regard itself as merely one way among others of rendering articulate such readiness to believe. It finds itself commanded to communicate itself to all. But for this very reason the problem of historical self-justification becomes most tryingly acute for faith.

Nonetheless, the structure of this justification does not differ from that which has been outlined above. It is a personal justification, which does not mean giving individual feelings and prejudice free rein, but it is of a personal, objective and historical nature. Take for instance the actual ("historical") relationships of contemporaries. Their openness for each other, and its justification, can be seen to be a combination of direct "personal evidence" and deduction from things done and said – a combination which is absolutely intrinsic to such contacts. The peculiar nature of such personal evidence with its combination of direct and indirect factors cannot be adequately described by the word "paradox". For at least insofar as paradox affirms an antagonism between the two factors and hence turns the difference into opposition, it fails to do justice to the essence of the personal which manifests itself precisely by self-communication by means of works, things and words. And then again, the special nature of such personal evidence is not properly understood if it is treated as rational verification and logical proof, since this would be to misunderstand the essential difference between the two spheres. The difference is of course admitted, and indeed gives rise to the very problem in question, namely, how even a fully valid proof on the basis of "facts" cannot be the foundation of the strictly personal assurance. But then the error is made of demanding for this personal assurance a proof which would be on principle of the same nature.

Even a personal relationship where a period of time intervenes is characterized by the twofold structure of its self-enlightenment. It differs, no doubt, from a relationship with contemporaries, but we must bear in mind that the contemporary relationship is not merely "subjective", direct, but also "objective", even in the sense of being determined by things and works; and that the historical relationship (to a figure in the past) is not merely historical, in the sense of involving also the records of the past, but also – inasmuch as a matter of history and records – direct, personal and "contemporary". This structure can be verified for the relationship established through the various degrees of mediation to the founder of the faith himself, and it also holds good for the channels of this mediation. These channels are witnesses whose testimony is given with probative force: with proofs personally and objectively "verifiable", just as the self-revelation of the founder himself is given in the power of the Spirit and of signs. While it is true that man is always predisposed to the experience of faith when thus addressed, his expectation is not simply the norm or law for such an utterance. The revelation fulfils his hope by going beyond it, and by doing so modifies it. In consequence, the Christian faith can point to the general structure of belief and the relevant reality justifying this readiness to believe in each case, when demonstrating against unbelief that its faith is reasonable. Nonetheless, it cannot strictly speaking justify its absolute claim and its validity in the eyes of others, since this claim of the reality to which the believer appeals can only be experienced by virtue of the reality itself and of the encounter with it (which, however, must be mediated through the testimony – a testimony once more both personal and embodied in things).

Thus the foundation of faith for the believer himself (and its justification as hope [1 Pet 3:15] with regard to others) must be distinguished from the "missionary" justification of the call to faith which he addresses to others. Nonetheless, this distinction is only a minor one in the framework of the problems envisaged here. In both forms of justification, the Christian must allow the factually historical its full rights and uphold its permanent significance for the faith (as against a merely "existential interpretation"). But then again, this factual history is only "probative" as a moment in a total personal relationship. This unity of the factual and personal is not confined to faith or the believing subject. It is also there, and functioning as the foundation, on the side of revelation – as the unity of the God who speaks in history and his *incarnate* Word. And these two aspects again, faith and revelation, must not be considered separately, but as moments of the identity-in-difference of the comprehensive event of grace in which God both imparts himself and enables man to respond to his self-communication. Hence in this complex event of revelation and faith, what is personal in the event comes about only through and in the fact, while on the other hand the "literal text" of the facts are at once read and understood in the "Spirit" – the Spirit who is both the spirit of the believer and the Spirit of God who frees and sustains him, who searches the depths (1 Cor 2:10), who is the Lord (2 Cor 3:17). In the light of his experience of this Spirit, the believer can now in fact go beyond the "justificatory" foundation of his own faith to "impose" on others the "missionary" foundation of his faith, since his faith gives him the conviction that this revelatory event – the structure of which has been described above – has already included all others within its scope, in a very fundamental way, in keeping with the universal salvific will of God.

From another point of view, the complex structure of the event as here revealed can again be demonstrated by the relationship between the *fides qua* and the *fides quae creditur*. The two acts are not to be opposed to one another but must be regarded as two intrinsically combined moments, not only in the individual believer but also in the social realization of these acts. This means that it would be wrong to contrast an existenti*el*-individual *fides qua* with some supposed opposite which would be a *fides quae* as a fixed deposit preserved by the Church. The personal and the ecclesiastical quality is proper to both these moments and in this way to faith as a totality. In consequence, the task of the justification of the Christian faith in its own eyes is never either merely the affair of the believing individual, nor again just that of the Church in its magisterium and (fundamental) theology. It is the common task of "both". This is true of the analytical, speculative foundations, of the self-justification of the truth which comes about as one "does" it (Jn 3:21) and of its attestation to those outside by means of mutual love (Jn 13:35). In this threefold self-justification of the faith, more is manifest than just the believer or the community of believers in the attestation of faith. He who is believed is also attesting himself, not just as the object of faith, but as once more himself the source of faith. In this testimony he is directly at work to convey his historical summons and to bring about the historical response of the believer in faith and in history.

Adolf Darlap

FAITH AND KNOWLEDGE

The relation between faith and knowledge is frequently formulated as follows: to believe means the same as not to know, or to know only provisionally, partly or superficially. This is not only an indication of the difference between the two spheres, but represents a definite characterization of faith as inferior. If knowledge is taken to mean well-founded and certain understanding, and if understanding indicates mental assimilation of that which is, and if the substantiation and certitude of understanding rests upon one's own insight and experience, then faith would appear to be hopelessly inferior to knowledge. Faith would then expressly mean the renunciation of one's own experience and insight and the acceptance of assertions and opinions on the basis of the authority and the testimony of another; it would appear that faith would then be greater the more it refused to see, the blinder it was. And finally, it would seem that the reality with which faith is concerned – especially faith in God and Christian faith – is the sphere of the invisible (cf. Heb 11:1), the inaccessible and the non-verifiable: all that which seems to border on the unreal.

For an individual in such a situation, however, there remain (we are told) but two possible ways of acting. He can practise a sort of double book-keeping in which truth would have two forms, or in which he would attempt so to separate faith and knowledge, both in the act and in the object, that a bridge between them would be impossible. The other and more cogent possibility (we are again told) consists in this, that one should attempt to elevate that preliminary and inferior understanding which faith offers to a knowledge based upon insight, and that one should relinquish all the assertions and claims of faith that are not capable of this or conflict with such knowledge.

1. *History of the problem*. It is significant that in the Bible, and especially in the NT, there is no evidence of such an opposition between faith and knowledge, in which the latter is taken to mean well-founded or certain understanding. On the contrary, faith and knowledge as they are represented in the Gospel of John, for example, are one; both concepts are alternately used and are interchangeable.

In the first centuries of Christendom, those Christians who came to the faith from philosophy understood faith as the true philosophy (Justin), or as the only proper knowledge. The theological thought of the Middle Ages formulated the proximity and inner unity of faith and knowledge in the well-known sentences: "I believe, that I may understand (comprehend)", and "I understand, that I may believe". Thomas Aquinas, who was sensitive to the difference between faith and knowledge, included them both in the unity and entirety of truth – truth cannot contradict truth – anchoring them both in God, the source and goal of faith and knowledge.

As this unified and ordered picture was more and more blurred toward the end of the Middle Ages and at the beginning of the modern period, and as tragic and painful conflicts broke out between theologians and the representatives of the new advance of the natural sciences (Galileo), the way was prepared for the mutual alienation and division between both. This division was decisively deepened and encouraged by the philosophy of early modern times oriented as it was toward the autonomy of reason. This was even more the case as knowledge and science in the strict sense came to be considered by philosophy to be possible only in the realm of experience, mathematics and the natural sciences, and as the natural sciences (and later also history) put forward "certain" findings as contradictory to the assertions of faith and of revelation. The programme of the critical philosophy of Kant, to limit knowledge "to make room for faith", expressly formulated, rationalized, and made effective use of such a dualism between faith and knowledge. Similar to this, though from other motives, was the intention of Jacobi, who wished to remain a heathen in his intellect, and a

Christian in his heart. The philosophy of German Idealism (especially Hegel), on the contrary, attempted to achieve complete speculative penetration of the Christian faith and to "sublimate" it in the form of knowledge and understanding. There were not a few theologians of this period who accepted this programme and who tried to support it from revelation. In the course of the 19th century, the separation, or at least the dualism, between faith and knowledge was upheld especially among the upholders of the theory of science, which claimed that knowledge is only possible in the spheres of mathematics and the natural sciences. Here eventually the natural sciences expanded to a scientific world-view and claimed to have the answer to any question. This was especially accentuated when a definite philosophy added its weight to these claims, or where the Christian faith was characterized as an ideology furnished with myths.

Our own day has seen a change in this approach insofar as natural science, through its foremost representatives, no longer claims to be a totally comprehensive view of life, and expressly recognizes its limits. Scientists claim competence only within that part of reality which is covered by the instruments and methods of science, and admit that science leaves room for an answer and, indeed, looks out for one, which it cannot of itself give.

No doubt, the answers to these questions are denied the character of true knowledge: they are relegated to a realm of faith distinct from scientific knowledge, or to that of a metaphysics which is discounted as merely subjective opinion. Present-day philosophy, especially existential philosophy, and personalism show ever more clearly what place and what importance is to be given to faith. From these points of view, however, Christian faith is again called in question as one kind of faith opposed to philosophical faith (K. Jaspers) and a new dualism of incompatibility is asserted because both are concerned with the ground and totality of existence.

2. *The notion of faith.* To see clearly in this matter, it is well to expound the genuine concept of faith. The basic form of faith is indicated in the statements: I believe you; I believe in you. To believe some*thing* is but the secondary form of this. From this it is clear that faith is primarily and properly not a relation of man to things, propositions, or formulas, but a relation to persons. And this relation is directed in particular to knowledge of the person. Faith is the manner and means by which we gain an understanding approach to a person. This is so true that without faith the reality and the mystery of the person remains closed in its most profound and real sense.

A person is not really known as he is by being taken under control and analysed by tests or experiments – such knowledge would remain more or less peripheral and superficial and could never lead to what is most significant: the person and his own unique existence. Knowledge of a person on the lines of mathematics or the natural sciences is inappropriate because such methods are inapplicable. A person in his true nature, in his very self, is only known if he allows himself to be known, if he discloses himself.

Faith opens the way to knowledge of the person. The one who believes shares in the self-disclosure of another, in his life, in his thought, in his knowledge, understanding, love and desire; he shares the manner and the way in which another sees himself and the world of things and of men. The "I believe you" necessarily includes certain particulars, in the form of: I believe what you say, what you ask, what you promise. Thus, faith implies also a faith in assertions, a faith in the sense of "holding to be true" certain statements and propositions of a very definite and concrete kind. But this belief in "truths" and "propositions", in "something", is not an isolated and unrelated belief; it is encompassed and sustained by the person who is believed. Whatever its particular object is, any related statement of the kind "I believe that . . ." is based upon the competence and the authority of the person at the centre of this belief, and upon the assurance derived from these.

Faith is therefore not a preliminary, partial, or approximate type of knowledge. It is authentic knowledge; it is understanding in that realm which is primarily not concerned with world, things, and objects, but with the person. Faith is not an unsure and unfounded type of knowledge. It is certain and well-founded: but it bases itself in the competence and trustworthiness of the one who is believed, and it is based on his insight and knowledge. From this it is clear how one-sided it is to consider knowledge as certain only there where one's own experience and insight can reach. With such a limitation, important areas of the reality of our knowledge would be eliminated or closed: the sphere of the person and of persons – consequently of men and of all that is human.

The discrediting of faith as a type of knowledge could only occur where reality was restricted to things, and these reduced to quantity and phenomena. This blindness to the reality of the person also occurred where knowledge was accepted only in the form of logic, mathematics, and the natural sciences. It is only possible to set faith and knowledge in opposition or contradiction when one is blind to the diversity and multiformity of what is, and when one lacks the realization that to the diversity and multiformity of what is, there corresponds not one but a multiformity of methods, of ways and approaches to knowledge.

Faith is not a compelling type of knowledge, though it is one that is thoroughly well-founded. It is founded on an act of confidence and dedication with regard to a person, who through his self-disclosure offers fellowship and participation with himself. But this act of trust must itself be grounded on something. It is grounded upon the credibility of the one to whom belief is given, on the extent and the manner in which he legitimates his authority and competence. He must justify his claim to be believed. The evidence of credibility is the condition and presupposition of faith and of the knowledge which it implies.

3. *Faith and knowledge in theology.* With this, the basic characteristics of faith are indicated and these apply also to what is called faith in a special sense – faith in God and Christian faith. This must be so if this faith is also to be a human act, as it claims to be. It is also true of Christian faith, and true in a particular way, that it is not primarily and originally a relation to things and propositions, but a personal act, a confrontation between the human "I" and the divine "You". Its primary formula also runs: "I believe you." This faith in God is definitely put forward as knowledge of the reality and of the mystery of God. There are indeed traces that lead from the world as a created reality to God himself. They lead to his existence and give knowledge of attributes of his nature. But, properly considered, these traces do not lead into the inner mystery of God himself, for the world is not God but only his work. And, what is even more important, creation is already and essentially a kind of revelation and self-disclosure of God (Rom 1:18). Faith is thereby already invoked as the manner in which we acknowledge in creation not only rational order and laws, but the very word of God.

If, over and above that, it is possible and essential to arrive at a knowledge of God as he is in himself, a knowledge of the inner being of God, of his life, his mystery, his eternal designs for our salvation, of what it means for man that God is the ground and last end of his existence – then this is only possible if God reveals and discloses himself other than in the way in which he does in creation. It is thus that we must understand the statement that is so important for the analysis of faith in God; God is not only the object and goal of faith, but he is, through his very self-revelation, its principle and ground.

If the revelation of God culminates in Jesus Christ, then faith as Christian faith means fellowship with the person of, and in the knowledge of, Christ. Faith is a pre-eminent way in which the biblical words are fulfilled: "It is no longer I who live but Christ who lives in me" (Gal 2:20). Christian faith is knowledge and understanding in the most eminent and elevated sense of the word: it is access to the reality of God who has spoken his ultimate word and accomplished his unsurpassable act of revelation in Jesus Christ. The Christian faith discloses a new reality for which a "conclusive" knowledge, which controls and checks on the basis of individual insight and experience and after the manner of mathematics and the natural sciences, is improper and incompetent. It is a reality which can neither be attained nor contradicted by such knowledge. To renounce or to exclude the knowledge which is heard and accepted in faith would mean that man robbed himself of his highest potentiality – and precisely with reference to knowledge. He would be barred from the supreme realization of his existence and personality and lose the possibility of expecting an articulate answer to the question of the principle and goal of existence.

In this act of faith the true existence of man is represented and realized: his existence as a created being capable of being addressed, as obedient, as a hearer of the word, and as man before God. From this one can form a definition of man: he is the being who is capable of faith. Faith describes the manner of human existence, the primary attitude of man before God, of the man who exists only through God. Only as a believer does man find himself.

If it is true that the confrontation of persons which is represented in the formula "I believe you" includes faith in certain assertions, it is true especially with reference to faith in God. It is all the more apposite in this case as the fragility, the limitation, the finitude and imperfection which are intrinsic to all men, even the greatest and noblest, are precisely what make possible, found and justify the unconditional and unhesitating character of faith. Faith considered as the acceptance of propositions is founded – and this is especially so of the truths of the Christian faith – upon the person who is believed. And in this way it does not have the isolated character of impersonal relations, the neutral and (non-existential) "it". Such truths are but a concrete and particularized form of how God expresses and communicates himself in revelation. From this it follows that faith in revealed truths is not founded primarily on the fact that they form a unified system and a structured whole which would be shattered by the denial of one of the statements, but on the fact that such a denial really signifies a mistrust and a non-acceptance, indeed, a rejection of God. It would call in question the basic act of faith represented in the form "I believe you".

If the presupposition of faith in general is the credibility of the person who is believed then it is necessary likewise to establish the credibility of the Christian faith. The whole question culminates in the question which runs through the whole event of revelation: "What do you think of the Christ? Whose son is he?" (Mt 22:42.) Is Christ one among many, or is he the unique revelation of God in his person, the Son of God in the exclusive sense – the Word made flesh who said of himself:

"He who has seen me has seen the Father" (Jn 14:9), of whom John said – and this is important to situate the question: "No one has ever seen God; the only Son, who is in the bosom of the Father, he has made him known" (Jn 1:18). Jesus Christ not only asserted the claim which is founded on the mystery of his history and his person, but rendered it credible. He did this through his life, through his destiny, through his word and work – and above all, through his death and resurrection to which the NT gives the testimony of faith and of history, and finally through his work in history up to the present day: the Church. Thus the question, "Who then is this?" (Mk 4:41), is answered, and the Christian's "I know whom I have believed" is given not a compelling proof, but a trustworthy basis and sufficient certitude. This still leaves room for the free decision of men to believe or not, and it demands – for the sake of faith – total commitment.

4. *Faith and science.* The question of faith and knowledge is especially acute and difficult with regard to the Church's pronouncements on faith and doctrine, and the conflicts with the assertions of the sciences which have actually arisen in the past and which in principle are always possible. Here we must note the following: the Church must not be separated from the revelation of God which culminates in Jesus Christ. The Church belongs to the concrete and particular element of revelation, it is part of the work of God who reveals himself in Christ and it is an object of the Christian faith. The Church is the work of Jesus Christ. In it Christ, through the Holy Spirit, is present and active in the world and in history in a new way. In the Church, the word and work of Jesus Christ are represented, actualized, and mediated in a new way in each age, so that men of every age may be contemporaneous with the revelation of God and with Jesus Christ. Christ promised to this Church that it would abide in the truth which he revealed to it, and that this his truth would abide in the Church. This enables us to recognize that faith in the comprehensive sense is made possible and mediated by the words and works of the Church. If the Church is all that is said of it here, then clearly it is above all the believing Church, indeed, the real subject of faith, and its pastors and teachers must be first and foremost listeners and believers. To try to attain revelation outside of the Church, whether it be simply without it or against it, basically rejects the concrete work and will of the God who reveals himself, and rejects the total dedication of faith.

It is also clear what the function of the Church is with regard to revelation. It has no new revelation to proclaim: it has rather to believe the revelation transmitted to it, to keep it, to guard it, to defend it. The Church must propose revelation and expound it anew in each age of history. In carrying out this task and performing this duty, the Church and its magisterium in the face of uncertainty, doubts and disputes, must express itself again and again in an authoritative way and articulate its pronouncements in the form of dogma. Such clear decisions are demanded of the Church and are part of its most essential tasks. It is also possible, nevertheless, for the Church as a whole to grow in the faith and in the understanding of the faith, to be led ever deeper into all truth in fulfilment of the promises which were made to it and to give testimony to this new understanding.

But when the believing and teaching Church proposes its doctrine, it is not lording it over or claiming to dispose at will of revelation and faith. It is a service in obedience to its Lord who called the Church to that activity and empowered it to carry it out. In the Church's obedient service of faith and revelation, which consists in its conservation, development and exposition, Christ himself continues his work: he keeps the Church true to himself and guarantees that the Church is the pillar and the ground of truth, against which the gates of death will not prevail. But because men carry out this work, and because Christ has entrusted his cause to men, this service will always fall short of its possibilities and will always be less than fully performed.

It is also especially true of the faith which the Church proposes for belief that such faith means both knowledge and understanding. It is the knowledge and understanding of that life and that reality which is opened up for us by the revelation of God in Christ for the sake of our self-understanding and salvation. It is also true here that between the faith and teaching of the Church, and the knowledge of natural reason and the sciences, there can be no final and insoluble conflict. If it nevertheless has actually arisen and threatens continually to break out anew, then the reason can only be that the perspective and different nature of the question in each sphere is not properly observed; it must be due to misunderstandings or trespasses with regard to the boundaries of faith or knowledge. In the case where conflict between the two has actually materialized, what is demanded is clarity concerning the real nature of faith and knowledge. It is necessary to examine whether or not the particular question is a genuine question of faith and revelation (here, for instance, the actual intention of the statements of Scripture are to be determined, the literary form and style, the difference between content, mode of representation, and means of expression). Likewise it is necessary to examine whether or not knowledge in such a case is really knowledge or only a hypothesis or opinion.

In principle, the conflicts can all be resolved, and the actual conflicts of past history could have been resolved. Burdensome though the past may be, it is a part of the way of faith and the way of man and of the Church. But there is a way out that leads to a possible solution and answer – and it is in the direction that we have tried to indicate here. Within the terms of the relations between faith and knowledge as they have been described here, a whole series of problems is eliminated from the very start, especially those that result from an inadequate conception of faith, or from a narrow and one-sided conception of knowledge, from a stunted conception of reality and above all from disregard of the person and personal activity. Problems are avoided which result from failure on one side or the other to observe the respective limits and spheres of competence. Finally, the problems are avoided which proceed from an incomplete or false understanding of what revelation is and of what faith intends to express in a particular and definite instance.

Heinrich Fries

FORMAL AND FUNDAMENTAL THEOLOGY

The special difficulty confronting dogmatic theology as a systematic scientific study of salvation history is that it has to combine science and history. It cannot be wholly concerned with a system of concepts, because it must address itself equally to God's saving activity in history. Nor can it deal adequately with this history in a static scheme, if it appeared (as Thomas Aquinas, for example, saw it formally in his *Summa*) to be a mere execution and application of such a scheme, because the essence of history, in which the formal element is revealed, is not really expressed in this way. On the other hand, it cannot simply be a pure report of the history of salvation, because a precondition for real historical understanding is an *a priori* sphere of essential insights, especially if a long history has to be understood as a single history. It cannot, moreover, simply report history because the preparation of this sphere of understanding in dogmatic theology cannot be carried out by a different and subordinate science and because, in the eschatological phase of this history, the supporting structures revealed in history (the hidden plan of salvation) have already been to a very great extent disclosed and have thus been made essentially intelligible. In this way, dogmatic theology is essentially an original unity and an irreducible duality of essential and existential knowledge, in accordance with man's being in history and God's free activity with a being capable of reflection. In any concrete presentation of this science, the duality and unity can possibly be made clearer if the systematic statement about the essence (which has eschatologically entered the final phase of revelation) of God and his plan of salvation (freely bestowed, but imparting a unity to history) is outlined first, followed by the historical report of the events in the time and space of salvation. If this is not done, experience has shown that sometimes the essential theology and at others the existential theology suffers. That part of dogmatic theology – or the aspect of the study under review – which considers the whole body of theological statements under the first aspect may be called "formal and fundamental" theology. This would distinguish it, on the one hand, from *fundamental* theology (the theological study of the rational justification of faith with reference to the datum of the Christian revelation) and, on the other, from "special" dogmatic theology as the theological presentation of the history of salvation as such. This formal and fundamental theology would be "formal" in its elaboration of the final, lasting basic structures of the history of salvation (the fundamental relationship between God and the creature, the concept of the personal revelation in word and deed as such, the concept of redemptive revelation, and so on). It would be "fundamental" in its provision of these formal categories as a means of understanding the history of salvation and – possibly in a special section and in close proximity to fundamental theology proper – if it confronted this universal and formal essence of Christian revelation with the formal structures of man's spiritual life. This history of salvation takes place, after all, within the life of man's spirit – as the "foundation" – and penetrates deeply into it. It is also from man's spiritual life that access to the history of revelation has to be established (but this has to be done, not as in fundamental theology proper, but in regard to the formal structures of this access).

Karl Rahner

FORM CRITICISM

I. Form Criticism

Contemporary scientific views on the literature of the Old and New Testaments are to a large extent based on the results of the form criticism of our own century. This state of affairs makes it incumbent upon all who intend to adopt a responsible attitude toward the Bible to acquire a basic knowledge of the "methods of form criticism", as well as of the results achieved by means of them for the "history of forms" in biblical writings. The official teaching of the Church lays upon scholars the task of scientifically investigating and interpreting sacred Scripture in order "that as many ministers of the word as possible may be equipped to impart the nourishment of Scripture to the people of God in a truly beneficial manner". It enumerates a series of "suitable methods" by which this task is to be accomplished, and in particular the method of form criticism (cf. Vatican II, *Dei Verbum*, arts. 23, 12). For our understanding of the synoptic gospels the form-critical approach is the "indispensable key". It may be said without exaggeration that "unless we begin by determining the form and history of the individual units of tradition in the synoptic gospels, we can achieve no understanding of them whatever" (I. Herrmann).

1. The place of form criticism in the history of biblical scholarship lies between the period which was dominated by literary criticism and the new phase which has opened, characterized by the "history of redaction". About the turn of the century a certain "discontent with mere literary criticism" (H. Zimmermann), together with a new awareness of the linguistic aspects of the biblical texts, which were derived for the most part from religious and popular traditions, led to a preoccupation with the pre-literary stage of tradition. NT scholars followed the trail which OT scholars (especially H. Gunkel and his school) had already blazed. These NT scholars adopted a new approach, investigating the texts from the aspect of oral tradition, the form in which they had initially been transmitted, and the marks of which they still bore. This approach was used especially in research into the synoptic gospels.

a) At the beginning of the present century J. Weiss declared explicitly that the investigation of the literary forms of the gospels and of the individual groupings of material in them was one of the "tasks for contemporary scientific research into the NT" (*Aufgaben der neutestamentlichen Wissenschaft in der Gegenwart* [1908], p. 35). But his predecessor, J. G. Herder, had already "recognized for the first time the problems involved in form-critical research into the gospels" (W. G. Kümmel). Another predecessor towards the end of the previous century was F. Overbeck, who had called for "a history of the forms" of "the primitive literature of Christianity" (*Historische Zeitschrift* 48 [1882], p. 423). Before the First World War two classical scholars, P. Wendland (*Die urchristlichen Literaturformen* [1912] and E. Norden (*Agnostos Theos. Untersuchungen zur Formengeschichte religiöser Rede* [1913]), set in motion form-critical researches into the NT in certain important directions. After the War, the period of the form-critical approach really began.

b) K. L. Schmidt paved the way to the analysis of forms in the individual pericopes with his work on the "framework of the history of Jesus" (1919). This work showed that the gospels were edited compilations of previously isolated pieces of tradition, and also of earlier partial compilations which had been handed down either orally or in writing. Next the methods of form criticism were perfected, especially by M. Dibelius (*Die Formgeschichte des Evangeliums* [1919; 4th ed., 1961]) and R. Bultmann (*Geschichte der synoptischen Tradition* [1921; 6th ed., 1964], E. T.: *The History of the Synoptic Tradition* [1963]). By these means an attempt was made to establish the laws of oral tradition by which the individual units of tradition had been developed and had acquired their distinctive shape. "To trace these laws back, to make the emergence of those small units comprehensible, to work out and explain their characteristics, and in these and similar ways to arrive at an understanding of the tradition – this is what it means to investigate the gospel form-critically." (M. Dibelius) R. Bultmann, whose approach is more strongly influenced by comparative religion and historical criticism, formulated the truth "that the literature in which the life of a given community, even the primitive Christian community, is reflected, springs out of quite definite social conditions and needs, which produce a quite definite style and quite specific forms and categories" (cf. E. T., p. 4). In the past fifty years the methods of form criticism have been tested over wide areas of Old and New Testament texts. Today reliable instruments are available to the practitioners of form criticism in the manuals of K. Koch (*Was ist Formgeschichte? Neue Wege der Bibelexegese* [1964]; this work is orientated more strongly towards the OT) and H. Zimmermann (*Darstellung der historisch-kritischen Methode* [1967]). Both authors provide full and detailed accounts of the "history of redaction", which currently appears as a supplement to the form-critical approach, and which enquires into the literary form and theological meaning of the final redaction of the gospels or other NT writings.

2. The following points may be mentioned as instances of the most important *aspects and results* of the work of form crticism today. For the understanding of biblical literature, of the process by which it emerged, of its transmission and its content, a knowledge both of the smallest units ("formulae") and the slightly larger ones ("forms"), as well as of the larger literary forms which embrace these ("types", literary genres), is indispensable. Once light has been thrown upon the history of the genres as well as on the "form" of the smaller units, the possible or probable *Sitz im Leben* ("social setting", actual community background) of these can be determined, and this in turn lead to a reconstruction of the history of their transmission, and thereby to a history of the development of the biblical writings as a whole.

a) In OT research the study of types of psalms, for instance, has led to a deeper understanding of the praise of God offered by the people of the old covenant. Once we have established that these chants belong to the various ceremonies of Israelite worship, to royal feasts or to the sapiential tradition, we learn to understand the situation of the psalmist in each case, the atmosphere surrounding him as he prays and other points. The prophetic writings can be more effectively interpreted if we pay attention to the various forms of discourse which are employed (messenger-sayings, narratives in the first and third person, reproaches, threats, exhortations, promises, etc.). We can gain a deeper insight into the transmission of ancient Israelite law if we notice the various forms (including those used by other nations) in which they are couched (for instance, apodictic or causuistic formulations).

b) In the treatment of the NT writings the form-critical approach has also proved fruitful. Among the four categories of NT writings (gospels, acts, epistles, apocalypse) two are of Christian origin: "gospels" and "acts of the apostles". The individual synoptic gospels are actually considered by the more recent exponents of the "history of redaction" as each belonging to a particular genre of its own (Mt: βίβλος; Mk: εὐαγγέλιον; Lk: διήγησις). There is some hesitation as to how form-critical methods should be applied to the Johannine writings (the most important applications are to Rev with its hymnic, prophetic and apocalyptic forms), but side by side with this goes more intensive work on the *Corpus Paulinum* (epistolary forms, thanksgiving, autobiographical passages, ancient formulae, proofs from Scripture, doxologies, hymns, lists, etc.; cf. B. Rigaux, *Saint Paul et ses Lettres* [1962]). This has yielded copious information, so that a comprehensive form-critical account of the Pauline writings has become a real *desideratum*.

c) Up to the present it is the traditional material of the synoptic gospels that has been most clearly defined. This material has been divided into the two basic categories of sayings and narrative tradition. In the transmission of sayings a distinction is drawn, e.g., between prophetic sayings, wisdom sayings, legal sayings, parables, "I" sayings, "Imitation" sayings, and also composite sayings. In the narrative tradition one distinguishes paradigms, controversies, miracle stories, historical narratives, the Passion narrative, and also composite narratives (cycles, summary narratives, etc.). The basic insight that it is real life (i.e., as regards the tradition of the primitive Church, the complex forms of life in the early Christian communities) which creates the variety of forms permits us to deduce from the distinctive kind of form its *Sitz im Leben*, though admittedly it is not always easy to determine this, especially as it may have changed several times in the early stages of transmission, e.g., when an isolated unit of tradition was subsumed under a more comprehensive category, or even as soon as a saying of Jesus was made to serve the early Christian preaching. Today in general a threefold *Sitz im Leben* can be deduced for the "Jesus" tradition: Jesus himself, the tradition of the primitive Church, the gospel redaction. Again for each individual *Sitz im Leben* various factors corresponding to the forms can be recognized. For instance, in the case of Jesus one may think of a dispute with his adversaries or the instruction of his disciples. In the case of the tradition of the primitive Church one may think of its missionary, catechetical, disciplinary or liturgical interests. In the case of the evangelists one may think of the literary and theological aims which they set themselves, these again being also determined by the needs of the ecclesiastical region in which each evangelist lived.

d) For the historical reconstruction it is important that one should carefully trace one's way back from the most recent *Sitz im Leben* to the earliest (which can be established at times not only for the evangelists and the Church tradition, but even for Jesus and his immediate disciples). Here the distinction between the literary form and the historical testimony it contains must be strictly observed, especially as the tradition has been shaped more by theological interests than by historical or biographical ones. The question of the historicity of the material handed down is rendered neither superfluous nor impossible by the form-critical approach to the text, but is assigned its proper place as the last question. In view of the kerygmatic interests of tradition, the historical question is not the most urgent theological one.

e) Form criticism has shown that the NT writings as a whole documentate the preaching Church and are the testimonies of faith. Thus by their very nature they demand to be investigated for their preaching message, for the faith to which they bore witness. Form criticism can sketch at least in broad outline the history of early Christian preaching and early Christian witness to the faith. Thus it contributes not only to our understanding of the NT (like the OT) writings but throws light also on the beginnings of the community of believers which produced these writings and is responsible for guarding them to this day. In this sense it also contributes to the Church's present understanding of itself.

Rudolf Pesch

II. Genus Litterarium

1. *Definition.* The problem of the *genus litterarium* of a writing is not confined to biblical exegesis. In French literature, for example, in the 17th and 18th centuries, the theory of the *genres littéraires* and of the distinctions between them occupied an important place. In this context lyrical, dramatic, epic, comic and tragic *genres* were spoken of. The "classicists" attempted to lay down exact rules, against which the "romanticists" protested. Today an attempt is being made to reach back beyond the literary to the "social phenomenon". The *genus litterarium* is regarded as "a collective form of thinking, feeling and self-expression which reflects a whole

civilization" (A. Robert). Thus it corresponds somewhat to style in the plastic arts, which is a function of a whole complex of circumstances (materials employed, predominant conception, etc.) which every architect, painter or sculptor must necessarily take into account if he is not to meet with incomprehension. The genre evolves with the life of the milieu with which it is so closely linked. When a work belongs to a civilization other than our own, it is dangerous to pass judgment upon it in terms of the literary genres which are familiar to us and it becomes very necessary to determine the laws which govern the genre in question.

2. *History of the question of literary genres in biblical exegesis.* No exegete has ever questioned the existence of various *genera litteraria* in the Bible: lyrical, didactic, historical, etc. No one has ever denied that the truth of a poetic composition, a parable or an allegory is one thing, while that of a historical narrative is another. Many scholars have set themselves to determine the laws of these different genres among the ancient Semites. It has been noted, for instance, that the psalms contain chants of various kinds, which are subject to rules determining their style, structure and content, rules which are also found more or less universally throughout the ancient Near East. In the same way the legal texts, the covenant formulae or the preaching of the prophets follow norms which are more or less fixed, the study of which is indispensable to exegesis. Certainly biblical revelation very often breaks out of this basic structure, but it is precisely when we compare biblical forms with the others that the originality of the former are thrown into relief (cf. J. Harvey in *Biblica* 47 [1962], p. 195), the more so since "views which are very different in themselves can lie concealed under external forms which are identical", or better, perhaps, "almost identical" (Robert–Feuillet, I).

3. *The magisterium of the Church.* a) *Before the encyclical Divino Afflante Spiritu.* In practice among Catholics the question has been put forward principally, if not quite exclusively, in relation to the books which are presented in the Bible in the form of historical narrative. Formerly certain exegetes appealed to the literary genre to assimilate a number of biblical narratives to "myths" in the sense of the term then generally understood, or to fables devoid of any historical value. The magisterium of the Church at first showed itself extremely reserved; yet as early as the encyclical *Providentissimus Deus* Leo XIII (1893) had promulgated the principle by which Catholic exegesis was to be guided. St. Augustine had provided an excellent formulation of it long before. On the subject of the manner in which the Bible speaks of the "shape of heaven" he explains that "the sacred authors have omitted to treat of these problems of the scientific order because they do not impart to those who recognize them any information which is useful for the life of blessedness". More precisely, Augustine admits that the hagiographers know these things but says that "the Spirit of God who spoke by their mouths did not wish to teach men matters the knowledge of which could not be in any way profitable for salvation" (*De Gen. ad Litt.*, 1, 9, 20; *PL*, XXXIV, col. 270; *Enchiridion Biblicum*, no. 121, recalled by *Divino Afflante Spiritu, Enchiridion Biblicum*, no. 539, and by Vatican II in *Dei Verbum*, ch. III, no. 11, n. 5). The point of importance here is not so much the particular application as the reason which is adduced; according to the still clearer formulation of St. Thomas, "The Spirit did not wish to tell us through the authors whom he inspired any other truth than that which is profitable for our salvation" (*De Ver.*, q. 12, art. 2 corp., likewise adduced by Vatican II, *ibid.*). Certainly there is no

question (though this has sometimes been alleged) of restricting scriptural inspiration to certain privileged parts of the Bible. The point is rather to define exactly the end which God had in mind when he inspired the hagiographers, and in consequence the sense of Scripture as a whole. In technical terms the "formal object of revelation defines the object of the teachings provided by Scripture" (P. Grelot). This was in the very nature of things to point to one of the essential characteristics of all inspired Scripture precisely as inspired, and to define in some fashion what might be called, if the expression were not equivocal, the "inspired *genus litterarium*". (The formula comes from L. Billot, *De inspiratione Sacrae Scripturae theologica disquisitio* [4th ed., 1929], p. 166. By this he meant to rule out any recourse to the *genera litteraria* in order to interpret the narratives of the Bible.)

In 1905 the Biblical Commission visualized a possible application of this to history: in certain rare cases, not to be admitted as such except on the basis of solid proofs, the hagiographer could perhaps not have intended to relate history truly and properly so-called, but rather a parable, an allegory under the form and appearance of history, or rather to give his narrative a meaning which was far removed from the strictly literal or historical sense of the words (*Enchiridion Biblicum*, no. 161). Again in 1909 the Biblical Commission admitted, for instance, that in the narrative of the creation the sacred author had presented not scientific teaching as the "concordist" explanations supposed, but rather a popular description (*notitiam popularem*) adapted to the intelligences of the men of that period (*ibid.*, no. 342).

The expression *genus litterarium* had not yet been coined. It appeared for the first time in the encyclical *Spiritus Paraclitus* of Benedict XV (1920). Certainly the passage in question is intended directly to exclude "the *genera litteraria* which are incompatible with the full and perfect truth of the divine word"; but the encyclical only condemns an "abuse"; when it recognizes explicitly the "justice of the principles, provided that they are contained within certain limits", it seems to have in mind among others the principle of the *genus litterarium* (*ibid.*, no. 461).

b) *Pius XII and the encyclical Divino Afflante Spiritu.* The whole question was to define those limits, and specifically the extent to which the Catholic exegete could have recourse to the *genus litterarium* in interpreting a historical narrative. It is this problem that the encyclical of Pius XII (1943) *ex professo* investigates: the official introductions in introducing the passage actually employ a significant subtitle: "The importance of the *genus litterarium*, above all in the case of history".

After having defined what it called "the chief law of all interpretation", which is to "recognize and define what the writer intended to say" (*ibid.*, no. 557), the encyclical states that "in order to determine what the authors of the ancient Near East intended to signify by their words" it is not enough to have recourse to "the laws of grammar or philology, nor merely to the context". It is "absolutely necessary for the interpreter to go back in spirit to those remote centuries of Eastern history, and make proper use of the aids afforded by history, archaeology, ethnology and other sciences in order to discover what literary forms the writers of that early epoch intended to use, and did in fact employ" (*ibid.*, no. 558). The reason for this is also given: "To express what they had in mind the writers of the ancient Near East did not always use the same forms and expressions as we use today; they used those which were current among the people of their own time and place." Now the encyclical goes on to explain that it intends to refer not only to "poetical descriptions" or to "the formulation of rules and laws of conduct" but also to "the narration of historical facts and events" (*ibid.*). Nor does the encyclical hesitate to make this "investigation into the *genus litterarium* employed by the hagiographer" one of the most important tasks, and one which "cannot be neglected without great detriment to Catholic exegesis" (*ibid.*, no. 560).

c) *From the encyclical Divino Afflante Spiritu to Vatican II.* This directive, however, which has been called "one of the most striking innovations of the encyclical" (J. Levie), was deliberately confined to affirming the principle. In 1948 the Biblical Commission made an initial application of this principle to two problems, which were disputed at that time: the Mosaic authorship of the Pentateuch and the historicity of the eleven first chapters of Genesis. In this they took up and made more precise the replies given in 1909, which were concerned only with the three first chapters. In this connection the Commission declares that "the literary forms of these chapters do not correspond to any of our classic categories, and cannot be judged in the light of the Greek or Latin *genera litteraria*, or those of modern times". In consequence "their historicity can neither be denied nor affirmed *en bloc* without making an inappropriate application to them of the norms of a *genus litterarium* under which they cannot be classified" (*ibid.*, no. 581).

Two years later – and, moreover, in the course of referring to these declarations – the magisterium made a declaration which was still clearer and gave encyclical authority to its declarations (*Humani Generis*, 1950). With regard to these same eleven first chapters it declared: (i) that they "do not correspond in any strict sense to the concept of history upheld by the authorities of our own time"; (ii) that "at the same time they do belong in a true sense to the category of history"; (iii) that this sense "still remains to be explored and determined more precisely by exegetes" (*ibid.*, no. 618).

Thus for the OT the question of principle, and one of its most delicate applications, was virtually solved. But up to the present no application had yet officially been made to the NT. Many even denied explicitly that this principle could be applied to it. Hence the instruction of the Biblical Commission of 14 May 1964, *De historica Evangeliorum veritate*, begins by recalling the duty of the Catholic exegete concerning "the investigation of the *genus litterarium* employed by the sacred writer". It explains that this statement of Pius XII enunciates "a general rule of hermeneutics which must be observed in interpreting the books both of the Old and of the New Testament, given that the writers in composing their works had used modes of thought and writing which were current among their contemporaries". It then applies to the gospels the positive results which Catholic exegesis has achieved by using with due prudence the method of "form criticism".

It shows in particular how at each of the three stages of the transmission of the gospel message one has to take the *genus litterarium* into account. In fact even "when he was expounding his teaching by word of mouth the Lord followed the modes of thought and speech appropriate to his own time, and adapted his words to the mentality of his hearers". The apostles in their turn "bore witness to Jesus" and "faithfully related the events of his life and his words" but "with the fuller understanding which they themselves had enjoyed after having been instructed by the glorious life of Christ and enlightened by the light of the Spirit of truth". Furthermore they too, like Christ, "taking the condition of their hearers into account in their manner of preaching, adapted to that condition the terms in which they interpreted the words and actions of Christ". Thus, as the instruction says, they had recourse to various "modes of expression" (*variis dicendi modis*), some of which it enumerates: "catechesis, narratives, testimony, hymns, doxologies, prayers and other literary forms of this kind, which sacred Scripture and the men of that time were accustomed to use". Finally, the third stage, "this preaching, at first orally transmitted, was subsequently committed to writing in the four gospels for the good of the Churches according to a method adapted to the particular end which each evangelist had set before himself". For "the teaching and life of Jesus were not simply related merely for the sake of preserving the memory of them. They were preached in order to provide the Church with the foundation of its faith and the basis of its moral teaching".

Under these circumstances the exegete finds himself faced with the following task: his first duty will be to "investigate what the intention of the evangelist was when he related a given episode or recorded a given saying in a particular way, and again when he set these in a particular context, for the meaning of a statement also depends upon the context in which it is placed". It would be difficult to throw into stronger relief the importance of studying the *genus litterarium* in order to arrive at an accurate interpretation of the gospels.

d) *Vatican II and the constitution Dei Verbum.* This is the doctrine which the Council has recently confirmed in its Dogmatic Constitution on Divine Revelation, in ch. III with regard to the inspiration and interpretation of Scripture and in ch. V with regard to the historicity of the gospels.

The first passage treats *ex professo* of the *genera litteraria* of the Bible, and the terms in which it does this are particularly striking and clear. Having recalled the traditional doctrine concerning "the truth of Scripture deposited in the books of the Bible for our salvation" (art. 11) the constitution enounces the principle which the encyclical *Divino Afflante Spiritu* called "the chief law of all interpretation" and which precisely gives rise to the necessity of taking the *genus litterarium* into account: "Since God speaks in sacred Scripture through men in human fashion, the interpreter of sacred Scripture, in order to see clearly what God wanted to communicate to us, should carefully investigate what meaning the sacred writers really intended and what God wanted to manifest by means of their words" (art. 12). Now it would be impossible to establish what this intention of the writer was without "among other things having regard for the 'literary forms' ". It is in fact not only clear that "truth is proposed and expressed in different ways according to whether it occurs in a historical narrative, a prophecy or a poem", but the constitution speaks explicitly of "texts of history of one kind or another" (*textibus vario modo historicis*), thus affirming that there were many ways of relating a "historical" event. In other words, there were several historical genres. The controversy which had long set certain Catholic exegetes in opposition to one another on this point was solved.

It follows that the interpreter must "investigate what meaning the sacred writer intended to express and actually expressed in particular circumstances as he used contemporary literary forms in accordance with the situation of his own time and culture", and the reason for this is likewise given: "For the correct understanding of what the sacred author wanted to assert due attention must be paid to the customary and characteristic styles of perceiving, speaking and narrating which prevailed at the time of the sacred writer, and the customs men normally followed at that period in their everyday dealings with one another."

Finally the last paragraph (art. 13) discloses the ultimate basis on which this doctrine rests: it is a corollary of the mystery of the incarnation of the Word of God himself, an incarnation which took place at once in human nature and in human words: "The words of God expressed in human language have been made like human discourse just as of old the Word of the eternal Father, when he took to himself the weak flesh of humanity, became like other men."

In ch. V the constitution applies these principles to the gospels, taking up what is essential in the instruction of the Biblical Commission on the historicity of the gospels, a résumé of which we have given above. The Council asserts their historicity unambiguously, but at the same time it explains the sense in which it intends this term to be taken: for the evangelists are not content to record mere facts; their purpose was to show at the same time the significance of those facts as they themselves had perceived it most of all in the light of the event of Easter: "What Jesus said and did the evangelists handed on to their hearers with that clearer understanding which they themselves enjoyed after they had been instructed by the events of Christ's risen life and taught by the light of the Spirit of truth." (art. 19.) Further, "they have selected some things from the many which had been handed on, reducing some of these to a synthesis or developing some in view of the situation of their Churches, always in such a fashion that they told us the honest truth about Jesus". Thus the Council defines to some extent the essential characteristics of the literary genres of the gospels.

4. *Conclusion.* While therefore the constitution *Dei Verbum* envisages a study of the literary genre chiefly in its bearing on the inerrancy of Scripture (art. 12) or on the historicity of the gospels (art. 19), nevertheless it goes beyond the strictly apologetic attitude with which the problem had usually been approached up till then. In fact the exegete's reason for having recourse to the literary genre is not simply that he wants to solve the difficulties to which certain historical narratives in the Bible can give rise. In reality the study of the literary genre has a contribution to make to the exegesis of the Bible as a whole, that of the psalms, for instance, which occasioned the researches of Gunkel and of the prophetic or sapiential books or again the legal texts in the Pentateuch, and of course the Song of Solomon. Furthermore, a given book does not usually present only one literary genre, but is composed of elements which fall under widely different genres, to each of which special attention should be paid.

If, then, the meaning of words or formulae is always more or less conditioned by the literary genre of the passage in which they are found, as recent research has shown more and more clearly to be the case, it can be understood that the exegete, anxious as he is to obtain an accurate grasp of what God wished to say to us through the medium of the inspired writer, counts the study of the literary genre as one of his primary duties (*Enchiridion Biblicum*, no. 560). His faith in the inspiration of Scripture, the Word of God, far from deflecting him from such a task, makes it still more incumbent upon him.

FREEDOM

I. Philosophical

A. On the General and Philosophical Notion of Freedom

1. The concept of freedom is an analogous one, predicated in different ways of beings of very different types. The

various forms of attribution all agree, however, to a certain extent, not by defining the same specific content, but by indicating a formal relation which remains the same. This relation can be put negatively or positively. Negatively, freedom means "being free from", i.e., the relation of not being bound (to a given being or law), of being independent from something and of not being determined by a given principle of determination (*libertas a coactione*, freedom in the sense of not being forced). This negative concept is also a relative one, because every finite being belongs to a world and is related to other beings in the world. It may be free from direct relationships to this or that, but only because their places are taken by others. Beings, for instance, which are not inserted into civilization and history, which are therefore "free" from these relationships, are all the more fully involved in nature and the universe. Men who are free from links with the past are all the more fully asborbed by the demands and goals of the present. A being fully free in the negative sense could not be a being in the world: without relationships, fully isolated, it would be based on nothing and be nothing. Negation is always relative and presupposes a positive. If relative, negative freedom were conceived as an absolute, such a fully indeterminate being would be without a world and reduced to nothingness, or its complete indetermination would have to be replaced by full self-determination. If negative, relative freedom is thought out to its logical conclusion, it becomes the mere obverse of positive, absolute freedom; and such a being would be God.

2. Thus in contrast to the negative, relative concept, there is a positive, absolute concept of freedom. A being is positively free insofar as it is in possession of itself and possesses in this relationship the sufficient condition for all its being and relations. Here freedom means self-possession, being completely present to oneself, complete self-sufficiency. This was called by the Greeks autarky, the condition of having within oneself one's principle and goal, one's beginning and end. The Latin *libertas*, as *dominium in actus suos, dominium super se ipsum*, corresponds to the Greek autarky.

The decisive point is that autarky, not mere independence, but a positive relationship to self, is now the basis of selfhood and self-determination in the sense of being fully at one with oneself. It then becomes distinctive for the concept of person, which was developed in Christian thinking to designate this condition. A being is a person inasmuch as it is in possession of itself and is not possessed by another. For the Greeks, the freedom of autarky was a sign of the divine – that which, "thought of thought" (νόησις νοήσεως), thinking itself, is its own sufficient reason and end and hence is fully "blissful". Among the non-divine, man approaches this state most closely in "theoria", the pure state of blissful contemplation which is its end in itself. In Christian thought this mode of freedom was described by "hypostasis" and "'persona". Thus freedom and personality can be primarily predicated only of God, but secondarily of man as the being who in spite of being finite has a certain possession of himself and so participates to a certain degree in absoluteness. In this freedom of self-possession he is the *imago Dei*.

3. Human freedom is clearly neither merely negative and relative (*libertas a coactione*) nor fully positive and absolute (*dominium super se ipsum*). Man has some dominion over himself (*dominium super actus suos*) and so also over parts of the world. But he is nonetheless inserted into the world and dependent on the beings among which he finds himself, upon which he exercises his faculties and dispositions, while he is also dependent on the laws of the world to

which he remains subject in all his lordship.

Thus freedom – which may also be attributed in a certain negative and relative sense to infra-human beings, while as positive and absolute is proper only to the infinite person of God – is an analogous concept in general. But so is the concept of human freedom in the strict sense. Here too it has many senses, which are again united by the double relationship – the negative one of a certain isolation with regard to other beings and to oneself, and the positive one of a certain dominion over other beings and oneself. This combination of isolation and power, being "free from" and "free to" constitutes human freedom in its many different aspects.

4. The basic mode of human freedom may be called *libertas transcendentalis*, transcendental freedom, which is the fundamental propriety of man by which he alone can say "is". He can contrast all things with himself as "beings" and so comprehend them "in being", while he can also contrast himself with all things and comprehend himself as this other who is contrasted with all beings. Man has the faculty of "distancing" all things from himself and himself from all things and even from himself. He can objectivate all things and even himself. This universal distance is at once transcendence, "being over and beyond" every individual being and even himself qua individual. It is the possibility of absolute reflection, a possibility which presupposes a footing in the absolute. Such freedom is identical with man's being as spirit. This freedom or spirit is the "light" by which man can illuminate all things, including himself. This light means that in finite man there is a formal absoluteness, which is called *participatio quaedam infiniti* by Thomas Aquinas. This formal, that is, empty transcendence of man is the fulfilment of negative freedom in a positive, though merely formal sense. This empty distance does not overcome or eliminate man's material bondage, but it gives it a new meaning.

5. It follows that man can never be deprived of this transcendental freedom, which is part of his "equipment" as man. But its emptiness and impotence point on to another mode of freedom.

Man is not simply there, he does not simply grow: he has "to be", he is a task absolutely imposed on himself, he has to decide to be himself or what he will be and there is no way in which he can evade this decision. Man has to move out of the distance of transcendental freedom and give himself, out of this distance, his own concrete form. This mode of freedom is called *libertas arbitrii*, freedom of decision (or "existenti*el* freedom").

How does decision take place? Man "is" in as much as he acts, posits actions for which he might have posited others. None of the actual acts is necessary, that is, none is determined by definitely assignable causes and explicable only by their effects. Each act proceeds from a state of indifference. This state has also been termed "freedom"; *libertas indifferentiae* indicates a state in which man must always act (by deed or omission) but in which several possibilities of action are offered, with regard to which man is indifferent.

6. This is the point taken up by polemics against the freedom of the will. Determinism maintains that such "indifference" does not exist. Like every other being, in every moment of his being man is totally "determined", and for every transition from a given state to another there is a sufficient reason – an adequate "motive" or some other "cause".

Indeterminism maintains, on the contrary, that there is real freedom of action (*libertas actionis*). Man is not merely the product of preceding and concomitant, conscious or unconscious "efficient" or "final" causes. He is also, conditioned though he may be, unconditioned initiator. Freedom qua initiative is called spontaneity. Hence indeterminism explains freedom of action by having recourse to *libertas spontaneitatis*. But since everything in the world of space and time is within the series of cause and effect (nothing is simply first) and hence explicable through its preconditions, man, when understood as free, is inexplicable on principle and supramundane though existing in the world. In his *libertas spontaneitatis*, man is seen once more as the image of God, reflecting the Absolute as first cause. Hence freedom seen as spontaneity is not an intramundane factor. For Kant, it is not a "phenomenon" and hence not a possible object of scientific enquiry. It is prior in nature to the world, unconditioned – what Kant calls "noumenal". Hence it cannot be attained by scientific, objectivating knowledge, though it can be experienced and evident in the exercise of the act (*praxis*).

But when the freedom of the will, freedom of action and of choice, is thus reduced to *libertas spontaneitatis*, the structure of the actual choice, the actual decision in favour of certain actions, is not sufficiently explained. Man has merely been shown to be at once conditioned and unconditioned, a being at once of the world and outside the world or absolute, at once contingent and non-contingent, or in Kantian terms, phenomenal and noumenal.

7. Freedom of choice and action, which transforms the state or indifference of freedom into the act of self-differentiation, could not be called freedom if it were merely arbitrary and random when spontaneity determines itself and the empty distance is filled. An arbitrary freedom would be no freedom: a man "free" in this sense would be leaving his actions at the mercy of mood, whim or chance. The freedom of a libertarian liberalism is baseless. It stems without any intrinsic necessity from the empty distance of transcendental freedom and from the power of a spontaneous initiative, but between these and the actual action lies the gulf of random wilfulness. However, the necessary derivation of the free act, if it is to remain free, can only mean a necessity of meaning, a consequence in meaning.

8. The choice falls upon a particular object because it is seen as valuable and preferred to other valued objects. But a value is always "valuable to": when we allow our choice to be motivated and explained by something "valuable" – and determinism is right in affirming that even the free choice is always reasoned, never baseless – this value is valuable and a "motive" for us, because we realize ourselves in it, and hence our essence. Hence the choice of actions and of the beings towards which these actions are directed is preceded by a basic choice, the only one which we can call decision in the strict sense: the choice of what we really will to be, the sketch-plan of our own essential form.

It is only within the horizon of this prior decision that anything at all is allowed in as a motive. By "essence" or "basic form" we mean the fundamental meaning, the fundamental attitude of man in the totality.

This totality, the only possible situation within which essences limiting each other can exist (Plato: an εἶδος is only an εἶδος in the κοινωνία τῶν εἰδῶν), is what we call the "world". It is the scene of constant changes. But we only say that the world changes when the structure of the basic meanings of beings, the basic structure of values, changes.

Hence affirmation of essence is also affirmation of the world for the time being in which this essence has validity and meaning. The existenti*el* decision for one's own being and purpose is therefore decision for one's own basic form (essential or eidetic freedom as choice of basic mode of life); and it is also decision for the world for the time being, for a form within the total order of being (ontological freedom as prior choice of world and acknowledgment of a given total order of being).

Thus the free act is fully determined by its motive, but the motive is only a motive in the pre-determination which is given by the basic choice of free decision. This freedom of decision enshrines the real personal freedom in which man's transcendental superiority to the world and his spontaneous priority to the world become concrete in active moulding of the world by means of free affirmation of the world and of essence. Freedom is only freedom in the concrete sense when all these freedoms are combined.

B. Social Structure of Freedom

1. Since freedom is transcendental distance and transcendent spontaneity, it is essentially part of man. But this "primordial" freedom is still only the basis for "existenti*el* freedom", the realization of man as person; it is not yet this personal being in actual reality. Transcendental and transcendent freedom are actuated only in the decision of existentiel freedom for its own essence as basic form (essential or eidetic freedom) and for the world as total order and order of being (ontological freedom). But the reality of world and essence is given only in the individual acts, whose accomplishment ("ontic" or "external" freedom) is subject to a number of conditions imposed on the individual by society. This corresponds to the way in which the more internal freedom of the existenti*el* affirmation of the world and essence depends on the knowledge had of them through a "basic education" transmitted by society. It follows that freedom is indivisible. Universal distance (transcendental freedom) cannot be separated from basic spontaneity (transcendent freedom), and both are actuated only in the decision for the world as offered by education (ontological freedom) and for the essence as experienced and conceived (eidetic freedom). In this last aspect the voice of conscience tests a given action for its aptitude to fulfil the essence. But the concrete action, in order to be real, involves things (as provided by nature and culture) and knowledge of their use (as provided through general technical education in the most general sense). This principle of indivisibility or totality proceeds necessarily from the analogous unity of the notion of freedom. A mere inner freedom or a purely transcendental or transcendent one is impossible, just as a merely external technical command of things cannot be called freedom, if it does not proceed from and return to that inner relationship to self of which we have spoken.

2. It follows that human freedom can never be a simple state of man or a specialized propriety; but neither is it simply the actuation of selfhood, pure act without history like the divine freedom. On the contrary, human freedom is history by its very nature: transition from indeterminate distance to decision with regard to world and essence, transition from decision to concrete act, the productive act, that which produces works. Action makes use of technical procedures to produce technical works in our environment. It brings out the intrinsic connections of things in truth as the work of science and of knowledge; or it transforms them in beauty as the work of art. Out of the possibilities of life together the free actions of man produce the works of fellowship, marriage and the family, society and state; from the God-given possibility of standing before God man becomes "Church". Thus actions are ordained to the works of truth, beauty human unity and social links and so on, and in this ordination they are wholly regulated by what is to be produced and achieved, that is, by the objective laws of action. Man is wholly claimed by the works to be done and the states to be achieved. He becomes truly a person by going freely out of himself

to throw himself into the work to be done. Hence the first step in the realization of freedom must be alienation. But since self-possession is the essence of human freedom, the "objectivation" of freedom in work must be followed by a further movement: the return which is the fetching in of the work in the act. All works and objectivations can only be said really to "be" insofar as they are modes of life, vital acts, absorbed into a life of freedom which has become through them more than a merely individual life. It is a life in which prison and work, selfhood and world, have attained one and the same existence. Hence apropos of human free acts Thomas Aquinas speaks of a *redditio completa in se ipsum*, a complete return upon one's self. Return presupposes going out: the *conversio ad phantasmata* of Thomas Aquinas, a man's turning freely to the sensible world.

Thus human freedom is not a state, as it is in things (freedom from this or that compulsion), nor is it as in God a pure act of self-consciousness. It is this history of outgoing and return, which was later described dialectically by Hegel and Marx (each in his own way) as extrapolation, alienation and conquest of extrapolation and alienation by return or synthesis. Hence the second basic principle of freedom is its history and historicity. If there is only freedom *as* history, it must be always *in* history, that is, the modes in which freedom is realized as history of union with the world and of absorbing the world and its works, must take on forms determined by the total history of the human race.

Metaphysically speaking, the principle of identity is latent in the principle of historicity as regards freedom: action and effect, person and work are the same thing. Action takes place in the effect, work "is" only a mode of being which fulfils the free man (by being re-absorbed). It is the one and the same act (not two acts) by which I am posited in the work and the work in me. Note the gnoseological formulation of this truth in Aristotle and Thomas Aquinas: *cognitum in actu et cognoscens in actu sunt idem*.

3. From the principle of historicity, the third basic element of freedom may be deduced, the principle of sociality. Most works could never be done by one man alone – truth in philosophy and science, beauty in art and literature, mastery in techniques, society and State, etc. Where free persons unite – simultaneously or generation after generation – for a common purpose, a task that can be done only by division of labour (in historical succession and in simultaneous association), freedom is the integration of a multitude of free achievements. The mode of co-operation, however, cannot be brought about by compulsion, if freedom is to remain freedom and the person a person. Freedom without permanent alienation is only possible in common consent to the acknowledged need of common action. Hence the principle of sociality does not lead to a doctrinaire and mechanical socialism but to solidarity.

4. Work, then, is always the common work in which a generation, a people, a number of generations find themselves. Nonetheless, the essential agent in freedom is always the individual person who freely disposes of himself. The proper and ultimate subject of freedom is the free individual, as Kierkegaard maintained again and again against Hegel. For freedom is the history of a person's "coming to himself", which culminates in fully conscious self-possession. In the strict sense, only the individual is with himself: self-possession can be predicated only analogously of a community or a people. Mastery over nature or foreign peoples may be exercised by a community. Mastery over self can be exercised only by the individual, and it is by reason of this self-possession that the individual is

called a person. Hence we may speak of a principle of substantiality or personality as regards freedom.

5. All these principles recur in the principle which regulates the mode of realization of freedom: the principle of subsidiarity.

Freedom in act is identical with the personality of the person: it is the person's mode of being. This mode of being is at once individual and supra-individual, conditioned and unconditioned. Conscious selfhood, as an act feasible only to the self, makes the individual unique as a person. He does not merely exercise a function on behalf of the supra-individual, he brings back the supra-individual to what matters throughout: the individual person is the absolute why and wherefore of all action. The common works of the realization of the person – science, art, technology, economics, politics, etc. – are not merely helps and means towards the self-realization of freedom and the person. Such a view would render them valueless. These common works are modes of self-realization, of the reality of freedom and the person. But as such modes they are forms taken by freedom, and they retain their meaning and purpose only by being referred back to the person and its reality. The free person can never be a means to something else. He is always the end of all else, and hence absolutely an end in himself. This is what constitutes the inviolable dignity of the person, as both Thomas Aquinas and Kant affirm. The principle of subsidiarity acknowledges the person not only as the real subject, origin and goal of freedom, but also as the primary agent in freedom, which must itself act to fulfil itself, in spite of all the helps provided by society, State and Church. What the person can do as an individually free being may not be taken over by the community; what the smaller unit, in which the individual still acts as his own man, can do may not be taken over by a larger community. And what can only be done by the largest community – the State as *societas perfecta* – must always be carefully referred back to the self-realization of the individual person. It may not be seen in isolation as "functioning" on its own behalf. The individual as such necessarily has a function in society. But man is not just an individual and a "functionary". Working does not absorb his whole self, but his works are modes of his being, realizations of his freedom, and as such are inserted into the historical process in which he returns to himself. Since the outgoing action of achievement is also under the law of the homeward return, the principle of subsidiarity is absolutely valid.

These five principles of Christian social philosophy are the consequences of a notion of freedom based on all the elements here discussed and not confined to any one of them. In the light of the foregoing, the rights of man are seen to be the rights of freedom, which apply not to the individual but to the person, who only realizes his selfhood in the historical process of involvement in his works. The rights of man are personal, not individual. So too the basic duties can be deduced from personal freedom, but not from individual. They are not negative restrictions on the individual (demanded by the formal truth that it has to allow for the existence of the freedom of others) but positive means of the achievement of the person, deriving from its basic structure. For personal freedom can only be real in the service of the common work, in which it returns to itself.

The principle of subsidiarity does not indicate one of the structural components of freedom itself (like the first four principles) but is a guide-line to its realization indicated by the personal structure of freedom. This guide-line is always subject to the historical process in the actual distribution of tasks and rights to individuals, the freely-formed smaller units, the family, society, State and Church. What an individual or a small unit can really achieve, what they have to renounce or what would be a blameworthy weakness if they renounced it, always depends on the historical situation.

C. History of the Concept in the West

1. *The Greek notion of freedom.* It is to be noted that the Greeks did not think of freedom as the freedom of self-decision or the freedom of the will, but as the freedom of the State or of its citizens. The ἐλεύδερος was the free citizen, ἐλευδερία was political freedom. The freedom of the State was its "autonomy", the fact that a civic community could regulate its life in common by its own rules, decided upon in view of the common good of the citizens. And the individual member of the community was only positively free in relation to this community, in which he found his fulfilment, as it in him. To be free "from" the State was a misery – the lot of the felon or exile. The freedom of the individual was quite compatible with his being thoroughly bound up with society as a whole, the determining factor in all education and each way of life. The Greek was not free under a tyranny, where State and citizens ceased to be one, and freedom only perished when the two were sundered.

Freedom as autonomy is a reflection of the metaphysical notion of autarky. The πόλις is principle and end, origin and duty. The Greeks knew nothing loftier than this very fact of common life in which all individual lives surpassed themselves and found themselves.

In Aristotle this thoroughly political notion of freedom became a theological one. Freedom was the autarky of the divine. God the only truly free being who, having no goal and no ground outside himself, is absorbed in blissfull love of self and though loving nøthing outside himself is "loved" by all, that is, longed for as the perfect.

2. *The Christian notion of freedom.* A very different notion of freedom appears in the revealed religions of Judaism and Christianity. Elements occur, apropos both of divine and human freedom, which have given such a distinctive stamp to the Western notion of freedom that nothing comparable can be found in the other great civilizations. The Jewish-Christian heritage has made the freedom of the West unique.

As regards divine freedom, the God of the OT and NT is not merely free in the sense of Greek autarky. His freedom goes out of itself in the act of creation, where it works unhampered by anything prior, creating out of nothing. This combination of freedom and creativity is absolutely new. Freedom is seen as the absolute power to initiate and set in motion, as the sypreme mastery which begins by calling its subjects into being and thus justifies its absolute claim to lordship. Another notion also appears. When God creates, his creatures are not the necessary consequences of his being and nature, and they are not created merely in the order of creation, but also in that of redemption. When man "falls" – freely renouncing the fulfilment of his being in God, choosing instead a fulfilment of his being in himself: a basic choice with regard to essence and world, such as had been undreamt-of in Greek antiquity – God bestows on him a new potentiality which does not stem from the nature of creation or from the nature of God. The freedom of God in which he makes himself the partner of man, summons the existenti*el* freedom of man to try to find itself through and with God. In the OT, this possibility is bestowed on a freely chosen people which had in no way merited the choice, while in the NT it is bestowed on all mankind. "History" in the true sense begins for the first time in this interplay of divine and human freedom. It is the free decision of essential freedom confronted with absolute claims and absolute offers of help, uninterruptedly, a decision for or against but always in partnership with the absolute freedom of God. This notion of history as the history of the two freedoms was given its most magnificent expression by Augustine in the light of the Old and New Testaments.

Thus human freedom, in spite of being unconditioned, is finite in a double sense. It is always a response to the absolute freedom of God, which it is in need of as the goal of its free decision. And throughout history human freedom has always failed in the encounter with God. From the Jewish-Christian point of view, the beginning of history was original sin. Human freedom is fallen freedom. The fallen and sickly freedom of man cannot heal itself. The remedy offered by God in the OT was the covenant characterized by the "law", in the NT it is God himself in his Son Jesus Christ in whom God's free love is incarnate. But man cannot accept this offer without the grace of God: the decision of fallen man's failed freedom can only become free again with the help of the freedom of God himself.

There are three conclusions to be noted as regards the Christian view of freedom:

a) Even if we bear in mind the basic structure of freedom and its acts, we shall miss its full reality if we fail to note the religious dimension of freedom: that it is fallen freedom needing the help of grace. Man's freedom alone necessarily falls a victim to slavery. The conviction of the wounding (*vulneratio*) and the sinfulness of human freedom is the only preservative against utopian dreams of Christian freedom, and strictly divides the Christian view from that of liberal humanism.

b) The view taken of human freedom in the historical Fall – whether it was destroyed (*libertas destructa*) or only wounded (*libertas vulnerata*) – whether grace heals and helps or must simply create man anew – marks the deepest difference between the Catholic notion of grace and freedom and that of the Churches of the Reformation. But here too the theologies of all the faiths have a problem which cannot really be solved by the powers of human thought: for if the freedom which has been enslaved is to be free again, it must take up God's free offer as it actually comes. But of itself this enslaved freedom is incapable of giving its assent to its salvation. Only those who have received prevenient, helping grace, for the free assent to the grace which makes freedom free once more (*gratia sanans, gratia efficax*) can actually perform this act of dedication and remain healed in it and become holy (with the help of further grace, *gratia sanctificans*, which enables us to keep the moral law consistently and love its author in unwavering natural love). But this prevenient grace is given by God prior to all merit, in an unfathomable free act. "So then he has mercy upon whomever he wills, and he hardens the heart of whomever he wills" (Rom 9:18). Hardening comes upon those who have not received the prevenient grace for the assent to redemption. The mystery of "predestination" in relation to freedom arises here. Since the later Augustine Christian theology has been struggling here with the question of the (sinful) *servum arbitrium* and the (healed) *liberum arbitrium* – how it is that freedom itself is not free enough to liberate itself from the slavery into which it has fallen; how it is that only God can enable freedom to be itself, through the grace of his mysterious choice.

c) It is the freedom thus healed and restored through Christ and in Christ which is meant when Christian theology speaks of freedom in the strict sense, as was done most clearly by Paul, who called it "the freedom of the children of God". Sin was for Paul the real slavery, by which man was at the mercy of the "world", "this world" or aeon, seen as the sum total of what is here below. The free man is the man at one with God. Only if he abandons himself to God does he receive himself back as his own personal possession. Otherwise he is held captive by his "works" and the activities directed to them. When he is thus given back to himself, he receives all things and all is subject to him, everything is "open" to him. It is now true to say: "Dilige et quod vis fac!" – "Love, and do what you will" – because the man who loves God is governed by no outside law, his freedom being identified in love with the freedom of God.

3. *From antiquity to the Renaissance.* The concepts of freedom which were dominant till the Renaissance were either varieties of the two concepts which had been most highly developed historically, that of Greek antiquity and that of Jewish-Christian faith, or syntheses of them.

In the Stoic philosophy of later antiquity the ancient politically-orientated concept of freedom lost its political character. The positive assertion of autarky became a renunciation of the world, a withdrawal into isolation and a negative attitude. The key-terms were *apatheia*, impassibility, and *ataraxia*, impassiveness, and Stoic freedom became freedom from the world through a retreat into the inmost spiritual kernel of man. This was to ignore the principle of historicity, that the spirit can only be really itself by going out into the world and fetching it in to itself.

In the greatest days of the Middle Ages, Thomas Aquinas tried to synthesize the various concepts of freedom, using the schema of the different types of movement to describe the degrees and realms of beings as degrees and realms of various types of freedom. The lifeless object is moved only from without, but plants have a spontaneous organic motion from within. The animal has more freedom of movement, not being bound to a particular place, and can follow his instinctive purposes by moving around. Man is the one being in the world who goes beyond the free spontaneous outward movement to return within himself. In all his movements he comes back to himself. He is the first being capable of a *reditio completa in se ipsum*. The movement of the angels, however, and in a supremely pre-eminent sense, the self-moved movement of God do not pass through the process of outgoing and returning. Their presence to themselves is not dependent on outside factors but is a "self-sufficient circumincession" without any previous self-alienation. The free act by which God goes out of himself in creation produces created reality according to his own image. But this image is the Son, the Logos, the *verbum per quod omnia facta sunt*. This is the *intellectualism* characteristic of Thomism: knowledge is higher than all will and action, and here it is God's self-knowledge in the Son which is the ground and norm of all his action. With Scotism and the nominalism of Occam trends appear which could be called metaphysical and theological voluntarism. God's freedom is conceived as the *potentia Dei absoluta*. There are no norms for his creation and his act of creation, so it is no longer necessarily a reflection of the essence of God. All that can be still deduced from its contingence is the fact that it has been willed. The order of essences, the natural law and so on give way to world orders which merely reflect *de facto* decrees. It then becomes possible to affirm with Luther that the "harlot reason" cannot decipher the will of God from the cosmos. It can only be accepted by faith from revelation. The differences between metaphysical and theological intellectualism and voluntarism (or nominalism) are among the decisive factors in accepting or rejecting knowledge of the natural law (a law proceeding from the nature of freedom and absolutely regulating in turn this freedom). The strict Lutheran notion of freedom is based entirely on the religious conditions to which the Christian is submitted, entirely ignoring the possibility of genuine freedom outside this realm in which the relationship to God is restored by Christ.

4. *Secularist views of freedom.* The views taken of freedom since the Renaissance are no longer Christian in the strict sense, though after fifteen hundred years of Christianity they cannot be pagan. A new period began in which an effort was made to interpret in a purely immanent "secular" sense many phenomena of "Christian freedom". One could show that the Christian interpretation of freedom affected the fundamentals of the theory of knowledge in the *Meditationes de Prima Philosophia* of Descartes. In the fourth meditation, error is attributed to sin, to the infinite and absolute presumption of our will which trespasses beyond the bounds imposed on our knowledge and tries to assign to man an absolute essence and knowledge which does not pertain to him. The pagan Socrates had ascribed all faulty actions to errors in knowledge, but here all faulty knowledge is ascribed to the basic decision of the free will, which has been wrong since original sin. In contemporary English philosophy discussion was based only on the negative notion of freedom, sometimes on the notion of every man's hand being against everyone else in the unbridled egoism of self-assertion. This primitive freedom was then said to have imposed limits on itself by the foundation of the State as a free, rational consensus. This notion influenced even the *Contrat Social* of J.-J. Rousseau.

No major philosophy of freedom was proposed again till Kant. In the "*a priori* feeling" of "awe", the non-objectivated, scientifically unknowable, noumenal freedom of the will in action experiences itself in the action as its own law-giver and as an end in itself not dominated by other ends. Will is the will to will, freedom is freedom for freedom and it can only be attested as morality, in the elimination of all heteronomy. In such autonomy man's life is spontaneous and non-conditioned (not inserted into the causal sequence of the world), based on absolute spontaneity – which is ultimately the true "in and of itself". Fichte based on this his distinction between the thing done (*Tatsache*) and the action of doing (*Tathandlung*), envisaging the latter as the true being of man and the world since it was freedom realizing itself. For Hegel, world history is the history of freedom coming to (consciousness of) itself, the transition from slavery in the world of nature to absolute knowledge as identity of knowledge of self and of the world, as identity of possession of self and of the alien. Hegel's concept of the principle of historicity is applied magnificently to freedom, but the human person is just as consistently made the servant of the universal spirit, for whose freedom countless persons and peoples have had to sacrifice themselves and perish.

Marx objects against Hegel that in his system reconciliation after self-alienation does not take place in reality, but only ideally, in knowledge and consciousness. The self-fulfilment of man only takes place really in the common mastery of nature by a collective achievement organized according to a division of labour. In capitalism, one class alone enjoyed the fruits of the victory won by man the worker. But the products must go back to the producers. All goods must be at the free disposal of all in a classless society. Man will then be free – his being, work and his existence will be identical – but not as a single individual, only as a species, since it is only as a species that he succeeds in transforming nature into a world at his disposal. The concept of freedom as mastery (*dominium*) is erected into an absolute, while the other meanings of freedom are completely lost sight of. The work which man tries to fetch back is here simply the work of society and technology as producers, while all the works of the true, beautiful and good are reduced to "epiphenomena". Culture is regarded at best as a means to happiness, not as a mode of life. Further, in Marx the individual person has no subsistence as the agent of freedom. Freedom is exercised only by the human species in its organization as "society". And society, in the historical attainment of its freedom as societal freedom, is itself not free, being at the mercy of the laws of dialectical and historical materialism.

Max Müller

II. Theological

1. The elaboration of the ecclesiastical and theological notion of freedom was carried on from the start in a dialogue with the philosophical notion of freedom throughout its history. To a great extent the two concepts were almost indistinguishable, and they always acted and reacted on one another. For the moment, however, the influence of modern thinking on freedom – in the debate between metaphysics and "after metaphysics" – has only been felt here and there.

In the documents of the magisterium, freedom is usually understood as man's psychological and moral freedom of choice in general, but with particular attention to matters of sin and justification where it is regarded as the ground of responsibility before God. The precise nature of this freedom is not described but presupposed as known. The documents stress, however, that freedom does not merely mean absence of external coercion, but also absence of inner compulsion (cf. *D* 1039, 1041, 1066, 1094). Its existence can be known by the light of natural reason (*D* 1650; not a defined doctrine).

Accordingly, the Church regards freedom of choice as an inalienable and essential part of man's nature (*D* 160a, 348, 776, 793, 815, 1027f., 1065ff., 1094, 1388). The early Church condemned the determinism and fatalism of the Gnostic and Manichean systems, and any form of predestination in which God moved man to an evil act by suppressing his human freedom (cf. *D* 160a, 200, 300, 316ff., 321f., 348, 514). The Church solemnly defined that even under the influence of original sin man was in principle free, that he had to assent freely to the salutary grace which was both necessary and prevenient, and that he could really resist this grace, even where it was sufficient (*D* 792, 797, 814ff., 1039ff., 1065f., 1093ff., 1291, 1298, 1359ff., 1375, 1521, 1791, 2305). At the same time, the notion of freedom as (moral or psychological) autonomy with regard to God was excluded, and also the notion that freedom in fallen man was the power to act by virtue of an untrammelled and unthreatened self-mastery. Freedom is subject to the impulses of concupiscence, and is said to be diminished, weakened and wounded (*D* 160a., 174, 181, 186, 199, 325, 793). Furthermore, without the gratuitous grace of God this freedom is absolutely incapable of salutary acts (*D* 105, 130, 133ff., 181, 186, 199f., 300, 317, 373, 811ff.). Hence, though man remains responsible for himself by his freedom, his freedom is only enabled to perform the action in which it is most truly itself when it is set free for it by the free grace of God, to which man has absolutely no claim, since he is a mere creature and a sinful one. This gracious liberation of the will is regarded both as the gift of the possibility of the free act and – where it actually takes place – as the gift of the act itself (cf. *D* 177, 182, etc.). But it is precisely the gift of the free act to freedom itself.

How God can create natural freedom

in spite of its radical dependence and how the salutary act can be given as a free act by the grace of God – such questions are left to be freely discussed in the schools.

2. For a systematic theology of freedom which will go beyond the framework of the post-Tridentine systems of grace and free will, only preliminary suggestions are provided by modern philosophy. The basic principles of a theological anthropology will point the way to a deeper grasp of freedom. Just as in created being dependence on God and degree of being grow in equal and not inverse proportions, and the possibility of the creation of such being demands the unique intervention of divine power, so too with created freedom. It is a transcendental note of being in general which appertains to various beings in proportion to their degree of being. It is simply called freedom where the degree of being proper to the spiritual person is reached. It is responsible self-mastery, even in face of God, because dependence on God – contrary to what takes place in intramundane causality – actually means being endowed with free selfhood. In the present order, this created freedom is by God's decree the vehicle of the personal free self-communication of God to a personal partner in free dialogue of the covenant. But it exists truly in the mode of a creature, whose finiteness is known in its history and historicity, in its bodily nature and in its being subject to limitations by the force of power.

When freedom is seen as the free love of God in dialogue with the partner necessary to such freely given love, it appears as the essential dignity of the person. This view of freedom must be the foundation of the doctrine of a rightly understood freedom of conscience and of the right of freedom to room for is concrete realization in face of undue restrictions laid upon it by State or Church.

In such a concept of freedom, it would be seen to be in need of interpretation by God. It cannot "judge itself" because it is historical and hence while its process is still going on it can never be fully present to reflection. This interpretation by God must be seen as a verdict of guilty and a verdict of gracious acquittal passed upon guilty freedom. It will then be seen that the freedom of choice (of the Greek notion) stands in the same relation to Christian freedom, by reason of the liberating grace of God, as nature stands to grace. The former, while retaining its nature, is still frustrated of its true sense where it is not elevated and redeemed by the freedom of the children of God.

Hence the proper attitude of man to his freedom must be defined as thankfulness. It is a welcome gift which he gladly accepts, not something to which he is "condemned". And because his individual deeds and basic choice are in principle not amenable to full and certain cognizance, it is only by hoping in God that he can accept it without being plagued by scruples or threatened with self-righteousness.

Hence in theology freedom is understood as having its source and goal in God (who is its "object" and the "horizon" of all possible objects). In this way it is total dominion over the self, aiming at the definitive. It is self-mastery bestowed on man in the dialogue with God, where he is called to the finality of love's decision. Freedom always finds itself fettered in an irremediable situation of disaster and as it accepts this verdict in faith, always finds itself the recipient of liberty through Jesus Christ. But in this way – at a level on which the systematic theology of freedom must cancel itself out by finding itself safely on a higher plane – freedom is a mystery to itself and all others. It is mystery as the primordial dialogue, as freedom liberated from bondage and called into the absolute mystery.

Karl Rahner

FUNDAMENTAL THEOLOGY

Fundamental theology is the word now used for what used to be called apologetics. This does not mean that the subject-matter and goal of apologetics have been abandoned, but that they have been made part of a more comprehensive theological reflection, primarily a positive one, where apologetics plays a decisive role but is not the whole of fundamental theology.

If we start from the words themselves, fundamental theology means the investigations of the foundations in the realm of theology. These foundations are not artificially constructed like an ideology and they are not extrinsic elements. They are presupposed by theology and hence form part of it.

1. *Notion and object*. Theology, as the science of faith or of God's revelation to men, has various foundations. Fundamental theology does not claim to consider them all, but its approach is nonetheless definite and decisive. It may be described as a transcendental theology, inasmuch as it considers the nature and event of revelation as such, prior to all special theology or branches of theology. The question is: What is the basis and presupposition of all theology in each of its departments and what is its "overriding" determinant? What is the principle which provides beginning or end, according to the perspective chosen? What is the master-key which opens the way to each department? A theological science based on such considerations takes a place corresponding to that of ontology in philosophy and in the general scheme of thought.

The revelation of God who communicates and discloses himself is the foundation and principle and likewise the all-embracing truth which takes in all elements of revelation and hence all theological disciplines. Revelation supplies the premises and impulse for all theological argument. Its content is made explicit in the detail of its individual elements, but revelation as such, as the "transcendental" condition of possibility of theology, is presupposed, and cannot be interrogated in detail. J. S. Drey, the founder of the "Tübingen School", put the problem as follows: "Revelation, as the condition and determinant principle of all particular revelations, as that which mediates revelation into particulars, cannot appear as an object among the objects to which it has given rise: that is, the doctrine *de revelatione* cannot appear as one dogma among others. It is at the basis of them all as their presupposition." But this is precisely the object of fundamental theology as the theological science of foundations or basic science: revelation as the origin and heuristic principle and overriding unity of all branches of theology. In this sense, fundamental theology is basic and formal theology, postulated by theology itself, the result of its profounder reflection on itself. It is a constitutive and structural element of theology. Hence its central question is: What is the revelation of which the various branches of theology speak and which both founds and comprises all particulars of revelation? How does it appear, how is it to be understood? What are its structures and categories, how does it come about, how is it communicated?

Here the fundamental theology in question does not start from a general concept of revelation. It bases itself on the theological concept of revelation, as given, for instance, in the pregnant formula of Vatican I: "Deus se ipsum revelavit et aeterna voluntatis suae decreta" (*D* 1785). It is set the same limits by historical experience and transcendental *a priori* reflection to which the spirit is elsewhere subject as a being in history. Man accepts spontaneously a historical experience which is never fully amenable to reflection and investigates the *a priori* conditions of possibility of such actual experience, which is the only way to gain a real understanding of this experience. The question thus posed as to the nature and possibility of revelation has a number of implications which fundamental theology makes explicit: the absoluteness, the supreme power, the sovereign freedom, the personal nature of God.

This question entails another (whose purpose is to ask how the proofs can be given in articulate and methodical detail): Has revelation, as so understood and as so presenting itself, actually taken place? It is the question of the *de facto* occurrence of revelation. Are there proofs, reasons, credentials and testimonies for the revelation which came at a certain time and place? Are there proofs which can be tested? Are there testimonies which will satisfy the questing, questioning spirit that revelation is credible by nature, and as a happening and a reality? Have men reason to accept revelation in faith, so that they are intellectually justified in doing so and obliged in conscience to take this step?

Thus the task of fundamental theology is to describe the nature of revelation and to demonstrate its *de facto* existence by pointing to the criteria of revelation and the signs of its credibility. This is what gives this theological science its special character. It considers the basis for the various branches of theology and its own special perspective: the question of the credibility of revelation and the justification of faith which this contains. It has to show the justification of faith, in the act of faith itself, which here above all is a faith calling for insight: *fides quaerens intellectum*. It is the problem of the *credibilitas rationalis*.

Thus the legitimacy and the necessity of fundamental theology stem from the fact that God has disclosed himself for the world and man in his revelation, that this revelation concerns man, the question of whose salvation is posed and decided by it. But this is only possible if revelation of itself appears in this way, if it gives testimony before men, if it justifies and accredits its statement, if it is capable of meeting and addressing man in his inmost self, if it corresponds in some way to the potentialities of man, world and history, if it can fairly meet and persuasively answer the questions, objections and doubts which it raises.

The NT documents, in the form of living preaching, the revelation of God which culminates in Christ. But since it is testimony and proclamation about God's word and work, it is also testimony for men, and presents itself as such, arguing, explaining and substantiating its claims. It presents itself as a credible and well-founded answer by pointing to the credentials which the claim to revelation offers. These credentials, according to Scripture, are the "signs", the "works", the purpose of which is clear. The summary which forms the conclusion of St. John's Gospel expresses this intention clearly: "Now Jesus did many other signs in the presence of his disciples, which are not writen in this book; but these are written that you may believe that Jesus is the Christ, the Son of God, and that believing you may have life in his name." (Jn 20:30f.)

Like the preaching of Jesus, the apostles' preaching about Jesus Christ is always centred on and impelled by two components, as it were: God who has disclosed himself in his word, ultimately in the Word who is the Son (Heb 1:1), and man, who is to come in faith to this God of revelation, for whom the way must be made ready, who must be able to justify his faith.

These unquestionable and essential truths, attested by Scripture, which make it kerygma and not a mere formal record, justify fundamental theology and make it necessary. For it does justice to the situation involved: revelation – God disclosing himself to men – men confronted by God revealing himself – men confronted with revelation. Hence comes the specific method of fundamental theology. If it is to substantiate and justify revelation as such and faith, by the demonstration of credibility, it cannot argue from the truths of revelation and from faith. It cannot use dogmatic proofs. It must have recourse to rational, philosophical and historical argument: to metaphysical thought for the nature and criteria of revelation, to historical thought for the fact of revelation. Fundamental theology cannot use revelation as a middle term in its proofs, since revelation is the goal of its efforts and the source of its inspiration. Its efforts must be rational in nature. It appeals to the verdict of insight. Hence, for instance, fundamental theology cannot draw proofs from Scripture or the doctrinal decisions of the Church by virtue of their inspiration or infallibility, since the inspiration of Scripture and the infallibility of the Church have still to be demonstrated and cannot be assumed. Scripture and Church teaching are to be treated as documents and sources to be investigated by the methods of philosophy and historical criticism, insofar as the sources in question can throw light on the nature, fact and credibility of revelation as such philosophical and historical thinking demands. The Church is an essential theme in fundamental theology inasmuch as it has a transcendental dimension for theology. The Church is mediator and depository of revelation, and also *the* believer. Hence the Church is *the* condition of possibility of theology. This dimension and its claims must be explained and justified in fundamental theology as an intrinsic part of the whole.

2. *Methods and application*. But there is still another special sense in which fundamental theology has to be an investigation of foundations and a basic theological science. When it enquires into the conditions of possibility of revelation, it must consider how revelation which is "not of this world" is to come forward as revelation entering this world; how revelation, which as God's word is beyond space and time, can take place in space and time; how revelation, which does not stem from the mind and words of men, can still be word and event for men and their minds and their capacities as beings of this world and of history. Hence as science of foundations and basic theology, fundamental theology has also to consider whether divine revelation which presents itself in a certain way is possible in the world of beings and for man. The question can and must be put, whether the world in which man finds himself a being, and man's own existence and nature, are such that there is room, openness and possibility for revelation from God. For this must be a freely given revelation, beyond what is already given and recognizable by nature. And it must be such that it is acceptable by men as "revelation" in the world, in words and in history, while still remaining God's own most proper word. It must not come under the creaturely *a priori* of the finite spirit, under pain of ultimately not differing in quality from "natural revelation" given through the world and man's mind. This presupposes man's openness for revelation, without prejudice to the freedom of God in revealing himself, and without laying down beforehand inadmissible rules for the how and what of revelation. Then, the word of God himself only escapes being reduced to a word from God about God, in the *a priori* mental constitution of man, if God is himself a component, in the grace of faith (as "uncreated" grace), of the hearing of the word of God – which of course can only exist as heard and believed.

Clearly, in this sense too and in these perspectives there can be a basic science of theology as a fundamental theology. It will be guided by ontological and anthropological principles and it will furnish an indication of the credibility of (a possible) revelation which is most important by reason of its ontological, anthropological and existential roots – its reference to the components and structures of existence. Since revelation comes to man in the world, space and time, the world, space and time, and above all man himself and all that determines him, must contain the presuppositions and prefigurations which make revelation possible and are therefore produced beforehand by revelation itself. These very elements must be brought to light and expounded in a theological science which aims at being a principle and foundation; otherwise it would not make good its claims: it would not be "fundamental" enough.

We can therefore see in what sense fundamental theology is the foundation of theology. It would be too much to claim that the questions and answers of fundamental theology are the sole foundation of theology as a science of faith and revelation, or the sole foundation of faith itself. It might possibly be so, if faith in God the revealer followed with logical rigour or psychological compulsion from insight into the grounds of credibility, like the conclusion from the premisses. But such is not the case. Hence the notion of foundation in fundamental theology needs to be qualified. Faith in the true sense in the divine revelation as a definite concrete reality is a new act and a new decision on the part of man, posited because of the authority of God who reveals himself. The authority of the *Deus revelans* is the real motive of faith which produces the act of faith and its real ultimate foundation. Knowledge or the credibility of revelation and of the faith which corresponds to it, in the two ways described above, creates the conditions and presuppositions whereby the assurance of faith can be explicitly possible, justified and demanded. Insofar as these conditions and presuppositions are a foundation, fundamental theology is the foundation of theology. This was summed up by Augustine in the pregnant words: "Nemo crederet, nisi videret, esse credendum." The "videre esse credendum" is concerned with the broad ring of truths which have been spoken of apropos of the justification of faith and are ordinarily called the *motiva credibilitatis*.

The questions dealt with in fundamental theology, seen from the standpoint of supernatural faith, are preliminaries and not the main questions. But from the standpoint of the human being who is to be the site, recipient and partner of a possible revelation, they are in fact decisive. If they are not asked or if they are dismissed too quickly, then – as it is instructive to note – when man is trying to penetrate explicitly the grounds of its existence, revelation is out of the question; it does not appear as a question worth putting, as a possibility, as an invitation, as an obligation. And man does not "dream" of going into the matter of revelation. But by the believer who reflects on his faith and explores its presuppositions and possibility – for the sake of the wholeness of his faith – this question and above all its possible answer must be taken with the utmost seriousness. These presuppositions and conditions may well determine the destiny of a man's faith.

3. *The kerygmatic character of fundamental theology*. Discussion of the foundations and presuppositions of theology and faith brings out further aspects when the effort is made to apply fundamental theology to practice. There is first the missionary aspect.

Fundamental theology can become missionary theology, addressing itself primarily to men outside the faith or on the threshold of faith. Then, as the science of the encounter of revelation and man, it takes man as it finds him in his human nature, situation and existence and tries to put him in contact with revelation. It calls his attention to something within him which is open to the word of God, which transcends him, and addresses him without stemming from him, for the work of salvation offered him in that word of revelation. It shows him how truly he longs to hear it, how safely it can fetch him home, how receptive and ready he is for it, and how much he depends on it. It tries further to remove the difficulties which stand in the way of seeing and hearing God's revelation. In unfeigned solidarity, honestly trying to encounter and communicate, it enters into the situation of questing man. It asks his questions and pushes them further, and thus tries to go beyond man and his perhaps too hastily drawn boundaries and inadmissible restrictions. Its effort is to expound the word of God's self-revelation as the answer to man, as the full and definitive disclosure, illumination, fulfilment and realization of man, in the sense of the words: "What you worship as unknown, this I proclaim to you." (Acts 17:23.) It works on the theological principle of the theology of existence: "To speak of man is to speak of God, to speak of God is to speak of man."

It may be said of "missionary" fundamental theology that it is theology in the form of pastoral care, and pastoral care in the form of reflection (E. Brunner). It is the response to the command: "Always be prepared to make a defence (*apologia*) to anyone who calls you to account for the hope that is in you." (1 Pet 3:15.) Hope is characteristic of Christian existence, while "being without hope" is characteristic of existence apart from Christ. The account given of this hope to one who asks for it should be so revealing that the questioner can be gripped, moved and perhaps won by this hope and its setting. The approach recommended in the same text, "Do it with gentleness and reverence, since your conscience is clear" (1 Pet 3:15f.), is still valid today. It is incumbent not only on the faithful but on the theologian reflecting scientifically on his faith, and it is an encouragement to him. The goal of such efforts is described by Paul as "taking every thought captive to the obedience of Christ" (2 Cor 10:5).

Along with the missionary element, there is also the apologetic, in the strict, original sense of the word. In 2 Cor, a very personal letter, Paul speaks of the "warfare" which he has to conduct, and of the weapons of this war. The weapons of God "have divine power to destroy strongholds. We destroy arguments and every proud obstacle to the knowledge of God." (2 Cor 19:4f.) The first letter of Peter, having called for the Apologia of the Logos of hope, affirms confidently that those who revile the Christian life will be put to shame by the Christian answer. This does not amount to a biblical foundation of apologetics as a theological science. But it affirms unmistakably that defence against and above all offensives against hostile positions, accusations and distortions are among the functions and tasks of the Christian faith and its preachers. If this is so, it is a matter which must be carefully considered in the science of faith.

Hence apologetics as an aspect of fundamental theology is concerned with the defence of revelation as such, of its nature, existence, possibility, claims and credentials, against all that is brought up as objections, doubts, misgivings and attacks. Such misgivings are voiced in the name of man and human reason. There is hardly any position which has not been invoked, right down to the present day, to reject and combat revelation. To be silent or to surrender one's weapons would be a sign of weakness and faint-heartedness. There is a duty of defending the faith by giving the answer of faith, and this is best done not by grappling at close quarters with each attack, but by discovering its presuppositions, analysing its nature and trying to win it over.

At the present time, efforts are being

made to draw up a programme of a "new fundamental theology" (K. Rahner), which as a basic theological discipline and an integrating element of dogmatics aims at raising to an articulate level the pre-scientific understanding of the faith. Its aim is therefore to produce evidence for the inner credibility of the truths of revelation and to investigate the conditions under which these truths can be accepted by men existentially at any given moment of their existence. The effort is not directed towards the explicitation of the content of revelation in all its manifold aspects, but to concentrate it in the "mystery of Christ".

Heinrich Fries

G

GNOSIS

This is a manysided term but primarily indicates that aspect of human knowledge regarded by the historical movement of gnosticism as the essence of salvation. But the concept of gnosis (even when it does not mean simply "knowledge" in the same rather vague sense as the English word) can also be dissociated from its purely historical origin. In this second case, gnosis may occur in two possible forms.

1. There is a genuinely Christian gnosis in the sense of a charismatic knowledge included within the *agape* (as an aspect of faith which does not, however, go beyond faith). Paul ascribed this gnosis to those perfectly illuminated by the Spirit (pneumatically). It is the knowledge in which man grows more and more in his "understanding" (in faith) of the incomprehensible love of God revealed on the cross of Christ and thus allows himself to be grasped more and more by this love as something that is most real and definitive. This "existential" intensification of man's knowledge of faith (or of the result of this knowledge) could, in accordance with the Pauline terminology, be called gnosis, because there is no other simple word with the same all-embracing meaning, and the word has persisted with that particular meaning in Catholic usage. This gnosis certainly exists and is bound to be studied by systematic theology. There is growth in grace and growth in the grace of faith, in the grace of illumination, in the light of faith, in the instinct to believe and therefore also in the knowledge of faith, not only in the Church as a whole, but in the individual. This growth is not simply or even primarily a quantitative growth in a conceptual knowledge of as many different articles of faith as possible. On the contrary, in the *fides quaerens intellectum*, it is a growth in a unifying understanding of the whole of revelation as such and in a more and more personal orientation towards one's own existence. It can, for instance, be said without any reservation that a correct understanding of the real meaning of Christian mysticism may be regarded as the normal consequence (given by grace) of growth in grace. If that is so, then theological knowledge is essentially directed towards contemplation. It should also be supported by wisdom as a gift of the Spirit. It should consequently become a "charismatic" theology (in the theologian himself, not directly in his scientific work as such). It should also grow from the fullness of what is believed in the liturgy (*D*

139, 2200). In a personal "connaturality" with regard to the mystery of faith (*D* 2324) and occurring in love, this theological understanding will become a (correctly understood) kerygmatic theology. As a theological programme, gnosis in the light of this particular concept is basically a demand that theology should not overlook its saving function. A dogmatic doctrine of knowledge can, moreover, only be provided in this way when theology really strives to achieve a sanctifying wisdom.

2. The word "gnosis" also has a heterodox meaning, derived from the meaning of the word in gnosticism, but in which the term gnosticism is raised to the level of a universal concept in the phenomenology of religion. If an arbitrary use of this concept is to be avoided, we can only take various characteristics of "gnosis" as our point of departure. (We cannot, for instance, begin with the question as to whether radical dualism, antinomianism and so on are represented in the term.) In this sense, then, the word gnosis has four different meanings (occurring in isolation or together). a) Religious knowledge results from a special capacity which is given *a priori* (and is possibly present only in a few individuals) and is therefore not representative of the whole man (and thus also of his reason). b) It is a form of knowledge which is derived, not from a gratuitous, personal self-disclosure of God, but from man's being itself, which has to be discovered. It is therefore gnostic "self-consciousness" and not an obedient hearing of the word of God, in other words, faith. In the last resort, it is of little importance whether this emancipated knowledge of salvation is presented to us more in the form of esoteric mysticism (outside obedience in faith) or whether it occurs in a more rationalistic form (as in the case of German Idealism or in that of semi-rationalism). It is similarly a matter of indifference whether the form in which this gnosis is expressed is mythological (mythos), or whether it is conceptual and whether the content of that expression is cosmological or spiritualistic, monistic or dualistic, deterministic or indeterministic. Again, it matters very little whether this gnosis is won individualistically or with the help of a community (in initiation and the celebration of mysteries) or through a "redeemer", who only helps to press man down to his own dislocated being and does not bring him salvation as an authentic man in history, as the redeemer Christ does. We should finally not try by a process of demythologization to dispose of all the theological statements that are nowadays regarded as "mythological", calling them "gnostic" and thus rejecting them. c) Knowledge as such (because that which has to be known has to be discovered) is in itself redemptive. Love as a moral act is (if it is necessary) simply the obvious consequence of gnosis, which is in itself everything, salvation, so that everything is objectively *and* subjectively given and man ultimately does not realize, but finds the absolute, all-embracing unity of all reality in himself and knows that he is, in his pluralism as a creature, always orientated towards the lasting unity of the transcendent God and that a concentration on pure knowledge has to be resisted in his existence. d) Finally, knowledge often results in the construction of a "closed" system. This system reflects the logically and physically determined course of the world. As a result, it does not acknowledge personal freedom, historicity or uniqueness and does not take into account the mystery of the ground of being as the fact that the incomprehensible God has come closer to us in his revelation of himself. On the contrary, this closed system of knowledge regards the mystery of God as already unveiled and (at least in secret) overcome.

Karl Rahner

GOD

I. The Divine

1. *Revelation and the question of God.* Man as he finds himself includes a dynamism towards an absolute in being, meaning, truth and life. Christian belief in revelation has always designated this absolute by the term "God". The reality which it denotes is in the Christian view a primary transcendental datum of the human spirit which must be firmly maintained, even though in the history of religion the empirical derivation of the idea of God remains an open question. Here a purely evolutionary theory which assumes primitive origins still confronts the theory of an original monotheism (belief in a High God). Neither of these theories can give an exact account of the genesis and development of the idea of God, though in favour of the theory of primitive monotheism it may be said that an explanation of belief in God drawn from nature, magic and animism does not appear convincing. Belief in a primitive revelation, in which man was given the (unanalysed) knowledge of a personal divinity, is not a matter which falls within the scope of the methods of comparative religion. These can neither prove nor disprove it.

Christian thought is not absolutely tied to the findings of the history of religions, which always have to some extent an ambivalent character. Christianity is convinced that in the OT revelation a completely new and underivative awareness of God appears, even though in the historical emergence of what was new, the links with the old ideas of God can be traced, so that it is possible to speak of a "development" of OT monotheism.

For man to speak about God at all represents in reality an "impossible task", for according to the statements of revelation as well as the experiences of the profoundest religious minds of humanity, God is precisely the inexpressible, impossible to conceptualize and objectivate. On the other hand, man must undertake this task, because it is impossible to pass over in silence the question of God. Man's own personal existence intrinsically involves that question, which is precisely what makes human reality problematic. Even contemporary militant atheism must acknowledge this. Its denial of God testifies to the impossibility of ignoring the question of God, and so on the Christian side does the extreme "Death of God" movement, which replaces an allegedly unacceptable personal idea of God by referring to the normative consciousness of human freedom which appeared in Jesus and which must serve as a norm. Even the deliberately intramundane philosophy of modern times was not able to exclude this question, even when it disdained the term God and replaced it with the principle of the universe (G. Bruno), the absolute spirit (G. W. F. Hegel), life exulting in itself (F. Nietzsche) or the supra-worldliness of the power of being limiting man (M. Heidegger). Even J. P. Sartre's resolute atheism has to raise the question of God in order to make intelligible the titanic human decision in favour of absolute freedom.

An explanation of this question of God which is involved in man's very existence as a person is only possible by reference to man's constitution as partner in a dialogue. Fundamentally, man stands under God's call, and his primordial orientation is towards hearing God's word.

Purely theoretical philosophical thought will, it is true, never be able to make it perfectly evident whether this call really proceeds from something outside man, from an absolute, or is merely an echo of the voice of human reality moving with its finitude and fragility in an inescapable circle of immanence and endless monologue. Consequently man is ultimately certain about God only through acceptance of a revelation in which God discloses himself to man perfectly freely and by his own power, and thereby opens man's destiny to a partnership between God and man.

It is true that the assumption of the occurrence of a divine revelation of this kind, which brings the relation between God and man into the pattern of events of history and temporality, sets a new problem. Why does God still appear to man to be questionable and problematic in his action and being? This is connected with a right conception of revelation. Revelation, whether regarded from the side of the absolute God or from that of finite man, cannot bring about a complete disclosure of the mystery of God. Even for the prophets and the apostles, the actual witnesses to revelation, the revealer remains shrouded in the hidden character of his nature. And so the hidden character of the God of revelation has been a constant theme of all thought about God based on revelation, since the Greek Fathers and the "negative theology" which they inaugurated, through Augustine, German mysticism, Nicholas of Cusa (*Dialogus de Deo abscondito*) and Luther, down to Pascal and Newman. It is notable that the very nation chosen by the God of revelation could raise the question of the *name* of God. This was not done out of intellectual curiosity, but from longing for assurance that God was near with active help in the darkness of faith and the hazards of history, to which the immutable God, despite his most intimate proximity, must always remain transcendent (cf. Exod 3:1–15).

2. *Proofs of the existence of God and God's mysterious character*. Man's turning from God in sin, and the consequent clouding of his knowledge (cf. Rom 1:18–21; see also *Original Sin*) is the ultimate reason why he will always experience God's mystery as a kind of absence, and has to raise a question about him. But this clouding is not so radical that there is no receptivity left for the call of God which comes from the order of creation. This receptivity is also indispensable when "supernatural" revelation occurs (because it guarantees personal responsibility for acceptance of the Word of God). It must not, however, be declared to constitute a way of natural knowledge of God side by side and on an equal footing with the revealed knowledge of faith (*D* 1785).

These various reasons for the non-self-evident character of God also explain why human thought has always been concerned with the natural demonstrability of God's existence, and why conscious inquiry of this kind was taken over and sanctioned by Christian theology in the form of the proofs of the existence of God. These "proofs" have become problematical in some respects for people nowadays, even for people concerned about religion. Yet no less a person than Hegel (on the basis of his own philosophical conception of God, it is true) regarded a feeling of repugnance for proofs of God's existence as "acquired intellectual prejudice". Such persistent prejudice is also largely explained by a misconception of the particular structure and purpose of these proofs. In the details of their historical formulation (cf., for example, the *quinque viae* of Aquinas, *Summa Theologica*, I, q. 2, a. 3) they are certainly open to objection. But fundamentally they cannot be abandoned because they make clear the unconditional which lies at the basis of all contingent phenomena of the world and which is particularly apparent in man's awareness that an absolute claim is made on him. Otherwise the Christian belief in God would be exposed to the suspicion of illusion, and theology would dishonestly evade the ultimate question of truth in regard to its highest "object".

3. *The theological problem of atheism*. The hidden and non-evident character of the God of revelation, in conjunction with the clouding of human knowledge

and the brittle orientation of the will towards the perfect good, also provides a basis for judging the phenomenon of denial of God, atheism. This deformation is nowadays frequently attributed to failure in the Christian proclamation of God and to the absence of persuasive testimony to God given in people's lives. It is, of course, never possible to dispute such failure of practical belief in God, but it is clear that the problem is very superficially envisaged if atheism is regarded solely as a consequence of failure to give practical effect to the idea of God. If that were so, atheism could only be interpreted as a misunderstanding of theism, as criticism of an idea of God out of harmony with the age, and therefore as aiming in reality at a more genuine act of faith. This possibility may be conceded where people deny God externally, in words, but hold fast to an absolute principle or value, even if in doing so they merely endow something derivative and relative with the character of an absolute. And certainly such a possibility can be admitted when, as in some Eastern forms of religion, for lack of an explicit conceptual theology, the absolute which is affirmed and honoured is not given a doctrinal basis. In these cases it is not really possible or appropriate to raise the question of theism or atheism at all.

This conception also accords with the observation of Vatican II that even in non-Christian religions there is "perception of that hidden power which not infrequently implies knowledge of a supreme God or even of a Father" (Declaration on the Relationship of the Church to Non-Christian Religions, *Nostra Aetate*, art. 3), even though what is meant is not given adequate expression in personal terms. A corrective to the apersonalism which is maintained in theory is often found in the actual practice of popular piety, which develops a cult of gods and spirits and so creates a substitute for the monologue of an apersonalism which is unsatisfying for man as a person. For an attitude to be regarded as "veiled theism", one would also have to inquire whether it produces a total dedication of the will and the acknowledgment of absolute ethical norms. And do these find realization in an attitude to the world and in a spirituality which affects man in the very centre of his being and prompts him to an attitude of adoration? That will not be the case with an atheism which has reached the highest degree of intellectual self-awareness, and which, like the "postulatory atheism" of N. Hartmann, considers that the existence of an absolute "centre of values" must be rejected precisely because of the dignity of the moral person. Nor is it possible to explain as misunderstood theism that virulent modern atheism which, drawing on Hegel's dialectic of "master and servant", regards all theism as expressing an intolerable heteronomy of the "unhappy consciousness", which can only be abrogated by acknowledging the divine humanity of the mind in its development.

A transcendental deduction may demonstrate from the fundamental principle of a theoretical and self-conscious atheism that the very denial of the unconditional and absolute implies its affirmation as one of the conditions of its denial. Such atheism is therefore in contradiction with itself. But from the subjective point of view of the person concerned, atheism must be regarded as an accomplished fact. That also applies even though from the standpoint of the Christian belief in God it must be admitted that no logical argument for the non-existence of God is possible, and consequently that any subjective conviction to that effect can only be apparent. In general, of course, a proof of the non-existence of some being will only be conclusive if the contradictory character of the alleged existence can be shown in the form of a *reductio ad absurdum*. From the Christian standpoint, atheism is objectively without foundation. It cannot, therefore, annul the objective, ontological constitution of man with his orientation towards God and his condition of image and likeness of God. But to try on this account to speak of atheism being impossible, would fail to recognize that man by his very condition as a finite being and by a decision of his finite freedom is able to deny the objective order from which he cannot in fact detach himself. And this provides a sufficient basis for atheism.

It must also be remembered that it is never a question of an intellectual judgment alone, but also of a decision of the will. Atheism is not an exclusively intellectual problem. If it were, this would ultimately lead to the theory of a mere error of the understanding and therefore in fact the very possibility of formal atheism would be disputed. Since a moral failure is also involved, rooted in man's shutting himself off in himself and making an absolute of his own finitude, denial of God must be regarded as a wilful "suppressing" (Rom 1:18) of the idea and experience of God which press upon man. Its character as sin and guilt must therefore be taken seriously. This does not mean that the element of guilt can be affirmed and determined from outside in each individual case.

4. *The problem of speaking about God.* The purpose of theological endeavour, however, is not to inquire about God, but to speak correctly about God, and this is also a fundamental purpose of God's call. Such speech, however, aims at intimate personal converse with God as the absolute personal partner, and this in turn is to find its perfect accomplishment in the direct vision of God. Consequently the problem of inquiry about God turns into that of correct speech about him and to him. This problem arises from the fact that our words and our concepts with their limits and essential relation to finite objects, are not capable of grasping the divine, which by its very nature is unlimited and unobjectifiable, prior to every determination and as the "divine" God, is the primordial and comprehensive factor in all thought and speech *about* him. Early Christian theology (as we see particularly vividly in the Pseudo-Dionysius) on the basis of living experience of the absolute otherness and non-objectifiability of God, came to recognize a real inexpressibility of God, and only admitted negative statements about him. Behind this was the Augustinian principle that God is more known and acknowledged by non-knowing than by presumptuous human curiosity which can only lead to a human simulacrum of God. But this programme of a "negative theology" has never been carried out because, if pursued strictly, it would lead to complete silence about God. This would contradict the teleological character of the question about God inherent in man.

The same must be said of a modern form of negative theology which will only consider statements about God if they take the form of existential self-interpretation of the believer. This position may be based on a hidden agnosticism or on an extreme actualism and existentialism. In an indirect mode of statement of this kind, though God is still acknowledged, for example, as the force at the root of my preoccupations (H. Braun), God is no longer regarded as existing in himself. And this is where the demand is expressly made to forget the very word "God" (P. Tillich) and to formulate this word, as well as the demands of theistic religious feeling, in a new and "unreligious" way for modern man. Underlying this programme is the genuine problem of the relation between God's immanence and transcendence. In an unreflecting kind of faith, there was a one-sided tendency to the second pole of the dialectic, and the problem was over-simplified. But in the radically new approach, the dialectic between the "worldliness" and the transcendence of faith is once again unbalanced. Theology as speech about God threatens to turn into a "pistology", i.e., a doctrine of man's concern with faith, and into an existential interpretation of man. And it is impossible to say whether the latter has any further need for the objective reality and genuine partnership of God, or whether it ever reaches the point of acknowledging a personal God.

The same thing applies to attempts to think of God as only found in actual reality in the course of human personal relationships. Those who think in this way do not want to speak in so many words of a personal God (J. A. T. Robinson). Behind this is the objection that even the category "personal" is not appropriate to God; it is said to conceive God on the lines of a "highest being" *above* man and his world. The self-contradiction of this line of thinking will perhaps be clear from the substitute solutions proposed. The experience of God is said to be man's "being accepted" or as the experience of the obligatory force of the unconditional seen in the light of wholehearted love for the world and the neighbour. Such sense of "being accepted", whether as an experience of the human person or of the unconditional, presupposes a person who accepts man and imposes the condition. Consequently for man, since he is himself a person, God cannot be less than a person, unless man wants to exalt himself into being the only absolute reality he will acknowledge.

The biblical testimonies, though they do not use the term "person" as such, make it clear that human thought about God is obliged to use the category of the personal. But it is fully represented and its place taken by the idea of the "name" of God and by the use of the divine name sanctioned by God himself (cf., e.g., Exod 3:14; 6:3; Is 42:8). Holy Scripture makes it clear on the one hand that God cannot be designated and grasped under a single name. Tradition develops this in the idea of God being "many-named" and even "nameless" (cf. *D* 428). On the other hand Scripture shows equally clearly that the God of revelation makes himself known by his name as a determinate subject and individual reality, as an "I" of supreme concreteness and dignity, and that as such he enters into a personal relation with men. From the ontological point of view this relation is what ultimately makes possible the phenomenon of human personality and personal relations. God's personal character finds expression above all in the personal pronoun "I" which is applied to him innumerable times in Scripture. Reluctance to apply the category of the personal to God identifies such a procedure too readily with reification of God. But no such danger is present if we recognize that when God is said to be "personal", the term is not a univocal designation and that it does not involve any limitation of God. It does not mean he is a stronger but limited "I", and that we are fixed in a static relation to him. It points to God as the all-comprising, transcendent ground of all personality, the total reality of autonomy, self-possession and responsibility. Understood in this way, God as personal is also the transcendent pole and more comprehensive reality which includes the human I-Thou relation to God. He therefore means more than the mere function of providing the absolute ontological ground of men's personal lives and of their mutual personal relations.

5. *The ways of speaking about God.* The difficulties that arise here are those of correct thought and speech about God. Traditional scholastic theology sought a solution in the doctrine of the analogy of all statements about God. This presupposes that God is quite different from what our concepts and words are capable of grasping. On this

negative basis, which of course itself involves an implicit awareness of God's special character, the mind is impelled to the further step of articulating the positive cognitive element in concepts of God. By their very nature these concepts can represent the divine only in a way which is both dissimilar and similar to it (cf. *D* 432). Yet they nevertheless direct our statements towards God's mystery, and consequently give them a genuinely meaningful content. Thus statements about God as personal or about his attributes refer to and attain a genuine reality in God, but because of their dissimilarity in similarity they cannot capture and express the mode of the reality they point to. If this were not so, language about God would be completely pointless and meaningless. This would amount to a thoroughgoing agnosticism, and as regards God, such agnosticism always leads to atheism. But even with its proper mode of dissimilar similarity, analogical thought has a tendency to specify God too precisely and by univocity and one-sidedness to circumscribe the all-inclusive or to delimit parts in what by its very nature is indivisible. Consequently, analogical thought requires a complementary kind of language about God, the language of dialectical statements. These do not envisage the divine solely from one angle and under one aspect but, because of its illimitedness, address it from many, even opposite points of view and under various aspects. Analogical thought itself of course includes a dialectical element by its emphasis on similarity *in* dissimilarity. As a consequence, dialectical statements about God, which, for example, think of God's divinity both as hidden *and* manifest, as transcendent *and* immanent, as absolute *and* as a factor in history, and which proceed both theocentrically and anthropocentrically, cannot dispense with the analogical element in each of the particular designations they employ. Recognition of this would lead at the same time to a better realization that statements about God always belong to a particular thought-form and are therefore inadequate. They would then be kept open for supplementation by other thought-forms.

6. *The history of revelation as warrant for speech about God.* Thus even if man can only think of God mediately and can only speak of him in a fragmentary way, this possibility exists and is even obligatory through the primal word of God uttered in revelation. By this utterance, God himself has entered into human language and has permanently empowered it to express him. And so the scandal which dialectical theology still takes at language about God founded on the analogy of being, is removed by showing that there is an *analogy of faith* in which God himself from on high chooses and sanctions created language as a symbolic expression of his mystery. The high claim implied in this affirmation of the possibility of appropriate language about God, ought not to be countered with the objection that God is thereby anthropomorphically distorted and diminished. Serious consideration ought rather to be given to the fact that by his creation and endowment with grace man is a "theomorphic" being called to speech about God and with him.

But if such speech is not to fail in its purpose in regard to the absolute God, it must follow the path by which God himself came down to man in revelation itself, i.e., it must be in accordance with revelation. The God of revelation is not an abstract idea of the supreme being. He is the Lord who turns to man in history, giving him grace and saving him. For statements about God to be in accordance with revelation, it is not sufficient that all Christian speech about God should be based on the norm provided by the revealed testimonies of holy Scripture, which themselves find an expression appropriate to their epoch in dogma and the magisterium of the Church. It is necessary, in fact, that such speech should not give the first place to statements about God's metaphysical being in himself and their speculative deduction from a root metaphysical concept. That place must be taken by an account of the saving actions done for man. In these the God of revelation shows himself with his care for the world, his love, holiness and justice as man's "pro me", powerful on man's behalf. But the complete form of God's concern for the world, God's true "being along with us", has revealed itself in the incarnate Son, in Jesus Christ. Consequently, language about God which is in accordance with revelation must always remain centred on God's highest concrete expression which took place in the coming of the God-man. The light of the revelation of Christ must always shine on any idea of God that accords with revelation. What God's love, truth, holiness or justice is, in language in harmony with revelation, must shine forth "in the face of Christ" (2 Cor 4:6), and must be learnt there.

7. *God's being in himself and for us: the idea of God.* This of course raises for the thoughtful believer the question whether statements about God's being in himself, and therefore any use of metaphysical language about God in ontological categories, are not impossible and therefore to be rejected. Here what Scripture itself has to say should serve as a warning of the need for caution. Scripture in fact indicates that God's *action* in regard to the world also reveals a divine *being*, which a fully conscious (theological) faith certainly can and must take as the subject-matter of statements. For God does not consist solely of his relation to man in revelation or of his significance for man. A purely functional concept of God of that kind which sought wholly to eliminate God's intrinsic being would ultimately make God a human simulacrum. The God of OT revelation is not merely his nation's helper in its life and survival. Here and there in Scripture use is made of God's so-called absolute attributes, which cannot be inferred solely from his relation to the world but truly transcend it (cf. Num 23:19; Ps 102:28). Such investigation of God's being is not intended solely to protect God's relation to the world, and his benignity towards man in history, from the danger of an anthropomorphic interpretation which would make the personal God a mere higher demiurge or superior world-spirit. It also promotes recognition and worship of the deepest mystery of God, which does not consist solely of his gracious merciful action for the world, but is in his being, which is not exhausted or exhaustible by that action.

It is indisputable nevertheless that Christian discourse about God in accordance with revelation will prefer to speak of the active attributes manifested in God's history with mankind rather than to determine the metaphysical attributes of God's essence. Consequently it will speak chiefly of God as Lord, of the events of the creation and the covenant, of his glory, holiness, fatherhood and love, as they impressed themselves on biblical man. Of course the expression of the attributes which have a biblical basis and which are relative "ad nos" in revelation gives rise to the hermeneutical question whether their relevance to human existence can still be made clear to people of today in a changed sociological situation. Is it possible to bring out the individual relevance of the content of the theological message? Here translation is indispensable. But it will respect the conditions of genuine translation which are fidelity to the original and recognition of an inalienable identity of spirit. In ontological terms this means that such a translation cannot deviate from the principle that God himself does not alter even though human thought changes. Even if the concept of God changes with a new world-picture and understanding of being, it contains an immutable element, and something constant in man himself corresponds to this. If this assumption is not made, and it is asserted with D. Bonhoeffer, for example, that modern man has become formally godless and no longer acknowledges any religious *a priori*, there is no point of reference in man for those "absolute" attributes of God and a translation is impossible. All understanding of the original language has been lost. In that case, however, it is not only superfluous to "smuggle in" God as a "stop-gap" into extreme human situations from which there is no escape (Bonhoeffer); it is also impossible to confront man with God at man's "strongest point", i.e., "in the midst of life", in his "health, strength, certainty and simplicity". For according to this conception man is conscious of his maturity in a transcendental and radical sense and therefore can no longer stand in need of God. If intellectual honesty in the Christian "proclamation of God" is understood in this way, and if it remains logically coherent, it will finally be compelled to draw the conclusion against itself and completely eliminate the truth of God from man's mind.

When the inadequacy of such enthusiasm for the negative is once recognized, it becomes possible to indicate the existential context of the biblical concepts in the new world-picture. Then the God who reveals himself in the history of the Covenant as Lord does not entail man's tutelage and enslavement. He reveals man's vocation to a partnership in which equality of rights does not indeed prevail, but in which man, precisely by his awareness of infinite distance, experiences his own greatness which consists in transcending himself towards the infinity of God. Then God's holiness becomes intelligible to man in relation to man himself, as the plenitude which manifests man's need, as the grace which judges him but also raises him from his sinfulness, as the power which obliges him to profoundest reverence. It is then impossible to misunderstand God's fatherhood as if it meant setting up an external heteronomous authority. It is seen to point to a transcendental living dependence which is the ground which makes human freedom and dignity possible and makes man, as God's mandatary in the empirical domain of this world, grow to his full stature as a creature.

The unique love of God which is revealed in his fatherhood and which, according to 1 Jn 4:8, can even be understood as the decisive NT definition of God, can then be taken generally as the essence of the divine action in regard to the world, which has its supreme revelation in the Son's sacrifice as victim for sin (Jn 3:16). This also manifests directly the relation to the world of this essential attribute of God, which the Gospel deduces from God's act of revelation just as it does God's power over man. The very form of this merciful love, accepting and overcoming death, throws light on the fundamental enigma of human existence, that of evil. God in his merciful love here effects something higher than love of esteem or love of friendship (the distinction between eros and agape being duly noted). This is evident from the power with which love penetrates the dark mystery of sin and throws many points of light into its darkness, even if it does not illuminate it fully. This holds good not only in regard to the objective disposition of the order of salvation but also to the subjective experience of the redeemed human being. He experiences most profoundly the power of God's love when he is in the situation of the prodigal son (Lk 15:11–32).

God's love only appears in its full magnitude through the resistance of sin. But it seems, however, to lose its superior power at the end of history, where the mystery of evil flows into the mystery of reprobation. Here the love of God appears not to prevail over sin, and the highest purpose of God's active reality is apparently curtailed. The assumption of a double divine decree, predestinating some to salvation, the rest to perdition, as in Calvinism, would at once detract from the genuineness of God's all-embracing love. On the other hand it would be no solution to re-edit the doctrine of apocatastasis and regard evil as swallowed up in the end by divine power. K. Barth sees here an actual danger of curtailing the freedom and gratuitousness of divine love and of naturalizing it into a cosmic power. Certainly a faith which is convinced of the omnipotence and purposefulness of God's love which is so resplendent in revelation cannot discuss the phenomenon of reprobation by bypassing this love and taking no account of it. It will rather note that the freedom inherent in this divine love cannot nullify the decision of freedom even in man and the sinner, but can only keep on inviting it afresh. The mystery of the loss of the goal of beatitude cannot be attributed to the lack or lessening of divine love for particular human beings but only to a love which always respects created freedom and which bears and tolerates the sinner's self-hardening. Thus in the mystery of definitive loss of God, God's love shows itself to be a love which permits man's totally free decision and endures its resistance, just as the love of Christ on the cross not only overcame the sin of those who were converted but also endured the sin of the unrepentant and obdurate. Consequently even the mystery of reprobation is comprised within divine love, though this can only manifest itself to the reprobate in the dark glow of his own disordered self-love and obduracy in the misuse of his freedom.

Some light is thrown on the darkness of this mystery by the historical experiences which man has of God's love. He can recognize that in the revelation of God's love, justice also is achieved, the justice with which the Holy One must cast from himself the evil to which man clings, and which God must leave to its own futility. Even the divine justice, which according to the strong expressions of the OT is revealed in the wrath and jealousy of God (Exod 32:11; 34:14, etc.), must not, theologically speaking, be regarded as a by-way of the divine paths, running alongside but unconnected with the universal mainstream of divine love, even though its complete conceptual integration is impossible to human understanding. It is possible for us at least to recognize that God must measure and judge finite human love and its defective manifestations by the measure of his own love. All earthly love requires the observance of measure and order, and God's love is the universal standard for the love which is required of man, the standard by which its absence or defective forms can be recognized. Man experiences the nonfulfilment of the standard required of him as God's justice and punitive verdict. At the same time it must be remembered that for man in his condition as pilgrim, as the history of salvation supremely demonstrates, every such judgment given by God always includes an offer of salvation. Consequently the biblical concept of God's justice can also signify the constancy with which he asserts his saving and loving will in the world and obtains his "rights", that is, causes his grace to prevail. At the same time this means that, as its obverse so to speak, the divine justice which bestows salvation brings into operation the diacritical function also. This is displayed as judgment and condemnation when man resists divine grace and holds fast to this decision. Consequently God's justice itself may be regarded as an element of his love directed towards the world and therefore set up for man as a standard. Viewed in this way, love always remains, the all-inclusive and guiding principle of God's action in the world. Those who earnestly seek their salvation can therefore be convinced that God's justice can never stand *against* his love and that the greatest love possesses the greatest clarity of judgment.

Love as a warm affection for a beloved person only attains its full identity if it is welcomed and reciprocated by the beloved. Consequently even God's love which is intrinsically perfectly free from desire and need, objectively seeks the response of the creature's love. This is aroused and evoked by God's love itself, and while it consists primarily in the act of love of God it is inseparably linked with love of the neighbour (cf. Mt 25:40; 1 Jn 4:20). The reason for this unity does not lie only in the dynamism inherent in genuine love of God, which necessarily extends to all that God has created. It has even deeper roots in the social character of the individual human being, whose self-development is only possible through personal relations with his fellow men. The perfect love of God as the highest act of human self-fulfilment can therefore only be exercised in conjunction with love of the neighbour, and is impossible without the latter. A purely existential, anthropological interpretation of the love of God is therefore excluded. The human act of loving God is not identical with love of the neighbour, and love of God is not only accomplished in love between human beings. L. Feuerbach's transposition of the Johannine sentence (1 Jn 4:16) into "Love is God" turns God's inaccessible subjectivity into an attribute of man and leads to a purely horizontal religious spirit. Coherently developed, this can no longer maintain the reality of God and soon dispenses even with the name of God. Fundamentally it also destroys the special quality of Christian love of the neighbour. The source of this love is that prior to any human love God gives himself to man in incomprehensible grace. This alone is what enables man to love his neighbour in a way which far transcends any consideration of utility or any humanistic motives. Only those who have first known God's love in Christ can love their neighbour as God's image unselfishly and without reserve.

A purely horizontal interpretation of God's love which is identical with a total reduction of God's transcendence to human immanence, is excluded for Christian thought for another reason which points to the mystery of the Trinity. God's love for the world must not be regarded as a natural, necessary movement towards the creature, otherwise God will appear to be an indigent and dependent being. This impression is only to be avoided if the divine being is believed to be a movement of love even independently of any relation to the world and in itself. But this is only possible between persons. And so the recognition of God in his essence as love, independently of the world, leads to the assumption that there are personal relations within God, which constitute the mystery of the Trinity. Of course it is only possible to make this conceptual connection on the basis of a positive divine revelation of the three persons in God, such as is found in the history of salvation. The NT above all makes it clear that God's being in its relation to the world and as bestowing salvation finds its perfect revelation in Jesus Christ the Son of the Father, and that this revelation becomes in the Holy Spirit a permanent reality in the world which lays hold of man and fills him. Thus the revelation-event itself exhibits a personal linking of God's action with the unoriginated abyss of love in the Father, the perfect generation of this love in the Son, and its spiritual interiorization and its perpetual actualization in the Holy Spirit who as truth (Jn 14:17), love (Rom 5:5) and holiness (1 Pet 1:15) permanently transmits revelation as principle of life. In this sense belief in the Trinity would be genuine biblical kerygma, even though it could not be demonstrated beyond all dispute by trinitarian texts. A fundamental trinitarian awareness, expressed in many triadic formulas, is a very definite feature of the NT (cf. 2 Cor 13:13; 1 Cor 12:4ff.; Eph 1:3; 1 Pet 1:2). In it the plenitude of revelation present in Christ unfolds both (backwards) into the source of revelation hidden from us, and (forwards) into the presence of the revealing power dwelling in us in the Holy Spirit. Regarded in this way, the mystery of the Trinity is not a *mysterium logicum* merely imposing submission on the understanding. It is the mystery of perfect redemption in which the mysterious "God above us" (the Father) becomes "God with us" (the incarnate Son) and "God in us" (the Holy Spirit in grace).

It is true that such an account of the Trinity which follows the course of the testimonies of revelation in the economy of salvation, might give the impression that the true personal nature of the principles of the economy of salvation is not preserved and safeguarded. In fact, such safeguards are only possible in discussing the "immanent Trinity" if ontological terms (substance, relation, propriety) are also used. This doctrine, which took form in the Christological and Trinitarian controversies of the patristic period, is not a mere external addition to a kerygma of the NT essentially expressed in terms of the history of salvation (cf., for instance, *D* 39, 40). That is why even the early Trinitarian controversies had a soteriological purpose. It can be seen that a triadic economy, if not rooted in the immanent relationships of the three divine persons and their essential unity, would soon have had to be reduced to a merely apparent triad and the mere semblance of an economy. The triadic structure of sacred history and of the reality of redemption (which is not to be regarded as merely a temporal succession in the operation of the three persons), unless anchored in firm faith in an immanent Trinity of three essentially equal persons, could only be regarded as an appearance of the one God in various forms. Such a "modalism" in the economy of salvation could never support the weight of reality and salvation contained in the events of creation, redemption and eschatology effected by the Father, Son and Holy Spirit. Realizing this, Origen drew the conclusion: "(The believer) will not attain salvation if the Trinity is not complete."

The perfection of salvation and its intellectual justification is finally explicitated in the question of the indwelling of the Trinity in the justified. At the present time this is answered more and more often on the lines that a genuinely personal relation links the three divine persons and the grace-endowed human being. Thus the mystery of the intrinsic being of God over and above the transmission of the divine saving action to the world, truly finds its perfect counterpart in man, who is sealed with the life of the Trinity. Here the mystery of the infinite God is continued in the mystery of finite man, "theology" becomes "anthropology", without one cancelling the other or being in any way incompatible with it.

Leo Scheffczyk

II. Knowability of God

When the question of the knowability of God is consciously posed, it is seen to be inseparable from that of the proof of the existence of God, but not identical with it. It has the prior task of defining the framework within which alone a rational proof of the existence of God can be possible.

1. *In the Bible.* The texts which speak of a universal possibility of knowing God, even in non-Christians and pagans, are Wis 13:1–9 and Rom 1:18–21. Wis 13:1ff. affirms that God may be known from the greatness and beauty of visible good things, as Lord of all creation. Men's failure to acknowledge

God as Lord of creation is understandable but inexcusable. Paul writes in the same vein in Rom 1:18ff., "For the wrath of God is revealed from heaven against all ungodliness and wickedness of men who by their wickedness suppress the truth. For what can be known about God is plain to them, because God has shown it to them. Ever since the creation of the world his invisible nature, namely, his eternal power and deity, has been clearly perceived in the things that have been made (ἀόρατα . . . νοούμενα καθορᾶται). So they are without excuse; for although they knew God they did not honour him as God or give thanks to him, but they became futile in their thinking and their senseless minds were darkened." In conjunction with Rom 2:14ff., where it is said that the conscience of pagans and their words of self-accusation or excuse give testimony to the law written in their hearts, according to which they act by nature, we have here a clear indication of the universal knowability of God. But the knowledge is hardly meant as theoretical and conceptual. It is to grow out of man's conscience in his contact with the things of this world, which is a sort of medium through which it is obviously discernible. Being a practical and existential knowledge of God, it is not threatened by stupidity or deficiencies on the intellectual or rational level, but by the moral attitude, the refusal of truth, injustice. Whatever be the exact translation one adopts for these passages, one must be careful not to read into them philosophical principles which cannot be intended. The fact that they affirm that the godhead of God appears and is obvious through the medium of the created world need not be taken to mean an indirect knowledge of God through causality or deduction. Quite apart from the suppositions which can hardly be justified historically, this would be systematically to disregard the immediacy which – according to the text – must be displayed in whatever mediums are used, if one is to speak of the manifestation of the godhead of God in creation.

2. *In the magisterium.* The universal knowability of God, which was constantly presumed or propounded throughout the tradition of the Church, was first formulated as a definition at Vatican I, against positivism, agnosticism and an increasing tendency to traditionalism. It was defined that "the one true God, our creator and Lord, can be certainly known by the light of natural reason, through created things" (*D* 1806; cf. 1785; *DS* 3026, 3004). The actual process by which such knowledge is arrived at is not defined – how, for instance, we are to explain the mediated nature of this knowledge ("through created things") or whether and how it can be enunciated in the form of a rational proof. However, from earlier doctrinal pronouncements (against Bautain, *D* 1622, Bonetty, *D* 1650, and Froschhammer, *D* 1670; *DS* 2751, 2812, 2853), it appears that a *ratiocinatio* is meant, in the sense of a knowledge which is attained through conceptual proofs. On the other hand, the Church has insisted, against all exaggerations of Gnosticism and rationalism, on the necessity of the "moral" assistance of God, if he is to be really known in the concrete by individuals (*D* 1786; *DS* 3005).

3. *In systematic theology.* The Bible and the magisterium are not merely concerned with the possible knowledge of God in the sense of a theoretical and rational proof of his existence, but also and above all with the moral and existential knowledge of God which means acknowledgment of his godhead. Hence theology must distinguish clearly in each case how the knowability of God is understood: as (purely) theoretical or as existential. They are by no means the same thing, as will be seen.

Since patristic times, theologians have constantly been preoccupied with the problem of the rational proof of the existence of God. Two traditions, which sometimes cut across one another, may be distinguished. One is the proof of the existence of God, on the lines of a "clarification of the truth", which goes back to Augustine and ultimately to Plotinus or Plato. The other is that of Thomas with his famous "five ways" which are based on Aristotelian principles. The Augustinian tradition is concerned with the condition of possibility of all spiritual and moral life, a consciousness of truth which as life and light is the deepest *a priori* of all knowledge and will, a primordial source welling up within the inmost core of the human spirit and prior to all man's thoughts and deeds, of which it is thus the explanation just as it is the force and guide of his desire of God. Through all the variations, the general structure of the Thomistic proofs is to demonstrate, on the basis of empirically existing beings and their contingent actuality, that transitory contingent beings cannot be their own sufficient reason. This provides the metaphysical principle of causality ("that which does not exist of itself must exist through another"), which is then used to conclude to a first cause. After further analyses, this first cause is identified with God. What makes this type of proof problematical is that, on principle, all proofs of the existence of God must demonstrate God as a personal being or show that the relationship between man and God is personal. But this means a relationship between (at least) two "freedoms" or two "I's", and not between some other sort of *things*. But the astonishing thing about freedom is that it must to some extent be its own sufficient reason, otherwise freedom would not ultimately be responsible for its own decisions. It is likewise true that consciousness must also be in a certain sense its own sufficient reason, otherwise consciousness could not always be self-consciousness. This relatively self-explanatory personal freedom and consciousness still remains contingent, and there is the question of how we are to think of its being based on a reality outside itself, and indeed of what we are to think in general of the relative independence of the free spiritual reality. But it seems certain at any rate that to explain the relationship between man and God some principle of personal existence is necessary to show how freedom can be called to be and consciousness generated. The production of the person as freedom and consciousness cannot be the same type of causation as gives rise to facts and things. But if the person and its independence cannot be brought about in the same way as a material thing, the contingence of the person cannot be subsumed under the contingence for which the metaphysical principle of causality is valid, even when considered precisely as metaphysical and not physical. For if we do not find a new principle to explain the origin of freedom, the grounds of freedom or of the person would still be considered after the pattern of causality, even when metaphysical, and there would be no advance in the theological problem. Hence a complete justification of the Thomist proof seems to call for an examination of its traditional structure as a whole, to see how the contingence of finite beings can be grasped as the personal contingence of the free consciousness. One should then show how the person is founded on God's summons and how from this summons God may be proved to exist personally and absolutely. Whatever particular forms this transcendental reflection may take, it is clear from the start even in the ideal case of a fully thought out proof of the existence of God, we should have attained only a theoretical knowledge of God, which is logically secondary. If we refuse to admit that such theoretical knowledge is enough as the fundamental justification of human existence – as if we only had to "transpose" rational knowledge into life – then there must be a primordial way of knowing God, given immediately in the historical process along with man's very existence. This historico-existential knowledge must precede all merely rational and secondary mediation, but must, nonetheless, proceed from a truly mediated knowledge, since consciousness of God is not always clearly present as soon as existence is encountered. This primordial mediation of consciousness of God, which man himself brings about in his historical existence is in fact a reality – in personal love or dialogue. The dialogue which takes place in truth and love is the mutual apprehension of the "I" and the "You", where the "I" and the "You" come to consciousness of themselves, and also of their common ground, the love and the truth which becomes event in the encounter.

In the concrete reality of love between two persons, given and received, each loves the other – who loves the other. They love each other by loving their mutual love. Thus they not only love the reciprocity of their love, but much more – as the medium and basis of their reciprocity – love itself. In love as an actual event, both love this love in its intrinsic genesis just as love loves itself. Thus they experience love as origin in themselves. Thus in love there is a consciousness of existence in which the I and the You come to themselves and to each other as to their origin. The transcendence of freedom and consciousness which is "lived" by every "I", being the ultimate *a priori* of human existence, is not *ipso facto* an object of knowledge. But when this transcendence comes "from without" to meet the "I" in the "You", primordially and, as it were, "objectively", and fulfils itself in the encounter, that is, communicates itself in its own being, then, through the dialogue, it is both actual as historical event and consciously known as it primordially is. Where love is real and true as dialogue, the reality of freedom and consciousness in the "I" and the "You" is truly and consciously orientated to its transcendence, that is, to the love which as the light of all consciousness and the life of all freedom displays and attests itself as self-originating. The dialogue is the reflection of existence at its most original in the historic process, and it is also a revelation of transcendence. In this conscious apperception of existence as the act of transcendence, man at last understands what transcendence really is. For it is only in such an act that one grasps the unique quality of transcendence which can never be communicated on the level of theory: the power of love to bring about freedom and insight, the love which approves (or condemns untruth) and grasps existence in its profoundest depths, to ratify and justify it irrevocably in the supreme majesty of love. This is the only way to arrive at an existential knowledge of God. There what is immanent in reciprocal love is disclosed as absolute transcendence, which gives itself a name in its absoluteness and historically speaking can be termed God.

This is a clear demonstration of the value of existential knowledge of God in contrast to all merely theoretical or rational proofs of his existence. We can see why abstract rational proofs must be without effect on the immediate living of life. They lack the majestic conviction which only shows its power in the light coming with love. Rational proofs are inadequate to sustain the confidence of existence, but the existential proof of the dialogue, being actual event, can carry with it conviction from this basic experience. We can also see why sin and guilt are fundamental factors, because the revelation cannot come about where the truth is not willed in the dialogue. This does not mean that men who do not, or think they do not know God must be considered bad in philosophy, and treated for the moment as "psychological cases". The historical condition of the atheist can be shown to be determined by his being open or closed to the truth in the dialogue in question. When we know that true knowledge of God comes about in sincere encounter, we see that the existential force of the theoretical proof of God need not be exaggerated. At the same time we see that the all-sustaining knowledge of God needs to be actuated by man in historical dialogue, and hence that it is largely dependent on the historical situation and traditions in which each man develops. Whether grace is necessary for the apperception of existence which as an act of transcendence implies the knowledge of God may be left an open question, historically speaking. Even if – theologically speaking – grace must be supposed, the universal possibility of existential knowledge of God is not ruled out, since the theology of grace allows us to suppose that the universal salvific will of God is a determining factor and a force in the personal history of every man.

The knowability of God thus appears as the *a priori* condition of possibility of abstract rational proof and as identical with the act of existence as it takes place in the historical dialogue of personal encounter. The knowledge of God implicit therein may be further analysed as regards its conceptual structure, but its true and unique quality can only be known in the experimental proof which every man must set up for himself in life in the boldness of personal encounter.

Eberhard Simons

III. Doctrine of God

1. *Historical.* a) It has always been accepted (although not as a matter of course) in Christian theology that dogmatic theology, if it is to be at all systematic, must begin with the doctrine of God, just as all creeds do. The θεολογία was always placed before the οἰκονομία or doctrine of salvation in the earliest scientific studies. In Origen's Περὶ ἀρχῶν, for example, the doctrine of God is at the beginning of this first systematic synthesis. The medieval theologians, with their conviction that the formal object of dogmatic study was "God as such" (see Thomas Aquinas, *Summa Theol.*, I, q. 1a, 7) must have regarded it as even more obvious that the doctrine of God should be at the beginning of dogmatic theology. But even when they did not adhere to this principle in practice, they often (though not always or consistently) placed the doctrine of God at the beginning. They did not, in other words, commence with the reality of Christ, the Sophia or the kingdom of God, faith itself, man's religious subjectivity or some similar theme, although their view of theology as a whole would lead us to believe that they would. This is understandable in the light of the ultimate meaning of revelation. This is God's disclosure of himself in word and deed (without mediation on the part of any creature and therefore without the knowledge that is made possible by that mediation) as God in his own inner glory. It may not be necessary to place the doctrine of God before the other theological treatises (which fundamentally also deal with the same theme of God's supernatural communication of himself), but it is understandable that it should occupy that position, which is almost universally given to it in Catholic dogmatic theology. This practice is also quite justified (see LTK² I, p. 625; II, p. 1161ff; III, p. 450).

b) A more serious historical difficulty is the relationship between the general doctrine of God (*De Deo uno*) and the doctrine of the Trinity. No homogeneous view can be deduced from the history of theology. The usual sequence of treatises nowadays became the normal and universal practice of the Church from the time that the Sentences of Peter Lombard were replaced by the *Summa Theologiae* of Thomas Aquinas. The Apostles' Creed, with its trinitarian structure, can help us to solve the problem of the unity and the distinction of the two treatises only if the word "God" in the ancient θεός terminology were understood as Father and the whole "being" of God were dealt with in a Greek-orientated theology of the Trinity (orientated towards the world in a linear fashion) in the first chapter of a dogmatic theology about the Father. What is remarkable is that the Master of the Sentences included the general doctrine of God within and subordinated it to a doctrine of the Trinity (Grabmann regarded this as one of Peter Lombard's "main errors") and that there is no smooth division between the two treatises in the *Summa Alexandri*. On the other hand (although his reasons are not made clear – he may have done it in opposition to the Arabic systems or for apologetical or educational motives) Thomas Aquinas did not unambiguously (see the Augustinian and Latin system) anticipate in the general doctrine of God a doctrine of God the Father as the origin without an origin in the deity, but rather anticipated the doctrine of a God of all persons of a common nature (*ST* I, q. 2–25), and only after this began with a doctrine of the Trinity.

Generally speaking, the situation has not changed; one-sided defences of this method are still met with. It is only very recently (for example, A. Stolz and Schmaus) that it has rightly been seen as a problem.

c) It is also remarkable that there is always a section, in all recent dogmatic theologies, on man's knowledge of God. This is particularly surprising in view of the fact that the proper place for this section is anthropology. It would certainly be possible to justify this action if this section were taken to a more profound level so that it could be made clear that, in this case, knowing and what is known (faith and what is believed) are specially and indeed uniquely related in such a way that what is said about the first could really and essentially only be understood in the light of what is said about the second. This is analogous to the case of ontology, in which the doctrine of being and the doctrine of knowing about being form an inseparable unity.

d) As far as the inner structure of the treatise is concerned (when the doctrine of God and that of the Trinity are kept separate), it has for some time been usual, after presenting the problem of God's "being", to provide a treatise on his qualities (his attributes or perfections). In this treatise, themes are customarily discussed which might equally well be found in the doctrine of creation and grace – themes such as providence (the government of the world) and predestination. This treatise on God's qualities almost always follows metaphysical guidelines; they are divided into static and active qualities, the first being sometimes subdivided into transcendental and predicamental attributes.

These tangible aspects of the history of the inner structure of the treatise on the doctrine of God do not, however, provide us with any powerful impulse to understand the problem of the theological aspects of the doctrine.

2. *Systematic.* a) *The priority of the treatise.* As we have already seen, quite apart from the need to introduce dogmatic theology (which is practised everywhere) and apart from the possibility of its being used in fundamental theology and in formal and fundamental theology, the doctrine of God is always placed at the beginning of the "special" dogmatic theology of the Catholic Church. (This means that no prior decision is made concerning the questions to be outlined under paragraphs c and d.) On the one hand, there is revelation and the history of salvation (and therefore the formal essence of theology) as God's disclosure of himself. On the other hand, there is the transcendental and ec-centric aspect of man who is called to respond in faith

and obedience to this God who discloses himself and who is only truly himself when he finds God and who would not find God if he were considered simply in his *ad nos*. These two aspects make it necessary for man to speak first not about his own salvation, but about God. This does not, however, mean that the origin of our divine knowledge of Christ should be forgotten in the treatise on the doctrine of God, which should, on the contrary, provide a clear idea of God. This idea of God ought to take into account man's experience of God in the history of salvation and avoid the risk of silently accepting an abstract metaphysical structure as a *norma non normata* for who, what and how God "may" be.

b) The treatises *De Deo uno* and *De Deo trino* appear in this order, as though the second were simply a "completion" of the first and as though statements can only be made in the doctrine of the Trinity which go beyond metaphysics, although this has to be confirmed and guaranteed. In this order of presentation, the factual history of theology is forgotten, that is, the two possibilities provided by this doctrine of the Trinity – the Augustinian Latin tradition and the Greek tradition. The appearance of the two treatises in this sequence also wrongly suggests that the history of revelation itself followed this order, in other words, that God's being was revealed first and then the Trinity was revealed. We might just as well say that the history of revelation first disclosed God as a person without origin in his relationship with the world and then disclosed him as the origin of life processes forming divine persons. Whether these two treatises are allowed to follow each other in one sequence or another or whether they are merged together is not so much a question of principle as a question of teaching. In any case, it is important not to elaborate the doctrine of God, if it is separated from that of the Trinity and placed before it, as though the second did not exist. The God of history who communicates himself to man by progressively revealing himself (and this is, after all, clearly a theme of the general doctrine of God) is certainly the God who communicates and reveals himself progressively as the Trinity. From the theological point of view, God's "being" is only expressed if it is recognized as divinely communicable and this communicability is understood as resulting from the nature of the being dealt with in the doctrine of God itself.

c) It can be regarded as a positive achievement of the later scholastic tradition to deal within the doctrine of God itself with the doctrine of man's knowledge of God. (This doctrine is discussed in its natural and in its supernatural forms, both as a point of departure – natural creation and the history of salvation – and as an ability – reason and supernatural faith supported by grace – as well as in its stages of development leading up to the vision of God.) There is a unique relationship here between knowledge as a subjective act and what is known, which never occurs at least in principle elsewhere. This knowledge has several distinct aspects. There is the transcendental aspect (pointing to God) of man's knowledge of and a desire for any object. This is accompanied by the inevitability of an (implicit and non-objective) knowledge of God. There is also the distinctive characteristic of the religious act and the need which results from precisely this knowledge for a total personal participation (if the act of knowing in faith is authentic and long-lasting). All these aspects have the effect of bringing about a unique interdependence of man's reflective knowing about knowledge of God and his direct (transcendentally implicit and objectively direct) knowledge of God. The consequence of this is that reflection about the distinctive character of man's transcendent orientation in grace towards God as an essential mystery makes it clear who God really is (insofar as this can ever be expressed). This is why what must be presented in a section of this kind is not simply the fact that God can be known in this way (and only as "natural" knowledge), but also an exhaustive analysis of its essence and distinctive character, because it is only in this way that the essential being and the distinctive character of what is known will be made clear. It is even possible to ask whether the essential aspects of our spiritual and personal attitude towards God (going beyond a theoretical cognizance) should not be outlined at least briefly here, because they are not developed as a whole elsewhere (despite the treatises on faith, the theological virtues and so on). This question may be asked, even though it is true to say that it has to be answered fully within the context of moral theology. It is, however, not simply a question of the metaphysical aspects of transcendent necessity, but rather a question of man's most suitable reaction, as defined in positive revelation, to God's free attitude towards him in the history of salvation.

d) *Structure and theme*. (i) *Fundamental aspects*. In considering the inner structure and theme of the doctrine of God, we raise the whole problem both of the relationship of the supernatural order and of the reciprocal knowledge and also (and this is in both dimensions) of the relationship between essential and existential knowledge and of the two co-ordinated themes. In any attempt to solve this problem, it is clearly not enough to stress that dogmatic theology has to acquire its answers from theological and not from metaphysical sources, if systematic theology and questions are already extensively provided by (equally extensively Christian) philosophy and the dogmatic theologian's task of preparing the *dicta probantia* is therefore reduced. It would be quite untheological to do this, because it would be acting as though theology as a systematic reflection about revelation could dispense with metaphysics. In the theological doctrine of God, we are basically only concerned with the experience of God through his own historical witness to himself in word and deed. It is, however, in this experience and its expression that man inevitably fulfils his metaphysical existence. The more clearly he reflects about it and the more open he becomes to the witness that God bears to himself, the more purely he will be able to express it. This statement may include not only God's essential characteristics, but also the fundamental structures, which persist throughout the history of salvation, of his free attitude towards the world. (The whole area covered by these actions can only be expressed by dogmatic theology as a whole.) These two data are usually not distinguished clearly enough. Faithfulness, mercy, love and so on, which we experience and then express in this treatise, are not simply the (theologically attested) necessary "qualities" of God's metaphysical being. They are essentially more than this, for the simple reason that God could also refuse to show us precisely this faithfulness, mercy and love, which he in fact shows us, without ceasing to be faithful, merciful or loving in a metaphysical sense. It ought therefore to be possible, taking this as our point of departure, to gain an insight into the essential meaning of Luther's *theologia crucis*. God's actions (even more than his qualities) cannot, because their effects on us are plural, be expressed in one concept. All that we can do is to express formally, in a statement which a-symptotically alludes to the unity of God, the fact that God's actions must be one in God himself and that they are merged together in him in perfect harmony. For us, they cannot be synthesized materially. Their effect on us therefore has, in itself and in our reaction to them, a history. A metaphysical equilibrium cannot and does not even need to prevail in our attitude towards these actions in this history. We should, for instance, praise God's mercy more than we fear his justice, because he has let his grace rather than his anger prevail. These structures, which are present in the history of God's dealings with man, have a rightful place in the doctrine of God and prevent the doctrines of providence, of God's freedom in conferring effective grace and of the historical character of salvation from becoming merely static, empty and formal. (This would result in the emergence of a theological counterpart to Heidegger's profane concept of a "history of being".)

(ii) If God's *being* is presented in the theological treatise on the doctrine of God as absolute being, it should not necessarily be irrelevant theologically (however little it may be a real statement about faith). The question as to what the "content" of God's being is will only remain open as what it shows itself to us in the history of salvation, revealing itself to itself. Ought we not, in this case, on the one hand to go back to an inclusive interpretation of Exod. 3:14 and 1 Jn 4:16 and, on the other, to make it quite clear that the infinite fullness of being of the *actus purus* with its aseity can only be "understood" if it is worshipped as the holy mystery? Because the concept of the person is necessary in theological statements about the Trinity, a terminological "bottleneck" tends to develop in the general doctrine of God. The personal character of God (Schmaus) as such (which is included in the *substantia spiritualis* of Vatican I – see *D* 1782 – but which still remains to some extent obscure) could be elaborated more explicitly in this kind of definition of God's being (together with an attempt to overcome the difficulties experienced by modern man, with his sense of the absence of God). The doctrine of the "divine names" could also play a much more important part in this question of God's being as dealt with in the treatise on the doctrine of God, because the "physical being" of a person (as distinct from that of a thing) has to be understood not simply as the sum of his necessary qualities, but also as the concrete expression of his free understanding of himself with regard to us. This concretization is expressed in these divine names as abbreviations of man's experience of the history of salvation.

Karl Rahner

GOD, ATTRIBUTES OF

1. *The problem of treatment.* If revelation in sacred history is God's self-communication in word and deed, it is also the self-revelation of his living and giving, his "truth" (in contrast to any creaturely mediation and the knowledge which is thereby given), which are traditionally designated as the nature and the attributes of God. These topics are dealt with in the tractate *De Deo uno* (separately from the theology of the Trinity), though they are also treated under the headings of creation and grace. Insofar as revelation is not concerned with the imparting of metaphysical statements about being to a purely receptive and speculative reason, but rather with the evocation of the knowledge, freedom and faith which direct men toward God, the theological elucidation of the attributes of God is not so much concerned with a theoretical explanation of certain themes, as with the demonstration of the summons contained in these assertions (in spite of its being possible to misunderstand them in an objectivating sense). The treatment of the attributes of God should therefore not follow an abstract metaphysical principle (as in fact it

generally does), but the progressive self-revelation of God in sacred history. In this method of presentation, nevertheless, it must always be made clear that all experiences of God, including those of the OT, must be related to the experiences which Jesus had of God and are to be interpreted in the light of his experience. All the experiences of God which are recounted in sacred history are to be viewed against this horizon.

The question of the attributes of God cannot be answered, therefore, by a metaphysical sketch-plan of the idea or the "nature" of God, which (as a *norma normans et non normata*) would decide in advance who and what God "could be". The answer can only be given by God himself in the form of his own free and characteristic decisions in the events of revelation. That which occurs in the course of sacred history is not an instance of some natural law which must ever act in the same fashion; it is primarily an incalculable free act of grace. Nevertheless, the historical action of God has as a whole an inner relationship to the world and represents thereby a revelation of his "nature". Thus, the OT and the NT display a unity of action and an identity in the attributes of God. Yet this identity throughout the history of revelation must not be reduced to the necessity and static nature of a metaphysical image of God. God is the same according to both OT and NT, not because both ascribe to him a necessarily changeless being, but because the whole of sacred history represents the progressive revelation of how a free and historically active God chose to act in regard to his creation, and of whom he showed himself to be.

However, this revelation of God who is active in history addresses a world from which he was already not "far away" (Acts 17:27) but to which he had always revealed himself in "natural revelation" (and this revelation is known by Christian faith to have a supernatural orientation). Theology, as a reflection upon the revelation in Jesus Christ, thus includes in its understanding of this word the "preparatory word" of God concerning himself and explains it by means of a questionable pre-Christian natural theology. It is called upon to give such an explanation not only by the revelation in Christ, but by this natural theology itself. But this call can bring with it the temptation to make that "preliminary understanding" of the natural knowledge of God the criterion of his historical self-revelation. This unavoidable ambivalence of call and temptation is the basis of the legitimacy and the limitations of theological assertions about the attributes of God.

2. *The traditional teaching on the attributes of God.* By the attributes of God the traditional scholastic teaching understands the divine perfections which are really identical with one another, which make up the "physical nature" of God and which are founded in the "metaphysical nature" of God as the ultimate ground of the divine being from which the attributes can be said to follow as from a logically prior being. The nature and the attributes of God are completely identical by virtue of the absolute simplicity of God. The distinction between the individual attributes is only virtual. As God is ultimately absolute mystery, all the assertions which theology can make concerning his attributes are much more disproportionate than proportionate. This incomprehensibility of God is itself, according to Lateran IV, one of the attributes of God. "We firmly believe and profess with sincere hearts that there is only one, true, eternal, incommensurable and unchangeable, incomprehensible, omnipotent, and ineffable God." (*D* 428.) These affirmations are repeated by Vatican I in a somewhat more expanded form: "There is one, true, living God, Creator and Lord of heaven and earth, omnipotent, eternal

immense, incomprehensible, infinite in intellect and will and in every perfection. As he is one unique spiritual substance, wholly simple and unchanging, we must acknowledge him to be really and essentially distinct from the world, totally blessed in himself and of himself and ineffably elevated above all things which are and can be thought of apart from him." (*D* 1782.) Theology generally arranges these attributes according to negative and affirmative, communicable and non-communicable, absolute and relative, static and dynamic. The necessity of a doctrine of the attributes of God is founded on the nature of human thought which is incapable of adequately including and comprehending in one act the whole of a "higher" being in its unity and simplicity. When speaking of the attributes of God we must always remain conscious of the inadequacy and limitations of human expressions with respect to the divine mystery.

3. *The attributes of God and the biblical concept of God.* The scholastic teaching concerning the attributes of God can claim to be founded on the testimony of the Scriptures. Nevertheless, the extent of this testimony is very limited, for the teaching on the attributes of God is in the end the product of scholastic philosophy and not of biblical thought. Biblical thought is not concerned with a metaphysical knowledge of God. The question about an ἀρχή, an ἰδέα, a last and final unity, is not asked in the OT or the NT and therefore questions about the nature or the attributes of God are not posed. The existence of (*one*) God is spontaneously assumed in the Scriptures: there is no need to prove that God is, for he reveals himself to his people in the faithfulness of his interventions. Thus, the Scriptures do not ask *who* God is, but only *how he shows himself* in his actions with men. One can only conclude to the nature of God on the basis of his actions with men, and the Scriptures speak primarily about these actions of God in the history of salvation.

God revealed himself *gradually* to Israel in the institutions and promises of the covenant. This absolutely free and sovereign revelation and the knowledge of God which it imparts are given in history, i.e., this revelation contains surprises, new horizons, and developments. It was awaited by the men concerned in hope and openness for the future, that of God and their own. The definitive revelation in the history of God's self-disclosure is the revelation of the Father in his servant Jesus. Through his obedience Jesus has become the way to all knowledge of God.

As God revealed his countenance gradually in concrete historical actions, the biblical image of God is a dynamic one. Naturally, many statements of Scripture about the mode of God's actions can be taken as indirect statements concerning the attributes of God. The Scriptures themselves understand these statements, however, as the personal active revelation of the divine freedom. According to the Scriptures, it is only to a limited extent that this can also be verified in "natural" ways on the basis of the world and its structures. But even here assertions such as those concerning the eternity (Rom 16:26), immortality (Eph 6:24; 2 Tim 1:10), and invisibility of God (Rom 1:20 etc.) take on new significance in the light of God's redemptive action. They lose their abstractness and are experienced in concrete relations. For "the knowledge of the glory of God" shines "in the face of Christ" (2 Cor 4:6) and reveals itself in the Spirit in whom man is able to call God "Father". Hence divine predicates such as ἀόρατος (Rom 1:20; Col 1:15, etc.), ἄφθαρτος (Rom 1:23; 1 Tim 1:17), μακάριος (1 Tim 1:11), ὁ θεὸς φῶς ἐστιν (1 Jn 1:5) are less characteristic of Scripture than such as "the faithful God" (1 Cor 1:9; 2 Thess 3:3, etc.), the "God of peace" (Rom 15:33; Phil 4:9, etc.), "of patience"

(Rom 15:5), "hope" (Rom 15:13), "trust" (2 Cor 1:3) and "love" (2 Cor 13:11), or, in Johannine terms: "God is truth" (Jn 3:33). It is also said that God is merciful (Lk 1:72, 78, etc.), kind (Mt 19:17 etc.), forgiving (Mt 6:14; Mk 11:25), loving (Jn 3:16 etc.), the "saviour" (Lk 1:42; 1 Tim 1:1; Tit 1:3, etc.). This is a language which, in spite of its affinities with possibly similar assertions of a metaphysics or natural theology, is in the end only intelligible in faith.

Edward Sillem

GOD, GLORY OF

The phrases, "the glory of God", "give glory to God", "act for the glory of God", are part of accepted Christian usage but they need to be properly explained. Understood in too anthropomorphic a way, they fail to do justice to the divine transcendence and hence to the absolutely free and disinterested love of God in his dealings with the world.

1. *Scripture*. Radically, the scriptural notion of the glory of God, in the general sense of the "bright majesty" of God, goes back to the Hebrew כְּבֹד יהוה, which is translated as δόξα by the LXX. Through this translation, it clearly determines the usage of δόξα in the NT. In the Latin Vulgate כָּבוֹד and δόξα are translated by *gloria*. Both δόξα and *gloria* mean more than the English "glory". In many cases it would be better to translate them by "majesty".

a) *The Kebod Yahweh in the OT*. The original meaning of glory in the OT is not, as among the Greeks and the Romans, that of a repute which demands admiration and praise, an honourable fame (cf. Cicero, *Rhetoric*, II, 55). Glory is primarily the real value, the measurable power, the weight of power (כָּבֵד, "to be heavy, weighty"). This meaning goes hand in hand with the classic sense of the majesty of fullness of light, of wisdom or beauty, which are worthy of honour and praise. Yahweh both reveals and conceals his *kabod* in the cloud and in consuming fire (Exod 16:7f.; 16:10; 24:15–17; 40:34f.; 40:38; Deut 5:24), a fire as bright and powerful as thunder and lightning, testifying to the powerful, inaccessible and terrible majesty of God. For those who experience it, this manifestation of Yahweh means punishment or gracious help (Lev 9:6, 23f.; Num 14:10; 16:19, etc.), which inspire adoration and praise: Exod 15:1, "I will sing to the Lord, for he has triumphed gloriously"; Exod 15:7; Ps 29:1–9. As well as by the marvels, the *kabod* of Yahweh is also revealed by the natural course of the world, and it summons all peoples to the praise of God, Pss 57:6–12; 145:10–12; 147:1.

b) *The doxa in the NT*. The majesty of God has become visible in Jesus Christ. He is the radiance of the *doxa*, the image of God's being (Heb 1:3). The *doxa* of the Father is revealed in the incarnation of his Word (Jn 1:14). Hence the Gospel is the glad tidings of the *doxa* of Christ (2 Cor 4:4). Through Christ, God has illumined men's hearts with "the light of the knowledge of the glory of God in the face of Christ" (2 Cor 4:6).

The invisible presence of the δόξα in the tabernacle or temple of the ancient covenant (Exod 25:8), for the sanctification of men, is replaced by the incarnation of the Word of God, the personal and tangible presence of God among men (Jn 1:14, 16; 1 Jn 1:1–4). Just as the majesty was once concealed by the cloud, so too now by the humanity of the Word. The δόξα shines forth during the earthly life of Jesus only in "signs" and manifests itself only to believers (Jn 2:11; 11:40). In his state of lowliness, the Son "glorifies" the Father, consummating the work of redemption, and the Father "glorifies" the Son (Jn 12:28; 17:5). For Paul, the risen Lord is the

"Lord of δόξα" (1 Cor 2:8). In the parousia, the heavenly δόξα of Jesus will be revealed to all (Mt 24:30). Peter, James and John experience a foretaste of this glory at the transfiguration (Lk 9:32), as does Paul before Damascus (Acts 9:3).

The glory of the Son is shared by the children of God, whom he "leads to glory" (Heb 2:10), as partners of his glory (1 Pet 5:1–4). According to Paul, the justified already participate in the eschatological glory (2 Cor 3:18; 4:17), though in a hidden manner and essentially in hope (Rom 8:18). The whole creation longs and groans for this glory (Rom 8:19–23).

When Jesus appears in this world, the angels proclaim "glory to God in the highest, and on earth peace among men with whom he is pleased" (Lk 2:14). It is the will of God that the Father should be glorified in the Son (Jn 14:13; Phil 2:11), and that the Son should be glorified in men (Jn 17:1–6). The glorification of God, of Christ and of men go together (2 Cor 4:15), as the fruit of the growing love which comes to completion on the "day of Christ" (Phil 1:9ff.; 1 Pet 1:7; 2 Pet 3:18). In the heavenly kingdom of God, the liturgy will be in the form of adoration and thanksgiving in Jesus Christ (Rom 16:27; Jude 1:24f.; Rev 1:4–7; 5:13).

2. *Systematic theology*. God created the world "not to increase his blessedness or to acquire it, but to manifest his perfection" (Vatican I, *D* 1783, 1803). His glory is primarily his intrinsic ontological perfection and his loving possession of himself in his holiness. The creation in which he manifests himself is ordained towards this holiness and glory, and this manifestation is of itself at once the "external" glory of God, "objective" or *materialis*. But creation would be meaningless if there were not also beings who go beyond this "objective" or "external" glory to respond to the revelation of the majesty of God through their knowledge and free love. The "objective" glory of God is only really glory insofar as it is a summons to spiritual beings to honour God "formally" and subjectively. Thus man would deny his own being if he tried to restrict himself to the "objective" glory of God, that is, to the fact of his human existence as such. But when he gives glory to God, he fulfils himself and finds his own glory in participating in God's glory. Thus, on Prov 16:4, Aquinas says: "The Lord made all things, to communicate himself" (*Summa Theologica*, I, q. 44, a. 4). Irenaeus says: "To those who see God, his glory gives life . . . participation in the life of God is the vision of God and the enjoyment of his blessings . . . the glory of God is the living man, the life of man is the vision of God." (*Adv. Haereses*, IV, 19; *PG*, VII, cols. 1035–37.)

a) Hence, the external glory of God means primarily the subjective attitude of adoring acknowledgment of the majesty of God. It is an act of adoration before the absolute mystery.

b) This act is directed to God's self-revelation, insofar as it manifests the majesty of God in its power and splendour. This self-revelation takes place in and through creation which through its being and through its response reveals God's glory and finds its purpose there. The unsurpassable eschatological revelation takes place in Christ Jesus, as the climax of the history of salvation.

c) The manifestation of the glory of God in history is again based on his fullness of being, his intrinsic power and majesty, as known and affirmed by God himself. This cannot be impaired, extrinsically or intrinsically, and hence constitutes his holiness.

Humbert Bouëssé

GOD–WORLD RELATIONSHIP

1. The relationship between God and the world can be understood in various

ways: as a relationship of knowledge or being, between God and the world or between the world and God. In each case the significance and our certainty are different. The central problem today is the relationship of being (the real relation) between God and the world. The introductory remarks about the other relationships lead up to this.

a) *The relationship of knowledge.* In contrast to theology, philosophy is constituted by the fact that its knowledge ascends from the world to God. Basic notes of the deficiency, the contingency of the world or the transcendence of man in its tension between the finite and the infinite point to the Absolute and Infinite which gives meaning and purpose to the world and to man. Its divine nature is envisaged, strictly speaking, by philosophy only insofar as the interpretation of man's being and activity in his world demands this perspective, and hence makes it possible. In Christian revelation, however, which is the source of theology, the movement of knowledge takes the opposite direction. God reveals what could not be deduced from the ontological structures of the world, his sovereignly free gracious will to impart his own life to men in Jesus Christ, at the same time giving us knowledge of the profound mystery of his triune Godhead. The knowledge "from above" through the word of God criticizes and surpasses with liberating clarity and inexhaustible significance the knowledge "from below", what men learn from the divine works.

b) *The relationship of being*, by which the world is referred to God, is the basis of the relationship of philosophical knowledge between the world and God. There is a relationship of being, a real relationship, in the strictest sense of the word, since the being of the world in its entirety was not just brought about once and for all at its origin, but is produced and sustained by God in continuous creation throughout its continued existence. The being of the world *is* intrinsically a permanent relationship to God, and it is constituted at each moment by this relationship. But the efficient causality is not everything. The world-constitutive relationship should rather be considered for the most part in terms of its finality, by which it is ordained to God. The origin of the world is elevated and surpassed by its future. God freely makes the world exist for the ever greater bestowal of his own excellence and goodness. Its goal (the cause of causes, in the old doctrine) is the primary and ultimate dynamism in the ontological relationship of the world to God. This constitutive relationship, recognizable in philosophy, also concerns the Christian faith, with its message of grace bestowed on man, of which the centre is the personal union with God in Jesus Christ. For it is the fundamental presupposition and outline of the final end which is but general and unfulfilled.

What has been said hitherto about the relationship of knowledge, philosophically and theologically, and about the relationship of being, as between the world and God, is in substance common ground among Catholics. But as regards a real relationship appertaining in itself to the order of reality, between God and the world, i.e., relating God to the world, philosophy – and traditional theology for the most part – hold that this must be denied. Today, however, theological reflection is inclined to maintain the reality of the relationship of God, the God of grace, to man and the world.

2. We shall now try – without claiming to give a complete solution – to propound or indicate the grounds for and against, a) in philosophy, b) in theology, and c) take up a middle position which will be necessarily very fluid and open.

a) The philosophical reasons against a real relationship aim at preserving

God's absolute independence as regards all that is not God, and the immutability thereby involved. A relationship to the world would change God, because it would add something real to his being, like an accident. For all change and increase would imply potentiality and hence contingency and finiteness. To take an example from human experience: husband and wife become through generation and conception ("fundament of the relationship") subjects or bearers of the relationship to their child ("term of the relationship"), and as such subjects they are called parents. The relationship is accessory to the already existing "absolute" being of the subject, and is really distinct from it, which is the characteristic of real "predicamental" relationship. This implies that it is impossible in the infinitely simple, unchangeable being of God. God's absolute independence excludes the second type of relationship, the "transcendental", in which a being or a principle of being is of itself (without any additional predicament of relation, and hence transcendentally, that is, in a way pervading and surpassing all predicaments or categories) related to its term of relationship, without which it can neither be nor be thought of (cf. W. Brugger). Such a relationship, which is really identical with its subject, exists reciprocally between finite substance and its accidents, or between body and soul; and the real relationship of the creature to the creator is now generally included under this head.

The philosophers who reject the real relationship of God to the world (cf. Brugger on A. Brunner.) consider that a transcendental relationship implies dependence of the subject on the term even when (as in creation) the term only comes to be through the free decision of the subject. Hence in a transcendental relationship God would not be dependent on the world in the sense that the world was (partial) cause of his relationship to it. But a real relationship of God to the world would be dependent on the reality of the world as the necessary condition of the relationship. Hence God would not be the Infinite Absolute, utterly independent of all that is not God.

But the stringency at least of the argument may be questioned. The real relationship of God to the world would be conditioned by and dependent on the world (which would react, so to speak, on God himself) only if the world, as fundament and presupposition of the relation, were a real factor in the setting-up of the relationship (which would then be conceived as static). But would God be conditioned by and dependent on the world if his creative will, the free decision whereby he really and effectively wills from eternity that the world should be in time, is so purely dynamically and purposefully referred to the world that the world is, of itself, only consecutive to, and not constitutive of, the real relationship of God to the world? If freedom with regard to the existence or non-existence of the world is an intrinsic perfection in God, the necessary eternal exercise of this freedom, the free eternal self-determination, of which the immediate consequence is the existence of the world, is also a perfection. No doubt all this is absolutely identical with the one, simple, unchangeable, infinite will of God, which is his being. But does it follow that the creative will which constitutes the world must only be *considered* by us as a relationship to the world, though it *is* not really so? Even though it is the supreme instance of real self-reference, that is, the most primordial and totally creative? If this "instance" does not fit into the scheme derived from finite relations (especially the words re-lation, "bringing back to"), the terminology must be examined. Strictly speaking, the distinction between transcendental and predicamental relationship is that in the former there is real identity of the relation and its subject, and in the latter case there is not. But it is not simply true (even in *sensu diviso*) that the subject of every transcendental relationship "can neither be nor be thought of" without its term, which is not a constitutive note of transcendental relationship as such. God can truly exist without the world. He only cannot insofar (*in senso composito*) as he is the eternally free creator who wills the world to be real. This creative will as act is absolutely and really identical with God's being in, of and by himself. God in himself does not become different by this willed act (even if we suppose that it contains a real relationship to the world – which is the question).

b) The theological affirmation of the "reality of the relation of God to his creatures" (Schillebeeckx) is now based principally on the personal character of the encounter between man and the creator-God of free grace. The dogma of grace means real "intersubjectivity" between God and man, a living fellowship of love, not two "one-way streets", but a common current to and fro. That the relational can exist, without being relative in the sense of the imperfect, is attested by the revelation of the Trinity in God. Love is essentially a relational reality, and creation and grace are acts of love. Hence God really loves us, "and for that very reason God's mode of being, with regard to really existent men, is a transcendental relationship of love in a real partnership" (Schillebeeckx). Thus God's anger with sin, his joy at men's goodness, would not merely be ways of speaking of effects brought about in sinful or good men, but would be a real activity in God himself. The "absolute newness" of God would react really to human freedom in its history, to the prayer of petition, for instance. The focus of such encounter between God and man, in action and reaction, would be Jesus Christ: "To maintain that the change or becoming is entirely on the side of the humanity of Jesus . . . would be as much as to say that we are dealing with an 'impersonal humanity', not personalized by the Son of God himself." (Schillebeeckx.) An authentic theology, which does not take refuge from the discomforts of metaphysics in a mythologizing vagueness, knows very well (as does Schillebeeckx) that the supposition of a real relationship to the world may not affect the absolute independence of God; that his "reaction" to the actual exercise of men's freedom takes place in sovereign transcendence, which includes man's freedom to set himself free for himself; that, therefore, the "partnership" between God and the world cannot be an interchange on the same level. Otherwise God would not be God and man would not be man (for man, as a relative being, finding himself referred to God, implies intrinsically the absoluteness of God). But the immutability of God must not be confused with frozen rigidity. The mystery of the way God is immutable surpasses human understanding.

But here again a question may be voiced. Do we preserve the divineness of God's being-for-men in creation and grace if we imagine, too anthropomorphically, that God proposes something, then carries it out and finally waits for the actions of his creatures to react to them? God's willing of the world – eternally necessary as an act, eternally free as regards its being terminated in finite objects – identical with his being, has in itself no finite purpose for the world. It has simply an immediate result, arrived at without any finite mediation immanent to the divine will: the very reality of created nature and grace, down to its very core, the humanity of Jesus Christ, produced by its personal assumption by the Son-Logos (for the formal structure, see W. Brugger). God's Yes to the fellowship in love with man, insofar as it is distinct from God's own being, *is* nothing else than the being of man and the world, including the ultimate reality of the most free decision of the creature. Such immediate production of the "other", down to its selfhood and its own activity, is the most sovereign and efficacious, and also the most selflessly free, self-surrendering, self-abandoning affirmation of the "other" in love, purely for his own sake. Because the creative will of God, without the world as prior intrinsic term of relationship, causes world and man to be directly, man and the world, as creatures, belong to God (the more so, in grace, and most of all in Jesus Christ), as the "other", without which God would not be what he is, that is, he who thus loves man and the world. Thomas Aquinas says of God: "amat nos tamquam aliquid sui" (*Summa Theologica*, I, 30, 2 ad 1). Hence God becomes and changes, by creating the world and man with all the changes of his free history, and above all by himself becoming man (without its being necessary to ascribe to him a real relation to the world).

c) A real relation of God to the world cannot be the secondary combination of realities otherwise separate. Once it was misunderstood in this way, silently and commonly but nonetheless to some extent, it had to be rejected by philosophers for the sake of the sovereign independence of God, but it had to be accepted by theologians on account of the reality of God's fellowship in the incarnation and grace with his opposite, man. Whether or not one retains the term (properly understood) of a real (transcendental) God–world relationship, the intermediate position may be put as follows, in the terms now available: God changes because he becomes man; he becomes something else and exists otherwise by becoming and being man. But God, the Absolute, Infinite and Simple, cannot change intrinsically. Hence he changes, not in himself, but in something else belonging to himself. He becomes different, not in himself, but "only" in the otherness of himself. To put the emphasis in this way does justice to the element of truth in the philosophical denial of a real relation of God to the world. Nonetheless, God changes – in his own self's otherness. This does justice to the element of truth in the theological affirmation of a real relation of God to the world. God does not change in his being as it is for himself, but in his being for "the other". God's changing for others and in others does not imply any strict addition (in creation) or diminution (in the incarnation, as self-emptying). It is identical with the infinite living reality of God's own being. In a word, one could say that God changes in that which is other – not God. "God can become something, he who is changeless in himself can be changeable in something else." (K. Rahner, *Theological Investigations* IV, p. 147; see also p. 116, note 15, pp. 148ff., 295; I, pp. 194–206.) "He changes when in producing the derivative 'other' he himself becomes the derivative, without having to undergo the process of becoming in his own originating and original self." (K. Rahner, IV, p. 148.) God, the "self-determining subsistent" (Schillebeeckx), determines himself to becoming man and to creating the world, and becomes and is creator and man: he himself, in the otherness of himself, bringing this other continually to be, through himself, through the subsistent freedom which is his being. "Deus est in se, fit in creaturis." (F. Baader, after Scotus Eriugena, *Werke*, II [1851], p. 145.) Such a solution should not be considered as the mere juggling with words of a feeble dialectics. The two partial affirmations – God himself changes, but not in himself – cannot fall into place for us in a comprehensible – that is, Hegelian – synthesis. Since we cannot comprehend the internal possibility of incarnation and creation, the real solution of this problem of knowledge in our regard is only possible through its being absorbed into the mystery of the love of God, who answers the love of man, which man has because he is loved (1 Jn 4:10).

Walter Kern

GOOD

1. *Introduction.* The good is "the end which is the object of all desire", according to Aristotle, who puts this description forward as traditional (*Eth. Nic.*, I, 1–1094a). Scholasticism took over the definition (e.g., Thomas Aquinas, *Summa Theologica*, I, q. 5, a. 1). The primordial reality of the good allows of definition as little as does the notion of desire. It can only be described on the basis of the experience of the good, that is, on the basis of the self-experience of desire, and classified in the framework of this description. The philosophical tradition has found two perspectives important. One envisages the type and degree of desirability, and divides the good into the *bonum utile* (the useful and helpful), the *delectabile* (that which contents and delights) and the *honestum* (that which is valuable in itself, that which ought to be). The other envisages the reality or the realization of the good, and divides it into *bonum onticum* (or *naturale*, the goodness or appetibility which goes with being) and the *bonum exercitum* (attained, actualized or realized goodness). The latter in its purest form (that which is knowingly and freely willed) is called the *bonum formale* (the good in the strictest sense). The two aspects, the ethical and the ontic-ontological, do not coincide, but they are most intimately connected. The precise determination of their relationship, that is, the question also of their unifying original ground, from which the good first addresses us, so that our desire and reflection can respond, brings us to the history of this experience and the nature of its self-understanding.

2. *History of the concept.* Scholastic metaphysics makes *bonum* one of the transcendentals, along with *unum* and *verum*. Whatever is, is – according to its degree of being – of itself good for itself, and by virtue of common being also good for others. The degree in which being is possessed determines the degree of goodness. On the analogy of substance and accident, and on the analogy of the substantial entities themselves, which range from the *paene nihil* of *materia prima* to the *summum ens, esse ipsum*, goodness is also ranged in degrees up to the *summum bonum*, the supreme good. Goodness does not add a new determination to being. It merely explicitates one aspect of its intrinsic relationships, the reference to the faculty of desire (the will),

This concept gave rise to two controversies. There was the question of the relationship of *ens* and *verum* to *bonum*, in other words, that of knowing and willing. There was also the question of the possibility and reality of the bad, especially of evil. Appealing to Plato, the Augustinian and Franciscan schools attributed a priority to the will which made it the foundation of knowledge. The possibility and power of evil stood out all the more clearly. This is less clear in the Aristotelian and Thomistic school which emphasized the priority of knowledge. And though the primordiality and power of freedom, and the proper character of the good itself were definitely noted and thoroughly thought out, they also stood out less clearly.

This was the occasion of the real disappearance of the proper reality of the good in rationalism, which culminated in Spinoza's conception of the *amor intellectualis*. But it also gave rise to an irrational philosophy of values, which especially in its modern form separates *esse* and *bonum*, knowing and willing (or "feeling") in a dualistic way and never envisages the antecedent unity in being as well as in consciousness. The appeal to a merely irrational "feeling" is a simple rejection of a positivist denial of the objectivity of the good, but has no way of demonstrating its claim. It was in this type of controversy that the Aristotelian position was built up, in its endeavour to establish the ontological foundations of the good, in opposition to the Sophists. But the controversy also had the effect of restricting the general perspectives. The character of challenge or claim which the good presents was obscured by the description of the objective finality of the real, in terms of potency and act. This was then followed by an ethics for which the commonsense insight of the cultured was normative – insight into the relationship of end and means, for the attainment of happiness in the achievement of the perfect.

Thus in the Aristotelian-Thomist conception, the good is envisaged in the light of the *appetitus*, and regarded as that which fulfils, while the ethical perspective remains secondary and derivative. One can see how it may give occasion to the aberrations of hedonism and rationalism. In Plato the good is envisaged more authentically, and one might say that the ethical perspective is prevalent, if ethics is taken in a more primordial and comprehensive sense than in the Aristotelian system. In Plato the good is the ultimate principle of the κοινωνία τῶν ἰδεῶν, principle of being as well as of truth, of reality as well as of the response to reality. It is illustrated by the metaphor of the sun which gives light and life. All reality is considered a participation of this good, and hence (like the good itself) not only is or wills to be (in the *appetitus naturalis*) but is *rightly* so and wills to be what it *ought* to be (*Republic*, VI; VII; Philebus). The proximity to the Hebrew and Christian (biblical) experience is obvious. But the question comes up of the material object of the good, its concrete realization on the various levels of participation. The question is also relevant in subsequent forms of Platonism, as when Augustine lays down the principle "Love, and do what you will" (*In Jo.*, 7, 8; *PL*, XXXV, 2033). For its precise application he has, however, to call on theological data, such as he envisages when he says, "Love, but give heed to what love merits" (*Enarr. in Ps*, 31, 2, 5: *PL*, XXXVI, 260).

Consequent to the new approach of Descartes and Cartesianism, this view was given an "epochal" effectiveness by Kant. His basic principle, that nothing "can be considered good except the good will" (*Grundlegung zur Metaphysik der Sitten*, I [Academy Edition IV, 393], E. T.: *Fundamental Principles of the Metaphysic of Ethics*, tr. by T. Abbott [10th ed., 1955]) recalls the *bonum formale* of tradition – especially when one remembers that the latter should not be restricted to the "objective". In willing its object the will primarily wills itself; freedom chooses itself when it makes its choice. Kant takes the *bonum formale* in a more precise sense, since he does not mean what is *de facto* willed but what is rightly willed, what ought to be willed. His polemical situation forbade him an adequate grasp of the unity of the theoretical and practical reason, and he did not go beyond a formalism of duty – which explains the attacks of Hegel and of the proponents of the philosophies of value, though it does not justify the radical opposition of the latter. Here Fichte intervenes, to synthesize systematically the formal and material elements in Kant (the latter being quite adequately present), as well as the theoretical and the ethico-practical. Modern research has shown that it is as wrong to brand Fichte's (later) system as "subjective idealism", as it is conversely to label the Aristotelian-Thomist (and Hegelian) doctrine as ultimately a non-moral justification of the *de facto* process, supposedly taken as the norm.

After the descriptive efforts of the

phenomenology of values, and the challenge of existential philosophy, M. Heidegger deliberately renounced all ethical assertions. This was not because he denied that being presented itself as good and as challenge, but because he is aware of the inadequacy of the modes available to express this fundamental experience, which determines unmistakably his ontological thinking.

3. *The problem.* As it affected the thinking of an epoch, this basic experience was expounded in various ways, with the emphasis now on the ontic, now on the ethical, now on the value-laden character of reality, or again on the claim of the "ought". In none of the major forms of thought (that is, the ontological and transcendental) was a given aspect stressed to the exclusion of the other, but nowhere was justice done to both aspects at once. The same is true of the approaches which stressed the objective or natural and the subjective.

The good, as a transcendental and challenging reality, is at once that which rightly is and that which ought to be. As such, it cannot at once be visualized or sensed objectively and unconditionally, in a simply theoretical contemplation. It can only be experienced, in a radically willing opening of the person, which is less *desire* and striving than obedience and surrender. This does not of course constitute the good – since these responses are both demanded and evoked by the good – but in its concrete form they go to make up the moral "event". Just as in the case of truth the event is the common actuation of the knower and the known, so too the good is the event in each case of the one act of call (destiny) and response – in the individual and in the epoch – in the interpenetration of the rule of the good and of autonomy. Can this complex relationship be expressed without giving the impression of a relativism contioned by external processes or of a mythologization of reality or simple facts, of some type of humanism or the formalism of an empty "decisiveness"? Perhaps this embarrassment signals the intrinsic difficulty of thinking and speaking of the good – not that this makes the attempt any the less permissible or imperative. For as such, the good can only be willed and done, "loved" as it wills to be. Hence the good, as properly experienced – an experience which has been described above as both active and passive, since it is a laying hold of by allowing oneself to be laid hold of – can by its very nature be only partially and inadequately articulated. The experience of the good is fundamentally less amenable to full explicitation than even the experience of truth, knowledge or decision.

The "experience" of the good is the starting-point and constant guide of reflection. It is brought about both by the appeal of the good and by him who opens his heart to it. The two factors make it clear that this experience can have a history, though the good always remains the good. Being freedom in act its concrete form cannot be deduced in any particular case or positively defined – except in general as "love", which remains love in all categories of realization and may not become hatred. Negatively, it may be defined as excluding certain attitudes or acts.

Efforts have been made to define the good more precisely, chiefly from two points of view. One sees it as perfection or happiness, which of course for the free spirit implies love and goodness – not as means to the end, but as essential constituents. The other sees it as dedication and love, which for the free spirit means fulfilment – not as an end to be achieved in isolation, but as "accepted" and completed love. Behind these efforts lies the great reality which is not only the object of actual desire, but which *ought* to be accepted by virtue of its own majesty and splendour. It is that which is "good for me" but which is only so because it is incalculably "good in itself". It summons man to this response and enables him to make it, while holding him sharply and inexorably at a distance because of the inadequacy of his answer. "No one is good . . ." (Mk 10:18.) But since it is the good – and not merely the "ought" – it comes. as men know, once more to aid this weakness. It reveals itself gratuitously and unforeseeably as grace, in the full sense of all experience which claims "meaning" – from the simplest and vaguest assurances to the great testimonies of religious history. But here the good points on beyond itself to the holy.

Jörg Splett

GRACE

I. Biblical

1. *The Old Testament background.* The prehistory of the theological concept of grace is to be attached to the terms חסד and חֵן in the OT. Both appear as χάρις in the LXX. They do not signify proprieties or entities, but, like the OT concept of justice, a social attitude, and its deployment in action rather than merely the mental disposition. Hence the concepts of תם, צדקה and ישר are closely connected with them, as is also שלום. Hence, in contrast to our notion of grace, חסד may be attributed to both partners in the relationship between man and Yahweh. For it must be remembered that חסד is the unfailing duty of reciprocity which exists between relatives, friends, sovereigns and subjects, and above all, between the contracting parties in a covenant, since the covenant implies the obligation of חסד (1 Sam 20:8). Here חסד is often used in combination with a second term such as truth (loyalty), love, justice, rights or mercy. The relationship to God called for by the covenant is described in Exod 20:6; Deut 7:12; Hos 6:4 as חסד. Hence, particularly in later texts, the God-fearing are called חסידים. The way is really paved for the Christian concept of grace in the texts which speak of God's relationship to Israel in the covenant (1 Kg 8:23; Is 55:3; Ps 89:29, 50; 106:45). Here the covenant bestowed by God is in fact identical with the "חסדי" which he has promised. Man can ask God to remember his favours or to act in keeping with them, that is, he can appeal to Yahweh's loyalty to his covenant (Ps 6:5; 25:6f.). This occurs above all when man has violated the covenant and asks Yahweh to remain faithful in spite of the breach. Hence stress is laid on the close connection between Yahweh's חסד and the keeping of the commandments (1 Kg 8:23), while חסד takes on more and more the meaning of mercy (Is 63:7; Jer 16:5; Hos 2:21), as the failings of the people are stressed.

This is true not only of the prophets but also of later times, since LXX mostly translates חסד by ἔλεος. Where Yahweh's חסד is seen as a blessing to be hoped for in the future, its theological basis is sought in the past, either in the promises to David (Is 55:3; 54:8) or to the fathers (Mich 7:20); or man begs (in the Psalms) for God to act "according to the חסדי", that is, in keeping with his salvific actions in the past. No such historical roots are attached to the word חן (except in 2 Kg 13:23), which does not stem from the realm of social ethos but simply means "favour". In the Pentateuch it is used only by the Yahwist (except Deut 24:1), and is practically confined to the phrase "to find favour in someone's eyes". Thus it is often used apropos of the patriarchs. As the phrase is used in ancient narratives (1 and 2 Sam) to speak of subjects finding favour with the king or a wife with her husband, the application to the relationship with Yahweh is a transfer from the realm of the profane.

It means no more than that someone is pleasing to Yahweh. In the case of Abraham, the phrase was first given a theological sense by St. Paul (Rom 4:1). In the OT, חן is seldom used in the theological sense, that is, of favours bestowed by God; see Ps 84:12, where it is a protective gift of God along with glory, Prov 3:34, where God bestows his favours on the lowly. The verb חנן is found more frequently in the theological sense (to be kind, gracious, merciful), sometimes in connection with the "face of God" which man sees or which shines upon him when he has found favour in God's sight and is blessed by him (Gen 33:10f.; Num 6:25). When חסד is used, more stress is laid on the sovereignty of the liberality of God than in חן (Exod 33:19 and the psalms of petition in the first person singular). Hence חסד is closer to compassion and consideration for weakness than to the notion of loyalty to a covenant. Hence too the prayer for חן occurs more often in formulas where the individual appears rather than all Israel (but contrast 2 Kg 13:23; Amos 5:1; Mal 1:9).

The LXX translates חסד by χάρις only in Est 2:9, 17; Ecclus 7:33; 40:17, which is, however, the standard translation of חן. Hence in the theological language of Septuagint Judaism χάρις, except on very few occasions, only means the favour which man finds in God's sight. But God's saving action, in his fidelity to his deeds and promises at the beginning of history (חסד) is translated only by ἔλεος (of which there is an echo in Lk 1:72). In spite of this LXX usage, the NT writers used χάρις very widely to render the sense of חסד.

2. *New Testament beginnings of a theological concept of grace*. The fact that χάρις (with χαρίζεσθαι, χάρισμα) is practically confined to Lk, Paul and the epistles of a Pauline character shows that the term was a key concept for the salvation brought by Jesus only in certain sections of early Christianity. Since the usage is very frequent in comparison with the Jewish and Greek backgrounds, it must be regarded as a technical term from a certain type of missionary activity which was developed in particular by Paul. We can see at once that χάρις became a sort of slogan, if we compare the expanded form of greeting used at the beginning of the epistles ("grace to you and peace") with the normal opening of a letter. The Pauline usage is "the Christian community's transformation of the Jewish opening blessing" (H. Schlier; but see the opening of the letter in the Syriac Apocalpyse of Baruch 78:2, "Mercy and peace be with you"). One of the characteristics of χάρις in the NT is that it stands in general for the whole salvation freely bestowed by God in Christ. The precise theological content of it is not indicated, nor its place in the history of salvation. What is in the foreground is the notion that God, in his freely-bestowed love, has made good the relationship between man and himself. But in profane Greek χάρις already meant both the condescension of the giver and the thanks of the favoured, as well as beauty or winsomeness. Thus it pointed to a joyful openness for one another, freely given, unenforceable. When applied to the relationship between God and man it meant both the salvation granted by God and the thanks offered by man. The freedom of χάρις in contrast to wages or reward is already brought out by Aristotle (*Rhetoric*, 1385a).

In the synoptic tradition χάρις and χαρίζεσθαι are found only in Lk. Hence the terminology of Mt and Mk offers no points of departure for the development of a doctrine of grace. In Lk 6:32–34 we have the pre-Lucan usage of Q (par. Mt 5:44ff.: the specific μισθός) where χάρις is the heavenly reward, hence a salvation yet to come; in Lk 1:30; 2:52 (cf. Prov 3:4) the OT usage still survives. But in Lk's own style, χάρις is the salvation wrought by God since Jesus, particularly through the words of the Gospel. The offering of this salvation to men through the preaching plays a special role (Lk 4:22; Acts 14:3, 26; 20:24, 32), so that χάρις, as in Paul, implies above all the act of believing (Acts 4:33; 11:23; 13:43). Here χάρις functions as a force given by God, as the combination with "power" and "signs" shows (Acts 6:8; cf. Lk 4:22; Acts 4:33; 7:10). This force is a special characteristic of missionaries (Acts 14:26; 15:40). In some very typically Lucan texts χάρις appears as an independent active force, the salvation of God itself expanding in place and time (Acts 4:33; 11:23; 13:43; and especially 20:32 – the constructive work of the word of grace as it confers the inheritance). The salvific grace of Christians is linked with the person of Jesus only in Acts 15:11. But even there it is only the grace of the Lord in general, which according to Lk 2:40 is simply "with him". It seems on the whole that the terminology of Lk is not derived from Paul but reflects a wider tradition which is partly pre-Pauline.

We find Paul reflecting at length on χάρις for the first time in Romans, and here too the element of gratuitousness is brought out in particular. But the usage is already so well worked out that χάρις means the whole salvation bestowed through Jesus Christ, the blessings in general to which the Church is called (1:6). But χάρις indicates in particular the saving power by which the Apostle was appointed to his task (1:15) and the legitimate apostolate itself (2:9 cf. Rom 1:5; 12;3). Thus the Christians addressed by Paul can be called partakers in the grace of the Apostle in Phil 1:7. Hence the action of God in his χάρις is not confined to the general sanctification of all the baptized, but is an economy of salvation with a diversified inner structure.

It follows that χάρις has basically the character of salvation, in contrast to a past ruled by sin, and especially in contrast to the vain effort to attain justification by works done under the law (Gal 2:21; 5:4). In the realm of χάρις justice is attained through the Spirit and because of faith (Gal 5:4, 5). But this grace is not given at once to all, but only to those who are called and chosen to receive it (Gal 1:6, 15; Rom 11:5). And even here it does not come to all in the same way, but appears as charisms of various types.

The office of apostle in particular is a special mode of working of the divine χάρις, which elsewhere signifies in a very general way the divine act of mercy extended to man. Here χάρις appears, as early as Gal, as a region or realm, comparable to that of the law (Gal 5:4; cf. the notion of justification), and is therefore opposed to all that is ungodly, all that belongs to the realm of *sarx*, death and sin (2 Cor 1:12). This realm is opened up in Jesus Christ (1 Cor 1:4). To turn back to the law for salvation (Gal 2:21; 5:4) or to return to sin in general (2 Cor 6:1) is to offend against this gift of salvation. But the concept of χάρις has still further connotations in Paul. It also means thanksgiving to God and the loving gifts of the community – applications of the term which are not to be isolated from the meaning already given (cf. 2 Cor 8:7, 9; 9:8, 14, 15). Because of the χάρις of Christ, the community can and must bring about a χάρις, and because of the χάρις which God gave, χάρις is due to him (Rom 9:14, 15). This is not a play upon words, since χάρις is a relationship to another in loving compassion. The relationship is set up by God's mercy in the salvation which came in Jesus Christ. This is the basis and model for human compassion, and also the motive for thanksgiving. Thus the usage of the term χάρις shows that thanksgiving is the action corresponding to grace in this relationship. In 1 Cor in particular attention is paid to the embodiment of grace in charisms. Paul makes use of the different individual embodiments of grace to try to solve the problems of community discipline and ethics. The multiplicity of charisms is contrasted with the unity of the Pneuma (1 Cor 12:4). In Rom, Paul stresses the fact that grace is given through baptism, as a gift (3:24), which contrasts it with the works of the law as a way of salvation, since under the law rewards are calculated, while in the order of χάρις the fulfilment of the law is a gift bestowed in the charism of love. In the important text Rom 5:12–21, the fall of Adam and the grace which came (χάρισμα) in Jesus Christ are not simply opposed, for the efficacy and riches of the latter far exceed the former. Grace is greater than sin, and its conquering march cannot be held back by sin. Thus the multiplication of sin in the time of the law only served to demonstrate all the more forcibly the riches of grace (Rom 5:20). But this truth is no reason for abiding in sin to allow grace to display its riches more abundantly (Rom 6:1). Sin and grace are successive aeons or reigns. Transition from one to the other is made when one dies with Christ to the power of the ancient (Rom 6:2), which happens in baptism (Rom 6:3ff.). But the way of salvation which grace substitutes for the law does not mean new freedom to sin. It means being laid hold of by a new power (Rom 6:14ff.). What therefore has Paul done for the concept of grace? He did not describe the full theological concept, but linked its function indissolubly to the death of Jesus Christ in his notion of the history of salvation; then, he situated it for believers in the process of justification and baptism; and finally, he interpreted this χάρις as a call to special moral or apostolic service.

In the rest of the Pauline literature, these concepts make themselves felt above all in Eph, where we find similar stress laid on the richness of grace (cf. Rom 5), the special grace of the apostolate and the individuality of the gifts of grace (Eph 4:7) and on the notion of a divine dispensation of grace (Eph 3:2). As in 2 Tim 1:9, grace is contrasted with works in Eph 2:8. But these are not now the works of the law, but simply human action as distinct from the divine plan of redemption (2 Tim 1:9). In many places, χάρις appears beside δύναμις, and the dawn of the day of salvation is described as its epiphany (Tit 2:11). In Heb, χάρις is the salvation granted in the new order of worship centred on heaven which must never be abandoned (Heb 12:15).

Like Paul, John opposes grace to the law (Jn 1:17) and in 1:16 we meet the key-word of the fullness of grace, which is interpreted in vv. 14 and 17 as the salvific blessing of "truth" (an obviously Johannine mode of expression, which reflects, however, the OT combination of חסד ואמת. The term is used in a variety of ways in 1 Pet. It is important to note, for instance, that at 2:19f., the sufferings of Christians appear as grace. 1 Pet shows how wide the concept of χάρις was in the Hellenistic missionary area before, during and after Paul's work. If 1 Pet 4:10 reflects pre-Pauline tradition, the division of grace into a number of charisms could no longer be regarded as an original achievement of Pauline theology. In 1 Pet, grace can also be used simply to indicate Christian salvation as a totality (1 Pet 1:10, 13).

Klaus Berger

II. Theological

1. *Introduction.* This article, which presents the Church's doctrine, biblical theology and systematic reflection in a single unified account, must on principle be read in conjunction with others which deal with the doctrine of grace from other points of view: *Man (Anthropology)*, *Salvation*, *Order*, *Justification*, *Faith*, *Hope*, *Charity*, *Holy*

Spirit, Holiness, Charism, Mysticism, Beatific Vision, Sin.

The question arises from the start as to what is the right basis for such a survey. The customary post-Tridentine division of the treatise into actual grace and habitual grace will not do, because it makes questionable assumptions. The starting-point must be a theological statement about man in the unity of his whole nature. This must be the source from which the distinction between nature and grace and possible distinctions within the concept of grace itself are drawn, and which will themselves serve as principles on which a treatise of this kind can be composed. In this sense we are starting from the theological proposition (of dogmatic anthropology) that the human being who is a Christian believer must understand himself to be called in history to God's own most intimate life, by the effective word of God's free and absolute self-disclosure; and that he is so called in his character as creature, and despite it, and despite his recognition of himself as a sinner by his very origin.

The decisive feature of this proposition is that God does not bestow merely a certain kind of saving love and intimacy, or a certain kind of saving presence (such as ontologically is necessarily implied even by the abstract concept of a relation between Creator and still innocent creature). God does not confer on man merely created gifts as a token of his love. God communicates *himself* by what is no longer simply efficient causality. He makes man share in the very nature of God. He constitutes man as co-heir with the Son himself, called to the eternal life of God face to face, called to receive the direct vision of God, called therefore to receive God's own life. Here we really reach the heart of the Christian conception of reality. The true and complete relation of the Absolute and of what we experience as ourselves and our world and know to be finite and contingent is not a relation of identity or of necessary connection in which the Absolute unfolds and attains its own plenitude as in the various forms of pantheism. But neither is it the simple relation of an absolute efficient cause to its effect, which remains external to that cause. It is rather the free relation of the Absolute communicating himself. And this relation by creative, efficient causality posits the recipient of the Absolute's outgoing self-communication, in order to be able to communicate himself in the mode of free personal intercourse in dialogue, and by the incarnation and grace to set the created world free for its own history.

The Christian doctrine of grace (with its highest realization, when the divine Logos becomes a creature) is the genuine means of transcending pantheism and deism. For the latter may be philosophically surmounted but is not really overcome by postulating that God is merely concerned about the *machina mundi* which he has set in being and motion. And the Christian doctrine of grace transcends these two systems of the relation between Absolute and contingent, each claiming to be metaphysically necessary, even though it is a doctrine of freely bestowed love. And this love shows itself thereby to be the real essence of the absolute reality. The "necessary" structures of absolute reality do not determine freedom as if the latter were something secondary, but are the formal structures of free and absolute love itself. This love itself turns towards the contingent. Yet it need not, except by the "necessity" of freely-bestowed love.

2. *"Supernatural" grace and nature*. On this basis it is possible to establish in the first place the distinction between nature and supernatural grace and the character of the latter.

a) *The official teaching of the Church*. The doctrine of the supernatural character of grace (as God's self-communication) is *expressly* mentioned for the first time in an official pronouncement of the Church when in the Council of Vienne the vision of God is attributed to the (grace-given) *lumen gloriae* (*D* 475). It is then propounded expressly, and the term *supernaturalis* is employed, against Baianism, Jansenism and semi-rationalism (*D* 1017, 1021, 1023f., 1026, 1385, 1516, 1669, 1671). It is taught by Vatican I (*D* 1786, 1789) as the reason for the absolute necessity of revelation and as a characteristic of faith. Pius XII (*D* 2318) stressed the importance of not weakening it (in contesting the abstract possibility of a "pure nature"). It is only this supernatural character of grace which ultimately explains why in the Church's teaching grace is declared to be gratuitous, impossible to merit by man's own powers, so that of himself man can neither positively prepare himself for it nor obtain it by prayer (*D* 134f., 141, 176f., 797, 813, etc.). The fact that man is sinful cannot of itself be the total reason for this.

b) *Systematic theology*. (i) God's self-communication in his own divine life, both as given, and as accepted by man, is essentially God's free, personal, uncovenanted favour. In itself it is a free gift in relation to man, not merely insofar as he is a sinner (i.e., someone who culpably shuts himself to God's offer of himself and to God's will as this is expressed in the whole of human reality), but even prior to this. On the one hand for the creature to be endowed with God in a personal love which communicates God himself is an unmerited favour on the part of God himself. It is essentially a freely bestowed favour if a person discloses his own self. And on the other hand the spiritual creatures (even if we assume them to be already constituted) cannot receive this favour as posited or promised by their own (innocent) nature, but apprehend it as consisting of a genuine dialogue in time and history which therefore presupposes the existence of the person addressed. Consequently the spiritual creature cannot regard it as identical with its character as creature or as posited by this with ontological necessity. If through its acceptance on the part of finite man (in accordance with the essence and measure of a finite creature) this self-communication by God is not to be reduced to an event which remains in the domain of the purely finite (which would contradict God's self-communication as such), the acceptance precisely as such must have its ground in God in the same way as the gift itself. The self-communication as such also effects its acceptance; the actual and proximate ability to accept is itself a supremely free grace. That is very clear as regards faith. If revelation when heard is to remain truly *God's* word, and not to become a divinely-inspired word about God, known as such – the two are *not* identical – by falling into the created, finite *a priori* frame of reference, then God himself must, in the *grace* of faith (the light of faith), become a constitutive principle of the hearing of revelation. But grace as God's self-communication is not only a constitutive principle of the *capacity* for its acceptance (in what theology calls the supernatural *habitus* of faith, hope and love), but also of the *free act* of *acceptance*. It is so by what theology calls unmerited *efficacious* grace for the actual performance of the act. For this self-communication of God as the cause of its own acceptance is free even in regard to the production of its actual concrete free acceptance. Precisely because this act of acceptance is free and underivative in the concrete, such a self-communication can be accepted as a divinely personal one. Of course it may be said that the free effectuation of acceptance by God, the efficacious grace as such, is given in circumstances (whether these are explained on a Banezian or a Molinist basis) which can be distinguished from the supernatural self-communication as such. But even then it must not be overlooked that God's self-communication by the very fact that it is personal, free and unique in every instance requires these freely posited circumstances, which themselves are unmerited, as its own concrete conditions. The gratuitousness of efficacious grace as such is therefore required by the very nature of God's self-communication and only by it is the self-communication in each instance a unique event of love freely bestowed.

(ii) This free self-communication of God in Christ and his Spirit has to be accepted by the spiritual creature in a dialogue-partnership which itself is free. This presupposes that man is permanently constituted in a certain way (which of course was freely posited by God the Creator). Now this precedes God's self-communication, i.e., it is creatively pre-posited by the latter as the condition of its possibility. For this self-communication has to be received by man (as a partner already historically posited) as a free historical favour which cannot be reckoned with on the basis of the presupposed condition. In other words, it is not a transcendental condition of the self-realization of man, although man is essentially and obligatorily open to this self-disclosure of God (by the *potentia obedientialis* and supernatural existential) and if he refuses it his whole being is in ruin. On the other hand, that intrinsic constitution of man is such that it persists (if only in the form of absurdity and reprobation) if he shuts himself off from God's self-communication. This recipient of God's self-communication, which the latter presupposes as a condition of its own unmerited and solely self-initiated coming, is called in Catholic terminology the "nature" of man. The strictly *theological* concept of "nature" therefore does not mean a state of reality, intelligible in itself and experienced by us separately (apart from a grace inaccessible to experience) on top of which, according to revelation, an additional higher reality would be superimposed. Nature is rather that reality which the divine self-communication creatively posits for itself as its possible partner in such a way that in relation to it that communication does and can remain what it is: a free and loving favour. Nature in contradistinction to the supernatural is, therefore, understood as a necessary element in a higher whole, which is experienced in grace and explicitly declared in revelation. The difference between nature and grace must be understood on the basis of the radical unity of God's free self-communication as love. Nor does this theological concept of nature imply that it is identical with the domain of what can be experienced. That is ultimately a nominalist misconception. The case is rather that it is possible to experience what is not "nature" (cf., for example, Gal 3:1–5) and it is not self-evident *a priori* that everything in "nature" must *in fact* be experienced by man.

(iii) In this sense, the grace of God's self-communication is supernatural, in other words it is not owed to man (or to *any* creature) even prior to his unworthiness as a sinner. It is not posited with man's inalienable essence (his "nature"). Consequently in itself even in the absence of sin it could be refused to man by God (yet if offered it could not be refused by man without guilt). It is unmerited because it is a participation in the reality which in itself is solely that of God himself. Moreover, it can only be received if its very reception is made possible by God. And this again is not due to man. As well as the concept which we have just outlined of what is supernatural in itself and absolutely, and which transcends the essence, powers and intrinsic claim of every creature by the nature of the gift itself and not merely by the mode of its communication, theology also has a concept of what is "preternatural". This denotes a reality which indeed transcends the exigence of a given nature (e.g., of man in contradistinction to the angel) but which lies in some fashion within the domain (scope, aspiration) of a given nature. It cannot, however, be claimed as an appurtenance of the nature, either in itself or in the mode of its attainment (e.g., freedom from concupiscence; miraculous cure of an illness, etc.).

3. *Grace as forgiving.* All this does not mean that grace as forgiveness has been ignored or has become secondary. Man in the concrete always for his part finds himself in a doubly inescapable situation, as creature and as sinner. In concrete experience these two factors mutually condition and throw light on each other. The fallibility of the finite creature is of course of itself not purely and simply sin, but in sin that fallibility comes inexorably to light. And sinfulness inescapably compels man to understand that he is an absolutely finite creature for whom God's divinizing favour always and in every case is grace. To the extent therefore that divinizing grace is bestowed on the sinner and as the proffered self-communication of the *holy* God implies God's readiness to forgive and the acceptance of this (through grace) that grace is once again unmerited, by being conferred on one who is positively unworthy of it. Consequently, it is not surprising that the whole doctrine of justifying grace at the Council of Trent, though concerned with supernatural grace, is not conceived on the pattern of the "elevation" of a nature but of pardoning the impious (*D* 790f., 793–802). The real need for redemption extends just as far and as radically as does man's capacity for elevation into the life of God.

This pardoning grace and, consequently, elevating grace, when given to man in original sin, is purely the grace of Christ (*D* 55, 790, 793f., 811f., etc.). Moreover, it is quite arguable that the elevating grace of man's original state was the grace of Christ. For in a Christocentric view of all created reality it is quite possible to assume that the creation and fulfilment of the world through God's gracious self-communication were willed by God from the start as factors of a divine self-communication to the non-divine, reaching its culmination, its full essence and historical irreversibility in the God-man. The incarnation and grace-given divinization of the world can then be regarded as mutually and necessarily interdependent elements of this one radical self-communication. Both factors are *free* because the one whole self-communication in its entirety is free, yet the one factor does not have to be thought of as separable from the other. By this origin from Christ, grace even as divinizing has an eminently historical and dialogal character. It is God's favour which, despite the fact that in essence it concerns all men always at all times everywhere and is indispensable to them (cf. *D* 160b, 1295, 1356, 1414, 1518, etc.) is dependent on the "event" of Jesus Christ. Consequently it possesses an incarnational, sacramental and ecclesiological character and unites man in grace with the life and death of Christ.

4. *Uncreated and created grace.* On the basic principle chosen it is readily intelligible that "grace" (of justification) as such and as strictly supernatural is first and foremost God himself communicating himself with his own nature: uncreated grace. On that basis any conception of grace which would reify it or treat it as an object and place it at man's autonomous disposal is excluded from the outset. The teaching of the Council of Trent about grace "inhering" in the soul (*D* 800, 821) was not intended to dispute this and was not put forward in connection with the problem of the distinction between created and uncreated grace (the latter is mentioned: *D* 13, 799, 898, 1013, 1015); it was simply intended to state the truth that justification consists, through genuine rebirth, in the constitution of a new creature, of a temple really inhabited by the Spirit

of God himself, of a human being who is anointed and sealed with the Spirit and born of God; and that the justified person is not merely "regarded" forensically "as if" he were just but truly *is* so (*D* 799f., 821). Terms such as "inhering", "accidental", etc., in this connection can be understood entirely independently of the question of the distinction between created and uncreated grace. It is of course true that the concept of uncreated grace means that man himself is genuinely and inwardly transformed by this self-communication and that therefore in this sense there is a "created", accidental grace (i.e., not posited by the very fact of positing man's nature, but received by him). There is no agreement in Catholic theology on how exactly the relation between created and uncreated grace is to be determined. There is no unanimity whether created grace is to be regarded as effected by God (in the ordinary sense of efficient cause) as the presupposition and consequence of uncreated grace conferred by quasi-formal causality. (On this view it would resemble a material disposition for the "form" which, in communicating itself, actively produces this disposition as its own condition so that the two realities condition one another in reciprocal causality.) Nor is there agreement whether created grace is to be regarded as a factor necessarily accompanying uncreated grace (*actuation créée par l'acte incréé:* de la Taille). It is still disputed whether uncreated grace is to be regarded as more or less merely the consequence of created grace. This has mostly been the view since Trent but in a way that is surely inadequate and contrary to the trend of the later thought of Aquinas (cf. Dockx, etc.). The special "indwelling" is then regarded as posited by created grace as such. With due regard for *D* 2290, it is at all events quite possible to regard uncreated grace as primary and as the grace which is the essential basis of the whole of man's grace-given endowment and as what alone renders intelligible the authentic and strictly supernatural character of grace.

5. *Actual and habitual grace.* a) *Official teaching of the Church.* On the "*habitual*" *grace of justification*, see above 1–4. In the sense which will be more precisely delimited below in section b) the existence of *actual grace* has been defined, because against Pelagianism and Semipelagianism the absolute necessity of grace for absolutely every salutary act is a defined truth (*D* 103ff., 176ff., 811ff.). Contrary to Semipelagian doctrine, these salutary acts include all (positive) preparation for faith and justification, hence grace anticipates man in his saving activity without any merit on his part (*D* 797) ("prevenient grace"; on co-operation with this grace see below, 6). In view of God's universal salvific will and of the sinfulness of man, it follows that there is also an assisting grace which is offered but does not produce its effect and which is therefore merely "sufficient", the existence of which has been defined against Jansenism (*D* 797, 814, 1093, 1295f., 1521, 1791). The essence of grace cannot therefore be located in the irresistible omnipotence of God (*D* 1359–75). According to the (almost) universal teaching (both of Thomism and of Molinism, with regard to grace and freedom), and despite human freedom in acceptance and resistance, the distinction between merely sufficient and efficacious actual grace is prior to man's acceptance or resistance and has its ground in the sphere of God's election (otherwise the fact of final perseverance would not be a special gift of God: *D* 806, 826). It is illumination and inspiration (*D* 135ff., 180, 797, 1521, 1791). It is regarded not only as unmerited but also as supernatural in the same sense as the grace of justification (cf. *D* 1789ff.). This is also suggested by its absolute necessity for any saving act. It is not merely "moral" necessity which is in question, i.e., to make the saving act

easier. Consequently it does not consist merely in the outward circumstances shaped by God's providence which favour man's religious action, but concretely and as a whole it is interior grace in the same sense as sanctifying grace.

b) *In speculative theology*. On the basis of the fundamental anti-Pelagian doctrine of Western theology regarding the necessity of grace for the salutary action of man (in the form which derives from Augustine: grace as inspiration of justifying love), grace in the first place is assistance for action (perpetually bestowed or constantly offered by the salvific will of God) and in this sense actual grace. (The state of grace of baptized children who are free from the stain of original sin but who have not yet reached the use of reason is not examined in this connection.) We are not concerned here to describe why and how in the Middle Ages doctrine developed in such a way that the recognition of grace as supernatural concerned the "habitual" grace of justification, so that a salutary act and an act based on habitual grace were viewed as identical. At all events this fact shows that the concept of the supernaturally elevating assistance for every salutary act is not to be identified from the start with the concept of actual grace as this is almost universally understood today and deduced from the case of the grace-given act of preparation for justification. That view presupposes (without any real proof) that such acts cannot be performed on the basis of the antecedently offered grace of justification (a "habitual" grace in other words but dynamically actualized). It is also a fact that down to the present day no agreement has been reached whether a supernatural elevating actual grace over and above habitual grace is necessary in a justified person for every saving action, or whether habitual grace in itself is sufficient. If with the Thomists as opposed to Molina we assume the doctrine which, though disputed, is perfectly reasonable and indeed preferable, that the grace given for the act itself elevates the faculties of man (so that the salutary act as such is not only received but performed), it is possible to say that the Church's binding doctrine only imposes a distinction between actual supernatural elevating grace and habitual grace to the extent that it is certain by dogmatic definition that there are saving acts of not yet justified persons by which they prepare for justification with a prevenient grace which is absolutely necessary for them. There is no official pronouncement of the Church and no agreed teaching whether this necessary grace is the same as, or different from, God's self-communication which by giving itself also makes possible and effects its own acceptance. There is no decision, therefore, whether in adults habitual grace is the same as or other than that same communication of God when freely accepted. The sense of the distinction as far as it is a binding one is simply that grace is habitual inasmuch as God's supernatural self-communication is permanently offered to man (after baptism) and (in the adult) is freely accepted in the various degrees in which it is possible to accept it. The same grace is called actual inasmuch as it is the basis of this act of acceptance in which it actualizes itself. The individual action in the concrete is essentially progressive and susceptible of indefinite renewal. (This conception also corresponds to the Thomist view of growth in grace.)

It follows from all this that the customary division of the treatise on grace since the Council of Trent into a section on actual grace and one on habitual grace is a very superficial one which does not do justice to the unity and nature of the one grace which divinizes the essence, powers and activity of man. All "actual" graces refer to the one dynamism for human action of the one divinizing grace as offered (actual grace for justification) or as already accepted (actual grace for merit on the part of the justified person). They are only distinguished from one another by the different degrees of actual vital acceptance of this one grace by man (grace for mere faith, for faith in hope, for love which integrates faith into itself).

6. *Grace as liberating grace of the free man.* Despite original sin, and even with concupiscence, man is free (*D* 792f., 798, 814ff.); therefore he freely consents to prevenient grace or freely rejects it (*D* 134, 140, 160a, 196, 793f., 1093, 1095, 1521, 1791, 2305). Consequently we must speak of mutual "co-operation" (*cooperari*) (*D* 182, 200, 797, 814). However, that does not in any way mean a "synergism" dividing up the saving operation. For not only the capacity for salutary action (the infused *habitus* or the prevenient sufficient grace) but also the free consent itself is God's grace (as was taken for granted in the controversy on grace between Molinism and Thomism, which is why the Church did not have to pronounce in favour of either of the two parties) (*D* 176f., 182, etc.). It is therefore grace itself which sets free our (formal) freedom in capacity and in act for saving action, and heals it in itself. Consequently the situation of this freedom to say Yes or No to God is not that of autonomous emancipated choice (*D* 200, 321f., 325). When man says No it is his own work; when he freely says Yes, he must attribute this to God as God's gift.

7. *Medicinal and supernaturally elevating grace.* The two doctrines – that of the difference between nature and supernaturally elevating grace, i.e., which endows with the gift of God himself, and that of concupiscence (as a spur to sin even against the natural law) which can only be overcome by a special help of God (the absence of which does not mean that the unjustified human being sins afresh in every action) – slowly led to a distinction being drawn between the necessity of grace for the divinized salutary act and the necessity of God's help for the observance of the law of nature. This is the distinction between elevating and medicinal grace. Though this distinction is not clear even in the Council of Orange (A.D. 529) and is not really brought out at Trent, the doctrine of the medicinal function of divine grace was nevertheless already present all the time (*D* 103, 132, 135, 186f., 190, 806, 832, etc.), because of course this aspect of divine assistance is directly opposed to Pelagianism. The same is true of the doctrine that the substance of the natural law cannot in the long run be observed without this help (and in fact certainly is not). It had also to be maintained against the Reformers, Baius and Jansenius (see also the Augustinian school) that not only do persons who are not yet justified perform salutary acts with the help of grace, but also that the (presupposed) lack of it does not necessarily make every one of their actions a sin (*D* 817f., 1025, 1035, 1037, 1040, 1297f., 1301, 1395, 1409, 1523, etc.).

As a consequence the absolute necessity of salutary grace for a salutary act and the purely relative help for moral action in accordance with the natural law (the *actus honestus*) are not simply and solely two aspects of one and the same divine action in man, and medicinal help and supernatural grace must therefore be distinguished. From this it follows that the medicinal help can also be regarded as external and that it is still an open question in Catholic theology whether precisely as such (and even as purely sufficient) it is in every case gratuitous or not, and whether in every case it is to be considered to be a grace of Christ. The relation of these two kinds of assisting graces is not fully elucidated, however, by this necessary distinction.

Although the *possibility* of individual purely human acts in the domain of religious knowledge (*D* 1785f., 2320, 2317) and of action in accordance with the natural moral law cannot be disputed, the question whether *in fact* there are moral acts which are merely good and reputable in themselves, but without any positive significance for salvation, or whether all such acts if they actually exist are also, through an elevating grace, salutary acts, is still freely discussed, for the second view (in the sense of Ripalda or Vazquez) has never been censured by the Church. The answer to this question largely depends on the open question as to what faith (without which there is no salutary act and no justification: *D* 1173, 801, 789, 798) is required as condition and element of the salutary act. If a "virtual" faith (in the sense for example of Straub) is sufficient, then justification by a baptism of desire and consequently salutary acts are possible in every man of goodwill even before contact with public revelation. If a psychological effect is also attributed to elevating grace, or at all events if it brings with it, as the Thomist doctrine maintains, a new cognitive perspective (a special *obiectum formale*, even if this cannot be grasped explicitly by reflection), and if this new supernatural perspective in which natural moral and religious objects would be grasped, can be regarded as a ("transcendental") kind of authentic divine revelation and therefore (if affirmed nonreflexively) as faith, then the problem can be solved even more simply. Every radically moral act would then occur in a supernatural perspective because of the elevating grace offered because of God's universal will to save. Consequently it also would constitute faith (in a "transcendental" way). For both these reasons, therefore, it would be a salutary act, and so every moral act (*actus honestus*) would *in fact* also be a salutary act. If this is the case, however (and it corresponds very closely to the optimistic attitude of Vatican II in regard to salvation [cf. *Lumen Gentium*, art. 16; *Gaudium et Spes*, art. 22], because it teaches the possibility of salvation and faith even for those whom the message of the Gospel has not reached), then "medicinal" grace can in all cases be regarded as the dynamism of elevating grace and as its concrete accompanying (external) circumstances. Then, in the actual course of a totally Christocentric human history, medicinal grace would be an element in a coming of grace, which, through God's loving will to self-communication to the creature, aims at realizing all that is human and Christian in man.

8. *Further characteristics of grace:*

a) It can be lost: see *Sin, Justification, Penance.*

b) It can grow: see *Works, Holiness.* On its relation to consciousness, see *Mysticism, Grace and Freedom, Faith.*

9. *Grace and God's salvific will:* see *Salvation* I, *Predestination, Providence.*

Karl Rahner

III. Structure of De Gratia

1. *Definition and divisions.* a) The theology of grace (*De gratia*) is that part of a theological anthropology which deals with man as redeemed and justified. Rightly understood, therefore, this treatise should not speak in the abstract about grace but about man endowed with grace. For where man's reality is not envisaged in all its dimensions, the concept of grace in formal abstraction remains either an "experience" of the nature of man or a moral help to his moral life itself envisaged only in a very abstract way. The Church's proclamation is not adequately served by this, nor is full justice done to biblical theology which speaks of grace much more concretely. This part of an anthropology, dealing precisely with redeemed and sanctified man, has its natural place after Christology and ecclesiology, because these two treatises describe the cause, conditions and situation of man's justification. It is a secondary matter whether man's state as redeemed (as an

"existential" analogous to the situation created by original sin, and antecedent to justification) is to be dealt with in soteriology itself or in a treatise on grace. This treatise must above all constitute a doctrine of the divinizing and forgiving endowment of man with grace (in his being and action) in all his dimensions, in all the spheres of his life. It therefore includes as an integral part the doctrine of the theological virtues and as a whole represents the dogmatic foundation which is essential to a radically dogmatic moral theology (cf. the description of a moral theology for the present day in Vatican II, *Optatam Totius*, art. 16).

Grace is ultimately the self-communication of the absolute God to his creature, and this self-communication itself has a history, which reaches in Jesus Christ its eschatological, irreversible culmination towards which it tended from the start and throughout, and which determined and formed the basis of its whole course from the beginning. Consequently the theology of man redeemed and justified (sanctified) by grace should include also a doctrine of man who was thus justified before Christ's time (but *through* Christ) or who (to some extent only apparently) stands outside the domain of the historical Christian message of salvation.

b) The essential themes of the theology of grace are as follows. (i) God's actual trinitarian self-communication itself to man in its fundamental character. As the fundamental act of God in relation to the non-divine, this includes (but as distinct from itself) both nature and grace. Nature is posited as its own condition for its own purpose. Grace includes the supralapsarian grace of God in the original state, which itself was already Christocentric. It also includes the grace of the infralapsarian order, after (original) sin, which was only "permitted" by grace on account of the latter's own absolutely triumphant power.

(ii) From this fundamental conception we have to work out the idea of supernatural justifying grace, both as uncreated and as the created grace deriving from it. And this must not be done only in a formal, abstract way restricted to the subjective interior life of the private individual (forgiveness of sins, indwelling of God, adoptive sonship, holiness). The Christological and infralapsarian character of this grace must be brought out, Christological in its dynamism towards sharing in the mysteries and death of Christ, towards the imitation of Christ, infralapsarian as being grace which is always threatened yet increasingly victorious again and again in overcoming concupiscence. This grace of justification has also to be seen in the appropriate way in each case, as divinization and redemption (liberation) of *all* dimensions of human reality. In other words, the individual *and* collective (ecclesial), anthropological *and* cosmic character (grace as transfiguration of the world) has to be brought out. Grace has to be considered in accordance with the transcendental dimensions of man as truth, as love and as beauty.

(iii) To this must be added the doctrine of the actual working out of this supernatural grace in the dialogue relation between God and man. This is free on both sides and it is free on God's part once again in this respect also: efficacious grace. Consequently this section must include: 1. The doctrine of actual grace, what formally constitutes it, its relation to justifying grace. 2. The formal aspects of the life of the justified in Christ (gratuity of grace even in the actual working out of justifying grace as such; hidden character of grace; experience of grace; freedom under grace and liberation of man's freedom by grace; grace as liberation from the Law) and its material dimensions (the doctrine of the theological and moral virtues and their acts). 3. The beginning of the divine life of grace (process of justification), its growth (merit), and the perils which always beset it (the justified person's proneness to sin; loss of grace). 4. The ecclesiological aspect and mission in the world of the life of grace (charisms). 5. The perfection of the life of grace (mysticism; confirmation in grace; holiness; martyrdom).

2. *Brief history of the theology of grace.* a) The Apostolic Fathers and the theologians of the first two centuries repeat the doctrine of Scripture, soberly stressing its moral demands but also starting to use the Hellenistic terminology of "divinization". The first theological reflections are made on the possibility of losing and recovering the grace of baptism (*The Shepherd of Hermas*, Tertullian).

b) The first great controversy on grace had to be waged in the 2nd and 3rd centuries against Gnosticism, i.e., against its doctrine of divinization, which made salvation non-universal, non-historical and a matter of one's "essential" constitution. It eliminated man's free acceptance of the free grace of God in favour of a cosmic history of God himself (Irenaeus).

c) The great age of the Greek Fathers (from Origen onwards) developed a doctrine of grace on the basis of the Trinitarian questions of the period. Because the Spirit is truly God, man is truly divinized, and because man (without becoming God) is truly divinized, the Spirit must truly be God. As the Spirit is definitively inserted into the world by the incarnation of the divine Logos, the Greek doctrine of grace is optimistic about salvation. It also had to be on its guard against a kind of "actualism" in the doctrine of grace, which identified grace with an enthusiastic, mystical experience of grace (Messalianism). But it was familiar with a Logos mysticism which gradually introduced man in ecstasy into the incomprehensibility of God.

d) The Western doctrine of grace was less interested in intellectual divinization and its cosmic aspects and more moralistic in tendency. It was also orientated towards the history of salvation and of the individual by the struggle against Pelagianism. Grace is the unmeritable strength of love for God which by free predestination delivers some men in original sin from the *massa damnata* of mankind and from their own egoism, liberates their freedom enslaved to sin and so makes them capable of the faith which operates in love (Augustine). In his theoretical works of controversy, Augustine no longer recognizes an infralapsarian *universal* salvific will of God. On the other hand he is the great teacher of the Church on original sin, the gratuitousness of grace and of predestination to beatitude, and on the psychology of grace.

e) The later patristic period (while preserving the genuine substance of the doctrine of grace of Augustine and of the Council of Orange: *D* 178–200a) and the early Middle Ages overcame, in opposition to predestinarianism, the thesis of a merely limited salvific will of God which would positively exclude many from salvation prior to their guilt (*D* 160a; 300; 316–25). The great age of Scholasticism gave precise formulation by means of a new philosophical (Aristotelian) terminology (habitus, disposition, accidents) to the nature of justifying grace, to the process of justification and to the theological virtues. The concept of the strictly supernatural character of salvific grace was slowly elaborated. It was not merely gratuitousness in regard to the sinner.

f) As against the theology of the Reformation, of Baianism and Jansenism, it was necessary to defend (especially at the Council of Trent, sessions V and VI) the freedom of man under grace, the truly inward new creation of man by habitual grace, its strictly supernatural character (in the post-Tridentine period against Baius) and the universality of God's will to grace (against Calvin and Jansenius). The controversy "De Auxiliis", concerning the more precise theories of how to reconcile human freedom with the divinely efficacious power of grace (Molina, Bañez) was left undecided in 1607 (*D* 1090, 1097) and has remained so until this day. Another equally open question is the problem which has been discussed since Petau (d. 1652), under the renewed influence of the Greek Fathers, whether by sanctifying grace a special relation not simply by appropriation is set up to each of the three divine persons. At the present day theology is concerning itself with the use of personalist concepts in the doctrine of grace, with the unity of nature and grace, without prejudice to their distinction, and with a better understanding of the biblical teaching on grace and of the theology of the Reformers.

Karl Rahner

GRACE AND FREEDOM

1. *The problem.* a) The problem of the relation between grace and freedom, as a specifically theological question within Catholic theology, is how to maintain that man is really free in his salutary acts and could therefore refuse the grace offered for such an act, and that at the same time he necessarily requires interior divine grace for this salutary action. This grace does not become effective simply and solely through man's actual consent to it, but the consent itself is given by God's grace freely bestowed. God could also refuse precisely such an "efficacious" grace, without man thereby being excused if he sinned, because in any case he is capable (through "sufficient" grace) of performing the salutary act.

b) Beyond its attestation in Scripture, the problem of man's freedom and God's sovereign power and grace has its vital importance in the concrete: man cannot abdicate his own responsibility even in the matter of salvation, yet when he does act in a way ordered to salvation, he must give the honour to God and acknowledge that it is God in his grace who has given him the power to act and the very act itself.

c) Theology then gives the problem its full theoretical extension and expresses it formally as the question of the relation between God's action (in his concursus) and man's free acts (including then both naturally good and morally bad ones).

2. *The correct starting-point for a solution.* a) The relation between God and the world is necessarily mysterious because God is *the* mystery, mystery as such. Any discussion of the topic can only proceed dialectically, in that tension of twofold utterance which the very nature of analogical language involves.

b) The relation between God and creature is characterized, precisely in contrast to any causal dependence otherwise met with within the world, by the fact that self-possession and dependence increase in direct, not in inverse proportion. It is God's causality itself which posits genuine difference from God and constitutes the creation of what is independent and has its own being.

This relation of a transcendental, non-predicamental kind culminates, without discontinuity, in the relation between God and the free subject together with his free act. The transcendental origin of the free act from God is precisely what posits it as free, and transfers it to the creature's own responsibility for itself. This ultimate creation in the authentic sense of the term, in which the idea of creation is at last fully realized, is the mystery of the "co-existence" of God and the free creature, and it is not susceptible of further analysis.

3. *The classical attempts at a solution.* All agree in attempting once more to mediate the mystery of this relation by indicating some third factor (of an ideal or real kind) by which, since it is distinct from God and from the free act,

some intermediary may be found between the sovereignty of God's grace and independent freedom.

a) *Bañezian Thomism*. Bañez (d. 1604) claimed to be following Aquinas, but with what justice is disputed, for some consider that his teaching presents Scotist features. The kernel of his doctrine is the necessity and nature of *praemotio physica* for *any* action of a creature, not only for a positively salutary act. According to this view, a creature requires, in order to pass from potency to act, an absolutely indispensable "premotion", which consists of a transitory created entity produced by God *alone*, which is distinct from God (and his causality in respect of the act of the creature), and from the faculty and act of the creature, but which infallibly determines this act in its nature and actual existence. When it is a question of a free act, good or bad, the *praemotio physica* infallibly and antecedently moves to this action and its freedom.

God decides in predestination on a certain definite premotion, and so according to his own absolutely sovereign choice gives the creature the good or bad deed as the creature's own free act. Where this premotion by its own very nature moves to a positive salutary act, it is called efficacious actual grace, as opposed to sufficient grace, which is really distinct from it and confers the full power to act, but not the act itself.

Criticism. The proposition that God's transcendental causality of itself is also the cause of the free act formally as such in all its (positive) aspects, and that this causality, because divine, is logically prior to that of the creature as its ground, is certainly unassailable and necessary. But when with the *praemotio physica*, a finite entity, distinct from God and his transcendent activity, though caused by God, is introduced, and this entity, distinct from the free act of the creature, infallibly determines it and yet is supposed to cause it in its freedom, a contradiction is surely presented. A created reality which antecedently determines the existence of an act, abolishes freedom of choice.

b) *Molinism*. According to Molinism, God possesses sovereign freedom in regard to human freedom. Without detriment to it, he can direct it as he pleases, because in his *scientia media* he knows "conditionally future" free actions from their objective ideal reality. God knows what every free agent in every situation that God can bring about would freely do or will do, if God were to or actually does, by his own free choice, produce this or that situation, internal or external. If therefore God wills to elicit a certain free action of a creature, he only needs to bring about the situation in which he knows by his *scientia media* that the creature in question will freely posit the act in question. Logically prior to the actual free act, therefore, God knows and directs by his *scientia media* the creature's actual freedom without coercing it, because this direction itself is founded on God's knowledge of the *conditionally* future free decision of the human being *himself*, and the quality of this is not itself determined by God. If God on the basis of his *scientia media* selects and brings about a situation in which someone acts in a way ordered to salvation, this situation is in the Molinist sense an "efficacious grace", even if it is not intrinsically different from another, merely "sufficient" grace, with which the person concerned could have acted in a salutary way, but in fact does not, as God already knows, prior to the actual decision, as a conditional future.

Criticism. This rather over-ingenious solution of the problem does not answer the question of where the conditionally future free action derives its reality from (even if this is purely of the ideal order), if it is not to have it from God, and primarily from God. Moreover, it makes God's knowledge dependent on something not divine, and without postulating once again a ground in God himself for this non-divine element, not merely in its character as possible, but as a conditionally future free act.

If the very possibility of real freedom before God is grounded in its direct relation to God, rather than being restricted or threatened thereby, then neither a "conceptual" nor a "physical" intermediary can be inserted between it and God.

c) *Other attempts at solution.* These either attempt to explain the infallibility of divine grace from God's side, though without destroying human freedom, by declaring grace infallible, not as *praemotio physica*, that is, by reason of its ontological character, but as a psychological impulse, when it is conferred in sufficient strength to overcome concupiscence (Augustinianism of the 17th and 18th centuries). Or they are a syncretism of Thomism and Molinism, explaining easier initial salutary acts (e.g., to begin to pray) on Molinist principles, but more difficult ones on Thomist principles. Augustinianism offers a concrete description of the history of the human heart as it in fact occurs. But by conceiving efficacious grace as of such a kind that its psychological character in itself permits God infallibly to know how freedom will react to it, it presupposes a grace which no longer leaves a man free. The syncretist systems (Tournely, Alphonsus Liguori) of the 18th century combine the problems raised by the other systems, without preserving their advantages.

4. *Special problems.* The problem of the relation between human freedom and a grace which from God's side is certainly efficacious and which, without detriment to the freedom of the creature, permits this freedom to be within God's disposition, is linked in the various theories of grace with the question of predestination. The efficacious grace selected by God on the basis of *scientia media* can be chosen *because* God absolutely wills the salvation of the human being in question (predestination antecedent to foreseen merits in the Molinist congruism of Suarez) or independently of this consideration (simple Molinism with an absolute predestination to beatitude as such solely on the basis of foreseen merits). Bañezian Thomism always views its own system on the supposition of a predestination to glory, antecedent (logically) to prevision of merits, because the latter of course are constituted precisely by the divine choice of the *praemotio physica* of grace.

Criticism. The question of predestination to blessedness before or after the prevision of merits would appear to be wrongly stated. That is made plain, if by nothing else, by the difficulties caused by predestination to damnation which, if viewed as positive and antecedent to demerits, is rejected by the Church as heretical Calvinism (*D* 816, 827). The absolutely transcendent God wills in his primordial, absolutely one, absolute act, a manifold world, in which the various items have quite definite relations of mutual interdependence, and of which the objective order is willed by God. But that does not mean that this finite order of connection within the manifold of the world has to be projected back into God too, so as to set up an order of several distinct divine decrees.

5. *Conclusion.* a) The endeavours of the various theories of grace to analyse even further the relation between God's universal causality and created freedom, and to distinguish a number of factors which to some degree permit the "concord" (Molina's term) of these two realities to be grasped, do not lead to any satisfactory results, as is shown by the very fact that since the 18th century theological controversy on the subject has stagnated.

b) It is probably correct to say that in this matter an attempt has been made to go beyond a point at which a halt has to be made, not out of mental laziness or theological scepticism, but because the point can clearly be seen to mark a limitation of principle. The relation between God and creature is a primordial ontological datum not susceptible of further resolution. In the fundamental transcendental experience of man's orientation towards God as the incomprehensible mystery, both man's independence and his derivation from God are simultaneously given. This experience is the most fundamental datum of the mind and even if it becomes the object of explicit reflection only later and imperfectly, it is logically prior, as the condition of the very possibility of existence as a person with intellectual knowledge and freedom. It culminates in the experience of the independence yet derivative character of freedom, and this manifests its specific nature. Consequently the relation God–freedom must be taken as primordial; there is nothing "prior" to it by which it can be rendered intelligible, any more than we, having come to know God "from" the world, can then understand the world anew, with God as starting-point.

Two facts established with certainty may not be contested because we cannot infer them one from another or both from a third, or because we are not in a position to exhibit a third which gives the how and why of their co-existence. Total origin from God in every respect, and independent freedom, are facts of that kind.

c) That is also the case as regards morally bad actions. They are ineluctably ours, and yet in everything about them which requires origination, they come from God. The morally good and the morally bad action, good and evil, are not, however, in themselves, morally or even ontologically perfectly equal possibilities of freedom. Evil, in the source of its freedom and in its objective embodiments, has less of being and less of freedom. To that extent it can and must be said that in its deficiency as such it requires no origination by God. This observation does not "solve" the problem of the relation between God and wicked freedom, but does show the creature's capacity to retain "something" wholly its own, the responsibility for which cannot be shifted to God, yet which does not require (like a good deed) to be returned to him thankfully as his grace.

d) In order really to "understand" the problem grace–freedom, to let it have its proper weight and to accept it, it is necessary to return to the frame of mind of a person at prayer. He receives himself, is, and gives himself back to God, by accepting the acceptance as an element in the gift itself. If one assumes that attitude of prayer (and by so doing in fact accepts the "solution" of the problem), there is no begging of the question, nor flight from it. One is only accepting what one undeniably is, both real and yet derivative, a creature which produced in freedom and is produced as grace as it acts.

Karl Rahner

H

HELL

Doctrine

1. In the history of revelation the notion of hell as the place and state of those who are finally lost goes back to the OT notion of Sheol as the place and state of the dead – the "underworld". In a long, slow process of theological reflection, the state in question came to be understood differently of the good and the bad, in keeping with their life on earth. The "sheol of damnation" (1 Q *Hodayot* [Qumran Thanksgiving Hymns], 3, 19) was the final lot of the wicked (Gehenna; cf. *LTK*, V, cols. 445f., with bibliography). The notion of the fire of judgment burning in the Valley of Hinnom (Gehenna) (Jer 7:32; 19:6; Is 66:24) also influenced the development of the theme.

2. In keeping with the theology of his time, Jesus, like the Baptist, spoke in his eschatological menaces of hell as the eternal place of punishment, prepared not only for the devil and his angels (Mt 25:41) but for all who have rejected the salvation offered by God. It is the punishment of their unbelief and refusal to repent (Mt 5:29 par.; 13:42, 50; 22:13, etc.). He speaks of hell as a place where eternal, unquenchable fire burns (Mt 5:22; 13:42, 50; 18:9, etc.), where there is darkness, howling and gnashing of teeth (Mt 8:12; 22:13; 25:30, etc.). A similar description is found in Rev 14:10; 20:10; 21:8. St. Paul speaks of hell in abstract theological terms as eternal destruction, ruin and loss (2 Thess 1:9; Rom 9:22; Phil 3:19; 2 Thess 2:10, etc.).

3. In its official teaching, the Church has defined the existence of hell (*D* 16, 40, 429, 464, 693, 717, 835, 840) (on the interpretation see below, 4c) and its eternity against the doctrine of the apocatastasis as put forward by Origen and other ancient writers (*D* 211). Asserting implicitly an important principle of hermeneutics, the Church eliminated temporal patterns from the existence of the dead, by affirming against the doctrine of an intermediate state of the lost before the general judgment that entry into hell takes place immediately after their death (*D* 464, 531). A certain distinction is made between the loss of the vision of God (*poena damni*) and the pain of sense (*poena sensus*) (*D* 410), but apart from this there is no official declaration on the nature of the pains of hell, though the difference of punishments in hell is mentioned (*D* 464, 693).

4. In speculative and kerygmatic theology, the following points should be noted:

a) For a proper understanding of the

matter, all the rules for the hermeneutics of eschatological assertions are to be observed, as must also be done in all preaching on hell. This means that what Scripture says about hell is to be interpreted in keeping with its literary character of "threat-discourse" and hence not to be read as a preview of something which will exist some day. Insofar as it is a report, it is rather a disclosure of the situation in which the persons addressed are actually to be found. They are placed before a decision of which the consequences are irrevocable. They can be lost for ever if they reject God's offer of salvation. The metaphors in which Jesus describes the eternal perdition of man as a possibility which threatens him at this moment are images (fire, worm, darkness, etc.) taken from the mental furniture of contemporary apocalyptic. They all mean the same thing, the possibility of man being finally lost and estranged from God in all the dimensions of his existence. Hence it can be seen that the question of whether the "fire"of hell is real or metaphorical is wrongly put, since "fire" and suchlike words are metaphorical expressions for something radically not of this world. Hence they can never be described in terms proper to their own "phenomena" and even when they seem to be expressed in the most abstract terms, they can only be spoken of "in images". Even such a term as "eternal loss" is in the nature of an image. This does not mean that "fire" is to be given a "psychological" explanation. It indicates the cosmic, objective aspect of loss which is outside the consciousness. Just as the blessedness of the immediate vision of God also involves an openness in sharing love and bliss with the glorified environment, so too loss means a definitive contradiction of the abiding and perfected world, and this contradiction will be a torment. It also follows that speculations about the "place" where hell is to be found are pointless. There is no possibility of inserting hell into the empirical world around us.

b) As regards preaching, the following considerations are important. "Hence, the theological exposition of the dogma cannot be primarily devoted to an objectivating speculation on the other world. It must apply itself above all to bringing out the real relevance of the affirmation of hell to human existence. Hence it cannot be the task of theology to go into details about supposed facts of the next life, such as the number of the damned, the severity of their pains and so on. But it has the task of maintaining the dogma of hell in all the severity of its realistic claim. For without this claim it cannot fulfil its task as part of revelation, which is to bring men to control their lives in the light of the real possibility of eternal failure and to recognize revelation as a claim of the utmost seriousness. This salutary purpose of the dogma must always set bounds to and provide the guiding lines for all speculation in this matter." (J. Ratzinger in *LTK*, V, col. 448.)

c) Even in his "judgment-discourses" Jesus gave no clear revelation about whether men are actually lost or how many may be. That he restricts himself to the possibility follows from the real nature of these discourses, which is to be a summons to decision. For this reason, there are no decisions of the magisterium on the matter, since these pronouncements are to be read in the same way as the judgment-discourses of Jesus, which they reiterate. Hence the preacher who mounts the pulpit must not appeal to visions of the saints or private revelations in these matters. To deny or to affirm that any or many were lost would be to go outside the terms of reference set by these summonses to decision and would be an immediate contradiction of the statement involved in the discourses. We must maintain side by side and unwaveringly the truth of the omnipotence of the universal salvific will of God, the redemption of all by Christ, the duty of all men to hope for salvation and also the true possibility of eternal loss. Hence too light-hearted appeals to the dogma of hell, as for instance when preaching on sin, are to be deprecated, especially if they only induce a servile fear which is insufficient for justification and which is unconvincing today. Hence the preacher must try to bring home to his hearers the seriousness of the threat to eternal salvation, with which the Christian must reckon without any sly look at a possible apocatastasis. Nonetheless, the emphasis on the possibility of hell as perpetual obduracy must be paralleled by insistent encouragement to rely with confidence on the infinite mercy of God.

d) It is possible, and indeed necessary today, to explain the eternity of hell (with Thomas Aquinas) as the consequence of the inward obduracy of man, and not either as cause of it or as an independent element. This inner obduracy, the rejection of the grace which inspires a salutary act, springs from the essence of freedom and is not in contradiction to freedom. Freedom is the will and the possibility of positing the definitive. It is not the possibility of constant revision of decisions. And "eternity" is not the continued duration of time after the history of freedom, but the definitive achievement of history. Hence hell is "eternal" and thus a manifestation of the justice of God. Hell is not to be thought of as a most drastic but merely additional punitive measure of God's vengeance, punishing those who would improve but for the infliction of this punishment. The just God is "active" in the punishment of hell only insofar as he does not release man from the reality of the definitive state which man himself has achieved on his own behalf, contradictory though this state be to the world as God's creation. Hence the notion of vindictive punishment, such as inflicted by political society on those who infringe social order, is not at all suitable to explain the doctrine of hell.

Karl Rahner

HERESY

I. Canon Law

According to the present law, a baptized person is a heretic if while retaining the name of Christian he contumaciously denies or doubts a truth which ought to be accepted by virtue of divine or Catholic faith. The heretic does not abandon the whole truth or a fundamental truth of the Christian faith, in contrast to the apostate (cf. can. 1325, para. 2). According to this definition, the crime of heresy comprises three elements. First, only a baptized person can be a heretic. Those who are not baptized and hence are not persons in the Church of Jesus Christ cannot be heretics (can. 87). The existence of heresy depends on error or doubt with regard to revealed truth. Can. 1323, para. 1, defines the meaning of "fides divina et catholica": all truths which are contained in sacred Scripture and in tradition, and which have been proposed to the belief of the faithful by the Church, as revealed truths, either by the ordinary magisterium or by a solemn definition. The existence of heresy also depends on the contumacious will to remain in error or doubt. Error or doubt alone would not constitute heresy, for which *error voluntarius* is required (Thomas Aquinas, *Summa Theologica* II,-II, q. 11, a. 1). Hence there must be the free and deliberate will to reject a truth proclaimed by the Church, in spite of its being known. The ecclesiastical penalty for heresy is only incurred when contumacy in error or doubt is expressed externally, by words or signs. Inward denial of the truth is a grave sin against the faith (2 Pet 2:17; Jas 2:12ff.). Along with the penalty of excommunication laid down in can. 2314, the heretic suffers further notable restrictions on his rights of membership (can. 167, para. 1, no. 4; 188, no. 4; 542, no. 1; 646, para. 1, no. 1; 731, para. 2; 765, no. 2; 795, no. 2; 985, no. 1; 1060; 1240, para. 1, no. 1; 1453, para. 1; 1470, para. 1, no. 6; 1657, para. 1). The absolution from the excommunication in the inner forum is reserved in a special way to the Holy See, in the outward forum to the Ordinary (can. 2314, para. 2).

The distinction between those who were culpably outside the doctrinal fold of the Church and those who adhered inculpably to false doctrine was already familiar to the ancient Church (see Augustine). The principle of penal law, "nulla poena sine culpa", had to be applied to those who did not accept fully, but without deliberate contumacy, the truths which should be accepted by virtue of divine or Catholic faith. Thus the Church distinguishes between material and formal heresy or heretics. Material heresy is a denial of the truth which is not deliberate and conscious. There can be no contumacious adherence to an error in faith where a Christian, baptized outside the Catholic Church, has no knowledge and understanding of the doctrine of the Church. It is to be assumed, as experience teaches, that in the case of Christians living in a community separated from the Catholic Church there is no contumacy. Hence the Ecumenical Directory (14 May 1967, no. 19) points out that non-Catholic Christians who come to the Catholic Church as converts are not subject to the penalties mentioned in can. 2314. Hence there is no need to absolve them from excommunication. After their profession of faith, they should be at once admitted into the full communion of the Catholic Church, according to a rite laid down by the local Ordinary. The provisions of can. 2314 hold good only for those who have culpably separated themselves from the Catholic faith and the Catholic fellowship.

Vatican II avoided completely the words heresy and heretic. The decrees speak only of separated non-Catholic Christians or of separated brothers. In view of the *Directorium Oecumenicum* it may be assumed that the notion of heresy and heretic have changed since Vatican II. The view upheld by Augustine that those who are born (Christians) outside the Catholic Church are not to be spoken of as heretics seems to be prevailing once more. Hence the only heretics would be those who deliberately departed from the doctrine of the Church of Jesus Christ, and these would then be subject to the penalties of canon law.

Heribert Heinemann

II. History of Heresies

1. *Basic considerations.* a) The history of heresies is to a large extent parallel to the history of dogma. Most of what has to be said about it is in substance said in the history of dogma. It can therefore be regarded as historical writing about the historical course, doctrinal content and historical effects of heresy, and this historical writing in turn has its own history. It can, however, mean the actual course of the heresies themselves. If the word is used in this second sense, the question immediately arises whether, how and from what points of view this series of heresies can be conceived as one single history with an at least to some extent recognizable structure. If we recall that the history of dogma and the history of heresies are mutually dependent, it immediately becomes clear that this question is identical in the concrete with the similar question which arises in the history of dogma. The history of heresies is the critical and threatening factor in the history of dogma, its merely human side.

b) The real theological problem of a history of heresies is only apparent, however, when the ambiguous nature of heresy is taken into account. In the first place it is difficult to draw a precise dividing line between heresy and the complete denial of Christianity (apostasy). Heresy is defined as false doctrine, rejected by the Church and declared to exclude from the Church, held by baptized persons within "Christian" doctrine ("retento nomine christiano"). On that basis one cannot clearly determine what belongs to a history of heresies and what does not. All the more so because even an apparently totally unchristian ideology (within the domain formerly occupied by Christianity) has not really succeeded, since the coming of modern times or in the post-Christian era, in being anything but the heretical and at the same time secularized counterpart to the Christian understanding of the world and of man. It can of course remain an open question whether that must be so and whether it will remain so. Leaving aside the distinction between heresy and apostasy, it is also possible to lay down that heresy is present when a doctrine meets with definitive rejection by the Christian magisterium. This appears readily to determine the subject-matter of the history of heresies. But then two things have to be taken into consideration and they once more complicate the problem of the history of heresies.

(i) A serious and historically influential heresy has a long prehistory and history in the history of the theology and dogma of the Church itself before it is rejected by the magisterium and leads to schism on the part of the heretics. And this prehistory and history of the heresy within the Church will always or almost always be intelligible only as a (humanly speaking) unavoidable crisis of growth in the development of the history of dogma and in awareness of the faith in the Church itself. As a consequence, often the most tragic and guilty element in this history consists in its moving out of the Church's unity and its history of faith, and becoming isolated in ecclesiastical bodies of its own. This may come about through the heretical, schismatical impatience of those immediately involved, or through a justified but to some extent impatient reaction on the part of the teaching Church. For this history, in spite of its onesidedness and problematical questionings, should really attain its proper goal, namely a real growth in the *intellectus fidei*, within the Church. The positive function of heresy for the Church and its growth in the faith does not entirely come to an end for the Church if after mutual anathema the heresy accomplishes its history outside the Church. Now if all this is taken into account, a Catholic theological history of heresies (not one simply designed as a history of ideas) cannot regard that history as anything but a part of the history of dogma, treated separately for convenience. Otherwise such a historical account would miss the real nature, origin and significance of heresy in sacred history. This is particularly clear if we remember that God-given faith can never regard itself as merely in antithesis to a human error. It must see itself as the higher, more comprehensive truth, against a part of which an error shuts itself off by "selecting" (heretically) and "separating" (schismatically). Moreover, the historical influence of a heresy is never explained by the error as such (as a firmly held negation), but by the truth contained in the error, though onesidedly stressed. The Church has reason to confront its own full truth with the partial truth which is showing itself in a historically influential way in the heresy.

(ii) It is self-evident to a Catholic understanding of the faith that "in itself", i.e., for man in general (and so – realizing this abstract norm – for many individual men), the Catholic Church is recognizable in actual fact as the bearer of the one complete truth of Christian revelation. This does not mean, however, that that is evident to all men and for all Christians, when their actual historical and individual circumstances and limited span of life are taken into account. By "recognizable" here we are not referring only to a quality in the reality itself but are taking into account that the knowing subject's own characteristics contribute to constitute the reality known. For to be recognizable means to be recognizable by someone. To deny this would imply that no one without grave subjective guilt could fail to find the Catholic Church by the end of his life. But that is certainly an assertion which on a variety of grounds is absolutely to be rejected. A man's inculpable failure to attain a moral goal which in itself is binding demonstrates the impossibility of its attainment for the man in question, even if that impossibility is attributable to the subjective guilt of others, e.g., the first heresiarchs (though their guilt also is ultimately impossible to establish), and in this respect may be merely "permitted" by God. Even so a positive salvific meaning can be acknowledged in this impossibility of recognizing the Church permitted by God in an innocent person, without thereby contesting the importance for salvation of the unrecognized truth or denying that it is recognizable in itself. To some extent it is possible to understand the positive meaning for salvation, under God's providence, of this particular unrecognizability. Having regard for the "hierarchy of truths" in Catholic teaching which "vary in their relationship to the foundation of the Christian faith" (Vatican II, Decree on Ecumenism, art. 11), it is clear that certain human beings (by their general historical and psychological make-up) more easily succeed in fact (not *per se*) in grasping the most central doctrines important for salvation when they are not confronted with the whole of explicit Catholic Christianity. From this point of view, however, the history of heresies assumes yet another quite different aspect, provided it is not regarded simply as a history of ideas. The formal rejection of a Catholic truth as such cannot be approved, but in most cases it can be presumed to be only objectively erroneous, not subjectively guilty. When it lives on in the history of heresy, it embraces the various individual and collective forms in which *genuine* Christianity finds realization. This is analogous to the way in which various mixed forms of *fides explicita* and *fides implicita* arise as modes of the Catholic faith, even within Catholic orthodoxy, which vary widely when compared with the *per se* valid doctrinal system of Catholic Christianity. Thus the history of heresies becomes once again, in its historically important manifestations, an element in the history of dogma within the Catholic Church, showing what shifts of emphasis in concrete personal attitude and degrees of realization are possible in relation to the manifold reality presented by faith. In fact, of course, it is not very difficult to match the various heresies (particularly if envisaged from the point of view we have just described) with homologous structures within the Catholic Church (e.g., an orthodox Christology can be indicated which is akin to Nestorianism or to Monophysitism, and so on).

c) It is therefore clear that the history of heresies is best dealt with in the context of the history of dogma itself. There it has the positive significance of throwing light on dogma in its actual history both as regards its content and the actual religious and personal attitude adopted to it in the concrete. Insofar as a structure can and must be discerned in the history of heresies (which cannot be deduced *a priori*, yet is not a mere enumeration of errors), this structure and its principle are those of the history of dogma.

Furthermore, certain formal aspects can be seen to recur constantly in the history of heresies. One feature of heresy is that the whole of Christianity is still virtually contained in it, or in its whole conception of Christianity. On this basis the idea of a purely verbal heresy might be formed (cf., for example, certain forms of Monophysitism). This is in fact an erroneous non-conformity with the linguistic usage of the Church. It is really schismatic, linked with sectarian distrust that in the language of the great Church genuine Christianity may not find plain and unmistakable expression. It is also quite conceivable that in the course of its history a real heresy may, unwittingly, work itself back into a purely verbal one. Then, because doctrine and practice go together, there is another important aspect. (The patristic theology could not take it into account, because of the short period during which heresies had existed.) The possibility has always to be borne in mind that within the history of a heresy as a historically developing non-Catholic denomination there can be forms of Christianity in teaching and practice which are indeed always preserved and present potentially in the Catholic, i.e., true, comprehensive and historically legitimate form of Christianity, but which have not yet reached there the same explicit level of realization. These can form a stimulus to the development of doctrine and practice in the Church itself.

In this way they can exercise a positive function in redemptive history in relation to the Church. According to Paul, heresy comes under the principle of something which "must be" in redemptive history. Man's at least objective guilt in diminishing and narrowing God's truth remains comprised within the will of God for his revelation and its bearer the Church. And from this fact (which does not legitimate it as a human act) heresy receives a positive meaning which it has not in itself. It is the way in which God's truth, to the extent that it is man's truth, remains subject to lowliness and in fact grows in the mind of men as the "inevitable" basis of leading the Church into all truth. In that way it assumes a position in relation to the saving history of believed and known truth analogous to that of Israel in relation to the Church (Rom 9–11). Consequently it is not true that in face of heresies the Church merely statically defends truths which it has already grasped adequately. The Church learns to know more clearly its own truth by hearing and rejecting contradiction of its own truth and of its growing self-understanding.

A further aspect, however, is that the history of truth and its development (the development of dogma) is the history of discernment. It is the progressive, fuller and clearer rejection of heresy by the Church, the necessary discernment of spirits, the initial stage of God's judgment which sifts the truth and the error of men. The Church's judgment, however, concerns the historical expression of man's attitude to truth (an expression always ambiguous as regards the interior faith), and not the attitude itself and hence not man. In accordance with the genuinely historical character of the knowledge of truth even in the Church, and the dependence of the Church, in its struggle, on God's unforeseeable designs (cf. Lk 21:14), a genuinely *a priori* (not purely formalistic) outline of possible heresies, a corresponding anticipatory sketch-plan of the history of heresies and an unambiguous *a priori* exposition of the history of heresies which have already occurred (in the style of Hegel's philosophy of history) are not possible. That does not mean, however, that the history of heresies is simply an arbitrary list of contradictions of the various articles of the faith. It is also to a large extent a function of the general history of ideas (and their political and social presuppositions) the structural pattern of which is to some extent intelligible. Heresies, therefore, are almost always to be understood as views of the truth from a certain angle, which are given a falsely radical character and then "split off". They are formally comparable to the different theological schools within the Church, which even in their plurality have a lasting function in the Church and its theology and to some extent an indispensable place in the whole. Furthermore, there are certain fundamental formal heresies which are continually recurring in concrete cases (e.g., the denial of the analogy of being; of the Chalcedonian principle of "without mixture, without separation"; of the principle of the incompleteness of all human intellectual systems in face of the "ever greater God" [cf. *D* 432]; of the analogy of faith, etc.).

These and similar points of view fully permit us to go beyond a merely positivist inventory type of history of heresies. Though the question of the most appropriate terminology remains open, it must be admitted that even within the Church and for considerable periods of time there can be tendencies, attitudes, emphases, etc., perhaps in theory, but above all in spontaneous practice, which can only be characterized as latent, inarticulate but real heresies or as leanings to heresy (cf. the theological note: *sapit haeresim*). Such latent heresies and heretical leanings should really form part of the history of heresies, especially as they may generate similar or opposed heresies of an explicit kind. However plainly the history of theological schools within the Church is to be distinguished from that of heresies, the homology of their history with the history of heresies should be noted, because important insights follow from it for both.

2. *Some pointers on the history of heresies.* a) *Principles of arrangement of the history of heresies.* As stated above, the really theological principles of structure are those of the history of dogma, but negatively applied. They need not, therefore, be repeated here. The specific ways in which heresies accompany the movement of dogma (retarding or accelerating it) can perhaps, however, be formally distinguished, though in the same heresy several such modes may be simultaneously at work. There are "reactionary" heresies which shut themselves off from a historically necessary development in the Church and its teaching (so for example Montanism or Novatianism, which wrongly wished to retain systematically a severer previous practice of penance; an Augustinianism which was given a heretically absolute status in Jansenism and Baianism). There are heresies by "reduction", which seek either to give Christianity an existentially radical character or to relieve it of doctrines that are "not modern", by restricting it to doctrines declared to be the only important ones. A heresy by radical reduction was the older Protestantism with its triple *sola* (*scriptura*, *gratia*, *fides*), "Fundamentalism", heretical existentialist demythologizing, modernism, etc., seek to relieve Christianity of unwelcome burdens. There are (as has already been noted) verbal heresies which think they cannot recognize their faith in a particular ecclesial formulation, although they in fact say the same thing or advocate an interpretation of an article of faith which is tenable inside the Church (e.g., certain forms of Monophysitism). We might also speak of "contact heresies", i.e., attempts to assimilate non-Christian ideologies into Christian doctrine or to subordinate the latter to the former (e.g., the phantom heresy of Americanism). If we extend to some degree the concept of heresy, there is cryptogamic heresy (K. Rahner, *On Heresy*, Quaestiones Disputatae 11 [1964]), i.e., what is in fact a heretical attitude inside and outside the Church consciously or unconsciously evades reflection and conceptual formulation. Not every heresy in its history or in its doctrine leads to the formation of a Church, although many have done so. It is therefore possible to distinguish between Church-forming and non-Church-forming heresies. The latter are usually called "par-

ticular" heresies, because they concern a single particular point of doctrine. Church-forming heresies usually start (explicitly) from some particular heresy but generally develop into a fundamental conception which colours their understanding of Christianity as a whole. They become "universal" heresies.

If we remember that a true statement about God must always concede that God is greater than can be directly stated in analogous mundane terms, i.e., that any statement about God must be a dialectical one and cannot say anything positive which, taken by itself, could serve as an adequate principle of deduction for all other statements in that domain, we see that there can also be "anti-dialectical", systematically one-directional heresies. One of these was Predestinarianism and another Pelagianism, in the question of sovereign grace and human freedom. On the frontier of mere heresy, or already beyond it, are "secularizing" heresies, which retain more or less some formal structures of Christianity and of its doctrine, but transpose them into attitudes and doctrines which are secular, i.e., without relation to God. This is to forget that such formal structures ultimately wither away if deprived of their real historical manifestation and concrete embodiment (which was and is Christian). Many forms of modern humanism are secularizing heresies of this kind.

b) *On the history of heresies*. Obviously not all particular heresies are to be listed here, nor is it a question of a precise distinction between heresies and totally anti-Christian doctrinal systems and philosophies (within the limits of the historical domain influenced by Christianity). (i) At the beginning stands the reactionary heresy of Judaism (which Paul was the first to combat); this was a denial that Christianity should be detached from the religious situation in which it appeared. The extreme contrary of this is found in Marcion with his denial of any continuity between saving history in the Old and the New Testament. (ii) The great heresies of the 2nd to 4th centuries, Gnosticism and Arianism, were contact heresies, which endeavoured to fit Christianity into existing mental perspectives. In the panentheistic view of the God–world relationship common in Hellenism, the history of the created world becomes the history of a God who lives through his destiny in a dualistic world (Gnosticism), and the self-communication of the absolute God to created history distinct from him becomes the communication of lesser principles, only half-divine (Arianism: the Logos and the Pneuma are not really God himself). (iii) The Christological heresies of the 5th century (Nestorianism, Monophysitism, Monotheletism) were primarily particular and anti-dialectical heresies which tried to systematize one-sidedly the mystery of the relation between world and God, either rationalistically (Nestorianism) or undialectically in a mystical philosophy of identity. (iv) Pelagianism (5th century) and Predestinarianism (5th, 8th centuries; Calvinism) were likewise anti-dialectical heresies, at first particular ones, which in the grace–freedom relation attempted to dissolve the mystery in favour of one of the two poles. (v) As Protestantism has no unified, closed doctrinal system, but exhibits very many radically divergent ones, what they have in common might perhaps best be described as a universal reduction-heresy. Either, as in early Protestantism in particular, a reduction to the threefold *sola* (*scriptura, gratia, fides*) is undertaken so that everything else becomes unessential to Christianity, or is felt to be radically opposed to it. Or else other elements are rejected as unessential, especially those concerning the constitution of the Church (episcopacy, papacy, sacraments). (vi) Other forms of reduction-heresy are Modernism and the many forms of Protestant liberal theology: Christianity is reduced to the interpretation of man's experience of himself.

c) *The formal basic structure of the possibility of heresy.* Although the historical order of heresies cannot be deduced, all heresies can be understood as the possible ways of deforming the mysterious fundamental relation between God and world which can only be stated dialectically and can never be comprised in a single formula. Either the true reality of the creature disappears (the human reality of Christ, human freedom, the significance of ministry in the Church, etc.), in face of the sole causality of God, or the reality proper to the creature is deistically misconceived as independent (e.g., in Nestorianism or Pelagianism), so that God in the ultimate resort becomes the radiance of man himself as absolute (as in Modernism).

Karl Rahner

HERMENEUTICS

A. The Notion and Problem of Understanding

Hermeneutics is an aid to the *understanding* of something which is not – as in matters which are to be "explained" – indifferent and external to the mind, but which is pervaded by individual, collective, permanent and historically conditioned elements and thus belongs to the world of intersubjective agreement. This universal and primordial phenomenon of understanding as it occurs in general, scientific and inter-human experience should not be disguised by the much more striking forms of disagreement which are the occasion for the development of a hermeneutics. As long as "tradition" is accepted and transmitted without question – prescinding for the moment from the re-interpretations possibly concealed therein – individual "misunderstandings" and many "errors" arise, rather than fundamental difficulties of interpretation. But the sense of the passage of time, changes in vocabulary, concepts and thought-forms can bring about a break with tradition, which will now appear as "strange" and questionable. To ensure against particular mistakes and to provide the relevant application or normative repetition of tradition a regional hermeneutics is then worked out, as, for instance, in the rabbinical interpretation of Scripture. This hermeneutics has a concrete way of understanding in mind, for which it draws up a canon of rules with which to approach the tradition, especially the texts. In this sense there exists a (special) hermeneutics in the normative sciences of ancient and medieval theology and law. There were rules for "application", "spirit and letter", allegory, for filling in gaps in codified law, for the scholastic interpretation of authorities: *reverenter exponere* and so on. But such hermeneutics were simply the sum of concrete guides to right understanding derived from experience, and were mostly applied to fixed systems, of an acknowledgedly authoritative character, which aimed at right practice. They aimed at an elaborate "art" or technique of understanding, which is far from what is meant by a "theory of understanding" such as constitutes the modern concept of hermeneutics. Profound spiritual upheavals (as between the Sophists and Plato, or "la querelle des anciens et des modernes") and a break with all inherited tradition (as between OT and NT; between the Old Faith and the Reformation) are the necessary prerequisites for a clear sense of the great problems of hermeneutics.

B. Origin and Purpose of Modern Hermeneutics

1. While the Reformers still maintained on principle the unity of the canon of the Bible on dogmatic grounds, the 18th century began to consider sacred Scripture as a historical document, which was therefore to be understood according to the mind of the authors who wrote the books and in the light of

the ancient environment. Hence the interpretation should prescind from the immediate interests of later readers (so, e.g., J. S. Salomo, A. Ernesti). This "critical and historical" interpretation is the logical outcome of the Protestant principle of Scripture explaining itself (*scriptura sui ipsius interpres*). The return to the "historical" understanding of Scripture was used at first to get rid of traditions and to disown a present Church supposedly alienated from its origins. The history itself thus remained subordinated to an application which felt sure of itself. The demonstration of the historical gap reached its climax in the 19th and 20th centuries, when the interpreter could no longer identify himself "naively" with the contents and purpose of the text. When the interpreter became fully conscious of his task, the Christian thing itself became problematic.

2. The universal hermeneutical problem was felt more acutely as it became clearly necessary to find the broader historical contexts of statements which could no longer be treated in isolation. It was seen that a whole complex world of experience and the individual components of it had to be used to throw light on each other. Once Romanticism had ended in a total alienation with regard to tradition, a radical means of overcoming this alienation and the universal possibility of misunderstanding was called for. Only a sincerely methodical and scientific attitude can take the finished article from its original context in world history and reproduce it faithfully, by means of a sympathetic divination which enables one to imitate the creative act. The difference between linguistic-historical and theological hermeneutics vanishes. Schleiermacher designates special hermeneutics as an "aggregate of observations", while general hermeneutics is a "mighty motive for linking the speculative with the empirical and historical". This relationship between conscious knowledge and the living totality which is inseparable from it must always be kept in mind and then leads implicitly to freeing hermeneutics from being confined to history and theories of knowledge. "It is difficult to define the role of general hermeneutics" (Schleiermacher).

3. It was left to W. Dilthey to bring to light the profoundest philosophical role of general hermeneutics. The concrete cognitive subject is linked *a priori*, by identity of life and possibility of experience, with the past which is being expounded, though man's having to rely on creations ("expression") other than himself gives rise to real history and hence finally to a disclosure of the meaning of life. The first stage in leaving behind the psychological intentions of Schleiermacher's hermeneutics and in arriving at an expansion of the domain of hermeneutics is found in the term "expression". This now includes – along with the texts and the oral discourse which Schleiermacher favoured – anything and everything, even wordless happenings and the actions of history-making man. But Schleiermacher and Dilthey bog down in an obscurely pantheistic conception: that of the pre-established harmony and free union of all individuals, each of whom represents an epiphany of the "Living All", whose basic unity makes a connatural sympathy of understanding possible. This is a tendency which the "historical school" also fails to avoid. Its ultimate aim is not the "emasculated objectivity" of a fully depersonalized individual, but conscious alliance with the great permanent moral forces which guarantees a secret share in the totality of world history and allows one to sense the hidden meaning of the whole.

4. This is no longer as in the speculative dialectics of Hegel the transformation of the mind's objectivations into the original spiritual reality. But in the mind of the modern historian there are the same presuppositions – those of the absolute self-transparency of the spirit

and the supreme capacity of the reason to explain itself to itself. Hermeneutics thus becomes the great effort of a totally lucid universal understanding and only thereafter is it a "methodology". But the question is whether the historian, for instance, by virtue of the presence of the same "spiritual nature" in all human behaviour, can have an inward sense and sympathy even for the most distant past. Can the creative process be so imitated and re-constructed subjectively and objectively that the original purpose of a work re-appears once more? The work thus fetched back from its alienation in the past remains after all a mere concept and it is precisely the necessary communication with the present which is left unachieved. Hegel saw clearly the impossibility here involved. Further, it is doubtful whether the justifiable purpose of excluding or controlling the "prejudices" of one's own historical situation, in order to have an "objective" view of ancient testimonies, can be successful when essential phenomena in particular are involved. If understanding is arrived at to some extent through the concrete situation of the interpreter at the present day, the whole depth of the historical experience actually undergone could not be represented in the self-understanding of the historical method. But then the basic problem of hermeneutics, the relation of the thinker to the subject-matter, remains unsolved.

5. A radically new approach was that of M. Heidegger, whose critique of the ontological premisses of modern notions of subjectivity disclosed the intrinsic infinity of this basically idealistic notion of spirit in the midst of the "finite-historical-empirical" understanding. Heidegger refuses to admit that the historicity of existence poses limits to understanding or threatens objectivity. Hermeneutics is now justified as ontology. Prior to all philosophical and methodological interests, existence has already "understood" the world. Hence to understand, being "ability to be", "potentiality", is a primordial characteristic of the being of human life itself. Understanding, as "sketch-plan", implies no detached self-possession of existence; it must always find itself limited by the inescapable facticity of its being and moulded by history and historicity.

This basic principle of a "hermeneutics of existence" was then taken further, independently, by H. G. Gadamer. An adequate hermeneutics deals with history thus efficacious in the very act of understanding. It must therefore demonstrate how the thinker stands therein in a manifold complex of tradition (*Wirkungsgeschichte* – "the effective history" or history as impact). It must make the thinker acknowledge this presupposition consciously before turning to the individual objects and "objective" analysis. Hence every affirmation can be regarded as an answer to a question which is the more or less definable horizon of a "prior understanding" (mostly unconscious) and which implies a vital relationship of the interpreter to the matter involved. This "prior understanding" is provisionally acknowledged and then itself submitted to criticism in the further process of understanding. The thinker always finds himself caught up in a world which is in process of explicitating itself in detail. When this open horizon takes in a new experience which cannot be subsumed into familiar expectations and tendencies, it upsets the older "pre-understanding", accepts and assimilates the "alien" and thus expands and enriches the realm of its own experience of the world ("the merging of the horizons"). This inescapable interplay of an efficacious tradition and the movement of the understanding itself is a relationship which no longer falls under the categories of "subjective" and "objective". Even the formal characterization as the "hermeneutic circle" is misleading (though there is no question of a logical or methodological [vicious] circle).

The decisive point has still to be made clear, that the circle, by virtue of the acknowledged finitude of the mental horizon, leaves an opening through which one can be the victim of something "alien" which impinges on one from the realm of history. Such an experience is not to be explained as the action of the subject, or subjectivity actualized – nonetheless, it does not come about without the thinker, as may be seen from the fact that the true understanding of what has been thus appropriated only results from the interpretation translated into one's own language. Such "knowledge of the known" contains an element of self-conscious analysis (which is, however, never exhaustive), and hence may not be regarded as naive spontaneity.

The universal medium of such hermeneutics as the basic movement of finite-historical existence in general is language. For language conveys, conceals and reveals a whole understanding of the world and other unobtrusive anticipations and conditions which affect the understanding. Its structure, which is not independent of ethical and political action and public life, can convey to a certain extent phenomena like power and social interests which seemingly lie outside the scope of speech. Hence, formally, language can provide the truly universal aspect of a hermeneutics.

It has been said (e.g., by E. Betti) that the transformation of the classical hermeneutics, which aimed at objectivity of understanding, into a hermeneutics of existence is a subjectivist denial of the independence of the object of hermeneutics. But this objection is a fundamental misconception with regard to the hermeneutics in question, since "being conscious of historical impact is inevitably rather being than being conscious" (Gadamer). In practice, however, the hermeneutical principles of Gadamer and Betti are very much alike, though Gadamer does not try to produce a methodology of such "sciences of the spirit" as history. W. Pannenberg and (to some extent) J. Habermas try to extend on principle the horizon of the new hermeneutics to make it take in, hypothetically or theologically, an anticipatory theology structured in terms of universal history or again, a philosophy of history of a concrete type. The relevance of hermeneutics for the theory of the sciences is still to be examined (K. O. Apel).

C. Modern Hermeneutics and Catholic Theology

The working out of a regional hermeneutics in the individual theological disciplines is as necessary as the hermeneutical task of theology in general. The transcendental or phenomenological and hermeneutical horizon which gives the conditions of possibility for the dogmatic truth, and also the receptivity of man with regard to such truth, must be treated much more carefully and expressly – in spite of the positive concrete nature of the history of salvation and of the Church (K. Rahner). A thoroughgoing confrontation of Catholic theology with modern hermeneutics is a task still to be accomplished, for which the following guide-lines may be suggested.

1. The term "hermeneutics" must not be used in a sense which fails to do justice to the present-day problems of philosophical hermeneutics. It must try to grapple critically with the questions there posed.

2. Since theological discourse has to uphold an "objective reality" which limits, integrates and transcends the universal historical flux and relativity of changing views of the world, it cannot take over inconsiderately the post-Kantian ontology which is the recognized basis of modern hermeneutics. The crisis in metaphysics cannot be solved by falling back upon hermeneutics. Hermeneutics as the one universal ontology is still an impasse, or a poor substitute for metaphysics.

3. To explain the biblical texts simply as expressions of the human understanding of existence, by the use of a hermeneutics which blunts the edge of the affirmations about God, the world and history is always – in spite of the bearing of self-understanding on such affirmations – an illegitimate restriction of the biblical "pre-understanding", which is not merely anthropological. It also fails to do justice to what Heidegger originally meant by "existence".

4. Hermeneutics may not be used to favour limited formal categories such as "decision", "communication", "word-event", "language-event", to the exclusion of the concrete contents of the Christian message. In theology, the efficiency of hermeneutics is measured by its power to re-state in undistorted form the actual truth of faith.

5. Hermeneutics can give rise to an intellectually justifiable rehabilitation of Church tradition and authority, as necessary functional elements in the thinking out of the faith. A constant recall of the traditional and free acceptance of authority are the prerequisites of a "dogmatic" form of thought.

6. Within a theological hermeneutics, "tradition", being the all-encompassing hermeneutical horizon, must be given a concrete historical orientation, with all its constitutive elements.

7. While adhering as it must to the methodical scholarship of each individual theological discipline, hermeneutics can show what is prior to all the understanding attitudes of the subject, including the methodical approach of science, and what is "skipped" or "blurred" by such understanding: the original claim of the gospel and its truth. This claim, and the original understanding experienced in faith may not be subjected to a process of total alienation in scientific study. On the contrary, they must become fully articulate in a fundamental theology (of the phenomenological type). Hermeneutics is not exhausted by the immanent scientific function of the theological disciplines as known hitherto.

8. Once we have conceded that the hermeneutic problem is a universal one, the question remains as to whether present-day hermeneutics provides a universally valid basis for all understanding of being (including action and the religious reality) and whether language, as a universal hermeneutical medium, is the key to the understanding of all that can be understood. Some indispensable test-cases in theology would be: sacramental structures, miracles, the action that goes beyond the word, the definitive nature of the truth with which theology is concerned.

In the discussion of these and other problems the hermeneutical task imposes itself on all theological work with an urgency which it would be hard to overestimate. And the difficulties which it presents by reason of the subjects and the mental processes involved should not be underestimated or evaded by short-sighted "solutions".

Karl Lehmann

HIERARCHY

1. *Concept.* Etymologically hierarchy means holy origin (ἱερὰ ἀρχή), holy dominion and, since the time of Denis the Areopagite, it has been used to signify the order given the Church by the Lord. In ecclesiastical legal language the hierarchy is the structure composed of those who, according to the principle of unity of head and body, are called to represent the invisible Lord; more precisely, it is, in the objective sense, the institutional order within this structure, and, in the subjective sense, the totality of those holding sacred authority.

2. *Basis.* To sum up the teaching on the Church as offered by Vatican II in a short formula, one could say that the Church is the new people of God living in hierarchical order in the service of the kingdom of God. The hierarchical order

which goes with the distinction between clergy and laity is essential to the Church; therefore one speaks of the hierarchical structure of the Church, which excludes the acceptance of a charismatical structure. The hierarchical structure is a constitutive principle of the people of God and has its theological basis in the sacramentality of the Church. The Church is the sign of salvation erected by Jesus Christ for all men, "in Christ as it were, a sacrament, i.e., a sign and instrument for the innermost union with God as well as for the unity of the whole of mankind" (Vatican II, *De Ecclesia*, art. 1). This sacramental significance of the Church is bound to the hierarchical structure proper to the Church, i.e., the Church is only a sacramental sign by reason of the fact that the Lord, who is the invisible head of the Church, is visibly represented in the Church by men: for without a visible head the Church cannot be a visible representation of the Lord's body. This order of the Church is based on the will of the Lord who has determined to continue his work of salvation in the Church by means of authorized representatives. He instituted the twelve apostles, made them, as the word shows, his representatives in a legal sense and placed Peter at the head of the Twelve. With the continuance of the Lord's mission guaranteed by the apostolic succession, Jesus Christ himself lives on in the Church and is the animating and ruling head of all the members of the people of God, not only by reason of the invisible rule of the Holy Spirit, but also in the visible activity of the servants chosen and authorized by him.

3. *Unity in duality*. The ultimate purpose of the hierarchy is to represent the one Lord. It therefore seems strange that the hierarchy is divided into a hierarchy of orders (*h. ordinis*) and a hierarchy of jurisdiction (*h. iurisdictionis*). Corresponding to this twofold hierarchy is the differentiation between the power of orders (*potestas ordinis*) and the power of jurisdiction (*potestas iurisdictionis*), which are to be seen as complementary elements of the one sacred ecclesiastical authority. The *CIC* speaks in the singular of *sacra*, or *ecclesiastica hierarchia* (can. 108, no. 3; 109), a point which is rarely noticed, and thus testifies to the unity of the hierarchy, which, in regard to orders and office (*ratione ordinis – ratione iurisdictionis*), is differentiated into a hierarchy of orders and one of offices. The constitution *Lumen Gentium*, which presents the hierarchical structure of the Church's constitution in its third chapter, avoided mentioning expressly the distinction between the hierarchy of orders and that of offices; nevertheless it offers all the elements which are essential to the distinction. Therefore one cannot say that the distinction between a hierarchy of orders and one of offices has been abandoned. What stopped Vatican II from expressly making the distinction, besides the lack of clarity concerning the relationship of the power of orders and the power of jurisdiction, was an urgent concern for the unity of the hierarchy as well as of ecclesiastical authority; this unity had been overlooked to a great extent in the Latin Church and had been distorted to some extent into a real separation. The Council emphasizes, in contrast to this separatist trend, that ecclesiastical authority is sacramentally based on orders, but does not deny that the canonical mission is still needed in order to make the power which is ontologically based upon holy orders a power capable of being exercised. The distinction of the two hierarchies, which in the last analysis aims to guarantee the unity of the hierarchy, must be seen in this context.

The hierarchies of orders and offices are basically distinguished by the fact that entrance into the ranks of the hierarchy of offices – except for the supreme authority of the Pope and the college of bishops – is through canonical mission (can. 109), which is primarily the transmission of an office, though it also includes delegation of jurisdiction. On account of the indelible character which is given with holy orders, enrolment into the hierarchy of orders is irrevocable; in contrast, the canonical mission can be lost at any rank and can be withdrawn by the competent ecclesiastical authority. The fact that a consecrated minister can be deprived of his office and be completely excluded from the hierarchy of offices protects ecclesiastical authority, called to represent the invisible Lord, against human failings; and because the only true wielders of sacred authority are in both hierarchies, the ecclesiastical hierarchy preserves precisely through its duality its intrinsic unity.

4. *Ranks within the hierarchies of orders and offices.* Within the bounds of the hierarchy of orders as well as of the hierarchy of offices one must distinguish between the ranks of divine and of ecclesiastical law. In the hierarchy of orders the three sacramental orders (episcopate, presbyterate, diaconate) are ranks of divine law; the other ranks of orders, together with first tonsure, which precede holy orders, are of ecclesiastical law (in the Latin Church: subdiaconate, acolyte, exorcist, lector, porter; in the Eastern Church: for the most part the subdiaconate, plus one or the other of the minor orders). Within the hierarchy of offices the supreme pastoral office of the Pope, as successor to St. Peter, and of the college of bishops, which has succeeded the college of the apostles and which has the Pope as its head (Vatican II, *De Ecclesia*, art. 22), as well as the episcopal office which is subordinated to the two bearers of supreme ecclesiastical power mentioned above and which is related to the guidance of a particular Church, are of divine law. All other offices are derived from these and go back to ecclesiastical institution. The offices of the Pope and the college of bishops are, with their divine institution, concretely present in the Church and neither need an ecclesiastical institution, nor are they capable of such; on the other hand, the episcopal office, related to a particular Church, necessarily needs an erection by the competent ecclesiastical authority because it demands an ordination to a particular flock. The particular episcopal office is of ecclesiastical law, but the tasks and powers which belong to episcopal office thus made concrete flow from the episcopal office as instituted by God and are not derivable from the primatial power of the Pope (Vatican II, *ibid.*, art. 27; Decree on the Bishops' Pastoral Office in the Church, art. 8).

The presentation of the Church's constitution in *CIC*, which still does not take into consideration the doctrine of episcopal collegiality – except for the ecumenical council – is based on the notion of the Pope as supreme authority and of the bishop as ruler of the diocese. Derived from the office of the Pope are: a) its auxiliary organs for the administration of the whole Church (college of cardinals, Roman congregations, Curia offices and courts, papal legates); b) archbishops (patriarchs, primates, metropolitans); and c) the bearers of episcopal power for those areas in which an episcopate has not yet been installed (apostolic vicars and prefects, apostolic administrators, abbots and prelates *nullius*), as well as the heads of exempt orders of priests. Derived from the office of bishop are: a) the auxiliary organs for administering the diocese (vicars-general); b) the deans or archpriests as local organs of inspection for greater areas within the diocese; c) the parish priests as the responsible leaders of the parish communities.

Over and beyond all the ranks within the hierarchy of orders and of offices, we find both hierarchies connected indissolubly with one another in the episcopacy. The various ranks of episcopal service are based upon the office alone, and not upon the episcopal ordination, which is the same for all. The Church's constitution is thereby so constructed that the supreme pastoral office of the Pope and every archiepiscopal office (patriarch, major archbishop and metropolitan) is connected with a particular see. This characteristic of the Church's constitution, which has no secular parallels, is based upon the fact that a particular Church is not only a part of the whole, but represents the whole Church in its area; at the same time it is an expression of a collegial element in the Church's constitution, which has found its legal expression in the institution of the synod. The collegial element is an important complement of the hierarchical principle of the ecclesiastical constitution. It connects the individual bishops not only with the Pope, but also with all the members of the college of bishops. The vertical component expressed in the relationship of Pope to bishop is complemented by the horizontal union of all bishops who represent, in unity with the Pope, the whole Church.

Klaus Mörsdorf

HISTORY

I. History and Historicity

A. Terms and Concept

The words used throughout Europe for history come through the Latin *historia* from the Greek ἱστορεῖν, to know, investigate, except the German *Geschichte*. The former group indicates rather the study or science of history, while the German envisages rather the event itself, first the individual occurrence and then the individual life-process and the total world-process. The humanists used the German *Geschichte* in the definitely scientific sense of *historia*. But *Geschichte* always retained a special nuance of its own (which has become important in modern theology, and is often rendered by simply transcribing the German word as it stands into English and other literatures). The special connotation of *Geschichte* is that of the irresistible working of historical forces (almost like that of the ultra-modern sense of "happening") which is more emphasized than the sense of research and knowledge. The word is used in the singular (in the plural it simply means occurrences), but not in the sense of a single science. There is always the connotation of the one great comprehensive event, the *one* History (of which the differentiations, the historicity and transcendentality will be discussed in C below).

This history is one, being the one world of man in his historicity (the world being understood not just as a setting, but as a reality coming into being, not just as space but as order). Here historicity means the peculiar nature of human existence (gathering up world and time into one) by which man stands between a past which is imposed on him, with enduring effects and yet beyond his reach, and an outstanding future on its way to him which he must try to procure. It is only in this interaction of beginning and end, the essentially inter-personal tension of freedom and determinism that man attains his (contingent) selfhood and essence. By reason of this essential structure, man can only become aware of his history and historicity in the course of history and can only accept it and take it over in the historical struggle with it. As a spirit-being he possesses his history only by understanding it (a truth which is the basic unity of the two senses of history, as event and historical knowledge, *Geschichte* and *historia*). But this understanding has itself its history and its very change is a moment of the history in which man lives out his historicity. Throughout this article, the word history will be used predominantly in the sense of (total) event.

B. The Development of the Notion of History

Since man is inextricably involved in history and historicity, there are no peoples completely without a history, even where the origins and the future of a people (and the world in general, of which it sees itself as the centre) are presented in mythic narratives. In the Occident, this self-understanding became *historia* in the "Father of History", as Cicero termed Herodotus (*c.* 484–425 B.C.). Herodotus tries to trace one consistent law throughout the multiplicity of all that was said and done. He sees the decisive force in history as the confrontation of man who recognizes his limits with man who is carried away by the arrogance of his *hybris*, which always leads to the destruction of the immoderate by the gods. A different view is taken by Thucydides (*c.* 456–396 B.C.), who confined himself to a description of the Peloponnesian War and was the founder of political history as such. For Thucydides, history consisted of the conflict of interests, in which the stronger always imposes his law as the right – though even the stronger is not exempt from the hazards of inexplicable catastrophes. Hence the lessons to be deduced from this one war can be seen as a "possession for ever".

Polybius (*c.* 201–120 B.C.) uses the same approach to write the first great history of Rome. He links the effects of geography, climate and other impersonal causes with the initiatives of men and demonstrates for the first time how the destinies of the various nations are interwoven. Polybius also makes it clear that the writing of history can be made to serve a purpose. By displaying the rise of Rome as a sort of natural law, he tries to legitimate the power of the Empire and to justify the practical politics of his day. Sallust (86–35 B.C.) on the other hand uses history as a criticism of the decadence of his times, as does Tacitus (A.D. 55–120). But the moral appeals are of no avail. The natural experience of flowering and fading, transposed from the start to the succeeding epochs of civilization, leads to a pessimistic renunciation of the senseless recurrence of rise and fall.

This attitude is then confronted by Christianity with a completely different notion of history. For Israel, history is above all else the history of the covenant lived out along with the God of the covenant (as is discussed more fully in the article *Old Testament History*). The history of the world itself is the prehistory of the covenant towards which it moves. The covenant itself will finally be one with the history of the world. All the successes and reverses of history are phases of this dialectical process: sin, punishment, forgiveness, fidelity and fulfilment are the categories in which history is understood. In the experience of the messianic fulfilment of this history through Jesus Christ its dialogal interpretation is again confirmed. This event was first regarded as the end of history, but when the expectation of the imminent end was disappointed, a new and comprehensive conception of history was outlined, even in the books of the NT, especially in St. Luke's Acts of the Apostles. In the light of the Christ-event, world history from Adam to the hoped-for parousia was seen as the history of salvation, centred on the death, resurrection and missionary mandate of Jesus.

This interpretation found its great spokesman in St. Augustine (354–430), whose historical thinking (*De Civitate Dei*), as much as anything else, made him the "Teacher of the West". But it may well be asked whether his influence here was not due in part to a misunderstanding. The two cities (*civitas Dei – civitas terrestris*) are founded through the twofold Fall before all history in the ordinary sense. And their *finis sine fine* lies outside all inner-worldly happenings. But even their advance through history is not historical, that is, demonstrable, in the sense of *historia*. Just as the *Confessions* describe the conversion of the individual, so too the great historical work tells of the inward way of man before God, and this way cuts right across the historical events. Hence either the whole political sphere is in the power of the demons (Cain the first founder of a city, leading on to Babel, to Babylon and Rome); or the contrast between the two cities is itself seen in terms of polities, and then the Church, which is really the earthly Jerusalem, the image of the heavenly, becomes a theocratic power. Or again, the contrast is made in non-political terms, and then the history of the State ceases to have any significance for religion. In Augustine, this is all left undecided. But one can see how various developments were left open to his successors in the writing of the "theology of history". For Augustine at any rate the facts formed a sort of text whose spiritual sense he worked out according to the patristic method of interpretation. He sees in temporality, sin, death, the present duty of love and eschatological hope the existentials of human history.

The work of St. Augustine's disciple Orosius, *Historiae adversus Paganos* (417–18) was richer in concrete historical detail. Then, at the height of the Middle Ages, Otto of Freising (*c.* 1115–58) transposed the Augustinian concept on a grand scale to recent history, in an attempt at justifying the Hohenstaufen imperial ideas. The last great work on these lines was the "Universal History" of Bossuet (1627–1704).

But in the meantime, the understanding of history had undergone a decisive change. The notion of progress had taken the place of providence. The Renaissance and the Humanists discovered the delights of experience, the value of the extraordinary, the special rank of the earthly. Observation and experiment, doubt and testing are to make knowledge a pliant instrument of power. History, in spite of its duties to the Church, is pressed into the service of national and political interests. The notion of nationality becomes associated with the will to discover new worlds. Thus the ancient world's approach to history could once more be adopted, though again, in spite of the abandonment of the notion of providence, the question of the total meaning of history could never be totally silenced.

Humanist historiography differs from that of antiquity and the Middle Ages above all by its conscious attention to sources and ancient documents. But the quantity of the collected materials was far too great for the scholars' powers of synthesis. Highly imaginative and eclectic outlines of universal history and philosophy of history went hand in hand with thoroughgoing and accurate collections of sources, though these could not yet be put into any comprehensive order. There were critics of culture like Rousseau as well as its admirers, but nowhere was a real sense of the proper nature of past or foreign cultures. And though history was acknowledged to be of immense value in education and regarded as part of the bedrock of all culture, of the individual and of society – as for instance by Voltaire – what was sought in history was the universal rationality which it was supposed to display in ever increasing measure, in spite of passing set-backs, and not the uniqueness of each particular epoch as such. G. B. Vico, for instance, whose philosophy of history and historical insights, in spite of much that was arbitrary, anticipated the progress made in the 19th century, remained uncomprehended and without influence.

Nonetheless, the growing perception of the differences of cultures and of the distance of each historical culture from the ideal norms laid down by reason was preparing the ground for a new approach. There was a dawning sense of the historical relativity of every form of society, and also of every standpoint from which they were viewed. (Thus Leibniz attributed a peculiar perspective to each monad within the totality. This was taken over by M. Chladen [Chladenius, 1710–95] in his work on the "Universal Science of History" [*Allge-*

meine Geschichtswissenschaft] and explicitly said to be the "viewpoint", the "inner and outer condition" of the historian.)

The humanist view of all history as the process of educating man to the attainment of his true humanity was given its supreme expression in Herder, Goethe and W. von Humboldt. And at the same time, romanticism was finding its joys in the richness of individuality in persons and peoples, and bringing out the proper intrinsic value of the Middle Ages, so long neglected in favour of classical times.

Savigny and Hegel may be named as exponents of both trends, which united to give rise to the 19th century as the century of history. The mental paradigm of the first line is the living individual organism. History is the life of a "body of people" or rather "a body politic" and culture the expression of the people's soul. Hegel too, especially in his earlier writings, made use of the notion of the organism. But Hegel's basic term was "spirit". Just as the individual, even the "great man", serves the spirit of the people, so too the various national "spirits" are moments in the self-explicitation of the spirit as such – which is Hegel's way of contemplating world history. Thus every figure has its own proper value, though not strictly speaking as an independent organism. It is there as a moment which is merged and merges of itself into the totality of the self-realization of the world-spirit. World history is the growing consciousness of freedom – a progress which has to be recognized as a process of necessity. Its goal is the freedom of the knowledge of the spirit – the manifest identity of reality and reason. It is therefore the freedom of the universal, into which the freedom of the individual, freed from *itself*, passes. Hegel's was a grandiose effort of historical thought, which took in all the riches of the concrete historical material then known in an effort to comprehend it. But it provoked immediate criticism, because the individual, his freedom and history could only be comprehended at the cost of dissolving them into an idea. That is, they were grasped in precisely what was not their own nature.

Thus the Hegelian understanding of history was challenged by a positivist philosophy (such as Schelling's), the claim of the individual to existence (as in Kierkegaard), the effort to understand the concrete (as in modern hermeneutics). The place of speculative interpretation and neat arrangement is taken by the demand for "the naked truth without adornment", the effort to show things "as they really were" (L. von Ranke). The classical perfection which von Ranke's descriptive work aimed at was methodically attained in the history-writing of J. G. Droysen. Rejecting mechanistic natural causality and the organic thinking of the romantic movement, Droysen brought out the creative independence of the (ethically-minded) spirit. And this spirit cannot be grasped by disregarding the self of the researcher. It is attained by its being totally committed to "enquiring understanding".

The synthesis thus reached contained too many disparate elements to be stable. Positivism tried to reduce history to a natural science, after the analogy of the "natural history" of biological evolution. For Marxism, history is likewise an event determined by natural laws, but still the history of freedom coming to consciousness of itself. But freedom is not that of the Hegelian Absolute, it is that of man in his working struggle with nature and between the classes. Knowledge of history is itself an instrument in this warfare, at the end of which lies the perfect society without a history. Then there were the various interpretations of culture: a social and political notion of culture (L. von Stein, H. von Treitschke), a humanist view of culture (J. Burckhardt), a rejection of culture (A. Schopenhauer, F. Nietzsche), and the morphology of cultures (K. Lamprecht and others).

Towards the end of the 19th century all this merged into the problem of historicism. W. Dilthey undertook the task of producing a "Critique of the Historical Reason", in order to understand "life" by virtue of life itself, in a "psychology" which aims at grasping the historical developments and interconnections of life as the mode in which man really is. His thought was undoubtedly fruitful and has provided extraordinary stimulation down to the present day, but it cannot be said that he is entirely free from biological or rationalist approaches and he did not succeed in laying stable foundations in the flight of change. What Dilthey aimed at with his ultimately vague concept of "life" or "life-philosophy" was attempted by E. Troeltsch in theology, while P. Yorck von Wartenburg tried to work out the categories of a genuinely historical thinking. M. Heidegger, in the main statement of his thought, *Sein und Zeit*, stated that his programme was "to cherish the spirit of Count Yorck, in order to serve the work of Dilthey" (E. T.: *Being and Time*, p. 404).

With this, the problem of history was freed from the restrictions of a mere theory of the (human) sciences and made an analysis of man as such. The search for man's history was extended to take in the search for his historicity. (It is only on this basis that even a theory of the human sciences can be envisaged, since they deal with *de facto* particulars and hence cannot be validly based as long as the historical forms are understood merely as the second-rate, supplementary realization of a universal.) Thus with the search for historicity, an ontological question is raised prior to an epistemological one. It is the effort to attain a new ontology which will not eliminate the ancient ontology of metaphysical essences but seeks to get "the better" of it, in a mode of thought which does full justice to the concrete and individual and which therefore does not strive to grasp and master by technical methods, but accepts its own historicity and allows itself to be grasped and mastered by the "destiny of being".

To develop these brief indications, however, would be not merely to register the history of thought, but to discuss systematically and on its intrinsic merits the problem itself. (This is in fact one of the permanent acquisitions from the logic of Dilthey, that in philosophy – and in theology – the historical and the systematical approach cannot on principle be kept separate.) The discussion may begin with a consideration of the singular existence of man, since being is not only there principally *in* him, but only *for* him – and *hence* principally in him.

C. Basic Structures of Historicity

1. *Historical man*. Man has his essence (not as an abstract notion of essence, but as the concrete basic reality), the essence which dominates his history as norm and end, only inasmuch as he fetches it in by bringing it about. His essence is the law "according to which he proceeds", the previously demarcated ground of his history of freedom. It is also that which is at stake for him in his history – that for whose realization he has "to be concerned". In this sense, not in the psychological sense of being troubled and oppressed, his existence is characterized by concern. Here there is displayed an ontological dialectic between what is imposed as a prior datum and what is imposed as a task, where no absolute equilibrium is possible. In this simultaneity of life assigned and life to be assumed – of *datum* and *mandatum* – man cannot simply be thought of as self-sufficient and autonomous.

Not only can he not give himself what is given him as himself – as follows from the analysis of the terms – he cannot of himself achieve the fulfilment of the task which the gift of himself imposes – though it is he who must fulfil the task. The reason for this is that it is the gift (he himself) with which alone he can master his task, which imposes on him the task: because, therefore, the gift is only "incipient". Thus the dynamism of his essence, its goal and its force, must belong to him intrinsically but still cannot be a constitutive element of his own self. He is man, before he fulfils his task, indeed, precisely as he on whom this task is imposed. And at the same time, this task, which has still to be fulfilled and hence is still outstanding, is nothing else than his being man.

This peculiar structure of human existence is its temporality, in the three dimensions which are generally known as past, present and future. Since man always experiences himself as a given, finding himself in a given world reality and situation, he experiences in himself a "has-been" which determines his "essence" now by virtue of the past (as something derivative). Thus the past has not simply gone by but continues to be effectively present as what has been. But it is present as escaping him, as the ground of the present disposition over which one does not dispose. But the past is likewise present as within one's grasp, since the present decision is not concerned merely with this thing or that but ultimately with freedom itself, that is, with freedom as an arrival from the past. That past demands to be accepted. Its origin arrives at man as a task, so that it displays and opens up to him his future. Thus the future comes as a demand, one that has still to be achieved, and furthermore, as something which surpasses his capacities of achievement and therefore must be bestowed on him as a gift in spite of all his efforts. In this sense the future is present only as something still outstanding. In this way, freedom experiences the present as the unity of a past that is out of reach and within one's grasp, and a future which is arriving and outstanding. The twofold character of the two dimensions explains the possibility of different attitudes towards them.

Thus man can repress the past by way of protest or take it over freely in remembrance and recollection. This repossession takes place in an immediacy mediated by tradition, so that the original reality of the past – individual as well as collective – is not disguised but is permanently visible, in order that it may in fact be a task (to which the response may be either acceptance or the rejection of [self-]criticism). The "necessity" of history does not mean here only the fact that what is done cannot be undone. It also means that existence is in possession of itself only in constant recourse to what has happened (not independently thereof in a plan based on an abstract notion of essence). Finally, necessity signifies the inevitability with which the past in each new back-reference receives a new configuration – though precisely in order to remain itself. Historical recourse (*anamnesis*) is not a matter of a *per se* neutral existence returning arbitrarily upon a mere past event, as historicism supposes, but considering and accepting the claim of what has come to be. Hence the identity of the past does not consist of its being always described in the same way but in the fact that its claim is always different – and hence to be described differently – in keeping with the actual present situation, while remaining the same. This is the basic notion of the truth of tradition. There is therefore a certain relativity, not in the sense of relativism, but in the literal sense of the word – as forming part of a relationship. Impartially, what has come to be addresses each hour of history differently. In doing so it displays new "visages" – whereby no doubt misunderstandings arise, creative as well as destructive. But the most infertile of all misunderstandings would perhaps be the effort to register the past once for all in the colourless, dispassionate archives which would fix it finally. But these visages or aspects, being part of its "effective history" (H. G. Gadamer) also belong to the event. The future of the event belongs to the event itself – even though it is never brought about by the event alone but is co-effectuated by the concrete situation of this future and by the free act of remembrance. And conversely, the event itself belongs to this its future. And so one cannot – as actualism and existentialism suppose – live in the present as a completely new beginning. One cannot really repress the fact that the moment of the present is always the future of what has come to be.

Just then as the past demands to be accepted as something beyond one's reach and yet within one's grasp and imposed on one as a task, so too the future at the same time, as arriving and yet as outstanding, that is, in hope and openness. For it is not just the past that arrives in it but also the claim to its fulfilment. This opens up the possibility of holding the actual past at a distance, the possibility of taking it over in repentance and revolution, that is, in rejection of it.

If one denies the derivative nature of this future, the result is the mistakes of utopianism and permanent revolution, while if one denies the true futurity of the origins, the result is restorative tendencies and timid or comfortable conservatism. Hence the right attitude to the present is obedience to the summons of what has been preserved but is still on its way, and relaxed tranquillity as regards the hoped-for gift of what is out of reach and outstanding. This unity of obedience and tranquillity avoids both the activism which sacrifices the present to the future and the dilettantism which remains irresponsive.

2. *Historical being.* In the way thus described, man has never to do merely with himself. The individual is never really left to himself: a situation always involves others, the "hour" is the hour of other people's claim on him; past and present are never just mine, but always and primordially ours. And again, man has not merely to do with man. One and all, men have to do with truth, with goodness, with being. Change of the condition of the self, the environment and the world is always and indeed primarily a change in the relation of being. And here one must distinguish the change of the articulation of this relationship – as expressed, for instance, in the theses of an ontology – from the basic change of the relationship itself (in existence).

A certain detached knowledge of history is part of the essence of history, and since this aloofness is only possible by virtue of the transcendence towards being (the true, the good), the transcendence towards the Absolute and Unconditional is a constitutive moment of historicity. Knowledge of history and historicity can only be there – even when only implicitly apprehended – when sustained by absolute knowledge. But man "has" not this absolute knowledge, he cannot dispose of it, but lets himself be disposed of therein by the Absolute – to be thus enabled to dispose of himself and things to a certain extent. Being thus withdrawn from man's control, absolute knowledge is knowledge of being forced to rely on the incomprehensible mystery.

This knowledge is not a purely speculative act but a basic option in personal openness – a laying hold of while allowing oneself to be laid hold of. It is itself the historical free action: the constantly original event of history. Philosophy as reflection on such historical primordial attitudes (individual as well as age-long) is again itself historical free action. Hence metaphysics is always thought out within a certain horizon which while becoming historical remains beyond the control of metaphysics and of man himself.

The historical event, interpreted by the metaphysical pre-understanding, comes within a pre-determined mental horizon, but determines and modifies in turn, according to its capabilities, the horizon within which it is understood. Where the absolute mystery becomes absolute proximity in concrete history and itself effects its acceptation through the obedient openness of historical existence, the historical horizons of this acceptation are not stripped of their cultural diversity. They are surpassed and redeemed into an absolute proximity to the absolute mystery as such. Their unity, in spite of the impossibility of an adequate positive expression, is positively fulfilled – it is not the empty unity of merely being referred to the mystery.

But even before this incomparable fulfilment – and in any case "taught" by it – thought can affirm, on principle and in general, the real unity of the manifold of history as historically suprahistorical. Its suprahistorical character is expressed in the non-historical character of the laws of thought and of the prohibitions of the natural law. But these abstractions are not the essence of being, any more than the abstract definition of the nature of man (*animal rationale*) are his fundamental concrete reality. But it is part of the concrete reality of being (truth, goodness) to be known by man. If this knowledge is historical, then, inasmuch as the *cognitum* and the *cognoscens in actu* are identical, being, truth and goodness are likewise historical.

But this consideration must be taken still further. No doubt the traditional metaphysic of essences recognized that our knowledge has its history. But it made a sharp distinction between the historicity of this our concept of being (truth, goodness) and the non-historical character of being, truth and goodness in themselves. In this perspective, the affirmation just put forward, that historicity can be asserted of being itself, is guilty of a switch in suppositions. But it is only relativism which denies the *in se* of what is intended by these concepts. A historical ontology aims at grasping the concept, not just as produced by man, but also, and prior to this, as produced by the "sending" of being, especially as being does not here mean the *esse subsistens* but primarily the reality which is at the base of the "concept" of the *esse commune*. However, even with reference to the supreme mystery itself the affirmation has a good sense. The "hour" is not just the hour of our "willing or running" – our more or less successful exertions – it is an hour disposed and sent. Thus the "Lord of the hour" is suprahistorical but he is so in a sovereignty which may not shrink from the *kenosis*, the "death of history", but founds history as its Lord and hence may rightly himself be called historical. (The word is not used univocally but analogically, as is true of all terms used in natural theology. Nonetheless, it may be used because in the ontology now in question it is not identical with the negative, finite temporality of the traditional metaphysics, but is prior to such a concept.) His transcendence is so "immanent" to history that the message of the incarnation always remains unfathomable, a marvel and a scandal, but not an impossibility. It represents a fulfilment – even in the guise of a superabundant fulfilment – of a potentiality which may be predicated of creator and creature. And it is not merely the centre, as the supreme instance of creation, history and historicity at its culminating point. It is also the recapitulation of history, that is, where it comes to a head and finds itself once more in its summary.

Thus historicity is not merely the seal upon the finiteness of man, the experience of his non-identity, the pain of the futile and destructive *pour-soi*, and above all, not the painful laborious way of an absolute which has yet to come to (consciousness of) itself. It is much rather the seal upon the dignity of man as "freedom called out", as a person. And it is the only way in which God can exist, not merely *in* "the other of himself" but also *for* the other, positing out of himself purpose and multiplicity-in-unity, freely diffusing the suprahistorical "processional" character of his trinitarian life as the *bonum diffusivum sui*.

Thus the concept of historicity, which was necessary to the discussion of the concept of history, leads back once more to the latter, since historicity appears as the potentiality and actualization of history, as the existential structure whose meaning and content must be found in concrete, factual history.

D. History and Historicity

The meaning of historicity cannot be found there, but must be sought in history. The story of the philosophy of history is the story of the quest for this meaning. But the pure factualness of an (eternally) recurring set of cycles of history cannot answer the question, any more than a linear concept – either of ascending progress or of descending depravation – once the past is seen as merely the past. The growing conviction of the inadequacy of attempts – to say nothing of the ideological short-circuits of totalitarianism, racialism and the like – has led to a phenomenon not unlike that of ancient Stoicism with its ideal of "opting out" (λάδε βιώσας). There is at present an interpretation of existence-philosophy which suggests a withdrawal into the individual and his own personal decision. But such evasions do not eliminate the question. And it is also unsatisfactory to affirm that the meaning consists of "endowing the meaningless with meaning" (T. Lessing) by our own interpretation. Meaning cannot be decreed but demands to be found.

There is, however, some element of truth in this last conception, since the finding of meaning is not a speculative experience, but a giving and receiving. Meaning is experienced inasmuch as this experience is one of the factors which go to make up this meaning. Decision and knowledge penetrate one another in a way which admits of no rational demonstration. Nonetheless this does not represent an irrational decree, but an experience based on its own luminousness. Thus the experience of the meaning of history is itself a historical event where the structures described above are once more verified. The meaning of history itself is present as at once out of reach and within one's grasp, as arriving and still outstanding. This is true of the meaning of the individual history (of one's "life") and equally so of epochal history and of the one history which is the unity of the various regions of history. (Even the unity of the one history which we spoke of at the start is only consciously explicit historically, and its manifold changes – from mere neutral juxtaposition to the conflict of spheres of power within the "one world" and new differentiations within each of these very spheres – is characterized by the same dialectical double structure as is the meaning of any given history.)

But if this is so, the meaning of history can only be experienced and known – and also to some extent effected – in the double act of remembering and hoping. The duality of this attitude can be seen in the interpretation of national histories (see, for instance, the *Aeneid* of Virgil, or indeed the national feasts of the present day), and hence it is also true of the acceptance of the meaning of the history of man (as an individual but no less essentially as a totality), of salvation through the self-communication of the divine mystery. Just as Israel lived in the tension of *anamnesis* of the Exodus and expectation of the Day of the Lord, so too and above all the community of Jesus the Christ lives in the *anamnesis* of his death and resurrection, "till he comes", in the hope of the parousia.

The certainty and finality of this experience of salvation does not mean that history is already abolished – obvious though the temptation to quietism is – but that history is at last really set free to be itself, because it is only the certainty of meaningfulness that frees man for historical action. And since it is the certainty of faith and hope it actually demands action, since the meaning thus given must be assimilated in freedom by us and thus at last fully accomplished.

In this way historicity is fulfilled by a history which is incalculable, that is, not just in fact unpredictable, but nowhere predetermined even ideally, proceeding only from interpersonal event and its primordial decision. And not only is it fulfilled, it is also transformed (since the formal structures of historicity are not its concrete reality, any more than in the case of being, truth, goodness or man). And in transforming historicity, history is again historical: history is always the one thing, the history of man in this world and of his gift of transcendence towards the mystery, but never uniformly the same, just as man and his history in their identity are never the same.

There is a short-sighted way of applying categories to this identity which reduces it to a manageable uniformity where the differences are ignored as accidental. Against this, historicism takes a relativist view and denies the "transcendental" unity and identity through all categorical change. Against this denial again the Baden school of Kantianism (Windelband, Rickert) tries to safeguard the permanent in a world of values. But historical ontology tries to preserve the balance of the transcendental and the categorical, demanding that the transcendental be thought of not as non-historical sameness but as historical identity. It renounces the effort to distinguish neatly between identity and difference not merely because the distinction is not adequately accessible to us, but because it does not exist "in itself": the core of reality is not univocal but of itself analogous, that is, relational: the self-relationship of freedom. The identity-difference which runs through history and historicity is a sign of such freedom.

Adolf Darlap and *Jörg Splett*

II. Philosophy of History

The term "philosophy of history", coined by Voltaire, is used in modern times for a large number of philosophical and historical sketches. Hence we shall first consider the various ways in which the philosophy of history is understood, then consider the main historical movements which a philosophy of history must suppose, and finally sketch the development of the philosophy of history.

A. The Main Approaches

1. Philosophy of history is in general the effort to penetrate the meaning of the past and orientate oneself to the future, without being tied to the traditional patterns of the theology of history. It is therefore characteristic of modern man's effort to understand the world and his own autonomous place in it. History takes on the character of a process with definite direction, either in the form of a development or a cyclic, spiral ascent. History is always considered "as" something – such as the progress of civilization, while the question of history as history does not arise. This is because in this type of the philosophy of history man, conscious of his autonomy, presupposes his own existence, as an individual or as a society, prior to history, and by this presupposition determines the meaning in the light of which history is interpreted. History can be judged on the basis of an unequivocal measure. This type of the philosophy of history includes such diverse approaches as the *Essai* of Voltaire, the *Positive Polity* of Comte and Spengler's *Decline of the West*.

2. In contrast to this "immanent" type of analysis of history, there is another approach based rather on the critiques made by Kant. It tries to work

out a critique of the historical reason which will enable it to deal with a multiplicity of historical events which cannot be reduced to a system. It enquires into the conditions of possibility of historical knowledge in general, in order to define the nature and scope of historical research. This type of philosophy of history takes history essentially as a succession of facts from the past. The transcendental reason, as the *a priori* ground of historical knowledge and action, does not offer the possibility of fixing an ideal in the light of which history could possibly be explained. But since meaning is disclosed only in the succession of past events – the reason being only the ground of possibility – the meaning of history can only be worked out by history itself. The notion of a universal key to history is a guiding-line only, a limit notion which can never be realized. The philosophy of history is the "construction of the historical world in the sciences of the spirit" (Dilthey). This type of philosophy of history is found above all in the sphere of influence of neo-Kantianism. But it is also the basic attitude of many historians and theologians who do not recognize its provenance. This position is found in reverse, as it were, in structuralism, which offers a sort of objectivation of the transcendental reason. All the historical data which are accepted as such are treated in isolation from one another and examined individually for their proper constitutive laws. By reducing each element to its laws, the historical data are transformed into a "simultaneity of perspicuousness" – they are as transparent as they are contemporaneous.

Philosophy of history takes on a meaning different from that given it in 1 and 2 when man or reason is no longer presupposed as prior to history but when he begins to consider his own real historicity. All knowledge and action is then drawn into the ambit of history, in which man encounters the world in his knowledge and action. Hence history here is the all-encompassing, including the existence of the world as well as that of man. Everything is stamped with the mark of historicity, and history is no longer regarded "as" something. It is not the set of events which can be registered in the light of the transcendental reason. History is thought of as history where man is always in motion in self-awareness and in action, where the world is disclosed to him and where he can converse with men and the innerworldly reality.

When history is regarded in this way as the all-encompassing, there are two modes of the philosophy of history, according to the aspect from which the relationship between history and thought is viewed. (Here "thought" is not taken in the sense of theory in contrast to practice, but as the luminous act of existing in which that which is becomes lightsome to man.) Since thought is always the act of existence, self-conscious and lucid, the philosophy of history can be understood as history dawning in thought, concentrating itself in concepts (see 3 below). Or history is world and worlds, man and mankind, being given into selfhood, and thus is the immemorial endowment of thought with the power to actuate in history all that is (see 4 below).

3. The basis of the concept of philosophy of history in the first of these two senses is the grasp of the conceptual character of thought. Since man when thinking is there with that which is, he actuates it in regard to its being. Thus that which is actuated is brought in the luminousness of the act into the selfhood of thought and thus grasped as concept. In the concept the thing comes to light and thought takes possession also of itself. This process of the spirit's becoming master of itself in the all, which is the assertion of the purpose of the spirit, is history. Thus history coincides with thought. It is the "actuation" of the spirit as it encompasses and

becomes aware of itself and so of all things. Thought, as self-realization of the spirit, takes place as the sending to self of all that there is, in a series of historical dispositions. In the light of such a philosophy of history, history always has a universal character. Its course is composed of a series of major meaningful complexes which succeed one another while at the same time essentially comprising one another. For Hegel, whose philosophy of history is the great prototype of such explanations, world history is essentially the "explicitation and realization of the universal spirit" (*Grundlinie der Philosophie des Rechts*, para. 342, E. T.: *Philosophy of Right* [1942]).

4. The second of the latter two types is a correction of the third in which the basis is modified. Thought is still regarded as constructive: it produces beings. But this production, in which that which is dawns on man, is in itself something assigned to man, because it comes forth, in an incalculable way, from its own nothingness: *ex nihilo sui*. Man and the world, man and man encounter each other in an openness which is a supremely sovereign and unfathomable act of giving. Since man in his mundane existence is presented with himself to be taken over freely, he is intrinsically – like his world – ek-static in structure: he is always stepping out of the past, and his taking over of himself in the world has always the character of a surge forward into the future. Thinking is essentially thinking over, thought is always after-thought. In its identity each being which is thought of affirms itself as other than that very concept, by reason of its immemorial origin. All comprehension is based on a self-bestowal which changes the grasp, from within, into a grateful acceptance. In this way thought is both historical and dialogal. In this thinking, which is in the nature of an event which comprises within itself, as a derivative mode, all thinking which registers and calculates, the structure of the world and the worlds, of man and mankind, is disclosed. But this structure is released by and does its work in that openness which while giving still retains the structure within its immemorial concealment. History, being this structure, presents itself as the self-interrogating question put to the mystery which is the ground of all that is.

This basic understanding of history would comprise such approaches as Heidegger's notion of the history of being, Jaspers's concept of transcendence and Rosenzweig's dialogical thinking. This type of philosophy of history opens up perspectives which are based on the event of the openness in question as the lay-out of history. This philosophy of history finds its justification in the light thrown on such concepts of history by the event which they themselves attest, of creative openness.

B. The Great Modes of Experiencing History

1. *Myth and metaphysics*. The ancient view of history, as attested by Herodotus, Thucydides, Plato and Aristotle, forms a remarkable contrast to the preceding experiences of history among the Greeks. Earlier, God (θεός, a word without a vocative case) was the supremely primordial event, history. Θεός is expounded through verbs in the infinitive (Diogenes of Apollonia, Frg. 5, Diels [Pre-Socratics]); cf. Wilamowith-Moellendorff. In the *Helen* of Euripides, Helen cries out: "O gods! For it is God, when the loved ones are known." The event of recognition is θεός. It is only when one looks back on the occurrence that the gods appear with name and contour. History comes about in events, in each of which all is concentrated – world, men and gods.

Greek metaphysics takes the opposite view. There everything is traced back to the supreme ἀρχή, the principle beyond time, ground of all beings, itself conceived of as a substance. From this ultimate principle comes the all, as a well-ordered beautiful cosmos which is grasped by inerrant knowledge ("science" – ἐπιστήμη). In contrast to ἐπιστήμη, we have ἱστορία, the story of the item qua item, told in terms of what has been seen and heard (Aristotle, *Poetics*, 1451 b). It includes accounts of plants and beasts as well as news of men and events. History, as sheer multiplicity of items, is ἀμέθοδος ὕλη, *materia invia* (Sextus Empiricus, *Adversus Mathematicos*, I, 12, 254). Hence the aim of Greek history writing was to give instruction about the universal which manifests itself in the individual items: the power of the gods which brings everything into balance (Herodotus), the immanent laws of politics (Thucydides). History as a whole is the fragmented, blurred appearance of the cosmos, its purpose is the ascent to the principle (ἀρχή) in which history is left behind (Plato, allegory of the cave).

2. *The OT covenant.* Unlike Hellas, Israel experienced history as a covenant. The covenant is not, as it were, within history, it is the primordial, incalculable opening of history. Israel proclaims Yahweh as its God, the God who had turned to the fathers, rescued the people from Egypt and promised to be its God for ever (historical Credo, Deut 26:5–9). The event of the covenant throws open future and past in a special way: in view of the utterly unfathomable election in grace, Abraham is nothing but a man, called out of the ranks of mankind. Before Yahweh, the peoples combine into mankind. The universal history of Gen 1–11 forms the necessary background to the history of Abraham and the covenant. But God's promise of well-being which throws open the future is not confined to the people of the covenant. It is also the guiding-line and the norm of history in general (Dan 7). The God of the covenant is, in retrospect, the creator God, in prospect the judge of history, its promise of well-being. The justification of such hope is seen by Israel again and again in its own continued existence. Throughout the many worlds and world-pictures which come and go, throughout judgment and grace, the people survives at least as a remnant, and hence may understand itself as the people founded on the covenant and willed by God.

Here history takes place as the one enduring history of the covenant in the one but manifold history of mankind.

3. *The fullness of time.* The Christian community affirms that the Christ-Event is the fullness of time, where covenant history and world history are merged, submerged and subsumed. The salvation come in Christ is the salvation of all the world and all worlds, not a thing of the distant future but something to be grasped in time. Above and beyond all the ambiguity and obscurity of history, overflowing all its bounds in death and sin, God has bestowed himself as blessed fulfilment. Thus all time becomes his time, in all times hovers the fullness of time. This is attested by the Church, as the one Church of Jews and Gentiles which sees itself sent to the whole world and understands itself to be most fully at one with the poorest and the most abandoned. Hence in the fullness of time the fellowship of men from the most diverse worlds, world-views and views of history is an event which takes place in a way of unmistakable significance. At the same time, this one world history, as the history of many worlds, is totally given over to man, "desacralized", because God, the salvation of history, abandoned all historical form – in the death of Jesus.

C. Development of Modern Philosophy of History

The Christian thinkers of antiquity and the Middle Ages took an essentially theological view of history. They were more concerned with the meaning of the whole than the investigation of historical facts, as may be seen from the historical judgments of Augustine, Bonaventure or Thomas Aquinas. But with

Descartes the traditional concepts of the world and of history began to be radically challenged. Basing himself on Descartes but reversing his conclusions, G. B. Vico sketched his *Scienza Nuova*. Combating incidentally the pretensions of science, he affirmed that all history was explicable beyond doubt or hesitation by virtue of its origin, its human positing. Fixed principles were at work in this positing of history by man. Hence Vico sought for "an ideal, eternal history, according to which the histories of all people follow their course in time". A little later Voltaire, in his *Essai sur les Mœurs et l'Esprit des Nations*, sketched a new outline of human history. Its goal is the enlightened man. Voltaire began with China, rejected the chronology of the OT and spoke as a historian and philosopher, that is, as a man who did not believe in revelation.

The Encyclopaedists, Turgot and Condorcet, continued with the philosophy of history as the philosophy of human progress, while Rousseau defined history as the process of depravation of natural man, and his true nature. Comte's *Cours de la Philosophie positive* (1830–42) was the basis of all succeeding positivist and sociological interpretations of history, with its three stages of human history – theological, metaphysical and positive or scientific. History, for Comte, is a sort of social physics, to be grasped scientifically by sociology.

Examples of German philosophy of history during the Enlightenment include Lessing's "Education of the Human Race" (*Erziehung des Menschengeschlechts*) and Kant's "Plan of a Universal History in Cosmopolitan Perspective" (*Idee zu einer allgemeinen Geschichte in weltbürgerlicher Absicht*). In both of these, the notion of progress was predominant, to which Herder then added his discovery of the "inner-directedness" of the individualities of various peoples and eras. A unifying central meaning and impulse in history is the key to human life. W. von Humboldt described the goal and structure of world history as the revelation of the power of the human spirit. In his essay on the task of the historian (*Aufgabe des Geschichtsschreibers*) he gives the principles of historical method as they result from his own view of history. History writing is the re-creation of reality, inspired by the human forces which unite past and present.

Hegel went beyond the tentative efforts of Herder, Humboldt, Fichte and Schiller to interpret history as the manifestation of the spirit as it comes to comprehend itself in its various forms (see A, 3, above). The systematic character of universal history which resulted from this approach led historians in particular, like von Ranke and Droysen, to reject it. While Marx, in spite of his opposition to Hegel, retained his systematic approach to the interpretation of history, Droysen's *Historik*, a philosophical consideration of the nature of history and the methods of modern historicism, formulated the principle: "The essence of the historical method is to reach understanding through research."

Hence there is felt to be a contradiction between historical understanding and the ideal of scientific objectivity. Windelband and Rickert sought to escape the dilemma by their appeal to a theory of values, while Dilthey sought for a solution in hermeneutics (strongly tinged by psychology). In Dilthey, and even more so in P. Yorck von Wartenburg, the link between the scientific ideal and the tradition of metaphysical thinking is affirmed. In the light of Heidegger's notion of the historicity of the understanding of being, the previous sketches of a philosophy of history seem to be nothing but metaphysical interpretations of history (see B, 1, above), which presuppose the Jewish and Christian affirmations of history as salvation but distort them by making them metaphysical. The development of a non-metaphysical, historical thinking in more recent philosophies of history opens up a new approach to the understanding of the affirmations of faith. But the latest developments of a structuralist philosophy of history offer, on the contrary, a new reduction of history to metaphysics.

Peter Hünermann

III. Theology of History

A. Problem

1. *History*. History is one of the basic categories of biblical revelation. Revelation does not merely throw light on history, it also gives rise to it. The absolute gratuity of revelation brings with it its character of historical contingency. As an event which can neither be foreseen nor influenced revelation sets up new historical reality and gives a promise of a future. The new conditions of salvation thus brought about demand on the part of men conversion of heart and the decision of faith, and thus revelation also leads to a knowledge of the intrinsic historicity of man. It is this character of historical event which distinguishes the OT and NT revelation from the non-Christian epiphany religions, where revelation is understood merely as a hieratic manifestation of the eternal ground of being, and still leaves history as the cyclic return of the eternal self-same. According to biblical revelation, history is not a moment of the cosmos, but the cosmos is a part of history. The metaphysical and cosmological notion of "nature" is replaced by the thought of a universal "history", in movement towards a future.

Elements of a theology of history are to be found as early as the first Christian apologists. Justin and Clement of Alexandria defended against Jews and pagans the continuity and the pedagogical purpose of the salvific action of God, while Irenaeus upheld the unity of creation and covenant against Gnosis. Origen used the doctrine of the Logos to depict history as a unified whole. Eusebius and Orosius had a theology of the empire based on the *Pax Romana*, while Augustine stressed the ambivalence of political power in his *De Civitate Dei*. In the Middle Ages, as for instance by Charlemagne, the doctrine of Augustine and the theocracy of the OT were again applied to the actual course of history.

Along with a speculative tendency, some starts at a theology of the history of salvation may be noted in Scholasticism (Otto of Freising, Rupert of Deutz, Petrus Comestor, Stephen Langton and others). More important efforts were made by Alexander of Hales, Bonaventure and Thomas Aquinas, though their thinking is mostly dominated by cosmological and metaphysical categories.

Patristic and scholastic thinking was more interested in a theology of the history of salvation than in a theology of history in the present-day meaning. This only became possible when history in general was detached from the framework of history of salvation (Voltaire, Vico), and when history had also become a philosophical problem. This was furthered by a process of secularization which began within theology as the expectation of the imminent end was disappointed. Other factors were the influence of Joachim of Fiore, the resumption of non-Christian trends, as from Gnosis and the Kabbala (the theme of fall and restoration to pristine perfection occurring in J. J. Rousseau and romanticism), the collapse of the antique and medieval picture of the cosmos (Copernicus), and a historicizing view of a world brought under man's control, to which modern science and technology contributed. In Scripture, history had been part of revelation, but now revelation often became a moment of history, and history itself was seen as revelation (Herder, Lessing, Schelling, Hegel).

The theology of history must now be prepared to maintain itself against the competition from modern philosophies, ideologies, Utopias and programmatic views of history. In contrast to a theology of the history of salvation, it provides the framework of a theology of earthly realities.

At present there are various trends in Catholic theology. One, more optimistic, is orientated towards the incarnation (G. Thils, P. Teilhard de Chardin), another, more critical, is orientated towards eschatology (P. L. Bouyer) or a *theologia crucis*. Most theologians strive for a theology of history which will be an adequate synthesis (H. and K. Rahner, J. Daniélou, Y. Congar, H. U. von Balthasar).

2. *Method.* In the dialogue with modern philosophies and ideologies of history, theology must draw its inspiration from its own sources. This means that it must try to understand world history in the light of the history of salvation as interpreted by the word of revelation. This excludes on principle any theological interpretation of individual historical events outside the history of salvation. We may not draw any conclusions, for instance, as to wars, natural phenomena, etc., from their coincidence or combination with Church feasts or the like, since revelation in fact tells us nothing about them. For the same reason it is impossible to divide up the history of the world and the Church into periods with definite theological significance.

The prophetic charism of the Church, however, obliges it to address its message to each *kairos* as it comes. It must therefore speak in such a way as to be adequate to the times and do justice to history. It is not enough to be objectively correct. The Church must read the "signs of the times" (Mt 16:4). This calls for a logic of existential thought and of insight into each *kairos*, a discernment of spirits which can hardly be reduced to a hard and fast method. It can only be achieved by continuous obedience to the cross and by the daring of love.

In contrast to such legitimately prophetical views of history, the theology of history is a form of fundamental theology which ponders the basic, intrinsic structures of the history of salvation and tries to grasp their implications for the theology of history. Since it looks back constantly to the words of revelation, it is different from the philosophy of history, which must on principle regard the history of revelation and its understanding of history merely as one group of phenomena among others. Since the theology of history is based on faith, it must continue to build on faith, hope and charity, and not merely on knowledge.

B. Basic Theological Assertions

1. The *starting-point* is the primary mystery of the grace of the self-communication of God to man and hence to history. This has taken place once and for all in Jesus Christ, and will be fully manifested in a real future yet to come. This affirmation about the end of history is necessarily veiled, because it sees the fulfilment as the sovereign act of God, whose mystery cannot be anticipated by human knowledge. Both the apocatastasis and double predestination run counter to this principle.

But God is the end of history in the sense that he is also end-term and completion, because he assumes and affirms it "inconfusedly and undividedly" (*D* 302). This means that the consummation of history must not be regarded as coming only from on high, in the sense of a one-sided theology of the incarnation. It must also be regarded as a process of self-maturation accomplished from below. The acceptance of history by God in the incarnation has as its counterpart the acceptance of God by Jesus Christ in historical obedience and self-abandonment unto the death of the cross, which God takes up again in the resurrection and glorification. History only reaches its fulfilment by the way of the cross; its fulfilment is the passover mystery of Easter, a possibility of surpassing itself provided by grace. But this obedient Exodus out of history to God is not a negation of history, but again the fulfilment of historical *ex-sistentia*, man's power to be outside and beyond himself. The cross is also his exaltation.

2. *Extension by a theology of creation.* The theological doctrine of creation is given not at the beginning but within the description of the history of salvation. It is there to justify the universal and total claim of the history of salvation and the absoluteness of the promise. Because God is Lord of all by his creative word, he can expect the answer of faith from within history. History then appears as a dialogue composed of divine offer and response or refusal by man's belief or unbelief. History has the character of summons and decision. But since it is founded only on God's free word, its contingence is not the hazard of blind fate, but the expression of a historical providence which is responsible for everything that is. The voice of history is a doxology.

Like assertions about the last things, assertions about the first (protological) are not historical descriptions of paradise, original justice, etc., but pointers to God's primordial and therefore all-embracing and therefore eschatological plan of history. Protology, therefore, also remains wrapped in obscurity and mystery, being an aetiology and not a report on externals. It gives the basis and horizon of our present order of salvation.

The power of sin is also a factor in our present situation, and it has been one of the determinants of history from the start. It is the refusal to go out of oneself to enter into the dialogue, and hence a refusal of authentic history. It comes to a head in the principalities and powers, in original sin, death, suffering, concupiscence and law. Awareness of the presence of sin should be a warning against an unduly optimistic view of creation, but also against a grinding pessimism, since sin too has been caught up in God's plan of salvation in Christ, to which the whole of history moves.

The intrinsic unity of human history is based on its protology and eschatology. This unity (peace) is eschatological expectation, symbolically proclaimed already in the unity of the Church composed of Jews and gentiles, which charges Christians with a special responsibility for peace in the world.

3. History has its *ultimate roots in God.* The eternity of God does not mean primarily timelessness, as it did to the Greeks, but a time positively master of itself, and freedom to set up and enter into history, without being submerged in it. The Supra-temporal is, therefore, the Ever-present, immanent to each instant of time. All history is encompassed and determined by God, but not as a necessary pantheistic evolution. It is God's free decision, the *concretissimum universale* of the divine plan of salvation, on which all history rests, and which cannot be reconstructed in definable terms, without turning the theology of history into a determinism. God's plan of history is in accord with human freedom, without being dependent on it. Thus the relationship between time and eternity should not be taken as a static one. It unfolds historically. Though "each age is as close to God as any other", history is still only on the way to the point where "God is all in all" (1 Cor 15:28). This is the justification of a well-considered pluralism of the history of salvation, the history of the world and the history of religions. The effort to homogenize ("integralism"), to separate here and now the weeds from the corn, to turn the world into a monolithic Church, is basically presumption.

C. The Categories of the Theology of History

1. *Time and times:* see *Time*.

2. *Factors of history:* see *Original Sin, Death, Law, Angels, Demonology*; but also *Spirit*.

3. *Periods of history:* see *History, Salvation, Religion, Natural Law, Covenant, Church.*

4. *Patterns in the theology of history.* The best known are the pattern of the circle for the Greek view of history and that of the straight line for the biblical. But both are ambiguous and inadequate. The circle can depict the non-historical, the meaningless and the aimless (Origen, Augustine) or again, the course of history from God and to God (Thomas Aquinas). The line can indicate eschatological purposefulness and continuity, but not the discontinuity of sin and of the cross. Points could represent contingence and the element of decision, but not the prolongation; the swing of the pendulum could stand for the antagonisms of apocalyptic but with the risk of importing a dualistic misunderstanding; the spiral could recall the element of continuity and progression, but not that of decision; the image of the widening circle in water unites some of these elements (point, line of movement, extension and circle), but lacks the moment of dialogue; the triangular movement of dialectic fails to represent freedom. All these diagrams are better ignored, because there is an element of distortion in all of them.

The most suitable theological pattern is that given by the typological and sacramental thinking of Scripture and patristic theology. Like the history of the world and the history of salvation, individual events are related to one another like anticipation and realization. We may thus deduce three fundamental laws of the theology of history: a) the law of continuity throughout and in spite of sin and the cross, by virtue of the divine fidelity; b) the law of orientation to a new and greater future. The antitype is always greater than the type; the last things are not just the restoration of the first, but their Easter transformation; c) the law of solidarity between the particular and the universal. The individual is always called as one with and representative of the whole of humanity. History cannot be simply divided between salvation and disaster; before God, humanity forms a single whole, for weal and for woe.

5. *Basic attitudes.* This threefold law brings about three groups of basic attitudes when the Christian looks at history: a) Faith: through the eschatological act of God's salvation, his triumphant power has intervened definitively in history and has redeemed it from dissolution and failure, in the death and resurrection of Christ. History cannot now be basically a nightmare. The basic Christian attitudes are not anxiety and scepticism, but calm, courage, humour and alertness. b) Hope: this means yielding oneself boldly to the ever-changing newness of history, instead of clinging timidly, like men of little faith, to over-rigid and ultra-conservative traditions. But it also means patience and willingness to wait; it is a confidence in God which excludes a naive belief in progress as well as the fanaticism of the revolutionary millenarist. c) Love and solidarity: this means dutiful co-operation in the humanizing and pacification of the world, testimony in word, life and suffering, as representative of humanity.

Walter Kasper

HOLINESS

1. The ultimate source of all holiness is the holiness of God, whereby he is the "wholly Other". But even in the OT, God the inaccessible, "the holy one of Israel", is also the joy, force, support and salvation of the chosen people (Is 10:20; 17:7; 41:14–20). In the righteousness brought by the "holy servant Jesus" (Acts 4:27, 30), who "sanctifies himself" that his own may be "sanctified" (Jn 17:19), God imparts himself to man. He draws him by grace into his own personal life, gives himself as the

Holy One, and makes him holy through sanctifying grace in the Holy Spirit, called to "the holy city, the new Jerusalem" (Rev 21:2). Man is enabled to accept this self-communication of God and to respond to it through the supernatural ("infused") virtues, especially faith, hope and charity. These virtues direct his religious and moral action towards immediate participation in the life of the Trinity. Through them and in them God himself in his self-communication brings about the possibility and the free realization of participation in his life. Here the basic option for God which was already involved in baptism (*viventes autem Deo*, Rom 6:11) is constantly renewed as man dedicates himself totally to God and to an unqualified answer to God's offer of grace. This free self-dedication of man of whom God has taken possession in baptism (and substantially sanctified) is also moral self-sanctification, which, however, again presupposes the grace of God for its realization. This actual dedication to God, which makes the life of the Christian a cultic sacrifice (cf. Rom 12:1; Phil 2:17; 4:18; Heb 13:15, 16; 1 Pet 2:4f., 9) is, through Christ, service of God, union with him and assimilation to him who "hallows his (own) name".

2. More precisely, this self-realization of the Christian is love, which is found in all the diverse acts of Christian life (Mt 22:40), which is "the fulfilment of the law" (Rom 13:10) and includes the fulfilment of the other precepts (Gal 5:14) which it "sums up" (Rom 13:9). Only love can assign man totally to God, because only love binds the multiplicity of his being into inner unity and dedicates it to God. For man is only fully himself when he turns in love to the Other. It is in love that man is given to himself and in it alone can he truly fulfil himself. Love alone is the full answer due to God as person.

3. But man who responds to God in love is a being of many dimensions. Hence his moral and religious perfection takes on many different forms, in virtues such as justice, virginity, humility, love of the neighbour, etc. For God does not speak merely in the commandment of love. There are a number of particular precepts which correspond to the manifold nature of human reality. These virtues may be there without the full expressiveness of love, but only come to their full perfection in love. Though they imply at once a total commitment, this is only gradually achieved, and it is only in personal action that all human faculties and domains are fully integrated according to the potentialities of the individual. From this point of view, love is always pressing forward to a stage beyond what it has reached at a given moment. The individual is called by God in his uniqueness and cannot know beforehand what God may demand from him in the future (K. Rahner, *Theological Investigations*, V, pp. 494–517). The more love has found itself and informed the other virtues, the more perfect is holiness.

4. God, the goal of life in love, does not remain hidden as he acts on man in grace. His self-communication brings about in man the response of knowledge as well as love. This action of God in grace does not remain beyond the bounds of consciousness, but is experienced, not indeed as an object, not as something "seen", not in the sense of Ontologism, but as an unobjectivated light which illumines the "objects" of the supernatural acts. But it is not itself the object of such acts. Hence God cannot be attained through psychological introspection, but only as a concomitant experience linked with the objects of faith, hope and charity which are given objectively and linked with the sense of faith of the Church. The experience is all the stronger, the more man is familiar with and knows how to practise the natural transcendence of the spirit towards being in general, inner recollection, ethical action, aesthetic ex-

perience and so on. This experience, however, gives no certainty about the state of grace.

5. The love of God, as well as being "other-worldly", that is, the love with which God in his immanent trinitarian life loves his own perfection, is also "worldly", that is, God's redeeming love of the world (Jn 3:16). The supernatural love of man is participation in the love of God. Hence the Christian who really loves God also necessarily participates in God's love of the world. Hence love of God, sharing in God's love of the world, is primarily directed towards men. These are loved in the absolute love of God, but for their own sakes, in keeping with the commandment which makes love of God and love of man run parallel. But since man is loved as a person, and hence by reason of an absolute moral decision, love of the neighbour necessarily includes love of God, which is its foundation and support. In a certain sense this love of the world also includes the irrational creation and material reality, insofar as they are "goods which we wish to others... So too God loves them *ex caritate*" (Thomas Aquinas, *Summa Theologica*, II-II, q. 25, a. 3). They are lovable insofar as they are seen in combination with the beloved person.

6. Since true love cannot remain inward only but strives to express itself in action, to embody itself, as it were (*caritas effectiva*), true love of the world will also try to act visibly in an effort to order human society with regard to things and things among themselves. Thus love is exercised in "profane" action in the world as well as in the "cultic" action of the liturgy in its various sacramental forms. Thus all appropriate action of the man who loves, in work and leisure, in action and meditation, is love and holiness, since the basic intention which sustains and shapes this action is the supernatural dynamism of love, which radically alters man and hence his action (*D* 799f., 821). If love is the basic principle which forms, moves and guides all being and action, it is also implicitly actuated here and also finds its fullness of being in such modes of life (work, service of the world – as *caritas implicite actuata*). It too participates in the "knowableness" of grace as described above, which is concomitantly the consciousness of the presence and action of God (light, force, joy, tranquillity). Thus the ontic world of categories is met as a form of the ontological and transcendent reference to God, which is or can be experienced as such in an eschatological prolepsis – which is the Christian way of "flight from the world". The reason for this harmony between the natural and objective relationship to the world and a life of love and holiness is ultimately the fact that the natural order of creation is a presupposition and intrinsic moment of the order of redemption – since in the incarnation the redemptive reality provides itself with the natural order in order to be itself, and by giving it an ultimately supernatural meaning confirms it in its naturalness and heals it where it is wounded (K. Rahner, *Mission and Grace*, I, p. 63). Hence holiness is not rejection of the world but, of necessity, holy action on the world. When he makes love manifest, the Christian is fulfilling the task which is given him as a member of the Church which is in the world to give testimony in history to the grace of God.

7. Since holiness is a participation of the self-communication of God, in man it is a grace-given listening to God and a commitment to him, wherever his summons is heard. Hence it is very necessary to learn to understand the "language" of God, which has its own "idiom" corresponding to the transcendence of God, for which the discernment of spirits is important. Scripture tells us that there is such a thing as growth in grace (Mt 13:8; Jn 15:2; Eph 3:16–19), which is both granted to and demanded of man (Eph 4:15; *D* 803).

Because of the danger of a self-centred perfectionism, the focus of all holiness must be God himself, who rouses and sustains man's effort as he encounters him in grace and is ultimately the goal of this dynamism ("hallowed be thy name"). But here precisely God wishes man to co-operate freely (*D* 799, 850), so that the unity of creation and redemption may be preserved, without the natural structures being disguised, displaced or distorted. The natural values of thought, desire and feeling are to be sought after and realized as a condition and inner moment of grace. What is naturally valuable is not in itself a condition or inner moment of grace, since nature can never be a positive ground for grace. It is only such insofar as God freely pre-posits and accepts it as the condition for his action in grace. It is only in this sense that nature is the antechamber and place of grace. As experience shows, psychosomatic health is not always the point of insertion for grace. It is often linked with bodily illness and mental strains. But the Church struggles against the disruptive forces of temptation (the devil, evil, sin, etc.) by orderly thinking, helps to the will, etc., that is, by directing creation to its natural fulfilment. In the justified, natural values are of course sustained by grace and when they are achieved they are already elevated by grace and are the fruit of the Spirit (Gal 5:22–23).

Love as self-dedication to God is necessarily allied to Christian self-denial in the work of sanctification, as an anticipation of death along with Christ; it sustains this work and realizes itself there (*caritas crucifixa*). Since holiness involves many attitudes whose immediate goals diverge, it must be a dynamic equilibrium of many dialectical tensions, which must find their inner harmony in love: self-development and crucifixion of the "natural" strivings, renunciation of the world and formation of the world, self-respect and humility, the prudence of the serpent and the simplicity of the dove, freedom and obedience, resistance and patience, total confidence and anxious effort.

8. When man's response to the gift of grace is approximately total, so that while still an individual effort it is an epoch-making moment in the holiness of the Church as a whole, then the holiness of Christians reaches the height which is called "heroic virtue" in the process of canonization.

9. All Christians are called to holiness. "The great commandment of charity knows no bounds . . . everyone is commanded to love God as well as he can" (Thomas Aquinas, *Contra Retrahentes*, 6), according to the measure and nature of his gift of grace (cf. Rom 12:3; 1 Cor 12:11), in the concrete realization of love to which they are individually called. The "rich young man" was called to total renunciation of his possessions, others were called to other forms of unconditional following of Christ. A double morality which attempts to assign a minimum Christianity to the laity is theologically indefensible.

10. Vatican II's Constitution on the Church (*Lumen Gentium*, art. 15) affirms the existence of great holiness outside the Church. So too it is above all the Church itself, and not any particular institution in it, which is the great state of perfection, "established by Christ in fellowship of life, love and truth" and as "instrument of the redemption" (art. 9), including that of its members, to which it offers "so many great means" of sanctity (art. 11). Christians are "equipped to bear increasingly rich fruit of the Holy Spirit" (art. 34). The holiness of the Church expresses itself in various forms, though in a special way (*proprio quodam modo*) through the evangelical counsels (art. 39). The way in which holiness appears in this way of life is only one particular and special way. All Christians are to grow in holiness "according to their own special calling" (art. 35), "the ways proper to

each" (art. 41), using the means proper to each (arts. 11, 41) and above all by serving in love, which "guides, animates and makes efficacious" all means of holiness (art. 42) and is therefore the one great means, the "more excellent way" of 1 Cor 12:31. In the Church, all Christians are "most intimately united with the life and mission of Christ" (art. 34). The whole Church must be "virgin", "true to the truth which it has pledged to the bridegroom, pure and inviolate, imitating the mother of its Lord in the power of the Holy Spirit and preserving virginally a faith undiminished, a confidence unshakable and a love sincere" (art. 64). All Christians must "dedicate themselves to God alone with a single-minded devotion", though this is easier in celibacy (*ut facilius corde indiviso*) (art. 42). All share in the priestly, kingly and prophetic office of Christ (art. 31). All are "consecrated to Christ" (art. 34). The eschatological age is anticipated in all of them through the beginning of the future transfiguration which comes in grace; all are also witnesses to this grace and the future glory, which the Christian family proclaims "with a clear voice" (art. 35). They are not only guided by the outward institution of the Church, they are also "inwardly impelled by the Holy Spirit" (art. 40), and also enriched by charisms (art. 12), so that they may embody in their lives in ever growing measure the Church's evangelical message and hence the essence of Christianity (arts. 31, 38, 41).

Karl Vladimir Truhlar

HOLY

I. Phenomenology and Philosophy

1. *The question of the holy.* a) To reflect on the holy is not to think of holiness as an attribute of God or of holy beings, places, times or things; what is in question, therefore, is not the meaning of the adjective holy as a predicate that can be applied to someone or something. Nor is the holy a neutralizing collective name for the different forms whether personal or impersonal in which the highest principle is conceived. Concern with the holy rather means seeking the domain or dimension proper to the divine encounter in which the supreme principle shows itself.

b) But how, then, is the holy important for Christian theology? That theology knows where the divine principle manifests itself: in the unique and definitive revelation which takes place in Jesus. Nevertheless it needs to understand the holy. It would be useless to draw a system of correct propositions from revelation whose very correctness left the essential and appropriate encounter with the divine God and the grace of his redemption unexplained, or even threatened to obscure it.

c) The question of the holy is of its nature not something confined to Christianity. It is bound up with man's awareness of being and of himself, and develops in many human ways and forms. This very multiplicity is significant from the Christian point of view, for revelation presupposes an ontological openness of man to God's self-revelation, in other words, the horizon of the holy. Revelation addresses itself to this horizon, makes use of its particular human form. Within this horizon the one enduring message takes on the manifold forms of its historical expression.

Jörg Splett

2. *Manifestation of the holy.* Not every concept of being and of man is open to the manifestation of the holy.

a) The holy does not reveal itself to a purely theoretical interest. The fact that attention is directed away from itself towards measurable and verifiable results does not exclude *a priori* the knowledge that finite being is not its own ground. But it is not of itself capable of being affected by the holy. A new dimension of man's cognitive life is reached as soon as he comes to sense the inexorable and in fact absolute impact of truth.

b) Similarly the holy is not perceptible to purely aesthetic contemplation. The enchantment of the beautiful gives aesthetic activity certain features akin to those of religion. Where, however, it is a game to be enjoyed to the full without regard to the earnestness of personal existence, there is no sense of the other quality, the holy, which is nevertheless close to the surface of the beautiful.

c) The holy remains closed even to a purely ethical attitude. When faced with the inviolable and incalculable majesty of the good, the will turns back to itself as its own measure, the good does not reveal itself as holy.

d) The simultaneous presence of two apparently opposite characteristics distinguishes the religious attitude, which is open to the holy. One is the seriousness of personal existence: what is at stake is not any particular thing, but everything, myself, my salvation. But then the gravity of the concern for salvation causes the self to turn away from self, to transcend self and to trust to the infinitely other than itself. Where serious concern for self and open-hearted detachment from self coincide, access is thrown open to the holy. This, however, does not force the holy to appear. It gives itself only as a free gift.

3. *Fundamental characteristics of the holy*. In the many forms in which the holy appears, two polarities are generally present simultaneously.

a) It is the intangible which touches me deeply. The basic religious attitude reflects this polarity. The holy is in itself sublimely transcendent through its own inexplicable, independent and unconditional primacy and majesty. But this very sublimity makes it anything but neutral. It concerns me deeply. It is self-subsistent – but bears down on me. Of itself, that is, unrelated to me, it is the totally other and prior, but thus it comprises me, though not like a general concept of which I would be an individual instance. It moves me and knows me in my inmost depths. To move and to know are not additional activities of the holy but its own primordial force. It is not because of something it does that the holy concerns me, but because it is the holy. The precedence of the holy raises it beyond my grasp; it is intrinsically a limit and inviolable, once again not in virtue of external adjuncts such as a prohibition, for example, but simply because it is holy and inaccessible as that which is the prior concern of all.

b) It is awesome and beatifying. The first polarity, which is simply the force of the very nature of the holy, also includes a second, as the fundamental religious attitude also testifies. The holy both rejects and attracts. It withdraws itself inaccessibly from my grasp and as it comes it opens up the insuperable difference of the otherness at whose mercy I am and before which I am silent. Yet nothing but this other can reach and fulfil me interiorly; it is only in contact with the holy that I am blissfully and intimately liberated from the ambiguity and vacuity of my self. The duality of abyss and close presence once again does not signify a disharmony in the holy, but the oneness of its holiness where I am both a stranger and at home.

4. *The concept of the holy*. How is our understanding of being to do justice to the coming and the summons of the holy? Not by counting the holy among the topics which it has comprehended, but by submitting itself to the holy. With the coming of the holy, it is "beside itself" but at the same time still itself, for otherwise the coming would merely be a blind impact. But it is a gift which endows me anew with itself and with myself and with my grasp of being. My understanding gratefully transcends itself and thus finds itself at home with the holy, which it still recognizes as the prior and transcendent. This understanding follows the normal lines

of all questioning – to ask after nature and purpose.

a) When the question of the nature or essence goes beyond individual beings to ask what is the being of beings in general, it comes upon such primordial and universal notes as the true, the good and the beautiful. Is the holy to be numbered with these? Its closeness to them is apparent from the fact that it transcends all beings and yet pervades them all. It differs from them, however, more than they differ among themselves. Truth, goodness, beauty and the corresponding being are not exhausted by the beings to which they are communicated, but their immediate orientation is towards beings; they tend to become predicates of beings and hence to become that which beings are. But beings are not holy of themselves, but only inasmuch as they point beyond themselves. The true and the good and so on are reflected and re-presented in beings. But the holy is merely commemorated there. That beings should be, in face of the holy, is not obvious, it is a marvel. Beings, in this ambit, are what are allowed to be. The holy is not the comprehensive essence of being, it is not prior to beings, but being's grateful memory of the hidden origin of all.

b) This backward thrust of being, in which the holy shows its might, even goes beyond the question of "why", which is itself a step further than all questions about beings. In the question, "Why?", beings cease to be taken for granted, but the purpose of this incomprehension is to look for the cause. Once the cause is clear, so is the being which was in question. If the why leads to an answer, I know what is "behind" things, in their cause. But there is no "getting behind" the holy. As the memorial to the holy, as the site which testifies that it intervened, beings remain unfathomable, wonderful; thus and only thus am I content. In the domain of the holy, the question "Why?" is answered only by remaining an open question; the source is not a first thing, but a mystery disclosing itself out of free and incalculable favour. The reversal of being which occurs in the holy manifests the difference between the "God of the philosophers" and the living, the divine God.

II. The Holy in Revelation

Attestation of revelation is in essentials, if not in words, attestation of the holy.

a) Gen 28 and 32, Exod 3 and 19, and Is 6, for example, display the typical combination of remoteness and proximity, fear and joy in the holy. Peter's cry: "Depart from me, for I am a sinful man, O Lord" (Lk 5:8), and the other, "It is well that we are here; let us make three booths" (Mk 9:5), indicate the tensions within which the domain of the holy is revealed and in which meeting with the divine takes place. Similarly the OT passages referred to. This "domain" is the irruption of the divine God, his action itself. It contains nothing but himself, but he is there present as he who goes beyond himself, filling this "extra space" and showing himself there, but still, as the origin, always "behind" it.

b) In the definitive divine revelation of salvation in Jesus Christ, all becomes the one comprehensive holy place (cf., for example, Acts 10 and 17, 1 Cor 3:22f.; 10:26), while losing all "magical quality". It is given into the hands of men to be at their disposition (as what has been truly sanctified). The sacred and the profane character of the world become identical in the Christian view.

c) The domain of the holy in which the definitive memorial to God's coming is placed and where his coming is constantly to be re-enacted, is revealed in Christianity by the love of the Son of God giving himself to us in death: it is the human partner universally (Mt 25:40) and especially the fellowship of believers united in this love (Mt 18:20; Jn 17:22ff.; Acts 21).

Klaus Hemmerle

HOLY SPIRIT

I. Pneumatology

The teaching on the Holy Spirit developed very slowly in the faith of the Church from the indications of Scripture. Pneumatology always lagged behind Christology. This is all the more surprising because, according to Paul, the possession of the Spirit is characteristic of the justified and distinguishes him from those who are not justified. In general, Scripture speaks more of the Spirit's function in our salvation than of his nature. The activity of the Spirit (in inspiration) joins the OT and NT together as a unity.

1. *The Old Testament.* The OT speaks of the Spirit in many different ways which create a number of tensions, which cannot be reduced completely to a system. The terminology differs from that of the NT; the OT does not speak of the "Holy Spirit", but of the "Spirit of God" (Yahweh), whereas the NT uses "Holy Spirit". There is, however, no difference in meaning. The change of terminology is probably due to the efforts of late Judaism to avoid using the name of God and to use instead one of his attributes. The "Spirit of God" is a spirit different from the world and therefore rightly named "Holy" Spirit. "Holy" here means "of God"; it indicates the transcendence of the Spirit. In the OT, the "Spirit of God" means a divine power active in the world, or rather God himself insofar as he is acting in man and in the universe, in history and in nature. As the divine power is evident in a special way in the bringing forth and the maintenance of life, the Spirit of God is considered as the source of life (e.g., Gen 1:2; 2:7; 6:3; Ps 33:6; 104:29f.; 146:4; Job 12:10; 27:3; 34:14f.; Ezek 37:7–10). The Spirit of God works powerfully and holds sway in history (e.g., Exod 33:14–17). In the majority of the texts, the Spirit is imparted to specially chosen individuals, men equipped with tasks that affect the course of history, such as Joseph, Abraham, Moses, Gideon, etc. (Gen 41:38; Num 11:17; Exod 31:1–5; Jg 6:34; 14:6), and especially the Prophets (1 Sam 10:6; 16:14; 3 Kg 17–19; 22:22ff.; Mic 2:7; 3:8; Hos 9:7; Ezek 2:2; 3:12ff.; 8:3; 11:1ff.; Wis 1:4f.; 7:7; 9:17). Now and again the Spirit is praised as the cause of salvation for all the members of the people of God (Ps 51:12f.; 143:10). While the original expectations of the Spirit were centred on heroic feats, especially in war, on physical strength and special prudence, these hopes were later transferred more and more to the religious sphere. The Spirit plays a special role in the description of the coming Messiah, the prince of peace (Is 11:1f.; 32:15–18; 41:1ff.; 42:1ff.). In the period which he inaugurates, the possession of the Spirit will be a gift given to all (Ezek 11:19; 36:27; 37:14; 39:29; Jer 31:33; Is 32:15; 35:5–10; 44:3; Joel 2:28f.; Zech 12:10). The Spirit of God imposes the loftiest demands upon the people of Israel, but he also comes upon the people as a blessing (Is 44:3). God's fidelity to his covenant is guaranteed by the promise of his Spirit (Is 59:21). Because the Spirit of God is in the midst of his people, there is nothing to fear (Hag 2:5). Among the Rabbis and in the Targums, the Spirit of God is above all the spirit of prophecy. The Spirit is mentioned many times in these writings as the pledge of the bodily resurrection of the dead.

The most emphatic pointer to the new Messianic age is given by Joel (3:1–5). Salvation will be accomplished with the outpouring of the Spirit upon all. The meaning of this prophecy is, as the NT texts show, not that the Spirit comes upon all men, but that he is imparted to all the faithful within the believing community.

2. *The New Testament.* Corresponding to this prophecy, we find in the NT the conviction that the redeemed community (the Church) is constituted by

the Holy Spirit. First, John the Baptist resumes the inspired prophetic ministry of the OT. But he differs from the earlier prophets inasmuch as he saw the Messiah already present as the bearer of the Spirit and the giver of the Spirit to all (Jn 1:26). The incarnate Son of God was conceived through the Spirit; he was equipped with the Spirit at his baptism. He was driven into the desert by the same Spirit for his first decisive struggle with Satan. The Spirit is the moving power behind every activity of Christ. The opposition of men to the Spirit is called by Christ the unpardonable sin (Mt 12:31f.; Lk 12:10; Mk 3:29f.). According to Acts, Christ promised the Spirit to his own during the time of his absence (Acts 1:8). In the power of this Spirit they were then to be his witnesses in Jerusalem, in Judaea, in Samaria, and to the end of the earth. In fulfilment of this promise, the fundamental gift of the Spirit was given on the first Pentecost. In the miraculous events that accompanied it, it was manifest that the saving action of God in the world was pressing forward irresistibly (Acts 2:1–11). Those partaking in the event experience it as the definitive bestowal of salvation. Peter interprets it as the fulfilment of the OT promises. The pentecostal outpouring of the Spirit is the beginning of the communication of the Spirit which continues through all time. The Spirit henceforth leads and guides the Church and inspires all within it. He chooses Paul to preach the gospel to the heathens (Acts 13:2ff.). He is the unseen power behind the apostolic missionary activity. He sends the Apostle from the harvest fields of Asia to those of Europe (Acts 16:6f.). The Spirit foretells to Paul the sufferings of his imprisonment (Acts 20:22f.; 21:10f.). The Spirit will tell the faithful what to reply to their judges in the time of persecution, so that they need not be anxious about their answers (Mk 13:11; Mt 10:19f.; Lk 10:11f.). Because the redeemed community is led by the Spirit, the lie of Ananias and Saphira is an offence against the Holy Spirit, and is severely punished (Acts 5:3, 9).

It is the Pauline writings which contain the most comprehensive and impressive testimony to the Spirit. In the Pauline theology, the word covers a wide field and it is impossible to define exactly what Spirit (πνεῦμα) meant to Paul. The functions which the Apostle ascribes to the Spirit form a number of sharp contrasts. They were not invented by Paul, but were experienced within the community. The new and revolutionary element was that the baptized experienced effects which clearly come from God. Paul sought to describe in orderly fashion the rich variety of this activity. With O. Kuss, we may begin with the most striking phenomena to interpret Paul's notion of the Spirit and gain a general picture of it. The most strange and surprising gift of the Spirit is glossolalia, the gift of tongues, an unintelligible stammering in the enthusiasm of faith, in praise of God. Paul judges this phenomenon in a basically favourable light, but demands that it be exercised in an orderly way in the community. This demand supposes that the Spirit does not overwhelm the recipient, but leaves him free to control the effects of the Spirit. But then the danger arises that the Spirit will be deprived of his effectiveness by human opposition. The difficulties of the communities in this matter caused Paul to issue the anxious warning: "Do not quench the Spirit" (1 Thess 5:19). But there are other "charisms" of the Spirit which are better than these enthusiastic cries which no one could understand. One of the most important is inspired prophecy, i.e., the explanation of the word of God. These gifts bring about more easily and effectively the edification of the community which is the goal of all the functions of the Spirit. Strongly though the Apostle feels that the work of the Spirit should not be restrained, when he is faced with the confusion caused by the charisms at Corinth, he points out insistently that the Spirit works for unity and order. In this connection, Paul develops his personal doctrine of the Church as the body of Christ which the Spirit produces and animates as vital principle.

Even when the faithful are not gathered for worship, it is the Spirit who keeps alive their sense of dependence on God and urges them to live a life of the imitation of Christ. Paul teaches that the Spirit moves them to express their thanks and joy even in unintelligible sounds (Rom 8:26f.), but, above all, to call God "Father" (Gal 4:6). But the work of the Spirit is not confined to these extraordinary gifts. He is also active in the everyday life of the faithful. He is the foundation of a totally new life and activity. The baptized are a temple in which God dwells (1 Cor 3:16). Both the Church as a whole and the individual Christian are temples of the indwelling Spirit (1 Cor 6:19). The Spirit is a force which is active not only in passing moments of ecstasy, but everywhere and always in the life of the baptized. He is the first-fruit, the pledge, the handsel, the anticipation, the guarantee of the eschatological fulfilment. He moves and guides the preachers of the message and all other Christian believers. Paul too sees the possession of the Spirit as the fulfilment of the OT promises. The notion that the Spirit is already a foretaste of final salvation gains more and more importance in Paul as it becomes clearer that the resurrection of Christ which the disciples experienced was not identical with his parousia, but that there was to be a long interval between the resurrection and the consummation of all things. With the giving of the Spirit a beginning at least has been made of the final consummation.

In the life of the believer, the Spirit grants all the gifts of salvation for which the believer longs. He is the giver of life (Rom 8:10), a life which partakes of the dialectical tension between present and future (Gal 6:8; Rom 1:17; 2:7; 5:17; 8:11ff.). The Spirit gives life, but full life will come only in the future (Rom 6:4, 11, 13; 2 Cor 3:6). The Spirit brings about freedom, liberation from the servitude of the law, from sin and from death: the eschatological freedom (Rom 8:2; Gal 5:15; 2 Cor 3:17), the freedom of the children of God.

He brings about holiness (2 Thess 2:13), so that the believer "thinks the things of God". The believer lives in the Spirit. This is opposed to the sphere of "the flesh"; he who lives in this realm thinks of the "things of the flesh". But the believer is under the influence of the Spirit who dwells within him (Rom 8:11). There is still something "fleshly" in the believer, who is under the influence of both powers. But the Spirit is the predominant influence, and it is only a question of time until the "flesh" is completely eliminated.

The fact that the faithful are moved by the Spirit, that the whole redeemed community is constituted by the Spirit as its principle of life, is manifest in their behaviour. There are ethical criteria for the discernment of the possession of the Spirit (Gal 5:19–31; Rom 11:17; Gal 5:19; esp. 1 Cor 13). The sign of the new life is a new morality (Rom 8:6–11; 1 Cor 6:9ff.; 15:9ff.; Gal 1:13–16; 5:9–23; Eph 1:17ff.; 1 Tim 1:12–16). The gifts of the Spirit are an unforeseeable, heavenly, marvellous and overwhelming intervention into human life. But they must be accepted, and given effect to by men. Their purpose would not be fulfilled if they did not impel men to corresponding action. The deepest purpose of the Spirit is to be a Spirit of joy, of love, of service. Characteristic of Paul is the combination of assertion and exhortation, of indicative and imperative (Gal 5:25; 2 Thess 2:13–17) which has often been noted. There are two questions which especially arise with regard to the Pauline teaching on the Spirit: what is the relation of the Spirit to Christ? Is the Spirit to be understood as personal or impersonal?

In respect to the first question, the Spirit is called both the Spirit of God and the Spirit of Christ. Gal 4:6 asserts: "To prove that you are sons, God has sent into our hearts the Spirit of his Son, crying 'Abba! Father!'" "Spirit of God" and "Spirit of Christ" are interchangeable (as can also be seen from Rom 8:9ff.).

Christ is for the baptized the principle of life, since he gives them the Spirit (Eph 4:11–16). The meaning of the formula: "The Lord is Spirit" (2 Cor.3:17) is disputed. According to the obvious sense of the words it seems to identify Christ and the Spirit. But as Paul usually distinguishes Christ from the Spirit (e.g., 2 Cor 13:13; Rom 5:1–5; 1 Cor 12), this should only be interpreted as a dynamic and not an ontological identity. Christ is active through the Holy Spirit, so that Christ and the Spirit do not constitute two separate principles of activity, but combine as one. Christ accomplished his work of redemption "in the Spirit" and is present in the Church in the Spirit as he exercises his saving power. For in the resurrection, he himself became "spiritual". As regards the personal nature of the Spirit, Paul does not of course use the developed concepts of the later teaching of the Church and of systematic theology. He attempts again and again to describe the Spirit from different approaches, primarily his function, not his nature. However, one can infer the nature from the functions of the Spirit, especially when combined with the Pauline texts in which the Spirit is named in the third place beside the Father and the Son, and hence in which the Trinitarian structure of the divine life is hinted at (especially 1 Cor 12:4–11; 2 Cor 13:13). At any rate, the Pauline theology contains the kernel from which the Church's doctrine of the Holy Spirit as the third divine "person" could be developed. Paul's teaching is thus in agreement with the baptismal formula given by Mt (26:28), the Spirit is the third person along with the Father and the Son. We find an echo of the Pauline teaching on the Spirit in the First Letter of Peter (e.g., 1:1f.).

In Jn we find the personal nature of the Spirit more in evidence. According to Jn, Christ promises his own in the farewell discourse "another comforter", who will be his representative during his absence. He will remain with the disciples till the end of time and help them to continue the work and the words of Christ (Jn 14:16f., 25f.). He will convince the world that there is sin, righteousness and judgment (Jn 16:5–11). The Spirit gives testimony to Christ, makes his work continually effective and explains it (1 Jn 2:1).

3. *Tradition.* In the patristic period, the Spirit is named in the baptismal formula with the Father and the Son, and he is also mentioned with the Father and the Son in reply to the accusation that Christians were atheists. As in Scripture, the Spirit is still seen dynamically, as for instance in Irenaeus. He says (*Adv. Haer.*, II, 6, 4): "Lord, Thou the one true God, beside whom there is no other God, grant that the Holy Spirit may rule in us through our Lord Jesus Christ." Similarly, he explains in the "Proof of the Apostolic Preaching" (1:1, 6f.): "And the third article is the Holy Spirit, through whom the prophets prophesied and the patriarchs were taught about God and the just were led in the path of justice, and who in the end of times has been poured forth in a new manner upon humanity over all the earth, renewing man to God. Therefore the baptism of our rebirth comes through these three articles, granting us rebirth unto God the Father, through his Son, by the Holy Spirit. For those who are bearers of the Spirit of God are led to the Word, that is, to the Son; but the Son takes them and presents them to the Father, and the Father confers incorruptibility. So without the Spirit there is no seeing the Word of God, and without the Son there is no approaching

the Father; for the Son is knowledge of the Father, and knowledge of the Son is through the Holy Spirit. But the Son, according to the Father's good pleasure, administers the Spirit charismatically as the Father will, to those to whom He will."

Because of the unity of action of the Word and the Spirit in the work of redemption, it is not surprising that in this period while doctrine was still undeveloped, there were many uncertainties. Thus, for example, Theophilus identifies the Spirit and the Word, or the Wisdom of God (*Ad Autolycum*, II, 10; II, 15). Theological reflection turned in the 4th century to the Holy Spirit, as an after-effect of Arianism, which was condemned at the Council of Nicaea (325; cf. *D* 125f. [54]). In a logical development of their views concerning the Son of God, the Arians taught that the Spirit was created by the Son. Athanasius attacked this view in his four letters to Bishop Serapion of Thmuis. Similarly, the Subordinationist interpretation of the Spirit was rejected by the Cappadocian Fathers, especially Basil, and by Ambrose. The main proponents of the false doctrine were Bishop Macedonius of Constantinople (362), and then Bishop Maratonius of Nicomedia. The decisive condemnation was pronounced by the Council of Constantinople (381), which affirmed the true divinity of the Spirit and his consequent significance for man's life of grace: "I believe in the Holy Ghost, the Lord and giver of life, who proceeds from the Father. Together with the Father and the Son he is adored and glorified. He spoke through the prophets" (*D* 150 [86]; cf. also 152–77 [58–82], 151 [85]). A Roman synod under Pope Damasus I (382) gave a more detailed presentation of the Church's doctrine, which emphasizes the divinity of the Holy Spirit rather than his function in salvation. Thus the synod tended in the direction of a more metaphysical systematization of the doctrine (*D* 178 [83]). Later doctrinal pronouncements brought only one important change, the addition of the *filioque* to the creed of Constantinople, which was to be a source of discord between East and West, down to the present day (*D* 527 [277]; also *D* 188 [19]; 566 [294]; 573 [296]). The addition was first made in the 6th century in Spain (Synod of Braga, 675) and then in Gaul and Italy. When in 808 the monks of the Frankish monastery on the Mount of Olives near Jerusalem sang the *filioque* in the Creed, they were accused of heresy by the Greek monks. Pope Leo III declared that the procession of the Spirit from the Son was to be preached but that its insertion into the Creed was superfluous. Nevertheless, at the request of Emperor Henry I, the *filioque* was included by Benedict VIII in the Creed at Rome in the year 1014.

The Greek Patriarch Photius (1078) made the procession of the Holy Spirit from the Father alone a main dogma of the Greek Church. He thus supported with dogmatic grounds a division between the Eastern and the Roman Churches which was rather due to ecclesiastical politics. The obligation of faith with regard to the procession of the Holy Spirit from the Son was determined as follows by Pope Benedict XIV in the Bull *Etsi Pastoralis* in 1742: "Though the Greeks must believe that the Holy Spirit also proceeds from the Son, it is not necessary for them to acknowledge this in the Creed. However, the Albanians of the Greek Rite have commendably accepted the opposite custom. It is our wish that this custom be maintained by the Albanians and by all those other Churches which have already adopted it."

The foundation of the procession of the Holy Spirit from both Father and Son is seen by the Church as the unity of the Spirit with the Father and the Son in the economy of salvation. The sending of the Spirit by the Father and the Son proves the immanent origin of the Spirit from the Father and the Son.

Greek theology teaches a procession from the Father through the Son, in which the Son is understood not merely as a transit channel but also as an active principle. There is no point in trying to find a real opposition between the two formulae. They express the same fundamental concept with a difference of accent. The Latin formula, which goes back to Augustine in content, if not in express terms, emphasizes that Father and Son form one single principle; but it does not mean that the Son did not receive from the Father his propriety as origin of the Spirit, as indeed he ceaselessly receives it. The Greek formulation affirms that the Father is the origin of the two divine persons. It does not deny that Father and Son are one as principle of the Spirit. Augustine does justice to the Greek concept, in spite of his Latin approach, when he says that the Father is the origin of the Holy Spirit *principaliter*. What is foremost in the Latin formula is the unity; in the Greek, the difference of the persons.

4. *Later theology*. A closer description of the Holy Spirit was arrived at in Augustine's theology of the Trinity. By having recourse to the life of the Spirit and the soul in man, and also stimulated by some indications of Scripture, Augustine came to the concept of the Holy Spirit as the love which binds the Father and the Son. He originates therefore from the movement of love between Father and Son. The theology of the Middle Ages developed the basic idea of Augustine in an often very subtle fashion. The question was more clearly posed whether the Spirit originated from the mutual love of Father and Son or from the one love of the Father and Son directed towards the divine nature.

The theology of the Holy Spirit returned, once more, to the dimension of salvation when in medieval and modern theology the question of the Spirit's relation to grace was raised. This question is indissolubly connected with the problem of whether grace is to be viewed as an entity or as a more personal factor. Peter Lombard identified grace with the Holy Spirit. This thesis was thoroughly discussed in the 13th and 14th centuries. It was generally rejected; but it brought to the fore in the treatise on grace, that is, on the free self-communication of God to men, an aspect which could never be forgotten and remained a burning question. In scholastic theology it appears under the key-words *proprium* and *appropriatio*. Scholasticism, in view of the dogma of the unity of the divine operation *ad extra*, maintains that the indwelling of the Spirit in men which is attested by Scripture is only an appropriation. It is questionable, however, whether the dogma referred to necessarily implies such a view. There have been many theologians since the 18th century, especially those with a historical bent of thought (e.g., Petavius, Thomassinus, Passaglia, de Régnon, J. M. Scheeben), who have asserted that each of the divine persons takes possession of the justified according to their personal proprieties. The Holy Spirit lays hold of him and thus grants him a share in the divine nature which is identical with each of the divine persons. In the Holy Spirit the justified are united to the Father through Christ. The Holy Spirit, therefore, only takes possession of man for the Son and for the Father. This is the deepest reason why his union with man is not a hypostatic union. The sanctifying function of the Spirit is also affirmed, when, in Greek as well as Latin theology, the Spirit is called the gift, not in an immanent process but in the perspective of the economy *ad extra*. According to Augustine, the Spirit is the gift of God to his creation from all eternity, because it is of his nature to be a gift (*donabile*). Augustine's doctrine of the Spirit seems to imply an immanent proximity of God to the creature, particularly in history, though this was not worked out by the Church Father. When the orientation to creation which according to Augustine was an eternal constituent of the Holy Spirit was realized through his mission to the world, and especially to the Church, he became involved in a historicity like that of the incarnate Logos, since he is the vital principle of the people of God. He is the eschatological force and the evolutionary factor which impels the people of God, and through them the whole of history, on to the fulfilment. His onward-urging power continues to work after the stage of fulfilment is attained, since the perpetual intensification of the dialogue with God in Christ continues in the Holy Spirit.

Michael Schmaus

II. Gifts of the Holy Spirit

In Catholic dogmatic theology the gifts of the Holy Spirit are one of the elements of justification. The Council of Trent explains the gifts (*dona*) as part of the "interior renewal" (*D* 799). The liturgy speaks of the sevenfold gift of the Spirit, e.g., in the hymns *Veni Sancte Spiritus*, and the *Veni Creator Spiritus*, and in the rite of ordination of deacons. The biblical basis is the description of the presence and activity of the Holy Spirit in the just (Acts, Paul, Jn). To be united in faith to Christ is to participate in his Spirit and hence to be bearer of the Spirit. The notion that participation in the Spirit of Christ as head of the Church takes effective form in the gifts of the Spirit is based on Is 11:2, which says that the Spirit of the Lord will rest upon the coming Messiah, the Spirit of wisdom and understanding, the Spirit of counsel and fortitude, the Spirit of knowledge and piety, the Spirit of the fear of the Lord (the gift of piety is not in the Hebrew). For an understanding of the gifts of the Spirit, it should be noted that in the ancient Church, in the theology of the East and of the West, the scriptural doctrine of the Spirit was understood to be that the Spirit himself was given to the just by God.

Augustine enriched this concept by noting that the Holy Spirit is the love which proceeds from the Father and the Son and, for this very reason, God's gift to man, since the first gift of love is always love itself. Augustine saw the difficulty of making the personal Spirit a gift to man, since the notion brought with it the danger of giving the Spirit temporal existence or quality. His answer was that the personality of the Spirit came from its eternal immanent propriety as gift, and not from its being actually given in time. That this view might also imply the attributing of the relationship to creation to the personality of the Spirit seems to have caused Augustine no misgivings. Later theology, where it did not lose itself in speculation, likewise adopted these views without misgivings. If the Spirit himself is the gift of God to man, then the seven "gifts" are the salutary consequences and manifestations of the basic gift of salvation. The question of the precise nature of these consequences and the exact number of the gifts was given various answers in the course of theology, till finally, in the 19th century, the number seven was generally accepted and one particular explanation, that of Thomas Aquinas (*Summa Theologica*, II-II, q. 8, etc.). Here the gifts are created qualities by which man is enabled to follow easily and gladly the salutary impulses given by God, especially in obscure and complicated situations, to enable him to come to the right decision in spite of the confusing clash of reasons for and against. Behind this theory of Aquinas is the doctrine of the *potentia oboedientialis*, according to which man is open and receptive to divine inspirations by virtue of his character of creature. Hence the gifts are special salutary modifications of the openness for God which is intrinsic to human nature. They also hold in check the forces of self-assertiveness, selfishness and sloth (concupiscence) which resist the inspirations of grace. Since God is ceaselessly active, these qualifications for the acceptance of the divine in man's own action are constantly being created anew. They exist as qualities by being constantly created.

This objectivating interpretation which is current in dogmatic theology needs to be supplemented by the personal component, which will also throw light on the earlier elements. The personal component consists of the fact that the Holy Spirit, as God's gift to the justified, brings about both the inclination to salutary acts as well as justification itself, though man does not cease to be the agent of his own action. The Spirit, as "uncreated grace", works throughout as the one Spirit. But he works in such a way that different effects ensue as the historical situation in which man has to realize his relationship to God demands. The plurality is not in the Spirit of God but in man.

The question of whether this effectiveness was a *proprium* (personal propriety) or an *appropriatio* (a mere attribution to the Holy Spirit) was discussed in Western theology. Scholastic theology in general held it to be an *appropriatio*. But in view of the indications given in Scripture and the doctrine of the Eastern Fathers one should rather speak of a personal propriety of the Spirit, on the understanding that in the work of salvation Father, Son and Holy Spirit act in a way corresponding to their personal propriety. Further, it should be affirmed that the Spirit, on the analogy of the incarnation of the Word, unites himself personally and dynamically (not personally and ontologically) with the Church and its individual members of which he is the principle of life. The doctrine that the divine action *ad extra* is one and common to all three Persons is not affected by this thesis, since it does not imply efficient but formal (or quasi-formal) causality.

As regards the domain of the gifts, dogmatic theology usually thinks of the individual as the main field of action. But we must not forget that the individual whose salvation is his own destiny receives, nonetheless, the gift of justification as a member of the Christian community, that he is bound to it by many bonds and can serve or harm it by his action. Since the community is the sociological *a priori* for the salvation of the individual, the gifts of the Spirit further the life and growth of the community in its understanding of Christ and its love of Christ in each changing historical era. In 1 Cor the gifts of the Spirit (wisdom, knowledge, prophecy, speaking in tongues, i.e., inarticulate cries inspired by the enthusiasm of faith, and its interpretation) are given an "ecclesial" interpretation, and seen as manifestations of the one body of Christ and helps to its building up. The charisms are within the domain of the gifts of the Spirit. These unpredictable but nonetheless always indispensable gifts are meant for special tasks in special situations of Church life. The systematic treatment of the gifts in theology brought with it the tendency to treat them as private and individual gifts, but their "ecclesial" origin and orientation should not be lost sight of. In theology, the gifts of knowledge were distinguished from the inspirations of the will, a distinction which made for precision and showed where the emphasis lay in each case. But in reality, the whole man is affected by the salutary illumination of the Spirit in his act of faith. The gifts of the intellect are understanding, wisdom, knowledge and counsel. They are all within the domain of faith and its actuation in the world and history, and do not claim to substitute for the effort of scientific investigation of the world and its technological mastery. They give insight into the mystery of salvation, they orientate the Christian in the world towards the horizon of God, they sharpen his hearing for the will of God in all the situations where law and precept are inadequate but where the conscience trained on law and precept must decide. The gifts of the will are piety, fortitude and fear of the Lord. They have nothing to do with naturalism or magic, but enable man to love and adore the Father Almighty and to combine with other men to build up a brotherly fellowship. With the help of these gifts, he is steadfast in hardships, trials, and dangers without sullenness or the flight into false mysticism or despair, and he follows the demands of his historical situations which he has critically sifted to see there the demands of God.

Michael Schmaus

HOPE

A. The Traditional Doctrine

1. The ordinary presentation of hope was in the framework of the theological virtues, in dogmatic and moral theology. The theology of hope was worked out above all by Thomas Aquinas (*De Spe*, *Summa Theologica*, II-II, qq. 17–22). Hope is directed to a future good which is hard but not impossible to attain. It is elevation of the will, made possible by grace, by which man expects eternal life and the means to attain it, confident of the omnipotent aid of God. Hope is *the* great virtue of man in his *status viatoris*. It comes after faith, from which it receives its object. It is akin to the love of desire (*amor concupiscentiae*) and precedes perfect love. Man can hope only for himself and for those whom he loves. The extreme threat and direct test of hope is death. The sins against hope are despair, as anticipated failure, and presumption, as anticipated fulfilment. In both these cases man seeks to break out of his pilgrim existence and have his life otherwise than from the hand of God.

2. In the outline of hope thus presented, there is little explicit mention of the gospel message, the redemption through Jesus Christ, his resurrection and his enthronement as Lord. The foundation and object of hope are as a rule not notably Christocentric. It is also notable that most dogmatic eschatologies fail to discuss the virtue of hope. Not enough attention is paid to the way in which the universal biblical promises correspond to Christian hopes, so that hope is reduced to a personal and private matter. In moral theology, the three theological virtues make up a set of themes along with others in special moral theology, and this obscures the fundamental and all-embracing importance of Christian hope. The intrinsic connection between faith and hope has been obscured since the Reformation by polemics against the *fides fiducialis* of Luther. The relationship between this world's hopes and Christian hope was either glossed over lightly or judged to be negative. Hence preaching on hope came too easily to sound like merely consoling oneself with the promise of a better life elsewhere, or a flight from this valley of tears and its tasks. This occasioned the reproach of Karl Marx that religion is the opium of the masses.

B. Biblical Theology

1. *Old Testament*. The structure of hope is determined in the OT by a wide range of concepts: בטח, to be confident, to feel secure, קוה, to wait for, be tense, יחל to expect, hope, חסה, to fly to, take refuge in, חכה, to wait for longingly, שׂבר, to trust, and אמן, to be firm and consoled, to believe, trust, hope. Israel hopes for blessing, mercy, help, just judgment, forgiveness and salvation from Yahweh. False and empty hope builds on idols made with hands, on men, riches, power, religious practice. More important here than a list of texts is a grasp of the structure of the OT relationship to God. Israel's faith is based on historical experiences which it regarded as the *magnalia Dei*. Israel's hope was directed to a future in history of which the horizon was constantly broadening. The unifying bond between past and future was the fidelity of Yahweh. Israel recalled his *magnalia* in

its liturgy, to reinforce its pleas for help and to strengthen its own hope. Thanksgiving for the mighty works of Yahweh which Israel has experienced becomes a confession of hope. Yahweh himself is the hope of his people (Jer 17:7; Ps 60:4; 70:5). The words in which the Protector God of the patriarchs presents himself: "I shall be [with you] as he who I shall be [with you]" (Exod 3:14) point to the future as the setting of man's knowledge of God. He who believes in this God is sent forth at his command to act mightily on history, with the hope of God's promised help. This faith enables man to take the risk of history with this God in the strength of hope. The bearer of the promises is not primarily the individual but the people, the covenant, the remnant (in the prophets), and only the loyal individual in apocalyptic. But at the same time the horizon of hope becomes more universal. Every hope fulfilled opens up new and greater hopes, till the whole cosmos and all peoples are embraced. Hope is the bridge between the Old and the New Covenants, since hope does not try to determine how God will show himself but remains open for all new and astonishing manifestations of love.

2. *New Testament*. The range of concepts identifying hope in the NT include ὑπομενεῖν, be patient, endure, and γρηγορεῖν, be watchful, as well as ἐλπίζειν, to hope. In Jn and to some extent in the Synoptics, hope coincides with faith, in 1 Pet faith coincides with hope, in Rev, hope with patience. Hope takes on different forms in the NT writings according to the various eschatological concepts which are taken as models.

In the NT, likewise, a look at the structure of hope is more enlightening than a listing of the texts. The lordship of God which has come in Jesus Christ, in his life, death and resurrection, is the basic experience of faith for NT man. But he has not possession and control of this lordship, which is his only as a heritage, in the form of a pledge or handsel, through the Spirit. The power of death, sin, the elements of the world, the principalities and powers and fear have been broken by Christ. The new freedom to which the Christian has been set free is freedom to live the new life in the hope of glory. In spite of (and because of) the known love of God, in spite of (and because of) the gift of God's life and Spirit, the believer lives only in hope. The contact with salvation is so close that the believer feels keenly the contradiction between it and the present which still persists and must be endured, and so tries to make his hope concrete in the expectation of an imminent end or substitutes for it a fanatical enthusiasm. The various eschatological concepts and paradigms are to be explained in the light of this situation, and none of them is to be erected into an absolute. The tension between the experience of the present and the salvation believed in, like the tension between justification and sanctification, must be sustained in hope. The ordinary way of explaining this tension, with the help of the concepts "Already" and "Not yet" in combination risks dividing salvation in the sense of a *partim – partim*. The justification of the sinner is a definitive gift of God which takes man into God's service and starts him on the way of fulfilment. Justification itself is thus promise of fulfilment. In the fellowship of Christ the faithful share the old experience that each stage of fulfilment is itself a new and greater promise: "Christ in you, the hope of glory" (Col 1:27). From this it follows that hope is identical with the New Testament relationship to God: a heathen can be described as one who is without hope (cf. 1 Thess 4:13; Eph 2:12). Faith is confidence and conviction about a hoped-for but unseen future (cf. Rom 8:24f.; Heb 11:1) which is described in terms of social well-being, such as peace, justice, forgiveness, conquest of suffering and death, resurrection of the flesh, marriage feast, heavenly Jerusalem, new heavens and new earth. Since his hopes are so universal, the believer is called upon to furnish an account of its justification before the whole world (cf. 1 Pet 3:15). The bearer of this promise and the provider of this justification is the community, the new covenant, the Church in intersubjective structure. Hope does not finally become possession pure and simple. It remains intrinsic to the eschatologically permanent form of the relationship to God (1 Cor 13:13), since it is always openness for the "always greater God" and the free gift of his immediacy.

C. Progress and Hope in Present-Day Thinking

When Christians, distrustful of the future offered within the world, put their hope in God, they need not be surprised that others set out to realize the world's hope without reference to God. We observe today a widespread atheism with regard to the setting of man and his future. This has led to the "great schism" of the modern world, the schism between "religion and revolution, Church and Enlightenment, divine faith and future purpose, reliance on salvation and responsibility for the world" (J. Moltmann). Karl Marx maintained that religion had to be eliminated if man was to be liberated from his alienation, oppression and slavery.

Ernst Bloch sees "the principle of hope" as the driving force of all human initiative, and from it he looks for the coming of the new, the never-before, the undreamt-of (hardly even in men's religions). What is primarily decisive for the present is not the past but the future, since the present is the seed-bed of the tendencies and latent urges which open out on the future and which man must seize upon and develop.

The question still remains, however, as to whether Bloch's theory really explains the presence of the truly new in the future. Is not the future, as he explains it, still merely the unfolding of what is already latent? And does he explain how there is still hope for each personal human being, and not just for "humanity"? Is not God who as regards the world is always "in potency", the sole guarantor of a really new future, for men and for mankind?

The "evolutionary humanism" of Julian Huxley, which is generally accepted on an atheistic basis, presents itself as a new system of ideas, an order of values open to and in need of further development, which is the instrument to man's hand as he masters his great task of directing an evolution which he himself has taken over. Evolutionary humanism rejects all dogmatism of principles or rules, since it would hinder evolution. It sees its own efforts as an aid to the better development of man as he is today and will be tomorrow, to the provision of a wider space of freedom. These efforts include practical initiatives such as help to developing countries and regulation of births. This humanism is to some extent combined with a new form of faith in science, which relies on technology for the solution of all questions. In view of the risks which it involves as regards the positive course of further evolution, evolutionary humanism must be characterized as a system of "hopeful knacks".

In non-Marxist philosophy, hope is seen as a good by G. Marcel in his reading of man as *homo viator* and by O. Bollnow in his effort to go beyond existentialism, while it is rejected by K. Löwith, who sees progress as a menace and hope as an illusion. Hope is left its place in the open dialectics of T. W. Adorno.

The present conjuncture forces man to ask the question of the meaning of hope and of progress and to examine his motives as he tries to dominate a baffling future. A new relationship between theory and practice is taking shape, since the future cannot simply be contemplated, but must be channelled. It is not enough for theologians simply to point to the biblical origins of hope and of the will to the future. The challenge to the Christian faith and the Christian hope which the modern consciousness contains is not thereby answered. The imposing and fascinating response attempted by Teilhard de Chardin suffers from the lack of an adequate distinction between evolution and history. He does not seem to take seriously enough the component of freedom, including the freedom of the will to evil and to self-destruction.

D. Theological Principles

1. *General.* The basis and centre of Christian faith is the message of Jesus and its promises, and Jesus' being raised up by God. But these two things, the message and the resurrection, are not really themselves in their entirety without the return of Jesus, without the resurrection of all flesh (cf. 1 Cor 15), without the new heavens and the new earth (cf. Rev 21:22). Hence faith in the resurrection of Jesus means hope in the universal consummation which is promised and pre-figured by this resurrection. All theology is discussion of how the resurrection and future of Christ affects us (J. Moltmann). W. Pannenberg sees the end, the consummation or fulfilment, as already realized by anticipation in the resurrection of Christ, where it can already be deciphered.

In hope, the believer pierces the gap which has been opened up by the cross and resurrection of Jesus. Faith and hope are two inseparable moments of the one act, of which (initial) love is the integrating centre. The juxtaposition of the three theological virtues caused a certain amount of obscurity with regard to this intrinsic unity of the three theological virtues. There is no truth or blessing of faith which is already fully and finally complete in the past and which one can secure merely by a faith which looks backwards. Hence a treatise on God, his nature and attributes (*De Deo*) cannot be presented as complete in itself at the beginning of theology, since it is only from creation, redemption and fulfilment that we see who God really is. God is always the "God in front of us" (J. B. Metz). He is the "absolute future" for man (K. Rahner).

For the same reason, the treatise on creation can never be fully rounded off, since we will only see from the new heavens and the new earth what God really meant by the first creation. The reason why so many questions about nature and grace bogged down hopelessly was because creation has been so thoroughly thought out that grace could only come as an accessory, as it were from outside.

The incarnation is not understood when the formula of Chalcedon is interpreted statically. It must also include the thought of the future of this Jesus of Nazareth, cross and resurrection, second coming and lordship, the permanent significance of his humanity for the fulfilment of man (K. Rahner), if even the incarnation is to be given its true meaning.

The inclusion of the eschatological dimension preserves the Church from identifying itself wrongly with Christ or the kingdom of God and hence from all "triumphalism". It shows clearly the limits imposed on the Church by its provisional character, and prevents the sacraments from being misunderstood as magical signs.

Discussion of the meritorious nature of works could be formulated in more biblical terms, and thereby become more readily acceptable ecumenically, if one emphasized the element of confidence and hope which is inspired by God's promises and fidelity.

The full application of the structural principle here set forth would mean the excision of eschatology from theology as a separate treatise, but would restore the eschatological perspective to all the other treatises by being seen at last in its true and comprehensive character. Hope is the advocate of the immense openness of the promised future amid the reality of faith and the reality of salvation in history. These are the two dimensions – truth and history – in which the theology of hope must now be expounded more precisely and its consequences noted.

2. *Hope and truth.* The truth of faith can only be grasped in the perspective of hope, not just in the sense that hope only has the notion of its goal from faith, but rather in the sense that hope is the inner force of faith which enables man to give himself to the "ever greater God", in confident dedication, in view of the promised future. There is no formula of human language which can ever adequately express revelation as promise, or interpret it definitively. Not even Scripture can do this, or a summa of dogmatic theology. Every closed system breaks down in face of the fullness and the futurity of the gospel. The whole of history will be needed, including its permanent fulfilment, to display this fullness. Dogmas are indications of the truth which is Christ, not the truth itself. This helps us to see what is meant by saying that all truths of faith are known by analogy. Hope is the safeguard of the *maior dissimilitudo* throughout all possible *similitudo* of the affirmations. The imagery of eschatological truth is a valid utterance, which cannot be wholly exhausted by demythologization and existential interpretation and is quite adequate to safeguard the openness for futurity, for the fullness of salvation – and hence to provide a new future for each stage of knowledge achieved. Through hope, faith avoids the mistake of taking the hiddenness of God for absence. Confidence in the fidelity of God enables faith to accept him as the principle and promise which sustains the immeasurable fullness. Through hope, the believer finds the strength to hold out even in the profoundest darkness, without despairing or giving up. Hope reminds the believer of the never-failing promise which was given in Christ. It is not hostile to past tradition but favours and promotes tradition as the "eschatologically-orientated transmission" of the redemptive works of God (G. Sauter). At the same time, it prevents tradition from hardening into an ideology, since it makes it impossible to take faith and Christian life for granted, as they are constantly threatened with being in the sphere of Christian traditions. Hope makes dialogue with unbelievers possible, because it recognizes that the believer himself is still on the way to the fullness and hence can make room for the experiences and findings of the unbeliever in its own discovery of truth. In the final fulfilment, hope is not eliminated but made fully manifest in its basic structure, as marvelling and trusting dedication to the ever greater God and the freedom of his love.

3. *Hope and history.* There is no truth for man except that which is mediated by his historicity. In this connection the distinction between history and evolution, between futurity and goal, is of decisive importance. Not all that happens merits the name of history, and not all that is yet to come merits the name of futurity. Evolution is a fixed process. The predetermined goal anticipates the whole process and determines it as its final cause. Evolution can only bring out what is already present and latent. We can only speak of history when the specifically human intervenes: freedom, responsibility, decision, possible failure in the individual and inter-subjective spheres. Freedom is the key to the new, to the coming of what never was before. History is played out between the freedom of God, the ground of all, and the freedom of man. Christian hope fixes its gaze on the futurity which this play of freedoms makes possible and not on the predetermined goal of a development. Hope looks to history that is to come.

God gives salvation in such a way that it has also to be achieved by man. Hence man goes towards the future which he hopes for from God by advancing towards his inner-worldly future. His inner-worldly hopes are the place where he practises Christian hope and the channels through which it is bestowed on him. They are not merely rivals. Hope does not render effort superfluous, but demands it. It is the way in which hope realizes itself and takes on its responsibilities. Man hopes for God's justice and peace by striving now for their anticipation. The Christian "must constantly make the correctness of his faith come true in the correctness of an action determined by the last things" (J. B. Metz). Though hope is just taking the next step (K. Barth), each present step is weighty because it helps to decide the definitive future. Hope is not the opium of the people but an impulse to change the world in the perspective of God's promises, a revolutionary force which strives to create conditions favourable to the men most loved by God, the poorest and the weakest. Christian hope is the driving force of all inner-worldly hopes, which are penetrated and carried on beyond the scope of their own powers in reliance on the mercy and omnipotence of God. He who loses his life in such loving service gains it before God. Death itself, which still must be suffered in its bitterness, has been opened up inwardly by Christ to the fullness of God. Hope confirms man's right to seek salvation in the new, but frees him from the burden of having to create this newness himself while it takes him into its service on behalf of the promised future. J. B. Metz calls for a "creative eschatology" which will be conscious of the social and political responsibilities which flow from the universality of the promises. And here hope must reckon with the meagreness of its knowledge of the future. Often it can only aim at its desires by simply criticizing or negating existing conditions but without being able to put forward positive suggestions. This safeguards it from the danger of being a totalitarian ideology. The heavenly Jerusalem comes down from heaven. It is the gift of God. The peoples bring in their riches – the fruits of love active in hope (cf. Rev 21:10, 24). Hope abides in the fulfilment as readiness to accept these fruits of its own love and hence God himself as the eternal gift of his love.

Ferdinand Kerstiens

HUMAN ACT

A. Origin and Primary Characteristics

1. When described empirically, "human" or moral action must be said to begin with the personal (free, conscious) reaction to the conflict between the urge to instinctive self-satisfaction and the claims of society. It supposes the development of the consciousness of self as distinct from and opposed to the surrounding world, which is experienced as a set of claims contrary to the needs of an immanent self-fulfilment. The human act in the child occurs when he makes the experience of being loved, as he is accepted and helped by his mileu. Thus the child denies himself instinctive satisfactions if they are contrary to his affectionate union with his mother which he naturally values highly. Where the conflict is not felt, the coming of the moral act is delayed.

The next stage of consciousness is that the need of self-realization, to which the setting is felt to contribute, leads to an uncritical adoption of the views of the environment. There ensues, in fact, an "introjection", by which the conduct of others, normally the family, is adopted as the pattern of behaviour, by a process of identification. As the child's world is enlarged and his critical faculties develop, new conflicts arise. He meets patterns of conduct which are mutually contradictory and must decide which to follow. Here his own needs are not the sole factor. He comes to see more and more the purposefulness of what is done and demanded of him. The strength of his affective attachment to certain models plays, of course, a large part.

Once the child can see that certain actions, such as telling the truth, are intrinsically rational and that they are demanded of him because they have a value of their own, he can accomplish inchoative human or moral acts. He is now able to demarcate immanent and spontaneous instincts so clearly that he can compare them with the claim of "duty" and react freely on the basis of this insight. In favourable family circumstances this occurs normally between six and seven years of age – the "age of discretion" when he "comes to the use of reason". But this stage can also be much delayed.

This critical detachment from the received norms of the environment and the instinctive urges of the ego is, of course, very restricted to start with and can only develop gradually, since conscious reflection and attitudes must always be a function of direct knowledge and deliberate decision, and these constantly change their character as the personality develops. They can never be fully perspicuous. Hence deliberate moral action cannot be fully and clearly distinguished from uncritical reactions and always depends on the firmness of the development of the personality. And the personality itself is often influenced by the ethos implicit in the super-ego, so that genuine moral choice is harder, since absolute value may be ascribed to traditional notions without sufficient reason, sometimes merely as the result of education.

An essentially higher stage is reached when a young person can decide freely and responsibly not only with regard to individual acts, but also with regard to himself, when he takes an attitude – definitive so far as he himself is concerned – towards the essential aspects of his environment. For this he must first have an adequate concept of the bearings of his action and, secondly, the objective self-consciousness must be well enough developed to allow of a definitive subjective self-determination. And effective personal relationships must be strong enough to allow of a subjective grasp of the absolute nature of moral obligation, so that to go against it is felt as something which makes man himself bad and not just the individual act.

Personal maturity in this sense allows of the human act fully worthy of the name. It presupposes a) a sense of one's own irreplaceable identity, normally induced by the conflicts set up by the awakening of sexuality and its concomitant phenomena; b) the power to see sufficiently well the bearings of one's action as it affects definitively one's own life and one's relations with the world. The essential future implications must be seen. The adequacy of such insight depends on experience and education. c) It also presupposes a recognition of the dignity of the person. This must be strong enough to make the young person respect and love it for its own sake. He is so far emancipated from egoism that he can see and accept the claims of others as persons. But this power of discernment and, above all, this capacity to love do not usually coincide with the end of physical puberty and should not be ascribed too hastily to young persons.

2. From the point of view of philosophy, one can speak of moral action or human acts when the personally conscious subject acts as such by means of his free decision, as he takes on responsibility for himself and others. Thus a human act demands consciousness and free will, regard for the other persons with whom the subject is always involved and responsibility with regard to their self-fulfilment. They are seen to have a right to an answer and an explanation. This means that there is no human act that does not involve an attitude to-

wards the transcendental norm of morality, towards perfection and the striving after it. Thus it is always a summons to metaphysical faith, hope and love. In other words, the human act is formally good when it recognizes God as the supreme good and hence believes, when it expects salvation from God and hence hopes, when it accepts God as the supreme good and hence loves.

For an act can be judged good or bad only insofar as it is seen to be in keeping with or contradictory to being. But this knowledge is only possible in proportion to the evidence with which being in itself appears. And this evidence summons us to believing acceptance of being in itself, because this is both the necessary precondition of all we know and yet is not grasped in itself, but is to be presupposed. Here it can be rejected by the will, though it is grasped by the reason as something which ought to be affirmed. This means that every morally good act is an act of faith.

It is also always an act of hope. For a conscious act can make man better or worse only insofar as it appears to him as reasonable or unreasonable and hence arbitrary. But this again is only possible insofar as a given line of action, which is in keeping with being, is recognized as absolutely obligatory. But knowledge of the reasonableness of action is a transcendental condition of conscious action, since this is necessarily purposeful. And the basic acknowledgment of the reasonableness of action in keeping with being is a free act of hope, since the proof of the rightness of this fundamental acknowledgment is awaited only from the future, and hence can be freely accepted or rejected.

Finally, when man makes a decision with regard to something recognized as obligatory, he is following or refusing to follow the moral summons, and hence to love the good in itself or to reject it wilfully and lovelessly. For in his conscious action man both necessarily strives after the perfect and hence the good in itself, and must still decide in favour of the good in itself, since the good in itself is only grasped by us in a limited way and hence can be rejected in favour of an arbitrarily chosen good.

Hence the starting-point for the determination of the human, moral action must be the transcendental relation to God. This relationship is only developed enough to enable us to speak of a moral act when man is so referred to God that he either accepts him in faith, hope and love in the moral decision, or rejects him in unbelief, arbitrarily and hence ultimately despairingly and selfishly. The relationship to God need not be consciously reflected on (*in actu reflexo*). It is enough that it be really there (*in actu exercito*) in the actual exercise of the act. This relationship to faith, hope and love is transcendentally necessary in the human act and in the present order of salvation it has been given in fact a supernatural extension. This threefold transcendental and supernatural relation of the human act to God will be discussed in the following.

B. Relationship to the Transcendental Norm: Faith

1. It follows that the prerequisite of a human act is that it be recognized as good or bad. This means both the knowledge of the norm of morality and of the relationship of the act to the norm. All that is meaningful in itself and hence ought absolutely to be is immediately desirable and hence objectively good in the moral order. Hence the ultimate criterion of morality is the orientation to the perfection of God, in whom alone we can find our ultimate fulfilment. We are objectively fulfilled by the perfect love of God and subjectively by our perfect adaptation to his will.

Everything else is good insofar as it is ordained to a goal which transcends it and which itself has an immanent purpose within it. For in this way everything is affirmed and accepted insofar as it partakes of God's perfection, and hence striven after in keeping with (its) being. The perfection of God is participated in by beings endowed with spirit (angels, men) in such a way that they both have an intrinsic purpose which makes their self-realization meaningful, and that this self-realization cannot be attained except by their being ordained to their transcendent goal, that is, towards that which is meaningful in itself and hence has a character of absoluteness (and insofar as it has such a character). But this means that the morally good is what promotes man's being man in accordance with other men and this accord insofar as it is in accord with God. Hence directly good acts are those which perfect the agent in his relationship to God and to man. In other words, ultimately goodness is what promotes inter-subjectivity, persons in relation to one another, in all its dimensions.

But since infra-human creation has no other end than to serve the self-realization of man, orientation towards it is morally good objectively insofar as it can be made to serve the development of man. This means that the material reality which is infra-subjective and hence objective and hence categorized can only be indirectly good in the moral order – "materially".

Hence an act is morally good subjectively insofar as it is consciously ordained towards the self-realization of the agent in accordance with God and the neighbour, and takes material reality into the service of inter-subjectivity.

It follows that the first prerequisite for moral action is an adequate knowledge of the incommensurability of persons with the infra-human, and hence of human and material values. One who cannot sufficiently distinguish persons from objects is not morally responsible.

The required knowledge of the good in itself can be more or less clear. It need not be fully conscious and articulated. But it is there as soon as one has direct if confused knowledge of certain values – truth, perfection, justice and freedom – in a word, as soon as one sees that virtues are desirable for their own sake. The virtues are always values which serve the development of "inter-subjectivity". Thus they are necessarily transcendent values. This means that the subject who aims at them is necessarily perfected, conditioned as he is by this "inter-subjectivity".

It follows that man cannot err in his grasp of virtues and vices. They always make him receptive to the good as such. By their very definition, that is, of their very nature, they point out a well-ordered or disordered inter-personal relationship. This means that man can never go wrong in deciding whether an act is permitted, forbidden or commanded, since he is necessarily ordained by his reason – and instinctively or freely by subjective disposition – towards the truth as such, in an act of the will; and he has evidence of his personal and inter-personal character ("inter-subjectivity") in spite of this being given him as the experience of objects ("objectivity"). For thus lawfulness or otherwise is referred directly to the subjective acceptance or rejection of persons, that is, to attitudes which are good or bad in themselves. Like the act of faith in the assent of faith, the moral act, in its intrinsic attitude to the norm, to the good as such, has a formal structure and is correspondingly certain. It is self-authenticating, because it is an act of direct inter-subjective communication, the structure of which is directly known by man – though not necessarily brought before the articulate consciousness – just as is the communication itself. Since it aims at the true and the good, the absolute in other words, it is directly ordained to God, even if something else is expressly affirmed, since the transcendental relation to the absolute is ordination to God, though its translation into propositions may be faulty.

But man has to interpret his inter-subjective attitudes in action. There must be external, objective and hence transcendent actions. This is achieved when man uses his bodily nature and the goods of this earth as means of self-expression and self-realization, referring them for this purpose to the demands of "inter-subjectivity". Here he is involved in the proper laws of these realities and their categories, but influences them so personally that he determines what they must be, and they are no longer simply the results of causes independent of him.

When man comes to weigh the proper laws of things he can err. In other words, he can err about the things which he permits, forbids or commands, that is, in the concrete objectivation of his attitudes. That his "objective" interpretation of his "subjective" attitudes can be erroneous is due to the necessity of abstraction and the necessity of forming a judgment. The former is by definition an imperfect knowledge of the essence of things, since the essential unfolds only in the historical process and thus is not definitively displayed. We grasp it selectively, by prescinding from certain characteristics. In the judgment, we pass a transcendental verdict on what comes under categories, since by means of the copula we link the transcendental concept with its realization in categories. Error is possible here, since the identity between subjective and objective is grasped by us only in their difference.

Further, though the mind is of itself necessarily ordained to truth, knowledge depends to some extent on the disposition of the subject. Our grasp of the truth is limited and "objectified", and we are always free in the attitude which we adopt to the truth as concretely grasped, since it is something open to interpretation. Hence our actual grasp of truth depends to some extent on our instinctive attitudes and our love of truth – which is a free act. Hence failure to grasp the truth can be due not merely to the limitations of reason, but also to the disposition of the will.

We conclude that moral judgments can adequately render the morally permissible, etc., or more exactly, the will of God. They are imperfect because they are abstract, and because of the limitations of the mind's ordination to truth in its actual efforts. And they are sometimes erroneous. But they render infallibly the will of God insofar as we are ordained to the truth as such. This ordination to the will of God, being a free act, always implies a "metaphysical act of faith", because the acceptance of the true and the good, though within the framework of the transcendental conditions of our knowledge and will, can only take place in an act which is not transcendentally necessary and hence is free.

2. Thus our assertions about the nature of objective realities and the purpose of our dealings with such categories can be positive, but can never be exclusive or definitive. In the same way, our assertions about the goodness or badness of such actions, being general and objectivating, can be positive assertions, but they cannot be exhaustive or definitive. We can define them materially, but not formally. In other words, the nature of an action concerned with categorized objects, of an *opus operatum*, may have been rightly grasped, but may still have an aspect which has escaped us, and the act may have a purpose which we have not grasped. This means that there are external acts of which on principle we cannot say that they are always and under all circumstances formally good or bad, morally speaking. It can only be said that they are materially so. And this means again that the act once done has an aspect materially good or bad which it does not lose even if it must be regarded as possibly objectively ambivalent, morally speaking, on account of other possible purposes in it.

According to the subjective intention, an act may be called objectively and formally good or bad, and not merely subjectively and formally so, though this does not eliminate the material finality of the act, which may be to the contrary. Hence, for instance, unjustifiable homicide is objectively and formally always murder. But homicide in legitimate self-defence has an objectively ambivalent moral finality, one which formally justifies the act and one which is materially bad, not formally but nonetheless objectively intended. Hence that murder is always formally bad is not due to the objective external act of homicide, but to the inward attitude, which is necessarily bad because by virtue of its presuppositions it is unjust. We must distinguish further the materially indifferent acts which in the concrete are objectively – and not merely subjectively – good or bad. This depends on the end which they are made to serve by the actual intention of the doer.

C. Relationship to Transcendental Perfectibility: Hope

1. If an act is to be a moral one, it must appear as good or bad for me. The recognition that an act, the good in itself, is suitable or unsuitable on the level of personal action and reaction does not at once mean that it is recognized as what ought to be done. Its obligatory character ensues only from the recognition that the act seen as good or bad is beneficent or pernicious for the doer or for others and hence that the doer must account for it to himself or others. He sees that the act ought to be done and that he is thereby responsible. Responsible action is, in fact, deliberately rational action. But deliberately rational action is only possible when one refers oneself to an acknowledged goal which is meaningful in itself and hence is an end in itself. Deliberately purposeful action is not necessarily responsible action because one could aim at arbitrary goals. The deliberate choice of an arbitrary end is, however, not only pointless, but irrational and absurd, since conscious intention is always directed to the fully self-comprehensive and self-justifying. Hence if the deliberate choice of a goal is to be rational, the goal must be grasped as something of itself desirable to the doer. The goal must be its own sufficient reason and the pursuit of it must be appropriate to the seeker.

It follows that man can only have responsibility with regard to the order of things which are amenable to the categories insofar as these things, with their physical laws which man cannot abrogate, are brought into the sphere of inter-personal relationships by the personal action of man. The realities of categorized experience have of themselves only the function of means to the self-realization of man. They cannot ordain themselves to an end, but must be given a direction by man to help him fulfil himself, since otherwise they would be pointless. If they are given arbitrary goals by man, a potential sinner by reason of his limitation, they are pointless insofar as they are referred to no rational end, but they are not absurd, since they retain their own proper meaning, which is to serve the self-realization of man. But man has responsibility with regard to selfhood consciously grasped, since this "subjectivity" is always meaningful of itself. Further, he must have grasped in the concrete the rationality or otherwise of the act with regard to himself or others, whereby he also recognizes its obligatory character.

It follows that there is a transcendental necessity that "subjectivity" should always strive for self-fulfilment. By definition, the realization of the subject is always self-realization. And hence deliberate self-realization is self-realization in responsibility to oneself. Thus even selfless love is only possible when it is seen as meaningful for the man himself and tending to perfect him. Indeed, he could only commit suicide with the intention of finding therein a self-fulfilment corresponding to his circumstances.

The ultimate reason for this is that all our potentiality can only be actuated by what is actual on at least as high a level, and ultimately by the activation imparted by God which alone makes our self-realization possible. Thus our productive activity consists in grasping the offered potentialities and not in primordially creative achievements. The only possibility is that bestowed on us, and our originality comes into play only in each attitude which we take up to the ever-changing possibilities. Thus it is that man is radically an individual and a social being, a creature who can only say "I" insofar as he can say "You" and ultimately "my God", original only in his unique self-realization in the historical process.

Hence self-realization can only mean the right ordering of life in dependence on others. This becomes moral purpose only when the action involved is seen to correspond to the meaning of life in general and when it is recognized as something that ought to be done. This is the case when persons and their attitudes to persons and categorized reality are referred to persons. But we know our subjectivity in an interplay of persons ("inter-subjectivity") which is channelled by objectivations whose transparency is limited because temporal-spatial. Thus we know our subjectivity and our inter-subjective dependence only by distinguishing it from objectivated past, present and future and at the same time referring it to the changing realities of such objectivation. But since moral action is always that of the subject, it can only exist insofar as the doer, in his objective action, can take an attitude towards subjectivity – which, by the nature of things, cannot be fully at one's disposition but which can dispose of the objective reality. Hence every moral act has a unique aspect, since every objective situation to be confronted is unique by reason of the persons involved, and every action stems from the uniqueness of the subject.

This means that man can only give an account of his action where his subjective attitude, mediated by objective reality, is referred to subjectivity. Responsibility can only exist where man has grasped the purpose of his own or others' subjectivity and the relationship of his own action to this end.

If man is to grasp and aim at such a goal, his future must appear meaningful in a certain manner, and his answer likewise. This presupposes transcendental hope of a meaningful and hence "salutary" future. Man must expect something from the future and so welcome it, while also recognizing that he can make this future his own by a certain personal attitude. If he freely affirms and accepts this ordination to salvation, he has the virtue of hope. This is the prerequisite of free, selfless and hence virtuous love, since man can only give himself insofar as he has become master of himself and accepted himself.

If he rejects the future as allotted to him and tries to give it an arbitrary meaning, he acts irresponsibly. His action does not correspond to the meaning of subjectivity and inter-subjectivity, which is known and demands acknowledgment. It corresponds to his own wilfulness and hence is irrational.

2. Insofar as one is responsible to oneself, we speak of autonomy, while where responsibility exists with regard to others, we speak of heteronomy. But since man is responsible both to himself and others, he is at once autonomous and heteronomous, though under different aspects.

Man is autonomous insofar as he must render an account to himself, to show that his subjective action corresponds to the acknowledged end of his subjectivity. The reason for this sense of being responsible to himself is that his free and deliberate action on his instinctive desires is such that they are no longer determined as such by causes independent of him, but become expressions and fulfilments of his self-understanding and autonomy. The sense of responsibility to self also arises from the fact that man's moral action is decided on the basis of his existing past and his links with the present, in view of a future which he sees as significant for his own well-being. Being thus original and goal of his action, he is responsible towards himself.

Man is heteronomous insofar as he must render an account to his neighbour and to God, to show that his subjective action corresponds to his subjectivity. Referring his actions to others, he discloses – within the range of his moral responsibility – the effects on the well-being and personal development of those involved and hence on his own salvation, which he can only hope for in reasonable accord with others. He is therefore heteronomous by reason of his dependence on others, since his self-realization demands that the proper laws of other beings be respected where he is dependent on them.

The human act is always part of the unique historical process. Hence the necessity of being able to take moral decisions in the light of conscience, which is legitimated by the love of truth as such and the resulting ordination of the judgment to the good. For in the verdict of conscience the act is judged, in the light of the good as such, subjectively, that is, as it is for the doer in its uniqueness. Thus in the measure in which truth is loved, knowledge is ordained to the good as such and the act to rational self-realization. This does not mean that objective error is excluded or deprived of its objectively evil effects, but it must first be regarded as the expression (though an inadequate one) of a good and loving attitude and a true and purposeful self-realization. The possibility of error always remains. This does not mean that the value of conscience is diminished (Vatican II, Pastoral Constitution on the Church in the Modern World, art. 16) because its ordination to the true, meaningful and good in itself remains.

If, however, the error in conscience is due to culpable lack of ordination to the truth, and hence to culpable lack of love of truth on the part of the agent, self-realization is striven for in a disordered and irresponsible way. Man's disordered love has failed to actualize the love of truth which he knew to be due and proper. The error was willed in the cause.

When man responds to his necessary ordination to truth and consciously refers himself to the truth, he orientates himself to the good as such, and consequently grasps, as the meaning of his existence, that it is his task to adapt his actions and his whole life to the claims of futurity. This is done by taking a responsible attitude to one's acknowledged duty with regard to self-realization in dependence on others. Hence, objectively, there is a morally responsible action in the strict sense when one takes a definitive subjective attitude, a morally responsible action in the broad sense when this subjective attitude is provisional. The first case is concerned objectively with a righteous deed – or grave sin – or an act which changes substantially one's own personal condition or intersubjective relationships (as in sin or repentance). In the second case we have an act which causes only a partial change in subjective or inter-subjective relationships, that is, under certain aspects, but without affecting them radically.

Subjectively, there is a moral act in the strict or in the broad sense, according to whether one uses a fundamental sketch-plan or merely a partial one to implement or alter one's subjectivity – and hence inter-subjectivity. We have a fundamental plan when one decides about one's subjective final end in connection with one's inter-subjective dependence. Thus fully moral action is only possible where one has grasped subjectivity or inter-subjectivity and their goals so well that one can take up a definitive attitude to them. This does not of course exclude the possibility of future objective conversion or perversion. We have a partial plan, when one decides about a particular act in relation to an existing fundamental plan; or again, when the definitive relationship to one's own subjectivity (or to inter-subjectivity) is fixated by emotional urges, but individual aspects of subjectivity or inter-subjectivity are well enough grasped to make a responsible attitude to them possible.

D. Relationship to Transcendental Perfection: Love

1. The human act by which man aims at salvation ordains man to perfection, since perfection ordains him to the fullness of reality. But if man is to realize himself as this fullness demands, the moral act must be free. Only where it is possible to take up an attitude freely is it possible to free oneself from the slavery of the various urges which one finds within oneself and which of themselves demand immediate satisfaction without regard to the total perfection of the person. With the help of reason, we can hold ourselves aloof from the fascination of these individual urges, and so liberate ourselves from their claim to satisfaction. This is done by refusing to act and then deciding on the basis of considered motives. Hence our freedom lies radically in our reason. This freedom makes it positively possible to ordain individual urges to the needs of subjectivity and inter-subjectivity insofar as we know them. Thus we are free to make them serve love or sin.

As the freedom to serve love and hence perfection, moral freedom is essentially a dynamic entity and never a static achievement. It ordains autonomy to heteronomy and hence knows no limits, but bursts out of the limits set by immanent necessities and external coercion, giving access to an existence which is all the more human, the more fully it is realized. For thus man strives more and more strongly for self-realization, not as simple identity with himself, but as acceptance of inter-subjective and objective dependence, and hence in accordance with the fullness of reality.

In sin, however, man refuses to accept himself as he is and hence says No to the full reality. He seeks his perfection only in identity with himself – where it is not to be found. He undertakes an effort which is foredoomed to failure, since he tries to transcend his contingence by claiming to be absolute.

What is the condition of possibility for such sin, which erects itself arrogantly into an absolute? It is a sufficient knowledge of the truth that man is a value in himself, that the dignity of the person is inviolable, claiming and meriting our reverence and loving protection and aid. We cannot dispose of its destiny arbitrarily. Thus we are fully morally responsible only to the extent in which we are capable of recognizing the inalienable rights of man as such.

Hence moral freedom imposes no external limitations on psychological freedom. It merely excludes misuse of this freedom, by giving a validity to the structures of transcendental freedom and so enabling this freedom to develop dynamically, it being its own end, since it is the transcendental presupposition for the fulfilment of love.

2. Man makes his individual urges serve love by orientating them as well as he knows how to, to the perfecting of his own subjectivity. This he does by directing this subjectivity to the affirmation and promotion of existing inter-subjective relationships within the framework of justifiable subjective interests. This means promoting subjective, interests insofar as they are compatible with inter-subjective claims.

It follows that the various virtues are virtuous insofar as they ordain certain modes of personal conduct to love.

Obedience is virtuous insofar as it submits one's own will, as love demands, to that of another who has authority over one. In this sense, love may be termed the form of all virtues. Sins, on the other hand, are sinful insofar as they are offences against love. For the distinction between theological, cardinal and other virtues, see the article *Virtue*.

The good as such, to which man is ordained by love for the truth, is inexhaustible, because the objective possibilities of man's perfection are of themselves unlimited, on account of his being ordained to being as such. But the concrete possibilities of perfection and hence of moral decision are limited, on account of the limited nature of man. Hence responsible action must always be directed in accordance with these concrete possibilities, while maintaining the mental orientation to the absolute possibilities, through love of the true and the good as such. Thus moral action continually opens up new and unforeseen possibilities of perfection, which ultimately are bestowed on man as the gratuitous gift of God.

E. Summary

The human moral act opens up to man the possibility of subjective personal fulfilment. This man achieves by turning to God and his neighbour as he makes his external works serve the subjective and inter-subjective perfection of those whom his acts affect – by their performance or omission. Here we must remember that when he turns to God in love, he can only "perfect" him *ad extra*, which is the way in which man himself attains his own supreme perfection.

Hence the human act is at once egocentric and altruistic, and formally good insofar as the transcendentally necessary self-affirmation is transcended in free outgoing ("ek-static") love for the persons affected by the act. The human act is formally bad when the necessary self-affirmation of free self-transcendence is made an absolute, so that man himself, his neighbour and God are only affirmed insofar as they are made to serve a self-realization which is arbitrary because in contradiction to reality.

In this formal structure, the moral act, *qua* immanent, is infallible in its commands, permissions and prohibitions, because here it necessarily takes a free, responsible attitude to consciousness, the claim of the person and perfection. The transcendent act arising from this moral stand has its formally moral quality from the intention of the doer. He can contradict its objective and material quality because of the human possibility of error in judging the laws of categorized reality, which man can bend freely to his service in an irrational way, precisely because he is finite and contingent. The human act, through its transcendental orientation, is capable of being informed by grace.

F. The Theology of the Human Act

To describe the human act theologically, we must start from its relationship to union with God in grace in the vision of God, to which all men are called according to the universal salvific will of God. This means that an act is human or moral insofar as it is proportioned to salvation.

Theologically speaking, therefore, deliberate, responsible and free acts which are not informed by grace can only be called moral in an indirect sense, since they provide at most an indirect disposition (*dispositio negativa*) with regard to grace and hence with regard to salvation. The question of the existence of such merely natural moral acts is generally answered in the affirmative by theologians. This is because they feel bound to maintain the distinction between the natural and the supernatural order, and particularly, the distinction between faith in the broad sense (*fides late dicta*) and the acts preparatory to faith (*initium fidei*). But this answer need not be taken as final, since the assertion that there are moral acts which have no significance for salvation is not without its problems from the standpoint of a theological anthropology.

Hence the starting-point of the theological determination of the moral act will be that the degree of the information of the act by a sufficient grace determines its positive morality, while its relationship to the supernatural virtues of faith, hope and love determines its inner structure. Thus a moral act in the broad sense will be one which makes possible a positive disposition to justification, or a modification of some particular relationship to salvation in the justified. A moral act in the full sense will be one which makes justification possible or can essentially alter the relationship of the justified to salvation.

The attentive consciousness required for the moral act begins with the possibility of the *initium fidei*, and attains the maturity required for a fully moral act when the faith required for justification is possible. Such requisite moral consciousness is present insofar as salvation is expected from God's turning to man in grace, insofar as the response to God's will to grace is recognized as an absolute "must", and hence insofar as man becomes capable of hope. Finally, the requisite moral freedom is there to the extent to which man is capable of supernatural love.

Here it should be noted that this ordination to the supernatural end need not necessarily be consciously articulate. It may be there merely implicitly, without being reflected upon – though it can be actually accomplished by "atheists".

The moral act implies an attitude to the order of creation in its incarnational and historical process of salvation. Thus it has an ecclesial structure corresponding to authority in the Church. Man's natural power of moral action is brought to fulfilment in a supernatural and hence incarnational way. Hence the moral act presupposes and implies this natural power.

Theologically speaking, therefore, the good moral act is always a matter of the reasonable obedience of faith, conscious of its radical obligation to the God who imparts himself in grace and comes to us in the incarnation, and responding in the love of God which embraces men as brothers and is thereby full of hope of salvation. A morally bad act is always a type of unbelief, rejecting in arrogant self-assertion God's offer of grace and hence the comradeship of mankind and so placing itself in a situation of menace and disaster.

Waldemar Molinski

HUMANISM

I. General

1. *History of humanism.* Humanism as the deliberate effort to justify the Renaissance arose in the 14th and 15th centuries as an intellectual movement among the nobility, especially the merchant aristocracy of the Italian city-states. Within the traditional framework of the medieval order, this new social class did not regard itself as bound to any existing pattern of life and could therefore develop its courtly patrician style of life into an original and autonomous mode of vigorous intellectual existence (alongside the scholastic culture of the clergy and the chivalric culture of the court). This mode of life (connected with the medieval tradition of the *artes liberales*) was based on a scholarly, religiously neutral and hence unprejudiced contact with the culture of antiquity, in a form untouched by Scholasticism. It regarded itself and its ideal of the *uomo divino* as a revival of the classical *humanitas*. Petrarch, the real founder of humanism, appealed to Cicero and his efforts to "humanize" the Roman *virtutes* by means of Greek music, mathematics, and especially literature, which was regarded as the model in both form and content, and thus produce the virtues of philanthropy, tolerance, and wisdom.

This direct aestheticizing embodiment of the classical spirit (differing to this extent from the medieval classical revivals, which had been much more strongly influenced by Christianity) dominated the private culture of the aristocratic and episcopal courts, even north of the Alps. It gained entry to the Papal court under Popes Nicholas V, Pius II, Sixtus IV, Julius II, and Leo X. An appreciable stimulus was given to humanism by the confrontation of the Western intellectual world with the original texts of Greek philosophy, to which it was introduced by Greek scholars at the Union Council of Ferrara-Florence (1438), and above all after the fall of Constantinople (1453); this encounter resulted in the revival of every variety of classical philosophy (of special importance was the Platonic Academy of Florence – Giovanni della Mirandola and Marsilio Ficino) and thus introduced the new intellectual attitude into the universities.

By the time of Erasmus of Rotterdam, humanism finally dominated the cultured world of Europe. It had ceased to be simply the cultured view of life of a new social stratum and was now a far-reaching scholarly movement. This movement not only led to a considerable intensification of linguistic and literary education in the *studia humanitatis* but also opened the way to a fresh start in many other fields (natural philosophy, historical research, political theory and practice.

Above all, abandoning the scholastic synthesis of Christianity and philosophy and relegating this synthesis to the status of a "middle age" in the essentially continuous history of thought from ancient to modern times (a threefold scheme which first appears in Flavio Biondi), humanism posed afresh the problem of reconciling the autonomous culture of classical paganism with the Christian culture based on revelation. In this connection not only Plotinian and Cabbalist mysticism (in the Florentine Platonists) but also the ancient Church Fathers down to Augustine acquired new relevance; in Petrarch, for example, who based his mediating formula, *Christus est Deus noster, Cicero autem princeps nostri eloquii*, on Augustine; even more so in Erasmus's efforts in the direction of a *philosophia Christi*. This effort to link up with Plato, the Stoa and Cicero, which had already been made by Origen, was intended not to provide a system but to point to a certain means of self-education as the divinely-willed preparation. By reaching back behind Scholasticism to the sources of faith (the efforts to provide exact original texts of the Bible were typical) humanism paved the way for the Reformation and also demonstrated the ambivalent relationship between itself and the religious approach. The absolute religious confidence of the Reformers, based upon a sense of being laid hold of by God's Word and not upon a linguistic, aesthetic interest in the Bible, is in the sharpest contrast with the humanist basis in a scholarship of an aesthetic trend, and with a correspondingly conciliatory diplomatic view of religion (cf. Luther's controversy with Erasmus). As an independent movement, humanism ended with the Reformation. The controversy between the new confessions left no room for any neutral ground of esoteric neo-classical intellectual culture. Although the rival parties adopted certain humanistic principles and educational methods (cf. Calvin's Stoic humanism as "handmaid" of the new theology, Melanchthon's humanistic Aristotelianism as framework for Lutheran dogmatics, and, on the other side, the use made of humanist education in the baroque scholasticism of the Jesuits), these hardly constituted any longer an independent form of intellectual life.

2. *Enlightenment and neo-humanism.* Following developments which may be termed humanist in a broader sense – the *humanisme dévot* (an anti-Jansenist

movement in France) and French classicism – the philosophical and theological problem of humanism, how to reconcile autonomous self-understanding with the understanding imposed on man by revelation, was raised anew in the Enlightenment. But now the criterion was "reason" rather than the ideal of ancient *humanitas*. At times the Enlightenment did no more than merely rationalize theology in favour of or in opposition to religion. But as early as Lessing, and still more in Kant and the transition to German idealism, it made a considerable contribution to the problem by its study of the human spirit in action, of the "practical reason" as the sphere of religion and the judge of its truth, i.e., of its compatibility with responsible self-understanding. It was, however, in the aesthetic theory and the philosophy of history characteristic of German classicism and romanticism that humanism, in reaction against the rationalism of the Enlightenment, experienced a conscious renaissance in the late 18th and early 19th century (in Winckelmann, Herder, Schiller, Goethe and F. Schlegel). This neo-humanism, with its wholly new understanding for Greek culture, took as its ideal the blending of all the manifold riches of the human individuality into a harmonious work of art in which artist, creative process and product are one. In contrast to the one-sidedness of rationalism, the "humanity" of the Greeks became the norm. With W. v. Humboldt and others (e.g., F. J. Niethammer, who in 1808 coined the term "humanism"), this educational ideal (in opposition to the utilitarian education in the non-classical secondary schools of the Enlightenment which was designed to produce functionaries for society) became influential in secondary schools and so spread widely (but very thinly) a humanist outlook among the middle classes down into the 20th century.

In the form known as the "third humanism", there was a further flowering of the West's enthusiasm for classical antiquity during the period between the World Wars (W. Jaeger, K. Kerényi).

3. *Marxist humanism*. To some extent related to this neo-humanistic self-understanding, a philosophy of history developed among the radical Hegelians which, without reference to classical *humanitas*, regarded itself as humanism in virtue of its hope in man's complete realization of all given possibilities (the thorough penetration of matter by the spirit being seen as the medium of man's self-realization).

This new movement acquired the form in which it remains influential to this day following its fusion with political economy in the work of Karl Marx. According to Marx and modern Marxism (chiefly represented outside the Soviet Communist area by R. Garaudy and E. Bloch), man is his own creator in the sense that all objective reality (including man's own reality) is simply the product of his own labour. (This production is achieved through the division of labour; in pre-communist forms of society it is taken away from the creating agent and thus alienated.) This state of affairs determines the task: namely, so to remove this "dehumanizing" alienation (of the subject from the objective world and so of men from each other) that each may find in social relationships the adequate medium for the mutual affirmation of all men (who acquire in this way their *raison d'être*). Humanism thereby becomes the successful implementation of "the ways of life through which the inward can become outward and the outward the inward" (Bloch); or, in concrete terms, humanism becomes social policy which, by purposeful planning of production, prepares the soil for the ideal of the person at one with himself and in harmony with others – the "total" man.

This classical Marxism is at present experiencing a further development in the "second Enlightenment", as represented for example in T. W. Adorno and M. Horkheimer. Their humanism rejects as inhuman the elaboration of any positive social goals at all, on the ground that man never adequately projects the truth about himself in such abstract ideals but simply the distorted counterpart of his own alienated situation. The really humanizing achievement is a persistently negative criticism, which will use all the tools of modern sociology in an incisive demonstration of the symptoms of self-alienation in society. (This important development is often echoed among a wider public in such groups as the Humanist Association and in sociological currents which, by their "militant humanism", convert the methodical principle of critical de-ideologization into a new ideology.)

4. *Existentialist humanism.* In part closely related to this neo-Marxist theory and in part as a reaction against it, "existence" philosophy also regards itself as humanism. Sartre, for example, dissociates man's freedom (as responsibility for himself) from any sort of belief in pre-existent norms and makes it wholly dependent upon itself. It is to produce its own concrete expression in freedom and as freedom, in the resolve which recognizes its absolute responsibility to all in face of a given decision. From this initially purely formal principle of a heroic, tragic humanism, Sartre develops formal and material criteria for testing the authenticity of the exercise of freedom. He finds in these criteria the way from complete arbitrariness in the content of self-creation to Marxism as the only possibility of genuine self-fulfilment of freedom in the present situation. Heidegger ("Brief über den Humanismus") discusses this concept in terms of the being of selfhood. And here the strict logic of the absolute freedom of the individual culminates in the absorption of subjective existence into the self-realization of the truly authentic self of being. The I, at the most radical moment of its "ek-sistence", that is, at its greatest openness for being as pure "it-self", is now the scene of the apparition of the being which is absolutely prior to all metaphysical disjunction between being and essence. In the light of "humanum" in this sense, where it is the realm of the event of being – situated, according to the later Heidegger, less in the vital resolve than in language, the purest revelation of being – true humanism is allowing oneself to be opend up to the "thereness" of "being", to the "realm of the coming of the wholly sound".

5. *Christian humanism.* To basically non-Christian varieties of philosophical humanism, other variants could be added, from the positivist religion of Comte to the medico-biological "evolutionary humanism" of the Ciba Foundation. Indeed, they could be increased, also almost at will, since every new standpoint taken up in the present discussion of practical philosophy claims to be a form of humanism because of the general terms of the dialogue. Christianity could never be uncritical in their regard, because it regards the truth of human existence as the eschatological transformation of man by God which surpasses even the greatest possibilities of man's self-realization within history. (In this sense, humanism in the Christian view is also, in the words of Karl Barth, the humanity of God, namely the kindness whose free gifts alone enable man to be really himself.) But Christianity could not remain neutral and indifferent to non-Christian humanism, for Christianity does not see itself as an extrinsic alien imposition upon man but rather as God's summons to man which is mediated through, and begins its transformative work at the very point where the hearer of the call is most authentically and responsibly himself, and hence "human" in the highest sense. Hence in striving for a Christian humanism, in face of the present state of the problem and aware of the ambivalence of its task, Christian thought is following a law of

its own being as the incarnation of salvation. It is also following a tradition which reaches back to Erasmus (explicitly) and (in substance) to the early Christian apologists and the medieval syntheses, and goes on, down to J. H. Newman in the English-speaking world, E. Przywara, T. Haecker and H. U. v. Balthasar in the German-speaking world, and J. Maritain, H. de Lubac and Y. Congar in the French-speaking world. In this sense, Christian philosophy (G. Marcel) as well as Catholic (K. Rahner) and Protestant (R. Bultmann) theology accept the humanism of the philosophy of existence which affirms that *humanitas* (and therefore the place of revelation) is realized not in the fact as such (i.e., in particular social orders) but in the act, i.e., in the resolve in which freedom is both realized and exteriorizes itself in the fact; in the (unobjectifiable) proper being of the self.

Christian theologians have also entered into discussion with Marxist humanism, not only as individuals, but on a wider scale (as in the "Paulus-Gesellschaft"). Like Moltmann in discussion with Bloch or Teilhard de Chardin in the field of natural philosophy, they have attempted very far-reaching syntheses of Christian eschatology with the Marxist hope of a salvation within history. They have sought for a synthesis of sacred history with an evolution aiming at universal integration.

To remain at the height which discussion has now reached, Christian humanism must undoubtedly use the various types of humanism which consider themselves atheist to correct one another. This means that it must clearly face the truth that the inability of man to achieve his humanity (and hence his openness for God) except in dialogal confrontation with others and in an integrated society poses an inexorable dilemma. For man has no other medium of interpersonal harmony than social reality, since freedom never exists purely as such, but can only be concrete and communicated through its objects. And this is why the humanism of the social utopia has a certain claim to be considered. But then again, man can never sublimate this social reality into unmistakable fact. There will never be a successful "communion of saints". And this is why the consistent reduction of the significance of the factual to the intention behind it has a certain justification. On the basis of this insight a Christian humanism – at one in this respect with the "second Enlightenment" and with Sartre as possibly the most honest presentation of the human predicament – must accept this dialectical oscillation between a positive mediating reality (which, if it is turned into an independent fact, is distorted into an ideology and actually hinders understanding) and a critical rejection of that reality (which, as mere negation can, of course, exist only in virtue of the positive). On the other hand, by accepting such criticism of the real (of the supreme attempt of humanity to secure its own salvation for itself dialectically), Christian humanism, being *Christian* humanism, will not fall into the absurdity of an endlessly open dialectical future. On the contrary, in the light of the cross, it is precisely this unending, impotent process of self-sanctification in a society in search of its *humanitas* which is seen to be an initial stage of the absolute judgment upon history and its illusory efforts to end man's self-alienation. The negative criticism (made very real by the very course of history) is interpreted by Christians as an element in an absolute judgment, which assesses particular forms of alienation as expressions of an alienated condition impossible to end within history and thereby, in principle, relativizes every form of humanism. And hence, the future appears as the hope of an absolute infinity in which the ambivalence of inter-objectivity and the fragility of inter-subjectivity therein revealed are finally removed (and it would be ideological naivety to expect this in human history itself). Christian humanism looks to a personal mediator in whom the reality of love between persons is definitely presented in an adequate social reality (bodiliness) and imparted as universal integration.

This salvation, the transformation of man himself, is the absolutely transcendent goal of our continuously self-judging history, and as such is certainly not purely other-worldly. On the contrary, despite the utter impossibility of expressing it concretely in any particular system or in any utopian programme for the future, it provides a point of reference for present action in the actual world; it is the real partner already present in the dialogue between each particular present and its future. Its presence makes it possible for the *humanum* to come about as it patterns itself (in faith, in the hope against all hope, and in love, in spite of all disappointment and tragedy) on the true *humanitas* of God.

Konrad Hecker

HUMILITY

1. *The term.* The English word "humility" derives from Latin *humilis*, "lowly" ("near the ground", *humus* = earth). In the OT (LXX: ταπεινός) the dominant note is the elemental human experience of not having given ourselves existence, and therefore of not being necessary, which thrusts itself upon man in the pointlessness of life (cf. the sapiential books), in guilt, sickness, and death.

2. *Scripture.* a) *Old Testament.* Since Yahweh, the Creator God, has given man existence and keeps him in being, since Yahweh also rules the history of the Jewish nation and of the individual, and imbues the history of his chosen people, of each individual and all mankind, with meaning as the giver and the gift of eschatological salvation, humility is the only fitting attitude before him. Thus humility is one of the basic characteristics of the pious in the OT; cf. Num 12:3: "Now the man Moses was very meek, more than all men that were on the face of the earth." The prophets call again and again for humility towards Yahweh lest his wrath be kindled against Israel (Amos 6:8; Jer 13:16; Is 49:13; 61:1f.; Mich 6:8). The bearer of eschatological salvation is pictured as a humble figure: "Lo, your king comes to you, triumphant and victorious is he, humble and riding on an ass" (Zech 9:9). Since here, as with Moses, humility is demanded even of those who share God's authority, the NT notion of humility is already signalled. The Psalms too abound with the assurance that Yahweh upholds the humble (Ps 25:9; 131; 149:4). In the sapiential books humility chiefly means fitting into Yahweh's cosmic order (Job 22:29; Prov 3:34; 11:2; 18:22; Ecclus 3:17ff.; 3:20; 19:26), so that humility also means forming a just estimate of oneself: "My son, glorify yourself with humility, and ascribe to yourself honour according to your worth" (Ecclus 10:28).

b) *New Testament.* Faced with the dawning kingdom of God and God's free condescension to him, man can only be humble as a child (Mk 10:15 par.) if he would be justified (Mk 12:38 par.; Lk 1:48; 14:11); and no man has any more merit than another unless it be the merit of greater humility (Lk 18:9–14). Jesus himself shows the right attitude: just as he, the envoy of the Father, humbly does the Father's will, so men must be humble before the Lordship of God which came with him: "Learn from me, for I am gentle and lowly in heart" (Mt 11:29), "For I have given you an example, that you also should do as I have done to you. Truly, truly, I say to you, a servant is not greater than his master; nor is he who is sent greater than he who sent him" (Jn 13:15–16). Decisively new here – though hinted at, undoubtedly, in the prophets' message about God's unfailing concern in Hosee and Ezek 16 – is that God himself showed himself humble in Jesus Christ. This gnosis is the reason why Christians must strive for the same attitude towards each other (Phil 2:5–11). Humility, which is intimately bound up with love (1 Cor 10:24; 13:4), must become a basic attitude towards the brethren (Rom 12:9f.).

3. *Theology*. Christian doctrine on humility grew out of constant struggle with the contempt for humility which prevailed in the ancient world (doubtless to be accounted for by social conditions). St. Augustine's profound definition, based on the sinfulness of man, "Tu homo cognosce quia homo es. Tota humilitas tua ut cognoscas te" ("Human, know that you are human. Your whole humility is to know yourself") (*Tract. in Joh.*, 25:16), exposes the shallowness of the ancient idea of humility. St. Thomas tried to link up humility with Aristotle's doctrine on magnanimity (*Summa Theologica*, II-II, q. 129, a. 3 ad 4). And in fact, Christian humility should be defined not in terms of lowliness but of selflessness. Christ is the supreme and inimitable model of humility in the inimitable greatness of his *magnanimitas* ("greater love has no man . . ."). Since all human virtues can become vehicles of self-assertive pride as well as of self-emptying love, humility is the peculiarly Christian virtue. This does not exclude the truth that charity is the *forma omnium virtutum*, since it merely declares that humility is the distinctively "Christian aspect" of charity. This is already suggested by the contrast between *eros* as the love which strives upwards and *agape* as the love which humbly condescends. The attitude of the ancient world to humility was passed on to the modern world (cf. Nietzsche) chiefly by means of the Renaissance. Man's growing power to master and manipulate his destiny and the pressing need to do so in this age of technology, nourish a cast of mind which gravely obscures the values of humility. But they could also pave the way to a comprehensive humility of a Christian inspiration, since man also experiences more clearly his limitations and his perilously exposed state.

Alvaro Huerga

HYLEMORPHISM

1. Hylemorphism is strictly characteristic of Aristotelian scholastic philosophy. It is an effort to explain the nature of inner-worldly things. All bodies are essentially composed of matter (ὕλη) and form (μορφή) which in the concrete thing combine to make a unified whole. Hence hylemorphism is opposed to the various forms of atomism and dynamic monism which ultimately assume one single essential basis of beings. It is also opposed to a dualism which would suppose in living beings, and especially in man, two entities united to each other by mutual causality but nonetheless independent substances.

2. Hylemorphism is a fundamental element in Aristotle's theory of being and is a direct consequence of his doctrine of act and potency. Aristotle arrives at this duality-in-unity of things on the basis of ordinary observation. Changes can be seen to take place. In the realm of art, for instance, a statue is formed out of a block of marble, and in the realm of nature water becomes vapour. Since such changes are not completely new creations and not annihilations – notions which would be hard to imagine, since there is always something to start with and something always remains – all changes of a thing must be based on a common substratum which remains throughout. This *materia prima* is itself completely undetermined but is determined as this or that through the form which it receives and the cause which produces the form. – Aristotle comes to a similar result from reflection on the judgment: something is always predicated of something. And once

more, all assertions suppose an ultimate substratum which is completely indeterminate, of itself pure indetermination but in potency to all possible determinations (forms).

Medieval Scholasticism adopted this view and developed it systematically. The accent, however, was displaced from the perspective of Aristotle, which was naive in the best sense of the word, to metaphysical discussions and speculation. But since even in Aristotle the notion of matter and hence the definition of the form was not quite clear, differences of opinion soon arose. Grave difficulties appeared above all when living things were considered and the question of the soul and entelechy arose. While Thomas Aquinas and the Thomists adhered strictly to the pure indeterminateness and potentiality of matter, Scotus and then Suarez allowed matter a certain actuality, which needed, of course, further determinations. Hence Aquinas maintained the unicity of the form from which all actuality and essential determinations flowed, while the others admitted a multiplicity of essential forms in living things.

In the Kantian and post-Kantian philosophy of the subject hylemorphism was not explicitly considered. It was not till the present century that renewed efforts were made to understand it, when dialectical materialism and the theory of evolution brought up the problem of matter and consciousness in all its acuteness. Mention should be made here of the view of Teilhard de Chardin that every "corpuscle" has two aspects, that of complexity externally ("matter") and the inward aspect of centering ("consciousness"), the inward aspect, which corresponds to some extent with the classical "form", "ascending" constantly in the course of evolution.

In theology, hylemorphism was invoked from the 12th century on to explain theological data, since medieval theology was strongly influenced by scholastic philosophy and found it applicable to the Eucharist, grace, the body–soul relationship, and so on. In sacramental theology in general, the sign was analyzed strictly in terms of hylemorphism: the material element (water, bread, oil) and the ritual gesture were considered the "matter", which was only constituted as a full sacramental sign by the "form" of the words, which determined the matter and gave it its meaning.

3. The history-centred thinking of modern times finds considerable difficulty in the way of a sympathetic understanding of hylemorphism, which is undoubtedly a somewhat static concept of reality. Not merely does the terminology appear hard to justify, but the Aristotelian concepts themselves, which have a certain justification in a limited field, seem to be transferred indiscriminately from one field to another. A distinction may be made between the matter and the form of a statue, but the application of these terms to other spheres only causes confusion: "matter" is not considered in a meta-physical sense but merely as an empirical datum ("ultimate substratum") which seems to exist in the same way as matter is understood to exist in ordinary conversation and in the sciences. Then too, the designation "form" seems to provide a world of degrees of being where each essence is neatly demarcated from all others. But this is a model of reality in which there is no place for evolution and a dynamic interweaving of things. But in spite of such justifiable criticism from modern philosophy the real concern of hylemorphism still has something to teach us. Underlying it is the question of the condition of the possibility of finite beings and of the finite spirit. Such beings, according to hylemorphism, are not "simple" but "mediated", at once active and passive. We can see most clearly what this being mediated means if we start from our own human action and production. We remark that there are always two aspects: the action is my

action but it necessarily affects others. This identity which involves non-identity at the same time is verified in all acts, even the most "inward". Man is forced back upon this outgoing, this self-estrangement, in order to be able to express himself as man, that is, in order to realize his essence.

Merely to turn in on himself would be the equivalent of emptiness, loss of selfhood. Thus it is of the essence of man to be referred to the other than himself and to be determined by it on the vegetative and biological plane as on the mental plane. His essence brings with it something which makes it possible for man to go out of himself and exteriorize himself in this way. But since in this expression of himself he is determined by others and causes himself to be determined by others, the principle in question can only be receptive or potential, that is, it must be material, the possibility of being-with-others. This material nature of man is expressed in his bodily and sensible structure which is the necessary precondition of his action. The predominant characteristic of the bodily sphere is its passivity, its capacity to receive and accept what comes "from without". However, man never surrenders himself totally to the other because he remains, after all, identical with his own action. He has given himself over to others, but always in such a way that he still is in possession of himself. For even the seemingly total receptivity of the sense is conscious, that is, even in his sensible acts man betakes himself back into himself. This is the aspect of recollection, of self-possession, where man is actively "with himself", spontaneous, self-determining. This principle is, as it were, the formal (i.e., form-giving) element which penetrates and stamps all action (thought, will, and work). The individual activities, which take man out of himself, are gathered to the centre of the conscious self-hood. Man is, indissolubly, both: receptivity to determination from outside and self-determination from within. Man as spirit mediates himself to himself by expressing himself in outward, perceptible action, in order to come to himself through (and only through) this self-alienation. "Matter" as man's being outside himself and "form" or spirit as his being within, aware of and in possession of himself, form a polar tension which cannot be reduced either to one extreme or the other. Both are equally primordial, since we never come upon ourselves except as body-soul. In spite of their being equally essential, there is a certain difference of rank: spirit as the determining element stamps matter as the determinable. Sensible knowledge, as self-mediation of the spirit, is always dependent on and formed by the consciousness. Nonetheless, it must not be forgotten that the receptivity of the senses demands a mediation of the human spirit through the material. For in this way consciousness, as constitutive principle of man, remains a human, finite consciousness, not purely creative and spontaneous, not pure self-transparency, but receptive spontaneity, a self-possession which is mediated by the non-self.

If these considerations, which arise immediately from our knowledge of human action, are applied analogously to other things, a certain parallel appears in the realm of living things. The determinative principle, the form, diminishes in range and function the lower we descend the scale, till it has entirely vanished in otherness in inorganic things. Self-possession is reduced to being merely different from other things, which are no longer fetched back into a self. Since these things are the objects of human action, they must also be hylemorphic in structure.

Herbert Scheit

I

IDEALISM

A. General Notions

In philosophy, idealism is the general term for the speculative position which may be described as follows:

1. When considering the similarities and diversities, the identities and the differences of which reality is composed, its intention is always directed to the universal, to what is common in the manifold individuals. It looks to the dominant factor which embraces the many and subsumes them into the whole of reality. It aims on each level at the single concept which will make the multiple comprehensible. It regards the universal as the permanent and essential in contrast to the transitory and contingent individual and hence assigns it priority in being as well as in knowledge.

2. On the analogy of bodily sight, it interprets this universal as *form* (*eidos, idea*), the immutable basic pattern which underlies its many manifestations, the permanent aspect disclosed to the spiritual gaze which looks beyond the sensible world. Thought is regarded primarily as pure vision, in contrast for instance to the biblical "hearing", and the concept is the fixed outline of the essence as it presents itself to the spiritual view. The insight thus immediately presented to thought in sensible experience renders it possible and necessary to link the objects of experience in mutual relationships. And the relationships discovered between the individual things serves once more in its turn to make the order of essences "evident".

3. The attitude is based on the speculative supposition that sight and insight, conceptual essence and spiritual vision, thought and form, are identical in act, because being itself, as spiritual being, is the "light" which illuminates both the form and the thought. Being diffuses and limits itself in the many "essences" which are the basic modes of existent reality: but in face of this reality, that is, in the ontological reflection which philosophy calls "spirit", being restores itself at once to its unity and illimitation. This still leaves open the question of the place where being and spirit hold sway in the supreme fullness of their identity, that is, to whom the form shows itself primarily as such, and who the thinker primarily is (the divine, the transcendent God, the thinking subject in the world and so on).

In this general sense, idealism is the basic form of Western metaphysics. When this philosophy asks about the being of beings, it looks – by virtue of the light of "being" or "reason" – beyond the existent being to its sufficient reason, and seeks above all to trace the essence of beings and establish the order of their essences as a whole. In this sense, idealism includes what is called "realism", insofar as realism considers the existent being as "res", that is, as the individual realization, in independent subsistence, of a universal entity. See St. Thomas Aquinas, 1 *Sent.*, 25, 1, 4c: "a quidditate sumiture hoc nomen res." This idealism also determines such reactions as conceptualism and nominalism, which put a radical cleavage between the order of being and the order of human thought, and treat the universal merely as a concept framed by finite thought, or as a generalizing name used to cope with the multiplicity of reality. But these systems remain tributary to idealism, because they still accord binding force, of a secondary order, to concept and name, which remain necessary for the ordering of human existence. The radical contrary to idealism is "materialism", whose dependence on the idealistic mode of thought may be seen in its attempts to understand itself and trace its own foundations, as in dialectical materialism. This denies that spiritual being is the real foundation of, and is prior in rank to, material reality. But by reversing the relationship, it retains the formal difference and the mediatory function of the ideal order. The basic forms of reality and its mutual relationships are no longer the ideal *a priori* aspects of a spiritual principle prior to and transcending the world, but the reflection of matter in human consciousness, as it attains self-awareness in the medium of human thought ("ideology"). This reflection remains more or less distorted till it is perfected in the dialectical-materialist truth.

B. Historical Survey

The history of idealism begins with the ontological idealism of Plato. For Plato, the changing sensible things in the world of perception (κόσμος αἰσθητός, the region of coming to be γένησις), which are only imperfect representations of their forms, do not really deserve the name of "beings". The real beings, in complete separation (χωρισμός) from these, are the forms themselves (idea = ὄντος ὄν; Platonic or extreme realism). The forms receive essence and reality from the supreme form of the good (the ἀγαθόν as εἶδος εἰδῶν) and form together the eternal intelligible world which is the true object of spiritual vision (κόσμος νοητός, the region of being, οὐσία). In the light of the good, and according to the model of the forms, the corporeal world was moulded from spatial chaos. Knowledge is only possible in the light of the good, and as a recall (ἀναμνήσις) of the pure forms originally present to the soul. Thus knowledge is a purgation (κάθαρσις) which frees the soul from the distraction and impediment of the senses and leads it to the pure contemplation where alone the soul can find its happiness. All action too is determined by this last end, especially in the social form of the State, which corresponds exactly in its hierarchical structure (ruler, guardians, workers) to that of the soul (reason, courage, desire) and must serve the common good by educating the citizens for happiness. This Platonic view of the State, which made it strictly subservient to an ideal order, became the foundation of the many Utopias of Western political philosophy.

The theological idealism of St. Augustine links up partly with neo-Platonism, partly with Stoicism, transforming both in the light of the Christian experience of God and revelation. It considers the forms as the eternal thoughts (*rationes aeternae*) of the transcendent God (the form of forms). As such, they are the source of all temporal things, and the reason why these are really knowable, in the light of the truth with which God enlightens man. (St. Thomas Aquinas combines this theological idealism with Aristotelian or moderate realism: the universal is prior to the thing, *ante rem*, as an exemplar in the mind of God; cf. **2** *Sent.*, 3, 3, 2 ad

1; *Summa Theologica*, I, 44, 3 c, in the thing, *in re*, as in the singularity of the existent being, consequent to the thing, *post rem*, as the conceptual universal which the human spirit attains by abstraction.) The forms (eternal thoughts) as a whole constitute the plan of creation and salvation, now understood as the provident provision made by God, who created the world and wills to lead men by his grace from the one beginning to the one end: to see God himself as the Truth, "face to face".

Modern philosophy is largely the secularization of Christian ideas about God and thinking about history. Psychological idealism separates radically the "world of consciousness" from the "real world" beyond consciousness, and treats the forms as innate (R. Descartes) or as acquired by experience (empirical idealism, J. Locke, D. Hume), but in any case, as subjective "representations". Questions can now be asked for the first time about the criteria of certainty. Epistemological idealism asks whether and in what conditions the idea corresponds correctly to the "external" object, and acosmic idealism can go so far as to deny the reality of the so-called "external world" (G. Berkeley). For the first time also, the philosophy of history can see the natural process of human thought and action as "storia delle idee umane" (G. B. Vico), with terms of reference different from the realization of the divine plan of salvation in history.

The transcendental or critical idealism of I. Kant "goes beyond" the world of consciousness of the empirical subject, but not to the ideal order either of an "external world" (of beings in themselves) prior to human consciousness, or of a "higher world" (of the thoughts of God) which surpasses the external. Kant goes back to the structure of the finite subjectivity of each human subject, to reach the pre-conscious subjective conditions of possibility of human thought and action. Knowledge does not attain existent beings as they are in themselves, by virtue of their essence or their form, but only as they are met with as objects, that is, in the unity given each by the categories – conditioned by the understanding – which determine them. When Kant speaks of the "idea" he means a non-objective totality, "the world", for instance, which cannot as such be the object of experience and hence cannot be theoretically known. It remains, however, a regulative idea, a principle of order, for the theoretical reason, and so a necessary condition of possibility for progress in intellectual knowledge. In the field of moral action, the ideas are "postulates" of the practical reason, which, to give meaning to morality, demands belief in freedom, immortality and God, as guarantees of the "highest good", the unity of perfected morality and merited happiness in the "kingdom of God". History consists of an unending progress to this "ideal" end.

Developing the movement launched by Kant, German idealism takes the subjectivity to be the infinite principle of unity, from which then proceed the empirical subject and object, the ideal and the real order, spirit and nature, thought and being. In the subjective idealism of J. G. Fichte, in the Ego, in a primordial "pre"-historical act, the Ego poses itself and the non-Ego, being or the world. This is the concrete, palpable sphere of duty, where moral action has to prove itself historically in freedom. In this conquest it returns to itself in act, once it has understood itself as that which it necessarily is, in intellectual self-contemplation, on the level of pure reflection.

The objective idealism of F. W. J. v. Schelling takes an absolutely undifferentiated subject and object as the source from which proceed freedom and necessity, consciousness and unconsciousness, spirit and nature. Just as nature is the self-revelation of the absolute in manifold forms, so spirit is the medium of the self-contemplation of the absolute, the total identity where all finite forms are comprised and absorbed. In the absolute idealism of G. W. F. Hegel, the principle of unity is the idea, which realizes itself by becoming other, that is, nature, and returns to itself from this otherness, as spirit. The supreme mode of this spiritual return is the absolute knowledge of philosophical "logic", in which the absolute idea understands itself as such through its historical manifestation (the phenomenology of the spirit). There, delivered from all exteriorization and from all the historical effort of its return, the idea achieves absolute selfhood, as logos.

The neo-idealism of the late 19th and the first quarter of the 20th century sought to overcome positivism and empiricism by a new effort of thought. Sometimes it linked up with Fichte, as in Rudolf Eucken's philosophy of the absolute life of the spirit as the unity of consciousness and action. Or it linked up with Hegel, as for instance Benedetto Croce and Giovanni Gentile in Italy, F. H. Bradley, B. Bosanquet and E. McTaggart in England. In Germany, the universalism of O. Spann is a noteworthy example of a doctrine influenced by the Hegelian notion of the absolute spirit. But the major impulse came from the transcendental philosophy of Kant, though indeed its metaphysical basis and horizon were deliberately disregarded, since Kant was seen only as the philosopher who had conquered and destroyed metaphysics. The neo-Kantianism of the Marburg school, founded by Hermann Cohen and Paul Natorp, took the exact sciences as its model and sought to establish the logical conditions for true – in this case, correct – knowledge and will. These conditions, normative of all experience, were supposed to be pre-contained in the structure of the "pure consciousness". Interest was thus centred on "theoretical reason" but this approach also dominated the treatment of aesthetic, religious and moral problems. Cohen had already stressed the importance of the social elements in Kant's doctrine, and Karl Vorländer took up the point, trying to form a synthesis of Kantian ethics and Marxist socialism. On the basis of the doctrine of the conditions of possibility of knowledge Rudolf Stammler outlined a philosophy of law which proposed a doctrine of "correct law" or "the right rights". The Baden school in South-West Germany, under the leadership of Wilhelm Windelband and Heinrich Rickert, attacked directly the questions arising from the "practical reason". The decisive elements in real life are not logical preconditions but duties based on judgments of value. The consciousness recognizes that it is orientated to absolute values and summoned to realize them. Hence they are not merely "subjective", that is, they do not derive from the consciousness itself. But since they are not real, neither do they "exist" objectively. But they "hold good" absolutely. The distinction was made between natural sciences which took no account of values and cultural sciences which were determined by values. And the cultural sciences which used generalizing (Rickert) or nomothetic (Windelband) methods, trying to establish laws, were distinguished from the cultural sciences which used descriptive or individualizing methods. These distinctions came to be important for the theory of sciences, especially the human sciences. The influence of the Baden school was decisive in the philosophy of E. Troeltsch and M. Weber.

C. The Characteristics of Idealist Thinking

To form a judgment on idealist thought, the following basic characteristics must be kept in mind.

1. Its principle ("ideation") allows it to see the question of the essence of any reality whatsoever as the quest for its "idea". Thus it can ask what idea is

verified in things, groups of things, and their mutual relationships. It can also ask what is the idea governing human attitudes and relationships such as law, love, the State, marriage, and so on. It can ask what is the idea of man and what happens to him, with him and through him in time – the idea which directs his history. Finally, it can ask after the idea of the whole and the highest, of being and of God himself.

2. The ideas are the basic determinants and relationships of the realm of reality. But they are also ordained to each other in a set of reciprocal determinations and delimitations, which may be called an "ontological" systematization. This has as its counterpart, on the level of reflective thought, the logical systematization of idealist thought. Such thought displays itself as the constructive force of the concrete intelligent consciousness, which must learn to know *the* world as *its* world, use this knowledge to construct itself and direct its action according to the knowledge.

3. A difference is experienced between the perfection of the basic form and the finite reality, between the measure and what is measured, between the order of things and the elements inserted into that order, between the absolute pure idea and the imperfect reality. This experience gives rise to the idealist ethic which recognizes in the idea the obligatory ideal, that which ought to be, the "value", and dedicates itself with all its might to the realization of the ideal (practical idealism). Now the pure idea is the measure and principle of order which allots the real its place in the whole. But the idea itself, in its perfection, can never be met with in any place accessible to immediate experience. It is "homeless" with regard to space and time – and therefore can be denied, when its mode of being is misunderstood. In this sense, therefore, idealist thought is essentially "Utopian", and in this type of thinking the man who goes beyond immediately perceptible reality (*mundus sensibilis*) to return to the region of its ideal causes (*mundus intelligibilis*) remains necessarily a "Utopian being".

The significance of the idealist position may be described as follows. Against all forms of irrationalism, it maintains that the nature of reality is intelligible. Against all forms of relativism, it defends the unconditional obligatoriness of a clearly recognizable order (and hence all thinking which recognizes norms and orders of things in natural law and social relationships is tributary to idealist thought). Against all forms of analytical positivism it retains the power of a synthetic vision of the whole and asserts the meaningfulness of the world and of human existence. And above all, against all forms of pragmatism, it affirms that the truth of the whole, knowledge of being, idea and value, are not merely means whereby man becomes in fact master of his existence in his struggle with the individual realities which he encounters. It recognizes that man is meant to transcend himself and individual entities in his orientation to the absolute, and that only in such transcendence can he hope to preserve his dignity and find his fulfilment.

The temptation besetting idealist thought is to try to conceive as an idea that which can never be an idea: the absolute and incomprehensible mystery which is at the root of being. And it may forget that man, since he is essentially referred to this mystery for his origin and meaning, must likewise remain a mystery and be incomprehensible. It is further tempted to take the order of essences, which comprises and determines all things, as itself a comprehensible whole. Hence, while looking to the ideal order, but being "blind" to reality, it often tries to force into a final "closed system" that which can never be coerced or encompassed.

The proper limits of idealist thought are set it by its experience of history, when this is taken seriously. History is not the accidental and somewhat unsatisfactory realization of the eternal, unchanging ideal order. Nor may it be conceived of as the reality which is the necessary self-understanding and self-development of the absolute idea. It is the activity of human freedom in its world, an activity obscure in origin, open and indeterminate as to the future. Hence history is a process of change which is utterly unamenable to theory and irreducible to concepts, the continuous remoulding of man himself, of his world, and of the whole order of beings, which never ceases to present new aspects. And here the question arises as to how the history of man and his "world" may be conceived, without dissolving the intrinsic enchainment of the changing, epoch-making order of things into the mere happenings. It is the question of the unconditional claim of the essential, the idea, the order and the norm, and of how this claim can be reconciled in each age with the insight that in the historical process of the "world", the order of essences itself, in things and in man, is always changing.

Alois Halder

IDEOLOGY

1. *Concept and problems.* The term ideology first appears in the discussions carried on by the French Enlightenment with Napoleon Bonaparte. The "Idéologues" were looked on by the political reactionaries as unworldly doctrinaires. But the general view is that "ideology" has a history going back as far as Bacon. It is still hardly possible to give a strict definition of ideology. The term is used in many ways – from the popular way of identifying ideology with programmed lying, the sceptical treatment of all non-empirical knowledge as ideological to the later Marxist identification of the class-determined consciousness with ideology. A definition could be sought in terms of psychological studies of projections and wish-fulfilment, the sociological theses on the determination of all thought by its environment or the positivist definitions of the theories of the sciences. But in each case one would have to include the philosophical, sociological or psychological school in question. This is true above all when assessing criticisms of Christianity as an ideology. The formal notion of ideology is part of the critique of knowledge.

Long before the term was coined, there were phenomena which could have been treated as objects for ideological criticism, the union between religion and the ruling powers, for instance, and so too it can be said that a partial critique of ideology was practised as early as the age of the Greek Sophists. But the actual historical appearance of ideology and critique of ideology was a consequence of the modern approach to science and the analysis of the bases of political and social order in post-medieval thought. As long as there was a principle of unity for the world with a philosophical basis and a theological guarantee, a principle which could be held to be binding on all, it was possible to derive axioms for the natural sciences and norms for social life from the *a priori* deductions of contemplative knowledge. But when the assumed unity of subject and object was called in question by nominalism and finally rejected, the ensuing crisis opened up the way to ideology and critique of the same. The shattering of this unity brought down with it not only the systematic fundamentals, theological and philosophical, of the Christian *ordo*, but also the identity of method in metaphysical and scientific study. In France and England especially, the claims of the inductive, empirical, experimental method prevailed against the deductive and speculative. Hence knowledge was valued not as theoretical contemplation, superior by reason of its intrinsic, non-utilitarian ends to *actio* and τέχνη, but as the analytical process of research into nature. Philosophy should in no way fall short of the natural sciences in its exactness, and for this new methods of reflection were necessary. Knowledge must prove itself in practice and thereby show its power: "tantum possumus, quantum scimus." This approach to the acquisition of knowledge influenced more and more strongly the political and social order as time went on. Principles of organization based on theology and metaphysics gave way to principles based on the pure light of reason which sought to press education and science into the service of the State and society. These non-theological, anti-metaphysical principles were called "ideas". The critical methods whereby grasp of the ideas could be safeguarded against inadmissible interference from outside and intrinsic sources of flaws were known as "ideology".

2. *History of the concept.* Francis Bacon (1561–1626) in his *Novum Organum* cast doubts on the methodical stringency of the traditional Aristotelian logic, since it seemed to provide no adequate protection against dogmatism and the distortions of the fallacies which he termed *idola.* The *idola* of Bacon were called *préjugés* by the French Enlightenment. Ideology is a doctrine of ideas, in the sense of being guidance as to how to distinguish correct ideas from false. Bacon acknowledged in the true ideas the "vera signacula creatoris super creaturam" – the hall-mark of the Creator – which were to be brought out by the inductive method and the critique of *idola: idola tribus*, the idols of the tribe, the sources of error innate in man's nature; *idola specus*, the idols of cave, the weaknesses inherent in the knowledge of the individual; the *idola fori*, the idols of the market-place, the confusions due to human means of communication and conventional terms, and finally the *idola theatri*, the idols of the theatre, the false maxims and syllogisms deriving from philosophical tradition. Bacon's criticism of religion was to have grave consequences. He distinguished philosophy from theology, no doubt, just as he distinguished theology from superstition. But unfortunately, in the time of the wars of religion of the 16th and 17th centuries, his theme of the idols proved to be an effective instrument in the hands of irreligious criticism. This was not the only case where Bacon's theories were taken over and put to uses foreign to their original intent, by controversialists dipping eclectically into the *Novum Organum*, of which the chapters on the idols had been designated by Bacon as the "pars destruens". Unlike the approach of the French Enlightenment, Bacon's critique was confined to psychology. He did not deny the general correspondence between being and thought, nor did he affirm that consciousness was subject to a material determinism. He saw philosophical truth as the mirror of nature. But the human mind was a mirror with a rough surface and to counteract its distortions strict methodical rules were needed. Bacon did not foresee the application of his scientific method to theology and politics, but once he had laid down his principles for science, the theme of science and politics was already intoned. The Enlightenment did not keep theory apart from practice in this realm, as did Bacon, but affirmed that a rational order based on natural law could be discerned and put into practice with regard to State and society. Only prejudices stood in the way. With this transformation of the discussion of the "idols" into a general critique of prejudices, ideology entered the field of political and social struggle.

Condillac (1715–80) and de Tracy (1754–1836) began by giving the psychological critique of the "idols" the radical form of a sensualist materialism. The spirit consists of sensible perceptions which are co-ordinated by an associative psychological mechanism of the consciousness. If this "science des idées" could attain the pure knowledge of the ideas, it would at last be possible to set up a just and rational order among mankind, without having to have recourse to metaphysics and religion for the "mystère de l'ordre social". The institutions of Church and State, which were both equally affected, struggled fiercely against this rationalism. Hence Holbach (1723–89) and Helvetius (1715–71) logically recognized in the alliance of Church and State a pact in defence of their common interest in the maintenance of the existing order. The two institutions could only cling to power as long as they deliberately kept men in ignorance. Religion was said to sanction the rule of the State by invoking a God whose existence could not be proved. Since then, ideological critique has been polemics against religious and socio-political prejudices at once. The source of untruth is not now in the psychological shortcomings of man, but in manipulation from outside in the defence of various interests.

These are the presuppositions – along with the materialistic critique of religion and Hegelian idealism by Feuerbach – on which is based the ideology-critique of Marx, the most important hitherto produced. For Marx, ideology means a false concept of reality, the separation of theory and practice (activity), neglect of the material, social and historical conditioning of thought. Like Feuerbach, Marx saw Hegel's systematic conception of the unity of reason and reality as a paralogism. Reality as a whole is as little rational as reason has really realized itself. Where the idea has been separated from its concrete material, social situation, ideology has taken over. And the presence of ideology is a symptom of social disease. In bourgeois capitalist society ideologies coincide with the interests of the ruling class. But the whole process of existence, torn in several directions at once by the division of labour and alienation, results in a set of ideologies, since the mind of the producer cannot recognize itself and realize itself concretely in the wares produced. Thus an antagonism is set up between production and (mental) reproduction, between thought and action, subject and object, idea and reality. The Christian religion presents a classical form of ideology, because it tries to justify unreconciled reality by an unreal reconciliation. Such ideological fetters can only be burst asunder by revolution. This is not just an interpretation of reality but so radical a transformation of it that the whole process of the life of society can be accomplished rationally, perspicuously and hence freely. The agent of revolution in the 19th century is to be the proletariate, which is in such dire need of the revolution. It is impossible to say, however, how far Marx's critique of ideology contains deterministic traits. The later developments of the theory of ideology in Marxism take very different directions. In the orthodox communism of today, the Marxist dialectic of theory and *praxis* has been replaced by the schema of infrastructure and superstructure. Communist doctrine is the ideology of the proletariate and hence true doctrine, while bourgeois ideology is false by reason of its basis. Other Marxists, such as Lukács, Bloch, and Lefèbvre, distinguish between ideologies linked to the infrastructure and utopian ideologies, which are also to be found in bourgeois society. The valuable elements in art, science and religion, for instance, need only be set free to be themselves by Marxism. Neo-Marxists in the West, such as Adorno, Horkheimer, and H. Marcuse, criticize ontology, existence philosophy, and positivism in dialectical and psychoanalytical terms, treating them as modern forms of late capitalist ideology.

The characteristic link between ideology and revolution in Marxism, like its social and economic determinism of the consciousness, was modified by K. Mannheim and M. Scheler, and was now presented as a sociological history of the spirit which took place on a level superior to all parties. Scheler attributed different thought-forms to each social class, but from the point of view of history as of empirical sociology these theories of upper and lower class thought must remain mere hypotheses. Mannheim, however, with his affirmation of the determinism of thought by virtue of being and situation, which reminds us of Marx, represented in fact a sociological modification of historicism. To escape the relativist consequences of his theory, Mannheim demanded that all ideology should be deemed suspect and postulated a group of "free minds" hovering outside the range of determinism. Philosophies of value, Fascist doctrine to some extent and positivism tried to escape the dilemma presented by the sociological theory of knowledge. Thus Scheler, Husserl and N. Hartmann sought to give absolute values a philosophical bedrock. Pareto declared that all dominant social elites and values were merely reflections of whatever political party happened to be stronger for the moment. M. Weber and T. Geiger dismissed on principle all concepts of value and purpose as unscientific, non-empirical speculation. These are the presuppositions on which the present-day discussion of ideology is to a great extent based.

3. *Christianity and ideology*. Whether Christianity is called an ideology or not will be decided according to the concept of ideology which is presupposed. That certain particular ideologies have been and still are influential in the activity of the Church cannot be doubted. But it is another question when the general suspicion of ideology is applied to theology and the faith. When ideology is taken to designate every thesis which goes beyond the realm of the empirically verifiable and linguistic analysis, the faith must lose the appearance of scientific demonstrability. But this does not eliminate the fundamental necessity of having to take radical decisions about the purpose and activity of one's own life. In this sense, Christian faith can be called an ideology. Since Christianity must be embodied in the concrete in historical and social forms, it is always involved in a certain ambiguity, where ideological elements in the strict sense cannot always be excluded.

The Marxist criticism of Christianity as an ideology is a consistent theory which offers no loopholes. It can only be refuted in actual political and social activity, by permanent criticism of all attempts to set static, finite bounds to man in his history, and by the practical effort to eliminate inhuman conditions. Christianity finds the justification and the criteria for such effort in its eschatological promises.

Werner Post

IMAGES

The image is a figure which is so constructed that it enables something to be really present. Hence the concept of image is not identical with that of a work of art. It is philosophically more comprehensive. In its theological form the concept is very close to that of a sacrament, since the sacrament likewise uses an outward sign to bring about the presence of another reality, grace. In the history of thought, the notion of image has been of paramount importance at one time: it was the point at which human minds diverged.

The metaphysical meaning of image is clear at once when the heathen worship of divine images is considered. The response of the Bible is to forbid the making of images: "You shall not make yourself a graven image, or any likeness of anything that is in heaven above or that is in the earth beneath, or that is in the water under the earth; you shall not bow down to them or serve them"

(Exod 20:4f.). But the Bible also says: "God created man in his own image, in the image of God he created him" (Gen 1:27). St. Paul writes that Christ "is the image of the invisible God" (Col 1:15; cf. 2 Cor 4:4). And he also declares that "now we see in a mirror dimly, but then face to face" (1 Cor 13:12).

The essence of the image may be considered to be a created reality (man or heaven), the Word made flesh, or simply a work of art. The character and significance of the image will change accordingly. An idol has its own intrinsic value (it is "ad se ipsum"). The Christian image points to something else ("ad aliquid"). This was the distinction made by apologists in late antiquity and the early Middle Ages, which, while it does not always do justice to the heathen image of God, correctly describes the essential traits of idolatry. The idol tends to have an independent life of its own (for a people or a locality), while the image determines the nature of man, according to Gen 1:27 and 1 Cor 13:12. This structure of the image gives rise to a debate which has lasted to the present day.

The first stage of the conflict (in the history of salvation) starts with the prohibition of images in the OT. This precept did not forbid works of art. There were works of art of one type or another all through the history of Israel: decorated veils such as the veil of the temple depicting cherubim, images on coins and seals, wall-paintings (Ezek 41:17–20; 25:1; cf. the catacombs and the synagogue of Doura Europos) and even images of God (Exod 32; Jg 17; 1 Kg 12:28; 2 Kg 21:7; Ezek 8:3). The prohibition affected above all monumental statuary and cultic images. The intention of the law was to reserve the character of image to the primary realities of creation, man and heaven – in contrast to the secondary reality of the work of art. Plato and Plotinus also understood by image not the work of art but the cosmos and the heavens in particular. They were suspicious of the "shadow-like images" produced by the artist (Plato, *Republic*, 598b).

The early theologians accepted this view in principle. Hence Irenaeus (*Adversus Haereses*, I, 25) condemned the images in use among the Carpocratian Gnostics, and Origen told the pagan Celsus: "Christians and Jews are mindful of the commandment, 'Thou shalt not make thee an image' . . . Hence they detest temples, altars and images and are even ready to die if necessary, rather than debase the notion which they have of God Almighty by any unlawful action" (*Contra Celsum*, VII, 64). Along with the decalogue, theological reasons from Christology are invoked to reject images. Writing to Constantina, the sister of the Emperor Constantine, who had asked for an image of Christ, Bishop Eusebius explained that Jesus, who had been radiant with divine majesty even in his earthly life, could not be represented "by means of lifeless colours" (*PG*, XX, col. 1545). But under the influence of Plato, Philo, and Plotinus and inspired by the symbolism of the ancient East and of Hellenism, a theory of images was developed which gave a theological foundation to religious art, especially to painting. The mystery of the incarnation was the starting-point of the theory, which regarded knowledge of images as of the essence of the human spirit. "The Son is the perfect image of God, the Holy Spirit is the image of the Son. Ideas of things are images, man is the image and likeness of God; the word is the image of thought; memory of the past and preconception of the future are images. Everything is an image and the image is everything" (A. Harnack, *Dogmengeschichte*, II, p. 457). This type of speculation distinguishes between likeness (ὁμοίωμα), relationship to origin (ἐκτύπωμα), and revelatory character as elements of the image.

This predominantly Byzantine theory which flourished in the early Middle

Ages underestimated the proper value of created things. In the West, St. Gregory the Great rejected the *adoratio* of images, though without distinguishing between *dulia* and *latria* (reverence for images and adoration of God alone). St. Gregory stresses above all the educative value of images: "The image is to the illiterate what Scripture is to those who can read, for in the image even the illiterate can see what they have to imitate: there those who have never learned to read are able to read" (*Ep.*, 11, 13). The thesis formulated by Nilus was meant to mediate between the two positions: images should exist "so that those who cannot write and who are also unable to read the sacred Scriptures may by contemplating the images be reminded of the justice of the true servants of the true God and so be inspired to imitate the great and glorious works of virtue by which these exchanged earth for heaven, as they preferred the invisible to the visible" (*Ep. ad Olympiodorum*, 4, 61; *PG*, LXXIX, col. 577). According to these theories, the image determined relationships to God. The growth of the cult of images finally brought on the conflict about the image.

The iconoclast controversy in the Byzantine Church began with an edict of the Emperor Leo III in A.D. 726 and came to an end with the "Feast of Orthodoxy", instituted by the Empress Theodora in 843. The controversy came to a climax in the General Council of Nicaea in 787, which approved the reverence paid to images (Mansi, XII/XIII). The theologians of Charlemagne wrote against this council in the *Libri Carolini*, 790 (*Monumenta Germaniae Historica*, Concilia, II, suppl.). Along with political rivalry against Byzantium, the starting-point of the conflict was the concept of adoration. The Carolingian theologians rejected adoration of images but paid too little attention to the fine distinction between *latria*, the adoration due to God alone, and *proskynesis*, the reverence paid to the image. So too the West emphasized more strongly the proper value of the work of art, though negatively, to begin with. According to the *Libri Carolini* the image has no relation to the *forma prima:* it is non-spiritual and material (lib. II, c. 16; lib. I, c. 7; lib. II, c. 30). In Bishop Claudius of Turin we meet a Carolingian iconoclast, who was opposed by Dungal and Jonas of Orleans (d. 843). This discussion brought the Carolingian theologians closer to the position of Nicaea. Thus the Romanesque period which followed saw a flowering of the production of sacred images.

A new conflict began with St. Bernard of Clairvaux. He looked on the riches of Romanesque art as the quintessence of luxury and a danger to the spiritual life. Poverty is strongly urged. The observation of social distinctions is counselled: works of art are permitted for bishops (cathedrals), but restricted for monks (as in the austere forms of Cistercian art). St. Thomas Aquinas distinguishes between a *latria absoluta* due to God alone, and a *latria relativa* which is accorded to the image of Christ (*Summa Theologica*, III, 25, 3). This classical solution is endangered by the overabundance of works of art in late Gothic spirituality, and by the new evaluation of art in the Renaissance. Discussion of the theological problem is accompanied by the conflict in the philosophy of art ("il paragone") about the priority of the word or the image. Leonardo could still describe painting as a science: "Painting in the true and scientific sense begins by ascertaining what is the body that casts a shadow, and what are primordial and derivative shadows, what is lighting, that is, darkness, light, colour; what is body, figure and posture, what is distance and nearness, what is movement and rest. These things are grasped by the spirit alone without the hands being engaged, and that is the science of painting, which remains in the spirit of those who meditate upon it" (*Libro di pittura*, I, 33 [19, 2]).

The Reformation provoked a new controversy about images. But the attitudes of the Reformers varied. In his *Abtuhung der Bilder* Karlstadt called for their removal (1522). Calvin condemned them in his *Institutio* (1529). For Zwingli (in his "Answer" to Valentine Compar, 1525, and his *De vera religione*) an image in church is equivalent to idolatry. In Switzerland, France, the Netherlands and also in Germany, numerous works of art were destroyed. Luther's initially hostile attitude was directed rather against the false idea of faith which thought it could amass merit by endowments for churches and images (v. Campenhausen). He treated images, even in church, as "adiaphora", "neither good nor bad".

The Council of Trent, while striving to suppress the abuses connected with images, retains the traditional doctrine. "I firmly hold that images of Christ, of the ever-virgin Mother of God and of the other saints, are to be kept and preserved, and that they are to be paid due honour" (Tridentine Profession of Faith). St. Robert Bellarmine (*De reliquiis et imaginibus sanctorum*, cc. 5–25: *Controversiarum liber*, IV/2) distinguishes between reverence paid to the image and reverence paid to the person represented. In contrast to St. Thomas, he holds that reverence for images is inferior to reverence for persons. Commentaries on Trent dealing with the theory of art (J. Molanus, *De picturis et imaginibus*, 1570; G. Paleotti, *De imaginibus sacris et profanis*, 1594; G. Ottonelli e. P. Berettini, *Trattato della Pittura e Scultura*, 1652; Interian de Ayala, *Pictor christianus eruditus*, 1730) demand that images should be perfectly true, and that "venustas spiritualis" should replace "procax venustas".

The most important attack upon images was launched in modern times by the Enlightenment. In the French Revolution, a number of churches and their contents were destroyed, and the goddess "Reason", a woman, was installed in the cathedrals as the embodiment of the modern concept of the world and science. Very many works of art were destroyed in Germany during the Secularization (three hundred monasteries and eighteen universities were suppressed). The world is no longer looked on as the image of a creator. It is understood by scientific observation as a storehouse of energy. The theological and mythological programmes of the baroque period were abandoned. Realism erects the visible into the norm of artistic work. Art itself becomes autonomous and loses contact with theology, even in the Church. Its reality is based on society and the person. The personalism of the artistic will brings about the isolation of the artist from society. The era of mental breakdown and suicide sets in for artists. In the course of the 19th century, the artistic mentality finds itself more and more in conflict with official taste (in a society of the masses). About 1910 the artistic movements of the 20th century begin, with cubism, surrealism and abstract art, which de-personalize art and make it anonymous. In Germany, the iconoclasm of National Socialism launches a merciless campaign against "inartistic art", as does Soviet socialism in the East. Inspired by the idea of a Gothic supposed to remain eternally valid, or searching for a basic religious style (Beuron, French symbolism), Church circles likewise opposed the modern forms. After 1945, there was a swing over to the opposite attitude. The productions of abstract art, cubism and surrealism – often tastefully embellished – are admitted into the churches, which now become miscellanies of the various styles. Thus the most recent writings and projects call for a Church art without decipherable content. It means the disappearance of the Church tradition. And the replacement of the great personal art of the moderns by a manneristic formalism at second hand. Modern art, which tries to mould its experience of materials and of energy along with its unconscious processes, calls for a reappraisal of the notion of image in Christian circles also. To give it a proper basis, it will be essential to recall that the world is the vehicle of a communication of its creator to his creatures.

Herbert Schade

IMMANENTISM

Immanentism is the name given to the doctrine or attitude which excludes transcendence, that is, the reference to "the other" in any form whatever, on the grounds that this other is to be found equivalently in the subject itself. Immanentism, therefore, substitutes a false concept of "inwardness" or of commitment to the world, to eliminate the authentic religious attitude, which is the adoring recognition of God as the "wholly other", and the thankful acceptance of the surprises of his grace throughout history.

1. *The forms of immanentism.* The normal distinction is between epistemological and metaphysical immanentism. The former ("gnoseological") holds that human knowledge only attains the thought of its contents, not their being; the latter refuses to consider God as the wholly other beyond the world. Both forms have been chiefly developed in modern philosophy, by an exaggeration of the notion of immanence fostered originally by Christian thought.

a) The concept of immanence is derived from a twofold train of thought. One element, based on such texts as 1 Jn 4:12, was the indwelling of God in the Christian sanctified by grace, and then that of the creator in the creature (the *Deus interior intimo meo* of St. Augustine). The other element was the concept of *actio immanens*, which was chiefly worked out from the consideration of living beings as whole units realizing themselves from within themselves as their own proper ends. Knowledge is *actio immanens* in the fullest sense (as is also will), since it makes no changes in the thing known, but assimilates the knower himself to the thing as known – which again can only be done by an act of self-realization on the part of the knower. Since all knowing involves this inner self-realization, the act of faith includes among its presuppositions the rational *praeambula fidei* and the inner light of faith – neither of which are possible except by virtue of immanence in the first metaphysical sense. Thus the Christian doctrine of immanence stands or falls with transcendence, that is, with the existence of "another", which is so fully self-subsistent that it remains "other" when it subsists in another. It would be immanentism, however, to hold that the "one" and the "other" within man are only two aspects of the one reality, or two poles of the same act of thought.

b) Epistemological (gnoseological) immanentism is of only indirect interest for theology. It includes the relativist theory of knowledge on which Modernism is based, the term immanentism having apparently been forged in connection with Modernism. This theory of knowledge invokes the stage of philosophical reflection arrived at with Descartes and Kant, according to which knowledge is originally concerned only with the content of thought, so that henceforward the necessary ("transcendental") structures of thought itself must be the object of philosophical investigation. Modernism sought to escape the resulting agnosticism by a vitalist theory of religious knowledge which made it a matter of psychological attitudes. Instead of transcendent, authoritative truths, "religion" now becomes the norm, religion being understood as a vital urge within man. Reflection discloses that "the divine" is needed to satisfy this urge. "Impelled by our need of faith in the divine", as the modernist programme says, we can accept historical facts as unavoidably necessary for religious experience, and are enabled to "re-mould" them accordingly, and thus make progress in the knowledge of faith and in dogmatic formulations. The essence of this immanentism consists, therefore, of the fact that the true direction of religious dependence is inverted. "The God who matters to me" now becomes dependent on the religious needs of man – a perversion present in its initial stages wherever the acceptance of religious truths or the performance of practices commanded are made to depend on their "meaning something to me".

c) Metaphysical immanentism strictly speaking is pantheistic in tendency, because it assumes that worldly reality is ultimately self-sufficient. In this form it can hardly be said to exist today. Much more widespread, however, is "historical immanentism", which recognizes nothing beyond and outside history and the time of the world, and holds that history and human life, if they reach their goal at all, do so within history. Thus Marxism expects to arrive at a final happy period through a series of dialectical switches which are all forms of the one reality; so too all types of evolutionary theory, insofar as the end-term is regarded, not as a pre-existing goal, as in Teilhard de Chardin, but as already contained in germ in the process of development; so too, finally, the denial of immortality, in theory or practice. The seeds of such immanentism can also be present in Christianity, wherever so much stress is laid on the salutary force of quasi-sacramental signs, such as brotherliness, the eucharistic meal, the preaching of the word of God, that Christians forget that these things point on beyond themselves and are efficacious only through the free intervention of God's grace. As the industrialized world grows more and more self-sufficient, and the sense of metaphysical realities is blunted by a predominantly "matter of fact" education and outlook, this historical immanentism is likely to continue to spread in the future.

2. Theologically, *immanentism is to be overcome* by the vigorous affirmation of the Christian doctrine of immanence, which must appear less as a sort of impersonal indwelling of God (which could easily degenerate into immanentism) than as a Christological truth. The doctrine of the two natures is a guarantee of transcendence, while incarnation and transubstantiation give genuine value to the whole reality of the world. In philosophy and apologetics, the effort to arouse a sense of transcendence must be made a sort of propaedeutic to the faith. The method of immanence must be used to alert men to their primordial and continual orientation to the absolute You.

Peter Henrici

IMMORTALITY

By immortality is meant, in general, endless life. It is said absolutely of a being who cannot die (gods, God) and then of a being who survives in a changed form after death. This survival can be thought of as personal or impersonal (supra-personal), as bodiless or in some way bodily, as a lower or a higher plane of existence.

1. *Comparative religion.* Belief in life after death is attested, even before the funeral rites and the cult of the dead in primitive religions, by the burial procedures of the earliest cultures. In view of the burial gifts, the "books of the dead" and the myths, the life in question seems mostly to have been considered as an only slightly altered form of earthly life. Differences were supposed also to continue among the dead. The rank after death could be determined by the moral qualities of the dead

person or by those of his relatives, by the burial rites or the type of sacrifice offered, by the nature of his death or simply by the rank he had held in earthly life. Rewards and punishments, linked with the notion of gradual purification, are the specific features of the doctrine of the transmigration of souls, though the ultimate end may differ – entry into *Nirvana*, into the *Brahma* or into a state where the soul is free of everything corporeal, as in Orphism.

2. *History of philosophy*. The Orphic tradition was adopted by Plato, who laid the foundations of the Western thinking on immortality by defining the soul as the element which survived the dissolution of the body at the moment of "separation of soul and body". But the soul was not merely part of man. "Man is nothing else than his soul" (*Alcibiades*, 129e, 130c). The immortality of the soul, according to Plato, is based on the cyclic character of nature in general and the doctrine of anamnesis: the survival of the soul corresponding to its pre-existence. More stringently, Plato argues from the simplicity of the soul, which cannot therefore be dissolved, and from its ability to grasp the eternal forms of the true, good and beautiful. Since like is known only by like, the soul must be of the nature of the forms. Finally, he argues from the nature of the soul as principle of life, in the *Phaedo* – an argument also taken up in the *Phaedros*, 245c–246a. The Aristotelian notion of matter and form guaranteed a closer and more organic unity of body and soul, but made it more difficult to accept the immortality of the soul. According to Aristotle, only the supra-personal intellect (νοῦς) was immortal.

The Platonic and Aristotelian approaches were combined in various ways in later philosophical schools. Plato was the great master here for Christian thought. Augustine, for instance, proves the immortality of the soul from its faculty of grasping the truth. The theological (and ethical) arguments also are emphasized. The adoption of Aristotelianism then became the mainspring of the strictly philosophical discussion, but with the rejection of Averroism by Albertus Magnus, Thomas Aquinas and the Fifth Lateran Council (*D* 738, *DS* 1440) the hylemorphism of Aristotle was given a Platonic interpretation. At the time of the Renaissance, the immortality of the soul was one of the major subjects of debate between the Platonists and the Sceptics, as it was among the Aristotelians between Averroists and Alexandrists. But with Leibniz in particular, it was treated as the "central dogma" of the Enlightenment, at least in Germany. In France, as represented by Voltaire and the *Encyclopédie*, and in England as represented by Hume, the Enlightenment showed itself rather sceptical and hostile to the notion of immortality. The reaction gave currency in Germany to the influence of Swedenborg, whose "dreaming" was attacked by Kant. Kant rejected the rational value of the traditional proofs as paralogisms, but postulated immortality on ethical and practical grounds, since man could only attain the end of his nature by endless progress and because the moral order of the world demanded that man's destiny should correspond to his virtues. For Fichte, immortality is already there with the acceptance of truth, which is the "blessed life", whose outcome can only be understood as transformation into still more perfect love. As against the more emotional humanism or personalism of a Herder or a Goethe, and the theosophist speculation of the later Schelling, the thought of Hegel was later influential – or rather, the interpretation of his own ambiguous position as the denial of personal immortality in view of the history of the World-Spirit. This Hegelianism of the left and the crude materialism of a mainly biological type were opposed by the Hegelians of the right and speculative theism. In the philosophy of the present day, death is one of the predominant themes, but no more interest is taken in proofs of immortality than in proofs of the existence of God, whether immortality is rejected, left an open question or accepted.

3. *Theology.* The key-word here in the anthropology of biblical theology is not immortality but the resurrection of the flesh. Thus in the OT, there is survival in Sheol. But what survives is not the soul as part of man and still less the soul as the real being of man. Only man's "shadow" survives, and this might possibly be called immortality. But this mere survival is completely insignificant in comparison with the loss of earthly life, as also in comparison with the growing hope of being raised up by God. The influence of Hellenism can be already noted in the post-exilic period, and then patristic theology took up explicitly, as has been noted above, the Platonic conception, which it combined with faith in the resurrection as expressed in the later books of the OT and in the NT. But just as the descriptions of the body-soul relationship by the magisterium in terms of hylemorphism do not erect Aristotelian philosophy into dogma, so too the official declarations on eschatology (*D* 530, *DS* 1000) and against Averroism (*D* 738, *DS* 1440) do not give any particular philosophical explanation of immortality any status as part of the faith. While rejecting false interpretations of the faith, they used a ready-made philosophical terminology as a handy way of allowing the faith to find self-expression.

Present-day Protestant theology has to a great extent rejected all such aid. H. Engelland, in the *Evangelisches Kirchenlexikon*, III, cols. 1579f., gives three reasons for refusing to work with the concept of immortality: "For the sake of the divineness of God, who alone has immortality" (1 Tim 6:16; cf. 1 Cor 15:53); "because of sin", of which the origin is not in the body but in the soul; "because of the unity of man". But there are also signs of a more moderate position (cf. *RGG*, VI, cols. 1177f.). And in fact, faith in immortality is not necessarily linked with a dichotomy between body and soul. It could be shown that the classical proof from the incorruptibility of a simple spiritual being, and from the necessity of eternal sanctions, is only a certain way of articulating the immanent basic experience of freedom itself. Freedom experiences itself in the experience of the unconditional claim of truth and of good. It recognizes that it could never escape itself, not even in death, and hence that it must resolve and decide, and that it must be fully itself by definitively accepting itself. At the same time, it experiences the "dialogal" nature of its situation. Immortality in the full sense of the word is not within its power, nor even merely a task to be laboured at. It is also a gift to be hoped for – a point at which it is well to recall the analogy with the proofs of the existence of God. That immortality is beyond man and yet man's gift is not a contradiction and not even a mere paradox. The two are indissolubly one, an identity in difference, by virtue of the essentially interpersonal nature of freedom as seen above all in the body and in language. In this sense, therefore, without any concessions to a rationalistic self-assurance or to an irrational hope which can give no "account" of itself (1 Pet 3:15), one can accept the quotation from Kierkegaard with which J. Pieper ended his book on death and immortality: "The question of immortality is of its nature not a scholarly question. It is a question welling up from the interior which the subject must put itself as it becomes conscious of itself" (*Concluding Unscientific Postscript*, p. 164).

Jörg Splett

INCARNATION

A. Introduction and Preliminary Remarks

1. The teaching on Jesus Christ is the central mystery of Christianity, which of course takes its name from him. The doctrine of the one God who, as an infinite transcendent person creates, conserves and guides the world to its goal, the doctrine of the nature and dignity of man as a free person with an eternal, blissful destiny, and the doctrine of the unity of love of God and the neighbour as the ultimate purpose and saving activity of human existence, are also of course doctrines which are fundamental to Christianity and the Church and are fundamental to the hierarchy of truths which constitute the one message of Christianity. Yet these three doctrines receive their specifically Christian content and their ultimate ground from the message regarding Jesus Christ. Only in him, and in the union and distinction between God and the world found in him, is the God-world relationship and, as a consequence, God's very essence, made clear as self-communicating love. In Christ man's highest dignity and ultimate nature as radical openness to God is manifest, together with the guarantee and historically tangible demonstration that man's destiny is attained. In Christ the love of God and the neighbour acquires in the person of the one God-man an "object" of the highest unity, and as a consequence love for man attains its supreme dignity.

2. The connection between the doctrine of the Incarnation and Christian belief as a whole may be made still clearer at the start. Christianity is the eschatologically historical event of God's self-communication. This means that the really fundamental Christian conception of the world (including spiritual persons) and of its relation to God is not to be found in the doctrine of creation, fundamentally important as this is. It is based on the history of salvation, which shows that the absolute, infinite and holy God wills in the freedom of his love, to communicate *himself* by grace *ad extra* to what is not divine. That is why he has creatively brought the world into existence as the recipient of his self-communication in such a way that this self-communication is God's fundamental purpose, but is not something to which the finite creature has a right. It remains a free grace of God's love. God creates the *ad extra* in order to communicate the *ad intra* of his love. This *ad extra* is not something presupposed and independent of God, but the possibility, effected by his own freedom, of his own self-communication. Its difference from himself has its origin in himself. Like the world and the spiritual creation, God's self-communication has a history. This self-communication is indeed the basis of world history because it is its ultimate meaning and its (grace-given) entelechy from the beginning. But it also has its own history within world history, attains clearer and clearer manifestation in it and reaches its culmination and irreversible manifestation precisely in the eschatological phase of the history of salvation which is constituted by Jesus Christ.

a) Viewed in this light Jesus Christ as the incarnate Logos of God is God's supreme self-communication. This takes place in the Incarnation. For here God is so much the self-bestower that the "addressee" of God's self-communication is posited by God's *absolute* will to his effective, i.e., accepted, self-communication (*ipsa assumptione creatur*, as Augustine says). The self-communication itself posits the act of its acceptance (as a created spiritual substance and its free and definitive act) and thus appropriates this latter wholly and makes it the manifestation precisely of God's will – identical with God himself – to self-exteriorization. (Further and more detailed treatment of this is to be found in Section D.)

b) Since this created spiritual reality,

posited by the very acceptance which itself receives, is by its very nature a part of the *world*, this self-communication of God as accepted by the creation in Jesus Christ means that the world is in principle accepted by God for its salvation. And this acceptance by God in Christ has become historically tangible and irrevocable. In the Incarnation (which also includes Jesus' human life, his death and resurrection), the history of the world has been decided as a victorious history of salvation, not of perdition, and has been made manifest as such.

3. The Incarnation is a mystery because the possibility of God's self-communication to the finite is a mystery. It is also a mystery that the possibility of such self-communication can find its culmination in the Incarnation. Finally, the irreducibly contingent fact of the Incarnation's having occurred precisely in Jesus of Nazareth is an aspect of this mystery in the concrete. Yet the freedom of the Incarnation can certainly be regarded as one and the same freedom as that of God's gracious self-communication to the world. For the essence of the assumption of a reality belonging to the world and its unity, in the Incarnation, itself implies God's fundamental will to sanctify and redeem the world as such. And conversely (cf. Section C below) the historically definitive manifestation of God's will to a self-communication to the world accepted by the world, that is, the absolute, eschatological mediator of salvation already implies Incarnation.

4. That the historical Jesus' self-awareness was materially identical with what is meant by the Incarnation of the Logos is expounded in the article *Jesus Christ*.

It is hardly necessary to stress that the experience of Jesus' resurrection was of essential importance for the interpretation of the witness Jesus had borne to himself. That is, of course, the reason why in the account of his words and deeds the pre-paschal Jesus' interpretation of himself is rightly given from the standpoint, and as a part, of the kerygma concerning the risen Christ. The resurrection is not to be understood merely as an external miraculous attestation of Jesus' words, without any intrinsic connection with them. It is itself the eschatological, fundamental saving event which, if precisely and fully interpreted, shows Jesus to be the absolute bringer of salvation and hence implies what is meant by Incarnation.

B. Jesus in the New Testament

1. The doctrine of the NT regarding Jesus (beyond the historical Jesus' own witness to himself) need only be presented briefly here. It is not a particularly difficult problem to verify the identity of the Church's dogma with the Christology of the NT. For on the one hand the latter expressly teaches Christ's pre-existence, and on the other all the NT "Christology of Ascent" (Jesus as the Servant of God and Messiah raised up by the Father through the Passion and Resurrection) is certainly implicitly contained in the classical doctrine of the Church, provided this is not misconstrued in a more or less Monophysite way.

This does not mean, however, that within NT Christology there are not very different, though not mutually incompatible, fundamental Christological conceptions according to whether an ascent or descent schema is preferred (gnoseologically and ontologically), and according to the precise way in which the starting-point is determined within such a schema. It goes without saying, too, that within the history of Jesus and NT Christology, certain terms (Son of God, Son of man, Messiah-Christ, etc.) themselves have a history of more precise interpretation, deepening and unfolding, and cannot therefore be taken as having everywhere the same meaning.

2. For the rest, cf. the article *Jesus Christ*.

C. The Official Teaching of the Church

1. *Its preparation in the history of dogma.* The NT texts regarding Christology of Descent, e.g., Gal 4:4; 1 Cor 2:8; Phil 2:5–11; Col 2:9; Heb 1:3; Rom 1:3f.; Jn 1:14, etc., show how increasing experience concerning the man Jesus was translated even in the NT period into the article of faith regarding the pre-existent Son of God coming in the flesh. It is therefore not difficult to understand that while early Christology down to the 4th century had no difficulty in overcoming an ancient *truncated* Christology of Ascent (in which Jesus was, ultimately, merely a human Messiah, as for the Ebionites), the Christological controversies of the first centuries, surprising as this may seem, were more concerned with the question of the relation of the pre-existent Son to the Father (in Arianism, Sabellianism, Modalism) – which does not concern us here – or else raised the question of how exactly we are to think of the "flesh" in which God's Son appeared as revealer of the Father and mediator of salvation. In Docetism this is volatilized entirely. In the East the Logos-sarx theory whether extreme (Apollinarianism) or moderate (Athanasius), either denied the human intellect of Jesus or at least did not do justice to it as a theological reality. In the West, from Tertullian to Novatian, Ambrose and Augustine, the explicitation of the mystery of Christ in theological concepts developed relatively without friction into the standard formulation of Leo I in the middle of the 5th century. The one *persona* (Tertullian already uses the term) has a double status (*spiritus* [divinity] – *caro:* Tertullian) and is *unus*, even though possessing (Ambrose) *utrumque* (*divinitas – corpus, caro, nostra natura*), and even though it was still often said (without thereby denying the unity of person) that the Word of the Father had assumed a "man" where we today would simply say a "human nature". The course of development in the East was more difficult. It is true that as early as Origen we find the axiom that man is only completely redeemed if the whole human reality, *soul* and body, is assumed by the Logos. But the conceptual grasp of the union between the Logos and the "flesh" (man, humanity), and consequently the communication of properties, caused considerable difficulty. The distinction between ὑπόστασις and φύσις was only slowly worked out in the theology of the Trinity and it was even longer before this distinction came into general use in Christology. Πρόσωπον (as principle of union in the school of Antioch) could easily be misunderstood as a principle of merely "moral" unity, in which statements about Christ would have to be divided between two subjects different in substance. This tendency found decisive expression in Nestorianism. On the other hand the older conceptual models which represented the union of divine and human as a "mixture" or thought of it on the pattern of the union between soul and body (as Augustine did in the West; cf. *D* 40) were not really very suited to bring out with equal force the union and distinction of the divine and human in Christ. In the struggle against Nestorianism, Alexandrian theology endeavoured to express the real substantial unity of the one identical Christ, God and man, by means of the term φύσις (or by other words which at that time were still identical with it: ὑπόστασις, πρόσωπον). And so in a formula which derives from the Apollinarian Logos-sarx Christology, Cyril of Alexandria and to some degree the Council of Ephesus could speak of the one physis (nature) of the incarnate Logos or of his incarnate nature, of a ἕνωσις φυσική (cf. *D* 115; 117), without any intention of denying his complete humanity and its distinction from the divinity. But the formula was then misused by Monophysitism (Eutyches). Not until the Council of Chal-

cedon was the terminology clarified: πρόσωπον, ὑπόστασις, *persona* were taken as identical in meaning and used of the substantial subject and (in this case) the principle of union of the natures; φύσις (οὐσία, *natura*) from the point of view of terminology was no longer taken to have the same sense as hypostasis or person but (as in Trinitarian doctrine) was understood as signifying the principle of objective specification of an ultimate subject and as the principle of specific activity. At the same time it must be observed that this terminology was not precisely fixed and methodically developed, but was employed forthwith as occasion offered in Christology.

As a consequence it is not surprising that much remains obscure even to this day and is left to the philosophical and theological interpretation of individual schools and theologians. Consequently if the *theologically* binding meaning of these terms is to be rightly ascertained, positively and negatively, we must repeatedly take our bearings from the simple insight of faith that precisely this concrete individual who acts and encounters us, is true God and true man, that these two predicates do not mean the same, yet both are the reality of the one and the same being. The history of Christology after the Council of Chalcedon includes the dogmatic conflict with Monotheletism; otherwise, however, it is almost solely history of theology, not of dogma. Efforts are made to define more precisely the terms made use of. Subtle variations can be observed between a Christology which stresses the difference of natures and one which stresses the unity of both in a single person. The consequences of the hypostatic union for Christ's human nature are considered – his grace, his knowledge, the mode of influence of the hypostasis on the human nature, the question of Christ's "consciousness", the possibility of a human freedom under the dominion of the Logos, etc. There are attempts to conceive the "unity" of the divine person as the consequence of some other ontological reality, e.g., in modern Thomism, where the existence of the Logos itself confers real existence on (achieves or brings into the real order) Christ's human nature and thereby unites this to itself. All this, however, only concerns the pastor to the extent that it shows that while the formula of Chalcedon remains the standard and valid statement, theology, preaching and piety should nevertheless not consider that all they are permitted to do is to repeat that standard formula.

2. *The actual official teaching of the Church.* a) *General characteristics.* The Church's official doctrine is formulated objectively and ontically, i.e., it is a concrete factual statement about Jesus Christ in himself. There is no explicit reference to the question of how we meet him in historical experience and in faith, or how this peculiar encounter (as the ultimate and absolute encounter with God, as he is in himself, in the midst of our history at its most concrete) can be used to establish this ontic Christology and understand it better. The key concepts of Church doctrine are the distinction between person and nature and the doctrine of the hypostatic union, as expressed by the Council of Chalcedon in terms which have never been improved on.

b) *The basic doctrine.* By the hypostatic union (*D* 148, 217) the eternal (and therefore pre-existent) Word (Logos), the Son of the Father as the second person of the Trinity, has united as his nature with his person in a true, substantial (*D* 114ff.) and definitive (*D* 85f., 283) union (against Nestorianism) a human nature created in time with a body and spiritual soul from the Virgin Mary, his true mother. The effecting of this union is common to the three divine persons (*D* 284, 429), but the union of the human nature is with the Word alone (*D* 392; against the Patripassianists). Even after the union the unmixed distinction between his divine and his human nature is not affected (against Monophysitism). Thus the Word became true man. Consequently to one and the same person, the Logos, there belong two natures, the divine and the human, without mixture and without separation (*D* 143f., 148); one and the same person is God and man. We can affirm of one and the same subject the realities of both natures and consequently, in a communication of properties (perichoresis: *D* 291), we can predicate of this one subject named on the basis of one of the natures, the characteristics of the other nature. This hypostatic union belongs to the absolute mysteries of faith (*D* 1462, 1669).

c) *The true divine sonship of Jesus Christ.* If this one and the same Jesus Christ is named, therefore, we must say that he is true God (*D* 54, 86, 148, 224, 290, 994, 2027–2031); the consubstantial (*D* 86, 554) Son of the Father (*D* 1597); his Word (*D* 118, 224), God from God, begotten not made (*D* 13, 39f., 54), the only-begotten (*D* 6, 13, 86); a person of the Trinity (*D* 216, 222, 255, 708); creator of all things (*D* 54, 86, 422), eternal (*D* 54, 66), incapable of suffering (*D* 27); because he is true and consubstantial Son, he is not (in addition) an adopted son (*D* 299, 309f., 311ff.) like us (against Adoptianism, and a certain form of Assumptus-Homo-theology). The divinity of Christ is the presupposition of his role as mediator in the redemption, of his offices and of the privileges which distinguish him from us even in a human nature essentially identical with ours, and even though these characteristics also belong to him inasmuch as he is man.

d) *This same Jesus Christ is true man.* (i) He has a true body capable (before his resurrection) of suffering (*D* 13, 111a, 148, 480, 708), not an apparent body (*D* 20, 344, 462, 710) or a heavenly one (*D* 710). This was united to the person of the Logos from his conception (*D* 205) and has a rational spiritual soul as its essential form (*D* 216, 480). Accordingly he possesses a human, sensible and spiritual soul (*D* 13, 25, 111a, 148, 216, 255, 283, 290, 480, 710), created, not eternally pre-existent (*D* 204). Consequently all forms of Docetism and any extreme Logos-sarx Christology (e.g., Apollinarianism: *D* 65, 85) are heretical. Jesus Christ is, therefore, consubstantial with us (*D* 148), a son of Adam, born of a mother in true human fashion, related to us by blood, our brother (*D* 40, etc.). In contradiction to Monotheletism, therefore, we must acknowledge the real free created will, energy and operation (*D* 144, 148, 262–269, 288–293, 710) of the man Jesus Christ, a will distinct from the divine will of the Logos but fully in harmony with it (*D* 251ff., 288ff., 1465). In its activity he stood truly God-fearing (*D* 310, 343, 387) under God's rule (*D* 285).

(ii) In this humanity (not in virtue of it), Jesus Christ is the natural Son of the Father, worship is due to him (*D* 120, 221, 1561) (also in regard to his heart: *D* 1563; so too the blood of Christ). In his humanity he also possesses impeccability (*D* 122, 148, 224, 711; *Collectio Lacensis*, VII, cols. 560f.), holiness (substantial by the hypostatic union and accidental by sanctifying grace) and integrity (freedom from concupiscence), power to work miracles (*D* 121, 215, 1790, 2084) and an infallible knowledge appropriate to his mission (including the vision of God from the beginning: *D* 248, 1790, 2032–2035, 2183ff., 2289; against the Agnoetes), but not, before the resurrection, an absence of the capacity to suffer (*D* 429, 708) or the *defectus Christi naturales* (Aphthartodocetism). In his humanity certain offices or functions belong to him.

e) *Official pronouncements* of the Church's solemn magisterium concerning the life and work of Christ are relatively few, except as regards the doctrine of the redemption. They are mostly dealt with by the ordinary teaching of the Church in its transmission of the statements of Scripture.

D. The Doctrine of the Incarnation in the Preaching of the Faith at the Present Day

1. The Incarnation is a mystery of faith and therefore involves all that a mystery implies: the impossibility of compelling the free assent of faith, the "paradox" involved in any formulation of such a mystery, the character of being a stumbling-block to the pride of a rationalism autonomously accepting only what is fully comprehended. But a mystery is not a myth or a miracle, i.e., it is not, and ought not to be understood and preached as something which within a man's own realm of experience cannot seriously be taken as possible and believable even by one who does not arbitrarily restrict the range of experience in a rationalist and scientific way to what can be experimentally demonstrated. That means that the mystery must possess for man a genuine intelligibility and desirability, even if in some cases this mental framework must first be brought to light precisely by actual encounter with the mystery and its proclamation. In presenting the faith we must to a greater degree than in earlier times avoid giving a mythological flavour to the expression of this mystery. But that always happens if Christ's human nature is made to look like God's livery, which the Logos puts on to make himself known, or if it seems to be a sort of passive marionette manipulated from outside and used by God like a mere thing or instrument to attract attention on the stage of world history.

2. This, however, presupposes that the human nature of Christ, of the person of the Logos, must be understood in such a way that Christ in reality and in all truth is a man with all that this involves: a human consciousness which is aware in adoration of its own infinite distance in relation to God; a spontaneous human interior life and freedom with a history which, because it is that of God himself, possesses not less but more independence, for the latter is not diminished but increased by union with God. For union with God and independence are in principle realities which grow in direct, not inverse proportion, as Maximus Confessor already emphasizes (*PG*, XCI, col. 97A). The divine act producing the union is itself formally one which posits the created reality as free for its active independence in regard to God. This means that present-day Christology (in preaching and theological reflection) must as it were re-enact (and preach!) that history of the Christology of Ascent which in the NT itself, between the experience of actual contact with the historical Jesus and the descent-formulas of Christology in Paul and John, was transformed with remarkable speed into a doctrine of the Incarnation of the pre-existent Son and Logos of God. Preaching must speak of the Incarnation in such a way that experience of the actual historical Jesus is so profound and radical that it becomes the experience of that absolute and definitive presence of God to the world and to our human reality in Jesus, which is only consciously accepted without diminution or reserve when the classical formulas of Christology remain valid and are properly understood. It is, therefore, quite possible at first to come to know and regard Jesus as a human "prophet", who in a creatively new way was moved by the mystery of God and at the same time lived as a matter of course with his roots in the history of his own world, who preached God as the Father and announced the impending coming of God's reign. Even within orthodox Christology we can and may perceive in Jesus a genuinely historical consciousness, because the ultimate spiritual, ever-present transcendence of his being towards the immediate presence of God (in scholastic theology: the immediate vision of God by Jesus' soul), as the

ultimate horizon and fundamental disposition of his human existence, does not exclude a genuinely historical character from his religious life in relation to God. But this "prophet" knew that he was not merely one of the many who had time and time again during a history open towards an indeterminate future, perpetually come to reawaken a genuinely religious and radical attitude to God. He knew himself to be the final and absolute bringer of salvation, in whose person, death and resurrection the definitive covenant between God and man was realized, and was known as such through his resurrection. He knew himself to be not merely the prophet of a still awaited, purely future "reign of God", nor of one which would constitute salvation independently of his person and about which he could therefore only speak. He himself *is* the reign of God, so that the relation to his very self is what is decisive for the salvation of every human being. A saviour of this kind, however, implies precisely what we mean by Incarnation. For "salvation" is understood here as the eschatological finality of history against the background of a history which in itself could always be different and continue indefinitely and in the presence of a God of, "in himself", unending possibilities. Why the concept of an absolute saviour implies God's "Incarnation" will now have to be discussed rather more closely under another aspect (under point 3).

3. In the history of ideas the situation since the beginning of modern times has been characterized by a turning away from Greek cosmocentrism, with its thought based on things, objects, to modern anthropocentrism which in the question of being in general takes as the paradigm case the subject who knows and wills things. In order the better to understand classical Christology, therefore (without annulling it or doubting its permanent validity), it is possible and advisable to transpose ontic Christology into a transcendental, ontological Christology. Expressed as simply as may be, this means that man from the depth of his being *is* the absolutely limitless question regarding God. He does not merely pursue this question as one particular possible occupation among others. That is seen by the fact that his transcendental ordination, in knowledge and freedom, towards God – as a possibility permanently opened out by God, not as autonomous "subjectivity" – is the non-explicit but ever-operative condition of the possibility of all human knowledge and free action. This transcendence finds realization, it is true, in a multiplicity of "accidental" human acts in space and time which constitute his history, but this very multiplicity itself is grounded in the fundamental act of transcendence which constitutes the essence of man. This fundamental act (insofar as it is antecedent to the exercise of man's freedom) is at once total origin from God and movement of return to him. It is the openness to God perpetually opened out by God in the act of creation, an openness which is a question addressed to the freedom thus constituted as to whether it will accept or refuse its transcendence. That openness is also the *potentia obedientialis* for God's *self*-communication as the possible but free and radically highest answer of God to the question which man himself *is*.

In this perspective, what is called in ontic terms the hypostatic union may be expressed in ontological terms as a union of question and absolute answer, on the following suppositions. The positing of the question which is constitutive of man, and the acceptance of this interrogative character, come creatively from God himself in such a way that the question is posited precisely as the condition of the possibility of the answer being given by God's self-communication to mankind. Moreover, this happens in such a way that the will to this self-communication and to its acceptance on the part of man, being absolute, not merely conditional, itself posits the *potentia obedientialis*, the unlimited question, because the will to answer is absolute. Finally, it happens in such a way that the absolute conferring of the divine self-communication on the spiritual creature (which implies its formally predestined acceptance) appears in a historical, irreversible manifestation. Then if all this is the case, the "question" (which man is) is an intrinsic component of the answer itself. In fact if this answer is not something which simply comes from God as its author but is most truly God himself, and if the question (as self-accepted in freedom, receiving the answer, allowing itself to be answered) is posited precisely as an element in God's giving of *himself* as answer (by self-communication), then the positing of the "question" as intrinsic component of the answer is as such a reality distinct from God and yet one which most strictly belongs to him, and is proper to him. On this basis it could then be shown in greater detail that the difference "without mixture" between divine and human in Christ derives from the unifying will of God's self-communication that the creation of what is human here (as Augustine already says) takes place through the "assumption" itself, and that the "covenant" is the ground of the creation (as Karl Barth is in principle correct in stressing). What has just been said can only be rightly understood and judged when taken strictly ontologically. Mind, self-consciousness, freedom and transcendence are not accidental epiphenomena "in" something which happens to be there (which at bottom is thought of in a reified way), but form the real nature of being, which in the individual existent is only hindered from attaining its true identity by the "non-being" of matter: "actus de se illimitatus limitatur potentia realiter distincta", the Thomist would say (cf. *DS* 3601ff.; 3618). On that basis it is also understandable that God's self-giving (his irreversible and victorious self-communication) takes place to the *world* (in divinizing grace) and so has its historically irreversible and victorious manifestation and presence in redemptive history in the unique God-man. It then becomes clear that the God-man belongs to the one history of redemption precisely as a unique event (God's descent into the world happens "propter *nostram* salutem"). But it is also true that the God-man does not represent a special "degree" of divinization, without which the divinization – through grace – of others, on a lower level, should still be conceivable. Finally, in this way it is also clear that the mystery of the Incarnation fundamentally lies on the one hand in the mystery of the divine self-communication to the world, and on the other in the fact that it took place in Jesus Christ. The former aspect, however, is "thinkable" through man's fundamental tendency towards absolute closeness to God, a tendency based in fact on God's self-communication. This preserves the mystery of the Incarnation from giving the impression that it is a sort of marvel or something heteronomous.

4. It is also possible to attain an understanding of the Incarnation (which does not of course evacuate the mystery) from another point of view, which must be taken into account when this mystery has to be announced to the unbelieving "heathen" of the present time. People today have an evolutionary view of the world. They see themselves and mankind inescapably immersed in the current of history. The world for them is not a static reality, but a world in process of becoming. Natural history and human world-history form a unity. And this single total history is experienced and regarded as a history with an upward orientation, however the formal structure of each higher phase of this history is in fact described, e.g., growing interiority in self-consciousness; increasing mastery of reality as a

whole; growing unity and complexity of individual beings. If this history is to produce something really new (i.e., higher, of greater ontological intensity, not merely different) and yet do so by its own action, then the transition from one form and phase of history to another can only be characterized as "self-transcendence". This self-transcendence in the direction of what is higher, although *ex supposito* it is produced by historical beings themselves, can, however, take place only in virtue of the absolute being of God, who, without becoming a constituent of the essence of the finite existent in process of becoming, produces the self-transcendence of the finite being as the latter's own action. He does this by his creative conservation and concursus and as the future which impels and is aimed at at least asymptotically. If this idea of self-*transcendence* is conceived as a divine motion and the divine motion is conceived as conferring *self*-transcendence, the development of the material-spiritual world can be understood as a single history, without its being necessary on this account to deny or overlook the essential difference of kind within this one world and history. As we know from God's revelation expounding man's ultimate experience of grace, the highest, absolute and definitive self-transcendence of created being which is the foundation of all preceding acts of self-transcendence and gives them their ultimate meaning and goal, is the self-transcendence of the created spirit into the direct reality of the infinite mystery of the being of God himself. This self-transcendence requires God's "concursus" in an absolutely unique sense. From this point of view, such a concursus is God's gracious self-communication. The history of the world and of mind which takes place in hierarchically ordered self-transcendencies of created beings has its ground in God's self-communication. A factor of this, which posits what it requires as its own condition, is the actual creation of what is other than God. Then in the world as it in fact exists, God's self-communication itself is the first cause and last goal. The ultimate and highest self-transcendence of the finite, and God's radical self-communication, are the two sides of what happens in history. In this regard two things must always be remembered. In the first place the goal of this ultimate self-transcendence is always the unfathomable mystery of God. This characteristic of the goal therefore contributes to determine the whole way into the future. It is a path into what is unknown and open. All self-transcendence is therefore hope and loving self-abandonment to what is absolutely beyond man's control and communicates itself as incomprehensible love. Furthermore, the history of self-transcendence is a history of freedom, and therefore a history of the possible, and actually realized, guilt and refusal of this dynamism of history, or of the false (i.e., autonomous) interpretation of self-transcendence, a history of the possibilities of the absolute and final failure to attain the last end. Within such a double possibility in the history of freedom, renunciation, the "Cross", and death have a necessary place.

This history of God's self-communication and of the creature's self-transcendence, which is the history of the increasing divinization of the world, does not take place only in the depths of the free conscience, but because of man's unity in plurality and the dynamic tendency of grace towards the transfiguration of all creation, has an actually concrete historical dimension. It is manifest and assumes concrete form in what we call history of salvation in the proper and usual sense, and this latter, a concrete history in space and time, is the history in which God's self-communication and the self-transcendence of the creature (i.e., man) takes place. Where God's self-communication and man's self-transcendence reach their absolute and irreversible culmination, i.e., where God is simply and irrevocably "there" in time and space and consequently where man's self-transcendence also attains a similarly complete self-giving to God, we have what in Christian terms is called the Incarnation. This indicates the Christocentricity of the world both on the cosmic plane and on that of the history of freedom. Not that the world attains its absolute self-transcendence "only" in Christ. It attains it as a whole, insofar as all that is material transcends itself into the domain of the spiritual and personal and will finally exist in the final fulfilment only as a factor of what is spiritual (in angels and men), and insofar as absolute closeness to God, to the absolute, infinite being, will be attained in the perfected spiritual creation. And so Christ does not really represent a "higher stage" of the spirit's self-transcendence and of God's self-communication. If this were so, we should have to ask why it only occurred once and why it is not attained in all spiritual creatures in a "panchristism". The incarnate Logos is the culmination and centre of the divinization of the world rather because as an "individual" he is necessarily present when the divinization of the world in grace and glory reaches its irreversible culmination and historically manifest victory. Because God gives himself to the *world*, there is Christ. He is not simply a possible mediator of salvation if he wills to accomplish this mediation, but is this mediation itself as irrevocable and as historically manifest. And this does not render the event of the cross and resurrection superfluous but actually implies them (see *Salvation*).

5. As regards the question why Christian dogma declares that the Son of the Father, the divine Logos as the second person of the triune God, and not another divine person, became man, reference must be made to the article on the *Trinity*. The two statements mutually condition one another's intelligibility. Because the Trinity of the economy of the redemption *is* the immanent Trinity (and conversely), the "Word" in which the Father (God without origin), without ceasing to be the uncircumscribable, utters *himself* to us (so that the Word must be consubstantial with the Father) is necessary for our understanding of the immanent Logos of the Father and the converse is also true.

6. By these and similar considerations which it has only been possible to indicate very inadequately here, because of the present state of theological reflection, preaching today must create in the hearer of the Christian message the necessary presuppositions so that the doctrine of the Incarnation can "make an impact" and not give the impression of being a merely mythological conception.

Karl Rahner

INDIFFERENCE

Indifference is an aspect of the Christian's attitude to the world.

1. There is no single word in Scripture to designate indifference. But the attitude grows from Christ's liberation of man from the powers of this world, so that he lives in expectation of the Day of the Lord (cf. Rom 8:18–39; 14:8–12; 1 Cor 4:9–13; 7:27–39; 2 Cor 4:16–5:10; Tit 2:12f.; Heb 10:32–39). Expectation of the eschatological event implies a freedom which enables the Christian to keep his correct distance from inner-worldly things and still be involved in history as he ought (see especially the ὡς μή formulas of 1 Cor 7:29–32).

2. In the spirituality of the Fathers, less emphasis was laid on the biblical and eschatological aspects of indifference. The influence of contemporary philosophy, such as the Stoic doctrines of indifference to pleasure or pain

(ἀπάθεια), impassivity under pleasure or pain (ἀταραξία) led to indifference being presented rather as a taming of the passions, which was to bring about the dispassionate repose of the soul which claimed to guarantee full freedom from created things in the vision of God.

3. In medieval German mysticism, the notion of indifference was rendered as "composure", "unconcern", which was essentially correct, but still could suggest a misunderstanding of indifference as a Stoic detachment, a cold aloofness from all that was not God.

4. In Ignatian spirituality indifference became a key-term. In the *Spiritual Exercises* of St. Ignatius Loyola, indifference is the indispensable precondition for going on to the central and decisive moment of the Exercises, the "Election" or choice (*Exercises*, no. 179; cf. also no. 166). The theology of indifference is indicated in the "Principle and Foundation" which is placed before the Exercises proper. From the end of man and of all created things it follows necessarily that "we must make ourselves indifferent to all created things, insofar as this is allowed to our free will and is not forbidden" (no. 23). If one notes the examples where indifference is to be brought into play according to Ignatius (the urge to be strong, to possess, to dominate, to exist, nos. 23, 166), it will be seen that these are fundamentally concentrated in man's effort at self-assertion within this world as a closed system. The object of "indifference" is to break through this shell, so that man can come face to face with the will of God (in the resolution or decision taken, for instance, in the "election" of the Exercises). But indifference, in the sense of detachment, is not the last word on the relationship of Christians to the world. The sphere and function of indifference are limited by the second conclusion drawn in the "Principle and Foundation", which is that we must "choose that which brings us more fully to the end for which we were created", and also by the link between indifference and decision ("election"). When the theses of the Foundation are interpreted Christologically, in keeping with the basic principle of Ignatian spirituality, it is seen to contain the eschatological perspective of the dynamism of history which Scripture uses to determine the Christian's attitude to created things. Hence indifference is the negative aspect of a courageous and confident commitment to history, of a definite position taken up in the dimension of the visible, in Church and world. This commitment is the choice to be decided on in the "election". The "outward gaze" which the Christian is to practise integrates indifference into Ignatian spirituality as a whole. Hence it is not a neutral aloofness from history but a constant effort to go beyond the restrictive set of circumstances which hedge in every human decision and to reach a greater openness for the purpose of all created things. Indifference means being wholly open to the claim of God's will, which is disclosed to the believer by the movement of his history towards its eschatological goal. In the vital integration of indifference and choice, of freedom and active, decided commitment to history, of hearing and of loving response, this detachment is the opposite of a cold and aloof scepticism, or a weary resignation, and is absolutely contrary to all indifferentism.

Ernst Niermann

INDIVIDUALISM

Individualism can stand for a large number of highly divergent views and attitudes, of which the highest common factor is the effort to make the individual stand out in bold relief against the background of society, community, group, collectivity and general setting. The meaning of individualism in any given case must be sought in the actual context. There is no systematic philosophy of individualism which the representative upholders of individualism possess. It is rather a matter of individualistic tendencies appearing in the train of other philosophical conceptions such as eudaemonism, nominalism, scepticism, subjectivism and existentialism. Here to some extent the individual is taken to be the goal and norm of ethical, political and anthropological knowledge in general and to some extent the individuality, in the metaphysical and logical sense, is given pride of place in contrast to the universal and the ideal, being considered as objectively prior, or as the only thing knowable or even real.

Individualism, however, is not necessarily at work every time that stress is laid on the individual or the individuality. It would be foolish, for instance, to see the Sophists and Socrates as representative stages on the way to individualism; it is even more aberrant to see Jesus as "the real initiator of religious individualism" (cf. *HERE*, VII, p. 219). Nonetheless, Socrates, the prophets, the Buddha, Confucius and Jesus (cf. K. Jaspers, *Socrates, Buddha, Confucius, Jesus* [1966]) and many others after them belong to the great individual figures of humanity; it is true to say that a history could be written of the flowering of consciousness as the personal self-awareness of the individual. But its stages would not be initial forms of individualism or preludes to it. Individualism, as a theory or as an attitude to life, is rather a one-sided overemphasis laid on the individuality. Abelard, St. Thomas Aquinas, Eckhart, Luther, Calvin and St. Ignatius Loyola are not "individualists", though they were – also – great individual personages. Hence the term individualism is unsuitable and should not be used to characterize the appeal to the individuality or personality in the metaphysical or ethical sense, that is, the appeal to the dignity, responsibility and freedom of man. For this it would be better to use the word personalism, in the metaphysical sense, though this again should be filled out by the (newer) concept of personalism, understood as an existential activation of the personality.

Though the term individualism cannot therefore be used for any philosophical theory, the concept seems to be most enlightening and useful to characterize a certain attitude to life and way of behaviour. In this sense, individualism is a modern phenomenon, which is usually associated with the Renaissance, the Reformation, the rationalism of the Enlightenment and the great revolutions. The individualistic attitude can express itself in an astonishingly large number of variations. It includes the appeal to reason, conscience, personal freedom as well as a total or partial resistance to traditional culture, beliefs, political and ecclesiastical institutions.

To show the whole wide spectrum of possible individualist attitudes in all their shades of colour, one could quote such names as Montaigne, Hobbes, Locke, Rousseau as well as Kant, Goethe, W. von Humboldt, Schiller and the economists A. Smith, Bentham and Ricardo; then there are figures like Bakunin, Carlyle, M. Stirner and Nietzsche and finally Christians like Schleiermacher, Kierkegaard and Newman. The term individualism is hardly applicable here because it is so equivocal. The above should be contrasted with figures like Hegel, Comte and Marx, as well as the upholders of socialist and collectivist theories in general and of fascist nationalism, and also those whose philosophy of history and especially of the State is dominated by an organic determinism. "Individualism" is often reproached with depreciating the State and society, whereas it gives in fact their proper value to State and society, which is a relative one. Liberalism, the "social contract" and democratic institutions are not simply to be branded as symptoms of individualism. On the contrary, they voice powerfully an understanding of the individual which can be ultimately justified only on biblical and Christian principles, and uphold the individual against the pressure to conform unduly to the anonymous mass, whether in the State and society or in the Church regarded merely as an institution. Where, however, emphasis on the individual becomes rejection of political responsibility, anti-social and egoistic (cf. its extreme form in M. Stirner, *Der Einzelne und sein Eigentum* [1845]), it leads ultimately to anarchy and the absurdity of solipsism.

The solution of the conflict between individualism and collectivism – in the fields of (social) ethics, politics, pedagogy, culture, religion and law – is to be sought in a correct understanding of personalism and solidarity. Actually, there is still plenty of room for individualist attitudes in the mass society of a technical age, and this type of "individualism" should be encouraged today. It is not the preserve of the rich, nor of the intellectuals and artists. At the present day, everyone has to foster a certain individualism or search for privacy, as a necessary and possible line of self-defence against the encroachments of publicity and the world of work. And such an individualism is one of the conditions of reciprocal personal relationships. The rights of the individual need to be stressed today as much as the rights of the person, if man is really to be himself.

From the theological point of view it should be noted that individualism, whatever its form, can only exist by virtue of the intervention of Christianity, since the consciousness of selfhood and individuality has its bases in the biblical experience of man's relationship to God. Within Christianity, however, it has happened that too much importance was attached to the subjective effort to attain salvation. The Christian thing is not the individual but the universal character of salvation. Piety, liturgy, the self-understanding of the Church, pastoral care and moral direction are now turning more and more away from individualism to enter more deeply into the spirit of eschatological brotherhood. Basic words like "the individual", "the heart" and "the person" point indeed to the inviolable dignity of each single historical human being, which can never be renounced and which sets up within the Church a fruitful and sometimes painful tension between authority and freedom. Theologically therefore an extreme individualism is also absurd, though the dignity of the individual can only be fully recognized in the light of faith.

Heinz Robert Schlette

INDULGENCES

The question of indulgences offers dogmatic, psychological and pastoral difficulties. To have a sound basis for discussion, we begin with the teaching of the Church, always bearing in mind, however, that most of the declarations of the magisterium (all, in fact, except the Council of Trent, which is very reserved) are not irreformable decisions and that they are often the echo of a theology which is not in all respects of a strictly binding character. As regards the notion of temporal punishments due to sin, reference must be made throughout to the article on "Sin" since otherwise misunderstandings would be almost inevitable.

A. Official Teaching of the Church

The fullest description of indulgences by the magisterium is found in *CIC*, can. 911 (similarly Leo X: *D* 740a): the remission before God of a temporal punishment for sins of which the guilt has been forgiven (at least by the end of the work to which the indulgence is attached: can. 925), granted by ecclesiastical authority out of the Treasury of the Church, to the living by way of absolution, to the dead by way of suffrage. Though the details of this description have not been defined, it has been defined as a doctrine of the faith against Wycliffe, Huss and the Reformers that the Church has authority (*potestas*) to grant indulgences and that they are to be retained in the Church and are salutary for the faithful (Trent: *D* 989, 1471; cf. also *D* 622, 676–8, 757–62). The pronouncements of the magisterium also indicate that in addition to the state of grace (cf. *D* 551, 676) further conditions are required for the gaining of an indulgence: baptism, freedom from excommunication, performance of prescribed work, and at least a general intention of gaining the indulgence (*CIC*, can. 925). Indulgences relate not only to the Church's canonical penalties but to the punishments due before God for sins (*D* 759, 1540). They are granted by the Church out of the "Treasury of the Church", which consists of the merits of Christ and of the saints (this was first declared by Clement VI in 1343: *D* 550–2; cf. 740a, 757, 1060, 1541, 2193). The power of the Pope (and, in dependence on him, that of other ecclesiastical authorities: *CIC*, can. 912, 239 §1 n. 24; 247 n. 2; 349 §2 n. 2) to grant indulgences is designated simply as *potestas* or as "power of the keys" (*D* 740a), which last term must doubtless (because of indulgences for the dead) be understood in a broad sense. There is no binding official declaration of the sense of the terms "per modum absolutionis", "per modum suffragii".

Theologians interpret the first in various ways (formerly, by reference to the remission of what are now hypothetical ecclesiastical penalties from which "absolution was given"; "payment" [*solutio*] of punishments in purgatory out of the Treasury of the Church; direct release from punishment, etc.). As regards the "per modum suffragii", cf. Sixtus IV: *D* 723a. The practice of the Church shows that there is a scale of indulgences, some of which are characterized by the provisions of the ancient canonical penances of the Church and are called "indulgentia partialis" (*CIC*, can. 921 §2), while the others are called "indulgentia plenaria" (l. c. and can. 926). A strictly official definition of the precise sense of this distinction has never been given by the magisterium. It is still disputed among theologians whether the plenary indulgence is simply the remission of all canonical penalties with an effect in purgatory which cannot be determined more precisely (Cajetan and a few others) or is intended directly to remit all punishment for sin before God (most theologians), though whether this intention is fully achieved in the individual instance remains quite undecided (cf. *CIC*, can. 929; Gregory XVI, in Cavallerra, n. 1273). It is certain that indulgences for the dead are of benefit to them "per modum suffragii" (Sixtus IV, 1476: *D* 723a, 740a, 762, 1542; *CIC*, can. 911). No authoritative decision has been given regarding *the way* they help the dead. In order to understand indulgences, reference must also be made to the doctrines of the temporal punishment due to sin and of purgatory. The Council of Trent defined that guilt (*culpa*) and punishment incurred by sin (*poena*) are not identical and are therefore not necessarily remitted simultaneously (*D* 535, 807, 840, 904, 922–925). There is no official explicit and definite doctrine regarding the more precise nature of punishment due to sin.

B. Scripture

As will become even clearer later, it is not correct to try to draw a scriptural proof in the proper sense from Mt 16 and 18. These passages, which are classical texts for the sacrament of penance, would prove, if they proved anything about indulgences, that in the sacrament of penance all punishment for sin can be remitted judicially, which is heretical. It is rather to be noted that a) it is a familiar idea in Scripture that the overcoming of the whole culpable alienation from God of a human being in his whole many-sided nature can be a long moral process ("to seek" the Lord; long practice of penance; penitential liturgy; dependence of the remission of all "guilt" on subsequent manner of life, etc.). This is all the more so because guilt can have consequences which are not simply extinguished by conversion to the God of mercy, so that the seriousness of penance can even consist precisely in the humble, deliberate acceptance of judgment (1 Cor 5:5; 1 Tim 1:20; 1 Cor 11:32; Rev 2:22f.), which one does not simply escape by conversion, for in fact the latter can even be the consequence of the former (*TWNT*, IV, p. 983). If according to Scripture there are in fact punishments imposed by God for sin which are not cancelled when the guilt is forgiven (cf. Gen 3:17–19 with Wis 10:2; Num 20:12 with 27:13f.; 2 Sam 12:10–14), then at all events it cannot be a fundamental and consistent norm that God's forgiveness of guilt involves *ipso facto* remission of the consequences of guilt and therefore of punishments due to sin. b) The Church can support this long process of reconciliation by its prayer. This is shown by the liturgical penitential prayers of the OT including those for the dead (2 Macc 12:43–46). The NT also bears witness to this (Mt 6:12; 1 Jn 3:20–22, 5:16; 2 Tim 1:18; Jas 5:16, etc.). c) A prayer of the Church as the sacred community of God's victorious mercy, made in the name of Jesus, has the firm promise of being heard (Mt 18:19f.; Mk 11:24; Jn 15:16; 1 Jn 5:15; Jas 5:16, etc.), to which the only limits are those set by the nature of God who hears prayer in his own sovereign way, and the willingness of the person for whom the prayer is offered.

C. Tradition

As the nature of indulgences is complex, having grown historically from various factors, we must first see how indulgences arose in the course of history (and were not simply discovered).

1. The Church's most ancient theology of penance clearly implies that a) the blotting-out of post-baptismal sins is not simply "remission" of sins, as in baptism, but presupposes a severe personal penitential activity of the sinner, even though (as Augustine clearly states) this activity absolutely requires to be based on the grace of Christ. Though in antiquity no terminological distinction was yet drawn between guilt and the penalty it entails, the foundation for the distinction was laid, for from the very beginning of a man's conversion no more doubt was felt about his salvation, yet a long penance was considered necessary (the distinction is in fact found substantially in the Protestant distinction between justification and sanctification). At least from the 2nd century onward, the Church supervised this subjective atonement by the sinner and regulated it according to the gravity of his guilt, and so the consciousness of possessing authority to determine works of penance, individually or generally, and to adapt them to the individual sinner, was very early taken as a matter of course. Severe penances being the rule for each sin, the coming of frequent confession in the early Middle Ages brought with it the counterpoise of "redemptory" works in individual cases. b) This process of purification could be supported by the prayer of the Church (whether of a more official, or a more private kind, the intercession of the martyrs). Such intercession took place in an officially regulated liturgical manner (by bishop and people) and was certain of being heard, insofar as the hearing depended on it. This intercession was not primarily the "form" of the sacrament of penance. That form consists of reconciliation with the Church and so with God. The intercession supported the subjective endeavour of the sinner to make atonement.

2. In the period of transition from

public to private penance (6th–10th century), a) reconciliation was gradually brought forward to the beginning of the Church's sacramental penitential discipline and yet a personal performance of penance was required, subsequent to reconciliation. That inevitably underlined the distinction between guilt and punishment. b) Even independently of the actual penitential proceedings, the sinner was assured of the Church's intercession in solemn but not in the proper sense jurisdictional forms (the original meaning of the absolutions from Gregory the Great onwards). c) Through the practice of commutations and redemptions of canonical penances (scale of penances), which was not a purely disciplinary measure but concerned the Church's insistence on undergoing the punishment due before God for sin, there was inevitably an increased awareness that the various ways of promoting the process of recovery of spiritual health and of sanctification are interchangeable.

3. Through the amalgamation of these traditional elements, the first actual indulgences appeared in practice and at first without theological reflection in France in the 11th century. The Church (bishops, Popes) assured believers in solemn and general form of its official intercession, and on that account, by an act of jurisdiction, simply remitted part or all of the particular person's canonical penance. The latter is not replaced by some other work of penance, even a more lenient one, as had been done in the remissions of penance for pilgrims to Rome in the 9th century. These must be regarded as redemptions. In contrast, the indulgenced work must rather be regarded merely as the ground of the special intercession-*absolutio*. The indulgence took place outside the sacrament of penance by a general offer, in the conviction that the efficacy of the intercessory prayer for propitiatory sanctification of the sinner was the same as would have resulted from his doing penance on his own behalf.

In this sense the first actual indulgences were on the one hand a true act of jurisdiction (remission of a real canonical penance) and yet from the start were regarded (on account of the "absolution"-intercession linked to this act of jurisdiction) as effectual non-sacramental remission before God of temporal punishment due to sin. From the point of view of historical development it is the linking of these two acts which constituted indulgences as such. The connection of indulgences with the priest's intercessory prayer in the sacrament of penance and with the practice of redemptions and commutations explains why indulgences were not at first regarded as the Pope's prerogative but were granted by bishops and confessors in carrying out their office. The slow transition from redemptions conceded very leniently, to indulgences, explains why the performance of some work was always insisted on as an indispensable condition of an indulgence. It also explains why even into the 13th century indulgences were regarded as a concession to the imperfect, which better Christians should not claim. In the transitional period it is not always possible to distinguish between a lenient commutation and an actual indulgence. Once the various elements had coalesced to form the firm concept of an indulgence, it was no longer to be expected that attention would be explicitly directed towards the *intercessory* absolution. There was simply an awareness of the power to remit punishment due to sin, without much reflection on the mode of its operation.

4. It was not till the 12th century that theological reflection was focused on indulgences. At first it was opposed to them. Abelard contested the bishops' right to grant indulgences. The Synod of Sens censured him on that account but on grounds that are not clear. Similar opposition was shown by Peter of Poitiers and other early scholastic theo-

logians. From the end of the 12th century onward the attitude of theology gradually became favourable, the chief argument being actual practice. With Huguccio (d. 1210) indulgences appear for the first time as an act of jurisdiction regarding the actual punishment due before God to sins. For a long time it was not clear why the suffrages of the Church were an adequate substitute for the effect that would have been produced in the next world by the remitted canonical penance. Nor was it clear what relation there was between the good work imposed as a condition, and the efficacy of the indulgence. Was it to be regarded as a redemption, or as a mere condition of an effect which itself derived exclusively from the power of the keys? Before the great age of Scholasticism the prevailing opinion seems to have been that indulgences possess their transcendent efficacy not because of a direct power of the Church to absolve, but only *per modum suffragii*. A new phase in the doctrine of indulgences arose when the idea of the Treasury of the Church was explicitly worked out (it is found in Hugo of St.-Cher, 1230). This made it possible to indicate more clearly what replaced the remitted penance. When it was added that the Church had a lawful claim to this Treasury and had jurisdiction to carry the claim into effect, the former difficulties appeared at an end, and the doctrine of indulgences as we still know it today could be developed. Previously the Church had only prayed for the remission of temporal punishment due to sin, and had excused a canonical penance on that account. Now, however, the remission of punishment could be regarded as occurring in an act of jurisdiction administering the Treasury of the Church authoritatively – as an owner disposes of his property – and consequently with unfailing efficacy (Albert, Bonaventure, Aquinas). On this basis it was possible for the relation between indulgences and the remission of canonical penances gradually to become so tenuous that at least some theologians (Billot, for example) excluded it entirely from the essence of an indulgence. For the same reason, after St. Thomas's time, the granting of indulgences became increasingly independent of the sacrament of penance, and a prerogative of the Pope, because only the Pope (or those empowered by him) could administer the Treasury of the Church. Earlier, when it had also (not solely!) been a question of remitting canonical penance, all who imposed such penances (confessors or, at least, bishops) could grant indulgences on their own authority. On the other hand, if the Church can administer the Treasury of the Church juridically, it becomes more difficult to solve the problem why and to what extent some good work is required as a condition for gaining an indulgence. This was really only intelligible in connection with the old commutations and redemptions of canonical penances, but not in the new jurisdictional theory.

5. Subsequent development of practice in the Middle Ages bears the following marks. a) Multiplication of indulgences accompanied by continual lessening of the indulgenced works. It is true that it was maintained that some work was a necessary condition on the part of the Church, though any reasonable cause could be considered sufficient for granting an indulgence (*Summa Theologica*, Suppl., q. 25, a. 2). b) The appearance of "plenary" indulgences. Towards the end of the 11th century the Church began to promise the Crusaders complete remission of punishment for sin (Urban II; Mansi, XX, 816), and in this way plenary indulgences arose (Boniface VIII: first Jubilee plenary indulgence, A.D. 1300). c) Since theologians and canonists from the 13th century onwards had been teaching the application of indulgences to the dead (cf. St. Thomas in IV *Liber Sententiarum*, Dist. 45 q. 2, a 2 sol. 2; *Summa Theo-*

logica, Suppl., q. 71, a. 10), genuine papal grants of indulgences for the dead are made from the middle of the 15th century. d) The use made of indulgences for fiscal purposes. In view of the biblical and traditional praise of alms-giving, there could be no intrinsic objection to alms-giving as the good work prescribed for gaining an indulgence, and in fact indulgences for alms-giving are found as early as the 11th century. In the later Middle Ages, however, on account of their material usefulness for Church purposes, such indulgences were multiplied beyond all measure, and were regarded as a convenient source of money to be tapped at will. This was often exploited simoniacally by those who preached indulgences in a theologically frivolous and exaggerated way, as the Council of Trent expressly observes (Mansi, XXXIII, 193f.; cf. also *D* 983).

D. Theological Interpretation of the Nature of Indulgences

It is permissible to doubt whether an adequate theological interpretation has yet been achieved. That is not surprising, because practice was in advance of theory and the reality involved is a many-sided one.

1. Negatively it may be said, contrary to the view of the vast majority of present-day theologians, that the Church's power of granting indulgences (even to the living) is not a power of jurisdiction in the strict sense, as regards the temporal punishment due to sin in the eyes of God, and that the appeal to Mt 16 is, therefore, not well-founded. Otherwise as regards the punishment due to sin, the Church would be able to do more outside the sacrament of penance and its judicial power than within it, yet the remission of such punishment is one of the very purposes of the sacrament. Nor would it be clear why the Church should not link the two powers so as to remit guilt and punishment entirely in every sacramental act. But that is contrary to tradition and to the teaching of the Council of Trent. Besides, indulgences for the living and for the dead would be different in kind. That does not mean that we deny that an act of jurisdiction was originally involved in indulgences, i.e., the remission of canonical penance. Nowadays, of course, this is merely hypothetical, and simply serves to express the different degrees of intensity with which the Church promises its intercession. It would also follow from the jurisdiction theory that the remission of punishment for sin in the sacrament of penance is less extensive, less certain and less readily to be assumed, than in indulgences. But that is contrary to the dignity of the sacrament and contrary to the fact that an indulgence, historically speaking, is simply that part of the sacrament which the Church can perform apart from the sacrament, and which consequently can be given distinct form. Besides, the theory which we are rejecting had to accept the difficulty and improbability that an (*ex supposito*) independent jurisdictional authority of the Church, derived from Christ (cf. *D* 989), was not exercised at all during 1000 years. For the regulation and mitigation of canonical penances, which always existed, is not the same thing as the granting of indulgences.

Finally, we must bear in mind that two formally and totally distinct causes cannot be assumed for the one effect. But it cannot be doubted, and has always been admitted in theology, that a charity which is perfect in all respects, which is not merely initially present in the intention but strives to integrate into itself the manifold dimensions and efforts of man's being – and hence is not necessarily there even at the death of the justified – means the remission of all the "temporal punishments due to sin". But if this principle is correct, then an indulgence can be nothing else than a (very important) aid accorded to the repentant sinner, to enable him to attain this charity which blots out everything but which is not necessarily present at the moment of justification. It is an (intercessory) aid for the gaining of the grace needed for such charity. In this way an indulgence ceases to be envisaged as a juridical process which is completely or to a great extent independent of the progress of man to maturity in morality and holiness and which would therefore deal with a restricted relationship of man to God. The notion of such a partial relationship was unhappy, since it implied that it could be regulated independently of love of God, whereas in reality the whole relationship to God is determined by charity. This way of integrating indulgences into the one process of faith and love which embraces the whole man and is therefore multidimensional, does not diminish the significance of indulgences, as will be made still clearer below. But this interpretation can resolve the justifiable inhibitions which are often felt today with regard to the conventional theology of indulgences – and a resulting practice which is often a matter of crude calculations. This approach also enables us to see clearly – as is *not* the case in the ordinary theory in spite of its well-intentioned efforts to do justice to this view-point – why indulgences are not in any way detrimental to the true spirit of works of penance. This last is what the help of the Church precisely aims at, because the integration of the whole reality of man into charity, which is perfected in this way, necessarily implies penance in the sinner.

2. The nature of an indulgence consists, then, in the special intercession continually made by the Church, in its liturgy and in the prayers of its members, on behalf of the complete reconciliation of its members, an intercession which by an indulgence is solemnly and in a special way applied to a particular member. Because that intercession is the prayer of holy Church itself and concerns a benefit which is indubitably in harmony with the will of God, it is in itself always certain of being heard, unlike the prayer of an individual sinful human being who does not know whether he is asking as he ought for what he ought; its only limit, but a real one, is therefore the receptivity of the person for whom it is made. If one remembers that even a "prayer" – as in the case of the anointing of the sick – can be an *opus operatum*, that only "actual" graces are asked for in indulgences, that every *opus operatum* is limited by the disposition of the recipient, then in the theory of indulgences here put forward there is nothing to prevent our granting the character of an *opus operatum* to an indulgence, as is generally done today in theology – though without making it sacramental.

On this basis, too, there is a difference between indulgences for the living and for the dead. The latter are not only beyond the Church's jurisdiction, but in other respects are in a special position, which means that the efficacy of the Church's official expiatory intercession for them is of a different kind. It is only indirect, through the merit of the living gainer of the indulgence, and through the recipient's merit, acquired earlier in life but no longer susceptible of increase, in relation to this indulgence (cf. Sixtus IV in *D* 723a).

3. On this basis the role of the "Treasury of the Church" in indulgences becomes clear. If we were to suppose that it is utilized by an act of jurisdiction, this would amount to "paying off" the individual items of punishment due, by partial reparations thought of in an equally fragmentary way (cf. Billot). On closer examination, such a conception is an impossible one and is rejected nowadays (e.g., by Galtier). But when the Church intercedes, it necessarily does so as the Body of Christ in union with the dignity and sacrifice of its head, and as the Church which is holy in all its "saints", that is, it "appeals" to the Treasury of the

Church. Nothing is in the proper sense "paid out" of that Treasury, but appeal is always made globally, and consequently it is not lessened but increased thereby. Galtier is therefore right in emphasizing that the recourse to the Treasury of the Church is made in every case of remission of guilt and punishment, and is therefore not something peculiar to indulgences. Hence the "Treasury of the Church" is nothing else than the salvific will of God, which aims at bringing all men to perfect charity. And such charity includes reparation and the elimination of the "punishments for sin", since this salvific will exists as centred on the redemption wrought by Christ and the holiness of the whole Church which depends on this redemption but is also present through it. And this holiness implies a dynamism which tends to the perfect charity which eliminates all the consequences of sin in every member of this Church.

4. The manner in which this intercession of the Church is to be considered efficacious in remitting the penalties of sin, and how exactly the certainty of an indulgence's efficacy is to be estimated, essentially depends on the precise idea formed of the nature of punishment for sin. If this is viewed solely as retribution, brought about by the justice of God specially for that purpose, but without significance for the moral purification and perfection of man, its remission would have to be viewed as God's simply waiving its actual infliction. As regards the way of representing the efficacy of indulgences, that would mean that on the part of the person gaining them, the only condition to be taken into account would be the cessation of actual attachment to sin. In that case indulgences would be an easier and more certain method of effacing the penalties of sin than personal penance and growth in holiness. If, however, the penalties of sin are regarded as various features of a person's interior and external condition brought about by sin, which are not removed or overcome by the first conversion (remission of the stain of guilt), and if these, through their disharmony with the whole objective, divinely-created reality (as the external instrument of punishment), both here and after death, produce suffering which is both retributive and in itself medicinal, then the remission by indulgences of the temporal punishment due to sin must be regarded as a divine help to discharging more rapidly and salutarily the "real" penalty of sin, in the sense defined. On this view, more conditions have to be fulfilled for this laborious conquest and total inner purification. And this latter does not necessarily imply an increase of merit and grace, but simply their increased influence on a person's whole state, such as can also be thought to occur in purgatory. An indulgence is only effective inasmuch as the willingness is there to undertake an ever deeper and sanctifying purification of the whole person, over and above the remission of the stain of guilt as such. This view makes it clear why indulgences and personal penance are not detrimental to each other, because an indulgence is seen as the Church's help to more intensive and consequently more rapid and salutary penance, not as a substitute, lessening the need for penance.

E. Consequences for Pastoral Theology

1. The first thing is to note the fact, soberly, that interest in indulgences is largely diminishing in the Church, even in circles where religion is devoutly practised. The genuine religious concerns of Catholics have profoundly changed in form, being transferred to the celebration of the Eucharist, personal prayer and a truly Christian steadfastness in face of the tragic hardships of ordinary existence. It may also be noted that people today find it harder to feel a share of responsibility for their dead relations and friends. This may be

due to the individualistic attitudes of modern culture (cf. K. Rahner, "Verehrung der Heiligen", *Geist und Leben* 37 [1964], pp. 325–40). It is unlikely that official commendations of indulgences or the granting of new ones would do much to change this situation.

2. Nonetheless, if indulgences are to be really retained, as the Council of Trent teaches, and not just officially upheld, the following points should be noted.

a) Efforts in this direction, justifiable though they be, should be prudently restricted, since otherwise too much pastoral time and energy would be consumed which should today be devoted to other objects.

The actual forms of the granting of indulgences (their frequency, the use made of them to recommend other secondary goals such as particular devotions, the number especially of "plenary" indulgences) need to be courageously though prudently revised. An obvious question, which should not cause much alarm, is whether the distinction between plenary and partial indulgences should not be abandoned. In any case, the various degrees of partial indulgences seems to have lost all religious significance today, though they still have a strange vogue, behind which no genuine principle can be discerned. Plenary indulgences at any rate – supposing indeed that the term should be retained – should be linked with an act of religion which really corresponds to the significance of such a grant.

b) The doctrine of the communion of saints, of the veneration of saints, of the punishments of sin, of the necessity and blessing of personal penance and finally of indulgences should be preached in such a way that it fits into the whole framework of the Christian life. The doctrine of indulgences should be made really intelligible in this whole context and hence "practicable". A formal juridical notion of indulgences would not lend itself to this end.

c) Forms and practices should be devised, such as prayer of intercession, penitential devotions, etc., which will help the faithful to recognize through their concrete experience that the Church, as the body of Christ and fellowship of seekers of salvation, is always interceding by its prayers for the individual members in their perils and struggles. Once this task of the Church, which is also that of the individual, is brought home to the faithful in the concrete, they will once more be able to see the meaning and the blessing of what we call indulgences. For they are one way in which the Church, in its concern for their salvation, thinks of them and prays for them.

Karl Rahner

INERRANCY

Inerrancy may, on the one hand, apply to knowledge of a spiritual subject as a whole or to individual knowledge of that subject. On the other hand, it can be regarded as the factual state or as a fundamental freedom from error. In both senses, inerrancy may, on the one hand, proceed from the very being of the spiritual subject concerned. (This may be a question of all knowledge: that is, God; or it may be a question of a certain sphere: for example, a knowledge of man with regard to certain ultimate ontological and ethical principles, or a knowledge of angels with regard to their knowledge of their own being.) On the other hand, however, it may be already given in certain circumstances ultimately brought about by God. As a concept, inerrancy should not be confused with omniscience or with the absolute adequacy of knowledge with its object. (In other words, it should not be regarded as identical with a knowledge that completely exhausts all that can be known about a given object. This would mean an ultimate objective identification of inerrancy with omniscience, since every object forms part of the whole of reality and is orientated towards the infinity of God, so that it can be adequately known together with everything.) The inevitable inadequacy of finite knowledge, however, is one of the causes of error and is (both subjectively and objectively) often difficult to distinguish from error itself, since error is frequently no more than a (guilty and sectarian) enclosing of oneself in the (inevitable) inadequacy of knowledge. Inerrancy, then, is often simply an openness to the inadequacy (which can frequently only be clearly known by others) of true (but historically conditioned) knowledge with regard to the greater (but unknown) extent of the object of that knowledge. There is also the Thomist metaphysical question of knowledge and freedom, in which an existentially different depth and firmness of consent (opinion – firm judgment) and a possibly contradictory difference between that to which implicit (but really also subjective) consent and that to which explicit consent is given are acknowledged. For this metaphysical tension, even in the case of an explicit error of opinion committed by one who is justified, without guilt and in a state of grace, it is possible for inerrancy to exist with regard to existentially meaningful truths because of an implicit knowledge to which a more radical consent has been given (see 1 John 2. 20, 27; John 16. 13). Insofar as inerrancy is an expression of the Spirit as truth and an existential communication of the subject with reality itself, it is a value, an object of moral will and a saving possession (to the extent that it is possible to achieve inerrancy as a whole through correct moral decisions and God's disclosure of himself in grace). Hence, in its various ways (in its varying object, its varying regional extent and its varying degree of certainty), inerrancy appears as a theological theme in the context of God's omniscience, Adam's knowledge in the first state, Christ's knowledge, Holy Scripture, the infallibility of the Church's magisterium, and the question as to whether for man there can be an atheism without guilt and absolute moral error.

Karl Rahner

INFALLIBILITY

A. Notion

The term infallibility very often is understood to imply also sinlessness, a mistake which had to be denounced by Bishop Gasser as the official *relator* at Vatican I (see Mansi, LII, 1219). "Inerrancy" might be better, but this is usually reserved for the same quality in Scripture. The positive content of the term infallibility is simply "truth" or "truthfulness". In the following exposition we continue to use the word infallibility.

Infallibility must be distinguished from inspiration, which is attributed only to the attestation of revelation in the Church of the Apostles and the canonical books of the Old and New Testaments. Infallibility is an element of the "*assistentia*" *Spiritus Sancti*, granted to the Church of post-apostolic times.

Since the closing of revelation does not mean that providence ceases to watch over the further progress of Church history and the history of dogmas, infallibility may be regarded as a corollary to the development of doctrine. If we further consider "truth" in its biblical sense of fidelity, the fidelity with which God makes good his promises in history, the infallibility of the Church can then be provisionally described as the historical form which the fidelity of God takes in being true to his historical revelation which was brought to its unsurpassable conclusion in Christ, since he uses the Church to this end.

B. Theological Context

Though infallibility is predicated of the Church, it should not be treated as one of the attributes of the Church, since it is rather the general condition of their possibility, especially of the indefectibility. Hence infallibility must be linked with the possibility of the Church in general. Since the Church is the recipient and mediator of revelation, which means that theological knowledge has an ecclesial dimension, infallibility is a transcendental element in theology. It is related to theological knowledge in general as the guarantee of dogmatic security. Hence the question of infallibility belongs to fundamental theology, from the point of view of theological methodology.

The relevant notion of truth here, and the treatment of infallibility in fundamental theology prevent over-hasty applications of the notion in particular cases, either by restricting it to special regions in ecclesiology or to particular organs of the Church. In principle, the whole Church must be envisaged when infallibility is spoken of. When the concept is taken in this wide sense, limited only by its being distinguished from revelation and from the inspiration which is ordained to revelation, all the historical statements can be integrated with no need to range them at once under the heading of any specific notion of infallibility, such as that proposed by Vatican I.

C. Biblical Foundations

The starting-point can only be the promise of the Lord, who is himself the truth (Jn 1:14; 14:6; 1 Jn 5:20) and who entrusted to his community the word of truth. The farewell discourses in Jn, especially the promise of the Paraclete as the Spirit of truth (Jn 14:17; 15:26; 16:13), are the most important proofs. The Spirit leads the disciples to all truth, remains with them and enables them to remain in the word and in the truth (Jn 8:32; 14:17; 17:17; 2 Jn 1–3; see also Mt 28:19f.). Pauline theology provides the notion of the "Gospel", which is God's word and power (Rom 1:16; 2 Cor 6:7; 13:8; Gal 1:7; 1 Thess 2:2), and which may never be falsified (2 Cor 11:4; Gal 1:6; 2:5). According to 1 Tim, the Church is the "pillar and the ground of truth" (3:15). In the synoptic Gospels we read of the teaching commission given to the disciples, with whose words the Lord ultimately identifies himself (Lk 10:16) and whose faith is to be strengthened by Peter (Lk 22:32). To sum up, it may be said that the post-Easter community reflected on the reliability of its faith and preaching, and took cognizance of the promise and of its duty to remain in the truth.

D. Historical Perspectives

The history of the development of the notion of infallibility in dogma has yet to be written, though there are a number of special studies and surveys which open up valuable perspectives. Infallibility was not treated of for its own sake in the patristic age, though the allusions to the "rule of faith", the "deposit of faith" and the Apostolic Succession show how closely the notion of "Church" and "truth" were linked, as also appears from the practice of excluding heresy (see especially Tertullian, Irenaeus, Vincent of Lérins). The obligation of the Church towards the truth of the Gospel is brought out in particular at the Councils. As regards medieval theology, the change of meaning in the terms *fides* and *haeresis* is to be noted, and also the rareness of the occurrence of the term infallibility, mostly used in a non-technical sense. But the teaching of theologians on the reality of infallibility must also be noted (e.g., Thomas Aquinas, *Summa Theologica*, II-II, q. 1, a. 2, 10; q. 2, a. 6 ad 3; *Quodlibeta*, IX, q. 1, a. 7). The Councils of Constance and of Basle are of importance, not merely because of the respect in which they were held and their continuing influence, which can still be seen to be at work in the 19th century, but also because of their permanent intrinsic importance as a counterpart to Vatican I in the history of the Councils. In the Conciliarist controversy the word infallibility was used in approximately the modern sense (J. de Turrecremata).

The Reformation stimulated reflection on infallibility, not merely by its opposition, but also by such positive approaches as that of Calvin. The controversial theology after Trent developed dialectically the notion of infallibility, through the Gallicanism of a Bossuet as well as through the works of J. Driedo, M. Cano and R. Bellarmine (among others). At the beginning of the 19th century the infallibility of the Church was universally taught, though the infallibility of the Pope was considered an open question in some quarters. That the whole people of God, including the laity, was involved in the real infallibility of the Church was clearly seen by such great theologians as Möhler, Newman and Scheeben. In the years preceding Vatican I the attribution of the most unrestricted form of infallibility imaginable to the Pope became the most widely held position. Vatican I had prepared a schema on the infallibility of the Church (Mansi, LI, 542f.; cf. LIII, 312–14), but succeeded only in defining the infallibility of the papal magisterium, in the dogmatic constitution *Pastor Aeternus* (*D* 1832–40, *DS* 3065–75). This result was due to some extent to the influence of the minority and to what R. Aubert calls the "third party". For the definition was that of infallibility and not that of the infallibilists. After the Council both supporters of the text like Manning and opponents like Döllinger went beyond the definition to underline one-sidedly the doctrine of infallibility (as the infallibility of the Pope). Vatican II re-affirmed the doctrine of Vatican I, but integrated it into the doctrine of the collegiality of the bishops united with the Pope and the doctrine of the Church as the people of God (*Lumen Gentium*, arts. 12, 18, 25).

E. Theological Explanation

Theological reflection on infallibility may well start with the constitution of Vatican II, *Dei Verbum*, on revelation, which considers the whole Church as the "hearing Church", *ecclesia discens*, prior to all differentiation (of offices etc.). In this sense, the infallibility of the Church in general can be described as "passive": it is the fact of the Church being rooted in and living by the word of God in the eschatological revelation which will never be withdrawn from the Church, since God remains faithful. The primary activity of the Church is "hearing", accepting the revelation which was given in words and events and which still resounds in the present day. The preaching, and especially the definitive preaching, is the second stage. The preaching, along with the promise of infallibility, forms as it were a testimony to an auditive experience.

1. From this point of view we may now ask who is the subject or who are the subjects of infallibility. The classic formulation of Scheeben is of interest here: "Infallibility belongs *radicaliter* only to the Holy Spirit who animates the whole body. It flows from the Spirit both into the teaching body and the body of the faithful". Hence the human subject so to speak of infallibility is the Church as a whole, because the Spirit lives and works in the Church as a whole. Since there is a certain order in the Church, infallibility conforms to the structure of the Church: the *whole Church*, in the organic unity of its parts, is subject of infallibility. Basing itself on the general priesthood of all the baptized, the Church is the hearing and teaching Church, and therefore the infallible Church, in all its members and offices up to the college of the bishops and the visible head of the Church, the Pope. It is the organized Church, with its various structures, equipped with hierarchical offices and urged on or criticized by the charismatic, which has received the gift of infallibility.

At this stage of reflection the question of an "inadequately distinct" independent or dependent infallibility of the episcopate as a whole may seem to be already superfluous, and the unity of the subject to be granted. But if we have to name the particular organs of authoritative teaching (see below, 3), we can deduce from the structure of the Church that they are the episcopate as a whole, in union with the Supreme Pontiff (or the Pope in union with the episcopal college of which he is the head). When these organs of the Church teach, the Church recognizes that it is *represented* in them. This is true of the ordinary and universal magisterium, with regard to the *ecclesia dispersa*. But this representation of universal Church is verified also in a special way, with regard to infallible teaching in an extraordinary way, when the organs of the teaching Church gather together as the *ecclesia congregata*, that is, when the bishops meet in a General Council. Both as regards convocation and assembly analogies may be drawn between Church and Council. The General Council, being the assembly of all local Churches to represent the unity of the "hearing" and the teaching Church (see *Dei Verbum*, art. 1) possesses the gift of infallibility. This does not mean that every Council must culminate in infallible truths of faith, that is, must strive to reach the heights of infallible pronouncements, as may be seen from Vatican II. Since the Council is to be regarded as representation of the whole Church and of each local Church, the dioceses are represented in the bishops, in the sense of being personified there, not that the bishops are merely deputies of the dioceses.

Though the Councils have been considered as representations of the Church since Tertullian (*De Paenitentia*, 13, 6–7), this way of understanding the infallibility of the papal office was slow to find acceptance. The main reason for this is to be sought in the preludes to Vatican I, in the ambiguities of its texts and a one-sided exposition of its doctrines. But as long ago as the early part of the 19th century, J. S. Drey could affirm that the Pope was "the one factor representing the whole Church" (*Apologetik*, 2nd ed., III, p. 311), while even at Vatican I Bishop Gasser gave an "official" explanation of infallibility which affirmed that the Pope was infallible only when exercising his supreme doctrinal authority, "ergo universalem ecclesiam representans" (Mansi, LII, 1213). When the Pope teaches infallibly (and certain conditions have to be fulfilled if the infallibility is to take the form of definitive infallible pronouncements), he speaks as an organ of the Church, which is represented, concentrated and manifested in him.

This throws light on the much-debated statement, "Romani Pontificis definitiones ex sese, non autem ex consensu ecclesiae irreformabiles esse" (*D* 1839; see *Lumen Gentium*, art. 25). Its anti-Gallican background and the actual teaching of the Church (see, for instance, on General Councils, *CIC*, can. 228, para. 1) allow us to bring this affirmation into line with our considerations on how the Church is represented, even with regard to the definitive truths of faith pronounced by a General Council. This helps us to understand better that such infallible pronouncements are testimonies to the faith of the Church, and so draw on the *sensus ecclesiae* whose norm is Scripture and the tradition which expounds Scripture. They can never be isolated from the Church. This is true not only of the source of these pronouncements, but also of their goal. The end and object of a truth of faith is "that you may believe" (Jn 19:35). And thus infallibility does in fact aim at the *consensus ecclesiae*, and lives by it. This means that the "non ex consensu ecclesiae" must be restricted to exclude only a juridically verifiable act of ratification, a consensus formally expressed by the whole Church which alone would make the pronouncement infallible. In view of the theological and historical context, the statement in question means more precisely "non ex consensu subsequenti formali ecclesiae". Understood in this way, Vatican I leaves the way open for a proper appreciation of the nature of the acceptance of an infallible doctrine by the believing Church. It takes place primarily as a "real consent" (Newman): it is a process of understanding which passes through the stages of reflection. There is a formation of consensus in a historical process, with theology having a hermeneutical function. The infallible pronouncements come from the whole Church, challenge it by their "ex sese . . . irreformabiles" and are assimilated by its conscious faith. This consensus develops in the historical framework of the Church's perception of revelation and its authoritative exposition, a situation which both promotes and demarcates the consensus. The infallibility of the Church as a whole is also shown by the fact that the *charisma veritatis* is given by the Spirit not merely to buttress the authoritative formulation but also to help the Church to understand the truth in question. This is also part of the general promise of assistance.

2. Though the Church is led by the Spirit of God and is infallible in its teaching on account of the divine assistance, it is still necessary to define as closely as possible the extent of this infallibility. Here too the historical development has been such that the most detailed treatment is to be found under the heading of papal infallibility. The application to General Councils and to the teaching of the episcopal college in union with the Pope in its universal and ordinary magisterium may be taken to be parallel. Vatican I affirms that in the cases considered the Pope possesses "the infallibility with which the divine redeemer wished to have his Church endowed for definitive decisions in matters of faith and morals (*D* 1839; *DS* 3074). Infallibility is promised for the preservation and the explanation of revelation. It is therefore concerned with revelation (cf. *Lumen Gentium*, art. 25), the content of which is indicated by the formula "matters of faith and morals". This is to acknowledge on principle that infallibility is determined by its object, hence that its importance and significance are determined not only by the subjects of infallibility but also by the object. When therefore the Second Vatican Council's Decree on Ecumenism bids Christians to bear in mind that there is "an order or 'hierarchy' of truths in Catholic teaching, since they vary in their relationship to the foundation of the Christian faith" (art. 11), more light is thrown on infallibility. A pointer is given to theological reflection, which is warned not to treat infallibility superficially by applying it to a series of truths all on the same footing. The point is to see how dignity accrues to infallibility from the heart of the kerygma, from "the foundation of the Christian faith".

This will help theologians to allot their proper places to the so-called secondary objects of infallibility, the "Catholic truths" which are closely connected historically, logically or practically with the truth of faith (dogmatic facts, theological conclusions, canonizations and so on). It follows that the Church does not teach authoritatively that infallibility includes such matters, though they are of great importance within the framework of the ordinary magisterium (*Lumen Gentium*, art. 25). As a corollary, the theological "notes" or qualifications need to be carefully considered.

3. The infallibility of the Church does not mean that every single utterance of the organs of the Church is infallible and must be believed "fide divina et catholica". The form in which Church doctrine is proposed is also decisive. In the ordinary case, in the "ordinary" teaching of the Church, infalli-

bility is as it were built into the life and preaching of the Church, especially the liturgy, though not all the individual statements could claim infallibility. If one then recalls that kerygma is objectively prior to dogma, it is not surprising that there can be true and infallible preaching in the Church on many matters and over a long period, without this being affirmed in particular for given propositions. And since dogma itself is ultimately doxology and always aims at being such, the intention of dogmatic definitions to be believed absolutely by all may not be present – as for instance in the dogmatic constitutions of Vatican II.

Hence it does not seem advisable to give more precise form to the "general and ordinary magisterium", which is endowed with infallibility, than that which it has achieved in the last hundred years. The essence of this teaching is precisely its relative lack of formal precision, which makes it difficult to grasp in meditative detail, but in no way lessens the importance of such infallible doctrine. The classical example in this matter is the Apostles' Creed. The moral unanimity of the consensus of the whole Church does duty for the formal statement of a truth of faith.

Dogmatic definitions which are binding on all the faithful aim at posing limits, that is, at marking off true doctrine from false. Hence they have mostly been given in answer to a threat to the faith. They are pronouncements of the "extraordinary magisterium". The infallibility of the Church comes to a head in them. They are "limit cases on the upper level" (M. Löhrer). They are linked to strictly defined conditions, each of which represents a limitation. They must be proclaimed by those who represent the whole Church, a General Council or the Pope speaking as universal teacher of the Church, *ex cathedra*. They are confined to matters of faith and morals. The definition must be addressed to the whole Church. This last condition shows that the infallibility in question is a matter of single acts, which are only made possible when all the conditions are verified. Finally, an utterance intended to be a dogmatic definition must be clearly recognizable as such. In contrast to a tendency observed in some quarters to extend the notion and application of infallibility beyond its due limits, especially with regard to the ordinary papal magisterium, the texts of Vatican I and II note that infallibility should not be ascribed too readily to papal documents. *Lumen Gentium* confines itself to urging a "religious submission of will and of mind" with regard to the authentic teaching authority of the Pope (*Lumen Gentium*, art. 25).

F. Ecumenical Aspects

The doctrine of the infallibility of the Church, especially in the form given it by Vatican I, has been subjected to much criticism by Christians separated from Rome, and expressed in a very pointed way by Protestant theologians such as K. Barth, E. Brunner, and G. Ebeling. Their general tendency is to denounce the apparent claim of the Church to be superior to Scripture, the "potestas Papae" over the gospel, the seeming identification of revelation and Church. Ultimately, however, many of the misgivings are connected only with the danger of abuse of papal authority and look for stronger assurances that the Pope and the teaching Church will not trespass beyond the limits and conditions laid down for them. A characteristic statement of the Protestant notion of infallibility may be found in P. Althaus: "What the promise of the Spirit to the Church means is this: God will never let the Church die of its own mortality, of its own sins and impotence. Somewhere in the Church the Spirit of God sends out truth and life anew for the whole Church. Somewhere he raises up prophets and reformers. This is the 'evangelical' notion of the guidance of the Spirit and the 'infallibility' of the Church" (*Die Christliche Wahrheit* [4th ed., 1958], p. 526).

In ecumenical discussion of infallibility, a comprehensive historical and theological exposition of the Catholic position is necessary, but as regards particular points the following truths may be given special emphasis on account of their ecumenical relevance.

a) Absolute infallibility belongs to God alone. The Church cannot have infallibility at its disposition, as a "work" which it produces, since it is always a gift, the *charisma veritatis*.

b) The magisterium is not above the word of God, but is at its service (cf. *Dei Verbum*, art. 10). Infallibility is exercised in the service of the word, and dogma is under the word of God. This characteristic of service and the responsibility which it involves must also be clearly seen from the forms and language of the teaching Church. There is no room for "dogmatic imperialism" and "triumphalism".

c) Infallibility helps the Church to be *ecclesia vera;* it makes it the Church in which the gospel is truly preached.

d) The infallibility of the Church means that the members of the Church join together in brotherly service in the finding of the truth. In this way the Church sees itself to be the Church which sustains and is sustained (J. Ratzinger).

e) Even with regard to infallible decisions on truths of faith, the conscience of the individual Christian is not excluded. It remains the immediate norm for his decision.

f) The solemnity and the definitively binding character of a definition does not mean a "thus far and no further" in preaching and teaching. The language of the definition is conditioned by its times, and possibly "contaminated" (K. Rahner) by the world image of the men who pronounce it.

g) The history of the infallible Church and the treatise *De Infallibilitate Ecclesiae* must be balanced by a realistic view of the *fallibilitas ecclesiae*. It must be granted that alongside of and outside the scope of the promised and actual infallibility, there can also be human error within the Church (as in the history of religious freedom).

h) The infallible dogmatic definitions represent a climax and also an extreme case of ecclesial infallibility. They cannot be given at will and without pressing need. Infallibility was not given to the Church to enable it to transform the whole kerygma into infallible dogmatic propositions.

i) The infallible dogmas are not ultimates, but milestones in the development of Church doctrine. They are manifestations of the truth in provisional stages, as follows from the fact that the Church is on pilgrimage. Dogmatic definition cannot blind us to the fact that faith only becomes vision in the kingdom of God.

j) When the Catholic Church speaks of the universal Church and attributes infallibility to the Church as a whole, it undoubtedly means primarily its own Church, but it must always consider this in relation to the separated communities which Vatican II also declares to be "Churches".

Heinrich Fries and *Johann Finsterhölzl*

INFINITY

1. *Meaning and history of the concept.* The word "infinite" appears for the first time as an attribute of formless "first matter". Later it became one of the most pre-eminent attributes of God. Anaximander is the first to speak of the infinite (ἄπειρον), which he makes the inexhaustible ground of the becoming and passing away of things. According to the Pythagoreans and Plato, things are composed of one element which is indeterminate (ἄπειρον) and another which is a determination (πέρας, limitation). Aristotle undertakes to solve the

difficulty posed by the fact that material things are limited and still divisible *ad infinitum*. He uses the distinction between the infinite in potency and the infinite in act, that is, between that which can be conceivably or possibly multiplied or divided endlessly, and that which is really and actually unlimited. Nothing actually infinite exists. The potentially infinite is the endless multiple in quantity and the endlessly divisible in space. Time is infinite in both these senses. Since along with time the movement of the world is endless, the obvious thing would be to deduce that the ultimate unmoved mover of all that moves, God, is actually infinite. But Aristotle does not take this step. The reason for his refusal is to be sought in the nature of Greek thought, as displayed further in art and ethics, for which the perfect is the measured harmony, while the formless and undefined is the inferior. The real, which is also the true and the good-beautiful, is the well-defined and demarcated. This is a type of thinking which is supremely confident of the power of reason with its conceptual definitions.

This assessment of the infinite was altered as neo-Platonists and above all Christians began to take a special interest in that pole of being opposed to the materially infinite, the divine. It was affirmed that the divine could certainly not be finite. As a being beyond our comprehension, it had to be without limit, and the sum of all perfections since it was the inexhaustible source of the world's riches. The Greek Fathers made "infinite" one of the pre-eminent attributes of God. According to Thomas Aquinas, (first) matter and form limit each other mutually as they constitute individual beings. But in this hylemorphism, the form perfects matter, while matter is no more than the limiting principle of form. Hence though both principles are of themselves unlimited, matter can only subsist in beings, while the form is of itself capable of being. The form of being subsisting purely in itself (God) is therefore actually infinite by its own virtue. Further, the infinite is not only prior as being, it is also prior as known, though only of and for itself and not to us. But since being is the image of God and is also that which is best known to our mind, hence in a certain way, God is also the first known for us. This conclusion was explicitly enunciated by Descartes: the finite thing and the indefinite world are knowable only against the background of a pre-knowledge of the infinite God. Hence the notion of the infinite is essential to the human soul, which is therefore itself in a certain way infinite. A similar line of thought had already led Nicholas of Cusa to place between the infinity of God and the infinity of matter a world really infinite in space and time, which he regarded as the explicitation of the richness of being existing in a compact way (*complicite*) in God.

Subsequent thought brought the infinity of the soul and the world and God closer and closer together, till they ultimately came to coincide in the thought of Spinoza and again in German idealism. Such efforts to "hypostatize" the infinite by separating it from the endless process of human enumeration or measurement were subjected to criticism by Locke, which was followed by the development of the infinitesimal calculus by Leibniz and Newton. Kant was inspired by a similar line of thought when he affirmed that all the objects given us were finite, but that all the objectives imposed on us were infinite – the task of continuing the synthesis of condition and conditioned, of dividing or enumerating. Hence the infinite is never a real object of knowledge but only the regulative idea of scientific research or the postulate of moral striving. Hegel was the last great philosopher of the infinite, his principle being that it would be a contradiction to assert the self-sufficiency of the finite, which he defined as that which was not identical with its concept. For everything finite is, as such, limited by another finite being and hence transcends itself. This shows that the finite strives to be once more that which it originally was, the infinite. But the true infinity is neither this endless process of going beyond the limit, nor a self-contained infinity with the finite outside itself – since such a "spurious" infinity would be in some way determined by the finite and hence again be itself finite. The true infinity is the identity of the divine being or idea (concept) with itself which is maintained throughout all dissociation and movement. In contrast to this type of the metaphysics of the finite, Heidegger tries to delineate a finiteness of being and of man which can be understood in the light of its own nature, without the presupposition of an infinity, which would be in contrast to the finite.

The mathematician Georg Cantor (d. 1918) introduced into his set theory actually infinite (transfinite) numbers which designated a constant and yet augmentable quantum which is greater than any finite quantity of the same nature, and hence greater than the (non-existing) greatest number of the natural series 1, 2, 3, etc. – e.g., the multitude of all finite numbers. The "Platonizing" concept of number as an ideal object which seems to underlie the theory of multitudes is contested by a more Aristotelian, "operative" line of thought in basic mathematics.

2. *The significance of the concept of infinity in theology.* In sacred Scripture little attention is paid to the designation of God as "infinite". Where the notion occurs, it means that God's incomparable power is to be praised, as displayed in the works of creation and his beneficent action in the history of salvation. The attribute always has the connotation of the impotence of man to comprehend God. These two notions remained of primary importance when theological speculation took up the attribute of infinity. Theology, which has to transmit the message of revelation in our thought-form (which is fundamentally Greek) can hardly do without the important contribution made by the notion of God's infinity. Without the doctrine of the infinity of God in the background, there is a danger that the message of God's loving care for us, expressed in personal categories, might lose its seriousness. Only a God whose being is infinite can be present to the limitless reach of man's spirit in such a way that he is still hidden. Only the infinite does not at once, like every finite object proportionate to man's knowledge, pass over into the state of appearance which must let itself be inspected whether it wishes it or not. That is, only the infinite can freely reveal itself and still, in the very act of revelation, preserve its supreme transcendence – as mystery – over all human knowledge. So too creation, which is the free active positing of finite being in its own independent subsistence, is only possible when the creator is so supremely and infinitely sovereign lord of all that is, that not merely can there be nothing which would be independent of him, but that the creature can exist in itself – not in spite of, but by virtue of this dependence.

Gerd Haeffner

INSPIRATION

"In many and various ways God spoke of old to our fathers by the prophets; but in these last days he has spoken to us by a Son, whom he appointed the heir of all things, through whom also he created the world." This opening passage of the Letter to the Hebrews at once fixes the Christian idea of inspiration as a saving mystery. Christ is the centre – the total, definitive Word, the fullness of revelation – round whom we find the concentric circles of the Son's creative activity, his manifestation in the universe, and the many words God sent from time to time as forerunners of the Word that crowns them all. The revelation Christ announced is echoed by his apostles: "It was declared at first by the Lord, and it was attested to us by those who heard him" (Heb 2:3). Thus we must think of inspiration within the context of the central mystery, the Incarnation, as part of the mystery of the word, something bound up with the cosmic order that is eloquent of God its Creator. In Christ all things hold together, including the inspired books. It is the common teaching of the Fathers that the whole of OT revelation has to do with Christ: "In his igitur Verbum versabatur, loquens de seipso. Iam enim ipsum suus praeco erat" (Hippolytus, *PG*, X, 819). Just as the Incarnation is the work of the Holy Spirit (Lk 1:35), so the mystery of the many and various words is the work of the Holy Spirit's manifold activity: the very term "inspiration" refers us to the "Spirit". The inspiration of Scripture, then, must be something living, active, piercing. The "breath" of God that was breathed at creation, that gives man life, that raises up heroes of salvation, also inspires the prophet, the "man of the Spirit"; and since this Spirit is a living, life-giving one, the inspired word too is something living and active (Heb 4:12). Charisma is the name usually given to the action of the Spirit in the economy of salvation. Inspiration must be seen in the variegated setting of the charisms, as part of the total experience of Israel and the Church.

A mystery of the word and a mystery of life, inspiration can be more precisely defined as verbal revelation. Every operation of God *ad extra* manifests him on one of three planes. In nature, organized being, a little thought enables us to trace the finger of God, a certain reflection of himself. (St. Paul calls this kind of thought *nooumena*, Rom 1:20). On the vast stage of creation God intervenes in human history, working signs and wonders, doing specific things, so that man may gain a closer knowledge of his Author. And within history God speaks to man: this is the fullest manifestation of God, revelation by his word. Nature tells us something about the being and attributes of God; from history we learn something of the ways of God with men; but verbal revelation gives us personal access to him. The personal revelation of the word sheds a flood of light on nature and history: they become transparent, God's revelation through his word unlocks the secret of the universe (cf. Ps 104, for example); in God's word man knows himself for what he is, so limited, torn between two poles (Ps 139), a sinner (Ps 51); that word shows beyond a doubt that history is the history of revelation.

We could imagine God causing the air to vibrate at the frequency of an address or a poem: words would sound in human language, Hebrew or Greek, but they would not be spoken by men; they would be appropriate to a particular age and society but transmitted mechanically. (Anyone who feels that such a revelation would be simpler and purer lacks an incarnational cast of mind.) The mystery of inspiration is precisely that God has chosen to speak through men, to "incarnate" his word: the word of God is truly a human word, it is spoken – not merely repeated – by men of a particular age and society, with a personality of their own.

A human word. Even in his language, man is the image and likeness of God. The creation of an orderly world shows us what God is like; and man, recreating the world through his words, shows what he is like. God incarnates himself in man, his image, he incarnates his word in language, the image of man and the second image of God. Language is communication, and the fullness of language is dialogue. This being so, language enables and compels man to know himself: having to express himself, man looks at himself, finds words for his experiences, thus taking reflex possession of them; stores them away in his memory, where they will be ready when needed. Dialogue is more than the sum of alternate communications, for in dialogue these communications become more and more enriched, more fraught with meaning. So it is with the language that God uses in his dialogue with men. This disclosure of God, of course, does not perfect him; but dialogue with God does exalt and perfect man, not only when he listens but also when he responds. The Psalms are a human response, one inspired by God, revelation embodied in dialogue: "Perpendat unusquisque nos per prophetarum linguam audire Deum nobiscum *colloquentem*" (St. John Chrysostom: *PG*, LIII, col. 119). When he must answer God, man comes to know himself; answering God in words that are inspired, divine, man knows himself in the light of God, of the divine word.

Language is a social and a historical thing. There are two ways in which it transcends the individual who speaks it. Since speaking actualizes language, when we speak we do not express our personal ideas by a process of elimination or purification, we take over the language of the society we live in with all its riches and variety, its overtones and atmosphere. In a sense the society speaks through the individual and the individual speaks in the bosom of his community – in its presence, on its behalf, for its benefit. This social dimension of language enters into inspiration. There is a second dimension, the historical one. A language both precedes and survives those who speak it; it endures and changes in strictly historical fashion, with its set forms, the evolution of its meanings, and the rest. This dimension too is subsumed by inspiration: when it appeared that the continuity of inspired language was going to be broken, that Hebrew would be displaced by Greek, God saw to it that a Greek translation of the OT provided a bridge between the two. We must not think of the inspiration of Scripture as a series of individual acts on the fringes of society, nor yet as isolated interventions on the part of God. Though the inspired writers are discontinuous in the sense that they are real individuals, inspiration uses them to express itself in language that is a social and a historical reality (and here one should not think merely of dictionaries and grammars, of Hebrew and Greek in the abstract).

We are acquainted with many inspired writers, men moved by the Spirit (2 Pet 1:21); some we know only through their books, others by name as well; and we must admit that the language they speak is thoroughly human, at times intensely so. Yet at the same time we believe that these words are literally the words of God, "qui locutus est per prophetas". How can one and the same word be both human and divine? Here is the great theological problem of inspiration, crucial because it takes us to the heart of mystery. The first thing to do if we wish to make sense of this mystery, or any other, is of course to refer it to the central mystery of the Incarnation, as the medieval authors recommend: "Verba quae multa locutus est, unum Verbum sunt; unum inquam quod et ipse caro factum est" (Rupert of Dietz, *In Jo*, 1:7). Pius XII himself follows their advice: "As the substantial Word of God became like man in all things except sin, so too the words of God, expressed in human language, are like human speech in all things except error" (*Divino Afflante Spiritu*).

The question still remains: what is the nature of this action of the Spirit that makes a human word a divine word? At what point does this action take effect? We cannot suppose that a purely human word becomes a divine word. Being acknowledged and received by the Church cannot make a divine word of what in itself is a purely human word (Vatican I); the Holy Spirit does not assume and elevate a human word that already has an independent existence, any more than God became man by assuming a complete human being already in existence. We must recognize that this word, this piece of language, is inspired from birth, indeed from the moment of its conception. The author's materials, to be sure, are another matter, whether these be experiences and intuitions, for example, that have not yet been formulated in language, or words already in existence which he turns to good account in new expressions, a new work of art. Like the sower's seed, the organic matter which the Spirit will form into the body of Jesus is not made out of nothing, nor even out of inorganic matter. It is in this way that we must think of inspiration, as operative from the moment when a concrete literary work begins to take shape. How does it take shape? This is not properly a theological question, having more to do with the psychology of language or literary creation. But these sciences can shed light on the way inspiration works.

Inspired writers. What immediately strikes us here is variety: inspiration is vigorous, complex, flexible. In the OT one first distinguishes between prophets and sapiential writers. The prophet receives a divine impulse, and contributes his own artistry to the work: the divine impetus may be like an unquenchable fire in one's bones (Jer), like a book that is digested before becoming a prophetic message (Ezek), like a lion's roar that is echoed in words (Amos), or a fleeting intuition (Jer 1).

The divine impulse sets the author to work on his book; and the whole task, from beginning to end, is guided by the Spirit. No less so is the literary labour of the sapiential writer; but he is not conscious of the action of the Spirit; he feels no superhuman impulse, claims no divine revelation; he seems to proceed entirely on the basis of his own thought and experience. The historiographer may work in both these ways; relating events or studying official records, he may be enlightened from above as to their meaning. In any case, he too writes under the constant influence of the Spirit. What all three write is the word of God, and we must not make too much of the distinction between *verba Dei* and *ipsissima verba Dei*. In the NT we encounter a new factor, because all the preaching and writing of the apostles merely echo the words of Christ (2 Cor 13:3; 2:17). If this is so, it is not because they were men with an exceptional memory. The apostles echoed Christ the Word, concretely embodied in the words of Christ, by the action of Christ's Spirit, who is sent by the Father and the Son (Jn 14:26; 16:13). Let us not make a fetish of the *ipsissima verba Christi* as though the rest were not really his word.

The inspired writers may also be classified according to literary genre. Examples abound in Scripture of the "many and various ways" God speaks. One book will be characterized by intellectual detachment, another by compelling emotion, another by traditionalism of form or content, yet another by literary artistry. Or we may distinguish these authors from the point of view of their social circumstances: some speak for the group to which they belong, others admonish rulers (Is), some are dogged fighters (Jer), some are men in advance of their time, some are isolated nonconformists (Eccles). But all offer scope for the operation of the Holy Spirit. We might set forth this plurality under the headings "intellectual element, volitional element, period of composition"; but perhaps pride of place had best be given to multiplicity, leaving us to marvel at the work of the Spirit that breathes where he wills.

Theologians have had recourse to various metaphors in an attempt to explain how a human word can also be a divine one. The metaphor of the instrument has enjoyed a great vogue (cf. *Divino Afflante Spiritu*): both *homo faber* and *homo ludens* know from elemental experience what an instrument is. The Fathers were very fond of the image of the musical instrument, with its suggestion of immediacy, of oneness with the artist, the blending of melody and tone. St. Augustine gives us the image of a bodily organ, such as the mouth or hand, alluding to the idea of the mystical body (*PL*, XXXIV, col. 1070). This image leads the Schoolmen into a metaphysical discussion of the efficient instrumental cause; St. Thomas himself, however, recognizes the limitations of the image and prefers to speak of a "quasi-instrumentum". The image of "dictation" is borrowed from the world of chancellories and literature: it has not the modern sense of writing down what another says (something that will soon be done by machines) but means the intelligent assistance of a secretary, artistic collaboration in finding the exact wording desired (cf. the evolution of the word *dictare* into *indite*). Politics and diplomacy give us the image of mission: the sacred author is a messenger, he does not merely parrot what he has heard but conveys the message as a responsible person. Besides these three traditional images, there is one drawn from the world of literature that helps to illustrate the mystery of a word both human and divine: a poor novelist or playwright can put his own words into the mouths of his personages, which are nothing but marionettes; whereas the good novelist or playwright is not merely the creator but also the servant of his personages, he cannot do as he likes with them, what he has each one say must be "in character"; and the reader can rightly say that such words are both the personage's and the author's. Obviously if this analogy were strained it would lose its point, just as if we reduced the human instrument to an inert machine, the messenger to a parrot, the writer to a mere typist. But what these comparisons all show is that we are justified in saying that God is the principal author of the inspired books, and man their secondary author.

The inspired books. We have considered the nature and working of inspiration in its human term, the inspired writers (cf. 2 Pet 1:21). Scripture tells us, however, that the books they wrote are also inspired (2 Tim 3:16). Or rather we ought to say that the authors are inspired in view of the word, which is a communicable objectification that exists in view of some action, the final object of the whole procedure. The Fathers much prefer the second expression, "inspired Scripture". If we have dwelt upon the role of the human authors, it is in order to make it quite clear that inspiration is not something added later to a finished piece of writing. Next it behoves us to examine the inspired reality that is still preserved to us in the Church: "Now these things (that) happened to them ... were written down for our instruction, upon whom the end of the ages has come" (1 Cor 10:11). We profess our faith that God speaks to us, that his word reaches us; Pius XII tells us that God uses language which is "completely human, error only excepted" (*Divino Afflante Spiritu*); and therefore we feel justified in discussing God's word by analogy with certain aspects of the human word.

Language (according to K. Bühler) has three dialogal functions: to inform, to express, and to impress. In the first case the speaker states facts, ideas, doctrines; in the second he reveals his inner life, his feelings, his experiences; in the third he acts upon the person he is speaking to. These three functions are of course intermingled in practice, but it is useful to distinguish one from the other. Now if we consider the divine word, we may say by analogy that it informs by making known the deeds by which we are redeemed, the truths we must believe so as to be saved; that it expresses by disclosing to men God's nature and knowledge; that it impresses by exposing the hearer of the word to a divine influence. What we are considering here are only three aspects of a single reality, not three different phases or areas. It would not do to suppose that inspiration, in the Christian view, enters the picture only when doctrinal truths are formally taught: were such the case a great deal of the Bible, being repetitive, would be superfluous; indeed we could well dispense with the Bible altogether since the truths it teaches are more clearly stated in the catechism. When God instructs us, he does not lecture like a remote academician, he speaks to us lovingly as a father to his son (Deut 8:5). The human word possesses a native power to stimulate, move, impress the hearer (though not an infallible power, since the hearer may resist it if he chooses). At least the same efficacy must be granted the word of God, but on the plane of salvation where his word operates. This efficacy of the divine word should not be confused with that of the sacraments, nor explained as a parallel movement occasioned by reading Scripture in the proper dispositions; such an explanation falls far short of the lapidary formulae "able to instruct for salvation, profitable for training in righteousness" (2 Tim 3:15–17), "living, active, piercing" (Heb 4:12), and conflicts with the doctrine and practice of the Fathers. Scripture is efficacious on the plane of the word; its acceptance is efficacious on the plane of faith.

There are three basic levels of language: the common, the technical, and the literary. The common level is that of personal communication. When this kind of language has undergone a process of purgation in the interests of the utmost possible precision of thought and terminology, the result is technical language – impersonal, objective, in a sense absolute. Literary language, exploiting all the half-used or untouched resources of common parlance to dilate, enrich, intensify it, abounds in suggestive imagery. It is fair to say that literary language is much more opulent than technical language and much less accurate. On which of these three levels do we find the inspired word? On all three, of course, since God has spoken "in many and various ways". A good deal of common parlance occurs in Scripture, and there are lengthy passages of technical language (ceremonial, legal, and so forth). On the whole, however, it is literary language that sets the tone, as we might expect. What more fitting to convey the riches of God's own life, his unfathomable designs, the plenitude of mystery, than an exalted imagery? Much mischief has come of treating biblical language as though it were technical (the language of astronomy, physics, or genetic history). Once we grasp the literary character of Scripture some important corollaries emerge, first of all the inexhaustible riches of Scripture. The delight of medieval writers (who called Scripture a treasure, a forest, a banquet, an ocean, a torrent, an abyss), they are now being rediscovered by the modern biblical movement. Secondly, we must do what we can to bring these riches to light and make use of them. That task, though a never-ending one, must be undertaken, in harmony with the Bible and the institutions based on it, under the guidance of the Spirit who inspired the Bible. Tradition is the name we give to this continuous, undeviating work of formulating, gathering, meditating on the treasures of God's "living, efficacious word", and the final guarantee of its soundness is the magisterium.

Language is either spoken or written. The spoken word is primary: writing is a convention that has become necessary in our culture if the works of men are not to be lost. Composition is either oral or written: neither lies beyond the scope of inspiration, and we may not suppose that a psalm, for example, that was not the word of God, became such merely because it was soon written down. On the other hand there is no reason why oral composition could not be supplemented by a composition set down in a different context. Scripture is the form in which God chose to have many inspired books written and to have them all preserved in the Church (2 Cor 10:11). But let us remember that Scripture is only notation, a score that needs to be interpreted, a word that returns to life through a new creation. When a person reads a literary text properly he revives it, calls it into existence once more: and when the reader gives the inspired word intellectual life, the life of the Spirit is imparted to him. It is well, too, to bear in mind that the utterances of the prophets were God's word before they were committed to writing; that a large part of the NT first existed as the word of Jesus, as the oral tradition of the primitive Church. Word of mouth does not die when it is written down; it goes on living parallel to, linked with, its written form.

As a rule biblical language hardened into literary works and did not remain an indeterminate flow of words. Together these works form a structure of massive proportions. A book of the Bible can belong to one literary genre, yet take up various traditional literary themes; blending artistic inspiration with the skill of many schools of writing, it may use a variety of styles; it speaks for the author, being his work, yet in a way transcends him because the language used evokes a whole society, a host of traditions; shut in upon itself as a complete book, it can nonetheless open the door to a new and higher context; though identical with itself, its character undergoes a change each time it is renewed by a reader's active co-operation; rooted in the life of one people and generation, it may be relevant to other peoples and generations.

These literary qualities are neither destroyed nor damaged by inspiration, which rather endows them with new vigour, meaning, and potency. Since the biblical book is a unit, it also follows that its parts exist for the whole and not vice versa. For this reason it is an error to regard the Bible as an enormous collection of propositions, each of which could be understood in isolation. Before we can expect to interpret any sentence, any word of the Bible, we must consider the book in which it is found, the character and intentions of the author, the age he lived in, and the whole context of divine revelation. Similarly, given the higher unity of Scripture, we must see each book as open to, in relation with, the rest, as part of a temporal process, a debate (Eccles, Job), and the whole of the OT as open to its fulfilment in the NT.

The inspiration of the Holy Spirit has certain consequences (which some authors call "effects"). The first effect of inspiration is to make the inspired language the word of God: the expressions "inspired word" and "Word of God" are practically synonymous; the former merely draws more attention to the Spirit, the latter to the Logos. Since Scripture is the word of God, it has a saving power of its own which operates in liturgical observance, in the preaching of sermons, in reading when one receives in faith those things that are "able to instruct for salvation through faith" (2 Tim 3:15). Being the word of God, Scripture teaches the doctrine of salvation in its own particular way: this doctrine is sought out, formulated, explained, and proposed to our belief in dogmatic definitions, the teaching of the magisterium, the teaching of theologians, and the catechism. All this requires certain adjustments of language and constantly poses the problem of how far such change should go. How far may theologians depart from biblical language? Should the catechism use the language of the Bible or of dogmatic theology? Let us simply recognize both the need for modification and the dangers it involves, keeping in close touch with the language God has inspired. A Christian child nurtured in this language is in touch with the real religious world, with the language of true dialogue with God. Of course flexibility is necessary in this matter. But it seems very unwise to bring up children in peaceful ignorance of inspired language. Since Scripture is inspired by God, it follows that it cannot assert any falsehood: otherwise God himself would be commending falsehood to us on his own authority. In negative terms, this characteristic of Scripture is called inerrancy. The inerrancy of Scripture has always been taught by tradition and must, of course, be associated with its positive correlative, truth. Truth is a doctrine, a revelation, a light to our eyes: of the inspired word of God, too, we may say: "In thy light do we see light" (Ps 36:10.)

Luis Alonso-Schökel

J

JANSENISM

Jansenism, a movement within the Catholic Church of the 17th and 18th centuries, especially in France and the Netherlands, represents one effort to solve the problem with which all Christian life is faced – that of reconciling the fundamental antagonisms inherent in Christianity. There is the acceptance of the world which has as its counterpart a condemnation of the world, and there is the necessity of working out one's salvation responsibly while always knowing it to be a freely bestowed gift, beyond all man's merits. The antagonism cannot be left as a dualistic discord, and it cannot be resolved into a monism where one or the other side alone remains in possession. The attempted middle position taken up by Jansenism was rejected as one-sided by the magisterium of the Church.

1. *Jansenistic doctrine*. The main initiator of this new effort to articulate the self-understanding of Christianity was Cornelius Jansen (the younger) (d. 1638), who had studied in Louvain and Paris, taught theology at Louvain and was Bishop of Ypres from 1636 on. His views were chiefly propagated through his *Augustinus seu doctrina S. Augustini de humanae naturae sanitate, aegritudine, medicina adversus Pelagianos et Massilienses* (published posthumously, Louvain, 1640ff.).

This work took up the themes of the right notion of divine grace and its relationship to the free will of man which had become once more burning questions among Catholics, under the influence of the Reformation and the controversy between Molinism and Baianism. The argument, in deliberate opposition to scholastic tradition as well as to the humanist notion of man's shaping his own religious and human destiny, relied so exclusively on patristic theology and on St. Augustine in particular – especially his controversy with Pelagius – that Jansenists could call themselves "friends of St. Augustine". Indeed, the whole movement could be described as a modern form of Augustinianism. It was on an Augustinian basis that Jansenism developed its own theological system, in the light of a threefold division of the history of salvation. In the first stage, the state of "innocent nature", "Adam" was so free and so much master of himself that he could freely bring about his own salvation – with the assistance of the *adiutorium sine quo non*, a grace indispensable for the supernatural end, but due to him and as it were at his disposal. But with original sin, man lost his self-mastery so completely that he has lost all sense of the religious and moral value of his actions, is totally incapable of a personal, responsible decision for the good and is completely at the mercy of "concupiscence triumphant". His will is therefore determined by the attractions of created things and so always sinful in all its actions. Every effort, no matter how well meant, to amend by his own forces, either in practice by the exercise of the virtues generally recognized as such, or in theory itself by the analyses of philosophy, can only be "splendid vices" in the service of evil desires, since man is so thoroughly at the mercy of the *libido sentiendi, sciendi, excellendi.*

Against this totally negative background of the loss of freedom, redemption is not presented as the restoration of freedom and new responsibility, but as a new determination of the will. But this time it is the heavenly joy which is the determinant. This is a re-orientation of the will towards its salvation, towards love of the divine instead of love of the created. There is an *adiutorium quo* which is in no way mediated by human assent, but is efficacious by its very nature and absolutely irresistible. An extremely literal interpretation of the antithesis between the "slavery to sin" and "slavery to Christ" presents Christian freedom not as inner freedom in and before the freedom of God and his love, but at the very most as freedom from outside constraint. For his salvation, man is abandoned to a totally arbitrary election on the part of God. He is treated as an object, not as a counterpart (relatively) to the divine will.

The logic of this position brought with it a point which was to be one of the most essential and highly controverted of Jansenist views – the *a priori* restriction of the salvific will of God and the redemptive value of Christ's death to those who were in fact predestined to salvation. Thus there was a sharp contrast between human corruption – the total extinction of responsible self-determination – and redemption (the arbitrary determination of some people, through a "triumphant concupiscence" now directed to the divine). This dualism remained the basic conviction even of later Jansenism in France, where it was less a theological system than a practical way of life.

2. *The spread of Jansenism in France.* This view of the history of salvation became of practical importance first in France, where it was to be at its most influential. The large convent of Cistercian nuns of Port-Royal, with two foundations in and near Paris, adopted a reform inspired by the Jansenist understanding of Christianity, chiefly under the influence of Saint-Cyran (Jean-Ambroise Duvergier de Hauranne [d. 1643]), Abbot of Saint-Cyran, a friend of Jansen in his student days at Paris. The Abbess of Port-Royal, Angélique Arnauld (d. 1661), was mainly instrumental in implementing the reforms. "Petites écoles" were set up, and hermitages provided for those who wished to retire from public life to devote themselves entirely to God and his new creation which was the negation of the old world. From these bases Jansenism gained great influence on French society, among its most notable conquests being Racine and Pascal, who came into contact with Port-Royal through his sister Jacquéline who entered the convent in 1642. Controversy ensued, chiefly with the Jesuits, the Jansenist spokesman being the youngest brother of Angélique Arnauld, Antoine (d. 1694), sometime member of the Sorbonne and later head of the movement.

Thus Jansenism took on the contours of a party in the Church. In the realm of morals and asceticism, it strongly opposed the broad-minded "Probabilism" of Jesuit casuistry by putting forward the severest demands with no room for compromise. Jansenism called for complete certainty about the lawfulness of an action before it could be performed ("Rigorism"); for perfect contrition based on love of God, not merely on fear of the punishment of hell, as precondition for the sacrament of penance ("Anti-attritionism"); for supreme reverence for the sacrament of the altar, which was to be received only on rare occasions (contrary to the Jesuit recommendation of frequent Communion), while the priesthood was considered to be a task of enormous daring. These were the theses of the controversial writings of Arnauld, especially his *De la fréquente communion*, and of Pascal's *Lettres à un Provincial*, whose sharp and witty polemics did much to discredit the Jesuits. This ideal of strict religious observance was put into practice in small groups, which were kept as intimate as possible – parishes, monasteries and oratories. Jansenism followed the trend in Church politics which opposed the centralism of the religious orders, mostly of international character, which sought as far as possible to be exempt from all jurisdiction except that of the Pope. It favoured the relative independence of dioceses and parishes. Most of its numerous supporters belonged to the upper middle class. These had had in the Parliaments (courts with legislative powers to some extent competing with royal legislation) a certain political instrument, but they had been discarded by the monarchy as soon as the power of the common enemy, the ancient "military" nobles, had been broken. When the monarchy now favoured the court nobility, descendants of the ancient feudal nobles, but now entirely dependent on the king, the upper middle class lost all hope of political power and was ready, in its disappointment, to see all purely human religious endeavour discredited. It was ripe for a doctrine which sharply opposed the true order of values, that of grace, to the natural and worldly order.

3. *The stages of the controversy.* Conflict with the magisterium of the Church broke out with the publication of the Bull of Innocent X *Cum occasione* (1653), which condemned five propositions of Jansen on the relationship of grace and freedom (*D* 1092–1096, *DS* 2001–2007). These propositions were not taken word for word from the *Augustinus*, but were formulated in keeping with its principles. The Jansenists acknowledged the justification and authority of this decision, and hence the *quaestio iuris*, but denied the *quaestio facti* – that the propositions in question were to be found in Jansen. They also refused to recognize the authority of the Church to decide on such "facts" which were not revealed facts, and claimed that in this matter the magisterium was entitled to no more than *silentium obsequiosum* from Christians. In 1657, the general assembly of the French clergy called upon them to subscribe to a formula of submission which acknowledged the *de facto* heretical status of Jansen and the authority of the Church in such matters of fact. A similar formula was also proposed by Pope Alexander VII in 1664. In the subsequent quarrels, many Jansenists, including Arnauld and Paschasius Quesnel, were forced to seek refuge in the Netherlands. There was a temporary peace after 1667 (the "Clementine Peace" of Pope Clement IX) and the conflict ceased to be a major preoccupation when the Roman and the French Church clashed on Gallicanism (the Jansenists being mostly on the side of Rome, defending the independence of the Church as regards the State). But after the settlement between the papacy and the monarchy, the conflict broke out again in still more acute form. The Bull *Vineum Domini* appeared in 1705 and led to the suppression and destruction of Port-Royal (1707–12). But the persistence of Jansenism may be seen from the condemnation of 101 propositions of Quesnel by the Bull *Unigenitus* (1713) and its counterpart – the demand for a General Council to decide this

new controversy. The promulgation of the Bull *Unigenitus* as French law finally brought Jansenism to an end as a movement. Organized Jansenism survived only in the Netherlands, where it still exists as the "Church of Utrecht", now united with the Old Catholics.

The whole controversy between the Jansenists and the magisterium has a strange twilight element. The longer the controversy continued, the less was it concerned with definite doctrines. Jansenism was a complicated matter, based rather on a certain mentality and spirituality than on an explicit dogmatic theology. It was an effort at Church reform in the spirit of early Christianity, which was asked to declare itself heretical, though this was the last thing which it wished to be. It is hard to avoid the suspicion that the reaction of the magisterium to this undoubtedly very serious-minded effort at Christian self-understanding really created the opponents whom it then condemned so severely as Jansenists.

4. *The relevance of Jansenism.* In the perspective of the great movements of the human spirit, Jansenism may be seen as a reaction, in line with that of the Reformation, affirming the Christian consciousness of election against the highly conciliatory intermediate position of Renaissance humanism. It undoubtedly highlights the central problem of Christian self-understanding – as Christian humanism did from the opposite standpoint – but seems as little helpful as the arguments of its opponents to the type of theological discussion which is now prescribed by the progress of philosophical reflection since the Enlightenment, transcendental philosophy, idealism and existence-philosophy. Above all, the great problem which is at the base of all the others, how to reconcile divine grace which is absolutely gratuitous and beyond merit with personal human responsibility, religiously as well as theologically, can hardly be solved along Jansenistic lines. The Jansenist abstractions concerned with an *adiutorium quo* effective of itself and of the nature of a "quality", and with a freedom of choice which is basically impotent, hardly allow us to pose the question properly, much less to solve it. It is a problem to which we can only hope to do justice if we treat it in the categories of interpersonal mediation, which will allow for the dialectic of individual personal originality within the framework of interpersonal originality. We must recognize, in fact, that responsible freedom can only be brought into existence by the creation of this dialectical tension and harmony with its opposite free counterpart. This dialectic must be basic not only for the limit notion of a "pure state of nature" but above all for the theological exposition of the mystery of redemption (insofar as it is a summons to use the liberty which it alone confers).

Konrad Hecker

JESUS CHRIST

I. Biblical

The following may be listed as assured findings of scholarship: a) No doubt is cast on the historical existence of Jesus by any serious scholar. Now that the debates raised by Bauer and Drews about Christ being a myth have died away, there is wide agreement about the historical fact of Jesus. b) The old-style attempt to construct "Lives of Jesus" has failed; even recent books of this kind (e.g., Stauffer's book on Jesus) are interesting for details but are no longer in harmony with the present state of scholarship as a whole. c) This is due to the character of the sources for the life of Jesus; the NT writings, even the gospels, being kerygmatic in purpose, are not strictly historical sources but testimonies of belief.

The present article assumes agreement on these points. It deals with problems of fact (A) and of method (B), the message and mission of Jesus (C), questions concerning the Passion and Easter (D), and NT Christology (E).

A. Questions of Fact

1. The few non-Christian sources merely confirm that in antiquity it never occurred to any one, even the bitterest enemies of Christianity, to doubt the existence of Jesus (cf. Bornkamm, *Jesus of Nazareth*, p. 25). These sources are: Tacitus, *Annals*, 15, 4 (Christ condemned to death by Pontius Pilate under Tiberius), Suetonius, *Claudius*, 25, 4 (a certain "Chrestus" caused disturbances in Rome; uncertain whether Christ is meant), Pliny the Younger's letter to Trajan, *Epistola* 10, 96 (Christ revered as a god), Josephus, *Antiquities*, 20, 200 (James, the brother of Jesus who is called the Christ). The authenticity of the *Testimonium Flavianum* (Josephus, *Antiquities*, 18, 63f.), which had long been recognized as a Christian interpolation, yet usually considered to derive in substance from Josephus, has been contested again recently. H. Conzelmann detects in the passage the Lucan pattern of the Christian kerygma and therefore considers that it was "subsequently interpolated in its entirety" (*RGG*, III, col. 622). The Talmud references and the apocryphal gospels likewise add nothing to our knowledge of Jesus.

2. The Christian sources comprise a few indications in early credal formulas (birth, death on the cross, resurrection), and above all the books which are expressly concerned with Jesus, i.e., the gospels. Nevertheless it is generally admitted that they do not satisfy the ideas and demands of a modern historian. The classical quest of the historical Jesus still thought it possible to draw from the gospels a psychologically and historically incontestable picture of Jesus. When the special character of the fourth gospel was recognized and the Two Sources Theory was worked out for the Synoptics, the attempt was made to reconstruct a life of Jesus on the basis of Mark's Gospel. Wrede, however, showed that Mark himself possessed no clear picture of the life of Jesus but arranged his gospel from dogmatic points of view; Schmidt established the secondary character of the framework. This excluded the last "historical" source, i.e., Mark's Gospel in its present form, for a reconstruction of the life of Jesus. These conclusions still remain substantially valid. Form-criticism made it clear that the beginning of the tradition concerning Jesus – if we leave brief credal formulas out of account – is the independent pericope. This is not a section of a larger whole, but contains the whole revelation of Jesus. The intrinsic interweaving of report and confession of faith prevents direct access from the individual pericope to the historical, earthly Jesus (see below, B). The NT writings take into account the new situation after Easter; they do not describe Jesus κατὰ σάρκα and are only interested in his earthly life to the extent that it is the necessary condition of the confession that "Jesus is the Christ, the Kyrios". But even if the character of our sources is taken into account (message, not report), the following biographical details among others can be established: Jesus' Galilean origin, baptism by John, execution under Pontius Pilate.

3. The chronology of Jesus' life, like the routes of his journeys, is uncertain The NT writers are not interested either in an absolute chronology or in synchronizing Jesus' life with the secular history of the age. Only the late passage Lk 3:1f. inserts at least the public ministry of John the Baptist into the framework of Roman and Jewish history. (The 15th year of Tiberius lasted according to Roman reckoning from 19 August 28 to 18 August 29, and according to Syrian reckoning from 1 October 27 to 30 September 28; the

second is now regarded as the more probable.) The year of Jesus' birth is also uncertain. The difficulties can only be briefly indicated: Jesus is said to have been born under Herod the Great when Quirinius was governor of Syria (Lk 2:1). But there is no evidence that Quirinius was governor during Herod's lifetime. None of the explanations of this contradiction so far suggested is satisfactory. All that is generally accepted is that Jesus was born before 4 B.C. (death of Herod). More precise details cannot be drawn from the infancy narratives of Matthew and Luke.

The most important chronological problem is the date of Jesus' death and, as a consequence, of the Last Supper. The paschal lamb was killed in the afternoon and eaten in the evening of 14 Nisan, and on 15 Nisan the festival of the Pasch was celebrated in memory of the deliverance from Egypt. According to the Synoptics, Jesus celebrated the establishment of the new Covenant within the framework of a paschal meal (14 Nisan) and was executed on 15 Nisan; according to the Johannine dating, Jesus was put to death on the eve of the feast-day, i.e., 14 Nisan, and Jesus' Last Supper has no connection with the paschal meal, which in John's Gospel is not eaten until after the Crucifixion. The controversy over these conflicting data has not been resolved to this day. Even the solar calendar discovered in Qumran does not make it possible to harmonize the Synoptic with the Johannine chronology. Moreover, both in Mark's and in John's indications of time, theological interests have to be taken into account. For Mark, the old commemorative meal is replaced by a new one; Jesus himself is the paschal lamb which is eaten; for John, Jesus is the true paschal lamb which is slaughtered. Once this theological purpose of the dates is recognized, it becomes of secondary importance to fix the actual day. The majority of exegetes take 15 Nisan (=7 April), A.D. 30, as the probable date of Jesus' death, but they are aware that this is hypothetical (cf. Trilling, *Problème*, p. 64).

4. The person of Jesus must be seen against the background of his age and environment. Since 63 B.C. the Jews had been politically subject to Roman sovereignty. Although these foreign rulers made considerable allowance for the national and religious susceptibilities of the Jews, there was in Jesus' time a widespread expectation, fanned by the fanatical Zealots, of a political Messiah. It is evident from the gospels that Jesus took no stand on burning political problems; they seldom mention a political group as hostile to him (except on the question of taxation), whereas they devote much space to religious controversy with the Pharisees. How far Jesus is to be brought into connection with the Essene movement, on which new light has been thrown by the finds at Qumran, is still disputed. Scholars seem to be agreed that the points of contact are substantially fewer than was first thought when the discovery of the scrolls was announced. There is no longer any question of direct dependence on Jesus' part. The Qumran community regarded itself as an organized community of salvation with a hierarchical structure; by its obedience to the Torah and the observance of prescriptions of ritual purity, it was fitting itself to be the eschatological "remnant". Jesus, on the contrary, addressed himself expressly and without distinction to the whole nation.

The Jews jealously defended their religious and national traditions; Hellenistic influence was therefore very slight in Palestine as compared with the Judaism of the diaspora. Jesus shows no sign of Hellenistic influence. His speech is Aramaic, his parables are drawn from ordinary Jewish life, his controversies with opponents concern the OT idea of God, the interpretation and observance of the Torah. His actual home, Galilee, was despised by the purely Jewish population of Judaea and the capital on account of its mixed population, as was its half-pagan neighbour Samaria. Although the geographical outline of the earliest gospel belongs to the Marcan editorial stratum, it is very probable that Jesus began his public ministry in Galilee (Lake of Gennesaret, Capernaum).

B. Problems of Method

1. The first problem is where to insert Jesus' earthly life. What place does Jesus occupy in an account of NT theology? Whereas one school of thought among exegetes (e.g., Meinertz) places Jesus at the beginning of NT theology, another (e.g., Bultmann) puts Jesus before the beginning of NT theology, as its presupposition. Even if Jesus knew himself to be the Messiah and called for faith in himself as such, he cannot be described, according to Bultmann, as a sharer of the Christian faith, of which he is none the less the object (cf. *Verhaltnis*, p. 8). Bultmann therefore deals with Jesus among the presuppositions of NT theology, but as a historical presupposition within its framework. A third school, however (e.g., Schlier), excludes Jesus completely from NT theology. These exegetes recognize that the NT presupposes Jesus, his words and deeds, and that without them there would be no NT. But the theology of the NT writers is not simply a continuation of Jesus' theology. The historical figure of Jesus cannot be drawn from the gospels, which throughout are an interpretation of his history by believers. The historical figure is a condition of NT theology but as such should not be made a part of NT theology itself (Schlier, *The Relevance of the NT*, p. 11).

There would probably be general agreement that Jesus may be termed the presupposition of the development of the NT kerygma. The further question whether he is to be dealt with within the framework of NT theology is of secondary importance.

2. A second, more important problem is the transition from the earthly Jesus to the Christ of faith, i.e., the problem of continuity and discontinuity raised by the dividing-line of Easter. The longer scholarship pursued the "quest of the historical Jesus", the more it emphasized the discontinuity between the "earthly Jesus" and the "Christ of faith". This development reached its culmination in Bultmann's theology. From the fact that only Jesus and the NT kerygma are historical elements, Bultmann concludes that only Jesus and the kerygma can be in continuity with one another, but not Jesus and the Christ of the kerygma, who is seen as outside history. Consequently no path leads from Jesus to the Christ of the kerygma. The kerygma is said to presuppose the sheer fact that the historical Jesus existed, the fact of his life and history on earth but this "fact that . . ." has no saving significance of any kind. Consequently it is said that the believer cannot believe in the earthly Jesus; the latter has no significance for one's own personal life; only the Christ of the kerygma can encounter the believer in the kerygma, in the word of the Church spoken today. The continuity between Jesus and the kerygma, which is inconceivable without Jesus' earthly existence, is acknowledged; but an agreement in content is not admitted, for the kerygma does not simply take over Jesus' message, nor did Jesus' me sage already contain the NT kerygma (e.g. the Christological kerygma had no place in Jesus' teaching).

With Bultmann, who is here representative of other exegetes, emphasis on the discontinuity between Jesus and the kerygmatic Christ reached its culmination. Hand in hand with it goes a serious concern for continuity; continuity stands in the forefront of inquiry for a whole line of Bultmann's pupils. The problem is acute because an explanation has to be found why the disciples and with them the NT do not simply repeat Jesus' message. The faith in God's action in Jesus evoked by the appearances of the risen Lord led, in a long process of reflection, inspired to some extent by passages from the OT, to the interpretation of the death of Jesus as redemptive. As this understanding gradually became more explicit (cross – glorification – baptism or birth – pre-existence), the whole of Jesus' earthly life was drawn into the post-paschal proclamation of Christ. This process is visible, for example, in the increasing interest shown in Jesus' earthly life. To explain the continuity as a linear extension, so to speak, without taking into account the Easter events as a radical dividing-line, would not do justice to the significance of the Resurrection. In any case an explanation acceptable to all theological schools of thought is not to be expected in the present state of research.

C. Jesus' Message and Mission

In the centre of Jesus' message and mission is the reign and kingdom of God (1); its proximity determines the uncompromising demand for immediate conversion (2); it is the absolutely sovereign and freely offered gift of God's grace to his chosen people (3).

1. Jesus' teaching on the reign of God shows that God is the centre of his thought. Men do not have to do something first in order to receive God's gifts, nor is God under an obligation to reckon up man's precise merits and reward them accordingly. Jesus declares war on piety of that kind. God is the only actor who really matters. The "kingdom of God" or "reign of God" therefore does not mean a merely static condition, but God's dynamic action also. The reign of God is a reality opposed to the present aeon, and signifies that the dominion of Satan is ended (Lk 11:20=Mt 12:28).

The reign and kingdom of God is the theme of many of Jesus' parables. The "parables of growth" (to which the term "contrast-parables" is now preferred because of their point) show that that reign can only be brought about by God, but that he will bring it about despite all obstacles (Mk 4:26–29, 30–32 par.; Mt 13:33 par.). These contrast parables are aimed in particular at the impatience of those who wish to bring about the kingdom of God by force (Zealots) or their own achievements (Pharisees). Such people are told that it does not depend on them, because the kingdom of God is the action and gift of God alone.

The controversy about Jesus' conception of the reign of God has led to agreement on a middle position. Neither thoroughgoing eschatologism (J. Weiss; A. Schweitzer) nor realized eschatology (C. H. Dodd) has prevailed. According to the first of these two extreme positions, Jesus expected the reign of God as a strictly future reality which would come in his lifetime (before the completion of the disciples' mission to Israel). According to the second, the reign of God is already present. With various modifications the prevailing view today is that Jesus regarded the essentially futuristic reign of God as extending into the present through his coming and as particularly manifest in his exorcisms and miracles.

From the post-exilic period onward Israel expected that God would inaugurate his reign with a day of judgment. The nations will be annihilated in battle (Joel 4:15f.; Ezech 38:22) or judgment (Dan 2:34f.; 7:9f., etc.) or must be subject to Israel (Psalms of Solomon 17). Israel as the chosen people of God enters into the kingdom of God. This self-confidence had already been opposed by John the Baptist (Mt 3:7ff.). Jesus even threatens that the kingdom will be taken from the Jews and given to others (Mk 12:9; cf. Mt 8:11f.).

2. The call for conversion inspired

by the proximity of the reign of God leads to an intensification of the demands of the Torah and also to the suppression of certain precepts which misrepresent the genuine will of God. Jesus' attitude to the Law is the point which provoked the hostility of the Jews, because they saw in it an attack on God. Among the precepts which are made more radical are the prohibition of divorce (Lk 16:18; cf. Mk 10:1–12; Mt 5:31, against the practice of the note of dismissal), the honest observance of the fourth commandment (Mk 7:10–13, against the usage of the "Corban"), the antitheses of the Sermon on the Mount (Mt 5:21–42) and the unqualified requirement of love of enemies (Mt 5:43ff.). Jesus is not concerned about literal fidelity in the fulfilment of a precept but about the will of God himself. Consequently he directly attacks the Law where that will was concealed by the "hedge about the Law". This is particularly clear in the disputes about the Sabbath (Mk 2:23–3:6); in this sense, Jesus' attitude is certainly correctly described by the saying, secondary in character, at Mk 2:27.

The insistence on the true will of God stands in direction connection with the message of the imminent advent of the reign of God. Jesus knows he is a voice calling at the last hour, consequently he lays down no law with detailed prescriptions but demands penance and conversion to God himself. This is seen in the herald's cry which sums up the whole of Jesus' proclamation (Mk 1:15). Because the reign of God comes solely by God's power and grace, man can only pray for it ("Thy kingdom come") and recognize the present as a sign calling for conversion (Lk 12:54–59; 10:23); it is now that the uncompromising decision for or against Jesus must be made.

The saying about confessing and denying (Lk 12:8ff.) shows that the positive or negative response to Jesus' message and person is decisive for membership of the eschatological community of salvation. Anyone who accepts Jesus' message now, i.e., fulfils God's will to salvation and holiness now in the radical way proposed by Jesus, has qualified as an heir to the promises.

3. The expectation of the imminent advent of the reign of God also inspires Jesus' endeavour to prepare the whole of Israel to inherit salvation. Jesus regards the empirical Israel of his time as the chosen people of God, i.e., in accordance with the history of revelation, he respects the prior claim of the people of Israel as the bearer of the promise of salvation. Consequently Jesus restricted to Israel his own work and later that of his disciples who were co-operating in his own mission (Mt 10:5f.; 15:24ff.). All the more weight attaches to the cures of pagans which are reported as exceptions (Mt 8:5–13 par.; Mk 7:24–30).

The summons to the whole of Israel finds expression in characteristic features of his preaching. A first typical feature is that there is no trace of flight or separation from the world. Unlike John the Baptist in the desert, Jesus sought public places in order to reach all Israelites with his message. In contrast to many movements of the age (Essenes, Qumran), Jesus did not want to gather together the holy remnant and separate the pious from the sinners. For Jesus, all Israel is a scattered flock without a shepherd (Mich 5:3; Mt 9:36; 10:6). God's goodness is shown by his not excluding even sinners and outcasts (Lk 15), and so Jesus too converses with the religious outcasts and sits at table with them. Access to the kingdom of God is offered to all Israelites on the single condition of readiness for conversion. Jesus' refusal to segregate and gather together repentant Israelites into a special Messianic community is shown both in his words and his actions; he avoided all contemporary ecclesiological references and terms. Even on the supposition that there was a circle of the Twelve before Easter, this is to be regarded as representing not the holy remnant but the whole of Israel, the twelve tribes of the nation. The number twelve unmistakably expresses Jesus' claim to the whole of Israel. The refusal to divide the good from the wicked is explicitly emphasized by the parables of the fishing-net (Mt 13:47–50) and the weeds (Mt 13:24–30).

The reserve shown by Jesus in speech and action results from the fear of misunderstandings: a) to gather the remnant into an organized community (cf. Qumran) would merely have been regarded as entering into competition with the "sects" of the day; b) Jesus does not simply demand the correct observance of the Mosaic Law; going beyond and partly cancelling the old Law (especially the ritual precepts) he teaches an ethics which is clear and uncomplicated compared with legalistic casuistry; with a special separate community there would be a danger of a new sectarian juridicism; c) the refusal to set up a special community is also consistent with the new relation between God and man; whereas Jewish sects claimed to do more than fulfil the Law and viewed their relations with God in the categories of achievement and reward, Jesus wished to manifest God's justice and mercy; all men are sinners before God. If Jesus had formed a separate community, this aspect of his message would have been less prominent: d) since Jesus laid down only one condition for entry into the eschatological community of salvation, namely decision for him here and now, the immediate urgency of this demand would have been unnecessarily weakened by the provisional foundation of a special community. These and other reasons explain Jesus' reserve with regard to an organized community of the heirs of salvation.

So far only the Israelites have been referred to as candidates for salvation, but something must also be said on Jesus' attitude to the pagans. Despite the recognition on principle of Israel's prerogative, Jesus' conception of salvation also has room for the pagans. Jesus excludes the idea of revenge from his teaching (cf. Lk 4:19 with Is 61:2) and at least in isolated cases allows pagans to know of the dawn of the reign of God which he has inaugurated (Mt 8:5–13 par.; Mk 7:24–30). Furthermore, it appears possible to show that Jesus had in mind the idea of the eschatological pilgrimage of the Gentiles (Mt 8:11; cf. J. Jeremias, *Promise to the Nations*). This would not imply a mission to the pagans, but would affirm their eschatological participation in salvation.

D. Questions concerning the Passion and Easter

It is possible to assume without serious difficulties that Jesus himself saw his passion coming as a reaction to his preaching about God and the kingdom of God, or even consciously went to meet it. Among the problems connected with the way Jesus regarded his death is the question of the historicity and origin of the λύτρον-saying (Mk 10:45), and the even more decisive question of the words used at the Last Supper on the pattern of various OT themes (Ex 24:8; Is 53; Jer 31:31–34). It is difficult to reconstruct the original form of words because the accounts of the Last Supper as we have them probably also reflect the post-paschal understanding of the Eucharist. Differences have long been observed between the Matthew-Mark version and the Luke-Paul version. Furthermore, two separate traditions concerning the Last Supper are involved: an account of the Supper which is eschatological in outlook, and an account of the institution (of the Eucharist). We can scarcely expect to reconstruct the original wording with certainty *in detail*. Nevertheless it is possible to follow the Semitic tradition very far back; at all events the themes of vicarious death and of the Covenant cannot be derived from Hellenism. It is also difficult to judge the prophecies of the Passion and Resurrection (Mk 8:31; 9:31; 10:32–34). These are considered by the critics to be *vaticinia ex eventu*; it is generally recognized that at least in their present form they are secondary in character. Consequently they cannot be quoted in isolation as evidence for the way Jesus envisaged his death. From the whole pattern of Jesus' claim to a divine mission, however, it appears at least probable that within the circle of his disciples Jesus spoke of his death as a divine "must" (Lk 12:50; 13:32f.) and accordingly understood it as a new means of salvation. It must also seriously be asked whether he cannot have been capable of discovering the divinely-willed meaning of his death in the function of the vicarious suffering of the Servant of God who suffers "for many" (Is 53:4–12), i.e., as a new gracious act of God for Israel and the Gentiles (Is 42:6f.; 49:5–8), especially as the thought of the vicarious and expiatory significance of the sufferings of the just man had been current since the time of the Maccabees (E. Schweizer, *Erniedrigung*, pp. 24–26). The idea of atonement can be supported at least by the logion of the baptism of death (Mk 10:38 par.) which is not open to suspicion of being post-paschal interpretation based on biblical theology.

The question of Jesus' understanding of his death is of secondary importance from the point of view of post-paschal faith, inasmuch as this death was overcome by God's action and the history of Jesus began anew on another plane. According to the convergent testimony of old formulas of belief and the Easter narratives in the gospels, the disciples were convinced by the apparitions that God had crowned Jesus' death by a new act of revelation, the miracle of raising him from the dead. He who had been executed shamefully was raised up to be the heavenly Kyrios. The markedly divergent Easter narratives of the gospels and Acts 1 are, of course, not to be regarded as a detailed report reproducing the actual course of events. But as "interpretations" of God's saving action they are valuable expressions of the primitive Church's belief in Jesus' resurrection and in its reality and significance for Jesus himself and for the continuation of the work of the redemption. Attention is rightly drawn to the contrast between the multiplicity of Easter accounts and the unity of the Easter message (Bornkamm, *Jesus*, p. 166). Catholic and Protestant theologians are agreed that not the Resurrection as such but the Easter faith, the disciples' personal conviction, is accessible as a historical event in the strict sense (Trilling, *Problème*, p. 152; Kolping, in *Handbuch theologischer Grundbegriffe*, I, p. 141).

With faith in Jesus' resurrection there begins a gradual unfolding of the Christ-event and a retrospective interpretation of Jesus' life; these are visible very early, particularly in kerygmatic formulas and Christological titles, and are finally incorporated in the gospels.

E. New Testament Christology

It is generally agreed that Jesus did not make his own person a main theme of his message, and that on account of the special nature of his eschatological claim he could not apply to himself any of the existing terms used to denote bringers of salvation, at least not to the extent to which they are now found in the texts (e.g., Son of Man). It is therefore possible that titles such as "Messiah", "Son of Man", "Lord", perhaps also "the Son", were first used by the primitive community to characterize Jesus' consciousness of his mission or the claim which his mission implied, and to express its own faith in him. The resurrection of the crucified Jesus to heavenly power must be regarded as the basic starting-point and guide-line of NT Christology.

1. Probably the earliest stratum of the NT is the "Exaltation Christology". In conjunction with theocratic messianic prophecies (2 Sam 7:14; Ps 2:7; 100:1), the Resurrection was interpreted as installation as Messianic Son of God, as sitting at the right hand of God and as enthronement as Kyrios equal to God. It is a very instructive fact that the primitive community, according to the most probable meaning of *Maranatha*, prayed for the coming of the era of salvation, not directly from Yahweh but from the heavenly Jesus. This is only meaningful if the Resurrection or Exaltation was not regarded merely as a transitory assumption but as the installation of Jesus with heavenly power to save. This faith in the Resurrection made Jesus the Saviour the centre of the preaching, instead of Jesus' message. In the light of the Exaltation Christology, the post-paschal message becomes the message about Jesus (the Gospel of Jesus, objective genitive [Rom 15:19; 1:9; 1:1–3]).

2. The message of salvation, first proclaimed on Jewish territory, spoke for missionary reasons in the first place of what God had done in Jesus. The divine confirmation of the Crucified was the primary reason for speaking about the redemptive meaning of this death (cf. the pre-Pauline formulation at 1 Cor 15:3f.). As well as the fact that the death was in accordance with the Scriptures (see also the OT allusions in the accounts of the Passion), the idea of atonement as well as the redemptive power of Jesus' death was also envisaged (Gal 1:4; 2 Cor 5:14f., 21; Rom 4:25; 8:32).

3. Another possible interpretation of Jesus' death is shown by the frequent linking of brief formulas concerning it (including the idea of atonement: Rom 5:6, 8; 1 Pet 3:18; being raised up by God: 1 Cor 15:3f.) with the title of "Messiah, Christ". The title of Messiah was not tied in Judaism to a particular bringer of salvation, and Jesus did not apply it to himself because of its political colouring. Even if the disputed saying before the Sanhedrin (Mk 14:61f.) is not historical, it may be considered certain that the Roman procurator condemned Jesus to death as a political claimant to Messiahship, at the instigation of the Jewish leaders (cf. the inscription on the Cross). Hence the apostolic preaching probably used the title of Messiah to affirm that the execution of Jesus as a messianic claimant was a divinely-willed redemptive death. Reserve regarding the title of Messiah consequently disappeared in the primitive community in the situation after Easter, and in fact "Messiah" became the most frequent way of designating Jesus' function. Then when it was used by Greeks for whom it did not designate a function, it became a proper name. Thus, to put it in a simplified form, the Palestinian profession of faith "Jesus is the Christ" became in Hellenism the proper name "Jesus Christ", and this then became an element in a new profession of faith, e.g., "Jesus Christ is Lord" (Phil 2:11).

4. The profession of faith in Jesus as the Messiah was linked in Palestinian circles with proof of his Davidic descent. The appeal to Jesus' ancestry, as in the ancient formulation at Romans 1:3, was used to prove the Messianic character of the earthly Jesus and this was linked with the Messianic enthronement as Son of God which took place in the Resurrection.

The reference to Jesus' Davidic descent in the oldest kerygma is due less to interest in biography than to the proof from prophecy (2 Sam 7:12; Is 11:1); it expresses the claim to the Messianic throne of David. On account of its strongly national colouring, this title meant little to Gentile Christians and soon disappeared.

5. Since the theological affirmation of Davidic sonship links Jesus' Messiahship with his ancestry and birth (cf. the opening chapters of Mt and Lk), the question of Jesus' pre-existence arose when recourse was had to what Jesus was before his birth. As the historicity of the Synoptic logia in which "the Son" is used absolutely (among others Mt 11:27 par.) is contested, as is the existence of the myth of the Anthropos (*Urmensch*) Redeemer at the time, preference may be given to the explanation that the Jewish-Hellenistic doctrine of the Wisdom which was prior to the world led to faith in Jesus' pre-existence. (Phil 2:6ff.; Rom 1:3; 8:3, 29, 32; 1 Cor 8:6; 10:4) and so to the affirmation of the Incarnation (according to Phil 2:6–11, even before Paul). The pre-existence Christology, i.e., belief in divine being as always belonging to Jesus Christ, was more precisely expressed in Jewish-Hellenistic Christianity with the help of the title Son (of God); for genuine Jewish thought, this is only a messianic royal title. Whether the use of the title Son of God to denote the pre-existent only came in with Paul (Gal 4:4f.; Rom 1:3a), or was already pre-Pauline, must remain an open question. But it is certain that the OT concept of Son of God had no connection with pre-existence and certainly not with metaphysical sonship of God. It was rather the notion of election for a special task and of strict obedience to the divine call (cf. Cullmann, *Christology*, p. 281). Similarly the term "divine man" among the Greeks, even when birth from a God is mentioned, contains no hint of metaphysical sonship. The divine man (ruler, philosopher, poet, doctor, wonder-worker) was a supernatural being (θεῖος) but not a god (θεός). But the primitive Church understood Jesus to be the true and only "Son of God" in an absolute sense, and on this account the apostolic message could also be termed "the gospel concerning his Son" (Rom 1:9; cf. the variant readings at Mk 1:1, which place the whole gospel under the confession of faith in Jesus as the Son of God). Even if Jesus did not use the absolute term "the Son" of himself, some explanation for the term may be found in the uniquely direct relation to God which Jesus claimed for himself as the final spokesman of God's will to save and sanctify.

6. Special problems are raised by the title "Son of Man" which historical research claimed most persistently for Jesus. Since it is improbable that Jesus used the title himself as frequently as it occurs in the texts, three groups of Son of Man sayings are now distinguished in the synoptics: sayings about his future coming, about his suffering and resurrection, and about his present work (Bultmann, *Theology*, I, p. 30). In the third group (Mk 2:10, 28; Mt 8:20; 11:19; 12:32), the title at least is almost universally regarded as secondary by exegetes (contrast E. Schweizer). In the second group (Mk 8:31; 9:31; 10:33 – not in Q) it is regarded as secondary by a large number of exegetes. At present the main debate is about the Son of Man sayings found in both Mark and Q (Mk 8:38; 13:26f.; 14:62f.; Mt 24:27, 37, 39, 44 par.)

Until a few years ago the only question was whether Jesus meant himself or someone else when speaking of the *coming* Son of Man. But today distinguished representatives of critical scholarship point out that Jesus could not have announced the imminence of God's reign, while at the same time expecting a new mediator of salvation before the judgment (Vielhauer, Braun, Käsemann, Bornkamm). Hence they hold that the primitive Church was the first to draw on the apocalyptic image of the Son of Man coming from the hidden world of God and carrying out the judgment in God's name. These were the only terms in which to explain an advent of the saviour from heaven, in other words the parousia of the Messiah, Jesus, for the judgment, on the basis of an existing form of eschatological expectation. But even on this assumption, the belief of the primitive community in Jesus' parousia would be anchored in an act of revelation by God; once again the importance of the Easter faith for the post-paschal gospel would be exemplified.

7. The title "Servant of God" plays as prominent a role in critical scholarship as that of Son of Man, since it is used to prove that Jesus was conscious of making vicarious atonement (Cullmann; Jeremias).

Of the four Songs of the Servant of Yahweh (Is 42:1-4; 49:1-7; 50:4-11; 52:13-53:12) the last in particular is relevant because of the vicarious atonement of God's Servant. The traditional view claims that Jesus himself had this in mind ("παῖς-consciousness" instead of "Messianic consciousness"; cf. Cullmann, *Christology*, p. 81). On the other hand, one should note two texts of Matthew (12:18 = Is 42:1-4; 8:17 = Is 53:4) which emphasize Jesus' quiet activity or his miracles but not his expiatory sufferings. Would this theological interpretation have been possible for Matthew if Jesus had plainly regarded himself as the Servant of God making vicarious atonement? Nevertheless the other extreme must also be excluded, namely that Jesus could not have understood his violent death as expiatory in the sense of the Servant of Yahweh of Deutero-Isaiah.

It is to be noted that Judaism did not think of the figure of the Servant of God as a single reality; the Servant Songs were not yet recognized as a thematic unity. Judaism did indeed attribute expiatory power to the death of a martyr, but not on the basis of Is 53 (e.g., verse 10). Moreover, the thought of vicarious expiatory suffering was not yet linked with the Messiah (Cullmann and others, against Jeremias). On these grounds a vicariously suffering Messiah could not have been deduced from Is 53. When the NT linked suffering with the Messiah, this was an absolute novelty, the explanation of the scandal of the Cross. It is also conceivable that Jesus selected the trait in Isaiah which corresponded to his special awareness of his mission (cf. Is 53:12; atonement). But even if Jesus did not regard himself as the Servant, this would not prove that he did not understand his death as expiation "for many" (Mk 10:45 and the words at the Last Supper, Mk 14:24; Mt 26:28; "for you", Lk 22:20, are secondary).

8. A frequently used title, particularly in primitive Christian worship, and one which expresses Jesus' installation as universal ruler, is the name Kyrios. Here we can trace in the texts the development from the Marē'- (Kyrios) of the liturgical intercession *maranātha* to the absolute ὁ κύριος in Greek-speaking circles or to the form of confession which was possible there: "Jesus is Lord" (1 Cor 12:3; Rom 10:9). This development was probably due in part to the use of the term Kyrios in Hellenism to denote a ruler honoured as divine, as well as to its use as the name of God in the Septuagint, even if Jesus was not honoured as Kyrios-Yahweh in the full sense. At all events the liturgical invocation of Jesus as Lord facilitated the transference of the Septuagint title "Lord" to him. In contrast to the pagans, the Christian confesses only one God, the Father, and one Lord, Jesus Christ (1 Cor 8:5f.). The function of this Lord consists in the present guidance of his Church (1 Thess 3:12f.; Rom 10:12), in the exercise of a cosmic dominion over principalities and powers (1 Cor 15:25ff.) and in the last judgment on the "day of the Lord", which is now attributed to Jesus (1 Thess 5:2; 2 Thess 2:2; Acts 2:20). Profession of faith in the exalted Lord is given its most magnificent expression in the closing words of Matthew (Mt 28:18). Jesus is also retrospectively called "Lord" (1 Cor 2:8;

9:5; 7:10, 12), but on the whole it is the post-paschal profession of faith which this title summarizes (Acts 2:36; Phil 2:9–11). Brief indications of other bases of Christology: Paul contrasts Christ as the second Adam and ancestor of justified mankind with the first Adam and ancestor of sinful mankind (Rom 5:12–21). Hebrews compares Jesus' function as mediator to that of a heavenly high priest. The Logos-Christology of the Johannine prologue sets special problems, and its origin (Gnosis? Wisdom?) has not yet been fully explained.

9. *Summary*. NT Christology as it has been exemplified here on the basis of certain titles inquires first and foremost not into the divine or human nature of Jesus Christ but into the significance of his person in the history of salvation; consequently most titles are words which denote functions and express some particular aspect of his activity as mediator of salvation. The full development of the ontological concepts of dogmatic Christology is not to be expected from the NT, since its interests lay elsewhere and its language was still uninhibited.

Ingrid Maisch and *Anton Vögtle*

II. Quest of the Historical Jesus

Historical investigation of the life of Jesus is inspired by the desire to establish a critically reliable picture of Jesus. From the time of the Synoptics and John's Gospel onward there have been portraits of Jesus coloured by the spirit of their age and the theological perspective of their authors. The scientific quest for the historical Jesus is, however, a phenomenon of modern times. It has developed since the Enlightenment, side by side with historical criticism and in particular with the emergence of historico-critical theology. If lives of Jesus in earlier times can be called critical at all, the critique was theological, not historical. Theological critique even seems to have determined more strongly the mode of presentation in the gospels themselves than it did the later arrangements of the canonical writings into gospel harmonies, poetical adaptations of the gospel materials, epic, dramatic and edifying representations of the life of Jesus (Tatian, Juvencus, Sedulius, the *Heliand*, Otfried, Ps.-Bonaventure, Ludolf of Saxony). The discovery of the theological critique of the evangelists and, as a consequence, the different pictures of Jesus presented by them, belongs in its acute form to the most recent phase of research (form-criticism). The recognition of the evangelists' theological critique by the historical criticism of modern scholarship marks an important dividing-line or even the end of the scientific "quest for the historical Jesus" of modern times. A brief account of its course and chief stages must be traced by a retrospective glance at the history of scholarship, with a brief sketch of the pictures of Jesus proper to each period.

The course of research into the life of Jesus was described at the beginning of the present century by Albert Schweitzer in his *Quest of the Historical Jesus* (1st German ed., 1906; E. T., 2nd ed., 1926) "as the inspiring and splendid history of the consciousness of truth in Evangelical theology" (C. H. Ratschow, in *RGG*, III, col. 655). "The quest of the historical Jesus is a monument to the veracity of Protestant Christianity" (A. Schweitzer, Preface to 6th German edition, p. XVIII). It can be properly understood only in the wider perspective of the general history of ideas and of theology in modern times. "In the great debate on the meaning and significance of the Bible, which began with the emergence of modern Western thought, the chief positions were already marked out by 1680. The Enlightenment changed the historical stresses, but contributed nothing essentially new" (K. Scholder). The Enlightenment, however, extended rational criticism, gave it a more radical tone and applied it to the gospels in order to attack the traditional dogmatic account of Jesus. The first important thrust against the orthodox biblical conception of Christ came from the Hamburg Orientalist H. S. Reimarus in his *Apologie oder Schutzschrift für die vernünftigen Verehrer Gottes*, from which G. E. Lessing published the *Wolfenbüttel Fragments* (1774–78). Conflict between "reason" and traditional "faith" over the figure of Jesus set in and has continued (disastrously) down to our own times in the form of a controversy between historical science and traditional notions of faith. Its solution will require considerable efforts in philosophical and theological hermeneutics. In view of this, the history of research into the life of the historical Jesus may also be regarded as a history of biblical hermeneutics.

Reimarus and Lessing introduced into the rationalist theology of the Enlightenment the historical element which was to contribute to its downfall. Reimarus's criticism of tradition was intended to shock. He regarded Jesus as a Jewish national Messiah inspired by strong apocalyptic expectations, whose disciples invented the legends of Jesus' resurrection and ascension in support of their expectations of the Parousia. This raised the fundamental problem of the distinction between the historical Jesus and the dogmatic Christ. In one form or another it has remained decisive for subsequent research.

The next important impulse came from D. F. Strauss (cf. the title *Der Christus des Glaubens und der Jesus der Geschichte* [1865]), who in 1835–36 brought out in two volumes his *Leben Jesu, kritisch bearbeitet*. The advance of intellectual emancipation from religious and dogmatic conceptions allowed Strauss systematically to apply the idea of "myth" to the forces which shaped the evangelical picture of Jesus. For Strauss the idea of the God-man as the goal of humanity and of each individual is what is unshakably real in the person of Jesus and cannot be contested by historical criticism of myths. The equally sharp criticism which Strauss applied both to the supernaturalist and to naturalist and rationalistic accounts of Jesus is, it is true, only made possible by a "mythical interpretation", but it opened out new paths to later research by its more complex view. The transformation of the tradition concerning Jesus into kerygma seemed to become intelligible, and a way had apparently been found to locate the "historical" Jesus. Strauss himself, however, drew a picture of Jesus on liberal lines in his *Leben Jesu, für das deutsche Volk bearbeitet* (1864), in which he rather clumsily spiritualizes the Jesus of the Synoptics. Here he followed the tendency of liberal theology to "modernize" Jesus and, with the help of psychological explanations, drew a great number of relatively consistent and often extremely subjective pictures of Jesus as exemplar, reformer and great man.

The pictures of Jesus in liberal theology were based on source-criticism. Since Strauss, this had become indispensable and was intensively pursued. The basis was recognition of the priority of Mark and of the importance of the older Palestinian Logia-source (Q). Mark's Gospel provides the outline of Jesus' life, Q that of his teaching. Historical imagination, the art of psychological composition and "the conviction that historical reconstruction can be the basis of present-day world-views" (H. Conzelmann, col. 620) guide the descriptions of Jesus as teacher and model for humanity. For Schenkel, Keim, Holtzmann, B. Weiss and Beyschlag, Jesus as a "personality" was primarily a "spiritualizer of the idea of the Messiah, a profound thinker and founder of a present Kingdom of God" (A. Schweitzer).

Trust in the sources for the life of

Jesus was shaken at the beginning of the present century. In the course of the last sixty years, form-criticism and history of redaction have taught us to regard the Synoptics themselves as preachers and theologians, and their gospels as the theological redaction of kerygmatic traditions of many kinds. The framework of the story of Jesus presented in the gospels has proved to be a secondary, literary composition, from which no conclusions can be drawn with certainty about sequence of events in Jesus' life. Even until recently, research was dominated by the 19th-century picture of two periods in Jesus' work, the Galilean spring-time of success, and the subsequent crisis and the end in Jerusalem; but fundamentally judgment had been passed on "biographies of Jesus" by W. Wrede at the beginning of the present century: "Present-day study of the gospels starts from the assumption that Mark had more or less clearly before his eyes, though not without gaps, the real circumstances of Jesus' life. It presupposes that Mark thinks in terms of the life of Jesus, bases the various features of his story on the real circumstances of this life, on Jesus' real thoughts and feelings and that he links the events which he describes in a historical and psychological sense . . . This view and method must be recognized to be false in principle. It must be plainly stated that Mark no longer has any real picture of the historical life of Jesus".

The results of more recent criticism, supported by the school of history of religions, which rejected liberal attempts to modernize Jesus and opened out new ways to a deeper historical understanding of the NT, were regarded as destructive by the "life of Jesus" type of theology (whether of the liberal or the conservative kind). They were felt as a liberation by dialectical theology, however, which seeks to make the Christ of faith wholly "independent" of the historical Jesus. The abandonment of the "historical Jesus" by R. Bultmann must therefore at bottom be regarded as an ultimate consequence of liberal theology. Bultmann's book on Jesus (1926) no longer draws any picture of Jesus. It attempts to clarify and translate Jesus' call for decision, Jesus' significance. With Bultmann's programme of demythologization and existential interpretation of the NT, study of the life of Jesus has also reached its most important hermeneutical phase. The antagonism between "facts" and "faith" in regard to Jesus was suppressed by Bultmann onesidedly in favour of faith (or to its disadvantage). At the same time, however, the possibility of a more reliable solution was opened up through reflection on the nature of historical understanding. It will not be possible to overcome the "historicism" which still strongly influences NT studies by a fundamentally unhistorical "existential" interpretation, but only by a historico-theological exegesis determined by a new way of thinking. The question of Jesus can no longer be taken up again as a new quest of the historical Jesus in the same sense as the old. But in the form of inquiry into the figure of Jesus as this is critically accessible to us, into Jesus' programme, into Jesus' action as attesting and calling for faith, a question seems to emerge which is susceptible of historico-theological understanding. This question also preserves the rights of both faith and historical criticism; for the former needs the latter in its own interest. The theology which kept historical criticism at a distance, or the kind of historical criticism which in the form of a quest of the historical Jesus despised theology, are both at an end today in the light of the testimony to Jesus contained in the gospels. A new historical understanding guided by testimony must re-state the old question regarding Jesus.

Rudolf Pesch

III. Christology

A. Historical Survey

1. *Early Christianity*. Though it is true that the Christian community broke out of Judaism by professing that Jesus is the Christ, that Jesus Christ is the Lord (Rom 10:9; Phil 2:11), and though it is also proper to say in this sense (but only in this sense) that the original profession is a "purely Christological formulation" (O. Cullmann), this profession of faith is nevertheless meant as an affirmation of the saving activity of the one God, who is the God of the OT and who established Jesus as the Christ and Lord (Acts 2:36). This profession is, therefore, embedded in faith in the one God of creation and of the whole history of salvation (and has thereby a higher unity); but it also indicates that the one God has his absolute and definitive representation in the world through Christ, and in the Church through his Spirit. And hence the whole proclamation of what God is for us can be articulated in a threefold scheme of a Trinity that is primarily conceived of in terms of the economy of salvation (Mt 28:19). In this scheme Christology is peculiarly subordinated to the profession of the one living God of the world and of history, but contains within itself the whole, since it is the very centre of that profession. This is the abiding problem of the nature and place of Christology.

2. *The patristic age*. Though in the Apostles' Creed various originally Christological assertions are inserted into the part of the creed which speaks of the Son, there is no change in the old tripartite scheme. It rather underlines the proper (that is to say, the comprehensive) meaning of these assertions about Christ. Although this basic form is primarily simply that of the profession of faith in the three divine agents in the one salvific activity, reflection upon their relation to each other (which had already begun with the μονογενής of the Apostles' Creed) was bound to lead soon to the developing of *theologia* in distinction to *oikonomia*. And we already find in the *De Principiis* of Origen that the teaching on the Trinity (book 1), and therefore an immanent Christology, is separated from the teaching on the incarnation which is only treated at the end of book 2, so that the two tractates are separated by those on creation and sin. The danger of a theology concentrated on the immanent life of God, and of a Christology that is only one part of an *oikonomia* instead of containing both *theologia* and *oikonomia*, is already very real. But the comprehensive view is already unmistakable, shortly before Nicaea, in Eusebius of Caesarea, though with a subordinationist tendency. The Council itself (325) rather emphasized the distinction between *theologia* and *oikonomia*, without, however, separating them absolutely. A more extensive survey of the doctrine of the Fathers would not change this picture very much, even though they differ so much otherwise (e.g., the great catechetical discourse of Gregory of Nyssa, *PG*, XLV, cols. 9–105; Theodoret, *History of Heresies*, book V: *PG*, LXXXIII, cols. 439–556; John Damascene, *De fide Orthodoxa*; Augustine, *Enchiridion*). The "total" Christology is divided up into a first part on the Trinity, without much elaboration in terms of the plan of salvation, and a Christology which only comes after the teaching on creation and sin. This division is in danger of isolating and levelling out Christology strictly speaking, especially when it is taught that each of the divine persons could "become man" (cf. *DTC*, VII, cols. 1466, 1511ff.). Fulgentius of Ruspe (*De Fide: PL*, LXV, cols. 671–706) presents, however, a unified doctrine of the Trinity and incarnation before speaking of creation, sin, baptism, and eschatology. The patristic scheme does not mean that its theology was not Christocentric, but only that

its systematic presentation made this character less clear.

3. *Early and classical scholasticism.* a) The sequence Trinity-creation-fall-incarnation, etc., basically a historical sequence, was generally taken for granted and it became all the more significant with the beginning of systematic theology as such. This is evident as early as the *Elucidarium* of Honorius of Autun (where the mysteries of the life of Jesus are also dealt with) or in the *Sentences* of the school of Anselm of Laon. (Christology is treated in the 3rd book among the remedies for sin.) In the *Summa Sententiarum* of the school of the Victorines we find again the approach of Gennadius and Fulgentius. The Trinity and the incarnation come first, though now the teaching on redemption is almost eliminated. In the *Sententiae Atrebatenses* we have, as against the scheme of the *Sententiae* of Anselm, perhaps for the first time a clear emphasis on the section *De Christo Redemptore* which is here placed before the other aspects of the "redemption". It is, therefore, the beginning of the separation between Christology and soteriology (cf. R. Silvain), although at the same time there are *Sentences* from the school of Abelard in which Christology is treated under the heading of "beneficia" and thus seen almost from the point of view of the Reformation. In the *Sentences* of Peter Lombard Christology (in book 3) follows the teaching on the Trinity (book 1) and treats of how Christ (and the virtues, which are, however, hardly developed out of the Christology) leads man on from the "utilia" of creation to the "fruibilia" of God (Augustine). This Christology is notable for the fact that the mysteries of the life of Jesus are presented in historical order within a systematic theological survey. The teaching on the sacraments (book 4) refers back to Christ only in one sentence (dist. 1 c. 1). It is no wonder that the commentators on the *Sentences* made little effort to develop a Christocentric doctrine of the virtues and the sacraments. While Robert Pullus, Gandulph, Peter Lombard, *et al.*, at least placed the teaching on the virtues after Christology, the Christology of Peter of Poitiers in his *Sententiarum libri quinque* is preceded by the treatment of grace, justification and merit (though in the Christology Christ is represented as the *caput ecclesiae*) – a systematization which was taken up by others (Grabmann, *Geschichte*, II, p. 515).

b) In the *Summa*, part III, Thomas may be said to divide Christology – as usual, treated apart from the "theologia" of the Trinity – into two parts. There is an abstract and speculative Christology (one that was traditional, but better structured and hence valid to the present day) in which the inconsistencies of Peter Lombard are overcome with the help of a clear theory of subsistence. And there is a concrete Christology of the mysteries of the life of Jesus (entrance into the world, life, death, glorification). He represents, then, in his treatment of the person at the centre of Christology a sort of return to the early Christology, in which abstract *theologumena* are developed in the light of the life of Christ as depicted in the NT. For Thomas, the place of Christology within the whole is of course determined, as for the other Thomists, Henry of Ghent, Scotus, *et al.*, by his conception of the object of theology (God as God: *Summa Theologica*, I, q. 1, a. 7). A different tradition which extended from Augustine through Cassiodorus to Robert of Melun, Robert of Cremona, Kilwardby, Robert Grosseteste, and finally to Gabriel Biel and Peter d'Ailly (cf. E. Mersch) saw the object of theology as the "Christus totus", "Christus integer". This could have prepared the way for a very Christocentric orientation of the whole of theology, though from this point of view it had in fact great difficulty in attaining a real synthesis.

But when the object of theology, as in Thomas, is God in himself, and the God who is attainable by the creature in supernatural immediacy, theology and *oikonomia* are grasped as a unity. The going forth of all things from this God and their return to him, the triune fullness of life who communicates himself and not only created realities, can be taken also as the basic conception of the whole history of salvation. In such a system, a Christology could also be incorporated which would be conceived as absolutely neutral, as soon as Christ is clearly enough considered as he in whom all things proceed from and return to God. But the question is whether in the concrete development of this system Christology does not appear too late in Thomas, as the whole Christian anthropology and the teaching on grace and Christian life have been elaborated previous to the Christology. Here, of course, the question about the systematization is of necessity a question about the content itself, about the Christocentric nature of all reality and the precise explanation of the predestination of Christ.

The rest of Catholic Christology cannot be discussed in detail here. It is really a history of commentaries upon the *Summa* of Thomas, with new recourse to the patristic inheritance (Petavius, Thomassin) but without any change in structure. Christology and soteriology draw farther and farther apart. Suarez still has a detailed tractate entitled *De Mysteriis Vitae Christi*. But in the time of the Enlightenment it disappeared almost completely from the theology of the schools.

B. Christology Today

The impulses which led to the revitalizing of Christology came from inside and outside Catholicism.

1. *The place of Christology.* a) *The present approach to the question.* In the course of its historical elaboration, Christology came to contain two parts which were not always very organically connected: Christology in the narrower sense (the doctrine of the person of Christ) and soteriology, which based its central theme – the satisfaction offered by Christ to God – upon the doctrine of the person of Christ as a divine subject of infinite value and dignity. This is only a part of Christology in the whole of Catholic theology. Fundamental theology treats of Christ as the bringer of revelation and the founder of the Church. Moral theology is trying (for the first time, or once more) to show how its teaching can be linked up with Christ and that it must develop its own approach (cf. J. B. Hirscher in the 19th century; and today, for example, F. Tillmann and B. Häring) since traditional Christology offers nothing explicit in this direction. Till recently, the theology of the life of Jesus has largely been left to pious literature on the margins of research (new attempts to treat of the life of Jesus specifically in dogmatics: B. M. Xiberta, *De Verbo Incarnato*; J. Solano, *Summa*, III). A part of Christology, then, has established itself outside of dogmatic theology.

It is also necessary to examine to what extent Christology is present or absent in the other treatises. The treatise *De Deo Trino* has, in its teaching on the processions and missions (and here precisely through the sending of the Son) a constitutive importance for Christology. However, the connection between these two important mysteries does not in general come clearly enough to the fore. There is a levelling effect resulting from the problematic assumption that any of the three persons could have taken on a human nature (cf. St. Thomas, *Summa Theologica*, III, q. 3, a. 5). Apart from the fact that reflection upon a purely "possible" order is very problematic, and that the possibility of incarnation in one hypostasis in God cannot be simply transferred to another, since "hypostasis" is precisely the source of differentiation in God, and cannot be applied univocally to the three persons, the relative proprieties of each person, as revealed in the *oikonomia*, must be given more weight in the solution of this question. Is it so clear that the *innascibilitas* of the Father is not incompatible with an earthly birth as Thomas asserts (*loc. cit.*, ad 3)? Does not the relation of the mission of Christ to that of the Spirit show that the one *oikonomia* has two totally different aspects? In the Son it is realized as a historical-objective work; in the Spirit that which was accomplished by the Son is inwardly appropriated by the redeemed. The roles are not interchangeable. The same is true of the Father, who would come appropriately as the "unborn" if a human reality could really become a presence that would be revelatory of him, insofar as such a "coming" (that is, outside of his coming in the Son) is at all conceivable. The human birth, therefore, has an inner and not merely a factual relation to the "Son", though it remains true that the incarnation as such is free. If there was such a thing as the incarnation of the Spirit, he could not accomplish the work of inner spiritual assimilation which is proper to the Spirit. Thus the order of the missions corresponds to the divine relations between the persons, and hence it seems that Thomas and his commentators could have linked the Trinity and the incarnation more closely.

The absence of Christology is especially noticeable up to the present in angelology and in anthropology (Suarez, however – contrary to Thomas – speaks of the grace of the angels as the grace of Christ). The teaching on the sacraments is fortunately taking on a new orientation. While Peter Lombard, for example, only mentions their institution by Christ, the sacraments today are seen more and more clearly as the sign of the effective continuation of the death of the Lord and thereby of his whole history (especially baptism, Eucharist and penance; cf. Thomas, *Summa Theologica*, III, q. 60, a. 3: *signa rememorativa*). And ecclesiology, which had already been treated of under its Christological aspect in the *Eludicarium*, is once more being developed in these terms, after many interruptions. The most complete example is perhaps that of chs. I and II of the Constitution *Lumen Gentium* of Vatican II, on which see the detailed commentary by A. Grillmeier in H. Vorgrimler, ed., *Commentary on the Documents of Vatican II*, vol. I (1967). The Council links Christology, soteriology and ecclesiology to an extent which had previously been unknown in such documents. The Christological re-moulding of eschatology is also given conciliar form in ch. VII of the same constitution. For earlier attempts see, for instance, J. Alfaro in *Gregorianum* 39 (1958), pp. 222–70. One of the most important tasks of present-day theology is, no doubt, to help to make good the claim of Christology to dominate the whole sphere of the *oikonomia*, from creation to the last things.

b) *Principles determining the place of Christology*. We have, at the very beginning of the history of Christology, had to do with the inter-relation of *theologia* and *oikonomia*. This relation means everything for Christology. The whole *oikonomia* is the Christ-event. Within it Christ does not share himself with the Spirit, but the whole belongs to him (as an objective, historical work, as described in the Creed), just as it then also belongs wholly to the Spirit who is the Spirit of Christ, as something which is to be imparted to the community of the redeemed. They were acquired in Christ and are now to be fully formed in the Spirit. This *oikonomia* derives its form and meaning from the very nature of its origin in the *theologia*. It is true that the early Fathers only came to the *theologia* by way of their analysis of the order of salvation. But then their interpretation of the *oikonomia* itself was reconsidered in a new light. In any systematic exposition, therefore, the treatises *De Deo Uno* and *Trino* must precede Catholic Christology. In this anticipatory synthesis of what is experienced of God in himself in the course of the history of salvation, the theologians of the early Church had already – in their opposition to the Gnostics – accomplished one of the greatest and most lasting achievements in the history of Christian thought. Within this synthesis, they included the work of creation and the divine missions, though their thinking verged on subordinationism (cf. G. Aeby). Thus Christian theology was early on the way to a system of an interpretation of the world (relation between God and world) such as was aimed at – in their own way – by the neo-Platonists and later by Schelling and Hegel. It is only on the basis of a fully developed *theologia* (of course joined to the *oikonomia*) that Christianity can counter such competition, by putting forward a non-Gnostic and non-Pantheistic "system" (which is an actual personal exigency as well as a general Christian one). This great Christian tradition and unavoidable task will prevent theology being dissolved into a purely "ad nos" preoccupation or attempting a Christology without a preceding tractate on the triune God.

But the basic decision about Christology must already be made in the *De Deo Trino*. The clearer the precedence accorded to the (Thomistic) formal object of theology (and hence also of trinitarian theology), the more important it is to bring out "the undivided" element of both tractates. The interpretation of the processions within the Godhead must, then, also include their possible (free) relationship to the world and to history. On the exact nature of this relationship there are still great differences of opinion. They centre on the question of the "motive of the incarnation" and on the relation between creation and incarnation. K. Barth's standpoint is resolutely and radically Christocentric: creation (i.e., the order of nature) is the "extrinsic basis of the covenant" (Dogmatics, III/1, pp. 103–58); the covenant (i.e., the order of the incarnation and the redemption) is the "intrinsic basis (necessary or freely given?) of the creation" (*ibid.*, pp. 258–377). On these grounds, in a way which not all will find convincing, the article on creation in the creed is inserted in the second place (cf. above: Fulgentius, *Summa Sententiarum*) in a sort of Christological strait-jacket. Since the light of knowledge is kindled only in the act of revelation in Christ – in the same way both for the knowledge of the Trinity and of the world – it follows that the "undivided" is preserved for *oikonomia* and *theologia*, in the strictest possible way. But the "unmixed" is endangered, because this obscures the fact that we encounter Christ within the totality of a history which reveals its Christocentric character only slowly, since otherwise the inner distinction between nature and grace within the one order of Christ is in danger of being lost. And so, no matter how strongly the Christocentric is stressed for the sphere of the *oikonomia*, one will always place the tractate on the incarnation after that on creation (which will, however, remain very formal for the moment).

The full Christological implications of the teaching on creation (angels, men, world) can also be indicated if it is retained in its historical place, and Col 1:15 taken seriously. The second article of the creed does in fact throw light upon the first (Trinity) and subsumes it within itself, so that its contents are already Christology of "Advent". But then the tractate on the fall (of the angels and of man) which goes with *De Deo Creante* must also be developed in advance with reference to Christ. The supernatural elevation of man, which is presupposed by natural creation as the condition of its possibility (so that creation appears in fact only as the place where God communicates himself in Christ), is an inviolable covenant established in Christ from the very beginning. The same is true then for the Christological character of the remaining theological tractates which display in full the sphere of the *oikonomia*. This need not be further developed here.

2. *The structure of Christology*. Here there are two things to consider.

a) *The relation between Christology and soteriology*. As we have seen, the separation into Christology and soteriology has existed from at least the 12th century. It was above all the satisfaction-theory of Anselm of Canterbury which promoted this development. Here too the "unmixed" and the "undivided" must go hand in hand. Catholic theology – at least since Scholasticism, but in a certain sense also since Hellenism – likes to go from "being" to "action". Hence the strong development of Christology in the narrower sense. We must, however, advert to the fact that Western subjectivism, as it was expressed in Augustine and then accentuated in the Reformation, opened up aspects which Greek theology, objective in spite of all mysticism, could not see (cf. A. Malet, *Personne et Amour* [1957]). The *pro nobis* characteristic of Christ was retained in Western theology from Augustine to the Scholastics, but only in modern times has it again been deliberately stressed, to some extent on account of the over-emphasis laid on it by R. Bultmann and F. Gogarten (cf. J. Ternus: *Chalcedon*, III, pp. 531–611, especially 586f.). Catholic Christology can, without detriment to its tradition, bring out more clearly the *pro nobis*, if soteriology is already prepared in the stricter Christology (e.g., by the treatment of the knowledge and power of Christ, his Sonship, his offices, in the light of the history of salvation). Since Chalcedon, Christology in the East and the West has been built up on a few concepts – the two natures, the one hypostasis, and the assumption of human nature by the person of the Word. Doubtless, it was precisely through the elaboration of these concepts, together with the efforts to interpret the mystery of the Trinity, that the imposing structure of Christian theology took shape. Nevertheless, the danger of a narrowing of perspective must be avoided (cf. K. Rahner, *Chalcedon*, III, pp. 3–49) if all the riches of the Christological utterances of Scripture and tradition are to be fully exploited. We shall deal with this briefly, taking Christology and soteriology separately.

b) *The intrinsic characteristics of the two groups of notions*. (i) The bond of union between Christology and soteriology will be provided *ipso facto* by the notion of the revelation of God in Christ. But revelation must not be discussed merely in terms of fundamental theology. It must be given a strictly theological development, such as is provided by Vatican II in the first two chapters of the Dogmatic Constitution on Divine Revelation (see R. Latourelle, *Théologie de la Révélation* [2nd ed., 1966]; H. Vorgrimler, ed., *Commentary on the Documents of Vatican II*. vol. II [1968]). In keeping with tradition, the concepts nature and person will furnish the indispensable structural schema for Christology, in the ordinary Christology of "descent" in which a human nature is taken on by the person of the Logos, Yet these basic concepts must not be presented as abstractions which can be presupposed as clear and obvious, needing only to be applied to the question in hand. It must rather be demonstrated that they follow necessarily from the words of revelation in Christ and about Christ. Hence the history of the development of these concepts must be creatively re-traced. In this process it would be necessary to presuppose certain formulas of Christology (as they appeared in the course of history) which preceded this "nature and person" Christology. Just as we cannot confine ourselves to these earlier formulas (in order to eliminate the Christology of Ephesus and Chalcedon as a metaphysical aberration, or a Hellenization of Christianity or religiously irrelevant), so also is it impossible for the Catholic theologian to assume tacitly that this metaphysical formula is the primordial Christology. Scripture speaks very differently. It is very necessary to investigate carefully these original formulas, with regard to their potentialities, scope, their possible "full" meaning and content (in the light of the present nature–person schema), and their present kerygmatic adaptability. We too must pose the question of the "meaning of NT Christology", even though we do not answer it like R. Bultmann (cf. H. Braun in *Zeitschrift für Theologie und Kirche* 54 [1957], pp. 341–77).

The same is true for soteriology. The biblical categories should not be all swallowed up by the theory of satisfaction. The total situation into which man has been brought by sin must be considered, e.g., his being doomed to, his being a prey to "principalities" and "powers", to the law, etc., and the act of redemption and its effects must also be considered under all these aspects. A theological analysis of the existential ontology of death must show why we are redeemed through *death*.

Anselm here points the way to a very progressive theology. The (self-)sacrifice of death is of such supreme importance, because it is the total (irrevocable) dedication of human existence, Christ's, in fact, who is the man of the highest worth and dignity (*Cur Deus Homo?*, II, 11; see also K. Rahner, *On the Theology of Death*, Quaestiones Disputatae 2 [rev. ed., 1965]). This is the place for dogmatics to include the mysteries of the life of Jesus from his birth to his exaltation. Here too the theology of the offices of Christ must find a place, and in this regard we have much to learn from Augustine (cf. also Luther and Calvin). It is true at any rate of Christology and soteriology that neither the mere "person and nature" schema nor the mere theory of satisfaction are sufficient to encompass all the riches of Christ and his actions as reported in the gospels and interpreted in both Scripture and the Fathers, though these aspects must remain directives for the thinking of the Church.

(ii) In such a presentation one will have to reckon with a tension which is typical of this tractate, the tension between Christology "from above" and "from below". It must first be shown how "God is in Christ" (cf. H. Vogel); Christology must be able to presuppose from *De Deo Trino* a real doctrine of the Logos and Son of the Father. He is not only "one" of the three divine persons, but he in whom "God" (as the unoriginated Father) expresses himself, if the Logos expresses himself within the world as the self-communication of God. "Word" and "Son" are capable of a reference *ad extra* and to birth, which is not proper to the other two persons. The Apologists of the 2nd century had already grasped this. To this Christology "from above" (which has also many other aspects) there must correspond another "from below". It still is so palpable in the gospels and the Acts that it often led to an Adoptionist misinterpretation. Here we have to show that we come to knowledge of the presence of the Son himself because this knowledge affirms something essential about the object of cognition itself. This knowledge is not only a conceptual acceptance of Christ's self-affirmation in his testimony to himself (though this remains an essential element in that knowledge). It also contains other elements which may not be merely characterized as the "knowledge of faith" in general. For in Christ and with Christ, man has an experience – on the cross and in the resurrection – which is not only external testimony to an affirmation, but is itself intrinsically connected with the presence of the God-man. The "experience-in-faith" in Jesus is here "a unity without confusion" which is both dogmatic theology of Christ and of the presence of God in the world, and a fundamental theology in the light of the real history of Jesus (since Christ is not merely the preacher but the object of the preaching; not only the motive of faith but also its content). The experience in faith reaches its culmination in Christ and is, as an experience of the real presence of God, not only one case of the general experience of faith but its comprehensive fulfilment.

Within such a Christology "from below", the affirmation that "Christ is man" cannot remain merely formal and abstract. He is a man, not a woman, not married, capable of suffering, in the middle of history and not at its beginning, etc. It is, therefore, impossible to deduce all that can be said about him either from the Godhead or from his humanity, taken in its formal sense. All further affirmations are about the Logos himself and must therefore be taken seriously. The Christology "from above" and "from below" brings with it a double form of soteriology. The redemptive coming, suffering and death of Christ are first of all to be shown as the initiative of the merciful God, as 2 Cor 5:18 says: he has reconciled us to himself, so that in a certain sense, even before our own personal decision in Christ we stand before him as "justified". This "from above" is also decisive for the work of Christ, so that every kind of soteriological Adoptionism is excluded. Nevertheless, redemption is the work of the man Christ, so that man has really satisfied the demands of God. This gives scope to a Christology which has taken the humanity of Christ seriously and which still derives all the value of his actions from his Godhead.

Alois Grillmeier

IV. History of Dogma and Theology

A. Jesus Christ in Classical Fundamental Theology

1. Fundamental theology traditionally considered Jesus as *legatus divinus*, i.e., as one of many bearers of revelation who confirm their message by miracles and are therefore worthy of credence. The miracles of Jesus were invoked in the same way. Among these miracles added extraneously to the prophetic message, the miracle of his resurrection was certainly given particular emphasis. Nevertheless it was treated simply as one of many external "wonderful works", evaluated solely from the apologetical point of view and therefore in their formal character as miracles. The essentially unique character of NT miracles was not brought out, which consists in the unity of God's final eschatological saving act and its self-attestation. Jesus having been once recognized in this way as *legatus divinus*, the argument immediately moved to his founding a Church, and to its teaching authority (and that of holy Scripture). After that the actual doctrine concerning the divine and human reality of this *legatus divinus* could be left entirely to dogmatic theology strictly so-called. The latter is based on the Church's magisterium and the Christology of Paul and John and is not a theme of fundamental theology itself. Within such a dogmatic theology the question is raised again, but at the most as a secondary one, whether it can be shown that the mind of the "Jesus of history", especially in the Synoptics and before them, was in continuity with ecclesiastical and NT Christology. This traditional method has of course the inherent advantage that in its own way it does distinguish between the Jesus of

history and the Christ of faith. It is nevertheless open to considerable objections.

2. *Critical objections to classical fundamental theology.* a) Even on general grounds we must insist on greater unity between fundamental and dogmatic theology. The fact that a divine revelation has taken place (and in Jesus Christ in particular) can probably only be shown to be credible today by continual reference to what has been revealed and as such appears credible. In our context that means that the credibility (*credibilitas* and *credentitas*) of Jesus is from the start that of the eschatologically absolute saving event and bringer of salvation (see below F 2b). And the distinction between the notion of *legatus divinus* and that of the absolute bringer of salvation who is the "Son of God", though logically and formally conceivable, cannot in fact simplify the situation of fundamental theology.

b) The traditional method of fundamental theology underestimates the difficulty of establishing precisely how the Jesus of history regarded himself. Yet precisely in its character as fundamental theology (and therefore distinct in a certain respect from dogmatic theology, though this cannot be gone into here) it cannot evade that question. Even if the continuity between the self-understanding of the pre-paschal Jesus and the post-paschal Christ of faith is not denied (and precisely in fact because of the findings of historical inquiry; see *Jesus Christ* II), nevertheless it is only in the light of Easter that the scope and implications of the pre-paschal Jesus' conception of himself can become clear to us. This was the case for the original community itself.

c) From the start, therefore, Easter must not be regarded merely as the miracle of the restoration to life of some man or other, but which provides no indication of who this man really is. The Resurrection must be seen from the start as the event in which God by his self-communication victoriously and definitively accepts the world (in the fulfilment of the Incarnation). It must be understood as the event in which this eschatological action of God for the world is manifested, and in which – despite the knowledge we necessarily have of how the pre-paschal Jesus regarded himself – it only really becomes fully manifest who he himself is from the beginning. Even from the standpoint of fundamental theology, Easter is intrinsic to the revelation of Jesus as the Christ. It is not merely its extrinsic attestation.

d) The other miracles of Jesus have not the same rank in fundamental theology *for us.* Precisely because they are reported in the NT as manifestations (rather than as external attestation) of the fact that with Jesus the reign of God is present, producing a situation of absolute decision and making the most urgent demands, their character as miracles in the traditional sense cannot so easily be proved "historically" for us. As compared with the Resurrection, they have not for us here and now the same relevance to our personal existence in its fragility and its expectation. Consequently they have not the same central importance for our human reality as the Resurrection.

B. New Approaches

A contemporary fundamental theology of Jesus Christ must assume or take into consideration the following.

1. *Its purpose and the persons for whom it is intended.* Salvation and faith, being an all-embracing event of the whole human being in his unity and totality, cannot possibly be built up in their entirety by mere reflection (after the fashion of a particular branch of knowledge). By the very nature of the case reflection, whether everyday or scientific, cannot wholly capture and render explicitly conscious our existence, and man never lives solely by reflection. The same thing therefore also applies

to Christology, if this is a central factor in Christian salvation and faith. In fundamental theology a Christology may not and need not proceed as if it had to synthesize faith in Christ (*fides qua* and *fides quae*) in the retort of scholarship by means of pure reflection (see the article *Faith* I). That does not mean that there can be a Christological fundamental theology *only* as *apologia ad intra*, i.e., as justification of belief in Christ within faith itself, but not as "rendering an account of faith" to others, *apologia ad extra*. It means that the *demonstratio christiana ad extra* of fundamental theology is directed to a human being whom it presumes to be of morally good will. It therefore assumes him to possess the interior grace of God in Christ and to have already given an interior unanalysed assent to Christ. Moreover, it does not matter whether he knows this or not, or whether the *demonstratio christiana* has expressly taken this into account during its course, if this proves successful.

2. *Abstract Christology and Christology in actual practice*. It follows from this that the Christian may and must unaffectedly and courageously accept the "Christology" which he acts on in his own life: in the one faith of the Church, in the worship of its risen Lord, in prayer in his name, in sharing in his lot to the point of dying with him. The confession of faith of Gal 1:8–9 applies to this global experience, which certainly cannot be exhaustively analysed but which carries its own evidence with it. And in regard to it the Christian can still say, even today: "Lord, to whom shall we go? You have the words of eternal life" (Jn 6:68). Reflection on the liberation, vivifying support, and all-inclusive concentration of mysterious and unfathomable meaning which comes to the believer from Jesus Christ, may in the first place (as reflection) apprehend faith in Jesus Christ merely as one of several abstractly conceivable possibilities of coping with life and death. But reflection as such need not achieve more. It lays hold of this possibility as present, already realized, salutary; it sees no other better concrete possibility; that is sufficient for the believer, beyond the scope and possibilities of reflection, to allow himself to be laid hold of by Jesus' absolute claim which faith, not reflection, answers with an absolute assent.

3. *Christological arguments appealing to present-day conceptions of human reality*. From what has been said above, B 1, it also follows that the Christology of present-day fundamental theology, as well as using the traditional arguments which have always been and still are valid, can also appeal in three ways to the global sense of human reality which through prevenient grace is already "Christian". It is not of course totally accessible to reflection, but it can be appealed to. This would mean carrying out one side of the "transcendental Christology" (see below, C 3; F 1–2) in a rather more deliberate and explicit way. These three arguments are all based on the principle that if man resolutely accepts his own existence, he in fact acts upon what may be called an "inquiring Christology". They all aim simply at making this anonymous Christology rather clearer. The conviction that this inquiring Christology will find what it seeks precisely in Jesus of Nazareth and is not simply "waiting for him who is to come", must of course supervene on this appeal to the spontaneous, unanalysed "inquiring Christology" really operative in each human being. In this respect we should simply have to ask where else an inquiring Christology of that kind is to find what it seeks, and what it affirms at least as a hope for the future, and whether Jesus and the faith of his community do not provide adequate grounds for the act of faith that he indeed offers what is always sought.

a) *The summons to absolute love of the neighbour*. Here we should have to take with radical seriousness what is affirmed in Mt 25. We should have to work this out from below, on the basis of actual love of the neighbour, not simply interpret it from above. If we do not turn Jesus' saying that he himself is truly loved in each of our fellow-men into an "as if" or a mere theory of juridical attribution, then this statement, when interpreted on the basis of the experience of love itself, means that an absolute love bestowed radically and unconditionally on a human being implicitly affirms Christ in faith and love. Now that is the case. For since a human being is merely finite and always untrustworthy, he cannot of himself meaningfully justify the absolute love bestowed when someone commits himself unreservedly and entrusts himself wholly to another person. Of himself he could only be loved conditionally, with a love in which the lover would either have reserves or else entrust himself absolutely to what may possibly be meaningless. To overcome this dilemma solely by recourse to God himself as guarantor and limit of the absolute character of such love would perhaps be possible speculatively and abstractly on the basis of the general concept of absolute love. But the love whose absolute character is experienced (even though it only becomes fully aware of itself in view of its radical unity with the love of God through Jesus Christ) involves more than a divine "guarantee" which remains transcendent to it. It requires a unity of love of God and of the neighbour in which love of the neighbour is love of God, even if only implicitly, and only thereby is fully absolute. By that very fact, however, it seeks the God-man, i.e., him who as man can be loved with the absolute character of love for God, and seeks him not as an idea (because ideas cannot be loved) but as a reality, whether present here and now or still to come. This argument presupposes of course that human beings form a unity, that true love does not shut itself off individualistically, but that in spite of its necessary particularity it is always ready to include all. Conversely it implies that love for all must always take concrete form in love of the concrete individual, and consequently that the God-man makes possible within the unity of mankind the absolute character of love for the concrete individual.

b) *The argument from readiness for death.* Ordinary preaching is too much inclined to treat Jesus' death, despite its radical importance for salvation, as a particular event in this world which took place along with many others on the world's stage. It presents it as an event with its own special features but not really as one which manifests and brings into operation very much of the innermost nature of the world and of human reality. This is so if for no other reason than that attention is too quickly directed to the external cause and violent character of that death, and the "satisfaction" theory then regards it as a purely external meritorious cause of the redemption. A theology of death, however, can link more closely the event of Jesus' death and the fundamental structure of human reality. Death is the one act, pervading the whole of life, in which man as a free being disposes of himself in his entirety. And that active disposition is (or should be) an acceptance of being absolutely disposed of in the radical powerlessness which is manifest and suffered in death. But if the free and willing acceptance of radical powerlessness by a free being voluntarily disposing of himself is not to be an acceptance of the absurd, which in that case might with equal justification be refused under protest, then that acceptance implies that man obscurely expects or affirms the existence of a death (whether it has already taken place or is hoped for in the future) in which the dialectic of activity and powerless suffering (which with us always remains an empirical fact) is reconciled in death.

But that is only the case if the dialectic is resolved by being identical in reality with him who is the ultimate ground of its duality. For man does not affirm abstract ideas and norms as the ground of his nature, but a reality which is already, or which will be, present in his own, historical existence.

c) *The appeal to hope in the future*. Man hopes. He moves towards his future, planning it, yet at the same time exposing himself to the unforeseeable. His advance into the future is a constant endeavour to lessen his inner and external alienations from himself, and to lessen the gap between what he is and what he wills to be and should be. Is absolute reconciliation (individual and collective) only the eternally distant goal aimed at asymptotically, only exercising its attraction from a distance? Or is it a goal which is attainable as an absolute future, but which, even when attained, does not involve the suppression of the finite, swallowed up in God as the absolute? If God's absolute future is really our future, is that reconciliation the goal as something which still lies entirely in the future? Or is it the goal of history because history already bears within it the irrevocable promise of the goal, so that history even now, though still pursuing its course, is in this sense already moving within its goal? The human being who really hopes must hope that each of these questions is answered by the reality of history in the sense of the second alternative. This hope provides the Christian with a certain understanding of what faith in the incarnation and resurrection of Jesus Christ professes as the *irreversible* inauguration of God's coming as the absolute future of the world and of history.

The content of these three arguments of a present-day Christology for fundamental theology can be summarized by saying that man is on the look-out for the absolute bringer of salvation and affirms, at least implicitly, in every total act of his nature directed by grace to the immediate presence of God as his goal, that he has already come or will come in the future.

C. Preliminary Considerations of Principle regarding a Contemporary Christology

1. *Its main apologetical purpose*. The most urgent task of a contemporary Christology is to formulate the Church's dogma – "God became man and that God-made-man is the individual Jesus Christ" – in such a way that the true meaning of these statements can be understood, and all trace of a mythology impossible to accept nowadays is excluded. The attempt may first of all be made radically to avoid mythological misunderstanding by the following operation. In the ancient and orthodox Christology of the Church, the meaning of the "is" – the predicating synthesis in the fundamental Christological statements – does not expressly represent that logical synthesis of two formalities which is normally taken for granted in affirmative statements, and which is founded on their real identity. The meaning of the copula "is" rests here on a unique union (such as is not found elsewhere and remains profoundly mysterious) of really distinct realities: Jesus in his humanity and in virtue of his humanity is not God, and God in his divinity and in virtue of his divinity is not man. The sentence "Peter is a man", on the other hand, posits a real identification of the contents signified by the subject and predicate terms. Consequently the "without separation" (ἀδιαιρέτως) of the unity must only be understood in conjunction with the "without mixture" (ἀσυγχύτως) of the distinction (*D* 148), even though the "is" in the fundamental Christological formulas says nothing explicitly about this. This first consideration, which classical Christology already stated in essentials, does of course formally exclude erroneous identification which would inevitably

involve mythological misconceptions. But it does not itself perform two other essential functions.

a) The centre of unity itself (in the sense of what gives unity and at the same time is the unity thereby constituted), namely the "person" of the Logos, remains very formal and indeterminate. This centre of unity may be called the "hypostasis" or "person" of the Logos. If the term "hypostasis" is used, which denotes the "bearer" of the divine and human reality ("nature") of the concrete One who "is" God and man, then what is meant by saying that the hypostasis is a "bearer" and "possessor" remains very formal and abstract. Or else when the attempt is made to elucidate it further, it easily reverts to the simpler fundamental affirmations of Christology so that nothing more is achieved than a verbal safeguard against the tendency to explain away these affirmations rationalistically. If, however, this centre of unity is termed "person", we must expressly state that this word is to be construed in the sense of the Christological "hypostasis" and this of course is then immediately forgotten. Or else the word "person", because of modern usage, represents a constant danger that the Christological statements will be misunderstood in a Monophysite or Monothelite sense. It would then be overlooked that the man Jesus in his human reality faces God with a creature's active and "existential" and absolutely distinct centre of activity (adoring, obedient, with a history and development, freely deciding, etc.). In this case, however, we should have a fundamentally mythological view of the Incarnation, whether this view were refused as mythology or "believed". Finally, there would also be the fact that if, as centre of unity, "hypostasis" or "person" makes intelligible and brings home to us the saving significance of this union "for us", it does so only with great difficulty and, at most, indirectly.

b) The Christological "is"-statements – "one and the same" is God and man – are exposed to the perpetual risk of false interpretation because of their resemblance to the "is"-statements of everyday life. The identity which the form of words suggests, but which is not really meant at all, is not excluded clearly and radically enough by the explanation, which inevitably comes second, and in any case because secondary is soon forgotten. That is not an argument against the justification and abiding validity of these Christological "is"-statements. But it is obvious that they involve the danger of a Monophysite and therefore mythological misunderstanding. If, for instance, someone says today, "After all I cannot believe that a man is God, that God has become a man", the immediate correct Christian reaction to such a statement would not be to think that a fundamental Christian dogma has been rejected. It would be to answer that the rejected statement and the construction apparently put upon it do not in fact correspond to its real Christian meaning. The true Incarnation of the Logos is indeed a mystery which calls for the act of faith, but it must not be encumbered with mythological misunderstandings. Though the Christian dogma has nothing to do with the god-men myths of antiquity, one can nevertheless admit without hesitation that some formulations of the dogma elaborated in terms of this particular historical form of thought (e.g., God "comes down", "appears", etc.) were used and accepted much more unquestioningly as helps to interpretation than is possible to us today. Even today Christology has an urgent task. It cannot be accomplished merely by verbal repetition of the old formulas and their exposition, which in any case is only carried on in the domain of specialist theological study. Nor, on the other hand, for many reasons which cannot be gone into here, can it consist in abolishing the old formulas. But a certain broadening of horizons, of modes of expression and viewpoints for the statement of the ancient Christian dogma is an urgent necessity, even if here we can only offer a few pointers and initial sketches which cannot be condensed into fixed formulas of a permanent kind (cf. K. Rahner, *Theological Investigations*, I).

2. On the *methodological and theoretical problems of Christology* in past and present, see above, *Jesus Christ* II.

3. *The double structure of Christology (transcendental and categorial) and its unity.* If a historical event is to mean the salvation of man in his entirety, it must possess an intrinsic structure which claims man in his entirety. This is so despite the event's historical character and despite the fact that it is freely effected by God and cannot be deduced. It must therefore concern man's essence, including his existentials, which in relation to his "nature" may be free dispositions of God. And it must therefore also be susceptible of elucidation by a "transcendental" method (see article on *Transcendental Theology*; cf. K. Rahner, *Schriften zur Theologie*, VIII, pp. 43–65). That does not exclude, on the contrary it implies, that man's "transcendental" orientation towards such a historical redemptive event is only explicitly reflected on when man meets with this event in history (cf. K. Rahner, *Theological Investigations*, V). That also, and primarily, applies to the Christ-event. For its complete comprehension it requires a "transcendental" Christology. In this the fact and intrinsic structure of the following truth must be elucidated: Thanks to his essence qualified by the supernatural existential, man is a being who is oriented towards a saving event which is possible to expect; as an absolute and definitive saving event, its content is precisely what Christian faith professes as God's final promise in Jesus and as "incarnation" or "hypostatic union" (cf. Rahner, *Theological Investigations*, I). A transcendental Christology must, however, also endeavour as far as possible to make it clear how it is that Christ's human reality (his "nature") has a *potentia obedientialis* for the hypostatic union. For it is evident that not just anything at all in the category of "substance" has the possibility of "subsisting" in the hypostasis of the Logos. Nor can this *potentia obedientialis* be regarded as a purely negative absence of contradiction. It must be inherent in the essence of man himself to *be* this *potentia obedientialis,* at least in the line of a conceivable and hypothetical prolongation of a spiritual being who is essentially and ec-statically oriented towards God. These two aspects and conditions of a transcendental Christology of course belong together and mutually condition one another. On the basis of such a conception, the content of the Christological dogma might become more intelligible and existentially assimilable.

Conversely it also follows that such a transcendental Christology only becomes historically possible and necessary when man encounters the factual Christ-event in his own empirical, "categorial" experience. This categorial experience requires in the first place a Christology "from below", for man, of course, first meets the human being Jesus. If he believes in him as the Christ, he does not do so solely because he hears Jesus' spoken testimony to himself and recognizes it as confirmed by miracles, but because he comes to know him in his resurrection as absolute saviour, as simultaneously the object and ground of faith, and translates this realization itself – and rightly so – into the classical statements of Christology. From that standpoint, the classical Christology of pre-existence, of the one divine person and the two natures, of the Incarnation and the hypostatic union, is a sort of mid-point between a transcendental Christology (i.e., of a transcendental ordination of man in his history towards the absolute saviour) and a categorial Christology "from below". As a Christology of descent "from above" (such as is already found in Pauline and Johannine theology), that classical Christology involves more explicitly and more directly than a Christology from below various metaphysical notions, terms, presuppositions, which can practically only be verified by a transcendental method. Yet it concerns the concrete Jesus of Nazareth who is known *a posteriori*. In this sense it is a categorial Christology (i.e., thought in the ordinary categories of experience).

4. *The unity of ontic and soteriological, ontological and functional Christology.* It has already been pointed out that classical Christology in its explicit formulation (i.e., in the doctrine of the one divine "person" and the two "natures") does not clearly express the soteriological significance of the Christ-event (cf. K. Rahner, *Theological Investigations*, I). This applies particularly to the Western conception which, probably because of Western individualism, is, of course, rather far from the idea of the "assumption" of all humanity in Jesus' individual human reality. Consequently, in this intellectual perspective the hypostatic union consists in the constitution of a person who, if he posits moral actions and if his performance is accepted by God as carried out vicariously in the place of mankind, accomplishes a redemptive activity; but he does not himself in virtue of his very existence signify salvation as such (see *Salvation*). On the basis of the statements of Scripture and our present ideas, however, even prior to any explicit and specifically soteriological affirmations, a formulation of the Christological dogma is desirable which would directly announce and express the redemptive event which Jesus Christ himself *is* (cf. Rhaner, *ibid.*). And this in turn might help to avoid Monophysite and therefore mythological misunderstandings in the formulas eventually chosen.

5. *The starting-point of systematic Christology.* Pauline and Johannine Christology is already "theology" (cf. Rahner, *ibid.*, V), though of course binding on us. It is reflection in faith in the light of the Easter experience on the implications of the historical Jesus' own understanding of himself. Nevertheless, a systematic Christology at the present time cannot take as its starting-point this theological understanding of Jesus Christ as a matter of course. This also applies to the oldest pre-Pauline Christological statements of Scripture. A systematic theology adapted to the contemporary outlook must retrace the theological path to the point at which these Christologies themselves arise, however historically basic they may be. Nor can the starting-point simply be the statements of the historical Jesus about the Son. In later tradition and in scholastic theology, these were for the most part read too quickly – which need not necessarily mean falsely – in the sense of a pre-existent Son consubstantial with the Father. In the mouth of Jesus, however, they have a meaning which is much more difficult to grasp. Certainly we may not exclude from them from the start the man Jesus' relation as a creature to God. Nor, however, is their meaning to be restricted to what is common to all men in their relation to God. Jesus' historically ascertainable understanding of himself must not be heard and read on the tacit assumption that for one reason or another (e.g., adaptation to his environment) it was less clear and explicit than the Christological dogma of the Church. The believer himself would after all expect Jesus' own statement about himself to appear to us today to express his *homoousia* with God the Father less clearly and radically than the Church's dogma, because his words are more comprehensive and complex.

For that very reason, however, they do not run the risk of a Monophysite, mythological misunderstanding of the classical Christological dogma. Because we are accustomed to think almost entirely on the basis of these dogmatic formulations, Jesus' statements seem less clear to us. But even apart from the impossibility of Jesus' having spoken in terms drawn from late Hellenistic philosophy, we cannot of course assume that the formulas of the ancient Church are the only possible and the clearest possible.

The starting-point of a systematic Christology cannot be a single biblical predicate applied to Jesus (e.g., Messias, Son of God, Kyrios, Son of Man, Logos, etc.). Such a single predicate taken by itself either cannot be shown to have been used by the historical Jesus or its exact sense is difficult or impossible to determine. The function of a systematic Christology is to show that classical Christology is well-founded, and to produce a sound and progressive understanding of it. But at the same time the whole of biblical Christology cannot be expressed in it.

It will be best to start from an understanding of Jesus' eschatological function in sacred history, attested by the OT and the historical Jesus. That is, we should start with the event which was brought to completion, and not merely externally confirmed by the Resurrection, namely, that in him God promised himself to the world in judgment and mercy, definitively, supremely and irrevocably. This could also be expressed by saying that Jesus by his Cross and Resurrection is the eschatological redemptive event, and in this sense is the absolute bringer of salvation because the Cross is not a mere passively endured occurrence but is his own act. It must not be overlooked that the historical Jesus understood himself in this way, and the full depth of that understanding of himself was disclosed and became credible to his disciples in the Easter experience. Such a starting-point is probably more assimilable today than if we simply say at the outset that God became man.

But when we say that "In Jesus, God's absolute, merciful self-communication to the world in a historical event is not only taught but in truth is eschatologically and definitively accomplished and present", such a statement depends for its understanding on the realization that man in virtue of his history and his temporal character seeks the ultimate and definitive fulfilment of his existence precisely in history (where the same things do not always happen and what is final can occur), and on the realization that such an ultimate fulfilment cannot take place without involving the abiding mystery of his existence. This starting-point is not open to the suspicion of mythology, unless of course any doctrine about God as salvation is regarded as mythology. And it has nothing intrinsically incredible about it. For this starting-point merely says that God exists, that he freely wills to be man's salvation, in himself, not merely by his finite gifts, and that this definitive and irrevocable gift of himself is made in history and has been accepted in history on man's part. The decisive question for a Catholic Christology which chooses this approach is naturally whether the classical, orthodox Christology can be arrived at on such a basis (see below, F 2).

6. *The relation between expression and reality in Christology*. What has been said so far, and in particular the distinction between an objective starting-point implicitly containing the whole of Christology, and the classical Christological statements, already points to a legitimate difference between the Christological formulas of the official pronouncements of the Church and the reality which they denote. And this concerns not only the reality in itself, but also the different ways in which that reality can be grasped by faith.

a) This is already evident in the fact that there are early Christological formulas, e.g., "Jesus is the Christ", "Jesus is Lord", which do not merely say the same thing as the classical formulas but in different words. Yet they do really permit the believer to attain the reality designated by the classical formulas.

b) Another variant of the distinction between formula and reality is shown by the difference already referred to between the "objective systematical starting-point" and the classical Christological formulas of the ancient Church.

c) A further point of legitimate difference is also found in the fundamental possibility of a "consciousness-Christology" in addition to the classical Christology (cf. K. Rahner, *ibid*., I). There was of course in the Protestant theology of the early years of the present century a consciousness-Christology, a sort of new edition of the Nestorian "confirmation" Christology, which was in fact heretical. That is to say, wherever by reason of a merely human reality, secondary and therefore derivative contents of a human consciousness arise and can be combined (e.g., a particularly intense trust in God) and these attitudes or mental contents are asserted to be what is really meant in Christology, there is a rationalistic and therefore heretical Christology. As well as an "ontic Christology", i.e., a Christology which makes its statements with the help of terms ("nature", "hypostasis") which can also be derived from concrete realities, there could also in principle be an "ontological Christology", i.e., one whose concepts, patterns, etc., took their bearings from strictly ontological realities and the radical identity of being and consciousness. Here, in some respects it would be much easier from the start to avoid the danger of a Monophysite and mythological misunderstanding than in an ontic Christology. An ontological Christology of this kind presupposes the realization that being and consciousness in their ultimate meaning are identical, that being is present to the degree that a being is "intelligens et intellectum" ("ens et verum convertuntur": "in tantum aliquid est ens actu, in quantum est intelligens et intellectum actu"; the degree of "reditio in se ipsum" is identical with the degree of "esse actu" and vice versa). This presupposition cannot of course be further justified here (see articles on *Spirit*, *Ontology*, *Being*). If it is legitimate, however, we can say that in principle an ontic Christological statement must be translatable into an ontological one. This principle is of practical importance, e.g., for the interpretation and justification of the scholastic doctrine that Jesus always possessed the immediate vision of God; probably much in the Johannine Christology (cf. the "I-sayings") could be made more precisely intelligible exegetically and objectively on the basis of a consciousness-Christology; similarly the connection between "transcendental" and "categorial" Christology could be demonstrated more clearly.

A more precise proof of these interconnections would have to undertake the following analysis: The man Jesus lives in a unity of will with the Father which totally dominates his whole reality from the start in an obedience from which he derives his whole human reality; he receives himself purely and simply and permanently from the Father. Always and in every dimension of his existence he has given himself over totally to the Father; by this self-dedication he is able, under God, really to do what we cannot do at all; his fundamental attitude and condition (as radical unity of being and consciousness) is radically complete origination from God and dedication to God. If these statements were worked out in detail, it would certainly be possible to translate them back into classical ontic Christology. (This of course would need to be shown in detail.) On the assumptions mentioned and if properly understood, such statements would no longer be the expression of a heretical consciousness-Christology but of a possible ontological Christology. By virtue of the ontic Christology, it would always have to be true to its own ultimate consequences, but could itself legitimately translate the reality denoted by ontic Christology and could lead to a better understanding of the ontic statements.

The primary purpose of all this has been to show in some detail, from the possibility of a legitimate pluralism of Christological statements, that there is a legitimate difference between Christological formulas and the reality they denote. Consequently dissatisfaction with classical Christology, because the changelessness of its formulas may easily seem lifeless, need not represent the unvariable condition of an ecclesiastical Christology.

D. Perspectives in Dogma and the History of Theology

The actual development of Christology can only be outlined in essentials here (but see *Jesus Christ*, III). The survey which follows is chiefly concerned with the historical development of dogma regarding the centre of unity of God and man in Christology.

1. *The central problem of the incipient Christology of the ancient Church: the union of God and man in Jesus Christ.* a) The decisive step in the development of this truth was taken in the NT itself, for even though a Christology "of ascent" (knowing the man Jesus as the presence of God for us in the crucified and risen Christ) is presupposed, a Christology "of descent" is also present, though of course in various forms: the incarnation of the pre-existent Word of God in Jesus, of the "Son" absolutely (see above, A 3, and below, F 3).

b) As a consequence, Ignatius of Antioch already affirms that salvation is only ensured if Christ is truly man (against Docetism) but also truly God. The question how he can be true God without this conflicting with monotheism as a fundamental Christian dogma or without teaching Patripassianism in a Sabellian or modalist way, was a problem which had to be answered more precisely on the basis of the Nicene Creed in the struggle against Arianism in the history of the dogma of the Trinity (3rd and 4th centuries). The problem that Christ is true man and how this is so was the subject of the struggle against Gnosticism (2nd century) and Apollinarianism, the latter asserting that the Logos took the place of Jesus' human soul. Although Origen had already affirmed that the whole of man would not have been redeemed if God had not assumed the whole man, a Logos-Sarx-Christology (though not a heterodox one) is to be found even in Athanasius and other representatives of the Alexandrian school of theologians. The central problem of Christology is how "one and the same" can be God and man. Since this problem involves the ultimate datum of faith in Jesus Christ, it cannot of course be solved in such a way that behind the unity affirmed by faith, another reality and mode is discovered from which the union appears to derive as a consequence and is thus explained. All the formulas which emerge in the course of the history of the Christological dogma are intended as a logical, not an ontic, explanation of the union (on this distinction in general see K. Rahner, *ibid.*, IV, pp. 300ff.). That is to say, what is in question is the history of the search for formulations intended to maintain and defend more clearly and effectively the simple statement that this Jesus is God and man in the face of misunderstandings and theories which explain it away. It is important to realize this, so as not to underestimate older expressions or to overestimate more recent ones.

2. *The first more elaborate expressions*

of the unity of the God-man. Down to the Council of Chalcedon (*D* 148), the Fathers always measured a Christological statement by the simple formula: "One and the same is true God and true man." This truth already had a basis in Rom 1:3f. and Jn 1:14, and then in the Nicene Creed, and can be elucidated by the *communicatio idiomatum* which justifies the title Θεοτόκος (mother of God) and is itself further explained thereby. At the same time the unity itself was also expressed in formulas and images which later proved inadequate (e.g., "mixture", "glowing iron", "Logos in the flesh", "Spirit, pneuma = [divinity] in the flesh", etc.). As the terms of Trinitarian theology had been worked out earlier against Arianism, they could gradually come into use in Christology. Thus Tertullian already speaks (though only for the West) of the one *persona* in which without mixture, but linked, there is a double *status*, two *substantiae*. This line continued in the West through Ambrose, Augustine, Leo I: one person, two natures. At the same time, however, the problematical comparison with the union of body and soul was retained (*D* 40: Quicumque) or the formula that the Logos assumed a "human being". This was not far from a more Antiochene Christology which in Nestorianism became heretical and lived on in the so-called "Assumptus-homo Christology".

In the East the development was more complicated. Πρόσωπον need not necessarily signify what "persona" means in the West (a subject ontologically one). On the other hand, φύσις was also used to denote the ultimately single subject and was not at first contrasted in Christology with ὑπόστασις. As a consequence, the Alexandrian school of theologians, influenced by Apollinarianism, speaks of an (incarnate) *physis* of the incarnate Logos in order to emphasize the identity of subject.

Even at the Council of Ephesus (*D* 115) expressions of this kind were used against Nestorianism, without any attempt at conceptual clarification of the unity and distinction in Jesus Christ.

3. *The classical Christological formula of Chalcedon.* At the Council of Chalcedon (451) the classical Christological formula of the ancient Church was established. The formula of Cyril of Alexandria (with its latent danger of Monophysitism) was replaced by a doctrine of two natures (φύσις) which are "unmixed", and respectively make Jesus identical in essence with God and with us, so that φύσις (and οὐσία) can no longer be used as synonymous with ὑπόστασις. The centre of unity in which the two realities meet and are therefore realities of the same subject, is called "ὑπόστασις" (πρόσωπον, *persona*). These terms are not given further philosophical explanations. No further attempt is made to elucidate how the hypostasis of the Logos assumes, appropriates and unites to itself the human φύσις (which of course cannot be thought of as if it were a thing, if we are not to think monophysitically or monotheletically). The difference between the relation of the divine hypostasis to the divine φύσις (real identity) and the relation of the same hypostasis to the human φύσις (real distinction) is not brought out by the formula "one hypostasis, two natures". The conciliar "unmixed and undivided" will always remain a fundamental (dialectical) formula not only of Christology but of the Christian conception of the relation between God and world generally. But because of the "and" which cannot be elucidated further and which links and opposes the two statements, it will always confront man with the mystery of God himself. Consequently in that way it will always be a new starting-point for further theological reflection (K. Rahner, *ibid.*, I.).

4. *Later elucidations and refinements of the basic formulas.* a) In the late patristic

period there was a (mostly purely verbal) Monophysitism and a simple maintenance of the formula of Chalcedon; the so-called neo-Chalcedonians interpreted the formula of Chalcedon more on the basis of Cyril's Alexandrian Christology. In East and West the attempt was made to grasp philosophically the more precise sense of "hypostasis" ("being *in se*"; "existence *in se*") and *persona* (Boethius: "persona est naturae rationalis individua substantia", a formula which raised problems of which Scholasticism was later conscious); the concept of *enhypostasia* was developed, and the idea of *perichoresis* taken from Trinitarian theology was put to good use in Christology.

b) The post-patristic and scholastic period in the West slowly refined the terminology even further. The word *subsistentia* was coined as an equivalent to "ὑπόστασις", so that *substantia* and *essentia* were now generally used only as equivalent to οὐσία; *persona* and *subsistentia* were made unambiguously equivalent. In the 8th century a form of Adoptionism was rejected; it was not in itself very virulent. Without influencing the official doctrine of the Church, Baroque Scholasticism speculatively investigated in particular the nature of the hypostatic union, inquiring into what constitutes this union itself. For Suarez, a substantial mode; for Cajetan, the actuation of the human *essentia* by the *esse* itself of the Logos; for Tiphanus, the referring of the *subsistentia* of the Logos to the real created human *essentia*. In modern times, the Church rejected rationalist and psychological theories in Christology, in opposition to Günther and Rosmini (e.g., *D* 1655, 1917). The Christology of early Protestantism was based on that of the early Councils, and differences from Catholic Christology mainly concerned soteriology. From the Enlightenment onward, within Protestantism the old Christology was increasingly rejected, with Schleiermacher in favour of a consciousness-Christology; K. Barth and E. Brunner, however, fully accept the dogma of the ancient Church. But they are rather exceptional as compared with the prevailing tendencies to demythologization of Bultmann and his school and to fundamental criticism of the Christology of the ancient Church. Nevertheless the World Council of Churches (1948) professes its faith in Jesus Christ "as God and Saviour".

E. The Official Doctrine of the Church

Comparison must be made with the article *Incarnation* as regards the Church's official doctrine on the true divine sonship of Jesus Christ, his true humanity, his life and work. The meaning of the key terms "person", nature", "hypostatic union", which were elaborated in the teaching of the Council of Chalcedon is not determined more concretely by the magisterium. The question of the precise sense of these terms must be pursued in a process which of its very nature is very complicated, and has to be guided by the meaning the terms possessed even before they were employed in Christology. At the same time it must be noted that when *philosophical* terms are taken over, and rightly so, they always revert to some extent to their meaning in common speech. Moreover, their further definition must also receive its orientation from the elucidation given to these terms by the Fathers and theologians, even though they are not always unanimous, and above all from the use made of them in the Christological statements themselves. This is possible if attention is paid to what they are designed to affirm, i.e., the one and selfsame in whom God and man are present for us.

Since the Council of Chalcedon and the rejection of Monotheletism, the official Church Christology in the narrower sense has undergone practically no development. Even Vatican II had scarcely anything to say on the question how the dogma of the ancient Church can be made credible to people today. Vatican II repeats the old doctrine, sees in confession of faith (in the Trinity and) in Jesus as God, Lord, redeemer and sole mediator – a formula similar to that of the World Council of Churches – the specific character of all truly Christian Churches (*Unitatis Redintegratio*, arts. 1, 20). It gives this doctrine a certain relevance to more recent problems: Jesus Christ as answer to the questions of existence (*Gaudium et Spes*, arts. 10, 22), as head of a renewed mankind (*Ad Gentes*, arts. 3, 8), as linked to the whole of mankind by the Incarnation (*Sacrosanctum Concilium*, art. 83; *Gaudium et Spes*, art. 22), as culmination of sacred history (*Ad Gentes*, art. 3; *Gaudium et Spes*, art. 45). By these and other expressions the predominantly concrete, existentially Christocentric character, centred on sacred history, of most of the conciliar texts concerning Jesus Christ is plain. They also display a certain reserve in regard to the classical Christological formulas, though not of course any suspension of assent to them.

F. Problems and New Questions

Only a few of the new questions can be selected and presented here in outline. The exegetical aspect and biblical theology of such reflections must be assumed from the exegetical section of this article.

1. *Christology in a comprehensive view of man's reality in the perspectives of evolution and sacred history.* The miracle of God's incarnation is an absolutely free act of God himself. But once it has taken place and is known by faith, it is possible to recognize that that incarnation can be brought into positive relation with the perspectives of man's knowledge of himself and the world. It is true, of course, that by insertion into these contexts, the intellectual perspectives themselves are given a radically different character.

a) We assume that there is such a thing as an evolutionary view of the world and that it is objectively well-founded (see the article *Evolution* II). This presupposes a unity of spirit and matter. The essential difference between them is not denied, but in view of the common origin of both from the same creative ground (God as the one Creator of matter and spirit), matter cannot be a reality totally different in kind from spirit. The same conclusion follows from the substantial unity of spirit and matter in man and from the ultimate teleological unity of the history of nature and the personal history of spirit and freedom. The history of the one world of matter and spirit may be regarded as the temporal history of "self-transcendence". What is earlier and lower rises above and beyond itself into what is later and higher (higher through its greater complexity and through growing self-consciousness in the individual and therefore of the world as a whole), and does so in virtue of the dynamism communicated to it by God's absolute being (*creatio continua*) as the innermost centre of the world (and therefore superior to it). If this is so, then the last, highest, unsurpassable instance of such self-transcendence – under the necessary divine dynamism which in this case is called "grace" – is the coming of the material-spiritual world into immediate relationship to God. This immediacy guarantees that God is not merely the original ground, the self-supporting dynamism of the world and its history, the ultimate goal which it always pursues, though only asymptotically. It shows that he does not merely create the world but that he himself is the perfect fulfilment of the world through his self-communication in grace and glory, that is, by a quasi-formal, not merely efficient causality. This divinization (which does not mean a pantheistic identification with God), in an absolute final culmination of the history of nature, spirit and freedom, is the self-transcendence of the world; and in it God himself (through his free act) is not merely the cause but the actual reality of the world's perfect fulfilment. (See the article *Grace*.)

b) If that is so, the process of divinization of the world is the history of all mankind as a unity in space and time. The essence of its history is present from the start and consists in a movement towards the immediate presence of God through God's free self-communication by grace, in a history which is perfectly fulfilled and known by us in that history. Consequently there must be in that history an event – whether it has already taken place or is still to come is irrelevant here – in which the essence of history understood in this way becomes irreversible and is manifested to us. This event, since it has already occurred in history, is what we call, in Christian terms, God's incarnation.

c) This is equivalent to saying that the really fundamental purpose of God's incarnation should not be regarded as a new and higher level of self-transcendence, of the divinization of the world, taking place only in a single individual, but as the centre and irreversible manifestation of the divinization of the created (material) spirit as such. This indeed only occurs in an individual, and in comparison to other factors of the one divinized mankind and its history, it is higher in kind. But it is essentially a factor in the one history of mankind that is to be divinized through grace and glory. That is its definitive meaning. "Propter nos et propter nostram salutem." This conception presupposes that we assume the necessary unity of the divinization of the world and the Incarnation as two correlative factors of God's one free self-communication to the creature. It presupposes that the grace of the angels is *gratia Christi* and that the angels are essentially related to the material world, so that their salvific history too can and does culminate in the Incarnation. Thus the question cannot arise why God "only" became man and not angel as well.

2. *Christology "from below"*. a) In a "transcendental Christology" (see above, C 3), it is possible to develop the idea that man is the being who has the "desiderium naturale in visionem beatificam". It does not matter here to what extent and in what sense the ontological ordination (*desiderium*) to the immediate presence of God belongs to the nature of man as an abstract entity or to his historical nature elevated by grace (by the supernatural existential, which, however, is an ontological feature of his fundamental condition). It is also possible to develop the idea that this orientation, since it is that of man who experiences and realizes his deepest essence in history, must find historical manifestation, must await and seek God's promise in *this* dimension if it is to achieve its valid realization through God's free action (on the historical *a posteriori* realization of this "transcendental Christology" see above, C 3).

b) On this basis it is possible to arrive at the concept of the absolute saving event and of the absolute bringer of salvation as two aspects of the one occurrence: a historical event of a personal kind, not merely a word added extrinsically to reality or a merely verbal promise, in which man experiences his essence (in the sense explained above) as really confirmed by God's absolute, irreversible ("eschatological") gift of himself. And every aspect of man is affected by it because only in this way is salvation a fulfilment of man as a whole. This personal and absolute saving event and the saviour who constitutes it, who *is* salvation and does not merely teach and promise it, must be God's actual and irreversible self-giving to mankind, not a merely provisional and conditional one; and it must be historical, because nothing purely "transcendental" can be definitive, unless it is already the vision of God or unless it were possible for man's transcendent character to be fulfilled without affecting his history. At the same time that absolute event and saviour must also be a free acceptance of God's gift of himself, which must be effected by the latter itself. And it must take place not merely in thought but by the activity of a whole life. For this too belongs to the saving event. At the same time the latter and its structure must not be regarded as absolute in the sense that it is identical with the perfect fulfilment of mankind in the direct beatific vision of God. Otherwise history would have already reached its consummation. It must be a really irreversible movement towards this consummation, of such a kind that the future of the individual as such is left open.

c) We assume here in the first place (see sections A, B above) that Jesus of Nazareth understood himself to be this absolute saviour and that his resurrection established and manifested that he really is so. Of course he did not employ the abstract formalization by which we try briefly to define and suggest the notion of an absolute bringer of salvation. But he certainly did not regard himself as simply another prophet to be followed in the still indefinite course of history by other acts of divine revelation which in principle would call in question and supersede what had gone before, and open out new epochs in redemptive history. On the contrary, man's relation to him is decisive for the salvation of man as such, and his death founds the new and eternal covenant between God and man.

In the second place we also assume that this view of himself is worthy of belief (see articles *Faith* III, *Revelation*) and that its content is not only attested as credible by the Resurrection but that it there definitively fulfils its redemptive function and reaches completion.

d) Such an absolute saving event and the absolute redemptive mediatorship of a human being will mean precisely what the Church's doctrine calls the Incarnation and the hypostatic union, provided that the implications of the first of these terms are carefully thought out, and that the second is not misunderstood monophysitically and mythologically. We also have to be clear about the special nature of a "real" act of revelation by God. This is never merely in the line of the empirical, but always has an ontological character. That is to say, its existence is that of a created reality of self-consciousness and language, and therefore of conscious relation to God. God's saving action, his "behaviour" in contradistinction to his metaphysical attributes, is free, and as such has a truly infinite range of possibilities. Sacred history is therefore always open to advance, and therefore each event in it can always be superseded; each is conditional, subject to reservation. This is all the more so because saving history is also the history of created freedom facing a future which is unplanned and cannot be calculated with certainty from what has gone before.

It is therefore impossible to determine in advance what will follow from the interplay of these freedoms. A mere "prophet" (or a "religious genius" as effective pattern for a certain religious relationship between God and man) can in principle never be the last. If God nevertheless does posit his uttermost, ultimate, unsurpassable and definitive redemptive act (though of course finite, because it is only one of many possibilities), then this act cannot have the same essentially provisional, temporal character as other instances of his revealed "word" (which of course itself consists of action and language). And the provisional character itself cannot be eliminated by a mere verbal "declaration" by God that he will "not speak any more" but will rest content with what he has said. For such a declaration would itself be marked by the conditional and provisional character of an utterance of that kind. Moreover, such a declaration would decree that redemptive history is closed, without actually bringing it to a genuine intrinsic goal. It would allow that history to pursue its course as the mere implementation of what had gone before, and this would destroy its true historicity. An absolute (eschatological) redemptive action must therefore have a really different relation to God from any other saving act of God in the course of redemptive history. Unlike anything else that is other than God, it cannot consist merely in the difference between God and created reality or in the difference between something real, but more restricted, and something greater that would have been possible. It cannot simply be the history which we ourselves carry forward under God's guidance and by his power. In the absolute saving event, God must act out its history as his own and maintain it definitively as freely posited. Otherwise it will be provisional and not binding on him in any sense. Only if this event is his own history, definitively determined in itself (because posited by divine and, of course, also by created freedom) and therefore irrevocable, can there be any question of an absolute, eschatological saving event. God's gift of himself, manifested in history and irrevocable, must consist in his own reality, not merely as regards divine origin but in its created character. And precisely this reality which is his, which he cannot set aside as superseded, must stand on our side, as our real salvation, on this side of the difference between God and creature. This provides a first basis for a Christology "from below", but objectively identical with the Church's classical Christology "from above". And this can also help to display the unity of incarnational (ontic) and soteriological (functional) Christology.

3. *The question of Christ's pre-existence.* The question of the necessity of Christ's pre-existence for an orthodox Christology has been raised anew at the present time and doubt has sometimes been cast upon it, at least as a necessary implication of the Christological dogma or if it is intended to be more than simply a representational model. On this point the following may be noted.

a) If Jesus Christ is the absolute eschatological self-expression and self-giving of God – and without this a Christology is not Christian – and, in conjunction with this, is the free created acceptance of that gift effected by the gift itself in formal pre-definition, and if only in this way can he be the absolute saving event, then he who is giving and expressing himself, namely God, is "pre-existent". And this is radically different from the case when God pre-exists to some other temporal creature which is not his *self*-utterance.

b) Exegetes can and must be left free to inquire without hindrance whether what Jesus meant by Son of the Father is simply identical with the God who is expressing himself in time and therefore expressing himself as pre-existent, or whether it also contains a factor which is not identical with this God and so is not itself "pre-existent" (cf. *Mysterium Salutis*, II, cols. 356–9). Even the second possibility does not exclude the pre-existence of the divine subject who is expressed and whom the classical terminology calls Son and Logos.

c) This question is a problem of Trinitarian theology rather than of Christology and is connected with the necessity and difficulty of speaking of three "persons" in God. If we understand by the three persons (i.e., more precisely the "person"-forming and "person"-distinguishing formalities) three ways in which the one God subsists, and regard the second as identical with God's historical expressibility which precisely as such is immanent to God and essentially belongs to him within the immanent Trinity (cf. *Mysterium Salutis*, II, cols. 327–99 *passim*), then we can and must speak of a pre-existence of the subject self-expressed in Jesus Christ. And this need not cause the difficulties which are obviously the cause of present-day hesitation and questions about pre-existence.

4. *The use of the term "person" in Christology*. The official statement of the Christological doctrine of the Church uses the term "person", "hypostasis" (of the divine Logos) to speak of the ultimate centre of unity of God uttering himself and the created utterance in which and through which the utterance takes place. That is legitimate, if for no other reason than that God's self-utterance in sacred history would not be conceivable at all if the unity of God and man in Jesus Christ were only the result of the uniting of two previously existing elements. Such an extrinsic union of two realities would be a third reality, not God's self-utterance. But we must also bear in mind the danger of misunderstanding. The fact of the single purely divine "person" has nothing to do with the heresy of Monotheletism, according to which Jesus' human reality was only the passively pliable instrument of the divine Logos. The *anhypostasia* of the human nature (or its *enhypostasia* in the divine Logos) must not be misunderstood. There does intrinsically belong to that nature as such, a personal (in the modern sense) centre of action of finite self-consciousness and created freedom. Created and "unmixed", this confronts God. The appropriation of this active centre by the divine Logos does not suppress its own character, if for no other reason than that closeness to God and active independence of a creature grow in direct, not in inverse proportion. Conversely, that means that the freedom of the creature – even in its substantial ground – is perfected by being totally given over to God. And the radical measure of its appropriation by God is determined by the particular ontological relation of its ground to God. Consequently Christ's human nature is the most independent, the freest and, in the modern sense, the most "personal", in its actual humanity.

It should also be remembered that in the Trinity, "person" denotes what is absolutely incommunicable, in its radical uniqueness and distinction. This cannot therefore be subsumed under a genuine universal term as if it were realized univocally three times over. It follows that even if in Jesus Christ the hypostasis of the Logos is the ultimate subject, it cannot at all be inferred that a different divine hypostasis could be the "bearer" of a human nature, so that it was only because of a particular decision of God that in fact the second hypostasis in God took over the function. Even leaving out of account the variety of Scholastic theories on the precise nature of the *unio hypostatica*, the representational model in which the second hypostasis in God is the "bearer" of the human nature, must be employed with the greatest care. For even in general it is not very easy, especially in the Trinity itself, to think of the hypostasis as the "bearer" of a nature. (In the Trinity, of course, what is in question are three ways of subsistence, each of which is really identical with the divine nature. Now when two realities are identified in reality, it is very difficult to conceive of one as the bearer of the other.) In Jesus Christ, however, the reality (human nature) which is "borne" by the Logos is only too easily interpreted monotheletically as a thing, a passively manipulated reality. The hypostatic function of the Logos in regard to the human reality of Jesus Christ need not, however, necessarily be thought of as formally identical with what hypostasis means within the

Trinity (Cajetan, for example, does not think of it in that way).

All this should make us realize that when the official Church doctrine speaks of the one divine person in Jesus Christ, we have not the right arbitrarily to attribute to the word "person" in this statement a meaning which is neither guaranteed and precisely defined by the magisterium nor really unanimously accepted in theology. Nor can we draw conclusions from it which lead us into conceptual difficulties or else wrongly make the matter too clear. Objectively the affirmation of the one divine person in Jesus Christ can with certainty only mean that the (in the modern sense) personal, human reality of Jesus Christ has entered into such a unique God-given union with God that it became God's real self-utterance and a radical gift of God to us. In other words, it was not merely made into a psychological unity subsequently. On this basis it also becomes intelligible that, correctly understood, a consciousness-Christology (an "onto-logical Christology") could be a serious aim of present-day Christology. It could describe and think the union between God (divine Logos) and Jesus as man (in his humanity) in categories which in a special way make unity and difference intelligible in an equally radical way (cf. *Mysterium Salutis*, II, cols. 331–99 *passim*).

5. *Jesus Christ's knowledge and freedom in his human reality*. An undefined doctrine of the Church attributes the direct vision of God to Jesus' human soul from the beginning of its existence. We can understand this thesis on the basis of the fundamental ontological condition which necessarily belongs to Jesus' human reality. For since being and consciousness are correlative, the ontic union of his humanity with God inevitably entails such an immediate relation to God. Even leaving out of account the fact that this direct vision of God must not simply be identified with the beatific vision of the risen Christ, such a fundamental and in a certain sense "transcendental" condition (existence on the basis of a most radical and unique link with God) does not entail that it must always have been explicitly reflected upon in all its implications and conceptually objectified. That would be simply incompatible with an honest exegesis of Lk 2:52; Mk 13:32; Mt 16:28. Nor does it mean that this fundamental condition, which is always the basis on which Jesus speaks, can be explicitly reflected upon, conceptually objectified and translated into language, except in contact with his historical experience, with the terms and concepts of his environment, and so with the human openness of his history. On that basis it is not impossible to assume a development in this "translation" of his fundamental condition, which may even still be recognizable in the Synoptics. Only in this way is it possible to attain a correct understanding of Jesus' immunity from error, one which does not do violence to the texts. This is a problem analogous to the question of the inerrancy of Scripture. The texts in question, especially Mk 9-1; Mt 10-23; Lk 9:27, must be read in their whole context, which is not just a collection of statements. The context is the individual's temporal process of translating his radical self-awareness into language through encounter with his open history. In such a context an imminent expectation – similar to that of the primitive Church – may be the only way in which truth is historically grasped, i.e., in this case with a certain imprecision of outline. The statement must not be described as erroneous, because in it a truth appears which is essential even for Jesus' human consciousness, namely, that in Jesus Christ, the Son of Man, the Kingdom of God is irrevocably taking possession of the world.

God is not a force competing with

others in the world; he is primarily the ground which establishes the world in its own reality. Consequently it should be clear that God's closer proximity does not absorb the creature but makes it more independent. It will also be plain that the absolute redemptive event requires a free acceptance of God's self-communication by man. If in this way all Monotheletism, even of a hidden kind, is avoided, then the created freedom of the man Jesus in face of God and his will presents no new problem (see the article *Grace and Freedom*).

6. *Jesus' death as the death of God.* Christology at the present day must reflect more closely on Jesus' death, not only in its redemptive effect, but also in itself. Not in order to countenance a superficial and fashionable Death of God theology, but because it is called for by the reality itself. For death is not a merely biological event but concerns man as a whole. If it is said that the incarnate Logos died only in his human reality, and if this is tacitly understood to mean that this death therefore did not affect God, only half the truth has been stated. The really Christian truth has been omitted. The immutable God in himself of course has no destiny and therefore no death. But he *himself* (and not just what is other than he) has a destiny, through the Incarnation, in what is other than himself (cf. Rahner, *ibid.*, IV, pp. 112–20). And so precisely this death (like Christ's humanity) expresses God as he is and as he willed to be in our regard by a free decision which remains eternally valid. In that case, however, this death of God in his being and becoming in what is other than himself, in the world, must clearly belong to the law of the history of the new and eternal covenant in which we have to live. We have to share God's lot in the world. Not by declaring with fashionable godlessness that God does not exist or that we have nothing to do with him. Our "possessing" God must repeatedly pass through that deathly abandonment by God (Mt 27:46; Mk 15:34) in which alone God ultimately comes to us, because God has given himself in love and as love, and this is realized and manifested in his death. Jesus' death belongs to God's self-utterance.

7. *Supplementary theses.* a) It has only been possible to indicate, not develop, the soteriological aspect of the Incarnation and hypostatic union as such (see *Salvation*).

b) However unacceptable the Nestorian confirmation-Christology may be, in which Jesus only became the Son of God in the course of his history, it must nevertheless be realized that God's saving will applies to Jesus Christ inasmuch as he carries out and suffers his history in accordance with the universal relation between essence and history. History is not a mere epiphenomenon of an essence which abides statically and unaffected; it is the history of the essence itself. Consequently the life, death and resurrection of Jesus are the history of the hypostatic union, even though the latter constitutes the real "law" of this history from the start.

c) A Christocentric view of all the reality of the world and of man (such as was at work in principle in Vatican II) cannot wholly succeed if the human reality which Jesus assumed and thus established with its own intrinsic reality and preserved "unmixed" is regarded solely as something intrinsically alien which the Logos merely "assumes". The Augustinian *assumendo creatur* needs to be taken seriously (cf. F. Malmberg, *Über den Gottmenschen* [1960], pp. 32f., 37ff.): Jesus himself is what comes to be if God wills to express and communicate himself "externally". God's self-utterance (as content) is the man Jesus, and the self-utterance (as process) is the hypostatic union. Christology is the most radical anthropology (effected by God's free grace).

8. *Christology and actual belief in Jesus*

Christ. Some people who reject the orthodox formulas of Christology (because they mistake their meaning) may nevertheless in fact actually exercise genuine faith in the incarnation of the Word of God. If in view of Jesus' cross and death, someone really believes that the living God has uttered in Jesus his ultimate, decisive, irrevocable and comprehensive Word and so has delivered man from all the bondage and tyranny which are among the existentials of his imprisoned, guilty, deathward-bound existence, then he believes something which is only true and real if Jesus is he whom the faith of Christendom professes. Such people believe in the incarnation of the Word of God whether they explicitly realize this or not. That is not to deny the importance of an objectively correct formulary which is the ecclesiastical and sociological basis of common thought and belief. But only a heretic who equates the circle of those who really believe the saving truth in the depth of their heart with the circle of those who profess the orthodox formulas of the Church (the Catholic cannot do that) can deny *a priori* that someone can believe in Jesus Christ even though he rejects the correct Christological formula. In the living of human life, it is not possible existentially to adopt just any position, however theoretically conceivable. Consequently anyone who does allow Jesus to convey to him the ultimate truth about his life, and professes that in him and in his death God conveys the ultimate truth in view of which he lives and dies, by that very fact accepts Jesus as the Son of God whom the Church confesses. And that is so, however he himself expresses that active faith practised in his life, even if theoretically it is an unsuccessful formula, or even conceptually false.

It is possible to go even further. Some encounter Jesus Christ yet do not realize that they are coming into contact with someone into whose life and death they are plunging as their destiny. Created freedom always involves the risk of what has been overlooked, what is inwardly hidden in what is seen and willed, whether that is realized or not. It is true that what is absolutely unseen and purely and simply alien is not appropriated by freedom when it grasps something specific and clearly defined. Nevertheless what is unexpressed and unformulated is not necessarily absolutely unseen and unwilled. God and Christ's grace are in everything as the secret essence of all reality that is an object of choice. As a consequence, it is not very easy to seek anything without having to do with God and Jesus Christ in one way or another. Even if someone who is still far from any explicit and verbally formulated revelation accepts his human reality, his humanity, in silent patience, or rather in faith, hope and love (however he may name these), as a mystery which loses itself in the mystery of eternal love and bears life in the very midst of death, he is saying Yes to Jesus Christ even if he does not realize it. He is entrusting himself to something unfathomable, for God in fact has filled it with the unfathomable, i.e., with himself, for the Word became flesh. If someone lets go and jumps, he falls into the depth which is actually there, not merely the depth he has measured. Anyone who accepts his human reality wholly and without reserve (and it remains uncertain who really does so) has accepted the Son of Man, because in him God accepted man.

We read in Scripture that those who love their neighbour have fulfilled the law. This is the ultimate truth because God himself has become that neighbour and so in every neighbour it is always he, one who is nearest and most distant, who is accepted and loved (cf. Mt 25:31–46). The reality which the Christian confesses to be that of Jesus Christ is not truth and redemptive reality for him alone, it is salvation for all, provided it is not rejected in personal guilt. It "holds true not only for Christians, but for all men of good will in whose hearts grace works in an unseen way. For, since Christ died for all men, and since the ultimate vocation of man is in fact one, and divine, we ought to believe that the Holy Spirit in a manner known only to God offers to every man the possibility of being associated with this paschal mystery" (Vatican II, *Gaudium et Spes*, art. 22).

Karl Rahner

JUDAISM

I. Judaism from Ezra to A.D. 70

1. *The concept.* Early Judaism (sometimes called "late Judaism", by comparison with classical OT times) is understood in various ways. As a period, it is sometimes taken to run from about the date of the composition of the Book of Daniel (*c.* 160 B.C.) to the end of the Jewish wars under the Emperor Hadrian (A.D. 140). Others take a longer period – from the time of the activity of Ezra and Nehemiah in Jerusalem (*c.* 450 B.C.) to the final formation of the Talmuds (*c.* A.D. 500). For others, early Judaism is the time of the second temple (*c.* 500 B.C. to A.D. 70). Others think of the period from the conquests of Alexander *c.* 330 B.C. to the fall of the temple. In any case, early Judaism is seen as a period which supplies Christian exegetes and historians of religion with much comparative material for the study of the OT and NT. It is relevant as a movement deriving from the OT, preceding, accompanying and opposing the NT and persisting after it.

But for many authors early (or "late") Judaism is not merely a way of speaking of a historical period. It is also a value judgment, depending on the notion that the only legitimate heirs of the OT are the NT communities – even on the plane of the history of religion. This is, however, to take an unjustifiably low view of Judaism after Ezra and Nehemiah. Hence the term "late" Judaism (mostly confined to continental scholars), though Judaism, as the religion and practice of the Jewish people, was still in an early stage of its evolution. Thus Bousset, *Religion des Judentums* (3rd ed., by H. Gressmann [1926]), can speak of "late Judaism" (the period now in question) as a time of inflexibility, petrification, legalism, ritualism, casuistry and superficiality, when the OT law was swamped by traditionalism and foreign influences. In this approach, Phariseeism and apocalyptic come in for some of the severest criticism. Very often this is done merely to bring out the uniqueness and absoluteness of the words and deeds of Jesus.

For a correct orientation here, it will be well to eliminate entirely the term "late Judaism" in this connection. Early Judaism is the correct term, and it is best taken as running from *c.* 500 B.C. to A.D. 500 (see above). It falls into two main periods, 500 B.C. to A.D. 70, the time of the second temple, early Judaism in the strict sense, and from A.D. 70 to 500, the age of the Mishnah and Talmud. This whole period is characterized by a growing tendency to centre religious life on the local synagogue, rather than on the central shrine at Jerusalem. Then, it will also be well to work out correctly the various relationships between OT, early Judaism and NT. As regards the NT, for instance, it should be noted that it must be read to a great extent in the light of early Judaism, while there is no correspondingly comprehensive view of early Judaism which can be gained from the standpoint of the NT. Finally, attention must be paid to the fact that NT statements on early Judaism are primarily and on the whole theological – not psychological, sociological or purely historical comment.

2. *Trends in early Judaism.* These may be distinguished as official, unofficial and separatist or heretical (early) Judaism. Official Judaism embraced those who were active in the government and religious life of the Jewish people. Unofficial Judaism held aloof. The others sharply opposed the official trend. It should be noted, however, that these notions apply differently before and after A.D. 70, since the hierarchical structure of early Judaism underwent a profound change after the destruction of the temple. Before that, the high priests, mostly Sadducees, were the hierarchical heads, while after A.D. 70 there was the patriarch in Palestine and the Resh Galuta ("Head of the Exiles") in Babylon. Before A.D. 70, no single party had been strong enough to force its own way of thought on the others as the prescribed norm. But after A.D. 70, the rabbinical schools, based on Phariseeism, became normative.

a) Official Judaism before A.D. 70 was represented above all by the religious policy of the Sadducees and Pharisees, and to some extent or for some time by the ruling families of the Maccabees and Hasmonaeans and the house of Herod. The two main religious parties had a common forum in the sanhedrin or council (of 71 members) which met in the precincts of the temple. The powers of the sanhedrin were, however, constantly more and more restricted by the actual rulers. Outside the sanhedrin, Sadducees and Pharisees had little in common. The Sadducees, according to Josephus at least denied that providence could be reconciled with human freedom (though here Josephus is probably importing terms from Hellenistic debate). The Pharisees, however, admitted providence and freedom, and also the resurrection of the dead, the existence of angels and the last judgment (cf. Acts 23:6–9; Josephus, *Antiquities*, 18, 16–17). Their views, perpetuated in the rabbinical schools, became normative for all Judaism after the calamity of A.D. 70, since Phariseeism had striven for peace with the Romans and had been severely critical of messianic pretenders and thus emerged less compromised from the war. But above all, its loyalty to the Torah and tradition and its religion of the synagogue made it the only practical way of life once the temple was no more. The compilation of the Mishnah and the Talmud provides clear instructions on the keeping of the OT law, but it also shows the range and vigour of rabbinical Judaism in discussions of the problems of election and suffering, evils within Judaism, pagan oppression and eschatological hopes. As a consequence of the shattered economy of Palestine, the main centre of Jewish learning shifted more and more perceptibly from Palestine to Babylon.

b) Unofficial Judaism was composed of groups which held aloof from the religious policies of the ruling classes, though without breaking formally with them. They would include the Amme-ha-arez (literally, the country people), various apocalyptic conventicles and – before A.D. 70 – militant groups of rebels against Roman rule. Rabbinical literature describes the Amme-ha-arez as ritually impure, uncultured, careless about the Torah and hence "provincials" who were to be avoided as far as possible (Mishnah, Demai 2, 3; bBerachot 47b; bPesachim 94b; see also the commentaries on Mt 5:3 and Jn 7:49). As far as one can see, they were not simply the common people who were unfamiliar with the niceties of the law, but probably representatives of an interpretation different from the official one, and it was this which made them the object of polemics.

There were many apocalyptic circles in early Judaism where esoteric speculation was encouraged, and especially the hope of an imminent coming of the *eschaton*. The most important works of early Jewish apocalyptic were *Enoch*

(Ethiopic) (2nd to 1st century B.C.), *4 Esdras* and the *Apocalypse of Baruch* (Syriac) (1st to 2nd century A.D.). Their influence can be traced in rabbinical writings, especially in the Midrash echa rabbati (on Lamentations) and the Pesiqta rabbati. – In spite of its radically negative attitude towards tense expectations of the imminent end, which it had inherited from Phariseeism, rabbinical Judaism of the second and third centuries A.D. could not always clear its mind of apocalyptic eschatological thinking, even in militant terms, though at first it was opposed to military action. The revolt of Bar-Kochba, for instance, had a messianic motivation which inspired it to take up arms (bSanhedrin 97b; pTaanit 4 [68d]).

The eschatologically orientated groups of rebels who launched the Jewish war could not have been excluded from Judaism before A.D. 70, firstly because there was no "normative" Judaism, and secondly, because their theocratic ideals were firmly rooted in the OT. The uncompromising rebels were not the criminals whom Josephus described them to be. They aimed rather at establishing the absolute sovereignty of Yahweh over Israel in all its rigour. It was an ideal which necessarily included revolt against Rome as a religious duty, since Rome treated Judaea as the appurtenance of a pagan emperor. After A.D. 70, the number of the revolutionary-minded was so greatly reduced that all that rabbinical Judaism had to do to counter them was to give a spiritual and pacifist interpretation to the OT texts which the rebels had used as a military ideology. (Mechilta d'Rabbi Ishmael, Tractate Shirata 3, on Exod 15:2; Tractate Amalek 3, on Exod 18:1.)

c) Separatist Judaism comprised groups which abandoned voluntarily official Judaism as corrupt, or were "excommunicated" by official Judaism. The typical representatives of voluntary separation were the members of the Qumran movement, which was headed by dissident priests of a radically eschatological mentality. The Qumranites considered themselves the only legitimate inheritors of the religion of Israel (1 QH 4–8; 1 QM 1; 1 QS 6–8, etc.), and hence may be regarded as a sect. After A.D. 70, certain groups and individuals were excluded from official and authoritative Judaism, and mostly given the somewhat ambiguous names of heretic (*min*) and Sadducee. The *minim* were chiefly the Samaritans, Judaeo-Christians and Gnostics (Mishnah, Sanhedrin 10, 2; bBerachot 28b; pTaanit 2, 1 [65b]). The Sadducees were considered as typically heretical on account of their denial of the resurrection of the dead and their rigid interpretation of the Torah (Mishnah, Makkot 1, 10; bJoma 19b).

Thus early Judaism appears as a composite movement containing various conflicting trends. Its historical development must be considered by students of religion and exegesis as a phenomenon almost entirely independent of the NT.

Clemens Thoma

II. Origin and History

A. The Correct Approach

Judaism is a very complex phenomenon, embracing religious, social, political, ethnic and historical elements. There are three main difficulties in the way of seeing it clearly as it really is. Firstly, each of the components mentioned cannot but involve the whole phenomenon of Judaism, so that there is an immediate danger of distortion if, say, the religion or the social structure of Judaism is taken in isolation – as is done by some authors who look on "early Judaism" as a religiously inferior form of the OT. Secondly, the whole notion of Judaism has undergone profound variations in the course of its history, and even today there is no general consensus as to how the nature, tasks and significance of Judaism are to be conceived. But thirdly and most important, ever since Judaism was born in OT times, it has been the object of fierce polemics from within and from without Judaism, so that a dispassionate and valid judgment is hard to arrive at. Existing Jewish and non-Jewish writing, either pro-Jewish or anti-Jewish, is to a great extent a reflection of attacks upon Judaism, or groups within Judaism, launched by religious or political movements, and of Jewish reaction to such attacks. Hence the most important prerequisite for a just and valid judgment is a correct estimation of biblical (and post-biblical) polemics. To avoid the temptation of either anti-Semitism or an uncritical admiration for the Jews, one must begin by forming a clear idea of the historically conditioned and hence relative nature of such polemics as occur in the Bible, and also of its formal nature, that is, of its function as a literary genre. The OT contains sharp denunciations of the Jews on the lips of prophets and teachers. Terms such as "a rebellious people" (Ezek 2:5–7) or "a stiff-necked people" (Exod 32:9; 33:3–5; Deut 9:6) are typical but stereotyped expressions of ancient polemics.

Nonetheless, the OT polemics is to some extent quite understandable, and can be positively evaluated as the frank and lofty self-criticism of the ancient people of God, and thus given its proper relevance. So too confusion is impossible when one observes critically the real intentions of the two parties involved in the opposition of paganism to Judaism which has flared up again and again from the 5th century B.C. down to our own times. But Jewish and anti-Jewish polemics always became overheated when it was a question of groups breaking away from Judaism and taking with them as their own inheritance the religious claims of Judaism (as in Qumran and indeed in Christianity). It is of particular importance today that Christians should take note of the historical conditions, the literary genres and the susceptibilities at work in general when they try to form a judgment on Judaism in the light of NT polemics. The importance of allowing for the historical situation can be seen from a comparison between Mt 23:35–39 and Ezek 22:2, 23–31. Both texts speak in similar tones of a blood-stained and sacrilegious Jerusalem, but in Ezekiel it is polemics within Judaism itself, while in Matthew it is the polemics of a Christianity in the process of freeing itself from Judaism.

B. General Characteristics

Judaism in the broad sense goes back to the establishment of the Amphictyony of the twelve OT tribes in the course of the conquest of Palestine (14th or 13th century B.C. onward). For its further development the history of Judah (after David) was of decisive importance. But strictly speaking, Judaism only exists from the 6th century B.C. on. The exiles who returned from Babylon were mostly recruited from the descendants of the tribe of Judah (see Ezra 1 and 2). They saw themselves as the purified "Remnant of Israel", that is, as the part of the Twelve Tribes which had survived the catastrophe of deportation and had submitted to it as the judgment of God upon their guilt. With this idea in mind, the Jews of the time sought to uphold the Mosaic traditions by a new Exodus which would bring them once more into the devastated land of Israel, there to make a new beginning in the hope of serving faithfully the God of the covenant. There is a very vivid expression of this feeling of being the "remnant" or true representative of Israel in Ezra 6:13–18. The consecration of the new temple included the ceremony of sacrificing "twelve he-goats as a sin offering for all Israel, according to the number of the tribes of Israel" (v. 17). See also 2 Kg 19:31; Is 41–55; Jer 40:11; 42:15; 44:12; Ezek 9:8; 11:13, etc.).

The story of the foundation of Judaism as given here in Ezra already manifests the most central feature of Judaism. At all periods of its existence and throughout all adversities it saw itself as the people of the covenant in a special collective relationship of service and partnership towards the God of the covenant. The basic creed of the people may be expressed as follows: Yahweh is the God of Israel, Israel is the people of Yahweh (cf. Exod 19:4–6; Jos 24). The promises of descendants to the patriarchs are to be understood ultimately in the light of this covenant (Gen 13:16; 15:5; 26:4, 24; 28:14; 32:13, etc.). The thought of being the people of the covenant determines the nature of the historical activity of Judaism in the world. As the appointed heir of Israel, Judaism strives to embody and give testimony to the God-given doctrines, commandments and events of salvation. From this union as a people with God results the ideal of a political, social, cultural and economic solidarity among the beneficiaries of the covenant. There is a desire to see ordinary profane activities penetrated by the thought of the kingship of God, which is always present but must be realized more and more effectively.

Another general characteristic of Judaism is its relationship to the land of Israel as promised by the God of the covenant. Though the "land of Israel" has seen too many historical changes in its boundaries to be exactly described as a geographical entity, and although at all times there were Jews living outside it, either voluntarily or in forced exile, the claim to the promised land has never been abandoned by Judaism to the present day. It is inspired in this claim by religious and ethnic motives, and the land has often had extraordinary qualities attributed to it (cf. Deut 11:10–12; Judah Halevi, etc.).

A third characteristic which is generally observable is that Judaism tries to live out the present, especially when it seems dark and sorrowful through trials imposed on the faith, by reflecting on the glorious past of the people and the future salvation to be hoped for. Thus Judaism has a double perspective to inspire it – the hope of the restoration of the past and the hope of an eschatological salvation which goes beyond all human limits. Both memories of the past and hope of the future can take on various nuances. At times the nationalistic element prevails, at times the universalist, sometimes earthly and sometimes heavenly hopes. To illustrate these tendencies reference may be made to the biblical expositions of God's sworn promises to the patriarchs (Gen 24:7; 50:24; Exod 13:5, 11; Num 14:16; Deut 4:31; 6:23, etc.). Typical too are such rabbinical expressions as "for the sake of the merits of the fathers" (bRosh ha-Shana 11 a, etc.) and discussions of the days of the Messiah and the world to come (bSanhedrin 97 a–b). We can see at once that the messianic hopes of Judaism are subordinate to the general eschatological expectations. Intense messianic expectations played a considerable part at times in Jewish history. This is particularly true of the period from about 170 B.C. (the time of the Maccabees) till A.D. 70 or 73 (suppression of the Jewish revolt by the Romans), and again of the rebellion of Bar Kochba (A.D. 132–5) and the period of the messianic pretender Sabbatai Zewi (1626–75). But in these and other periods of intense messianic expectation there was never any consistent or ideologically fixed notion of the concrete duties of the Messiah in the time of final well-being. As a rule, the Messiah appears only as the representative or protector of a well-being which has come or is about to come. He is not thought of as redeemer in the Christian sense.

One might also possibly adduce as a permanent characteristic the loyalty of Judaism to the languages of the Bible and the Talmud. No doubt many Jews, at all periods of the history of Judaism, did not know the languages in question (Hebrew and Aramaic, but above all Hebrew). But it was constantly felt to be a religious duty to learn Hebrew, and the modern slogan of "Yehudi, daber ivrit" (Jew, speak Hebrew!) was constantly given religious and national motives.

These essential bonds with covenant, land and past (and perhaps language) do not mean, however, uniformity, but leave room for strong polarities. The assertion of Leo Baeck, that Judaism has always been "bipolar" – he meant above all the polarity of diaspora Judaism to Judaism in the land of Israel – is true in many ways of the relationship of Judaism to the covenant. The people of the covenant feels itself, as the chosen people and the envoy of the God of the covenant, in a permanent state of tension as regards the peoples of the world. And at the same time, Judaism has to do justice to the fact that within the people and among those who profess the Jewish faith there are members who are not loyal to the covenant.

As regards the relationship of Judaism to past and future, tension arises above all from the different attitudes of various groups of Jews to their origins, present position and future fulfilment. The contrasts, for instance, between the strict orthodox in the present State of Israel and certain other groups, especially in the Kibbutzim, show that Judaism is elastic enough to allow one to feel oneself a Jew and still be without faith in God, attachment to tradition or messianic hopes. On the other hand, it is also possible to accept all that is genuinely Jewish in the religious sphere and still refuse to commit oneself to the concrete politics of the Jewish State.

Popular presentations of Judaism are very much given to ascribing peculiarities to Judaism for which there is little if any foundation. It is incorrectly asserted, for instance, that Jews are a homogeneous or singular race. It is common knowledge today among students of racial questions that within the Mongolian, Negro and European types of race only mixed forms occur or can occur. In any case, neither the Bible nor post-biblical Judaism gives occasion for affirming the superiority, inferiority or even unity of the Jewish race. There are, no doubt, strong tendencies to ethnic segregation in Judaism. The tendency was already prevalent in the 5th century B.C., in the age of Ezra and Nehemiah, and also in the age of the Mishnah and the Talmud. The existence of the Jewish ghettoes was not due solely to the desire of Jews to escape from anti-Jewish attacks. Their existence was due in part to the genuinely Jewish need for local isolation, in order to be more easily able to fulfil the mission of Judaism. But such tendencies always had their counterparts (even if we prescind from the divergent ethnic origins of Judaism) in outward-looking movements which sought for contacts and even assimilation with their surroundings. Thus at the same time that the group around Ezra and Nehemiah was dominant in Jerusalem, the Book of Ruth was written, to praise a foreign (Moabite) woman as the ancestress of the Jewish king David. The Book of Jonas is also inspired by such universalist religious motives. The OT itself already denounces clearly and firmly the notion that precedence in election involved superiority on the human plane. The OT makes it clear that the people of the covenant was not chosen on account of its qualities, but rather in spite of its obstinacy and rebelliousness – merely by reason of the sovereign love of God (Deut 7:6–9; 9:4–9).

One must also be careful not to attribute an absolutely special and unique thought-form to Judaism. It is certainly quite wrong to affirm without qualification that Jewish thought is concrete, dynamic, lacking in speculative power, ethnically introvert and so on – in contrast to Greek (and hence the Christian) thought which is supposed to be abstract, static, speculative and universalist. There is still less justification for saying that there is little or no possibility of reconciling the two thought-forms. Even in OT times the Septuagint translation and such achievements as the very successful harmony of Jewish and Greek sapiential thinking in the Book of Sirach (Ecclus) tell strongly against such "psychologies" of religion and people. An even more telling example against the creation of such categories is the work of the Jewish philosopher, Moses Maimonides (d. 1204), with his notable contribution to classical scholasticism.

In conclusion, one could describe Judaism in general as an ethnic fellowship with the God of Israel, based on the covenant, looking on the possession of the land of Israel and the mastery of the language of Israel as its essential features, along with the constant actualization of past blessings and future hopes in each present moment. These features may include certain national peculiarities which are often designated as typically Jewish. But it should be noted that these secondary features are allowed relatively little value within Judaism itself and are often cancelled out by strong tendencies in the opposite direction.

C. The Main Divisions of the History of Judaism

1. Early Judaism in the strict sense *began with the Babylonian exile* (*587* B.C.) *and ended with the fall of the second temple*, A.D. *70*. The earlier Jewish State became at the beginning of the Babylonian exile and in the course of the post-exilic period an ethnic fellowship of worship (a union in prayer, sacrifice, religious study, meditation and assembly). The vitality of Judaism manifested itself in three main ways: as hierocratic restorative tendencies, as eschatological movements and as biblical learning. The restorative efforts were chiefly carried on by the priestly circles of Jerusalem and the ancient Jewish nobility. These strove to set up once more the conditions of liturgical and political life which had existed in particular under David and Solomon. Eschatological hopes were particularly lively from the end of the 3rd century B.C., as a result of the apocalyptic movement among priests and laity (especially those of the country-side, who were less well off).

As time went on, these hopes were expressed more and more forcefully. Among the Hasidaeans (cf. 1 Macc 2:42–48), the Qumranites (or Essenes) and other groups the notion of the imminence of final and universal salvation was less tinged with national and political hopes than among the Maccabees, the Hasmonaeans and many of the rebels in the first Jewish war against Rome (A.D. 66 to 70 or 73). The Scripture scholars, or rather "doctors of the law" in early Judaism, recognizing that inspired prophecy had ceased (i.e., prophecy acknowledged as inspired by the people of the covenant) [bJoma 9b; bSanh 11a], that it was impossible to restore the past adequately and that the future was impenetrable, turned to the task of collecting national traditions and expounding the law for everyday needs (with the help, at times, of Wisdom speculation). It became clearer and clearer that study of the Scriptures, which was in fact mainly study of the law, provided the most solid basis for the shaping of Jewish social and private life. And here the Pharisees seemed clearly to offer the most desirable alternative to the Sadducees allied to the priesthood, temple and landed gentry, to the fanatical groups of eschatologically-minded "seers" (apocalyptic), the conciliatory Tobiades and Herodians, the uneducated masses of the people (am-ha-arez). Phariseeism must not be judged exclusively in the light of NT polemics. In the course of its history it strove constantly and vigorously to do justice to the law by bringing it into relevant relation with contemporary needs, it was a peace-making force and also the educator of the Jewish people at prayer and at study. Present-day Judaism is essentially based on the spiritual and religious principles of Phariseeism.

2. *Early Judaism of the period of the Mishnah and Talmud.* This was a period in which the Jews were without a temple and politically insignificant, under Roman and later under Persian rule. But Jewish life and religion flourished, especially in Galilee and in Babylon, and displayed its vigour above all in houses of prayer and of study, which to some extent were looked on as definitely replacing the temple (Pirke Aboth 5, 16; bMeg 29a; Mechilta Rabbi Ishmael, Tractate Bakodesh 11 [on Exod 20:24]). Leadership of Judaism was in the hands of the rabbinical sages, who imposed their pharisaical principles and norms on all Judaism. The synod at Jamnia (*c.* A.D. 90) became the basis of Judaism, which now sought to maintain itself, without temple and without political and religious independence and security, in the midst of the "peoples of the world" and in the face of new rivals in religion, especially Christianity and Gnosis. The most important products of Jewish efforts in late antiquity are undoubtedly the Mishnah and the Talmud (described under *Judaism* III). The repression of repeated Jewish revolts took a high toll of bloodshed. Judaism suffered very severe blows before, during and after the two revolts against Rome (A.D. 66–73 and 132–5), which were partly inspired by messianic hopes. They led to sharp religious and political persecution and to deportations. But there were also some successful efforts, especially in the 3rd century A.D., to work out a *modus vivendi* with the oppressive powers of the world.

3. *Medieval Judaism.* By this we understand the period from the end of the compilation of the Babylonian Talmud (6th to 7th century A.D.) to the Jewish "Enlightenment" of the 18th to 19th centuries. In Western Europe it took the form of individual assimilation, in Eastern that of a national Enlightenment movement, the Haskala. But there are authors who say that the modern period of Judaism should be considered to have begun with the expulsion of the Jews from Spain in 1492. Medieval Judaism appears on the one hand as stamped by the spirit of the Talmud, and a constant tendency to form groups, just as constantly repressed by external forces. But on the other hand, it also appears as a pioneering force in spiritual and religious matters, at least outwardly, since its debate with antiquity, Islam and Christianity helped it to work out a lofty religious philosophy (especially in Avicebron and Moses Maimonides). To a great extent, it was overshadowed and even oppressed by the medieval Christian world with its discriminatory legislation, ghettoes, persecutions and horror-stories. Late medieval Judaism was marked by the growing importance of East European trends such as those of the Chasidim and Mitnagedim and also by persistent messianic revivals in the middle of the seventeenth century (the Sabbatians and the Frankists), with no sense of political realities.

4. *Modern Judaism.* There are four main forces at work in modern times: a) Sacred Scripture and Talmudic tradition; b) Enlightenment and emancipation; c) Zionism and d) the foothold gained, not without new dangers, in the ancient land of Israel.

a) Traditionally-minded religious Judaism is chiefly represented by orthodox and conservative Judaism. But Scripture and Talmud play an important part in the thinking of all Jewish groups, even of Reform Judaism and of circles very far to the left.

b) The Haskala, the Jewish Enlightenment, was chiefly represented by Moses Mendelssohn (1729–86) (see, for example, Lessing's *Nathan the Wise*). It was chiefly inspired by a growing need for a relaxation of the traditional Jewish way of life with its quite totalitarian claims, and for closer cultural connections with the non-Jewish environment. It urged the Jews, especially in Central and Eastern Europe, to rid themselves of expendable elements of tradition in order to share fully the culture of the peoples among whom they lived. Since Jewish emancipation, especially in German-speaking countries, evoked anti-Semitic reactions, and since the Haskala in Eastern Europe did not meet with the desired success, the Zionist movement began.

c) Zionism may be divided into three main streams which are not entirely separate: (i) the Chibat-Zion Movement founded by Leon Pinsker (1821–91) which set out to organize all Jews who wished to go to Palestine; (ii) the political Zionism of Theodore Herzl (1860–1904); (iii) the Zionut Ruchanit, a religious Zionism, represented in particular by J. M. Pines (1844–1914) and Achad Haam (1856–1921).

d) The independent State of Israel (1948) may be said to be the fruit of the direst persecutions in history, under National Socialism in Germany. While it claims legitimation to some extent from its ancient rights, Judaism recognizes that in the eyes of the world this claim can be fully legitimate only if Israel extends to the non-Jewish inhabitants the toleration and citizenship rights which it so energetically defends for itself. There is also a hope among the Jews that the State of Israel is the "beginning of the dawn of redemption".

Clemens Thoma

III. The Religion

1. *The situation of Jewish religion.* In contrast with Christianity above all, with Islam and with Buddhism, the Jewish religion remained throughout its history almost exclusively the property of one people, the Jews. This concrete link with a definite people and the resulting fewness of the adherents makes it impossible to designate Judaism as a world religion. All that can be said is that it is not merely a national religion, since it possesses some emphatically universalist traits, and has attained world-wide significance through its "offshoots", Christianity and Islam.

The term "Mosaic religion", coined during the Enlightenment, does not go to the heart of Jewish religion. Jewish tradition looked on Moses as the founder of the Jewish religion, as prophet, teacher and leader of the people, but as such he was only a pointer to the heart of the religion, which was neither a human personality nor human nor even divine doctrine, but the historical presence of the God of Israel, powerful among his people (Is 45:14). It would also be incorrect to describe Jewish religion without qualifications as a hard and fast rule of the law. The law or Torah is no doubt an essential constituent of Jewish religion, but it is not the be-all and the end-all and must not be isolated from its many contacts. Along with pious exposition and observance of the law, important roles are also played by messianic hopes and mystical trends such as the Kabbala, the Chasidim and the Mitnagedim. The Jewish religion may indeed be called the great "religion of reason" (Herman Cohen, after Moses Mendelssohn and others), on account of the supreme importance attached to the law. But since it is so closely connected with what has sometimes been described as the "mystery" of the people of Israel, it cannot simply be contrasted with religions which appeal to mystery, though it remains resolutely opposed to all religions of myth and Gnosis.

Since the Judaistic religion is the

forum of endless, comprehensive, subtle and often unsolved discussions about OT law and its practical implementation, there is every reason for designating it as a religion of law. But one must always bear in mind the evident truth that to the Jewish mind the demands of the God who chose Israel are behind the law. Beyond the nomocracy there is the theocracy. Finally, it may be remarked that according to the Jewish mentality, the question of Jesus Christ is only incidental to Jewish religion. Christians who assign to Jesus Christ a role in Jewish religion, either as the "cornerstone" or as a permanent reproach, are possibly misinterpreting the almost total silence of Jewish literature in his regard. It should also be considered that the Jewish attitude to Jesus Christ is not always simply total rejection and that there is a sense in which even a positive acceptance of Jesus need not mean rejection of Judaism.

The Jewish religion is an ethical monotheism connected with the historical destinies of the Jews. The diverse individual features of this monotheism are displayed in the religious history of the Jews.

2. *Sources.* Judaism relies on the divinely-revealed Torah ("proclaimed by the Holy Spirit") for the justification of its creed and its existence. The Torah has been transmitted orally and in writing. The written Torah is identical with the Tanach (OT) which according to the shorter canon used in Jewish reckoning consists of twenty-four books. The oral Torah has the same divine origin as the written law (bShab 31a; bNed 35b–37b). It is to be found above all in rabbinical literature, especially the Mishnah (compiled *c.* A.D. 220 by R. Jehuda Hanasi) and the Babylonian Talmud (finished in the 6th or 7th century A.D.). The Mishnah (literally, tradition, repetition) is the official commentary on the OT law and the traditions. It is chiefly due to the efforts of the Tannaites (transmitters, the five generations of rabbis from A.D. 70–220), whose interests were mainly legal. It contains 694 commands and prohibitions. Since the Mishnah left many applications open, the need was soon felt to collect the rabbinical discussions about the Mishnah. The commentaries of the Babylonian sages (Amoraim, the speakers) were compiled as the Babylonian Talmud, the last official expression of the oral law. The rabbis looked on their work of preserving traditions and expounding the law – which included the safeguarding of the text of the Bible – as the "rediscovery" of what was revealed by God on Sinai. It was all "already revealed to Moses on Sinai" (bNed 37b).

The rest of the rabbinical literature also exercised a lasting influence on Judaism. This is true above all of the Jerusalem or Palestinian Talmud, which comprised the discussion of the Mishnah carried on in Palestine and was finished in the 5th or 6th century A.D. Other important items are the Midrashim and the prayers used in the synagogues. The Midrashim are homilectic ("haggadic") or juridical ("halakic") reflections on biblical texts, of which the hidden meaning is sought in order to re-interpret it for the present time and for practical action. The process and the end-product are comprised under the term Midrash (searching). The halakic Midrash on the normative parts of the Torah is of far greater importance in the religious life of Jews than the haggadic Midrash which is mostly legend.

Among the prayers of early rabbinical times the Shemone Esre ("Eighteen Prayer") holds pride of place. It was compiled at the end of the 1st century A.D. It contains praises of God and the prayers and hopes of the oppressed Jewish communities. Pious Jews recite it three times a day, facing in the direction of Jerusalem.

The possession of the written *and* the

oral Torah is a "nota" of Jewish religion, to the mind of the Jews, which distinguishes it from all others. Even the Tanach (OT) is said to indicate the divinely-willed function of the oral Torah, and hence of the Mishnah, Talmud and other main Jewish traditions. Texts such as Deut 17:8–11 and Haggai 2:11–14 are invoked.

3. *Religious outlook and practice*. Doctrines have not the same place or meaning in the Jewish religion as dogmas in Christianity. They are norms and inspirations for the practical life of the Jews. From this point of view, the Jewish religion is a system of conduct which directly affects the Jewish people, of which it is the mainspring and the formative element: "Our people is not a people, except in its doctrine" (Saadia Gaon, A.D. 882–942). Systematic expositions of Jewish religious teaching are mostly wrongly interpreted by Christian readers whose approach is that of dogmatic theology. The Jewish doctrine of God, for instance, can only be said to be identical with that of the dogmatic treatise *De Deo Uno* if one remembers that Judaism does not aim at producing consistent formulas – except those already given in the Bible – and is rather intent on the concrete "hallowing of the Name" (*Qiddush ha-Shem*) as outlined in the law. There is a contrast to Christian teaching in anthropological principle, where Judaism rejects the notion of original sin, instead of which it has the doctrine of the good and the evil urge in man. The evil urge can be mastered by effort, with the help of God; for this view Ps 8, Zech 1:3; Mal 3:7 are invoked in particular. This favourable view of human potentialities goes hand in hand with a strong emphasis on this life in general. The other life has little place in religious discourse, as compared to Christianity. This neglect of the other world is due to some extent to the unhappy experiences of the Jews with over-excited groups intent on eschatological and messianic hopes, or on esoteric speculations about the beyond.

Thus the religious Jew is a man who feels himself bound in all his actions to the God of Israel with his claims and promises, and to the people of Israel with its privileges and expectations (cf. Deut 6, the OT missionary precept). A visible symbol of this centring of the life of Jewish men and boys on God, tradition and community is circumcision (cf. Gen 17; Deut 10:16; 30:6; Jer 4:4; Ezek 44:7–9). For religious Jews in general the observation of the sabbath and feast-days, the recital of prayers, the keeping of the purity laws, the maintenance of ancient Jewish tradition, the hope of eschatological salvation and so on mean that they are bearing the yoke of God for the sake of the kingdom of heaven, that is, that they are being true to the obligations of the covenant.

Clemens Thoma

IV. The Philosophy

1. *Introduction*. There is no Jewish philosophy as such. There are only Jewish philosophies. All of the emphases and modulations of Western philosophy – Greek, Hellenistic, Christian scholasticism and Moslem rationalism and scepticism, German idealism, and contemporary existentialism have been registered within Jewish thought.

The Jewish people did not begin to philosophize because of an irresistible inner compulsion to do so. Rather it may be argued that the history of Jewish philosophy reflects the effort of successive generations of Jewish thinkers to come to terms with the challenges and assaults of foreign ideas and traditions, to apprehend their methods and principles, to assess their relevance to Jewish concerns, and – where possible – to accommodate them by rethinking and transforming inherited and traditional categories of Jewish thought. Judaism has been singularly capacious and latitudinarian, therefore, in its response to foreign philosophies, primarily because its concern, after A.D. 135, was no longer to maintain an apologetic or missionary stance before the non-Jewish world, but to endure within an essentially hostile environment. Where Philo of Alexandria and Josephus were prepared to make use of the intuitions of Hellenistic philosophy and culture to establish Judaism as a religion in which reason and the Holy Spirit were conformed and the canards and blasphemies of paganism overcome, the speculations of the rabbis of the Talmudic Age were more concerned with the definition of the practical theology of Jewish life, the setting forth of the limits and bounds of permissible experience, and the provision of differentia by which Jewish life might remain secure in a politically, intellectually, and religiously inhospitable world. When Judaism ceased to be religiously aggressive before the pagan world, the uses of philosophy as missionary apologetics languished. It was only later when Judaism once more came under the attacks of its own dissenters, the Karaites, and received the glancing blows launched by the Mu'takallimun against the orthodox of Islam that it began to philosophize once more.

2. *The biblical origins of Jewish philosophy*. There are many philosophies of Judaism because there is but one revelation of God which Jews accept as authentic, preserve, and transmit. Judaism and Jewish philosophy begin therefore with the presumption of the biblical absolute: God covenanted his person to Israel, revealed to it his way, and instructed it that it might become a holy community. All of the formulations by which later Jewish thought sought to interpret, rationalize, and accommodate the biblical reality to the demands of non-Jewish traditions must reckon with the primacy of revelation. Indeed, it may be argued that the very multiplicity of authentic styles and emphases in Jewish philosophy – the absence of any normative Jewish philosophy or authoritative philosophical school – arises from the fact that the biblical datum is in no wise theoretically challenging. The God of the Patriarchs, of Moses, and of the prophetic and Wisdom literature is one who discloses himself under the aspect of nature, society, and history. The biblical writ is thus a refracted and refracting document. It is never fully open, for God is never wholly present. It is proper then to describe the Bible as a document, eminently anthropomorphic (in that man always sees in God that which God has already given to man) and theomorphic (in that God always offers to man that which man has already sought from God). Such anthropomorphism (or as it has been more vividly called by the contemporary thinker, Abraham Joshua Heschel, "anthropopathetism") presents the image of God as a translation of his mystery into the accessible arena of human passions and actions. What is crucial is not the biblical translation of the revealed God into man apotheosized. The Bible is rather, as Heschel has observed, God's anthropology. God reads man in God's terms in precisely the same sense in which man reads God in his own.

What is decisive, therefore, in the biblical account of the relations of God and man, of God and world, and especially of God and Israel, is that the person of God and the corporate life of Israel are marked by a continuous dialectic tension of the holy and the unredeemed. Indeed, if one were to formulate the essential intuition of Israel about the character of God, it would emerge in the form of a theology of the holy. All other theological virtues and all other theological *realia* would turn upon one's understanding the nature of the holy.

Rabbinic Judaism (135 B.C.–A.D. 1035) is founded upon the characteristic emphases of biblical faith. Where it differs from biblical Judaism is not in the substance of its thought but in the attitudes and approaches by which the rabbinic mind sought to rationalize the biblical encounter with the holy. Rabbinic theology (for it was not properly philosophy) begins with certain "givens", with experienced realities about which the rabbis had no questions – the creation of the world, the gift of the Torah to Israel, the giving of the Land to the wanderers of the desert that they might inhabit it and fashion there "a kingdom of priests and a holy nation". These are the urgent data of Jewish faith. Beyond these, the God who created, revealed, and bequeathed is a God of mercy and justice, who is concerned with his creatures, gives them instruction and reproof, delivers to their keeping and transmission a regimen of conduct that channels intention, inspires right action, and inhibits their impulse to infidelity. The theology of the rabbinic world was pragmatic; however, its pragmatism was dependent upon a cluster of primary realities available only to faith.

3. *Religious philosophy of Hellenistic Judaism*. If we leave aside the influence of Greek ideas upon Ecclesiastes and the Apocryphal literature (which were at best slight and marginal), it may be said that the first significant meeting of Judaism and external philosophy occurred and would continue to occur only within a diaspora where contact and communication between Jews and non-Jews, even if not free and unrestricted, were at least possible. Jewish philosophy did not flourish within the confined precincts of the Academies of Palestine and Babylonia nor within the ghettoes of Europe. It flourished only in cosmopolitan centres where an aristocracy of learning was permitted to mature, indifferent to the anti-intellectual bias of the narrowly orthodox. The Jews who lived in Alexandria and within the diaspora accessible to Greek culture regarded their religion as a philosophy and developed an apologetics which sought to unfold the philosophical character of the Jewish idea of God and the humanity of Jewish ethics. Hellenistic Jewish thought was characterized therefore by the attempt to supply a philosophical form for the intellectual substance of Judaism. In some Greek modes of expression only a superficial patina for Jewish ideas was provided, but in others – most extremely in the case of Philo of Alexandria – Jewish ideas were transformed by Greek ideas into what Julius Guttmann has called "a radical philosophical sublimation". Sincerely believing that he was in no wise misrepresenting the intention of Scripture, Philo extracted from the Bible a complete philosophy. Unlike the pantheism characteristic of the Stoics, Philo's God was absolute in his transcendence and utterly immaterial. In divesting God of every trace of anthropomorphism – exalting him above all knowledge and virtue, indeed, above all perfections conceivable to the mind – he laid the foundations for what would become in later times the distinctive emphases of negative theology. However, not content with defining a radical incommensurability between God and man, Philo developed a doctrine of mystical ascent whereby the knower might come to union with God. In seeking, by allegorical interpretation of Scripture, to bring together human knowledge and divine revelation, to effect a reconciliation of mystical wisdom with *scientia*, Philo posed for the first time the problem which was to remain basic to the philosophy and theology of monotheistic religions.

4. *Medieval Jewish religious philosophy*. Jewish philosophy in the Middle Ages arose within the cultural world of Islam and was profoundly influenced by Islamic thought. Its original stamp was defined by the religio-philosophic ideas of the Islamic Kalam, and even after it had come under the influence of

neo-Platonism and Aristotelianism, its connection with Islamic thought was maintained. Jewish neo-Platonists were dependent upon sources made available to them by Moslem translators and Jewish Aristotelians took up interpretations of Aristotle advanced by Alfarabi, Avicenna, and Averroes. Even later, when Jewish philosophy had spread to Christian lands, notably Spain, Provence, and Italy, the influence of Islam remained dominant, Christian scholasticism remaining a negligible and subordinate factor in its development.

The rise of Jewish philosophy within Islam is due to the fact that Judaism was obliged to defend itself, both by the heretic denial of the rabbinic tradition advanced by Karaism within and the energetic refurbishment by Moslem enthusiasts of old attacks against Judaism from without. In their effort to counter a rising tide of criticism from non-monotheists in the East and sceptics and unbelievers within Islam, there arose a school of believing rationalists, the Mu'tazilites who sought to supply a conceptual framework for the Kalam. Less adventuresome than Islamic thinkers who willingly entertained all kinds of philosophical and scientific questions, Jewish philosophy was content to rely upon Islamic thinkers for considerations of general philosophical questions, undertaking for its own part to inquire primarily into more specifically limited religio-philosophic issues. The primary concern of Jewish philosophy was the justification of Judaism. As Islamic thought expanded with the appearance of Al-Kindi's and Alfarabi's Aristotelianism at the end of the 9th century, so too the neo-Platonism of Isaac Israeli, the first Jewish philosopher, gave way to the thought of Saadia b. Joseph (882–942), a follower of the Kalam. Saadia's doctrine of the relation between reason and revelation affords him the foundation of his religious thought. Religious truth originates in revelation and becomes thereby a distinct form of truth. The conflict between reason and revelation does not emerge for Saadia as a specific problem of human consciousness, but is posed rather in terms of the relation of reason to a specific religion claiming to speak the absolute truth. Jewish religion, in such a view, is radically different from others which are human creations, speaking erroneously of God and his nature. Saadia's view had the positive advantage of enabling reason to apprehend, through its own powers, the content of revelation as being without contradiction with the findings of reason. To be sure, it will be asked what need there is for revelation if reason, unaided, can achieve the presumably superior knowledge provided by revelation. Saadia's answer – one that became commonplace among later thinkers – was that revelation is an expeditious and efficient pedagogue of man, who is liable by the limits of his creatureliness to inconstancy, confusion, and misapprehensions.

The followers of the Kalam, extending and embroidering the insights of Saadia, gave way a century later to an impressive period of Jewish neo-Platonism, the most notable representatives of which were Solomon ibn Gabirol (1026–*c.* 1050), Bahya ibn Pakuda (*c.* 1080–*c.* 1156), and that unique and only tangentially neo-Platonic thinker, Jehudah Halevi (1085–1140). Jehudah Halevi's *Kuzari* (The Book of Argument and Proof in Defence of a Despised Faith) does not, like earlier efforts, seek to identify Judaism with rational truth. Denying rational certainty in metaphysics, Halevi argues that philosophical doctrine is as arbitrary and dogmatic as it claims assertions of revelation to be. His concern, however, is not to destroy philosophy as such, but rather to undermine its pretensions. God, world, and man, as separate and uncorrelated facts are demonstrable by reason, but their connection, their intimate relation, is not available to reason, but to revelation alone. Halevi refutes the supposed opposition of reason to revelation by exposing the casuistry of the claims of reason. His method of argument is dialectical, rather than expository, for Halevi is not asserting the autonomy of religion as regards reason but a supernatural conception of revelation.

It was in the middle of the 12th century that Aristotelianism displaced neo-Platonism as the dominant style of Jewish philosophy. Abraham ibn Daud of Toledo (d. *c.* 1180), whose work *The Exalted Faith* (*Emunah Ramah*) exhibits the apparent harmony of Judaism and Aristotelian doctrine, is actually a commonplace presentation of the major characteristics of Avicenna's reconciliation of religion and philosophy. It was only when Maimonides (Moses ben Maimon of Cordova, 1135–1204) published his classic *The Guide of the Perplexed* (Arabic: *Dalalat al-Hairin*; Hebrew: *Moreh Nebukhim*) about 1190, that the issue between philosophy and revelation was squarely put. Although Maimonides sought to reconcile the apparent contradiction between philosophy and revelation and hence reassure those who might come to doubt either the truth of faith or the propriety and significance of philosophic inquiry, Maimonides did not conceive his task as the reunion of irreconcilables, but rather the demonstration of their essential conformance and identity. Unlike his predecessors, who held similar views to his own, Maimonides did not seek *only* to prove that the content of philosophy and revelation was the same, but that philosophy was the only proper means for the apprehension of revealed truths. For Maimonides, religious faith was a form of knowledge. Whereas it is the task of tradition and the continuity of historical faith to provide an external, and therefore indirect, form of knowledge, the internal apprehension of truth – an apprehension which is direct and unmediated by external forms and customs – is made possible by philosophical knowledge. Such an intellectualist concept of faith aims at making the inwardness of the believer dependent upon the deepening of philosophical understanding. The philosophical enterprise is essentially religious; and the pathos of religious rationalism is given an articulate and definite form in Western philosophy.

It can well be imagined that such a thoroughgoing intellectualism in religion, conjoined, as it was in both Jewish and Christian minds, with Averroist Aristotelianism, produced a considerable reaction within the exposed and vulnerable Jewish communities of Southern European Christendom. The 13th century witnessed in consequence a violent controversy, not only about Maimonidean rationalism, but about the right of philosophy to exist at all. The controversy itself eventually acquired a philosophic form, with anti-Maimonideans either opposing philosophy as such, or else defending Averroes against Maimonides's strictures, or, as did Levi ben Gerson (1288–1344), undertaking to recapitulate and strengthen Maimonides's criticisms of extreme Averroism. The response of the 14th century, as evidenced by Moses ben Nahman of Gerona (1184–c. 1270) and Hasdai Crescas (*c.* 1340–*c.* 1410) was to undertake, in the case of Nahmanides, a supernaturalist critique similar to that of Jehudah Halevi against theistic rationalism, or, as did Crescas in his *The Light of the Lord* (*Or Adonai*, 1410), the construction of an anti-Aristotelian dogmatics in which ultimate religious values were preserved beyond the precincts of reason.

5. *The emergence of modern Jewish philosophy*. The cleavage of Jewish life from the intellectual currents which bathed Christian Europe was not bridged until the middle of the 18th century. Although the course which 18th and 19th century Jewish philo-

sophy was to take cannot really be discussed independently of the movements of secular humanism and Enlightenment, the rise of extra-ecclesiastical culture, and the political struggle for civil emancipation in Europe, it may be said that the issues which had once defined the ambit of Jewish (and Christian) scholasticism were to wane in importance as the challenge and promise of secularization materialized. Moses Mendelssohn (1729–1786) most conspicuously set the tone which was later to find particularly meaningful expression in the work of *Wissenschaft des Judentums*. Although Mendelssohn preserved many of the distinctions developed by medieval Jewish philosophy, he established in common with the optimistic rationalism of the Enlightenment a view of Judaism in which reason became the sufficient arbiter of faith; in which both pure and practical reason might judge the relevance and universality of intellectual and moral truths. Judaism became a religious polity which might within a messianism of reason provide salvation (liberation from error) for all mankind.

It should not be surprising that the legacy of Mendelssohn (although surely not Mendelssohn alone) was one of dissolution within Jewish intellectual life. Although Nahman Krochmal's (1785–1840) *Guide for the Perplexed of Our Time* (published posthumously in 1851) undertook to provide an internal historico-philosophic justification of Judaism on the grounds of idealist (but anti-Hegelian) impulses and Samson Raphael Hirsch (1808–1888) was to defend Judaism in his *Nineteen Letters* by utilizing Hegelian models to elevate and incorporate Judaism into the rhythm of the unfolding logos, it was not really until Solomon Formstecher (1808–1889) published his *The Religion of the Spirit* (1841) and Solomon Ludwig Steinheim (1789–1866) his eccentric *Revelation according to the Doctrine of the Synagogue* (published between 1835 and 1865) that Judaism found two more or less congenial philosophers. Formstecher offered a rationalism with which Judaism (albeit one reformed) could survive and Steinheim, in almost violent opposition, a Judaism in which religious truth was once more grounded in revelation.

It is with Hermann Cohen (1842–1918) that Judaism is set forth in a manner compatible with the putatively best in European culture – German idealism and liberal religion. Cohen's works, *The Concept of Religion in the System of Philosophy* (1915) and *The Religion of Reason drawn from the Sources of Judaism* (1919) expound a consistent and plodding rationalism in which no other religion than that of reason is to be considered; moreover, he finds that Judaism, notably prophetic Judaism, is that religion in which reason, the moral direction of man, and a God of ethics and humanity are united. In the present century, Franz Rosenzweig (1886–1929) and Martin Buber (1878–1965) proclaimed an opposition to the rationalism dominant within Judaism as well as within Western religious philosophy generally. For Rosenzweig, the existential particularity of the living subject addresses the facts which are God, world and man and defines through them and before them the relations by which they are bound to one another; while Buber has formulated the dialogal principle of I–Thou in such a manner as to disqualify intermediating and objectifying discriminations which depersonalize the relations of man with man and silence the ultimate Thou of which all human beings are particularizations. Rosenzweig and Buber reopened the question of being within Judaism on grounds of existence in the world, rather than from the more conventional epistemological perspective. The train of thought which Rosenzweig and Buber have developed within Judaism is at present finding expression in Israel and the United States among thinkers for whom the reality of Jewish existence is being sought in a renewal of the connection between the existential-historical situation of the Jew and the problematic reality of a God who lives, but speaks not. It is not surprising, given the events of recent decades, that for Jewish thinkers such as Nathan Rotenstreich, Steven Schwarzschild, Will Herberg, Emil Fackenheim, Arthur A. Cohen, and others the relation of God, evil, and history is of particular importance.

Arthur A. Cohen

JUSTICE

I. Scripture

1. *The social sense of justice in the Old Testament.* The OT idea of צדקה (usually δικαιοσύνη in the LXX), unlike justice as conceived of in terms of objective theological principles, is not determined by permanent and immutable norms of human behaviour such that a man is accounted just when he acts in conformity with them. Throughout the whole of the OT in general, צדקה is a style of action, in a relation of fellowship between partners, which is the permanent constituent of this relationship and hence has its norm in the very existence of this relationship. Now since man is involved in various relations of fellowship there are various modes of justice which must be exercised between the parties as the basis of their partnership. Hence too there is no negative or punitive aspect in the OT idea of justice. The punishment of offenders is not numbered among the activities proper to the just man (with Cazelles and against Nötscher). The idea of the "justice of God" which appears especially in the apocalyptic writings and later in Paul (the corresponding idea in the OT is the just action of God conceived of as the deeds of salvation performed by him for Israel) suggests that in relationships between men justice can also be described as an act directed towards others and positive in its effects, by which one accords to them some advantage or opportunity which helps them and (thereby too the doer of justice) to preserve fellowship. Hence without justice to each other, fellowship between partners is impossible. This applies both to fellowship between men and fellowship between men and Yahweh. To be just, therefore, means to be free from any fault which would damage fellowship. To make just is to remove the obstacles set up by the other party (e.g., Is 53:11).

In the relationship of men to one another justice can denote a favourable attitude towards the innocent in judgment (thus in the series of "prohibitives" forbidding men to base their ethical conduct on their social rank in Exod 23:6–8; cf. Deut 25:1, where, accordingly, the hifil of צדק is used to signify: "to let the innocent have his due," to "justify him"). But the concept extends far beyond the forensic sphere. Especially at the beginning of the series dealing with the social order (e.g., משפט, Ezek 18:5) justice appears combined with משפט as an expression of the totality of the prescribed social attitudes towards those in a lowly walk of life. In relation to these groups the right, that is, the just attitude is one which extends beyond the basic requirements of mere giving and taking, and imports sympathy and compassion. The just man of the Wisdom literature is he who conducts himself so prudently in his dealings with his social equals and with those of lower station that he can obtain profit by it in the end. In antithetic proverbs he is often set in contrast to the "wicked", who is therefore also the foolish, for the comparison embraces both behaviour and its outcome. The just, however (in the course of the theological development this becomes clear), are rewarded with what is conceived to be true happiness. In later books this means that the just obtain not earthly riches (the unjust are requited with these) but eschatological or heavenly recompense. In Proverbs the just is the prudent man who bears in mind the outcome naturally to be expected of things. In passages influenced by the liturgy, however, the just man is one whose relationship with Yahweh is right, one who joins in his worship (Ps 15), one, therefore, who obtains from Yahweh the title of "righteous" and the promise of life (Ezek 18:9). Again the fact that faith is counted as justice (Gen 15:6) must represent an extension of the idea of ratification originally belonging to the sphere of worship (von Rad). Evidently those taking part in the liturgy were first subjected either collectively or individually to an examination as to their loyalty to the commands of the covenant bestowed by Yahweh (cf. Ps 24). Since one was either qualified to take part in worship or not, there was no intermediary position between justice and lack of justice.

In the psalms in particular we frequently find the צדיק described in quite general terms as one who takes joy in Yahweh's will and his precepts, with no mention of any concrete individual commandments. (We often encounter a similar phenomenon in parenetic discourse addressed to the just in later literature: cf. Ps 1 with the parenetic sections of Enoch.) The just man is pronounced blessed not by reason of what he does but in view of his life as a whole. Not until later, in the rabbinical literature, do we find a notably different concept of justice. Here it is the sum total of a man's acts of obedience to individual precepts (D. Rössler). In the apocalyptic literature, on the other hand, a sharp distinction is drawn between the just and the unjust (as in the Wisdom literature), and the just are consoled by parenetic discourses for their present unavoidable sufferings, and warned against apostasy.

While in the later literature it came increasingly to be doubted whether Israel could be just before Yahweh at all (Ps 143:1; Dan 9:18), Yahweh himself remains absolutely just towards Israel. The deeds of salvation which he has performed on its behalf are called the "manifestations of Yahweh's justice" as early as Jg 5:11 (cf. 1 Sam 12:7; Mic 6:5; Ps 103:6; Dan 9:16). This justice of Yahweh is not only often set side by side with the concept of חסד (faithfulness, love, "grace"), but also finds expression in the commandments which Yahweh gives to Israel, which are therefore considered to provide the possibility of salvation (Zeph 3:5; Ps 50:6). Even before the prophets, therefore, the justice of Yahweh is used as a synonym for the salvation bestowed by Yahweh (von Rad), and, furthermore, that salvation as applied to the individual.

Finally, a point to which so far too little attention has been paid is that justice is frequently spoken of in connection with the kingship (1 Sam 24:18; 26:33; 2 Sam 8:15; 1 Kg 3:6; 10:9). Justice is not only attributed to individual kings, but is actually the essential quality of the work proper to their state. The theology of the royalty may have been an important factor in the OT concept of justice. Hitherto the analysis of its cultic roots has often overlooked the fact that the texts in question (Ps 89:15; 97:2; 85:14; 89:17) have been applied to Yahweh only at a secondary stage, and analogously. In the context of sacred kingship justice is originally the proper attitude towards God, towards one's social equals and towards those of the humbler classes. In Is 11:1ff. the accomplishment of justice is attributed particularly to the son of David who is to come. Hence Jesus is called the "holy and righteous (just) one" in Acts 3:14.

2. *Justice in the theologies of the New Testament.* In the NT concepts of justice elements from the OT, Judaism and Greek popular philosophy are com-

bined. For Paul and Matthew in particular "justice" has acquired a primary significance, and in both of them with reference to the end or judgment shortly to come. For both authors justice is required from men at this judgment. For both, man can obtain this justice by deciding to embrace the message of Jesus and the community belonging to him. For this is the community of the just. In concrete terms this is achieved through faith and baptism. By these means man ceases in principle to belong to the unjust, unless he proves himself by his conduct to be not yet just or unless he falls away. For at present the community possesses justice only in a "provisional" and veiled manner. For Matthew as for Paul, therefore, the fulfilment of the ethical commandments is not the *condition* of justice but rather an *expression* of the justice which has been obtained by baptism and must therefore be preserved until the judgment. Thus the norm of judgment is the fulfilment of the law (for Matthew as for Paul this consists in the fulfilment of the social commandments), but the just are those who in principle have entered into a state in which they are capable of such fulfilment. In Matthew this is because Jesus is the teacher of justice for his community (the Sermon on the Mount), and because the baptized possess the Spirit. In Paul it is because justice has been imparted through the Pneuma in such a way that by it love, precisely the fulfilment of the law, is bestowed as a charisma (1 Cor). Certainly Matthew too recognizes that justice does have this character of a gift (18:23–35), but justice for him consists primarily in being free from sin, whereas in Paul the predominant idea is that of being in Christ as being in the justice of God (2 Cor 5:21, etc.). In particular Paul's thought is dominated by the idea of the indwelling Spirit, by which justice is affirmed as something present, as a gift and as a force.

For *Paul* the question of the relationship between the justice required of man and the justice of God is vital. Paul takes over the idea of the justice of God from the apocalyptic literature (cf. also Deut 33:21). For Paul too justice is not one of the attributes of God, but a gift manifested in God's actions towards man. God opens up a cosmic sphere of power in which the just are included. This sphere is somewhat like the Pneuma, for it signifies the sphere of the salvation bestowed by God. Hence the believers themselves become "the justice of God in Christ" (2 Cor 5:21). Here the new being is designated by the name of the power which constitutes and defines it (Stuhlmacher). This justice of God is revealed in Christ (Rom 1:17f.), in contrast to the injustice of Jews and Gentiles, which, when measured by the standard of the law, is shown to be such. This justice of God bestowed upon man in Christ is nothing else than the faithful execution of God's promises to the fathers (Rom 4:9–11). For this reason justice can only be obtained through a faith such as Abraham too possessed (Rom 4), and now, therefore, this must be faith in Jesus Christ. This connection between "justice" and "faith" was taken over by Paul from Gen 15:6 (elsewhere in the OT only Hab 2:4), and this is because on the one hand the justice of God for him consists in the fulfilment of the promises to the fathers, while on the other he feels compelled to connect this indissolubly with faith in Jesus Christ. Faith here as the way by which justice is to be obtained (according to Gen 15:6 the justice of Abraham, but for Paul God's own justice) is contrasted with the traditional way of the Jews, who seek to obtain justice by fulfilling the law. According to the Jewish notion, justice was obtained by fulfilling the commandments. As a possible way to salvation this law was linked with the Jewish people; as a gift of God bestowed in the course of the history of salvation it was a distinction. But in the light of the faith now required of man it represents a temptation to pursue one's "own" justice (Rom 10:3; Phil 3:9), that is, by the exclusively Jewish way of the law. But in the justice that comes by faith, the distinction between Jews and Gentiles is actually removed, and thus the universal way of salvation is revealed which alone can correspond to the universal, eschatological salvation in Christ. Hence the justice of God has now been revealed without the law (Rom 3:21). In concrete terms justification is achieved through the death of Jesus, the primary function of which is to take away sins. In the OT too justice did indeed mean to a large extent freedom from sin, but this was in the context of a relation of fellowship, and so signified that this relationship was still intact. Now in Paul over and above this the possession of justice is characterized in positive terms by the possession of the Spirit and the life which proceeds from it.

In the Gospel of Mark, the term justice is not found. But it appears in the Lucan writings, in Lk 1:75; Acts 10:35, where it is combined, in a manner characteristic of Hellenistic thought, with the fear of God (as the sum total of human duty), and elsewhere in Luke is used to designate the whole moral well-being of man, as the prior condition for the reception of the Spirit. In Matthew all the passages in which justice appears are of redactional origin. Here too justice is a collective concept, one namely which stands for all that constitutes the "religion" of the community henceforward separated from Judaism. The apocalyptic pattern of the division of mankind into just and unjust is adhered to. The Jews now become the types of the unjust, and among them the Pharisees in particular, by reason of their hypocrisy, will not survive the judgment, and will not obtain any heavenly reward (5:20; 6:1). Man becomes just through baptism, by which he already obtains the fullness of justice (Mt 3:15), although he still remains in danger of losing this by apostasy. According to the ideas of the apocalyptic tradition the just must necessarily endure persecution (Mt 5:10, etc.). This traditional principle also provides the background to earlier interpretations of the death of Jesus as that of the suffering just man (Ps 22 as cited in the Passion narrative; Mk 8). The justice of the community is contrasted with that of Judaism by being brought into relation with the βασιλεία (Mt 6:33), and by the fact that it will be revealed as justice in the judgment to come. As the parables of the weeds in the wheat etc. attest, the justice of the just is thought of solely from the aspect of the judgment. The sharp dualism between just and unjust is not to be understood in the sense of an available criterion, for both groups live together in the world. But the just are persecuted here, and thereby their difference from the unjust becomes ever more apparent and the reward they are to receive to compensate for their sufferings is prepared.

In the Letter of James justice is likewise brought into connection with the idea of retribution at the judgment. Justice before God (1:20) is bestowed as a fruit (3:18) growing out of men's actions (2:23). It was not by faith alone that Abraham obtained his justice. Rather he was called "friend of God" only after the sacrifice of Isaac, and hence it is only here that Gen 15:6 was fulfilled.

In the rest of the NT writings the idea of justice as a sphere of salvation as in Paul is to be found here and there. The saved are taken into this sphere. Thus according to 2 Pet 3:13 justice dwells in the new heaven and the new earth as a blessing of salvation which permeates the whole. According to 2 Pet 1:1 the justice of God is a sphere within which faith in God and Jesus Christ has been bestowed. In conformity with the special concept of miracles in Heb 11 the work of justice on earth belongs, according to 11:33, to the special deeds of the just which transcend this world and cause astonishment to men. Elsewhere too in the Letter to the Hebrews justice is orientated to the heavenly world. The "word of justice" is only for the perfect (5:13). The high priest Jesus is the completely just one who has loved justice (1:9), and to whom Melchizedek pointed by his name. As in Jas 3:18, so too in Heb 12:11 justice and peace are combined as mutually complementary blessings of the eschatological age. Thus for Hebrews justice is a power reaching into the world through Jesus and through faith in him, and it is also an eschatological gift. 1 Pet 2:24 clearly stands in the line of the Pauline tradition. The sacrifice of the body of Christ means for believers that they are separated from sin, and that it is possible to "live to righteousness". But this is not understood in the light of the justice of God as in Paul, but rather, as the context shows, is already (or perhaps still?) primarily ethical. Then in the Pastoral Letters we find a concept of justice which is still more remote from that of Paul, for here it is regarded as one virtue among others. Frequently emphasis is laid upon the doing of justice (1 Jn; Rev; Tit 3:5). Here what justice actually consists in is either left undecided or is defined as brotherly love and compassion. (This is connected with the usage of later Judaism, in which צדקה meant alms; cf. δικαιοσύνη in Josephus.) Thus in the non-Pauline writings the ideas which are most emphasized are: the doing of justice and the insertion of justice into the list of the virtues. There is little or no link with the justice of God, with the idea of justice as the heavenly reward (2 Tim 4:2) or with the person and work of Jesus (2 Pet; Eph 4:24).

Klaus Berger

II. Moral Theology

The notion of justice is fundamental to the human spirit. All men have some sort of aspiration, at least obscurely, towards justice. From the beginning, the notion of justice has been attached to the sphere of religion, as may be seen in Plato's *Gorgias*, 507b, and *Republic*, I, 331a. In the most ancient texts of the Bible, the first monuments of supernatural revelation, there is also a bond between justice and religion (in the covenant by which Israel was bound to Yahweh). "Abraham believed the Lord; and he reckoned it to him as righteousness" (Gen 15:6). In the Book of Proverbs, the "just" is frequently contrasted with the "impious" (or the "wicked", the "foolish", in a profound and complex religious sense). See Prov 10:11, 20f.; 11:10, 23, 31; 12:3–13; 5:13, 9, 21, 25, etc.

1. *Uncertainties and errors.* This undoubted sense of a salvific and transcendent justice, this demand for justice in the mutual relations of men and in the order of the city did not free men from profound uncertainties as to the nature and meaning of justice. In the dialogues of Plato, various speakers are criticized for concepts of justice based on a purely hedonistic, utilitarian or materialistic outlook – that, for instance, justice is merely the law of the stronger. There is the radical relativism of Protagoras and the theory of justice as a social compromise to avoid greater evils. Avoiding such errors and incertitudes, the profound humanism of Aristotle, in the *Nicomachean Ethics*, crowned a long process of secularization of the concept of justice. Medieval scholasticism took over the heritage of Aristotle and transformed its spirit, in the concrete and in the theory of ethics. The notion of justice came to be placed within the horizon of religious transcendence. For the ethical thought of Thomism, along with biblical and Augustinian influences, the impact of Stoicism, through the Latin writings of Cicero etc., was very important. Thomas Aquinas, while remaining faithful to the Aristotelian concept, was responsive to the strong

social trends which are at the heart of the patristic tradition on justice and the proper use of goods.

Then once more, in the great process of the secularization of thought which came to a climax in the 18th century, the notion of justice was deprived of its transcendental roots. In much more profound and complex forms, in keeping with a much more highly evolved thinking for which the progress in the new positive methods of science was decisive, the errors and uncertainties of ancient Greek thought appeared once more. They are to be found in Hobbes, Nietzsche and the many forms of positivism and sociological theories of justice which multiplied at the end of the 19th and the beginning of the 20th century. Faced with the uncertainties as to the content of the notion of justice, some were tempted to accept a purely relative system of values. Hence came the tendency to take refuge in a purely formal concept of justice. On account of the value of "security at law" and the universal character of law itself, there was a tendency to reduce justice to the virtue of impartiality in the general application of the one law, leaving aside as insoluble the problem of "natural justice".

2. *The impact of the "spirit of capitalism"*. This whole modern picture of deviations and uncertainties with regard to the ever-imperative ideal of justice was coloured throughout the 19th century by the "spirit of capitalism" (see the encyclical of Paul VI, *Populorum Progressio*, art. 26). Its influence on the ideals and concept of justice were deleterious. Economics attained the rank of ultimate and absolute values and claimed to be ruled by its intrinsic and wholly autonomous laws. *Homo economicus* was bound to aim, as the ultimate goal of his activity, at the maximum quantitative development of the economy. Economic ethics were rationalistic and individualist, like the political liberalism of the age. The central point in this concept of economic life was profit, which came to be radically separated from all demands deriving from the solidarity of an *ordo amoris* and from all metaphysical, ethical and religious bonds. Economics became a world with a law of its own independent of all other norms. The individual in the system followed only the dictates of his individual interests (gain), as rationalized by foresight and calculation, and thus inserted himself and his activity into the "natural order" of the world of economics.

The "classical" school of economics, drawing on a philosophy of a very special type and on historically-conditioned experiences, produced the new "economic science" and gave the "spirit of capitalism" its final perfection and consistency, consummating the breach with all moral norms transcending the internal laws of the economic system. What remained of the concept of justice in this outlook on the world and life? The whole notion of social justice was eliminated. Justice became commutative justice which obeyed no other law than the conventions of negotiated contracts within the framework of the law of supply and demand, with no restrictions on individualistic enterprise. The function of the State was to allow free play to the forces of individualism by enforcing public order and the fulfilment of contracts, while remaining rigorously neutral as regards their contents. This was the general notion of justice in liberal capitalism. The aberrations of the "spirit of capitalism", along with another complex series of factors, produced the ideas of Marx and Engels and the movements which flowed from them. Marxism is a tragic contradiction between a messianic aspiration after justice – raised to its highest coefficient of secularization in the form of a systematic atheism – and the acceptance of an immanent natural determinism in economics. It substituted, no doubt, for the atomistic mechanisms on which classical economics were based a dialectic and historical materialism. But this was no less a renunciation of the whole transcendent ideal of justice. This is the historical context in which the Christian of today has to ask himself about the ideals and concept of justice.

3. *The comprehensive and religious sense of the idea of justice.* The Bible constantly uses the word "justice" in a sense which is at once ethical and religious. The OT already puts forward the idea that this justice cannot come to man through his own strength but is a gift of God. This order of ideas is developed more and more fully in the NT, the supreme revelation of the salvific grace ("justice") of God.

Though on an essentially different plane, since the supernatural revelation of the "justice of God" is lacking, the Platonic concept of justice has a comprehensive character and a religious colouring. It is immediately related to the supreme form, that of the good. The form of the good in Plato is the supreme principle, the initiative behind all initiatives (cf. *Republic*, VI, 508b–510b). It is the *logos* of all things, not only in the sense of their explanation but as the inventive and efficient cause. Everything that exists is essentially ordained by it, according to Plato, to a function which derives directly from the form of the good. The functional purpose of the essence demands that things be intrinsically structured in such a way that they are apt to fulfil their function. This principle of functional structure applies both to individual things and to organic compositions. Any of them can pervert their structure and render themselves unable to perform their function. This deviation and decadence, when the realities affected are the soul and the State, is for Plato the constitutive element of injustice. Justice is the structural equilibrium (rectitude) of the soul (personal justice) and of the State (political justice), which has to secure their functioning in the best possible way, in accordance with an order of functions determined by the illuminating radiance of the supreme form of the good.

4. *Comprehensive (religious) justice and general justice.* This fundamental tendency to identify the ideal of justice with full religious and moral rectitude and – in a more genuine religious way of thinking – with a salvific realization of the good (justice) in man by a free intervention of God which justifies, has gone hand in hand from the beginning with the tendency to conceive justice as a characteristic virtue, qualitatively distinct from the other virtues. The Bible speaks of justice not only in the comprehensive sense mentioned above, but also with reference to a characteristic virtue distinct from the others. Sometimes justice has a juridical colouring and means conformity with a legal norm (Prov 11:4,19; 12:28; 16:8; Deut 1:16; 16:18; 25:15). In the historical and prophetic books, justice is often the equivalent of due rights (Hos 10:12; Is 9:6; 11:4f.; 16:5; 32:1; Jer 22:3f.; 23:5; Ezek 45:9f.; 2 Sam 8:15; 1 Kg 10:9; 1 Chr 18:14; 2 Chr 9:8). Jeremiah denounces the injustice of riches accumulated by paying starvation wages (Jer 22:13–15). In this context the prophets sometimes call the oppressed poor the "just" (Amos 2:6; 5:12; Is 1:17, 23; 3:4f.; Lam 4:13); Jas 5:6 speaks in the same way. The Wisdom literature teaches that justice demands rectitude in the mutual relationships of men (Job 35:8; Eccles 5:7) and in the concrete, rectitude in the exercise of judicial functions (Ecclus 45:26). Justice is used as a synonym of benevolence (ἐλεημοσύνη in the LXX) (Tob 7:6; 9:6; 12:9; 14:9–11; Ecclus 3:30). This identification of justice with beneficence (alms) is given great prominence in the patristic age (e.g., Basil, *Hom. in Lk*, 12:8, no. 7: *PG*, XXXI, cols. 276f.; Ambrose, *De Nabuthe*, 12, 53, *CSEL*, XLVI, p. 426, *PL*, XIV, col. 747; John Chrysostom, *Hom. 12 in 1 Tim*, 12, 4;

PG, LXII, cols. 562f.; Augustine, *Sermo 50*, 2, 4; *PL*, XXXVIII, col. 327; id., *Epist. 153*, no. 26, *CSEL*, XLVI, p. 426, *PL*, XXXIII, col. 665). In the NT justice also appears as a virtue distinct from others (Act 24:25 along with self-control; 1 Tim 6:11 along with piety, faith, charity, constancy and mildness; 2 Cor 9:9f. a synonym of beneficence, almsgiving; Rev 19:11 the virtue of just judgment).

Can the comprehensive religious idea of justice and the idea of justice as a particular virtue be reduced to some type of unity? Aristotle introduced the concept of legal justice (an integral or general justice embracing all the virtues) and that of particular justice (equity in the attribution of ownership among individuals), cf. *Nicomachean Ethics*, V, 1129a–1131a. In both cases justice involves a relationship to others (*ad alterum*), in the first to the common good, in the second to the good of an individual. Legal justice includes the exercise of all the virtues insofar as they bear on the common good (integral justice) but maintains the character of relationship to others which is characteristic of the special idea of justice. No doubt the Aristotelian concept of legal justice is completely secularized and purely political. It is the civic virtue of observing the positive law of the State (in the context of the strong community spirit characteristic of the Greeks). In Scholasticism, which based itself on the notion of the eternal law of God, in which all other laws participate, legal justice includes the civic virtue of observance of positive law but goes beyond it to become once more a comprehensive justice under the sign of religion.

But why is it called "justice"? The solution seems to lie along the line of an idea much favoured by the Fathers. Man does not belong to himself but to God. Hence all virtue is giving God his due. But God is Father, and his love binds us in solidarity. It is therefore a duty in justice to work for the common good, and especially – from the standpoint of the Fathers – to aid the neighbour in his needs and not to use one's goods as if they were absolutely and exclusively one's own. See, for instance, *Letter of Barnabas*, 19, 8; *Didache*, 4, 8; Clement of Alexandria, *Paedagogus*, 2, 12 (*GCS*, Stählin, I, p. 229); Tertullian, *De Paenitentia* 7 (*CSEL*, XLVII, p. 11, *PL*, I, col. 1261); Lactantius, *Epitome Institutionum Divinarum*, 5, 14; 6, 11–12 (*CSEL*, XIX, pp. 445ff. and 519ff., *PL*, VI, cols. 596ff. and 671ff.); Basil, *Hom. tempore famis*, 8 (*PG*, XXXI, cols. 324f.); Gregory of Nyssa, *De Pauperibus Amandis*, 1 (*PG*, XLVI, col. 466); Ambrose, *De Officiis Ministri*, 3, 3, 19 (*PL*, XVI, col. 150); Jerome, *Epist.*, 120, 1 (*CSEL*, LV, pp. 476f., *PL*, XXII, col. 984); John Chrysostom, *Hom. 10 in 1 Cor*, 3 (*PG*, LXI, col. 86); Augustine, *De Trinitate*, 14, 9, 12 (*PL*, XLII, col. 1046); Leo I, *Sermo* 10, 1 (*PL*, LIV, col. 164).

5. *General and particular justice.* We may now attempt a synthesis. Justice is always fidelity in giving (*reddere*, rendering) to another what is his due (cf. St. Thomas, *Summa Theologica*, II–II, q. 58, a. 1). There is a radical and comprehensive justice, of a religious character, which consists in man's "surrendering" himself to God. Hence every sin is really an injustice (*iniuria*) to God. On this level justice and love are inseparable. In a general way, the NT sets up an existential dialectic between love (supernaturally "open" to God and to the neighbour, and inseparably so, cf. 1 Jn *passim*) and justice, though love alone is capable in fact of accomplishing adequately all justice, in freedom of spirit. To justice in the religious sense general justice is intimately linked, its object being the general good in all its aspects and implications, with no other limit than the due proportion between one's own needs and those of others (cf. 2 Cor 8:13–15 and the patristic texts referred to above).

For this general or social justice has as its immediate object a common human good which is transcendentally ordained to each man (Thomas Aquinas, *Summa Theologica*, II–II, q. 58, a. 5).

Hence social justice can take the form of obligations in justice towards certain persons in need of aid. But this grave obligation in justice does not entail (except in the case of extreme necessity) the right of the individual to claim directly for himself the good due to him, if it is due in virtue of social justice. Social justice involves particular justice – the accomplishment of which is always a social value – which is divided into distributive and commutative justice. The former is the proper distribution of the goods and offices of common life among the members of the community, which suffers unjustly in the goods proper to it if the distribution in question is not in keeping with the capacities, needs, functions, sacrifices and merits of the various subjects. The latter (so called by Thomas Aquinas, whereas Aristotle spoke of "corrective justice" – τὸ ἐπανορθωτικόν) governs exchange of goods between individuals and, in general, their mutual relations with regard to the goods belonging to or due to each, when the individuals are on a footing of equality (Aristotle, *Nicomachean Ethics*, 1131bff.). The immediate object of particular justice is "the property of the individual" (*Summa Theologica*, II–II, q. 7; cf. q. 61, a. 1). Goods are the object of commutative justice insofar as they are related to the needs of the persons who enter into relationships. Justice demands mutual equilibrium in the satisfaction of their needs by each party concerned (*Nicomachean Ethics*, 1133a–1133b). On the other hand, commutative justice, which cannot be embodied in the concrete without its tending to social justice (cf. *ibid.*, 1159b–1160a) needs to be completed by aspects of distributive justice (*ibid.*, 1131b).

These various types of justice must be considered to be aspects of one fundamental demand, which takes on various forms in concrete relationships. In the comprehensive sense, justice, in a given situation, is the concrete accomplishment of the fundamental imperative which calls for positive respect for the dignity and rights of others and contribution in solidarity to the meeting of human necessities. John XXIII (in *Mater et Magistra*) recalled repeatedly the demands of "justice and equity" and emphasized the comprehensive character of justice in the concrete, very much in keeping with the patristic notion. Vatican II spoke in the same sense (*Gaudium et Spes*, arts. 23–32; 63–72).

José María Díez-Alegría

K

KERYGMA

1. *Concept.* The Greek term κηρύσσω was adopted by the NT writers (mostly in the form of the noun κήρυγμα) and used to signify in a specifically biblical way a central reality of Christianity. It can indeed be regarded as one of the key concepts for the description of revelation. Neither the OT (where the most frequent corresponding term was קרא) nor the NT explains the term explicitly, but the usage is clear enough. The word, as a substantive, denotes both the act and the message, and ranges in meaning from "address" and "call out" to "summons"; in English the word is either transliterated or rendered as "preaching", though for this latter, which has in general the implication of a doctrinal and moral exposition, the word "proclamation" is often used.

2. *Scripture.* In a remarkable departure from the ordinary approach to reality and from the traditions of classical philosophy, the NT writers are profoundly inspired by the conviction that "salvation" is essentially linked with the "word". And there the "word" is not just information about a salvation which might be in itself and in its manifestations "wordless". Salvation is understood as the reality of the word: God himself in his epiphany is word and expresses himself as such. In this sense, kerygma is the word of salvation, understood as the word which is constitutive for the coming of salvation. The challenge of the OT prophets and finally and supremely that of Jesus of Nazareth and his envoys was not merely that they spoke of God's name or in God's name, but that God himself spoke in their words – in such a way that all, speakers and hearers, understood that salvation or loss depended on responsive self-commitment to the word of God. This coming of the word, understood as coming of salvation, is given more or less prominence and expressed in various ways in the NT writings. But in general it may be said that kerygma is the proclamation of salvation *as* the real coming of the kingdom of God (Mt 4:23; Lk 9:12). It is deliverance (Acts 8:5; 9:20), grace (Acts 20:32), reconciliation (2 Cor 5:19) and truth (Col 1:5; Eph 1:13) for men. Whatever forms the kerygma takes, it is always the expression of one thing only: the "word of Christ" (Rom 10:17), which is the origin and medium and object of the whole kerygma (as event). Since the Lord himself presents himself in the kerygma, it judges and justifies and is bringer of salvation. Hence as it affirms itself as true and life-giving, it can also summon to confident faith and then empower those who are

convinced of and filled by this word of the Lord to speak in turn in the same way, so that their mission is summed up in the words: "He who hears you hears me" (Lk 10:16). In this way the kerygma is constitutive of the Church as the fellowship of those who hear and follow the word of God (Mt 8:12). Hence the kerygma, as an event which takes place in and through the "word of Christ" is at once historical and supra-historical. It is the presence of the past and the future, of the temporal and the eternal. It is the one Lord who did his work as Jesus of Nazareth, who dwells as Spirit in his own and is to come as the Lord of glory. In this threefold way the Lord is the living and present though hidden Lord in the kerygma.

3. *Theological reflection.* These basic characteristics of the NT understanding of the kerygma at once throw light on the comprehensive nature of the kerygma as a dialogal and dialectical reality. The Lord is the subject and object and medium – in an analogous way: in one way as Jesus of Nazareth "obedient in the flesh" and in another way as the risen Lord. So too those who preach in Christ are themselves in their own way subject and object and medium of the kerygmatic event. Paul, for instance, is the subject who preaches, the medium of the preaching and also, in an analogous way, the object of his preaching, inasmuch as he has recourse to his experiences with the Lord. In this twofold mediation, already of itself analogous, which not merely takes place in the kerygma but is itself actually the kerygma, there takes place the free act of God and the free act of man as a totality interwoven in each other. Thus the twofold mediation proves to be once more mediated. This dialectic of mediation, which is personal as well as instrumental, and which may be termed dialogal, is a kerygmatic event both in the sphere of metaphysical principles and of the concrete historical.

Hence, qua historical, and thus involved in the contradictions of history by virtue of original sin and guilt, the kerygma is submitted to a new dialectic: the tension – in terms of glory as well as of logic – between true mediation of salvation and culpable barring of salvation. The primordial salvific and kerygmatic mediation through the cross and resurrection of Jesus, when historically mediated as kerygma, is once more crucified by history and must rise again in this dimension, if the message of salvation is to be fully unfolded. Resurrection and cross, as dialogue and dialectic, combine once more on the plane of history to give at last the fullness of the dimensions – dialogal and dialectical – of the kerygma. They are the dimensions of a dialogal and dialectical historical mediation where there is an interplay of the eschatological and the linear, the doxological and the objective, the personal and the material, the socially public and the pneumatically charismatic, the officially determined and the creatively free. All these elements of the kerygmatic event act and react on each other and are finally to "sublimate" all contradictions in a genuine harmony. Hence the kerygma is a reality which is at once its own subject and object in the medium which it itself is. It forms – in the metaphysical and in the historical and dialogal dimensions described above – a reality which mediates salvation and which understands itself as such. It sees its origin and its goal, its being and its purpose and thus its subject, object and medium – its whole nature as mediation – as given in the "word of Christ", its only possible ground.

It is understandable that the many dimensions of this dialogal and dialectical reality should have been approached on many levels and in different ways by the NT writers. And it is still more readily understood that the subsequent practical exercise of preaching in the history of the Church should always have been and be in danger of a one-sided self-understanding, not merely theologically, but with reference to its own life and origin. There is a tendency to simplify a gift and a task which is multi-dimensional. The act of preaching may be misunderstood. A one-sided emphasis may be laid on the act of preaching as merely the work of God. Its dimension of personal dialogue and pneumatic dynamism may be obscured by that of its merely factual occurrence. On the Protestant side, there is a tendency, on the public level, to an altruism centred on God in the preaching which may occasion a non-dialogical dualism. On the Catholic side, in modern times, there is a strong tendency towards an institutional and factual historicism. Such erroneous trends are numerous and could be verified in the history of the kerygma in the Church (and the Churches). Fundamentally, they coincide with the great public or cryptogram heresies or reflect them on the kerygmatic level.

The question of the nature and the reality of the kerygma has become much more acute today, when the preaching is faced with a situation which is becoming more and more difficult. And there are philosophical complications. Some are the heritage of German idealism, with its understanding of the constitutive contribution of consciousness to reality in general, which raised still more sharply the whole question of the possibility of revelation. Others arise from existentialism, with its view of the constitutive nature of concrete historical self-understanding for the understanding of reality in general. Finally, there are the questions raised by the historical criticism and exegetical discussion of a relentless biblical research. But all this has helped in fact to show the problem of the kerygma in its true light, since it now appears as the question of revelation in general, its historical mediation and its self-understanding in ecclesiastical, biblical and dogmatic contexts.

In this situation, where the Protestant preaching of the faith seemed to have reached an impasse, R. Bultmann sought to find an answer with the aid of existential philosophy, in an effort to do justice to the understanding of man and the world conditioned by present-day science and technology, and also to the demands of historical exegesis. His "existential interpretation" which undertook a systematic "demythologizing" of the NT, succeeded in fact in depriving revelation of its historical content. Revelation, as mediation of salvation, became essentially the summons given here and now in the actual preaching, the summons itself being the "Christ-event" which calls the hearer to decide in the act of faith. The consequences of this principle are not taken to their logical conclusion by Bultmann, and it is hard to say what precise theological meaning he attached to this "Christ-event" as the act of preaching. But it is certain that the kerygma is now given a very definitely central place, which involves a very definite theology of the kerygma. However, the complexity of the notion of kerygma, as propounded in the NT, is certainly deprived of its full dimension when the kerygma, as in Bultmann, is viewed merely as the event of the summons in the here and now of the preaching, since its mediated character, historical both dialogically and dialectically, is not sufficiently taken into account, and the material content of its traditional character also suffers.

But this theology of the kerygma has the merit of excluding an objectivating misunderstanding of the kerygma which would reduce the word of God and its mediation to a mere report supplying information about the past. The kerygma ceases to be the abstraction of mere narrative of the past as such, and appears emphatically as the event of the word of God, a salvific event of personal attestation, pneumatic dynamism and eschatological presence. But to arrive at this it was not necessary to exclude *a priori* the historical content of the NT and its transmission in the Church as unimportant or not part of the data. No doubt there is a dialectic in the public, social, official and institutional mediation of the kerygma-event, as there is in the apostolically authorized ecclesiastical form of its legitimation. In spite of authorization and legitimation from the official Church, the kerygma can be distorted and diminished by the preachers, not so much in the letter as in the spirit. But such possible tension cannot be obviated beforehand by simply excluding the historically objective and hence also official and institutional dimension of the kerygma. This dialectic is not set up for the first time by Church preaching in the wider sense. It has its origin in the initial commitment of the word of God to writing as sacred Scripture. This is a clear proof that the full understanding of the kerygma is ultimately dependent on the understanding of the incarnation and of revelation in general.

The discussion launched by Bultmann still goes on, even among Catholics. But if theological thinking is to make an advance in this sphere, it must first leave behind the ill-considered and inadequate contrast between "act and content" in the kerygma. To counter the revival of the "subject-object-transcendence" schema in existential philosophy, it must develop a dialogal theory of history of salvation which will throw more light on the historically objective as the medium of intersubjectivity and hence as medium of the history of salvation. Such a theory, embracing all the dimensions of the kerygmatic event, will at last be able to throw light on the glorified body as medium of the historical coming of salvation, and hence the significance of the glorified body for the kerygma. This would lead to a better understanding of the relationship of word and sacrament in the mediation of salvation and kerygma. Whatever form this dialectical theology of the history of salvation may take, Catholics will see the kerygma in the actual life of the Church as a mediation of salvation which takes place essentially in a sacramental event which is also the action of the word. Its supreme form is the liturgy, especially the celebration of the Eucharist in its framework of prayer, Scripture reading, exhortation and homily: the most real presence possible, in the "time of the Church", of the crucified and risen Lord and of the salvation of all in him.

Eberhard Simons

KNOWLEDGE

A. Knowledge as a Problem

1. *The self-acceptance of knowledge and of scepticism*. The question of the "nature" of knowledge, as posed in philosophy, is itself aimed at knowledge, that is, at knowledge about knowledge. If it is posed as a meaningful and rational question, it positively anticipates the possibility of knowledge, and accepts itself as knowledge and has thereby begun to give concrete reality to the nature of knowledge. To put the problem and solve it by denying that knowledge is possible in any identifiable sense is to pretend to know and understand what knowledge is, and at the same time use it to maintain that it does not exist, concluding that the problem of knowledge is not merely insoluble but non-existent. Hence absolute scepticism cancels itself out. Its intrinsic contradiction has been constantly proved against it in the course of the history of philosophy, in classical form by Augustine (*Contra Academicos*; *Soliloquium*, II, 1, no. 1; *De vera religione*, 39, no. 73; *De Civitate Dei*, XI, 26; *De Trinitate*, X, 10, no. 14; cf. Descartes, *Medita-*

tiones de Prima Philosophia; Kant, *Logik*, Introduction, X). The decision of the spirit to evade all effort to attain knowledge of reality does not lead to the concentrated repose of self-possession. It is the abdication and self-dissolution of the spirit. For the spirit would be unreal and futile if it did not know what really is and could not know its own existence and nature in such knowledge of reality.

But it is legitimate to be (relatively) sceptical with regard to particular forms of knowledge which claim in fact to be valid, and with regard to the self-analyses of these particular forms. Even in such analyses there is always the danger of not getting behind the naive claim to validity and testing it against its valid foundation. One could remain at the stage of naive reflection, where the theory of the validity of such acts of knowledge would be merely dogmatism. Hence it is legitimate to enquire into the particular structure of the various forms of knowledge, their relevant fields and the sources from which they derive their effectiveness. But all such questions are combined in the basic question as to the extent, nature and unifying origin of all knowledge qua knowledge.

2. *Epistemology as the logic of ontology.* Hence it would be just as absurd as absolute scepticism to seek even a positive solution from a standpoint outside knowledge, that is, "to try to know ... before one knows". "The examination of knowledge can only take place in acts of knowledge", as Hegel said, trenchantly underlining the fact that all questions about knowledge are themselves knowledge (*Enzyklopädie*, § 10, in the course of an objection, too severely framed to be sustainable, against the critical philosophy inaugurated by Kant). "Total absence of presuppositions" in the investigation of knowledge can only mean that the process presupposes nothing but knowledge itself (*ibid.*, § 78). It must admit such presuppositions as stem intrinsically from knowledge as such and its individual forms, and hence must be accepted by it as its own presuppositions. With this, Hegel has only said in his own way what Western philosophy has been aware of from the beginning: that the question of "what is" always included the question as to what knowledge itself was and what the spirit itself was in such knowledge of "what is".

It is true, however, that the question only became fully explicit and of primary interest when philosophy took its transcendental turn in modern times. The "ignorance" which Socrates and Plato put at the beginning of all knowledge, including philosophy and epistemology, does not mean that the mind is totally sundered from the reality which is to come to it in knowledge. It is the initial stage of this coming, as knowledge, the veiled but irrecusable presence of what is to be known: a dawning knowledge which is still ignorant, or an ignorance which is dawning knowledge. Later efforts of theories of knowledge to get behind all knowledge and try to see whether and how the "subject" supposed to be closed in on itself can emerge from the immanence of its "consciousness" and attain knowledge of an "object" transcending it (reality, being), are mistaken from the start. For spirit is by its very nature a thinking relationship (intentionality) to beings, the gathering-in (*logos*), the co-ordination (*cogitatio*), that which "takes in" beings and hence the most primordial "onto-logy". And it is of the nature of spirit to bring this ontological thought-relationship to beings out of the generality of thought into the determinateness of knowledge. But such knowledge, the determinate presence of beings and the determination of the spirit itself, could not be attained unless spirit of itself were with beings as the general presence of beings, if it were not being-with-beings. And this general being-with-beings which the spirit essentially is, as thought, would not be complete, if it did not arrive at itself, if it did not become knowledge of itself, since each determination it takes on is a degree of knowledge.

The two together – being something and at the same time having come to self-awareness – is metaphysically the supreme meaning of both being and spirit: truth as presence, and self-transparency, in the uttermost determinateness.

Thus the problem of knowledge, at its most radical, necessarily leads to the basic question of metaphysical ontology. The philosophical doctrine of knowledge proves to be the "logical" aspect of metaphysical ontology, the "logics" of ontology. And any given theory of knowledge which tries to present itself explicitly as non-ontological and anti-metaphysical is merely suppressing inherent implications of an ontology and metaphysics which are nonetheless amenable to explicitation.

3. *Formal logic and the real logic of epistemology.* If the philosophy of knowledge is basically the "logic" of ontology, it is a "material" or "real" logic in contradistinction to "formal" logic, which merely investigates the "formal rules" of all thought couched in propositions. Formal logic analyses the laws of "how" articulate thought connects its possible content – in the formation of concepts, judgments and conclusions – in order to be in harmony with itself, logically "true" or, rather, "correct". It prescinds from the concrete content of its thought, from the relationship of the proposition to "what" (elements of reality) should be comprehended. Thus a proposition may be correct in formal logic but not necessarily in accord with reality and hence not necessarily knowledge, for which it displays the indispensable conditions without being the adequate cause. Such logic considers the thought of the knower "one-sidedly", from its formal aspect, though with its own stringency.

Epistemology as material or real logic investigates the "conditions" for knowledge from the point of view of its concrete content, by which it is grasp of a real "something" if it is knowledge, and hence also comes under the conditions of the object known. But epistemology also obeys the laws of formal logic, not just spontaneously, but with the most rigorous attention. For the basic principles of propositions, which are abstracted by formal logic, are now interpreted in the sense in which they are "also" principles of being in things themselves. This identity is investigated as the ultimate source of the possibility of knowledge – the source which as formal is also real. And the logic which confines itself to the abstract, formal aspect of thought is likewise not merely logically accurate. It is knowledge, the real grasp of formal rules, the abstract aspect of all comprehension. As conscious reflection on itself, this logic is more than the thought on which it reflects. When formal logic is made to reflect comprehensively on itself, it must also explain the sense in which its rules are "given it", in what sense these formal laws "are there". In such reflection it ceases to be merely formal logic and becomes real, it is epistemology as metaphysical and ontological philosophy of knowledge. When formal logic, in the legitimate pursuit of assurance of accuracy, merely reflects one-sidedly on itself, that is, when it restricts itself once more to the formal and abstract aspect of the knowledge which it actually is, it begins a regressive process of self-formalizing and becomes a meta-logic etc. of itself.

4. *The primordial nature of epistemology and its link with historical tradition.* Epistemology, intent though it is on taking cognizance of its present object, is likewise orientated to its own historical past. Like all philosophy, it must

always begin anew, and still be mediated by tradition, since there are no fresh starts and new perspectives simply in immediate contact with the object. They must also be won through the critical examination and the transformative reception of the history of philosophy. Epistemology too has a general understanding of itself and its object, knowledge, from history, an understanding which it must accept or transform critically, but cannot simply skip. The supposedly fresh start from a zero unaffected by history is merely the naive concentration on a conceptual knowledge of which the traditional character is not recognized, and to which it remains willy-nilly tributary, merely by speaking of "knowledge", "philosophy of knowledge", "principles and methods of knowledge", or by contrasting abstract and concrete, subject and object, consciousness and reality and so on. Hence insight into the historical character of the philosophy of knowledge, of philosophy and of knowledge as such in all forms is part of epistemology today.

B. Nature and Forms of Knowledge

The basic self-understanding of knowledge, as investigated and explained in the metaphysics of knowledge and as maintained peremptorily throughout its history and its various interpretations, is the understanding of being and spirit as identical: τὸ γὰρ αὐτὸ νοεῖν ἐστίν τε καὶ εἶναι (Parmenides, Fr. 3; Diels-Kranz, *Fragmente der Vorsokratiker*, I [11th ed., 1964], p. 231); "cognoscens ens in actu est ipsum cognitum in actu" (Thomas Aquinas, *In Aristotelis librum de anima*, II, lect. XII; cf. Aristotle, *De anima*, III, 5; 430a, 20, τὸ δ' αὐτό ἐστιν ἡ κατ' ἐνέργειαν ἐπιστήμη τῷ πράγματι; "the conditions of the possibility of experience of objects are the conditions of the possibility of the objects of experience" (Kant, *Critique of Pure Reason*, B 137); "the real is the rational" (Hegel, *Philosophie des Rechts*, E. T.: *Philosophy of Right* [1942], preface).

It is the same with the basic divisions of the forms and degrees of knowledge. The particular historical forms of epistemology can be given their proper place in the history of metaphysics when we see what forms and degrees of knowledge obtained some predominance through them, or became patterns for the interpretation of knowledge in general. In the light of history, the anti-metaphysical epistemologies appear as fixations of a type of knowledge or of a partial moment of it, and sometimes as epistemologies which deny that knowledge can be meaningful in itself. Thus they deny that knowledge is simply the presence of the thing known to the knower and vice versa, that it consists of this common, reciprocal presence and is truth in, of and for itself. They try to have all possible knowledge, that is, actuation of presence and truth, referred to an end outside itself and measured by its adaptability to this end (as, for example, in pragmatism).

1. *Sensible knowledge, perception or experience in the strict sense*. Knowledge begins with its most obvious and everyday form, man endowed with sense-perception encountering consciously a concrete object, a being perceptible to the senses which is "outside" as something else. This is the perception of external data, or, since it is in a certain manner man himself, as a bodily being in his interiority, it is the perception of his "inner" state. This perception, the "external" and "inner experience" or sensible knowledge, is not simply bombardment by a disordered multiplicity of stimuli and hence the structureless reception of a chaotic mass of sensible data. Nor does such a process of reception of a mere multiplicity of elementary data precede temporally and objectively the perception as such and condition it, as the atomizing psychology of the 19th century supposed. If so,

perception would only be the aggregate of such elements combined according to certain laws which again would need repeated perceptions and the comparison of their similarities and dissimilarities before they could be recognized (associative psychology). But the multiplicity of sensible elements and the mere mass perception corresponding to it are in fact secondary abstractions from the one concrete act of perception and its object, which is immediately perceived as this or that in such and such a determined form. It is perceived as a "sensible thing" comprised by a unifying "spiritual" meaning; it is perceived *as* some thing (identical with this meaning).

No doubt such perceptions "as" this or that have different degrees of definiteness, attentiveness or "consciousness" in various acts in the course of human life. Particular objects of perception can stand out or recede among the field of perceptible things. But an isolated process of "mere" sense-perception is not an independent primary element of human perception. If it did occur, it would be a radical destruction of the human character of sense-perception. Even in infra-human, animal "perception" we must not suppose such feelings as primary processes to be taken in isolation. They must be supposed to be comprised and permeated by a prior "instinctive meaning" which is a factor of their constitution, given in the sense-structure of each different animal. In human perception too the encounters by which it is affected are mostly taken in their significance for the "sensual", instinctive life of man – as helpful or not towards a particular end serving the general maintenance and promotion of "vital" (biological) existence. But first of all, human perception can detach itself from the bond of this "vital structure" and concentrate its attention solely on the aspects of the thing perceived which are independent of its possible relationship to any particular sensual and instinctive complex. And secondly, in human intercourse with reality, even the "vital" relevance of what is encountered is based on a self-disclosure of what is encountered. It displays what it means in itself, prior to any vital relevance, which is, therefore, based on perception in the strict sense, as acceptance of the arrival itself as presence. For the setting-up of vital relationships in man is not an automatic and instinctive process. It is mediated and determined by this acceptance, which is the perception of a sensible arrival, but also of some thing significant in itself. ("Because the arrival is this and that and does such and such, it is suitable or useless for this or that purpose which I undertake.")

Perception as acceptance is not a merely "sensible" passivity, receptivity to impressions. It is also actuated by an active anticipation (spontaneity) with regard to this possibly significant something, by an outgoing expectation of a possible "nature" proper to the arrival itself. It is only by reason of this factor of expectation that the arrival can display itself as the presence of a determinate being in perception. If this active expectation of essential significance is understood and characterized as a moment of the spirit, then, in the one act of perception, the sensible and the spiritual are not to be considered as two ingredients which were once realities in themselves. They are such that they are what they are only in this reciprocal reference and their common and indivisible actuation. Just as that which is met with in perception is never totally indeterminate matter to which later a certain meaningful form can be imparted (εἶδος, μορφή, *forma*, significant content), but of itself is an informed and structured material thing; so too human sensibility is never a "pure" sensibility (only conceivable in the abstract and as a limit-concept) and never a purely instinctive and biologically determined sensibility. Of itself it is always "more" than instinctive or pure sensibility; it is "spiritual" sensibility. Hence men's instincts cannot be analysed merely by comparison with those of the brutes, but must further be seen in the setting of the "spiritualized" sense-perception of man, which likewise runs through his instinctive effort to survive and expand. In the same way, man as spirit is intrinsically and indissolubly a sensible being.

Hence the first act of his "spiritual sensibility" (or spirit in sense), perception, is at once the identification of "this" which arrives with its essential meaning ("what this is"), an identification which combines "in the consciousness" what is understood as occurring together in the thing perceived, in its "being", and which can be expressed in the perceptive apprehension. Hence too the process of knowledge always begins with perception, with this identification explicit in the apprehension, the σύνδεσις which claims to correspond to the σύνζεσις in the thing perceived itself and indeed to be "identical" with it. Hence reflection on knowledge implies ontological theses from the start (with regard to the structure of beings insofar as they are met with in perception and "as what" they are so met). And there are also anthropological theses (with regard to the structure of man as sense-spirit, insofar as he knows beings in perception and in what guise). When *Gestalt*-psychology, in opposition to the atomistic and associative (and their repercussions on epistemology) stressed the character of wholeness, form and significant content in human perception, and the meaningfulness of the objects of perception, it was really enriching once more the psychology of perception with an insight traditional in metaphysics from the start and which had always had to defend itself against similar objections and distortions, such as those of the atomist theories of antiquity and of later sensism.

The first traits of beings present to perception are their temporal and spatial ones. In view of what has been said, the spatial and temporal characteristics of the thing perceived are not just extrinsic properties adhering to a merely material aggregate object, or forms applied by a disparate, "abstract" sensibility in the subject, but constituent notes of the beings perceived and known, and modes of presence of the rational-sensible beings, men, who perceive and know. The critique of Kant distinguishes sharply between the faculties of receptive sensibility and spontaneous spirit (intellect, reason), though they only bring about perceptional knowledge in co-operation. For Kant, space and time are not significant forms of the spirit or understanding, but primarily only forms of the "mindless" receptive sensibility. Their "common root" with the spiritual must be divined, but remains unfathomable. In spite of this isolation and the obscurity of the supposed common ground, Kant considers the (spatio-temporal) combination (σύνδεσις) in sensibility as the effect of spirit (intellect) on sensibility (cf. *Critique of Pure Reason*, B 152).

Anthropologically, this separation and inexplicable relationship of spirit and sense in Kant means that man is treated as a spiritual and also sensible entity, while knowledge strictly speaking is only perceptive knowledge or is restricted to the reality of perception and to reflection on and explanation of the perception of reality (i.e., to theory). But the reality in question is not really the homeland of man, and the knowledge is not really a human act. And again, the essentials of man are confined to the spirit, which is an entirely non-sensible realm above and beyond sensibility. Indeed, the truly human act is spiritual representation devoid of sensible elements, and this realm of presence is man's true homeland. But it is a realm which is apart from the reality of things, and what comes to be present there is not knowledge in the strict ("theoretical") sense, but "only" in a practical sense.

Ontologically it follows that the beings met with in perception are not beings as they are in themselves ("the thing in itself"), but only as they are for the sentient subject: not that that makes them different beings, since they are the beings themselves, but only in their appearances (as phenomena). The phenomenon-reality of perception is not the essential reality, but the reality amenable to physics and mathematical sciences in spatio-temporal relationships. And the phenomenal (and hence knowable) spatial and temporal relationships of a being are not significant elements of its (unknowable) essence. Pre-critical (and likewise post-Kantian) metaphysical philosophy interpreted sensibility as a mode of being of spirit itself in the oneness of man, the perceptible appearance of a being as something belonging to what it was in itself, and spatio-temporal relationships as properties of its essence. They were "qualities" of the thing perceived which combined with other qualities to make up "what" it was and show how it was partly of the same nature as other beings and partly different. Hence the qualities, as moments and consequences of the essence, are "concepts" which, in perception, are attributed to what is met with as specific proprieties, constitutive of and consequent to its substantial nature, in which it coincides with other beings of the same nature. And they are also attributed to it as individual and changeable, and hence as "unessential" characteristics of its nature, differentiations by which it stands out from its class.

Hence perception is always the identification of what is met with with generalities already understood and known "in concepts". Nominalism and conceptualism treat these generalities as "mere" names and "pure" concepts. They are just convenient labels, individual or collective, to help one to master the multiplicity of things. But the concept is not something that appertains merely to the ("subjective") mind in a wrongly understood immanence, and the common essence is not something that appertains only to things in their wrongly understood transcendence. And hence if the concept is the "there-ness" of subject and object combined, the "presence in essence" of the knower and the known, the question now is how the essence is actuated in the concept and the concept in its essence. It is not only a matter of individual acts of perception, in which an arrival is perceived "as" this or that, identified with some generality already known. It is a matter of how this universal essence can become known, how this grasping of the essence is itself possible. The answer of empiricism (positivism) is that the so-called essence only exists through perception itself, that conceptual knowledge of essence only comes about as a consequence of perception and as perception in the comparison of perceptions. But all comparison of perceptions ultimately presupposes something that cannot be simply explained as perception.

2. *Experience in the wider sense and scientific experience*. Experience in the strict sense, individual perception or sensible knowledge, is the estimation of something that shows itself directly here and now, to the effect that it is and is thus and thus behaves. The estimation, which may be formulated in the percipient judgment, has the character of immediate certainty and validity, momentary and localized (in the individual subject) though it be. Hence it cannot be directly affected by another judgment, but only contradicted, modified or confirmed by further perceptions. The comparison of similarities and differences in a number of perceptions, the memory of past perceptions and the expectation of perceptions only now taking place or still to come, con-

stitute experience in the wider sense. It is not the knowledge that something met with is there, is just so and behaves just so, but knowledge of natures and rules of behaviour as they are interconnected in a whole realm of possible objects of the same or similar type. It can be formulated in a "judgment based on long experience". It has the character of a certainty transmitted by such a process of experience, of an assurance of consistency in significant relationships, results and patterns of behaviour. It provides a "pragmatically" adequate insight, since it alone guarantees realism and hence success in adapting to various ends what may and usually does happen in a given sphere. And this insight can be transmitted as a set of propositions, and even to a certain extent be taught to others, discussed and enlarged. In this sense we speak of practical professional knowledge, especially in handicrafts, of knowledge of men, experience of life and so on.

Based on experience in the strict and wider sense, but on a higher plane, there is the knowledge of scientific experience. It is not the immediate grasp of something "there" by grasping "how" it presents itself. It is not the necessarily somewhat naive acquaintanceship with the significant relationships and regular laws of a given field of possible objects of experience. It means knowing "why" these possible objects must so appear and behave, "how" they may be met with in individual perception and also referred to each other in general experience. Scientific knowledge is objective knowledge of causes and effects in their necessary links. Hence it is not merely possible and useful to formulate it as a judgment, but it presents itself expressly as a self-explaining judgment which is the justification of its strict scientific certainty and inter-subjective validity. This justification is twofold. It is the appeal to facts and ostensible causal connections which can be verified by repeated experiment. It is also – since even these experiences are comprehended in the judgment – an appeal to further judgment on which a scientific judgment is based. Just as the matter considered is in co-ordination with other matters, so too the scientific judgment is subsumed into a co-ordinated group of judgments, that is, into a "system" of scientific knowledge, the science of the subject in question. The facts of experience are not ascertained in the more or less random way of individual occurrences, and then linked together as in general experience. They are traced and arranged according to a planned perspective of research and expressly ascertained rules. Scientific knowledge is knowledge methodically gained. In the judgments of immediate perception and general experience, the concepts used for the characteristics considered are derived from the sense mainly expressed in ordinary language, and hence there is a wide variation in the meaning of the words used for them, because this vocabulary has to be able to meet all possible situations. But the meaning of scientific concepts and terms is strictly confined to the limited possibilities of the scientific field in question. The scientific judgment aims at the greatest possible clearness (univocity) of its concepts.

Even individual perception does not apprehend the whole nature of the beings it encounters with the same intensity as regards all their significant elements. It emphasizes this or that trait of the thing. So too in general experience in a given field. There is no comprehensive grasp of the common nature of possible occurrences in this field, but certain characteristic structural essentials are more strongly grasped than others. Scientific knowledge, on the other hand, confines itself from the start to a possible field of experience (the "material object"), which it envisages only in the perspective of a chosen set of characteristic notes and relationships. And this choice is strictly defined and unified from a certain aspect (the "formal object"). The scientist prescinds from all other possible traits of the material object, though such traits can be then taken as the formal objects of other sciences of the same material object. Thus the formal object of a science does not coincide with the "concrete" fullness of meaning in its object; and this means that even in the hypothesis of a completed science we should not have exhaustive knowledge of the "whole" essential meaning of its object. The self-restriction of a science to a definite section of the totality of meaning is what provides it with a clear set of concepts to work with, and with its specific method. Even if we suppose that all experimental knowledge has the same material object, the objects of possible perception, and that a plurality of material objects (scientific fields like "nature" and "history") only comes from a preliminary singling out of aspects ("formalizing") when, for instance, the object of perception is taken "as" having come about naturally or "as" having been produced by men in history: even then the sciences are fundamentally distinct, at least according to their formal objects (their basic interest) and hence in method and conceptual framework. Hence no method or mental frame can claim "universal validity": we cannot speak of *the* scientific method or mind. The effort to reduce all scientific method and concepts to one single type (the so-called monism of method and concept) would not be helpful. It would be the pruning away of possible knowledge to leave only one possibility, which would be to renounce the multiple access offered by knowledge to the richness of meaning of beings.

On the other hand, the fact that each science is restricted by its sectional formal intention to being "partial knowledge" does not mean that the mere sum of the findings of particular sciences or a subsequent systematic effort to combine them provides at once "total knowledge" of a field of scientific reality. An attempt, for instance, to integrate all historical disciplines into one general history does not furnish knowledge of "all" history and historical reality as a whole. So too with the natural sciences. This is not merely because, as in the case of history, the object of knowledge is not (yet) finally there, or because, in general, scientific findings can and must be expanded and are never rounded off. It is primarily because the aggregate and systematic combination of the formal objects, of natural science and history, for instance, never gives the full essence of nature and history, much less of "beings in their totality". Conscious experience, in the strict and wider sense, of nature and history, in spite of the different emphasis resulting from more or less accidental occurrences, in spite of its dependence on the various individual qualities of the multiplicity of reality and on the individual personal interests of the observers, is always "more" than scientific knowledge can present to the "inter-subjective" consciousness, even through an organized division of labour and its co-ordinated and definite acquisitions.

3. *Knowledge of essence and a priori knowledge*. Empirical knowledge, as it appears in the judgment, is the conceptual, generalized and permanent mode of presence of possible individual items (of the knower and the known) which enter and disappear from this presence. Empirical scientific knowledge gains its definite validity by doing its utmost to restrict its concepts to such significant moments as occur in strictly the same way in each experience, and hence can be verified by repetition of the experience. Hence this knowledge consists of the formation of concepts, insofar as it is the demarcation and clarification of concepts against the back-

ground of less restricted, more comprehensive, "more general" concepts. But it is not the pure and simple production of concepts. Empirical knowledge, especially in scientific experience, has also presuppositions which it recognizes but cannot work at with the concepts and methods of its own discipline – because knowledge of the suppositions cannot come in the same way as what is known on the basis of these presuppositions. These are "subjective" and "logical" as well as "objective" and "ontological". The more comprehensive concepts presupposed in all the restrictive judgments of scientific knowledge, especially the notion of a field of experience such as "nature" or "history", represent the mental horizon within which scientific knowledge works to form and combine concepts. But this mental horizon as such is not explained and interpreted in its totality by the science in question. The natural sciences, for instance, investigate what can be found in "nature" under various restricted aspects. But they do not investigate the more comprehensive notion of "nature" here presupposed. So too history of art is preoccupied with the events of the "history", but not with the notion of "artistic happening" as such. And all such self-limiting scientific knowledge proceeds with an inkling, a proleptic notion of what "knowledge" in general means, but is unable to explain the concept of "knowledge" in its full significance. On the contrary, it restricts it to certain determined processes of registering knowledge.

The self-understanding of conceptual knowledge includes the insight that the concepts do not merely mean themselves, but that they bring the beings referred to into the presence of knowledge, with regard to certain of their essential characteristics. So too the more general concepts in the presuppositions include, as present in consciousness, the integrating totality of the "essence" of the being in question (e.g., the "essence" of nature, of inanimate beings, of plants and animals, the "essence" of art, history and so on). This knowledge of essences and the formation of such "essential concepts" as are always presupposed in the conceptual knowledge of scientific experience, do not proceed in the same way as the formation of concepts within a science. And the general, necessary essence of a field of reality cannot be "objectively" ascertained in the same way as certain notes and proprieties comprised in the essence.

For Plato, the essence, the truly universal, was the noetic prototype (ἰδέα) which was represented in sensible beings by participation (μέδεξις) in the "form". But this essence ("form") was already contemplated by the knower's mind. Knowledge of the beings of sense-perception was therefore being reminded (ἀνάμνησις) of the original knowledge of their essence. Their encounter in perception was primarily only the occasion of re-possessing the already (we should say *a priori*) known and contemplated essence. In contrast to the Platonic tradition which presented knowledge of essence as "intuition", the Aristotelian and Thomistic tradition interprets it as "abstraction". The general essence is inserted into the individual things themselves and is really there. It can only be derived from them, by means of the encounter with concrete beings. Hence knowledge of essence is not *a priori* but completely *a posteriori*, a knowledge to be gained empirically, though it can only become explicit in an empirical approach which does not concentrate on this or that essential element in the beings in question, but remains perceptive and open for the essential unity of all the moments there encountered. A similar "experience of essence" is taught by Husserl in his *Phenomenology*, which, however, does not attribute the formation of the concept of the essence to abstraction, but, more in the Platonic tradition, to intuition, contemplation of essence and description of the essence contemplated. Husserl also developed the fundamental notion of a multiplicity of ontologies for various fields ("regional ontologies"). He spoke of sciences of the essence in contrast to the individual sciences at work within each realm of essence. But implicitly, in the experience of beings in everyday life and in the individual sciences, the experience of the essence common to such and such beings is included, being communicated in the experience of concrete beings, which is a factor in its genesis. And implicitly too, in all detailed conceptual knowledge of beings, the general essence which demarcates the realm of similar beings is included as a "horizon", which one may intend at least to turn into a concept, by means of an explicit "science of essence". This will not be in the nature of a particular science, but will be philosophical in type, method and concepts.

The essence is the "more general", in relation to beings in their individuality, and to this or that typical characteristic; and according to Aristotelian and Thomistic epistemology it is grasped by abstraction. But this does not mean that it is in all respects more meagre in content than beings in their real individuality, and that the concept of the essence is more "abstract" in the sense of being more one-sided than the concepts formed within the given horizon. On the contrary, the concept of the essence is more comprehensive, because less limited and less selective, and the essence is richer than any portion of the elements which it comprises.

Thus in all experimental and scientific knowledge essence and concept of essence of similar beings are present factors. They demarcate the "objective" field of knowledge and provide the "subjective" horizon of knowledge. But there is a further presupposition. Knowledge of essence is only possible and practicable by virtue of a "premonition" which reaches out beforehand to the highest modes of mutually exclusive being (self-sufficient being and contingent being; categories), and also to the highest modes of mutually inclusive being. These latter are aspects of what is one and the same, and import no differences, no division, into the multiplicity of beings (i.e., anything that is, any being, is one, something, good and valuable, etc., according to its degree of being; transcendentals). And in all this there is also the consciousness that the possible composition (σύνδεσις) of the moments of knowledge will be in accord with the composition of the moments of being in beings themselves. The "logical" laws of knowledge are at one with the law of being of beings, of the "ontic", in ontological identity.

The traditional metaphysics of knowledge understood the categories (and the concepts of essence within the categories) as univocal concepts, distinguished, however, from the concepts of essence ("empirical categories") by their character of being *a priori*. And only the (likewise *a priori*) transcendentals were regarded as analogous concepts, which did not apply to all beings in the same sense, but in keeping with their similarity which was also dissimilarity, spoke of them in various senses which were still not wholly distinct from one another. Now modern science consists of a number of disciplines, in which the individual science remains separate by virtue of its univocal set of concepts. But in spite of such differences, they are not entirely dissimilar in their categories of concepts and they remain connected. Indeed, it is only through what is common in the variety of their concepts that the common "marginal problems" as such can be investigated from different angles. Hence we have to ask whether and how the categorical concepts themselves are to be considered analogous: in an analogousness not simply of a uniform type, but "analogous" to that of the transcendentals. For instance, time and space mean different things for physics and for biology (here living-space and time lived), but still not something radically different. "Final causes" do not mean the same thing in biology and in scientific history, but they are not entirely unconnected.

Further, the traditional epistemology has accepted the number of *a priori*, though not empirical categories as fixed once and for all – though the number and enumeration of the categories has not in fact been entirely consistent throughout the history of the doctrine. Here too we must ask whether and how, in the course of human knowledge, new approaches may be opened (as for instance, undeniably, in the foundation of new independent scientific disciplines), and how new *a priori* concepts may be formed there. This is not irrational when one remembers that the *a priori* categorical concepts do not derive "from experience" – by abstraction – in the same way as the concepts of essence. And they are not formed in the same way as the empirical concepts of science within a horizon of essence, where their bearing is strictly limited, and where they can be repeatedly confirmed by (verifiable) "experience". From the point of view of their justification, the *a priori* categories, on the contrary, precede experience of essence and experience of concrete beings "as" this essence. They are, to use the terms of Kant (who, however, denied the experience of essence as a constitutive of concrete sensible-spiritual knowledge), "*a priori* conditions of possibility" of ordinary and scientifically verifiable experience. Nonetheless, just as we may speak of an "experience of essence" in contrast to experience of concrete perceptible beings, so too we may speak of "basic experiences of categories". Modern interpretations and developments of Aristotelian and Thomistic metaphysics and epistemology reject a rationalist view of being which takes it merely as the "primary concept", and hold that the *conceptus entis* only becomes possible and actual through a primordial experience (*conceptio*) of being and its self-deployment in the transcendental analogies. Hence we should look to an experience of the basic modes of being of the categories which gives rise to a conceptual knowledge of the *a priori* categories. The concept of "experience" itself proves to be not merely univocal but analogous, like that of knowledge, of method and of the concept itself in all "analogous concepts". Hence no one mode of knowledge, no one method or world of concepts, no science or type of science can claim to be exclusively valid.

In all knowledge that which is encountered is at once transcended to reach its essential notes, its essence which links it with similar beings, its *a priori* categorical structure and the truth that it is in fact a being in the variegated unity of its transcendental modes of being. Each degree of knowledge points of itself to the other gradated basic forms of knowledge and to the analogous unity of all forms of knowledge, though this unity cannot be expressed in a single act of knowledge, through any one method and in a concept of "higher" univocity which would comprise all analogy. (This in fact is what the "identity philosophy" of Hegel tried to carry out, treating knowledge, method [dialectic] and concept as the same, and identifying them with absolute "science", which had nothing but itself to bring into the presence of its knowledge – no "other", no beings and being prior to itself; science was both being and beings).

And at every degree of conceptual knowledge in the judgment it is also recognized that the σύνδεσις ("composition") in the judgment seeks to be the equivalence, the representation, that is, the presence of the σύνδεσις in the object of judgment itself. Knowledge is *adae-*

quetio rei et intellectus in the judgment, and the judgment is the true seat of knowledge because it is the "logical" concretion of the truth. But logical or mental truth is based on the truth given in experience. This is ontic truth since it is the disclosure of the beings met with and their general essence. It is ontological truth as the categories and transcendentals in which being is disclosed to the spirit, which knows because it experiences.

4. *The historicity of knowledge.* All knowledge is based on experience, *a posteriori*, ontic knowledge on the sensible perception of this or that individual being, *a priori*, ontological knowledge on the categorial and transcendental experience of essence and being. This raises a number of problems.

a) What being and its most primordial explicitation signify, the "meaning" of being and of its essential articulation is not on principle at once in the possession of the spirit in the act of knowledge. Knowledge of being and of essences in general is not simply the *de facto* explicitation of an implicit body of knowledge, of an immutable though mostly unarticulated deposit of consciousness – as in the metaphysics of consciousness in modern rationalism. The essential significance of being is something imparted to the spirit, and spirit is a participant in being. But this again does not imply a disclosure of being and a constitution of spirit which has taken place once and for all. Ontological knowledge is not just the more or less accurate re-enactment of a permanently identical (because always already actuated) grasp of being on the part of the human spirit – as in the participation theory of the classical metaphysics. The primordial event of truth, the illumination of spirit by being and the acceptance of being by spirit, is always a new "encounter", ontological "experience". But this means that ontological experience, like all experience, is temporal and historical in character, and indeed is so in a more primordial sense than any ontic experience. There is something more, therefore, than the ontic history of changeable beings and their various relationships, of the *de facto* and *a posteriori* and its "empirical" experience. This ontic history is itself based on an ontological history of the changing meaning of being and its most essential order, the history of the *de jure* and *a priori* and its "transempirical" experience. The fundamental history is that of the epochal changes of meaning of the "being" of beings in the totality, the world, and of the being of man in his changing world, his "time".

The unity of being and time was first considered by Hegel, who, however, could only treat the historical present as a necessary grade of being in an immanent dialectical system of development through which the Absolute became for itself what it had already always been in itself in an absolute past. This view ignored the precisely characteristic element of historical time – its non-deducibility from past moments, and its vulnerability to incalculable future happenings. The historico-temporal character of world-disclosing being and of world-knowing spirit then began to come to the fore in reflection on the basic elements of (narrative) history in the late 19th century (Ranke, Droysen) and in the theory of the human sciences (Dilthey), to receive its strictly philosophical emphasis from M. Heidegger. Since then the notion of the history and historicity of being and its truth, of the spirit and its knowledge, is unavoidable. It does not solve the problem, but it sets the terms of reference. The effort must now be to explain conceptually the experience of the historical consciousness which has come to the fore in a way which can no longer be ignored. It is now a matter of trying to understand the unconditional claim of being and truth on the spirit, and at the same time the historico-temporal conditioning and ever new and unique concrete form of this claim. It is a matter of seeing the connection between the tradition of the past and each new historical task set for the future. We cannot take up the historicist position which makes all bonds merely relative or indifferent and reduces history to a set of disconnected items. But neither can we relapse into a non-historical substance-and-accidents schema of nature and cosmos, where history can only be the accidental and indifferent recurrence of the realization of an inviolable and immutable substantial order.

b) All knowledge, including the ontologically conceptual, is based on experience, and first and last on the ontological experience of the truth of being and essence. But conceptual knowledge does not exist on its own. It is interwoven into a complex of basic acts, the living totality of the experience of truth. Conceptual knowledge, the "logical" crystallization of truth, is not the sole crystallization. Truth is also concrete in the moral act, in personal love, in the works of art, in the action of religious faith. The question then arises as to whether conceptual logical knowledge – in its scientific and philosophical as well as in its ordinary form – is not only not the sole form of knowledge, but not even the most perfect crystallization of knowledge. The perspective of this living historical experience and interpersonal consciousness may lead one to reject the priority of conceptual knowledge which has been maintained more or less explicitly since philosophy first took shape in the West. But the new perspective is not irrational or anti-intellectual and does not set up an opposition between conceptual "knowledge" and "life". It is an effort to do justice to the free and therefore more than conceptual decision of conscience in personal responsibility, to the work of art, to the word of the poet, to the symbol of religious faith. For none of these may be totally submitted to the norm of the concept and its crystallization of truth, as if ethics, the conceptual theory of moral action, was "truer" than this action itself, as if aesthetics and theology were "truer" than art and faith. This is the proper modesty of the concept, which is not master of truth and time but can be the servant of these fundamental modes of truth in their self-elucidation, and has constantly to renew its structures in their light. No doubt, the traditional priority of conceptual knowledge has reasserted its claims in modern times. The sciences are concentrated forms of it, and man's attitude to the world is predominantly an effort to master it by the concepts and weapons of scientific technology. The steady growth of the power of this knowledge to manipulate the individual elements of the world is as obvious as its bewilderment when trying to cope with existence as a whole.

Alois Halder

L

LAITY

The Layman in the Church

Since it is impossible to discuss here all the possible aspects of the word "laity", this article will confine itself in the first part to a survey of the mind of the Church on the subject, as it developed in the course of history. The second part will be an attempt to assess systematically the declarations of Vatican II on the laity. If the laity is to play its proper role in the Church, this will not be the result of pastoral encouragement and organizational measures. It depends above all on the mind of the Church, which again depends primarily on the theological self-understanding and self-realization of the Church.

A. Historical Survey

1. The NT speaks of the Church as a fellowship which is contrasted with the world by its special relationship to God through Jesus Christ. The members of this fellowship – called κλητοί, ἅγιοι, μαθηταί, ἀδελφοί – are singled out from the world and formed into a special "people" by the call which went forth in Christ (cf. 1 Pet 1:10). This people and all its members are given the epithets which were used in the OT to describe the special standing and holiness of the OT worship and its ministers: holy priesthood, priestly kingship, spiritual temple (cf. 1 Pet 2:9f.; 1 Cor 3:16f.; 2 Cor 6:16f.; Eph 2:19–22; Heb 10:21f.). The special character does not mean separation from the world, but holiness on behalf of the world and testimony to the world. The NT notes that there are differences within this people. They differ according to charisms (1 Cor 12:7; 14:26) and again according to authority: there are ministers (1 Cor 4:1; 2 Cor 3:6; 6:4), presidents (Rom 12:8; 1 Thess 5:12; Heb 13:7, 17, 24; Acts 13:1; 20:28), pastors (Eph 4:11), elders (Tit 1:5) and teachers (Acts 13:1; 1 Cor 12:28). Stress is laid on the fact that these special gifts and ministries serve to build up the community and are tributary to the community (cf. 1 Cor 12).

2. The primitive Church knew what it was to be a "little flock". Christians were the object of persecution, and individuals suffered martyrdom. The sense of being singled out and of being a closely-knit fellowship grew. Parallel to this came the sense of the special role of the hierarchy of the community as the reflection of divine order and as the representation of the authority of God and Christ. In the letter of Clement of Rome (*c.* 95) we meet then for the first time the term λαικός, applied to the ordinary faithful in contrast to the officials. The Latin translation *plebeius* then led to the

notion of the laity as the mass of the people with no special competence. This was due in part to the profane usage of the word, and chiefly to a change in mentality (Congar).

3. The further development in the Middle Ages was determined in the main by the various circumstances which brought about a gradual interweaving of the Church and civil society. The tension and opposition between the Church and the world was transferred to within the Church itself. The *spiritual* man, such as the monk, is contrasted with the man who is occupied with the things of this *world*. The contrast is not so much historical and eschatological as moral. The world of the Spirit finds itself opposed to the world of the flesh, which appears as a menace. Thus true Christianity appears above all as detachment from the world. The Church, the one stable factor in the upheavals of the barbarian invasions, has to take upon itself the burden of upholding the earthly and political order among the young nations. The mission of the Church is combined with political action in a very special way which had been hitherto foreign to Christian experience.

For the holders of office in the Church, this development brought with it an approximation to the monastic form of life, as in the matter of celibacy, while the Church hierarchy became a distinct sociological entity, with special dress and the tonsure, which had certain effects in civil law. The contrast of the worldly and the spiritual became an element distinguishing the ordinary faithful from the clergy.

Pastoral work in the Middle Ages paid special attention to the layman. The duties of his state in life were kept before his eyes, to help him to lead a Christian life within the world, though always in terms of a Christian ideal which was monastic in flavour. He was ἅγιος only in a metaphorical sense, by having a religious element in an otherwise neutral life. The great representative of the laity was the prince and the ruler, whose formation was taken very seriously, and whose work was regarded as real service of the Church, as may be seen from the rite of the consecration of kings. This dualism within the Church is clearly reflected in the changes which took place in the liturgy during the transition from antiquity to the Middle Ages. The action is carried on by the clergy, while the ordinary faithful are reduced to a community of "hearers". A veil is drawn between them and the mystery – as by the liturgical language, the canon of the Mass pronounced inaudibly, the rood-screen across the chancel, the decrease in the frequency of Holy Communion.

4. Humanism, the Reformation, and the French Revolution which ended the Middle Ages and brought in a new organization of the political world, the broadening of horizons in the ages of discoveries and the transition beyond the borders of the Christian West – these were the factors which produced the epoch of emancipation, when the world was set free from Church tutelage and became conscious of its own intrinsic value and autonomy. For the first time in the course of its history, the Church was confronted with the world in the full sense of the word: a world of incalculable dimensions, fully self-conscious, in which Christians were once more a little flock. The first reaction of the Church in this encounter was an intensification of its effort to assert and defend itself. The pastoral work of the 19th century was mainly organized with a view to maintaining little islands of the older Christendom within this new profane world. Relations between Church and State were envisaged from the point of view of defending the regions of freedom allotted to the Church, as in the Concordats. The layman, being regarded as an expert in this matter of dominating a more and more complicated world, was sought out and wel-

comed as a helper in these efforts. But his services to the Church had still to be distinguished – in keeping with a still medieval mentality – from the level of the ordinary Christian life. Solutions were found to explain his special relationship to the Church, but they were all clearly tentative: a mandate from the episcopacy, a combination of a worldly form of life with certain monastic ideals, Catholic Action and so on.

B. The Second Vatican Council

These transitional forms were, however, unavoidable stages in the development of an understanding of the Church which took the autonomy of the world more and more seriously and could not but have consequences in the ecclesiastical sphere. The tension Church-World begins to regain its eschatological component in the climate of historical thought, and loses its one-sided moral quality. The defensive mentality yields to a sense of the mission of the Church in the world. At the same time, the tension Church-World ceases to work so strongly with the Church: there is less sense of hard and fast lines being drawn between hierarchy and faithful, and less danger from clericalism and anticlericalism – which had not been without effects even within the Church. The laity have a new sense of their proper role in Church life. These new stirrings – which had not of course been equally marked in all parts of the Church – were recognized and ratified by the Second Vatican Council, which saw there the "unmistakable work of the Holy Spirit" and gave it expression in its teaching. The doctrine of Vatican II as a whole, and not merely in the sections which dealt expressly with the laity, provides a large number of important elements for the further development of a notion of the Church which gives the laity its due place.

1. Chapter ii of the Constitution on the Church develops, on the basis of 1 Pet 2:9–10, the doctrine of the unity of all members of the Church. This unity is founded on the common baptism, confirmation and call of all, and on their participation in the triple office of Christ. This unity is prior to all distinctions, as may be seen at once from the place allotted to this chapter in the constitution in the course of the discussion in the Council.

This people of God exists, however, in historical fact, as an articulated fellowship. There is the "common priesthood" of all the faithful – a clear allusion to the doctrine of the universal priesthood formulated in the Reformation, which had been constantly invoked as an argument against it in preconciliar discussions among Catholics. Then there is the "ministerial or hierarchical priesthood", distinct from the former in essence and not only in degree (*Lumen Gentium*, art. 10). This ecclesiastical ministry is "divinely established" (*ibid.*, art. 28).

Other distinctive elements are the special gifts of the Spirit, the charisms, which are distributed throughout the Church. They are signs that the people of God is animated by the one Spirit, but they differ in their concrete historical forms. Common also to these different gifts and offices is their function of service in the Church, by virtue of which the ordination of these various services to each other can be emphasized (as in arts. 7 and 10).

2. Chapter iv of the same constitution discusses the special place of the laity in the Church as a whole. This is the basis of the Decree on the Apostolate of the Laity. The layman is distinguished from the hierarchy and the religious state not by a lesser degree of participation in the Christian life, but by his position in the world, as is clear, for instance, from the description of the "layman" in *Lumen Gentium*, art. 31, and from the repeated stress on the calling and dignity common to all. But the Christian call is always a summons

to a "participation in the saving mission of the Church itself" (art. 33); the "right and duty to exercise the apostolate is common to all the faithful, both clergy and laity" (*Apostolicam Actuositatem*, art. 25). The call to the "apostolate" is given in baptism and confirmation, and not by a special mandate of the hierarchy which singles out some of the faithful from others. One may contrast the ironical notion of the "professional Catholic" or the unhelpful notion of the "militant Catholic" as occurring in certain countries. To describe this activity of the laity, the texts of the Council use the traditional expression "lay apostolate", though in a sense which departs so much from the original usage that it needs to be carefully explained, if the danger of restricting it to "spiritual co-operation" is to be avoided.

In view of these texts, the role of the laity cannot be based on a dualism of priests and faithful, or an opposition between the spiritual and the worldly. The Church as a whole is in the world, and not the laity exclusively. The laity is only "of the world" in a special way (*Lumen Gentium*, art. 33). The primary element must always be the one Christian quality which is common to all and the mission given to all. This is the framework within which the differences between the various services must be discussed.

Clergy and laity must rely on each other for help, if the common goal is to be attained. Hence the Council exhorts the pastors to humility, since they must remember that "they themselves were not meant by Christ to shoulder alone the entire saving mission of the Church toward the world" (*Lumen Gentium*, art. 30). The prerequisite for the fruitfulness of the work of the laity is their "living union with Christ", which means that they must go to the pastors who are the servants of the word and the ministers of the sacraments (*Apostolicam Actuositatem*, arts. 4, 28, 29). The laity must be receptive to the testimony of the religious state "that the world cannot be transfigured . . . without the spirit of the beatitudes" (*Lumen Gentium*, art. 31). In the light of this unity and mutual dependence, in the spirit of brotherhood (*ibid.*, art. 32), respecting each other's special gifts and talents and the freedom resulting therefrom (cf. *ibid.*, arts. 25, 37, where the duty of obedience incumbent on the laity is carefully circumscribed), Christians are to work out the various forms of organization in which the laity co-operate in the life and mission of the Church. The Council alludes to such forms in several places (cf. *Lumen Gentium*, art. 33; *Apostolicam Actuositatem*, arts. 15–27; *Christus Dominus* [on the bishops], arts. 10, 27; *Ad Gentes* [on the missions], art 21). But it refrains from giving detailed precepts and thus leaves Christians free to find solutions which can be adapted to varying circumstances. This does not mean of course that the line of least resistance should be taken, or that there should be uncritical efforts to follow out political models and slogans. Whatever the form of organization, it must do justice to the special constitution of the Church.

The sense of the unity of the people of God will depend to a great extent on the success of the reform of the liturgy. It envisages the "full, conscious and active participation of all the faithful", and its various stages – simplicity and intelligibility of the rites; use of the vernacular; sharing of the liturgical functions – are both spurs to development and a way of measuring how much has been attained or missed.

3. Another important element in forming the ecclesiastical consciousness of the laity is the delineation of their own proper mission. This was attempted by the Council on several occasions, though in the line of a description rather than that of a precise definition. The Council speaks, for instance,

of "the effective presence of the Church in the world"; of "testimony in faith, hope and love" – either through the laity's own words or through the preaching of the word of God in the work of evangelization; of the "ordering of temporal things"; of the "sanctification of the world". These indications are to be understood in the light of the relationship of the order of creation to the order of salvation. The missionary character of the Church is emphasized in the definition of the Church given at the beginning of *Lumen Gentium*, where it is described as the sacrament, that is, the sign and instrument for intimate union with God, and for the unity of all mankind (cf. art. 1). This definition is then elaborated according to its historical and eschatological aspects (art. 48) and in its cosmic dimensions (*Gaudium et Spes* [on the Church in the Modern World], art. 45; cf. also art. 39). This incarnational recapitulation of human effort and world history in Christ (in the light of Eph 1:10) rules out any dualism which would divide the two orders, juxtapose Church and world as if indifferent to each other, or blur the newly won vision of the unity of the Church. The Church cannot be divided into specialists for nature (the laity) and specialists for supernatural matters (the clergy). There is an implicit rejection of the "two-storey" theory of nature and grace which makes it clear that the activity of the laity in the world, as described above, is to be understood in the light of the history of salvation. The "ordering of temporal things" and the "testimony" or evangelization are not two distinct activities, but must take place at one and the same time in the same human effort. Only the rejection of such dualism will make it possible to give full effect to what the Council says about the laity's task in shaping the world (*Gaudium et Spes*, arts. 35, 43).

The unity of the two orders, however, is that of a common end and that of the divine plan of salvation. It is not an actual fact of the present time. Further, the convergence of the historical dynamism of mankind upon Christ is endangered by sin (*Gaudium et Spes*, arts. 37, 45). Hence the Council affirms the "rightful autonomy of earthly realities" (cf. *Gaudium et Spes*, art. 36). For Church and world are not identical, but penetrate one another in a mutual dialogue (*Gaudium et Spes*, art. 36). This imposes on the layman the special task of recognizing the true and peculiar nature of the world and of working together with the rest of men at its development (*ibid.*, art. 43). He is in conscience bound to bear the burden of the conflicts which are imposed upon him by his membership of both civil and ecclesiastical society (*Lumen Gentium*, art. 36; *Gaudium et Spes*, art. 43). He can expect help from his pastors, but not concrete solutions. For the Church is not tied to any particular form of civil society, and hence cannot allow itself to prescribe any models of political, economic or social order, just as it may not betray its mission by giving it the form of earthly sovereignty (*Gaudium et Spes*, art. 43). When Christians, in their judgment of a given earthly situation and the line of action to be adopted, reach their own independent solutions, "as happens frequently, and quite legitimately" (cf. *Gaudium et Spes*, art. 43), they are free to do so as far as the Church is concerned (*Lumen Gentium*, art. 37). Hence such terms as "the ordering of earthly things" and the "sanctification of the world", as used by the Council, need to be properly interpreted in the light of the normative force of revelation and the forces of salvation at work in the history of the worldly world. But they may not be interpreted in terms of any particular "Christian political programme" or "Christian social order" in the popular sense of such terms.

Ernst Niermann

LANGUAGE

The study of language is now fundamental to many of the human, and particularly the social, sciences. The causation of utterance and its functions (expression, evocation, reference, and so on); the respective situations of the speaker and the interpreter; the genetic or social origins of language-patterns; the socially restrictive or socially adaptive components, and the creative, communitarian or propagandist effects of language: these and other aspects of language-genesis and language-use are obvious elements (so it now seems) of any proficient assessment of the nature of symbolism and sign-systems, communication between persons or institutions, worship, and necessary propositions: to name only a few major elements of theological concern. The choice of a symbolic or expressive language adequate to conviction, to new human experience of that which is most worthwhile, and to knowledge or experience of God, is obviously central to religious choice and experience.

Theologians have looked to linguistic philosophers, and recently to linguisticians, for help in studying theological questions: this despite the generally known logical "oddness" of the language of systematic theology. To some extent, this is a process of refreshment, of clarification, perhaps because linguisticians contend that no effective examination of religious language is possible apart from an examination of language itself: in other words, religious language has to be studied as an aspect of language as a whole.

Awareness of the complexity and relatively undecided nature of linguistic discussion has tended to replace an initial euphoria among theologians newly conscious of the subtleties of the linguistic sub-disciplines: sociolinguistics, psycholinguistics, computational linguistics, metalinguistics and so on (each allowing new insights but inevitably new conundrums in the corresponding areas of theological investigation). Comparative stylistics and the use of the computer, for instance, seem to offer rich possibilities in establishing the authorship of literary (biblical and conciliar) texts and the dominant function at some time in the past of credal or catechetical documents. But in some cases the reformulation of existing theological problems in terms of language-theory does not solve them; instead the novelty and authority of a new scientific terminology make the theologian falsely confident; and the new discipline or language-game merely detaches him from the experiential context in which his question was first asked, and in which his religious decision was first evoked. If that situation was not essentially a *linguistic* situation, it can be quite futile (because inappropriate to the religious dimension in which he has always conceived of himself as working) if the theologian translates his concern and his questioning into the terminology proper to goal-indifferent and value-neutral linguisticians, psycho-linguisticians, and so on.

Sometimes a particular linguistic survey or statistic is seized on for (supposed) confirmation of a particular "conservative" or "radical" conception of man, or of man's relationship with God. Hence the generative grammar of Noam Chomsky could be thought (simplistically) to confirm an inherited but unassimilated Platonism or Jungianism ("pre-existent" but divinely endowed and unchanging "forms" or "archetypes" of the mind). Even though Chomsky declares: ". . . the processes by which the human mind achieved its present stage of complexity and its particular form of innate organization are a total mystery, as much as the analogous questions about the psychical or mental organization of any other complex organism," he also talks of the research in which he is engaged as probably bringing to light "a highly restrictive schematism that determines both the content of experience and the nature of the knowledge that arises from it, thus vindicating and elaborating some traditional thinking about problems of language and mind". Without a thorough grounding in and knowledge of the openness of the science, it is possible to shift from the notion of the principles of a universal determinative grammar to the notion of a universally determinative theological or ecclesiastical formula.

If study of the distinct nature of religious utterance and decision is not confused with study of the basic technics of all human utterance and capacity for decision, then linguistics can make a valuable contribution to theology. The language of religious or sectarian activity, of services and documents specific to a church or sect, or that language generally accepted as inducing or proper to religious experience, or a religious disposition, or religious emotion, can and should be examined with the categories of linguistic science in order to determine its appropriateness to context, or, more accurately, the half-hidden and extra-religious (political or social, dominative or submissive, and so on) suasions governing its use. An important verification process is that in which religious talk (and theological discourse) is judged by individual experience of typical human contexts as well as typical religious contexts.

Until theologians began to interest themselves in the generative grammar of Chomsky, the sociolinguistics of Basil Bernstein, the structural linguistics of de Saussure, the "efficacious tradition" of Gadamer, and so on, it was the logical positivism of the Vienna School, or the "language-games" of Wittgenstein, to which they turned for enlightenment about the basic rules of the common language of their talk and other forms of discourse, in order to discover if theological statements were "true to reality". That could mean accepting the notion that a propositional statement is the proper locus of meaning – a philosophic position rather than one proper to religious discourse. In addition the new interest in semiology (Roland Barthes) has tended to focus on the prime importance of codes rather than on language alone, and to stress the study of *signification*; even then ". . . it appears increasingly more difficult to conceive a system of images and objects whose signifieds can exist independently of language: to perceive what a substance signifies is inevitably to fall back on the individuation of a language: there is no meaning which is not designated, and the world of signifieds is none other than that of language" (Roland Barthes). And yet: "The language of a living religious faith is judged for syntactic adequacy by reference to internal language-norms. For Christians these language-norms are basically scripture and church traditions, creeds and authoritative declarations" (Frederick Ferré). It is also judged for mystery, poetry, satisfying profundity and glorious oddness: that "transcending of meaning" (Jean Ladrière) essentially characteristic of religious utterance. This kind of swing away from reductionism has been noticeable recently in theological discourse on language; there has been an increasing concern with uniquely deviant forms of religious discourse, those which are more like literary uses of language when they try to express profundity or to predict a harmony as yet unexperienced in its fulness and therefore to some considerable extent outside the discussion-net of ordinary language: "The wider the spectrum of language a man employs . . . the richer is the world in which he finds himself" (Van Buren). "Behold I make all things new."

J. Cumming

LAST THINGS

1. In religious language, especially in catechetical instruction, we find the term "the last things" (*novissima*) used to designate the realities which form the limit – or lie beyond the limit – separating time, history of salvation or loss and free acts from their definitive and eternal fulfilment. Hence the last things are the various partial aspects of the one total definitive state of man, as individual before God, as member of humanity and as mankind entire. This total, definitive state of history can be in the form of positive fulfilment or radical, final and permanent disaster. There are the personal aspects of death, particular judgment, beatific vision or hell (*D* 175, 530, 693, 983), as the final destiny of the individual. And there are the general aspects of the return of Christ in the parousia, the resurrection of the flesh, general judgment and kingdom of God, as the cosmic fulfilment of mankind. As the limit of history and as the fulfilment, there is a formal element common to these realities, in spite of their being so radically diverse as loss and salvation, so that they can be called the "last things". The term does not merely embrace disparate realities under the one formal concept of an abstract finality or fulfilment. For if the whole reality of creation forms a real unity in which each element has a relation to the whole and depends on the whole, this is also true of the fulfilment of this one totality.

2. The hermeneutical principles for the understanding of eschatological assertions, as the doctrine of the last things, are dealt with under the headings of *Eschatology*, *Afterlife*, *Millenarianism*.

3. If man is really a manifold reality – as for instance in the body-soul relationship – and is thus a unity in which each element of this manifold reality is determined by all the others, without being simply identical with them, the multiple ways in which tradition speaks of the last things cannot be simply and on principle reduced to one and the same "de-mythologized" meaning. Nonetheless, they cannot be clearly distinguished from one another. No assertion can be understood except in connection with the others, and even in their content they cannot be fully and neatly distinguished from each other. This becomes even more evident when one recalls that very great prudence is needed when speaking of the "time" of the "intermediate state", "between" particular and general judgment, beatific vision and resurrection of the flesh, beginning and end of purgatory. It is certain that this "interval" cannot be regarded as a continuation of time as we know it. This makes the definition of the relationships between the last things all the more difficult to attain. Is it right, for instance, to imagine that the particular judgment on a person who dies today is separated from the general judgment by a length of time which runs in this world from now to the end of history? If this is unthinkable, the relation between particular and general judgment is hardly capable of positive definition. It may be said that the particular or personal judgment is primarily concerned with the destiny of the individual insofar as he is not just an element in the collectivity of mankind. The general judgment speaks of the fact that mankind and its history, as a collective unity, comes under God's judgment. But one should not try to dovetail the two statements by attaching a positive definition of their meaning to two given points of the one system of temporal co-ordinates.

4. Since man already lives through Christ in an eschatological situation, the last things should not be regarded merely as future events which are only anticipated in thought. They are not just events to which man moves. They are already proleptically real in grace, in the yes or no to grace, in faith and

hope. In faith and hope the future judgment and salvation are already realized (Jn 5:24; 12:31; 16:8; contrast, for example, Heb 9:27; Rom 8:24, etc.). The Pneuma which transforms the lowliness of our fleshly existence is already given (Phil 3:21; Rom 8:23) and with him the resurrection has already taken place (Jn 5:25, 28, though not simply empirically, 2 Tim 2:18). The doctrine of the last things thus appears as the doctrine of an eschatological presence of the last things in the life of man. This is not to deny that the present does not exist except in the tension in which it aims at a future different from itself.

The doctrine of the last things has, therefore, relevance to society as well as to the individual and his private "interior" life. For Christians must seek to implant their eschatological hope (which can only bear ultimately on the last things) into the social structures of the world (Vatican II, *Lumen Gentium*, art. 35). This means that even in the social order the Christian cannot merely be "conservative", since his eschatological hope means that any given condition of things must be only of relative value in his eyes, and the same hope which gives the present its true proportions tries to manifest itself in the structures of human society. By his hope of the last things which God himself will bring about, the Christian is set free from the principalities and powers of this aeon (Rom 8:35–39). For he knows that even though he must feel their impact, they cannot, in the last resort, do him harm. And further, he knows that he can and must actively and creatively criticize them and try to transform them, even at the cost of his life.

5. As a rule, the description of the last things can easily appear rather pallid, giving the impression of a purely philosophical discussion. Unwittingly, they are presented as deductions from a philosophical doctrine of the immortality of the soul and of the freedom of man to make definitive decisions. The further elaborations added to this philosophical kernel then give the impression of merely embellishing it with elements of biblical imagery, in terms of the parousia, Antichrist, the resurrection of the flesh understood as that of the body. This can only be avoided by bringing the doctrine of the last things into connection with the relevant dogmatic treatises, more explicitly than is usually done. Thus death is or should be participation in the death of Christ. Judgment is the visible manifestation of the judgment – primarily acquittal – which took place in the cross of Christ (Jn 12:31f.; Rom 8:3; Gal 3:13, etc.). The consummation of the world is the disclosure of God's acceptance of the world in the incarnation of the Son of God. The doctrine of purgatory can only be made understandable by a profounder analysis of concupiscence and the punishment of sin. The parousia of Christ must be seen more clearly as the final stage of the one coming of Christ which began with the incarnation of the Word of God, continued with the descent of Christ into death (cf. Mt 12:40) and initiated in the resurrection and in the outpouring of the Spirit the transformation of the world. Hence the "return" of Christ is the arrival of all things at their destination in Christ.

Karl Rahner

LAW

I. Biblical

A. Old Testament

1. *The character of the Old Testament collections of laws.* As used to designate certain sections of the OT the term "law" is derived from the rendering of תורה by νόμος in the LXX and NT. Originally *torah* means direction and instruction in general. Thus it is found in the Wisdom literature in the sense of instruction given by elders (Prov 1:8; 6:20) and

sages. In the earlier strata of the Pentateuch the word occurs only in Exod 13:9; 16:4, passages which O. Eissfeldt assigns to the "Lay source" (Yahwist). This is already the *torah* of Yahweh. Hos 4:6; Jer 2:8; 18:18 are early passages which bear witness to the fact that this *torah* of God was entrusted to the lips of the priests, and thus contrasted with the knowledge bestowed by God, the counsel of the wise and the word of the prophets. According to Is 8:16, 20; 30:9 (cf. 1:10), on the other hand, the *torah* is the message of the prophets by which Israel must guide its actions. In Hos 8:12 *torah* already stands for written "commandments". But it is only in Deut that the designation becomes frequent, and here in fact it is used alike of individual precepts (Deut 17:11) and of Deut itself, which is referred to as the "book of the *torah*" (Deut 17:18f.; Jos 8:32).

In the Deuteronomist writings it is chiefly Deuteronomy itself which is designated by this term, but it can also be used quite generally of all that God has commanded. In the work of the Chronicler, the entire Pentateuch is designated as *torah* ("*torah* of God, *torah* of Moses, *torah*"). This usage is reflected in the division of Scripture into "law and prophets" found in the writings of later Judaism and in the NT. Thus *torah* originally signified an individual precept, then Deuteronomy, and finally all the writings attributed to Moses. Since over and above Deuteronomy the rest of the "collections of laws" in the OT were also regarded as binding and valid norms of behaviour, *torah* came to designate the totality of all the divine precepts in the Pentateuch (thus in 2 Chr, Neh, and certain of the psalms, cf. Ps 1). In particular the fact that this word is translated by νόμος in the LXX makes it clear that at this period the emphasis was laid upon the aspect of norm. These norms are to be found in the Pentateuch in the Book of the Covenant (Exod 21–23), Deut, the Holiness Code (Lev 17–26) and the ritual laws in P. These sections consist of collections of individual clauses of extremely varied origin incorporated in the narratives of Moses.

The distinction between apodictic and casuistic law was introduced by A. Alt, who maintained that there was a fundamental difference between the two. According to Alt apodictic clauses are those which contain a bare directive formulated for the most part in the negative and without any punitive sanctions attached (e.g., "Thou shalt not steal"). Casuistic clauses, however, are formulated as hypothetical cases with "if . . ." and with concrete legal decisions attached to them. According to Alt the apodictic clauses are typically divine law in Israel, for behind the phrase "Thou shalt . . ." stands the authority of Yahweh. By contrast the content of the casuistic clauses is to a large extent common to Israel and the surrounding peoples, and is derived from legal decisions. The distinction drawn here by Alt has on the whole proved too inflexible to fit the facts, and with regard to the origin of the apodictic clauses it has been shown to be questionable. The works of Rabast, Reventlow, Kilian and Feucht threw light upon the problems of literary criticism, and then Gerstenberger solved in a new way the problem of how the apodictic clauses originated. Taking as his starting-point the observation that these clauses are handed down in lists (sometimes as decalogues and duodecalogues), he found that the content of these clauses suggested they once comprised sage rules such as the fathers of the tribe handed down to their sons by way of instruction in the context of the clan (Lev 18:20 may be an allusion to this). The attribution of these to Yahweh would have been secondary.

A more far-reaching solution to this problem has been proposed by W. Richter: he suggests that the designation "apodictic", which is derived from the content, should be abandoned, and that in its place the designations "prohibitive" (negation with לא), "vetitive" (negation with אל) and "imperative" should be introduced. Richter has established parallels, often of considerable extent, between the content of the lists of "prohibitives" in the collections of laws and the "vetitives" contained in the Wisdom literature. From the aspect of the history of forms the "vetitives" belong to the sapiential exhortatory proverbs (*Mahnsprüche*) which are always accompanied by a motivating clause. In "prohibitives" such motivating clauses are always secondary. Both forms are expressions of an educational system in which those belonging to the upper classes, especially officials, were brought up. (This is to be deduced both from the content and from Egyptian parallels.) The "prohibitives" are collected into series on the basis of a common theme (persons who are sexually *taboo*, judges and judgment, commerce). This ethos would have applied to priests also. It is not law or justice that is in question here but an ethos which in the "prohibitives" is "applied to public and professional life" and "is intended to regulate behaviour in a circumscribed sphere of life". By contrast the "vetitives" of the Wisdom literature are more concerned with interior motivation and the formation of disposition and character. Thus the "prohibitives" of the classic decalogue also embody an ethos pertaining to a particular class. It is the free, male and property-owning Israelites that are envisaged.

Furthermore, we can plainly recognize how law and ethos are related in the decalogue: for the "prohibitives" of the decalogue precisely as "prohibitives" are not concerned with juridical practice. The crimes listed here are rather of a kind which cannot be brought home to the offender in the law-court, so that in order to prevent them the ethos has to be appealed to. Thus the ethos of the "prohibitives" blocks up a loophole at this point in the maintenance of social order which the juridical case-law is unable to cover.

The cultic procedures prescribed for individual crimes in the Priestly laws (6th–8th commandments) represent secondary developments. Secondary and subsequent also is the process by which the ethos of these decalogue "prohibitives" is made subordinate to the worship of Yahweh by the "prohibitives" which have been placed before the third commandment: in this way a new basis could be provided for the ethos. In later strata the earlier "prohibitives" are further developed by the addition of positive clauses (cf. the commandment to love one's neighbour in Lev 19:18 in the light of its context), and in the "imperatives" thus formed special value is attached to man's interior disposition and attitude. But even the casuistic clauses were not simply law from the start. If we take, for instance, the group of "if-thou" clauses established by Feucht, we can say with certainty that they are not intended to prescribe for particular cases, but were rather the expression of reform movements of a social and humanitarian kind. The special interest apparent in these clauses is also to be found in the prescriptions of the so-called "social" lists. What we have here are lists of exhortations to the upper classes and property-owners in order to make them treat the humbler classes (widows, orphans, strangers, day-labourers) justly, and to accord them due respect as members of society.

In terms of content exhortations of this kind are also to be found in the "collections of laws". But it is not until the preaching of the prophets that we find actual lists. (Here, therefore, is an important area in which the preaching of the prophets overlaps with the "legal" tradition contained in the Pentateuch.) This category is especially developed and extended from Ezra on. The opening and closing clauses contain, as a rule, general formulations concerning justice and judgment and the relationship to Yahweh. Each of these enumerations of rules of social conduct is a summary of what is demanded by Yahweh. A series of double catalogues in the Priestly tradition contain in the first section a list of social crimes, in the second a list of cultic ones. The fact that this category appears so frequently is due to the necessity of summing up ethical exhortations concerning social behaviour, which as such are often incapable of being enforced by law.

A special kind of legal clause is that characterized by the so-called מות יומת formulation ("Shall be put to death"), which probably did not intend to impose the death penalty, but merely constituted a special kind of curse. The death which is to overtake the perpetrator of the crime consists in the withdrawal of life by God. The criminal has fundamentally transgressed the rules of communal life and thereby has set himself outside the sphere of life bestowed and protected by Yahweh (cf. Lev 20:10 with the 6th commandment of the decalogue). It is not until post-exilic times that formal excommunication from the community in the form of the "ban" is found in the practice of the synagogue, at Qumran and in Christian circles.

In reality, therefore, only a minor part of what we describe as "law" really deserves to be called so. It is chiefly concerned with crimes against property, which are always formulated casuistically, and such crimes as are requited by fines or corporal punishment. The Priestly prescriptions regulate sacred matters in particular, which are envisaged as the decisive instruction delivered to Moses by Yahweh; for the dwelling of God in Israel and the manifestation of his glory commenced with the revelation at Sinai: "Thereby Yahweh drew near to Israel in a manner which made necessary the comprehensive cultic rules and safeguards" (von Rad, *Old Testament Theology*, I, p. 180).

Little light has yet been thrown on the manner in which these various clauses came to be combined, formed as they were from exhortations based on ethos in general, or on the ethos pertaining to a particular class, or deriving from writings envisaging particular occasions and circumstances, laws of property and cultic laws. The procedure is similar in all the collections and is often based on "catch-words", which have broken up older groupings. The two versions of the decalogue have a role of their own.

2. *The theological function of law in the Old Testament.* Probably none of the individual forms which have been mentioned bore originally any theological implications (although in particular cases they may have been theological in content). The theological element is located in the motivations and the framework of such clauses. Thus, for instance, the reference to the slavery in Egypt ("For you were a slave in the land of Egypt") is a motivation for clauses designed to protect slaves. This was the model for the motivations which contain references to the "stranger" (cf. Lev 19:34 with Lev 19:18 and Deut 12:12–15). The concluding formula, "I am Yahweh" set at the end of a list, which is probably intended to bear a meaning similar to that of Exod 20:2 (". . . who brought you out of the land of Egypt") is also an instance of the process of theologizing. Other motivations are, for instance, Deut 14:21: "For you are a people holy to Yahweh", or the classification as "an abomination to Yahweh". Deut imparts a deeper meaning to these motivations by the demand it lays upon men to love Yahweh with their whole hearts. But the most comprehensive way of subsuming the prescriptions under the Yahwistic faith was to bring them into connection with the event of Sinai and the person of Moses. Everything which could be described as a norm of behaviour is firmly anchored

here in the revelation of Sinai (in contrast to the prophets, who represent such demands as proceeding immediately from God in the present).

Appealing to Exod 20:2 von Rad offers the following interpretation of the process by which the laws were anchored in the Sinai revelation: "The proclamation of the divine will in law" is "like a net thrown over Israel", "the process by which it is made over to Yahweh as his own". This event the OT itself already interpreted as the establishment of the covenant (with the constituent elements: proclamation of the covenant prescriptions, establishment of the covenant, blessing and cursing). Israel understood these commandments as life-giving (Ezek 18:5–9), as a guarantee of the election, which is for Israel's own good (Deut 10:13), but not as a sort of ukase where all that mattered was the work of obedience as a human achievement. This view of the law, according to von Rad, is not found before the post-exilic development in which the law lost its function of service. As against this view, we may point to the parenetic elements, especially in Deut and the Holiness Code, which make the possession of land in particular dependent upon the fulfilment of the commandments.

From Ezra on the concept of *torah* or *nomos* undergoes a development in which it becomes the sum total of what the external onlooker might describe as the "Jewish religion". *Nomos* becomes identified with the Jewish way of life as a whole, which man abandons the moment he ceases to observe "the laws". D. Rössler showed that in the language of apocalyptic "law" is used in a comprehensive sense, and seldom defined in more concrete detail. The "law" does not merely regulate religious conduct, but is actually identical with it. This led at the start to a universalization of the law. It is seen as the order which is eternal, and which alone brings salvation, which was given to Israel as its light, and which gives it a central place among the peoples of the earth. And if this is true, then it was also contained in the basic plan of the world. It must already have been known to the patriarchs, and, in its minimum demands, even to the Gentiles. Thus the OT law becomes the eternal law written upon heavenly tables, which is identical with the natural law, and according to which even the course of the stars is directed. Another process, likewise arising from the universal meaning attached to *nomos*, results in a reduction of the contents of OT law, and it becomes identified to a large extent with social commandments in general (the writings of later Judaism, and, so far as Jewish, the *Testament of the Twelve Patriarchs*). This process by which the law becomes detached from the actual contents of the *torah* of Moses is also presupposed in the synoptic tradition, and wherever it is found possible to sum up the "law" in the "love of neighbour" or the "golden rule" (Mt 7:12), disregarding the cultic and legal elements of the OT. What is presupposed here is a concept of the law which includes only the worship of the one God, the social commandments and the combined Jewish and Greek catalogues of vices from Hellenistic Judaism.

B. New Testament

1. *The position of Jesus in regard to the law.* None of the gospels attributes Jesus' death to his attitude to the law. (According to Mark the causes of Jesus' death are the envy of the leaders of the people and the blasphemies attributed to Jesus.) Citations of the law are attributed to Jesus by the Synoptics: the two chief commandments, the social commandments of the decalogue in the pericope concerning the rich young man, the commandment to honour parents in Mk 7, Moses' commandment concerning divorce and the sixth commandment in the pericope on divorce, and the fifth and sixth commandments of the decalogue and a series of formu-

lations similar to commandments in the "antitheses" of the Sermon on the Mount. But they cannot be attributed to Jesus in this form. The first area which these interpretative citations are to be found in Mark is the secondary and anti-Jewish stratum of the Marcan controversies, which contains other citations from Scripture also directed against the Jews. Secondly it should be noticed that the formulation of the social commandments of the decalogue, together with the two commandments of love, is common to the Marcan tradition and to the popular theology of Hellenistic Judaism which precisely regarded this combination of decalogue and chief commandments as the most important part of the law (Philo).

In the formulation of the antitheses in the Sermon on the Mount this tension between the community and Judaism, which appears in the Marcan controversies, is intensified. The remnant of OT law which is regarded as still in force, and which is defended as Christian in the community against the Jews, is nothing else than the conservation of specific Jewish-Hellenistic or Jewish-apocalyptic positions of the 1st century. This finds expression in Mark and Luke in the fact that only the commandment of love and the social commandments of the decalogue have been retained, and in Matthew over and above this, in a concept of law which includes only social duties towards one's neighbour so that the law can actually be summed up in the golden rule. Again for Mark the reason for restricting the law to the commandment of love and the decalogue (for him no other commandments are in force) was the same peculiar concept of law characteristic of later Judaism, which only included duties towards one's neighbour. When this concept of law came into contact with apocalyptic traditions, these invariably had the effect of establishing a relationship between the duty of fulfilling the law and the judgment according to works: either the law must be fulfilled in such a way that a heavenly reward is obtained (antitheses 1,5 and 6), or a special act must be performed which went beyond mere fulfilment of the law, so that it was through this act that the heavenly reward would be obtained (Mk 10:17–21).

Apart from this conclusions are to be drawn concerning the attitude of Jesus: a) from the clauses concerning the preservation of purity which constitute the basis of the three earliest antitheses in the Sermon on the Mount. Of these Mt 5:28–32 constitutes an interpretation of the sixth commandment inserted into the actual clause itself, while Mt 5:34–37 constitutes a remote interpretation of the second commandment. Since these clauses can hardly have had their origin in Jewish or Hellenistic circles, they may be taken to approximate most closely, relatively speaking, to the actual message of Jesus himself. The clauses in Mt 5:28–32 are cast in the form of Wisdom teaching, and lay down that the impurity entailed in looking lustfully at a married woman or in marrying a divorced woman is so great that it constitutes a transgression of the sixth commandment. The ancient tradition of the purification of the temple might be adduced as evidence of the fact that an interiorized conception of purity of this sort is not strange or unprecedented in the preaching of Jesus. b) Conclusions can be drawn concerning the attitude of Jesus to the law on the basis of a series of individual logia which constitute the basis of the Marcan controversies (Mk 2:17a, 19, 27; 3:4b; 7:15; 10:9). The structure of these clauses is that of the Wisdom literature. Their mode of thought is clearly different from that of the cultic tradition, and they display a definite "realism". In the pericopes under consideration there are two elements: the actual maxims laid down and the questions which prompt them, and which are introduced and "framed" by references to some practice of the community. Now this practice of the community always reflects a considerably lower moral standard of behaviour than that prescribed in the maxim, so that the question as to what is permitted by the law envisages customs which are only slightly different from the practice of the Pharisees. But the reply to this question contained in the key clause of the pericope concerned is more universal in character, and goes far beyond what was initially envisaged. These pericopes, therefore, have to some extent been supplemented by secondary interpretations of the law. The basic maxims, however, which may be ascribed to Jesus himself, are distinguished by the fact that they convince the hearer by their compelling intrinsic logic, and not initially by reason of the authority of the Lord who utters them. Just as in the case of the Sabbath healings, it is not so much the law as such that is being called in question and re-evaluated. Rather, questions concerning the practice of religion in daily life are being answered with a definite measure of liberalism and an evaluation, which is emphatically unritual in character, of what is right for man. On the whole it was probably only because of the death of Jesus that a cleavage arose between the community and the Jews on the question of the law. The circle of the "Hellenists" in the primitive community upheld positions on the question of the law which must have been quite similar to those of Jewish Hellenism. These positions only became anti-Jewish when Judaism itself, in the course of the 1st century, withdrew more and more from these positions as the rabbinical view prevailed.

2. *The law in Paul.* In his conception of the law Paul shows close connections with the thought of later Judaism in two respects: where he has occasion to speak of the content of the law (Rom 13:8–10; Gal 5:14) he points to love of the neighbour as its essence and designates social commandments of the decalogue as its expression. Other commandments too could only be regarded as relevant here in that they are concerned with one's attitude to one's neighbour. Then, both Paul and Judaism see the law as an independent theological entity: according to the claim of those who submit to it, it is an independent way of salvation, in competition with faith in Jesus Christ. While Paul leaves untouched the social conception of the law upheld in Judaism, the salvific function of the law becomes a problem for his theology. It is axiomatic for him that salvation can be obtained only through faith in Jesus Christ, and this applies to Jews and Gentiles alike. Although the demands of the law (as understood by Paul) remain in force, and although man will one day be judged according to the works of love for his neighbour which he has performed, the law as a way of salvation must be excluded. Salvation consists in the justice of God, i.e., in the fulfilment of the promises made to the patriarchs. Whereas in Judaism justice is achieved by the fulfilment of the law, Paul goes back to the close connection of justice with faith in Gen 15:6 (Abraham) and, with the help of scriptural proofs, is able to show that the promises, and therefore their fulfilment also, are linked to this justification by faith. The law, therefore, as a way of salvation is excluded because those who observe it hope thereby to achieve righteousness, whereas Scripture demonstrates that righteousness is linked with faith. Law and faith (faith here being understood as faith in Jesus Christ) are made exclusive alternatives. Paul goes on to demonstrate that man could never have obtained righteousness by the way of the law, for no one (as Paul postulates) can fulfil it completely (Gal 3:10; 5:3; cf. 6:13). Hence all men come under the curse which is the penalty threatened in Deut 27:26. But Jesus alone can free man from this curse, for in him is promised the opposite of the curse, the blessing for all peoples already prom-

ised to Abraham. Man attains this blessing, however, only by faith and baptism, since it is by these that he puts on Jesus and is so identified with him, the seed of Abraham, that the promises given to this seed now apply also to all believers.

In order to safeguard the universality of redemption, Paul shows in Romans that the Gentiles like the Jews had sinned against the law, which must therefore have been known to them (Rom 1:18f.). Paul probably regards the law by which the Gentiles are to be judged as an interior norm which corresponds to the Mosaic law, and which, if actually expressed in words, would coincide with the Mosaic law. By the acts which they have committed against the law men have fallen into the realm of the *sarx*, sin and death. So long as they remain in this realm they will never be able to fulfil the law, for this belongs to the opposite realm of the Pneuma (Rom 7:14). It is only when man has been raised into the realm of the Pneuma that he can conform his actions to this "spiritual" law. Now man attains to this Pneuma through Jesus Christ, as the fulfilment of the promise. From the time of Adam until Christ the power of sin prevailed, activating the sphere of the *sarx*, and bringing the sinful works of the flesh to light (von Dülmen), so that the power of sin signified both the sinful act itself and also the state of bondage to sin, while law assisted sin to gain power and life (1 Cor 15:56). For with the advent of the law all became guilty of transgression. In contrast to sin, however, law is only destructive in its effects and function, not by nature. Sin avails of the law in order to kill. The law is the catalyst which reveals the ruinous and hopeless state of man. But when the curse of the law is concentrated upon Jesus he endures the penalty of death, and thereby sets aside the demand of the law. For this reason, and also because the law is no longer used to demonstrate the presence of sin, Christ is the end of the law. Henceforward by the gift of the Pneuma Christ makes possible a life in which the law is fulfilled. Christ, therefore, does not put an end to works of every kind, but only to those works which are the result of accepting the law as the way of salvation instead of faith in himself. The ἐν Χριστῷ brings the ἐν νόμῳ to an end. For just as the law was the decisive factor in the old dispensation, so Christ now becomes the decisive factor in the new aeon (von Dülmen). Paul regards love of the neighbour as summing up the whole of the law, yet at the same time includes it among the charismata. For him, therefore, the fulfilment of the law is a gift of the Pneuma.

At present the law only has a part to play in bringing out the obstinacy of the unbelieving section of Israel, which opens the way for the Gentiles to be taken into the community (Rom 9:11). Thus the law of Israel was bestowed for such a purpose and in such a manner so that its function in the history of salvation might contribute to the attainment of the promise by all.

3. *The law in the other New Testament writings*. In the Gospel of John, in contrast to Paul and the synoptics, the law is no longer regarded as a norm of action for the community. The requirement that men shall love one another, the new commandment (Jn 13:34f.), does in fact originally stem from Jewish tradition, but it is no longer connected with the authority of the law. Its sole basis is the work of Jesus. The possession of the law is confined to the Jews ("your law"). The law of Moses (which does not mean merely the Pentateuch: Jn 10:34) finds its most positive function in the fact that it bears witness to and promises Christ. Jn 1:17 presents the overall pattern: the law and Moses are contrasted with grace and truth and Jesus Christ, and thereby the imperfect revelation in the Jewish religion is contrasted with the revelation which comes

through Jesus (Grässer) (cf. 9:28). According to 19:7 Jesus has to die because of the law against blasphemy. Thus the law itself derives from an imperfect stage in revelation. The fact that it pointed to Jesus went unrecognized by the Jews, and it was used as an instrument against him.

The Letter of James presupposes the same late Jewish concept of the law as the synoptics and Paul. According to Jas 2:8–16 the command to love one's neighbour sums up the content of the law. It is the word of salvation which can save souls and is the royal and perfect law of liberty (1:21, 25; 2:8). The question may be left open as to whether the law has these characteristics because it is not merely an OT summary of individual prescriptions, and is to be applied by the individual freely according to the standard of love (Gutbrod), or whether it is simply a law which does not impose Judaism and circumcision. Ch. 2 is concerned not with the contrast between faith and law, but only with the manner in which faith and works are related to one another, which is also a problem for Paul.

The concept of law in the Letter to the Hebrews is similar to that in the Pauline letters inasmuch as the law, as a way of salvation, is set aside by the death of Jesus. Here, however, the law does not regulate the moral conduct of men, but is chiefly concerned with cultic and priestly precepts. The concept of law in Hebrews, therefore, has its origin in the Priestly tradition. The priesthood of Jesus is based not upon a law consisting of earthly commandment, but on the power of eternal life (7:16). Because it is only the high priest Jesus Christ who has brought true purification, the law of the OT was not able to achieve this; for the priests instituted by it were only mortal. It is not because man cannot fulfil it (Paul) that the law is incapable of causing salvation, but because only mortal men fulfil it (cf. Gutbrod). The priesthood of Christ in the form of the priesthood of Melchizedek had always been in competition with the Levitical priesthood according to the law (Heb 7).

Klaus Berger

II. Theology and Moral Theology

1. A consideration of the notion of law in moral theology must start with the moral law and then proceed to the other types of law. The laws of nature and positive laws then appear as deficient modes of the moral law. By laws of nature we understand a rule for what must be, which those subject to it must follow by an intrinsic necessity. By positive laws, those which are imposed on man from outside, we understand a rule for what ought to be, to which those subject to it freely adhere, according to the will of the law-giver. The free will of those who are bound in such a way is not subject to the law by intrinsic necessity but by reason of their own free decision or external compulsion. The moral law, on the other hand, is both a rule for what must be, which man obeys by an intrinsic necessity and also a rule for what ought to be, to which he freely adheres – though from a different aspect. Hence the moral law combines the perfections of the two types of law: accord with nature and free self-determination. For when he acts morally, man is subject to the claims of the moral law by an intrinsic necessity, since moral action is only possible on the supposition that something is recognized in one way or another as what absolutely ought to be, that is, as something to which he must freely take up an attitude. Thus, through the moral law, man is obliged to follow an order of things which alone makes free individual and social life possible and whose claim forces itself on the reason. On the other hand, he must freely take up an attitude to this necessarily recognized obligation, since he must himself freely decide whether he will bind his freedom

to the claim of what ought to be, or act contrary to what he recognizes as imperative. Thus he must himself decide on the order of things to which he is bound, and thus freely acknowledge it. The refusal of this acknowledgement is seen by theologians as the sin against the Holy Spirit (Mt 12:31ff. and parr.; Acts 7:51).

The moral law, however, points to the divine law-giver who establishes it, since the life endowed with reason and freedom according to the image and likeness of his orderly perfection (*lex aeterna*) is produced by him (*lex naturae rationalis*) and enriched with the dynamism of his free self-communication (*lex gratiae*).

Accordingly, the moral law is formally a necessary rule of free moral action, whose claim that man ought to do this or that is absolutely binding, but to whose content man can freely take up an attitude. The obligation imposed on the moral subject by an absolute ought is always an obligation imposed by God himself, whether it is recognized explicitly or only implicitly, since absolute obligation can come only through God, who binds men by granting an external and internal participation in his absolute perfection – the former by creation, the latter by grace – and hence concretely imparts himself. Man may only bind himself in the moral law to this communication of the divine law, insofar as he recognizes it explicitly or implicitly as the radiation of the divine "ought". This means that subjectively and in the concrete the content of the moral law is that which the moral subject recognizes in one way or another as what absolutely ought to be and hence implicitly or explicitly as the obligatory will of God, so that the subject is guilty of a moral failure if he does not respond to the known claim.

2. As regards the content of the moral law, it does not follow from what has been said that the content of what has been recognized by the moral subject as divine law is definitely willed by God, independently of the subjective decision and hence in this sense objectively. For what appears to man as obligatory moral law is infallibly at one with the divine order only from the formal aspect of absolute obligation to God. As regards the content, the contingence of man is such that under the appearance of accord with divine order there may in reality be a link with mortal disorder, by reason of error or sin. Hence, as regards content, there is only accord with the divine law when what appears to man subjectively as divinely established order is also such independently of his subjective opinion and thus corresponds objectively to the divinely established order of nature and grace.

This order of divine law, as Christians hold, consists of the self-realization of man by his living for his fellow-men and so for God. This involves observance of the known laws of nature and civilization which make the development of man possible, and which he must apply in such a way as to serve the development of the person as such, that is, the realization of love of God and of the neighbour. What this precisely means man may learn from the revelation proposed and interpreted by the Church and from the laws of nature and civilization as formulated by philosophy and the sciences according to their various stages. In this way, reason enlightened by faith has objective knowledge insofar as it measures the contribution of various actions to the perfection of the moral subject by using norms independent of the subject.

However, the channels through which revelation comes expresses the content of the divine law in a limited and conditioned way, imperfectly therefore, though sufficiently. Further, the laws of nature and of civilization can be influenced by men's free decisions and are also imperfectly known. Thus the content of the divine law which is incorporated in the natural and supernatural order is only accessible to men in a limited way. But though we may therefore speak of development and corrections in the knowledge and formulation of the content of the divine law, the content itself cannot change. But the subjective obligation towards this content can change, which means that there is a development of the moral law. For the moral law only exists insofar as it is known concretely and subjectively as binding, for freedom is only effectively under an obligation where it has to react existentially to an obligation imposed on it. But knowledge of these obligations is subject to constant change on account of our being involved in historical change and differs in the case of each individual according to the formation of his conscience.

3. As regards obligation, the following is to be noted. Since law always has two aspects which influence each other, the formal attitude of the person involved and the material content of the ordination of the moral subject to his fulfilment, it must be affirmed, both from the existential and the essential point of view, that the divine law obliges in analogous ways.

a) If the fulfilment of a concrete law is so necessary for the realization of the content of divine law, subjectively or objectively, that without it the order seen as the content of the divine law is essentially disturbed, then one is obliged *sub grave* to keep this law. If man offends in such a case, he takes, by the very fact of doing so, a fundamental decision against God, because he deliberately violates God's will which is recognized as essential.

b) If without the observance of a given concrete law the integral maintenance of the order in question is disturbed, one is obliged *sub leve*. An offence in such a case does not affect essentials and hence is not a fundamental decision against God.

c) If the observance of a given concrete law makes possible a more perfect fulfilment of the order of love, while the neglect of such a law (which in such cases is called a counsel or a work of supererogation) does not positively disturb the order of love, one is obliged only *sub perfectione*. One knows that to follow the counsel is to avail of an opportunity offered by God, but to fail to use the chance does not mean that one turns away from God.

Hence, contrary to the opinion of some modern theologians, it can scarcely be said that the notion of counsel or work of supererogation is confined to the order of essences, while in the concrete order one either sins or acts meritoriously. For it is impossible to consider the absolute claim of the "ought" apart from the content of the law. A prescribed action is formally God's law and existentially of obligation because and insofar as it is seen, from the point of view of its content, as divine law. But that which subjectively or objectively, *sub grave*, *sub leve* or *sub perfectione* appears formally as divine law, is only analogously divine law according to its content.

To sum up: God desires man to be freely his partner. He only judges him insofar as man judges himself by turning away from the one source of life or by turning towards it imperfectly. Once Christian existence has been established, it will to a considerable extent work out in a region where only a greater or less perfection is at stake, and not salvation or loss. The divine law (*lex aeterna*) consists of all that corresponds objectively to man's perfection. This obliges man insofar as it is recognized by him as the moral law. Hence the will of God is materially the divine law and formally the moral law. The communication of the divine law in the moral law takes place in the *lex divina supernaturalis* (*lex gratiae*) and the *lex naturalis* (the *lex naturae humanae rationalis*). The law of grace and the law of rational nature are formulated in concrete terms in the organs of revelation (*lex positiva divina*) and the rules of ethics (the *lex naturalis* formulated in the moral law). The divine law, as grasped existentially, is only rendered imperfectly here because apart from the reasons given above they also comprise it in a way which is independent of the subject, while, however, the existential dependence on the subject is essential to the *lex gratiae* and *naturae rationalis* in the concrete. It must be maintained, nevertheless, that at least the positive divine law interpreted by the Church by virtue of the assistance of the Holy Spirit always renders sufficiently the will of God. The moral law is inscribed subjectively in the conscience, which alone binds absolutely, because in it alone there ensues a direct confrontation with the will of God as grasped in the concrete.

4. It is only in this context that the question of the moral justification and the possible extent of positive human law can be asked, with regard both to ecclesiastical and civil law. The answer must be based on the truth that a human law obliges to obedience insofar as the human law-giver partakes of divine authority and represents it. How far this is true depends on the function to be exercised by the authority in question with regard to the persons entrusted to its charge when this function is exercised in the service of the good which it upholds by virtue of divine mandate. This means that human law is only morally justified insofar as the human law-givers exercise their specific function of service. Thus, for instance, the civil power may only make laws insofar as this is demanded by the common good of the citizens. This is also true, *mutatis mutandis*, of the Church, parents and so on. To determine whether there is justification for making a given law, and whether it is to be obeyed for moral reasons, it follows that objective criteria must be applied to the material contents of the law, to see whether it corresponds to the demands of the limited values to be upheld by the human authority. If this is the case, the law also binds morally.

Hence the theory of purely penal laws needs a certain modification. According to this theory, if the law-giver does not wish to bind in conscience, in the case of laws which are not absolutely necessary, the subject need only be ready to pay the penalty attached to a breach of the law. This theory does not take into account the fact that the human law-giver can never directly bind in conscience and that the indirect obligation in conscience stems exclusively from the intrinsic aptness of the law to attain its end – for the good reason that the moral obligation always derives formally from God and always derives, as regards the material content, from the objective aptness of the law with regard to its end. But the theory sees correctly the intrinsic importance of authority as such, in cases where respect for the law is not called for by intrinsic material reasons. And thus it affirms the obligation of being ready to suffer the penalties for breaches of the law, since the just dignity of authority cannot be preserved otherwise. For it is the objective intrinsic end and goal of human authority as such that has been opposed. This means that the human law-giver, if he is exercising his charge justly, always binds morally, indirectly, because he either makes apt regulations or exercises his office aptly. Only when the law is inept is the punishment of the justifiable violation of a legitimate but incorrect law unjust.

5. It is impossible to judge the aptness of human law merely on ethical principles. But from the point of view of morality (or politics) it is possible to decide, with the help of prudence, a) what value the law ought to serve in the concrete situation; b) what formal principles ought to be observed if a law is to be just, i.e., to serve the value in question with due regard for other relevant values; c) whether an order can

justly claim the character of a law. The canonical directives for the interpretation of the law (*CIC, normae generales*, especially can. 8–24) and the rules of jurisprudence comprise the detailed principles which are to be observed in judging universal laws.

The following points are to be noted with regard to all laws, whether universal laws or personal precepts: a) whether the law-giver is entitled and empowered by virtue of office and authority (jurisdiction) to make a given law, who precisely are affected by it, where and how long it is valid; b) what precisely is the content of the law, whether it has been regularly promulgated and how it is to be interpreted; c) whether the dispositions of the law correspond to the just end which the law-giver ought to serve, or whether it is dishonourable, unjust, superfluous, or impossible to fulfil; d) how important the commands of the law in question are for the maintenance and furthering of the order of things in question and hence how far it binds morally, by permission or prohibition, or again, how far there are grounds for exceptions, impediments, excusation or rejection, or how far a law ceases to exist or is invalidated. The objective criteria which are to be observed in the drafting of apt and hence morally justifiable laws are derived from experience. They correspond to the intrinsic demands of the matter in question as studied by the relevant scientific disciplines and are therefore unaffected by moral values. Neglect of these objective demands for aptness in practice must *eo ipso* be detrimental to the moral value which a law should promote, since a law is objectively just only by being of proper service to the value in question. Thus if a just law is to be drawn up, there is need both of a well-ordered moral or political will to serve the value in question, and also of expert experimental knowledge of the matter under legislative treatment. The synthesis of these two conditions always remains imperfect on account of our human imperfection.

6. It must therefore be noted that the moral law must always appear as in a state of tension and in a certain aloofness with regard to positive human law. This recognition of the "relativity" of human law, whose moral aims should often only be indirect, prevents its being overhastily charged with moral values and perhaps being transformed into something alien to its proper nature. It also makes it impossible to identify morality too hastily with positive law, which can never do more than reflect imperfectly the demands of morality. This clear distinction between morality and positive law opens up the possibility of showing the faithful that the claims of the divine law are not adequately met if one restricts oneself to positive laws. In this way the divine law appears as a force which is always working for the reform of human law. Thus the formulation of the moral law can be freed from the suspicion of being abused as moral coercion to help to establish or confirm earthly interests in power to which their claim is unjustifiable.

J. Heckel

LAW AND GOSPEL

A. State of the Question

1. *The practical problem.* The distinction between law and gospel helps us to define Christianity: it is regarded as the distinctive feature of the Christian faith as contrasted not only with Judaism but also with all pagan religions, with philosophy, ethics, and the like. Today, as in St. Paul's time, that distinction is still an important matter for the Church's mission and its relationship with the world; on it depends the Christian character of canon law, dogma, and moral teaching, which must hold a middle course between the opposite extremes of an antinomian spiritualism on the one hand and legalism on the

other. In short, it prevents Christianity becoming either secularism or Churchmanship.

2. *The historical problem.* The distinction between law and gospel derives from Jesus' denunciations of legalism in the Judaism of his day, his criticism of the pious people of his time, and St. Paul's struggles with Judaizing tendencies in the early Church which seem to him little different from the legalism of pagan (Gnostic) religion. Nevertheless the Church presently had to set its face against the dualism of Marcion, so that a synthesis emerged (a dialectical one, to be sure). Luther made the distinction between law and gospel the main theme of his theology, emphasizing the difference but never himself misinterpreting it in an antinomian sense. Calvin, on the other hand, stressed the facet of law in the gospel. Unfortunately the theme of law and gospel never became a major one in Catholic thought. The Council of Trent dealt only marginally with the doctrine of the Reformers on this point, emphasizing once more the harmony between the two elements. A reconsideration of the matter in the light of Scripture and tradition is greatly needed.

B. The Doctrine

1. Law in this context does not mean human law, designed to secure the common good, but the disclosure of God's will by the natural law he has written in the hearts of the Gentiles (Rom 2:15f.) and by the word of revelation in the history of salvation. In the OT this law, regarded as a token of election, is seen in the context of God's promised salvation. Christ himself acknowledges the law (Mt 5:17), restores it (Mt 5:31–42; 19:8), indeed radicalizes it (Mt 5:20); and Paul says that it is just, good, and holy (Rom 7:12, 16). Law, then, does not necessarily mean human regulations. Only in Judaism did it harden into a self-assertive, legalistic human system, interposing itself between God and man and leading to the idea of righteousness by the law.

This attitude, which may be found in any age, takes God's will not too much but too little to heart, confining it to set commandments in which casuistry then finds convenient loopholes. Above all, such righteousness wholly mistakes man's position before God, assuming that it is possible to "reckon" with the Almighty (Greek νομίζειν θεούς). This is how the law provides an opportunity for sin, which kills (Rom 7: 10ff.). Under a law that he cannot observe, sinful man becomes aware of his impotence. So the task-master law is pointing on to Christ (Gal 3:24).

Natural law, as well as the law of the OT, can be thus misinterpreted, in which case it turns into "principalities and powers" that hold men in bondage. We find this kind of law where people are enslaved under abstract laws by institutions, principles, or ossified traditions instead of responding to the personal will of God. From the theological point of view, law can only be rightly understood in relation to the promise of grace as fellowship with God. Of its nature, then, law is ordered to the gospel.

2. For Scripture, the gospel is not primarily a doctrine to be believed, much less a new law, nor again a purely inward law of grace as contrasted with external law. Rather it is the proclamation of God's kingship which has dawned eschatologically in Christ and demands men's radical obedience. Since the gospel is essentially a personal summons, the antithesis of "law and grace" does not quite express our theme. It is from this point of view, too, that we must understand Jesus' criticism of the law: a man's salvation does not depend on his attitude towards the law but on his attitude towards the person and word of Christ. Accordingly, St. Paul does not contrast law with grace, but the works of the law with hearing in faith (Rom 10:17). Such faith has noth-

ing to do with a desire to excel in observance of the law; it is an unconditional surrender of self to the dominion of God in Christ, who has fulfilled the law for us once and for all. That is why the law is not a means to human salvation.

Scripture itself, however, condemns misinterpretation of the gospel in an antinomian sense. Far from annulling God's will, the gospel makes it more peremptory; only now that will no longer addresses men from without, it is written upon their hearts (Jer 31:31ff.); the imperative follows from the indicative, from our status as sons of God. Faith works through love (Gal 5:6). Thus we are no longer under the law, but in the law: we are ἔννομοι Χριστοῦ (1 Cor 9:21). Only in this analogous sense can we speak of the law of Christ, of Christ as a law-giver (*D* 1571). Accordingly, the dictum that the gospel abolishes the ceremonial and judicial law of the OT, but not its moral law, is an inadequate attempt to express the fact that under the Christian dispensation law (even the moral law) retains only an analogous validity.

If the gospel reveals a God who always transcends any idea we have of him, then he must also be more demanding than we can ever imagine; man is always an unprofitable servant (Lk 17:10), in concrete reality always both just and a sinner. God's will, then, cannot be objectified and defined: dogma is not "the" word of God, canon law is not justice itself, office is not the Spirit. Law no longer sets a fixed goal of achievement which can be attained by fulfilling it. It is a summons (parenesis) towards a point which always lies beyond our grasp, a call to perfect love with our whole heart and soul, as in the Sermon on the Mount. The function of law is to show how serious a matter is faith, to embody faith in concrete form as a safeguard against sentimental enthusiasms.

3. Within history, as we have seen, law and gospel are permanently balanced against each other in a tension that is not to be resolved in any higher synthesis.

a) We must not conceive of law and the gospel primarily as two eras of the history of salvation, nor as two different kinds of divine revelation (sometimes a temptation for Protestants). In the OT as in the NT, law and gospel are always elements of the one word of God, though their mutual relation is always a dialectical one: "Lex data est ut gratia quaeretur, gratia data est ut lex impleretur" (St. Augustine). Grace fulfils the law in such a way as to deprive it of its legal character.

b) The *primum in intentione* is the gospel of grace, as Karl Barth in particular has forcefully reminded us. This means that not only the OT but also creation itself is ordained to Christ; that the foundations of the State and of human culture are Christological. On the other hand the gospel remains transcendent: by showing us that law is "mere" law the gospel strips the world of its numinous character, of its pretensions to divinity. Thus it comes about that the distinction between law and gospel preserves the specific nature of both Christianity and the world and their ordination to each other.

c) Law and the gospel, however, also stand in historical relation to each other; the history of salvation advances from the law to the gospel.

No doubt the OT too is gospel, but its promise may mean either judgment or grace. No doubt the NT too is law (analogously) but it is a law that has yielded to grace – a verdict of death and condemnation that has been quashed. Thus the distinction between law and gospel points on to the ever greater mystery of God and the full revelation of God's kingdom, one only to be looked for at the last day, when there will no longer be any need of an external law (Rev 21:23; 22:5).

Walter Kasper

LIBERALISM AND LIBERAL THEOLOGY

A. Origins and Social Meaning of Liberalism (19th Century)

Liberalism, which dominated much of the thought and social endeavour of European middle-class life in the 19th century, stemmed in the main from the great spiritual impulses of the 17th century which are only partly comprised by the Enlightenment and the French Revolution. There was the broader, more general recognition that freedom gave man the chance and the task of self-determination, while this responsible "self" on which so much depended was chiefly if not exclusively "reason". The dominant note was the rational, analytical insight into all factors of life from the laws of nature to morality. This epoch-making view of freedom and reason was really first developed by Spinoza and Leibniz, who took up the thought of Descartes. Philosophy became basically an experience of the self which prescinded from all material reality. The self was a sort of otherworldly *a priori* reality which was to be regained from the world of objects and then be set free to follow its own autonomous laws of thought. In this way it was to re-discover all reality for itself and re-build it anew. This "egological" principle set social philosophy the task of explaining the possibility and the norms of intersubjective unity in the light of the same immanent laws and needs of the Ego. The political and legal theorists of the epoch started from here to set up a liberalistic individualism which could only see society as a secondary contract entered into freely and all social authority as strictly subordinated to the rational autonomy of the individual. This notion of freedom did not remain confined to the professional philosophers. It was already at work in the "Declaration of Rights" of 1689 and the growing influence of the Whigs in England, in the American constitution of 1787 and very decisively in the French Revolution. It may be said to have been one of the main factors in social history and must be presupposed in all analyses of modern social thinking.

The new wave of humanism and the Romantic Movement of the beginning of the 19th century saw things differently. They recognized that where "reason" was set up as the only valid judge, it readily degenerated into an alien and stifling domination of a really much more complex individual. The ideal of freedom was retained, of course, as inviolable, but less stress was laid on finding the truth of the authentic self in the reason. It was replaced by the notion that life should be lived to the full. The many sides of personality, now seen to be highly complicated, were to be freely developed, almost to the limits of anarchy. There was a "pre-established harmony" which would enable men who gave their individualities free rein in this way to do justice to their real selves and hence be free. It was this notion of "liberty" which dominated all realms of social life as the ideal in the liberalism of the 19th century.

An important consequence of this notion of liberty as regards social practice was the separation which now ensued between State and society. In the new relationships now set up, civil society was regarded as the more or less mechanical coupling between self-centred individuals who lived only for themselves. In this marvellous play of forces of a totally unrestricted *laissez faire* which automatically ensured fair shares for all, the State had merely to be a sort of "night watchman", ready to intervene if the process of social development was menaced. The State was regarded merely as a secondary function of social aggregation and was to regard itself as such, not claiming legitimacy from a higher authority of a questionable nature, but relying on the automatic conjunction of the wills of the individuals in a freely elected parliament. This upheaval in social thinking, and consequently, in political and economic practice (the latter based on the theories of Adam Smith and similar liberals) eventually brought to light the intrinsic tensions of the liberal notion of freedom. How could the claim to be free from State interference be reconciled with equal freedom for all? The older liberalism found itself in conflict with the democratic theory which it had itself to some extent fathered. This democratic theory sought for the benefits of social order not from the very dubious workings of spontaneous free wills, in harmony without a tuner, but from the State. Social organization was to be assured through political institutions on an egalitarian electoral basis. But the real conflict came with socialism, which extended the egalitarian system of democracy to take economic life as well.

The relationship between the Church and a society which was gradually "liberalizing" itself in the sense described above took on various forms. In Protestantism especially, but also in the Catholic lands, movements arose within the Churches to shake off all tutelage of believers by the State or by a quasi-statutory hierarchy. This was a corollary of the general political reaction against the omnipresence of civil authority. There were a number of emancipation movements, mostly in connection with liberalism in theology (see below). In France at the beginning of the century there was the mostly lay movement grouped around the periodical *L'avenir*, and at the end of the century *Le Sillon*. In German-speaking countries there were the "Eos" group in Munich, the "Protestant Union" of 1863, the Swiss "Union for Free Christianity", and also the "Protestant Friends" who had been forced out of their Church by disciplinary measures. In Italy there was the "Democrazia Cristiana" of Romolo Murri.

But then, in the second place, since the Churches often identified themselves with the reactionary forces in politics, the opposition of liberalism to alien authorities was also and indeed above all directed against the political and social potentiality of the Christian Churches. Liberalism became the demand for the total restriction of religious life to the private sphere. Finally, the State itself, especially in the Catholic countries where liberalism had come to power against clerical conservative opposition, took forcible or even violent measures to restrict the social influence of the Church. So, for instance, in Latin America, especially Mexico, in southern Europe and in another way in Germany, in the *Kulturkampf* of Bismarck.

Within the Catholic Church, all demands for liberalization, for the separation, for instance, of Church and State and for a withdrawal of the Church from political life were met by sharp opposition from Rome. Gregory XVI in the encyclical *Mirari Vos* (1832), Pius IX in the *Syllabus* (1864), Leo XIII above all in *Libertas Praestantissimum* (1888) and Pius X in *Lamentabili* (1907) condemned liberalism as the effort of civil society to set itself free of the authority of God which was embodied in the Church. It is only in the present day that the *de facto* development of society has brought about a change in the attitude of authority. The Church is gradually beginning to reconsider its role in society, and to see its specific task less as a doctrinaire guidance of society, either inside or outside of the Church. Here there seem to be the beginnings of a tangible liberalization of Church life.

B. Liberal Theology

With the coming of liberalism, then, a notion of liberty which was basically individualistic penetrated all civil society in the 19th century. Theologians were inevitably confronted with the problems arising from this liberalistic individualism. How could Christianity be justified, not just rationally, as on the whole intellectually satisfying and useful to the common good, but in face of the Ego of freedom which saw itself as absolutely free and comprehensively responsible?

1. In Protestantism, Schleiermacher (d. 1834) worked out what was to be the decisive way of seeing the problem for a whole century of liberalism. He placed the Christian faith within the framework of the transcendental philosophy which understood reality as primordially "spiritual" or determined by the consciousness – and hence as the reality of freedom. Applied to theology this new philosophical approach meant that it too should not seek understanding in an effort to rationalize subsequently a rigid positive fact. All understanding must be "genetic", a dissolution of facts back to their transcendental conditions of possibility and constitutive elements. These include the concrete and historical as well as the *a priori*, and aim at the primary origin of consciousness and reality. From this point of view, Schleiermacher investigates the Christian faith, not primarily as it appears historically and objectively in its contents (*fides quae creditur*) but as the *fides qua creditur* which contains the former as its objective counterpart. The question now is: What is the real situation of the *fides qua?* How can it be genetically exhibited in the light of freedom as the primordial and normative disclosure of meaning?

The origin of "faith" – in the verbal sense – appears to Schleiermacher as the wholly personal "feeling of absolute dependence". Feeling here is not taken psychologically as a mere mental state. It is the immediate and irrefutable self-presentation of existence, with the claim of transcendental experience involved. On these principles, the articulation of faith as doctrine can only be the conceptual self-interpretation of the subject in the light of his truth-disclosing "feeling". And hence theology must take the same view of the faith of the Church as presented in Scripture and doctrinal tradition. When then dogmatic theology still normally speaks of the believing Ego, the world as seen in the light of faith and the "divine attributes" as apparently distinct realities, this can only be legitimate when Christian faith is reabsorbed into the act of self-consciousness as consciousness of God. But then we have the acute problem of how to reconcile this luminous inwardness with the historical person of Jesus as the Christ "outside" us. (The orthodox viewpoint is that it is only in and through Jesus that the relationship to God is possible which Schleiermacher affirms is directly realized in the "pious consciousness" itself.) It is the problem of what Lessing called the "troublesome gap" between eternal truths of reason and contingent truths of history. Schleiermacher's solution was to give the theological significance of Jesus a drastically new interpretation. "The redeemer . . . is like all other men, by virtue of the identity of human nature, but differs from all others by the persistent force of his consciousness of God, which was a true existence of God in him" (*The Christian Faith*, para. 94). For this reason, the "ecclesiastical formulations" concerning the person of Christ are to be constantly revised in a critical spirit. Jesus is redeemer and mediator insofar as he is the supreme model who stimulates, impels and guides men, in repentance and conversion, to self-knowledge as knowledge of God. "The redeemer imparts to believers the force of his own consciousness of God. This is his redemptive activity" (*ibid.*, para. 100).

2. With this interpretation of Christianity, the 19th century was faced with the systematic problem, at its most acute, of reconciling self-understanding (as self-justificatory) with the mediatorship of Jesus. And the way was also paved for the effort which liberal theology then saw to be its real task, and where in fact it was to make its most

important contributions: the critical investigation of the historical sources of the Christian faith. This effort took three forms.

First there was the critical research into the texts, for which the way had been prepared by the similar projects of rationalism (J. S. Semler, d. 1791). Text-criticism was inspired now by the transcendental approach, which sought to reduce the whole of Christian revelation to the perspicuousness of the "pious consciousness". Thus it had a theological function, inasmuch as it broke down the resistance of the texts to the proper grasp of them, and so prepared the statement for its integration into the act of faith. Then, the principle of liberalism was also a justification of the critical sense in historical research, not merely, as in rationalism, to help out when exegesis broke down, but as in principle the true and adequate method of theological exegesis in general. In consequence namely of the fundamental sameness of Christ and Christian, the self-communication of Jesus which is the awakener of faith cannot by its very nature proceed otherwise than does the self-communication of historic personalities in general. Hence the method by which their history is investigated must likewise be the means of encounter with Christ. Finally, the liberal principle did not merely allow critical historical research to be generalized and made the exclusive principle of theological exegesis. It actually demanded such research if its "pious consciousness" was to continue at all to understand itself as specifically Christian. For since all that the Christian preaching has to say is absorbed and transformed into intrinsic evidence, the function of Jesus is restricted to his stimulating example. But this can only make an impact when his person is known, and this can only be through critical historical research. Hence the "quest for the historical Jesus" became the most burning question of liberal theology in the 19th century and its real theological interest.

With this re-valuation of historical criticism, the historical conscience of the exegete was now endowed with a really independent criterion of theological truth. The sense of the truth of history freed itself from its roots in a set of principles which also underlay to some extent, as a philosophy of religion, the classical dogmatic theology. Historical research could then become a court of appeal against all concrete pre-sentiments about the true content of Bible and dogma, whether these attitudes came from religious experience or from orthodox tradition. And in fact the whole history of liberal theology is dominated and stimulated by the action and reaction between an intrinsically evident religious *a priori* (however derived) and the content of the sources proved most reliable historically. The main interest was always the image they presented of Jesus.

3. The first phase of liberal theology was characterized by the effort to link up with the "lived theology" (*Erfahrungstheologie*) of Schleiermacher and the historical speculation of Hegel. It was always an endeavour to master the problem of uniting the concrete content of faith and the positive historical material of faith. In Switzerland, A. Biedermann (d. 1885) was for long the dominant figure in theology, following to some extent the subjective principles of Schleiermacher's experiential spirituality. German Protestantism, however, was in the main under the influence of the so-called "Younger Tübingen School". Its founder, Ferdinand Christian Baur (d. 1860), sought to reconcile the dogmatic content of Christology (and hence theology as a whole) with history by means of a philosophy of history which was derived from Hegel. The genesis of the truth of the absolute in the consciousness was considered to be both historically mediated and to include Jesus as a decisive moment in this

historical genesis. This was a view which was to be maintained above all as a hermeneutical principle in the historiography of dogma and of Church life. But Baur's disciple, D. F. Strauss (d. 1874), abandoned entirely the historical figure of Jesus, as non-essential for Christianity. In his epoch-making *Life of Jesus* he described the figure of Jesus as totally overgrown by myths, and buried so deeply under secondary theological and mythic interpretations that even in the Bible it was no longer historically attainable. Baur and Strauss for the first time used the method of historical criticism not merely to rationalize away the miraculous elements in biblical narratives but as a theologically decisive criterion. They thus became the founders of the exegetical tradition of liberal theology.

The problem of modern mediation was also taken up on the Catholic side, chiefly at Tübingen, by Catholic professors such as J. A. Möhler and J. E. Kuhn. An effort was made to solve it in terms which would do justice to the Catholic notion of dogma – and may still perhaps be used as directives today. It was an effort to grasp dialectically and dynamically the findings of positive, historical theology as moments in the universal dialectic of perceptible "immediacy" and conceptual "universality". This dialectic was seen as moving towards Jesus Christ by an intrinsic necessity, since he is the Idea in the concrete. And thus the dialectic moves towards the synthesis of self-understanding and understanding of history in the Christian faith in the history of salvation.

4. At the middle of the century, liberal theology in Germany received a major new impulse from A. Ritschl (d. 1889) and his disciples. He declared that practical love of the neighbour, realized very concretely in social life and in one's calling, was the true and only meaning of the love of God. Hence it was the heart of Christianity, and when given adequate extension could be the reality of the "kingdom of God", in the form of a cultured and ethical society. Jesus Christ was seen as the original bringer of this very worldly kingdom of God, since his life was exemplary as regards the love of God now seen as requisite. His example enables the moral life to be lived by those who trust in him in spite of all their consciousness of guilt and all their despair of fulfilling this precept of love. Thus God is understood as the reality of this love which has become manifest and efficacious in Jesus. With this theological conception, Ritschl and his extensive and influential school abandoned all philosophical speculation on religion in history or the consciousness and placed their dogmatics squarely on an ethical foundation. They claimed to have derived the criteria for this ethics from historical biblical criticism and the resulting scientific picture of Jesus. The same criteria were then widely used as hermeneutical keys in exegesis and history of dogma.

This broad mainstream of liberal theology, of whom the most important representatives include W. Hermann, A. von Harnack, Holtzmann, Wellhausen, Duhm, Weizsäcker, Jülicher and Schmiedel, had its strongest repercussions among the middle-class Protestants of Germany, but also had parallels and effects outside. In France, for instance, there was the "(Symbolo-) Fideism" of A. Sabatier and E. Ménégoz. Then there was the "Social Gospel" movement on the non-theological level (in America and England), which stressed the ethical example of Jesus and the optimistic view of society as embodying the kingdom of God, with a view to social reform. It was one of the factors in the rise of Christian socialism. In France in particular liberal theology penetrated Catholicism, especially through its exegetical findings, and so contributed essentially to the rise of modernism.

5. But there was also persistent criti-

cism of liberal theology itself from the "left". Taking its principles to their radical and logical conclusions, critics like the later D. F. Strauss, Gottfried Keller, Jacob Burckhardt, E. von Hartmann and Franz Overbeck denounced a lack of honesty and consistency in the liberal spirituality which remained centred on Jesus while destroying Bible and dogma by its historical criticism. New approaches, partly inspired by liberalism itself, brought about a major crisis in the classical liberal theology at the turn of the century. The exegetical studies of younger scholars, especially those of the "school of history of religions", itself a product of the Ritschlian school, demonstrated the close connection between the biblical affirmations and their ancient religious environment. This was the work of such scholars as Eichhorn, Gunkel, Bousset, Wrede, Weiss, Wernle, Heitzmüller and Troeltsch, with the support of A. Schweitzer. It was evident that there was an immense distance between the Scriptures, and especially the biblical picture of Jesus, and the optimistic social ethics of liberal theology and its notion of humanity. The Scriptures and their Jesus seemed to lose their claim to absoluteness and even any claim to special force of obligation. But there was also a trend in the opposite direction, inspired by the controversy with the school of historicism. The need was felt once more of a philosophy of religion which while allowing for the many-sided relativity of Christianity, would still demonstrate clearly the proper nature of religion and the uniqueness of what was specifically Christian. Hence Otto, Bousset and Troeltsch in particular introduced once more into theology the questions raised by metaphysics, epistemology and religious psychology. What was finally fatal to the old liberal theology was the collapse of a bourgeois historical optimism and its ethics with the First World War. This crisis found its exponents in the school of dialectical theology, which reproached the liberals with having merely projected their own humanistic ideals, no matter how valuable, into the Bible and their image of Jesus. By contrast, these theologians stressed the "otherness" of God and the uncompromising verdict on the world through his paradoxical manifestation in Jesus Christ. This did not fall within the bounds of any human certainty or *a priori*, of a speculative, religious or ethical philosophy. Under National Socialism in Germany, the "Confessing Church" of Protestantism was impervious to the old liberal theology, and so its last defendants could survive only in Switzerland (where it is represented in a certain way by M. Werner, F. Buri and U. Neuenschwander).

6. Liberal theology was right in seeking to disclose a way to the Christian faith which would be justifiable in the eyes of modern men, once they had been led by modern philosophy to recognize explicitly and consciously their fully personal responsibility to their conscience in the matter of the truth. Its legitimate interests are recognized on the Catholic side as well as the Protestant (there especially in the school of Bultmann), in the effort inspired to some extent by existence-philosophy to base exegesis on a concept of history and of understanding which is philosophically alert and no longer the naivety of historicism. There is an effort to develop a corresponding theological hermeneutics which will demonstrate the point of contact and unity between the historical person of Jesus and the "pious consciousness" of the modern man whose existence is wholly responsible to itself and thus – and only thus – given a religious dimension. Only such a philosophy of historical existence, as (logically) the theology of the history of salvation, can bridge – if anything can – the distance between a liberalism which has ceased to be Christian and an ideological "Orthodoxy".

Konrad Hecker

LIFE

I. Natural Science

1. Scientifically speaking, no valid answer can yet be given on the question of life. But its characteristics can be described in great detail. Life is linked to protoplasm, the substance which is the highest known form of organized matter. The protoplasm is basically a system of structures and functions in which nucleic acids, carbohydrates, fats, hormones, vitamins, and enzymes occur. This living matter never occurs, even in its simplest forms, except in a cellular organization. The cellular schema means that life is only present in an individualized form. We can distinguish in the cell, which can range from .001 mm to 500 mm in size, a membrane, a nucleus and the body of the cell with its organelles or suspended granules. The most important elements of the composition of the cell are the basic substance (hyaloplasm) with its inclusions, which are of great importance for the chemical processes, and the nuclear matter (caryoplasm). Along with water and the ions of inorganic compounds, the hyaloplasm is chiefly composed of organic compounds, mostly in the form of proteins. These proteins result from the immense number of combinations possible for the twenty or so amino acids, whose number and sequence constitute the various macromolecular structures and can thus bring about the various specific proteins. The caryoplasm, which occurs in the form of effector and transport structures, is composed of proteins and the typical nucleic acids DNA and RNA (desoxyribonucleic and ribonucleic acid). The basic units of the nucleic acids are the nucleotides, which consist of a purine or pyramidine base, phosphoric acid and a pentose sugar. Over 100,000 such nucleotides are here polymerized to polynucleotides, and offer innumerable possibilities of combinations.

The precise structure of these polynucleotides has been visualized by the Watson-Crick model, which shows that they have the form of two helices wound round a common axis. Each of them fits the other like key and lock, according to the given possibilities of pairing off determined by the bases. These polynucleotides of the nucleus undergo a change of form when passing from their steady or working state to that of division. Under the light microscope they can be seen at various stages of the division of the cell as chromosomes. The number and form of the chromosomes is constant in each species. The vital processes take place in and through these structures of the cell (of which only a selection has been given). The basis of the vital processes is the metabolism of the cell, an interchange of materials which may again be divided into a metabolism of nutrients and energy. Building materials external to the cell are assimilated from the environment and become matter proper to the cell.

The metabolism brings about as a rule a synthesis of simpler materials in more complicated forms. From one half to two-thirds of these synthesized products are enzyme proteins. The rest of the synthesized protein serves as building materials or nutrients, and continues to undergo constant transformations and finally dissolution (katabolism; the formation process is called anabolism). The anabolism is an energy-consuming process, which is fed by a metabolism of energy-producing factors, in which the furnisher and storehouse for the necessary energy is ATP (adenosine triphosphate). The most important source of energy is the respiratory function of the cell, the biological oxydation, through which the nutrients absorbed – autotrophically by plants, heterotrophically by animals – are turned into the requisite energy, insofar as they do not enter into the anabolism. The metabolism of the cell means that the organism is in a constant relationship to its environment and that it is in a position to develop and preserve the capacities for the maintenance of life. These may be briefly characterized as follows. Living matter forms a continuous system in time, both as regards the individual and the species. The anabolism means among other things that growth takes place which remains true to the original pattern. This is the basis of the formation of new cells by division (mitosis). The living matter also remains continuously homogeneous throughout the reproductive cycle, which makes it potentially "immortal". The DNA is the main bearer of the hereditary information which preserves the identity (of the organism). It can transmit (this information as) identical copies by means of replication in the mitosis and the reproductive process. But the constancy of the hereditary information in the DNA is not absolute. It is subject to "mutations" by which the information is suddenly altered at a statistically measurable rate, but mostly by small stages. This is the basis of evolution in living things.

The metabolism of the cell means that the living thing is in active movement, that is, it is empowered to bring about the contractions of its macromolecular elements which are the basis of all active movement of the organism. The mobility is specified by the differentiation of the cells and the resulting tasks allotted them. The fundamental process is the transmutation of the chemical energy supplied by the ATP into mechanical energy. A further property of life is its specific irritability or response to stimuli. This enables the organism to maintain itself (within limits) as individual or species against its environment. In living systems there is no opposition or juxtaposition of structure and function. The living thing is always a constant flow of activity. Living forms cannot be said to be: they rather take place. They form a perpetual flow of matter, energy and information. This flow is kept in harmony in a regulated "flowing equilibrium", sometimes called a steady state of non-equilibrium. This steady state makes the living organism an open system which is involved in a constant interchange of matter, energy and information with its environment, a process in which it remains constant over long periods. Possibly analogically open systems are also to be found outside the typically living thing. This steady state with its input and output holds good of all levels of living things, even up to the level of "psychic" behaviour. This equilibrium enables the organism to adapt itself and hence safeguard its continued existence and its individual and specific development The process which takes place in this open living system is irreversible. The second law of thermodynamics is not applicable in its usual form, since it constantly receives and must receive an input of energy, which enables it to continue to work. In the more highly organized individuals a number of causes which are still not fully explained lead to the dissolution of the system in death. Meanwhile the steady state can only be maintained by a complicated system of regulation which follows essentially cybernetic laws, as modern research sees more and more clearly. The enzymes (and the nervous system, where it exists) play a role in this regulation. A rigid machine-like regulation occurs relatively seldom. What is preponderant in directing the systems are the feed-back mechanisms which are often intermeshed. It seems that life is inconceivable without regulation by such feedback mechanisms as a basic principle.

2. The question of life in natural philosophy has been, as a matter of history, restricted to the specific aspect of one question of being. Do organisms, in contrast to non-living structures of matter and functions, form a special level of being which cannot be derived from the lower degrees of being, or is the special treatment of organisms ultimately a convention which allows a line of de-

marcation in research between the disciplines? Has life, qua life, special laws of its own or is it subject exclusively to laws outside itself? Are the ultimate presuppositions of the theory of the inorganic sufficient to explain the typical characteristics of the organic (metabolism, reproduction), or must there be special presuppositions, not required by general physical and chemical theory?

In the course of a controversy extending over the centuries, this question of the degree of being of living things has been intrinsically linked with more general problems of philosophy such as the body-soul relationship, monism, dualism, theology and ethics. It seems in the process to have been given a special importance which it hardly has of itself. The wide range of answers given to the question may best be illustrated by the theses of mechanism and vitalism. Mechanism views the laws of physics and chemistry as the effective laws of life and also often holds that the genesis of the first living beings can be explained on the basis of a continuous transition from the non-living. Vitalism attributes to life a principle of operation which is wholly its own, and which cannot be identified with the laws of the non-living. Hence it refuses to allow the origin of life from the non-living. Neither of these schools has been able to prove its thesis either by empirical or logical analyses. The sometimes passionate discussion was often confused by a lack of adequate methodological distinction between what is the criterion of life and what is the explanation of it. Mechanism is inclined to deny the experiential traits of order in the vital processes or to disregard them and leave them outside the boundaries of research. Vitalism is inclined to hold that it has demonstrated the irreducibility of life when it has registered its typical characteristics. The strongest argument against the whole controversy and against the extreme positions taken up by some debaters is probably the fact that the standard of comparison for the organic order, the physico-chemical theory with its notion of matter, has undergone a profound change, so that its significance as regards reality of being or degree of being is not now definable.

The controversy between mechanism and vitalism is today an anachronism, though the psychological situation which has all along been to some extent characteristic of research means that continual vigilance is called for. Otherwise the importance of causal and analytical research may be underestimated, and the way thrown open to fantasies and speculation such as the natural philosophy of Romanticism indulged in. Or again, exclusive attention to physico-chemical analysis may overlook what is typical in the process of life.

In view of these facts, modern theoretical biology tries to find a way which will eliminate the blind spots of the problem-makers. Its research is characterized rather by heuristic principles or working hypotheses rather than by "statements about reality". It avoids any metaphysical interpretation of experimental science in the direction of any given form of philosophy. What were formerly seen as "ontological" assertions about "degrees of being" are now merely provisional characterizations of various regions of being, while the problem of explanation is left open. The task of natural philosophy today in its consideration of life is not so much to take up a more or less well founded attitude towards the various classical explanations of life, as to keep the question open. For this is undoubtedly the only way in which even in biology due attention can be paid to man, whose existence represents a life which ranges from what are certainly inorganic natural processes to an ethical behaviour which is determined by values and by the consciousness of responsibility.

Werner Bröker

II. Moral Theology

1. *The right and duty to live.* When moral theology considers the right to life and the duty to live, the necessity and value of preserving life, it has to examine how life can best and adequately serve the love of God, the neighbour and oneself. Its starting-point must be that the Bible and theology consider life to be a participation of man in the life of God, in such a way that earthly life makes possible and prepares for participation in eternal life. Since the definitive attainment of salvation presupposes the maturation of earthly life, the latter is an intrinsic moment of the development of the religious and moral personality. Hence fundamentally all men have the same right to life and the duty to preserve life as long as it can be reasonably thought to serve the development of the person. This right to life is limited by the rights of other men and above all by the right of God, to whom alone it belongs to dispose freely of life. Hence life must be preserved as long as it can be reasonably put at the service of love. Since the necessity of placing life at the disposition of love admits of various degrees of urgency, there are also various degrees of obligation to preserve life. Hence earthly life has not an absolute value but merely a relative one, since it is there to serve the religious and moral personality (cf. Mk 8:35).

Hence it follows that all men have fundamentally the same right to as much medical care and protection of health as society at a given state of development can reasonably supply. In addition to this, each one has the right to use all the means within his power to protect his health, insofar as this can be done without detriment to his social obligations. But he is only obliged to do so within the bounds of what is possible and reasonable.

The justification of the artificial prolongation of life in its terminal stages must therefore always be judged in the light of how far the prolongation of life, in the service of the person in question, is compatible with his links and duties to society. Thus artificial prolongation of life, where it may be imposed on the dying person, may be appropriate as a service to science. But it would not be fitting to prolong life artificially at the cost of necessary efforts on behalf of others who are urgently in need of help.

Experiments to produce human life in test-tubes and artificial insemination are forbidden insofar as according to human estimation life so engendered opens up no proper possibilities of a development in keeping with human dignity.

But just as responsible parenthood in marriage cannot be considered as a violation of the sovereignty of God, so too the responsible efforts of science to trace the biological laws of living organisms cannot be considered as an unlawful effort to intervene in a field reserved to the authority of God. Man is merely trying to learn the structural laws implanted into life by God, in order to use them in the service of life. Such efforts are only forbidden when they lead to a manipulation of life which is no longer in the service of the worthy development of the human person.

2. *The crime of murder.* It follows that man may only dispose of earthly life when its preservation cannot reasonably be compatible with love. Hence the fifth commandment (Deut 5:17), as understood by the Church and its theologians, forbids all killing on one's own authority which cannot be reconciled with the demands of love. This is the grave sin of murder or suicide because it is interference in the sovereign decision of God on one's own authority.

If no relationship between human life and eternal life is acknowledged, the wrongness of murder can only be based on the equal right of all men to life, without respect of persons. The prohibition of euthanasia and suicide can then only be based on possible duties towards others and on the consideration that it is irrational to throw away incalculable chances of self-realization.

Such merely immanent justifications of the prohibition of murder, euthanasia and suicide lack the stringency given by the theological proof. Hence it is difficult, if not impossible, to reach a consensus between believers and non-believers in difficult marginal cases, where it is a matter of the morality of killing men whose lives, according to human estimation, are no longer worth preserving (or worth living). It will be impossible to persuade non-believers that in extreme cases suicide is forbidden or euthanasia, if the person in question assents.

3. *Indirect killing*. All voluntary homicide is not necessarily murder. If one defends one's own life or that of another against arbitrary attack, even by killing the arbitrary aggressor (when there is no other effective means), one is not arbitrarily preferring one life to another but deciding in this case for the life of the innocent to the detriment of that of the arbitrary aggressor. This may be called indirect killing, because the intention is the preservation of (innocent) life and it directly serves this preservation. It is allowed by theological tradition, because love will seek to protect life against irrational destruction, if necessary at the cost of the life of the aggressor.

This argument is all the more stringent, the more people there are who can be protected from arbitrary death in this way. Thus in the case of a heavily-armed killer who is running amok, there is an obligation to kill him rather than to allow unresistingly many others to be killed by him. But this argument does not prove that there is an obligation to kill an arbitrary aggressor rather than to allow oneself to be killed, since well-ordered love does not need to prefer one's own life to that of another. We are rather invited to follow the example of Christ and surrender our own life rather than take that of another (Jn 15:13; cf. Mt 16:25; Jn 12:25). But one still has the right to prefer one's own life to that of an arbitrary aggressor. However, it is already questionable that the killing of an innocent should be permitted, if it can be prevented by the killing of the arbitrary aggressor.

From this point of view, it is doubtful whether the death of two innocents may be permitted, where neither of them is an aggressor against the other and whether the killing of one could save the life of the other. The Holy Office declared (*D* 1889, 1890 a–c; cf. Pius XI, *Casti Connubii: D* 2242–44; Pius XII, *AAS* 43 [1951], pp. 838f., 857ff.) that the permissibility of killing the child in the womb, and in particular craniotomy, could not be safely taught even where it could be foreseen with certainty that both mother and child would die ("tuto doceri non potest"). But the ruling also made it clear indirectly that in this case the prohibition of craniotomy cannot be regarded as certain. Similar problems about the inviolability of human life have been recently presented to moral theology by the fact that it is impossible to say with absolute certainty when life has ceased, while vital and viable organs can be transplanted from dead or dying people and effectively used to sustain the life of others.

Rational consideration seems to suggest that it is part of the rational service of life that where death is directly and inevitably supervening, life should be allowed to perish, where, according to human estimation, it can no longer be the vehicle of a worthy human existence, and where it can save another life which cannot be saved otherwise. The difficulty is that man seems here to arrogate to himself the decision about life and death. In such extreme marginal cases, it is practically impossible to decide when exactly the independent, responsible application of reason swings over to the arbitrary disposition of human life. The limit between the direct killing of the innocent, which is always forbidden, and indirect killing, which may be permitted in the service of life, is clear in theory but cannot be neatly drawn in practice. In any case, killing is only justified insofar as it serves the optimum expansion of life and does not arbitrarily sustain one life at the expense of another. It is scarcely possible to say definitely that this is so in the case of craniotomy and the transplantation of certain organs.

Since man's right to life is not given him by man, and man has the duty of placing himself as fully as possible in the service of life, the killing of men when forced to defend oneself can only be done within the limits of the absolutely necessary, that is, insofar as it serves the optimum preservation of life. Hence even a defensive war is unjust where the protection of the lives of the attacked is out of all proportion to the destruction let loose by the war. For the same reason, passive resistance is to be preferred in the first place to violent revolution. But even revolution may be permissible when it is the means of averting a worse reign of terror. Under normal circumstances the death penalty is likewise to be rejected as unjustifiable.

4. *Protection of embryonic life*. The protection of human life raises special problems in the case of the embryo. From the scientific point of view, it must be assumed that human life begins with the fertilization of the ovum. Hence means of birth control which allow the ovum to be fertilized but not to be implanted in the womb cannot be regarded as means of avoiding conception but only as causing abortion.

From the anthropological point of view, it is still possible to ask whether such a fertilized egg is already a human person, since a successive animation – as taught by Aristotle and medieval theologians and more and more widely once again today – seems to correspond better to the evolutionary mode of thought (J. Feiner in *Mysterium Salutis*, II, p. 581). The question as to the exact moment of the animation of the human embryo has not been decided by the magisterium of the Church (cf. G. Siegmund, "Beseelung der Leibesfrucht", *LTK*, II, col. 294). In 1679, Pope Innocent XI condemned the opinion that animation took place only at the moment of birth (*D* 1185). In 1887, Leo XIII condemned the view of Rosmini, who held that animation only took place with the first intellectual act of the child (*D* 1910). The opinion is sometimes heard today that personal life need only be assumed to begin when the brain has developed enough to serve as the substratum for specifically human activities. The persistence of personal life on earth is said to be amenable to the same criteria.

But it would be wrong to derive from such arguments the practical consequence that abortion may be more widely permitted in certain cases (cf. *CIC*, can. 2350, §1). On account of the inviolability of the human person, one must be certain in practice that there is no human person in the embryo, when it is not to be allowed its full rights to personal integrity. Otherwise the killing of the embryo would imply the readiness to sacrifice the life of a person if necessary for the sake of values not vital to life. But it is not at all certain that the embryo, at the moment of fertilization, is not a human person.

Nonetheless, the circumstances are different in the killing of unborn and born life, since in the case of unborn life, the dependence on the mother is qualitatively different, as compared with the child once born. Hence in general abortion is not as grave a sin as murder. Hence too the State for the most part provides much more definite and comprehensive legal protection to born than to unborn life. The neglect of the State to proceed against those who arbitrarily kill embryonic life can hardly be justified either on juridical or on moral grounds.

Nonetheless, civil law and moral theology must allow for the possibility of intervention to bring about indirectly an interruption of pregnancy, if this is the direct means of preserving life. First, it is a debatable question, whether abortion is ruled out if there is danger of both mother and child dying. Then, the Church is not in a position to give a clear and definite answer to the question of how far the exercise of the right to self-preservation, e.g., by the use of medicines with abortive side-effects, justifies an indirect interruption of pregnancy. Here a grave task is imposed on the responsible conscience. But it may be affirmed as a principle that the right to life of either cannot be sacrificed merely to the well-being of the other. Economic and social needs must be catered for by economic and social measures. They do not justify the elimination of existing life, even if it is in a state of dependence. Even the life which results from a rape comes from God and has its own right to free development. To destroy it irresponsibly is sinful.

5. *Principles for the estimation of values.* Since life is the presupposition of all salutary action of man, it must ultimately take precedence of the preservation of all other values whose immediate acquisition is not necessary for the attainment of salvation. This means that the preservation and development of life, if it is to be morally justified, always implies an estimation of values. Consequently, man must renounce life if its preservation would bring him into direct opposition to the attainment of salvation. This would be the case if one had to turn away from God or commit any other formal offence against charity and so sin directly in order to preserve life. In such a situation man should be prepared for martyrdom, since it is irrational to try to preserve earthly life at the cost of turning away from eternal life.

On the other hand, even high moral values whose realization is not immediately called for must be renounced if they can only be attained at the cost of life. Hence duelling, which endangers life, cannot be regarded as a legitimate means of defending honour, though personal honour is a higher good than earthly life. The redress of insults must be sought within the provisions of law.

So too what is useful and pleasant in life may not be sought and developed at the expense of what is necessary to life. Life must be protected even at the cost of very great material values, provided that the loss of these goods does not mean indirectly the loss of the necessities of life for a large number of men. Above all, luxuries must be renounced to provide the necessities of life for others. It must, however, be remembered that a certain standard of living may well serve the optimum development of life.

The optimum preservation and development of life are only possible if one is prepared to take calculated risks with regard to the loss and the maximum development of life. This must be allowed for in the estimation of values. Hence, for instance, sports such as motor-racing can be regarded as in the service of life, even though such activities cannot be carried on without more or less danger to life and health. Consequently, their effects on life and health must be assessed, as far as is reasonably possible, and then risks more or less dangerous to life may be undertaken, insofar as they are seen as on the whole of service to the optimum development of life. Accordingly, one must be neither too light-hearted nor too timid about the preservation of life, since either attitude would be detrimental to the optimum development of life. Relatively little consideration has yet been given to the rules to be observed in the calculations of such risks.

Waldemar Molinski

LIMBO

1. *Notion.* Limbo (Latin: hem, edge, etc.) is a technical theological term for the place and state of the dead who are neither in heaven nor in hell nor in purgatory. A distinction is drawn between the *limbus patrum*, i.e., the place and state of the pre-Christian just, who could not enter into eternal happiness before Christ's descent into hell and his ascension, and the *limbus infantium*, i.e., of the human beings who on earth never attained the use of reason, and to whom the sacrament of baptism was never administered, although the gospel was sufficiently proclaimed in their countries for the possibility of their sacramental incorporation into the Church not of itself to have been excluded.

2. *History.* Neither revelation nor the oldest Christian tradition deals expressly with the eternal lot of unbaptized children in general, or with their limbo in particular, though they both particularly stress that our salvation in Christ depends on belonging to the Church, and that this depends on baptism. It was only when Pelagianism denied these fundamental Christian truths, and asserted in proof of its views that God does not deny access to the kingdom of heaven to unbaptized children, that this specific problem was envisaged. Augustine put forward the doctrine, which went uncontested for centuries, that these children are condemned to the real (though mitigated) pains of hell. Anselm of Canterbury and after him the great Scholastics firmly held with Augustine that these human beings remain excluded from eternal beatitude, but they also postulated for them the existence of a place and final state of their own, that is, limbo. The nature of this limbo, however, was differently conceived in the course of the centuries and in general was interpreted more and more benignly (intellectual sadness – unawareness of the loss of the beatific vision – purely natural happiness).

3. *The modern discussion.* In present-day theology the existence of limbo is questioned by many, including some distinguished theologians and historians of dogma, and there is much discussion whether the assumption behind all teaching on limbo, namely that the persons in question are excluded from the beatific vision, is in fact a theologically irreformable, established doctrine. Representatives of the new and so-called liberal tendency appeal in particular to the dogma of God's universal salvific will, to the unity and solidarity of the human race which as such was called to the supernatural and redeemed by Christ, as well as to the possibility of a special kind of baptism of desire, which would make it possible for those persons sufficiently to enter into relation to Christ and his Church. Within this school of thought, however, opinions diverge at many points, especially the following: a) the degree of certainty with which the concrete possibility of salvation for children who have died without baptism is maintained (extending from tentative hypothesis to the affirmation that this doctrine is implicitly revealed); b) the range of its application (all such persons – children of Christian parents – unborn children, etc.); c) the actual concrete mode in which the baptism of desire, universally considered necessary, is regarded as realized (by the intermediary of the Church, or the parents, or through those persons' attaining the use of reason at the moment of death and being made capable of a supernatural act of love for God through special actual graces); d) the theological methods employed (more speculative considerations – critical, historical research into the contrary and supposedly theologically binding "tradition"). In view of the fact that theology, as the science of faith, not only takes its starting-point in the content of revelation, but also finds the

norm and limit of its endeavour in authentic tradition and the binding interpretation of the Church's magisterium, it is evident that the elucidation of the last question ("tradition") is of the very greatest, and indeed decisive, importance for the problem of children dying without baptism and consequently for the question of limbo. It is not in accordance with the spirit of genuine theology to hold fast uncritically to inherited doctrines and opinions, but it is equally untheological to set aside a doctrine that for many centuries has been held practically universally in the Church to be a binding one, and which as such as been taught to the very widest extent in the Church's catechesis.

As regards the present state of the relevant and extremely complex learned researches, it must be noted that a) opinions still differ very widely among specialists; b) those who hold the liberal view have been able to establish many important items in their favour; c) conclusive proof of the theological tenability of their views has not even yet, however, been provided. The Church's magisterium has so far not favoured the liberal opinions but allows inquiry to continue without hindrance. This being so, in preaching the faith any categorical or even polemical pronouncement must of course be avoided and caution must be observed in every respect. It remains obvious that the persons in question are to be baptized without delay if this is at all possible. (Suprema Sacra Congregatio S. Officii, 18 February 1958: *AAS* 50 [1958], p. 114.)

4. *Pastoral theology*. The pastor can and should tell the Christian parents of children who have died without baptism that there is no definite doctrine of faith regarding the fate of such children, and that consequently they can entrust the final lot of their child to the mysterious but infinitely kind and powerful love of God, to whose grace no limit is set by the earthly circumstances which he in his providence has allowed to come about.

Peter Gumpel

LITURGY

I. The Liturgies

A. Definition

The word λειτουργία in classical Greek means a function (ἔργον) undertaken on behalf of the people (λαός): fitting out a ship, preparing a feast or doing any public service.

In the Greek Bible, the word is regularly used of divine worship, to speak of the sacred ministry with which the priests and levites of the OT were charged. In Heb 8:2 Christ himself is designated as λειτουργός. The word remained current among Greek-speaking Christians, first to indicate the ministry of Church officials in general (for instance, *Didache*, ch. 15), and then divine worship in particular. As early as the 4th century it was restricted to meaning the Mass. This is the sense in which it is used at present by the Greeks and the Eastern Slavs. The word went out of use in the West till it was revived by the Humanists of the 16th century. In the official terminology of the Church it reappears only in the 19th century.

No complete agreement has been reached about the definition of the liturgy. This is because different elements may be stressed in the group of ecclesiastical institutions which are generally classed as liturgical. Some have proposed to understand by liturgy simply the outward forms of divine worship, or the sum total of regulations which govern the Church's worship. This would be to restrict the concept to an aesthetical or juridical approach. In contrast to such views it has been maintained, especially since the beginning of the liturgical movement, that by liturgy we are to understand the worship offered to God by the Church itself (L.

Beauduin). This view is also presupposed in the encyclical *Mediator Dei* (1947), when the liturgy is taken to be the "whole public worship of the mystical body of Christ, head and members".

Within this worship, however, it is still possible to emphasize in particular the priesthood of Christ which underlies the action of the Church (R. Stapper) or again, the trinitarian structure of Church worship (H. Schmidt); or emphasis may be laid on the redemptive act which becomes a present reality in it (as in the mystery-theology of O. Casel). Or one can stress in particular the sanctifying work of God which accompanies the worship of the Church (J. Vagaggini).

It should not, however, be necessary to stress such particular aspects when merely giving a definition. It should be enough to say that the liturgy is the worship offered to God by the Church, provided that we give their full force to the concepts used in the definition.

But we must also note an important difference in the usage of the word, as it occurs in canon law.

According to *CIC*, can. 1057, the regulation of the "liturgy" is a matter reserved exclusively to the Holy See. Vatican II affirmed the rights of the bishops in this matter. By a declaration in the *Instructio de Musica Sacra et de Sacra Liturgia* of 3 September 1958, it has been established that according to the terminology of Church law, only such acts of worship are to be regarded as "liturgical", as are performed according to books approved of by the Holy See. These alone are subject to Roman regulations, while the bishop is put in charge of all other devotions, holy hours, processions, etc., which are regarded as *pia exercitia*. Thus the concept was restricted to a narrower usage in the terminology of Church legislation. Historically speaking, so narrow a concept would be applicable to the liturgy only from 1568–70 on, since it was only after this time that books approved by the Holy See were prescribed for use in the whole Latin Church. A more general view of the liturgy, which must take in all ages since the foundation of the Church, and all areas, including those of Eastern Christianity, would find the canonical concept inadequate. We hold therefore that the liturgy is the worship offered to God by the Church: "cultus Deo ab Ecclesia praestitutus".

This definition calls for a closer explanation. Not all divine worship is liturgical, but only such as is offered publicly by the Church as such. Beside it there exists the worship offered privately by the individual faithful. The NT itself speaks of personal prayer, for which the individual goes "into his room" (Mt 6:6), as well as the public worship of God in the Temple and then the celebration of the Eucharist as enjoined by Christ (cf. Vatican II, *Sacrosanctum Concilium*, art. 9).

The Church is only at worship, that is, we only have liturgy, when divine service is held by a legitimately assembled group of the faithful (from parish, religious order or ecclesiastical institute), under the leadership of someone holding office in the Church. Here the Church becomes visible, here it is "Event". When the Church is gathered to pray and celebrate, its prayer will necessarily take on a form which is not only worthy of such an assembly – whence the liturgy makes use of noble art – but is also a very faithful mirror of the nature of the Church. This Church is the people of God, because it is the community of those who are redeemed by Christ and sanctified in the Holy Spirit. In the liturgy, therefore, the word "we" will predominate, not the "I" of the individual, and the Christological and trinitarian character of its basic attitude will come to the fore.

These essential traits must find expression in every actual liturgical institution. It belongs to the Church authorities to lay down the rules for such institutions: the Pope for the whole Church, and the bishop for the sphere assigned to him by law. Juridically there is a difference between a liturgical action prescribed by the bishop and one prescribed by the supreme authority of the Church. But it does not alter the religious and theological value of the worship offered. In the first case the liturgy exists by episcopal right ("Sacra exercitia", according to Vatican II, *Sacrosanctum Concilium*, art. 13), in the second by papal right, a liturgy universally valid.

Liturgy is in the last resort always a sacred ministry directed to God. A prayer, rite or devotional gesture can in fact be addressed immediately to a saint or Mary or Christ, but ultimately its object is always the Father of our Lord Jesus Christ.

The worship of the Church is accomplished most perfectly in the celebration of the Eucharist, because the Church is "gathered" most intensively in the one bread of the Eucharist and so is most truly itself. There the Church fulfils the inmost law of its being and thus God is supremely glorified through Christ and in Christ.

The concept of liturgy is also verified in another way in the sacraments.

The celebration of the Eucharist is only possible on the basis of the other sacraments, which form its substructure to a certain extent. They prepare the holy people in baptism and confirmation, they purify it in penance and anointing of the sick, they sanctify the means whereby it is perpetuated from generation to generation, and equip the ministers of the altar for their sacred service (matrimony, orders). Further, the sacraments are accompanied by various forms of the prayer which pervades all liturgy.

But Eucharist and sacraments do not cover the whole field of the liturgy. Prayer is also asked of the Church outside the Eucharist, if the Church and not just the individual is to "pray always and not lose heart" (Lk 18:1). Such prayer has in fact been offered in the Church since the earliest times. It accompanied the reading and preaching of Scripture, or it stood more or less on its own in the form of psalm-singing, or it was offered for various necessities and wants.

The most important manifestation of the Church at prayer is the canonical hours or office, by which certain hours of the day, especially morning and evening, are sanctified. The contrast of one time of day with another was enough to suggest that the form and content of prayer should vary with the hour of the day. A similar change extending over longer periods was found desirable for another reason. Since the worship of the Church is based on the divine dispensation of salvation, it was necessary to recall continually in the Eucharist not only the climax of redemption, but also the stages of its development as given in the Scriptures.

The recollection of the most important events in the history of salvation was then spread over certain dates in the year, given further development and finally combined with the anniversaries of the great heroes of the faith. Thus the liturgical year took shape.

B. Historical Survey

The liturgy is necessarily as old as the Church. But only the innermost nucleus of Christian worship was enacted by Christ himself and thus not left subject to alteration. All other developments were to be the work of the Church and of the forces within it which change from age to age, always fertile in new forms and always seeking still more. On the other hand, the liturgy is of its nature conservative, since it is a sacred ministry. Forms once laid down appear to be somehow sacred, and hence are preserved and transmitted unchanged as far as possible. Thus no understanding of Christian liturgy is possible unless it is considered in its historical development. In the primitive Church, divine worship was restricted to the celebration of the Eucharist, which being the memorial of the Lord took place every week on Sunday, the day on which Christians recalled the completion of redemption through the resurrection, called the Lord's Day as early as Rev 20:7 (κυριακὴ ἡμέρα). On certain occasions there was also the evening *Agape*, when food was distributed to the poor, a function accompanied by psalm-singing and prayer at which the clergy presided. Traditions from the way of life of pious Jews (such as Qumran) are seen to be at work here. The heritage of the synagogue also makes itself felt in the stylization of prayer: the introduction with the greeting "Dominus vobiscum" and "let us pray"; the conclusion with the affirmative "Amen" of the people.

At least from the 2nd century onwards, the Church celebrated Easter every year. It was a nocturnal celebration, in which the transition ("passover") was made from the memory of Jesus' passion to the joy of the resurrection. The baptism of converts also took place on the night of Easter, a procedure which gave apt expression to the truth that the baptized shared the resurrection of Christ and became partakers of his divine life. Further, Easter was considered to be the continuation as well as the fulfilment of the OT Pasch. Hence efforts were made to keep to the Jewish lunar calendar in fixing the date of Easter. However, after some wavering on the point, the rule prevailed, from about A.D. 200 on, that Easter was to be celebrated on a Sunday.

Thus the thought of Easter pervaded the life of early Christianity and strengthened it in the tribulations of persecution.

Fixed liturgical texts did not yet exist. A typical formula for the celebration of the Eucharist, which was recorded by Hippolytus of Rome about 215, the text of which has been preserved, states expressly that any bishop who might wish to use it is not bound to follow it word for word. Some centuries later, in the manuscript tradition of this work, the "not" was eliminated from the remark, and thus the set form of words was made into the norm. From the 4th century on, fixed texts became more and more the rule, as indeed they probably also became a necessity with the continued expansion of the Church and the waning of inspiration. It was the same with the places where the liturgy was held. The primitive Church displays no interest in special places of worship, least of all in the type of temple which the pagans had and the Jewish people once possessed. These were majestic buildings enshrining only a tiny inaccessible sanctuary. In complete contrast to this, the community of the faithful knew that it formed a living temple. All the congregation needed for divine worship was a room large enough to hold it, which it found at first in the dwelling-houses of the well-to-do members of the community.

With the freedom granted by Constantine, and under his generous patronage, came buildings designed for worship. The basic structure was that of the "Basilica" (Palace, hall) as developed by Roman architecture. About this time the Hellenistic culture of the surrounding world also began to exercise other notable influences on the shape taken by the Christian liturgy. Indeed, the liturgy has preserved since then many features which belonged to the culture of that age. This is true of liturgical vestments. These are, not only in the Roman liturgy but also in the Oriental rites, a slightly elaborated form of the dress worn on festive occasions in late Roman antiquity (a tunic with a girdle; a *paenula*, cloak, which became the chasuble). Further, some insignia belonging to the higher state officials of the time were taken over for the bishop's dress in particular (the maniple, stole, pallium and episcopal shoes). Forms of court ceremony were also adopted by the liturgy. It was, for instance, the privilege of the highest officials to be preceded by torches and cressets on solemn occasions. From this arose the custom of carrying candles and incense before the bishop, and later before any celebrant of solemn High Mass: two elements of liturgical solemnity which were later used to advantage mainly as marks of adoration offered directly to God.

The religious rites of antiquity on the other hand supplied only marginal items to the Christian liturgy, when indeed they did not give rise to counterparts which were rather in the nature of protests. The origin of Christmas is a case in point. Towards the end of the 4th century the feast in honour of *Sol Invictus* had been raised to the status of an imperial holiday. In opposition to this the feast of the Nativity was introduced, to celebrate the birth of him who rose upon the world as its true sun. In the cult of the dead, however, the choice of certain days had become deeply embedded in popular paganism, and these dates managed to survive into Christianity. It was the custom to pay honours to the dead and to try to help them by sacrifices and funeral banquets, not only on the day of burial, but also on the third, seventh (or eighth) and thirtieth (or fortieth) days. Of these dates, the third, seventh and thirtieth days are still regarded as privileged days for Requiem Masses in the regions of the Roman rite; in the East they are the third, ninth and fortieth days.

The years of the 4th to the 5th century were also the time in which what had hitherto been a fundamentally uniform liturgy, though with some local differences, split up into the sharply distinct liturgies which survive to the present day. A variety of languages had of course been used from the very start. Divine service had invariably been held in the vernacular of each region. It was, however, supposed, if for no other reason than that the liturgy necessarily included sacred Scripture, that the language in question had reached a certain stage of development and could be put to literary uses. This principle was not indeed always observed later, as, for instance, at the beginning of the Chinese missions. During the early days of Christianity the three languages used in the inscription on the Cross, "Hebrew" (Syriac), Greek and Latin, were of primary importance. With these one could make oneself understood in any part of the world of the time.

In the East, beyond the Roman frontiers, Syriac became fundamental. This is the liturgy which still survives today as the Eastern Syrian, which comprises what is known as the Chaldaean inside the Catholic Church, as well as the Nestorian, and the Syro-malabar of India.

Greek predominated in the eastern part of the Roman Empire. Latin prevailed in the West after the strengthening of the Latin element in the Christian communities from the 3rd century on. Within the Greek-speaking area, however, from the 4th century on, various centres stood out which proceeded independently of each other in establishing their liturgical institutions. One was Alexandria, which held the leadership in the Egyptian area and developed a liturgy known as the liturgy of St. Mark. Another was Antioch, which dominated the Hellenized area of western Syria, though in liturgical matters it soon had to abdicate its leadership in favour of Jerusalem, which had been flourishing again since the days of Constantine. The liturgy here developed is known as that of St. James.

The third centre, which made itself felt at once, was the new imperial city on the Bosphorus. It took up and developed further the liturgy of Antioch, forming from it the Byzantine liturgy. Favoured by the political authorities, the Byzantine liturgy spread in the course of the Middle Ages over the whole remaining territory of the Greek empire, took in Antioch as well as Alexandria and finally covered the whole eastern Slavonic area, following the Byzantine missionary effort. Among the Russians, Serbs and Bulgarians it is celebrated in old Slavonic (Church Slavonic), among other peoples of this area in the language proper to each. The originally Greek-speaking population of the regions of Antioch and Alexandria, who had remained within the sphere of the Byzantine Empire and Catholic Church – known by the Syrians as Melchites ("royalists") on account of their close connections with the imperial court – also went over to the Arab language in their (Byzantine) liturgy after the triumph of the Arabian peoples. The western Syrians, however, in the hinterland of Antioch, who had liberated themselves more and more from Byzantine influences after the Council of Chalcedon (451), and had developed a national consciousness of their own, gradually went over to Syriac in their liturgy. This is the liturgy of St. James, still used by the Jacobites and Maronites.

The same thing happened in Egypt, where a Coptic and an Ethiopian liturgy, each in the native language, grew out of the Greek liturgy of St. Mark. And then the Armenians, exposed to Byzantine and Syrian influences, drew on both sources to build up a liturgy of their own, which has been celebrated in Armenian since the 5th century, by which time it had become a literary language. All these rites survive to the present day and are grouped under the heading of Oriental liturgies. They have many typical features in common, which are most strongly marked in the Byzantine rite. Characteristic is the lengthening of the preparatory part of the Mass, which is composed of a number of preludes, and above all, the great solemnity of the rite, which comes from the thought of its being a participation in the heavenly liturgy of the angels. Several forms of Byzantine court ceremonial are used, such as the προσκύνησις. The two processions of the eucharistic liturgy are notable features. In solemn train, first the sacred book and then the offerings are carried into the sanctuary (the little and the great entry). Where a number of priests are present, a Mass read in silence by each priest is unknown in the East. In such cases the rite is performed by all together (concelebration), though the words of consecration need not be pronounced by each individual, except among the Russians and in the Uniate Churches. An attitude of profound submission and humble adoration in face of the divine majesty was further reinforced by the fact that during the long defensive struggle against Arianism, the thought of Christ as mediator was forced into the background. His role of mediator remains undoubtedly an aspect of his historical work as Saviour, but for fear of misinterpretation, it is no longer considered as part of the function exercised by Christ in his humanity at the right hand of the Father. So prayer is no longer regularly addressed to God "through Christ", which was the style of liturgical prayer in the preceding centuries and still characterizes the Roman liturgy. Prayer is directed to Christ himself or to the triune God, whose praise resounds in the doxologies with which each prayer is concluded. A strong Marian note, which is heard above all in many hymns (*theotokiae*), provides a certain substitute for the recessive mediatorship of Christ. The Epiclesis after the words of consecration, a solemn invocation asking for the descent of the Holy Spirit upon the offerings, also stems from a line of thought which is predominantly centred on the Trinity. A sense of holy awe in face of the divine mysteries is expressed in the veiling of the sacred species, and especially in the marked distinction made between the sanctuary and the nave of the church. The original barriers have been extended upwards in course of time to form a lofty partition covered with images (iconostasis). This cuts off the view of the altar, and only the voice of the celebrant maintains the connection with the faithful.

All Oriental liturgies, on the other hand, make provision for the ministry of the deacon. He assists beside the celebrant at various points of the liturgy, and also intones the litanies in non-eucharistic services, where each invocation is answered by the people. The *Kyrie eleison* which is common to all rites is one of the oldest forms of such acclamations by the people. This ensured an intensive participation of the people in the liturgy, even though at a certain distance from the heart of the process, and did much to link it to the life of the people and sustain Christianity under a hostile pressure lasting a thousand years. Much as was done for the vernacular, no general effort was made to grasp the exact meaning of the words in the various elements of the liturgy or to understand objectively the real and original meaning of each rite. As early as the 5th century, an allegorical interpretation took its place (ἄλλα ἀγορεύειν, that is, reading something else into the actual rites). The liturgy is taken as the earthly projection of the heavenly liturgy, or as a representation of the decisive events in the work of salvation: the incarnation, passion, burial and resurrection of Christ.

In contrast to Western usage, it is characteristic of all Oriental liturgies that in the Mass and the Office the prayers of the priest remain unaffected by the liturgical year. Only lessons and chants follow the cycle of the year and the festive seasons. However, some changes were provided for in another direction. For the principal part of the Mass, the Anaphora ("Oblation"), which followed the introductory Scripture readings, a number of formulas are provided in which the Canon and its immediate setting are treated differently. Only two such formulas exist, however, in the Byzantine liturgy, the "liturgy" of St. John Chrysostom and the "liturgy" of St. Basil.

There are three in the East Syrian liturgy, three in the Coptic, and only a few more in the Armenian, while seventeen have been traced in the Ethiopian. In the West Syrian liturgy, the number of formulas for the Anaphora rises to around eighty, though only some of these are still in use today.

Towards the end of Christian antiquity, several liturgies had also been evolved in the West, on the basis of a common structure which originated no doubt in Rome. It is due to this common structure that, Latin being retained of course everywhere, the prayers of the priest in these liturgies changed with the feasts and seasons of the year, as well as other parts of the Mass. Beside the Roman liturgy, with which the North African was closely akin (as far as we can tell: it is mainly known through St. Augustine), we have to distinguish a Gallic type of liturgy, from which stem further the old Spanish, Milanese (Ambrosian), Gallican and Celtic liturgies. Of this group, the last two are merely ways of classifying texts from the British Isles and Gaul in which some kinship can be descried. They have been preserved only very haphazardly. But complete liturgical books have been preserved from the old Spanish liturgy, while the Ambrosian survives to the present day, though strongly penetrated by later Roman elements. The Roman liturgy finally prevailed all over the West in the course of the Middle Ages, and on the whole, without any particular pressure from the part of Rome, apart perhaps from the intervention of Gregory VII in Spain.

The Roman liturgy came into the British Isles along with the Roman missionaries sent to the Anglo-Saxons by Gregory the Great. But it was only centuries later that it succeeded in penetrating Celtic Christianity also. In Gaul, the native forms of the liturgy had lost the esteem of their own clergy, since liturgies varied from place to place, were open to every outside influence, especially from the East, and hence presented a very disordered picture. The Carolingian rulers Pepin and Charlemagne, who wanted a uniform Church order throughout their dominions, were thus able to suppress them completely without much trouble and introduce the well-ordered Roman liturgy as part of their reforms. The ancient Spanish Church on the other hand had evolved in the 6th to the 7th century a rich and fully elaborated liturgy, when the Moorish invasion arrived, to destroy the kingdom of the Visigoths and arrest the flowering of the Spanish Church. As the country was reconquered from the north, the Roman liturgy was also introduced here. The old Spanish liturgy survived till the end of the Middle Ages, but only in the parts still subject to the Arabs. This is the origin of the name "Mozarabic" given to the liturgy, meaning the liturgy used by the "Arab" Catholics of Spain.

Finally, the old Spanish liturgy is characterized by a peculiar trait. It was coming to full flower at the time when the Spanish Church was engaged in sharp controversy with the Arianism of its Visigoth neighbours. Hence reaction to the denial of the true Godhead of Christ led to similar results in the liturgy as we have noted in the East. And the powerful influence of the flourishing Spanish Church spread through Ireland to the Anglo-Saxons and ultimately into the Carolingian Empire, to make this anti-Arian strain of Christian piety one of the essential elements in the religious culture of the Middle Ages.

We may now concentrate our attention on the Roman liturgy. In the Eternal City, Christianity was at first predominantly Greek-speaking. Only when the Latin elements had grown strong enough to compete with the Greek could a Roman liturgy in the Latin language take shape. It is only in the 6th to the 7th century, however, that the Latin liturgy of Rome appears in its full development, enshrined in complete liturgical books. The manuscript witnesses date only from the 8th to the 9th century, the time when many scribes were hard at work in the Frankish scriptoria, naturalizing the Roman liturgy in their own country. The form fixed in Rome during the last centuries of antiquity was preserved almost without exception in the Roman liturgy till modern times, only partially embroidered with additions that came in later on Frankish soil.

The most ancient books of the Roman liturgy were not divided, as they are today, into Missal, Ritual and Breviary, according to the sphere of worship in which they were to be used: the division followed the character of the officiant. The Sacramentary contained the prayers to be said by the Pope and the bishop, at Mass, at the administration of the sacraments and at the Office. The *Liber antiphonarius* contained the chants for the choir during Mass, the *Liber responsorialis* the chants for the Office. Lectionaries provided Scripture readings, though a Capitulary, or list of chapters to be read on each occasion, was enough for the gospel readings, which were mostly taken from a complete codex of the gospels. Finally, the cleric who was a sort of Master of Ceremonies in charge of the general arrangements was provided with an *Ordo*.

At the start, before these books had been filled out in each case to meet the requirements of the annual cycle, help was provided in the form of single libelli, small books of texts containing some suitable formularies for each occasion. This is still to be seen quite clearly in the sacramentaries, of which three Roman ones are known. The oldest of them, the *Sacramentarium Leonianum*, is in fact merely a loosely-assembled series of such libelli, from the 5th to the 6th century, covering the whole year. One of these libelli, for instance, offered a choice of several sets of prayers formulated to suit the feast of the Princes of the Apostles; another gave texts for Paschal time or for a certain group of functions such as the conferring of major orders.

Another sacramentary is the so-called *Gelasianum*, which already displays an arrangement worked out to suit the whole liturgical year. It was likewise composed in Rome in the 6th century, but was later expanded in France, where it was given a strong Frankish tinge, which is the form in which it has been preserved.

The third is the *Sacramentarium Gregorianum*, which is attributed to Gregory the Great (d. 604), and on which the texts of the prayers in our present-day Missal are based for the most part. A little later than the sacramentaries, the books giving the chants and order of lessons in the Roman liturgy were composed, each book providing for the whole annual cycle. The 7th century also saw the appearance of the oldest Roman Ordines, which describe the outward procedure in the more complicated rites of the liturgy, such as the "Stations", the liturgies of Lent and Easter, the rites of baptism and of ordination.

These were the books which the Frankish clerics and bishops sought after with ever increasing zeal from the 8th century on, and which they took as the basis of the new order of their worship. As was to be expected, it was not the pure Roman rite which was observed in the Churches of the Carolingian Empire, but one which had been interpreted in the spirit of their own tradition interspersed with existing native customs of many kinds, and even misunderstood at certain points. This was almost inevitable, as the directions given by the books were often vague, and the rare traveller to Rome could only report what he thought he saw, which was a very meagre help. Furthermore, the directions on which the Franks had to rely catered almost exclusively, especially in the Ordines, for the solemn liturgies of the major feasts and it was very difficult to apply them to the ordinary occasions of popular worship. A shift in meaning was also imposed by the fact that many of the piously preserved rites of antiquity no longer suited the new circumstances. And the Latin of the books was no longer understood in its new environment, either by the Romanic or the Germanic populations. The liturgy became the preserve of the clergy. The long series of rites by which the adult catechumen had been prepared during Lent for baptism at Easter were now condensed into one single act, and finally combined with baptism itself, though they no longer had much meaning, since baptism was now administered only to children. The people continued indeed to frequent the daily services in which they had once taken part, morning prayer and evening Vespers (the former, Matins, corresponds to our Lauds; daily Mass was not yet the custom). But the prayers were offered by the clergy alone, and then expanded to form the full diurnal cycle of the canonical hours (Breviary). Under the growing influence of monasticism, the clergy of the great ecclesiastical centres, since Chrodegang of Metz (d. 766) and Benedict of Aniane (d. 821) in particular, had adopted not only common life but also the monastic form of the office, which was said in common and distributed over seven canonical hours. It became thereby all the more remote from the ordinary world of the faithful. So in many places in the later Middle Ages, the logical step was finally taken, and the choir where the office was chanted was completely divided from the nave of the Church, by means of a choir-screen, where it was not simply transferred to the "Chapter-house".

Since it was almost impossible for the people to follow the words of the Mass, its visual possibilities were at once exploited in Frankish lands, enriched by dramatic elements and interpreted allegorically. Solemn High Mass in which all the clergy participated was long predominant. At the beginning of Mass and at the beginning of the Offertory the altar was incensed from all sides. Differences of rank as between the lessons were stressed, epistle side was distinguished from gospel side, and the gospel surrounded by a number of marks of honour. Every movement of the congregation or of the priest was now given a special meaning in the allegorical explanation of the liturgy, which was worked out systematically by Amalar of Metz. The great acts of the history of salvation were re-discovered in the ceremonies of the Mass, from the cry of the OT patriarchs in the Introit and Kyrie to the birth of the Saviour in the Gloria and so on to the last blessing, which represented the blessing given by our Lord to the apostles before his ascension. Thus the congregation was relegated to the role of reverent onlookers. The weakening of the bond between altar and people is also exemplified by the fact that prayers to be said only by the priest, on his own behalf, were now introduced at all parts of the liturgy where the action or process had hitherto been performed in silence: at the beginning and end of Mass, during the preparation of the gifts, before and during the Communion. In the eucharistic prayer, the Canon was explained as the sanctuary which the priest alone could enter; its words were therefore to be pronounced softly.

The meaning of the word *Praefatio* was misunderstood, and so it was taken to be a mere preface to the Canon, instead of the first section of the great prayer which should have been uttered out loud "before" the people and before God: *praefatio* is the same as *praedicatio*.

This is the form in which the Roman liturgy, transformed in fact into a Franco-Roman liturgy, made its way back to Rome from the 10th century on. During the "dark ages", traditional Church order and liturgy had fallen into decay and disintegration in Rome and Italy. So when the German kings, starting with Otto I, appeared in Rome in the company of numerous prelates, and undertook in their role of Roman emperor to set up a new order, it was also the liturgical books and institutions of the north which regulated divine worship henceforth, even in the centre of Christianity. The monks from Cluny, the starting-point of the inward renewal of Church life in the 11th century, also worked in the same direction. The Cluniac reform, however, did not result in a set of strictly uniform institutions. All through the Middle Ages the principle was indeed maintained that each Church should conform to the Metropolitan of the province to which it belonged. But very often not only the various provinces but even the individual Churches of bishop or monastery observed their own particular customs. The liturgical books, which had of course to be copied out by hand in each case, were subjected to a constant process of expansion and transformation, which affected especially their later parts, dating from Carolingian times. Only some leading centres, and the religious orders then beginning to flourish, tried to establish firm and obligatory institutions on their own behalf.

This epoch also gave rise to the special forms of the Franco-Roman rite which still survive today among the Carthusians and Premonstratensians, in the ecclesiastical provinces of Lyons in France and of Braga in Portugal. The special forms then established for the Cistercians, various Benedictine abbeys, the Churches of Cologne, Trier, Mainz, Liège and elsewhere, were abandoned in favour of the post-Tridentine reform after the Council of Trent.

Only one important change has come into general use since the 13th century, the elevation of the host and chalice at the consecration of the Mass. This provided an unmistakable climax in the Canon which met medieval man's longing for contemplation, and the sight of the sacred host also furnished him with a certain substitute for sacramental Communion, then rarely permitted and even more rarely practised. Otherwise, the end of the Middle Ages was not only a time of liturgical variations; it was also a time of many abuses and superstitions. The violent assault of the Reformation, which with its principle of "the Bible alone" rejected not only obvious abuses but even the Canon of the Mass, was the occasion for the "Catholic Reform" of the liturgy, which was demanded by the Council of Trent and carried through by the succeeding Popes, beginning with Pius V and his editions of the Breviary and Missal (1568 and 1570).

At the same time the principle was laid down which was expressly formulated later on, in *CIC*, can. 1257: that in matters liturgical the Roman See was the only competent instance in the Latin Church. A strictly uniform liturgical practice now became possible with the introduction of printed books. It was further supervised by the Congregation of Rites set up by Sixtus V in 1588 and was maintained successfully from then on, down to the 20th century. The first notable changes in this somewhat rigid liturgical order were instituted by Pius X. He led the way back to the early Christian practice of frequent Communion by his decree on Holy Communion. He also made new regulations for Church music and introduced a new arrangement of the psalms for the Breviary. Another factor of change was the liturgical movement, which strove hard to bridge the gap, grown wider with the years, between the altar and the people in the liturgy. A radical reform was started under Pius XII with the new liturgy for the Easter vigil (1951) and for Holy Week (1955). The Second Vatican Council has provided for the extension of the reform over the whole field of the liturgy (decree *Sacrosanctum Concilium*). As sub-divisions of the liturgy are treated in special articles, we have now only to speak of the structural laws and the most important constitutive elements of the liturgy.

C. Structural Laws

Sacramental actions form the heart of the liturgy, and their climax is the celebration of the Eucharist. Obviously, the liturgical setting of each sacrament can only take the form of an extension of the sacramental sign. It will prepare for its enactment, aid its understanding and ensure the disposition of the recipient. Prayers will be offered for the efficacy and persistence of the sacramental effect. The various blessings in the liturgy will follow more or less similar rules. But no such obviously obligatory norms exist to direct worship when it consists merely of prayer. It can only follow out the laws of its own being.

Every time Christians meet to pray, their assembly should reflect the relationship in which the Church stands to God, by virtue of the Christian order of salvation. If full expression is to be given to this relationship, the word of God will come at the beginning, either in the form of Scripture reading, or in the form of a sermon which proclaims the word. For it is God who calls the Church together. And we can only answer when we are called by God's grace.

The word of God must then resound in our hearts. This could be in silent meditation. But in the assembly of the Church the echo in the hearts of the faithful will mostly try to express itself in some outward form. It will manifest itself in song. Only then comes the prayer. And since it is precisely a community which has gathered for prayer, the community will now speak, either in silence for the prayer of each one's heart, or in a common invocation, and above all in alternating prayer. Prayer, however, will culminate in the formal *Oratio*, the "Collect", in which the representative of the hierarchy "brings together" the prayer of all and puts it before God.

This sequence is in fact presented more or less clearly by all the liturgies, but above all by the Roman. Here it determines the structure of the second part of each canonical hour: a *capitulum* or short reading from Scripture to begin with, followed by a hymn or a responsory. The *oratio* of the officiant forms the conclusion, which on certain occasions is still introduced by the alternating prayer of the congregation, as was formerly always the case.

The same sequence could be repeated several times if a longer period was to be filled out with prayer, as was the case in the ancient Christian vigils lasting all the night. So we find it repeated six times in the first part of the Mass for the Saturday of Ember Days, and twelve times in the liturgy of Holy Saturday, the former Easter vigil, as it was conducted up to 1955. In both these cases each *oratio* is introduced by silent prayer, to which the individual is summoned by the *flectamus genua*.

The word of God in the form of Scripture reading has its most honourable place in the Mass: but lengthier readings from Scripture could find a place only in the Office.

In many medieval monasteries, the whole of Scripture was read each year. But under the regulations in force since then, the Bible is read through every year in selected portions. The reading does not follow automatically the order of the books, but is so adjusted that certain books with relevant themes are arranged around the two cycles of feasts.

For the Church's song, after a first brief period when the hymn flourished, the psalter has always been favoured, ever since Christian antiquity, and it has remained the primary song-book of the Church. The psalter is the inspired word of God and as such superior to any human creation. Its OT matter may not always have corresponded to the language of the people of God under the new covenant. But there did not seem to be any difficulty in reading its obscure allusions in the light of fulfilment. The words of the psalmist were taken to be the voice of Christ or of the Church redeemed, where they were not used as an invocation to Christ himself.

The recitation of the psalms took two forms in the Church. In early times, the responsorial method was predominant, where a precentor recited the psalm and the congregation answered each verse or section of the psalm with a refrain, a verse given out at the beginning of the psalm. The so-called responsories used today, where the former text has been shortened and the melody enriched, are a remnant of this method. But ever since the early Middle Ages, the antiphonal method of recitation has prevalied. Here the two halves of the choir alternate verse by verse, and the verse used as a framework, the antiphon, melodically more richly developed, is sung only at the beginning and the end.

The early history of this type of chant, which begins in the 4th century, and even the original meaning of the word "antiphon", are, however, still a matter for controversy among the historians of music.

In the canonical hours of the Byzantine rite, the chanting of psalms was again almost entirely eliminated at an early date by a rich flow of hymns. But in the West the hymn could only succeed in establishing itself after strong opposition. It was adopted into the liturgy of the city of Rome only about the 12th century, under northern influences. Needless to say, the ordinary hymnbook must in principle be allotted the same role as the Latin hymn, especially in vernacular worship. It must, however, be noted that in a large number of the compositions which we have inherited from the last few centuries, the richness of religious thought has been far too much restricted to narrow fields where subjective feelings held sway. Hence severity must be exercised in their choice.

As regards the type of music used and the executants, the widest possible choice is offered: from simple unison to the riches of polyphony, accompanied or unaccompanied. The principle, however, should be that except on very special occasions which suggest or necessitate a display of artistic brilliancy, community hymn-singing is what corresponds best to the nature of the Church.

As already suggested, alternating prayer, where the congregation responds with short invocations to the words of a spokesman, seems the most suitable form for the prayer of the people. The typical example of such prayer is to be found in the litanies. We might take as a model the form given in the oldest section of the Litany of the Saints, where the people respond to the petition mentioned by the officiant with: "We beseech thee to hear us." Still older tradition was used to the same effect by the *Kyrie eleison*.

Other forms of prayer suitable for congregational use have been evolved in the so-called *preces*, which now precede the *Oratio* in the Office when "prayers" are indicated, and which regularly preceded the *Oratio* in former times. The intention is expressed within a summons to prayer addressed to the community: "Let us pray for our absent brothers." In response, the verse of a psalm is used for preference: "Save thy servants, O Lord, who trust in thee" (Ps 85:2). The communities of long ago, well-versed in the Scriptures, rightly felt that texts from Scripture were particularly apt, even though their intention was only imperfectly expressed in the verses used. This procedure supposes a certain knowledge of the Bible which we can of course no longer count on in the average faithful of today.

This form of prayer can be seen in a further stage of development in the various litanies, where, however, the principal thing is to recite with reverence a list of holy names and titles of honour. These have now become independent prayers, with ecclesiastical approbation.

The prayer of the Church comes to a conclusion, and is also given its most perfect expression, in the prayer uttered by the priest (or, as the case may be, by the leader of the liturgical assembly). It begins, according to primitive Christian tradition, with a greeting to which the congregation responds, followed by a summons to prayer. Two basic forms of this prayer exist, corresponding to the occasion on which it is offered: the Preface for the prayer of thanksgiving, the *Oratio* for the prayer of petition. In thanksgiving, the summons to prayer is: "Gratias agamus Domino, Deo nostro." The supreme expression of all thanksgiving is the "Eucharist" itself, the Canon of the Mass with its Preface. But the structure found in the Preface is also used at other important acts of consecration: for the consecration of persons (deacon, priest, bishop, abbot, abbess), and of objects (chrism, baptismal water, paschal candle, church, altar, cemetery).

It begins by praising the salvific action of God and then passes on as a rule with an *igitur* or *qua propter* to the petition, in which God's blessing is asked for the occasion in question.

In a petition, the summons to prayer is usually short: *Oremus*. But in many cases, as for instance in the *Orationes* of Good Friday, the particular object of the petition is also indicated. In our Roman liturgy the prayer itself is usually very distinctive. It is in fact absolutely characteristic, especially where the intention has already been mentioned in the summons to prayer or in the preliminary supplications, that the prayer with which the priest appears before God as the appointed spokesman of the people, does not lose itself in fluent rhetoric or indeed in poetry. The prayer pronounces the essential in a few well-ordered words, as is in fact the case in the Roman *orationes* as they have come down to us. Clearly, these are laws to be observed also when new prayers are composed, which may well be called for in a vernacular service. The important thing is not to give a copious exposition of our human needs, but to make sure that our prayer is in conformity with the great ordinances of God. Hence the prayer is directed, not to any of the heavenly powers, such as the saint whose feast we may be celebrating, but to God himself. And it ends as a rule by looking to Christ "through whom we have obtained access" (Rom 5:2) to the Father. The "amen" of the people responds to it and confirms it.

Part of the constitutive elements of all liturgies, along with the words, are the external rites, the gestures, the well-ordered movements. One remains standing before a superior; hence well into the Middle Ages, standing was the predominant posture at prayer. This was also explained, especially in early times, by saying: We rise to our feet, because we have risen with Christ. For the same reason it was emphasized that standing was the only possible posture for prayer on days connected with Easter: Sundays and Paschal time. In antiquity it was also thought important that prayer should be made facing the East, the direction of the rising sun. This was again in memory of Christ, in whose resurrection the sun rose upon us. The easterly direction is still favoured today as far as possible in the orientation of Church buildings. Later on, kneeling became more and more prevalent for prayer, a posture expressive of submission. It had always been in use for the prayer of petition from the earliest times, as the "Flectamus genua" shows. Where the element of adoration is emphasized, it has also been the practice, from ancient times, to fall on one's knees before the divine majesty. This is particularly true of the awesome moments when God comes so close to us in the mystery of the Incarnation. Till the recent reforms, it was usual to kneel at the words "Et verbum caro factum est", at the "Et incarnatus est", and also before the Blessed Sacrament.

The reposeful attitude of being seated seems indicated whenever it is a matter of listening receptively. So we sit down for the lessons, except when they are taken from the gospel, and for the sermon. Sitting is also normal during pauses in the liturgical action; such moments of rest are in fact provided by the longer chants. It has also become usual to sit down for the chanting of the psalms, so that the lengthy service may not prove too tiring. Prayer also demands that the hands should be held properly. In Christian antiquity, the usual practice at prayer was to spread out the hands, pointing upwards, ready to offer and to receive. This is the attitude of the *Orantes*, familiar to us from the paintings of the catacombs, and still taken by the priest at the present day for all the prayers of the Mass which come from ancient tradition. Germanic usage favoured bringing the hands together. In the feudal system, the vassal placed his joined hands in the hands of his liege lord, as a sign of submission and obedience. The gesture is still used today by newly-ordained priests as they make their promise of obedience to the bishop. This way of holding the hands also gained prevalence in the liturgy from A.D. 1000 on, under the influence of the northern countries. The hands are either intertwined, or laid palm to palm, as is done by the priest at the altar.

The laying on of hands is an important liturgical symbol, whose use extends to the administration of the sacraments. It serves above all to signify the transmission of authority, at the conferring of major orders; but it also signifies the bestowal of grace (when the priest raises his hand in the sacrament of penance) and blessing.

In recent times, however, the sign of the cross has become the chief symbol of blessing. The priest makes the sign of the cross over persons and objects, and one signs oneself with the cross when receiving a blessing and beginning a prayer or a sacred action.

Joseph Andreas Jungmann

II. Liturgical Language

1. *The data of comparative religion.* Most religions hand down their sacred teachings and hold their sacred rites in sacred, cultic languages. Sometimes these are merely severely classical or literary forms of the ordinary language, from which they can be sharply distinguished. Where a strictly cultic language is used in worship it is usually an earlier form of the living tongue (as among the Romans); often it is the language of a former culture, since displaced by "more modern" languages (as Hebrew was by Aramaic among the post-exilic Jews); often it is no longer intelligible even to the priests (in Rome, for example). Cultic languages exist because of a belief that the gods can be reached only through "their own language" (thus the ancient Germans), a fear that speaking of holy things in ordinary language is a profanation which will incur the divine wrath, a sense that the numinous and awesome may only be approached by means of extraordinary words; because of the solemnity with which cultic language invests an occasion, or because of reverence for and a desire to preserve the linguistic form in which a saving event has taken place (Hebrew as the language of the OT). These sacred languages are static in character; apparently beyond the reach of historical change, they express the timelessness of revelation and prayer, at once protecting and bringing home to men the unfathomable mystery of the divine, the *arrheton*, the ineffable. They spring from a conviction that the divinity can only be addressed "divinely", that compared with the otherness of God and his holiness human words are blasphemous (cf. "holy silence"). Since the very existence of cultic languages, then, betokens a definite idea of God, the problem they pose is more than a rubrical one; it is theological.

2. *Christian liturgical languages.* The liturgy of the Church uses cultic languages at the present day: Latin in the West, various "ecclesiastical languages" in the Eastern rites (hardly any of which use the current vernacular). In the course of four centuries the English of the *Book of Common Prayer* and the German of Luther's Bible have also hardened into sacred languages. The Roman Church in particular has cherished Latin as "the language of the Church" and stoutly defended it down to our own day, almost as if it were part of the Church's nature. But liturgical Latin was never a completely foreign language: the Church has always been concerned that liturgists, at least, should understand it. (Thus in 1949 Mandarin Chinese – not the vernacular – was again sanctioned for use in the Missal, as had been done in 1615.)

3. *Theological analysis.* Any critical discussion of the language of Christian worship must start from the following premisses: Jesus Christ is God's unsurpassable, definitive Word to mankind, which, though prepared and uttered in a particular historical setting, so far transcends it – given God's universal salvific will and the consecration of all that is human by Christ's incarnation and resurrection – that the historical forms of the Jewish-Hellenistic world have no abiding validity. Much less, then, need we cling to the forms of any other culture: man is constantly summoned anew to final decision. Since Christ is God's definitive Word to us, a valid answer is possible only in Christ and according to Christ (that is, we must now speak to God in human words,

not "divine" ones): so that in Christ every possible form of worship has been superseded. Until the end of time the only appointed temple of God's Word and man's answer is now the Church formed by the new people of God who are called out of every tongue, in permanent diversity (cf. Acts 2:4–11). The people of God adore him in the spirit and the truth that are Christ himself, by accepting the salvation he has wrought and praising him for it. Here, in this Church, each in his own mother tongue, every human being is entitled to hear God and respond to him. What this means is that there are no longer any strictly cultic languages, nor even any specifically "sacred languages" which ought to be the vehicle of God's Word and man's response. Now every human language is potentially a liturgical language once it is used to proclaim the gospel and to embody the decision of faith. The seriousness of the content will, however, give the language of liturgy a special style (for example "Christian Latin") that sets it apart from ordinary speech, just as the utterances and decisions of poets and philosophers go beyond the language of business and practical needs.

4. *History of Christian liturgical language*. Ancient Christianity, unlike other religions, made free use of the vernacular in its worship: Aramaic, Greek (at Rome as late as the 4th century and even in Gaul [Lyons]), Latin (first in Africa). The extemporaneous character of the ancient liturgy, whether charismatic glossolalia or the "official" anaphora, necessarily presupposed use of the mother tongue. The witness of faith at Christian worship is "sine monitore, quia de pectore" (Tertullian, *Apologia*, 30). But just as the gospels, confessing the way of salvation that history has established, bore traces of their origins ("Abba", Mk 14:36; "Eloi, Eloi, lamma sabacthani", Mk 15:34; cf. Mt 27:46 and other texts), so too the worship of the Church: "Amen", "Hosanna", "Alleluia" from the temple liturgy, "maranatha" (Aramaic) from the primitive Christian community of Palestine (1 Cor 16:22; *Didache*, 10, 6), Greek "Kyrie eleison" (and at one time, perhaps, Latin formulae). If special liturgical and ecclesiastical languages nevertheless came into being, the reason is to be sought outside the liturgy. The barbarians who invaded the Empire adopted the culture of nations who saw in Old or New Rome the model of all civilized practice, even where religion was concerned: it was only natural to adhere to those centres of worship and missionary activity. While the Greek of Byzantium, however, did not spread as an ecclesiastical language, the Latin of Rome became the liturgical language of the new medieval Church. No doubt the Roman liturgy if not "understanded of the people", did endow the West with a noble example of the solemn worship of God, for which we must be grateful, and the problem of having the liturgy in a foreign language only emerged in modern times, when Latin had ceased to be familiar to the learned world. Those who early perceived the "latina miseria" of the Christian people (an expression used by the Italian Camaldolese Giustiniani and Quirini, addressing Leo X in 1513) were doomed to remain isolated, since Latin had acquired an almost dogmatic importance in reaction against the principle of worship in the vernacular upheld by dissidents from the 13th to the 16th century (Catharists, Waldensians, Hussites, Reformers). Yet the Council of Trent made no positive statement on the value of Latin in Catholic services: its use must simply be recognized as legitimate, even though one function of the liturgy is to proclaim God's word (*D* 946, 956; the actual decrees are a good deal more cautious in tone than the texts originally submitted to the Fathers). The arguments advanced in favour of liturgical Latin by apologetics and on occasion by the magisterium it-

self (those cited in section 1, above, are found in a letter of 1080 from Gregory VII to Vratislav, king of Bohemia; Mansi, XX, 296 f.) are either inadequate ("Latin is the vinculum unitatis Ecclesiae" – contrast Acts 2:4–11), or unsound ("changeless Latin safeguards the purity of doctrine" – compare the Latin of the Roman Missal with that of the 13th century Scholastics): they fail to carry conviction. Taking its cue from Trent, the Second Vatican Council did not merely grant that the mother tongue was a handmaid of, or a poor substitute for, Latin (thus the instruction of the Congregation of Rites as recently as 3 September 1958), but recognized its complete suitability for liturgical use (Constitution on the Liturgy, arts. 36, 63 and 14, 26, among others). This means more than permission to use accurate vernacular translations of the liturgy to which we have been accustomed: in effect the Council said that the vernacular would be meaningful – as Latin once was – only in the setting of a liturgy that was modern in the best sense of the word, one that for the people of God today was eloquent of his saving deeds, and in which it was natural for them to declare the obedience of their faith. To work out such a liturgy will be a task requiring great patience and constant meditation on the nature of Christian salvation. And its language will always be a task calling for new effort.

Angelus Häussling

III. Study of Liturgy

Liturgical science might be taken to mean a purely theoretical study of the many different forms of worship that Christians have used in the course of two millennia – a branch, in other words, of cultural history and archaeology. But such a view would fail to do justice to liturgies as an ecclesiastical science, which for all its interest in historical forms is ultimately concerned with interpreting the contemporary liturgy.

This task is of considerable importance for the reason that liturgy is naturally conservative: it tends to cling to established forms even after these have grown unintelligible to a changed world. Non-Christian rites, as comparative religion shows, often deliberately renounce intelligibility; but Christians may not be content to persist with the unintelligible, because they must adore God "in spirit and in truth".

First of all, the existing liturgy must be made as comprehensible as possible; then its original form and basic principles must be rediscovered, so that it can be suitably restored or adapted.

There was no need for a science of liturgy in the early Church. The forms of Christian worship were drawn from contemporary culture and the people shared in a service that was held in their own language.

As early as the 4th century, however, we find explanations of the liturgy, forms of catechesis on baptism, confirmation, and the Eucharist, which the bishop gave neophytes in Easter week – only, however, after their reception of the sacraments on Easter Eve. It was taken for granted that the direct sense of word and rite would be grasped without difficulty; only afterwards came a deeper religious interpretation. Among such catecheses – which contain important data on the liturgy – we should mention those of St. Ambrose, St. Cyril (or John) of Jerusalem, and Theodore of Mopsuestia.

By the early Middle Ages, however, the need was felt for an explanation of many traditional forms. But recourse was had to allegory, instead of the original sense: that is, a sense different from the original was read into the liturgy. These allegorical interpretations, beginning with St. Isidore and reaching a climax in Amalarius of Metz, prevailed throughout the Middle Ages. St. Albert attacked them in vain. Some few attempts at sober interpretation date from this period: we should mention Florus of Lyons, the opponent of Amalarius; Strabo, Abbot of Reichenau (d. 849), whose book bears the striking title *De exordiis et incrementis quarumdam in observationibus ecclesiasticis rerum*; and Berold of Constance, who wrote his *Micrologus* about 1085.

Only when the Humanists had awakened a sense of history and the Reformers had made the liturgy a subject of controversy can we speak of a strictly scientific treatment of the matter.

First some important source material was printed by Catholics in defence of their liturgical inheritance. In 1565 Jacobus Pamelius, Archdeacon of Bruges, published two quarto volumes of ancient liturgical texts (antiphonary, sacramentary, lectionary). Three years later Melchior Hittorp, a canon of Cologne, published a selection of early medieval liturgical commentaries, together with a collection of Roman Ordines and a Pontifical which, as M. Andrieu has shown (1931), dates from about 950 and subsequently became the standard Roman Pontifical for Germany.

The second period of liturgical scholarship is dominated by the "Maurists" (French Benedictines of the Congregation of St. Maur), who methodically collected and published liturgical manuscripts together with the results of their exhaustive research. Specially notable among the Maurists are Hugo Ménard (d. 1644; edition of a Gregorian Sacramentary); Jean Morin (d. 1639; studies and liturgical texts relating to the sacraments of penance and holy orders); Jean Mabillon (d. 1707; Roman Ordines and early Gallican liturgy); and above all Edmond Martène (d. 1739), whose four volumes *De antiquis Ecclesiae ritibus* are still a mine of information on the wealth of liturgical forms that existed north of the Alps during the Middle Ages. We are indebted for similar labours to the Cistercian Abbot John Bona, the polymath Muratori, and Martin Gerbert (d. 1793), Abbot of St. Blasien; in the case of the Eastern rites, to Eusèbe Renaudot (d. 1720) and the Assemani brothers.

With its lack of interest in history, the Enlightenment was not an age favourable to liturgics. About the middle of the 19th century commenced the period in which we still find ourselves, thanks to the renewal of theology that was by then under way and especially to the revival of patristic studies and Christian archaeology. Impressive general surveys now appeared, histories of the liturgy as a whole, like those of Ferdinand Probst of Breslau (d. 1899) and the ecclesiastical historian Louis Duchesne (d. 1922), or studies of special subjects – of the Breviary, like that of Dom Suitbert Bäumer O.S.B., of the medieval Mass or Benediction, like that of Adolf Franz (d. 1916). E. Bishop's *Liturgica Historica* (1918) was reprinted in 1962.

The sources too were being methodically collected, in Italy by Adalbert Ebner (d. 1898), in France by Victor Leroquais (d. 1946). On the Protestant side the Henry Bradshaw Society in England began publishing liturgical source material, British and Continental, on a large scale. Of F. E. Brightman's projected *Liturgies Eastern and Western* only the first volume was published (*Eastern Liturgies*, 1895). Anton Baumstark (d. 1948) also did much for the advancement of Oriental liturgical studies; and much light was shed on the transition from antiquity to Christendom, so crucial for the liturgy, by the research of Joseph Dölger (d. 1940) and his school.

Over the past century or so there has been a series of discoveries of basic liturgical source material from Christian antiquity (the *Didache*, the *Euchologium* of Serapion, the *Pilgrimage* of Aetheria, the *Testamentum Domini*). Analysis of Church ordinances for the ancient East has made it possible to reconstruct one of their sources, Hippolytus's *Apostolic*

Tradition, which dates from about the year 215 and gives us a general picture of liturgical practice in the Roman Church at that time.

The research carried on by the monks of Maria Laach and the Abbot, Ildefons Herwegen (d. 1946), is of great importance – the two collections (afterwards merged) of *Liturgiegeschichtliche Quellen* (1918ff.); the *Liturgiegeschichtliche Forschungen* (1918ff.); and the *Jahrbuch für Liturgiewissenschaft*, largely directed by Dom Odo Casel (d. 1948), begun in 1921 and reappearing since 1950 as the *Archiv für Liturgiewissenschaft*.

It was Odo Casel who first gave deliberate consideration to theological questions in the light of liturgical history. He put forward a "mystery-theology", which was afterwards much disputed. In Christian worship, he held, more precisely in the sacraments, the saving act of Christ that happened only once in history is made present, so that the faithful may enact it with Christ and share the fruits of the redemption. Although this thesis has had a persistent influence on the theology of the sacraments, complete synthesis does not appear to have been reached.

But there is now general agreement that the liturgy demands more than mere historical consideration and that it must be studied from a theological point of view. Theology had already begun to include such study, especially under the stimulus of the liturgical movement. But the liturgical movement itself only became possible because the investigation of the nature of the Church as the community of the faithful in contrast to a purely hierarchical conception was pursued in particular by German theologians, after the first studies of J. A. Möhler (d. 1838) at Tübingen.

It was left, however, to a Roman Benedictine, Cipriano Vagaggini, to treat the matter comprehensively in his book *Il senso teologico della liturgia*. Here the liturgy is seen as the continuation of saving history: the Church, sanctified by God through Christ in the Holy Spirit, responds by offering its worship through Christ.

Other major theological problems bearing on the liturgy are: the nature of Christian worship, Christ as high priest, worship and Church fellowship, the explicitation of the sacramental sign. The communal character of the liturgy is a central issue. Here there arises the further theological question of how far the liturgy coincides or can coincide with the life of piety in the Church, and how far the personal religious life of the individual is demanded by it or even indispensable to it. Then there is the question of how the communal character of the Church can or ought to be developed within the liturgy. This last question calls for a close scrutiny of the various pastoral and liturgical interests to which more and more study has been devoted in the literature of recent years. They are such matters as the active participation of the people in worship, the position of the laity, the language of the liturgy, the role of Church music and ecclesiastical art, popular devotions and their connection with liturgy, the rights of the bishop and the episcopate within the liturgical framework laid down by Rome.

All these, obviously, are important practical problems that must be clarified at least in principle. Light will only be thrown on some of these questions by the course of history itself. Where the liturgy is concerned history and theology must always go hand in hand.

As to the future, the liturgical sources must be brought to light with the aid of the appropriate sciences (paleography, philology, and the like) and modern techniques (such as the photography of palimpsests), and important texts published in critical editions.

For the West as a whole this task is fairly complete; but in particular areas, not least in Germany, the sources have by no means been exhausted. For the

East, outside the Byzantine area, little has been made available in European languages except the eucharistic liturgies. Research based on these will require help from the biblical sciences and comparative religion, patristics and Christian archaeology; the cultural history of antiquity, and Oriental philosophy and literature; the history of the kerygma, dogma, and spirituality; the history of art, iconography and musicology. If these studies are to be fruitful for the liturgical life of the Church, surveys must be produced summing up and interpreting the findings of the scholars. Thus too the way will be opened to further reforms. Such books will practically always raise theological questions.

It is hardly necessary to point out that the reforms we have already seen in this century – from the revival of Gregorian chant by Pius X, on the basis of the research done at Solesmes, to the restoration of the Easter Vigil – were only possible thanks to labours undertaken in liturgical science. So too the reforms launched by Vatican II.

The new appreciation of the Oriental rites, and the abandonment of efforts to reduce them to uniformity along Latinized lines, are due to the relevant studies in liturgics. Sound developments in the worship of the Church will only be possible if liturgical science continues to fulfil its tasks. Prospects that it will do so have brightened in the past few years with the foundation of liturgical institutes (one at the Institut Catholique in Paris and one at Sant' Anselmo in Rome) and the decision of the Second Vatican Council to include liturgics among the *disciplinae principales* in faculties of theology.

Joseph Andreas Jungmann

M

MAGISTERIUM

A. History of the Doctrine

The history of the doctrine concerning the magisterium is in the concrete almost identical with the history of the self-understanding of the Church itself, which cannot but understand itself essentially except as the bearer of the gospel message. To ask about the bearers of the message in the Church and their right to demand faith is always a question about the essence of the Church, and vice versa. Hence as regards the history of dogma and of theology in this connection, it will suffice to a great extent to refer to the articles *Church* II, III, *Word of God, Bible* I, *Tradition, Ecclesiastical Authority, Apostolic Succession, Hierarchy, Pope* I, *Bishop*.

At the end of the apostolic age, the monarchical episcopate was firmly established as the decisive court of appeal in the Church, in contrast to a class of enthusiastic prophets. And the doctrinal authority thus reserved to these bishops was understood as the mandate of handing on the doctrine of the apostles. Hence there are two elements in tradition. One is the material element, the doctrine of the apostles about the Christ-event (in the broadest sense of the word) which is handed on and given the expression corresponding to the needs of the times. The other is the formal or active element, the claim of the bishops to demand faith as they testify in the name of Christ and with the assistance of the Holy Spirit. Tradition is both something transmitted and the action of transmitting it. This tradition involves a number of moments which act and react upon each other in a relationship which cannot be reduced to any one single element. The Christ-event attests itself and demands faith, and in doing so also establishes the "authority" of the witnesses. But it attests itself on the lips of the qualified witnesses and envoys themselves, in the authority which is thereby given them, and which is handed on from witness to witness in a historical continuity of a juridical type. If one also considers that the Church of Christ understands itself to be the community of faith in its Lord, the pillar and the ground of truth (1 Tim 3:15), against which the gates of hell cannot prevail (Mt 16:18; cf. also Gal 1:8), one must undoubtedly acknowledge with the ancient Church that the episcopate as a whole possesses an "infallible" doctrinal authority, in all cases where the whole episcopate teaches a doctrine as part of its actual testimony to Christ, to be accepted with an absolute assent of faith (cf., e.g., Rouët de Journel, *Enchiridion Patristicum*, nos. 204, 209ff., 242, 296, 298; C. Kirch and L. Ueding, *Enchiridion fontium historiae*, nos. 124ff.). This is also attested by the early efforts – as in Ignatius of Antioch, Hegesippus, Irenaeus and Tertullian – to register the consensus of the ancient episcopal Churches and to use lists of bishops to establish the formal aspect of the apostolic succession and the authority of the bishops. Hence too the unquestionable authority of general councils in the early Church is at once understandable. In spite of the denial of the infallibility of general councils by the Reformers (and by some few precursors such as Wycliffe and Huss), the only point that can be open to debate within the Catholic consciousness of the Church is how this universal episcopate is to be understood as a unity, since it cannot be merely the sum of the individual – fallible – bishops. From this point of view, the history of the doctrine concerning the magisterium of the Church coincides with the history of the doctrine concerning the primacy of the Pope, as the concrete centre of unity and head of the whole episcopate. The development of the doctrine concerning the inner structure of the magisterium, against Conciliarism, Episcopalism, Gallicanism and Febronianism, reached a high-point in the dogma of Vatican I on the infallible doctrinal magisterium of the Pope. This was completed by the doctrine of Vatican II on the infallible doctrinal authority of the episcopate as a whole with and under the Pope. But this does not mean that all the questions as to how the primacy of the Pope is related precisely to his function as head of the whole episcopate have been given a generally accepted solution.

B. On the Basic Notion of the Magisterium

1. In a theology of the ecclesiastical magisterium, it will not do to start at once with the simple notion of a transference of formal authority from God, imparted to a man in such a way that he is clothed with this authority as he confronts other men "from outside". In such a pattern of thought, which is very common in fundamental theology, it is inexplicable, for instance, that a doctrinal authority such as is found in the Church of the new covenant should not have existed under the old covenant, though the need for certainty as regards the truth of revelation was then equally desirable. For a proper theological understanding of the (infallible) magisterium of the Church, one must begin with the eschatological triumph of the Christ-event as such. Part of its intrinsic composition is the word in which it testifies to itself. It can only remain eschatologically triumphant and present in the world if it does not falter and fail in the word of its self-attestation. This word of testimony, by which the Christ-event becomes historically present to all ages, is uttered primarily by the whole community of Christian believers, by the Church as such and as a whole. Hence the action of the Spirit is from beginning to end directed to this Church as a whole, which is preserved in the truth of Christ by the Spirit (cf. *D* 1821, 1839). But this Church which is the historical presence of Christ preserved in the truth of Christ, through which the truth of God is offered to the world, accepted in faith and manifested in historical confession, is essentially something more than the mere sum of individual believers, totted up as it were from below. It is not just a meta-historical fellowship, but a historically-structured society with a confession of faith and a doctrinal authority. Hence in the last resort, the precise nature of this authority is only to be explained in terms of the eschatological nature of the Church. While the actual teachers do not receive their authority by being appointed by the members of this community as the sum of the individuals, still, their authority and its "infallibility" are only conceivable within this eschatological community of belief. It is a moment of the implementation of the decree of God in Jesus Christ, by which

he willed that the salutary truth of the Christ-event should remain historically present in the world. The Church would not be the eschatological community of salvation if it were not in "infallible" possession of the truth of Christ. For the Church proclaims that the grace of God – hence also the grace of truth and faith – is not merely constantly offered anew, but that this grace of truth in the Church always remains in fact triumphant there, and that this triumph remains tangible and manifest in the historically concrete Church, and hence also in its confession of faith.

2. When we speak of the magisterium of the Church, we should not forget the inner unity of the offices of the Church. Vatican II speaks frequently, especially in *Lumen Gentium*, of the three offices of Christ and of the hierarchy, though this threefold division is comparatively recent in the history of theology, and cannot be easily harmonized with the classical teaching of canonists on the two powers in the Church, the power of sanctification (*potestas ordinis*) and the power of government (*potestas iurisdictionis*). All these offices (*munera*) and powers (*potestates*) can be comprised within the one authority of the "creative" word of God, which does not merely notify what is said, but actually brings into play (*verbum exhibitivum*) the grace, presence and power of God. It is the word which judges and sanctifies as it is uttered into the concrete presence of man and of the Church. As anamnesis, it re-presents perpetually the one, single past event of Christ's salvific deed, and as prognosis anticipates the promised future in hope. In keeping with the nature of man and the diversity of his history, this one word has necessarily various degrees of intensity. It ranges from the seemingly merely doctrinal proclamations of the magisterium, and the directives which define a Christian task in a given situation of the Church and the individual, to the word which is the "form" in the sacrament and makes the grace of God historically present and effective *ex opere operato*. This is the basis of the unity of offices and powers in the Church, and it must be carefully considered, if the magisterium of the Church is to be rightly understood. Thus the magisterium is not strictly speaking the authority to teach abstract doctrines for their own sake. It is the guarantee that the salvific word of Christ will be really addressed to the concrete situation of a given age, in view of Christian life. And this forms the history of dogma, not just the history of theology. The magisterium as thus understood does not replace the work and rule of the Spirit, through whom it lives and to whose guidance it is always subject. But the magisterium is the concrete form in which the guidance of the Spirit, as the Spirit of Christ who gives the Christ-event historical presence, maintains historical continuity with Jesus Christ.

3. In spite of the individualism of later days, which is still very much the prevailing temper of the West, a new understanding for the magisterium of the Church must surely now be possible, in view of our knowledge of the man of today and tomorrow. Man cannot possess his truth as an isolated individual, since he is no such thing. Hence there can be truth for the individual only in inter-communication with other men – especially if the truth is that of the one and total existence of man. And such fellowship can only be realized in a society with concrete institutions. The truth of man would be dissipated into the hazard of private opinions which the self-doubting man of today would not take particularly seriously if in free and inevitable resolve he did not allow himself to be corrected by the truth which is not *a priori* his own but which comes to him as that of a socially instituted fellowship. Truth of its very nature has to do with fellowship, society and institution, even though the precise relationship of an individual and

his truth to the truth of a fellowship and society differs essentially according to the nature of the society in question. But in a post-individualistic epoch new possibilities of understanding may be opened up, even for the understanding of the magisterium in the Church.

C. The Magisterium on the Magisterium

1. The doctrine proposed by the magisterium about itself is to be found in its fullest and most authentic form in the third chapter of Vatican II's Dogmatic Constitution on the Church (*Lumen Gentium*, especially arts. 24–25). This whole chapter must be kept in mind throughout, though there will be no need to refer to it constantly for the points of doctrine now to be proposed. Most of the references in the following will be to earlier pronouncements of the Church on its magisterium.

2. We need not go into detail here about the concrete manner of the origin of the Church from the historical Jesus (for which see *Church* I–III). We may refer to the biblical justification of the magisterium given by Vatican II, which needs, however, some further nuances from the point of view of historical criticism, since it deals with the connection of the Church with the pre-Easter Jesus. Otherwise the teaching of the magisterium is as follows. In the college of the apostles (*D* 1787, 1793, 1798, 1828, 1836, 2204) Jesus Christ endowed the Church which he founded with a permanent magisterium (*D* 1821, 1837, 1957). This magisterium is authentic, that is, demands assent by virtue of the formal authority confided to it and not merely by virtue of the contents of the message (*D* 1800, 1839), and is also essentially infallible (*D* 1800, 1839). This magisterium has authority with regard to the rest of the faithful, in keeping with the constitution of the Church (*D* 1958, 2313), without prejudice to the infallibility of the believing Church as a whole (cf., for example, Mansi, LI, 542, 552, 1214; *Lumen Gentium*, art. 25: "charisma infallibilitatis ipsius ecclesiae"). This doctrine is already implicit in the doctrine of the Church on tradition, the apostolic succession and dogma. It was also propounded against the Reformation (*D* 765ff., 769f., 783, 786, 1788), defined in substance by Vatican I (cf. also *D* 1957f.), and reasserted by Vatican II.

3. As has already been remarked, there is still no absolutely clear and unanimous doctrine in Catholic theology about the ultimate essence of the possessors of authentic and finally infallible doctrinal authority in the Church. The point at question is the precise nature of the relationship between the whole episcopate with and under the Pope, without whom it is not a college, and the Pope as wielder of the same supreme doctrinal authority such as is proper to the whole episcopate. Two wielders of the supreme doctrinal authority in one and the same society is inconceivable, and the usual solution of text-book theology, that in this case there is only partial non-identity, while correct, does not really solve the problem. The question was also finally left open by Vatican II. With this reservation in mind, it may still be affirmed that the wielder of the supreme doctrinal authority in the Church is the college of bishops, as the legitimate succession to the college of the apostles, with and under the Pope as its head. This college can act through the ordinary magisterium, which can be quite well considered as a collegial act, though it may not be a *new* collegial act, and accordingly may be referred to an explicit act of the whole episcopate or to an act of the Pope as head of the whole episcopate. This college of bishops can also act when it assembles as such in one place in a Council or when it is represented by the Pope. For the Pope, in the exercise of doctrinal primacy, acts as head of the whole episcopate, though the juridical validity of his act does not

thereby depend on the previous assent of the other members of the episcopal college. But this again does not mean that the Pope is independent of the college in the discovery of the doctrine taught and for the moral justification of his act. On the ordinary magisterium, see *D* 1683, 1792; *CIC*, can. 1323; *Lumen Gentium*, art. 25. For the authority of a Council, see *D* 54, 212, 349, 691, 792a, 810, 873a, 882, 910, 929a, 1000, 1781, 1821; *Lumen Gentium*, art. 25. For the doctrinal authority of the Pope, see the articles *Pope* I, *Infallibility*; *D* 1839; *Lumen Gentium*, art. 25.

4. The object of the magisterium is the content of Christian revelation and all that is necessary or useful for the preaching and the defence of this revelation. In determining the content of revelation and demarcating it off from matters on which the magisterium is not competent, the magisterium is itself the judge of its own authority. That the magisterium does not go beyond its powers when demanding the absolute assent of faith (at any rate), is guaranteed, according to the Catholic faith, by the assistance given to the Church by the Spirit. This is the one ultimate guarantee, but it is sufficient.

a) Hence the primary and direct object of the magisterium are the truths of Christian revelation which are revealed *per se* (for their own sakes, and not for the sake of revealing something else). This is the *depositum fidei*, the doctrine on faith and morals (*D* 1792, 1800, 1836, 1839; *Lumen Gentium*, art. 25). This principle does not solve at once the question of the precise explanation of the divine revelation itself as to its origin, unity and essence. Hence the principle must not be taken to mean that the deposit of faith contains divine revelation in the form of a number of individual propositions (no matter how numerous) which are to be authoritatively taught by the magisterium as purely doctrinal propositions.

b) The secondary or indirect object of the magisterium are other truths which, though not revealed *per se* or explicitly, touch matters of faith and morals directly or indirectly. This may be by their logical connection with revealed truths, of which they may be the presupposition or the imperative consequence – and thus "virtually revealed". Or they may be "dogmatic facts", e.g., the legitimate authority of a given Council. Or they may be propositions of purely "ecclesiastical faith", in contrast to the truths of "divine faith" which are revealed *per se*. They would be doctrines taught with absolute binding force by the Church, when the Church does not claim that they are implicitly or explicitly revealed by God, but finds them necessary for the safeguard and the effective and relevant preaching of the faith strictly speaking (*D* 783, 1098f., 1350, 1674ff., 1710ff., 1798, 1817, 1930a, 2005, 2024, 2311f.). This affirmation of a secondary or indirect object of the magisterium is put forward rather as a matter of principle. Whether and where such statements of the magisterium occur, and how they share in the magisterium and the quality of propositions of faith strictly speaking, is, it seems, to a great extent an open question.

5. The source of the magisterium of the Church and its ultimate norm is the divine revelation in Jesus Christ, which on account of its eschatological fullness was closed with the apostles (*D* 2021). It is not augmented by the magisterium, but transmitted, given relevant expression in each age and in this sense, developed (for which see *Dogma* II; also *D* 783, 1800, 1836, 2020f., 2145, 2313; Vatican II, Dogmatic Constitution on Divine Revelation, *Verbum Dei*, arts. 1–10). Revelation is given in the apostolic tradition, which again crystallizes in Scripture and "oral tradition" (*D* 783, 1787, 1792, 2313f.; *Dei Verbum*, arts. 7–10; see the article *Scripture and Tradition*). The content of this divine revelation, as preserved by the magisterium of the

Church and the faith of the Church, can be seen – primarily by the magisterium itself, secondarily by individual believers and theologians – by referring back to the expression of this revelation at any period of the Church's history. Recourse is had for this to the consensus of the Church Fathers and theologians. In this recourse to the *loci theologici*, however, careful note must be taken of the exact degree of insistence with which the Fathers and theologians proclaim that the doctrine in question is really an attestation of the divine revelation in Jesus Christ.

6. The magisterium can propound its doctrine as obligatory in various degrees. Even where it does not demand an absolute and irreformable assent of divine faith (or of purely ecclesiastical faith, if there is such a thing), it can of itself and normally demand interior assent (*D* 1350, 1683f., 1698, 1722, 1820, 2007f., 2113, 2313; *Lumen Gentium*, art. 25). The degree of obligation towards the doctrine of the magisterium is expressed by means of the "theological notes". See further under E below.

D. The Scriptural Doctrine

Against the background of the biblical doctrine of the magisterium, as propounded by Vatican II in *Lumen Gentium* and *Dei Verbum*, we may confine ourselves here to some general indications of texts which affirm substantially, though often relatively implicitly, what the ecclesiastical magisterium teaches about its own nature. The Church, the community necessary to salvation, knows that it is the fellowship of the one faith (Eph 4:5) and the one confession, and hence in touch with the salvific reality of Christ. As was said above under A, the real nature of the magisterium derives from the Christ-event, which is eschatological triumph and possesses in the Church and its confession of faith its permanent presence. If the Church is the pillar and ground of truth (1 Tim 3:15), and if it has a social constitution and hence sacred offices, among which, primary and fundamental, must be the authority to preach salvation in Christ and demand belief, then this office is to be explained by the very nature of the Church. Its doctrine is not an innovation to be discovered by the office or the community. It is that which has been received and handed on, the tradition which is defined by its necessary relation to the one and unique salvific event (1 Cor 11:2, 23; 15:3; 2 Pet 2:21). This teaching is handed on (1 Tim 6:20; 2 Tim 1:14) by envoys who are sent by Christ as witnesses, with authoritative power (Mk 16:20; Lk 24:48; 2 Tim 1:13; 2:2, 15; see the article *Apostle*), to all nations. In Peter and the college of the apostles, and, since the Church is to endure to the end of time, in the primacy of the Pope and in the college of bishops, this Church has an authoritative government by mandate and mission from above (Lk 10:16; Jn 20:21; Rom 10:15). This mandate is handed on in the apostolic succession. And since the Church finds its being in the doctrine of the apostles (Acts 2:42; 2 Jn 1:9), the college of bishops with the Pope at its head has the mission and authority to hand on the doctrine of the apostles. This is a mission with an authority which cannot be overwhelmed by the gates of hell (Mt 16:18), since the Church is eschatological in nature. Its mission and authority is exercised with a sense of absolute claim (Mk 16:16; Mt 10:14ff.; 16:19; 18:18; Gal 1:18), because it knows itself sustained by the permanent assistance of Christ (Mt 28:20; Lk 24:47ff.; Acts 1:8; Jn 14:16) and of the Spirit (Jn 14:16, 26; 15:26; 16:13). This absolute claim would be irrational and immoral if the Church could fall away from the truth of Christ and hence destroy itself as the historically tangible community which confesses Christ, at the very moment when it commits itself with all its might to its doctrine and demands an absolute assent of faith.

E. Various Questions

1. As regards the definitive decisions of the magisterium, while they are "irreformable", they are also subject to the created dimensions of human statements and the historicity of human knowledge of the truth – into which too, however, the Word of God became incarnate, without ceasing to be the Word of God. When we say that a doctrine is irreformable, we mean that in its true and proper meaning it can never be rejected as erroneous: it is not revocable as regards the past. The creatureliness and the historicity of dogma mean that it can and must be interrogated age by age and confronted with the mental horizons and the knowledge of each age. The various dogmatic expressions must be constantly related to each other in new ways, which is one way by which marvellous insight may be gained into them and their knowledge renewed (see *D* 1796). In this sense a dogma is always "reformable" in the forward direction – though in "eodem sensu eademque sententia", *D* 1800 – and indeed it can be a real duty for the Church not simply to repeat monotonously its ancient dogma but to rephrase it in such a way that earlier and possibly misleading overtones or outdated forms of thought may be excluded, and that it may cause no more difficulty to faith than is intrinsic to the mystery contained in revelation. The permanent identity in the varying utterances of the history of dogma can and must be investigated historically. But ultimately the presence of this identity is an element of the faith of the Church in its identity throughout history, which cannot be adequately grasped in conscious reflection.

When a dogma is to be taught by the ordinary magisterium of the whole episcopate, without conciliary or papal definition – as is quite possible – it is not enough that a doctrine be propounded with moral unanimity by the whole episcopate. It is further required that the doctrine be explicitly propounded "tamquam definitive tenenda" (*Lumen Gentium*, art. 25). Hence mere *de facto* universality of Church doctrine related to the faith is not enough. It has often been assumed in the past, with practical effects, that a doctrine is irreformable in the Church simply because it has been generally taught without clearly notable contradiction over a considerable period of time. This view runs counter to the facts, because many doctrines which were once universally held have proved to be problematic or erroneous, and is fundamentally unsound. It follows that though the notion of authentic doctrine as opposed to definitive is not to be rejected or made light of, we may expect a greater "reformability" in Church doctrine than was counted on in modern times, before Vatican II.

2. Unquestionably, the attitude of Catholics, even of non-theologians, to the *per se* authentic pronouncements of the magisterium, the non-defined statements, has become more critical. This is due to the experiences of the last hundred years. It cannot be denied that the practical preaching of Church docrine often unduly blurred the basic and acknowledged differences between doctrinal utterances, as regards their binding force. In the preaching of doctrine in the Church today this distinction must be clearly brought out. The normal duty of inner assent to non-defined doctrinal pronouncements of the magisterium (*Lumen Gentium*, art. 25) is not to be propounded in such a way that in practice an absolute assent is still demanded, or as if there were no instance in which one of the faithful might withhold his assent. Reference may be made to the pastoral letter of the German bishops of 22 September 1967, where this difficult question is frankly and soberly treated. The pastoral says:

"At this point we must soberly discuss a difficult question, which in the case of many Catholics today, much more than in the past, either menaces their faith or their spontaneous confidence in the doctrinal authority of the Church. We are thinking of the fact that in the exercise of its office, the doctrinal authority of the Church can be subject to error and has in fact erred. The Church has always known that something of the sort was possible. It has stated it in its theology and developed rules for such situations. This possibility of error does not affect doctrines which are proclaimed to be held with absolute assent, by a solemn definition of the Pope or of a General Council or by the ordinary magisterium. It is also historically wrong to affirm that errors of the Church have subsequently been discovered in such dogmas. This of course is not to deny that in the case of a dogma growth in understanding is always possible and always necessary, the original sense being maintained while previous possible misunderstandings are eliminated. And of course the problem in question must not be confused with the obvious fact that there is changeable human law in the Church as well as divine and unalterable law. Changes in such human law have nothing to do with error, but simply raise the question of the opportuneness of legal dispositions at different times. As regards error and the possibility of error in non-defined doctrinal pronouncements of the Church, where in fact the degree of obligation can vary very widely, we must begin by accepting soberly and resolutely the fact that the whole of our human life in general has also to be lived simply 'according to the best of our knowledge'. We have to follow our conscience according to our lights, which cannot be justified with absolute intellectual certainty but still remain 'here and now' the valid norms to be respected in thought and action, because for the present there is nothing better. This is something which everyone knows from his own experience. It is a truth accepted by every doctor in his diagnosis and by every statesman in his judgment of a political situation and the decisions to be taken in view of it. The Church too, in its doctrine and practice, cannot always allow itself to be faced by the dilemma of either giving an absolutely binding doctrinal decision or simply remaining silent and leaving everything to the personal opinion of the individual. To safeguard the real substance of the faith, the Church must give doctrinal instructions, which have a certain degree of obligation but not being definitions of the faith, have a certain provisional character, even to the extent of possible error. This is a risk which must be taken, since otherwise the Church would find it quite impossible to preach its faith as the decisive reality of life, to expound it and to apply it to each new situation of man. In such a case, the situation of the individual with regard to the Church is somewhat like that of a man who knows that he is bound to accept the decision of an expert, even though he knows that this is not infallible.

"There is no place, at any rate, in sermons and religious instruction for opinions contrary to such provisional doctrinal pronouncements of the Church, even though in certain circumstances the faithful should have the nature and the limited scope of such provisional pronouncements explained to them ... The Christian who believes he has a right to his private opinion, that he already knows what the Church will only come to grasp later, must ask himself in sober self-criticism before God and his conscience, whether he has the necessary depth and breadth of theological expertise to allow his private theory and practice to depart from the present doctrine of the ecclesiastical authorities. The case is in principle admissible. But conceit and presumption will have to answer for their wilfulness before the judgment-seat of God."

F. Present-Day Problems

The development of Western theology with regard to the magisterium was influenced by the formal juridical thinking of the Latins. This led to very precise and juridical formulas in answering the question: by whom and how is a doctrinal pronouncement to be made in the Church, so that there can be no doubt of its legal validity and hence of its binding force? The question of the formal juridical structures of a doctrinal pronouncement completely overshadowed the question of its nature and of its concrete historical and sociological (ecclesiological) characteristics. Even in Vatican II, little attention was devoted to such non-juridical questions of doctrine. There is a brief statement, for instance, to the effect that the Pope and the college of bishops, when considering how their doctrine is contained in revelation and tradition, must be zealous in using the necessary means to answering this question. But theologians gave little thought to how this is to be done in general and how in particular it is to be done in the social and spiritual situation of the present day. In this matter, Vatican II hardly went beyond what Bishop Gasser had already said in Vatican I. Nonetheless, there are very many problems behind these simple questions. It is quite possible, for instance, to think that the magisterium would no longer be morally justified today, when trying to fulfil its duty of informing itself before making a doctrinal pronouncement, if it simply followed the procedures which were formerly the best available and also adequate. One reason for this is that the magisterium must not aim simply at material accuracy, but also at the greatest possible efficacy in its declarations. Hence, in face of the *ecclesia discens*, the Church to which instruction and enlightenment is due, the magisterium cannot just appeal to its formal authority. The faithful must also be able to see clearly in any given step taken by the magisterium that the magisterium sees itself as organ and function of the Church as a whole, that it not merely offers men doctrine true in itself but tries to bring them into contact with the very reality of salvation and its salutary force. And since the magisterium receives no new revelation when making its pronouncements, it must make every effort to explain intelligibly to the educated faithful *how* it arrived at its decision in the light of the totality of the one revelation which is the life of the Church.

The question of the "opportuneness" of a doctrinal decision, especially in the case of a definition, must not be lightly dismissed by saying that the question is already solved if the decision in question is correct in itself. Even when a doctrine is true (in the ultimate sense and when properly interpreted), it can be uttered too hastily, couched too harshly, be of too little use for the real life of Christians or formulated against certain backgrounds of thought which make the obedience of faith unjustifiably difficult. Even in the Church too much reliance must not be placed on formal authority. In an atheistical age, when the faith is being radically threatened, important decisions of the Church, including definitions – and new ones may be given in the Church of the future – will have to be less a matter of the further material explicitation of revelation and rather aim at safeguarding the basic substance of the Christian faith and seeing that it is presented in new ways in the living preaching of the Church. Finally, the theology of the magisterium should reconsider the fact that beyond studying the eternal truth of gospel revelation, the magisterium may have the task of addressing a prophetic word of directive to the Church for its inner life, and also to profane society, as the Church discharges its task in the world. These are tasks which need to be precisely envisaged today, and are difficult to bring within the competence of the magisterium as it is normally conceived, or within the pastoral office, as it is commonly understood.

Karl Rahner

MAN (ANTHROPOLOGY)

I. Philosophical

Anthropology is man's explanation of himself, the reflection of his own being, a being that is never simply at hand as a given datum, but has always presented itself as a question, and (whether this is explicitly realized or not) has always had its existence merely as its own answer at any given time to that question. Here is not a matter of the content of this answer, or of the "object" of question and answer; the point of concern is rather the theoretical, scientific reflection on the different ways in which this question and answer have found historical expression.

1. *History*. Man has always been a source of enquiry to himself. The earliest answers are contained in the prehistoric myths and legends of origin of the so-called primitive peoples and of the early civilizations. It seems likely that, in the beginning, man was explicitly conscious neither of the question nor of the answer; both take shape in the rites, the place and the instruments of religion: they come to verbal expression in myth, in which religion seeks to explain itself – until such time as this way no longer suffices. Then the question is seen to be a rational and philosophical one seeking for a consciously theoretical answer.

In the West, after the early beginnings in the pre-Socratic period, attention was first focused on man in a decisive way in the time of Socrates. While the Sophistic Enlightenment declared man to be the measure of all things, tragedy (Sophocles) and metaphysics (Plato, Aristotle and the Stoa) place him, precisely as a rational being, under the universal law of the cosmos. Judaeo-Christian thought, meeting with this tradition, regards man as one called in an absolute, personal way into a unique historical process of salvation (*Heilsgeschichte*). Not the nature of man but his salvation, that of the people as of the individual, is sought for here (prophets, Paul, Augustine). While Greek thought in general dominates scholasticism (but, besides other incipient manifestations, note especially the teaching on the absolute binding force of conscience from the time of St. Thomas), the special place of the person as an individual comes to the fore in Eckhart and especially in Nicholas of Cusa. In contrast to the Renaissance cult of the hero and the genius, the question of the special place of man was felt in the Reformation period (and in a similar way by B. Pascal) as an urgent problem. The theoretical correlative to this desire for certainty is provided by the philosophy of Descartes, laying the foundation for the modern distinction between subject and object, between man and the world and, in its distinction of *res extensa* from *res cogitans* in man, setting the course for the future development of anthropology.

The term anthropology first appears at the beginning of the 16th century in a work on physiology by the Leipzig scholar M. Hundt. In 1594–96 O. Casmann published in Hanover his two-volume *Psychologia anthropologica sive animae humanae doctrina. Secunda pars anthropologiae: hoc est Fabrica humani corporis*. Here, as subsequently, anthropology consists in a combination of physiology and psychology on the one hand and ethics (especially theory of the emotions) on the other. This is true of the English as well as the French and German Enlightenment, up to Kant who distinguishes a pragmatic and a physiological anthropology. More comprehensive is the picture of man given in German classical literature, in the pedagogy of humanism and in the philosophy of German idealism according to which man is the seat par excellence of the general reason (*allgemeine Vernunft*) and of the absolute spirit.

Kant's reference to research into races and peoples was taken up by Blumenbach, thus giving modern anthropology a decisive turn in this direction in the second half of the 18th century. As well as this research which concerns itself with the earliest archaeological discoveries, modern anthropology devotes its attention to the doctrine of evolution and today in the Anglo-Saxon countries consists for the most part of ethnology and the morphology of culture.

In Germany in particular, especially through M. Scheler, anthropology freed itself after World War I from its limitations to the biological and developed into philosophical anthropology. Here the opposition, different in each case, of Feuerbach, Marx, Kierkegaard and Nietzsche to German idealism takes its effect in the study of man as he is, real and historical. This study starts from the phenomenon of culture and history (Dilthey, Rothacker), from biology (Plessner, Gehlen) and medicine (Weizsäcker, Binswanger, Frankl) and takes distinctive shape from existential philosophy. In this sense Heidegger's *Sein und Zeit* (1927) has been of decisive importance (even though it was by way of a one-sided interpretation of his intention) even for modern theology both Protestant and Catholic.

2. *Questions and tasks.* More than anything else, the impossibility of giving a final answer to the question about man – and this was already apparent in antiquity (Heraclitus Fr., 78, 101, 115) – has once again become evident. For here it is not a matter of making a statement about a given object the nature of which is clearly outlined; the statement is itself an element in the self-articulation, the free self-shaping of the "as yet undetermined animal" (Nietzsche), so that only on looking back at the objectivations of his freedom, at his history, can man say what and who he is, and even this answer is not definitive, since his history is not ended and besides, his statement is itself always a free act of this history.

From the point of view of the theory of the sciences the problem here is to find an adequate dividing line between anthropology and the other philosophical disciplines. On the one hand anthropology is a necessary aspect of ontology, cosmology, natural theology and ethics, and these are on the other hand necessary aspects of a philosophical anthropology. Yet all philosophy cannot and should not be reduced to anthropology. So too it is hard to determine the relation of philosophical anthropology to the individual sciences (anthropology, biology, history, medicine, psychology, sociology, linguistics, etc.). It cannot simply build on them "inductively" by interpretation and synthesis, nor can it attempt to plan and structure them in an *a priori*, deductive way.

The same question arises in the relation of anthropology to the culture and life of an epoch. On the one hand it is conditioned by its times just as conversely it conditions them. From this point of view a historical review remains always questionable, since anthropology in itself, not only in the content of its answer but even in the nature and meaning of the question itself, does not always mean the same thing (and therefore it is not without significance that the name anthropology – and the discipline itself, as a defined science – came only so recently into use). On the other hand it must rise above its times to a validity which neither derives merely from the point of view of the particular period nor is able *a priori* to limit and relativize it using a concrete, suprahistorical knowledge. Anthropology must therefore avoid a rationalistic and unhistorical notion of the nature and existence of man no less than an ideological fixation in a particular concrete historical or social view of man (an ideology). Yet it must not restrict itself to recording man's self-interpretation in a relativistic and positivist presentation of facts (as in historicism). It cannot – turning the temporal, historical aspect into that of material content – present an abstract notion of man nor a collection of the results of the individual sciences. It must rather be built up as a unity, which being itself independent and irreducible, must be accepted as historical, although the acceptance of this historicity does not imply the renunciation of critical reflection on it, nor of knowledge and truth. Here we find, in fact, the same form of analogy that we have in being where the attempt to extract a univocal nucleus misses the transcendental unity just as completely as does the assumption that being is merely equivocal. (See the articles *Spirit* and *Being; anima quodammodo omnia.*) Justice is not done to this unity of man – whether considered as genus or as individual (against the Cartesian body-soul dualism) – merely by distinguishing it from the brute and its proper environment. And the theory of the degrees of being does not grasp the unity of man except as something statically objectivated. It does not encompass it as the operative process of living of a being that becomes itself only in the other and has its existence only in this process of self-deprivation and self-acquisition (*reditio*): in an indefinable "between" – between the basis of freedom (little more than a point) in the person and the pluralism of the relations in which he lives and realizes his existence.

Thus by a variety of approaches philosophical anthropology has to secure an understanding of man: from the point of view of a philosophy of the spirit and of freedom, in the light of culture, history, religion, ethics, aesthetics, economics and technology, politics and biology; and in these his "eccentricity" and transcendence are to be demonstrated. This is done by interpreting (through hermeneutics) man's epochal condition (and, at least for Western man, Christianity is an essential element in it), because it is the context in which absolute meaning is conferred on man, the apprehension of which is what makes him human in the first place. Thus man's questionableness is revealed and his answer sought for, in the entire process of his living (especially in the religious act) as well as in theoretical reflection, in anthropology.

Jörg Splett

II. Biblical

1. *Preliminary questions of hermeneutics.* None of the writings of the Old or New Testament represents a conscious attempt to produce a systematic anthropology either from the scientific, the philosophical or the theological point of view. In view of the complexity of the material covered by anthropology, which embraces the most disparate periods and branches of tradition, it is especially important to determine the line of approach of the interpreter who is looking for a self-consistent anthropology in the Bible. The nature of the evidence in Scripture, primarily religious in intention as it is, makes it futile to put questions to it which properly belong to the realm of metaphysical psychology, or still more to those of scientifically or bio-psychologically orientated phenomenology. The analysis of existence (*Dasein*) inaugurated by "existence" (existentialist) philosophy can be considered more fruitful to the extent that it is based upon the following correct position. Every historical (*geschichtlich*) understanding of "the world" has prior to, but inseparably connected with it a corresponding self-understanding of man. Thus this understanding of self acquires a central importance as the standpoint from which all anthropologically relevant statements must be understood. Admittedly in the case of the Bible the question of its anthropology must be understood as

essentially a theological one, and must be investigated on that basis. But since in the case of the biblical evidence theological and anthropological lines of investigation can be shown to be one and the same, it seems possible to fulfil this requirement. For statements about God and Jesus Christ, creation and redemptive history, life and death, sin and justification, salvation and judgment all involve in the last analysis an understanding of man and his situation (which in the Bible is never considered in itself but always in relation to God) as a factor most intimately connected with them. To the extent then that this "explicitation" of man's understanding of himself (as existing by and for God, or else as having fallen away from him) has the character of revelation in the Bible, its statements about man are made "with absolute binding force". It is because of this too that "they claim to be first and alone in bringing man to an experiential knowledge of his proper (concrete historical) nature, which would otherwise remain hidden from him" (K. Rahner in *LTK*, I, col. 619).

2. *Old Testament*. The hermeneutical presuppositions of our investigation having been indicated, we must consider first the various statements of an anthropological nature to be found in the OT. The importance to be attached to these varies considerably. *Fundamental themes* are: man's wholeness as person, his relationship with God as covenant partner and as member of a community, his creatureliness, his responsibility, his consciousness of sin and his hope of salvation.

a) Regarded in his relationship with God and the world, man, the creature who has historical (*geschichtlich*) existence is essentially a creature of God subject to earthly limitations (Gen 2:7). As such he is seen as a *living personal whole*. In this view man is considered under various of his principal aspects as "flesh", as "soul" or as "spirit" (בָּשָׂר–נֶפֶשׁ–רוּחַ) but not as a compositum with these as his parts. The theological significance of this integral view of man is shown by the fact that well-being or calamity affects the entire man as an indivisible whole. As "whole person" in this sense (represented especially by the heart, לֵב as the seat of the faculties of feeling, understanding and willing), with "will" as his definitive aspect, man does not "have" a soul and body, he "is" soul and body. Thus in the later OT period the hope of salvation is expressed in terms of hope of the resurrection of the body (Is 26:19; Dan 12:2ff.; 2 Macc 7:14), a conception which is taken up and developed in the NT (Mk 12:18f.; Jn 6:39ff.; Acts 24:15; 1 Cor 15). The idea of the immortality of the soul (Wis 2:22f.; 3:4) is derived from a way of thinking which is of Greek provenance and which is anthropologically speaking completely different. It is not developed in the writings of the later OT period or in the NT.

b) OT anthropology is concerned not with the concept of man "in himself" but with man as *a creature of flesh and blood*, that is, as socially involved in family, tribal and national relationships; with the solidarity of men under blessing and curse. As a member of the community man feels himself related to God as gracious Lord of history, as covenant partner and as guide. Involved by his very nature in the community, man is also committed to his fellow man by his relationship with God. For by the terms of this relationship his fellow-man is not only equally powerless in the face of God's transcendence, but also possesses equal value as himself. He is presented as a brother who in virtue of a right deriving from God must be protected, and in virtue of a love of neighbour commanded by God must be cherished (Lev 19:9–18, 34; 25:35–38). The responsibility of man for man is especially inculcated by the prophets (cf., for example, Is 3:13ff.; Amos 8:4ff.), and the *Torah* becomes in a certain measure the form in which the dialogue between

God and men is crystallized" (V. Warnach in *Handbuch theologischer Grundbegriffe*, II, pp. 149f.).

c) In addition to the aspects of covenant partnership and dialogue, the portrayal of man in his relationship with God is dominated by an awareness of his *creaturehood*. While as derived from dust (Gen 3:19) he is absolutely impotent and dependent, this does not exclude his dignity as image of God (Gen 1:26f.) and the position of dominance which he occupies in the world (Ps 8). The two creation narratives (Gen 1–2) convey the idea of man's nature by describing how he came to be. Pre-eminent among creatures (Gen 1:26ff.; 2:7), he is endowed with the godlike faculty of speech (Gen 2:19f.). He is God's representative in the world below, and as person, in spite of all his defectibility, he is the "thou", the partner in relation to God. Created male and female (Gen 1:27; 2:18, 21ff.), man is most deeply "himself" as the "thou" in a relationship of personal love.

d) Called into life by a word ("by his name", Gen 35:10; Exod 31:2f.; Is 45:3f.) which occurs once and for all in history, but which once uttered is irrevocable, man has an *inalienable responsibility for his own acts* (Gen 2:16f.), and finds himself summoned to a decision and a response or "counter-word" (*Ant-Wort*). By his basic involvement in (salvation) history and covenant partnership, no less than by his relationship as creature and his openness to dialogue, man is the being confronted with a decision, the being who refuses, repents and finally proves himself in virtue of a saving pardon. Responsibility is intensified too in view of death, which is set before him as the strange and inexorable boundary to life, and also in view of the fact that time is bestowed upon man as *kairos*, opportunity. But in spite of all menaces and shadows (and so far as the OT is concerned, death is the ultimate shadow), a life lived responsibly, that is, in obedience to God, will in its innermost depths be joyful (1 Kg 4:20; Ps 43:4). (In the NT this joy is based upon the "joyful tidings" of definitive salvation.)

e) In his state of freedom and responsibility man has decided to refuse and to set himself in "contradiction" to himself (because – and in consequence – in contradiction to God). The OT sees *man as sinner*. Although it has not developed the idea of original sin, it designates all men as sinners (Gen 8:21; Ps 143, 2, etc.), because their hearts are filled with pride and disobedience and they refuse the claims of God and of their neighbour. Gen 3–11 depicts the outbreak and the swift spreading of sin (man's "refusal") in the world as a prelude to the vicissitudes of Israel's covenant history. Yet so far as the Bible is concerned the advent of sin is "not so much a temporal event as an ontic one, having significance for the theology of salvation" (H. Haag, *Biblische Schöpfungslehre und kirchliche Erbsündenlehre* [1966], p. 57). The guilt and liability to punishment which all men have in common is not thought of as transmitted through the medium of biological descent.

f) Suffering and death are regarded in the OT as conditions of nature rather than as punishments for sin. It is by the ordinance of God that birth is followed by death, a state in which life is reduced to a minimal, shadowy and enfeebled form of existence (Is 14:10; Ps 88:5). Indeed this can no longer be considered as life in the true sense, in which the praise of God is an essential element (Is 38:18f.). The *hope of man* is orientated towards a joyful, "replete", "worldly" life on this earth, graciously made possible for him by God, who is faithful to his promises of favour. Hopes for a saviour and a time of salvation, for resurrection and new life are only very gradually explicitated from the covenant promises of Yahweh. They develop concomitantly with a deepening of the consciousness of sin (Jer 13:23), which looks for a renewal of the heart only from God (Jer 31:31–34), for he alone could "change the human heart and so bring about perfect obedience" (G. von Rad).

3. *New Testament.* In the NT "man" stands commandingly at the centre of things in the person of Jesus Christ. In him the "new man" of the promises is present, mankind constituting the new body and he the head. For the rest, NT anthropology (only the essential outlines of which can be sketched in here) is based upon the ideas of the OT. The problem of man is presented as essentially concomitant with the question of sin and redemption, and is treated of chiefly by Paul and John.

a) The vision of *Jesus* points in the same direction as that indicated in the message of the prophets but goes beyond it. He regards all men as sinners, and subjects them all to God's demand for a radical conversion (Mk 1:15), which is also, for the moment, the salvation which he himself offers. Man now stands irrevocably "between" salvation and perdition. Thus Jesus discloses the paradox of man's existence before God as judge and as gracious father (cf. R. Bultmann). He does not describe the "nature" of man in abstract terms (so no superiority of the soul as opposed to the body can be deduced from Jesus' preaching), but brings man to the crisis of decision, and thereby (through the medium of his own offering of salvation) to his authentic existence. Jesus does not paint any picture of the ideal man (nor does he present himself as such an example). True to the tenor of OT thought he finds reality in the true sense in history. It is with man as he exists in concrete history that Jesus is concerned, and it is to him that his claims are addressed. This emphasis on man as he exists in concrete history is most clearly exemplified in Jesus' radical interpretation of the command to love one's neighbour, in which even enemies are regarded as neighbours (Mt 5:43ff.). The claim of God summoning him to a decision reaches him in and through the concrete demand represented by the continuous presence of his neighbour to him in the world (Mt 25), and it is by his response to this that he stands acquitted or condemned. With Jesus' preaching, salvation as well as the possibility of perdition are in the world and among men. The position of man "between" salvation and loss is reduced to its basic anthropological dimensions. In Jesus himself – as preached by the Church after his death and resurrection – the character of absolute salvation in this intermediate position is revealed. The new man belongs entirely to God: he is Son of God and child of God.

b) *Paul,* in the perspective of the death and resurrection of Christ, makes more explicit the theological anthropology latent in the preaching of Jesus. He is able to sustain the dialectical tension involved in statements about man, in spite of his dualistic and Gnostic environment, precisely because of the perspective of redemption in Jesus Christ. Just as his Christology is at the same time soteriology, teaching about the redemption of man, so "Paul's theology is, at the same time, anthropology" because "every assertion about God is simultaneously an assertion about man" (R. Bultmann). It is in a soteriological sense that Paul develops (although unsystematically) his anthropology in statements about the condition of man as he was before the coming of Christ, unredeemed, and man as he is in Christ, redeemed, about man as he was, under the law, and man as he is, in faith, man as he was, subject to the dominion of sin, and man as he is, enjoying the freedom of a child of God. In the light of the gospel of grace all individual, social and national distinctions lose their ultimate significance. The Christian message is concerned with a new man in a new community, the Church. Although Paul takes over concepts from Greek tradition (νοῦς, διάνοια, συνείδησις, etc.), he adheres to the line of thought of the OT in refraining from speculations about the nature, elements and properties of man. Hellenistic dualism, which had infiltrated into Hellenistic Judaism, is no less foreign to his thought, as is attested by his statements concerning the body. For him the hoped-for resurrection is to involve a transformation of the body (1 Cor 15). Among Paul's anthropological concepts (σῶμα, ψυχή, πνεῦμα, ζωή, νοῦς, συνείδησις, καρδία, σάρξ) is the broadest in extension and the most complex, while *sarx* is the most important and the most difficult. These therefore deserve special attention.

The body (σῶμα) for Paul is intrinsically necessary to the being of man (1 Cor 15:15ff.). "Body" is not just how man appears: it is often used to describe the person as a whole. Man is body (Rom 12:1; 1 Cor 7:4; Phil 1:20). As such he can view himself objectively in his active and passive roles, be at one with himself or divided against himself, this relationship with himself always ensuing from, and being an expression of his relationship with God. For the unavoidable necessity of taking a decision before God (laid upon him as creature) affects man as a whole. Man finds himself a sinner in this world, in the power (σάρξ) of alien forces, in the domain of the flesh considered as human self-sufficiency and self-seeking, which is rebellion against God (Rom 8:6f.; 10:3; 2 Cor 10:5). When he is considering man as alienated from himself and in opposition to God, Paul calls him flesh, the sinner. Flesh is "put off" at baptism (Rom 8:9f.), while body, man as a physical whole, is transformed at the resurrection (1 Cor 15:44; Phil 3:21). The "old man", man as he was prior to Christ's coming to him, whether he is under the "law" (which does not prevent sin) or "without the law", is in a state of radical division which prevents him from achieving a free and integral existence (Rom 2:12ff.). Only when he believes in Christ and so turns his attention from his own righteousness (always presumed in his "glorification of self") to the mercy of God, is he set free with the freedom of authentic existence, at peace with God and thereby free too for a life in which he is united to his fellows in fraternal love. But man continues in the state of eschatological tension, awaiting the completion of salvation; for although this has already "taken place" and "been appropriated", it is for all that not yet fully accomplished and bestowed. The freedom of the children of God is either achieved in its fullness or else lost once more to the power of sin, which works through man's self-seeking. The position of man is characterized by the imperative no less than by the indicative of salvation (cf. Gal 3:27; Rom 3:14; Col 2:12, 20). But in faith in Jesus Christ the possibility of fully personal (eschatological) existence is given; that is, of an existence in the midst of this world which has still been emancipated from this world. In this faith there is no more fear of death, but rather hope for the "appearance in glory" (Col 3:4) and the love that is man's response to this (Col 3:14).

c) The statements concerning man in *the Johannine writings* are couched in terms which are still more explicitly Christological in import. The existence of man is determined by his origin: man is "of this world" considered as the domain of Satan, of evil, darkness and the lie. Man is closed in on himself in the darkness of self-assertion manifested in disobedience, unbelief and hatred towards his brothers. For John as for Paul the cosmos is above all the world of men who, by reason of their wickedness, would be lost, were it not for the coming of the revealer, the Son. By sending his Son the Father does indeed bring the world to a crisis, but from the motive of love (Jn 3:16f.). He sends him not to judge the world but to save it (1 Jn 4:9, 14). For man in his self-assurance and in his desire to confine himself to the sphere of the self-evident (in which the peculiar "extravagance" of man stands revealed) is imprisoned within the domain of evil; and he can be freed from this only by the "birth from above' (Jn 3), of God. By believing in the sending of the Son man receives a fresh possibility of life starting from a fresh source. This implies a withdrawal from the world amounting to the "shattering . . . of all human norms and evaluations" (R. Bultmann). This new life is the eschatological existence in which the believer becomes a stranger in the world, yet finds a new home in the community of the faithful by his freedom from sin as well as by the love of his brothers, in which he proves his sinlessness (1 Jn 3:14–18; 4:19ff.). It is not for man actively to decide whether he will be born again or not. This is achieved rather by his "submission" (by submitting himself to be "drawn" by the Father, Jn 6:44) in the act of faith as an act of radical "self-surrender". With regard to the Christ-event, the claim which the revealer makes upon men introduces a crisis into their lives and by the immediate decision which he educes from them to believe or to disbelieve reveals them for what they are, either children of Satan "from below" or children of God "from above". Human existence does not thereby cease to be a time for decision. Rather this aspect of its significance is brought to the fore. As believer man must abide in Jesus' word and act according to Jesus' command (1 Jn 1:6f.; 2:3ff.). Naturally man is anxious to find out about future salvation, but in John the strong emphasis upon eschatology as a present fact finally draws man away from all speculations concerning the "when" and "how", and concentrates his mind on the "that" of future glory. Though this is a truly "future" reality, man finds it in the unity of life with Son and Father which he achieves by faith in the here and now (cf. 1 Jn 1:2f.; Jn 17:3). The message of the Bible is that to be a man means in its deepest sense to live by grace.

Rudolf Pesch

III. Theological

Among the things directly spoken of by the word of God is man's knowledge (e.g., Rom 1:19ff.; *D* 1806); it follows that methodological reflection by theology on its own activity is itself theology. What is intended here is, therefore, a *theological* reflection on theological anthropology, not on the secular sciences which in their various ways deal with man *a posteriori* and not on the basis of the revealed word of God. How a theological anthropology is distinguished from an *a priori*, transcendental understanding of man by metaphysics, cannot be laid down beforehand by definition. That is a question which belongs to theological anthropology itself. In this perspective a glance at the history of theological anthropology shows that it has not yet been worked out in Catholic theology as a coherent, comprehensive unity and that for that reason what is said here inevitably consists chiefly of preliminary reflections.

A. History

In these historical notes it is not a question of the history of dogma regarding the various propositions which theology expressly lays down as theses concerning man: the creation of the first human beings, the spirituality, individuality and immortality of the soul, its relation to the body, original sin, redemption, grace, justification and all that is said of man in moral theology and eschatology (for which the relevant articles may be consulted). Here it can only be a matter of indicating the questions which orientate these various branches of knowledge towards an originally unified anthropology.

1. *Scripture*. Divine revelation in the Old and New Testaments contains of

course statements about man and these assume absolutely binding force and claim alone to bring man to an experiential knowledge of his own real (concrete, historical) nature which otherwise would remain hidden from him or be his only in a repressed way – "suppressed" (Rom 1:18). Man is the being who is without parallel in his world, so much a personal subject that he is God's partner, in comparison with whom everything else is by its nature only man's environment. Man's subjectivity as mind, freedom, eternal individual significance and value before God, constitutes his capacity for partnership with God in an authentic dialogue, which makes possible a "covenant" (a genuine, responsible reaction to God despite his universal causality), and extends even to the absolute intimacy of "face to face" in inaccessible light and the "sharing in the divine nature", in knowing as we are known. It even constitutes the possibility of God's expression of himself in the incarnation. And it makes man truly a being who, ultimately, is not a mere part of a greater whole, the world, but who is himself the whole in a unique way in each individual, in other words, a person, a personal subject, authentically "existent" as opposed to merely "there". As a consequence the genuinely historical, i.e., unrepeatable, non-cyclical history of the cosmos is, in its ultimate significance, from beginning to end a component of the history which takes place between God and man; the history of man is not an element in a comprehensive cosmogony. The world is, therefore, only the preparatory basis which renders possible the history of man (and of the angels) and has the ultimate ground of its own possibility in that history; the goal of the cosmos is determined before God by the history of man. From these and other reasons it follows that the statement of what man is, when theologically made, is not a proposition in one branch of study alongside others, but the statement of everything that has to be said. For there is no domain of reality (at least since the Incarnation of the Logos) which does not formally (and not merely indirectly and by reduction) enter into theological anthropology. This is what constitutes the special character of such an anthropology: it is also the whole of theology.

Nevertheless this revealed affirmation of radical personal subjectivity as fundamentally expressed in Scripture is not itself an anthropology such as is meant here, and this in two respects. In the first place, Scripture does not attempt explicitly and systematically to organize the data on the basis of a conscious principle. Secondly, the categories used in the statement of this direct anthropology are to a large extent those of the world of things, of mere objects, and of the ontology that can be derived from it, and so the danger remains of mistaking the special theological character of man and of regarding him as an item in a world of objects having only the reality of things.

2. *The Fathers*. Patristic theology represents an advance to the extent that it makes the first attempts at systematization (Tertullian's *De Anima* is the beginning) and seeks more clearly for unifying principles, for example, the idea of man as image and likeness of God, that of the history of the universe and of mankind as the history of divinization, that of the spiritualization of the universe, etc. In all this, however, essentially the same state of development remains. In fact the persistent latent danger continues that the distinction and union between man and the God who is communicating himself to man are either reduced to an opposition and union of spirit and matter (so that with one part of his nature man from the start stands on God's side: Greek theology) or of the sinner and the merciful God (Western theology: Augustine). In that way the beginning (the Garden of Eden) and the end (eternal life) are de-

prived of their profound unity-in-opposition, because the history of the world is only the history of its restoration, not the free history of God himself in the world.

3. *The Middle Ages*. As regards medieval theology, an indication that no decisive advance towards an independent anthropology had yet been made can be seen in the fact that the various components remained dispersed among very disparate treatises, despite all the systematization of the Summas. The reason is that man, overlooking his own subjectivity, in which alone he possesses and knows everything else, saw himself as one creature among others about which he "naively" made his statements one by one, without recognizing that in doing so he always implicitly affirms and strives towards himself and his own mystery (that is, God himself). Consequently in these medieval treatises the various creatures are simply listed one after another (angels, corporeal world, man). This "objective" view could not do full justice to the special character of man. The Garden of Eden was taken as the starting-point from which to speak of man, but not on the principle that such teaching about man's original condition is based on aetiological retrospect, and is ultimately intended to say something about our own situation. That is also evident in other features, of which a few may be mentioned as examples: to a large extent reflection was lacking on the history of salvation; the necessary categories were scarcely developed beyond the data already expressly contained in the original revelation. An analysis of faith and in general an existential description of the process of justification were still largely lacking; what was found interesting about the latter was what could be comprised within the categories of the various causes. The doctrine of grievous sin as essentially distinct from venial sin had not yet inspired an existential analysis of human action in general. There was not yet really any theological analysis of fundamental human experiences: anguish, joy, death, etc. The individual human being was still too much a mere "instance" of the universal idea of man. The world as such (in contradistinction to the Church) and as much more than simply the scene of concern for human necessities, as a condition of attaining salvation, scarcely really existed yet. The world was something ready-made by God, in which man works out his salvation; and it was not yet explicitly something which by God's command had still to be brought about.

Yet there are already signs that the mind of man was moving towards a genuine anthropology. The question of the history of individual salvation was propounded and answered in more individual terms: beatific vision even before the general judgment; the doctrine of the *votum sacramenti* and, therefore, of a non-sacramental possibility of salvation; the inviolability of the conscience. The profound difference in nature and consequences between original and personal sin became plain. Through a clear grasp of the really supernatural character of grace and of the last end even in relation to the spiritual creature in the state of innocence, the Greek and Western danger (to which we have already referred), of misconceiving the fundamental relation between God and man, was in principle eliminated. The growing recognition of the relative independence of philosophy in relation to theology, of the State in relation to the Church, of the domains of culture in relation to religious life, did not simply produce a dangerous impression that religion is a partial section of human reality, but (in the long run at least) compelled reflection on the reason why that is not the case: the transcendental subjectivity of religion, which can be merely a sector in its predicamental zone without thereby ceasing to imply the whole and to penetrate and determine it. Scholastic ontology, as a doctrine of being and mind, provided what was in fact a true basis for the recognition of genuine subjectivity, for it noted that anything is or has being, in proportion to the degree in which it is subjectivity in possession of itself, *reditio completa*.

4. *Modern times* are the centuries-long process of man's understanding himself as subject, even when he will not admit this. From the standpoint of the theology of history the process is something that had to be (δεῖ) – and from the start a "fall of man". We mean that the process never in fact took place except as a fall, though it "could" have been otherwise. It was a fall in which a very radical religious subjectivity before God was isolated in abstraction against Incarnation, Church and universal essence; a fall in which an individualistic subjectivity closed in upon itself and set itself up as independent, without transcending itself towards God. But the same process is also found, even if more hesitant and anxious, in the development of the Church and its awareness of its faith. It shows itself for instance in the factors to which we have already referred, in the course of Church life and orthodox theology. The *analysis fidei* becomes a problem. Historical theology is founded. Recognition of the wide possibility of salvation increases. Nature and supernatural grace are more sharply distinguished. World, culture and State are more clearly left free as the scene and objects of independent responsible lay action not directly and in the concrete subject to the Church. The question of God's mercy "to me personally" is raised just as radically within the Church as with Luther (Ignatius Loyola, Francis de Sales). A logic of concrete individual knowledge of the particular will of God here and now precisely for me personally is developed (the *Spiritual Exercises* of St. Ignatius). But there is no actual construction of an anthropology. Teaching about man is still divided between the various treatises and the systematic basis of anthropology as a whole is not explicitly worked out. Anthropology in the sense intended here is, therefore, a task which theology has still not fulfilled. It is not, of course, the case that the various propositions that such an anthropology would contain have still to be found, for of course they are the statements of revelation concerning man. Nevertheless Catholic theology has not yet developed a systematic anthropology corresponding to the knowledge man has attained of himself as a "subject".

B. Attempt at a Systematic Outline

1. *Basis*. Only a theological affirmation can enter into consideration for this fundamental principle, for one of any other kind would make theology intrinsically dependent on other doctrines of man. Consequently what man knows about himself "naturally", i.e., independently of the historical revelation of God's word, must be drawn from this fundamental starting-point, otherwise it would be without importance for a theological anthropology as such, even though theology itself leaves man free to take seriously such secular knowledge of his own nature. A possible fundamental theological anthropology is subject to the same conditions as fundamental theology in relation to revelation and theology generally. The presupposition on which it is based is one laid down for theology by theology itself as a comprehensive whole, not an *a priori* foreign to it. The light of faith is the comprehensive factor which, from the moment theology is pursued at all, "supersedes" the light of reason while preserving this as a component of itself. The basis which we are seeking, since it is a theological one, and therefore implies a believer who has heard it, can certainly be regarded as *a posteriori*, i.e., as contained in what is heard in the historical message of faith. That message, being from God himself, presents itself by the very nature of its source (and despite its historically *a posteriori* character) as com-

prehensive and regulative. How that is possible despite the fact that what is heard *a posteriori* seems to fall under the measure of man's *a priori* self-understanding, is a question which it is precisely the task of a genuine theological anthropology to elucidate and one which is decisive for its own very existence. It is the question why an interpretation of man which comes from outside, in a historically contingent way, must not by that very fact always come too late to figure as a fundamental interpretation of man (which, as a theological one, it tries to be and must be). For man is a being primordially in possession of himself, a personal subject. Ultimately the solution is that man's adequate *a priori* knowledge of himself includes the light of faith as a "supernatural existential". Man, therefore, does not approach the *a posteriori* revealed doctrine of man with an *a priori* norm alien to theology. Moreover, by his very nature man is necessarily orientated towards what is historically *a posteriori* and cannot simply reject this in a rationalistic way as non-essential. As, however, in all his reflection man always finds himself historically conditioned, he can never fully and explicitly formulate this concrete historical situation by any process of reflection (called science). It remains part of himself as he accepts himself confidently and spontaneously, though understandingly. For that reason it is quite legitimate to begin with the factual self-knowledge obtained from faith heard and historically exercised, provided that this starting-point stands up to explicit reflection.

The Christian man knows that despite his being a creature and despite his sinfulness – and in fact in it – he is a person spoken to by God in history, in the word of God's absolute, free self-disclosure in grace. This affirmation is directly intelligible for the Christian as a summary of what he hears in faith about himself, and is also suitable as a fundamental principle of theological anthropology. (That of course is not intended to deny the possibility of a more clearly defined and simpler approach. It merely indicates the basic self-understanding of the Christian.)

2. *The development* of this basic principle into a Christian theological anthropology can only be sketched in rough outline here. For we are merely trying to indicate the nature and method of a theological anthropology which does not yet exist; we are not trying to construct one.

On the basis of this fundamental idea the most comprehensive definition of man would have to be worked out: the fact that he is a creature, a determining characteristic which comprises the distinction between nature and grace. It is true that what primarily would have to be envisaged would be man's character as a created personal subject. (The created character of mere things is a deficient mode of such personal existence.) It would be the limitless receptivity to God in one who is not God, a determination both positive and negative, both aspects of which increase in the same proportion before the incommensurable God.

It might then be shown that, despite the possibility – which need not be further defined here – of recognizing by natural reason the fact of revelation, its true hearer is he who accepts it in the absolute (and therefore loving) obedience of faith in such a way that the quality of the word of God as God's revelation of himself is not lost or, through the (necessary) *a priori* of a finite human being's capacity to hear it, reduced to a human utterance on the merely created level. From this theological starting-point, it would be possible to establish the root distinction between nature and grace without having antecedently to assume the purely natural concept of "pure nature" as a fixed philosophical norm – instead of as a concept regulated by theology. Grace is the condition of the possibility of the capacity for connatural reception of God's self-manifestation in word (faith – love) and in the beatific vision; nature is the constitution of man which is presupposed by, and persists in, this capacity to hear. That nature persists in such a way that the sinner and unbeliever can shut themselves to this self-manifestation of God without thereby implicitly affirming what they are overtly denying (as in a man's culpable refusal of his metaphysical nature). Nature also persists in such a way that this self-communication, in relation to man as already created, can still appear as the gratuitous marvel of personal love which of "himself" (= nature) man cannot demand, although he is essentially open to it (nature as positive *potentialis obedientalis* for supernatural grace). On the basis of this nature one could seek a theological understanding of all that man implies as "spirit": absolute transcendence, freedom, eternal validity (immortality), personality.

On the basis of the historicity of the hearing of the word of God, it would be possible to bring out the theological thesis of the historicity of man himself with its full content and significance: his intrinsic situation in the world as his environment, his corporeality, the racial unity of humanity of which he is a part, his sexuality, his social orientation (family, State and Church), the character of his existence as a test, as historically conditioned and incalculable. And there is the incalculable pluralism of his nature, which means that though he is primordially one and not a subsequent sum total, he cannot dominate this unity in the concrete, but must constantly strive anew to attain the obligatory form of his existence.

It would in itself be possible to bring the whole of dogmatic theology into theological anthropology, in view of the fact that man is endowed by grace not only with something created but with God himself. This, however, is not advisable for various reasons, ultimately based on the inescapable dualism in spiritual creatures between what belongs to their "essence" and what to their "concrete existence". Hence theological anthropology will only include statements which characterize man in every situation of his history, whether these characteristics are natural or supernatural existentials. It will therefore be appropriate to assign separate treatises to the history of salvation (or perdition), moral theology and the prospective aetiology of the *eschata* on the basis of the eschatological situation as it is "now". And separate treatment will certainly be reserved for doctrines directly concerning God. Not as though God (one and triune), of whom theology speaks, could be spoken of without something being said about man on whom by grace that God is bestowed. But because man is the being who by his very nature has his centre outside himself, in God (and only in that way is truly at home in himself), his statements about God should be made outside theological anthropology, in a theology which must never forget the actual concrete situation of man.

3. Special attention must finally be given to the *relation between Christology and theological anthropology*. In earlier times this problem was not perceived as a problem in the methodology of theology. People already knew what "man" was when they set about saying that Christ is a true man. It was, therefore, at most a question of considering in Christology what this statement did not include in the case of Christ. In addition they were clear that Christ is man in an "ideal way" and so is an example to men and the ideal model for a theological doctrine of man, but a model which, strictly speaking, was not required by anthropology. At the present time, since K. Barth and K. Heim, the problem of the relation between the two treatises must be given serious attention. In the first place Catholic theology must reflect on the fact that a good

number of its statements about man (resurrection of the body, divinizing grace) are only possible since the existence of Christology. This at least suggests that such statements were not merely contemporaneous, and that this part of theological anthropology which gives every other part its deep significance and measure should be considered objectively as an effect of Christ's reality (and not merely "by way of merit"), and subjectively as a consequence of Christology. If furthermore the Logos himself became man, that statement is not understood if all that is seen in it is the affirmation of the "assumption" of a reality which has no intrinsic relation to the person assuming it and which could just as well have been replaced by something else. On the contrary, the Incarnation is only rightly envisaged if Christ's humanity is not only, ultimately speaking, a merely extrinsic instrument by which a God who remains invisible makes himself known, but is rather precisely what God himself becomes (though remaining God) when he exteriorizes himself into the dimension of what is other than himself, of the non-divine. Even if it is obvious that God could create the world without the Incarnation, it is nevertheless compatible with that statement that the possibility of creation has its ground in the radical possibility of God's self-exteriorization (for in the divine simplicity different possibilities cannot simply be juxtaposed without connection). In that case, however, the ultimate definition of man is that he is the possible mode of existence of God if God exteriorizes himself to what is other than himself; man is the potential brother of Christ. Precisely if the *potentia obedientalis* for the hypostatic union and for grace (that of Christ) are not merely capacities among others but human nature itself, and if the latter (nature = *potentia obedientalis*), which is not something self-evident, is known from its actuation, then it will appear most clearly and reveal its true mystery only in its highest actuation: that of being the other mode of existence of God himself. As viewed both in relation to God and to man, Christology therefore appears as the most radical recapitulation and transcendent culmination of theological anthropology. Consequently though theological anthropology would need at least at some point to have Christology as its criterion and guide, it is nevertheless not appropriate to sketch out theological anthropology solely on the basis of Christology. It is true that we never find man outside of a situation of partnership with the word of God, and this partnership does in fact only disclose its ultimate meaning in the God-man, in whom speaker and hearer, word expressed and total attention are one and the same person. Nevertheless we encounter this unsurpassable culmination of the history of that partnership within our human history as a whole in which we come to know man. And we already know something of man – partly by revelation – when we meet Christ and understand that he is a man. It would therefore lead to a limitation of theological anthropology if we tried to pursue it solely on the basis of its goal, Christology, for the ultimate experience does not annul the earlier.

Karl Rahner

MARIOLOGY

I. Biblical

Mary, the "mother of Jesus" (Mk 6:8; Mt 13:55; Acts 1:4), does not figure largely in the NT writings. The testimonies of faith in her regard take on greater extent and depth with the growing interest in the life of Jesus, the death and resurrection of Jesus being the event first and primarily proclaimed in Scripture. In the letters of Paul, which are earlier than the gospels, Mary is mentioned only in Gal 4:4. But the important truth is already uttered here. Paul speaks of the Messiah by speaking of Mary, though without mentioning her name. "But when the time had fully come, God sent forth his Son, born of a woman, born under the law." According to this text, Mary is the place in which the Son of God entered human history. The birth from a woman guarantees the true humanity and historicity of the crucified and risen Lord whom Paul preaches, and excludes all "spiritualizing" tendencies. When Christians began to have recourse to the life and actions of Jesus before his death and resurrection, the mother of Jesus who was part of his life began to play a greater role. This new interest was satisfied most fully in the gospels of Matthew and Luke (about A.D. 80), which narrate the conception and birth of Jesus and do not confine themselves like Mark to scenes from the public life of Jesus. According to the gospel of Mark (3:20f.; 3:31–35), Jesus' relatives, and also his mother – whose participation, however, was merely that of a silent bystander – sought to fetch Jesus back home, since his activity was arousing the crowds and drawing attention. Mt (12:46–50) and Lk (8:19f.) present this text in such a way as to lessen the awkwardness for Christian readers. Lk gives another scene from the public life of Jesus. He relates that when a woman praised his mother, he responded by saying, "Yes, blessed indeed are they who hear the word of God and follow it" (this translation is more correct than "No, blessed rather . . ."). Interest in the beginning of the life of the Messiah led to the composition of the infancy narratives in Mt 1 and 2 and Lk 1 and 2. They diverge from each other in many points, especially the genealogies, so that the stories cannot be fully harmonized. The two evangelists were obviously drawing on different streams of tradition. Further, each evangelist had a theological purpose, which meant that the traditions were placed in a theological perspective. Both infancy narratives have OT and Jewish traits. The influence of the story of Moses is recognizable in Mt. His text is interwoven with OT quotations and composed as the fulfilment of OT promises. The Aramaic background is also perceptible in Lk. Both narratives are in the line of popular traditions, recounting, for instance, many apparitions of angels, in contrast to the other parts of the gospels. But the historical kernel remains. We learn that Mary came from Nazareth and that she was espoused to Joseph, of the house of David (Mt 1:18; Lk 1:26f.). Whether Mary herself was of the house of David is not clear from the text. Joseph's ancestry was enough to make Jesus legally son of David. Before Mary had been brought to Joseph's house as his married wife, the angel Gabriel announced to her (Lk 1:26ff.) that she was most highly favoured and that the Lord was with her. She was to conceive and bring forth a son whom she was to call Jesus. Her motherhood was not to come about through human intervention but through the action of the Holy Spirit (Mt 1:18; Lk 1:35). The heavenly message telling her that she was to be the mother of the Messiah prompted her to pay a visit to her cousin Elizabeth. The evangelist attributes to Elizabeth, to Mary herself and to Simeon, as he greets the Messiah in the temple, hymns of praise and thanks which are mosaics of OT elements. The birth takes place in Bethlehem (Mt 1:23; 2:1; Lk 1:27; 2:4). Shepherds come to pay homage to the child, and wise men from the East. Herod's murderous intentions force Mary to take refuge in Egypt. When the family returns, Mary lives at Nazareth with Jesus and Joseph (Mt 2:23; Lk 2:39). Jesus was circumcised and presented in the temple according to the prescriptions of the law (Lk 2:21–40). Only one other scene from the childhood of Jesus is narrated, the visit to the temple in Jerusalem (Lk 2:41–52). It is a striking scene, because instead of joining the returning pilgrims and without warning his parents, Jesus stayed behind. And when his parents found him after an anxious search, he gave them the astonishing answer, "How is it that you sought me? Did you not know that I must be about my Father's business?" As the evangelist says, Mary and Joseph did not understand, but Mary kept all these things in her heart, to meditate on them in faith.

One particular question forces itself upon our attention in the story of the infancy. It is that of the virginal conception and birth. Since Augustine (*De Sacra Virginitate*, 4, 4), theologians in general were convinced that Lk 1:34 meant that Mary must have made a vow of virginity. But this traditional view has been criticized in recent years. Why should Mary have let herself be espoused if she had no intention of leading a married life? Hence many theologians now assume that Mary resolved on a life of virginity only at the moment of the annunciation. She then dedicated herself exclusively and without reserve to the service of the divine plan of salvation. Through this dedication, she conceived the Son of God in her spirit as well as in her body. The Holy Spirit is here represented not as the father who begets Jesus, but as the active force which brings about the conception. The notion of a procreation without a father is foreign to the OT. It also differs essentially from pagan mythology, according to which a god unites himself to an earthly woman and begets a child like an earthly father. Hence the virginal conception and birth of Jesus must be considered as a revelation proper to the NT. Nonetheless, this revelation was prepared for in the OT narratives in which great men were born of mothers who were humanly speaking doomed to sterility (Gen 18; 1 Sam 1). The promise of the Messiah in Is 7:14, which speaks of the bringer of salvation and his birth from a woman (*almah*) was probably already understood by the Greek translators of the Septuagint as a prophecy of the virginal birth. This, at any rate, is the meaning given to the text of Isaiah in Mt. The view that the texts of the infancy narratives deal only with the hearing of prayer does not do justice to the actual words and overlooks the decisive elements. If one asks why Jesus should have been virginally conceived, the answer is not that an earthly father would have been a sort of unwelcome rival to the heavenly Father of the preexistent Logos. Nor is it that conception in the course of marriage would have been unworthy of the eternal Son of God. The reason is the transparency with which the virginal conception and birth lets the creative power of God and his sole initiative in the work of salvation shine through. It is occasioned by no human deed. It is part of the most ancient faith of the Church that after the birth of Jesus, her first-begotten (Lk 1:7; cf. Mt 1:25), Mary renounced married intercourse with Joseph, in consequence of her total dedication to the charge given her by God and hence to God himself. The "brothers of Jesus" who are mentioned several times in Scripture (Mk 3:31; 6:3 par.; Jn 2:12; Acts 1:14; 1 Cor 9:5; Gal 1:19) could be the actual brothers of Jesus as far as the literal sense of the texts is concerned, but according to biblical Greek they need only have been cousins of Jesus (Gen 13:8; 14:14). The latter meaning is taken by Catholic exegetes. Then, according to Mk 6:3; 15:40, Mary, the mother of the brothers of Jesus, is different from the mother of Jesus himself.

Further information is provided by the Acts and the Gospel of St. John. According to Acts, Mary was with the disciples of Jesus at Jerusalem as they awaited the coming of the Holy Spirit promised by Jesus (Acts 1:14). According to John, Mary took part in the marriage feast of Cana (Jn 2:1–11). She asks Jesus to come to the aid of the hosts, whose wine has run out. Jesus first refuses his mother's request and then grants it. Mary appears here as the lady of the house. It is obvious that at the time when the fourth gospel was composed, Mary's place was fully recognized in the Church (Bultmann). Under the cross (Jn 19:25ff.) she is told by her dying Son that she is now to consider the beloved disciple as her son. The disciple is told by Jesus that he must consider Mary as his mother. The transparently symbolic character of the fourth gospel allows us to conclude that the words of Jesus go beyond the purely historical and point to the relationship between Mary and the Church. It is difficult to say whether Mary is meant by the woman of the Book of Revelation. The woman probably stands primarily for Israel and then for the Church itself.

In post-apostolic times the indications of Scripture are developed more and more fully. The basic notion throughout is that of Mary's motherhood. The actual title of Deipara, the bringer-forth of God, seems to be found for the first time in Hippolytus of Rome, at the beginning of the 3rd century. The sense of the term became clearer and clearer in the Christological controversies of the 3rd and 4th centuries and became so well established that the Council of Ephesus could use it as the hall-mark of orthodox Christology in contrast to Nestorianism, which endangered the unity of the structure of Jesus. The term expresses the personal unity of Jesus, and represents a confession of faith in the true humanity of Jesus against Gnostic spiritualizations, and in the true Godhead of Jesus against Judaism. The method of the communication of idioms was employed in the use of the term Deipara. By reason of the personal unity, the personal self of Jesus is possessor both of the divine nature and of the human nature born from Mary through the action of the Holy Spirit. When the term Deipara, bringer-forth of God, was used in a heretical sense by the Monophysites, it was displaced by the term Mother of God, which had been coming into use over a long period. It was a term which brought out better than Deipara the fact that Mary's function was not merely physiological but also spiritual and personal. It paved the way for the concept of Mary as the spiritual mother of all the faithful.

Patristic theology understood Mary as the virgin mother of the Lord. The virginity was primarily regarded as *virginitas ante partum* (Ignatius of Antioch, Justin). As regards the perpetual virginity of Mary there was no fully general consensus before the Council of Ephesus. It was not taught by Tertullian, Origen or Jerome. But it was upheld by Irenaeus, the apocryphal writings of Clement of Alexandria, the *Consultationes Zacchaei et Apollonii*, and Gregory of Nyssa. The virginity of Mary *in partu*, after the birth of Jesus her first-begotten, was taught by Origen, Peter I of Alexandria, Gregory of Nyssa, Hilary and Jerome. Basil held that the contrary opinion was not against the faith. The most powerful defenders of the virginity of Mary in and after the birth were John Chrysostom, Ephraem, Ambrose and Augustine. The conviction of the virginity of Mary soon grew into belief in her perpetual virginity. From the 4th century on, her perpetual virginity is often mentioned. After the 7th century (Lateran Synod of 649), the formula of "virginity before, in and after giving birth" came into use.

The antithesis "Eve – Mary", stemming from the proto-evangelium and developed by Justin and still more by Irenaeus, proved very fruitful. It was for a long time the keynote of Mariological thinking on the faith. The unbelief and disobedience of Eve brought ruin, the faith and obedience of Mary brought salvation. Another theme, also developed by Irenaeus and then by Hippolytus and Tertullian but above all by

Augustine, was the comparison of Mary's role in the history of salvation with that of the Church. The Church here appears as the mother of the faithful by reason of its preaching of the word and also by reason of baptism. Mary brought forth the head of the Church. This identification suggested that many traits of the personified Church should be transferred to Mary. After some uncertainty about the holiness of Mary, inspired by Lk 2:48, and indeed some negative pronouncements (Cyril of Alexandria), the absolute sinlessness of Mary was taught for the first time by Pelagius and Augustine. This thesis was soon expanded into the freedom from original sin which was then attributed to Mary. In the East, something similar was taught by Andrew of Crete and John of Damascus. No express testimony to Mary's freedom from original sin is found in the West before about A.D. 1000. Bernard of Clairvaux, a fervent admirer of Mary, and Thomas Aquinas remained doubtful. Theologians could not harmonize the universal necessity of redemption with the thesis being developed of Mary's freedom from original sin. In the course of the controversy William of Ware (*c.* 1300) and Duns Scotus developed the notion that Mary remained free from original sin by virtue of Jesus' redemption, while the rest of mankind was freed from it. This view makes Mary a subject of the law of original sin, but it did not actually take effect in her, simply by reason of a special divine decree. Mary too was redeemed, but in a more excellent way. Pope Sixtus V recognized the general conviction of Catholics in this matter and forbade the opponents and the upholders of this mystery to brand each other as heretics. The doctrinal declaration of the fifth session of the Council of Trent on original sin stated that it was not the intention of the Council to include Mary in its teaching on the universality of original sin. In the 19th century, faith in the freedom of Mary from original sin had matured so widely that Pius IX could teach it as a dogma in 1854. The freedom from original sin had wide bearings on the whole spiritual life of Mary. According to the doctrine of tradition, Mary was also granted the gift of preternatural integrity which was man's before the fall. This meant that she could integrate into the wholeness of her dedication to God even the spontaneous emotions which precede every human decision. This was also true of the sufferings which she had to undergo, and of her death. Her death was very often regarded as the pure absorption of her life into the love of God. But this does not mean that her death was not as a consequence of illness or old age.

In the development of the faith after the patristic age the thought of the divine motherhood of Mary was completed by that of her participation in the cross of Jesus. Her salvific function is considered here. As mother of the Redeemer Mary herself is called Redemptrix, from the 9th century on. This term was changed into Co-Redemptrix in the 15th century. In the 17th and 18th centuries Mariology was strongly determined by feelings and polemics – "no praises too great". A Mariology founded on the patristic data was introduced by J. H. Newman and M. J. Scheeben. The main questions centred on Mary's share in the redemption. The problem crystallized in the question of Mary's relationship to the Church and vice versa. In 1950 Pius XII defined the doctrine of Mary's bodily assumption into heaven.

If we sum up the gradual development which was accepted as authoritative in the Church and leave aside the far-reaching speculations and theologies which sometimes overshot the mark, the doctrine of the Church emerges as follows: Mary conceived Jesus the Messiah through the Holy Spirit and is therefore truly bringer-forth and mother of God. In and after the birth of Jesus she remained a virgin. From the

3rd century on, the general doctrine of the Fathers of the Church and the theologians was that the birth took place without pangs and without bodily lesions in Mary. But this cannot be regarded as dogma. In recent years theologians have been discussing the question, on which the Church has made no pronouncement, as to whether a birth in the ordinary sense necessarily involves a lesion of virginity and whether virginity is not adequately preserved if one accepts that Mary's giving birth to the child is not a sign of previous sexual intercourse as in the case of ordinary births. It may be affirmed that Mary's giving birth was a fully human and personal act and that even as a bodily process it was entirely determined by the grace of her motherhood, though it is impossible to indicate precisely the nature of the virginity in the birth. To sum up, it may be said that Mary conceived Jesus of the Holy Spirit without a male principle of generation. It is the constant teaching of the Church from the beginning that she gave birth to Jesus without violation of her integrity and that she remained ever virgin. Though there has been no formal definition on the subject, but only non-infallible declarations of the Church in the course of Christological assertions (Lateran Synod of 694: *DS* 504; Constitution of Pius IV, *Cum quorundam*, 7 August 1555: *DS* 1888), the perpetual virginity of Mary is certainly part of the faith and preaching of the Church.

Mary's election as mother of Jesus brought with it so high a degree of union with God that she was preserved from original sin. Her closeness to Christ brought with it according to God's eternal plan of salvation her assumption, body and soul, into heaven (Constitution of Pius XII, 1 November 1950: *DS* 3900–4), that is, this union with Christ worked out as the transfiguration of her body. There is no formal testimony to this effect in Scripture. Patristic testimony begins only in the 6th century. But the picture of Mary in Scripture indicates that she is most intimately united to the risen Lord. Her bodily transfiguration is the supreme degree of that "conformity" with her Son Jesus which grew steadily closer during her life. The similarity linked her to God in love and penetrated the whole of her existence. Thus she became, as Pius XII said (Constitution *Ad caeli reginam*, 11 October 1954: *DS* 3913–17), "Queen of Heaven". This title, which comes from mythology but is used in a non-mythological sense, indicates the lofty position of Mary in the divine economy and in the historical course of salvation. A number of important theological questions such as the body-soul relationship, the beatific vision and the resurrection of the dead are involved in the dogma of the transfiguration of Mary.

A general survey of the main points which emerged in the course of the historical development might take the following form. The fundamental truth is the virginal motherhood of Mary. All the other Mariological assertions can be derived from this, not with logical necessity but as a well-founded development. The fundamental grace given to Mary was embodied in each of her actions in the history of salvation. When discussing the greatness of Mary's role in the history of salvation, theologians have brought to bear on the doctrine of the divine motherhood of Mary many considerations which have led to too widely divergent views. The question can only be satisfactorily solved by a sober theological exposition of the testimony of Scripture as laid before us by the Church. It would be most inappropriate to judge the various opinions from the point of view of maximizing or minimizing assessments. The question of Mary's participation in the work of salvation may be divided into two parts. The first is: what share had Mary in the redemptive work of Jesus Christ? Was her participation a constitutive or an integrating element in the work of salvation? The second is: what share has Mary in the appropriation of Christ's salvation by the men to whom it is ordained? Is Mary the "mediatrix of all graces"? Nothing has been proposed as of faith in this matter by the Church, though Mary is several times described as co-redemptrix in the doctrinal pronouncements of the Popes. Pius XII was reserved with regard to requests to have the function of co-redemptrix defined. Those who maintain this doctrine must explain it in such a way that the clear doctrine of Scripture on the unique mediatorship of Christ is neither denied nor obscured, so that any salvific function which may be ascribed to Mary can only be understood as a derivative one, depending on the saving action of Christ. Mary's task is in any case a subordinate one (Vatican II, *Lumen Gentium*, art. 62).

Vatican II declared that it had not the intention of giving a complete doctrine with regard to Mary or of deciding questions which were not yet fully clarified by the work of the theologians (*ibid.*, art. 54). As regards the texts which were issued, it is important to note Paul VI's comment on the theological notes of the conciliar decrees, in his speech at the last public assembly on 7 December 1965. The Council, he said, has propounded no new dogma and did not aim at any such (except on the sacramental character of episcopal ordination). This does not mean, however, that the Council confined itself to pastoral exhortation. "Its texts, according to their literary form, have serious claims upon the conscience of Catholics; their pastoral dispositions are based on doctrine, and their doctrinal passages are suffused in concern for men and for a Christianity of flesh and blood in the world of today. This Council is 'pastoral' in its fusion of truth and love, 'doctrine' and pastoral solicitude: it wished to reach beyond the dichotomy between pragmatism and doctrinalism, back to the biblical unity in which practice and doctrine are one, a unity grounded in Christ, who is both the *Logos* and the Shepherd: as the *Logos* he is our Shepherd, and as the Shepherd he is the *Logos*" (Joseph Ratzinger's commentary on the Dogmatic Constitution on the Church in H. Vorgrimler, ed., *Commentary on the Documents of Vatican II*, vol. I [1967], p. 299).

Mary entered into the process of salvation through her faith. As the Fathers frequently affirmed, she first conceived the Son of God and saviour in her heart through faith, and then in her body. By her Fiat to the divine message Mary contributed to salvation, just as Eve had done to man's ruin (*Lumen Gentium*, art. 56). This does not mean that God made his plan of salvation dependent on Mary's consent but that according to the eternal plan of salvation man for his part was to assent to his salvation, through divine grace. Humanity's Yes to God and to Christ the saviour is summed up in Mary. In her Fiat of faith, she received salvation for all. "She embraced the salvific will of God with her whole heart, unhindered by sin, and gave herself wholly as handmaid of the Lord to the person and work of her Son. Thus she was united with him and under him, and with him in the grace of the most high God, to the mystery of redemption" (*Lumen Gentium*, art. 54). Mary's participation is founded on the fact that she gave life to the historical bringer of salvation and followed his work in faith and love to the death of the cross. But this was not all. The salvation brought by Christ is ordained to man by its very constitution. It calls for acceptance and assimilation. This is where its essential purpose is fulfilled. Mary was the primary recipient of this salvation, which she took to herself in the most excellent way, not only for herself in individualistic isolation but with a willingness and an openness which were orientated to all men. Her personal appropriation of salvation has ecclesial significance. The salvation of Christ is concretely embodied in the sacrament of the Church, as *Lumen Gentium* affirms (art. 59). Salvation is present and accessible in the Church, and Mary is the first and most privileged member of the Church.

This notion of the ecclesial significance of Mary's appropriation of salvation is based on a definite interpretation of the notion of the Church, as given by St. Paul. The Church is the body of which Christ is the head, and the Church is the bride of whom Christ is the bridegroom. The first image is not meant to point to a natural but to a personal relationship, and the second is even more explicitly personal. They both mean that the Church, the fellowship of the faithful, is called to bring about and maintain the saving bond with the saviour, and that this is its responsibility. But Mary was the type or model of all in pronouncing her Fiat, both of those who already belong to the Church and of all others insofar as all are called to the Church, that is, to Christ. But it would be wrong to see Mary's role in such a way that the immediate relationship to Christ and in him to God would be obscured. The function of Mary means that dedication to Christ in faith has a Marian colouring but not that it loses any of its directness. Mary is where the salvation of Christ came to man in the world, not just as an objective entity but as the movement of Christ towards man. That this is involved in the relationship of Mary to Christ is particularly clear from the fact that she was with the disciples in Jerusalem awaiting the descent of the Holy Spirit (Acts 1:14). She was not invited to the Last Supper, but her presence is noted with some emphasis as the Holy Spirit was awaited. She knew from her own experience since the annunciation the power of the Spirit. In the Spirit Jesus himself remained present, in the fellowship of the Church. That Mary was there when the Church was constituted in the Holy Spirit, in the Spirit of Christ, is significant for the whole course of its history. When she died, and above all when her body was glorified, her heavenly existence was stamped for ever by her earthly role in the work of salvation. Her "assumption into heaven" did not mean that she left mankind far behind, but that she came all the more personally close to them. Her loving gaze is fixed for ever on her risen Son and on his brothers and sisters. But her whole glorified existence is also praise, thanks and intercession before God. What she is, she is through Christ. What she does, she does through Christ. Vatican II avoided speaking of her universal "mediation of grace". But the truth behind such terms is taught with reserve, while the mediatorship of Christ is strongly stressed and all Mary's activity is seen exclusively in the perspective of Christ. If, nonetheless, the mediatorship of Mary is affirmed, this is in order to bring out a fundamental thought from the Bible, the solidarity of all men. Men do not receive salvation as individuals or monads in isolation from each other, but as social beings. Each one who receives the gift of salvation becomes himself a source of salvation. The good of one is fertile in good things for the other. This general principle holds good for Mary in a special and comprehensive way. Hence Mary's mediatorship is to be understood on the level of the solidarity of all mankind which is in need of redemption, to which she herself belongs, and not on that of the one and only saviour (O. Semmelroth). In the light of the thesis that Mary's glorified existence is that of intercession, and that this is essential for her, the much discussed question of whether Mary's function is sacramental or petitionary seems to be given too much superficial prominence. Mary's heavenly life of dedication to Christ is marked by her care for the brothers and sisters of her Son who are still on their pilgrim way to the Father. Her existence is perfect exchange of love and also hopeful concern.

The function of Mary in salvation determines her relation to the Church. At a very early date, though the doctrine was first propounded explicitly by Ambrose, Mary was regarded as the type or model of the Church, and the Church as the image of Mary (*Lumen Gentium*, arts. 60–65). Mary is type or model in her motherly fruitfulness and virginal integrity. In the tradition of the Church, especially in Augustine, Mary's motherhood of Jesus expands to the spiritual motherhood of all the faithful. Her virginity is displayed in her total dedication to God. The Church in turn mediates the salvation of Christ through its preaching and the sacrament of baptism. It thus brings forth the Son of God by grace in men, as is affirmed with especial emphasis by the medieval mystics. The Church is virginal because it remains true in faith, that is, in the loving acceptance of God mediated by Christ. Hence the Church has a Marian life inasmuch as it contemplates, grasps and proclaims the salvation of Christ realized in Mary.

In a work attributed to Ambrosius but actually written by Berengarius of Tours in the 12th century, Mary is termed mother of the Church itself as well as mother of the faithful united in the Church. In an anonymous work from the beginning of the 13th century the mother-child relationship between Mary and the Church takes on a twofold aspect. From one aspect, Mary is mother of the Church, from another the Church is mother of Mary. Vatican II avoided the title of "Mother of the Church". But the term was used by the Pope in his speech at the end of the third session. The formula had not a prominent place in theology before the Council, but was often used in preaching and even in theology without any exact definition. The term is in any case a metaphor. It can be understood in two ways, according to two ways of looking at the Church. The Church may be understood as a community which is prior to any individual member of it. Here Mary's relationship is that of mother, because she gave birth to the head from whom flows the existence and life of the community, and also because she accompanies the life of the community by her fruitful intercession. The Church can also be regarded, though less aptly, as the hierarchically constituted multitude of all the individual faithful. Mary is mother of the Church under this more individualistic aspect, since she is effectively concerned for the salvation of each individual (O. Semmelroth).

Michael Schmaus

II. Theological

A. The Problem

Mariology concerns us here not in the sense of theological reflection on the person and character of Mary, her role in the history of salvation and the orderly presentation of the results, but as reflection on these primary theological truths. Hence our primary interest is not the content of Mariology, but the ranging of this content in its place in theology as a whole. But the two elements cannot be kept totally separate, since the place of Mariology in theology is determined by the nature of its assertions. The solution of this theoretical task is only now taking definite shape. Up to the present, theologians have been content in general with working out the contents of Mariology in systematic form. But they thereby prepared the way for the general theological assessment of Mariological treatises. The problem falls into three parts:

1. Should there be a special Mariological treatise at all, drawn up on the same lines as the other treatises of dogmatic theology such as Grace, the Last Things or Christology? No one can doubt that Mary played a role of her own in the history of salvation. But the

question is whether the perspectives and aspects which it implies should not be inserted into the conventional treatises which have prevailed almost universally since Peter Lombard. Or should they be combined into an independent presentation of the whole of Mariology? The first method is that of the Fathers and also of medieval theologians on the whole, though particular questions such as the virginity, assumption and immaculate conception of Mary were sometimes treated separately. They were dealt with at times in special works like sermons, allocutions, homilies and monographs or discussed in the course of other works such as commentaries on Scripture. The advantage of this method is that it avoids isolating Mariology from the rest of theology and hence eliminates all distinctions between theology and Mariology. Further, the matter of the other treatises such as Grace or Eschatology can then be illustrated by the supreme example of its realization. The theologian can demonstrate all that Mary has in common with the rest of the redeemed and also the special nature of the redemption as imparted to Mary. The disadvantage is that then Mary is not seen as a whole in the fullness of her role and her person, and the intrinsic connections between the various Mariological assertions are not brought to light. The second method avoids these disadvantages but loses the advantages of the former. And it can easily fall victim to an isolated Mariology, which mistakes its allotted theological boundaries and can give the whole of theology a lopsided appearance. If, however, one opts for the second method, its inherent dangers can be avoided if reference is made to Mary in the usual treatises and if the Mariological treatise shows how Mary is inserted in each case into the process of salvation – redemption, justification, consummation – as it affects all men. In this way, the treatises can be integrated with one another, without making too much or too little of the treatise on Mariology.

2. The second part of the problem is the legitimate place to be assigned to any such Mariological treatise within the whole framework of theology. Since Mary and her work are entirely dependent on Christ, the Mariological treatise can be an appendix to Christology. But since Mary is the spiritual mother of the faithful, the most excellent member of the Church and indeed the beginning and the archetype of the Church (cf. Rev 12), the Mariological treatise can also be prefixed to ecclesiology or appended to it. When medieval theologians made Mariological assertions within the framework of systematic theology, such assertions were inserted into Christology. See, for instance, Thomas Aquinas, *Summa Theologica*, III, q. 27–30, or the *Commentaries on the Sentences*, where Mariological questions are dealt with in the third book. The plan of Thomas Aquinas is to discuss the hypostatic union and its salvific consequences and then to deal with the life and actions of Jesus. The Mariological assertions are meant to throw light on part of Jesus' life, his entry into the world. The doctrine of his conception and birth as well as that of his work demanded some knowledge of the woman in whose bosom the conception took place. It was necessary to know the special nature of her place in the spiritual and religious world, and also the consequences which her function with regard to Christ had for herself.

3. The third part of the problem is concerned with the basic principle of Mariology. To be precise, one should here distinguish between the basic reality of salvation as applied to Mary and the basic perspective of a Mariological treatise. Though the basic reality of Mary must be reflected in the basic notion of the Mariological treatise, the latter need not coincide fully with the former. In consequence of Mary's place

in the whole plan of salvation, the basic notion can be prior at least to the basic reality and be its theoretical presupposition.

B. The Answer

1. The general possibility of Mariological assertions is based on Scripture. It is particularly clear from Gal 4:4 and from the gospel texts which deal with Mary. Mary is included in the testimony of Scripture to the Son of God made man, not accidentally, so to speak, in the way in which the Lake of Genesaret is mentioned, but in the essential sense in which the assertions about the historicity of Jesus are linked indissolubly to the assertions about his mother. Everything, no doubt, which is said of Mary occurs in a Christological context. But one cannot reasonably speak of the Son of God made man, of his belonging to the human race, of his situation in human history, without thinking of how he was inserted into history, of his continuity and his discontinuity in its regard. This is particularly clear from Matthew and Luke. Truths of faith with regard to Mary form part of the truths of faith with regard to Christ, as may be seen from the articles of the creeds of the Church which speak of Jesus Christ as "born of the Virgin Mary". Here the assertions of the faith of the Church with regard to Mary are clearly linked with Christology. That Mariological assertions should occur in theology from the earliest times is quite understandable. Such assertions are concerned with particular questions and are often not the result of scientific thinking of the faith but the expression of pious veneration. Hence they often have the character of poetic intuition and enthusiastic exuberance, which means that they must be interpreted by a method appropriate to such literary forms. Even Albertus Magnus, who was formerly considered the greatest Mariologist of the Middle Ages, is not a Mariologist in the modern sense. The *Mariale* represents in fact the first systematic effort at a theology of Mary, inasmuch as all assertions about Mary are reduced to one single principle, that of the all-embracing fullness of grace. The principle, however, cannot be sustained and is not without dangers. And the *Mariale* itself is not a work of Albertus. Mariological reflection did not go beyond particular questions and the effort to introduce some order into them, till after the Reformation. Independent treatises were then drawn up, by Peter Canisius, Francis Suarez, Charles Vega and others. Very soon, however, individual problems came once more to the fore (mediation of all graces, co-redemption). These brought with them the danger of isolating Mariological assertions from their basis. Having first appeared only as intrinsically connected with Christology, there was a tendency to make of them a Mariology equal in rank with Christology and ecclesiology. At present, the dialectical law of thesis and antithesis seems to have brought about a synthesis, the main principles of which are to be found above all in the Mariological texts of Vatican II. The development of dogma seems to have shown that the revelation in Mary implicit in the self-disclosure of God allows us to state a number of truths of faith as regards Mary. These may then be built up into an organic whole or rather combined to form a part complete in its kind within theology as a whole. This is the ground of possibility of a Mariological treatise or at least of a presentation of Mary on the lines of a treatise.

2. The second question is concerned with the place of the Mariological treatise within theology as a whole. Medieval theology, when it took up Mariological problems from a systematic viewpoint, always dealt with them within Christology. But this is not a decisive argument for a Mariological treatise which would be exclusively Christocentric. It was impossible in the

Middle Ages to give Mariology an ecclesial stamp, since there were no fully developed treatises on ecclesiology in existence. But in any case, a Mariology inserted into or appended to Christology should never be treated simply as an element or annexe of Christology. Mariology is more than a developed Christology, just as ecclesiology is more than a developed Christology. The opposite approach would lead to an identification of Christ and Mary or to a volatilization of the Mariological element. After long discussions, the Second Vatican Council adopted an intermediate position. It declined to answer all problems of Mariology, but gave a coherent presentation of it on the lines of a brief theological treatise, which it then inserted into the Constitution on the Church (*Lumen Gentium*, ch. viii). Thus the ecclesial perspective of Mariology appears at once in a clear light, while the Christocentric quality is given due attention. The two aspects appear as indissolubly linked, though the ecclesial is the more immediately prominent. The Church is considered only in the light of Christ. Hence, though it is described as the people of God, its special characteristic as people of God is that it is the body of Christ, of which Christ is the head. The liturgy of the Church, which is an expression of the faith of the Church, brings out the unity of the ecclesial and Christological aspects in the canon of the Mass: "Communicantes, et memoriam venerantes, in primis gloriosae semper Virginis Mariae, Genitricis Dei et Domini nostri Jesu Christi." The difficulties inherent in the ecclesial approach will have to be accepted. They arise from the fact that not all Mariological assertions fit in logically with this arrangement (as, for instance, Mary's share in the objective redemption).

3. The third problem posed by the treatise on Mariology is that of its basic principle. By this we mean the basic notions or perspectives from which all the assertions of the treatise on Mariology can be derived – not by logical necessity, but with some sort of reasonable coherence through which their unity is assured. The answer will of course be determined and coloured by the basic principle of theology as a whole. The particular solution applied to Mariology will vary according to whether one takes as the basic principle of theology "God as God" or God as self-communicating, or again, if one takes the Church or the consummation of the world and man in the glorified body as basic principle. In the course of history the following notions have come to the fore as characteristic of the basic principle of Mariology: Mary as the second Eve, Mary as the most fully redeemed, Mary as archetype of the Church, Mary as mother of the Church, Mary as bridal mother of God or Mary simply as mother of the Son of God made man. What is most in keeping with the Marian tradition is the notion of the maternity of Mary and of Mary as archetype of the Church. But it would seem that the notion of the divine motherhood is what answers best the demands which must be made on the basic principle. It seems also the notion which represents most fully the perpetual mind of the Church in its faith and theology. It contains within itself the theological elements comprised within the other proposals, but also lays the emphasis in the proper place, according to the role of Mary in the history of salvation, while remaining closest to a sober and concrete assessment of reality. The other proposals come, no doubt, to the same thing ultimately, but need more copious explanations and contain many more abstract elements. When we speak of motherhood here, we mean it in a comprehensive, personal and existential sense. It is not considered merely as a biological process in which both human dignity and dedication to God in faith are reflected. Motherhood here includes the

loving, obedient acceptance of the divine charge. It includes readiness for commitment to God's plan of salvation and to the life-work of Jesus. This readiness is an intrinsic and indissoluble element of Mary's motherhood. In Mary's assent, which was predefined by God, humanity itself accepts the grace of redemption. When Mary's motherhood is understood in this way, the other Mariological assertions can be derived from it – freedom from sin, bodily glorification, participation in the event of salvation – according to the various methods of logical explicitation, the theological analogy of reference to Christ, the due and fitting, etc. This notion of motherhood lends significance to the other assertions in the order of salvation. It gives them their proper co-ordinates in Mariology and indeed in theology as a whole. It also contains the principles of Marian devotion, for which it provides both legitimate grounds and boundaries.

Michael Schmaus

MARRIAGE

I. Institution and Sacrament

A. Sociology and History of Religion

1. Sociologically speaking, marriage is a sexual fellowship, the structure of which varies considerably according to general social conditions. Modern field-work in anthropology rebuts 19th-century evolutionary theories (especially that of Morgan) to the effect that marriage gradually developed from primitive promiscuity through various stages of group marriage (sexual relations of all the men with all the women in a group) and polygamy to monogamy. On the other hand it cannot be denied that extraordinarily various forms of marriage in fact exist and that the Catholic definition of marriage as a life-long, indissoluble union between one man and one woman is recognized, in this strict form, only by Catholics themselves. Monogamous marriage however, though dissoluble in certain circumstances, is very widespread indeed and associated with no particular form of culture. Polygamous marriage is favoured by complex social conditions where there is a particular demand for female workers, or where prestige and the desire for numerous offspring is involved. Polyandry is very rare; it is favoured by a firm rule of primogeniture, whereby the younger sons acquire marital rights only in the marriage of their eldest brother, or else a shortage of women.

The factors which determine the concrete structures of marriage can never be sought merely in terms of sex-life and sexual hygiene, or merely in terms of the relationship between man and woman. They are above all the needs of the family and society – that is, the demands of education, economics, property, social security, public morals and the like; because in the long run general social conditions are decisively affected by married life and family life. So we can readily understand why marriage has never been regarded as the private business of the two partners, but has always been fitted into the supra-individual, general human contexts of morality and religion and always considered to exist in view of the family, law, morals, and ethical rules concerning themselves more with this ordination than with the exigencies of marriage as such.

2. Hence it is not surprising to find that marriage, in the history of religion, is an objective, prescribed order which involves the partners in cosmic relationships. It is often held to have been instituted by the Supreme Being as a special stage of life that can only be entered upon through ritual initiation. Wedding brings a new status; it is a turning-point in the life of man, like birth, puberty (admission among adults), and

death, and determines whether we can speak of marriage or not. As a rule the marriage-rite is celebrated only once between one man and one woman, although a wider range of sexual relations of one sort or another is often permitted. In any case the wedding makes marriage valid in the eyes of the community. There is really no personal relationship that can compare in importance with this state of marriage created by the wedding. When intercourse is allowed, for example, with the wife's handmaid because the wife is barren, so that she may be given children (Gen 16:1–6; 30:1–13), this is considered to happen within the existing marriage, not to constitute a new one. And so we see that the idea of marriage as something willed by God is more deeply rooted in men's religious consciousness than one might at first suppose, considering the wide range of sexual relationships permitted in various cultures. In order to gain as clear an insight as possible into marriage as the Church understands it, with all it involves in the fields of theology and natural law, we must realize what a multitude of forms marriage may take and at the same time bear in mind the features common to those many forms.

B. Marriage in Historical Revelation

1. *Old Testament.* a) *Creation narrative.* The Catholic view of marriage stands in direct relation to the OT, Hebrew view. Marriage was given its basic law in what the creation narrative says about the relationship between man and wife, but because of the hardness of men's hearts – according to the words of Jesus which have been handed down to us (Mt 19:6) – the principle was never fully developed during the history of the chosen people. The creation narrative, then, says that woman was created for man's sake, man being in need of help and completion. Woman is created as a suitable helper for Adam, as it were "opposite him". She is to be his lifelong companion. So a man leaves father and mother for his wife's sake and becomes one flesh with her, precisely because it is only in her that he finds all of himself – only with her can he enter a union which has no parallel in the human order, which is even closer than the bond of descent with his father and mother. And man, created male and female, is instructed to be fruitful and to fill the earth.

Then in the NT conception of marriage another feature of the creation narrative plays an important part: the affirmation that the sexes are "hierarchically" ordered one to another (Reidick) – that Adam's nature is the measure of Eve's nature. This primordial priority and subordination underlie the whole relationship between the sexes, making their union possible. The priority therefore does not aim at favouring an individual but completion in oneness: and the difference in position as between man and woman is to be appreciated in terms of the oneness that is its goal and fruit. That difference gives each sex its own dignity and at the same time presupposes equality of value. Man's dignity consists in being woman's head, woman's dignity in being the brightness and the glory of man. This priority and subordination is part of the order of creation, and the judgment pronounced upon woman (Gen 3:16) does not turn it into a moral and juridical subordination but simply recognizes a fact – that as a consequence of sin woman will not only find many a burden in motherhood but will also be subjected to violence and exploitation at the hands of man. This is not a rule of conduct, implying that things ought to be so.

b) *Old Testament tradition.* Against this background marriage primarily figures in OT tradition as an institution for the preservation of the husband's clan. The idea is not to found a new family but to continue one that already exists. Hence children are a blessing and a gift from

God; childlessness is a disgrace and a chastisement; unmarried people are a sign of national decadence; and virginity as a consecrated state of life is unknown. Mutual help and support, and joy in sexual life, are also regarded as the meaning and purpose of marriage. It is an institution pre-ordained by God, yet not really something sacred. Accordingly the structure of marriage is altogether determined by the needs of the clan, which quite overshadow the interests of the partners. For the sake of the race, and in view of social and economic conditions, certain forms of polygamy and of concubinage with slaves are allowed (cf. Exod 21:7–11 and Deut 21:10–15, for instance), and when a woman marries, her family hand her over to the husband to be his property, in return for payment of the bride-money or other services. Not that the bride becomes her husband's slave; he cannot do what he pleases with her; she remains a free person and must be respected as his wife. But adultery with the woman is now considered a violation of the husband's proprietary rights. Even when intercourse with a virgin is forbidden, the reason given is that it lessens her value. So logically enough a man can only violate someone else's marriage, and a wife only her own. This of course involves a certain sexual freedom. Also because the needs of the clan are the main consideration, marriage can be dissolved, at least by the man, not only for childlessness but also for dislike, incompatibility, and adultery. But if the wife cannot reasonably be expected to continue the marriage, she can also demand release from it. Thus the Hebrew notion of marriage was "naturalistic", which looked with favour on marriage, children, and intercourse within the limitations set by the force of circumstance.

2. *New Testament.* a) *The Synoptics.* In the NT Jesus deepens the Hebrew conception of marriage in two respects: on the one hand he spiritualizes it, not only forbidding the dismissal of the wife as an offence against the basic law of marriage contained in the creation narrative and ingrained in human nature, which makes man and wife one flesh, but also teaching that divorce does not sever the marriage-bond, since he declares that the re-marriage of divorced persons is adultery. Thus he indicates that the deepest purpose of marriage in God's eyes is the oneness of man and wife. St Matthew's Gospel seems to interpret this doctrine practically, without weakening it, when it allows separation for adultery, but declares re-marriage adulterous because the marriage-bond is still there. (In this case Mt 5:32 is to be read in the light of Mt 19:9, so that Jesus is re-interpreting as a separation *a mensa et thoro* the dismissal which the Jews took to be a divorce giving the right to re-marry [Dupont]. This view is disputed. On the other hand Jesus consistently states that marriage is a kind of life proper to this age, which will pass away with it. In heaven there will be no marrying, and those who have risen from the dead will be as angels (Mk 12:25 and parallels). Compared with the kingdom of God and its demands, marriage becomes a matter of secondary importance, so that it is better for those to whom the mysteries of the kingdom have been revealed, not to marry. And the concerns of marriage must yield to the claims of the parousia (Lk 14:20; cf. also Mt 24:38f.; Lk 17:27). Given his essentially eschatological outlook and expectation, Jesus doubtless had this relative conception of marriage (with respect to the end) in the foreground of his mind, yet not in such a way as to lose sight of the value which marriage represents in its own right. Rather that value, which God himself gave it, was set in a special light, and at the same time it became clear that the value of marriage is a limited one when we consider the kingdom of God.

b) This ambivalent view of marriage emerges even more forcefully from the *writings of St. Paul*, the next most important source we have for the NT doctrine on marriage. On the one hand he is intent on seeing the basic law governing the relations of the sexes, as contained in the creation narrative, in the light of NT anthropology. Significantly, 1 Cor 6:12–20 tells us that sexual union is not merely a marginal erotic function, but an act which by its very nature so absorbs and expresses the whole personality as to be an entirely unique kind of self-revelation and self-commitment. And then he stresses the spiritual equality of man and woman, and makes it clear that in Christ the differences between the sexes, with all that they entail, are relatively unimportant. It is significant that 1 Cor 11:3–15 discusses the disciplinary question of women's head-covering in church, which concerned Christians at the time, in the basically theological terms of relations between the sexes. Above all, Eph 5:21–33 interprets Christian marriage as mirroring Christ's marriage with the Church, which in turn is foreshadowed by Adam's relationship with his wife (Adam being a type of Christ). Now this means that in their marriage man and wife preserve the relationship between Christ and the Church and reflect it in their relationship, so that the union of man and wife is not only compared to Christ's union with the Church but actually based upon it. Thus when husbands love their wives as their own flesh they are only doing what Christ does with the Church. But this great mystery of the love of Christ for the Church is mysteriously prefigured, according to Eph, in the text of Gen 2:24 about the mutual relationship of the sexes, and goes to constitute Christian marriage. Accordingly the relationship between man and wife is theologically set apart from all other human relationships – that, for example, between children and parents – of which it is only said, for instance, that they should be "in the Lord". And thus we are given a view of marriage which makes it possible and necessary to regard marriage as a sacrament in the dogmatic sense. According to the same text of Eph, conduct must agree with the relationship: wives are to be subject to their husbands "in all things". This subjection, however, is to the husband who for his wife's salvation must be lord like Christ. Only when he is lord unto her salvation does obedience become wholly possible. So the injunction to love one's wife is correlated with the injunction to obey one's husband (H. Schlier, *Der Brief an die Epheser* [2nd ed., 1958], pp. 252–80). Similarly Col 3:18f. warns wives to be subject to their husbands as to Christ, and men to love their wives in a Christ-like way. (1 Pet 3:1–7 says that by an exemplary fulfilment of the duties of their state in a Christian spirit, husbands and wives must win their partners over to the faith.)

Marital relations were bound to be affected by the fact that in the Churches founded by St. Paul women enjoyed a favoured position, considering the outlook and standards prevalent at the time. He asserts their equal dignity and equal rights as had never been done before, raising marriage from the all too material state in which he found it onto a spiritual and personal plane. His letters contain the definite beginnings of a specific Christian spirituality for married people, of which too little was made later.

On the other hand in 1 Cor 7 Paul wishes that the faithful would renounce marriage in favour of virginity because he thinks the Lord will soon return and fears that the hazards of this life may engross them to the neglect of the only things that really matter. True, not everyone has a vocation to virginity and there is no sin involved in marrying; but the married man is more tightly bound to the world by the nature of his life, less able to devote himself to Christ than is the unmarried man, who is not deceived by the appearance of this fleeting world and gives himself up altogether to the service of the Lord. Here Paul reduces marriage to something of secondary importance in view of the parousia, and stresses the dangers of married life. Whereas the creation narrative says that "it is not good that the man should be alone", St. Paul counters with "it is well for a man not to touch a woman". But he is not carried away; he does not condemn marriage. His pastoral wisdom and theological insight make him affirm that marriage is necessary on account of the structure of man, and that to avoid disadvantages married people should not abstain from intercourse except for a sound reason and a short time. Because husband and wife no longer belong to themselves, they may not refuse each other except by mutual agreement, and by Christ's command neither must leave the other. Only by the death of one of the partners is the marriage-bond dissolved. Thus Paul not only spiritualizes the "naturalistic" Jewish view of marriage but shows how fragile it is.

C. Marriage in the History of Theology

1. *The Fathers.* After the apostolic age this ambivalent attitude towards marriage grows more pronounced. Whereas the creation narrative had represented marriage as a glorious divine institution which fell into the realm of human distress because of the fall of man – whereas Jesus had shown marriage to be an indissoluble bond willed by God, and yet an ordinance of this aeon that will pass away with it and must be subordinated to the exigencies of the parousia – whereas St. Paul had laid the foundations for a specific spirituality of Christian married people, at the same time insisting on the dangers of the bonds between marriage and this world: now marriage is seen more and more as the justification of the use of sex which has been infected by original sin. And so marriage ethics, the doctrine on the subjective motive for the marriage act, comes to determine to a great extent the end of marriage and dogmatic teaching on marriage. The trend reaches a certain climax in St. Augustine from whose theological views later ages found it hard to break away, as is well known.

Now Augustine assigns sexuality to the animal domain, seeing no specifically human aspect in it at all. The purpose of marriage is the begetting of offspring. Sexuality has been deeply wounded by original sin, which expresses itself in concupiscence. This truth is most evident from the fact that the sex organs move spontaneously, that the will cannot control orgasm, and that venereal pleasure is so intense. This means that sexuality can diminish and overwhelm the spirit, so that even an act of procreation good in itself must always involve a degree of "animal excitement". He went so far as largely to identify original sin, concupiscence, and venereal feelings; and then concluded that while marital intercourse is theoretically good, any concrete instance of it must be considered at least materially evil, so that one can say that every child is literally begotten in his parents' "sin", because procreation is only possible with the seductive aid of fleshly lust. Still, since God wills that children be born, it is a sort of permissible or tolerated sin; and so the marital act, subjectively directed to the begetting of children, is morally justified. The same is true of doing one's conjugal duty, because by marrying each partner has given the other a right to his body. Such conjugal embraces as are not motivated by either of these explicit intentions but do not interfere with the natural consequences of coitus, are "venial" sins, because one of the purposes of marriage is the abatement of sexual desire. Given the testimony of Scripture and the tradition that has been built upon it, Augustine will not deny – is not tempted to deny – that marriage is an honourable state, in some sense a sanctifying one; but this, in his view, is precisely because of the "goods" that excuse it, and especially the spiritual love between husband and wife. These goods – offspring, faithfulness, sacrament – he explains as follows: "Fidelity means that one does not have intercourse outside the marriage-bond with another man or woman. Offspring, that one lovingly accepts the child, and brings him up kindly in the fear of God. And the sacrament, that the partners shall not be divorced ... This is the fundamental principle of marriage, since it ennobles the fruitfulness willed by nature and at the same time keeps perverse desire within its proper bounds" (*De Genesi ad litteram*, IX, 7, 12).

It may be that this altered view of marriage came in because the Fathers were influenced by Hellenistic dualism, which considered the essence of the good life to be ἀταραξία – the Stoic ideal of tranquillity, keeping oneself fully under control, especially in face of sensation, of which the keenest is sexual sensation. It was Encratist and Gnostic forms of this dualism in particular which could find allies in the Christian conception of marriage. While the perfectionist instinct of Encratism, with its over-emphasis on the ascetic principle of ἐγκράτεια, self-control, continence, was to over-exalt virginity and depreciate marriage, the dualistic premiss of Gnosticism that matter is evil provided Encratism with something like a dogmatic basis. Gnosticism maintained that marriage and sexual intercourse only served to imprison more souls in the flesh; and recommended continence in order to thwart this purpose of the demiurge and to subject the flesh to the spirit. Now this doctrine was an approach – though a heretical one – towards the Christian idea of the dangers of sex because of sin and the secondary position of marriage vis-à-vis the claims of God's kingdom. So it is understandable that the Fathers, with the emotional attitude they generally had towards marriage and intercourse, should have been much influenced by the spirit of the age in which Christian tradition took shape, especially as most of them lived in close touch with their environment. The limitations of their time became their own as well. Nevertheless they never went so far as to betray the substance of Christian tradition, and over the centuries they defended the basic value and sanctity of marriage in terms like those of 1 Tim 4:1–5. This is not to deny that the Fathers had a negative influence on the medieval theology of marriage and on preaching in general.

2. *Scholasticism*. Hence it is not surprising that marriage was readily accounted one of the seven sacraments when the idea of a sacrament in the present dogmatic sense was worked out in the 12th century, even though not all the Schoolmen agreed at first as to whether or how the sacrament of matrimony conferred grace. Thus Abelard (d. 1142) says of matrimony, which he groups with baptism, confirmation, Eucharist, and the anointing of the sick: "Among them (these sacraments) there is one that does not avail unto salvation and yet is the sacrament of a weighty matter, namely matrimony. For to bring a wife home is not meritorious for salvation, but it is allowed for salvation's sake because of incontinence" (*Epitome theologiae Christianae*, 28: *PL*, CLXXVIII, col. 1738).

But the sacramental character of marriage was soon embodied in pronouncements of the Church's magisterium: the decree for the Armenians (1439), of the Council of Florence, plainly teaches that this sacrament contains grace and communicates grace to those who receive it worthily (*D* 695, 698), and the Council of Trent expressly defines against the Protestants that matrimony is a sacrament.

D. Systematic Theology of Matrimony

1. *Dogmatic theology*. This doctrine that marriage is a sacrament affirms and

guarantees that the married state is a lawful, and even salutary one; it ensures that it will not be wrongly seen in a profane light. The doctrine means that through marriage man must in some way share in redemption, since every sacrament conforms us after its own fashion to Christ and his saving deed – which neither man himself nor the sign of itself can do, but only God's grace bestowed on us through Christ. Now since that grace is henceforth attributed to marriage as such, it follows that only the marriage of baptized persons is a sacrament – that is, bestows *ex opere operato* the grace proper to marriage, provided no obstacle is placed in its way such as would destroy the disposition necessary in the recipient for the sacrament to take effect. Moreover, only marriage between baptized persons can be – at least in full measure – that sign and witness which conformation to Christ by grace enables marriage to be. Only such marriage, then, can so fully represent the bond between Christ and his Church that the mystery of God's incarnate love itself will become operative in it.

Accordingly the contracting of marriage between Christians is a sacramental sign. That bond comes into being when the will to marry is made known (*matrimonium ratum*), and reaches fulfilment in complete marital dedication (*matrimonium consummatum*). The declaration of willingness to marry must, however, be made in the form prescribed by canon law, because marriage as a sacrament is also an ecclesiastical act and therefore the Church can and must regulate it according to the mind of the Church and the role of marriage in the Church. Canon law for its part must further the Church's work of vicarious sacramental sanctification.

Now according to Eph 5:21–23 marriage is a certain image of Christ's "great marriage" with the Church. So Christian married people are in duty bound to present an unmistakable image, for the world and above all for their own children, of the love between Christ and the Church, so that we can say the *res et sacramentum* of marriage consists in the visible bond of ultimate, indissoluble love between the partners till death do them part. That is why being in the state of Christian marriage gives one a "right" to the constant help of grace – grace to do one's duty as a Christian husband or wife and do it well – if we can call a right a claim upon God that he has freely given us apart from any deserts of our own. In this sense the marriage-bond can be compared to the other sacraments which found a state of redemption. By living their marriage, therefore, and so showing forth a mystery of redemption in their own way, Christian couples have a salvific function, which is why the Church has the right and duty to make suitable arrangements for the form in which marriage is contracted.

The grace bestowed by the sacrament (*res sacramenti*) consists in this: the mystery of God's incarnate love becomes so efficacious in the husband and wife who do not close themselves against it that they are supernaturally united with God and each other as Christ is united with the Church. True, baptism itself gives the whole Christian life a sacramental character; the grace of baptism has already put all our relations with God and man on an entirely new footing. But over and above this, marriage brings one into the mystery of redemption in a new, more perfect way. Now when the grace of marriage conforms one to Christ over and above the conformation wrought by the grace of baptism, one is of course linked in a new way with Christ's salvation and glory, to which the cross and death are a prelude. The grace of marriage too involves the cross. And so faith alone can look on this grace and the responsibility which it brings as ultimately a beatific gift. Since grace does not destroy our nature but fulfils it by transforming it on a nobler plane, the grace of marriage is not to be thought of as something that completes and perfects marriage as it were from without, but as a dynamism within marriage that penetrates and transforms its created nature, to make it not only a state of the redeemed but also a redeeming state. The created nature of marriage is not thereby abrogated or destroyed: it is fulfilled in Christ's way. This fulfilment means that Christian marriage is penetrated through and through, in a new and unique way, by the love that grace has shaped – the love that unites Christ and the Church (Volk).

Accordingly, husband and wife are rightly said to be *ministers* of the sacrament. We should of course remember that the Church's intervention – normally through an authorized priest – is essential for the contracting of marriage, even though the Church may participate more or less explicitly and though the manner of its participation has greatly varied in the course of history and still does so. Now there are certainly cases where bride and groom contract a marriage without thereby wishing to confer and receive a sacrament; and so the question arises whether Christians can marry without the conferring of the sacrament. This question was long and sometimes angrily debated in connection with the problem of who the minister of the sacrament is, especially after the Council of Trent, but was then settled in harmony with ancient Christian tradition by doctrinal pronouncements of Pius IX and by the Code of Canon Law (can. 1012), which says that among Christians the marriage contract as such has been raised to the dignity of a sacrament; so that by the very fact of marrying one receives the sacrament. Hence, according to whether one intends to contract a sacramental marriage or to exclude the sacrament, a marriage comes into being or fails to do so. Thus the sacrament is conferred by the giving and receiving of consent and a bond is created on terms which the partners to the contract cannot fix, because they are fixed in advance by the nature and purpose of marriage.

This nature and purpose subject the marriage contract to the requirements of natural law, Church, and State, in such a way that if a marriage does not duly satisfy these requirements it will be illicit or even invalid. We are dealing, then, with a contract *sui generis*. In particular, the continuance of the marriage does not depend on the continued will to be married, as Roman law supposed; for a marriage can only be contracted if one intends to bind oneself for life and regardless of what may happen in the future. Only such an intention accords with the nature of the marriage bond.

Such being the case, we can say that according to Gen 2:18 and Eph 5:21–33 the nature of marriage is a mutual completing and perfecting of the marriage partners through their union, which reaches its high-point in its sacramental elevation and perfection, and finds its strongest expression in sexual encounter. But the immanent meaning of marriage points beyond itself to a transcendental purpose – personal and physical fruitfulness arising from the union and therefore common service of the world, especially begetting and bringing up children – the family. This purpose, intrinsic to marriage and yet transcending it, flows from the way in which man and wife are ordered to each other in marriage, and necessarily follows from the nature of their union and of sexuality, which are ordained to fruitfulness. For being married perfects man and woman not only in their manhood and womanhood but also in the oneness that is proper to marriage. Now since any perfecting of the person makes him more open to God and neighbour, the personal union which is marriage must also order the partners more fully to God and neighbour. But that union, which embraces every dimension of the personality, has a sexual dimension and therefore includes the ordination of sex to fruitfulness. Marriage being thus intrinsically ordered to fatherhood and motherhood, sexual love exhibits fatherly and motherly characteristics from the very first, as sexual behaviour shows. By giving men a human share in God's creative power, consummated union orientates the partners to the human beings it brings forth. We must not, however, conclude, from the fact that marriage is ordered to the child, that marriage apart from children is meaningless or even non-existent. In that case all marriages which were known in advance to be childless, or which eventually proved to be such, would be invalid. This is admittedly wrong. On the other hand marriage is ordered not only to sexual encounter but also to procreation, and that so essentially that it is also agreed that no one can contract a valid marriage on the understanding that there shall be no sexual union or no children. Even where the partners *intend* to abstain, the *right* to sex is admitted; and the exclusion of children on principle invalidates matrimonial consent.

This interpretation of the nature and purpose of marriage seeks to avoid the widespread tendency to assert a "hierarchy" or a "dualism" in respect of the ends of marriage. The matter is a weighty one, considering the problems of moral theology that are involved. Whereas in the "hierarchical" view marriage exists primarily for the sake of procreation, only secondarily and derivatively for the sake of the marriage partners, the "dualist" view is always tempted to treat the child as an end that is really extrinsic to marriage. But in fact the procreation of children and the perfecting of the partners are not so much subordinated or diverse "ends" of marriage as co-ordinate structural principles of one total entity, marriage. This view of the nature and purpose of marriage is made possible, and indeed suggested, by certain utterances of Vatican II (Pastoral Constitution on the Church in the Modern World, arts. 47–52), which regard mutual love as the norm and meaning of marriage and at the same time affirm the ordination of marriage to the child who arises from the core of this love. Nor does this interpretation conflict with traditional doctrine as laid down in the Code of Canon Law (can. 1013) and other documents of the Church's magisterium, since that doctrine never divorces the purely biological ordination of sexuality to procreation from the total personal encounter of the sexes, much less subordinates the encounter to procreation. Indeed one is compelled to say that such a moral interpretation would falsify the purpose of sex by treating a personal value as a means to a biological end. Precisely to forestall such an interpretation Pius XII declared artificial insemination unlawful (*AAS* 41 [1949], pp. 557–61; 47 [1956], pp. 467–74).

The nature and purpose of marriage – especially as a sacrament – account for its necessary unity and indissolubility. By unity, we mean an exclusive and total union between one man and one woman. And indissolubility means that the union is lifelong. These characteristics derive from the natural ordination of the partners to one another, antecedent to the sacramental nature of marriage, for marriage is of itself a total surrender of each partner to the other for life. Given our frail, earth-bound, historical nature, a conditional dedication would be plausible, for when it comes to complex moral decisions we are our own masters subjectively but not objectively. For we can revoke our decisions, and we can neither foresee all that they imply for the future nor be fully aware of how past experiences shape our present motives. Nevertheless only an unconditional dedication quite befits the dignity of the human person, since it alone fully affirms and accepts the partner in a way appropriate to the total union and completion of body and soul in marriage. Polygamy and bigamy, therefore, reflect a shallow, actualistic attitude towards common life and sexual dedication. Generally speaking they are more unfavourable to the woman, who finds it much more difficult – because she is more inclined to give herself wholly, because her maternal task ties her more closely to the family and because of her role in society – to break away from one set of social circumstances and adapt to another. Unity and indissolubility follow still more emphatically from the sacramental character of marriage, since marriage not only fully represents Christ's union with the Church but as a sacrament creates so intimate a supernatural bond that the partners are taken up into the mystery of redemption in a unique and specific way. When this sacramental marriage is consummated, the marriage bond acquires a new strength and perfection. Despite wearisome medieval discussions of the subject, however, the theological significance of the consummation of marriage has not been fully worked out even today.

For these reasons the Church teaches that marriage is intrinsically indissoluble – that is, that married people, whether Christian or not, can never abandon their own marriage and then lawfully contract a new one. Common life, however, can be given up for grave and just reasons (separation from bed and board – *separatio tori, mensae et habitationis: CIC*, can. 1128–32) so as to avoid a greater evil – that is, if continuing to live together as befits the nature and purpose of marriage as such, would in the actual circumstances be contrary to the dignity of either party or the good of the family or both. The right of the innocent party to a separation is limited by the duties of love, because marriage is a total dedication – which of course does not involve, but excludes, self-destruction.

The Church also teaches that sacramental marriage, once consummated, is indissoluble from without: that it can be ended by no power on earth, only by the death of one partner (*CIC*, can. 1118; cf. *DS* 1805–7). Apparently the reason is that in sacramental terms this marriage represents without restriction the union Christ has consummated with the Church. Further, "becoming one flesh" brings about a union in grace with God and each other, of divine origin, which no human intervention can affect. All other marriages can in certain circumstances be dissolved "extrinsically", that is, by human authority. Thus the unconsummated marriage of a baptized person can be dissolved by the solemn profession of religious vows. By the Pauline privilege even a consummated marriage between pagans can be dissolved if one partner is converted and the other will no longer live with him in the spirit of the natural moral law (*sine contemptu creatoris*). By the Petrine privilege the Pope sometimes dissolves a marriage between unbaptized persons or between baptized and unbaptized persons on other weighty grounds in the interests of the faith.

The Church has not always seen the problem of the extrinsic dissolubility of marriage in the same light, and has still not worked it out in every detail. We must say that the problem was an unimportant one for the Church in the first millennium. Originally, no doubt, stricter notions prevailed on the indissolubility of marriage, so that the permission given in Mt 5:32 and 19:9 to dismiss a spouse for unchastity at first applied to adultery alone, extending only by degrees to other offences against marriage. Even the Pauline privilege was not originally understood to allow a dissolution of marriage from without, but a separation from bed and board; only with the reforms of Gregory VII and the consequent recasting of canon law did the present interpretation win general acceptance. Doubts which arose before that time in some areas – notably in the Eastern Church, and then later among the Anglo-Saxons, Franks, and Germans – about how to treat people who, after a separation for some reason or another, entered upon a new union, were based on pastoral rather than dogmatic considerations, since remarriage, though admittedly against the divine law, was held to be the lesser evil in some cases. Thus from the early 4th century down to the present time there have been certain differences between the Eastern and the Western Church in the disciplinary treatment of separation and remarriage.

If the matter of the extrinsic dissolubility of marriage was not much gone into in early times the reason probably was that the Church only recognized more clearly after A.D. 1000 its competence and duties with respect to marriage and then began to take more of an interest in the law of marriage. This development was fostered by the legalistic thought which so strongly marked the Middle Ages, and its desire to create an orderly society; and concretely by the Church's assumption of full jurisdiction as regards marriage. Whereas marriage had earlier been regarded as a more or less private concern of the two partners in which of course they were subject to God's laws, now much more was made of the Church's right and duty to control the institution of marriage. The development of our modern dogmatic concept of a sacrament also helped the process along a good deal. So laboriously and by degrees, with much fierce argument among theologians and canonists, it was finally established that the sacrament comes into being through the partners' matrimonial consent, but the external indissolubility only through consummation of the marriage. At the same time it was not only agreed that other marriages could be dissolved in the interests of the faith (*in favorem fidei*), but the validity of the contract was considerably restricted by legislation and the multiplication of impediments. Theological discussion of the Church's role in the contracting of marriage and in its external dissolubility continues. It is clear that the intervention of the Church in certain specific ways is essential for the contracting and continuation of sacramental marriage. It is also clear that the Church exercises jurisdiction over non-sacramental marriages only in relation to the faith. It is not quite clear how far non-Christian religious bodies and civil society have jurisdiction over non-sacramental marriages. And the precise explanation of the jurisdiction of the Church with regard to sacramental marriages is also obscure. How widely the *in favorem fidei* is to be interpreted is a matter that will need further study – not least in view of what the Second Vatican Council says about the orientation of non-Catholics to salvation.

2. *Moral theology*. a) *The ends of marriage and matrimonial ethics*. Matrimonial ethics must be deduced from the nature and purpose of marriage and the basic structures of marriage which result therefrom. This point must be particularly stressed because, as we have seen, the Fathers and especially St. Augustine proceeded in the opposite direction; working from a negative kind of sexual ethics, they developed the idea of the *bona excusantia*, the goods of marriage which made it a respectable state. True, St. Thomas makes these the intrinsic structural principles of marriage, but he is still so dominated by Augustine's rigorist, pessimistic, narrowly sexual view of marriage that he too places the problem of whether the sexual act is lawful in the foreground of his matrimonial ethics. For him too the basic thing in marriage is the procreation of offspring. This profound and fundamental element is constantly elevated to the higher planes of matrimonial common life and the sacrament, there acquiring an ever richer and more meaningful reality. But these levels still remain a "circumstance", a "superadditum", with regard to the more primary

and "natural". Only in this context can we understand why the doctrine of the goods of marriage faded into the background from the 16th and 17th centuries onwards, leaving the *copula per se apta ad generationem* as the decisive standard of matrimonial ethics. This isolated stress on sex restricted considerably the perspective of matrimonial ethics. Even in the assessment of the marriage act, the accent was placed too one-sidedly on the formal structure of the physiological process. Thus a comprehensive matrimonial ethics, aiming at the intrinsic purpose of marriage, was not envisaged. Accordingly, neo-Scholastic matrimonial ethics – especially by introducing the notion of the *actus perfecti et imperfecti* – is largely a matter of analytical casuistry and prohibitions: nothing must be done contrary to the "natural" use of marriage. Now matrimonial ethics must not be reduced to mere sexual ethics; even though the latter is essential to the former, it is only a part of matrimonial ethics. And if matrimonial ethics is not to be mutilated, it must be related to matrimonial dogma with all the latter's anthropological implications. Only thus shall we find an ethics which does justice both to the dignity of this sacrament and to the reality of this state, since the various dimensions and levels of marriage can be brought into the closest possible harmony only if we order them all to the nature and purpose of marriage.

b) *The married state and the ideal of perfection.* We must start from the premiss that marriage is a saving state through which those called to it are to reach their appropriate Christian perfection. That is, married people must regard the opportunities and tasks which marriage alone brings them as an essential part of their striving towards perfection; so that their perfection is to be achieved only through marriage, not outside it. All religious decisions taken by the partners must take their marriage into account, so that they gain an entirely new perspective on their fully individual salvation, having to include the salvation of the partner in all their decisions. Hence it can rightly be said that marriage really becomes the saving state for the partners, the way to their perfection. It directly perfects a man who lives it according to its nature and purpose, and yet does not perfect him absolutely. For what grace does through sacramental marriage is to make a man more like Christ in one particular respect. Naturally this must not be understood to mean that marriage is the absolute way or even the most privileged way to human perfection. For perfection embraces every aspect of man's being and is therefore inexhaustible. We can attain it only to a limited extent, because our contingency, individuality, and particular circumstances mean that we never realize all our potentialities to the same degree and in perfect harmony. Thus marriage makes a man more perfectly human, but only in a way that is proper to marriage, not in every possible way. And so marriage as a state that leads to religious and moral perfection should not be contrasted with virginity. Each perfects man in its own way; and when all the concrete circumstances are right, virginity is better able to lead us to perfection as such, to total union with God. But virginity is not the best road for every individual to his own particular perfection; it is only best for those called to it. For the married, virginity should be a heartening example of self-denying love, just as the married should be a privileged example of self-sharing love. In this context marriage and virginity do not clash, but each sets off the other and makes it fruitful.

Though Scripture gives the principles of such a view, it is only in our day that theologians have become conscious of marriage as a state which actually leads those called to it to salvation and Christian perfection. Now we are witnessing the growth of an independent, positive spirituality for married people. We are shaking off the idea that marriage must be accepted because of the contingence and frailty of human nature but is rather a hindrance than a help to moral and religious perfection.

c) *Mutual completion.* If marriage is seen as a saving state which leads to religious and moral perfection, then its fundamental law must be the duty of the partners to do whatever will foster the love that completes and unites them, and avoid whatever will frustrate or destroy it; to orientate themselves as companions to the transcendent purpose of marriage which their complementing union makes possible – fruitfulness not merely biological but also moral and religious thanks to their new religious situation.

The final criterion of what concrete acts foster or frustrate marriage must always be what acts befit the partners as such. The specific possibility of union and completeness in marriage has a sexual component. But sexuality determines in various ways the totality of human nature. For men can only realize their nature in a sexual way, though on the other hand it is human nature that makes sexuality possible.

Completion means concretely that the husband helps his wife to be a woman, and the wife helps her husband to be a man. So the partners are to affirm each other in their difference, each thus helping the other to find selfhood. Now the specific completion which marriage offers is of a sexual nature, and must therefore also be sought in the realm of sex. But it must be remembered that while sexuality is directly biological, it is indirectly affected by sociological, economic, and psychical factors – and therefore also by spiritual and religious factors. And so completion is to be sought in all these domains, in the way appropriate to each; and the same with selfhood. However much it unites the partners, marriage must not impose uniformity but help each towards real manhood or womanhood – which are always intrinsically ordered to fatherhood or motherhood. One of the major problems in our modern spirituality of marriage is this: that for historical reasons access to the specific roles of man and woman, particularly that of woman, has become more difficult. Many marriages go through crises because the difference between the sexes is practically ignored, or is interpreted in an out-of-date way, and therefore it is most important for matrimonial ethics to ascertain how the sexes should complete each other today, so that marriage partners can act accordingly.

On the other hand completion presupposes a harmonious understanding, above all in matters that are specifically human, and therefore religious and moral harmony but also psychical, social and economic, and also biological harmony. Hence the choice of a partner must be made with care, taking everything into account, from religion to eugenics. In view of advances in medicine and the mounting scale of mutations it is all the more vital to consider eugenic factors; for the equilibrium between mutations and elimination in man now seems to be not far from the point where any further burdening of the inheritance might well jeopardize the continued existence of mankind.

d) *Mixed marriages.* Marriages between persons of different religions present a special problem in this respect. They are inevitably on the increase, because of the evolution of society and religion alike, and yet always make the common life of the partners considerably more difficult, the more so in proportion as the partners have firm religious convictions and are conscious of the religious dimension in marriage. The sacramental structure of marriage does not give it religious relevance, but simply makes that relevance crystal-clear. Marriage already has a religious character in that it embraces the total human being, including his moral and religious dimensions. On the other hand, marriage as a total claim and an intimate communion is particularly vulnerable to sin and its consequences. For that reason excluding the religious element, or relegating it to the background, must always prove detrimental to the whole marriage. As a rule one cannot simply say that difference of religion between the partners need not matter if only they are tolerant of each other; for tolerance makes co-existence possible but not oneness. By the nature of the case the disadvantages of a mixed marriage are even plainer when the marriage is blessed with children. For the child is not only the fruit of physical union; the development of his personality is decisively affected by the totality of the unity of his parents' marriage. So it is a mistake to look on mixed marriages as an admirable field for missionary work, for the attainment of each partner's special perfection presupposes common thinking and feeling to a very high degree. It will be all the more effective, the more the partners have humanly in common. The same ways of thinking and acting are more a foundation of marriage than a result of it. Thus 1 Cor 7:16 warns against false self-assurance as to the possibility of converting the unbelieving partner. On the other hand Paul stresses in the same context that the unbelieving partner, if he is prepared to live with the Christian one, will be sanctified by the believer (cf. also 1 Pet 3:1: wives must try to win over their unbelieving husbands to the faith by the silent example of their manner of life). Mixed marriages come nearest to being justified where there is no religious prejudice – a different thing from tolerance – and especially where the lack of prejudice is combined with a receptiveness to religion. So one must not hastily generalize about the difficulties involved in mixed marriages or make too much of them; not only because doing so makes the pastoral approach unjustifiably difficult and increases the danger of excluding religion from mixed marriages, but above all because given an unprejudiced outlook these marriages can prove sanctifying.

e) *The union of husband and wife* calls for a partnership so intimate that it is neither possible nor desirable outside marriage. It means strict solidarity and absolute faithfulness and the closest intimacy at every level including the bodily one. This is what makes adultery so grave at its various levels, just as it emphasizes the various degrees of "obligation" to conjugal dedication. A common house, table, and bed are as desirable in general for the sake of union as are common planning, finances, and action. Priority and subordination can be meaningful within this partnership only insofar as they contribute to union. Matrimonial modesty is to protect intimate union against misunderstandings arising from without, and against undue strain from within. And sexuality should be used in this encounter between partners to the extent that it will foster union, and subordinated to the extent that it would hinder it. That is the law of marital chastity. Of course this fellowship is only possible and desirable insofar as it fosters the dignity and personality of each partner, or at least does them no harm. Partnership and independence do not conflict in marriage; they nourish each other because love addresses the other person in his freedom and tries to persuade, not to coerce, when sacrifices are necessary for the sake of the partnership. It follows that partnership ceases at the point where either partner attempts to abuse the other for selfish ends. Any such attempt, and any readiness to let oneself become the slavish instrument of the other, is sinful, the more grievously so the more personal judgment, freedom, and responsibility are violated. The duty of marriage partners to integrate all the many dimensions of marriage into their personality so far as possible often encounters great difficulties in the sexual sphere, for the management of this emotionally explosive force demands great personal maturity and is often made more difficult by the concrete conditions of civilization. All the same we should beware of trying to lay down in objective detail what befits the dignity of the human person and what does not, for that often depends on very individual factors; and we should be still more hesitant to say how far a person is responsible in a concrete situation and how far the situation arises from prepersonal factors. We must also remember that difficulties of adjustment in other aspects of marriage may result from differences of origin or upbringing, ingrained habits, crowded living conditions, insufficient acquaintance with one another and so on, and can only be overcome by a gradual growth in understanding and love. A matrimonial ethics that is no longer narrowly sexual has to call attention to the moral significance of all these factors in marriage; for the success of a marriage will often depend precisely on them.

f) *Marriage looks beyond itself*, and first of all requires the partners not to suppose that their exclusive, lifelong partnership shuts them off from God and all other people. Marriage must not be lived as a solitude for two, for the completion and union marriage brings tends of its own nature to make the partners more open to God and their neighbour. Since marriage of itself enables one to be more human in a specific way, and as a sacrament draws one deeper into the mystery of Christ, and therefore of God, it demands that one live in union with God and man and affirm both. But complete physical dedication to everyone cannot be what is meant by that greater capacity which we objectively receive and which should make us subjectively more disposed to love. For being bodily and temporal, we can make a complete and ultimate gift of ourselves only once, since, unlike spiritual values, spatio-temporal things can only be at the disposal of one person by being withdrawn from others. Spiritual values can be shared with others without thereby being divided or diminished, and in fact they count more by being thus shared. But a spatial object can be possessed only by one person at a time: no one can make use of it while it is in another's hands. Now in marriage a person gives himself completely and finally together with his bodiliness, so that to make himself available to a third person would be to withdraw the gift from his partner. Moreover, we can never realize our existence definitively in any given moment, but only step by step, so that the definitive gift of ourselves can only be made, in the concrete, by a lifetime of devotion. Being more open must therefore mean that because of the new and deeper self-discovery a person has made in marriage, in the union of man and wife, he is better able and more disposed to affirm all others in their otherness, to love them as they are, and also to accept himself with his limitations – even with his limited capacity for love.

Moral and religious fruitfulness, when the circumstances are right, should also take concrete shape in physical fruitfulness, marriage widening out into the family. The aim must not be to produce as many children as possible but to found a family which will be qualitatively the best possible. For personal responsibility must always be the proximate norm of specifically human, and therefore moral, acts. In the case of marriage, this means that the right number of children is the number which will best favour the personal development of all members of the family, at the same time taking account of the wider interests of society. Regulation of births will thus be necessary generally speaking. But it should always be inspired by a generous spirit of self-giving love in accordance with the purpose of marital fruitfulness. If marriage is divorced from its purpose – which of course transcends physical fruitfulness but includes it within the bounds of what is physically possible and morally responsible – its nature, "dualistically" split off from its purpose, will also be misunderstood and the result will be a group selfishness hostile to life. If the purpose of marriage is misinterpreted in "hierarchical" fashion, so that the greatest possible number of children actually becomes the ideal, then in sexual union one partner cannot "intend" the other for his own sake, as a person, but only "use" him as a means to a physiological end. Further, in such a case the right of the children already in the family to live and develop – and perhaps the rights of society as well – would be irresponsibly infringed: marriage would become a mere institute for the breeding of children.

3. *Canon law.* Canon law as it relates to marriage must so dispose the faithful for the salvation to be communicated by marriage that the pastors of the Church can help them not to misunderstand or abuse marriage but to live fittingly in that state. Matrimonial law must therefore regulate for marriage, the social dimensions of which bear so directly on salvation, to further the common good of the people of God and the moral and religious advancement of individual Christians. Civil society attends to those aspects of marriage which affect the temporal common good.

a) *Marriage in the CIC.* The present law on marriage is substantially contained in can. 1012–1143 of the *CIC.* It codifies in a legally binding way the nature and effects of marriage, the rules of matrimonial consent, the impediments to marriage, the form for the celebration of the marriage and the laws on separation, so that the juridical norms for the regulation of sacramental marriage are ready at hand. For pastoral reasons a clearer and more compact arrangement would be better. These rules are not directly dogmatic but pastoral in nature. They were drawn up against the background of conceptions of marriage and the Church which have now in part been superseded by the findings of contemporary theologians and the declarations of the Second Vatican Council. As the expression of a mentality not abreast of the times, these juridical formulas often conflict with pastoral needs, causing real or psychological difficulties when there is no necessity to do so either by the nature of the case or for the sake of clarity. A comparison between can. 1013 and 1081, §2, for example, and what the Pastoral Constitution on the Church in the Modern World has to say about marriage (art. 48), or between the canonical rules on mixed marriages and the present ecumenical spirit, will give some idea of the difference in point of view between the *CIC* and the Second Vatican Council. Considering the new understanding we have of the Church, and the needs of our time, the centralizing tendency in the regulation of matrimonial law seems questionable. A certain shift in emphasis from legislation to judicial rulings would seem more appropriate to our present idea of personal responsibility, and would make fairer decisions possible in cases that have not been, and could not be, foreseen, without any need for too frequent changes in the law. Again, various provisions are based on sociological and pastoral assumptions that have been overtaken by events. In this connection it would be well to reconsider without prejudice the civil laws of matrimony, which could not hitherto be done because of various obstacles (cf. can. 1016). It is therefore very important that we gain a deeper insight into the function of matrimonial law, so as to know how it can help solve pastoral problems, and be better able to judge the limitations of the present matrimonial law. This last is particularly desirable in view of the reform of matrimonial legislation which has been initiated by the Holy See.

b) The canons on the *nature and effects of marriage* set forth the differences between sacramental and non-sacramental, contracted (*ratum*) and consummated, valid and invalid marriage; they enumerate the "goods" of marriage and the effects of marriage as to unity and indissolubility, and the rights and duties of the partners. Can. 1111 affirms the wife's strict equality of rights as regards physical partnership. But as regards common life, can. 1112 provides that she shares the status of her husband, with regard to canonical effects, unless special provision has been made to the contrary. Thus the husband is given priority in the guidance of the family. The rights of the wife should also be expressly set down; suggestions of male domination should be eliminated.

c) The juridical implications of *matrimonial consent*, which constitutes marriage, are the subject of can. 1081–93. For a marriage to be validly contracted, they provide (i) that the matrimonial consent must be actually present on both sides; (ii) that both parties must be able to marry; and (iii) that their consent must be expressed in the legally obligatory form. The consent itself must (i) relate to the nature of marriage, (ii) relate to a particular person, and (iii) be freely given. The law then determines in what circumstances these conditions for matrimonial consent are presumed to be verified; what minimum knowledge and acceptance of the nature of marriage are presupposed; it introduces the notion of error with regard to the person and "simple error"; and says when unjust external coercion, or grave fear induced within, makes the consent juridically invalid.

It is often difficult to apply these canons in a given case at law, because the criteria for the presence of an adequate consent are only adequate within limits, and because the purely legal presumption of a consent which is not actually present seems questionable in many respects when we consider how marriage bears on salvation. Perhaps the main difficulty is that nowadays the needful maturity for marriage cannot be so readily and so generally presumed as is done in the *CIC*; for on the one hand it has become extraordinarily difficult for many people to recognize and grasp personally that marriage is indissoluble, on account of the widespread errors touching the substance of marriage, and the *de facto* breakdown of marriage in so many cases; and on the other hand, the findings of modern psychology and sociology show that the personal moral maturity presupposed in the total obligation of marriage is more often and more seriously retarded than one was inclined to think in earlier times. Moreover, the conceptual difference between error with regard to the person and error with regard to the qualities of the person is perhaps too formal and not always very convincing. Serious vices, or circumstances altogether different from what the person represented them to be, and which, had they been known, would have precluded the marriage, do not seem to have been properly allowed for here.

d) The provisions on *impediments to marriage* recite factors which either because of natural law or because of a divine command exclude the possibility of marriage (diriment impediments of divine right are: an existing marriage, impotence, blood relationship in the direct line and probably in the first degree of the collateral line) or limit its lawfulness. Then come the impediments to marriage which the Church has laid down. These prohibitions of marriage are more or less obvious ones. Ecclesiastical prohibitions of marriage may restrict the natural right to marry, one of the fundamental human rights, only for weighty reasons. On the other hand the pastors of the Church have a duty to establish such impediments to marriage insofar as called for by the common good of the people of God and the good of individual Christians. Undoubtedly the scheme of impediments in force at the moment needs adaptation in the light of present-day pastoral needs, so that the natural right to marry may be limited as little as possible and only as far as necessary. Modest beginnings have already been made with the instruction of the Congregation for the Doctrine of the Faith dated 19 March 1966. It seems questionable whether the principle of the utmost possible legislative uniformity for the whole Church should apply to matrimonial impediments (cf. can. 1038–41), and one may hope that greater clarity and compactness will be attained in the diriment impediments. For example, why does the diriment impediment of abduction (can. 1074) appear again in quite another connection in can. 1087, where the Church declares that external coercion and grave fear invalidate matrimonial consent? Again it seems unnecessary to make impotence a separate impediment (can. 1068) when can. 1081. §2, provides that there can be no matrimonial consent in such a case. There would appear to be more reason for making a special impediment of homosexuality in cases where the man is sexually potent but cannot take a sexual interest in a woman. Under certain circumstances eugenic considerations might make it necessary to limit the right to marry. At least in the more advanced countries people should be asked to provide a sufficient account of their heredity and genetic prospects.

The Church cannot dispense from the natural moral law or from divine positive law, but not every offence against these will invalidate a marriage. Thus a mixed marriage contracted in disregard of conscience is morally illicit, even if the Church dispenses from the canonical impediment, but not invalid. In principle all ecclesiastical impediments can be dispensed from; but the Church never dispenses from the impediment arising from episcopal consecration, and hardly ever from the impediment of public conjugal murder, affinity (by marriage) of the first degree in the direct line after consummation of the marriage, or priestly ordination. The practice of dispensing so as to regularize invalid marriages (*ad convalidandum matrimonium*) was established as early as the 6th century, but that of dispensing beforehand so that a marriage can be contracted (*pro matrimonio contrahendo*) dates only from the 11th or 12th century. To this day it is not usual in Greek Orthodox canon law to dispense from impediments to marriage. Dispensations are granted according to whether impediments are public or secret for the external or merely internal forum, by the appropriate authorities. Details of procedure are very complex. Where the diriment impediment ceases to exist in an invalid marriage, the marriage can be regularized by renewal of consent (can. 1133–7), or in the case of *sanatio in radice* (can. 1138–41), where the consent continues, even without explicit renewal of the consent.

The distinction between impedient and diriment impediments does not refer directly to dispensability but to the canonical validity or invalidity of marriage. It follows that matrimonial impediments may have the indirect function of dissolving marriages (from without) which for some reason are thought undesirable. For this very purpose the impediments to marriage were greatly widened when matrimonial law was recast and expanded in the Middle Ages. Even in our present law some traces remain, such as the impediment of affinity (can. 1077) and that of spiritual relationship (can. 1079), both of which used to extend much farther than they now do. The reason to some extent for these impediments was a mistaken attitude to physical sexuality: it used to be assumed that becoming one flesh with the marriage partner established a metaphysical bond, in the nature of kinship, with the partner's relatives and that standing sponsor at a baptism (rebirth) also created a quasi-parental bond, the basis for all sorts of metaphysical relationships that ruled out marriage. We must therefore ask how far it now serves any useful purpose to keep traditional impediments in being which a different mental and social context produced and made meaningful. Similarly the impediment of "mixed religion" (can. 1060–4) derives in part from a background of solidly Catholic or Protestant regions (*cuius regio, eius religio*) and a closed society that has quite changed today with the great mobility of population and with spiritual pluralism.

The impedient impediments have much the same effects as the prohibitions of marriage, which, for example, forbid marrying lapsed Catholics and members of proscribed societies (can. 1065) and affect the marriage of a public sinner or someone under certain censures. In individual cases a prohibition of marriage may make up for the lack of a matrimonial impediment (cf. can. 1039).

e) The Church's right to determine the *form of marriage* follows from its duty to regulate marriage, including its social aspects, by taking steps appropriate to the nature of the Church to prevent bigamy, arbitrary dissolution of marriage, and the like, so far as may be necessary or desirable; and from its duty to make it clear in fitting ways that marriage is a sacrament and that God joins the marriage partners together. So on the one hand it must beware of abetting moral abuses in the common life of the sexes, such as sometimes prevailed in the Middle Ages, by doing too little; and on the other hand it must not interfere with the freedom to marry, or obscure the fact that bride and groom themselves contract the marriage, by any undue perfectionism. In this connection many question the wisdom of the present regulations for mixed marriages.

Historically speaking, the prescribed form of marriage has evolved from the liturgical rite of betrothal. Its main features are that the bridal pair freely bind themselves together, and that God joins them together as testified by the presence of the Church. The former feature was sometimes so much overstressed in the Latin Church, to the neglect of the form for contracting marriage, that clandestine marriages abounded. But only since the decree *Ne temere* of 2 August 1907 has the active, not merely passive, presence of the priest as the Church's representative been normally necessary. Since then the theology of the Church's necessary part in the contracting of marriage has been considerably deepened. In the Eastern Church, by contrast, so much is made of blessing the bridal pair that they were sometimes not even asked whether they wished to marry and so a certain clericalist distortion of the sacrament was not excluded. Under the law now in force (can. 1099; motu proprio of Pius XII, 1 August 1948), the Church requires all who were baptized Catholics and all converts to the Catholic Church to use either the ordinary (can. 1094) or the extraordinary form (can. 1098) for contracting marriage. Except in case of emergency, marriage is celebrated according to the matrimonial rite (can. 1100). Non-Catholics, whether baptized or not, who have never belonged to the Catholic Church are not bound to this form when they marry among themselves. In the ordinary form (can. 1095–9) marriage is contracted before the competent priest and two witnesses. Under Oriental canon law the nuptial blessing is also necessary to the validity of the marriage, except in case of emergency. When marriage is contracted in the extraordinary form, the presence of a competent priest is not necessary: here the Church is present only in its prescriptions. Marriage may be contracted in this extraordinary form only when a competent priest cannot attend, either through physical impossibility or because grave detriment would result for him or Christian people; and, except in danger of death, only when it is prudently judged that the emergency will last at least four weeks.

f) The rules for the *dissolution of marriage* first lay down the circumstances in which the marriage-bond can be extrinsically dissolved – where the main consideration is *in favorem fidei* –, and then what is involved in separation *a mensa et thoro*. There must be grounds for separation so serious that it is too much to expect a person to continue common life, and the interests of the children must be safeguarded so far as possible. Can. 1132 insists that in all circumstances the Catholic education of the children must be guaranteed.

g) Then can. 1960–92 deal with *matrimonial causes in Church courts*. Here many details call for reform. More must be done to safeguard the rights of the person involved, and especially to see that the parties involved take a more personal and responsible part in the exercise of their rights. Oriental canon law agrees with the Latin on all essential points (*Ius Orientale matrimoniale*, can. 1–131; *Ius Orientale iudiciale*, can. 468–500).

4. *Pastoral theology*. The most urgent task of pastoral theology is to strengthen the awareness of Christian people that marriage is a saving state which leads those called to it to their due perfection. The existing principles of special spirituality for married people must be further developed. In particular we must not minimize the tension between the "secular" and the sacred in marriage, but rather see that we acquire a better grasp of its full range – which always involves correlation between the two. Much can be done to that end by overcoming anti-sexual prejudices which are still widespread. We must warmly welcome modern advances in sexual knowledge and sex instruction. It would be a great pity if disagreeable overtones in this accelerating process of enlightenment caused us to suppress the hopeful beginnings that have been made towards banishing a misguided taboo, especially since repressed sexuality would then break out in unruly and unhealthy forms. Many, even many married people, have not acquired the art of speaking and communicating with each other in a way which befits the dignity and realities of sexuality, and this circumstance often creates grave difficulties in marriage. In particular, the notion of woman's role in marriage and the family needs fundamental revision. Moreover, a great many married people will inevitably be alienated from religion unless unnecessary harshness and false emphases in the law of marriage are corrected, and unless a suitable pastoral approach is worked out for couples of different religions and couples who have drifted away from religion. Courses for engaged couples and the development of Catholic marriage-guidance councils, staffed by qualified experts, may be a beginning. The recognition that the multi-dimensional development of society has increasingly involved marriage and the family in a complex social network should help us to acknowledge that it is now more often appropriate to make use of social workers to solve matrimonial problems. The Church should direct more attention to the problems of a choice of partner, early marriage, and the physical and mental health that marriage calls for, even sometimes at the sacrifice of familiar and cherished ideas that do not square with reality. Training of conscience, the practice of the confessional, and methods of pastoral dialogue will all have to be adapted to the deeper insights we have gained in our day into sacramental marriage, which shapes and claims the whole human being.

Waldemar Molinski

II. Parents

A. Parenthood

1. When parents bring a child into the world, they make use of their ability to

participate in God's creative power, which they do in a human and therefore analogous, but nevertheless unique manner. In giving new life, they share the work of the ultimate giver of all life. They are made more perfect through parenthood, as the child that has been given life opens up the well-springs of maternal and paternal love. Like God, who in his wisdom created us out of pure love, they not only take upon themselves the responsibility of passing on life in wisdom and love, but also the duty to care for their children. God brings his creation to fulfilment by ordaining the infra-human to man, and through his providence self-revelation and grace enable man to work with the help of the Church, freely and responsibly, towards his own salvation; similarly, parents must bring up and educate their children, giving them the material things they need and enabling them to make the best use of their physical and mental abilities, so that as the result of parental education, supplemented by that of the Church and society, they become capable of making their own free responsible decisions.

2. In parenthood parents participate in the authority of God as origin "from whom all fatherhood in heaven and earth takes its title" (Eph 3:15). This authority is unique and takes precedence before any other. It is above all the result of actual parental care and is generally greater than any other authority, as is clearly shown by the limited influence of other authorities, such as school or Church. Thus St. Thomas Aquinas, for instance, regards parents as the child's natural and total principle of existence, describing the child as "part of the father" and the family as his "spiritual womb" (*III Sententiarum*, 4, 2, 1 ad 4).

Parents exercise an authority over their children that is subjective and objective, personal and *ex officio*, based on their personal superior position and their educational task. The exercise of parents' authority should, as befits its personal nature, emanate mainly from their care and love, while their *ex officio* authority is primarily and directly a matter of the objective rightness of the institutional aspect and only indirectly personal. This shows that parents have a primary authority, while that of Church and State is secondary, and typologically exemplified in parental authority.

The responsibility of parents arises from the fact that they have given life to the child, which has come helpless into the world, entirely dependent on loving care. Children do not only owe their existence to their parents, but also hereditary traits, and their later development will be decisively influenced by pre- and post-natal factors to which they are inevitably exposed. They need parents to maintain them and help them in their development as human beings. They need particularly their religious example, as faith can only be fostered by bearing witness to it and removing obstacles, as faith is always in danger and unable to establish itself unaided because of our human limitations and sinfulness.

As parents have given the child life, they must *provide* for all his needs. The child will turn spontaneously to those who love and cherish him, to find support and help in taking his place in society. The relationship between creator and creature is therefore the eminent typological example of the parent-child relationship; thus arises the relationship of authority and subordination which is basic to any educational process.

The basis of parental authority is therefore the dependence of the child on his parents. Its content is determined by the needs of the children with regard to their parents. Their authority is therefore substitutional and a guardianship, that is to say, they must try through their independent parental acts to help the children as much as possible towards independence. There must also be an appropriate order and *ex officio* authority because the family community needs a certain "division of powers and functions". But the *specific* parental task is responsible care for their children in their minority. The duties and rights of parents extend as far as is necessary to ensure the development of the children into responsible adults. There are also secondary rights and duties which arise from an ordered communal family life. If for some good reason any parental functions are being exercised by foster-parents, parental rights and duties will pass to them to the same extent.

This exercise of care for their children is the basis of the parents' right to be honoured and cared for by their grown-up children if they should be in need of it and can claim it on the grounds of their own behaviour towards their children.

3. These parental duties and rights, based on the order of creation, are raised to a higher level through grace. Since God wills all mankind to be orientated towards salvation and since marriage is orientated towards participation in grace in God's union with redeemed mankind, the parent-child relationship is thus placed on a supernatural level, giving parents the task of disposing their children, as far as they can, towards salvation. They will receive the grace they need for this, if they do not refuse God's call. This supernatural dimension of parental duties and rights finds its sacramental expression and fulfilment in baptism and matrimony. As God wishes all men to be saved, parents have the duty to give their children a religious upbringing in accordance with God's will and they therefore may count on the necessary grace by virtue of the divine promises. They are, however, unable to give natural life by themselves and even less able to give supernatural life; they can only dispose hearts, for God alone is the source of grace.

By virtue of the call to supernatural salvation, parental rights and duties have an importance which can be fully grasped only in faith. One cannot therefore expect that non-believers will grasp the gravity of parental responsibility, especially in matters of religion, in the same way as believers.

4. As the children are born of both parents, it follows that in fulfilling their parental functions, both parents have equal duties and equal rights. But as the two parents play a different role in the begetting, rearing and education of their children, a certain division of labour naturally occurs and therefore a certain division of parental duties and rights. This division of tasks between husband and wife which applies only to a limited extent and is not at all easily defined, arises out of the "nature" of fatherhood and motherhood, and also out of the specific function which each status brings with it in their particular society and which, like society itself, is subject to change.

If a division of tasks has not arisen naturally or has not been agreed upon, the necessary decisions must be taken jointly. If no agreement is reached, no one partner has any overriding right, as parental duties and rights derive directly from the parental status and are therefore of the essence of parenthood and inalienable. In such a case the superior communities of Church and State would, as subsidiary authorities, have to render aid and protection. Any precedence on the part of the man, that is, any hierarchical order, can only apply within home and family. The man represents the family unit within family and society, within which the woman is his helpmate (Eph 5:21–33; Col 3:18f.; 1 Pet 3:1); but this in no way affects basic personal rights, including the inalienable right to provide for the education of the children according to the dictates of conscience. Thus one cannot accept, for instance, any exclusive right on the part of the father to determine the children's religion, because both parents have equal rights and because of the tolerance demanded by religious freedom of conscience.

Since rights and duties correspond, and as the duties are not cancelled if one of the partners forfeits his rights because of a neglect of duty, it can happen that one parent loses the right to control education, if by a breach of duty he does not provide a suitable education for his children. However, a breach of duty, in bad faith, cannot be presumed, but must be proved. If the conscience is erroneous regarding education, no compulsion must be used, because of the right to religious freedom, unless overriding necessities of the common good or the welfare of the individual give the State a right to intervene. The Church, in accordance with its spiritual mission, can only use spiritual appeals to the faith of the parents to have the children educated in the faith and can, if necessary, apply suitable sanctions.

If a parent forfeits his rights, he is not thereby absolved from his duties; this can be important in the case of illegitimate children, for instance, or divorce.

B. Parental Duties and Rights

1. As parents participate through their parenthood in God's creative power and since their children depend on them, parental duties (as stressed by *CIC*, can. 1113) imply the following:

a) Responsible assumption of parenthood. This means that they may only bring a child into the world if they have reasonable hopes that they will be able to rear and educate him in a way worthy of a human being. Here the family is the natural framework, willed by God. Thus procreation outside marriage must be regarded as impermissible. One might even say that, because children are dependent on the two parents and the family, procreation outside marriage is a greater wrong than to use illicit methods of birth control, as these do not normally have such far-reaching deleterious effects as illegitimate birth. Hence it would also seem that it would be wrong for a condemned man to beget a child, since the child also has a right to paternal care as far as is reasonably possible.

The problem of how many children one can reasonably bring up and educate depends on so many factors, which vary from case to case and family to family, that only the parents themselves can decide when they can undertake the responsibility to bring a new life into the world (cf. Vatican II, *Gaudium et Spes*, arts. 50–51). Church and society can, however, provide valuable assistance in the formation of consciences. It is necessary to pay special attention to the health of the parents – including hereditary factors – and the needs of children already born, but one might also have to consider population factors, the economic and social situation, such as living conditions, professional obligations, etc.

b) Because they have brought children into the world, parents also have a duty to look after them in a manner worthy of a human being, which includes their bodily needs: food, clothing, health, etc. This means that parents must only have as many children as they can hope to feed and they would be doing wrong if they did not make suitable provision for their children. But parents need not take upon themselves any greater – or any lesser – sacrifices than they expect of their children, but should take into account the individual needs of the various members of the family. It is also part of the parental duty to help the children found their own homes when the time comes.

c) But parents have a duty, above all, to educate their children to the best of their ability and to look after their spiritual welfare, for the proper development of the children's personality is the foremost work of care and love and the parents are, because of their status, the immediate representatives of God to their children, though of course analogously. Parents are absolutely bound to provide education and formation, making the best of their children's capabilities and their own opportunities. They must protect their children from moral dangers with which they could not be expected to cope themselves because of their immaturity. They must foster their ability to make moral decisions and support them in the good they do. Hence the right balance must be found in giving children protection and allowing them to fend for themselves.

A special duty in this connection is that of providing religious education. This is because the child is ordained to religion as to the highest fulfilment of man. It is not enough to confront the child with religious problems when he is of an age to make his own decisions, since psychological reasons and God's claim to our religious allegiance demand that religious education must start as early as possible. In any case religious problems and influences cannot be kept from the children.

Of course parents can only provide a religious education within the possibilities open to them, but as it is so important, it should be as comprehensive as possible. Parents will fulfil this duty if they are following their sincerely formed conscience, since in this way they are directing their own and their children's lives to God. Parents, of whatever religious creed, who permit or even actively encourage a religious education against their conscientious convictions, fail very gravely. A marriage where husband and wife have different religions or belong to different denominations within Christianity can raise such great problems in this respect that the Church has decided to forbid such marriages in general, reserving dispensation to the competent authorities and making such dispensation dependent on the provision of safeguards (cf. instruction of the Congregation for the Doctrine of the Faith, 18 March 1966). There is, however, some doubt about the pastoral advisability of such legal measures in our present age, considering the modern conditions of faith and marriage, because attempts to force religious decisions on a conscience by law can easily have a deleterious effect on the desired religious education, which today depends more than ever on the personal religious commitment of the parents. This is often more likely to be endangered than fostered by any legalism, especially with people whose links to the Church are not very strong.

d) Parents must not delegate their educational duties and rights without good reason, for example send their children to a boarding school merely for the sake of their own comfort, as their responsibility is basic and inalienable. Nor is it at all easy to replace the natural ties of the parent-child relationship, as is shown, for instance, by experiences in orphanages.

Parents must therefore see to it that anyone who takes their place pays due regard to their wishes. It would be an offence against parental rights if a State or Church institution were to assume that it was carrying out the parents' wishes without having the support of some kind of parental consensus of opinion. Institutions must take care that sufficient regard is paid to parental co-operation in the way they are educating the child. It is of course important to maintain a proper balance between parental wishes and educational expert opinion, for any one-sided influence either on the part of the parents or of the institution would be equally harmful for the child. Clearly, parental influence on institutions will be advantageous only if based on real parental responsibility; a planned schooling for parenthood must be an urgent objective of adult education.

If parents neglect their duties, they can be forced to carry them out. They can, for instance, be obliged to provide higher education, within their means, for children who are apt for it.

If, for reasons beyond their control,

parents are not in a position to discharge their duties, they should be helped to help themselves as far as possible, and in the meantime the necessary services should be rendered to the children by the competent "subsidiary" authority. Thus, for instance, the school can give sexual information and education, if the parents have failed to do so and if disadvantages to the children might otherwise result. But the school also has the duty to do all in its power to ensure that the parents themselves can undertake this task.

2. Parents' duties are balanced by rights:

a) Man has an inviolable right to marry and have children as long as he can undertake the responsibility of founding a family. This means that Church and State must not set up arbitrary obstacles to marriage, nor must they demand or enforce a limitation of the number of children, except insofar as is absolutely necessary for discharging their own tasks, for the rights of parents are absolute, though limited by the rights of their children and of the societies within which they live.

b) As the right to marriage is inviolable – although one may of course decide not to make use of this right – it follows that man also has a right to an income sufficient to maintain a family, insofar as he does not culpably neglect his duty of self-formation and work. The way this family wage is to be achieved will vary with different economic and social systems, but there can be no doubt that there is a parental right to an income sufficient to maintain a family. It is not only a question of personal dignity, but also of the service parents render to society by bringing up and educating their children. It is against distributive justice if responsible parents are expected to accept a lower standard of living than childless people of the same social group. In fact, a higher standard of living for parents would be easier to understand in view of all the additional work and trouble they have taken upon themselves, especially if those without children are not making any particularly outstanding social contribution.

c) Finally, the parents' duty to bring up children is balanced by their right to do so, and they can decide on the form and content of their education according to the opportunities available. Only in this way can they do what their conscience demands of them. It follows that, to safeguard their basic rights, parents should be associated as far as possible with educational work which they cannot carry out themselves, such as school education. Educational tasks which are beyond parental scope must always be carried out with the rights of the parents in mind. It is therefore a parental right that any task not delegated by the parents, but stemming directly from functions proper to Church or State, should be carried out as far as possible with parental co-operation. To ignore the will of the parents in educational matters without good reason is an offence against a fundamental human right, and the State may only use compulsion as far as this is absolutely necessary in carrying out its own task. The Church too can only play a subsidiary part in religious education, reserving to itself those functions which parents cannot or do not carry out. A monopoly in education must therefore be regarded as indefensible, or at best only to be tolerated if sufficient scope is given to all justified parental wishes, in other words, if integration has been achieved freely, and the common good absolutely demands integrated education.

There is a particular parental right to determine their children's religious education, for its foundations must be laid by the parents. The negative reason is that neither Church nor State is in a position to do so on its own. The State is not in a position to do so, because its concern is with man's temporal welfare. It must respect every man's right to religious freedom and must remain neutral in such matters. The Church is not in a position to do so, because religious education must be an integral part of a child's education and it is not the Church's business to provide an integrated education, but only a religious one, and that only as far as men are prepared to open themselves to it of their own free will or through their guardians, as revelation should be accepted with morally legitimate faith. In particular one must remember that the less mature the children are, the more must religion be integrated in their general education, if it is to be at all effective, for the younger the child, the more dependent will it be on an integrated approach. And the older the child is, the more directly must it be led to a personal decision of faith by the discussion of other convictions. From the positive point of view, parents have a right to determine their children's religious education because they brought their children into the world and are therefore responsible for them, a responsibility of which they cannot be relieved by either Church or State, whose responsibilities are limited to their own specific spheres. Neither Church nor State may obstruct any religious education desired by the parents; they may not refuse any help it is in their power to give, if parents want to bring up their children according to their convictions. Thus the State must not place any obstacles in the way of religious instruction in State schools, but must co-operate, without of course interfering with the freedom of religious teaching.

d) When parents exercise their rights, they must bear in mind their obligation to love their neighbour, so that insistence on their own rights does not prejudice the rights of other parents. This could happen if, for instance, one type of schooling, which is perfectly good in itself, were to be given undue preference at the expense of other children's opportunities. Undue preference given to State schools can have this effect just as much as undue insistence on the right of denominational schools, if this would interfere with other educational necessities.

C. Limits of Parental Duties and Rights

Parental duties and rights are directly correlated to the duties and rights of the children, and indirectly to the duties and rights of others, such as the superior communities of Church and State on the one hand and, on the other, school, relatives, etc., who have their own basic responsibilities towards the children. The duties and rights of parents are therefore limited by the duties and rights of others. The inner reason for this limitation of parental responsibility is of course that their basic authority is derivative and therefore limited.

a) Parental authority is limited by the rights of the children, as children are not their parents' property, but in principle equal partners with equal and inalienable human rights. The degree of dependence on their parents determines their duties towards them, and the degree of independence determines their rights. Thus they owe obedience to their parents to the extent to which they are not yet capable of making their own decisions and taking full responsibility for their own actions, but parents may only expect obedience to that extent and no more. Parents must not attempt to limit or influence their children's wills except as far as is necessary in the children's interest, properly understood. This applies particularly to important things, such as choice of occupation and marriage, but also to unimportant matters such as fashion. Physical force may only be used in self-defence or if urgently necessary for the good of the child. In religious matters particularly the child's freedom must be respected to the greatest possible extent, but he must also be faced with the necessity to make a decision, for religious education can only be a shaping of conscience, and any other approach will not only fail to be helpful to a genuine religious development, but will actually be a hindrance. Parents are of course their children's natural guides and advisers and must object in a suitable manner if the children offend against God's law.

b) Church and State also have certain rights within their own sphere, especially regarding education, for the parents are not in a position to provide everything the children need: they must have subsidiary, indirect help from superior communities, especially State and Church, and this gives the helpers corresponding rights. Thus the State is entitled, for instance, to insist on proper schooling, though compulsion must not go beyond what is absolutely necessary. The Church, in order not to go beyond this point, tends to leave preparation for first Communion at the right time as far as possible to the parents (cf. *CIC*, can. 854, §4). Church and State, in discharging their own functions, also have a direct, basic, natural or supernatural right to influence the children. Thus the State can insist on compulsory schooling and an educational standard appropriate to the age and its culture, without infringing parental rights, as long as it leaves as much free scope as possible within the compulsory framework; similarly the Church is entitled to an appropriate share in religious instruction, and parents do wrong if they refuse. But, unlike the State, the Church must only use moral means of persuasion.

c) School, relatives, etc., apart from any rights delegated by the parents, also have rights of their own which limit parental rights. Thus the teacher in the school carries out his own educational task of integrating the child into the larger community, a responsibility which is not merely based on delegation by parents and State, but is also his own specific task. The same is true of all others who provide some service for the children which only they and no one else can provide within a framework of authority, which is always a sort of relationship of origin.

d) Parental duties and rights, therefore, are to be clearly distinguished from the rights and duties of others, but they cannot be separated from them, as they are all rooted in the indivisible personality of the child in its various aspects. The needs of this personality can be formally decided *a priori*, but the details can only be decided *a posteriori*, as these will depend on continually changing personal attitudes and the resulting needs of the child. The functions and rights of those who stand in some relationship to the child are also subject to change. Thus the actual concrete demands of parental responsibility are continually changing and cannot be described once and for all.

But one can lay down a general rule that the relationship between parental rights and duties and those of other responsible people must be balanced in such a way that any rights over the child are limited as far as possible and extended as far as necessary, because otherwise authority over the child, in the service of the child, turns into manipulation and thus treats man as an object or thing and not as a person. Power over anyone and force can only be justified within the context of genuine preservation and development of the person concerned or of the person exercising the power or force. Only if this truth is understood and observed is it possible to make a proper assessment of parental responsibilities, their extent and their limits.

As parental rights are subject to historical change under changing conditions, they need to be formulated by *positive law*, which must not, however, be formulated independently of the various holders of authority.

Waldemar Molinski

III. Family

The Church's teaching on the family, if it is to meet present-day needs, must present an up-to-date realistic approach together with a deeper theological outlook. Over-romantic, patriarchal or sentimental ideas of family life no longer carry conviction. Neither can the picture we give be an over-abstract one, divorced from the actual realities of modern families. It must rather take sympathetic account of the nature, difficulties and opportunities of the family as it is.

A. The Family in the Order of Creation

We lay particular stress on those facts which are of special importance in the Church's preaching and teaching.

1. *Family and marriage*. The family has its origin in marriage; marriage is directed to the family as its goal. In earlier, more primitive times, even in the OT, the emphasis was on the family community, with a view to the continuation and growth of the greater community (clan, tribe), and the individual was almost entirely absorbed in the family (as in ancient China). Nowadays the marriage itself and the personal relationship of the married couple are increasingly seen as the real heart of the family on which the children depend for growth and support. This view of marriage, already clear in Gen 2 and Eph 5, is expressed too in the pronouncements of Vatican II's Pastoral Constitution on the Church in the Modern World, arts. 47–52. In this important document emphatic and detailed stress is laid on married love, without omitting, however, a corresponding emphasis on its expression and development in the family and the children. "... While not making the other purposes of matrimony of less account, the true practice of conjugal love, and the whole meaning of the family life which results from it, have this aim: that the couple be ready with stout hearts to co-operate with the love of the Creator and the Saviour, who through them will enlarge and enrich his own family day by day ... Marriage, to be sure, is not instituted solely for procreation; rather its very nature as an unbreakable compact between persons, and the welfare of the children, both demand that the mutual love of the spouses be embodied in a rightly ordered manner, that it grow and ripen. Therefore, marriage persists as a whole manner and communion of life and maintains its value and indissolubility, even when, despite the often intense desire of the couple, offspring are lacking" (*ibid.*, art. 50).

2. *Family and community*. The family (not marriage) is the primary unit of community living. It binds the sexes as well as the generations and introduces the young people into the life of the community. It brings into existence on a minute scale an astounding variety of relationships since it encompasses the members entirely and binds them together in love.

The proper development of this variety of relationships needs corresponding need for space (housing!) and time, as well as an alertness and sensitivity of spirit. Pastoral care must help to unfold and realize these riches and must not one-sidedly moralize or sacralize – otherwise even the laws of unity and indissolubility of marriage and of piety between children and parents carry no conviction and are not capable of being put into practice.

3. *Family as fellowship*. These relationships include the following:

a) *The sex and blood relationship*. The intimate relationship between husband and wife affects both, physiologically and biologically, but especially the wife, through the exchange of semen and hormones, as well as through the life of the senses. The laws of heredity too have confirmed the experience that the children are physically and therefore in their basic temperaments formed by both parents. The parents pass on life, their life, to the children and see in them both the fruit and the continuation of their own life. Blood relationship in the descent from Abraham (*semen Abrahae*) plays a decisive part in the history of salvation in the OT. Even Christ's own genealogy is given twice in the NT. In the NT, to be sure, blood relationship is no longer of decisive significance, its place being taken by higher bonds (cf. Rom 4; 5; 9). Yet as a fact of the created world it has not entirely lost its meaning.

b) *The primary economic community*. In the family we have an intensive exchange of goods and services which is not commercial but based on love: perfect communism according to the classic formula: from each according to his means, to each according to his needs. Such perfect communism is possible only here, for nowhere else do we find such deep and intimate personal relationships. This "communism of love" carries at the same time an urgent appeal, an earnest demand for selflessness, self-giving, readiness for sacrifice, self-conquest.

c) *Community of mind and spirit*. In daily living, based on love, trust, esteem and respect, there is also an exchange of ideas, convictions, values and attitudes, a sharing of the experience of joys and sorrows, successes and trials, such as we find in no other group. The mysteries of human life have from the earliest times made the family a centre of religious cult (the sacred hearth). Although the essential sacrifice of Christianity does not take place in the family but in a public and specially consecrated community room, since it has its source not in man but in the only begotten Son of God, yet the family remains a holy place in which religious sentiments and convictions are cultivated in common, passed on to the coming generation and above all carried into the realities of everyday life. In the family the child is baptized and receives the first introduction to the truths and realities of faith.

d) *Educational unit*. Modern psychology and pedagogy confirm the traditional judgment that man's decisive formation takes place in the earliest years of life, long before his intellect is capable of critical discernment, first of all because he is most impressionable at this stage and secondly because it is then that facts and attitudes are conveyed to him in the most intimate and personal way, in love. Man takes in best what comes to him by way of the heart. Thus it is also of decisive importance for pastoral work that the family and family living be shaped and surrounded by a religious atmosphere that is healthy, mature and responsible. Family education, however, relates not only to the children but also to the parents: "As living members of the family, children contribute in their own way to making their parents holy" (Pastoral Constitution on the Church in the Modern World, art. 48).

e) *Meeting of the generations*. The most fundamental and most intensive meeting of the generations comes about through birth, and shared living. Yet in a dynamic society age has not the commanding position it held in earlier times. Nowadays the knowledge and experience of earlier generations are handed on not merely in the family but also in the school, as well as through organizations, books, libraries and museums, press and radio. The older generation has become more independent of the help of the younger generation in material matters. Savings, life insurance, public welfare institutions, hospitals and old people's homes have in many cases taken over the services formerly provided by the children. The duty of children to provide for their aged parents has ceased to a great extent to be a matter of necessity. Nevertheless the meeting of the generations in the family retains its importance, especially in the realm of the mind and the spirit.

4. *The change in family life in industrial society*. Industrial society has made an enormous change in the external form of family living, nor has the inner structure remained unaffected. The essential elements remain, but take on in many ways a new form and undergo a shift of emphasis. For pastoral work and religious education it is important to note these changes and not cling to outmoded images. Careful consideration must be given to the question as to which of these changes represent a decline, which are merely a transition from one historical situation to another, and which even imply genuine progress in the light of true Christian values.

a) *Disappearance of the former economic independence of the family*. On the farm the family produced almost everything that was needed. What was produced was for the most part used by the family itself. This naturally made for a certain simplicity and restricted the circle of acquaintances, but resulted too in a considerable independence of the market and of contact with other people, of competition and the changes of fashion. More than anything else, life on the farm implied a common work and a common destiny. The farm was at once the provider and organizer of work, hospital and health insurance, pension fund and old people's home, vocational guidance (insofar as this was in any sense called for!) and centre for training, marriage counselling and match-making, etc.

This meant that there was a great need for members of the family to help with the work: each child was, even while quite young, an economic asset; large families were economically and socially valuable. Thus in all the rural cultures of the world, in China and Africa as well as in Russia and Patagonia, large families were the normal thing. This was also a necessity because of the high death rate among children and for the growth of the human race. This was not so much a question of morals as of economic and social trends. The present-day family in industrial society has suffered socially and economically a considerable loss of function and has taken a turn in the opposite direction. The consequence is that greater emphasis is laid on the cultural and spiritual functions of the family.

b) *The self-sufficiency of the ancient family was also great in spiritual matters.* At a time when there were no schools, organizations, press, radio or TV, the children learned almost everything from their parents. It was thus comparatively easy for the parents to hand on their views and convictions about life to their children. Today a multitude of outside influences affect the members of the family and the family itself. The force and significance of tradition have diminished. The call for discussion, personal assimilation and independent conviction is incomparably greater.

c) *The number in the rural family* was greater in two respects: the number of children and the number of relatives who lived under one roof or at least in close proximity. The relationship of the generations (parents, grandparents, even great-grandparents and children) was also a matter of course and strengthened the force of tradition. In the nature of things kinship played a greater role socially and politically. Today relationship in both directions plays a far smaller part: the social pressure of the family has grown less, the freedom and independence of the individual has grown greater and more demanding.

d) With the high degree of socio-economic and cultural self-sufficiency came the *very influential position of the father of the family* in respect to his wife and to the children. It was the patriarchal age, based less on moral and religious convictions (these only in a secondary, indirect way) than on social and cultural factors. The father was at once manager of the family business, work director of his "people", master of apprentices, administrator of the family possessions, etc. Today the father's authority rests not so much on his economic functions (these are in fact specifically laid down by law and made legally binding) as on his personal qualities of mind and character.

e) A further factor to consider is *the local, social and mental immobility* of the traditional family in contrast to the mobility of industrial society. This latter in fact weakens tradition or makes it partly impossible. In the city the same life cannot be lived as in the country neither occupationally nor economically, neither from a cultural nor a religious point of view.

f) In addition, partly as a consequence of the changes described above, *the consciousness of individuality and the desire for freedom* have a much greater influence nowadays, bringing a new pressure to bear on the family, even to the extent at times of breaking it up. There is "emancipation" in all spheres and greater exposure to the multiple influences of the larger society. This situation can, however, also lead to a mental development of the individual and to better human relations.

5. *Some characteristics of the modern family*. From all this it follows that the traditional family was anchored much more securely in its economic, social, cultural and traditional functions, whereas the modern family is far more dependent on its mental, cultural, moral and religious powers. This involves a greater vulnerability and insecurity but also a greater opportunity and task from the personal and pastoral point of view.

a) Both for the protection and orderly development of the family, in moral and religious questions as well as in matters of authority, there is need of a more intensely personal commitment. The family is not sufficiently secure, either socio-economically or legally (possibility of divorce). All the more earnestly must those forces be developed which are calculated to strengthen families and hold them together. Pastoral work must also lay less stress on commands and prohibitions and more on the development of the inner forces of selflessness and readiness for sacrifice, of responsibility and fidelity freely chosen.

b) In this respect particular importance attaches to the role of the woman and her training for that role. It is especially the woman's task – and her potentialities make her capable of it – to bring the spiritual forces to their full development. It is a matter for urgent consideration whether the education and training we give to girls take sufficient account of this fact. In our preoccupation with mental and occupational training for girls (not to speak of competitive sport) do we not perhaps give far too little attention to the training of the heart, the sensibilities, the awakening of love? The extension of the education and training of girls, the approach to equality with men in this regard, their increased independence are to be welcomed. But in all this the basic vocation of woman, to be a life companion and mother, should not be pushed too far into the background in a reaction against the former patriarchal social order. As well as the similarity, the dissimilarity (not inferiority, not subjection) should not be eliminated or neglected. This would be to subject the special qualities and task of woman to harmful pressure.

c) The man's position and task, as husband and father, call for special qualities of mind and character. Perhaps a new meaning should be found in the saying of St. Paul that the husband is head of the wife, to the effect that man is not so much the head of the wife but rather the natural head of the marriage and of the family community. This gives the justification for his position as well as setting the limits of his task. It signifies no right of precedence but rather an obligation of service. The man has the amount of authority which is called for by the needs of the marriage and family, of the wife and the children.

That will vary with age and other circumstances.

d) The children are, through the school and social conditions, State law, and social security, less dependent on their parents. This makes education more difficult but also more human. The basis of education has to be trust and service, rather than authority and obedience.

e) The circle of relatives is smaller, the relationships are fewer and above all less taken for granted. They should not be neglected, especially as a protection against isolation and as an enrichment of life, but they should be cultivated on a new basis and in greater freedom and independence.

f) Similarly, aging parents have become more independent materially of their children and relatives. Young families have a right, indeed a duty, to direct their lives in a freer and more independent way. Yet a warm and intimate relationship between the generations, with respect for freedom on both sides, can be of great human and spiritual value. The duties to the aged must be re-formulated.

6. *The special task of the family in industrial society*. Since industrial society threatens to become a mass society, mechanized, de-spiritualized, anonymous and atomized, increasingly bureaucratic and subject to the extension of public power, the family has a providential task as a place of refuge and protection for the soul and mind of man, for personality and individuality, for freedom and morality, for the direct responsibility for others and for religion.

B. The Theology of the Family

A specific theology of the family has not yet been written. Yet a beginning has been made in some important respects.

1. Since marriage and the family derive clearly from the order of God's creation, there is a special dignity and sacredness about them. They are much more closely connected with man's nature and existence than, for example, the State. Thus they are also more directly determined and regulated by nature and its Creator.

2. The priority of parenthood over married union is biblically and theologically untenable. Gen 2, as well as Eph 5, tells against it. Marriage is a sacrament for the consecration not of parents but of the husband and wife; it refers directly and in the first place to marriage and married love, and only secondarily and indirectly to parenthood. However, since marriage is a permanent sacrament and since married love naturally unfolds in parenthood, the latter shares too in the dignity and grace of the sacrament. Fruitfulness pertains without any doubt to the essential function of marriage in the biblical and theological view.

3. Attempts to deduce the notion of the family theologically from the Blessed Trinity must be regarded as a failure. Life, love, fruitfulness and community living have indeed in a general way their source in the life, love, and fruitfulness in the divine Trinity, but the attempt to establish this in detail is theological speculation, which, however ingenious and even correct and valuable it may be, departs too much from Scripture to be theologically capable of proof.

4. *Order in marriage and the family*. Study of holy Scripture has led to the realization that many directives of Scripture on authority and obedience, on the order of ends in marriage, the position of the wife, etc., contain formulations that are a product of the age in which they were written. Scripture experts are endeavouring to extract the permanently valid core from those elements which merely derive from the culture of the period. Something of this has already been mentioned above under A.

5. *Vatican II* emphasizes both in the Decree on the Apostolate of the Laity and in the Pastoral Constitution on the

Church in the Modern World (arts. 47–52) the special significance and mission of marriage and the family for the individual as well as for society and the Church. Art. 47 of the Pastoral Constitution says: "The well-being of the individual person and of human and Christian society is intimately linked with the healthy condition of that community produced by marriage and family." Cf. arts. 50–52, and Decree on the Apostolate of the Laity, art. 11: "Since the Creator of all things has established the conjugal partnership as the beginning and basis of human society and, by his grace, has made it a great mystery in Christ and the Church (cf. Eph 5:32), the apostolate of married persons and of families is of unique importance for the Church and civil society . . . The family has received from God its mission to be the first and vital cell of society." Therefore the family must not close in on itself in an egoistic or timid way, but must exert its influence on the Church and society (*ibid.*). Those who have the care of souls must in their turn have a special care for the family (Pastoral Constitution, art. 52; Decree on the Apostolate of the Laity, art. 11) and help it to overcome difficulties. "It devolves on priests duly trained about family matters to nurture the vocation of spouses by a variety of pastoral means, by preaching God's word, by liturgical worship, and by other spiritual aids to conjugal and family life; to sustain them sympathetically and patiently in difficulties, and to make them courageous through love, so that families which are truly illustrious can be formed" (Pastoral Constitution, art. 52). Pastoral care has in many cases fallen a victim to one or other of two extremes: on the one hand it has been over-individualistic in its care for various groups (children, men, women, young men, young girls) and has only seldom seen the family as a community; one need only think of the arrangements for Mass and the sacraments, of the confraternities and their effect on the family, on the reluctance to make house visitation. On the other hand pastoral work for the family has concerned itself too exclusively with morality (sex morality and number of children), with sacramentality and with the question of authority, while giving too little consideration to the total human reality, especially to the value of married love in its true depth and variety. There are here, especially in the light of the Pastoral Constitution on the Church in the Modern World, big gaps to be filled in preaching and pastoral care.

6. If man is in a certain sense a summary of the variety of existence, so is the family in a special way the living synthesis and harmony of multiple tensions: matter and spirit, natural tendency and free choice, sex and love, personality and community, the past (in the forefathers) and the future (in the children), tradition and individuality, self-realization and self-giving, nature and grace are brought in the family in a unique, personal and yet socially valuable way to a fruitful unity, both bringing life to be and shaping its development. The seemingly most trivial things in the family come to have the greatest human and spiritual significance as symbols and expressions of love and fidelity. Diversity and tensions are here not so much a source of conflicts as of fruitfulness. Since the sacramental consecration of married love is the foundation of the family and comes in it to full development, the entire order of creation becomes here in a sense the vehicle for sacramental grace and a means of salvation.

Jakob David

MARTYRDOM

1. *The concept of martyrdom.* Since most of the aspects of the original concept of μάρτυς in dogmatic theology are dealt with elsewhere, the concept of martyr-

dom is treated here in the sense of dogmatic and fundamental theology, where it has above all to do with the free acceptance of death for the sake of faith (including the moral doctrine of faith) as a whole or with regard to individual doctrines (although these should be seen in the context of the whole of faith). It is only by analogy that a death *in odium fidei* which is not consciously accepted (for example, the death of children in religious persecution) can be called martyrdom.

2. *The theology of martyrdom.* a) Martyrdom is Christian death in acceptance of the death of Christ, and as such is the supreme act of love (Jn 15. 13; *Summa Theologica*, II–II, q. 124, a. 3, c). It places man completely at the disposal of God, radically unifying an act of love with the act of being taken from oneself in confrontation with man's incomprehensible, but very powerful denial of the love revealed by God. Martyrdom is the perfect manifestation of Christian death as such. b) This death is therefore a witness on the part of faith to a totally resolute act including the whole of man's being, based on God's grace and experienced in a deep inner and outer impotence patiently accepted by man. This witness is a total realization of faith and testifies not only to faith, but also to the reality of what is believed. The attainment of what is believed, which characterizes faith and distinguishes it from any other kind of "conviction", because it is marked by grace, reaches (primarily in the case of the martyr himself) a climax in martyrdom (cf. Viller and Rahner). c) The doctrine of martyrdom as a baptism of blood bringing certain justification and the fact that martyrs can be canonized show that Christians have always been convinced that, in his predefinition of effective grace, God never allows the inner attitude of being turned in faith and love towards him to be absent or to be replaced by pure fanaticism or obstinacy when the outward phenomenon of martyrdom is really present. Finally, we should note that, as *quasi ex opere operato*, martyrdom brings justification.

3. *Martyrdom as a (fundamental) theological (or apologetical) witness to the truth of Christianity and the Church.* Because of its frequent occurrence in the history of the Church up to our own times and its concrete character (both sexes, all classes and ages, without fanaticism, in patient resignation, the cruel circumstances, the acceptance of martyrdom as the fulfilment of Christian life and so on), martyrdom for the sake of the Christian and Catholic faith has always, since the patristic period, been regarded in the theological tradition as a miracle (because it transcends man's normal moral strength) and therefore as an argument for the divine origin of Christianity (*D* 1683, see also 1794), especially since it does not occur in this way and so frequently in the history of religion (outside Judaism and Christianity). The continuation of this argument is not easy. It is made more difficult by the fact that Christians have persecuted Jews and put them to death and because of the cases of martyrdom that individual Christian confessions of faith in defiance of death have inflicted on each other. The whole complex of a phenomenon that has many aspects in time and space has to be kept in mind and this should be compared with other similar phenomena. This objectively valid procedure is, however, difficult to imitate, because the individual confession made in defiance of death does not in itself guarantee the correctness of the doctrine. The miracle of many cases of martyrdom in an accumulation of individual acts of martyrdom in time and space is also something that can only with great difficulty be historically assessed as a miracle. It is, moreover, not denied in the fundamental theology of the Catholic Church that the freely accepted death of a non-Catholic Christian for

his faith may as such be martyrdom for Christianity (the Protestant martyrs of Uganda in 1885 are examples of this). Nor does the Catholic Church dispute that the continued confession of an erroneous opinion until death (although this happens relatively rarely) in fact draws its strength from the whole of Christian faith and grace as in other cases of an objective erroneous confession made with a subjectively good conscience.

Karl Rahner

MARXISM

System and History

1. *Concept and general problem.* a) Marxism is the philosophical term used to describe not only Marx's teaching but also the numerous additions, developments, revisions and immanent criticisms of that teaching. Marxism is thus a collective concept under which many individual Marxisms may be subsumed, although they differ from one another, sometimes even considerably. Thus the name Marxism-Leninism is given to the modification and application of the Marxist teaching in the Russian Revolution; heretics are called revisionists; there are left- and right-wing deviationists, and finally there are numerous national (e.g., Chinese, Yugoslav, etc.) versions of Marxism. Formally this multiple interpretation of Marxism raises a primary fundamental difficulty of Marxism: the problem of an authoritative exposition in practice for any particular historical or social situation. The root of this difficulty lies in the specific nature of Marx's work itself. Theory and practice affect each other dialectically, philosophy does not rest content with the interpretation of historical phenomena, it must be implemented; and vice-versa, every theory must draw into its reflections the concrete social situation in which it is dialectically involved. Thus with a change of historical and material conditions, the theory itself changes. Marx never reflected systematically enough on this scientific method of his for a heuristic principle to be derived from it for the process of the internal revision of Marxism itself.

b) A second problem lies in Marx's choice of the proletariat for the role of revolutionary leadership in the liquidation of the bourgeois-capitalist class-war, and the actual absence of such a revolution. Marxism, it is true, showed itself extremely effective for the international organization of workers, for founding trade unions and for decisive improvements in conditions of industrial work, yet the revolt of the proletariat foretold by Marx did not in fact take place. Rather has the improvement in living standards had the effect of repressing the development of revolutionary thinking. The Russian Revolution was the work of Lenin with a few hard-core professional revolutionaries, and took place in a feudalistic monarchy instead of in a capitalist industrial State; these conditions as well as the early rise to power of cadre and functionary had to have an extensive legitimation. This resulted in large-scale modification of Marxism: Lenin's voluminous writings brought the first justification of national distinctions and a revolutionary doctrine which placed heavy emphasis on the tactics and techniques, more important for the political and strategic application of Marxism than for its philosophical interpretation. It can be taken as certain that in the modern Western neo-capitalistic countries there is no question anywhere of a revolutionary-minded proletariat, in spite of all the political propaganda which, because of party dogmatism, refuses to accept this. In this respect the Marxist prognostications have been shown to be false, although modern Marxism has not drawn the appropriate consequences from this fact.

c) Through the political developments, above all after World War II, there arose in the opposition between East and West a classical confrontation of capitalism and socialism, which since then, however, has notably diminished, partly as a result of the risk of atomic war if world revolution was pursued, partly because of the rise of a neutral "third world", and finally because of a partial assimilation of capitalism and socialism to each other. This global inter-dependence enforces coexistence at least in practice, and also endangers the permanency of the Marxist doctrine, inasmuch as capitalism, in spite of all prognoses, has not succumbed to its inner contradiction; it has rather endeavoured, by partial assimilation of elements of Marxism, to integrate it and to give it a new function, thereby ushering in a new phase of the class dialectic, the theoretical and practical mastering of which becomes the source of new inner-Marxist controversies.

d) Some philosophical problems, regarded as essential by Marx and the Marxists, have since lost much of their relevance or must be approached from a very different point of view. Thus the opposition between idealism and materialism has become much less important after Husserl, Heidegger and Wittgenstein and the natural philosophy of Planck, Heisenberg and Weizsäcker; the notion of ideology has become in many ways detached from the Marxist context and translated into terms of sociology of knowledge, of psychoanalysis and of positivism; political philosophy and jurisprudence have abandoned the Hegelian position and are rightly uninterested in certain Marxist posing of alternatives about State and society; in social economy the Marxist theory of labour value has not succeeded in establishing itself; the traditional Marxist criticism of religion has been subjected to correction from the point of view of philosophy, theology, and the theory of religion, and this with the approbation of Marxist theoreticians.

These are only a few of the points in which a tension has arisen separating Marxism both from the teaching of Marx and from the realities of modern life. They explain too the reasons for the many versions of Marxism obtaining today.

2. *Doctrine and development.* The philosophical teaching of Marx took shape above all in his grappling with the system of Hegel. Marx took over at first the materialist principle of Feuerbach and some other left-wing Hegelians, to criticize the idealistic assumptions of Hegel, the intellectual monism, the conceptual identity of subject and object, the synthesis of reality and reason as theology; to expose the apparent reconciliation and the abstract ideology; and instead of it to formulate the new task of philosophy after Hegel, namely, to bridge the real gulf still remaining between being and consciousness. To achieve this, philosophy must cease to wish to remain merely philosophy and must rather translate the reality of meaning into meaningful reality. Marx, in the "Eleven Theses on Feuerbach", made an essential modification of the materialism taken over as part of this synthesis from Feuerbach, inasmuch as instead of the uncritical, mechanist, metaphysical notion of matter, he identifies matter as a *social* reality and thus brings being and consciousness into the dialectical process of theory and practice in human society. The gulf between thought and reality, and in particular ideology, is seen to be the consequence of social alienation, the analysis and removal of which becomes thereafter the chief aim of Marxism. At a very early stage Marx entered the sphere of political philosophy and jurisprudence, and in these areas too he attacked the use of Hegelian assumptions found in Prussia; increasingly, however, his attention was given to the classical doctrine of social economy, the results of which occupy by far the greater part of his entire writings. In this, the chief effort was

devoted to proving that capitalist society would destroy itself through class war in which the proletariat, being subjected to a progressive pauperization, would carry the banners of revolution and, realizing their momentous role in events, would become conscious agents in the process of world history. Specially characteristic of the Marxist doctrine is the fact that all empirical economics, sociology and political criticism remain within a systematic philosophical framework, making secure the continuity of earlier and more recent work without at the same time dogmatically preempting the empirical analysis. In all his writings the philosophically formulated purpose remains the free self-realization of man and his emancipation from historically conditioned alienation which Marx saw as caused principally by the theory of exchange value, which was raised to the level of an abstract natural law in the capitalist society centred on the market, together with the division of labour deriving from this and from the private ownership of the means of production; in the later writings especially there are extraordinarily sceptical expressions about the power of the "Kingdom of Necessity" in the "Kingdom of Freedom". The first distortion of Marx's doctrine was caused by Engels, partly with the concurrence of Marx. It finds its clearest expression in "Anti-Dühring". Engels applies Marx's dialectic of the historico-social process to nature, thus falling back into the naturalistic materialism previously rejected by Marx. With this Marxism becomes a closed systematic *Weltanschauung*, providing, with the help of materialist metaphysics, a universal, coherent explanation which subsumes the social dialectic under the natural and from then on involves the danger of totalitarianism.

In the succeeding period Marxism was philosophically much neglected; it was swept along in the wake of the factional squabbling and internal rivalries of the Socialist and Communist Parties. Lenin's copious writings too were concerned chiefly with questions of practical politics and of tactics; he was the first to attempt the application of Marxist doctrine to an unforeseen situation, but also gave Marxism an aggressively militant and extremely technological direction. Through the establishment of a corps of functionaries bound to the party and to the orthodox party-line teachings, as well as through his ruthless handling of opponents, Lenin opened the way to Stalinism. Concurrently, the dialectic of theory and practice gradually degenerated to a mere empirio-critical realism, under the formula of basis and superstructure, thus mechanically over-simplifying all tension between subject and object. On this reduction of Marxism abbreviated to "Diamat", Stalin was able to establish the Soviet claim to leadership within Communism with the appearance of ideological legitimacy.

Yet, even if there were no other proof, the continuing stream of criticism by Marxists themselves is sufficient to refute the view that a direct line of development leads from the early writings of Marx to Stalin's reign of terror. In *Germany* Rosa Luxemburg and Karl Liebknecht raised severe objections to Lenin's bureaucracy of party functionaries and demanded instead, as orthodox Marxists, the participation of the entire proletariat consciously and willingly in the revolution. Karl Korsch and Georg Lukács attempted to breathe new life into Marxism by reverting to Hegel. The National-Socialist persecution of Socialists and Communists brought Marxist research to a standstill.

In *France* the lectures on Hegel by Kojev resulted in a philosophical acceptance of Marxism, the effects of which are still in evidence and which is represented by names such as Merleau-Ponty, Sartre, Lefèbvre, L. Goldmann, etc. Merleau-Ponty sees in the proletariat a group with inter-subjective authenticity whose action gives meaning to history; the latter is to be brought to realization by creative effort, and thus contingently, not deduced as part of a blind process. It is questionable, however, whether Merleau-Ponty's concept of the historicity of the subject before all history does not remain irreconcilable with the Marxist notion of history, and thus whether an essential limit is placed by Marxism on the transcendental, ontological philosophy of history. Sartre came from an existentialist concept of revolution to an acceptance of Marxism to the extent that he regards existentialism as an essential corrective to Marxism, since this tends to dogmatism and to the reduction of man to a mere object. Severe inner-Marxist criticism is expressed by H. Lefèbvre, expelled from the French Communist Party in 1955: "l'expérience d'aliénation" as a beginning and "l'homme total" as the asymptotic end mark the road of Marxism. The crisis about objectivity affected Marxism also – in place of the flight into rigid dogmatism, Lefèbvre recommends the concrete, critical dialectic of daily life. Besides the confrontation of Marxism with existentialism which has hitherto set the tone, the debate with structuralism begins to take on more significance.

In *Italy* there exists since A. Gramsci (d. 1937) a form of Marxism which is closely tailored to Italian circumstances: undogmatic, nowadays partly pragmatic, it openly advocates parliamentary democracy, dialogue with the Church and ideological tolerance. As L. Lombardo-Radice expressed it, the basic philosophical principle is that men are in a position to recognize their problems and to solve them in the course of history. In *West Germany* there are the hesitant beginnings of a renewal of Marxist research. As well as the investigations into basic sources, Catholic and Protestant theology have made special efforts to come to a right interpretation of the early writings of Marx, with the frequent tendency, it is true, to interpret them in ontological or anthropological terms, as, for example, when the notion of alienation is taken as a basic anthropological category, instead of arising from transitory, socio-economic conditions. The Frankfurt school with Adorno, Horkheimer, Habermas, etc., attempts to understand Marxism as a critical, dialectical social theory, with some emphasis on cultural criticism and psychoanalysis. Habermas in particular takes Marxism as philosophy of history with a practical intent and as a logic of the social sciences. E. Bloch relates Marxism and a cosmological philosophy of history to an utopia of identity strongly reminiscent of Schelling. In *the Communist countries*, above all in Poland, Yugoslavia and Czechoslovakia, a revisionism emphatically existentialist and positivist has won attention as a result of the criticism of Stalinism with its neglect of the individual in theory and practice. Thus Kolakowski distinguishes between institutional and intellectual Marxism, i.e., between its dogmatic form and existential adaptation. However, this revisionism threatens to depart so far from Marxism that Marxism shrinks to a mere scientific methodology.

A. Schaff poses the question of the place of the individual, of the scientific nature of Marxism and its ability to deal with subjective, personal problems. More remarkable than the results (social eudaemonism, socialist humanism) appears the recognition that even in a socialist society not all conflicts at once disappear, i.e., that the needs of the individual reach beyond the status of unquestioning welfare even in an optimally organized socialist society.

3. *Marxism and Christianity*. Marxist criticism of religion is based on Feuerbach's thesis of the projection of human concepts on God. Marx explained this projection by the social alienation which demands and even enforces an abstract, ideological consolation, since the

thought and being of man are torn apart in the wage relationship, instead of being reconciled. Religion protests against the misery, it is true, yet its primary effect is to find, by means of its consolation, a justification and explanation for the present evil, thereby stabilizing it. In the Communist society religion dies of itself; Lenin holds that an extirpation is called for. Even in the early stages of socialism (Fourier, Buchez, Weidling, etc.) and in religious socialism (Tillich, Steinbüchel) the first contacts began between Marxism and Christianity. The weakness of the Marxist criticism of religion is nowadays admitted by the Marxists themselves; it consists above all in its hypothetical character; no precise description of the phenomenon, use of categories false to the history of religion, methodological inconsequence. The thesis about the withering away of religion is established by methods indefensible even by Marxist standards. For Christianity the question arises to what extent the Marxist axiom of the total identity of history and society bears an ideological character. The less true this is, the more easily can Christianity come to a reconciliation with Marxism and in a freer society hope for a form of the faith that would be less endangered by ideology. An acceptance of the permanent difference between the kingdom of the world and the Kingdom of God appears for the moment more possible in practice than in theory.

Werner Post

MATERIALISM

The term "materialist" first appears in Robert Boyle for the older "Epicurean". While some historians of philosophy regard the existence of "materialism" as being as old as philosophy itself (so, for instance, the Marxists), and find it clearly propounded by the ancient Greek philosophies of nature, as in Democritus and Epicure, others date materialism, in the strict sense, only since the concept was "clearly demarcated by Descartes" (R. Eucken). The older philosophies of nature contained so much myth that at the most "only a tendency to materialism can be found there" (A. Müller). According to Eucken, "the English have provided the cleverest, the French the wittiest and the Germans the bluntest defenders" of materialism.

Materialism is an attitude to life and an explanation of the world based on matter. It views matter as corporeal, like the world of bodies which is made from it, and takes various views of what the corporeal is like. This attitude or explanation can be spontaneous and uncritical or thought-out and made a considered theory. Practical materialism, the principle of which is material possessions, comforts and sensual pleasure, is often unreflecting and naive, and can be linked with a theoretical idealism, just as practical idealism is compatible with theoretical materialism. Materialism as a philosophy can be either total or partial. Total materialism considers matter as the principle of all reality, either equivalently or causally, that is, either in the sense that there is nothing but matter, or that matter is the efficient cause (mechanically in metaphysical materialism, dialectically in dialectical materialism) of everything, actual or otherwise. Partial materialism sees matter as the exclusive principle of certain realms of being. It may be an element of a total materialism, but may also be combined with non-materialist convictions. Boyle and Newton were materialists in scientific matters, for which they often appealed to Gassendi, but recognized the limits of this materialism. Boyle compared the universe with the famous clock in the Strasbourg Cathedral. It was a mechanism which presupposed an intelligent cause, like the clock.

The attractiveness of total materialism is due to that of the natural sciences, which rests on the experimental study of matter. In contrast to an infantile and fantastic materialism whose notion of matter is often highly imaginative and which is often the basis of philosophical speculation, this materialism is technically competent and investigates the relationships of matter (Bachelard). It is methodical, and prescinds from other causal factors, in order to test the validity of material explanations.

The question of the structure of the universe was answered by 18th-century science by the principle that it resulted from various combinations of matter which could be analysed and grasped in terms of space and time. The common element of the various materials involved was mass, which is given momentum by energy. The product of mass and momentum gives the amount of the energy acting on mass.

The success of the mechanical explanation of nature led to mechanist materialism, which was accepted by most of the cultured classes and became in the hands of the bourgeois, especially in France, a political instrument, a lever, in the struggle against throne and altar. Confidence, however, that the material world or even reality as a whole could be explained exclusively by matter and the laws of mechanics was shaken by the progress of science. Acoustics, optics and thermodynamics might be amenable to mechanical treatment, but it became clear that alongside of matter, mass and energy there was a physical reality, the nature of which remains obscure to the present day, a something which had to be assumed to render intelligible the action of the various parts of matter on each other. This was the "field" – a field of gravitation, and also an electro-magnetic field which is essentially different from the former, and since the investigation of the atom, a nuclear field, once more essentially different, the existence of which has now to be assumed. It also became clear that the laws of physics which held good for the realities dealt with in classical science and which had seemed to be of universal validity, were actually confined to the level of ordinary quantities and could not be applied without more ado on the cosmic and atomic levels. It was the end of the total domination of mechanistic concepts in physics, where they had gained such brilliant successes and which had been used to build up a universal mechanistic world-view. The physicist, faced with the discovery of infinitesimally small quantities (10^{-13}) in the nucleus of the atom, finds himself forced to use concepts which seem to depart definitely from the realm of the mechanistic. Today more than thirty elementary particles are known to exist in the atomic nucleus, appearing and disappearing with extreme rapidity and changing into other particles. Hence W. Heisenberg could say: "All elementary particles are made of the same matter, which we may call energy or universal matter. They are only the different forms in which matter can appear. If we compare this situation with the concepts of matter and form in Aristotle, we might say that the matter of Aristotle, which was essentially *potentia*, i.e., possibility, should be compared to our notion of energy. Energy appears as material reality through the form, when an elementary particle is produced" (cf. W. Heisenberg, p. 131). H. C. Oersted, the discoverer of the relations between magnetism and electricity, pointed to law as the perpetual, unchangeable essential core of things, and hence called for a combination of materialism and spiritualism even for the realm of physics (see his *Soul in Nature* [1852], E. T. of *Der Geist in der Natur* [1850]).

It is still impossible to determine whether matter can be seen as a sufficient explanation for the phenomena of life (changes of matter and form, growth, evolution, perception of stimuli). The nucleic acids (micromolecular combinations) and the proteins (macromolecular combinations) are prerequisites for the coming of life. To explain the appearance of life, some biologists assume the existence of a spiritual principle of organization, while others try to produce life from matter itself. In 1953 Stanley Miller in Chicago used the play of electric charges on an artificially prepared atmosphere to produce amino-acids (micromolecular). Up to the present no such experiments have been successful in the synthesis of the proteins. And even so, amino-acids and proteins are not life. For life, there must also be the major factors of spatio-temporal organization, the co-operation of the various materials in the service of self-sustenance and the preservation of the type. Theologically it hardly seems to matter whether life may be explained on the basis of the intrinsic laws of highly complicated material or the influence of a distinct spiritual principle of organization. God could have produced life equally well through the general laws of nature alone or by means of a special vitalist principle of organization (cf. K. Wacholder, in *Naturwissenschaft heute* [1965], p. 49). Like life, consciousness is also different from matter. Heat as a physical process is "a disorderly movement of the atoms", while heat as sensation is a type of experience which presupposes this movement of the atoms. The eye does not see light-waves but colours. The ear does not hear wave-lengths but sounds. The material basis of the process of consciousness is the nervous system. While sensible knowledge rests on perception, intellectual knowledge becomes independent of its material basis and displays a unity which is alien to matter. Comparison between various impressions, memory, the act of judgment – all surpass the possibilities of material and spatial reality. Taken along with the phenomenon of psycho-physical causality, the nature of life on the higher levels of the soul point to the independence of the physical and psychic spheres.

In their struggle against materialism, philosophers and theologians have often been so much carried away by their zeal that they overlooked the valuable elements which it contains. They forgot that one must often wait patiently to see how much may be accorded to material forces as the explanation of phenomena, that sound material relationships, while not representing the supreme values, still are fundamental, and that the dignity of human existence is often only possible on the basis of their adequate realization. Theology must pay greater attention to the creational character and hence the high value of matter, of the material and sensible world.

Marcel Reding

MEANING

A. Introduction

The discussion of "meaning" may well begin from one of its synonyms: "sense", where the difference between the subjective ("feeling", "opinion", "discernment") and the objective stands out at once – "that which is reasonable" – as in the common phrase: "that makes sense". So too "meaning" can be either subjective – "that which is in the mind or thoughts" – or objective, "that which has significance" or purpose, as in the phrase once so common as the title of books – "the meaning of life". The present article treats only of the latter, objective sense, but even here it prescinds from certain extensions of it. Thus it omits the questions of analytical philosophy (linguistic philosophy), "meaning" as the significance of the spoken word, and such specific studies as those of structuralism, "meaning" as interconnection and analysable structure.

We are therefore concerned with "meaning" in the objective sense – which of course includes and primarily affects the subject – of purpose, value, worthwhileness or usefulness. In this sense, something has meaning when it is justified by its appropriateness (as "way") to a goal. But if the goal itself is meaningless, pointless, it calls in question even the limited meaningfulness of the way. A way only has real meaning when the goal also has it. Thus we arrive by the degrees of higher and wider sets of goals to a notion of meaning which determines it not by virtue of its "in-order-to" but by virtue of its having meaning in and of itself (καθ' αὑτό) absolutely, without reference to anything else. When something is meaningful of itself, it need not be taken as the ultimate and all-embracing. Even the particular and provisional can have meaning in and of itself. On the other hand such a determination of the meaningful also includes the notion of purpose, since every meaningful goal – even when not considered as an intermediate goal on a way which goes further – gives sense and purpose to the way or ways thither.

This formal definition must now be given some fullness of content, as far as possible, in view of what is to be said later. The filling out with content is here part of the concept itself, since meaning or purpose considers not just the goal *de facto* envisaged, but the justified goal, its justifiability. There is meaning, sense or purpose in that to which man can say, "Yes, be it so". And he finds this Yes possible where he is in agreement or harmony with his world and it with him, and he is "identical" with himself in this mutual agreement. "Meaningfulness is the possibility of my finding myself in agreement with myself in such a way that it is in agreement with my world" (cf. B. Welte, *Auf der Spur des Ewigen* [1965], p. 20). This takes place in the meaningful moment of a particular agreement, but is ultimately in the perspective of the whole which embraces all particulars. "Something has meaning, when it may lead to my finding myself in agreement with my being as a whole in such a way that it is in agreement with beings as a whole" (*ibid*., p. 22). The actual eventuation of this possible agreement is what is then meant by speaking of the absolute, ultimate meaning. With the concept so determined, it is clear that meaning cannot be merely – or properly – discussed theoretically. There can be no "abstract" understanding of the question of meaning or the possible answers. To ask after meaning (purpose, sense) is to ask what is the point for me and for us, in such a way that in the question of the "meaning of life", life and existence itself are under examination.

B. The Question as to Meaning

Actual meaning itself, the moment of "identity" and agreement, poses no questions. Hence when one asks the meaning of something, it has already become of questionable worth. The fact of asking after the sense shows the absence of agreement, either because it is not yet or no longer there. Thus widely different experiences of "non-identity" have given rise to the question of meaning. And the more unambiguous and deeper the experience of non-identity, the sharper and more urgent is the question of meaning.

The many impulses to questioning may perhaps be summed up under four headings (cf. H. Reiner, *Der Sinn unseres Daseins* [2nd ed., 1964]): (i) The lack of apparent meaning in the experiences of suffering, pain and misfortune; (ii) the evasiveness of meaning in the slack and joyless boredom of life; (iii) the destruction of meaning by the menace of death; (iv) the sense of responsibility for new life which may be produced. Here it is no longer a question of finding a meaning *for* an already existing life, but the meaning of life in general. These impulses, especially the last, make themselves felt with most force in times when life is much pondered. Men feel themselves bound to perpetual questioning instead of surrendering themselves confidently according to their most basic urge. They think that the "risk" of seeing and accepting meaning is something which they may not undertake.

However, as has been stressed by M. Müller ("Uber Sinn und Sinngefährdung des menschlichen Daseins", *Philosophisches Jahrbuch* 74 [1966–67], p. 8), these impulses to question are not *ipso facto* arguments against the presence of meaning. Suffering and happiness cannot be weighed quantitatively against one another. Here a "moment" can outweigh years or a whole lifetime when "time and eternity coincide" in it, that is, the absolute justification is "incarnationally" present (see below, D). Even death does not simply destroy meaning. It also makes room for it, by making the endless flux of time the decisive "hour", the moment of decision in which something must "set", if it is to be at all, instead of offering unlimited chances (where meaning would slip away into the world of the "immaterial", because always equally available). So too there could be no such thing as a tragic experience in a world of total absurdity. For it is only an overriding, comprehensive sense of meaningfulness that makes the painfully irreconcilable clashes of life's plans and purposes appear at all as painful – prior to making them bearable (though only in hope [see E below], and even there without positive reconciliation). Even in the senselessness of evil there is still some meaning, not just in the promise of forgiveness but even in the gift which the persistence of the demands of the good represents, and in the task of repentance (which means that all time is "time of grace" because the time in which constant claims are made on man). Thus meaning (purpose, sense) is not ruled out because questions are provoked. But the pointers sketched above make it equally clear that it is really called in question.

C. Answers

It would be impossible here, and indeed unnecessary, to register all the attempted answers (see *Evil*, *Dualism*, *History* I, II, III). But the types of would-be answers which are fundamentally unsatisfactory must be mentioned. They are the answers which in one way or another deal only with a truncated version of man's question.

This happens, for instance, when the world of coming to be and passing away, man's bodily and worldly dimension, is treated as insignificant, and the meaningful is considered to reside in a timeless, supramundane beyond, to which man must find his way by freeing himself from his present situation. (This is sometimes called the metaphysical solution. Whether the title is justified, and how far such a solution is to be attributed to metaphysics as a whole, need not be gone into here.)

Another answer is to ascribe meaning to the greater whole, in order to justify partial, individual absurdities as necessary moments of the whole. This is sometimes done from a static point of view, in "aesthetic terms", as when it is said that the dark patches go to build up the picture, that God's justice can be revealed on the wicked and so on (Augustine). Or the process may be viewed dynamically, as in a philosophy of history which marks the individual down for sacrifice for the sake of the end result. (This is true of Hegel and Marx, and to some extent of Teilhard de Chardin.) Or all these questions may be by-passed in the message of a "nonmoralizing" ecstasy in undifferentiated unity.

The opposite approach transfers meaning to the individual person and either reserves it for the great man, the superior personality, or ascribes it to each man as a (private) person. In the first case, the claim to meaning is given more content, but then restricted to a minority. In the second case, the lifting of restrictions is paid for by a further watering-down of the claim to meaning. Here, then, it may be said that the mere possibility is accepted as sufficient meaning instead of its full realization.

This appears most clearly where the experience of the moral claim, the "ought" as such, is asked to guarantee the meaning. It is not merely a case of virtue being its own reward, but of the mere duty of virtue. (This retreat from reality, the "withdrawal-effect of the ought-category" [Marquard] was the object of protest from both Hegel and Scheler, each in his own way.) Why are these answers to be rejected as unsatisfactory? Not from an absolute viewpoint which could indicate the positive content of what meaning involves and say what should be there if life is to be called meaningful. They are unsatisfactory in the light of the very demand for meaning which is inspired by the occasions in question. For all these answers do no more than follow the counsel which says that when one cannot have the happiness which one desires, one must desire the happiness which one has – apropos of which Augustine said (*De Trinitate*, XIII, 7, 10: *PL*, XLII, col. 1021) that he did not know whether to laugh or weep at such happiness.

Nonetheless, it is no empty desire which provides this norm, but the goal of the desire – though the goal is never adequately objectifiable. It can only be hinted at in presentiments, in the combination of ("mythic") image and abstract formula, which is the only form in which it presents itself as the possible object of search and hope (see below, E). And this goal is not merely present as the (non-objectified) object of search. It already imparts itself (partly but really), it appears, fleetingly and fragmentarily no doubt, but not merely apparently, in the "hour" when meaning is experienced.

D. The Experience of Meaning

B. Welte speaks of the high-points of man's being, the supremely integrating moments beyond all calculation and control, at which lucid meaning dawns (*op. cit.*, p. 135). He names love and death. M. Müller lists six manifestations: (i) The moments of truth (the meaningfulness of arriving at or resting in the "theoretical" truth, theory here being taken in the full Aristotelian sense of contemplation [θεωρία]); (ii) moral action in which the personal deed and the acting subject (as the goals of this action) are there "for their own sake", not as means but as possessing their own acknowledged worth; (iii) the relationship of love, which considers each partner in his own proper being and by that very fact releases them into their "betweenness" (M. Buber), the instant of insight into each other which cannot be held; but that it has come remains, and gives absolute certainty of meaning; (iv) the appearance of truth and meaning in works of art, appearance not in the sense of a reflection from a world beyond, but as the "incarnation", the coincidence of truth and image in the peremptory form; (v) the forms of religious worship, inasmuch as they go beyond instruction and mutual aid, and even beyond the purpose of salvation to be achieved, and are the scene of the non-utilitarian meaningful "play" (R. Guardini) of man before his God and in harmony with him; (vi) political institutions, understood not as the technique of public co-operation but as the life of fellowship – as a form of εὖ ζῆν, the good life.

But perhaps all these notions are a little too "lofty". In fact meaning is constantly met with on a much more modest scale. There is no question of the withdrawal spoken of above. No concessions are made, though the tone is kept low. In the Bible, the answer comes to Elijah not in the storm or the fire but in the murmur of the breeze (1 Kg 19:9–13). E. Bloch gives as intimations and signs "the way the pipe lies there, the way the lamp shines on the road and so on" (*Die Spuren* [1959], p. 71). M. Proust "recovers" time, that is, finds himself "in agreement" with the identity of meaning, in the tinkle of a spoon and the taste of tea through a cake. The later Wittgenstein, who feels everything fragile, also speaks of a sustaining power when he says that "a good angel will always be necessary, whatever one does" (*Bemerkungen über die Grundlagen der Mathematik* [1956], V, 13). Kirillov, in Dostoevsky's *The Possessed*, looks at the sun shining through an autumn leaf and says: "No allegory. Just a leaf. A leaf is good. All is good. – All? – Yes, all." However, interpersonal experiences of meaning must have an absolute precedence, since they are also rationally founded, in contrast, for instance, to psychedelic experiences. See, for instance, R. C. Zaehner, *Mysticism, Sacred and Profane* (1957). Here nothing can be proved, since it is a matter of seeing. Any demonstration can only be in the nature of an indication of what can only be seen with one's own eyes – though the indication may be enough to make one open one's eyes for the first time.

But there is another element here. Not only must each one experience meaning for himself – to learn *about* it is not enough – but he cannot even come upon it as ready-made. To "see" is one of the very constituents of meaning. Meaning is not man's creation, in the sense of being imposed on the meaningless by man's own law, as T. Lessing held. On the contrary, it must "give" itself, or be given to him. Nonetheless, it does not exist independently of man's (active) experience. When meaning is defined as my finding myself in agreement with myself and my world, such agreement cannot simply be registered *post factum*, it must be actively co-produced and realized. The identity of the *cognoscens* and the *cognitum in actu cognoscendi* extends also to the *volens* (*ponens, agens, assequens*) and the *bonum* – though this active identity is always due to the ultimate meaningfulness. Thus the experience of meaning is also the positing of meaning in a unity of acceptance and establishment, knowledge and decision-for. It is a unity intrinsically indissoluble, since it does not consist of two acts, even in "synergistical" combination. It is one single act, a differentiated unity. Man accepts himself and his world and so makes himself and his world his own – and hence really "acceptable" for the first time. But what he makes his own is not something alien. It is himself and his world, in an act which is again given him.

Here we see that the difference to be bridged (and so preserved) is not between the I and the world or the spirit and sense. It is prior to and runs through all these derivative distinctions. Identity and difference are in the dimension of freedom, that is, interpersonality in the widest sense. This is not only the I-You relationship or the far-ranging relationships of political and social freedom. It includes the "field" of these relationships, which cannot be considered as an impersonal field of possibilities, but must itself be real freedom: the "light" of truth, the "life" of goodness, creative freely-communicating radical freedom. Meaning is not just therefore agreement with the manifest purpose: it is also the participative, symbol-laden concordance of meaning as manifest and the grounds – or fathomless grounds – of meaning. This primordial agreement is what first makes meaning meaningful. But even this most primordial agreement does not simply happen and is not merely received as something assigned by the ground of meaning. It is also actively co-produced.

This may help to show more clearly why the answers to the question of meaning cited above were considered unsatisfactory. They broke out of the totality of freedom which is poised in fluid equilibrium, so to speak, between two poles, and falsified it by coming down firmly on one side. And the proper approach to the question of meaning and its answer should now be somewhat clearer. It was clear from the beginning that the question was never put merely theoretically. But the questioner is not always convinced that the answer too cannot be ready-made theory. Ultimately, he himself must give the answer – no matter where the prompt may come from – and give it by accepting it, not hypothetically, but as certain of the gift received, while still positing it as his thesis. He decides in favour of the Yes of which we spoke at the start, Yes as Amen, that is, so it is and so be it. It ought to be, inasmuch as it is, and it is inasmuch as it ought to be, not just on my say-so, but in any case, by virtue of the "light" of truth and its "life". This fundamental Yes was described as a two-part harmony by F. Rosenzweig (*Der Stern der Erlösung* [3rd ed., 1954], pp. 294ff.). If the due differences are preserved, and not allowed to fall apart in a wrong and as it were "tritheist" equality, one could speak more comprehensively of a trinity of this harmonious Yes and Amen. For freedom and freedom in the affirmation of meaning join in in harmony with the ground (and abyss) of meaning and freedom, and only by virtue of this concord are in harmony with each other and with themselves.

It must also be noted, however, that this gives new sharpness and depth to the question of meaning, which is to be answered by the appeal to such experience. If meaning and purpose is only given in the full sense with man, and not without him, its questionableness seems more constant and radical than ever. It might be objected that – as the full sense – it has already been definitively nullified by the No of finite freedom which has been uttered from the start.

E. Meaning and Salvation

When this more forceful objection is urged, it is often answered by the appeal to the *felix culpa* experience, the superabundance of grace of which Paul spoke where evil had abounded (Rom 5:20). These are experiences which are not confined to the religious, much less Christian, dimension, but can be met with in the whole region of human encounter. The experience is undeniable. But must not then the recipient of the grace of pardon become really conscious of the absolute senselessness and absurdity of his sin – precisely because forgiveness alone makes him fully conscious of what sin is? This is not to say that he must wilfully and rigidly hold fast to his guilt, instead of humbly accepting pardon. But he only really receives the non-exigible grace of pardon as grace, when he does not try to give his fault any sort of surreptitious merit.

The full notion of meaning pure and unalloyed must be retained, and also the absolutely undeniable senselessness of sin and evil. This has been insisted on in particular by R. Lauth in his book on the meaning of life. The fact that "even sin" can be absorbed is not denied, but, like the corresponding message of Scripture, it must be carefully explained. Formally, one might say that the principle in question is positively but not exclusively valid. The fault has become a happy one through grace, but to say so is only saved from being blasphemy, and the fault only remains really sinful and evil when it is also affirmed that innocence would have been happier. C. Péguy in particular, in his *Mystère* poems and in his prose writings, maintained the incomparable excellence of original innocence against the view of the fall which was given its clearest expression in German Idealism, where sin appears as the necessary exit from the "garden reserved for beasts" (Hegel), and the serpent as "the chrysalis of the goddess reason" (Bloch). There is not even a hint of the "mystery of iniquity" in such systems. It is not necessary at this point to discuss the real existence of original innocence (see *Original Sin, Man*). The point is simply to use it as a standard to see things as they really are: a reality which is believed to be and also experienced as good, though its goodness does not justify evil, the sin in this reality. But then it is not merely in the present or from now on that we must reject the suggestion, "Are we to continue in sin that grace may abound?" (Rom 6:1). Logically, the "by no means!" holds good also of the past. He in whom grace has in fact shown itself the stronger will proclaim his sin as inexcusable from first to last, as absolutely senseless. (It is true that in the actually faulty act there is an element of genuine accomplishment and not just sin and senselessness [cf. K. Rahner, *Theological Investigations*, III, ch. xiv]. Nonetheless, the really sinful element of this whole remains undisguisably – sin.)

How is it then with the meaning of things? It is impossible to claim a surreptitious meaning for evil by considering it as requisite and serviceable on principle. Nonetheless, positively and factually, there is the happy experience to be proclaimed, that truth and love have power to give meaning, strong enough to overcome even sin, in an incomprehensible but real way, and to make "all things good". But the same principle must be applied to this experience as was already laid down apropos of the experience of meaning. It is perception as co-realization, knowledge as decision, certainty as risk. The essential note of this experience, as was again maintained by Péguy, even more effectively than later by Bloch and his school, is the daring of confident hope. Man hopes in fact for a wholeness of well-being without restriction or exception, in which he and all things are fully saved.

The question must now be raised as to the criteria and justification of the hopeful affirmation of meaning. It is certainly true that the full defence, when one is called on to account for the hope within him, can only be made by appealing to Jesus Christ (1 Pet 3:15). He alone gives us real grounds for hope beyond death (see *Resurrection*, *Immortality*), and (the more daring and even more seriously longed-for) hope of salvation in spite of undeniable sin. He does not merely promise to wipe away all tears. He has the creative power to make the promise: Behold, I make all things new (Rev 21:4f.).

According to Vatican I, men can know God as their creator, but are *de facto* forced to rely – with "moral necessity" – on revelation (*D* 1786, 2305). In the same way, if they cannot call upon the promises of Jesus Christ, perhaps hope can hardly hold its ground against the suspicion – voiced from outside or within the hopeful themselves – that they do not take death, and above all, evil, seriously enough. But just as the appeal to Christ leaves hope in the state of hope and does not raise it at once to security, so too a hope which does not explicitly appeal to this promise (though it too lives by it, the believer will say) need not collapse in total uncertainty. Hence philosophy, being precisely reflection on basic experiences, cannot be merely questions about the whence and why, the origins, and not merely a question which refrains on principle from giving any answer. We may recall here the intrinsic connection noted by Heidegger between "think" and "thank", which are etymologically connected. Such thankful (re)thinking can well reflect experiences, as has been shown in part above. Thinking does not merely reflect experiences of the "salvation gap" (B. Welte, *Heilsverständnis*), but also of its promise-laden, anticipatory bridging: as in compensatory moments of happiness, in signs of death-defying union (G. Marcel) and in the meaningful advent, ever newly incomprehensible, of creative forgiveness. (This can come perhaps even in sleep, from which Faust could wake up "newly alive", and be anything from the chance of a new shot at life, where everything seemed to have been fooled away, to the actual personal encounter where a love can be in fact "renewed", that is, not merely re-started but above all felt as the morning of a coming day.)

It is, therefore, not true that philosophy has nothing to do but ask new questions. Even in philosophical thinking a self-accepting questioning has (necessarily and obligatorily) to become a reflective acceptance. This is not out of disgust for or weak capitulation before the "effort of thought" but by virtue of the very essence and act of thought, which is to be reflection on experience and so related to what is encountered in experience and subject to its norms and laws. Nonetheless its thankful utterance remains hovering questioningly. But then again the theologian or the believer will never be able to boast of security in his answer to the question of meaning. He knows whom he has believed (2 Tim 1:12), but he also knows well who he himself is and what it can mean in the sight of the pure majesty of his Lord, that "if we are faithless, he remains faithful", that is, "cannot deny himself" (2 Tim 2:13). Just as the believer is not sure of his own salvation (*D* 804, 810), so too he cannot rationalize his hope for others by assuming an apocatastasis. Nor, as happened in the course of tradition, will he try to reconcile hell positively with the happiness of the blessed. Here hope in the strict sense – no more and no less – must really be the hermeneutical principle for the statements of revelation (cf. K. Rahner, *Theological Investigations*, IV, pp. 331f.). But the believer, though he cannot claim to be secure, has the certainty of the promise of God, whose righteousness was revealed by his justifying the sinners, in Jesus Christ (Rom 3:21ff.). They are redeemed only in hope (Rom 8:24). But in this hope they can and ought to confess: "He who gave up his own Son for us all – will he not also give us all things with him?" (Rom 8:32.) But this means really all: the Yes and Amen (2 Cor 1:19f.) of an all-embracing harmony of freedom, of absolute meaning.

Jörg Splett

MEDIATORSHIP

1. The reality denoted by the term mediator is of central importance for the Christian faith. The OT people of God was aware that its relation to God passed through intermediaries. The form of mediation changed in the course of history, assuming different forms in the patriarchs, national leaders such as Moses, Joshua, judges and kings, prophets and levitical priesthood. Religious mediatorship received its fullest expression in the incarnate Son of God; the faith of the NT people of God is therefore essentially a religion of the mediator.

Mediatorship denotes a position and the function resulting from it. It creates between two personal realities facing or opposing one another a link which they did not yet possess, although they had a tendency towards it. For "an intermediary implies more than one; but God is one" (Gal 3:20). In what follows, we do not envisage mediatorship generally and theoretically, but in regard to Christ, in whom the essence of mediatorship is most perfectly realized and whose position and function in the order of salvation are best characterized as mediatorship.

2. Christian faith is centred on the person and work of Christ because as mediator between God and man he is the foundation of our redeemed life.

a) It may seem rather surprising, in view of the dominating importance of Christ's mediatorship, that the term mediator is only applied to Christ four times in the NT: 1 Tim 2:5; Heb 8:6; 9:15; 12:24. The use of the term is also rare in the official pronouncements of the Church's magisterium. It is only found in Leo I (*D* 143), in the Councils of Florence (*D* 711) and Trent (*D* 790). The reality denoted by mediatorship does, of course, from various points of view govern the whole doctrine of faith regarding Christ and his redemptive work. And on closer inspection we must also say that this concept is the most specific expression of Christ's function. The terms redeemer and saviour, which are much more frequently used in the Church to describe Christ's saving function, in fact characterize less distinctively Christ's role in the saving event. The concept of saviour or redeemer (σωτήρ) is also applied to the Father (1 Tim 2:3); mediator, on the other hand, exclusively denotes the role of Christ. How central it is, is shown by the use made of it in Hebrews, where the mediator is spoken of in connection with the new and better covenant. Now the new covenant (Lk 22:20; 1 Cor 11:25) essentially means the new relation to God established by Christ's saving work and his fulfilling the OT economy of salvation.

b) In the patristic, and above all the scholastic tradition, Christ's mediatorship was regarded ontically, in an apparently static way. The fact that in the God-man, divinity and humanity are hypostatically united, appears to form the basis of mediatorship. Behind it, however, lies a dynamic conception. Christ's theandric state is regarded as the result and therefore as the pledge of an event which has led to the union between divinity and humanity. Or else, since the time of medieval scholasticism, the Incarnation has been regarded as the condition of the possibility of his acting as mediator for us before God. The hypostatic union makes his sacrifice for man so precious that it merits salvation for us before God. These two views must be taken together as complementary.

3. The term mediator expresses the dialogue character of Christ's redemptive work. The mediator who, even before he begins his action, stands on God's side, must first come to sinful men and, in a second, corresponding movement, give himself to God.

a) This double, communicative function is expressed in what tradition describes as the triple office of Christ as king (or shepherd), prophet and priest. This involves a duality which corresponds to Christ's mediatory work. Christ's kingship or pastoral office should probably be regarded as the comprehensive function which is exercised through his prophetical and sacerdotal actions. His prophetic and his priestly office are both royal. By his intermediary action as prophet and priest, Christ is the agent of God's royal reign over men.

b) The Son of God exercises his mediatorship when, as sent from the Father, he comes to men as the reconciling Word. He continues it in his teaching about the Father, in which he vindicates the rights of God and summons men to respond by gathering round him in belief. He gives the answer as sacerdotal head of the human race by a life of obedience even to death on the cross for men. The two together constitute his work of communication as intermediary.

4. Christ's mediatorship is described in the NT as the sole mediatorship "between God and men" (1 Tim 2:5). This, however, does not exclude mediatorship within human society. This is not meant in reference to the mediatory activity of the Church's spiritual ministry. This is not really a mediatorship, but a sacramental representation of the sole mediator, Christ. Mediatorship properly so called is exercised by one person on behalf of others in human society. Mary's position in particular is relevant here. She "is invoked by the Church under the titles of Advocate, Auxiliatrix, Adjutrix and Mediatrix" (Vatican II, Dogmatic Constitution on the Church, art. 62). It is not incompatible with the sole mediatorship of Christ to regard Mary as a figure representing the community of believers, and giving her receptive consent in faith, not only for her own benefit but for that of the community of the redeemed. Thus in a true sense she has become a mediatrix for other human beings, even

if she does not really stand "between" God and men. Fundamentally, any saving decisions made by human beings have a kind of mediatory significance for the community to which they are united, even if it is not possible to determine the effect of this mediatorship. And in comparison with Christ's mediatorship, it is derivative and analogous. But its reality is brought about by the operation of the redemptive grace of Christ which, of course, is not received merely passively by man but empowers him actively to share in Christ's redemptive action.

Otto Semmelroth

MERCY

God's mercy is described as the readiness of God to come to the aid of his distressed creature out of free grace. Man's primal experience of God as the God of mercies, compassion, and forgiveness is recorded in many ways in the books of the Old and New Testaments (on the biblical doctrine see *Charity*, *Grace* and *Salvation*). In theology mercy is axiomatically predicated of God as one of his essential attributes, because being infinite in every perfection (*D* 1782) his just and holy nature precludes all cruelty and unfair severity. Moreover, mercy is an actual attitude of God towards sinful man, who truly merits the divine judgment, an attitude that man can only become aware of through historical experience of the God who reveals himself as merciful. It is disclosed in God's universal salvific will in the redemptive action by which he takes the world to himself, in the incarnation and glorification of his Son, in the justification of the individual, and in the eschatological consummation of the world. God's love and his mercy interact. They are themselves definitively and irrevocably present in the world in the mercy of God's incarnate Word (cf. Heb 2:17; 4:15f.). As a free attitude of God, his mercy is *a priori* incalculable – incalculable as to the forms, the manner, the conditions, and the measure in which God is pleased to bestow it on individuals; and therefore it cannot (as to its effects) be "taken for granted" like other attributes of God (justice, longanimity). Here men cannot count on what God will do. Indeed God's mercy is not really acknowledged until it is accepted as incalculable, and so man must not sin against it by presumption. How God's mercy can be reconciled with evil in the world, with judgment and damnation, reduces itself to the mystery of the holy God's sovereign freedom (Rom 9–11) which will only be elucidated at the end of time (2 Cor 4:14). When God shows mercy he does not thereby defeat his own justice; but by transcending it and turning a sinner into a just man, he displays the fullness of justice (St. Thomas, *Summa Theologia*, I, q. 21, a. 3), and so mercy enables God to be just to the man that he has made just. As a mode of God's love for his unprofitable creature, mercy is presupposed by God's just judgment and his just rewards. The prayer of petition is man's appeal to and praise of God's mercy.

All human mercy is founded and summoned forth by that of God. It can only be called mercy (in an analogical sense) as a response, because it knows that its own self and all it has to give are always received by way of a loan; so that human mercy does not give of its own but only what it has received, and that not at will but because God's mercies to a man always compel him in turn to show mercy. Mercy sees the distress of others as its own. There is a solidarity in which both giver and receiver have received of the same fullness. He who shows mercy receives more than he gives – the clear vision of his own emptiness, which alone prevents his losing the fullness he has received. – On the tension between mercy and justice in human affairs see the article *Poverty*.

Adolf Darlap

MERIT

The theological question of merit is concerned with the question of whether man can gain merit before God by his moral acts, especially when these acts are inspired by grace. One of the aspects of the problem is how far such a notion, which stems from human relationships, can be applied to the relationship of man to God. To avoid misunderstandings about the theological applicability of the concept, some remarks on how merit works between men may be desirable.

1. In human relationships, merit is understood as the claim for recompense which arises from actions performed on behalf of others and the amount of recompense involved. The actions which are recompensed according to their merit can be morally good or evil. But the expression merit is mainly reserved for good deeds, which can be objective, like work done or things supplied, or subjective, like mental acts. The claim to reward for a good deed may be based on grounds of justice or equity. In the former case, we speak of merit in justice (*meritum de condigno*), in the latter of merit in equity or decency (*meritum de congruo*).

Where merit is a matter of justice, the service performed and the reward bestowed are more or less equivalent. The reward is really "earned". Where merit is a matter of equity, there may be a certain relation between the service performed and the reward for it, but the reward surpasses the actual value of the service. Hence merit in equity is only analogously merit, compared with merit as a matter of justice. The proportion in which reward stands to merit is therefore either quantitative and strictly measurable or qualitative and only subjectively estimated. The moral value or merit of the act is assessed differently according to the type involved. When an act is designed and apt to be of benefit to others, it is potentially meritorius (*meritum in actu primo*). But a corresponding obligation on the part of those who reap the benefit arises in fact (*meritum in actu secundo*) only when the beneficiaries cannot reasonably refuse the proffered service because it is for their real good, or when it is freely accepted by them.

2. a) The application of the concept merit to the relationships of man to God is problematic, since man is never an independent partner on the same level as regards God, but exists only as God's creature, and child by grace. There is no way in which he can merit to be created in the first place, or to be favoured with grace and redeemed. So too he cannot in any way merit the first efficacious grace and final predestination. All this is the completely free gift of God, inspired only by the communicative love which has its foundations within God. In view of these gifts, which alone constitute man as man and as a child of grace, man at once owes God as perfect a service as possible, because God has so radically "merited" it that every good deed starts from him and is perfected by him (cf. Jas 1:17). Hence any good which man does is only the discharge of his duty towards God. Further, God has no need of man's service for his own perfection. Hence there is no need for him to reward man for what man already owes him and which is of no advantage to him. Scripture therefore represents the election of Israel as completely unmerited (e.g., Exod 20:2; Deut 7:7f.; Jer 31:36f.; Ezek 16:3f.), and all reward is purely a matter of grace (e.g., Is 49:4; 61:8; Mt 20:1–16). This truth leads Paul to affirm that no one can be saved by the works of the law (Rom 3:9–20). Those who seek justification in this way are under a curse (Gal 3:10), since the law "was added be-

cause of transgressions" and for no other reason (Gal 3:19).

When, in spite of all this, theology took over the term merit, it was primarily to speak of Jesus' moral acts and in particular of his sacrifice in the "service of reconciliation" of man with God. By virtue of the dignity of his divine person, Jesus makes satisfaction in the strict sense on terms of equality with God. He expiated vicariously the sins of mankind as their representative and thus strictly "earned" their redemption once and for all.

b) Luther took his stand on this basis. And on the supposition that all mention of merit of man before God leads to misapprehension of human action, either in the sense of the Pharisees that God owes a reward to service done, or in the sense of the Pelagians that man can achieve something before God by his own efforts, he denied that man could have any possible way of gaining merits before God. Luther was convinced, on the contrary, that man was justified purely extrinsically by grace through the merits of Christ. By this he meant that while Christ's merits are imputed to men for their salvation, men themselves cannot perform any salutary works. This notion of a purely extrinsic justification had been prepared for by Nominalism, with its theory that God, by virtue of his supreme independence (*de potestate absoluta*), could accept even the works of the non-justified. It stems more directly from two ideas of which Luther was convinced, firstly that human nature was totally corrupted by original sin and concupiscence, and was not changed by justification; secondly that any assertion of human merit before God contradicted the truth of faith that God alone is the sovereign author of all salvation. Hence justification consists of the fact that the believer trusts firmly that God does not impute to him the sins which stem from his corrupt nature and confers salvation on him independently of his own merits.

3. The Catholic doctrine of justification, however, affirms that man is intrinsically changed by justification. By virtue of this transforming grace man himself is now enabled to do something valuable in the eyes of God and hence gain merit. As man participates in the merit and work of Christ, as son in the Son, the grace accepted by man is changed in the exercise of human freedom into his "merit". It remains entirely the grace of God, merited by Christ on the cross. But it becomes man's own by the free act of faith and justification and is regarded by God as meritorious by virtue of the Yes of grace and freedom. In man's participation and union with the risen Christ, his brother, it is rewarded graciously and justly by God.

a) This is the sense in which the definition of Trent is to be understood. There it is said that the justified can truly merit (*D* 801, 803, 809, 832, 834, 842), because through sanctifying grace he has been taken in to full partnership with God. From the history of the Council it is theologically certain that this true merit is to be taken as merit in justice (*de condigno*), as was also affirmed by Pius V against Baianism. The object of such merit is the increase of (sanctifying) grace (*D* 803, 832, 834), and probably also, concomitantly, of the infused virtues (cf., for instance, Ripalda and K. Rahner), and also of glory (*D* 809, 842). As against the view of many theologians, it seems that merit *de condigno* must be based on serious moral actions as well as on justification. Consequently, venial sins can cause the loss only of the acquired virtues, not of the infused virtues. There is a further debate among theologians as to whether meritorious supernatural acts need to be motivated by faith as well as being elevated. The answer should be in the negative, insofar as supernatural moral acts necessarily include a recognition of God's self-communication. This necessarily presupposes a direct and implicit consciousness of the object of faith. Beyond this, no express and articulated motivation of faith is necessary, since the faith on which merit is based consists at once of the direct assent to God, who addresses himself immediately to the person.

b) In the supernaturally elevated acts of the non-justified, the supernatural transformation is essentially inferior and in a certain sense peripheral, as contrasted with the acts of the justified. Hence on principle the non-justified can only gain merit by equity (*de congruo*) from their supernatural acts (*D* 797, 801). And efficacious grace (except the very first efficacious grace, which by its nature cannot be merited in any way by man), final perseverance (*D* 806, 826), the restoration of lost justification and graces for others can only be the object of merit *de condigno*, which God, however, has not promised to reward.

c) The purely natural acts of man, being without any possible proportion to the supernatural order, can in no way merit supernatural grace. The question therefore arises as to whether man performs good acts which are not, however, meritorious, because not supernaturally elevated. Various answers are given by theologians, but the answer should be in the negative.

4. This doctrine of the Church is well founded on Scripture. Scripture speaks of a growth, of progress in justice, grace, faith and love, of a constant renewal of the inward man, etc. (Prov 4:18; Lk 17:5; 2 Cor 4:15–17; 9:8–11; 10:15; Eph 4:15; Phil 1:9; 3:12f.; Col 1:10; 1 Thess 4:1; 2 Pet 3:18; Rev 22:11).

Eternal beatitude is represented as a reward (Wis 5:16; Prov 11:18; Is 40:10; Mt 5:12; 20:1–8; 1 Cor 3:8; Rev 22:12), as a prize to be won (1 Cor 9:24f.; Phil 3:14; 2 Tim 2:3, 5; 4:7; Jas 1:12; Rev 2:10) and as a remuneration (Col 3:23f.; Heb 10; 35; 11:6, 26). Through his good works, man becomes worthy of eternal beatitude (Wis 3:5; Lk 20:35; 2 Thess 1:5; Rev 3:4). God recompenses them because he is the just judge (2 Tim 4:8; Heb 6:10), in keeping with the effort made (Mt 16:27; Lk 19:16ff.; Rom 2:6ff.; 1 Cor 3:8; 2 Cor 9:6; Rev 22:12). The reward is contrasted with the punishment for evil deeds (Mt 25:34–46; Jn 5:29; Rom 2:6ff.; 2 Cor 5:10; Gal 6:8). Mt 6:20 urges men to lay up treasure in heaven. The data of Scripture were soon elaborated into a systematic doctrine of merit, to some extent by the Fathers of the Church, especially the Latins, but above all by later theologians.

5. For a proper understanding of the doctrine of human merit, two things must be kept in mind. One is the extent to which human merit is impossible before God (see 2a above). The other is the principle laid down by Thomas Aquinas (*Summa Theologica*, I–II, q. 114, a. 1) that all merits of the creature can only be called merit in an analogous sense: "non simpliciter, non de ratione iustitiae, sed secundum quid." The ground of the possibility of man's gaining merit before God is his likeness to God (see the article *Potentia Oboedientialis*) and the transforming grace of God's self-communication, by which he is made a true, though not equal, partner of God, in an analogous way, on a lower level. This partnership does not supervene by virtue of man's independence of God and in autonomy as regards God, but by virtue of his being called by God and in keeping with the particular call of each individual.

a) This doctrine is an expression of the truth that man is created by God and elevated by God's grace in such a way that he really can perform something valuable and meritorious in the sight of God. God, of course, gains nothing intrinsic by creating man and giving him grace. But he freely makes and enriches man in such a way that man is an irreplaceable person before God and his supernaturally loved partner, one with intrinsic value. Man himself has a sort of direct experience of this, that is, the doctrine of merit is an assertion of the intrinsic value of man.

b) The doctrine also affirms that man – with God's help – can perfect himself. The very fact that he is a person enables him to transcend the existence of infra-human nature with its mere succession of non-historical moments. His personal acts sum up his past and present with a view to the future, momentarily no doubt, but nonetheless purposefully and progressively – and hence historically. As he realizes himself progressively in keeping with or contrary to his being and his grace, he perfects himself positively or negatively with regard to his definitive salvation. Hence the doctrine of merit means that this life is to be regarded as the preparation of the life to come and is constantly being sublimated into it. The doctrine makes for a theocentric orientation of the effort at self-fulfilment and obviates fatalistic misapprehensions of the doctrine of grace, as in quietism.

c) The danger of the doctrine is that it easily leads to Phariseeism and Pelagianism, since the notion of merit is very easily linked with the notion of claims which can be asserted, and also readily suggests that man is in some way independent of God. It can thus promote a fundamental misunderstanding of religion. Further, the doctrine can easily obscure the sense of the ambivalent character of the content of the formally good moral act, since it determines the merit of the moral act merely according to formal aspects. It may thus possibly promote a one-sided ethic confined to attitudes, to the detriment of an ethic with a considered sense of responsibility, which must always bear clearly in mind the materially bad effects of even formally good actions. Some theologians hold that the external act must be accorded a merit of its own. But this view should be rejected, on account of the ambivalence of the effects of the external act, from the aspect of what is materially moral.

Hence it is absolutely necessary to see the doctrine of merit in the perspectives of the whole doctrine of creation and grace, and a corresponding ethical doctrine. In such a context the doctrine of merit will be given the subordinate position which is proper to it.

Waldemar Molinski

METAPHYSICS

1. *The ancient origins.* "After physics", τὰ μετὰ τὰ φυσικά, was originally a heading in a catalogue of a library. When editing the *Corpus Aristotelicum*, Andronicus of Rhodes used this heading to range "after the writings on physics" the fourteen books in which Aristotle developed a "first science" (πρώτη φιλοσοφία) distinct from all other sciences. This placing of the subject was possibly inspired by pedagogical motives, to suggest that this supreme science could only be properly dealt with and assessed after the treatment of scientific subjects. At any rate, metaphysics soon came to mean a branch of knowledge whose place in the process of thought was after the investigation of the various realms of nature, since it was devoted to the realm which transcended and united all the realms of nature. But since it was the basically unifying principle, it was objectively prior and primordial, and hence knowledge of it was the "first philosophy". Hence the natural sciences, being "second philosophies", point by their very nature to the first, and no cognizance can be taken of the expanse of nature without an initial understanding, prior to science, of what binds nature together. But all scientific knowledge (ἐπιστήμη), in contrast to mere sensible perception (αἴσθησις) of temporal changes, is knowledge of the permanent grounds and causes, a knowledge "for its own sake" and not a utilitarian one, like knowledge of trades and art (τέχνη). But the "first philosophy" is the knowledge, su-

premely meaningful for its own sake, of the permanent "first causes and principles" (αἰτίαι καὶ ἀρχαί) of all that is – of beings not just in a given realm of nature, but in the most general sense of "beings qua beings" (ὂν ᾗ ὄν). The inquiry into beings as such leads to a super-excellent being, and the search for the many "first" principles to an ultimate ground: the divine (θεῖον) which is thought thinking of itself in pure contemplation (θεωρία). Thus in this science of Aristotle which is entitled metaphysics, theology and ontology are linked in a primordial unity, though the name "ontology" in turn only came into use in the 17th century. Since onto-theological metaphysics strives to bring into the region of conscious and articulated knowledge the general determinations of beings, that which is primarily and always pre-recognized and thus makes the encounter with this or that being possible, metaphysics may be regarded as on principle "transcendental" even in Aristotle. But the transcendental character of philosophy only came to the fore with the growth of methodological reflection in modern times, and then took on in fact a decidedly new form. Finally, it is true that transcendental onto-theological thinking goes beyond the beings of the various phenomena of the realms of nature to reach the general determinations of beings as such. And hence it goes beyond the partial knowledge of the natural sciences, "physics", to become metaphysics as universal knowledge of being. Nonetheless, in the very process, metaphysics still remains linked to the beings of nature and to scientific knowledge of them. It is the metaphysics of physics. And conversely, scientific knowledge has of itself a prior relationship to its metaphysical grounds of possibility and is thus orientated to metaphysics. It follows that the "natural science" which Aristotle considered as deriving from and pointing to metaphysics is in a completely different order of meaning than modern science. Aristotelian metaphysics does not try to reduce the phenomena of nature to non-metaphysical, immanent and mathematically measurable laws, but goes back by onto-theological processes to the laws of essence and being. One may recall, for instance, how Aristotle explained the circular motion of the stars or the fact that lighter bodies tend to rise.

Aristotle reached this form of metaphysical thinking by taking up, criticizing and transforming the pre-Socratic tradition, and in particular the Platonic view of the problems envisaged in this tradition. The pre-Socratics had already made the transition from "myth" to "logos", from the salvific religious truth mediated only historically to the possibility of a self-communicable and purely cognitive truth. Plato's immensely influential achievement was to distinguish sharply between perception and thought, between perceptible beings with their changing appearances, their process of becoming, and beings knowable only to thought in their permanent, suprasensible, essential being. What comes to be and appears is a being (ὄν) but also a non-being (μὴ ὄν). But beings are only truly beings in their suprasensible essence: the εἶδος is the ὄντως ὄν. And the most essential of all essences is the being of the good: the ἀγαθόν is the εἶδος εἰδῶν, form of forms. Being, as the Good, is also light. By communicating essences to beings, it provides them with participation in itself and thus illuminates them and makes them knowable to thought. Just as the light of the sun enables the eye to perceive appearances, so too the light of being enables thought, as "spiritual seeing", to have knowledge of beings in their essential being. Plato made all metaphysics a metaphysics of illumination and a more or less strongly accentuated participation. With his doctrine of causes and principles, Aristotle undoubtedly added to and modified considerably Plato's doctrine of participation and his teleology. But even for Aristotle the supreme and most essential of beings remains the ἐρώμενον, the desired, of all beings, and this relationship is only intelligible in the light of Plato's doctrine of participation. Further, in solving the problem of knowledge, he opposed abstraction (ἀφαίρεσις) to the anamnesis of Plato. And he introduced – though here again linking up with Plato – the distinction between the categorized, univocal concept and the transcendental analogous concept. Important as were these and other ways in which Aristotle completed or even departed from Plato's thought, and thus set up a double current in metaphysical tradition, more important still was that Aristotle explained the supreme and most essential of beings – called the Good by Plato – as thought itself, as reason, spirit. On this principle, the essences communicating being could be regarded as the thoughts of the spirit exteriorized and at the same time submerged in sensible beings (which can thereby really be said to be and not merely not be). This view was all the more influential because it affected both streams of tradition – in the Middle Ages, chiefly visible in the Platonism of the Augustinianists and the Aristotelianism of the Thomists, though neither could be depicted as composed of exclusively Platonic or Aristotelian elements. After all, even Aristotle himself cannot be understood except in the light of the Platonic elements in his philosophy. But Aristotle made all metaphysics a metaphysics of the spirit in the sense that the being of all beings is to be spirit, to be thinking and to be thought of.

2. *Basic characteristics of metaphysical thought.* The twofold origin of metaphysics in Plato and Aristotle was basically decisive for metaphysics, and all later epochal developments were determined by this origin in the directions they took. But this basic characteristic does not mean that all subsequent forms were merely corrections and hence prolongations of the earlier, or that they could all be simply deduced from the initial impulse of the Greeks. But the relation between metaphysical thought and metaphysical tradition, that is, between system and history, can, it seems, when it ever appears as a problem for metaphysics itself, only be interpreted as a progressive "correction", or as a necessary development from the initial stage. Thus Leibniz could write *De primae philosophia emendatione* and Hegel's dialectic presented itself as the identity of system and history. This way of looking at the relationship from within the perspectives of metaphysics was imposed, as it were, beforehand, by the distinction between essential, supra-temporal being and the contingency of its temporal realization in nature. The supra-temporally perfect "disciplines", first fully demarcated by C. von Wolff as *metaphysica generalis* or ontology, *metaphysica specialis* or rational (natural) theology, cosmology or natural philosophy and anthropology, were seen in the same perspectives. There were interruptions and menaces, but never total abandonment. The attitude is still maintained insofar as the supreme and primordial being to which the ascent of metaphysics leads, always appears as the essential and unlimited fulfilment of "reality" and "truth", as the identity of "being" and "thought" (reason, spirit). By virtue of this absolute identity, which is at once extremely general and extremely simple, any non-absolute being only "is" at all in proportion to its relation – however conceived – and hence is knowable only in the same measure. Its "being", being merely relative, then involves non-being and unknowability. In its oneness, it is not as much one as the absolute. In its identity, it is not so much itself as is the absolutely self-identical. Thus from the start, metaphysical thought finds itself involved in a peculiar tension with regard to the worldly, the singular, the multiple,

whose irreducible, non-absolute independence it acknowledges, while seeing it merely as poised over nothing. It appears as emptiness by contrast with the absolute fullness, in Plato's "space", Aristotle and Thomas's "matter", even Descartes's "extension" as radically distinct from thought.

This tension is only resolved in Leibniz, and fully so in Hegel, by consistently equating the nothing (and hence the being) of the relative with the mere thought of nothing (and of being). The singular, the relative, really "is" not at all, but only "apparently" a being. The only concrete is the universal, of which the so-called individual is merely a necessarily emergent moment, which as necessarily disappears. In the light of the metaphysically absolute identity of being and thought (reason, spirit), man too is ultimately considered the being whose "real" reality is singular and relative, but whose "real" potentiality – as in the Aristotelian-Thomistic doctrine of the *intellectus agens-possibilis* – is universal and absolute. The intrinsic tendency of his being and knowledge is to transcend the finiteness (matter) of things and of his own self (his sensibility) and to become in fact so absolutely spiritual as he already is in principle. It is this absolute identity alone which gives significance to the basic metaphysical distinction which differentiates the permanent and intelligible essence and being from the changing sensible appearance, the suprasensible spiritual (thought) from the sensible (perception), and hence eternity from time. The world is thus a manifestation of God, God not as eternally himself but in his temporal appearance. And man who knows all things and in knowing becomes all things is microtheos as well as microcosm. This is the foundation of the precedence of theory (contemplation) over the practical and productive virtues (praxis and poiesis). From the point of view of metaphysics, the latter are in the service of the former, because theory, as self-constituting (self-basing) and self-inspiring (self-determining), fulfils the meaning of poiesis and praxis. By its essence and being, all reality that comes about is for the coming about of truth. All truth that comes about is under the sign of conceptual, scientific knowledge. All scientific knowledge tends to exhaustive comprehension. In all action, the goal is the pure (divine) knowledge which determines all action, and hence the at least approximative *deificatio* of man, as time is reduced to eternity, sense to spirit, appearances to essence and being.

3. *Present problems*. All efforts to give a new foundation and development to metaphysics in terms of the modern mind are faced with problems which cannot readily be fitted into metaphysical thinking "in general" – wide though the term "in general" is. The problems mark at any rate a more decided caesura in the history of metaphysics than earlier turning-points in metaphysical thinking. And they also serve to place in a truer perspective questions raised in earlier times to which justice was not fully done, or which were perhaps not even adequately formulated, such as the "nominalism" and "voluntarism" which challenged the Middle Ages. Such problems emerge today on the side of modern science, not so much by reason of its direct assertions about nature, but because natural science no longer needs any metaphysical foundation either in ontology or transcendental logic, and provides itself with the necessary presuppositions, basic definitions and verification of results. It performs itself its progressive self-correction. On the whole, science challenges philosophical reflection less with regard to its own cognitive bases as by virtue of its significance and technical effects. And then again, history offers a challenge, both because the history of the past is less and less experienced as "tradition" and appears rather as communicated by historical science; and also

because the vision of the enormous upheavals in the ever-widening horizon of the past has gravely shaken the conviction that there are laws of essence and being independent of history. A reconsideration of what is normative and what is factual, of "eternal" claims to validity and "temporal" limitation is called for, for which the distinction between the substantial (being and essence) and the accidental (appearance) can no longer be adequate (see *History* I). Then, the philosophical problems of language raise the question of whether words are fundamentally to some extent interchangeable, merely furnishing us with an ultimately inadequate but actually unavoidable means of presenting externally the unchangeable concepts. Is the word merely the external reality of thought which is its essence, as it is regarded in traditional metaphysics? Or is all conceptual thought to be understood as essentially and basically a linguistic matter? In general, the question must be seriously considered as to whether thinking knowledge essentially tends to be "comprehending" knowledge. Is "truth" in the supreme sense the truth of the concept, so that all other mediation of truth, as in the artistic vision or religious faith, is to be regarded as a merely provisional and imperfect form of knowledge? Or are there types of truth of equal primordiality, each of course with its particular sphere of universality, its own sort of evidence and its own criteria – none of which types of truth can be played off against another? If so, what new definition must be given of scientific, and in particular of philosophical or metaphysical comprehension, and what is its "fundamental" and "universal" character as knowledge? Finally, the question then arises once more as to the essence of man. Is the human in man, his "being", to be sought for in his reason, the power of knowing and comprehending, compared with which the sensibility of man, which is undoubtedly part of his being, is a medium of his self-realization on a lower level of being, a hindrance as well as a help? Or must we take a completely different view of the relationship between sense and spirit, and hence between action, which is always centred on the particular, and knowledge, which aims at the universal, between appearance and being, between reality and essence, between historical change and permanent characteristic – without simply reversing the relationship? The efforts which have been made to formulate these problems, in particular by Kierkegaard, Marx, Nietzsche and Heidegger, and by the dialogal and personalist philosophy of the present day, have done much to give philosophy a new orientation. But such reflection cannot be carried on without deliberate recourse to history, to the basic origins of metaphysics and the new impulses it received in each epoch.

Alois Halder

MIRACLE

I. Theological

1. *Hermeneutical considerations.* a) Every attempt to give a theological definition of miracles must start from those described in the biblical tradition. This follows at once from the unique theological dignity which is accorded these miracles in the teaching of the Church (cf. *D* 1790, 1813). Then there is the well-founded presumption in theology that the real miracle must be closely and intrinsically connected with the unique historical coming of the revelation of God in Jesus Christ. (This suggests the further principle that miracles will be "sparingly used" in the "time of the Church".) The fact that the theological concept of miracle must be based on the biblical tradition provides a decisive hermeneutical insight, namely that theology does not deal directly with miracles, but with testimony to miracles

or miracle-stories. Since G. E. Lessing's book on the power of the Spirit (*Vom Beweis des Geistes und der Kraft* [1777]), the analysis of this "historical difference" has been explicitly discussed in attempts to determine the theological notion of miracle. The abstract and metaphysical analysis of miracle, based, for instance, on the notion of an intervention in the laws of nature, is a fundamental abandonment of the hermeneutical starting-point. The theological investigation of miracle is primarily concerned not with nature but with history. The marginal cases which it deals with are concerned with historical rather than natural science.

b) Historical information only makes an impact on man when it presents itself as an answer to an inexorable question which affects his future. But today above all, when men's world-view is dominated by the categories of natural science, the vital relevance of the historical has been largely lost sight of. Hence theology, in the form of fundamental theology, part of whose subject-matter is the miracle-stories of the Bible, must try to reveal to man his fundamental and to some extent *a priori* openness to the miraculous. This affinity may be shown first of all by bringing out the sense of wonder (θαυμάζειν) behind all particular forms of settled self-understanding: man's questioning and insatiable astonishment at the "wonderful" mystery of his historical existence, which inspires and centres on itself all man's questions. Then there is the permanent and fundamental openness of man for the strange, the unforeseeable and the indomitable, even in an increasingly "humanized" world of matter whose behaviour can be calculated and manipulated. Finally, it must be clearly shown that the world, in its character of history, is essentially based on human intersubjectivity. Hence it can never be reduced to descriptions of mere objects and information given in totally objectivated moulds. The world as history means that man is caught up in genuine "traditions" and interpersonal connections, and that he can never objectivate himself in such a way as to free himself and his future from his historical existence.

c) The application of form criticism to the Bible has provided a criterion for the literary genre of the miracle-stories of the NT. They are not the reports of a detached observer, but the testimony of believers, orientated to the kerygma and theologically determined. From this formal character and the description of the miracle itself, both as an element of the actual promise and as an element of the proof of credibility of the promises, it follows that the wonders narrated are not simply "marvels", (natural) events which could be registered by detached and objective observation. The miracles, by their very nature, must be considered as "signs", which affect human existence inasmuch as they bear on each man's future, on the very salvation which he seeks as an interested party. Hence for their general accessibility, the fact that they are attested by those who are subjectively affected (in contrast to mere reportage) is not accidental, but essential.

2. *Definition and explanation.* a) From the theological point of view, miracles are authenticating signs. They display the promised lordship of God as actually and effectively present. They accredit the historical figures through whom these promises come true: the patriarchs, the prophets, and Jesus Christ. In this perspective they have the function of a call which arouses men and directs their attention to their fundamental search for meaning and happiness – an existential which makes itself felt openly or obscurely, and is welcomed or repressed in all man's programmes, as it strives to find articulate historical expression. Hence a miracle is not an arbitrary exhibition of God's omnipotence. It is embedded in the general historical context of the promises, since it is an

anticipatory revelation of God's eschatological power to heal and save. In Jesus Christ and his resurrection this power has begun its definitive work as the future of mankind.

b) A miracle is not a natural or "physical" phenomenon to which a certain significance is subsequently added on. It is a "sign" by its very nature, by virtue of its own proper constitution, in every aspect. This "identity" of sign and fact may perhaps be compared to the experience, not reducible to the categories, in which men as persons encounter each other (cf. B. Welte, *Auf der Spur des Ewigen* [1965], pp. 337–50). A miracle is a sign which does not simply demonstrate in a purely intellectual way the thing signified, but is meant to make it *credible*. Theologically speaking, therefore, it cannot be a sign which compels assent. It does not make the thing signified a perspicuous and manageable truth. It is a sign which is a summons. Its promise appeals to the element of man which daringly strives to attain the full future of his existence as man with men (and man is in fact always taking this risk, explicitly or implicitly). Hence the miracle as such can never occur within the horizon of a world whose programme excludes *a priori* (or perhaps merely methodologically, as in the natural sciences) this orientation of existence where freedom is the sustaining and determining factor.

c) Hence the primordial situation in which a miracle may be experienced cannot be the field of methodical observation in the scientific sense. The natural sciences work on the methodical presumption that reality is fundamentally calculable. They assume a sort of "methodological determinism", which is the only possible basis of their process of observation, since it allows reality to appear in its physical factuality. And it is legitimate as long as it does not go beyond its own categories and does not erect itself into an absolute. Hence too in the natural sciences there is no such thing as an existentiell impact, but only embarrassment – which merely inspires the scientist to seek for a new set of explanations. For these and other reasons (especially the ambiguity of the terms "nature" and "natural law") it is better not to define a miracle (negatively) as a "breach" or "violation" of the laws of nature. It is a (positive) sign of the fact that all reality is included in the historical dispensation of God. It can be seen by all whose outlook on the world is dominated by interpersonal relationships in their basic search for the meaning and wholeness of life.

Johann Baptist Metz

II. Miracles of Jesus

A. Biblical Theology

1. *Miracle and message.* In the public life of Jesus as recorded in the gospels, the miracles occupy an important place, not only because of the number that are reported, but also because of their significance. They do not just appear as a profusion of wonderful happenings, on the margin of the message of salvation. They are themselves part of the gospel, the message of salvation in action. Though the synoptics practically always use the word "mighty deeds" (δυνάμεις) to describe them, it is better to translate this as "manifestations of power". The term "power" is not meant to stress the exceptional character of the manifestation or belief in the transcendent intervention of God, but the *saving* presence, the triumph over the "principalities and powers" of evil. As a sign of salvation, the miracle takes on its full meaning and is perfectly realized in Christ, the fullness of the saving presence and the definitive "yes" of God, in whom all the divine promises become a reality (2 Cor 1:20). All the great themes of the prophets and of the messianic activity of Jesus are expressed in his miracles in a striking series of lessons in action: the pre-eminence of the Kingdom over material

concerns (the tribute taken from the mouth of a fish); deliverance from sin (the paralyzed man let down from the roof; the woman bent double for eighteen years); victory over the devil (exorcisms); victory over death (Naim; the daughter of Jairus); the paradox of the cross and glory (the walking on the waters; the stilled tempest); the barrenness of those who reject salvation (the withered fig-tree) and the blessings of those who follow the way of salvation (the miraculous draught of fishes; Peter walking on the waters). Jesus himself, in the synagogue at Nazareth and in his reply to the messengers of the Baptist (Lk 4:16ff.; 7:18–23), specifically associates his miracles with the messianic prophecies of Isaiah where the material gifts symbolize the salvation and riches of the Kingdom.

Thus all the miracles of Jesus are the prelude to his own resurrection, which was the decisive triumph of the "power" of God and the eschatological reality beyond all signs. But for the Church, which still lives in expectation, the signs are the empty tomb and the appearances of Christ. To the pilgrim Church the risen Christ further promised that it would be accompanied by signs to the end of time (Mk 16:17; Mt 28:18). And this reveals the ultimate meaning of every miracle: to be the anticipation and the token of the final parousia, an initial realization of the new heavens and the new earth. But the Church has no resting place here, because it must continue on its way to the final promise. In the Gospel of John the character of the miracles as significant acts is even more strongly accentuated. For Jesus himself, the miracles are part of the "works that he accomplishes" (ἔργα) and which he did not even once describe as "my works" (7:3–8:16) but always as "the works of the Father who has sent me" (cf. 5:36; 9:3;10:32). So it is the Father who through these works manifests Christ as his Son and reveals himself as God the Saviour. When the evangelist is no longer reporting the words of the Saviour, but rather developing his own theological insights, to describe the miracles he uses the word "sign" (σημεῖον) which has a very special meaning for him. In Jn the sign is a guarantee of the divine testimony, a theophany of the glory of the Father in the Son, a symbolic illustration of the Son's saving work and of his struggle against the prince of darkness and the murderer from the beginning (sight for the man born blind; the resurrection of Lazarus), an archetypal figure of the sacramental universe (the wine at Cana, the multiplication of bread, the water of Bethzatha) and a prefigurative symbol of the fulfilment and of the eschatological judgment (the wine of the eternal nuptials, the living water springing forth unto life eternal, the light without shadows, the resurrection unto life eternal). That is why Christ always relates his miracles to his "hour" (e.g., 7:3–8) and to the definitive sign of his exaltation, on the cross and in the glory of the resurrection.

2. *Miracle and faith.* As a divine testimony, a significant action combining with and confirming the significant word (Mk 16:20; Jn 10:25; Heb 2:4), the miracle is one of the most important meeting-places of the message and faith. To recognize the significance of the miracle is not necessarily to believe. It is to be brought face to face with the divine invitation and forced to make a choice (Jn 10:37f.; 15:24). For the miracle is a sign which invites, but does not compel. John's terminology is very precise when distinguishing the various stages involved in this encounter with the signs. It is possible "not to see" the miracle: that is, to see the material wonder without grasping what it means (Jn 6:26). On the other hand, "to see" the miracle is to have discerned its salvific meaning and by this very fact to have found oneself challenged by the summons to faith (John expresses this seeing which precedes faith by using the

aorist εἶδεν). Men respond to this insight either by an act of faith (καὶ ἐπίστευσεν repeated like a refrain, 2:11; 4:53; 11:45; 12:42, etc.) or by a refusal to believe (8:47; 12:26f., etc.). So the act of faith is more than a mere recognition of the fact that the sign is an authentic reference to some further reality; it is the abandonment of one's whole being to the person who is signified and to his saving embrace. Once consent has been given, faith leads men to "see" the miracle in a completely new way: through the sign, they contemplate the glory of God revealed in Christ (John uses the perfect ἑώρακα to describe this seeing, 9:37; 17:7, 9; 19:35; 20:29). The miracle now is much more than an invitation to faith; for the believer it is an impulse to life in the spirit, of his intimate familiarity with the Father in Christ. Refusal to believe can have many shades and proceed from a variety of reasons: spiritual dullness (Jn 6:15, 26; Lk 17:11–19); human respect (Jn 12:42); political interest (Jn 11:48, 53); legalistic arrogance (he healed on the Sabbath day – Mk 3:1–6; Lk 13:10–16; Jn 5:10; 9:16); clerical jealousy (Jn 12:11), etc. This refusal to believe can even distort the meaning of the signs and attribute them to Beelzebub (Mt 12:24–28). And above all, an attempt is made to submit God to conditions laid down by men and to make faith depend on a "sign from heaven" (Mt 12:38–39; Mk 8:11; Jn 2:18), a complete contradiction of the Johannine "sign": some prodigious display without any intrinsic connection with the message, imposing itself by its sensational character, furthering political dreams and a kingdom of temporal power. Such a sign, so obstinately demanded by the Jews (Paul describes the Jews as those who "demand signs", 1 Cor 1:22), Jesus just as persistently refused to give, because their demand for such a sign comes from a previous refusal to believe.

The faith aroused by the miracle is not itself at once perfect. Like the word, a miraculous sign is a seed which bears fruit according to the type of ground in which it is sown: the fickle faith of the crowds; the hesitant faith of Nicodemus; and on the other hand, the faith which is longed for or professed even before the sign is performed (the paralyzed man let down through the roof; the father of the epileptic boy, Mk 9:24) and which Jesus surprisingly finds above all in foreigners (the Canaanite woman, the centurion). From this we can see that for Jesus the miracle is not the only way towards faith, nor even the more perfect (Jn 4:48). It is only the fringe of his garment: the encounter with his teaching and above all with his own person is a much more effective way of bringing men to faith. Many of those who were the most closely bound to him in faith – the first disciples, Matthew, Mary Magdalen, Zachaeus and many others, his mother most of all – came to him by other ways than that of miraculous signs. "Thomas, blessed are those who have not seen and yet believe."

B. Apologetics

Unless even the possibility of miracles is rejected *a priori*, it follows from all that we have said that it is not possible to eliminate the miracle from the gospel or to "demythologize" it without touching on the substance of the message. No doubt it is essential to examine each pericope in the light of form-criticism so as to determine its historical kernel and separate it from later retouches and additions such as kerygmatic and liturgical developments. But the substantial historicity of the miracles of Jesus is guaranteed by the nature of the apostolic testimony. All the NT authors insist on the fact that the saving action of God in Christ was worked out and declared itself in history; and this coming of salvation they expressly attest to be historical (Lk 1:1–4; Jn 1:1–4; 2 Pet 1:16–20).

The miracles are of value as signs only

if they are accepted as being on the same historical level as the person of Christ and his teaching; and the evangelists see themselves definitely as eye-witnesses of miracles. Further, even his enemies never seem to have denied the actual fact of Christ's wonderful deeds. There is no trace of such a denial either in the gospels or in the Jewish rabbinical polemics of the early centuries. To estimate the narratives, they should be compared above all to the wonders of the Apocrypha or the pagan wonder-workers like Apollonius of Tyana or the mythologies which are meant to give religious and historical authenticity to them. There is on the one hand a remarkable sobriety, austerity and simplicity which contrasts with the showmanship and the fair-ground atmosphere on the other. The dignity, seriousness, the self-forgetfulness of Jesus, the atmosphere of prayer, contrast with the trances, the fantasies, the trickery and the greed of the wonder-workers. In the gospels there is no miracle which is futile, trivial or unwholesome, such as abound in the marvels of mythology. Nor are there miracles which inflict punishment on anybody. No frantic thirst for the marvellous; no miracles in the gospel of the infancy or in the account of the passion; no miracles attributed to such a mighty figure as John the Baptist (just as one finds in Acts a purely historical treatment of a number of events – 14:20; 20:10; 28:5 – which appear to lend themselves to legendary embellishment). By contrast, in the accounts of the miracles there are a number of details which have too little interest to have been invented and yet, on the other hand, are so human and true to type that they suggest the presence of an eye-witness. The narratives are perfectly consonant with the person of the Lord, with his message and his work of salvation, with the symbolism of the sacraments and the language of the parables.

Louis Monden

MISSION

The word "mission", much used today, represents one of the most decisive but also complex themes within Christian belief and life. Its primary meaning is "sending", and in the deepest thrust of biblical and Christian religion there has been a repeated sense of the sending of men by God to do his business in the world. It is this which has provided the Church both with its sense of having authority and its deliberately expansive character. It has been "sent" by God to the world. The prophets were the first to be so sent and their mission to proclaim and live his "ways" was continued and fulfilled in that of Jesus Christ, who was supremely the sent one, the "apostle" (Heb 3:1) of God, for that is the meaning of the word. To define his mission, Jesus in Luke's gospel applied to himself some words of Isaiah: "The spirit of the Lord has been given to me, for he has anointed me. He has sent me to bring the good news to the poor, to proclaim liberty to captives and to the blind new sight, to set the downtrodden free, to proclaim the Lord's year of favour" (Lk 4:18).

These words give some sense of the range of mission; its purpose is no less than the proclamation and immediate inauguration of salvation, seen as a divine gift of liberation both spiritual and temporal. God's mission to the world, the "missio Dei", is manifested above all in the full round of the life and teaching of Jesus Christ. The task of the sent one is to proclaim the word of God, to enact his works, and by so doing to generate among men a fellowship which is in some way already the society of God. The works of God are the works of justice and compassion whereby men are liberated here and now from some of the immediate physical hardships or injustices pressing upon them and are thereby enabled to experience what is truly a certain beginning to the liberty of God's full kingdom proclaimed in his word. The message (kerygma), the human service of temporal liberation (diakonia), and the building up of a fellowship understood already as a sharing in the life of God (koinonia) go necessarily together. The three constitute an indivisible unity, the matter of "mission", whereby God's love and concern are pointed to and made explicitly present in the world.

This mission Jesus Christ passed on to his disciples: "As the Father sent me, so I am sending you" (Jn 20:21). All four gospels close with comparable passages whereby the mission of Jesus is handed on to his disciples, in particular the eleven who are the immediate recipients of his power. It is, therefore, somewhat misleading to say that the Church has a mission, as if the existence of the Church comes first. In truth it is because of the mission that there is a Church; the Church is the servant and expression of this mission. The mission consequently dictates the nature of the Church and in so far as the Church fails to live up to the demands of mission, it is effectively failing to be Church. In this perspective it is quite misleading to say that the purpose of the mission is the expansion of the Church; in the fullest sense of mission the Church cannot possibly be its end. Rather is the Church called into being by mission for the sake of salvation.

The nature of this missionary task is essentially a universal one. The "all the nations" of Mt 28:19 represents an absolutely decisive dimension for both mission and Church. The latter in the process of history quickly came to be called "Catholic" (universal) not because it really was present all over the world, but because by its deepest nature it required to be so and could not properly exist at all if it did not exist universally. The mission had to explode into new areas and groups of people if it was not to be unfaithful to itself. Hence, while mission is indeed the Church's task everywhere – in old Christian communities as well as "virgin soil" – the test of its vitality came to be seen, rightly, in regard to its expansive character. The word "missionary" then came to be restricted to this expansive activity ("foreign missions") exclusively, and this was mistaken. As a consequence both the theology and the organization of "missionary activity" came to relate only to the "foreign missions" and the establishment of the Church in places where it did not previously exist.

This kind of work is a vitally important ministry within the total mission of the Church, and in some sense the very spearhead of the whole, but it cannot simply be identified with the whole without a dangerous and misleading restriction in the overall understanding of mission.

One of the most important developments in modern theology and church life has been the re-establishment of a sense of the unity of mission. At the same time it is most important to define precisely the proper character of that particular ministry which has often simply been allowed to monopolize the name.

In many ways mission in places where there has hitherto been no church represents the nature of mission in its fullness. Failure to embark upon it, involving a limitation of the Church's ministerial activity to people already members or living in places where the Church is already established, would be indicative of the contemporary Church's failure to take her catholicity with sufficient seriousness; such has clearly been the case at certain periods in her history.

At the same time the missionary task within societies where there has hitherto been no Christian presence, and undertaken by people who are foreigners to that society, requires a particularly clear understanding of what mission and Church truly require and what they do not. In every society there is a natural tendency for Christianity to take on the characteristics of a local culture, and ministers working within their local church seldom note how far their own form of Christianity has been shaped by the secular cultural history of their society.

But when men go out from their own local church, as representatives of Christ and the universal Church, to preach the gospel and implant the *Catholica* in a different society and cultural milieu, they have to see themselves as servants of a new local church reflecting a different culture and national tradition, and so avoid imposing the traditions of the home church in a form of ecclesiastico-cultural imperialism. Unfortunately they have seldom succeeded in this. The task of "missiology" in its narrower sense is precisely to help missionaries understand the basic theological and sociological character of the ministry to which they are committed.

To conclude, the understanding of mission involves: 1: the sense of participation within a movement of "being sent", which extends the whole length of biblical and ecclesial life and vastly transcends the purpose of "implanting the Church"; 2: a sense of the content of mission as consisting of an integral combination of three elements: proclamation, service and fellowship; 3: a sense of the particular exigencies of mission when carried out, not within one's own natural society and local church, but by those who have been called to leave the latter in order to bring into being a new local church, growing out of and witnessing to a different socio-cultural milieu, and while retaining full communion with the wider body of the Catholic Church, yet possessing from the earliest possible moment the proper characteristics of a local church – self-ministry, self-support and ecclesio-cultural particularity.

Adrian Hastings

MODERNISM

A. The Term and Concept

Modernism, in the strict theological sense, is a general term for the manifold crisis in the doctrine and discipline of the Church at the end of the 19th and the beginning of the 20th century. In its extreme forms it was the occasion of the condemnation pronounced by Pius X in 1907, in the decree *Lamentabili* and the encyclical *Pascendi*.

The term "modernism" was in use since the 16th century to characterize the tendency to esteem the modern age more highly than antiquity. In the 19th century it was used by some Protestants in a religious sense, to designate the anti-Christian tendencies of the modern world and also the radicalism of liberal theology. When at the end of the century there was a movement in the Catholic Church urging reform of the Church and its doctrine in the sense of adapting them to modern needs, the term modernism was at once applied to it by its opponents, first of all in Italy. It was taken up in a much more precise sense in the encyclical *Pascendi* of Pius X (1907). Here it means a complex of clearly defined heresies which form the logical conclusion of the heterodox trends within the movement in question, which took in fact many forms and was in many respects legitimate, but which was also simply imprudent and given to wild exaggeration. In connection with modernism and the reaction to it, the term was often applied without distinction to all who refused to adopt a strictly conservative standpoint. Such heavy-handed criticism made it easy for opponents of the Church to reproach it with being impervious to all modernizing efforts.

Even when reduced to this technical usage, the notion of modernism is hard to define. It was a "direction" (P. Sabatier), a "tendency" (A. Loisy), rather than a set of definite doctrines. It showed itself in fact at the beginning as a movement which sought to remain in the Church but was still ready to accept from the modern world all that seemed irrefutable in the realm of thought and healthy in the line of institutions, so that Catholicism could adapt itself to an altered world and rid itself of apparently contingent and outmoded elements. The idea was that in this way men would be kept loyal to the Church or won back to it. But no notice was taken of the danger that under the pretext of making the Church adapt to the times, it could be forgotten that the modern age also needed to be brought into line with the demands of the spirit of Christianity.

These tendencies had already shown themselves in liberal Catholicism about the middle of the 19th century. There were basically two forms. One was the effort to change the traditional discipline of the Church, the other was the claim of almost absolute freedom for Catholic scholars with regard to the magisterium – upheld, for instance, by Rafaele Lambruschini, Ignaz von Döllinger and Lord Acton (among whose activities was editorship of *The Rambler*). The tendencies made themselves felt more strongly than ever after 1890, and in much more daring forms, in such different fields as exegesis, philosophy of religion, apologetics, political and social action, as well as in the question of the reform of Church discipline. Even though the papal condemnation rightly articulated a number of principles which were at the base of the heterodox forms of this multifarious movement, it remains true that modernism, before it became a heretical system, appeared in its historical development as a totality of different basic attitudes which were spontaneous and unplanned.

B. Origin and Development

1. The first and main centre of the crisis produced by modernism was in France. Firstly, there were certain philosophers – such as L. Laberthonnière, C. Denis and M. Hébert – who were under the influence of post-Kantianism and thought that they could claim M. Blondel as their patron, though they falsified his ideas. They tried to replace scholastic intellectualism by a doctrine which would involve the forces of the heart and the concreteness of actual life. In the religious realm in particular they called for a moral dogmatism, by striving to derive moral certitude not from theoretical argument but from action itself. In apologetics they were immanentist, inasmuch as they sought to deduce religious truth from the needs of the subject and tried to find the mainspring of supernatural grace in the intrinsic tendencies of nature itself, instead of the "extrinsicism" which saw the supernatural as working from outside nature. Under the confusing influence of religious symbolism, in the wake of Schleiermacher, and of the evolutionist thinking of Spencerian and Hegelian origin, they even went so far at times as to demand that all unchangeably fixed concepts should be rejected, and that contact with the ceaseless flow of life should be maintained by constantly changing interpretations.

Then, parallel to this movement in philosophy, the most important organ of which was the *Annales de philosophie chrétienne*, younger theologians discovered biblical criticism. They noted that German scholars using the principles of historical criticism had once more called in question traditional interpretations of Scripture and of primitive Christian history – chiefly as regards the Pentateuch, the religious history of Israel, the teaching given by Christ and the life of the first generations of Christians. They were faced at once with the problem of how far the Catholic faith could be reconciled with the results of modern exegesis. Some, like M.-J. Lagrange and P. Batiffol, tried the following way. They distinguished what were really truths of faith and what were merely incidental and eventually revisable views in the traditional doctrines. And they also closely scrutinized the very unequal results of rationalistic criticism, distinguishing between the real findings of literary criticism and the historical or theological consequences which were too lightly drawn from them. Others, however, in direct contradiction to the teaching of the Church, thought that they had to accept many conclusions of German liberal exegesis as definitive, scientifically established truths. From then on the problem of adapting apologetics to the new age presented itself to them in a new light.

This task was taken up by the French exegete Alfred Loisy (1857–1940). After publishing several articles under the *nom de plume* Firmin in the *Revue du clergé français*, he published in November 1902 a little book, *L'Évangile et l'Église*, which he supplemented in the following year by an explanatory volume, *Autour d'un petit livre*, which gave the book still more weight. Loisy himself presented his work "firstly, as an outline and historical explanation of the development of Christianity, and then as a general philosophy of religion and an effort to interpret the dogmas, the official creeds and the definitions of the Councils, the purpose of which is to reconcile them with the realities of history and the mentality of our contemporaries, by sacrificing the letter to the spirit" (*Revue d'histoire et de littérature religieuse* 11 [1906], p. 570). Hence his view of history and his exegetical positions were based, according to his own statement, on a certain view of the philosophy of religion. He starts from the principle that the exegete must prescind entirely from any preconception about the supernatural origin of holy Scripture, which is to be interpreted like any other historical document without reference to the magisterium of the Church. Loisy thus called in question the notion of revelation from without: "Dogmas are not truths fallen from heaven" (*L'Évangile et l'Église*, pp. 202f.). He held in consequence that one could rightly assume a profound development not merely in the formulation but in the meaning of ecclesiastical dogmas, as also in the organization of the Church.

These revolutionary ideas, which were often rather suggestions than firm assertions, found a lively echo in certain intellectual circles, especially among the younger clergy, who believed to some extent (wrongly, in fact) that they could appeal to the authority of Cardinal Newman and his theory of the development of Christian doctrine. Loisy's ideas were also taken up favourably by certain Christian democrats (P.-A. Naudet and his periodical, *La justice sociale* [1893ff.], P. Dabry and his periodical *La vie catholique* [1898ff.], M. Sangnier and his organization, "Sillon", founded in 1894). These saw in Loisy's claim for the autonomy of science as regards theology a parallel to their own demand for the autonomy of the lay people and civil society as regards "clerical autocracy".

2. Loisy withdrew from the controversy, to avoid clashes with ecclesiastical authority. (As regards his real attitude to the Christian faith at this stage, the researches of E. Poulat have shown that the categorical assertions of his *Mémoires* cannot be accepted without reserves.) But then a new centre of the modernistic movement appeared in England, of which the moving spirit was the ex-Jesuit George Tyrrell (1861–1909), who had shown himself to be an apologist of rank. His own mysticism and his intuitive rather than intellectualist mentality were stimulated by his encounter with the philosophy of M. Blondel, to which he was introduced by F. von Hügel, and then by the criticism of Loisy. Tyrrell proceeded to combine the scattered suggestions from the works of his French master into an organic theological system. The thesis of his writings (especially *A Much Abused*

Letter [1906], *Through Scylla and Charybdis* [1907]) is that Christ did not present himself as the teacher of an orthodoxy and that Catholic theologians would be very wrong to understand faith as the assent of the intellect to the historical and metaphysical assertions of a "revealed" theology marvellously preserved from errors, since theology – by which he meant in fact dogma – was only a human effort to grasp in intellectual terms the divine force working in man. Less cautious disciples took their symbolism and immanentism much further than Tyrrell, and came ultimately to the verge of a pantheism, according to which the divine, immanent in history, seeks itself in and through successive religious symbols and reveals itself through them.

E. Le Roy, a philosopher close to Bergson, did not go so far in his article "Qu'est-ce qu'un dogme?", *La Quinzaine* 63 (1905), pp. 495ff., which attracted much attention. According to Le Roy, the essential purpose of dogma was not to enlighten the spirit but to guide religious activity. In a purely pragmatic perspective, he placed the moral aspect of revelation on a higher level than its intellectual significance.

3. This current of thought spread rapidly from France to Italy, chiefly under the influence of F. von Hügel. Lectures by brilliant though less original speakers and some periodicals (*Studi religiosi* by S. Minocchi; *Rivista storico-critica* by E. Buonaiuti) disseminated the exegetical views of Loisy, the modernistic conception of the history of dogma or the doctrines of immanence and moral dogmatism.

In Italy, however, more than elsewhere, what has been called a social modernism developed, particularly round Romolo Murri, a young priest with Christian-democratic ideas. Murri sought to build up political and social action, in an atmosphere of complete intellectual and disciplinary freedom, apart from all control by the hierarchy. The extraneous influences finally combined with a reform movement within the Italian Church, which was given a particular stamp by the famous novel *Il Santo* (1905) by A. Fogazzaro. In the beginning of 1907 a group of young lay people in Milan founded the periodical *Il Rinnovamento*, which spread the ideas of political and religious liberalism. But this was rather an extremist reform movement than a definitely heretical modernism. It was a legitimate but insufficiently mature effort to react against the backwardness of ecclesiastical sciences in Italy and to build a bridge between Catholicism and the pretensions of the modern world.

4. The same is true of the *Reformkatholizismus* in Germany, which followed F. X. Kraus in its opposition to ultramontane tendencies. But unlike the actual modernists, it did not envisage a "modernization" of the basic structure of the faith and the Church. In Holland, the socially active priest Fr. Poels was also unjustly accused of "social modernism" by his opponents, simply because he favoured the formation of vocational organizations on non-denominational lines.

Though geographically modernism was restricted to France and Italy (apart from some small circles in England) and sociologically embraced only a few priests and educated laymen, it found such a strong echo that it threatened for a while to be a great menace to the Church, and would in fact have been so, had it been taken up by the clergy in great numbers. But the radical measures taken after the condemnation in 1907 broke up the movement in a few months. There were a few attempts at resistance, especially the manifesto drawn up by Buonaiuti, *Il programma dei modernisti*, and the anonymous books on the history of dogma (by J. Turmel). The quick collapse indicates that the roots had not gone very deep. Nonetheless, it was important that all obscurities should have been cleared up. Unhappily, the justifiable suppression of the movement was accompanied, especially after 1910, by a very distasteful conservative reaction, which is known as integralism.

C. Ecclesiastical Condemnation

Leo XIII could never bring himself to take strong measures, which might have given the impression that he was summarily condemning the progressive biblical movement. When the danger had grown acute, Pius X did not hesitate. At the end of 1903 the most important writings of Loisy were put on the Index and subsequently various other characteristically modernist works. Then, from December 1905 on, a number of episcopal pastorals were also directed against Italian modernism. In July 1907 the Holy Office published the decree *Lamentabili sane exitu* (*D* 2001–65), which had been drawn up after several years' work on the basis of a list of propositions from the works of Loisy produced by two Paris theologians. The decree condemned sixty-five characteristic propositions of biblical and theological modernism. A few months later came the encyclical *Pascendi*, published on 8 September 1907 (*D* 2071–2109), a much more thoroughgoing and solemn condemnation (not, however, a definition of the infallible magisterium of the Church). It begins with a comprehensive presentation of modernism and reduces its specific errors to two fundamental philosophical ones: agnosticism, which denies the validity of rational argument in the religious sphere, and immanentism, which derives religious truth from the intrinsic needs of life. This philosophical approach leads to a certain theology: faith is the perception of the work of God in human consciousness. This gives rise to dogma, which is formed in the course of an intrinsic development of life on the basis of an exploitation of this fact of experience by the human mind. So too the sacraments come from the need "of giving religion visible form". Holy Scripture is a collection of the religious experiences of the Jews and the first disciples of Christ. The Church is the outcome of collective consciousness, and the sole function of authority is to help to give expression to the religious sense of the individual. The encyclical also rejects the modernistic conception of biblical criticism, the methods of a purely subjective apologetics and the demands for reform put forward by the modernists. It ends with indicating practical measures to be taken against the spread of the evil, particularly in the seminaries. Since a number of modernists, inspite of their condemnation, still claimed to belong to the Church while secretly continuing to make propaganda for their ideas, Pius X thought it necessary to take further measures. In the motu proprio *Sacrorum Antistitum* of 1 September 1909 he required all the clergy to take the "anti-modernist oath". This was a profession of faith, drawn up in the light of the various forms of modernism already condemned, which supplemented the *professio fidei tridentina* of Pius IV. The first part affirms in most explicit terms the demonstrability of the existence of God, the value of the rational and historical foundations of faith, the foundation of the Church by Christ, the unchangeableness of dogmas and the role of the intellect in the act of faith. It goes on to proclaim submission and assent to the decree *Lamentabili* and the encyclical *Pascendi*. Without adding anything essential, the text presented, so to speak, a solemn summary of the decrees of Pius X, with a view to demanding formal acceptance from all the clergy and hence exposing crypto-modernists. The clergy as a whole submitted without much outward resistance. There were only some forty exceptions in the whole Church. Nonetheless, the measures provoked a strong reaction in Germany in the name of scientific freedom, and finally, at the request of the German bishops, Catholic university professors were absolved from taking the anti-modernist oath.

The modernists at once reproached the encyclical with drawing up an artificial system of modernism which could be found as such in no given author. In fact, the encyclical is a schematization, "using a process of abstraction to work out a general basic idea implied in a large number of individual propositions" (J. Rivière). But, as the Anglican A. L. Lilley pointed out, once the various movements had proved to be inspired by a common principle and goal, it was to some extent normal and right that the authority which condemned them should envisage them under a common denomination and impose on them a common censure.

As time goes on, the actual error of modernism appears more clearly. It was undoubtedly the merit of biblical modernism that it called attention to the law of the development of dogma and the need of including the historical method in dealing with the texts of Scripture. But its principle was to leave entirely out of account the supernatural and inspired character of the scriptural testimonies, and also the interpretations suggested by tradition and the magisterium of the Church. Further, historians are now becoming more and more alert to the fact that the notion of history used by Loisy and many of the modernists was dependent on the positivist notions of the end of the 19th century, which are today undoubtedly outdated in many respects. Theological modernism started with a partial truth, which it then exploited in a one-sided and intemperate fashion. It is undoubtedly true that the inner religious experience is an essential element of the life of the spirit and in many cases the psychological source of faith. Dogmatic formulas always remain inadequate to their object which is the mystery of God. Revelation is first and foremost to direct our religious life, rather than to satisfy our speculative curiosity. The message of revelation was only gradually unfolded by the Church, and in many respects only after several trials. But it is not true that religious experience is the only way to know anything of God. Dogmatic formulas are not completely devoid of objective content. The development of dogmatic formulas does not take place according to a purely natural process which expands inordinately the original message of Jesus and even deforms it, so that it needs to be adapted to new historical realities.

As regards the so-called "social" modernism (even if one can regard it as and early and rather clumsy effort to strengthen the autonomy of the intramundane), it is important to note that its followers saw the Church less as a supernatural institution for the attainment of salvation than as a factor of the civilization and moral progress of this world. They thus ran the risk of falling into the fundamental error common to all modernists, which F. von Hügel characterized as follows: "The main and decisive difference now appears to me to be the difference between Religion regarded as a purely intra-human reality, its only evidence being confined to the aspirations of the human race; and Religion seen as manifesting its own evidence, metaphysical, the effect in us of something more than us – of more than any purely human facts and desires" (Baron Friedrich von Hügel, *Selected Letters, 1896–1924* [1927], p. 334) (original in French).

Roger Aubert

MONOGENISM

1. *Notion.* Monogenism is the doctrine which affirms that the whole of mankind, at least those who lived after original sin, stem biologically from one single pair of ancestors. Monogenism is thus opposed to polygenism, according to which the evolutionary transition

from beast to man took place in a number of cases, though it is assumed that the starting-point in the animal world was one and the same species. Thus the differentiation of the various races of man took place solely within the biological history of humanity. But monogenism is opposed above all to a polyphylism which would derive man from various species of animals and tries to explain the difference in human races – at least to some extent – on the same terms. Or it assumes that the concrete, present-day unity of mankind is due to a long evolution from various starting-points. One also finds isolated instances of a form of monogenism which takes "pre-Adamites" into account. But there is no need to consider this here, since the hypothesis of pre-Adamites not elevated to the order of grace, who died out before the "Adam" of original sin, the head of the humanity of salvation and perdition, works with too many arbitrary and unjustifiable postulates. It is a mere theory artificially constructed to meet certain difficulties, and would imply a divine decree in which not all spiritual creatures were called to the vision of God by grace.

2. *Scripture and tradition.* a) There can be no doubt that Scripture (Gen 2:5; 3:20; Acts 17:26; Heb 2:11) speaks of Adam as numerically one. But the question is: What is the pattern of representation behind such assertions and what is really meant, what is their real statement? For in Gen 2 (ha-adam, with the article) Adam means *man*, representing thereby also a "corporate person" – mankind in its unity. This unity of origin, kinship and goal has many aspects and remains a reality even when a precisely monogenist origin is not asserted. The monogenism of Scripture can also be the imagery with which it affirms the unity of mankind as a historical reality coming from God, in salvation and perdition. More will be said later about biblical "monogenism" in connection with original sin.

b) The declarations of the magisterium, if we prescind for the moment from the doctrine of original sin as such in *Humani Generis*, simply speak like Scripture of the man Adam (e.g., *D* 101, 130, 174, 228a, 717c, 788, 790, etc.). They do not envisage any explicit position with regard to monogenism. It is undeniable that a few secondary texts (*D* 228a, 717c) go further than this. And a canon in favour of monogenism had been prepared for Vatican I, while there was also a pre-conciliar draft to the same effect at Vatican II. But it is clear from all this that no definitive decision has been given with regard to monogenism.

An explicit position with regard to modern polygenism was taken up by the encyclical *Humani Generis* of Pius XII (*D* 2328; cf. also *D* 2123). Polygenism is rejected, because and insofar as it is not at all clear how it can be reconciled ("componi queat") with the ecclesiastical doctrine of original sin. This statement bars the way to a polygenist view of the origin of mankind, as long as its compatibility with the dogma of original sin is not established. But one may well hold that in the meantime the development of Catholic theology has advanced so far that the compatibility of polygenism and the dogma of original sin has become gradually clearer. Hence in spite of *Humani Generis*, some form of polygenism may be prudently maintained.

3. *Monogenism and science.* The scientific reasons for and against the theories of monogenism and polygenism cannot be discussed here. (It should be noted that monogenism would have to be discussed on the supposition of a biological connection between man and the animal world; cf. *D* 2327.) Scientifically, the question is not yet finally decided, though scientists, who are not much interested in this particular question, mostly assume that the question has been settled in favour of polygenism, wherever the origin of man is

thought of at all in evolutionary terms. But even today there may still be many scientific arguments in favour of monogenism, when one recalls the complicated and hence certainly rare macromutations which were necessary for the genesis of man. One may also reckon with the possibility that a first pair of human beings might have been able to maintain themselves and multiply within an animal milieu. And it is impossible to draw an *empirically* clear line – by means of primitive tools, fire, upright walk, volume of the brain? – between man and the (extinct) species closest to him, on the grounds of paleontology. In favour of polygenism there is the parallel of animal evolution, where few could envisage a monogenist origin for the arrival of a new species. Then there is the fact that biologically speaking only a population can be envisaged as the milieu for the conservation and increase of the individuals of a species. Finally, it should be remembered that it is becoming more and more difficult to try to think, even hypothetically, of the "cradle" of mankind as confined to a small circle. This, however, makes the question of a form of polyphylism to some extent more serious, though the unlimited possibility of inter-marriage among men of all races makes scientists slow to envisage such a hypothesis.

4. *Monogenism and the dogma of original sin.* In the present state of the question, the one real theological problem is whether or not the dogma of original sin necessarily implies monogenism. The answer should be in the negative, and hence the declaration in *Humani Generis* (*D* 2328) should not be considered to be the definitive position of the Church. For a proper understanding of this matter, the following points should be borne in mind.

a) Even without the presupposition of a biological monogenism, mankind forms a true unity. All men have their origin in the one God with his one plan for the history of mankind and his universal salvific will, through which all individuals are already members of the one mankind in the sight of God. They have a common essence. They are all *de facto* interdependent on one another in the one spatio-temporal history. All are concretely ordained to the one Christ. All have the same goal, the kingdom of God.

b) In and through this unity, the actual religious situation of each man is co-determined by the personal decisions of all. For none remains in the mere interiority of the individual. All are inserted into the ambit of the existence of the one mankind and of men's mutual intercommunication.

c) In the history of this "situation", in which each one works out his salvation or perdition in personal freedom, there must necessarily have been a transitional phase in which a still wholly innocent mankind became a mankind living in a situation determined to some extent by the existence of guilt. Such a transition was necessary, since the "sin of the world" (Jn 1:19; 16:8; Rom 5:12f., etc.) is there, and cannot have "come into the world" through God's creative act, but only through the free will of man. Since all men are in need of salvation, this transition must have taken place at the very beginning of human history. This can and must be affirmed, even though we cannot know the concrete circumstance of this sin. It can only be postulated on account of the situation of all men "from the beginning" with regard to salvation and perdition. And we must work with a retrospective aetiology, starting with what we know to be our own situation.

d) Original sin, *peccatum originale originatum*, that is, as "inherited", means the following. (i) God gives each man sanctifying grace, as the means of salutary action, not on account of his belonging to this one race of men, but simply because of his infralapsarian ordination to Jesus Christ. (ii) This membership of the race has no (other) causal or mediatory function for the individual in the reception of grace. (iii) But humanity as such, and hence the individual, according to the original will of the creator, should have had this grace, and have mediated it to the individual by belonging to humanity. This is implied in God's will to give grace to humanity and *thereby* to each member of it. (iv) This membership of the race, which should have meant mediation of grace, has now lost its function, for mankind universally (because from the beginning) exists in a situation of freedom, one of the determinants of which is sin. (v) The absence of sanctifying grace, because contrary to the will of God, means a state of guilt, even though this state is only analogous to that which comes about through personal decision against the will of God.

e) For the establishment of this primordially guilt-laden situation of freedom, which eliminates the grace-bearing character of membership of the race for the individual, it does not matter whether it came about through the will of one individual or through the sin of many, especially as it is not the *actual* sin at the beginning which is inherited or imputed to the descendants. Ultimately, it does not much matter whether we consider the "many" of the beginning – who would be relatively few, so that their general personal guilt is not an irrational hypothesis – to have been identical with the whole of *humanitas originans* or to have formed only a group within it. For in any case, the grace of the members of *humanitas originans* who on the latter supposition would not have sinned can be understood as the grace of Christ, so that these too would have their salvation in Christ. Further, there is no need to ask here whether the sinfulness of *humanitas originans* is sufficient of itself to eliminate the grace-bearing function of membership of the human race, which is the traditional conception of original sin, or whether that sin is merely to be considered as one (specific) moment of the "sin of the world", which latter, as the totality of "original sin", is the disqualification (Schoonenberg).

f) To sum up, it may be affirmed that for the nature of original sin it does not matter whether "Adam" was an individual or a word for *humanitas originans*. It does not matter whether the sin which set up a situation of blight from the beginning was committed by an individual or by many among this *humanitas originans*. It follows that monogenism is not a necessary element of the dogma of original sin.

Karl Rahner

MONOPHYSITISM

Monophysitism is the doctrine that there is only "one nature" (φύσις, ὑπόστασις) in Christ, as developed in discussion of the relationship between Godhead and humanity in Christ from the 4th to the 6th century, chiefly on the basis of Alexandrian presuppositions. The starting-point is the kerygma about Jesus as the one Son of God become man, or the profession of faith in the true divinity and true humanity of the one Christ. Theological reflection tries to explain how this unity in diversity exists. Monophysitism (on the whole) then emphasizes, particularly in opposition to Nestorius, the oneness of Christ, to the detriment of the differences.

1. *Forms of Monophysitism*. a) *Arianism and Apollinarianism*. The Arians, at least the second generation Arians, as also the Apollinarianists, used the Logos-Sarx schema, strictly interpreted, to explain the constitution of Christ. Christ is Logos and Sarx (flesh, body) without human soul. The Logos, who is a higher, but still created being for the Arians, but God in the strict sense of Nicaea for the Apollinarianists, takes the place of the "soul" and becomes the vital principle of the flesh of Christ and

the source of all his spiritual and bodily acts. Logos and flesh together form the "one nature (*physis, hypostasis*) of the Logos incarnate" – the main formula of the "Apollinarianist-errors".

b) This Apollinarianist one-nature formula was taken up by Cyril of Alexandria in his controversy with Nestorius, but given its correct interpretation. Cyril affirms that there is a human soul and a true human nature in Christ, but does not explain the unity and difference in Christ by a distinction between person and nature. Hence this Christology remained open to Monophysite exploitation, as Eutyches and the further history of Christology were to show. Without this distinction, the "essential" or substantial unity of Christ can only be explained in terms of the natural unity found in various categories of things. This is what is intended by the patristic comparisons which suggest that the divinity and humanity in Christ are like soul and body in man, that they penetrate each other like fire and glowing iron (or coal), or like fire and wood in the "burning bush" (Cyril), or that they are merged like a drop of vinegar in the sea (Gregory of Nyssa). Since such comparisons are based on the Stoic doctrine of *krasis* (mixture), they guarantee the distinction between divinity and humanity, but remain open to misunderstanding.

c) *Classical Monophysitism.* This took shape in opposition to the Antiochene and then the Chalcedonian Christology, the doctrine of the "two natures" in Christ.

(i) *Strict Monophysitism.* Only a few theologians can be suspected of affirming a real mixture of the divinity and humanity in Christ to produce a third substance, or the absorption of the divinity in the humanity or vice versa. In most cases their formulas have been misunderstood by their opponents, as, for instance, by Leo I and the Popes of the 5th and 6th centuries. A more correct view was taken by Vigilius of Thapsus (*PL*, LXII, col. 110) and by John Damascene (*PG*, XCIV, col. 741): see *LTK*, VII, cols. 563f.

(ii) *Verbal Monophysitism.* This was upheld by theologians who were Monophysites only in the formulas which they used. They remained in fact within the framework of the pre-Chalcedonian or Cyrillic Christology. Their chief representatives are Severus of Antioch (the Severians), Philoxenus of Mabbug, Timothy Aelurus, James of Sarugh and Peter the Iberian. The deficiencies of the pre-Chalcedonian statement led to continuous splintering into sects (listed in *PG*, LXXXIII, col. 53), especially in the controversy about the passibility (natural corruptibility) of the body of Christ, which was denied by Julian of Halicarnassus (the Aphthartodocetes). A verbal Monophysitism is still maintained by the Coptic, Ethiopian, West Syrian (Jacobite) and Armenian Churches, which separated from the Byzantine Church after Chalcedon. Union with the Greek Orthodox Church is being discussed.

2. *Assessment.* a) Arian and Apollinarianist Monophysitism, with its synthesis of natures between divinity and humanity, is a strict violation of the transcendence of the Logos and a distortion of the God-world relationship. (Arius was guided by the neo-Platonist schema of ἕν – νοῦς – πνεῦμα – σώματα.)

b) But even verbal Monophysitism does not provide sufficient safeguards against a misinterpretation of the unity of divinity and humanity in Christ, as is clear from the history of Monotheletism. The only way out is the Chalcedonian doctrine of the one person (*hypostasis*) and two natures, though this too continually demands new efforts of understanding. The Chalcedonian doctrine of "inconfused and undivided" must also be applied to ward off "Monophysite" modes of thought in other theological fields, wherever in fact there is question of God and man together and the interpretation seems likely to fail to do justice to the human element. There is room for the Chalcedonian principle in such matters as the notion of the Church, inspiration (God's word in human word; inerrancy of Scripture), grace and freedom, Church and world (the autonomy of the secular), history of salvation and profane history. But a "Nestorian" division must be as carefully avoided.

Aloys Grillmeier

MONOTHEISM

Monotheism in general means an understanding of "the divine" (or the transcendent, the *numen*, the metaphysical first cause), in which its mysterious nature is represented as personal, accessible to prayer, essentially *one*, whose being is only remotely similar and comparable to the beings of the world. This description of monotheism stems from the historical forms it took in the great religions of Judaism, Christianity and Islam, where we find a notion of God which is expressed most explicitly and clearly in monotheistic terms. It is methodologically important to bear this characterization of monotheism in mind, when one takes up the much-debated problem of the origin of monotheism. Though the meaning of monotheism is most clearly expressed in the above-mentioned religions, this does not exclude the possibility of finding monotheism and monotheistic tendencies elsewhere. Meanwhile we are provided with some distinct concepts, indispensable if confusion of terminology is to be avoided in the philosophy and science of religion.

Historical research into the original form of religion started from *a priori* principles, either evolutionist or monotheistic, and led to contradictory positions. That monotheism developed out of polytheism was maintained by P. Lafitau, C. de Brosses, D. Hume, J. J. Rousseau, A. Comte, etc. B. Tylor started with animism instead of polytheism. Voltaire, however, put monotheism at the beginning. This view received confirmation through Andrew Lang, but above all through W. Schmidt and his school, who thought they could prove the existence of a primitive monotheism, in keeping with the traditional understanding of Genesis. As a result of deeper ethnological studies, the view of the historical problems is now more nuanced. It is now admitted that the widespread archaic belief in "High Gods" is not yet monotheism, since it admits the existence of other numinous beings, although on a lower level. Nor has it been proved, as R. Pettazzoni in particular has demonstrated, that belief in a High God leads on without a break to monotheism, as the evolutionary theory would have to suppose. Further, belief in the High Gods is not a uniform phenomenon. According to Pettazzoni, its predominant symbols emerged in close connection with primitive cultures and ways of social life. In the pastoral cultures the High God is the "heavenly father", at the agricultural stage "mother earth", in the presumably older stage of hunting (and collecting fruit, etc.) the "lord of the beasts". In weighing these facts, belief in the High Gods ought not to be considered apart from the fundamental attitude of their worshippers to the world, which they understood to be pervaded by the numinous. Pettazzoni points out that wherever monotheism prevailed against polytheistic (and "High God") concepts, it was always thanks to the decisive intervention of a particular religious figure (such as Zarathustra, the prophets, Jesus [?], Mohammed); and in this sense he speaks of monotheism as revolutionary (so too now Holsten and Ratzinger). This fits in with the thesis of Mensching that all monotheistic religions have been "founded" – though such foundations must not be considered as having taken place at too precise a point of time, or too deliberately launched.

Though the question of the nature of primitive religion may now be considered historically insoluble, it must be noted that Pettazzoni's thesis undoubtedly involves an element of evolution (which was always at work to bring about the revolution of monotheism). No valid arguments can be found against a theory of evolution which stresses the historical growth of monotheism, but there are strong objections to an ideological theory of evolution of a rationalist and deterministic type (as in Comte's law of three stages of progress). From the point of view accepted here, one can observe monotheistic phenomena even outside the great religions named above. But the question remains as to whether we are really dealing with monotheism and not with mere henotheism or with monistic conceptions, where the divinity is not a person or not independent. Thus it is hard to decide how far one can speak of monotheism in Egypt (Amen-hotep IV), in Socrates and Plato or in the worship of Vishnu and Shiva.

Pettazzoni's view receives a welcome confirmation from the OT. This is important theologically, as well as from the point of view of the history of religions. Israel begins with the common faith of the tribes (cf. Jos 24:13–25) in the God Yahweh. Other peoples have other gods, but Israel knows that it is bound to worship Yahweh alone ("monolatry"), whom it considers the greatest and mightiest of the gods (Exod 15:11f.; 20:3; 22:19; 23:13; Deut 4:19; 29:25; Jg 11:24; 1 Sam 26:19f., etc.). This "mono-Yahwism" (Vriezen), which is a practical monotheism, becomes theoretical monotheism under the influence of the prophetic movement (Is 40:21–28; 43:10f.; 44:8; 45:5f., 14, 21f.; 46:9, etc.). It is a "logical development" (V. Hamp, *LTK*, VII, col. 568). That the designation אֱלִילִים for the gods (Buber: "non-gods") implies their non-existence in the actual ontological sense (cf. Is 2:8, 18; 10:10f.; 19:1, 3, etc.) seems doubtful in view of the Hebrew concept of being. It is, however, possible that the impotence of the gods which is certainly expressed in this term came gradually to be understood as non-existence. The priestly writings are dominated by theoretical monotheism (cf. Gen 1:1–2:4).

Theoretical monotheism is also the doctrine of late Judaism and of the NT. In particular, it is not in the least affected by the preaching of Jesus. Jesus does not proclaim the Trinity as such explicitly, but the eschatological lordship of the one God of the world and of history. The faith and understanding of the Church (cf. Jn 14:20, 26), enlightened by Jesus' testimony to himself, discovers expressly the triune personal life of the one God. With this mystery, the faith is opposed not only to polytheism, but also to (Greek) henotheism, such as that of Plotinus, as later to Mohammed's insistence on the singleness of person in Allah.

Christian monotheism therefore appears always as trinitarian; but the principle of unity remains inviolate, all the more so as it is fundamental to ecclesiology (cf. Eph 4:5f.). However, the dogmatic assertions *De Deo uno* and *De Deo trino* must also be taken together because otherwise the Christian faith can easily degenerate into a monotheism of the type favoured by Deism, where the one God appears as "the supreme being". Further, the trinitarian structure of monotheism prevents a misunderstanding of the personal nature of God such as can arise when analogy is disregarded. Many objections against theism and monotheism (cf., for instance, J. A. T. Robinson) seem in fact to pay no attention to the principle of analogy. The comparison between the divine and the human person is pushed so far that no dissimilarity is allowed for, and then theism is found to be a scandal. However, distaste for a monotheism which represents God anthropomorphically as a super-person is perfectly justified;

Tillich warns us against allowing monotheism to sink to the level of a "henotheistic mythology".

From all this it follows that from the point of view of the philosophy of religion, the monotheistic position is by no means obvious. The intuitions of metaphysics show no doubt "monistic" leanings. The unity of the ontological principle of being has always been maintained in Western thought since the pre-Socratic philosophers, against the temptations of dualism. Monotheism therefore has the support of metaphysics, inasmuch as by discussing, for instance, the problem of the proof of the existence of God, it has helped to create a type of thinking which leads in formal metaphysics to the concept of a "mono-archy" or single principle of being. It can hardly be maintained, however, that philosophy itself, without recourse to theological or perhaps mythological sources, attains the concept of God as a person in the sense of a fully-constituted monotheism. Nor is one obliged to deduce from *D* 1785 that philosophy does so. Philosophy can concede the personal nature of the transcendent, inasmuch as the principle of the human person's existence must itself, as is clear, actually have within itself that which constitutes a person. But since this consideration presupposes the concept of the human person, which could not have been attained in philosophy without the help of Christianity, it seems that philosophy stops half-way along the road to the solution of the problem. Hence the most that can be done in philosophy with the opponents of monotheism is to persuade them to acknowledge a metaphysical monoarchy. That this points on to monotheism as its goal can only be seen by reflection on a religious experience of a certain type. This thesis corresponds to the findings of the history of religions, according to which monotheism was not the result of correct philosophical thinking, but the fruit of a historic revolutionary struggle, carried on with passion in the field of religion.

Heinz Robert Schlette

MORALITY

I. Concept

The way the good is experienced depends to a large extent on the fundamental structure of the environment, society and community and on the whole view of life. The derivation of the word "morality", as a comprehensive term for the human good, from the *mores*, customs, reflects a historical situation in which a uniform social milieu was universally recognized as setting the standard. A person who allowed himself to be guided by prevailing custom was moral. That does not necessarily mean that no interest was taken in the good as such. It may reflect the more or less well-founded confidence that tradition and society are men's best guides to the knowledge of the good. Regard for prevailing custom can gradually become an expression of responsibility for the community if the concept of morality and the way it is experienced are broadened and deepened.

Even narrower than the identification of *mores* and morality is the juridical misconception of morality. This places legal norms and sanctions in the forefront of "moral" consciousness and conduct: what is morally necessary must be imposed by law and enforced under supervision; what is not subject to legal sanction is not regarded as morally important. Similar to this misconception is a one-sided emphasis on priestly supervision by means of laws and casuistic models which make it possible to tell everyone what he must do, and which above all make it possible to supervise and measure morality. What is mistaken here is not that this concept of morality attributes value to law and legal sanction and supervision, but that morality is almost exclusively identified with it.

The good or morality only comes fully into view when there is a genuine experience of conscience. This occurs when the human person, endowed with reason, and free, becomes aware of the claim of the good, the liberating and joyous character of goodness for its own sake, a claim made by what ought to be even apart from prevailing custom or sanctions.

1. *The claim of conscience.* Conscience is more than a central office which records, with or without temporal sanctions, that "one" does this and avoids that. In his conscience a human being experiences existentially – in a way which demands a real emergence, *ex-sistere*, from narrow egotism – that his own integrity, wholeness and authenticity are bound up with the good and the claim it makes. "Conscience is the most secret core and sanctuary of a man. There he is alone with God, whose voice echoes in his depths" (*Gaudium et Spes*, art. 16). In the experience of conscience man is aware of his inner conflict if he does not obey the claim of the known good. In peace of conscience he experiences something of the beatitude of those who listen to the voice of the true and the good and put it into effect, and the misery of the refusal of the good and of action contrary to his understanding of the good.

Where there is an honest search for the true and the good, there is genuine morality, even in the case of error. "Conscience frequently errs from invincible ignorance without losing its dignity. The same cannot be said of a man who cares but little for truth and goodness, or of a conscience which by degrees grows practically sightless as a result of habitual sin" (*ibid.*, art. 16).

One of the important questions is: how does man come to know the good? A particularly important part is played by persons who rank as models and by the values and norms convincingly lived and protected in society. But the knowledge does not come from outside in a purely intellectual way. Man's conscience recognizes the good in a way which expresses his own intimate bond with it in freedom. "In a wonderful manner conscience reveals that law which is fulfilled by love of God and neighbour" (*ibid.*). The fundamental value is always the human person with his or her capacity for love and the relation between person and society. All genuine norms of morality express the essential requirements of love and justice. Since morality is always ultimately concerned with the relations between human beings, and between person and society, it is inevitable that the moral knowledge of the individual will largely depend on the moral level of his milieu. A merely servile submission to prevalent custom and legal sanctions is, however, not the true expression of men's conscientious obligation. Genuine enrichment through custom, example and law occurs where obligation arises in an upright search for the true and good. "In fidelity to conscience, Christians are joined with the rest of men in the search for truth and for the genuine solution to the numerous moral problems" (*ibid.*).

2. *Religion and morality.* Since the experience of conscience is an inescapable one, the question arises as to what justification there is for the claim of the good. What connection is there between that part of morality which regulates a man's relation to other persons, to the community and to himself, and the religious mystery? It cannot be denied that the claim of moral value and duty is also experienced by human beings who have not yet or not yet fully found their way to faith in a personal God. Phenomenologically – in the realm of experience – morality is not always expressly connected with the "holy", with religion. But no explanation of morality is satisfying or leaves its deepest experience intact if it omits or indeed denies the link between religion and

morality. In genuine moral experience a human being who is prepared on principle to live according to conscience, is not ultimately dealing with a mere principle or merely concerned with his own fulfilment. He knows that ultimately he is in relation with a Thou who can unconditionally give and demand.

3. *Characteristics of Christian morality.* The depth and authenticity of the experience of conscience and of actual moral practice link the Christian with all human beings who seek and strive honestly and conscientiously. Nevertheless Christian morality has a distinguishing characteristic which is not found, or only implicitly, outside the Christian faith. The believer experiences moral obligation wholly and entirely in the light of God's gift, the light of God's grace and love. It is an obligation under the lordship of God who is wholly and entirely love and who wills to save and direct the world by his grace and love in his only-begotten Son. Moral obligation is experienced as a call to imitation, and in such a way that obligation can never be the primary factor. What is fundamental is the gift of God's friendship and sonship, the love and attractiveness of Christ's personality as ideal and model. It is a morality of the imitation of Christ, of close communion with him in life and love; a morality of the covenant, in which the fact that the covenant is freely bestowed is the most pressing motive for fidelity to the covenant; a morality of fellowship (κοινωνία), in which consent to the covenant with God is united with consent to the people of the covenant. The Lord of the covenant wills that we should show our love for him above all by love of our neighbour and by sharing in responsibility for the welfare of the people of the covenant. The morality of the new covenant includes a mission and obligation in regard to all men. NT morality rests even more clearly than that of the OT on a faith which bears fruit in love, for the life of the world. Morality, like faith, is dialogue and response. Man exists and truly attains his identity in speech and in love, in hearing and perceiving, in loving response and responsibility.

Fundamentally the Christian does not stand under a regime of law, but of grace (Rom 6:14). Seen in a Christian way, therefore, morality is dynamic like God's giving, and like God's self-revelation which impels to a response of love and adoration. The measure of obligation, the living norm, is given simultaneously with the measure of grace, of the genuine possibilities bestowed. Consequently for Christian morality those commandments that concern the goal, which indicate the obligatory direction, are more characteristic than the limiting precepts which state the minimum or limit beyond which a complete contradiction to the essence of true love and justice becomes plain. Morality in the full sense means a perpetual journey. Self-satisfaction and self-righteousness contradict the nature of man and of human society, which is to change and develop. Since we stand in the tension between the sinfulness of man (the old aeon) and his redeemed condition (the new aeon), morality understood in a Christian way means not only constant striving, but also to some extent a constant, a constantly deeper conversion. Human morality is characterized by man's historical situation. Consequently there is no closed system of natural law, though of course, as well as his permanently and essentially temporal and historical character, man has other enduring essential features and relationships.

In concrete terms, the natural moral law is the reality of man as temporal, historical and living in society, with his concrete possibility of self-knowledge and consequently of knowledge of the good. Since man historically is always in movement, so too morality, man's knowledge of morality, its function and mode of realization, are always in movement. Both the factor of continuity and that of discontinuity have to be kept in view. There are far-reaching conversions of individuals and of whole societies which represent a most fortunate discontinuity. But there is also the possibility of the decline and decay of morality.

A Christian understanding of morality includes both an ethics of interior disposition and an ethos of responsibility. Interior disposition and intention is more radical and decisive than any particular action. But since genuine intention essentially implies openness to others and the community and to every value, a genuine ethics of intention and disposition is inconceivable without the spirit of responsibility, readiness to devote oneself to others and to the community. Anyone who grasps the importance of the whole environment for morality cannot envisage a genuine reform of men's dispositions without striving for a corresponding reform of existing conditions.

4. *Dialogue with secularized morality.* In view of the universalist tendency of the ethics of the new covenant and in view of the pluralist and largely secularized state of mankind, what is chiefly needed is for us to work out those aspects of Christian morality which unite us with all the valuable aspirations of the secularized world and which may promote dialogue and collaboration. These points of contact consist chiefly of concern for man, for human things, because morality is always a consequence of the conception we have of man. We might also mention the desire for unity in multiplicity, for solidarity, for the development of all men, the consciousness of movement and change, a historical conception of humanity and morality and, not least, respect for honest conscience.

Bernhard Häring

II. Moral Law

When we think of the moral law, we are led to ask what is the force of the word "law" in this context. Originally law (Greek νόμος, Latin *lex*) was an ordinance (command) directed to the wills of the citizens, regulating their lives as a community and claiming their strict adherence while leaving it possible for them to disobey (enacted, "practical" law). Later the notion of God, who as supreme power orders and directs not only the lives of all men, but also the entire universe (OT, Stoa), led to the idea of a law, not subject to human will, which regulates directly all nature and events, so that the idea of deriving it from God's special decree became secondary or disappeared entirely (law of being itself, "theoretical" law). The strict binding force of law in the first definition is paralleled here by the completeness of its validity (actual effectiveness).

The moral law can be taken theologically or philosophically. Theologically the Decalogue presents itself as moral law; and here it is enacted, practical ordinance (moral commandment). Mostly, however, moral law is taken to mean an ordinance, the content of which does indeed correspond to the chief commandments of the Decalogue, but the justification for which is independent of the Christian faith, and which is recognizable by all men and valid for all. Thus it is of a philosophical nature. The content is then derived, not from the decree of another coming from without (command), but rather from the nature of things, which includes a law in the theoretical sense and which the individual sees as presenting a valid claim on his will.

The moral law so understood was at first and for a long time discussed under the name of *lex naturae* or *lex naturalis* (natural moral law). St. Thomas Aquinas developed what was to become the classical doctrine on the subject from beginnings made in antiquity (Plato, Aristotle, Stoa, Cicero). The following account takes up the Thomistic teaching and develops it critically with the use of modern terms. The law of being which is at the basis of all doctrine of the moral law is given by the structure of human action. According to St. Thomas, this consists in the fact that all action springs from a desire (*appetitus*) of the subject, aimed at securing a missing good (*bonum*) as a state of being (*ens*). The activity is therefore directed towards self-perfection (*perfectio*). The *bonum* in question has a) as *ens*, the character of a *perfectum* (i.e., in modern terms, an "absolute", "self-contained" value, Scheler, N. Hartmann), b) insofar as it leads the being of the subject towards *perfectio*, that of a *perfectivum* (i.e., a "relative", "need-filling" value, Scheler, Hartmann, Reiner), c) insofar as the *appetitus* is desirous of fulfilment, that of *appetibile*. The *bona* desired by the *appetitus* in this context range from the simplest pleasure to the highest practice of virtue. The goal of the *appetitus*, and therefore of all activity, is the entire satisfaction of all desire, and includes the elimination of all personal, ontological deficiencies, *beatitudo*. The *ratio* must decide in the light of this ultimate goal in cases of conflict among various immediate goals.

Consideration for the nature of others and their needs or natural deficiencies and indeed regard for God himself, come in this system only indirectly into play by way of the effort (under the direction and positive impetus of the *ratio*) towards the inner perfection of *one's own act* seeking its appropriate (*conveniens*) external object, or through the call that comes with the notion of law (with a break-through as regards the initial principle) to direct one's activity to securing the common good (*bonum commune*). However, even our natural sympathies tell us that the good or bad fortune of other people, even strangers that cross our path, call directly too for their own sake for our active response; and Jesus taught this expressly (e.g., in the parable of the Good Samaritan, Lk 10:33ff.). The Christian also knows that he must seek God and serve him loyally, for his sake and not only as a means to his own perfection and happiness.

From this it follows that *bonum* as *perfectivum* is to be sought both for the sake of one's own *perfectio* (*bonum proprium*), i.e., as a "personally relative" value, meeting personal needs (Reiner), and also as *bonum alterius* with the purpose of the *perfectio* of the other, i.e., as a value "relative to the other", as a "fulfilment of the needs of the other". Further, *bonum* as *perfectum* ("absolute value") can be the object of action insofar as we seek to preserve, protect, respect or honour it (e.g., the glory of God). Thirdly, the general definition of *bonum* as *appetibile* is thereby seen to be untenable, since this is only indirectly true of the *bonum perfectivum alterius* and not at all of the *bonum perfectum* in another person. Rather, in view of our evaluation, *bonum* in general must be considered as *laetabile* (delightful, gratifying). In the case of *bonum* as *perfectum* (absolute value), its existence is in itself gratifying and in the case of *bonum* as *perfectivum* (relative value), its possession. The absolute values are, then, apart from concrete *entia* such as people, animals or works of art, certain qualities or ideal states of being such as the virtues or the law. At the same time we find a double relationship of the *bona* to the acting subject. Inasmuch as a *bonum* is considered as *bonum proprium* (personally relative value), it has an *attractive* quality; inasmuch as it presents itself in the form of a *bonum alterius* (value relative to another) or as a *bonum perfectum* (absolute value) it *demands* (respect, realization or protection).

The objects of desire (*bona* as *appetibilia*, relative values, fulfilling needs) normally also serve the natural purpose of self-preservation or self-realization (*perfectio*) or the preservation of the species, and thereby serve the realization of absolute values, though they are not primarily or usually sought after for this purpose. Indeed they do not even in all cases promote this purpose; they can be indifferent with regard to it or an obstacle to it; thus, for example, eating and drinking to excess or just for the satisfaction of the palate, or to satisfy harmful desires which are not natural but acquired, for example the habit of smoking. Here our needs aim at values (*bona*), which, since they serve only our own satisfaction, are "only subjectively significant" and therefore capable of being forgone. On the other hand, the value desired has "objective" significance insofar as it claims our will either as a value for others (*bonum alterius*, value relative to others) or as an "absolute", "self-contained" value (*bonum* as *perfectum* or *quoad se*). Thomism has met this situation only imperfectly (through the distinction of *verum* and *apparens bonum*).

In this situation the demand arises, whenever we are in a position to work with some prospect of success for values objectively important for reality, that we do this, even if it requires a sacrifice of values which are only subjectively significant. If we act accordingly, our behaviour is good, if not, it is evil. Evil usually occurs in the pursuit of a value that is only of subjective importance, i.e., from "egoism". In rarer cases there is "evil" strictly speaking: an objectively important value is destroyed for its own sake. Hence the difference between good and evil is dependent on the will and even the most limited intelligence is conscious of this.

In many cases, however, there is a question of choice between a number of objectively significant values. Here the choice does not essentially lie with the will and is thus not really a choice between good and evil, but a matter of sound judgment of what is morally right. This is determined partly from general points of view such as the level, number or urgency of the values on either side, and partly from individual or personal capabilities or concrete prospects of success. What then appears to be morally right is spontaneously done as long as subjectively important values do not intervene. But to decide what is objectively moral, there is often need of prudence and of experience. Also in many questions the help of various sciences such as economics, sociology, medicine and psychology is needed. Such questions (e.g., whether the charging of interest is justified, whether co-education is to be recommended, whether craniotomy or atomic armaments are morally justifiable) are partly to be dealt with in special or supplementary disciplines such as economic ethics, medical ethics, pedagogy, or moral casuistry. Since the facts with which these questions are concerned are subject to historical change, the method of treatment needs to be examined and renewed from time to time. Even with this, there still remains, as far as individual aspects of what is morally right are concerned, a residue not capable of being handled in a general way and this gives situation ethics its very limited justification.

But the distinction between what is morally right and wrong can now be connected with the distinction between good and evil. This happens when, in the choice between several objectively important values, a subjectively important value is connected with one of them. Then the question as to which is the morally right choice takes on this form: Is the choice which includes the subjectively important value morally *permissible* or not? This it is, if the value with only subjective importance is connected with the objective value which is judged to be preferable. But my choice is morally good only if I make it for the sake of the objectively important value, and morally worthless (yet morally correct and in itself not evil) if I choose it solely for the sake of the subjectively important value. If, on the other hand, the subjectively important value is connected with the value that is objectively not preferable, then the action directed towards it is not permissible, and my choice of it is not only morally wrong but also evil.

The "natural" moral law derived in this way gets not only its content but also the gravity of its obligation in the first instance from the importance of the real goals and consequences which present themselves to our eyes to be attained or avoided. The importance and binding force of the law varies according to the nature of these goals. In many cases too we expect others to act along these lines, thus expressly or implicitly recognizing the validity of the demands made. We are then bound to them ourselves with at least the same strictness with which we make such definite demands on others, e.g., that they respect (our) property (Reiner: *Die goldene Regel*). For Christians finally this obligation is supplemented and essentially strengthened by the majesty of the creative will of God.

Hans Reiner

MORAL THEOLOGY

I. Catholic

Since some people regard the casuistic and canonist text-books of moral theology as a permanent and classical expression of Catholicism, we must first note that the Church managed for more than fifteen hundred years not only without that type of moral theology, but even without moral theology as a separate discipline at all. Was the Church less perfect or less concerned for the authenticity of Christian life when it did not possess any self-contained branch of study of that kind?

Scripture does not resemble a text-book of dogmatic theology nor one of the classical handbooks of moral theology. It demonstrates in concrete history the radical unity of the truth of salvation and the way of salvation, of the good news and the summons to a life in harmony with the good news. Of course there are shorter or longer passages in Scripture chiefly concerned with instructions on conduct, e.g., the Decalogue in the OT or the Sermon on the Mount in the NT. But even passages containing direct moral teaching are characterized by the way they combine covenant and law of the covenant, saving event, saving truth and way of salvation.

In the patristic period, teaching about Christian conduct was mainly presented during the preparation for baptism and the Eucharist. Typical examples are the catecheses attributed to Cyril (or John) of Jerusalem on the sacraments, and on a Christian life corresponding to the sacramental reality. None of the great Fathers of the Church or of the medieval theologians can be termed a moral theologian or even a moralist in the modern sense of the word. Perhaps Gregory the Great might be regarded to some extent as an exception. He did not draw up a complete system of moral theology or aim at doing so, but his interest was predominantly directed to practical questions of conduct and concrete spiritual difficulties.

1. *Antecedents of moral theology*. The early Middle Ages saw the rise of the *libri paenitentiales*, chiefly within the sphere of influence of the Irish Church, and in the late Middle Ages the *summae confessariorum* quickly became popular. But no one thought of regarding these as handbooks of Christian morals. The former were exclusively concerned with the amount of penance to be imposed, the latter were mostly alphabetically arranged reference books for confessors, containing questions of canon law and doctrine, and solutions to cases of conscience.

Long before moral theology, moral philosophy developed in the Middle Ages, chiefly by discussion of Aristotelian ethics. The Fathers themselves, e.g., Clement of Alexandria or Ambrose, had drawn on Stoic ethics or developed their own ideas in critical confrontation with the Stoics. Thomas Aquinas represents a decisive turning-point. On the one hand he embodies the whole previous development in a synthesis in which saving truth and way of salvation are dealt with together. On the other hand he gives a systematic treatment of many moral questions in the Second Part of the *Summa*, basing himself to a large extent on Aristotelian ethics. But Aquinas had no thought at all of presenting this part of his *Summa Theologica* as an independent treatise on Christian ethics. This part of the *Summa* has meaning and function only as part of a systematic presentation of theology as an indivisible unity. Many questions, e.g., the virtue of penance and the whole morality of marriage, are dealt with in the Third Part in connection with the sacraments. The influence of St. Thomas was at first considerably restricted because of the condemnation of his works by the Bishop of Paris. After the Thomist renaissance of the 16th century, however, a development of moral theology took place in which currents as various as the *libri paenitentiales*, the *summae confessariorum* and the predominantly Aristotelian perspective of the Second Part of the *Summa Theologica* converged. The difference between these currents was very considerable, but they had one feature in common: the almost total absence of Christ. Aquinas cannot be held responsible for this, for he did not regard the Second Part of the *Summa Theologica* as in any way an independent structure. Nevertheless, at the end of this development we can with justice ask whether it was really appropriate to deal in the *Summa* with fundamental questions of Christian morals, before Christ had been presented as the way, the truth and the life.

2. *History of moral theology*. The actual history of the moral theology which is so often referred to as traditional begins in fact after the Council of Trent. This very fact obviously presents an ecumenical problem of the first order. In the course of the Catholic reform, the Council of Trent gave a new impulse, new forms and prescriptions for the administration and reception of the sacrament of penance. Confession of all grave sins before reception of the Eucharist, their accusation according to species and number, were inculcated afresh. The chief purpose of the Tridentine seminary was to train good confessors.

The *Ratio studiorum* of the Society of Jesus met the new situation by introducing a special course of moral casuistry for confessors. The great perspectives of Christian conduct at first continued to be dealt with in conjunction with the truths of faith, within a theology regarded as an indivisible unity. But more and more a new systematization grew up, centred on questions concerning the practice of the confessional. Very soon theologians, now called dogmatic theologians, excused themselves from handling questions of Christian conduct on the plea that this after all was dealt with in casuistry, i.e., in moral theology.

In accordance with the special purpose of this new type of moral science, the chief concern was how cases of conscience were to be decided by the confessor, and what and how the penitent had to confess. Consequently conscience became the focus of attention, but in a quite special sense and in a very typical mentality. Sometimes the Thomist perspective, directed towards the *finis ultimus*, final fulfilment, was extrinsically linked with this new type. But since one of the main purposes of this new discipline was the regulation of decisions of conscience by the confessor, the question of the static, legal norm inevitably came to the fore. Hence the problem of legal obligation in cases of doubt assumed disproportionate importance in the controversy concerning moral systems.

3. *Presuppositions of traditional moral theology*. It need hardly be emphasized

how much the whole outlook of moral doctrine was bound to be affected once it was directed towards the confessional. Furthermore, the conception of the role of confessor and penitent was coloured by the historical context. Theology in all ages necessarily has a function within the history of redemption; it has to answer the practical questions of contemporaries in a system of concepts which are intelligible to them. Theology inevitably bears the mark of its age. In order to understand the radical changes in the whole conception of moral theology, we must be fully aware of the actual environment of theology at any given time. Only the most important lines can be indicated here.

A significant part was played by the prevailing style of social life and authority of the period. The age in which the style of casuistic moral theology was established was characterized by the patriarchal family and a paternalism accepted with real gratitude. In the family, the father ruled more or less as the sole authority. The cultural and social élites were not numerous. The great majority of people had no idea of rising socially or culturally. It was the accepted thing for responsibility to be in the hands of a few. A combination of feudalism, absolutism and centralism prevailed to a large extent. The Counter-Reformation, the more or less static nature of the social order and the tendency of the clergy and of the dominant social élites generally to support the *status quo*, encouraged a static view of moral doctrine. This explains the way in which the question of conscience was envisaged chiefly within the perspective of exact obedience to law and the orders of superiors. In addition there was the lasting influence of the Roman doctrine of natural law and of the ancient Germanic ideal of a retainer's absolute fidelity. The doctrine of the natural moral law had been worked out in Greece and in Rome chiefly within the horizon of the State and in the political interest of its preservation. It is not surprising that moralists had recourse so readily to the old doctrine of natural law, in text-books orientated to the sacrament of penance.

The identification of the Church with the hierarchy (or, at best, with the clergy) worked in the same direction. The Church appeared more evidently present in its own statutory enactments than in the gospel. All this explains the frequently quite uncritical juxtaposition of canonical precepts, State laws, principles of natural law and quotations from the Bible. This state of affairs was very appropriately indicated by H. Jone in the title of his moral theology: *Moral Theology with special reference to Canon Law and German, Austrian and Swiss Law*. Legally established structures were very much in the foreground in this type of moral theology.

On the other hand, it must be remembered that the best representatives of this type of moral theology did a great deal to make legal burdens and restrictions more endurable. This purpose was served by the appeal to natural law in opposition to the arbitrary will of princes, by the theory of the purely penal law and by the "moral system" of probabilism.

Emphasis and viewpoint were largely determined by the themes of the Reformation and the spirit of the Counter-Reformation. While on one side the slogans were "faith alone", and "grace alone", the legalistic type of Catholic moral theology almost completely avoided speaking of the relation between faith and its fruits. There was a one-sided emphasis on the works of the law, and grace was only mentioned incidentally, as far as it was a help to fulfil the requirements of the law. It was typical that morals were not dealt with in the light of the Sermon on the Mount, but that the Decalogue was expounded first, then the sacraments, the latter almost exclusively from the point of view of a new set of duties. If the Reformers one-sidedly stressed "Scripture alone", moralists of the Roman type took the decretals of the Popes and formulations of natural law as almost the sole starting-point. If the Reformers stressed the universal priesthood of the people of God, the Catholic moralists laid all the more stress on the subordination of the laity to hierarchy and confessor. An individualistic trend of thought, which also found expression in the religious sphere, for example in the leitmotiv "Save your soul", was counterbalanced by legal controls and sanctions, while the individualistic attitude itself was an over-compensation for legalism.

The security complex of a society and Church preoccupied with self-defence produced a kind of collective scrupulosity, exemplified, among other things, by the concentration of the energies of several generations of moral theologians on the set of problems connected with the moral systems, and in particular by tutiorism and probabiliorism. Under the menacing ubiquity of the Inquisition and later, in rather milder form, of the Holy Office, and with the very strict civil and ecclesiastical censorship, little room was left for creative thought. The great figures of the patristic era, and above all St. Thomas Aquinas, had engaged in fruitful dialogue with the intellectual currents of their age, but now it was considered "safer" to hold fast to traditional formulas. Even the theses of the natural moral law often did not incorporate new knowledge of human history, psychology, sociology and anthropology. It was considered "safer" to cling to traditional formulas and solutions. And so the gap widened between moral theology and the attitude to life and human problems of the scientific age.

In reaction against the Reformation, emphasis was laid on the official priesthood and the religious state. The inherited privileges of the clergy were maintained in an outmoded class-society. Hence little question was raised about dividing off moral from ascetic and mystical theology. The former was for the laity, who were to be guided by the law, the latter for members of the "state of perfection" who had somehow monopolized the vocation to perfection.

It must be emphasized, however, that this development in the Catholic Church was never unopposed, and was subjected to a certain amount of correction. It is sufficient to point to the French school of spirituality in the circle of Cardinal Bérulle; here the sacraments as signs of grace and love occupied a fundamental place in the whole perspective of the Christian life of all. Alphonsus Liguori, whose vast *Theologia Moralis* belongs to the classical type of moral treatise for confessors, wrote several very widely-read works on the Christian life, addressed to all Christians and characteristically based on the Augustinian principle: *Dilige et fac quod vis*, e.g., *La pratica di amare Gesù Cristo* (E.T.: *The Practice of the Love of Jesus Christ* [1854]). In Germany in particular, under the influence of the Enlightenment and then of the Romantic Movement and of a first early springtime of ecumenism, a quite different type of moral theology arose. This deliberately engaged in dialogue with the intellectual currents of the age and the concerns of the Protestant Churches, and consequently took more account of biblical foundations. Among the numerous pioneers it is sufficient to mention Johann Michael Sailer, Johann Baptist Hirscher and Magnus Jocham. Unfortunately they could not exercise any lasting influence beyond the borders of Germany. Even in German-speaking territories the Latin type once again gained the upper hand in the second half of the 19th century, if we leave out of account a few great individuals such as Franz Xaver Linsenmann, whose great concern was the Pauline conception of freedom and the "law of the spirit". Pioneers of a renewal in moral theology in the present century, such as Joseph Mausbach, Otto Schilling and, in a quite special way, Theodor Steinbüchel and Fritz Tillmann, could link up with a great tradition.

4. *The new presuppositions of moral theology*. Vatican II marks the transition to a new epoch in moral theology just as plainly as it does to a renewed understanding by the Church of its own nature. In order to comprehend this changed awareness and to recognize more fully the direction in which efforts are being made, it is necessary to take account of the new context, the new world, in which and for which moral theology will have to perform its function. Johann Michael Sailer addressed his *Handbuch der Christlichen Moral* (1817) not only to "future pastors" but also and equally to "all educated Christians", as he said significantly in the subtitle. The decisive perspective of the moral theology of today and tomorrow is no longer the confessor and confession alone, but the Christian as such, the people of God on pilgrimage, striving for maturity and solidarity.

On the one hand the "discernment of what is Christian" in face of the pluralist, partly unbelieving world of today becomes more urgent than it was in a society which regarded itself as Christian. At the same time, in relation to the Eastern Christians and the Churches which owe their origin to the Reformation, the emphasis falls more on what is common than on what separates. And the discernment of what is Christian will have to be pursued in such a way as to promote dialogue with all as far as possible. Even in the necessary rejection of atheism, the chief concern will be to investigate and overcome the hidden forms of unbelief in ourselves, in our formulas and our conduct, that is, to seek the causes of unbelief and remove them as far as possible. A moral theology intended to promote dialogue and serve in the conduct of life in a pluralist Christendom and world, will exhibit much greater breadth and variety, despite the unity given by faith, than a morality of the confessional which corresponded to a Mediterranean culture and a Church intent on maintaining the status quo.

In a world of specialization and differentiation of functions, of management and the machine, the part of mankind which will decide the future is experiencing a positive thirst for totality, unity and synthesis, for an existentiell and personalist conception of life. Any effective presentation of moral theology will have to take this into account. Only those who base themselves on and are inspired by this kind of experience of life will be capable of sketching a moral theology which will influence such people. In this sphere of synthesis it will be a question of rethinking the great themes of post-Tridentine theology: creation and redemption, faith and reason, gospel and natural law, grace and the historical nature of man.

"The human race has passed from a rather static concept of reality to a more dynamic, evolutionary one" (Vatican II, Pastoral Constitution on the Church in the Modern World, art. 5). This will have to find expression in the whole presentation of moral theology. One of the fundamental themes will be: flexibility and fidelity in regard to the living God, the Lord of history. Hence, fundamental ideas such as readiness for change, growth, constant conversion, renewal, reform of structures, reconciliation, courage to take risks, will receive a new tone and emphasis and find a new place in the whole.

Students of the Bible and of the natural law are becoming more and more conscious of the history and historicity of man. Readers, observers and thinkers are fully aware of the context. More and more efforts will be made to exploit anthropology, cultural studies, psychology, and sociology, especially the sociology of knowledge, for the Christian view of man and therefore for Christian ethics. Despite our emphasis on the absolute uniqueness of God's revelation in Jesus Christ, there is a sense in which we can speak of a continuing revelation of God in his work, in history; for God's works bear the character of speech, message, summons. The language is obscured in many ways by our sins, and so we can only interpret it in the light of the revelation in Jesus Christ and in docility to the Holy Spirit. The question of how we can understand the "signs of the times" is of fundamental urgency.

Modern sociology and social psychology have taught us the power of the environment. We shall speak less abstractly of the "salvation of the soul" or of the "soul" itself. Our theme will be man in society and in the world. Sin will not be regarded solely as the transgression of a commandment or as a refusal of the gracious call of the Holy Spirit, but also as being carried away by the unenlightened environment, as lack of responsibility for the world, as enslavement to the collective powers of darkness. The result of redemption will be displayed by sensitiveness to the longing of creation for the freedom of the children of God, by a good use of individual and communal freedom in our own milieu, and by the responsible shaping of personal and social relationships and structures.

5. *The self-understanding of the Church and moral theology.* The casuistic and legalistic moral theology sprang to a large extent from a mainly institutional and static conception of the Church, and crystallized and confirmed that conception. Similarly, the renewal of moral theology during the last thirty years probably contributed to the view of the Church which gained authority at Vatican II. This will be reflected in the moral theology of the coming age.

If the Church views itself essentially as a fellowship of love, devoted in faith to Christ and gratefully docile to the action of the Holy Spirit, moral theology will clearly confess Christ as centre, and honour the Holy Spirit, who wills to mould our life into conformity with Christ, as the decisive reality in the law of Christ, and it will comprise everything in the gift and task of love. If the Church understands itself in its dedication to Christ as the sanctified, priestly, messianic people of God, the chief subject of moral theology will be "the sublimity of the vocation of the faithful in Christ" (Vatican II, Decree on Priestly Formation, art. 16). The whole of morals must be stamped by the truth of faith, that those who are "in Christ" allow themselves to be led by the Spirit of Christ and so have chosen Christ as their true law. Christ is the summons which gathers them together. Anointed by the Spirit, a sacrificial victim in the Holy Spirit and glorified by the power of the Holy Spirit, he gives the Church and each believer life and unity. Moral theology must mirror the following central truth of ecclesiology: "In their diversity all bear witness to the admirable unity of the Body of Christ. This very diversity of graces, ministries and works gathers the children of God into one, because 'all these things are the work of one and the same Spirit' (1 Cor 12:11)" (Vatican II, Dogmatic Constitution on the Church, art. 32).

The institutional side of the Church, law, administration, use of earthly means, need to be tested. The norms are the presence of the Holy Spirit grasped in faith, and the mission of manifesting Christ's love to all. So too moral theology must be careful to explain the meaning and correct use of the explicitly formulated law within the decisive perspective of the dynamic presence of Christ and of the operation of the Holy Spirit.

The Church understands itself to be a community adoring and loving in faith and as such sent to serve man and world. A purely intellectual conception of faith has been superseded as a result of the biblical and liturgical renewal. That will benefit moral theology in a quite special way. Dogmatic theology is gradually finding its full dynamic relation to life, and moral theology is returning to a clearly grasped and articulate basis in a dynamic conception of faith. Consequently future moral theology, in close association with the Bible and the Fathers, will once again represent the "law of faith" (cf. Rom 3:27–31), that faith which "bears fruit in love for the life of the world" (Decree on Priestly Formation, art. 16).

The Church began its work of renewal in Vatican II by giving new life to the liturgy, overcoming a dangerous formalism and legalism in the liturgy. The conclusion of the Council was the Pastoral Constitution on the Church in the Modern World. It is probably true to say that a view of moral theology which takes as its starting-point the saving mysteries (i.e., the sacraments viewed in the widest sense, with Christ as the primordial sacrament), and regards the people of God as the *sacramentum mundi*, will be more and more widely accepted. The Church knows that it is on pilgrimage, as the eschatological community of salvation seeking to interpret the signs of the times in gratitude for the great saving events, and with its eyes turned towards the expected fulfilment. The eschatological hope itself causes it to take very seriously the service of man here and now. In this respect moral theology will represent a holy secular spirit and will work out standards by which this can be distinguished from unholy worldliness and godless unworldliness. A morality rooted in the sacraments will to a large extent rid itself of an unhealthy preoccupation with juridical validity and will link more closely the sacraments and bearing witness before the world. The sacraments of salvation impose an obligation on the whole people of God to combine the message of eternal salvation with opportune concern for the well-being of man and his world.

Moral theology after Vatican II is not only addressed to the laity, but requires their collaboration. Only if laymen with a thorough knowledge of the various spheres of life and of modern knowledge in all its branches collaborate in the further development and renewal of moral theology, can it make close contact with real contemporary life. "It is to be hoped that many laymen will receive an appropriate formation in the sacred sciences and that some will develop and deepen these studies by their own labours" (Pastoral Constitution on the Church in the Modern World, art. 62).

In all ages Christian morality is distinguished by the fact that faith is a response, a dialogue relationship. The dynamic and pluralist character of our present society demands in a quite special way a morality of responsibility. This is only possible if the necessary measure of freedom is permitted to the moral theologians who bear such a heavy responsibility and if there is also candid mutual criticism. "In order that such persons may fulfil their proper function, let it be recognized that all the faithful, clerical and lay, possess a lawful freedom of inquiry and thought, and the freedom to express their minds humbly and courageously about those matters in which they enjoy competence" (*ibid.*).

Bernhard Häring

II. Protestant

Ethics, as treated in Protestant theology, offers at first sight no very consistent picture. The specific interest taken by the Reformation in this matter showed itself above all in polemics. The Reformers attacked the notion of merit arising from good works, and denounced all "holiness of one's own making", on the ground that man is of himself impotent to love God and do his will. But ethics was of minor interest to them compared to dogma. As an independent discipline it was late on the scene – after the separation of ethics from dogmatic theology by G. Calixt (1586–1656). But then older elements were also pressed into service, from pre-Reformation times – an after-effect of the "ethical" Aristotelianism of Melanchthon.

But the initial stages of ethical thinking are clearly to be sought in the doctrine of "good works", where the approach is not merely negative. The necessity of good works was never contested, and extremist positions, such as that of N. Amsdorf, who maintained the "harmfulness" of good works, as obscuring the pure grace of justification, were unanimously and decisively rejected.

The law of God which is binding on all men is no doubt prior to the gospel, but good works can be done only by the regenerated. The moral acts of Christians, properly speaking, neither cause nor contribute to justification. Christian morality is the fruit of justification and has the nature of a "corollary". The classic statement of this position is to be found in art. VI of the *Confession of Augsburg*, "de nova obedientia", where good works are described as the fruit of faith. They come about spontaneously, as it were. But the *Confession* also uses the word *debet* here, implying that the commandment is effectively at work to direct and instruct. The *Heidelberg Catechism* (1562), the most widely used confession of the Reformed Evangelical Church, treats the whole question of morality, as exercised within the framework of the divine commandments, in the third part of the section on "Thankfulness". Thus ethics appears once more as a corollary. We even find in question 86 the particular doctrine of the Reformation, in the "practical syllogism": "that of ourselves we can be certain of our faith from its fruits".

In the 19th century Protestant ethics was often extended in scope to take in a whole programme of culture. The process began with F. Schleiermacher, whose great work on Christian ethics (*Die Christliche Sitte*, published posthumously by Jonas in 1843) formed a triptych along with his works on Christian doctrine and philosophical ethics. It was a majestic presentation, quite modern in outlook, of the doctrine of family and society, Church and State. He was followed by R. Rothe of Heidelberg, who put forward a speculative system of ethics (5 vols., 2nd ed., 1867–71) in which by an inverse procedure dogmatic theology was incorporated into ethics. These influential works, to which may be added that of the Danish Bishop Martensen (3 vols., 1871–78), prepared the way in essentials for the social ethics of the present day. They also provided the classic foundations for the much-discussed "Protestant culture", whose epoch only ended in the stormy days of the First World War.

To risk a generalization, we may say that the theological ethics now current in Protestantism fall under four heads. In the first school, the influence of I. Kant may be still felt, combined effectively with themes from Luther's doctrine on the Law, as was done by Wilhelm Hermann in his *Ethics* (1901). This line of thought has led many Protestant theologians to question the very existence of an independent "Christian" ethics. The essence of morality is seen in an imperative immediately valid for all men, to which the gospel also points as part of its universal message (Gogarten, Løgstrup). This Kantianism is today mostly proposed on the basis of an existentialist theology. The second group is formed by the upholders of an untroubled biblicism, more or less fundamentalist. Of all the groups, it is the least influenced by philosophical considerations, taking its directives unquestioningly from the commandments of God, as they are given in the Scriptures and as they are applied there to the various aspects of human life – marriage and family, people and State. This type of Protestant ethics is characterized by dislike of philosophical influences, great simplicity of systematization and the predominance given to problems of social ethics (A. de Quervain, H. van Ogen, H.-G. Fritsche). A third group takes the law of God, as given with creation, as the starting-point of its ethical thinking. This law is recognizable in the "institutions" of human life and is seen to be confirmed by the revealed law. It calls us to take responsibility for our actions (P. Althaus, W. Elert, W. Künneth) and takes the theologically pregnant concept of righteousness as the supreme criterion (E. Brunner). In its social ethics this group is predominantly conservative, and it has a certain tendency to think in terms of natural law, though some decisive features of the traditional concept are missing (the reliability of the knowledge gained by reasoning; authoritative exposition of the law), and the doctrine of "law and gospel" forms the horizon of its thinking. The fourth and last group is that of K. Barth and his followers, whose influence is important. Barth's ethics is entirely incorporated into his *Church Dogmatics* (I/2; II/2; III/4), from which the Lutheran dialectic of "law and gospel" is excluded. Though particular questions are impressively dealt with on their own merits, Barth's ethics is an ethics of the kingdom of Christ, which would be a challenge to non-Christian ethics, except that in Barth's Christology, the whole world is already subjected to Christ, either openly or secretly. If the ethics of "institutions" looks back to the original creation, this "Christological" or even "Christocratic" ethics looks forward to a future – already in force – in which the "law of Christ" will rule. See E. Wolf; O. Cullmann on the State; W. Schweitzer; also N. H. Søe. These groupings, which do not of course exclude mutual influences of many kinds, reflect some very important questions which are also debated in Protestant theology.

Three principal sets of problems affect the issue: a) Must theological ethics take philosophical ethics into account and give weight, say, to its existential analyses and the fact of a universally valid "ethical evidence" (Ebeling, Løgstrup, Trillhaas), or exclude it in order to be true to itself and the principle of "revelation alone" (biblicism and the school of Barth in the widest sense)? b) Can ethics be based on the unity and concrete simplicity of the "Word of God", or does not ethical thinking itself force upon our attention the dialectic of law and gospel, the interpenetration of the old order and the new, the law of the world and the commandment of love (the "Two Kingdoms" doctrine of Luther)? c) In opposition to an ethics tending to fixed categories of thought, and to which a basic conservatism can appeal, the "ethics of the situation" also finds supporters in Protestant ethical thinking. They point to the profound changes which have modified the data of social ethics in the modern world (H.-D. Wendland; W. Schweitzer) and try to find solutions to ethical problems by examining limit cases (H. Thielicke). Freedom of discussion, boldly availed of, has always been the pride and at times the strength of Protestant theology. In ethical thinking, the clear principles of the Reformation remain a clear and lofty goal, but they impose no effective limits. They do not otherwise affect the effort to systematize, to make contact with the world of reality, to counter the influence – unrecognized at times – of contemporary philosophy, to grasp fully the message of the Bible. We may therefore without misgivings use some negative statements to give the ground common to modern Protestant ethics in spite of the variety of approaches. This will help to characterize the "credal" nature of Protestant ethics.

The positive affirmations of the statements will be readily seen when examined favourably. (i) Apart from the commandments of God and rational insight, Protestant ethics recognizes no "ecclesiastical" norms of morality. The Church, the community of Jesus Christ, is undoubtedly an important theme of Christian ethics, but it has no norms of its own to contribute to the rules of moral behaviour. The moral principles which are valid in the Protestant Church can never claim the character of "commandments of the Church", especially as the Protestant Church recognizes no particular doctrinal authority, apart from the word of God and its own common faith. (ii) In spite of the conviction that the commandments of God oblige all men and that God has intimated his will in his creation, Protestant ethics has no developed doctrine of the natural law. This remains indeed, since it raises the question of the "just law", an ever-pressing problem, but it provides no court of appeal to which one could turn for a clear and final verdict, according to Protestant ethical thinking. (iii) Protestant ethics has always refused to engage itself in casuistics. This is partly due to the fact that it refuses on principle to be an "ethics of law", that is, to prescribe any particular course of action. The Christian attitude of love of God and the neighbour, of loyalty and responsibility in the sight of God, can express itself by different actions in various situations, sometimes even by actions diametrically opposed to one another. Situations are so different that it is impossible to comprise them within a system. This explains the tendency of recent Protestant ethics to develop an "ethics of the disposition", an ethics of love, which can also appear as an ethics of duty in the sense of Kant. (iv) From its beginnings in the time of the Reformation, all thought of merit has been banished from Protestant ethics. All expectation of gaining benefits, even indeed the benefits of salvation, by means of moral acts, clouds the purity of the moral will, just as it calls in question the sovereign majesty of divine grace. However, gratitude for the gift of divine sonship will naturally call for a fully moral service, "not for the sake of reward and thanks, but inspired by thankfulness and love" (W. Löhe). (v) In Protestant ethics, all attempts to fix degrees of moral goodness are excluded on principle. It recognizes no difference between ordinary and higher principles, and does not reflect on "degrees" of virtue, contrasting, say, holiness with virtuousness. Goodness is an indivisible unity, and there is only one sort of good will or love of Christ. To pass judgment on our deeds and the value of our actions is reserved to God alone, where the verdict is a theological, that is, an absolute one. (vi) An explanation of Protestant ethics in the technical terms of philosophy might speak of an autonomous morality which includes, however, a "heteronomous" element. The conscience of the Christian in his moral actions is subjected to no man, and yet is completely dominated by the word of God. Protestant morality is marked by a great simplicity, which is justification enough for the often childlike ethics of the biblicists, and the endless meditation of the Decalogue offered by sermon and catechism. This does not exclude notable varieties of deportment within the rich variety compatible with the specifically Protestant way of life. We may contrast the frugal Puritanism of certain Calvinist ethics with the grateful enjoyment of the earthly gifts of the creator in Lutheranism. But then again, Lutheranism betrays the tendency to be content with good citizenship without any great display of zeal, while the Calvinist tendency is to strive to subject the world to the divine ordinances and make public institutions serve the glory of God.

Wolfgang Trillhaas

III. Moral Systems

Soon after the development of a new type of moral theology in the 17th century, where confessional practice was the main interest, the attention of theologians was concentrated on the "moral systems". How did this come about? The law of Christ, as typified above all in the Sermon on the Mount, puts the accent on the commandments of perfection. This is the orientation to the end and goal which the seven times repeated "But I say to you" contrasts with the merely or mainly limited objectives of "the men of old". But post-Tridentine moral theology envisaged a supervision to be exercised by men, in view of the granting or refusal of absolution. Such supervision is only possible by virtue of a command which lays down a limit. With this in mind, a large number of moralists came to adopt, consciously or unconsciously, certain definite attitudes. One of their principles was that the conscience is only involved in the case of a prohibitive law which is clearly formulated. Sin, for all practical purposes, was equated with the transgression of a limiting precept, to the neglect of the "law of grace" and the commandments of perfection which, according to the Sermon on the Mount, have real normative value (according to the measure of grace received). But since the command to aim at perfect fulfilment does not provide a norm which can be checked by a human judge, moral theology of the type in question was entirely concentrated on the limiting commands. And these often seemed to come into conflict with one another, especially when the command of love was treated merely as one among many and likewise as setting a definite limit to be achieved. Under the influence of the jurists of Bologna, theologians had long since ceased to take really seriously the law corresponding to the gospel of Christ and the natural law, unless it could be formulated as firmly and precisely as the norms of statute law. It was typical of this situation that the treatise *De Justitia Commutativa* was given disproportionate attention, since here everything could be reduced to the equivalence of performance on either side. There was little room for social justice and love in such a mentality.

1. *The objectives of the Probabilists.* Even within a predominantly legalistic mentality, Christian mildness and a spirit of understanding were at work. Confessors and the moralists whose chief aim was to be at the service of confessors were not merely concerned with the fact that decisions had to be taken in conscience in face of frequent conflicts between the claims of laws. The legal situation was anything but perspicuous. In their effort to formulate the moral laws as precisely as possible, the moralists – happily – did not always come to the same conclusions.

Strictly legal precepts, and the claims of gospel and natural law as formulated in precepts which were rigidly handed down, often failed to meet the demands of charity in changing social, economic and cultural conditions. The discomfort was felt most acutely in times of major social change and in places most open to progress. The moralists lacked a philosophy of language and a sociology of knowledge which might have helped them to distinguish the permanent core of a moral principle from the conditions of its formulation in a given place and time. Both civil and ecclesiastical law were on the whole authoritarian, which meant that moralists rarely dared to call in question the justice of many laws and legal formulations of the natural law. The Inquisition, for instance, often reminded theologians of the ancient decrees which inflicted imprisonment on those who questioned the prohibition of usury.

It was in this situation that Probabilism came to the fore. It was an effort to leave room for doubt, and hence to provide some relief for the over-burdened conscience. The great principle invoked was: "a doubtful law does not bind in conscience", doubts being chiefly raised about interpretations and applications in the case of laws which were in themselves certain. The procedure was justified above all by the principle that liberty is in possession till the opposite is proved.

To the Tutiorists, the Rigorists and the Probabiliorists, for whom the terms of the law and the divine will were absolutely identical, this must have seemed almost blasphemous, since man apparently claimed to be "in possession" as regards the sacred will of God. Most Probabilists were in fact concerned with setting man free for a Christian life of joy, which would still be alert to its true needs and possibilities. But since discussion was carried on within a moral theology orientated to the confessional where the "judicial office" of the confessor was the centre of interest, decisive arguments such as the "law of grace", the diversity of gifts, the law of growth and openness for the demands of the hour and the signs of the times could not effectively be invoked. The Probabilists were forced to defend the liberty of the gospel with the weapons of the legalists. This was at times debilitating and even really dangerous for the seriousness of morality. Mildness could be misunderstood as yielding to influences "from below" and as putting the law at the mercy of the subjective and arbitrary. The spiritual and social background of the discussion must be borne in mind. The Probabilists were themselves the whole-hearted children of a Church which had been in the main thrown back on the defensive since the wars of religion. They too suffered from a safety-first complex. The threats from without made men seek a higher degree of security than is really due to man. The Probabilists also tried hard to have the authority of the well-known theologians of the past on their side, though this effort often led to doing violence to the texts. As regards the administration and reception of the sacraments, they too laid the main stress on a juridical conception of "validity". Nonetheless, their efforts were in general a sound reaction against the all-pervading safety-first complex of the schools.

2. *The moral systems* – which we should prefer to call "systematized rules of prudence" – deal chiefly with the hesitations of conscience when faced with a good action not strictly prescribed by the law, and an action whose legal obligation is doubtful. Doubt can arise about the law itself: has it come into force, does it still hold good, how far does its scope extend? Or the doubt can be concerned with the facts involved: does the undoubted obligation actually apply in a given instance? It is the question of how the tension between the law and the "freedom of the children of God" is envisaged within this limited sphere. The mentality behind the various systems of prudential rules may be roughly sketched as follows:

a) Rigorists, Tutiorists and to some extent Probabiliorists of the older type are above all custodians of the law. Since for them the whole will of God, and their own security and the security of existing institutions is primarily and exclusively to be sought in formulas of universal legal validity, they decide in favour even of a law which very probably or more probably does not bind – as long as there is no definite legal prescription on the other side. To seek the will of God in the light of the graces and needs of the hour hardly enters their minds.

b) According to the Probabilists, the spontaneous and creative freedom of man is of course bound entirely to the will of God, but this freedom is "in possession" from the start with regard to any purely legal obligation. In reaction against too many legal burdens, the "law" (with no distinction very often between positive law and divine law as presented in static formulas) is primarily regarded as a restriction of freedom. But Probabilism sometimes took the form of a mere reaction against legal rigorism. The "innovator" remained within the vicious circle of the system and merely tried to lighten the burdens of the law without making watchfulness as regards grace and the signs of the times a positive programme. Where Probabilism was really concerned only with the primacy of the law of grace over the letter of the law, with openness for "the hour" to the exclusion of scrupulous legalism, it often failed to enunciate its intention in a theologically convincing way. The arguments were still confined to the theology of the confessional.

c) Moderate Probabilism, which took refuge in the name of Equiprobabilism mainly under the aegis of Alphonsus de Liguori, after the suppression of the great champions of Probabilism, the Society of Jesus, in 1773, may be characterized as follows. The freedom of the children of God welcomes the revelation of the will of God whether it comes in the form of a law or not, and hence always decides in favour of the action for which the reasons seem stronger. It is a matter of prudent judgment, in which the maturity of the Christian and the dangers to the general good or to spontaneous and creative initiative play an important part. According to Equiprobabilism, it is more prudent to abide by the demands of the good as legally formulated, as long as there are not equally or approximately as good grounds for thinking that a spontaneous action not prescribed by a universal law is equally good or better. And even if a spontaneous, creative act of love is not for the moment at stake, Probabilists and Equiprobabilists hold that it is important not to make too many legal demands on freedom in cases of doubt, so that men may be able to meet spontaneously and joyfully the demands of a given situation.

d) Laxism, finally, urges a liberty which does not find its ultimate inspiration in the revelation of God's will, and is therefore more or less wilful or slothful.

3. *New perspectives on an old problem.* The search for helpful rules of prudence in the moral endeavour is by no means outdated. But it must be carried on in the light of modern circumstances and present-day systems of moral theology. Moral theology is not a search for hard and fast rules to be applied by the "judge" in the confessional, though the office of the confessor, who proclaims peace and the messianic order of peace – the great mystery and command of love – is to be highly esteemed. What is wanted now is a morality of responsibility to be practised by Christians who are called to live in a dynamic and pluralist society and Church. It is seen more clearly that moral laws, rules and precepts formulated in different ages and cultures bear the marks of their times and need to be re-thought and revised in the light of modern problems. It is also clearer that action on a safety-first basis in times such as ours entails the greatest of all risks, that of offering men the image of life at a stand-still and of faith in a "dead God". The cross-currents of modern life and the advance towards a future of undreamt-of possibilities and dangers demands more subtle thinking and a very great effort to combine courageous enterprise with the necessary prudence. Further, moral theology must be concerned with preserving the balance between the forces of revolution and of restraint in Church and society.

The question of genuine, that is, of feasible probabilities poses itself in quite a new way in an age of reforms long overdue, in the age of ecumenism and so on. One need only think of the liturgical revival, which had to struggle for so long (and still must, in certain ways) against the resistance of considerable forces in the institutional Church and the impediment of a legislation which, to say the least, lagged behind. One must ask oneself what sort of courageous maturity is called for with regard to laws and precepts when circles in the institutional Church try to confine life in a strait-jacket of laws, inspired either by a sort of panic or by a programme of counter-reformation. There is the question, for instance, of how probable in practice is the view of birth control now held in wide circles of educated laymen and theologians. It has often been stated that birth control is not a matter of free opinion, and the view in question is now clearly in opposition to the pronouncements of the papal magisterium (cf. *Humanae Vitae*, 29 July 1968). But it finds support in the declarations of several episcopates. The situation is therefore somewhat like the absolute prohibition of usury in earlier times, to which the Probabilists responded with great skill for many centuries. It is different, however, insofar as the theologians who now express themselves with such timorous caution and contortions as the moralists of the 18th and 19th centuries in the matter of interest on money, are now simply treated with intolerance. The narrowness of the channel between the Scylla of total incredibility and the Charybdis of the undermining of the magisterium is something completely novel, all the more so if one persists in trying to answer the new questions with the tools of the 18th century.

Bernhard Häring

MYSTERY

1. The word "mystery" is certainly one of the most important key-words of Christianity and its theology. Vatican I expressly declared (*D* 1816; cf. 1671–3; 1795f.) that there are mysteries properly so called which can only be known through actual revelation by God (against Gnosticism, Rationalism and Semi-Rationalism). It follows that revelation and faith cannot be superseded and abolished by philosophy and understanding. Vatican I also affirmed that, despite their abidingly mysterious character, realities and truths of that kind are accessible through revelation. The dilemma presented by every kind of rationalism therefore simply does not arise, whereby, at least in principle, something has to be either clearly intelligible and susceptible of fitting plainly and totally into the formal perspectives of human understanding and subsumed under man's logical principles (brought into his "system"), or is something which is of no concern to man at all, so that he cannot deal with it or make any pronouncement on it (as Wittgenstein says in the *Tractatus*, no. 7: "What we cannot speak about, we must be silent about"). Vatican I also stated that the existence of mystery (that of God and of his free action in regard to man) is the reason why revelation as such is necessary (*D* 1786, *DS* 3876) (and consequently, sacred history in the strict sense, which is only conceivable in conjunction with the history of revelation), if God precisely as mystery is to approach man at all (cf. also Vatican II, Dogmatic Constitution *Dei Verbum*, arts. 2–6). Vatican I also declared (*D* 1782; cf. 428) (with Scripture) that God is incomprehensible and that this is one of the essential predicates which characterize God as God in contradistinction to everything else. Because of what God is, it is evident that his incomprehensibility essentially belongs to him and is not something which ceases with the beatific vision. These are the two fundamental principles from which all theological reflection on the nature of mystery must start and to which it must return.

2. Christian tradition has always attested this experience and doctrine of the incomprehensible God who comes to us as mystery. But it cannot be said that the mystery was always emphasized enough. There was always the danger of regarding God's mystery as something that will be overcome, at

least in the beatific vision, instead of as precisely what will endure and will constitute our perfect happiness when we are immediately united to God in ecstatic love. Moreover, the existence of mystery is usually explained by man's pilgrim state (cf., for example, *D* 1796). In Scripture itself God is he whom no one has seen (Jn 1:18; 6:46; 1 Jn 4:20); he lives in unapproachable light (1 Tim 6:16), and his free action in regard to man is a "mystery" (Mk 4:11 par.; 1 Cor 2:7; Eph and Col, *passim*). The darkness on the mountain into which Moses entered to converse with God was a figure of all man's knowledge of God (Gregory of Nyssa); in the struggle against Gnosticism and the rationalism of Arianism (Eunomians), the Fathers of the Church emphasized the incomprehensibility of God the Father; the patristic period and the Middle Ages developed the *theologia negativa* "per modum negationis et eminentiae". Even for the Fourth Lateran Council (*D* 432) the unlikeness between God and creature is greater than their likeness, and Thomas Aquinas could write, "Man's utmost knowledge of God is to know that we do not know him" ("quod [homo] sciat se Deum nescire": *De potentia*, 7, 5 ad 14; cf. Pieper). Nicholas of Cusa praises *docta ignorantia* and *aenigmatica scientia*. The *theologia crucis* of the Reformers also included a protest against any tendency to subject God to systematization. In the 19th century the Church struggled simultaneously against theological agnosticism, on behalf of the "natural knowability of God" (*D* 1785f.; Vatican II, *Dei Verbum*, art. 6) and against a theological rationalism which subjects God to man (*D* 1786; Vatican II, *Dei Verbum*, art. 6). If the battle against present-day atheism can only be correctly waged if it is also understood to involve the destruction of false and primitive ideas of God (Vatican II, *Gaudium et Spes*, art. 19), then a theology of mystery is an urgent task. In Protestant theology (e.g., Ebeling) an attempt is being made to deal with it by theological hermeneutics. It also calls for much more concentrated attention on the Catholic side than it has so far received. Jesus Christ in his human reality shares our relation to God's incomprehensibility (Thomas Aquinas, *Compendium Theologiae*, 216). Consequently, as man, he also stands in that position of the creature where it must freely decide whether it freely accepts the absolute mystery with the adoration of loving ecstasy, or wills to be atheist.

3. If we leave out of account what is simply unknown about God and also what is grasped in analogous but philosophical concepts about him, scholastic theology distinguishes between mysteries in the strict or absolute sense and mysteries in a wider sense. The use of the plural as a matter of course is itself noteworthy. The former are realities (or statements about them) which even when revealed cannot be fully understood in their essence or intrinsic possibility. The existence of the second kind of mysteries is not accessible to man unless they are made known to him by revelation (e.g., God's free decisions) but their essential meaning can be understood once they have been made known. This distinction may be quite clear formally and logically, but it does not take us much further in the real question at issue. For one can at once ask whether we have to reckon with just any number of mysteries (in the plural). This may be doubted. It is of course conceivable and in accordance with experience for there to be many realities which for all kinds of particular reasons are inaccessible to human knowledge. But in principle, on the Thomist axiom that objective and subjective truth are proportionate to the degree of being of object and subject, we must surely admit that a finite being as such can never transcend the ontological scope of a spiritual cognitive faculty of unlimited transcendence (such

as that of man) to such an extent as to constitute a mystery in the strict sense. If such a mystery is in question, therefore, God as such must be involved, in himself and in his relation with man. This makes clear the inner connection between the two fundamental principles which we referred to above. The essential and permanent incomprehensibility of God precisely as such must be the real reason why there is such a thing as mystery (or mysteries). And there can only be mysteries of faith in the strict sense where God as God, i.e., as incomprehensible, communicates himself. This real self-communication (as an event which simultaneously makes itself known) necessarily shares in the character of incomprehensibility which belongs to God. For he communicates himself, not something finite and other than himself.

4. Before we can advance from this starting-point, the epistemological basis for the theological conception of mystery must be examined. Radically and intrinsically man is not a being who employs the *idea clara et distincta* (in the sense of Cartesian rationalism), nor is he the subject of an absolute system in which alone he and reality in general attain their conscious identity definitively (in the sense of German Idealism). The unlimited transcendentality of the finite human subject in knowledge and freedom, theory and practice, consists in going beyond any comprehensible statement and raising a further question; and likewise in having further and further questions put to it and being led into precisely what we call mystery. This orientation towards mystery is not a mere residue of what for the moment is not yet known, nor is it something which is found side by side with what is clearly known and with what can be clearly investigated. It is the innermost essence of transcendence in cognition and freedom, because it is the condition of the very possibility of cognition and freedom as such. Consequently it is the ground of man's personal life as such; man's ground lies in the abyss of mystery, which accompanies him always throughout life. The only question is whether he lives with mystery willingly, obediently and trustingly, or represses it and will not admit it, "suppressing" it, as Paul says. Transcendence is transcendence into mystery. Analogical knowledge (*analogia entis*) is not the limiting case of a knowledge which in itself is univocal and which brings the particular object of knowledge into a firm and humanly intelligible system of co-ordinates (of the *prima principia*). It is the fundamental open and upward movement of the spirit towards the uncircumscribed mystery. This transcendence must always be understood totally, with all its dimensions: transcendence back into the inaccessible beginning, transcendence towards what is at root the single totality of possible objects of knowledge, transcendence beyond the always particular object of freedom into its accomplishment, transcendence above and beyond the manageable future (in absolute hope), transcendence of personal intercommunication beyond the actual individual partner who simply as such always represents promise, never absolute fulfilment. Mystery is the ground throughout, yet withdraws all the more; it is the foundation throughout but does not come under our control; it gives itself as all-encompassing and abiding mystery; we can speak in reaction to it but never really about it.

5. It is possible on this basis to form a clearer idea of what is really meant by the mysteries of the Christian revelation. At bottom there is only one mystery: God's incomprehensibility as God is not simply the remote horizon within which our existence moves, or the infinitely distant point towards which the multiplicity of finite realities move asymptotically as towards a single inaccessible unifying point; without ceasing to be that, God gives himself to us

without intermediary; he himself as he is becomes the innermost reality of our being. The one mystery is that this is possible, real and known to us through grace in faith. And this one mystery has a double aspect: God himself as mystery and God's self-communication to us, through which as abiding mystery he becomes our innermost reality. Moreover, he does so himself, not through some representative gift which as such in principle would ultimately be without mystery. And this self-communication (uncreated grace) makes us able to accept it.

It is impossible to resolve the dialectic of the simultaneous affirmation that God's most immediate self-bestowed presence is the vocation of the spiritual creature, and that mystery essentially characterizes him as God. This dialectic is the most radical ("supernatural") form of the analogical structure of transcendence. The unity of this dialectic is only grasped, without annulling its mystery, through the affirmation of that mystery in love. Ultimately love alone is able to leave what is other (here, the incomprehensible God as such) in its own reality. God, for example, who is love, makes the creature a real being which is different from him and which has its own independent reality, and so freely gives himself to it. This mystery, formally one and the same, is found in all the Christian doctrines which are declared to be the (absolute) mysteries of Christianity. a) The mystery of sanctifying grace and the beatific vision of God as the two stages of the personal history of the acceptance of God's self-communication and its definitive state. b) The mystery of the radical, unique culmination of this self-communication of God to humanity in the incarnation of God's Logos. In this, God's movement of self-communication to creatures reaches its highest pitch, its entelechy (*causa finalis*) and its eschatologically definitive historical manifestation. c) The mystery of the Trinity which is the Trinity of the economy of salvation under the double aspect of God's self-communication in Pneuma and Logos from God as incomprehensible and inexhaustible source (God the Father). Because this is true self-communication, it is also the mystery of the immanent Trinity of God in himself. (Cf. *Mysterium Salutis*, II, cols. 317–97.) It is not possible here to show in detail that whatever else is described as mystery in dogmatic theology can be reduced (if absolute mystery is really in question) to this triune mystery. The really mysterious character of original sin, for example, has its ground in the mystery of grace. The lack of grace as the communication of the essentially holy Pneuma can alone be the ground of a sinfulness which is antecedent to personal decision. Transubstantiation in the Eucharist need not be regarded as a particular instance of a wider possibility by which God can transubstantiate anything into anything else. It can be regarded as only found with Christ (in a way that would have to be explained), by reason of his unique redemptive function and hypostatic union. In that way the mystery of transubstantiation would be traced back to the mystery of the Incarnation.

6. The doctrine that mystery characterizes the content of the Christian message and the special way in which it is known, is of fundamental kerygmatic importance. a) It can explain how it is that atheism, if inculpable, does not really deny the God of the gospel, but rejects ideas of God which falsely present him as finite (Vatican II, *Gaudium et Spes*, art. 19), or for a great variety of reasons, individual and social, is unable to express objectively man's permanent ordination towards God which presents God in a quite different way from all other known realities. b) It links up with the Christian message man's ever-present, if not always expressly conscious, fundamental experience of his exposure to a mystery which pervades his whole

reality. It makes clear that the Christian message is the one answer to this experience of his own exposure: the incomprehensibility of the ground of human existence is the mystery of God who gives himself in love in the most immediate, beatifying presence, and does not simply rule man's existence in remote detachment and judgment. c) It makes clear the intrinsic unity of the Christian message, which does not consist in communicating on divine orders an arbitrary number of obscure propositions which have little or nothing to do with man's experience of his own reality. It is one single but comprehensive explanation of man's reality which is already fulfilled by grace, that is, by God himself.

Karl Rahner

MYSTICISM

Nature and History

A. Theory and Technique

From the theological point of view, mysticism may be regarded as consciousness of the experience of uncreated grace as revelation and self-communication of the triune God. The task of a "theology of mysticism" is to give a scientific and theoretical account of its presuppositions and principles, using the methods of theology. It is not possible to start with a definition of mysticism, since the definition has to be worked out in a theology of mysticism, of which it forms the content which it thus demarcates against similar subjects. Neither the etymology of the word "mysticism" nor the series of meanings which it took on in the course of history can provide information about the meaning and structure of the subject in question. In contrast to asceticism and ascetics, which are used to mark the difference between practice and theory, mysticism stands for both the theory of scientific investigation and the practice or art of training and experience. This is one of the reasons why it is so difficult to reach agreement about the basic reality involved and the explanation of mystics' writings. The theology of mysticism cannot confine itself to one single theological theme, such as certain chapters from the treatise on grace. It must also envisage the fundamental mystery of the "Trinity of the economy" (salvation), which is identical with the immanent Trinity where God communicates himself in freedom personally and fully, not by way of appropriation, while remaining always the same. Nonetheless, the special character of mysticism leads from a diversity of themes to one single theme whose simplicity is such that it is open to everyone, just as the Christian receives in the Creed an enlightenment from God which tells him what he is and what he is to become. This point is of importance for the consideration of method. In his created nature, and in spite of his sinfulness, man experiences himself as constantly addressed by God. For God communicates and discloses himself in a very intimate way to the spiritual being of man, drawing the whole world of man into the horizon of the "supernatural existential". God gives himself in goodness and love, so that he is the ground of man's existence and the real truth of his life. He divinizes man according to his own likeness, by inherent grace, not by imparting created signs or through a representative, but by his own personal presence. This is done in full and absolute freedom, hence in the mode of grace, so that his offer and his divine word may also meet with a response which is full and free dedication and a divine hearing. This can only be in faith, which receives God's word as the word of God. But grace, the light of faith and the light of grace, the *scintilla animae*, is not merely knowledge. It is prior to and higher than knowing and willing. It is where the soul is a unity before developing in multiplicity and not just the comprehension and acceptance of a multiplicity of truths; where the soul exists not in the disjunction of multiplicity nor even in the special choice of some among many. Grace claims and summons the whole man and his whole life to strive to grasp and penetrate ever more deeply the hidden truth of the mystery, to a constant dedication in faith, fidelity, hope and love. Man's light and dedication will be in proportion to God's own self-disclosure in his permanent action, provided that man is humble and resolute enough to remain true to the basic initial realities. This then is the proper theme of a theology of mysticism, because God's revelation is also a statement about man, to be sought in all theological statements about the triune God, his creating and sanctifying, the incarnation, life and suffering of his Son, the Church and the sacraments, grace and the beatific vision: just as all this proceeds from the one mystery, is contained in it, and leads to its ultimate disclosure. This does not mean that theology can become mysticism, any more than mysticism can become theology. But (at least more than normally hitherto) it will be part of the real task of theologians, and indeed of all who reflect in Christian and theological terms, to turn to this prayerful, "adoring" theology. No theme of theology can remain untouched, any more than moral theology and ascetics can proceed with theories and doctrine without a constant reconsideration of their statements and demands.

A theology of mysticism will also have to include in its investigations the radical subjectivity of man as the recipient of grace. Here an adequate theological anthropology becomes of equally great importance. Its task is to probe theological assertions for the spiritual meaning which expounds and explicitates the religious reality in terms of the world of objects and in intramundane categories. The theological relevance of man thus shows that mysticism properly so called is also a speculative process (Thomas Aquinas, *Summa Theologica*, I, q. 1, a. 10). Further, reflection on the religious act under the special aspect of profound interiorization will bring to light its mystical element, to display the structure of the supernatural being of the soul in grace – not the psychology of mysticism or the mystic – and to offer an interpretation of it. But there is nothing except faith, and hence grace, which could or should be the medium of the beatific vision. This perspective once more throws light on the triad of nature, grace and glory, which makes it possible to have a true understanding of the unity in content and method of the theological disciplines. This is undoubtedly one of the reasons, if not the main one, for giving respectful consideration to non-Christian mysticism, an element which cannot be neglected by any theology of mysticism. Finally, mystic knowledge has no other goal or end than itself: it reposes in itself, in the fullness which is fulfilment and more than fulfilment (Jn 10:10; Rom 5:20; Eph 1:8; 1 Tim 1:14).

In asceticism, the call to practice is predominant. As regards the practice and technique of mysticism, the call may be said to be included in the exhortation to "pray always", prayer here being understood in a very wide and radical sense – as *lectio, studium, meditatio, contemplatio*. Nonetheless, there seem to be direct imperatives, such as 1 Cor 12:31; 14:39. In the dialogue of the soul, when we pray, we speak to God, when we read and hear (Scripture), God speaks to us. Mysticism is not confined to a privileged few. Mystical being corresponds undoubtedly to the absolute and free will of God, and also to the free acceptance and reception of the divine self-communication in faith and love, no matter how fragmentary and variable all this may be in its successive moments and its incalculable character.

Mysticism cannot be reproached with being aloof from or hostile to the world.

It affirms God and all his creatures, seeking and finding God in all. The truly mystical event is to be understood dialectically: no grace received is empty, idle or futile. Further, mysticism is the truly dynamic element in the Church, which transcends the mere observance of the letter of the law and gives the sacramental and institutional the full richness of the inward spirit which promotes their efficacy. The Church is never without the mystic element. It has never made any universal and binding declarations on the exact nature of true mystical experience. Revelation and the Church remain a *norma negativa* for mystical assertions. But the Church has pronounced on erroneous conceptions in the realm of the inner religious life (which by that very fact betray themselves as pseudo-mysticism), where their presuppositions or consequences involved errors in the doctrine of faith. Disapproval was expressed of the Messalians, the Brethren of the Free Spirit (*DS* 866), the Béguines and Béghards (*D* 471–9) whose errors show a remarkable similarity to those of the Alumbrados of the time of Ignatius of Loyola, the Quietists (*DS* 2181–92) and Michael de Molinos (*D* 1221–88; *D* 1243, "mysticis"; *D* 1246, "mystica"; *D* 1281, 1283, "mors mystica"; see also *D* 1341, 1342, 1343, 1347, "sancti mystici"). By urging the faithful to a life of profound faith and prayer, the Church promotes indirectly the mystical life, as in Vatican II, the Dogmatic Constitution on the Church, arts. 12 and 15, the Decree on Priestly Formation, art. 8, the Decree on the Ministry and Life of Priests, arts. 9 and 22, the Declaration on Non-Christian Religions, arts. 2 and 3, the Dogmatic Constitution on Divine Revelation, arts. 2, 3, 19, 25. (The encyclical *Mystici Corporis* of Pius XII, *AAS* 35 [1943], pp. 193–248, in spite of apparent similarities under a different terminology, was actually interested in other matters, as the circumstances of the times demanded.) These calls to a "new spirituality", which were inspired by the inward dynamism and charisms of the Church, undoubtedly mean that theologians, preachers, pastors and layfolk must seek to rekindle a mystagogical piety which even in everyday life lives out the faith which also loves the earth and knows that the mystery of the God who comes and gives himself is present even in the seemly insignificant.

As regards the authenticity or otherwise of mystical phenomena, two points are to be noted. The first is that one must prescind from outward and merely accidental concomitants, which are not the core and the essentials of the mystical happening, but are rather a distraction which impedes the view. Then, an experience of divine grace taking place in the depths of the spirit may be interpreted subjectively in a wrong and misleading way. But it never includes the privilege of an assurance of individual justification. Here, in the various grades and kinds of "knowledge and wisdom" (1 Cor 1:5), the discernment of spirits (cf. 1 Cor 12:10) has an essential task to perform (cf. also 1 Cor 12:31ff.).

B. Mysticism and Scripture

The whole of sacred Scripture is open in a very special way to a mystical interpretation. It appears, in particular when we recall the element of human causality in the production of the various books, that God freely creates the ground and possibility of his personal communication and its acceptance and experience. He discloses it progressively and, remaining unchanged, maintains it, manifesting his intimate presence, at various times and in many ways (cf. Heb 1:1). And since his word and divine action, his free willing and creating are identical (cf. Gen 1:3; Ps 32:9), he can also address the "object" as his personal You, his own, his friend and not an alien. Without detriment to its historical character, it becomes a means and mirror of the divine "theophany".

It must therefore be presupposed that under the husk or rind of the letter (*sub cortice litterae*) lies a spiritual and finer sense, the mystical sense, so that the true gnostic and mystic finds and adores God "in spirit and in truth" (Jn 4:23). In this perspective Gen 1:1 and Jn 1:1 go together, throwing light on each other as elements of the history of creation and the history of salvation, as the beginning which is also the end (cf. Rev 21:6; 22:13). Hence a genuine theology of mysticism is justified in starting with man, who is described as "Adam" at his origin, taking him not as an individual but with his uniqueness, his special quality as exemplar, his closeness to God and his awareness of it and of his likeness to God. High-points of this encounter with God, which leads to the "covenant" (Gen 15:18; 16:2ff.) and then to the *consortium sermonis Dei* (cf. Exod 34:29; 2 Pet 1:4), can be seen in Abraham, who is guided and instructed by God (Gen 12–22), in Yahweh's dialogue with Abraham (Gen 22:1–18), in Jacob's vision (Gen 32:25–31; 35:9–15), in the revelation of the name of Yahweh as he who is who he is (Exod 3:14), in God's speaking to Moses in general (cf. Exod 6:2ff.; 19:3ff.; 33:18ff.; 34:6–35), in God's commands to Moses (Lev 1:1ff.; Num 1:1ff.), in the transmission of God's word and its meaning (Deut 1:6ff.), in the words of the Lord to Elijah (1 Kg 19:8ff.). The theophanies of Yahweh granted to the prophets are always visions, and also a vocation and charge with regard to others (e.g., Is 1:1ff.; 6:1–13; Jer 1:4ff.; Ezek 1:3ff.). The lyrical form of the psalms expresses both the nearness and the word of God and their reception by the men so favoured, taking the form of thanksgiving, praise, repentance and prayer. The Song of Solomon has always made a special appeal to mystics and was the starting-point of all bridal mysticism. Throughout all the books of the OT the spiritual interpretation came upon the self-revelation of God, which was always historical, verbal and u[...] going from the individual addr[...] a wider circle and finally to the [...] people, and to mankind through [...] covenant. From the beginning, it was eschatologically orientated to the end.

In the NT, what was hitherto shadowy and provisional becomes lightsome and definitive reality. God's self-communication in the incarnational epiphany is linked with the blessed experience of union with God in faith. This is particularly clear in the Johannine perspective. The contents of the dialogue with Nicodemus (Jn 3:1–21) and with the Samaritan woman (Jn 4:7–26), the emphatic "I am he" (Jn 8:24) which challenges the You of the vis-à-vis (cf. Exod 3:14), open up the possibilities of an encounter, so that ultimately "rivers of living water" (Jn 7:38) flow from the believer and learner himself (cf. Jn 6:45). This "I am" is the one open door (Jn 10:7), the bread of life (Jn 6:35, 48, 51), the light (Jn 8:12), the resurrection and the life (Jn 11:25), the way and the truth and the life (Jn 14:6). And the bridal theme is also to be heard (Jn 3:29; Mt 9:15; 25:1). The experience of God's self-communication must be accepted gratefully and humbly (Mt 11:28). No one is excluded from the offer, which takes in the poor, the hungry, the afflicted (cf. Mt 5:3ff.), the heathen (cf. Mt 9:13; 11:19). The indications contained in the synoptics, hints as it were in a number of parables which demand further explanation, point in the same direction: a knowing in unknowing, an unknowing in knowing, seeing and not seeing, finding in losing. But this is combined with the question of decision and discernment, of those who see and are blind, of those who do not see and still can see (cf. Jn 9:39). There are those who are "outside" (Mk 4:11), those who do not listen to his voice, who do not retain his words as a permanent possession, who search the Scriptures but whose will is not such as faith demands (Jn 5:37ff.). And there are others who are and will be given the gift of understanding the mystery of the kingdom of God (Mk 4:11) under the outward cloak of the letter, the image and the parable. For Paul, the mystery of God is decisive, the mystery of Christ, of the gospel, of the faith, which is also the mystery of piety (1 Cor 4:1; Col 2:2f.; 4:3; Eph 1:7ff.; 6:19; 1 Tim 3:9, 16). He sees his office and his task as the proclamation of the revelation of the mystery which had been kept secret, but which is now disclosed and made known to all peoples through the prophetic writings, to obtain the obedience of faith (Rom 16:25ff.). To Paul, as the least of all, the grace was given to announce to all the mystery hidden in God since the ages of the world began (Eph 3:4–5, 7–9). The Apostle accepts this grace and becomes familiar with it through λόγος and γνῶσις (1 Cor 1:5). He can speak wisdom among the perfect, a wisdom veiled in mystery (1 Cor 2:6), but the distinction remains between the earthly and the spiritual, the babes are given milk, while adults get solid food (cf. 1 Cor 2:14f.; 3:1f.; Heb 5:11ff.). With good reason, Paul at once warns against misunderstandings and abuses and recommends a holy soberness (Rom 12:3).

C. History and Tradition of Mysticism

Though the mystical life was never absent from the Church, its forms and manifestations always varied considerably. All forms of genuine mysticism will have a trinitarian structure, just as their foundations will be biblical. They will also be characterized by their Christological, ecclesial and eschatological elements. Images and symbols come to the fore in the language of mysticism – the "dark night", for instance. Various ages and circumstances will produce representatives of monastic (religious), liturgical, world-orientated or cosmic mysticism. A history of mysticism would have to depict the flowering of individual elements of mysticism. These would appear as the materially and formally diverse moments of the one mystical idea, displaying itself through the successive phases of its historical manifestation. In such a history the individual mystics will only appear as the representatives of various spiritual trends, the literary spokesmen of movements and "schools" or as systematizing theologians.

It is characteristic of the patristic age that the theory of mysticism remained at the stage of hint and allusion, linked in particular with the image of God in man, after Gen 1:26f., or developed the theme of the divine birth in the soul. The theological effort to formulate clearly trinitarian and Christological truths and to justify them against heresy also produced new and fruitful suggestions, couched in the language of Hellenistic philosophy and drawing on non-Christian tradition. Here it would be hard to overestimate the influence of Origen on Western spirituality. Among the great figures, Gregory of Nyssa stands out. He has been called the "father of mysticism", and indeed the most recent research has come to surprisingly new conclusions, to the effect that the influence of Eastern mysticism on the medieval West was very far-reaching. The figure and the writings of (pseudo-)Denis the Areopagite had extraordinary effects, some of which were disproportionate. While the thematic structure of his little work *De Mystica Theologia* is centred on knowledge of the divine mystery, in a very sober exposition of the matter, the influence which it had through the mass of commentators in the Middle Ages, and above all since Baroque scholasticism, can hardly be estimated. Thomas Aquinas did not expound any personal theory of mysticism, but the question of prophecy and charisms (including *raptus* and *excessus*) come much more clearly to the fore, as indeed in medieval scholasticism in general. It remains to be noted that Thomas and the medieval theologians presuppose the notion of the "supernatural existential": "Beyond this general mode of presence there is a special one which appertains to the rational nature, in which God is said to be present like the known in the knower and the loved in the lover ... The rational creature attains to God, there being a special mode according to which he is said not only to be in the rational creature but to dwell in it as in his temple ... But to have the faculty of enjoying the divine person comes only from sanctifying grace" (*Summa Theologica*, I, q. 43, a. 3). "Through the gift of sanctifying grace the rational creature is perfected in such a way that he can not only freely use the created gift itself, but also enjoy the divine person himself" (*ibid.*, ad 1).

Down to the present day, the influence of Spanish mysticism has had a disproportionately strong effect on theological study. This meant that the true visage of mysticism was seen in too individualistic a way. There was an unnecessary and unjustifiable stress on what was psychological and subjectivist, the realm of feeling and of private experience. This restriction has made it difficult to overcome a theoretical view which was very much a child of its times. And it also has the disadvantage of giving absolute value, as it were, to what are merely moments in the whole of spirituality, positive though these elements may be. A theology of spirituality has to make special efforts to counter such one-sided views.

D. Future Tasks

As in every new approach to scientific questions, the theory of mysticism will be concerned first of all with the choice of starting-point and method. As an introduction to its impenetrable dimensions, it will be well to systematize in terms of the given state of theological research, in the realm of the theology of grace, for instance. A distinction between mysticism in the wider sense (treating it more or less as "normal") and in the strict sense (treating it as a privileged state) would cancel itself out. For ultimately, the giver bestows himself in the gift, though in the average religious life, for various reasons – hindrances from without and within – not all the potentialities are realized by all. And it must be conceded that a further and more precise explanation of "experience" would have to be worked out, through which, with the help of speculative psychology, the experience of grace as created reality in all its interchangeable variety and subjective condition would be distinguished from the genuine though mediated experience of encounter and communication with the personal God. Mystical data must also be clearly distinguished from all types of transcendental experience in philosophy. And there is always the need to determine more precisely the relationship of mysticism to Gnosis, esoteric experience and charismatic endowment – the last being of particular interest in the ecclesiastical sphere, where charisms are bestowed for the benefit of others. The distinction to be made here is already foreshadowed by the contrast between *uti* and *frui* in Augustine and the medieval scholastics.

In this connection two particularly pressing questions arise. How does one determine the relation between asceticism and mysticism in the synthesis offered by a theologically-minded spirituality? And what is to be said about the possibility or existence of a non-Christian mysticism? The presence of mystical phenomena outside the Church, in Judaism and Islam and in the religions of the East, is undeniable. But the theories put forward to explain them differ widely. Some suggest the common "nature" of man as addressed by the divine, others the receptivity of the *anima naturaliter christiana*, others explain them by the "analogy of faith" which obviously comes to mind here. But even apart from such refinements, the general interest in mysticism implies that the hour seems to have come for a confrontation between Christian and non-Christian mysticism as part of the encounter of religions (H. de Lubac).

Now the presence of mysticism is not primarily manifested in written or oral communications. The mystic often lacks the power to reflect articulately on his experience or to express it in apt forms of communication. This is important to note for the interpretation of "mystical" texts. The word "mysticism" has been so widely profaned and secularized – as for instance when it is replaced by myth or when the *horror mysterii* makes it total unknowing and an ambiguous negative theology – that a critical hermeneutics is urgently required, especially for all types of merely "literary" mysticism, if it is to be approached with the necessary predispositions. This study would then also include investigation of the authentic form of the texts, the tradition of the individual texts, their literary genre, the culture and psychology of the authors, linguistic influences such as neo-Platonic terminology, images and symbols, combination or confusion with subjective experiences. However unprejudiced one may be in assessing the phenomena of mysticism, a critical and well-informed theological attitude will be an indispensable element in the final "discernment of spirits".

Heribert Fischer

E. Theological Interpretation

According to the Catholic understanding of the concepts of mysticism on the one hand and of revelation and faith on the other, there can be no absolute dilemma between them. Mysticism is, after all, not a pantheistic experience of identity with the absolute. In those cases in which mysticism is simply the person's experience of his own pure spirituality, it is as provisionally open and ambiguous as all of man's other experiences of himself in an encounter with the living God. On the other hand, however, revelation is not possible in the original bearer of revelation without the occurrence of what may be called "mysticism as the experience of grace". What is more, as the giving and the attestation of this experience of the living God, the "prophetic" element can (it does not have to) be connected with mystical experience. According to the Catholic understanding of faith, this includes inner grace and therefore also the experience of grace, the light of faith and the meaning of faith as an inner aspect. Faith would therefore be a mere human opinion and not the reception of God's word as such, if this came simply from outside in a mere "word". On the one hand, the point of departure for a theological consideration of the mystical phenomenon would have to be a concentration on the empirical aspect of mysticism. Mystical experiences would consequently be thought of as "essentially" different from the normal Christian experiences of a person who has received the gift of grace from the Spirit and therefore as a special grace. On the other hand, however, it is important to bear in mind that it is not possible for a real theology of grace to insert, between faith and the experience of grace on the one hand and glory on the other, an intermediate state which on the one hand transcends the giving of grace to the Christian in the real sense of the word and on the other is not a (transient) participation in the beatific vision of God. Man's deification and possession of uncreated grace cannot, in the real sense of the words, be surpassed by anything that is not glory. Moreover, it cannot be assumed that mystical experience leaves the sphere of faith and becomes an experience that is no longer faith. Mysticism occurs, on the contrary, within the framework of normal grace and within the experience of faith. To this extent, those who insist that mystical experience is not specifically different from the ordinary life of grace (as such) are certainly right. Any other theory of Christian mysticism would undoubtedly be either gnosticism or theosophy and either an overestimation of mysticism or else a fundamental underestimation of the real depth of the "ordinary" Christian life of grace. It should also not be forgotten that mystical experience as such and statements made about this experience, which of necessity make use of terms derived from other spheres of theology, psychology and so on, are two quite different things. What is more, even a genuine mystic is not always capable of describing his own genuine experience in appropriate language. There are quite striking differences between these descriptions and they cannot be explained in any other way. There is, however, no reason to doubt the existence of these mystical experiences themselves. On the other hand, mystical theology can, in its attempt to surpass parapsychology, be simply an aspect of dogmatic theology, at least according to dogmatic principles. We are therefore bound to conclude that the psychological character of mystical experiences (at least insofar as mysticism is not "exalted" by grace in the same way as man's "normal" spiritual life) is in itself confined to the purely natural sphere and is simply a special kind of natural transcendence and a "return" to oneself. Insofar as it occurs in connection with the whole spiritual activity of man as the recipient of grace and is itself raised up by grace, this natural experience can, like every natural pre-condition of supernaturally "exalted" acts (consciousness, freedom, reflection and so on), be of great significance to man's salvation, be experienced as grace (with regard to man's freedom from guilt and his orientation towards his goal), and allow the supernatural act (of faith, love and so on) to remain even more deeply rooted in the person's innermost being. Theology as such cannot provide an answer to the question as to whether this greater personal depth of the mystical act, which is in itself natural, and the greater reflectiveness and purity of the transcendent experience, which accompanies it and which is in itself also natural, although it is exalted by grace, are in themselves wonderful (praeternatural), or naturally attainable by practice (or possibly both, according to the level at which the phenomenon occurs). This question may simply be regarded as open, in which case mysticism may occur as a natural, pure experience of transcendence when the mediation of categories either partly or completely ceases and the old question is raised once again. How, in other words, can the incarnate structure of any Christian religious act be preserved in the mystical experience, since, according to this structure of incarnation, "secularity" has been made essentially Christian by God's assumption of human flesh? This question can only be properly answered by reference to the "pure" transcendence in mystical experience of Christian openness to the absolute mystery of God (which communicates itself to the world while still remaining a mystery). This pure mystical transcendence is also a participation in the death of Christ in love for the world. It is therefore not a process of "desecularization", but a saving transfiguration of all reality as created by God.

Karl Rahner

MYTH

A. Definition

"Myth" meant originally (Greek μῦθος) word, news, language, message, but could also mean an event and history. The word and message of myth are concerned with life, the world and things as a totality, describing their origins, relationships and meaning. More precisely, myth is characterized by the fact that it sees the empirical world and its happenings, and above all man and his action, in the light of a reality which constitutes them, makes them a unity and at the same time transcends them. This reality is that of the gods. The message which comes in the words of the myth deals with the action and influence of the gods. It is mostly in narrative form, a story which is a "sacred word" and hence traditional and authoritative. But myth should only be called "stories about the gods" insofar as the gods in such stories are regarded as the real origin and true ground, an effective reality which is also the norm which determines human action and earthly events. In myth, therefore, the adventures of the gods are inextricably interwoven with man and his destiny, and man and the world are drawn into the sphere of the being and actions of the gods.

Hence the function of myth is the explanation of origins, in the sense of a principle and foundation which "concurs" in the events of earth and cosmos and in human action, and is effectively at work therein. The events in the myth are "the origins of a given condition and the model for further developments, and myth as such is explanation" (J. Slok in *RGG*, IV, col. 1264).

It follows that myth was not regarded as fiction and fancy, but as a hereditary experience of reality, as word about true being and the all-sustaining event, not merely in the causal sense, but in the sense that it gave meaning and purpose to all actual being and happenings. This reveals a definite characteristic of the *time* proper to myth. It is remote, primordial, pre-historic, or again, the end of time, but distinct in any case from historical time, upon which it nonetheless acts. It thus brings about the beginning of human and earthly happenings, and points them towards their end. The mythical events are normative and appear as prototypes of all happenings. It may be said of myth, therefore, in a transferred sense, that "it never happened but it is always there".

The all-embracing original, fundamental and constitutive reality of the myth is living and active in religious worship. Here the protological or eschatological events become effective within time. The liturgical action recalls the mythical event and repeats and represents it in symbolic signs, actions and gestures. The words which accompany the cultic action repeat the words of the myth and release the forces which it contains.

B. Types

Within this basic structure, it is possible to classify certain types of myth, all of which exemplify the general structure. Cosmogonies tell in mythical form how the world began. The supreme being created it, or a number of gods worked together, or it resulted from war or conflict among the gods, or by emanation from a heavenly being and his members and parts, which are thought of as human in form. The anthropogonies, which tell of the origin of man, may be classed under the same heading. The story of man's being made from a mixture of material substances is very widespread. Myths of the original state describe the conditions which obtained after the world came to be, pointing out the grounds and origin of human existence and of the conditions, experiences, obscurities and riddles which it imposes on him: life, sex, suffering, evil, sin and death. Here we find the myths of the golden age, of paradise and of the change from the original state of well-being to the present situation. Thus the transformation myths tell of seduction and fall and of the flood. As a counterpart to these we have the soteriological myths of the coming saviour. Finally, the eschatological myths tell of how the world is destroyed by catastrophes at the end of time and then renewed, with the dead rising to life.

C. Presuppositions and Assessment of Myth

W. F. Otto has described myth as the primordial speech of the peoples of prehistory. But this is not altogether correct, since myth presupposes a definite epoch and an advanced stage of culture. Myths can only be composed when speculation on reality has attained a certain structure. At the stage of animism or pre-animism, where appearances and events themselves are regarded as the immediate vehicle of divine or diabolical powers, with no intermediate stages, myths cannot be elaborated. The distinction must be worked out between the sacred and profane. The world must be regarded as a cosmos. Man must have developed the faculty to differentiate and be able to distinguish the human from the divine, to see transcendence and immanence as contrasts, in spite of his tendency to unification. Only then are the conditions present under which myth can arise (J. Slok).

Various assessments are made of myth. Myth may be regarded as a comprehensive vision of the world, as an effort to give it meaning and purpose within the framework of the divine, the gods and the story of the gods, who are the ground, origin and end of all things and of all events. Such myth, as a "transcendental basic apperception", is assigned to the childhood of the race, the naive, pre-scientific and uncritical early stage of humanity and its history. Myth is said to owe its existence to the fact that man had no true notion of causality at this stage of his history. Those who are ignorant of natural causes and relationships but seek for explanations, attribute everything to the gods and their action. The mythical explanation replaces, obscures and hinders the discovery of empirical causes.

A critique of myth on the grounds that myth, in its narrative form, in its images, symbols, personification and dramatizations, is merely fiction which embodies no real knowledge, is already to be found in Greek philosophy as it passed from myth to *logos*, from image to concept of essence, from contemplation to knowledge. In contrast to the Sophists, who rejected all myth in the name of their Enlightenment, and to Aristotle, who assigned myth to the realm of poetry, Plato sought to free myth from its current inadequacies and repulsive elements and to look for its *logos*, its meaning and function, for the hidden truth which could be extracted from the myth itself. Above all, Plato called upon the myths in the service of human discourse about divine things and being as a whole.

Modern science, and above all the exact natural sciences, supersede myth by discovering and identifying the verifiable and calculable intramundane causes which not only render the myth and its explanation of things superfluous, but even impossible and outmoded. Similar conclusions result from the explanations of the origins, motives and interplay of historical events and human action, as offered by psychology, sociology and critical historical science.

Finally, modern philosophical anthropology takes a completely unmythical view of man. He is not the plaything of forces outside himself, divine or demonic. He is responsible to himself, master of himself, aware of his power over all things and of his initiative in the happenings of history.

This minimizing view of myth has not been allowed to pass unchallenged. The critique of myth as outlined above has been described as rationalistic, positivist, and superficial. Efforts have been made to bring to light once more the profound and imperishable meaning of myth.

The Romantics led the way, especially Görres, Schelling, Creuzer and Bachofen, who saw myth as the expression of the oldest and earliest experiences of mankind, with a genuine and undeniable relation to truth, communicating a perspective of reality to which empirical and positivist, abstract and rationalist concepts remain blind. Myth, according to this view, gives expression to the meaning which underlies all being, seeing the dimensions of the world and its events in depth. Hence the superseding or elimination of myth and its associated thought-form and language is not a mark of progress, but the loss of a major experience in the comprehension of reality. There can be no question, therefore, of downgrading or writing off myth, but only of interpreting it. "Mythical thinking has not passed away, it is proper to us in every age. We need to regain the mythical way of thinking in our assurance of reality" (K. Jaspers).

Myth is also given positive value in the modern study of religions, for example by such scholars as M. Eliade, R. Pettazzoni, W. F. Otto, K. Kerényi and L. Lévy-Bruhl. The endeavour is to show that the myths and their associated worship are by no means absurd, confused or unintelligible. The myths and the relevant cults represent on the contrary an experience of the mystery of reality and all that happens. Hence they are fully within the scope of human understanding, insofar as man is true to his human reality and does not try to "reduce it to the tyranny of technical, mechanical and logical causality" (A. E. Jensen).

A positive attitude to myth which has become very influential at present is to be found in the psychology of C. G. Jung. According to Jung, there is a "collective unconscious", the psychic background and matrix which is common to all men, though at the same time supra-personal. Here his analysis discovers archetypes, "forms or images of a collective nature", which are present and active in every mind, remnants of "historical mental states" which have been transmitted by tradition, migration and heredity. Closer inspection reveals that these archetypes are identical with the themes of myth. But then, the myths are really projections of the mind, more precisely, of the collective unconscious. Nonetheless – or rather, according to Jung, for this very reason – the myths, like the archetypes, are phenomena outside the scope of our arbitrary efforts and inventions. The reciprocal relationship between archetypes and myths gives myth an intense human interest, and indeed a truth, the only significance of which for Jung, however, is the sheer fact of its existence. In myth, man re-discovers himself. Myth is therefore to be accounted for and explained only in terms of psychology, not historically, rationally or sociologically. Any tendency to downgrade or eliminate myth can only appear to Jung as an impoverishment or indeed a destruction of man and of his soul.

D. Mythology

Mythology can be taken to mean either a collection of myths or the theory or science of myth and the myths. It can also mean the effort to bring out and articulate the statement, the *logos* of the myth. Mythology means further, as contrasted with *logos* as abstract, conceptual science, the special thought-form, perspective and language of myth. It means speaking with visualizations and images; calling on symbols, the language of things, using their character of sign and reference; using in particular spatial representations – above and below, height and depth, this side and the other side, in keeping with the various world-pictures. In this sense it is true that myth speaks of the beyond in terms of the here and now, of the unworldly in terms of the world, of the divine in terms of man (R. Bultmann). Mythology in this sense includes the (dramatic) narrative form and the tendency to personification.

E. Theological Assessment of Myth

Here the following viewpoints may be developed:

1. The express revelation of God, which culminates in the historical epiphany of Jesus Christ, came to and still comes to men who know of God and

the Godhead in a mythical way in historically and sociologically conditioned religions. Nonetheless, revelation as event and word is not to be derived from myth, to which it is explicitly opposed.

2. Since the definitive historical revelation is an event and a word which springs from the free decree of God's love, that which can be known and expressed of revelation is *formally* akin to what myth is trying to say: to its statement, given in discourse and concepts full of action and vivid imagery, about God and the Godhead and the relationship to the world and to men determined thereby. Without the vivid imagery of mythical notions, the knowledge of God's saving act, which passes from myth to *logos* and surpasses while absorbing both, would remain an empty thing. And such knowledge is desirable and necessary for the sake of truth. To this extent, therefore, the mode of apprehension proper to myth, when properly understood, is not in opposition to knowledge of revelation, but is ordained to it, as the *logos* is, and partakes of the analogous character of that knowledge. It is in fact a mode of knowing that which surpasses all comprehension and expression and which can be known only "in a mirror dimly".

3. The revelation culminating in the incarnation of the Son of God supersedes and surpasses the combination of Godhead and world, of divine and human action, which myth described in many ways but without clear distinction, and hence rather surmised than grasped. Myth is predominantly dramatic, vivid and concrete. But these qualities are supremely present in the epiphany of God in the man Jesus and his history, in whom all promises can be fulfilled, who is the image of the invisible God and of whom it can be said: "He who has seen me has seen the Father" (Jn 14:9).

It is therefore possible to say that the elements stated in many myths are applicable to Jesus Christ. Mythical traits, images and notions may be drawn upon to expound the mystery of Christ and the meaning of his deeds and words. Such expositions do not turn the revelation in Christ into a myth, but relate myth to revelation in a way paved by revelation itself. Hence it follows that not only is revelation not myth, but that where it has occasion to reflect explicitly on myth, it takes a clear and definite stand against it, as in 1 Tim 1:4; 2 Tim 4:4; 2 Pet 1:16. But the faith which reflects on revelation and the preaching which communicates it may make use of myths. The insight given in myth is invoked to lend apt expression to the dimensions of the universal salvation given in revelation. When myth is thus related to the person of Jesus Christ and his historical work of salvation, myth is at once abrogated and fulfilled, its end in Christ being also its perfecting.

4. From this we can deduce how revelation is the crisis of myth and the judgment upon it. Revelation is the rejection of the univocal and undifferentiated treatment of the relationship of the divine and human. Confession of faith in the triune God – in contrast to the gods – expresses the absolute transcendence, sovereignty and freedom of God with regard to the world, and sees this world, in a wholly non-mythical way, as the work of God, the creation. And this again means that the world itself is emancipated to be its own non-divine self. Revelation is the negation of myth, since in contrast to myth it recognizes the non-recurrent and irreversible character of history, historicity and time as a determinant of revelation, and the Christ-event within time as having taken place once and for all. Myth contains and welcomes many gods and many stories about them. No concrete detail is obligatory, much less exclusive to any myth. Myths appear in many variations and combinations. But revelation claims to be obligatory and exclusive. It is the concrete decisiveness of

God in Jesus of Nazareth which has a universal power of attraction and demands a personal answer and an existentially founded decision in faith.

Man, as described by revelation, is not, as in myth, a nature subject to the forces of destiny and unable to determine his own fate. He is a person, a being living in history, a being who takes responsible decisions in history and recognizes the work of Christ as a deed which sets him free for himself and frees him from the gods, elements, lords, powers and fatalities of which myth is full. Thus revelation is the horizon within which man finds his true place and his real meaning.

Heinrich Fries

N

NATURAL LAW

Natural Law (Moral)

1. *The notion.* Natural law is here the natural moral law, using a broader sense of the word "law" than in the physical "laws of nature", where it is natural necessity, the order of non-rational nature. There the natural laws of physics and biology are at work, which are studied by the natural sciences. Such law makes no claims on man's freedom and hence has no moral character. But the natural moral law in a wide sense embraces the whole field of morality. It is understood as the order of things assigned to man by his creator for the development of his human qualities. This order is to be rationally known and used as the basis for free action. At least among Catholics, natural law in the strict sense deals with the moral law as affecting the due order between man and man, and man and society. It comprises the realm of moral obligation which can be determined in the form of norms for the minimum standard of moral behaviour and also be enforceable as law. In non-Catholic thinking, however, law is not always considered part of the moral realm. Hence the notion of natural law is often used in various senses, although the function of study of the natural law seems unambiguous enough. It is to describe the dignity of the person, the rights of man, and give them validity in social life. No strict distinction is made in ecclesiastical pronouncements or theological writings between natural law (in the wider sense) and natural rights (natural law in the strict sense). Here, therefore, natural law is taken in the wider sense, as the more comprehensive term. The answer to the question of the foundations of natural law, its knowability and content, its universal validity and changeability presuppose a certain understanding of the world, man and God.

2. *Ontological starting-point.* The doctrine of the natural law is an established part of Catholic moral theology. Since the words of scriptural revelation alone do not suffice to establish ethical norms, recourse must be had to the being or nature of man. The key concept of nature opens the way to moral directives which are binding on all men. The Christian story of creation provides the foundation, and a theistic world-view sees a strict relationship between the creator God and all created things. There is a divine thought at the root of all created things, which is to be respected by man. Man finds the law of his moral action primarily in the truth of God's creation – in the nature and essence of things. Thus the philosophical axiom *agere sequitur esse* comes into play.

The "ought" is founded on the "is". The principle only implies, to begin with, a close connection between being and obligation, ontology and ethics, being valid also for the realm of grace – every gift bestowed by God on man becomes a task. The principle suggests that for man the demands of morality are not merely juridical but stem from the structure of his being, his nature. Hence natural law is not a heteronomous morality but the structure of moral order which is assigned by God to man in creation and imposed on him as the goal of self-fulfilment. But all this as yet tells us nothing about the universality and unchangeability of such norms.

But the norm for moral behaviour is neither human nature in the state of original justice nor in the state of original sin. It is that residual state of man which always remains the same independently of each historical mode of existence – or any other – and which underlies all the historical reality of man. It is the metaphysical nature of man, that is, what necessarily belongs to man at all times, as such. Nonetheless, this notion of human nature is an abstraction. It has never in fact existed. Using this notion of nature and under the influence of Stoic thought one would arrive at a static concept of nature and an absolute unchangeability of the natural law, in spite of the historicity of man.

3. *Knowability*. The mentality of most peoples points implicitly to the existence of a natural law, which is there before all positive human legislation and appears to be knowable to man, at least in certain outlines. This capacity for moral knowledge should not be denied to man on principle, otherwise he cannot be held responsible for his actions. Nonetheless, he has not an exhaustive knowledge of it, and he can only know the truth from certain perspectives and in its actual historical relationships. It is impossible to say with absolute certainty how far man can penetrate to the structures of his being, to the order of nature as proper to man.

The Church has often affirmed – at Vatican I as also in the encyclical *Humani Generis* – that in spite of the wounds of original sin man can know the basic principles of natural law, though the help of revelation may in fact be morally necessary (*D* 2305f.; 2320ff.). Since in the logical order man can know the norms of morals and rights independently of the words of revelation, the doctrine of the natural law is one of the foundations which Christians can use to discuss ethical questions with all men. The history of cultures and ethnology show that all peoples attain a certain moral order, though the content is not everywhere the same. The ontological basis and the knowability of the natural law give it universal validity and make it the criterion of all legislation. And the Christian order of salvation did not abrogate the natural law, but rather integrated and elevated it. A pure nature independent of any grace of God has never existed.

4. *Content*. With the help of his reason, man seeks for concrete norms, the content of natural law, which will serve his effort at self-realization, and reject those which radically contradict it. In its recognition of what is natural law, reason is not autonomous. There are data which man must necessarily take into account. His "natural inclinations" give a first general orientation as to the goals to which human conduct should be directed.

Though in the OT morality is primarily based on the word of God and his covenant with Israel, while the ten commandments bear on the history of salvation and not on natural rights, tradition has nonetheless to a great extent regarded the "second table" of the Decalogue as natural law. It appears chiefly in the absolute limits which cannot be violated without detriment to human dignity, e.g., the prohibition of murder. Paul concludes from the behaviour of pagans that they have implanted in them by nature a sense of a standard by which they know what they ought to do. The Apostle also holds that the pagans know a certain number of basic norms, which are in substance the same as part of the Decalogue.

Much of what was long regarded as the unalterable order of nature is now seen to be a historical form, and sometimes a specifically Western form of human self-fulfilment. Thus the subordination of woman to man demanded in Eph 5:24 is no longer regarded as a basic relationship between man and woman, demanded by nature and ratified by Scripture. It is seen as a historically conditioned element of Western patriarchal society. The personal nature of man, his call to shape the world, his social character, are undoubtedly basic postulates founded on the nature of man and always recognizable by man. But in each age he has to learn and decide anew how far he can claim mastery over the infra-spiritual reality and over "nature" within man himself. It is also part of man's nature to be a social being. But just as society goes through history and developments, so too man. His social nature points at once to history and development. Hence the actual actions of man cannot be determined merely in the light of an abstract metaphysical nature. His historical nature as it has come to be in the present, and his situation, must also be envisaged. Thus the natural law takes on a necessary relation to the situation. All human action must be orientated to its present moment.

5. *Historicity*. The static view of nature is foreign to the mentalities of the OT and the NT. Scripture attests the intervention of God in the history of man. It gives testimony to a history of salvation. All its moral directives are orientated to men in the concrete and have the character of a "situated" ethics. Without denying the existence of timelessly valid and unchangeable norms, one may renounce Scripture as a proof for the unchangeability of the natural law. Hence the natural law must always be seen with reference to the concrete man. Definite basic structures of human existence may no doubt be deduced. But a code of fixed norms of natural law would be in constant need of questioning or testing. For the NT mind, history is the proper dimension of man and his intrinsic constitution. The being of man and his proper nature is a task which has to be understood and accomplished in the course of time. Hence human nature does not merely develop (independently of human freedom). It also has a history and makes progress. The potentialities of the realization of the being of man expand. Simultaneously, the responsibility and perils of man grow greater. This development does not merely take place in a straight line as a process which unfolds automatically. In keeping with man's freedom of decision there are also leaps, backward steps and slowing down. Man does not merely have a history: he *is* history. He realizes his being by mastering nature and making it serve him, he shapes things and gives himself values and goals. This purposefulness indicates an orientated historical development of the moral consciousness. Its goal is first a clearer consciousness, reflective awareness, but hence also a greater distance and freedom with regard to involvement in nature. In this development of freedom and the resulting responsibility and morality, man strives to attain a higher degree of personalization, but at the same time a greater degree of social commitment – where, however, the dignity of the individual may not be violated, though the play of freedom undergoes some restrictions for the sake of society.

Today man understands his task of shaping the world as to some extent including the possibility of changing his "nature". Interventions in the course of nature are in fact to a great extent desirable for man's existence. Hence they are not *ipso facto* immoral. But they must not be detrimental to man's dignity. The set of problems which are now posed arise from the phenomenon of history and historical change, which means that all reality is understood radically as in historical process. Hence too a dynamic view of natural law. But the historical viewpoint in ethics does not lead to an unbridled relativism. Through all changes and developments man remains ultimately the personal subject who is capable of history and is historical. There remains further the endless task of describing exactly the really unchangeable element of the being of man. Even if something appears empirically as universally valid, as belonging to the nature of man and unchangeable, this does not yet prove that it belongs absolutely to the nature of man. Nonetheless, the student of ethics must be content with this type of knowledge, which is always in need of supplements. His task is always to pose further questions and to strive for a more profound foundation for his norms.

Knowledge of the abstract metaphysical nature of man, which is the basis of the natural law, must therefore be supplemented by the elements which determine man in his nature as historically conditioned. Along with his "changeless" nature there is a dynamically changing nature. There are many changing levels of the human person which possess more than "accidental" significance. They are rather forms and expressions of man and his development. The process of hominization is by no means finished. Hence in the justification of its norms, moral theology will have to take into account the historical changes of human society and of mankind as such. It cannot say what tasks will be proposed to it tomorrow as it unfolds anew, in the light of man's being, the potentialities of man. So too the actual state of the natural law does not determine finally all the moral demands which may be made on man.

It would be an illusion to think that man has grasped exhaustively the essence of man and the natural structures of his conduct. Human knowledge being historically conditioned, limited, and always confined to certain perspectives, we are justified in speaking of a history of human knowledge of truth. Knowledge of the natural law is also a historical process. Hence we may speak of a change in the natural law from three aspects: on the basis of profounder insight, on the basis of changing situations and on the basis of change in man himself. Progress in knowledge means that ethical assertions are made more precise or altered. This historicity of human knowledge brings with it fragility and new perspectives. Even knowledge of the natural law suffers the general fate of being provisional.

Along with the development of theoretical knowledge, change in the actual conditions of life also modifies the moral demands made on man. Duties which arose out of a particular age or culture have sometimes been too hastily declared to be timelessly valid. Things have been declared to be unnatural, as contrary to the nature of private property, money, woman or marriage, which were in fact only historically-conditioned and changeable moral issues. Altered conditions have considerably modified our views of private property, interest, the just war, the death penalty, sexuality and marriage.

But the gravest of changes takes place in man himself. He has the task of realizing and constantly developing his own nature. In the evolution of the whole cosmos, but above all in the planned shaping of the world by man, changes take place. Just as the individual remains the same personal subject, but is assigned different tasks in childhood, youth, maturity and old age, with different rights and duties, so too with the maturation of human society as a whole. There should be changes in the obligations arising from man's being. If history is an essential dimension of man's being, human nature must also be understood historically. We must envisage the nature of man as changing and being subjected to changes. Such change must always be in the service of a still greater measure of self-fulfilment (see *History* I).

6. *Natural law and eschatology*. The historical understanding of man and its application to his nature makes it impossible to speak simply of a predetermined essence, a "nature" from which the whole future development could be deduced. Hence the notion of nature now needs to be given a certain orientation to the goal and end of man. For a theistic world-view, this at once implies an orientation to a goal beyond this world. Since for Christians history is already history of salvation, now that the kingdom of God has already dawned with Christ, though not yet consummated, it is now impossible to make a strict division between nature and grace or to prescind from the supernatural end. Hence human nature in all its complexity and all the goals set before it are decisive for the deduction of moral norms. Hence the principle that the "ought" is founded on the "is" includes consideration of the end of man, of whose transcendence man has only a vague surmise without recourse to revelation. Hence the natural law is related to eschatology.

In the light of the goal towards which man is always only on the way, many positive "natural" obligations, such as the demands of love, take on the character of a command to attain the final end. The individual always fails to satisfy fully such a command. But on the other hand – and this is how ethics is referred to the present moment – the actual "condition of being" is the basis of the duties of the moment which the individual must be well able to perform. The tension between what is actually to be done and what is ultimately to be aimed at – between what is basically possible to man at this moment and what is held up to him as an unattainable goal – is intrinsic to the earthly life of man. This should help one to see that man is only on his way to the goal and is always a debtor before God, as Protestant ethics particularly underlines. Nonetheless, though not without the help of God's grace, he can fulfil the demands of ethics to some extent. This is true above all of prohibitions.

7. *Protestant theology and natural law*. Very often Protestant theologians understand by nature the basic rectitude of man as yet unspoiled by sin. In general, they flatly reject the Catholic doctrine of the natural law. The profound opposition between Protestant and Catholic here is chiefly based on the doctrine of the total corruption of man and the resulting blindness to knowledge and values. This scepticism appears in various degrees in Protestant theologians, from a radical rejection of all natural law and knowledge of it (H. Thielecke) to the positive attitudes of P. Althaus, E. Brunner and D. Wendland. But the term natural law is mostly replaced by other expressions such as orders (of creation etc.) or institutions, which are used to make place reluctantly for the permanent values of the natural law theory. Even the radical thesis of the totally existentiell lack of order in the world, at the basis of the thinking and theology of H. Thielecke, cannot be carried through consistently. He too finds it necessary to attribute to reason the power to distinguish between objective and unobjective, true and false. Hence the assertion that Protestant theology rejects all notion of natural law cannot be maintained. Criticism of Catholic views of natural law is often directed against certain one-sided views which may still survive or have in fact been abandoned, against false ideas of it

or against a non-historical rigidity noticed there. The Catholic theologian will do well to note the justifiable interests which underlie such criticism (see *Ethics*).

8. *Natural law and ecclesiastical magisterium.* In its pronouncements on the natural law, the Church has always taken up a protective attitude, maintaining that there is a true natural law and hence moral duties deriving from the nature of man which are knowable by human reason at least in their fundamental structures. In view of a number of authentic pronouncements of the magisterium on problems of the natural law, as for instance in the matter of regulation of births (cf. the encyclicals *Casti Connubii* and *Humanae Vitae*), the question arises as to the right of the Church to intervene to impose theological obligations in the matter of natural law. The appeal to the infallibility of the Church in matters of faith and morals overlooks the truth that this infallibility in the strict sense is related to the "deposit of faith", the actual content of faith and revelation. The Church has constantly claimed the right – most recently in the encyclical *Humanae Vitae* – to make authoritative pronouncements in matters of natural morality. But it has been objected (J. David) that the Church can make no authoritative and infallible pronouncements on the contents of the purely natural law, since propositions of purely natural law come perhaps under the competence of the jurisdictional or governing authority, but not under that of the doctrinal. However, the sharp distinction here made between the scope of the doctrinal office (merely the doctrine of the faith) and the pastoral office (government and education) is not convincing. The question further arises as to whether there is such a thing at all as a "purely natural" realm of moral law, where the Church would have no authority, since the whole man as such is included in the process of redemption. This thesis is certainly correct in asserting that in non-theological matters the Church must invoke the aid of the relevant sciences. The matters must be discussed primarily in the light of reason, since the Church has received no direct revelation about them. Hence false presuppositions stemming from the conditions of a given historical period can bring about erroneous conclusions in the authentic declarations of the magisterium. Examples of this could be given from the history of matrimonial ethics.

Since the whole man is embraced by the order of salvation, the Church rightly claims the right to speak authoritatively in questions of the natural law – not merely as pastoral directives, but as doctrinal assertions. Nonetheless, the theologian will examine carefully the notion of nature supposed in such declarations and test its validity in the light of the acquired results of the human sciences. For in the past, the order of nature was mostly identified with the order of God's creation, and man was asked to recognize his place in this world order, to take over in his freedom and to realize those goals of nature which the rest of creation aimed at instinctively. Without contesting the validity of this principle, it may be affirmed that man now takes a much freer attitude to the natural order. He knows that he is charged with shaping the world, not merely by accepting passively the goals of creation, but by giving this very nature goals and ends. It is certainly his task to shape and manipulate nature rationally. Hence, within certain bounds, he may interfere with the course of nature. This particular notion has hardly received proper attention up to the present in the pronouncements of the Church.

In Catholic theology today, discussion of natural law is more and more open to arguments from Catholic social theory, and is to some extent being replaced by such thinking. The gospel is being investigated as to its social ethics and its dynamic tendency to change society.

Johannes Gründel

NATURAL THEOLOGY

A. The Philosophical Problem

1. *The history of natural theology.* The extremely complex nature of the problems set by natural theology (or "philosophical theology") may be seen from a critical examination of some aspects of its history. The traditional philosophy in question was orientated apologetically in the Church, and its scholastic inheritance was elaborated into a special discipline of natural theology at the beginning of modern times. From the time of the early Christian apologists of the 2nd century it has been asking "whether" God exists. In doing so, it presupposed a general understanding of "what" God is, and some general understanding of reality which made such an enquiry reasonable. Historically, the result of putting the question of natural theology in this traditionally abbreviated way was that "God" appeared as a special object of metaphysical enquiry along with others. And hence very generally, since Christian Wolff (d. 1754), the question of God was treated in "special metaphysics", instead of in general metaphysics, which is its objective and historical place. In this distortion of the metaphysical perspective it was easy to assign God a place in the realm of being. It was a transcendence understood as a beyond with no relationship to the world (so Deism), and God's action, in spite of the critique of Kant, was implicitly assimilated to the particular causes registered by science. Thus, for instance, proofs of the existence of God were based on natural science, with appeals to the beginning of the world or the constant increase of entropy. In contrast to this impoverishment of the question, natural theology now has recourse to the scholastic sources, particularly to Thomas Aquinas, and interprets metaphysics in the light of modern thought, particularly along the lines of transcendental philosophy and existential ontology. But in view of the deepening of the philosophical bases of the problems, it cannot attempt to give any answers or offer any proofs without having first considered the intellectual framework, the purpose and the linguistic field of metaphysics. It must show that the fundamental questions about being and God are primordial, meaningful and necessary questions of human existence. This justification will be hermeneutical and transcendental.

2. *The possibility of natural theology.* a) *The opening up of the horizon.* The questions of being and of God ultimately derive their force and orientation from man's question about himself. Man is only himself in his openness to being in general and hence to the absolute ground of the whole. This basic (religious and philosophical) relation of man to the absolute is expounded by metaphysics and philosophical anthropology in terms of their poles – man and absolute being. If the origin and purpose of man, like those of his world, are defined by their relation to the absolute, man must himself have knowledge of the absolute, if he is to know his own nature and that of the world. Hence man's search for self-understanding, of which the question of his understanding of the world is part, culminates in the question of God. At heart, it is in fact the same question. It is one question which appears on many levels and inevitably challenges man. Since he is an incomplete spiritual being, he is himself radically a questioning search for the absolute through which he can be fulfilled and find wholeness. He cannot but decide in face of the absolute, in the practical self-determination of conscious freedom, which includes the moment of theoretical self-interpretation and world-view.

b) *The epistemological foundation.* Human knowledge, especially metaphysical knowledge, being finite and questioning, cannot on principle constitute its object by producing it from the autonomous spontaneity of the subject. Man has contact with reality in knowledge only insofar as he allows himself to be determined by this contact in experience and its insights. So too philosophical knowledge of God must rest completely on the openness of God, who freely discloses himself in human experience. Natural theology, however, in its strictly traditional form, begins its demonstration of the existence of God by deferring to the needs of the rational verification and communicability of the process of thought. Hence it does not start with religious or existentiell experience, but with everyday, indubitable phenomena, such as change. Or when it aims at a purely metaphysical or transcendental proof in the strict sense, it begins with the necessary structure of beings directly experienced as such, or with that of the experiencing spirit. But in all these approaches, the presence of God in the empirical foundation of the demonstration is so little clear it can hardly be strictly and evidently demonstrated by an analysis of experience. It must rely on rational deduction, which rests on insight into the metaphysical dimension.

But the plus of the metaphysical dimension over the empirical data of the senses can only be understood and demonstrated as true and real if it derives not merely from the subjective spontaneity of human thought, freely confident or necessarily affirming, but is due as a whole to the receptive encounter of knowledge with reality itself. The plus stems therefore from experience. All that the constructive activity of metaphysical thinking does, in analysis and abstraction, synthesis, demonstration and deduction, is to disclose and illuminate reflectively the realm of receptive spiritual perception. Further than this it does not go, though it does undoubtedly go beyond what is immediately and articulately accessible to the direct view of experience. Since, however, the metaphysical principles (of deduction) are not merely ontologically valid but logically inevitable, and hence belong to the essence of thought, the experience which founds the principle is not an extrinsic and accidental addition to thought, but is prior to it as its origin.

This transcendental experience is the primordial clarity of the act of spiritual selfhood and being. Man comes to consciousness of himself in this light, by recognizing himself as present by consciousness to the all of reality. Thereby he experiences himself and the whole of the world as founded and called by the absolute. This basic experience, explaining itself and appropriating itself personally and deliberately, produces from within itself the explicit act of thinking in its essential reality. This thought is first articulate in the form of a question, but since it is the question of the ultimate ground, the absolute meaning and unconditional truth, it already formally programmes the one adequate answer. But the answer is only explicitly given when thought and the basic experience within it comes upon the concrete intramundane object – which may only be thought itself – and by virtue of its own illumination discovers levels which were not directly definable in the experience of the object alone. What now appears is the contingent being of the object and its dependence on God, and here thought finds itself concretely ratified and fulfilled. The question of the ground or sufficient reason is therefore a necessary, *a priori* structure of man, but his essence and dynamism are constituted by the previous experience of the unconditioned ground, and are verified in the thought which makes contact with the world.

Since human knowing is in a tension between experience and articulate concept, natural theology is by its nature exposed to a double peril. It may neglect the strict logic of analysis and synthesis, a conceptual process which is an intermediate one, and therefore positively mediating, for the sake of proximity to experience – as when a merely existentiell indication is offered. Or the formal logical development may fail to prepare for the ontological and existential understanding of the concept through a phenomenological interpretation of the experience.

3. *The development of natural theology.* a) In the basic experience, ontologically and in the metaphysics of knowledge, the impact of the absolute is the ground for man's being opened out to the whole of reality or being in general. But in the theory of knowledge, dealing with express and explicitating knowledge as it gropes its way back to its origin, being, as the ontological horizon of the world, is prior to subsistent being. Hence in explicit knowledge the absolute can only be attained through the unlimited ontological realm of reality as a whole or of being. Otherwise it would be conceived of merely as the highest of beings, which participated with other finite beings in the same (univocal, rationalistically conceptualized) being, instead of providing by its gift the realm of participation for all the finite, itself unoriginated and its own ground. If then natural theology is not an independent discipline, by the interpretation of being in the light of its absolute ground, and hence merely ontology taken to its utmost conclusions, the interpretation of being in its general sense, forming thus general metaphysics, its primary task must be to expound the meaning of being, along with ontology and philosophical anthropology. The interpretation given to being will determine whether God can be known, and how properly known and under what aspects.

Since God's transcendence cannot be grasped exhaustively by finite thinking, the fundamental understanding of being rightly undergoes historical change. New aspects of the "image" of God come to the fore, and analogous changes take place in the "image" of man, the empirical starting-point of knowledge of God (as the privileged place of God's showing through in the world), the principle of the transition to God (and so the definition of the God-world relationship), and likewise the conception of "proofs" of the existence of God. Hence, for instance, efficient causality, unity, truth and goodness, ground and goal, purpose and fulfilment, blessedness, justice, love or summons can be keys to the understanding of being and God, the various aspects of which are held together, beyond any formally conceptual mediation, by the identity of the one absolute God who shows through the various modes of experience. The "history and historicity" of the understanding of being, which is prior to metaphysics, does not exclude the necessary investigation of the permanent basic structures. But it means that natural theology, if it is to be intelligible and effective, must try to speak in terms of contemporary understanding of being, and hence must also find the relevant starting-point in experience and correspond to the given historical self-understanding of man.

b) The systematic structure of natural theology explains the absoluteness of being along the threefold way of negation, affirmation and reference to the mystery (in negative theology). It thus leads to the centre and ground of being in the absolutely subsistent being of God. Here the demonstration of the reality of God already includes in principle the whole philosophical definition of the essence and action of God. The traditional structure of natural theology – the existence of God, the essence and attributes of God, the action of God – may be didactically helpful as a way of conceptual demarcation, but obscures the radical unity of the philosophical knowledge of God, to which

God's existence and nature are accessible only as a unity, from his action, his finite works. Hence the central effort of natural theology must be directed to the demonstration of God, and especially to its foundations, but not to the broad development of the logical consequences. In this demonstration, God is not merely seen, along the lines of scientific explanation, as the possible, hypothetical, explanation. He is recognized as the necessary condition without which the finite itself could not exist.

The metaphysical proof of the existence of God sees the concretely-given beings, by virtue of their "ontological difference" from the illimited, unconditional nature of being, as finite and contingent. Hence they are ontologically secondary and based on another – by causality – which as the adequate ground must itself be infinite and nonconditioned. The metaphysical proof can take on various forms, not only in the empirical starting-point for the exhibition of contingence, but also and especially, as the variously accented understanding of being demands, through the various conceptions of the basing of the finite by God, which is not confined to efficient causality.

Since the contingence and dependence of the finite can only be known by the spontaneous, implicit pre-orientation of the human spirit to being and God, the metaphysical proof includes epistemologically a transcendental moment. Hence even when it begins with the infra-personal, it is always radically personal. And conversely, it is the presence of non-conditioned being, irreducible to man, which enables the transcendental proof to pass from the immanence of consciousness and from the concept of God to God himself, as the proof exhibits God as the condition of possibility of human spiritual activity. Hence metaphysical and transcendental proof go together, completing each other.

4. *The purpose of natural theology*. Philosophy is neither first nor fundamental in placing man before God and hence in the essential framework of his humanity. For man starts out by experiencing himself as constitutively touched by God in the ground of his being. And this experience he explicitates spontaneously, though imperfectly, in the forms of understanding embodied in language and concept. Hence theoretical knowledge is a primordial and essential element of human life, which strives to grasp and guide itself in full awareness. Man wishes to know explicitly that in believing in God he is taking his stand on the truth, and as a social being, he wishes to give an intelligible and well-founded account of the view of the world which he holds in faith. He must be able to have a rational understanding of himself and the world in relation to God, if his faith in God is not to evade encounter with the world and hence slip into the sentimental or the inauthentically existentiell. Since the basic experience is obscured and the spontaneous comprehension still imperfect, and since man is also faced with the task of responsible and therefore informed and alert living, which is always in danger from ideologies and errors, there results the inescapable obligation of seeing through to the end the spontaneous grasp, in a deliberate effort to have sure knowledge of the nature and purpose of reality, in other words, to philosophize. Here again knowledge of God is the fulfilment of the inner dynamism of philosophy.

Such knowledge does not ordinarily issue in the form of a fully elaborated natural theology. But this is a scientifically correct and defensible form of it, which is extremely important for the scientific cast of modern thinking, which is exposed to such a pluralism of world-views.

Nonetheless, even a natural theology which knows its own processes does not provide man with an objectifiable assurance, such as was attempted in the mathematical proof, where he could use his acquired knowledge of God to defend himself against the claim of the real God. The power and stringency of the metaphysical proof, which testifies indirectly to the absoluteness, universality and inexorability of the divine claim, depend on basic insights which are only fully perspicuous when the whole human person is committed, when receptivity has been purified by the moral will and when there is an existentiell openness to the absolute.

B. Natural Theology and the Theology of Revelation

The magisterium of the Church (*D* 1622, 1650, 1670, 1785, 1806, 2145; cf. also 1786), relying on Scripture (especially Wis 13:1–9; Rom 1:18–21) and tradition, maintains the possibility of a natural knowledge of God, and hence a double knowledge, one based on historical revelation and the other founded directly on rational insight. Their scientific forms are theology (of revelation) and natural theology. This double knowledge is only possible and meaningful if the two types complete each other in an articulated unity. If theology is not to come under a rule alien to its nature in natural theology, the structural principle of the unity in question must be derivable from theology as the goal and fulfilment. It must be sketched in the light of God's self-communication in grace.

Since grace has a revelatory character, so too human nature, the intelligent spirit, is orientated to grace, that is, to God. It is *potentia oboedientialis*, since otherwise grace could not come in its revelatory character. Hence the human spirit, whose knowledge is centred on the God who can freely communicate himself, is the condition of possibility for grace and revelation, a condition set up in its autonomy by revelation. This transcendental ordination of the human spirit to God as unoriginated origin, and hence presumably to God the Father, founds and begins the explicit knowledge of God which is naturally and even philosophically attainable. But the *de facto* concrete totality of this knowledge may have already been influenced by grace, by virtue of God's universal offer of grace.

The natural knowledge of God does not stem from the self-assertion of the creature which tries to master the transcendence of God by way of a natural *a priori*, a being common to God and to itself, as maintained by K. Barth and dialectical theology. Natural theology is to be understood as a presupposition and intrinsic moment of the historical self-disclosure of the Father in Christ. It has knowledge of the incomprehensible transcendence, the all-encompassing activity and the personal nature of God. And these (in spite of shifts in the historical knowledge of them) form the permanent, supra-historical ground and horizon which alone make it possible to reckon with an intervention and appearance of God in history without his being absorbed in history. This first permanent stage of the knowledge of God is based on God's free self-revealing act of creation, and hence on the Logos, in whom all things are created. And this is true not merely of the beings of the world from which God is known, but also of the human faculty of knowledge, whose exercise is activated by God.

The progressive self-revelation of God in the history of salvation, especially in the OT, should not – e.g., in the theological treatise *De Deo Uno* – be interpreted as the illustration and repetition of natural, metaphysical knowledge of God but as the history of the self-disclosure of God which prepares directly for the historical revelation in Christ. It shows God not just in his appropriate, metaphysically knowable being, but in his historical action, as he freely wishes to be for man.

The theological place of natural theology must be defined in view of the several levels on which the one historically developing revelation of God exists. It appears as an essential, pre-theological function of theology itself and must take a central place in the formation of theologians, for the sake of the unabridged totality of the (self-)utterance of God, and for the preaching which introduces men to the faith. Since it is a preparatory and remote introduction to the revelation in Christ, it must not be in opposition to the God of revelation, either expressly or implicitly by virtue of its field of vision. It prepares for the God of revelation by a philosophical concept of God which is at least open to a possible revelation. But then again, natural theology must not pre-determine and limit the nature of revelation, by appearing rationalistically as the fully-formed basis of the "religion of reason". Nor must it anticipate it, by presenting the content of revelation as its own and naturally knowable. The "image" of God in natural theology is abstract and relatively indeterminate. Positively, it throws open the basic existentiell question of man about salvation or the God of grace, and negatively, it leaves it open. Hence it must be distinguished from the "image" of God in revelation, so that by virtue of this difference, in which the freedom of revelation appears, the God of the philosophers is correctly said to be not (yet) the God of faith.

Klaus Riesenhuber

NATURE

I. Philosophical and Theological

The Theological Concept

1. Since the 13th century, Catholic theology has systematically had recourse to the notion of nature to explain the transcendence and immanence of grace in man. Except for the Nominalists of the 14th to 16th centuries, there was always fundamental agreement about the concept, which has been reconsidered in depth during the past fifty years. The notion of nature is almost totally absent from the Eastern Orthodox theology of grace and has met with strong opposition from Protestant theology. It is a not unimportant concept both within Catholic theology and in the ecumenical dialogue. In the treatises *De Trinitate* and *De Verbo Incarnato* nature is contrasted with person. Here we consider it only as correlative to grace.

Nature is not a biblical concept, but results from theological reflection on a primordial element of the NT (especially in the writings of Paul and John), "the grace of God through Christ". Man, subjected to the dominion of sin and death, is called to share in the glory of Christ and through Christ in the life of God itself. This participation has already begun with man's justification by faith and will reach its eschatological fulfilment by union with Christ through the resurrection and the vision of God. A number of points must be noted in this revealed truth. (i) There is no other grace for man than the grace of Christ. The primordial intention of God in creating the world and man is the direct communication of himself to Christ and through Christ to the world and men. (ii) The grace of Christ is for sinful man. But grace is not exclusively liberation from sin. It is principally communion of life with God through Christ. (iii) Justification brings with it the interior transformation of man by the Spirit of Christ who produces in him faith, filial confidence in God and love of men. (iv) The presence of the Holy Spirit in man is the vital principle of the resurrection. All creation will share the glory of Christ the Lord with and through man.

From Irenaeus on, the Greek Fathers understood this participation of the life of God through Christ as a true "divinization" (θείωσις) of man. The Latin Fathers, especially Augustine and Leo the Great, adopted this concept, which came to be the foundation of the whole theology of grace in the Middle Ages, especially in Thomas Aquinas. The Oriental liturgy as well as the Western reflects the theme of the divinization of man by participation in the glory of Christ. The magisterium of the Church, especially the two Vatican Councils, expresses the essence of grace in the same terms (*DS* 3005, *D* 1786; Vatican II, *Lumen Gentium*, art. 2; *Dei Verbum*, art. 6; *Gaudium et Spes*, art. 21; *Ad Gentes*, art. 2).

The gratuitousness of grace and hence the gratuitousness of the divinization of man, that is, of God's self-communication to Christ and so to men and the world coincides absolutely with the gratuitousness of the incarnation, which is the supreme personal gift of God himself. The full explanation of this truth inevitably raises the question: Would the creation of man and of the world for man be meaningless without the divinizing grace of the incarnation? Does the existence of man as "spirit-in-world" necessarily imply his call to share in the life of God itself, that is, the self-communication of God to man in his Son made man? It would be irrational to maintain that man, in his fundamental structure as "intellectual creature in the world" necessarily includes his destination to divinization. The absolute freedom of the self-communication of God in Christ forces us to conclude that though God made man and the world for Christ (that is, to give himself to the man Christ and through him to man), he could have created man without necessarily including in his intention the personal communication of himself which is the divinization of man through the incarnation.

Hence the theological concept of nature is the following: man in his fundamental structure of "bodily-spiritual creature", is intelligible and potentially real without the grace of divinization: the creation of man and the world is possible without the incarnation. It is a limit-hypothesis, demanded by the total theological explanation of the proper gratuitousness of the incarnation and the divinization of man, in contrast to the gratuitousness of creation. The whole self-communication of God *ad extra* is free. But his self-communication through the incarnation entails a special gratuitousness inasmuch as it entails the divinization of the intellectual creature. Hence the existence of man non-divinized by grace is a possible hypothesis.

Nature is a theological concept which stems from reflection on the revealed truth of the divinization of man by the grace of Christ. The possibility of the state of nature is a conclusion whose affirmation is only justified insofar as it appears necessary for the full understanding of the strict gratuitousness of divinization. The conclusion is not reached by starting from an abstract consideration of the possible, but from the data of revelation and from the economy actually established by God, that is, the divinization of man through the incarnation.

Hence nature is a "vestigial concept" (*Restbegriff* – K. Rahner), arrived at by abstraction from divinizing grace in man. It is certainly not a purely negative concept, since it implies the rationality of man in the constitutive dimensions of his finite spirit and his fundamental relations to God, men and the world – implying the absolute possibility of natural religion and ethics (cf. *D* 1785, 1786, 1806; *DS* 3004, 3005, 3026). The theological concept of nature is not necessarily linked to any given philosophy, though its appearance in the history of theology is due above all to the influence of Aristotelianism. Philosophical reflection can arrive at a concept of human nature. But the theological concept is different from the philosophical, not merely in the mental processes from which it stems, but also in its content, which includes the radical capacity of man for the divinizing grace of the incarnation. This fundamental aspect of the theological concept of nature is not within the reach of human reason.

2. The historical genesis of the theological concept of nature will throw light on the meaning of the term here. The Greek Fathers contrasted "image" and "likeness" (εἰκών - ὁμοίωσις) to designate respectively the state of man in his creation and his progressive attainment of perfection. But the "image" already contains the initial grace and hence is not identical with the nature of man. It is rather the nature of man in the history of salvation. There are undoubtedly some isolated reflections on man as an intellectual "creature", elevated to the grace of divinization (Athanasius, Gregory of Nyssa, Didymus of Alexandria, Cyril of Alexandria: *PG*, XXVI, col. 173; XLIV, col. 1280; XXXIX, col. 791; LXXIII, col. 153). But Maximus the Confessor forms a remarkable exception, since he uses the philosophical concept of nature (in the Aristotelian sense) to explain the divinization of man by grace (Stoeckle, *Gratia supponit naturam*, pp. 91–98).

St. Augustine mostly considers the nature of man in the history of salvation: man as he was *in fact* created by God (in the situation of grace) or as in fact he comes into the world (in the situation of sin). But in some cases he applies to man the concept of nature in its strict sense, prescinding from sin and in contrast to "grace" (*PL*, XIII, col. 352; XXXII, cols. 597, 1203; XXXIII, cols. 767f.; XXXVIII, col. 173; XLI, col. 357; XLIV, cols. 272–6, 744, 896; XLV, cols. 51, 53, 59, etc.). Man receives from Christ the grace of divinization, in his nature as a spiritual creature. This twofold concept of nature in Augustine (with the former sense predominating) was reflected throughout the works of the Latin Fathers and remained in vigour at the commencement of medieval scholasticism. With the coming of the 13th century (Philippus Cancellarius etc.) the theology of grace was based systematically on the Aristotelian notion of nature. Thomistic theology attained a notable depth and equilibrium along these lines. But it must be emphasized that St. Thomas radically modified the Aristotelian concept in the light of the revealed truth about the grace of divinization. Man is nature precisely through the illimited opening of his mind to the Absolute Spirit, that is, through his fundamental capacity for the vision of God. The Thomistic explanation of the proper gratuitousness of the divinization of the intellectual creature (*indebitum naturae*) logically implies the possibility that man might not have been called in fact to the vision of God. This conclusion was explicitly drawn in the 14th and 15th centuries (Thomas Angelicus, Dionysius the Carthusian) and further developed in the 16th century by Cajetan. In his effort to underline the reality of original sin, Michael Baius affirmed that man had necessarily to receive in his creation the gifts of "original justice", which appertained to the integrity of his nature. He ignored the divinizing function of grace and explained its gratuitousness solely in terms of man's being a sinner: it was not gratuitous with regard to man as an intellectual creature (*De prima hominis iustitia*, IV, VIII, XI). Jansen rejected categorically the possibility of the state of "pure nature". By reason of his being an intellectual creature, man could not be created without being destined to the vision of God (*De statu naturae purae*, Liber I, caput 15; Liber II, caput 1).

Post-Tridentine scholasticism (with the exception of some theologians of the Augustinian school) developed the theology of grace within the hypothesis of *natura pura*, considered as necessary to explain the gratuitousness of the elevation of man to participation in the divine life. But there were a number of theologians of this period who put forward a notion of nature which could neither explain the immanence of grace nor the internal character of original sin. They (unconsciously) considered *natura pura* as a real situation of man.

The magisterium of the Church has maintained against Baianism and Jansenism the legitimacy of the concept of grace as "not due to human nature" (*indebitum naturae*, *D* 1021, 1026, 1516; *DS* 1921, 1926, 2616). The encyclical *Humani Generis* of 1950 affirmed explicitly that the gratuitousness proper to the supernatural order cannot be rightly explained unless it is admitted that God could have created intellectual beings without ordaining them to the vision of God (*D* 2318; *DS* 3891).

3. It must undoubtedly be emphasized that though the concept of nature (in the sense explained in 1 above) appears necessary for the full explanation of the divinization of the intellectual creature by the grace of Christ, it still has its limits and dangers. The rationality of man in his nature as such does not constitute the gratuitousness of his divinization, which is merely a consequence of it. Grace does not bring with it the divinization of man because it is not due to the nature of the intellectual creature. It is *indebita* because divinizing. The "supernaturality" of grace does not express what grace is in itself, the self-communication of God in himself to man and the participation of man in the life of God. But it does signify the absolute freedom of God and of his giving of himself to man. The term "supernatural" is necessary and legitimate, but it is insufficient to express the transcendence of grace.

On the other hand, the origin of the notion of nature in cosmological thought brings with it the permanent danger of the "reification" of the relation of man to God. It may be forgotten that man is open to grace precisely because he is not simply nature, but personally responsible in face of the call of God. Theological reflection on grace as fellowship of life between man and God must employ at once the concepts of nature and person. Otherwise it will be radically defective.

The deviations of some post-Tridentine theologians remind us of the continual danger involved in thinking of the nature of man as a factual situation and of grace as merely "added" to or superimposed on nature (*superadditum naturae*), while nature would be supposed to remain intact in itself under the "accidental" modifications induced by sin or justification. It cannot be denied that the presence of the concept of nature in the explanation of grace can lead to a dualistic vision of the existence of man in his relation to God – who is so to speak on the one hand his creator and on the other his saviour through Christ, with a different relation to man in each case. Hence the importance of the theological problem of "nature and grace".

Juan Alfaro

II. Naturalism

1. The term "naturalism" is employed in so many different senses, both in technical language (scientific, philosophical and theological) and in current usage, that it is impossible to reduce them to a common kernel. Perhaps its main characteristic may be described as a tendency to think of all reality exclusively or predominantly in terms of concepts and images derived from the world of things, while denying or ignoring the transcendent dimension of the person and his liberty. Such a tendency inevitably affects the solution of the fundamental problem of man – the meaning of man and the world. Is man's existence limited to an intra-mundane horizon or is there an opening towards an absolute and personal being greater than the world – or rather to a personal absolute depth as the intimate foundation of man's own inwardness? The problem of man as "spirit in the world" is ultimately the problem of the personal God, at once transcendent

and immanent to man and the world.

In the sphere of philosophy, the most radical form of naturalism is monistic materialism, which reduces all reality to one material principle whose inexhaustible dynamism is deployed immanently, determining all the phenomena of the world, of life, and even of the highest forms of thought. The Stoic concept of God as the "soul of the world", that is, as vital principle absolutely immanent to the world, is a form of naturalism and is in principle indistinguishable from monistic materialism.

Some religions and philosophical systems contain traits of a spiritualistic naturalism, which is basically a monistic view of reality. Either they do not underline sufficiently the personal distinction between God and man, or they foresee the ultimate absorption of the spirit of man in the Absolute Spirit (as in Hinduism, Buddhism, Idealism). Even though they put the return of man to God after death, both the process and its term are natural. All reality, or at least all spiritual life, is ultimately reduced to the immanent evolution of the Absolute Spirit.

The Deism of the 17th and 18th centuries implied a naturalist concept of God, as non-personal cause of the world without any actual relation to the world or man. God (*natura naturans, Deus sive natura* – Spinoza) and the world (*natura naturata*) are comprised within a fixed system of causality which excludes the possibility of revelation and grace and reduces all positive religion, especially Christianity, to the elements proper to natural religion. The biblical concept of God (as in Islam, Judaism and Christianity), of which the specific note is the absolute freedom of the personally transcendent and his manifestation in history, is radically incompatible with Deism, which is basically an acosmic naturalism but does not really exclude atheism (Hegel).

The Deistic position should lead to a more attentive reflection on the proofs of the existence of God starting from the world. It is only when such proofs are mediated by the spiritual illimitation of man (to whom the world is ordained and in whom it has its immediate meaning) that they can effectively lead to the affirmation of a personal God, that is, of the truly transcendent. Only man is the "image of God". He can only find in the depths of his own inwardness the created reflection of the personal Absolute.

Scientific naturalism, which confines itself to taking as a "working hypothesis" the possibility of explaining intramundane phenomena within the schema of "space-time", prescinding from the need of an ultimate explanation of the world and man outside the region of pure experience, does not of itself exclude authentic Theism. It only becomes atheistic when it goes beyond the proper field of the experimental sciences and pretends to reduce all reality to what is verifiable by experimental methods, as in positivism.

2. In the field of theological reflection (centred on the primordial revealed truth of salvation as personal dialogue between the absolutely free love of God in Christ and the responsibility of man), naturalism has left certain traces. These have sometimes been expressly condemned by the magisterium of the Church, as in the case of Pelagianism and Semi-Pelagianism. In other cases they remain concealed in certain positions which are freely debated.

Both the presence of original sin in man and the insertion of grace into his natural finality have been explained by some theologians as if the nature of man remained intact in itself under the accidental superimposition of sin or of grace. Once the illuminating function of grace is rejected, it is logical to affirm that apart from some privileged cases the Christian's experience of his spiritual depths is the same as it would have been in the state of "pure nature", that is, simply that of finite spirit and not that of being called to fellowship of life with God. The natural and the experiential are absolutely identified in the ordinary religious life of the believer. This is to forget that the existentiell position of man before God is intrinsically determined by grace as invitation to filial intimacy, and that every other attitude as regards God is excluded *a priori* (as existentielly unrealizable) by this interior invitation. It is to ignore the fact that the interior attraction towards God has made impossible in the concrete a merely natural love of man for God (and every purely natural moral act). This is not because original sin has totally corrupted human nature, but because man only exists in fact insofar as he is challenged by the grace of Christ.

Forgetfulness of increated grace, of its primacy with regard to created grace and of their mutual indissolubility, has contributed to a dangerous tendency to naturalism in the discussion of created grace. It is sometimes treated of as if it were merely a higher type of nature ("supernatural"), one of the things possessed by man, of which he disposes in his free acts to move God to grant him new graces. It should be remembered that the absolutely free personal self-communication of God brings about created grace, and is definitively achieved in the free acceptation by man, whose response does not in any way modify the absolute gratuitousness of all grace.

Juan Alfaro

III. Nature and Grace

1. The problem of nature and grace is implicitly present in all theological reflection on the salvation of man, and is strictly related to a series of basic themes such as creation and covenant, creation and incarnation, natural knowledge of God and revelation, reason and faith, philosophy and theology, law and gospel, freedom of man and God's gift of himself, history of the world and history of salvation, progress and the kingdom of God, ethics and the law of Christ, humanity and the Church, State and Church, etc. The formula "nature and grace" means man before God, as he reveals and gives himself through Christ. God saves man by the communication of himself, revealed and realized in Christ. Man is saved by freely accepting the gift of God through Christ. Salvation, already begun by justification in faith and definitively achieved by the vision of God in Christ, is fellowship of life between God and man, a personal dialogue inasmuch as God communicates himself and man receives the gift of God himself and so participates in his life. It is the encounter of God's love and man's responsibility in face of the summons given by God through Christ. Thus the problem of nature and grace is: What are the necessary conditions for the encounter of man with the God of love, that is, for man's being really able to receive the communication of God in himself? Since the self-communication of God is absolutely transcendent – though we can undoubtedly conceive that it is not impossible for the Absolute Spirit to communicate itself to the finite spirit – we must ask ourselves above all about man himself in his radical capacity for accepting freely the gift of God in himself.

2. The problem of nature and grace must be examined within its fundamental perspective, that is, the Christocentric character of the created world and of man (1 Cor 8:6; 15:24–28, 44–49; Rom 8:19–23, 28, 30; Eph 1:9–10, 19–23; 3:11; Col 1:15–20; 3:4; Phil 3:21; Heb 1:2–3; Jn 1:3; 12:32; Vatican II, *Lumen Gentium*, arts. 2, 3, 7, 48; *Gaudium et Spes*, art. 22). In the divine intention, creation is for the covenant and definitively for the incarnation. The existence of man, and the world for man, is sustained by Christ and ordained to him. This "Christian existential" constitutes the most fundamental di-

mension of man and of the universe (through man). The incarnation of the Son of God is the foundation on which creation rests – indeed, it might be said that the very possibility of man and the world is founded on the possibility of the incarnation. There is no other God for man than the God of revelation and grace, "the Father of our Lord Jesus Christ" (2 Cor 1:3; Eph 1:3; 1 Pet 1:3, etc.) This means that all the relationships of man's existence in face of God, and of the world through man, go through Christ. There is in fact no merely natural relationship of man to God. Man does not exist at all except as justified in the acceptance of the grace of Christ or as a sinner in refusal of such grace. In either case he is called interiorly to participate in the glory of the Lord (cf. Vatican II, *Lumen Gentium*, arts. 13–17; *Gaudium et Spes*, arts. 19–22). The intrinsic orientation of man in Christ radically excludes any dualism between nature and grace. The merely natural relationship of man to God, possible in the abstract by virtue of his fundamental structure as "spirit in the world", does not and cannot exist in fact, because man does not exist except as ordained at the deepest level of his spirit and in the unity and totality of his corporal spirituality to fellowship of life with God through Christ. The natural capacity for knowing God (Rom 1:18–28; Acts 17:24–27; *DS* 3004) which is identical with the spiritual being of man, and the exercise of which implies the intervention of his freedom, cannot be existentielly activated except by the grace of Christ. Man is responsible only before the God of grace.

3. By sin, man refuses fellowship of life with God and becomes absolutely powerless to return to it of himself. Only Christ through his Spirit can restore the relationship of son with regard to God. Grace is an interior call to conversion and thus presupposes in the sinner a radical capacity for being summoned by God. Otherwise his conversion would be absolutely impossible and his responsibility before the permanent invitation of the God of grace would cease to exist. In a word, the sinner would not really be "called" to fellowship of life with Christ (1 Cor 1:9; Gal 2:20; Rom 8:28–30). If the faith which justifies implies man's obedience to the saving word of God in Christ (Rom 1:5; 10:16; 16:26, etc.), man cannot be fundamentally incapable of knowing the God of revelation and of accepting the God of grace. Otherwise the word and the grace of God would cease to be word and grace of God for him. The call of God is meaningless unless there is a destination for the call. Grace supposes even in the sinner the radical capacity to receive it. This capacity is identical with the limitless openness to being, and ultimately to the Absolute, which constitutes man as "spirit in the world". Grace supposes the nature of man. But his nature is the radical capacity for grace, that is, the transcendental condition (Bouillard) for the possibility of grace, as grace, for man.

The real intention of the Catholic teaching on the non-total destruction of the freedom of man by original sin (*DS* 1521, 1555) and on the natural capacity to know God is not so much to describe the nature of man, to affirm the permanency of his responsibility before the grace of God which he accepts or refuses freely (*DS* 1525, 1554), and his fundamental capacity to receive divine revelation (*DS* 3005, 3008, 3009, 3016, 3028, 3034). Faith is indivisibly the gift of God and the free response of man (*DS* 1526, 1553, 1559, 3008, 3010, 3035). The nature of man is of interest to Catholic theology primarily, and in a certain sense, exclusively, by virtue of its radical capacity for God – its *potentia oboedientialis*. (Luther, and especially Melanchthon and Calvin, would admit that original sin does not destroy totally in man the capacity to know God; see M. Lackmann, *Vom Geheimnis der Schöpfung* [1952], pp. 320–67.)

We must not forget, of course, that if grace supposes nature, nature – in its own way – supposes grace, insofar as the grace of Christ sustains man in fact and orientates him to his end, and all creation through man, in his very nature. The personal gift of God to the man Christ through the incarnation, and through Christ to humanity and the world, is the ultimate foundation of the very existence of the world and man.

4. Catholic theology sees in the openness to the illimited horizon of being, which is constitutive of man as finite spirit, the fundamental capacity for receiving the gift of God himself, begun in faith and consummated in vision. This capacity of man's nature for the vision of God has been interpreted in different ways, either as a mere non-contradiction between nature and grace, or as a "natural desire" for direct union with God. The second interpretation, suggested by Augustine, was thoroughly analysed by Thomas Aquinas and accepted – under a diversity of forms and terminology – by the major part of scholastic theologians, both medieval and post-Tridentine. In recent times it has been given new depths by J. Maréchal, P. Rousselot and their followers. By its very ordination to the illimitation of being, the human mind cannot but strive and seek indefinitely, as long as it has not attained direct knowledge of the ultimate foundation of being, which is called God. It is only in the vision of God that it can satisfy fully and definitively the illimited aspiration to know which is identical with the spirituality of man. No finite reality totally satisfies man's radical tendency towards his limitless perfection. It is only in the personal encounter with the Absolute in itself that he finds definitively the depths of his spirit (*intimior intimo meo* – Augustine) which are always sought for and always hidden. Hence in his very nature man is ordained to the vision of God as to his one "perfect happiness" and his one absolutely final end. But by his own proper dynamism he cannot transcend the horizon of being and attain the absolute mystery in itself. Within his condition of creature, he would remain indefinitely in a progressive development and would enjoy only a "happiness in movement", corresponding to his finitude and potentiality. Of himself he could never go beyond his creaturely dimension. The existence of man in his nature – in his created spirituality, non-divinized by grace – would, however, not be absurd. By his nature, man is ordained to the vision of God as grace, that is, as the absolutely unmerited and gratuitous personal gift of God in himself. Participation in the life of God brings with it a duration beyond the creaturely ("participated eternity", according to Thomas Aquinas), that is, a divinizing self-possession in the consciousness which is determined by the immediate presence of the Absolute Spirit. Hence the vision of God represents for man his supreme and absolute possibility, but which God alone can actuate by the free gift of himself. The nature of man cannot be given a definitive end and goal except in the vision of God. But it is not of itself ordained towards that vision. It is only grace which begins the divinization of man and ordains him effectively to immediate union with God. Thus all dualism between nature and grace is eliminated. Man does not exist except as intrinsically ordained by grace to the vision of God as his end, which is the only absolutely final end of that very nature. There are not and cannot be in man two definitive finalities merely juxtaposed to one another. The notion of the nature of man as capable of attaining its definitive fulfilment by its proper dynamism is radically excluded. On the other hand, the transcendence of grace remains intact. The created spirituality of man does not necessarily imply ordination to the vision of God, since of itself it cannot give itself an absolute end.

This explanation of the relationship

between nature and grace needs to be completed by some further remarks. Man is essentially a spirit incarnate. His eschatological salvation is only complete in the totality and unity of his corporeal spirituality. This is the ground of the "eternal function of the humanity of Christ" (K. Rahner) in the vision of God. The nature of man, as "spirit in the world", is by that very fact ordained to union with the glorified Christ and in him to the mystery of God in himself. The "natural desire" of man awaits the vision of God in Christ. And just as the world has no meaning except insofar as it is ordained to man – the human finality of creation is the leitmotiv of the evolutionary concept of the world – it is exact to say that in man the whole universe aspires to the grace of the incarnation as to its definitive perfection – absolute and absolutely gratuitous.

Above all, it must be borne in mind that the existential situation of man prior to grace is not simply that of his nature, but that of his condition of sinner who *has lost* his fellowship of life with God. His intimate yearning to go to meet God is quickened by a sort of nostalgia (R. Guardini). The situation of sin implies a pre-understanding (*Vorverständnis* – R. Bultmann) of reconciliation with God by his grace.

5. If grace is inserted in the profoundest depths of man, ordaining him internally to the vision of God through Christ, we have to try to explain further what are its precise effects in the spirituality of man and what are its repercussions on his existentiell relationship to God. This is also a problem where Catholic theologians have held various positions. Up to the 14th century Augustine's doctrine of the "interior teaching" of grace was predominant, and was understood as an internal "illumination" which elevates the spirit of man to participate in the life of God through faith, hope and charity. This concept of the proper function of grace attained its highest development in Thomistic theology. Duns Scotus limited considerably the interior illumination of grace, and the Nominalism of Occam arrived at a radical "extrinsicism". Grace brings with it absolutely no internal modification in the natural spiritual dynamism of man. This extreme position was abandoned by post-Tridentine theology. But some theologians reduced the internal action of grace to the juridical and entitative elevation of supernatural acts, which did not otherwise surpass the natural dynamism of man.

A better knowledge of the biblical doctrine – especially that of Paul and John – apropos of the action of grace in man, and a profounder reflection on the transcendental dimension of the spiritual dynamism of man brought about in 20th-century theology a decided return to the Augustinian and Thomist position. This has been ratified by Vatican II (cf. *Lumen Gentium*, art. 12; *Dei Verbum*, art. 5).

The notion of grace as the internal illumination of man in the depths of his spirit is already found in the OT. In the new covenant, announced by Jeremiah and Ezekiel, God will give man a "new heart", that is, will create in it a new personal attitude through knowledge of the saviour God and submission to his law (Jer 24:7; 31:31–33; Ezek 11:19–21; 36:26–28). Paul attributes the conversion of man, as he passes from ignorance of and hostility to God to knowledge and love of him, to the action of the Spirit sent by the glorified Christ (Gal 1:21; 4:8–9; Eph 4:18; 5:8; 2 Cor 4:6; cf. Acts 16:14). Only the interior illumination of the Spirit of Christ enables man to grasp through faith the mystery of Christ's death and resurrection (1 Cor 2:2–16; 12:3; Eph 1:17–18; 3:14–17; Col 2:2). The attitude of son towards God is brought about in man through the Holy Spirit (Rom 8:14–17; Gal 4:6). The believer receives a "new life", which is participation in the very life of Christ (Rom 6:5–10; 8:4–18; Gal 2:20;

5:5; 2 Cor 5:17; Eph 2:10; 3:17). The existence of man in the Spirit tends towards union with the glorified Christ by the resurrection, in order to share through Christ the very life of God (Rom 8:11, 19–23, 29; 1 Cor 6:15–20; 2 Cor 5:7–8; Phil 1:19–23; 3:19–21; 1 Thess 4:17). In the Johannine writings grace is described as an interior "attraction", by which man is taught to know Christ (Jn 14:15–23; 15:15, 26; 16:13), as participation in his filial knowledge of God (Jn 6:44–46, 56; cf. Mt 11:27), and also as a "faculty of knowing" (διάνοια) (1 Jn 5:20; cf. 3:6; 4:7, 8), by which man is given "fellowship of life" with God through Christ (1 Jn 1:3, 6; 3:3, 5–9, 15, 24; 4:12–16). Even at present the believer possesses eternal life (Jn 3:16–17, 36; 5:24; 1 Jn 3:15; 5:12–13), which consists of knowing Christ (Jn 17:3) and which tends towards its fullness in participation in the life of the glorified Christ and through him in the very life of God, that is, in the vision of God through Christ (Jn 17:24, 26; 1 Jn 3:1–2). Modern exegetes unanimously teach that according to the theologies of Paul and John the action of the Spirit imprints in the profoundest depths of man the call to intimacy of life with God through Christ, and finally to eschatological participation in the very life of God, through the union of man raised from the dead and the glorified Christ.

The importance of this illuminative function of grace is obvious when the problem of nature and grace arises. The natural dynamism of man, as "spirit in the world", receives a profound novelty from grace, and man is given an intrinsic orientation – in his unified totality of spirit and body – towards final and immediate union with God through Christ. Grace touches man at the deepest level of his nature, that is, in his fundamental structure as spirit and person. It is the internal invitation, in the profoundest depths of man's consciousness, to existentiell decision in face of the self-communication of God in Christ. The free answer of man cannot exist without the free acceptance or refusal of God's love. There is no other existentiell relation of man to God. The moral law, known by each man expressly or not, impressed on his heart by the Holy Spirit, is the interior law of filial love for God and of fraternal love for men: in a word, the law of the love of Christ (1 Cor 16:21; Gal 2:20; 1 Pet 1:7; Jn 14:15, 23; 15:9–15; Mt 25:40–45).

The internal illumination of the spirit of man by grace and his final end in the vision of God through Christ imply that the whole universe is destined to eschatological participation in the glory of Christ (Rom 8:19–23). The ordination to the vision of God which grace implants in the profoundest depths of man, orientates the existence of man, and hence that of the world, to transcend time in order to share in the divine eternity. The time of man and the world moves to a state beyond time, to the dimension of the eternal. The future of eschatological salvation is already present in man's destiny, immediate union with God through the grace of Christ. The history of the world is not the movement of indefinite progress, but an advance towards the absolute future, the definitive revelation of God in the glorified Christ.

6. If grace supposes in man the radical capacity for accepting freely the gift of God in Christ, and is inserted precisely in the responsibility of man prior to the absolutely free gift of God in himself (M. Blondel), it must be admitted that grace supposes man not just as nature but also as person. The formula "grace supposes nature" should be completed by the affirmation that "grace supposes the person". The two expressions necessarily evoke one another, inasmuch as the human person includes his nature and the nature of man includes his personal character. Man is open by his nature to the "I-You" relation with

man, and definitively with the Absolute. Grace realizes this relationship in the intimate dialogue with the God of love. In his acceptance of grace as the personal gift of God in himself, man takes up by faith, hope and love his authentic personal attitude and realizes himself progressively as person. In the vision of God through Christ he will receive fully the personal gift of God and will in turn give himself fully to God in himself. He will then achieve the fullness of conscious self-presence, that is, come fully to himself. When the mystery of God is immediately present to the interior of man, man will be fully present to himself, and participate in the eternal duration of God. He will then receive from grace his fullness as person in the totality and unity of his spiritual corporality, that is, in his relation to the world, men and God as he is in himself: in a word, in his relation to Christ. The human community will receive from Christ its supreme unification, and history will be given its definitive meaning.

Juan Alfaro

NEO-PLATONISM

Neo-Platonism is not simply a revival of the original Platonic philosophy. It is a remoulding of a number of Platonic, Aristotelian, Stoic and neo-Pythagorean propositions and themes. The process of assimilation was guided by a principle of its own which gave rise from the start to a clearly envisaged "system".

The following principles were taken over from Plato: the first three hypotheses of the *Parmenides*, which were expounded as the three hypostases on which all reality and degrees of reality were based: the One, the spirit (νοῦς) and the soul; the One of the *Parmenides* could thus be identified with the absolutely transcendent Good of the *Republic* (509b: πέκεινα τῆς οὐσίας). The five basic categories of the *Sophist* – to be, identity, other, permanence and movement – became structural elements of the timeless (absolute) spirit. They make spirit intelligible as an intrinsically organized totality which *is* (παντελῶς ὄν). The fundamental movement of thought in the *Symposium* and *Phaedrus* supplies the principle that Eros is the moving force in the dialectic ascent of thought, and also, in its aspect of function as the Beautiful, the upward-leading mediator of truth and knowledge. The *Phaedo* and the *Theaetetus* indicated the way and the goal for neo-Platonism: the "purification" of thought as abstraction from the sensible world, and reflective familiarization with the unity of the One. The end is "similarity to God" (ὁμοίωσις θεῷ), the equivalent of the flight of the human soul into its true home – the Ulysses motif. Finally, the *Timaeus* was responsible for the solution adopted for certain problems of cosmology: the intelligible world (the forms) was the "model" for the creative activity of the Demiurge, who is not identical with the supreme principle; the dialectic of being and becoming, archetype and image; the sensible world as positive μίμημα, imitation of the intelligible world; time as the life of the World-Soul in contrast to eternity as the life of the Spirit. The Platonic philosophy, especially in the hands of Plotinus, became rigorously spiritualist and individualist, as may be seen particularly from its abandonment of political thought, which was still integral to Plato's philosophy.

From Aristotelian psychology and metaphysics came the notion which was constitutive for the neo-Platonic concept of spirit, that in non-material being thought and the object of thought are identical and hence that God, as pure act and immutable life, thinks himself, being thought of his own thought (Aristotle, *De Anima*, 430 a; *Metaphysica*, 1074 b). But this self-thinking God was not considered the first principle in neo-Platonism. In general, the neo-Platonists considered Plato and

Aristotle as two forms of the one philosophy (so, for instance, Ammonius Saccus, the teacher of Plotinus; the neo-Platonic commentators on Aristotle; the same tendency was apparent as early as Antiochus of Ascalon).

The Stoic notions of the mutual relationships of all things (συμπάθεια τῶν ὅλων) and of the *ratio seminalis* (λόγος σπερματικός) were taken over in the neo-Platonic concept of the world, which was regarded as an organic whole, existing on various but not discontinuous levels and analogical in nature to its ground. The same influence may be seen in the notion of the One as the principle which is present and active in all beings.

Finally, there was the neo-Pythagorean theory of principles, derived from the oral teaching of Plato and from the early Academy. In various forms, it became the basis of the neo-Platonist dialectic of "unity" and "indeterminate duality".

In addition to these active elements from philosophical tradition (which were also influential in a number of problems for Philo of Alexandria, Middle Platonism [Gaius, Albinus, Celsus] and Numenius), there were the religious sources regarded as authoritative. These were the Orphic traditions, the Chaldaean Oracles and mythology in general. The first two groups were sometimes regarded as sacred and unchallengeable revelation and hence interpreted philosophically, as by Porphyrius, Iamblichus and Proclus. Mythology was subjected to a method of abstraction and systematization by which it was reduced to an allegory and metaphor for philosophical thought.

It would be a mistake, however, to try to arrive at the structure of neo-Platonism merely by adding together these philosophical and religious elements. They have rather a maieutic function in the understanding of how the neo-Platonists integrated the heritage of the past with their own thought to form a new philosophical pattern.

The basic religious trend of neo-Platonism is due less to its authoritative religious sources than to the rational end (*telos*) which determined each of the systems: union with the divine origin. Hence after Porphyrius (234–*c.* 305) especially, philosophy becomes a way of salvation, along which one is impelled, however, not by a non-rational certitude of salvation, but by thought and reasoning. But doubts may already be noted in Porphyrius as to the all-sufficiency of the rational method. This diffidence crystallized later in various forms of theurgical and magical practices, which made genuine philosophizing at least questionable, though it did not deprive this type of neo-Platonism of its logical and metaphysical starting-points.

Neo-Platonism in the strict sense begins with Plotinus (203–279). It is characterized by a strongly monistic basic trend. The One is the first hypostasis, the supreme ground and origin of all beings, but also identical with the Good, and hence the universal end and cause of motion in all beings. As the absolutely simple (non-multiple) it is transcendent to the act of being, which is multiple, and even to that of thought, since reflection on self posits difference and hence multiplicity in thought. It is utterly different from all that proceeds from it and hence is outside it. Being "nothing of the kind" it is by its nature only knowable and expressible for human thought, which is marked by multiplicity and finiteness, by means of the *via negativa*. In spite of its transcendence, however, the One is the ground which is at work in all beings – being "everywhere and nowhere" – the prime mover of their intelligible return from multiplicity to their ultimate origin.

The One emits the spirit (νοῦς) as the second hypostasis, without being in any way diminished in its power by this emanation (or "radiation" of its "light"). The metaphors of source, root and seed are used to explain the One in this connection, though they cannot or do not try to explain *why* the One goes out of itself at all or *why* there is anything other than the One. In the procession of the Spirit from the One the principle of "indeterminate duality" is at work. It is through this principle alone that the Spirit becomes and is multiplicity and otherness. But it is unified multiplicity, oneness in otherness or one in the act of being – in contrast to the One which transcends the act of being – by virtue of its immediate conversion to the One in the timeless moment of its outgoing. Thus the One remains its centre. The Spirit is the quintessence of all multiple reality. Its nature is to be the identity of being and thought. The being which it thinks are the ideas ("forms") but it is itself the ideas (*Ennead*, V, 5: "The intelligible [the ideas] are not outside the Spirit"). In the ideas therefore, each of which differentiates the Spirit as a whole and is the whole, the Spirit thinks itself. This identity of being and thought, as Spirit itself, is its life. The dialectical unity of being, thought and life is its truth – in the ontological sense of the conformity of absolute thought with itself (*ibid.*, V, 2, 18f.).

The Spirit emits the soul as the third hypostasis (sometimes understood negatively as a "Fall"), which then brings about the sensible world and sets it in motion in the mode of time. The soul embraces all that is animated: world-soul, souls of stars, men, beasts and plants. By virtue of its spiritual element, the soul is the substance which links all sensible beings with their intelligible ground. The transcendent spirit ceaselessly at work in the human soul, though at first unnoticed, is what enables us to return, through introspective thought, to this its noetic ground and so transform ourselves into it (νοωθῆναι) by transcending ourselves. The act of the soul's transcending itself is prepared by ascetic abstraction from the sensible world and takes place in a knowledge which is constantly expanding through dialectic and eros. It is perfected by the ecstatic, supra-rational union with the One itself. In contrast to Spirit and soul, matter is the absolutely formless and undetermined, and hence, in Plotinus, the "primary evil", a notion decidedly modified by Proclus, who distinguished matter from evil and explained the latter as merely a "par-hypostasis".

Neo-Platonism after Plotinus (e.g., Porphyrius, Iamblichus, Syrian, Proclus, Damascius, Simplicius) modified the metaphysical basis laid down by Plotinus by propounding the realms of the Spirit and the soul in terms of intermediate beings. This emphasized still more sharply the subordinate structure of beings in general and the aloofness of their origin. This notion was developed most consistently by Proclus (410–485). To explain the transition from the absolute One to the many, and indeed from any higher degree of being to a lower, he begins with the procession of the "Henads" from the One itself. The first, in which unity still predominates, is the multiple unity which first gives rise to multiplicity in the strict sense. This multiple unity is understood by Proclus as the gods or divine numbers. Then come the two principles of limit and illimitation (the indeterminate), which co-operate to constitute being, then life, and spirit. This subordination of spirit to life and being is foreign to Plotinus, but his identification of being and thought is retained, as fundamental to the understanding of the nature of spirit. The identification, however, is now dynamic or relational, and not absolute. The dimension of the spirit and of the soul emanating from it is treated most emphatically as a triad. The logical and ontological law of this triadic form is "subsistence – procession – return", which determines the formal structure of each triad and re-unites beings as a whole with their one origin. Thus the system is a sort of moving "circle of circles". Every degree of this continuous subsistent being is identical with a godhead, so that philosophy is equivalent to theology by virtue of its ontological principle. The "flowering" of the Spirit, the "One in us", allows man to be always united with the One and enables the negative dialectic to be resolved through the *negatio negationis* of the *unio mystica*.

The obverse of the anti-Christian attitude of neo-Platonism – particularly active in Porphyrius and Julian, after Celsus – is the importance of neo-Platonist themes in the theology of Origen, Gregory of Nazianzus, Basil, Gregory of Nyssa, Maximus the Confessor, Ambrose, Marius Victorinus, Augustine and Boethius. The authority of the writings of Pseudo-Dionysius the Areopagite meant that Proclus in particular had an immense direct and indirect influence on the metaphysics and mysticism of the Middle Ages, especially in John Scotus Eriugena, Meister Eckhart, John Tauler and then Nicholas of Cusa, who had a good knowledge of the actual texts of Proclus. Through the *Liber de Causis* also, first thought to be Aristotelian but deriving substantially from the *Elementatio Theologica* of Proclus (translated in the 12th century by Gerhard of Cremona from Arabic into Latin, and then the subject of many commentaries) essential elements of the ontological axioms of neo-Platonism influenced medieval theology.

Werner Beierwaltes

NEW TESTAMENT BOOKS

I. The Synoptic Gospels

The first three gospels are called the synoptic gospels because, in announcing the gospel of Jesus Christ, they follow a common pattern of exposition, as may be seen at once from a "comparative view" (Greek *synopsis*). To understand their individual theological viewpoints we must investigate each of these gospels in their relation to one another and to the pre-synoptic tradition.

1. *The pre-synoptic tradition.* a) *The synoptic fact.* (i) *The data.* The triple or Marcan tradition (pericopes with three witnesses) extends to more than half of Mk and to about a third of Mt or Lk, while the double (or Mt-Lk) tradition is seen in about a fifth of Mt or Lk. As regards the matter which appears only in one witness, Mk has about 50 verses, proper to himself, Mt about 330 and Lk 550. So it appears that Mt and Lk have a common basis (represented by Mk because of the centre position it holds between Mt and Lk and because of its substance, which is contained in Mt and Lk) to which many other individual traditions are added. However, if we examine the common matter more closely, we can see that it also includes wide divergences. How does this come about? If we deny all mutual literary dependence, how are we to justify the many agreements? If we assert the mutual dependence of the texts, how do we explain the additions and omissions? Is it enough to appeal to the particular point of view of the individual author and to the preoccupations of his readers?

(ii) *The arrangement.* The facts of the gospel are distributed in the three synoptics according to four principal divisions: the preparation (Mt 3:1 – 4:11 = Mk 1:1–13 = Lk 3:1 – 4:13), the ministry in Galilee (Mt 4:12 – 18:35 = Mk 1:14 – 9:50 = Lk 1:4 – 9:50), the ascent to Jerusalem (Mt 19:1 – 20:34 = Mk 10:1–52 = Lk 9:51 – 18:43) and finally the passion and resurrection (Mt 21–28 = Mk 11–16 = Lk 19–24). Within this general arrangement there are many variations: the missionary discourse before or after the parables; Mt, unlike Lk, does not follow the sequence of Mk 1:21 – 6:13; the sentences common to Mt and Lk are either grouped together (Mt) or widely dispersed (Lk). Within the great sequences we can sometimes find agreements in a broadly different context (for instance, Mk 1:21–45 and Mt 7:28 – 8:16) and sometimes disagreements when the grouping is identical (Mk 1:40–45 placed by Mt before Mk 1:21–39). Finally, even within the same episode, there are sometimes quite astonishing transpositions (Mt 4:5–10 = Lk 4:5–12), showing a great freedom in treating the elements of the traditions. And so the question arises: if the generally identical sequence reflects a close and common dependence in regard to the same schema, how are the numerous transpositions to be explained? Are they all to be explained by the literary workmanship of the evangelists?

(iii) *The expression.* Here again the agreements necessitate literary contact between the synoptics. But once again, the disagreements (compare Mt 25:14–30 = Lk 19:11–27; Mt 22:1–10 = Lk 14:16–24; Mt 8:15 = Mk 1:31) tell against immediate literary dependence of the different texts between themselves.

b) *The interpretation of the synoptic fact.* Oral tradition, interdependence and documentary sources are the three elements which are to be found in varying proportions at the basis of the various hypotheses seeking to explain the synoptic fact. But all are now agreed that no satisfactory solution is to be found in the direction of harmonies of the gospels (cf. the *Diatessaron* of Tatian). Indeed their whole idea was to reduce the differences at all costs, even if this meant doing violence to the literary evidence. It was only towards the end of the 18th century that the synoptic problem began to emerge (Lessing, Storr, Griesbach, Herder); but during the 19th century it was treated in very systematic fashion.

(i) According to the system based on *oral tradition* (Gieseler, Godet, Soiron, Gächter), all the synoptics, and each quite separately, depend on oral tradition alone. This theory starts off from an established fact, namely, the part that oral tradition undoubtedly played at the beginning and even while the gospels were being set down in writing. But on its own it cannot explain the close literary contacts that are evident from the texts themselves.

(ii) Passing to the other extreme, critics have also systematized the relations between the synoptics, in terms of *interdependence*. Only two among all the various genealogies of the gospels which have been suggested merit our attention. The sequence Mt→ Mk→ Lk (Butler) is commonly rejected; for Mk is independent of Mt and Lk, while Mt and Lk are mutually independent. The other hypothesis has today almost attained the status of a critical dogma: Mk is at the origin of both Mt and Lk. The supporters of this theory are of the opinion that Mt and Lk possessed either Mk's actual text (the majority of the supporters of the two-source theory) or a "Proto-Mark", a Protean form of Mark's gospel which changed according to the needs of Mt or Lk (see Bornkamm). In actual fact, this dogma is only an opinion, and to our mind is a serious oversimplification of the literary evidence.

(iii) Other critics have moved in a different direction and held that at the origin of the synoptics there were *source-documents.* An Aramaic Mt, for example, was the basis for the triple tradition (Vaganay); but no one has ever reconstructed its content. A complementary document (Logia-source) has been suggested as the source of the double tradition. But this document appears to lack homogeneity, definable extent, clear arrangement and even historical foundation. Like the Proto-Mark it usually disintegrates into numerous subdivisions according to the different uses made of it. Many critics also dispute its documentary character, regarding it only as a useful label serving to group together various heterogeneous materials (e.g., Jeremias, Barrett). By appealing to a second source (S – different from Q), Vaganay' hypothesis suffers from the same difficulties as the system of the two-sources.

(iv) Faced with such uncertain results, other critics have had recourse to *multiple documentation*. First presented under the form of *diegeseis* or short summaries gathering together a number of small literary units (Schleiermacher), this system, which is undoubtedly more flexible than its predecessors, runs the risk of not facing all the aspects of the problem presented by the evidence, at least in that it does not take into account the probable existence of a much larger document than the others (Gaboury): after mentioning John the Baptist, this document continued with the visit of Jesus to Nazareth and then through the long development of the ascent to Jerusalem. On to this basic outline were added more or less extended documents dealing either with the ministry of Jesus in Galilee or the logia of the double tradition.

(v) None of these different theories solves all the problems. As a consequence, one cannot say for certain that the theological attitudes of the synoptics are derived from some extended document of great length, or from the alleged *Quelle* which probably never existed as a separate document, or from Mk which was possibly not directly used by Mt or Lk. On the other hand we are on certain ground if we start with the pre-synoptic tradition which can be discovered with the help of form-criticism.

c) *The theological outlook of the pre-synoptic tradition*. Before the gospels were committed to writing, the Church preached the gospel in line with the theological notions and presuppositions that we can discover behind the stereotyped formulas of the NT (hymns, confessions of faith, etc.), and behind the sources of Acts and of the gospels. At the origin of the proclamation of the gospel stands the faith of Easter: the history of salvation has been accomplished in Jesus, who became Lord on Easter Day. The paschal event, through the light thrown on it by the biblical prophecies (cf. "according to the Scriptures": 1 Cor 15:3–4), gives a fuller understanding of the actions and words of Jesus and inspires the believer to await the coming parousia (1 Thess 1:10). These are the "last days" as recognized in the light of the paschal faith. But though the paschal faith, which relates all to Christ, effects an inner unification of all the different elements of the gospel tradition, it cannot be expressed independently of the whole complex of the life of the community (liturgy, catechesis, mission); under their influence the form of the presentation takes shape and a choice made from among all the different memories. The light of the paschal faith and the influence of the life of the Church are the determining factors behind the theological attitudes assumed in the little literary units and the first groupings which lie at the origin of the synoptic gospels.

Here are a number of examples of pre-synoptic interpretation, first of all as it influenced the literary units. As spoken by Jesus, the parable of the murderous vinegrowers announced the fate of Israel (Mk 12:1–9 par.); but the Church, by adding Isaiah's saying about the stone rejected by the builders (Mk 12:10 par.), orientates it towards the destiny of Jesus himself, and more precisely towards his resurrection. Elsewhere, the paschal symbolism explains the meaning of an incident such as a healing, by the choice of a word with rich overtones: *egeirein*, meaning both "to rise" and "to raise to life" (Mt 8:15; Mk 1:31). Then, a catechetical application attaches a moral significance to the parable of the sower (Mk 4:13–20). The eucharistic liturgy colours the accounts of the multiplication of bread. All these are ways of attaining the unique person of Jesus, the Lord of faith. Similar ideas are to be recognized in the *grouping together* of memories and words. For example, the missionary catechesis associates the stilling of the tempest with the exorcism of Gerasa (Mk 4:35 – 5:20 par.). A eucharistic purpose gives unity to the "section of the bread" (Mk 6:31 – 8:22). By simplifying the historical facts, the pre-synoptic tradition illuminates Jesus' progress to the cross through the certainty of Easter and makes a theological composition of the ascent to Jerusalem: the catechetical purpose relates the fate of the disciple to that of the Master (Mk 8:34 – 9:1 par.). Finally, a biographical interest soon appears, probably as a result of non-Jews embracing the Christian faith, as well as of the passage of time. Once it began to be influenced by the paschal faith, the gospel tradition (whose only source is Jesus in person) was given a theological orientation and it was on this foundation that the theological attitudes of each of the individual synoptic gospels were based.

2. *The Gospel according to St. Mark.* The first gospel to be drawn up was finished before the siege of Jerusalem (67). It is attributed by tradition to the John Mark who is mentioned in the NT (Acts 12:12, 25; 13:5, 13; 15:37; 1 Pet 5:13; Col 4:10; Phm 24; 2 Tim 4:11).

There have been many attempts to interpret Mark's theology on the basis of one particular aspect thought to be fundamental: a preface to the account of the passion and the resurrection (Kähler); the book of the secret epiphanies of the Messiah (Dibelius); a description of the triumph of Jesus over Satan (Burkill); the eschatological perspective of the event proclaimed, the messianic secret (Wrede), etc. But this involves stressing one aspect of the evidence which in no way excludes the others. All these different approaches can find a place within the main purpose of the gospel as it is clearly set out by Mark at the beginning of his book: to write a gospel with the purpose of proclaiming that Jesus is the Son of God.

In fact, the first characteristic to note about Mark is that he is the only one to use the substantive εὐαγγέλιον without some explanatory attribute. While Luke intends to write as a historian and Matthew to fulfil the task of the alert scribe (cf. Mt 13:52), Mark simply wishes to present a "gospel", not in the sense of a writing, but as the Good News proclaimed kerygmatically (Marxsen). No man recognizes this proclamation until the death of Jesus, and then the man is a pagan (Mk 15:39). Before this it is only God who proclaims it, at the baptism (1:11) and the transfiguration (9:7), or the possessed (3:11; 5:7). Jesus himself imposes secrecy as regards his own person: a secret which is imposed on the devils (1:34; 3:12), those miraculously healed (1:44; 5:43; 7:36; 8:26) and on the disciples (8:30; 9:9). Even his parables are intended to hide the mystery from those who are unworthy (4:11). As for the disciples, they appear as lacking comprehension when faced with the situation (4:41; 6:51–52; 8:16–21; 9:33–34; 10:35, 41–42). This is the doctrine of the "messianic secret" which Mark uses to show how the gospel was proclaimed before Easter (Sjöberg). Here he expressed systematically, though imperfectly (cf. 2:10, 28; 10:47–52), an element of tradition to which Matthew is also a witness and which through the help of the literary device of "now hidden – now revealed" fits in with Jesus' own original purpose: to remain faithful to the conditions imposed on the revelation of the mystery of his person which cannot be summed up in one particular "title", and in this way avoid a carnal interpretation of his divinity. A pre-paschal gospel, but proclaimed after Easter, Mark's is also a paschal gospel.

The way in which the narrative is distributed reflects the pre-synoptic tradition. It appears to be subordinated to the events of the passion which is the culmination of Jesus' life. After an opening triptych (1:1–13), there are two parts. In the first, Jesus presents himself first to the people (1:14 – 3:6), then to his own (3:7 – 6:6) and finally to his disciples (6:6 – 8:26–30). Each of these sections opens with a summary and closes with the description of an attitude; each time Jesus puts a question to his contemporaries: What is this man? Is he not the Messiah? The second part (8:27–31 – 16:8), after the section about the bread, describes the ascent to Jerusalem, ending with the passion and the resurrection. These two periods signal the purpose and the economy of the revelation. Before Peter's confession, Jesus shows himself as the awaited Messiah and imposes secrecy. After this he shows his uncomprehending disciples the way to be trodden by the Son of Man. Thus Jesus dies in complete solitude (Lohmeyer).

The geographical framework has also a theological significance. Galilee, without necessarily being the place of the parousia (Marxsen), is that of the eschatological revelation (1:9, 14, 16, 28, 39; 3:7; 9:30; 14:28) and the starting-point for the mission to the pagans (7:24; 14:28; cf. 4:35; 13:10; 14:9). Jerusalem is not only the place of the death of Jesus, but also that of the obduracy of the Jews (3:22; 7:1; 10:33; 11:18). In this way an element of the tradition is given justification: the gospel passes from the Jews to the pagans (3:6; 7:6, 8; 8:31; 9:31; 10:33; 12:12; 13:2; 14:41; 15:38). Within this geographical framework a drama unfolds: Jesus as the Son of God, clothed with divine power (1:8, 10, 12; 3:29–30), does battle against Satan (1:11; 3:11; 5:7), especially in the exorcisms which triumph over the prince of death, but also in the controversies and the healings (2:1–12; 3:1–6, 22–30). Clear sayings (e.g., 2:10, 19–20, 28; 3:28–29) affirm his power.

The gospel is "actualized" for the reader who sees himself invited to reply to the summons of Jesus. The chapter of the parables is conceived in terms of a theology of the word to be listened to, which is exclusive to Mk (4:3, 9, 12, 13, 23, 24, 25, 33–34), so much so that the Good News addresses directly every reader throughout the whole of time. The same effect is produced by the schematic nature of the narratives, which, compensating for an impression of "reportage", imbues what could have been a mere anecdote (e.g., the call of the disciples) with a significance which transcends time. In fact, Mark's book bears the mark of a twofold origin: a witness who recounts what he saw and a community which passes on what it believes. This characterizes all the gospels in varying proportions.

3. *The Gospel according to St. Matthew*. The first gospel was addressed to the "believers who came from Judaism" (Eusebius, *Historia Ecclesiastica*, VI, 25, 4). Matthew had at his disposal other sources than those used by Mark, in particular traditions about the words of the Lord and the infancy of Jesus. These are all taken and moulded together in the light of a theological insight which often enables him to rediscover the original meaning of the events and of the words of Jesus. This gospel integrates the many insights and attitudes of the early Church into a vision which concentrates principally on the two great themes enunciated in the final words spoken by the risen Christ to his disciples (Mt 28:18–20): the role of Christ and the role of his Church (Trilling).

Like Mk, Mt tells of the Good News of Jesus, but he has a more developed Christology and he is at pains to fill out the picture of Christ as seen by his Church when it confessed its faith in him. He has little interest in the "messianic secret" (9:30; 16:20; 17:9) which he transposes into the idea of a retreat or withdrawal (12:15–21; 14:13). On the other hand, for catechetical reasons, he has a whole catena of titles which he applies to Jesus: Emmanuel (1:23; cf. 28:20), Jesus the Christ (1:1, 16, 18; 16:20; 27:17, 22), the Son of David (only in Mt 1:1, 20; 9:27; 12:23; 15:22; 21:9, 15), the Son of God (4:3, 6; 14:33;

16:16; 27:40, 43). The naive realism of Mark gives way to a more hieratic presentation of Jesus (under the influence of the liturgical background, though not a liturgical edition, as Kilpatrick suggests). There is the elimination of feelings which could appear too human, a more dignified tone, especially in the account of the passion. Described for Jewish Christians, the mission of Jesus is set within the framework of God's majestic design as seen through the prophecies; explicit quotations from the prophets continually punctuate the narrative of events which are difficult to understand and give an apologetical explanation of the life of Jesus: his birth from a virgin (1:22–23), at Bethlehem (2:5–6), his flight into Egypt (2:15), the massacre of the innocents (2:17–18), his life at Nazareth (2:23), his ministry in Galilee (4:14–16), his bearing as the servant of Yahweh (8:17; 12:17–21; 13:35), his entry into Jerusalem (21:40). Without going so far as to speak of a "school of Matthew" (Stendahl), we must recognize that here we have an interpretation of the gospel by a scribe discerning in his use of the Scriptures. This Christ foretold by the prophets is the Lord in whom the disciples believe, the Kyrios: announced by the prophet Daniel, he receives universal authority not from Satan (4:8–10), but from his Father (28:18).

The Lordship of Jesus holds sway over all the nations: through this universality, Israel is brought to fulfilment, but only through the mediation of the Church, because of the rejection of Jesus by the Jews. The Church is the true Israel. This involves a more profound conception of *ecclesiology*, which is achieved through the introduction of the term ἐκκλησία (16:18; 18:17) and by virtue of a theology of the kingdom (51 times). In Mt, this term becomes a category of thought (used without explanatory attribute, 4:23; 9:35; 13:19). "Kingdom of heaven", probably an expression from apocalyptic, indicates in Mt the divine kingdom which exists in heaven, is realized on earth in image and anticipation, and will finally be consummated in heaven at the end of time. Being both present and future, it constitutes the newness of the era inaugurated by Jesus. The kingdom is taken from Israel to be given to another people (21:43): the future of the kingdom is bound up with the destiny of the speaker, the destiny of the kingdom is entrusted to the Church itself. The history of Jesus shows that, by rejecting their Messiah, the Jews have enabled the gospel to spread to the whole universe. Time and again Matthew takes pains to show how both the justice spoken of by Israel (5:17) and the new community, constituted by the Twelve gathered around Christ and which announces the future Israel, are brought "to fulfilment". These disciples (who receive little blame, if Mt is compared with Mk) are initiated step by step into the secrets of the kingdom (13:11) and are called prophets, sages, and scribes of the new law (13:52; 23:34). They are invested with the authority and the power given to the Son of Man (9:6, 8) and are to manifest this in their exorcisms (17:16, 19).

As a consequence, the gospel materials are more clearly grouped and distributed around the rejection of Jesus at Nazareth. In the first part, Jesus presents himself to the Jewish people who refuse to believe in him. After a triptych (3:1 – 4:11), where we see John preaching, Jesus coming to be baptized and then triumphing over the devil, three major subdivisions can be distinguished: Jesus, all-powerful in works and words (4:12 – 9:34), the disciples sent out by the Master (9:35 – 10:42), the choice for or against Jesus (11:1 – 13:52). The second part describes the passion and the glory of Christ. Jesus ceases to teach the crowds (cf. Mk 6:34; Lk 9:11) and devotes himself to the instruction of the disciples. He forms them and strengthens them (14:1–16:20), reveals to them the mystery of his passion and teaches them the law of brotherly service (16:21 – 20:28). This arrangement shows very clearly how the proclamation of the kingdom of heaven eventually passes from Israel to the nations (24:14; 26:13; 28:19).

Ecclesiology and Christology are not treated in a theoretical fashion. The catechesis is not turned into a kind of catechism illustrated with a few well-chosen examples to accompany the discourses of Christ. It announces a new life which has doctrinal implications. So Matthew makes the events of the past actually present by the way he makes his Christian reader a party to the narrative. The more extended compositions reveal the inner meaning of the life of Jesus in the form of an authoritative catechesis (the five discourses). The hieratic character of the narratives helps the reader to react just like those who lived long ago. Already the disciples speak to Jesus as to the Kyrios (8:2, 6, 21, 25; 9:28; 15:27; 17:15; 20:30, 31, 33). In this way the believer sees himself raised by the merciful hand of Jesus, like Peter's mother-in-law (8:15) or the three prostrate witnesses of the transfiguration (17:7), called to follow him (8:22, 23; 9:9), to enter with the disciples into the boat which signifies the Church (8:18; Tertullian; Bornkamm). On every occasion he asks himself who is this Lord with whom he journeys (8:27). We can speak of a Matthaean theology of the "little faith" (Held), which reflects a traditional element (Lk 12:28 = Mt 6:30). Unlike Mark, who shows the disciples as completely lacking in comprehension (Mk 4:40), Mt perceives in the pre-paschal attitude of the disciples what was later to be proclaimed by the faith following on the events of Easter. By following Jesus, they already believe, but they have still to live this faith: to judge by the way they behave, their actions do not yet correspond to what they confess with their lips: they lack confidence (8:26; 14:31; 16:8; 17:20). The believer must allow himself to be penetrated by the continual presence of his Lord (28:20). Finally, we must note the significant way in which Matthew groups his materials. Thus when he incorporates the sentence on the rejection of the children of the kingdom into the story of the healing of the centurion's son, he transforms this miracle into a paradigm of the coming of paganism to Jesus (8:5–13 = Lk 7:1–10; 13:28–29). The warnings which Jesus addresses to the unbelieving Jews still resound throughout the Church which, like every organized society, is threatened by a spirit of self-sufficiency and conformism. More generally one can say that if the pre-synoptic tradition reflects a time of crisis, Matthew tries to make the words of Jesus practicable and adaptable. In the Sermon on the Mount he shows the way that the new Israel must follow, in contrast to the codification of the Jewish synod of Jamnia (W. D. Davies). All the same, he does not substantially alter tradition, but brings out what was potentially contained in the teaching of Jesus, who was himself a great moral teacher. By introducing the Sermon on the Mount into a gospel, Matthew relates it to the person of Jesus and so prevents the reader from reducing the gospel to a merely superficial moralization or to a kerygma devoid of any interest in the problems of morality.

4. *The Gospel according to St. Luke.* Luke is a man of tradition. Like Mark, he writes for Christians of pagan and non-Palestinian origin, about the year A.D. 80. He respects the distribution of his sources better than Matthew. He preserves the pre-synoptic schema, although he introduces into it the many sources which he had collected himself: the words of the Lord and other particular traditions. The view he takes of the gospel is determined by the fact that he also composed the Acts of the Apostles. He proclaims the Good News of salvation for every man, provided

that he is humble and repentant (5:32; cf. Mk 2:17). He writes a "book" and sets down a scripture which is to serve in the teaching mission of the Church. This gospel, which was composed at the close of the apostolic era as an addition to the original catechesis (1:1–4), is the result of reflection and meditation when compared with the early witnesses (Schürmann). Luke is the theologian of the history of God's plan. His intention is to span the history of salvation from the coming of Jesus upon the earth (Jesus, the son of Adam:3:38) up to the extension of the kingdom to the ends of the earth, and to arrange it around two central axes: Easter and Pentecost. For Mt and Mk, the life of Jesus appears as a central point which unites and divides the two major stages of the history of salvation: the time of the promises and the time of their accomplishment. For Lk, the accomplishment itself takes place in two stages: the time of Jesus and the time of the descent of the Spirit whom the Father promised upon the disciples. The binary schema of promise and fulfilment is overlaid by a triple division: the time of Israel, the time of Jesus and the time of the Church. As a result the life of Jesus has a meaning and importance in itself and for ever. It is not only the source engendering pardon, the essential prerequisite for the coming of the Spirit or of entry into salvation: it is the image and the pledge on which the hope of the believer is established (Conzelmann). The time of Jesus, who was preserved from temptation, is the prefiguration of heaven: the kingdom is not only near, it is actually there, in Jesus. The Christian life consists in looking back towards the Jesus who has come and lived among us, and looking forward to the Jesus who is yet to come.

This theological conception is balanced by a very practical concern for catechetical presentation, which shapes the third gospel into a rule of life: the teaching on riches and poverty (1:52–53; 6:20; 12:13–21; 16:15) and on renunciation (12:22–34; 14:26–33; 18:29); the disciple of Christ must take up his cross "every day" (9:23). The life of Jesus has opened up a new era in the life of the world: the era in which we now live. Every man is invited to discover a meaning in his own life by continually relating it to the life of Jesus himself. Even more than Mk, Lk shows how the human life of Jesus was a continual struggle against Satan. As a sign of contradiction (2:34), Jesus fought the good fight. He exorcized those who were possessed, and healed "all those who were oppressed by the devil" (Acts 10:38); thus even the healings were exorcisms (4:35, 41; 8:24; 9:42). He knows that the Son of Man must suffer much and be rejected before appearing like the lightning (17:24–25). For Lk, the ascent to Jerusalem is not only given prominence through the threefold prophecy, arranged with careful and detailed illustration (the great interpolation, 9:51 – 19:27); it carries the reader forward towards the glory which comes through the cross. The account of the passion does not picture a hero to be imitated (Dibelius), but an eschatological person to whom we can and must unite ourselves: the Servant of God, the innocent victim (23:4, 14, 15, 22, 47) who, with the weapons of gentleness (22:48, 51, 61; 23:34, 43), triumphs over the powers of darkness (22:53; cf. 22:3, 31).

In his own confrontation with Satan (8:12), in his trials (8:13) as in times of persecution (12:12), the believer discovers within himself the dynamic force of the Spirit, the most excellent gift (11:13; cf. Mt 7:11), the power come from on high (Acts 1:7–8), the Spirit whom he sees acting in John the Baptist (1:15, 80), in John's parents (1:41, 67), in Mary (1:35), in Simeon (2:25–27) and even more in Jesus himself (4:1, 14, 18; 10:21; cf. Acts 10:38). He is invited to breathe the air of the gospel which for Luke, as a witness to the early Church's experience of the Spirit, becomes a universe of praise (1:46ff.; 1:64, 68ff.; 2:13, 20, 28, 38; 5:25–26; 7:16) in joy and in prayer (in addition to Mt and Mk: Jesus at prayer 3:21; 5:16; 6:12; 9:18, 28–29; 10:21; 11:1; 22:32; 23:34, 46; 24:30; teaching on prayer: 11:5–8; 18:1–8; the Spirit and prayer: 1:15–17; 3:21–22; 10:21; 11:13). If Luke was concerned to spell out in detail the practical demands made by the gospel message, at the same time he shows the Spirit at work in the life of the believer, a life now enlightened by joy.

This catechesis which sheds the light of the gospel beyond the confines of Israel shows that for Lk universalism is an evident truth, not the surprising outcome of some tragic drama as in Mt. The rejection of the Jews is simply the signal for the spread of the Good News. The evangelist of mercy (Lk 15) omits traditions that are coloured with Jewish preoccupations (Mt 15:1–20 par.; 15:21–28 par.), and brings out the universalism latent in certain traditions (2:14, 32; cf. Mt 8:11–12; Lk 3:6; 10:25–37; 17:11–15). The herald of the saving mercy of Jesus towards sinners, strangers, and women, and the witness to the brotherly love inspiring the life of the community of Jerusalem, Lk is also the first historian among the evangelists. He is not content to be just a writer setting down the apostolic tradition. He exploits the theology of history implied in the kerygma, and by marking out the three great periods in the history of salvation and relating them together, discloses God's universal plan of salvation in its mysterious dimensions.

II. The Gospel of John

1. The fourth gospel provides in 20:31 a statement on its purpose: "These (signs) are written that you may believe that Jesus is the Christ, the Son of God, and that believing you may have life in his name." The use of the title "the Christ" means that the great question which moves all men has been posed, as in the other title used in 4:42, "the saviour of the world". It is the question of where the ultimate deliverance and well-being is to be found. The gospel's answer is: in Jesus, whom God sent into the world to be its saviour (cf. 3:17). The religious and secular background reflected in the fourth gospel casts light in two ways on this question and answer. It points out the way in which the seeker will find the answer to his question, and it also rejects misleading answers, such as the suggestion that salvation is to be found in a timeless region, like Gnosticism, devoid of all reference to the historical action of God in the "Word made flesh". Hence the gospel insists that the seeker must concentrate on a historical person, Jesus of Nazareth, the incarnate Logos. This is also the real reason why the kerygma is not given in the form of credal statements, but as a *Vita Jesu*, through which the answer to the question of salvation is propounded in detail: Jesus' words and works are salvation and the way to salvation. But this again does not take the form of a word for word and day to day reporting of the life of Jesus. Taking the synoptic type of gospel-writing a stage further, it is done by transposing the life of Jesus into kerygmatic form, which makes this life the gospel tidings for the world. This necessarily brings up the hermeneutic problem of the fourth gospel: how is the historical event of the coming of Christ seen and understood in the gospel? What is the perspective of the author? The answer may be found in the special terminology, characteristic of the fourth gospel, used when speaking of knowledge – the terms "see", "hear", "know", "attest", "remember". The Johannine perspective is that of a witness who believes, knows and loves, who "remembers" and "sees" the historical Jesus of Nazareth in such a way, under the guidance of the Paraclete, that the hidden depths, the mystery of the divine

Logos who is by nature Son of God, become "manifest" and can be expressed in the kerygma for the benefit of the Church. Hence this seeing is also a creative process. It makes it possible to transpose the insights thus acquired into the attestation of the kerygma, which takes form in the Church as *anamnesis*. In this kerygma Jesus, as the glorified Lord, continues to live and to speak through the Paraclete.

Hence the Johannine kerygma, as found in the fourth gospel, is the product of the Johannine perspective. And thus the fourth gospel gives testimony to the history of Jesus as it was known and seen in faith. This causes a certain merging of temporal horizons, because the time of the historical Jesus and the time of writing, that is, of the Church and the kerygma, are projected into one another, though without being confused. This process of transposition and merging goes so far that the Johannine Christ, as appears from a linguistic investigation of the fourth gospel, speaks a Johannine language. Thus the historical Jesus speaks in the fourth gospel as the glorified Lord addressing himself to the Church. The vocabulary of the Johannine Christ is that of dualism, from the point of view of comparative religion (life – death; truth – lie; light – darkness; above – below; God – cosmos); but the antithetical dualism is not that of the abstract and non-historical which is so characteristic of Gnosis. It is linked inseparably to the historical epiphany of the Logos and Son of God in the world. And hence the language is full of concepts which bring out the notion of epiphany – δόξα, φῶς, φαίνειν, φανεροῦν, φανεροῦσθαι, [ἐξ]-έρχεσθαι, καταβαίνειν, ἀποστέλλειν, πέμπειν.

The presence of such terms is a corollary of the appearance of the Logos Christ on earth, to which "seeing" and "hearing" in faith correspond on the part of men, as in the theophanies described in the OT. It is in fact because the coming of Christ is seen very much as a "vertical" event, one proceeding from heaven to earth, that it has the character of an epiphany. An event of this nature is above all something "seen" (1:14), and what is "seen" and "heard" there in faith is more than the outward happening: it is the heavenly doxa of the divine Logos himself. Thus the understanding of the coming of Christ in terms of an epiphany, kerygmatically translated in the fourth gospel, becomes a gospel "testimony" formulated in terms of an epiphany. And thus it becomes the answer to the questions which called for explanation in the Church at the time of writing (between A.D. 90 and 100), chiefly questions of Christology. The Gospel of John takes an existing tradition about Jesus and his words and works (possibly going back to the Apostle John, the son of Zebedee, cf. 3 below) and makes it relevant for a certain epoch of the Church, and – as a gospel received into the canon – for all ages of the Church.

2. Though the Gospel of John is a definite and very special interpretation of the existing tradition about Jesus, this does not mean that it claims to be the product of a sort of "private Gnosis" detached from the Church, composed, say, to counteract the gospel-writing of the synoptics. The author may indeed have been someone endowed with charismatic gifts – "the beloved disciple" – but he does not exploit his charisms against tradition. On the contrary, and especially in Christology, he maintains the tradition which was taught "from the beginning" (cf. 1 Jn 1:1; 2:24; 3:11), though envisaging it at a decidedly deeper level, through the insights of his faith. This sense of being tributary to the community and tradition is expressed in the Johannine writings chiefly by the use of assertions in the first person plural, which are found both in the gospel (cf. esp. 1:14) and in the first letter (1:1–3; 4:14–16). Hence the kerygma of the fourth gospel is specifically presented as a lasting prod-

uct of the eye-witnesses' contact with Jesus, the Logos incarnate, as a community product which lives on in the Church as apostolic tradition. It is true that the vision of faith "is not limited to (Jesus') contemporaries, but is communicated by them to all succeeding generations. Nonetheless, it is only through them that it is communicated, since it is not a matter of something timeless, a valid eternal truth, but of the ὁ λόγος σὰρξ ἐγένετο" (Bultmann) – the doxa of the incarnate Logos. This link with a concrete person and his history, never lost sight of in the fourth gospel, maintains the "seeing" and "hearing" of faith in constant dependence on tradition and its source, the ecclesiastical community. While the heretic, according to 2 Jn 9, does not "abide in the doctrine about Christ" transmitted by the apostolic circle in common, and underlines the "independent" nature of his private Gnosis by speaking in the first person singular (ἔγνωκα αὐτόν, 1 Jn 2:4), the author of the fourth gospel speaks in the plural: "we have seen", "we have known", "we believe". Hence the Church did not hesitate to receive the fourth gospel into the canon of normative gospels, in spite of some resistance, as the history of the canon shows. The Church recognized thereby that the figure and history of Jesus of Nazareth were correctly interpreted in it. Nonetheless, the deliberate adherence of the fourth evangelist to tradition does not mean that he took it over mechanically and merely repeated it. His work was a creative and highly independent interpretation of it, as demanded by the theological and ecclesiastical situation of his times.

3. Is the Apostle John, the son of Zebedee, behind this interpretation? The question cannot be answered definitely. Since narrative and theological interpretation are mingled in a very special way in the fourth gospel, we may assume that it comes as the end of a long process of the evolution of tradition, and that though the Apostle John may well be the "narrator" behind the recital, the narratives were given a consistent theological purpose and linguistic form by a circle of disciples who shared his inspiration. They adopted the perspective of the Apostle's faith and took it to its greatest possible development. In this "Johannine school" (whose historical setting escapes us) the "seeing", "knowing" and "hearing" of the apostolic witnesses who heard and saw became an experience which was shared by all. The narrative became kerygma in an unmistakably "Johannine" form, in which the epiphany character of the coming of Christ was given its adequate literary expression.

III. Acts: see *Apostle*.

IV. The Letters of Paul

The twenty-seven "books" of the NT include twenty-one letters. This feature is to be explained by the literary customs of antiquity, especially in the environment of the NT, where letters and collections of letters were often used to propagate philosophical, ethical, political and artistic views. Thus we have collections of letters which were ascribed to Plato, Aristotle, Cicero, Epicurus, Seneca, Horace and Ovid. In the Church, the collection of Pauline letters was followed by the letters of Ignatius, Cyprian and Augustine.

Conventional forms develop with the writing of letters. The ancient letter first gave the name of the sender, then named and greeted the recipient, and ended with good wishes and greetings. Paul used the standard formula, but often modified it considerably. But his letters are not systematic treatises, like so many in the collections mentioned above. They are real letters, inspired by the duty and the needs of the Apostle, who cannot be everywhere along with his communities, as he would have wished (2 Cor 1:15; Gal 4:20; 1 Thess 2:12f., 18). He sends instead a fellow-worker (2 Cor 2:13; 5:6f.; 8:6; 1 Thess 3:1), or at least a letter (Gal 6:11). The letters cater for particular historical occasions, with which the original readers were familiar, but which are obscure or unknown to us. Hence the interpretation of certain matters remains uncertain.

We have not all the letters which Paul wrote, and perhaps only a small selection of them. The surviving letters are from about A.D. 50 to 60, and are all to communities, except the personal letter addressed to Philemon. The two canonical letters to the Corinthians show that he wrote them at least four letters. A letter to the Laodiceans mentioned at Col 4:16 is also lost. Some decades after his death, all the available letters of Paul were collected from the archives of the Churches. The editors may have tried to preserve everything they found, combining together fragments and portions in the process. Possibly some of the existing letters – like 2 Cor, Phil and perhaps others – owe their present unity only to the activity of the editors.

Fourteen letters are given under the name of Paul in the NT. Thirteen name him as the sender. (On Heb, see below.) Many writings have been preserved from antiquity under fictive names. Publishing under another name was a recognized feature of literature, more or less like our use of *noms de plume*. Philosophical schools, for instance, published their writings under the name of their founder or an authority, to signify that they owed their views to the predecessor in question. Outside the canon we have a third letter of Paul to the Corinthians, a letter to the Laodiceans and even the correspondence between Paul and Seneca. These letters are certainly not authentic. Exegetes could not avoid posing the question as to whether all the canonical letters ascribed to Paul stemmed directly from him. It is now recognized that Rom, 1 and 2 Cor, Gal, Phil, 1 Thess and Phm are unquestionably authentic. 2 Thess, Eph, Col and the pastoral letters are the subject of controversy and are held to be to some extent post-Pauline. These are not questions of faith but of literary history. The importance of "genuinity" in general should not be exaggerated. All the writings of the NT are genuine witnesses to the faith and life of the NT Church. In all the ancient manuscripts, the letters of Paul are arranged in descending order of size, with a second letter to the same recipients joined in each case to the first. Here they will be dealt with according to the probable dates of their origin.

1. *Thessalonians*. Paul had founded the Church in Thessalonica on his second missionary journey (*c.* 49). His companions were Timothy and Silvanus. Paul wrote the two letters to the Thessalonians, *c.* 50, at Corinth, after receiving good news from Thessalonica through Timothy (1 Thess 3:6). Hence his letters are full of joy and thanksgiving. Like the whole Church of the NT, the Christians of Thessalonica awaited the early return of Christ with earnest hope. Meanwhile some Christians had died. Were they to be pitied because they had not experienced the great fulfilment? Using the notions of his day, Paul sketches a picture of the last day with the resurrection of the dead, the coming of Christ and the general judgment. Finally, he utters the consoling words: "We shall always be with the Lord" (1 Thess 4:17). Those who have been laid hold of by Christ and who have laid hold of him can never be deserted by his love, which is powerful and faithful, able to bring them through death to life. The certainty of being responsible before God should make Christians sober and serious in their moral endeavour (1 Thess 5:6–11). In the second letter (3:6–12) Paul again calls for soberness, work and patience in face of eschatological expectations. Before the return of the Lord, the Antichrist will come, who is already secretly at work, though restrained by

another power (2 Thess 2:3–12). It is not clear what Paul means. Thessalonica, like the Church down the ages, had its share of overheated enthusiasts, such as some sects represent. They are serious in their professions and have faith and love. The Church may often find it hard to disown them. But it must live in hope, without succumbing to blind enthusiasms. Large parts of the two letters belong to the apocalyptic genre, which is represented in the NT by other sections of the Pauline letters, by sections of the gospels (Mt 24 and 25 and parr.) and by the book of Revelation.

2. *Galatians*. This letter was probably not sent to the Churches of the province of Galatia in the south of Asia Minor, but to the Galatian peoples of the north. Paul had evangelized them during his second and third missionary journeys (Acts 16:6; 18:23). The letter was written possibly in 44, but more probably in 55, during his long stay at Ephesus (Acts 19:21). Like the other Churches, the Galatians has also received from Paul the gospel of grace and with it the message of freedom from the law. But now "false brethren" from Israel were demanding that all Christians, including those of Gentile origin, should be circumcised and keep the whole OT law, as practised among the Jews, if they were to be saved (5:2f.; 6:12). Paul's answer is vigorous and passionate, torn between anger and love. There is nothing to be gained by works of the law which is not already there for faith in Christ. To turn halfway away from Christ in the hope of a different and better justice is to lose Christ totally (3:5; 5:2). The only purpose of the law was to educate men for Christ and guide them towards him (3:15–29). The Galatians must not exchange their freedom and sonship for serfdom under the law (4:8–11). But the law of love remains, which is always valid (5:6). Here, as elsewhere, Paul makes use of rabbinical methods to propound his arguments. But he gives a permanent answer to questions which are always being posed to the Church as to what is essential and valid: the rigidity of tradition or the creative freedom of faith, law or Spirit, restrictions or freedom, works or grace, achievement and reward or faith and its gifts, ultimately man or God. Paul spoke out decisively for the freedom of faith, for grace and Spirit. His answer was not inspired by human boldness. His doctrine of justification is essentially the same as Jesus' teaching, that the kingdom of God is given to the child. The letter is of great historical importance as the charter of the freedom of the Church. Without this freedom Christianity would have remained a Jewish sect and would not have become a world Church. The letter did not merely give a ruling to suit a special occasion. It excludes all empty legalism in the Church.

3. *Corinthians*. Paul stayed in the Greek city of Corinth for a year and a half during his second missionary journey, probably from the autumn of 51 to the spring of 53. He founded there a community of considerable proportions with a very active Christian life (Acts 18:1–18). During his third missionary journey, Paul was in Ephesus (54–57), maintaining contacts with Corinth across the Aegean Sea (Acts 19:1–20:1). Letters and messengers went to and fro. Paul wrote at least four letters to the Corinthians, of which two survive. They give a picture of the Christian mission in the Greek world. The meeting with a new way of life and a new mentality posed many questions.

a) The first (surviving) letter to the Corinthians was written in Ephesus (1 Cor 16:8). Paul first had to see that harmony reigned in the Church. Like the schools of Greek philosophy, groups and parties had been formed in the Church of Corinth. Some demanded wisdom of a higher type and cut themselves off from the simple faithful (1:10–4:21). Paul reminds them that there is only one wisdom, the divine foolishness of the cross (1:18–2:16). But the whole community belongs to the one Christ as Lord of the Church, and Christ to the one God (3:1–22). All this forms a text on Church unity – like Jn 17; Eph; Jud; 2 Pet – which is of particular interest today. Corinth was notorious for its licentious way of life. There were moral failings even in the Christian Church which had to be denounced and corrected (5:1–13; 6:12–20). Questions of civic life had to be settled, since Christians were bringing their disputes before the pagan courts (6:1–11). A large portion of the letter (7:1–15:58) is taken up by answers to questions put by the Corinthians. In the over-wealthy and almost over-refined culture of antiquity, ascetical tendencies, as often happens under such conditions, grew up, calling for abstinence from the world. Some felt that marriage and sex might be evil and that sexual continence might be a duty. Paul defended the principle of marriage against such false asceticism. In marriage, the unbelieving partner is sanctified by the believing one, for which reason the children too are holy (7:14). Hence marriage is a permanently holy act, like a permanent sacrament. Paul warns against all ascetical experiments or enforced continence (7:9). But the vocation to celibacy in the Church is a sign of its eschatological expectation (7:29–31). Another question was whether a Christian could buy and eat meat sold in the market, if it had been slaughtered in a religious rite. (In ancient religion, life was sacred to God and animals could only be slaughtered in view of sacrifice.) Paul gives the very liberal answer that the earth and its fullness belong to the Lord, and hence to the Christian. He is under the power of God and the protection of the one Lord Christ and need not fear any powers that demons might be supposed to have (8:1–11:1). The regulation of divine worship called for strong measures from the Apostle. The Eucharist was being endangered by the arrogance of some who were turning it into a luxurious banquet. Paul reminded the Corinthians of the seriousness of the meal. The broken bread implies the body of the Lord, broken in death, and the wine in the chalice his outpoured blood. The meal proclaims the death of the Lord (11:17–34). Finally, Paul speaks of the resurrection. Greek philosophy taught the immortality of the soul, but that the body was the prison of the soul. The Corinthians thus found it hard to understand the resurrection of the flesh. Paul expounds the resurrection of Christ as the ground of Christian faith and life (15:1–58).

b) Between 1 and 2 Cor, grave disputes arose between Paul and the Church in Corinth, which had to some extent at least accorded entry and influence to false apostles. It seems that these also upheld the claims of the OT law, but with the addition of some Gnostic doctrines. Paul's adversaries may therefore have been Judaistic Gnostics. They attacked Paul's personal character and tried to turn the Church against him. In 2 Cor, Paul had to defend his call to the apostolate and his ministry.

His defence produced a comprehensive and penetrating theology of the office in general. He propounds the nature of the office in the NT by means of a comparison with the office in the OT (3:1 – 4:6). He then describes the NT office as above all service of the word. The word effects what it signifies. In the word of the Church God himself is at work (5:19f.). Paul is constrained by the opposition to speak of himself and his ministry. He speaks of his weakness, indeed of his perpetually dying state (4:7 – 6:10), and also of the supreme revelations which he was granted. In no other letter does he speak of himself so often as in 2 Cor, which is therefore a highly important autobiographical document. Like other letters, 2 Cor shows how Paul fought for his

Churches. He is not trying to retain their personal allegiance, but to win them for Christ (2 Cor 11:2). But Paul, the tireless and homeless wanderer, had nothing but the communities which he had created by his preaching of the gospel and which he served with the utmost dedication. Any loss or lapse of confidence between him and the community must have been a source of deep personal pain to him.

4. *Romans*. In the winter of 57–58, Paul wrote from Corinth (Rom 15:25f.; 1 Cor 16:6) to the Christians of Rome, to announce his near arrival. Many roads had led Christians to the great capital city of the Empire, and there was already an imposing Christian community in Rome. Paul did not intend to do missionary work there. But since he had been charged with the mission to the Gentile world, he had finally to visit its centre (Acts 19:21; 23:11). His intention was then to proceed from Rome to Spain (Rom 15:24). The letter was to introduce himself to the Roman Church. Hence he presented the main lines of his teaching and preaching, in the form of a programme. The main theme of the first part, which is predominantly doctrinal (1:18 – 11:36), is the justice of God and of man. The second part (12:1 – 15:33) contains exhortations for the whole community and for each individual. The first part is a close and comprehensive study of the theme of justification which was outlined in Gal. Hence Rom represents the fierce controversy between a religion of justice from works, which Paul depicted in Judaism, and the gospel of justice from grace. Paul finds his doctrine already expressed in Hab 2:4, "The righteous by faith will live" – as Rom 1:17 quotes the text. Paul may have given the words a profounder meaning than the prophet, but his interpretation is a perfectly correct understanding of the tendency and purpose of the OT, inasmuch as in the course of its development down the centuries the OT came more and more to point away from the work of man to the grace of God. When Paul speaks of the futility of paganism and Judaism, he is not speaking of things of the past. Every religion is always tempted to paganism, that is, to natural religion, insofar as man is always tempted to find God by his own virtues and to try to become just before God through his own effort. Every religion is also faced with the temptation of Judaism, inasmuch as it constantly tries to have God in its debt, by fulfilling the law. Paul affirms that both types of effort are in vain, since man as a sinner can do nothing to help himself. There is only one justice and one salvation for man, that which is God's free gift.

5. *Letters of the captivity*. Phil, Phm, Col and Eph, according to their headings, were all written when Paul was in prison, though they do not say where. It need not have been the same place for all these letters. Acts (23:35 – 26:32; 28:16–31) tells of long periods of imprisonment in Caesaraea and Rome. Paul himself mentions other occasions, which are otherwise unknown (Rom 16:7; 2 Cor 11:23). A large number of scholars assume that Phil was written in Ephesus – 1 Cor 15:32 may allude to an imprisonment there – and that the others were written in Rome. Hence Phil is dated to 54–55, the others to 62–63. All these letters come from prison, which was then much harsher than deprivation of liberty today. But they all attest Paul's freedom (Phil 4:10–13) and even joy (especially Phil 1:4, 18; 2:17f.; 3:1; 4:4). Phil is a letter of friendship and union between Paul and a Church particularly dear to him, which he thanks for help sent to him in prison. In 2:6–11 he takes up a hymn of the Church which speaks of the divine being of Christ before time, his emptying himself and being crucified, and then exalted to glory. Paul invokes the hymn to urge the community to harmonious service and obedience. Paul again warns sharply against Judaistic-

Gnostic heresies (3:1 – 4:1). All they offer is valueless, since Christ is the only prize to be won (3:18). The truth of the gospel and purity of doctrine are to be maintained undiminished.

According to Col, strange doctrines were being taught at Colossae, probably tenets of Jewish Gnosticism. Christ was debased to the rank of one of the intermediate beings between God and the world. In discussing this doctrine, Paul provides a further development of Christology. Christ is higher than all powers. The fullness of the Godhead dwells in him. He is mediator of creation and now head of the Church (Col 1:13–23). Here Paul is taking up Gnostic slogans, which he does not dismiss as sheer heresy, but recognizes as genuine questions, which indicate a yearning and a demand for truth which should be satisfied. He can promise all such longing that it will be fulfilled in Christ.

Eph was probably a circular letter to the Churches of Asia Minor. It speaks of the immeasurable depths and heights of the redemption (Eph 3:18). Christ is the head and beginning of a new humanity (Eph 5:23). In the Church, the body of Christ (Eph 1:10), the unity of mankind is restored (Eph 4:3–16). To be in the Church is to be in Christ.

In the short letter to Philemon, Paul intercedes for Onesimus, a runaway slave, but now a follower of the Apostle. Severe punishments awaited the slave, according to the law. Paul acknowledges the existing legal order, but goes beyond it in calling the slave "a beloved brother . . . both in the flesh and in the Lord" (Phm 16). The letter is a manifesto for the abolition of slavery, not through force but through Christian love.

6. *Pastorals.* The two letters to Timothy, bishop at Ephesus, and the letter to Titus, bishop in Crete, are known as the pastoral letters, because they give advice and exhortation on the exercise of the pastoral office. The offices – bishops, priests, deacons and also widows are mentioned – have undergone development and are of considerably greater importance than in the older letters. In doctrine too the accent is placed differently at times, and it appears more clearly as established dogma. Hence most exegetes consider that these letters can hardly stem from Paul as directly as the older letters. The explanation is sometimes offered that a disciple and secretary of Paul composed the letters himself, though charged to do so by Paul. But the clear development which is reflected in the letters suggests rather that a later author used the pseudepigraphical genre to give directives and exhortations to the Church in the spirit of Paul and on the basis of his genuine letters. The author was familiar with the Pauline letters and used them intelligently, though at times over-simplifying matters. Paul appears as the generous helper of his friends, the father of his disciples, a founder and director of Churches, a great man and saint who is unbowed by suffering. In prison he prays, and meditates on sacred Scripture (2 Tim 4:13). Finally he is Christ's witness before his judges (2 Tim 1:16f.; 2:9; 4:16f.). All Christians must be ready for such trials and persecutions (2 Tim 3:12). Are these allusions to be taken to mean that the Church expected pressure and persecution in the near future, and that Paul was to be held up to Christians, especially the heads of the communities, as the model of a true witness? If so, the pastorals probably date from the time of the beginning of persecution, the last decades of the 1st century.

7. *Hebrews.* In the liturgical and other official books of the Church, Heb is also given under the name of Paul. The letter itself does not mention any author. It is written in polished Greek with sonorous rhythms. Some 140 words in the letter are foreign to the vocabulary of Paul. The OT is expounded by a skilful use of allegory. Christ appears as the

high priest who intercedes for men in the heavenly sanctuary. The differences between Heb and the Pauline letters are undeniable. Heb probably came to be attributed to Paul because of the mention of Timotheus, 13:23, which suggested the circle of Paul's friends. From the 3rd century on, the Greek Church considered the letter to be Pauline, but the Fathers already noted the differences and expressed doubts about (direct) Pauline authorship (Clement of Alexandria, Origen, Tertullian, Augustine). It is now generally considered to be the work of an unknown author. It comes from Jewish-Christian circles of Hellenistic culture. The enlightened doctor of the Church took up the gospel on his own behalf, mastered it thoroughly and taught it convincingly. The letter gives us a glimpse of the riches of knowledge and eloquence with which the Church was endowed along with the primitive apostolic testimony. Heb is a homily in the form of a letter and as such should be treasured as an early example of a Christian sermon. It gives much earnest attention to the interpretation of the OT. The method often differs from that of the present day, but its love for Scripture makes it precious to readers of the Bible today. And it is precious to the Church and important for dogmatics by reason of its profound doctrine, copiously expounded, of the sacrifice and priesthood of Christ. The author, noting signs of weariness, urges Christians very earnestly to steadfastness and loyalty (6:12; 12:12f.). The letter stands like a beacon before the coming persecutions under which the Church must prove itself (10:32–39): "For our God is a consuming fire" (12:29). This situation presupposes a long period of Church history. Hence Heb may be dated to A.D. 90 or so.

Paul, when teaching and governing the Churches, was convinced that he was one who by the Lord's mercy was trustworthy (cf. 1 Cor 7:25), having the Spirit of God (cf. 1 Cor 7:40) and expounding the precepts of the Lord (cf. 1 Cor 14:37). This conviction also underlay his letters, which, however, he intended to be of service to the Churches and individuals in their given historical situation. It was not his intention to produce permanent works of literature. The Spirit which inspires the Church recognized the same Spirit in the writings of the Apostle (1 Cor 14:37), and took them into its canon of Scripture. Thus they are a permanently basic and inexhaustible source for faith and theology. Nonetheless, a later document of the NT can already say that the letters of Paul were being misunderstood and misused. From the beginning, the questions and difficulties of their interpretations laid burdens on the Church (cf. 2 Pet 3:15). This remains true to the present day. The letters of Paul are not easy and comfortable reading. But for this very reason the Church must always take pains to listen to their teaching and exhortations, to be judged and tested by their words, but also consoled and healed.

Karl Hermann Schelkle

IV. The Letter of James

The Letter of James was probably written by James of Jerusalem, "the brother of the Lord" (cf. Gal 1:19; Josephus, *Antiquities*, XX, 200) in the early sixties A.D. It is among the most important documents of the early Church and of the NT canon. For it insists, perhaps more strongly than any other NT letter, on the necessity of putting the "implanted word" into effect in a Christianity of action: "Be doers of the word and not hearers only, deceiving yourselves" (1:22). This Christianity in act manifests itself according to James chiefly in the following respects:

1. *The eschatological orientation of the Christian's whole existence.* James is convinced that human existence is radically temporary and transient in character

(1:10; 4:14; "You are a mist that appears for a little time and then vanishes"). He is also convinced that "the last days" have already begun, and the parousia of the Lord is close at hand (5:4, 8f.). He therefore warns the communities against relying upon their own power in planning their lives, and against every kind of boastful project (4:13–16). Every plan in the life of the believers should have the proviso: "If the Lord wills" (4:15, the so-called *conditio Jacobea*). The time which the community still has at its disposal is chiefly a time of "temptations" in which the community has to prove itself in "steadfastness" and faith, and in which it must wait patiently for the parousia of the Lord (1:2–4, 12; 5:7–11). James repeatedly draws his readers' attention to the approaching judgment (2:12; 4:12; 5:9, 12), but also, hopefully, to the "crown of life" (1:12). Thus time as James understands it is simply the "interval between". He makes no allowance for the communities' needing to "establish themselves" in the world.

2. *The renunciation of any "double standard of happiness" and an emphasis on "wholeness"*. James follows Jesus closely in upholding the biblical idea of "wholeness". Proving oneself in temptations, prayer, control of the tongue, patient waiting for the return of the Lord, and the works of love which, as "the perfect law of liberty" (1:25), it demands from men – these constitute the pre-eminent way of attaining to this "eschatological perfectionism".

3. *Trustful prayer*. He who prays must do so "in a simple manner", "in faith, without the least doubt" (1:5f.; cf. also 4:3). In particular he must also pray in times of misfortune (5:13). "The elders of the community" must pray for a man when he is grievously sick. James views man as an integral whole, and as one who must bring all the circumstances of his life and bodily condition, all physical and spiritual needs before God to the accompaniment of petition and praise. In this James is wholly in line with the tradition of the OT and Judaism. The dualistic anthropology and piety of Hellenism are alien to him.

4. *Faith and works*. In order that Christianity may become a Christianity in act James insists very strongly, particularly in the central section of his letter (2:14–26), upon the necessity of making faith live and endure by works of love towards one's neighbour, and of obedience towards God. In this he is clearly rejecting a doctrine of "faith alone". He affirms that faith alone cannot justify man before God if it is not combined with and fulfilled by the works of love. To prove his point here he invokes the examples of Abraham and Rahab. In doing this he is reacting against "a certain person" who has clearly drawn false conclusions from the preaching of the Apostle Paul on the freedom of Christians from the law, to the effect that mere faith alone is the one way to achieve justification. Against this James requires "works", but by this he does not in any sense mean "the works of the law", which, according to Paul, are of no avail for justification. The only works which James has in mind are the works of love.

5. *Social justice*. This constitutes a special preoccupation for James. It belongs to the essence of true piety (1:27). For this reason his condemnations of the rich with their feverish striving appear sharp in the extreme. He warns them that God's judgment upon them will be strict (1:11; 5:1–6). He requires the communities to have special care for the poor because God has "chosen those who are poor in the world to be rich in faith and heirs of the kingdom" (2:1–12). A further point, connected with this, is that James rejects every kind of "cult of personality" in the communities (cf. 2:1, 9).

6. *Poverty of spirit*. James reaffirms constantly the traditional ideal of "the poor man" as practised from ancient times in certain circles of Judaism. He

equates "poor" with "humble" (cf. 1:9–11). For him "poverty of spirit" is the right attitude for man before God. It is an attitude which is also adopted, for instance, by the Essenes of Qumran, but in James the idea of a "holy war" which the "poor" are to wage at the end of time against the "sons of Belial" (cf. 1 *QM*, XI, 8f., 13, *War Scroll, Qumran Cave* I) is absent. Instead James looks for help for the poor only from God or from the Lord at his return.

7. *Warnings concerning the tongue.* James regards the tongue as the source of manifold evil, and in this he is again following ancient ethical traditions (cf. 1:26: "If anyone thinks he is religious and does not bridle his tongue ... this man's religion is vain"; 3:1–11); he calls the tongue "a fire", "an unrighteous world", "a restless evil full of deadly poison" (3:5, 8).

8. *Wisdom and peace.* He who is truly religious must entreat God for wisdom (1:5), and this appears above all in virtuous conduct and in the rejection of ambition to teach, of jealousy and of factional intrigue in the communities. Wisdom loves peace (3:13–18).

9. *Unreserved truthfulness and the avoidance of swearing oaths lightly.* "Above all ... do not swear either by heaven or by earth or with any other oath, but let your 'yes' be 'yes' and your 'no' be 'no', that you may not fall under condemnation." In this James follows Jesus faithfully (Mt 5:33–37).

10. *Confession of sins and intercession. Spiritual help for the brother who has gone astray.* James's mind is wholly preoccupied with the idea of one's neighbour, especially in the context of the community. Help is to be given to him in every need of the body as well as of the spirit or of the mind. This must be one's attitude to widows and orphans (1:27), the poor (2:15f.), the sick (5:14f.), the brother who has gone astray (5:19f.). The spiritual unity which exists between brethren must also be manifested in the communities in mutual confession of sins and in prayer for one another (5:16).

Thus James is constantly preoccupied with the sincerity and genuineness of the confession of faith. He regards the Christian communities only as communities of brethren, and in this he also provides an important pastoral directive for our own times. A "pastoral programme" which would have immediate relevance to the present might be developed from his letter. James was not merely a "brother of the Lord" in the physical sense, but in a spiritual one as well. Many of the exhortations contained in his letter have their parallels in the principles of right living taught by Jesus, especially as these have been handed down in the Sermon on the Mount (cf. Mussner). James saw with complete clarity that the "newness" of Christianity consists in the fact that all that God requires of man is gathered up in the commandment of love, which he calls a "royal law" (cf. 2:8), in this too following Jesus. Hence the Letter of James in a special measure "inculcates Christ", which Martin Luther unfortunately denied.

Franz Mussner

V. The Letters of Peter

A. 1 PETER

1. *Literary history.* The letter, according to its heading, is written by the Apostle Peter (1:1), from Babylon (5:13), i.e., Rome, to the Church of Asia Minor (1:1). Babylon, the worldly and ungodly city of the prophets (Is 13; 43:14; Jer 50 and 51) is certainly taken as standing for Rome (cf. Rev 14:8 – 18:2; *Sibylline Oracles*, 5, 134 and 158f.; *Apocalypse of Baruch (Syriac)*, 11, 1; 4 *Esdras*, 3, 1). This agrees with other ancient mentions of Peter in Rome, where he is also supposed to have died. But it is not generally accepted that Peter wrote the letter. The writing shows a firm grasp of Greek style. The OT is quoted frequently, and always according to the

LXX. Could Peter have been so much at home in things Greek? Certain thoughts and elements of vocabulary are modelled on the Pauline letters (e.g., the theology of the passion 1:9; 2:24; 3:18; 21; 4:13); submission to the civil authorities 2:13–17; the formula "in Christ", 3:16 etc.). Could Peter have been thus tributary to the theology of Paul? At the time of the letter, the Church anticipated persecutions in Rome and in Asia (2:12; 3:13–17; 4:16f.). Can these menaces be explained by the persecution of Nero, which was confined to Rome and was an isolated incident? General persecution of Christians did not begin till under Domitian. If this is meant, the letter would be from about A.D. 90. It indicates in 5:12 that it was actually written by Silvanus, who had been with Paul in Asia Minor (Acts 15:40; 18:15; 1 Thess 1:1). Possibly Silvanus wrote at Peter's wish, but with a certain amount of independence, and was responsible for the link with the Churches in Asia Minor. It may even be that Silvanus or someone else wrote the letter after the death of Peter, convinced that he was following out his wishes. Or it may have been written at the request of the Roman Church, which felt itself to be one with Peter. Hence a large number of exegetes hold that 1 Pet is pseudepigraphical, published as representing the spirit and heritage of the Apostle.

2. *Contents and theology*. 1 Pet is a valuable piece of early Christian paraenetic writing, showing the faith, liturgy and doctrine of the early Church. The Church has been chosen out of the world (1:2) and hence is a stranger there (1:1). It has neither the right nor the means to exercise power there. Its actual distress is taken to be of the essence of its permanent situation (4:17). It is always following its Lord through suffering to glory (3:13 – 4:6; 4:12–19). The Church is a "royal priesthood" (2:5–9; cf. Exod 19:6; Is 61:6; 62:3), and as such has the task of preaching (2:9) and sacrificing (2:5). Like Rev 1:6; 5:10, the letter points to the general priesthood of the faithful. Some hold that it represents a baptismal sermon, but this is not likely, though it refers to baptism (3:21) as re-birth (1:3, 23; 2:2). The grace and sanctification experienced in baptism are to be put into effect in life (2:1–10; 3:21f.). A list of household virtues (*Haustafeln*) (2:13–3:12) forms along with similar lists at Eph 5:22–6:9; 1 Tim 2:8–15; Tit 2:1–10, etc., an early attempt at enumerating Christian social duties. Such lists combine elements of Greek ethics and Jewish tradition with Christian precepts. The sections 1:18–21; 2:21–25; 3:18–22 are signalled by their succinct style and rhythmic parallelism, as well as by the similarity of their contents, which is the Christian kerygma. They represent the initial stages of the formation of creeds, and are also examples of ancient hymns to Christ (cf. Phil 2:6–11; 1 Tim 3:16). In 3:19f. Jesus' descent into hell is probably meant to express in imagery the truth of his human death. The "spirits in prison" are now generally taken to be the "sons of God" who sinned according to Gen 6:1–6, fallen angels according to late Jewish midrash and also NT tradition (Jud 6f.; 2 Pet 2:4, 9). This would then be a "mythic" way of saying that the royal power of Christ extends universally and redeems all sin.

B. 2 Peter

1. *Contents and theology*. The letter is addressed to all the faithful (1:1), being a doctrinal piece in letter form. It is meant to strengthen the faith of the Church against dangerous errors (1:12f.; 3:2). The heresies in question are probably Gnostic. Since Gnostics sometimes curtailed the canon of Scripture and sometimes extended it unduly, and in any case misused Scripture for their own purposes (3:16), the letter takes up the question of Scripture. This needs proper interpretation, which is given in the Church through the Spirit (3:19–21).

The apocryphal and mythological elements employed in Jud 6, 7, 9 are deliberately omitted by 2 Pet. Hence the (OT) canon is restricted, and within the NT canon one book is criticized by another and indeed "demythologized".

Some Christians deride the eschatological hope of the Church. But in spite of all the questions which this poses to the Church, it still firmly believes that the last time has come (3:3). The letter uses OT and Jewish terms to describe the eschatological events, and also contemporary notions of the conflagration of the world (3:10–13). But since the new creation is described by saying, rather abstractly, that justice dwells there (3:13), it may be considered doubtful that it wishes to cling to apocalyptic descriptions. It is the beginning of an apologetical and systematic theory of Christian eschatology. Its problems are still felt by the Church and theologians today.

Heretics come forward arrogantly in the Church (2:18). They confuse freedom with licence (2:19). They deny the power and holiness of the angels (2:10f.) and the Lordship of Christ (2:2). They show traces of a Gnostic libertinism. Unlike Paul and John, who treat errors dialectically and try to win over opponents, the discussion here is confined to fierce reproaches. The letter is strongly concerned with upholding strict norms of moral behaviour. A Christianity which tried to be only Gnosis and spirit would be a lie. It is also essentially an ethical way of life. The letter shows that the Church from the time of the NT on could not realize the ideal of the one *holy Church*. Here it is already weighed down by the sins of its members, its unity threatened and weakened by sectarian doctrines and divisions (2:3). The Church already recognizes the need for and the difficulty of interpreting the Scriptures (3:15f.). The transition to "early Catholicism" is already apparent. The doctrine of the apostles is already a definitely fixed tradition (2:21; 3:2). The NT canon is in the process of formation (3:15f.). There has been terminological progress in the statement of the truths of faith and also development of their understanding (1:1; 1:11; 3:2). Faith is now not so much a personal act as the sum of the truths of faith (1:1). The demands made on man's own effort are emphasized. Terms and concepts from Greek philosophy are used in teaching the faith (1:3–7).

2. *Origin*. The letter bears the name of Peter as its author (1:1), and the author claims to have been present like Peter (Mk 9:2) on the mount of the transfiguration (1:16–18). But the letter cannot have been written by Peter. The circumstances of Church history and doctrine as supposed or described by the letter point to a later date, probably towards the end of the first century. The letter is an example of pseudepigraphical literature (see *New Testament Books* IV). The author wishes to make the apostolic preaching understandable in his day, and hence uses the name of the first apostle, Peter. He makes use of the Letter of Jude (2 Pet 2 = Jud 4–16), as another piece of apostolic writing. He appeals to the Apostle Paul, whom he calls his brother (3:15f.). Thus Peter and Paul ultimately appear together as teaching the Church and the world from Rome (where the letter was probably written, cf. 3:1). The same notion is found in 1 *Clem*, 5, 3–7; Ignatius, *Ad Romanos*, 4, 3; Irenaeus, *Adv. Haer.*, 3, 1, 1; Eusebius, *Hist. Eccles.*, 2, 25, 8). This is the beginning of the Roman Catholic Church in the NT, with Peter and Paul, as the princes of the apostles, as its pillars and teachers.

Karl Hermann Schelkle

VII. The Letters of John

While 2 Jn and 3 Jn are really "letters", the first letter should rather be considered as a "manifesto" – "a tractate intended for all of Christendom, an encyclical directed to all fellow believers"

(W. G. Kümmel, *Introduction to the New Testament* [1966], p. 307). But from the point of view of the subject-matter, 1 and 2 Jn go together, while 3 Jn deals with a particular problem of some acuteness. But the doctrine of all three letters is of permanent significance and validity for theology and for the Church.

1. Though 1 and 2 Jn give no references to concrete details, such as the sender and the recipients, the interests of the author, who is probably identical with the author of the fourth gospel, can be clearly seen. He writes to denounce very firmly some heretical views on Christology and ethics, which may be briefly summed up by saying that they put asunder what is essentially joined together, the unity of Jesus of Nazareth with the heavenly redeemer, and the unity of knowledge (faith) and love.

a) "Who is the liar but he who denies that Jesus is the Christ?" (1 Jn 2:22); "every spirit which dissolves Jesus is not of God" (1 Jn 4:3a, Vg). This denial and dissolution is the work of heretics, who have therefore the "spirit of antichrist" (*ibid.*, 4b). The heretic is one of the "many deceivers" who have left the Church and gone out into the world, because they did not confess that the coming of Jesus Christ had taken place in the flesh (cf. 2 Jn 7). Orthodox believers, however, confess that "Jesus Christ has come in the flesh" (1 Jn 4:2b) and believe that "Jesus is the Son of God", who came "in water and blood" (4:15; 5:5f.). Thus orthodoxy clings fast to the reality of the incarnation of the eternal Logos of life (1 Jn 1:1) in Jesus of Nazareth, to the uncompromising truth of his bloody death on the cross and of his being made known to Israel at his baptism in the Jordan (cf. Jn 1:31). But all this is denied by the heretic, who thus separates Jesus from his unity with the Christ and Son of God, as taught in the Church "from the beginning". He "does not abide in the (traditional) doctrine of (i.e., about) Christ" (2 Jn 7). The community is therefore told: "If any one comes to you and does not bring this doctrine, do not receive him into your house or give him any greeting; for he who greets him shares his wicked work" (2 Jn 10f.).

b) The heretic, proud of his freedom as a "spiritual" man, appeals to his own particular Gnosis: "I know him (Christ)" (1 Jn 2:4a). But he does not keep Christ's commandments and hence he is a liar and the truth is not in him (1 Jn 2:4b). The heretic is so proud of his "knowledge" that he no longer feels himself bound by the commandments of the Lord which are taught and handed on in the Church. He maintains that he is "in the light", but since he does not love his brothers, he is really "in the darkness" (1 Jn 2:9, 11). The community acknowledges its own sinfulness and hence can be urged to sin no longer; but if it does sin, it knows that its sins are forgiven on account of his name (cf. 1 Jn 1:9; 2:1f.; "for his sake", v. 12). The heretic, however, is arrogant enough to believe that he has left sin behind him. Thus he suffers from a great self-deception and the truth is not in him (cf. 1 Jn 1:8). He makes God a liar (1 Jn 1:10). No doubt the Church can claim to have "known" God and his Son, but it has the touchstone for true knowledge in its consciousness of its sinfulness before God and of its obligations towards the commandments of his Son, especially that of love.

This is the message which the Church has heard from the beginning (1 Jn 3:11; 2 Jn 5) and it knows that in keeping this commandment it has passed from death to life (1 Jn 3:14). For only he who loves his brother is "born of God and knows God", for "God is love" (1 Jn 4:7f.). Thus the indissoluble unity of love and knowledge is also part of the traditional doctrine.

2. In 2 Jn 9, the heretic who refuses to abide in the doctrine which comes from Christ and speaks of Christ is de-

scribed as προάγων – "he who goes ahead", a "progressive". This is clearly said in view of the liberty which he claims with regard to the apostolic tradition which has lived on in the fellowship of the Church "from the beginning" – the tradition of Christology as well as ethics. Orthodoxy, on the other hand, which lives in the "fellowship" (κοινωνία) of the apostolic eye-witnesses (cf. 1 Jn 1:1–3), is characterized in 1 and 2 Jn by the fact that it "abides" in that which was taught "from the beginning" (cf. 1 Jn 2:7, 24; 3:11; 2 Jn 5 f.). Thus the Church is clearly referred to *tradition*, against the views and teachings of the "progressives", a tradition which goes back to the beginnings of the Church and is ultimately rooted in the incarnate Logos of life himself (1 Jn 1:1f.). In other words, 1 and 2 Jn already invoke against heresy the principle of tradition, a typical characteristic of early Catholicism, which is concerned to preserve inviolate the apostolic tradition in the Church. But, what is theologically very important, tradition is not felt as in opposition to "Spirit". The authentic possession of the Pneuma comes out in the community's loyal adherence to the traditional doctrine (cf. 1 Jn 4:1, 6; 3:24; 5:6c, 10).

3. The doctrine in force "from the beginning" is not that of an individual, but of a fellowship. This is brought out in 1 Jn by the term κοινωνία and also by the frequent statements in the first person plural, in which the author associates himself with the apostolic eyewitnesses (cf. 1:3, "What we have seen and heard we proclaim also to you"; cf. 1:5 and 4:14, "and we have seen and testify"; 4:16, "we know and believe"). What is thus attested and proclaimed by the witnesses who have seen and heard is the normative doctrine which is in force "from the beginning" and which must be "preserved". Hence the fellowship of the Church, which recognizes the authority of the apostolic tradition, is an extension of the group that says "we"; to join this group and share its faith is to acknowledge the doctrinal tradition of the Church. The heretic, on the other hand, who does not abide in the "doctrine about Christ" handed on by the apostolic circle which speaks in the first person plural, has a special vocabulary for his "independent" private Gnosis. His formula is in the first person singular, "I have known him" (1 Jn 2:4), by which he deliberately opts out of the apostolic group which speaks in the plural. Hence his doctrine is devoid of all normative character.

4. 3 Jn also deals with the problem of ecclesiastical fellowship, but from another aspect. In this letter, "the elder" first praises a certain Gaius for the hospitality which he has extended to the "brethren" (missionaries and wandering preachers) on their travels, and urges him to continue to do so (1–8). Then the author denounces a certain Diotrephes, an authority in the community, who refuses to acknowledge the authority of the "elder", and not content with refusing to welcome the "brothers" himself, "stops those who want to welcome them and puts them out of the church" (9f.). The circumstances of the composition and the historical situation which underlie the allusions of the letter remain somewhat obscure. But the letter clearly teaches that there should be no communities in the Church which cut themselves off from the others. Each community must be ready to help the others and offer hospitality, so that the Church's testimony to the truth may be acceptable to the world. No community exists just for its own benefit. This has been recognized by Gaius, but not by Diotrephes.

Franz Mussner

NEW TESTAMENT ETHICS

1. *Jesus*. The new religious message of Jesus is closely linked to a new ethics, which is fully understandable, however,

only against the background of the OT and the eschatological mission of the Messiah.

a) *Relationship to Old Testament and Jewish ethics.* All Jesus' ethical thinking takes the OT as its base. The will of God remains for Jesus the supreme norm of moral action (Mt 6:10; 7:21; Mk 3:35 par.; Lk 12:47; Jn 7:17), and hence obedience to God, service of God with undivided heart, is the decisive attitude called for from man (Mt 6:24; cf. Deut 18:13; Lk 11:28; 17:7–10; Jn 6:45). Jesus reaffirms the Decalogue (Mk 10:19 par.), links up with the preaching of repentance (*metanoia*) by the prophets (Mk 1:15; 11:13f., 20f.; Lk 13:1–5, 6–9; 10:13–18 par.; 11:31f. par.; 15:7, 10) and proclaims an interiorized ethics as they did (Mk 7:6f. par.; 12:33; Mt 23:23, 25–28). Thought and act form an indissoluble unity (Mt 6:1–18, 22f.; 21:28–31; Lk 6:45). The motive of action is purely religious: God's perfection is the supreme model (Mt 5:48; cf. Lev 19:2), his heavenly reward (Mt 5:12; 6:4, 6, 18; Lk 6:35; 12:44, etc.) and his eschatological kingdom (Mt 5:3–10; Lk 12: 32, etc.) await those who seek and love God, while his anger and judgment threaten the wicked (Mt 5:21f., 26; 11:22f.; 12:36; 18:34f.; Mk 9:48; Lk 12:46, etc.). Even the Sermon on the Mount, if one considers merely the material content of its demands, does not go beyond the possible exigencies of OT and Jewish ethics, and has certain parallels in some rabbinical utterances (cf. G. Kittel, *Die Probleme des palästinischen Spätjudentums und das Urchristentum* [1926], pp. 96ff.). In enforcing radically the strict demands of the law, without detriment to moral disposition, and in practical austerity, the community of Qumran seems even to go further than Jesus (cf. 1 *QS;* on which see H. Braun). The novelty of his ethics lies elsewhere and its import is different.

b) *The unique significance of Jesus' ethics* comes from the fact that it is the eschatological message given with messianic authority. It is the proclamation of the will of God as the last days of salvation dawn, forcing men to decision (Mk 1:15; Mt 7:24–27; Lk 12:54ff.; 17:26f.). Men must first seek the Kingdom, subordinating to it all earthly cares (Lk 12:31 par.), indeed, sacrificing everything to it (Mt 13:44ff.), to make the supreme effort of entering in by the "narrow gate" (Lk 13:24 and the other sayings about "admission"). Since Jesus is God's fully authorized and final envoy (cf. Mt 10:40 par.; 12:41f.; Lk 12:23f. par.; 16:16), he proclaims the will of God in a new, authoritative and radical way, with no regard for earthly relationships. But because he is the Messiah, who promises God's mercy, help and salvation, and makes them tangible in his works, he can also dare to make these absolute demands on men. Hence his sovereignty with regard to the old law ("But I say to you . . ."), his superiority with regard to Moses (cf. Mk 10:1–9 par.), his abrogation of human statutes (Mk 7:8–13 par.), his call for a greater justice (Mt 5:20). He demands an inward dedication hitherto unattained (Mt 5:28; 18:35; Lk 6:45; Mk 7:20ff.), action of the most radical nature (Mk 9:43–47 par.), and a love extraordinary enough to go beyond those near to us and even take in enemies (Lk 6:27–36). Thus the ethics of Jesus transcends all nationalism, particularism and egoism, and is perfectly universal in a way that surpasses Judaism (cf. Lk 10:25–37). For the concrete realization of the NT ethics of the Kingdom, Jesus demands adherence to his own person. Discipleship in this sense is new to Judaism and can only be explained by his claim to Messiahship. The notion of following Jesus, which originally referred to the disciples in the stricter sense, those who shared his life of travel and took over his missionary task, applies basically in fact to all who believe in him (cf. Lk 14:25ff., 33; Mk 8:34 par.), and hence appears in a new form in primitive Christianity. Following now means placing the whole of the believer's life under the direction of the exalted Lord (Jn 8:12), taking with him and after him the same way (which Paul calls dying and rising with Christ; cf. Larsson). It includes readiness to follow Jesus in suffering and on the cross and produces new and specifically Christian motives, but is also combined with the idea of imitation which comes from the Greek notion of conformity to an ethical exemplar (A. Schulz).

c) *Incorrect interpretations.* Hence we must reject all interpretations of the ethics of Jesus which prescind from his religious message and isolate and erect into absolutes individual aspects which are liable to be misunderstood apart from his religious interests: upheaval or reform of the social order, renunciation of rights in favour of love, conquering through patience, disregard of cultural values, etc. But we must also reject all "idealistic" interpretations which disregard the concrete messianic message of Jesus and try to understand his doctrine as the climax of the religious and moral development of man, the ideal of a filial relationship to God and brotherliness among men and so on. Mistakes can also arise from wrong ideas of Jesus' message of the Kingdom. Thus for the eschatologists the ethics of Jesus is only an "interim ethics", while for others its demands can only be fulfilled in the coming Kingdom. Finally, we must reject the interpretation of modern "existence theology", which sees in Jesus' ethics only a call to decision and radical obedience, with no specific content to the demand (cf. Bultmann, *Jesus*); nor can the norms laid down by Jesus be volatilized into a mere "ethics of the situation". Nonetheless, the ethics of Jesus must not be petrified into a new code of law or reconciled with a "middle-class morality" which can be comfortably accommodated to the conditions and demands of this world.

2. *The primitive Church.* The primitive Church understood Jesus' ethics as a summons to act, his demands as concrete obligations. It accepted the tension with regard to "the world" in keeping with its own eschatological attitude, but drew strength from its faith in redemption through Christ and took up the struggle against the destructive powers within and without, knowing that it possessed the Spirit.

a) It is quite clear that in moral as in other matters, the Church adhered to Jesus' words, interpreting them to apply to its own situation. Matthew orientates the ethical programme of the Sermon on the Mount towards his Jewish-Christian readers in particular, as may be seen from the exhortations to keep the law, the antitheses, the treatment of pious practices, the warnings against false prophets and the threats against miracle-workers who are morally blameworthy. The missionary discourse (ch. 10) includes a collection of precepts and directives for preachers, demands fearless confession of faith, unwavering courage before tribunals, detachment from the bonds of family, material support for Christian missionaries. In a sort of "community catechism" Matthew draws up rules for the behaviour of Christians to one another, to the "little ones" and to the "brothers", making service, unity and forgiveness the supreme law of Church life (ch. 18). The question of poverty is particularly instructive for the understanding of the words of Jesus in the primitive Church. Luke (who gives special matter on the subject in Lk 16) describes in Acts how the primitive community at Jerusalem "pooled" all its property (4:32ff.; 5:1–11), which is neither a fiction of Luke nor simply a borrowing from Qumran, but an effort to put Jesus' command of love into practice. James, hard-headed and downright, with his spirituality of action in works, must also be considered a witness of how the words of the Lord were accepted and interpreted in certain circles in the primitive Church – no matter how the circumstances of his authorship are to be determined. And Paul does more than transmit occasionally a moral directive of Jesus (1 Cor 7:10f.). In the paraenetic parts of his letters, he constantly interprets the ethics of Jesus, especially by giving the central place to the commandment of love (cf. Rom 12:9–21; 13:8ff.; Gal 5:14; 6:2; Col 3:12ff.; also the great canticle of love, 1 Cor 13). But the great interpreter of Jesus' command of love is John, who in his theological insight into the theme of love succeeded in making it in fact dominant and central in his exhortations (cf. Jn 13:34f.; 1 Jn 2:7–11; 3:11–18; 4:7–21; 5:1ff.; 2 Jn 5). The contrast between the disciple of Christ and the world, which was expressed paradoxically by Jesus, is quite clear to all the NT preachers and is inculcated in their exhortations (cf. Rom 12:2; 13:12ff.; Eph 5:8–13; Phil 2:15; Heb 11:13; 13:14; Jas 4:4; 1 Pet 2:11; 2 Pet 1:4; 1 Jn 2:15ff.; Rev *passim*).

b) But the ethics of the primitive Church also displays new features, due to its situation in the history of salvation and revelation. Thus, with the redemptive death of Jesus and the mission of the Holy Spirit in mind, it proclaims that men can be saved only through repentance (*metanoia*) and baptism (Acts 2:28, 40; 3:19; 17:30f.; cf. Mk 16:16), that forgiveness of sin and salvation can be attained only through Jesus Christ (Acts 3:26; 4:12; 5:31; 10:43; 13:38f.). This places moral effort on a new basis. The certainty of being the eschatological community of salvation produces a new sense of fellowship in the primitive Church, with corresponding obligations of communal life (Acts 2:44f.; 4:32–37) and common worship (2:42, 46; 5:12; cf. 4:24–30; 12:5, 12; also Heb 10:25). Baptism, from the start, has the two-fold function of conferring salvation and incorporating the baptized into the community of salvation (cf. Acts 2:38, 41, 47; 8:12 with 14ff.; 19:1–7). There is a corresponding development of the baptismal homily (Eph, 1 Pet), explaining how the sacramental foundation of salvation makes Christian conduct possible, and at the same time demands it. Here special emphasis is laid on Christian motives and precepts: eternal election by God, his gracious call to salvation in Christ, hope of full and final salvation; the following of Christ, constancy, patience; temperance and detachment from the world; kindness and gentleness, brotherliness and love of enemies. And the primitive Church is fully aware of what it means to live between the first and second coming of the Lord; the lively expectation of the parousia provides strong impulses for moral conduct (cf. Acts 3:19f.; 10:42; 1 Thess 5:1–16; Rom 13:11–14; 1 Cor 7:26–31; Phil 1:10; Jas 5:8; 1 Pet 1:13; 4:13; 1 Jn 2:28; Rev). Further, since Jesus had not elaborated an ethical system, the primitive Church found itself compelled to answer the new questions forced upon it, such as the continued validity of the Jewish law, a hostile State demanding worship of the emperor, the problem of slavery, marriage and the family, and ascetical tendencies. The lack of uniformity in the answers attests a certain *libertas in dubiis*, which goes hand in hand, however, with an attention to the voice of the Holy Spirit (cf. 1 Cor 7:40) which can amount to a conviction of his authoritative guidance (cf. Acts 15:28f.).

c) Paul is of particular importance for early Christian ethics, with his clear grasp of the intrinsic connection between salvation by grace and the obligation to a moral life, which he expressed perhaps better than any other NT writer. We are reconciled with God through Christ, but we have still to reconcile ourselves with God (2 Cor 5:18ff.). Our old sinful self has been destroyed (in baptism), being crucified together with Christ (Rom 6:6); but we are also to divest ourselves of our old self and its deeds and put on the new

(Eph 4:22ff.; Col 3:9f.). We live in the Spirit but we are also to make the Spirit the rule of our conduct (Gal 5:25). Thus the moral imperative is intrinsically linked to the indicative of salvation. Moral action is impossible without the divine life given in grace; but this life is only there to be realized in moral action. The driving force of the new life, according to Paul, is the (divine) Spirit who is given in baptism and now impels the Christian to abandon the works of the "flesh", to root out evil passions and lusts and to produce the fruit of the Spirit (Gal 5:16–24; Rom 8:12ff.). Thus the weakness of the "fleshly" man is overcome (Rom 8:3), the tyrannous might of sin is broken and the slavery imposed in practice by the old law is eliminated (Rom 7:14–24). The Christian gains true moral freedom (Rom 8:2; Gal 5:1, 13), which means being free to do what is good, to serve God (Rom 6:16ff.). This profound and basic concept which Paul stated so courageously was misunderstood even by some of his contemporaries (Rom 6:1, 15), but remains a pointer to the essential connection between Christian ethics and the doctrine of redemption.

A further merit of Paul is to have recognized that conscience plays the decisive role in moral matters. As the innate sense of moral values, it holds the same place in the life of pagans which the positive divine law has for the Jew (Rom 2:14f.). In Christians too it has the function of the ultimate court of appeal in doubtful matters (cf. 1 Cor 8:7, 10; Rom 14:20, 23). But conscience, as the faculty of moral judgment, can also be formed and educated, a process in which love and consideration for weaker Christians are to be primary (1 Cor 8:9–13; Rom 14:15f., 19ff.).

d) In some matters, early Christian ethics was affected by outside influences, as in the drawing up of lists of household virtues (*Haustafeln*) and in a liking for lists of virtues and vices. The pastoral letters draw up lists of qualifications for candidates for Church office and canonical virtues for various groups in the community. There is undoubtedly a certain tendency to treat earthly conditions as normal and to adapt to them; but the spirit of resistance and the eschatological perspective are maintained (cf. 2 Tim 2:3–7 and 10ff.). The influence of Stoic ethics has often been over-estimated, as has the tendency to come to terms with "the world", which is sometimes supposed to have set in early. Heb and the letters in Rev 2–3 are examples of powerful exhortation inspired by specifically Christian motives, uncompromising and full of the authentic spirit of penance. Rev itself is permeated by the spirit of the Church of the martyrs, tried by suffering, but unbroken and sure of victory, a Church which produces true witnesses and disciples of Jesus.

Rudolf Schnackenburg

NEW TESTAMENT THEOLOGY

I. Data and Methods

Theories as to how a NT theology should be constructed in the concrete continue to this day to differ widely. Nevertheless the programme outlined by H. Schlier would meet with a wide measure of agreement: NT theology has "the task of bringing out the theological ideas which have been expressed either explicitly or implicitly in the NT, to set these in order, and to present them in their intrinsic connection with each other" (H. Schlier in *LTK*, II, col. 448).

1. *The history of New Testament theology*. The process which led up to a theology of the NT was exclusively Protestant (cf. H. Riesenfeld, cols. 1259f.; H. Schlier, *loc. cit.*, cols. 444–7). One reason why Catholics joined in only at a relatively late stage is that originally the effort was very strongly influenced by anti-dogmatic tendencies. Catholic interest in NT theology, chiefly stimu-

lated by the encyclical *Divino Afflante Spiritu* (1943), which called for work on the theological content of the individual passages and books (*Enchiridion Biblicum*, no. 551) found expression in an increasingly theological orientation of the commentaries. Then along the same lines as Protestant work came monographs on concepts and themes of the NT which are theologically significant (Kingdom of God, Church, Redemption, *Agape*). Studies appeared on particular areas of the NT primarily the theology of St. Paul (e.g., F. Prat, L. Cerfaux), and finally isolated treatments of the theology of the NT as a whole. Dictionaries of biblical theology appeared alongside the *TWNT*, though more modest in scope (J. B. Bauer; X. Léon-Dufour, etc.). (On the work of both Catholics and Protestants in the field of biblical theology, cf. R. Schnackenburg; W. G. Kümmel in *RGG*, I, cols. 1227–50.) On the Catholic side, general surveys of NT theology were produced, in French by A. Lemmonyer (1928; 2nd ed. by L. Cerfaux, 1963) and J. Bonsirven (1951), and in German by M. Meinertz (1950). The progress which has been made since then has been surveyed and critically evaluated by R. Schnackenburg in a sketch of "New Testament Theology" which itself represents an advance in the field.

2. *New Testament theology as an independent discipline.* As an attempt to reflect methodically upon the revelation of Christ as attested in the NT, and upon the faith which is a response to it, NT theology presupposes the exegesis of particular books and groups of books. In common with exegesis, this discipline makes use of the methods of scientific history, and of its progress in factual knowledge. Just as NT theology, with its concern for the general message of a book or group of books can guard exegesis against isolating and over-emphasizing a particular passage, so conversely progressive exegesis can exercise a critical function with regard to the effort of theological generalization. The contrast with the dogmatics which illuminates the whole faith of the Church is not that NT theology dispenses with *ratio* – the intellectual effort to explain, deduce and arrange in categories. This effort continues, but the difference is that NT theology deliberately confines itself to the facts, themes, thought-forms and expressions of the NT. And these again need not coincide with those of later theology. From the nature of NT theology as indicated here, we can already see that it has certain limitations but also special advantages. In comparison with subsequent theological developments NT theology is "still incipient, embryonic and undeveloped, but it has the power of the root and the fruitfulness of the source" (Schnackenburg).

3. *Differences in method and approach.* In the more recent comprehensive presentations the same differences and contrasts of method are apparent as in the rest of NT scholarship. Their various advantages and weaknesses bear witness to the difficulty of producing an objective NT theology. Works in which the approach of the "history of religions" school is predominant (such as that by H. Weinel, the subtitle of which is *The Religion of Jesus and that of Primitive Christianity* [1911; 4th ed., 1928]) laid such emphasis on the links between the origins of Christianity and the culture and religion of its environment that they tended to reduce NT revelation "to an expression of immemorial convictions of man in terms conditioned by its own day" (R. Schnackenburg). Authors like A. Schlatter and T. Zahn, who recognized that the NT message was concerned with revelation and faith, opposed to such efforts a positive and biblical description of the "doctrines" of the various books. But they, like J. Bonsirven and M. Meinertz, who followed as closely as possible the "historical" sequence in their presentations, failed to do justice to the real historical

and theological problems. Against R. Bultmann, E. Stauffer has put forward a *Realtheologie*, that is, a "Christocentric theology of history". He, and O. Cullmann (the chief representative of a "theology of salvation-history"), working from the correspondence between "promise and fulfilment", take as their basis conceptions which to a large extent have proved to be untenable schematizations, and in many respects fail to recognize the real differences of doctrine in the NT. R. Bultmann's *Theology of the New Testament* combines the critical approach of the "history of religions" school with presuppositions drawn from existential philosophy. It attempts to trace and to give expression to the development of the early Church's understanding of itself by faith, and the significance which this bears for mankind today. It has achieved an outstanding analysis of many basic concepts of Pauline and Johannine theology, and has shown incontrovertibly that a true understanding of human existence is an essential element in the NT concept of faith. For all this, however, it has not done full justice to this concept. Bultmann's existential theology raises problems, the force of which has been felt even by his own disciples. Its problematical character appears not least in the fact that on the basis of his hermeneutic principles Bultmann has been able to discover the true Christian kerygma only in Paul and in (a revised) John.

4. *The primary tasks for a theology of the New Testament.* The NT consists of a series of writings which differ widely in literary form, origin, aim, content and importance. For this reason one of the tasks with which a NT theology indisputably finds itself confronted is that of isolating and describing in appropriate terms the theological contents of the particular writings or groups of writings. This task gives rise on the whole to the least difficulties, especially in the case of the Pauline letters (these being recognized as genuine in their existing form or their essential elements). The certainty we have about the essential stages of the spiritual development and work of Paul makes it easier to understand certain basic themes in his theology, such as justification and works, grace and faith, the universal necessity of redemption and its overflowing fullness of grace, the emphasis on the resurrection of Jesus considered as the eschatological new creation, and on the glorified Christ as Lord of the faithful and of the Church, who exercises his power through the Spirit to bestow life and to bring a new creature into being. For a long time scholars were content to distinguish between three main branches of theology, Pauline theology, the theology of Hebrews (which interprets the death of Jesus primarily from the standpoint of the high-priesthood of Christ), and Johannine theology. Today, however, a richer and more nuanced picture is presented. Other groups, with special theological significance, are the deutero-Pauline letters and the Catholic letters. The first of these, which may include Colossians, develops fully the cosmic and ecclesiological significance of Christ, and his significance for mankind as a whole (Col and Eph). The pastoral letters are concerned with the preservation of the *depositum fidei* and the strengthening of ecclesiastical organization. The Catholic letters likewise attempt to overcome problems of the post-apostolic age, threatened as it was by the growth of heresy (cf. also 1 Jn). Such problems are that of faith and works (Jas), the upholding of the Christian position against Gnostic and libertine heretics and against those who were opposed to the expectation of the parousia (2 Pet) – in a world which was already hostile (1 Pet). They appealed either explicitly or implicitly to the apostolic tradition, and became important for the Church as it found itself after the death of the apostles in a world unexpectedly durable (cf.

also Rev, with its Christological and ecclesiological interests).

Since the methods of source criticism and form criticism have rightly been supplemented by that of "history of redaction", the synoptic gospels have come increasingly to be recognized as theological works of a high order. Jn had always been esteemed for its highly developed Christology, in the light of which Jn interpreted the whole work of Christ, including the present work of the glorified Christ. It has been possible to check and evaluate a considerable part of the work of Mt and Lk (as distinct from the first gospel writing by Mark) by the sources which they used (Mark and Q or the "*logia*-source"). The result of this has been that the theological concerns of the two later synoptics have emerged more clearly. The Gospel of Luke aims at giving an account of the apostolic tradition of Jesus in a form which will strengthen Christian faith and life. Thus it depicts Jesus primarily as the true and promised bringer of salvation to the whole of mankind, which languishes in the grip of sin, sickness and misery. In Acts, the sequel to Lk, the significance of the life of Jesus as a pattern for the post-apostolic era is emphasized, and also the victorious progress of the Church pressing irresistibly forward under the leadership of the charismatically endowed apostles. Matthew's doctrinal work, explicitly catechetical and apologetical, presents Jesus chiefly as the promised Messiah and Son of God, destined primarily for his own people, who culpably fail to recognize him. He proclaims the definitive will of God, and summons men to follow him. He is the founder and teacher of the true Israel, the Church, the new people of God which embraces all nations. The question of the "theological" intentions of the earliest of the evangelists had already been raised in W. Wrede's book on the "messianic secret" of Mark, a subject not yet done with. Mark presents Jesus as the secret Son of God who announces the kingdom of God, acts in the power of and by the authority of God, and prepares his disciples for their mission to the world. "His mystery, which went unrecognized by the world, was only accepted by the disciples by faith, in following him on the way of the cross" (R. Pesch). Recent works point out the great theological achievement of the creator of the genus "gospel" (in addition to the bibliography provided by R. Schnackenburg, cf. E. Schweitzer, *Markus* [1967]).

5. *Basic questions and conclusions*. The discipline which we are considering is *the* theology of the NT, as its name implies. We are still far from having established such a single theology when we have merely surveyed the theological contents of the various NT books. Here questions arise to which various answers have been proposed, and which to some extent still await a genuine solution. These are concerned above all with what the content and structure of a NT theology really should be.

a) All NT writings presuppose a more or less lengthy development of tradition, mostly oral but sometimes also written. There was Pauline theology, no doubt in a less developed form, before 1 Thess (A.D. 52), and there were theological assertions about the Christ-event before Paul, as is proved above all by his use of the paradosis of 1 Cor 15:3ff. in his theology of the resurrection. In view of the state of the sources, the singling out of archaic traditions behind the developing theology, which appear in stereotyped truths of faith, credal statements and liturgical fragments, is a difficult task, especially for the synoptic gospels. Nonetheless, much of the work has been successfully accomplished. It is undoubtedly the work of NT theology to try to trace the primitive apostolic preaching and its possible developments – along various lines – inside and outside Palestine. This would show the earliest stage of the theology of the primitive Church.

b) The most highly controverted question is whether or not the history or at least the preaching of Jesus, as such, is part of NT theology. Neither Bonsirven nor Meinertz had any misgivings. Meinertz began with the doctrine, person and history of Jesus, and Bonsirven included that of the Johannine Christ. But later authors have proposed other approaches, since it has been established in the meantime that even in the synoptic gospels the tradition of Jesus' life ("Jesus-tradition") and the post-paschal interpretation of it are closely interwoven and amalgamated. H. Schlier, for instance, admits that the life and death of Jesus, his words and his actions, are directly or indirectly the source of all theological reflection in the NT authors. He also holds that decisive elements of the history of Jesus can be historically reconstructed. He affirms nonetheless that on theological grounds a NT theology can, and even must, prescind from such reconstructions. Otherwise the impression might arise that there could be a Jesus otherwise than through the words of the Church's preaching – as though alongside the only legitimate interpretations of the ῥῆμα Χριστοῦ in the four gospels there could be another, the image which the historian forms of this event. Schlier, though in a different sense than Bultmann, makes the history of Jesus a "presupposition" but not a part of NT theology. This appears as only a half-truth to R. Schnackenburg, whose own position endeavours to meet the demands of both extremes. His proposal is that the message of Jesus and the saving events of his life, as given in the synoptics, should be regarded as a stage of the common primitive preaching and theology, difficult though it is to extricate this clearly, as he himself stresses. It would coincide "in essentials" with the primitive apostolic kerygma, which would have been dealt with at an earlier stage. This "synoptic theology", so to speak, would then be prefixed to the subsequent "theology of the individual synoptic gospels".

In all such procedures we have to resist the inclination to try to establish the greatest possible material identity, explicit or implicit, between the Jesus who preached before Easter and the Jesus who was preached after Easter. Firstly, we must take into account the undoubted progress in the revelation of Christ, and primarily the revelatory importance of the Easter "experience", on the basis of which – with the help of Scripture and in dialogue with history – the meaning of the whole Jesus-event, culminating in the divine marvel of the resurrection of the crucified, was explicitated with regard to Jesus himself and the new type of preaching addressed to Israel and the nations. And then, in view of the firm conviction of the apostles that God answered the execution of the authorized eschatological announcer of the dawning kingship of God by a new act of revelation, we may in fact expect such problems as the Christological titles and even the exact notion which Jesus had of his death and of the future (involving his parousia for judgment and his exaltation to a divine existence in the meantime).

c) The main difficulty of the theology of the NT which has in fact to be worked out is the unquestionable *multiplicity* of different theologies, which are rarely actually "propounded". H. Schlier holds that a presentation of NT thinking on the faith would offer only a number of fragmentary theologies, very different in content and form, with the added difficulty that they are hard to measure against one another, since their extent, degree of explicitation and intrinsic importance are hard to define. This diversity within NT theology with its fragmentary character, which limits it to certain aspects and fails to co-ordinate it systematically, may be explained by various factors. The authors differ in origin, experiences, training, world of imagery and concepts. And their writings are orientated to and conditioned by their times. They were more or less occasional writings, but in any case were "written sermons" catering for definite needs, questions and menaces, which again were conditioned by the varying cultures and changing situations of the recipients. Thus the methodological question arises as to how and in what measure the unity, and above all the material uniformity, of these different theologies can be brought out. The most viable method seems to be to concentrate on the at least fundamental unity, using some major theological themes like God, the reign of God, Jesus Christ, his death and resurrection, the Spirit, faith and the new life (Schlier) or more systematic sub-divisions like Christology, ecclesiology and the Christian state of salvation (Schnackenburg). It should be a recognized principle that in doing so the admitted peculiarities of the various theologies should not be blurred for the sake of a superficial unity. Nor should the theology of one book or group of books be made explicitly or implicitly the norm according to which all other theological concepts are censured.

d) Another principle is that the relationship between NT and systematic, especially dogmatic theology must be characterized by mutual interrogation, stimulation and critical examination. NT theology may be impelled by dogmatics to pose its questions to the texts in a more nuanced way, while dogmatics may hope for many benefits from a fountainhead of theology which is authoritative for further development of the faith. It will be led to reflect, for instance, on basic biblical concepts and truths which may have been long in the shadow or even forgotten. It may note principles not yet fully exploited or even "gaps". But here one must not lose sight of the limits set to the critical and normative function of NT theology or theologies, with regard to the dogmatic theology which deals with the whole faith of the Church in its contemporary visage. As has been said above, NT theology is historically conditioned and its assertions should not be reduced overhastily to a system.

Anton Vögtle

II. Pauline Theology

The faith of Paul, and his theology as his reflection on his faith, are founded and centred on the vision of Christ before Damascus, in which Paul recognized the Messiah, now exalted as Lord (1 Cor 9:1; 2:2; Gal 1:16), the crucified Jesus whom he was persecuting. This revelation illuminated history and present reality for Paul. A presentation of his theology must therefore be founded and centred on Christology (cf. 1 Cor 2:2). Formal elements and the structure of Pauline theology stem to a great extent from OT and rabbinical tradition, to a much less extent from the Hellenistic environment. But Paul also uses stereotyped traditions and formulas of the Christian Church, from confessions of faith, hymns and the liturgy, expounding them and adapting them to his thought.

A. Jesus Christ: His Person and Work

Paul was not himself a disciple of Jesus, but since he persecuted the Church, he must have had some information about Jesus. It is questionable that he ever saw him. Nothing can be deduced on the matter from 2 Cor 5:16. But these are not essentials. Paul's own conviction was that he gained his knowledge of Christ from the apparition before Damascus. Long accounts in Acts describe it as a visible and audible process. Paul speaks of the event as an inner experience. God revealed to him his Son (Gal 1:17). Paul enumerates the apparition before Damascus as one of the Easter apparitions of the risen Jesus (1

Cor 15:8). It revealed to him that God had sent Jesus as the Messiah, thereby ending the way of salvation of the OT law and throwing open the way of faith to all, Jews and Gentiles alike (Phil 3:7–9). Theologians, historians and psychologists have asked whether the experience could not be wholly or at least partly explained by natural causes. Paul might have been subconsciously impressed by the faith and dedication of the first Christians, and been finally won over by his memories of their devotion. Or Paul might have already been cherishing doubts as to the possibility of justification by the works of the law – though according to Phil 3:5 he was a convinced Pharisee. The NT sources allow only the interpretation that Paul, contrary to all expectations, underwent the experience of conversion and call through the risen Christ.

Having become a disciple of Christ through this revelation, Paul became a member of the Church in Damascus (Acts 9:19). He shared its faith, its doctrine and its liturgy. It should be noted that he did not join the primitive community of Jewish Christians at Jerusalem but a community in the diaspora, where Jews were freer in their attitude towards Jerusalem and its temple and more open to Hellenism. Such diaspora communities may have developed certain features. Possibly more stress was laid on the sacraments of baptism and the Eucharist than in the strict Jewish homeland. Three years after his conversion Paul stayed for fifteen days in Jerusalem, meeting Peter and James (Gal 1:18). He was not looking for confirmation of his gospel – which, as an apostle called directly by the Lord, he did not need – but he undoubtedly sought the fellowship of the community which in his eyes was the Mother Church (Rom 15:25–27; 1 Cor 16:1–4; 2 Cor 8:1–4).

1. Paul speaks little of the man Jesus. The problem thus posed has at times been exaggerated into the affirmation that Paul created a new Christology of the exalted Lord, with no connection with the historical Jesus. But it must be remembered that the preaching of Paul, after Easter and Pentecost, could not simply repeat the words once spoken by Jesus. It had always to include the affirmation that this Jesus had been shown to be Messiah and Son by the resurrection and was now enthroned as Lord. The words of Jesus pointed on to the turning-point of history by proclaiming the imminent kingship of God. The post-paschal preaching looked back, after the turning-point, to the revelation of salvation in Christ. Then, the letters of Paul do not repeat his missionary preaching but deal with the conditions and problems of existing communities. The life of Jesus may have played a greater part in the missionary preaching. (In 1 Jn, there is hardly any mention of the historical Jesus, in contrast to the Gospel of John.) And the letters show that Paul spoke of Jesus in his preaching. He alludes to his entry into history (Rom 15:8; Gal 4:4), his origin from the house of David (Rom 1:3), his family (1 Cor 9:5; Gal 1:19). He also speaks of the mercy of the redeemer (Phil 1:8), his mildness (2 Cor 10:1), his poverty (2 Cor 8:9), his love (Rom 8:35, 37; 2 Cor 5:14f.), his truth (2 Cor 11:10), his holiness (2 Cor 5:21), but above all of the saving event of the death and resurrection of Christ (Rom 8:34; 1 Cor 1:18, 23; Gal 3:1, 13; Phil 2:6–8). He also quotes sayings of Jesus, to decide questions of fundamental importance such as the nature of marriage (1 Cor 7:10f.), the form and meaning of the Eucharist (1 Cor 11:23–25) and the regulation of the mission (1 Cor 9:14). The Apostle's own exhortations echo the words of Jesus, as in the liberating statement on the clean and unclean (Rom 14:14), the need to pray for enemies (Rom 12:14) and in the command of love as the great commandment (Rom 13:9; Gal 6:2).

2. Paul uses many metaphors, images and considerations to interpret the life

and work of Jesus, mostly drawing on the OT. He continues the proof from Scripture which the primitive Church had begun to use (Gal 3:13 etc.). The saving death of Christ is explained in terms of Jewish worship. His death is an expiatory sacrifice (Rom 3:25; 5:9), a covenant sacrifice (1 Cor 11:24f.) and passover sacrifice (1 Cor 5:7). The briefest formula is that Christ died for others (Rom 5:6) and for sins (1 Cor 15:3; 2 Cor 5:21). The death of Jesus frees all those who had been slaves to law (Gal 3:13; Col 2:14), sin (Rom 5:15; 6:10), death (Rom 6:8) and all the powers of this world (1 Cor 2:6; Col 2:15). The miserable past is hypostatized in its forces. But Paul follows (and enriches) the tradition of the primitive community which was convinced that it for its part was handing on the interpretation which Jesus had given of his death (Mk 10:45; 14:24).

Existence in Christ is described in OT terms as reconciliation (Rom 5:11; 2 Cor 5:18), justice, sanctification and redemption (1 Cor 1:30), peace (Rom 5:1; Col 1:20), salvation (Rom 1:16). The adoption of OT terms is not mere literary embroidery. It is a way of affirming that the hopes and strivings of Israel have been fulfilled.

Paul explains the salvific import of the death of Jesus in another way when he speaks of the faithful being united with the death and life of Jesus. Baptism extends the death and resurrection of Jesus to the believer (Rom 6:3f.). The sacramental event must be acted out in personal moral life (Rom 6:11). The Eucharist is constant growth in fellowship with the Crucified. The chalice is participation in the blood of Christ. The bread, as the body of our Lord sacrificed on the cross, brings about the reality of the one body of the Church (1 Cor 10:16f.). The question has been raised in exegesis as to whether Paul used terms from Oriental and Hellenistic religions, the mystery religions perhaps in particular, to explain the sacraments. This was the accepted view in the school of comparative religion, but it is now somewhat dated, and modern exegesis finds it questionable. It now tries to explain the NT understanding of the sacraments rather in terms of OT presuppositions.

3. *The figure of Christ.* In interpreting Christ's work of salvation, Paul also describes the doer of the work. Christ appears as man, but his humanity is not the ordinary one. He is not merely a lofty figure, like an extraordinary man who stands out among his fellows. He is mysteriously singled out from humanity. He differs from man as being the one sinless man (2 Cor 5:21). Jesus did not simply take on a body and humanity subject to sin, but only the "likeness" of man (Rom 8:3; Phil 2:7). Christ belongs to the generations of man, but is greater than all historical figures, not merely in degree but as it were in kind. The only possible comparison is with the prototypical man, Adam (Rom 15:21; 1 Cor 15:45). Adam is father of mankind, but Christ the beginning of a new mankind. Both bear within them the destiny of mankind, Adam decisive for death, Christ for life. All who believe, all who are redeemed are contained in Christ and embraced by him (Gal 3:27–28). Christ is head of the body. This body may have originally been understood to be the universe (Col 1:19f.; 2:17–19), but in a further development of the thought, the Church is the body (Eph 1:23f.).

Christ and the eternal God are joined in an incomparable unity, intimacy and exclusiveness. In a crescendo such as 1 Cor 3:22f., "All are yours, and you are Christ's, and Christ is God's", Christ is, it seems, subordinated to the Father, but associated with him in a way which far transcends all created beings (cf. 1 Cor 11:3). He is the "image of God" (2 Cor 4:4; Col 1:15), that is, the revelation and epiphany of God in the world and time. God was (2 Cor 5:19) and is in Christ (Rom 8:39). "In him the whole fullness of deity dwells bodily" (Col 2:9). Before his incarnation he was a heavenly being "in the form of God" (Gal 4:4; Phil 2:6). He was already active in the history of Israel (1 Cor 10:3f.). He was and is the Son of God (Rom 1:3, 9; 8:3). Now he has been exalted with God and is "Lord" over the Church and the world. He will come again as judge (1 Thess 1:10). He has the attributes of divine eternity, dignity and power. It would have been possible to go on to the explicit assertion of eternal, divine existence. But it is not certain that Paul actually made this assertion, since Rom 9:5 is not absolutely clear. The phrase "God who is over all, blessed for ever" may refer to Christ, but may also be an independent doxology.

These sublime assertions of Paul appear in his letters in older formulae of faith which he has taken over (Rom 1:3f.; 10:9; Phil 2:6–11). The Aramaic prayer, "Maranatha" ("The Lord is there", or, "Come, Lord", 1 Cor 16:23) shows that the Aramaic-speaking primitive community already revered Christ as the Lord, as also appears from the prayer of Stephen, Acts 7:59. The Christology of Paul is that of the Church before him and around him.

Paul uses another mode of describing the lordship of Christ when he speaks of Christ and the faithful being in each other. Christ is in the believer (Rom 8:10; Gal 2:20; 4:19). The redeemed, the Church and the whole creation are in Christ (Rom 6:11; 12:5; 2 Cor 5:17; Gal 1:22; 3:28; 1 Thess 2:14). This mode of being is finally summed up by Paul in the words, "The Lord is the Spirit" (2 Cor 3:17). In this Spirit-existence and this Spirit-power, Christ fills, possesses and rules all.

B. The World

Paul explains and fits together the phenomena of the world and history in the light of the figure and work of Christ. As a Jew, Paul sees the world as God's creation (Rom 4:17). Paul takes Israel's faith a step further by his Christology of creation: "the Lord Jesus Christ, through whom are all things, and through whom we exist" (1 Cor 8:6; Col 1:16–19). (This Christology of creation is further developed in Heb 1:2, 10; Jn 1:3; Rev 3:14.) The NT doctrine of the creation in Christ is to be understood as a truth of faith expressed in the light of the end. Christ is now Lord. He will come again as judge (1 Thess 1:10; Phil 2:10f.). From the beginning he must have had his place in the plan of God. This deduction made by faith had been prepared for by the sapiential teaching of the OT, according to which Wisdom was with God from the beginning, and was already there at the creation of the world (Prov 3:19f.; 8:22, 27–31; Ecclus 24:5). Christ is the revealed Wisdom of God (1 Cor 1:24–30). The predicates of Wisdom in the OT are attributed to Christ in the NT. The redemption is also seen as a new creation in Christ (2 Cor 4:6; 5:17). Thus Christian faith in creation is not ultimately founded on Gen 1 and 2, but on faith in Christ. Christ as the revelation and word of God sustains faith in creation and gives it its fundamental certainty. Faith in creation is not, therefore, merely a pious Israelite speculation or, still more uncertain, an attempt at a religious and mythic explanation of the world. It is a Christian truth. Christ is the centre from which the whole of history, from creation to fulfilment, is to be understood as a unity.

C. Israel

The phenomenon of Israel's history is an oppressive burden for Paul. Its refusal to believe is a tormenting question (Rom 9:2). He was proud of belonging to the chosen people (Rom 11:1f.; 2 Cor 11:22), of being an Israelite more zealous than many others (Gal 1:14; Phil 3:5). Israel's law was the gift of God and as such holy, just and good (Rom 7:12). It was not a burden for Israel, but a grace, a mark of election (Rom 2:20–24; 9:4). Israel owed to the law its pure faith in God in the midst of pagan idolatry, its orderly life and fellowship in the midst of pagan immorality. The OT and Judaism often proclaim the joy of possessing the law (cf. Ps 119). Can any man, especially a pious man, or the Church, dispense themselves from the law of God? What could ensue except general collapse and disaster? Nonetheless, once the exalted Lord had appeared to Paul before Damascus and given him his mission to the Gentiles, the principle was already implicitly asserted, that the OT law was no longer valid in such a mission. The question was solved for Paul in the light of the cross. The crucified Christ, hanging on the wood, is judged and condemned according to the law (Gal 3:13, after Deut 21:23). As the Holy One, he cannot rightfully come under such punishment. He bears it for others, for sins committed in terms of the law. Thus the curse brought down by the law has been satisfied. Indeed, the law and its claims have been done away with. Christ is the end of the law (Rom 10:4). To acknowledge the law and at the same time to confess one's faith in Jesus who had been crucified in accordance with the law was an intolerable contradiction. But now the revelation of salvation in Christ shows up the misery of the earlier age (2 Cor 3:16). The Church is free from the law, or, more precisely, it is now enabled to fulfil the real and essential demand of the law, which is love (Rom 3:31; 8:4). Nonetheless, Israel remains under the call of God, for "the gifts and call of God are irrevocable" (Rom 11:29). Paul is certain that all Israel will be saved at the end of time (Rom 11:26), though he undoubtedly hoped that the time was near. Israel was soon to be redeemed.

D. Man

Paul's description of man and his teaching on man also transform the traditions of Israel in terms of Christian faith. As the new Adam (Rom 5:12), Christ is the beginning and the foundation of a new humanity. While the first Adam was earthly and transmitted animated life, the last Adam is life-giving spirit, and comes from heaven (1 Cor 15:45–47). The ancient doctrine that man was the image of God is also given a Christological interpretation. In Christ man is created anew to be truly in the image of the creator (Col 3:9–11). The old Adamite man was a prisoner of his lusts. The new man is newly created to life in justice and holiness (Eph 2:10). Christ is now "the first-born among many brethren" (Rom 8:29). The redeemed will be finally transformed by a glory like that of their prototype, Christ (1 Cor 15:49; Phil 3:21). The new being in Christ brings with it a new way of being, a new style of life which ought to follow. Of the basic attitudes which ensue, faith, justice, freedom and hope must be mentioned.

1. Faith acknowledges and lays hold of God's action in Christ. "We know that a man is not justified by works of the law but through faith in Jesus Christ, (therefore) we have believed in Jesus Christ, in order to be justified by faith in Christ" (Gal 2:16; cf. 2 Cor 3:4). That faith is centred on Christ is also said in Rom 10:17. Faith is not human merit, but God's gift to man (Phil 1:29). When God acts, man is not deprived of his responsibility but summoned to take it on (cf. Phil 3:12). Faith, as decision, is also a human act. Man is obedient to the word of God which reaches him in the preaching of the Church (Rom 1:5; 1 Thess 2:13). Faith must prove itself in the deeds of love (Gal 5:6). It is obedience, but not a blind obedience. It has its own "knowledge", since it has recognized the work of God (cf. Rom 6:8f.). The believer gains a new self-understanding and a new insight into existence (Rom 5:3; 14:14; 2 Cor 1:7; 5:6; Phil 1:19). Faith is not forbidden to put questions. It is to advance constantly in knowledge and understanding of God

(Col 1:9f.). Faith and knowledge are opposites which form a unity. Faith is the powerful conviction of a man seized by God. But it always has an object to which it is referred. It is faith in and confession of Jesus Christ (Rom 10:9, 14; Gal 2:16; Phil 1:29; 1 Thess 4:14). Norms and rules of faith are already taking shape, and the creed of the Church is already being established (cf. 1 Cor 15:3; Rom 12:6; Gal 1:23; Eph 4:5; see further the pastoral letters, 1 Tim 2:7; 3:9; 4:6; Tit 1:1).

2. Justice is bestowed on faith. Israel had striven to obtain righteousness from God, working tirelessly and suffering patiently to this end. In NT times, the community of Qumran was working hard for the strict observance of the law in a new way. But the pious psalmist of the community was well aware that he depended on God for the gift of righteousness: "My justice is in the righteousness of God" (1 *QS*, XI, 12). Paul promises that this effort and this hope will be fulfilled. Like all Jews, he is certain that God is just (Rom 3:5–8). Hence for Paul the notion of the justice of God contains a juridical element. The all-decisive point for man is whether he can prove himself just before God. "He who through faith is righteous shall live" (Rom 1:17). In a lengthy proof, Rom 1:18–3:23, Paul comes to the conclusion that righteousness before God had never existed. This is true both of Jews and Gentiles. But now there is one single possibility of life offered to man: "The righteousness of God is revealed" in the gospel (Rom 1:17; 3:21). God is revealed as he who is just and justifies (Rom 3:24, 26). The righteousness of God demanded the expiation of sin. God made Christ "to be sin for us, so that in him we might become the righteousness of God" (2 Cor 5:21). The righteous is now he who acknowledges and accepts God's salvific will and work. "(I have not) a righteousness of my own, based on law, but that which is through faith in Christ, the righteousness from God which depends on faith" (Phil 3:9). Faith is not justification, but the acceptance of the gift of God, after the confession of poverty and the abandonment of self-asserting boast. This is the "obedience which leads to righteousness" (Rom 6:16). Though righteousness is not moral effort but a gift, it becomes the source, when it is accepted, of a new ethics. It must produce its "fruit" (Phil 1:11). The just requirements of the law must now be fulfilled (Rom 8:4). The judgment will one day show how genuine this righteousness has been (Rom 2:13; Gal 5:5). It has been already bestowed, but it is still something expected in the future, since it will be assigned in the final judgment. The preaching of Paul is a summons to a continuous encounter with the judgment of God and the grace of God. In making righteousness a central theme, Paul has added nothing alien to the gospel. He is in accord with the synoptics though offering a continuation of them after the cross and resurrection. God's "kingdom and his righteousness" (Mt 6:33) have now come. Righteousness is now really assigned without works (Lk 18:14).

3. Freedom is one effect of righteousness. Man finds himself under the slavery of the law (Rom 7:23), sin (Rom 6:20) and death (Rom 6:23; 8:2). Powerless to help himself, he is freed through the act of Jesus Christ, who took his place and took sin and death upon himself for the sake of man (Rom 8:3; 2 Cor 5:21; Gal 3:13). "For freedom Christ has set us free" (Gal 5:1). Freedom becomes a reality in the believer as he hears the call to freedom and follows it (Gal 5:13). Freedom does not mean lack of all restraint or rule. It is not so much being free from something as being free for something. It means being free from the law to follow the gospel; from the flesh to follow the Spirit; from sin to follow grace; from death to life, free for the neighbour (Gal 5:13) and for God (Rom 6:22). The new

existence is according to "the law of the Spirit of life in Jesus Christ" (Rom 8:2) and means fulfilling the "law of Christ" (Gal 6:2). The Letter of James also sees that freedom from the law is only true and real in the fulfilment of the law of freedom (Jas 1:25). Freedom is now displayed in particular in the confident boldness of faith as it speaks out before God (2 Cor 3:12; Eph 3:12) and before men (2 Cor 7:4; Eph 6:19). The fullness of freedom is a gift reserved for the end. It is liberation from the slavery of the perishable to the freedom of the glory of the children of God (Rom 8:21). The great importance attached to the term and the notion of freedom in the NT and especially in Paul is due to the attention which they paid to the contemporary Hellenistic world, where freedom was regarded as a precious possession and a prize to be sought after in philosophy, ethics and religion. Contact with the surrounding world led the NT authors to recognize that true freedom was to be found in the gospel. It was a point at which the world and the gospel met and parted. In the former, in the Stoa, for instance, freedom is won by the wise man's own effort. In the latter it is the gift of the liberating grace of God.

4. Hope is so essential to faith that Paul can describe Christians by saying that they "rejoice in hope" (Rom 12:12), while the pagans are those "who have no hope" (1 Thess 4:13). The biblical God is the "God of hope" (Rom 15:13), and hope has its roots in faith (Rom 4:18), being likewise a gift (2 Thess 2:16), and likewise founded on God's work of salvation in Christ (2 Cor 3:9). Hope is strongly forward-looking, its object never being experientially present. Otherwise it would not be hope but possession. This does not diminish the blessings of hope but guarantees their greatness and value. Hope does not choose the visible as being apparently more secure while considering the invisible uncertain and discarding it. Hope may never be directed to the visible, since all that is visible is transitory (Rom 8:24; 2 Cor 4:18). It is directed to the future, which is God, and its objects are so far beyond man's reach and calculation that the world sees it as the paradox of "hoping against hope" (cf. Rom 4:18). But hope has its own certainty, in keeping with the outpouring of God's love through the Spirit into the heart of each Christian (Rom 5:5). If present tribulation does not shatter faith, it is because it awakens hope (Rom 5:4), while hope brings courage (2 Cor 3:12) and joy (Rom 12:12). Hope is an existence rooted in God and not in the world (Tit 2:11–14). It comprises the whole creation. Anxiety and longing are now palpably the lot of all living things. This condition is not due to God's original work of creation but a state of guilt, for which sinful man is to blame and not the irrational creation. The lament of creation is a sign that it waits and hopes for redemption and transfiguration (Rom 8:20). Its hopes will not be frustrated. Man's redemption, according to Paul, is not redemption from the world – which may have been the Oriental or Platonic notion – but redemption with the world. Creation began in Christ (see above), it has its existence in him and it is fulfilled in him, at present and in the future (Col 1:16f.; Heb 1:2f.). It is universally true that "Christ (is) in you, the hope of glory" (Col 1:27).

E. The Church

The messianic community takes form in the letters of Paul as the Church. It uses many titles to express its self-understanding and its riches. Christians call themselves "the saints" (Rom 1:7 etc.), indicating their call and consecration, and "brothers", indicating the closeness of their fellowship (Rom 16:14; 1 Cor 16:20; 1 Thess 5:26). The community is God's special people (Rom 9:25f.; 1 Cor 10:11; 2 Cor 6:16). The messianic community had already been described by the prophets as the people of God

(Hos 2:25; Deut 7:6), and hence the Church fulfils the hopes of Israel. The Church is the new and authentic Israel (Gal 6:13; Phil 3:3), the spiritual Jerusalem (Gal 4:26), the new covenant set up by God (1 Cor 11:25; 2 Cor 3:6). The name by which Paul prefers to designate the community is *Ecclesia*, Church (of God) (some 100 times). Since the term takes up once more a title of the old covenant, it describes once more the new community as the true Israel. The Church means primarily the whole world-wide fellowship of the elect and sanctified, not the local community. In each local Church, however, the whole Church is present and manifest. But Christians are not in the Church, nor is the Church something in contrast to the faithful. The faithful are the Church. Paul is intensely interested in preserving and strengthening the unity of the Church (Rom 12:5; 1 Cor 10:17; 12:9–20; Eph 4:4–6). He uses a non-biblical image to describe the Church. It is the "body of Christ" (Rom 12:5; 1 Cor 12:27). The real body of the crucified Lord, the sacramental body in the Eucharist and the body which is the Church form a profound unity (1 Cor 10:16f.). The concept is further developed in later letters (Col 1:24; Eph 4:16; Christ is the head of the body). The question arises here of the possible influence of Gnostic notions of the primordial cosmic man (*Urmensch*). No clear expression of them can be found till after the NT period. Many offices and ministries are envisaged in the community (Rom 12:6–8; 1 Cor 12:7–11, 28; Phil 1:1). They are charisms, understood as creations of God (1 Cor 11:28–31), gifts of Christ (Eph 4:11f.) and effects of the Spirit (Rom 12:6; 1 Cor 12:11). The ministries are instrumental in the proclamation of the word in which God's word is audible and effective in the Church (1 Thess 2:13; 2 Cor 5:18f.; Phil 2:16). This word does not just tell of a salvation which was effected in the past. In the preaching itself salvation is present. Thus the word of reconciliation (2 Cor 5:18f.), of salvation (Acts 13:26), of grace (Acts 14:3; 20:32), of life (Phil 2:16) effects what it proclaims. The word has sacramental force. (One may recall that Vatican II speaks in the same way of the power of the word, e.g., Constitution on the Liturgy, art. 7.) The word is also uttered in the sacred celebrations of baptism (Eph 5:26) and the Eucharist (1 Cor 11:26). The Church exists by the word and the sacraments.

F. The Consummation

Paul also speaks, though comparatively seldom, of the royal lordship of God which is so essential to the synoptic preaching. This "kingdom of God" is already present in the Church (1 Cor 4:20; Col 1:13), but is also future, as the goal of faith and life (1 Cor 6:9f.; 15:50; Gal 5:21; 2 Thess 1:5). The synoptic preaching of the reign of God was orientated to the futurity of salvation. This is now already a reality in Christ. Hence the message of the kingdom is overshadowed by the gospel of Christ. Like the early Church in general, Paul expected the speedy return of the Lord, to inaugurate the final stage and fulfilment of all things, which begins with the resurrection of the dead. He uses the apocalyptic imagery and notions of his day to describe the last things (Rom 13:11f.; 1 Cor 15:23–28, 35–53; 1 Thess 4:14–18). The precise date is not essential to the Christian expectation of the imminent end, but it means constant preparedness (1 Cor 16:23) and detachment from the world (1 Cor 7:29). Paul is well aware that the description of the eschatological event is beyond human powers, since that world is invisible and unimaginable (Rom 8:24f.; 2 Cor 4:18). Here the mystery of God takes over (1 Cor 15:51). Questioning can be foolish (1 Cor 15-36). The traditions of the OT and Judaism are applied to Christ and given a new foundation in him. The resurrection of Christ is the pledge of our hope of resurrection (Rom 8:11; 1 Cor 15:22; 2 Cor 4:14; 1 Thess 4:14). In life as in death the Christian is united to Christ (Rom 8:38; 1 Thess 4:17). The dead too are "in Christ" (1 Cor 15:18; 1 Thess 4:16). To die is to go to the Lord (Phil 1:21–24) and to be at home with the Lord (2 Cor 5:8). The Christocentric perspective leads on to the theocentric God, who is the fullness of life and ensures that death is not the end. "We rely on God who raises the dead" (2 Cor 1:9). Finally, God will be "everything to everyone" (1 Cor 15:28).

The passages 2 Cor 4:17–18 and 5:1–10 form a remarkable contrast. In the latter the apocalyptic scene is the traditional world-picture. In the former, eschatology is given a mystic and personal form and interpreted as a present factor. Paul first says that in our daily dying union with the Lord Christ only grows stronger and more intimate (2 Cor 4:11, 16). But then he says that life in the body means separation from the Lord (2 Cor 5:6–10). In the first passage he speaks confidently of the conquest of death as already certain, and even accomplished (2 Cor 4:16f.). In the second he speaks with dread of death which still has to be overcome (2 Cor 5:2–5). He can use very different modes of thinking and teaching to treat of the same subject-matter.

G. God

Finally, Paul's Christology also determines the notion of God. God is he who is revealed in Christ. He is the "Father of Jesus Christ" (Rom 15:6; 2 Cor 1:3; Col 1:3). His glory has appeared on the face of Christ (2 Cor 4:6). Belief in the one God is an unquestionable certainty in the light of Israel's history: "We know that there is no God but one" (1 Cor 8:4, after Deut 6:4; Rom 16:27; Gal 3:20). Paul shares the gratitude of his people for this faith, in the light of which he condemns pagan idolatry (Rom 1:18–32). This faith is not a merely theoretical confession, God's being "for us" (1 Cor 8:4–6) is an essential. Those who confess the one God may have no gods beside him – obviously, no idols (1 Cor 10:21; 2 Cor 6:16), and then not even any type of recognition of alien powers is possible, either through fear (Col 2:8, 20) or through a secret respect (Rom 1:25; 1 Cor 8:5).

The strictly monotheist confession of faith is regularly linked with the confession of Christ, by virtue of the unique but permanent coming of salvation. This gives two-membered formulae such as "Grace to you and peace from God our Father and the Lord Jesus Christ" (Rom 1:7; 1 Thess 1:1), which are then developed as three-membered formulae such as "The grace of the Lord Jesus Christ and the love of God and the fellowship of the Holy Spirit be with you all" (2 Cor 13:14; Rom 15:30; 1 Cor 12:6; Gal 4:6; 2 Thess 3:13; cf. Mt 28:19; 1 Pet 1:2). Such utterances form the basis of the later trinitarian theology of the Church, which was elaborated with the help of Greek philosophy. The NT does not make assertions about the immanent metaphysical essence of God. It speaks in terms of the history of salvation: the eternal God was and is revealed in his Son Jesus Christ, who is present in the Church through the power of the Holy Spirit.

The theology of the Apostle Paul is essentially Christological. Hence it may be summed up in the text: "He who descended is he who also ascended far above all the heavens, that he might fill all things" (Eph 4:10).

Karl Hermann Schelkle

III. Johannine Theology

A. General

There is a "Christological concentration" in Johannine theology which is unparalleled in this form elsewhere in the NT. From the point of view of Church history and theological development, this is due to the fact that the problems at the time of the composition of the fourth gospel were chiefly Christological. The chief question, as may also be seen from 1 Jn, was one which is again highly relevant today: Is the crucified Jesus of Nazareth identical with the heavenly redeemer? Heretics of a Docetic-Gnostic type seem to have maintained that Jesus Christ did not really "appear in the flesh", as had been taught "from the beginning" in the Church (cf. Jn 1:14, which is polemical; 1 Jn 2:22–24; 4:2f.); he did not reveal himself in water and blood (cf. 1 Jn 5:6). These heresies were answered by the evangelist in the epistles, and also in a *Vita Jesu* in the form of a gospel, where Jesus of Nazareth and his history were interpreted in such a way that "the doctrine about Christ" proclaimed "from the beginning" (cf. 2 Jn 9) was clearly affirmed and the Christological misinterpretations of the heretics were refuted. Thus the Christological programme of the fourth gospel can be put briefly as follows: Jesus Christ is to be shown to be the incarnate Logos, that is, both Logos and Logos made man, but in their unity. This also means showing how his Doxa became "visible" in Jesus Christ for the apostolic eye-witnesses (cf. Jn 1:14; 1 Jn 1:1–3). The resulting "Christological concentration" affects not merely the Christology, but also the soteriology, "mysticism", eschatology and even ethics. The unmistakable Johannine imprint may also be observed in the formal principles of structure. These are mainly:

a) The principle of dualism, which appears in the frequent antitheses, such as life – death, light – darkness, spirit – flesh, truth – lie, (from) above – (from) below, heaven – earth. The divine sphere of life is sharply contrasted with the cosmic sphere of death. The world is irreparably lost. There is no possibility of salvation unless heaven intervenes; deliverance can only come "from above". This dualistic schema gives its special character to Johannine theology and terminology, which is very different from that of the synoptics. There results a certain formal resemblance to Gnosis. But the dualist schema is used in Jn to develop the principle of grace: the salvation of the world comes only "from above", and not from the depths of its own being.

b) The principle of the ambiguous expression, such as ἄνωθεν γεννηθῆναι, meaning to be born again or from on high. This technique enables the evangelist to take a problem a stage further in a discussion and to offer an explanation occasioned by the preliminary misunderstanding. Theology can thus be examined "in depth".

c) The principle of "kerygmatic stylization" (Strathmann). The discourses, meditations and symbolic actions ("signs") are all made to serve the kerygma about Christ. This explains the frequent absence in the fourth gospel of what is called in form-criticism (Dibelius) the "novelistic" element. The narrative takes in only what serves the kerygmatic purpose. There is little interest in incidentals.

d) The use of a special terminology with regard to knowledge. Terms like "to see", "hear", "remember" or "give testimony" have a special significance in Jn with regard to the process of knowing. "To remember" is always more than a mere mental reproduction of the past. The historical event which is "seen", "remembered" or "attested" discloses its deeper dimension in the act of "seeing", "hearing", "remembering" or "attesting". This is the way "knowledge" is gained of what was first hidden and transcendent in the background of the event; the "mystery" is disclosed and can be formulated in the kerygma.

B. The Main Themes of Johannine Theology

1. *Christology*. a) *Formal elements of structure*. (i) *The Logos principle*. This is an organic component of Johannine dual-

ism. It is only through the Logos that a real relationship exists between the transcendent world of God and the cosmos. The Logos, by virtue of his being mediator of creation, has an essential, "intrinsic" ordination to creation. The universal and exclusive mediation of the Logos continues to function in the Logos made flesh, who is the sole mediator of salvation (φῶς and ζωή). Hence Jesus, the incarnate Logos, is the only "way" and the only "door" to salvation.

(ii) *The Christological polemics.* In the fourth gospel, charge and countercharge, in the style of the law-courts, serve to propound Christology (cf., for instance, 5:16–47; 6:26–52; 7:15–30; 8:12–59; 9). They are all concerned with the question of who Jesus is, what is the basis of his claims, whence he comes and whither he goes. These discourses are the creation of the inspired evangelist, but they have their historical occasion in the controversies carried on by Jesus with his opponents, according to the synoptic tradition. Here too the ultimate issue is the person of Jesus and the claims he put forward in Israel.

(iii) *The self-predications of Jesus (the ἐγώ εἰμι formulae).* These are very emphatic ways of affirming Jesus' exclusive claim as revealer, often in terms of a sharp contrast to the expectation of salvation then current. They express what Jesus means to the world. There are seven in all: "I am the bread of life"; "I am the light of the world"; "I am the door"; "I am the good shepherd"; "I am the resurrection and the life"; "I am the way, the truth and the life"; "I am the vine". The stress is on the subject, while the predicate signifies the salvation present in Jesus, in images not directly "messianic" but familiar to all religious language and hence universally understandable. Nonetheless, "they are distinguished from the self-presentations and self-revelations which occur in OT, Indian and Mandaen literature by having a further clause which speaks of salvation, e.g., 11:25b, 'he who believes in me, though he die, yet shall he live', promising it to those who accept Jesus in faith. In the non-Christian parallels, the self-predication of the god or the 'divine' king consists of an accumulation of titles and an enumeration of mighty feats. Here the additional clause makes the self-predication a discourse of salvation" (W. Grundmann).

(iv) *The confessions of faith in Christ.* These represent the answer of faith (in the community) to Jesus' claim. They begin either with "This is ..." or "You are ...", but also appear as vocatives and as acclamations. The titles used are mostly taken from traditional usage (among the Jews and in the primitive Church): "the Messiah", "the king of Israel"; "the holy one of God", "the saviour of the world"; "the Son of God".

(v) *The "signs".* These are means of demonstrating vividly and concretely the meaning of the revelation in the "I am" words of Jesus, and are inseparable from his words. They also demonstrate that Jesus has in fact the power to make good his claim to be saviour of the world, as put forward in the revelation discourses. The words of revelation and revelation in action form an indissoluble unity in the fourth gospel, which in this respect is very like Mk.

b) *The Christology.* The Johannine Christology is not metaphysical and supra-historical, but orientated to the concrete action of God in salvation, as uniquely revealed in the sending of the eternal Word and Son of God into the world. This is true even of the predicate of Logos, which is used absolutely in the prologue of the fourth gospel. The "Logos", echoing the OT assertions about Wisdom, is visualized particularly in its relation to creation and the salvation of man (cf. Jn 1:3, 4, 10, 12, 14; 1 Jn 1:1). The affirmation that the saviour is the eternal Logos, of like being with God (Jn 1:1f.) implies his absolute spirituality and sovereign freedom. The affirmation "all things were made through him" implies the *bonitas* and *unitas* of creation, an anti-Gnostic note which shows that the Johannine dualism is not radical. Further, the Logos predicate combines many lines of religious and philosophical thought of very different origin and character. There is the OT doctrine of the creative word of God, by which all things were made according to Gen 1, and which later in the OT was identified with the divine Wisdom. There were also the Greek notions of the Logos in the world (Heraclitus, Plato, the Stoics), which were taken up by Hellenistic Judaism (Philo). Hence the Johannine "Logos" completes and explains the notions which human religion and philosophy had attached to the concept. In the fourth gospel, the initial adoption of the concept of Logos already points on to the incarnate Logos as the incomparable bearer of revelation – the "truth" – since he is *the* word of the Father to the world, bringing tidings of the Father (1:18; 3:11, 32ff.; 7:16; 8:26, 28, etc.). Since the incarnate Son, as the Logos, has always been the link between the transcendent God and the world, Jesus is always seen in relation to the Father, who sent him into the world to accomplish everything which the Father commanded (10:18; 12:49; 14:31; 15:10). It is this notion of mission that links the work of Jesus with the Father, who then has the functional attribute of "him who sent me (Jesus)", while Jesus is he "whom the Father has sent". The mission is incomparably higher than that of the OT prophets, because in Jn it is the eternal Son of God, of like nature to the Father, who is sent (1:14b, 18; 3:16–18, etc.). His mission fulfilled, the Son returns to his glory with the Father. Thus it is a mission from "above" to "below" and from "below" to "above", which from the point of view of comparative religion recalls the Gnostic schema of descent and ascent. In Gnosis, however, this is intrinsically connected with the cosmic process and also with the question of where man comes from and whither he goes, which is not raised in Jn, which is concerned rather with the mystery of Jesus Christ – *his* origin and destiny. The answer given by the Johannine theology is not new, being derived from the existing faith of the Church, but in the expression of the Christological mystery it seems to have drawn upon its environment for some of the formulae, as is again apparent in the Johannine interpretation of the traditional Son of man Christology (cf., for instance, 3:13f.; 6:62). Jesus' way to his glory passes, according to Jn, through his death "for the life of the world", and the fact that for Jn the glorification of the Son already begins with his being lifted up on the cross shows both the deliberate adoption by the fourth evangelist of the existing kerygmatic tradition of the primitive Church, and a new interpretation of this kerygma by virtue of the presuppositions and teachings of the Johannine theology. The "vertical" and "dualistic" cast of thought is very marked, as in the mission "from above" and the return of the envoy to "on high". But the "horizontal" component of the history of salvation is equally evident, since according to Johannine theology Jesus is of course the Messiah, while Moses, "the Scriptures" and the Baptist have already given testimony to him (5:33, 39, 46). But here the main point is that the Johannine Christ combines and fulfils in himself many eschatological expectations which were linked with the cultus in Judaism. He is the eschatological "tent" (dwelling-place) of God among men (1:14), the new order taking the place of Jewish ritualism (2:1–11), the pneumatic temple of the time of salvation, the source from which flow all blessings (2:13–22; 7:37–39; 19:34), the eschatological place for true adoration of the Father (4:20–23), the paschal lamb of the new covenant (19:33, 36) and the high priest of the last days (6:69; 17:19; 19:23f.). One may therefore speak of a "cultic background" to Johannine Christology, where something undreamt of and incomparably new appears because Christ changes the old order radically, but where the continuity is still maintained with the old, with the time of promise and expectation. This brought with it a strong "cultic concentration". Christ is now absolutely central in the worship of God; the whole content of the cultic realm of the ancient covenant is now realized in Christ.

2. *Soteriology*. In Johannine theology soteriology is indissolubly connected with Christology, because Christology is wholly orientated to soteriology. This can be demonstrated most clearly from the basic soteriological concept in Jn, ζωή, "life". For Christ does not merely bestow life, he is himself life as the pre-existent Logos of life who is from the heavenly world of God and has become incarnate (Jn 1:14; 1 Jn 1:1). "I am the life" (Jn 11:25; 14:6; 5:26). He is the bread of life from heaven (6:35, 48), who is sent to bring life to the world (3:15f.; 10:10). To "believe" in him, to "see" him, to "know" him, to "have" him, is to "have" already (cf. especially 5:24; 1 Jn 3:14) "eternal life" through him (Jn 3:15f., 36; 5:24; 6:40, 47; 10:28; 17:2f.; 20:31; 1 Jn 5:12). Salvation, which is essentially fellowship with Christ (cf. 15:1–5), is imparted to believers in the sacramental birth from God through the Spirit (Jn 1:13; 3:5f.; 4:14; 7:38f.; 1 Jn 5:6ff.), by Jesus' death "for the life of the world" and its representation and application in the eucharistic gift (6:51c–58), and by the obedient faith which accepts his life-giving words (5:24; 6:63, 68; 8:51). Faith, as in Pauline theology, is the way to salvation. And faith is taken in the full existential sense of total, decisive dedication of the person with all its powers to the saviour Jesus Christ. In Johannine theology *he* is always the object of the decision of faith. In contrast to the Pauline theology of faith, the problem of the law has disappeared from view, which is likewise due to the "Christological concentration" of Johannine theology. What is at stake now is not the question of the significance of the "works of the law" in the attainment of salvation, as in the middle of the 1st century, but the "object" of faith – Jesus Christ as the sole "way" to salvation, in comparison with which all other ways of salvation, past, present or future, are radically eliminated.

3. *Eschatology*. The eschatological salvation is so radically and decisively linked with the saviour Jesus Christ, the Logos of life who has already appeared in the world, that salvation and perdition, life and judgment, have already been projected out of the future into the present time of faith. "He who does not believe is already judged" (Jn 3:18); "he who has the Son has life" (1 Jn 5:12); cf. also Jn 5:24; 1 Jn 3:14. This gives the "Now" of the world's time a special and unique character. It is the time for the irreversible decision which brings with it salvation or perdition. This eschatology is not completely new in the NT, since the synoptics and Paul already saw that salvation had already begun to be present in Jesus (cf., for instance, Mt 12:28; Rom 3:21; 5:9 ff.; 6:22; 7:6). But it is taken to its most radical conclusion in Jn, since Christ is understood as *the* eschatological event, so that salvation and perdition are decided not merely in the future but here and now. Salvation, however, does not simply consist of gaining a "definitive self-understanding" (as Bultmann holds), It also means the mystery of fellowship with Christ, bestowed by the Father, which is the source of life; it means "abiding" in Christ – the "Johannine mysticism". But this is not an illusory anticipation of the future or its total elimination. The Johannine theology also contains a future judgment (5:27–29; 15:6) and points on to a full flowering of the gift of life when the disciples

share manifestly the heavenly glory of the exalted Lord, after the resurrection of the dead (cf. 14:2f.; 17:24, 26), and contemplate the glorified Christ with face unveiled (17:24).

4. *Ethics.* John is the great interpreter of the command of love given by Jesus, "by which the Johannine theology is so thoroughly penetrated that it becomes in practice the central and dominant point of all exhortations (Jn 13:34f.; 1 Jn 2:7–11; 3:11–18; 4:7–21; 5:1ff.; 2 Jn 5)" (Schnackenburg).

5. *Ecclesiology.* Though the term "Church" (ἐκκλησία) does not occur, the matter itself is treated both as a theological and an institutional entity. The Church appears as the flock gathered and led by Jesus, who gives his life for it as the good shepherd (Jn 10:1–18) and who appoints Peter as its shepherd after his own departure (21:16f.). The members of the Church are the branches of the vine which is Christ (15:1–5), though this does not automatically guarantee their salvation. The branches must "abide" in him and "bring forth fruit" if they are to endure (15:4, 6). Further, the nature of the Church is also demonstrated in the use of "We" in so many affirmations. The plural points to the κοινωνία of a common faith and tradition, where the normative "doctrine about Christ" which goes back to "the beginning" is faithfully "preserved". And this fellowship has a highly developed sense of community according to Johannine theology, since the community is in the world but not "of the world" (17:11–19). It is persecuted by the world (16:33), but is still full of the peace, joy and love bestowed on it by its Lord (16:33; 17:13, 26). Thus everything is reduced in Johannine theology to an almost "dualistic" opposition between the "world" and the community of believers in Jesus. This is one more instance of the uncompromising nature of Johannine thought.

Franz Mussner

NOMINALISM

The nature of the problems usually raised under the heading of "Nominalism" and also their impact on the history of thought can be best described by examining their historical origins and suggesting a possible response to them at the present day.

1. The word "Nominalism" indicates the controversy which arose in the 11th and 12th centuries apropos of the ontological or metaphysical value of the general concept, the "universal". It was a revival of the debate which had been left open by Porphyrius (d. 304) in his introduction to Aristotle on the Categories – a work known in the Middle Ages through the translation of Boethius (cf. *PL*, LXIV, cols. 84ff.). Are *genus* and *species* "real" or are they only present in the intellect? Are they distinct from the sensible or are they *in* the sensible? It is easy to recognize here a crystallization of the whole philosophy of Plato and Aristotle in its confrontation with the various forms of scepticism. Though in the discussion prior to Roscelin de Compiègne and in Roscelin himself and above all in Peter Abelard the linguistic and logical problem is in the foreground, it is clear that the ontological or metaphysical question, which represented a fundamental critique of the philosophical and theological tradition, was a basically dangerous and shocking one.

Reliable historical information about Roscelin is lacking. The general view that he maintained that the *universalia* were nothing but a *flatus vocis*, words empty of all but the sound of breath, is due to the account of him given by his adversary Anselm of Canterbury (*De Fide Trinitatis*, 2; *PL*, CLVIII, col. 265). Though it would therefore be unsafe to range Roscelin among the main protagonists of Nominalism, his "anti-realism" may well have initiated and inspired the scholastic attack on the *réalisme outré* of the "Platonists" (understood in the widest sense of the term) (M. de Wulf). Nor was the radical *flatus vocis* theory of Nominalism upheld by Roscelin's follower, Peter Abelard (see especially his *Nostrorum Petitioni Sociorum*, ed. by B. Geyer). His formula, "universale est sermo" or "nomen" (not just "vox") indicates his rejection of a crude sensualism and points to a "conceptualism" (so Reiners, Vignaux, Gilson). This is still an ontologically based logic and epistemology in which the actively productive role of the human mind in the formation of concepts and the discovery of truth is allowed more play than in the Platonizing type of "realism", while the over-simplification of the *flatus vocis* theory has been left behind. Thus Peter Abelard already shows a tendency to adopt a critical Aristotelianism or what might be called an intermediate position, such as is taken up later by Thomas Aquinas (cf. *De Ente et Essentia*, c. 4). William of Occam is clearly a conceptualist (Böhner). He is mainly concerned with the conditions to which knowledge is subject and with the human activity involved in the process, that is, with the question of subjectivity in general. On questions of detail, commentators are divided.

The analysis of the historical data shows that Nominalism is a vague term and now of highly questionable value. In all probability, no one ever upheld a thoroughgoing Nominalism. It was rather a theoretical position stylized by the "realists" as a negative limit. But in this form, as a constantly menacing phantom or chimera, "Nominalism" influenced persistently the philosophy of the Middle Ages and even of modern times. The critical approach of all empirically-orientated modern thought is necessarily along the lines of the Nominalist position and sometimes expressly claims to be a Nominalism. In the latter case, "Nominalism" signals the rejection of the ontological priority of essence in general (of the Idea, the Form) and also of metaphysics.

Particular mention should be made of the broad current of philosophy and theology in the 14th and 15th centuries which understood itself as the *via moderna* outlined by William of Occam and became widely influential. Here too Nominalism is used in a very wide sense to cover positions as different as those of Nicholas d'Autrecourt, Peter d'Ailly and Gabriel Biel (cf. J. Auer in *LTK*, VII, cols. 1020–3). The theological problems of this "Nominalist scholasticism" – of which Luther was an adherent – stemmed from the epistemological critique of metaphysical and biblico-dogmatic language in general. This was no longer regarded as the direct or at least analogous rendering of an ontological content, but merely as a form of discourse orientated rather to human understanding than by the "object" itself. Those who took up this position could not but regard the traditional views of the relationship between language (thought) and being, knowledge and faith, philosophy and revelation as questionable. The development may be described in general terms as leading to a stronger emphasis on subjectivity, will and freedom, as also on the empirical and the individual positive fact as the historical.

2. The attitude of Catholic philosophers and theologians to Nominalism has been predominantly negative up to the present day (cf. Grabmann, von Balthasar, etc.). An over-simplification has made Nominalism responsible for the Reformation and its (non-ontological) theology, for the critical and anti-metaphysical philosophy of modern times and indeed for modern emancipation. In the same way, the so-called "resurrection of metaphysics" and the re-discovery of "values" in the first half of the 20th century have been acclaimed as the long-awaited anti-critical and anti-Nominalist reversal. But it should be calmly recognized that the revival of the traditional philosophy, especially of classical scholasticism, has not succeeded

in spreading beyond the confines of "Christian philosophizing". The linguistic philosophy of logical positivism, existential philosophy and Marxism are all decidedly on the side of Nominalism. Since Nominalism, no matter what form it takes, always brings with it the metaphysical problem, while metaphysics comes to a stand-still or even succumbs before the difficulties which it poses, the central issue of Nominalism, the ontological validity of the concept, cannot be definitely solved. But if one considers the historical progress of philosophy, it is not difficult to recognize that Nominalism – even in its chimerical form – has been and still remains a liberating force. It is therefore necessary to try to reach a positive assessment of Nominalism – or rather, of Conceptualism – without flinching before the difficulties posed to metaphysics and surrendering theology to a "dialectic" where decision is its own and only motive. Hence the wide range of problems suggested by the term "Nominalism" retains its relevance, even though the term itself has proved to be historically and objectively inadequate.

Heinz Robert Schlette

O

OBEDIENCE

1. For modern man with his belief in autonomy, obedience largely appears to be merely a necessary evil, not a virtue. In other words, people realize that without some obedience education and social life are impossible, but they would like to see it reduced to a minimum, on the ground that man's goal should be maximum possible self-determination. This ideal can on this view only be attained if obedience is rendered superfluous.

Such a conception of obedience stands in sharp contrast to the conviction, springing from Hellenistic philosophy, especially neo-Platonism, that man attains perfection only by giving up his own will and submitting to God's heteronomy and to divinely-established authority, because only in this way is man's dispersion overcome by recollection. Ideal obedience therefore carries out an order for the order's sake.

Some features of this metaphysics of unity have left their mark on the ascetical language of Catholic writing on obedience. For example, obedience is sometimes represented one-sidely as the abandonment of self-will, self-determination appearing as something which by its very nature separates from God. In this perspective, to obey seems better than to command, blind obedience which carries out the command for its own sake appears to be the ideal form of obedience, and the obedience of members of religious orders seems more perfect than that of those who are not so vowed to obedience, precisely because religious have renounced self-determination. However, the classical theological writings on obedience lend themselves to this interpretation rather because of their terminology than their doctrine. Their language was influenced by many historical factors of their day.

2. The word for obedience, both in the Semitic and in Indo-European languages, is derived from the word "to hear" and always denotes a readiness to listen to what other people say and to do their will. A clear distinction must be drawn between readiness to obey God and to obey men, for the first must be unconditional, whereas the second can only be conditional. Readiness to obey comes naturally, because of the instinctive need to rely on authorities. It becomes morally relevant in proportion as submission to authority becomes open to question on the part of the obedient person, who in consequence is capable of coming to a free decision about it.

a) In the history of religions, obedience is only important in the higher stages of religious feeling where relations with God are practised in a personal way. Initially what is demanded is almost exclusively ritual obedience. In the higher religions, obedience to God is central to the religious attitude, because it appears as a response to the claim of the "holy" and expresses submission to the will of God whose creatures, subjects and children men are. The explicit use of the category of obedience to interpret man's personal relation of dependence on God is, however, liable to considerable historical changes, for that category expresses only one aspect, not the whole, of that relation. Consequently, in the history of religions obedience is chiefly regarded as an expression of the religious life of the community, where it denotes submission to the spiritual and hierarchical authorities, particularly in cultic matters. This aspect finds its highest development in the monasticism and religious orders of the higher religions, where the further relation of spiritual child and disciple to superiors is also important.

Even within the revealed religions, obedience to God is not always clearly distinguished from faith, humility, imitation, etc. It is therefore not surprising that when Aquinas discusses obedience, what he chiefly has in mind is obedience to human beings, that he counts it among the social virtues, regards it as part of the virtue of justice and explicitly stresses that our relation to God is not to be reduced to obedience, and that the latter is not the highest virtue (II-II, qq. 104 and 105).

b) In the OT, morality essentially consists in obedience to the will of God (Deut 1–4; Eccles 12:13). Religion is expressed by obedience to God's revelation in the word of the law and the prophets (Is 1:2; cf. 1:10; Jer 2:4; 7:21–28). Consequently men are repeatedly charged to observe the commandments and precepts of the Lord (Gen 17:9; Exod 19:5f.; 24:7f.; Ps 119; 2 Mac 7:1–42). The fulfilment of the promises of the covenant is conditional on such obedience (e.g., Exod 15:26; Lev 20:22ff.; Deut 5:32f.; 6:1; 8:1; 28:1–4 [15–69]). Disobedience, on the other hand, is threatened with a curse (Deut 28:15; Jer 11:2ff.); the very essence of sin consists in disobedience, as can already be seen from the account of the Fall (Gen 3:1–7). Faithful observance of the commandments, however, strengthens the nation and preserves it from distress (Deut 6:17f.; 11:8f.; 28:1f.; Jos 1:7f.; Pss 119:1; 128:1). Obedience is rooted in fear of God (Deut 5:29) who is the only Lord (Exod 20:2; Kg 8:23). God responds with his love (Is 1:18f.). This in turn makes obedience possible out of love of God (Jos 22:5; Ps 119), so that love of God consists in love of the law. Hence obedience is ranked higher than sacrifice (1 Sam 15:22; Jer 7:21ff.). In the post-exilic period, the precise fulfilment of the letter of the law comes more to the fore, instead of the direct relation of God to his people. The law is no longer envisaged primarily in relation to the people as a whole but in regard to the individual (Prov 1:33; Ps 128:1). The fourth commandment (Exod 20:12) assumes in the OT a large role (Prov 1:8; 23:22). The mother was considered as equal in personal dignity to the father. Transgression of the fourth commandment was severely punished (Exod 21:15–17).

c) In the NT, categories other than obedience are obviously used more frequently to determine man's relation to his creator and redeemer, e.g., love, faith, etc. Nevertheless the concept of obedience is of great importance in the interpretation of our relation to God. Thus, according to the synoptics, Jesus subjected his whole life obediently to God (Mt 5:17; 17:24ff.; 26:39, 42; Lk 2:49), and precisely by obedience stood the test in temptation (Mt 4:1–11; Mk 8:33). He obeys his parents and legitimate authorities as a matter of course (Lk 2:51; Mt 17:27). Himself obedient to God, he is obeyed by the demons (Mk 1:23ff.; 5:12), illness, even death (Mk 5:41) and nature (Mt 8:27 par.). He expounds the law of God for men in a binding way (Mt 5:21–48; cf. 7:21; Mk 3:31ff.), calls men to imitate him and submit their will to him (Mk 8:34ff.).

The acceptance of his message demands that the will of God should be accomplished on earth as it is in heaven (Mt 6:9–13). And so the obedience of the Christian is freed from the legalism which prevailed among the Pharisees and which Jesus opposed all his life (cf., for example, Mk 2:27; Lk 14:1ff.). Conscience decides how the law is to be followed (Mt 15:1–20), because the personal relation to God is deepened and takes concrete form in the imitation of Jesus (Mt 6:9ff.; Mk 14:36).

According to John in particular, the love of God is expressed and proved by obedience to the will of God (Jn 14:31). Christ did not come to do his own will, but the will of him who sent him (Jn 4:34; 6:38; 9:4; 10:18; 12:49; 15:10; 17:4). Paul accentuates this theology of obedience. By Christ's obedience, man is saved from the disobedience which came into the world through Adam (Rom 5:19; cf. Gal 4:4). His obedience led to his death on the cross (Phil 2:8; cf. Heb 5:8); and so, according to Hebrews, the life of Christ is a sacrifice of obedience (Heb 10:5–10; cf. 1 Sam 15:22). Redemption by Christ comes to men (Rom 10:3, 16; 2 Cor 7:15; 2 Thess 1:8) in the "obedience of faith" (Rom 1:5), so that Christians are men of obedience (Rom 2:7; 2 Cor 9:13; 10:5) and Jesus Christ is their only law (1 Cor 9:21).

Obedience to human beings and the established order is divinely willed because men share in divine authority (Rom 13:1ff.; cf. 1 Pet 2:13ff.), and obedience is "in the Lord" (Eph 5:22; 6:1; 6:5; Col 3:18ff.). Special emphasis is laid on the obedience due in the family (Eph 5:22; Col 3:18, 20), that of slaves (Eph 6:5; Col 3:22; Tit 2:9) and obedience to the State (Rom 13:1ff.; Tit 3:1; cf. Mk 12:13–17; 1 Pet 2:13ff.).

The NT view of the limits of obedience is summarized in the phrase of Acts 5:29: "We must obey God rather than men" (cf. Mt 12:46–48; Mk 12:17; Lk 2:48; Jn 2:4; Acts 4:19; 1 Pet 2:17).

3. In accordance with the scriptural data, therefore, obedience in its theological sense primarily and in general consists in the determination to accomplish the will of God in all things as it is revealed in his law. As a word-directed being created by the word of God, man is essentially ordained to listen to God to whom he belongs and whom he must obey in all things. In this formal sense, obedience is a general virtue and the foundation of all the moral virtues, for in that formal sense it is always morally good to obey. Such obedience makes man actualize his own being, for the root of action is in freedom, which is only exercised in commitment to one's fellow human beings and to God.

The problem of obedience of this kind consists, however, in its content. How does man recognize what is the will of God for him personally? Moral theology attempts to answer this question. Starting from the principle of God's universal salvific will, it analyses man's personal encounter with God in the religious and human act in which man conscientiously makes a decision in regard to God's law, the claims of brotherly love and, through this, the love of God.

Within this framework a special problem is set by the question as to how far obedience to human beings is compatible with the will of God. The basis for an answer is that man as a communicative being only fulfils himself through personal relations with his fellowmen. Being one of them, he is dependent on them and must obey them in proportion as he recognizes that their orders are directed to the welfare of the community and the individual, for that is the extent to which human orders express the will of God. But the will of God is our perfection.

Orders of this kind can be issued by means of a representative and co-ordinating authority, which aims at the education or collaboration of human beings and consequently at the development of their potentialities. Well-regulated obedience therefore offers man favourable opportunities, the neglect of which would inevitably lead to his impoverishment. Proper obedience is therefore not a necessary evil but a virtue. It does not demand self-abandonment but makes self-realization possible. For unless the pupil relies on the teacher, he cannot achieve his full capacity, and without orderly co-ordination of the activities of individuals there can be no successful development of the potentialities of the individual. It must be noted, however, that obedience to an educator is only meaningful to the extent that the latter is superior in attainments to the pupil. Obedience to co-ordinating authorities, on the other hand, becomes all the more necessary the more complicated the requirements of collaboration become. The latter in turn make possible greater self-realization of those involved.

Human action is only virtuous to the extent that it is free. Consequently, in order legitimately to obey, man must always have sufficiently recognized that a given command is in the service of man. That, of course, can be verified in a great variety of ways. A child, for example, cannot judge the implications of an order, but only needs to know that its parents want the best for it. Ideally, however, obedience is not this kind of formal and implicit obedience for obedience's sake; it springs from fully explicit awareness that what is commanded does in fact stand in the service of man. For in this way the content of the will of God is known more fully and therefore more perfectly and becomes the object of man's own will.

This means, however, that human beings can and should be obeyed only to the extent that they share in the authority of God. For the end of man can never be simply man, but is always God, despite the fact that man has his end in himself and possesses an absolute value. Consequently, in the Christian view there is no hierarchy of persons, but only of functions and the services which follow from them. Hence man may never subject himself to other human beings as such, but can submit to them only to the extent that they stand in the service of a divinely-willed goal. Otherwise the personal dignity of the giver of the order would be placed above that of the person obeying, and so the latter would be diminished.

Furthermore, since the various human authorities share in the authority of God in different ways, obedience to them takes different forms. The child, for example, owes obedience to its parents within the framework of their authority as the source of its life, i.e., because they act on behalf of the child, assisting it to develop its own personality. Their authority also extends to the tasks involved in ruling the family, i.e., within the scope of their functions in the service of the family community. The pupil owes the teacher obedience within the range of his work of promoting the child's education to social life. The employer has to be obeyed as far as obedience is necessary to the correct performance of the work. The citizen owes obedience to the State within the framework of the constitutional laws, i.e., as far as the organs of the State carry out their functions in the service of the common good. The Church can demand obedience within the framework of its office of sanctifying, teaching and pastoral care in the service of salvation. The individual may, of course, have bound himself to a more far-reaching obedience through acceptance of official ministry in the Church or by taking solemn vows. This ecclesiastical obedience has always an aspect of the mysterious, since the Church itself can only be grasped through the mystery of revelation.

Obedience to the various human authorities is, therefore, not only different in degree, but assumes different forms corresponding to the different functions of the various authorities. By the nature of the case the relation which links the will to that of the "superior" in the child, employee, soldier, citizen, believer, etc., differs in structure in each. What is essential is that the required bond of obedience should be formed with the greatest possible freedom, and that obedience should be exercised as far as possible on one's own responsibility. This does not diminish obedience, but makes it more personal and therefore more valuable. It also ensures that obedience will not mean the abandonment of one's own will, but its more perfect adjustment to the requirements of self-realization. This will be attained by putting one's own will at the service of the needs of the social community, for the purpose of commands themselves is to serve the development of the subjects.

Ascetical or educational obedience in the service of self-perfection, and functional obedience in the service of the community, are therefore not attitudes opposed to obedience, but are complementary. Educative or ascetical obedience is necessary if functional obedience is to be achieved as perfectly as possible, while functional obedience always has an educational or ascetical effect. Obedience in imitation of the crucified Christ therefore never demands self-sacrifice for its own sake; it calls for renunciation, which is justified by the objective requirements of love.

Most of the lack of balance to be found in Catholic writing on obedience is caused by the fact that the relation between self-sacrifice and self-realization, the educative or ascetical and the co-ordinating function of obedience, is seen as an opposition instead of as a polarity. The reason for this is that the relation between God's will and human laws and precepts is sometimes over-simplified through inadequate understanding of the way the divine will finds embodiment, as though men in virtue of their participation in God's authority were actually God's personal representatives. But they only represent his authority in different ways in virtue of their function and real superiority. The imbalance is also due to the distorting influence of a concept of man coloured by Hellenism which sees the ideal of human behaviour in an unworldly, angelic life instead of in activity which integrates bodily and spiritual capacities.

A consequence may be drawn in regard to the right and duty of resistance. Man may obey other men only to the extent that an order is recognized to be meaningful: purely blind obedience is unworthy of man. So-called blind obedience has, however, a certain justification because the individual can often recognize the reason for obedience without being able to see the point of the order. For the individual may lack the competence necessary to judge the appropriateness of the order given, yet have sufficient grounds for assuming sufficient integrity and competence in the commanding authority. Within the framework of educative or ascetical and of co-ordinating functions, with their regulative principles deriving from the intrinsic nature of the activity in question, obedience for obedience's sake is possible and meaningful. For in this case authority as such is necessary. On account of the fundamental importance of freedom for man, however, resistance to authority is justified when it is seen to be more imperative than recognition of authority.

4. Education in obedience must therefore aim on the one hand at conveying to men as much insight as possible into the meaning of obedience.

The different functions of human authorities, their character of service and their limits, must therefore be explained. At the same time the value of the obligation imposed on freedom by obedience must be made clear. That is, one must show that the ties of obedience and freedom itself do not contradict but condition each other. On the other hand, education must likewise see that freedom is actually submitted to authority as such, because the virtue of obedience consists in the well-regulated binding of one's own will to the will of legitimate authority. This, of course, has to take place as rationally as possible. The aim of Christian education in obedience is, therefore, neither man's untrammelled self-determination, nor his self-surrender in obedience. It is man's self-realization through submission to authorities which represent and take the place of God, and therefore through submission to the will of God to which alone unconditional obedience is due.

Waldemar Molinski

OLD TESTAMENT ETHICS

OT revelation has its historical origins and progresses gradually. Incomplete in itself, it finds its conclusion and completion in the NT. There is a corresponding development in OT ethics. It is seen from the outset to be inseparably connected with OT religion and to be fundamentally aimed at making human behaviour conform to the will of Yahweh. The more clearly God's personal will is recognized in its authoritative claim upon all spheres of life the more exalted does the ethical message become. Since in respect of its content the religion of Yahweh does not enter history as a ready-made whole, the OT does not offer a closed system of ethics. It found customs and ways of life ready to hand, some of which could be taken over and adapted to the worship of Yahweh, but some of which had to be rejected and fought against, since they were irreconcilable with the OT idea of God. A few examples may serve to make this clear. The duties to God and to one's fellowmen recognized by all men as belonging to the natural law are formulated apodictically in the Decalogue (Exod 20:2–17; Deut 5:6–18). Now it is remarkable that the desires which precede actions are also placed under divine sanction. The consciousness of solidarity prevailing among members of the same tribe is a sociological fact among nomads; one expression of it is the blood feud. It still exercises an influence long after the nomadic stage has given place to sedentarization. Hence the principle of the talion has been taken over both in cuneiform codes and in the laws of the OT (Gen 9:6; Exod 21:12–23; Lev 24:17–21; Num 35:16–33; Deut 19:11ff.), while two traditions which have been more precisely determined are the principle of collective responsibility (Exod 20:5; 34:7) and the duties of the *goel* (= the nearest relative of an afflicted person, responsible for upholding his rights: the Levirate law, Deut 25:5ff.; redemption, Lev 25:25, 48ff.). In fact the entire covenant relationship of the OT people to God is rooted in the concept of solidarity (Lev 26:3–45; Deut 30:15–20). Like other ancient peoples Israel also believed in the power of the spoken word, especially in the form of blessings (Gen 49) and cursings (the cursing psalms: against private opponents, Ps 7:10ff.; 58:7ff.; 109:6ff., or national enemies, Ps 83:10ff.; 129:5ff.). But the OT idea differs from that found among extra-biblical peoples in that the blessing or the curse is not a magical instrument whereby the deity can be forced to intervene, but an appeal to God as sovereign. The ritual of sacrifice (Lev 1–7) and calendar of festivals (Exod 23:10ff.; Lev 23) exhibit parallels with the peasant culture of Canaan, but in the OT they do not represent attempts to influence the powers of fertility by means of magic. Their function is rather to acknowledge God as the dispenser and sustainer of life. All other customs which infiltrated into Israel from the surrounding world and endangered Yahwistic monotheism and the ethical standards relating to it were relentlessly resisted (idolatry, Lev 20:2ff.; Deut 13:6ff.; sorcery, Exod 22:17; invocation of the dead, Lev 20:27; sacral prostitution, Deut 23:18, etc.).

1. *Traditions in Genesis.* Without entering into the distinction of literary strata in Gen the following factors relevant to OT ethics may be deduced: man is answerable to God for his actions (Gen 2–3); God's will is the highest ethical norm (Gen 6:9; 7:1); God provides laws to protect life, for this belongs to him (Gen 9:4–7; cf. 4:10). The patriarchs recognize God as holy, patient, righteous, omniscient (Gen 18:16–19; 39:9; 41:16), that is, as a religious and moral power which demands perfection (Gen 17:1). Sin is a violation of Yahweh's will (Gen 13:13; 20:6; 38:9ff.); in fact the patriarchs do strive, in spite of occasional lapses, for true devotion (Gen 28:20ff.; 32:10–13). They offer sacrifices (Gen 31:54; 46:1), are themselves submissive to God (Gen 22:1–14), practise hospitality (Gen 18), recognize the duty of protecting their guests (Gen 19:8) and sometimes evince a heroic love of their neighbour (Gen 13:8ff.; 14:14ff.).

2. *Legislation.* The personal will of God, the claims of which extend to all spheres, is made known in the OT law, and salvation is declared to depend upon observance of the law (Exod 15:26; Deut 28:1–14). In the oldest section of these laws, namely the Book of the Covenant, idolatry (Exod 22:19), murder (Exod 21:12ff.), harming and cursing parents (Exod 21:15, 17) and the stealing of a man (Exod 21:16) are forbidden under penalty of death. Measures are also taken for the protection of the fellowman (Exod 21:18ff.) and his property (Exod 21:33ff.), the truth in causes at law (Exod 23:1ff.) and the rights of the poor, widows, orphans and strangers (Exod 22:20ff.). These penal laws enacted in the name of God show a particularly humane conception, which one looks for in vain in the corresponding laws of the ancient Near East. Deuteronomy, which is rooted in ancient tradition and influenced by the prophetic preaching of the 9th to the 8th century, emphasizes above all the command to love God (6:4ff.), for a merciful God (5:10) chose Israel of his free grace and love (7:7f.). Hence all Israelites are brothers (15:7 etc.), who must hearken to the voice of God (13:19), support one another (15:7–11) and be especially careful to protect the weaker members of society (15:12ff.; 24:12ff.). Here then the commandments affect man's innermost dispositions. He must cherish them in his heart and put them into action (30:11–14). The Code of Holiness (Lev 17–26), which was composed by priestly circles of Jerusalem, seeks to raise man to God by inculcating loyalty to the traditional prescriptions: "Be holy for I am holy" (Lev 19:2; 20–26, etc.). The various groups of laws concerning moral life (Lev 19), marriage (Lev 20), priests (Lev 21f.) and the festal calendar (Lev 23) are directed towards this goal of sanctification, for holiness must permeate the entire life of the faithful, and in the cultic community one "loves one's neighbour as one's self" (Lev 19:18). The priestly laws with their rituals of sacrifices (Lev 1–7) and their rules of purity (Lev 11–15) were compiled in the 5th century at the latest. These served to make Israel aware of the transcendence of God and of its own special position among the peoples. Faithfulness to the law was to be above all a demonstration of obedience to God.

3. *Prophets.* Since all laws are an expression of Yahweh's will, in the OT all ethical behaviour is referred to God.

This intrinsic connection between ethics and religion is upheld above all by the prophets, who free religion from mere cultic externalism and root it in the moral dispositions of the heart (Jer 4:4). God is absolute perfection, ontological holiness (Is 6:3; 57:15; 66:1). He loves his people and demands loyalty from them. Hence the prophets present Israel's relationship with God under the image of marriage (Hos 1–3; Jer 2; Jer 31; Ezek 16; cf. Song). Ritual acts of repentance without a purpose of amendment are meaningless (Amos 4:6–11; Is 58:5ff.). God rejects sacrifice without interior devotion (Hos 6:6; Is 1:10–15). Faith must be living and must take effect in daily life (Is 29:13f.). Hence the prophetic movement fights against social injustice (Amos 4:1ff.; 6:1–11; 8:4–7; Mic 2:1f., 8ff.). Isaiah regards unbelief (Is 1:2ff.; 2:8, 18; 8:5–8), that is, the rejection of God's just dominion, as the root of all immorality. Ethics does not consist in the observance of particular commandments, but results from a theocentric disposition translated into action (to do good, Is 1:17; justice, love and humility, Mic 6:8). Hence in the last analysis there is only one evil: to reject the will of Yahweh (Is 24:5; 46:6–9), which is at the same time folly in the face of the divine wisdom (Is 29:14). Thus the prophets lead to a deeper understanding of ethics, even though the people are slow to respond. Jeremiah reproaches them with moral and religious superficiality (Jer 5:21; 6:10). Ezekiel offers what is almost a systematic treatment of sin (Ezek 18:6–9; 22:6–12). The fulfilment of all the commandments constitutes in the last analysis a single act of faith and obedience, for which the individual is responsible (Ezek 14:12–20; 18:10–20). The history of Israel is, however, a series of infidelities (Ezek 16; 20; 23). God alone is able to convert this people and to impart his spirit to them (Ezek 36:17–32), i.e., man can never fulfil the claims of God of his own strength, or point to his own merits or achievements. Salvation and justification are the exclusive gift of God.

4. *Psalms and Wisdom literature.* Naturally the moral and religious formation of OT man by the law and the prophets found expression in the psalms. The content of these is as varied as life itself, and in them the most diverse aspects of OT ethics in their concrete application are reflected. Thus to be just, pious, wise, holy, upright and perfect, to seek, fear, love God, etc., all ultimately signify the same thing, namely the fulfilment of Yahweh's will. At this point only a few examples can be adduced: the summons to the praise of God and to the love of God (Ps 47; 96–100; 134–136; 147–150), to integrity of life (Ps 112; 128), to righteousness (Ps 15; 18; 21–25; 82, 3f.), to love of the law (Ps 119), etc., while conversely to have the love of God is recognized as the highest good (Ps 73:25). Psalm 51 is worthy of special note since it evinces a clear ethic of interior disposition; justification and forgiveness of sins presuppose repentance and acknowledgement of guilt as well as a purpose of amendment. In spite of their practical outlook the rules of life inculcated by the wisdom teaching of the OT are not ethically neutral as are, for the most part, those of other peoples of the ancient Near East, but permeated by a deep faith in God, and hence morally and religiously orientated. Thus, for instance, the Book of Proverbs emphasizes that every good derives from God (10:22), that the fear of God is the beginning of wisdom and justice (1:7; 14:2), and that man must love and observe the law (29:18). Love of one's neighbour (11:17; 14:9, 21; 17:17; 21:3) and almsgiving as well as the forgiveness of injuries draw down God's blessing (14:31; 19–17; 22:9; 28:27). Here too we find a rejection of vices (Pride: 6:17; 11:2; 16:18; 25:6ff.; avarice: 23:4f.; 10:12; unchastity: 5:1–14; 6:20ff., 27; envy: 14:30;

drunkenness: 23:29–35; anger: 15:18; 29:22; sloth: 6:6–11; 26:13–16; 24:28–34), while conversely the cardinal virtues are listed in Wis 8:7. In particular folly is equated with godlessness and sin (Prov 9:6–12; Wis 1:3; 5:4–14), and wisdom with the fear of God (Ecclus 1:16–20), that is, with a way of life that is theocentrically directed. The exhortations to humility (Ecclus 3:17–21) and temperance (Ecclus 37:27–31) are based on the same grounds. The summary of duties towards one's neighbour runs: "What you hate, do not do to any one" (Tob 4:15; cf. Mt 7:12).

Walter Kornfeld

OLD TESTAMENT HISTORY

Palestine is strewn with pre-historic sites. They go back at least to the second-last interglacial period (the Mindel-Riss period), though this, according to the new radio-active carbon method of dating, is only about 100,000 B.C.

1. However, the history of the Israelite people does not begin here, but at the beginning of the 2nd millennium B.C., with its ancestor Abraham, though it is difficult to determine his date precisely. He lived first in Ur, in southern Mesopotamia (Gen 11:28–31). Probably the Semitic tribe of the Terachites was one of many nomadic tribes from the west (=Amurru) which had been attracted thither by the rich civilization of the third dynasty of Ur. The Terachites did not remain uninfluenced by the worship of the national gods there (Jos 24:2). In the course of the wars following the downfall of the third dynasty of Ur, the tribe migrated to Harran in northern Mesopotamia, that is, to the plains between the Euphrates and the Tigris. Several of the names of Abraham's forebears, and many of the stories in the first eleven chapters of the Book of Genesis (for instance, the Tower of Babel and the Flood) still bear traces of the culture and mythology of Mesopotamia. Some time in the second period of the middle bronze age (about 1850 B.C.) God "called" Abraham to leave his home at Harran (Gen 12:1). As an alien leading a semi-nomadic way of life he entered the land of Canaan. Thence he journeyed southwards in a time of drought to the fertile delta of the Nile, still maintaining, however, connections with his Mesopotamian homeland. Later, when Jacob, subsequently named Israel (Gen 32:29), returned from Mesopotamia with his numerous sons and their families, the consciousness of being a distinct people had already begun to emerge. Once the Hyksos, a mixed race of Indo-European and Semitic stock, had seized dominion in Egypt (about 1720 B.C.), the "children of Israel" or, more probably, a part of them, were able to establish themselves there. Under the eighteenth dynasty (from 1550 B.C. onwards = the late bronze age) Egypt freed itself of foreign rule and the power of the Pharaohs was increased in a manner hitherto unprecedented. In the 13th century B.C. Pharaoh Ramses II was foremost in oppressing the descendants of Jacob, who had in the meantime greatly multiplied. Probably it was under his successor, Merneptah, that Moses appeared. The earliest mention of Israel in writing is found on a victory stele of Merneptah set up about 1220 B.C. and it appears here as a conquered tribe or ethnic group.

2. In the wilderness the tribes, who were once in bondage, feel themselves to be the chosen people of God. Henceforward Israel is conscious of being the vassal people of Yahweh, i.e., of the God of Abraham, Isaac and Jacob considered as a royal overlord. From now on Israel and Yahweh are united by a sacred covenant. The people have undertaken as their primary duty not to honour any other gods besides Yah-

ment: the people must cleanse themselves of idolatry once and for all. But they must also cease to rely on human strength and to interpret revelation mechanically – they must learn to begin afresh. They will penetrate the mystery of the God whom they seek and find in "Scripture", and live in ever keener expectation.

Luis Alonso-Schökel

ONTOLOGISM

1. *Meaning.* Ontologism is the doctrine propounded under this name by V. Gioberti (1801–52) according to which human reason first grasps intuitively infinite being, though not in the same way as in the beatific vision. Being is grasped not as an indeterminate abstraction but as supremely real, containing within it all determinations, even though they cannot be distinguished by earthly knowledge. This being (*essere* – also called *ente* by Gioberti, "that which is") is perpetually present to the human mind, and it is only in the light of this being that existing things are known, which remain on the level of sensation as they impinge on experience. Knowledge is a philosophical reflection on the relationship present in the mind between existing things and this being, by virtue of which they exist. They are not part of it, as in Pantheism, but they are created by it. Hence the act of creation is present to the human mind in its origin, being as creating, and is re-enacted along with it when the mind knows in thought the existing things which are only felt in experience. Hence knowledge may also be called "co-production" and every judgment may be regarded as the particular application of a basic judgment of which the "ideal form" would be "That which is creates that which exists" ("L'Ente crea l'esistente"). In this way the movement of human knowledge follows the order of real being. What is first in the order of being (*primum ontologicum*) is also first in the order of knowledge (*primum logicum*). This is the only way, according to Gioberti, that the real value of rational knowledge can be guaranteed.

2. *History.* Gioberti, who was himself influenced by Hegelian thought, developed his system as a reaction against post-Cartesian philosophy, which he rejected as a psychologism since it was based on the "Cogito" of the subject and led to subjectivism and scepticism. This he opposed by an onto-logism of which the starting-point was being and which could therefore safeguard the truth of human knowledge.

If ontologism is defined as Gioberti understood it, it is impossible to range other theories of a similar nature under the same heading. Only some of his disciples or followers can be called Ontologists. Nonetheless, Gioberti claimed to be in the tradition which went back through Bonaventure to Augustine. But he disregarded the distinction between the Augustinian doctrine of God as the light in which the *rationes aeternae* of created things can be known, and the Ontologistic opinion that infinite being, God, is the first and intuitively grasped object of thought, with all other things only known in the light of this intuition.

Malebranche, however, may be regarded as a precursor of Ontologism, since he also assumes a vision of all things in God, who is in fact for him the only direct object of human knowledge. But since his starting-point is totally different from that of Gioberti (an occasionalism which denies the relation of knowledge between created things), he can only be called an Ontologist in a very broad sense. Nor can Gioberti's contemporary, A. Rosmini-Serbati, be taken as a representative of Ontologism, since he does not regard the primary object of knowledge, being, which is always present to the human mind, as the presence of God.

weh. Henceforward this practical monotheism sets Israel apart from all other peoples of the Near East. Although it is uncertain which route the people took at the exodus from Egypt, there are sound reasons for believing that the crossing of the Red Sea took place at the southern end of the Salt Lakes. But the question of how many Israelites entered Palestine from the east under the leadership of Joshua towards the end of the 13th century B.C. (=the end of the bronze age) remains obscure. Some tribes or parts of tribes could have returned by another way, or may never have migrated to Egypt at all.

3. The entry of the children of Israel into Palestine coincides with the political upheavals which were caused throughout the entire Near East by the incursion of the "Peoples of the Sea". As the "Philistines" (from whom the name Palestine is derived) these were to become, in the two centuries which followed, the mortal enemies of the twelve tribes. From time to time charismatic figures emerged from the individual tribes to lead the struggle against the Philistines and other hostile neighbours. Since they sometimes intervened vigorously to uphold law and order, they were called "judges". However, once the confederation of the twelve tribes had encountered the political and military unity of the Philistines, the call for a king in Israel became louder and louder.

4. The effect of the newly established Davidic monarchy (from 1000 B.C. onwards) was that the opposition between Judah, the tribe from which David came, and the northern tribes became, so to speak, constitutional. For the first king, Saul, had been chosen from the tribe of Benjamin. In the mighty "empire" which David founded these tensions were, it is true, to a large extent transcended. But immediately after the death of his son Solomon (990–930 B.C.) the kingdom split into two. The northern kingdom, to which the name "Israel" was henceforward exclusively applied, acquired its own sanctuaries at Bethel and Dan as the counterparts of the Salomonic temple at Jerusalem. The form in which Yahweh was honoured in the northern kingdom, as a young bull, was derived from Syro-Canaanite religion. Thus a religious cleavage followed upon the political one, and Israel was laid open to further influences from the fertility religions of the Canaanites.

5. The downfall of the northern and subsequently of the southern kingdom must be seen against the background of the political developments in Mesopotamia. In the second half of the 8th century B.C. Assyria came to the fore under Tiglath-Pileser III (745–727 B.C.). The peoples menaced by him combined under the leadership of Damascus in an anti-Assyrian league and made war on Judah (the Syro-Ephraimite war) to force it to join. Judah called upon Tiglath-Pileser III for help, and thereby became his vassal and liable to pay tribute to Assyria. It was in these years of the "war of nerves" that the Prophet Isaiah emerged in Judah, calling for confidence in Yahweh. Tiglath-Pileser III was succeeded by Shalmaneser V. Samaria, the capital of the northern kingdom, fell in the final year of his reign (722 B.C.). Tiglath-Pileser had already begun the deportation of the tribes of the northern kingdom, and Sargon II (722–705 B.C.) now completed this. In the meantime Egypt was stirring up hostility against Assyria. Babylon attempted to rebel, and Judah, still liable to tribute, made overtures to the Babylonian king, Merodach-Baladan (2 Kg 20:12f.). But Sennacherib, the Assyrian king, first subdued Babylon in 703 B.C. and then waged a triumphant campaign against the west, without taking the city of Jerusalem (701 B.C.). For all this period it is possible to compare the account in the Bible with the Assyrian war records inscribed in cuneiform on cylinders and prisms. In

the 7th century B.C. the Assyrians were occupied with Egypt and Babylon. Judah continued to be a vassal of Assyria, a circumstance which, from the religious aspect, had evil effects, above all under the reign of Manasseh.

6. Towards the end of the 7th century Babylon, under Nabopolassar, undertook together with the help of the Medes a successful rebellion against Assyria. Niniveh, the capital of the Assyrian empire, fell to the allies in 612. Neche II of Egypt decided to hasten to the aid of Ashur-Uballit, the last of the Assyrian kings, now broken and fleeing. King Josiah, who had been able to carry out a religious reform in Judah and also in the northern kingdom, failing to realize the new situation in world politics, set himself in his path. In 609, at Megiddo, he was utterly crushed. Soon afterwards Jerusalem was taken by Nabuchodonosor II (Nebuchadnezzar). According to the Babylonian cuneiform texts this was on the 15th–16th March in the year 597 B.C. (cf. 2 Kg 24:10–16). In 586 came the final destruction of the city and the second deportation into Babylonian captivity (2 Kg 25:8–11). Babylonian cuneiform tablets actually tell us the food rations allowed for the captive king of Judah at Babylon. Before the catastrophe the prophet Jeremiah had called upon the people to repent. During the exile it was chiefly Ezekiel who strengthened his fellow Israelites, and towards the end of the exile it was the great unknown author of Is 40–55 who consoled the humiliated people.

7. In the year 539 B.C. the fortified city of Babylon fell without a struggle to Cyrus, king of the Persians. This brought to a close the period of Semitic dynasties in the east. Henceforward Judah was subject to Persian, Hellenistic and finally Roman dominion. The religious tolerance of this new epoch made the return possible. The tribe of Judah turned this opportunity to good account. It was the birth of "Judaism". Since the exile this people had been dispersed through the entire world, becoming the Judaism of the diaspora. For the future its power was to lie not in the political strength of a royal house but in the religious sense of the individual Jew. From this period onwards the synagogue structure was the mainstay of its religion.

8. In the 5th century the Greeks brought the Persian onslaught on the west to a halt. In the meantime in Palestine, which had, for purposes of exterior politics, been absorbed into the system of Persian satrapies, the Jewish people consolidated their position. The building of the "Second Temple" was on a modest scale. In the middle of the 5th century B.C. Nehemiah, followed by Ezra, probably at the beginning of the 4th century, renewed the liturgy, strengthened the hierarchy and the sense of nationhood, and deepened the people's love for the sacred Scriptures, which were now assembled and edited.

9. After Alexander the Great had conquered Darius III (at Issus in 333), Hellenism dominated the east in the political, economic and cultural fields, and to some extent in the sphere of religion. However, the Jewish people had in the meantime so recovered their strength that they were able to absorb the new intellectual impulses without losing their special religious character. In the 3rd century the Jews of the Diaspora in Alexandria acquired the Greek translation of the Bible known as the Septuagint. It was at this time too that the Wisdom literature came to the fore. In this period of the Diadochi Palestine changed its political masters five times. Finally, in 200, after the Battle of Paneion (later Caesarea Philippi) it finally passed from the Ptolemies who resided at Alexandria to the Seleucids with their seat at Antioch on the Orontes. These ruled over Asia Minor, Syria and Mesopotamia. But from 190 onwards they were exposed to pressure from the kingdom of Pergamum, which was

already in alliance with Rome. Then Antiochus IV Epiphanes, ruling over a kingdom which was more Oriental than Greek, turned once more against Egypt and tried to force his own national and religious culture on his Jewish subjects. He imposed his will on Jerusalem, but the country areas were roused to active hostility against him.

10. Under the leadership of Mattathias, a priest of Modein, and his five sons, one of whom Judas, was called the Maccabee ("hammerer"), the people launched the "holy war" (167–164). On the 25th Kisleu, exactly three years after the temple at Jerusalem had been profaned (cf. 1 Macc 1:59 with 1 Macc 4:52), the monotheistic worship was restored. To this day the memory of this event is kept alive among the Jewish people by the feast of the dedication of the temple (cf. Jn 10:22). The primary purpose of the Maccabean rebellion, namely the right to practise the Jewish religion freely, was achieved. This religious war was now followed by a war waged with great strategic and diplomatic skill for the restoration of Jewish power in Palestine and the extension of Jewish territory. By an adroit exploitation of the struggle for the throne in Syria, and by a policy of alliance with Rome, which had in the meantime subdued Greece, the Maccabees were able stage by stage to loosen the ties which bound them to the kingdom of the Seleucids. From 142 onwards, under the leadership of Simon, who was at once high priest and military and political leader, the political independence of the Jewish nation was an accomplished fact. Politically powerful, but not over-scrupulous in religious matters, this newly established dynasty of the Hasmonaeans ruled the Jewish nation and enlarged its territories southwards (Edom) and especially northwards. Now (*c.* 100) for the first time since Tiglath-Pileser III under whom its population had been deported, Galilee became once more a Jewish possession (cf. Mt 4:15; 26:73). But after the death of Alexander Jannaeus the house of the Hasmonaeans was divided against itself, and the Roman general Pompey, who was just then advancing into Syria, exploited this. In the year 63 he entered Jerusalem in triumph.

11. Twenty years later Herod I, known as the Great, the ambitious, cruel but politically adroit son of an Edomite master of the palace, was actually able to raise the Jewish nation once more to a certain degree of independence. In 40 he was crowned "king of the Jews" at the Capitol in Rome. His power, however, remained continually restricted and under the surveillance of Rome. At his death in 4 B.C., he bequeathed his divided kingdom to his sons Archelaus, Philip and Herod Antipas, who was to become the overlord of Jesus. After only ten years (A.D. 6), Archelaus was deposed by Rome for bad government (cf. Mt 2:22). He was succeeded by Coponius, the first Roman procurator, who took over the government in Judaea and Samaria. Normally residing at Caesarea, the city which Herod I had recently built by the sea, on festival days he would appear in Jerusalem, the religious capital of the region over which he ruled. Under one of his successors, Pontius Pilate (A.D. 26–37), Jesus of Nazareth began his public ministry. According to the most soundly based method of calculating, it was on Friday 7 April of the year 30 that he was crucified by the Romans at the instigation of the Jewish authorities. The most important extra-biblical source for this event is the Roman historian Tacitus, who records in his account of the persecution of "Christians" by Nero in 64 that "this name derives from Christus, who suffered the extreme penalty during the reign of Tiberius, at the hands of the procurator Pontius Pilate" (*Annals*, XV, 44).

12. In 41–44 the period of the procurators was briefly interrupted by the

reign of the Jewish King Agrippa I, a friend of the Emperor Caligula. After his death the Roman procurators took over the entire territory, including Galilee. It was here precisely that the "first Jewish war" broke out in 66 (so called to distinguish it from the "second Jewish war", A.D. 132–35). The aim was to restore the dominion of God over his people. But in A.D. 70 Jerusalem was conquered by Titus, the temple was destroyed, and sacrificial worship finally brought to an end. This marked a turning-point in the history of the people. Even Jewish historians can hardly fail to recognize it as such. Early Christianity, which had at first counted as one of many Jewish sects, was now recognized even among pagans as a religion distinct from Judaism. The Christian Church felt itself to be the true people of God, the new Israel whose king is Christ, the Messiah promised by the prophets (cf. Rom 11:26; Rev 7:4–8; 21:12).

Benedikt Schwank

OLD TESTAMENT THEOLOGY

1. *Historical background.* For over a thousand years Christian theology was predominantly, almost exclusively, biblical. In the 12th century a less biblical theology began with Peter Lombard and the Victorines. By the mid-13th century Bacon was complaining that the *Liber Sententiarum* had displaced the *Liber Historiarum* (Petrus Comestor) as a textbook. But to teach theology was still to expound Scripture: "magister theologiae legit sacram paginam". Such also was St. Thomas's view, though his compendium or *Summa* paved the way for an independent science of theology that was to depart more and more from Scripture. Even though the Protestants proclaimed the supremacy of Scripture, their theological tractates are quite speculative in character. For his part, Melchior Cano lays down the method of theology in his book *De Locis Theologicis*. Scripture is the first source or "topos" where we find arguments to be used in controversy and scholastic disputation. With the ascendancy of the controversial approach in theology, Scripture was relegated to second place and theological science felt less and less need to be biblical. The first Protestant reaction against a too speculative theology took place in orthodox circles in the 16th century, when Cocceius (Koch) advocated and elaborated a "covenant theology" (*theologia foederalis*). In the 18th century, instead of *dicta probantia, dicta improbantia* were sought against a dogmatic theology.

J. P. Gabler was the first to announce the programme of the new science: "Oratio de iusto discrimine theologiae biblicae et dogmaticae regundisque recte utriusque finibus" (1787). The former is historical and sets forth the thought of the biblical writers. The latter is dialectical and sets forth the thought of contemporary theologians. The two complement each other. This notion of biblical theology as a historical and descriptive science became predominant with rationalism, and led to a type of "history of the religion of Israel", which was the negation of theology. The descriptive work was either systematic or chronological. Some extracted the underlying rational principle of the Bible, others registered the ideas and experiences of the biblical authors. Some merely described, others systematized on the basis of some philosophy – especially Hegel's. Believers, like Stendel (1840), Hävernick (1848), Oehler (1845, 1873), and J. C. F. Hofmann (1841, 1852), were exceptions and do not change the general picture. Critical study of the Bible finally (with Wellhausen) established a new and more accurate chronology and fortified the rationalist and purely descriptive approach to the religion of Israel: Smend, Giesebrecht, Marti,

Budde, etc. Karl Barth's admonitions and the situation after the First World War paved the way for a return to biblical theology. First there were a few articles (Steuernagel, Eissfeldt), Hänel's essay and the teaching of Procksch (whose works were published posthumously in 1949). In 1933 Sellin's short book and Eichrodt's monumental first volume appeared, followed by Köhler (1936), Eichrodt's second volume (1939), and Heinisch (1940). Biblical theology has flourished since the Second World War, with O. J. Baab (1949), Procksch (1949), T. C. Vriezen (1949), G. E. Wright (1952), E. Jacob (1955), von Rad (1958, 1960), G. A. F. Knight (1958), and others. At present the field is dominated by Eichrodt and von Rad, the protagonists of two fundamentally different methods. Eichrodt tries to make out a strict pattern, starting with the covenant as a historical and constitutive fact, its prescriptions, its organs and its fullness (the second volume does not achieve quite the cohesion of the first). Von Rad says that there can be no system, because Israel's religious life is essentially dynamic, the continuous actualization of its traditions, so that the theologian can only recount the process, and the reader is shown a procession of OT theologians, major and minor, Yahwist and Deuteronomist, Isaiah and Zaphanaih. Vriezen constructs a more systematic order: God – man; relations between God and man; relations among men; God, man and the universe now and in the future.

2. *Method.* a) Biblical theology, being theology, starts with the faith. Not that it claims to discover the faith in its present state in the OT – since revelation is historical and dogma evolves – but it works within the living context of the faith, the faith is its light and guide, the driving force behind its search.

OT theology tries to understand organically the revelation imparted by God in the historical economy of the OT and registered in the canonical books of the OT. Since that revelation is essentially historical and since history is the channel of revelation, OT theology must bring out the historical aspect of revelation. And so it uses the data provided by historical criticism in order to set the process of revelation in its proper historical context. OT history is not mere succession, it is movement towards a goal which determines that movement. Accordingly, OT theology must not describe the process of revelation in terms of mere genetic development, taking a profane view of the evolution of doctrine, but recognize how revelation moves towards the goal that draws it on: Christ, the synthesis and crown of revelation. A complete theology of the OT must include this Christ-directed dynamism. Being an economy that has been translated into words, the OT is intrinsically bound up with religious life: the life of Israel as "the people of God". The word is something active, a part of history, an authentic expression of that life. So OT theology will not merely catalogue theories or isolated thinkers. Becoming God's word through the charism of inspiration, the OT economy takes on all the qualities of God's word, one of which is the power to appeal to men of every age: "The word of God endures from generation to generation." OT theology must make that truth clear. Like all real theology it starts from the faith and returns to the faith.

b) As biblical theology it is distinguished from dogmatic theology because it deals with the documents of the OT: the formularies in which the faith has been couched down to the present time and the elaborations of dogmatics enlighten and guide biblical theology but are not the material it studies. Comparing its findings and formulas with the formulas of dogmatics is a secondary matter for biblical theology. Its business is not to supply arguments for a dialectical theology to use in polemics or disputation. On account of its time-conditioned character, going hand in hand with the process of revelation, the OT formula cannot always be reduced to the modern formulation, and it is not the task of biblical theology to do so. Its help is called for on a different, deeper plane – as the bridge between exegesis and dogmatic theology. First, because it selects: exegesis must cope with a great many factors, whereas theology selects "theological" data to work on; second, because it takes thought, asks questions, draws conclusions, works out new formulae that are more accurate or less complicated; third, because it organizes material in partial syntheses or complete ones. The results of this labour necessarily benefit dogmatic theology, which in its turn asks biblical theology valuable questions and offers general orientations.

c) OT theology is part of biblical theology, not simply in the quantitative sense but very much in the qualitative as well: such is the bond between the two testaments, as economies and as books. The NT makes abundant use of the OT: by way of messianic argument, to illustrate its own doctrine, or to probe into the mystery of Christ.

This use is not always equivalent to a critical interpretation of a text in its primary meaning. But the NT is the destination of the great movement of the OT, and therefore those who elaborate OT theology must bear the NT in mind, while differentiating critically between them.

d) Besides God's revelation in an initial state, the OT also contains much human theological reflection upon that revelation, reflection which is trustworthy because it too is the word of God. We may speak of a theological activity within the OT, of a theological concern which many of the sacred writers had to delve ever deeper into the meaning of God's saving deeds. To distinguish clearly between direct revelation and the thoughts of men in the OT is very difficult, and perhaps not always necessary. But it is always necessary to examine the techniques by which the various authors hand on God's message, whether in prophetic utterance or human meditation. Among the tools of the inspired theologian is symbolism. A great deal of prophetic literature is poetry, and the poet naturally thinks and speaks in symbols. Moreover, the historical books tell of institutions that have a symbolic function. Much of this symbolism is embodied and expanded in tradition. The themes are less fixed than the symbols and offer more facilities of systematization to the investigator (Guillet). There are also a number of concepts which are progressively spiritualized, or defined, or altered, or which fall into groups. These are exploited by dictionaries of biblical theology (Kittel, Bauer, Léon-Dufour). In the OT we often encounter literary units with well-marked structures, some of them purely formal but many full of theological significance. So it is essential to discover, examine and explain these structures, which show on the level of the inspired book internal relations with the mystery of salvation (the literal sense). Deut 26, for example, is built about the key-word "enter". There are concentric devices in poetry and prose, refrains appended to the narrative, schemes of literary genres used in the matter proper to them or transferred to other matter. These structures, genres, and so forth contain formulae, either fixed or slightly variable, which sometimes have or acquire a theological significance. Biblical theology can accurately determine the purpose behind the constructions of some sacred writers and the main ideas of others, disclosing partial syntheses within the OT. But the total synthesis will be the work of the investigator, and so there will be various theologies of the OT. What matters is that the system is not altogether alien to the inspired book, artificially imposed on it from without, but flows in some sense from the broad outlines of OT revelation.

3. *A synthesis.* Israel's religious life starts from an encounter with God: God intervenes in history to bestow salvation. Instructed by the mediator's words, Israel comes to know this active presence of God as "salvation". New saving deeds, perceived to be such, mark a continuing revelation, a salvation that lasts through history, preparing a decisive new encounter in institutional terms: the covenant. God offers Israel a religious life with him which makes it "the people of God", specially appointed to receive, guard, and hand on revelation and salvation.

The covenant embraces the basic elements of religious life.

a) *On God's part.* (i) *History*, that is, the saving deeds of the past, accumulated during a historical process, falls into a coherent pattern and forms the basis of God's offer. This formal offer that God makes is a summons, a demand, and at the same time gives men the power to accept or reject it as they will – only it does not leave them indifferent.

(ii) *Rules for living with God.* The holy God reveals the order through which he wills to save man. Thus law, or commandments, are part of the covenant, the living revelation of divine love, able to create new history in a new order.

(iii) *Blessings and curses.* In this form the goods and ills of life and history enter into the basic framework of religion. They are part of living with God; as reward and punishment they become a revelation and direct the course of history.

b) *On the people's part.* The people's response to the offer of the covenant must be a thoroughgoing acceptance: the basic act of faith, total surrender, responsible assent to the commandments. This basic attitude is particularized in active recollection (especially that of worship) of God's saving deeds and in the observance of the commandments.

In the properly religious sphere, Israel must offer God an exclusive worship of prayer and sacrifices (without images).

(i) *Prayer* begins with invocation of the name: God reveals his name so that man may call on him, and promises to hear. Man speaks the name either to glorify God, e.g., in hymns of praise and thanksgiving – or beg his help, in lamentations and supplications.

(ii) *The sacrifices* must embody man's real sentiments; only so do they please God and nourish man's religious life. They may express either homage, or thanksgiving, or expiation.

Profane life is not neutral ground. It is closely bound up with religion. The people have their political life, but they are the people of God, above all through the assembly for worship. They till the soil, but it is God's soil, promised and bestowed by him, watered by his rain – his blessing. The weekly cycle leads smoothly to the Sabbath rest, and the yearly cycle moves round from great feast to great feast.

c) *The people*, and the individual member of the community, may react to the covenant in the wrong way: forgetting God's benefits, ceasing to trust in him, transgressing the commandments which Israel has undertaken to keep.

That is sin, an intensely personal thing: not the violation of a purely objective order but an offence against a person, which "provokes" God and stirs up his wrath. God's wrath fully revealed and deployed is "eschatological" punishment, final exclusion of the individual or group from the covenant, through tragic, untimely death, or exile and the loss of national identity. If God's wrath is confined within the covenant, punishment becomes salutary, an invitation to repentance, a disclosure of the malice of sin and the patience of God.

It is necessary for God to take the initiative before anyone under wrath can return to favour, passing from sin to grace. This may take the form of a salutary chastisement or lesson, a call through the prophets or a list of charges in divine worship. Worship has its set means of restoring the people or an individual to grace: days of expiation, and sacrifices. But these must issue from the heart and not be empty forms that leave man unconverted.

As sin and forgiveness follow one upon the other, a pattern may become established: blessing – sin – chastisement – forgiveness – blessing tempting us to see history as a chain of almost natural or unfailing cycles. But the passage from sin to grace remains manifold and unpredictable, revealing the sovereignty of God.

The covenant is at once stable and dynamic. It grows because redemptive history evolves through new deeds of God. It grows by adopting new laws – even purely human and profane ones – to regulate the life of the people of God. It grows because the people acquire an even deeper understanding of their God. It grows by adopting a human wisdom which it links with and subordinates to revelation.

Living with God, the people steadily discover, experience, and penetrate the perennial features of God's works, his "ways": mercy and faithfulness, closeness and remoteness, love and wrath, might and wisdom, holiness. Moreover, they come to know themselves better before God: their own frailty and sinfulness, the meaning of life, values and historical destiny.

When the people have known their God as the author of history, they are able to gaze beyond the context of their election. Then what was revealed in germ begins to unfold.

(i) Henceforward the history of the deliverance is prefaced by the history of the patriarchs, now regarded as the pre-history of salvation: it reveals a current in history towards a future that has become the present.

(ii) The people look back in time beyond the patriarchs to the origin of man and the origin of the universe: their God is the creator of the world. In the spatial order God appears as Lord of all the nations, whom he rules and judges in history.

(iii) This wider vision of God also enriches the people's vision of themselves. Israel has a better grasp of its missionary task among the other peoples, its function as witness to the Lord. Moreover, it understands the fact and origin of man's universal sinfulness. It invites the universe to glorify the Creator.

Two striking facts stand out in the history of salvation and the people's grasp of it: one is grace, and the other is chastisement.

A king and dynasty are chosen for mediation and continuity. Raised to a sovereign dignity by his anointing, the king is identified with the people of God and responsible for them. Within the assimilative context of the covenant, the monarchy absorbs and embodies a number of potent symbols connected with priestly mediation and royal deliverance. Symbols native and foreign and a variety of historical experiences gradually form a complex image in the king's sacred person.

Dynastic continuity also acts as a constant reminder of God's faithfulness. It develops and purifies Israel's consciousness of history as a movement towards a future. The association of glorious symbols with crushing calamities, of poetic visions with the bitter experiences of history, produces a maturer expectation, a yearning for the future, and redirects the religious life of Israel. Continuity points to a consummation, the person of the king foreshadows a Saviour.

Exile is the great historical chastise-

It is an indeterminate ideal being (*essere ideale indeterminato*) which is distinct from God.

But the central notions of Ontologism are in fact to be found in many Christian philosophers who came into contact with the thought of Gioberti in the middle of the 19th century. It was a time when with the earlier forms or Christian philosophy devalued by Kant, and the inadequate efforts of the Traditionalists rejected by the Church, an effort was being made to find new bases for Christian philosophy. Hence Gioberti's ideas found a ready welcome, first in Italy (T. Mamiani della Rovere, *Dell'Ontologia e del Metodo* [1841]) and then in Belgium (G. C. Ubaghs, *Essai d'idéologie ontologique* [1860]), where Gioberti was living in exile. Ubaghs, who came under censure for the ontologist nature of his lectures at Louvain after 1840, resigned his chair in 1866. From Belgium, the doctrine spread quickly in France about the middle of the century (L. Brancherau, *Praelectiones Philosophicae* [1849], J. Favre d'Envieu, *Défense de l'ontologisme* [1861]). When Ontologism was condemned by the Church in 1861, it represented the predominant trend of Christian philosophy.

3. *Ecclesiastical condemnation.* Since Ontologism was regarded as containing the dangers of pantheism and rationalism, the Holy Office condemned seven theses in 1861 as "unsafe to teach". They were: (i) Immediate knowledge of God is essential to human understanding. (ii) The being, without which we know nothing, is the divine. (iii) The universals are really identical with God. (iv) We know implicitly in God all other beings. (v) All other ideas are only modifications of this idea. (vi) Created things are outside the indivisible God but still as it were parts of him. (vii) God creates a creature in the same act by which he knows and wills himself as distinct from it. Though some Ontologists had to recant explicitly, most of them did not feel that they came under the condemnation, since the theses in question were felt to be a distortion of Ontologism. It was not till the publication of the encyclical *Aeterni Patris* in 1878 had helped neo-scholasticism to establish itself that Ontologism ceased to be propounded as a system.

4. *The real issue.* It is possible to invoke Bonaventure for something similar to Ontologism when he says that it is the divine being which "is first seen by human reason, and without this it can see nothing" (*Itinerarium Mentis ad Deum*, c. 5). But Bonaventure cannot be said to have had the context of 19th-century philosophy in mind, and the formulas of Ontologism are to be rejected insofar as they affirm the perpetual presence of God to human reason in the form of an object. Nonetheless, there is a justifiable purpose behind this assertion, one which was native to the Augustinian tradition and to which Christian philosophy is again devoting its attention today. It is the effort to explain how the non-objectivated grasp of being, which is characteristic of the human mind, is related to the knowledge of God, "self-subsistent being", and whether this does not imply a non-objectivated experience of God prior to and at the basis of all proof of the existence of God.

Albert Keller

ONTOLOGY

1. *The term.* The term "ontology" is first found in R. Goclenius (*Lexicon Philosophicum*, 1613). The usage spread (J. Clauberg, *Metaphysica de Ente* [1656], J. B. Du Hamel [1678]), and came to be a technical term in philosophy through the writings of C. Wolff (*Philosophia prima sive ontologia* [1729]). According to its Greek components (τὸ ὄ, λόγος), it means the doctrine about that which is.

2. All sciences treat of beings, since they take various realms of beings and investigate them under certain aspects. But ontology differs from all other sciences insofar as its object is not a limited field of beings but that which is, as a totality, treating it not from a limited aspect but precisely insofar as it is. Hence ontology may be defined as the science of that which is as such. Ontology then seems to coincide with metaphysics or indeed philosophy in general, whose various regions such as ethics or epistemology would then merely be sub-divisions of ontology. But in the course of philosophical thought they have been distinguished from it in various ways.

3. *History*. In classical times, philosophy, which was still considered as the comprehensive heading for all systematic knowledge, was divided by the Platonist Xenocrates into dialectics, physics and ethics – a division still accepted by Augustine (*De Civitate Dei*, 8, 4). Dialectics had the task of going beyond the world investigated by physics to the order of the forms or ideas, the realm of that which really is (the ὄντως ὄν), so that what was later known as ontology should be ranged under the heading of dialectics. Aristotle, however, regarding dialectics as a logical procedure which was rather a prelude to philosophy itself, assigned his "first philosophy" or "theological science", dealing with that which is as such (ὂν ᾗ ὄν, *Metaphysics*, 6, 1), to theoretical philosophy. Here it is contrasted with the "second philosophy", sub-divided into physics and mathematics. It was later called metaphysics. Scholasticism followed in general the division of Aristotle. It is clear throughout the whole of this pre-Cartesian philosophy that ontology, already described by Aristotle as the doctrine of that which is as such, was not distinguished from metaphysics. And metaphysics always treated of God as the ground of all beings, as that which most supremely and truly is, or as being itself.

After Thomas Aquinas, and under the influence of Avicenna, being understood as the existent was contrasted with essence, whose relation to it was contingent (Suarez). It was then possible to establish a science of beings which prescinded from existence and dealt with beings insofar as they at least *could* be (*ens nominaliter sumptum*). This was general metaphysics, contrasted with special metaphysics which treated of beings which actually were – God in natural theology, the soul in psychology, corporal things in cosmology. This division became the ordinary one under the influence of Wolff, who also called general metaphysics ontology and hence fixed for a long time the meaning of the word and its demarcation as regards metaphysics.

Kant also treated ontology as part of metaphysics. But it was no longer concerned with beings in themselves. It was the science which was "a systematizing of all concepts and principles, but only insofar as they are concerned with objects presented to the senses and are hence verifiable by experience. Ontology is not concerned with the suprasensible, which is the ultimate goal of metaphysics. It belongs therefore to the latter only as propaedeutics, like the entrance-hall or forecourt to metaphysics itself, and is called transcendental philosophy, because it contains the conditions and first elements of all our *a priori* knowledge" (*Über die Fortschritte der Metaphysik*).

Hegel also was familiar with Wolff's division and called ontology, which was the "first part of metaphysics" in this division, "the doctrine of the abstract determinations of essence" (*Enzyklopädie*, 3.3, paras. 33–36). But for Hegel himself, logic takes over the tasks of ontology, since he affirms that "the rational is real and the real rational" (*Philosophy of Right* [E.T., 1942], Introduction): the structures of thought are those of the Absolute and hence of being.

Ontologism has a certain affinity with this way of thinking, while the rest of post-Hegelian thinking in the 19th century mostly eliminated ontology from "scientific philosophy".

After Husserl, however, who divided up ontology (the "eidetic" science or the "science of essence") into various regional ontologies corresponding to the various "regions" of empirical objects (*Ideas*, I, para. 9), the reaction against neo-Kantianism brought about in the present century a "rebirth of ontology", as it has been described by N. Hartmann. Hartmann himself is one of the most important representatives of this "new ontology". The main difference between this and the older metaphysics, according to Hartmann, is the new way of solving old questions, since it no longer claims to attain the intrinsic, unchangeable structures of being, which are said to be for the most part irrational. Ontology merely tries to analyse the changing world of phenomena, the only real world, into its categories, degrees and relationships. In contrast to this ontology, entirely orientated to objects, there is the fundamental ontology of Heidegger which starts from (human) existence. Its "existential analysis" is to show that being in the existent is the ground of the understanding of being (cf. M. Heidegger, *Kant and the Problem of Metaphysics* [E.T., 1962], no. 42). In addition, neo-scholasticism has an ontology inherited from the Middle Ages, which is rooted in the pre-Socratics but was greatly modified in the course of history and enriched with new findings and questions. Efforts are made to insert it into present-day philosophy, but success will undoubtedly depend on further transformations.

4. *Systematic survey*. a) *Its place in philosophy*. Ontology considers that which is as such, not primarily in its relation to human knowledge or will and desire, as in epistemology or ethics, and prescinding for the moment from the fact that being, its formal object, is only known insofar as man is orientated to it (see *Psychology*), and insofar as it is mediated by the world (see *Natural Philosophy*).

Insofar as this formal object itself is considered, ontology becomes the philosophical doctrine of God, with which it was originally identified (see *Natural Theology*). But it is also difficult to make a sharp distinction between ontology and the other philosophical disciplines, of which the most important traditional ones have been mentioned above. For it leads naturally to these considerations of how beings as such are related and appear, even though the specific task of ontology is to consider that which is as such, that is, prescinding from such further relationships.

b) *Possibility and method*. True assertions about that which is as such must be valid for all beings. Hence the possibility of ontology depends on whether true universal propositions are possible for an unlimited field of objects. At any rate, they could not be shown to be true for us if they had to be arrived at inductively from experience (they include, for instance, future events). Ontology can only be a science if we dispose of insight into necessary truths, valid always for their whole field of objects, prior to experience. And the propositions in question cannot be merely analytical, if ontology is to be more than meaningless tautologies. The accessibility of such synthetic judgments *a priori* must be demonstrated by epistemology.

c) *That which is, from the aspect of being. Principles and transcendentals*. Our insight into synthetic *a priori* judgments is based on a knowledge of being which makes human experience possible, and does not therefore result from experience, though it only becomes conscious knowledge through experience. Our possession of such knowledge is evident from our knowledge of the metaphysical principles or transcendental "notes" of being. In the principle of non-contradiction, which includes the principle of the excluded middle and of identity, we express, for instance, our insight into the truth that being, and only being, excludes non-being and only non-being. When this is applied to beings it means that it is impossible for something not to be, insofar as it is. This proposition is so evident that it can hardly be said to have ever been contested. But it does not stem from our empirical experience, which can never provide us with absolute impossibility. We know *a priori* that being has the "note" of excluding non-being. Since judgments expressing such *a priori* truths are the starting-points for further knowledge (and every conclusion not only itself represents such an insight into a necessary sequence of truths but also demands, by virtue of its validity, that at least one of its premisses go back ultimately to such a judgment), they are called principles. The "notes" which necessarily belong to being are called transcendentals.

The most important *a priori* judgment for our knowledge is, after the principle of non-contradiction, that of causality, i.e., that everything, insofar as it has being contingently (=not necessarily), has it through a cause. For it is only through the principle of causality that it seems possible to deduce from the (contingent) existence of a being the necessity of the existence of another.

The transcendentals are the various notes of being either in itself or in its necessary relationships. Apart from those expressed in the principles (which are often not considered as transcendentals), it is generally taken that unity is the characteristic of being in itself, truth the characteristic in relation to knowledge and goodness or worth in its relation to the will. When applying this to beings, we say: Each thing that is, insofar as it has being, is one, true and good. Other transcendentals may be envisaged, but they all form a unity, since they add nothing real to being but only explicitate it, since being, without non-being, comprises in itself all positive determinations.

d) *Finiteness, analogy, categories.* By virtue of this positive non-limitation of being, being must be distinguished from (finite) beings (the "ontological difference"). Such beings only participate or share in being – they do not have, of course, "part" of being. Being is theirs not simply and strictly but only analogously, that is, inextricably linked with non-being. This merging of being and non-being is the condition in which finite beings exist in their multiplicity and mutual exclusivity. Since even in abstraction their being cannot be clearly distinguished from non-being, individual beings are at one only in analogous being, not in having the same being. Hence all efforts to divide up these beings into a number of neatly defined categories are always to a certain extent arbitrary and do not find general acceptance. The division which was maintained most persistently was that of the categories of Aristotle, centred on the distinction between substance and accident, that is, on beings existing in themselves and the modifications inhering in them. But even here it is hard to say which determinations inhere and which are substantial. Nonetheless, our language still has to make use of some such division of the realm of beings – the categories, even in Aristotle, are primarily types of propositions – since language can only take in this realm with the help of universal concepts. It can only indicate the singular but not express it, since the singular cannot be exhausted in any general concepts and is only to be known in actual encounter.

Hence the more ontology is confined

to the universal, the easier will the intellect be able to deal with it; but it will remain in the same proportion aloof from the special character of the individual and the concrete historical situation. It will be all the more laborious, the more it deals with these latter and confronts the empirical. The most pressing task of ontology today is to face this painful task without shirking.

Albert Keller

ORDER

I. Concept of Order

1. *Meaning*. Order is a unity of many elements systematically referred to each other. These must be different from one another but they must be in a possible relation to each other and in a real order also existent (Thomas Aquinas, *De Potentia*, q. 7, a, 11, c.). The unity need not be rounded off, but may be open – as in the series of natural numbers. The rule which determines how the elements follow or proceed from each other in a dynamic order is called for preference law, or, in planned action, method. When the rule lays down the situation of the elements in a static order, it is rather called the schema, pattern or disposition. The formal aspect produced by this principle of order in a dynamic order is called its direction, finality or entelechy. In the static order it is called the structure or – with reference to perception – the form (*Gestalt*).

2. *Classification*. According to the various relationships which they have to the orderly spirit of man, three main groups of order are distinguished: the natural order (the cosmos), which is there prior to man and which he needs only to discover; the ethical order and the logical order which are imposed on him and whose norms he recognizes as pre-existent but must explicitate and follow in his thinking and willing; finally, the order of culture and technology which man develops according to his needs, primarily in the light of the prior order of ethical norms (the order of law) or of laws of nature (technical structures), or again – as he sketches out according to his disposition – games with rules, clothing according to the dominant fashion, even works of art according to canons of style.

The peculiar nature of the members of an order also determines its structure. If the order is a closed unity, of which the members are not independent but can only be seen as parts of the order, we speak of a whole or totality, of which the organism is the most impressive example. If the structure combines the various elements in a way which corresponds to our aesthetic sense, we speak of a harmony. According to the principle of order, the point of view according to which the elements are arranged, the primordial form of which is precedence and posteriority (simple juxtaposition is not an order), we distinguish the spatial order (according to distance in like or various proportions from a given point, or conformity with a given plan or model); the temporal order (simply continuous or periodically returning sequence); the order of rank (according to the dependence of elements from one another or their conformity with a prior order of values); the causal order (according to the various types of causes and the relationship of cause and effect); the highest is the order of finality, the order of ends, which for man is the archetype of all order, since by virtue of his rational action he sees in the structure of order a goal attained or to be attained by the combination of the elements. Finally, the orders must be distinguished according to the (human) faculty which can discern them, as, for instance, the rational order, beside or in contrast to the "ordo amoris" (M. Scheler) or "ordre du cœur" (B. Pascal).

3. *History*. Since order is so important in human life, it is not surprising that the problem of order has been one of the great preoccupations of philosophy since the beginning. Mythological thinking began by trying to grasp the origin and structure of the world and the meaning of human destiny by linking them to orders and images transferred from human life into the sphere of the divine. Pre-Socratic philosophy sought for the ἀρχή which determined an orderly world, as they experienced it. Among the Pythagoreans, for instance, number was the principle of order, while for Anaximander the Illimited (*apeiron*) was the orderly material of the cosmos. It is precisely the order of the world, not the presence of matter (which was the material prior to the world and hence of itself totally disordered) which Plato and Aristotle sought to explain by the organizing power of the Demiurge – like the Logos of Heraclitus – and the form or idea as the principle of order. Order is structure, but it is above all the ordination to the good to which it is subordinated (cf. Aristotle, *Metaphysics*, XI, 1075a). Since for Christianity, matter itself is created, there is nothing outside the range of order. Creation is a comprehensive order, as is already clear from the creation narrative in Genesis, particularly in the imagery of the six days of creation. Hence the conviction that all things are good, in contrast to the Greek tendency to see matter as a principle of disorder and then of evil, since evil is departure from the norm, the obligatory order, and matter is prior to the order imposed by creation. But then evil is an especially grave problem for Christians, who are convinced that all is ordained by God. Augustine's *De Ordine*, one of his early works, is chiefly preoccupied with this question. The Middle Ages took over from Augustine and the neo-Platonist tradition the notion of the hierarchical structure of the world, in which everything has or strives for the place assigned to it in the eternal plan of creation in the mind of God. Since the supreme good to be realized in the world is the whole order which corresponds to this plan, an evil can still be meaningful if it serves the realization of the universal order (cf. Thomas Aquinas, *Summa Theologica*, I, q. 49, a. 2).

In modern non-scholastic philosophy, the most important contribution to the discussion was made by Kant. According to Kant, sense perception with its *a priori* of space and time and the intellect with its categories import into nature the order which man finds there. The correct observation, that order depends on spirit, which was developed in German Idealism to the principle of the identity of the order of thought and the order of being, often led to the inclination, encouraged by Kant, to reduce all order to the human spirit, though the causal structure of nature – the natural constants in the inorganic and their development in the region of the vital – make the presence of a pre-existent order unmistakable. But even in these spheres an order of ends is denied, and the effort is often made to explain particular ethical norms as merely human conventions or the like and not as an order imposed on man. Such efforts have to leave unexplained the absolutely binding character of ethical norms.

Following Hegel, historical materialism sought to discover a fixed order of development in history. This view is in accord with the human conviction which naturally seeks to find order everywhere, so that thought may have a realm on which it can to some extent count. But the justification of historical materialism is still more questionable than the corresponding Christian effort of Teilhard de Chardin, who sought to indicate an intra-mundane goal to which the history of the universe was ordained as to its fulfilment. Such a view entails the risk, at the very least, of treating existing man as a mere transition to something future, whereas each human person is in himself the goal of world-order, and has to realize in himself a God-orientated order which is through man the ultimate order of the world.

4. *Significance of order*. Hence if man is to live properly in the world, he must take into account the order which he discovers there and then extends, since otherwise he could neither plan his life nor adjust to the world and still less adapt it to his own purposes. And he must also arrange his life with other men into social forms and his knowledge into science, since otherwise life and thought would be unmanageable guess-work. But above all, he must ordain life and thought themselves according to a norm, if they are to be meaningful – ultimately a norm prior to and imposed on him. For it cannot rationally be in the last resort a matter of arbitrary choice, since every rational choice can only be made in each case in view of a goal which is set it beforehand. Understood in this way, the principle of Thomas Aquinas (*Contra Gentiles*, I, 1), which ultimately goes back to Aristotle (*Metaphysics*, I, 982e), "sapientis est ordinare" contains the authentic programme of human life. It is the task of man to realize in himself and hence in the world, the right order.

Albert Keller

II. Order of Creation

This highly controversial term is used in modern Reformed theology to designate a number of social relationships such as marriage and family, people, State and economy (also the Church, according to Bonhoeffer) where everyone finds himself, including the Christian, prior to and independently of his being a Christian, so to speak, and where he is subject to the commandments which God gave as creator and to which he obliges all men (Lau, col. 1492). The content is more or less in line, therefore, with what Catholics understand by the *societas naturalis*, the natural law and the order of nature. To some extent, the concept of "order of creation" is more adequate to describe what is meant than that of natural law (Ratzinger, col. 465). It points explicitly to God the creator as the ultimate reason for the obligatory character of such orders of things, and avoids the danger of a purely static conception such as is implied in the concept of nature. It is significant that Vatican II also speaks of the laws and values which appertain to created things and societies, and which are to be acknowledged, used and put in their right hierarchy (Constitution *Gaudium et Spes*, art. 36).

But the concept is as problematic as the Catholic notion of natural law. According to the Catholic view, there is in fact no such thing as *natura pura*, because nature is entirely ordained to supernatural salvation and hence only exists as the refusal or the acceptance (at least implicit) of this salvation. So too the order of creation is entirely ordained to the God-man. The question arises, therefore, as to whether we are not always dealing with a reality comprised by grace, and one which is constantly being perverted by sin (as, for instance, in war or the death penalty). And there is the further question as to whether and how far man can recognize the order of creation without the light of revelation, or follow it out without the grace of redemption. This does not mean, however, that it may be reduced to positive theological law.

Pieter Smulders

III. Supernatural Order

1. "Order" may be understood to denote an interrelated system of distinct realities differing from one another in various ways, in which interrelation the individuals achieve the fulfilment proper

to them (to their "essence"), mutually contribute through their interdependence to this fulfilment of their nature, and so form a meaningful whole. The problem of order is therefore ultimately that of unity in multiplicity and multiplicity in unity. All order is based on the fundamental Christian principle that everything ultimately derives from a radically primordial unity, God, who, though absolutely One, is nevertheless able to create a genuine multiplicity. The one world is in fact such a multiplicity, in which each is related to all, constituting a unity held together as such by God. Order accordingly appears as the necessary presupposition of the world of becoming and as a goal in process of development and fulfilment (see *Order* IV, *Reign of God*). If plurality is real and not merely apparent, yet nothing can be purely and simply disparate, so that difference as such implies unity, then the concept of order is one of the fundamental features of a Christian conception of the world and of man. If an adjective is added to the word "order", it either denotes a particular domain of realities in contradistinction to others, with the order that it entails (e.g., political order), or it means the objective viewpoint and structural principle under which a plurality of whatever kind is thought of as ordered. This latter is what is meant by the supernatural order. This term indicates that in fact the whole multifarious reality of the world (of mind-endowed beings, including the angels) has the "supernatural" as its inner structural principle. This determines the beginning and end or goal of the whole "world" distinct from God, determining of course each of the various realities in the world in accordance with its own particular character.

2. *Content of the concept*. The meaning of the term is therefore primarily determined by the concept of the "supernatural" (see *Nature:* these provide the proofs for what is said here). By "supernatural" in the strict sense we mean God's free and unmerited self-communication, for this is neither necessarily entailed by the finite essence of any created spiritual being, nor can it be validly claimed from God's wisdom, goodness and justice. It is the miracle of God's sovereign love bestowing himself, not merely a created gift, and so constituting himself the creature's innermost reality and goal. The relation of gratuitous gift to its recipient characterizes God's self-communication not simply in regard to creatures envisaged as possible, but also in regard to real creatures, and even in regard to a real creature who freely and culpably has made himself positively unworthy of God's self-communication.

3. The supernatural order therefore involves the following: a) The world as a whole belongs to this order. The world itself of spirit and matter forms such a unity that the material world is not merely the external stage on which the history of the spiritual creature is deployed without itself being affected at all by that history. The unity of spirit and matter at least in man (and perhaps in an analogous essential interrelationship between world and angels) constitutes an intrinsic factor in spiritual history itself (see *Resurrection* II). Furthermore, God's supernatural offering of himself to the created spirit is the innermost and ultimate characteristic of this spirit in its total reality (not something added to whatever else it has) and decides its final condition of salvation or perdition. On this basis it can also be said that creation in the sense that it constitutes what is other than God, is in fact (by the free decision of God, in no way due to the created) to be understood from the outset as the condition and a factor of God's self-communication *ad extra*. God in fact created the world in order to have those to whom he could give himself. Nevertheless he could have created it even without the intention of com-

municating himself and even though he is free in regard to what he has in fact created in the world. The creation as it in fact exists is an element in the fundamental miracle of divine love in which God wills to give himself. Despite its supernatural character, therefore, the order of grace is not, in respect of the world as it in fact exists, a supplementary orientation added afterwards, directing towards higher, but extrinsic, goals. It is the world's innermost characteristic from the outset, not because it is demanded by the world's constitution but as self-transcendence, above and beyond what it is, towards immediate relationship with God. Such self-transcendence is a real possibility of the creature because from the start God willed and created it in the free act of a love in which God wills to give himself. In this way, however, the "supernatural" is precisely the first and ultimate characteristic of the created spirit and, in and with this, of the world as a whole. Everything proceeds from this saving will of God and is objectively directed towards the goal of that will, everything according to its kind.

b) The supernatural order therefore cannot be evaded. In the first place human knowledge cannot evade it. The spiritual creature must, it is true, come to know and acknowledge, explicitly or implicitly, as a gratuitous grace, its ordination towards God's self-communication. It must know its supernatural vocation to be a gratuitous grace. Consequently the elaboration of the concept of "pure nature" as a limiting case is possible and justified as a means of elucidating what actually exists. But our cognition always occurs within the order of grace and we cannot really escape from the dynamism of grace even in cognition, whether we are consciously aware of it or not. Consequently we cannot form any positive and unmixed idea, full, definite and certain in content, of what would still be found in a *natura pura* and what would not. We cannot, for example, know and state with absolute precision what in a purely natural order would remain of what we know as the spontaneous and unanalysed experience of freedom, guilt, etc. For these concrete realities are always experienced within the supernatural order. Nor is it necessary for us to be able to do so. We must therefore always have to take into account that even in regard to the objects and themes of philosophy, implications are involved which belong to the supernatural order, even if that is not known in explicit concepts (see *Philosophy and Theology*).

Above all, however, the supernatural order is inescapable for human action, even where man is not explicitly aware of this and does not realize that the presuppositions and goals of his action are constituted by God's supernatural saving will. In his action man cannot leave the order which is established from his beginning, the law according to which he has set out, the goal towards which he is directed by his actual concrete (and therefore supernaturally determined and orientated) nature. He can freely reject that supernatural order, but precisely by doing so he is adopting an attitude to it. He implicitly affirms it by the very act of rejecting it, just as a man affirms logic even if he rejects it by scepticism or relativism. In this sense the supernatural order, although freely established by God, has the character of "transcendental necessity" for human action.

c) The supernatural order is a personal order, an order of love in faith and hope. For of course the spiritual creature must be set in order by the integration of its whole reality and its historical activity into that love of God in which God himself makes himself man's innermost reality on man's behalf. This order is not first constituted by man's free action, firstly, because man's finite freedom has a nature and situation given it beforehand by God, and secondly, because man's freedom, which is always in the nature of a response, can only answer God because God gives himself in grace and thus again efficaciously makes possible what is most the creature's own – the loving obedience of its free acceptance of God. Nevertheless the supernatural order is a personal order because it signifies the real situation established in fact by God, that of personal loving freedom on the part of God and creature. That does not mean that the supernatural order can be reduced merely to a relation between God and man determined simply by the abstract, formal concept of personality. For "personal" and "constituted by grace" are not identical concepts. Nevertheless the supernatural order is only correctly viewed if it is understood not as if it were concerned with things, but as an order of which the personal as such is an essential formal characteristic.

d) The supernatural order is a historical order. That means that it constitutes the permanent structure of the history of salvation. From the outset the spiritual creature is inescapably orientated towards "participation in the divine nature". The history of that creature through all the "growth" and guilt of history consists, if the very essence of history is not missed, in the actual attainment of God's definitive self-communication in the beatific vision. All that happens in the history of the individual and of mankind has a closer or remoter connection with this ultimate determination and "teleology" of man, present from the beginning and constituted by the supernatural order. The historical character of the supernatural order also means that this order itself is not only the abiding structure of the history of salvation and consequently of the history of the world in general, but itself has a history. God's self-communication, which is what the supernatural order ultimately is, actualizes itself, has its own culmination in history, in the incarnation of the Logos. By this, God's self-communication becomes irreversible and the history of God himself appears and finds its perfect accomplishment in the kingdom of God in which God will be "all in all". The supernatural order is therefore not the extrinsic law of a history, but the abiding structure of the history itself, and reaches its own fulfilment in that history.

e) Since the supernatural order constitutes the structure of salvific history as it ought to be, as the history of finite freedom before God, directed towards direct union with him, it makes demands on man. Man has freely to accept and make his own the given and inescapable order of his history. To that extent, therefore, it has the character of law. But ultimately it has the same character as the demand involved in the personal offer of the love of God himself seeking to communicate himself. Such a demand is ultimately quite different from law in the sense of an objective norm distinct from the law-giver himself. The law of the supernatural order is one which is identical with the law-giver and his personal love; it is giver and gift in one. Here "Law and Gospel" are identical, and the gift becomes an external demand (a threatening law) only for those who have not responded to it and accepted it with love.

f) The supernatural order is a Christological order. Although it is a theologically controverted view, it can nevertheless be postulated that God's original intention in his self-communication, which gave the history of salvation its structure even before the Fall, was directed to the incarnation of the Logos as its historical, eschatological culmination. The incarnation, therefore, together with the glorification of Christ, which because of sin takes place through death, both manifests the supernatural order absolutely in history and definitively establishes it in the world. In other words, it is permissible to assume with Scotism that even supralapsarian grace was the grace of Christ, and that the supernatural order as such is Christological. Christ does not become and remain head and goal of saving history only when he enters into it because of sin. The supernatural order present in the history of salvation is from the outset of such a kind that God willed to communicate himself to the world in Christ in the Incarnation. That does not exclude, but includes, the fact that that history of salvation was likewise willed by God from the outset as the history of God's victorious self-communication to a world guilty of refusing him. God, that is, permitted sin in order to show the radical greatness of his self-giving love, by which he offers himself once more to man despite his rejection, and shows himself as greater and victorious in relation to man.

g) Because this victory of God's love takes place on the cross of the incarnate Son, the supernatural order is also always a "staurological order", an order of the cross. In its concrete realization, in the history of salvation, it is not purely and simply "growth" but a history which leads through cross and death. Here the supernatural order appears to disintegrate in an illusion which as the terrible reality of defeat can be grasped and accepted by man only by a greater love made possible by God himself.

Karl Rahner

IV. End of Man

1. *Introductory: the notion of "end"*. a) Man first learns what an "end" can be from his own immediate internal experience. He strives for a certain good (value) which he has before his mind and which he wills to attain. He chooses appropriate means – possibly by co-ordinating a number of parts into an instrument or machine – and sets them in motion towards the end in view. He sets himself an "end", consciously and deliberately chosen, and realizes it.

b) He then recognizes in the course of reflection that his deliberate choice of end or goal is submitted in his "faculties" and their structures to an *a priori* law which predetermines the direction and limits of his deliberate efforts (though leaving open a certain amount of variation). Since such a faculty (of biological or other character) is a complex system, it can be understood (on the model of a machine) from its performance, or, conversely, one can deduce from the structure of the complex system the "reason why" it is there. This "natural" end, and the direction towards the end ("finality") in a "natural" system, understood here simply as one not produced by man, throw light on each other and form a unity. The givenness of the end-directed system, and its power to come to terms with outside influences and so to maintain itself, make the "end" of the system appear as something which "ought" to be. The natural end appears as the full actualization of the structure ("essence") of a given (complex) system.

c) On this basis the living being (on the biological or conscious level) can be seen as a totality. As such, as one and as whole, it has a "natural end", the full development and actualization of the structures of its (complex) system.

2. *Formal application of the concept of end (and finality) to man.* a) From what has been said above, one could already make the formal affirmation: the ("natural") end of man is the full actualization of his being. This description (rightly) takes man's end as a unity, in spite of the plurality of his reality and in spite of the experience of disintegration (in concupiscence, illness and death). The goal is a single actualization in which the plurality of man is fully integrated. This end is "natural" (prescinding for the moment from the dis-

tinction between nature and [supernatural] grace), since, like the structures of man himself, it is there prior to man's free choice of goals. Hence to miss it must be harmful and destructive for the allotted reality of man and therefore also for the free choice of goals. But this notion of end, stemming primarily from mechanical and organic models, is not adequate of itself to determine the formal concept of the end of man, for reasons explained below.

b) In the analysis of the notion of the end of man, the peculiar unity in man of predetermined and freely chosen goal must be borne in mind. Man's "essence" sets his knowledge and action a predetermined goal, a "natural" end, which is more radically and essentially an "ought" (see below, d) than can be affirmed of any "end" of a mechanical or organic (biological) character. But the "end" of man, the content and mode of the self-understanding which he wills for himself as a totality, cannot simply be seen as one of a number of possibilities such as are given with the "nature" of any other (mechanical or organic) reality, and any of which ultimately corresponds to *such* "natural finality". Man, as personal consciousness and freedom, does not merely "work" a ready-made "machine", at most for better or for worse, productively or harmfully, while it remains otherwise the same prior datum, really only the substratum of its actuality (its *actus secundus*). Man disposes over his own *self*. He produces creatively the definitive nature of his being (see below, e). His essence is not just predetermined but a task set before him. Hence too his end is something which he not merely achieves but sets himself creatively in the concrete. His predetermined (natural) "end" is the charge of giving himself freely his own end. This "charge" is certainly not a mandate to be purely arbitrary. It does not open up a space of limitless and empty possibilities. But neither is it the programming of a course where all that remains in question is how far it really corresponds to the programme. The charge is precisely to be free, so that failure to carry out the charge consists precisely in not recognizing this freedom. (Since "sin" contradicts the essential finality of man, it is the refusal to deploy the whole unlimited range of freedom in the love of God as the infinite "good" – it is the restriction of freedom to a finite category of "good".) The predetermined end and the freely chosen end are intrinsically united in a mutal relationship.

c) The formal definition and the material description of the end of man (or of the morally relevant finality of a particular element of his being) must always take man's "intentionality" into account. This purposeful dynamism of intellect and will provides a critique of the organic and mechanical key-patterns and also a satisfactory answer to the question of the end (goal, meaning). Otherwise this question would have to be restricted to functional and provisional particulars (which serve the general end *once* this is presupposed as an ought) and would have to be declared meaningless with regard to the being as a totality. The "end" of an essentially purposeful ("intentional") being can only be determined by the "Whither" or goal of this intention. But if this intentionality is unlimited in knowledge and freedom, the intentional possession of reality as such (a possession which is very "real") is the end of this being, an end which is *quodammodo omnia*.

The end is therefore the limitless fullness of reality, i.e., "God", though this does not mean that the end is simply extrinsic, a ready-made goal lying ahead of the purposeful striving (see below, e). If then being and possession of being in consciousness (knowledge) and love are "meaningful" (and they are affirmed as such in every act, with transcendental necessity), i.e., if they are an end which does not merely function once more as a means to a further (wilfully chosen) goal, the question of the end finds a satisfactory answer.

d) In man – in contrast to biological finality and the patterns of representation stemming from it – the transcendental character of the ordination to the end must be taken into account. This alone gives the end the character of an absolute "ought", and makes it possible to see the attainment of the end as "salvation" in the strictly theological sense (and vice versa). This means that inasmuch as the ordination of the spiritual person to the end is again implicitly affirmed by him even when freely turning away from it, the end in question (and hence man's ordination to it) is not merely a "fact" (like subordinate goals which always remain provisional) but something necessarily affirmed. It is an "ought" with a moral claim (the *bonum honestum necessarium*), from which every other "ought" derives its value and obligation (as a means and partial realization). We may already note that even the "supernatural" end freely set before man by God is also transcendentally necessary. Through God's self-communication in grace, because of his universal salvific will, it is implanted in the being of every man prior to his free decision. (It is the "supernatural existential".) It is there in man either in the form of acceptance in faith and love, or in the form of rejection in sin. It can never be simply just something externally commanded, which can become immaterial to him through his freedom of indifference, as lying outside his movement towards his end.

e) A further aspect of the end of man must also be considered, if the ordinary patterns are not to hide its true nature. The unlimited transcendence of man and God's self-communication in grace to man mean that God is the (intended) end of man, which therefore precedes his free realization of his goal. It is predetermined and not that which man sets himself and produces. But this only means (in scholastic terms, see under 3) that the *finis qui* is simply predetermined, but not the *finis quo*, the actual possession of God, who furthermore takes this *finis quo* to himself as his own determination. (Here we must reflect on the mystery of the incarnation and on the fact that God is not merely the transcendent first cause but the subject of a history of salvation which is his own.) The end realized or to be realized in freedom and the predetermined end (see above, b) as the self-realizing end (*finis quo*) has to be set by the free act, creatively, in continual hope. Hence it cannot be simply regarded as the actuation of a potentiality, such as takes place outside the field of freedom. It is not just the evolution and flowering of what is already there. The goal of freedom, even where God himself is the end and absolute future (at least as the *finis quo*), is in the concrete the new goal freely chosen among many possibilities and creatively mapped out. The past, even as potentiality, is left behind by this incalculable future, in the light of which man understands himself creatively. Thus the end, in the case of historical freedom, cannot be merely the unfolding and actualization of the potentiality of the past. It is not a "return to paradise", the recapture of the past or the fetching home of the "essence" (see *Creation* IV). It cannot be so above all because the "new earth" is part of the absolute future (see K. Rahner, *Schriften zur Theologie*, VIII, pp. 580–92). The kingdom of God is the consummation of history itself and not just a subsequent reward of past history. God himself, through the incarnation, completes his own history in the completion of history. The end of man's history of freedom is not simply the goal which is set him, but the goal creatively sketched. Though he has a predetermined "essence", this "essence" (see above, b) is itself to some extent constituted by the "essence" of personal, historical freedom, which is not just an "accidental" determination added to a predetermined, ready-made subject but actually produces the reality of this subject. Indeed, since all causality except that of personal freedom only produces transient phenomena, which can be constantly replaced and surpassed by other phenomena, freedom is the only action which produces definitive meaning. Hence the free realization of the end is actually the only way in which a real "end" in the strict sense of the term can be brought about (see *History* I).

3. *Further distinctions and principles.* The distinction between the *finis qui* and the *finis quo* has already been mentioned. A further notion is often added, that of the *finis cui*, the subject for whom something is an end, for whom the end means full actualization. It is also obvious that an end in general can be something to be produced or to be achieved (*finis efficiendus* – *finis obtinendus*). One can also distinguish between the ultimate end, which means the full actuation of the being in question, and the particular end which is a means to or a moment of the all-embracing ultimate end. The end aimed at by an agent (*finis operantis*) need not coincide exactly with the end (usefulness) of what he produces (*finis operis*). Scholastic philosophy also affirms that God cannot have an end distinct from him which could move him like an external cause (*causa finalis*). (See *God, Glory of.*) This does not make God an "egoist". In his creative and grace-giving action he wills himself *as* the selfless goodness which can impart itself. The end exerts real causality. It is not merely the result or aim achieved or to be achieved by an action or process. It actually sets this action in motion, above all where the action is conscious, intentional. Contrasted with this, "teleological" processes of an unconscious character are to be interpreted as deficient realizations of being. A being which has no consciousness of itself is "still" a being, but its being is determined and limited by a real negativity. The end as the moving cause must, however, be understood in the sense explained above (see 2e).

4. *"Natural" and "supernatural" end of man.* (See *Nature* III, *Grace.*) The vision of God, the absolute future which is God himself in immediacy to man, and the ordination of man by grace to this final future are "supernatural". That is, they are a free, gratuitous act of God, not only with respect to man as a "possible" (who has to be "freely" created) but with regard to man in the concrete – prior even to his sin. But then this future becomes "obligatory", and without it man fails and is "lost". Hence the (real) end of man must be designated as "supernatural" (*DS* 3005, *finis supernaturalis*; *DS* 3891). The term "supernatural end" has been current since the 13th century. Nonetheless, one can only speak of a "natural end" of man with extreme caution. If a *natura pura* had ever existed, it would have had a "natural end" (which would have been completely different from the actual end of man, not just materially but also formally). And in the real order, as man now actually exists, there are elements which on this unreal supposition *would* belong to such a "natural end". But this does not justify one in speaking of a "natural end" of man as he actually is. Thomas Aquinas's language does not make the natural end an alternative to the supernatural end. The term in question always seems to suggest that man could decide at will for one or the other end. But the (last) "end" in the strict sense can only be the end which is actually proposed to man's freedom, which is to be realized by his freedom, which if missed is man's ruin. But this is the "supernatural" end. It can quite well be understood as supernatural and as intrinsic at the same time. For the "essence" or "nature" of man is that of a purposeful free being, whose "nature" it is to be open without limit

to the free disposition of God (as *potentia oboedientialis*). And the finality of man is not mechanical, organic or static, but must be seen from the outset in terms of a dialogal relationship between divine and human freedom. These constitute the end, so that the "nature" of man is only a formal and permanent pre-view of this relationship, but is not something which of itself constitutes this end. For the self-communication of God (grace), in spite of being supernatural, is the very "heart" of man.

5. *Systematic assertions about the supernatural end of man.* a) Man has an "end". This Christian conviction is the first thing that must be affirmed. It is not self-evident, least of all today. Present-day man is easily convinced that the "history" of the world and above all of man are the product of hazard in the interplay of causes. Many partial series of causes have in fact the character of hazard, that is, their result cannot be identified *as* something which the interplay of causes *aimed* at (so Darwinism). But even the dialectical materialism of Marxism secretly gives a definite direction to "evolution" and proclaims its goal as an "ought" which will certainly impose itself. For Marxism, the liberation of man from his self-alienation is a real end, not an accidental result, which is already sketched in the dialectical "wisdom" of "matter". In theism, with its doctrine of providence, there is one first ground of all reality, the God who exists in infinite spiritual self-possession – and his free act; so the world necessarily has a goal. A personal spiritual act necessarily involves a goal. "Hazard" and its results can be only predicated of particular combinations of causes. It is there a token of materiality, which brings an element of indetermination and hence of *de facto* failure into the deployment and interplay of causes. Finality is recognized (at least in its formal nature) through the transcendental experience in human knowledge and above all in freedom. Man recognizes that he is a self-determining, responsible being, acting necessarily in the light of his future, a being who must act freely and who always critically surpasses his present in his action. But if there were no true future, no true goal, if one runs in vain (cf. Phil 2:16), one would have the right to do what one cannot: to cling to the present as the definitive or – what is ultimately the same – to protest against the absurdity of life, where one is forced to run with the conviction that one will arrive nowhere, or to find "meaning" in the course itself, the eternal spinning of the wheel of change (cf. Jas 3:6) (see *Meaning*).

b) But this finality is that of a personal history of freedom (of divine and human origin) for the simple reason that a genuine and ultimate end can only be found there. Hence this movement towards the goal must not be reduced to the organic type, the mere evolution and unfolding of what was "always there" in potency (see above, 2b and e; *Creation* III, *Eschatology*).

c) The fulfilment, the definitive end of man (and his world) is not to be regarded as the last stage of a "development". It cannot be planned, since it is not produced from within the world by the combination of the manifold intramundane causes. The kingdom of God is the gift of God and is not earthly time filled with earthly happiness and endlessly prolonged. This does not mean that the goal, the endpiece, is attached externally to the historical movement. The God who is the fulfilment and who gives himself as the absolute future, is the God who is himself the inmost principle of the end-ward movement, through his self-communication in grace (and the incarnation). Hence the goal can be both the free gift of God's unique power and the yield, the fruit, of history itself. This is so because the "co-operation" of the freedom of God and of man in history must not be regarded as an external association, a "synergism" where each is a partial cause. The free grace of God releases the freedom of man for its supreme possibility, that of achieving the end himself, as his salvation. But salvation is only achieved through the fulfilment of an intramundane task – which may even be renunciation, asceticism, "flight from the world", since none of these alone can make up a whole human life and they have in any case a genuine function in the service of the world when this is properly understood. In a word, there can be no love of God (i.e., no will to the eschatological goal) which is not, in the concrete, love of the neighbour and which can be restricted to a private realm. Hence the God-given nature of the eschatological goal does not diminish the importance, the seriousness, the obligation of man's dedication to intramundane, i.e., particular and provisional ends, in all realms of human existence (see Vatican II, *Gaudium et Spes*, art. 43). Hence the eschatological hope has also a bearing on the world and a critical function with regard to society.

d) For a description of the concrete "content" of the end or goal, reference must be made to many other articles which cannot be repeated here. They appeal to the positive sources of revelation: *Reign of God*, *Salvation* II, *Beatific Vision*, *Resurrection* II, *Eschatology*, *Last Things*. When the end of man is described in the concrete according to the Christian faith and its hope, Christianity is clearly seen to include all the proper features and dimensions of man in its vision of fulfilment – in spite of Mt 22:30. No dimension of man which is now essential for his existence is disdained and excluded from the final fulfilment. Hence it includes the resurrection of the flesh, a new earth, an eternal fellowship of the saints after a general judgment, etc., as well as the vision of God in a new heaven after a "particular" judgment of the individual. And Christianity holds that all the elements of this final fulfilment (and not only certain ones), divided by the boundary of death from our present experience, will be absorbed into the mystery, the incomprehensibility which is so radical because God himself, the absolute mystery, is in himself this absolute future, this goal. This God of the incomprehensible mystery does not consume the creature by his coming, his eschatological immediacy, but imparts his own incomprehensibility to the fulfilment of all the dimensions of the creature (see, for example, Vatican II, *Gaudium et Spes*, art. 39).

e) This end is what ought to be, absolutely (see above, 2d). This character of obligation arises from the absolute self-communication of God. Since this is the personal love of God, given without reserve, it is what ought to be in the highest thinkable form. The will of God the creator and Lord in the form of law is only a formalized and ultimately derivative formulation of this "ought". And God's law, if not referred back to this, its real nature, can easily be misunderstood as the expression of a will which only imposes an obligation on man by the threat of punishment and only succeeds by coercion and force.

f) It follows that by its nature this end is such that to miss it (see *Sin*) would be absolute disaster (see *Hell*). The transcendental ordination of man (see *Existence*) to this goal means that to miss it brings man into radical and final contradiction with himself. He cannot end this situation by renouncing this end. He still affirms it in the definitive No of his freedom. And it is this which is the real nature of damnation.

g) When the relationship between the goal and fulfilment of the many individuals and the goal of humanity as such is analysed, one must keep in mind the relationship between individual and society, where the spiritual person is not merely an element in the service of the society or community, and the community is not just the sum total of the individuals. See *Reign of God*.

h) The end of man (men and humanity) has two aspects in its attainment: the "glory" of God (see *God, Glory of*) and the "blessedness" of man. The fulfilment of creation in its goal reflects the reality of God (*gloria Dei obiectiva*), which it also sees and acknowledges as the personal spirits who belong to it (men and angels) refer the created reality expressly to God in knowledge, love and adoration (*gloria Dei formalis*) (*D* 1805). But it thus gives perfect glory to God because and insofar as it is itself perfected, at its goal and hence transfigured and itself "blessed". This one *finis operis* of created reality with its two inseparable aspects is to be distinguished from the "end" or purpose of God (*finis operantis*), which God himself "pursues" in the creation of the world. This end is God himself as self-communicating goodness (*D* 1783).

Karl Rahner

ORDERS AND ORDINATION

I. Institution

A. Problems of Terminology

The various changes, which the terms used for orders underwent, could suggest a number of changes in emphasis or even in theological intention. But the data must be interpreted cautiously, bearing in mind the remote and immediate context, both in the text in question and in the minds of the authors who prefer one set of terms to another. During the early centuries of the Church, even after the Edict of Constantine and the ample "prerogatives" accorded to the clergy by the Christian emperors, the context is primarily biblical, and, in particular, that of the OT. H. U. Istinsky, E. Stommel, J. Gaudemet and R. Gryson have challenged the rather sweeping assertions of G. Dix and the thesis of T. Klauser, accepted too uncritically by P. M. Gy, to the effect that the *ordo promotionis* in civil life had rapidly given rise to a hierarchical institution modelled on that of the Empire.

The term *clerus* is found from the 3rd century on, a neologism from the Greek κλῆρος, with levitical connotations which remained perceptible for a long period. Cyprian uses *clericus*, Hilary *clericalis*, Jerome, Siricius and Augustine *clericatus*. These terms contrasted the clergy with the *plebs* or *populus* which had already been assigned the attribute *λαϊκός* indirectly by Clement of Rome (*1 Clement*, 40, 5). From Tertullian on, *ecclesiasticus* meant "Christian", but was used for *clericus* by Jerome, Priscillian and the Ambrosiaster. Tertullian chose *ordo*, probably under the influence of the "sacerdos secundum ordinem Melchisedech" of Ps 109:4 and Heb 5–7. It means either the clergy as a whole or the various degrees of orders, for which latter, from Cyprian on, *gradus* was also used. The meanings attached to the word *ordo* in modern times date only from the Middle Ages. From Tertullian and Cyprian on, *honores* and *dignitates* came rapidly into widespread use, but were not part of the very detailed and rigid protocols by which the imperial nomenclature was regulated. *Meritum* in the sense of function and *militia* in the sense of a corporation, not necessarily military, did not become widely current.

As regards the grades in ecclesiastical orders, it should be noted that ἄρχων (Origen) or *princeps* meant at the start only the "first", not "prince", which latter sense emerged only later, in the feudal terminology of the Middle Ages, in the classical contrast between the *principes ecclesiastici* and the *principes saeculares*. In the early centuries, the terms *princeps sacerdos*, *princeps sacerdotum* and *sacerdos magnus* were strictly reserved for Christ. The bishop, a modern term derived from the Latinization of ἐπίσκοπος was also commonly called *sacerdos* (or *summus sacerdos*), though *sacerdos* could also be used of the priest. *Pontifex* was used more sparingly, because of its pagan associations, though it is already found in Jerome. The priest was called *presbyter*, a term which has passed over into most modern languages. *Senior* was sometimes used, as in Ambrose. The διάκονος was usually called *minister*, as being charged with the *ministerium*, though like *sacerdos*, *minister* and *ministerium* could have the more general sense of "ministry", which is found in the NT. The terminology of the minor orders varied very widely in the early centuries of Christianity (Lennerz).

The Syrian Church retained certain symbolic titles of biblical origin: "the chair of God", or "of Moses" (cf. Mt 23:2), while the term "second thrones" was used of the priests (cf. Dan 7:9; Mt 19:28).

A development appears in the use of the terms signifying the rite of consecration. The "laying on of hands" (cf. 1 Tim 5:22) is very ancient, while χειροτονία signified primarily the election or nomination. It was used of the rite from the 4th century on only along with χειροθεσία. In the same way, *ordinare* originally meant "designate", the rite being called in Latin *benedictio* or *consecratio*. The *ordinatio* of the priest was not distinguished from the *consecratio* of the bishop till the 12th century.

In the course of time, the corporative sense of *ordo* was gradually lost sight of. During the discussions connected with Vatican II, patrology helped the re-discovery of the term *collegium episcopale*, which had been introduced by the Africans in the 3rd century and accepted at Rome in the 5th by Celestine I. Ambrose for his part preferred *sacerdotale consortium*. These terms designated a richer and more complex reality than the juridical notion accepted reluctantly by the minority at the Council, since it was something live and actual, ordinarily expressed in the early centuries by the frequent use of *frater* and the many composite words with the preposition *co-*, such as *coepiscopus* and *copresbyter*, which were already used in the NT.

These remarks show how prudent one must be in interpreting ancient texts. Even when dealing with certain seemingly "evident" expressions, one must guard against over-hasty and generalized conclusions, which seem to be too readily accepted in this age of turmoil.

The problems of interpretation are not confined to terminology. They are still more urgent with regard to the reality of orders as "lived" at a given epoch. We are now in quest of a "new image" of the priest and bishop. The "image" is the identity, meaning and value in the socio-psychological order attributed to a person exercising a function in a community. By means of this image, the others affirm that they accept and acknowledge this person and his function in the group, while the person in question finds there the foundations of the self-respect without which no man can survive. A change of identity or image is a common enough phenomenon in eras of such profound upheavals as our Western culture is now undergoing. The image of the woman, the parent, the politician and the military man is changing. But such a loss of identity is experienced perhaps nowhere so painfully as in the priest. The bishops feel it less, though their image is also evolving rapidly. Obviously, to clear up these questions the theologian must pay attention to the objections and the urgent suggestions of the sociologists and the psychologists. But it would be an illusion to think that such problems can be solved with the aid of sociology and psychology alone.

If it is true that the priesthood was entrusted by Christ to his Church from the start, it is also clear that this "idea and reality", to be assimilable, had to be integrated into the social and cultural structures of a given epoch. For the priesthood is a function to be exercised in a human community. Hence it has to accept the functional structures of this community. And this is in fact what took place under the Empire, in the feudal society of the Middle Ages and again later on. The "image" of the priest and the bishop never ceases to evolve.

To understand the evolution of orders in the Church, two elementary principles must be borne in mind. The first is that this "real idea" of Christ, this basic or seminal idea, contains by virtue of its divine riches more potentialities of concrete realization than the Church could ever implement. The second is that this "real idea" must necessarily express itself in the context, ambiguous because human, of a given epoch. This necessary insertion cannot but pose limits to the original idea, and indeed, because of the presence of sin in the Church, cannot entirely escape the charge of inauthenticity, though within the framework of the substantial indefectibility of the Church on its way to God through history. But the important point to remember is that any concrete realization on the human plane carries with it advantages which are visible above all to contemporaries, and disadvantages which are felt above all by subsequent ages. This is true of many of the "images" of the priest which the Church has known in the past.

Hence the Church will always have to re-think and remould its concrete and historical notion of orders, orientating it again and again on the evangelical ideal of Christ. This is why, ever since the OT, the institutional priesthood cannot preserve its authenticity without acknowledging the ministry of the prophet who continually reminds it, in the name of God and of his living faith, of its true vocation. Orders must inevitably institutionalize themselves, but all institutional processes lead to rigidity in "religion" and hence to "the system". Without prophetism, the OT would have been doomed to betray its original inspiration. Without the prieshood, prophetism is doomed to anarchy. The "institution" and the "charism" are not mutually exclusive, as liberalism and modernism held, but sustain each other.

Hence on the plane of theological reflection one must distinguish the "real idea" at the start, as willed and hence founded by Christ (*substantia sacramenti*) or perhaps the rite intended by Christ (*substantia ritus sacramenti*), from the concrete, historical realization of this idea by the Church at a given epoch (*essentia sacramenti*), and in turn perhaps from the *essentia ritus sacramenti*, which would be the symbolic expression of the intention of the Church and of its faith, in the rite of consecration. This technical distinction is an aid to interpretation, especially in the study of the past, where the theologian may discover, with the help of comparative studies, the permanent and primordial inspiration beneath the many forms of historical expression, subjected to a continuous movement of evolution under the impulse of the evolution of human culture. But it would be a simplification to think that it is easy to separate the pure idea from the pure element of concrete realization. This is particularly difficult at the present time. For the notion willed by Christ cannot be expressed in the concrete for the present or the future except in terms of notions and images and socio-cultural structures which belong to the language and patterns of behaviour of our own time and culture. That the purity of the evangelical idea can be attained is an ancient and tenacious illusion, but still a mistake. Christ himself had to embody his idea in the images and language of the OT and the Judaism of his day, and in accordance with the social structures of the Jewish environment in which he lived. The same is also true, *mutatis mutandis*, of the apostles after him (see E. Schillebeeckx and P. Schoonenberg in H. van der Linde and H. Fiolet, eds., *Neue Perspektiven nach dem Ende des konventionellen Christentums* [1968], pp. 69–161).

B. The Teaching of Scripture

1. *The institution of the Twelve.* Most exegetes seem to agree that during his public life Christ gathered round him a more or less stable group of disciples, according to rabbinical usage, "to be with him" (Mk 3:13–14). Very early, probably during the lifetime of Christ, they were named "the Twelve", a symbolic title which envisaged the origins (the patriarchs) and the end of time (Mt 19:23; Lk 22:28–30), and hence also signified the new people of God (the twelve tribes). They were Christ's helpers in the preaching of the kingdom (Mk 6:7–13; Lk 9:1–6). Their mission was confirmed after the resurrection and then became universal, as is very clear in Mt, where stress had been laid on the fact that Christ's own mission was confined to the chosen people. See Mt 28:16–20. Their mission was also unique in a certain sense, since they were the privileged witnesses of the life, death and resurrection of the Lord (Lk 24:48–49; Acts 1:4–11).

But some points remain debatable. a) Did Christ himself call them apostles (Dupont)? But it seems that this notion was worked out by Paul, along the lines of the prophetic office in the OT. b) Did the rabbinical institution of the *sheluchim* ("envoys") influence the actual form which the ministry of the Twelve originally took? But there are no clear proofs that such an institution existed in Judaism before A.D. 70. c) Some recent Protestant authors hold that the institution of the Twelve was the creation of the Church and not of Christ. But this question must be solved by a careful study of history, and above all by the "history of redaction" of the synoptic texts.

2. *The mission of the Twelve.* We note first that the synoptic gospels attribute a special mission to the Twelve, which cannot however be neatly distinguished from the mission of others who believed in Christ. Thus Mt, in the discourse edited by the evangelist and addressed to the Twelve (9:35–11:1), incorporates a number of sayings which in a different redactional context (e.g., Mt 18, context of the Christian community) refer to all the faithful. Hence the notion of orders cannot imply too harsh a separation between the Twelve and the other believers. One might also point to the pericope proper to Lk, that of the 70 or 72 disciples (10:1–24), a text which is difficult to interpret, but which Lk has undoubtedly placed at one of the high-points of his gospel – between the counsels given to the Twelve (9:46–62) and the "hymn of jubilation" (10:21–24). Exegetes agree in general that the number 70 (or 72: six twelves) implies an institutional authority (cf. the 70 "elders" of Moses, Exod 24:1; Num 11:16, the symbol and tradition persisting in Judaism to the time of Christ; cf. Qumran) – or a universal authority (the world has 70 peoples or 70 languages). (See also the reply to the article of B. Metzger in *New Testament Studies* 5 [1959], pp. 299–306, by S. Jellicoe, *ibid.* 6 [1960], pp. 319–21, who suggests that the notion of world-wide preaching is based on the *Letter of Aristeas* concerning the miraculous origin of the Septuagint.) Lk may have been wishing to justify the government of the Pauline Churches by *episcopi-presbyteri*, or rather, as seems more probable, he was thinking of the universal apostolic mission of the people of God. Then the famous text, "He who hears you hears me", which is applied so frequently to the episcopal magisterium, would refer in this context to

the prophetic testimony of all the faithful before the world.

The same ambivalence recurs in the word by which the synoptics mainly define the ministry of the Twelve, the *diakonia*. Christ's mission is a *diakonia* (e.g., Lk 22:26f., where the normal and original meaning of the word is still recognizable: to serve at table). So too is the mission of all the faithful, since they are the "servants of God" and of men, inspired by charity (e.g., Mt 23:11f.; Jn 12:25f.). But the ministry of the Twelve is described with a special insistence as "service": Mk 9:35 10:43f.; Mt 20:26–28.

The special mission of the Twelve is to share in the mission given to Christ by the Father: the preaching of the kingdom. This is asserted by the three synoptics, Mk 9:32–42; Mt 10:10–42; Lk 9:46–50. And if Lk 10:1–24 envisages in fact the *episcopi-presbyteri* of the Pauline Churches, the same assertion is found in 10:16, in a form adapted to Greek readers. John repeats it in another form at the end of his gospel (20:19–23), where this mission is explicitly linked with the gift of the Holy Spirit in view of the remission of sins – equivalent to the *metanoia* preached in the synoptics in view of the kingdom (but see *Penance* II).

The same notion of participation in the mission of Christ seems to us to be expressed in concrete symbolism in the three images of the servant or child, shepherd and rock. According to M. Black, the Aramaic *talia* can mean both "child" and "servant". The rabbis called themselves the "great" and their disciples the "little ones" or the "children". In the Septuagint, the עֶבֶד of Deutero-Isaiah is translated by παῖς and by δοῦλος, while in the Psalms the translation δοῦλος is preferred. Thus when sharing in the mission of the "Servant of God" the Twelve are compared to "children" or "little ones". (Christ shows them a child, which is a parable in action.) Throughout this context it is notable that Christ contrasts the exercise of the Twelve's authority with that of the great ones of this world and of the rabbis, but does not speak of that of the priests of Judaism. It seems therefore that the evangelists paid no attention to the position of priests in Judaism, where, in any case, except for the social standing of the high priests in the Sanhedrin, they do not seem to have had authority in matters of doctrine or government.

Christ is the good shepherd. Peter (Jn 21:15–18), the Twelve Mt 9:35–38) and the other ministers (1 Pet 5:2) are also shepherds. Christ is, after Yahweh, the rock of Israel. So too Peter is called Rock (Mt 16:13–20), and the Twelve are the "columns" or the "foundation" (Eph 2:20; Gal 2:9; Rev 21: 14). Christ is to suffer for the kingdom; so too the disciples. Christ is the prophet, and they too are to preach the kingdom. Christ is the new Moses, and the disciples are to be his "seventy elders" (according to a probable interpretation of Lk 10:1–24).

II. The Ministry in the Theological Reflection of the Church

A. The Apostolate

The re-thinking of the original fact of the Twelve as envoys of Christ in terms of the new notion of "apostle" is probably due to Paul and Luke. In the strict sense of the term, an apostle is a witness of the life and death of Christ, by virtue of the gift of the Spirit, by which he receives a universal mission (Acts 1:21f.). This unique role is extended to Matthias (Acts 1:24ff.), to Paul and to James, the brother of the Lord, who did not, apparently, belong to the college of the Twelve. For such an extension, it seems to us that Paul and Luke presuppose a direct intervention by God (through the casting of lots) or a vision of the risen Christ. Later on, the word apostle is used in a wider sense, which seems to be based simply on the notion of universal preaching. It is an analogous and subsidiary use of the title. See further the article *Apostle.*

B. The Various Ministries in the Apostolic and Sub-Apostolic Church

The institution of orders as a sacrament by Christ is different, strictly speaking, from the institution of the Twelve. We do not feel bound to affirm that there is no relation between them. Nonetheless, it is difficult to show how orders derive historically from the apostolate. It follows that the dogmatic truth of the institution of orders must be taken up from an angle different from the classical approach. This started from a notion of the Christian priesthood current in the Middle Ages, which was too strongly cultic. It therefore linked the institution of orders by Christ mainly to the institution of the Eucharist, especially to the words of Christ, "Do this in remembrance of me" (1 Cor 11:24; Lk 22:19), and also to the power of forgiving sins (Mt 16:19f.; 18:18; Jn 20:22; cf. the Council of Florence, *DS* 1326, and the Council of Trent, *DS* 1764, 1771). (See H. Denis, "Vatican II, Les prêtres", *La vie spirituelle* 118 [1968], pp. 193–232.) The historical and dogmatic question is more complicated, at least by the fact that the meanings of the words "priest" and "priesthood" evolve in terms of the religious and cultural context in which they are used. In this matter, which is of such importance in the life of the Church and ecumenical dialogue, it is important to avoid hasty conclusions, which might also tell against the scientific probity of Catholic theologians. In the revealed religion of Christianity, where revelation is linked to historical facts, it is most important to acknowledge historical realities. Our theology has too often succumbed to the attraction of the abstract, a tendency which can lead to theological myths.

1. *The origin of the ecclesiastical hierarchy.* On the historical plane, it seems impossible ever to arrive at definitive conclusions as to the concrete origin of the ecclesiastical ministry as we now know it. No one doubts the importance of the Twelve. But soon afterwards, other "apostles" were added, whose authenticity seems to have been recognized by all, but for reasons which mostly remain unknown to us. Others were then joined to these, with an authority at the beginning very like that of the apostles, the "prophets and teachers" (1 Cor 12:28; Acts 13:1; 15:32; Eph 2:20; 3:5; 4:11). They soon yielded their authority to others. Their successors seem to have had an authority based rather on an institution than on a charism, though the distinction should not be overworked. There are προϊστάμενοι ("superiors", 1 Thess 5:12) in a position of authority (Rom 12:8), sometimes called κυβερνήτεις ("guides", 1 Cor 12:28; cf. Acts 27:11; Rev 18:17) or ποιμένες ("pastors", 1 Cor 12:28; Eph 4:11). Paul only mentions the ἐπίσκοποι (bishops, Phil 1:1) once, before the "deacons". The title is probably of Hellenistic origin (Acts 20:28 – where the office is compared to that of a shepherd). At an early stage, the apostles at Jerusalem called in the "Seven" as helpers (Acts 6:1–6). These are traditionally the first deacons. But they seem rather to have been the first type of "presbyters" or elders, modelled on the Jewish institution. These elders formed a governing body, a type of religious authority fairly widespread in the Jewish diaspora, to which a parallel may be found at Qumran. The elders as such are first mentioned at Jerusalem (Acts 11:30; 15:2–23; 16:4; 21:18; 22:15), then later in other places (Acts 14:23; 20:17–35; Jas 5:14; 1 Pet 5:1, 5). Later still, they are under the authority of a disciple of the Apostle Paul (1 Tim 3:5; 5:17, 19, 22; Tit 1:5).

These are scattered and fairly disparate indications. With only this to go on, the historian can hardly venture very far. But it is fairly clear, nevertheless, that the apostles claimed at a very early stage the right to call on "helpers" whose responsibilities are not very well defined, while reserving to themselves the general direction of the Churches which they had founded. One may also distinguish in this development a Palestinian tradition, also called Johannine because of certain indications in Rev (the "angels" of the Churches) and some later testimonies. Beside this tradition from Asia Minor, one might suppose a Pauline tradition, sometimes called "missionary", in which the Churches founded by Paul and others, like the Church of Rome, gradually came to have a governing body, called elders (πρεσβύτεροι) and later bishops (ἐπίσκοποι), as in Acts. Here Jewish-Christian influence may be assumed. These Churches developed more slowly towards the monarchical structure adopted in Asia Minor. This delay seems to be attested by Clement of Rome and in *Hermas*, and still later in the customs of the Churches of Alexandria and perhaps Lyons, where the installation and ordination of the bishop was the work of the elders. These customs may have lasted till the 3rd century.

This evidence does not permit us to affirm that the hierarchy of orders, i.e., monarchical bishop, college of elders and deacons, was a divine institution in the strict sense, or even an institution of the apostolic Church, considered as a norm for later Churches. The Council of Trent may have envisaged this possibility, since in can. 5 of the session on orders it chose the formula "divina ordinatione institutam" instead of "divina institutione" (*DS* 1776; cf. 1768; *D* 966, 959). Vatican II undoubtedly affirmed that the bishop is given the fullness of the priesthood as member of the episcopal college by the fact of his ordination, and that the priest is ordained as "helper" of the bishop. But as we see things, the Council did not decide whether the matter in question was a dogmatic definition of a revealed reality or an act of "the ecclesiastical economy". An ancient controversy, which had gone on till the time of the Council, was thus in fact closed, but not *de iure*.

2. *The primitive ministers as priests.* The question is now being posed, with a certain amount of disquiet, as to whether the apostles or their "helpers" considered themselves as "priests". Before taking up the fundamentals of the question, we must obviously have a clear notion of the semantic problem. What was the concrete reality evoked in each case by the words כֹּהֵן (*qohen*), ἱερεύς, *sacerdos* or *pontifex*? And what concrete reality have we in mind when we now acknowledge or reject a "sacerdotal" dimension in the ancient or modern developments of the Christian ministry? As regards the basic question, it seems that the biblical data tell in favour of a negative answer. But every historian knows that the argument *ex silentio* must be wielded with extreme delicacy. In the time of Christ, the words in question had a well-defined sense, the result of a long religious, cultural and hence semantic evolution in the Jewish and pagan world. In view of this well established linguistic usage, it was impossible to recognize in the ministries of the early Church these "images" of the priesthood universally accepted but foreign to Christian experience.

The letter to the Hebrews interpreted the heavenly role of Christ by means of the symbols of the liturgical priesthood of the temple and the feasts of expiation. In this context, the priesthood of Melchizedek was used to distinguish the unique and transcendent reality of Christ at the right hand of the Father from his liturgical "type" in the OT. It cannot even be said to be improbable that the author of Hebrews wished to exclude all notions of an earthly priesthood, to reserve the priesthood to Christ alone, just as Paul in Rom rejected justification by works to retain only justification by faith. But the conclusion is not evident.

The NT also shows some after-effects of the OT tradition (Exod 19:6), when a "royal priesthood" is attributed to the people of God (1 Pet 2:4–9). Rev 1:6; 5:10; 20:6; 22:3–5 seem, however, to draw their inspiration from Is 61:6, 21. The influence, negative or positive, of the "sacerdotal" spirituality of Qumran cannot be excluded as a possibility, e.g., in Heb. We should not wish to discredit in any way the value of this biblical teaching on Christ but it should be evident that semantically we have here a transposition on to a spiritual plane of a meaning and use of words as they were familiar to the early Christians from their reading of the Bible.

Those who reject or invoke certain expressions by which Paul describes his apostolic ministry as a sacrifice or liturgy (Rom 1:9; Phil 2:17; 15:15–16), without excluding the life of other believers (Rom 12:1; Phil 2:17; 4:18; cf. Jas 1:26f.) show at the same time that they are really thinking of a cultic and liturgical priesthood. There is a text in Acts (13:1–3) which can hardly be interpreted in a purely spiritual sense, but it deals with "prophets and teachers" such as we have spoken of earlier. But this text presents us with another problem, which is also suggested by other texts in the NT, that during the 1st century no ordination was necessary in order to preside over a liturgical service, whatever its nature (O. Casel, *Jahrbuch für Liturgiewissenschaft* 9 [1929], pp. 1–19). Nowhere is it clearly stated who must preside at the eucharistic repast.

But to return to the notion of priesthood. Is not the notion of mediation between God and man more fundamental (e.g., 1 Cor 4:1–5; 2 Cor 3:6) than presiding at the liturgy, which is only one of its many manifestations? The evolution of the notion of priesthood in Vatican II shows that the ministry of the word, the government of the community and, above all, participation in the mission of Christ for the building up of the Church as the body of Christ – the Church itself being orientated to the world in the spirit of service and testimony – can also be an expression of this same office of mediation.

However this may be, Clement of Rome is the first to compare the ministry of the apostles and their successors with the Jewish hierarchy (*1 Clement*, chs 42ff.). Ignatius of Antioch clearly underlines the office of the bishop as president of the liturgical worship. Tertullian is the first to give the bishop the title of *summus sacerdos*, while Hippolytus of Rome gives it to the apostles. Eusebius has preserved the testimony of Hegesippus about James and of Polycrates of Ephesus about John, where the two apostles are accorded the dignity of the high priest in the OT (*Historia Ecclesiastica*, II, 23, 6; V, 24, 3). Hegesippus and Polycrates, of whom little is known, seem to have belonged to the Jewish-Christian world. But it is obvious that this evolution was not influenced by Constantine, or, if one prefers, this deformation of the ancient Christian tradition.

We do not claim that these few remarks can resolve the modern controversies. The facts can be explained in two ways. The vocabulary attached to the "priesthood" may have been gradually taken out of its cultural and religious background in Judaism and paganism, so that it could be used in a new and Christian way, after a process of refinement. Or the cultural environment, strongly imbued with "religion", determined a pernicious orientation towards the "sacred" in the Graeco-Roman concept of the Christian ministry. It seems to us that this problem cannot be solved by purely historical arguments bearing on an epoch which was unaware of our modern problems.

And hence we shall make every effort in the course of this article to speak above all of realities and concrete functions, before diverging to discuss a terminology which has taken on such different and debatable senses in the course of time and again in our own day (see J. Colson, *Ministres de Jésus-Christ, ou le sacerdoce de l'Évangile* [1966]).

3. *The laying on of hands*. The laying on of hands (the *semikah*) was a fairly widespread rite in Judaism. It is interesting to note that Jewish priests were not consecrated by a *semikah*. Nonetheless, in Num 8:5–11, the whole tribe of Levi is set apart for the service of the covenant by the imposition of hands – that of the whole people. The "priestly" strand of the Pentateuch speaks of Moses having laid his hands upon Joshua, whereby Joshua was filled with Moses's spirit of wisdom (Deut 34:9) or invested with some of his authority or dignity (הוד) (Num 27:15–20). At a certain date the scribes or doctors of the law, the heirs of the authority of Moses, must have adopted this collegial rite (cf. Num 27:22) in order to transfer their authority to their disciples. The rite was juridical, but had also a quasi-sacramental character, since the disciple received in this way the "spirit of Moses". Possibly Exod 18:13–27; Deut 1:9–18; Exod 3:16; 24:1–14 and above all Num 11:16f., which speak of the transmission of the spirit of Moses to the elders, influenced the rabbinical tradition. The question has been raised finally as to whether the rabbis' *sheluchim* (envoys) were confirmed in their most specific mission by a laying on of hands (E. Lohse).

The NT shows that Christ, and later the apostles and the "Seven", used this symbolical gesture as a sign of blessing and healing. The rite was employed very early, it seems, for the transmission of the "gifts of the Spirit" (see *Confirmation*).

The laying on of hands (ἐπίθεσις τῶν χειρῶν) is mentioned in a number of NT texts with reference to the handing on of a mission in the apostolic Church. It is still debated whether Acts 13:1–3; 6:1–6; 14:22, 20, deal with truly priestly ordinations. The texts are too short to allow of a definitive conclusion. There is hardly room for doubt about 1 Tim 4:14 and 2 Tim 1:6, when taken together; and 1 Tim 5:22 and Tit 1:5 may refer to an ordination. Only the apocryphal *Actus Petri*, 10, says that Christ laid hands upon the apostles, as Chrysostom says of James of Jerusalem (*1 Cor, Homily* 38, 4). But these texts do not seem close enough to the primitive Church to allow us to conclude with certainty that Christ or the apostolic Church instituted this as the rite of ordination. The *rite* cannot be identified with sufficient probability till near A.D. 200. It may therefore be presumed that the laying on of hands is not a "substantial" element of the sacramental rite, but a rite instituted by the Church.

C. Orders in the Life and Thought of the Church

1. *The evolution of the "image" of the priest in the course of history*. The life of the Church, the *praxis ecclesiae*, embodies the faith of the Church in the course of history. This *praxis* is a *locus theologicus* for theological reflection. It is important, though difficult, to interpret, as we have seen in the initial section on the problems of interpretation.

Modern Christianity is searching for a new "image" of priest and bishop, including that of the Pope. It is impossible to prepare the future without knowing the past. The study of the past should help us to discover what seems "substantial" in the ecclesiastical ministry and what has often changed in the course of centuries. This should help us to understand the present and prepare the future. But it would be extremely difficult, if not impossible, to sketch here in a few lines all this complex history. It is not even possible to refer the reader to a synthesis of the matter, since such a comprehensive study does not exist, though there is a general survey in the popularizing work of X. de Chalendar, *Les prêtres* (1963). Hence the outline given here must necessarily be somewhat superficial, though it should be enough to show that in this very complicated evolution, biblical and dogmatic themes and the purposes of the ecclesiastical dispensation ("economy") are combined with preoccupations of a social, economic, psychological and even political nature.

For the Church of the martyrs, the *sacerdos* is primarily the bishop. At a time when salvation was undoubtedly lived as a spiritual reality, the authority of the bishop is strongly affirmed, as for instance by Cyprian. The "authoritarian" attitude is corrected by a profound sense of fellowship between the bishop, his priests and his people, and between the bishops of the various Churches all belonging to the *ecclesia Dei*. Further, the "pneumatic" inspiration of the episcopal mission was strongly felt, 1 Cor 2:14ff. being often applied to the bishop. The role of the priest emerges only marginally in history, since he remained in the shadow of the bishop as a member of his council.

The Church of the Fathers was faced with a different situation. Constantine proclaimed Christianity as the religion of the Empire. The clergy received many "privileges", being dispensed above all from municipal duties. The priesthood inevitably took on a new image. An attentive study of the texts shows that the development was influenced less by the example of imperial institutions than by those of the OT. The phenomenon of cultural osmosis in this Graeco-Roman world is another matter, which is very difficult to trace exactly. A strong monastic movement in the Church countered the process of spiritual entanglement. In the East, it seems that it soon reserved the sacrament of penance to the monk and the spiritual man. It ended by becoming part of the spiritual heritage of the Byzantine Church. In the West, the influence of the monastic movement was prolonged, especially in the Celtic Churches, till the 11th century. The Church made the movement its own by choosing its bishops from among the "spiritual men" of the time, such as Ambrose, Augustine, Chrysostom and Gregory, mostly in fact monks. The priests were in the entourage of the bishop, as his counsellors, exercising a special authority only in his absence or with his permission, as when the priest Augustine inaugurated in Africa the custom of preaching before the bishop. However, from the 3rd century on, the *tituli* (parishes) came into being and multiplied, especially in distant hamlets outside the towns where the bishops resided. It was perhaps in the countryside that priests received for the first time the "care of souls"; probably also in some great cities with several basilicas or churches.

Between the 6th and the 9th century an important development took place in the notion of Church, Empire and priesthood (see Y. Congar, *L'ecclésiologie du Haut Moyen Age* [1968]). Against the background of the heavenly majesty of Christ, the Church and the Empire, both Byzantine and Carolingian, appear as the visible image on earth of the heavenly kingdom. The *potestas sacerdotalis* and the *potestas regalis* share the forms of spiritual authority and competence. The power of the keys is conceived above all as the power of opening the gates of heaven to the faithful. With the break-up of the Empire in the West and the weakening of the papacy, the great patriarchates developed in the East, and a regional episcopate in the West. Charlemagne exercised in his empire an ecclesiastical jurisdiction very like that of the "basileus" in

Constantinople. The power of the bishops was understood above all as moral and spiritual. The Church of Rome, for its part, after an eclipse due to internal struggles, gradually worked out more juridical structures of fellowship, including a primacy of jurisdiction. The priests, scattered through the countryside, were gradually absorbed into the feudal system which was taking root in Europe. They were chosen by the lord of the domain from among the inhabitants of the village, and ordained by the bishop for the service of the liturgy. A capitular of 779 made the tithe obligatory, a custom inspired, like so many others, by the OT. It was soon to weigh heavily on the clergy because it added to their cultic functions the charge of collector of taxes, which was to last for more than a thousand years.

From the 9th century on, the West worked out an ecclesiology which departed more and more from that of the East. While in the East the "symbiosis" of imperial and episcopal power prevented the secularization of the State, the first clash between Church and State in the West during the investiture strife inaugurated a very long evolution which was to lead to the separation of the two powers after centuries of struggle. Meanwhile this struggle for a sort of spiritual hegemony of the ecclesiastical over the temporal power provoked a campaign for ecclesiastical rights such as had been unknown in antiquity. This had a deleterious influence on the development of ecclesiology, inasmuch as the wholly spiritual mission of the episcopate and the Pope was mainly considered under the aspect of a *potestas* with a tendency to surround itself with a system of ecclesiastical and civil privileges. (See Y. Congar, *Problems of Authority*, ed. by J. M. Todd [1962], pp. 119–50.) Henceforward the struggle for regions of authority became a normal part of the Western world. These politico-religious tensions were complicated by the fact that the politico-social structures of the feudal system were to a great extent decisive in the distribution of Church functions within the Church itself. The bishop, who during the barbarian invasions had had to assume many civil charges, entered the feudal system as a *princeps ecclesiasticus*. The priests, who had formerly been the bishops' men, often came under the authority of the lords who founded or owned the benefices by which the priests lived. The cathedral chapters, once the ancient *presbyterium* around the bishop, became, like the abbeys, the prey of the nobility or the kings, precisely because of their wealth. In reaction against the abuses of episcopal power or riches, of which many complaints were made at the epoch, the monks, and later the mendicant orders, developed a priestly and missionary activity which escaped to some extent episcopal jurisdiction by means of papal exemption. The Pope had to defend them against undue interference from local authorities, ecclesiastical or civil. A similar phenomenon may be noticed, due to the same reasons, at the origin of the great universities of Bologna, Paris and Oxford.

A common law gradually took shape, extremely complex, including social and financial privileges based on a rural, territorial and patriarchal concept of authority, which was thereby linked to possession of or jurisdiction over a clearly defined territory. Though present canon law has renounced many concrete applications which have become outmoded, the fundamental principles of this ecclesiastical law still depend to a great extent on a view of human society which has now entirely lost its relevance, at least in the Western world.

While the East always preserved a cultured laity, the West could not save Latin and hence ecclesiastical culture except through the agency of the clerics. The introduction of ecclesiastical celibacy, where some see the influence of a Manichaean notion of marriage and of the sexual act, finally constituted a caste of priests, often very strongly committed to temporal responsibilities, but with a position of privilege unparalleled in the Western world.

Thus the priesthood, implanted in a society issuing from the barbarian kingdoms, having undoubtedly profited from its involvement in the world around it, began to display more and more clearly after the dawn of a new epoch, that is, after the end of the 14th century, the profound defects of its accommodation to the barbarian world. It could even be maintained, though with the necessary modifications, that from this epoch onwards the history of the priesthood has been reduced – apart from some periods of reform and intense renewal – to a slow process of disengagement in which it strove to free itself from a shell which had become a yoke. The structures and forms of life which had brought it close to the world now separated it more and more from a world whose evolution was constantly accelerating.

The first crisis, prepared by a growing tension of about two centuries duration issued in the outbreak of the Reformation. The Reformation had a profoundly religious impulse, but at a distance of four centuries it is obvious that it was above all a protest against a notion of the priesthood which was compromised by forms of life and authority too widely removed from the gospel ideal. Undoubtedly, the Counter-Reformation inaugurated a deep renewal of priestly life and activity, of which Charles Borromeo, Francis de Sales and the founders of religious orders in the 16th century offer remarkable examples. It could even be said that Ignatius Loyola had a presentiment of forms of priestly life for modern times, but here he was not followed by the order which he founded. The priesthood did not in fact succeed in freeing itself completely from a notion of the priesthood and of ecclesiology which dated from the Middle Ages. The bishops retained too many links with the royal power and the nobility, which prevented the Council of Trent and the succeeding ages of Gallicanism from solving the urgent problem of the relationship between the episcopate and the papacy. The mystique of the Holy Empire was replaced by the sacred union of the "altar and throne", a more secularized form of the *respublica christiana* of the Middle Ages. The priest remained above all the accredited dispenser of the sacraments and the celebrant of the Eucharist, which was characteristic of the priestly spirituality of the Counter-Reformation. Nonetheless, the 17th century saw a renewal of preaching and a missionary movement embracing the whole world. But as the controversy of the Chinese rites was to show, Europe refused to allow the missionaries forms of life and piety unknown to the West (see M. Hay, *The Failure in the Far East* [1956]).

The priestly world went through another crisis in the 18th century, culminating in the French Revolution with its fierce anti-clericalism, which has remained widely characteristic of the epoch which is now only slowly disappearing. The priestly renewal under the influence of Vincent de Paul, Bérulle and Oler gave rise to the seminaries of Saint Sulpice, whose influence extended to the U.S.A. (see J. T. Ellis, *Essays in Seminary Training* [1967]). No one would deny the spiritual depth of this revival of spirituality which affected above all the diocesan clergy and which found its ideal in the Curé d'Ars. Nonetheless, the reform did not succeed in restoring the priest to the world in which he ought to have fulfilled his mission. A too cloistered formation, a too individualist piety, a notion of the Church and the priesthood which was too much on the defensive, prevented the priest too often from breaking out of the circle of the devout. In Continental Europe, the Church lost the world of the workers. It was losing the world of the intellectuals while the priest could not regain contact with these de-Christianized milieux.

A third crisis, more profound perhaps than the others, is affecting the priesthood at the present day. It was inaugurated by the Second Vatican Council. This time at last it came from within the Church. The Council called in question the "closed" concept of the Church and its Western monolithic structure. Paul VI himself has several times admitted that the papacy, under its present aspect, is a major obstacle to the union of the Churches. The same could be said of many notions, still common, of the episcopate. But one still has the impression that the value of the testimony contained in some objections put by the separated brethren is not always perceived, in spite of the expressions of esteem otherwise accorded them by the Church of Rome. For the moment, the priesthood is in a state of crisis. Vocations are falling off nearly everywhere. The seminaries are emptying. Many priests renounce their vocation and those who remain faithful are tormented by anguish, uncertainty and doubt. It is urgent for the Church to reflect on the meaning of the priestly vocation, at every level of holy orders. Such reflection cannot dispense with the lessons of the past.

2. *The liturgical expression.* The liturgy is fundamentally the symbolic expression in word and gesture of the "faith of the Church", a notion absolutely common in the theology of the sacraments down to the Council of Trent. What takes place in the celebration of a sacrament is by no means evident. By the liturgical celebration the Church confesses its faith in the presence and activity of its Lord. Hence the study of the liturgy should help us to rediscover the "substantial" notion of the priesthood.

Hippolytus of Rome (*c.* 230) has preserved for us in his *Traditio Apostolica* the first text of a liturgy of which the terminology and inspiration is already well established. No doubt we cannot be sure of how well this liturgy represents the faith of the Church in the 3rd century, but its influence was very great. The bishop is the *sacerdos*, the successor of the apostles. He is elected by the people, but receives the imposition of hands from another bishop. The priest is ordained by the bishop, *contingentibus etiam presbyteris*, with the other priests joining in, as one who is *particeps consilii in clero*, a clerical counsellor, while the deacon is ordained by the bishop alone because he is ordained to the "service" of the latter. It is interesting to note that the rite of consecration for the bishop is inspired rather by the NT, while the ordination of the priest is frankly inspired by the OT. This anomaly might be a confirmation of our earlier suggestions about the probable origins of bishop and presbyter (see II B, 1, above).

At Rome, between the 6th and the 8th century the *Sacramentarium Leonianum* and the *Gregorianum* take up the same themes, enhancing the "mystical" character of the Christian priesthood in contrast to that of the OT. The presbyters are ordained formally as *cooperatores ordinis nostri*, probably in reaction against the presbyterial theories of Jerome and others in the 5th century (B. Botte). The episcopal office is a charge of intercession. Later the ministry of the word and of reconciliation is added.

The East adapted the *Traditio Apostolica* in the eighth book of the *Constitutiones Apostolicae*, which was the model for all the Eastern liturgies, examples of which may be seen in the *Euchologion* of Serapion (which may not deal with the Church of Egypt, cf. B. Capelle, *Travaux Liturgiques*, III [1965]) and the *Testament of Our Lord* (from the Church of Syria). The Byzantine liturgy also drew its inspiration from the same source. From the Council of Nicaea on, each bishop had to be consecrated by three bishops. The laying on of the holy gospels was added to the laying on of hands.

At the beginning the number of minor orders, some of which were open to women, varied between two and eight. But the Byzantine Church soon ceased to recognize any but subdiaconate and lectorate (H. Lennerz; R. Gryson in *Revue Bénédictine* 76 [1966], pp. 119–27).

Ordination, both in the East and in the West, bound the ordinand to a given Church ("relative ordination"), a system confirmed by the sixth canon of the Council of Chalcedon (Mansi, VII, p. 361).

In the West, liturgical development was far from at its term. It may be seen in the *Ordines Romani* of the 8th–9th centuries. After the Council of Arles in 314, three consecrating bishops were necessary for the consecration of a bishop. The ritual of minor orders was still very simple. Only the subdiaconate seems to have been given a universal statute which is reflected in most Churches.

In the Frankish Churches of the 7th and 8th centuries new rites were added. For the bishop there was the anointing of the head with the holy chrism, the giving of the crozier and ring, and the enthronement. For the priest there was the anointing of the hands, the giving of bread and wine and a second laying on of hands in view of the absolution of sins. This development reflects Germanic customs, which attached great importance to the transmission of the emblems of power, a "princely" power for the bishop and a cultic power for the priest. Towards the 10th century this liturgy was merged with the Roman tradition in the *Romano-Germanic Pontifical* of Mainz (*RSR* 32 [1958], pp. 113–67). "Absolute" ordinations, not tying a priest to a diocese, were still forbidden for priests and minor orders in the fifteenth canon of the Synod of Piacenza (1095), but were permitted by the sixth canon of the Synod of Rome in 1099 (Mansi, XX, pp. 806, 970). In France during the 10th century a new liturgy for minor orders was worked out under the influence of the *Statuta Ecclesiae antiqua* (Gaul, 5th century) and the theological reflection of Isidore of Seville and the pseudo-Jerome (*De septem ordinibus ecclesiae*, Spain, 7th century; *PL*, XXX, cols. 152–67; *Revue Bénédictine* 40 [1928], pp. 310–18). One may find there practically the same rites as are now in use for the porter, lector, exorcist, acolyte and subdeacon. Here too the *traditio instrumentorum* (investiture) holds pride of place in the ritual, under the influence of Germanic law. Towards the 12th century the tendency to allow the subdiaconate the dignity of a sacrament appears (*DS* 711, 1765; here the "ecclesiastical economy" is at work). The Council of Trent did not succeed in restoring minor orders, which had become merely juridical grades of preparation for the priesthood (*CIC*, can. 978). The Second Vatican Council decided to restore the functions of the deacon (*Sacrosanctum Concilium*, art. 35; *Lumen Gentium*, art. 29; *Optatam Totius*, art. 12; *Orientalium Ecclesiarum*, art. 17), and also decided in principle on a revision of the liturgy of orders (*Sacrosanctum Concilium*, art. 76; *Orientalium Ecclesiarum*, art. 17). The diaconate was recognized as having the nature of a sacrament (*Lumen Gentium*, arts. 28, 29). Henceforward all bishops present are to join in the rite of episcopal consecration (*Sacrosanctum Concilium*, art. 76). On 18 June 1968 Paul VI promulgated the Apostolic Constitution *Pontificalis Romani*, introducing a new rite for the ordination of deacons, priests and bishops (*AAS* 60 [1968], pp. 369–73).

3. *The ordinary minister of orders.* Ignatius of Antioch already reserved most of the sacraments to the bishop. The bishop has remained the ordinary minister of confirmation (in the West), and also of orders. But there are traces in history of exceptions to this rule, which was also accepted in principle by the theologians and canonists of the Middle Ages since Huguccio, with no reserves except for papal permission.

The other exceptions may be divided into three groups. The first contains the cases which are almost impossible to interpret because of their antiquity and our inability to see what pastoral or theological motives may have been at work. We have already mentioned the customs of the Church of Alexandria (possibly also followed by Lyons) as late as the 3rd century, when the bishop was consecrated by the college of presbyters. Cassian admits that he was ordained by the priest Paphnutius in Egypt (*Conferences*, IV, 1). The Synod of Ancyra in 314, can. 13 (Mansi, II, p. 518, original reading), touches on the thorny problem of the *chorepiscopi*, whose status and powers are not exactly known. The second group contains some cases of ecclesiastical jurisdiction exercised by Charlemagne, who ordered the priests Willehald (d. 799) and Ludger (d. 785) to ordain other priests in the missionary territories of Frisia and Saxony. The third group is of cases duly documented from authentic sources, the papal bulls. Boniface I, in *Sacrae Religionis* (1 February 1400), gave permission to the Abbot of S. Osith in Essex to confer all orders up to and including the priesthood. This was revoked by the bull *Apostolicae Sedis* (6 February 1403), at the instance of the Bishop of London, who felt that his jurisdiction had been interfered with by the abbot. The revocation was not therefore on dogmatic grounds. See *DS* 1145f. Martin V, in *Gerentes ad vos* (16 November 1427), also gave permission for orders up to the priesthood (*DS* 1290) and Innocent VIII, in *Exposcit* (9 April 1489), up to the diaconate (*DS* 1435). G. Vasquez mentions similar privileges accorded by the Pope in the 16th century in favour of Benedictine abbots or Franciscan missionaries, but has not preserved for us the official text of the papal bulls (cf. J. Beyer in *NRT* 76 [1954], pp. 361–7). Vatican II recognizes the bishop as the minister of episcopal ordination (*Lumen Gentium*, art. 21) and as the dispenser of holy orders as part of his general responsibility for the sacraments (*ibid.*, art. 26).

Only the Council of Florence says explicitly that the bishop is the "ordinary" minister of orders (*DS* 1326; cf. 1777; *D* 701, 967). This restriction was not reaffirmed by Vatican II, though it corrected the usual terminology with regard to confirmation by saying that the bishop is the *minister originarius* (*Lumen Gentium*, art. 26; cf. art. 21).

4. *Episcopal and presbyterial tendencies.* Two tendencies may be noted in the West, one "episcopal" and the other "presbyterial": the grace of the priesthood, received in the sacrament of orders, is fundamentally realized in the bishop or in the priest. And in fact, as regards the government of the local Churches, the prerogative of the bishop was never in doubt, except perhaps in the Celtic Churches, where the government was in the hands of the abbots of the great monasteries. The relation of this "princely power" to priestly ordination as such was never very clear, so that it could sometimes even seem that this "power" was independent of all priestly ordination. The causes of this diversity of opinion in theology are complex, and not always of dogmatic inspiration. It seems clear that the vagueness of the NT terminology as regards *episcopi* and *presbyteri* was often at the root of the discussion.

The first signs of this presbyterial tendency are seen in the 4th century.

An Arian called Aerius affirmed the equality of bishop and priest (Augustine, *De Haeresibus*, 53; cf. G. Bardy, *Miscellanea agostiniana*, II [1931], pp. 397–416). In the same work (*De Haeresibus*, 27), Augustine deals incidentally with the Montanist heresy of the Pepuzians or Quintilians, who conferred the priesthood on women. But presbyterial tendencies come to the fore even in orthodox circles, as in Chrysostom and the *Canons of Hippolytus* (B. Botte, *Mélanges Andrieu* [1956], pp. 53–63). The authors who exercised a decisive influence in this matter on the Middle Ages were Jerome and the Ambrosiaster, the latter being identified with Ambrose all through the Middle Ages. Both writers appeal to the NT terminology. However, this theological stand of Jerome cannot be disassociated from his attacks on the growing power of the deacons at Rome and his angry clashes with John, Bishop of Jerusalem (Lennerz, nos. 50, 71–76).

The authority of Jerome and "Ambrose" had a deep influence on the theological reflection of the Middle Ages. Being entrusted above all with the administration of the sacraments, the priest was seen by his contemporaries mainly from the cultic aspect. His mission was defined by his *potestas in corpus eucharisticum* and his power to remit sins. The effect of this impoverishment of the priestly image was to make it very difficult to see how the bishop was different from the priest by virtue of his ordination. Hence this presbyterial notion of orders became very common. The bishop retains as his own only the *potestas in corpus mysticum*, a certain "princely power" (*principalitas*). There is a debate as to whether in some theologians, e.g., Thomas Aquinas, this "princely power" did not retain a quasi-sacramental character. Nonetheless, the canonists in general maintained the strictly sacramental quality of the episcopate.

The controversy between the two tendencies was revived in the middle of the present century. In Belgium and France, where there has been a broad movement for the renewal of the spirituality of the diocesan clergy, which had been too much neglected in the manuals of scholastic theology and in historical studies, efforts have been made to underline the role of the clergy as helpers of the bishop, in a highly "episcopal" perspective (e.g., C. Journet in *Revue Thomiste* 53 [1953], pp. 81–108). Typically, a large number of the books defending this point of view have been written by bishops. Other authors like H. Lennerz, followed by C. Baisi and J. Beyer, base themselves on the facts and doctrines of history to maintain a frankly presbyterial position. (The principal historical points have been touched on above.) Others again try to present the teaching of Thomas Aquinas in forms which avoid over-simplification, hoping thus to escape from over-rigid positions (e.g., Y. Congar in *Maison-Dieu* 4 [1948], pp. 107–28; H. Bouëssé in *RSR* 28 [1954], pp. 368–91).

It might seem that Vatican II has ended this ancient controversy by adopting a frankly "episcopal" doctrine. But the presbysterial tendency does not seem to have disappeared. The doctrine of the scholastics is no longer at the centre of the debate. Some writers, like H. Küng and E. Schillebeeckx, pose the fundamental question as to whether the distinction between episcopacy and priesthood is of divine institution. A closer study of the NT and of the historical evolution of the ministries in the primitive Church, along with ecumenical preoccupations, have led some authors to question the very nature of episcopacy, at least in its present form. (See Bernard Dupuy, "Is there a Dogmatic Distinction between the Function of Priests and the Function of Bishops?", *Concilium* 4, no. 4 [1968], pp. 38–44.) For the first time in the history of theology the debate is taken up by students of the sociology of religion, who are prepared to allege that the present structures of Church government are no longer adapted to the conditions of modern life and to the mentality and mode of work of modern man.

5. *Crystallization of Church thinking in the magisterium.* The Councils of Florence and of Trent simply sum up the *fides* of the Church with regard to orders, as it was understood in the Middle Ages. In the Decree for the Armenians, the fathers of the Council of Florence follow the text of Thomas Aquinas in his *De articulis fidei et Ecclesiae sacramentis* (*DS* 1326, *D* 701). The Council confined itself to determining the forms of the *traditio instrumentorum* according to the principle established by Thomas Aquinas, that "quilibet ordo traditur per collationem illius rei quae praecipue pertinet ad ministerium illius ordinis". Where Thomas says, "Minister huius sacramenti est episcopus", the Council adds the further precision that he is the "ordinarius minister". It is clear that the Council defines the priesthood as the "potestas offerendi sacrificium in Ecclesia", citing the text of the *Pontificale Romanum*. The episcopacy as a sacrament is not mentioned. The bishop is simply recognized as the ordinary minister of orders.

To escape these difficulties, especially that of the reduction of the essential rite of ordination to the *traditio instrumentorum*, contrary to the ancient practice of the Church, theologians have suggested that the Decree for the Armenians was merely disciplinary and did not intend to treat of matters of faith. But this is not convincing. The suggestion is in fact contradicted by the acts of the Council, which clearly show that the declaration treats a matter of *fides*, since it bears directly on reunion with the Roman Church. This is also suggested by the choice of the text of Thomas Aquinas bearing the title *De articulis fidei*. However, close studies of the usage of the word *fides* up to Trent have shown that in the epoch in question the word was used in a wider sense (A. Lang in *Münchener Theologische Zeitschrift* 4 [1953], pp. 133–46). It seems to us that the conciliar magisterium was confirming the opinion of the nature of the priesthood generally held at the time. But there was no intention of defining a matter of faith formally revealed by God.

When we come to Trent, it must be noted above all that Trent regards Florence, including the Decree for the Armenians, as an important witness to the "faith" of the Church. And it should also be noted that the fathers of Trent took a definite interest in the nature of the episcopate. The question was raised from the very beginning of the Council and the crisis which it caused in the third session was so grave that the Council nearly broke up. (See H. Jedin, *Krisis und Wendepunkt des Trienter Konzils* [1941].) But it was mainly the bishops of Spain, France and the Empire who were defending the divine right of the episcopate, especially with regard to the duty of residence, in opposition to the papacy. According to Charles Borromeo, Secretary of State at this period, Pius IV felt that the crisis could become like that of the Council of Constance.

But when one reads the introductory chapters and the canons (*DS* 1763–78, *D* 956a–68), it is clear that the essence of the priesthood is defined as the power to consecrate, offer and administer the body and blood of Christ, and also to forgive or retain sins. The episcopate is dealt with at the end of each text, to affirm that it is part of the *hierarchicus ordo* (without mention of the Pope), that it is superior to the priesthood (*DS* 1768, 1776, 1777, *D* 960, 966, 967) and that its authority is "legitimate" (*DS* 1778, *D* 968). The Council does not formally assert that the episcopate is a sacrament. The omission was deliberate, since the matter was an object of controversy (A. Duval, *Études sur le sacrement de l'ordre* [1957], pp. 277–324; id., "Le sacrement de l'ordre", *Bulletin du Comité des Études* [*Saint Sulpice*] 6 [1962], pp. 448–72). One could follow H. Denis ("Les prêtres", *La vie spirituelle* 118 [1968], pp. 193–232) in saying that Trent used two views of the priesthood, one strictly cultic and the other hierarchical, without really uniting them. For the interpretation of the Council it is important to note that the introductory chapters intend to do no more than give a general survey of the doctrine of the day as commonly held in the Church (H. Jedin, *Begegnung der Christen, Festschrift O. Karrer* [1959], pp. 450–61). And the Council declined to present a complete doctrine of orders, especially in the canons. It merely intended to condemn such opinions of the reformers as appeared "heretical", this word being also used in a wider sense than now. (See the instruction of Charles Borromeo to the legates, of 26 June 1563; J. Susta, *Die römische Kurie und das Konzil von Trient*, IV [1914], p. 100.) These remarks are important for the correct interpretation of another point now in debate, which was not envisaged by Trent in the way in which it is now propounded. This is the question of a temporary priesthood (*DS* 1767, 1771; *D* 960, 961). Trent meant merely to deny that the priesthood could be linked simply to the preaching of the word in such a way that the minister who ceased to preach automatically returned to the lay state.

The theological perspective was profoundly changed by Vatican II. First of all, it restored to the priesthood its true Christological and ecclesiological context, as witness to the paschal mystery (*Lumen Gentium*, arts. 19–29, *Presbyterorum Ordinis*, art. 2). Under the influence of the biblical movement and the ecumenical dialogue, the Council desired to stress the apostolic importance of the ministry of the word, but without abandoning the ministry of sanctification and of authority.

The episcopate is a true sacrament, the "fullness of the priesthood". By virtue of his ordination the bishop is co-opted into the episcopal college united to the Pope. Ordination is the basis of all the other powers. Before the final vote, at the request of the fathers, a statement was added to the effect that the office of priest was "ordini episcopali coniunctum" (*Presbyterorum Ordinis*, art. 2). The priesthood was thus described as in dependence on and conjoined to the episcopate.

As is well known, the Council did not wish to give dogmatic definitions. This means that it laid down the official doctrine of the Church without trying to distinguish formally between dogma and general theological opinion. In view of the controversies preceding the Council, the attitude adopted has the value of a directive. But one can still ask whether this directive bears on a matter of principle (a dogmatic declaration) or a simple point of fact (of the ecclesiastical "economy"). Theological and ecclesiastical reflection after the Council will have to solve the question, if possible.

For a better understanding of the episcopal magisterium, it is important to note how these three ecumenical councils, whose attitudes towards orders have been described, tried in each case to sum up and express the actual life of the Church in this matter, the "instinct of faith" as felt at a given epoch. For the Middle Ages had preserved a realistic notion of the role of the magisterium. It is an exercise of community activity, which does no more than confirm the faith which lives in the Church (cf., for example, *DS* 1405, 1406, 1398; *D* 723a).

A final point of interest is that on 30 November 1947, Pius XII decreed that henceforward the rite of ordination for bishops, priests and deacons would include the imposition of hands and part of the Preface of the rite, without prejudice to previous opinions and practices (*DS* 3857–61; *D* 2301; F. Hürth in *Periodica* 37 [1948], pp. 9–56). This was implicitly a preparation for Vatican II, since the episcopate was considered as a sacrament of orders.

6. *Canonical ordinations and the need for reform.* Since Pope John XXIII ordered a revision of the canon law in force since 1918, the canonical legislation on orders has been called in question in varying degrees. Further, Vatican II decreed certain changes and adumbrated new structures of government which will have to be incorporated into the reform of canon law. The rediscovery of collegiality in orders and of its social roots in the people of God has led to a reinforcement of the synodal structure of the Church and orders: the episcopal synods representing national episcopates at Rome (*Christus Dominus*, arts. 5, 36; *Ad Gentes*, art. 29); national or regional episcopal conferences (*Christus Dominus*, arts. 18, 37, 38); the diocesan pastoral council (*Christus Dominus*, arts. 27, 29) and the parish council (*Apostolicam Actuositatem*, art. 10). The decree on the pastoral office of the bishops (*Christus Dominus*) contains a number of general directions which will have to be put in practice and hence receive a canonical statute, like the reform of the Curia (*Christus Dominus*, arts. 9, 10), diocesan organizations (*ibid.*, art. 17), the independence of the Church in the nomination of bishops (*ibid.*, art. 20), the retiring age for bishops (*ibid.*, art. 21), the demarcation of dioceses (*ibid.*, art. 23), diocesan responsibility for Christians of other rites (*ibid.*, art. 23), the status of coadjutor and auxiliary bishops (*ibid.*, arts. 25, 26), the new organization of the diocescan curia and pastoral councils (*ibid.*, art. 27), the reform of incardination (*ibid.*, art. 28), the reorganization of the parish clergy (*ibid.*, arts. 30–32), relations with religious (*ibid.*, arts. 34–35), reorganization of synods and provincial councils (*ibid.*, art. 36) and the erection of ecclesiastical districts under a metropolitan (*ibid.*, arts. 39–41). In the meanwhile, "directories" are to be drawn up giving specific directives for the inauguration of the work of reforming the canons, a task which will no doubt take many years (*ibid.*, art. 44).

There is no need to summarize here the present canon law on ordinations. Excellent surveys are given in recent encyclopedias (*LTK*, VII, cols. 120–2; *Dictionnaire de Droit Canonique*, VI, cols. 11, 25–32, 1145–55). Some dispositions are no longer observed. Others, like the age of the ordinand (can. 975), the usefulness of certain canonical irregularities, partly inspired by the OT (cans. 983–91), the canonical titles for ordination, partly deriving from the Middle Ages (cans. 979–82), tonsure and minor orders (can. 949), education in the seminary *a teneris annis* (can. 972), and the liturgical times for ordination (can. 1006) are subjects of discussion and call for reform.

Other more essential dispositions will remain. The ordinary minister of ordination is the bishop (can. 951), without prejudice to the rights of the Holy See (cans. 952–3). The bishop is to judge the aptitude of candidates for the diocesan clergy (cans. 956–63). Regulars are presented by their major superior (cans. 964–7). A candidate may not be forced to receive orders against his will, or be prevented if he is apt (cans. 971–3).

The code of canon law will probably have to solve fairly quickly some much more urgent and difficult questions: the ordination of women, ecclesiastical celibacy or ordination of married men, the highly controversial notion of the part-time priest. These questions do not appear to be dogmatic. They should be solved in terms of the real needs of the people of God at this epoch, and not by virtue of abstract principles. They are matters of "ecclesiastical economy" (cf. *DS* 1728, 3857; *D* 931, 2301) which, being pre-eminently pastoral, should be given a "pluralist" solution, that is, one adapted to the situation of the Christian people in a given region.

The most urgent question is the crisis of authority in face of the anachronistic forms of its exercise: vertical in the extreme, with a dubious use of secrecy, a lack of respect for the human person inspired by a mythical confusion between the will of God and the authority exercised by man, even within the structures instituted by Christ. Communications now seem to be disturbed between the Pope (and the Roman Curia) and the bishops, between the bishop and his priests, between the clergy and the faithful. It is symptomatic that in some countries the priests have felt the need of forming as it were trade unions to defend their rights, that some priests and lay people have formed a sort of underground Church. This type of crisis cannot, of course, be solved by canonical legislation. What is needed is a climate of confidence and sincerity, a psychological re-education and, fundamentally, a conversion of heart in keeping with the gospel. Nonetheless, it would be well if canon law could provide certain synodal and other structures which would facilitate relationships between the various members of the ecclesiastical hierarchy, set up channels of communication and establish guarantees against abuse of power by the local authorities. This has always been one of the traditional functions of the papacy, and it would be failing its mission of testimony to unity at an essential point if it now renounced this responsibility and enclosed itself in a more and more tragic isolation.

III. Theological Synthesis

A. Questions of Method

1. *Terminology*. Many technical terms of theology, especially in the matter of orders, are being called in question at the present day. We shall therefore try to discuss the realities in question, avoiding as far as possible the technical terms whose scope and meaning are debatable and debated.

We omit therefore the triple division of the priestly mission as the power of order (the priestly power of sanctification or "ministry"), the power of the magisterium (prophetic office) and the power of jurisdiction (kingly power). It is now fashionable to stress the "prophetic" mission of the bishop or priest. We omit this category because in the Bible prophetism has a well-defined sense. Prophecy is a religious fact essentially linked to a personal vocation by the Spirit and a profound docility of soul in a commitment of faith which escapes all institutional forms. One is not a prophet because of one's function in the Church, but by a special vocation. To postulate that a man receives a prophetic mission by his ordination is to falsify the biblical meaning of the word and, worse still, to lead the person in question into error. Many bishops and priests are far from being prophets, though they are excellent priests. In other words, the ministry of the word and the prophetic charge are two different vocations, though they may, of course, co-exist in the same person.

Another example of the evolution of terminology is provided by the new *Ordo Baptismi* for adults, published at Rome *ad experimentum* in 1966. This *ordo* avoids using the term "celebrant" for the minister, since all the members of the ecclesial community participate actively in the conferring of baptism. Only the term specific to the function is retained, that of "priest".

Instead of the word "power", we prefer to say "priestly function", while recognizing the possible dangers. There is a certain ambiguity, since when taken in the ordinary sense it lacks ontological depth. But we should wish to avoid in any case all suggestions of a "metaphysical clericalism" which would place the priest on a higher level of being than the faithful. Hence by function we simply mean that the Christian who has been ordained remains fundamentally one of the faithful, a brother "among brothers" (*Presbyterorum Ordinis*, arts. 3, 9), who has received from Christ a specific mission of service, service of Christ and of the community. We do not exclude the fact that ordination disposes the priest "ontologically", that is, that his specific mission orientates his whole person and hence his whole life towards this service. When God calls us, our whole person is engaged or "touched".

2. *Christological and ecclesiological structures*. Orders are not a self-subsisting reality. They are unthinkable outside their dogmatic context of Christology and ecclesiology.

a) *Christological context*. This is the most fundamental, not merely as a principle of synthesis in an abstract theological system, but as an existential truth which should be given expression in the whole of a life. Our only priest is the risen Christ. The priest, along with the faithful, is a witness to this paschal mystery in the world. His specific mission is to share in the mission of Christ, the envoy of the Father, in the power of the Spirit, for the building up of the Church as sacrament of salvation for the world.

b) *Ecclesiological context*. Outside the Church the priest has no meaning. Vatican II has radically changed our concept of the Church. A theology of orders not integrated into this new image of the Church would be inadequate. The new dimensions of the Church may be summarized as follows.

(i) First and foremost, the Church is not a static reality, fully achieved. It is "event". The Church is, so to speak, a matter of "continuous creation", produced by faith and charity, expressed above all in the sacraments. Further, it is in movement, towards God, on pilgrimage towards God throughout history, always alert to the divine invitation which comes to us in the "hour" of grace present in the world. Ordination places the priest squarely within this region of responsiveness.

(ii) The Church is a hierarchy, but not on the model of a pyramid, where authority descends vertically from the top to the base. The people of God is the reality of the Church. Within this fellowship of faith there is a hierarchy of service and ministry. No one in the Church has a monopoly of the Spirit, who is given to each Christian according to his charge, his function and his personal vocation.

(iii) Hence the Church is a fellowship of faith and charity. The collegiality of orders, the decisive rediscovery of Vatican II, is nothing else – contrary to certain exclusively juridical interpretations – than sharing in this fellowship on the level of a ministry of authority. Hence the collegiality in question cannot be exercised independently of this fellowship in faith of the people of God. There is a continuous osmosis or interpenetration between the fellowship of faith and the college of those in orders. This is not the same thing at all as the democratic systems of our age, though the democratic spirit may have favoured the rediscovery of the community dimensions which were already outlined in the NT.

(iv) Hence the Church is above all the sacrament of salvation. The community of the faithful united with its pastors is the visible and efficacious sign of the life-giving presence of the risen Christ in this world, uniting us to the Father by his Spirit. This life of grace is present and active in all men and in all men's forms of religion ("the anonymous Christians"), but this presence is signified and actualized by the Church which is part of this world. At the same time, however, as well as being a mystery of salvation, the Church is also a visible organization of men with an authority proper to it. These two aspects of the Church, its sacramental reality and its sociological and institutional character in the world, are inseparable, though distinct. The main source of the woes of the Church at the present time is the continual confusion, a legacy of the Middle Ages, between the authority exercised by men and the "theandric" reality of the paschal mystery which gives life to the Church and to the world, from within. This confusion of ideas and practical principles is at the root of the confusion between morals and canon law, between the fully free and personal will of God and human authority in a religious society founded by Christ. This confusion gives rise to the strange anomaly that in Vatican II the Church delared that it recognized liberty of conscience outside the Church, while it still seems incapable of devising structures within which a similar liberty will be allowed to its members and its priests.

We must finally mention a point which lends itself to many misunderstandings today. It is generally expressed by affirming a unity-in-distinction of the vertical and horizontal lines of religious existence. In past centuries, stress was laid almost exclusively on the vertical dimension between God and man, under two aspects: from God to us (less happily called the male dimension) and from us to God (still more unhappily called the bridal dimension). In our own times there is a reaction which tends to consider only the horizontal dimension. These words, especially the mention of the "vertical", have at the most symbolic value. God may be considered as "beyond this world" or "above us" or perhaps as "within us" or as the "grounds of our being" (P. Tillich, followed by J. A. T. Robinson), as "before us" (J. Moltmann) or "behind us" (M. Bellet). In each case we have an image which tries to correct other images, but in all cases they refer to the same reality, the truly personal relation which the religious man has with his God. This relationship with God has to be embodied on the horizontal plane, which is that of human existence. This is the problem of theology when considered as religious anthropology. Since the priest has to represent the divinity in a certain way, he must inevitably express in his activity the immanence of this divine presence in our lives. It would be calamitous if the mutism of our epoch with regard to the divine mysteries should develop in us a negative attitude which would reduce Christianity to a vague humanism of brotherly solidarity. The same tendency seems to be at work in a number of authors who seek a solution for our modern difficulties only in studies of the sociological and psychological aspects of the priesthood. These studies are very important. The distinction we make in the unity of the ecclesial reality between the Church as mystery and sacrament of salvation and the Church as institution and human organization lends these studies more value than formerly in theological reflection. But we must refuse categorically to reduce the theology of the priesthood to a treatise on religious sociology.

B. Priestly Functions

In expounding these functions we shall respect the ecclesial structures which we have analysed above.

1. *The Church as the paschal mystery of salvation*. The Church is continually embodying its being and action in the sacraments, especially the Eucharist (K. Rahner, *The Church and the Sacraments*, Quaestiones Disputatae 10 [1963]). The sacraments are inseparable from the faith, the "faith of the Church", and hence the faith of the community which celebrates the mystery of salvation and the faith of the person who receives a sacrament (E. Schillebeeckx). Hence the celebration of a sacrament necessarily includes the

proclamation of salvation by the ministry of the word (the sacramental homily and the sacramental prayers as confession of faith), for its fullness. The sacraments are celebrated by the community of the baptized believers, under the presidency of the priest who represents it. But the priest represents still more our unique priest, Christ. Hence he acts *in persona Christi* in a strict sense. His priestly activity is the sacramental visibility of the "theandric" initiative of Christ. To represent Christ entails a certain depersonalization, which is expressed in liturgical symbols. But Christ cannot be fully represented in his sacramental visibility without a personal commitment in faith on the part of the priest. Hence the priest acts *in persona Christi* both by his work of sanctification (from God to us by the ministry of the sacramental celebration and preaching), and by his task of presiding at the prayer which is an expression of ecclesial faith (from us to God in the sacramental prayers: the prayer of the priest being the sacramental visibility of the "per Dominum nostrum Jesum Christum" in which our liturgical prayers end). This task is confided exclusively to the priest, though in certain circumstances the ecclesiastical economy permits lay people to participate in it, as for instance in the celebration of marriage.

2. *The Church as a human institution.* The Church, as we have seen, is a human organization which cannot live and perpetuate itself without an authority recognized by all. By reason of the most profound reality of the paschal mystery and the sacrament of salvation, this authority has always been acknowledged to reside in the college of bishops, united to the Bishop of Rome. The bishops delegate this authority in part to the priests, their helpers in the sacramental ministry, and to the lay people, members of the Church of Christ with full rights. It is not impossible that a larger share of authority may be accorded to the lay people in future, in a process of declericalization. This authority is not exercised *in persona Christi*, that is, its decrees, decisions and directives are not identically the expression of the will of God. The authority is *in nomine Christi*, that is, it is willed by God in itself, and it entails some degree of indefectibility (a better term than infallibility here). For it cannot, in essential questions, separate us from God, because of the inspiration of the Spirit expressed in the priestly collegiality, which is intimately united to the fellowship of faith of the whole Church. This authority is unique in a certain sense. It cannot be reduced to any form of purely human authority, and hence can be incorporated in patriarchal, aristocratic or democratic structures, adapting itself in the matter to the sociological structures of community and authority in the humanity in which and for which it was established. Hence it is also in this sense a ministry of authority. We may not erect into dogmas concrete forms of the exercise of authority in the past, for the Church continues to belong to the world in which it lives. Its faith does not imprison it in outdated forms of authority.

3. *The expansion of the actual life of the Church.* Since therefore the Church is both a sacrament of salvation and an institution it has two poles or centres of activity from which it acts upon the whole concrete life of the Church.

a) *The sacramental centre.* The sacramental reality of the Church radiates its influence through the sacraments and the preaching of the word. The administration of the sacramentals is normally reserved to priests, on the analogy of the sacraments, though Vatican II foresees forms of administration to be confided to lay people (*Sacrosanctum Concilium*, art. 79). Obviously, the ministry of the word is of extreme importance. The Church lives by faith, which must therefore be constantly nourished, enlightened, guided and strengthened. The ministry of the sacraments imposes on the priest one of his most exacting tasks. He has to prepare the faithful for the sacraments, and confirm the graces bestowed through them, by preaching in all its forms: as proclamation of salvation, instruction, consolation, spiritual direction, personal testimony and fraternal partnership in the common search for the will of God in actual life. This ministry is chiefly exercised by priests, both as regards the members of the Church and those who are outside it (missionary activity). Their preaching has a special note of authority, based on the apostolic mission which they received at ordination. Nonetheless, the renewed sense of the apostolic mission common to all the members of the Church ought to bring with it a great increase in the number of such tasks entrusted to lay people. Like priests, they have the duty of giving testimony to the faith which lives in them, and they have at their disposal many occasions of helping their fellows to a better knowledge of the faith and a more personal dedication in that faith. By the help they can give to underdeveloped countries, they can do much more than before to collaborate with the immense missionary task of the Church, directly or indirectly.

b) *The institutional centre of authority.* The authority of the priesthood in the Church is deployed at various levels. The Church is directly responsible for the purity of the faith, both on the doctrinal and practical level, in a spirit of fidelity to its saviour. Hence the episcopal college has the right to regulate the public formulation of the faith, the public teaching of the faith in theology and catechesis, the editing and publication of liturgical and religious books, the administration of the sacraments and liturgical prayer. The secondary question remains, however, as to whether the exercise of this authority should not search for forms which will be more respectful of the individual conscience and of the cultural and religious pluralism inherent in the community of man. On the plane of morals, the Church is directly competent only in the preservation of the gospel message, which should inspire, purify and orientate the ethical behaviour of a given culture. In this complex and difficult work of the humanization of life and the adaptation of morals to the principles of the gospel, the Church, and hence too the priesthood, recognizes the scientific and practical competence of men, even of those not belonging to the Church, as has been explained most strikingly in one of the most revolutionary documents of Vatican II, *Gaudium et Spes* (Pastoral Constitution on the Church in the Modern World). Finally, the Church undoubtedly has the right to control the forms of life in its own fellowship, to pass laws and impose sanctions, and to determine its relationships with the State and with other religious bodies. This authority is often entrusted to priests, such as the nuncios, but it is obvious that apart from certain prerogatives reserved to the college of bishops and the ministry of unity belonging to the Church of Rome, many of these tasks could be carried out by lay people whose technical competence would be greater.

C. The Effects of Ordination

Vatican II threw new light on the decisive role of sacramental ordination. Fundamentally, the specific mission of the priest is conferred by ordination. But its role had been obscured by a too individualistic notion of the sacraments as privileged means of grace, and by the predominance of a juridical notion of the Church, as though the kingly powers of Christ were delegated to bishops, priests and faithful through the agency of the Vicar of Christ, the Pope. In this way, the Church seemed to be established primarily on the primacy of jurisdiction of the Roman Pontiff, a doctrine completely foreign to the gospel and Christian antiquity. – By the effects of ordination we mean the sacramental "character" and the sacramental grace.

1. *The sacramental character.* A number of misconceptions still persist in this matter, due to wrong notions of theology and history. There is no common doctrine of the character in theology. The most restrictive definition makes it simply the impossibility of re-ordination, while the tendency to enhance it has produced a sort of complex metaphysical superstructure, due, as we think, to a very jejune theology of grace. The trinitarian and Christological aspects which the latter tendency gladly discovers in the character are already fully realized in the riches of the mystery of grace. The tendency in question has promoted a mythic theology of the priesthood which places it on a higher level of being than the rest of the faithful, a metaphysical clericalism which is responsible for barring the way to many reforms at the present time. The study of the development of this doctrine reveals a number of further anomalies. When Augustine, who initiated the doctrine of the character, speaks of its "inviolability", he is thinking simply of the inviolability of the confession of the Trinity, even if made in a Church separated from the Catholica. When Augustine speaks of the effect of a sacrament which remains, independently of personal sins, he uses other expressions such as *sacramentum manens*, *consecratio* or *ordinatio*. The character, for Augustine, remains the external rite in which the Trinity is invoked, that is, the visible and audible expression of "the faith of the Church". Its inviolability consists of the fact that the ordinand is adopted into the "ordo" of the Church ministry.

For Thomas Aquinas, like the other theologians of classical scholasticism in the Middle Ages, the character is still the external rite inasmuch as it is the basis, in the eyes of all, of the legitimacy of ordination in the Church. "Hence the character is primarily the rite by which one is given a certain situation, and not the fact of being in a certain situation" (E. Schillebeeckx, *Tijdschrift voor Theologie* 8 [1948], pp. 424–30; id., *De sacramentele heilseconomie* [1952], pp. 489–91; N. Haring in *Mediaeval Studies* 14 [1954], pp. 79–97; id. in *Scholastik* 30 [1955], pp. 481–512; 31 [1956], pp. 41–69, 182–212). But in early scholasticism a tendency may already be noted to include in the description of the character the effect of ordination (legitimate membership of the college of ministers) as well as the simple rite which hitherto had "characterized" the ordinand. This development was embodied in the now classical formula which affirms that the character is *sacramentum et res* (sign and hence rite, and the effect of the rite), while the grace is *res tantum*. For Thomas Aquinas, in the early stages of his teaching, this second meaning was secondary and metaphorical (cf. E. Schillebeeckx, *De sacramentele heilseconomie*, pp. 505–10). He soon added the *deputatio ad cultum*, which assimilated the character to an interior disposition in view of liturgical worship. The essentials of the doctrine of Aquinas are simply that ordination places the ordinand "in face of the community in the name of Christ". Subsequent scholastic theology, however, translated this notion into ontological terms.

The Councils of Florence and Trent do no more than repeat this theological notion which had become more or less general. The character is a "signum quoddam spiritale et indelebile; unde ea iterari non possunt" (*DS* 1609; cf. 1313; *D* 852, 695). But the scope of Trent's definition is different from that of Florence, though the enunciation is the same. Trent was concerned above all with defending the reality of the ministry against certain reformers who wished to suppress the distinction between the community and the minister. But it would be an abuse of the text and a disregard of the intentions of the Council to take this definition as a dogmatic crystallization of scholastic speculation. Some of the fathers of Trent were against any definition of the nature of the character by the Council, which is understandable when one remembers that Scotists and nominalists were in the majority at Trent, and they did not accept the Thomist tradition. In any case, no objections were raised when, at the beginning of the present century, Cardinal Billot proposed a new interpretation of the character, which reduced it to the right to the actual graces proper to the sacrament. Finally, it may be noted that both Aquinas (*Summa Theologica*, III, q. 63, a. 2 ad 3) and Trent refused to affirm the "eternal" nature of the character. It has no meaning except in this earthly life, a view which has been confirmed by Vatican II (*Lumen Gentium*, art. 48).

This glance at the evolution of the doctrine of the character is of importance at the present day. A supposedly classical and common doctrine of the character is in many ways a hindrance and a block to the concrete adaptation of the priesthood to the religious needs of the Christian people. If some theologians are hesitant when sociologists and pastoral needs suggest the institution of part-time priests, it is primarily the scholastic doctrine of the character which causes difficulty. But a scholastic tradition, adopted without critical study of its content and its historical evolution, should not be allowed to brake the pastoral reform of the priesthood.

We believe that the more realistic notion of the character as held in ancient times should be taken up again. The character is above all the visible rite of ordination by which the ordinand is legitimately incorporated into the college of his "order". This incorporation implies a number of rights and duties. Its principal element is the mission of service with regard to the community of the Church and of all mankind. The priest, sharing in the mission of Christ, should live and die "not for the nation only, but to gather into one the children of God who are scattered abroad" (Jn 11:52). Finally, this incorporation may be called a consecration. By belonging to the order for which he was ordained, the ordinand is "set apart", but not "separated" from men, who are his brothers (*Presbyterorum Ordinis*, art. 3). The main effect of this consecration is that it is definitive. No priest may be re-ordained. This aspect of the character may be based on the fidelity of the divine election rather than on an ontological quality taken separately. In this view, the main meaning of the character is retained, that is, it retains a symbolic function – *sacramentum et res* – with a reference to the divine promise which guarantees us the fullness of its graces. But there is nothing to prevent the Church freeing a priest temporarily or permanently from the obligations of his ordination to return him to the condition and life of the laity. This is a pastoral, not a dogmatic question.

2. *The sacramental grace*. Sacramental grace cannot be different from the fundamental grace of justification, brought about in us by the inhabitation, proper to each, of the three divine persons. At the present time, its eschatological character may be underlined, since this trinitarian presence is given us in the form of a dynamic attraction towards its final realization in the kingdom of God. All the sacraments are celebrations of our Chritian hope "until he comes" (1 Cor 11:26). This is also true of ordination. The process of justification is not mechanical. It is divine, and hence sovereignly free and personal. Hence the grace of orders is a deepening and a re-orientation of baptismal grace in view of the specific mission and service of the priest. It thus allows for the development of a truly

priestly spirituality, fundamentally identical with that of the rest of the faithful in the brotherhood of the same faith. This grace also unites the priest to the other members of his order in the brotherhood of their common mission. For all are called to share together in the same mission of Christ, to represent the same Christ in the celebration of the sacraments and to speak in his name in the same ministry of authority. The bishop or priest who detaches himself from the other members of his order no longer possesses the same guarantees for the efficacy of his ministry. This is ultimately the reason why we are so interested in the restoration of the ancient theology of the character. This theology affirms more strongly that the grace of the sacrament is linked to a great extent to the faithful exercise of priestly collegiality.

IV. Conclusion

In conclusion, we may mention the main pastoral problems which arise at the present day with regard to the priesthood and its future in the Church. What will be the image of the priest? As E. Schillebeeckx says, we do not contemplate the future, we fashion it. Right practice in a sincere fellowship of faith is the best guarantee of future orthodoxy. Hence it is the task of all of us, together, to construct the future image of the priest.

Secondly, it is important in this effort at renewal to distinguish the truly dogmatic arguments from those of the "ecclesiastical economy" or dispensation. The "substance" of the priesthood is very rich, but at the same time very simple. As history shows, it allows of forms of exercise which vary very widely. Most of the arguments derive from reflection on pastoral needs.The main concern of the Church in such pastoral reflection is the good of souls. Very often, supposedly dogmatic objections or arguments obscure the primordial fact that the *sacramenta sunt propter homines*. The principle that the sacraments are for the good of men holds true above all for the priesthood.

Piet Fransen

ORIGINAL SIN

1. *Introduction.* a) The fundamental Christian doctrine of original sin meets with a threefold misunderstanding today.

(i) It is felt to be in contradiction to that present-day conception of man in which he feels himself from the start, by his very nature and essence, to be good, sound and whole. Men regard the existing individual and social defects of man (sickness, crime, inner or social disharmonies) as merely secondary products of civilization and society or as progressively eliminable phenomena of friction in the development of men and mankind. Men accordingly strive for a fortunate condition of freedom from all these defects (from "alienation from self"). And this condition is regarded as belonging to this world and as attainable by man's own power. All this would be contradicted, it is thought, by original sin as an abiding existential of man.

(ii) Original sin (usually of course expressed in other terms: absurdity of human existence, etc.) is regarded as purely and simply identical with the (tragic) nature of man (his finite character, etc.), as a reality impossible to abolish, constitutive of man's very nature, a reality which cannot therefore be referred back to a primordial historical event at the beginning of mankind, but which means that man as such is flawed, a tragic and insuperable contradiction (all forms of pessimistic existentialism).

(iii) Original sin is sometimes regarded in a univocal way even by Christians, misinterpreting the Church's teaching, as the same as personal sin, if not in its cause at least in its nature (as "habitual" sin). The problems thus created (a collective guilt produced by someone else) then cause original sin to be either accepted as a "mystery" or rejected as an intrinsic contradiction. (Other secondary misconceptions or inadequate views will be mentioned later.)

b) In this situation of the doctrine of original sin at the present day, it is understandable but not on that account excusable that the doctrine plays a very small part in the contemporary presentation of Christianity. It is of course not denied in the Church (though the case is to some extent different in Protestant theology). But it is atrophied and largely a catechism truth, mentioned at its place in the system and then forgotten in daily life and average preaching. Unfortunately it no longer has any really formative influence in contemporary man's vital conception of human reality. That is also due to the fact that concupiscence and death are felt as a matter of course to be so natural that an experience of man's original sinfulness can only be linked to them with difficulty. Moreover, baptism is regarded as annulling original sin more or less in such a way that the latter is only felt to be a vital problem as regards unbaptized children. This average state of preaching must be considered a serious minimizing of the Christian doctrine of original sin. This does not mean, however, that the actual earlier concrete attitude of Christendom to the doctrine, extending from Augustine deep into the age of the Reformation and into religious feeling coloured by Jansenism, must be a norm and pattern for us in every respect today. From Augustine onwards this doctrine was in fact linked with pessimistic feelings (a tragic conception of man) and with a view of salvation as restricted in extent, which was not identical with the doctrine of original sin itself. Original sin was not taken as designating a feature in the constitution of human reality which is always and from the start comprised within God's salvific will for all and the powerful grace of Christ, but as the situation of all, out of which a subsequent grace saves only some; the universality of original sin was clearer than the universality of man's redeemed condition, chiefly because it was not clearly seen how the universality of God's saving will and the fact that Christ died for all men could be translated into a structural feature intrinsically characterizing the personal life of every man even prior to his justification. Consequently the universal redemption by Christ was regarded as affecting the individual only when the process of justification itself or baptism took place.

2. *On the history of the dogma of original sin.* The teaching of Scripture about original sin, which is very brief and sporadic (see below), was not developed until Augustine (with the term: *peccatum originale*). The Greek Fathers with their incarnational theory of redemption and in their struggle against the pessimism and determinism of Gnosticism and Manichaeism were not very interested in the doctrine of original sin (though it is not absent). Augustine appeals to Scripture and the practice of infant baptism in his controversy with Pelagianism, which denied original sin. He stresses the doctrine of original sin as a dogma binding in faith, and its universality. He sees its nature in the concupiscence which turns men from God, to the extent that, and as long as, this inherent stain of guilt is not destroyed by baptism. He regards it as transmitted by the *libido* in the parents' love by which a human being comes into existence. This teaching is linked to a view of salvation as limited in range: most men are left by God's just judgment in the *massa damnata* constituted by original sin. To the extent that concupiscence infects all the acts of the sinner, all his acts are "sin" (which does not mean that they

are *new* sins). Augustine does not work out the intrinsic difference between original and personal sin because the consequences in the next world are the same. In the Middle Ages from Anselm of Canterbury onwards, supernatural and habitual grace was clarified as sanctifying grace and by a more precise doctrine of *iustitia originalis* (placing its fundamental basis in sanctifying grace). The essence of original sin was increasingly situated in the lack of sanctifying grace for which Adam's actual sin was responsible. Concupiscence now appeared simply as the consequence or as the material factor of original sin (Aquinas) and so it became more intelligible why original sin is really blotted out in baptism, although concupiscence remains. The Council of Trent defined (with the Reformers) a real inward original sin in all (except Mary), which is caused by Adam's sin, is really effaced by justification and (against the Reformers) does *not* consist in concupiscence, since this persists in the justified, but in the lack of original righteousness (justice) and holiness, which the Council regarded as constituted by the grace of justification as interior and habitual. Post-Tridentine theology developed various theories as to why the factual lack of this grace in us, as descendants of Adam, is not simply a consequence of sin, merely negative absence, but is something *in us* which ought not to be, or theories why it would be possible to impute the sin of Adam to us. For a long time now theology has taught and emphasized the merely *analogous* similarity between original sin and personal sin, although in systematic theology this recognition has not always been sufficiently maintained.

3. *Systematic theology.* a) *Preliminary considerations.* (i) Original sin is certainly a mystery which is not to be rationalistically disintegrated. We must inquire, however, what objectively and epistemologically is the real ground of this mystery. Its nature need not consist in an unintelligible imputation of the sinful *act* of the first man, nor in "collective guilt", since both of these lead to contradictions and are not required by the dogma of original sin. The genuine ground of this mystery lies in the fact that sanctifying grace is a mystery, because it is the self-communication of the essentially holy God. This self-communication of the God who alone is essentially (ontologically) holy is, as grace, antecedent to the free decision of a creature who is ambivalent and therefore not holy by his very essence. By it, therefore, there is a holiness of man which is *antecedent* to the moral goodness ("holiness") of the free decision, and (where it is accepted in freedom) confers on this decision and the condition that ensues from it a holy quality which it does not possess of itself. A lack which ought not to exist of a "holiness" which is antecedent to moral decision (the lack of endowment with the holy Pneuma of God) therefore posits a state of unholiness which is antecedent to the individual's moral decision. This assumes that it is possible to make it intelligible how the divine obligation of this holiness is conceivable in respect of the individual without its becoming a directly *moral* demand on the individual, which would be meaningless if addressed to a person who inculpably cannot fulfil it. The fact that the mystery of original sin has its ground in the mystery of the bestowal of sanctifying grace also explains why the actual doctrine of original sin only appears in Scripture when the divinization of man by the Pneuma of God is explicitly grasped.

(ii) The mere analogy which holds between the concept of original sin and that of (grave) personal sin as "sin" is not seriously contested by any theologian and is not excluded by the teaching of the Church. It must, however, also be firmly and clearly maintained, as will be made even clearer below. The analogous character applies from the start, therefore, to all the elements which constitute the nature of habitual "sin": its cause (another's decision – one's own); its inner nature (its pre-existence as the situation of freedom – lasting character of the free decision); its consequences ("punishment" of sin only in an analogous sense as resultant phenomenon – punishment for sin as reaction to personal decision oriented towards finality); its relation to the will of God (will of the Creator – will of the legislator imposing personal obligation); its relation to the situation regarding salvation (dialectical relation between two existentials – non-dialectical relation of a free decision in Yes or No).

(iii) Original sin cannot be regarded as more universal and efficacious than the effects of redemption deriving from Christ (cf. Rom 5:15–17). It is ultimately not prior *in time* to redemption. Adam's sinful *action* was prior in time to Christ's redemptive *action*. But original sin and being redeemed are two existentials of the human situation in regard to salvation, which at all times determine human existence. It may be assumed that sin was only permitted by God within the domain of his unconditional and stronger salvific will, which from the very beginning was directed towards God's self-communication in Christ.

b) *The testimony of Scripture*. Although in the aetiological OT account (Gen 2:8–3:24) the loss of familiar intercourse with God by our first parents, as well as hardship, suffering and death, are explained by the (first) sin of these first parents, the OT is not yet aware of original sin in the strict sense as the consequence of the first sin. In the gospels also there are only hints of the fall of man; a condition produced in all men by the fall is nowhere perceptible. The decisive biblical statement is found in Paul: 1 Cor 15:21f. and, above all, Rom 5:12–21. In the latter passage Paul speaks of original sin (cf. the Tridentine decree, *D* 787–92) by first drawing a parallel (verse 18) between Adam and Christ (or the effect on all men of Adam's action and of that of Christ) and deduces from both a situation of disaster or salvation which indeed is ratified by individual human beings (by their own sin or faith), but is antecedent to this decision and really and intrinsically affects man, making him through Adam a sinner without the Pneuma (verse 19) and through Christ, a person sought by God's active salvific will (one who, objectively, is redeemed). Catholic theology certainly would need to view more clearly than is usually the case this objectively redeemed condition antecedent to faith and sacrament, in a Pauline way, as an existential intrinsically characterizing man. Only in that way is the precise parallel made clear between the situation of perdition deriving from Adam and the situation of redemption deriving from Christ, as well as the way in which in each case the situation is prior to personal decision, which then ratifies it by personal sin (which Paul also envisages in verse 12), or by faith.

c) *The Church's teaching*. Original sin (already taught at the Council of Carthage, A.D. 418; *D* 101ff.; cf. also *D* 174f.) was treated in detail and in doctrinal definition by the Council of Trent (*D* 787–92): existence of a personal actual sin of the first man, by which his original holiness and righteousness was lost, which brought about in him the domination of the devil and death and which brought him into a worse condition in body and soul; he lost precisely this holiness and righteousness for us also, so that consequently not only death but also sin (as habitual) passed to all men; this inherited sin (which is inherited through common descent, not by imitation) is in origin one, but is truly proper to each and is only removed by Christ's redemption, so that for this reason the baptism of infants is important for salvation; the stain of guilt of original sin is not identical with concupiscence since this remains in those who are justified. Pius XII emphasized the importance of monogenism for the doctrine of original sin (*D* 2328).

d) *Synthesis of the doctrine of original sin.* (i) The fundamental conviction of Christianity about redemption and grace is that all men are offered divinizing and forgiving grace but in such a way that it is given to all only through Christ, and not simply because they are human beings or members of mankind (if this is thought of without Christ) and it is given to all as forgiving sins. That is already implied by Jesus' own interpretation of himself and his expiatory death "for all". The NT simply expounds this, but does not substantially expand it.

(ii) This means that a man lacks God's sanctifying Penuma (as offered and accepted), *precisely because* he is a man and member of the human race. In regard to man, however, the will of God is that man should have the divinizing Pneuma. (This will is an element of God's will to a creation divinized by his self-communication.) And that will (as the actual concrete creative will) is antecedent even to God's moral demand on the freedom of the individual. Consequently if the divinizing Pneuma is not there, this is only conceivable because of guilt freely incurred (otherwise its absence would be unintelligible, in view of God's will). Yet the absence is contrary to God's will, even where the responsibility of the individual free being is not in question (because he is not culpably responsible for its absence). This lack which in this sense ought not to exist, of a divinizing holy grace atencedent to personal decision, has therefore in an analogous sense the character of a sin. It is a state which ought not to be (and ought not to have been). (This in itself would have been true of a mere *consequence* of sin opposed to the creative will as such.) It is also a state in which ontological holiness is lacking, antecedent to personal decision, but which in contra-distinction to the other consequences of sin which cannot deprive their subject of holiness, must be characterized as sin. This deprivation in the descendants of the first man also of course presupposes that it is brought about by guilt, since it is something that ought not to be. In that case it can exist as a consequence of sin *contrary* to God's creative will. This in turn presupposes as its condition that God was willing to give grace (in subordination to and in dependence on Christ) to man in the unity of the human race and its original "covenant" with God, precisely inasmuch as men are the descendants of the first man endowed with grace. It presupposes that since God owes grace to no one, he could link it to any meaningful condition, and therefore to the steadfastness of the first man. If this condition is not verified, then men receive the offer of the divine Pneuma not as "children of Adam" but only because of Christ to whom as head of mankind the will of God remains attached even despite sin. As children of Adam standing in a physical, historical connection with the beginning of humanity, men do not have the divine Pneuma. They "inherit" *generatione* the "origin-sin". The mode of that connection, normal (libidinous) generation, or artificial insemination, has no significance.

(iii) Since this lack (which ought not to exist) of the Pneuma is in each instance an inner condition proper to men – precisely because they belong to the fellowship of the human race by physical descent – we can rightly speak of an interior original sin proper to each.

(iv) The Pneuma as salvation of the *whole* human being has a dynamic tendency towards the overcoming of death by the transfiguration of the body (Rom 8:11; 1 Cor 15:45), of death in the comprehensive sense ("second death"), which also includes the concrete mode in which human life ends. Consequently the lack of the Pneuma means the lack of a dynamism which overcomes death, an absence which affects even the concrete form of death. That does not mean that we need to be able to say exactly what, in regard to what we experience as our death, is the necessary end of this life following as a matter of course from the nature of man as a biological organism and as a being endowed with freedom, and what is the particular form of death which would not exist if the pneumatic life had been able to operate from the first unimpeded by guilt (Adam's and ours). That must be presupposed when we say that death is the consequence (and manifestation) of original sin. It is not thereby denied that death is *also* the "wages" of our own sins, nor is it asserted that without sin man would have experienced no end to his biological life (cf. 1 Cor 15:50–53). It is not denied that death (even in its concrete form), measured by our nature, is "natural" (*D* 1024, 1026, 1055), nor that death in the form it actually takes is transformed, in the justified, by grace from a manifestation of sin into suffering with Christ as a means of overcoming sin and the results of sin.

(v) Precisely what has been said about the relation between original sin and death also holds good of the relation between original sin and concupiscence. In both cases it must be considered that death and concupiscence are indeed natural, if measured by man's "nature". But that does not exclude the fact that both are in contradiction to what man is in the concrete, to the extent that they are indices of the as yet incomplete victory of grace. For they both stand in opposition to the supernatural existential of (proffered) grace as this ought to be. Moreover, grace with its dynamism towards overcoming death and concupiscence now in the infralapsarian order begins the historical process of its development and reintegration of human reality at a point where death and concupiscence are not yet eliminated. Even if, therefore, man remains under original sin what he is by "nature" (*D* 1055), he can nevertheless realize that he is "wounded" and "weakened" in his natural powers (*D* 788) when he experiences and measures himself by the "claims" which are made on him by the supernatural existential of orientation by grace, and the (non-explicit) experience of grace, towards the life of God himself.

(vi) Since the possession of grace in this life is a condition of final salvation, the blotting out of original sin is necessary for the attainment of salvation (*D* 791). We have not to inquire here into the various ways in which this can be done: see *Baptism* I, II, *Limbo*.

(vii) Despite its character as a real, interior sin (but sin in an analogous sense), original sin (with concupiscence and death) can be termed man's "situation", if we wish to refer to it briefly and intelligibly in what distinguishes it from personal sin. For, of course, a situation characterizing man's very existence as such does not necessarily mean something external to man but includes everything which is antecedent to the decision of freedom, as its condition and "material". It is part of this situation in which the free decision is made, whether for salvation or ruin, that because of Adam grace is not at man's disposal as the content and means of the decision about salvation which is required of him. That is the essence of original sin. Moreover, this decision about salvation, which is possible for man through the grace that comes from Christ, has to take place under concupiscence. By this the "Law" cannot be simply an expression of intrinsic pneumatic will, and therefore has to be experienced as a servile necessity. The decision also has to take place in the perspective of actual death. As a result, even when justified, man always stands in temptation from these two "principalities and powers" of ratifying his Adamite lack of grace by personal sin and of making it the real meaning of his existence. By the very fact that even the justified still remain in the situation of death and concupiscence, even though by grace and its acceptance they no longer have original sin as a state of guilt, they in their actual concrete personal life are still directly concerned with original sin.

(viii) In speaking of original sin it must always be borne in mind that the factual situation of ruin which it expresses is always different (because of God's universal infralapsarian salvific will), from what it would have been if man were nothing but a descendant of Adam as a sinner. God's offer of self-communication to man remains in force because of Christ and in relation to him, despite man's descent from Adam. This saving will of God not only holds good in regard to all men in God's "immanent" intentions, but also implies ("terminatively") a permanent existential, a factor in every man's situation in regard to salvation. It is expressed in the fact that to every man in a situation of moral decision the possibility of a saving act is assured by that offer of grace. Antecedent to the decision, therefore (whether to faith and love or to personal guilt), man's situation in relation to salvation is dialectically determined: he is in original sin through Adam and redeemed as orientated towards Christ. In personal free decision the dialectical situation of freedom is annulled in one or other direction. Either a man freely ratifies his state of original sin by personal sin or by faith and love freely ratifies his condition as redeemed. By either decision the existential against which the decision has been made is not simply suppressed, for man in this life always remains in the situation of concupiscence and death and in that of having been redeemed. But according to the particular decision, by his acceptance of one or other real antecedent situation, man becomes either simply (undialectically) good *or* bad before God, and consequently determines by his freedom the real antecedent situation itself.

(ix) Even for the baptized, original sin is not simply something which belongs to the past, because superseded by baptism and justification. It has abiding significance, indicating that salvation and grace are unmerited favour not only because of their transcendental origin from God but also in their objective historical dependence on Christ. It indicates that this grace occurs historically and is not an existential which it would be inconceivable for men to be without. It shows that this grace comes from Christ as the goal of history, not from the beginning of history, from Adam, and that the goal of history therefore really transcends its beginning. Original sin is also the abbreviated Christian formula for the fundamental truth of a theology of history, namely that the situation of death, concupiscence, law, futility which guilt contributes to create and of the empirical inseparability of good and evil which concupiscence imposes on us, cannot be abolished in history, because it permanently belongs to the constitutive features of all history, even of the future, because it belongs to the beginning. The Garden of Eden is not an attainable goal in this world any more; the utopia of attempting to establish it would inevitably produce the opposite, because it would be guilty hubris. That does not mean that the Christian is condemned to passive resignation, individual or collective. For on the one hand the eschatological power of grace to overcome suffering and death is already operative everywhere. And on the other hand the Christian, by his active planning and shaping of the future in justice and love, must produce a concrete historical manifestation of this presence of grace. The doctrine of original sin is a warning that this task is a duty but cannot be completed in this world.

(x) When the connection outlined above between original sin and personal sin is clearly envisaged, it will be recognized that original sin has a history, which is to be read in the history of the "sin of the world", though this does not mean that original sin is merely the sum total of all sin. And today it is perhaps easier to see how the "sin of the world" directly affects human existence, while original sin as such is less easily noted in this role. Hence the "sin of the world" could well be the starting-point for a treatise on the sin of man, which could then be the vantage-point for an examination of original sin, since this is the "beginning" of the sin of the world. But it is a beginning which is not merely the first temporal moment (see *Creation* IV) and one which is unique in its kind.

Karl Rahner

P

PANTHEISM

1. Pantheism is not a special and self-contained phenomenon in the history of religions, but a constantly recurring tendency which appears in almost all religions, cultures and philosophies: the tendency to define the relationship of God or the absolute to the world and the cosmos as that of unity. It is difficult to reduce its various manifestations to one common definition, since they developed in each case on the basis of various concepts of God and the world and in terms of various epochs in the history of thought. The basic structure of all types of pantheism is the negation of an essential difference between God and the world, or the affirmation of their complete unity in a being which underlies the whole of reality. This being is defined by Spinoza as immutable substance, by Hegel as the absolute reality of spirit, by Schelling as pure, free and absolute will. God is not distinct in being and essence from the world (cf. Vatican I, *D* 1782, 1802). The human person and the intrinsic value of the things of the world are ultimately eliminated.

2. This affirmation of the essential unity of God and the world gives rise to two main trends in pantheism, according to whether in the affirmation of this unity the accent is placed on God or on the world. In pantheism properly speaking God is absorbed in the world in a pancosmistic perspective. But then there is the panentheism (πᾶν ἐν θεῷ) in which the world is ultimately only God's mode of manifestation, and the "theopanism" in which the all is absorbed in God "who is and contains within him all things". Panentheism is acosmistic in trend, while theopanism is a definitely acosmistic mysticism.

A similar distinction may be made between immanentist and transcendent pantheism. In the former, which ultimately appears as atheism, God enters fully into the world, so that no reality but that of the empirical world is acknowledged. In the latter, a mystical form sees God only in the inmost being of things, and an immanent-transcendent form affirms that God is realized and manifested in things.

In the emanationist forms of pantheism, things come to be by proceeding from the immutable, absolute being. In the evolutionist types of pantheism the self-realization of God takes place in a dialectical process of world-evolution.

3. The notion of an all-pervasive force, an all-embracing being which is the impersonal principle underlying all reality is to be found in all religions of nature. In India, since the *Upanishads*,

the *Brahman* immanent to the world and the *Atman* animating man have been regarded as a unity. Pantheistic notions may also be traced in Buddhism, which refuses to affirm either the world or the personality of man, and in the polytheistic system of Egypt, according to which man is united after death to the divine All. In the monotheistic religions the notion of the universal presence of God provides constant occasions for pantheistic trends.

In the philosophies of the West such tendencies have been present from the beginning. According to Xenophanes, the world of appearances is absorbed in the all-embracing cosmic being, which, like Parmenides, he sees as immutable and identical with the world. The emanationism of Plotinus, according to which the νοῦς, the world-soul and matter proceed from the absolute One by intrinsic necessity, was taken up by Denis the Areopagite and then in the 9th century by John Scotus Erigena. Pantheistic notions are met with in the Middle Ages in the school of Chartres, in Amalrich of Bène and David of Dinant. The philosophy of Spinoza is a pantheistic monism. There is only one substance, in which all beings are perfectly identical. Earthly, empirical things are only *modi* of this substance. In German Idealism and in the classical and romantic literature of Germany, the search for a comprehensive view of the world and history produced a rational, world-centred pantheism. Fichte sees absolute being as the unifying ground of the I and the Not-I. According to Schelling, it is the total undifferentiated identity of subject and object, while Hegel sees the world and history as the absolute in its dialectical explicitation. Herder, Goethe and Schleiermacher, like romanticism, substitute a "natural piety" towards the world, a pantheistic sentiment, for the religious attitude of Christianity.

4. The reason for the fascination of pantheism is to be sought in a number of problems and basic questions posed by philosophical and theological thought. a) A natural human conviction, supported by reason and the experience of the order and harmony of the cosmos, leads to the assumption of a principle immanent to nature which conserves it in its being and directs its development. Nature does not appear as a mechanism guided from without, but as being given out of its own innermost being a self-contained but progressive development. In pantheism this essential note of nature and hence nature itself is identified with God. b) Pantheism is also a testimony to the dynamism towards the absolute which is proper to man. Man's constant experiences of himself and the world awaken in him, as do change, temporality and contingency, the question as to the presence of an unchangeable ultimate reality in the things themselves. c) The problem of God's presence in the world, of the relationship of God to the world, was always a preoccupation of theological and philosophical thought. Christianity teaches that creatures, though essentially different from God, have received their being through participation in the infinite being of God and have been made in God's likeness. The relationship between God and the world, between creator and creature, is characterized in Christian thought as unity which is also difference, and hence left in a tension – the analogy of being – which cannot be fully resolved conceptually and rationally. Pantheism seeks to eliminate this tension in favour of the total immanence of God in the world or of the world in God.

5. The solution attempted by pantheism leads to atheism, at least according to the Christian viewpoint. For the equation of God and the world means ultimately the reduction of God to the world and the denial of a transcendence which goes beyond this world. The Christian notion of God is

gained from historical revelation, but pantheism derives its idea of the God-world relationship from an *a priori* concept of being, and by equating God and the world eliminates the notion of God. The contrast between pantheism and theism or Christian faith is ontological and religious. And in both cases there is no absolute antithetical opposition. From the Christian viewpoint, the basic impulse of pantheism is taken up and away in an adequately considered notion of the God-world relationship. For here – not in spite of, but because of the pneumatic "unity" of creator and creature "*in* the Holy Spirit" – the relationship may be primarily defined as that of dialogue between the God who reveals himself in grace and man who responds in faith, hope and love.

Ismael Quiles

PAROUSIA

1. The parousia, as understood in theology, is the permanent blessed presence of Christ in the manifest finality of the history of the world and of salvation which is perfected and ended in the destiny of Jesus Christ. It is the fullness and the ending of the history of man and the world with the glorified humanity of Christ – now directly manifest in his glory – in God (Mt 24:36; 25:31ff.; 1 Thess 5:2; 2 Thess 2:2ff.; Rev 20:11ff.; 22:17, 20). The resurrection and ascension of Christ and the sending of the Spirit are the beginning of a process already irreversible, in which the history of salvation, mankind's and the individual's, goes on and comes to an end and fulfilment in what Scripture calls the parousia. The consummation of this process, whose duration in terms of world-time is unknown because it is the free and incalculable act of God (Mk 13:32), is called the parousia of Christ. It reveals to all – because all have achieved the God-given finality of their salvation or loss – that the beginning and driving force of the process, its orientation and climax as well as the permanent ground of its consummation is the reality of the risen Lord, who comes again inasmuch as through his act all attain their consummation in salvation or loss. This return is to judgment (*D* 6, 40, 86, 429). It cannot really be thought of apart from the judgment, which is simply the definitive crystallization and manifestation of the eternal results of history. For this manifestation makes it clear that history is the work of God, whose purpose is centred on Jesus Christ.

2. Judgment, therefore, this final judgment, must be seen as one with the consummation of the world and history as a whole: as an intrinsic moment of the parousia of Christ and the resurrection of the flesh. It is an intrinsic element of this consummation that the completion of the whole history of the world's freedom be radically made manifest. And further, this consummation is not just the result of the immanent development of the world. It depends on the sovereign disposition of God, having an end given to it and not just aimed at from its beginning. For these reasons the consummation is called the judgment of God. Since its nature is ultimately determined by the action of God in Jesus Christ, the consummation is called the judgment of Christ. Since this consummation embraces all – in their mutual relationship, as both good and evil are brought to their finality – it is called the general judgment. Since it is the definitive consummation which ends history, it is called the last judgment.

The relation between the general and the particular judgment, and hence too in part what must be said about the last judgment, must be determined in the light of the general principles of eschatological utterances. The "nature" of man calls for a dialectical unity of assertions about the one being of man. The elements of these assertions cannot be adequately balanced against one another or neatly distributed as between the two "parts" of man (body and soul). Man is always a unique spiritual being "subsisting in himself" – and hence not to be reduced to a mere moment of the cosmos and its history. But he is also a social entity of the world, "subsisting in matter", permanently caught up in the destiny of the one world and mankind. The unity of these two groups of sayings being dialectical, neither reducible to a higher unity nor divisible between two realms, since the "parts" of the substantial unity of man are real principles of being and not entities existing in themselves, the consummation of this unity (man) can on principle only be expressed in statements which are dialectically contrasted and connected with each other. This will take the form of an individual eschatology – that of death – and a cosmic eschatology. This rules out the (modern) attempt to reach a purely individualistic eschatology by a process of "demythologizing" where the statements of the universal eschatology are treated as images and metaphors for individual eschatology. It also rules out an inclination noticeable in the history of dogma before Benedict XII and persistently recurring in Reformation theology: to skip the individual eschatological assertion in favour of the cosmological, where the individual is only a moment in this event. Neither attitude does justice to the nature of man and his consummation, since he is not divisible into parts, though he is multi-dimensional. There can be no justifiable attempt – or demand – to indicate neatly and clearly which particular elements in the consummation of the individual belong to one or other of two definitely distinct events, separate in time and unrelated to one another. The consummation of man as a social being and part of the world (the "resurrection of the flesh", for instance) is a moment of the consummation of his uniqueness. Even as spirit he is only fulfilled in this event. And the consummation of the individual as his own very self (the vision of God, for instance) is a moment of the history of the cosmos. This fundamental relationship between what is distinct and still not adequately divisible in the statements of universal and individual eschatology also holds good of the general and particular judgments.

3. But the parousia of Christ to judgment is the revelation of the love of God, since God judges the world in an act of love which fetches home all that will let itself be fetched home, and which bestows this very will according to a disposition as yet unknown to us but revealed at the parousia of Christ, with its purpose again centred on Jesus Christ. There are dogmatically certain principles of hermeneutics for eschatological assertions which can be applied to the parousia as depicted in Scripture and tradition. When correctly applied, it appears that our eschatological assertions are not an anticipatory report of future events, but the extrapolation of our present salvation, the situation experienced in faith, into the mode of its completeness. It may therefore be inferred that hardly anything more can be said with certainty of the parousia of Christ than what has just been formulated in such abstract terms. It should, however, be noted that this parousia whose nature has been determined in the abstract will have a concrete form of being, though one which at present escapes our understanding

What has been said above may be summed up as follows in terms of the doctrine of the magisterium. It is a truth of faith that Christ will return in glory to judge the living and the dead (*D* 6, 40, 86, 429). It is certain doctrine that the hour of this parousia cannot be reckoned beforehand (*D* 2296). The so-called presages of the parousia which were constantly adduced in tradition (the preaching of the gospel in the whole world, Mt 24:14, the conversion of Israel, Rom 11:25f., the appearance and successes of Antichrist, 2 Thess 2:3, cosmic transformations, Mt 24:29f.; Lk 21:25, etc.) must be treated with critical prudence in the light of the hermeneutic principles for eschatological assertions. Statement is to be distinguished from world-picture.

Empowered by the example of Jesus, the Church anticipates and foreshadows in the celebration of the Eucharist the communion of saints with the risen Lord of glory.

Karl Rahner

PARTICIPATION

A. History of the Problem

Like such terms as being, unity and analogy, participation has had a major role in the metaphysical and theological thinking of the West, where it has been used to reflect on the Greek and biblico-Christian experience of reality. Hence the understanding and critical assessment of the notion of participation, with the possibility of rethinking it on one's own behalf, involves an interpretation of Western metaphysics which is particularly concerned with its origin and the fateful encounter between the Greek and the Christian experience of existence.

Plato was the first to place participation (μέθεξις, μετοχή, μετάληψις) at the centre of his thought, so that the notion has always been linked with his name. But the significance and scope of this step can only be seen when we envisage the change which occurred between the pre-Socratics and Plato in the experience and understanding of the unity and difference of all reality. The key-words of early Greek thought – εἶναι, φύσις, ἀλήθεια, λόγος, etc. — show that being was always experienced as a dominant unity, comprising, extrapolating and reintegrating the difference. This early Greek experience of the unity and difference of being crystallized in grammar in the form of the participle (Greek μετοχή) which designates a "duality" (Heidegger: *Zwiefalt*) based on identity. Thus the participle comprises the duality or difference between beings and being (the "ontological difference", i.e., between each being and the being which is its ground). In Plato the difference appears in the form of a split or separation (χωρισμός) between that which truly is (ὄντως ὄν) and non-being (μὴ ὄν). This separation is determined more closely by Plato as the gulf between the forms, as perpetually changeless beings, and being which come to be and pass away (ὂν γιγνόμενον) – between spirit and sense, between eternity and time, etc. How the original unity shows through this separation (χωρισμός) and that it does so, is expressed by Plato in the notion of participation. The μέθεξις combines the separated in unity. How this combination (participation) takes concrete shape is determined by the way in which the difference and the differentiated are displayed. Since for Plato the difference implies a gulf between ὄντως ὄν and μὴ ὄν, participation can only take the shape of the relationship of archetype and image – a notion which remained determinant in many forms throughout the whole of the classical metaphysics of the West. But it must be further affirmed that though Platonic and Western thought speaks of and makes use of participation, its real nature was not considered. The different terms considered as archetype and image were orientated to one another in the combination of relationship, but the relationship itself, that is, the event of the unity-in-difference, or, to put it still more radically, the event *qua* unity-in-difference was not considered (see below, under B).

How little the problems set by the original unity and difference were felt and analysed subsequent to Plato may be illustrated in particular by Aristotle's critique of the notion of participation. For Aristotle, participation is no more than a new word (*Metaphysics*, I, 987b 7–14). This is understandable, inasmuch as participation does not readily fit into his system of causes – though Thomas Aquinas was later to try to combine the notions of participation and causality. In the tradition tributary to Plato, especially in Plotinus and Proclus, participation is explained as the process of emanation from the primordial One. The "relationship", or the basic unity *qua* guaranteeing difference is taken so little into consideration that participation risks being misinterpreted as a vertical, rectilinear process of identity.

To throw light on the Christian reception of the notion of participation, recourse is usually had to texts of Scripture which speak of "sharing", "partaking". Thus, for instance, the OT is quoted to the effect that men are created according to the image and likeness of God, that through the covenant they partake of the fullness of Yahweh's blessings: "The Lord is my chosen portion and my cup" (Ps 16:5). In the NT, the notion of participation is said to be found in sayings such as those about entering into the kingdom of God, the eschatological banquet, the promises and beatitudes, in the terms fellowship (κοινωνία), divine sonship (υἱοθεσία), in the formulas "in" and "with" Christ (ἐν, σὺν Χριστῷ), abide in (μένειν ἐν), be in (εἶναι ἐν), have (ἔχειν), and explicitly in Heb 3:14 (μέτοχοι τοῦ Χριστοῦ, "share in Christ") and 2 Pet 1:4 (θείας κοινωνοὶ φύσεως "partakers of the divine nature"). While it is admitted that these last terms come from the religious philosophy of Hellenism, the NT authors are said to have transformed the concepts radically. In this connection it should be noted that while such individual assertions undoubtedly explain some aspects of the Christian reception of the Greek notion of participation, the phenomenon as a whole, especially as regards its broad implications and the problems posed thereby, remains unexplained. For no account is made of the fact that the Greek notion of participation stems from an understanding of being which is basically different from the biblical-Christian experience of being. For here the three great characteristics are grace, freedom and history (event) – keywords which have no place in the Greek understanding of being. We are dealing therefore with the encounter of two basically different experiences and understandings of being: an encounter which still determines our thinking today, and indeed more than ever today.

How this fateful encounter proceeded may be best seen from Augustine and Thomas Aquinas. When Augustine replaces the noetic world of (neo-) Platonism by the *verbum aeternum*, in whose *rationes aeternae inmutabilesque* our knowledge participates, we see that Greek, Platonic thought retains the upper hand, though in many respects Augustine also expounds and emphasizes specifically biblical and Christian elements (see *Spirit*). But it is only with Thomas Aquinas that the notion of participation received from the Greeks becomes the universally fundamental and dominant thought-form. Aquinas thinks of being in terms of participation, as may be seen from his two central assertions: God is *esse per essentiam*, the creature is *esse per participationem*. The same schema applies to all other perfections such as truth, goodness, knowledge and life. In the precise explanation of participation as offered by Aquinas two forms may be distinguished. In general, he uses the schema of composition. Something (a subject) participates in a perfection (form) by receiving the perfection and thereby limiting it (participation by composition). The most important "instance" of such a mode of participation is the real composition of all finite beings from essence (as "potency" and "subject") and act of being (as the perfection of being which is participated). This mode of participation, when considered the primary or indeed the only one, involves an impasse: since the "subject" enters into a composition with the perfection received, it remains an extrinsic principle – a co-principle, in fact – with regard to the perfection. The result is a metaphysical dualism which is incompatible with a genuine doctrine of being, much less with any Christian doctrine of God. But Aquinas is also aware of another mode of participation, which functions, however, rather as a background to his thought. It is participation as a hierarchy of degrees (of being) on the basis of a deficient likeness (*similitudo deficiens*): finite beings participate in being, by representing the deficient (finite) modes of the "realization" of the perfection of being, which means its presence. This type of participation is therefore better fitted to explain the original presence of the "whole" in the individuals.

In the scholasticism subsequent to Aquinas, the notion of participation became more and more formalized, its central position in the thought of Aquinas being thereby gradually lost sight of. In modern non-scholastic philosophy the term participation is rarely used – which does not mean that the notion itself is absent. The term itself, however, is found in writers like L. Lavelle, who uses it to expound the relation of consciousness and being, and M. Buber, who uses it of the interpersonal correlation of the I and Thou.

B. Intrinsic Assessment

The question of whether and to what extent the notion of participation can claim validity today cannot be decided *a priori*, but only in the light of its original content, its origin and its historical interpretations. From what has been said above, it appears that participation was always understood more or less explicitly as a solution of the problem of the identity and difference of being as a whole. The basic intention of the notion was to give articular expression to the fact, necessity and mode of the presence of the whole in the particular or the insertion of the particular in the whole. The notion of participation strives to safeguard both for the whole and for the particular their own way of be-ing (understood as a verbal form). Or, to speak more precisely and trenchantly, it means that the whole (the unity) only exists and appears *as such* when the particular (the "different") does not disappear in the process but actually comes into its own there. It means then that identity and difference, the whole and the particular "grow" (reveal themselves) in like and not in inverse proportion.

These seemingly very abstract considerations are the key to a possible understanding and rethinking of the classical notion of participation which might be used to expound Christian revelation in terms of present-day awareness of problems. For it is of the essence of participative unity that the "whole" appears as truly whole insofar as the particulars (the different) attain their own proper selves. This means that participation is not to be regarded as a static structure, as if the whole and the particulars appeared at once and once and for all in their own proper nature. Participation must be regarded as an *event*, the event of the self-disclosure of the whole through and in the self-realization of the "parts", that is, of the different particulars. Participation *is* history. If, then, one considers the Christian experience of the "whole", it is clear that this history is not just any anonymous happening, in the form, say, of a mythical or natural "event", but a process of events of which freedom is an essential component. The event thus made possible, mediated and sustained by freedom is the disclosure of the meaning of the identity-and-difference of God and the world-and-man. The more God reveals himself *as* God, that is, the more the difference stands out, the more radically he displays his all-penetrating and all-encompassing rule of man and world, in other words, the dominant unity which stems from himself. The unique originality of this understanding of reality, in which biblico-Christian thought has adopted the Greek notion of participation, is that the event is regarded as a radically personal exercise of freedom. And man can appear as the freely-acting partner of God because he is admitted from the start into the dimension of freedom's dialogue which is previously thrown open by God himself. This is the deepest meaning of participation and is only to be grasped in terms of Christianity. Thus the "whole", which has hitherto been spoken of in an indeterminate way, now appears as the unique and ultimately single event of the self-imparting of God and the partaking of man. It is the original unity which alone manifests and actualizes the immeasurable difference between God and man-and-world.

All this would have to be applied in concrete to all the "totalities" which "particularize" our reality in so many different modes and degrees: the person and work of Jesus Christ, the history of salvation, humanity, Church, society, State and so on. Wherever and in whatever degree a totality appears, it must be considered as a participative unity, that is, as a unity whose nature or purpose only comes to its own proper fulfilment in the establishment and liberation of its "parts" (particulars, differentiations). If the totalities are not taken as participative, they remain abstract and ineffectual – as would be, for instance, a sealed-off and clericalized Church – or they become totalitarian organizations, inasmuch as the individuals are inserted into the whole by coercion and repression, and not by means of genuine participation. Thus the notion of participation is of supreme importance not only for the solution of speculative questions but also, and in a very special way, for mastering the concrete problems of Church, State and similar matters.

Lourencino Bruno Puntel

PASSION OF CHRIST

1. *Terminology*. In the expression "the passion of Christ", the passion means not only the sufferings which preceded the death of Jesus but above all his death itself. This usage is scriptural, insofar as the death of Jesus is often indicated as his πάσχειν (Lk, Acts, Heb, 1 Pet) in the NT. The usage probably goes back to Jesus himself (Michaelis). Since Ignatius of Antioch the substantive πάθος has been used as a fixed expression for Jesus' death. The corresponding meaning was given in early Christian Latin to the words *pati* and *passio*.

2. *The passion in the early Church*. The death of Jesus was one of the dominant themes in the thought, teaching, and life of early Christendom. This was due especially to dogmatic and apologetic considerations. The cross was the great enigma with which the Church had to grapple (cf. 1 Cor 1:23). The figure of a suffering Messiah was foreign to the Judaism of that time, and hence the passion of Jesus must have seemed to them to be a proof against his messianic claim (Lk 24:14f.). And even more, on the basis of Dt 21:23, the crucified was supposed to be cursed by God (Gal 3:13; 1 Cor 12:3). Similarly, in the non-Christian world, death on the cross was considered ignominious (Tacitus, *Hist.*, IV, 11), and for this reason opponents of the Church such as Celsus, Porphyrius and Lucian mocked at Christians for having one who had been crucified as the object of their faith and worship. The

Church, on the other hand, sought to show that the passion was part of the eternal saving plan of God. The proof of this was first and foremost the fact that God raised up the crucified and so accredited him as his Messiah (Acts 2:23f.; 2:36; 3:13, 15; 5:30f.). Hence in the earliest credal statement (1 Cor 15:3–5) and kerygma (Acts 17:3; 26:23), the death and resurrection of Jesus are mentioned together. At the same time, there was an effort to show how the passion corresponded to the Scriptures. If it could be shown that the passion was already prophesied in the OT and that these prophecies were fulfilled in the death of Jesus, then the cross would be a proof in favour of, and not against, the messiahship of Jesus. The fact that Jesus was not surprised by the passion but had foreseen, foretold and freely endured it served further to alleviate the scandal. Finally, the scandalous character of the passion was removed by its salvific meaning being stressed and elaborated (as in the theology of St. Paul; cf. Mk 10:45; 14:24).

The passion also assumed an important place in the liturgy. The passion-hymns contained in various letters (1 Tim 3:26; Phil 2:6–11; 1 Pet 1:18–21; 2:21–24; 3:18–22) witness to the early liturgical worship of the crucified and glorified Christ, as do those texts in Rev which treat of the heavenly liturgy of the worship of the lamb (5:6–14 etc.). The sacraments were related to the death of Christ: baptism was understood as a dying and a rising with him (Rom 6:2–11), the Eucharist as the representation and application of the fruits of his redemptive death (cf. 1 Cor 11:26). It is probable that in the first Christian communities the account of the passion was read on the day of the annual commemoration of the Lord's death, as in the Jewish custom whereby the father of the household used to explain the origin and meaning of the Passover celebration in the *Haggada*. It was not long before the passion was used for the purpose of ascetical pedagogy: the Christ of the passion became the prototype and exemplar of Christian behaviour, and the account of the passion became an effective appeal to follow Christ upon his way of humility, obedience, self-denial, loving service, and the giving of his life (Mk 8:34; letters of Paul; 1 Pet, Heb).The passion eventually assumed a permanent role in the polemic of the early Church against unbelieving Judaism. Reference was made to the events of the passion in which the guilt of certain Jews and Jewish groups was evident, in the hope that Israel would understand, be converted and believe (Acts 2:22f., 30; 3:13f., 17–19; 4:10f., 25:28; 5:28, 30; 7:52; 10:39; 13:27f.; 1 Thess 2:14f.).

3. *The passion according to Mark.* The oldest passion account known to us owes its form to these considerations. It is not meant as a complete account of the facts (the name of Caiaphas is never mentioned, for example). It is not concerned to show the motives of the people involved (e.g., those of Judas); and neither is it concerned with the arousing of any feelings of sympathy, repentance, gratitude, etc. (The crucifixion itself is mentioned in three short words.) The dogmatic and apologetic aim is clearly visible already in Mk, i.e., the effort to show the passion as being in harmony with the Scriptures and as thereby corresponding with the saving intentions of God. Such references to the OT are mainly represented by words of Jesus. The scriptural citation, however, is only once given as a citation (14:27); usually the quotations are implicit (14:18, 24, 34, 62; 15:34), and twice the passion is referred to in a general way as corresponding to the Scriptures (14:21, 49). In the narration itself there are three OT texts not actually named as quotations (15:24, 29, 36) and two features which recall Is 53:7 (14:61; 15:5). In the passion as a whole these texts take up little space, so

that the proof from prophecy cannot be said to have played a predominant role in the shaping of the passion narrative. That Jesus had foreseen his passion is mentioned several times (14:8, 18–21, 27, 30f.). Ascetical and paraenetic interests have left little trace. But the inclusion of and the form given to the "agony in the garden" may perhaps be due to such interests (cf. especially 14:38), and likewise the denial of Peter. What is especially evident is the intention to show clearly what persons and what authorities were responsible for the death of Jesus and the extent of their guilt. This explains the information given about the members of the Sanhedrin (14:1, 43, 53, 55, 63–65; 15:1, 10f., 31f.; contrast 15:43–46), Judas (14:10f., 18–21, 42, 45), the crowd (14:65; 15:8, 11–15, 29f., 35; cf. 15:40f.; 16:1–8; 15:21), Pilate (15:2–15, 43–45) and the Roman soldiers (15:16–20, 21–27; cf. 15:39). But this intention could only be realized by means of a connected narrative, and this is the main reason why the passion-narrative was formed and handed on as a continuous story, with unity of time and place. Critical research holds, and certainly with reason, that the passion-narrative is the part of the gospel tradition which was given the earliest fixed form. Mk already had before him such a relatively fixed account from oral tradition, as the insertion of 14:3–9 into the older account shows, and he enlarged it with further matter, e.g., with "memoirs" of Peter (apart from 14:3–9) such as the account of the denial (14:54, 66–72). But not only the passion-narrative proper treats of the death of Jesus. In 3:6 the plot to kill Jesus is already mentioned. More especially, Mk has Jesus prophesy his passion (with the resurrection) early in the gospel, as his divinely decreed messianic destiny, chiefly in the three great prophecies found in 2:19f.; 9:12; 10:38. For these reasons the Gospel of Mark has been called, not unjustly, "a passion-narrative with a long introduction" (M. Kähler).

4. *The passion according to Matthew, Luke and John*. The motives determining the form of the account which are discernible in Mk are even clearer here. We find in Mt further elements which are presented, partly explicitly (27:9f.), partly implicitly (26:15; 27:34, 43) as fulfilled prophecies. Jesus' rejection of the attempt to defend him (Mt 26:54) is explained by his assertion of the necessity of fulfilling the Scriptures. In two additional episodes, the guilt of the Jews is stressed (27:19–24); and by the account of the fate of Judas in 27:3–10, the execrable nature of the betrayal is illustrated.

In Lk interest in the proof from prophecy comes less to the fore (23:49; 24:26). There is an apologetic intention behind the changed form of the exclamation of the centurion (23:47). What is new in Lk, outside of the motif of satanic influence upon Judas (22:3; cf. also 4:13; 22:53), is the edifying tendency: the inner struggle of Jesus in Gethsemani appears less tense; the flight of the disciples is not mentioned; Jesus is mourned over by compassionate women (23:27, 31); Jesus prays for his enemies (23:33); he promises the repentant thief a place in paradise (23:39–43); he dies with a final word of trust in God (23:46, after Ps 31:6).

Jn also shows a great interest in the proof from prophecy (15:25; 19:23f., 28, 36f.). As in Lk, Satan's influence upon Judas is affirmed (13:2, 27). For the rest, the image of Christ in Jn is full of royal dignity. The crucifixion appears not as defeat, but as victory: the last word of the crucified is the triumphal cry "it is accomplished" (19:30).

5. *Historicity*. In view of the fact that the passion-narrative is not a simple factual report but also an interpretation, the question of its historical veracity arises. The assertion that the passion-

narrative is legendary by reason of this characteristic must be rejected. "To fabricate a history and to narrate a history with a particular purpose in mind are two different things" (P. Wernle). The proof from prophecy influenced the choice of material and the manner of its narration; that it was the cause of historical fabrication cannot be proved. It is to be noted that the motifs characteristic of the Jewish martyr-literature are lacking in the passion-narrative. As far as it has been possible to compare the particulars of the account with the history of NT times, the results are surprisingly positive. Thus, the widespread rejection of the account of the trial before the Sanhedrin has been shown to be unwarranted by recent studies in the history of law. The fact that Mk 14 and 15 juxtapose items which sometimes agree and sometimes disagree with the requirements of the Mishnah was hitherto felt puzzling. The explanation is that the Sanhedrin was at that time bound by the Sadducee law, which agreed with the Mishnah only exceptionally. But if Mk 14 and 15 were a legendary construction, it would be hard to explain how the author, supposedly so uninterested in historical fact, managed to be so accurate with regard to the legal customs: to the unlikely extent, that is, that the actions of the Sanhedrin only agreed with the Mishnah when the provisions of the latter coincided with those of the Sadducees, and not otherwise. There are, however, elements of the various traditions whose historicity may be doubted. Catholic exegetes are inquiring today whether, for example, Mt 27:51–53 might not be a "midrash" to illustrate the idea that with the death of Jesus the "last days" have begun; or whether the detailed exchanges between Pilate and Jesus (Jn 18 and 19) are not merely interpretative expansions; or whether the words of Jesus on the cross found in Lk and Jn are authentic or put into his mouth on the basis of the evangelists' interpretation of the crucifixion.

Josef Blinzler

PASSOVER

1. *Mysterium paschale*. a) The expression *mysterium paschale* is used repeatedly by Vatican II as a pregnant designation of the Christian redemption in its essential aspects. It is the Easter mystery of the passion, resurrection and ascension of Christ, the salvation prefigured in the OT, consisting of the conquest of death and the gift of life (Constitution on the Sacred Liturgy, art. 5), hence the origin of the Church and of the sacraments, especially baptism and the Eucharist (*ibid.*, arts. 5, 61; cf. arts. 10, 47). This gives the Christian life a paschal character. It is the sacramentally existentiell participation in the Passover mystery of Christ, into which Christians are inserted by baptism and the Eucharist (*ibid.*, art. 6) and which they have to re-enact in daily life, by virtue of a link with the Christ-event by which even non-Christians are in some way affected (Pastoral Constitution on the Church in the Modern World, arts. 22, 38, 52). The example has been given by the saints (Constitution on the Sacred Liturgy, art. 104). This is made possible by the liturgy, whose two focuses – the Sunday Eucharist and the yearly Easter feast – celebrate and re-present the Passover mystery (*ibid.*, arts. 106f., 109; cf. art. 102). Bishops and priests are to familiarize the faithful with this mystery in their preaching (Decree on the Bishops' Pastoral Office, art. 15; Decree on the Ministry and Life of Priests, art. 8; Decree on the Church's Missionary Activity, art. 14).

b) The Christ-event has an Easter colouring in the NT itself. (i) A Jewish Passover was the "hour" fixed by the Father for Jesus, towards which Jesus consciously moved, according to the gospels. (ii) Jesus died as our "paschal lamb", our Passover (1 Cor 5:7; cf. Jn 19:34, 36; 1 Pet 1:18). The OT Passover terminology provided many of the soteriological themes and terms (e.g., the group of words "redeem") in which the salvation brought about by the NT Passover is expressed. (iii) Jesus' farewell meal, on which is founded the eucharistic anamnesis re-presenting the Christ-event, is brought into connection in the synoptics with an OT Passover meal of the Jews. This theological context is important. Whether the Last Supper was in fact a Passover meal, and whether the synoptic and Johannine chronologies can be reconciled on the basis of different calendars in use in the time of Jesus, is of minor importance.

c) Along with these points of contact which are expressly mentioned in the NT, there is a profound and instructive similarity of structure between the OT Passover and the salvific event of the NT, extending to the resulting state of salvation and to the re-presentation which activates the state of salvation. The following sketch of the main structural lines of the Passover theology is meant to throw light on the Christian theology of the *mysterium paschale*.

2. *History of salvation as basis.* a) The OT and Jewish Passover theology is centred on the fundamental saving acts of Yahweh, and hence is essentially stamped by the history of salvation as revealed in Israel. Its central interest is the salvation (or "redemption") of Israel, as may be seen from the narrative of Exod 12:1 to 13:16 (or to 15:21). (The narrative is mainly Yahwist and Priestly: a cult aetiology interspersed with ritual precepts, some of which show Deuteronomist redaction.) There are three phases or aspects: Israel (or its first-born male children) is spared death by virtue of the blood of the Passover lamb, used as a protective sign (12:13, 27); Israel is led out of bondage in Egypt (12:42; 13:8); Israel passes through the Red Sea – another rescue from death – and is finally delivered from tribulation (13:17–15:21). Life is the goal: from death to fullness of life, since deliverance from bondage is redemption (ransom) and includes the transition into the domain of the redeemer, Yahweh. It is God himself who directly procures salvation – as indeed for the most part in the NT also – by himself rescuing and ransoming. (The LXX uses the terms σῴζειν, ῥύεσθαι, [ἀπο'] λυτροῦσθαι which became basic to the NT vocabulary of redemption.) But Yahweh also uses a mediator and a means of salvation, with functions which are transferred to Jesus in the NT: Moses his servant and the sacrificial lamb or its blood.

b) As thus described, the Passover salvation is a departure (exodus) and a transition (διάβασις, in which Philo sees the essence of the Passover, spiritualized as the transition from sin to virtue, from the material to the spiritual; he calls it τὰ διαβατήρια, the sacrifice of transition – cf. the Johannine "crossing over" [μεταβαίνειν] of Christ and the Christian from death to life, from this world to the Father). Then there is the further Passover-event, the culmination of the whole movement of salvation, the entry into the land of promise and into "rest" (cf. Heb 3:7–4:11 etc.). According to Jos 5:10ff. – again a cultic aetiology – the Israelites celebrated the first Passover of the promised land in Gilgal, immediately after the crossing of the Jordan, which is viewed as analogous to the passage of the Red Sea.

c) OT Judaism in particular regarded a series of further events as Passover-events, so that the Passover was increasingly considered as the compendium of the history of salvation. Noteworthy for their theological importance and by reason of their pre-Christian origin (cf. especially the Palestinian Targums on Exod 12:42) are the creation of the world and man (Gen 1f.), Yahweh's covenant with Abraham (Gen 15; 17) and the sacrifice of Isaac (Gen 22), to which rabbinism attached a manifold and far-reaching soteriological function, often on the same lines as the sacrificial death of Jesus.

3. *The background in comparative religion.* a) The Jewish Passover combined two different celebrations: the feast of the Passover at home in the evening and the seven-day feast of the unleavened bread (mazzot) as the end of a pilgrimage. Both Passover and mazzot were of pre-Israelite origin. The Passover was originally a rite of nomad shepherds, performed in the night of the full moon at the spring equinox for the protection and well-being of themselves and their flocks (note the apotropaic significance of the blood), before leaving their winter for summer pastures (i.e., from the steppe to the cultivated lands). But the mazzot belonged to the culture of farming populations, who marked the break between old and new at the beginning of the harvest by eating unleavened bread which contained no flour from the crops of the previous year. Hence Passover and mazzot were two nature-feasts which were "historicized" by the Israelites when they were adopted as memorials of the history of salvation. (A similar process of historicization underlies some Christian feasts such as Christmas.)

b) But the connection with the process of nature was not entirely lost. This is particularly clear from the fact that in the OT the notion of the sacrifice of the first-born was still combined with both mazzot and Passover. The theme of the first-born is an integral element of the Passover (cf. Exod 12:12 and 13:11–16 etc.). And the feast of the unleavened bread, which was the first loaves of the new harvest, included the offering of the first sheaves (Lev 23:9–14; in the NT Christ is the first-born and the first-fruit, Rom 8:28; 1 Cor 15:20, 23 – in a paschal context). First-born and first-fruits were regarded as the most precious and vital elements of all they represented – family, flock, harvest. Their sacrifice gave hope of well-being and fertility – in a word, of life. Thus the theme of life was already part of the background of the Passover in the nature religions. In the non-Israelite religions some authors have traced spring festivals of dying and rising vegetation gods, which would then also have had life for their theme. It is of central significance in the NT Easter: the risen Christ is the source and cause of the life imparted through the paschal sacraments.

c) The Passover thus appears as part of the ritual surrounding the new year in the ancient East. This included fertility rites – the cult of the vegetation gods and the "sacred marriage" – and also a re-enactment of the cosmogony or creation. This latter was viewed as a theomachy, in which the victorious god attained to royal power over the world of gods and men. It may be due to these themes, directly or indirectly, that Judaism chose the Song of Solomon, with its bridal allegory of Yahweh and Israel, as the Passover pericope in the synagogue. This may also explain why even in the OT the (paschal) creation of the world was regarded as the Passover-event by which Yahweh became king, and why it was described in terms borrowed from the mythical struggle against chaos (cf., for instance, the Passover canticle Exod 15:1–18; see also 6a, below). The ancient East also associated with these themes the inthronization of the earthly king, who was viewed as the representative of the godhead. There may be an echo of this context of ideas when Judaism expects the coming of the Davidic, messianic kingship at the Passover, or when the NT sees Jesus as made "Kyrios and Christus" through his paschal resurrection (Acts 2:32–36; 13:33f., alluding to Ps 2 and 110).

4. *The liturgical and sacramental aspect.* a) The Passover was essentially a memorial celebration: "This day shall be for you a memorial day" (Exod 12:14; cf. 13:9). The great saving acts of Yahweh and the resulting salvation for Israel and the Israelites were recalled in recitals (the "haggada") and hymns of praise (especially the Alleluia psalms). But this liturgical anamnesis was not just thinking of past history. According to the biblical notion of memory, it was a "revival", at once subjective and objective, of the *per se* unique past happening, both in the Israelites who celebrated the feast and in the God who was celebrated (cf. the prayer "Remember, O Lord . . .", in connection with the role of sign for Yahweh which the Passover blood had in Exod 12:13, 23 and in Judaism). Thus at each actual feast the celebrants have a re-actualization of the Passover salvation: "This day you are to go forth" (Exod 13:4, 8). The rite is performed "for the sake of all that Yahweh did for *me*, when I went out of Egypt" (cf. Mishnah, *Pesachim* 10, 5, etc.). So too in the NT celebration of the Eucharist: it takes place with recital and thanksgiving, as the kerygmatic eucharistic anamnesis which re-presents the fundamental past action of God in Christ (cf. 1 Cor 11:23–27; Lk 22:19).

b) The Passover anamnesis was not merely a mental and verbal recall, but also a ritual symbolic re-enactment. The "night of watching" (the origin of the Christian vigils) corresponded to the watch kept by Yahweh and the Israelites at the first Passover (Exod 12:42); the travelling-clothes (Exod 12:11) symbolized the readiness to depart. (In Judaism, the restful position at table signified the freedom from bondage already attained.) But the element of anamnesis was attached above all to the meal, the interpretation of which was to provide the starting-point for the kerygmatic catechesis in Judaism (but see already Exod 12:26f.; 13:7f.). Like the bitter herbs, the unleavened bread, the "bread of affliction" (Deut 16:3), signified the time of bondage, but also the exodus (more precisely, the unexpected haste in which it took place, Exod 12:34, 39), and then, along with the wine which played an important part in the Jewish Passover, though not mentioned in the OT, the happy possession of the promised land (cf. Jos 5:10ff.). Further, the bread and wine, over which the blessing was pronounced by the head of the group, could be considered by the partakers not merely as an expression and realization of brotherly fellowship, but also at times as to some extent vehicles of blessing. Here again the analogy with the NT Eucharist is noteworthy. It too consists of an "action", and bread and wine are vehicles both of anamnesis and of salvation (cf. especially 1 Cor 10:14–22; 11:23–32).

c) The OT Passover was also a sacrificial meal. As at the peace offerings, the Deuteronomist centralization of the cult meant that at the "post-Egyptian" Passover (cf. Deut 16:1–8; 2 Kg 23:21ff.; 2 Chr 30:1–27; 35:11–19; Ezr 6:19–22) the lamb or kid to be eaten at home was first sacrificed in the temple. The father of the family or his delegate slaughtered the lamb, and the priests offered Yahweh his portion, by burning the fatty parts and pouring the blood on the altar. Yahweh and the sacrificers partake of the same repast. Then, like all sacrificial blood according to the view of the later books of the OT and Judaism, the Passover blood had expiatory value. It could make expiation for those for whom the lamb was offered, that is, blot out sin in the genuine biblical sense (see, for example, bPes. 61b; 65b). Against this background it is understandable that the notion of sacrifice was associated with the NT Eucharist and that redemptive power was attributed in particular to the blood of Jesus (1 Pet 1:18f.; Rev

5:9, 12; 7:14; 12:11; cf. Jn 19:34, 36, the blood of the [paschal] lamb), precisely in connection with the Eucharist (Mt 26:28, "for the forgiveness of sins").

5. *The ecclesial components.* a) Though the Passover-salvation was for everyone personally ("what Yahweh has done for me"), the Passover, as saving event and liturgical celebration, was essentially a community matter. At the time of Jesus, the community celebrating the Passover liturgy took two forms: that of a small household party and the great community of the people. The liturgy of the meal (the "seder") took place within the family at home, or among a small group (חֲבוּרָה, φρατρία), such as the disciples at the Last Supper. This corresponded to the original character of the Passover. But at the same time, the fusion of the Passover with the feast of the unleavened bread which brought the pilgrims to Jerusalem, and the fact that the centralization of the cult meant that the lambs could be sacrificed only in the temple, made the Passover a feast of Israel which took in the whole people as a community (the קָהָל, the ἐκκλησία), see 4c above; also Jos 5:10ff.). The twofold structure occurs again in the NT in a notably similar way. Here too the liturgy is celebrated both by the whole Church as the people of God and by the local Church as household fellowships gathered in various houses (Acts 2:46; 5:42, κατ' οἶκον as Exod 12:3, LXX).

b) The Passover was not merely one of the feasts of Israel. It was the great feast of Israel as such, and was celebrated in all probability in this way about the beginning of the Christian era, having been for some time challenged by the autumn festival. According to the rabbis it was "the birth-day of Israel". This was correct, because the action of God in the Passover, expressed in the central truth of faith, that Yahweh had led Israel out of Egypt, was regarded by Israel as "the foundation of its existence and of its special place among the peoples, and was used for preference to designate the beginning of the history of 'Israel'" (M. Noth). Here too there is an obvious parallel with the NT. The Church is the community of God, "which he obtained with his own blood" (Acts 20:28, cf. Rev 5:9f. and Jn 19:34, 36. The formation of Eve from Adam's side, which the Fathers compared with the origin of the Church from the side of the crucified, was dated by Jubilees 2, 14; 3, 8 to the Friday after the Passover full moon, that is, the day on which Jesus was crucified.)

c) All this suggests a certain link between Passover and covenant. And in fact the OT often mentions the covenant "which the Lord made with them when (on the day that) he brought them out of the land of Egypt" (Deut 29:25; 1 Kg 8:9; Jer 31:32; 34:13). It also seems as though the renewal of the covenant was sealed for preference by a solemn Passover (2 Kg 23:23, 21f.; cf. 2 Chr 35:1–18 and 30:1–27). According to Wis 18:6–9 (possibly part of an Alexandrian Passover haggadah), the Israelites met on the night of the Passover and offered sacrifices and "with one accord agreed to the divine law" (διατίθεσθαι), "in sure knowledge of the oaths in which they trusted", i.e., the promises to the fathers (cf. Gen 15:13–18). This is an allusion to the covenant with Abraham, which was supposed to have been given at the time of the Passover, according to non-biblical Palestinian texts from about the same period as Wisdom (see above, 2c). Hence too parallels were readily drawn between the Passover blood and the blood of circumcision, which was identified with the blood of the covenant (circumcision, often closely connected with the Passover in the OT, is in fact the sign of the covenant; cf. Exod 12:44, 48; Jos 5:2–10 and Gen 17:10–14, etc.). This may partly explain how the NT could call the eucharistic blood of Jesus the "blood of the (new) testament" (Mk 14:24 par.), precisely in the framework of the Passover.

6. *Eschatological perspective*. a) Even in the OT, the Passover and the salvation which it brought were seen as a type or prefiguration of the last things and final salvation. The future salvific event came to be looked on more and more definitely as eschatological and was described as a new Passover. It was to be the new intervention of God to protect and save (Is 31:5; cf. 30:29) and above all a new exodus (e.g., Is 35:1–10; 43:16–21; cf. earlier Hos 2:16f.), at which Yahweh's struggle with the mythical powers of chaos was to be finally decided (cf. Is 21:1; 51:9f.; Ps 74:12ff.; 89:10f. and Rev 12:3–17). The same theme is used to link protology with eschatology, and both with the Passover. And then again, as may be seen in particular from the Book of Wisdom, eschatological traits were added to the ancient Passover narrative, so that the historical events of the Egyptian Passover were transposed into the supra-historical domain. The NT used this Passover eschatology, as further developed by post-biblical Judaism, to proclaim and expound through its concepts and images the final salvation already brought in and through Christ, in its actual or still outstanding phases.

b) But Judaism did not merely use the Passover as an analogy for the final event. The final event was to be itself a Passover, inasmuch as the great climax of all God's saving acts was to take place on a Passover. Thus according to the LXX translation of Jer 31 (38):8, Yahweh will gather together the Israelites from the ends of the earth on the Passover feast, in order to make the "new covenant" with them (31:31–34). The hymn of the four great nights of salvation added by the Palestinian Targums to Exod 12:42 praises the last Passover night still to come as the night at the end of time in which the yoke of calamity will be finally broken and the Messiah appear. According to the NT, Jesus was in fact exalted as Messiah at Easter (see above, 3c) – to come again in his royal glory on another, final Passover, according to an early Christian expectation still attested by Jerome (Homily on Mt 25:6).

c) The Passover of the Jewish OT was undoubtedly the seed-bed and site of this eschatological Passover hope. As human plans and institutions and saviours brought only repeated disappointments, it was inevitable, especially in times of oppression (cf. Josephus), that at the celebration and anamnesis of the divine redemption in the past the hope of a new and definitive intervention of Yahweh should be enkindled and nourished. This brings the liturgical meal of the NT once more into close association with the Passover. At the Eucharist, which is also to have its still awaited fulfilment in the salvation of the heavenly banquet (Lk 22:14–18 etc.), the paschal death of the Lord, for the moment both present and absent, is proclaimed "until he comes" (1 Cor 11:26).

Notker Füglister

PASTORAL MINISTRY

A. Introduction

The "pastoral ministry" is the expression now preferred for the "cure" or "care of souls", the "spiritual charge", formerly too exclusively regarded as a clerical task (see *Pastoral Theology*). It is really the "ministry of salvation" (Vatican II, *Christus Dominus*, art. 35.), in the service of all men (see *Salvation* I), the basic charge of the Church (see *Missions*), and incumbent, according to their various states of life and offices, on all members of the Church. See *Church* II–IV, *Church and World*.

B. The Agents and Objects of Pastoral Care

The recognition of the fact that the

"shepherds" cannot be simply and totally distinguished from the "flock" is of great significance in modern pastoral work. Since Vatican II, the Church has, as it were, thrown itself open to lay people, Protestants, pagans and atheists. Hitherto, these classes seemed to be rather the passive or reluctant objects of the work of "the Church". That they had something of value to say on their own about Christ and man was hardly considered. But the modern Christian has a deeper sense of the unity between the person and his environment, between the Church and the world, between the office-holders and the people of God, between clergy and congregation. The ministry of salvation is a work done in partnership, where the agent and the object re-act upon one another. Full justice can be done to this situation only in the actual encounter, where each partner is ready to criticize and be criticized as they examine together the real situations.

1. *Religious orders and congregations.* Religious must today be ready for and welcomed to closer co-operation with diocesan plans, and aim at greater mobility and flexibility. The reform of religious life called for in Vatican II (*Perfectae Caritatis*) stresses the need for adaptability and a strong ecclesial sense. Orders and congregations exist primarily to serve the Church, not to further the particular ends of an order (cf. *Christus Dominus*, arts. 33–35). Nonetheless, religious cannot be wholly absorbed in parish or similar work. The orders represent the charismatic and prophetic element of the Church, on an institutionalized level, which must not be diverted from its proper purpose. Vatican II noted this specifically, apropos of the exclusively contemplative orders (*Christus Dominus*, art. 35, para. 1).

2. *Laity.* The laity are "in their own way sharers in the priestly, prophetic and kingly functions of Christ" (Vatican II, *Lumen Gentium*, art. 31). Hence the "pastoral" ministry of salvation would be essentially deficient without them. This appears more clearly than ever in the "special circumstances of our time" (*ibid.*, art. 30). The Church is more clearly devoted to the world which it now esteems expressly as the world, and it is the layman who redeems the world from within, as it were, while the priest's vocation is "chiefly and professedly to the sacred ministry" (*ibid.*, art. 31). Then, only the laity can remain in touch with the swiftly changing problems of the day, with direct knowledge of them. Finally, the general structure of modern society tends to the democratic. The Church is not "simply" a democracy, but neither is there any known form of earthly "monarchy" which could be a direct parallel. The clergy has to strive to find the true form of the ministry or service which it is empowered to exercise by Christ. The laity must find the true form of obedience, freedom and responsibility. The lay "service of salvation" has two main forms: the general apostolate of the laity, basically being a Christian in the world, and the various forms of "Catholic Action" (cf. Vatican II, *Apostolicam Actuositatem*, art. 20). In either case, the model for the laity is not the hierarchical office, but the relationship of the Church to the world. In this service of salvation, no attempt should be made to differentiate on principle between men and women.

Here the provision of "adult education" is the main necessity. Education is no longer confined to children in any case. And the religious and theological education of adults is demanded by the fact that the adult is the fully developed person, the pillar of the family and the congregation, the shaper of the world. Provision is now being made in many countries, in the form of university extension lectures, theological and biblical academies, degrees at theological faculties, etc., but much more remains to be done. This is especially true of the type of "education" to be offered. It can no longer be simply "lecturing", but demands active participation, criticism and dialogue – study "circles" in the strict sense, where all points are joined. Indeed, this problem must solve itself, if it is to be solved at all, since the clergy will hardly have sufficient spare resources to offer "expert tuition" even in Scripture and theology, to say nothing of the many allied disciplines, from psychology to history, with which the "educated laity" need to have some acquaintance. The full implementation of the mission of the Church to the world will be the work of the adult and educated layman as much as of the clergy. See *Laity*.

3. The *family* forms a very special area of ministry. See *Marriage* II, III, *Education, Catechesis, Sex*; cf. Vatican II, *Apostolicam Actuositatem*, art. 11 ("The apostolate of married persons is of unique importance for the Church and civil society") and *Gravissimum Educationis*, art. 3. But the family cannot exist in self-protective isolation. It creates for itself a circle of like-minded neighbours and thus helps to build up a Christian milieu where the weaker members of the community find encouragement. And the family is homogeneous and self-perpetuating by nature: over 80% of the members follow the family religion.

a) The child is at its most receptive, especially for the fundamental symbols of Christianity, up to the age of seven. Instruction in the "wonderful works of God" must clearly distinguish the Scripture miracles from the fantastic magic of fairy-tales in which children take delight. Children readily accept the distinction between what is "really true" and what is "just a story", told to stimulate the imagination and to amuse. They should be given the critical approach from the start, with no attempt to exploit their infant credulity for the sake of the miraculous. Where religion is taught in the schools, the family must ensure that it is more than a school subject – by example, prayer and the liturgy, rather than by emphasis on moralistic implications. The faith must not be invoked as an educational sanction, i.e., God's displeasure should not be used to reinforce the parents'.

b) During puberty and adolescence, the main effort will be to bring children to an attitude of personal commitment and to help them to take their place normally among the adult Christian community. The three main stages here have been described as (i) the discovery of the "I" and inner difficulties, (ii) the discovery of the social world, and the ensuing conflicts, and (iii) the discovery of the "You" and the sexual difficulties which precede maturity. The appropriate sacramental helps are the Eucharist (Thomas Aquinas, *Summa Theologica*, III, 72, a. 9 ad 1, 2), confirmation and matrimony respectively.

c) Today youthful "contestation", the generation gap, the rejection of so many material and social values which have been taken for granted in the consumers' society, leave priests and parents at a loss. It may be true that total abandonment of authority would be as little welcome to the young as are the formal modes of its ancient exercise. But for the moment, the dead weight of the ancient "establishments" needs to be counteracted by a readiness for discussion, both of means and goals, and a sharing or sanctioning of authority, which many of the older generation cannot but find disconcerting. There are no rules for such unforeseeable crises, only the sincere love which can safely risk its dignity and authority for the sake of true partnership in the one human affair.

Where schooling is continued at secondary (high school) and university level, there are many opportunities of stimulating or channelling Christian interests by means of voluntary associations, from the St Vincent de Paul

Society to Pax Romana, etc. Elsewhere the ages from about 15 to 25 can form a sort of pastoral vacuum. Here the family is the only direct means of access and influence, though with the earlier age for marriage, counselling courses should always be available. See further *Marriage*, *Celibacy*.

d) Bachelors, spinsters and unmarried or divorced mothers present special pastoral problems. First, they must be reassured, if necessary, of the normality of their status: there is no more obligation to marry than there is to celibacy. Where they have not, as so often, undertaken serious family obligations of one sort or another, they are free in a special way for the apostolate. Nonetheless, for lack of inner security, many unmarried women turn to the priest for help. This is pastoral work which must not be shirked, but undertaken in a relaxed way. Priestly celibacy demands a detached maturity, without which even sheer flight is compromising.

e) The elderly are as difficult to generalize about as any other human "grouping". Their supposed unwillingness to unlearn the old and accept the new cannot be universally verified. But there is a general trend to separate the older generations from the younger, sometimes in institutions which have been analysed with most insight by the novelists (e.g., M. Spark, *Memento Mori*; J. Updike, *The Poorhouse Fair*). Such institutions provide captive audiences for pastoral work, but the trend cannot be accepted uncritically by Christians. With the elderly too, there is interreaction between subject and object of the pastoral ministry, wisdom from one side, encouragement from the other. The great Christian ministry here is to ensure that the old do not feel lonely and unwanted. Here charity more than any theory of pastoral ministry or homiletics for the aged is the great guide.

4. *The various callings in life and professional groupings.* These form areas of ministry which are important because of their influence in forming the milieu and their direct contacts with the world of work. In many countries, e.g., France and South American countries, the "workers" are to a great extent estranged from the Church, and hence present missionary rather than pastoral problems. Elsewhere, as in the English-speaking countries, the general trend in pastoral work is to encourage "(Catholic) Workers' Colleges", where both employers and employees, at all grades, can study trade union and business law as well as Christian social principles. The trend is away from "Catholic" trade unions, such as existed in some countries. "Guilds" exist for Catholic doctors and other professional men. One of the most fully developed approaches has been that of the "Week-end (or longer) Retreat" in *ad hoc* houses where groups with like interests come together. More attention needs to be paid to the social ethics of each group, since very often the grouping was merely the occasion of preaching a rather individualistic conversion or perseverance, with the minimum reference to the specific duties of a given state. In most advanced countries, special "sodalities" or the like cater for the needs of night-workers, policemen, teachers and so on. The farming population presents particular problems by reason of the new mobility forced on it by changing economic conditions, which vary so much from countries with a third or more of the population engaged in farming (as in France and Germany) to countries like England where only some five per cent are engaged in agriculture. The "Jeunesse Agricole Chrétienne" and similar organizations have done invaluable pastoral or missionary work in Belgium, France, Germany, etc. Elsewhere, as in Ireland, country-folk's institutes have avoided "denominational" lines, and sought rather to better the conditions and

enhance the personal dignity of country life by co-operatives, university extension lectures and other cultural aids.

5. *Special situations* such as life in the diaspora, where Christians are isolated and do not even form contiguous minorities, immigrant labour, university students, especially guests from the developing countries (cf. Vatican II, *Gravissimum Educationis*, art. 10), tourists, the religiously and socially isolated of all types, e.g., drug addicts, alcoholics, need specialized forms of pastoral care, which are now being more or less rapidly developed along the lines of the "non-territorial" parish which will be more and more a feature of the modern Church.

a) The (physically) sick have always been the object of special pastoral care. But here again the more or less helpless state of the patient should not be exploited for pastoral ends. The sick are a captive audience, and it is not always easy to respect their spiritual freedom when the agent of the ministry (priest, nurse or doctor) tries to bring home to them the positive role of sickness in the fulfilment of human life – which is the specific task of the pastoral ministry here.

b) Work for prisoners must not be allowed to appear as part of the prison or penal system. Much depends on the tact and ability of the chaplain, etc., who must make clear the difference between divine and human judgment. But the task of rehabilitation in family and society is incumbent on others as well as the prison chaplain and welfare officers. Without the full co-operation of the (Christian) community, restoration to normal or full Christian life is impossible.

c) Specially skilled efforts are called for on behalf of the mentally ill. The main effort (to be undertaken only according to expert advice) is to distinguish authentic culpability from the neurotic. With some hysterical and scrupulous people, firm directives, rational recreations, elimination of one-sided legalism and general sympathy may be partially successful, but each case must be judged on its merits, which supposes some elementary knowledge of psychopathology on the part of the would-be helper.

d) Non-practising Catholics, apostates, the invalidly married, etc., must at least not be neglected. There is the danger of their being lost sight of in the larger urban parishes, where indirect contacts may still be possible through families and friends. As far as discretion allows, they should be notified of parish and missionary projects and fund-raising activities, which are so many reminders of the claims of the love of God.

e) As regards Christians of other Churches, Vatican II has noted that "ecumensm" is one of the great graces of our times. It presents a challenge to the inventiveness as well as the charity of clergy and laity. See *Ecumenism*.

f) Converts remain a special pastoral situation, even though the ecumenical movement takes precedence over individual conversions. The individual must weigh his own duty in conscience. Instruction should be "global" in the Catholic faith (and life), not centred on controversial points. In mixed marriages, a dispensation is preferable to a hurried course of instruction and reception into the Church. Instruction can come later, in common with the marriage partner, and sincerity will be the better assured. Converts who can work for the unfulfilled interests of their original Church can make a special contribution to the renewal of the ministry of salvation in the Catholic Church. But they must not equate their particular form of faith with the absolutely necessary. As regards the sects, it should be recognized that their often bigoted if not slightly pathological sense of mission makes pastoral work with them difficult. It is probably more important to provide the faithful with the spiritual and historical resources to engage successfully in controversy with them.

Non-believers are now rarely such by reason of personal decision. They are mostly born into their particular religion, and must be handled accordingly. This is also true of atheists. Few have the Promethean feeling of having robbed heaven of its secret, and hence, being less aggressive, are more open to the mission of the Church (see *Atheism*). In many parts of the world, the pastoral task of the Church will be determined in future by its atheistic setting. This may result in repressed "disbelief" among the faithful, inasmuch as it may often be impossible to find a style of life determined in its totality by Christian principles. All forms of the ministry of salvation will have to pay attention to such defects and gaps in the faithful (cf. Vatican II, *Gaudium et Spes*, arts. 19–21).

6. *Other fields*. a) The press, cinema, radio and television must be provided with attractive matter (liturgy, sermons, discussions, etc). The pastoral ministry must not be content to counteract possible damage, just as it must not rest content with supporting such government censure as may exist in moral matters. The object here must be to train experts who can impart some critical principles and guidelines of "taste" to the public. Here the primary work must be done by the family, as the intimate reach of television proves. In face of such all-pervasive influences, the Christian who has not been trained to critical maturity in all fields will hardly resist. See Vatican II, *Inter Mirifica*.

b) The coming of the five-day week, paid holidays, sick pay, redundancy and unemployment pay, and earlier retirement, in ever wider measure, means that a large new sector has to come under pastoral care. This is the area of recreation, free time, amusements. Here again, in normal circumstances, it cannot be a pastoral task to initiate, direct or influence leisure any more than work. But since leisure is now rightly recognized as an intrinsically formative element, and not just as an interlude in "the serious business of life", it is part of the Church's mission to man to explain the nature and responsibilities of leisure, to stress the true cultural values, to counteract the emphasis on material goods in the advertisements of the consumption society. Whether the morality and economics of such a society should be challenged by the Church is a question which arises with special emphasis when the pastoral approach to leisure activities is studied.

C. The Activities of the Pastoral Ministry

The service of salvation is actively embodied in the proclamation of the faith, the liturgy, the Christian service of the world and the government of the Church.

1. *The proclamation*. The necessity of faith for salvation (*D* 801) and the fact that faith normally comes by hearing (Rom 10:17) means that the proclamation of the gospel is the primary pastoral ministry (Vatican II, *Lumen Gentium*, art. 25). It is the authoritative attestation of the saving acts of God, primarily the Pasch of Christ, building up the body of Christ for the parousia.

a) The first phase is preaching. See *Kerygma*, *Word of God*, and Vatican II, *Sacrosanctum Concilium*, art. 23. The goal of preaching is neither pure biblical commentary nor moralizing timeless truths, but to make the word of God audible in a given situation. The situation is described in the light of the word of God, which then summons man to detach himself from egoism and slavish worldliness, and to turn to God in reverent faith, hope and love (*D* 798). The real problem is less biblical exegesis than the changing understanding of man and the world. The effectiveness of the preaching will depend on the intrinsic vigour of the attestation of the truth rather than on the intellectual effort, though to shirk the latter is to tempt God.

b) Preaching is accompanied by planned fundamental instruction (see *Catechesis*).

c) Many men can be reached only by (religious) dialogue, which priests may perhaps initiate by district visiting. Otherwise it is the authentic form of lay preaching. The confirmed are empowered to profess their faith "quasi ex officio" (Aquinas, *Summa Theologica*, III, q. 72, a. 5, ad 2), and this will be the main instrument of the dialogue between the Church and the world (Vatican II, *Apostolicam Actuositatem*, art. 14; cf. *Gaudium et Spes*, arts. 3, 43, 85, 90, 23, 28, 21). In a democratic society and a pluralist world, the official forms of preaching will depend to a great extent for their fruitfulness on this sort of dialogue.

2. The liturgy, with the preaching of the word, is the climax of the life and ministry of the Church (Vatican II, *Sacrosanctum Concilium*, art. 10) and hence of the life of the pastor (Vatican II, *Presbyterorum Ordinis*, arts. 5, 14). Christ is "proclaimed" in the liturgy (1 Cor 11:26) which means that it must open to the world – intelligible (1 Cor 14:23ff.), at suitable hours and with a missionary component (as at marriages and funerals). As thanksgiving and transformation, the Eucharist is an assertion in a godless world of the transcendence of God against self-sufficient humanism. See *Eucharist* II, *Liturgy* I, *Sacraments* I.

3. The Christian ministry in the world, a basic function of the Church, was rather neglected in the one-sidedly clerical view of pastoral action. It is simply the everyday life of the Christian – which St. Paul calls "worship" (Rom 12:1). There is a worldly realm, which must be recognized as relatively autonomous, and which is "Christian" when properly managed (see *World, Church and World, Secularization* I, II). The fact that all things are ordained to Christ does not mean that bishops and priests can be the practically unique caretakers and moulders of the world. There is a "worldly world", beyond their *de facto* and *de iure* reach, which the Church can accept tranquilly. Nonetheless, even in the world the Church is mysteriously apart, and is the framework of Christian life, which may be inserted into the world in such "worldly" forms as schools, academies, hospitals and social welfare.

The clerical service of the world includes example and testimony, various contacts and visits, the formation of a missionary-minded kernel in the parish. But the laity's range is more universal. The world can hardly be reached from a distance – from the altar, pulpit, confessional and synod. See above B, 2–6; Vatican II, *Gaudium et Spes*.

4. The government of the Church, with its lawful directives through law, precept, custom, courts, etc., is also a form of pastoral activity. The hierarchical (pastoral) office is active when it ordains, gives mandates, directs, imposes sanctions and defines formally the channels of salvation. It confirms the reality of conversion by the absolution of the individual, excommunicates or admits, disposes of Church property, etc. All these exercises of authority must be seen as pastoral service (Mt 20:24–28; Jn 10:1–29) in the Spirit of Christ, whose law is self-dedicating love and only then demand. The tension between office and charism, love and law, is essential to the pilgrim Church, though it is the duty of all to reduce this tension to the minimum. The complications of real life make it difficult for the office-bearers to give precise directives. This means that in the reform of canon law, the laity

should be part of the juridical order of the Church, and share in the government, precisely as pastoral ministry. Here again all clericalism is to be avoided. Tasks for which the laity are better equipped should be handed over to their independent responsibility.

Viktor Schurr

PASTORAL THEOLOGY

1. *Basic remarks on the history and nature of pastoral theology*. The need for systematic doctrine and practical, up-to-date guidelines for the exercise of the pastoral ministry led to the development of pastoral theology as a separate discipline within theological studies. This took place from about 1770 onwards, at first in Austria, and shortly afterwards in Germany and neighbouring countries. The individual pastor was alone regarded as the agent of the Church's pastoral action. Consequently he and his activities alone formed the subject-matter of pastoral theology. The more the "pastor" became the focus of pastoral theology and of pastoral activity as that theology envisaged it, the more the exaggerated clericalist conception of that state of life and ministry was strengthened. In the end, the individual clergyman was defined as the historical continuation of the person and function of Christ ("Christ's representative", "God's viceroy", "channel of all graces", "shepherd of the flock", etc.). And the individual Christians and the Church congregation stood before him passively, as something "directed", "led", and indeed "sanctified" by him.

In the last few decades it has become more and more clearly evident that in the light of a theologically correct view of the Church, this "obstinate misunderstanding" (Arnold) of pastoral theology can no longer be maintained. As a consequence, the very name itself becomes open to question, for it constantly encourages the misconception that pastoral theology is purely and simply a doctrine of the priestly office, or even that the Church's work is a matter of transitive pastoral action carried out on a passive object. It is therefore reasonable, and in the last few years has become widespread in practice, to speak of "practical theology" to denote the practical theological discipline which deals by the methods of scientific theology with all that constitutes, conditions and makes possible the action incumbent on the Church from day to day. This name had already been suggested in 1841 by A. Graf under the influence of the Lutheran and Catholic theological schools of Tübingen.

Such a "practical" pastoral theology would necessarily have to comprise all those practical theological disciplines which are concerned with some fundamental function of the Church (liturgy, catechesis, etc.) but which developed separately from the old-style pastoral theology mainly because of its non-ecclesiological basis. The name "pastoral theology" could then be used as a meaningful and legitimate term for that domain of practical theology which deals with questions of the pastoral ministry as one element in the total activity of the Church.

It is not difficult to show that practical theology is a necessary branch of theological study. The systematic, dogmatic disciplines study the abiding essence of the Church and God's self-communication to man which becomes historically tangible and effective in it. The fixing of that self-communication in the words of Scripture, and its development and realization in history, are the subject-matter of the biblical and historical sciences. The situation in which the Church here and now has to fulfil itself, i.e., its own nature, which is identical with its function, together with the structure, demands and opportunities of that situation which are not contained in dogma or in canon law, require for their methodical, socio-theological analysis and for the working-out of the principles of "pastoral" action which they imply, a branch of study which is truly theological and at the same time truly practical, in other words, practical theology.

2. *The material themes of pastoral theology envisaged as practical theology.* In contradistinction to dogmatic or essential ecclesiology, the object of which is the abiding, transcendental and sacramental nature of the Church, practical theology deals with the Church as a reality with a social and historical structure, and therefore concerned with empirical data. This reality of the Church has to be actualized here and now at any given moment in order really to be what it is and achieve its purpose. Pastoral theology understood in this way could rightly be called "existentiell ecclesiology", especially since one of its specific tasks would be to work out principles and prescriptions for the necessary activity of the Church imposed on it at any particular moment. The fundamental theme of the Church's activity gives rise to the following developments:

a) All the agents of that activity must be dealt with in relation to the task and place of the Church as a whole in the world of today; the nature and function of the various Church ministries: the bishop and his diocese, the Pope as principle of unity of the Church and the organization associated with him in the government of the whole Church; the ecclesiastical functions of each individual Christian and, not least, the functions of the various members of the diocesan *presbyterium.*

b) All the fundamental functions which follow from the Church's essential mission have to be dealt with, but in the way in which they must be carried out in a particular contemporary situation, which is not simply known all along, yet always conditions the performance of those fundamental functions. In this sense we have to speak about the liturgy as a celebration of the mystery of the Church, about the proclamation of the word (as missionary preaching, as preaching in the Christian congregation and as catechesis), about the activity of the Church in the sacraments, about Church discipline, corporal works of mercy, and the Christian life of the individual inasmuch as the Church finds tangible historical expression in him. Consequently it is not necessary or useful in this connection to deal with the whole of liturgical science or catechetics; if only on didactic and methodical grounds, they can and must remain distinct daughter sciences of practical theology as a whole.

c) All the social and sociological factors and aspects of the Church must be taken into consideration because, of course, only against that background is it possible to recognize the relevance of the socio-theological analysis (cf. below, 3).

d) The fundamental formal structures of ecclesiastical action and life have to be dealt with; the various possible legitimate and contemporary kinds of spirituality; the differences between the sexes and their significance for the life of the Church; the discrepancy between theoretical and actual morality in contemporary life; the difference between the Church's mediation and the personal appropriation of the salvation which is present in the Church and which has continually to become effective in its various activities.

3. *The formal point of view of pastoral theology.* The formal point of view, from which the subject-matter of practical theology as we have outlined it must be envisaged and dealt with, is the conditioning of the Church's activity by the particular situation at any given time. Since it came into existence, pastoral theology has been interested in the special needs of the age, the changes in some of the conditions

of pastoral work. Because of its clericalist approach, however, that interest was directed solely to the situation of the individual "pastor" and his activities. The contemporary scene with its actual social and cultural structures was to a large extent regarded merely as external, resistant material, or simply as "the world", against which spiritual pastoral activity had to work. The pastoral theology which we have in mind here, however, can only regard the contemporary situation at any given time as the inescapable summons of God to the Church, reminding it of its ever new task of formulating and announcing the gospel of Jesus for – not against – human society as it exists here and now, in other words, for the world which God always loves, not for itself. The present time, therefore, has to be understood as the particular configuration of that abiding historical and consequently changing background against which offer and acceptance of God's free self-communication to man take place. Furthermore, such a contemporary situation always determines not only the human being to whom the Church at any given time seeks to convey its message, but also the Church itself and the various agents who carry out its various functions.

The analysis of the contemporary situation postulated here presupposes of course a comprehensive description of the most important structures and structural changes of contemporary society. It therefore represents not merely a permanent formal point of view from which the various factors and possibilities in the Church must be studied, but material which practical theology has to supply.

4. *On the method and systematic structure of pastoral theology*. The definition of the material and formal objects of pastoral theology which has been given above clearly indicates its necessary and specific task in theology as a whole. It must not be overlooked, however, that a pastoral theology at the present time has necessarily to deal with questions which really belong to essential ecclesiology, but have not yet received proper treatment there. Nevertheless they are necessarily presupposed if practical theology is to do its work properly. An example of this would be the definition of the nature of the Church, the question of the ultimate, indispensable and therefore truly permanent essence of the Church's worship, or of the "sacramental" nature of the Church's saving mediation. It will probably only become clear in the future how exactly essential ecclesiology can be separated from existentiell ecclesiology. For there is no doubt that pastoral theology, by giving expression within theology generally to the contemporary world situation, involves a perpetually new inquiry addressed to theology. As a result, the statements of theology, especially of ecclesiology, on the plane of essences are only genuine and adequate answers if the questions which practical theology has formulated (in the name of the world) have been heard and treated with respect. To that extent, therefore, pastoral theology envisaged as practical theology would have a hermeneutical function for theology as whole. As regards the method of pastoral theology, this would mean that in its inquiry into existing reality it always questions the known facts and forms of the Church and its pastoral action – always, of course, with the constructive purpose (see below, 5) of establishing principles for the Church's relevant and effective actualization of the gospel.

5. *Remarks on the analysis of the contemporary scene*. The various sociological questions can of course be formulated in the first place on the basis of a theological pre-comprehension of the Church, its fundamental task and possibilities. A merely secular sociography which tried to leave out the Church as a factual datum, would never make

possible or directly provide a conclusive and practical answer to the questions which practical theology has to raise. The nature of the questioner means that the sociological question always has a theological character. To what extent do the actual structures of the Church, its administration, regional organization, the mode of formation of its congregations, its relation to secular society, the concrete forms, language, words and signs of its preaching, catechesis, administration of the sacraments, etc., follow necessarily from its abiding nature? How far do they result merely from its exposure to temptation, its pilgrim lot, over which it has no control, which can never be perfectly elucidated but only accepted in patience? To what extent are they merely the consequence of blind and guilty petrification of the expressions and forms of its life? Precisely these questions must be answered, however, before pastoral theology (in one special section of its work) can set about formulating principles and, above all, prescriptions for the activity incumbent on the Church at the present time.

Three groups of questions in particular would have to be distinguished and explicitly treated in the socio-theological analysis of a pastoral theology in the sense we understand it here:

a) Those questions which concern the situation and structure of the contemporary world as a whole. The Church has become a world-wide Church as never before, and can therefore only understand its specific task in relation to the world as a whole. It can only plan its world-mission in a really strategic way if it has recognized what the tendencies and basic structures of the present day are. This planning can and must to a considerable extent be methodical and scientific, yet without leaving out of account the charismatic initiative of the individual, of missionary societies and religious orders.

b) Those questions which concern the situation and structure of the various societies and groups of the contemporary world; for in regard to the latter, the Church is merely one among many religious societies and institutions. Among these, however, it has an uncontested and even a pre-eminent place. But it has perpetually to reconquer this consciously for itself in order really to hold it. And with other religious societies the Church shares, for example, the problem of religious freedom, tolerance, world peace, the universal human ethos, and also the situation of increasing secularity, religious pluralism and indifference.

c) The questions which concern the condition of the individual in the world of today. Since from the start he is a member of secular society, he is the first to be affected by a change in its structure. Certainly these questions seem to be the most urgent problems of pastoral work as previously practised. It would be false on principle, however, to separate the situation of the individual from that of the Church as a whole. Otherwise the result would be a pastoral tactics instead of a strategy of the Church's action as a whole at the present day, which is what the real goal of pastoral theology ought to be.

6. *Purpose of pastoral theology*. The primary aim of pastoral theology as we understand it here is, as has clearly emerged, the planning of the Church's action for the present and the future. This distinguishes it decisively from the kind of pastoral theology which chiefly aimed at the training and practical equipment of the individual pastor. Such practical, pragmatic initiation into the spiritual ministry will, of course, always have its place in the formation of the future clergyman; as such, however, it is not what we are calling pastoral theology here. But practical theology cannot only explain the sense of the Church, scientifically grasped, in its necessary action here and now. It can also work out principles and prescrip-

tions for the Church's present action. But it does not itself constitute the Church's pastoral action. Pastoral theology in the sense intended here is therefore a theological, and therefore inevitably theoretical discipline; but without solid theory, solid practice is not possible.

Theology as a whole must probably expect that in the future its relative self-sufficiency, its systematization and the relevance of its previous theses will be called in question. This applies not least to previous views of the Church's jurisdiction and legislation. It is obvious that pastoral theology as we understand it is ultimately a precondition of future canon law. For canon law studies have of course to interpret the law as it actually exists. If they are not to abandon their methodological basis, canonists cannot themselves analyse the preliminary domain where it is decided what reaction, what norm of behaviour, what law is adequate and meaningful in view of the contemporary situation as it exists here and now.

In all this it must not, of course, be overlooked that the planning of the total activity of the Church, so far as it belongs to the function of pastoral theology, remains contingent in principle. It must, however, be accepted in a positive spirit by the Church as a whole, by all bearers of office and theorists, as well as by individual Christians. The Church as it reflects on its own present and future must submit its planning to the essentially hidden providence of God, at the same time clearly distinguishing it from any utopia of this world, and also from any kind of ecclesiastical "planned economy" which would like to foresee and plan everything by an *a priori* pastoralism.

Heinz Schuster

PATROLOGY

The study of the Church Fathers is briefly known as patrology. It embraces all ancient Christian writers down to Gregory the Great (d. 604) or Isidore of Seville (d. 636) in the West, and John of Damascus (d. 749) in the East. In our own days, the study has been pursued with a new attentiveness. In theology, a one-sided effort to exploit the Fathers according to scholastic viewpoints has given way to a more scientific investigation of their proper interests. A blind faith in authority has yielded more and more to the view which sees the Fathers primarily as witnesses to the faith of their times in the fundamental epoch of the Church. Classical studies have finally overcome a distaste for the Fathers which was a legacy of the Renaissance and are investigating more exactly the language and concepts of the Fathers. Students of history of religion find the Fathers excellent sources for their researches into the problem of "Antiquity and Christianity". Patrology has thus become an independent science for the study of late antiquity and early Christianity.

The process of emancipation was slow. The name patrology is of comparatively recent date. It was coined by the Lutheran theologian J. Gerhard when he published his *Patrologia sive de primitivae Ecclesiae christianae Doctorum vita et lucubrationibus* in Jena in 1653. Here patrology was the study of the life and doctrines of the Fathers, though the Fathers meant all ancient Christian writers, including heretics, since patrology embraced all theological writers of antiquity. At the beginning of the 20th century the precise aim of patrology became a matter of lively discussion – of which the protagonists were O. Bardenhewer and A. Harnack – as to whether patrology was the history of ancient "Christian" or ancient "ecclesiastical" literature. It was merely a question of terms, since in patrology and in "patristics", which is sometimes distinguished from it, the theological viewpoint predominates. "Patristic" comes from the dogmatic textbooks of the 17th century, which distinguished between biblical, patristic, scholastic and speculative theology. In the 18th century this *theologia patristica* gave rise to the section of history of dogmas which uses the Fathers as sources for proof-texts for dogmas.

The notion of a history of ancient Christian literature written largely from a theological standpoint is much older. It goes back to Eusebius of Caesarea, who in his history of the Church (*Historia Ecclesiastica*, I, 1, 1) did his best to list all the ancient Christian writers and their works, orthodox and heretical, with long quotations from many of them. Thus Eusebius is one of the most important sources for patrology, since many of the works quoted have been lost and Eusebius remains our only source of information for many ancient writers. The first real patrology was produced by Jerome, whose *De Viris Illustribus*, a catalogue of writers which he composed at Bethlehem in 392, was an effort to rebut the accusation of cultural inferiority levelled against Christians by pagans. There are 135 sections, giving biographies and critical evaluations of the ancient Christian writers from Simon Peter to Jerome himself, who lists his own works down to 392. The work is modelled on one of the same name by Suetonius. This work of Jerome remained the basis of all study of ancient Christian literature for more than a thousand years and is still the most important source for its history. This does not mean that the work has not many defects. There are inaccuracies and some unfortunate prejudices, apart from the fact that it includes Philo, Josephus and Seneca among ancient Christian writers. A valuable continuation of this work was provided by the semi-Pelagian priest Gennadius of Marseilles, who wrote a work with the same title about 480 (*PL*, LVIII, cols. 1059–120). Of lesser interest are the *De Viris Illustribus* of Isidore of Seville, *c.* 615–18 (*PL*, LXXXIII, cols. 1081–106), and Ildefonsus of Toledo (*PL*, XCVI, cols. 195–206), which are informative about Spanish writers in particular. The only non-Spanish author mentioned by Ildefonsus is Gregory the Great. The next effort to bring the work of Jerome up to date was made by the Benedictine Sigebert of Gembloux in the 11th century. His *De Viris Illustribus* (*PL*, CLX, cols. 547–88), which closely followed Jerome and Gennadius, first gave biographies and works of ancient Christian writers and then more meagre information on the Latin theologians of the early Middle Ages. No Byzantine writers are mentioned. Similar compendiums of the history of theological literature were produced by Honorius of Autun (*c.* 1122), in his *De Luminaribus Ecclesiae* (*PL*, CLXXII, cols. 197–234), and by the Anonymus Mellicensis about 1135, in his *De Scriptoribus Ecclesiasticis* (*PL*, CCXIII, cols. 961–84), who wrote, however, not in Melk (Lower Austria) but at Prüfening near Regensburg. A sounder work is the *De Scriptoribus Ecclesiasticis* of Abbot John Trithemius (*c.* 1494) which provides information about 963 writers, including non-theologians. But Trithemius too was practically confined to Jerome and Gennadius for his knowledge of the Fathers.

It was important for the East that a Greek translation of Jerome's catalogue had been provided very early. It was long attributed to Sophronius, who translated many of his writings into Greek, as Jerome relates (*De Viris Illustribus*, 134), but seems to be of later date. The anonymous reviser of the *Onomatologos* of Hesychius of Miletus (*c.* 550) drew on this translation, and the *Onomatologos* itself was used by Photius and Suidas. Photius composed his *Myrobiblion* or *Bibliotheca c.* 858, a mine of information on ancient literature, containing summaries with long extracts of some 280 classical and

Christian works from his library. The work shows great erudition and independence of judgment. Without it, many works would have been entirely lost or remained quite unknown. Valuable information on patristics has also been preserved in the *Lexicon* of Suidas, *c.* 1000. Finally, there is a catalogue of Christian authors who wrote in Syriac, composed by the Nestorian Ebedjesus bar Berika *c,* 1317, which contains important items about many ancient Christian authors.

The Renaissance brought with it a new interest in patrology. The humanists brought to light a large number of hitherto unknown writings of Greek and Latin ecclesiastical authors. The Reformation and the Counter-Reformation alike appealed to the Fathers for their different views on the doctrine and structure of the early Church. A good introduction to patrology was provided by Cardinal Bellarmine's *De Scriptoribus Ecclesiasticis* (Rome, 1613), which dealt with Christian writers down to the year 1500. A new era in patrology began with the work of the Maurists, who produced in the 17th and 18th centuries editions of the Fathers which were exemplary for their age, and provided scholars with enormous amounts of source-materials. The sixteen volumes of *Mémoires pour servir a l'histoire ecclésiastique* (1693–1712) by L. Du Pin and S. de Tillemont rendered great service to patristic chronology. After a brief recession in the 18th century, new advances were made in the middle of the 19th. Between 1844 and 1866, the Abbé J.-P. Migne published his *Patrologia Latina* in 161 volumes and his *Patrologia Graeca*, with parallel Latin translations, in 221, a collection unsurpassed for completeness down to the present day. They were reprints of all known patristic texts, containing many mistakes, no doubt, but ample and accessible enough to give a mighty new impulse to patrology. The call for better texts became insistent, and led to the two great undertakings of the Vienna Academy and the Berlin Academy, the *Corpus Scriptorum Ecclesiasticorum Latinorum* (*CSEL*, 1866ff.) and *Die griechischen christlichen Schriftsteller der ersten drei Jahrhunderte* (1897ff.) respectively, which have been publishing full critical texts. Critical editions of the newly-discovered Oriental Fathers were published in France from 1907 on, in the *Patrologia Syriaca,* the *Corpus Scriptorum Christianorum Orientalium* (1903ff.) in Syriac, Coptic, Arabic and Ethiopian series, and the *Patrologia Orientalis* (1907ff.) which also includes Armenian and Georgian. In England there were the great series of translations, the *Library of the Fathers* (45 vols., 1838–88) and the *Ante-Nicene Christian Library* (24 vols., 1866–72), and in the United States the *Select Library of Nicene and Post-Nicene Fathers* (28 vols., 1886–1900). Similar series in Germany were the *Sämtliche Werke der Kirchenväter* (39 vols., 1830–54), the *Bibliothek der Kirchenväter* (80 vols., 1869–88) and the new *Bibliothek der Kirchenväter* in two series (61 vols., 1911–30) and 20 vols. (1932–39). Comprehensive surveys were published by A. von Harnack, *Geshichte der altchristlichen Literatur bis auf Eusebius* (3 vols., 1893–1904) and O. Bardenhewer, *Geschichte der altkirchlichen Literatur* (5 vols., 1913–32, reprinted 1962). A new era of international co-operation began after the Second World War, as may be seen, for instance, in the five "International Conferences on Patristic Studies" at Oxford (1951, 1955, 1959, 1963, 1967), the contributions to which are published in the nine volumes of *Studia Patristica,* edited by F. L. Cross and K. Aland (*Texte und Untersuchungen* 63, 64, 78, 79, 80, 81, 92, 93, 94) (1957–66). There is also the *Bibliographia Patristica*, published by the patristic commission of the Academies of Göttingen, Heidelbert, Munich and Mainz, edited by W. Schneemelcher with an international team of helpers. The resumption of the series published by the Vienna Academy and the Berlin Academy has been accompanied since 1953 by the great undertaking of the abbey of St. Peter at Steenbrugge in Belgium, the *Corpus Christianorum*, a new Migne, which will reprint all patristic texts in a *Series Latina* and a *Series Graeca*. Important preliminary work for this *Corpus* is done by the *Clavis Patrum Latinorum* of E. Dekker and A. Gaar, which lists the best editions of the Latin Fathers (1951; 2nd ed., 1961). New series of texts and translations were launched in France with the collection *Sources chrétiennes* and in the United States and England with the *Ancient Christian Writers*, the *Fathers for English Readers* and the *Fathers of the Church*. The finds of Nag-Hammadi provide patristic studies with many hitherto unknown Gnostic texts which throw new light on the history of Gnosticism and the beginnings of Christian theology. Since 1961 the *Greek Patristic Lexicon* has been in course of publication at Oxford (edited by G. W. H. Lampe, 4 fascicles, 1961–65), which will be indispensable to patristic studies (5th and last fascicle, 1968).

Johannes Quasten

PELAGIANISM

Pelagianism designates in theology a heretical position with regard to the problems of grace and freedom. It goes back to the British monk Pelagius ("Morgan") who about the year 400 preached in Rome a strictly biblical spirituality with strong emphasis on the human will. It was disseminated by his disciples Caelestius and Julian of Eclanum. Augustine played a decisive role in the Pelagian controversy, whose historical course need not be pursued here in detail. Like the Stoics, Pelagius thought that one could obtain every good by prayer except virtue. Once having received the gift of free will, it is man's responsibility to make good moral use of it. He is responsible for his actions and, if only he has the courage to will it, there is no height of sanctity which he may not attain. Having read in the *Confessions* of St. Augustine, "Da quod jubes et quodvis jube", "Lord, command what you wish, if you give me the power to accomplish it", Rome's popular spiritual director was scandalized. Later on, Julian of Eclanum, one of his disciples, expressed his doctrine in an even more characteristic way: "By free will man has become adult; he has been emancipated by God" ("Libertas arbitrii qua homo emancipatus est a Deo").

This affirmation of the freedom of man as a created but fully autonomous power of self-determination, who can observe the law of God by his own powers, was a denial of the necessity of grace for the natural and salutary observance of the moral law and hence disregarded the doctrine of original sin and of the consequences of sin (concupiscence). Undoubtedly, nature, law, providential occurrences, and the gift of freedom itself, are God-given graces in the broad meaning of the word. But in the strict sense, grace is something different. It is a supernatural gift, an interior assistance by means of which God himself acts at the very heart of our liberty so that we may put it to good use. According to Pelagius, God gave me existence and it is my responsibility to sanctify myself. Augustine referred him to the words of our Lord, "Without me you can do nothing" (Jn 15:5). And he comments, "Christ did not say: Without me it will be hard but: Without me you can do *nothing*."

To support his thesis, Augustine appealed to several texts of Scripture: "The king's heart . . . is in the hand of the Lord" (Prov 21:1); "God is at work in you, both to will and to work for his good pleasure" (Phil 2:13); "Not that we are sufficient of ourselves to claim anything as coming from us; our sufficiency is from God" (2 Cor 3:5). He argued that perseverance in good is still more obviously a gift of grace. He recalled with particular warmth (Sermon 290) the parable of the Pharisee and the publican (Lk 18:9–14). During the controversy, Augustine several times compared the Pelagians to the Jews spoken of by St. Paul who, not knowing the true justice of God, sought to establish their own (Rom 10:3). He stressed the opposition between the OT, directed towards the realization of temporal promises, and the grace of the NT – an interior grace which leads us towards an eternal inheritance (see the letter to Honoratus, *Ep.*, 140). The old law, he said (still following the Apostle of the Gentiles), could only make one aware of sin, without at the same time bestowing the power to fulfil the law. The Pelagians pretended that there could be sinless men. Augustine for his part, invoking St. Paul, confessed his own wretchedness and cried out to God for mercy (Sermon 154).

Pelagianism stemmed from too narrow a concept of revelation, and so fell victim to a philosophical error. Stoicism, from which its ideas were more or less consciously derived, contrasted the greatness of heroes with the meanness and torpor of the ordinary man. It was unable to appreciate that the moral stature of heroes is measured above all by their dependence on God. Of this Augustine was well aware. "God, who made us without us, will not save us without us", he said. But he went on to add that he saves us by communicating his power to us. "Nothing can exist", St. Thomas Aquinas was to say, "which is not at every instant dependent upon the first cause. For the creature, creation is a relationship of dependence which keeps it in being after existence has been given to it" (*Summa*, I, q. 104; *De Potentia*, q. 5). *In ipso vivimus, movemur et sumus* (Acts 17:28). But since it is a positive, vital reality, the good use of free will supposes a new relationship with God. When I say "my action is my merit", I must always imply that, without my ceasing to be a responsible being, this free act is a gift given me by God, except in the case of sin of which I am the principal cause and which in moral terms is a non-entity. The Council of Orange said with St. Augustine, "No one has anything of his own save sin and the lie." "Man can do no good without God. God does great good in man without any action on man's part, but man does no good which God does not enable him to do" (*D* 193, 195).

This metaphysical reality must, however, be expressed in terms of a vital relationship between man and God. Hence Pelagianism is an ever-recurring temptation. The moral teaching of Kantianism, with its emphasis on duty and its majesty, is in its own epochal form a Stoicism which asserts that man is the sole master of his own destiny. The philosophy of Fichte laicizes the Christian idea of grace and eternal life. The atheistic existentialism of today, broadcast in so many plays, novels and films, is inspired by the same principles. It is a reaction against the psychological and social determinism of the 19th century. As Taine put it, vice and virtue were natural products. The failure of particular individuals was explained by representing them to be the slaves of an environment, or socially deprived through no fault of their own. For Sartre, in contrast to Zola, every man is free and responsible for his life. If there are heroes and cowards, if there are courageous and sluggish souls, he says, it is not the result of temperament or environment. One is not born a hero or a coward, one becomes either one or the other, and there always remains the possibility of failure or recovery. Like that of Pelagius in the 5th century, this is a healthy reaction. But contemporary existentialism, which is often an atheistic existentialism, is more dangerous than the teaching of Pelagius. At least he believed in God. Man is at the centre of nature, all alone, with no other finality than that which he gives himself; with no other support than that of his own freedom. On the other hand, this philosophy of man leads yet again to pride and self-satisfaction. Nietzsche dismisses Christianity as having produced only unredeemed men and looks for a morality of the superman. Pelagius set man alone before the law of God, and one day God would ask him to render an account of his life. Atheistic existentialism, which views all moral codes with suspicion, has not been able to develop an objective ethics, but aims at an ethics which will be subordinated to man qua man.

What has been called the conflict between the humanisms, the conflict between Christian humanism and Marxism or atheistic existentialism, shows the permanent interest of the controversy between Augustine and Pelagianism. Pelagius appears as a Christian still under the spell of the OT. He has not understood what grace means theologically, and understands grace, in keeping with his pragmatic understanding of Christianity, as an external aid for the action of man. He does not seem to have considered the doctrine of the mystical body of Christ, the social nature or solidarity of man in sin and in salvation. The inward grace which he refuses to admit is in reality the grace of Christ. Christ merited salvation for us through his sacrifice of reconciliation, but he is also the head of a living body, vivified by the Holy Spirit. If we need an inward supernatural help for the right use of our freedom, this is because we do not exist as self-contained monads but in union with other men and with Jesus Christ, the head and redeemer, as members of his body. He who cuts himself off from the body by sin becomes a dead member. A living root can send forth another shoot instead of the one which is cut off, but the shoot cannot live without the root (cf. *D* 197). The Pelagian controversy made it possible to formulate the doctrine of the necessity of inward grace. But the doctrine of the absolute necessity could only be formulated in the context of its supernatural character and goal.

Henri Rondet

PENANCE

I. Virtue of Penance

1. *Essence.* Penance as a virtue denotes the morally and religiously appropriate human attitude, bestowed by the grace of Christ, in regard to one's own sin and to sin generally. Its central act is contrition in its various forms, but its full nature includes not only the specific act of contrition as a turning to God and away from past personal sin, but also all the other interior and external Christian attitudes to sin: courage to face the fear of God and the truth of one's own existence without "repressions" – the only way true responsibility for one's past can be assumed; grace-given readiness to allow oneself to be convicted of sin by God's revealing word, by destruction of pharisaic self-righteousness; fear of the constant threat of sin, and the fight against it by the penitential works of mortification (biblical "watching", fasting, alms-giving, etc.; cf. *D* 806); serious and active will to amendment, with confidence in the grace of God which proves victorious in man's powerlessness; the struggle against concupiscence and the world; the will to receive the sacrament of the forgiveness of sins; readiness humbly to suffer the consequences of sin which remain even after it is forgiven (*D* 906, 923); co-responsibility for the struggle against sin in Church and world; a share in bearing the burden of sin which finds embodiment in general unhappiness and distress; the determination to make satisfaction (*D* 904f.) and atonement.

All these acts are to be understood in the same way as Christian activity in general has to be. Without detriment to human freedom even in fallen man, they are initiated by the grace of God which cannot be merited; first and last they are his gift to us, concrete acts of justifying faith, a participation in the cross of Christ. What is true of contrition also holds good for the wider act of penance. It is in principle, as a formal act, necessary for salvation for those guilty of personal sin, precisely because it is the way in which God's free mercy grants salvation to the free creature (*D* 797f., 811ff.). The concept of penance implies the freedom of the salutary act (*D* 814). Precisely as God's gift, penance is a human act (not merely passively experienced: *D* 897, 914f.), in which a man turns away from his past, rejecting it permanently in the free spiritual act. (In "pain" man acknowledges the inviolable validity of God's order and in "detestation" of sin he freely fulfils that order itself once more.) It includes recognition in faith that it is God's action in us which forgives sin, not our contrition (to the extent that this on our part must be distinguished from God's action), and that that action is first accepted in hope. Finally, it includes recognition of the created, ontological and existentiell plurality of man, which itself determines and demands a plurality of human acts in this respect also (interior and external works of penance, faith and love, contrition and satisfaction, revolt against the past, anticipation of the future by the firm intention of amendement).

2. *History of the concept.* a) In the OT and NT: see *Contrition*.

b) Doctrinal differences as compared with the doctrine of the Reformers: see *Contrition*.

3. *Systematic theology.* a) Systematic theology asks whether penance is a distinct virtue (*virtus specialis*) or merely a collective name (*virtus generalis*) for the other virtues. Every virtue in fact does by its very nature contradict the sin opposed to it. This question has its importance for religious instruction, for if the second view is correct the explicit and special cultivation of a penitential attitude is less evident than if the first is true. It is generally said that penance is a distinct, special virtue (with Aquinas, against William of Auxerre, Gabriel Biel, Cajetan, etc.). In the question as to the particular "formal object" of this special virtue, opinions are again divided, e.g., in Duns Scotus the good is the readiness to accept punishment for sin; in de Lugo, the good is peace with God; in Aquinas, Suarez, etc., the good is the removal of sin which, as an offence against God, is opposed to the holy God and his right to honour from his creatures. In accordance with this last view, penance is usually regarded as a "potential part" of the cardinal virtue of justice. Penance in the narrower sense (formally) can only exist as a virtue in those guilty of personal sin. Consequently it cannot be attributed to Christ (S. C. Inquisitionis, 15 July 1893: *Acta Sanctae Sedis* 16 [1893–4], p. 319) or to Mary, although they are "maximum exemplum paenitentibus" (Aquinas, *Summa Theologica*, III, q. 15, a. 1, ad 5). Furthermore, the questions concerning virtues in general are also raised about penance (infused and acquired virtues, loss, acquisition, growth, relation to the theological virtues and to the virtue of religion, etc.).

b) Sin has an existentiell dimension in depth. It is not merely a temporary misfortune which happens "to" a man who still remains fundamentally good, merely attributed to him juridically. It springs from his "evil heart" and is "radically evil". But then, the "metanoia" of the NT and the "rebirth" must be regarded as a unique intervention of the creative power of God, which affects the whole existence of man. Hence systematic theology must envisage two aspects of penance. It is fundamentally the work of God who alone can give a "new heart". And the individual moment in which penance takes place is integrated into a life which is one whole act in spite of its being spread out in time, while the whole of life is immanent in the single moment of it. These aspects must be worked out in existential ontological terms. (See *History* I.)

Karl Rahner

II. Sacrament of Penance

Penance is the sacrament in which, through the authoritative pronouncement of the priest, the Church removes, in the power of Christ, the sins of the repentant sinner which he committed after baptism.

A. The Church's Teaching

The most important pronouncements of the magisterium on penance are contained in the condemnations of Montanism and Novatianism, in the doctrine of the Fourth Lateran Council, in the medieval doctrinal decisions regarding the existence of the seven sacraments, and above all (after the rejection of the teaching of Huss), in the 6th and 14th sessions of the Council of Trent, when the denial or misinterpretation of this sacrament by the Reformers of the 16th century was rejected and the Church's teaching expounded in detail. This teaching of the Church, defined in essentials, though not in all points, may be briefly summarized as follows.

1. *Existence*. There exists in the Church a sacrament of penance (*sacramentum paenitentiae*, μετάνοια), instituted by Christ, which is one of the seven sacraments (*D* 402, 424, 465, 699, 807, 844, 894, 911, 913, 2046), and is distinct from baptism (*D* 807, 866, 895, 912), though it presupposes and is based on baptism (*D* 696, 894, 895).

2. *Necessity*. The reception of the sacrament of penance and, therefore, as its condition, confession of sins, are necessary for salvation as a means prescribed by God (*D* 574a, 670, 699, 724, 895, 901, 916f.), for all those who after baptism have sinned gravely (i.e., in a way that involves the loss of sanctifying grace). The necessity is like that of baptism: in an emergency, desire for the sacrament (*D* 807) can replace it.

3. *Nature*. The nature of this sacrament is described as "aliud ab ipso baptismo sacramentum ad remissionem peccatorum . . . quo lapsis post baptismum beneficium mortis Christi applicatur" (*D* 894; cf. also the definition in *CIC*, can. 870). The remission is through a judicial pronouncement of the Church (*actus iudicialis, iudicium, sententia*; a precise definition of this authoritative act has not been given). It concerns a person who by baptism has been made subject to the Church's authority and has incurred guilt (*D* 895, 902, 919) towards God (and the Church: *D* 911; Vatican II, *Lumen Gentium*, art. 11). This pronouncement of the Church does not merely declare that forgiveness of guilt and reconciliation with God have taken place, but actually effects this forgiveness (*D* 699, 896, 902, 919, 925, 1058). This reconciliation is also "reconciliatio cum Ecclesia" (*Lumen Gentium*, art. 11), and admission to the "communio sacramentorum" (*D* 57, 95, 146, 247; F. Cavallera, *Thesaurus Doctrinae Catholicae* [2nd ed., 1936], 1250, 1253), especially as those in mortal sin are excluded from the Eucharist, the mystery of the Church and its unity (*D* 880, 893, 1138; *CIC*, can. 856). With the forgiveness of guilt, the sinner is freed from the penalty of eternal damnation (*D* 807, 740, 925) and from the power of the devil (*D* 894), but the consequences of guilt, the temporal punishment due to sin, are not always completely effaced, as in baptism (*D* 535, 807, 840, 895, 904, 922, 925).

4. *Extent of its power*. Against the heresies of Montanism (*D* 43) and Novatianism (*D* 55, 88, 94, 95, 97, 894), the Church teaches that its authority is unlimited (the Christian's conversion in

faith and contrition being presupposed), both as regards the kind of sins to be forgiven and the frequency (possibility of repetition) of this sacrament (in contrast to baptism which cannot be administered more than once) (*D* 430, 540, 839, 895, 903).

5. *The sacramental, efficacious sign* consists above all in the priestly absolution, which must be imparted orally (*D* 695). As a judicial sentence it has an indicative meaning and in fact in the Latin Church a form in the indicative mood is now obligatory. The optatives and other prayers here no longer belong to the necessary sacramental sign. But the earlier (*D* 146) impetratory form of absolution (e.g., penitential rites) in the Eastern Churches is certainly permissible and valid (and presumably would be still valid even in the Latin Church, though not permissible) (*D* 699, 896). In addition to the priest's absolution, the sacramental sign comprises as *quasi-materia*, or as further *partes*, the acts of the penitent, which belong to the *integritas* of the sacrament: contrition, confession, and satisfaction (*D* 699, 745, 896, 914). Accordingly, the following must be affirmed:

a) Interior contrition based on faith is a necessary (formal) condition of the sacrament's validity and efficacy (see *Penance* I: *D* 699, 751, 807, 817, 896ff., 914, 1207, 1210, 1214); contrition must be manifested in some way to the priest by the penitent in the sacrament (*D* 754); imperfect contrition or attrition is a sufficient condition of the efficacy of the sacrament (*D* 898, 1146).

b) Confession of all grave sins which have not yet been directly forgiven in the sacrament is required by the very nature of the sacrament, and is therefore of divine law. This obligation to confess extends to grave sins, as far as the penitent is conscious, after serious examination of conscience, of being guilty (even subjectively) of them, but it extends only to them. And then the obligation extends to all such sins, even secret and interior ones, according to their actual species (with any circumstances that alter their nature), and their number (together with those which were forgotten in a previous confession: *D* 1111) (*D* 699, 748, 899f., 916ff., 1208). This confession is protected by the seal of confession which also follows from the nature of the sacrament (*D* 145, 438, 1220, 1474). If a particular sin is inculpably omitted (merely formal integrity of the confession), it is nevertheless forgiven by the sacrament (*D* 900). Since the Fourth Lateran Council, positive Church law has imposed the strict obligation of making a valid confession each year if one is conscious of serious sin (*D* 437, 901, 918, 1114). Venial sins and sins already sacramentally forgiven can with profit (but do not have to) be confessed as sufficient matter of the sacrament (*D* 470, 748f., 899, 917, 1539; *CIC*, can. 902; confession of devotion). Sacramental confession (by word or signs) can only be made if penitent and priest are physically present (not by letter or messenger, for example) (*D* 147, 1088f.).

c) *Satisfaction.* As an element of the power of the keys, the priest has the right and duty to impose with spiritual prudence on the penitent a penance (satisfaction) which corresponds in some degree to the gravity of the guilt and the spiritual capacity of the penitent (*D* 699, 905f., 923, 925), and which can also be performed after absolution (*D* 728, 1306ff., 1437f., 1534f.). The reason for this imposition of a penance is that forgiveness of sin after baptism does not involve *ipso facto* (as baptism does) the cancelling of all consequences, and penalties of sin (*D* 807, 840, 895, 904, 922). But through the inescapable but patiently accepted penalties of sin and by the discipline of penance voluntarily assumed or imposed in the sacrament (both of which constitute satisfaction: *D* 906, 923), man experiences the seriousness of divine justice and the gravity of sin, is preserved from further sin in the struggle against proneness to evil and shares more deeply in the passion of Christ which overcomes sin. And all this springs from the grace of Christ (*D* 904, 923f.). (In fact all that is to be said of the good works of a justified person as the fruit of grace, applies here.)

6. The minister of the sacrament of penance is a priest who has received the necessary authorization (faculties to hear confessions) to exercise the power of order in this sacrament (*D* 146, 437, 670, 699, 753, 902f., 920, 957, 1113, 1116, 1150, 1537). It follows that the Church for grave reasons can impose restrictions in granting this authorization (except in case of danger of death: *D* 903). For example, certain sins may be reserved to another higher penitential tribunal or to special jurisdiction (*D* 903, 921, 1104, 1112, 1545).

B. The Teaching of Scripture

1. It must not be overlooked in the first place that the reaction of holy Church to the sin of its members is not limited to penance in the narrower sense. The entire existence and activity of the Church is a negation of sin. The Church functions as the judicial and forgiving presence of Christ in the world of sin. It is the minister of the word of reconciliation, exhorting the sinner to allow himself to be reconciled to God (2 Cor 5:18ff.). Baptism is the fundamental sacrament of forgiveness (Acts 2:38; Rom 6; 1 Cor 6:11). The Eucharist is the anamnesis and proclamation of the death of the Lord for the forgiveness of sin (Mt 26:28; 1 Cor 11:26). The Church confesses its guilt (Mt 6:12) and does penance in prayer and fasting, in watching and almsgiving (Mt 6:1–18; 9:15; Mk 9:29). Then, turning to the individual in his concrete situation, it prays for the individual sinner (1 Jn 5:16), gives fraternal correction (Mt 18:15) and may "note the sinner" through one of its officials (2 Thess 3:14). If fraternal exhortation is not enough, the Church may give an official reprimand (1 Tim 5:20). Finally, it may bind and loose the sinner, in an act which is the Church's strongest judicial reaction, but which is still, as far as possible, an act of grace and favour.

2. Since the practice of excommunication existed in the synagogue and in the Qumran *Rule of the Community* (*1 QS*, VI, 24 – VII, 25), it was to be expected that exclusion and readmission would be provided for in Jesus' community. Its actual meaning and true nature can, of course, ultimately only be determined from what Jesus' "Church" knows itself to be from its Lord, through its unity with him and through the fact that this new covenant was founded by him: this must be taken for granted here. As the Church is the presence of Christ and his grace in the one Now of this aeon, it can only expel with the intention of pardoning and saving (1 Cor 5:5; 1 Tim 1:20), and this deeper purpose can only be frustrated by the sinner's obduracy; as the Church is *holy* Church, it must react to the sin of one of its members, for sin is incompatible with its nature. The Church is the effective presence of victorious grace, the eschatological community of those called out of the world to the forgiveness of sins and reconciliation with God. In its totality, therefore, it can never be such only in appearance, only in claim and intention. It is the fundamental sacrament of Christ's grace in the world. Consequently, reception into the Church (baptism) or reconciliation with the Church is a tangible expression of reconciliation with God in which this reconciliation effectively takes place, and is, therefore, a sacrament. The ideas and practices of Jesus' environment suggest *a priori* that he would have given such power to ban and re-admit to the Church (which he founded, as is shown at least by the account of the Last Supper). If so, the

extent to which the "theology of the community" may have operated on Mt 16 and 18 is not of great importance.

3. What can at least be surmised in the light of Jesus' institution can also be deduced from the positive testimony of Scripture.

a) Peter and the apostles, as authorized leaders of the Church of Jesus, received power so to "bind and loose" that their sentence is valid in "heaven". The conception of the verdict of an earthly court having an effect in the other world with God and in God's eyes was current at that time and need therefore cause no surprise (cf. Billerbeck I, 741–4). In this "binding and loosing", the original and universally current sense of the expression must not be lost sight of. Jesus (Lk 11:20 etc.) regarded his authority as a power, victorious over Satan, of "binding" (Mk 3:27), which "looses" (1 Jn 3:8) from Satan's fetters and he gave the disciples a corresponding ἐξουσία (Mt 10:1). Paul interprets excommunication in the same way (1 Cor 5:5; 2 Cor 2:11; 1 Tim 1:20). And Mt 18 clearly shows that there is authority to impose and lift a ban in respect of a brother who by his actions obstinately and in principle contradicts Jesus' holy community or, as the case may be, as a penitent is reconciled once again to it. The authority conferred on the apostles here, which must not be regarded as simply identical with the function of the Rock or the Power of the Keys as conferred on Peter, but as the authority which characterized the apostles generally, is therefore the authority to exclude the guilty person from the community in a way that has real significance even before God himself, removing the guilty person from the saving domain of the Church and banishing him to the devil's domain. Or it is the corresponding authority, valid before God, to receive him once more into the Church, withdrawing him from the devil's power to destroy. In fact, therefore, the saving authority to loose has the effect of forgiving the sin on account of which the exclusion was imposed. Anyone who is reconciled to the Church on earth, so that he stands within God's saving domain and is so free from the power of the devil (who himself is now "bound") that the kingdom of God is really open to him through his peace with Jesus' Church, has thereby attained forgiveness of guilt in God's name. Such authority to impose and lift excommunication from the community with effect in the next world before God is a power which by the nature of the case can only belong to the authorized leaders of the Church. (No doubt their action is the action of the Church [Mt 18:17], but the Church acts only with and through its leaders [1 Cor 5:3f.]) Consequently it is a power of jurisdiction, judicial in nature. If the efficacious and productive, i.e., sacramental word, which makes the individual experience what it promises to him, is not to be eliminated from the theology of the NT, then the efficacy of penance for salvation presents no greater difficulties than the word of baptism or the word of celebration of the Lord's Supper. If there are sacraments at all, then the word of reconciliation, authority for which is bestowed here, is one of them.

b) What is expressed in Mt in rather archaic terms recurs in another and more popular from in Jn 20:19–23, which is quite in harmony with Jesus' language, and not even particularly "Johannine". In continuance of Jesus' mission, the apostles (it is they who are addressed, not everyone) are endowed with authority to forgive individuals their respective sins (τινων τὰς ἁμαρτίας), just as the Son of man has power on earth truly to forgive sins, although only God can do this (Mk 2:1–12 par.). Or they can retain them, that is to say, "note them" and ban the sinner because of them. Both acts involve as a *conse-*

quence that what the apostles declare is truly so before God; they do not merely register existing facts. A double power of this kind in regard to the individual, which includes a decision between two possibilities with effects in the next world, can neither be the mission to the universal preaching of the gospel of reconciliation (as the Council of Trent understood the doctrine of the Reformers: *D* 894, 902, 913, 919), nor the power to baptize. He who is outside is not judged, i.e., excluded by excommunication (1 Cor 5:9–13), and so nothing can be "retained" in regard to him. It is, therefore, a question here quite simply of what the text says: power by a judicial decision either to forgive the sins of a member of the Church, so that they are also forgiven before God, or to allow sins to take effect as a reason for the ban. More recent theology (in contrast to antiquity and the Middle Ages but in agreement with the Council of Trent; *D* 894, 913) sees in these words a form of institution of the sacrament of penance which is clearer *quoad nos* ("praecipue"). This is not to deny that the same fact can also be recognized from Mt, and consequently as a common element of apostolic tradition. The question of the precise literary character of the Johannine discourses of Jesus therefore does not need to be raised at all here. Nor is it denied that the way in which, in the sense of Jn 20, sins are forgiven and retained, that is, through imposition and lifting of a ban, can be more clearly gathered from Mt. Since in Mt 18 and 1 Cor 5 the exercise of authority supposes that a "brother" is concerned, the explanation that has been given does not mean that the mortal sin, or the expulsion which is here in question (and which is not to be identified with excommunication as present-day canon law understands it), necessarily eliminates membership of the Church. The magisterium declares, against Huss, etc. (*D* 627, 629, 838, etc.), that this membership persists, even for the sinner. Since the Church is not simply an external religious organization, but the body of Christ vivified by the Spirit (*D* 2288, etc.), the loss of grace inevitably means a change in the (enduring) relation of the sinner to the Church, which is "noted" by the ban as exclusion from the Eucharist in every case of mortal sin.

4. The correctness of this interpretation is confirmed by apostolic practice.

C. The Teaching of the Fathers

1. *The 2nd century* developed the practice of the apostolic period. With Hermas we have a first theological reflection on this practice, in obscure and figurative terms. As long as the Church of this aeon is still growing, the baptized person who by sin has moved away from the Church can be reincorporated into it and so find salvation (*Similitudines*, VIII, 11, 3; IX, 21, 3f.; *Mandata*, IV, 1; *Visiones*, III, 7, 6; *Similitudines*, IX, 14, 2, etc.). Because of the close proximity of the end, Hermas proclaims that penance is still possible one more time, but he does not open this door for the first time, as if previously it had not been there. The impossibility of penance more than once, as taught here (*Mandata*, IV, 1, 8; 3, 6), was later separated from its original foundation and became a principle of penitential discipline but not, properly speaking, a dogmatic principle, for the whole patristic period in the West, from Tertullian (*De Paenitentia*, 7, 11) to can. 11 of the Third Synod of Toledo, A.D. 589, but in the East only in Alexandria, in Clement (*Stromata*, II, 13, 57, 1), and Origen (*In Leviticum Homilia*, 15, 2). The practice of only one penance was defended as a barrier against ecclesiastical laxity, but the possibility of salvation for a sinner who fell again was not thereby denied. Nothing in Hermas (*Similitudines*, VIII, 11; *Mandata*, IV, 1, 8; 3, 1–7, etc.) or elsewhere (Ignatius of Antioch,

Dionysius of Corinth, Polycarp, Justin, Irenaeus, Clement of Alexandria, etc.) indicates that even schismatics, apostates and fornicators, if truly repentant, could not be reconciled with the Church. It cannot be shown that there were any capital sins unforgivable in principle. It is perfectly arbitrary to try to introduce into the practice and theory of the 2nd century a distinction between a forgiveness granted by God but refused by the Church for its forum. Where the Church knows that God forgives, it knows in principle that it is entitled to give full ecclesiastical pardon. And the view that God always forgives the truly repentant is everywhere clear and unmistakable. That does not exclude the fact that the various local Churches used their own discretion to a very large extent in the matter of granting or refusing reconciliation. Proof of repentance was not very readily accepted, and the ecclesiastical discipline of that age made readmission to the congregation, even of the penitent, seem undesirable. It must, therefore, be admitted that individual Churches (in Africa: Cyprian, *Ep.*, 55, 21; in Spain: Synod of Elvira, and as late as A.D. 380, of Saragossa; cf. also *D* 95) even down to the 4th century refused reconciliation to certain sinners, even when this was not called for by their subjective impenitence. But this only became a dogmatic question when the right of the Church to reconcile grievous sinners was contested in principle. Yet in general the refusal of a (first and only) reconciliation even on the death-bed was regarded, with the Council of Nicaea (*D* 57; cf. also *D* 95, 111), as Novatian cruelty, and rejected. The case of Cerdon (Irenaeus, *Adv. haer.*, III, 4, 3) does not prove the possibility of repeated reconciliation in the West.

2. a) *The 3rd century* produced two at first purely Western heresies in regard to penance, the Montanism of Tertullian and Novatianism. They were not a defence of an ancient rigorism against the gradual abolition of the principle of unforgivable capital sins (unchastity, murder, apostasy), but a new theory (admitted by Tertullian to be such), which intensified the old possibility of rigorism in discipline and practice into an absolute dogmatic obligation of the necessary and permanent expulsion of capital sinners. The Catholics appealed to the baptismal parallel (Tertullian, *De Paenitentia*, 12, 9), to ancient practice and to the authority of Christ from Mt 18 (not yet to Jn 20) (Tertullian, *De Pudicitia*, 21, 9), and fixed their ancient practice by explicit dogmatic pronouncements, such as a decree of a Metropolitan of Carthage (*D* 43) and the synodal decrees of Carthage and Rome in the middle of the 3rd century. The protracted and circumstantial synodal legislation in Cyprian's Africa was concerned (apart from the rejection of Novatian), not with the question of the possibility in principle of reconciliation for apostates (which was taken for granted), but with the practical administration of penance in distinguishing the various cases, duration of penance, speedier reconciliation in danger of death, before martyrdom, etc. In the conflict of Hippolytus with Pope Callistus I, the issue apparently was merely that the Pope was receiving schismatic Christians into the Church without their performing further penance, without reference to whether they had committed other sins while in schism (Hippolytus, *Philosophoumena*, IX, 12). The liturgy of Hippolytus recognizes that the bishop, by the authority of Christ given to his apostles, can loose every bond of evil (G. Dix, *The Treatise on the Apostolic Tradition of St. Hippolytus of Rome* [1937], p. 5).

b) *The sacramental form of penance in the 3rd century* was still determined by the notion of excommunication. The sinner was identified by the Church as being what his sin made him, that is, a person who had placed himself in opposition to the Church and was consequently excluded, at least from the Eucharist. If he confessed his sins privately before the bishop (possibly after asking someone else whether his sins were actually mortal and hence demanded canonical penance: Origen, *In Ps. 37, hom.*, 2, 6), and if he was really repentant, he was admitted to canonical penance. This was itself an act of grace on the part of the Church, but did not yet signify reconciliation with the Church. The penitent was marked out as such by his clothes, by his special place at divine worship, and by the penances imposed on him, such as fasting. After a certain time he was reconciled by imposition of hands by the bishop (and the clergy), accompanied by prayer. In the East anointing was sometimes added and in some places in the East this later led to the idea of a repetition of confirmation. The duration of the penances varied, from those which only ended on the death-bed (e.g., Synods of Elvira, 306, Ancyra, 314, cf. Toledo, 400; Pope Siricius, *Ep.*, 1, 3 and 6, etc.), down to some of only a few weeks, which, however, were presumably preceded by a period of amendment (*Didascalia Apostolorum*, II, 16, 2). The reason given for the necessity of this long personal penance is not very clear. It is that baptism alone, administered only once, is an absolute decree of pardon (ἄφεσις). Hence in this sense later sins "cannot be *forgiven* in the Church" (Hermas, *Mand.*, IV, 3, 3f.; Tertullian, *De Paenitentia*, 7, 10; Origen, *In Ex. hom.*, 6, 9, etc.), but must be atoned for through personal penance (μετάνοια) before God. (That is also the sense of Origen, *De Oratione*, 28.) There was, however, sufficient awareness of the sacramental nature of ecclesiastical penance. The necessity of public canonical penance was stressed (Tertullian, *De Paenitentia*, 10–12), reconciliation with the official Church was considered necessary for salvation, even for a sinner suffering martyrdom (Cyprian, *Epp.*, 65, 5; 55, 17; 72, 2; Origen, *In Jos.*, 3, 5; *In Ps.*, 36, 2, 4, etc.), and the re-endowment with the Holy Spirit was attributed to the rite of reconciliation, not to personal penance (Cyprian, *Epp.*, 57, 4; cf. also *Epp.*, 15, 1; 16, 2; 17, 2;Origen, *In Lev. hom.*, 8, 11; *Didascalia Apostolorum*, II, 41, 2). Admission to this reconciliation with the Church which makes peace with God took place through the bishop (cf., for example, Cyprian, *Epp.*, 17, 2; 43, 3). The intercession of confessors of the faith supported the sinner's personal penance and was of importance for the question of how soon reconciliation could ensue. But it was subject to the bishop's final decision, for at that time the Churches already had a quite definitely episcopal structure. There is no indication of "private" sacramental penance. Only the degree to which penance was public varied according to circumstances. The efficacy of official ecclesiastical reconciliation with God was explained (without precise definition) by reference to the infallibly efficacious prayer of the Church (Tertullian, *De Paenitentia*, 10, 6), or to the Church's authority from Christ (Tertullian, *De Pudicitia*, 21, etc.) to forgive sins or to confer the Spirit. Delinquent clerics were still treated like other sinners. As regards the range of sins subject to canonical penance, it was recognized in theory that these were all sins which destroy baptismal grace (cf., for example, Tertullian, *De Paenitentia*, 8; *De Pudicitia*, 9), but in practice the tendency was to consider only capital sins since penance was severe and could not be repeated. It is true that a wide view was taken of these, and it was not only complete apostasy, murder and formal adultery which were accounted such, for Cyprian (*Epp.*, 16, 2; 17, 2; 4, 4) and Origen (*In Lev. hom.*, 14, 2), for example, include other, even secret sins.

3. *The patristic age.* a) What is new

in this period is the intense legislative activity of synods, individual bishops in the East (*epistolae canonicae*) and Popes, in questions of penitential discipline, particularly in regulating the duration of penances and other casuistical questions (*DTC*, XII, cols. 789ff.). Then a scale of penance was established in the East, i.e., degrees of exclusion from, or readmission to, divine worship and to the Eucharist (only with the latter can there in fact be total readmission to the Church, so that all the stages are varying forms of excommunication). Finally, canonical penance in the West took on lasting consequences even after reconciliation, e.g., prohibition of marital relations, ban on morally dangerous professions, impediment to becoming a cleric (cf. Poschmann). As a consequence, the duration of the actual penance was of less importance. In the West it seems to have shrunk to Lent (except in cases of quite exceptional transgressions) when the Church's penitential rites were stated at the beginning of Lent (Innocent I, *Ep.*, 1, 7; Leo I, *Sermo*, 45; 49, 3). The conversion of the sinner had probably already taken place.

b) The external form of penitential discipline was, as before, excommunication. It is not possible to regard as a truly private sacramental form the *correptio secreta* referred to by Augustine (*Ep.*, 82, 8, 11). This dispensed with the public liturgical reprimand, but it is uncertain whether the canonical penance was dispensed with altogether, because impossible to carry out, or whether the normal *paenitentia publica* was performed, but without the reprimand. Nor is such a private form to be found in other practices which were either adaptations of the *paenitentia publica* to particular circumstances (immediate reconciliation, because there was no real guilt, in the case of material heretics, etc.; penance in sickness), or which cannot be shown to have been sacramental, such as spiritual direction in monasteries, or the charismatic promises of forgiveness by "spiritual men". The range of sins dealt with by excommunication and penance was the same as before. The Eastern penitential legislation in particular shows that the term capital sins must not be taken too narrowly; it included everything that even today can be presumed in the average man to be grave sins, even subjectively. The canon of sins indicated the wide range of the possibility and obligation of canonical penance.

c) The confining of penance to one occasion only was maintained in principle in the West (Jerome, *Ep.*, 80, 9; Ambrose, *De Paenitentia*, 2; Augustine, *Ep.*, 153, 3, 7; Siricius, *Ep.*, 1, 5). Here and there casuistical skill introduced an alleviation of the principle in marginal cases, but that was all. (Perhaps even the *viaticum* was given at death, but then without "reconciliatio absolutissima" [cf., for example Siricius, *Ep.*, 1, 5, 6; Innocent I, *Ep.*, 6, 2; Leo I, *Epp.*, 108, 4; 167, 13 .) The practical consequence was that Church penance was postponed until the death-bed or old age. Express approval was given to this practice (Caesarius of Arles, *Sermo*, 258, 2; Avitus, *Ep.*, 18, etc.) and synods (e.g., Council of Agde, A.D. 506, can. 15; Third Council of Orleans, A.D. 538, can. 24) warned against granting ecclesiastical penance before a ripe age; since it was only possible to receive it once, insoluble conflicts inevitably arose.

d) Special forms of penitential discipline developed. For clerics there was deposition from office (without other acts of penance) and admission to lay communion (e.g., Siricius, *Ep.*, 1, 14, 18; Basil, *Ep.*, 188, *c.* 3; Leo I, *Ep.*, 167, inquisitio 2). There were various kinds of reconciliation of heretics, in which those who were born in heresy (but only they) were reconciled by imposition of hands without further acts of penance (Council of Arles, A.D.

314, *c.* 8; *D* 55; Siricius, *Ep.*, 5, 8; Augustine, *Ep.*, 185, 10; Leo I, *Ep.*, 167, inquisitio 19).

e) The sacramental nature of the penitential discipline is clearly testified, though generally the term sacrament was not used. The Church can reconcile all repentant sinners. Novatianism was definitely considered a heresy after Nicaea (*D* 55; cf. also *D* 88, 99) and was explicitly opposed by the Fathers. The authority to forgive sins, bestowed on the Church by Christ, was emphasized and confirmed by the parallel with baptism (e.g., Ambrose, *De Paenitentia*, I, 8, 36; Pacian, *Ep.*, 3, 7; Jerome, *In Or.*, III, 12). Penance and reconciliation efface sin (and Augustine, *Serm.*, 96, 6; *In Joann. tract.*, 49, 24, expressly attributes remission of the stain of guilt to the Church's action). The (visible or secret) disturbance of the relation to the Church by sin forfeits salvation and hence reconciliation with the Church is sought, especially before death (Celestine I, *Ep.*, 4, 2; Innocent I, *Ep.*, 3, 2; Augustine, *Ep.*, 228, 2, etc.). The Church's efficacy was sometimes explained simply by reference to Christ's command, but otherwise the interpretation given to the *pax cum Ecclesia* (as is particularly clear in Augustine) made it a medium of reconciliation with God. For the intention of reconciliation always included peace with the Church, and the "impetratory formula of absolution" is to be regarded as support given by the prayer of the Church to personal penance (cf., for example, *D* 146). The bishop's action reincorporates the sinner fully into the Church, in which, even if the bearer of office as such is without the Spirit and so cannot give the Spirit, the sinner receives the Holy Spirit because the Church is the Church of the *sancti spirituales* (Augustine, *Serm.*, 99, 9; *In Joann. tract.*, 124, 7; *De Civitate Dei*, XX, 9, 2; *Serm.*, 71, 23, 37). Here and there (Jerome, *In Mt.*, III, 16, 19, *Consultationes Zachaei et Apollonii*, n. 18, and, later, Gregory the Great, *In ev. hom.*, II, 26, 6) a conception of the Church's action which seems purely declaratory may be met with, unless such texts simply stress subjective penance as a necessary condition for effective reconciliation.

f) In the East, the intensive legislation and theological discussion down to the end of the Empire show that public penance persisted in theory and to some extent even in practice (Holl), even after Nectarius (Socrates, *Hist. Eccles.*, V, 19; Sozomen, *Hist. Eccles.*, VII, 16) had abolished the special priest-penitentiary for Constantinople (A.D. 391) and so left it to the individual's conscience to decide whether he had to submit to the bishop's official penitential discipline or not. But the tendencies towards mitigating the duration of penance and its public character gradually prevailed. Among the Syrian Monophysites, public penance seems to have fallen out of use about the 8th century, and was slowly replaced by private confession to a priest, optional at first, but late obligatory (De Vries). The old teaching that the physician of the soul must be holy, the practice of spiritual direction by the abbot in monasteries and by monks generally, the need to be assured, through charismatically enlightened encouragement, that sins had in fact been forgiven, and to have the proper penance imposed, led in the East (apart, presumably, from cases in which even the laxest practice required official public penance) to the practice of confession to a monk (Holl; Hörmann). This is the less surprising, because in Palestine, for example, in the 6th century, the abbot of a monastery exercised penitential discipline even in regard to capital sins (Holl). Sometimes little attention was paid to whether the monk-confessor was a priest or layman (as early as the 5th and 6th centuries), but this drew a protest from Psuedo-Dionysius (*Ep.*, 8). After the Iconoclast controversy

(8th century) only the priest-monks had in practice the right to hear confessions. With Simeon the New Theologian (d. 1022) (*Ep. de confessione*: text in Holl). and John of Antioch (*PG*, CXXXII, col. 1128), it is then taught that the power of forgiving sins has passed from bishops and priests to the monks (Balsamon, *PG*, CXXXVIII, cols. 42, 972f., Nicephoros Chartophylax, *PG*, C, cols. 1061–4). Simeon of Thessalonica (*PG*, CLV, col. 861) and others, however, opposed this abuse, which seems to have persisted until about the 14th century. It is said never to have existed in the Russian Church (*DTC*, XII, col. 1134). In medieval negotiations for reunion between East and West there was agreement on both sides about the sacramentality of penance (*D* 465; M. Jugie, *Theologia Dogmatica Christianorum Orientalium ab Ecclesia Catholica Dissidentium*, III, pp. 15–25, 333). Cyril Lucar (d. 1638) was the first to contest it; but it continued to be recognized in confessional writings. The only differences of opinion between East and West concern the nature of the penance imposed (Jugie, *op. cit.*, III, pp. 342–62).

4. *End of the patristic period and transition to a new system of repeatable aural confession.* a) At the end of the patristic period we at first see the persistence in theory of the old "public" excommunication-penance which could only be received once. It is still defended, for example, by the Synod of Toledo, A.D. 589 (can. 11). But generally it was insisted on by the Church, as long as the sinner was in health, only if there were public scandals; otherwise it was received in the form of penance of the sick, on the death-bed. From the 6th century onwards this was in fact gradually received by all Christians (including saints, Isidore of Seville, for example, the first saint of whom we have evidence to this effect: *PL*, LXXXI, cols. 30–33). It even appears as a legal obligation (Synod of Barcelona, A.D. 541, can. 9; Isidore of Seville, *De Ecclesiae Officiis*, II, 17, 6), so that this kind of death-bed penance lost its defamatory character, though in itself it was simply a variety of public penance. Where the ancient penitential discipline was still practised, the form, duration and penances imposed were the same as before. At most, in Gaul and Spain, from the middle of the 5th century, exceptional cases had to be expiated in a special group of penitents similar to the penitential grades in the East (Felix III, *Ep.*, 13; Grotz). At this time (6th century) the excommunication seems in certain cases to have been separated from the general rite, as a purely ecclesiastical penalty, and to have been imposed and lifted independently, without imposition of the actual canonical penance. This in fact had still to be performed on the death-bed although the excommunication had already been lifted (cf., for example, Avitus of Vienne, *Epp.*, 15 and 16). Lasting consequences of being admitted to penance remained and are attested by Spanish councils as late as the 7th century. Only when canonical penance had been undertaken without necessity (in danger of death), could such a "penitent" still become a cleric (e.g., Synod of Gerunda, A.D. 517, can. 9; Fourth Synod of Toledo, A.D. 633, can. 54).

b) A new and special form of penance was that of the *conversi*, monastic penance: entry to the ecclesiastical order of monks and ascetics, which also was lifelong in duration and under the Church's supervision. This form is readily intelligible, for the penitent in practice had lasting obligations in any case which made his life resemble that of a *conversus*. The *benedictio paenitentiae* (the liturgical consecration of a *conversus*) was regarded as equivalent to the rite of reconciliation, but presented the possibility of avoiding the disgrace of public penance, for the status of the *conversi* was in itself very honourable (Gennadius *Liber Dogmatum*, 43; Faustus of Riez, *Serm.*, 3; *PL*, LVIII, cols 875, etc.). Whether such a form of penance is to be termed sacramental is hard to say; whether it is called "public" or "private" is again only a question of terminology. It is the origin of the Merovingian practice of banishing a sinner to detention in a monastery.

c) *The emergence of new forms of penance*. It has to be accepted as a fact, the causes of which have not yet been properly explained (intolerability of the permanent disadvantages, influence of confession to monks, etc.), that among the Irish and Anglo-Saxons of the British Isles from about the 6th century onwards, canonical penance was not practised as something that could be undergone only once in life (*Paenitentiale Theodori*, I, 13). This was a deliberate departure from continental practice. In this situation it was not possible to impose a penance with life-long consequences (the order of cause and effect may have been the other way round). At the same time it seemed the obvious course to submit lesser sins also to canonical penance, and in that way it was possible to use the Church's penitential process actually during life, and not merely at death. The sacrament could be brought back into ordinary life without much change in the old practice (heavy penances, long period of atonement, lapse of time between confession and absolution, impetratory formula of absolution) or in theory (reconciliation with the Church and with God). The continuity with the old form of canonical penance was therefore perfectly clear, particularly as the ancient legislation of the Church regarding duration of penance etc. was applied to the new form. But there was, of course, one new element present from the start: the repeated absolution was given in a simpler form by the priest, no longer solemnly by the bishop, and on any day, not only on Holy Thursday. In this sense it was no longer "public". The frequency of confession and the variety of sins confessed called for a more discriminating allocation of the satisfaction (as regards gravity and duration). The old periods and kinds of penance had to be adapted by commutations and redemptions and so the new literature of penitential books came into existence. With the missions of the Irish monks the new system of penance came to the continent in the 7th century. The first testimony to it is perhaps the Synod of Châlons between A.D. 639 and 654, can. 8 (but see C. Vogel), and in any case it is exemplified in the *Paenitentiale* of Columbanus. As the old form was used almost only for the dying, the new met with almost no resistance. The penitential books show that in the 8th century the new practice had already spread everywhere on the continent.

D. The Theology of Penance since the 12th Century

Only a few fundamental themes and lines of development can, of course, be indicated.

1. *The question of the efficacy of the sacrament*. From the time that the doctrine of the seven sacraments was proposed, in the process of defining the notion of sacrament as there supposed, i.e., from the middle of the 12th century, penance has been one of them. Alger of Liège (*PL*, CXXX, col. 886; B. Geyer in *Theologie und Glaube* 10 [1918], p. 329) already counts penance as belonging to the sacraments as he understands the term; Robert Pullen expressly proves that penance is a sacrament (*Sententiae*: *PL*, CXXXVI, col. 910). When the present-day concept of a sacrament is used, as in the *Sententiae Divinitatis*, in Simon Magister and the Glossators of Gratian's *Decretum*, it is explicitly taught that penance is a sacrament (Geyer, *loc. cit.*, pp. 341ff.). In local synods of the first decades of

the 13th century, the doctrine is already taken for granted (Mansi, XXII, cols. 1110, 1173ff.; XXIII, cols. 396f., 448). On the basis of the ancient tradition there was never any doubt in practice that this sacrament was necessary and obligatory for the mortal sinner, though the theoretical explanations given for its necessity varied. Testimonies to this (Anciaux, *Théologie*, pp. 31–36, 164–274, 392–490) are found, for example, in Bede (*PL*, IX, cols. 39f.), Alcuin (*PL*, C, cols. 300–37), Jonas of Orleans (*PL*, CVI, cols. 151ff.), Rabanus Maurus (*PL*, CVII, cols. 331f.), Godfrey of Vendôme (*PL*, CLVII, col. 199), Theodulph of Orleans (*PL*, CV, cols. 203, 206f.), Peter Lombard (*IV Sent.*, d. 17, 1–3), Hugh of St. Victor (*PL*, CLXXVI, cols. 549–55), Anselm of Laon (F. P. Bliemetzrieder, *Anselms von Laon systematische Sentenzen* [1919], p. 124), Abelard (*PL*, CLXXVIII, col. 668), Roland Bandinelli (A. Gietl, *Die Sentenzen Rolands* [1891], pp. 243ff.), Robert Pullen (*PL*, CLXXXVI, col. 896) and others. There are, it is true, a few sentences of the Synod of Châlons-sur-Saône (can. 88, Mansi, XIV, col. 99), which then continued to be quoted by canonists such as Burchard of Worms (*PL*, CXL, col. 1011), and Gratian (*De Paenitentia*, I, can. 90), regarding the questionable necessity of private confession as long as the older form of penance still existed, or concerning the view that forgiveness already takes place through sorrow for sin before the (nevertheless indispensable) sacrament is received. The question of some canonists of the 12th century was at the most whether the *paenitentia solemnis* alone was an authentic sacrament. The undisputed acceptance of the sacramentality of penance did not, however, prevent scholastic theology down to the middle of the 13th century (*not* down to Aquinas) from contesting that priestly absolution effectively influences the forgiveness of guilt as such (the *reatus culpae*). All theologians of the 12th century were in the first place convinced that true contrition achieves forgiveness of sins before confession (though in conjunction with the *votum sacramenti*). This contrition was not further analysed. And emphasis was laid on it, especially after Abelard, as the act which effaces sin, in contrast to the penitential works of the patristic age, once absolution was moved forward. Thus Anselm (*PL*, CLVIII, col. 662), Bruno of Segni (*PL*, CXV, col. 137), Abelard (*PL*, CLXXVIII, cols. 664f.), Roland Bandinelli (Gietl, p. 248) and the whole circle of the Victorines (e.g., *PL*, CLXXVI, col. 565).

In the great age of Scholasticism, therefore, down to and including St. Thomas, it was considered normal and even a matter of duty for the penitent to be justified before the actual reception of the sacrament. That is the basis of the various inadequate theories as to the effect of priestly absolution. One "declaratory" theory is found as early as Anselm (*PL*, CLVIII, col. 662), then in Abelard (*loc. cit.*) and his school and down through Peter Lombard (*IV Sent.*, d. 17, c. 1) to the 13th century with William of Auxerre (V. Heynck, *Franziskanische Studien* 36 [1954], pp. 47–57f.), Alexander of Hales (P. Schmoll, *Die Busslehre der Frühscholastik* [1909], pp. 146–50), and Albert the Great (*ibid.*, pp. 133f.). The theory was that the priestly absolution is the authoritative declaration of the forgiveness already conferred by God alone. Some theologians added that it could fix the right satisfaction, remit temporal punishment due to sin, admit to the sacraments, exercise psychological effects on contrition, etc. The other theory, that of the Victorines, postulated an effect of absolution in the next world; the Church does not forgive the guilt, but remits the debt of eternal punishment (Hugh of St. Victor: *PL*, CLXXVI, col. 564) or changes the conditional forgiveness of sin by

God into an absolute one (Richard of St. Victor: *PL*, CXCVI, col. 1165; Praepositinus, cf. Schmoll, pp. 83–88, etc.). It was only with William of Auvergne, Hugh of St.-Cher, William of Melitona, Bonaventure and Thomas that forgiveness of guilt was considered to be an effect of the sacrament as such (see V. Heynck, *Franziskanische Studien* 36 [1954], pp. 1–81, for references, covering also what follows). This has since been the general opinion. Theologians first appealed to the influence of absolution on contrition, which had long been taken into consideration, but was now thought of no longer as merely psychological, but as having a grace-giving, sacramental efficacy. Absolution could then be conceived to be effective for forgiveness without eliminating or by-passing contrition. The question was further complicated by the different theories in general sacramental doctrine regarding the causality of the sacraments in relation to grace (physical disposition theory, intentional disposition theory, efficient causality theory). And so down to and including St. Thomas, the personal and the sacramental event still remained interwoven (grace *for* contrition). It was only with Scotus that absolution, with sufficient sorrow (attrition) merely as a morally necessary condition, effects the "infusion" of justifying grace, which is no longer communicated and accepted through the medium of an act (of actual contrition) that corresponds to its nature. In this way the theological progress attained in the 13th century became clear and was permanently consolidated, but probably at the cost of an understanding of the significance of the person in the theology of grace and the sacraments which at the present time needs to be recovered with the help of Aquinas.

2. *The doctrine of Aquinas.* For Aquinas, as for one line of tradition before him, the sacramental sign consists of the acts of the penitent as matter and the absolution as form; but it is only in the *Summa Theologica* (III, q. 84, a. 1–3; q. 86, a. 6) that he concedes to the matter in this complex any causality in relation to grace. The *paenitentia interior* is the *res et sacramentum*. This had also been the view of Guido of Orchelles, William of Auxerre, Alexander of Hales, William of Melitona, Bonaventure and Albert the Great. The penitent must in the normal course approach the sacrament with such sorrow that he is already justified. In that sorrow the power of the keys makes its influence felt in advance (Albert the Great too held this view as against Alexander of Hales and Bonaventure). If, however, a penitent in good faith does not yet have such contrition, but has a serious aversion from sin, which places no impediment, his sorrow is seized upon by the justifying grace conferred by the sacrament and transformed into contrition (based on the motive of love): *ex attrito fit contritus* (an almost universal doctrine at that time, e.g., *IV Sent.*, d. 22, q. 2, a. I, sol. 3). Since the *paenitentia interior*, as contrition which justifies, must be inspired by justifying grace, and indeed consists in the actual acceptance of the infused grace, which is communicated by the medium of this act, this (instrumental) causality of the sacramental sign, if properly thought out, cannot relate to an *ornatus animae*. (In his earlier doctrine of the sacraments in general, Thomas had held that this *ornatus* was the *res et sacramentum*, as the direct [dispositive] effect.) The causality can only relate to justifying grace itself (but as the grace which is actualized in contrition). Consequently place is left for the *res et sacramentum*, despite the literal tenor of Thomas's text. This must either not exist (as really distinguishable), or it must be something other than the *paenitentia interior*. This is also more in accord with the fact that, in the *Summa*, Thomas seems to have abandoned the dispositive theory

of sacramental causality in favour of a theory of instrumental efficient cause.

On St. Thomas's doctrine on penance, see: R. M. Schultes, *Reue und Busse: Die Lehre des heiligen Thomas von Aquin über das Verhältnis von Reue und Busse* (1906); P. de Vooght in *ETL* 5 (1928), pp. 225–56; 7 (1930), pp. 663–75; 25 (1949), pp. 77–82; R. Marine, "La reviviscenza dei meriti secondo la dottrina del dottore Angelico", *Gregorianum* 13 (1932), pp. 76–108; H. Bouillard, *Conversion et grâce* (1944); G. N. Rus, *De munere sacramenti paenitentiae in aedificando corpore Christi ad mentem S. Thomae* (1944); M. Flick, *L'attimo della giustificazione secondo S. Tomaso* (1947); C. R. Meyer, *The Thomistic Concept of Justifying Contrition* (1949); P. Letter in *Bijdragen* 13 (1953), pp. 401–9.

3. *Confession.* In the patristic period the necessity of confession as an indispensable condition of the Church's penitential process was explicit after Tertullian, and repeatedly inculcated. Yet a certain change in attitude is unmistakable. In the age of the Fathers, confession was regarded as a matter of course as a condition for undertaking canonical penance. It was this latter to which attention and exhortation was directed, and which constituted the "exhomologesis". But when the sacrament of penance was received more frequently, which involved the confession of smaller and more secret sins, the confession itself was felt to be of greater weight and more arduous, and so became almost the actual penitential work itself (even to the point that repeated confession could be made the satisfaction prescribed in the sacrament): the shame of the avowal becomes the expiation of what is confessed. So while in the time of the Fathers satisfaction was the fundamental theme of penance, from the 8th century onward it was confession (and the priest was the father-confessor), and this remained so in practice and was emphasized anew in the Reformation period. The sacrament of penance becomes "confession" (*Confessio Sacramentalis* as the title of one of his writings is found in Peter of Blois: *PL*, CCVII, cols. 1077–92). The basis suggested for the obligation of confession was for a long time very uncertain (e.g., from the OT or from the Letter of James, ch. 5) and at all events it was far from always being the *ex institutione sacramenti* of the Council of Trent. In some canonists, as in the *Glossa Ordinaria* on Gratian and in Nicholas de Tudeschis, the only basis of the duty of confession is the Church's precept (Anciaux, *Théologie, passim*). From the 12th century onward, contrition and its interconnection with absolution were the fundamental themes of learned theology.

4. *Contrition and the sacrament of penance.* See the articles *Contrition, Penance* I.

5. It is also relevant to note briefly that all the early and classical Scholastics hand on the patristic doctrine that one of the effects of the sacrament is reconciliation with the Church. This is universally the case in the 11th and 12th centuries (Anciaux, *Théologie, passim*; cf. also M. Landgraf in *Scholastik* 5 [1930], pp. 210–47). But it is still the case with Bonaventure (for whom the indicative part of the formula of absolution has precisely this significance), in Hugo Ripelin's *Compendium Theologicae Veritatis* and in Thomas Aquinas (*IV Sent.*, d. 16, q. 1, a. 2; q. 5 dubium), whereas after Aquinas the idea was neglected, though not opposed. The affirmation (against Wycliffe and Huss) that the sinner still belongs to the Church seems to have made that view hard to conceive for a mode of thought tending to rigid categories. Yet Luther himself (*Weimarer Ausgabe*, I, p. 539) was still aware of the ecclesiological aspect of sin and its forgiveness, and its connection with the theology of these realities. This idea is once again to the

fore at the present time (B. Xiberta, B. Poschmann, M. de la Taille, H. de Lubac, M. Schmaus, etc.) and was sanctioned by Vatican II.

E. Systematic Theology

1. The treatise on penance in its customary form has one intrinsic advantage over the other treatises on the sacraments: it nearly always includes some consideration of the subjective side of the sacrament, the virtue of penance. This procedure could serve as model for other sacraments, and would probably also lead to abandoning the custom of dealing with the various sacraments one after the other simply on the same pattern. In a treatise on sin and forgiveness in the life of the baptized, various subjects should, or at least could, be dealt with which are passed over in the usual treatises on penance: temptation, the experience of forgiveness (cf. *D* 896), penance of everyday life, and much that belongs to the Church's fight against sin (see above, B, 1).

2. For a comprehensive approach and a better understanding of the history, it would be no harm if the treatise on penance made it clear once more that even nowadays, as from the very beginning, the power of "binding" is still exercised in regard to the sinner. He is excluded from the Eucharist and is obliged to confess his sin. This deprives him of the illusory appearance of being a "living" member and so places a certain distance between him and the Church. The essential element of excommunication-penance is, therefore, retained, though this ban has to be distinguished from the present-day censure of excommunication, the supplementary penalties of which concern only certain sins and are not a necessary consequence of the nature of sin itself. It would be objectively correct and in keeping with the character conferred on the soul in baptism, if the *pax cum Ecclesia* were regarded as the *res et sacramentum* and if with Augustine we were to continue to say: *pax Ecclesiae dimittit peccata* (*De baptismo contra Donatistas*, III, 18, 23) or were once more to speak with Cyprian of *accepta pace recipere Spiritum Patris* (*Ep.*, 57, 4). The objection that all this does not apply to the forgiveness of venial sins, which, nevertheless, may be sacramentally forgiven, is not decisive; for every theological interpretation of penance must solve the problem of how it is possible to speak of the judicial power of the Church in this case, where the Church cannot after all bind, and in fact cannot even absolve except what is already forgiven. The difficulty is not insoluble if it is realized that even venial sin (though in only a remotely comparable way) involves injury to the Church, because it lessens the *fervor caritatis* which is important for the whole body of the Church.

3. Since Duns Scotus, the combination of subjective and sacramental event in penance has been viewed too extrinsically. The unity of the one way to salvation is not made clear enough (see *Baptism* II). The sacrament appears (explicitly from Scotus onwards: Krautwig) as a divine institution which does not indeed replace actual personal assimilation of forgiveness in faith, but allows the latter to be underestimated. It should rather be seen to confer, as God's action in man, precisely what is needed (grace and its full appropriation in love) by a person who, though placing no obstacle, does not himself already bring to the sacrament the full achievement of personal assimilation of grace and love. A return to Aquinas would be appropriate here. If a distinction is drawn between a disposition sufficient for the reception of the sacrament and a disposition suitable to the definitive reception of the grace of the sacrament, Thomas's view can be followed without abandoning Attritionism.

4. It is generally, and rightly,

assumed that in absolution the *potestas ordinis* conferred at ordination is actively exercised, and is not a purely static condition for the exercise of "jurisdiction". But the jurisdiction which is in any case required for absolution is then generally regarded either as an active power which in conjunction with the other produces the one sacramental effect, or as the necessary allocation of "subjects" to the power of the keys conferred on the priest by ordination. But if on the basis of modern historical research it is realized what great power the Church possesses in regard to determining the conditions for the validity (not merely the permissibility) of administering the sacraments, it is simplest to regard the "jurisdiction" required for valid absolution as a "setting free" of the *potestas ordinis* which alone is effectively exercised in absolution, but any act of which without such authorization by the Church would not only be illicit but invalid. In this way it would also be easier to explain how a priest in schism or *in articulo mortis* can have "jurisdiction" although he is not to the full extent a member of the true Church. He retains his *potestas ordinis*, the Church gives him no further new positive power, but allows him, for good reasons, the valid exercise of the *potestas ordinis*.

5. The theology of the satisfaction that has to be imposed in the sacrament of penance depends to a large extent on how the temporal punishments due to sin are understood. If they are the connatural results of man's sinful decision, whose repercussions affect all the dimensions of his existence and are not simply obliterated by conversion in the kernel of the personality, it seems reasonable to think that the complete overcoming of sin requires more than mere repentance and reconciliation with God in the kernel of the personality, and that all grace, even of the sacrament, signifies precisely the strength and the obligation to integrate the whole reality that has been injured by sin into the new fundamental decision by a genuine exercise of penance, and so to obtain that "love" to which all is forgiven.

Karl Rahner

PEOPLE OF GOD

1. *Preliminary note on method.* "People of God" is a biblical term, recently brought to the fore again in the Second Vatican Council (*Lumen Gentium*, chs. i and ii). It characterizes the relationship between God and a certain group of men – Israel, the Church, humanity. "People" is of course a profane reality, part of the order of creation, produced by God like all primordial human realities. But this of itself does not justify the formation of the phrase "people of God" in scriptural and ecclesiastical language. For this, "people" has to be used in a transferred, metaphorical sense, which must never be forgotten when further deductions are to be made from the notion. Thus it does not follow that when applied to the Church it can reveal or be made to imply all the actual attributes of the Church. This consideration is already enough to show that there is little point in arguing which if any of the many images which can be used to explain the nature of the Church – especially people of God and "body of Christ" – has theological precedence as the key-notion.

2. *People of God in Scripture.* Israel calls itself the people of Yahweh (God) in the OT, since in its experience of faith – through the passage through the Red Sea and the giving of the covenant – it owed its national and religious existence to Yahweh and his historical action. For this reason, and not by virtue of any natural endowment, it was his creation and special possession. Hence "God" in "people of God" is a genitive of authorship (through action in the history of revelation) and of pos-

session. The relationship thus expressed in the term "people of God" obliges the people to loyalty to this "concrete" God of its history: the Ten Commandments are the statutes of the covenant. Likewise, as people of God, they can hope in his promise. He will always be true to his historical deed in creating this people and hence will always be on their side. The community of believers in Jesus knows itself to be the new covenant founded on his blood, the new Israel in the Pneuma, to whom the promises to the fathers have been transferred. Hence it affirms that it is the real, true and definitive people of God. It knows no national bounds but seeks to embrace all nations, being based not on membership "according to the flesh" but on the Holy Spirit and faith. But it does not think of itself as a completely new institution. It is the legitimate successor of the ancient people of God, which is related to it as a shadowy promise (*typos*) to the definitive reality (cf. Mk 14:24; Acts 3:25; Rom 1:7; 4:16f.; 9:6, 27; 1 Cor 1:21; 2 Cor 6:6, 18; Gal 3:7; 4:24; 6:16; Eph 1:18; 2:21; 5:27; Heb 2:16; 8:8ff.; 13:15; 1 Pet 2:9; Rev 1:6; 2:9; 7:4ff.; 13:7; 14:1ff.). This enables us to understand how some – not all – of the imagery once used of Israel, the ancient people of God, is applied to the Church. It is the "new Jerusalem", the "holy city" (Gal 4:26; Phil 3:20; Heb 11:10; 12:22; 13:14; Rev 3:12; 11:2; 20:9; 21:2ff.; 22:17) or the "bride" (Mt 9:15; Jn 2:1ff.; 2 Cor 11:2; Eph 5:30ff.; Rev 19:7ff.; 21:2, 9; 22:17) – because the OT people of the covenant had a "bridal" relationship to Yahweh. This also explains the typological application to the Church of Israel's experiences in the history of salvation (1 Cor 10:1–12, 18; Gal 4:21–31, etc.). Hence too, on the analogy of Israel's sojourn in the desert, the Church is seen as the pilgrim people of God (Heb 4:9).

3. *Dogmatic meaning.* Thus it is relatively simple and easy to determine in ordinary ecclesiastical terminology the certain dogmatic content of the term "people of God" as applied to Christians. God has chosen men for salvation. (Whether this predestination comprises many, few or all, in comparison with the totality of mankind, does not affect the notion here.) His salvific will chose these men not as isolated individuals, each called to salvation on his own, but in the network of historical and social relationships by which they are bound to each other, and which also has a function in the mediation of salvation, at least because of the unity of love of God and of the neighbour. Beyond their historical and social unity, these men have also an inward unity in the freely-accepted self-communication of God, in grace. This unity was manifested historically and became eschatologically irreversible in Jesus Christ and his resurrection. This gives the self-donation of God which unites these men, and hence this unity itself, a historical and social tangibility, even though for us this group, called and united in the Spirit of God, is not clearly discernible from other men. In this sense, therefore, there is a people of God (see also *Salvation* III).

4. *The people of God and the Church.* It is more difficult to determine the relationship between the people of God and the Church. Just as when speaking of the Church and membership of the Church, this question is a matter of the terminology used. But one should be clear on the terminology which one chooses, and define it clearly in order to avoid misunderstandings.

a) It is possible, with regard to the NT time of salvation, to regard the people of God as a socially constituted people (in the sense of a *societas perfecta*) and hence simply identify the people of God (materially) with the Church. This has the advantage of providing a simple and clear terminology. But the disadvantage is that then some important theological realities, which do not simply coincide with the notion of the hierarchically constituted Church, must be deprived of designations which are kerygmatically easy to manage and traditional. Further, ordinary modern profane usage distinguishes people and State (the people socially constituted) as two interrelated but formally and materially (inadequately) distinct things. This suggests that when the terms are used in a transferred sense, an analogous distinction should be observed.

b) It seems therefore desirable, and it is quite feasible, to understand the people of God as the pneumatically united sum of all who are justified. This would include those who are not yet "fully" incorporated in the social bond of the hierarchical Church. Understood in this way, the people of God attains its full "visibility" and social constitution in the one, visible, hierarchical Church, but would also include those who are not yet fully "incorporated" into the Church. Within the framework of this terminology one might also formulate matters as follows: the people of God includes all (and again in different ways) who in any way (at whatever degree) belong to the Church. Thus there would be a distinction between the people of God and the Church, and the many difficulties which this terminology still involves would be avoided. Thus, for instance, the baptized sinner in the Church belongs *corpore* (as Vatican II says: *Lumen Gentium*, art. 14) to the Church and hence also to the people of God, though again not *corde*. To put it in another way: membership of the Church can be at various levels, and hence the notion of the Church admits of degrees. It can be taken in a broad or a narrow sense. If one speaks of the "Church" without qualification, one might therefore confine oneself to the strictest and fullest sense of the word "Church". This is the Catholic usage, as reflected in *Lumen Gentium*, art. 8, where it is said that *the Church* "subsists" in the Catholic Church. It would then be most desirable to use the term "people of God" to designate the further implications of the notion of Church, taken in its widest sense. But even then the question still remains as to whether baptism must be included among these necessary factors, or whether justification is sufficient, this being possible without baptism of water.

c) One could also quite well envisage the possibility of calling humanity itself the people of God. It is not just the natural substratum of the people of God, in whatever sense one takes this term. Humanity is a unity by reason of its origin and its supernatural destiny. It has only one history, to which Jesus Christ belongs. All men are comprised in the supernatural universal salvific will of God. They are redeemed – as the prerequisite of their justification – the supernatural existential. The movement of man's history is sustained by the offer of the divine self-communication. This one history has already felt, in Jesus Christ, the impact of that which formally predefines the *blessed* outcome of this history (as such). Hence mankind as a unity and a totality, prior to the personal decision of the individual and prior to the formation of the Church, is something constituted by the gracious act of God in Jesus Christ. If one wishes to find a name for this fact, "people of God" suggests itself.

Karl Rahner

PERSON

I. Concept

1. *Etymology: history of the concept*. The word "person" comes from the Latin *persona*, usually derived from the verb *personare*, "to sound through", though this is not certain. In medieval philosophy it was sometimes said to come from *per se una*, which is certainly false.

Modern philology links it with the Etruscan *persu*, a word found written beside a representation of two masked figures. It was used to translate the Greek πρόσωπον, face, first in the sense of the actor's mask, which designated his role.

The theological and philosophical concept of person remained unknown to ancient pagan philosophy, and first appears as a technical term in the early Christian theology of the Trinity and Incarnation (cf. Tertullian, *Adversus Praxean*, 12; 27). The first formal ontological definition of person comes from Boethius (*De duabus naturis*, 3): "persona est naturae rationalis individua substantia". In this form, and with the modifications given it by St. Thomas Aquinas ("incommunicabilis", *Summa Theologica*, I, q. 30, a. 4 ob. 2; "subsistentia", *Summa contra Gentiles*, IV, 49) and especially by Richard of St. Victor ("intellectualis naturae incommunicabilis existentia", *De Trinitate*, IV, 22, 24; a similar definition in Duns Scotus, *Sententiae*, I, 23, 1), the definition was not only valid for medieval Christianity and its theological and philosophical tradition: it still determines modern thinking to a great extent, especially in the field of philosophy and social ethics. Person does not mean "essence" or "nature" but the actual unique reality of a spiritual being, an undivided whole existing independently and not interchangeable with any other. This reality is the reality of a being which belongs to itself and is therefore its own end in itself. It is the concrete form taken by the freedom of a spiritual being, on which is based its inviolable dignity. This is but a formal concept of person. Clearly, what it implies in the concrete can only be learned from the "nature" of the spiritual being in question, and from the degree of reality which its freedom attains essentially, that is, by virtue of possessing such a nature (see 3a).

2. *The historic experience at the origin of the concept of person and the modern state of the question.* Ancient metaphysics understood man as a being at once finite and infinite, in which the spirit, that which is universal and supra-individual, is limited and individualized by its embodiment in matter. Thus understood, man is, in a word, an individual. He is the representative of a species, in whom the universal as such is really threatened with destruction. He represents a fallen state, from which the spirit frees itself once more at death, to attain its essential universality, its unlimited totality, its untrammelled existence and its divinity. The perspectives of Christian theology and anthropology are different and are opened up by another type of experience. God's freely uttered word, addressed to man as precept and promise at once, calls man and his responsive liberty to be partaker of his own living reality. The infinite transcendent God and finite, passible man are partners. This partnership of unconditioned and contingent freedom constitutes man as such, and thereby unites him to others who share a common destiny. And partnership with the infinite God does not eliminate the peril which is intrinsic to man's situation as a finite creature. Rather, it is only in the light of this partnership that man's situation is clearly seen. He is challenged and he cannot but respond: and his free decision itself determines its final reality. And thus finite man, as an individual, is still of absolute value and significance, so much so that God himself became man for the sake of his salvation, that is, of the realization of his freedom. This religious experience of faith disrupts the categories of ancient thought with a twofold paradox: the authentic incarnation of God who remains God, and the absolute, infinite significance of the finite individual man, who remains finite, in a common destiny with men in general. This experience alone makes it possible and necessary to form the concept of person as that of the spiritual

being who freely disposes of himself and who is of absolute significance. And on this basis too, though God is and remains first to last the absolute and incomprehensible mystery, we are entitled to designate God as a person, to call his relationship to man a personal one, and to think of his life as the immanent perfection of his being, accomplished not in a simple but in a multiple personal act.

Here, then, is an experience of the person which began in the Jewish religion, found initial expression in the "metaphysics of the exodus" and came to its fullness in the Christian faith. Searching for articulate self-expression, it could turn at first only to Greek philosophy, but with its new perspectives it brought with it certain changes and clarifications in the ancient concepts. The concepts of φύσις, οὐσία, ὑπόστασις, their Latin counterparts *natura*, *substantia*, etc., and the distinctions and relationships between them were affected. A Jewish-Christian "metaphysics of the exodus", orientated towards a historic experience, confronted a Greek metaphysic of being, orientated towards universal processes. It was therefore only to be expected that the resultant concept of person should not range it among other intramundane entities, even as the highest of them, but should see it on the contrary as that which basically determines the world and the beings within it, with regard to what and how they are and appear. Man, as a person, was seen as something "prior" to all beings in the world or as something "escaping" its structural framework: because, as a personal being, he is and is what he is by virtue of the very way in which he "takes place", he is not merely determined by essence and nature.

This is in fact already expressed in the classic metaphysical definitions of person: the person is the permanent *de facto* unity – a contradiction in formal logic – of the absolutely individual (a freedom which can be exercised by none but itself) and the most comprehensively universal (the spiritual); of immanence and transcendence; of what modern philosophy calls in-sistence (subsistence in self) and ek-sistence (openness to the world of being). In this unity the universality of spirit, *qua* being and essence, is not totally submerged in the individual, nor is the individuality dissolved and merged in a greater whole. The person is the effective realization of a permanent ontological difference.

Wherever man is understood as such an exceptional unity, and not reduced to a mere individual or an element integrated into a whole (either *de iure* spiritual or *de facto* collective), and wherever he is experienced as someone faced by an absolute claim not entirely explicable on intramundane grounds: we must call such thinking "personalist" – insofar as it is conscious of, and gives effect to, the contradiction inherent in this unity and to the claim made upon it. This is true even if the terms person and personality are not expressly used.

We may still ask, however, whether by themselves the classical definitions give fully adequate expression to the religious experience which underlies them. Do they do justice to its structure, which is accessible even to natural philosophy through the experience of conscience? Subsistence and incommunicability are expressed, but what of the other essential elements of the experience of the person and its freedom? Do they bring out well enough the elements of real historical activity and of partnership between person and person? For it is in these that the person as such, even the divine, primarily discloses and presents itself to others. There is a personalism which considers the person primarily as substance, and a personalism which is more existentialist, considering the person rather in its activity: the latter is in the line of tradition which goes through St. Augustine, Eckhart, Nicholas of Cusa, Pascal, Kierkegaard and others down to the present day, less concerned with the classical concepts and definitions, and markedly personalist in its outlook. (For a general survey and classification cf. G. Gloege, "Person, Personalismus", in H. Brunotte and O. Weber, eds., *Evangelisches Kirchenlexikon*, III [1959], cols. 128ff.) Such personalist thinking was undoubtedly furthered by the theology of the Reformation, and in recent times by the philosophy of "existence as dialogue" put forward by F. Ebner, M. Buber and others, by existentialism, by dialectical theology, and also by the new attention paid in Catholic circles to the biblical foundations of the Christian faith. Its main concern today is to oppose and overcome the individualistic or collectivist view of man, society and history, by exposing them as one-sided interpretations of a common original experience.

3. *The meaning of the concept of the human person.* a) *Person and nature.* If man is to be understood as person, that is, as he really is in the free achievement of his *nature*, it should be recognized that this nature is not a purely (limited or unlimited) spiritual and simple one. Man as a spiritual being is likewise localized in space and time in his bodily reality. His nature is of many dimensions and subjected to many restrictions by reason of its "spiritual and psychic capability", its bodily vitality, its corporeal materiality. This complex and therefore finite nature, with its many levels and their intrinsic, unalterable structural laws, with its constitutive elements of vitality and materiality, is always prior to and imposed on the human person as something not its own choice, which is to be freely brought to full realization by that person. If man is to be properly understood as a person, that is, above all in the *actual* free realization of his nature – which is a historical, not a natural process, since it is freedom in the concrete – we must further recognize that as far as we and our fellow-men are concerned, this realization is never achieved at the level of full freedom. Man never actually fully possesses and disposes of himself. His finite nature is never completely integrated into the unity of personal being. The material element resists, the vital functions fail, the mind forgets, and can be unconscious of the content of its spiritual and psychic processes. There are, on the other hand, means of counteracting such resistance. The realization of the person in freedom may be intensified, or enlarged in scope, by the various stages of the formation of the personality. This formation takes place through exercise and through omission; through the free acceptance or rejection of what, apparently, "impinges from without", through its absorption into the inwardness of personal, "fateful" experience, or again, through its elimination; through decisions which constitute the permanent reality of a personality either fulfilled or defective. And there are degrees of intensity in the build-up of the person: not every act affecting mind and body, not every deed or omission makes the same important contribution to the realization of the person. Man the temporal never fulfils his nature in a single act, but in the developing series of his historical acts, as he does and suffers, strives or omits to strive. In the course of his history, man as a person can never quite "catch up with himself" as nature, and take definitive possession of himself, neither in knowledge nor in will nor in action. Man's historicity (see *History* I) stems essentially not from his nature's being finite, but from the painful discrepancy between nature and person, which he tries to overcome.

In spite of this discrepancy, we must not think of man's nature as primarily an intramundane individuality, and only secondarily and potentially a person. No doubt the various dimensions and possibilities of man's nature follow their own laws, and it is legitimate to distinguish hypothetically and methodically these various levels in the necessary divisions of anthropological studies. But from the very start, man's nature is subjected to the claims of the person, which not merely embrace it but actually constitute it as nature. Science may indeed systematize the various "departments" of man's nature, and the practical needs of education, culture and vocational adaptation may call for a precise grasp of the particular gifts, likings or handicaps of any given subject. But we may not lose sight of the indissoluble natural bond between the various elements, nor above all of the personal quality of man's nature and dispositions etc. as a whole. This quality is based on the fact that man's nature, once it is there at all, and no matter how situated, already exists in the essential and actual unity of the person. For the same reason, the natural law cannot be deduced from man's nature considered in the abstract. It is basically a law deriving from the rights of the person, and hence can only be derived from the fact that man's nature as such is subject to the claims of the person, to its self-imposed exigencies. It does not matter how well or ill man's nature can display its ability to cope with its inexorable task, or how much of it he actually undertakes or evades. From this absolute claim of the person stems the right at least to exist, to have real possibilities of existence: which holds good too for the mentally deranged and the helpless aged. For the same basic reason, the other fundamental rights and positive law are not to be based on nature in the abstract, where man appears either as an isolated individual in perpetual conflict with others, or as a mere component in a collectivity, an *animal sociale*, which as far as this takes us is no better than the inhabitant of an ant-heap. The other fundamental rights, and positive law as guardian of rights, are rather based on the self-realization of the person, on the ever-disparate, gradual actualization of the persons and the groups which constitute human society. Hence it is only in the light of man's being a person that his relationship to his fellow-men, to the community, can also be properly understood (see 3c).

b) *Person and world.* Just as the "departments" of corporeal, psychic and spiritual life are in each case the interlocked dimensions of the *one* human nature, so too human nature as such is related to "nature" in the broader sense which is its setting – to beings in general. The relationship is triple. With other particular beings man's nature stands in a causal connection on the material plane. With its own special milieu it has a vital relationship. With the *one* "world", it is involved in the relationship of spiritual communication which surpasses and assimilates to itself all particular beings and its own milieu. Man is a bodily entity, localized in a given point of history and the universe. But the transcendence of the spirit takes in the past, cosmic distance and the future, and sets him in the one world which is always a historic, significant presence, and is man's true and proper "place". And just as man's nature is prior to and imposed on its own finite, free self-realization, but only exists at all, being human, within this process of realizing the person: so too the world is prior to and indissolubly imposed on the person, as the medium of his whole personal existence, a medium which is *a priori* constitutive of man's (psychosomatic) being, and not merely a subsequent participant in its development. Thus the historic realization of man's being takes place both as the development of his "natural gifts" and as the moulding of the world. Wherever this moulding of the world is seen in its essential unity with the self-realization of man, we have a relationship of man to the world which, because *human*, recognizes the *objective* law and significance proper to each level of beings as a whole. It sees that the world of things is not there just as a means to an end, to sustain man's life, but that each has its essential place and significance in the whole and for the whole – though the use and consumption of things to sustain and intensify man's life is unavoidable. But just as the realization of man's being is not simply identical with the maintenance and enhancement of life, so too man's work on the world is not done when he has provided himself with goods to use and consume. His effort only reaches its climax when in obedience to the transcendence of the spirit man goes out of himself into the vastness of the universe, to crystallize and present the world in a unit of being, understandably, plastically and symbolically. This he does in the great achievements of perception and communication (language), of truth (science), beauty (art), worship (liturgy), mastery of nature (technology), mastery of men for their common end (State), etc. It is only by officiating in the "service" of such works that man realizes himself and displays himself to the full ("objective" culture). But these works collapse into nothingness and insignificance if they are allowed to remain external, isolated from their living source. They are and remain realities only by being constantly reabsorbed into the inwardness of man. Just as the development of man's nature is and remains real only by being integrated into the selfhood of the person, so too the "figure of the world" is and remains a reality, when represented by the works, only insofar as these works and the totality they portray are constantly brought back to their origin in the person. This recall and appropriation of the transfigured totality, its orderly insertion into the reality of personal fulfilment, is what we call culture (in the "subjective" sense). The spirit's transcendence, involved in what is common and universal in the one world, demands to be reinstated in the immanence of freedom, which remains singular, unique and irreplaceable in this process of development. And vice versa, this immanence of freedom demands such transcendence of spirit. The moulding of the world and the fulfilment of self, the flux and reflux, differentiation and reintegration, are moments of one and the same happening, divided in time, but still aspects of the self-realization of the human person in history. And likewise: just as throughout its history the human person can never adequately "take in" its own nature which is prior to it and imposed on it (though at the same time always overtaken by it), so too no human person in history can ever totally "take in" the world, so as to mould and appropriate and master it in history once and for all. This permanent historical difference between person and world is the basis of man's "historicity" in understanding and mastering the world: the fact that tradition is inexhaustible, the present fluid, the future unforeseeable and uncontrollable, culture an unending process.

c) *Person and community*. Just as no one man is alone and self-sufficient, but must work in and with society if he is to do his work, the world, that is, and his own self-realization thereby, so too the culture that returns him to himself can only exist and develop by common effort, determined by the historical tradition and the actual constitution of society. And this social quality is necessary, even though culture ultimately means a liberation only to be achieved by and for each person alone. And vice versa, this personal, unique self-fulfilment of developing freedom is and remains one of the factors which determine effectively the nature of society in its actual form and future history. For the reality of human social life is not the arithmetical total of juxtaposed "natural individuals", nor is it an independent organism unfolding itself in its various single members. A common social life, human and worthy of human beings, is only achieved and preserved in the achievement and preservation of each member's personal life of the spirit. Since social life is the common spiritual product and setting of each single member, whatever each one does, even in the most private sphere, is of real importance, in varying degrees, to society. So too all "public" social activity affects private behaviour to a greater or lesser extent. For this reason, there is a real distinction between the common good and the good of the individual, which is manifested in their different immediate goals. But there can be no essential opposition between the two, as if in certain cases the common good could be achieved only at the cost of the good of the individual and vice versa. Utilitarian restrictions of the concept of the general and private weal are to be rejected. The personal foundation of both must be kept in view. Hence it must be affirmed that renunciation and sacrifice, for instance, as in limitations imposed on the exercise of power or of freedom, need not be just extrinsic (painful) means of gaining the greatest possible benefit. They can be intrinsic constituent elements of personal achievement for the individual and for society. And it is only on this condition, namely that they *can* be inwardly accepted and not just enforced from outside, that such sacrifices are really tolerable and hence truly legitimate. However, in the absence of theoretical and *a priori* norms, it is always difficult to determine, in any concrete historical situation, what exactly constitutes the common and the private weal. Hence there is no easy way of justifying thereby any given measure or procedure.

Why is man a social being? Why is he only capable of existing as a single person when upheld by a shared reality? The reason is not the interplay of causes on the material level, nor men's biological needs and mutual dependence. It is man's spiritual nature, his historical openness to the past, to the presence of the world and to the future. In the division of labour, in his insertion into society's accomplishment of the common work, each single person is necessarily claimed by a function: he serves the work, he is a "functionary" of society. But it is equally necessary that each one, in the process of the formation of the person, should make the general and total achievement his own, by subsuming it into his own independent freedom, which always remains distinct from the common social reality. The totalitarian State, with its emphasis on the training and development of the individual, achieves by compulsion the total insertion of each subject into the functions and processes of its endeavour, and is thereby undoubtedly capable of producing the most imposing works of the spirit. But the totalitarian State strives at the same time to hinder culture, the process whereby the person withdraws himself and returns to himself, since the possibility of criticism is involved. It restricts personal freedom and endeavours to eliminate it.

If our thinking and decision with regard to the future is to be responsible, we must recognize that the "threat to the person", constituted by the growing comprehensiveness of socially-organized life, does not come from the absence of the spirit or from hostility towards the spirit. It is on the contrary the spirit and its very universality which primarily threatens the person and the unique freedom of each. For today the spirit is giving effect to its remotest possibilities, so that the attainment of personal freedom was never so much endangered as at present. And what is the supreme achievement of the spirit? It is to reduce everything mysterious to explicable causes. It is to organize all diversity into unity, to perceive, as the spirit alone can do, a universal order in history and nature, and by comprehending this order, to dominate it.

The domination of this order only becomes possible, however, when we fit ourselves entirely into it as its servants. All particular tasks become one single task. All that can be organized is subsumed into the organized state of the one world. "No man is an island." The tendency seems to be that there should be no more "islands" at all, either in quality or in quantity: that all is to become one. The barriers between ways of thought and life are being broken down, in the same way as the bounds of intimacy, familiarity and public knowledge are being blurred. The possibility of acting on one's own within a relatively narrow circle is disappearing. And universal teamwork has begun. This universal teamwork seems to signify the end of the "personality" in the Romantic sense. What remains is the task of preserving the person, which will have to realize itself in the future under a new form, of which the outlines are as yet scarcely perceptible.

Max Müller and *Alois Halder*

II. Man

A. Philosophical

1. *The question posed by the definition.* The best-known definition of man is *animal rationale*, which probably goes back to the Peripatetics. According to Iamblichus (*De Vita Pythagorica*, 31), the definition was already given by Aristotle himself. It was adopted by the scholastics, e.g., Boethius, *Isagoge Porphyrii, Commentarium, editio prima*, I, 20 (*PL*, LXIV, col 35); Anselm of Canterbury, *Monologion*, cap. 10; *De grammatico*, cap. 8; Thomas Aquinas, *Summa Theologica*, II-II, q. 34, a. 5; *Summa contra Gentiles*, II, 95; III, 39; *De Potentia*, VIII, 4. It has held its ground down to modern times, and was discussed by Kant in his *Die Religion innerhalb der Grenzen der blossen Vernunft* (1793, E. T. by T. Greene and H. Hudson, *Religion within the Limits of Reason Alone* [1960]). In neo-scholastic manuals the definition is considered both classical and evident.

In the 19th and 20th centuries, new principles and aspects have been considered in philosophical anthropology which without contradicting the definition are nonetheless hardly deducible from it. It appears therefore that *animal rationale* is incomplete. New aspects were brought out by Marx, to some extent in dependence on Hegel, in his analysis of work and alienation, whereby man was regarded as essentially sociohistorical. Dilthey also found that the notion of "historical" was one of the characteristics of man, which had been neglected in the one-sidedly "cosmological" approach of earlier philosophy. Kierkegaard viewed man as existence and as an individual. As existence, man is a relation which refers back to God who posited this relation. Nietzsche defined man as the will to power, not in a merely psychological sense, but in the sense of the basic urge to produce the superman. Heidegger describes the unity of the being of man as existence (*Dasein*), using the older "existentia" only in the sense of "happening to be there" more or less automatically like inanimate objects. Jaspers sees man as poised in the tension of existence and reason. He uses Kierkegaard's notion of existence to answer the Kantian question as to how and why reason is to become practical. In contrast to the dualism of Descartes, modern philosophy insists on the unity of man, emphasizing historicity and language. This is a development which was heralded by Vico and Rousseau, became explicit in Herder and then dominated the philosophy against German Idealism.

The misgivings against *animal rationale* as a definition of man may be summed up by saying that it does not do justice to the historical and linguistic structure of man. Further, the old definition can easily, though not necessarily, be understood in a dualistic sense. Finally, the possibility of ever adequately defining what man "is" has now become fundamentally questionable.

2. *Historical survey*. The question of the nature of man is linked with the problem of the unity of man in his diverse elements. The question has been raised and answered in very different ways since classical antiquity. For Plato, man is really man only in his soul, which is not truly and essentially united to the body. He distinguishes three parts of the soul: the spiritual (λογιστικόν), the courageous (θυμοειδές) and the passionate (ἐπιθυμητικόν) (*Republic*, 441e; *Timaeus*, 77e). After death the spiritual soul survives, set free from the body. There is a further element of obscurity in the relationship between the human soul and the "world-soul". The notion of the soul as a spiritual substance has been part of Western philosophy since Plato. Aristotle regarded the soul as the first entelechy of a physical organism (*De Anima*, 412b 4). The soul is the form or determining principle of an organism. But in man there is also the intellect (νοῦς) which is the faculty of the higher level of knowledge. The ancient commentators of Aristotle were already divided as to whether th e νοῦς was individual or supra-individual.

The fact that the soul, in the biblical usage of the word, was often interpreted in a Platonist sense by the Fathers led to a one-sided evaluation of the soul as opposed to the body, which was also reflected in early scholasticism. Augustine, for instance, regarded man as a unity, but left the unity unexplained in ontological terms (*De Moribus Ecclesiae*, I, 4, 6: *PL*, XXXII, col. 1313; I, 27, 52: *ibid.*, col. 1332; *In Johannis Evangelium*, XIX, 1, 15: *PL*, XXXV, col. 1553; *Confessiones*, X, 20, 29). For Hugh of St. Victor, the personal nature of man still stemmed from the soul (*De Sacramentis Ecclesiae*, I, 2; I, 6). Thomas Aquinas found a new solution, by applying the definition of the soul as entelechy to the spiritual soul and regarding it as the one single form of man. Man does not then consist of soul and body but of matter, regarded as real potency, and the spiritual soul. The corporeal nature of man is at once formed by the soul in each case (*Summa Theologica*, I, q. 76, a. 1). This doctrine was rejected by other schools of scholasticism, since it appeared to endanger the immortality of the soul. Against Thomas Aquinas, Duns Sctous maintained the multiplicity of forms in man, in order to explain his diverse modes of being (*Opus Oxoniense*, IV d. 11, q. 3, n. 46). The modern perspective of the creativity of man is prefigured in the teaching of Nicholas of Cusa. Descartes regarded man as the *cogito* and so came to a radical dualism between *res cogitans* and *res extensa*. The unity of man could only be upheld by having recourse to a philosophical notion of God, and this theory was further elaborated in the occasionalism of Malebranche and taken up again in the "pre-established harmony" of Leibniz. Pascal, however, introduced an analysis of the being of man in which the intrinsic oppositions and tensions were insistently stressed. The importance of Pascal could only be seen after Rousseau, Herder, Dilthey and Kierkegaard had introduced a new approach which interpreted man as a historical entity.

Kant made a sharp distinction between the pragmatic and the physiological knowledge of man. The latter is concerned with what nature makes man, the former with what man makes of himself, or can and ought to make of himself, as a free agent (*Anthropologie in pragmatischer Hinsicht* [1798]). The way was thereby paved for the philosophical anthropology of the 19th century, which was to interpret man as a self-forming and purposeful being.

The main influences were Kant's *Critique of Practical Reason* and Herder's *Outlines of a Philosophy of the History of Man* and his essay on the origin of language. Herder's influence has reinforced that of Kant in this matter down to the present day. The animal lives with its instinct in a narrow environment, whereas man is free, and disposed by nature to reflect and consider. German Idealism discussed the question of man in terms of a more highly developed transcendental philosophy (Fichte) or of a dialectic of the absolute Spirit (Hegel). The critiques of Feuerbach, Marx, Kierkegaard and Nietzsche placed man in the centre of philosophical thought. Feuerbach distinguished man from beast, but explained freedom and culture by man's sensible nature. Marx first followed Feuerbach but then abandoned him, insisting that philosophy must be practical and pursuing his own dialectic of society and history. Max Scheler (1874–1928) is considered the founder of modern anthropology. He came from phenomenology to an Augustinian and Christian view of man, but then abandoned this again in favour of a purely intramundane anthropology, of which his *Stellung des Menschen im Kosmos* (1927; E. T.: *Man's Place in Nature* [1963]) is typical. Man is not simply at the mercy of his urges and instincts. He can say No, and the spirit is the principle of this refusal. All the force of the spirit comes from the vital instinct, but the spirit cannot be reduced to urges and instincts. As a person, man is a principle of action and hence raised above slavery to his environment. H. Plessner's biological and physiological approach, in which he also availed of the perspectives of the human sciences of the 19th century, enabled him to depict man in such a way that the unity of human life could be deduced from human behaviour. A. Gehlen also regards man as a totality with a special place in nature, who would be inadequate under natural conditions. He compensates for his inadequacy by his faculty of action. Gehlen explains this power of acting and the freedom of man's decision on the basis of his intrinsic vitality, in the analysis of which he departs markedly from Scheler. Lévi-Strauss has taken ethnology as the positivist basis of his "structuralist" anthropology. Mention may be made finally of the various answers to the question of man given by Marxism, Existence Philosophy, Sartre, Camus and Teilhard de Chardin.

3. *The characteristics of man.* The divergences of views in modern anthropology should not be looked on as completely unpromising. Some attitudes and principles may well be very prejudiced. This is often the case when the question is approached exclusively from the point of view of a restricted field of sciences and their specific methods, such as biology, sociology, empirical psychology and linguistic analysis. In contrast to all schematic surveys and too narrow bases, it seems important that certain aspects of man should be considered and their significance assessed.

Language is the medium of all interpretations of man. Man enters upon this process not as a consciousness detached from the world but as a being-in-the-world. Man is thus seen in his wholeness as a bodily being, who represents the climax of a long evolution which now proceeds through him and from him. Hence the question of what man is necessarily involves the historical viewpoint, as well as the existential hermeneutic question. Man points beyond himself and his given situation and as being-in-the-world is also deathward being. Selfhood is at once the existence of man and the fulfilment to which existence tends. On these grounds it can be shown that a purely biological analysis is insufficient. The analyses of depth psychology, empirical psychology and ethics all point to a centre of action which we may designate as the person. But the very notion of person is a debatable question in modern anthropology and needs to be referred back to the totality of man's being. In its actual life, this totality displays a certain compact unity which is not as such communicable, and is also characterized by a primordial spontaneity by which man can be distinguished from other living beings. Freedom and necessity are neither merely demands nor extrinsic properties. They represent intrinsic determinations of man's being, which is realized in terms of language and history. The relationship to the You and society arises from the very being of man. Man knows himself from the start as open to the world and in communication with his fellow-men, though at the same time as different to others. This openness of man for his fellows and for the world also contains implicitly an openness for something higher. The question of how man realizes this relation in the form of religion is one which belongs to philosophical anthropology but at the same time points beyond it.

Joseph Möller

B. Biblical

1. *The Old Testament.* According to the OT, in the tradition seen mainly in the priestly writings, man is created by God, Gen 1:27; 5:1–2; 6:7; Deut 4:32. This assertion which is accepted as binding in all the OT writings stresses the dependence of man on God. Man is part of creation, taken from the earth (Gen 2:7) and like all created things is perishable. The OT makes use of a number of terms to speak of man's autonomy and dependence, of his vitality and mortality. Above all, man is "flesh". This designation, used both of animals (104 times) and man (169 times), is the favourite way of expressing what is typical of created things. It can mean the skin (Ps 102:6), the material substance (Gen 41:2ff.), and the body of man (Lev 13:2–4; Ps 63:2), and is used above all to designate man as such (cf. the common phrase "all flesh"). The element of creatureliness is always implied in such assertions: Gen 6:3; Jer 17:5; Ps 41:6; 56:5; 78:39; Job 10:4; Dan 2:11. But creatureliness means dependence on the creator, or transience and mortality, Is 31:3. This means that man, who is essentially "flesh", needs the "power of God" if he is not to be merely "flesh". Without the breath of God (Gen 2:7) which is the life-force (רוּחַ, Gen 6:17) animating and sustaining man, he is only dust, "power"-less and dead, inert and lifeless. When Yahweh imparts to the thing of dust (Gen 3:19b, c) his life-giving force, man becomes a living being (נֶפֶשׁ). "Flesh" and "soul" ("life-force"), בָּשָׂר and נֶפֶשׁ, are often synonymous and interchangeable terms (Ps 63:2; 78:50; 88:4f.; Job 13:14), which reflect different aspects of the same reality. Man is "flesh" in his transitory and mortal aspect, "soul" when he is seen rather from the aspect of his vitality and activity.

The important thing is that Hebrew thought is not pessimistic as regards man. Even at the time of the exile and in the post-exilic epoch, when contacts and encounters with other cultures influenced to some extent the Hebrew understanding of man, Israel preserved its optimistic outlook on the nature of man. One reads, no doubt, throughout the whole of Scripture that man, as flesh, is powerless and mortal, but this is always said of the whole man, and when man is spoken of as "soul" and "spirit". For the Israelite, a pessimistic attitude implying the moral inferiority of the "flesh" was inconceivable, since though convinced of man's dependence on his creator, he recognized no metaphysical or anthropological dualism, such as was propounded in particular by Greek and late Hellenistic philosophy. Man in the OT stands before God not as an independent, sovereign being but as a creature. No doubt Scripture recognizes man's temptation to renounce God and shape his life independently of God, as the prophets' call for conversion shows. But the cause of "apostasy" from Yahweh is not the wickedness of the "flesh", the sinful, sensual body, "something" in man which acts as an evil principle to draw him down to perdition, but the "heart" of man. And this, in Jewish thought, is the inmost core, the centre of man's being, from which come the evil inclinations and desires which go against the order of God, Gen 6:5; 8:21; Exod 4:21; 7:13; Is 29:13; Jer 4:4; 9:25. One may compare the distinction made in rabbinical Judaism between the "good and evil urge". The OT picture of man is characterized not by the anthropological dualism of body and soul which occurs in Greek philosophy or the metaphysical dualism between spirit and matter which dominates the Gnostic systems, but by the relationship of man the creature to his creator. Hence sin is an offence against the divine ordinance whereby the history of the people is governed in this world: Hos 2:10ff.; 4:1; 9:17; Is 5:18ff.; 6:9f. For it is in this world, according to the OT, that the destiny of man is played out. Israel's understanding of existence is dominated by the sense that man has to live successfully, competently and prosperously in this world, crowned above all by great age. Death is man's inexorable destiny (Gen 2:17; Ecclus 8:7) and OT man does not envisage life after death. Expectations of future life and well-being can be traced only in the Judaism of the time of apocalyptic (Ezek 37:1–14; Dan 12:2). Early death is the punishment of culpably wrong behaviour, Gen 47:9; Deut 24:16; Ps 102:24f.; Jer 17:11. On the other hand, however, the promise, "Do not fear, you shall not die" (Jg 6:23; 2 Sam 12:13) is one of the most important announcements of blessing (cf. Ezek 18:23, 32; 33:14). For this life (in this world) is the most supremely desirable good (Prov 3:16). "All that a man has he will give for his life", Job 2:4).

Though the prophets warn against wasting life in idle pleasures (Is 22:13), the attainment of a great age, full enjoyment of earthly goods, to be gathered tranquilly to the fathers after a long evening of life (cf. Ecclus 1:12f., 17; 30:22ff.) is the great goal. Thus we are told that Abraham, to whom Yahweh had personally promised long life (Gen 15:15), died "an old man and full of years" (Gen 25:8). Jacob too was "old and full of days" when he was gathered to his fathers (Gen 35:29). In contrast to a Job who sees no promise in life and therefore yearns for death, the optimism of his friend Eliphaz is typical of Israel as a whole: "You shall come to your grave in ripe old age, as a shock of grain comes up to the threshing floor in its season" (Job 5:26). But then Job himself died "an old man, and full of days" (Job 42:17, cf. Ps 91:16). Further, the reward of a long life is a constantly recurring Deuteronomist theme (Deut 5:16; 16:20; 30:19), and the prophets also promise long life to those who seek Yahweh and strive for good instead of evil (Amos 5:4, 6, 14; cf. Ezek 18:23, 31f.; 33:11; Hab 2:4).

Thus the meaning of man is to be found here below, according to the OT, in the sense that man belongs wholly and undividedly to this world, that he is to seek and find the fulfilment of his existence in this world, an existence, however, which has been given by God's power and is regulated by God's ordinance.

2. *The New Testament*. Few sayings or discourses about the nature of man are to be found in the synoptic gospels. Jesus expresses himself in the terms, notions and images of the apocalyptic Judaism of his day. His call for conversion (Mk 1:15; Mt 4:17; 11:20) is directed to all men and shows that each

man has need of conversion and penance, since men are evil (Mt 7:11 = Lk 11:13), a wicked and adulterous generation (Mk 8:38; 9:19, etc.). Matthew in particular gave this verdict of Jesus special emphasis in his gospel. Hence in keeping with the petition of the Our Father, Matthew several times inserts into his gospel the plea that God may forgive men's sins and have mercy on them. Against this background it is understandable that the most important element of the preaching of Jesus and his disciples is the assurance of the mercy of God for all who are in need of mercy. This mercy which Jesus showed to religious and cultic outcasts (so Mt in particular) and to the socially oppressed and lowly (so Lk in particular), is also demanded of his disciples. For mercy takes precedence of obedience to cultic precepts and the Torah (Mt 9:13; 12:7), since "all the law and the prophets" depend on the two commandments of love of God and of the neighbour (Mt 22:40). Jesus' polemics against the responsible leaders of the people and the polemics of the primitive community against the Pharisees and doctors of the law (cf. the synoptic controversies) underline the necessity of a re-appraisal of the meaning of the Torah, which determines the relationship of God to man. Man is fundamentally bound to obey the Torah, but from the preaching of Jesus he knows that he is primarily bound to show mercy and love. But the decisive element in the messianic message is that man must detach himself from this world (Mk 8:36), since man's earthly being is no longer decisive and definitive as in the OT. It is only transitory, the passage to a new life, Mk 8:36; 9:43, 45; 10:17, 30. Hence the demand for *metanoia*, for penance, for detachment from things of this world, occupies a position of decisive importance in primitive Christian preaching (Mk 9:43, 45, 47; 10:30; Lk 12:13–21). The terminology and the psychology (cf. Mk 7:20–23) of the OT understanding of man are retained and not further analysed. Nonetheless the eschatological stamp of the promised salvation gives expression to the really "Christian" element of the primitive Christian message, which distinguishes it radically and finally from that of the OT and of Judaism. The imagery may derive to a great extent from Jewish apocalyptic, but detachment from the world for the sake of the kingdom of God, the only good that matters for man in the preaching of Jesus (Mt 6:33), is the strictly new element in the synoptic gospels.

Paul takes a way which is not affected by these assertions. And in terms and concepts he follows the OT and Judaism in his understanding of man. But in reality he sought for a new understanding of man (cf. Rom 7). His verdict on man is decisively coloured by his preaching of the death and resurrection of Jesus, who had appeared in the world in the form of sinful flesh in order to overcome sin (Rom 8:3). The gift of the Spirit (Rom 8:4) breaks the power of sin in man, so that he need no longer live "according to the flesh" (Rom 8:12, 13; 1 Cor 3:1–3; Gal 3:3, etc.), but "in the Spirit". Through faith in Christ and in the power of the Spirit, the destructive forces of sin, law and death have been themselves destroyed. It was the law above all which enslaved man, subjected him to the rule of sin and delivered him over to the power of death. Every effort of man to find redemption through his own achievement and the strictest obedience to the law reveals the inmost nature of sin: it is a power which enslaves all men without exception. Paul is enraptured by the possession of the Spirit and the certainty of the imminent coming of Christ and hence of the proximity of the end of this aeon. For Paul, this aeon, the world, the wisdom of this world, boasting according to the flesh are disposed of: all that matters is what is to come. No doubt the redeemed and Spirit-filled man still lives in the "flesh" (Gal 2:20; 2 Cor 10:3), but this life is not really life, since only the (new) being in the Spirit has significance for salvation. But the Spirit, as Paul affirms, must already bear fruit in man at the present time: love, joy, peace, patience, kindness, goodness, faithfulness, gentleness, self-control (cf. Gal 5:22).

The Pastoral Letters consider man from quite another aspect and one that is very different from Paul. They see him as belonging to a Church which is no longer dominated by the expectation of the imminent end. It has been "sobered" by the non-appearance of the Lord and has established itself in the world. The picture of man brings out more strongly the "pastoral" elements, that is, the features which go to form a community, such as conduct, Church discipline, hierarchy of office. Man is a being who must be distinguished by his exemplary conduct, who needs to have sound doctrine and do good works, so that a stable order may be established in the Church.

The Gospel of St. John, to which a late date must be assigned, stresses very strongly the connection between man and the world (κόσμος). But the Johannine cosmos is radically evil, inasmuch as it is ruled by the darkness (8:12; 12:35, 46; cf. 1 Jn 1:5f.; 2:8f., 11) and the prince of this world (12:31; 14:30; 16:11) has gained mastery over the cosmos. If then man not only lives in this cosmos (13:1; 17:11; cf. 1 Jn 4:17) but has himself become part of the cosmos (3:31; 8:23; 15:19; 17:14–16; 18:36; cf. 1 Jn 2:16; 4:5f.), he is at enmity with God. For he has not accepted the revealer sent by the Father and hence is not "of the truth" (18:37; cf. 1 Jn 2:13; 3:29), not "of God" (7:17; 8:47; 1 Jn 3:10). If man does not recognize the hour of judgment as the hour of decision, he becomes an enemy of God like "the Jews", who in the fourth gospel are generalized into types of all enemies of Jesus. Thus the judgment of the world which is to be expected loses in Jn much of its futurist character, since it is the hour of the decision of faith and so already present and actual in the individual.

The NT assertions about man show a relative consistency, by reason of their links with the writings of the OT and of Judaism, when they are considered from the "anthropological" and "psychological" points of view. But this is unimportant and without significance when compared with the theological and above all the Christological aspect under which the picture of man is viewed. But here there are considerable differences between the NT writers, which arise from the fact that as well as different "theologians", communities of various theological orientations were at work in the effort to answer the one important question, that of the salvation or ruin of man.

Alexander Sand

C. Theological

1. *The teaching of the magisterium.* a) Man is a creature of God. (i) This affirmation is usually made, explicitly or implicitly, in connection with the affirmation of the creation of the world in general. It often includes the assertion that man is in a certain sense the centre of the material and spiritual world (meaning the angels), and that his body too partakes of the goodness of creation (*D* 236f., 242, 421). So in the professions of faith and the Councils: *D* 428, 706, 1783, 1801, 1802, 1805, 2123. Man shares the task and goal of creation in general (*D* 1783, 2270) and is under the providence and the law of God, not an impersonal fate (*D* 1784, 239f., 607).

(ii) Man is a creature in both soul and body. This includes the first man, though this does not exclude a theory of evolution with regard to the body of the first man (*D* 2327). Little express heed is paid to the creation of the bodies of the descendants of Adam. But the creation of each individual soul is affirmed (*D* 170, 527, 2327); it is not "generated" by the parents (*D* 170, 533, 1910ff.). Monogenism is taught in *Humani Generis*, but may now perhaps be considered an open question.

b) Man is multiple but still truly and essentially one being. He is of "soul" and "body" (*D* 255, 295, 428, 481, 1783, 1914), but still a substantial unity in which the soul is essentially and of itself the "forma corporis" (*D* 255, 480f., 738, 1655, 1911f., 1914). The unity between *spiritual* soul and body is assumed to exist even before the child is born (*D* 1185). The precise moment of time at which the ontogenesis begins to be directed by a spiritual principle has not been determined.

c) The soul of man is described as rational and intellectual (*D* 148, 216, 255, 290, 338, 344, 393, 422, 480, 738), though no precise definition of this intellectuality is directly attempted. It is ultimately described most clearly in the doctrine of the intellectual knowability of God (*D* 1806). But it is affirmed with the weight of a definition that the spiritual principle in man is itself individual (*D* 738). So too the freedom of man's spirit, even in his relationship to God, is affirmed again and again with force (*D* 129f., 133ff., 140, 174, 181, 316f., 322, 348, 776, 793, 797, 1027f., 1039, 1065ff., 1093ff., 1291, 1360f., 1912, 1914). The "soul" of man, as so defined, is "immortal" (*D* 738).

d) Man's social nature is affirmed (*D* 1856, 2270), since it is the presupposition of original sin and the redemption of all by Christ.

e) Vatican II, *Gaudium et Spes* (chapter I, arts. 12–22), offers a survey of the anthropology now envisaged by the Church. In contrast to earlier pronouncements, man appears more clearly as a "person", as the "image of God" in the unity of his natural being and endowment with grace, and in the radical questionableness of his existence, which only finds its ultimate answer in the paschal mystery of Christ. The social nature of man is developed at some length in chapter II of the same constitution (arts. 23–32). The introduction (arts. 4–10) gives a sketch of his existentiell situation.

f) Since his original state (*D* 788) man has been called by God, freely, to supernatural fellowship with God in revelation and grace (*D* 1001–1007, 1021, 1671, 1786). This call is not revoked by the situation of original sin and its consequences (*D* 174, 788f., 793, 1643ff.). It is permanent, and has become eschatologically valid through Jesus Christ and his redemptive act. This call is the innermost directive force of the history of salvation and is perfected in the vision of God.

2. *Systematic presentation.* a) *Preliminary considerations.* To make a truly theological assertion about what and who man is, the general principles of theology, the hermeneutics of theological assertions, must be taken into account, but there are two further points to note.

(i) One could quite legitimately presuppose the distinction between nature and grace, the natural and supernatural order, and then start with a "regionally" organized anthropology. It would start with the body and the bodily origin of man, the spirit (immortal soul) of man, his creation, and the unity of the two realities (all together making up man's "nature"). It would then go on to treat of man's supernatural call in grace to participation in the life of God. But this is not methodologically desirable. Inevitably, there would have to be a protology (of paradise) to treat of man's original state. This would then go beyond the "essential" analysis of man and take up an "existentiell' anthropology and man's history. Hence a better approach is to start with the concrete unity of man, individual and collective: man an essentially unitary being, before God who reveals himself in the one mankind of history. Such an initial assertion will comprise the distinction between nature and supernatural endowment, explicitate it from its own content and so make it intelligible.

(ii) The second point, which will be developed more fully later, is that man is a being, individually and collectively, whose selfhood is a goal to be attained in knowledge and freedom. He *becomes* what he is, because this self-realization is not simply the addition of something external to a static and ready-made substance, as in the "accidental" modifications of "things". It is not there to be taken, so to speak, but as history, whether individual or collective, it has to occur and is still far from reaching its end. Since, then, man *is* as he knows himself and acts – though in various degrees – a full anthropology in the theological realm must include the history of salvation (with protology) and eschatology. This reserve must always be kept in mind, if an abstract theological anthropology of essence is propounded, which is either the formal precipitate of a full anthropology or merely propounds what can be known from the modest experiences of man alone. If then man "creates" his concrete nature in a history which is still taking place in fear and hope, this does not of course mean that this history has not a beginning and an end which are prior to this history of freedom, being the ordinance of God. And of course one may, with good reason, call this preordained horizon of the history made by man his "immutable essence". But then one must be clear that one runs a great danger of thinking of man in terms of a pattern which is appropriate to "things" but not to man. "Things" are never ultimately affected in their "essence" by their "action" – not really and definitively.

(iii) Man's knowledge of himself, which always aims at a unity of knowledge since man is a unity, is always conditioned by a plurality of experiences which can never be adequately synthesized by man himself – all the more so, since this multiple experience is not yet rounded off. Hence theological anthropology must always be propounded with the reservation that its assertions, true though they may be and true as they are in fact in their "defined" substance, must always be reappraised and better understood in the light of what continued historical experience will add. And the natural anthropological sciences will be an element in this history. Hence one should not be surprised that historically the anthropology propounded by the Church has in fact (without detriment to its ultimate "substance") been greatly dependent on profane anthropology and has sometimes offered ideological justification of an ostensibly theological nature for the profane self-understanding of man.

(iv) There is a mutal relationship between theology (strictly speaking) and anthropology. We have only reached the stage of a theological anthropology when we affirm that man is a being who has to do with God. And what "God" means can only be expressed by having recourse to an experience – transcendence or whatever one may call it – within which that which is called God is found, as its goal. Hence an anthropological assertion is only theological when it contains implicitly or explicitly a reference to God, and is not merely taken as a regional assertion of some fact about man's being. Every theological assertion about man is made at that indefinable point where man vanishes from his own eyes into the mystery of God, and where, nonetheless, many precise statements are to be made about man, to prevent the concrete experiential determinations of other anthropologies becoming so rigid and immovable that they cannot escape him into the mystery of God.

b) *The basic principle*. (i) Man is a being who is referred to "God", whose self-understanding must be based on God and point towards him. This must not be taken as a "regional" assertion which says "something" about man to which much else could be added. Where man has not grasped this reference or where he has freely rejected it, he has lost sight of himself, of his essence as a whole, of what distinguishes him from an intramundane thing. In the light of what was said under a, iv, above, this truth could also be formulated by saying that man is referred to the absolute mystery. This means that in his self-knowledge and freedom he necessarily experiences himself – this being the condition of possibility of all actual and required knowledge and freedom – as at once translated beyond what is knowable (by clearly definable elementary data of experience), manageable and feasible into the region of the indefinable and incalculable. He realizes that it is in the light of this reference to the indefinable that he grasps and does the definable and thus differentiates himself as subject from the definable. This reference to the mystery is not a subsequent expansion of a perspicuous and manageable (and expanding) existence, but its condition and presupposition (in an inarticulate way), since it is only in this way that the gap between object and subject, subjectively realized in thought and action, is at all thinkable. The acceptance of reference to the mystery is the – implicit or explicit – acceptance of the existence of God as the perpetual ground of man's existence, since no finite being (because always at once transcended) nor "nothing" (if the term is not distorted by mystifications so that it no longer means nothing) can found this openness.

(ii) This reference of man to the mystery determines all the historical dimensions of man as subject. His perpetual relationship to his past is thereby displayed as his origin from a beginning not made by himself or within his own power but sent him freely by the mystery itself. His present is now the moment of free, responsible decision about the particular thing to be done here and now and hence about man himself. The future which he plans and must believe in is always a mere provisional stage in relation to the mystery. It is the question, unanswerable to man, as to how the mystery in which God presents and conceals himself, will freely and finally behave towards man.

(iii) The Christian faith professes that God is not merely the God far off, the unattainable though ever more approachable goal which summons and moves human existence. God wills to be, in self-communication, the "content" and future of man. With this, the Christian faith articulates the concrete reality and the ultimate meaning of man's being referred to the mystery, a reference experienced by every man and in the whole history of mankind (revelation considered as universal, and co-existent to the whole history of humanity). The distinction between nature and grace is made inasmuch as man experiences this self-communication of God as a free happening in his regard, as a marvel of God's personal love, while he also (being free with regard to his own existence) can culpably close himself to this self-communication of God. He thus recognizes the self-communication of God as "supernatural grace", and his own human reality, persisting even in saying no to the self-communication, as "nature".

(iv) Man achieves in the world and in history this essence which is demanded by the self-communication of God. Just as the reference to the mystery is the condition of possibility of the subject's mundane self-experience, so too conversely this reference is mediated by the world and history, since it is to be activated in freedom. This circle is endless. Man can never break out of it. He has its individual moments only in the constantly renewed achievement of the whole "circle" of his existence. Historical, mundane existence implies space, time, body, sex, society, though such concrete "existentiells" need not be deducible from the abstract notion of world and history as the permanent mediation of this relationship to God. It is precisely in their concrete, non-deducible factuality that they are mediation to God.

c) *The various aspects of human "nature"*. (i) Man is "spirit" or soul. This means that he is a reality which cannot be adequately described by the concepts and methods of natural science. He is "subject", that is, a "system" which is once more confronted with itself as a whole, and hence cannot simply be thought of on the lines of a computer made up of different parts, which, in spite of all built-in controls, cannot once more manipulate itself as a whole. Man is consciousness of self, knowledge whose horizon is in principle limitless, and freedom. This description of man as spirit should not at once be associated with the notion of a "part", which would, for instance, be the uncertain and questionable element, in contrast to the "material", scientifically verifiable reality of man, which, if its existence were granted, would live "in" the concrete matter of man. The declaration of the Council of Vienne that the *anima* is the *forma corporis* must be taken seriously. Man is really "substantially" one, and not the final addition of two beings, which could be thought of, at least, as originally existing in themselves. All man's characteristics, despite their real differences, must always be considered as determining the one man, and none of them can be adequately grasped except as applying to the whole, that is, when they are taken beyond themselves in an assertion which aims at the whole man. Hence man as spirit comes to be, phylogenetically and ontogenetically, through the creative act of God (see *Evolution* II A), in the sense that the self-transcendence of the material (biological) reality towards a spiritual corporeality and a corporeal spirituality is sustained, through the creative act of God, by the profoundest impulse of finite reality.

(ii) Man is "immortal" inasmuch as he is a spiritual subject. This means that the end of his spatio-temporal history really makes this history definitive. Here too it would be dangerous to confine the statement *a priori* to the "soul", as if it were a being-in-itself instead of a meta-empirical principle of being in the one man. Death is the end of the history of the whole man, since with it the history of his freedom ends. And the real completion of this history of the one man takes in (in his own way in each case) both what we call the immortality of the soul in the traditional sense and what is called the resurrection of the flesh in biblical and ecclesiastical terms. Both concepts envisage the definitive state of the free subject who has completed his history. We may or perhaps must suppose a "temporal" interval (as we have to imagine it) in the process of this one completion – a difference between personal completion as such and "bodily" completion, the latter being the completed manifestation and expansion of personal definitiveness into the "worldly" dimensions of human existence. But this is a question which need not engage our attention here.

It may perhaps be affirmed, with all due caution, without coming into conflict with the Fifth Lateran Council, that the immortality of "souls" which never were in a position to make a radically personal decision may be left an open question – which does not mean that it is to be answered in the negative. No one can say with certainty that there are such "souls", which never came, in any imaginable way, to a personal act of self-disposition ("adulthood"). But then, all "rational" arguments for the "immortality of the soul" always and necessarily envisage a spiritual subject which is responsible for itself before God. These are arguments which can only be applied with extreme caution to a mere "spiritual substance". We must finally consider that at least on the supposition (itself uncertain) that the spiritual soul comes to be at the moment of conception of new life, the vast majority of mankind would attain an "eternity" which is not the definitive result of a history of freedom. (We argue here on the general supposition that a personal human act is possible only when a certain age has been attained.) But this again is a very doubtful proposition, especially as we cannot say that eternal life acquired in freedom is less a grace than where (*ex supposito*) the completion is attained without passing through a history of freedom.

(iii) Man is a free being. See the article *Freedom*.

(iv) Man is both an individual personal subject with a unique history of freedom for which no one else can deputize, and at the same time a social being who can only have a history in the unity of the one humanity. He is never merely a numerical "case" of the collectivity, and he is never so much an individual that he could be himself without inter-communication with his fellows, without his "world". Both aspects bear upon each other. Inter-communication and self-realization, self-possession, grow in principle in like and not inverse proportion. Man's social orientation, taken in its totality, is not "subsidiary" in relation to the uniqueness of the individual free person but equally primordial and essential to it. And the social nature of man is again multi-dimensional: personal inter-communication (fellowship) in love, communication in the same truth and common cultural values and acquisitions, institutionalized society, biological and economic interdependence and so on. A single such dimension may no doubt be considered as subsidiary with regard to the human person as a whole. Antagonisms and conflicts occur between the various dimensions and "levels" of man as "individual" and between individual men (and so too with humanity, people, society, group and State). Their concrete mutual relationship is one of perpetual historical change.

(v) So too man is a sexual being. His sexuality should not be assumed from the start to be a regional faculty, that of generation in this case. It is a quality which affects all the regional determinations of man, in a different way in each case. Hence it too exists on many levels and shares in the historicity of man and his "indefinability", as spiritual being whose historical self-interpretation makes up his concrete essence but loses itself constantly in the mystery of God.

d) *The "supernatural" in man*. (i) The origin and goal of man's existence is the self-communication of God. See *Grace*, *Virtue*, *Salvation* I, III. This free self-communication of God, when consistently thought out in relation to the nature of historical man, has its own history. Hence it must reach a phase of victorious irreversibility, and has in fact reached in it in Jesus Christ. Hence it aims from the start at this point as its final cause, and so this self-communication is always (even in the supralapsarian order) Christological. Man was always willed as member of a humanity and sharer of a human history which attain their most proper structure and real hope of the future in the incarnation of the divine Logos, the eschatological climax of the divine self-communication.

(ii) The divine self-communication, as the free history of God himself, is also the ultimate ground and content of the history of man's freedom, in acceptance or rejection. But this is so only in the sense that while the outcome of the history of salvation of the individual remains open, the positive outcome of the collective history of man's salvation in Jesus Christ is already assured (cf. Vatican II, *Lumen Gentium*, art. 48). Man as such, mankind in its history, moves within the historical reality, already made manifest, of the absolute salvific will of God. The real self-alienation of man, who is only in possession of himself when attained victoriously by the self-communication of God which brings about the positive Yes of his freedom, has been fundamentally overcome since Jesus Christ. The individual's hope is assured when he inserts it into the sure hope of mankind, which is definitively triumphant in Christ.

Karl Rahner

PHENOMENOLOGY

1. *History of the concept.* The terms "phenomenon" and "appearance" contain a remarkable duality: *something* makes its *appearance.* We distinguish between what something is in and for itself (and for others) and the manner in which it shows itself to us. The phenomenon points back to a being ("in itself") which is different from the appearance, while the identity and difference which dominate this combination constitute the very nature and the problem of the phenomenon. Must we look to that which is, in and of itself, more than appears or is displayed to us – or *is* that which appears the being in question?

For the Greeks the phenomena were all that are immediately to hand or can be made such. Phenomena are met in the field of sensible perception (αἴσθησις) and have the mode of existence of the perceptible. Whether they are reliable or not is as yet undecided. A being can show itself other than it really is: "It only looks like that or as if." In this sense the phenomenon is also the merely apparent or illusory. Plato tried to decipher the "natural" mingling of being, appearance and illusion by defining being as the imperishable and infallible. In the medium of the *logos*, the "forms" "themselves" are revealed and distinguished from the changeable, manifold "appearances". Aristotle, more strongly orientated to the experiential, gave phenomena a new value. The phenomenal character forms the criterion in the realm of nature for the correctness of the assertions of the *logos.* Metaphysics and the "sciences", each in their own way, "clarify" the apparent disorder of the phenomena and explain them as a form in which the ideal or mathematical orders display themselves ("saving the phenomena").

Modern philosophy, partly in view of the change from mere observation to methodical experiment, mostly regards phenomena as the "objects" of the natural sciences. The phenomenon, within the terms of reference of the system of any given science, is the fact – which under certain methodological and technical conditions and modifications has sometimes to be produced for the first time. The phenomenon is then inseparable from the totality of the determinations which constitute it, so that it cannot be examined to see what it is "in itself" and without reference to the plurality of concomitant phenomena. The phenomenon is then purely "relative to . . .", without the least regard to its own reality. But this purely extrinsic reference is hardly thinkable in philosophy. The phenomenon is related to something "inward", the indeterminable "thing in itself" which is the ground, though not accessible at this level. Or, if this "transcendent" realm is negated, it represents the reality of consciousness, where the phenomena remain merely "the notions of something". Husserl put the relationship of that which appears and appearance into a new perspective, in which objects were to be explained through the mode in which they are given us in our consciousness (see 2).

The term "phenomenology" was apparently first used by J. H. Lambert, as the title of Part 4 of his *Neues Organon* (1764). This "doctrine of appearances" was to provide a clear distinction between truth and error. Herder, Novalis, Kant, Hegel, Blondel and others used the term in sometimes very different senses. Brentano and the early Husserl identified phenomenology with "descriptive psychology". The Husserlian schools of Göttingen and Munich regard phenomenology as a descriptive investigation of beings directed to objects. Husserl's own view must be understood from the start in terms of his "subjective" orientation. "The phenomenology of knowledge is the science of the phenomena of knowledge in a twofold sense: science of knowledge as appearances, representations, acts of consciousness, in which various objects are present, become conscious, passively or actively; and science of these objects themselves as they thus present themselves" (*Husserliana*, II, 14). Phenomenology has a special note of genuineness and strictness. It aims at returning to the originality of immediate experience. It seeks, for instance, the origin of (undemonstrated) logical concepts in a return to intuition. "We refuse absolutely to be content with 'mere words', that is, with a merely symbolical understanding of words . . . We wish to get back to the 'things themselves'" (*Logische Untersuchungen*, II, 1,5). On the history of the term "phenomenon" (Phenomenalism, etc.) see H. Barth, *Philosophie der Erscheinung*; on the history of phenomenology, see H. Spiegelberg.

2. *The phenomenology of Edmund Husserl.* The correlation between knowledge and knowledge of objects is the basic theme of Husserl. The "intentionality" (reference to object) in consciousness is not a subjective type of attention or the purposefulness of a conscious act. *In* our acts, we at once take cognizance of a "mateiial content" – an object. Phenomenology analyses this systematically as various modifications of intentionality (cf. also love, hatred, etc.) and also examines the various modes of presence of the object, as "intended" in each act. When a being is considered as it is given "in itself" in consciousness, the intentional analysis shows that each perception includes a number of "potentialities" not hitherto grasped reflectively by the consciousness. Their performance, "functioning anonymously", helps to adduce the whole object with its "environment" (*Umwelt*). Thus, for instance, every external perception includes "a pointer which goes from the aspects of the object actually grasped to facets as yet unperceived but only anticipated in expectation and for the moment in a non-intuited emptiness, coming nonetheless in perception: a constant 'pro-tention' which takes on new meaning with each phase of perception . . . a past horizon potentially full of memories to be awakened . . ." (*Husserliana*, I, 82). Consciousness is therefore knowing the further meaning of what is recognized (*Meinung seines Gemeinten*), going at every instant beyond its explicit content. Further analysis penetrates more and more into this hidden "life" of the anonymously functioning intentionality.

The results of this elementary analysis are as follows. a) We have no isolated sense impressions (cf. Kant), delivered as it were by purely receptive senses. b) The field of conscious "performances", along with the implications of its horizon, as opened up by the intentional analysis, allows of no "objectivism", goes at once beyond all simple schemas of subject-object, and allows no conclusion from the evidence (truth) to the truth of a proposition (factual). c) The many levels and fluidity of intentionality show that the *intentum* can "be a-being" in many ways, which means that there are many regional ontologies or that ontology has many dimensions. "Constitution" is the designation of intentionality, when it is radically grasped in its function as ground. The "how" of the given is not a raw datum in empirical observation. What is constituted is primordially there only *in* the synthetically structured act, wherein alone it can "build itself up". Hence constitution is anything but the "production" of idealism.

The more clearly reflection concentrates on the act itself – not on naive observation – the more urgent it appears that one must abandon the "natural" attitude. Consciousness is methodically consistent in refusing to use the positive and "worldly" elements of knowledge – including that of itself. In the various stages of "bracketing" (*epoche* – prescinding from) the mundane coefficients and in the reductions which reach the "absolute ego", a fundamental "transcendental re-appraisal" comes about. The newly-won "ground of being" of the absolute consciousness is open-ended and yet self-contained. It is a sphere in which all possible phenomena are "represented", as in the "primordial phenomenon".

Critical consequences of this development of phenomenology. a) The more the world is universally referred to the subjectivity of the consciousness, and the more the latter excludes itself and its relationship to the world, the greater is the problem posed by this transcendental consciousness which is prior to the world. What is its mode of being? "Who" is that? b) The question is not solved by the fact that the (temporal) self-constitution of the transcendental subjectivity takes place in the "living stream of the present" – the "passive genesis of self" – "transcendental life". Heidegger takes up the unexplained structural unity of the phenomenological subject and tries while investigating the mode of being of the "productive" subject to find also the "place" of the transcendental. Further problems posed by Husserl are: the possibility of an ultimate explanation within phenomenology; the relapse of what is transcendentally disclosed into the mode of being of the "positive" by the nature of its "positing"; the primacy of the explicitly envisaged in the investigation of the constitutive experience. Heidegger asks: What is the (mode of) being of the beings in which the "world" is constituted? Husserl gives no ontological analysis of "*being* conscious". Heidegger answers: The nature of human existence (which is more than just "concrete" consciousness) is precisely the mode of being which makes possible the transcendental constitution of the "world". Human existence is "being-in-the-world". But the analysis of existence depends on previously working out the question of the meaning of being. (A fundamental ontology is required.) The self-disclosure of phenomena for the phenomenology of conscious acts, and the "business itself" which must be interrogated according to the principles of phenomenology, is no longer consciousness and its objects but the being of beings. (This is a recourse to Aristotle and the problems of metaphysics.) The fundamental Cartesian attitude of Husserl made it impossible for him even later to exploit fully his analyses of "living-world", "historicity", "intersubjectivity" and so on. In greater or less proximity to Husserl and Heidegger, the phenomenology of the concrete consciousness has been extended by Sartre and Merleau-Ponty. A typical example is the analysis of corporeality and of bodily consciousness.

Phenomenology rightly considers itself an ontology. It cannot simply be extended into metaphysics, or skipped to reach metaphysics. The phenomenon must not be understood as an ontological devaluation because of its dependence on consciousness. There is always a great temptation to attribute to the "thing in itself" – whatever significance or substitute function is attributed to it – all being and the "highest" being, and to depreciate the "phenomenon" ontologically till it is a "mere representation". In some ways philosophy has never taken the phenomenon fundamentally enough – as the analysis of the "everyday world" and the problem of the constitution of the "thing" demonstrate. The exact relationship of phenomenology to a radically altered form of metaphysics has not yet been made clear.

3. *Phenomenology and theology.* Theology must not dismiss too quickly the notion of phenomenology, which is more than the mere observation and direct description of the raw materials of experience. But it is not a matter of breaking through to the "real" behind the phenomenon, with a supposedly theological thrust. Phenomenology will analyse the strictly religious act and experience to see how they grasp consistently the data of their objects. See *Experience*, *Mystery*, *Faith and Knowledge*, *God* I, *Holy*, *Revelation*, *Religion*.

Since phenomenology and hermeneutics can adapt themselves more fully to the various "modes of givenness", e.g., in the act of faith, they will prove to be methods of great importance to a future theology. They have their feet well enough planted on the ground, so to speak, of the actual phenomena of living faith, and will not dissolve it into an *abstract* transcendence. They can bring out the proper worldliness of faith without recourse to ideologies. Phenomenological and hermeneutic thinking has many advantages over the deductive style of formal logic. The recourse to the "evidence" is not to assure the truth of an experience assumed to be meaningful or to base it on a principle. The constitutive analysis brings out the meaning of the truth step by step from the *de facto* experience. Hence phenomenology does not really offer grounds from outside the thing itself, but effects the presence of the "business itself" in its own proper medium. "Thought" has then to secure for the assertion the conditions of intelligibility which are proper to the thing affirmed, bring its evidence directly to light and from the new encounter open up for itself unknown horizons, not merely applying pre-understanding. This then allows of a more radical approach to the word of the poet, the work of the artist and also to the original thought: the canon of themes and the "material" of theology are enlarged. Possibly too the adoption of these elements of construction can produce a reconciliation between methodological approaches which are as yet in conflict with each other – the anthropological, existential, theocentric and so on. Basically of course all great theologies have had a phenomenological perspective, even though they may have unduly obscured once more their experience by clothing it in an inappropriate language and world-view (see *Demythologization*). But now phenomenology has become an indispensable methodological tool of theology (see, for instance, B. Welte). When phenomenology is combined with hermeneutics (and linguistic analysis), it is preserved from a non-historical notion of essence, while hermeneutics can avoid a merely formal interpretation indifferent to the real content – a process which merely arouses historical memories but fails to transmit any universal claim or meaning.

Karl Lehmann

PHILOSOPHY AND THEOLOGY

A. Introductory

It is hard today to define philosophy. Any answer to what philosophy is proves to be itself one of the many philosophies which now exist. Naturally

– because philosophy differs from "regional" thinking by including its own nature in its thought and hence neither can nor will exclude anything from its questioning *a priori*. (Hence it can on principle take in a self-understanding of man based on revelation, since philosophy finds it at least a datum of history.) Then again, in spite of its claim to absolute "universality" in its object and methods, the historicity of man and the endless multiplicity of his (sources of) experience suggest strongly that there will be more than one philosophy (quite apart from disagreement among philosophers). And this pluralism is again a matter of conscious reflection, prior as such to the question of the truth of any particular philosophy. There are so many different themes, starting-points, terminologies, relationships to other sciences, and to philosophical tradition that no individual or small (efficient) team can take in the whole of philosophy, though they know that other philosophies exist besides their own. The question arises at once as to how theology is to deal with this – at least *de facto* – pluralism. Another question at once involved is how philosophy and theology can co-exist, since both claim to be basic sciences, that is, to throw light scientifically, methodically and consciously on existence as such and as a whole and hence to be universal. How can this be, when faith – and hence theology – judges all things and is itself judged by no man (cf. 1 Cor 2:15), while the same faith in its Catholic understanding rejects fideism and traditionalism and so recognizes a natural knowledge of God, a fundamental theology (preambles of faith) prior at least in a certain sense to the decision of faith, and (hence) philosophy as an independent activity of man (cf. *D* 1799 etc.)? The solution given by Vatican I, that the truth in both cases comes ultimately from the same God and hence cannot be contradictory, is not enough when taken by itself. For then it is postulated that the same results will be arrived at, but philosophy and theology are not shown to be reconciled in their claims to be sciences and methods, each universal in its own field. It is not clear whether one can be both a philosopher and a theologian or whether a choice has to be made. This is still true when one affirms that faith has a "healing" function, not only in the realm of moral action but also in the realm of natural knowledge, to counter its *de facto* errors, and that the Church has the right to claim that its magisterium is at least a negative norm for the Christian philosopher and his philosophy (*D* 1619, 1642–5, 1674, 1710–14, 1786, 1798f., 1815, 2085, 2146, 2305, 2325) – which would still leave room for a positive assessment of philosophy (Vatican II, *Gaudium et Spes*, arts. 44, 57, 62; *Optatam Totius*, arts. 14, 15). In answering this question, one should not be tempted to try to set a higher value on the independence of theology by stressing the discredit which now attaches to philosophy – "the end of metaphysics". At the very least, one would merely transfer the problem to the realm of science, inasmuch as it claims to be the heir to classical philosophy. The other problems which have to be discussed will be immediately clear.

B. The Fundamental Relationship between Philosophy and Theology

We prescind for the moment from the at least *de facto* pluralism of philosophies today, among which even the Church can no longer simply choose one particular philosophy as the only true one (in spite of what will be said under D below on "Christian philosophy"). We also prescind from the fact that philosophy cannot today be the only means by which the theological relevance of the "world" can be made clear to theology. The basic question is the possibility of the co-existence of two fundamental sciences in the Christian.

1. In approaching the question, it should first be noted that Catholic theology makes an essential distinction between nature and grace, and hence between natural knowledge of God and revelation. Hence by its very essence, it not merely tolerates philosophy but actually calls for it. Revelation and faith are not built up on the absolute incapacity of man (the sinner), and the failure of his thought. Then, it is a matter of history that theology has always used philosophical instruments in its thinking, and against modernism and all religions of feeling Catholic theology maintains that this historical process was justified. Revelation and grace are addressed from the outset to the whole man, and hence to the thinking man, and this claim to human thought is not a subsidiary element in the nature of religion. The believing Christian is as such always inspired by the conviction that spirit, nature and history are the creation, revelation and possession of God, who as the one truth is the source of all reality and truth and who has also given revelation by his words in history, to perfect and surpass the creation which is his own. There are things which lie outside the realm of reality in the world demarcated by historical revelation, the Church and theology. But the Christian does not see them as outside the realm of his God. Hence he may not and need not set an absolute value on theology, to the detriment of philosophy. If he did, he would be confusing his theology with his God. But the Christian in particular recognizes that there is a pluralism in the world, the unity of which is mastered positively and adequately by no one (apart from God), not even the Church and its theology. This is not, of course, to suggest that there could be a "double truth" in the sense of assertions which simply contradict one another while still remaining true.

On the other hand, if philosophy is to be the intellectual grasp of human existence as it actually is and in its whole breadth and depth – and even purely transcendental initiatives in philosophy have to have regard to the history of the spirit – philosophy cannot overlook the phenomenon of religion. Even where atheism is extolled as the true interpretation of existence and hence as "religion", religion remains everywhere and at all times part of the fundamental structures of human life. A philosophy which did not in some way include "philosophy of religion" and "natural theology" would be a poor kind of thing, since it would not be looking at its own subject-matter. (A tranquil atheism which behaves as if the religious question no longer existed either does not know what we mean by God or is a transparent technique of flight from God – and a pose.)

2. This second point, however, is decisive. Insofar as philosophy tries to be systematic transcendental reflection (and if it does not, it now falls under the heading of a non-philosophical discipline), it cannot by its very nature claim to be a concrete, salutary and adequate interpretation of existence. Hence it is impossible for it to claim to replace the concrete and historical reality of religion – and so its theology.

Philosophy might try to be more than such transcendental reflection ("mediation"), and attempt the concrete introduction into real existence, which can never be exhaustively analysed but still remains as such imperative and inexorable. This would be an effort to generate an actual religion, and philosophy would then be the manifold unity of theology and philosophy. It would be both *a priori* self-understanding and revelation, under the guise of philosophy – or it would be a false theology, because mostly secularized. It would then be a question of terminology and of the correct analysis of the one comprehensive attempt to master existence. The analysis would show that this existence was something which could never be adequately mastered by reflection – the unity of the *a priori* of the spirit and of history, of reason and revelation, of theology and philosophy.

But if, in keeping with its whole tradition, philosophy regards itself as transcendental reflection, it can never materially embrace the whole concrete nature of existence, even though the concrete is known to be a ground of existence and not regarded as an indifferent residue. Historicity is less than real history, concrete love is more than subjectivity formally analysed ("one can and ought to love"), experienced dread is more than the concept of this basic condition in which man finds himself. But such assertions are self-determinations of philosophy. They are therefore among the fundamentals of philosophy, inasmuch as it is the "first" (basic) science, to which as such no other science can be prior (as ground) – nothing in fact except the actual reality which is greater than it. But then philosophy, as the doctrine of the transcendence of the spirit, points on to God as the absolute mystery "in person". As anthropology and philosophy of religion, it makes man a possible "hearer of the word" of this living God (perhaps already under the influence of the supernatural existential). And as pure reflection and never-ending mediation it sends man – who finds himself historically and not merely reflectively – to history itself for his real existence. Hence philosophy, by nature, is not the type of basic science which would claim to be the sole illumination and master of the concrete existence of man. If it rightly understands itself and its own freedom (freed by the secret grace of God), it is the first conscious light on existence which gives man courage to take history and the concrete seriously. But then it opens up for man the possibility of finding God in concrete history, where God has communicated himself to man in the incarnation.

3. Revelation in the concrete, and hence the Church and its magisterium, make the claim – necessarily, by their nature – to represent the whole of reality (as supreme principle and salvation of all things). By virtue of the unity of his existence, therefore, the Christian qua believer, living this unity and hierarchical gradation in faith, cannot treat the doctrine of the Church as simply indifferent and irrelevant to him qua philosopher. For his philosophy as such this doctrine is not a source of truths, but it is at least a *norma negativa* (cf., for instance, *D* 1675, 1703f., 1711, 1714, 1810). In view of the permanent distinction between philosophy and theology demanded by theology itself, this does not mean that there must always be a positive synthesis (comprehensible in terms of the historicity of man) which man must be able to grasp as he gives himself to philosophy and theology. He may and must leave the ultimate unity of his philosophical and theological destiny to the one God of philosophy and theology, who is always greater than either or both.

C. Philosophy in Theology

We prescind here from what is no doubt the more important problem philosophy in the original revelation. Its first utterances and the traditions by which they were handed on were in human concepts and propositions, within mental frames of reference, which existed prior to and independently of (the word of) revelation, though they were no doubt also modified by that revelation. These concepts, propositions and mental horizons involve a certain historically generated self-understanding of man which is due in part to philosophy or is the material of philosophy in a spontaneous, pre-scientific state. This self-understanding may be termed rightly a pre-scientific philosophy.

Leaving this aside, we must at any rate note that theology – in contrast to revelation and preaching – is a reflection on revelation and Church preaching. The theologian, questioning and critical in both directions, confronts revelation with his whole understanding of existence, on which he has also reflected philosophically to some extent. This confrontation, in the concrete situation, is to help him really to assimilate revelation, to interpret it as it affects him, to eliminate misunderstandings by an effort of criticism – and vice versa, to allow his own pre-existent mental horizons to be called in question by revelation. This means that in theology one necessarily "philosophizes". Such "philosophical" self-understanding (implicit or explicit) which the theologian brings with him is (at least) one of the forces which divide theology from revelation and set it in motion. This philosophical start of theology is possible because revelation is a call to and a claim on the whole existence of man and is therefore open at once to the self-understanding of man. And revelation itself also contains some such self-understanding, philosophical, pre-philosophical or originally philosophical but having relapsed into the apparent obviousness of ordinary life and common sense. Those who think that they must not "philosophize" when doing theology merely fall victim to a dominant philosophy which is unconsciously accepted or confine themselves to edifying discourse which does not discharge the theologian's task. To do philosophy in theology does not mean that a closed philosophical "system" is presupposed as permanently valid and directly applicable. Philosophy may in fact be somewhat "eclectic" in reflecting the unsystematic pluralism of the history of human experience and thought, and it must be ready to undergo changes in its theological use.

D. The Problem of "Christian Philosophy"

If such a thing exists at all, it must remain philosophy in principles and method, and aim at being nothing else. Otherwise it would not be philosophy as a fundamental science. Philosophy can be the "ancilla" of theology, that is, a mere element in a higher totality towards which it points of its own nature, only if it remains free. Theology too must not be afraid of open-ended dialogue, not steered in a certain direction from the outset by man himself and the Church. Theology must also be prepared to listen to things that it does not know *a priori*.

The philosopher can be "Christian" inasmuch as he accepts his Christian faith as a negative norm. This is not contrary to philosophical principles, as has been shown under B above.

A philosophy can be called Christian inasmuch as it received impulses from Christianity to do its own work. Without such impulses it would not have been what it is in fact.

A philosophy will also be Christian when the philosopher who is a Christian strives for the greatest possible convergence between his philosophy and his faith, and so with his theology, without overlooking the essential difference and disproportion between the two realms, and hence the asymptotic nature of his effort. Such effort prevents his assuming a harmony between philosophy and faith with no threat of tension, and also forbids him to take refuge in a "double truth".

A philosophy can also be Christian when it uses philosophical methods – with the help of the history of religion – to analyse Christianity as a *de facto* phenomenon in the philosophy and phenomenology of religion. This is legitimate, since philosophy is essen-

century. The first half of the 18th century was its heyday but it made itself felt in 19th-century revivalism and is still a force even today (e.g., among the Moravian Brethren and some types of Methodism). Pietism does not look on the Reformation as a mere occurrence in the past that is now embodied in an institution, but as an event that the Church must constantly actualize if Christ's kingdom is to be a living reality. The substance of all pietism is a longing for *praxis pietatis*, the "exercise of godliness". For pietism, the real purpose of redemption is to bring the religious subjectivity of man into lively, spontaneous play, and such is also the main interest in theology. There is no difficulty in the old-established Protestant denominations about stressing a subjective approach, but radical pietism has the effect of loosening Church bonds.

Calvinist pietism derives from 17th-century English Puritanism. John Bunyan (d. 1688), author of *The Pilgrim's Progress*, held that salvation is communicated in a "break-through" which one feels happening at a particular moment. Preachers driven from England brought this Puritan idea to Holland, where it soon spread. J. Labadie led the first group of pietists who formed a separate Church (1669). Calvinist pietism was sustained through the efforts of Gerhard Tersteegen (d. 1769), composer of many hymns, Samuel Kollenbusch (d. 1803), G. D. Krummacher (d. 1837), and H. F. Kohlbrügge (d. 1875).

P. J. Spener's *Pia Desideria* (1675) marks the first appearance of German Lutheran pietism. He set down the classic programme of pietism in his six proposals for reform. The *collegia pietatis* which he founded soon proved to foster separatism, and therefore met with much opposition from the authorities of the official Church. Spener's work was continued in the pietism of Halle, notably by Spener's disciple August Hermann Francke. Being a professor of theology (1691) and the founder of an orphanage with a college attached to it (1695), Francke was able to exert a very pervasive influence on the religious, intellectual and social life of his time. His orphanage contributed towards shaping the spirit of Prussia and the minds of many philosophers of early German Idealism. It soon became a centre for foreign and Jewish missions, for the distribution of the Bible, and for the care of the Protestant diaspora in South-Eastern Europe and North America. Francke gave pietism an educational theory of its own; guided by the experience of his own conversion, he educated children in view of leading them to conversion.

Count Nikolaus Ludwig of Zinzendorf, who had been a member of the Halle group, created an independent pietist body by founding the settlement of Moravian Brethren at Herrnhut. They adopted an imaginative form of religious life, blending pre-Reformation traditions with the spirit of Luther (their own calendar of feasts, congregations divided into choirs, etc.). The zealous life led at Herrnhut left a mark on Protestant piety that has endured to the present day (the "watchwords of the Brethren"). Pietism in Württemberg powerfully affected the existing Church there. In J. A. Bengel and F. C. Oetinger it was combined with mystical speculation (from Jakob Böhme, E. Swedenborg) to produce a devotion based on literal interpretation of the Bible. It greatly influenced German Idealism and 19th-century Protestant theology (J. T. Beck, d. 1878; Adolf Schlatter, d. 1938).

Compared with these schools of thought, radical pietism had only a transitory influence, owing to its anti-ecclesiastical enthusiasm. Still it can boast a number of important personalities, above all Gottfried Arnold (d. 1714). His *Impartial History of Churches and Heresies* (1699) is the first large-scale attempt to present the history of the Church since NT times as the progressive decay of Christian life.

Pietism in general must be seen as part of the great process whereby modern man has been discovering his own autonomous subjectivity. Pietism is a grandiose attempt to refer this process back to the sources of Christian life. Emancipated from tradition, autonomous man is to decide the shape of his own religious life by confronting the Bible and contemplating the situation of the primitive Christian community. No doubt the understanding of faith largely in terms of religious life, as it can be actually led and experienced, released considerable moral and religious energies and ensured that pietism would make its mark on the history of the spirit. Protestantism is indebted to pietism for more than stimulation of missionary activity, of religious instruction and education, and thus of personal piety. Having to conduct controversy with the impatient and lively pietist mind gave official theology a flexibility in its understanding of religion that enabled it more than anything else to enter upon constructive discussion with the post-Christian intellectual life of modern times. In particular, by reviving appreciation of Scripture, pietism helped to pave the way for modern biblical science. Thus it ultimately helped to liberalize the rigid outlook of the various denominations.

Stressing, however, subjective independence at the expense of tradition, pietism was always in danger of forgetting that the life of faith is an open-ended discussion with history. All forms of pietism are prone to look on religious subjectivity as the actual source of religious life, so that doctrine becomes a purely pragmatic function of that life. Looking for verifiable conversion in the Christian, regarding the converted person as an *ecclesiola in ecclesia*, imperils the concept of grace, makes the Christian fellowship an arbitrary association of religious individuals, and at worst leads to separatism. The heir of pietism and the champion of modern Protestantism, Schleiermacher, has drawn the logical conclusion as instructively as could be wished: religious experience becomes the criterion according to which one selects such points of tradition as one cares to consider still valid. The ambivalence of pietism shows the task which the preaching of the faith will have in coping with modern subjectivity.

Wenzel Lohff

PLATONISM

A. Meaning

The meaning of Platonism depends on how the work of Plato is assessed, and which elements are considered essential and characteristic. Till the beginning of the 19th century, Plato was considered above all for his contribution to ontology, natural theology and cosmology. This was the view transmitted through the interpretation and continuation of Plato's philosophy by his pupils Aristotle, Speusippus and Xenocrates, by Middle Platonism (Plutarch, Albinus, Apuleius, etc.) and by neo-Platonism. The *Timaeus*, which deals with cosmology (Latin translation and commentary by Chalcidius, 4th–5th century A.D.) was probably the dialogue which had the greatest influence down to the Middle Ages. The effort to understand Plato independently of the neo-Platonist tradition began with Schleiermacher's translation and commentary. The writer, artist and the philosophical significance of the dialogue form came to the fore. Plato was seen as the setter of problems and dilemmas rather than as the constructor of systems. Stress was laid on his dialectic (Hegel), his epistemology (neo-Kantianism: Natorp), and his political and pedagogical theories. Recent research points to the historical justification of the neo-Platonist and medieval interpretations. It does not base itself solely on the dialogues, like Schleiermacher, but also on the lecture "On the Good", preserved only in the later writings of his disciples. The work had considerable influence on the traditions of the school. It is not certain whether the work was first produced in Plato's old age or whether the system here apparent was already at work behind all the dialogues.

B. Basic Themes

1. *The form* (*idea*). Plato's starting-point was the ethical investigations of Socrates, whose debate with the relativism of the Sophistic Enlightenment was concerned with the establishment of an inviolable norm for moral action. Man cannot be good, just, brave, and so on, unless he knows what is the goodness, justice, courage, etc., which remains the same in all situations. Hence Socrates sought for definitions of the general concepts of ethics.

According to Plato, the moral norm cannot be derived from experience. For no particular good action is good from every respect. The good man is not necessarily always good. The action is good and the man is good, but they are not the good. There is need of a spiritual vision which grasps the good in its perfect and unchangeable "form" (εἶδος, ἰδέα). Plato then transferred this doctrine from the ethical to all predicates. Their application to visible things, in the judgment, presupposes an *a priori* knowledge of them. In the proposition, "These two pieces of wood are the same size", the concept of equality cannot be derived from experience, since this only offers objects of approximate equality. But the presupposition of this knowledge of "equality itself" is that it has an object. Hence ideal essences must exist apart from perceptible things. In contrast to the changing visible things which include a variety of aspects, the forms are unchangeable, simple and true reality, which remains constantly at one with itself (ὄντως ὄν) (*Phaedo*, 74a–75c).

2. *Participation and analogy*. If the vision of the forms is to give us a true judgment of the things perceived through outward show, the world of the forms (κόσμος νοητός) cannot be fully separated from the visible world (τόπος ὁρατός), in spite of the difference of being. The thing participates in the form (μέθεξις, participation). The being which is immutable and necessary is present in the changeable and contingent (παρουσία: immanence of the transcendent). But it is a being (οὐσία) which is realized only in an imperfect way in the visible thing. Since the form represents the good, all things "strive" to be like it; it is the archetype and goal (τέλος) for whose sake they exist. The various degrees of participation set up an analogy between beings, which is illustrated by means of a line in which two unequal divisions are made. The smaller represents the realm of the visible, the larger that of the intelligible. The sections are then divided again in the same proportions. The lower sections of the visible stand for shadows and bodily things, those of the intelligible for mathematical proportions and forms (*Republic*, 509d–511a). The meaning of the simile is that the visible and the intelligible are as different from each other (χωρισμός) by virtue of their being as shadows and reflections are from real things. But just as the thing is reflected in the shadow, so too the intelligible appears in the visible (μέθεξις). The visible has only the being of a reflection, but as an image, it points to the archetypal being. The shadows (or words) can lead to sight of the things, the things to knowledge of mathematical laws and these to the vision of the forms.

The analogous participation brings

about degrees of being, which the *Symposium* (210a–212a) expounds with reference to the beautiful, which is the only form which can be grasped in sensible as well as spiritual vision. The beauty of individual beings is a less perfect presence of the form of the beautiful than the beauty of all bodily things. This again is only a stage which leads to the beauty of morals and laws, which point in turn to that of the sciences and through them to the unchangeable ultimate beauty. The lecture "On the Good" illustrates by analogy and participation the model of the mathematical sequence of the one (ἕν) and the dyad (δυάς) (the latter as the principle of multiple positing of the one) – numbers – lines – surfaces – bodies. The principles of unity and duality are present in all subsequent "dimensions" and also transcend them. So too the higher are contained in the following "dimensions".

3. *Ascent and dialectic.* The human soul possesses an *a priori* knowledge of the mathematical proportions and the forms, of which it had vision in a pre-existence and which can be awakened through instruction and sensible perception (ἀνάμνησις). Hence man can know the structure of being at the level of the forms. Plato distinguishes the method of mathematical knowledge (διάνοια) from that of edietic (νόησις or ἐπιστήμη or dialectic) (*Republic*, 510b–511e). The mathematician starts from untested presuppositions (ὑποθέσεις) from which he draws conclusions. He proceeds deductively. He cannot reduce his axioms to some ultimate principle. And he must also invoke the aid of sensible intuition. The dialectician examines the conclusions from his hypotheses to see if they are free from contradiction. If they are not, he rejects the hypothesis and proposes another. Otherwise he looks for a higher hypothesis which is contained in the previous as its presupposition and from which the latter can be deduced as its consequence. The procedure is continued till a first principle (ἀρχή) is reached which has no presuppositions and cannot be derived from anything else. This is the form of the good (ἀγαθόν) or the One. The dialectical ascent takes place without the help of the visible. From the form of the good the dialectician can then descend to the individual forms. The good itself is beyond the forms (ἐπέκεινα τῆς οὐσίας, *Republic*, 509b). Each form partakes of the good (just as in its quality of ideal number it partakes of the One) and is ordained to the good as its end or goal, as is particularly clear from the forms in the ethical realm. Thus the relation of things to the forms as their exemplars and goals has a parallel in the relation of the various forms to the good, the One, as the Absolute. The seventh epistle (341cd) describes the knowledge of the highest beings in the language of later mysticism: through long familiarity with the truth, a light is "suddenly" enkindled in the soul and this light then nourishes itself.

The dialectical ascent is not to be separated from its ethical goal. Man is to know the good in order to be himself good. Knowledge serves the "assimilation to God" (ὁμοίωσις τῷ θεῷ) which consists of man's growing just and pious through insight (*Theaetetus*, 176b). The philosopher is to return from the vision of the good to political reality. The dialectic of the later dialogues (*Phaedrus*, *Sophist*, *Statesman*, *Philebus*) displays greater interest in logic. It is concerned with the division of concepts (διαίρεσις), their hierarchical arrangement and the possibility of uniting them in the judgment. Plato shows in the *Sophist* that there is non-being even in the realm of the forms. The identity of each form with itself implies a difference as regards the non-identical forms and hence that it "is not – they.

4. *Soul, State, cosmos.* Since the unchangeable forms have no efficient

causality, another principle is needed to co-ordinate the world of becoming with that of being. This principle is the soul. It moves itself and the inert, and is therefore immortal (*Phaedrus*, 245c–e). Plato compares it to the objects of mathematics. Like them, it is between the form and the appearance. The totality of beings is reflected in the soul as in the realm of mathematics. Hence it can know all beings. As Eros, the soul is the desire of ascending to the eternal essences and of rendering them visible in the world of becoming. Since it is a principle of movement it can bring about participation. The threefold division of the human soul expresses its intermediate position. The rational or spiritual soul is endowed with thought, and its function includes that of guiding the other parts of the soul. Its immortality and its affinity with the forms is proved in the *Phaedo*. The lowest part is the instinctive passionate soul (ἐπιθυμητικόν), while the courageous (θυμοειδές) is the bridge between them. Plato's myths of the other world affirms the freedom and responsibility of man. The Platonic State follows the structure of the soul. There are three corresponding classes: the ruling class of the philosophers, the warriors and the providers. The analogy of structure is based on the common end: both soul and State are to realize the good in the visible order. Each part of the soul and the State is ordained to a virtue: the first to wisdom or prudence, the second to courage and the third to self-discipline. The co-operation of the parts leads to justice. The harmonious movement of the cosmos is ascribed to the world-soul. According to the myth of the *Timaeus*, this is directly created by the Maker of the World (δημιουργός), who arranges the all according to the ideal pattern of the "perfect soul", since he is good and without envy and wishes that all should be as like him as possible. Through the world-soul, divine providence (πρόνοια) makes the world an animated and rational living thing. The demiurge uses the rest of the matter from which he made the world-soul to make the immortal part of the human soul. Since Aristotle and Xenocrates the question has been asked as to whether the myth of the Timaeus teaches that the world had a beginning in time, or merely its dependence on a cause. But the debate is of secondary importance compared to the central philosophical assertion that the visible world participates in the good. It is an image of the order of the forms and so has the good as its end and goal. The rational soul is the cause of this participation and finality. The order of the cosmos is knowable because the law of the cosmos is also the law of the human spirit.

Friedo Ricken

POLITICAL THEOLOGY

The term "political theology" is used in present-day theology in the context of a definite set of problems and ideas. This context must be taken into account, because the term could be ambiguous and misleading, as well as being historically "loaded". The actual term comes from Stoicism which divided theology into three parts, mythical, natural and political (cf. Varro in St. Augustine, *De Civitate Dei*, VI, 5). In Rome, political theology took precedence over natural theology (in contrast to the Hellenistic tradition). Here it was used to justify theologically the primacy of politics and the "absolute" claims of the State. This political theology of Rome was revived in the Renaissance. It was championed by such writers as Machiavelli and Hobbes, and by the French traditionalists of the 19th century with their notion of restoring the "Christian State".

1. This notion of political theology was in force until Romanticism, when social conditions forced it to take on a

restorative and integralist tinge or voluntarist traits. But in present-day theology, when dealing with the hermeneutics of basic problems, it has the two following aspects.

a) Political theology is a critical corrective of a certain tendency to confine theology to the realm of the private and personal, as in its transcendental, existential and personalist forms. There is a tendency to reduce the heart of the Christian message and the practical exercise of faith to the decision of the individual standing apart from the world – a reaction to the separation between religion and society as suggested by the Enlightenment. Here political theology intervenes, not in the sense of a spontaneous, pre-critical identification of religion and society, but as a new deliberate effort to define the relationship.

In this effort at critical correction, political theology aims at "nationalization" – taking theological concepts, and the language of preaching and spirituality out of the private realm. It tries to overcome the exaggerated esotericism of discourse about God, the stubborn opposition between private spiritual life and social freedom, which is obviously widening the universal gap between what theology and preaching put forward as peremptory and what the Christian in fact lives by and surrenders to.

b) Political theology is now also the effort to formulate the eschatological message of Christianity in the conditions of present-day society, taking into account the changes of structure in public life. In other words, it is an effort to overcome a purely "passive" hermeneutic of Christianity in the context of present-day society. Society is not regarded as a secondary object of Christian activity. And it is not a matter of the Christian claim to be heard in public on the local, national and international level – a claim which seems always to be more or less coloured by the desire for political power. Human society is seen primarily as an essential medium for the discovery of theological truth and for Christian preaching in general.

2. In this sense, political theology is not primarily a new theological discipline among others, with a regional task of its own. And it is not simply a sort of "applied theology" – theology applied to politics and human society. It cannot then be simply identified with what is called in theology "political ethics" or with what was aimed at by the laudable movements of a social theology or the "Social Gospel". Political theology claims to be a basic element in the whole structure of critical theological thinking, motivated by a new notion of the relation between theory and practice, according to which all theology must be of itself "practical", orientated to action. Only when this fundamental interest of political theology is ignored can it be mistaken for a theology dabbling in politics, i.e., in direct contact with socio-political public life, which would be wrong. It is in fact one of the aims of political theology and its society-directed thinking to prevent the Church and theology being saddled as it were unwittingly with this or that political ideology.

3. This political theology sees everything in the light of the eschatological message of Jesus. But it takes the new standpoint provided by the critical reason, for which the way was paved by the Enlightenment and which was given articulate expression at least since the middle of the 19th century, since Hegel and Marx. In the wake of the purely Idealist and then the personalist and existentialist traditions, the value of this approach had long been underestimated or obscured in the eyes of theologians. The distinctive feature of the new starting-point is the fundamental relation between reason and society, the society-directed character of critical

reflection, the compulsion felt by the critical reason to consider itself in the light of society and the impossibility of the critical reason's justifying its claims "on the level of pure reasoning". Thus the classical problem of the relation between faith and reason appears once more in political theology on this new plane. And the basic "hermeneutic problem" of theology is not primarily the relation between systematic and historical theology, between dogma and history. It is rather the problem of the understanding of faith and society-directed practice.

a) *The new theory-practice relationship, theologically*. In the context of new developments in Protestant theology after Bultmann, especially in J. Moltmann and W. Pannenberg, political theology stresses the basic nature of eschatology and brings the eschatological message of the kingdom of God into the foreground of theological thinking in a new way. It thus tries to do justice to the close and intrinsic link between God and the coming reign of God in the NT tradition. The futurity of this lordship of God is an intrinsic and permanent element of theological assertion about the Godhead of God. The category "future" and the society-directed category of "kingdom" and reign of God become fundamental in all theological reflection. For if the promised "new world" corresponds to the Godhead of God, the truth of God's Godhead cannot in any way be adequately conceived under the conditions of the present. The world as it exists at any given moment cannot be a sufficient basis for the understanding of this truth. Only a change of the present age and of the conditions which make its insights possible can give access to the future truth of the Godhead of God. A theology which takes seriously the eschatological nature of its "object" is necessarily orientated, as a condition of possibility of thought, i.e., transcendentally, to an articulation of its self-understanding which will be directed to action (J. Habermas).

This is the perspective in which political theology regards the new theory-practice relationship as propounded in the dialectical philosophies of history (with the history of revolutions in mind) in the 19th century, especially since Hegel, and in the tradition of the Hegelian Left. It does not see it as a poor version of Christian eschatology in popular terms, as the degradation of this eschatology into blue-prints of a self-contained world history and social utopias. It sees it as a token that the eschatological sense of crisis here becomes part of historical (world) consciousness (cf. J. Habermas). Thus political theology undertakes to confront critically a philosophical tradition which was too little considered in modern theology. Recent systematic theology (and Catholic theology chiefly where it broke out of the neo-Scholastic system) debated the transcendental philosophy of Kant, German Idealism and its successors in personalism and existentialism. But the tradition of the Hegelian Left with its characteristic sketch-plans of the philosophy of history was more or less lost sight of. Political theology also takes up the discussion with the critique of religion based on this philosophy, where it appeared as critique of ideologies. Religion was there seen as a derivative function of certain social practices and power groups. The notion of "false conscience" was used to explain the religious believer in terms of a society as yet unaware of its nature.

b) *Public affairs, theologically*. Taking into consideration the world situation which has felt the impact of the Enlightenment and secularization, political theology tries to study afresh the relationship to public life and human society which is implicit in the NT message of salvation, forgiveness and reconciliation. It insists that the trial is on, on a capital charge, between the eschatological message of the kingdom

tially a fundamental science. But in practice, the distinction between such philosophy and a theology working philosophically will be fluid.

E. Philosophy, Theology and Modern Science

The *de facto* relationship between philosophy and theology has been changed by the extensive pluralism of present-day philosophies, which in this age of historicism, of the "one world" and the greater range of communication media is perceived at once as existing and irremediable. But the relationship has also been changed by the fact that philosophy is no longer the unique and not even in fact the primary mediation of the "world" for theology, whose work is done in contact with the world. Here too philosophy is now accompanied by the modern sciences (of history, nature and society). And these do not consider themselves branches of a single philosophy, though they undoubtedly recognize philosophy as their origin. But they do not allow philosophy to prescribe to them their self-understanding, their nature and their methods. They are rather inclined to regard philosophy as superfluous for contact with existence, or as an afterthought which analyses formally the methods of the autonomous sciences. Whether this self-understanding of the modern non-philosophical sciences is fully justified or not is another question. But the fact is there, and theology has to take it into account. The sciences are also partners in a dialogue which has effects on both sides. Theology has then to consider the various methods and results of these sciences, and as well as this, the basic mentality of modern science and its titillating situation with regard to knowledge (an irreducible pluralism of sciences). Theology must also try to help the scientist to maintain his human dignity in face of this situation of concupiscence (which can at times be a spiritual schizophrenia).

F. Philosophical Teaching in the Church

In spite of the pluralism of philosophies today, which will never be thoroughly synthesized, and which also evokes a parallel pluralism in theology, certain points must be maintained. The *one* Church with the one confession and the one magisterium for all its members cannot but have a theology which is to some extent identical throughout. The Church needs it for the interpretation and preservation of the one confession of faith, and it can even imply a certain regulation of terminology beyond what is demanded by the nature of the matter in question. Such a standard theology, homogeneous to some extent, in terminology and so on, at the disposal of the magisterium, implies also a certain teaching philosophy, standardized in methods, in concepts, presupposed as accepted and current, etc. – in spite of remaining in the stream of historical development. It may of course be asked whether such a Church philosophy is still philosophy in the strict sense, or is really nothing more than a language and mental horizon which may indeed have been taken over from philosophy but now represents only the general mentality of an epoch in its unreflecting and non-systematic state.

But this stock of standard philosophy does exist. It is necessary in a theology which is demanded by the oneness of the confession of faith. It must still be respected and cherished, though this ecclesiastical teaching philosophy cannot close its mind to outside factors or claim to call itself the *philosophia perennis* in the manner of the neo-scholasticism of the last century (cf. Vatican II, *Optatam Totius*, art. 15).

Karl Rahner

PIETISM

Pietism is a comprehensive term for a widespread and manifold movement within Protestantism in the early 17th

of God and any given form of social and political life, in its various historical changes. It does not deny the legitimate individual relationship to God (as an element of the NT in contrast to OT tradition), but it affirms that the central promises of the reign of God in the NT – freedom, peace, justice, reconciliation – cannot be made radically private affairs. They cannot be entirely interiorized and spiritualized as corresponding to the individual's longing for freedom and peace. They make the individual free with regard to the political society around him, in the sense of committing him to it in a free critique of it. The view of the society-directed, "public" character of the gospel promises can be distorted in two main ways.

(i) The first mistake is to follow the type of political theology which was worked out in early Christian tradition under the influence of the metaphysics of the State in Rome. It becomes a "political Christology" (H. Schmidt) or a "political monotheism" (E. Pedersen), in which a dangerous fallacy turns the kingdom of God into a political entity. This meant, in the Constantinian age, that political theology could be the direct successor of the religious ideology of the State in ancient Rome. This way of giving the Christian message a political bearing has had a detrimental effect up to the present day, distorting the fundamental society-directedness of the NT message and barring the way to an unambiguous use of the term "political theology". Indirectly too this line of tradition had questionable effects. Particularly since Augustine, there was an understandable critical reaction to this ideological degradation of Christian eschatology. The content of the promises was unduly interiorized, spiritualized and individualized.

(ii) There is another misapprehension which hinders a proper grasp of the "public" nature of the eschatological message. Its critically negative function – negativity which is a liberation – is commonly overlooked. When the public element of the message is emphasized, the spectre of a Christian or ecclesiastical neo-integralism is conjured up, as if political theology sought to undermine a secularized and religiously emancipated society and infiltrate it with "restorative" tendencies. But in fact political theology tries to take this "secularized" world seriously, as the starting-point of theology and preaching. This does not mean "emancipating it" unconditionally by eliminating the social bearings of the eschatological message, as in many modern theological theories of secularization. It means that it asserts its essentially universal categories "only" as a negative critique in this society. Being a particular element in society, Christianity can only formulate the decisiveness ("absoluteness") and universality of its message without falling into an ideology when it formulates it as critical negation (of and in given situations).

This shows that when political theology brings out the public nature of the Christian message, it does not relapse into a direct challenge to the socio-political world. There are two reasons. One is that Christianity and its message cannot be simply identified with a given political institution (in the narrow sense). For there is no political party which can be merely such a critique. And no political party can take as its platform – without falling in the end into Romanticism or totalitarianism – that which forms the horizon of the critical stipulation of Christianity: the totality of history as reserved eschatologically to God. (The "whole of history under the eschatological reserve of God" sums up the negative critique. There is nothing intramundane which can be identified as the motive force of all history, so that it could take the coming of all history as the programme of its political action.) On the other hand, the "negative conscience", the critical attitude to society in which the public claim of the gospel makes itself heard, must not be underestimated. Its critical contestation of socio-political conditions is a "determinate negation". It flares up in criticism of very definite conditions. Being a critical attitude to society, it may well take the form, under certain conditions, of revolutionary protest.

This negative voicing of the gospel is not the void and vagueness of the "purely negative". It has within it a powerful force for the positive. New possibilities are opened up in and through this critical negation, though only by going right through and out of it (a strictly dialectical process). It gives contour to the formal figure of Christian hope, inasmuch as the promised fulfilment in the resurrection of Jesus Christ can only be attained through the "death-dealing" negation of the existing world, such as is expressed in the message of the crucifixion of Jesus.

The other reason why political theology is not a direct challenge to society is that problems of political rule can never be strictly reduced to the single dimension of technological rationalization (cf. H. Marcuse). The political decision itself – above and beyond all technological planning – remains orientated to debatable goals. The process of rationalization undertaken by political action itself always has a certain horizon of utopian interests. This may be denied by the pragmatism that takes decisions in the dark, but the horizon cannot be eliminated and must be answered for ("dialectically"). If this is regarded as the site of the theoretical decisions of Christianity's critique of human society, its utterance cannot be open to the suspicion of being a direct and therefore misplaced challenge to the social and political realm.

4. Political theology as described above could also be termed "dialectical theology", in view of its methodology and the historical problems which form its context. But it is not a dialectical theology in the sense of the early Barth, where it indicates that the God-man relationship is a paradox which cannot be resolved (and hence too works non-historically). It is dialectical theology in the sense of a historical communication of the biblical message, in which communication of the message attests its transcendence in a critical, liberating "over-riding" of existing conditions.

5. Political theology can and must also propound the central truths of theology in the light of its statement of the relation between faith and society-directed reason. It displays the Christian faith in the form of freedom to be critical of society, and the Church as the homeland of this freedom to which the Christian knows that he is called in face of the eschatological message.

a) *Faith, hope and love as the form of freedom to criticize society.* "Dogmatic faith" appears here as acceptance of doctrinal propositions in which a perilous past is remembered and revived, which means that the claim of promises held out and hopes experienced are called to mind to break the spell of the predominant mentality – and its "repressions" – by a critical thrust. Hope appears as the protective criticism which liberates the individual so that he can definitely reject any totalitarian view of history and society. For in the foresight of hope, the totality of history is reserved to the eschatological action of God. Love is not merely an interpersonal happening. It is a social matter, being the unconditional and selfless resolve to work for freedom and justice for others. This could be the point of insertion for theological discussion of revolution.

b) *The Church as the place and institution for socio-critical freedom.* This tentative definition of the Church is not an adequate dogmatic definition of its essence. But the Church in action (in preaching, worshipping and sacraments) and in its central task of reconciliation and forgiveness may take the direction of social criticism. This description of the Church implies above all a new hermeneutic of the Church in society. This will explain the role of tradition and institution in the *post-histoire* society; how the ecclesiastical institution, conscious of its own provisional status, does not repress critical freedom but makes it possible, this being the formal contour of the "servant Church"; how criticism is part of the public life of the Church; how partial identification with the institution is to be positively treasured; how rights and freedom in the Church are not merely constitutional problems but elements of the process of attaining knowledge in the Church's theology; and so on.

Johann Baptist Metz

POPE

I. Theological

A. Definition

The Pope is the vicar of Jesus Christ, the successor of the Apostle Peter, the head of the Catholic Church and also Bishop of Rome, Patriarch of the West, Primate of Italy, Archbishop and Metropolitan of the ecclesiastical province of Italy, Sovereign of the Vatican City (cf. *Annuario Pontificio*). In ancient times, the title "Pope" ("Father") was given to bishops. It was widely used in monastic circles and became the ordinary title of a priest in the Orthodox Churches, as also in the Romanic parts of the Roman Catholic Church. In Egypt, it was the prerogative of the Bishop of Alexandria. From the middle of the 6th century on, the title came to be restricted in the West to the Bishop of Rome. This usage was juridically established by Gregory VII.

B. Biblical Foundations

The papacy can only be understood in the framework of the Church as a whole and in connection with the hierarchical structure of the Church. The Church cannot be properly understood either as a papal or as an episcopal Church. But it does not exist except with the Pope as the visible representative of Christ, the invisible head of the Church. According to Catholic faith, the papacy grew out of the mission of the apostle Peter, who, according to reliable testimonies (not, however, universally accepted), ended his life in Rome. In the NT, Peter appears as the first of the apostles in rank. The gospels show him as their spokesman (Mk 8:29; Mt 18:21; Lk 12:41; Jn 6:67f.). In the lists of the apostles given in the synoptics he is always named first (Mk 3:16–19; Mt 10:1–4; Lk 6:12–16; cf. Acts 1:13; Mk 1:26; Lk 9:32; Mt 16:7). A most important point is that, in what is obviously a traditional formula, Peter is named by Paul as the first to whom the risen Christ appeared, though chronologically he was not the first (1 Cor 15:5). The Easter apparition is a revelation of his call. Since the formula in 1 Cor 15 is a very ancient piece of tradition, it is an expression of the primordial conviction that Peter was the primary witness to the resurrection. Three texts in particular bring out specifically the special place of Peter: Mt 16:13–19; Lk 22:31f.; Jn 21:15ff. In the first text, the authenticity of which as part of the gospel cannot be seriously doubted, though its place in the arrangement of the text is perhaps due to the redaction, Jesus gives Simon a new and symbolic name, by calling him *Petros* (Kephas = Rock). Jesus promises the apostle that he is to be the rock foundation of the Church which he planned. Peter is to guarantee stability and security, permanence and unity. Christ is himself the foundation of the Church, but this foundation appears visibly in Peter. The other apostles are also included in this function (Eph 2:19f.). One must also remember that according to the Letter to the Ephesians, the Church is also founded on the prophets, i.e., the charismatics. None of these elements should be overlooked. Though Peter alone was given a special charge, it is clear that he can only exercise it in unity with and in conjunction with the rest of the apostles, and indeed, with the Church as a whole.

The function of the rock foundation is further defined by Jesus as the power of the keys and the power to bind and loose. In the house where Jesus is the householder, Peter is given authority to rule as representative of the master. The formula also includes authority to teach and to impose doctrine. The metaphor of binding and loosing means to exclude from the community and to re-admit, also to impose an obligation and to release from it, finally, to declare something lawful or prohibited. This triple function is also assigned by Jesus to the other apostles (Mt 18:18), but it is clearly Peter's in a special way which is his alone. The Gospel of Matthew does not explain what the primacy of Peter consists of. But the twofold conferring of authority does not make sense unless a single function is meant, though shared at various levels.

According to Lk 22:27–32, a quarrel among the disciples inspired by ambition and desire for power gave Jesus the occasion of proclaiming the law of the kingdom of God, readiness to serve the brethren. And here Jesus gave a special task to Peter, promising him his prayer to enable him to fulfil it. According to the words of Jesus, Satan was to bring the disciples into a situation of severe trial for their faith. This took place in fact at Jesus' death. And even Peter was not to be spared this crisis of faith (cf. Lk 22:33f.). But the prayer of Jesus, offered for Peter in particular, was to help him to recover, and it would then be his task to provide support for his "brothers", that is, for the whole community. Peter is to be a stronghold of the faith.

According to Jn, Jesus fulfils his promises and completes his transmission of authority after the resurrection. It is understandable that the confirmation of the authority should be after the resurrection, since the existence and life of the Church are linked to the resurrection of the Lord. Peter is made shepherd of the flock. This metaphor, common in the OT and NT, comes from an agrarian culture and is based on the notion that the shepherd has to find pastures and watering-places for the flock, to defend it against attack and to preserve due order within the flock. What is meant therefore is that the Lord who will no longer be visibly and historically present appoints a representative who has to mediate Christ's salvation, the life of salvation, by preaching the word and establishing salvific symbols. He must also protect this life from all threats from within and from without.

In the Acts of the Apostles, Peter appears as the head of the young Church, conscious of his responsibility and full of the power of the Spirit. He is the successful, enterprising and courageous preacher of the gospel. He is equipped with authority to combat anything unholy within the Christian community. It is he who breaks through the bounds of Judaism into the universality of the message of salvation. He is the pace-maker for the mission to the world. This is all described without any effort to glorify him or to gloss over his weaknesses (cf., for instance, Acts 1:15–26; 2:14–40; 3:1–26; 4:8; 5:1–11; 5:29; 8:14–17; 8:18–25; 9:32–43; 10:15). The importance and the limits of Peter's authority are shown in the dispute between him and Paul at Antioch when the question of the persistence of the ritual law of the OT arose (Acts 15:7–12; Gal 2:11–21). And in general, it was only normal, in view of the simple, rudimentary and hence undeveloped organization of the primitive Church, that the exercise of the Petrine functions should have been on a modest scale. Further, according to the words of Jesus, the authorities were to see themselves and to behave as the servants of the rest and not as their lords (Mt 20:26ff.; Lk 22:25ff.; Jn 13:1–20). The primacy of Peter was not in any way diminished by the fact that he exercised his function of head by keeping in touch with the consensus of the Church and remaining in loving fellowship with it. He remained head of the Church when he left Jerusalem and went to Rome (cf. Acts 12:17; 1 Pet 2:11; 5:13; Heb 11:13).

C. Historical Development

Jesus himself did not appoint successors either to Peter or to the other apostles. The succession follows from the nature of Peter's mission (Mt 28:18ff.), which is to the ends of the earth and the end of time. The succession to Peter is not on the same lines as succession to the other apostles, since he can have only one successor at a time. According to the faith of the Church, this is the Bishop of Rome, since Peter was in Rome and suffered a martyr's death there. Sufficient proof for this is given in Ignatius of Antioch (*Ad Romanos*, 4, 3), Dionysius of Corinth, the Roman presbyter Gaius and Irenaeus of Lyons. Peter's going to Rome must be ascribed to the impulse of the Spirit pervading the Church as well as to Peter's own decision. And it is not impossible that the link between Rome and succession to Peter was based on a decision of the Church towards the end of the apostolic age. The Roman papacy passed from a rudimentary to a fully-developed stage. Under the stress of circumstances, in the course of history, many alien tasks accrued to the Popes, including the government of the Papal States. Then as political, cultural and social conditions changed, the Popes freed themselves once more from such tasks, though only slowly, hesitantly and often unwillingly, fearing that the loss of worldly power might involve restrictions on their spiritual mission. The changing shape of papal power corresponds to the changes in the whole Church. It is determined by political and cultural shifts in the course of history, though also by the personal character of any given Pope.

In the early centuries, there are many proofs that the Church was conscious of the primacy of the Roman Pontiff, but the testimonies are in germ, so to speak, and not fully explicit. The first is provided by a letter of Bishop Clement of Rome to the Church in Corinth at the end of the 1st century. Quarrels have broken out in Corinth, and Clement acts as peace-maker. He does not intervene authoritatively, but displays a deep sense of responsibility for the whole Church. It is this sense of responsibility which inspires his initiative. The spirit, the force and the claim of the Roman Pontiff are heralded in the letter, which was held in extraordinarily high esteem throughout the Church in the 2nd century.

Ignatius of Antioch says that the Roman Church is "president of love", that is, first in the realization of the new principle introduced by Christ into history. He goes on to say that the Roman Church teaches others but does not itself receive instruction. He begs it to take care of the Church in Syria. The reason for Rome's precedence, as explained by Ignatius, is that Peter and Paul lived in the Roman Church and preached the gospel there.

Irenaeus of Lyons defends tradition against Gnosticism. To establish what the tradition is, the local Churches founded by the apostles are the competent witnesses. The apostolic succession guarantees the truth of the doctrine. In such a matter sufficient proof has been given when it is shown that in the greatest and most ancient Church, one universally known and founded by the glorious apostles Peter and Paul, its line of bishops goes back to the apostles and that its doctrine is therefore apostolic. "With this Church, on account of its more primordial authority (or: more effective priority, 'propter potentiorem principalitatem') all other Churches in every place cannot but agree, since in it the Christians of all places have preserved the apostolic tradition" (*Adversus Haereses*, III, 3, 3).

Tertullian and Hippolytus regard Peter as the first in the line of Roman bishops. Cyprian sees the unity of the Church as founded on Peter. The link with Peter provided by succession to the episcopal office is, according to Cyprian, the fundamental justification of all episcopal power and likewise determines the unity of the Church universal. When Peter settled in Rome, the primitive Church embodied in Peter also settled there. Hence the Roman Church is the *ecclesia principalis*. Optatus of Milevis (d. before 400) held that communion with the Roman Church guaranteed the legitimacy and divine authority of the other Churches. Ambrose (on Ps 40:30) says: "Where Peter is, there is the Church." Augustine in his struggle against Pelagianism strove with growing vigour to gain the support of Rome, because, as he said, only the verdict of the Apostolic See could give the proper emphasis to the decision of the African bishops (*Epistle*, 172, 29).

From the 2nd century on, the Bishop of Rome was asked to decide in questions of controversy, e.g., the date of Easter (see the accounts of the numerous journeys to Rome in Eusebius's *History of the Church*). From the 4th century on there is the fact that bishops look to Rome for protection of their rights, and that Rome is the court of appeal in matters of law, while appeals against its decisions were held to be inadmissible. The Roman baptismal Creed came to be authoritative. Rome played an essential role in the fixing of the canon of Scripture, as also in the struggle against Gnostics, Marcionites and Montanists.

In the Middle Ages, the papacy was discussed only incidentally, in connection with other problems such as the manner of ordination of priests, the analysis of faith and especially in solving the questions raised by the founding of new religious orders in the 13th century. These orders wished to be dependent only on the Pope, and not the bishops, especially in financial matters. Religious thus became in a special way the "sons of the Pope". A tendency in the opposite direction has only set in recently. In late scholasticism, the pressure of historical circumstances, i.e., the occupation of the papal throne by rival Popes, gave rise to the "conciliar theory", which made the Council and not the Pope the supreme authority in the Church (see *Schism*). The conflict between Conciliarism and the doctrine of papal primacy went on for centuries, in spite of the condemnation of the theory at the Council of Florence, till the First Vatican Council, at which the question was decided in favour of the papal primacy. But at the Second Vatican Council a certain synthesis was arrived at, without prejudice to the primacy of the Pope.

Thomas Aquinas used ancient Greek notions of monarchy rather than biblical ones to justify the papal primacy as the most perfect form of government. It guaranteed the unity and peace of the Church. According to Bonaventure, there is a first and supreme principle in every realm, to which all particulars can be reduced, and from which in turn all particulars derive. The Pope is the summit of the whole hierarchical structure of the Church. All duly constituted power in the Church stems from him. This was a consideration inspired by neo-Platonist thinking, and led Bonaventure to a view of the primacy which differed considerably by its exaggerations from what was later defined as Church doctrine. Peter John Olivi came in the course of his defence of the Spirituals against the Curia to hold the view that the Pope was Antichrist. Here he anticipated one of the theses of the Reformers. In theology after the Council of Trent, as the concept of the ecclesiastical hierarchy, especially that of the magisterium, was worked out in opposition to the Reformation, the doctrine of the primacy was given a more and more systematic form till it finally reached the stage in which it was adopted by the First Vatican Council.

The way in which the Bishops of Rome understood their universal mandate is instructive. To some extent, such self-interpretations were included in the declarations of the First Vatican Council. This is true, for instance, of the declaration of the papal legates at the General Council of Ephesus (431; cf. *DS* 3056), which was acclaimed unanimously by all the fathers present. So too the profession of faith of Pope Hormisdas, which was subscribed to by some 250 Eastern bishops and thus ended the Acacian Schism (484–519; cf. *DS* 3066, 363). It was also accepted by the eighth General Council, Constantinople IV (869; *DS* 128). So too finally the profession of faith of the Emperor Michael Palaeologus, which he made as representative of the Eastern Church and swore to through his legates at the Council of Florence. Mention may also be made of a pronouncement of Pope Siricius (384–98; *DS* 181), which says that it is the task of his office to bear the burdens of all, since "the blessed Apostle Peter bears them in us" (*DS* 181) and thus protects his heritage. Innocent I (401–17), in the course of a letter written at the instigation of Augustine to the bishops of Africa during the Pelagian controversy, wrote as follows: "In your search for the things of God... you have followed the examples of ancient tradition . . . and confirmed the strength of your faith in true insight, since you affirmed that the matter in dispute among you should be referred to our judgment, knowing as you did what was due to the Apostolic See. For from this See comes all episcopacy, and all the authority which goes with this title" (*DS* 217). In 1302 Boniface VIII declared in the bull *Unam Sanctam*: "Therefore this one and only Church has not two heads like a monster, but only one body and one head, Christ and his vicar Peter and the successor of Peter . . . For all men, it is absolutely necessary for salvation to submit to the Roman Pontiff. This we declare, affirm and proclaim" (*DS* 872; *D* 469). Wycliffe's spiritualizing image of the Church and the views of Huss, who was theologically dependent on Wycliffe in many respects, gave rise to a number of papal condemnations of theses in which the papacy was rejected or underestimated (*D* 633, 635–9, 646–50, 652, 655; *DS* 1207, 1209–13, 1220–3; 1226, 1229). Other important affirmations of the primacy include that of the Council of Florence (17th General Council, 1438–45), the Lateran (18th General Council, 1512–17), the bull *Exsurge Domine* of 5 July 1520 and the rejection of Gallicanism and Febronianism, two movements in which the Conciliarism rejected by Florence lived on.

A distinction must be made between the dogmatic statement of the primacy, ie., explicit faith, and the actual exercise of the office, though there is a close connection between affirmation and action. In the first thousand years the exercise of papal primacy took the form of arbitration. Later the Popes themselves took the initiative more and more in making decisions. For a long time they exercised their authority by means of fraternal admonitions. But as early as the 2nd century, it also took the form of juridically binding precepts.

Pope Victor (189–98) gave forceful expression to the primacy. The Churches in Asia Minor had refused to accept the Roman dating of Easter. In face of the resulting disunity, Victor excommunicated them, not just by breaking off his own communion with them but by expressly excluding them from the fellowship of the whole Church. In doing so he appealed to the fact that the graves of the Apostles Peter and Paul were in Rome. Pope Stephen I, the first, as far as we can see, to appeal to Mt 16:18ff., demanded of all the acceptance of his doctrine on the baptism of heretics and threatened those who opposed it with excommunication, appealing to the authority conferred on the Apostle Peter, which he claimed had been transmitted to Peter's successors. From the 4th century on the Roman Pontiffs, Siricius (384–98), Innocent I (402–17) and Zozimus (417–18) in particular, claimed the primacy in more and more explicit terms. Leo the Great was especially clear and definite on the matter. Human and subjective elements may have played a part, but their action was primarily inspired by the conviction that as successors of Peter they had a task to fulfil which was committed to them by the Lord of the Church. That the claim of Rome was fully in keeping with the mind of the whole Church was clearly manifested at the General Council of Chalcedon, to take one example. When the letter of Pope Leo was read to the Council, the fathers cried out: "This is the faith of the Fathers. This is the faith of the apostles. Peter has spoken through Leo." The letter sent by the Council to Leo describes the Pope as the interpreter of the voice of the Apostle Peter. Gelasius (492–6) laid down the basis of the theory of the two powers which led in the Middle Ages to the subordination of the temporal to the spiritual power (Innocent III, Innocent IV, Boniface VIII).

If the affirmations and exercise of the primacy in Christian antiquity are compared with the doctrine of the First Vatican Council and subsequent practice, the extent of the development cannot but be apparent. Nonetheless, there is an undeniable continuity between apostolic times and the present day. In action and reaction, both the Bishops of Rome and the Church universal became more and more clearly conscious of the primatial position of Rome. For the organization of the wide-ranging Church provinces, the patriarchate structure was historically characteristic. This form was undoubtedly affected by the development of papal authority, but it was not eliminated. For in general, this structure only came into play in its function of supreme judicial authority, even in matters of faith. In later history, since the beginning of the Eastern Schism (1054), patriarchal authority in the West was absorbed into the primatial. Bishops are appointed directly by Rome and are directly subject to the Bishop of Rome, without the intermediate authority of a metropolitan.

The First Vatican Council determined the full extent and also the limits of papal authority, against episcopalist tendencies on the one hand and integralist tendencies on the other. The Council aimed at stating its faith in such a way that the total self-understanding of the Church could find expression in it. By reason of external circumstances and also of the immaturity of ecclesiology, only part of the problem could be dealt with, that of the papal primacy. As regards the bishops, the Council was content to put in a saving clause, which was meant to ensure that no detriment should be done to the ordinary power of the bishops, given them by Christ. The strong emphasis on the primacy launched a line of development which took the concrete form of Roman centralization and which now prompts a search for a form of exercise of the primacy which will allow the bishops, not merely in theory but also in practice, the freedom of movement which properly belongs to them. The most important text of Vatican I is as follows:

"We teach and declare that the Roman Church has the primacy in ordinary authority, by the disposition of the Lord, over all other Churches. This jurisdictional power of the Roman Pontiff, which is truly episcopal, is direct. Towards this authority the pastors and faithful of every rite and rank, both individually and collectively, are bound by the duty of hierarchical subordination and true obedience, not only in matters of faith and morals but also in matters of discipline and government in the Church throughout the whole world. By maintaining the unity of fellowship as well as of the same faith with the Roman Pontiff, the Church of Christ is thus one flock under one supereme pastor ... The authority of the Supreme Pontiff does no detriment to the ordinary and direct power of jurisdiction by which the bishops, the successors of the apostles, appointed by the Holy Spirit, are truly pastors of the flocks assigned to each of them to rule and feed. It is, on the contrary, acknowledged, strengthened and defended by the supreme and universal pastor, as was affirmed by St. Gregory the Great when he said: 'My honour is the honour of the universal Church. My honour is the vigorous strength of my brothers. I am only truly honoured when due honour is paid to each of them ...' Because the Roman Pontiff is, by divine right of the apostolic primacy, head of the whole Church, we also teach and declare that he is the supreme judge of all the faithful, to whose judgment appeal can be made in all matters which come under ecclesiastical examination. But the verdict of the Apostolic See may be rejected by no one, since there is no higher authority, and no one may pass judgment on its judgment. Hence they stray from the right path of truth who affirm that it is permissible to appeal to a General Council against the judgments of the Roman Pontiffs, as if the General Council were a higher authority than the Roman Pontiff.

"If anyone therefore says that the Roman Pontiff has only the office of supervision and guidance, but not full and supreme power of jurisdiction over the whole Church, not merely in matters of faith and morals but also in matters of discipline and government in the Church throughout the whole world; or if he says that the Pope has only the major share but not the whole fullness of this supreme power; or that this power is not ordinary and direct over both the Churches individually and collectively and the pastors and faithful individually and collectively: let him be excluded" (*D* 1827–31; *DS* 3060–64).

Other statements about the papal primacy are to be found in the encyclical of Pius XII *Mystici Corporis*, 29 June 1943, and in many texts of the Second Vatican Council.

The primacy of the Pope defined by Vatican I refers not to the power of orders (*potestas ordinis*) but to the pastoral power (*potestas iurisdictionis*). The teaching authority, the magisterium, which is often, though incorrectly, regarded as a distinct type of authority, should be ranged under the pastoral or jurisdictional power. (See *Magisterium*.) As regards the power of orders, the Pope is not superior to the bishops. Nonetheless, power of jurisdiction and power of orders are linked very closely to the Pope, since his supreme pastoral power is based on the fact that as Bishop of Rome he is the successor of the Apostle Peter. Even though a baptized person when elected Pope at once possesses papal power when he accepts the election, episcopal consecration, by virtue of the link between power of orders and power of jurisdiction, is essential to the taking up of supreme power in the Church. The two powers form an organic unity, though they need not come at the same time.

In the realm of jurisdiction, the Pope possesses supreme, full and universal power in the Church. It is truly episcopal and takes in every member of the Church. Its extent is determined by the revelation which took place in Jesus Christ. The Pope has no authority in purely worldly matters. Claims of such a nature put forward in the Middle Ages were due to historical circumstances and did not derive from the primacy proper to the Pope. According to the teaching of Vatican I, the papacy is to be regarded as instituted by Jesus Christ and not as the result of historical developments or even as the outcome of intrinsic necessities in the Church. The Pope is not given his mandate by the Church, and he is not the delegate of the bishops, even though he acts in the name of the whole Church and of the bishops representing the whole Church – as he does, even when acting on his own initiative. The election, which has gone through many changes of form in the course of history, though now long since stabilized, serves to designate the holder of the office. But the papacy itself is based on the commissioning of the Apostle Peter, though the Pope is not the Apostle Peter, any more than the bishops are apostles. The main difference is that the apostles were at once the (direct) bringers and witnesses of revelation, while the bishops are (indirect) transmitters of revelation.

Vatican I gave no formal explanation of how the succession to Peter actually came about in the course of Church history. The Christological perspective in which the Pope was placed is of particular importance. The Church does not have two heads, but only one, inasmuch as the invisible head, Christ, is represented by the Pope as the visible head. The emphasis on the relation to Christ, so far from excluding, rather presupposes the spontaneity, freedom and individual qualities of each wielder of the primacy. In the activities of the primacy, Christ comes to the fore precisely in the fragility of men. The personal character of each Supreme Pontiff is fraught with consequences, in spite of his call to be the instrument of Christ. Nonetheless, the authority of the Pope is ultimately the authority of Christ. When the Pope exercises his power of jurisdiction, his pastoral office, he is owed internal and external obedience. Since it is Christ who acts in the primatial actions of the Pope, the papal power is rooted in the sacramental character of the universal Church (cf., for example, Jn 20:21–23). Normally, only those united with Christ in the Spirit are called to transmit to others the salvation given by Christ. According to Jn 21:15ff., Peter's love of Christ is the presupposition of his being charged to feed the flock of Christ. The wielders of spiritual authority are to live in peace with God and with the brethren. The Church had indeed to learn by experience in the course of history that union of heart with Jesus Christ can be lacking, but that this does not mean the loss of papal authority (against Wycliffe, Huss and Luther). The primacy would in fact be null and void if it were dependent for its value on something which could never be definitely ascertained, like the mind and heart of the holder of the office. Nonetheless, the normal situation is that the representative of Jesus Christ lives in union with Jesus Christ. Otherwise not only would the salvation of the Pontiff himself but that of the whole messianic community be endangered. Hence too it has always been the conviction of the Church that a Pope who fell into heresy would lose his office. But the question has yet to be solved as to who should determine the fact of heresy in such a case. In any case, a sinful holder of the primacy is a grave scandal. The intrinsic bond between power of orders and of jurisdiction shows that the actions of the Pope, even in juridical matters, are concerned with salvation and sanctification. The reason why Christ combined the full and supreme pastoral power in one member of the Church, the Bishop of Rome, seems to be that the continuity and unity of the Church are guaranteed and displayed in this office. Communion with the Pope brings out the full membership of the saving community, the *communio sanctorum* as communion of saints and communion in the holy, in the most visible and reliable way. Hence the institution of the primacy appears as a manifestation of Christ's concern for the inner unity and the reliable proclamation of the message of salvation both within and without the people of God.

The universal episcopate of the Pope naturally brings up its relationship to the episcopate. The question is all the more important because Vatican I affirmed that papal power was truly episcopal. In spite of the division into local Churches under the personal rule of a bishop, the Pope is universal bishop, so that the whole Church appears as comprised within one diocese. Though the pope is not superior to his fellow-bishops by virtue of the power of orders, he is, in this view, by virtue of his power of jurisdiction and its primacy, bishop over all members of the Church, both bishops and faithful. And he can make use of this episcopal power in any part of the Church. Nonetheless, there are not two bishops in each diocese, the local ordinary and the universal Pontiff. In spite of the direct episcopal power of the Pope, the local bishop remains the immediate pastor of the flock entrusted to him. It seems impossible to reduce the relationship between the universal episcopal authority of the Pope and the local episcopal authority to a satisfactory juridical formula. But it is certain, at any rate, that the universal episcopal authority of the Pope does not entitle him to intervene at will. In particular, he could not abolish episcopal rule in the Church. "The right of the Pope to intervene in the government of a diocese rests therefore not on an authority of like nature to that of the local ordinary, and one which would be in competition with it in every way, but on a higher right which is prevented by the principle of subsidiarity from intervening except when the ordinary competent organ fails" (K. Mörsdorf). But here again it is for the Pope to judge when such a situation has arisen. The primacy lays in fact grave obligations on the holder. He is not free to remain silent when he ought to speak, and again, he may not speak out of turn. There is much in all this which remains and must remain the decision of the Supreme Pontiff himself, but he is nonetheless inexorably bound to the charge given by Jesus Christ. This charge means service of the people of God and hence of the salvation of the individuals. The Pope is appointed as member of the Church on behalf of the Church. His actions, by virtue of Christ's dispositions, stem from the Church and in turn serve the Church. Pope and Church do not face each other like strangers who come from different parts. On the contrary, the Pope speaks as a member of the Church to the other members, though as one equipped with special and indeed supreme authority. And the Church in turn is a brotherly fellowship within which the Pope lives as brother and father. Highly as a member of the Church may be placed by the primacy, he is just as profoundly at the service of all. Thus the primacy may mean supreme authority, but its truest meaning is the most intensive service (*servus servorum*). The Pope has to answer to Christ for the way in which he serves the salvation of all (1 Pet 5:1–4). Thus the primacy is itself also a form for the expression of love, placing itself at the service of men in obedience to God's eternal plan of salvation (1 Cor 13:13). But the love of which we speak here is of such a type that it cannot connive at or confirm man's self-assurance or selfish ease, his worldly longings or his enslavement to the world. It has to tell the arrogant and self-centred to go out of themselves and find the liberty of the children of God, freedom from anguish and freedom in joy. For man, this often means disquiet and disturbance. He shrinks from taking the step across the abyss to God and hence finds the challenge to do so an imposition. Hence an institution which binds him formally by law to go out of himself and give himself to Christ is for him a scandal. While it is true that all the efforts of the Church can become a scandal, the character of scandal is concentrated in the papacy as in a focus, because from it comes the supreme statement of the obligations which are intended for man's well-being but can nonetheless be felt as threats to earthly self-assurance and appear furthermore at times in forms which are not consistently understandable, since they have to pay the tribute of human frailty. At the same time, these considerations show that the exercise of the primacy is determined as to its necessity, its proportions and its limits, by the approach of the reign of God and by the salvation of men. It cannot be used to train men in obedience for the sake of obedience. Hence it must respect human freedom, which is man's highest natural good and takes priority in doubtful cases, since man in his freedom is analogously the image of God. Hence the primacy cannot restrict man's freedom except to the extent that such restriction is necessary for his salvation.

Vatican I left the question open as to how the relationship between primacy and episcopacy should be determined. The solution given by Vatican II was the affirmation of the collegiality of the bishops. It was not the intention of Vatican II to limit the primacy, but to complete the affirmations of Vatican I and supply what was omitted there. The collegiality of the bishops is to be understood in a broad sense. Vatican II used great emphasis and piled up formulations to point out that the college of bishops essentially includes the Bishop of Rome, the Pope, and that as head of the college he is so much part of it that without the Pope there is no college of bishops, and that the college only possesses spiritual authority inasmuch as the Bishop of Rome is a member of the college and is over it as its head. Without his membership, the college would be reduced to a sum total of individual bishops. An exceptional situation occurs when a Pope becomes incapable of acting as Pope, as for instance when he is mentally ill or falls into heresy or has died. In such an exceptional case, the college of bishops would not cease to exist as a college. It would not disintegrate into a number of individual bishops, because important factors of unity remain effective – unity in confession of Christ, unity in the Spirit, in love, in the celebration of the memorial sacrifice. These factors are also effective and play a decisive role in normal times, when the Pope presides over the college of bishops as its head. And these factors make it clear that the unity of the college is not just an external juridical bond. Its basis must be understood as sacramental. That the Pope is essential to the constitution of the college is the visible manifestation of a unity which is ultimately based on the sacramental element. For the rest, in an abnormal and exceptional case the Church is obliged to give itself a head once more. This is done by the election of a new Pope.

The collegiality of the bishops in the context of the primacy presents theology with a difficult problem. Vatican II declared that the Bishop of Rome, by virtue of his office as vicar of Christ and as pastor of the Church universal, has full, supreme and universal authority, which he can exercise always and everywhere without needing the consent of the bishops. This affirmation corresponded to Vatican I. But Vatican II supplemented it to the effect that the college of bishops, in common with the Bishop of Rome as its head, is also (*quoque*) holder of full and supreme power over the Church universal. The Council thus affirmed with regard to the college of bishops a doctrine which had already been universal in the Church with regard to the General Councils. The statement on papal power includes the word "universal", which is not used in the Council's statement on the power of the college of bishops. But this does not change matters in any way. Though the relationship between the holder of the primacy and the college of bishops (with the Pope as its head) is made quite clear in the texts of the Council, the "Nota Praevia Explicativa" added to *Lumen Gentium* (cf. H. Vorgrimler, ed., *Commentary on the Documents of Vatican II*, vol. I [1967], pp. 297ff.) put the matter beyond all possible doubt by saying that the distinction is not "between the Roman Pontiff and the bishops taken collectively, but between the Roman Pontiff by himself and the Roman Pontiff together with the bishops. Since the Supreme Pontiff is *head* of the college, he alone can perform certain acts which in no wise belong to the bishops, for example, convoking and directing the college, approving the norms of action, etc." But it is worth noting that the introductory explanation says that the Pope can use various methods in making these decisions, as the circumstances of the times demand. He need not confine himself to a form laid down once and for all. The Pope being entrusted with the care of the whole flock of Christ, it is for him to judge, as the needs of the Church change in the course of time, the manner in which he will exercise this charge, either personally or collegially. Though the final text of the Council does not say so, it may be assumed that even when the Pope acts on his own initiative, without the suggestions of the bishops and without their co-operation, exercising his authority for the whole Church, he then acts as head of the college. For he always speaks in the name of the Church as well as for the Church. When he acts as Pope, he never acts as a private person, but always as successor of the Apostle Peter, whose task it is to give effect to what has been handed down in the people of God. The college of bishops possesses full and supreme power not because this has been given it or conceded to it by the Pope, but by virtue of its own competence, in consequence of Christ's institution. But since the Pope, his characteristic membership, is essential to the constitution and effectiveness of the college, the consent of the Pope is required for every decree of the college of bishops. This consent is to be taken in the strict sense. It is not a subsequent confirmation, but an element intrinsic to the decree from the start and indeed a vital element. This is so even if the consent of the Pope only comes in the external form of a subsequent approbation. The same conclusion may also be drawn from the formulas used in the publication of the decrees of Vatican II since the holding of the Council.

But the manner in which the Pope exercises his function as chief member of the episcopal college can vary very widely. Here the actual situation can be of extreme importance. The participation of the Pope can range from a voluntary or even silent acceptance of a decree of the bishops to a solemn promulgation. And the Pope can decide which form he chooses. In view of the historical facts, especially the proceedings of the ancient Councils, we are justified in assuming that the way in which the Pope exerts the rights or authority which are his by divine institution, is dependent on human factors and historical circumstances – so much so, that the observer who does not view the processes in the light of faith may be able to see only the human and historical factor.

The fact that the Pope with the college (or the college with the Pope as its president) possesses full and supreme authority in the Church, while the Pope alone also does so without the college, leads to a question which seems to be insoluble and indeed to contain an inner contradiction. The question is: are there two supreme powers in the Church, in rivalry with one another? Or: is not the college of bishops once more stripped of its power by the fact that the Pope exercises supreme power, even without the bishops? The Council itself left the question open. The traditional answer is that there are two inadequately distinct organs of supreme ecclesiastical power: inadequately distinct, inasmuch as the Pope is himself a member of the college of bishops. Another view is that there is only one wielder of supreme authority in the Church, the college as constituted under the Pope, the holder of the primacy. To avoid prejudicing the primacy of the Pope, the supporters of this thesis add that even when the holder of the supreme authority is so defined, a distinction must be made between actions which the Pope alone performs, without the college, even though in the name of the college, and actions which have a strictly collegiate character by virtue of authoritative papal participation.

To proceed according to the strict logic of law, it would perhaps be more correct to say that the Pope is the one organ of supreme authority, and then add that he can exercise this authority either alone or along with the bishops in a collegiate act. This thesis would appear most suitable to ensure the unity of the Church insofar as it stems from the supreme living authority within it. But the unity is also assured by the supposition of two inadequately distinct organs, since the two organs are combined together in unity by the fact that the Pope is head of the college. Parallel to this is the truth that the primacy suffers no detriment or danger when the supreme authority of the college of bishops is affirmed, with the due precautions. It may well be that in deciding for one or the other solution, psychological and jurisprudential factors may be more strongly at work than strictly theological ones.

What is always true is that the Pope is never alone, but is always in essential union with the bishops. Even if it is undeniable that he can always exercise freely his supreme authority, nonetheless, by virtue of his responsibility for the unity of the Church, he is perpetually being thrown back upon his unity with the bishops. Rather than being a "free" agent, the Pope, like the college of the bishops, has to adhere to divine revelation, as attested in Scripture and tradition, as handed on incorrupt through the apostolic succession and in particular through the concern of the Bishop of Rome, and as preserved in its purity and faithfully interpreted in the light of the Spirit of truth in the Church (Vatican II, *Lumen Gentium*, art. 25). The activity of the Bishop of Rome must be directed to the well-being of the Church (*ibid.*, Introductory Explanation, art. 3). Hence not only the bishops but also the Supreme Pontiffs are bound to take adequate steps, by appealing, for instance, for help to theological science, by exploring the faith of believers, to strive to ascertain correctly the revelation attested in Scripture and also to find the way to present it in adequate terms. This effort is an intrinsic element of the power of jurisdiction belonging to the Pope. He has not therefore just a formal authority, but one which is also determined as to its content. If it is to be exercised in accordance with the will of Christ, it must, like the exercise of the freedom which is man's right, always submit itself to the true message which comes from God, that is, to what is attested in Scripture. But then, it is the Holy Spirit who is at work in the Church universal. It is he who links the faithful who discharges a spiritual office with the faithful who have not such an office, binding them together in a unity which is often full of tension.

Georg Schwaiger

POSITIVISM

I. Philosophical

1. *Concept.* Positivism is not a definite doctrine which can be assigned to any particular epoch of philosophy, but a certain attitude towards science and theory. It is always characterized by distaste for traditional philosophy, with especially sharp criticism of metaphysics, not only with regard to certain tendencies or results, but even with regard to its basic problems and methods. It is further characteristic of neo-positivism, as the genuine development of older positivist principles, to make philosophy a science directed by the methods of the exact natural sciences. This does not lead to a categorical rejection of philosophy, but to the effort to set up a "new", "different" philosophy, purified from all unscientific, speculative or metaphysical elements.

The starting-point of positivism, epistemologically, is that the only possible source of knowledge is the empirically tangible datum, by which is understood the multiplicity of sense impressions. All the assertions of traditional philosophy which go beyond this cannot be verified in the light of given facts and hence are not objects of science. The human ego is ultimately the sum of a number of regular psychological, logical and other relationships. Its independence with regard to the world, in the sense of its being a person, cannot be deduced from the data and hence is not an object of human knowledge.

2. *History.* There were positivist tendencies in ancient scepticism, in Epicurus and the nominalism of the Middle Ages (in the controversy about universals). But the English empiricists are regarded as the real founders of positivism. F. Bacon (1561–1621) sought to base all human knowledge on experimental and inductive science. T. Hobbes (1588–1679) rejected all metaphysical bases of law and only recognized law as laid down by the State. But the most decisive contribution to the development of positivism was that of D. Hume, who held that human knowledge could only rest on mathematics or on the sciences dealing with empirical facts. His discussion of the principle of causality is typical. Experience tells us nothing of an intrinsic connection between cause and effect. We can do no more than register how often the same result follows the same cause and apply our experience to natural phenomena in the guise of "laws" recognized by us. Causality is not an objective link between cause and effect, founded on being, but a subjective recognition of temporal succession which is arranged systematically with the help of psychological associations. Hume divides the data accessible to our experience and knowledge into two main groups: impressions, which arise both from sense perception and our experience of our outward and inner states, and ideas, which are reflections of our impressions.

Positivist notions came to the fore in France with the Encyclopédistes (D'Alembert [1717–83] and Turgot [1727–81]). They also demanded that scientific activity should be restricted to what is perceptible by the senses and rejected all speculative and hypothetical knowledge which went beyond the domain of experience. The sociological positivism of A. Comte (1798–1857) was the most influential of all. Applying the notion of science as concerned with facts to history, he divided it according to the three scientific stages of humanity into the ages of theology, metaphysics and positive sciences. In this process man frees himself from the bondage and tutelage of faith in God and the gods, then from the fruitless effort of philosophy, and finally attains to independence and to mastery over nature, whereby he creates for himself the possibility of intervening in the course of the world to change and improve it ("voir pour prévoir, prévoir pour prévenir, prévenir pour pouvoir").

The basic positivist attitude was given a new orientation in the neo-positivism which originated in the Vienna Circle. It is distinguished from the older positivism by the shift of philosophical enquiry to the realm of logic and linguistic research – the instruments of scientific assertions. The most important representatives of this trend are M. Schlick, L. Wittgenstein, R. Carnap, O. Neurath and B. Russell, one of the main proponents of symbolic logic. The task of philosophy is not the investigation of facts, which are left to the exact sciences, but the logical analysis of the units of language (words, propositions, speech as a whole) with which we speak of the world (investigated by science). Neo-positivists allow only two types of meaningful propositions: propositions about factual relationships stemming from experience (*a posteriori*) and verifiable by experience; propositions about purely logical relationships which provide no knowledge about facts and hence are valid independently of experience.

The logical analysis of these propositions, which are made with the help of language, is the task of philosophy. According to Wittgenstein, philosophy is not a doctrine but an activity. It results not in "philosophical assertions" but in the clarification of propositions. Language can be reduced to "elementary propositions" deducible, as logical constructions, from elementary sense-data, and the effort is to give them the greatest possible consistency and exactness. This also helps to show that all the traditional problems of philosophy are either strictly scientific ones or are actually meaningless, since the exact investigation of the logical structure of language ultimately eliminates all false views about the object of scientific research.

3. *A critical discussion of positivism* must start with its claim to make philosophy an exact science. The positivist attitude is induced by the scandal of disagreements in philosophy. In contrast to the natural sciences, with their constant gaining of ground, philosophy gives the impression of being at a standstill. The problems which philosophy took up at the beginning of its course still remain unsolved. Positivism draws the conclusion that whatever be the interest of philosophy, it provides no access to knowledge in the sense of science.

The preference of positivism for the purely factual and experimental is in keeping with the mood of modern times. But while positivism boasts of its objectivity, it represents in fact an arbitrary and unjustified restriction both of the object and method of enquiry. Its method is to determine beforehand what can be accepted as real, thereby forbidding reality to display itself in its full ambit. Experience is more than what is equally available to all. Experience of the given is only open to us within a transcendental horizon. If philosophers failed to reach agreement, it was not from lack of proofs, but because their approach was dictated by different presuppositions in each case. Positivism fails because it lacks openness to experience in all its dimensions including the religious and metaphysical, from which synthetic *a priori* judgments could be justified. This want of openness means that positivism, in spite of its humane intentions, is silent in face of the great human problems.

But the verdict on positivism should not be entirely negative. Without its restrictive negations it can be salutary. When it insists that knowledge must build on human experience, it is a sharp reminder to the philosopher that his task is to explain and change this world and not to construct possible worlds. Further, its unconditional demand for proofs of a statement forms a good counterpoise to the dogmatism which can appear in philosophy. The nature of truth is not just to satisfy the mind. It must express the reality which is displayed in experience. Positivism has also a contribution to make to theology. It reminds the theologian that faith and redemption are not so much a matter of theory as of history and experience. If theology is taking on a new form today, it is partly because it recognizes that its first task is not the erection of a logical system but the patient investigation of what God has revealed.

Robert O. Johann

II. Moral

1. *The concept.* Moral positivism is not just the denial of universal, objective and changeless norms in the moral order. Whenever the good is reduced to definable norms and not left in the state of a general exclusion of the bad, there is always some change in standards. But moral positivism also rejects all absolute imperatives in morality, which might then in turn be formulated as changeless norms. No human acts are essentially good or bad, absolutely imperative or forbidden, and hence possibly so for all men. The objective morality of an act and the moral obligation in its regard do not depend on the mentality and on the object of the act, but on something which is outside the object and can be subject to change.

2. *Types.* Two kinds may be distinguished. a) Theonomous moral positivism holds that the moral order depends for its structure and obligation entirely on the "absolutely" free will of God. It is not founded on the nature of God and a reality formed according to his "image". Good is whatever God decrees is good, evil is whatever God decrees is evil. Moral values depend entirely on God's free will. This view, held by Occam and the nominalists, is based on the assumption that there is neither good nor evil prior to the decree of the divine will, which is absolutely free to decide one way or the other.

b) Autonomous moral positivism holds that moral norms are not derived from the nature of things or of man, or from divine revelation. They are rather "invented" than "uncovered", their purpose being to regulate social life in its various political, economic and human relationships. This notion of the moral norms was already put forward by the Sophists of antiquity, who held that the difference between right and wrong, good and evil, was based not on the nature of things but on human convention (so Protagoras, Aristippus and Gorgias). Montaigne and Hobbes likewise held that nature provides no universally valid norms. The only general rules are those laid down by the law of the State.

With the progress of the empirical sciences, ethnology and comparative religion, more was learned about the differences in the moral laws as formulated among various peoples. Doubts were expressed about the existence of general and objective norms recognizable as such. Developments were also noted in the course of the history of ethics, which suggested that morals, like the rest of culture, had evolved from primitive starting-points.

3. *Critique.* It cannot be denied that morals differ from people to people. And the differences are due to the various social, economic and political conditions in each case. But the question remains as to whether the conclusion

drawn from these data by the moral positivists is valid. Morality is reduced to an empirical problem. Nonetheless, it is more than a question of statistics and history – not in the sense that there is a supra-historical world of values, but because of an unconditional dimension in moral reality, which remains beyond human measure even though it takes concrete form in the historical. It is given with the essence of man and the nature of things. Man's self-realization as a person and in society, his shaping of the world or his dealings with it, confront him with an "ought" in the demands of morality which is not at the mercy of his arbitrary will. The obligation is to be defined for each concrete situation, but is of itself prior to each historical situation. The fact that this claim of morality is given different answers at various times and in various places is simply due to the "historicity" of man – the fact that he is conditioned to some extent by his culture. But his history is what it is not just by the favour of man, but because it is "the hour" of the good itself. The very changes which ensue, being changes of what is permanently the same, point not only to the opposition between an abstract, non-historical "rationalistic" morality and the relativism opposed to it, but, above all, to the contrast between a concrete, "incarnational" morality and a moral positivism which is in fact amoral.

The contrast therefore is not between rationalism and relativism, but between the comprehensive truth and one-sided falsifications of it. Moral positivism has a real task to perform, but in a new and legitimate sense. The changeless good has in fact to be realized differently in time and place, on the social as well as on the individual plane, and there is always need to establish new positive norms. In this sense, the task of moral positivism is both to maintain the permanent claims of the "principles" and to aim also at the "applications", the "discernment of spirits", the "prophetic" formulation, the moral "imperative".

Ireneo González

POSSESSION

The existence of non-human, personal evil "forces and powers" with an effect on the world is a truth of faith (*D* 428, 806, 894, 907, 909), and the theoretical possibility of diabolical possession must therefore be described as at least theologically sound teaching. Nevertheless, the concept of possession, unlike temptation by demons and other sorts of real influence on men, is not very clear, is only relative, and includes a wide range of variables, since even the most external influence (such as a drug) affects man's personality, and the most intimate creative intervention still leaves the deepest core of the responsible person free. Even Scripture (e.g. Lk 13:16; Hab 2:14; 1 Thess 2:18) implies that the assumption of demonic influence should not start at the point where reason and this-worldly empirical methods find "abnormal" phenomena. On the contrary, Scripture regards the very "normal" and "naturally" explicable course of events in nature and history as the object of the action of demonic powers. A theology of evil would in fact stress that the aim of these powers is an autonomous *perfection* of the natural qualities of the world without God, and that all merely destructive tendencies reveal the failure of this claim to autonomy rather than the original intention of making it fail. In this view illness, death and self-destructive tendencies in human existence can and should in every case be seen as also an expression of the power of demonic forces, even when they have natural (proximate) causes and can and should be fought by natural means. From the religious point of view, it is therefore neither possible nor particularly important to draw a precise distinction between possession and natural illness, particularly since illness can be both a symptom of and a point of entry for possession (cf., e.g., Aquinas, *S.T.*, I, q. 115, a. 5). The radical dilemma of whether to fight the phenomenon by exorcism or medicine also disappears from this viewpoint, since every Christian should pray for health even in the most "natural" of illnesses. The concepts of "toleration" and "punishment" may have a place in the description of possession, provided they are not given too anthropomorphic an interpretation (i.e. as a some sort of miracle under the influence of evil), but even in cases where a phenomenon may correctly (according to the rules given above) be regarded as possession in the strict sense, the correct view would be that it is a manifestation of the underlying realm of diabolical forces which enters our perception only as a result of the situation which exists (is "tolerated") here. Such a phenomenon should be regarded as merely revealing something which is permanently present in the world, and therefore does not exclude natural causes but merely makes use of them for its own ends. For a sober assessment of possession, and to avoid rationalist objections, it should be remembered that any observed phenomenon (as in the case of, e.g., visions) is itself a synthesis of, on the one hand, demonic influence and, on the other, the conceptual and imaginative world of an individual or period, individual temperament, possible illness and even parapsychological capacities. A clear division is neither necessary nor possible. Attempts by students of comparative religion to reduce states and experiences such as prophetic inspiration and mystical ecstasy (where these are genuine) to a common denominator with possession ignore an essential difference between the two sorts of phenomena. Possession has a destructive effect on the human person, while mystical and prophetic experiences work on the spiritual centre of the free person, even when they are experiences as the inescapable grip of divine power.

Karl Rahner

POVERTY

I. Christian Poverty

Poverty is a lack of the means of subsistence (food, clothing, shelter, and so on). But besides privations of this kind, poverty also connotes helplessness when faced with the demands of life: ignorance, weakness, bondage, isolation, defencelessness against injustice. Such poverty is more or less relative. The most radical experience of poverty is the absolute destitution of death.

1. *Scripture*. Revelation gives poverty its full meaning both as inescapable distress which opens a man for God, and as the humble, loving abandonment of one's own rights.

a) Though the OT often represents wealth as a blessing and poverty as divine chastisement and retribution, the rich man as godly, the poor man as a sinner, the prophets and post-exilic thinkers began to realize that the rich man is all too likely to harden his heart at the distress of his neighbour, to succumb to self-righteous "impiety", ruthlessly using his power to exploit others, whereas personal experience of distress often fosters solidarity with one's fellow-sufferers (in exile, for instance). It was the humiliating experience of want and servitude in Babylon which chiefly made poverty a religious term, synonymous with "humility" and "piety" (Isaiah, Psalms, Zechariah, Proverbs). For Isaiah the "poor" are simply oppressed Israel, which finds refuge only in its God (14:32; 25:4; 49:13). God's kingdom is preached to these, "Yahweh's poor", and they are exhorted to await his coming glory with perfect trust.

b) *New Testament.* It is only with Christ that the religious significance of poverty becomes fully clear. His unbounded abnegation and self-sacrifice unto death reveal the glory of the Father (Phil 2:5–11). Sharing men's distress unto the end, Christ made the living God present by his death and resurrection. So seriously did he take men's distress that he proclaimed the poor blessed and promised that they should have their fill (Mt 5:1–12). He promised salvation (Mt 11:1–6) to all who in their need should trust him, not presuming to shut themselves against him (Mt 9:12). The "food" which Jesus promises the hungry is the kingdom of God. Thus he does not come as a social revolutionary. He loves the poor because they embody men's sheer need of deliverance, and because in their distress they are prepared to listen to his message. He shares their poverty, requiring the same poverty of those who would follow him (Mt 8:20 par.; 19:12–21 par.), so that they may devote themselves wholly to God's kingdom. Jesus does not commend poverty out of contempt for wealth or for purely ascetical reasons (cf. Mk 14:3–9; Lk 8:2f.; 10:38). Christ makes love for our suffering brethren meaningful (Mt 25:31–46) as a disclosure of the Father's perfection and glory (Mt 5:16, 48). The *familia Dei* (Jn 15:9–71) is grounded in helplessness freely accepted and sincere altruism. Acts 4:32 ("they had everything in common") does not mean that the primitive Church rejected private property; it explains the preceding statement: "The company of those who believed were of one heart and soul." In the NT only the Letter of James actually condemns possessions and riches. Jesus' attitude, especially the sacrifice of his life for his brethren, reveals the soteriological character of his poverty. In him, all poverty is a sign of man's forlorn and needy state, and at the same time a possible way of salvation.

2. *Moral theology.* Poverty must first be recognized by the sufferer as a fact. By nature every form of poverty demands admission of one's own inadequacy. It is part of the human condition that distress can never be altogether abolished, whatever our efforts, whatever the successes of civilization and technology, that each advance, each new development brings new problems and dangers – or first makes us aware of them. Man can never make his life perfectly secure. Certain privations are thrust upon us; certain others must be "voluntary" in a special sense – the sacrifice of our life, or something precious, if the good of our neighbour or of the community requires it, or if we know we are called to follow Christ and serve God's kingdom.

a) *Material poverty.* In the Western world only isolated individuals lack the bare necessities of life. The understanding of poverty has largely disappeared from these countries. Instead of material poverty we often find other forms of poverty – desolation of heart, a sense that life is meaningless, anxiety, isolation – which must be interpreted as a kind of longing for redemption and love. A Christian who finds these things in himself or in others must accept them in the spirit of Christ as a means of encountering God, as a call to travel new roads in loving our neighbour.

Besides such distress, there is the appalling poverty of Asian and African peoples, which demands an enormous extension of Christian love. We may no longer confine it to a narrow circle of people close to us, we must love people afar, everywhere. For if voluntary poverty can be a redemptive thing, destitution can beget hatred, bitterness, and despair, and be a sign that men have not found love. Particular works of mercy alone (almsgiving and works of "supererogation") can no longer cope with world-wide poverty. Rational planning is necessary. Christians must realize once more, as the primitive Church did, that private property is a trust, given us to be intelligently used for the needs of all in accordance with "social justice". This may mean renouncing personal wealth and the power it brings. Certainly we must consider how far certain economic systems (such as economic liberalism and uncontrolled capitalism) can be transformed so as to satisfy justice and answer contemporary needs. No effective help can be given in modern mass societies without soundly organized, well-directed co-operation.

b) "*Spiritual poverty*" plays an important role in Christian life. It means trying to live "as one who hopes", humbly, in expectation of Christ's coming, learning to dismiss the cares of this aeon in Christian detachment. The Christian is undemanding, and frugal in managing his goods. Religious seek to practise a special form of spiritual poverty, the basis of which is the actual, voluntary poverty of individuals if not of their communities as such. St. Francis of Assisi gave this poverty its deepest and most beautiful form.

Constant readiness to serve the kingdom of God and the good of one's fellow-men, penitence, patience, love of one's enemies, are the fruit of spiritual poverty, which is the best cure for self-righteousness and pharisaic formalism, the touchstone of genuine spirituality, what makes our total expropriation at death a salutary testimony.

3. *The Church of the poor.* People sometimes speak romantically of the "Church of the poor". There are two dangers here. Firstly, Christians may be asked to live in a "Franciscan" way which is in reality only a dream of the past. This is to ignore the changed economy and manners of modern society, which is after all part of God's providence. Secondly, this romantic ideal could be used to evade the duty of alleviating (or even abolishing) distress to the extent which Jesus' command of charity imposes on his disciples. After all, man's increasing mastery of the world and his own political economy must be seriously acknowledged as a divine challenge, which summons Christians to be abreast of such developments in giving practical effect to their charity. Nonetheless, just as there is no ultimate security in human life, whatever man's technical achievements, so too in a deep theological sense the Church will always remain "poor" – men following the Lord who emptied himself, accepting in faith and confidence the abandonment into which Christ preceded them in his death.

Sigismund Verhey

II. Medieval Movements

Many currents in a complex and many-sided movement for renewal of the Church in the 12th, 13th and 14th centuries were stimulated and shaped by the ideal of evangelical poverty. The Church – not only or even mainly the hierarchy – was attempting to do justice to the contemporary situation, to find a form for itself that would both accord with its tradition and be appropriate to the times.

The original concern of the reform movement was to establish the "liberty of the Church", to free it from lay control as embodied in the system of imperial and proprietary churches. Its efforts to this end, first directed against the abuses resulting from too close an involvement of the Church in the world, led to a major separation of the spiritual domain from the temporal and fostered the ideal of a spiritual Church apart from the world (thus Joachim of Fiore, for example). The conflict between Church and Empire logically followed from the Church's growing sense of independence, its claim to primacy over the temporal power, and an associated idea of the Church that was rather narrowly clerical. Once disengaged from the structures that had hitherto given it support and protection, the Church itself laid claim to worldly powers, as was particularly clear in the centralization of the Roman Curia and the papal claims to universal rule, e.g., by Innocent III.

But the medieval Church, in spite of all its efforts, could not altogether separate itself from secular structures. The leading role in this Christian society increasingly devolved upon it, and even in the non-spiritual realm it had become part of the texture of the West. This may be seen from the impracticability of the solution to the Investiture Controversy proposed by Paschal II and the unsuccessful pontificate of Celestine V. At the turn of the millennium, to be sure, the compenetration of the spiritual with the temporal power had been beneficent, and prince bishops (like Ulrich of Augsburg) were revered as the kind of saint appropriate to the times. Even when the papacy had triumphed over the emperor, the best representatives of the poverty movement did not object to the Church's temporal grandeur; and the mightiest of the Popes, Innocent III, recognized the legitimacy of evangelical poverty. Moreover, the Crusades were motivated not simply by the Church's new consciousness of power but to a great extent by religious enthusiasm as well, and there is no doubt that they helped to turn the renewal of medieval piety in the direction of evangelical poverty.

On the other hand, the effects of the reform movement made themselves felt in the domain of secular politics, and not alone in the struggle for supremacy between Pope and emperor and in the tremendous influence of the Cluniac reform. Even the movement of the *Pauperes Christi* was not devoid of worldly interests. This is clear as early as the Patarines of Lombardy. Evangelical poverty influenced the Crusades and the foundation of the orders of chivalry. And it did not prevent St. Bernard of Clairvaux from intervening in politics. It sometimes threatened Church and State with near-anarchy (cf. Arnold of Brescia and Peter Waldo with the one-sided spirtualist conclusions they drew from the evangelic renewal; the Catharists with their unchristian dualism).

Nevertheless, the tendency to withdraw from the world, which for various reasons kept reappearing in one form after another, was basic to the medieval reform movement. Large numbers were attracted to the monastic life, and this flight from the world found characteristic expression in the eremitical movement, which combined the tradition of the Eastern anchorites with the cenobitical life, usually on the basis of the Rule of St. Benedict (for example, the Camaldolese and Carthusians). The simplicity and austerity of life in the wilderness were also found attractive, as by the Cistercians. The cases of St. Bernard, and of St. Peter Damian, who exerted a powerful influence as an ecclesiastical statesman and author, show that strict detachment from the world did not necessarily mean that one could not make oneself felt in the life of the Church.

The popularity of pilgrimage, which encouraged many to forsake all things, was another facet of flight from the world. This form of piety, which also contributed to the Crusades (cf. Peter of Amiens and his followers), took on a different character when the more mobile townsmen began to develop a monetary economy alongside the stable, localized, agricultural economy of feudal society. The new men of the rising bourgeoisie (rising both economically and socially) now take abandonment of the world to mean turning their custom of "travelling about the world for the sake of gain" (St. Francis of Assisi, *Regula non bullata*, cap. 8) into an apostolic way of life, and proclaim the gospel as itinerant preachers without money or possessions, living on alms (*ibid.*, cap. 9). No doubt, the beginnings of this movement are closely linked with the eremitical and monastic life. Robert of Arbrissel, for example, and Norbert of Xanten, with their followers, based their community life on the Benedictine or Augustinian rule, in accordance with the requirement of ecclesiastical authority that some existing rule be adopted (for example, Fourth Lateran Council, can. 13). But the later forms of the movement for poverty retained their own proper character – the Waldensians in opposition to Church authority, and the Franciscan Order as a renewal of Christian life accepted by the Church as thoroughly Catholic.

In this situation the dualistic rejection of the world preached by the Catharists was dangerously misleading. Their condemnation of the Church's wealth and worldliness sprang from such wholly unchristian principles that they even denied Christ's incarnation and the visibility of the Church.

Primitive observance was the criterion to which the reform movement characteristically referred, whether aiming at correcting abuses or at establishing new forms of life. Thus monks who adopted oriental practices and withdrew into desolate places revived the Benedictine rule in a new, austere observance, notably in the Cistercian reform. The case of St. Bernard indicates on what depths the renewal of religion drew, not motivated by the letter of the rule or human achievement but by the redemptive image of the incarnate Son of God who became poor for our sake.

Many clerics, too, no doubt influenced in part by the monastic revival, began to embrace a life of poverty. It was chiefly the Augustinian rule that commended itself to these zealous reformers. It became the rule, for example, of the Austin Canons and the Orders founded by St. Norbert (Premonstratensians) and St. Dominic. Laymen too were affected by the religious awakening: they entered monasteries as *conversi*, or formed secular brotherhoods associated with religious houses so as to live a semi-monastic life in the world. The orders of chivalry are notable examples.

Whatever part was played by the influence of the Crusades and by changing social conditions, the religious renaissance in the medieval Church sprang largely from new reflection on the gospel and the life of Christ, on the manner of life of the apostles (Lk 9:1ff.) and the primitive Church in Jerusalem (Acts 2:44ff. and 4:32ff.). The poverty and humility of Christ, the *vita apostolica* – already the theme of the new Benedictine piety, as in St. Bernard of Clairvaux – increasingly became the spur of reform, the standard in the light of which men judged the successors of the apostles, sometimes therefore the occasion of anti-clerical movements (the Waldensians, for example) in cases where the clergy were hostile to change. St. Francis of Assisi set the most felicitous example of holy poverty, combining affirmation of the world with utter self-denial in an evangelical life that he made acceptable to the Church of his time, without any suggestion of dualism or anti-clericalism. Quarrels among the Friars Minor (over the question of mendicancy and communal property) later led to institutional forms being imposed on the spirit of religious poverty in the Order of St. Francis and in the Church. The vital urge was thereby, no doubt, to some extent repressed or overshadowed.

Sigismund Verhey

POWER

1. *Nature of the question.* There are two theological reasons why it is important to understand what is meant by power.

a) Power is one of the primary religious ideas; mankind's awareness of God is an awareness of him as powerful. Power is one of the first of God's attributes. That is also the case in OT and NT revelation. The possibility and existence of the creation rest on God's omnipotence; the election and guidance of Israel are viewed as its manifestation in history; Jesus' good news concerns the reign and kingdom of God, that is, the perfect expression and exercise of his power; as Christ and Lord, Jesus shares in that power and even the new knowledge of the God who is love discloses this love precisely as the essential and central feature of God's power.

b) A right attitude to power is fundamental in human social relations. The Christian's citizenship in heaven (Phil 3:20), and the knowledge that to Christ the Lord all power is given in heaven and earth (Mt 28:18) and that he will return to establish and perfect God's kingdom, exclude any absorption in the possession of, striving for, exercise of or dependence on earthly power. Renunciation of force and the passive suffering of violence are imposed as an obligation on his disciples by Jesus' teaching and example. Nevertheless, power is to be exercised by God's commission for the sake of a well-ordered life in this aeon (Rom 13:1). Readiness to accept this aeon as the moment granted by God will lead to serious respect for power as well. In fact, out of charitable responsibility for others, the Christian must even be ready on occasion to assume and exercise power, though here too he will only hold it as though he did not (1 Cor 7:29ff.).

2. *Nature of power.* a) Power is chiefly in question in the sphere of human social relations, but it is also present in nature and indeed in all domains of reality. To exist is the most universal and primordial form of power; what is, in proportion as it is, is powerful; being and power are identical. Why then speak of power at all and not merely of being? Power is both identical with being and an intensification of being, a "plus" in being, always intended and striven for by being. At the very least it signifies that mysterious "plus" contained in the fact that the being of beings does not simply disappear and dissolve when it is contemplated, inquired into, grasped: it is "still" there, remains identical with itself, remains what it was despite the difference between later and earlier; man perceived it, inquired into it, dealt with it, but it proves resistant to his grasp, maintains itself against him. For power to be in question a "difference" must intervene, the possibility of negation, or otherness. The idea of power does not arise in the silent absorption of pure being; the latter has to maintain its unity with itself if it is to manifest itself as powerful. Power is unity of being with itself despite a difference, the presence of future being in present being.

b) Power exhibits three degrees. The lowest, which belongs to the being of beings, and is identical with it, has just been examined: power as persistence in being. The difference here, in face of which being persists, is external to it; being is called in question from outside and maintains its own identity. With the second degree, the difference enters into the being of beings itself: power as active self-preservation in being. This stage is met with when the being of beings goes out of itself, when this present being determines its future form. Such power only occurs where being is "present to itself"; then it attains the plane of self-determination and is an active potency and faculty, freedom. Yet power is only perfect and reaches its highest and authentic level, when being can determine not only itself, its own form, but can also determine what is other than itself which comes to exist by it, yet without its originator's ceasing to be one with itself and to endure. This is power no longer as persistence in being, nor as self-preservation, but as giving. Such power, however, annuls in itself the difference between present and future. It is the productive, creative power of being itself, thanks to which everything exists and is what it is, and by which everything ultimately – in the passive sense – can be, in other words, omnipotence.

c) All beings presuppose the omnipotence which causes them to be and determines their being. Such a power itself cannot therefore be a particular being, yet in order to be powerful it must absolutely and pre-eminently bear within it the degrees of power. Omnipotence must be thought of as an absolute source, in possession of itself and freely deciding what is not itself. By causing this other to be, it gives it a share in its power, empowers what is not itself to persist in being, freely to preserve itself and to transcend itself by giving. For finite being to transcend itself freely into what is other than itself, is only possible in social inter-relationships; here power has its authentic and highest place within the creation. Power is thus essentially identical with love: power, like love, is unity with itself in bestowing being on what is other than itself and allowing it to be and to be free.

3. *Political social power* is the will of individuals or groups exercising determining influence on the communal life of a number of people within a common living space or organized structure. Such a will is not powerful by the mere fact of willing, but because it imposes what it wills externally. This external domain is the living space shared by a number of people; they carry on their existence there, it is their "world", and at the same time it represents their will, by which they fulfil themselves in their world. If the powerful will works through the freely consenting will of others in a common domain of reality, power assumes the form of authority. If it acts directly on the external reality and determines the world of other people's wills from outside, it takes the form of force. The possibility of force belongs to power, but the latter is all the more powerful the less force it needs to employ and the more the power flows from within and not merely from extrinsic means. However, in the world as it is in fact, force cannot be entirely eliminated; in the widest and fundamental sense it is posited by the very fact of corporeal existence. The powerful will must not only be at one with the world and with the consenting will of the others who acknowledge it, it must be at one with itself. This demands that what it wills ought to exist and its act ought to be posited, i.e., power must be good and must be rightful. Finite will is not its own independent ground, consequently it must be responsible, and therefore good; it must be empowered to act and therefore rightful; in that way it becomes authority. The real purpose of power is the powerfulness of what is good and right, in the form of the common good. Power is therefore a harmony of the will with the world, "horizontally" in harmony with other wills in a society deciding and shaping a common world, and "vertically" in harmony with the norm of the good and rightful. In short, power is the effective ordering of human society as existence in the world.

4. *Power and powerlessness.* Power is at once persistence, self-preservation and giving. The dimensions which are coterminous in omnipotence, split up in the realm of the finite. By willing itself, power wills what is other than itself. The transition to the other, to allowing the will of others, to unconditional consent to the generosity of the divine will, demands of the finite will, which is not the source of its own power, a self-abandonment, self-sacrifice, self-mediation through weakness, by questioning its own power. That is why finite power is tempted to establish itself in self-assertion, to shut itself off in ostensible independence in face of the competition of other finite wills and against the claim of the absolute power. The redemption of power is the cross.

Supreme love, in Jesus' death, accepts self-abandonment to the will of the Father on behalf of many, to be confirmed and manifested by the Father in the resurrection as the supreme power of the Son. Nevertheless the cross of power involves for the Christian not only readiness for self-sacrifice, but willingness to accept power in its vulnerable earthly conditions. But even then it will only be accepted with detachment and will be valid only because it comes from God.

Klaus Hemmerle

PRAGMATISM

Pragmatism is the name given to a philosophical trend which appeared in the U.S.A. towards the end of the 19th century. Its founder was Charles Saunders Peirce (1839–1914) and its most important representatives William James (1842–1910), who helped to make it widely known, and John Dewey (1859–1952), whose long activity ensured its continuing influence. Pragmatism is the first great original American contribution to Western philosophy. It began by being a method of logical analysis, i.e., of explaining the content or significance of concepts and phrases and it went on to present itself in consequence of its analyses as a doctrine of the nature of truth, at least insofar as this is known by man. As a theory of truth and knowledge it found wide hearing at the beginning.

Pragmatism, as a theory of meaning, was first formulated by Peirce (*How to Make Our Ideas Clear* [1878]): "Consider what effects, that might conceivably have bearings, we conceive the object of our conception to have. Then our conception of these effects is the whole of our conception of the object." The notion of an object or event contains no more significance than that of the practical consequences to be considered, the attitudes and behaviour suggested, the experiences to be foreseen. If the concept is wrongly applied to a situation, the actual consequences will be other than those foreseen with and in the concept. If a number of concepts have the same results in practice, they are only different in name, but really mean the same thing. A concept without practical consequences, which means nothing for our actions, our expectations and possible reactions, has really no meaning.

This pragmatic rule for meaning, which included the reactions of our senses, was derived from scientific practice. In the theory of Peirce, it was primarily a means of analysing concepts and meanings which was also, to his mind, the first if not the only task of philosophy – compare the present-day "linguistic analysis" in England and the U.S.A. Nonetheless, Peirce also had in mind to re-shape traditional metaphysics, showing up its "verbalism and endless discussions" as meaningless by means of his pragmatic criterion of signification. This idea recurs in logical positivism in a still more emphatic form.

One consequence of the pragmatic criterion of meaning is that the truth of an assertion cannot be recognized through purely contemplative consideration or through comparison of the proposition with the object of which it is asserted. The assertion has to be tested in practice to see whether the empirical results coincide with the expected ones or not: the "testing of a hypothesis by its actual working". A judgment is true if it actually regulates our conduct, that is, if it leads to successful adaptation to the possibilities and demands of the matter in hand. As W. James and F. C. S. Schiller said, more succinctly than clearly, something is true if it is useful in life and brings about satisfactory results in practice. If faith in God is useful for life, one has the right to hold this faith as true.

But even Peirce and Dewey found

themselves forced to modify the formula suggested by James. They held that while all that is true is a good, it did not follow that all that is good is also true. Endless peace would be a good, but must it therefore come about? Truth and value are not to be identified. In particular, truth is concerned only with the "value" of thoughts. Dewey therefore suggested a correction which James afterwards accepted: truth is merely the value which is characteristic of thoughts which under practical testing lead to the expected experiences. A judgment about reality is true if and only if it is confirmed or is or can be verified by the further course of experiences, directly or indirectly. A judgment about the past is only indirectly verifiable, by means of the traces which the past has left and which can be registered in the present. But no verification of judgments of experience can ever be complete, i.e., check all implied expectations. Hence the certainty which they offer can never be absolute. Their evidence is never apodictic. They can give rise only to judgments of a possibly fallacious type – to what Peirce called "fallibilism". They are propositions for which there are good grounds or a certain degree of probability, but are not strictly speaking proved. They have what Dewey called "warranted assertibility".

Finally, it is characteristic of pragmatism that it does not consider knowledge as an independent function but as part of the process of life in the concrete. Knowledge and science are in the service of life. They are the most important means at man's disposal for adapting himself to his natural and social environment and for meeting successfully the difficulties and problems of daily life. Ideas, hypotheses and theories are so many "tools" for bringing about concrete aims in life. Hence Dewey could also term his theory "instrumentalism".

Pragmatism was applied to the field of social science by George Herbert Mead (1863–1931). He developed a theory of the genetic relationship of individual and society, according to which society can be regarded as a complex of social customs developed by man in order to master his environment. It is only by assimilating these social customs in his thinking, feeling and action that the individual develops spiritually and is enabled to become a "self". Ideas like those of Peirce were represented outside of the U.S.A. by such thinkers as F.C.S. Schiller of Oxford and W. Jerusalem of Vienna.

What pragmatism was trying to determine was not truth in the abstract, independent of the process of knowledge, but truth as it is also verified and justified in the actual process of living experience. But its upholders disregarded the important distinction between the element of validity or truth in itself, and the procedure by means of which this validity is established or this truth is recognized. Truth and knowledge of the truth must not be confused.

This obscurity is compounded by a further defect of pragmatism, that the method of establishing a truth is unduly empirical. The truth to be known and the field of meaningful discourse are restricted to what is given in experience or what can be tested by experience. This means the exclusion of all *a priori* or essential knowledge of a non-analytic, i.e., synthetic type. In consequence, there could be no metaphysical principles by virtue of which, in a categorically valid way, experience could be transcended and the suprasensible known. And there could be no absolute moral norms by which one could determine what is good in itself, independently of what "one" (individually or socially) wishes or likes or in fact pronounces good. An ethical relativism, extending to the order of society and the State, would be the inevitable consequence.

Clemens Schoonbrood

PRAYER

A. The History of Christian Prayer

Prayer, as generally understood, can take many forms. And it is significant that "in early times . . . the OT contains no general term for prayer" (*RGG*, II, col. 1213). This suggests that we should consider the subject, which is certainly a unified theme, from more than one aspect if we are to avoid over-hasty conclusions. There are two classical definitions. "Speaking to God" (or Christ) has been a spontaneous description of prayer since the Apostolic Fathers (διάλεξις, *homilia, conversatio*). But theology adopted another definition, generally attributed to John Damascene: the "raising of the soul to God". Undue stress on the notion of speaking to God (*DSAM*, II, cols, 1123–30) runs the risk of seeming to profane the divine mystery, of reducing the divine person to the level of other beings, of making the Absolute the insignificant nonentity of Deism or of thinking in terms of magical influences. Undue stress on "lifting up the heart", however, may easily obscure the fact that we meet God in the man Jesus Christ. The encounter may be treated as a pleasant occasion for indulging in pious sentimentality. Or there may be a "mystical" effort (see *Neo-Platonism*) to lead back the scattered multiplicity of the creature to the unity and recollection of the Origin.

1. *History of religion.* A glance at the history of religion provides examples of such errors. But in judging the prayer of the nations, there are two points to which more attention must be paid than was done by the historians of comparative religion. One is that prayer is not something that can be adequately described in equivalent terms from other fields of reality. The other is that prayer, of its nature, is an effort to give expression to a personal attitude which is only fully real in this effort at expression – while it can never find conceptual categories to comprise its total riches. It *must* be an effort to objectify something which cannot be fully objectified. It must be the impossible effort to translate the personal into terms of things. Hence we must "demythologize", reduce the many "alienated" forms to their ultimate content. This will undoubtedly bring to light the true attitude, which will be in some way theistic, even though combined with idolatry and badly disfigured by magical practices. The same process must be applied to the philosophical or "mystical" forms of prayer in the higher religions, where the encounter with God is vaporized in speculative thinking or nihilistic self-annihilation. Here too only extremely cautious interpretation will avoid confusing a profoundly religious act with its possibly atheistic form of expression.

2. *Old Testament.* Prayer in the OT shows with an astonishing clarity that all such errors, actual or possible, have been left behind. An examination of the initial stages, as disclosed by the sources, shows that magical practices, long since integrated into true prayer, are only marginal phenomena. The theological ground for the purity of this prayer is to be sought in Israel's experience of the saving deeds of God, who after the wanderings of the patriarchs and the trials in Egypt finally gave his people the covenant made with Abraham: "I will be with you and bless you" (Gen 26:3). The faithfulness of Yahweh (Exod 34:6) is the setting of all forms of prayer, which has three aspects. One is the memory of the past: "He has delivered his people from the bondage of Egypt" (cf. Exod 32). Then there is the present certainty: "He will not forget the covenant" (Deut 4:31) and finally the expectation of the great final

deliverance: "See, thy king comes to thee" (Zech 9:11). A large portion of Israel's prayers, as collected, for instance, in the Psalter, are inspired by the memory of God's great deeds in the past to beg for his help in present distress. Just as the prophets recall the past in their constant exhortations to repentance, so too the sapiential books may reflect on it in hymns of praise and thanksgiving.

This sense of the personal guidance of God pervades the prayer of the individual, and also that of the community. The kingship, the sacred precincts of the temple, the sacred times and rites, the prohibition of certain types of food and clothing embody the truth that Israel is a holy people (Lev 20:7). This basic assurance gives unity to the many forms which prayer can take: from almost disrespectful argument (Gen 18:23ff.; Jer 14f.) to peaceful confidence in God's providence (Ps 127), from ardent supplication to despairing protest (Ps 74:1ff., Job 31), from adoration, praise and thanksgiving (1 Chr 29:31) to humble repentance (1 Chr 21:17; Ps 51). There is no point in enumerating here the various forms, texts, gestures and postures (cf. Krinetzki). It is more important to insist on the all-pervasive attitude, which may be roughly described as confidence in the divine goodness, and at the same time a sense of awe before the divine majesty.

This basic attitude could undergo changes. The familiar conversation with Yahweh in early times appears later in reflections which may seem perhaps too sentimental – "When Israel was a child, I loved him" (Hos 11:2; cf. Jer 2:2; Is 5:1ff.). But in the disasters of the monarchy, the Babylonian exile and the dramatic struggles of Yahweh with his people it came to appear in a purer form as a reverent personal piety: "For thou hast no delight in sacrifice . . . The sacrifice acceptable to God is a broken spirit" (Ps 51:16f.). It was finally stabilized as prayer according to the law and the liturgy in the last five centuries B.C. ("Then wilt thou delight in right sacrifices", Ps 51:19). This shift of emphasis within the one basic attitude is associated with the growing sense of the majesty of Yahweh. Thus his proper name is not uttered in prayer, mediators such as angels intervene between him and his people, and a painfully meticulous legalism threatens to form a barrier, impeding free dialogue between them.

3. *New Testament and the primitive Church.* Though it was only in the course of Christian dogmatics that the traits of prayer described above came to stand out so clearly, the prayer of Jesus – inextricably interwoven in the sources with that of the primitive Church – may undoubtedly be regarded as a definitive stage in the history of prayer (cf. Lk 11:1). The Sermon on the Mount, in both redactions, shows Jesus' childlike confidence in the Father in heaven, his sense of security, his conversing with God as the child speaks to its father. Gethsemane and Calvary provide the clearest instances of the polarity of active and passive tension in the prayer of the Lord. It is a dialogue with God which can go so far as to beg that the Father's will may be averted, and also submit silently to the divine plan. Both attitudes are indissolubly one. We cannot tell whether the frequency with which our Lord is portrayed as praying in Lk is theological interpretation or historical fact. But there is no doubt that Jesus' prayer reveals the perpetual unity of his will with that of the Father (cf. the invocations before healing the sick or Mt 11:25ff.). In Jn this unity is so central that the prayer of Jesus, which could express some kind of subordination, is explained as merely uttered for the benefit of the bystanders (Jn 11:42).

The prayer of the primitive Church is inspired by the actual encounter with Jesus, the intercourse (*homilia*) with the Lord, as well as by his example.

The model proposed by Jesus is seen most clearly in the Our Father, though here as elsewhere (Jn 4:22 deals with another matter) Jesus distinguishes his own prayer from that of others. Two things were taken over by the Church from the Lord. One was an absolute confidence in the goodness and power of the heavenly Father. This was so dominant that the "certainty of being heard" does not seem to have been a problem in the early years. The other was the expectation of the parousia of the Lord. All prayer was focused on this. The certainty of being heard in all petitions was centred and founded on the "Maranatha – Our Lord, come!" (1 Cor 16:23; Rev 22:20; *Didache*, 10, 6). It echoes the preaching of the kingdom of God by the Lord.

But the NT also shows clearly how the intercourse of the disciples with Jesus, with the risen Lord and the Spirit of Christ, became the medium of prayer (cf. the development in the use of the title Kyrios). Closeness to Jesus gives access to prayer. This conviction, intensified by the experience of the Resurrection, underlies such texts as "Lord, teach us to pray" (Lk 11:1), the accounts of the sick kneeling to Jesus (especially in Mt) or the confessions of the demons. The classic expression of this conviction is the "through Christ" of the Pauline letters. According to St. Paul, it is the πνεῦμα Christi, i.e., the closeness of the Lord (gradually distinguished as a person) which enables us to pray. It is the Spirit within us who cries, "Abba, Father!" (Rom 8:15; Gal 4:6). The Spirit is the bond which unites the many forms of prayer in the primitive Church: charismatic stammering or choral hymns, cultic assemblies or private prayer, the high-point in the Eucharist or the everyday attitude expressed in the exhortation to "pray always". The Spirit bestows the new assurance which is expressed in ecstasies or again in the bold and frank approach to God (παρρησία).

Through the medium of the Spirit, with the person of the Lord as the historical focus, the three factors of Jewish prayer are brought to their fulfilment. There is the backward look to the historical action of God in raising up the Crucified – the supreme and all-embracing saving deed of God in history. There is the presence of the Lord in the Spirit in the Church, by which all the prayer of Christians is inspired. There is the expectation of the coming of the Lord. But his return was experienced day by day in its initial stage in the prayer of the Church, and was far more important to the Church than the expectation of the Messiah had been in the OT.

4. *Tradition.* We examine here the transmission of the biblical heritage merely to see how the innumerable manifestations of Christian spirituality, in its most personal act, that of prayer, can fertilize our present thinking. Prayer is not only part of Christian history, it is perhaps one of its main driving forces. Hence a sketch of the history of prayer must retrace the many factors of the history of dogma, which are here briefly summed up under a number of headings. We cannot of course attempt to describe the whole tradition, but in a negative way, by mentioning some of the main deformations, some notion of the true riches of Christian prayer may be given.

a) It is quite clear, and to some extent already visible in Scripture itself, that prayer turned from the *Jesus of time*, soon to return to judge the world (the expectation of the imminent parousia), or at death (theology of martyrdom), to the *Jesus of supra-temporal blessings*. Contemplation frees itself from past and future to sink tranquilly into itself. Historical expectations are sometimes revived in heresies (e.g., Joachim of Fiore). While the world-picture was symbolic, this static and spiritualizing tendency – the lingering look instead of the urgent expectation – was checked.

The inner unity of concrete reality and spiritual sense still linked prayer to time and place. But when the symbolic world-picture was "demythologized", prayer came dangerously close to a contemplation of the beyond, denying the world to cleave to the spiritual.

b) Equally obvious is the decline of the charismatic element, such as was apparent in the Church of Corinth with its prophecy, hymnic inspiration, etc. No doubt the religious orders must be regarded as a series of fresh charismatic approaches. But it is typical that the *Spiritual Exercises* of St. Ignatius, in which there is a delicate balance of the charismatic movement of the Spirit and the regulated procedure, were soon reduced to the element of "exercise". A number of developments fit in here. The charismatic element appears only in heresy or in private prayer, where the *gratia gratis data* for the sake of the Church becomes an individualistic mysticism. Public prayer is strait-jacketed by laws and becomes the prerogative of the hierarchy: the priest officiates, the faithful "attend". Increasing stress is laid on the formula, so that where faith is active it is misinterpreted legalistically, and elsewhere misused as a sort of magic.

c) In practice, from the Middle Ages on, the place of Christ in the economy of redemption, the biblical "through Christ", is hardly a real factor any longer, even in devotion to the Sacred Heart or the incarnation, as the latter was practised in the school of Bérulle (*École Française*). Indulgences, pilgrimages, adoration of the Host, and so on, which have no meaning except in relation to the historical humanity of our Lord, were accorded a sort of absolute value. Even if much Protestant polemic must be dismissed as mistaken, there is no doubt that in the practice of piety devotion to the saints and the Blessed Virgin often enough took the place of the humanity of Christ. The pendulum naturally swung also in the opposite direction. The ecclesial character of private prayer, which can only be offered *per Christum et Ecclesiam*, was lost sight of.

d) The temptation to spiritualize is intrinsic to all forms of piety, and its appearance in Christianity cannot be traced merely to Gnostic or neo-Platonist influences. Possibly the whole history of prayer is that of the struggle against such temptations. They suggest that prayer must be elevated to "pure prayer", since the prayer of petition is only for beginners and all emotions are unworthy. Gregory the Great's longing for contemplation reappears as the enjoyment of esoteric truth. As the effort is intensified, it becomes the purely intellectual intuition of the *apex mentis*, the *cime d'esprit*, the fine point of the mind; or it becomes pure darkness, the mystical obscurity in which man ceases to be the partner of God in dialogue. The final exaggeration is found among the followers of Evagrius of Pontus (4th century) as well as in the "Brethren of the Free Spirit" (13th century): man rids himself of all impurity, including that of prayer, and merges in sheer purity with God himself. We for our part seem to hear a faint echo of this movement when, for instance, as in Origen, St. Thomas Aquinas or O. Karrer, the prayer of petition is stripped of all real activity and is reduced to abandonment to the divine will.

e) When the degrees of the "way of perfection" were kept rigidly separate, perfect prayer was reserved for the *perfecti*, and the difference in state of life was equated with a difference in perfection. But since the basic sense of sinfulness before God, of humility, of always falling short of one's call belongs to the existentials of prayer, the too static notion of the degrees of prayer could be easily transformed, especially by seekers of perfection, into tormenting doubts about one's election. There is a wide literature to attest this – Luther being by no means a marginal case.

f) In the same way, the analysis of the various elements of prayer led to a series of "methods of prayer", where it could be too easily forgotten that no method was more than a handmaid to prayer. On the same principles, distinctions were made between Scripture reading and prayer, between the pursuit of theology and the longing for God, etc. At the opposite extreme, the reaction to this was to identify too readily the Christian attitude with actual prayer. Clement of Alexandria could say that the true Gnostic was always praying, Evagrius that true theology was prayer. Ebeling, following Luther, takes a similar position.

g) A similar principle is at work when St. Paul's "Pray constantly" (1 Thess 5:17) is turned into such exercises as the "Jesus Prayer" (incessantly repeated, cf. J. Salinger's "Franny and Zooey"). The "attitude" is identified with an "exercise". The true Christian attitude must comprise both things. The Christian prays and asks at regular intervals. He "lifts up his heart" to God afresh on each occasion. And he is perpetually in the attitude of prayer, which is what really makes a man a Christian.

h) A further splintering occurred when normal prayer was distinguished from the mystical. There were broad historical reasons behind this development, but the impulse also came from controversy within the Church ("May one, or must one, strive for consolation?") and from movements outside the Church (the Messalians holding that grace was vision of God). There are of course degrees of prayer, but the common ground, the experience of personal encounter with God, is greater than all differences. It is understandable that in view of such distinctions normal prayer should lose much of its freshness. To be truly addressed by God was reserved for the higher degree of prayer. Normal, everyday prayer was regarded rather as a duty to be performed and an exercise to be done, not as something also capable of soaring to the heights, under the impulse of the personal summons of God.

i) Many of these phenomena may be explained by the growing distinction between the subjective, the proper realm of prayer, from the objective, which means in Christianity Christ, Scripture, the Church, the sacraments, the liturgy, and so on. Thus, for instance, the same principle is at work when the Eucharist, the communion in common, becomes "private communion", when the strictly sacramental element is separated from the many other religious acts, and when adoration of the Blessed Sacrament is performed in isolation. One result of this development is the persistence of the notion that true prayer must be in private, a misinterpretation of "in your room" (Mt 6:6) which is not yet fully eliminated.

B. The Essence of Christian Prayer

1. *The concept.* An informed discussion of Christian prayer has to take into account the matters described above. The two classical definitions mentioned at the outset will also be important factors.

Prayer is *the* great religious act. What man really is in the depths of his being, something that cannot be static but must be realized in a fundamental activity in time yet transcending time – that is prayer. It is the acceptance of the prime fact of being created, not in a stupor of resignation, but alert to its coming from the Father's hands. It is committing oneself to the basic dynamism of the kernel of the person, wishing in a way to break through all limits of time and space, but still seeing its fulfilment not in infinite being, but in the Thou who speaks and answers and first calls. It is the all-pervasive longing for happiness, not seeking emotional satisfaction but personal fulfilment. It is the will to free action, which ultimately can only be realized in face of a person who is immanent to all possibilities of freedom and summons man to freedom. In a word, it is unconditional and therefore sensitive openness to the God who transcends all the encounters of everyday life but who uses them and goes beyond them to demand an answer to the basic question of our existence, the meaning of life. Hence tradition tries to define prayer as the "ascent to God" and Scripture speaks of "pouring out the soul before God" (1 Sam 1:15), of longing for God "as the hart longs for flowing streams" (Ps 42:1), of lifting up the heart (Ps 25:1), of taking refuge in the Lord (Ps 31:1f.). In modern terminology it can become "man's self-commitment to the transcendence of his own being, hence the humble, receptive and reverent admission of, and the re-active, responsive affirmative dedication to his call and destiny, the impact of the mystery of God as person on human existence, to which man cannot but be somehow sensible" (K. Rahner in *LTK*, IV, col. 543).

But it is equally important to recall the simple description of prayer as "the great art of conversing with Jesus" (*Imitation of Christ*, II, 8). It is like Abraham's negotiations with Yahweh (Gen 18:23–33) which strike us as very anthropomorphic, or the dialogue of our Lord in Gethsemane as he wrestles with the will of his Father, or the encounters with God of which we read in the lives or legends of the saints, and which we find so overfamiliar as almost to seem blasphemous. While the first definition strives to convey the majesty and universal omnipotence of God, the definition of prayer as "speaking to God" bears on the truth that God hears "me", that he has chosen "me" very personally, and that "my" casual steps are guided by his infinite wisdom. This truth is operative above all in the prayer of petition. The attempt to make abandonment to God's providence the quintessence of prayer ignores its character of dialogue. It stresses one truth, the immutability of God (which taken in isolation would mean that real prayer is impossible) and forgets the other, that God is "personally" concerned with our affairs. The immutability of God must not be reduced to a proposition which can be manipulated in the usual categories of human thought. It must be kept open for the truth of the incarnation and crucifixion, for the truth that God "changes" for the sake of man. This is the only possible source of a dialogal character of prayer.

In true Christian prayer, the granting or refusal of requests is not a problem. One need only think of the typical pilgrimage where the believer whose request has not been granted in spite of or because of his ardent prayer still gains the profound peace of answered prayer. This may be illustrated by an analogy from personal relationships. Any genuine request is always put forward as the minor wish in which the general plea for the other's favour is crystallized. But the Christian prayer of petition takes its impetus (i.e., has its certainty of being heard) from the saving gift of God to men, which is Jesus Christ.

2. *Basic forms.* If prayer then spans the whole distance between ascent to God (Bonaventure's *sursumactio*) and dialogue with God, its basic forms – adoration, praise, thanksgiving, petition, repentance, sacrifice, etc. – are seen to be its natural connotations. Adoration is undoubtedly closer to the "ascent", but without dialogal encounter there can be no adoration, just as there can be no genuine petition without the inward impulse of the Spirit of God, such as is expressed in the *sursumactio*.

This span is wide enough to take in much that is often too quickly rejected in the phenomenology of religion as un-Christian. Christian prayer, in which the intrinsic tension is again surpassed in the person of the Lord, who is God, filling all things while remaining the same, and man, limited and changing historically, appears even phenomenologically as the climax and fulfilment of the prayer of the nations. And this does not mean that non-Christian prayer must be at once branded as un-Christian non-prayer.

3. *The essential structures.* a) The first essential component follows at once from what has been said. Prayer is a grace, a gift of God, a response to something which was previously put on man's lips and in his heart. But prayer is also man's own free act. To have some idea of this mystery, we must first distinguish the aspect of what is given by God from the aspect of what is accomplished by man's own force.

All prayer is wholly the gift of God. There is nothing in it that we can keep for ourselves. There is no previous foothold that we can provide for God's action, and no later response that we can give of ourselves. But prayer is likewise human action. Man is not a machine kept in motion by God. He is free, and there can be no question of prayer unless it is rooted in man's freedom, an action for which he is personally responsible. These two aspects, which both take in the total act of human prayer, must be clearly distinguished. Only then can we truly admire the new mystery, that prayer is after all a response to the call of God, that cutting across the different levels, divine grace and human freedom still meet. This has been the bliss of great saints, often experienced in fear and trembling. But this interplay of call and response is at the heart of all prayer, even the prayer of petition, whose structure only seems to be different when it is considered superficially.

b) Prayer is also a unity of the inward and outer man. Man prays when he is inwardly and outwardly recollected, when he is himself. "Interior prayer" always seeks to express itself in word and gesture, while "external" or vocal prayer can influence the inner attitude when one is tired and distracted. The traditional distinction between "attention" and "intention" ir relevant here, and this is one way to understand the rosary (though there are also other approaches). But the practical consequences are more important. Prayer must of course aim at being "interior", but since man lives in the external world it must also be guided by external rules, postures and formulas and follow the cycle of feast-days and times for prayer. See *Liturgy*, *Worship*.

c) The importance of the link between the inner and the outer appears plainly in the third essential factor: prayer is always both individual and social. The theological reason for this is the unity of the Spirit, who is the Spirit of the Church and also animates each of the faithful. The Christian has both to praise God in a fellowship of prayer and formulate his own prayer for himself. But he must not forget that the prayer of the individual relies on the community which it serves, and that the only ultimate meaning of community prayer is to lead the individual to God. There can be no problems of precedence here, since each man is, irreducibly, at the same time both an individual called personally by God and part of the chain of mankind whose link with God is Jesus Christ. The closer it is to the Eucharist, the centre of prayer in common, the higher the degree of unity in prayer. The breviary is prayer in common in its own way, as are also congregational devotions. The same principle of social prayer also explains, for instance, the precept of going to Mass on Sundays, and the duty of praying for parents and relations. The notion of proclaiming fellowship before God can throw new light on a feature of the early Church, prayer as a confession of faith, which in turn may throw new light on pilgrimages and so on.

d) A further basic structure of prayer follows from the link between prayer and words, which in its highest form is identity. Language is the real personal bond of fellowship. It is the most perfect expression of the inward man. Language here means simply that the Word became flesh and encounters us in the word of Scripture and the articulate action of the sacraments. It is only today that this dominant role of language is coming into view. If prayer is really the basic religious act and the verbalization (its personal outcome) is not merely a vehicle of prayer but its essence – prayer is speaking to God – we can measure the responsibility of those who have to deal with the words. The verbal character also throws light on prayer as a confession of faith, since all honest language is at once the giving of testimony.

e) *The essential deficiency of human prayer.* These demands bring out one further quality, that prayer falls short of what it should really do. This is not a matter of sin, though closely connected with it, nor of incidentals which might be avoided, say, by greater recollection. Man, as he encounters God, is at once conscious of his darkness before the radiant light. This is not a matter of a mystique of sin or of fiducial faith, though the existentiell ground of such notions may well be found here. Man essentially receives at prayer, and prayer, with all the due reserves made above, is essentially a process of receiving. It has often been experienced as such by great men of prayer, who saw their own poverty better the more gifts they received. The prayer, "Lord, I am not worthy" is not just for beginners but also – to keep to the terminology – for the perfect. Penitential prayer, adoration and many other forms must be interpreted in the light of this principle.

C. Dogmatic Introduction

1. Essentially, prayer is the explicit and positive realization of our natural and supernatural relationship with the personal God of salvation. It realizes the essence of the religious act. It is man's entry into the transcendence of his own being, in which he allows himself to become receptive, humble and reverent, gives himself in a positive response, and is totally available and subjectively concerned in his whole existence with the mystery of God as a person. All positive religious acts which are directly and explicitly related, both knowingly and willingly, to God may be called prayer. Even sacrifice is essentially no more than prayer made objective by external presentation. The *a priori*, integral, rational, personal, categorical and incarnate structures of the religious act are therefore structures of prayer. As a response, Christian prayer is an acceptance of the transcendence directed towards the God of eternal life which is made known in grace by God's revelation of himself. It is therefore essentially an act of faith and hope which is fulfilled (when it is fully expressed) in total surrender to the love of God. It is therefore an act of salvation, borne by the grace of the Spirit, having God "in" Christ in view. Whether prayer is always an act of virtue of religion depends on our definition of the concept of religion. In other words, it depends on whether this is simply concerned with external acts of worship as such or whether it is concerned with full, inner worship of God. Insofar as prayer is an act of grace and is therefore "in Christ", it is also prayer "in Christ and in the Church" (see Eph. 3:21) and therefore it has an ecclesiological character. This character is of course much more explicit in the official liturgy of the Church and as such liturgical prayer, at least under similar circumstances, is more valuable and more effective. The commandment to love one's neighbour implies a duty to pray, at least in general, for one's fellow men.

2. *Qualities.* Apart from the fact that we may and indeed must, as created beings with a need to care for ourselves that is recognized and wanted by God,

pray for ourselves and for our own salvation, prayer also has, as an act of divine virtue, its own intentionality which in itself and for its own sake tends towards God. Because the man who prays forgets himself in this way and does not wish to assert himself, his prayer will inevitably be anthropocentric in the right sense. It will also have the objective merit, which is not sought as the first and the most all-embracing motive for prayer, of being a good work and an act of salvation. It will also lead to an increase of grace. It will similarly have the effect of satisfaction (*D* 807, 923). A theological distinction is made between this and the "impetrative" effect of the prayer of petition as a request for God's mercy. Prayer must have all the qualities possessed by the virtues of faith, hope and love – certainty, firmness and radical self-surrender. Just as there are saving acts which prepare for justification by preventive grace (*D* 797ff., 814, 817, etc.), so too is there the prayer of the penitent sinner and this is also a necessary disposition for justification. As a realization of man's being which is orientated towards God in dialogue and which God wished to create and to perfect by grace, true prayer is pleasing to God and acceptable to him; it is not merely anthropomorphic. As man's asking for God (a petition that is borne up by God's act itself) and for everything else only insofar as it forms part of this aspiring for God in accordance with God's unconditionally accepted plan, prayer is certainly heard by God. It is, moreover, heard whether we pray for ourselves or for others (see F. Suárez, for example, *De religione tract.*, 4, as opposed to Thomas Aquinas, *S.T.*, II–II, q. 81–5), although, even in prayer of the right kind, the way in which it is heard is left to God. Insofar as it is the prayer of faith in the grace of Christ (whether this is consciously and reflectively known or not) for salvation in Christ, all authentic prayer is made "in the name of Christ". Since prayer is fundamentally no more than the concrete realization of the religious act, it hardly needs to be said not only that it is a necessary means of salvation (at least for the mature believer), but also that its content as a necessary religious act can also be as clear or as indistinct as faith itself as a necessary means of salvation may also possibly be under certain circumstances (see *Cat. Rom.* IV, 1, No. 2). The necessity of prayer gives a concrete form to the need for an explicit and positive orientation of man's whole life towards God. This also determines its extent and presence – it is always practised wherever the explicit orientation towards God is threatened or suppressed. Because of the integral structure of every religious act, oral prayer (including the use of fixed formulae of prayer) has a positive meaning, so long as we are totally orientated towards God in every aspect of our being when praying in this way. It is possible to make a distinction between the individual types of prayer only in their various ways of making the realization (which is implicit in every saving act) of man's raising of himself in supernatural transcendence towards God concrete in different explicit categories. These different kinds of prayer are, however, essentially the same. (This is also true of the prayer of petition, whenever it is an authentic and absolute surrender to God's will; similarly, every prayer of man in his need is always a prayer of petition, even when that man is praising and giving thanks to God, since God is always asked, in prayer, for God.) Prayer to the saints is, correctly understood, a very complex reality. It is a legitimate "veneration" of the saints (*D* 941, 952), a legitimate petition for their intercession (*D* 941, 984) and a realization in this form of prayer of a fundamental intention directed towards God. It is therefore a realization of the being of God, since it is always God who really hears this prayer to the saints. Insofar as it is implicitly an orientation towards God, every saving act is really also prayer, although this does not mean that formal prayer, as an explicit raising of the heart to God, is superfluous.

Karl Rahner

PREDESTINATION

I. Concept and History of the Problem

Two aspects are to be clearly distinguished from the start: the divine prevision which belongs to the order of knowledge, and predestination, which involves much more. In the latter, God is envisaged as the creator and conserver of the world, the primary mover who moves all secondary causes, including the human will. He moves the will in such a way that its free decisions are ultimately effects of God's primary causality. This is as true of any human life as a whole as of each individual decision. Nonetheless, man remains free under the divine influence; see *Grace and Freedom*. These general statements may be confirmed and made more precise by the doctrine of Scripture.

The OT speaks again and again of the infinite wisdom of the creator. It also affirms his omnipotence, by which he can use his creatures as the instruments of his anger (Is 10:5f., 15) or of his mercy (Is 45:1). It shows him hardening the heart of the Pharaoh (Exod 7:3), but also insists on the freedom of man, and on the divine mercy which can create a new heart in man (Ezek 36:26). The NT also reveals God as hardening the sinner and punishing him with blindness (Jn 9:39), just as it also affirms the liberating grace of God (Jn 8:36). The most characteristic texts are to be found in the theology of St. Paul. God is absolutely sovereign. He has mercy upon whomever he wills, and hardens the heart of whomever he wills (Rom 9:14–18). No one can resist his will or demand an account from him. Like the potter, he is master of the vessel which he moulds (Rom 9:19–24). He loved Jacob and hated Esau, before they were born (Rom 9:11ff.).

The Greek Fathers interpreted these and other relevant texts mainly with a view to preserving human freedom. But these commentaries come from the time before the Pelagian controversy, and there was no precise terminology which would allow of an exact description of the relation between nature and grace, distinctions between the various aspects of grace and reflection on the problems of the *initium fidei* and final perseverance. As a result, charges of semi-Pelagianism have been brought against this author or that, though unjustly.

The problem of predestination was first envisaged and discussed in all its implications by Augustine. Though he affirmed the necessity of human co-operation in the business of salvation, he constantly insisted on the sovereign independence of God. At the beginning, he failed to recognize the need of interior grace for the call to salvation, but from 397 on (*Quaestiones ad Simplicianum*: *PL*, XL) he corrected this view. At this period most of the Fathers tended to link baptism with final perseverance, so that all Christians, except those who became heretics, schismatics and apostates, had the certainty of being saved. Augustine showed in his sermons and various treatises (*De Fide et Operibus: PL*, XL) that even Christians can be lost. The problem of predestination was thus linked with final perseverance. Towards the end of his life, when answering the questions of various monks, in *De Correptione et Gratia* (426; *PL*, XLIV, cols. 915–46), *De Praedestinatione Sanctorum* (*ibid.*, cols. 959–92), and *De Domo Perseverantiae* (429; *PL*, XLV, cols. 993–1027), Augustine defined more precisely his positions in the question of grace. As a consequence of original sin, mankind is assigned to perdition, but God saves from this *massa damnata* those whom he has marked out for salvation, and these are infallibly saved. The number of the elect is predetermined from eternity. God does not positively reject the rest, but permits them to assign themselves to perdition, because of their sins.

Though the Augustinian synthesis was accepted in principle in the West, it was a constant source of doctrinal controversy, as in the Carolingian controversy on predestination in the 9th century (Gottschalk of Orbais), in which two equally orthodox councils were opposed to one another (Quiercy and Valence, *D* 316–25). At the end of the Middle Ages, Wycliffe and Huss took up once more the thesis of Augustine, and used it to buttress their ecclesiological opinions. Thus a bad Pope or a bishop neglectful of his duties could not belong to the society of the predestined, and hence could claim no authority in the Church (*D* 588, 606, 646, 647, 648).

This view was applied still more widely by Luther, and above all by Calvin, in the 16th century. For Calvin, as for Augustine, some have been chosen and others reprobated from eternity. But Calvin considered predestination and reprobation independently of the problem of original sin. God, the creator and sovereign Lord of his creatures, disposes of them for his glory according to his good pleasure ("supralapsarian predestination", *Institutes*, III, 21–24). The Arminians rejected these harsh views, but the uncompromising Calvinists (followers of Gomar) gained the upper hand at the synod of Dordrecht (1618–19).

In Catholic theology, Jansenius sought to end the controversies about grace by appealing directly to Augustine. He did not take over the notion of supralapsarian predestination from Calvin, but based his system on the Fall, the impotence of man, the gratuitousness of grace and the absolute sovereignty of God. This view resulted in a denial of the active universal salvific will of God. Against this inhuman assertion the Church declared that Christ died for all men and not only for the predestined, and not only for the justified or believers (*D* 1096, 1294, 1379).

Post-Tridentine scholasticism was much preoccupied with the problem of the efficacious grace, predestination and reprobation. But the problem was approached from too narrow an angle. The general view was that heretics, schismatics and unbelievers were condemned to the punishment of hell. In this framework, the discussion bore on whether the just were predestined before any prevision of their merits, or, on the contrary, with their merits taken into consideration. The latter position was upheld by Lessius. This view, which was rejected by Bellarmine and Suarez as well as by the Thomistic school, ultimately prevailed among the Jesuits and many other theologians. The Dominican school, which was more strongly orientated to Augustine, emphasized above all the prevision and omnipotence of God and, in particular, that the merit of man was itself the fruit of grace and final perseverance a special help of God's grace. But the Dominican school was also inclined to admit a negative reprobation of those who did not come under predestination to glory, which was of its nature gratuitous. The great interest of theologians of this school is to avoid any suggestion of God being in any way dependent on man. In their view, the choice lies between a God who (sovereignly) determines and a God who is determined (by the creature).

The best representatives of modern Thomism consider that this perspective on the problem should be abandoned. For God is not in time. His transcendence places him in an eternity which has neither past nor future, but only an eternal present, though even this concept is inadequate. Augustine had already drawn attention to this truth, but was forced by the needs of controversy to adapt himself to the problems of his opponents and to speak as though God had chosen Jacob and rejected Esau *before* the historical event. But this priority is admissible only in the metaphysical sense, not the historical. Thomas Aquinas says: "Just as God sees all things in his own essence, in one act of knowledge, so too he wills all things in his goodness in one act of his will. Just as in God knowledge of the cause is not the cause of knowledge of the effects, but God knows the effects themselves in their cause: so too to will the end is not in God the cause of willing the means to the end. Nonetheless, he wills that the means to the end should be ordained to the end. Hence God wills that something should be for the sake of another, but he does not will that something because of another ("Vult ergo hoc esse propter hoc, sed non propter hoc vult hoc") (*Summa Theologica*, I, q. 19, a. 5). The relationship between grace, merit and glory is explained on this principle (*ibid.*, q. 23, a. 5). But the conception must also include the intercession of the saints, to whose prayers the possibility of mediating with regard to predestination is assigned (*ibid.*, q. 23, a. 8). When it is affirmed that the number of the elect is fixed immutably, this only means that God does not need to wait for the end of the world in order to know the final destiny of each man. Even Aquinas was unable to carry out his basic principle consistently in this question, since he sometimes uses formulas which falsify the perspective and suggest that God had sketched a programme for the world in his mind, before time began. In this picture, the light called for the shadows (*ibid.*, q. 23, a. 5 ad 3). Further, the real problem is our inability to express in human terms the *mode* in which God, the first cause of all that is, works through the secondary causes, in particular, our freedom, when creating a world in which some save themselves and others condemn themselves, though no one can accuse God of injustice or favouritism (*D* 142, 2007, 805f.).

Like the Church itself, spiritual writers do not shrink from anthropomorphic language. As Bossuet says, they hold the two ends of a chain, without seeing all the links between them (cf. *The Imitation of Christ*, book I, ch. 25, no. 2). What appears primarily as an abstract metaphysical truth is in fact the concrete yield of the subtle interplay of grace and freedom. In the 17th and 18th centuries, some theologians held that God, growing tired of the resistance of sinners, could abandon them and leave them to their fate of self-condemnation. This was to draw over-hasty conclusions from the Augustinian formula which had been reaffirmed by the Council of Trent: "Deus neminem deserit nisi prius deseratur" (*D* 804). We now understand more clearly that the assertions of Scripture with regard to the omnipotence of God and the efficaciousness of grace must be kept in equilibrium with the assertion of human freedom and the infinite mercy of God.

The theology of predestination must bear two elements in mind. All the good which we do comes from God. In a supernatural order, nothing good can be done without grace. And the call to salvation, perseverance in the grace given in the sacrament of baptism or regained in the sacrament of penance are also gifts of grace. Further, it must be maintained that final perseverance is a greater gift than all the others taken together (cf. *D* 806). Our life as a whole is in fact in the merciful hands of God. Our spiritual life is a dialogue with a personal God, not a mere relationship to an absolute being.

These considerations bring us back to the problem of the redemptive incarnation in connection with the problem of predestination in general. It is enunciated by Aquinas, when he speaks of the predestination of Jesus Christ and of our predestination in Jesus Christ. "If in predestination one considers the act of predetermining, the predestination of Christ is not the cause of our predestination. For God predestined him and us in one and the same act. But if one considers the end and object of predestination, the predestination of Christ is the cause of ours. For God has ordained from all eternity that our salvation should be brought about by Jesus Christ. For eternal predestination involves not merely that which is to come about in time, but also the manner and order according to which this is to take place in time" (*Summa Theologica*, III, q. 24, a. 4).

Henri Rondet

II. Theological explanation

Predestination is only one aspect of the mystery of the universal causality of God in relation to the independent freedom of the creature. It is merely the application, on the level of action, of the mystery of the co-existence of the infinite divine reality with created beings which really *are*. They are genuine realities, different from God and valid even before him, and *as* such utterly and entirely upheld by God. Thus predestination means the eternal "divine" decree, ordained to the supernatural goal of each individual insofar as this final state – and the events decisive in its regard in the history of man – are absolutely willed by God not merely as something desirable but as in fact to be attained. Here predestination is understood either in the sense that it includes reprobation, along with predestination to glory, as a type of predestination, though not on the same level, or it is merely predestination to glory, understood as in contrast to reprobation. Since God is the absolute ground which bestows reality on *all* things by his free act, he is not merely an onlooker at the course of the world, but must will each movement, if it is to come to be. This divine will takes in reality as a whole from the start and is immediately effective at every moment of reality. This will cannot be determined except by God's own wise and holy freedom, which is necessarily incomprehensible and unappealable. The creature only has the proper religious attitude to God as *God* when he acknowledges this unfathomable freedom which is the ground of all things. Hence there is a predestination to glory for those who attain bliss, since this is the climax and end of the history of man and the world (*D* 805, 825, 827). Insofar as predestination envisages the totality of human salvation as such – arising from morally good decisions and/or salvific situations, both made possible by God's efficacious grace, from perseverance and the resulting glory – the sole cause of predestination is the free love of God. But as such it wills the glory of man (in the case of those who have come to the use of reason in freedom) in dependence on his moral decision (but see *Limbo*). God's unfathomable love wills a salvation whose elements explain one another. The predestination to glory for the spiritual creature as a whole has already become a manifest eschatological reality in Jesus Christ. For each individual man on his pilgrimage, predestination, as it refers to himself, remains unknown, but is an object of hope and prayer. Predestination does not eliminate the freedom of the creature, its responsibility, its dialogal partnership with God, but is the basis of all this, because the will of God can and does aim, in the transcendence of its causality, at the constitution of the free man and his act.

If predestination is understood as the elimination of human freedom and responsibility in the working out of salvation – theological determinism –

we have the heresy of predestinarianism (*D* 300, 316ff., 320ff., 816, 827). There is no positive and active predestination to sin, that is, to the misuse of freedom. It would be incompatible with the holiness of God and his universal salvific will, and is unnecessary theologically, since the sinfulness of the sinful deed as such, being a deficiency in being, needs no positive divine causality. God does not will sin, even though he foresees it, permits it and wills positively the punishments of sin (predestination to perdition as punishment). For these punishments are the consequences of sin, and not the ground of the divine decree to permit sin (*D* 300, 316, 322).

Karl Rahner

PRIEST

A. Concept

It is important to bear in mind, in the following discussion of the applicability of the terms "priest" and "priesthood" to the office-holders in the Church, that the NT does not use the terms ἱερεύς, ἱεράτευμα, to describe ecclesiastical office. They occur, however, in the interpretation of Christ's work of salvation and in the description of the NT people of God.

The Letter to the Hebrews, in the perspective of the Jewish-Christian community and its interest in OT tradition, works out a theology of Christ's work of salvation which presents it as the exercise of the high priestly ministry of the OT. This is the only text of the type in the NT. It sees Christ's work as the definitive fulfilment of the promises contained in the cultic order of the OT, and also as the ending of the OT sacrifices, which can henceforth neither be repeated nor surpassed. On the basis of Ps 109:4, OT assertions are transferred to Christ which display his "priesthood" as immeasurably surpassing all types of priesthood in the people of Israel (Heb 7:3; cf. 1:2–13; 3:6; 4:14; 5:5; 7:28). The crucifixion is seen as the consummation of his self-sacrificing obedience (9:12ff., 28; 10:8ff.). His mediating action is complete and supreme, in the forgiveness of sins, sanctification, and the opening up of access to God, and this mediation is there "once and for all" through Christ's sacrifice on the cross (7:27; 9:12, 25–28; 10:10–18). Seen from the standpoint of Christ's salvation, the OT dispensation is merely a shadow (8:5; 10:1) and a parable (9:9) of the true salvation.

Where the terms which have to do with priesthood are applied to the NT people of God, as in 1 Pet 2:5, 9:; Rev 1:6; 5:10; 20:6, they are used to express the self-understanding of the Church in its future eschatological form as well as in its present incarnational form. And here it should be noted that the term sacrifice, a necessary correlative to priesthood, is also used in a transferred sense (cf. Heb 13:15f.; Phil 4:18; Jn 1:27; Rom 12:1). Thus the whole Church, and in it each individual Christian incorporated into it by baptism and confirmation, is the historically visible and tangible representation of the priesthood of Christ. Hence it can, by invoking the unique sacrifice of Christ, have direct access to God, share in his holiness and surrender itself as a sacrifice to the divine disposition.

If the question is now posed as to the possibility and legitimacy of explaining ecclesiastical office through the concepts of priest and priesthood, the NT material and the obvious opposition to the OT priesthood show that the question cannot be answered by having recourse to OT models. And the other priesthoods known from the history of religion are still less relevant. The questioner must confine himself to NT sources, and patterns which are suggested or intruded from outside can only be used with the utmost critical prudence.

B. Historical Development

If we now consider the historical development in which ecclesiastical office was interpreted by the use of the terms priest and priesthood, three stages may be distinguished, though only in a very summary way. They are the early Church, the medieval Church and the modern Church with its crisis and reconsiderations.

1. *The early Church*. The call and mission of the "Twelve" is of decisive importance for the understanding of the office in the Church. The characteristic of the Twelve is one that is already clear in the lifetime of Jesus: their intimate connection with the saving work of Christ. They carry out the charge which was given to Christ. Their destiny is like that of Christ. Their words and actions have the power and authority of his ministry behind them. Their later title of apostles points in the same direction. They are dependent on Christ and charged with the preaching of the gospel. The intimate connection between office in the Church and the mandate of Christ was maintained after his departure by faith in the risen Lord, who was thus known to be present to his Church, and through the confirmation of the mission in the events of Pentecost. To the charge of preaching, that of ordering the growing communities was added, these being the visible representation of the risen Lord. And this again was part of his charge. Further expansion made the appointment of helpers of the apostles necessary. They received their authority from the apostles. The legitimacy of its exercise was based on their dependence on the apostles. Thus were formed the colleges of the elders (πρεσβύτεροι, which gives the English "priest"), within which the office of their president or head developed (ἐπίσκοπος, English "bishop"). A third office also appeared, that of the deacons (cf. Acts 6:1–7, διάκονοι).

Parallel to the external differentiation of the ecclesiastical office there was also a development in the understanding of it. It was seen as service or ministry. It was thus distinguished from all other political and religious notions. It was a service of authority over the unity and order of the communities through the preaching of the word, the administration of the sacraments and personal action. The holders of office were endowed with power to govern and to act and speak with authority in the name of all. It was a collegiate constitution with a monarchical head. It acted by Christ's mandate and as his representative.

The stage of development shown in the Pastoral Letters is that this official authority is permanently transmitted to individuals. This is done in a cultic framework and the action is understood as sacramental. A ritual of consecration is indicated 1 Tim 4:14; 2 Tim 1:6. In accordance with the basic structure of the office, the direction of cultic and sacramental actions was associated to the function of preaching the gospel (e.g., Acts 2:42, 46; 6:4; 13:1ff.; 8:15–18; 19:6; Jas 5:14; 1 Cor 11:25; Lk 22:19).

As ecclesiastical office came to be understood in this way, it became possible to explain its function by the terms and concepts of priest and priesthood, once the interpretation of Christ's work of salvation as the exercise of a priestly function had prevailed. But the official priesthood in the Church must be defined more closely in terms of the NT material outlined above. Its activity is a participation in the one, definitive priesthood of Christ and not an independent entity beside it. It gives actual force and effect to this work of Christ, but adds nothing new to it. It is an activity within the Church and within the priesthood of the Church, as constituted by the baptism and confirmation of its members. Hence it is not opposed to the general priesthood. It does not diminish the priestly character of the people of God but serves its historical realization. Since this official priesthood is permanently bestowed, it gives rise within the Church to a special priestly existence, whose testimony to Christ in and for the world can be distinguished from that of those who do not hold office – the laity. This testimony consists precisely in the exercise of these official functions in the Church. Since the ministry acts in the person of Christ, it needs for the legitimation of its claims and activity the due insertion of each of the office-holders into the historical sequence of those who were installed by Christ himself at the beginning of the chain; see *Apostolic Succession*.

In sub-apostolic times the external differentiation in the ecclesiastical office crystallized firmly. Ignatius of Antioch testifies to the distinction between "bishop", "priest" and "deacon", and already develops a theology of the episcopal office. A theology of the priesthood was also developed, appearing for the first time in Clement of Alexandria, and then more clearly and firmly in the *Traditio Apostolica* of Hippolytus, in Tertullian and Eusebius, as the eucharistic celebration came to be analysed more profoundly in theology.

2. *The medieval Church*. In the time between Constantine and the Reformation, many factors were at work in the shaping and the self-understanding of the official priesthood in the Church. They brought with them some valuable contributions, but undoubtedly led here and there to some loss of insight into the proper, NT principle of the priesthood. The accent was shifted to one single function, even though the highest of priestly functions, that of offering the eucharistic sacrifice. The priesthood was then defined as *potestas in corpus eucharisticum*. The other functions receded into the background. The concept of the "power of orders" was distinguished from that of the "power of jurisdiction", which had certain consequences for the way in which their intrinsic relationship was understood.

The office of deacon became colourless in contrast to the priesthood, with its exclusive power to consecrate, and was reduced to a mere transitional stage. The office of bishop, the *potestas in corpus mysticum*, was primarily regarded as power to govern. Its sacramental character was denied here and there, and the relationship between bishop and priest unduly restricted to the jurisdictional plane. The rise of monasticism and the adoption of its forms of life by the official priesthood, as in celibacy, reinforced the charismatic character of the priestly office. But once the notion had crept in that the *homo spiritualis* was of higher moral value than the man in the world, the official priesthood was exposed to the danger of losing its original unity with the laity, when indeed it was not simply seen as its contrast. Sociological factors contributed to the rise of a special caste or class of clerics, underlined by the privileges allotted them in civil law. The territorial parish came into being. The political power intervened in the organization of pastoral work, using its authority as landlord to claim the right of patronage and to consider churches the personal appanage of the ruler. All this led to an increasing independence of the priest with regard to the bishop.

3. *Crisis and reconsideration in modern times*. The modern crisis in the traditional understanding of the official priesthood was first signalled by Luther's protest against the gulf between clergy and laity which he regarded as an accomplished fact in the medieval Church. He recalled once more the general priesthood of the faithful. This was not to deny the existence of a spiritual office as the ministry of the word and sacraments, nor its institution by Christ. But Luther denied the necessity of any special religious qualification, bestowed in a sacrament of orders and enshrined

in the law of the Church, to equip the baptized and confirmed Christian for the exercise of this function. The call was enough. The basic qualification was provided by baptism and confirmation. The denial of the sacrificial character of the Eucharist implied that the office of celebrant was not a priestly one. As against this position, the ecclesiastical magisterium affirms, especially in Trent, that there is an external, visible priesthood in the Church, instituted by Christ (*D* 949, 957, 961, 963), transmitted by the sacrament of orders and independent of the will of the State or of the people of the Church (*D* 2301). Further, it is proper to the official priesthood, in contrast to the general priesthood of the faithful, that only the priest can celebrate the Eucharist in the name of Christ and so truly offers sacrifice and is therefore "priest" (*D* 957, 961, 2300). In the same way, certain other sacramental powers are reserved to him; see *Penance* II.

There were also other developments which had weighty consequences for the traditional notion of the priestly office. There was a transformation in the society which had given a stamp to the clerical state and way of life. There was a movement towards secularization which eliminated sacred institutions in society in favour of purely utilitarian forms of organization. There was a change in the situation of the Church in the modern world, where it found itself more and more in the situation of a diaspora, but for this very reason activating all the members of the "little flock", stressing their unity and concentrating more on what was common to them than on what distinguished one from another. Finally, there was the influence of democratic political practices on the common life of the Church and on the acknowlegment and exercise of Church authority.

C. The Doctrine of Vatican II

Directives for the necessary rethinking of the essence of the NT priesthood are to be found in the declarations of the Second Vatican Council, especially in the Constitution on the Church, *Lumen Gentium*, arts. 10, 28; Decree on Bishops, *Christus Dominus*, arts. 15, 28–32; Decree on Priests, *Presbyterorum Ordinis*. The Council reaffirms the existence in the Church of a true official priesthood, which owes its origin to divine institution and is exercised in various "orders" (bishops, priests, deacons) (*Lumen Gentium*, art. 28). Formally, it is there to bring about Christ's presence in his Church (*Lumen Gentium*, art. 21; *Sacrosanctum Concilium* [on the liturgy], art. 7), to share Christ's office of mediator, shepherd and head (*Presbyterorum Ordinis*, art. 1; *Lumen Gentium*, art. 28), with authority "to act in the person of Christ the head" (*Presbyterorum Ordinis*, art. 2). The description of the actual functions of the office takes in a very wide field. "Those who are consecrated by holy orders are appointed to feed the Church in Christ's name with the Word and the grace of God" (*Lumen Gentium*, art. 11). Within this wide framework there is room for the preaching of the gospel, pastoral work for the faithful and celebration of divine service (*ibid.*, art. 28). These texts prevent too narrow a view being taken of the official priesthood, such as was suggested by the undue emphasis on its cultic function, and show that its full significance is not perfectly rendered by the term "priests", if the notion is adopted too literally and uncritically from the OT tradition, and above all from comparative religion. The priesthood of the NT is exercised not merely in worship (sacrifice and sacrament), but also in the preaching of the word and in authoritative government. Hence the priesthood must be completed by such notions as that of the prophetic ministry.

The "fullness of orders" is found in the episcopal office (see *Bishop*; Vatican II, *Sacrosanctum Concilium*, art. 15). In the light of history, this is a noteworthy demand that its significance should not be restricted to the power of jurisdiction. As regards the shaping of the relationship between bishop and priest, it follows that the priest is not merely his subject but above all his co-worker (*ibid.*, art. 15). He shares the fullness of the bishop's power of orders, and in accordance with the proper constitution of the Church, exercises it in the fellowship of the *presbyterium* (cf., for example, *Lumen Gentium*, art. 28; *Christus Dominus*, arts. 15, 28). Finally, the restoration of the diaconate "as a proper and permanent rank of the hierarchy" (*Lumen Gentium*, art. 29) contributes to a better understanding of all that is implied in the ecclesiastical office.

The official priesthood is distinct from the common priesthood of the faithful "in essence and not only in degree" (*ibid.*, art. 10). Hence its powers are conferred by a special sacrament and its ministers are distinguished by a special "character" (*Presbyterorum Ordinis*, art. 2). Nonetheless, priests are not ordained for their own perfection, but for the service of their brothers (*Lumen Gentium*, art. 18). Hence the official priesthood does not intrude between God and the priesthood common to all the faithful, but prepares the way for the latter to its eschatological fulfilment.

Ernst Niermann

PRIVILEGE

1. It is difficult to define "privilege", because of the disparate notions which it suggests. In Roman law, which provided the basis for the notion, it meant a favour bestowed by the lawful authorities on certain persons. But post-classical Roman law also used the term to designate "personal law", truly juridical norms applying only to certain categories of persons, who had special rights in comparison to their fellow-subjects under the ordinary law. This ambiguity persisted throughout the Middle Ages, and in some regimes down to the 19th century. It survives in the Code of Canon Law, where *De Privilegiis* includes those granted "per modum legis" (can. 71; 74 para. 2) and those granted to particular persons (or affecting certain things) (can. 72, para. 2). The difficulty is that the term combines two disparate notions. Privilege is both general law aiming like all law at the general good, but it is also a means of favouring individuals for their own particular benefit, and as such is not general law.

This rules out the classical definition as given by Isidore of Seville: "Privilegia sunt leges privatorum, quasi privatae leges" (*Etymologiae*, V, 18, 1), because it does not express the notion of favour, which has been there since Roman times. The only common and distinctive criterion seems to be "favor specialis". When some prerogative, some special favour is bestowed either on certain individuals (by a particular procedure or decree) or on a group (by law or custom), privilege comes to be.

2. We must, however, distinguish between a privilege and a dispensation. If a dispensation is defined as "contra ius", a breach of the law, and a privilege as "praeter legem", law on a different level, at least the privilege which is "contra ius" becomes a dispensation. This is what Suarez holds (*De Legibus*, VIII, 2, 10) in the case of a dispensation being granted not for a single occasion but permanently.

The present-day tendency is to hold that a privilege is or sets up an objective norm, even if only in favour of one person, while a dispensation is merely relaxing the law or, in another view, a purely "subjective" justification for acting against the general law. This is the only way to explain the enduring validity which is proper to every privilege (*CIC*, can. 70). In a given case, the recipient of a privilege is allowed an objectively valid type of action, that is, a norm which takes the place of the one which would have been breached by it. Otherwise a privilege would have to be considered as contrary to the law, a "vulnus legis", which would be abolished, like a dispensation, when the reason for it ceased. The definition also explains why a privilege is traditionally termed a "law" in the formal sense (=norm) and hence comes from a legislator. A permanent line of action in the juridico-social realm, even if confined to one person and in the nature of a permission, must be regarded as a law, a norm given by the legislator.

Under these circumstances, a privilege may be defined as a valid provision which sets up an objective norm of behaviour for certain persons or groups, granting them a "special favour" in contrast to others.

3. Since the Church is a fellowship of salvation and the people of God, such legal institutions as privileges are of especial importance. The task of the Church is not primarily to uphold a given juridical order for its own sake, but to lead men to the gospel, which is the goal to which all the laws of the Church, and above all, privileges are and must be directed. But too many privileges could be a danger to the order of the Church, on the inward or outward level.

Olis Robleda

PROPHETISM

1. *The concept.* The figure of the prophet, in various modifications, is a phenomenon in the history and sociology of all religions which are constituted within a major cultural potential. In spite of a certain possible fluidity of roles, and an actual identification at times, the prophet is different from the priest, who is the minister of divine worship. Worship is in more or less set terms and gestures, its validity is established by tradition and it can be passed on to new officials in an institutionalized way. The prophet, on the contrary, always comes forward with a new message. He has to produce his own credentials. His task cannot be, strictly speaking, institutionalized. Where mention is made of "disciples of the prophets", these are followers and assistants, but not really prophets in the course of formation. Hence the uniqueness of his vocation is essential to the prophet. He is the envoy of God. He is always to some extent the religious revolutionary, and since religion and society form a unity, he is often the ciritic of society speaking in the name of his God. Thus he proclaims a message which makes demands, and does not confine himself to truths which become perspicuous as they are propounded. Those who merely propound "wisdom", who offer initiation in mystical experience, who display mantic powers in developing certain techniques for oracles and divination, should not be called prophets. The prophet is the "bearer of revelation". He claims to be the envoy sent directly by God, the *legatus divinus* of Catholic fundamental theology, with a primordial relationship to the word of God. He is convinced that what he proclaims is the word of God himself. He feels himself the instrument not of a numinous power but of a personal, "living" God who freely reveals himself. The message which he brings is not really meant for himself alone. It is primarily for others – for those to whom he is sent with a mandate. Hence the actual nature of any given prophet must be seen as intrinsically connected with his message, with his "concept of God". And this affects again his relationship to the priesthood and the institutionalized religion within the ambit of which he appears. The "word" is constitutive of the prophet and his task, so that it is not a merely neutral record, but a criticism of religion and society, an interpretation of historical events, and indeed, as such,

an intrinsic element of these events, because giving them their real depth and truth and allowing them to exert their full force.

It follows from what has been said that the prophet does not make predictions in the sense of an oracle or clairvoyant. This would be a very secondary restriction of the concept. Nonetheless, since he creates a new and forward-looking situation in the history of salvation by his criticism of society, he is essentially associated with promises and the future. Furthermore, since the prophet's words are not to be just doctrinal propositions but are to be translated into real action, he will himself nearly always be the leader and organizer of religious and social changes. He himself "institutionalizes" his message, in a strange, dangerous but necessary paradox which conflicts with his own nature.

To sum up: prophetism – where the word does not merely mean the prophetic office – may be said to exist wherever a religious society accepts on principle the possibility of a prophet, where the coming of a new prophet is reckoned with, where prophetic criticism of traditional and institutionalized religion, of "a Church", is not ruled out from the start as irreligious, where religion is understood as much in the light of its future as of its past, where prophetic criticism is acknowledged to be an intrinsic element of religion itself.

2. *Dogmatic principles with regard to prophets and prophetism,* a) The prophet is constitutive in a religion which is convinced that it is established by a historical revelation given in words. Hence he is essential to the history of OT and NT salvation.

b) This proposition does not mean that there were no true prophets outside the OT and NT. There is a general, genuine, grace-given history of revelation (see *Salvation* III), co-extensive with the history of mankind in general because given with the perpetual and universal self-communication of God in grace, by virtue of his universal salvific will. And this "transcendental" revelation is inconceivable without being in some way consciously objectivated in words, a process which is necessarily the history and mediation of this "transcendental" revelation itself. Thus the phenomenon of prophecy must occur again and again in this general history of revelation. This does not mean that there cannot be simply "false prophets", who speak only in their own name. And it must also be considered that the translation into words of the general revelation (which is there with grace), and its actualization, may be partially defective or may be relevant only within certain areas and certain periods.

Nonetheless, such wholly or partially genuine prophets, who came forward by a truly divine disposition outside the OT and NT, can be essentially distinguished from the prophets, as *legati divini*, in the OT and NT. For these have a palpable historical connection, acknowledged as legitimate, with Jesus Christ. They are his acknowledged "precursors", while Jesus Christ is the vehicle of the pure and eschatologically unsurpassable revelation of God, present in him as event, and in his words as going to constitute this event.

It is therefore impossible to provide a clear and definite criterion for true and false prophets outside the OT and NT, or for what is genuine and what is merely human and erroneous in a prophet who may eventually be recognized as on the whole genuine; see *Revelation*. But this need not stop us from recognizing on principle the existence of true prophecy outside Christianity and its immediate pre-history – the OT as an element in the history of salvation. This means primarily pre-Christian times, but it should be remembered that this "pre-Christian" period need not have ended chronologically at the same time in all the regions and situations of salvation.

c) The relation of the hearer to the

prophetic message and to the prophet who comes forward claiming the obedience of faith is dealt with relatively precisely in fundamental theology; see also *Faith*, *Miracle*, *Word of God*.

d) In contrast to medieval theology, the present-day theology of the schools pays relatively scant attention to prophetism. Points to be discussed would include the prophetic vocation, the coming of revelation to the prophet himself, the growth of his inner certainty that he is uttering and must utter the divinely revealed truth, the various types of the prophetic word – imagery, apocalyptic discourse, promise, threat of judgment, etc. Here grace, the self-communication of God, would have to be considered as revelatory by its very nature. The unity and the difference between such revelation and revelation in words would have to be treated expressly. One would have to consider the circular process in the prophet himself, in which the mission and the content of the message legitimate each other. If mysticism, in the full sense, is not experience of one's own "numinous" inwardness, but the experience of grace, revelatory in character, there is no absolute opposition between mystical and prophetic experience. But then there is much in the theology of mysticism about mystical experience, about the criteria to be used by the mystic and others to test such experience, which could be applied to the theology of the original prophetic experience in the prophet himself. According to what has been said under b) above, there is no need to assume *a priori* that parallels between prophecy in non-Christian religions and in the OT and NT will not throw light on the question.

e) Jesus Christ is *the* great prophet, the absolute bringer of salvation. This does not mean that prophecy has simply ceased (see below, under 3). But the only prophets are those who strive to uphold his mesage in its purity, who attest that message and make it relevant to their day. Since Jesus Christ is *the* prophet, and since the notion then coincides in fact with that of the absolute, eschatological bringer of salvation, the content of this notion, with its two aspects, can be seen to be identical with the dogmatic statements of the Church on the person and work of Jesus Christ. But he is the eschatologically final prophet, *the* prophet as such, who cannot be surpassed in the further history of revelation and salvation, not because God arbitrarily decided that no prophet (to surpass him) should be sent, but because his task and his person are identical (though he explains himself in the light of the presence of the Kingdom of God rather than vice versa). He brings the absolute immediacy and self-communication of God, not just a particular message and promise, couched in ordinary categories and addressed to this nation or that age. Through his death, the elimination of all intramundane goals, his entry, by the resurrection, into full immediacy to God, he created and manifested the situation in which "*after* him" there could only come the consummation of history by its absorption into the immediate presence of God. When God responded to his prophetic destiny with the resurrection from the dead, he became the final prophet, the one real prophet in the full sense of the word, and was manifestly revealed for what he was. All other prophetic words either point to the (unanswered) question of death or to a coming prophet, and so remain "precursors".

3. *Church and prophecy*. a) Prophetism is not alien to the Church, because the Church itself is the permanent presence of the word of *the* prophet, Jesus Christ. It is the Church in which the word effects what is signifies and is therefore a prophetic word. For the sacraments of the Church are also the supreme actuation of the efficacious word, both as regards the ministering Church and the recipients of grace. The "closure" of its

apostolic kerygma and the permanence of its basic institutions are not due to a refusal of prophecy, but to its belief and hope that Jesus Christ is the one incomparable prophet, and that the Church is definitive (in this age), inasmuch as it holds firm to the definitiveness of Jesus Christ and is again given this steadfastness by him.

b) Within this fundamental prophetism, there is again a prophetic element, inasmuch as the charisms are of the essence of the Church, in spite of and throughout all its institutions. Of their nature, the spontaneous charisms which work in and for the Church are prophetic. They do not cease to be prophetic because they must remain within the "order" of the Church, though possibly only at the cost of grave conflicts. For the "order" of the Church is itself nothing else than a participation in the prophetic charge of Christ. This charismatic prophecy in the Church helps to make the message of Jesus new, relevant and actual in each changing age. It does not matter whether the representatives of this charismatic prophecy in the Church – the authors of religious renewal, the critics of the Church and the society of their day, the discoverers of new tasks for the Church and the faithful – are called prophets or are given other names. They are mostly comprised under the title of "saints". If such men do not merely reaffirm general principles and apply them to new cases, but display in their message something creative and incalculable, with the force of historic turning-points, so that they are legitimate and effective in the Church, we may say that the Church has had a "major" or a "minor" prophet.

c) The ecclesial and theological reality of private revelation is to be discussed in this framework.

d) It may even happen constantly in the Church, without detriment to the ultimate promises to the Church, that true prophecy may be repressed by the holders of office or the indifference of the faithful. And there may be false prophets in the Church, and indeed difficult or even impenetrable mixtures of true and false prophecy. The "discernment of spirits", by the defence of genuine prophecy against a conservative establishment, or by the unmasking of false prophecy in the Church, can itself be a prophetic mission.

e) In the light of the prophetic element in the Church, the official priesthood must be subjected to a reappraisal. The priest is essentially the preacher of the word, and never a mere administrative officer in a religious society. And his cultic function is not the offering of a new independent sacrifice each time, but the re-presenting of the one sacrifice of Christ through the efficacious words of the Eucharist. Hence the priesthood should be understood rather in the light of the prophetic than the cultic element, a matter perhaps of some practical importance. This approach should not be excluded *a priori*, since in the Church the "office" and the prophetic charism are not elements which can be totally and neatly distinguished from each other.

Karl Rahner

PROTESTANTISM

1. From a Christian point of view mere rejection of unity with the Catholic Church obviously cannot create a *Christian* Church or any sort of unity. The same is true of baptism pure and simple, for since it is given the most various and contradictory interpretations, it alone cannot form a Church.

2. The Catholic recognizes that his own post-Reformation Church must at least be presumed to be the true Church of Jesus Christ (until the contrary is proved), because its historical continuity with the Church of the past is without doubt more substantial than that of the Protestant Churches, since it preserves

the unity of the episcopate and communion with the Roman See (which characterized the pre-Reformation Church), and since Protestant Christians themselves can only be a legitimate Church to the extent that the old Church is also their Church. Accordingly, a Catholic could only concede an objective right to secede from the traditional Church if the points of difference between Catholics and Protestants were all entirely irrelevant to salvation before God, and we were divided on no matter about which we ought to agree (which no Christian can seriously maintain, for otherwise intercommunion would be the universal practice), or if it were certain that a Protestant Christian found the Catholic Church patently denying a truth which his Christian conscience would have obliged him to continue to profess at the time of the rupture.

But a Catholic Christian cannot agree that this second supposition is verified, for: 3. The doctrine of the all-sufficiency of Scripture (*sola Scriptura*) can certainly not be allowed to mean that the living preaching of the word of God did not precede the written word of God in the Church, demanding the assent of faith and efficaciously at work before Scripture existed; Scripture objectifies this spoken word and therefore is permanently sustained by the authority Christ bestowed to proclaim the word of God with binding force. Otherwise the fact that the Church fixed the limits of the canon of Scripture is really unintelligible. This is not to deny that the later Church – whose doctrine can contain nothing but the apostolic preaching and can be judged by no other standard – finds in Scripture the normative source of the faith and the permanent criterion of the (necessary) development of its doctrine and the fresh actualizations which it must constantly be given. But by the nature of Scripture this criterion is to be used by the Church as a whole, not a decisive critical weapon with which the individual can attack the Church's interpretation of Scripture.

4. The Catholic Church too accepts the doctrine of *sola gratia* if it be rightly understood. For from first to last every salutary act of man without exception is the fruit of gratuitous grace; whether it be the capacity for such acts or the free act itself or the liberation of freedom for divine faith, hope and love, all comes from that grace which indeed is meant for all but which none can claim of right. Now this grace really happens, so that God by a true interior transformation makes man, who otherwise would be Godless, his own dear child – man is no more what he once was (or otherwise would be). Yet man cannot boast of this grace as his possession. For he hopes in faith that he possesses it, but can never be certain that he does. Daily tempted and sinning, he daily flees anew from himself to God's mercy, because he never knows for certain whether his temptations and the sins he hopes are venial may not forbode or conceal a real rejection of God. Thus the Catholic Christian also admits he is a sinner while clinging to God's grace as grace that alone can save him. But because grace truly transforms the justified, whatever he does in the Spirit of God deserves the reward of eternal life – gains that merit of which Scripture is eloquent. This doctrine is a statement of fact in praise of divine grace, not a statement of Christian motivation, for in order to find God one must love him for his own sake and not simply be preoccupied with one's own blessedness.

5. If, as most Protestants acknowledge, there are sacraments in the Church, that is words which when spoken by the Church in a sacred rite issue into act in the individual's concrete religious situation and what is proclaimed becomes in him by God's act (baptism, Lord's Supper); if on the other hand, as Catholic doctrine affirms, the sacraments vary in rank and dignity

and are not all equally necessary and, needless to say, do not effect in adult man what they validly pledge unless they are received by (or produce) a repentant believer; if, finally, as Protestants believe, God's word spoken by the Church is not a mere abstract statement but the actual happening of what it announces, then it is difficult to see why Protestants should not agree with the Catholic Church that all those words in which the Church engages its whole being – as the sign of the fulfilled promise of grace – and pledges God's grace to the individual at decisive moments in his life, should be called sacraments. Especially since the words of forgiveness addressed to the sinner (Mt 16; 18; Jn 20), the bestowal of the Spirit by confirmation (Acts 8), the anointing of the sick (Jas 5), the transmission of office by the laying on of hands (Acts 6), are well attested in Scripture and St Paul considers marriage to be the token of Christ's redemptive love for his Church (Eph 5). See *Penance* II, *Confirmation*, *Marriage*.

6. If Protestant theology does not wish to transform the Church which is a tangible reality in the world, confessing Christ its Lord before the world, into a purely invisible community of grace (which is not generally the case today at least); if *this* Church, despite all weaknesses and betrayals, has received the promise that the might of grace will always defend it against all the powers of death; if this Church, in order to be such, must exhibit a certain order and organization, that is, office invested with Christ's authority (however that office and authority may be interpreted in detail): then this Protestant theology must acknowledge that when it repudiates with all its strength unbelief or false belief which would dissolve its very being, founded as it is on personal faith in the apostolic kerygma of Christ, it must be able to pronounce a No that is absolutely final and permanently binding, though it must always fall short of the fullness of lived witness to Christ (not only must be able to but in fact intends to do so and does it – and this anathema and *damnamus* was uttered by the fathers of the Reformation and during the struggle against National Socialism); and that this No, if it is not to dissolve the Church as true witness to Christ, must be kept from going astray by the power of the Spirit, that is to say, it must be "infallible" (which does not mean "plenary"). Protestant theology must also recognize that this magistral No must be pronounced by appointed office in the Church if it is really to speak in Christ's name and by his commission. If this office of the Church is permanently organized in a college which succeeds by right to the apostolic college, under a personal head who perpetuates the office of Peter in the apostolic college, then this supreme authority (the universal episcopate in the Church and its personal head) must be invested with this power to pronounce "infallible" judgment in matters of faith when it acts on behalf of the Church as a whole in the authority of Christ. In other words, if the Church, whose faith is always threatened, is also constantly protected by grace, must constantly announce new historical articulations of the faith, and if its authority is vested in certain persons, then there must be a supreme teacher in the Church whom the divine mercy preserves from error when he engages his full authority as supreme teacher of the Church. Here reference should be made to what was said above under 1 b), and we ought to add that the Church, which must at least be presumed to have been founded by Christ, has definitively made its own this conception of the permanent Petrine office, which at any rate is no more unscriptural than the doctrine of the infallibility of Scripture.

Though a Catholic feels he is in the comfortable position of being able to presume that Christ founded his Church, and, as a believer who has experienced the faith of his Church "from within", to perceive that nothing un-Christian can be found in his Church's idea of itself which would compel him to abandon the presumption, nevertheless it is his duty, and the Church's duty too, continually to rethink and pray over its interpretation of the faith and to elaborate it, asking himself what it is about Catholicism which makes it difficult or impossible for other Christians of good will to recognize it as the pure, complete development of that Christian faith which they too profess and practise.

On the other hand it is obvously the duty of non-Catholic Christians not to attempt to justify the old separation by constantly devising new and more complicated theological formulae, but to consider how their own convictions can be expressed so that the old Church – which after all is their mother Church – may recognize these as deeper insights into its own faith.

But the Catholic Church must fully realize that unity of faith and unity of the Church in and under the primacy of Peter does not mean uniformity in discipline and theology for the churches so united. – See also *Schools, theological.*

Karl Rahner

I. Self-Understanding

The following article is an attempt to describe the essence of Protestantism as understood, at least implicitly, by Protestants.

Protestantism is a general term for all the Christian Churches and communities which hold themselves consciously aloof from the Roman Catholic and Eastern Orthodox Churches and in general repudiate the notion "Catholic" in the traditional sense. Protestants have a definite view of the Church, a particular view of faith and a chosen way of life, so that they cannot be merely described in a negative way as "non-Catholic" Churches. Some of them go back directly to the Reformation and can trace their genealogy to the work of Luther, Zwingli and Calvin themselves, while others owe their origin to the Reformation Churches of more recent date. These have retained characteristic traits of their past, but are so strongly marked by the problems of modern times that they have ways of life and forms of faith which do not allow of their being called Protestant in the strictly historical sense. Old Protestants may therefore be distinguished from New Protestants. The term "neo-Protestantism" may also be applied to the Churches stemming directly from the Reformation because they have been so strongly influenced by the problems and insights of modern times that their main doctrines have undergone a basic modification. Their ancient Protestant traits have little vitality or appear simply as rudiments owing their survival to a lack of resolution.

If one decides to continue to use this general term to characterize the Churches and communities which are neither "Catholic" nor "Orthodox", it will be well to distinguish two aspects in Protestantism. Firstly, it is a certain attitude in matters of faith and the Christian life. Secondly, it is a definite verdict on the basic problems which are posed by the existence of the Church, e.g., with regard to the relation between Scripture and magisterium or with regard to the instruments which the Church uses in its work, but above all with regard to the meaning of ecclesial actions and the factors, personal and supra-personal, which determine the Christian life of believers. Seen from these aspects, i.e., as an answer to the questions raised by the existence of the Church in general, and as a definite way of faith and life particularly evident in the individual Christian, three approaches are opened up. One is the question of its Confessions of faith, the second its special position within the ecumenical movement, the third the strongly marked differences between the Churches and communities which claim to be or are considered Protestant. Under these aspects, it is legitimate to speak of "World Protestantism". This concept may be used in its widest sense, so that – like "Catholicism" – it is not just a confessional demarcation, much less merely "non-Catholicism", but a Christian way of faith and life which has highly characteristic and inalienable traits, just like Catholicism. Protestantism and Catholicism would then be distinguished and correlated as two manifestations or possibilities of being Christian.

Recently, the Eastern Orthodox Churches have begun to describe themselves as "Catholic". This is a non-denominational use of the term. It is a general characteristic of the Christian Church. But it is then given a particular stamp by the Churches which see themselves as "Catholic" and thus define the general term "Catholic" in a particular concrete way. So too with the term Protestantism. But here it is not the equivalent of an assertion made solely in view of the phenomenon "Church". It is an element of self-understanding which means both a Christian attitude and a definite understanding of faith and fact. But then there can be no question of the "essence" of Protestantism or an indispensable "Protestant principle". An effort must be made to define the general term according to its full content, which need not be applicable or confined to all the Churches and communities which call themselves Protestant. From this point of view, there are Protestants not only in specific denominations, but also such as are to be so termed, by reason of their form of faith and way of life, in other Christian Churches, even though they see themselves as Orthodox or Catholic.

1. *Concrete description.* a) As regards the characteristic Protestant mentality, there is a wide spectrum of judgments within Protestantism on the problem posed by the existence of the Church as such. The main point is the relationship between the essence and the outward form of the Church. From Christian tradition as well as from its own history, Protestantism is aware of the tension between the spiritual essence and the empirical manifestation intrinsic to the very being of the Church. The tension is a basic theme of its own history, so that one might even say that wherever this tension is felt and extrapolated to the real forms of life in the Church, a "Protestant" attitude to the basic questions of Church life is ultimately manifested. St. Augustine had made it clear in his doctrine of the Church that there is an irreducible dialectic given with the being of the Church as such. The Church is the fellowship of faith and love. In all its manifestations and in all its members it is the work of the Holy Spirit, of special divine actions which are beyond all human grasp and all earthly power. But it is also an earth-bound historical institution through which and in which the fellowship of faith and love has to take concrete form in each period. This tension is intrinsic to Protestantism from the start, and felt so deeply that it carries to its ultimate consequences the protest against a type of Church which does not acknowledge this tension, represses it, or thinks to resolve it either by a one-sided spiritualization or institutionalization of the Church. Any attempt to enclose this fellowship of love and faith within history, i.e., any identification of it with an empirical entity or institution eliminates this tension. But the tension is there once and for all with the very existence of the Church. Indeed, it is already built into the preaching of Jesus himself, since the eschatological nature of the kingdom of God and the call to a very real discipleship in the following of Jesus involve this tension and perpetuate it in history.

Hence Protestantism is not to be taken as a mere No to the Church, or as the mere "individualism" as which it was formerly regarded. It is the No to a Church in whose self-understanding the essential notion of tension between the spiritual essence and the empirical form has been eliminated. The retention of the polarity is of decisive importance for the actual, empirical manifestation of the Church, for its encounter with the world and for its very understanding of the world. The recognition and the conscious retention of this tension necessarily brings with it a certain attitude to the world and a corresponding approach to the world. Protestantism arose as soon as this tension was consciously felt, affirmed as an essential ingredient of the Church's self-understanding and allowed to shape life. This also explains the multitude of Churches and communities to which Protestantism has given birth, and which is regarded by most non-Protestants as a destructive splintering. But this multiplicity is a way of protesting against the neglect of these principles within Protestantism itself. It is therefore the consistent acceptance – even though telling against itself – of a perpetual element of unrest and disquiet in the very life of the Church. The phenomenon of self-multiplication which has so often been lamented and has caused Protestantism to be reproached with its inability to form a Church, is ultimately based on the effort to find a way of life adequate to the self-understanding of the Church.

b) This also provides a solution for another question which stems from the existence of the Church, that of the relation between Scripture and ecclesiastical magisterium. In former times, and down to the present day, on the Catholic and the non-Catholic side, these two things have been regarded as either incompatible or as absolutely necessarily linked together. But now it must be recognized that there is no question of the Church coming down firmly on one side or other, as if it had to choose *either* Scripture *or* magisterium as the final court of appeal. It is not a question of the magisterium alone being competent to expound Scripture or of the magisterium only being acceptable as long as it subjects itself entirely to Scripture. The point is that the two are in a relation of indissoluble polarity. They function in a sort of feed-back circuit without which Scripture is never really present in the Church or community, and without which the magisterium as such cannot be exercised with definite objective loyalty. Scripture is first made to function by being believed in the Church or community, by being used for instruction and as the guide of life. But this instruction and doctrine and application to life can in turn only be directed to what is given and laid down in Scripture itself. Hence the magisterium is not to be considered so much from its institutional aspect, but above all with reference to its functions which in fact are at work in every Christian Church or fellowship and are exercised in varying degrees, at the level of the local Church or the synod or the whole Church, or by godparents or the recognized teachers and pastors of the Church. Hence Protestantism exists wherever men recognize and put into practice this polarity between the bond to Scripture and the necessity of actualizing its contents, the teaching function, in itself very manifold, belonging to the members in various degrees of responsibility. It cannot therefore simply be said that there is Protestantism wherever the "magisterium" is renounced. Protestantism also exercises the functions of the magisterium, though its various degrees are determined by the spiritual status of the faithful and not as an official hierarchy.

c) The material criteria of Protestantism also include a certain notion of Church action and a definite assertion as regards the means through which the Church acts. Here the relation between word and sacrament comes up. The Churches belonging to Protestantism cannot be described as those who are equipped only with the word or hold only the word in high estimation, in contrast to the sacraments, while the Catholic and Eastern Orthodox Churches would be distinguished by being the "Church of the sacraments". Such a distinction between a "Church of the word" and a "Church of the sacraments" is now theologically impossible, and above all with regard to Catholicism after the Second Vatican Council. Word and sacrament are so intimately related that they both live by the presence of Christ, though a clear distinction must be made between this presence as encountered in the word and as experienced through the sacrament. The sacrament is, no doubt, the word being rendered visible. Nonetheless, there can be no sacramental efficacy without the accompanying word. Ultimately, the difference here between Protestantism and other Churches is that it reduces the number of the sacraments to two, baptism and Eucharist, and explains them, in the light of their biblical foundation, as special gifts of Christ through which he gives himself. What other Churches consider as sacraments in addition to these two, Protestantism regards simply as actions of the Church which can only be legitimated by the word. Hence one cannot – though this has been done by many fellowships within Protestantism in a very misleading way – affirm that a low estimation of the sacrament in contrast to the word is a general characteristic of Protestantism. In this regard, it is characteristic of Protestantism that the word is seen in its proper function as the specific means of applying the blessings of salvation to the community. But this does not mean that the sacrament has not a corresponding significance, which is, however, basically distinguished from that of the word. This is due to the different way in which Christ is present in the sacrament. Hence in Protestantism, apart from baptism and the Eucharist, the various actions of the Church are given their particular meaning by the words which constitute them. It is consistent with this attitude that these actions are always referred back to their biblical foundations to determine whether they are truly ecclesiastical and "genuine" usages. Thus there is no place for a rigid traditionalism in Protestantism, though here the Protestant Churches themselves may have been at fault. It cannot be conservative about human and historical additions which may have been made to the sacramental actions in the course of history. It is prepared to examine their justification in the light of Scripture. A critical factor is constantly at work, striving to test the legitimacy, in the light of Scripture alone, both of discourse about God and of the visible deployment of this word in the customary Church actions. It is true, then, to say that constant reformation, necessary at all times by reason of the human and historical elements in the Church, is undoubtedly a Protestant principle: *Ecclesia reformata semper reformanda.* But it does not follow that Protestantism is essentially the "protest against forms", since such an attitude of protest always presupposes that the process of setting up forms is necessary and is always going on. Otherwise no protest against it would be possible.

d) Protestantism may therefore be characterized as a definite view of life and action, which displays itself in such a range of variations that no single Protestant Church contains them all. But it is also characterized by a certain understanding of faith. It recognizes its total dependence on supra-personal elements, divine grace and the Holy Spirit. At the same time, it stresses the reception of grace and the Spirit by men and strives to grasp the precise nature of this reception. This personal appropriation of the supra-personal gifts is the basis of the true spiritual life of the Christian, which is then to be manifested as such in all realms of human life. What constitutes the special significance of Protestanism and its position in Christianity is that it stresses this personal element, showing its existentiell significance for Christians and giving it a theological interpretation. Since Christian faith can only be fully realized in this personal appropriation, even Protestants have held that its key-note was "individualism". But this is only a half-truth, an effort to say that Christian faith is intrinsically ordained to taking shape in and giving shape to the personal act of man. It would be wrong to say that Protestantism attributes absolute value to the individual traits of faith. But it is certainly true that the recognition of the importance of the personal element in the appropriation of faith had far-reaching consequences for the discovery of the laws of development of human individuality in general.

Hence Protestantism is characterized by a very definite notion of life and action, as also by a notion of faith which sees it as the individual's concrete realization of the faith imparted by God as a gift.

e) If then one considers Protestantism according to its material principles, its understanding of the Church, particularly the obligation of the Church and all its members to Scripture as the normative and critical *a priori* for Christian faith and theological opinion, it should be clear that the Protestant Churches are distinguished rather by the multiplicity than the uniformity of the doctrines held in faith. It is in fact characteristic of Protestantism that it shrinks from erecting any single doctrine of faith into an absolute and thus succumbing to the temptation of a new set of laws, giving a juridical structure to the Christian life of faith. Hence there is a wide range of variations within Protestantism with regard to the notion of the Church. Some Churches uphold the "historical episcopate" or the offices mentioned in the Bible as absolutely constitutive of Church and community. Others recognize only one single office belonging to the whole Church, though it may give rise to other offices, all of which, however, have the same eminent role in the preaching of the word or the administration of the sacraments. It is perhaps a note of Protestantism that should be expressly mentioned here that it does not recognize the "sacramentality" of the office and of the sacramental actions performed by the ministers. It sees the office as founded on the Christ-event and the "word of reconciliation" (2 Cor 5:18f.) which expresses it. (The office is not as it were a creation of the community, though ultimately discharged only by virtue of the charge which it personally determines and gives to definite persons.) The office-holder within all the Protestant Churches and communities is and can only be a "minister", a "servant" who has to serve the community which has called him to its service. This does not mean that the community can do as it likes about the existence of the office and its occupation. There are Churches within Protestantism which hold on to the apostolic succession in the office of bishop, though without making it constitutive of the Church in their ecclesiology. Here the Anglican Communion forms an exception, but in any case its relationship to Protestantism is not quite clear. And there are Churches, especially among the Presbyterians or "Reformed", which consider the presbyteral and synodal order as an essentially constitutive element of the Church without which it cannot exist. It is held to be based on the apostolic Church order and hence to be one of the necessary and indispensable notes of the Church.

f) Another characteristic of Protestantism follows: its specific notion of the relation between the Church and the world. There is no idea of running the State (legislation, judiciary, etc.) along Christian lines. The world is always the place of alienation from God and distance from God. The Church, and the local Church representing it, is sent there, like the individual Christian, to make clear, by their symbolic activity, that God loves the world and the men who turn away from him again and again. They try by their action to win new individuals to the Christian fellowship of faith and so help them to limit the social effects of the world's apostasy or indeed to eliminate some of them, no matter how provisionally. This type of work in the world is definitely just a token for Protestantism, or to put it theologically, it holds that the kingdom of God, which is not of this world, can never be brought into the world, much less set up as a "kingdom" within the world. It is therefore common to all Protestant fellowships to repudiate any qualitative superiority of the Church over the world, of the spiritual over the earthly. The world with all its distinctive qualifications remains the basis of the tokens of redemption given by faith.

These material determinations which go to make up Protestantism in all its variety are arrived at by examining the concrete forms of fellowship in which Protestantism is displayed. Each of them makes some contribution to the typical traits of Protestantism described above, though no one Protestant body can be said to be the Protestant Church *par excellence*. When Protestantism is embodied in the concrete, the same problem arises as is posed on another level when one considers the nature of the Church of Christ and its concrete realization and manifestation by one of the "confessional" Churches. None of them, in spite of the claim to be comprehensive, represents fully and perfectly the Church of Christ. Their efforts are always thwarted by the elements of historicity. So too with Protestantism. It is never represented perfectly by any Protestant fellowship. It is limited by historical, cultural, national and sociological conditions.

It takes shape in Protestant Churches which primarily describe themselves negatively, i.e., as non-Catholic and non-Orthodox, though in fact they are positive but fragmentary embodiments of definite truths, as we have tried to show.

2. *Historical*. The name "Protestant" arose on the occasion of the Diet of Speyer (1528), to designate the Christians within the Catholic Church at the time who protested against a majority decision in matters of faith and Christian life, maintaining the direct personal responsibility of each individual before God. This undoubtedly underlined at the very beginning of Protestantism an important and indeed characteristic element, whose theological significance was studied in the following centuries and whose consequences in all realms, Church and world, were more and more clearly grasped. It only became clear after the Diet of Speyer and its continuation, so to speak, in the Diet of Augsburg (1530), that these "Protestants" were united in a notion of the Church which distinguished them from the Catholic Church of the time, so that a special Church, deliberately set apart from the Catholic, became inevitable. But it is also clear from the beginnings of Protestantism that this notion of the Church and a notion of faith embodied in the personal element were intrinsically connected and could issue primarily only in a confession of faith, which was again a rediscovery of an essential element of Church life. This does not mean that the Church is to be based on the confession of faith by its members. It means that its concrete presence in the world can be recognized through the confessions of its members, and hence that such confession is an expression of the self-understanding of

the Church and of Christian existence. Thus Christians were at first distinguished only as "Catholic" or "Protestant", till the recognition of the special ecclesial character of each group prevailed. This came with the more or less final forms of the Protestant confessions (the Book of Concord [1580]; Synod of Dordrecht [1618]) and the demarcation of the Roman Catholic faith at Trent (1545–63).

This crystallization into particular Churches started more or less at the same time at various points of the Church in the 16th century. But the developments within Lutheranism had a certain priority, which was soon overshadowed by others. In Germany, the Lutheran Churches were the main representatives of Protestantism. In Switzerland another independent Church was formed, first under the aegis of Zwingli, but given its definitive form and doctrine by Calvin. It influenced strongly the continent of Europe and later played a considerable role in North America. Protestantism also took root in England in connection with the reform of the English Church, which never lost certain conservative features inherited from its medieval form. The Anglican Church itself, at first decisively influenced by Calvinism and Lutheranism, only took on its definitive form after long years of internal controversy.

In Germany, Switzerland and England Protestantism in the main took the form of Churches, and as such lives on in these regions to the present day. But alongside this came a Protestantism which repudiates the Church as it came to be in the Lutheran and Presbyterian Churches or the (Established) Church of England and affirms the autonomy of each local community in which the Church is embodied ("Congregationalism"). It has gone so far as to deny every sort of communal life and issued in a Christian individualism and spiritualism, which must undoubtedly be included among the general phenomena of Protestantism.

Just as Pietism undertook this process of interiorization of faith and Church in the Lutheran and Presbyterian realms, so too Puritanism had deep effects in the realm of the Church of England. These Dissenters of various types, denied legal status as Churches, found a new home in America, where they made a decisive contribution to the modern world of capitalism and democracy. There is no doubt that one must include within Protestantism the various groups which brought about the separation of Church and State in various regions or countries, some even rejecting for themselves the title of Church or community. These have stressed one-sidedly certain elements of Protestantism. Some were convinced, like Congregationalism, that the Church can be present only in the form of independent local communities. Others, like the Baptists, hold that the Church only comes to be by the free association of its faithful, the Baptists also having a special notion of baptism and its administration. Others have emphasized re-birth and the striving for sanctity as the criterion of true Christianity, like the Quakers and Mennonites. But the Free Churches formed in England and Scotland in opposition to the established Anglican and Presbyterian Churches are also typically Protestant phenomena in the Anglo-Saxon countries, where they claim freedom of faith for the Church even in its relation to the State. They feel unable to recognize the Church except in a self-determining community independent of the State. On the other hand, they lay so much stress on the free faith of the individual that the Church takes on the character of a voluntary organization which can never oppose the freedom of the individual in his faith but has to respect it to the utmost. The groups which stem from the Free Churches of Scotland, like the "Churches of Christ" or the

"Disciples of Christ" are also part of Protestantism, since they portray typical traits of it for the modern world. This is also true of the Free Churches stemming from Lutheranism and Presbyterianism, such as the "Old Lutherans" as they were once called or the various other movements inside and outside the Protestant Churches.

Finally, it must be recognized that a number of Churches and communities have been recently formed on the American continent, to some extent as a protest against the lack of universalism in the Church outlook of the European Churches and communities. These American Churches have undoubtedly also been one-sided in stressing some features of Protestant self-understanding, but they undoubtedly belong to Protestantism and represent a typical aspect of it, however narrowly, in the world of today. The main examples are the Churches which belong to the Pentecostal movement. But even such phenomena as the Christian Scientists, the Mormons (the Church of Jesus Christ of Latter-Day Saints) and the Jehovah's Witnesses must be accounted Protestant, even when they have gone beyond the bounds of a Christian fellowship. Some have supplemented the biblical revelation by new non-biblical documents. Others have attached absolute value to certain interpretations of human experience. The universal scriptural foundation of Christian faith has been automatically pushed into the background, possibly by the hypertrophy of some single doctrine which has been made the centre of Christian preaching. But in the Protestant attitude to such associations, an essential trait of Protestantism must come into play. They must be recognized as Christian brethren who grew up on its native soil, and are to be regarded not so much as alien as alienated by the Church of their time. The narrowness and one-sidedness of their doctrines and practice put a critical question to the Christian Churches as regards the fullness of their testimony, which these Churches cannot ignore. But they therefore also display distortions which show clearly the dangers to which a wrong understanding of freedom is exposed in Protestantism.

Thus modern Protestantism is characterized by its multiplicity and variety. But this also gives it a special and a very difficult position within the ecumenical movement, so that it is justifiable to speak of "World Protestantism", in spite of the difficulty of an exact definition of the term. Protestantism as a whole has the vocation of representing its specific self-understanding within the ecumenical movement and of asserting its own way of faith and life in face of other types of Christianity. Its future is not to be a negation or protest against a certain notion of Catholicism or Orthodoxy. Its future is the consistent development of its own specific way of faith and forms of life, in the form of a Protestantism constantly reforming itself. This will make it appear even more convincingly as hitherto as a manifestation of Christian faith which is by no means identical with its denominational bounds but attains its fulfilment in the fact that it is also acknowledged, after its justification, by other Churches. This means that there could be "Protestantism" within the Roman and Orthodox Churches, if certain truths and ways of believing were accepted and expressed in a typically Protestant way – the converse also being true. The ecumenical problem can be solved only in this way, and not by any attempt to confine it to the study of denominations. But this means that within Protestantism itself doctrines and attitudes must be recognized and treasured as typical manifestations of the Christian faith, though hitherto they may have been regarded as typically Catholic or Orthodox. Such matters are not to be received as institutions but to be valued and applied according to their functions. Hence in the ecumenical movement of the future Protestantism has the important task of uniting, not dividing the Churches.

Peter Meinhold

II. Church Constitutions

1. *History*. The earliest Protestant Church order was established in 1528 for the Duchy of Brunswick, which had become Lutheran. Similar arrangements for worship, religious instruction, the erection of parishes, and the administration of Church property and funds were decreed by all the Lutheran princes or civic authorities during the first half of the 16th century, and during the second half in Calvinist areas such as Switzerland and Holland. These arrangements were not the work of the Churches as autonomous bodies, or of individual congregations, but were made by temporal rulers, since the diocesan powers of the Catholic bishops had passed to Lutheran or Calvinist "established" Churches.

2. *Juridical structure*. Originally the chief concern of the Reformers was to repudiate the jurisdiction of the Pope, the hierarchical principle in Church government, and sacramental ordination. Distinctive Protestant doctrines, like the priesthood of all believers and the autonomy of the congregation, hardly entered the picture. (Only today are they being recognized as underlying principles common to the Churches of the Reform in the ecumenical movement.) Confessional differences were the primary factors distinguishing Lutheran and Calvinist constitutions. In England the Reformation produced different forms, both in Anglicanism and the Free Churches that broke away from it. Finally, in the movement for reunion during the 19th and 20th centuries, forms of Church government were devised that combined Lutheran and Calvinist elements.

3. This historical background explains the great variety of outward form which marks contemporary Protestantism. It also explains the far-reaching dialectical "unity *in* difference" within the Protestant world. The "World Council of Churches", founded in 1948, has since evolved the principles of an ecumenical Church government on federal lines.

4. Thus Protestant ecclesiastical constitutions tend to fall into two main categories. One is rather episcopalian, stressing Church offices and confessions of faith, authoritarian, institutional and juridical in outlook, of the type of an established Church. The other is rather presbyterian, congregational, autonomous and egalitarian, more pneumatic, more ecumenical than confessional in outlook. Four centuries of historical evolution, as well as theological reflection and missionary experience, have extended and refined institutional organization. Extensive alliances for practical purposes have also been formed.

5. There is a growing trend towards autonomous, ecumenical alliances for each region, rather along the lines of the great denominational families such as the Lutheran World Alliance, World Alliance of Reformed Churches (=World Presbyterian Alliance), and the Anglican Communion. The World Council of Churches is also important as a model for constitutions. But a Protestant world Church in the sense of a single constitutional organization will never result from this ecumenical movement, because its watchword is "unity *in* difference". Its object is an alliance or confederation of Churches, each of which retains its own confession, doctrine, and constitution. Accordingly the World Council of Churches is neither a super-Church nor a union of Churches. When even the episcopalist Lutheran World Alliance and the presbyterian World Alliance of Reformed Churches are decentralized confederations, we need hardly say that

the congregationalist world organizations of the Methodists and Baptists are such. Nevertheless – like the "National Councils of Christians", bodies in Africa, Asia, and Latin America, and the "Council for East Asia" set up in 1959 – they provide a pattern for possible co-ordination of the Protestant Churches.

6. The theological interpretation of Church order among Protestants is generally of the Lutheran or the Reformed (Presbyterian) type, both of which of course have undergone a good many changes since the 16th century.

a) Luther's version of St. Augustine's doctrine on the two kingdoms and the dichotomy he introduced between "law" and the "gospel" led the next generation to spiritualize divine law on the one hand and de-spiritualize natural law on the other. The result was a repudiation in principle of the attempt to base Church constitutions on the Bible, and later even the denial of the spiritual character and autonomy of Church law.

b) Calvin, in accordance with his doctrine of God's absolute sovereignty and a *Regnum Christi* already ruling this world, stressed the necessity of a *Politia Christiana*. He recognized scriptural principles fixing the form of Church government, and stressed the kerygmatic role of "law" and the divine covenant of election. This initial "covenant theology" soon developed into a *Ius Divinum* governing worship, Church office and Christian living. Zwingli similarly taught that law and gospel are dialectically one (*lex est lux*).

7. These basic differences in theological approach produced not only different views of the nature of Church law among Lutherans and Calvinists, but also two types of ecclesiastical constitution which remained markedly different from the beginning down to the 19th century. Today, however, some Lutheran Churches are organized on distinctly Presbyterian lines (no bishop, a governing synod, elders associated with the minister), for example in the U.S.A., while many Presbyterian groups among the younger Churches have a Lutheran type of constitution (with the office of bishop, and appointed consistories instead of elected synods).

8. But most Lutheran Churches, unlike the Presbyterian, still retain a distinctive notion of the "threefold office of Christ", though since the 16th century all the Churches of the Reformation attest more or less emphatically the doctrinal, priestly and pastoral (governing) office in their confessions of faith.

a) In principle the Lutheran Church order admits only *one* office in the Church. The "teaching office" is associated with the ministerial office (the office of public preaching); only the regional Church, not the local congregation, can take doctrinal decisions. The "priestly office" is regarded as an institution of divine right founded by Christ. Hence the office-holders are subject only to the discipline of the Church, not of the congregation. Ordination, which is irrevocable, confers spiritual authority on the minister (office of public preaching), which limits ecclesiologically the theologumenon of the priesthood of all believers. According to the doctrine of the episcopal office, the supreme government of the Church must be entrusted to bishops. The "pastoral office", which locally belongs to the parish clergyman, is part of the episcopal office at regional level. Laymen co-operate as members of consistories, but in practice are excluded from exercising the "ministry of the Word". The "spiritual office" allows of helpers (lectors, cantors) but not of genuine sharers among the lay people. Its main duties, preaching and administering the sacraments, cannot on principle be exercised by the non-ordained.

b) In the Presbyterian Churches, the office can function on four levels. Those mentioned in Scripture – the office of pastor, deacon, elder, and teacher (which were not introduced in every Calvinist congregation) – are seldom found complete nowadays; the office of teacher is rarely a separate element in the ecclesiastical constitution. But even where it lacks this recognized legal form, the "teaching office", often exercised by leading theologians, is considered one of great authority because of the ecclesiastical discipline (including doctrinal discipline) which is urged in the Confessions and vests in the community. The "priestly office" (the term is not used), i.e., the ministry, is on principle the same everywhere and is not considered superior to other offices; in exceptional cases it may be exercised by persons who are not ordained. Ordination is simply the appointment of qualified preachers, not the gateway to a "clerical state". The ministry is conferred by mandate of the congregation. Accordingly it is not bishops but a collegiate body that rules the whole Church; the "pastoral office" belongs to the elders of the local congregation and to the elective regional synod. National Synods, or General Assemblies, look on themselves as "governing congregations". The membership is composed of ministers and laymen, the latter at least in equal numbers.

9. In practice such points of difference are gradually being diminished through ecumenical unions and as an effect of collaboration in the World Council of Churches, the more so as even the confessionally-minded members of the Churches concerned no longer feel that the theological reasons for these differences are compelling, and everywhere tend to regard themselves simply as "evangelicals"; apart, that is, from relatively small areas that have been spared the convulsions of the 20th century, where old confessional traditions still prevail.

10. Mixed constitutions, first seen in the "United Churches" of Germany (Prussia 1817, Baden 1821, Hesse 1837), and later set up (from 1910) in Canada, U.S.A., India and Japan, have to a great extent displaced the purely confessionally based constitutions even in areas where the Reformation originated. Where Churches have amalgamated in the same confession (not simply joined together for administrative purposes), such constitutions are also theologically demanded.

11. Other antiquated differences, such as that between a "spiritual" and a "juridical" form of Church order, are also disappearing in the most recent constitutions of Churches that have ceased to model themselves on the political constitutions of States – whether authoritarian or democratic – especially those in Europe which had to contend with National Socialism between 1933 and 1945. Promising efforts are being made to see that Church order and its functioning reflect the life of faith. Thus "office" is now seen less as a bureaucratic institution than as diaconal and missionary "service", and juridical forms are being adapted accordingly.

12. Protestant ecclesiastical constitutions today stress what unites them with rather than divides them from other Churches, not excepting the Roman Catholic Church. There is general agreement on the binding force of the two Testaments of Scripture in the original texts and the translations approved by the Church authorities. In the elaboration of constitutions the other two theologoumena of the traditional trio *sola Scriptura*, *sola fides*, *sola gratia* are to a great extent yielding to the "scriptural principle" (not least in the interests of ecumenical *rapprochement* with the Orthodox and Anglican Churches). This latter provides a basis on which all Protestant Churches can organize themselves in the spirit of fraternal Christocracy, leading ecumenically to a recognition of the Church as a Christocratic brotherhood. Like the ancient Church, the Church of the Reformation regards itself as an

indissoluble society founded by Christ, that is not at the disposal of men, and therefore tends to hold that a member can neither "leave" the Church nor be lawfully "excommunicated", from the point of view of Church law.

Erik Wolf

III. Confessions of Faith

The "Confessions" in Protestantism are written summaries of doctrine which purport to contain the revelation contained in Scripture, as norm of public preaching. Three factors were operative in their formulation. (i) The belief of the Reformers needed justification in the face of the existing authorities and of Christendom as a whole, and so the attempt was made to show its agreement with Scripture and the ancient Church. In this regard the Confession of Augsburg is especially important. (ii) Binding principles of doctrine and order were needed for the exposition of the faith and the organization of the communities of the Reformation Churches. The Lutheran catechisms, as well as the greater part of the Presbyterian Confessions serve this purpose. (iii) Doctrinal disputes within Protestantism required decisions based on the principles of the Reformation and the general ecclesiastical tradition. Documents belonging to this class, e.g., the Formula of Concord on the Lutheran side and the Dordrecht Canons of the Calvinists, have received, by common understanding, only a limited recognition.

Of the numerous confessional formulas only a few have eventually attained more than regional recognition. Here we must distinguish between the local and the dogmatic authority. The development of the former was determined by a principle upheld in post-Reformation times, that of the confessional unity of a given territory. This led, especially in Lutheran circles, to the drawing up of the *Corpora Doctrinae*, i.e., collections of Confessions in which the prevailing doctrine was registered. The juridical significance of these Confessions is perpetuated in the ordination of ministers in which even today, as a rule, they are obliged to certain Confessions which are to be the norm for preaching.

Independent of this formal obligation and more extensive than it, is the dogmatic authority of the Confession of faith. It consists in the fact that the teaching formulated in the Confession is understood as a binding interpretation of the revelation contained in Scripture. The Confession is therefore the *norma normata* of the faith through the *norma normans* of Scripture. The believer is to gain his understanding of revelation in the fellowship in which the doctrine of the Confession is taught. In this dogmatic meaning, the authority of the Confessions is not subject to territorial or temporal limits. This is the essential effect of the Confessions on the Protestant understanding of faith.

1. *Lutheran Confessions.* There are seven classical Confessions which were included in 1580 in the *Book of Concord*, and which have prevailed to a great extent among Lutheran bodies. The three "Ecumenical" Creeds (the Apostolic, the Nicene-Constantinopolitan and the Athanasian) are basic and the Lutheran Confessions must be read in the light of this confession of faith in the one Church of Jesus Christ. They appeal to Scripture and the Fathers to propound the Protestant doctrine, with an eye to controversial theology.

a) By far the most important was the Confession of Augsburg, presented to the Emperor in 1530. This document, composed by Melanchthon, comprises 28 articles divided into two parts. Arts. 1–21 develop (appealing in art. 1 to the Nicene Creed) the basic dogmatic teaching on the Trinity, justification, ecclesiology, the sacraments, eschatology. Arts. 22–28 endeavour to show that the apostolic discipline has been preserved, or rather restored, in the rites of Protestantism. This Confession, in Melanchthon's altered version of 1540 (the *Variata*, spiritualizing the sacraments), penetrated the Presbyterian Churches and attained general recognition among Protestants. Strict Lutheranism returned in 1577 to the *Invariata* of 1530.

b) In 1530–31 Melanchthon composed the *Apology* on behalf of the Confession of Augsburg. This considerably more comprehensive work follows the structure of the Confession which it defends in the light of the Protestant doctrine of justification.

c) The Schmalkaldic Articles were drawn up in 1536 by Luther for the assembly of the Protestant Princes and theologians who met at Schmalkalden in 1537 to discuss the Council called by Paul III for Mantua. Its three parts deal with the articles common to all Christians, the central doctrines of the Reformation, and finally disputed questions of the doctrine of salvation. This work only gained the status of a Confession later, unlike Melanchthon's *Tractatus de Potestate et Primatu Papae* which was presented at the same time.

d) Luther's Large and Small Catechisms appeared consecutively in 1528–29. Similar in outline, they treat, in five main parts, of the Decalogue, the Apostles' Creed, the Our Father, baptism, and the Lord's Supper, in the form of question and answer. While the Large Catechism served to instruct preachers and catechists, the other, intended for children and laymen, became a popular religious book which also influenced Presbyterian circles.

e) The *Formula of Concord* was the common work of theologians from Württemberg and North Germany and originated in long deliberations from 1573 to 1577. It served to settle inter-Lutheran controversies. From the *Solida Declaratio*, the result of preparatory studies and numerous amendments, J. Andreae prepared a concise extract (*Epitome*). In the twelve articles of both versions, the first six attempt to solve the misunderstandings with regard to the Lutheran doctrine of justification (I. Original Sin. II. Free Will. III. Justification. IV. Good Works. V. Law and the Preaching of the Gospel. VI. *Tertius Usus Legis*). The remaining articles include a rejection of the spiritualizing tendency of Melanchthon's followers with regard to Christology and the sacraments. They also reject "double predestination". The authors of the *Formula of Concord* included these together with the older Lutheran Confessions in the *Book of Concord* (*Concordia, Liber Concordiae*), which was published in Dresden in 1580. Even though it did not prevail in this form in all Lutheran territories, the credal books which it contained remained the doctrinal basis of Lutheranism, especially the Confession of Augsburg and the Catechisms of Luther. The latter were spoken of in the 1947 constitution of the Lutheran World Alliance as the fundamental Confession.

Lutheran Confessions which did not attain general recognition include the Wittenberg Concord of 1536 and the Württemberg Confession of 1551; the *Confessio et Ordinatio Ecclesiarum Danicarum* of 1561 (Danish); and the Church Order of Laurentius Petri of 1571 (Swedish).

2. *Presbyterian ("Reformed") Confessions*. There is a much wider variety of Confessions among Presbyterians. This is due to the special character of their understanding of faith and their high regard for doctrinal formulations. While doctrine depends exclusively on Scripture, the Confessions only serve the organization of the community. The Confession relates not primarily to dogma but to the Church order, which for Presbyterians represents the third "note of the Church" beside Word and Sacrament. Conversely, Church order itself ranks as a Confession. This explains why the authority of the Confes-

sions is limited to the regional Churches comprised within them. Further, the Presbyterian Confessions, unlike the Lutheran, did not arise more or less simultaneously from among a localized group of theologians. They were the result of historical developments. And, there was no official collection of credal books. However, the sixty or so Confessions which became authoritative show a remarkable affinity in their formulation of characteristic Presbyterian beliefs. Some have attained special prominence and a supra-regional importance.

a) The Geneva Catechism of 1545 was written by Calvin after his return from Strasbourg to reorganize Church life in Geneva. In 373 questions and answers, he treats systematically of the principal tenets of Calvinism and then of questions of pastoral care and Church discipline.

b) The Second Helvetic Confession of 1562 was written by Bullinger as a private Confession but was then subscribed to by the Swiss groups, as also by others (in Scotland, Hungary, Bohemia, Poland and Holland). It thus became a source of unity within the Presbyterian (Reformed) Church. Characteristic features are the enumeration of the Ten Commandments according to the OT and the emphasis given to the prohibition of images.

c) The Scottish Confession, from a draft by J. Knox, was accepted by the Scottish Parliament in 1560. Following the structure of the Apostles' Creed, its twenty-five articles propound a doctrine uncompromisingly Calvinist, including the characteristic teaching on civil authority. While obedience to authority is the service of God, the elimination of tyranny is a good work.

d) The Belgic Confession, written in 1561 by Guy de Brès, was largely influenced by the *Confessio Gallicana* written in 1559 by Calvin for the French communities. In 37 articles, it presents the Calvinist theology (from natural knowledge of God) to eschatology, with many scriptural references.

e) The most important and most widely read was the Heidelberg Catechism. At the instigation of Frederick III, the Elector of the Palatinate, it was composed in 1563 by the followers of Melanchthon, Ursinus and Olevian. It became the classical Confession of the German "Reformed Churches", and was also disseminated in many European languages and lands. Its three parts treat of sin, redemption, and life in thanksgiving, developing Presbyterian doctrine from the point of view of life in faith. (The first question is characteristic: What is your one consolation in life and death?) This practical orientation of faith is combined with a strongly Christological dogma, with many references to Scripture.

Besides these main Confessions there were also regional ones. Hungary had the Erlauthal Confession of 1562, and the Hungarian Confession of the same year. In Poland there was the *Consensus Sendomiriensis*; in Bohemia, the *Confessio Bohemica* of 1609. In the English-speaking world there were the Westminster Confession of 1647, and the Larger and Shorter Westminster Catechisms of 1647, which were widely accepted by American Presbyterians. In German-speaking countries there were the Confession of the Frankfort Fremdengemeinde of 1554, the Emden Catechism of 1554, the Consensus Bremensis of 1595, and the Staffort Book of 1599.

The Canons of the Synod of Dort (Dortrecht) (1618/19) are of special importance. They represent an attempt of the Dutch National Church to establish the strict Calvinist doctrine against the more moderate positions of the Humanists and Arminians.

3. *Other Protestant Confessions.* Churches stemming from Calvinism mostly adopted Presbyterian types of Confessions, e.g., the Congregationalists (the Cambridge Platform, 1648;

Statement of Faith [Grand Rapids], 1944); the Baptists (the London Confession [of the Calvinistic Baptists], 1644); the Baptist Confession, 1688, the Philadelphia Confession, 1742, the New Hampshire Confession, 1833. The Episcopal Methodists (U.S.A.) (Doctrines and Discipline [1924]) belong here.

While the status of the Confessions, as long as the established Churches lasted, was generally unchallenged, especially in Lutheranism, the Enlightenment and neo-Protestantism undermined their authority. In the latter, the validity of the tradition of the faith itself was limited and conditioned by the individual certitude of the believing subject. A new sense of the value of the Confessions came with the "Restoration" in the 19th century. In Germany, the struggle against National Socialism lent great weight to the Barmen Declaration of 1934. The ecumenical movement bore fruit in the Christological Confession of Amsterdam, 1948.

One rarely finds nowadays any tendency to make the Confessions into absolute norms or exhaustive formulas. It has been checked by the Confessions themselves which claim validity only through their scriptural content. Hence they really should serve to bring about a consensus through the interpretation of Scripture and thus make possible a new and better testimony to the message of revelation.

Wenzel Lohff

IV. Theology

1. *Historical survey*. The function assigned to Protestant theology depends on the view taken of the nature of Protestantism and its ecclesial character. This is fully confirmed by the way the history of Protestant theology has been dealt with so far. In selection and characterization, it has always depended on such conceptions. Hence it is always an expression of the position adopted by the writer in regard to Protestantism even if he views the latter from inside. More clearly than other branches of Church history, this fact exemplifies the principle that a Church's view of itself is chiefly manifested in its interpretation of its history. Consequently, with the awakening of historical awareness in theology in modern times, the "history of Protestant theology" developed in the 19th century into a separate discipline within the framework of Protestant historical writing. Intended to clarify Protestant theology's conception of its own nature, if has always been an expression of that conception. It is not possible, therefore, to speak of the present-day function of Protestant theology unless one has previously surveyed the historical accounts which have been given of it so far.

The principles laid down in the 19th century as the basis of such accounts are still regarded, by both Protestants and Catholics, as the characteristic distinguishing marks of Protestantism as such. In other words, their authors measure the phenomena of Protestant theology by what seems to them to be its function at the present time. This argument in a circle is clearly unavoidable in historical theology, which judges the historical phenomena by criteria which it establishes for itself, and in this way seeks to provide itself with historical justification. This is a further sign of how history-writing is both determined by the writer's assumptions and made a vehicle for propounding them. The present survey, while incomplete, shows how some characteristic historians regard their history: as a consistent or erroneous development, as the justification of their own position or of the ecclesial or non-ecclesial character of Protestantism.

The presentation of a history of Protestant theology has the additional function of being the history of dogma which Protestants obviously could not write. The views of dogma current at the end of the 19th and the beginning of the 20th century restricted such history to the early Church, though sometimes including the Middle Ages and the initial stages of the Protestant Confessions. Consequently the formation of Protestant doctrines was linked with the history of dogma in the early and medieval Church. It is clear, however, that this view of "dogma" and the history of dogma (as found in existing works on the history of dogma) only left open a "history of Protestant theology" or of specifically Protestant doctrines.

The first comprehensive effort was that of Wilhelm Gass (1813–89) in his *Geschichte der protestantischen Dogmatik*. He restricts himself to ecclesiastical or ecclesiastically approved systems, using them to trace the formation of doctrine in Lutheranism and the Reformed (Presbyterian) Church. The "Protestant sects" are omitted as not amenable to the ecclesiastical type of doctrine. To what extent even they reflect a certain kind of Protestant theology and "Churchmanship" or otherwise is not examined. Gass endeavours to connect up the various dogmatic systems by applying to them his conception of Protestantism. For him, Protestantism is "the vindication of the equal claim of all Christians to the highest good and their equal need of it". This aspiration emerges from the innermost depths of the conscience. "Protestantism" is therefore implanted as it were by nature in all men, in the striving of conscience for the "highest good". Once the existence of this desire has been established, it is completed by the principle of appropriation which Gass lays down. This gives formal expression to what Protestantism is, namely, the "free appropriation" of Christian salvation through belief in the divine grace revealed by Jesus Christ. Since this revelation is contained in Scripture alone, the latter must provide the norm for the manner and extent of appropriation.

Gass is of the opinion that Protestant theology or dogmatics has developed from this principle. This process is to be presented in conjunction with the general scientific ideas of the various periods. Luther represented the "Protestant principle" in general without giving it didactic form, but Melanchthon was the real originator of the Protestant doctrinal system. Gass follows its development down to the middle of the 19th century. His presentation of the "history of Protestant dogmatics" encouraged the elaboration of a more comprehensive history of Protestant theology as a systematic account of the development of the typically Protestant doctrines.

This work inspired by Gass was carried further by the Bonn theologian Isaak August Dorner (1809–84) in his *Geschichte der protestantischen Theologie*. Dorner too understood this to be the history of the "Protestant principle", which, according to Dorner, is the "subjective and objective assurance of salvation". Dorner supports this principle by a comparative study of denominations. The purpose of all history of Protestant theology is to justify the emergence of Protestantism as opposed to Catholicism and to Eastern Orthodox Christianity. Protestantism or the "Protestant principle" made its appearance in Christendom at a providentially appointed time. The way for it was historically prepared both negatively and positively. At the time fixed by God the "universal Church" of Protestantism appeared by the side of the Greek Catholic and the Roman Catholic Church. This universal Church is one in the "Protestant principle" laid down by Dorner, and "the Church" has thereby assumed a new form for the subjective and objective appropriation of salvation. Historically speaking, therefore, Christendom has reached a higher stage as compared with the two other forms of the Christian Church. According to Dorner, the task of a history of Protestant theology is to exhibit the unfolding of this "Protestant principle" in the Protestant understanding of doctrine. It will then become evident that with Protestantism a higher historical stage has in fact been attained. Although in Dorner the ecumenical and universal Christian functions of Protestantism are stressed, they are at the same time coloured by his particular view of the Reformation. It is "the greatest work of God since the days of the apostles". But since it arose in Germany and chiefly developed and exerted its influence there, German theology and the German nation have a God-given place in the history of Christianity. Dorner endeavours to demonstrate this from the history of Protestant theology. In this way also the necessity of the emergence and development of the Protestant principle down to the form it assumes at the present day is to be justified.

Of course this way of looking at the matter stands or falls with the "Protestant principle" employed as a criterion. By it is meant a general formula by which the nature of Protestantism can be stated, its different manifestations comprised in a unity and distinguished from Catholicism. Catholicism is regarded as the absolute contrary of the supposedly Protestant principle of an objective assurance of salvation appropriated through Scripture.

Gustav Frank (1832–1904) proceeded like Dorner, but taking as the Protestant principle "the free dedication of the self-determining subject" to true Christianity as the "ideal religion". He also stressed its embodiment in outstanding personalities.

A new link was forged with the general history of ideas when Otto Pfleiderer (1839–1908) traced the development of Protestant theology in Germany since Kant and of Anglican theology from 1825 on. He did not use a "Protestant principle" but noted the influences of philosophy.

In order to link the history of Protestant theology more closely with the history of dogma and to remedy the faults of earlier accounts, Otto Ritschl (1860–1944) produced a "History of dogmas in Protestantism". Protestant histories of dogma had mostly ended with the Reformation and its Confessions. Ritschl refused to confine dogma to ecclesiastical propositions as did, more or less, A. von Harnack, F. Loofs, R. Seeberg and W. Köhler. He took his idea of "dogma" from jurisprudence, science and modern philosophy, where he saw it as the "general idea" of these disciplines. In theology this would be the history of ideas of a dogmatic character but not the history of ecclesiastically sanctioned doctrines. And so Ritschl regarded the history of Protestant theology as the methodical "history of the dogmas of Protestantism", according to its general ideas, e.g., the relation between Scripture and tradition, the understanding of faith and its appropriation, etc. There is no doubt that Ritschl took an important step in the history of Protestant theology – the only way to overcome its isolation from the dogmas of the early and medieval Church. But this would only be a success if a unified concept of dogma could be laid down. For in fact the history of Protestant theology implies the history of dogmas of the early and medieval Church. The problem which Ritschl thus set still persists, because of his own unsatisfactory concept of dogma which was too general and untheological. Recent reflections within Protestantism on the nature of dogma and the function of the history of dogmas may help.

The works mentioned so far deal with the history of Protestant theology since Luther. They either suggested or took for granted a certain homogeneity in the understanding and formulation of dogmas. In modern times Schleiermacher's theology has been seen as a turning-point, whose influence has to be depicted. Schleiermacher defined the essence of Protestantism and Catholicism by saying that Protestantism posits a direct relation between Christ and the believer, whereas Catholicism sees the Church as the intermediary without which no relation to Christ is possible. Ferdinand Kattenbusch (1851–1934) was convinced of the importance of Schleiermacher. His history of Protestant theology took in the beginnings of dialectical theology and ended with a pointed question. How far has modern Protestant theology done justice to the fundamental purpose of the Reformation and so fulfilled its own proper function, which is to encounter the revelation of God contained in Jesus' preaching, and to express it otherwise than in the terms of the ancient and medieval Church, which refracted it through notions borrowed from antiquity?

Horst Stephan (1873–1954) took a similar line, but began with German Idealism, as the overthrow of Enlightenment Deism. He also recognized the importance of Albrecht Ritschl (1822–89), so that theology was Ritschlean to World War I, but then simply "post-war". There was no unified conception, but simply a description of names and themes. The superficiality is ultimately due to the lack of a definite notion of Protestantism.

K. Barth's (1885–1968) history of Protestant theology is no better. Barth was notoriously sceptical about the value of Church history, which he treated as the handmaid of exegesis and dogmatics, having no legitimate theological function of its own. In his own historical writings he then tried to present the various Protestant theologies as culture-conditioned discourse about God. Man makes history, and so history must be there to tell about men. This principle was decisive in his treatment of the Protestant theology of the 19th century. There is no attempt to determine the overriding problems which divided or united theologians, simply a characterization of each unit. The debate is conducted from the standpoint which Barth held, that theology is discourse about God and has to legitimate its discourse. This critical principle did not allow of a balanced presentation. The emphasis was on the Enlightenment and Idealism and their pernicious influence on discourse about God, as understood by Barth. The 19th century became the sad pre-history of dialectical theology, of which Barth himself was the great exponent.

The latest history of Protestant theology, by Emanuel Hirsch (b. 1888) also surveys all that has been said about "Religion, Christianity and Theology" in non-theological circles, insofar as it has basically affected theology. The result is a broad and detailed canvas of the history of ideas since the 17th century, the age of discovery as regards history, nature and the non-Christian religions. But again there was no overriding theme, such as these discoveries might have suggested. Hirsch ends with the 19th century and the influence of Idealism on theology. In contrast to Barth, with his critical principle as regards legitimate discourse about God (raising problems which cannot be dealt with here), Hirsch applies no critical principle to the essence of Protestantism.

This brief survey of the main exponents of the history of Protestant theology naturally leads to the question as to what is the task of Protestant theology at present.

2. *Content.* If we now attempt to define the function of Protestant theology, we have to postulate a connection between Church and theology with which Protestantism is obviously still not familiar. But Protestant theology does not live in a vacuum of pure learning. It is not an end in itself and certainly not a merely academic matter. It springs from the life of the Church, and all its work is meant to serve that life. Hence the ecclesiastical function

which Schleiermacher assigned to Protestant theology and which Barth also brought out in his own way continues to exist. But the field which it has to cover today is very much more extensive. Earlier it was limited to five branches of study (OT, NT, Church history and history of dogmas, dogmatics, practical theology), but the problems of modern life call for more. Theology today has to deal, for example, with man's relation to his environment, *de iure* and *de facto*. It cannot now leave out the ecumenical question – how the Churches and their claim to truth stand to each other, which at bottom is the question of the justification of their plurality in the pluralist world. It has to examine the significance of the special characteristics of one Church for another. It must take in comparative religion, quite deliberately, since the theology of the history of religions was guillotined by the recent theologians who affirmed that Christianity was not a religion but the critique of all religions. If theology is thus regarded as at the service of the Church of its age, the perspective of the various disciplines is altered. This is most evident in biblical studies.

a) These have to use the methods of modern historical study to examine the claim of the Bible to be testimony to the word of God uttered in history through historical persons. In this domain, modern Protestant theology has developed the principles of hermeneutics (theory of the interpretation of a given text and its unique claim) with all their linguistic and historical prerequisites. Furthermore, it has taken account of the critical principles of modern historical science and has been remarkably faithful to the historical mode of inquiry in regard to the Bible. It has done this in order to trace a picture of Jesus and his teaching capable of resisting historical criticism and not coloured by contemporary thought. In this connection the relation between history and Church proclamation, between fact and kerygma, has become a problem of particular concern. At first it was thought that the problem could only be solved by opposing the two terms. This failed to recognize that there can be no historical fact without interpretation and no historical Jesus without the kerygmatic declaration which interprets him. The two are so linked that one cannot exist without the other. The kerygma would be an illusion if it lacked sure historical foundation, and on the other hand this latter only becomes "historic", decisive for man universally, when it is interpreted by the kerygma and its existentiell content made plain. These dominant problems of Protestant theology sufficiently indicate that it draws its meaning only from the service to the Church which both prompts it and is its goal. It is of course intrinsic to Christianity to ask what history means to man here and now, i.e., to inquire into the existentiell aspect of the events. This question is not met with in the same way outside theology, and cannot be, because the Church alone offers scope for the realization of that aspect with all the problems it involves. For it is here alone that historical fact and kerygma go together.

b) Church history is a comprehensive study and therefore has to investigate and sum up the whole life of the Church. It must relate the history of theology and of the ecclesiastical understanding of the kerygma to the general history of ideas. It must show their ecumenical significance. The critical principles of its work are inherent in it. Every history of the Church looks back to the past, especially to the beginnings of the Church. Hence its view of history is critical, because it asks how far the Church in history has remained true to its beginnings, or how far it has been distorted by the admission of elements of piety or philosophy not really compatible with its nature so that its later form no longer corresponds to the principles of its historical being.

Moreover, Church history has always to direct its gaze towards the future, for Christian faith from the start aims at transmission and tradition, i.e., the road to the future. Furthermore, the work of Church history is determined from the very beginning by the question of the Parousia, its delay and the ensuing development. As, therefore, in the Christian view of time, the history of the Church moves towards an end determined by God, the other critical question for the ecclesiastical view of history arises: how is the relation between tradition and progress to be conceived? Tradition here is not to be thought of merely as the accumulation of matter handed down. It must be understood as the critical principle by which the movement towards the future is to be examined. The Church view of history, therefore, contains its critical principles within itself. To the extent that it employs the critical methods of general historical study, it is simply using the auxiliaries which the particular age provides. Church history does not thereby become a discipline in theology doing a work of criticism. The critical principles which Church history must always use are rather contained in the very nature of Church history itself. This ensures its independence of any other kind of view of history, and at the same time gives it its legitimate theological function.

Protestant theology of the present time has in fact to a considerable extent been concerned with the new conception of the role of history in theology. It had become so dependent on the secular historian's way of looking at Church history that Karl Barth and his friends could even call in question the theological character of Church history and claim that it is simply an auxiliary science of dogmatic theology. Church history, however, is a genuine theological discipline, because it has its own distinctive questions: the Church's insertion into the world, the interlocking of Church history, world history and redemptive history, the non-arrival of the Parousia, the problems of Church and State, the adoption of the language and thought-forms of each age for the Church's preaching, etc. And so Church history as such has its own special function to fulfil in theology in accordance with its own intrinsic critical principles, in contradistinction to the questions proper to the biblical disciplines and to dogmatics.

c) The function of dogmatics in Protestant theology today cannot consist simply in systematizing the existing teaching of the Church. There are now two kinds of Protestant theology, with two distinguished exponents. One was Karl Barth, with his enormous output, where he showed himself far from being the destructive critic of theology which he was often thought to be. On the contrary, he revived Protestant theology in a way which passed all denominational barriers. He took the word of God as the sole source of theology and defined the task of the latter as that of making and maintaining the legitimate ecclesiastical statement of that word. Consequently, the line of thought established by Barth, impressively represented by his vast *Church Dogmatics*, gave Protestant thought more substance and depth. It prompted new questions in almost every field – with the exception, of course, of Church history and comparative religion, whose proper problems he did not grasp.

Paul Tillich has also been a distinctive representative of Protestant theology in our age. He assigned it the function not of being the Church's pronouncement, but of assisting man generally to a new understanding of his being in relation to God. With this purpose in mind Tillich made philosophical affirmation fruitful for man's understanding of himself. In that way he enriched theology considerably, widening the field of vision rather than indulging any theological isolationism, and in particular he defined anew the "principle of Protestantism".

Work done in Protestant dogmatic theology of the present day can be divided between these two representatives, though there are, of course, many nuances and overlaps, and older approaches are still at work. At all events, these two also represent tendencies which have become influential across all ecclesiastical frontiers, and are not in any way limited to German Protestantism.

d) There is no doubt that Protestant theology needs to develop, in addition to the disciplines so far mentioned, three new branches of study if it is to do justice to the present situation of Christianity in the world. The first need is to develop Christian social doctrine to meet the problems of modern mass society. Here the Church has the task of incorporating the functional man of this society into the brotherhood of the Body of Christ. In face of the problem of the masses, which in any case the Churches also have to deal with within their own walls, as may be seen from the multiplication of sects and societies looking for true fellowship, the Churches have to show that they themselves have so many social forms and levels that the structure of the Church may appear as degrees of service. Furthermore, in modern mass society theology has to help the Church to preserve a domain in which men can develop their personality in complete freedom. The plurality of Churches in the mass society has to be paralleled or justified by the plurality of Christian service.

e) Finally, Protestant theology will have to deal afresh with the problems of comparative religion and make it again a special discipline, to some extent because of the discussions about religious freedom, which involves freedom of unbelief and of anti-religious propaganda. The mass society with its communications media will gain new perspectives on the co-existence of the many religions. It will no longer be a question of truth as between denominations, but of the truth which stands or falls with religion in general. Protestant theology must renew the study of comparative religion, which has assumed new importance for the Church's mission itself.

f) Finally, theology must develop a special branch of study which might be called ecumenical ecclesiology. Its purpose would be to investigate the co-existence of the Churches and all their claims, and to examine the question of what the co-existence of Churches means for each of them and how each has attempted to cope with it. It must note how well they develop their forms of life and their elements of truth. It must show that the new theological orientation of the Churches can also guide interdenominational relations into new paths. Consequently, problems between Churches will cease to be matter for "controversial theology" but will be dealt with in the perspective of this "ecumenical ecclesiology". It has to take the ecclesial character of the other Churches seriously and deal with the consequences for the particular Church which it serves.

The Protestant theology of the present time is therefore struggling to reshape what the Church has to say. Its tasks have been extended and deepened in accordance with the Church's position in the world. It must be able to claim that in a changing world and in the crisis which has befallen the universities, it is the faculty from which flow the strongest forces in the moulding of history and mankind, because it propounds the question of truth and its vital significance. In any case, the future role of Protestantism will not be externally very brilliant. It will be the way of the cross, of persecution and inner and outer trials. It is precisely here that the task of Protestant theology must be fulfilled, today, as always, critical in its questions and constructive in its work.

Peter Meinhold

PROVIDENCE

The notion of providence sums up God's relationship to the world as he knows, wills and executes his plan of universal salvation and leads the world to the end decreed by him.

1. *Providence in non-Christian beliefs.* Greek philosophy concluded that providence watched over men, because it saw the world as a rational, apt and purposeful order. This order was seen as the work of a divine Spirit pervading all things and guaranteeing the well-being of man. The word πρόνοια (providence) appears for the first time in the 5th century B.C., and from then on stands for the work of a divine Spirit or for the Godhead itself. The doctrine was given a special meaning in Stoicism, above all in ethics. A non-personal divinity pervades the world and guides all things to their end. This divine reason (or divinized rationality) in the order and movement of the world also takes in man and his salvation. It gives him security by integrating him into this cosmic harmony.

Being part of the universal harmony does not leave room for man's freedom, but it gives him the ataraxia (imperturbability) which enables him to bear the slings and arrows of outrageous fortune with detachment. The harshness of destiny is only a transitory illusion.

The Stoic doctrine of providence and its ethical consequences could be left to historical scholarship, except for the fact that its basic themes continued to go hand in hand with the Christian faith in providence. They still form the background against which that faith is understood and exercised, and indeed influence it and sometimes distort it. The influence began to work as soon as the eschatological nature of the world (the end-directedness on which faith in providence is based) was explained in terms taken from the Hellenistic philosophy of the ancient environment. There have been times when spirituality (not so much doctrine) should have been much more clearly conscious of how it differed from notions which had little but the name in common with Christian faith in providence. And at such times the influence of Stoicism has been more marked, e.g., in the theodicy of Leibniz, who sought to justify the ways of God to men by invoking a pre-established (rational) harmony; in deism; in the optimism of the Enlightenment with regard to progress and history which affected the 18th and 19th centuries; in Hegel's world-reason, in the Marxist interpretation of history, in the abuse of "providence" as a cloak for power politics in totalitarian systems. The necessity of the distinction becomes absolutely clear when protests are raised about such "providence" in the name of freedom and autonomy, or because false hopes have been shattered by historical catastrophes. Even the God of Christianity becomes a scandal when he is thought to govern the world along the lines of secularized notions. So in Voltaire's *Candide*, Feuerbach's *Essence of Christianity*, Camus's *The Rebel*; see the article *Religion* I B. In view of such questions and their background in the history of the spirit, Christian preaching must envisage clearly the foundations of the Christian faith in providence and give them their distinctive expression.

2. *The biblical foundations.* The term "providence" only appears in the later pages of the OT and then under Hellenistic influences (Job 10:12 [LXX], Wis 6:7; 14:3; 17:2). But it was always clear that God was powerful, wise and good in foreseeing the path of man and his world and guiding it to an end. This marvellous history, inspiring admira-

tion and confidence, begins in the OT with creation itself. It continues in the election and guidance of Israel to the promised goal, these manifestations of God's goodness. This experience is voiced in the Psalms (e.g., 9:2; 26:7; 40:6; 71:17; 72:18) and is summed up by Isaiah in particular in his view of history as the saving action of God (Is 9:5; 28:29; 29:14). Hence the OT faith in providence is based on the experience of God's action in history and on his promise. It presupposes a personal God and his free, historical creative act, which is precisely why man can be free under divine providence. The crisis of faith at the exile opened up a new perspective on providence, which was now regarded as embracing the individual as well as the chosen people. There was a new sense of the mystery of the divine goals, as something beyond man's calculation and reach.

The NT also speaks of God's tireless regard for his creatures (e.g., Mt 6:25–34; 10:29–31). The traditional faith in providence is given its final stamp by the revelation of Christ's saving work. The kingdom of God which he announced is awaited in faith and hope, not as the consequence of the laws of nature but as the free, historical intervention of God. But the beginning of this eschatological fulfilment does not take place in the beyond, outside world history. It is within history and recognized as present. What the Lord underwent in this world – crucifixion – and the way in which the world opposed him showed that even the shadows which fall on man and his history (sin, guilt, failure, agony and death) are comprised within God's plan of salvation. The acceptance of this truth, so hard to grasp, is expressed in the NT by the repeated affirmation of the Must of the history of salvation (δεῖ), as in Lk 24:26: "Was it not necessary that the Christ should suffer these things and enter into his glory?" It is central to the preaching of the primitive Church that the death of Christ is the revelation of God's plan of salvation and shows his goodness and wisdom (e.g., Acts 2:23; 4:28; Eph 1:3–14). The sense of being safe in the hands of providence is given to men not by rational insight into the harmony of the universe but by the following of Christ, who accepted freely and obediently the destiny which befell him as the loving summons of God and thus transformed and disarmed it.

3. *The theology of providence*. Christian theology later tried to define exactly the relationship of God to the world which is expressed by the term providence. The main notions invoked were "the conservation of the world" and the "joint action" (*concursus*, concurrence) of God. The "conservation of the world", its being constantly upheld in being by God, stresses the radical dependence of the world on God. The dependence does not cease after the act of creation, as suggested by deism. But the continual activity of God in grounding existence is not to be understood as a perpetually new creating, which would deprive intermediate causes (*causae secundae*) of their significance. Only the sense of this continual conservation of the world prevents its being regarded as a fully closed system and makes possible the personal relationship of man to the God who plans and guides.

The *concursus* of God, the divine action which goes with every free act of man, means that all his actions are encompassed by God's providence, both as regards their presuppositions and their effects. All that men propose and achieve thus becomes secondary, provisional, subordinate to the goal set by God. But the divine co-determination does not mean that human freedom is eliminated and that its acts under providence are valueless. There is no rivalry or competition in the relation between divine and creaturely freedom. Divine freedom is the transcendent cause which enables the creature to be

free. The exact nature of this relationship is a controversial question in theology (see *Grace and Freedom* and *Predestination*). The magisterium of the Church – in particular, Vatican I – defended and affirmed the doctrine of God's providence against atheism, deism, fatalism and dualism: *D* 1784; cf. *D* 421, 816, 1702, 2305.

The scriptural foundations and the teaching of the Church on the providence of God may be summed up – in the light of the historical background – as follows:

a) God's rule, in which he guides the world to the end foreseen by him is not an immanent element of a natural order. It is the free, historical intervention of God. It comprises creation as *creatio ex nihilo*, and the eschatological fulfilment as again the free act of God, outside the reach of man and the laws of nature (*causae secundae*). The eschatological nature of the world cannot be adequately described in terms of teleological thinking (final causes).

b) The relationship between God and his world expressed in the term providence comes to a climax in the personal relationship to a personal God who gives man's freedom a beginning and an end. Hence the freedom of the creature does not cease to depend radically on its ground of possibility, and is not eliminated by the will of the providence which brings about its own goal. The free act of man is not a factor which competes with this providence but an inward element of the plan of salvation; see *God-World Relationship*.

c) God's goodness, wisdom and power can be known to men both in the history of salvation and in the promises. Both coincide in the saving work of Christ. Providence embraces man insofar as he is exposed to this world, its destiny and unpredictability.

d) The goodness of God, which plans and implements, needs the interpretation given by the word of revelation and is known in faith and hope – not by rational insight into the world-reason. Hence the assumption of this providence is exposed to the challenges by which all faith is assailed.

e) The indifference of the Christian which goes with faith in providence is not the Stoic ataraxia, which stems from the sure insight into the rationality of the world, contemplating the great drama there played out from the detached viewpoint of the mere spectator. It is to believe and know that man is freed from the "principalities and powers" of this world, and the hopeful expectation of the "Day of the Lord". The Christian is emancipated from the bondage of the world, while still throwing himself courageously and happily into the action.

f) Faith in providence is exercised in prayer, not only in praise and thanksgiving for the goodness of Cod already experienced, but also in the petition for the fulfilment of the promises. In face of a personal God who acts in history, the prayer of petition is not superfluous, though again it does not try to force God to fit into human previsions and projects. The words of Jesus: "Father, all things are possible to thee; remove this cup from me; yet not what I will, but what thou wilt" (Mk 14:36) embrace in a seeming contradiction the whole range of human supplication. It is the expression of human need which is commended to God's care, and the radical, actual acceptance of dependence on God, confident that "everything works for good with those who love God, who are called according to his purpose" (Rom 8:28).

Ernst Niermann

PSYCHOLOGY

Psychology is first and foremost determined by the criteria which define science in contradistinction to all other

forms of knowledge. The notion and definition of science as such are subject to historical changes. On the model of the exact natural sciences, the prevailing empirical scientific psychology sometimes, like radical behaviourism, regards the "organism" as empty, i.e., regards it purely from outside through the stimuli and the reactions they provoke. But even when it also considers interior determinants as necessary to explain its behaviour, it is concerned to break down the psyche in an atomizing way into a minimal state of fictitiously generalized, irreducible, qualitatively invariable and mutually independent factors (basic psychological elements, primary traits or mental abilities, etc.). These are then worked up into correlation units (as opposed to units of meaning: Merleau-Ponty), into factor-profiles and interdependent systems of vectors (as psychological forces: Lewin). The aim is, as in physics, to find a "field quantifier" which will link this quantum-theory of the psyche with the apparently incompatible continuum theory (Lewin, Köhler, Koffka). This ideal of an "objective psychology" is best realized by the objectivation of psychological indicators (trait-indicators) through measurements. Through the instruments used and their laws of mass and measure, everything psychological assumes objectively definable attributes.

This aim imposes the obligatory use of objective nomothetic test procedures designed for psychometric measurement of performance, behaviour and personality. For the conception of science which finds expression in such principles, requirements and methods, there are only two forms of indubitable certainty: logico-mathematical and that "bodily evidence" of sense experience which makes tangibility and verifiability the exclusive criterion of reality ("finger and thumb philosophy of metaphysics": Woodger). Consequently, it is concerned with the empirical registration and mathematical treatment of psychical behaviour. In other words, it is concerned, in the style of logical positivism, with a calculus of sense-data (Hobbes) as the only legitimate method. Mere facts are to be transformed into a calculus of logico-mathematical systematic and dynamic structures. This is "psycho-logicism", which rationalizes the psyche into a mathematical manifold and thus reduces its reality to that of a mere *modus cognitionis*. This fundamental attitude of maximum precision in registering facts void of meaning and value, "the matter of fact sort of way", decrees that the psyche is wholly a quasi-physiological or quasi-physical reality. This is evident, for example, in its conception of thought as subvocal speech (or as inhibited speech reflexes) including the muscular movements and glandular processes as reactions to external stimuli, so that thought and learning are based solely on a conditioning of the motor habits or reflexes involved in speech (Pavlov, Watson; motor theory of thought: Washburn). In the same line of thought, operationism (Bridgman) forms the logical counterpart to behaviourism by its excessive emphasis on activity and the "nonsensical" (G. Bergman) reduction of all cognitive acts to practical ones (perception, thought=action, speech; Skinner). According to this, every concept denotes a particular class of operations ("operational concept") and every definition is the description not of an object but of the procedures and manipulations which have to be used to register it.

The objections to this psychology which claims to be specifically scientific, concern the general conception of science represented by inductive and logical positivism. They are primarily directed against the limiting of scientific knowledge to two sources regarded as autonomous and fully sufficient: immediate sense-perception and logical self-evidence. To make an absolute of external sense perception dictates rejec-

tion or at least depreciation of introspection, and with it of actual lived experience, which is represented as an exclusively heuristic and fictive process, but never scientific knowledge. Such a standpoint necessarily entails absurdities, though it is one which is perpetually defended. This is so whether it is put forward in its radical form or in a milder form. Thus, for example, every analysis of factors (variables etc.) presupposes for their definition when they are introduced and for their interpretation when they are applied, a knowledge of these primary forms of performance, attributes, motives, etc., drawn from experience. But the singling out of psychologically relevant facts from the universe of existing things is only possible because of prior (initial) knowledge of mental reality by which alone the distinctions can be made. The prescientific world of life provides the absolute condition, starting-point and constant basis for the general pursuit of science (Husserl, Merleau-Ponty, Litt, Dingler, etc.), for it is the one universal world of experience (cf. Allon; E. Strauss), and all scientific methods, results and laws are necessarily related to it.

Similarly, psychology is based on the pre-psychological empirical dealings of human beings with themselves and others, i.e., on their everyday, actual mental life.

Psychology can be divided in a variety of ways. According to the conception of science and method, for example, it may be divided into phenomenological, introspective, rational, descriptive, comparative, analytic, explanatory, purely empirical and inductive, experimental, operational, nomothetic, ideographic, speculative, theoretical psychology, or, comprehensively, psychology as a natural and human science. According to its various aspects, psychology may be divided into the psychology of experience, behaviour, attainment or performance, of the conscious and the unconscious. According to the fundamental psychological facts or functions, it may be divided into the psychology of the senses, or of perception, memory, thought, learning, will, feeling, conation, needs, motivation, etc. According to its principles and so-called fundamental laws, it may be divided into the psychology of association, reflexes (stimulus-response), elements, factors, vectors, totality; structural, Gestalt and field psychology, etc. According to the concept and significance of man, it can be divided into anthropological, individual, personal, impersonal, collective, naturalistic, deterministic and existential psychology. According to its tasks, it may be divided into diagnostic, aptitudinal, educational, therapeutic and prophylactic psychology, the psychology of advertising, psychological techniques, etc. According to the various domains of reality, there is human, animal, plant, social, cultural, economic and industrial psychology, etc.

Since in spite of all declarations of independence, psychology can still be divided up according to non-psychological standpoints, it is obviously dependent on metapsychological principles, hypotheses, experiences and theories, and seems bound to remain so, like all other sciences of man. The result is that there are so many different trends that one cannot speak of psychology as a single science with homogeneous axioms, principles, basic concepts, methods and so on. Hence "the difficulty of taking the first step" in this science (J. Cohen). In what direction? As an introduction to what psychology?

Edward Zellinger

PURGATORY

1. *Hermeneutical basis for understanding the Church's teaching.* The true meaning of the doctrine of purgatory can only

be understood within the framework of a general account of eschatology. Only the idea of the eschatological as such, as the transcendental condition of all eschatological phenomena, makes it possible to conceive a condition which has its special theological significance precisely "in the end". This is so both formally, i.e., in regard to the necessity of any statement about it, and materially, i.e., in regard to its meaning and factual character.

The eschatological, however, affects the whole of reality, and this is mirrored in the destiny of the individual. In principle, therefore, the domain of the individual as an integral part of the whole can be described in terms of the fundamental, eschatological structure of the whole. The final destiny generally is mirrored and reproduced in the death of the individual. There is in fact an essential connection between the two, even though they do not coincide in every respect.

The eschatological situation of believing humanity, characterized by finality of decision, also includes the personal life of those dead who, as part of the world – like the Church itself – can only attain their complete fulfilment gradually and in the midst of distress and affliction, because of their condition, which is marked by the concupiscence resulting from sin.

The doctrine of purgatory therefore forms an essential part of a systematic Christian eschatology conscious of its own presuppositions. It may not be superseded either by the theory of a general resurrection of the dead here and now (Barth), or by the theory of a general sleep (Cullmann). The first is not seriously compatible with the multiplicity and futurity of human deaths, while the second does not take the personal character of death seriously enough. Moreover, both theories overlook the fact that death as death belongs to the intermediate state, that precisely by it Christian existence as a whole comes to maturity, and that while the resurrection can be thought of as an individual event, it is only the outcome of the final victory of divine grace.

2. *History of revelation and of dogma.* Outside Christianity it is characteristic that all the dead without distinction are located in the same place (Hades, Sheol). It is only within this framework – according to the particular eschatological or mythological conceptions current at the time – that they are distinguished from one another according to their merits, sometimes after a long struggle and after passing through an "ordeal by fire" (e.g. "transmigration" of souls) and with the help of the prayers and sacrifices of the living. In the OT, or at all events in its later phase, this is what happens (2 Macc 12:42–45) in regard to the resurrection, to which at first only certain human beings (special figures, the just), but finally all, are admitted.

For the NT, the eschatological situation was more acute, because Jesus himself, and then the original community (see *Resurrection* II, *Parousia*) considered that the dawn of the Kingdom of God had already come. In accord with the definitive character of the Jesus-event, the specific hope of the Christian was directed towards an immediately imminent, general and universal consummation. (In the individual domain notions of Sheol are still operative [Lk 16:19–31]). The real testing of faith and its works is expected in the "fire" of the Last Judgment (1 Cor 3-12–15).

Justin and Tertullian still shared this perspective in the 2nd century and teach that the dead are waiting "in the grave" for the consummation. Irenaeus took a dynamic view of this state (*Adv. Haer.*, IV, 37, 7: *PG*, VII, cols 1103–4), and Origen, in the framework of his universal eschatology (apocatastasis) worked out a doctrine of a particular purification for each individual (*In Lucam Hom.*, XXIV: *PG*, XIII, cols.

1864–5: baptism of the spirit takes place in the baptism of fire), and thus developed in germ the doctrine of purgatory. Nevertheless, until the 4th century the idea of the direct combination of purgatory and judgment prevailed without exception.

In the West, however, Augustine emphasized that all the just (not only the martyrs) immediately attain the vision of God and do not have to wait for the end in some indeterminate place. The eschatological process thus essentially includes an individual element. As a result, the doctrine of purgatory is detached from that of the universal eschaton. The reference to 1 Cor 3:12–15 lost its direct application; the purifying fire of the judgment – Augustine himself still hesitates – becomes the *ignis purgatorius*, and now appears as an actual intermediate realm for man in death. The very fact of not yet being totally with God constitutes a punishment (Gregory the Great, *Dialogorum Lib.*, IV, 25; *PL*, LXXVII, col. 357).

The Middle Ages followed Augustine's line of thought and also emphasized the penal and expiatory character of purgatory. At the Second Council of Lyons (1274) and at the Council of Florence (1439), the Latin position (*D* 456; *Locus purgatorius, ignis transitorius*; cf. also *D* 570f.), strengthened even further by Benedict XII's definition (*D* 530–1), had to be explained in face of the Greeks, for on the basis of their tradition they contested the existence of the *fire* of purgatory and any *immediate* retribution after death (*D* 535).

Both sides recognized the utility of prayer for the dead and the fundamental difference in their condition (see *Hell*). But because the Greeks regarded the universal last judgment as the only consummation, they could only attribute relative importance to the decision regarding each individual. For them, as had been the case in Sheol, the good and wicked were still essentially in the same place. For there was only one fire, that of the Last Judgment. In that regard, the saints were already purified (and in the exceptional case even the damned); nevertheless all (*D* 535, including Mary and the apostles) had to undergo the final judgment (Mansi, XXXI A, 485–94, especially 488). The Greeks, therefore, could accept, though with reservations, the dogma of the particular judgment after death (*D* 693), also the doctrine of the *poenae purgatoriae* (*D* 464, 693). They could not accept a separate fire, for they regarded it as an Origenist doctrine of a fire in which all were saved. On this basis they formulated the Church's doctrine at Lyons and Florence in collaboration with the Latins.

The Reformation brought another element into play. Against the background of Western development, which even by the union with the East was not to be detached from its own more and more materialized representations (purgatory as a place of torment), the Reformation now called in question precisely what so far had remained unquestioned, the utility of prayers for the dead (see *Indulgences*). Luther as well as Melanchthon and the Confession of Augsburg, at first very reserved (*D* 777–80), finally, from 1530 onwards, rejected the doctrine of purgatory. Zwingli and Calvin had done so from the beginning (see *Predestination*).

In reply, the Council of Trent defined the distinction between *reatus culpae* and *reatus poenae* (*D* 807, 840) and the propitiatory value of the sacrifice of the Mass (*D* 940, 936), even for the dead. Otherwise, however, it only says (in terms of Latin thought): "purgatorium esse, animasque ibi detentas fidelium suffragiis iuvari" ["Purgatory exists, and the souls detained there are helped by the prayers of the faithful"] (*D* 998, 983). Also worthy of note, however, is the warning that all that does not serve to edify, but only encourages greed, curiosity and superstition, must be avoided by preachers (*D* 983). Bellarmine and Suárez then gave the theological treatise *De Purgatorio* its standard form.

3. *The Church's teaching.* The doctrine of purgatory is an essential element in the belief of the Christian Church. Formulated dogmatically for the first time in the Middle Ages (*D* 464, 693), later pronouncements do not go beyond this position (*D* 983, 998, 723a, 840, 2147a).

The core of the Church's teaching is that there is a purification (the term *purgatorium* is expressly avoided for the sake of the Greeks) for all who "vere paenitentes in Dei caritate decesserint, antequam dignis paenitentiae fructibus de commissis satisfecerint" ["who died truly penitent in the love of God before satisfying for their sins through worthy fruits of penance"] (*D* 464). This doctrine is connected with the utility of prayers for the dead (*D* 464, 693, 983), and is seen against the background of a profound conviction of the seriousness of death and of the multiplicity of individual eschatological acts (*D* 840; see *Penance*) in which death itself represents a salutary burden: *poenae purgatoriae.*

The decisive documents do not impose any obligation as regards fire, a place of purification, or the duration, kind and intrinsic nature of the punishment.

4. *Preaching the doctrine of purgatory.* a) Against the background of the eschatological presence of God in the Church, it must first be emphasized that death itself stands in the perspective of hope. The very separation it involves has a purifying power. For in the judgment, death radically detaches man from himself, and so frees him from his sinful subjection to the world. The immediate relation to God also intensifies its purifying character and turns the very happiness of the saved into a cleansing grief.

b) It is only possible to speak in objective terms about this condition on the basis of Christ (and his descent into hell). His destiny was to overcome death to the point of resurrection. Consequently he "incorporated" all modes of human existence into himself. As the explicit object of our faith, he alone makes possible explicit reflection on death in faith.

c) In virtue of the union with Christ which constitutes the Church, the Church is essentially linked with its dead members (see *Communion of Saints*). Consequently its central act of faith and worship necessarily affects their life. All prayer for them is meaningful if it actualizes the Church's essence. Attempts to make direct contact with the dead would be absolutely unchristian and uneschatological, and would amount to spiritualism. The Reformation protest was rightly directed against such a magical conception.

d) Eschatology itself is constituted by events, because absolute salvation as such is historical in character. Although the classical tradition is silent about it (Mt 27:53?), the question ought certainly to be raised (in line with Latin theology which regards the beatific vision as intervening between purgatory and resurrection) as to whether individual fulfilment does not imply an individual resurrection, on the same presuppositions as and strictly parallel to the general final consummation. Purgatory would then in principle be the state in which those who have died in the Lord wait for the individual and universal consummation. Prayer for the dead in purgatory would thus in another form be prayer for the second coming of the Lord (Rev 22:17). As such it would possess an individual meaning in the highest degree.

Elmar Klinger

R

RATIONALISM

1. *Meaning.* Rationalism is a self-understanding of the spirit which defines itself on the one hand by the positive content of its spiritual existence, and on the other hand, by the type of reflection in which conscious being gives an account of itself. In the latter sense, the rationalistic mentality, the temper of a whole epoch, is characterized by the effort to reduce the whole spiritual being to concepts in a conclusive and perspicuous coherence – as Wittgenstein said, whatever can be said at all, can be said clearly. In contrast to this, a positive concrete rationalism claims to explain the whole life of the spirit through the autonomous spontaneity of the understanding and intellect. The first ("formal") rationalism, the effort at rational self-explanation, does not coincide with the second ("material") rationalism, the effort to attain the concrete content of the spirit as the ground of such explanations. On the contrary, this latter, intent on the concrete content of the spirit, finds in formal rationalism its main opponents – sensualism or empiricism in epistemology, eudaemonism in ethics, classical liberalism in economics and politics, certain types of supranaturalism such as agnosticism or scepticism in religion and metaphysics. Hence rationalism is a constantly ambiguous term and must be defined in each case by its opposite.

2. *Rationalism as the mentality of an epoch.* Rationalism in the general formal sense of the effort at clear, definite conceptual self-understanding represents a certain stage in the self-awareness of consciousness. Mind for the first time detaches itself from its dedication to the known object and turns back on itself in a fundamental effort of reflection. Mind abandons its naive immediacy to its reality, that is, to its existing determination by its content (historical experiences in the widest sense). It distinguishes its content as such from itself, and so attains a critical aloofness from it. Mind is independent enough to test its content, free to accept it or reject it.

Historically, this stage of reflective self-awareness in rationalism is the conscious emancipation of the individual or society from an authoritative explanation of reality – or perhaps a merely habitual one – dominating practice and thought out in programmatic world-pictures. In any case, the explanation had forfeited its claims by its inability to meet new problems, or by its own catastrophic consequences. The emancipation takes the form of rational certainty as to the categories and norms of one's own existence, these being attainable in clear concepts and demonstrable by rational evidence.

In this sense, a rationalism has nearly always signalled the questioning, crisis-laden end of a successful epoch of social integration by means of unquestioning sensible experience. As such a revolutionary crisis, rationalism last appeared – and in some ways irreversibly – in the 17th and 18th centuries. It was the answer to the physical and moral catastrophes of the Christian Churches in the Thirty Years War. It was the answer to the helplessness of orthodoxy in face of the dimensions of the world discovered by the modern sciences. It was the explicit liquidation of an age in which Christianity took itself for granted, being philosophically integrated in scholasticism and perfectly established socially.

3. *The rationalism of the 17th and 18th centuries.* The rationalistic impetus of this epoch-making movement is often summed up under the heading of the Enlightenment (for historical details, see *Enlightenment*). It appeared first as the destructive criticism of questionable world-pictures and as the draft of various systems of explanation. It sought to reduce reality to a few easily comprehensible premisses, among which some traditional Christian principles came to the fore once more in a very different guise. Theology too was essentially rationalist in its approach to religious tradition. It saw this tradition as training for a rational mode of life, in keeping with the universal finality and rationality of nature. It used a similar, very tangible moral interest as a hermeneutic principle to assimilate Christian doctrine, critically investigating it for its contribution to a universal morality. The Bible was given a moralizing interpretation or subjected to historical criticism in order to keep it in line with the moral *a priori*. This was done most consistently by the Protestant "Neologians" between 1740 and 1790, and a little later, by the "Christian Rationalists". But even outside these schools and also in many parts of Catholicism, the keynote of theology was the same. The presupposition was the demonstrable correspondence between the maxims of reason and Christian doctrine. The procedure was the tacit correction of the latter by the former, or the *de facto* reduction of the Christian message to rational principles.

But the rationalism of the 17th and 18th centuries did not become a turning-point because of the popularity and keen-sightedness of formally rationalistic world-pictures. The main thing was that it was the first really strict attempt to make reason fully perspicuous as its own explanation, not that it constructed a coherent model of reality on simple premisses which were ultimately non-rational. Rationalism, strictly speaking, made thought so directly its own object that the act and content of the mind, thought and that as which it thought itself, were identical in total communication. This is an integral formal and material rationalism, the absolute self-possession of the intelligent mind, not a mere challenge to the attempted systems of formal rationalism, but a new, decisive, irreversible reflection, attentive to the necessary identity of thinking and the thing thought in the self-determination of the spirit. It was propounded in an exemplary way by Descartes in the *Meditationes de prima philosophia*. He showed that truth is ultimately based not on something distinct from thought but on the act of thinking itself and its necessary implications. This autarky of reason as regards truth, founded on the *sum cogitans*, was seen by Descartes and subsequent rationalism as the absolute self-immediacy of thought which excludes any non-subjective mediation, including the intervention of an omnipotent deceiver. In its self-interpretation as to its content it is guaranteed by an *a priori* consciousness of God. It is a power of mathematical combination which draws only on its own resources. This absolute lucidity of the spirit in pure autonomy sets up both a formal criterion of evidence and a material principle of knowledge (Descartes's *ideae innatae*) which represent the necessary and sufficient condition of all meaning and hence the logical and ontological premisses of all sensible reality.

4. *The crisis of rationalism and present problems.* Every type of rationalistic mentality brought with it – with dialectical necessity – an anti-rationalistic movement. Against the effort to gain a conceptually certain and comprehensible view of the world, the as yet unamenable multiplicity of the world appeared as an absolutely unfathomable deep, the abyss of reason. This mostly took the form, and in the reaction to the rationalism of the Enlightenment above all, of a romanticizing recourse to tradition, which had rather been dismissed than overcome by rationalism. The new formal and material rationalism countered this "irrationalistic" objection to the comprehensiveness of the reason by a more than *de facto* external opposition. Since the grasp of the absolutely self-mediated nature of understanding as the essence of subjectivity made the autarky of reason the basis of a universal system, it had to take up on principle the problem of the mediatedness of spiritual existence, its obvious limitedness, the dependence intrinsic to its spontaneity. The real acuteness of the problem came to the fore in the question now posed for the first time, as it now only could be against this background, of the whole possibility of revelation. For this presupposes the essential meta-rationality of a realm of truth, or the dependence of the spirit on principle on certain historical experiences. It was the problem which Lessing called that of the "yawning gap" between the "eternal truths of reason" and "contingent historical facts". See *Faith and History* and *History* I.

The weakness of the rationalism tributary to Descartes was due to its predominantly scientific perspective. It reduced the problem to the objective connection between the mind and a sensibility conceived of as a mechanism. The solutions – the theory of the pineal gland, occasionalism or psychophysical parallelism – were very inadequate in view of the real problem, which was the dialectic of the self-immediacy of spiritual existence and its *de facto* mediatedness. The dependence of the mind on sense-perception is merely the most palpable indication of this dialectic, which shows its full significance only in the claim of revelation to be a communication of truth inexhaustible by reason. The real problem of rationalism was first put by Kant, who saw that the theoretically evident *a priori* of the self-immediacy of the Ego in Cartesianism was really the problem of freedom as the real act of the immediate, autonomous self-determination of the mind. The autonomy of thought was primordially not a theoretical datum but a "categorical imperative", the regulative idea constitutive of practical existence. Theoretical or intellectual knowledge took place on principle only as the mediation of *a priori* formal elements through empirical contents.

With this the real question was put. Hitherto the question of the unity of self-immediacy and mediatedness had been projected "outwards", on the lines of natural science. It had been the question of the possibility and guarantee of the objective coincidence of "thought" and "being" – the mediation between a "spiritual" and an "extended substance". Now it was the question of the autonomy of practical freedom (self-immediacy) and empirical rational knowledge (mediatedness), the problem of the constitution of reason itself in its effort at absolute self-explanation. The rationalistic dilemma of the self-determining spirit which had also to see itself as finite, conditioned and hence non-autonomous thus became the problem of "absolute reason" as the unity of theoretical and practical rationality.

This no longer merely led away from a rationalistic thought-form to its "shadow", an anti-rationalistic concern with the dimensions of reality which had been closed to reason. An intrinsic logic led rationalism to the full problem of mediation which became the central theme of "romantic" philosophy and German Idealism. There it led to the epoch-making discovery of inter-personality as the absolute integral of self-mediation and mediatedness. Society was the total and universal logical and ontological *a priori* of all meaningful reality. The way was prepared for considering history as the absolute medium of meaning.

This new level of speculative reflection superseded the disjunction which had enabled rationalism to be both (formally) the alternative to the surmises of a sense of self as incomprehensible and (formally and materially) the radical effort at self-explanation by the mind. Rationality was given a fundamentally new meaning, that of the historical and social reason. It was a definite function in the process of social mediation. Rationalism in its classical form became philosophically outmoded. So too the great question of the philosophy of religion, first really posed on principle by rationalism, must now be orientated to the possible meaning and communicability of revelation, directed to the social and historical nature of the mind, as the constitutive categories of human existence.

Konrad Hecker

REALITY

The "real" and the "actual" are often used synonymously and the general term "reality" applied to both. But they were distinct concepts originally and in the course of history, though as central philosophical terms not readily definable.

In medieval terminology, *realitas* was one of the transcendentals convertible with entity, unity, goodness, etc. It means that anything which has being in any sense at all has a concrete content, determination and essential constitution (see St. Thomas Aquinas, *De Veritate*, 1, 1c: "nomen rei exprimit quidditatem sive essentiam entis"; cf. *1 Sententiarum*, 25, 1, 4: "quidditatem vel rationem"). As a transcendental note of being, reality is therefore prior both to the distinction between potency and act (*potentialitas* and *actualitas*) and the categories of substance and accident, and applies to all these throughout. Hence it also comprises the distinction between "being" and "thought" (thinking; see *Spirit*), since absolute being, the unlimited fullness of all essential determinations (*ens realissimum, omnitudo realitatum*) is the perfect thought of all these determinations (cf. St. Thomas Aquinas, *Summa Theologica*, I, q. 44, a. 4, "rationes omnium rerum . . . ideas . . . formas exemplares in mente divina exsistentes". In this metaphysics, which goes back to antiquity, "being" is interpreted in terms of actual identity with absolute thought, reality in terms of the absolute idea; so too even in the Identity-Philosophy of the 19th century, cf. Hegel, *Enzyklopaedie*, para. 553, "The concept of spirit has its reality in the spirit." It follows that all metaphysical realism determined by this tradition is essentially a metaphysical Idealism (see *Metaphysics*).

In finite being and thinking, reality and idea are distinct as "esse in re (extra animam, extra mentem)" and "esse intentionale (in anima, in ratione)". But since reality is a transcendental, the idea must here be regarded as a type of reality. Thought in finite thinking is referred to being as its measure and fulfilment. See Aquinas, *1 Sententiarum*, 25, 1, 4c: "nomen rei (se habet) *et* ad id, quod est in anima . . . *et* ad id, quod est extra animam, prout res dicitur quasi aliquid ratum et firmum in natura." This natural division of reality between thought ("ideal" reality) and being, the object of thought ("real" reality), is hardened in Descartes into the distinction between *realitas obiectiva* (meaning reality merely subjectively *represented*) and *realitas formalis sive actualis* (true reality, given in the solidity of things themselves). It is only on the basis of this Cartesian distinction that the problem of the "reality of the external world" could arise (which, however, was only felt later as an acute one). In Descartes its reality was still assured along with the certainty of the actual reality of God, since his objective (intentional) infinite reality in finite thought surpasses the material powers of this finite thought itself. Kant took the separation of being and finite thinking a step further. Being becomes a "thing-in-itself" which is never knowable as an object by finite thought and whose reality is never demonstrable to it. It must remain only marginally thinkable, a mere (though necessary) subjective idea. This is the transcendental idea as Kant conceives it. In the same way, the precritical situation of the transcendental idea in the absolute idea (thought) of the infinite divine thinking (*Critique of Pure Reason*, V, B, 139) must remain a pure idea. "Objective reality", reality demonstrable to finite thought, does not appertain to the thing-in-itself. It is "theoretical reality", appertaining only to sensible representations (phenomena) mediated in the intuitional forms of space and time; or it is moral, practical reality, appertaining only to the representations which refer not to sensible experiences but to the pure moral experiences of reason which are the law for moral action (the one "fact of the pure reason", *Critique of Pure Reason*, para. 7, note). All representations in terms of objects (categories of the intellect) have objective reality, reference to reality, only in this *a priori* relation to the realm of sensible experience or as the case may be the realm of moral conscience and action. In this way, "reality" loses its character of a transcendental determination of being, and is critically reduced to an intellectual category (the quality of that which is given in experience), because Kant reduced experience itself primarily to what he held to be alone relevant in science (theory); sensible experience, or again, the pure experience in conscience of the unconditional moral imperative – though the latter, by comparison with the paradigm of sensible experience had "only" practical relevance.

This approach had the merit of bringing out very clearly that reality can be mediated to thought only by experience and can never be the product of thinking alone. But it was itself uncritical in neglecting the problem of how far thought itself (and not just thought as mediated by sense-perception) is an experience of reality, i.e., of being, and has to understand itself as such. This problem of an experience of being in thought (not just a sensible and not just a moral one) had been clearly posed in the history of metaphysics under the heading of *participatio, illuminatio, lumen naturale*, etc. (see *Participation*). However, it had not been consistently worked out. And the metaphysical and theological identification of the transcendental ontological reality with the absolute idea of the infinite divine thought did not take the problem any further to a solution.

If reality then means the objective significance as a transcendental determination of being prior to all sub-divisions and definitions, actuality means the true state of reality in which reality is fully "there" and given. Hence the actuality of reality has always the time-related sense of a "presence". And the absolute actuality of all reality as such (*actus purus*) is its eternal divine presence to itself (*aeternitas, nunc aeternitatis*). And since this unlimited self-realization (in both senses of the word) of all reality takes place as infinite thought (idea), this means, in the traditional identification of the real with the ideal, that infinite thought is the perfect reality of all objective truth or content: the idea is the actuality of reality. Just as it is only in finite being and thought that the real and the idea are disjoined, so too with actuality and potentiality.

Here all substantial or accidental reality is the coming about (in merely temporal presence – *nunc temporis*) of a possibility which precedes the real and so represents its "past" and which also represents its "future", being the task of this realization. In the history of metaphysics, it had always been noted that actuality, as *perfectio* and *consummatio* of reality, was not itself a merely real element of being, but the problem was not kept consistently enough in the foreground. The critique of Kant was directed against the supposed reduction of actuality to an element of reality, of reality to an essence (and hence according to Kant, to a conceptual content), a process particularly clear in the ontological proof of the existence of God (implied in all empirical proofs).

Kant also helped to show that actuality cannot merely come from the act and deduction of subjective thought. It displays itself by bringing about an impact on man, an experience of man. But when it was primarily restricted to sensible experience, actuality – while retaining its character of transcendental being – was deprived of any mode of being beyond the categories and reduced to an intellectual category (a modality of the relationship of the representation to the faculty of knowledge). This makes it clear on the whole that actuality is only there in experience, and that the objective content (reality) can only be mediated to thought through such actual experience. One can see why "reality" can be used to designate both the actual (the full presence of reality) and the real itself (the content which is "there" in the experience of this presence). But it must be noted that experience embraces the many ways (beyond mediation by sense-perception) in which man is met by reality (the actual and the real) and realizes himself by his response to this impact. Hence reality is the correlative concept to experience as the total life-activity of man.

Alois Halder

REFORMATION

The Reformation was a many-sided event, not merely a religious one. Martin Luther, the *homo religiosus*, was undoubtedly at the centre, but many non-theological factors (Humanism, politics, economics) contributed largely to its origin, form and extent. It was part of the shift in European thought and experience which had begun in the 14th century.

Nonetheless, at its core it was a religious movement, and also a theological event, in the great trends launched by Luther, Calvin and also Zwingli. Thus the Reformation is not just a chapter of world history. To an important extent it is a chapter in the history of theology and hence must also be seen in theological perspectives.

Agreement has not been reached about all the points of contention which then attached to the central question. But it is now possible to do justice to the central interests and formulations of the Reformers in such a way as to make scientific and theological dialogue valid and possible. The following account does not deny the Catholic standpoint, but still claims insight into and sympathy with Protestant verdicts.

The authors and protagonists saw the Reformation as the recovery of the pure revelation of primitive Christianity, the "word of God undefiled", while the Catholic Church of the time saw it mainly as a rejection of Christian truth.

It was a challenge like that of Gnosticism in the 2nd century, a threat to the foundations. But it may now be said that wherever the fault lay, it was a *felix culpa*, since the Reformers sought for the pure gospel and succeeded in fact in presenting it to Christians in the face of grave deformations. In many ways they reasserted the ancient Catholic truth.

The Reformers had not the heroic humility which would have enabled them to preserve the unity of the Church. But historically and theologically, it is also important to see the guilt of Catholics. It is generally agreed that the Catholic Church was partly to blame. But even after 1517, the bishops and theologians were unable to accept the new contribution even after critical examination. Today, when the Catholic truth is more profoundly and fruitfully grasped (see *Church* II, III; *Sacraments*, the Catholic element of the offer can be more clearly seen. It was missed in the 16th century, partly because of the false interpretations with which it was combined and its massive onslaughts on the Catholic Church.

A. Notion and Causes

The word *reformatio* was used in all realms of political, cultural and ecclesiastical life in the 15th and 16th centuries. It became a "keyword" (Peuckert) in the 15th century. In Church history *reformatio* also meant *renovatio*, renewal in the double sense of "back to the original form" and "a new start" (cf. Jer 1:10; Rom 12:2; Gal 6:15; Rev 21:5). The story of the monastic orders which had fallen away from their first fervour gives clear instances of this notion of reform. In the 15th century the pressure for reform, inspired by such eschatological and apocalyptic themes as fear of an ultimate calamity, hope of a new creation, Antichrist, appeared in some radical trends. Luther does not often use the word "Reformation", but it appears nonetheless in the course of his first public moves (*Works*, in the *Weimarer Ausgabe* [= *WA*] [1883ff.], I, p. 627). He used it to sum up his programme of *metanoia*, the restoration of the ancient Christian truth by serious attention to the living word of the Bible. Since corruption had extended into the very essence of the Church according to the view of the Reformers, "Reformation" was the watch-word of a religious movement for renewal which did not aim at creating a breach, much less at political revolution.

The impact on world history was due to the condition of the Church itself. In Germany, France and Switzerland, three very different Reformers with a similar intensity of religious purpose achieved revolutionary results of a lasting nature, whose influence was felt far beyond their homelands. The following flanks were exposed to attack: clerical life, which fell short of true Christian standards on all levels (worldliness, pleasure-seeking, immorality, lack of pastoral zeal, simony); theology, where Thomism was still active here and there but was on the whole in decay. It was the heyday of Nominalism where the faith was subjected to logic-chopping in a decidedly non-biblical form of thought. The starting-point of the *potestas Dei absoluta* could swing over into exaggerating the role of human forces in salvation. It was a perilous Pelagianizing of justification which Luther was to denounce as "fooling with works". Theology lost its substance inasmuch as it departed from the central questions. Like redemption, faith and justification, the discussion of the Church as a sacramental and spiritual institution was almost entirely lacking. The sacraments were envisaged in a very material way. Mass was a "good work" of man, of finite value, whose fruits were distributed piecemeal to the hearers. The result was the effort to have as many Masses said and heard as possible. The doctrine of indulgences was seen in a very dubious light, with the Pope disposing of the "treasury" of the Church. Even in mysticism the sense of living by the sacramental reality of the Church had dwindled to a dangerously low point. The valuable *devotio moderna* (cf. Th. a Kempis, *Imitation of Christ*) enriched Eucharistic piety, but expressed itself above all in the dialogue of the individual soul with God. It influenced Adrian VI, Erasmus, and also Luther, who spoke warmly of the *theologia germanica* which it breathed.

At the papal court as in the bishops' palaces the theory and practice of "curialism" were predominant. The power of the keys was taken primarily in a juridical sense (hence fees, taxes, traffic in benefices).

The theological obscurities which were still being lamented at Trent reached a degree of opaqueness which we now find difficult to imagine. And the lack of orientation was made more painful by another complicated factor, Humanism.

Where Humanism had a neo-Platonist tinge, the doctrine of redemption and of the sacraments was at once distorted (Pico della Mirandola, d. 1494). Sound efforts like those of Nicholas of Cusa (d. 1494) were not followed up. Humanism was characterized by an often exaggerated enthusiasm for pre-Christian antiquity. But it was not essentially pagan. In some of its representatives (Quirini, Giustiniani) it was a component of the Catholic reform. Another important factor which had a wide influence on Christendom was the style of life of the Renaissance, which was markedly hedonistic. The Renaissance produced a great treasury of Christian art, but even this was to a considerable extent of a worldly tinge. In philosophical and theological circles there were radicals like Eoban Hessus of Erfurt who inclined to scepticism in the matter of dogma and the Church.

Erasmus of Rotterdam (d. 1536) was the central figure of Humanism. His great memorials are the first printed edition of the Greek NT, and his many editions of the Church Fathers, with Introductions. Dogmatically correct, he lacked dogmatic fullness, and indeed his grasp of the Catholic faith was often endangered by his lack of practical and speculative interest in dogma. Recent efforts to rehabilitate his religious qualities break down at the simple comparison with the force of the gospels and St. Paul, which can also be felt in Luther. His scriptural principle allowed in theory the authority of the Church, but in practice worked only with an eye to the magisterium of scholarship. His malicious criticisms of monks and bishops, like his *Epistolae Obscurorum Virorum*, reinforced the tendency then widespread to hold inwardly aloof from the Church, and paved the way for the exodus of the Reformation.

The Church was especially weakened and its position undermined by the condition of the papacy. Alexander VI could be personally amoral and still proceed against the justifiable efforts at reform made by Savonarola (burnt at the stake in 1498). Leo X set out to "enjoy the papacy", but with no corresponding sense of the priestly and pastoral nature of the papal office, and with a far from adequate will to reform. The demand for reform had long been normally voiced as a general criticism of the papacy (pioneered by Marsilius of Padua, d. 1343, and William of Occam, d. 1347), and after the deeply disturbing experiences of the great Western Schism, worked out as a corrosive uncertainty which penetrated every nook and corner of Christendom.

The papal curialism was opposed by Conciliarism, which had been defeated but not disarmed in the 15th century. The constantly reiterated appeal from the Pope to a General Council became one of the weapons of the Reformers. The answer of the Curia was typically reactionary: too much insistence on authority and too little real action. There were of course zealous bishops and well-meaning priests, but the general trend was to enjoy the benefice rather than to discharge the office. The clergy on the whole were more or less unfit for their task. The cathedral chapters were mostly occupied by noblemen's sons, with no call to the priestly life, and living in concubinage. The lower clergy were uneducated, received orders without probation, were poorly off and multiplying rapidly, a sort of spiritual proletariat: monks and priests formed as much as ten per cent of the population in some places, not including the nuns. The lower clergy were generally despised and being free from taxes were an economic competitor of the burghers.

Nonetheless, religious yearnings and concern for the salvation of one's soul were dominant traits of the times. This may be seen from the many costly votive offerings and the decoration of the churches. But Church life was often an almost exclusive preoccupation with gaining foreseeable merits through the accomplishment of precepts. Confraternities offered a way of sharing in countless good works, Masses, indulgences, etc.

The great Reformers were not just inspired by the abuses, but this "pitiable condition" (Zwingli) made it easier to fall in with their grave criticism. The credibility of the Church had suffered. The theses of the Reformers repeated, especially at the beginning, reproaches or demands which had long been heard. Many, including well-educated monks, made common cause with the Reformers out of a desire to live religiously. A reformation in the sense of a radical critique had become historically unavoidable.

Non-theological, social and political factors contributed to the spread of hostility to Rome. The provincial or national Churches which had been supported by the papacy in pre-Reformation times, for political and pecuniary ends, and for reasons of Church politics, such as the need to find allies against Conciliarism, made intervention in Church affairs by the local ruler easier. "The Duke of Cleves is Pope in his land." This was later to be of service to the Reformation (as to the Counter-Reformation). So too the city councils had gained more and more hold over the Church even in Catholic times, which made it easier for them to intervene in the Reformation period to seize Church property and dissolve monasteries. (One example, with concomitant rioting, was the Poor Clare convent of Nuremberg, which, like many others, was condemned against its will to extinction, though even Melanchthon recognized the truly evangelical spirit of the nuns.) Social tensions also benefited the Reformation.

B. Martin Luther and the Beginnings of the Reformation

The Reformation in Germany was given its essential stamp by the personality and activity of Martin Luther. Since the twenties of the 16th century down to our own times his figure has given rise to controversies which seem almost insoluble, even on the Protestant side. The reasons are as follows. His own accounts of his life are inconsistent. He left no general survey of his theology, least of all a systematic one. Nearly all of his enormous output were occasional writings, in which his explosive temperament was to an extraordinary extent the prisoner of his own emotions and the external polemical situation. The paradox was his natural form of expression, often compressed into a forceful series of contradictions, with an exaggerated use of superlatives and little concern for exact terminology. Thus he appears to waver and contradict himself: "Lutherus septiceps" (Cochlaeus), "As many Luthers as books by Luther" (H. Boehmer). Studies of Luther always follow up some special line or other: forensic justification; Luther, the supposed upholder of the autonomy of conscience; Luther, the revolutionary; the theology of the word.

Martin Luther, b. 10 November 1483, was the son of a miner. He was brought up hard, and this affected his notion of God: "I could not but blench . . . when I even heard the name of Christ . . . whom I took to be a stern and angry Judge" (*WA*, XL, I, p. 298). This explains the suddenness of his entry into religion, a step which no one had foreseen. (He had vowed to do so in a thunder-storm at Stotternheim, July 1505, in his anxiety to save his soul.) His life in the monastery was a soul-shaking combat for the grace of God, accompanied by scruples of high religious value. He learned to know the Bible very closely, and soon came to an extraordinary personal relationship to it. He spoke of the Letter to the Galatians as his "bride". This new, creative contact with the words of the Bible and the life-engendering thought-form thus produced are the core of the Lutheran reformation.

But was he a "hearer of the word"? The subjective character of his discovery and its application is unquestionable. He sees some texts in a completely new light, but is blind to others, which he knows but does not attend to equally. He is eclectic with Scripture. His own experience of Christ ("was Christum treibet" – what serves Christ) is the norm of all that is to be learned from Scripture. He attached far less importance to the synoptics and John than to "his" Paul.

He said his first Mass, plagued by scruples. At the Philosophical Faculty of the University of Erfurt, he came into contact with Nominalism, teaching the arbitrariness of God's will. The irreligion of this theology caused him to "lose Christ" (*WA*, II, p. 414). He had no feeling for the sacraments. He lived in fear of the anger of God. His anxiety cast him into the "despair" which was constantly evoked even later, and then to his liberating "Tower-experience" with Rom 1:17. The text meant for him not the wrathful but the saving justice of God. In his great retrospect of 1545, he claimed to have discovered for himself a new truth. But as Denifle has shown, it was not new, but an ancient Catholic truth to which he penetrated in spite of Pelagianizing misinterpretations. This great experience of the reformer cannot be exactly dated. The late date 1518–20, which has been so circumstantially maintained of recent years, presupposes an experience other than that expressly described by Luther in 1545. But in any case, Luther's discovery need not have been disruptive of Church unity.

Both St. Thomas Aquinas and St. Bernard of Clairvaux used the Lutheran expression *sola gratia*, and many prayers of the Roman Missal are inspired by the same conviction. But Luther maintained all his life that the Pope taught that forgiveness of sin and justification came by man's own work. This means that "in this main chapter" Luther was not combating the teaching of the Church but a widely-held opinion of the Schools and a Church practice of his times. Luther preached magnificently throughout his whole life the doctrine of the merciful justice of God, with an inexhaustible richness of exposition. It was a life chequered by the above-mentioned "despair", and tirelessly bent on study of the Bible text, and it also brought out consolingly the joyous sense of sonship of God, the freedom of the Christian man, in word and action. There was also a Luther at peace.

But justification is now through the "alien justice" of Christ, as Luther calls it. It is attributed to us, is merely imputed to us, but is to become our own not merely extrinsically and forensically but by God's creative word which accomplishes what it affirms. Here the terminology fluctuates. Justification is a process of healing which has begun but is never finished before death. It takes place in the hospital of the Church.

There is a difference between the forgiveness of sins and their total obliteration. The expression "simul iustus et peccator" can be admitted by Catholics. Luther creates difficulties by taking being sinful as *totus peccator*. His assumption of a double justice is of slight importance as soon as it is seen that he teaches that grace truly transforms us and demands that we co-operate with our justice which comes from without but becomes our own. Luther adopted as one of his favourite sayings the words of St. Bernard: To stand still is to go back. This is not concerned so much with actual daily sins as with the basic sinful attitude. It is a summons to repress this through the grace of Christ.

Indulgences. A jubilee indulgence granted by the Pope in favour of the rebuilding of St. Peter's in Rome was used in favour of the newly elected Archbishop of Mainz, Albrecht of Brandenburg, by the Curia, which linked it in a shameful way with a financial affair and indeed made it an item of barter in a piece of big business. The doctrine of indulgences as propounded by Albrecht in his *Instructio summaria* was theoretically correct within the framework of the current opinions. But the possibility of buying a "bill of confession", which could be used later to confess all "reserved sins" to any priest, led to the postponement of penance. The "buying" of a plenary indulgence for the dead (only *per modum suffragii*, by way of supplication, but "very efficacious and sure"), and the exaggerated commendation of this "supreme grace" could not but lead the people to a non-biblical notion of sin and guilt.

The effects of Tetzel's preaching came to the notice of Luther in the confessional. Thereupon he addressed himself to the local ordinary and to Albrecht of Mainz. Only when the bishops failed to answer did Luther decide to put his theses forward for discussion among scholars inside and outside Wittenberg. There was no nailing-up of theses. This is an important instance to show that Luther did not aim at a break with the Church but became unintentionally a reformer, for serious Christian reasons.

The theses themselves did not contradict the teaching of the Church as then put forward as binding, though it is impossible not to notice a dangerous trend towards disregard of the magisterium. Their value is in their religious richness, which speaks out in extraordinary pastoral force against non-Christian and un-Christian expressions which had become common in the Church. It is summed up in the first thesis, which is a sort of motto for Luther's whole view of the Christian life: "When our Lord Jesus Christ said, Do penance, he meant that our whole life should be penance." The secret of their rapid dissemination was that they came with forceful eloquence at the precisely right historical moment, when they could speak to a widespread and to some extent radical discontent, and do so from the very heart of conscience. Luther had not foreseen what the impact would be. He tried to give a detailed theological justification of his views in the *Resolutiones disputationum de indulgentiarum virtute* (*WA*, I, pp. 528–628) (1518). In the covering letter he affirmed his orthodoxy and his readiness to come to an agreement with the Roman Church.

Like the *sola gratia*, the dispute about indulgences need not have been disruptive, if the call for reform had been taken up on the side of the Church, and if Luther had managed to be heroically patient and been ready for a major act of obedience. Archbishop Albrecht denounced Luther to Rome in December 1517 for spreading new doctrines. Leo X, a pleasure-seeking, nepotistic fund-raiser, preoccupied with the danger from the Turks, considered the matter to be a monkish quarrel. The general of the Augustines, Gabriel della Volta, was delegated "to soothe the fellow". But the order backed Luther. At the disputation of Heidelberg, April 1518, Luther defended a number of radically paradoxical theses from his *theologia crucis* and won a number of his later disciples, including Martin Bucer, Johannes Brenz and Erhard Schnepf. In August 1518 Luther was invited to Rome by Cardinal Cajetan, then in Germany. At Luther's request the Elector Frederick saw to it that the case was heard in Germany. Luther's discussion with Cajetan, who had made himself well acquainted with Luther's works, ended fruitlessly. Cajetan declared that the subjective certainty of salvation demanded by Luther was "the equivalent of founding a new Church". He noticed correctly the neglect of the role of the Church in the transmission of faith, but probably "maximized" Luther's views, being misled by a case one-sidedly overstated in polemical terminology.

Luther appealed to a General Council, but when pushed by John Eck at the Leipzig Disputation of the summer of 1519, he questioned on principle its validity. Then came the writings on reform: *Of the Papacy of Rome* (*WA*, VI, pp. 285–324) (1519); *To the Christian Nobles* (1520); *Of the Babylonian Captivity of the Church* (in Latin, 1520). He denounced unyieldingly the doctrine of the sacrifice of the Mass, but maintained the real presence of Christ in the sacrament. Only baptism, the Eucharist and penance were admitted. He rejected in particular the sacrament of Orders and hence the sacramental priesthood. On the contrary: "All that has crawled out of baptism can boast to be Pope, bishop and priest." This made it clear to many Christians that Luther was not merely launching the long overdue reform but proclaiming fundamental dogmatic differences, that is, heresies. The same year 1520 saw the appearance of the very valuable book, *The Freedom of the Christian Man*, where he brought out a central biblical truth and made it normative for his theology. In the same year 1520, after the election of the Emperor and hence after Luther's own ruler had ceased to be of political interest to the Curia, the charge of heresy was taken up again, the summons to recant was issued and excommunication was threatened (in a far too general formulation, where the errors imputed to Luther were not clearly evaluated). Luther reacted by burning the bull which threatened excommunication, December 1520. The excommunication came into force on 3 January 1521.

C. Advance of the Reformation and Ecclesiastical Changes

Luther had become so clearly the spokesman of the German nation that the existing canon and civil law could not be used to enforce the excommunication by outlawing him. He had to be negotiated with. Invited to Worms for the first Diet of the new Emperor Charles V (April 1521), he stood over his writings and refused to recant. On his way back, he "slipped away to the Wartburg". The imperial edict against Luther came only on 25 May 1521, after the departure of most of the members of the Diet, but still valid at law. Charles, who in spite of his youth had shown in his own personal statement at Worms (in French) – still impressive today – that he was the only peer of Luther, had to go back to Spain because of the threat of war from France. In the decisive years when the Reformation was taking root, he was absent from Germany for nine years. Further, he needed the support of the Estates friendly to Luther for his wars against the Turks and the French.

At the Wartburg, perhaps stimulated by doubts of conscience, reinforced by his isolation, he produced an amazing mass of deeply religious books: the commentary on the Magnificat, the Postillae on the Church, Confession (in favour of private but against compulsory confession) and a polemical work against the Louvain professor of theology, Latomus, on the central theme of his theology, "the persistence of sin":

sins are fully forgiven but not totally obliterated. The most important literary production of the time at the Wartburg was the translation of the NT into German, a work of immense religious impact. It swept into sheer oblivion the fourteen printed editions which had appeared in High and Low German before Luther.

Meanwhile there were disturbances in Wittenberg – the Mass publicly denounced, monks renouncing their vows, etc. To throw light on the matter, Luther wrote his *De Votis Monasticis* (*WA*, VIII, pp. 573–669). A vow against freedom is invalid. The religious life is unnecessary. Marriage makes it possible to fulfil the command of chastity. There was a mass exodus from the monasteries. At the same time the liturgy was being transformed at Wittenberg, though without the consent of the Elector. Private Masses were abolished, Communion given under both species, vestments, statues and side-altars were eliminated. Melanchthon and the town council, no longer able to control the situation, begged Luther to return. Without the consent of the Elector, he left the Wartburg and preached, in monk's hood and with a fresh tonsure, for one of the weeks of Lent, 1522, "against the fanatics". Thereupon some of the old customs, but not private Mass, were brought back. This caused the breach with Carlstadt, his colleague and ally. Luther now had him expelled by the Elector, as a "factious spirit".

The most important of Luther's helpers (among whom were N. von Amsdorf, J. Jonas, J. Bugenhagen and G. Spalatin) was Philip Melanchthon (d. 1560), a grand-nephew of Reuchlin. His *Loci Communes* (1521) made him the theologian of the Reformation. His effort to combine Humanism and Reformation has been judged in different ways down to the present day. He suffered much from Luther's temperament and complained bitterly, without wavering in his loyalty.

The under-privileged classes had got the impression from Luther's writings that he would meet their social programme or hopes. This was a mistake, since the freedom of the Christian man which Luther had insisted on was not meant in a political or social sense. But then he had also made radical onslaughts on Church authority, and in his demagogical way had sown the seeds for a general contestation. The "Revolutionaries" now looked to him – the knights (1522), the peasants (1524–25), Hutten and Sickingen (1523).

The Peasants' Revolt was mainly to redress social grievances, but received a religious tinge through the fanatical elements. Luther was undoubtedly unjust to them, especially where he included Carlstadt in his condemnation. Since their scriptural interpretation was so wild, so much a breach with tradition in the appeal to the "Spirit", Luther cannot be accused of inconsistency in condemning them, except perhaps on grounds of pure logic. Thomas Münzer, highly gifted and cultured (1488/89–1525) who took the side of the peasants, was an inspired preacher, but the longer he was at work, the more clearly he appeared as a fundamentally destructive force. He was executed in 1525. The peasants looked to Luther, who responded with a "Plea for Peace", directed both to the peasants and the nobles. But as early as May 1525, shaken by the abuse of the gospel by Münzer, he published the horrifying tract *Against the Predatory and Murderous Faction of the Peasants* (*WA*, XIII, pp. 357–61), in which he urged the nobles to slaughter them mercilessly. The nobles followed his advice and the peasants' revolt was suppressed with the utmost savagery. Luther was often blamed for the atrocities. His answer was: "I struck down all peasants in the revolt . . . but I leave the responsibility to our Lord and God, who commanded me to say such things" (*WA*, Table Talk III, 75, no. 2911a).

The Reformation now became the concern of the princes and burghers. It had ceased to be the popular movement it had been before. In the middle of the dreadful months of the Peasants' Revolt Luther married, much to Melanchthon's distress. His bride was the former Cistercian nun, Catherine of Bora. The same year saw the great clash with Humanism. Erasmus, typically prudent, had tried for a long time to avoid the issue. Luther prized him for his work on the Greek Bible, and in general for his high degree of culture. But he had sensed early on that Erasmus could never be a kindred spirit. Finally the "Prince of Humanists" published in 1524 his book on free will. Luther answered in 1525 with his *De servo arbitrio* (*WA*, XVIII, pp. 600–787), which he always maintained was his best book, since it really dealt with "the heart of the matter", that in the work of salvation all is absolutely dependent on God. But it is impossible not to notice that Luther here goes beyond the main elements of his doctrine of the faith, by introducing a new notion of God (*Deus ipse, non revelatus*), not used by him elsewhere, and which contradicts his other theological work. And he was not quite just to Erasmus. Even many followers of the Reformation could not adopt Luther's radical view of predestination.

D. The Reforming Princes and the Regional Churches

In spite of the Edict of Worms, the Reformation spread in Germany, favoured by conflicts between the Pope and the Emperor. In the person of Adrian VI, the former tutor of Charles, a blameless and deeply pious priest came to the papal throne in 1522. As his legate Chieregati read out at the Diet of Nuremberg in the following year a public confession of guilt, made above all on behalf of the prelates and "this Roman Curia", it seemed that the interests of the Reformers were to be met on the religious plane and that the movement could become once more a Catholic reform. But Adrian died in 1523, unsuccessful. The following Pope, Clement VII, a Medici (1523–35), supported France, which was co-operating with the Turks. Charles had a war on three fronts on his hands and could not intervene effectively in religious matters. The following Diets temporized accordingly, while the religious trends built up more and more strongly into political power-groups. The danger of a war of religion could be scented for the first time.

The second Diet of Spires (1529) called for a halt to innovations and the right to celebrate Mass in peace. The protest made against this demand by the reformed Estates caused them to be known as Protestants. They demanded tolerance, but were themselves unready to accord it.

Luther's notion of the Church. For Luther, the Church was neither the sacral organization nor the external hierarchical authority but the fellowship of true believers in Christ. He preferred the word "community". The Church is constituted by the gospel mediated in the word of God and the sacrament, and is the "creation of the word", which takes precedence over the sacrament. Every baptized person has the right and duty to teach and spread the word of God. It was merely "to avoid unhappy disorders in the people of God" that all were not charged with this ministry. Thus the community calls ministers to act in its name. It has no earthly head. Institutions and ceremonies are insignificant. The preaching creates "of itself" the necessary outward forms. The essential for Luther was merely the continuity between faith and the word of God, and to this extent it is unfair to Luther to charge him with intending to found a new Church. But his doctrine on the Church is ambiguous, not consistently sustained and at times overstated in polemics. At any rate, it is not merely invisible, though also object of faith. It can be known by the word of God and the sacrament. The main problem is his concept of the ministry or office (the divine mandate is in the foreground in the Confession of Augsburg and the later Luther). The congregational type of Christianity first envisaged by Luther proved unworkable. The Church of Orlamünde, which had chosen Carlstadt as minister, refused at once to allow Luther the right to set up such a type. Experience with the fanatics showed that Church discipline was indispensable. The obvious depositary according to late medieval developments seemed to be the regional Church, i.e., the authorities who had become Protestants. This made it difficult for Luther to draw a clear distinction between the secular and the spiritual government.

Luther's doctrine of the Two Kingdoms was partly inspired by his experiences with the fanatics, the war against the Turks and the action taken by Catholic princes against the Reformation. This resulted in exaggerations and ambiguities which he could not later defend. The two regimes are different ways in which God governs the world. The secular authority wields the sword, since "the world cannot be governed by the gospel". Everyone must obey his superior – even among the Turks – except that no Christian should let himself be used in the struggle against the gospel. Against unjust governments there are ways of non-violent active resistance by means of instruction or blame, or passive resistance in the form of suffering injustice or taking to flight. The secular government is from God but is in no way a help towards salvation. The Christian is under the secular government (which includes marriage, parenthood and calling), because even as just he is also a sinner.

Ecclesiastical government. As time went on, Luther's calls to the Protestant authorities to break resistance to the gospel became more insistent. Even in ecclesiastical matters the Prince is to help "as a Christian member". He calls the rulers "Notbischöfe", "emergency bishops", but control did not devolve upon the Church in the course of time. The local rulers became the "supreme episcopate", as Melanchthon had demanded. Even in the Lutheran communities the development was not what Luther had expected. He lamented the "unspeakable disregard for the word of God". Even preachers and rectors of parishes took only from the gospel "a lazy, damaging, disgraceful fleshly freedom" (*WA*, XXX, I, p. 125). An order had to be drawn up for divine service. In 1526 the "German Mass" and the order of divine service appeared and the baptismal booklet was translated. In 1529 the marriage booklet appeared, saying, however, that marriage was a worldly business.

Visitations and the Church Order were imposed in 1527 by the Elector John and put into force by his officials. But the Visitors examined doctrine as well as finances and public morality. Those who refused to take Christian instruction as offered by the authorities were to leave the country. The detailed instructions for the implementation of the Church Order were put together by Melanchthon in 1528, and Luther wrote the preface: "It is the office of bishop to be the inspector, but since none of us are called to this or have a certain precept . . .", he turned to the Princes. The consistory set up by the local ruler later took the place of the missing bishop. The visitations showed that there was great ignorance among the people. Luther composed his Catechisms to remedy this (1529). The Large Catechism presents the individual items in the form of preaching and instruction, while the Small Catechism was a series of questions and answers formulated with a remarkable sureness of touch and in an easily memorized way. This and his hymns made Luther the great religious instructor of the masses.

E. The Reformation in German-Speaking Switzerland

For similar reasons but independently, reform movements started in south-west Germany and Switzerland which made it impossible for the Reformation to appear as a unity. The protagonists were Martin Bucer (1491–1551), John Oecolampadius (1482–1551) and most important of all John Calvin (1509–64). They worked mainly in the cities, which meant that the local community was of greater importance. Zwingli, who was strongly influenced by Humanism, had been parish priest at Glarus since 1506. Study of the Church Fathers and Scripture strengthened his religious armoury. From 1518 on he was in Zurich as a secular priest. A grave illness (1519) and acquaintance with Luther's writings helped him to reach a decision. At the end of 1520 he renounced allegiance to the papacy, but only gave up his priesthood in 1522. The town council provided him with a position as preacher. In this capacity he paved the way for the Reformation which was introduced by the town council in 1523 after a debate for which sixty-seven theses of Zwingli provided the basis. The charitable institutions of the Church were sequestrated and taken over by the administration of the city. Statues, pictures and relics were removed from the churches in the summer of 1524. Mass was abolished in April 1525. On Holy Thursday the "Lord's Supper" was celebrated for the first time as "thanksgiving and remembrance of the Passion of Christ".

Zwingli's reforming activity was strongly marked by his Federal patriotism. He had no sympathy with Luther's attempt to distinguish the Christian from the political. His aim of making the Confederation independent and powerful coincided with the effort of Philip of Hesse to unite all Protestants and free them from Hapsburg domination. Zwingli became a member of the council at Zurich and practically Minister for External Affairs and Home Secretary, while Joachim Vadian worked along the same lines at St. Gall, like Oecolampadius at Basle and Berchtold Haller at Berne. The triumph of the Reformation at Berne gave it a tremendous fillip, but increased tensions in the Confederation, since the ancient cantons kept to the old faith. After the first war against the Catholic regions (ended in 1529 by the Peace of Kappel) Zwingli joined with Philip of Hesse in an effort to come to an agreement with the reformers of Wittenberg. After some polemical writings, discussions were held at Marburg 1–3 October 1529. According to Zwingli's Eucharistic doctrine, the words of institution were purely spiritual, since the saving body of Christ is enthroned in heaven and hence cannot be in the host. He could find no meaning in a "spiritual eating". The Eucharist was only a memorial, a confession of faith acted out by the community, a reminder of the past sacrifice of Christ.

Luther took his stand on the literal interpretation: "The words, 'This is my body', held me spell-bound." It was not just a single truth of faith which was at stake. The whole basic religious structure was different. Zwingli continued to defy the Hapsburgs on the political level and tried to draw France into the contest. New disputes broke out among the Swiss in 1531. At the Battle of Kappel, 11 October 1531, Zurich suffered a grave reverse and Zwingli fell. His successor was Henry Bullinger (1504–75), who was, however, restricted by the city council to the preaching of the word of God. The *Consensus Tigurinus* of 1549, bearing on the Eucharist, united Zwinglianism with the powerful upward surge of Calvinism.

F. Catholic Writings against the Reformation

For the general Catholic response to the Reformation in the first half of the 16th century reference may be made to sections Hand I. Here are some supplementary notes on the situation in Central Europe. Of the 260-odd writers who took up the pen against Luther, an astonishingly large proportion are from Germany. They give a vivid insight into the powerful religious and intellectual forces which confronted Luther. His earliest opponents found themselves in an especially difficult position, and their work had to be done under unfavourable circumstances. It was often the best of them who saw in Luther the force which was to bring about the long overdue Reform. Men like John Eck, on the contrary, who maintained inexorably the charge of heresy, could only seem like trouble-makers. Another difficulty was that the movement could not be adequately described by the negative term of heresy. The just and central demands of the Reformers had a rightful place, by the nature of things, *within* the Church. The Catholic faith should have been put forward positively and independently, with religious force, and taking into account the central interests of the Reformers. But the Catholics remained on the defensive, refuted the Protestants thesis by thesis, but failed to reach the heights of true preaching. Luther had the appeal of novelty, made justifiable criticisms of abuses and had the advantage of getting in the first blow all the time. The long-standing anti-Roman emotions of the masses also worked against the defenders of the ancient Church. And the forcible religious preaching of Luther made the complicated systems and the intellectualist terminology of scholasticism seem bloodless by comparison.

Scholastic theology was ill-prepared for such a conflict. The sacrifice of the Mass had hardly ever come up for discussion in the 14th and 15th centuries. Interest in the Eucharist went above all to transubstantiation and the connected problems of natural philosophy. Nominalism, bogged down in formal problems, raised the Reformers' ire and offered a definitely poor basis for apologetics. One of the main causes of the Reformation, lack of dogmatic clarity and religious drive, hampered in turn the defence. The principle of *sola Scriptura* which Luther upheld so radically presented a grave methodological problem. Was one to adapt oneself to the opponents or include tradition? Was a scriptural proof enough or – like Zwingli later and Melanchthon, more than Luther – should the Fathers of the Church and the Councils be appealed to, as was the custom in the ancient Church? Schatzgeyer, for instance, tried to manage with scriptural proofs alone in his *Scrutinium*. But most Catholic writers kept to the traditional method, without sufficient discussion of the scriptural nature of tradition, or without distinguishing sufficiently between tradition in keeping with Scripture and compromising distortions.

The first and relentless opponent of the Reformation, the best-known and the most hated, was the professor at Ingolstadt, John Eck (1486–1543). At the Disputation of Leipzig, 1519, he had demonstrated clearly that Luther had given up the full Catholic notion of the Church. With his sermons and translations of Scripture he joined the main stream of internal Catholic reform. But his contact with the many texts which he cited was not creative enough. Hence his great literary output is theologically inadequate. He did not probe sufficiently the depths of Luther's concerns, which were often enough distorted beyond recognition by Luther's polemics. Jerome Emser (1478–1527) and his successor John Cochlaeus (1479–1552) worked at the court of the Archduke of Saxony. Emser never got beyond mere refutations. Cochlaeus, selflessly devoting his whole life to the task, made a more positive contribution. One of his main works was the first large-scale biography of Luther, a distorted picture which has obscured the Catholic image of Luther down to the present day.

The other Catholics engaged in controversial theology were overshadowed by the figure of Cardinal Thomas de Vio Cajetan (1469–1534), the most important theologian of the day. He had already treated of indulgences before he read Luther's writings or met the Reformer at Augsburg. Without recourse to polemics, he was able to defend both the papacy and the unity of the Mass with the sacrifice of the Cross on theological grounds. This answer to Luther was not listened to in Germany and also had little influence at the Council of Trent.

The irenically-minded Provincial of the Franciscans, Caspar Schatzgeyer (1463–1527), likewise failed to make any impact. But his presentation of the Catholic doctrine on the Church and the Mass was such that while refuting errors, it also clearly displayed the justifiable interests of the Reformers in the whole Christian truth. A writer of the next generation from Cologne, John Gropper (1503–59), was more successful, and he preserved Cologne and the North-West for the old faith. He was even suspected of heresy. George Witzel (1501–73) also led an unsettled life, full of privations, being distrusted by both sides. He first upheld Luther, but after profound study of the Fathers abandoned the Reformation to devote himself to preaching and to a fruitful catechetical endeavour. In the line of Erasmus, he pleaded for reforms, but without lasting effect.

History unfortunately did not at once give the lie to Cardinal Stanislaus Hosius (1504–79), who accepted the split as a *fait accompli* and sharply underlined the contrasts. Affirming clearly the divine authority of the Church as essentially *one*, he sought to win back the waverers and confirm them in the faith. His Latin confession of the Catholic faith (1552–3) brought the series of Catholic enchiridia to a close.

G. Protestant Confessions

Written confessions of faith were first composed by the Reformers as a defensive measure. The Articles of Schwabach (1529) were directed in part against the followers of Zwingli. They served as a basis for the Confession of Augsburg (1530) which was presented to the Diet there. Here the Lutherans had a double objective – to disassociate themselves from Zwingli, and to show that they upheld the old Catholic faith in its purity. Luther, being "outlawed", did not appear at the Diet, where Melanchthon upheld the cause of the Reformation. The Estates who favoured the Reformers put before the Emperor and the Diet the *Confessio* drawn up by Melanchthon. Its effort to reduce the whole conflict to a few misunderstandings made Luther remark that the Confession of Augsburg "trod delicately and lightly". It affirms that agreement on the central truths of the gospel is enough for Church unity. Customs can vary. Melanchthon was reserved about the old Church, but outspoken against Zwingli and the fanatics (Anabaptists, etc.). The cities of Upper Germany presented a confession of their own, the *Tetrapolitana*. Zwingli sent his *Fidei ratio ad Carolum imperatorem*.

Melanchthon continued to strive for reconciliation and was ready to submit to episcopal jurisdiction and finally even to retain public Masses if Communion could be administered under both species and the marriage of priests permitted. No one wished to hold dogmas which differed from the Roman Church (which was a pretence that doctrinal differences were negligible). The Confession was answered by a *Confutatio*, of which the sole drafter was John Eck. The Emperor rejected the first draft as too long and too polemical. A shortened and amended version was read to the Diet on 3 August, but not handed to the Protestants. The *Confutatio* is an important witness to the interdenominational controversy, but not a full answer to the debated questions.

The Emperor held that the Confession had been refuted by the *Confutatio* and expected the Protestants to submit. They refused. The effort to settle the dispute by means of the Emperor's arbitration had failed. Forceful intervention was ruled out by the Turkish threat. The *Confutatio* was countered by an Apologia composed by Melanchthon. But the Protestant-minded Estates were less conciliatory than the theologians. Above all, they refused to submit once more to episcopal jurisdiction. Melanchthon remarked: "They are not concerned with religion and doctrine. They think only of independence and power." Negotiations about Communion under two species, Mass, celibacy, Church property and monastic vows broke down. The further developments were determined by this failure, and not by the consensus which had been to some extent arrived at on doctrine.

The Diet again broke up with the matter adjourned as a compromise, and the reiterated call for a General Council, which had long been demanded by all religious men in the Church. Unfortunately, Rome, the Catholic States and the Reformers had very different ideas about its nature.

Melanchthon then revised his Apologia, which was adopted along with the Confession of Augsburg as part of the professions of faith at Schmalkalden in 1537. It brings out doctrinal differences more sharply than the Confession of Augsburg. The fourth article, on justification, promoted the one-sided forensic view of justification. It speaks no doubt of regeneration and new life, but the merely imputative declaration of justice comes out as the more decisive element. The attacks were directed against "Scholastici" who were no longer in existence – the *Confutatio* having expressly rejected the opinion that man could merit eternal life by his own efforts, without grace. See also *Protestantism* III.

H. The Reformation as a Political Tool

One of the first results of the Diet of Augsburg was that the Reformation became largely a political weapon. The day after the Diet broke up, the Elector of Saxony started negotiations with a view to a political league among "all Protestant Princes and Cities of the Empire". (Luther changed his mind about the right of resistance: the Electors are not subjects of the Emperor, so that his military proceedings are not executive acts of authority but war.)

On 27 February 1531 the Schmalkaldic League was set up (the Electorates of Saxony, Brunswick-Grubenhagen, Brunswick, Lüneburg, Hesse, Anhalt-Bernberg, Mansfeld and eleven cities including Strasbourg, Ulm and Bremen). After the death of Zwingli the cities of Upper Germany also joined. The League focused all anti-Hapsburg forces, not just anti-Catholic ones. It had contacts with France and England, and for a time with Bavaria. The danger from the Turks forced the Emperor to purchase an armistice from the Protestants. The Nuremberg agreement of July 1532 assured the Protestants that no law-suits would be pursued against them before the General Council or the next Imperial Diet. Protected by this assurance and by the Schmalkaldic League, the Reformation spread further. Several cities and States of the Empire went over. Duke Ulrich introduced it into Württemberg, and the Archduke Ferdinand had to agree to it, in return for recognition of his sovereignty and help against the Turks. Here Lutheranism and Zwinglianism came together in the "Concordia of Stuttgart". But relations remained strained. New negotiations between Melanchthon and Bucer in 1534 prepared the way for the "Concordia of Wittenberg" in 1536, in which the Upper German cities acknowledged with Bucer that "the body and blood of Christ is truly proffered and received at the Lord's Supper". The

Swiss refused to accept the Concordia, but it strengthened the influence of Lutheranism in southern Germany.

On 2 June 1536 the General Council was finally convoked for the following year. The Protestants who had demanded it so loudly now refused to participate. The Schmalkaldic Articles of Luther now presented a summary of non-negotiable truths of faith (justification, rejection of the sacrifice of the Mass and the papacy) and others which could be debated. On the papacy they were downright: "And so we are and remain separated for eternity." In the year 1538 a defensive league, not very strong, was formed between Charles, Ferdinand, the Dukes of Saxony, Bavaria and Brunswick, the Archbishops of Salzburg and Magdeburg. Saxony dropped out again on the death of Duke George (1539).

The discussions of 1539–41. Since the Council was postponed anew, and Charles was prevented from intervening by political reasons, negotiations had to be resumed. Discussions important in the history of theology then ensued. The negotiations of Hagenau, 1539, which had taken a not unfavourable course, were transferred by the Emperor to Regensburg, for the Diet. Meanwhile promising secret talks had been going on, Gropper and the Imperial Counsellor B. Veltwyk representing the Catholics and Capito and Bucer the Protestants. Philip of Hesse was very interested, his bigamous marriage having placed him in a difficult position. A comparative table was drawn up, the "Regensburg Book", which the princes of Hesse and Brandenburg agreed to, while Luther was sceptical. The papal legates, of whom one was Contarini, accepted it as the basis of negotiations, as did Melanchthon and his companions. This was a unique combination of conciliatory forces. Agreement was reached astonishingly quickly on the first four articles – the state of original justice, free will, the cause of sin, and original sin. Article 5 was on justification. Eck and Melanchthon first rejected the draft, but after several days' discussion agreement was also reached here, to the general delight (justification of the sinner through living and efficacious faith, confidence in the righteousness of Christ alone). There was no question of a "double righteousness" but only of the one righteousness, that of Christ the mediator. But though passions had once been kindled by the doctrine of justification, it was not here that the talks broke down, but on the notion of the Church (interpretation of Scripture, administration of the sacraments). The most determined seeker of union, Contarini, stood firm by the formula of transubstantiation, because it had been defined by an infallible General Council. The articles of agreement on justification were completely rejected by the Curia and by Luther. The Emperor's policy of reunion had again foundered.

This made the matter of reform within the Church all the more urgent, as Contarini warned. The bishops insisted on the necessity of a Council, which the Pope promised once more. But the Emperor decided that force was the only solution, feasible, it appeared, since the weakening of the Schmalkaldic League by the bigamy of Philip of Hesse. But Charles's hands were tied by foreign affairs. The Pope still refused to convoke the Council, to help against the Turks, a greater menace than ever, or to support the Emperor against France. The usual concessions had to be made to the Protestants in 1541, 1542 and 1543. But Charles was able to defeat the Duke of Cleves, whom the Schmalkaldic League failed to help, won the province of Gelders and blocked the spread of the Reformation in north-west Germany. But it continued to make progress. The League conquered the Duke of Brunswick and introduced the Reformation into his duchy, Luther agreeing because of the Duke's "blasphemy, tyranny and wickedness". The duty of hindering idolatry also led the League to try to reform the bishoprics of Naumberg and Meissen.

The struggle for the Archbishopric of Cologne was of the greatest importance. The Archbishop, Hermann von Wied, not a theologian, invited in Bucer and tried to introduce the Reformation. The cathedral chapter, advised by Gropper, Billik and Kalckbrenner, resisted vigorously. The Pope did not depose the apostate till 1546, and Wied did not withdraw till the help of the Imperial army was called in. The west and north-west of Germany were thus retained in the Catholic allegiance.

The Schmalkaldic war. After long diplomatic negotiations and subterfuges, and sometimes dangerous compromises, Charles felt himself, after a rapid and successful campaign against France, in a position to conquer the Protestants by force of arms. First there was another Diet at Worms (spring 1545), at which the main business was the war against the Turks, while the religious question was adjourned till the Council, which had now been convoked. But the Protestants refused to recognize the Council. The papal legate, Cardinal Farnese, nephew of the Pope, then entered upon an alliance with the Emperor in view of common military action against the Protestants.

The Pope supplied money and troops, while the opening of the Council was to be postponed till the war was settled. Ferdinand made an armistice with the Turks, and Bavaria, hitherto undecided, was won over by a Hapsburg marriage. Duke Maurice of Saxony was promised the dignity of Elector and the protectorate of the bishoprics of Magdeburg and Halberstadt. The Schmalkaldic League was now isolated. But the Emperor wished to avoid the appearance of a war of religion, and declared war on Hesse and the Electorate of Saxony as an executive measure within the Empire. After initial successes by the League, the Emperor seemed to be master of the situation. At this juncture the Pope, fearing that the balance of power would come down too heavily on the side of Charles, withdrew his troops. More could not well have been done to save the Reformation. Charles, suffering gravely, hastened to the front in person and won the Battle of Mühlberg, 24 April 1547. The Elector John Frederick was captured and forced to renounce his territory and dignity. But he refused steadfastly to recognize the Council, and remained a prisoner, like Philip of Hesse, who submitted to the Emperor. Charles V then seemed to be absolutely victorious. But "the quarrel which then broke out between the Emperor and the Pope was the salvation of the German Protestants in their hour of direst need". For the Council, which the conquered Protestants were to be forced to attend, had been transferred with the consent of the Pope to Bologna, where the Protestants would never go, since it was within the Papal States. Charles had to try to solve the religious situation in Germany without the help of the Pope. But at the "court-martial" Diet, September 1547, only the "Augsburg Interim" could be hammered out, which was accepted by the Diet on 30 June 1548. There was no more question of the return of Church property. Its confession of faith upheld the teaching of the Church without omissions, though striving to do justice to the interests of Protestantism. They retained the right to have married priests and Communion under the two species. But now the Catholic Estates refused to agree. And so this last attempt to save religious unity failed. The Emperor issued decrees for the Catholics calling for the reform of the clergy (formation, conduct, obligation of pastoral ministry), the use of the vernacular in the sacraments, the holding of reforming synods. In August 1548 the Pope ratified the Emperor's measures. But the Emperor could not enforce the Interim on account of the resistance of the Protestant theologians.

Meanwhile a front had been formed among the princes against Charles, who, contrary to previous agreements, now wished to secure the imperial succession, after Ferdinand, for his son Philip. The German Estates were roused against this "calf-like servitude to Spain". Maurice of Saxony was resentful. He was considered a "traitor". His hopes of greater power had not been fully satisfied and he had not succeeded in securing the liberation of his father-in-law, Philip of Hesse. He became the rallying-point of the discontented. They entered into an alliance with the king of France, who was promised Metz, Toul and Verdun for hard cash, while the Turks were incited to attack Hungary. Charles was in Innsbruck, to be close to the newly assembled Council. Maurice stormed the Ehrenberg Pass, the gout-ridden Emperor fled over the Brenner, the Council broke up again (spring 1552). At Passau, the Protestant princes demanded the withdrawal of the Interim, permanent religious peace and undisturbed possession of Church goods. Charles agreed to the *status quo* only till the next Diet. He was deeply shaken by the treason of the princes, who had allied themselves with France against the head of the Empire. His conscience would not allow him to make the concessions to the Protestants. After a last unsuccessful effort to force back the French, he handed over the Empire to Ferdinand at a memorable session in Brussels, a centre of his Burgundian heritage, and returned to Spain for good. He had made a declaration – the impressive counterpart to that at Worms at the beginning of his struggle – in which he protested beforehand against anything "whereby our true, ancient Christian and Catholic faith might be harmed".

The Peace of Augsburg. Few of the princes appeared at the Diet of 1555, and negotiations were carried on by the counsellors. The time was not ripe for a real religious peace. The Protestants demanded unrestricted freedom but were not ready to grant it themselves, either to Catholics or Anabaptists. Only Cardinal Otto von Waldburg, Bishop of Augsburg, spoke on behalf of the Catholics – uncompromisingly. He left the Diet after the death of Julius III, to go to the conclave. The Curia was not represented at the decisive negotiations. There was little theological argument. The discussion was concerned simply with ways and means of making a lasting peace between the religious trends. The difficult questions were Church property, episcopal jurisdiction, the "spiritual reservation" (a prince-bishop lost his power by becoming Protestant) and the "free choice of religion" (prince-bishops were to grant religious freedom to their nobles). Ferdinand's ratification of this last item was against the wishes of the Catholics and was therefore not inserted into the acts of the Diet. The "spiritual reservation" was inserted, with the clause noting that the Protestants did not agree.

The religious Peace of Augsburg was promulgated on 25 September 1555. It included only those who belonged to the Confession of Augsburg and the free choice of religion was only for the nobles, not for their subjects ("ubi unus dominus, ibi una sit religio"), who were granted the right to migrate. Prince-bishops could only go over to Protestantism as private persons, without obliging their subjects to follow them. In the Imperial cities the two denominations could co-exist. Spiritual jurisdiction was not to be exercised over the nobles accepting the Confession of Augsburg. Church property was to remain in the *status quo* of the time of the convention of Passau. The peace was to last till a final settlement between the religions, and if this failed to materialize it was to continue as "permanent and continually valid peace".

The obscurities of the Peace of Augsburg led to many conflicts, especially the "spiritual reservation". The secularization of the bishoprics and foundations in northern and central Germany continued well after 1555. The Imperial cities often failed to protect the minority religion. The Presbyterian ("Reformed") Churches in Switzerland etc. soon came to enjoy *de facto* the benefits of the Peace, and *de iure* after 1648.

This compromise struck at the heart of the notion of the Empire, which was now no more than a federation of territorial States. It was only logical that Charles V should resign the imperial crown in 1556. The Curia contented itself with deploring the Peace, but made no formal protest.

Luther could take no part in the dramatic events which followed Charles's attack on the Schmalkaldic League, when there was a mortal threat to the Reformation. After a series of astonishing achievements in pastoral, administrative and theological work (where in the wisdom of age he laid new stress on faith as a reality, an activity) and after giving vent several times more to his hatred of the Pope in unspeakably crude terms, he died in the town in which he was born, Eisleben, on 18 February 1556. His last notes, written the evening before his death, contain the words, "We are beggars, that is the truth". – On the enormous historical contribution of John Calvin to the Reformation, see *Calvinism*.

I. The Reformation in Western and Southern Europe

1. In the strongly centralized kingdom of France the king had acquired in the course of time so many rights over the Church that the decision for or against a religion was mainly his alone. Small groups of reformers first gathered at the cost of their lives and property in some cases. The official Catholic life was anaemic and could not satisfy religious needs, especially in the burghers of the cities. A biblical Humanism had long been active in small circles (Lefèvre d'Etaples being one of the leaders, d. 1563), which either ended in Catholic reform or prepared the way for the Reformation. In France the Reformation could also find a stay in the Waldensian tradition and its translations of the Bible. When attacks were made openly on the Mass, the king reacted sharply with the setting up of the Chambres Ardentes, which pronounced five hundred condemnations in three years, sending sixty-one victims to the stake. The first preachers of the secret "communities" came from Strasbourg (influenced by Calvin) and then directly from Geneva (88 ministers between 1555 and 1562). Fifty communities were represented at the Paris synod of 1559. A legate of Calvin ratified the *Confessio Gallicana* (de la Rochelle) where the Real Presence is not accepted. After Henry II, the struggle was carried on under his weak sons by the nobles, who used it as a political weapon against the absolutism of the Catholic King. The discussion of religion at Poissy (1561) was still seeking for an agreement. Administrative concessions were soon suspended. The uncompromising religious policies of Catherine de Medici were followed by an attempt to destroy the new believers by force. The Massacre of St. Bartholomew in 1572 claimed 3000 to 4000 victims. The Pope had nothing to do with it, but greeted the news in a way not in keeping with the spirit of the gospel. Henry IV (1589–1610) granted wide liberties, religious and political, to some 1,200,000 Huguenots, mostly peasants and artisans with some of the nobles at their head. In later repression, some trades vanished and took on new life in the lands to which the Huguenots emigrated. The schools were the important factor in establishing Protestantism in France. There were some 1000 Protestant schools in 1578, with their centre at the Academy of Ortley.

2. In the Spanish Netherlands the Reformation went hand in hand with the struggle for political independence,

especially among the nobles. French missionary communities helped to further the national revolution. The *Confessio Belgica* was the Calvinist creed. The Counter-Reformation of Philip II had no pastoral concern for the religious acquisitions of the innovators and therefore had little effect. Opposition hardened when under the Duke of Alba (from 1567 on) there were many executions, including those of a purely political nature. A wave of migration was followed by successful wars of freedom and a split between the Catholic south and the Protestant north. After the political peace of 1581, theological disputes arose within the Protestant States on the question of predestination. The national synod of Dordrecht (1618–19) fixed the Calvinist confession definitively. Later in practice tolerance was widespread.

3. In England the Reformation came, on the whole, through political coercion, a process favoured by the special traditional powers of the *Ecclesia Anglicana*. Proceedings were taken later not under heresy laws, but on grounds of high treason, which was the charge for which St. John Fisher and St. Thomas More were executed. The split was occasioned by the question of Henry VIII's marriages. Protestant creeds were admitted or rejected as the political needs of the hour demanded. The Book of Common Prayer was made the basis of the new liturgy: the edition of 1549 being still strongly in the line of the old Church, while that of 1552 had certain Calvinistic accents. After efforts to restore Catholicism, partly by force, under Mary Tudor (1553–58) the Reformation was re-introduced by Elizabeth I (1558–1603), purposefully and resolutely. At the end of her long reign, the Anglican Church was an institution of a special type.

4. In Scotland too, politics, ecclesiastical and national, combined with religious forces. The main agent was the fiercely anti-Anglican John Knox (d. 1572). His successor, Andrew Melville, had also done his studies at Geneva and later established the Presbyterian Church system. James VI (1578–1625), King also of England (1603–25), supported an episcopalian system for political reasons, but failed in Scotland.

In Ireland, the Reformation remained an English thing, like its importers. After surviving attempts at religious genocide under Elizabeth and Cromwell, beside which a Bartholomew's Day pales into insignificance, the Irish remained impervious to persecution and blandishments, to be the main factors in the establishment of the immense block of U.S. Catholicism.

5. In Italy and Spain there was no anti-Roman feeling. Abuses either could not be exploited against the Church or were overcome by such reforms as that of Cardinal Ximenes in Spain. The Spanish rulers had inherited a militant Catholicism from the long struggle against the Moors, while the Italians depended either on the Pope or the Emperor.

But in both countries no slight amount of Lutheran writings were circulated, with a corresponding influence. Little centres were formed in Venice and Milan, Seville and Valladolid. The boundaries between Catholic Reform and Protestant Reformation remained unclear, at least for a long period (cf. Juan Valdès, d. 1541). Important Italian Protestants include Bernardino Ochino (d. 1564), formerly an influential Capuchin, Pietro Vermigli (d. 1562) and Pietro Vergerio (d. 1565), formerly nuncio and bishop. All three had to flee. The newly established Inquisition struck hard, especially in Spain (in 1559–60 well over three hundred were tried, and many sentenced to death). In Italy, the Reformation could find a stay in the tradition of the Waldenses. After the Inquisition struck, the little communities survived underground. The religious reaction of the Curia was inadequate.

6. In the Nordic lands, little trace of longing for reform can be noted before the event. Its progress was determined primarily by political forces and national rivalries. Under Frederick I (1523–33) Denmark favoured Lutheranism. The Diet of 1536 made it the only legitimate religion, also that of the State. Bugenhagen composed the Church Order of 1539 on which the national Church was based. Soon there were many Danes at work who had studied at Wittenberg.

Norway and Iceland were under Danish rule. But some bishops defended steadfastly the Catholic heritage. In Sweden, Church property, which was taken over by the king in 1529, played an important role. Gustav Vasa went to work purposefully to build up the Lutheran Church. The last monastery, at Vadstena, a foundation of St. Brigid, was suppressed in 1595.

The development in Finland mostly followed the course of things in Sweden. Here too former students at Wittenberg played a leading part.

7. In eastern Europe the multiplicity of nationalities and types of society favoured the introduction of the Reformation but meant that it took different forms. Many of the smaller groups received their first literary monuments through the Reformation. The nobility and the burghers of the German towns were most accessible. Kings, princes and peasants mostly remained Catholic. In East Prussia and Poland students and merchants were the pioneers. The first communities were in the University towns of Cracow and Königsberg. The Reformation spread most strongly in Poland under Sigismund II (1548–72), but split into many groups, including anti-Trinitarians. No broad levels were affected. Under Sigismund III (d. 1632) and Cardinal Stanislaus Hosius (d. 1579) large numbers of the nobility were won back, with the help of the Jesuits.

The German parts of Hungary were mostly pro-Lutheran. John Hunter worked in Transylvania. Catholicism was forbidden in these regions in 1566. While the Hungarians as a whole remained Catholic, there was a strong Calvinist (and anti-Trinitarian) minority, as well as the smaller Lutheran groups.

J. The Struggle for Orthodoxy in Lutheranism

Luther's preaching, so highly coloured by his personality, and his lack of terminological precision gave rise to conflicts among his adherents even during his lifetime. John Agricola (d. 1566) tried to banish the law entirely from the preaching to leave the gospel alone in force. In his own fierce battle against the "Antinomians" Luther drove them out of Wittenberg. When the great prophetic authority was no more, these tensions could not but increase. A group deriving from Melanchthon understood grace and free will as partners, each contributing its share (synergism). Luther had strongly emphasized the impotence of the will, but still demanded human effort in the striving after salvation. The disputation at Weimar in 1560 was the high-point, at which the *sola gratia* triumphed over synergism. Against G. Major (d. 1574) Melanchthon demanded that faith should produce fruits, in a Humanistic sense. Other disputes concerned the persistence of ancient Catholic customs which Melanchthon tolerated. The last of such debates is linked with A. Osiander (d. 1552), because he pressed for private confession and stressed the transformative power of grace. In the debate on the "Real Presence", the "denial" of which came into Lutheranism from Calvinism, Melanchthon sought to reconcile both parties but only added fuel to the fire by his reserve. Luther had taken the elements as the sacramental sign. But Melanchthon rather stressed the eating and drinking. He could thus maintain the Real Presence without linking it to the bread and wine. After the death of

Melanchthon, a crypto-Calvinism and even an openly Humanistic spiritualism asserted themselves. In spite of the Formulas of Concord of 1577, these tensions remained.

K. The Forming of Denominations in the 16th and 17th Centuries

Each "confession" understood itself at first as the universal Church. It was only very gradually that the division of the Church and the existence of two confessions (of almost equal size) were seen and accepted. They both opposed the "fanatics".

The formation of the confessions depended largely on the local ruler, but his influence was stronger in Lutheranism than in Calvinism. After the beginning of the 17th century the population was frequently unwilling to change its faith along with its ruler. The particular forms of each confession were more strongly established. Nonetheless in the case of a number of changes old customs were preserved to make the transition easier, or indeed to disguise it.

The adoption of a catechism was the criterion of belonging to a confession. Fixed dogmas were necessary to avoid uncertainties of doctrine, and polemics demarcated one particular set of beliefs from others. The time of conciliation ended with the second half of the 16th century. There is a denominational pride on all sides, with a note of militancy and defiance.

L. The Essence and Effect of the Reformation

It may be said to sum up that the kernel of the Reformation is its positive preaching, which thrust forward to simple structures, the words of Scripture and the general priesthood of all believers. Faith was at the centre, faith in the "man on the Cross". In spite of the *sola Scriptura*, the ancient creeds and the ancient Councils were retained as obligatory. This search for the sources led in fact to a fundamental weakening of tradition and continuity. The apostolic succession was not preserved, which is not just a question of the interpretation of the sacrament of Orders. It mainly concerns the magisterium. The tragedy of the Reformation was the unresolved tension which arose from the fact that the interpretation of the obligatory fundamentals of faith was left to an unsure and changing Church government and its theologians. Since there was no ultimate court of appeal, "a subjective principle" came in (von Loewenich) which made for growing divisions. The Reformation was radically a Christian, religious reform which did not restrict itself to morals. Later this essential priority of religion over morals was largely lost sight of.

Since Luther is the truest and fullest expression of the Reformation, the tensions and contradictions can be most readily disclosed by an examination of his own life. But even this is problematic, inasmuch as he was always affected by the situation and his partner in the dialogue. Hence, though well acquainted with the tools of late scholasticism, he developed no system. Theology was for him a "sapientia experimentalis, non doctrinalis" (*WA*, IX, p. 98). In his prophetic confessions of faith, throughout his preaching, he preserved much in common with the ancient Church and this assured an intrinsic cohesion.

The basic problem of Luther research today, when the old and younger Luther are distinguished, or the differences at each stage, is whether his doctrine forms a strict unity. Since the terminology varies, the matter must be distinguished from the theological formulation. The problem is rendered more acute by the use of paradox. Does the dialectic guarantee a higher unity, as W. Maurer affirms, or are there real contradictions? Perhaps the realms must be distinguished. There seems to have been a strict unity only in the kernel of the doctrine: that of justification, as propounded and constantly held by Luther, with the inclusion of a specific notion of God, Christology, soteriology and anthropology. His sacramental doctrines and ecclesiology are more on the periphery, where Luther often wavered. Calvin was more orderly and consistent in the doctrine of faith, as indeed were many Anabaptists. But here the system is maintained at the expense of the substance – and proximity to tradition.

While Luther's paradoxical and dynamic diction often bewildered both friends and enemies, so that they missed the kernel, Zwingli aimed above all at the simple and intelligible in doctrine and spirituality. Luther meant by justification a really new creation. Behind the "simul iustus et peccator" is the fellowship of the Christian, ontic and moral, with Christ. Sin is here a lack of fullness in love. Righteousness and new life already grow in secret. But in spite of the moral seriousness, the insertion of morals into theology was far from sufficiently successful. Zwingli saw a society strictly ruled by law as the "situation" for service of the glory of God. In Calvin, a sense of election displaced the notion of justification, bringing with it strong moralistic traits.

In contrast to such often artificial nuances, the preaching of the German Reformer contained much that was common to all Christians and hence Catholic. This provides the chance of a theological agreement today – though now endangered by the effort to evaporate the notion of the oneness of truth and the *fides quae* which Luther maintained. He was convinced that his interpretation of Scripture was the only true and salutary one. Here must be posed the question of the magisterium. If Luther is seen outside the polemical situation, where he appears as interested solely in justification by faith to the elimination of justice by works, agreement with him on a magisterium does not seem hopeless, in spite of all his condemnations of the papacy.

The spread of the Reformation was rapid and not merely superficial. The real force was the spirit of God's word. Since Luther first came forward as the reformer of the ancient Church, the split which was beginning was not noticed. It was only for this reason that the establishment of the Reformation in a way which split the West was possible. It was also helped by the politics and Church politics of the rulers, who had a Christian responsibility in the matter, according to Luther. Since the ministers of the Church had no concern except with spiritual matters, Luther had no fundamental objections to secularizations. Apart from strengthening in this way the local rulers, Luther, who thought in terms of a patriarchal agrarian culture, displayed no great political drive, while the ecclesiastical principles of Calvin, on the contrary, became a supreme political force. The many dedicated champions of the Reformation who were ready to accept persecution and death for their faith did much to spread the Reformation. The emigrants in particular formed many new communities in many places. The spirit of faith in the leaders could sweep the masses along with them.

In noting the effects of the Reformation, the religious realm must be carefully distinguished from the cultural. The religious fruitfulness is unquestionable. The establishment of the Reformation was always the great stimulus of religious movements and trends. After Protestant orthodoxy and Pietism, and the liberal Protestantism of the 19th century, the 20th century again saw a religious encounter – as in the work of S. Kierkegaard and K. Barth. Nonetheless the effects of the Reformation were also multivalent. Many lines lead to the Enlightenment and Idealism, even though the end-product here was often the total inversion of the starting-point. Faith was deepened and enriched, but weighed down by the contradictions of the confessions. Hence the most far-reaching effect of the Reformation was the division of the Church. On the Catholic side this meant a loss of powerful forces, a retreat on to the defensive, a restriction on freedom. Few Catholics are found in the first flight of thinkers of modern times. But the positive effects on the Catholic Church were also notable: the Reform and the theological explanations (Trent) were almost exacted of it. Catholic theology in its present form would be unthinkable without the impulses, questions and examples from the Protestant side. But it can also be noted that certain principles of the Reformation were better preserved on the Catholic side than by their direct heirs.

The cultural effects of the Reformation have at times been exaggerated. Much had already been there in Catholic life and came only to fruition on the Protestant side. An exclusive primacy of the religious element could also be inhibiting. Thus cultural consequences were often rather permitted than aimed at. Nonetheless, the great release of spiritual forces also meant the release of great cultural drives: a paradox comparable to the cultural fruitfulness of the medieval monks' flight from the world.

In Protestantism, freedom of conscience also gave the impulse to deeds of daring in non-religious fields. But the tolerance and freedom of the Reformation was a limited affair, since very harsh measures were often taken against Catholics and fanatics. The laws on heresy were, however, applied rather against denial of the Trinity. The Reformation was only a very remote preparation for civil tolerance, which only won the day under the Enlightenment. Luther's importance for science is most marked in the field of language. What he did for his mother-tongue can hardly be over-estimated; and the effects on school reform and exegesis must also be mentioned. The Reformation was to a great extent a movement affecting the schools, rooted in and carried on by outstanding achievements in education. It was especially fruitful for music. Architecture benefited only later. In the plastic arts much still derived from Catholic roots. Here Luther denounced the "glitter". He had something correct in mind, from the religious point of view, but it was a field in which he had no competence.

The national States were essentially affected by the Reformation only in the Netherlands and Scotland. In other places, though the Reformation helped decisively, the struggle for political freedom must be distinguished from that for religious freedom. They did not go hand in hand.

Daily work and professional calling were not first given religious roots by the Reformation, but some new emphases appeared. But in some parts there was a lowering of moral standards, as Luther himself complained. Being a good businessman only appeared among Calvinists as a sign of election in the U.S.A. In spite of repeated assertions, the principle does not go back to Calvin. Insofar as modern civilization is religiously valuable, the precedence of Protestants over Catholics in its creation is unmistakable. But then fidelity to the intrinsic interests of the Reformation is often lacking. Its individualism and subjectivism had much to do with the negative sides of modern civilization.

The full picture could only be given by a penetrating view of the real challengers of the Reformation, Charles V and Philip II, Ignatius Loyola and the Society of Jesus. The Catholic Reform – for whom Seripando and Pole may stand, to omit many others – was an abiding force through which many individuals were helped to follow the Crucified and overcome by holiness the pagan side of the Renaissance.

The goal of the Reformation, a purified Christianity in the one Church, was not attained. This goal is a permanent task. Though it cannot be brought about by men, it will not be granted without them. Courage is needed and the selflessness of love and service.

Joseph Lortz

REIGN OF GOD

The message of the kingdom of God (βασιλεία τοῦ θεοῦ), which mostly appears in Mt as that of the kingdom of heaven (βασιλεία τῶν οὐρανῶν), is the central element in the preaching of Jesus. Mk sums up his message in the words "The time is fulfilled, and the kingdom of God is at hand; repent, and believe in the gospel" (Mk 1:15). This announcement of the kingdom of God, more precisely, of the lordship or reign of God, since βασιλεία means primarily the exercise of royal power, sovereignty and dignity, and only secondarily the realm or territory, must be understood in the light of the OT expectations of the kingdom of God. The death and resurrection of Jesus put his message into a new and higher context, with the result that Jesus' words about the kingdom of God are no longer at the centre of the Christian preaching in Paul and John. In the course of the history of theology, the interpretation of the term constantly changed, in ways which echoed the spirit of the age rather than the original meaning of the words.

A. The Kingdom of God in the Old Testament

The notion of God as king was widespread in the ancient East. The godhead exercised lordship over its city, realm, princes and people. It was the owner of the land, the giver of prosperity and blessings, of chastisement and disaster. The ruler was the shepherd chosen by God, to whom everything was subject (cf. F. König, *Christus und die Religionen der Erde*, II [2nd ed., 1956], pp. 386–498). The God is unthinkable without his kingship. If his sovereignty is destroyed, he is himself reduced to impotence. The earthly kingdom is the epiphany of the lordship of God. It was natural for an Israel living in such a cultural milieu to begin to call Yahweh its king, from the period of the monarchy on. There were older titles such as the "God of the fathers" (cf. Exod 3:13), but the title of king quickly prevailed, as in the hymnic psalms (e.g., Ps 29; 103), or the narratives of the prophetic visions (Is 6:1; Ezek 1). As against the thesis of M. Buber that the covenant of Sinai was granted by Yahweh as king, recent research has shown that that title only came into use for Yahweh after Jerusalem had been made the king's capital (J. Schreiner). This was probably partly due to the Canaanite notion that the royal dignity of a god was only really proved by the building of a temple (W. Schmidt).

Though the notion of Yahweh as king was not part of the most ancient faith of Israel, it fitted in smoothly with the basic experience of the people, as reflected, for instance, in the canticle of Exod 15: Yahweh is the Lord who saves, incomparably greater than the gods. He leads his people by wonderful ways, and Israel can trust in Yahweh (cf. Deut 8:14f.; Jer 2:6f.; Mich 6:4). The ark of the covenant is the throne of God and as such the pledge of his mighty presence (Num 10:35f.). He is the "Lord of hosts", the "King of Israel". Balaam blesses the camps of Israel's soldiers, where the "shout of a king" is heard, i.e., the acclamation of Yahweh as king among them (Num 23:21). Samuel condemns the people for asking for an earthly king, because Yahweh had made Israel his special possession (1 Sam 8:7; 10:19; 12:12).

With the theological development of its faith in creation, which Israel obviously only learned to link gradually with its faith in the God of the covenant and salvation, the notion of Yahweh's kingship took on a deeper meaning. Yahweh is king of the world. His lordship of the world is based on his act of creation (Ps 24:1f.; 95:3ff.; 96:5, 10) as is also his function of judge (Ps 58; 12; 76:9ff.; 94:2ff.). The notion of the creator god and the universalism which it implied was part of the religious world of Canaan, within which the OT theological statement of the lordship of God was developed, but Israel was very far from simply taking over myths of creation. Creation was regarded as a historical work of Yahweh, that which really opened up the prospect of history (cf. von Rad *Old Testament Theology*, I, pp. 135 ff.). The Lord of history who is so close to man is also creator of the world (cf. Ps. 74:12–17).

This historical and universal kingship of Yahweh becomes specially concrete in the social realm. Since the God of the covenant is King of Israel, the earthly king is "son" of Yahweh (cf. 2 Sam 7:14), obedient to the spirit and law of the covenant. He must cherish and protect the people entrusted to him (cf. 2 Sam 12:1ff.). He must not let himself be intoxicated by his power, keep large stables of horses, amass gold and silver, have many wives and let his heart "be lifted up above his brethren" (cf. Deut 17:14–19). The poor, widows, orphans, labourers and immigrants are assured of the king's special protection. Israel is to remember that it too was once subjected to forced labour in exile, and hence it must be kind to the weak and oppressed (Deut 24).

Homage was paid to Yahweh in the liturgy as King of Israel. The "accession" or "enthronement" psalms, e.g., Pss 47; 93; 96–99, with their acclamation, "Yahweh reigns!" were hymns for a (postulated) feast of the enthronement of Yahweh. They were probably chanted during cultic celebrations in the temple, possibly dating from after the exile. Since they praise the living God who rules the events of history, and not the mythical godhead returning in the cycle of the events of nature, these hymns seem particularly vivid, fresh and actual. Memories and future hopes are gathered up into the "today" (Ps 95) of the supreme encounter with the King of heaven and earth.

Israel's faith in the promises was given a peculiar turn by the prophets. From Amos on, they proclaimed judgment on Israel, North and South alike. Israel had culpably set aside the grounds which justified its existence. "The only thing (Israel) can hold on to is a new historical act on the part of Yahweh" (von Rad, II, p. 117). The God who led Israel out of Egypt can say: "Remember not the former things, nor consider the things of old" (Is 43:18). The only other prophet to speak so trenchantly is Jeremiah (cf. Jer 31:31), since the prophets in general assume some sort of continuity for the ancient covenant (but see, e.g., Amos 8:2, Mic 3:12). This divine judgment comprises the nations as well as Israel (Amos 1–2; Is 13ff.). The prophets rarely mention Yahweh's kingship. (Is 6 is an exception, and the term only reappears in Deutero-Isaiah). But they are deeply concerned with the truth which the term expresses. Israel discovers through its prophets the hopelessness of its historical existence. As the national State is destroyed, the temple razed and the surrounding peoples overwhelmed by catastrophe, Israel learns that this is the manifest judgment of God on sinful man. And it is in this situation that the prophets hold out hope of a new and all-embracing salvation. The imagery in which this salvation is announced is taken from the ancient traditions of the "mighty deeds of Yahweh", but leave them far behind in content. Hosea speaks of a new possession of the land, rich in blessings (2:18ff.; 14:6). Isaiah proclaims the peaceful kingdom of a new David in Zion (cf. the Immanuel prophecies, Is 7–11), Jeremiah of a new covenant by which men's hearts will be changed (Jer 31:31ff.), Deutero-Isaiah of a new exodus, in which Yahweh will show himself once more as King of Israel, the Holy One, the Creator (Is 43:15). This is the framework into which the Servant Songs are inserted, with their individual and collective traits. The new reign of Yahweh is described as unmixed happiness, which is imparted through Israel to all the nations, brings about an inward transformation and takes in the whole earth in which man lives, and indeed the whole creation (Is 34; Mic 4; Is 9:25). Finally, this promise of salvation also includes doing away with death (cf. Is 25:6ff.). The kingship of Yahweh is thus understood as eschatological.

B. The Kingship of God in Later Judaism

In later Judaism (i.e., the late OT period, really "early Judaism"), the notion of God's kingship underwent characteristic changes. A "national" eschatology came to the fore in wide masses of the people. Such expectations are exemplified in the Psalms of Solomon, e.g., Psalm 17: 23–51, in which the Messiah is described as a political liberator and the founder of a new State of Israel, in the Shemone Esre (the Eighteen Prayer), or certain passages in the gospels (Lk 24:21; Mk 10:37). The notion of taking up arms to establish God's kingdom was easily associated with this line of thought, as may be seen from the War Scroll of Qumran, the political history of the Zealots and the revolt of Bar Kochbah, A.D. 132.

The rabbinical tradition was forced to reconsider the role of Israel, and came to the conclusion that Israel's immediate task was to attest the kingship of God in the world by its adoration of the true God and the faithful observance of his commandments. Israel had to take upon itself "the yoke of the kingship of heaven", till the day on which God would reveal himself to all the world. Contrary to the doctrine that God would set up his kingdom by the sole decree of his sovereign will, some rabbis held that the kingdom of the Messiah, the prelude to the full kingship of God, or indeed the kingship of God itself could be brought on by penance, study of the *Torah* and works of charity.

In apocalyptic thinking still another type of hope was cherished. The kingdom of God is the world transfigured and taken up into heaven. This expectation is still temperately expressed in Dan, but the "parables" of *Enoch*, the *Ascension of Moses* and the *Syriac Apocalypsis of Baruch* give vivid descriptions of this kingdom and the judgment. The history of the world is divided into periods (Dan 2:37–45; 4 Esdras chs 11f.), the weeks of years till the Day of the Lord are calculated (*Enoch*, 93). Such doctrines were handed on to some extent as secret and esoteric. J. Moltmann explains the main difference between prophetic and apocalyptic hopes as follows: in the prophetic message, the hopes of Israel have to wrestle with historical experiences, and the history of the world comes to be seen as leading up to Yahweh's eschatological purpose, while in apocalyptic, historical eschatology wrestles with cosmology, and so explains the world as the historical process of the aeons, where age succeeds age, in apocalyptic perspective (cf. *Theology of Hope* [1967]).

C. The Kingdom of God in the Message of Jesus

The preaching of Jesus is the proclamation of the imminence of the kingdom of God: it is "at hand" (Mk 1:15; the expression "kingdom of God" occurs nearly a hundred times in the synoptics, though mostly as "kingdom of heaven" in Mt). In the preaching of the historical Jesus, the kingship of God is never the eternal rule of the creator, but the eschatological kingship which has intervened in these very days, without cosmic transformations or the political reconstitution of Israel. Jesus' message is characterized by a supreme urgency: the moment has come (cf. Lk 12:56). The parables of "crisis" (Lk 13:6–9; Mt 22:1–14), the judgment-sayings and threats (Lk 10:10–15), the radical moral imperatives of the Sermon on the Mount (Mt 5–7), are only intelligible in the light of the coming of the hour of grace.

Jesus promises the kingdom of God to all – tax-collectors and prostitutes, the ill and the poor and the little children (Mk 2:15; 10:15f.). It is salvation for men, not judgment. God rejoices in forgiving sinners (Lk 15). And hence Jesus keeps company with sinners. God's favour presupposes nothing. It only asks for assent. This response must bear the mark of the unconditional (Lk 6:27–38). Without limits, in the divine way, men must forgive one another (Mt 18:21f.). Separation and judgment come only at the end (Mt 13:24ff.). The good news is for Israel (Mt 10:6), but also for the nations: "Many will come from East and West and sit at the table with Abraham, Isaac, and Jacob in the kingdom of heaven" (Mt 8:11). Jesus' wonderful works underline his preaching. His healings and exorcisms are signs of the kingdom of God which has come nigh in Jesus: "But if it is by the finger of God that I cast out demons, then the kingdom of God has come upon you" (Lk 11:20). The relationship of the healings to the preaching of Jesus is explained in the message to the Baptist in prison: "Go and tell John what you hear and see: the blind receive their sight, and the lame walk, lepers are cleansed and the deaf hear, and the dead are raised up, and the poor have the good news preached to them" (Mt 11:4; par.; cf. Lk 4:18). Jesus sets himself above the law and the prophets (Mt 5:20ff.; Lk 16:16). The disciples are congratulated because they hear and see what many prophets and kings longed to see (Mt 13:16). By virtue of a unique relationship to the Father (Mt 11:25–27 par.), Jesus claims a mysterious "immediacy to God" (A. Vögtle). He calls men to follow him (Mk 1:16ff.; 8:34ff.). But the kingdom is not simply Jesus', its construction is not his work. It is the kingdom of the Father (Lk 12:32; 22:29f.), who alone knows "the hour" (Mt 24:36 par.). The kingdom of God "comes", it can only be received, it must be prayed for (Mt 6:10; Mk 10:15; Lk 11:2). God's kingship is there in Jesus, and hence now, while it is also still to come. The sovereign freedom of God's intervention is manifested, as it were, in the paradoxical language used to describe it. Neither the thesis of a fully-realized eschatology (C. H. Dodd) nor that of a purely futurist one (J. Weiss, A. Schweitzer) can be sustained without reserves on the basis of exegetical findings. The same is true of the affirmation of Jesus' expectation of the imminent end (W. G. Kümmel) as also of the supposition that any such expectation can only be ascribed to the primitive community. The sayings and the parables of the gospels cannot be brought into total harmony: some sayings indicate a term (Mt 10:23; Mk 9:1; 13:30), others reject all attempts to fix a date (Mk 13:32 par.); some parables speak of growth (Mk 4; Mt 13:24–30, 47f.), others of admission (Lk 13:24; Mt 7:13). This may very well be due to the nature of the kingdom of God as preached by Jesus. It is an event which rounds off history definitively and thus penetrates constantly into every situation, so that it can only be expressed in temporal categories which clash with one another. Realities within history can in the long run only be deficient signs of the reign of God, no matter how full of meaning. These sayings escape the grasp of human system and science. They are in a sort of "eschatological disequilibrium", which only proves to be a steady support when grasped in the spirit of repentance. It is basic to the message that the world and its situation are understood in the light of God's kingship, while the kingship is not a projection of anything of this world. If this is correct, we can understand why Jesus made no descriptive utterances with regard to the kingship of God, but spoke in parables (Mk

4:33f.), similes, summonses and maxims which gave hints of that transcendent reality. We can also understand why the group of disciples which formed around Jesus and the college of the Twelve are not simply identical with the fellowship in the kingdom of God.

D. The Kingdom of God as Understood in Early Christianity

The NT credal formulas and professions of faith show that the primitive Christian preaching was centred on faith in Jesus Christ, the Lord, the Son of God (Rom 10:9; 1 Jn 5:1; Jn 20:31). The formulas have been divided into two classes (W. Kramer), one dealing with faith in the person of Jesus, the other with his works – his mission, passion, death and resurrection, his exaltation and return (1 Cor 15:3–5; 1 Pet 1:18–21; 3:18–22). Both types of formula speak of God's eschatological action. Peter's address to the crowds at Pentecost ends with the words: "Let all the house of Israel therefore know assuredly that God has made him both Lord and Christ, this Jesus whom you crucified" (Acts 2:36). The installation as Messiah and Lord, the proof of his being Son of God, come through his resurrection from the dead (Rom 1:3). But the resurrection follows his passion (Phil 2:9). The Risen Lord who has overcome death is the first-born of many brothers (Rom 8:29). Jesus' message of the reign of God at hand is absorbed in the Christ-event as thus sketched. The post-paschal faith sees the passion and death of Jesus as a salvific event of the reign of God proclaimed by Jesus. Jesus, in whom the kingdom was at hand, is the exalted Lord in his death, clothed with the splendour of the royal lordship of God. "The great event of the coming of the kingship of God bears his name."

One of the major types of this new understanding of the kingdom of God, profounder but still the same, is given in the Pauline theology. St. Paul speaks only rarely, and then in a futurist sense, of the kingdom of God (1 Cor 6:10; 15:50; Gal 1:5, 21), as the heritage of the faithful. Eph 5:5 speaks of "the Kingdom of Christ and God". In Pauline theology, the kingship of God is realized fundamentally in the Lordship of Christ (1 Cor 15:24; cf. Col 1:13). It is present in the faithful (Col 3:1–4), in the Church (Col 1:18, 24; cf. the Body of Christ), in the work of the authorized officials and charismatics (Eph 4:11–16). This is a "fragrance" which is spread among the pagans by the preaching of the Church (2 Cor 2:14). The triumphant quality of the life of faith shows how Jesus Christ has reduced to impotence the powers of this world, each region of which had its own *kyrios*, according to Hellenistic beliefs. The exalted Christ exercises his cosmic sovereignty through the Church (Eph 1:21ff.; 3:10; 4:8–10), and his lordship comes to its perfect fulfilment at the parousia, the conquest of all enemies of God and of death itself, when God will be all in all (cf. 1 Cor 1:24–28). The early letters of St. Paul show a sense of the end being imminent. But for the most part, he refrains from all efforts to picture or represent the future glory (cf. 1 Cor 2:9). Statements bearing on personal fellowship with Christ and the faithful are always kept central (cf. 1 Cor 15:35ff.; 1 Thess 4:17).

Except for the one text Jn 3:35, the term "kingdom of God" is not found in the Johannine writings. The message of Christ is characterized by an eschatology – of life, death, judgment, joy and peace – which has been made a present reality (Schnackenburg). At times there are glimpses of the future: the resurrection of the body and judgment (Jn 5:28f.), eternal life (12:25). This aspect is brought out still more clearly in 1 Jn (1 Jn 3:2; 4:17). But in Rev the eschatological Kingdom of God is identical with the kingdom of Christ (Rev 11:15), and through Christ the Church has become the kingdom of

God (Rev 1:6; 5:10). History is the battle-field where the hostile powers fight against this kingdom, which triumphs in the end. The theme of the thousand-year reign of the Messiah appears at Rev 20:4.

Study of the "history of redaction" has enabled us to see the contours of the theologies of the synoptics more clearly. Mk uses the doctrine of the messianic secret to link Jesus' message of the reign of God with the post-paschal faith. He draws on apocalyptic notions (Mk 13), and reflects on the relationship between the Church and the kingdom of God (Mk 4:11). In Mt, the kingdom has already become a standard concept in ecclesiology (Mt 13:52). It means the heavenly reality of the fulfilment of the will of God (Mt 6:9, 10). Hence righteousness ("justice") is the condition of entry into this kingdom (Mt 5:20). The kingdom comes fully into its own in Mt through the return of the Son of man and the universal judgment (Mt 25:31).

In Lk, the history of salvation appears as divided into periods. The time of Jesus' activity is the middle of time, and thus distinguished from the time of the Church (H. Conzelmann), which ends with the parousia. Through the history of salvation, the presence of the Church loses in a way its eschatological character (P. Hoffmann). The later writings of the NT show at times a tendency to give a Hellenistic colouring to the "kingdom of heaven", i.e., it becomes literally another world of the present day, e.g., 2 Tim 4:18; Heb 12:28; 2 Pet 1:11, just a heavenly reality, so to speak.

E. History of Theology

Early patristic theology was profoundly influenced by the notion of the lordship of Christ and the expectation of an imminent parousia (cf. Ignatius, *Ephesians*, ch. 11; Pseudo-Clement, 2 *Corinthians*, 6, 12). Then there were such apocalyptic notions as that of the thousand-year reign (Justin, *Trypho*, 80f.; Tertullian, *Adversus Marcionem*, 3, 24). In some writers, immortality is the one great blessing of salvation (Theophilus of Antioch, *To Autolycus*, II, 27). The expectation of the imminent end in Tertullian was reinforced by an enthusiasm inherited from Montanism and was linked with moral rigorism (cf. *De Monogamia, De Corona*). The reign of God in Clement of Alexandria and Origen is somewhat spiritualized. Christ is praised as the *Logos* who divinizes men (Clement, *Paedagogus*, 3, 1f.) and prayer for the coming of the kingdom is a request for wisdom and knowledge (Origen, *On Prayer*, 13). This strongly interiorized notion of the kingdom of God came to prevail to a wide extent in the East, with a basic conceptual schema derived from the neo-Platonic notion of flux and reflux, from God and to God (cf. Gregory of Nyssa, *De Hominis Opificio*, 17). Eusebius of Caesarea used elements from Origen to propound a sort of political theology, in which faith in the one true God was linked with the earthly Roman empire. The republican city-state was polytheistic, while Constantine's kingdom of peace was an image of the kingdom of God. In the West, the Church came to be more and more identified with the kingdom of God (e.g., Augustine, *De Civitate Dei*, XX, 9). The Church is the *regnum Christi* and the *regnum coelorum*, which is still, however, the *regnum militiae* and waits in longing for its fulfilment. It is the thousand-year reign of Rev 20:4, the sixth "age" of the world which is the last form of the *civitas Dei peregrinans* (ibid., XV, 20).

A still more thoroughgoing identification of the kingdom of God and the Church, with a corresponding view of the Petrine office, is found in the succeeding centuries, in such Roman writers as Gregory the Great, who interpreted Lk 9:27 ("the kingdom of God") as the Church opposed to the "power and the glory" of the world (*PL*, LXXVI, col. 32). Once the Franks came to power in the West, this ecclesiastical interpretation of the kingdom of God was completed by a political one. Charlemagne was the new David who had taken over the reins of royal lordship in the Church, allowing the Pope the role of a Moses at prayer (Letter to Leo III: *PL*, XCVIII, cols. 907ff.), while remaining himself the sovereign who participated in the reign of Christ and God (cf. Alcuin, *PL*, C, cols. 301ff.; the coronation liturgies in P. E. Schramm, *Die Ordines der mittelalterlichen Kaiserkrönung*). This notion of the reign of God was also one of the inspirations of the crusades, and was seen as a reason for the investiture of the bishops by the king. "Since the kings reign with Christ, they bestow with him and exercise with him all the powers which belong to the kingdom of Christ" (The Anonymous of Yorck). Apocalyptic notions were then added to the political. Adso of Montieren counted the kingdom of the Franks along with that of the Romans as the "third kingdom" (cf. Dan 7), after the Greeks and the Persians, and awaited a last ruler who would restore the empire to its glory and lay down his crown in Jerusalem, before the onset of the time of the Antichrist (E. Sackur, *Sibyllische Texte und Forschungen* [1898], pp. 97ff.). The most radical formulation of papal opposition to the imperial notion of the reign of God is undoubtedly the bull *Unam Sanctam* of Boniface VIII: "Porro subesse Romano Pontifici omni humanae creaturae declaramus, dicimus, definimus et pronuntiamus omnino de necessitate salutis" (*D* 469, *DS* 875). Joachim of Fiore (d. 1202), for whom the way had been prepared by such writers as Rupert of Deutz, Honorius of Autun and Anselm of Havelberg, proclaimed the coming of a kingdom of the Spirit which was to precede the definitive kingdom of God. Francis of Assisi was regarded by the Franciscan Spirituals as the new Baptist or Elias, the "angel with the sign of the living God", who ushered in the age of the Spirit (cf. Bonaventure, *Legenda Maior*, Prologue). It gave signs of its presence in the various religious brotherhoods. This view of the reign of God was still effective in the brotherhoods of the late Middle Ages and the Reformation, as in the Bohemian Brethren and the Anabaptists.

Dominican mysticism such as that of Meister Eckhart saw the kingdom of God as "God himself with all his riches" in the depths of the soul, but in contrast to this there was the theology of the lordship of Christ in ecclesiastical and political society as put forward by Savonarola, Bucer and Campanella which was sometimes expressed in the form of Utopias (More's *Utopia* [1516] reappears in large portions of Bucer's *De Regno Christi* [1550]; cf. Campanella's *Civitas Solis* [1623]). Luther's doctrine of the two kingdoms stands out in sharp contrast both to sectarian excesses and the theocratic notion of the Church held in some Catholic circles. God's reign is essentially invisible and spiritual. It is justification by faith in the preaching of the gospel, while the law is the affair of the secular power. Christians, while upholding the independence of the secular power, have to exercise or submit to it in faith. "The kingdom of heaven is one and the same, and there is only one original parable of it, though this can only be expressed in a multitude of diverse parables ... This is what was meant by Zeno, by Parmenides, by Plato and by all who spoke of the truth. They all looked to the same One and gave it expression in different ways" (*De Filiatione Dei*). This system, a breach with the medieval ontologies of substance, became the basic pattern of a series of presentations of the "Reign of God" in secularized or partly secularized dress. The reign of God was identified with the reign of spirit. In Descartes God is the immanent guarantor of the self-evident structure of systematic reality. In Leibniz, the existing order is the best of all possible worlds, where a pre-established harmony, based on the rationality of God, reigns throughout.

In such systems, the sciences, ethics, metaphysics and theology form a unity. But Kant separated the theoretical and the practical reason. The reign of God comes about through the establishment of human society according to ethical laws, which are seen as divine because they appear as morally obligatory. Society thus constituted – the Church – starts in fact with belief in revelation, but must become pure belief in religion. The religion with the closest affinities to such pure religious faith is Christianity. The reign of God comes closer and closer, the more thoroughly religion is purified. The notion of an eschatological fulfilment is "a beautiful ideal" (*Religion within the Limits of Pure Reason Alone* [1960]). Fichte's approach was more aesthetic. He drew a picture of the rational State of the future, the kingdom of liberty and individuality which would be the beautiful harmony of all and so reveal the universal as the manifestation of God. Scholars and artists would have the role which formerly fell to priests and prophets. Hegel's theory of the kingdom of the Father, Son and Spirit is the final stage of his theory of the forms of outward manifestation in which the spirit comes to full consciousness of self. Beyond the kingdom of the spirit – the community which has grasped that it is identical with the State – there is only self-intuitive knowledge. Thus the reign of God is the supreme form of the spirit, in which are displayed the essence and the history of the world. It comprises the full exercise of freedom and the highest morality.

This way of thinking of the kingdom of God is also at the base of such divergent types as the Marxist theory of communist society and Ernst Bloch's philosophy of Utopia. Both approaches have the pretension to be purely philosophical, to the exclusion of all theology. In contrast to the types of thinking outlined in the foregoing section, the future now becomes the decisive dimension, constantly changing *praxis* takes precedence of theoretical consideration. But the future remains as much at the mercy of man's intervention as in the other systems the essential structures were open to the penetrating gaze of man. In none of these views is the reign of God the incalculable and impenetrable irruption of grace in love. It is always the self-understanding of human existence.

Along with these types of notion, where the reign of God is the ultimate cognitive framework of human science, there were approaches in which the reign of God was kept in the basic framework of faith. Leaving aside systematic philosophy, Pascal could confront the growing challenge of modern science with his doctrine of the various orders. This was an attempt to define philosophically the realm in which it could be meaningful to speak of the kingdom of God and Christ. It was the *ordo caritatis*, which takes man out of himself, where he experiences the forgiveness of sin and begins to taste the hidden bliss of God's friendship. The doctrine of the kingdom of God became a structural principle of theology in the Catholic Tübingen School, the lead having been given by B. Galura. J. S. Drey, in his *Introduction to the Study of Theology*, describes the notion of the reign of God as "the idea of Christianity which contains and produces all others". The "noumenon" (cf. Kant's "thing-in-itself") is the doctrine of the Trinity which contains the whole economy of the reign of God. Extending throughout the stages of history of salvation, the reign of God has appeared as death and reality in Jesus Christ. It is also the grace-given end of history and so is also the revelation of the finiteness of all history. Hence it can only be accepted by man as he grasps in faith and hope the finiteness of his own being. J. B. Hirscher took the reign of God as the "basic idea" from which he developed his "Christian Morals". The human faculties were described as essentially the disposition of being able to belong to this kingdom. Entry is conversion and the kingdom is the rule of God in all realms of life.

Among Protestants, the reign of God became a central concept among Pietists. Through the conversion of individuals to the Christian life, which was nourished in "conventicles" by Bible-reading, the world was to be transformed into a place where God reigned. Highly divergent notions of the reign of God developed among Pietists. Some even envisaged a rule of Christ on earth. Orthodox Churchmanship came in for heavy criticism. Messianic hopes were emphasized and educational and social work developed. Schleiermacher, rooted in Romanticism and with a Pietist education, defined the kingdom of God as the "free fellowship of pious faith" (Works, III/2, p. 466) in which each member develops his individuality and makes his life a work of art. This self-fulfilment was to be based on Jesus Christ as the great exemplar of mankind through the purity of his harmony with God. From the ethical point of view the kingdom of God, in this sense of the expansion of the higher powers of man in the Christian community, was the supreme good.

The "liberal" theology of the 19th century in general (F. D. Maurice in England, A. Ritschl in Germany, etc.), using the terminology of the synoptic gospels but mainly interested in the principles of the Enlightenment, explained the reign of God as the fellowship of moral endeavour founded by Jesus Christ. Men united in love exercise their lordship of the world by their work in life and help each other to perfection. In most cases, the ideal may be said to have that of the respectable bourgeois. This notion was corrected by the exegetical work of J. Weiss and A. Schweitzer who rediscovered the eschatological character of the message of Jesus. K. Barth then propounded a Christocentric and eschatological notion of the reign of God in which he brought out the gratuitousness and incalculability of its grace, the comprehensiveness of the bestowal of salvation which takes in the whole of the world and history.

Peter Hünermann

RELIGION

I. Concept of Religion

A. Religion in General

There can be no easy-going approach to the subject of religion today, above all if one considers it the quintessence of one's relationship to God. The word religion seems to have fallen into discredit. But if one refuses to accept this devaluation, one must analyse the difficulties involved in the term and then offer philosophical and theological reasons for continuing to use it.

1. *The notion and its difficulties.* The question of the theology of religion is now put explicitly, since so many authors give the impression that the notion of religion is purely abstract and can hardly be verified in the concrete forms of religion. And it is even maintained that religion, as a human attitude, is anti-Christian.

a) In the study of religion, the philosophy of religion has worked out eight methods of finding formal and material criteria for the notion of Religion.

The method of abstraction: Some historians try to prescind from all the particularities of the individual religions to attain the essence of religion. But the abstract generalizations thus arrived at make no contribution in practice to the understanding of concrete religious attitudes.

The additive method: On the principle that the essence of religion should be comprehensive and concrete, other scholars tried to construct the essence of religion by combining the positive assertions of all religions. This was to ignore the fact that the essence of religion is not attained at once by adding up all positive notes. It must be an *a priori* notion enabling one to distinguish the accidental from the essential.

The method of subtraction: While the additive method assumed progress in historical development, Rationalism excluded the historical religions from its consideration, on the ground that they were decadent, and sought for the genuine "essence", the spiritualized "truth" in religion. The resulting notion of religion is so unworldly that it cannot explain how religion is historically relevant and appealing to man.

The method of identity: This is likewise non-historical. It is used in traditionalist orthodoxy and in certain sects. It maintains that the essence of religion is there once and for all and hence allows of no variation of expression conditioned by time or space.

The method of isolation: Since Schleiermacher (as also R. Otto and A. Nygren) there has been a tendency to isolate a certain aspect of religion, e.g., the religious experience or feeling; the holy. This was made the motive of religion, and the motive was identified with the essence. The advantage of this method was that it concentrated on appealing motives for education to religion. Its disadvantage was that it did not do justice to the notion of essence. It excluded other religious motivations, such as reason, which also form part of religion.

The evolutionist method: Used with various aims by Feuerbach, Freud and Jung, the evolutionist or genetic method assumes that at a crucial point of individual or sociological development, non-religious phenomena mutate into religion. It is the moment when man can no longer bear his dependence, anxiety and poverty. He covers up his misery by means of a projection of a divine power, which can reward man in the afterlife for the misery he endures here. This is what Feuerbach meant by saying that "the poor man has a rich God". This psychological aspect of religion may have therapeutic value, but it is unfortunately generalized into a mandatory pedagogy, under the illusion that religious men are to be freed from their self-alienation by the suppression of religion. The descriptive "religion is the opium of the people" is dogmatism as an assertion of principle and is no proof of how hope and fear become religion.

The method of interpretation: Gnosis, and later Hegel, saw religion as confidence in the transcendence of one's true being and as dedication to it. Their attitude is positive, but they held that this confidence and dedication only really appeared after reason took the place of its "prelude", religion. Thus the Gnostics interpret religion as only finding its true being in philosophical knowledge. Kierkegaard attacked this hermeneutic as making religion an asylum for the feeble-minded. But in any case it is impossible to show why reason alone can lead to the freedom of limitless openness and communication (K. Jaspers), if religion can be described as total reliance on the transcendence of man. The total claim of religion can preserve man from ideological shortcomings and loss of freedom better than a total claim of reason which is realized only in the absolute spirit.

Finally, the functional method: This links up with the historical approach and notes the functional components which are at work as they change from age to age. But the method does not supply the structural principle behind these functions and hence is unable to exclude a number of functions which are associated with religion but which could be the object of reforms.

b) This survey of the various methods used to determine the notion of religion shows that it is not enough to produce formal criteria. This may be why the etymological interpretation of the word religion still enjoys a certain favour.

"Religion" comes from the Latin *religio*, which describes the religious act, the three verbs *relegere*, *religari* and *reeligere* being possible derivations. The fluidity of the derivation need not cause misgivings. Since *relegere* means "constantly turn to" or "conscientiously observe", the object of concern must merit and indeed demand man's careful attention. This claim brings up automatically the second derivation, since *religari* can mean "binding oneself (back)" to one's origin and goal. Finally, since man can live in culpable oblivion of his origin and goal, he can then "choose again" to live religiously by his origin and goal (*reeligere*). The possible derivation from the three verbs thus offers converging perspectives, which are more than an etymology, since they describe possibly religious attitudes. But this etymological approach to the phenomenon of religion is unsatisfactory. It is only possible in Latin, and it is impossible to overlook the fact that the religious phenomenon appears in widely different linguistic dress. Thus we have the paradox that the *Encyclopedia of the Jewish Religion* does not contain the word "religion" in the index. And the absence is justified inasmuch as Judaistic thinking cannot attain the pregnancy of the comprehensive *religio* but can only describe the phenomenon in a series of approaches.

c) This example brings us to the difficulties of the comparative method which needs a universally valid definition of religion, if it is not to peter out into Relativism. Even if the concept is kept very general, as for instance when religion is said to be belief in transcendent powers, comparative religion shows at once that the definition fails. Buddhism and Taoism must be regarded as religions, but have not the notion of higher powers still involved in the process going on in the world. If one were then to cast one's net wider and try to subsume the object of all religions as the "holy reality", the concept would remain empty unless one resolved to determine which reality is to be named "holy".

2. *Theological and philosophical approach.* a) It may well be held that in the philosophy of religion in the West since Plato and Aristotle and down to our own days, "the holy" stands for the reality meant by religion (see *Holy*). But it must be noted that a theoretical interest, an aesthetic sympathy and ethical holiness merely touch on the main concept of "the holy" without comprising it. Interest, aesthetics and ethics remain under the control of the faculties which we call intellect, feeling and will, as long as these three powers are not absorbed in man's total self-dedication. This is so serious that it overwhelms man, because he knows that all is at stake, the wholeness of the holy, and not just some particular interest.

b) The totality of the claim which the holy makes on man, and this total *engagement* (G. Marcel) were studied by the philosophy of religion, as understood in the patristic and scholastic eras, in their effort to do justice to the phenomenon of religion.

c) Thinkers of the ancient Church like Justin, Tertullian, Irenaeus, Clement of Alexandria and Origen were well aware that the thought is prior to the word in philosophy, since philosophy is a reflective process which is finally expressed as well as may be in words. But they also knew that faith, and hence religion, were not the creation of the brain, but something addressed to man, something not produced or fully analysable by thought but impinging, summoning, imposing obligation. (J. Ratzinger, *Einführung in das Christentum* [1968], pp. 50, 62). They recognized the difference between philosophy and faith, as revealed in the different role played by the "word" in each, but they also recognized the link between philosophy and religion, as given in the "Logos" (see *Philosophy and Theology, Theology*). They knew that the meaning, the Logos, on which we base ourselves must be truth, because a meaning which was not truth would be meaningless. The Logos, as the principle of revelation in religion, here attained universal significance as the giver of meaning. Wherever man's actions are determined by the Logos, hence also in philosophy, the *ratio seminalis* (λόγος σπερματικός) is at work as the gift of God. It is the dawn of religion. But when men desert the Logos to rely (illogically) on demons, or even make themselves slaves to the irrational, they at least fall away from the "natural" religion of the philosophers. Falling into idolatry they are in fact, though not *de iure*, in a state of blindness or distraction by futilities which has no eyes for the dawn of the full religion in philosophy.

This view of the "Logos" in the patristic era was both a condemnation of debased forms of religion and an assertion of the dawn of religion in philosophy. St. Augustine still echoed this affirmation when he wrote: "That which is now called the Christian religion already existed among the ancients, and was never absent since the human race began, till Christ appeared in the flesh. From then on the true religion, which had always existed, began to be called Christianity" (*Epistola*, 102, 12, 5).

d) In scholasticism, St. Thomas Aquinas took over the positive estimation of the rational structure of the world from the Fathers. With the help of his anthropology, he reduced further the gap between non-Christian thought and faith. He was then able to justify religious freedom. Religion, in Aquinas, had the role of embodying man's ordination to God. He could deduce that all who ask after the ultimate ground and goal of the world link it with the name of God (*Summa Theologica*, II-II, q. 81, a. 1; cf. I, q. 1, a. 2) and hence are religious. The "natural" intellect of man can recognize the effects of God's action, (though not his essence), and hence can speak analogically of God as his end, and therefore be truly religious (*ibid.*, I, q. 1, a. 7, ad 1). Knowledge of God in the various religions and philosophies is one of the *praeambula fidei* and is to be accepted as religious by Christians, since it opens up the way to faith.

e) In combination with the transcendental method in philosophy, authors like J. Maréchal and K. Rahner linked the anthropological perspective of St. Thomas with the Logos speculation of the Apologists in a certain way. Man as "hearer of the word" is presented as simply transcendental. But this characterization of man is not simply derived from the transcendental philosophy which can show that man's dynamism takes him beyond any achievement and finally beyond himself. It is not merely derived from the structure of human thought which strives towards the one beyond multiplicity and, finding that it cannot attain in itself the totality of this one whole, must postulate the ground of unity beyond its thought, in the transcendent God. The transcendence of man can also be noted in his action – as Blondel showed – which must always point beyond itself if it is not to fall victim to a superstitious and ideological cherishing of any given achievement, which would be to devaluate the dynamism to the level of one of its milestones, though it was the law which set action on the move towards this supposed limit. In other words, the transcendental view of man takes the wholeness which it offers to thought and action more seriously than does any other humanism. It unsettles any human tendency to rest content with itself. It helps to give a positive answer to the biblical question: "Is it not written, 'I said, you are gods'?" (Jn 10:34, cf. Ps 82:6). For it answers with Pascal (*Pensées*, no. 434) that man can surpass himself. He is not merely capable of going the way of religion. He is summoned to do so.

Obviously, this extension of St. Thomas's principles in transcendental philosophy does justice both anthropologically and theologically to the religious phenomenon. This is also the view of Vatican II when it affirms that all men, as persons, are "at once impelled by nature and also bound by a moral obligation to seek the truth, especially religious truth" (Declaration on Religious Freedom, *Dignitatis Humanae*, art. 2).

f) Meanwhile, while recognizing this general anthropological basis of religion, it must also be noted with Vatican II that to master the world man has fashioned closed systems of knowledge of temporal things, whose "autonomy" comes with insight into their laws and verification in practice (*Gaudium et Spes*, art. 36). But these achievements of the human mind which favour man's further manipulation of the world bar the way, as closed systems, to the personal search for truth which seeks to move on under the religious imperative. Anthropologically, the anti-religious fascination of the systems comes from the fact that in his search for truth man relies always on the real, which he meets first in his world, and acknowledges what he can verify. An outlook on the world which makes it the verifiable has produced both the phenomenon of the non-religion, the "absence of God" (Heidegger), the "darkness of God" (Buber), the "adult world" (Bonhoeffer), and the phenomena of ersatz religions masquerading as the "death of God" theology.

g) It is certainly not a liberating answer when K. Barth assigns the concept of "religion" to such ersatz religions, calling "religion" an artefact of man's effort to assert himself against God and interpreting Christianity as the judgment which condemns all religion. It seems more honest to treat with utter seriousness the anthropological law of all initial progress, in the name of man's freedom, even where it leads to world-views which bar the way to religion.

But of course the positive assessment of progress here suggested remains problematic, because Christians now live in a religionless world which solves the necessary problems of progress without the "working hypothesis of God", and induces Christians to live in such a way that they can deal with life without God (D. Bonhoeffer, *The Worldly Christian* [1967]). But it is still doubtful that this service of man, this "secularization inspired by faith", can give itself out as a "religionless Christianity". Barth's own objection (*Epistle to the Romans* [1933]) still has force. Man the sinner remains tied to the forms which his religion has created, until the eschatological fulfilment. Their function of allusion, even according to H. Cox's *Secular City*, may take strange forms but are there for the sake of hope.

If hope is to become practice, one must agree with P. Tillich when he says: "The divine No to religion is only perceptible where religion exists." This is the proper approach, critical but not negative. But the question remains as to whether the religionless faith which could reject all alienations in the Christian Churches is not rather an abstraction than an ideal. No one could live by this abstract "pure faith". Human history, seen steadily and whole, still poses the question as to where man could find in the world he makes the courage to accept "man's relation to his own being" without further ado (Feuerbach). But such acceptance would be the only possible ground for action.

It would be certainly wrong (as was pointed out by the critique of religion offered by a "religionless Christianity") to try to introduce God on religious terms as a stop-gap in defective systems or as a projection of the wishful thinking of man's independence. This would in fact be an artefact. But this cannot be purified or reformed by the religiously inarticulate "pure faith" of a religionless Christianity, because it is an abstraction which cannot crystallize in action. Unless of course it made itself socially articulate, which would mean surrendering the purity of its abstraction.

In the programmes for a religionless Christianity drawn up by philosophies of religion and by pragmatism, for the reasons set out above "pure faith" is replaced by "service". Service in the world may perhaps be understood in terms of a post-Theistic outlook and feel detached from any confession or religion. But it must be emphasized that service, as a function in the social group, remains related to the group. Sooner or later it must adopt the category of Christian "representation" and become a new confession with new religious forms. One may try for "secularization" on the grounds of Christian faith, to save oneself from the slavery and hence the inhumanity of the secularism of systems. But one cannot evade the basic question of religion, as to how God is in the world. In all honesty, one should try to bring about not a religionless Christianity, but a radically new religious Christianity. Even such a Christianity will remain religious. The question would be whether such an active group could still call itself Christian, not whether it would still be religious.

It seems unthinkable that Christians serving men, and hence active, should be religionless. If so, it is right to oppose the notion of "religionless Christianity" by stressing the service to freedom, in the framework of the very religion which is represented in Christianity.

h) Man's transcendental way to the "absolute future", which God alone can be, shows clearly what religion is, if we note the "inability to be sorry", as it has been termed, which is intrinsic to all the systems. If one is to remain in movement, one must rediscover the capacity for regret, the "hidden inwardness" of man (Kierkegaard), as the sense of guilt. But as Kierkegaard also noted, the sense of guilt may be a change *in* the subject, but it does not free him from his sadness. It is the sense of sin which is a change of the subject himself, and this, the overriding of the philosophical "absurd", can lead to religion. Consciousness of sin points away from itself to the truth that there must be a power outside the individual which shows him that by becoming what he is he is other than he was. He has become a sinner. This power is God. (This is the theme of Kierkegaard's *Concluding Unscientific Postscript* [1941] and the *Philosophical Fragments* [2nd ed., 1962].)

In other words, if one is not to remain a prisoner of the closed system and incapable of regret, if one is not to be grimly conscious of guilt and a victim to *Weltschmerz*, the "sadness of the world", one can face guilt as sin before God and hence find in religion freedom from self and freedom for God. The way to God which we call religion is necessary for the sake of human freedom. Hence religion is judgment on enslavement to systems and the sadness of the world. And as judgment it is also herald of the redemption which sets man free for himself, because it makes him free for God who gives himself in revelation. Hence the future of religion is the *ordo ad Deum*, the orientation to God, which as natural religion is fulfilled in the Christian revelation. Christianity, it has been said, is the redemption of religion, but it is true even of Christianity that it contains the fulfilment of religion in the state of promise and not as perfectly achieved. Religion is human action on the way to God who comes towards man to draw him to him with many helps. In his religion man says, "Lord, show us the Father" (Jn 14:8), because this alone can satisfy man.

Norbert Schiffers

B. Critique of Religion

1. *Notion, problems and method.* Just as there is no generally accepted defini-

tion of religion, critique of religion is also hard to describe exactly. It can be theoretical (in philosophy, science of religion, etc.) or practical (in propaganda, persecution, discrimination). Along with criticism from outside, the critique immanent to religion plays a great part. It ranges from the revision of outdated theological formulas to heresy. A distinction must also be made between criticism of religion on principle and *de facto* criticism mostly restricted to the gap between the essence and the actual phenomena of a religion. A critique weighs heavier on a religion the more binding its doctrinal and practical orthodoxy claims to be. The more a religion is studied and expressed in conceptual terms, the more flanks it exposes to attack. On account of the love-hate relationship of belief and unbelief, the historicity of truth and the historical contingency of all religion, critique of religion is on principle constitutive of religion.

A cursory survey will be given here of the internal critique which appears in similar forms in nearly all religions. The external critique is mostly exemplified from Christianity, as representing the form of religion which has up to the present been most thoroughly reflected in conceptual form. The question as to whether Christianity may be subsumed at all under the heading of religion need not be discussed here.

2. *Immanent critique: history and development.* a) No adequate history of religion has yet been written. The material is so vast that we must restrict ourselves here to a few indications. Certain patterns are more or less faithfully repeated everywhere. An enthusiastic beginning with wide missionary success is followed by a phase of consolidation during which doctrine is defined and groups which look on themselves as an élite break off. The establishment of dogmas, the incorporation of the masses and popular piety lead to a predominance of ritual and law, to compromises and exteriorization, with ensuing crises and manifestations of debility. This is countered by reform movements aiming at interiorization. Mystical trends arise. Modern religious practice is characterized nearly everywhere by the problems of secularization and demythologization. Trends towards rationalistic enlightenment come into conflict with the conservative and orthodox.

b) In ancient Greece, the Pre-Socratics formulated the first criticisms of the Homeric mythology. The Sophists are the classical model for the "enlightened," rationalistic critique of religion. Plato and Aristotle superseded this criticism by providing methodical criteria to distinguish myth and philosophy. Plato himself used the genre of myth to articulate what was indefinable in terms of concepts and thus gave myth a restricted validity. Greek religion then declined and was absorbed into the syncretism of Hellenism.

In the Judaism of the OT the internal critique was mostly the work of the prophets. They were quick to denounce symptoms of decay, accommodation to neighbouring religions, political surrenders or power politics which failed in loyalty to the covenant given by Yahweh. The sense of being a political and religious élite excluded the assimilation of alien cults and even benevolent contemplation of them, though there were in fact many examples of tolerance. Many reforming groups are known from the time of Jesus, inspired by mixed political and religious motives. Some criticized existing conditions by an appeal to a more rigorous legalism, others in terms of an apocalyptic world-picture. After the destruction of the temple there was a spread of Hellenistic influences but the institution of the rabbinate maintained its predominance in the preservation of tradition and creative development of it. Sociologically the rabbinate is an instance of sustained theological reflection. In the Middle Ages and at the beginning of the modern era there were Jewish reform movements, especially in Spain (the cabbala, Ben Jehuda, Juda Halevi, Maimonides), which revived long afterwards in Hasidism (Eastern Europe, 16th–18th century). This was ended by the excesses of Zaddikism and the gradual secularization of Judaism after emancipation was finally granted in Europe and the U.S.A. Critique is now exercised in Judaism from the completely liberal to the ancient orthodox wings.

Unlike Judaism, Islam mostly adapted itself to the conditions of the lands where it spread, with an attachment to the Koran which left little room for creative tradition. In the 7th century three rival schools were formed, which still exist today in a vestigial form – Sunnites, Shiites and Charidjites – the question being the legitimate succession to Mohammed as leader of Islam. The last great reform movement was about 1100 (Sufism, al-Ghazzali). It aimed at a Humanism and an interiorization of religion. With the end of the Crusades and the break-up of the Gnostic-Hellenistic syncretisms, critical self-analysis almost disappeared till the modernism of the 19th century. This was an effort by Islamic intellectuals to get rid of the dead weight of a rigid teaching system and link up with rational scientific thought. The gap is still wider than ever at the present day. A militant attitude was adopted to other religions only in political conflicts, as a rule. In general, militancy was confined to apologetics, and minorities of other faiths were always tolerated.

The immanent critique in Hinduism is too vast and many-sided to follow, since no creeds were imposed on all, and much of the history is buried in obscurity. The notion of critique is further complicated by a tolerance of verbal differences, which Western minds find hard to follow. This tolerance is itself a critique of missionary aggressivity, religious bigotry and fanaticism. One can regard as internal critique the movements in Hinduism from the 19th century on which sought to eliminate social abuses based on religious motives (the caste system, etc.). A Hindu humanism in the form of an Enlightenment philosophy occurs in Indian Hinduism (S. Radhakrishnan, etc.).

The Buddha is often considered a reformer of Brahmanism. Here too there are many divisions, e.g., Hinayana and Mahayana Buddhism, with the Hinayana movement again divided into conservative groups whose ethical standards are very austere (monks; the Theravadins ["old school"]) and a liberal popular group (the Mahasanghika ["great community"] and the Vajrayana ["diamond vehicle"]). After the 8th century A.D., Buddhism split into innumerable individual groups, while in China a Taoist form developed, and Zen Buddhism in Japan. Here too the main problem of religious critique, as known to the West, that of orthodoxy, played little part. At present, particularly in Japanese Buddhism, there is a tendency to evade the growing wave of criticism by magic and ritual practices.

c) The history of Christianity and its theology is a perpetual history of religious criticism. Elements of it are to be seen in all theological schools, all apologetics, all conciliar decrees and all confessions of faith. It is not necessary here to characterize the various epochs in detail. Ever since the age of Constantine, epochs of decadence alternate with thrusts forward, tendencies to superficiality in the masses are followed by reform movements among the élite. Schism, anti-Popes, Reformation and heretical breakaways are the concrete historical forms taken by internal criticism. On the other hand, even in patristic times, efforts were made to include critique of religion as part of theology. The principle ("sic et non") was one of the main helps in developing the scholastic method, but was later restricted in apologetics. This restriction was partly the result and partly the cause of the growing estrangement between science and theology at the beginning of the modern era. In recent times the rivalry between Catholic and Protestant theology took on far-reaching importance as critique of religion. But in general modes of thought have become so secularized that a critical attitude has become more or less habitual everywhere. Theology itself reflects this factor in new reforming trends: dialectical, personalist, transcendental, existential theologies; demythologizing; death of God theology; exegesis versus dogmatics; ecumenism; religionless Christianity; political theology; see the corresponding constitutions of Vatican II. The polarity of office and charism, in which internal critique mostly takes shape, now threatens to be resolved finally in favour of the office. The greater sociological consistency of the institution tends to give predominance to law and ritual, against which the charism of the individual has a chance only in exceptional circumstances.

3. *External critique*. Historically and formally, external critique recurs again and again in the shape of intellectual and socio-political criticism. The former is concerned with the relation of faith and knowledge, the latter with the relation of religion and power. In each case, it ranges from a fundamental to a merely *de facto* criticism.

a) Intellectual criticism takes up the question of the existence of God (as an absolute, transcendent and mostly also as a personal being), the possibility of revelation (on the part of God and on the part of man), and the linking of this revelation to a certain religious community (the Church). Fideism, Pietism and the like refuse *a priori* all rational critique, while fundamental theology is faced with the difficulty that the *fides quae* is not the object of empirical verification and direct experience. It has to work with derivative concepts, while at the same time the *fides qua* is buried in obscurity. Since the Sophists' critique of the myths, these problems have been exploited to prove the irrationality of religion. These misgivings of the critics have not been removed either by proofs of the existence of God, the concept of analogy or the metaphysics of the *philosophia perennis*. And since Kant assigned religion to the practical reason, the "truth-value" of religious thought has been widely denied in philosophy, the scholastic method being rejected along with the "theological" syntheses of Fichte, Schelling and Hegel. This, however, is equivalent to the admission that religion, in its principles and concrete forms, cannot be fully reduced to philosophy, ethics and so on. The reaction to the great syntheses and to classical metaphysics took the form of the proclamation of the "death of God" (Nietzsche), the postulate that all theology was to be deciphered as anthropology (Bayle, Feuerbach, Marx), Historicism and Relativism (Dilthey, Troeltsch), Vitalism (Darwin, Driesch), Life-Philosophy (Eucken, Bergson, Spengler) and Existentialism (Kierkegaard, Sartre, Camus, Jaspers). The tradition of scepticism running from the ancient suspension of judgment (ἐποχή) via Hume, Locke, Kant and the French Enlightenment down to modern positivism and pragmatism is summed up in respect to the critique of religion when Wittgenstein says: "What cannot be spoken about must be left in silence" (*Tractatus Logico-philosophicus*, p. 7).

b) Socio-political criticism is not confined to the denunciation of compromising alliances between Church and State or of theology as the tool of the powers that be. It takes up in general the social origins or specific social traits of all religions (Durkheim, M. Weber), the general trend to bigotry in religious thought (Holbach, Helvetius), the ideological bondage of theology and faith (Marx, Engels, Lenin). The argument is mainly directed against the notorious hostility of orthodoxy to science as a matter of history, the selfish favouring of "restorative" tendencies in socio-political matters, the resistance to secularization or the "desacralization of the world through science", the obstacles placed in the way of emancipation by a heteronomy in anthropology and finally the flight from the world in introvert subjectivity. The Marxist critique has proved particularly effective in its claim that Christianity in the bourgeois age played a decisive part in the alienation of man in capitalism, whose contradictions it embodies, expresses and even justifies. The really emancipated man will therefore be religionless. Just as sociological criticism opposes the social conditioning of religion to its claim to be a primordial experience, so too psychoanalysis points to the unconscious roots of the religion of the individual. Finally, there is a growing contrast which opposes an enlightened, profane Humanism which works for freedom, critical reflection and free democratic government to the religions, which lay the predominant stress on order, obedience, traditions and hierarchical organization.

4. *Conclusions.* The religions, including Christianity, have too often met criticism with inadequate weapons. Opposition was forcibly repressed or sanctions imposed on the indocile, or the labour force was badly employed, controversy being assigned to some particular discipline, while the rest of theology held aloof and indulged in abstractions which also included an unreal view of history. The ground-swell of the demand for a legitimation of Christianity was only ignored, not stayed. Vatican II, however, was a triumph for the essentials of a theology which sought "dialogue" with non-Christians, not just as a necessary evil or for missionary purposes, but in the hope of new lights from the other side and with the intention of joining as partners in the humanization of the world.

Werner Post

C. Philosophy of Religion

1. The philosophy of religion is not a timeless phenomenon. It is possible and necessary only under certain historical conditions. It is not a discussion of eternal problems but of such as arise in a given epoch of emancipation and enlightenment. This may be seen from its history and subject-matter. They are phenomena which first appeared in the modern world of science and political and social life, which since the 17th century has been taking the form, first in Europe and then outside it – in spite of many tensions and conflicts – of the "One World".

The term "philosophy of religion" came into use only at the end of the 18th century. It has been a special discipline in philosophy or theology only since the Enlightenment. But from the start it was quarrelled over. Hegel found the term equivocal and "slanted". There has never been agreement about the function of the philosophy of religion in philosophy and theology, in science, Church and society.

Nonetheless, it may be affirmed as a start that the philosophy of religion is possible and necessary when the religious doctrines and institutions of the Jewish and Christian tradition find themselves in a state of schism from the modern world, and when the critical reason, noting this division, feels the need of insight into the truth of religion. Where the division does not yet exist or the need is not felt, or when both cease to exist, the philosophy of religion is not possible or necessary.

Since the actual historical notion of philosophy of religion was due to specific circumstances, there is no point in using the term to describe earlier notions and theories. Not all analysis of religion and not all critique or justification of it is a philosophy of religion. Discussion of religion within the "primitive" societies or within such non-European societies as the Indian and Chinese with their written traditions, starts from suppositions other than those of the European Enlightenment and hence cannot be adequately described with its concepts. And when Greek philosophy criticized the myths, when Plato and Aristotle described their philosophy as contemplation of the divine, or when the Hellenistic world distinguished between mythic, natural and political theology, they started from suppositions which are no longer generally admitted, after Christ and above all after the Enlightenment.

So too discussion of the historical revelation of God in the Bible, in antiquity and the Middle Ages, was not philosophy of religion in the modern sense. No doubt the exposition of biblical texts and their application to the present with the help of philosophical notions, above all those of Plato and Aristotle, were part of Christian tradition from the start. And in the old society of Europe, Church and individuals always sought to apply various thought-forms to make the Christian revelation persuasive. But this was theology, not philosophy of religion. This only came in when the subjective and critical reason had "a need to understand" religion in the course of the emancipation and Enlightenment. This is Hegel's starting-point when he describes the post-Enlightenment era by saying: "The Church or the theologians, though seeing philosophers not hostile to religion, simply trying to fathom its truth, may reject their efforts with proud irony and laugh at the manufactured truth. But this contemptuous attitude is no longer a help, and it is futile, once the need to understand and the split from religion have been recognized. Here insight has its rights which cannot be denied it."

Very different reasons led as early as the 17th century to this split between the Christian tradition and the emancipated world which makes the philosophy of religion possible and necessary. Only a few need be mentioned. The historico-critical investigation of the Bible showed clearly the gap between the world-picture of the Bible ("mythological") and that of modern times. It was greater than previous exegesis had supposed. So too the exact sciences led with intrinsic necessity to a "demythologizing" of many religious notions. Then the critique of the rational metaphysics of scholasticism and the critique of metaphysics in general questioned the philosophy with which it was thought that religious doctrines had been propounded and justified once and for all. Finally, the modern State developed as the guarantee of freedom and law. The modern society developed as a system of creating and contenting needs. Thus the old moral, social and political institutions with which the Church had often too readily identified itself were altered or even swept away. For these and other reasons the persuasiveness of Christianity, hitherto channelled by tradition and society, has been declining since the Enlightenment. At the same time, the tension between an interiorized, critical subjectivity and religious institutions losing their functions has been growing steadily greater. Since the 18th century, "the need to understand and the split from religion have been recognized", and the process of enlightenment which now affects more than the "cultured", has become irreversible. Even inside the Church there are more and more who can only partially identify themselves with the Church, its doctrines and its directives.

2. The philosophy of religion has three main interests. Some pursue it because they feel they must criticize and reject the Christian tradition, for the sake of full emancipation. Others aim at defending this tradition, and religion in general, in a world which is emancipating itself. Finally, those who think that the emancipation is complete, and feel no need either to criticize or defend, merely investigate religion empirically and without value-judgments, to de-

scribe and compare its phenomena. Hence the philosophy of religion has hitherto been a) either a total critique of religion in the name of nature and society, or b) an apologia for religion in the name of a given natural theology, a transcendental, personalist or existential philosophy; or c) the empirical registration and analysis of religious notions and institutions.

a) The radical critique of religion starts from nature outside man or a prehistoric natural state of man. It sees the (Jewish-) Christian tradition as a false and alienated notion of nature in and outside of man. This was the approach of Helvetius, Feuerbach, Nietzsche and Freud. It went over into Marxism and evolutionist philosophy, where it takes two forms. There is a romantic form, as in Feuerbach, which begins with the notion of a sound, non-alienated natural life of man. There is a sceptical form, as in Freud, which hopes that finally in the future, when all religious illusions and taboos are gone, man will be able to limit and manage, with the help of science and reason, the inevitable conflict of anarchical drives.

All this radical criticism in the name of nature hopes that enlightenment about the causes of religious alienation will bring about a change in human consciousness. The false religious consciousness is due above all to lack of knowledge of nature, lack of technological mastery of nature, lack of insight into the complex of unconscious drives in man, and into individual and social projections and neuroses. Forms of therapy are suggested in keeping with the diagnoses and the various views of nature. Religion will be conquered by a growing mastery of nature and further manipulation of human nature; or by a return to the Greek interpretation of the world as nature, which has been obscured by Christian tradition, European philosophy and the "historical" consciousness (Nietzsche, Löwith); by a return to the immediacy of the senses, natural sex and the direct I-You relationship (Feuerbach); or by the formation of a new religion of evolutionary Humanism (J. Huxley).

The starting-point and guideline of this radical critique – the notion of nature in and outside man – has become vague and ambiguous in the scientific and technological world of today. It had to, because that notion of nature meant the cosmology of the Stoa, a vague evolutionary process of heaven and earth, a romanticized immediacy of the senses, etc. Nature was a Dionysiac primordial unity, conjured up with anti-Christian passion, and the will to power. It was the wordless world of nature sought in scepticism (Löwith). The notion of nature is so wide and vague that this sort of critique must now be at least revised.

Another form of radical critique is put forward in the name of society. This too is forced, above all by the real development of modern society, to revise its starting-point and guidelines. Condorcet and Comte, the Hegelians of the left, and above all Marx criticized Christianity and religion in general as an ideology and as a reactionary social and political institution hindering the progress of man and the realization of a truly human society. Religion either justified inhumane social and political conditions or tried to make them tolerable by an illusionary reconciliation and holding out hope of another world.

This critique was plausible as long as the hope of a more humane society through further emancipation was plausible. But such hope cannot now be based on the historical processes on which the Enlightenment theories of progress relied. Man's mastery of nature, on which Condorcet and Comte pinned their hopes, has in the meantime been vastly extended. But as the world of science and technology in socialist and capitalist society shows, it is no sufficient guarantee of a more humane society and politics. Marx based his analysis of his times on the unresolved social tendencies of bourgeois society, a transformed Hegelian philosophy of history and a modified materialism. He thought he could detect in the proletariat's class-consciousness the objective tendency to revolution, and hence that the proletariat could be enabled to be the agent of revolution. But Marx's idea lost its force both in theory and practice as time went on and had to be transformed in various ways. Neither in the capitalist and socialist societies nor in the Third World does it offer a pattern for the reforms and revolutions now possible and necessary if freedom is to come about. And, as the experience of this century shows, it does not guarantee that it will not itself be abused, like religion, as an ideology in the service of the rulers. For these and other reasons, the radical critics of religion on the basis of society are forced to revise their arguments.

b) But the split between traditional religion and the emancipated modern world also engenders the apologia of religion. The apologists in question have this in common with the critics that they are often blind to the complex nuances of the new socio-political, scientific and spiritual reality, and to the questions which the critical subject can and must put. They are often not open to the possibilities offered to religion by the process of emancipation itself, though these possibilities are historically substantiated in the positions which they attack. Further, as Lessing saw, the mere apologia does not avoid being infected by the heterodoxy of the enemy in the uncritical use of its arguments. The limits of a mere apologia are particularly clear when one considers natural theology, the philosophy of religion put forward by transcendental philosophy, and that of an existentialist or personalist philosophy.

The natural theology worked out in the 17th and 18th centuries, e.g., by Deism, and in later times especially by neo-scholasticism, bases itself on the rational nature of man, understood teleologically, to make statements permanently valid *a priori* about the nature of God, the world and man. Reason can thus give a new justification for religion which will be clear and acceptable to all. It often thinks that it has thus preserved ancient and medieval metaphysics in a way which is now convincing.

But this is not so. Now that historical research has disclosed the variety of philosophical and theological traditions in antiquity and the Middle Ages, and the growing differences in methodical reflection in European metaphysics, it is useless to conjure up the supposedly sacred tradition, Christian Platonism or Thomism, as a block. The presuppositions of the natural theology of reason are no longer obvious. It is no longer accepted that man can and needs to grasp what ancient and medieval metaphysics called eternal being, the Absolute, and that Christianity is justified if it contains timeless truths. Such natural theology is logically indifferent or even negative as regards historical tradition, the present and the future. Deism, for instance, took from Christianity only what could be reduced to a system of permanent metaphysical and moral truths. It found the historical element of Christianity and all that was channelled by tradition and institutions as purely historical, purely "positive" and so fundamentally equally valid or invalid. Such detachment from the historical now signals the limits of all apologias of religion in the line of rational natural theology. Not even believers agree on the supposedly timeless propositions about God, man and the world. And the apologia which started from supposedly timeless presuppositions is now seen to be itself historically conditioned.

Transcendental philosophy's justification of religion, in the sense of Maréchal and his followers, is also defective.

Like the natural theology of reason, it is ultimately non-historical in its presuppositions and goal. The transcendental Ego remains ambivalent. It is to be distinguished from space and time and all historical mediation, but is still to be my "I". Its form of apologia is based on the claim that even without reflection on the contents of religious tradition man can be shown to be formally open to the Christian message. It speaks of the *anima naturaliter Christiana* as though this were still a perspicuous truth, without reflection on the present forms of religious tradition. This type of philosophy of religion may have been plausible as long as the Christian world survived relatively intact, stamped by tradition and environment. But once the break with tradition has become clear, this philosophy of religion is inadequate. It remains formal, a stage on the way out of the natural theology which claimed to make eternal assertions about God, the world and man. It remains formal, even if it starts not with the transcendental Ego but with the "historicity" of man, because this is not reached through real history, past, present and future.

The philosophy of religion in existentialism and personalism likewise has axioms which are no longer self-evident. After the First and Second World Wars, these approaches undoubtedly had a legitimate critical function in the history of science, theology and sociopolitics. Personalism in Catholic theology was and is, for instance, a necessary corrective to neo-scholasticism. Existential and dialectical theology was and is a corrective to the liberalism of the 19th and 20th centuries. But they started from a primordial religious act, an anthropologically significant relation to the holy and numinous or from the abstract antitheses between I-You and It-World, between intersubjectivity and moral, social and political institutions. And the philosophy of religion was then necessarily a private and unworldly matter, abandoning what it now tries to hold on to. The attitude of existentialism and personalism to the new scientific and social possibilities which the world holds out to Christianity is entirely negative. Or they leave this world as "secularized" outside the scope of their reflections. They fail to see that man now lives not just in the immediate I-You relationship, but in mediated and objectified institutions. They fail to realize that where the pre-modern religious institutions are more and more losing their reality and functions, while the explicit forms of religious and Church life are becoming more and more inadequate to the totality of society, the critical subjectivity and the new socio-political world are the indispensable prerequisites for all living forms of religion. The tensions which the critical subjectivity must endure and live by are reduced in existentialism and personalism to an unworldly interiority, decision for the sake of decision – to a subjectivity out of touch with the present reality. They ontologize that which man must take up and away if he is to reach true freedom and his supreme fulfilment. Since today the worldless interiority is collapsing and being manipulated, it can no longer provide a satisfactory justification for religion.

c) The third form of philosophy of religion was mainly worked out since the end of the 19th century in Northern and Western Europe and the U.S.A. It is the historical, sociological, psychological and phenomenological or linguistic analysis, in empirical procedures, launched by Max Weber, Troeltsch, Lévy-Bruhl and others. These investigations are not based on the notion of a split between Christian tradition and the modern world, but on the conviction that society is totally emancipated from this tradition. They claim neither to criticize nor justify Christianity or religion in general. In general they are deliberately detached from all critique or apologia and hence often avoid using the term philosophy of religion. They restrict themselves to the description and analysis of religious phenomena and structures, trying to reach by comparative and typological methods some general definitions of the essence of religion. Many arguments and themes derive in fact from the criticism or defence of religion. The main difference is that they see present-day society as the result of the previous process of secularization or confine themselves to purely formal statements on the phenomenon of religion.

Today the notion of secularization is often used as fundamental in the debate about the legitimacy or otherwise of the modern. Where philosophy and science of religion suppose that modern society is the result of legitimate secularization and emancipation from the Christian tradition, they imply that one must choose between tradition and the modern. Tradition is only a history of past ways to the present. The surviving forms of religion are merely marginal or vestigial phenomena which can be of only partial and private interest in view of the secularized religionless society.

Where the philosophy and science of religion work with a formal notion of religion, gained inductively from the various historical religions, they seek historically etc. the structures common to all religions. But the concept of religion is so formal that while it can be applied to all historical phenomena of religion and pseudo-religion, it is useless in interpreting a given historical problem and as a concrete critique. Hence the "empirical" philosophy of religion is even less competent than that of the 17th and 18th centuries to resolve the tension between Christianity and the modern world. It cannot cope with such questions as the modern debate about the nature of the Church and Christianity, the antithesis between Christian faith and religion as put forward in dialectical theology, the demand for a "religionless Christianity", the critical function of the Church and theology as regards society. If the choice between Christianity or religion in general and the modern were in fact as radical as the secularization theory supposes; or if present-day society were as irreligious and as detached from history as many philosophers of religion and others assume; then theology and the philosophy of religion would indeed be literally without an object, or a mere memory of the past and perished. As Kant said, the "business" of "biblical theology" and "philosophical theology" would be finished and theologians and philosophers of religion would be what they were accused of being by many from the Middle Ages to the 18th century: deceived deceivers. But perhaps the process of emancipation and enlightenment is only now reaching its high-point, both in the Church and theology and in society and the life of the individual.

3. There are reasons to think that philosophy of religion, in the forms which it has taken hitherto, is finished and outmoded. But this does not mean the end of all philosophy of religion. If, as we suppose, it discusses the problems posed by emancipation and enlightenment in the Churches, sciences, society and the individual life, there is much to be said for it today, as the process of emancipation and enlightenment takes in ever wider circles. But less than ever can it be merely a special branch of philosophy and theology. It must also be reflection on individuals and individual sciences and an inter-disciplinary discussion. It has a double function.

a) It must criticize the religious notions and the arguments of the abstract and hence unenlightened enlightenment, since they can no longer be convincing to the critical subject. It must show, for instance, that today many religious concepts explicable by psychology and sociology are no longer convincing. It must also show that for present-day questions the alternatives fixed by the Enlightenment between immanence and transcendence, nature and supernatural autonomy and heteronomy are invalid, as are the standard proofs of the existence of God and the death-of-God theory directed against them.

b) It must formulate the questions now put by the individual, the Churches and society and try to answer them if possible. But even if the philosophy of religion can do no more than disclose criticism and the negations arising from unsolved or unsolvable problems, it remains for all a necessary tool for understanding the truth.

Such a philosophy of religion, with such concrete and historical presuppositions, is distinct from "biblical theology". The latter, as Kant showed, must proceed from its own specific bases: the belief of the Church in the historical revelation attested in the Bible and Jesus Christ. But this philosophy of religion must also be distinguished from the "impartial" sciences which do not (at least deliberately) base themselves on the historical religion of Europe, but describe and analyse with empirical categories and principles of verification and falsification the various forms of religion.

Three unsolved problems, already raised by Lessing, Kant and Hegel, may be mentioned in conclusion.

(i) The "yawning gap" between religious tradition and the experiences of the critical subject in the developing world of philosophy, science, sociology and politics has been constantly widening since the Enlightenment. Where this split is recognized, all forms of reconciliation are ineffective which do not link up with these experiences of the critical subject. Religious tradition can only be relevant if it continues the process of enlightenment which has been begun. It will not help to conjure up what was once taken believingly on trust. Only critical remembrance can preserve what the unenlightened Enlightenment fallaciously abandoned. Critical remembrance and re-presentation and reform of the tradition is now the only way to preserve it credibly and vitally. The critical mind can accept as tidings of revelation only the tidings which show it to be the answer to its still unsolved questions.

Hence even in religious tradition the process of enlightenment is dialectical, both destroying and preserving. It sweeps away, for instance, certain notions of God. He can no longer be used to explain processes of nature and history which science sufficiently explains. The notion of God has become unacceptable which is used to sanction moral doctrines and political systems which are unacceptable to present-day morals and politics. But the process of enlightenment can also lead to a refinement of the notion of God and a new insight into revealed truths. The experience of the distance of God and his silence can explain, for instance, aspects of God's revelation in the Bible about which the Church and theology have said little as yet. But even if the philosophy of religion cannot say as much about God as traditional theology, and serves rather to sift out unacceptable notions of God, it is today an instrument for understanding the truth.

(ii) The relationship of Christianity to the non-Christian religions is a second urgent problem. Christianity is no longer as in the medieval *respublica cristiana* the integrating force of all society, so that the heathens are "outside". And one can no longer consider that metaphysical considerations and a philosophy of history with "ages" and "periods" are adequate to explain to all the relationship of Christianity, as the one true religion, to the others. If Christianity, which now appears as one religion among others, is to continue to make its claim to truth and universality in a way universally intelligible, it needs other patterns of thought than those of the traditional metaphysics and philosophy of history. For the critical mind, the relationship of Christianity to the non-Christian religions cannot be adequately explained by affirming that all historical religions are ideograms of a philosophical faith or that all non-Christians are anonymous Christians.

(iii) The place and function of religion within the new political and social world is a third unsolved problem. Since the Enlightenment, which made freedom the principle of ethics and politics and demanded institutions which would guard the freedom and the rights of all, the relationship of religion to politics and society cannot be explained along the lines of the political theology of antiquity and of medieval notions. As the politics of Romanticism showed, these led to a combination of politics and theology which was pernicious to both. Even in modern times religion and the Churches can offer, by virtue of their own presuppositions, certain motives and arguments for moral and political life which are different from those of other social groups. But when justifying their directives, they must take into account the concrete social and political conditions. Where, for instance, the State has in fact become the sum-total of the institutions which guarantee the rights and freedom of man, religious freedom and the separation of Church and State must be accepted, if religion wishes to speak of political and social action. Where society has developed into a system of needs and satisfaction of needs and as a system of scientific and technological mastery of the world, religion, by virtue of its own specific principles, has also a contribution to make to the creation and safeguarding of a life of human dignity.

A philosophy of religion, as Hegel said, is not a sermon. It cannot produce religion in a man and a society which is so to speak without religion. It cannot import something substantially new and foreign into man. Its specific task, in dialogue or if necessary in controversy with the Churches, science and society, is to expose the problems which arise for religious tradition if it is to be propounded in a vigorous and plausible way in a given state of emancipation and enlightenment. As long as the need to understand religious truth persists, the philosophy of religion has its rights which cannot be denied it.

Willi Oelmüller

II. Science of Religion

A. Introduction

1. *The "science of religion"*, a term first used by the Oxford professor Friedrich Max Müller (1823–1900), is the scientific discipline, often called "comparative religion", whose task is the empirical investigation of all religions, from those of the advanced cultures to those of the "primitives" (rather, non-literate peoples). It takes in all their past and present forms, and their relationship to civilization, landscape, ethnology, society, politics and economics. It is divided for practical purposes into several disciplines, and uses other branches of science which can help it to fulfil its proper task.

All science of religion is based on the study of religious history, which deals with the fundamental factors of the genesis, growth, beliefs, cultus and ethics of the various religions and examines the contacts between religions. The phenomenology of religion is concerned with the various forms in which religion manifests itself, e.g., holy objects, places, times, sacred traditions, oral and written, holy men and religious communities. To grasp the essence of its subject-matter, it compares these phenomena of the various religions while "bracketing out" historical incidentals. The psychology of religion is concerned with man's personal religious life, religion in the subjective sense. The sociology of religion is a relatively recent discipline, which investigates the social aspects of religion in the realms of religious institutions and the mutual relationships between religion and society. The geography of religion has hitherto been more or less confined to merely descriptive work. Systematic efforts to work out interdependence between landscape and religious phenomena are only at the initial stages.

Not all would agree that the philosophy of religion is part of the science of religion. Since it is a normative discipline which makes a philosophical analysis of religion, it has not the empirical character of the science of religion. Nonetheless, philosophy of religion must rely on the science of religion for its facts. There is a similar situation as regards the theology of religion. But work on it is much more urgent than formerly, now that the contact between the various religions is so much closer. On the basis of the new One World, human societies are interlocked, materially and culturally, as never before, and the ecumenic encounter of religions is becoming a dominant factor in the spiritual situation of the world.

The demand that cognizance be taken of the findings of the science of religion in the solution of problems of the theology of religion leads to a new stage in the relationship of theology and religion, which has hitherto been ambivalent. The science of religion had been developed without the tutelage of theology. Nonetheless, there was always a close connection between the disciplines, because the science of religion used the approach of historical theology to develop its methods, which meant that it applied frequently to the phenomena of other religions certain categories which had been evolved in theology.

However necessary theology may be, it is not the sole prerequisite for the science of religions, which cannot work in isolation any more than the other sciences. It needs to draw on expert knowledge of languages above all, which is the only key to the sources in their original form. Other relevant disciplines are archaeology, history of art, culture, economics and politics, psychology, ethnology, geography, sociology and philosophy.

2. *History of the science.* All encounters between religions always gave rise to some sort of scientific discussion. Historians and philosophers treated such themes in antiquity. Christian theologians in late antiquity and the Middle Ages who dealt with ancient religions, including the German and the Slav, or Judaism and Islam, were preoccupied with apologetics. The Enlightenment aimed rather at a detached and critical investigation of strange beliefs. Here the basic supposition was that there was an "innate" religion, first outlined by Lord Herbert of Cherbury (1583–1648). This ideological basis for the study of religions was extended in the second half of the 18th century by a new element, the opening up of the archives of the non-European religions, which began with the translation of the basic texts of the advanced religions of India and Iran. The deciphering of old Oriental scripts and a constant stream of archaeological finds (texts, temples and ritual objects), which has gone on to the present day, led to a further increase in the subject-matter.

At the universities, study of religion was first done by members of the theological and philosophical faculties, who occasionally lectured on the subject. The first chair of comparative religion was set up at Geneva in 1873. Boston University introduced the subject in the same year. Chairs were set up in the Netherlands in 1876, at Amsterdam, Groningen, Leiden and Utrecht. The Paris University followed suit in 1879, Brussels in 1884. The science of religion was introduced at the University of Uppsala in 1893 by the classical scholar

S. Wide. Under N. Söderblom (1866–1931), who taught the subject from 1901–14 at Uppsala, the Swedish school of comparative religion became important internationally for the first time. The subject had been lectured on at the University of Rome since 1886, but it was only with Raffaele Pettazzoni (1883–1959), who became professor there in 1924, that the Italian school gained international standing. The first chair in Asia was at Tokyo in 1903. In Scotland, Lord Griffith (1820–87) founded chairs for "Natural Theology" at the universities of Aberdeen, Edinburgh, Glasgow and St. Andrews. The first chair of "Natural and Comparative Religion" was set up in Oxford in 1908. The science of religion was made an academic discipline at Berlin in 1910 and at Leipzig in 1912. Chairs were set up in Copenhagen in 1914 and in Oslo in 1915. Today many universities offer the subject, sometimes in conjunction with the philosophy of religion, OT theology, missiology or an Oriental language.

3. *Schools of thought.* a) *Evolutionism.* This was the most persistent of the theories which treated religion as a derivative and determinable phenomenon. Its approach betrays the influence of the positivism of Comte and the application of Darwinism to human history. It was ultimately based on the agnosticism of Herbert Spencer. Evolutionism, with its effort to deduce religion from impersonal experiences, was the common factor in many theories, which then made very different assumptions about the earliest stages of religion. In the animism of E. B. Tylor, man's experience of his soul led first to belief in spirits and finally to belief in gods. The "Dynamism" chiefly propounded by R. R. Marett, based on a misunderstood letter from the Melanesian missionary Codrington, saw the earliest stage of religion as belief in an impersonal power (*mana*).

b) *Astral mythology.* Another effort, which was relatively well represented in the early part of the 20th century, was the astral mythology which attributed the formation of myth to the effect of watching the movement of the heavenly bodies. It again treated religion as a derivative phenomenon, to be explained not on its own terms, but in terms of some outside elements. The Pan-Babylonianism of A. Jeremias and H. Winckler stood out in particular.

c) *The psychology of myth.* Even more than by Freud himself, this school was influenced and moulded by his disciple C. G. Jung, who regarded myth as the expression of archetypal, supra-personal vital truths. Some major works on mythology were essentially or to some extent based on this notion. Its influence can also be seen, though again not everywhere, in the Eranos circle of Ascona; see the *Eranos Jahrbuch* (1933ff.).

d) *"The holy" in comparative religion.* In the twenties and thirties of this century, discussion centred to some extent on the notion of the "holy" or "numinous". This was mainly due to Rudolf Otto's *Das Heilige* (1st ed., 1917; E. T.: *The Idea of the Holy*, 1923). Rudolf Otto (1869–1937) strove to establish the absolute independence of the religious sphere and its fundamental difference from all secular phenomena. His book was primarily an analysis of the psychology of religion. It was this methodological basis which evoked lively criticism. Otto's preoccupation with the religious subject evoked misgivings, as did also neglect of the moral element, which is essential to the holy.

e) *The High Gods.* The theories which treated religion as a secondary and derivative phenomenon, or subordinated it to the notion of the holy, were most vigorously opposed by the representatives of a school which produced proofs of early belief in a "High God". It is significant that the essay on evolutionism by G. Widengren, one of the leading representatives of the new school, was one of the main factors in the abandonment of evolutionist theories. The school of W. Schmidt (1868–1954) had wide and deep influence. It was firmly opposed to the application of evolutionist schemas to the history of religion, and also to the importance attributed by R. Otto and his followers to the impersonal notion of "the holy". The effort now was to show that belief in a personal High God, monotheistic in nature, appeared very early. See especially *Der Ursprung der Gottesidee*, by W. Schmidt, 12 vols. (1926–55), for the findings of this school of "primitive monotheism".

f) *History of cultus*. Evolutionism was also opposed by the upholders of the "cultic history" method. This was directed also against an unduly individualistic concept of religion and stressed its social character. Hence its investigations were primarily concerned with the ceremonies of the social celebration of the cultus. There are two main trends here, one the Scandinavian school, which goes back mainly to the Danish scholar W. Grönbech (1873–1948), and the British Myth and Ritual school, in which S. H. Hooke was a leading figure. Noteworthy also was an intensive study of "sacral kingship", partly occasioned by the cultic history method, but to some extent independent of it. The protagonist here was J. G. Frazer (1854–1941) with *The Golden Bough*, 12 vols. (3rd revised and enlarged ed., 1911–15).

g) *Symbolism*. The studies of E. Cassirer and M. Eliade gave the main impulses to the intensive effort to disclose the meaning of religious symbols, These include all the phenomena of place, time, nature and human life where their symbolic character makes the world transparent for the experience of transcendence.

Günter Lanczkowski

B. History of Religion

1. *Method*. To begin with, one has to be convinced that it is possible to have some real understanding of other religions (cf. J. Wach). Where a religion is documented in literary form, scholarly research provides the readiest access. This means study of the language concerned, since language is the most direct expression of mentality and is at least partially determined by religious influences. The real meaning of religious traditions can only be attained through studies in their original language. The notorious *traduttore-traditore* should warn the researcher from swearing allegiance to the scholarly expert, since his translations inevitably contain an element of interpretation.

But the history of religions cannot be content with philological research. One of the characteristics of its approach is that it tries to see life from its religious aspect. This quality demands of the student of religions, in contrast to the linguistic expert, a general view of the whole history of religions. From the point of view of method, restriction to the study of one or two religions is inadequate and leads to unsatisfactory findings.

But knowledge of languages is not the only technical requirement. The monuments of a religious epoch are found in works of art, general culture, political and economic developments as well as in strictly religious documents and profane literature. In the case of non-literary peoples, linguistics helps only insofar as the religions in question have been preserved in written form by researchers. Otherwise the sources must be the "Relations" of European and American observers, which are often due to missionaries interested in ethnology.

2. *Division*. The attempt to survey the religions of the world as a whole has to find some system of classification. There are considerable difficulties here, from the points of view of science, philosophy and theology of religions. The scientific study of religions generally proceeds by reducing very complex structures to a few characteristics which

are made the basis of the systematic presentation. A simple numerical or geographical approach leads to the division between world religions and local religions, which are sometimes then called inexactly national religions. The cultural approach distinguishes the religions of the advanced civilizations from those of the "primitives", this distinction being also applied to various features of religions. The qualitative approach can lead to an arrangement according to the nature of belief in God: monotheistic or polytheistic religions. So too religions can be classified according to their ethical values. This history of origins can be used as a principle of classification, as when religions whose traditions show no traces of a founder are distinguished from religions which have been "founded". The latter can then be classified as prophetical religions, though this term can also be used to form a contrast with mystical religions.

The problems which arise from a one-sided application of certain characteristics are further complicated by the overlapping which ensues when several such characteristics are considered together. There can be prophetism in local religions and in world religions, in the higher religions and the "primitive". The contrast between local and world religions does not coincide with that between monotheism and polytheism, etc.

In the philosophy or theology of religions, all systematization from the point of view of history is problematic, because this implies a sort of verdict on them, or at least can be understood as such. It must then be the urgent task of theological reflection to divide religions into historical periods in the perspective of the religion in question. This is relatively easy in the case of some schools of Oriental mysticism where all religions are regarded as equally acceptable ways of attaining mystical union, though some less perfect than others. Religions founded in modern times have often subsumed the traditional religions into a framework of progressive religious enlightenment, at the climax of which they themselves come. In Islam, the supreme value attached to written revelation led to a theologically consistent division of religions which distinguished the possessors of divinely-inspired scriptures, the "peoples of the book", from the faithful of non-scriptural religions.

As long as there is no such accepted classification among Christian theologians, with regard to non-Christian religions, the task of the historian of religions must be to present the material as neutrally as possible, in the face of the problem of a Christian theology of religion. Hence the following obeys a neutral principle of geographical distribution, combined with the historical approach, since a special treatment of modern religious foundations, living religions and religions which have disappeared as complex wholes will serve to underline systematically the difference in the actual significance of these groups. Hence too the religions of the non-literary peoples ("primitives") will be dealt with separately.

3. *Religions of the past.* a) *Ancient East.* (i) *Egypt.* Since Champollion succeeded in 1822 in deciphering the ancient hieroglyphics of Egypt, the primary sources in inscriptions and papyri became available as well as the accounts of ancient writers like Herodotus, Strabo and Plutarch. Its changing course of many thousand years of history could now be followed, while the ancient accounts had dealt with a late period only, and hence given undue prominence to the worship of Isis and Osiris, as also to the worship of gods in animal form, by which pagans were amused and Christians angered. The original documents are so numerous, thanks to the extraordinary readiness of the ancient Egyptians with pen and chisel, that a full picture can now be sketched.

The religion of the Old Kingdom (*c.* 2778–2263 B.C.) was characterized by the notion of "sacral kingship". The king is the divine and supremely powerful centre of the whole cosmos. He alone, in the older view, has access to the gods, though in practice the growing number of sanctuaries compelled him to appoint priests as his delegates. The king is surrounded by a strict ceremonial hedge. He is a power-centre, taboo to ordinary mortals. Along with the documents, the most impressive proof of this is the pyramids, those enormous tombs of dead monarchs which testify to faith in the inviolable divine nature of the king. This monumental form of tomb, which developed from the rectangular burial mound with sloping walls, the *mastaba* in Arabian, is characteristic in particular from the third dynasty on. The sacral character of the king comes from his relationship to Maat, (goddess of) the cosmic, ethical and ritual order of the world. Maat is the norm of truth and justice which holds good for the divine and human world and to which all men must bow. But the king is the "Lord of Justice" (of Maat) and the embodiment of Maat. The divinity of the king, who is called the "Great God", also appears from the fact that he was regarded as a form of manifestation of the falcon-like god, Horus, the last of the series of gods who were the rulers of Egypt at the start of its history (see especially the Royal Papyrus of Turin). The sacred status of the king was diminished in the 5th dynasty, when worship of the Sun-God Re became the State religion. Instead of being identified with the ruler god Horus, the king was now regarded as the son of the Sun-God Re.

The first Intermediate Period (2263–2052) comes between the catastrophic breakup of the Old Kingdom and the establishment of the Middle Kingdom. The catastrophe left its mark on the spirit of the era, with its conflicting trends, sceptical and hedonistic, but also prophetical, where a monotheistic faith was linked with ethical demands.

The Middle Kingdom (2052–1786) had a monotheistic ideal, which from the 12th dynasty on acknowledged officially the God Amon, who was also the supreme God in the New Kingdom (1580–1085) which flourished after the Hyksos period (1785–1580). The only break with the established religion was in the time of the "heretic king", Amenhotep IV, the husband of Nefertiti, who proclaimed the sun disc Aton as the sole God. He changed his name (meaning "Amon is happy") to Akh-en-Aton ("Pleasing to the Aton"), left the royal city of Thebes and built a city at the present Tell el-Amarna, which he called Akhet-Aton, "Horizon of the Sun Disc".

The established religion of the one High God was accompanied by a *de facto* polytheism. This goes back to the earliest days of the kingdom, when the small political units of territory were united to form the State of Upper and Lower Egypt. The gods of the various districts were combined in a pantheon which gave rise to syncretistic developments.

In the Old Kingdom, ethics was the embodiment of Maat. A personal ethical decision is demanded for the first time in the texts of the first Intermediate Period. The Wisdom literature and the exculpatory formulas ("negative confessions": "I have not done violence to a poor man", etc.) which are found in the mortuary texts (the "Book of the Dead") and biographies are fundamental acknowledgments of a moral order and its claims.

The moral life was also to some extent essential in determining the form of one's afterlife, with which the Egyptians were preoccupied more than any other people. But later, these ethical strivings yielded to preoccupation with magical practices, to which numerous mortuary texts bear witness. This trend apparently became dominant through the place given to Osiris in the afterlife. The judgment of the dead, originally attributed to the God Re, was transferred to the underworld where Osiris reigned.

The later period of Egyptian religion was marked by a pessimistic sense of decline and fall. Under the Romans, the last believers lamented the imminent downfall of their religion with the words: "The time is coming when it will seem that for all their zeal and piety, the Egyptians worshipped the Godhead in vain."

(ii) *Mesopotamia*. The cuneiform which the Sumerians had developed by stylizing an older pictographic script was the most widely used form of writing in the Near East in antiquity. It was used for the Sumerian, Akkadian (Babylonian and Assyrian) and Old Persian, and for Ugaritic and other languages in Asia Minor. When it was deciphered in 1802 by G. Grotefend, the primary sources became available for the study of Mesopotamian religion, which had hitherto been known only through such writers as Herodotus and Strabo, and by the fragments of Berossus, a Babylonian priest (c. 300 B.C.).

The most ancient advanced civilization of Mesopotamia was that of the city-states of the Sumerians (from *c.* 3000 B.C.). Their political power was broken by the Akkadians, Sargon I and his successors, *c.* 2360–2180. The Sumerians were finally conquered by the old Babylonian empire, with a West Semitic dynasty of which the most notable king was Hammurabi (*c.* 1700). The Babylonian empire was brought down by the Cassites, who ruled in Mesopotamia from *c.* 1600 to 1170, and were in turn succeeded by the Assyrians, who had formed an empire in northern Mesopotamia. From *c.* 1100 B.C. the Assyrians were the great power in the Near East. The fall of Niniveh (612 B.C.) came with the rise of the new Babylonian empire (612–538), which was conquered by the Persian king, Cyrus.

The cultural achievements of Sumer and Akkad were undoubtedly great, though the Pan-Babylonianism of some Assyriologists, especially *c.* 1900, with its exclusive emphasis on the importance of Mesopotamia for human religion and culture, represents a one-sided and overstated case. The break which came in the political history of Mesopotamia when the Semites replaced the Sumerian rule by their own did not mean a similar break in the history of civilization. The Akkadians took over much of the spiritual heritage of the Sumerians, in spite of ethnic and linguistic differences. Though there were profound differences in religion, the Semites took over Sumerian elements which they developed independently.

Sumer. Like the Egyptians of the Old Kingdom, the Sumerians recognized no purely worldly realm. Religious interests predominated in the structure of the State, and the Priest-King of the city-states, with the title of *lu-gal* ("Great Man"), combined theocratically the functions of ruler, judge, general and high priest. The highest priestly task of the king was the "sacred marriage" which he and the high priestess enacted at the New Year's Feast, functioning as representatives of the god Dumuzi and the goddess Inanna. The cultic action was a fertility rite which was to ensure the new life of the spring vegetation. In spite of his cultic importance, the king was not considered a god, but only the son of a god.

There were huge numbers of gods and goddesses. The Sumerians said they were 3600 in all, meaning an endless number, this being the square of the basic figure of their sexagesimal system. A system was gradually thought out, along the lines of human kinship, which embraced these man-like gods in a pantheon. The sky-god An, with his wife, Ki, the earth, came at the head, though in actual religious life they played little part. Their son was Enlil, the "Lord of the Storm", the god of the air and catastrophes, the author of the deluge. His wife was Ninlil, the "Lady of the Storm". The piety of the Sumerians went above all to the kindly god Enki, the "Lord of the Below", of the abyss of waters which gave earth life. Enki was also the Lord of Wisdom. His wife was Ninki, the "Lady of the Below". The Sun-god Utu, the moon-goddess Nanna and the god of hunting, Ninurta (biblical Nimrod), were also important. The rulers of the underworld were Nergal and his wife Ereshkigal. Sumerian and Near Eastern art in general displays motifs which link Inanna, the goddess of love, the Babylonian Ishtar and Dumuzi, the Babylonian Tammuz. The themes are concerned with the cycle of vegetation. The notion of the tree of life is often linked with Dumuzi.

The Sumerian religion, in contrast to that of the Semites, lacked the notion of sin. The underworld of the afterlife was a desolate place from which there was no return. The frequency of prayers for long life underlines this notion.

Babylon and Ashur. Many gods of the Assyrian and Babylonian pantheon are modelled on the Sumerian. Anu corresponds to the Sumerian An, Ea to Enki, Ellil, the lord of earth and mountain, to Enlil, the Sumerian god of the air. The moon-god Sin with his son, the sun-god Shamash and his daughter Ishtar, formed a cosmic triad. The dynasty of Hammurabi raised Marduk, the city god of Babel, to the status of universal god, with the name Bel – *the* "Lord". In the Babylonian epic of creation he conquers Tiamat, the power of chaos, from whose giant body he makes heaven and earth.

A power corresponding to that of Marduk under the Hammurabi dynasty was attributed in Assyria to the national god, Ashur, who legitimated the wars of the Assyrians. Ashur represents the main special element in Assyrian religion, which was strongly coloured by the Babylonian.

Babylonian and Assyrian religion centred its cultus, prayer and ethical behaviour on this world. There was no belief in an afterlife. This explains the extraordinarily wide gap between gods and men, voiced by the pessimism of the Gilgamesh epic, where the hero seeks in vain to attain immortality.

The effort to foresee human destiny was a special feature of Babylonian religion. The stars were supposed to influence the destiny of earth. Hence astrology was supreme among the arts of sooth-saying.

(iii) *Ugarit*. The excavations at Ugarit, present-day Ras Shamra in northern Syria, occasioned by an accidental find in 1928, led to the rediscovery of Canaanite religion and mythology, as contained in alphabetical cuneiform texts of about the 15th century B.C. These are important sources, because they give a much more exact view of ancient Canaanite religion than could be gained from ancient writings such as the OT. They are also of keen interest to OT scholars, since they show the religion of Canaan when the land was being taken over by the Israelites. Myth and ritual at Ugarit is centred on the religious effort to secure the fertility of nature. The supreme God was El, but he was far surpassed in importance by the younger god, Baal, who displayed his power in the thunderstorm and bestowed fertility. In the heat of summer, Baal is conquered by his rival Mot and suffers death. Baal's virginal sister Anat helps him back to life at the beginning of the rainy season.

(iv) *The Hittites*. Excavations at Boghazköi, east of Ankara, in 1906, revealed cuneiform texts in a language hitherto unknown. The Czech orientalist B. Hrozný deciphered them in 1917, and recognized in "Hittite" an Indo-European language, with a vocabulary partly non-Indo-European. The Hittite kingdom (*c.* 1900–1200 B.C.) had its centre at the great bend of the river Halys. It was a combination of various ancient Eastern peoples under an Indo-European ruling class. The religion reflected both the variety of peoples which went to make up the State and the tolerance of the Hittite kings towards the religions of their peoples. The most important divinity was the Sun-goddess of the city of Arinna. The non-Hittite god Teshub (Tessub – a Hurrian god), god of the weather, played a leading role. His wife was Chepat, likewise Hurrian. The myth of Kumarbi relates how various gods succeeded each other as lord of the gods. The rites and language of worship differed according to each people in the kingdom. Its aim was to bring down blessing on the king and people. The king was divinized only after his death. The personal religion of the Hittites was marked by a deep sense of sin which found expression in prayer. Information about their ideas of the afterlife is scanty.

b) *Europe*. (i) *Greece*. The primary sources are the Greek historians, philosophers and poets, especially Hesiod and Homer, with the innumerable ancient inscriptions. Interest in an unprejudiced view of Greek religion began in the Renaissance; cf. the *De Genealogia Deorum* of G. Boccaccio (1313–75).

The Greek notion of God appears as less grand and exclusive than that of the monotheistic religions. The Greeks' power of plastic visualization and their tendency to personification expressed themselves on the religious plane in anthropomorphic representations of the gods. The goal of man could be seen in a way which Plato called ὁμοίωσις θεοῦ, man's assimilation to God, and could be embodied, so to speak, in the cult of the Heroes, demi-gods or "divine men", which developed perhaps from the cult of the dead, especially that offered to the great lords of Mycenean times whose feats had an aura of the preternatural. Nonetheless, the gods are greater than men. They are the "higher powers" (κρείττονες) possessing all the Greek ideals of beauty, wisdom and power. And human destiny falls short of that of the gods, since they are the immortals.

Zeus, the Father of the Gods, is clearly supreme. They assemble on Mount Olympus in Thessaly, a notion undoubtedly pre-Homeric. He is a sky-god (Uranian), and hence appears as the weather-god, manifesting his power in thunder and lightning. His ethical nature appears in his concern for order and justice. The Greek ideal of wisdom is expressed in the notion that the supreme God of the polytheistic pantheon possesses prudence and insight. His wisdom takes in the future, and hence he is the great source of oracles. One of the two brothers of Zeus is Hades, the lord of the underworld, a colourless figure who rules with his wife Persephone over the desolate dwelling-place of the dead. When the realms of divine rule were distributed, the lot of Hades was the underworld, while the other brother of Zeus, Poseidon, had the waters as his lot. In the myths, his palace was in the depths of the sea, and hence for the seafaring Greeks Poseidon was of great importance. This "Shaker of the Earth" with his trident could have baneful aspects, as when he raised tempests and caused earthquakes and seaquakes.

Zeus had also a sister, Hera, who was also his wife. As queen of heaven, enthroned on Mount Olympus, she appears primarily as a lordly being, her marital relationship with Zeus being secondary. She watches jealously and often unsuccessfully over the fidelity of her husband. For men, she was the guardian of marriage and its laws. Demeter was also regarded as sister of Zeus. This goddess of the fertility of the fields derives from the pre-Indo-European religion of the Aegaean (Crete).

After his father Zeus, Apollo, who always appears in his youthful prime, was the most important of the Greek gods. His function was the warding off of evil in general, and in particular he had the power of healing and discharging from guilt. Justice, law and order in the State go back to him. He is the god of wisdom and the lord of the Delphic sanctuary and its oracles. His twin sister Artemis is goddess of hunting and in general the πότνια θηρῶν, the "Lady of the animals". Aphrodite and her son Eros were the divinities of love. Hermes, a son of Zeus, was the messenger of the gods. Since he characteristically knows the ways and roads, he knows the way of mankind into the beyond and hence is the guide who leads mortals to the underworld.

Athena, protectress of Athens, though probably originally a palace goddess of Crete, became essentially Greek in quality. She is goddess of wisdom, of war, planned and rational like the works of peace, protectress of the olive-tree, handicrafts, art and science. Hephaestus has an affinity with Athena since he was revered as the god of manual workers. He is linked with the crafts, especially that of metal-working because his power over fire is his main attribute.

The god Dionysus has traits which make him seem alien and disturbing in the world of Homer and the Olympian gods. His cult is marked by the orgiastic element of wild enthusiasm and even frenzy. The human longing for redemption is linked with the aspect of disorder and intoxication which Dionysus displays in the myth when celebrating his feasts among satyrs and beasts.

Greek religion was the social one of a city-state. Citizenship was the prerequisite for admission to public worship. The sacrificial rites, with their expiations, petitions and thanksgivings, were centred on the sacrificial meal, the purpose of which was fellowship. In the sacrifices of the Homeric heroes men received the edible portions of the victim, while the bones which contained the marrow were given to the gods. The central place of Greek worship was the temple, the shrine of the images of the gods, which was served by a priesthood. Delphi, the "navel of the earth", was the most important Amphictyonic sanctuary.

The mysteries of Dionysus contained cultic practices which deviated from the classical forms of Greek religion. Another mystery religion was Orphism, which spread over Greece from Thrace. It had rites of initiation and purification which aimed at freeing men from an anthropological dualism in which divine and titanic forces were in conflict. It taught the transmigration of souls. The mysteries of Eleusis near Athens, in honour of the goddess of fertility, Demeter, seem to have been rites to celebrate and ensure the growth of vegetation.

(ii) *Etruria.* The ruling, cultured class of the Etruscans probably reached Italy by sea from Asia Minor. It dominated Tuscany from the 9th century B.C. on, reaching the height of its power *c.* 600 B.C. Decline then set in, and was hastened by conflict with the growing power of Rome. The Etruscan city of Veii was captured in 396 B.C. by the Romans, and the end of Etruria, announced in 44 B.C. by an Etruscan seer, coincided with the period in which Rome ceased to be a republic and became a monarchy.

Ancient writers who discussed the Etruscans include Herodotus, Dionysius of Halicarnassus, Livy and Cicero. Modern research on the Etruscans began with the Renaissance. The archaeological monuments are more revealing than the literary, which are in an idiom whose philological affinities are still the subject of debate, and are mostly concerned with burials.

The Etruscans, whose religion was a syncretism of Greek elements and old Italian traditions, were considered most pious by the writers of antiquity, while Christians called Etruria the "genetrix et mater superstitionis". Its religion gained enduring importance by the Roman conquest. Typical of the way Etruscan gods were taken over is that the Roman general who took Veii brought the statue of the goddess of the city, Uni, to Rome, in solemn procession, where a temple was erected for it. The Roman Juno corresponds to the Etruscan Uni, Minerva to Menrva, Saturn to Satres. Typical features of the Etruscan Sethlan were taken over by the Roman Vulcan, of Turan by Venus, of the Etruscan god of the dead, Charun, by the Roman Dispater.

For training in augury and sacrificial rites, the Romans sent their priests to the Etruscan Cerveteri. Divination in Etruria was a secret discipline, studying the flight of birds, thunderstorms and the livers of animals. The funereal traits by which Etruscan religion was so strongly marked found entrance into Rome in the form of gladiatoral combats, which were a survival of the human sacrifices of the Etruscans, later officially declared games, in imperial times.

The "disciplina etrusca", as the Romans called it, was a specific element of Etruscan religion. It was supposed to derive from Tages, the grandson of the supreme god, the king of heaven, Tinia. It taught that periods of decline were allotted to the Etrurians, within a span of eight to ten centuries.

(iii) *Rome*. The continuity of documentation of Roman religion ("religio") was never completely interrupted. Scientific study of it dates from the Renaissance.

There was a triad of gods at the head of the Roman pantheon, first Jupiter, Mars and Quirinus, then Jupiter, Juno and Minerva. Jupiter, the sky-god, always first in the lists, dwelt on the mountain-tops. He is thus the storm-god and one of his epithets is *fulgur*, the lightning. As Jupiter Stator and Jupiter Victor he gives warriors steadfastness and victory. His ethical functions include guardianship of loyalty and justice. Mars was the real god of war in Rome. Quirinus, worshipped on the Quirinal, was very like Mars. Juno, the wife of Jupiter, was guardian of marriage and had strongly marked maternal traits. Greek influence meant that the originally Etruscan Minerva was largely identified with Athena. Similar influences were at work on other Roman gods, so that the Roman god of water, Neptune, corresponds to Poseidon, and the Roman goddess of love, Venus, to Aphrodite. Diana was identified with Artemis, Vulcan with Hephaestus, Mercury with Hermes, the latter's function of patron of merchants being particularly emphasized. Ceres corresponds to Demeter, while Liber and Saturn took on Dionysiac traits.

The numinous protectors of home life were characteristic of Roman religion: Vesta, the goddess of the hearth and the home-fire, who became a goddess of the city of Rome, Janus, the god of the doorway (*janua*), and the Penates, the spirits watching over the pantry. Abstract notions were also made into deities at Rome. Fortuna was the happy lot, Victoria victory, Spes hope, Concordia harmony, Fides loyalty, Mens intelligence, Securitas safety, especially that of the State, Aeternitas eternity.

The most important act of religion at Rome was the *sacrificium*, "consecration, dedication, sacred offering". The gifts were animals or corn. In historical times there were no human sacrifices in Roman religion. Prayer and the ritual of sacrifice had set formulas and ceremonies. The high priest of the Roman State was the Pontifex Maximus, the "supreme bridge-builder", a title going back to the religious conditions for placating the river-god when a bridge was built. The Vestal Virgins were women priests. "Pietas" (reverent loyalty) was the key-word for the attitude of the individual and of the community to the gods. As an ethical attitude it meant honouring obligations between men, and hence comprised in particular the virtue of love as between parents and children.

Worship of the emperor became a

new element in Roman religion in imperial times. His divinization in the later phases took on overweening proportions.

(iv) *Oriental religions and Hellenism.* The worship of the emperor marked in fact the end of the real separation of Roman religion from the spiritual trends of the epoch which is termed "Hellenistic" (300 B.C. on). It was an epoch of syncretism, when Eastern and Western religions combined and Gnosticism came to the fore. See *Gnosis.*

The Egyptian divinities Isis and Osiris became the objects of mystery-cults, in which Isis was far more important than her husband Osiris. Isis, whose cult was introduced to Rome *c.* 70 B.C. and definitively tolerated by Caligula (A.D. 37–41) was allotted a cosmic role as "Mother of All Things" and "Queen of the Elements". She had also a humane aspect, in which she was portrayed as the goddess with the child Horus. A third element which became important was soteriology. Another cult of Egyptian origin was that of Sarapis, a godhead combining Egyptian with Greek elements. His place of honour was due to the religious policy of Ptolemy I Soter (323–285 B.C.).

Further contributions came from the Near East and Persia. The myth and cult of the vegetation-god Adonis spread from Byblos over the world of late antiquity. Similar notions and practices were attached to the Phrygian Cybele, the Magna Mater, whose cult had gained entry into Rome during the calamities of the Second Punic War (*c.* 200 B.C.). Ecstatic frenzies were part of the worship of the Magna Mater and her paramour, Attis, a typical representative of the dying vegetation-gods who reappeared each year.

Mithra was originally a Persian god, whose cult became widespread in the Roman Empire from the 2nd century A.D. onwards. He was the favourite of the legionaries. Sanctuaries of Mithra, "Mithraions", were to be found above all in the garrison towns along the military frontiers. They were underground constructions. Mithra was a bringer of salvation. This was imparted to men through the killing of a bull, which was the source of all fertility by virtue of its origin in the realm of the moon.

Along with the mystery religions, Gnostic trends characterize the Hellenistic era. They aim at imparting a "Knowledge" which will free the initiated from the bonds of matter. In Manichaeism, Gnostic ideas were built up into a world religion. In the 4th century it was a serious danger to the Christian Church. Its great Christian opponent was St. Augustine, who was himself a Manichee from 376 to 384. Though the Manichaean Church in the West broke up in the 4th century, Manichaeism reappeared in the 12th century under the guise of Catharism in Provence and Upper Italy. Another form of it was practised by the Bogomiles in Bulgaria from *c.* 950. In Asia, Manichaeism became the established religion of the Uigur kingdom, and maintained itself in parts of China till the 14th century.

(v) *The Celts.* From the beginning of the 6th century B.C. onwards, the Celts' migrations carried them over immense areas. They penetrated eastwards through Thrace and Macedonia to Galatia, where they set up an independent kingdom. In the West they entered Italy and spread from Gaul over the Iberian peninsula. They settled in the British Isles from *c.* 400 B.C. on, where branches of their (Indo-European) language are still spoken in some parts. The sources for Celtic religion are difficult to exploit. Beside the indications in ancient writers, there are only a few authentic inscriptions, which throw little light on the archaeological remains. Irish poetry, coming at a late stage of tradition, can only be used with caution.

Teutates ("King of the People") was a god revered perhaps by all Celtic peoples. The god of learning, eloquence and poetry was Ogmios, portrayed as a bearded ancient. In Ireland he was called Ogma Mac Elathan, "Ogma, son of learning". There was an ancestral divinity, also the god of the dead, known in Ireland and Scotland as Donn. In classical authors, the gods Esus and Taranis are mentioned as the harsh exactors of human sacrifice. Dagda was revered as a kindly god, and appears in late Irish tales as a hero skilled in magic. Lug was revered as the inventor of all arts and crafts. His main centre of worship in Gaul gave its name to the city of Lyons (Lug-dunum, the fort of Lug). Manannan Mac Lir, "Manannan, son of the Sea", was god of the sea and of the Isles of the Blessed. Brigid or Briganti, the goddess of poetry and learning, was the daughter of Dagda. Celtic goddesses often appear on the monuments in groups of three, the "Three Matrons", probably as divinities of rivers and vegetation.

The Druids ("sages") held a position of high rank and great power among the Celtic peoples. They were probably priests, but certainly exercised judicial and mantic functions. Human and animal sacrifice was under their control. The Celts believed in the survival of the soul after death. Some hold that their burial practices point to a belief in the transmigration of souls of the Indian type, but this is strongly controverted.

(vi) *Germans*. Caesar and Tacitus give comprehensive accounts of the Germanic religion. Then there are archaeological remains, runic inscriptions, the Eddas, sagas, and the descriptions given by Christian missionaries. Scientific study began with J. Grimm (*Deutsche Mythologie* [1835]).

The great figures were the gods Odin (Wotan, cf. Wednesday), Tyr (Ziu, cf. Tuesday) and Thor (cf. Thursday). They were of the younger race of gods, the Aesir. Wotan (cf. German *Wut*, anger, in the sense of ecstasy), leading the wild chase by night on horse-back, represents the functions of the overlord and is especially the lord of the scalds (bards) and the warriors who enter Valhalla (the hall of the fallen) after death in battle. Tyr is the sky-god. Thor is a god of war, who conquered the powers of chaos with the hammer Miollnir. Frey (cf. Friday), who took precedence in Sweden over Odin, and the earth-goddess Nerthus, who appeared in Scandinavia as the male god Njörd, were gods of fertility. The female divinities, among whom Freia stands out, were primarily goddesses of fertility. Loki was the great trickster, who leads the forces of destruction when the world collapses into ruin (Ragnarök, the "doom of the gods" or Ragnarökkr, the "twilight of the gods"). His adversary was the god of light, Balder.

Worship took place at first in sacred groves, later in temples. The great shrine in the north was the temple of old Uppsala, where there were great sacrifices every nine years. Humans were sacrificed as well as animals. Honour was the key-note of Germanic morals and was linked with the duty of the blood-feud. No consistent picture can be formed of the fate of the individual at the end of the world.

(vii) *The Balts*. The main sources are ancient chronicles, accounts from missionaries, Church documents and folklore. The ancient Prussians, Lithuanians and Letts spoke languages which were closely related, of a branch which is closest to the original Indo-European, cf. modern Lithuanian. Their religion was characterized by the agrarian nature of its beliefs and cultic practices. The sky-god, an important figure, was often depicted with a heavenly court. All the Balts revered a god of thunder (Old Prussian Percunis, Lithuanian Perkúnas, Lettish Pérkons), and a goddess of fate, Laima. The sun was also worshipped. The cultic cycle was agrarian, feasts being celebrated in spring and autumn.

(viii) *Slavs*. Our acquaintance with

the ancient Slav religion is fragmentary, since here, as with the Balts, there is no literature from pre-Christian times. Mother Earth and Fire were considered sacred. The Russian epic of the "Campaign of Igor" shows that the East Slavs revered a god of thunder, Perun, and a Svarog, of whose functions little is known. Triglav, the "three-headed", was revered in the region of Stettin. Another West Slav god, Svantevit, had a temple at Arcona near Rügen. Originally the Slavs seem to have revered divinities of nature, and the demons of the cult of the dead and of fate.

c) *Ancient America.* The religions of the advanced civilizations of ancient America are known both from archaeology and from pictographic documents from equinoctial America. Then there are the accounts given by the Conquistadores, who conquered Mexico in 1521, traversed the Mayan regions in 1523 and were in the domains of the Incas by 1532. The most important material is in a Roman script where native traditions were written down in the original languages. These include the copious "Relations" of the Franciscan Bernardino de Sahagún about the Toltecs and Aztecs, drawing on accounts given by Indian priests and nobles, and the *Popol Vuh*, the "Book of Counsel" in the Quiché language, containing the sacred traditions of some of the Mayans. This literature lay mostly neglected in European archives till scientific work on them began with W. von Humboldt (end of the 19th century), the "Rediscoverer of America". E. Seler made an important contribution at the beginning of the 20th century, and the work is now being carried on systematically in Mexico.

(i) *Equinoctial America.* This title is not the same as "central America". It is confined to the regions in which there were advanced civilizations at the time of Indian independence. The Mayas in the damp tropical forests of Guatemala ruled the Old Kingdom from 317 to 981 A.D. and established a New Kingdom (*c.* 1000–1441) in the rocky uplands of Yucatan. The religion of the Mayas of Yucatan was strongly influenced by that of the Nahuas, of whom the great representatives on the central Mesa, the uplands of central Mexico, were the Toltecs and the Aztecs. The Aztecs, who set up a kingdom in the 14th century A.D., felt themselves the spiritual heirs of the Toltecs. But the warlike spirit and the cruel religious rites were specific to the Aztecs.

Toltecs and Aztecs. At the time of the conquest by the Spaniards, the Mexican religion was polytheistic. The real tribal god of the Aztecs was the warlike Huitzilopoktli (the "Serpent of the South"). Tezcatlipoca, (the "smoky mirror") was also warlike, but was also considered the omniscient god who punished, rewarded or forgave sins. Tlaloc ("the Sprayer") was lord of the rain and thunderstorm, Xiuhtecutli (the "turquoise-coloured lord") was a fire-god, Tonatiuh ("giver of warmth") the sun-god, Cinteotl the corn-god (cintli = maize). Mictlantecutli was lord of the world of the dead, Mictlan.

Behind this well-populated pantheon of the Aztecs, which had multiplied by the adoption of tribal gods and the personification of divine attributes, there was originally the religion of a one High God. He was the godhead proclaimed by Quetzalcoatl (the "green-feathered serpent"), Priest-King of the Toltecs *c.* 1000 A.D. in the Toltec city of Tollan (now Tula), who was later divinized. He practised a religion excluding human sacrifice and was later forced into exile by the upholders of sacral homicide. Ancient prophecies foretold that he would return one day.

As well as offering human sacrifices, the Aztec priesthood, who lived in monastic fellowships, were the guardians of science, especially that of the calendar and of oracles. The Aztecs had the concept of sin and its earthly punishment by illness or calamity. But man's destiny in the afterlife depended on his manner of death. Most of the dead came into the gloomy underworld of Mictlan. Those who died by drowning or lightning came into the paradise of Tlaloc on the mountains. The souls of fallen warriors and of those offered in sacrifice lived in the realm of the sun-god.

Maya. In contrast with the religion of the leading Nahua peoples, that of the Mayas is less well known. The frequency with which the rain-god Chac occurs in the manuscripts suggests that he was the most important of the gods. Itzamna was lord of the heavens. The figure of Kukulkan, whose name is a translation of Quetzalcoatl, suggests Mexican influences. Ixchab seems specifically Mayan. She was the goddess of suicide, which gave immediate entry into paradise.

Mayan religion was less bloody than that of the Aztecs. The sacrificing priests played a subordinate role. The priestly sciences of astronomy and the calendar, medicine and architecture, were highly developed. Entry at death into the heavenly paradise or the underworld was determined by moral behaviour in this life.

(ii) *The Incas*. The Incan kingdom of Peru, which grew in power from the end of the 12th century on, had a State religion given its main features by the ruling tribe of the Incas, at the time of the Spanish conquest. It seems to have been "established" by the ninth Incan ruler, Pachacutiv (1438–71), the great turning-point of Incan history. The figure of the creator-god, Pachacamac or Viracocha, is here overshadowed by his son Inti, the sun-god, with whom the Incas felt closely linked. The reigning Incan king was considered the "Son of the Sun", Intip Cori. The reigning queen was considered to be an embodiment of "Mother Moon", Mama Quilla.

The temple of Curicancha was the central place of worship. It enshrined a golden disc representing the sun and the mummies of dead kings seated on thrones. There was a well-organized male priesthood with a strict division of functions, and also "elect women" (aclla), priestesses, who lived in convents. Human sacrifice was rare. The Incan religion is characterized by lofty moral demands. Survival after death depended apparently on the preservation of the body.

4. *Religions of the present*. The living religions may be divided historically into three groups, within which a geographical distribution may be followed. The first group are the traditional religions. These include the "religions of revelation", Christianity, Judaism, Islam and Parsiism; religions of Indian origin, Hinduism, Jainism and Buddhism; Chinese religion and the Shintoism of Japan. The second group are the "new" religions, and the third that of the non-literary peoples, whose history cannot be traced by written documents.

a) See *Christianity*, *Judaism*. (i) *Persia* (*Iran*). The ancient religion of Iran, in which the god Mithra had a predominant place, has been preserved down to the present day only in the form given it by the preaching of the priest and prophet Zarathustra (Hellenized as Zoroaster, Latinized as Zarathustra). The dualism and eschatology attributed to him influenced Judaism in a way which also affected Christianity and Islam. The importance of the religion of Zarathustra at the present time is far slighter. Only small groups of the faithful are to be found in Iran. When the Sassanid kingdom was conquered by the Arabs in A.D. 642, most of them emigrated and settled in north-west India, mainly near Bombay. Their name, "Parsees" and the name of their religion, "Parsiism", point to their Persian homeland. The Parsees are known from their way of disposing of their dead (exposure on high trestles) and their regarding fire as a means of purification and holiness. They do not adore it, however, and "fire-worshippers" is a misnomer. The religion of Zarathustra was known in the West at an early date through Greek, Latin, Arabian and Syrian authors. Scientific work began on the original sources with the French scholar A. Duperron, who published the first European translation of the sacred books of the Parsees, the *Avesta*, under the title of *Le Zend-Avesta, ouvrage de Zoroastre* (Paris, 1771).

Little is known of the life of Zarathustra, and his dating has ranged from 1000 to 600 B.C., though scholars now incline to put his *floruit* nearer 500. The Gathas, "preaching verses", the oldest sections of the *Avesta*, probably go back directly to Zarathustra. They proclaim an ethical dualism, based metaphysically on the opposition between Ahura Mazdah (later Ormuzd, Ormazd), the "Wise Lord", the good god, and Ahra Mainyu (Ahriman), "The Evil-Minded". The battle between these two eternal forces is fought out on earth, where man has to opt for *asha*, in a "good choice", i.e., for the right order, the truth, the principle of Ahura Mazdah, or for *drug*, the lie. One of the main concrete demands made by Zarathustra is the care of cattle. This shows his high esteem for the peaceful work of the cattle-raiser and also implies a challenge to the ritual killing and eating of cattle in the nocturnal sacrifices of the prophet's opponents. There is an eschatological judgment in which each individual is rewarded or punished for his behaviour. Zoroastrianism also teaches a universal eschatology. The good are finally separated from the bad by a flow of molten metal, at the judgment and consummation of the world.

(ii) *India. Hinduism.* Ancient authors, especially Megasthenes (*c.* 300 B.C.) gave accounts of Indian religion, but like the Persian, its scientific discussion was mainly furthered by A. Duperron, who in 1801–2 published at Strasbourg a Latin translation of the *Upanishads.* But this was from a Persian version, not from the original Sanskrit. The most ancient religious literature of India, the *Rig-Veda*, was revealed to the West by the first reliable scholarly edition in 1849, under the charge of F. Max Müller (1823–1900); cf. F. Max Müller, ed., *The Sacred Books of the East*, 50 vols. (Oxford, 1879–1910).

Due no doubt to a certain sense of timelessness in Indian history, exact dating of the Vedic period, so called after the sacred book of the *Veda* ("Knowledge"), is impossible. It may have begun about 1500 B.C. The *Veda* reflects an early stage of Indian religion. The myths describe a pantheon of many gods, among whom Indra, Varuna, Mitra and Agini stand out. The magical power of the priestly word and the intoxicating cultic drink *soma* play an important part in the lengthy ceremonies. The priests (Brahmans) gradually came to be supreme in the Indian caste system, which had a religious basis.

Brahmanic wisdom is reflected in the *Upanishads*. The title of these texts (*Upa*, near, *ni-shad*, sitting down) indicates the position of the pupil by the teacher and hence the imparting of esoteric knowledge. This sequel to the *Veda*, unlike the *Veda* itself, is pessimistic in outlook. The sadness of life is underlined by belief in a cycle of rebirths (*samsāra*), understood as the necessary consequence of each man's *karma*, his "work" of good or evil deeds in each period of his life on earth. Salvation is possible only through mystical absorption in the knowledge of the one true reality, the Absolute, Brahma.

Brahmanic religious philosophy was harmonized with popular forms of religion by Shankara (*c.* 800 B.C.), who taught a doctrine of a higher and a lower truth. This was decisive in the further development of Hinduism, where Brahma the creator, Vishnu the preserver and Shiva the destroyer head the pantheon. Of the various forms in which Vishnu appears on earth (the *avatāra*, descent), that of Krishna has great importance. It is as Krishna that he appears in the *Bhagavad-Gita*, "The Song of the Majestic", a didactic section of the Indian epic *Mahabharata*. Here he proclaims religious and moral truths. The pre-eminence and religious influence of the *Bhagavad-Gita* in modern India is unchallenged. Along with the Sermon on the Mount, it was the favourite reading of Gandhi.

Jainism. Jainism appeared, like the Buddhism which was its contemporary, as a heretical religious order, whose monks and nuns were joined by lay followers. While the Brahmanic counter-reformation and the Islamic invasion swept away almost completely all influences of Buddhism in its homeland, Jainism retained its hold, but failed to become a world religion, remaining confined to India. Jainism and Buddhism both rejected the religious authority of the *Veda* and the gods of the Indian pantheon. Both movements were a revolt against the religious predominance of the Brahmans and a rejection in practice of the caste system. The founders in each case were of princely rank.

European scholars date the life of the prince Vardhamāna, founder of Jainism, later given the titles of Mahavira, "the great hero", and Jina, "the victor", between 539 and 467 B.C. At the age of twenty-eight, he left his family and homeland to lead a life of ascetical pilgrimage and to proclaim his doctrine of salvation. It teaches the existence of infinitely numerous individual souls weighed down by matter and evil *karma* who can attain salvation only by a life of absolute asceticism. Jainist asceticism is more rigorous than that of Buddhism. The precept of *ahimsa*, not to kill or injure living things, is of primary importancy.

In the 1st century A.D., the Jainist order split into the Shvetambaras, "the white-robed", and the Digambaras, the "air-clad", who originally went naked and whose asceticism is now the stricter.

Buddhism. Siddharta Gautama, of the princely line of the Sakyas, who later received the title of the Buddha, the "enlightened one", lived in north-east India between 560 and 480 B.C. On sorties from his father's palace of Kapilavastu on the borders of India and Nepal, he encountered human misery in the form of a helpless old man, a victim of grave sickness, and a dead body. On his fourth sortie, he saw for the first time in his life a wandering beggar-monk. Though newly married and the father of a little son, he chose at once to live this life of the homeless ascetic. When he took food again, after a vain effort to find the way of salvation by means of self-chastisement, he received the *bodhi*, enlightenment, as he was sitting one night under a fig-tree on the bank of the river Neranjara. He proclaimed the revelation in his first sermon at Benares as *dharma*, the doctrine of Buddhism. It teaches that man can break out of the grim cycle of rebirths and attain *Nirvana*, a sort of "dissolution" or "vaporization" (in ecstasy?), by going the "middle way", avoiding the extremes of total absorption in the world and aimless self-torture. *Nirvana* as the goal of salvation implies the conquest of all desire and the invalidation of the law of rebirths according to one's deeds.

The Buddha gained his first adherents after his preaching at Benares. He thus instituted the second element of Buddhism along with the doctrine (*dharma*), the community of the members of his order (*sangha*), comprising only monks at first, but later also nuns. These were joined by lay followers. Differences of opinion about doctrine led to a split in the 1st century A.D., the stricter observance being Hinayana, the Buddhism of the "Little Vehicle", which allows entry to *Nirvana* only to those who follow the strict precepts of monasticism. In Mahayana Buddhism the influence of the layfolk is obvious. It leads to an altruistic ethics and holds that salvation is open to all who revere faithfully the many earlier Buddhas and the Buddhas yet to come, the Bodhisattvas, the inheritors of the Buddha's qualities. This doctrinal schism marked the spread of Buddhism. Hinayana Buddhism is called "Southern Buddhism" because it gained Ceylon, Burma, Thailand and Cambodia. Mahayana or Northern Buddhism is mainly represented in Central and East Asia.

(iii) *Tibet and Mongolia*. The original religion of Tibet is called "Bon", meaning perhaps the invocation of gods and spirits by magical sayings. Magic and the occult predominate in Bon. There was a host of helpful or harmful spirits with whom the (priestly) shamans could enter into contact in a state of trance. Later developments were perhaps influenced by Manichaeism. Bon then influenced Buddhism, which was preached in Tibet from the 7th century A.D. on. This gave rise to the form of Mahayana Buddhism which is known as the "Diamond Vehicle" (*Vajrayana*). Another particularity of Tibetan Buddhism is expressed in the title "Lamaism", which comes from the Tibetan *bla-ma*, the title for clerics, and underlines its function in the formation of a Church and the affairs of State. To secure the necessary continuity in the government of the State and the great monasteries, Lamaism upheld a series of incarnations, called after the Mongolian word *chubilghan*, transformation. The great lamas of Tibet, especially the Dalai Lama and the Panchen Lama, are the reincarnations of a Bodhisattva and a Buddha. Tibetan Buddhism reached Mongolia, where its missionary work was completed in the 16th century. The Chutuktu of Urga is the supreme reincarnation in Mongolia.

(iv) *East Asia. China*. Taoism, the ancient religion of China, is a numinous notion of order, *tao*, "the way" in which macrocosm and microcosm move ("universism"). The *tao* comprises a male, active principle (*yang*) and a female, passive principle (*yin*). Man must live in harmony with the order of the world as it is determined by the *tao*. There were also gods who were persons, Shang-ti, the "Ruler Above", heaven, being the loftiest.

Cung-fu-tse (551–479 B.C.), Latinized by the Jesuit missionaries of the 17th century as Confucius, came forward as the upholder of tradition in a time of decline. He made a collection of the ancient writings and transmitted them to posterity with his own interpretation of them, which had an ethical bent. This, with the dialogues (*Lun Yü*) transmitted by his disciples, made Confucius the great teacher of China. His ethical interests centred on *jen*, "humaneness". The right order dictated by *tao* is maintained by the accomplishment of the rites (*li*). The rites performed by the emperor, the Son of Heaven (*tien-tse*), are essential for the security of the State.

Lao-tse was formerly regarded as an older contemporary of Confucius. Recent Sinologists are inclined to put him later. In the Tao-te-king, the booklet of Lao-tse, *tao* becomes a mystical quality. The concept designated by Lao-tse as *te*, virtue, comprises not only the ideals of peace and humaneness but also and primarily the demand to tread a mystical way by means of *wu-wei*, nonactivity.

Along with Confucianism and the Taoism of Lao-tse, which was continued by Lie-tse and Chuang-tse but later debased to magical rites, northern Buddhism became important. The first contacts were made in Central Asia when the Chinese Empire was extended westwards under the Han dynasty. But details about the time of the introduction of Buddhism into China are lacking. The first certain date is 67 A.D., when an edict of the Emperor Ming-ti proclaimed toleration of Buddhism. The Chinese were allowed to set up Buddhist monasteries only in A.D. 355. This made the normal practice of Buddhism possible and helped its spread. But Confucianism, with its ideal of the social life in family and clan, remained hostile to Buddhism.

Japan. The authentic religion of Japan is generally called Shinto, a Sino-Japanese term, of which the Japanese equivalent is *Kami no michi*. Both expressions mean the way (*to*, *michi*) of numinous beings (*shin*, *kami*). Shinto is essentially a polytheistic religion with a simple cultus of nature. It was the established religion, assuring the worship of the emperors, who according to tradition had ruled Japan since 660 B.C. The emperor was sacred because he descended from the sun-goddess Amaterasu, who symbolically bestowed on him the mirror, the sword and the jewels. The temple complex of Ise is the central shrine of the imperial cult. Three periods are distinguished in the history of Shintoism. The early period was followed by one in which there was a far-reaching amalgamation with Buddhism, which was introduced in the 6th century A.D. The third period is that of the restoration of pure Shintoism, in the Meiji era (1868–1912).

Buddhism reached Japan through Korea in 538 A.D. It was admitted into the national institutions after being given a Japanese form in various sects. The sect of Jodo promises entry into paradise, the "pure land" of the Amida Buddha, to those who trust in his grace. The Nichira sect, so called after its founder (1222–82), tried to make Buddhist doctrine practicable for all men through meditation of the "Lotus of the Good Religion" (Hokkekyo), a Buddhist book in which Nichira considered the core of Buddhism was contained. The practice of meditation is central in the many schools of Zen Buddhism, which reached Japan from China and deeply influenced its culture.

b) *Modern religions.* Most of the "modern religions" have come into being since about 1850, though some are older. Mormonism, founded by Joe Smith in 1830, with its own sacred book, the *Book of Mormon*, and its own theology of history, both very far removed from Christianity, is held by some to be still a Christian sect. Some of the new religions were ephemeral, e.g., the Cargo religion of New Guinea and the Melanesian archipelago, which combined secular and religious hopes, and foundered with the former. There were Indian religions founded in North America, which lasted only for a short time and mostly within the limits of some Reservations. But the Ghost Dance Religion spread for some time over wide regions of the Middle West and California.

Another group is still in existence. It is most numerous in Japan, where the official statistics include 160 new religions, mostly of syncretist character. The Tenrikyo, the "Doctrine of the Heavenly Origin", founded in 1838 by Miki Nakayama, "The Foundress", is important. The Sokagakkai, the "society for the creation of values", which is deliberately based on Nichiren Buddhism, is politically very active.

In South Korea an anti-Western and especially anti-Christian religious movement began in 1860, called Tong-hak, "Eastern teaching", which sought to reactivate the ancient religion of Korea, a monotheistic adoration of the god of heaven, Hananim. In South Vietnam the mandarin Le-vantrung founded Caodaism in 1925 (*Cao-Dai*, the great palace, the notion of God in this religion). In its teaching it describes itself as the fulfilment and higher stage of all religions. In practice it is characterized by spiritualism (mediums, etc.).

The Sikh religion is comparatively recent in India, being founded by Nanak (1469–1538) to combine Hindu and Islamic doctrine in a monotheistic confession of faith. Its sacred book, the *Granth* ("Book"), is almost religiously worshipped. The Indian reform movements of the Brahma-Samaj and the Arya-Samaj are monotheistic, and resulted from discussion with Christianity. The Yoga of Aurobindo (1872–

1950) tries to produce the superman by a synthesis of the Indian and Western mentality.

Bahaism (cf. Islam), moulded by Ali Muhammed (1820–50) and Mirza Hussein Ali (1817–92), who called himself Baha-Ullah, "The Brightness of God", has its centre at Haifa. It is strictly monotheistic, with a humanitarian emphasis on social ethics, and very active in its missionary work.

Two religious movements in North America are marked by the special claims of their founders. The Peace Mission, which strives to bring about a religious utopia on earth, honours its founder as the "Father Divine". The Black Muslims regard their founder, Elijah Muhammed, as the "Envoy of Allah".

The Voodoo cult of Haiti contains West African notions transferred to the Caribbean. This is also true of a number of religious movements in Brazil, comprised under the name of Macumba. They identify African gods with Christian saints and sometimes with Indian divinities.

c) *Non-literary religions* ("*Primitive*"). The term "primitive religion" is often used for the beliefs of peoples without a written tradition, but this term too easily suggests an evaluation of them. European scholars first came to know about them in the age of discovery, mostly through the narratives of missionaries and the accounts of their travels. A distinction must be made between the present position of these religions and their interest for the study of religion.

As independent religions, they steadily lost ground to the Christian missions, and, in Africa in particular, to Islam. Contact with Western civilization in general had a disintegrating effect on them. But they have still had important influence in the foundation of modern religions.

The study of religion, insofar as it used the non-literate religions as material for phenomenological research, and particularly as a means of access to the earliest religious ideas, has reached a sort of provisional conclusion. Evolutionist theories, which sought to trace the growth of the notion of the "High God" from primitive beginnings, are now considered invalid, since belief in a High God has been shown to be extremely widespread among the non-literate peoples. Scientific accuracy in describing the notions of the "Great Spirit" in the various cultures can be attained only in respect to the relatively brief period when these religions could be observed by Europeans. In the hunting cultures, a more primitive form of religion worships a "Lord of the Beasts", while a higher form believes in a sky-god or heavenly god. The worship of an earth-goddess seems to be characteristic of agrarian cultures.

Günter Lanczkowski

C. Phenomenology of Religion

1. In the study of religions, the phenomenology of religion, unlike history, does not try to trace its growth and changes, but to bring together similar religious phenomena while omitting their historical situations and connections. It is then strictly "comparative" religion, basing itself on the findings of history of religions, to present the phenomena in terms of analogies and summaries. The aim is to understand, not to evaluate these phenomena. It is therefore an empirical procedure, methodologically close to the history of religions, inasmuch as its *epoche* – "bracketing out" – precludes the application of preconceived judgments. The researcher becomes a "hearer of the word", i.e., the facts of the religions which from his own standpoint appear as alien.

The special task of phenomenology here is to arrange and display the extremely diverse concepts and manifestations of religion. The phenomena of religion include all the ways in which it impinges on the profane: in space –

rivers, seas, groves, caves, mountains, etc., which as holy places are the meeting-point of heaven and earth; in time – consecrated by feasts and seasons. Manifestations of the holy can also include objects: stones, astral phenomena, beasts, trees and plants, idols and fetishes. So too man: the priest, monk, mystic, prophet and sacred king, and also society as consecrated in marriage, the family, clan, caste and religious order. Then there are the rites of purification, sacrifice, prayer, mystery-cults, liturgy, the sacred word in myth, legend, blessings and incantations, and also the canonization of sacred traditions in "scriptures". The sense of the sacred space is expressed in the consecration of houses and towns, and especially temples. The world of religion includes belief in god(s) and teachings about the beginning and end of the world and the afterlife.

2. *History of the subject.* The encounter and confrontation of various religions led at once to the comparison of the phenomena, but in the sense of polemics and apologetics, not scientific understanding. As a scientific discipline, the writing up of the phenomenology of religion is a modern science. In 1933, in the first edition of his *Phänomenologie der Religion*, G. van der Leeuw pointed out (p. 653) that while the history of religions was a recent science, their phenomenology was still in its infancy, its first steps being guided by Chantepie de la Saussaye (1887). In the first edition of his book on the history of religions (1887), the latter had stated that his aim was to group religious phenomena, without imposing a doctrinaire unity on them, in such a way that the most important aspects might be projected by the matter itself. But this section was omitted in the next two editions and reappeared only in the fourth, edited by A. Bertholet and E. Lehmann, in a chapter on the "phenomena and ideas of the religious world" re-written by E. Lehmann (Lund). Pioneer work for the recognition of the subject was done by Gerardus van der Leeuw in his *Phänomenologie der Religion* (1933), which has been several times re-edited and translated into other languages. This had been preceded by a work of the same author in Dutch in 1924 on similar lines. Other phenomenological presentations followed by the following authors, listed according to the date of the first edition of their books: C. J. Bleeker, E. O. James, A. Bertholet, S. Mowinckel, G. Widengren, M. Eliade, K. A. H. Hidding, W. Brede Kristensen, F. Heiler and H. Ringgren.

Contributions were not confined to overall presentations of the subject. Individual phenomena were studied in monographs. These are so numerous that mention can be made here only of some works whose continued importance is unquestionable. One was R. Otto's study of the notion of the holy, which led to lively controversy. F. Heiler's first book was a comprehensive study of prayer, which he tried to present phenomenologically while at the same time working out the differences between mystical and prophetical religion. On the idea of God the works of N. Söderblom and A. Bertholet were influential, as was the phenomenological approach to the typical omniscient God as presented in Pettazzoni's last work. A comprehensive view of worship was given by R. Will, of priesthood by E. O. James.

The sociology of religion, which received its main impulses from J. Wach, E. O. James and A. V. Strom, has been gradually developing into an independent discipline in the study of religions. A phenomenological approach to geographical factors in religion was initiated by H. Frick.

3. *Controversial points.* The phenomenology of religion met with a very mixed reception. Some scholars like A. Jepsen greeted it as the authentic type of research to be done in the study of religions. Others, especially R. Pettaz-

zoni, G. Widengren and P. Lambrecht, made the critical reserve that it could only be studied in close connection with the history of religion. The singling out of phenomena from their living context gave, they maintained, a non-historical view which neglected the changeability and grasped them only at a particular point of their situation. Another danger in the sifting out of phenomena from various religions was that such isolation of them could miss the actual meaning of them in the framework of the religion to which they belonged. Criticism has also been voiced with regard to the deliberate reserve or neutrality of the phenomenologists: their omission of evaluations. Such a bracketing out of the subject can be at best only approximative. Some value-judgments are already embodied in the structure and arrangement of the material, as also in the singling out and underlining of certain phenomena at the cost of a much more cursory treatment of others.

Günter Lanczkowski

D. Psychology of Religion

The psychology of religion can be taken as part of the science of religion or as part of scientific psychology. To subsume it under the heading of science of religion means that the *factum religiosum* is to be investigated, here with the help of scientific psychology. If its logical place is taken to be psychology, it means that the problem of the soul is to be investigated, and that for completeness' sake the sphere of piety (the soul in its religious activities) is to be interrogated. Both approaches are defensible, though the history of psychology of religion makes it clearly a branch of the science of religion.

The psychology of religion is an empirical science, to be distinguished from the phenomenology of religion which discusses the meaning of religion, and from the philosophy of religion, which discusses its truth – its basis in the nature of man. The restriction to the empirical, however, does not exclude the need to grasp the significance of the religious experience in its orientation to "transcendence" as an objective realm of value and being. This is, on the contrary, included, since the psychological fact of religion exists precisely in this framework.

The psychology of religion studies religion in the subjective sense, i.e., spirituality or piety, the character of religion as act and the behaviour of man in the religious sphere. Its inquiries are centred on what happens in man when he has the experience of religion. Its answers are based exclusively on the reality of (possible) experience. It gathers its materials with the ordinary tools of psychological method, though adapting its procedures to the particular nature of the object to be investigated. Research is given its general distinctive traits by this latter factor.

The science in question is relatively recent. There are very impressive descriptions of mental processes in St. Augustine, St. Teresa of Avila, St. John of the Cross and many other writers, especially mystics, but methodical and scientific research began only towards the end of the 19th century. Attention was first aroused in America by the researches of James H. Leuba, Edwin D. Starbuck and William James. Starbuck developed a system of questionnaires and recognized the limits of his procedures (the number and the peculiar character of his subjects). But the material gathered by this inductive method was given a one-sidedly immanentist and biologist interpretation which showed that Starbuck was a prisoner of his assumptions. Leuba and James made their researches on ideal, i.e., especially interesting cases. They claimed simply to register facts and to prescind from judgments of value. But what they actually offered was a pragmatist, naturalist interpretation of religious experience in a philosophical perspective. In the main, what they investigated was the phenomenon of conversion. In Switzerland, Théodore Flournoy (1854–1920) developed a procedure designed to investigate the inner religious experience. It was applied to the realm of the morbid, and the interpretation was predominantly positivist and pathological. It is not surprising that he ranked mystical experience along with epilepsy and hysteria, and that he was also preoccupied with parapsychological phenomena.

In the German-speaking world Wilhelm Wundt (1832–1920) gained widespread attention with his huge collection of materials for a history of the development of mankind. But his method of "ethnological psychology" was a product of the evolutionism then in vogue and with its law of "four stages" – primitive man, totemism, heroes and gods, development into humanity – was a preconceived system. What Wundt described as the origin of religion was afterwards described by W. Koepp as "a speculative mastery of pure empiricism without waiting for its pure results" (*Einführung in das Studium der Religionspsychologie* [1920], p. 67). The first real progress was signalled in 1914 with the foundation of the *Archiv für Religionspsychologie*, by W. Stählin and K. Koffka. The methodical research here demanded was given exemplary form in the experimental findings of K. Girgensohn (*Der seelische Aufbau des religiösen Erlebens* [1921] and W. Gruehn (*Das Werterlebnis* [1924]). Their verdict was that there was no elementary religious feeling, but that religious experience was a complex process, including the intellectual moment as a dominant factor, and always an "I-function", i.e., emphasizing the totality of personal involvement. This was equivalent to a scientific refutation of Schleiermacher's attempt to reduce religion to an ultimate feeling of total dependence.

Alongside these developments, the psychoanalysis of Sigmund Freud (1856–1939), the individual psychology of Alfred Adler (1870–1937) and the analytical psychology of Carl Gustav Jung (1875–1961) led to special types of approaches. But the methodological boundaries were constantly overstepped, which could only awaken distrust of "depth psychology". Freud forced the religious phenomenon into his philosophical system of psychic life and designated religion as a "universal compulsive neurosis" which he assumed would one day disappear like an "infantile neurosis". Adler regarded God as a basic force, not infinitely high above us (transcendence) but a drive deep within us (exclusive immanence). Jung allowed God and religion validity as "Archetypes" intrinsically constitutive of the human consciousness, important not as to their content but merely as to their functions.

If a distinction is made between the scientific findings of depth psychology which are strictly respectful of facts and the *a priori* philosophical theories which appear to be projected into the results, a good deal of useful knowledge may be gained. Much has already been done in this direction. But it must be noted that when depth psychology and theology come together, it is generally on the level of mental therapy in pastoral work, while the psychology of religion is only vaguely considered or completely disregarded. Nonetheless, the psychology of religion and pastoral psychology are basically distinct. The former tries to throw light on the psychological processes of religion or piety. Pastoral psychology is an effort to draw on modern psychology to help the priest in his task of counselling.

Methods, as efforts to go *after* and trace the often highly complicated psychological processes, are intrinsically of limited value. No method can keep all the factors in view and hence all need to be completed. New methods must always be welcomed, whether developed in the various branches of psychology or derived from the psychology of religion itself. The psychology of personality has given new impulses. It helps to concentrate less on the phenomenon than on the person which is the source of the phenomenon. Role psychology, a combination of apperceptive psychology and the social role theory (from sociology), promises to fill up certain gaps. The "role" can provide the frame of reference for perceptions and thus make it possible to anticipate the attitude of one's partner (God, in the religious sphere). The examination of multiple data by means of computers makes it possible to pursue further their various connections, using scientific methods. Factor analysis, polarity profiles, projective techniques, thematic apperception tests are some of the methods not yet adequately used in the psychology of religion.

Since drugs can bring about "psychedelic" experiences, and mescalin and LSD (lysergic acid dethylamide) in particular bring about visions, the question of the significance of the hallucinogenic drugs in religious experience arises, "religion from the test-tube" and manipulations of "religion". See the last three volumes of the *Archiv für Religionspsychologie* and the studies in A. Godin, ed., *De l'expérience à l'attiude religieuse* (1964).

For methodological clearness, the question of meaning should be omitted from the psychology of religion. And it cannot be admitted, as theologians often object, that true religious experience is ultimately "grace" and being "supernatural" is outside the scope of experimental science. Even in the experience of supernatural grace nature is not simply excluded or stifled, but retained, transformed and elevated. It is precisely the persistent natural components of the religious act of the human person which are the subject-matter of psychological research.

Wilhelm Keilbach

III. Theology of Religions

A. The Plurality of Religions

The fact that after vigorous discussions Vatican II on 28 October 1965 voted a Declaration on the Relationship of the Church to the Non-Christian Religions represents a very important event in the history of the Church. In view of the past history of the Church's attitude to these religions (which cannot be gone into here), which for dogmatic, psychological, social and cultural reasons had been entirely dominated by condemnations, disqualifications, ignorance and incomprehension, the conciliar declaration *Nostra Aetate* represents both in tone and content a decisive and even unique advance. The implications of this document justify the expectation that, both in theory and practice, the Church is willing and able to make its contribution to a world united in fraternity and peace. Since the conciliar declaration deliberately deals with the Church's *habitudo* (relationship), which means that it largely omits questions of systematic theology, it will be advisable in the present article to point out, like the Council, mainly practical points regarding this set of problems. On the theological problems, see III B, below; on the science of religion (including the history and characteristics of the various non-Christian religions) see *Religion* II.

The tenor of the declaration *Nostra Aetate* had been prepared by decades of intensive dogmatic studies as well as researches in the philosophy of religion and of civilization. Prominent among the topics of such inquiries were the questions of relativism and the absolute claim of Christianity; the difference between natural religion and positive, historical religions and between natural religion and supernaturally revealed religion; toleration and religious freedom; the salvation of "pagans" (i.e., the unbaptized), and in particular of children dying without baptism; the general view to be taken of the world outside Christendom, and of "nature"; conversion, the mission and finally "history of salvation" and "world history". It was a slow process to turn from an ecclesiastical attitude which was unfavourable to the non-Christian religions not only theoretically, but in practice. In the meantime, readiness to reflect afresh on the Church's practice and attitude in regard to non-Christian religions and also to undertake actual practical steps led to the foundation of a special Secretariat for the Non-Christian Religions (1964).

The importance of the declaration *Nostra Aetate* lies chiefly in the fact that it was promulgated at all. The statements actually contained in the five chapters of the document differ in weight. When the declaration alludes to theological assertions, it has in mind the position represented in pre-conciliar theology, frequently with reference to the *logos spermatikos* speculations of the Greek Fathers, especially Clement of Alexandria (cf. de Capéran, Harent, Karrer, de Lubac, Ohm, etc.; for greater detail cf. the survey given by H. Nys). From the point of view of the history of salvation and of the related concept of special revelation, it is regrettable that in the end the Council gave its views on the Jewish religion, and in particular on anti-Semitism, within the framework of this declaration and under the title it bears. Yet if we leave out of account Chapter IV of the declaration, which is devoted to Judaism, the text loses considerably, not only in bulk but in content and weight.

a) The general points of view expressed by the declaration concern the unity of history, God's universal salvific will, developments leading in the direction of the One World, the non-Christian religions as answers to the metaphysical and existentiell questions regarding the meaning of life (art. 1). There is "perception" and "acknowledgment" of the divine everywhere in mankind. Religions must be counted as social forms which embody religious experience. The true, good and holy is to be met with in them (art. 2). In this respect *Nostra Aetate* is very different from the unfavourable judgments of "dialectical theology" (cf. the questions which Karl Barth formulated in regard to this conciliar text in *Ad Limina Apostolorum* [1967], pp. 38–40). In particular *Nostra Aetate* rejects all *discriminatio* or *vexatio* by reason of race, colour or religion (art. 5).

b) These general principles and admonitions, which are also found in other conciliar documents, especially in *Lumen Gentium*, *Gaudium et Spes*, and in the encyclicals *Ecclesiam Suam* and *Pacem in Terris*, are not left purely abstract and formal, but receive an initial concrete embodiment in brief references to some particular non-Christian religions. These direct references (Hinduism, Buddhism and Islam are named) deserve special attention because such a demonstration of sincere respect (*aestimatio*) was not customary in previous official documents of the Church.

The declaration devotes only one sentence each to Hinduism and Buddhism; nevertheless the pregnant formulas resume genuine specialist knowledge drawn from the science of religion. Reference is made to the great variety of schools of thought in Hinduism, in particular to the difference between popular, mythological Hinduism and liberal, rationalist, philosophical Hinduism. As modes of the Hindu quest for "liberation", the declaration rightly names ascetical practices, meditation and "love of God". No mention is made of the problem of the identity of *atman* and *brahman*, i.e., the problem of pantheism or monism, which is raised especially by the *Upanishads* and the speculation connected with them. Consequently, the view of Hinduism is probably still too much coloured by Christian theism. As regards Buddhism, it is said that in its various forms, i.e., chiefly Theravada and Mahayana, it starts from the radical insufficiency of this changing world, and teaches a path (*via docetur*) by which men can attain a state of perfect liberation (*perfecta liberatio*) or supreme enlightenment (*summa illuminatio*). It may be asked whether further statements would not have been appropriate here, bringing in central Buddhist ideas such as suffering (*dukka*), thirst (*tanha*), *nirvana*, and above all introducing the name of the Buddha. The terms "liberation" and "enlightenment" used in this purely formal way are not very informative, and tend rather to mislead by suggesting questionable parallels.

In art. 3, Islam is dealt with in relative detail. In traditional Catholic views of the non-Christian religions, Islam had always occupied a special place, for historical and theological reasons. This is shown, for example, by the division into "pagans, Jews, Mohammedans" (still found in T. Ohm, *Machet zu Jüngern alle Völker: Theorie der Mission* [1962], pp. 146–57). Stress is laid on monotheism, belief in the day of judgment, religious duties, and also the special position accorded to Abraham, Jesus and Mary in Islam. The text recalls the numerous conflicts in the past between the Church and Islam. All are admonished to collaborate peacefully in the social and political domain. Once again it is to be regretted that the name of the prophet of Allah is not mentioned.

The declaration *Nostra Aetate* has faults and is not all of equal quality. Furthermore, it goes considerably less far than what Catholic theologians and specialists in comparative religion had long been saying about "encounter" and discussion with the non-Christian religions. Nevertheless, there will be no hesitation in rating very highly the value of this document. It is irenic and calls for genuine contacts to be made. The willingness for a new relationship of the Church to other religions was stated solemnly and convincingly. At the same time the Council of course maintains here (art. 2) as in other documents (*Lumen Gentium*, arts. 16, 17; *Ad Gentes*) the duty of the mission which constitutes the very nature of the Church. Consequently, the new relationship to the non-Christian religions which is aimed at can only be convincingly achieved on all levels of human and social life if a new theological interpretation of the non-Christian religions and of the mission is worked out in harmony with it. Fundamentally this means a renewed understanding by the Church of its own nature. Nor should the aim be simply a united front of all religions against atheism. This can easily occasion theological and even political misconceptions. The common challenge to religions by secularization demands rather a reflection which makes plain the structurally Christian character of the modern conception of the world. The desired exchange with the non-Christian religions must also be viewed in connection with the conciliar Declaration on Religious Freedom. Equality with the partners in a dialogue must be guaranteed, without detriment to the views which the various religions hold about themselves and other religions, and without prejudice to the claim implied in their conviction that they are the truth.

Heinz Robert Schlette

B. Theological Synthesis

1. *Theme and method.* The discussion of religion in Parts I, II and III A must now be completed by a survey from the point of view of Christian theology. How does Christianity judge the religions which exist outside itself, including its own prehistory, the OT? The answer given here can only be very general and formal, since the essential differences which the various religions display in the concrete cannot be brought out here. They must rather be reduced to a common denominator and viewed in the light of Christianity. The method will be to present the main

assertions of dogmatic theology with regard to non-Christian religions in an objective sequence.

The subject is clearly important, since the answer determines to a great extent the actual missionary procedure of the Church (See *Missions*). It may be recalled incidentally, that this Christian doctrine has also undergone historical development. But at the present time, as the One World crystallizes, when the new unity of world history is making the history of the nations the relevant setting of the universal Church, when the universal Church is as it were a diaspora nearly everywhere in a pluralist society, the question and the answer may be drawn up more appropriately. The data of tradition, often very varied in character, can be used more adequately to solve the problems. The history of the development of the doctrine must, however, be omitted.

2. *The obsolescence of the other religions, in Jesus Christ.* The attitude of Christianity to the other religions is determined on principle by the self-understanding of Christianity. Since it proclaims the universal salvation which has come eschatologically in Jesus, and knows itself to be, in the Pneuma, the presence of this salvation for all men, and preaches Jesus "to all nations" in this sense, it is, at least where the mystery of God in Christ is actually proclaimed, the announcement of the abrogation of all religions. The abrogation is not merely a judgment, it is also the answer to their questions. In this sense Christianity legitimately entitles itself a religion, and not merely faith as the dialectical counterpart to them. From this moment on, the religions, as social historical realities, must recognize the claim of Jesus to judge and save them, and are no longer "legitimate religions". Dogmatic theology usually makes this moment begin for all men with the descent of the Spirit to form the Church (Pentecost). This is the *promulgatio legis* for all, though the *divulgatio legis* is a charge still to be carried out in (world) history. In spite of the difference indicated by the two traditional terms – the difference between the beginning and the divulgation of the beginning – it is better to take the promulgation itself as a long historical process. It should only be considered to penetrate the dimension of the public history of salvation where Christianity is so adequately embodied in a given people and epoch that it really constitutes a challenge in the order of salvation. Hence Christianity and its claim have themselves a history, and so too the process of becoming illegitimate in other religions. It is certain that the process is not yet complete, even though we cannot say what precisely constitutes an adequate historical presence of Christianity in a given place and time.

3. *The religions as implicitly, on principle, Christian.* God's universal salvific will is valid in the concrete historical ("infralapsarian") order. It is possible on principle for all men to attain supernatural salvation: "God our Saviour desires (i.e., wills) all men to be saved and to come to the knowledge of the truth. For there is one God, and there is one mediator between God and men, the man Christ Jesus, who gave himself as a ransom for all" (1 Tim 2:3ff.; on which see also Vatican II, *Lumen Gentium*, art. 16). The grace of justification, the possibility of salutary acts, is perpetually offered and at work, prior to its acceptance by the man who is thus personally justified and prior to its rejection by the man who is thus personally culpable, whether it coincides with its effective historical manifestation (see *Baptism*) or still merely aims at this in its intrinsic dynamism. Prevenient grace, the supernatural existential not owed to man but nonetheless given to all by virtue of the universal salvific will, is therefore at work in every man, whether it is accepted or rejected, and strives to express itself in the concrete, because man's inescapable reaction to it is necessarily his-

torical, embodies itself, finds expression in an individual and social form. Since it is always the grace of Christ, every man is a "secret" or "anonymous" Christian. And every religion must likewise give some expression to this grace. Religion is necessarily social. Man is necessarily a social being in his religion (cf. Vatican II, *Dignitatis Humanae*, art. 3). He cannot be his real self in interior isolation. Hence the socially-constituted religions must also be structured on the supernatural existential and the acceptance or rejection of grace must find outward expression. (This does not, of course, mean that such objectivations are consciously such or exist separately from the acceptance or rejection of grace.) The religions cannot therefore merely be "natural religion" – based on purely natural knowledge of God – shot through with human depravation. The religions and their manifestations must contain or have contained a supernatural element, even though disfigured beyond recognition.

4. *The pre-Christian religions.* These may be considered on principle as the legitimate religions of pre-Christian man. By legitimate religion we mean that a socially constituted religion must be qualified theologically as the positive mediation of salvation for certain men, who were therefore entitled to regard it as on the whole willed by God for them, failing a better. There must have been such religions. a) Man can and must work for his supernatural salvation at all periods of history. But he cannot do so, on principle, except as a social being and in a social form of religion. b) The OT religion was not merely *de facto* incapable of reaching all men. On principle, it was not meant for all men. The existing religions could, on principle at least, exercise these functions. The legitimacy of a religion does not necessarily imply that it only contains elements positively brought about by God's salvific providence. It does not mean that it possesses and acknowledges explicitly a permanent institution to distinguish between God-given elements and human depravations. Even the OT lacked such an institution. The prophets exercised their critical function only intermittently, and this itself can only be distinguished with certainty as valid in the light of Christ. Then, the legitimacy of a religion does not mean that it had to be accepted by all to the same degree in all its aspects. And since everyone could criticize his religion, in the light of his experience, of movements for reform, etc., everyone could make an existentiell option in the direction of the perfect religion, by deciding for what was better in the context of his own religion.

5. *Theological characterization of the non-Christian religions.* The non-Christian religions reflect in fact the influences of "natural" knowledge of God, universal grace and the faults of individuals and (indirectly) society as exteriorized and institutionalized. This "mixture" is of course very different in the various religions. But they all are to some extent – not totally – an expression of man's sin, in their specifically religious forms – erecting certain forces into absolutes, striving for self-redemption and so on. And this element is not merely contrary to their religion, a depravation of the social and historical manifestation of the essence, as in the *ecclesia semper reformanda*. It is really part of it, at least because there is no authority in its social dimension which can distinguish the religion from the depravations, clearly and authoritatively. Hence the non-Christian religions also differ essentially from Christianity in this point. For in Christianity the definitive and unique principle of its salvific force, Jesus Christ, is the mainspring of the Church even in its historical and social dimension.

6. *Legitimate pre-Christian religions and the Old Testament.* The OT itself in its interpretation of history extends the principle of the covenant between God

and man to take in all peoples. As an institutional entity, it could definitively decide against God, in spite of its being a legitimate religion. As a social, historical entity, it could not define its stand clearly with regard to such depravations as Phariseeism or to strivings for reform. Thus the canon was not closed before the time of the NT. The OT did not claim to be the universal religion. Its effort was to be the religion which God in his saving providence had assigned to this particular people. Nonetheless, the OT was the immediate prehistory, profane and religious, of Jesus Christ, who now provides us with the critical principles to be applied to the OT. Two points follow.

a) In the light of Jesus Christ, the OT can be considered as one among many legitimate religions. This is not to deny it a relative superiority in many regards – monotheism, covenant principle, theocratic moulding of life – even though the superiority does not embrace all aspects – e.g., its restriction to one nation. It should not be forgotten that the other legitimate religions could also be tutors leading up to Christ (cf. Gal 3:24), though in very various ways and degrees, and disappear into Christianity (possibly bearing gifts). They are also the prehistory of the universal religion of Christianity.

b) Since for us the OT is the immediate prehistory of Christ, we are enabled to discern, from the Mosaic covenant on, the positive trend in its history and distinguish the salvific element from what is opposed to God's positive providence. In the light of Jesus Christ we can recognize a religion of the OT which is "fully" legitimate in the order of the history of revelation and salvation, though provisional. The main criteria are the establishment of the canon of the OT and the Christocentric hermeneutics of the OT as Scripture. This gives the OT a character which cannot be allowed in precisely the same sense to other legitimate religions.

7. *Post-Christian religions.* If we prescind from Judaism, which is a special case – a post-Christian OT rejecting Christ – the post-Christian religions are more and more influenced by Christianity, in the development of their doctrines and their religious acts. In Islam Christianity was at least partially constitutive of its original impulse. Hence even where they refuse to be absorbed into the message of Christianity, their hidden Christianity grows, embracing also the social and institutional sphere, just as the Christian Church is stimulated to further development and a clearer self-understanding by the impulses which it receives from these religions and their cultural background. Further, it is to be foreseen that the technology of modern civilization, the unification of world history and the process of secularization will mean the disappearance of the local religions of nature. There should be a far-reaching convergence and at the same time the continued separation of the great world religions. Christianity, in the light of its origin, can foresee no end within the world to its situation of struggle, which probably implies opposition from the other religions as well as from atheism. Convergence and separation will coexist with a world-wide atheism. The mission of Christianity must not be aimed merely at individual conversions, but must strive for the further convergence – from both sides – to meet the challenge of atheism, the anti-religion of the future, which owes its existence in part to Christianity. But what holds good for the continued existence of the non-Christian religions will be also true in a way of this anti-religion. As regards Vatican II, see III A; but the statements of the Council represent merely a stage in a process of theological reflection which is only starting.

Adolf Darlap

C. Theological (Normative) Concept of Religion

1. *The question.* How must religion be in order to be in reality what it ought to be? This question cannot (since it refers to a concrete situation) be given an *a priori* philosophical answer (although the Christian philosophy of religion cannot be entirely dispensed with in regard to this question). On the contrary, we are bound to make use of theology in this instance, with revelation especially in mind. The question cannot, however, be answered exclusively by theology with reference simply to Christianity as the only valid religion because of its claim to be absolute. This is principally because Christianity has not been in existence throughout the whole period during which religion has existed, some manifestations of which have been (according to God's universal will to save) legitimate and able to mediate salvation. Because too of the very special nature of the Old Testament (as a factor in the history of salvation), the faith of Israel could not be this religion for all men. It is, moreover, not simply to be assumed as a matter of course that Christianity has existed everywhere in the world for so long already that any earlier and possibly legitimate religion is ruled out for certain nations and people. This is not the case, since it is obviously wrong to assume that the promulgation of the Christian faith at the first Pentecost would result in obligatory Christianity throughout the world, and that the spread of Christianity was not a historical process. Again, it is very doubtful, to say the least, whether every individual encounter with Christianity makes the Christian faith obligatory for that person.

2. *The concept of legitimate religion.* We can, of course, express the question in this way and at the same time assess both the data of the history of comparative religion and the difficulty of obtaining *a posteriori* a concrete concept of religion. In addition, we can also consider the possibility of an implicit saving association with God and his will to save.

If all these dominant factors are borne in mind, no attempt will be made to fill the theological concept that we are seeking with a material content or to define it in such a way that we might have a criterion which would make, for *us*, an unambiguous division in the history of comparative religion between legitimate and illegitimate religions. In this case, all that we can say is this. Both for larger historical groups of a homogeneous nature (nations, peoples and cultures) and for individuals (even before their historical confrontation with the Christian message) the objectivizations of a religious and social kind are legitimate religions. These objective forms provide a better chance of an obligatory kind in the concrete situation of such people than other religions (even in the same environment) for existential acceptance of God's offer of grace and revelation by the individual. This is because they are more objective than other religions which may be present in the environment of the individual concerned. In any attempt to understand this statement, we must remember that, if a non-Christian religion is to be regarded as legitimate, it cannot be subjected to the dilemma of being either, on the one hand, a pure human invention or a corruption of a natural religion or, on the other, a pure historical and social objectivization of ("transcendental") revelation without any admixture of error or corruption. Even in the Old Testament (in the absence of an infallible institutional authority and in the situation where its canon had not been closed), that was not the case. We should, moreover, not forget that man cannot realize his supernatural, transcendental orientation towards God in freedom, unless he does it with reference to a historical and social matter which is suitable for the purpose, in other words, religion. Suitable and therefore legitimate religion, then, must always be present everywhere if we are to speak seriously of God's universal will to save. Viewed in this light, then, it is possible to regard even the Old Testament and its history of salvation as a paradigm for the pre-Christian history of religion, without needing to deny that in certain respects it is "preferable" to other religions.

Karl Rahner

RELIGIOUS FREEDOM

Religious freedom is the right of man, as a person, to decide freely for or against religion, to express freely his mind on religious matters, for or against, and to confess it openly by worship, propaganda, educational efforts and so on. Religious freedom is therefore a right which belongs not only to individuals but also to religious groups as such in their own way. It is primarily asserted against the State, and represents one of the fundamental rights of man, that is, one of the rights of the person, prior to positive law, which stems from his nature as a free and rational being. Since the 18th and 19th centuries it has become an element of nearly all the constitutions of modern States, and it is also enunciated in article 18 of the "General Declaration on Human Rights" of the United Nations. Its first explicit appearance seems to have been in the articles of agreement of the Irish Confederacy of 1641.

Though religious freedom is primarily a matter of civil or constitutional rights and is a problem to be discussed in the philosophy of law, it must also be explicitly discussed in theology. This is the task of a theology of religious freedom or of tolerance, which should use the ordinary methods of theology to demonstrate that the religious act is intrinsically and necessarily an act to be freely accomplished by the adult person. The social and political implications of this basic truth would also have to be discussed.

1. Historically speaking, religious freedom is the outcome of the fierce conflicts of the Christian confessions with one another (Lecler), and also of the conflicts between the Christian Churches and the Enlightenment, which worked for emancipation and secularization. "Religious freedom, which is now to a great extent taken for granted by Christians, owes its origins not to the Churches, the theologians or Christian natural law, but to the modern State, the jurists and the rational law of nations" (Böckenförde). In 1864 the *Syllabus* of Pius IX, like the earlier encyclical *Mirari Vos* of Gregory XVI (1832), condemned religious freedom along with freedom of conscience and other matters which are taken for granted today. This was chiefly because religious freedom seemed to conjure up the dangers of indifferentism, naturalism and liberalism (cf. Aubert). In A. Ottaviani's presentation of canon law, the recognition of religious freedom is still a trait of the "novissimus liberalismus catholicus". Even today Catholics very often use the term liberalism pejoratively to designate indifferentism. There is a certain irony in the fact that Ottaviani also ranged J. Maritain under this rubric. He also feared that even the *paritas cultuum* would favour indifferentism and hence atheism. In 1953, Pius XII, in his "Allocution on Tolerance", rejected religious freedom, basing himself on the primacy of truth over freedom and repeating the traditional opinion that only truth had rights, but not error. The sharp conflicts during the Second Vatican Council (see Pavan) still reflect the older views, and in view of this background it should be noted with a certain admiration that the declaration *Dignitatis Humanae*, with the carefully elaborated title, "De iure personarum et communitatum ad libertatem socialem et civilem in re religiosa", was passed

with relative unanimity on 7 December 1965, towards the end of the fourth session.

From the point of view of the history of ideas, and also from that of intrinsic coherence, religious freedom, like freedom in general, is founded on biblical anthropology, soteriology and eschatology, and on the resulting positive fundamental esteem for the individual as such. But various developments in history and the social order, which cannot be pursued here, had first to take place before the basic religious and theological convictions as to the dignity of the individual, of conscience, of freedom, of equality before God, of love (especially love of enemies), of brotherliness, etc., could have full play. It was only at the end of a long evolution that theologians grasped the full scope of the rights of the individual and of religious groups outside the Church, and hence the civil, political and finally the theological desirability of religious freedom.

2. We must pay attention to the position which as a result of the recent development of doctrine was adopted by the declaration *Dignitatis Humanae*. In the traditional doctrinal discussion, the main problem was that the revelation of God had been given authoritatively in history. It had to claim, through the Church as the authorized instrument, the obedience of all men. Hence a subjective, arbitrary choice or rejection of religion could not be admitted. This argument overlooks the fact that "revelation" is not as evident and assimilable as the theorem of Pythagoras, and also that it is precisely what gives man his full freedom, so that it presupposes, makes possible and expects freedom, particularly in such a fundamental demand as is made by religion. The Council's declaration, however, made a certain concession to the traditional views, insofar as it insisted on man's duty to seek for the true religion, that is, basically, the truth as such (arts. 1–3). This paves the way – without prejudice to "dogmatic intolerance" (Pribilla) – for the recognition of "civil" tolerance, which here means social and political tolerance.

Religious freedom is therefore understood formally as "immunity from coercion in civil society" (art. 1). This definition, which is clear in its purpose, but obscurely worded, has as its background (like the whole declaration) the difficulty of proclaiming religious freedom in such a way that States with attitudes as different to religion as the Soviet Union and Spain could be addressed at the same time (see art. 6). In spite of the remarkable diplomatic eloquence of the document it must remain debatable whether the language aimed at was successfully achieved. The terms "religion" and "society" are used in a sense which cannot be considered sufficiently clear. And the reflections on the philosophy of law and of society in the first part (arts. 2–8) are on a level whose intention is plain but whose argument could not be perspicuous and of wide appeal. Terms such as revelation, word of God, and *lex divina* only possess authority and motivating force within the Church, but not for "others". These difficulties primarily concern the methods.

When one envisages the series of problems contained in the justification of religious freedom, it may be said that the explanations are clear and apt for the pastoral instruction of Catholics. This is true especially of the assertion of the "social nature" of man (arts. 3 and 4). The terminology recalls the traditional teaching on natural law, but seems to exploit it rather phenomenologically and pragmatically. In any case, the right to religious freedom both of the individual and of the religious *communitates* – a formal designation which comprises both the non-Christian religions and the Christian denominations, with the Catholic religious orders and congregations – is justified or confirmed.

One element of religious freedom is that "in spreading religious faith ... everyone ought at all times to refrain from any manner of action which might seem to carry a hint of coercion or of a kind of persuasion that would be dishonourable or unworthy, especially when dealing with poor or uneducated people. Such a manner of action would have to be considered an abuse of one's own right and a violation of the right of others" (art. 4). This assertion represents a very grave warning, which affirms that all efforts at disseminating religion must conform to the criteria of freedom and honesty.

The declaration mentions specifically the right of religious bodies to organize their interior structure, to choose their own officials, to acquire property, to public worship, to educational, cultural and charitable activities (art. 4), and the right of parents "to determine, in accordance with their own religious beliefs, the kind of education that their children are to receive" (art. 5).

Certain privileges enjoyed by a religion thanks to the special (historical and cultural) situation of certain nations are left untouched, insofar as the right to religious freedom is acknowledged and granted to all citizens and religious bodies, i.e., to minorities (art. 6). All coercion and all impediments to religious practice from the side of civil authority are condemned (art. 6), but a warning is uttered about abuses which could occur under the cloak of religious freedom (art. 7). Where "genuine public peace" is endangered, the civil power must intervene for the sake of the *bonum commune* (art. 7). The considerations of art. 7 seem somewhat abstract and dangerous, because they open up a wide field of action to the State (Pavan). And it is not clear what is meant by the "iustus ordo publicus" (arts. 2, 3 and many allusions), of which it is said that it must not be endangered by the practice of religious freedom (see *Church and State*).

The second part of the declaration contains theological considerations. In conjunction with the reference to the growing interest in the person or subjectivity in the modern era (cf. art. 1), it is noteworthy that art. 9 says that religious freedom is only implicit in Scripture and became a clear principle of human reason only after the "experiences of centuries". This shows that the Council was aware of the difficulties of a traditional proof from history and tradition, and that it also recognized at this point the principle of "historicity" or of doctrinal development in the Church. The Council affirms that God asks for the free decision of conscience, that Jesus refused all means of compulsion, either by miracles or political power, but that consideration must be had for the weak (art. 11). Hence the approach which seeks to convert non-Christians is described by the metaphor of "invitation" (art. 14). This shows that the affirmation of the right to religious freedom throws more light on the theory and practice of the Church's mission than was possible in the days when religious freedom was not accepted.

The element of self-criticism in art. 12 is particularly noteworthy. In the people of God, in the course of its earthly pilgrimage, there were "at times" certain "ways of acting which were less in accord with the spirit of the gospel and even opposed to it". The statement is certainly to be welcomed, and must be read also between the lines. But in the light of the facts of history in many countries it must appear as very colourless.

With regard to the argument of the theological section of *Dignitatis Humanae* it has been rightly pointed out that the argument from the freedom of the personal act of faith to religious freedom in the sense of modern constitutions is not compelling.

3. It may therefore be said that the Council's Declaration on Religious Freedom has brought a most important

truth to the forefront in the mind of the Catholic Church (cf. the earlier *Pacem in Terris*, art. 14). The Church demands religious freedom not only for itself but for all men, as a fundamental human right (art. 6). It aims thereby at helping to produce a society universally based on true freedom, justice and solidarity, in which alone the sincere effort for (religious) truth can be made in fitting form, and in which the religious act – like the rejection of religion – can be truly itself, the free, responsible ("existentiell") "private affair" of each person. But the Council also considers the religious bodies as such and affirms their rights and duties on the human and political plane as well as on the religious. In this perspective, the Declaration on Religious Freedom forms a unity with the Declaration on the Relationship of the Church to Non-Christian Religions, the Dogmatic Constitution on the Church, the Pastoral Constitution on the Church in the Modern World, and the Decree on the Church's Missionary Activity. They form together the legal basis, as it were, on which a future may be possible in which man can seek for absolute (religious) truth and social justice, and can live in peace, free from all repression. But this possibility is still endangered by the very truth which *Dignitatis Humanae* presupposes and defends, that of human liberty.

It remains to be noted that the seriousness of the Council's statements with regard to religious liberty in particular will be measured by the readiness of the Church itself to allow room for "religious freedom" within its own walls. Will the Church really become a "free country" on the theological, spiritual, cultural, intellectual and psychological level? Or must freedom be sacrificed there on the altar of a truth formulated in the letter? Since the Church considers the "inviolable rights of man" (art. 6) as a fundamental prior datum, it cannot but assert and maintain such rights, even within its own realm. They are prior to positive law and hence, theologically speaking, of divine right. It must insert them in appropriate fashion into its own internal law, as a protection against all abuses. But if in the concrete life of the Church – whose theological self-understanding has been given such impressive and promising expression in *Lumen Gentium* – all of its members cannot be truly free, free from fear, suspicion and supervision, and protected against the dangers from "false brethren" (2 Cor 11:26), the Church in its role of advocate of social and civil liberties would have to remain suspect.

Heinz Robert Schlette

RELIGIOUS ORDERS

A. Origins of Monasticism

Religious associations such as existed in the Jewish or pagan world are no longer considered possible origins of Christian monasticism. And no continuity with the *vita communis* of the primitive Church can be demonstrated, though the asceticism of the early Church was often invoked in the course of monastic history as a model for reforms. The starting-points are rather to be sought in the ascetics within the Church, living alone or in groups, who appeared in the Near East and in Africa in the 2nd century and in the West at the end of the 3rd. The basic traits of their asceticism are depicted by Origen: constant meditation on the other world, aiming at a mystical vision of God (γνῶσις); renunciation of the world by abstaining from sexual intercourse, and from the exercise of a worldly calling and possession of goods; extreme austerity in the use of the necessities of life; the practice of the perfection of certain virtues, especially humility, self-denial and continence. Shortly after the middle of the 3rd century the ascetics in the East began to withdraw from inhabited places, and the withdrawal to the desert probably began about the same time. The external characteristic of the monk was his withdrawal from human society (ἀπόταξις).

Anthony was not the founder of monasticism but the continuator of an existing tradition. But the *Vita Antonii* by Athanasius gives us our first clear picture of withdrawal to the desert, though it is not wholly objective, as may be seen from the *Apophthegmata Patrum*. Life in the desert of Scete, with its biblical models in Elijah and John the Baptist, was considered to be the highest possible level of the following of Christ, a protection against unnecessary distraction and temptation. The cell ensured inward peace, primitive handicrafts occupied the burdensome body and there was enough contact among the hermits to provide the necessary brotherly aid. The most important principles of monastic life were thus established. The desire to imitate the primitive Church led to the founding of the first coenobium by Pachomius in Egypt (*c.* 323) at Tabennisi. The common order of the day in a settlement cut off from the outside world led to a greater degree of mutual aid and of obedience to the directions of the elders. The eremitical and coenobitical life were the two basic components which were to be reflected in various proportions in all later forms of religious life.

From the middle of the 4th century on, the ascetic in the community, the hermit in the desert and the coenobite in the monastery were firmly-established elements in Church order, the hermit being the most highly esteemed. A stay in the colony of hermits in the Nitrian desert was used by many as a trial period and a preparation for the much severer conditions of isolation in the desert of Scete. As the form of life practised in the colonies of hermits was taken up in Palestine (Hilarion in Gaza, Chariton in the Judean desert) and then in Asia Minor, it gradually crystallized into the coenobitic. Basil the Great opposed the total isolation of the anchorites as an ascetic ideal, on the ground that the commandment of love of the neighbour could not be fulfilled in it. He also held that only coenobites could be the beneficiaries of the charismatic gifts of monks. The principles of Basil – and of Dorotheus of Gaza (6th century) – were taken up again by Theodore of Studios (9th century). He too regarded common life as the ideal, and the code of rules which he drew up for his monastery were meant to safeguard the intrinsic values of the coenobitical life. The impulses given by Basil and Theodore led to the two main forms of monastic life in the East. But neither could totally repress the desire of the Eastern monk to seek his ultimate perfection in the asceticism of the hermit. The ideals of the Egyptian hermits and the counterpoise created by Basil gave rise to the extraordinary breath of variations in Eastern monasticism, ranging from charitable institutions to eremitical settlements in the precincts of most of the monasteries.

Familiarity with the *Vita Antonii* of Athanasius supplied important impulses to monastic life in the West. But its initial stages were not marked by the decisive step of withdrawal to the desert, and there was no clear distinction between a group of ascetics in the community and an eremitical movement away from the centres of population. Typical examples are already to be found in the Latin monasteries of Jerome at Bethlehem and Rufinus of Aquileia at Jerusalem at the beginning of the 5th century. They were coenobitical communities near the cities, with no thought of eremitical isolation, finding spiritual activities quite compatible with their special type of ascetical life. They had no noticeable influence on Eastern monasticism, but their translations made the thought of the Eastern Church accessible to the West. Jerome translated the Rule of Pachomius and Rufinus the Rule of Basil. The ideals of the fathers of the desert, in the theological form given them by Evagrius of Pontus (*c.* 500), became familiar to the West through the work of John Cassian. After long stays in Palestine and Egypt, Cassian founded a monastery at St. Victor of Marseilles, where he wrote the *Collationes Patrum*, 426–28, a collection, with commentaries, of the most important sayings of the desert fathers, which he presented to his monks to introduce them to the spirit of the *Apophthegmata.* Thus the notion of contemplative vision, as striven after by the anchorites, gained entry into Western monasticism. It may have been due to the inclination of the West to stabilize its asceticism within juridical limits that Cassian foresaw the realization of the ideal only within the framework of monastic life.

But it would be wrong to think that Western monasticism sprang only from Eastern asceticism. Along with the type introduced by Cassian, based on many generations of experience, which spread from Lérins up the valley of the Rhone, there was also a form of asceticism proper to the West. It grew out of communities of ascetics in the Church and took some time to recognize that the monastic state was a special form of Christian life. If one prescinds from the charge of heresy, this was the problem of the Priscillianists. Then there were groups of ascetics in northern Italy (one of whom was Eusebius of Vercelli) on which the monasticism of Augustine and of Martin of Tours was based. After 396, Augustine took his monks with him to the see of Hippo and expected all the clerics of his diocese to live in monastic communities. After 375, Martin transferred his see, for all practical purposes, to his second monastery at Marmoutier and used monks to carry out missionary work in Gaul. This pastoral activity so foreign to early monasticism in the East, and the lack of clear distinction between the monastery and the ordinary Church administration, were sharply criticized by the monks of Lérins.

With Caesarius of Arles and his Rule, the influence of Lérins was extended in the first half of the 6th century outside the valley of the Rhone. The decrees of the Council of Chalcedon, urging the rights of the bishops to the inspection of monasteries, were welcomed and supported by these monks. But the monasticism of Martin developed in the direction of Spain and very probably of Ireland. In the 5th century, Ninian was strongly influenced by the monasticism of Martin, as was Patrick by that of Lérins. It is known that Ninian carried on missionary work in Ireland from Candida Casa, but did not aim at setting up a regular hierarchy. In the 7th century the name of Patrick was linked to efforts to enhance the authority of the hierarchy, which suggests that the Church order introduced by Patrick had succumbed in the (poorly documented) interval to the missionary practice of Ninian. At any rate, in the 6th century the main pastoral work in Ireland was carried on by monastic communities, which included bishops, but under the jurisdiction of the abbot. Irish monasticism reintroduced to the Continent a pastoral ministry carried on by monks. The writings of Martin of Braga are clearly influenced by Cassian and Caesarius. But his monastery of Dumium, with its own bishops for the *familia servorum* after 559 is a late aftermath of the monasticism of Martin, which was to develop into a regular system under Fructuosus of Braga in the 7th century.

The *Collationes* of Cassian and the single text into which Rufin had combined the two Rules of Basil were still not really "Rules". They were merely general directives whose application was left to the abbot or the individual monk in each particular case. They were combined at times with other directives and rules which had the binding force of house rules, and thus provided an ideal of the monk. Sometimes parts of various Rules were combined into a new Rule. The origin of the *Regula Benedicti* in the second quarter of the 6th century is to be ascribed to this practice of the observance of *regulae mixtae*. It is still not certain that the text ascribed to Benedict of Nursia is really due to this author. But it has been proved that Gregory the Great, the biographer of Benedict, was not a Benedictine and hence that the monks whom he sent to evangelize Britain were not Benedictines. The spread of the Benedictine Rule presents unsolved problems since these findings. It is found in the centre of the Merovingian kingdom at the beginning of the 7th century, but always combined with the Rule of Columbanus. Columbanus had brought the main stream of the wandering monks from Ireland to the Continent at the beginning of the 6th century, founding Luxeuil as a model of rigorous asceticism. Luxeuil only became the centre of the Merovingian reform after 614, when abbots of Frankish origin linked the monastery closely to the court of Paris.

This was not the only place where the form of monastic life was subjected to tensions arising from the forces of the local Churches. From the Synod of Whitby on (663/4) monasticism of the Irish type among the Anglo-Saxons adapted itself more and more to the Benedictine form. The manuscript tradition of the Benedictine Rule in England goes back to the second half of the 7th century. But how it arrived there is still not known. In Italy too, the Benedictine Rule was first known only in combination with other Rules. In the Iberian peninsula, where the Benedictine Rule was still unknown, the diocesan bishop determined the monastic way of life. In the middle of the 7th century, Fructuosus of Braga sought to change this system by giving his monks a unified rule and placing them under the patronage of the royal court.

In France above all the monasteries developed into political strong-points of the nobles and took their distinctive character from this function. Once it was used as a means of partition or of political infiltration, the monastic rule ceased to maintain its diversity. The right of endowment was now the main factor, and the continuing process of combining Rules resulted in a general levelling out in which the formal victor was the Rule of St. Benedict. It is the only one mentioned by the Synods of Autun (663–80). Subsequently, however, its demands were only partially reflected in the juridical status of monasteries and in monastic observance. But in the east of the kingdom, with the support of the Carolingians, the Anglo-Saxon missionaries (Willibrord after 690, Boniface after 721) spread a type of observance which was strictly regulated. The Benedictine centres of Fulda for men and of Tauberbischofsheim for women were aspects of a reform which aimed at adopting totally a Roman or supposedly Roman type of observance. The *Concilium Germanicum* (743) declared that the Rule of St. Benedict was the only permissible form of monastic life. Thus the spread of the Benedictine Rule took two forms, one in the Frankish kingdom, as the mixed rules gradually became the Benedictine Rule, in a series of stages which are hard to trace individually; the other in the Eastern missionary territories, with a definite programme of the foundation of Benedictine monasteries which were to help the reforms of Boniface within the kingdom. Thus the day of the mixed rules was drawing to its close.

B. Benedictine Monasticism and Cathedral Chapters

Though monographs are lacking on the form of life adopted in common by the cathedral canons, it is clear that the boundaries between monastic spirituality and canonical choir-service in cathedral churches had become fluid. The Carolingian reformers tried from about 780 to distinguish the two spheres clearly, by pressing for the observation of the Rule in the monasteries, and by urging the "canonical" form of life on all communities which did not wish to submit to the demands of the Benedictine Rule. The findings of an enquiry completed by 813 were used in 816 by the Synod of Aachen as the basis for comprehensive measures. Meanwhile Louis the Pious had come to undisputed power, and Benedict of Aniane was enabled to extend his systematization of a purely Benedictine Rule throughout all the Frankish dominions, having first put it into practice in Aquitaine. The *capitulare monasticum* decreed by the Synod of Aachen was meant to further and symbolize the complete unity of the kingdom on religious and civil lines. With the help of a newly constituted royal protectorate, which ultimately sought to use ecclesiastical means of its own to obviate the disadvantages of monastic individualism, a number of royal monasteries were founded of the type of Aniane and Indes (present-day Kornelimünster), which were expected to be models of life according to the *capitulare monasticum*.

In the middle of the 8th century the "Rule of Chrodegang" had been drawn up for the canons of Metz. In 816, this was made the basis of the *Institutio canonicorum Aquisgranensis* (of Aachen) as a counterpart to monastic observance. But this only aimed at ensuring the regularity of the office in choir with the help of a *vita communis*. And the bishops of the eastern part of the kingdom were not prepared to dispense from the obligation of "poverty" monks who were entrusted with the cathedral office and who lived under the Benedictine Rule. Thus the form of life adopted by the cathedral canons did not attain such a degree of uniformity as that of monastic life in general. As the empire broke up and the power of the Carolingians declined, the throne ceased to be the guardian of uniformity of observance. Nonetheless, the common life of the cathedral canons and the monastic life remained till far into the Middle Ages the only basic forms and possibilities of "religious" life. And in monasticism the Benedictine Rule alone remained, though in varying forms of observance, which were to lead to the formation of new groups of monasteries.

The largest and best known of these is the association built up by Cluny from about 910 on. The original aim was the restoration of the Aniane observance, which had finally taken the form of a sort of monastic aristocracy with what may be called a hypertrophied liturgy. The not uncommon practice of associating monasteries, at least temporarily, with centres of reform when need arose, became a permanent juridical institution under Cluny. There were three forms of such association: priories directly under Cluny, abbeys incorporated but preserving old privileges, and abbeys merely under the supervision of Cluny, which in turn became centres of reform. In the 12th century, Cluniac monasteries could be found in all parts of Europe, from England to northern Italy and from Flanders to Portugal. They were characterized externally by the affirmation of monastic *libertas* with regard to proprietary (i.e., the "King's own" etc.) Churches, understood, however, merely as a privilege, in a world accustomed to think only in terms of proprietary Churches. Historians no longer agree that Cluny was the initiator and champion of the Gregorian Reform.

It has long been clear that the monastic reform movements of the Middle Ages had no unified inspiration, though many were influenced by Cluny or received the first impulses from it. There was no question of aiming at a uniform observance of the type of the reform of Benedict of Aniane. Like Cluny, St. Victor of Marseilles and Cava in South Italy set up juridical associations of monasteries, often with the help of the civil authorities who used them as political levers. But Brogne, Glastonbury, Subiaco, St. Vanne in Verdun and St. Benigne in Dijon formed associations linked merely by ideals, mostly inspired by the personality of a reformer and of brief duration. Not long afterwards, Gorze, near Metz, became the centre of a movement which had started in 933, inspired by the desire for an eremitical type of asceticism. Essentially, the movement took in the whole Empire, but the region directly influenced by Gorze was mostly restricted to Lorraine. Its reform spread, however, in a series of waves centred on such secondary points as St. Maximinus in Trier and St. Emmeram in Regensburg. No juridical links were formed, but monasteries were more or less affiliated on the basis of common customs, without attaining general uniformity. The sharp contrast which may be drawn in these terms between Cluny and the "imperial" monasteries associated with the Gorze reform has, however, been seriously questioned.

The Hirsau reform has a special importance, not because of its wide influence, but because of the new development which it reveals. On its own initiative, Hirsau tried in 1075 to assure the autonomous control of its property by a new system of appointment for the abbot and steward, modelled on that of St. Benigne. It was brought, however, by Gregory VII to disregard the juridical system of "proprietary" churches. Though Hirsau took over the customs of Cluny to a certain extent, it sought to avoid the exclusiveness which had given Cluny such a special position in the Church. It set up a new type of *conversi* ("lay brothers") which enabled it to aim at economic self-sufficiency, and envisaged a union of monasteries which would model their observance on that of Hirsau but would consistently avoid centralization of the Cluniac type. Here Hirsau was too far ahead of its times to find sympathy, and since the hierarchy of monastery, bishop and Pope could not be renounced, the monks of Hirsau became in the end the helpers of episcopal expansionism on the basis of proprietary Churches (Mainz, Bamberg). The reforming influence of Hirsau may not have directly affected the Cistercians, but it was undoubtedly continued there.

The origin of the Cistercians is still part of the initial stages of the formation of monastic unions. It was only in later times, as the contrast with the other Benedictine monks became marked, that the Cistercians became a religious order of their own in the present-day sense of the term. In principle, the foundation of Citeaux was an effort to return to the ideal of the desert fathers and was in the tradition which also inspired the foundation of the Camaldolese, the Vallumbrosans and the Carthusians in the 11th century. It was marked by the strict observance of the Benedictine Rule in its literal interpretation. Hence the monastery was in an isolated position, its buildings modest, its way of life simple, and manual labour became once more in principle a means of sanctification. (The *conversi* supplied its economic needs.) But since withdrawal into the desert, as interpreted by Athanasius, was not just a flight from temptation but a fierce struggle against the world of demons, the same struggle could also be carried on in the service of the Church. Hence the Cistercians found themselves torn between cloistered retirement and intense activity. This also explains the ease with which their missionary activity could become support for the Crusades, and the interest of certain Cistercians in the foundation of orders of knights. From St. Benigne, early Cluniac customs found their way into Citeaux and around 1114 Stephen Harding, like the monks of Hirsau, took up the idea of a union on the principle of the *linea*. Monasteries were founded from Citeaux which were independent as regards their property, but the abbot remained a professed of Citeaux. The abbot of Citeaux was in supreme control, with only minor powers allotted to the general chapter. It was only due to the personal authority of Bernard of Clairvaux that this system was gradually transformed, by the middle of the 12th century, into a collegiate rule by the five chief abbeys, with extended powers given to the general chapter. This may be deduced from the various forms through which the *charta caritatis* developed. The desire to mark the contrast with Cluny led eventually to Bernard's being considered the real founder in Cistercian tradition.

The form of life followed by the cathedral canons flourished with new vigour in Germany as early as the 10th century. Hildesheim was almost as strict as a monastery, and was taken as a headline by the Emperor Henry II when founding the cathedral of Bamberg, from which it was hoped that its influence would radiate to the other chapters of the cathedrals in the Empire. In France too from the early 11th century on there was a return to the *vita communis* among the canons, after the monastic model. This was inspired by a notion of restoring the *vita apostolica* which was to show itself in various forms till well into the 12th century. Rules of life were drawn up for the canons. The Lateran Synod of 1059 declared that the Rule of Aachen was inadequate. Urban II made a clear distinction between the *ordo canonicorum* and monasticism. Gregory VII had the Rule of Aachen revised. Ivo of Chartres drew up a Rule for St. Quentin in Beauvais and Peter de Honestis a *Regula Clericorum* for S. Maria in Portu at Ravenna. They all called for renunciation of personal property, obedience to a superior, *stabilitas loci* and life according to the canonry rules. In spite of the diversity of the Rules, the canons all felt that they were under the Rule of St. Augustine, since by living the *vita apostolica* they were following the example of the primitive Church in the way St. Augustine and his clerics had done. There were two contradictory forms of the Augustinian Rule, which posed an insoluble problem till it was recognized shortly after 1118 that only one form could be authentic. The Canons Regular of St. Augustine took the milder form as the basis of the *Ordo Antiquus*, retaining also some existing customs, while the Premonstratensians and others took the stricter form as the basis of the *Ordo Novus*.

As long as the *vita apostolica* only obliged to common life on the model of the primitive Church, the bishops were interested in the canons regular only as the basis for the reform of the clergy. But when after 1120 the *vita apostolica* also included the obligation of pastoral work, the bishops sought to make use of their services for the work of the diocese. The older centres of reform like St. Ruf at Avignon and Rottenbuch never did more than set up loose associations of communities observing the same Rule, but later centres like Salzburg, Arrouaise and St. Victor of Paris, belonging to the *Ordo Novus*, established juridical links. The largest of these associations was that of Prémontré near Laon under Hugo de Fosses, which followed closely the Cistercian system, once the founder, Norbert of Xanten, had become Bishop of Magdeburg in 1126. There had possibly been difficulties about the direction taken by the spirituality of his reform. The Premonstratensians formed an order of their own, distinct from the canons regular, along Cistercian lines.

C. Congregations and the Poverty Movement

New ideals as well as new forms of organization were introduced into the history of religious orders with the knightly brotherhoods. The development of knightly chivalry had led in the monastic spirituality of the 11th century to an assimilation of the spiritual "militia" of the monk to the worldly "militia" of the knight. Recourse to the model of the desert fathers took the form among the Cistercians of the notion of a fight on all fronts against the enemies of the faith. Leading Cistercians helped to found the spiritual orders of knights. Bernard of Clairvaux composed the *Liber de laude novae militiae ad milites Templi* and helped the Knights Templar to obtain a constitution of their own at the Council of Troyes (1147). The Portuguese Order of Aviz owed its foundation to the abbey of Tarouca. The Order of Calatrava was originally composed (1158) of Cistercians from Fitero and in 1187 actually linked up with the *linea* of Morimond. In 1218 this branch linked up with the Order of Alcantara (founded in 1157). In 1200 Theodorich, later abbot of Dünamünde, founded the Brothers of the Sword in Livonia. The Order of Dobrin probably goes back to the Prussian missionary Christian, about 1227. Another group is formed by the three great orders of knights in the service of the Jerusalem pilgrimages, the Knights Templar (above), the Knights of St. John (*c.* 1050) ("Hospitallers") and the Teutonic Order (*c.* 1130, in dependence on the Knights of St. John). These Orders, later "exempt", had charge of the route from Jaffa to Jerusalem and a hospital in Jerusalem. Under the influence of the armed Crusaders the Knights of St. John and the Teutonic Order became military Orders like the Templars. Thus the Orders of knights were neither monks nor knights, but religious of a special type, whose biblical model was the Maccabees.

War with the heathen and care of pilgrims became the main functions of the military orders. With their task thus restricted, the passage of time and changing conditions brought dangers to which the Templars were the first to succumb, in 1312 (under shameful circumstances). The constitutions were determined by their functions. It was no longer a matter of groups attached to a monastery, but of orders which formed individual brotherhoods, while the internal organization was modelled on that of an army. The need of conveying large quantities of supplies to the front meant that each order developed certain activities which finally became ends in themselves. The Templars invested the profits from their many sources of income in new commercial interests. The Hospitallers put their superfluous money into landed estates. The Teutonic Order sought to extend its possessions into vast dominions in the hinterland behind the fronts.

In the military orders, religious brotherhoods were identified for the first time with specific tasks. This led, at first sporadically (with the Trinitarians after 1198 and the Mercedarians after 1223 ransoming Christian slaves) and then on a wide scale, to justifying the foundation of new orders by the assignment of special tasks. There was no direct influence from the side of the military orders. The new constitutions, the transformation of older ones or the amalgamation of monasteries in general reflected a general tendency to centralization in the Church. The new orders were stubbornly supported by the Popes, not so much with a view to establishing juridically linked associations as to procuring conditions where direction and supervision would be possible. The process had been begun by the Cistercians by the powers given in time to the general chapter. At the urging of Bernard of Clairvaux, Benedictine monasteries of the province of Rheims held regular provincial chapters after 1131. The Fourth Lateran Council obliged all monasteries without distinction to provincial chapters (the basis of the regional congregations of today) and to submit to visitation by delegates of the order. In the second half of the 12th century, the Premonstratensians set up a network of visitation circuits which cut across the old system of affiliated monasteries and finally eliminated it. At the same time the dominions of the Templars were divided into provinces, those of the Hospitallers into "tongues" (languages) and those of the Teutonic Order into commanderies. The commandery, first a visitation circuit, finally became an autonomous corporation with landed estates. In the mendicant orders, the division into provinces was followed out purposefully. This brought about a certain similarity of structure in spite of the very different positions from which the various orders started.

With its prohibition of the creation of new Rules, the Fourth Lateran Council marked a further stage in the history of the orders. The intention was not to limit the many possible ways in which religious life could express itself, but to direct along traditional and manageable lines the unexpected response which the call to a return to the *vita apostolica* or the restoration of early eremitism had evoked, especially among the laity, since the 11th century. The demand for supreme poverty, the growth of wandering preachers and the literal understanding of the Bible had often resulted in heretical distortions. A spirituality mostly pursued by layfolk, seeking for new forms of life, showed itself till well into the late Middle Ages as a fertile field for aberrant speculations and fanaticism. Parallel to the Inquisition which was taking shape at this time, the Council's decree, evoked to some extent by the Catharist movement, was to maintain the religious impulse towards Church unity. In the end, new forms of religious orders were not suppressed by the decree but developed on the basis of older Rules towards a type of which the Franciscan order, founded before the decree, is the great representative.

The typical mendicant order, divided into men, women and a "third order" of lay-people, was already prefigured in 1201 by the Humiliati. But each of the orders began in a different way determined by the various circumstances. It seems that the Franciscans and Dominicans influenced each other, in particular through the intervention of the Cardinal Bishop Ugolino of Ostia, while the Carmelites and the Augustinian Hermits finally adopted constitutions which, by papal directives, were closely modelled on those of the Dominicans.

As regards the *quaestio franciscana*, the sources are in a state of confusion, due to the later controversies about poverty. But it now seems clear that the initial aims of Francis of Assisi were neither a radical renovation of Christendom in the sense of a social revolution nor a sort of "Third Order" without visible community bonds. It cannot be said that the movement he launched was transformed against his will, under exterior pressure, from Cardinal Ugolino, for instance, into institutionalized religious orders of men and women. What can be seen is the formation of a community of Friars Minor as an echo of the personal decision of the saint for a life of uncompromising poverty. From 1209 on, they put their own decision into effect in free association with the founder. In 1207 Francis, when making his decision, had renounced his native citizenship. This cutting off of earthly ties was reflected in the deliberate choice of material insecurity by the brotherhood. The Franciscan forms of community life became, no doubt, with the benevolent help of the Curia, a sort of safety-valve for a spirituality highly sensitive to revolutionary movements in favour of poverty. But the Franciscans were not conscious of the full extent of the issues. As early as 1210, Innocent III gave his oral confirmation to the kernel of a Rule, which had developed by 1221 into the fixed form of the *regula non bullata*. When this Rule was revised and made the *regula bullata* in 1223, the first conflicts arose. These were due partly to the difficulty of organizing a brotherhood whose numbers had swollen enormously, and partly to the fear that juridical restrictions could quench enthusiasm for the original ideal.

Poverty and itinerant preaching went hand in hand as demanded by the *vita apostolica.* But it is clear that poverty, as the expression of the highest perfection, took precedence over the preaching of repentance in the spirituality of the Franciscans, while in the Dominican order priority was given to the conversion of the misguided masses by systematic preaching. The difference of emphasis was due to a difference in the initial impulse. In 1206, Dominic had joined the campaign of preaching directed by the Cistercians in the South of France against the Catharists and Waldenses. It was to enhance the authority of his preaching that he had chosen a life of poverty under the spiritual direction of his bishop, Diego of Osma. While Francis, in consequence of the demand for total poverty, had refused to accept any fixed dwelling-place for his community and thus being without local allegiance could put his brotherhood directly under the jurisdiction of the Pope, the order of Friars Preachers began in 1214–15 at Toulouse with a house in its possession and a small but assured income, and had to restrict its activities at first to the diocese of Toulouse. A stricter rule of poverty *in communi,* without assured income but with house ownership, was only introduced in 1217 when the brotherhood was no longer confined to a limited field of activity. The standard of poverty was modelled on the constitutions of the Order of Grandmont. At the instigation of the Curia, the chapter of Pentecost, 1216, decided to adopt the Augustinian Rule according to the observance of the Premonstratensians. But the principle of *stabilitas loci* was modified in favour of a *stabilitas* within the order as a whole, so that the character of a personal association was maintained.

The second phase in particular of the origins of the Dominican order was characterized by deliberate planning, while the Franciscan order developed under the impulse of various spontaneous movements. This brought with it a much more rapid increase in the numbers of the Friars Minor, but also much uncertainty in the interpretation of the Rule after the death of the founder. The Friars Preachers on the other hand looked for consistent support from the papacy from an early date and appeared in consequence as a sort of flying column of the Popes against heresy and paganism – an impression reinforced by a type of bull favoured by Pope Gregory IX, that of *Quoniam abundavit.* The great days of the Cistercians were over. Large-scale preaching campaigns against heretical movements in northern Italy were now entrusted to the Dominicans, while the Franciscans took up missionary work in Islamic regions. In the middle of the 13th century, the Roman authorities were trying to amalgamate religious associations of a traditional character, and also to re-model them along the lines of the mendicant orders, in order to make use of them to greater advantage in pastoral work.

Between 1207 and 1210, the hermits who had been established on Mount Carmel since about 1155 were given a Rule by the Patriarch of Jerusalem. In the fifties of the 13th century, the threatening political situation forced them to migrate to Europe. Through the efforts of the Englishman Simon Stock, the order escaped dissolution, in spite of being so widely dispersed. Innocent IV confirmed their Rule at the Council of Lyons, but forced them to give up their purely eremitical structure (1247). By 1253, the Carmelites could be officially reckoned as one of the mendicant orders. It was also by order of Innocent IV that Cardinal Richard Annibaldi united various groups of hermits in Tuscany and gave them the Rule of St. Augustine (1243–44). These Augustinian Hermits became in 1256 the centre of the further amalgamation of associations which were to some extent quite disparate: the Wilhelmites, founded as hermits in 1153, who had followed since 1237 the Rule of St. Benedict according to the Cistercian observance while still remaining hermits, but who abandoned later the union of 1256; the Brictinians and Johannbonites, founded only in the 13th century, who had tried to combine an eremitical way of life with a style of poverty and of preaching modelled on the Franciscans. The Catholic Poor, followers of Durandus of Huesca, and really going back to the Poor Men of Lyons and the Waldensian movement, were amalgamated in 1272 with the Augustinian Hermits, though there was nothing eremitical about them. But a union of groups of hermits produced the Servites, at Florence, in 1240, the Paulines in Hungary in 1250 and the Hieronymites in Spain, *c.* 1350. They all adopted the Augustinian Rule and took up pastoral work.

The important mendicant orders, except the Carmelites, became the real pillars of Scholasticism, in favour of which even the older orders, in order to compete, had to abandon to a great extent their patristic interests in theology. And all the mendicant orders, except the Dominicans, had serious internal difficulties to contend with. We still do not know how the Carmelites managed the change from the eremitical to the monastic life. But in any case the symbolism of the scapular, reflecting the development of the privileges by which the order was constituted in its new form, seems to point to deep-seated controversies. Among the Augustinian Hermits, the eremitical type ot life had to be tolerated to some extent. The contrast was explained by saying that the juxtaposition of the two forms of religious life was the criterion of the *status perfectissimus*. Behind this propaganda was the question of which form of religious life realized most perfectly the *ordo monachorum* or *contemplantium*, prophesied for the age by Joachim of Fiore. In the quarrel about poverty among the Franciscans, the really explosive force came from the same direction, calling in question the efforts of Bonaventure (1260) and the Bull *Exiit qui seminat* of Nicholas III (1279) to canonize a middle position (an order of priests with tendency to stability). The "Spirituals" demanded the literal observance of the Rule and testament of St. Francis, "without gloss" even authorized by the Pope. They upheld the primacy of the contemplative life and rejected all scholarship. The poverty of the order was thus erected into an absolute and identified with the highest religious perfection. Hence John XXII, with the revocation of the Bull *Exiit*, deprived them of their juridical and theological arguments, by declaring that ownership of the Franciscan monasteries was not vested in the papacy, and that the doctrine that Christ and the apostles possessed no property, even *in communi*, was heretical.

Though the moderate "Conventuals" within the order, who were even ready for a compromise allowing for real estate and assured incomes, triumphed at the time, the Spirituals continued to survive till 1466, outside the order, under the name of the Fraticelli.

Under the pontificate of John XXII a change also came over the religious movement among women. The call to a return to the *vita apostolica* had evoked a wide response among women in particular, and there was a strong tendency to form religious groups with strict clausura inspired by the isolation of the eremitical life. They were usually closely linked to a corresponding order of men by obedience to the same superiors. In the course of this development the forms of religious life were changed in the existing monasteries and new secular orders were founded. In 1135 Gilbert of Sempringham founded a congregation of women with a form of life which was meant to meet the wishes of women intent on perfection. Each convent had its own Canon to supervise it. This institution was imitated in Scandinavia with the foundation of the Brigittine Order in 1369. Many Premonstratensian foundations consisted of two monasteries, one of men and one of women, from the start. Clare of Assisi was the first to be associated with the Friars Minor, and the new order of the "Poor Clares" grew up around her. To provide a way of life of equal austerity to the communities of women converted from the Catharists, Dominic founded at Prouille, during the course of his *praedicatio Jesu Christi* in the south of France, a convent of women which was to be the model for the Dominican nuns. But even in the second half of the 12th century the Premonstratensians were finding the annexed convents of women very burdensome, and they and the Cistercians sought from about 1230 on to break the connection with them. And very soon after that, the Franciscans and Dominicans were also working hard to separate from their feminine branches, since the large number of recruits alone presented great technical difficulties.

The opposition of the orders of men and the negative attitude of the bishops made it necessary to seek a compromise solution. Along with the Magdalenes, congregations which were particularly numerous in Germany after 1224, there were the Béguines, first established in Belgium in 1216. These were a novel institution, inasmuch as they took a *via media*, where women either lived alone or more or less conventually, but without linking up with an existing order and without adopting an approved rule, devoting themselves partly to contemplation and partly to works of charity. No uniform type of community life developed. In the Netherlands they mostly lived in Béguinages, in Germany in ordinary dwelling-houses. What was common to all was that they lived in urban surroundings and followed a life of poverty, which did not, however, exclude private property. They succeeded nearly everywhere in gaining exemption from parochial jurisdiction, and in linking up at least for pastoral purposes with the Dominicans and Franciscans in particular. This was another grievance to exacerbate further the already strained relations between the diocesan clergy and the mendicant orders. Since there were Béguines among the enthusiastic followers of Spirituals of Provence, the Council of Vienne condemned the "sect of the Béguines and Béghards" (the male counterparts of the Béguines). The accusation of indulging in theological speculation and reading religious writings in the vernacular, without being properly prepared, was a global attack on the *via media* as such. John XXII, though ordering in 1317 that communities which gave no grounds for suspicion should be left undisturbed, declared also that the *status beginarum* could not be considered to have official approval, since it had no Rule. From then on the movement was in decline. In the course of the 14th and 15th centuries most communities of Béguines and Béghards adopted some recognized Rule, mostly that of St. Augustine or that of the Third Order of Franciscan Regular Tertiaries. But they did not give up their contemplative and charitable modes of life. This was to give rise to the new type of congregation later to be found in the Brothers of Mercy and Sisters of Mercy.

D. The Catholic Reform and New Types of Congregation

As early as in the 13th century there was a reaction against the movement in favour of poverty, and all the orders were affected by it. In the older orders individual monks or nuns could have fixed dowries reserved for them, and as they did not lose the right to inherit from their family, the setting up of benefices became widespread. This led to a perpetual limit being set to the number in a monastery. At times it was reduced to a system for providing for the younger children of the nobility. The Canons Regular in particular failed often to resist the dangers which threatened the *vita communis* from within. Hence, for instance, the Premonstratensians lost their group of foundations in the Roman circuit. The efforts at reform of the Benedictines by the Fourth Lateran Council, which set up provincial chapters, supplemented by statutes of Gregory IX (1235–37) and Benedict XII (1336), had little success. This was partly due to the lack of a central government in the order, and partly to the practice which obtained from the time of Innocent IV to John XXII, of gaining dispensations from reforming measures. Further, papal reservations especially in the Latin countries gave rise to abuses of the commendam: when abbacies were conferred on persons not belonging to the monastery, it was not for the benefit of the religious, but to produce income for a papal Curia notoriously short of money. This must be regarded as the main cause of the collapse of religious discipline.

As well as the provincial chapter, each association of monasteries had a general chapter. The union of the Cluniac monasteries remained formally intact till the end of the Middle Ages. But the forces of reform came from new associations. The congregation of the Olivetans, which arose out of a number of hermits and was approved in 1344, was unique for its time and had a unique structure, being divided into provinces. The real reform of the Benedictines started about 1380 from Kastl in South Germany, around which some twenty-five monasteries were grouped. It was an aftermath of the Hirsau reform, which survived till about 1469. An association also without juridical bonds was the union of Melk, founded in 1418, inspired by the reforming efforts of the Council of Constance and also influenced by Subiaco. It spread throughout South Germany, Bohemia, Poland and Hungary. But the reform launched by St. Justina in Padua took the form of a congregation (1419), to which then nearly all Italian monasteries became affiliated. In the 16th century it named itself after Montecassino. In order to exclude the system of commendams, the congregation was the corporate owner of all the property of the monastery. Profession was made to the congregation, and all offices were held by mandate of the general chapter, *pro tempore.* The Bursfeld congregation, founded at Trier under the influence of St. Justina and St. Matthias, sought a middle way between the centralism of the Montecassino system and autonomy of the individual monasteries. It included a total of 111 monasteries, mostly in North Germany, and survived the disturbances of the Reformation. The congregation lasted till 1802. The congregation of San Pablo in Valladolid also shows traces of the influence of St. Justina, after 1505 or perhaps 1641. Its type of observance had already been taken up by other monasteries as early as 1436, and was made obligatory for all Spanish Benedictines in 1504.

In Kastl, Melk, Bursfeld and Valladolid, the impulse to reform was given by the local lords, as also in the Premonstratensians, where the reform started at Magdeburg in 1446. It led to a systematic set of visitations organized by Charles VIII of France which lasted till 1502. The political situation made it necessary to set up the English (1512) and Scottish, Netherlands (1552) and Spanish circuits (1573) as autonomous congregations. The beginnings of this reform had been influenced by the Canons Regular of Windesheim, founded in 1395 and incorporating 87 foundations by 1500. But their influence must have extended to some 300 monasteries in all. Their initially contemplative spirituality was very much akin to that of the Brethren of the Common Life, a community of clerics in existence since 1380, of the Béghardine type. They had no Rule, but a set of practical, religious goals by which they sought to instil an inward piety (*devotio moderna*) into secular life. From 1404 on the Canons Regular of St. George of Alga near Venice had a certain influence in Italy and Portugal.

After the relaxation of the rule of poverty with the intervention of John XXII, there were a number of independent movements in the Franciscan order which aimed at restoring the primitive observance, in Italy (1368), France (1372), Hungary (1380) and Spain (1397). In 1415 the Council of Constance allowed the French group to have a Vicar General and chapter of their own. The high repute of St. Bernardine of Siena (d. 1444) and St. John Capistran (d. 1456) enabled the growing number of "Observants" to form an opposition to the "Conventuals" who were against reform, especially as efforts at union failed or when accepted only partially led to the formation of new groups. A final effort ordered by Leo X brought about the union of all the groups of Observants, but confirmed the division of the order into Observants and Conventuals, with the Observants clearly predominant after Cardinal Ximenes de Cisneros had ordered the Spanish Franciscans to join the strict observance. But as the strict observance became more and more widespread, it lost some of its impetus, and the effort to reach a still higher degree of perfection led to the formation of new groups within the strict observance, the Riformati in Italy (1531), the Alcantarines in Spain (1540) and the Recollects in France (1592–1602) – all re-united with the Observants in 1897. The most important group was the Capuchin. Starting in 1525, this reform was taken in hand by Louis of Fossombrone, the real founder, who aimed at the re-enforcement of the Bull *Exiit* with a tendency towards an eremitical form of life. The reform received approbation in 1536, and in 1619 the Capuchins succeeded in freeing themselves of the jurisdiction of the Master General of the Conventuals and thus in forming a new order. From this time onwards they also devoted themselves more strongly to pastoral work, especially among the poor, and were particularly ready to join in the work of the Counter-Reformation.

All these reform movements are characterized by a trend towards eremitical retirement, so that we can note a number of efforts within the mendicant orders to return to their original form of life. The impulse came from contact with the Camaldolese or, in the case of the Hieronymite Observants of 1422, from contact with the Carthusians. The Order of Minims founded by St. Francis of Paola in 1454 in southern Italy (confirmed in 1493 by Alexander VI) was formed from a number of hermits who were living in hermitages. They were not originally Franciscans, but adopted the Franciscan Rule, though with the intention of leading a stricter life than Francis had prescribed for his Friars Minor. The Servites also went through similar stages of reform. A movement of reform started from Montesenario, the cradle of the order, in 1411, which was given a Vicar General in 1440. This did not, however, prevent the reform from splintering into new groups, such as the Observants of Corvara in 1491. All, including the final reform of the Discalced Servites, 1593, sought to reinstate the original eremitical ideal.

A move towards a strict observance was also set on foot in the Dominican Order by the General (of the obedience of Urban VI), Raymond of Capua. It started in southern Germany and was vigorously promoted in Italy by Catharine of Siena. Here too splinter-groups were formed, as for instance by Savonarola, after Sixtus IV in 1475–77 had given a general permission for the possession of real estate. But no definitive divisions ensued, because the Conventuals merged with the Observants, under pressure from Pius V.

The corresponding movement among the Carmelites was much more clearly a determined and persistent effort to maintain the ancient strictness of observance, a relaxation of which had been sought in 1430 from Eugene IV. The General Johannes Soreth tried to prevent the formation of splinter-groups by launching a general reform, 1466. This had no lasting effects, but led nonetheless to the formation of a feminine branch for the first time, when Béguines of Geldern linked up with the Carmelites in 1452, after a visitation held by Cardinal Nicholas of Cusa. The Carmelite nuns were responsible for a division throughout the whole order in 1563, due entirely to the vigour of St. Teresa of Avila. A type of clausura was introduced, in keeping with her mysticism, which provided for eremitical retirement. And this was taken up by St. John of the Cross, who set up a male branch from 1568 on, under great difficulties, which renounced pastoral work and preaching, though this latter element was re-introduced. The division of the order into Calced and Discalced Carmelites was completed in 1593 by the efforts of the reformers. At the same time the Augustinian Hermits also split up into the Calced and Discalced, the stricter observance having also given rise from the end of the 14th century to a number of different congregations, especially in Italy, Spain and Germany.

Significantly, the desire felt among most of the mendicant orders of returning to the original ideal of brotherhood and getting rid of the weight of accretions from the past had started at the end of the 14th century. It was rooted in the effort of the Church of the late Middle Ages to reform itself, and even among the last representatives of the reforming movements was not a reaction against the Reformation – which in fact saw itself as merely an effort to restore the original form of Christian existence. Though all the orders had much to suffer from the hostility of the Reformers to the religious orders, and though they suffered grave numerical losses, nothing in the nature of a decisive break in the development of the various orders can be traced. In contrast to the mendicants the reforms attempted by the older orders of monks and canons regular cannot be considered as a return to the primitive observance. They were rather deliberate efforts, dictated by expediency, to take advantage of the possibilities offered by unions of persons not tied to monasteries or cathedrals. They were efforts at adaptation for the sake of survival. Under the heading of this type of reform, less attached to the past, comes the creation of new orders in the context of the Catholic reform. Here the Jesuits (Society of Jesus) are the great representatives of the trend, and their origin had likewise no connection with the Reformation. The Brethren of the Common Life seem to have provided the prototype for this new form of religious life, even though no direct links can be traced. The Brethren had in fact only survived the disturbances of the Reformation in small and scattered bands.

The Brethren of the Common life took no interest in such burning questions as the extent to which eremitical retirement or poverty should be practised. Their basic interest was a profound spiritual life which would equip them to serve God in the visible Church. They regarded such readiness as the fulfilment of personal striving for perfection. The external form of life, and hence the form of the order, counted for little, as may be seen from the Oblates of St. Ambrose, a community of priests which placed itself at the disposition of the Archbishop of Milan for pastoral work from 1578 on, and lived either in groups in presbyteries or singly at their pastoral posts. The same line (without vows or Rule) was followed by the Oratorians founded by St. Philip Neri in 1564 in Italy, where the Oratories were independent of each other, and by the Oratorians of Pierre de Bérulle in France (1611), who were under one Superior-General. The congregation of the Theatines also began as an Oratory of priests and laymen, but under the founders Cajetan of Tiene and Gianpietro Carafa (later Paul IV) adopted the Rule of St. Augustine in 1524, with the privileges of the Canons of the Lateran, and thus became the typical form for the Clerks Regular. Traditional features are more marked among the Barnabites, who received a Rule of their own in 1533, and combined pastoral work with a life of penance and the solemn chanting of the office in choir.

The Society of Jesus was not the first order of clerks regular, but it gave this new type of order its decisive characteristics. It did not adopt a Rule in the sense hitherto known, but the founder, St. Ignatius Loyola, finally provided it with constitutions which comprised the *Examen generale* and the ten parts of the constitutions themselves. This constitution was approved in 1558. These external constitutions presupposed the individual encounter of each member of the order with Christ, the Spiritual Exercises devised by Ignatius on the basis of his own experience being the means to bring about this encounter. When Ignatius and six companions formed an association in Paris in 1534, their object was strictly limited, the preaching of the gospel to the pagans in the Holy Land. The political situation made this impossible, and the society placed itself at the disposition of the Pope. Its scope became thereby universal, with particular stress on the formation of the clergy, pastoral work at various levels (popular missions in the 17th century) and the foreign missions. The powers conferred on the general of the order, who was elected for life, which deprived the immediate superiors of many of their normal functions, made the centralized character of the personal union more marked than ever. After the members were divided, in 1546, into the professed with four solemn vows (the fourth being of special obedience to the Pope), and coadjutors with three simple vows (which bound the coadjutors to the order but not vice versa), the order became a sort of élite, above all when the numbers of the professed rose out of all proportion under the General Claude Acquaviva (1581–1615), as the number of the provinces rose to twenty-seven. Thanks to the thorough formation given to its members and the new pastoral methods which it developed (Spiritual Exercises, sodalities of the Blessed Virgin, catechisms, universities and high schools), the Society became one of the most important factors in the Tridentine reform.

The (very temporary) restriction of the first Jesuits to a special task was a significant characteristic from the start of the other congregations which came into being at the same time. The Somaschi were founded in 1532 for the care of the sick and the education of orphans, the Camillians (1584) also for the sick, the Piarists for the education of children, like the "Brothers of the Christian Schools" in 1681. The priests of St. Sulpice (1642) and the Eudists (1643) were led by their experiences of mission work in France to confine themselves to the formation of seminarists. They are regarded as the creators of the Tridentine type of seminary in France. The congregation of Lazarists (Vincentians) founded by St. Vincent de Paul in 1625 devoted itself to popular and foreign missions and to the education of the clergy. A fourth vow obliged the members to be faithful to these tasks as long as they remained in the congregation. They excluded education and the care of the sick, which they regarded as the special work of most of the congregations of nuns. The Salesian Sisters (Visitation order, Visitandines), founded in 1610 by St. Francis de Sales and St. Frances de Chantal, devoted themselves to the sick, and later to the work of education, when they became an order by adopting the Rule of St. Augustine.

An association became an order through solemn public vows, and a congregation through simple vows. The Society of Jesus combined both forms by its distinction between professed and spiritual coadjutors. This made little difference to the external structure of the order, since the taking of simple vows was acknowledged by the Church in 1550 and Gregory XIII (1583–84) decreed that the coadjutors were also religious in the strict sense. The persistence of ancient suspicions and of certain abuses had led the Council of Trent in 1563 to make clausura stricter and put all convents of nuns under control of the bishop. The Ursulines were founded in Brescia by St. Angela Merici for the education of girls. They had a Rule which did not entail common life. In 1568 they were invited to Milan by Charles Borromeo who introduced simple vows and common life in 1572. The Ursulines who followed the Italian model in France from 1596 only received a Rule, that of St. Augustine, with solemn profession, in 1612. The real conflict with the regulations of Trent came when the "Institute of the Blessed Virgin Mary" (the *Englische Fräulein*, English Ladies) was founded in 1609. Since they aimed chiefly at working in England, the foundress, Mary Ward, decided that the constitutions of the Society of Jesus were the best model to take for her congregation, for which she also demanded the absence of clausura. Urban VIII suppressed the institute in 1631 but allowed the community to continue teaching. Benedict XIV in 1749 forbade them to acknowledge Mary Ward as their founder. This was intended to underline the jurisdiction of the bishops of their dioceses. When the prohibition was revoked by Pius X in 1907, he really gave his sanction retrospectively to the type of congregation of women for which the English Ladies had paved the way. The next foundations were the Sisters of Charity (of St. Vincent de Paul) in 1634 and the Sisters of Charity (of St. Charles Borromeo), for the care of the sick, in 1652. It was typical for all such congregations that there were many with similar names and similar purposes which remained independent of each other because of their regional ties.

The final crystallization of the type of congregation already foreshadowed in the late Middle Ages took place with much less friction on the male side. The differences which remained were really only technicalities of canon law. The final transition stands out most clearly in the case of the Piarists. They were confirmed by Gregory XV in 1621 as an order with the Rule of St. Augustine and solemn profession. In 1645, as a result of internal disputes, they were reduced to a society without vows and then in 1656 were approved by Alexander VII as a congregation with simple vows. This was the form in which the Passionists were founded in 1725 for home and foreign missions, and the Redemptorists in 1735, with popular missions as their specific object. The Redemptorists became of great importance in the 19th century, thanks in part to the repute of their founder, St. Alphonsus de Liguori.

E. Secularization and Revival of the Orders

The process of secularization, which involved no simultaneous, uniform measures but took place at various levels in the course of more than a century, was already signalled in 1759, when the Jesuits were expelled from Portugal and its colonies. It was a complex combination of political, anti-Catholic and inner-scholastic theological interests which first led to the expulsion of the Jesuits from all the countries under the Bourbon dynasty (1764–68) and then finally to the suppression of the order by Clement XIV – to safeguard the necessary peace of the Church, as the papal bull put it. Even in this early period, the Redemptorists felt some of the weight of the hostility directed against the Jesuits, since the fact that they were a congregation gave the impression that they were particularly loyal to the Pope, an accusation under which all similar congregations had to suffer, even under the *Kulturkampf*. Under the Enlightenment, lack of understanding of the Catholic ideal of the religious life led to a partial secularization of monasteries in France in 1766, which bore on all types of religious. Partial secularizations in Lombardy under Maria Theresa and finally in 1782 in Austria and Hungary were directed against "useless and superfluous monasteries" which "led a merely contemplative life". The measures taken in Bavaria after 1769 were principally intended to weaken the mendicant orders. The general secularization in France in 1790 was inspired by the financial needs of the State, and also by the principle that there should be no positions of privilege. The secularization in Germany in 1803 was meant to provide funds for the ruling monarchs. The fundamental motives therefore varied widely, ranging from a sense of responsibility on the part of the State for the religious welfare of the people, to an anti-clericalism of principle. Otherwise it would be difficult to explain the equally effective decrees of closure passed in Spain (1821 and 1835), Portugal (1834), Italy (1866) and Switzerland (1805–74). The first effects of the *Kulturkampf* are already visible here.

The faithful themselves came under the influence of the Enlightenment. From *c.* 1700 on there was a sudden drop in recruitment even for the clergy to be appointed to regular benefices. And the trend to secularization made ground among Catholics. But the state of religious discipline nowhere justified intervention on such a scale. The Tridentine reform had brought about a lasting renewal of the non-mendicant orders, by reactivating the congregations which had been so hesitatingly formed and had remained to some extent ineffective in the Middle Ages. The congregations now had the character of juridical corporations, which had led in Italy and to some extent in France to considerable restrictions on the autonomy of the individual Benedictine monasteries. The high level of studies among the Benedictines (Maurists) and Premonstratensians and the Trappist reform of the Cistercians (1664) were among the fruits of the reform which could be widely recognized.

Only a few orders disappeared entirely as the process of secularization went on, but the general picture was fundamentally changed. Since suppressions did not take place everywhere at the same time, and the process of regeneration began once more in 1814, as Pius VII restored the Society of Jesus, the various orders were able to survive the storm as meagre remnants. The orders and congregations which were in the nature of personal unions with centralized structures succeeded gradually in re-establishing themselves and setting up new foundations. But the orders based on autonomous monasteries found things much more difficult, especially as they needed much wider economic bases. Hence the orders of monks and of canons regular took little share in the process of regeneration which went on in the 19th century. Since religious life in the 19th century was marked by the multiplicity of new congregations, secularization had brought about a fundamental change in the external manifestations but not in the general development of the religious life.

Apart from devotion to the Holy Spirit (Holy Ghost missionaries, 1848; Society of the Divine Word, 1875), no new trends of spirituality are noticeable in the new foundations. Devotion to the Sacred Heart, the Eucharist and the

Blessed Virgin was still the dominant note. Some definite task, for which the other orders had insufficient resources or none at all, continued to be the occasion of a foundation and the justification of its existence, with an emphasis on the apostolate which appeared one-sided. The foundations of the early 19th century concentrated on the traditional tasks of popular missions, seminary education and pastoral work among the poorer classes. In the second quarter of the century, attention was also paid to foreign missions (Picpus Fathers, Oblates of Mary Immaculate, Marists and Precious Blood Missionaries). In the wake of colonialism, the missionary activity of the Church took on dimensions of a hitherto undreamt-of size. New congregations were founded to meet the new demands (the Missionaries of the Sacred Heart, 1854; the Sons of the Sacred Heart, 1866–85; the White Fathers, 1868, and the Sacred Heart Fathers, 1877). Other congregations, like the Salesians of Don Bosco, the Salvatorians or Pallottines with their associates took up foreign missions only at the end of the century. The Assumptionists, founded in 1854, did very good work for the dissemination of literature and also by its contacts with the Orthodox in the Near East. But they form an exception within the general picture. Most of these congregations, which all arose in France or Italy, with the exception of the Society of the Divine Word, also provided for a corresponding congregation of nuns. So numerous were the foundations of congregations of women devoted to nursing the sick and educating children that it would be difficult to trace them all. They did not depart, however, from the traditional framework of such duties, nor did they spread beyond their own diocesan or regional boundaries.

As a type of religious order, each of these foundations of congregations of men or women remained in a direct line of development from the 18th century. Even the restored congregations of the strictly monkish or canons regular type – naturally few in number – linked up with the latest stage of their own monastic tradition as it was before the almost total breach. This was partly due to pressure from the side of the State, as in Bavaria, which made teaching obligatory, partly to the continuity provided by surviving ancients from the suppressed monasteries. This clinging to traditional ways was a reflection of the general attitude of the Church, which was itself in keeping with the restorative tendencies in the State. There were only a few exceptions, such as the Benedictines of Solesmes, Beuron and Subiaco, who deliberately by-passed later developments of monastic life and made a completely fresh start by adopting early forms. It is not astonishing that they became centres of renewal for monastic and liturgical life.

A fundamental change seems to be on the way in the present century. Formally, the secular institutes which were given canonical recognition by Pius XII in 1947 are a logical development of religious life in the 19th century, since the external form of life and hence the obviousness of the "state of life" play only a subordinate role. Here the roots reach back to P. de Clorivière, who founded in 1790 the "Société des Prêtres du Coeur de Jésus" and the "Société des Filles du Coeur de Marie". But since each member pursues his own activities, partly secular in character, the special field of tasks disappears as a significant characteristic. And since in the secular institute in the strict sense of the term obligation to a form of common life is also absent, the main stress lies on the independent and to a great extent isolated following of the evangelical counsels. Since 1933 something similar has existed among the "Little Brothers of Jesus" and since 1939 among the "Little Sisters of Jesus" who follow the example of Charles de Foucauld by sharing the ordinary life of those around them. They form small communities but each has his or her own secular occupation. Since 1956 the "Little Brothers of the Virgin of the Poor" have formed an eremitical branch. Meanwhile, at the urging of the Second Vatican Council, the older orders have been trying to abolish the partitions between each other, which had in any case ceased to have had very much significance. The main line along which they have been working so far is the setting up of common centres for studies. The Franciscans of the Netherlands have been experimenting with the dispersal of their students in various houses in suburban sites. This departure from conventual life seems to point in the same direction, which may well be characteristic of the future of the religious orders. Their effort will be essentially to bring about the presence of the Christian spirit among men, in the form of a special striving after perfection.

F. Canon Law for Religious

The Catholic notion of religious life is highly diversified and can only be understood in the light of its historical development. It began with the self-sufficient economic unit of the individual monastery, giving itself its own rule of life. The fact that a number of monasteries followed the same rule did not make them an order. Orders may be said to have been established for the first time when the Carolingians imposed a uniform observance on the Frankish monasteries. This was the principle on which distinct orders were constituted in the Middle Ages: each was a group of *monasteries* with a set of constitutions in common. In the same way, from the 12th century on, groups of *persons* combined to form distinct orders. But now their centralized organization and their lack of attachment to any particular locality along with a fairly even distribution throughout the whole of the West paved the way for a new notion of the religious life. Rule, constitutions and certain common external features (field of work, liturgy, habit, etc.) became the distinguishing marks of an order. And as this development went on, the older foundations of monks and canons regular were subsumed under the headings of the "Benedictine" order or the "Augustinian Canons". In this way the Camaldolese, Carthusians or Cistercians were fundamentally Benedictine by their Rule, but formed distinct orders by their organization and other characteristics. And an associated group of monasteries within the Benedictine order now began to be called a congregation, even though it had the same functions as in the era before the formation of the non-monastic orders (personal unions). The existence of associations without the three customary vows of obedience, chastity and poverty led in the late Middle Ages to the shifting of the centre of gravity to the characteristic of the vows. From the 15th century on, only associations with solemn and public vows were recognized as orders in the strict sense, while associations with simple vows were called congregations. Associations without vows had simply a status like that of the congregations. Since they all came under the *Congregatio Episcoporum et Regularium* when it was set up in 1601, and then under the *Congregatio super Statu Regularium* (1652), the *Sacra Congregatio negotiis religiosorum sodalium praeposita* (1908), reorganized as the *Sacra Congregatio pro Religiosis et Institutibus Secularibus* in the reform of the Curia 1967, the notion of religious order became more and more comprehensive. A further stage in this process of levelling came with the constitution *Conditae a Christo* of Leo XIII, 8 December 1900, which accorded general canonical recognition to the religious congregations. Vows and common life ceased clearly to be the characteristics of the religious life when the secular institutes were approved, with their renunciation on principle of common life.

Thus the law for religious has become applicable to all states of perfection in the Church. It includes canon law in general, which provides the general framework of the law for religious in *CIC*, canons 487–681, in the subsequent papal legislation and the authoritative decisions of the Congregation for Religious. To these must be added the particular law of the various institutes and associations, as laid down in their approved rules, constitutions, statutes and other regulations. The juridical persons or corporations come under these norms in such matters as the foundation or abolition of orders, provinces or monasteries, individual religious in such matters as admission to or dismissal from an association, the powers of the various authorities or superiors, the obligations arising out of profession, the possible privileges and special rights of an order with regard to studies and type of apostolic activity.

By virtue of the vow of obedience, the Pope is the highest superior of each religious. But since the Council of Chalcedon (451) each member is also subject, under certain conditions, to the authority of the local ordinary. In spite of this definitive ruling, many orders, especially in the Middle Ages, succeeded in obtaining exemption from episcopal authority. Exemption became in fact one of the main characteristics of the new non-monastic orders, but still remains an exception from the point of view of the law. Permission from the diocesan bishop, with the assent of the Holy See, is necessary for the foundation of a congregation; so too for the foundation of new houses by an exempt religious order. If a diocesan congregation wishes to set up houses in other dioceses, it must have the approval of its own local ordinary as well as that of the diocese where it wishes to set up a new foundation. If the constitutions of such a congregation are to be altered, the consent of all the bishops in whose dioceses it has foundations must be obtained. Only the Holy See can suppress a congregation, even if the congregation in question is a diocesan one. A diocesan congregation becomes a congregation of papal right by the *decretum laudis* by which power to propose changes in the constitutions is withdrawn from the bishops and reserved to the Holy See. After a further period of probation, the congregation may receive the *decretum approbationis instituti* and finally the *decretum approbationis constitutionum*, by which papal approval is bestowed on the rule of the order. The Congregation for Religious and Secular Institutes is the competent authority for all religious, either of papal or of diocesan right. But congregations of papal right must also have a Cardinal protector to look after their interests. All orders of men of papal right must also have a Procurator General residing in Rome to represent them at the Holy See. A papal indult is necessary if a congregation of women is to be attached to an order of men. Associations of tertiaries with common life must be affiliated to the First Order. A condition for entry into an order is a period of probation (a noviceship to which sometimes a preceding period of probation is also attached). The novitiate ends with the taking of vows (profession). A number of stages of profession may be envisaged. Final profession binds the religious to the congregation in perpetuity. The obligation can be ended only by a special indult in the form of exclaustration or secularization. Transition to another order is not excluded. All houses with common life have some sort of clausura, more or less strict, by which the part of the house reserved as living-quarters for the religious is demarcated. Strict or papal clausura obtains in all monasteries of clerks regular and all monasteries of women with solemn vows. It comprises the whole house apart from the church and guestrooms. The nuns in question are forbidden to leave clausura. Congregations and associations without vows have a less stringent form of clausura.

Odilo Engels

RESPONSIBILITY

1. Responsibility obviously has to do with answering (for something, to somebody). More profoundly, it means disclosing oneself when one's action and, through it, one's own self are called in question. Responsibility is therefore a specific personal attitude, since only a person can be called in question by another. There can be only indirect responsibility with regard to things, where one's treatment of things has to be answered for to another. Responsibility only enters in insofar as one can be called in question by another with regard to oneself and one's action, and insofar as one can answer this summons.

In the radical and definitive sense, man can only be responsible before God, since only God can call man totally in question, and man in turn may deliver himself up totally only to God. One can speak of God's responsibility to man only in an improper sense, since, though God discloses himself to man through creation and through his self-communication in grace, he cannot be called in question by man, but can at most be rejected. Responsibility towards oneself and one's fellowman can exist insofar as man can be called in question by himself or by others. But it is limited by one's power over oneself and others.

Theology asserts this truth in the doctrine of the scope and limits of certainty of salvation. It implies that only God can ultimately evaluate and pass judgment on man's answer to his offer of salvation, since he alone has total disposition over the answerer. The answerer is at his own free disposition to a certain degree, but he is not free as regards self-disposal as such, and once he has made his free disposition he has control of it only to a limited extent, dependent on its objectivation. So too man's subjectivity is accessible to his fellows, but only dependently on his objectivation in external and expressive action. Hence according to Trent man can have the certainty of salvation only in the broader sense (*D* 826). Man is forbidden just as strongly to try to judge definitively his fellowmen (Mt 7:1; Lk 6:37). But within the framework of mutual dependence, and in particular within the scope of his authority, he may call his fellowman to account and where necessity compels, even exercise power over him.

2. *Responsibility as dialogue*. Man's responsibility therefore consists in his being liable to be called to account for himself and his action. He is responsible insofar as he has to give an account of himself and his actions to God, his fellowmen and himself. He has to do so, insofar as he freely disposes of himself. For it is in proportion to his freedom that he is there, for those to whom he is ordained and on whom he is dependent, in a way which is significant to them. With regard to God, this significance consists in the acknowledgment of total dependence on him and the absolute binding force of his will, which is in turn fulfilled in the total self-realization of man. With regard to others and the responsible agent himself, it consists in the optimum development of his own being, in keeping with his ordination to others and his dependence on them (see *Human Act*).

Responsibility therefore supposes freedom. Man can act responsibly only insofar as he acts freely. But the essence of responsibility consists in the ordaining of the free action to the good of those affected by it. Hence the ground of responsibility is the respect due to the dignity of the person. In the concrete, it is behaviour in keeping with the dignity of the person of those affected. It is an expression of the dialogal nature of existence.

Scripture, in the account of creation, brings out man's responsibility by presenting him as one to whom God's word is addressed and who is claimed by God (Gen 1:28ff.; 3:9; 4:9; cf. Jn 1:1). Man is not dependent on God merely as his efficient cause, a relation expressed by the notion of creatureliness. By his responsibility he is called into a relation of partnership with God which Scripture comprises under such terms as "covenant" or "sonship" (cf. Rom 8:19). Since man is partner and hence "image of God" (Gen 1:27), he is called to be lord of the infra-human creation (Gen 1:26). He responds to this partnership by dedicating himself to God in and through love of his neighbour (cf. Lk 10:27). Hence man was created as a social being, in the form of man and woman (Gen 1:27).

3. *Ethics.* Responsibility is accepted by the free and deliberate direction of one's acts to the good of the persons involved. It calls for a judgment on the effects of one's actions to the best of one's knowledge, and a decision to act in a given way taken in conscience to the best of one's ability. But the decision must not be guided unduly by an interior value aimed at in isolation from all but the disposition. And it must not be guided unduly by the prospect of successful action as a means to a given end. Hence the *a priori* estimation of value must be weighed against the needs of the situation as gathered from experience. A compromise must be found which will do justice to the obligation of the moral value and the imperative of the proper laws of the factors determining the situation. The compromise must aim at the optimum realization of the moral value in question. The moral attitude which aims at the optimum compromise between mere interior disposition and mere exterior success was called the "ethics of responsibility" by Max Weber.

4. *Responsibility: indivisibility and differences.* As man takes on progressively responsibility for his actions, he decides, in keeping with his historical character, his definitive and total salvation or ruin. This means that man is made responsible not merely for his individual moral acts, but through these acts, progressively, for the kernel of his person. The person is there through its acts. In the measure in which man decides subjectively in view of his salvation, he is also responsible for his acts, so that his responsibility cannot simply be reduced to and identified with his individual free acts. Man is rather responsible for himself, as he freely ordains his acts to his fellowmen, and through them to God, and then to the world around him. Thus man himself merits by his good moral acts or becomes guilty by his sinful ones. The acts themselves are only conditional and limited expressions of responsibility.

If the responsible act is directly ordained to definitive salvation, it is said to be a moral act in the strict (or qualified) sense; if only indirectly, it is said to be a moral act in the broad (or simple) sense (see *Human Act*, C, 2). In the former case, one must distinguish between a responsibility which is provisional and conditional because the moral act in question is revocable, and a responsibility by which man seals his final salvation or ruin. It is true that man decides for or against his final salvation in every strictly moral act. But till he arrives at his fulfilment, he is a historical being who can express the laws of worldly reality only conditionally in his acts. Hence he can only identify himself with these acts conditionally and a revision of them remains always theoretically possible. This is only excluded when at the end of his earthly life man has decided definitively about all the chances of salvation offered him and exhausted all their possibilities. The theoretical possibility of a revision (of which one cannot say that it will ever be practical) makes the decision for or against salvation a merely preliminary one. Hence some theologians consider the possibility of a definitive decision distinct from the preliminary decisions for or against salvation (see *Death*). This decision makes man definitely and finally responsible for himself.

Thus man has responsibility for his individual acts only in the framework of a total self-understanding, a fundamental sketch-plan of himself. These acts can be attributed to man only insofar as they are ordained to or derive from such a plan. Hence indivisibility, differences and degrees of responsibility result from the subject-object tension in man and the limited capacity to master his own objectivity which results from it.

5. *Accountability*. Man is accountable insofar as he disposes of himself in his action. This is the measure in which he himself is good or evil. His acts are laid to his charge in the same measure. But it is not a matter of passing acts being attributed to him, morally or juridically, while he himself remains unchanged. Man's responsibility is never a mere accidental. It is from first to last a way of being.

Man is then responsible for his individual acts insofar as they express his way of being. And one can conclude to man's responsibility from his acts only insofar as they can reasonably be attributed to his way of being. This subjective way of being can only be grasped conditionally through its objectivation. Hence responsibility can be presumed in a given case only conditionally. Responsibility can be excluded insofar as an action can be sufficiently explained by motives over which it can be reasonably presumed that the doer has not sufficient control, since they obey laws which he cannot evade. This happens when someone – through inner compulsion or outward coercion – is left so limited a choice of motives that he has no power to choose a responsible mode of action, or only a very limited one.

6. *Education to responsibility*. Man becomes responsible by being entrusted with responsibility within the limits of his capacity. He is gradually introduced to moral action and his conscience is formed. Education is the progressive assignment of responsibility, aiming at making man able to act responsibly towards the persons affected by his actions. To this end, his sense of the dignity and value of human persons must be stimulated and deepened. He must be taught to calculate the effects of his actions, which can only be done by a grasp of the laws of earthly reality.

It is proper to charge someone with responsibility, the precondition of merit or sin, reward or punishment, when it can be reasonably presumed that he knows the value of the persons affected by his actions and can foresee the effects of his actions.

7. *Collective responsibility*. According to what has been said above, collective responsibility can only be improperly and derivatively such. A collectivity can be a "person" in an improper sense, insofar as it supports and becomes liable for the (subjective) actions of its members. There is ground for this liability, since the collective action gives rise to collective consequences which can only come about through the co-operation of the members. Responsibility for the consequences of a collective action cannot therefore be simply reduced to the responsibility of the members. Hence one may rightly speak of collective responsibility in a derivative sense. Individuals are personally responsible for the consequences of collective action only insofar as they are answerable for these consequences by reason of their personal action towards others. But they can also be made answerable for the collective consequences insofar as all members are liable by reason of their interdependence.

Waldemar Molinski

RESURRECTION

I. Resurrection of Christ

A. Preliminary Considerations

If the resurrection of Jesus is to be proclaimed credibly at the present day as a fundamental dogma of Christianity, then (logically) we must first establish the *a priori* horizon within which it can "dawn" intelligibly and credibly. This postulate cannot be vitiated by the objection that a "transcendental" question of this kind only arises *after* the historical experience, whereas the answer is supposed to provide the conditions of possibility of the experience. In fact such a mutual relation between actual experience and the establishment of its possibility is a constant feature of man's mental life.

1. Man is a being who looks to a future which is his fulfilment. Because man is a unity, he cannot at all events spontaneously think of this fulfilment, this goal of life, simply as a fulfilment of his "soul". His life is orientated towards fulfilment as a man even if he cannot imagine such fulfilment, or can more easily conceive certain features of it (e.g., fulfilment of personal spirit as such) than others. Moreover, for present purposes we can leave the question open whether the desired fulfilment represents the fulfilment of man's "nature" or of man's being as orientated (by the supernatural existential) towards fulfilment through God's self-communication, and implicitly experienced as such. If "flesh" in the biblical sense is understood as man's perishable being, it is quite possible to say that man turns in hope towards the "resurrection of the flesh" as the fulfilment of his existence. For that does not involve any concrete notion of how exactly this transfigured fulfilment is to be conceived (any more than the dogma of the resurrection of the body explains it: see *Eschatology*). It simply establishes that the substantial and actual unity of man forbids us for our part to exclude on principle certain domains of human existence, as being merely provisional, from the human fulfilment which is asymptotically striven for.

2. God's self-communication to man in grace has a history directed towards such fulfilment in which the Pneuma saves and transfigures the whole man. Man is constituted as supernaturally transcendent. Prior to any acts of knowing or willing, the human subject has a grace-given dynamic structure which directs his acts towards the self-communicating God and therefore, whether negatively or positively, towards supernatural salvation. Consequently in the historical unfolding of that supernaturally transcendent constitution, the "case" has to be envisaged in which the whole being of a certain man a) is perfectly fulfilled as the beginning and ground of the victorious, saving end of all history and b) is grasped precisely as such an event in the experience of faith. Such can be the goal of hope, the definitive culmination of that history, to be asymptotically aspired to.

3. It cannot be explained in detail here that (and why) this *first* saving event (always at least implicitly hoped for), the definitive fulfilment of a human being (if it is to be both experienced and the guarantee of the positive outcome of redemptive history as a whole), involves the idea of an absolute mediator of salvation, which again involves that of the incarnation of the Logos and the hypostatic union. Nor can it be shown at this point why we are entitled to believe that this "transcendentally" desirable culmination of saving history occurred in Jesus of Nazareth. This will be dealt with in Section II, even though the conditions of possibility and the problems of the knowledge of this "hypothetical" saving event are on practical grounds being envisaged in the light of Jesus' resurrection.

4. This line of approach, however,

shows what is involved here: a) The definitive fulfilment of a human being as known in experience (and consequently constituting the eschatological redemptive situation of those who experience it) is simultaneously the culmination of saving history and the supreme authentication of this history itself. Attestation (by miracle) and reality attested are here identical. b) It is already clear from this that knowledge of this event is of a unique character. By the very nature of the case this is the most radical instance of reciprocal conditioning of faith and the motive of faith. As the fundamental eschatological saving event, this resurrection is essentially an object of faith and consequently is attained only in faith itself, in the light of faith which, as divine self-communication, is itself the dynamism directed towards such fulfilment. At the same time in this saving event faith finds the historical ground which makes faith possible and legitimate. This "circle" does not preclude access "from outside" to the ground of faith, i.e., to the resurrection (shown in fundamental theology to be well-founded), because the circle is posited by grace (the proffered grace of faith, which by its very nature is the grace of belief in the resurrection). It therefore does not have to be formed artificially, by men, from a point outside it. Such a resurrection, into a human existence finalized and bringing history to fulfilment, is essentially an object of knowledge of an absolutely unique kind. It is essentially other than the return of a dead man to his previous biological life, to space and time, which form the dimensions of history unfulfilled. Hence it is not in any way an ordinary object of experience, which could be subsumed under the common conditions and possibilities of experience. It is an "experience" *sui generis* which, if possible at all, grasps in fact the definitive transformation of the historically knowable. Testimony and what is testified, faith and experience, are here by the nature of the case interlocked in a unique way. But this unity is not an undifferentiated sameness, which would allow one to say that we attain only the testimony itself and not its own proper structure in which the difference between experience and what is "objectively" experienced can be recognized.

Karl Rahner

B. Biblical Synthesis

In the minds of the apostles the resurrection of Jesus is the central fact of the history of salvation, the decisive event in the eschatological order of salvation. As such it forms, with the crucifixion, the central theme of the kerygma and of theological instruction.

1. *The kerygma.* In spite of the differences in NT formulations (cf. 1 Cor 15:3b–5; Acts 2:22–36; 10:34–43; 13:23–41, etc.; cf. Rom 1:3f.; 2 Tim 2:8) and in its literary "patterns" (cf., for example, 1 Cor 15:3b–5; Acts 3:12–26), the Easter message of the apostolic Churches exhibits in all its forms the same essential aspects – positive (historical), didactic and biblical. Since the Church recognizes no other norms or foundations in the proclamation of its message than the gospel of primitive Christianity as transmitted through tradition (cf. 1 Cor 15:11), it is appropriate to give a brief outline of these aspects at this point.

a) According to the principle stressed by Luke (cf. Lk 24:48; Acts 1:21–22, etc.), and already in force in the Aramaic-speaking Churches (cf. 1 Cor 15:3ff.; Gal 2:1–10), the kerygma is by definition a testimony to the resurrection of Jesus. It is not merely an expression of the Easter faith. It emphasizes first and foremost the fact that belief in the risen Christ is guaranteed by the collective and individual experience of the apostles immediately after the Passion.

The gospel narratives (cf. Mk 16:1–8; Mt 28:1–20; Lk 24:1–53; Jn 20:1–29;

cf. Acts 1:3–14; Jn 21:1–23; Mk 16:9–20) constitute the most eloquent witness for this. Varied as they are in origin and mode of presentation, they show in their very diversity that the apostolic Church did not omit to authenticate the kerygma by facts when it formulated it in view of new pastoral and missionary situations.

According to the earliest tradition in John and the synoptics the following events stamped in the main the Easter experience of the followers of Jesus. On the morning of the third day certain women, among whom Mary Magdalene is included (cf. Mt 28:1; Jn 20:1), set out for the tomb. While they are still far off they see that the "stone has been taken away from the tomb" (cf. Jn 20:1; Mk 16:4). Hastily they return and tell the disciples whom they meet what has happened (cf. Jn 20; Lk 24:9; Mt 28:8). At this news "some" run (cf. Lk 24:24) to the tomb (according to one particular variation of the tradition, Peter and John, cf. Jn 20:2–10; Lk 24:12). Unlike the women they actually enter the tomb and are confused to find it empty. The apparitions, however, allay the uncertainty of the apostles. These consist of a "seeing" and a "hearing" of the risen Christ (cf. Acts 4:20; Mt 13:16–17 par.), and are probably extremely similar to the Damascus vision of Christ (cf. Acts 9:3–7; 1 Cor 15:5–8). They are, individually or collectively, "recognition-scenes" (cf. 1 Cor 15:5a par.; Jn 20:24–29; 1 Cor 15:7a and *The Gospel of the Hebrews*, fragm. 7; Mt 28:9f. par.) or "mandate-scenes" (cf. 1 Cor 15:5b, 7b; Mt 28:15–20; Lk 24:36–49 = Jn 20:19–23; Acts 1:4–8; Mk 16:14–20). These apparitions are distributed unequally over a relatively long period (the limitation to the "forty days" was unknown to the ancient tradition), and, insofar as the places are mentioned at all in the text, they take place in Galilee and Jerusalem. The tradition attested in John (cf. 20:11–29), Luke (cf. 24:13–53; Acts 1:4–14) and in part in Matthew (cf. 28:9–10) of the appearances in Jerusalem is at least as important as the other tradition of the appearances of Christ in Galilee of which we are told in Mark (cf. 16:7, 14–20) and Matthew (28:7, 16–20).

In order to adapt these events to the mentality of their hearers and to emphasize the actuality of the message, they were interpreted in the later preaching by means of themes drawn from Jewish anthropology and especially from the biblical world of ideas: the angel at the tomb, the proofs provided by the risen Christ himself of his corporeal state and of his identity with the crucified Jesus. Finally, they were interpreted in the ecclesiastical and theological instructions which define more precisely the original missionary mandate and in fact expand it. All these elements, which are secondary in origin and importance, are meant ultimately only to bring out the truth of the kerygma and the conformity of the post-Easter Church to the will of the glorified Lord from a specific point of view.

Faithfulness to the witness of the disciples and adaptation of the message to the circumstances of the time are, therefore, the imperatives of the apostolic Church for the conduct of its mission. They explain the development of the tradition and permit us to make a correct evaluation of the various elements of the NT narratives.

b) As one who vouches for the glorification of Christ, the apostle is *ipso facto* God's witness. The resurrection is more than a historical fact: it is the decisive "word" in the dialogue which God conducts with the world, the chief argument by which he means to convince men of his faithfulness, his "wisdom" and his "power" (cf. 1 Cor 1:22ff.).

The Easter event is first and last the deed of the Father. Attested in the kerygma (cf. 1 Cor 15:4b; Acts 2:24a, etc.) and at the base of all the expressions of Jewish-Christian thought in the primitive Church (only from the fourth gospel, in which leaving the tomb represents the beginning of the "ascent" of the Son to his Father, can an argument be drawn for the "active" resurrection), this article of faith, as the foundation for the apostolic work, contains in germ all the themes of Easter spirituality and theology. For the biblical and post-biblical Judaism of Palestine the return of the dead to life in the eschatological age is the sign of the new creation. "To give life to the dead", therefore, is the prerogative of the Creator. The disciples apply this principle to the resurrection of Jesus and draw the following conclusions: In that the Father has raised Jesus from the dead "on the third day", he has, to the astonishment of the world, established his messianic title. Further, he has established him for ever as the redeemer. The work of salvation is not concluded with the act of atonement on the cross. It is brought to its fullness only by the resurrection in which all is made new.

The Palestinian and Hellenistic Churches give expression to these ideas in the various names which they give to the risen Christ in kerygma and prayer. Jesus is the "just one" (Acts 3:14; 7:52), the "holy" (Acts 3:14; Mk 1:24 par.; Jn 6:69; Acts 2:27 par.), the "Christ" (1 Cor 15:3b; Acts 2:36; 4:26f., 10:38), the "Son of man" (Acts 7:56), the "Son of God" (Acts 8:37), the "Lord" (1 Cor 16:22; Rev 22:20; Phil 2:11; Acts 7:59f.). According to other titles which have a specifically soteriological content, he is the "Prophet" (Acts 3:22; 7:37), the "Servant" (Acts 3:13, 26; 4:25, 27, 30), the "Saviour" (Acts 4:9–12; 5:31; 13:23), the "Leader" or the "Pioneer" (Acts 5:31; Heb 12:2) of "salvation" (Heb 2:10) and of "life" (Acts 3:15). The Christianity of apostolic times unfolds the doctrinal and religious meaning of these titles which derive chiefly from the OT and Judaism.

Finally, as the deed of the Father the resurrection of Jesus is a vital factor in the economy of salvation. It is among the decisive facts of saving history. The early tradition emphasizes this fact although it only sketches the rudiments of a theology of the history of salvation. To this end it employs the following themes:

The kerygma is characterized by witness or "proof" from Scripture (cf. 1 Cor 15:4b; Acts 2:24a, 25–31, etc.; cf. also Lk 24:7, 25ff., 32:44–47; Jn 20:9). Though the references are laconic, two groups of scriptural passages referring to the Easter event appear to be adduced: Hos 6:2 par. and Is 53:10–12 par. In importance, the references to the passages concerning the suffering and glorified "just one" come first. In addition to Is 52:13–53:12 and Ps 22:2–32 (cf. 1 Cor 15:3b, 4b; Acts 3:13–26; Phil 2:6–11) they refer chiefly to the fragments of Ps 18:5f. (cf. Acts 2:24a) and Ps 16:9ff. (cf. Acts 2:25–31; 13:35ff.), and what they purport to show is as follows. In the eyes of the apostolic Church the Resurrection is chiefly and pre-eminently the response of the Father to the submission of Christ on the cross (cf. Mk 15:34 par.), the "deliverance" of the Messiah from the snares of hell (cf. Acts 2:24) and indeed the reward which is imparted to the servant who has been "obedient" unto death (cf. Phil 2:9). As relics of an archaic line of thought these passages, which derive from a Palestinian tradition of preaching, seem to emphasize in their own way that in Scripture the Passion and Resurrection represent two inseparably united elements in one and the same "mystery". In this they are different from the prophecies which refer to the historic event of the third day. Hos 6:2 and its parallels gave little occasion to later emphasis (cf. 1 Cor 15:4b; Acts 10:40; Mt 16:21 par.). Apparently they refer simply to the direct nature of the intervention of God on behalf of the Messiah to deliver him.

As witnesses to a more developed stage in tradition the gospel narratives go beyond the salient facts as set forth in the primitive preaching. The argument from Scripture here is found only occasionally in the few passages which seek to give an archaic impression. In order to show the place of the Resurrection in God's salvific plan, the presynoptic record concerning the empty tomb employs the literary motif of the *angelus interpres* (cf. Mk 16:5f. par.). By this means it brings out (i) that the Easter event, the fulfilment of which is already indicated by the empty tomb, constitutes one of the most decisive turning-points in saving history; and (ii) that God is the author of the Resurrection and of the kerygma, which even in its formulation (Mk 16:5ff. par. = Acts 3:15 etc.) is transmitted by the angel to the women and indirectly too to the disciples (cf. Lk 24:44–48 par., where it is the risen Lord himself who formulates the Easter message). Behind this quite specific kerygmatic intentions can be discerned. The further the tradition is developed, the more it takes pains to insist upon its faithfulness to the testimony of the disciples. The subsequent preaching does not vaporize the original message, which remains its norm and basis.

2. *The New Testament theology of the Resurrection.* The reflection of the apostles upon what they have witnessed defines more closely the content of the kerygma. Reflection bears primarily upon the fact of the Easter event, but refers no less emphatically to its soteriological and messianic significance. The glorified Jesus appears not merely to be vindicated in his Christological prerogatives. It is equally true that he is the New Man, the author and exemplar of a new humanity.

a) *The redemptive resurrection.* Ancient prophetic tradition affirms that in the last days of Israel, which has been "mortally" laid low by its sinful infidelity to the covenant, God will give "new life through the Spirit". In other words, the messianic work is the renewal of humanity. Salvation of its essence signifies the restoration of the people of God and of the individual in the Pneuma.

A prophetic tradition which goes back to Ezekiel (cf. 36:25ff.; 37:1–14) and Jeremiah (cf. 31:31–34), and which is taken over and developed more fully by devout circles of biblical (cf. Ps 51:7, 9–14) and Palestinian (cf. 1 *QS*, IV, 18–26; cf. Mk 1:9ff. par.) Judaism is that of the Second Adam or the eschatological man. This finds its fulfilment in the Easter event, which right from the outset the primitive Church regards as the act of the new creation.

Through the resurrection Jesus has undergone a total "transformation" of his human nature. The two indivisibly united aspects of this are adduced in the apostolic texts, not without a certain inner continuity. (i) Henceforward Jesus is "Pneuma". According to the ancient credal formula cited in Rom 1:4, he possesses "the Spirit of holiness" (πνεῦμα ἁγιωσύνης), the source of moral and religious perfection through which man shares in the glory of the luminaries. According to the more synthesized presentation of 1 Cor 15:15–45, he is the "life-giving Spirit" (πνεῦμα ζωοποιοῦν) – in contrast to the first man, who was only a "living being" (ψυχὴ ζῶσα). These expressions, which proceed from a Jewish understanding of Gen 2:7, are certainly determined to a large extent by Palestinian anthropology with its dualism. Nevertheless they attest the fact that according to the ideas of Jewish and Gentile Christianity Jesus is in his renewed humanity divinely "pneumatic", and this finds expression chiefly in his power and holiness. (ii) The "body" is not excluded from this transformation. Since "glory", "power" and "immortality" characterize it, it is in itself "spiritual" (σῶμα πνευματικόν). Although the message of 1 Cor 15:42ff. (which incidentally corrects the apologetic presentation of the risen Lord in the pericopes concerning his appearances) is directed to the Greeks, it is in truth simply an application of the apostolic faith to the Jesus who has become πνεῦμα through the mighty deed of the Father at Easter.

But these prerogatives are not confined to the person of Christ. The salvific will of God has destined them for the whole of humanity. Jesus who has come in order to lead back humanity into pneumatic incorruption by a radical transformation is, as the "new Adam" (1 Cor 15:45), the "head" of a new generation, the exemplary and the instrumental cause of the eschatological new creation. The Resurrection is the prototype of the "transformation" of man. It is, moreover, its prelude and its inception. The "Pneuma of Christ", which is further bestowed upon the believers in the sacramental *anamnesis* of the Easter event at baptism (cf. Rom 6:3–11), is the foundation of the Christian life (of faith, of prayer and of the Christian way of life), and of the growth of the newly baptized in the Spirit. It is the life-principle of the Church which, in a certain sense, is the cosmic "body" of the risen Lord, while he is the Church's "head". It is the principle of the Christian dispensation in the world, and not least of the ordering of the whole of creation anew to glory (cf. Rom 8:19–23), as also of the resurrection of the body (cf. 1 Cor 15:12–57). Christ, who is the "Spirit" (cf. 2 Cor 3:17), "conforms" the faithful "to his own image" (cf. 2 Cor 3:18), and thereby leads them unfailingly to his glory as "the image of the Father" (cf. 2 Cor 4:4; Col 1:15). Finally, the Easter event has cosmic and historical dimensions. As the climax of the work of salvation it sums up the whole of the past and already includes ἔσχατον. Regarded in this light there is no doubt that it is "*the* mystery" in the absolute sense without which the experience of humanity in the OT, as also "our preaching", would be meaningless and vain (cf. 1 Cor 15:14).

b) *Christ the Lord.* The Resurrection is the definitive epiphany of the Messiah. Not only does it confirm his eschatological prerogatives, but it also points to his complete transcendence. It is this that is expressed in the second central theme of the kerygma (in its usual formulation) which primitive Christianity has tried to portray in a rich variety of aspects, which we cannot enumerate here.

Here we shall concentrate only upon the title "Lord" (*Kyrios*) which is applied to the risen Christ. Of all the numerous Christological titles used in the apostolic Church, this is certainly the most closely associated with the Easter event, and the most traditional. Rooted in the vocabulary which the disciples were accustomed to use in the company of their "Lord and Master" (cf. Jn 13:14), attested by the Aramaic-speaking Churches (cf. 1 Cor 16:22; *Didache*, 10, 6; Rev 22:20) and finally taken over and given prominence in Gentile-Christian circles, it constitutes a firm element in liturgical prayer and in eschatological expectation (cf. 1 Cor 16:22). It refers first and foremost to Christ in the Resurrection, and gives expression to his "sovereignty", which requires "obedience" and "submissiveness" on the part of the faithful. This attitude, therefore, is characteristic of the disciples who are witnesses to the appearances of Christ (cf. Phil 3:12). When fresh light is thrown upon the meaning of the title by Scripture (Ps 110:1; Acts 2:34f. par.), it is also an expression of Christ's equality with the Father or his divine transcendence. At the same time the cry "Lord Jesus!" implies an acknowledgment of Christ as God (cf. Jn 20:28).

In the awareness that the risen Lord is divine, the Church of the NT asks finally whether Christ possessed this perfection already on this earth. By considering the history of salvation anew in the light of the Easter event, it recognizes its true meaning: it is an eschatological theophany or the saving presence of God among his people (cf. Mk 4:41 par.), and among men (cf. 2 Tim 1:10 par.).

Joseph Schmitt

C. Fundamental Theology (Apologetics)

1. *The Resurrection as foundation of faith.* Jesus' resurrection (with the incarnation and crucifixion) is a central object of faith. In another respect, as an event which can be historically established, it is one of its decisive foundations. Although something that occurred "on the margin of history" (for in it Jesus left the domain of this world), and in its deeper nature a mystery, it nevertheless stands in such inseparable connection with a series of intrinsically historical facts that on the basis of the latter it is possible to attain what is at least in an analogous sense a historical certainty regarding the fact of Jesus' resurrection. To reject on principle any consideration of Jesus' resurrection from the point of view of apologetics (as is commonly done in non-Catholic theology) is in contradiction to the NT, which sees in Jesus' resurrection the decisive sign of Jesus' mission (cf. 1 Cor 15:12–19 etc.). For the rest, the relation between Jesus' resurrection as ground and as object of faith is the same as that between faith and recognition of credibility.

The starting-point has to be a "predogmatic" exegesis of the resurrection texts. For preference those texts should be used which can be regarded as the oldest and critically most certain, 1 Cor 15 and the discourses of Acts, which without doubt reproduce the fundamental features of the original apostolic preaching. The gospels only give sections of the complicated Easter events, partly in brief summary and from various points of view of composition or kerygma, partly with a certain freedom of presentation (cf. the reshaping of the reference to Galilee at Lk 24:6 as compared with Mk 16:7). Hence not too much store should be set by attempts at harmonization.

The ultimate attainable reality is not, as is sometimes said, the Easter faith of the disciples, but in that faith the appearances of Jesus which provided its basis, together with a complex of facts important for their evaluation. The whole is only intelligible, even from the historical point of view, if Jesus really rose from the dead.

a) The death of Jesus is established beyond doubt. The hypothesis of apparent death (H. E. G. Paulus) met with general rejection as completely aberrant.

b) *The situation of the disciples.* None (except perhaps John) stood by Jesus during the Passion. Peter's denial is typical of their failure. Their state of mind is aptly described at Lk 24:21, "We had hoped that he was the one to redeem Israel."

c) Jesus' burial is already mentioned in the early formula of 1 Cor 15:3ff. The more detailed accounts in the gospels in no respect give a legendary impression. Legend would not have introduced for the burial a man remote from the circle of disciples. The archaeological findings are in harmony with the gospel accounts (cf. J. Jeremias, *Golgotha*). The fact of the burial is important, for the apostolic preaching began in Jerusalem and therefore the question of the tomb must have arisen at the latest with it.

d) *The empty tomb.* This fact in itself is of course no proof of a resurrection, but it is not without importance. According to all the gospels, the tomb was found empty on the morning of the third day. A legend for apologetical purposes would not have made women discover the tomb, for in Jewish law they were not competent to give evidence. Apostolic preaching in Jerusalem itself would have been impossible if the disciples had not known for certain that Jesus' tomb was really empty. By that very fact, however, their preaching could have no more successful starting-point than Jerusalem. The objection of the critics that Peter's discourses could not have failed to mention the discovery of the empty tomb is groundless. The fact of the empty tomb did not require proof. The discourses take it for granted: cf. Acts 2:27–32. It must have become known in the city with the utmost rapidity. To mention the visit to the tomb was not advisable; the accusation of having stolen the body would obviously have suggested itself and had perhaps already been made. Paul too without doubt takes for granted the empty tomb, for in 1 Cor he is concerned precisely with the bodily resurrection of Jesus. The importance he attributed to it can be seen from the fact that his preaching in Athens failed precisely over this point: Acts 17:32. The comparison of baptism with the burial and resurrection of Jesus (Rom 6:4) presupposes his resurrection.

e) *The appearances.* The empty tomb alone is not an unambiguous event. What was decisive was that the disciples "saw" the risen Christ. The place, number, sequence and some circumstances of the appearances are uncertain; the fact and its essential content are indisputable. Can these appearances be explained as having a psychological cause, as "subjective visions"? From the point of view of fundamental theology, that is the decisive question.

(i) Liberal criticism explains the appearances as psychological effects of the Easter enthusiasm. But according to all the accounts, it was the other way round; the appearances caused the Easter faith. That alone corresponds to the situation of the disciples after the collapse of their messianic hopes. It would also be inexplicable that the appearances ceased when belief in the resurrection had triumphed in the Church.

(ii) Subjective visions would presuppose a certain length of time for the psychological development of the disciples. That contradicts the well-attested "third day" (earliest tradition, according to 1 Cor 15:4), which cannot be derived from Scripture. The scriptural proof adduced for it (Jon 2; Hos 6:2?) always presented difficulties.

(iii) Visions of purely psychological origin cannot explain the complete change in the disciples, their unshakable certainty and their readiness for sacrifice. The conviction of Jesus' resurrection was the foundation of their whole subsequent lives.

(iv) Although elsewhere in the NT there is mention of "visions" (the origin and significance of which need not be examined here), the disciples cannot be called "visionaries". Besides, the Easter encounters were always clearly distinguished in fact and in name from other visions. Paul speaks of the Damascus appearance as the last (1 Cor 15:8), even though he still had visions later.

(v) It is also an objection to a psychogenic explanation that appearances took place even to groups, once to more than 500 people together (1 Cor 15:6) and at least once to an opponent, Saul. Perhaps James too only found faith in this way (1 Cor 15:7).

(vi) The appearances were not simply an inner experience but must have had the character of events. Hence the apostles could come forward as "witnesses of the resurrection". That was their distinctive function (Acts 1:22; 2:32; 4:20, etc.). Paul holds the same view: "If Christ has not been raised, then our preaching is in vain ... We are even found to be misrepresenting God ..." (1 Cor 14:14f.).

(vii) The corporeal character of the appearances is supported by the fact of the empty tomb which is firmly established independently of the appearances. Suggestions of transfer, mistake, etc., are just as aberrant as the hypothesis of theft put forward by the Jews. The facts of the tomb must have been just as public as the taking down from the cross. After a person of consequence had buried Jesus (it is unlikely that anyone else would have had access to Pilate), the Jews no doubt kept the tomb under surveillance. On the other hand, it must not be overlooked that Jesus did not rise in a body belonging to this world. The older apologetics did not always take this sufficiently into account. The gospels note that Jesus was not at once recognized. On the road to Damascus he appeared in light, from heaven. In his glorified body he had to be made visible to men by God. The fourfold repetition of ὤφθη at 1 Cor 15:4–8 is probably to be understood in this sense (as a "theological passive"). Hence only those who were called saw the risen Christ. It is therefore possible to speak of "objective (divinely effected) visions", provided this expression is not intended to exclude the corporeal reality of Jesus' resurrection. Only with great caution can anything be said about the nature of that corporeal reality itself.

Werner Bulst

2. *The Resurrection and human experience.* What is the place of the Resurrection, as known to the disciples and men in general, in the whole understanding of existence? There should be no attempt to analyse the first Easter experience into its elements in order to reconstitute it subsequently. Here too the whole is more than the sum of its parts. This indivisible experience includes encounter with Jesus, who knew himself to be the Son of the incomprehensible mystery which he dared to call his Father with such astonishing assuredness, even in the dereliction of death. The experience includes the encounter with his love and fidelity, with his blameless obedience in the darkness of his death and with the Easter event itself. It is possible that at the present time we cannot clearly distinguish in the Easter event between Easter (the risen Christ) and the Easter experience of the disciples. That is to say, for us the Easter experience of the disciples is never merely a purely external means of communication (like telephone wires or telescope), which disappears as it were when we have the event itself within our grasp. The Easter faith and the Easter experience (faith and its ground) were inseparable for Jesus' disciples themselves; the ground of faith (the risen Christ) was experienced powerfully and compellingly as ground of faith only in faith itself. There are other instances of matters of experience which are really accessible, but only in the experience of another; this is all the more the case, the more important and vitally central to the individual the matter is. Indubitably we are dealing here with a different situation from that of a dependable and honest witness reporting, for example, that he saw someone jump into the water. In a case of that kind the possibility of such experience is known and intelligible to us from our own experience independently of the report. Consequently, the eyewitness's report establishes a relation to the event reported which can go beyond the equally intelligible reliability and honesty of the witness and to a certain extent becomes a direct experience. As regards Easter it is different. By the nature of the case this experience is *sui generis*. For the encounter with a person from the other world, who must "show" himself, who no longer belongs to our space and time, who on principle is not defencelessly accessible to perception on our part, is certainly not an occurrence which we can understand on the basis of our own experience. We cannot estimate its possibilities and conditions for ourselves, so as to be in a position to apply everyday criteria to decide whether we can accept it as it occurs and is experienced here and now. Reference to the empty tomb as an event of our normal world of experience accessible to everyone is of no real avail: an empty tomb cannot attest a resurrection to perfect fulfilment, because its cause can be conceived in a variety of ways. We have no experience of the same kind as the Easter experience of the first disciples,

at least if we leave out of account the "experience of the Spirit" (Gal 3:1ff.). We are therefore dependent on the testimony of the disciples in an essentially more radical sense than in the case of the acceptance of other ocular testimony. This is not to deny that that experience itself had a structure, that the disciples could therefore distinguish and express the actual ground of their experience from the process of the experience itself: "the ground shows itself to us and is not created by our experience". Nor is it denied that we can somehow establish this structural distance between cause of the experience and the experience itself: by the number of witnesses, the disproportion between their mental state and the experience undergone, the vital personal effect of the experience, etc. Nevertheless all this in no way alters the fact that the Easter experience had a unique special character absolutely incommensurable with man's other experiences, and that for this reason our relation to it cannot be classed with reports of eyewitnesses in secular matters. Without the experience of the Spirit, i.e., in this case without acceptance in faith of the meaningfulness of existence (as it is, that is, as a whole), trustful reliance on the Easter testimony of the disciples will not come about even though the former can in many cases draw its real strength from the latter and in any case only fully attains its own nature through the latter. Only those who hope can see the fulfilment of hope, and at the sight of its fulfilment hope attains the purpose of its existence. This "circle" neither needs to be, nor can be, broken. But men called to hope for the "resurrection" of their own flesh (which they are, and do not simply possess) can by God's grace spring into that circle. How could it be otherwise here where what has to be accomplished is a total personal commitment, not in regard to this or that matter among many others of equal importance, but in regard to what gives ultimate meaning to all human reality and which is manifested in history? Such a matter must bring its own foundation with it, even though it comprises many mutually conditioning factors, and so the experienced reality of the risen Christ provides the ground of the experience and conversely the event "manifests" itself only to faith. It should in fact never be overlooked that the perfect fulfilment, in immediacy to God, of a human existence cannot of itself be a datum which can enter into, and be happened upon within the realm of earthly experience in space and time, but at most can "announce" itself in face of the total decision of a human life and for it (in all its dimensions). Nor do we need to imagine what someone in the genuine totality of his human existence looks like, "with body and soul", as we say. We can calmly admit that we cannot imagine a corporeal resurrection because, unlike, for example, the raising of the dead to life, it is not and is not intended to be the restoration of a previous state but a transformation of a radical kind (of which Paul already speaks as the condition of perfect fulfilment), through which the free act of personal life must pass if it is to find its fulfilment through the overcoming of time and the maturing of time into eternity. When we say "bodily" resurrection, we are simply saying that we are thinking of the whole man as brought to perfect fulfilment and that in accordance with our own experience of human reality we cannot divide him into an ever-valid "spirit" and a merely provisional "body".

If this is considered, what ground could there be forbidding us in the name of our moral obligation to truth to trust to the Easter experience of the first disciples? Nothing compels us to believe them, if we do not wish to, and if we remain sceptical. But there is much to justify our believing them. What is required of us is something extremely bold yet quite obvious: to venture our whole existence on its being wholly directed towards God, on its having a definite meaning, on its being capable of being saved and delivered, and on precisely this having occurred in Jesus (as the exemplary and instrumental cause), so that it is possible to believe that with regard to ourselves as the first disciples did. In them there really occurred, and absolutely, to the point of death, what we should always "like" to do, i.e., believe. And from the depth of our being we seek the objective historical facts by which such belief can come about.

Have we a better solution of the fundamental question of the meaning of our existence? Is it really more honest or simply at bottom more cowardly sceptically to shrug our shoulders in the face of this fundamental question and yet to go on acting (by living and by endeavouring to act decently) as though the whole thing had meaning all the same? There is no need to assert that anyone who considers he cannot believe in Jesus' resurrection is not able to live with an ultimately unconditional fidelity to his conscience. But we do affirm here that someone who really does this, in harmony with or in contradiction to the actual interpretations he consciously assigns to his existence, does believe – whether he is explicitly aware of this or not – in the risen Lord, who for him is nameless. For, in the fundamental decision of his personal life, even a person of this kind aims at a whole and assured existence (in body and soul) as a transformation of its present temporal character. He therefore directs his aim into history and at most does not yet know whether history has yet reached the point which even a belief of his kind acknowledges as at least the future goal of history. In that case, however, such a belief, which we too share, need not shrink from confessing (in view of Jesus and the faith of his disciples) that the event has already taken place.

Karl Rahner

D. Theology

1. *General remarks.* The resurrection of Jesus in his glorified body is one of the fundamental truths of faith which is acknowledged in all the professions of faith from the beginning (*D* 2ff., 13, 16, 20, 40, 54, 86, 255, 429, 462, 709, 994, 2084). It is not only a decisive factor from the point of view of apologetics in the demonstration of the grounds of faith (*D* 20, 28, 36f., 86) (see above, C), but the central theme of faith itself (1 Cor 15:17ff.), in that it is the perfect accomplishment of God's saving action for the world and for man, in which he irrevocably communicates himself to the world in the Son whom the resurrection definitively identifies and acknowledges, and so admits the world to salvation with eschatological finality. All that still remains then is simply the carrying out and disclosure of what happened in the resurrection. All this involves an absolute mystery of faith in the strict sense. For the resurrection in its full concrete reality as the perfect fulfilment precisely of Jesus, can only be fully understood on the basis of the absolute mystery of the incarnation. Theologically, therefore, the resurrection of Jesus is ultimately not an instance of a general resurrection that is intelligible in itself, but the unique event consequent upon Jesus' very being and death, an event which alone is the ground of the resurrection of those redeemed by him.

2. *The Christological aspect of Jesus' resurrection.* The resurrection has both a Christological and soteriological aspect. The former means that Jesus with his whole, and therefore his corporeal, reality rose to perfect fulfilment in glory and immortality (in contradistinction to bringing back a dead man to life: Lazarus). This was properly his because of his passion and death, which produced this concrete fulfilment by intrinsic necessity. Despite the statements of Scripture concerning Jesus' resurrection, which make it rather passive, an

action attributed by appropriation to the Father, the developed doctrinal statement of the faith teaches that the Lord, as the Son of God who possesses life in perfection, rose from the dead by his own power (cf. Jn 2:19; 5:21; 10:17f.; *D* 286), especially as God's activity *ad extra* is a single work of the triune God in the unity of the divine nature (cf. *D* 281, 284, 421, 428f., 703). In accordance with Scripture (Lk 24:26), theology maintains that this glorified state of resurrection, to the extent that it is different from Jesus' state before his death, despite the beatific vision which he already then possessed, is the object of Christ's merit. (On the history of this doctrine, cf. A. M. Landgraf, *Dogmengeschichte der Frühscholastik* [1952ff.], II 2, pp. 170–253.) The doctrine of faith also stresses that it is a genuinely bodily existence of the "flesh" (*D* 344, 422, 429, 462, 707), the actual character of which is the result of the history of that body (Jn 20:27; Rev 5:6; marks of the wounds of the glorified Christ). It is, however, the transfigured difference which alone makes Jesus' resurrection to a definitive corporeal condition meaningful. Furthermore in this respect Jesus' resurrection corresponds to the resurrection of the flesh and the risen body in general. As regards the Christological aspect of the resurrection, it must also be noted that Jesus' death and resurrection form a single event, the phases of which are inseparably interconnected (cf. Lk 24:26, 46; Rom 4:25; 6:4ff.). Every man dies from within into his own definitive state, so that the latter is the fruit produced by his life of freedom in time and is not merely a period which follows in temporal succession, in which there could be something completely different in kind from what preceded it. For otherwise what comes "after" death would not be the final fulfilment of time which has been well lived through, but a new phase simply following on the one preceding and itself therefore temporal in an earthly, transitory sense. (If death itself in this way places man in his complete fulfilment and the latter is ontologically and not merely in a juridical and ethical sense the fruit of life in time, this is not to deny that, for example, the resurrection must be bestowed by God. For man's action itself is in every respect, the ontological included, an acquiescence in being at the disposal of what is other than oneself; cf. K. Rahner, *On the Theology of Death*, Quaestiones Disputatae 2 [2nd ed., 1965].) With Jesus, therefore, the resurrection must be the goal and fulfilment precisely of his death and both factors of the one occurrence must mutually condition and interpret one another. Consequently it is not a mythical expression but the actual truth, when Scripture and tradition view the resurrection as the objective acceptance of Jesus' sacrificial death, which belongs to the essence of the sacrifice itself.

3. *The soteriological aspect of Jesus' resurrection.* In this respect it is remarkable that theological reflection has not yet reached the desirable degree of elaboration, at least as far as speculative theology is concerned. In general, theologians emphasize that in contrast to the death on the cross, the resurrection is not a morally meritorious cause of the redemption, because in itself it is not a free moral action of the man Jesus. In this regard it must not be forgotten that Jesus' resurrection is an element in a single event in which the death is the first phase which goes to constitute the actual resurrection itself. Furthermore, the rejection of causality by way of merit does not necessarily mean the exclusion of an instrumental physical saving causality of Jesus' humanity, including his corporeal nature (cf., for example, Thomas Aquinas, *Summa Theologica*, III, q. 56, a. 1 ad 3, etc.). On this basis the soteriological significance of Jesus' resurrection and of the risen Lord would have to be thought out afresh. Jesus' corporeal humanity is a

permanent part of the one world with its single dynamism, a relation and unity which need closer examination. Consequently Jesus' resurrection is not only in the ideal order an "exemplary cause" of the resurrection of all, but objectively is the beginning of the transfiguration of the world as an ontologically interconnected occurrence. In this beginning the destiny of the world is already in principle decided and has already begun. At all events it would in reality be different if Jesus were not risen. (Thomas Aquinas, for example, *loc. cit.*, considers that even the resurrection of the damned depends on Jesus' glorified humanity as the efficient cause.) Where theology rightly, if not unanimously, postulates a physical instrumental causality of Jesus' glorified humanity for the supernatural life of man, a basis is available for a more precise interpretation of the soteriological significance of the risen and exalted Lord as such (even if so far the full content of that proposition in formal ontology has not advanced very far; cf. M. J. Scheeben, *Handbuch der katholischen Dogmatik*, V [2nd ed., 1954], 2, § 253; Patres S. J. in Hispania, *Sacrae Theologiae Summa*, III, pp. 138–48).

Such an endeavour would of course raise the question whether every strictly supernatural communication of God to a created spirit in grace and vision is not necessarily (ontologically and therefore morally) to be thought of as an element (provisional preparation and subsequent repercussion in the world as a whole) of God's personal self-communication to the world in the hypostatic union, which itself, as the communication of God himself to a historical reality, is only fully accomplished in the definitive fulfilment of that history which we attain in the resurrection of Jesus. Only on this basis would it perhaps be possible to indicate why Jesus not only *de facto* and by a certain extrinsic suitability is the first to rise to the definitive state of glory (Col 1:18; 1 Cor 15:20), but is necessarily the first. It would probably also be possible to infer that the occurrence of his resurrection created "heaven" (to the extent that this implies more than a purely spiritual process) and taken together with the ascension (which fundamentally is an element in the resurrection), is not merely an entry into an already existing heaven. Here too, therefore, in accordance with the nature of Christianity, the history of salvation is ultimately the ground of the history of nature and does not simply unfold against the background of a static nature unaffected by it.

On the basis of these reflections systematic theology might then show why Jesus as pledge and beginning of the perfect fulfilment of the world, as representative of the new cosmos, as dispenser of the Spirit, head of the Church, dispenser of the sacraments (above all in the Eucharist), as heavenly mediator and goal of hope, can only be fully grasped if he is known throughout as the risen Lord, and if his resurrection is not thought of as his private destiny after a work which alone had soteriological significance. It would also appear that the risen Lord, freed by resurrection from the limiting individuality of the unglorified body, has in truth become present to the world precisely because risen (and so by his "going"), and that therefore his return will only be the disclosure of this relation to the world attained by Jesus in his resurrection.

Karl Rahner

II. Resurrection of the Body

A. Biblical

1. *Old Testament.* Until a late period in its history the religion of the OT knew of no resurrection of the body. Human life is limited to this world. This does not mean that man ceases to exist altogether at death, when God withdraws from him the spirit by which he became a "living soul", i.e., a living being (Gen 2:7) and the body returns

to the dust from which it was formed (Gen 3:19). But the shadowy existence of the dead in Sheol does not deserve to be called life. The *earth* is the "land of the living" (Is 38:11) and Yahweh is the God of the living only, not of the dead. When the OT says that his power also extends to Sheol, the realm of the dead (Amos 9:2; 1 Sam 2:6; Ps 139:8; Job 26:6), it means to express belief in the limitlessness of God's power. In fact he has no further concern for the dead any more than they have about him. The dead no longer know anything of him and therefore do not praise him (Ps 88:11–13). It is particularly important in this respect, however, that the fate of the dead is considered to be final. Sheol is the land of no return. "He who goes down to Sheol does not come up" (Job 7:9; cf. 14:12). According to the OT doctrine, man is not a being composed of body and soul, but a body given life by the spirit of God. Man does not *have* a soul, he *is* a soul (Hebrew נֶפֶשׁ), i.e., a living being, an animated body. This distinguishes the OT view of man fundamentally from the Greek. Without a body there is no real life. Consequently the dead in Sheol are not the souls of the dead but only shadowy beings, in fact the shadows of the whole human being (1 Sam 28:14; Is 14:9). In the OT they are also called the "rephaim", "the weak, the powerless" (Is 26:14, 19; Ps 88:11; Job 26:5; Prov 9:18). Their existence is not a state of suffering but is nevertheless regarded as an evil, above all because the dead are for ever separated from Yahweh. This mortal destiny, to which all without exception are subject, was accepted by the pious Israelites with calm devotion. Accordingly their wish was directed to a long life and a share in the good things of this world, then, "old and full of years" (Gen 25:8; 35:29), "to go the way of all flesh" (1 Kg 2:2).

Even in the post-exilic period the OT continued for centuries to maintain this earthly standpoint. This is shown by various psalms, e.g., Ps 88, and in particular by the Books of Job and Ecclesiastes. On the other hand, the thought of the later period is distinguished from that of earlier centuries by the full development of individualism. The individual no longer regarded himself simply as a constituent part of the nation as a whole but was conscious of his personal value. And there was added to individualism in this period the full development of the religious idea of retribution. It corresponds to God's holiness and justice that he justly apportions the lot of individual human beings and that as a consequence it must go well with the pious and ill with the wicked. But precisely this belief was constantly belied by the experience of life. For the author of the Book of Job this unjust state of affairs actually became the problem of how to vindicate divine providence, and the desolate pessimism of Ecclesiastes is rooted in the constant injustice which he sees unceasingly and experiences for himself, and in the fact that he finds no difference between man and the beasts. "As one dies, so dies the other. They all have the same breath, and man has no advantage over the beasts" (3:19). OT religion with its still undeveloped eschatology therefore almost of necessity tended to move beyond the stage it had so far reached. The two chief motives in this were the OT conception of God, the belief in God's government of the world and in his justice, and the belief in retribution already mentioned, which set a problem regarding faith in God's moral government of the world. But the chief stumbling-block was the situation of the whole nation suffering under the domination of alien heathen nations. Belief in a different lot for the just and the impious in Sheol could *per se* have developed from the belief in retribution. But this would have involved a profound transformation of anthropology, which only took place a few centuries later under Greek influence.

The natural development of the Israelite-Jewish idea of just retribution did not take the form of a new idea of the state of the dead. It was that man receives another life and a different lot in a future aeon and is thus remade in his entirety as God created him. This presupposes that the dead are restored to life.

It is important to note that the first demonstrable appearance of this belief occurred in a time of grievous distress. In Ezekiel, where we first meet this idea, the resuscitation of the dead bones does not, it is true, signify the resurrection of the dead abiding in Sheol, but the restoration of the nation. It is only affirmed that in certain circumstances God can awaken even the dead, while in general it remains true that the dead do not return. But the revivification described by Ezekiel actually takes place in the living, not in the dead; for the dead bones signify the nation in the "dead condition" of exile, to which a return home is promised. In the other passages of the older literature which speak of restoration to life, what is meant is simply the cure of grave illness in which the breath of life (רוּחַ) appears to have departed (2 Kg 5:7; Is 38:10; cf. Baudissin). The oldest testimony which is still primarily a profession of joyful belief in God's just rule is found in the "Apocalypse" of Isaiah (Is 24–27), probably composed in the Hellenistic period (3rd century B.C.): "Thy dead shall live, my dead shall rise, the dwellers in the dust shall awaken and exult; for thy dew is a dew of lights, the earth will bring the shadows to light" (26:19). Hope for restoration of the dead to life is linked here with expectation of the time of salvation for the whole nation. To complete the redeemed community, the just dead must also be added.

A considerable further step is taken in the Maccabean period, in Dan 12:2: "Many of those who sleep in the dust shall awake, some to everlasting life, the others to shame and everlasting abhorrence. The teachers of the Law shall shine like the brightness of the firmament and those who have instructed many in righteousness, like the stars for ever and ever." This passage is not merely much more definite than the previous one. It is also distinguished from the former by the fact that not only just but also impious will rise again. The reference is to the martyrs of the time of persecution under Antiochus IV Epiphanes, when many Jews suffered death for their faith, and to their persecutors. There is no thought of a general resurrection, nor of the great figures of the ancient history of Israel. It is also clear that it is not God's power alone which is to be manifested thereby but also his retributive justice. There is a striking difference between the two Books of Maccabees. The first still retains completely the terrestrial standpoint (2:52ff.) (like Ecclesiasticus) and knows nothing of a resurrection. In the Second Book of Maccabees, however, the belief in a resurrection is clearly and distinctly expressed and, as in Daniel, is linked with the idea of retribution. The Maccabean brothers express it one after the other. "The King of the world will raise us up who die for his Laws in the resurrection of eternal life" (7:9; cf. 7:11). "It is consoling to lose one's life at the hand of man; for we have the hope given us by God that we will receive the resurrection from him. For you (Antiochus), however, there will be no resurrection to life" (7:14). The same Second Book of Maccabees is also acquainted with the belief that it is useful and meaningful to pray and to offer expiatory sacrifices for the fallen who in their life-time have sinned, "that they may be loosed from their sins". This "pious action" is motivated by belief in resurrection. "For if he (Judas Maccabaeus) had not hoped that they that were slain should rise again, it would have seemed superfluous and vain to pray for the dead" (12:44).

But once again there is no mention of a general resurrection even of the Israelites, and for the impious there is none (7:14). The question has been much discussed, and has often been answered affirmatively, whether the influence of Zoroastrianism was operative in the origin and particularly in the further formation of the Jewish belief in the resurrection. Belief in the resurrection of the dead in Zoroastrianism is attested in Greek sources from the 4th century B.C. (Theopompos in *Diogenes Laertius*, Proem 9). The principal argument for assuming Zoroastrian influence is the connection between resurrection and judgment found in both cases. The possibility of such influence is of course admitted in principle. It must, however, be remembered that the fully developed concept of retribution and the problems to which it gives rise in the actual experience of life, provided the conditions for the rise of belief in the resurrection, yet this belief only appeared in Judaism at a time when the Palestinian Jews no longer lived under Persian but Greek rule.

2. *Judaism*. After the Maccabean period the belief in the resurrection prevailed in Palestinian Judaism. Both the apocalyptic writings and the Pharisee rabbis attest it. And mainly through the influence of the Pharisees it became the general national belief and a dogma which was incorporated into the Shemone Esre (2nd Benediction) to be recited daily by every Jew. Yet its victory did not come about without resistance. The attitude adopted to it formed one of the most important doctrinal differences between Pharisees and Sadducees. The latter, as is demonstrated by the rabbinic literature and Josephus (*Jewish War*, II, 8, 14; *Antiquities*, XVIII, 1, 4) as well as the NT (Mk 12:18ff.; Acts 4:1f.; 23:6–8), were absolutely and actively opposed to this belief, which they regarded as contrary to reason and not attested by the *Torah*. The resurrection was also rejected by Hellenistic Judaism (see below).

In answer to the attacks of the Sadducee "freethinkers", the Pharisee rabbis endeavoured to demonstrate the resurrection both from the OT and on rational grounds (cf. the controversy of R. Gamaliel II with the Sadducees in *Sanhedrin*, 90b–91a and the summary in Billerbeck, IV, pp. 893–7). On the other hand, Judaism never reached agreement whether all men or only some will rise again. And even where a general resurrection is taught, it is only with the proviso that certain men or categories of men should nevertheless be excepted from it, as for example the race of the Flood, the Egyptians who died in the Red Sea or the desert generation. These are not to rise again, but remain in their place of punishment because they have already received their judgment. Where the resurrection of only a part of mankind is taught, Israel is primarily meant, and even here first and foremost the great figures of antiquity such as the patriarchs Moses, David, Hezechiah, and also the martyrs of the Maccabean period of persecution. Then the circle is extended to include the just in general, though once more the pious Israelites are meant. More important than the debatable question as to which human beings rise from the dead and which not, is the following distinction. Where the restoration to life is limited to the just, its purpose is for these persons to share in salvation. Consequently, in this connection there is no thought of the impious dead, who remain in their underground place of damnation (*Psalms of Solomon*, 3, 11f.; *Ethiopic Book of Enoch*, 22, 13). Since in the OT view of man there is no true life without the body, the resurrection of the body is necessary for sharing in the eschatological salvation. This is also the case for the time when under Greek influence the old "monistic" view of the nature of man was replaced by the dualist doctrine of the soul as a distinct essential part of man besides the body. The dead in Sheol were now no longer thought of as mere shadow beings but as real "souls", i.e., spiritual beings (*ibid.*, 90, 33), which, separated from the body after death, have a life of their own. According to the deeds which men have done during their earthly life, they are in separate realms of the world of the dead, enjoying a certain happiness or suffering punishment (cf. *ibid.*, 22). The just souls are to be resurrected to share in salvation and to be reunited with their bodies, so that the whole man as God created him will receive salvation. Where, on the other hand, there is mention of a general resurrection of the good and of sinners (certain particular categories of sinners excepted), what is in question is the resurrection to the eschatological judgment. Consequently, resurrection precedes the judgment. "All who are born are destined to die, and the dead are destined to live once again, and those who are restored to life are destined to be judged, so that it may be known, and announced and confessed that he is God the Creator, he who knows, the judge, and that one day he will judge" (*Mishnah*, *Sayings of the Fathers*, 4, 22). In this doctrine, resurrection and judgment belong together and inaugurate the future world (*4 Esdras*, 7, 29ff.; *Syriac Apocalypse of Baruch*, 30, 1–5; 50, 2–51, 3; 85, 18; on the rabbinic literature cf. Billerbeck, IV, pp. 971–3). For the various statements about general resurrection or that of the just alone, see Billerbeck, IV, pp. 1166–98, P. Volz, *Die Eschatologie der jüdischen Gemeinde im neutestamentlichen Zeitalter* (2nd ed., 1934), pp. 235–47. The oldest testimony to the view that all men, just and impious, Jews and pagans, will rise again, is *Ethiopic Book of Enoch*, 22, 1ff. But the Book of Enoch itself is not consistent on this point, any more than the apocalypses of Esdras (cf. Volz, *op. cit.*, p. 38) and Baruch (cf. Billerbeck, IV, p. 1170); in the rabbinic writings too, statements which speak of the general resurrection are found side by side with others which at least do not mention more than the resurrection of the just.

The teaching of most rabbis from the earliest Tannaite period onwards was and remained that *all* the dead are resurrected. The rabbis were not, however, always unanimous about the chronological moment of the resurrection. This is connected with the doctrine of the "days of the Messiah". The older opinion regarded these as already the absolute accomplishment of salvation, so that the resurrection of the dead must therefore take place in them. In the post-Christian period, however, the rabbis separated the messianic period from the future aeon and reckoned it as belonging to the present aeon. Consequently, they now linked the resurrection with the future aeon as its prelude (cf. the texts in Billerbeck, IV, pp. 971–3). In the 3rd century, however, the rabbinic scholars, taking as their starting-point the belief that the fulfilment of the OT prophecies is to be expected in the messianic time, returned to the old view to the extent that they now expected the resurrection of the just at least in this period, while that of the rest of mankind is only to take place immediately before the Last Judgment (Billerbeck, III, pp. 827–30).

According to almost universal Jewish teaching, the resurrection is God's prerogative, and consequently in the Shemone Esre (2nd Benediction) he receives the predicate "who gives life to dead" (cf. Deut 32:39; 1 Sam 2:6; 2 Kg 5:7; Tob 13:2; 2 Macc 7:9, 14; *4 Esdras*, 5, 45; Billerbeck, I, pp. 523f.). As regards the question how the resurrection takes place, it is significant that in the period when the belief in the resurrection assumed its full shape, the doctrine of man was also transformed by the spread of the Greek idea of the soul. This was now conceived as a second essential part of man besides the body. As a consequence a fundamental change ensued in the way the dead were thought of; they now lived a life of their own independently of the body, as real "souls". The older view was that the dead receive their bodies back again, which are vivified by the spirit of God, as happened when man was created. Once belief in the soul had been elaborated, however, the resurrection was regarded as taking place through the reception of a new body by the souls coming from the realm of the dead. Thus man is reconstituted whole and entire. This is important for the doctrine of man in Palestinian Judaism. The whole man is to share in the salvation of the world to come; that is what the resurrection means. There was no agreement whether the body which the dead receive at the resurrection will be entirely the old body which is restored once again, or one which is transfigured in some way, or an entirely new one. According to the *Syriac Apocalypse of Baruch* (50, 1–51, 10), as well as rabbinic teaching (cf. Billerbeck, IV, p. 1175), the earth gives up the dead precisely as it received them, for this is necessary to establish their identity, and only then does their transfiguration ensue (cf. on this Volz, *op. cit.*, pp. 249–55).

The teaching of Hellenistic Judaism was in marked contrast to that of Palestinian Judaism. Its doctrine of man was very strongly influenced by Platonism and Stoicism, which regarded belief in the resurrection of the body as ridiculous (cf. Acts 17:32). The chief but not the only witness to this Hellenistic Judaism is Philo. The Hellenistic influence is also exhibited in the Book of Wisdom, which expresses the Greek doctrine of immortality (1:16ff.). Retribution for the actions of men follows immediately after death (3:1ff.; 15:1ff.) and the souls of the just immediately attain a supramundane place (1:15; 15:3). The resurrection of the body is not contested, but neither is it ever mentioned. The Greek doctrine of immortality is also clearly represented in *4 Maccabees* (16, 13; 17, 5; 18, 23). Platonic dualism is most clearly expressed by Philo. According to him the soul is the part of man which originates from God, whereas the body, the animal part of man, is the source of all evil in him. It is the dungeon in which the soul is imprisoned (*De Ebrietate*, 101; *Legum Allegoriae*, III, 42), the corpse which it drags about with it (*ibid.*, I, 69), its coffin or tomb (*De Migratione Abrahami*, 16; *Legum Allegoriae*, I, 108), which impedes the free development of its powers. This is why those men who are philosophers strive to die to the life of the body (*De Gigantibus*, 14; cf. *De Vita Mosis*, II, 288). There is therefore no place in this view of man for the resurrection of the body. The redemption of man consists rather in liberating the soul from the prison of the body (*Legum Allegoriae*, I, 107).

With the destruction of Jerusalem, Sadduceeism disappeared from Jewish history and the Pharisee rabbis set up a new centre of teaching in the Synod of Jamnia. Through its patriarchs they succeeded in dominating Judaism throughout the Roman Empire and imposed their own doctrine as alone valid and as binding on all. In this way belief in the resurrection was taken over by all medieval Judaism, not excluding the Karaites. Maimonides expressly lists it among the 13 articles of orthodox Jewish belief which he enumerates, though others such as Ch. Crescas and Jos. Albo assigned a less important place to it. Maimonides, however, calls the life of the soul after its separation from the body "resurrection", thereby identifying the latter with immortality. As a consequence, he interprets Dan 12:2 metaphorically. Modern Reform Judaism has abandoned the doctrine of the resurrection of the body and replaced it by belief in immortality. It has accordingly paraphrased in terms of immortality the sections of the liturgy which speak of the resurrection of the body.

3. *New Testament.* In a discussion with the Sadducees (Mk 12:16–27),

Jesus refutes their denial of the resurrection by an appeal to the *Torah*, but above all to the power of God. At the same time he corrects the Pharisee doctrine that the resurrection meant a return to the conditions of earthly life. "When they rise from the dead, they neither marry nor are given in marriage, but are like angels in heaven" (12:25). In the synoptic tradition no mention is made of the resurrection of the impious. It is, however, implied in what is said about the judgment of all men. It will be more tolerable at the judgment for Tyre and Sidon than for the Galilean towns which have refused to believe in Jesus (Mt 11:22 = Lk 10:14; cf. also Mt 10:36f.; 12:41 = Lk 11:31f.; Mt 25:31–46). Consequently, Lk 14:14, where express mention is made of the "resurrection of the just" should not be understood in an exclusive sense. The resurrection is not mentioned in the Catholic Epistles. On the other hand, the Letter to the Hebrews (6:2) counts it among the elementary doctrines of Christian belief. Acts (24:15) speaks of "a resurrection of both the just and the unjust". St. John's Gospel speaks of the resurrection of the just (6:39f., 43f.; 11:25f.) and of the "resurrection of life" and "the resurrection of judgment" (5:28f.). A judgment of just and impious and consequently a resurrection of both is found in Revelation (1:7). This work is also the only one to speak of a double resurrection. The second is the general resurrection of all the dead at the Last Judgment (20:11–19), the first is reserved to the martyrs who will then rule with Christ for 1000 years (20:4–6).

Paul develops a real theology of the resurrection in his controversy with Christians in Corinth (1 Cor 15) who, under the influence of Hellenistic or Gnostic thought, denied the resurrection. He sharply dissociates himself from Hellenistic and from Gnostic thought for which the body is the tomb or prison of the soul and redemption consists in liberation from this prison. For Paul, redemption, the state of salvation, is only completed by resurrection in the new body. At the same time he dissociates himself from the Jewish, Pharisee doctrine, which had already been opposed by Jesus (see above). An incorporeal life in a denuded condition is obviously no true life in Paul's eyes. Consequently, in order to escape this intermediate bodiless state, he wishes to "put on" the heavenly body over the earthly one (2 Cor 5:3). He consoles the Thessalonians who were anxious about their dead, solely by means of the prospect of the resurrection, without making any reference at all to their lot until it occurs (1 Thess 4:13–18). In dealing with the Corinthians who denied the resurrection, he does not take into account at all the possibility of a disembodied state of happiness with the Lord but rather declares that if there is no resurrection of the dead, "We are of all men most to be pitied" (1 Cor 15:19); all his work and suffering as an apostle is in vain, life generally is futile and all that is left is the maxim "Let us eat and drink, for tomorrow we die" (15:32). In Philippians (1:23) he does indeed speak of his desire to depart and without a body "to be with Christ". Nevertheless even here the ultimate goal of his longing is the resurrection (3:21).

Fundamental to the Pauline idea of the resurrection is the connection which he draws between Christ's resurrection and that of Christians. According to Paul, Christ has been raised up by God as the "first fruits of those who have fallen asleep" (1 Cor 15:20), as "first-born from the dead" (Col 1:18) – the same idea is also found in Acts 3:15; 26:23. His resurrection is the beginning of the awakening of the dead (1 Cor 15:23) and its basis. Just as death came into the world through the first Adam, so the resurrection of the dead comes through Christ. "For as in Adam all die, so also in Christ shall all be made alive"

(1 Cor 15:22f.). The Christians have already been sacramentally buried and raised up in baptism (Rom 6:4f.; cf. Col 3:1; Eph 2:5f.). By this the expectation of the resurrection which is still to come is not annulled in a Gnostic way (cf. 2 Tim 2:18). The communication of new life is regarded rather as an anticipation of the final salvation which is still to come. According to Paul, the being "in Christ" produced by baptism is the presupposition of the future resurrection (1 Cor 6:14; 1 Cor 15:22). This being in Christ also includes the possession of the divine Pneuma, and this is precisely the power which produces the being in Christ and will also effect the future resurrection. "If the Spirit of him who raised Jesus from the dead dwells in you, he who raised Christ from the dead, will give life to your mortal bodies also through his Spirit who dwells in you" (Rom 8:11). For that reason Paul can call the Pneuma the "guarantee" of our clothing with the heavenly body (2 Cor 5:5; Rom 8:23).

In his controversy with the Corinthians who denied the resurrection, who considered anything of the sort to be impossible and who believed that the resurrection takes place in a spiritual manner at baptism itself (cf. 2 Tim 2:18), Paul also speaks of the condition of the risen body. He cannot indeed give a precise description of it. He calls it "pneumatic"; which does not designate the material of which it is made, but its quality. The risen body is different in kind from the fleshly or "animated" body, for it is imperishable, immortal (15:35ff.). Christ will transfigure the body in which we exist in a lowly condition and make it like the body of glory (δόξα) which he possesses since his resurrection (Phil 3:21). And just as the body of the risen Lord is identical with his earthly body, so also the Christians' heavenly bodies are identical with their earthly ones. That is already implied in the concept of resurrection, but is also confirmed by the image of the kernel of wheat (1 Cor 15:36–38) and the idea of transfiguration. The resurrection for Paul, as for the whole NT, is an eschatological event connected with the Parousia and Last Judgment and the end of the present aeon (1 Thess 6:16; 1 Cor 15:51f.). Like Christ's resurrection, it is an act of divine omnipotence (1 Cor 6:14; 2 Cor 13:4; Rom 4:25; similarly Acts 3:15; 4:10; 5:30; 10:40; 13:30, 37; contrast Phil 3:21; on John see below). It completes the conquest of the power of death (1 Cor 15:53–55).

Since, however, the transformation of the body is to take place at the Parousia (1 Cor 15:51), this excludes the opinion that Paul regarded the heavenly body as pre-existent and lying ready in heaven. The text of 2 Cor 5:1–4 does not demand such an interpretation. All Paul's statements referred to so far only hold good of Christians, because only they "are in Christ" and possess the divine Pneuma. Paul says as little about the resurrection of other human beings as the synoptic tradition does. This limitation is explained by the kerygmatic and paraenetic purpose of his letters. It would therefore be rash to infer that he excluded the rest of men, especially the impious, from the resurrection. The contrary must be assumed if only from the fact of his Jewish, Pharisee past. It also follows from his doctrine of the general judgment (1 Cor 6:2f.; 11:32; Rom 2:11, 12, 16; 2 Cor 5:10). The further question as to whether Paul taught a double resurrection, first that of the just, i.e., the Christians, and only then that of others, is not to be affirmed on the basis of 1 Cor 15:20–22, because τὸ τέλος does not mean the "rest" (contrary to the view of J. Weiss, Lietzmann, Oepke, in *TWNT*, I, p. 371; contrast W. G. Kümmel in H. Lietzmann, *An die Korinther* [4th ed., 1949], p. 193); as is usual in Jewish apocalyptic, it means the end of the present aeon.

The relevant statements of John's Gospel have special features. The Johannine Christ says of himself on one occasion, "I am the resurrection and the life" (11:25). But here "resurrection", like "life", is a term of the specifically Johannine "realized eschatology". This sense of the resurrection as already present is also contained at least implicitly at 5:21–25. Verse 21: "For as the Father raises the dead and gives them life, so also the Son gives life to whom he will." Verse 24: "He who hears my word and believes him who sent me, has eternal life and does not come into judgment but has passed from death to life." In these passages it is spiritual resurrection from the death of sin which is meant. Immediately afterwards, however (5:28f.), mention is made in plain terms of the resurrection of all who are in their graves, both the good and the wicked, by the Son of man "on the last day" (similarly 6:39f., 44, 54).

Whenever the NT mentions the resurrection, it speaks of the "resurrection of the dead", never of "resurrection of the body (of the flesh)", which is not found until 2 *Clement*, 9, 1, and Justin, *Dialogue*, 80, 5. What is always meant, therefore, is the whole man. For Paul, the term "resurrection of the flesh" would not have been possible at all, because for him the word σάρξ, in contradistinction to body, included the idea of something weak, perishable and sinful. That is clearly expressed at 1 Cor 15:50: "Flesh and blood cannot inherit the kingdom of God, nor does the perishable inherit the imperishable."

In the opinion of many Protestant theologians at the present time, death does not consist in the immortal soul's being separated from the body and continuing to live on its own. The total nature of death, as Paul understands it, demands rather that the whole man is shattered in death. Consequently, there is no intermediate state between death and resurrection, and the resurrection is a completely new creation. In this view man only lives on between death and resurrection *in mente Dei*, in God's remembrance. This opinion contradicts several passages in the NT. Paul knows of a "being at home" with Christ in a disembodied state between death and resurrection (Phil 1:21; 2 Cor 5:6–8; cf. also Lk 23:43f.; Rev 6:9; 20:4).

Josef Schmid

B. Theological

1. The biblical form of belief in immortality is the hope of the resurrection which, however, before long, in the Graeco-Roman world in which the Christian message unfolded, was no more conceived of in the totality of its claim. It was seen rather as a complement to the idea of immortality already at hand and which was based upon the concept of the immortality proper to the rational soul. Both of these concepts of immortality were considered to be half-answers to the question of the eternal fate of man, and were thus added together: to the Greek premonition of the immortality of the soul already present, the Bible joined the revelation that the body would also be raised on the last day in order to share for ever the fate of the soul – whether of damnation or salvation. From then on the whole theological problem was determined by this juxtaposition of antique and Christian ideas which was fixed in the Bull *Benedictus Deus* of Benedict XII (1336). Through the dogma that the *anima separata* is capable of entering immediately into the beatific vision or into hell, it put an end for the time being to the dispute concerning the relationship in this question between the Greek and biblical traditions.

Actually, what was originally involved were not two complementary notions, but rather two complete answers to the problem of the future of man. As its basis the Greek idea has the notion of two heterogeneous substances which have been added together in man, one of which decays (the body), while the other (the soul) is of itself immortal and thus able to continue existing in itself, independently of any other being; only then, in separation from its essentially alien and mortal body, is the soul able to achieve its full and proper self. In contrast to this, biblical thought presupposes an indivisible unity of man; for example, the Bible has no term which signifies only the body (separated and differentiated from the soul); vice versa the word "soul" always means the whole man existing bodily (J. Schmid). The raising of the dead (not the bodies!) which the Bible speaks of is thus not meant as simply a partial aspect of the hope of man, but concerns the salvation of man as *one* and indivisible.

2. It is not enough then, when trying to bring the Greek and biblical ideas of immortality into a proper relation, simply to join them together and thus do neither justice. It is rather necessary to distinguish more precisely the intentions of each idea, and then to ask in which way the Greek idea might be of help, both in thought and in language, in formulating the biblical notion. Concerning the latter, it should now be clear that its essential point is not that the body is given back (even though this method of presentation is found throughout the Bible). Its main point is best expressed by contrasting it with the dualistic conception of ancient philosophy already sketched above.

a) It deals with an immortality of the "person". In Greek thought the normal entity man is doomed to decay. The being as such does not live on, but goes two different ways according to its heterogeneous assembly of body and soul. But for the biblical faith it is precisely this entity man as such which, though changed, lives on.

b) It treats of immortality in a "dialogal" way (= resurrection), i.e., immortality is not simply derived from the evident impossibility of death in the indivisible, but from the saving act of one who loves and who has the power to bestow immortality. Man no longer faces the prospect of utter dissolution, because God knows him and loves him. All love desires eternity; God's love not only desires it, but effects it and is it. The biblical concept of the resurrection actually grew directly out of this dialogal motive: he who prays knows in faith that God will establish justice (Job 19:25f.; Ps 73:23f.); faith is convinced that those who have suffered for God will also participate in the realization of the promise (2 Macc 7:9f.). Because immortality as it is biblically presented does not proceed from intrinsic indestructibility, but comes instead from being included in a dialogue with the Creator, it must be called resurrection. And because the Creator does not simply have the soul alone in mind, but man as he actually unfolds himself within the concreteness of history, and because he also gives him immortality, therefore this immortality must be the raising of the dead = of man. (At this point it should be noted that the *resurrectio carnis* in the Creed still understands *caro* in the biblical sense, i.e., *caro* = the human world, and not in the sense of a corporality separated from the soul.)

c) That the complete resurrection on the "last day" is expected at the end of history and in the fellowship of all men indicates a further fact, namely the "social" dimension of human immortality, which always has a relation to the whole of humanity within which and in relation to which the individual has lived, and from which he is saved or damned. This is really only one consequence of the integrally human character of immortality as it is biblically presented. In the Greek notion, the body is completely external to the soul, and thus history also; the soul continues to exist apart, and has no need of any other beings. In contrast to this, being-with-others is constitutive for man thought of as a unity; should *he* continue living, then this dimension cannot be done away with. Thus the question often posed, as to whether after death there can be fellowship between men, appears from the biblical point of view to be solved. It was really only able to arise through a predominance of the Greek element at the initial stage. With the belief in the *communio sanctorum* the idea of an *anima separata* is finally superseded.

The basic elements of this biblical faith in the resurrection became still more concrete in the NT when it was referred back to Christology. The resurrection of Jesus became the guarantee and starting-point of the resurrection of Christians. To the believer the figure of Christ signifies in fact the incarnation of the divine dialogue with humanity. If this dialogue is the resurrection and eternal life of man, it follows that Christ himself may be called the Resurrection and the Life (Jn 11:25). That would further mean that the entrance into Christ, i.e., faith, gives in a well-defined sense entrance to that being known and being loved by God which is immortality: "He who believes in the Son, has eternal life" (Jn 3:36; 5:24; 3:15f.). From this is derived the "present eschatology" of John's Gospel, in the light of which it becomes clear that in accepting the world of faith the event of the resurrection becomes a present occurrence, insofar as it means living in the world of God and immortality. The relation of faith in the resurrection to Christology has the further effect that the two dialogal dimensions of human existence (cf. above, b and c), the theological dimension, which is directed towards God, and the co-human, which is directed towards social existence, are now seen to be deeply implicated in each other. Christ, who primarily represents the incarnate dialogue of God with man, is at the same time, as *Christus totus*, the radical unity of man as social being "in one body", and is he who through the whole of history waits for me and encounters me in my fellowman. The unified eschatology which thus results has been most strongly developed by John. He sees in Christ not only the resurrection, but also the judgment as already present (3:18f.; 5:24; 12:31; 16:8).

Seen from this Christological centre, the question is finally answered which was so often posed in the patristic age, later by John XXII, and again since Luther: the question of the "intermediate state", between death and resurrection. The being-with-Christ, which is established in faith, is a life of resurrection which has already begun, and which thus survives death (Phil 1:23). The eschatological reality, thus already present and thrusting itself into our actual life (cf. Jn), means that the idea of sleeping in death, considered by Luther and Lutheran theology (e.g., Paul Althaus), must be viewed as unbiblical (at least as found in the NT). Starting from a different approach we arrive at the same result: he who belongs to the body of Christ is already encompassed in the sphere of the resurrection and by his participation in this body takes part in the resurrection of Jesus, in which death is conquered for him.

3. At this point a certain *rapprochement* with the Greek concept of immortality, as well as its transformation into a Christian idea, becomes possible, despite the basic difference in their points of origin. This was attempted in the late medieval dogmas (*D* 738). This idea, despite its originally dualistic intention, can at any rate become an expression of that essential immortality which belongs universally to man on the basis of the special manner in which God has willed him to be and called him to be, and which finds its proper interpretation and fulfilment in the Christological declarations.

Since man is always called by divine love to give a blessed answer, even where he freely and finally fails this love, and since "soul" is the key-word for the personal unity of man as a supramaterial being, one can and must speak of the "natural immortality" of the spirit-person, and hence of that of the "soul" (*D* 738, 1622; *DS* 3771, 3998). Every truly anthropological assertion about body and soul means the one being of man, but in its intrinsic differentiation by virtue of a spiritual and a material *principle* of being. It means man as spiritual and as spatio-temporal. These attributes cannot be divided between two beings, but neither can they simply be identified. Hence to speak of an "intermediate state" of the soul, free from the body, "before" the resurrection means no more, theologically speaking, than the necessary difference between the two attributes, which are only true of the being of man and his fulfilment when taken together.

From all this it should be clear that cosmological, biological and physical speculations, inquiring into the possibility of a resurrection, are not dealing with an object proper to their disciplines and are thus meaningless. What must be held fast to is that the time of history, through the sovereign power of God, will come to an end, and that then, in the fulfilment of Christ's work, God will be all in all (1 Cor 15:28).

Joseph Ratzinger

REVELATION

I. Concept of Revelation

A. The Basic Notion

1. *History of religion.* a) Though the science of religion has not succeeded in proving the existence of a primitive revelation, it would be wrong to assume that all notions of revelation outside the Jewish and Christian religions are merely philosophy. Critique of religion may lead one to affirm that procedures aiming at self-deliverance, using either external or internal means, still fall short of being religious acts. It may nonetheless be affirmed against any negative attitude to the Jewish and Christian religions that revelation is part of the self-understanding of all religions which claim to be divine creations and not human constructions (*RGG*, IV, col. 1597). The phenomenology of religion confirms this statement.

b) Hence in Islam the author of revelation is the personal God and the content of revelation is his inscrutable will, whose decree governs all the realities of the world and displays itself as commandments. There is, however, no promise of a self-revelation of God and a participation in the divine life which would form the basis of a history of salvation.

c) Zarathustra also explains revelation as the act of will of a personal God. In later Persian religion this divine decision becomes a summons to ethical and spiritual responsibility which goes out to all men, who are chosen before the beginning of the dualistic world of history. History becomes a battle whose outcome is already certain as a triumph for God and for the men who have decided for him.

d) The Vedantic religion of India is also a religion of revelation. In the Vedas, an uncreated word is uttered which resounds in the world of man. In this self-utterance, the word remains the transcendent ground of being and as such it is mediated by revelation, which becomes the sacred law governing worship and the social order.

e) In the other religions outside Judaism and Christianity the revelational character is less marked, insofar as rational knowledge of the hidden laws of being or irrational participation in life itself predominate. Nonetheless, even in the archaic stages of religious consciousness there is a yearning to experience the primordial ground of the human world. And this is accompanied by revealed tidings of the first principle, presented in general as a comprehensive "something", more rarely as a person. This principle, being the goal of all induction, is what gives meaning to everything. Hence it is there not merely as a foretaste to be sought for, but as the way of salutary life which makes itself manifest.

The poverty of the Church demands that in loyalty to its sacramental universality it must assume the presence of non-Christian notions of revelation wherever these indicate and promote in their way the peace which comprises all men (Vatican II, *Lumen Gentium*, arts. 13–17; *Nostra Aetate, passim*). See K. Rahner, *Theological Investigations*, V (1966), pp. 115–34; G. Thils, *La valeur salvifique des religions non-chrétiennes* (1965), pp. 197–211.

2. *Revelation and self-revelation in biblical usage*. a) Since there are tendencies to positivist self-assertion in the Church and in men, Vatican II reminds the Church and the faithful of their place as hearers of revelation. This means hearing the Scriptures of the OT and NT as they point on to God who reveals his goodness and mercy. Thus Scripture can be looked to for divine revelation, because God speaks today to the Church and to men through Scripture (Vatican II, *Dei Verbum*, arts. 2, 8, 9, 25). In view of this function, Scripture may be defined as God's speech and action committed to writing for the good of man and the Church. It is God's revelation in self-communication through words.

b) The OT affirms that man of himself cannot know God. God is known only when he lets himself be known, when he decides to reveal himself (Deut 4:32–34), because he has shown himself to Israel (Ps 147:19f.). But since Israel lived with divine revelation, the later Wisdom literature could not imagine any real life without revelation (Ps 1:1–3; 19:8f.; 119). Revelation makes true life possible, and is indeed life. True to this notion of life, revelation in the OT is not registered as a noun, but described by verbs. And the three verbs, "disclose, announce, present something clearly to someone" are not reserved to divine revelation but also indicate the action of disclosing and learning in human intercourse (Est 3:14; Prov 20:19; Gen 31:20). The OT clearly takes the view that in spite of God's majesty his revelation and man's knowledge are not so far apart that God's revealing his name (Is 64:1f.), his power (Jer 16:21), his action (Hab 3:2) and his aid (Ps 98:2) remains merely the decree of his will. On the contrary, when God shows himself, it is not just that he acts in history and on man (W. Eichrodt, *Theology of the Old Testament*, I [1962]). His revelation is also understood by the men who hear and is put into practice or undergone as history (1 Sam 16:3; 2 Sam 7:21; Jer 11:18; Deut 8:19).

God's revelation takes place in history and the history of God with man is both the object and the means of his revelation. The history-centred nature of God's revelation is reflected in the forms in which God shows himself: the storm, pillars of cloud and of fire, the rustling of the trees and the whispering of the wind, the whole majestic work of creation. These are not magical revelations but appear as commentary on God's self-revelation in the world. They arouse attention, like the methods more fully laden with historic consequences, the inner perception when man is laid hold of, and tremendous eternal events (Exod 19:16; 14:24; 2 Sam 5:24; 1 Kg 19:12; Ps 8:4; 19:2; Job 38ff.). Here, as in the case of the pledges of revelation – ark, tent, temple, sacrifice – the prophets bring criticism to bear on the means of revelation (Is 28:7; 29:9f.; 30:10; Jer 23:16, 25; Ezek 13:6; Zech 13:4). It appears more and more clearly that the goal of revelation is the choosing of Israel to be the people of the covenant (at the Exodus and on Sinai). It is the revelation of God's will in history. By virtue of this disclosure of the will of God in history, as brought to light by critical reflection, history becomes the setting of human decision. Man is to respond, to accept God's purposeful guidance, to be thankful for this help and be ready to serve God's salvation in history. God makes history, with Israel as his partner, so that they "may know that I am Yahweh" (cf. Jer 31:34; Ezek 36:38; 37:28; Is 43:10).

The history of God with man is distributed among places of blessing (Sinai, the walls of Jerusalem, Egypt – Deut 33:2; 2 Sam 7:8–16; Is 11:11) and over periods of blessing and visitation (Is 9:1; 49:8; 10:3; 61:2; Jer 46:10; 50:27). But this makes recognition of God's revealed plan of salvation so difficult that a key is needed to read in the chequered course of events God's presence in the world, which is his revelation. In the OT human history as such is not recognizable even to the elect of Israel as salvation-history. It is only such when the key-experience of God's word comes into play – the word which created the world and man and which as word in action gives life, in a history which is interpreted on the part of God by the prophets and the law (Gen 1; Ps 147:15–18; Deut 8:3; Ps 106:9; 107:20, 25; Is 50:2; Jer 18:18; Deut 1:1, 18).

It may be noted that in Ezekiel historical events are presented, without words of interpretation, as revelations (Ezek 17:24; 29:6; 37:28; 39:7, 23; cf. R. Rendtorff, "Offenbarungsvorstellungen im Alten Israel", in W. Pannenberg, ed., *Offenbarung als Geschichte* [2nd ed., 1963]; on which see A. Gamper in *ZKT* 86 [1964], p. 186; English summary of the debate by J. M. Robinson, "Revelation as Word and History", in J. M. Robinson and J. B. Cobb, eds., *Theology as History* [1967], pp. 42–56). Nonetheless, one finds these events presented by a prophet, and the connection between word and history in the OT is that "the history of Yahweh with Israel is the setting in which the truth of his revelatory word in action is recognizable" (cf. W. Zimmerli, *Gottes Offenbarung* [1961], p. 22). God presents himself in words of revelation which appear within longer "cognition formulas" (i.e., predictions of God's action in which men are to learn that "I am Yahweh"). These "self-presentation formulas" (cf. Deut 7:8), enshrined as they are in promises, then have the value of "words of demonstration" (1 Kg 20:28; 2 Sam 7:12; Zimmerli, *op. cit.*, pp. 14, 41–119, 121). The word of God, working in history (Is 55:10f.), demonstrates that history is promise. It creates thereby in history what is all-important for the OT – the link between promise and fulfilment. This revelation of the divine will turns history into salvation-history. From Daniel on, it gives rise to an apocalyptic understanding of history whose influence is felt in the NT (A. Oepke, "ἀποκαλύπτω", *TWNT*, III, pp. 563–92).

But if the word of God in the OT becomes history and history becomes a demonstrative word pointing to God's revelation being fulfilled, the difference between seeing and hearing of revelation becomes of minor importance, in spite of the predominance of vision and images in Apocalyptic. God's revelation, still unimaginable to purely human thought, is experienced in the human action which is called history. According to the OT God reveals himself in history as a promise for the men of Israel and of all nations (Mic 4:5; 6:3–5; Jer 11:5; 33; Deut 4:37; Exod 32:13; Is 41:8–10; Gen 9:1). God reveals the goal of man and his history by showing himself as active in history.

c) In the NT, the terminology alone suffices to show that the concept of revelation differs in St. Paul and St. John. St. Paul describes revelation by the verbs "reveal" (Rom 1:17f.; 2:5; 1 Cor 1:7; Gal 3:23) and "manifest" (Rom 3:21; 2 Cor 4:10f.), which are also found in the OT. And he uses the noun "mystery" (Eph 1:9), which comes from the Wisdom literature and the Apocalyptic of Judaism (Wis 6:22–24; Enoch 9:6; 81:1; 103:2f.; 4 Esdras 2:1). But the theology of St. John, though permeated by the notion of revelation, does not use the noun revelation at all, and the verb only once, in a quotation from the OT (Jn 12:38). This, along with the absence of the terms "mystery" and "reveal" and the general use of "manifest", indicates a deliberate adoption of the vocabulary of later Hellenism. The starting-point is still Jewish, the essential "invisibility" of God (Jn 1:18; 6:46; 1 Jn 4:20). But the emphatic assertion that God is only visible and attainable in the incarnation of Jesus, in the words and works of Jesus (Jn 1:14; 1 Jn 1:1f.; 4:7–9; Jn 5:36; 9:4; 10:37f.; 14:10; 1:18; 3:11; 17:6–8), makes a clear distinction between the revelation of the OT and the revelation in Christ. In Jn, Jesus is the revealer, the light, the truth (cf. H. Schlier, *The Relevance of the New Testament*, ch. 18).

In St. Paul God remains the revealer, as in the OT. The mystery of his will had been hidden in him, till executed in time through the death and resurrection of Jesus, in his bond with the Church as his body, in the summing up of the universe in Christ (Rom 3:25; 16:25f.; 1 Cor 15:28; Eph 1:9f.; 3:9–11; Col 1:18). According to St. Paul, Christ is the content of the mystery of God (Rom 3:21–24; Gal 1:16; Eph 3:3, 5; 1 Tim 3:16) and he is not so much the revealer as the revealed.

Nonetheless, the distinction between "Jesus the revealer" and "Jesus the revealed" is not the whole story. It does not do full justice to John, for whom salvation is from the Jews (cf. Jn 5:39, 46f.; 8:56; 12:41), or to the synoptics (Mk 8:12; Lk 1:19, 72; 2:25, 38; 19:9) or the other writings of the NT (Acts 2:36; 13:32f.; 26:16; Heb 8:8ff.; 1 Pet 1:3, 10–12), or to Paul, for whom Christ is the end of the law (Rom 10:3f.). These texts, and the exegesis of the basic concepts common to the OT and the NT, such as "covenant, testament" (Jer 31:31ff.; Ezek 37:26–28; Heb 8:8–12; 10:16f.), "God the royal lord" (Ps 47; 93; Is 52:7; Mk 1:14f.), "people of God" (Exod 4:4f.; 5:22f.; 17:4; Num 11:31–34; 1 Pet 2:9f.), show that the notion of God from the OT and the promise of God from the OT are given in the NT, that is, in Christ (Eph 3:6), who is the fullness of revelation. This fulfilment cannot be demonstrated on historical and critical grounds from the typology appealed to in the NT proofs from prophecy (Zech 9:9, cf. Mt 21:5; Is 7:14; cf. Mt 1:23; Is 59:20, cf. Rom 11:26f.; Jer 31:31–34; cf. Heb 8:8–11). The fulfilment of all the promises of revelation in Christ does not make Jesus the "middle" of a cyclic or linear understanding of time in the history of revelation. And the fullness of revelation in Christ does not absorb eschatologically the history of mankind in the historicity of a definitive decision of faith. Such notions correspond rather to a philosophical pre-understanding – Stoic allegory, Hegelian philosophy of history or existentialist ontology. They do not do justice to the biblical understanding of the history of revelation.

When Rom 9–11 links Christ with the history of Israel, when Jn 5:39 treats the OT as testimony to the Son and when Gal 3:15 presents believers as the heirs to the promise made to Abraham, the doctrine of the NT is that Jesus, the revelation of God in the light of the OT promises, is the anticipatory fulfilment of all promises (W. Pannenberg, "The Revelation of God in Jesus of Nazareth", in J. M. Robinson and J. B. Cobb, eds., *Theology as History* [1967], p. 113). Jesus is the revelation of God because he is the fulfilment of all promises in a salvation-history. The events of this history, including works of God in the light of the OT, the decisive saving act of the resurrection of Jesus, the anticipatory realization of the future resurrection of believers, do not deprive the present of its value. They make it an openness to the future which springs from the present fulfilment of a past of promises (J. Moltmann, *Theology of Hope* [1967]). The message of the risen

Jesus takes the form of history being fulfilled in the resurrection of Jesus. The word of the resurrection becomes the bestowal of reconciliation, of the life and love of God himself, as they were revealed in Jesus Christ (2 Cor 5:20; 6:2; 1 Jn 1:2; 3:5, 8; 4:7ff.).

The resurrection of Jesus is the self-revelation of the living God who wills that man should have life. God reveals himself in the history which runs between word of promise and work of fulfilment and spans past and present and binds them to the open future of the definitive, salutary participation of man in the life of God. Revelation in the NT is salvation-history which does not go beyond Jesus, because it is fulfilled in him, but continues to work for man, whose salvation is promised in the triumph of Jesus. Revelation is God's word on history, and as faithful word, the history of God's word among man.

3. *Meaning of revelation-history.* Obviously, this biblical notion of revelation as ordained to the word and to history is only a start. The meaning of revelation is not yet worked out. For a meaningful statement consists of words, according to linguistic analysis. And history presents itself to criticism as individual items. In the concrete, here and now, the co-ordination of the existentiell subject with history only takes place in an overriding totality of all actions, since history is more than the sum of the expressive deeds of all individuals. If human conduct is considered, the totality of word and history, according to the methodology of science, cannot be arrived at by adding up words, data and individual actions, nor by mere induction without a principle for the process of induction. Without a principle, the understanding of revelation would lead to various positivisms with regard to revelation. According to the various approaches, the OT and the NT, and hence Judaism and Christianity, would be irreparably sundered. Or within Christianity, schools would be formed orientated to the word, to works or to existentialist anthropology. And this, as experience shows, hardens into opposing confessions. Schools of positivism with regard to revelation bring about and maintain the ecumenical problem.

The Church and theology take pains to avoid such fragmentation of the Church, which comes through fragmentation of the one revelation into revelations. They focus their gaze on Jesus Christ, in whom the fullness of revelation, as the self-communication of God, has appeared. If, however, in this context the unity of revelation, within a statement of system reduced to monotheism, was preserved only by virtue of its origin from the one God, revelation would be the promulgation of a decree, given for and through Jesus, which could be loyally executed but not fulfilled in free responsibility. With this merely juridical conception of revelation we may contrast Vatican II, which takes up the doctrinal articles of revelation, the "revelata", which Vatican I, after Trent, treated as intellectual information "to be held to be true", but subsumes them under the one "revelatio" of the fullness in Christ. Christ makes manifest the dialogue of salvation as communication from person to person. (Vatican II, *Dei Verbum*, art. 5, changes "revelata" [*D* 1789] into "revelatio"; art. 6, unlike *D* 1785f., speaks of "manifestare" and "communicare". See J. Ratzinger's contribution in H. Vorgrimler, ed., *Commentary on the Documents of Vatican II*, vol. III [1969], pp. 178–80.)

In this perspective, Christ as the Son of the Father is himself the utterance of God, because at the end of revelation God has expressed and shown himself in Christ (A. Oepke in *TWNT*, III, p. 594; Ignatius, *Ad Magnesios*, VIII, 2; Vatican I = *D* 1795; Vatican II, *Dei Verbum*, art. 4). Hence an isolated Christocentrism in the understanding of revelation has been left behind in favour of a trinitarian conception. The movement of revelation starts from the Father, meets us through Christ and gives us access to fellowship with God in the Holy Spirit (Gal 3:26ff.; Rom 8:9ff., 29; 2 Cor 3:17f.; Vatican II, *Dei Verbum*, art. 2; cf. W. Thüsing, *Per Christum in Deum* [1965]). If one accepts the trinitarian conception of revelation, then the obvious question is the meaning of revelation, in the sense of how God communicated himself to us in Christ. God remains – in accordance with the biblical understanding – inaccessible to man by his own efforts, since nature and history only teach us that we do not yet possess revelation when the fulfilment in Christ is not seen by all (J. Ratzinger, *loc. cit.*, pp. 170, 178). The question then becomes insistent: how can the inaccessible God communicate himself to us in such a way that we can have experience of him?

There is a positivism with regard to revelation which simply says, in the obedience of faith within the Church, that revelation is there at any rate as a fact, even if one cannot explain it. But this reply is obviously insufficient, because in the experience of revelation what matters is not explanations, but understanding: believers are called to give an account of the hope which they have from revelation (1 Pet 3:15; 1 Cor 14:20–25; I. A. Philips, *The Form of Christ in the World* [1967], pp. 156–72). This account must begin with the consummation of Christ's work, and hence with the resurrection of Jesus, because the new meaning given by God's interpellation to everyday life and extraordinary happenings is revealed in the risen Jesus. This may be seen from the final chapter of Jn, which begins in the style of revelatory discourse with the words, "After this Jesus revealed himself again", and goes on to tell of an unexpectedly large haul of fish and the new orientation given to the two men, Peter and John (Jn 21:1ff.).

Here then, as in other contexts of the gospels, the individual miracles are inserted into the one great marvel of God which is Jesus Christ, above all in his resurrection (1 Jn 1:2; 3:5, 8; 1 Pet 1:20; Heb 9:20; Vatican II, *Dei Verbum*, art. 4). But this reference to miracle in the course of revelation merely hints that Jesus "spoke the words of God" (Jn 3:34). It does not show that he revealed God the Father, as his Word, sent "as man to man" (cf. Jn 1:1–18; *Epistle to Diognetus*, VII, 4). If one is to give an account of the coming of God the Father in the Word which the Son is, and which the Holy Spirit expounds, one may point to two basic phenomena of human reality: language and history. As the horizons within which revelation may be understood, they are also realities of God's self-revelation in the world. One may follow R. Bultmann in recognizing that life is manifest in the word: but in the word which takes cognizance, life is condemned to death, though language also shelters the profoundest being of man which is existentially and historically orientated, that is, towards life.

This is something still understandable to every inward-looking man. But the preaching of the coming of revelation in the fact of Jesus is the paradoxical assertion that this historical event is also eschatological life which is manifest in the life of the risen Jesus and is already perspicuous and present for those who believe this word (R. Bultmann, *Existence and Faith* [1961]). The interpretation offered by Bultmann in terms of the word and existentialist philosophy provides an approach for a human self-understanding which feels the impact of the revelation of life from God, and so accepts here and now in faith the intellectual paradox of the victory of life over death. But whether or not Bultmann's understanding of revelation – if the paradox is maintained – declines into the problematic "anonymous Christianity", still, the act of faith as described by Bultmann rests on an existentialist individual decision. Revelation is reduced to a private matter of faith and understanding and is at least tempted to be blind to history (W. Pannenberg, "Heilsgeschehen und Geschichte", *Grundfragen systematischer Theologie* [1967], pp. 37, 72f.; cf. J. M. Robinson, *op. cit.*, pp. 22f.).

These misgivings about the privacy of revelation (reinforced by the fact that Christologically the OT history of revelation is treated as worthless – cf. R. Bultmann, *Glauben und Verstehen*, II [4th ed., 1965], pp. 32ff.) suggest reflection on history as a second basic phenomenon of human reality and the reality inherent to revelation. History is the setting of the individual decisions of man, and is therefore more comprehensive than any of them. And being a continuity or combination of traditions, it is a past in a present which neither brings history to a stop nor makes it perspicuous, but thrusts forward to a future which is the condition of new experiences. As this condition is still unknown, the future thus demands confidence of those who march forward (J. Moltmann, *op. cit.*, ch. 2). Such experience of history, available to all reflection as typical of the directedness of history (W. Pannenberg, *op. cit.*, pp. 26, 72f.), finds a hermeneutics which overcomes the modern disjunction of fact and meaning, by placing itself in the history of the transmission of traditions and making use of it (*ibid.*, pp. 88f.; cf. J. M. Robinson, *op. cit.*, pp. 82–92). But this hermeneutics is also applicable to the self-revelation of God, which comprises the promises of the "self-presentation formulas" of God in the OT, prophecy and apocalyptic and finally that promised future of which the prospect is offered in the fullness of Christ.

In this perspective, revelation is in a context of transmission of tradition – of divine directives and assurances – in the light of which events can be recognized as God's action and can be accepted in hope of the perfected, future participation in the life of God. The contradiction which the resurrection opposes to the cross turns history once and for all into the eschatology which makes the future articulate in the light of all the affirmations about Christ which say that "he is our hope" (Col 1:27). Hence what we have to expect from the self-revelation of God in the resurrection of Jesus is disclosed less in a "leap" of faith (an intellectual paradox) than in a confidence of faith which marches forward to an unknown goal. Hence it is not a doctrinal system, but the history of him who hopes (Moltmann, *op. cit.*, p. 13). Revelation is understood in the light of Christ, the first of the dead to be raised up, from the midst of history itself. This is not the ostensible knowledge of reality as a whole in a "universal history". Revelation is understood in the light of the condition of possibility of reality as history – a condition which on principle cannot be fully comprehended by man – the promise and fulfilment of an eternal divine life, which both sustain history and form God's self-revelation (H. Urs von Balthasar, *Prometheus* [1947], pp. 91ff.; J. Moltmann, *op. cit.*, pp. 38ff., 69f.).

Hence "history as such", in the sense of Idealism, is not yet the epiphany and revelation of God, any more than the "depths of man" or the "most human word" are of themselves self-revelations of God. But revelation as God's promise impinges on history, human nature and human word. And revelation is properly understood when it and these things are not sealed off in traditionalism, but orientated to the future, where they are still regarded as unfulfilled and hence as open. God's revelation comes as the word of God. The intellectual paradox, that in the fact of human existence there is still hope, because there is life, becomes the insight of hope which sees that life continually grows and grows in the world (H. Geyer in *Evangelische Theologie* 22 [1962], p. 103; W. Pannenberg, *Grundfragen systematischer Theologie* [1967], pp. 229ff.). Revelation as the self-revelation of God in the OT, in Jesus and in the apostles, does not define either God or man simply as "non-world" (K. Jaspers, *Philosophie*, II [1932], p. 1). It announces that God is in the world so that men may be ordained to God in history and be able to criticize their inherited traditions in the light of this orientation. Through the revelation of God, which is always present promise, the works, words and self-discoveries of men are under the judgment of God, just as they are also under the promise contained in this judgment, which was fully accomplished in the contradiction offered by the resurrection to the cross of Christ (Rom 1:17 – 3:20).

Revelation as the one word of God is always there in the form of "law and gospel", not as a timeless ideology but as a historical action of God which reaches men in this age and puts man in his place in the context of this history, as the setting of his salvation (cf. J. Ratzinger, *loc. cit.*, pp. 172f.). The revelation of God, as the "mystery of his will", is the proclamation of God's good pleasure in the world as the history of men. Revelation, as God's being-in-the-world, can be interpreted in ecclesiastical language, after Vatican II (*Dei Verbum*, art. 2) as the "sacrament" of his will for us, the fulfilment of the communication of the life of God himself in Christ. In Jesus, the promised and fulfilled Word of the Father, which the Spirit of God brings to mind in this age, to make acceptable history possible, God himself has become judgment and good news (gospel) for us. God himself became, is and will remain for us revelation so that in the world we as men may have hope.

Norbert Schiffers

B. Theological Interpretation

1. *Preliminary considerations on method.* The question to be answered concerns the theological meaning of revelation. How is it that revelation, despite its directly divine origin, can constitute the very core of human history? How can revelation be present everywhere at all times for the salvation of all men in all ages, without ceasing to be a free act of God which cannot be counted on in our view of history? For revelation is the miracle of God's grace in an event at a particular time and place, occurring once and for all in the flesh of Christ, in the voice of the prophet as he speaks, and in the letter of Scripture. The fundamental hermeneutical principle required for an answer to this question is to be found by considering the most general relationship between God and the world of becoming. God is immanent in the world yet precisely as such is absolutely superior to the world. He endows the finite being with a truly active self-transcendence in its becoming. He himself is the ultimate future and final cause, which is the true efficient cause operative in all becoming. To ask what revelation is, is thus equivalent to asking what is the highest and most radical case of that general relationship in which the actual coming to be of the higher from the self-transcending lower, is only one aspect of the one wonder of becoming and history, the other being its perpetual creation from above. Both aspects are equally true and real. This is the supreme instance of the truth that God in his free relation to his creation is not a "second" cause side by side with others in the world. He is the living perpetual transcendent ground of the world's own movement. This principle also applies *mutatis mutandis* to the relationship between God and man in the event and in the history of revelation. The principle in fact applies in the highest degree, because this history more than any other must simultaneously be God's action and man's if it is to be the highest reality in the being and becoming of the world.

These considerations make it possible

to overcome in principle the barren antithesis between the immanentism of Modernism and a merely extrinsic concept of revelation. For Modernism, at least in the systematized summary presented in the Church's condemnation, revelation is merely the inevitable development (immanent in history) of man's religious needs. Those needs find expression in an endless variety of forms in the history of religions, and gradually grow to greater purity and comprehensiveness until they find expression in Judaism and Christianity. The other term of the antithesis is a purely extrinsic concept of revelation. This regards revelation as a divine intervention coming purely from outside, speaking to men and conveying to them through prophets truths in the form of propositions which would otherwise be inaccessible to them, and giving moral and other commands which men have to obey.

2. *On the theology of revelation.* a) If theology takes seriously its own standard doctrine of divinizing grace, of God's universal salvific will, of the necessity of interior elevating grace for faith, and the Thomist doctrine of the ontological transcendental significance of entitative grace, and applies these doctrines to revelation, then it is quite possible, without falling into Modernism, to recognize that the history of revelation and what is usually called revelation as such, is the historical self-unfolding in predicamental terms, or, more simply and correctly, the history, of the transcendental relation between man and God which is constituted by God's self-communication. This communication is supernatural, grace-given, but made to every mind inescapably and always, and can itself rightly be called revelation. Transcendence only actually operates in history, and is always mediated historically. Furthermore, man is also transcendentally constituted by the permanent existential which we call divinizing grace, by God's self-communication (not by some other causal operation). Consequently this *absolute* transcendence directed towards the absolute presence of the ineffable mystery giving himself to men, has a history, and this is what we call the history of revelation (see *Salvation*).

Active revelation therefore always presents two aspects. On the one hand it constitutes man's supernaturally elevated transcendence as his permanent though grace-given existential, always and everywhere operative, present even when refused. It is the transcendental experience of the absolute and merciful closeness of God, even if this cannot be conceptually expressed at will by everyone. On the other hand, the active revelation-event is also a historical mediation and conceptual objectivation of this supernaturally transcendental experience. The latter takes place in history and, taken in its totality, constitutes the whole of history; the individual's own spontaneous theological reflection belongs to it, though it is not its primary basis and does not determine it. It is what is called the history of revelation in the usual sense when it really is the history of the true self-interpretation of this supernaturally transcendental experience, and not its misinterpretation, and when, therefore, it is really the result of God's transcendental self-communication in grace, hence under the will of his self-communication, in accordance with his supernatural saving providence, and is explicitly known as such. If this view is taken of the unity and reciprocal relationship between transcendental revelation and predicamental historical revelation, or, rather, between the transcendental and historical (mediating) factors of the one revelation and its one history, then a really primordial distinction is apparent in what is revealed.

God is revealed as communicating himself in absolute and merciful presence as God, that is, as the absolute mystery. The historical mediation of this transcendental experience is also revealed as valid, as bringing about and authenticating the absolute experience of God. The unique and final culmination of this history of revelation has already occurred and has revealed the absolute and irrevocable unity of God's transcendental self-communication to mankind and of its historical mediation in the one God-man Jesus Christ, who is at once God himself as communicated, the human acceptance of this communication and the final historical manifestation of this offer and acceptance. And in this unity of God's transcendental self-communication and its definitive historical mediation and manifestation, the fundamental mystery of the triune God is also revealed, since what is involved is the communication of God in himself. For this mystery is merely the ground of God's action on us – tne *in se* of the *quoad nos* of God – in history and transcendence, God in his incomprehensible primordiality, God in his real capacity to enter man's transcendence and history: Father, Son and Holy Spirit. Inasmuch as history mediates transcendence, the Son sends the Spirit; inasmuch as transcendence makes history, the Spirit effects the incarnation of the Logos; inasmuch as the appearance in history implies the manifestation of reality, the incarnate Logos is revealed as the self-utterance of the Father in truth; inasmuch as God's coming among us in the centre of our life signifies his love and ours, the Pneuma is revealed in his intrinsic reality as love. If through the intermediary of history we come to know the transcendental absolute presence of God in his self-communication, and accept it by means of itself, we know by the act of faith itself what we mean when we speak of the Trinity and thereby sum up the whole form and content of our Christian faith and its revelation and the history of revelation, and are baptized in those three names.

b) The fundamental concept of revelation having been indicated, a few further considerations may serve to throw light on its basis and consequences.

If what has been said is correct, transcendental and predicamental revelation and the history of revelation are co-extensive with the spiritual history of mankind as such. This is not a Modernist error but a Christian truth. This can be shown very simply, for it is certain that the history of supernatural salvation is operative everywhere in history. This has been brought even more clearly into the light of the Church's consciousness of its faith by the declarations of Vatican II (*Lumen Gentium*, art. 16). Now salvation is impossible without faith and faith is impossible without revelation strictly speaking. It is not necessary to explain this possibility of revelation and faith outside the OT and NT history of revelation and faith by some special theory, nor to have recourse to an explicit, empirical tradition deriving from primitive revelation, in which Adam's actual experience is supposed to have been transmitted in propositional, doctrinal form. That is hardly probable in view of our present knowledge of the history of religions and the duration of human history. It is only necessary to assume – and the data of present-day theology support this – that every human being is elevated by grace in his transcendental intellectuality in a non-explicit manner. This entitative divinization, which is proffered to freedom, even if it is not freely accepted in faith, involves a transcendental divinization of man's fundamental subjective disposition, the ultimate horizon of man's knowledge and freedom, in the perspective of which he accomplishes his life. Consequently, for absolutely every human being this supernatural existential itself constitutes a revelation of God through his self-communication in grace. And that grace-given fundamental subjective disposition which is directed towards the God of triune life, can quite definitely be regarded as a word of revelation, provided that the notion of "word" is not reduced to that of a phonetic utterance. It must not be forgotten that such transcendental revelation is always historically mediated, and that man's historical reality can never be without language. It never consists merely of dead facts; the interpretation of the facts is itself a constitutive factor of any historical event. No revelation in conceptual terms of any particular objects or propositions is given solely by this transcendentally experienced openness of man to the triune God of eternal life. What is given is something more, and this forms the basis of all the articles of faith and is the condition of their very possibility, alone making them really the words of God: the supernatural horizon of experience of an *a priori* kind, the light of faith as such, as tradition says. All this does not mean, of course, that this transcendental *a priori* openness of man to the God of eternal life and of absolute self-communication can be non-historical, isolated, pursuing some mystical existence or other of its own in individualistic introspection outside history. It is necessarily accomplished in the history of the action and thought of mankind, and may be so in a very explicit or in a very hidden way. Consequently there is never a history of transcendental revelation in isolation. History in the concrete, both individually and collectively, is the history of God's transcendental revelation. Of course, such concrete history is never revelation pure and simple. Revelation in ordinary history is always indissolubly mingled with error, misinterpretation, guilt, abuses. It is a history both just and sinful, for the history of sin and that of salvation are inextricably interwoven until God's judgment comes. That in no way excludes a genuine history of revelation in the whole history of humanity. In fact Christians, for example, are able to discern and distinguish in the religious history of the OT between the genuine history of revelation and a sinful, proud religious history, only in the light of Christ, never merely by standards provided by the OT itself. It is only in Christ that the OT scriptures possess an internal and external canon as a guiding principle of their own interpretation. Yet they have to be recognized by the Christian as a genuine history of the revelation of the Father of our Lord (see *Bible* I A, B).

c) Even those who try to work out the idea of revelation entirely on the basis of encounter with the word of God, preached or written, finally meet with the transcendental side of the revelation-event. For they require a canon within a canon; to them the spoken and written word only becomes the word of God absolutely as such in the interior grace-given occurrence of faith, and the external message of faith is demythologized into a transcendental form. If religious history is that part of human history generally in which the theological nature of man is not only accomplished in fact (as in all history), but also becomes the focus of explicit attention, then the history of religion is at the same time the most explicit part of the history of revelation and the intellectual region in which historical misinterpretations of the transcendental experience of God occur most plainly and with the most serious consequences, and where superstition most clearly flourishes. But it is always a case of both, and always in an ambiguity which for us is inextricable.

d) In the theology of the last centuries, in contrast to that of the Middle Ages, preferential treatment has been given to the question of the testimony paid to the messenger of revelation by miracles performed in the presence of hearers summoned to believe, but the question of the revelation-occurrence in the bearer of revelation, the prophet himself, has not been dealt with or has been dealt with inadequately (see *Prophetism*). From what has been said, it would follow that the theology of the act of faith and that of the revelation-occurrence are to a large extent identical. Fundamental theology is, therefore, entirely right from the point of view of method if it deals with the *analysis fidei* within its own sphere, on the condition that it does so where faith and the reception of revelation can still be seen in their original unity. For the transcendental side of the original reception of revelation and that of faith coincide: man is constituted (through grace) as determined by God's ontological self-communication and in radical freedom accepts this existential or constitutive feature of his human reality.

For Catholic theology, the question of demythologization is still largely the concrete problem of whether what fundamental theology calls miracles are possible, what their significance is and whether they can be recognized. On the basis of the fundamental idea which we have just outlined, should we not really lend greater weight to the view that the mediation of a transcendental experience of God cannot itself adequately be mediated once again, but is always the trusting awareness of the prior presence of the unmediated? Consequently it is impossible in principle to distinguish adequately and explicitly between mediation through the bare fact of so-called objective reality and mediation through the interpretative representation of that bare fact. Nor is it necessary, because the mediation has its ultimate truth in what is mediated. For that reason someone who, with the intention of demythologizing, distinguishes them purely and simply, and someone who posits both the mediation and what is mediated as equally absolute, both miss in the same way the ontological difference and unity between what is predicamental and what is transcendental, as well as the difference yet indestructible unity between the mediation of so-called historical fact and its interpretation. It must, of course, also be remembered that this mediation, being an historical one, is necessarily always social; it is "ecclesial" in the deepest sense of the word. It therefore includes an acceptance of the never totally explicit belief of the Church, the community of believers. That belief of the Church is always, whether in the Church or in the individual, a unity of sign and truth beyond man's disposal or decision. And as in the word of the sacrament and in the Word incarnate, sign and truth are given inseparably and unmixed, and are not merely brought together by the faith of the believer.

e) This will also explain what *fides implicita* is. Fundamentally it means that all explicit faith, as such, lays hold of a sign and is, therefore, truly faith only if it grasps the sign through being itself held in the grasp of the unutterable mystery of the presence of God mercifully communicating himself. It always has to be aware that the finite mediation has the character of a sign, and one that belongs to the Church and is found in the Church. And since the holy darkness of the incomprehensible God is not abolished but, rather, on the contrary, definitely established by revelation, and is accepted as it is with adoration and love, the "implicit" character of what is really revealed in the word of revelation, and the character of one's own faith as "implicit" in that of the Church, both belong to the very nature of revelation and faith and are not factors which are only present when the uneducated and simple hear revelation and believe.

f) This throws light on a well-known phenomenon of the history of religion and of Christian dogma: the continual attempt to reduce the totality of the many-sided and extensive dogmas and institutions of a religion to a kernel, to what alone is truly important, however this single decisive element is discovered and named. On this point it can now be said, on the basis of the unity of transcendental and predicamental revelation which we have indicated, that such a single essential element in religion does exist, but is not replaced by any reduction to categories nor is it thereby experienced more directly or with more certainty. Moreover, if Christianity is to be the absolute religion of all and is not to represent a particular covenant of a particular people with God, it must confess Christ as the mediator and bringer of salvation in such a way that he integrates in himself, in his truly corporeal nature present in this world, every conceivable mediation by all that is real, so that he relativizes it and at the same time definitively posits it as valid. There is therefore no point at which, in this mediation of his, other things have to be excluded entirely and on principle, whether they be word, liturgical sign, the Church's social reality, the ministry, imagery, or even secular things. Yet despite the plurality of the mediation, and despite the legitimacy of all its aspects and the obligatory character that *per se* belongs to it, the possibility nevertheless remains that, in the various times and places which the one God of grace has determined even under the new covenant, the urgency and perceptibility of various particular mediations may, even when they are enduringly valid, themselves possess a history. Such a history of the definitive revelation in Christ, within the final and eternal aeon, may still be mirrored even now, in its legitimacy as willed by God, in the tragical history of divided Christendom, whose divisions reflect the genuine multiplicity of the many mediations of the one revelation, and while they accuse us, nevertheless promise us the grace of God.

g) The unity and distinction between transcendental revelation and predicamental, historical revelation, which imply that the same distinction and the same unity are also found in faith, also indicate that the subjective disposition of the believer must be thought of as distinct from faith and yet as one with it. If we leave out of account for a moment the very incidental mention of grace which is all that is commonly found in theological descriptions of faith, the character of faith as coming by hearing is explained in such an empirical and *a posteriori* manner in relation to certain defined articles of faith, that the word of faith appears to be addressed to hearing almost as if the latter were a quite unexceptional formal capacity to grasp any true proposition once it is understood, and provided it is presented correctly with its proper grounds in an appropriate way. The *a priori* capacity to believe, i.e., the subjective disposition, is itself scarcely taken into consideration in theology. This *a priori* capacity for revelation and faith must not, of course, be thought of as a localized faculty side by side with others, as a sort of particular sentiment, an intrinsically limited "need". It should be understood as the union of what we have called the transcendental aspect of revelation with the *a priori* capacity (identical with the whole transcendental character of man), for God's self-communication in grace; for it is by these two that God's transcendental revelation is constituted. Moreover, both of these must be understood not in a merely ontic, factual sense, but in an ontological sense.

h) Every analysis of faith declares the "authority of God" to be the highest, ultimate and sole "formal object" and "motive" of faith. As often as not, inextricable difficulties then arise, because this "authority" is itself thought of as mediated empirically by *a posteriori* cognition, and so determined by the horizon of human knowledge. Yet it must go beyond such a horizon if the word is to remain really the word of God and is not to be reduced by the *a priori* conditions of human cognition to the purely created level. But if in revelation and faith God himself in his own self-communication is what is believed and is the *a priori* principle of belief, and if the logic of faith is not a predicamental logic learnt from without, but, like spontaneous natural logic, is the intrinsic ontological structure of the act of faith itself, and if the external message of faith does not supply the *a posteriori* motive of faith but brings the *a priori* motive directly into relation with itself, then the problem in question disappears. In that way it also becomes more understandable why a materially false act of faith can be a genuine act of faith and not just a human act of recognition of a formal object grasped *a posteriori* under merely human mental conditions.

3. *Revelation and magisterium.* Where the culmination and final form of God's eschatological self-communication and revelation in Christ is present explicitly and in a socially constituted form, we have what is called the Church. The Church receives and announces this absolute revelation. Inasmuch as this truth of God's absolute self-disclosure is definitive, and victorious, and not merely ideological but is really abidingly present in Christ, the Church is infallible in its confession of this truth. The objective and real truth of God's self-giving in Christ is present in its confession which cannot fail or err when it is done with the Church's absolute commitment. Otherwise the truth of Christ himself would no longer be present. Since this victorious character of Christ's truth in the Church is constitutive of the hierarchical Church, infallibility must belong to the hierarchical leadership of the Church, its magisterium (Pope and episcopate) in its function of service. Its role is to preserve the abiding presence of Christ's truth by actualizing and unfolding its truth for each successive moment of history.

Karl Rahner

II. God's Self-Communication

1. In order to explain what is meant by this expression in terms of traditional scholastic theology, we shall start with the theological doctrine (though not defined in all its consequences) of the immediate vision of God as constituting the content of eternal life. According to Benedict XII, God in glory is seen directly, and no created reality serves as "object" "mediating" this knowledge. There is therefore no finite reality which is known first and serves as starting-point of an inference or other cognitive transition and thus renders God present to human knowledge. For a Thomist metaphysics of knowledge, which in this connection at least is obviously well-founded, cognition does not occur simply in virtue of the fact that there is a knowable reality and a power of knowing, unless the two are identical from the start. Cognition is a real occurrence and presupposes the ontological conditions and grounds required for its actual accomplishment. In the case of the direct vision of God, however, the real basis cannot be a created reality, a created *species impressa*. The *species impressa* is of course a real ontological determination of the subject, who thereby becomes self-aware in cognition, and it presents the object, from which it originates, as an object of cognition. If a *species impressa* of this kind were involved, God would be known "mediante creatura in ratione obiecti". Hence Thomistic theology rightly affirms that in the case of the vision of God, God himself must act directly as the real ontological determination (*forma*, *species*) of the created cognitive faculty. Of course this does not mean he is totally identified with this function and becomes dependent on the subject thereby. God himself must be not only the immediate object of the vision but also its immediate ground. In this sense, therefore, by "self-communication", God himself must be the cognitive determinant of the finite creature by a quasi-*formal* causality, not by the kind of efficient causality by which he produces a created reality distinct from himself. The

difference and unity of the ontic and ontological aspects of this quasi-formal causality of God, in which God's "actus infinitus" itself becomes the "finite" actuality of a finite potency, cannot be further discussed here. This causality is not called "quasi-formal" as though it were merely metaphorical, but because the God who communicates himself, unlike any other "forma" in its formal causality, is not subordinated to the subject which he determines, and his own infinity is not limited thereby.

2. By taking the case of the beatific vision and extending it to a certain extent, it is possible to arrive at a definition of the concept of God's self-communication. It means not merely that it is possible and is in fact the case that God can and does creatively produce by efficient causality what is other and distinct from himself, but that he himself in his own uncreated divine reality can become the actual determinant of his creature ("finitum capax infiniti"), without thereby ceasing to be God, i.e., dependent on no other, remaining infinite and determined by nothing outside him. Self-communication therefore bears a fundamentally ontological meaning. It includes "communication" in the gnoseological sense but is even prior to this, for it is the condition of its possibility. The term self-communication also implies that God himself can really have a "history" of his own, and does not merely creatively posit it as distinct from himself. This cannot seriously be denied by anyone who believes in the incarnation of the divine Logos. It is often obscured, however, by an over-anxious scholastic philosophy under the impression that it endangers the dogma of God's immutability. Correctly understood, the idea of God's self-communication explains God's quasi-formal causality by maintaining the dialectical insight that God who "*in* himself" is unchanging ("quasi ..."), can have a change in the changeable creature ("... formal"), e.g., God's Word *himself* was made man "in time". Such a concept of self-communication avoids pantheism (and panentheism, etc.). But God and world are not thought of in crude over-simplification as subsisting side by side. Any such view forgets that the difference between God and man cannot itself ultimately be thought of as created; it is identical with God, and constitutes that ultimate unity which links God's self-communication and his creatorship. God himself is his difference from his creature; he does not create it. Consequently he can make himself with his whole reality a quasi-formal determinant (see *God-World Relationship*).

3. The idea of self-communication is capable of serving as a key-concept of theology in its attempt to express in conceptual terms the various metaphorical statements of revelation concerning the relation between God and the world.

a) It makes it possible to express more briefly and clearly the unity and distinction between the order of creation and that of grace. The order of creation is that of efficient causality, in which God makes what is other than himself, precisely as such. The order of grace is that of God's self-communication (see *Order* III). The unity of the two orders means that despite his infinity and self-sufficiency, God (as love) can communicate himself, that he freely wills to do so as his *first* decision *ad extra*, and that this is the reason why by efficient causation (as creator) he posits the other partner to whom his self-communication is addressed as "grace". This does not mean that God could create only if he willed his self-communication. The possibility of creation thus appears as a factor (condition of possibility) in self-communication. The latter itself is primary and wider: *Deus caritas est*.

b) Grace and beatific vision form a unity, in which grace initiates and has the same formal character as the vision of God, so that grace and glory are two historical phases of the one grace. Grace (justification) can and must therefore be understood as God's self-communication. What the doctrine of grace calls "uncreated grace", "indwelling of God", "participation in the divine nature", is simply God's self-communication in its first phase, when man's freedom is still running its course in history, the phase of man's free acceptance of God's self-communication.

c) God's free decision to communicate himself, and the communication itself, can be viewed as the reason for creation and the world as such. Consequently God's self-communication, as the freely posited ground of the world and world-history, and of the history of the world in its innermost essence, can be regarded as the history of the created acceptance of God's self-communication, and as constituting a history which is that of God himself (see *Salvation*).

d) Corresponding to the two Trinitarian processions, immanent in the Trinity and in the economy of salvation, incarnation and grace can be regarded as two self-communications of God, both having their ground in God's one free decision to self-communication *ad extra*. God's self-communication to the world in grace (as the innermost principle of the history of the world) has its historical eschatological manifestation in the incarnation, in Jesus Christ, and is directed theologically towards this as its goal.

e) The concept of self-communication also throws light on the nature of verbal revelation, the word of God. God is not merely the object and the efficient cause of a created utterance concerning him. By his self-communication as the grace of faith, he is the *interior* principle within man both of the occurrence and of the hearing of that utterance. Consequently God's self-revelation in his word regarded in this light, is of a specifically different, higher divine quality than it is in his "natural" indirect revelation through creatures. On this basis, therefore, it is possible to give an intelligible account of the difference yet necessary relationship between a general but "supernatural" revelation operative everywhere and always through God's grace-given self-communication to the world, and constituting the general history of salvation and of revelation on the one hand, and the special, "official" verbal revelation found in the NT and the OT on the other. In the latter, the general revelation attains full self-awareness in historically objective form, manifests itself explicitly in language and so authenticates itself.

f) This self-communication must not of course be thought of as simply the divine principle of the creature's knowledge of God. It is a dynamic principle which is the real ground of the world's hope, both individual and collective and cosmic; it is also the realization of God's love for the world and the principle of the world's love for him. God's self-communication is, therefore, the source of the world, the ultimate ground of world-history, and its perfect culmination is the goal of world-history and the content of its final conclusion. In it God himself really becomes all in all.

Karl Rahner

III. Primitive Revelation

1. *The history of the notion.* It is hard to tell when the term first came into theology. All that can be said is that it was in the modern era and that the theme was mainly expounded in the theological movements of the first half of the 19th century. But the notion itself may be said to have been "always there" in theology, when man was considered in his original state in the setting of paradise, and seen as equipped with preternatural and supernatural gifts, the background for discussing the consequences

of sin (See *States of Man* [*Theological*]). In this connection, theologians spoke of a special mode of the self-communication of God, in grace and revelation, to the first man. But the significance of this revelation at the beginning of human history, before the particular, historical revelation beginning with Abraham, was not made the subject of explicit reflection. It was understood as the introduction to the particular revelation which was to integrate and surpass it. It was the *revelatio ante legem*, which seemed to be of all the less intrinsic importance as the question of the historical development of revelation had been overshadowed by the notion of a propositional truth conceived of statically. This seemed further justified by the apparent possibility of making the interval between Adam and Abraham last no more than a couple of thousand years. There was also the belief that the Bible was the oldest book in the world, that all knowledge of God was given in one way or another through the Bible, and that the world was only the then known world.

When these last assumptions were called in question, as happened at the start of the modern era, and as the horizons of geography and history widened, new importance and an intrinsic interest were attached to the theme of a self-disclosure of God to man in the form of a primitive revelation, before and outside the particular historical revelation. The primitive tradition to be connected with the primitive revelation also came into view.

2. *Meaning – importance – application.* a) It was recognized that primitive revelation and tradition was an assumption designed to explain the phenomenon of the universality of religion in the newly discovered continents. Religion is never found in the abstract. It always appeared with concrete content deployed in general in the basic notions of salvation, grace, sin, judgment, reconciliation, redemption and re-birth, along with a number of ethical norms and duties. These notions and the rites, cults and myths in which they were embodied were regarded as signs of the primitive revelation given to man at the start of his history and preserved in the primitive tradition.

The traces of the primitive revelation and its main contents had not perished, it was assumed, in the course of history. They survived in spite of the "repression of the truth in wickedness" (cf. Rom 1:18). The thesis of primitive revelation was also used to determine the conditions and presuppositions of missionary work. It provided a foothold, so to speak, for the preaching. This gave rise to a further thought. Primitive revelation was the presupposition of a basic religion which all religions were rooted in. This explained the remarkable agreement of all religions in their main content.

Primitive revelation as the basis of primitive religion, primitive religion as the basis of the nuanced agreement of all religions – this thesis was first upheld by individual theologians like Lafiteau, Huet and Bergier, then by Traditionalism, most notably represented in France, and above all by J. S. Drey, J. A. Möhler and P. Schanz (cf. Tübingen School). It was confirmed by further reflection, especially by the principle that all knowledge of God and about God comes through God, that is, through revelation.

Knowledge about God through God, based on primitive revelation, corresponding to primitive religion, brings about the consciousness of God which goes with man, the innate idea of God. It is then taken over by man's reason, his perceptive faculty and organ. Man thus situated in his finitude is in contact with the origin, as primitive revelation, and also with the historical tradition which is one of his own determinants, since it determines his origin. For the same reason man is essentially part of the society which sustains his existence.

b) In the theology of Traditionalism and in the Tübingen School the idea of primitive revelation was generally understood as a necessary postulate or as a genuine aetiology. In the science and history of religion, efforts were made to prove it historically. At the beginning of the 20th century the main effort was made by the Vienna school of W. Schmidt and W. Koppers. Against the evolutionist theory which saw monotheism as the successor to polytheism at the end of a long evolution, W. Schmidt maintained the thesis of a primitive monotheism. Religion was not merely a primordial datum of humanity, but the way of religion was a descent from the original heights represented by monotheism. The argument for primitive monotheism, which was linked with primitive revelation, was drawn from the oldest primitive peoples then to be found on earth. Their religions contained such matters as monotheism, paradise, the story of the flood, and a relatively high standard of morals. Schmidt's thesis was generally rejected, as not doing justice to the history of religion which was a highly differentiated matter.

c) A further reason for the enunciation of the thesis of primitive revelation and its possible consequences was the question of the salvation of the pagans. New interest was roused in the question by the age of discovery, which demolished the supposition that the gospel had in fact been preached all over the world. Primitive revelation was then appealed to. It was attested by the Bible and presupposed by its revelation. It was the permanent, active presence of God and his grace in the world, in history, in the spirit and conscience of man. It was a legitimate theological explanation of the possibility of salvation in those whom the message of the Bible had not (yet) reached. It drew them into the possibility and history of salvation. In consequence, the religions were given a new positive co-efficient. In spite of their obvious deficiency and ambivalence, their prayers, sacrifices, feasts, rites and "sacraments of nature" could be regarded as concrete acts of religious faith and parts of the encounter between God and man, all with an intrinsic relation to salvation in Jesus Christ. This insight, which was explained in patristic times by the doctrine of the *ratio seminalis*, the λόγος σπερματικός, was interpreted in the light of primitive revelation in the modern era. The thesis was upheld by de Lugo, F. Collins, Bailly and others, and was all the more appealing because other theological explanations of the possibility of salvation for the pagans (such as Ripalda's) met with no success.

d) Romanticism and Traditionalism were part of a general historical reaction against the great guide of the rationalistic Enlightenment – the philosophy of the autonomous subjectivity and the critical, creative and normative reason (see *Rationalism*). The reaction was to make reason the perceptive faculty of the spirit, its supreme achievement being the reception of what is given, of what is not produced and posited by man. Tradition now gains new significance in the life of the spirit. It is the transmission of what one has received. It is handed on so that it can be again received. This presupposes the authority of the transmitter, who has direct access to the origin of the matter handed on. If the process is traced back to its ultimate origin, it ends in a primitive revelation and a tradition determined by this. The "sacred tradition" preserves these structures at their purest and clearest. This endows it with special authority.

It is not surprising that this new era, with its new estimation of tradition and revelation, enhanced by its being traced back to its ultimate source, should have brought about a reappraisal of the theological significance of primitive revelation. But it never became an official doctrine of the Church. Indeed, where an extreme Traditionalism seemed to exclude the fundamental possibility of man's natural knowledge of God, it was rejected by the Church (*D* 1622–7, against Bautain [1840]).

e) Protestant theology paid far less heed to the notion or term of primitive revelation. The term is found for the first time, and only here and there, in J. T. Beck, the notion then in H. Schlatter. Of later writers, the most noted upholders of primitive revelation have been P. Althaus and – to some extent – E. Brunner. It was used to oppose the "Christomonism" of revelation, chiefly as presented by K. Barth. Althaus understands primitive revelation as a primordial basic situation of man. Hence he speaks of a basic revelation as well as of a primitive revelation. Neither term is used in a historical sense, of a past event, but in the sense of a principle at work, in the present tense. The purpose is to give the conditions of possibility of revelation, as given with man's created being and the self-attestation of God which it involves: in conscience, in the structures of existence *qua finite*, in the sense of gratitude, of dependence, of self-transcendence, of historicity. Primitive revelation in this sense is the presupposition of missionary preaching of the new word of God in the revelation through Jesus Christ. It is a presupposition which offers both a point of insertion and a contradiction. G. Gloege (*RGG*, VI, cols. 1199–1203), while accepting the basic position of Althaus, reject the terms primitive or basic revelation and speaks of a revelation of the Creator (rather than a revelation through creation). It takes place in three components: creation, history and existence, with three encounters at each stage of the dialogue: God's saying, man's gainsaying and God's summons.

3. *Conclusions.* There can be no historical proof of primitive revelation any more than of the story of creation. Nonetheless, as a real aetiology or theory of causes it is both possible and rational. Since what is expressed in primitive revelation affects man as man in his primordial and perpetual situation and constitution, the element of temporal beginning cannot be eliminated from what is understood by primitive revelation.

Primitive revelation could be a way of saying that man is primordially and essentially – which also implies from the beginning – within the scope of God's universal salvific will. He is within the scope of the offer of grace, which raises him above pure nature and designates him as destined for supernatural fulfilment in the absolute future of God. Primitive revelation could then mean that man is conscious of this finality and also that when he offends against it he does so culpably.

Primitive revelation could be a description or interpretation of the "supernatural existential" (see *Existence*), insofar as this means that man is originally and hence always under the finality and the imperative of his supernatural goal. This structure is a real ontological determination of man, which is in his nature through grace, but is never absent in the real order. It remains as the inescapable horizon, even when man fails and refuses it.

Primitive revelation could also be a way of saying that – as follows from the above – the history of the world (i.e., the history of humanity) is coextensive with the history of salvation, and coincides with it, in spite of the major differences in particulars.

Primitive revelation and its implications offer a possible basis for a theology of religion(s) and hence a means of doing justice to their achievements and limitations.

Heinrich Fries

IV. Private Revelation

1. *The formal concept.* A negative definition is possible. Private revelation is

genuine revelation which is not addressed (directly) to the Church but to an individual. It imposes no obligation of belief on all. It is not given to the Church to be preserved and preached. Such private revelation is possible at all times. But it is usually only the object of theological reflection when it occurs within the Church. To deny the fundamental possibility of private revelation, one would have to be prepared to maintain that all revelation is impossible – which would be equivalent to a denial of Christianity – or that no revelation is conceivable except in a community and for a community. But this would not do justice to the importance of the salvation of the individual as such, and would be a failure to recognize that even "public" (ecclesiastical) revelation must be given to definite individuals (prophets, apostles). Further, the tradition and practice of the Church (in devotions, prophetic figures in the Church, acknowledged mystics) presuppose the existence of genuine private revelation. Then again, the "closing" of (public) revelation ("since the death of the apostles") must not be taken to mean that since then, in contrast to former times, the attitude of God to individual and collective history is silent and aloof. The "closing" of revelation indicates the absolute supremacy and permanent normative character of the Christ-event, which remains to produce new fruits of the Spirit in the Church.

To accept in principle the possibility of private revelation is not to deny, but rather to affirm, that it always is a "child of its times". It may appear today in a very different way, less spectacular and visionary, which may indeed be a criterion of its genuineness. For any given private revelation is always – as experience shows, in Scripture and in the Church – a synthesis in which the character of the recipient, as determined historically (theologically, culturally, etc.) and psychologically (or parapsychologically), is fused with the mystical or normal grace given to him in the depths of his existence. Hence one cannot exclude the possibility of illusions, misinterpretations and distortions even where there is genuine private revelation according to the ordinary criteria by which mystical phenomena are judged. In particular, the "visionary" element in private revelations has in fact very clearly a "contemporary style". The "genuineness" of a private revelation is a very variable quantity.

2. *The Church and private revelations.* That a revelation is "private" need not mean that it can have absolutely no relevance to the Church. Many examples from Church history (e.g., Joan of Arc, Catharine of Siena, Margaret Mary Alacoque, Lourdes, etc.) show that it can be of public importance. But where private revelation makes itself felt in the Church as a prophetic impulse, it must stay within the framework of the general revelation given to the Church, though this does not mean that the private revelation may not contain an imperative with a "new" direction. For private revelation, the magisterium of the Church is at least the negative norm (and often perhaps nothing more). Such revelations may be treated critically with regard to their human elements, even though they are fundamentally acceptable. Their relevance may be restricted to given places, times and groups in the Church. Indeed, one must reckon seriously with the fact that private revelations of ecclesiastical import – as prophetic directives and imperatives to the Church in a given situation – may be proclaimed in the Church – and be more important than others – without seeing themselves as private revelations, because less linked with visionary or parapsychological side-effects than other or earlier ones. (The theological and ecclesiastical nature of a private revelation can perhaps be rendered more purely in the figure of John XXIII or the *Populorum Progressio*

The Second Vatican Council re-affirmed these positions in various documents, especially in the Decree on the Church's Missionary Activity, the Declaration on Religious Freedom, the Declaration on the Relationship of the Church to Non-Christian Religions, and the Pastoral Constitution on the Church in the Modern World.

The Church considers it its duty to protect the rights of man (*Gaudium et Spes*, art. 41). The Church "is bound to no particular form of human culture, nor to any political, economic or social system . . . (It) has no fiercer desire than that, in pursuit of the welfare of all, (it) may be able to develop freely under any kind of government which grands recognition to the basic rights of person and family and to the demands of the common good" (art. 42). It regrets the discrimination against the faithful in certain States which disregard the basic rights of the human person (art. 21) and try to build up a society "with no regard for religion" (*Lumen Gentium*, art. 36). It demands religious freedom for all men (*Gaudium et Spes*, arts. 26, 73), as a claim which results from "a proper view of the relation between the political community and the Church" (*ibid.*, art. 76). It condemns all coercion and the use of any improper means in making conversions (*Ad Gentes*, art. 13). As a human right, religious freedom is something for which the Church must be concerned (*Dignitatis Humanae*, art. 6). It will act "lovingly, prudently and patiently" with regard to those who differ from it (*ibid.*, art. 14), in sincere and patient dialogue (*Ad Gentes*, art. 11), showing respect and charity everywhere, even with regard to opponents, since they retain their dignity as persons, even when burdened by false or less correct religious opinions (*Gaudium et Spes*, art. 28). It asks for frank dialogue in cases of difference of opinion (*ibid.*, art. 43) and calls on Christians to "respect their fellow citizens when they promote such views honourably even by group action" (*ibid.*, art. 75).

In particular, the Council calls for the protection of human rights in public life, including "the rights of free assembly, of common action, of expressing personal opinions, and of professing a religion both privately and publicly". Since man "stands above all things, and his rights and duties are universal and inviolable", he must have access to "everything necessary for leading a life truly human, such as food, clothing and shelter; the right to choose a state of life freely and to found a family" (*ibid.*, art. 26). There is special mention of "the inalienable human right to marry and beget children" (*ibid.*, art. 87), in view of the radical solutions to the problem of over-population envisaged by some States. Vatican II also mentions the right to "education, to employment, to a good reputation, to respect, to appropriate information" (*ibid.*, art. 26), and re-affirms the doctrine of John XXIII (2 b, above) on the right to free speech in various forms.

On education (*Gravissimum Educationis*), the Council insists again on the right of all men to education (art. 1), and goes on to declare: "Parents, who have the first and inalienable right to educate their children, should enjoy true freedom in their choice of school . . . It is incumbent upon the State to provide all citizens" with the opportunity of education. But the State "must keep in mind the principle of subsidiarity, so that no kind of school monopoly arises. For such a monopoly would militate against the native rights of the human person, the development and spread of culture itself, the peaceful association of citizens, and the pluralism which exists today in very many societies" (*ibid.*, art. 6).

Man has further the right to act "in accord with the upright norm of (his) conscience", which may possibly be equivalent to the right to be a "conscientious objector" as regards military service. The "protection of his privacy" is also one of man's rights. To sum up: "With respect to the fundamental rights of the person, every type of discrimination, whether social or cultural, whether based on sex, race, colour, social condition, language or religion, is to be overcome and eradicated as contrary to God's intent" (*ibid.*, art. 29; cf. *Nostra Aetate*, art. 5).

José María Díez-Alegría

S

SACRAMENTS

The Sacraments in General

A. Introduction and Historical Survey

The sacraments, in the sense here understood, and as defined in the theology of the Church, are the seven vital actions of the Church in its liturgy which are efficacious for salvation: Eucharist, baptism, penance, confirmation, orders, matrimony and anointing of the sick. The theology of the sacraments, which began in Scripture, was constantly developed in the course of history and was mainly stimulated by questions of soteriology, is not confined to the understanding of the individual sacraments as such. It is also concerned with the common element which characterizes all of them intrinsically, though this generalizing approach does not mean that the notion of sacrament is one that has been attained by mere abstraction. Still less may "sacrament" be regarded as an *a priori* notion, or one so determined in the history of salvation that it could be used to specify deductively the precise nature of each sacrament. The notion of sacrament when rightly understood participates in the special character of that of life. Life is an eminently concrete notion, but at the same time one which is "universal". For life unfolds in a number of individual acts, which must be grasped individually before one can "understand" and say precisely what "life" is. So too with the vital action of the Church in the sacraments. Originally one, this symbolic reality of salvific Church life, bestowed by God's grace, to be known and accepted by man in faith, unfolds in various actions which are individually perceptible. These – along with other modes of the mediation of salvation – are the sacraments, through which the Church, in its members, shares "today", i.e., at all times, in the triumphant eschatological salvation promised by God through Christ as his Word, and wrought by God through Christ as the incarnate Son of God and mediator. In this sense, the true notion of sacrament, though elaborated only at a relatively late date, is no secondary abstraction and not a purely speculative concept of theological ontology.

Undoubtedly, the term "sacrament" in this sense is not found in Scripture. But even in the light of Scripture it is a legitimate general term for the vital ecclesial actions just mentioned. For the biblical foundation, the first references must undoubtedly be to the articles on the various individual sacraments. But there are also adequate biblical indications for a theological grasp of the sacraments in general. Different judgments are possible as to the extent and value of this biblical theology of the sacramental self-realization of the Church, since this theology is present only in germ. Many factors will be at work: (present-day) preconceptions of the individual sacraments; theological positions already adopted, which must therefore be presumed to be at work in the theology of the sacraments, especially with regard to the doctrine *De Deo*, anthropology, the theology of grace, Christology, ecclesiology and eschatology. None of these approaches, however, should be allowed to inhibit the application of the *Analogia Fidei* to the treatises in question, in the light of the theology of the sacraments as validly elaborated. Further, it is always important to distinguish, when investigating the biblical foundation of the theology of the sacraments in general, and when studying its history, to make an adequate distinction between the history of the *word* "sacrament" (or its explicit concept) and the *thing* signified thereby. The latter has been at work in the Church from the beginning (though at various levels of intensity), the response of the Church's life to something which it receives and mediates.

It is clear from 1 Cor 10:1–22 that the primitive Church regarded at least the Eucharist and baptism as having a common aspect. They were "means of salvation" of a similar character, from the soteriological and pastoral point of view. Another instance of the same approach is Eph 5:21–33, where one may justifiably say that marriage is linked with baptism and the Eucharist under a common aspect (though this needs careful definition). There are other scriptural assertions along the same lines which furnish essential basic principles for later theology in its understanding of the sacramental life of the Church. The texts are discussed under the various sacraments. In the light of these and similar starting-points in NT theology one can understand how the Fathers, while not subsuming at once clearly and definitively the individual sacraments under the one heading of "sacrament" (or *mysterion* or the like), used each sacrament to throw light on the others, worked out what they had in common and their intrinsic unity, linked them in one way or another and so made constant progress towards the doctrine which became common theological truth in the Middle Ages. In the process, the term "sacrament" undoubtedly underwent progressive restriction. It was first applied in general – though in a specifically Christian way – to particular sacred realities such as Scripture, faith, the mysteries of faith and salvation, means of salvation, cultic rites and even to allegory and typology. It was finally restricted to the means of salvation which were termed emphatically, and with a certain exclusivity the seven (and seven only) sacraments.

The concept and theology of the sacraments were strongly stamped by the doctrine of Tertullian, St. Irenaeus and St. Cyprian. The great master was St. Augustine, though even he was far from giving a doctrine *de sacramentis in genere*. In the Greek world, the main figures are St. Gregory of Nyssa and St. John Chrysostom, who used the term *mysterion*, in a sense closely allied to that of *sacramentum*. It should be noted that the Fathers as a whole worked out their theology of the sacraments by depicting the realities given in the individual sacraments, especially the Eucharist and baptism. The patristic notion of the sacraments was transmitted to early scholasticism through the medium of St. Isidore of Seville and the Carolingian theologians. Here the main figures are Hugh of St. Victor, Peter Lombard and later St. Thomas Aquinas.

As in the elaboration of many other theological truths and technical terms, the process of progressive definition of the term led to a restriction and even an imbalance in the theological notion of the "thing" itself. This is apparent at once from a comparison between the Western theology of the sacraments and that of the Eastern Church. In recent times, however, under the impulse, for instance, of the liturgical movement and modern ecclesiology, a significant step has been taken towards the rediscovery of the real fullness of the sacramental life of the Church. This breakthrough has been ratified by Vatican II, though there is a certain resistance in modern thinking to the notion of the symbolic reality of the sacraments.

B. The Fundamental Pronouncements of the Magisterium

The history of theology and of the Church makes it clear that a common and comprehensive doctrine of the magisterium on the seven sacraments cannot be traced before the Middle Ages. The main statement of the doctrine, as it has remained in force to the present time, is given in the Council of Trent. It runs as follows:

1. Though the Church speaks of OT sacraments (which were valid in their day and efficacious for salvation after their fashion) (*DS* 1348, 1602), the decisive element in the NT sacraments is that they were instituted by Christ (*DS* 1601, 1864, 2536, 3439f.), according to their "substance" (*DS* 3857), over which therefore the Church has no power (*DS* 1728, 3857).

2. Though each of the sacraments is intrinsically a unity, they are "visible" signs (*DS* 3315, 3857f.) or symbols of "invisible" grace (*DS* 1639) which are composed of "matter" ("element", *res*) and "form" (words) (*DS* 1262, 1312, 1671, 3315). They are means of grace because they are "powers of sanctification" (*DS* 1639) or "instrumental causes" (*DS* 1529), signifying and "containing" (*DS* 3858) the grace proper to them in such a way that they mediate and produce it *ex opere operato* (*DS* 1608, 3544ff.), i.e., not by virtue of the personal merits of the minister or recipient. The precise mode of this "instrumental production" of grace is not stated. But, particularly in the light of the necessity for salvation which is sometimes attributed to the sacraments (*DS* 1604), it seems that a real (instrumental) efficient causality is intended. The *opus operatum* does not mean that the sacraments produce their proper effects in an automatic and mechanical way, or by some sort of magic. The mediation of grace, both in its actual occurrence and in its "measure", is also essentially dependent on the disposition of the recipient (which is a condition, not a cause). It depends on the faith of the recipient (*DS* 1528) as he lays himself open and surrenders to the sacramental grace, as also on the intention of the recipient (*DS* 782, 1806, 1877) and of the minister "to do what the Church does" (*DS* 1611f., 1617).

3. The grace mediated by the sacrament corresponds to what each sacrament symbolically signifies and contains (see articles on the individual sacraments). It is really the effect of the sacrament, though the sacrament is only the instrumental cause. The grace of the sacrament is either that of justification (*DS* 1604, 1606) or the development and growth of this grace (*DS* 1638, 1310–1313), and hence the grace corresponding to the symbolic reality of each specific sacrament (cf. *DS* 1310–1313). Further, some sacraments also produce a special sacramental "character" (*DS* 1313, 1609) which prevents their being repeated.

4. As regards the Church as a whole, the sacraments are of necessity for salvation (*DS* 1604), a necessity which in each of the members of the Church takes a concrete form which varies according to the specific type of membership obtaining in each case.

5. In keeping with the nature of the sacraments as means of salvation established by Jesus Christ, the plenipotentiary of God the Father (Mt 28:18f.; Heb 2:10; 5:10), and entrusted to the

Church as such, a member of the Church can administer a sacrament only by virtue of real authority coming to him from Christ or the Church (*DS* 1610, 1684, 1697, 1710, 1777). For the valid and efficacious administration of the sacraments the correct "matter" and "form" is also necessary, as well as the correct intention, though not the state of grace or right belief (*DS* 1310, 1612, 1617). Similarly, the recipient must have formed a sufficiently explicit intention of receiving the sacrament, apart from certain special cases, such as infant baptism. Different conditions are laid down for the explicitness of the intention in the various sacraments.

6. The number of the sacraments, in the NT and the Church, is "seven, no more and no fewer" (*DS* 1601); see A above. In the life of the individual Christians, however, they are not all of the same dignity and are not all of the same importance or necessity for salvation (*DS* 1603, 1639).

7. The basic statements of the magisterium as summed up above must of course be completed by reference to the official statements on the individual sacraments.

8. It follows from what has been said under A above that these doctrinal statements of the magisterium are to be understood in the light of the historical situations in the Church which gave rise to them. Many formulas and the problems which they echo are children of their times. They are today often palpably one-sided, and as such, a challenge today to reach a fuller understanding which corresponds to our present-day notion of the sacramental life of the Church. The necessary ground-work for such progress was already laid down in modern theology and has been taken over by the Second Vatican Council. Hence the declarations of the magisterium must now be completed by noting the most important assertions of this Council on the Church and its sacraments. Here it is undoubtedly of decisive importance that the Church is (once more) designated as being itself "in Christ, the sacrament, that is, the sign and instrument of the most intimate union with God as of the unity of the whole human race" (*Lumen Gentium*, art. 1). The individual sacraments are described as vital actions of the Church, whose mysterious essence it is to be "in Christ" and by virtue of Christ, the "primordial sacrament". And since the Church is regarded as a personal fellowship, that of a royal priesthood sanctified and organically constituted by God through Christ and in his Spirit, this primordial sacrament takes concrete form in the individual sacraments and through these affects its members, in its receptive and mediating character, and so lives for God the Father by virtue of the holiness thus attained, in its responsive character. In this perspective, the rather individualistic and materialistic-sounding view of the sacraments suggested in earlier declarations of the magisterium is at once fundamentally abandoned. In the theology of the sacraments there is a new openness, confirmed by the Church, for a more comprehensive view of the sacramental life of the Church, but it is only barely beginning to bear fruit.

C. The Theology of the Sacraments

1. *The problem of the theological starting-point*. The term "sacrament", as has been noted in A above, is not a biblical one, but is nonetheless a legitimately formed theological concept. Hence theology itself, and the various points of consensus reached and affirmed in the history of the Church, must determine to a great extent how wide or narrow and how rich in significance the term "sacrament" (and "sacramental") is, and hence the reality which it describes. But it is not a matter of fixing arbitrary boundaries. For though the notion of sacrament – if it is not to be defined without reference to its history – is relatively open, it would not be theologi-

cally justifiable to define it in the light of certain insufficiently analysed theological preconceptions or prejudices, and then to use such a pre-defined notion to try to determine as a consequence the nature of the various vital actions of the Church which are to be called "sacraments".

One must certainly begin with the seven sacred rites enumerated above. They must be considered in their character of ecclesial actions, both in themselves and as throwing light on each other. The comparison of the individual sacraments shows that there is a certain resemblance between them, modified, however, by a still greater dissimilarity. One cannot therefore expect to reach a single notion of sacrament which will apply with equal validity in all details to all sacraments. Nonetheless, an essential inner unity becomes more and more apparent which makes it impossible to see the sacraments otherwise than as the unfolding of the one ecclesial life bestowed by God's grace, growing out of its original unity. All the sacraments appear as "vital acts of the Church in the process of its self-realization as the primordial sacrament. In these acts the Church gives concrete form to its own essence, which is to be the eschatological, historical and social presence of God's self-communication to the world for the sake of individuals in the moments essential to their salvation" (K. Rahner).

But this definition is inadequate. A distinction is made, mostly, unfortunately, in the sense of a division, between sacrifice and sacrament in the Eucharist. If this possibly misleading distinction is abandoned and the Eucharist is left – as seen by the Fathers – in its wholly sacramental character, which holds good precisely for it as "sacrifice" (a perspective imperative today), another component enters into the notion of this sacrament which is scarcely less important for the others. The sacraments must not merely be considered as actions of the Church in view of the individual members. They must also be considered as means by which the Church in its members (and its members through the Church) lives and acts in thankful response towards God the Father. If in addition the notion of sacramental grace and its concomitant salvation is also seen in its ecclesial and historical dimension, the perspective ceases to be unduly restricted to the individual minister and individual recipient. The sacraments will again be seen in a Pauline way as the particular, actual concrete forms in which the fullness of life develops and multiplies. This is the fullness promised men by God in the Christ-event and imparted to them with eschatological definitiveness. Hence, because it is sacramentally perceived and received in the grace of a symbolic reality, it works out as a sacramental symbol of thoughtful thanks addressed to the Father, in eucharistic doxology and personal appropriation in the Church.

The whole point, therefore, is to see the sacraments (once more) as the *gloriosa commercia* – in various forms – between God and man. They are the real personal and concrete symbols of the personal life which stems eternally from God the Father, gives itself to man by God's Word and Spirit and is to be accepted by man personally in the Church and responded to gratefully. It is an exchange "between" God and man "by means of" the sacraments. By virtue of the Christ-event, all being and life must be analysed and understood in the light of faith in this event. This leads to the theologically fundamental truth that all the reality of created being – "natural" and "supernatural" – is *ipso facto* constituted as coming from the Father through the Word of God and as ordained to the Father in the Holy Spirit. Since, therefore, it exists through the Word and in the Word, it is itself – by participation – word, and as such each creature "symbolizes" and "proclaims" both itself and others (persons and things) in various particular ways, ultimately symbolizing and proclaiming God himself (cf. Ps 8; 19, etc.). The Christ-event means the mystery of redemption, and this presupposes creation, the grace of original justice and sin, all within the horizon of salvation-history.

But the eschatological salvation has been wrought, and irrevocably assigned to man and the world through the incarnation of the Son of God in sinful flesh, through the cross and resurrection of Jesus Christ. And the sacraments are the salvific act accomplished *in this way* and the real, present symbols which represent and apply its effect. Hence they necessarily share in the "foolishness of the cross" (1 Cor 1:23) and in the "power and wisdom of God" (*ibid.*, 1:24) which is attested and takes effect in the "weakness of God" (*ibid.*, 1:25). They are therefore vehicles of the hidden promise and revelation of meaning and being which is therein accessible to faith, by God's grace, participating in the promise and revelation of the God-given life – that of the time of the Church as of the age to come – which was bestowed in eschatological finality on his Church in the resurrection of the Lord.

In the light of Jesus Christ, the fullness of the mystery of creation and redemption is revealed. It is the salutary self-communication of God which founds and fulfils all, historically and eschatologically. With this in mind, theologians can avoid or overcome the extremes and misunderstandings which have constantly disfigured sacramental theology: a mistaken dualism of "nature" and "grace"; a magical mechanistic or materialistic approach; a spiritualism which is foreign both to man and to God because hostile to the body and the world; the materialism of a worldly heathenism; an un-Christian contrast between the preaching of the word, the gospel, and the sacraments; an exaggerated sacramentalism which forgets that the sacraments are not the only vital acts of personal Church life. There are others in which God also promises and imparts himself to men through Christ – other modes, just as imperative, of the Christ-like symbolic communication of God, such as Scripture, preaching, and the needy described in Mt 25:31–46.

2. *Basic outlines of a theology of the sacraments.* It should be clear from what has been said above that even at the present day there should be no more difficulty in grasping theologically the symbolic reality of the sacraments – once a sufficient basis in theological ontology and the notion of salvation-history is supposed – than in the Christian faith in general, when no unwarranted *a priori* restrictions are placed on the Christian view of reality.

a) There are undoubtedly difficulties in the way of an unprejudiced grasp and assessment of the symbolic reality of the sacraments of the Church. But anthropology seems to offer certain bases for the understanding of the sacraments which is appropriate to the Christian faith. One such element which has not quite been lost sight of today is the very human need of "expressing" oneself before others, as can be universally verified because constantly put in practice, consciously or unconsciously. Selfhood, one's own thoughts and volitions, seek "expression" in and through "another" in order to be themselves. The soul exists in its own being by embodying itself in its body as something other than itself – which is what makes it itself and gives its essence reality and action. So too "spiritual" or "mental" attitudes, movements and reactions only become real and effective on the human, personal level when they find expression in word and gesture and create something "other" than themselves. This is the meaning of "symbol" in the real and comprehensive sense. On closer inspection a number of other such symbols as the body come to light. They are part of the concrete being of man and make use of strictly human means of expression, such as bodily attitudes, the language of the hands or the face, the word which characterizes, contains and gives effect to the person. It should also be noted that personal intercourse and collective attitudes are expressed in (multi-) personal embodiments and are only truly real in this collective production. Further, in the historical progress of humanity, one can see that a number of symbols or means of self-expression have been determined by the human will and have become historical. Such expressions of the individual or the community, created collectively, are recognized as obligatory, and all the more so when they display universal human structures.

Another approach to the understanding of the sacraments is the recognition of the special character and the uniqueness of certain actions, days and times in life which are intrinsic elements of man's existence and which in themselves or in their commemoration are always actual and relevant. These include birth, death, marriage and family, meals and conversation and socially established institutions with their particular forms of functions and powers. It can be shown that the individual sacramental actions of ecclesial life correspond essentially to such forms of "natural" human life as it takes shape in various individual acts, though the sacraments do not fully coincide with them. There is a common element in all these expressions and symbols in which human life becomes real and effective by embodying itself in "the other". It is that in spite of the "positive law" which governs the various forms and structures, they always rest on basic human structures intrinsic to human nature as such, since they stem from the constitution of man as body-spirit and hence from the "positive" creative will of God.

b) Apart from these possible approaches to sacramental theology, there are the fundamental data of the special history of revelation and salvation. And these are "new" divine creations in history. If (special) revelation and hence the salutary self-communication of the triune God who is the loving and sovereign Lord of all being and life is acknowledged, the approach is open on principle to "positive" modes of self-communication freely and creatively established by God. Historically, the basis of all God's special graces is the covenant with "his people" Israel, freely and irrevocably constituted by God to be accepted and cherished by man. The covenant made Israel the people of God and a sign of salvation among the peoples. "Salvation is from the Jews" (Jn 4:22; cf. Rom 9–11). This covenant was instituted, implemented and expressed throughout the centuries in the paschal lamb, from the first passover on. The passover, like the other OT rites ordained to it, appears in the light of the NT as a provisional "sacrament", tending to the full eschatological and definitive grace of God in the new and eternal testament.

The OT sacraments actualized at each moment for Israel or the individual Israelites, in memory, hope and salutary efficaciousness, the provisional self-communication of God displayed in the saving works of God in the OT, e.g., in the liberation from Egypt. But behind the NT sacraments lies the triumphant eschatological fullness of the self-communication of God in the Christ-event. Here we have the historical culmination of the history of salvation, unsurpassable because eschatologically fulfilled, and hence the absolute self-communication of God. And as regards the mode of this reality and its form of application, it possesses the character of divine symbol and word, in the most radical sense, which is the foundation of all strictly "sacramental" and other modes of communication. For it came through the one, perfect Word of God, in whom God so perfectly expresses himself as author of all being and life that the Word is called Son of God and he himself is called Father (in the full NT sense), and that the interpersonal relation of Father and Son constitutes a divine personal "Other", the Holy Spirit, as the "expression" of divine love in a person. *This* primordial reality of communicated life in the divine *commercium* of a love constituted by and constitutive of persons, where this love represents itself perfectly in the Other, has in Jesus Christ, the Word of God made man, been given to mankind and the world in eschatological fullness. Hence the man Jesus Christ, instituted by God in theandric mediatorship through the hypostatic union, is the one mediator, the one absolute personal primordial sacrament of God and of man. By virtue of the Holy Spirit as the divine personal bond who dwells in Jesus Christ in divine fullness, the Spirit is present in him as man both in a mediated and primordial way. The Spirit, that is, the pledge and "soul" of all life, is present there efficaciously, perpetually poured out by God on mankind and the world, and expressing itself in responsive thanks to the Father in and through "another", *in* the Spirit and its "unutterable sighs" (Rom 8:23-27), and *through* the incarnate, Spirit-filled Word. This absolute self-communication of God was and is bound to the mode of being of the incarnate Son of God. In order that it could be personally and historically imparted to each man, Jesus had to "go away" (Jn 16:7). God made his mediatorship divinely eternal by exalting Jesus Christ through the resurrection and installing him in the fullness of divine power, so that he could pour out his Spirit as pledge and principle of life into "Another" which is his "body" and his "fullness". The other so formed and animated by the Spirit is the Church, the eschatological people of God which the Father instituted through Christ as a sign and as the primordial sacrament. This Church, as the body of Christ the eternal high priest in power and glory, performs in its many ways of giving itself vital expression all that it is commanded by its head. It acts as the "sacrament in Christ".

c) In this approach, where the Church is understood as the people of God the Father and the body of Jesus Christ, animated by the Holy Spirit, and as the primordial sacrament in Christ, the question of the institution of the sacraments coincides with that of the institution of the Church by Christ. For the sacraments as for the Church, Jesus Christ is the *mediator* who fulfils the will of the Father. Thus the Church and the sacraments stem equally and in the same fundamental way from the will of God the Father. And Church and sacraments are as fully "there", and as capable of vital action (that is, are instituted), as the Christ-event has been accomplished. It follows that Church and sacraments are only instituted with full validity and efficaciousness when the work of salvation has been accomplished by Jesus Christ and accepted and ratified by the Father, that is, after the resurrection and the sending of the Spirit. It is only on these terms that the question of the institution of the sacraments by Jesus is placed in the proper perspective.

This also shows how much the sacraments – at any given moment – partake of the mystery of the Christ-event and the exalted Lord. They are the ever-present process of the life bestowed on mankind and the world in the one saving act of Jesus Christ. They are this life in act, as it prepares for the fulfilment of the eschatological mystery of Christ, which it proclaims in hope as it remembers it with intimations of the future. They are preparations for the moment when the Church, finally built up into the perfect body of Christ, will place itself, through Christ its head, at the feet of God the Father as his people, in thanks and homage, so that God will be all in all (1 Cor 15:20–28). Thus the sacraments are vital ecclesial acts of this aeon, their efficacy *ex opere operato* following from the truth of the fully victorious saving act of Christ. For this is irrevocably potent and hence can only be thankfully received or perhaps rejected, but can need no human "complement" or "filling out". But again, like the Church itself, the sacraments have an essentially eschatological character. The fullness of grace bestowed in the sacraments shares and gives share in the eschatological Christian hope, whose work today prepares for and extends to the final coming of the Lord.

To sum up: the sacraments prove to be real personal and present symbols established by the creative power of God and moulded for man in the history of salvation in the Christ-event. They derive from the Church as the body of Christ and the primordial sacrament. Through them – along with other indispensable means of mediation of the form of Christ – it can and should be known, grasped and tasted who and what God is and will be for men's salvation. They are signs that the whole man has (again) been accepted and blessed by God in his personal bodily nature along with his material, spirit-pervaded world. They are also symbols and signs that man, blessed by such grace, can come in the Church to God the Father through his Word in the eternal life of the Holy Spirit.

Raphael Schulte

D. Sacramental Theology

In any scientific consideration of the nature of sacramental theology, an attempt must be made to define its relationship to the other branches of theology, and its own inner structure.

1. *Its relationship to other theological disciplines.* a) Insofar as fundamental theology presupposes dogmatic theology as its foundation, it is not only reasonable, but necessary to speak of a fundamental sacramental theology. This would be a theology of symbolism in general derived from a study of man concerned with the indissoluble unity and diversity of the existential ("inner"), religious act of freedom and its physical and social ("external") objectivization, in which the act of freedom can take place. From this point of departure, then, we have to go on to consider, in the light of the philosophy and history of religion and of theology, what is regarded in theology as a natural sacrament and is not an accidental appendix, but a presupposition based on the principles of fundamental theology for a sacramental theology. Anthropology should offer evidence of fundamental importance concerning the relationship between the existential act and its physical, social and cultic objectivization (the real symbol), the priority (in its various aspects) of these two elements, and the personal and cultic aspects of the sacrament. It is not a question here of possible natural sacraments in a naturally pure state, but of natural sacraments in the history of man's salvation. In this salvation history, man receives supernatural grace and God reveals himself transcendentally. This history is above all co-existent with the whole of man's history and is also the basic, inclusive sphere of the official history of revelation of the Old and New Testaments. In Scripture, revelation is given as a historical and social reality through God's supernatural providence.

b) *Sacramental theology and the theology of the official history of salvation of the Old and New Testaments.* The universal history of salvation draws on the dynamism of God's communication of himself in grace (as offered; supernatural, existential) and on God's supernatural providence, and makes itself "officially" objective in the salvation history of the Old and New Testaments (with the essential division made by the eschatological event of Christ). In very much the same way, the sacraments of the

Old and New Testaments can be regarded as objectivizations in the salvation history of the natural sacraments. Similarly, it is in this perspective that it is possible to define the relationship between sacramental theology and the theology of the history of salvation. In sacramental theology, the Old Testament sacraments have therefore to be seen as preparing the way for the sacraments of the New Testament. The latter should, moreover, not be seen simply in a positivistic light as directives given by God, but rather as the "sacraments" which were given when God's supernatural communication of himself in Christ reached its eschatological phase and was expressed in a historical and social context (of the Church) precisely as an eschatological reality. Only if the problem is approached from this vantage-point is it possible to understand what is meant by *opus operatum* and to make the essential (not simply the ceremonial) difference clear between the Old Testament sacraments and those of the New Testament.

c) *Sacramental theology and ecclesiology*. If we bear in mind that the sacraments cannot simply be dealt with individually, but have to be situated within the context of an anthropology of redeemed man living in the Church, we can see that sacramental theology in general is nothing more than an essential inner aspect of ecclesiology. The Church is the primordial sacrament, the historical and social concentration of God's eschatological (forgiving and absolute) promise made to the world. Since the Church exists in this sense (as the sacrament), there are sacraments in the New Testament sense. These sacraments should therefore be understood *in genere*, that is, in the original sense and not simply as an abstract concept derived later from the individual sacraments as we now know them, a concept which may also blur the essential differences (*D* 846, 876) between them. It is obvious, then, that what we have in a theology of the sacraments, considered *in genere*, is an aspect of the theology of the Church. The sacraments, in other words, are expressions of the life of the Church which at the same time constitute the Church as the primordial sacrament. They make the Church eschatologically, historically and socially present and actual as the visible reality of God's promise of himself to the world, especially for the individual in his concrete situation. This is also why each sacrament has an ecclesiological aspect. They are not simply distributed by the Church. They are an event of the Church. They relate each person who receives them in his own way towards the Church, so that *res et sacramentum* can be regarded as the relationship of the believer to the Church on the basis of the sacrament concerned. This is so because the character of the sacraments themselves at least implies a relationship of this kind. What is implied, for example, in the sacrament of penance is reconciliation with the Church. In the case of the other sacraments, there is only *res et sacramentum* if they can be freed from formal emptiness. (The Eucharist implies a deeper incorporation into the Mystical Body; marriage a situation of growth in the Church, *D* 1853, 2229; the anointing of the sick a reconciliation with the pilgrim Church – as a *consummativum paenitentiae*, *D* 907 – and as a sign pointing to the Church triumphant – as a *consummativum totius vitae*, *ibid.*)

d) What has been said above under c) clearly indicates the relationship between *sacramental theology* and *Christology*, *sociology* and the *doctrine of grace*. As the primordial sacrament, the Church is the constant presence in the world of the saving mystery of Christ and his grace. This relationship has, however, to be realized in sacramental theology, in which case the sacraments will be seen simply as "founded" by Christ or as the mere "infusion" of grace, understood purely objectively. They will rather be understood, in the light of a theology of the mysteries, as the mysterious presence, occurring in *anamnesis*, of the saving event of Christ that took place once in history (Christ's incarnation, death and resurrection), as real *signa rememorativa* and as a personal (intersubjective) encounter with the man Christ. (See Schillebeeckx, *Christ the Sacrament*, London, 1963; see also Ambrose, *PL*, 14, 916: Facie ad faciem te mihi Christe demonstrasti, in tuis te invenio sacramentis.)

e) *Sacramental theology and eschatology.* Thomas Aquinas made it quite clear that the sacraments were also *signa prognostica* of the completion of salvation. That, however, is something that has still to be learnt in contemporary sacramental theology. God's grace has a quality of irrevocable victory. This victorious quality is historically present in Christ and in the indefectibility of the Church. It also enables the ultimate state of definitive salvation to dawn here and now for believers in the sacraments. This, then, is the basis of the New Testament sacraments – their present reality here and now can only be understood in the light of the eschatological future.

f) *Sacramental theology and canon law and moral theology.* It is clear that the dogmatic theology of the sacraments is the foundation and the critical norm of the Church's law regarding the sacraments. In the light of sacramental theology, it seems very questionable to include the sacraments within the framework of the Church's law. The critical function of the theology of the sacraments with regard to canon law and pastoral theology (the frequency of reception of the sacraments, the age at which they should be first received, their liturgical framework, their significance at different stages in life, and so on) should also be given more emphasis and developed further. Insofar as moral theology can claim to be independent of dogmatic theology, the dogmatic theology of the sacraments is also the foundation and the critical norm of the moral theology of the sacraments. In this critical function, however, it is necessary to bear in mind that the sacraments should not simply be regarded as the primary and completely adequate guide-line for the life of the Christian as a whole. The Church is not simply a Church of the sacraments, nor does the sacramental life of the Christian comprise his whole life, nor has God identified his grace as a whole with the sacraments (Thomas Aquinas, *Summa Theologica*, III, q. 64, a. 7, c).

g) Consequently the question arises of the correct place for sacramental theology. This place is to be found in ecclesiology, which is closely linked to Christology and to soteriology as the doctrine of the historical and social presence of the event of Christ. Sacramental theology should therefore not be thought of as a teaching anticipated for didactic reasons, but as subsequent to the doctrine of the septenarium of the sacraments as a whole. On the contrary, it is an *a priori* justification effected in the case of the seven individual sacraments, of what the sacrament as such is, seen in the eschatological perspective of the life of the Church. It is possible to deal with the sacraments individually because ecclesiological principles are followed in the theological study of the life of redeemed man as an individual. Sacramental theology, then, precedes this doctrine of the septenarium, is able to justify it and does not have to remain tied to it, to the detriment of both. If they are separated, it ought for the first time in recent history to be possible to give a special place to the doctrine of the Eucharist. In this way, justice may be done to the distinctive nature of the Eucharist (*D* 846, 876), which will then receive the emphasis due to it as the Church's cultic expression of itself (as the community, the mediator and the fruit of salvation).

2. *The inner structure of sacramental*

theology. What ought sacramental theology to deal with, bearing in mind what has been said above under section 1? This question can be answered more easily if the relevant scholastic treatises are briefly indicated and for the sake of brevity only in headline form.

a) The "foundation" of the sacraments. "Foundation" is used here only in the most all-embracing sense, including the concrete definition of many sacraments (*institutio sacramenti in specie infima et immutabili*); the meaning of "foundation" is not confined to the institution of the sacraments, since the "foundation" of the Church by Christ forms the basis of all the sacraments and their "foundation".

b) The theological nature of the sacraments and the difference between them.

c) The septenarium of the sacraments and their organic interrelationship.

d) The way in which the sacraments operate and their effects; the relationship between the sacramental and the personal event.

e) The administration and the reception of the sacraments.

f) The sacraments as essential means of expression of the Church as the presence of the grace of Christ; sacramentals as a preparation and an extension of the sacraments; the basis of sacramental pastoral care.

g) The sacrament as the dawn of the eschatological completion of salvation.

Karl Rahner

SACRIFICE

I. Concept of Sacrifice

In the technical sense, sacrifice designates the attitude of man before God. The significance is twofold. Sacrifice is the expression of man's duty of total dedication to God, but it is only possible with regard to God. And again, sacrifice makes the special relationship of man to God visible in a way which excludes any one-sided humanization or secularization of the notion of God. While it is true that sacrifice can only be offered to God, the explanation of the attitude can only start from men's relationships to one another. In explaining the relationship of man to God in sacrifice by means of our experience of the relationships of men with each other, we are exposed to obvious dangers. Nonetheless, it opens up an understanding of sacrifice which has constantly to be reasserted, in view of the frequent questioning of the notion today.

1. When the formal notion rather than the material process of sacrifice is examined, it appears as a sort of confession of faith in the truth that man faces the personal reality of God, though the personal nature of God is supremely unique and incomparable to that of man. This type of confession, which mostly takes place through the giving of material things, can undoubtedly obscure a proper understanding of personal encounter with God. There is the danger of deposing God from his aloof otherness and drawing him, as it were, into the reach of man and his manipulation. Hence man must be highly vigilant with regard to the purity of his intention as he offers sacrifice. But the fact that dangers are involved does not affect the value of sacrifice in determining man's relationship to God.

a) Through the interpretation given it in the act of sacrifice, man's relationship to God becomes clear and concrete, in the light of men's attitude to one another. This is important for the religious act. The God-man relationship is experienced as an interpersonal relationship, such as men have in their intercourse with their fellows – be they good or bad. Their happy experiences in such encounters will point on to the fulfilment promised in encounter with God, while the unhappy experiences in human encounters enable them to hope that they will obtain from God what they have missed in their encounter with men.

The sacrifices offered to God by men correspond to the human usage of expressing affection by a gift. One's esteem appears in the gift as a sort of readiness for self-dedication – a token of one's belonging to another. Such gifts between men nearly always suppose that the giver has already been favoured in some way by the other, at least to the extent that he has experienced the other as lovable and life-enriching. Hence the human gift is always really a reaction, a response. There is a reciprocal relationship of receiving and giving between men who bestow gifts.

b) When man's offering of sacrifice to God is seen in this light, it appears as a confession of faith in the personal nature of God and in the nature of man's relationship to God. God is not a magic, impersonal power but a person whom man may come before with a gift. God is infinitely powerful but so loving that he allows man to give him gifts, though he has no need of them.

But in the relationship of man to God the gift offered in sacrifice has a meaning which transcends the gift. It is now an expression of man's total dedication, in acknowledgment of the infinite Lordship of God to whom man belongs and desires to belong. Hence it is generally said that the gift offered in sacrifice is an expression of *religio*. But it is also an expression of love. The gift of sacrifice to God must also be ranged within the personal encounter which is determined by mutual love, both between man and man and between man and God. Since this love is directed to the actual personal reality whom man faces, and includes therefore acknowledgment of his status and nature, loving dedication to God as creator and Lord takes on the quality which we designate as that of sacrifice and expression of *religio*. The fact that Christ, without denying the Lordship of God, proclaimed this Lord as Father is a confirmation of the truth that the *religio* given expression in sacrifice must be animated by the love which makes the sacrifice truly a gift.

Even more than among men, the (sacrificial) gift to God presupposes the belief that one has been enriched by God. It might then perhaps be affirmed that the presupposition is faith in the Lordship of the creator, which is acknowledged in sacrifice. But the truth of being created by God gives rise not only to the conviction of the Lordship of God but also to the sense of having been given gifts by God. Not only the grace which elevates man to supernatural participation in the life of the triune God but also creation itself is a free gift of God. *Agape* appears in the NT as the truth of having been loved and enriched by God – a truth of which man feels the impact and which impels him to response. In the light of this truth, a sacrifice offered by man to God seems actually unthinkable. For how could this love which descends from God be answered with a human gift? Hence there are only two ways in the NT order of salvation in which man can respond to his being enriched by God. There is the sacrifice which Christ offered once and for all as head of the human race, inviting men to share in it. And there is love of the neighbour, in which the love of God is passed on.

2. Sacrifice is usually offered by means of a gift which is withdrawn from human use, to symbolize its dedication to God. The insistence with which theologians have been preoccupied with the various modes of this symbolic treatment of the sacrificial gift – destruction, alteration, improvement – shows the perhaps exaggerated importance attached to the sacrificial gift in the act of sacrifice. Whether this preoccupation is justified is open to question, since in the most perfect of all sacrifices, the sacrifice offered by Christ, these categories are inapplicable. And in fact the real sacrificial action is the

self-dedication of man, which is willed in the very core of the person, though it seeks to include expressly all the dimensions of his existence as far as is possible.

a) We must start from the fact that sacrifice is the gift of man's whole self to God, to whom alone a person can totally dedicate himself. The dedication expressed in sacrifice is total, both in intensity and in extent. It is intensively total, insofar as man gives expression in principle, with the fullest sincerity, to the truth that he belongs to God, which he proposes to himself as the programme of his whole life. It is total in extent, insofar as all spheres by which the existence of man is determined are included as far as is possible in this dedication to God. The decision taken in the inmost depths of the person is embodied in the visible gesture, in the community – represented by the sacrificing priest – and in the gift which comes from the sphere of the world. The sacrifice is not upright if it is not offered in the core of the person. But it must also visibly demonstrate that man wishes to make his dedication to God effective in all dimensions of his existence.

b) Hence it does not seem apt to explain the use of the sacrificial gift as a sort of substitution or vicarious performance. It is not as though man found himself unable to give himself directly, as for instance in death, and then offered God a material gift instead of himself, as a symbolic sign of what he may not do to himself. If sacrifice in the strict sense is understood to be the action of the individual, in a community represented by the official sacrificing priest, through the use of material gifts, this is because sacrifice is dedication to God as the absolute Lord and must therefore include everything which characterizes the whole existence of man. In fact, man can dedicate himself totally to God without making use of material signs which "stand in" for him. But sacrifice is this act of dedication, which is also a programme of life, in its most forcible expression. It is this character of programme or design for living which makes it appropriate that sacrifice should be used to represent the wholeness of man's self-dedication, by bringing in visibly the plurality of the dimensions of man's existence – in the body, in society and in the world.

Hence there is sacrifice in the full sense when the free decision of the human heart is given bodily expression in the spoken word and (or) the symbolic action, among those who are united by the same purpose, through the offering of gifts from this world which is the nourisher of man's life.

3. Since the act of sacrifice is the encounter with God in which man gives expression to a certain mode of his existence, the question arises as to the precise content which is here expressed. This question is mostly dealt with under the heading of the "ends and objects of sacrifice", which is not, however, a very happy way of speaking of what is meant, since the personal encounter with which sacrifice is concerned is put too pragmatically on the level of purposeful action in view of things to be achieved. It would be more in keeping with the nature of sacrificial action to ask what man expresses thereby before God. The theories of the ends of sacrifice need further correction, in the sense that the various aspects of sacrifice should not be so unsystematically juxtaposed as is frequently done. They should be arranged according to a hierarchy of purposes, which should first be investigated.

a) The comprehensive meaning, which is essential to sacrifice, and which must therefore always be intended, is that of adoration, that is, the acknowledgment of the Lordship of God through the self-dedication, as a programme of life, of the sacrificing community. It is precisely this purpose which distinguishes sacrifice from other manifestations of man's position before God, and makes it impossible to offer sacrifice to anyone but God.

b) Those who sacrifice are men. They give expression in sacrifice to the dedication of their own selves. But they themselves are in constantly varying situations. Hence the permanent note of adoration in sacrifice takes on various overtones or calls for various accompaniments. Since man as a sinner has offended against the Lordship of God, the purpose of adoration demands that sacrifice should have the character of expiation. Since man experiences distress and helplessness, the acknowledgment of God's power and of his readiness to help takes place in the offering of the sacrifice of intercession. After experiencing the divine help, man expresses his homage in the sacrifice of thanksgiving. These meanings of sacrifice are not juxtaposed to its purpose of adoration, but are its concrete expression in terms of a given situation.

Otto Semmelroth

II. Substitution (Representation)

This notion derives in part from jurisprudence, where substitution ("proxy") means acting in another's stead. Reflection on this reality in human law shows that it has metaphysical implications which shed light on the primal religious value of the notion. Comparative religion shows that the idea of substitution is familiar not only at the (later) stage of magic (primitive totemism) but also in the sacrificial rites of the earliest peoples known to ethnology, as well as in the unbloody consecrations of men and the human sacrifices of advanced civilizations. Though we still find a certain echo in Israel of propitiatory substitution (vicarious expiation) in the shape of bloody (Lev 16:3, 5, 9) or bloodless (Lev 16:8, 20, 26) animal sacrifices, "the scapegoat", this fact is not to be explained in terms of general comparative religion. Substitution in the OT is determined both by a theology of history and by personal ethics. Already in the creation-narrative we see man, the intimate of God, given dominion over the whole world (Gen 1:26ff.), sharing a common destiny with the cosmos which turns out to be calamitous because of the fall of man (Gen 3:1–24; Rom 8:20ff.). Within mankind, too, Adam acts on behalf of all, as we see from the fact that all are now forfeit to the death which he incurred (Rom 5:12–21).

Throughout the OT the idea of substitution occurs in various forms: as a purely pragmatic replacement of one person by another (Cain by Abel, Esau by Jacob, Saul by David), as an act "on behalf" of another, and as something actually done or suffered "in another's stead". Substitution is not, however, conceived of in strictly juridical terms, but rather is based on an ontic solidarity ("corporate personality"). Thus a father stands for all his house (Noah: Gen 7:1), the prophet for the community (Jer 11:14, 18:20), the king for his people (1 Kg 14:16). This hierarchic or "vertical" aspect of the idea is completed by a "horizontal" one, when an equal acts to the benefit or to the ruin of his fellows (Rahab: Jos 6:23, 25; Judith: Jud 13:4; Dathan and Abiram: Num 16:27). Substitution is not merely incidental in the OT: together with the idea of election, it is part of the underlying law of the history of salvation. So in Abraham "all the nations of the earth are blessed" (Gen 12:3, 18:18, 22:18). Israel's election is for the benefit of all peoples, and even its infidelity becomes an incentive to the gentiles (Rom 9–11). When Israel as a whole abandons the covenant, the covenant passes to a "holy remnant" (cf. Is 1:9, 10:21); their vocation is embodied in the messianic figures of the "suffering servant" (Is 42:1–4, 53:11) and the "Son of man" (Dan 7:13ff.), which achieve historical realization in Jesus Christ.

The history of salvation thus shows

the progressive reduction of the vicarious mediators of salvation to the one perfect representative of mankind. So basic a law cannot cease to operate *after* Christ, though given his absolute primacy it must apply in a somewhat different way. Since Christ, no individual can assume his formal role of substitution. Accordingly, history from the incarnation onward towards the end of time again sees a growing number of those called to act as representatives: the apostles stand for the whole Church, the Church represents all mankind redeemed and to be redeemed, while mankind represents the whole cosmos (including the world of matter), which is also to share in the transfiguration of man.

Traditionally, theologians have exploited the notion of representation in purely soteriological terms. Then they went on to apply the idea to Mary. In soteriology the expression *satisfactio vicaria* took on a wholly juridical sense, which left no room for any organic, ontological view of redemption. The latter emerges only when substitution is linked with the idea that mankind is really "included" in Christ (1 Cor 6:15, 10:16f., 12:12–27; Col 1:18, 2:19; Eph 1:22f., 5:23), so that man not only enjoys the fruits of the redemptive act, but participates in it intrinsically and is affected by it in his being (even though it is not efficacious in the case of the individual without his free consent). The representative function of Mary is different. It is ascribed only receptive causality (as is clear from the Annunciation). Because the Church continues Christ's representative function, all its activity remains absolutely relevant to the life of the world, quite independent of the fact that our present age is characterized by a decline in the number of Christians. But "the salvation of many depends" on the activity of the individual Christian as well (encyclical *Mystici Corporis*). Even the traditional doctrine of grace tells us that the justified can win (*de congruo*) the first helping grace and the grace of conversion for others. This truth should make us realize that the Christian has an inescapable duty to co-operate in the work of redemption on behalf of the non-Christian. True, there is no strict substitute for the latter's own effort to save his soul and serve God, but the Christian can at least represent the non-Christian's interest before God and usefully intercede for him. Besides, the Christian will gratefully experience, in his non-Christian brother, the mystery of his own calling and sense more keenly his own responsibilities.

Leo Scheffczyk

III. Sacrifice of Christ

1. That Christ redeemed us through a sacrifice is most explicitly attested in the NT in the Letter to the Hebrews. Here its cultic sense is characterized as an expiatory sacrifice, as also appears from the description of the life and death of Christ as obedience to the Father and from the fact that Christ gave his life for the sins of men. In the other parts of the NT the sacrifice of Christ appears in the sayings about his expiatory death, an expiation which is vicariously performed "for many" (Mk 14:24 parr.; 10:45; Rom 3:25; 4:25). No explicit mention of sacrifice is made, but the memory of the blood poured out at the sealing of the covenant is evoked. Further, the sacrifice is at least suggested by the comparison of Jesus with the Paschal lamb (1 Cor 5:7; Jn 1:29, 36; 17:19; 1 Pet 1:19; Rev 5:8, 12; 7:14; 13:8), by the typology of Isaac (Rom 8:32) and by his being designated as a sacrificial gift (Eph 5:2). Hebrews explains to its readers the scandal of the crucifixion by displaying it as the fulfilment which outdoes the sacrificial system of the OT. This has been abrogated by the death of Christ, since this is the true sacrifice, towards which the OT sacrifices could do no more than point.

The statement that Christ redeemed us by the sacrifice of the cross needs some fuller explanation. If the notion of sacrifice is to be applicable to the NT order of salvation and the salvific action of the Church, it must be taken out of an over-narrow cultic context and understood in a broader sense. The cultic ministry of sacrifice is a symbolic pointer to the sacrifice of an existentiell nature which Christ offered. This significance of the cultic sacrifice is symbolic prefiguration, without intrinsic efficacy, in the worship of the OT or in the heathen religions. In the sacrificial meal celebrated as eucharistic memorial in the NT Church, the sacrifice is made present in the sign and is sacramentally efficacious. This sacrificial celebration in the liturgy is merely provisional, because it "takes on the appearance of this passing world" (Vatican II, *Lumen Gentium*, art. 48) and because it points beyond itself to the existentiell sacrifice of Christ which it contains according to the reality which is proper to the sacrament.

When we speak of Christ's death on the cross as a sacrifice, two further points must be noted. First, this sacrifice did not stand in isolation at the end of Christ's earthly life. It summed up the whole life of obedience which the Lord lived, and gave it its full meaning (cf. Phil 2:8; Heb 5:8). Then, the incarnation must not be regarded as merely a preparation for the redemption, as though in the incarnation the redeemer first entered history, in order to redeem man later in a sacrifice distinct from the incarnation. On the contrary, the incarnation, which is carried on and explicitated in the prophetic preaching of the Father by Jesus, is an essential element of the redemptive event. The sacrifice, which is dedication to the Father, has therefore the sense of a response, which leaves the initiative of the redemptive work with God.

If we were to try to describe sacrifice merely as a cultic, liturgical action with the help of material things, we could not really describe the redemptive death of Christ as a sacrifice. But the real justification for applying the notion of sacrifice to the death of Christ is that it is not itself a liturgical sacrifice celebrated with the offering of material gifts, but that very self-dedication for the redemption of men towards which all liturgical sacrifices point – either as prefigurations in the OT, or as sacramental memorials in the NT. When we speak of the death of Christ as a sacrifice, we do not speak of what is intrinsically characteristic of this death itself, but of its character as the fulfilment and the real content of what is depicted in the celebration of the cultic sacrifices in the liturgy. Hence the death of Christ may be called a sacrifice, though a number of elements which strictly speaking appertain to a sacrifice cannot directly be found there. Thus at the death of Christ on the cross, there was no visible, formal sacrificial action. Christ's being killed on the cross only became a sacrificial action because what was intended in a totally different sense by his executioners, was transformed into a sacrificial action in the heart of Jesus, which his words express. Then again, there is no gift distinct from the offerer himself, and hence nothing on which a symbolic action could be performed, to express self-dedication to God. Finally, there is no visible action of an official sacrificing priest at the head of his community. The community character of the self-dedication of Christ consists in the fact that it was vicarious expiation for sinful mankind, as whose head Christ suffered death and was exalted, for his own glory and for that of the redeemed. Hence the notion of sacrifice can be applied only analogously to the death of Christ. It is correct to do so because it is the fulfilment pointed to in the pre-figurative sacrificial actions of the OT and in the sacramental memorial celebration of the Church.

2. The significance of the sacrifice of

Christ can only be properly seen when its uniqueness is taken seriously. Outside and apart from it, there can be no sacrifice in the NT order of salvation. The "once and for all" which Hebrews affirms of the effect of the sacrifice of Christ makes any repetition of it impossible in the NT Church. Nonetheless, the Church knows that in the Eucharist it has a sacrificial celebration which can be performed again and again without denial of the sole validity of the sacrifice of Christ. This mystery is possible because the sacrifice of Christ faces towards this world inasmuch as it is death, while it has been fully accepted by the Father inasmuch as it is resurrection and ascension. And though numerically one, it has a threefold mode of existence.

a) The sacrificial act of Christ belongs to human history. Just as it is essential that the redemptive work of Christ should take place in the same history in which man rebels against God in sin, so too the sacrifice of Christ must appear as an event of history, even though it is not apparent from its historical form that the death of Christ was a sacrifice for the redemption of mankind. Even the disciples only grasped this meaning of the death of their master in the light of Easter.

b) Following the pattern of the OT sacrifice, in which the high priest entered the holy of holies with the sacrificial blood, Hebrews makes the entry of Christ into the glory of heaven, through the resurrection and ascension, part of the totality of the sacrificial action. In human concepts, which can only imagine the (eternal) continuation of a sacrifice offered once in a passing moment of time on earth as the existence of the victim, Rev 5:6 speaks of the slain lamb which the seer has sight of. The intercessory significance, however, is again expressed as continuous action, when Heb 7:25 speaks of the perpetual intercession which the heavenly high priest makes for us, or when 1 Jn 2:1 says that Christ is the advocate whom we have with the Father. This is the "heavenly sacrifice" of which some theologians speak, which can be described as "the one sacrifice of Christ, offered in the state of glory" (cf., for instance, V. Thalhofer). This approach was only rejected, it would seem, by many textbooks of dogma because it was misunderstood as implying a constant repetition of the act of sacrifice. It should, however, be noted that a "continuation" of the historical sacrificial act of Christ above, in participation in the eternity of God, must always be taken into account – because no one enters eternity without his history. He who enters eternity at death is marked by his whole history. Indeed, the whole history which here on earth was spread out over a succession of moments goes with him into eternity, where there is no such succession. "Their works follow them" (Rev 14:13). Hence Christ is eternally with the Father along with his sacrifice – which was the fulfilment of a whole life under the sign of obedience (Phil 2:8). His sacrifice has an eternal mode of being, a supra-historical as well as a historical one, though it is numerically the one sacrifice.

c) When Christ offered sacrifice "for us men", this was not merely because it was instead of sinners who were incapable of it and had to rely on the expiation made by Christ. Christ offered in history a sacrifice remaining actual beyond history, in order that men gathered round this sacrifice in the Church could make it their own. Without offering a new sacrifice of their own, they were to be able to offer this sacrifice to the Father, as the sacrifice of the Church, the community of salvation. This is possible through the third mode of being of the sacrifice of Christ, the sacramental. This consists in the fact that Christ is present in the memorial meal which he instituted as the victim in the consecrated gifts, and as the offerer in the celebrant "acting in the person of Christ" (Vatican II, *Lumen Gentium*, art. 28). He is present, therefore, with his sacrifice. In the celebration of the Eucharist Christ has "left to his bride, the Church, a visible sacrifice" (*D* 938, *DS* 1740), without detriment to the numerical oneness of his sacrifice. For it is the one sacrifice, offered in history and living in the eternal present of God, which is given into the hands of the Church in the sacramental representation of the eucharistic memorial meal, to be offered again and again by the Church to the Father.

Otto Semmelroth

SAINTS

History of Saints

1. *In the history of religions.* Among those forms in which the holy can be present, man has a central place: men in general, men in special circumstances or situations (children, the dying), men in special offices and functions (priest, prophet, warrior, king), and finally any individual, the saint, in whom the divine power is experienced in some special way (especially through miracles). This presence of divine power seems to have been understood at first not as something related to personal morals but to magical influence. According to van der Leeuw, "in the first place, a saint is a person whose body possesses divinely potent attributes", indeed, he is primarily revered "as a corpse or part of one", being thus more easily accessible. Saints are the mighty dead, whose tombs and relics are important. This is especially true in Buddhism and also in Greece (Oedipus at Colonus). But the divine power can also appear in the living man, though there are no discernible preconditions for such a presence; it may come with asceticism, continence, study, as well as by a call, consecration, through much suffering or through "uselessness" and a superhuman crime. There are examples of holiness ranging from the great founders of religions (Buddha, Zoroaster, etc.) to truly demonic figures. The saint is characterized by the same sort of ambiguity as the sacred power which is active in him.

2. *Christian holiness.* Insofar as "the holy", in the course of Israel's history, appeared so distinctively in the inviolable dignity and the overwhelming majesty of the "Holy One of Israel", the figure of the saint also took on characteristics which removed it from the twilight zone of its appearances in the history of religions. It was here that saintliness was revealed as the greatest realization of human existence.

a) *The holy one, Christ.* The "holy one of God" (Mk 1:24), in this sense, is the Son Jesus Christ. Whoever sees him, sees the Father (Jn 14:9); in him the mystery of God is present: the being of God in its unapproachable hiddenness and otherness, that at the same time desires to draw near and disclose itself. Just as in God himself his essential holiness penetrates his entire will and activity, so in Christ it is not only that the power and glory of the Father is present (as the "finger of God" in his acts of power, Lk 11:20), but that the splendour and the "truth" of this power shows through his words and actions: "which of you convicts me of sin?" (Jn 8:46).

b) *Christ, source and measure of holiness.* But Christ did not come for his own glory (Jn 8:50), but to "sanctify" those whom the Father gives him (Jn 17). The Law of Holiness in the OT (Lev 17–26) had already presented the demand: be holy as I am holy. The pious are called saints (e.g., Dt 33:3; 1 Kg 2:9; Ps 29:5). But they above all recognized clearly the impossibility of fulfilling this command of holiness. They awaited the "day of the Lord", the day when God would pour out his Spirit of holiness, his Holy Spirit, upon all flesh (Joel 3:1–5). It is Christ who brings this eschatological fulfilment, manifested in his resurrection and the events of Pentecost (Acts 2:14–36). This Christ-event is the centre and measure of all holiness, to the mind of the community.

c) *The holy Church.* It is as pointing to Christ that it sees the great figures of the OT, the "cloud of witnesses" (Heb 12:1) – the patriarchs, the judges, the kings and the prophets. What was then said only of a few chosen ones is now true of all. All the members of the community are called "holy and elect" (cf. the introductions to the Epistles), and the Church is believed in as the communion of saints, because of common fellowship and share in the holy – a *communio sanctorum* in the fullest sense.

d) *Saints in the Church.* Nonetheless there are different degrees of acceptance of the proffered salvation, different degrees of the gift of self in faith, love and selfless hope. There are different degrees of intimacy granted and of the level of the following of Christ. There are also degrees of the manifestation of holiness to the eyes of the Church. In the imperilled eschatological reality in which we now live, which is both there and not yet there, sin and apostasy are possible among "the saints", though the Church as a whole cannot fall away from the love and the truth of the Lord (as the synagogue did). But then there are men in the Church who manifest very luminously what is true of the whole Church: that Christ is present in it as the victor, that Satan's power is broken (Lk 10:18), that the Church has died to the world (Gal 6:14) and that Christ alone lives in it (Gal 2:20). The Church rightly looks to these men, with due respect, thankfulness and supplication. Among them Mary, the mother of the Lord, has a unique place. In her direct proximity to Christ and to his redemptive work, she is the beginning and the "archetype" of the Church (O. Semmelroth) and thereby the perpetual model of the "imitation of Christ", of Christian sanctity in all its historical forms.

3. *History of sanctity.* Just as Christ was the "faithful witness" (Rev 1:5), who made the "good confession" before Pilate (1 Tim 6:13), so the saints, manifestly filled with the power and holiness of God, are witnesses among and before their brothers in the community, which is itself, as a whole, an unmistakable testimony to the victorious love of God (Jn 13:34f.; Acts 1:8; *D* 1794).

a) *The martyrs.* The first and supreme form of this testimony is the testimony of blood, in the perfect following of the Lord. This was the perfection which Ignatius of Antioch (beginning of 2nd century) longed for. He entreated the community at Rome not to intervene in his favour with the authorities. The *Martyrdom of Polycarp*, Bishop of Smyrna (second half of the 2nd century), is the first documentation of the veneration of martyrs. From the middle of the 2nd century onwards the word martyr (μάρτυς – witness) was used exclusively for the testimony of blood. The history of the veneration of saints began with the cult of the martyrs. (The veneration comes in here, because the saint is not simply one who is [definitively] justified, but the justified Christian whom the Church expressly recognizes as having arrived at fulfilment and whom it singles out in a special way for veneration.) Since the 2nd century in the Eastern Church and since the 3rd in the West, the Eucharist was celebrated upon the tombs of famous martyrs. The victory of grace in them was especially celebrated on their 'birthday" (*dies natalis* – the day of their martyrdom). So strong was the conviction that the martyr was the perfect Christian, that the apostles and the first bishops were later all considered to be martyrs (even if they were miraculously saved, like John). In this veneration, the martyrs of the OT also had a place: Isaiah, the Maccabean brothers, and John the Baptist.

b) *Confessors*. As the time of the persecutions drew to a close and Christianity became an official religion, it was an advantage rather than a risk to be a Christian. New communities who had no martyrs of their own sought out as yet unknown martyrs or the tombs of martyrs already forgotten. But martyrdom was no longer able to represent in such a direct and real way the ideal of the Christian life. Though this was the absolute measure of such perfection, another and "more accessible" form developed. And so the sermons of the Fathers were wont to describe the uncompromising and radical Christian life as an unbloody martyrdom. In the first ranks were the virgins (men and women), then the widows. Both ascetical groups acquired a fixed institutional form. The confessors, then, were next in rank to the martyrs. If the martyr represents the final and fatal contradiction to the world, the confessor is a type of living contradiction to his "worldly" surroundings. This is most evident in the ascetics and hermits who have fled "the world". But outside of martyrdom, every other form of saintly witness remains, in a sense, only partial. It has not the unequivocal finality of martyrdom. Flight from the world cannot and should not be "individualistic" and radical. The relation to the Church and the world remains, as it must, and is expressed especially in petitionary prayer for the community or in acts of penance for others. The life of the hermit is understood as a battle which, in imitation of Christ (Mt 4:1–11), is carried out in the desert against the adversary, as by St. Anthony. But the same struggle is also to be waged in the world. It is taken up by bishops, princes and the founders of orders.

c) *Types of holiness*. Thus in the great saints of later times there is a sort of tension. Flight from the world and sanctification or transfiguration of the world are the two ways of combating the sinful world. Variations upon these two basic movements are endless. Though the holiness of the Church of Christ shows itself in a special way in the saints ("saint", and "blessed" were used as technical terms from the beginning of the 5th century), it is a holiness which is stamped by the historical circumstances of the Church of any given period. There is no *a priori* pattern to which history can be reduced, since it is the expression of freedom, as between man and man, or between man and God. All that is possible is a *post factum* survey of "historical figures", "epochs" which display distinctive characteristics. In this sense, a classification ("typology") of the saints would correspond generally to a classification of types of piety and the history of spirituality. The saints could be arranged according to their fate, their office or task (cf. Ecclus 44–50): martyrs, confessors, popes, doctors, kings, bishops, abbots, virgins, etc. (cf. the *Missale Romanum*). But they can also be considered from the point of view of their special function within the Church. From this point of view the great saints are the "creators of new styles of Christianity" (K. Rahner). Just as within the history of dogma there has been a living and growing assimilation of the truth of God, so also there has been an unforeseeable growth in the assimilation of grace in the history of saintliness. The great saints point out new possibilities to the Church, new ways of answering the demands of the world, new ways of answering God's call for the total dedication of man as he finds himself in this or that place and time. The founders of the orders responded to their times in a creatively new language: Saints Benedict, Bruno of Cologne, Bernard of Clairvaux, Francis, Dominic, Teresa of Avila and John of the Cross, Ignatius, Francis de Sales. But this is also true of great individual figures such as Catharine of Siena, Joan of Arc, the Curé d'Ars, Theresa of the Child Jesus. And individuals can also be important for the Church even though they do not belong to it. As the Spirit can also give his gifts and graces and "strengthen many even to the shedding of their blood" outside the Church (Vatican II, *Lumen Gentium*, art. 15) the special call of God for a given historical period can find expression in such representatives of Christian holiness. Thus one can speak of saints in Protestantism and even of "saintly heretics" (W. Nigg), who might include a Savonarola, a Wesley or a Kierkegaard.

d) *The "classical" image of the saint.* If one were to describe, with all due reserves, the typical saints of various periods, one could say of the Middle Ages that the interrelation and equilibrium of the two poles mentioned above stand out clearly. Flight from the world and transformation of the world was the aim: hermit, monk, scholar, missionary, king or prince – all saw the world as unholy and as something to be "sacralized". Both poles are represented, in the greatest and the most ordinary figures. Saints were chosen as models and as patrons of the various professions and guilds and as patrons of various virtues and good works. They were models, but primarily helpers to be invoked. In all these forms the same evaluation of "the world" is found. This was also expressed in the "institutionalization" of the veneration of the saints in the process of canonization. This process no doubt arose because of abuses. So too in the ancient Church the erection of tombs of the martyrs had to be reserved to bishops. The effect of this was also a certain "official take-over" of the saints. The saint was not only a clear testimony to the victory of grace in the eschatological holiness of the Church, but he was also the witness of a direct claim to leadership on the part of the official Church, the insistence on the need of a "sacralization", i.e., "churchifying" of the world.

e) *Sanctity today.* The Reformation marked a change. First of all, its repudiation of the veneration of the saints provoked a reaction, precisely in the form of an emphasis on the official character just mentioned. The world, the married state, and the various professions were reduced even more emphatically to a field where "virtue" could be tested. The saint was a sort of émigré – outwardly, in the "life of religion" (the orders) or at least inwardly. In both cases he seems to be stamped to a great extent by the poverty of mind and heart which marks most of the 19th century. Hence the great number of canonizations and beatifications in this period need not mean very much. But on the other hand, we have now learned to disregard the seeming pettiness of externals, and to find beneath it a new, if less spectacular, everyday form of "heroic" seriousness and dedication. The clearest example of this is the change in the image of the "Little Flower".

Such examples already hint at what has since become very clear: the abandonment of the idea of the "great", "heroic" or "noble" and the coming of a sanctity without glamour, but all the more deeply moving. This change is mirrored in the literature on the saints. Out of the "Acts of the Martyrs" and the accounts of their deaths, the legends of the martyrs were fashioned, in which (as in the apocryphal histories of the Apostles) the miraculous element was given the central place along with a stylized life of the saint. The development went on, taking in the "Lives of the Monks" (from the 4th cent.) to the legends of the Middle Ages. Scholarly hagiography began in the 16th century (the Bollandists). While the legend has now become a rather rare poetic genre (S. Lagerlöf, A. Curtayne, G. von Le Fort), books are being written about the saints which combine biographical exactness (even to the point of a "demythologizing" with all the means of modern psychology) with a no less exact and thorough account of the theological meaning of the message which a saint embodies, for all the basic questions in the self-understanding of the believer (cf. I. F. Görres, J. Brodrick, H. U. von Balthasar, W. Nigg, etc.).

This "decrease" (Jn 3:30) of the "personality", the witness vanishing as the light attested grows mysteriously stronger, is directly observable in the modern form of martyrdom in which the confessor suffers above all a sort of a spiritual death and extinction. It may be seen in the new forms of religious life, in the secular institutes, in the recognition of the intrinsic value of marriage and the various professions, in the new awareness of the layman's place, and in the attitude which recognizes values in the world and in its commitments which, as such (profane), are not to be "sacralized" but sanctified. This is done no doubt by the power of sacrifice, worship and meditation, but also by the very recognition of the proper function of those worldly values. This change can also be seen in the shift from a self-protective type of morality to a venturesome love, though all this is, of course, a matter of emphasis and not of exclusivity. With this movement away from the "officialized" concept of the saint there is, finally, another related fact: veneration of the saints in the form of the relation of patron and petitioner is diminishing in favour of a more fraternal type of interest, so to speak. Instead of stylizing the saint as a ready-made "type" of perfection, veneration includes an effort to share in the life of the saint, in his difficulties and struggles.

Types of holiness cannot, as we have seen, be distributed neatly among various epochs. They exist side by side at the same time, in different places and even where boundaries overlap. But the change indicated here is unmistakable. Its burden as well as its promise are the same as those of the changes of spirituality in general. The good and the beautiful are less striking, but to make up for it, the essential is unmistakably clear. It is the mystery of the God of holiness whose power in human weakness is the heart of all sanctity.

Jörg Splett

SALVATION

I. Universal Salvific Will

1. *Introduction.* The Christian doctrine of God, his infinite goodness and holiness (*D* 1782f.) and that of the total origin of all other reality from God by creation imply the fundamental Christian conviction that in itself the whole of reality is (objectively) "good", i.e., that it must be positively accepted as meaningful and worthy of love, in that fundamental act of our existence (in knowledge and love) which is known to us from our experience. On the other hand, in the Christian conception of human existence we are aware that the directly experienced, heterogeneous reality (of man and of the world) is finite and can only be affirmed with the appropriate reserve. The ontological difference between God and what is not God is prolonged into the very act of adopting an attitude to reality (if this is not to become an immoral and self-contradictory idolatry of cosmic reality). Moreover, there is in man, and consequently in the world, the mystery of sin and guilt, and consequently of evil and the absurd. These two fundamental facts cannot positively be seen to be compatible. Their compatibility is only to be assumed in the unconditional act of acknowledgment of God, of absolute goodness. For these two facts do really exist and the acceptance of their compatibility, without in any way ideologically arguing away one of them in favour of the other, involves the acceptance of man's createdness, of his not being God. For since man is not

the radical centre of reality, he cannot understand reality from the sole point from which in its unity all is intelligible. From this, two consequences flow.

a) The proposition that "everything is good" does not entail the invulnerability, nor even an ultimate and unquestionable security for the individual's personal life. Man's existence is threatened at its ultimate root (see *Sin*) and at its possible definitive condition (see *Hell*). Moreover, even in the decision of his very freedom as such and despite the impossibility of shifting his responsibility for his choice to the holy God when it is evil, man must know that he is comprised within the sovereign will of God, which cannot be put in the balance with the will of a creature. Consequently the vulnerability of his personal life means that he has to endure a situation of uncertainty as to whether God will finally be good and merciful to him, this particular individual. Of course we can and must draw the distinction between the antecedent, conditional will of God and his consequent, unconditional will. We can say that God in his antecedent (though conditional) will is certainly good to me, a particular individual, and that the only uncertainty is whether I, the individual in my freedom, will freely decide for God. We can say that that is why it is uncertain in my own particular case whether God will be good to me and will (i.e., can will) my salvation in that unconditional will of his which follows my decision. But this does not explain the relation between the meaningfulness of the good God, of his will and of non-divine reality on the one hand, and the absurdity of (moral) evil and its consequences (including possibly its irremediable consequences) on the other. It does not bring man peace by presenting him with something he understands and therefore has within his grasp. It may be held that one cannot speak absolutely in the strictest sense of a will of God as consequent upon a created reality. The Thomist school in fact explains this consequent will as referring only to a series of *signa rationis* within God, and makes it antecedent to any foreseen created reality. But even if this is left out of account, the uncertainty of the situation in regard to salvation is not removed by the classical distinction of antecedent and consequent will, correct and inescapable as it is.

In the first place, created freedom in its evolution (to which the uncertainty of the relation to the good God is transferred) remains impenetrable for the person reflecting on it. There is an uncanny threat there. Furthermore, the free subject knows of course that despite his freedom and precisely in his freedom, he is at the sovereign disposition of God, however little this may permit of his transferring his own responsibility to God. Where and when freedom accepts God's proffered salvation, this acceptance is itself an effect of the gratuitous grace of God (*D* 176f., 182, 193, 300, 322). The "antecedent" will of God itself, as good, is therefore once again intrinsically differentiated, as is shown by the common theological doctrine of the difference, effected by *God* himself, between merely sufficient and efficacious grace. And so it too becomes impenetrable. Whether even the antecedent will of God is in fact such that it establishes the ultimate and definitive meaningfulness of existence for the particular individual, no one can affirm absolutely on the theoretical plane, on the basis of the principle of the meaningfulness, the goodness, of reality generally.

b) This affirmation being impossible on the theoretical plane, some conception of the relation between meaning and absurdity (for us) in the domain of the non-divine has to be formed in some other way, because after all it is necessary to have some positive position regarding the question itself: I have to *hope*. This shows that hope, i.e., living by what is not rationally fully demonstrated, is a fundamental mode of human existence. Hope is not simply a self-evident, derivative function of cognition (including "philosophical" faith). It can only be shown philosophically that there must be hope on principle, but that does not make hope a secondary function of philosophical insight (in philosophical faith). For the concrete hope of a particular individual for *his* salvation (the ultimate goodness and meaningfulness of his unique existence) is indeed rendered legitimate before the tribunal of reason by such insight, but it cannot be constituted by it. It cannot provide the ground of hope, which is the efficacious salvific will, efficacious in the particular case, originating in God alone and remaining hidden in him.

2. *Fundamental basis*. This being presupposed, a real, genuine conception of God's salvific will has to be attained in faith. This will is the ground of hope precisely as hope, and this ground is only concretely attained in the act of hope itself. Hope, like every salutary act, has its ground in the "transcendental" capacity bestowed by grace, and also in the "categorial", historical call to hope, which comes in the offer of salvation through Christ, in the experience that "hope does not disappoint us" (Rom 5:5), and in the knowledge that such hope has already been realized in Christ's resurrection.

3. *Scripture and magisterium*. According to Scripture, God's salvific will is not identical with his metaphysically necessary goodness and holiness, nor something strictly derived from this. It is not a metaphysical attribute of God which can be established everywhere and always, but a divine attitude in the nature of an event, which has to be experienced and proclaimed in history. This free attitude of God, which is directed towards the salvation of every man, has only become a manifest principle, definitively and irrevocably, in Jesus Christ, but the individual experiences it as such only in hope. (If anyone thinks he can be sure from inner experience of this salvific will of God, the experience is due to the interior grace of Christ.) All have one saviour (1 Tim 4:10), all are enlightened (Jn 1:29; 3:16f.; 4:12; 8:12; 1 Jn 2:2). The classical text for the universal salvific will of God is 1 Tim 2:1–6. Other relevant passages are Mt 26:28 par.; Mk 10:45; Rom 11:32; Mt 23:27; Lk 19:41. Although Scripture praises in this way the mighty power of the merciful will of God, which comprises all and powerfully transcends sin (cf. Rom 5:17f.; 11:32), it has no theory of an apocatastasis. It leaves man confronted with two possible final states of his history, in salvation and perdition (Mt 25:31–45 etc.). It commands man to hope for himself and for all, but forbids him the certainty which would supersede "mere" hope by giving knowledge of what the comprehensive and definitive actually is. Consequently the magisterium only recognizes the intermediate position which hope can occupy between the doctrine of God's universal salvific will and ignorance of the concrete outcome of history for the individual as such. Christ died for all men, as the Creeds affirm. All the justified receive sufficient grace to avoid every formally (subjectively) grave sin and so attain their salvation (*D* 804, 828, etc.). It would be heresy to assert that Christ died only for the predestined (*D* 1096 etc.) and a theological error to say that he died only for believers (see *Atheism*) or that pagans, heretics, etc., outside the Church do not receive any sufficient grace (*D* 1294, 1376, 1646, 1677; Vatican II, *Lumen Gentium*, art. 16).

While therefore the absolute universality of God's salvific will in regard to all men (who come to the use of reason) has not yet been solemnly defined (as a result of the history of the development of dogma), that universality can nevertheless no longer be denied, all the more so as Vatican II envisages the possibility of salvation for "pagans" (*Ad Gentes*, art. 3) and even for those who inculpably have not yet attained an explicit recognition of God (*Lumen Gentium*, art. 16). No official pronouncement has been made on the question whether infants dying without baptism are also comprised in God's saving will (see *Limbo*). (A positive answer is to be given.) On the other hand the doctrine of apocatastasis is rejected (cf. *D* 209, 211). There is no positive predestination to damnation or to sin, antecedent to man's own guilt (*D* 160a, 200, 300, 316f., 321f., 514, 816).

4. *Tradition*. In the Greek and other Fathers before Augustine there is in principle no doubt about the universality of God's salvific will, though the concrete possibility of salvation outside the Church and baptism was scarcely made clear. The later Augustine (at least after 418) no longer recognized in theological theory a universal salvific will for the *massa damnata* of fallen man. God wills to manifest his just judgment by leaving many in the inherited ruin of sin. Fulgentius teaches the same. Prosper of Aquitaine once more teaches the universality of salvation, for this aspect of Augustine's doctrine was never regarded as binding (*D* 142, 160a–b). A not inconsiderable undercurrent can also be detected in the Fathers in favour of the apocatastasis of all. Later the principle of the universality of salvation on God's part remained in essentials undisputed. Exceptions are the priest Lucidus (5th century) and Gottschalk of Orbais. Only in the later Middle Ages (Thomas Bradwardine, Wycliffe and Huss) and in the theology of the Reformers (in Calvin but not in the Confession of Augsburg or in the Formula of Concord) and in Jansenism, was it thought that the supreme sovereignty of the will of God, the manifestation of his justice and the irresistible might of grace can only correctly be maintained by thinking in non-universal terms of salvation and by teaching as a consequence a positive predestination to damnation antecedent to fault (predestinarianism). In this question Karl Barth abandoned the classical teaching of Calvinism.

5. *Systematic theology*. a) This seeks to systematize the teaching of Scripture and tradition by means of the distinctions between conditional and unconditional, antecedent and consequent will of God. The universality of God's salvific will is construed to mean his antecedent and conditional will which need not necessarily apply to his consequent and absolute will. The various theological theories disagree, however, on the nature of divine predestination, and dispute as to the point at which these two "wills" are distinct (merit and fault of man or the will to manifest divine justice).

b) In expounding the universality of God's salvific will, it is said that God repeatedly gives every sinner, unbeliever and hardened person the at least remotely sufficient grace to attain salvation, so that this is even more the case as regards the justified, believers and those who inculpably have not yet come to believe. The question how God's salvific will can be serious and attain its purpose, when apparently not only baptism and membership of the Church, but also actual faith are, inculpably, not possible, has not yet received a comprehensive and clear answer (see *Atheism*, *Baptism* II).

c) A special problem is set by the question whether and how children who die in infancy without baptism, neither through their own fault nor that of others, are individually comprised in God's universal salvific will if, as the almost universal opinion of theologians holds, they are without supernatural beatitude (cf. *D* 693, 791, etc.) in Limbo (*D* 1526). The question of the condition of these children, and therefore of God's salvific will for them, has not found a really satisfactory answer, because it involves too many unknown factors. An answer is probably not to be expected because it calls for knowledge which is of no profit for Christian action.

d) God has empowered us and laid the obligation on us (in Jesus Christ and his experienced grace) of hoping for final salvation for all men, whom we must love, and consequently for ourselves. This means that we are to affirm the saving will of God which is implied and as it is implied in this act of hope. Hope here of course is meant in the sense already described, of an absolutely fundamental act of personal life.

e) That means that because hope has its ground in the eschatological saving event of Jesus Christ, his death and resurrection, salvation (as goal of hope and so of God's saving will) is in general (in the perspective of hope) not one of two possibilities, with the other, that of perdition, standing on an equal level with it, so that the free creature autonomously chooses between them. Existentially and ontologically the morally evil decision is not even formally on the same plane as the morally good decision. God by his own sovereign efficacious grace has already decided the totality of the history of freedom (which forms the domain within which the individual's free choice is made) in favour of the salvation of the world in Christ, and in Christ has already promulgated this event. Without detriment to its freedom the world as a whole is "conquered" and delivered by the love of God. That is the saving will of God with which Christian hope is primarily and fundamentally concerned.

f) On that basis alone there is no justification for speaking of a double predestination on an equal footing. It is impossible because in any case a consequent predestination (*post praevisa demerita*) already "presupposes" the creature's free refusal, which cannot be attributed to God (however impenetrable this impossibility may be from the ontological point of view) in the same way as the free Yes of the creature (as a manifestation of efficacious grace) must be referred back to God in praise and glorification of the grace of God. And it is impossible above all because the Christian (without of course being certain on this account of his individual salvation and so rendering hope superfluous) encounters God as one who wills the salvation of all men. In the concrete he cannot stand outside this situation without falling into an abstract formalism where the ground of hope can no longer be found – unless of course one were to consider egotism itself a sufficient reason for hope rather than despair.

In the case of a double and equal possibility of predestination and in mistrust of his own freedom, man would have just as much reason to despair of salvation as to hope for it. The concept of "consequent predestination to damnation" and the distinction between efficacious grace and merely sufficient grace do not limit God's concrete salvific will which man encounters and must encounter in hope (cf. *D* 1296). They are secondary means of making it clear that man encounters this saving will in *hope* and not in theoretical certainty, and that he may not attribute to God the shipwreck of hope which is to be feared. But that does not mean that in hope as such he encounters a doubtful or limited saving will of God or his hope can be any but a firm one (*firmissima spes: D* 806). A theoretical system of double predestination on the same level is also ill-founded because in the eschatological situation of Christ we know with certainty that there are those who are saved, but we must only fear (we do not know) that there are those who are lost. But precisely this fear which confronts a genuine and for us undeniable possibility, but one which is not demonstrated by its fulfilment, commands man to hope in the saving will of God. For this has already taken effect, even though it remains theoretically indemonstrable that it is effectively operative in one's own case.

g) It is evident that a human being, inasmuch as he hopes (with love), encounters the real, efficacious saving will. He is not meeting a will which carries a real possibility of damnation side by side with it, but one which excludes the possibility of a double predestination. But we can never tell ourselves with certainty whether we are really hoping. We cannot as it were step out of ourselves and look at ourselves from outside. We can only tell ourselves we hope by *hoping*, that is, by taking refuge in what is beyond our control. Hope creates its object because it is created by it. That is not a cheap paradox but simply another way of expressing the fact that one can only hope when this hope in God's saving will, which is God himself, is supported by God's prevenient, efficacious grace, which itself once again is God himself. It states the fact that hope (in love) hopes that the real saving will of God is truly operative, that it operates by being hoped for as incalculable. God's salvific will acts by causing it to be hoped for precisely as what is the incalculable. Because the salvific will wills a salvation which is God himself, he has made a creature to attain it.

Karl Rahner

II. Biblical Concept

1. The Hebrew expressions corresponding to the English word "salvation" show that the OT concept of salvation had its roots in concrete experiences and situations. Salvation for the psalmist is deliverance from mortal danger, healing in sickness, liberation from captivity, ransom from slavery, help in a law-suit, victory in battle, peace after political negotiations (Ps 7:11; 18:28; 22:22; 34:7, 19f.; 55:17; 69:2; 86:2; 107:13, 19, 28, etc.). This experience is also shared by the nation as a whole. As soon as Israel was conscious of itself as a nation, it understood its exodus from Egypt as the decisive saving action of Yahweh; God had become his people's salvation (Exod 15:2; cf. 14:13, 20). The outstanding men in the history of Israel, such as judges (Jg 2:16, 18; 9:15, 31; 6:14; 13:5; 1 Sam 7:8) and kings (1 Sam 9:16; 11:9, 13; 14:45; 23:5; 2 Sam 3:18) delivered the nation from distress and oppression and were regarded as instruments of God's saving action. But the biblical writers emphasize the predominant importance of Yahweh as the giver of salvation. Thus Gideon may lead only 300 men into battle so that the people may ascribe its deliverance to God and not to its own strength (Jg 7). Isaiah emphasizes: "He (Yahweh) became their Saviour" (Is 63:8f.; cf. Hos 13:4; 14:2ff.).

The experience of salvation as a concrete manifestation of help for the individual or the whole nation assumed a new form in the message of the prophets. After the destruction of Israel and Judah, salvation was viewed during the exile under the image of bringing home the "remnant". The home-coming becomes, like the exodus, a sign of God's saving action, cf. Jer 23:6–8. Israel and its life were spiritualized (Jer 31:7, 31–33). God is "salvation" (Is 12:2; 35). The newly granted salvation is realized in a kingdom of peace in which God reigns as king (Is 52:7). In the post-exilic period, there appears as well as God the figure of an actual bringer of salvation; cf. the prince of peace, Zech 9:9.

In contrast to the prophetical picture of salvation for all nations (cf. Is 45:22), the later books of the OT show the development of the idea that on the day of judgment Israel can expect final salvation but the (pagan) nations which have oppressed Israel must expect final perdition; expressed in individual terms, the just are allotted salvation, the wicked perdition (Wis 5:2; Joel 3:5; Dan 12:1f.). This restriction of the idea of salvation to Israel appears even more strongly in the non-biblical books of

Judaism, e.g. Jubilees, Psalms of Solomon, Enoch. They hold in common that the Gentiles were really created only for destruction.

Whereas the OT prophets summoned Israel to repentance so that for its part it might create the necessary condition of salvation (cf. Is 30:15; Jer 4:14), there was a shift of accent in later Judaism. The *Torah* was regarded as a saving gift because with its help men could faithfully fulfil the commandments and thus acquire merit for themselves. God must pay them a well-earned reward in the next world.

2. The Qumran community had not a consistent concept of salvation any more than the OT. The looked-for salvation was eschatological in character. When a decisive battle takes place in the last days between the Sons of Light and the Sons of Darkness, salvation consists in victory over the enemies (Gentiles) (1 *QM* [*War Scroll*], 6, 5f.; 18, 11), in the happiness of the good and in their rule over the rest of men (1 *QM*, 12, 12ff.; 19, 1ff.; *CD* 20, 33f.); salvation therefore is a state of earthly happiness.

According to another picture, man obtains a share in salvation when God pardons (literally "covers") his sins (1 *QH* [*Thanksgiving Hymns*], 2, 13; 16, 12; 1 *QS*, 11, 14). Salvation therefore consists to a greater extent in a sphere of conversion to God.

Whether it is a question of the eschatological battle or of purification from sins, salvation can never be obtained outside the community of Qumran. Only by strict observation of the rules within the community is the requisite conversion possible. Consequently the old antithesis no longer exists between pious Israelites and the rest of the world or Israel as a whole in contrast to other nations; the dividing-line now runs between the community on one side and those outside it on the other.

3. The NT uses for salvation the Greek term σωτηρία which can mean both bodily welfare and the corresponding state of spiritual life. In the NT the word salvation is a religious term and is almost never applied to purely earthly conditions (special context, Acts 27:20, 31, 34). Even where it is thought of as healing from illness, as help in a storm on the lake or as deliverance from mortal danger, it points to a profounder reality because of its connection with faith (Mk 5:23, 28; Mt 8:25; 14:30). In the light of biblical anthropology (body-soul totality) any healing is a sign of the bestowal of salvation by Jesus (cf. Lk 10:19; 18:42).

With Jesus, salvation has come to men, hence he says to Zacchaeus, "Today salvation has come to this house" (Lk 19:9). Salvation is often expressed by the image of the Kingdom of God. This is characterized by the fact that God's will is done (Mt 6:10). But where God is Lord, the dominion of Satan is at an end. This is indicated in particular by the driving out of demons by Jesus (Lk 11:20 par.; 10:18). Salvation is also manifested by Jesus' turning to sinners, the poor and the sick (Mk 2:1–12; Lk 7:36–50), whom he blesses in a special way (Lk 6:20f.); all who have strayed are received back (Lk 15). Because the content of Jesus' message is the salvation of men, the Gospel is called the "message of this salvation" (Acts 13:26; cf. 11:14), "the way of salvation" (Acts 16:17), "the power of God for salvation" (Rom 1:16).

A wealth of ideas serve to describe the content of salvation; its present and future character is particularly to be noted. Present salvation is the situation created by Jesus' redemptive death: liberation from sin and the law (Rom 6f.; 1 Tim 1:15; Eph 2:1–10), forgiveness of sins (Acts 10:43; 13:28), divine sonship (Rom 8:14–17), justification by grace (Rom 3:24; cf. 8:29). Future salvation consists in deliverance on the Day of the Lord (1 Cor 3:15; 5:5), from the wrath of God (Rom 5:9; cf. Mk 13:13), in sitting down at table with the patriarchs (Mt 8:11f.), in eternal life in the world to come (Mk 10:30); the call to salvation is a call to "obtain the glory of our Lord Jesus Christ" (2 Thess 2:13f.; Rom 8:30). The Christian's earthly existence is lived in tension between these two aspects. The Christian shares in salvation even now by baptism, and yet he awaits its full realization at Jesus' coming in the Last Days (Heb 9:28; Rom 8:24; 13:11; Phil 3:20; 1 Thess 5:9; 1 Pet 1:5). Statements about the author of salvation are not uniform; both God (1 Tim 1:1; Tit 1:3; 2:10) and Jesus (Tit 1:4; 2 Pet 1:11; Heb 5:9; Acts 4:12) can be called "Saviour". Man of himself can effect no salvation; even faith (Rom 10:9ff.), conversion (Acts 3:19, 26; 5:31), baptism (Acts 22:16; 26:18; 1 Pet 3:21) and constancy in earthly life (2 Thess 2:10) acquire for him no "right" to salvation, but are only its necessary presuppositions. Salvation is not restricted to particular groups, as in the OT and in Qumran, but extends in principle to all men because of the universal efficacy of Jesus' death.

Ingrid Maisch

III. History of Salvation ("Salvation History")

A. Theological Analysis

1. *Biblical approach: The genesis of "history of salvation" as a scriptural concept.*

a) An exegetical investigation of the concept of "history of salvation" must examine the relationship of a purely political interpretation of events to a theological one, in the various biblical traditions. No event is "chemically pure", but presents itself with various meanings. Since this is so, instead of asking about "subjective" or "objective", one must inquire into the intention of the author, determining his chosen genre, his stylistic instruments and likewise his political, theological and social attitudes. This will make it clear that his presentation of events as directly or indirectly caused by God is not merely a subjective reinterpretation of events, but the application of a traditional category, transmitted socially, to the telling of historical events in general. The author could not have done otherwise, in view of the systematic schooling under which he had been brought up, or his political position, e.g., as a court theologian at Jerusalem. Hence the exegetical inquiry into the history of salvation is not a matter of comparing "sheer facts" with their theological interpretation. It means pinpointing the theological element and its influence in history as interpreted by an author or a tradition, and comparing it to other factors of historical interpretation. It will be seen that we are not dealing with the contrast between immanent and trans-immanent interpretation of history, since this alternative was unknown to the biblical writers. They do not regard the intervention of God in history as a breach of its continuity, just as they do not regard "miracles" as breaches of the "laws of nature". Their theological style of interpretation simply sees the permanent action of God in all events. In the light of this deliberately "slanted" presentation, history cannot but appear as the history of salvation and perdition. The tendencies are variable, but the concepts by which history is theologically interpreted in the OT, late Judaism and the NT have certain common elements of structure on the literary and theological level. Apart from a general Yahwism imposed on all the matter, the elements are as follows:

(i) There is a tendency to universalize points of time. The theological interpretation is not applied just to one event (as for instance in the political appeals of the prophets) but is generalized as "patterns of history" – Yahwistic, Priestly, Deuteronomist.

(ii) There is a tendency to "archaeologize" and "eschatologize", which is a consequence of (i). The beginnings of the human race are presented by the Yahwist and the Priestly writings in the same way as the coming judgment on the enemies of Israel. This is then further developed in terms of a universal judgment.

(iii) There is a tendency to universalize in terms of space and persons. Notions of divine causality in the sequence of events are not applied simply to Israel and Palestine. All the nations are envisaged, at least as the ultimate horizon.

(iv) There is a tendency to see history in periods. In history as sketched by P for instance, it falls into periods according to the various covenants (with Adam, Noah, Abraham and Moses).

(v) There is the principle of attaching historical material to chosen (central) personalities. This is not the cult of personalities, but the standard process of the history of tradition, whereby originally alien matter crystallizes round great individuals. Thus we have, for instance, the "laws of Moses". These persons have mostly been called in a special way. (The literary genre of the vocation-narrative is applied.) This principle comes to the fore particularly in late Judaistic sketches of the history of salvation (e.g., Ecclus 44–50).

(vi) There is in general a progressive tendency to eliminate anthropomorphisms. Thus in the Elohist, the apparition of Yahweh himself, as given in the Yahwist materials, is replaced by the coming of Yahweh's messenger, the "angel of God". This tendency is continued in the LXX. The aim is not to keep God free of the sphere of history. It is rather a transfer of political and diplomatic protocol to the heavenly court.

(vii) There is a tendency to aetiologize. Present conditions are traced to some blessing or calamity in the past, and thus based on God's dispositions in the past. Thus the question of the existence of evil is explained by the story of paradise and the fall, and commandments are deduced from the order of creation, as in Mk 10:5ff. par., *Jubilees*, 3, 8; 4, 32. In late Judaism the *Torah* is regarded as the treasure amassed throughout the generations of Israel's history. The blessed past survives there in an enduring record of it (cf. *Apocalypse of Baruch* [Syriac], 85).

(viii) There is the tendency to revive the past ("actualize") in the service of paraenetic instruction. The great deeds of God in past history are used to provide consolation in the present (Heb 6:13–20) and the fathers are put forward as models of ethical conduct.

(ix) There is the principle of the historical connection between prosperity and the observance of the divine law. This schema was taken from "Wisdom" – the wise man prospers. The identification of wisdom and law gives rise to such sketches of history as those of the Deuteronomists and the Chronicler, which find this connection everywhere in the history of Israel.

(x) There is the tendency to typological presentation. New figures are described in terms of great traditional personalities who had a similar function. The great models are Adam, Abraham, Melchizedek, Moses, Aaron and David. The exodus from Egypt and the crossing of the Red Sea are constantly taken as images for new experiences of salvation. Writers use this method, along with the literary technique of allusions to or echoes of earlier writings and the schema of promise and fulfilment (and the reflective citation), to give a consistent picture of the history of salvation.

(xi) There is the tendency to affirm and bring out a continuity in the history of salvation (based on the "fidelity" of God to his promises to the patriarchs and to his covenants with the earlier figures).

A typical example of these procedures may be seen in the later tradition about Gideon as presented in Jg 6ff. (cf. Beyerlin). The traditional material speaks of a successful repulse of Midian intruders by the Abiezrites. The event thus depicted is then made the affair of the united tribes of all Israel and thus detached from its circumscribed local significance. It becomes an event which affects the twelve tribes.

Gideon's victory over the Midianites is then presented as a consequence of Yahweh's will to save which still persists (Jg 6:7–10; tendency i and viii). The event is presented as similar to the exodus from Egypt and Gideon is described with the traits of Moses (cf. Exod 3:9, 10 and Jg 6:13, 14; Exod 3:11 and Jg 6:15; Exod 3:12 and Jg 6:16; tendencies x and xi). These theological elements, which turn the story into history of salvation, primarily link the tradition to the great historical and theological complexes which made up the picture of the past as then seen by the cultic community of Israel. Older traditions of individual tribes had to be fitted into this centralizing schema. For the history of the cultic community of Israel, the exodus from Egypt was then regarded as the fundamental datum of salvation.

b) *The oldest sketches of a "history of salvation" and its "short creed"*. Basing himself on such considerations, G. von Rad singled out behind the confessional summaries of OT theology the following material kernel. There is a "short historical *Credo*" behind the traditions of the Pentateuch, which is the principle of the presentation. It embraced in a systematic time-schema the sequence of patriarchs, exodus from Egypt, desert wanderings and conquest of Canaan. This confession of faith was in use from ancient times, down to the time of Nehemiah (Neh 9). The main proof-texts are Deut 26:5–10; 6:20–24; Jos 24:2–13. But L. Rost has shown that Deut 26:6–9 is probably due to the Deuteronomist. W. Richter then showed that such systematizations are on the whole the product of a relatively late era and presuppose individual traditions which they systematize, but for which they did not provide a principle of presentation and composition. These propositions, which do not go back beyond the early monarchy, grow more and more obviously abstract and are purely theological constructions. The most frequent theological formula of this type is the "exodus formula", indicating that Yahweh (less frequently Moses) brought the children of Israel out of the land of Egypt. The verb is either עלה or יצא. According to Richter, the עלה-formula was associated with the holy tent (2 Sam 7:6), while the יצא-formula comes from the North. The formula is not older than the oracle of Nathan, the oracle of Balaam and J, where the formula does not occur in traditional material but in sections mainly formed by the Yahwist himself. The exodus-formula is not linked with Moses till E.

This formula was long understood as the fundamental assertion of Israel's history of salvation. But hardly anyone now supposes that there were twelve tribes in Egypt to be led out of it. And then, that the tribes which came out of Egypt bore the name of Israel is as uncertain as whether a union of the twelve tribes could have been formed so soon after the conquest. But if "Israel" was not the hero of the exodus and only came later to be a cultic community, the creation of the "exodus-formula" can only have taken place at a much later period (cf. W. Richter). The formula is linked with the desert wanderings for the first time in Amos 2:9ff. and Hos 2:17. In Jos 24:2–13 the formalized statements concern only the exodus and the list of battles. Hence instead of a *Credo*, this is primarily a composition which takes in the sequence patriarchs, exodus, encampments in the desert, schematic list of battles and finally conquest of the land. Thus the schema of exodus and desert wanderings given in Amos is already considerably expanded in the text specially elaborated for Jos (no doubt Elohistic), and the traditions of the patriarchs are connected for the first time in a temporal sequence with the exodus traditions. Mic 6:1–5 can still be explained without supposing an underlying creed, but it is there in Jer 2:2–7, for the first time, with three members – exodus, desert wanderings and conquest of the land. Special emphasis is laid on Israel's being led to a fertile land. The expansion of the exodus formula into a creed at Jg 6:8 (or 8b)–10 is secondary (Deuteronomic-redaction). In the formulas of the Deuteronomists the possession of the land, promised to the patriarchs and then come true, becomes the most important of Yahweh's saving acts, obviously because of Jeremiah and the Deuteronomists the loss of the land had become once more a major menace, after the fall of the northern kingdom. The conquest-formula stems from the promises of the land made in the histories of the patriarchs. A link with the exodus formula is already forged by the Yahwist in Exod 3:8, 17, which thus for the first time orientates the complex of patriarchal narratives to the exodus from Egypt. Here the giving of the land is a transference from the promises to the fathers. But then, according to Richter, there is no historical creed underlying the passage which is rather "a theological penetration of traditions, whose main themes are fixed on for the first time and arranged in order".

The Deuteronomists had recourse to this passage in particular when formulating the *Credo* for the conquest of the land, but were also influenced by Amos and Hosea.

c) *History of salvation as seen in J, E and P.* In contrast to the successive stages of reflection on history of salvation which could be traced in the growth of the short creed, the older strata of the Pentateuch already display an arrangement of materials which was only possible through the development of formulas and the thorough mastering of the subject-matter. And there are certain additions and compositions which follow one another in such a way as to suggest the thought of a temporal sequence. The individual strands of tradition were originally to a great extent independent of each other.

According to von Rad, we owe it to J that the tradition of the conquest was expanded by an insertion, an addition and a prelude: the Sinai tradition, the patriarchal tradition and the history of origins respectively. But since the patriarchal traditions originally saw the promise of the land fulfilled when the paternal gods were installed in the various sanctuaries, a conflict arose with the exodus narratives, according to which the land was given only after the deliverance of Israel from Egypt. But this conflict was also the reason why the patriarchal history was made part of the Pentateuchal tradition at all. The harmonization took the form of underlining the element of promise (of land and descendants) in the patriarchal traditions, while the element of fulfilment was eliminated from them and placed after the exodus from Egypt. This gave a theology of history embracing promise and fulfilment (M. Noth): the God of the fathers was identified with the God of the exodus and so all the narratives of the Pentateuch became a testimony to the one purposeful action of God in the history of salvation. Hence the theme of promise and fulfilment already embraces the basic compositional units of the Pentateuch.

Gen 12:1ff. then becomes the end of the history of origins and the key to it in J. The themes of "great nation" and "land" were already there in the patriarchal traditions, but the reference to "all nations" is typical of J (Gen 18:18; 27:29; 28:14) and has the function here of associating all nations with Israel: those who enter into fellowship with Abraham will be likewise blessed by God (J. Schreiner). Thus salvation becomes possible for all nations through the people of God, and Gen 12:2f. is the starting-point of the prophetic and eschatological texts which speak of the nations being converted to God (cf. Is 19:24). In the intention of the author, the text is connected with the theological problem of J, how to legitimate the boundaries of the empire of David. In this political perspective of the court-theologian the ancient territorial postulates of the patriarchal traditions are actualized. The programme of the Elohistic historiography is clear from what are presumably its beginnings in Gen 15:4a, 5, 6, 13 (minus "400 years"), 14, 16, where 13–16 explains the future destiny of the children of Abraham. In E the patriarchs are models, and hence the faith of Abraham is stressed as the model of the faith of Israel. The emphasis is not on the possession of the land but on the destiny of the people of God. E understands the history of Israel as a history beginning with Abraham and as the history of the children of Abraham, according to the divine plan already revealed to Abraham (vv. 13f., 16). Faith and not the land plays the decisive role.

It is surmised that the historical work of P provides the basic lines for the present structure of the Pentateuch. It runs from the creation of the world to Shiloh, divided into periods by the covenants. It could be represented by the image of a pyramid, at the top of which is Israel's worship as the goal and climax of the whole creation. The presupposition of man's acts of worship and hence of the further interventions of God in human destiny is the fact that man was created in the image of God (Gen 1:26f.; 5:1).

d) *Concepts of history of salvation not confined to the Pentateuch.* Along with the above-mentioned schemas, there are a number of similar interpretations of the whole history of Israel or at any rate of major periods. The Deuteronomic history begins with Moses and ends in 587. It is focused on the kings of Israel, in whose hearts the salvation or rejection of Israel was to be decided (von Rad), by virtue of their attitude to the law of Moses. The *Torah* of Moses and the Davidic royalty are the two elements which decide the fate of Israel. The catastrophe of 587 is the consequence of a series of violations of the *Torah.* The Chronicler's history goes from Adam to the period after Nehemiah. Here again the principle is that there is no sin without punishment, a very definite one for each generation. The Levites play a special role, including that of teachers of the law. A descendant of David is expected to appear in the future (1 Chr 17:11; cf. 2 Sam 7:12). The images of Moses and David are merged to some extent.

The prophetic concepts of the history of salvation cannot be discussed in detail here. Nevertheless, the outlines often follow closely those given above. Since the prophets stress the connection between apostasy from Yahweh and political disaster, threats and promises play a predominant role, mostly in the form of political expectations and probabilities for the near future. But while previous interpretations of history as salvation were orientated only to the past and related the present to the past, there is a fundamental difference in the prophets, inasmuch as their view of history is "eschatologized". The importance of this feature was first brought out by H. Gressmann. Here von Rad has rightly noted that God's action within history cannot be separated from his action at the end of history. While the prophets consider the time of the patriarchs and the exodus as a "saving period of history", they also interpret the present and the future disaster which looms on the horizon as the continuation, renewal and resumption in a much more powerful form of the same divine activity. The election and salvation of Israel are now made entirely dependent on what God will do in the imminent future. The new comes about in continuity with the old and hence on the analogy of the old. There will be a new Zion, a new David, a new covenant and a new exodus (Is 1:26; 11:1; Jer 31:31ff.; Hos 2:16f.; Ezek 20:33–38). The same categories as above continue to be applied to history of salvation (see on Jg 6ff.). But now the restoration of Israel in the fullest sense is expected from the future. In Jer and Ezek and also in late Judaism there is also the expectation of the gathering in of the twelve tribes, to be brought about by God or the new son of David or Elijah. Fundamentally, the ancient deeds of God are deprived of their actuality ("de-actualized", von Rad) by the new action in the future, and the relationship with the past is established by analogy and the concept of "remembrance" (דבר). In late Judaism, the mention of the covenant with Abraham is linked with formulas which pray for deliverance from danger in such words as "Remember, O Lord, the covenant which you made with Abraham, etc." The apocalyptic understanding of history of salvation is already foreshadowed in Gen 15:13f., where the divine plan is already laid down and is revealed beforehand to Abraham, God's elect.

e) *The function of history of salvation in the New Testament.* The understanding of history in the NT is fundamentally on the lines of the prophetic and apocalyptic tradition and starts with the same principles. The categories of the history of salvation which Jesus and the Church applied to his person and message are all traditional. This may be seen in the oldest narratives from the life of Jesus, the passion narratives, which are wholly in the style of apocalyptic historiography, as for instance in the indirect use of Scripture. It also appears in the pre-Pauline, Hellenistic and Jewish-Christian "exaltation Christology", which is orientated on the notions of the giving of the Spirit and the new covenant and law in the heart, as in Jer and Ezek. Typology, using the figures of Elijah, Moses, Abraham, Adam and the prophets in general, plays a large part, even in the older tradition. Jesus' own understanding of history is determined by the imminent expectation of the kingdom, but also by the emphasis on the present decision for the message of repentance. Salvation is decided by the attitude to God's envoy, Jesus (cf. Mk 8:38) and then to Jesus' envoys (Mk 6:11 par.). In the pre-Pauline Hellenistic tradition the decision with regard to the word of the envoys (see *Apostle*) is the way in which man himself anticipates the final decision as to salvation or perdition, because the resurrection of Jesus has brought on the final situation itself. But this means that with baptism (assimilation to the risen Lord) these Churches already possess the final blessings of salvation: peace, love, abrogation of the law, resurrection (2 Tim 2:18; καινὴ κτίσις, new creation) and knowledge of God by the gentiles (hence the mission to the heathen carried on by the envoys of Jesus). This notion of the end-time being already localized in the present, of which there are traces everywhere in the NT, especially in Jn, the pre-Pauline community at Corinth, in Paul and the synoptic missionary discourses, is what is really new in the notion of the history of salvation, from the point of view of religious history.

All later Christian theologies are essentially efforts to harmonize this radical conception current in the early post-Easter days with others which are more dependent on the cosmology of apocalyptic and only expect the moment of the end when heaven and earth actually pass away. The combination of these two currents gave rise to the "Already-Not Yet" of Pauline theology and to the later general Christian division of history into periods – the time before Jesus, the time of Jesus, the time of the Church and the time after the final judgment. This conception is well worked out in Lk, in which the time of Jesus is the "middle of the times", but also occurs in rudimentary stages which have affinities with the Pauline solution; cf. Lk 16:16f., where the message of the resurrection of Jesus (εὐαγγελίζεσθαι) has succeeded the OT word of God through the law and the prophets, and the mission to the heathens has begun (Lk 16:16b). Nonetheless, the law remains as the norm of judgment till the actual end of the world. Paul develops this approach, especially in his solution of the question of the law by primarily Christological categories. In the Letter to the Hebrews, the relationship between the resurrection and the last things is that Jesus appeared at his first coming in order to suffer, then became high priest and preceded the wandering people of God (E. Käsemann) of the two testaments into the heavenly sanctuary, and will appear a second time for his immediate work of salvation (9:28). Thus the various NT theologies give very different answers to the question of where salvation is. For Heb it is wholly in the future, since the present is still the time of promise, for Luke it is in the past in the time of Jesus, while for pre-Pauline and Johannine circles it is in the present possession of the Spirit. (Here U. Wilckens appeals to 1 Jn 3:2, where a future event is foreseen, but which obviously does no more than reveal what has already taken place.) Hence the relationship to the history of salvation up to Jesus is a matter of how radically the break brought about by the resurrection of Jesus is conceived. The continuity stands out most clearly in the texts which make use of the Deuteronomists' view of history to explain Jesus and his destiny (Mt 5:11f. par.; Mt 23:29–36 par.; Lk 13:31, 34f. par.; Mt 23:37ff.; Lk 11:49ff.). Here the death of Jesus is in line with the killing of the prophets, the destruction of Jerusalem follows the necessary pattern of punishment, the obduracy of Israel is the cause of its rejection and of Jesus' envoys' turning to the heathen (after the resurrection in Mt, after a second preaching of repentance in Luke's Acts). The working out of the reflective quotations in Mt (modelled in particular on the *Liber antiquitatum biblicarum* of the pseudo-Philo) is also due to the use of a category long familiar to the theology of history – that of promise and fulfilment. When the proof from Scripture is later used against Judaism (e.g., Mk 10:5f.), the discontinuity between Israel and the Church of the nations is stressed. It means that the obduracy manifested at the crucifixion of Jesus has long been seen as applying to other fields. It is now seen in everything which divides Judaism from the Christian harmonizations of present and future eschatology.

Klaus Berger

B. The Old Testament Period

Here we are concerned neither with the OT as Scripture nor with the history of the people of Israel in detail but with the nature of the period in "salvation history" which is designated by the term OT (ancient covenant) as this is to be understood, in the light of the NT, from the sources of dogmatic theology. Theologically speaking, the OT is the phase of the history of revelation and salvation which began with God's covenant with Abraham, had its centre (as the prophets teach) in the exodus from Egypt and the covenant of the chosen people of Israel under Moses at Sinai, and came to fulfilment in Christ's death and resurrection and the new and eternal covenant of God with the whole of mankind which they constituted. This epoch in salvation history had an anterior limit because the history of origins and the time before Abraham are regarded by the OT itself (even in the Yahwist tradition) as "pre-history" of a general (universal) kind, in which a special ("particular") history of salvation does not yet stand out, that is, one expressly distinguished by God's revelation itself from the rest of world history and salvation history and in this sense "public". The OT period was closed by the new covenant in Christ

Jesus. Spatially, the OT is limited, because grace cannot be limited to the OT, and with grace and in it, a revelation – apart from "primitive revelation" – though not strictly "public" and "official". This follows from Scripture itself (Ezek 14:14, 20; Jon; Ps 46:2f.; 101:16f.; 137:4f.; Mt 12:41; Jas 5:11), and the teaching of the Church (*D* 160 a–b, 1295; cf. also *D* 1379, 1647). And there is now the doctrine of Vatican II, especially in *Lumen Gentium* (on the Church), art. 16, and in *Ad Gentes* (on the Missions), art. 7, according to which it cannot be doubted that there is real and salutary faith even outside the OT and the NT preaching. On the contrary: wherever there is supernaturally elevating grace, there is a new formal object (motive) for a knowledge and action and in this sense, a transcendental revelation.

Consequently, from the present-day standpoint this period is very limited. In view of the antiquity of mankind and therefore the lengthy duration of the "status legis naturae", and in view of the brevity and restrictedness of the history from Abraham to Jesus in comparison with the whole of world-history, it rightly seems to us today a relatively short immediate preparation for Christ. And in many respects (not in all) it has the appearance of a paradigm of God's action in history generally, which providence has specially emphasized in revelation. The OT may be more closely characterized by the following features.

1. It is genuine supernatural history of salvation and revelation (in "word"). Consequently, since the discontinuity of history through the fault of men's unbelief has no power to disrupt the unity of God's saving action, it is the irrevocable prehistory of the definitive revelation of God in Christ. Salvation is from the Jews (Jn 4:22), God in the OT "in many and various ways spoke of old" to the fathers by the prophets (Heb 1:1). The NT writings (Mt 15:3f.; Mk 7:8; Lk 24:44; Jn 5:46; 19:36f.; 1 Cor 10:11; Heb 7ff., etc.), and the teaching of the Church (against the various forms of Gnosticism, Manichaeism, etc.) repeatedly emphasize that the history of the OT derived from the God who has revealed himself definitively in Jesus Christ (*D* 28, 348, 421, 464, 706), so that the scriptures of the OT and of the NT have the same author (*D* 783, 1787). The rejection of rationalist attempts (e.g., in Modernism) to reduce the authentic history of revelation to a purely natural, universal history of religion (*D* 2009–12, 2020, 2090, etc.), is also a defence of OT history. It must of course be noted that the divine authorship of this history does not abolish the fact that God's saving will and illumination were also at work outside this official history of redemption. Even outside the OT there has never been a purely natural history of religion anywhere. And in Jesus Christ God and man received an inseparable unity such as never existed before even in the OT.

This authentic OT history of salvation essentially consisted in the first place, according to the testimony of the OT itself, in being the history of an ethical and prophetic monotheism produced, maintained and even more, renewed, by God's own intervention. As such it consisted of the proclamation of the "experiences" caused by God's actual action in history, regarding God's free "actions", which go beyond rational inference of the attributes he necessarily possesses. In the second place, this history was such that the one true and "living God" (because and although Lord of all creatures) himself willed by his action in history to enter into the relationship of a special covenant with the people of Israel. He was not simply a "national God" from the start and inalienably, merely a numinous personification on the natural plane of the nation itself (cf. Vatican II, *Dei Verbum*, arts. 3, 14ff.). The two factors conditioned one another. Yahweh the God of the covenant was ever more clearly recognized and honoured as truly the only God, and as opposed to mere henotheism of fact it was ever more profoundly grasped that the God *of the whole world* had concluded a special covenant precisely with this nation, so that the ultimate purpose of the particular covenant was to be a universal one, as the promise in the OT of the future conversion of the Gentiles proves (Gen 12:3; Is 2:2; 11:10ff.; 42:4ff.; 49:6; 55:4; Ps 21:28; 85:9; Jer 3:17; Zeph 2:11; 3:9; Hag 2:7; Zech 8:20). When fulfilment had come it was possible to recognize that the historical covenant of God revealing himself in freely-bestowed favour was to find its supreme accomplishment when the two partners in the covenant, God and man, were united in the God-man, so that the former covenant was a preparation for this.

2. The OT was a "particular" history of salvation and revelation. This restricted history is chosen by the God of history from the whole of history, which is also willed and ruled by him. He has not revealed himself to all peoples and made a covenant with them in this way. What this implies, both positively and negatively, has already been noted above. This particularism has a universal meaning: if in addition to history in general there is also a *history* of salvation (and not merely a situation in relation to salvation which remains the same for all at all times), and if the actual redeemer is not mankind as a whole, but mankind – as a whole, however – is redeemed by one man, then the temporal and spatial setting of this historically one and therefore spatially and temporally located redeemer necessarily has its own determinate historical limits. It is planned by God with the redeemer in view and so shares in the supernatural character of the redeemer himself.

3. It was a history of salvation open to the future, not a definitive history. This open and provisional character was not a feature of the OT simply because everything historical is by that very fact transitory and always a provisional step towards something new. Even as God's action, imposing an absolute obligation here and now, it was understood to have a preliminary, preparatory function (which was all it was to have, and certainly by its own fault is all it had). This was understood to belong to its own nature because what was final, the eternal covenant, was still to come. Moreover, the ancient covenant, the existence of which was radically threatened by the moral infidelity of the nation, could and did fail, and God's fidelity which was greater for all that, even towards the unfaithful, as was slowly recognized, pointed to the new covenant, not the ancient. That was how the OT regarded itself and that is how it was interpreted from the standpoint of the NT. It was planned "from eternal ages" as a prologue to Christ. He is its secret entelechy (cf. Rom 10:4), manifesting itself, though still hidden, in the slowly developing expectation of the Messiah.

a) Consequently this period of the history of salvation is to be interpreted as "not yet eschatological". That is to say, God's free, radical and definitive, irrevocable self-revelation and self-communication in his word as victorious grace to the definitively accepted world is not yet seen in such a way that God has already given himself tangibly and irrevocably in the world. OT salvation-history was still in suspense between judgment and grace; the dialogue was still open and the conclusion had not yet been reached in the world (i.e., disclosed by an event) that the pardon of God and not man's refusal has the last word. Consequently the visible social form of this not yet eschatological salvation-history (i.e., the ancient covenant and the synagogue) could still be annulled by the unbelief of the human partner and so everything in it was still ambiguous and a revocable promise which could be made void. For that reason an OT sacrament was not an "opus operatum", i.e., there was no absolute and unconditional promise of grace on God's part (cf. *D* 695, 845, 857, 711f.). Since the OT was in this sense not yet the definitive reality but, precisely as something established by God in view of salvation, was subject to the temptation of regarding itself as absolute, a temptation to which through men's fault it succumbed, it was the covenant which was the "Law", requiring but not conferring the realities in view of which it made its demands (God's Spirit, his life, holiness and grace). It was merely external legality and Levitical sanctification, a servile bondage to what was other than God (the objective structures of the world, even the mediation of the Law by the angels), because it could not give what the world was really meant to be in the total order of salvation: participation in God's self-communication by grace and beatific vision. It therefore left man in an intramundane condition, even if one sanctioned by God. When as such (though divine and holy) it encountered sinful man, without conveying grace (and precisely to that extent) it produced servitude, it became a goad of sin, it meant death and the service of perdition. But in this way (since God of course ultimately decreed the "holy" Law with a positively beneficent intention for the salvation of mankind), and through the hidden grace that was given with the Law, though it did not belong to it, the Law in fact became a guide towards Christ (cf. Rom 3:19f.), though Paul mostly envisages only the calamitous (shadow-like: Hebrews) role of the Law, which consequently appears rather as a "tutor" *until* Christ appears (Gal 3:24f.).

b) On the other hand the OT is a manifest movement, guided by God, towards definitive redemption, the "shadow" cast before (1 Cor 10:6; Heb 10:1), which is there because the reality is on the way and creates for itself its prerequisites. To that extent there was already grace, faith and justification in the OT (Mt 27:52; Rom 4; 1 Cor 10:1–5; Heb 11; 1 Pet 3:19), not through what differentiates it from the new and final covenant, but because it already bore the latter hidden within it. Anyone who trusted himself in obedient faith to the saving action of God which took place in the OT, to the incomprehensibility of the divine dispositions and their hidden intention (and such obedience to God's unfathomable providence belongs to the nature of faith), entered into that hidden unity of God's redemptive plan, and was saved by hope (in this sense) of the promised future redemption (cf. *D* 160b, 794, 1295, 1356f., 1414f., 1519f., 2123) found salvation through Christ even in the OT.

The dialectic constituted by the fact that the OT could introduce one, by faith, which was always possible, into the reality which the OT itself was not, because it was provisional and only existed in virtue of what was to come, understandably made Christian theology waver in its verdict on the OT. (This was already heralded by the lack of a complete synthesis of the judgment passed on the OT by Jesus and Paul in the writings of the NT.) Much remained debated: whether the Patriarchs had already the grace of Christ, the value and meaning of circumcision and other OT sacraments, the precise principles of interpretation of the OT scriptures, the enduring validity or abolition of the decalogue, the differing "scale" of grace in the OT and the NT, the range of the content of faith (Trinity?) in the saints of the OT, the beginning of the "Church" in the OT (for example, from Abel onwards), the inhabitation of the Holy Spirit in the just of the OT, the precise nature (and limits) of God's authorship of the OT law, the exact moment of the abolition of the OT, when it became not only "dead", but "deadly", and so on.

4. It is a period in the history of redemption which is now fulfilled and ended by its fulfilment. Jesus said that his coming did not abolish the law but "fulfils" it (Mt 5:17) (by giving a radical character to the concrete demands of the OT law [Mk 10:1–12], by bringing it back to its essential core [Mt 22:34–40], and in that way finally abrogating the ceremonial law [Mt 7:15]) and cancelled the ancient covenant as such in its entirety in his blood (Mt 26:28 par.; cf. Lk 16:16). But Paul, without distinguishing between ceremonial law and moral demands, declared the ancient covenant ("the Law") to be abrogated, so much so that to continue to observe it as of importance for salvation amounts to denial of Christ and the unique significance of his Cross for salvation (Gal 5:2, 4). That abolition does not make the real past simply non-existent for Christians. Abraham is the father of all believers (Rom 4:11). The patriarchs of the OT are witnesses to the faith even for us (Heb 11). But so too are all other just men who, though more anonymously, are members and bearers of the whole history of salvation, extending beyond the OT, on which as a whole our salvation rests. That history is enduringly our own actual past. Seeing that the ontological and existential difference of the various realities involved has to be respected, it is not very easy to say what "still" remains because the OT is our valid past and what has simply been swept away because otherwise it would be denied that the ancient covenant is really past. The Law belongs to the second category; the holy Scripture of the OT, which is still our holy book too, belongs to the first.

5. As the prehistory of the new and eternal covenant, in which the OT has been annulled yet incorporated, it can only be fully and correctly interpreted from the standpoint of the new covenant, because its true nature is only disclosed (2 Cor 3:14) in the revelation of its τέλος (end) (Rom 10:4). To consider the OT merely as part of the "history of religion" would be a failure to recognize its supernatural character, as in Liberalism and Modernism. Attribution of a purely immanent significance to the OT (M. Buber), even if its special character as effected by God were recognized, would miss the truth that the OT only revealed its full nature in the NT, and that we cannot leave this out of account today, without missing the real conception which the OT had of itself, though of course that immanent OT conception of its own nature must be inquired into, to the extent that such a question can be propounded and answered by a later age.

Karl Rahner

C. The New Testament Period

1. NT history of salvation has two senses. The first is the time of Jesus Christ and the apostles, the primitive Church, which can be distinguished by some essential features from the post-apostolic Church, even though it is itself the beginning and the first period of the Church. The second is the period of the history of salvation which runs from the resurrection of Christ and Pentecost (taken as one salvific event) to the parousia, the return of Christ.

The "new covenant" or NT in the first sense differs from the second in the following respects. It is the time in which Jesus Christ was among men "in the flesh". *The* Christian revelation took place and was "closed", being henceforth "merely" handed on in tradition. Scripture, the inspired testimony to the original Christian revelation, was written. The Church was given its constitution *iuris divini*. But in spite of these features, the distinction is secondary. The main thing is the NT in the second sense, since Christ remains present throughout the whole of this time of salvation in his Spirit. His life on earth only means the beginning of his parousia, in which the kingdom of God will come definitively and in full openness. Hence the following considerations are confined to the time of the NT in the second sense.

2. According to Scripture, the NT is a unique phase of salvation, clearly distinguished from the previous one and running till the end of history. For in the NT Jesus Christ (even according to the self-understanding of the pre-Easter Jesus) is the absolute mediator, the eschatological coming of salvation, in whose death the new (and eternal, 2 Cor 3:11) covenant between God and all mankind is established (see *Eucharist* I). Scripture distinguishes this new covenant from the OT, partly by affirming its radical novelty and hence its opposition to the old, partly by affirming a certain continuity. From the first point of view, the NT, as the covenant of freedom from the law, of the Holy Spirit, of forgiveness of sins, of justice and the new fellowship with God, is distinguished by Paul from the OT, which is the time of the law and death, of the concealment of what the previous covenant really meant. From the point of view of continuity, the relationship of the NT to the OT is that of fulfilment to promise, but in such a way that the fulfilment surpasses the promise not only of the OT in the stricter sense of the Mosaic covenant, but of the whole history "since the beginning".

Scripture also shows why this strictly eschatological period cannot be succeeded by a new temporal period of salvation. The NT is radically open to the fulfilment. It is founded on the death of Jesus, the event which ends history, and on participation in this death, and thus has already left behind any possible inner-worldly future. It hopes for the kingdom of God, which is God himself, from God alone, and thus is forbidden to confuse any inner-worldly future with the absolute newness already at work within it, and with regard to which it is itself only promise.

3. From the theological point of view, the NT is the eschatological time.

a) This means that in the matter of salvation the history of human freedom as such is no longer simply open, an endless dialectic (for man) between salvation and loss. In the predefining grace of Christ, previous to the actual decision of man, efficacious without detriment to man's freedom, history as such is already decided, in favour of the love of God and the kingdom of God – though the history of salvation of the individual remains open.

b) This predefining, triumphant self-communication of God is not just secretly implanted in the world and its history as its ultimate end. It has been historically manifested in Jesus Christ, his death and resurrection, so that the ultimate ground of the history of salvation and revelation is present and active as an element of history. This is the specific element of the NT in contrast to the OT. The Church, the community which professes faith in, and makes memorial (*anamnesis*) of, this Christ is the presence of this ultimate ground of history. It is the basic sacrament of this predefined salvation of the world (a sign one with and differing from the thing signified). Hence the NT is the "time of the Church". The NT, as the eschatological phase of the history of salvation, revelation, grace, faith and hope as world history continues, is not just patient waiting. It in turn has its own history (see *Church History*, *Dogma* III), which is not simply identical with the history of salvation and of the world in general, but is the history of the articulate grasp of the ultimate nature and goal of the world.

4. Kerygmatically, two points may be noted.

a) The vast expansion in knowledge of a history of religion which has proved highly diversified leads to the temptation to co-ordinate the time of the NT with past and future religious history. Modern man is inclined to see it as simply a phase, though no doubt an important one, which can be left behind at some time, though perhaps only by a secularized future ("de-sacralization") in which Christianity dissolves into a worldly, profane self-understanding of man, where "togetherness" or the like reigns. This is a temptation which necessarily follows from the nature of Christian existence (cf. 2 Tim 2:18; 2 Pet 3:3f.). We must remember, nevertheless, that while Christianity has to take on historical forms (in propositional language and social contacts), it sees itself as the "taking up and away" of all worldly religious and anti-religious experiences, including those yet to come, into the mystery of God's incomprehensibility, in the death of Christ and in participation in this death. This is the only way in which the NT claims to be the eschatological time, during which it also criticizes itself in the hope of the kingdom of God. Thus it does not exclude the possibility of new religious and anti-religious experiences. It is ready to face the element of the unforeseeable in them and to integrate them into itself. But it also knows that it has already gone beyond them, not just in the formal dialectic of abstract concepts, but in real participation in the death of Christ. For here, when it is really accepted in faith and hope, the whole religious and anti-religious future of the world is already "passed over" (Jn 5:24; 1 Jn 3:14). The eschatological time has reached the God who is not just a moment of a history which would have to live by virtue of this history as a whole.

b) The modern impression is that history, after an almost incalculable lapse of time, is only now really beginning. There is a planned campaign for the elimination of the self-alienation which social conditions, according to Marxism, have brought about in man, and for the humanization of his environment. For the first time, there seems real hope of success. This could suggest that the time of the NT was a transitory epoch, already in decline, of which the greatest achievement was that it anticipated in abstract theory and mythological formulas what now lies within man's practical grasp. But here the following considerations are in place.

(i) Since God imparts himself to history as its entelechy and goal, this grace of the expectation of the absolute future is not the denial of the seriousness of (profane) history. For this hope – which the individual may refuse – means precisely that all history, and not just explicitly religious history, is concerned with the absolute future, salvation.

(ii) If the history which is now only beginning is *within* the time of the NT, it is actually accorded its greatest possible dimension. Its only limit is the illimitation of God, and its function is to mediate the acceptance of the absolute future of God. For every free act, and not just the religious and cultic act, being salutary because positively moral (though perhaps mostly not recognized as such) serves to mediate the acceptance of the absolute future. This history as a whole, because embraced by the time of the NT, is given the promise that it is not bound for the nothingness of death. And what takes place in it will become, though by means of a radical transformation (1 Cor 15:35–58), the concrete fulfilment in which God will be "all in all" (1 Cor 15:28). The time of the NT proclaims that death will remain in history as its "last enemy" (1 Cor 15:26), but that history is still not bound for death, but for the glory of God, which in the resurrection of Jesus has already begun to take possession of the world. This faith and hope offer the world a standpoint from which to criticize false conservatisms and utopias, to which history might otherwise fall victim.

Karl Rahner

IV. Theology

A. Redemption

1. *The fundamental problem.* a) Redemption objectively presupposes a need of redemption and subjectively the admission (the acceptance) by man of his need. The starting-point must therefore always be the question whether there is such a need of salvation, what constitutes it and how man can be brought to take an honest attitude to this fundamental fact of existence.

(i) In the first place this need for deliverance signifies the condition in which man inescapably finds himself in his own experience, and which he feels to be incomplete, ambiguous and full of suffering. And he feels this to be so in all the dimensions of his reality so that the experience of this state, as both individual and collective, is practically identical with his existence itself. For the Christian interpretation of man, however, this condition does not consist solely in the unavoidable frictions of material, biological, social and personal development. It does not consist solely of social grievances or the finite character of human existence (biological or spiritual). This condition must not, however, be falsely exaggerated to the point of denying the very capacity for salvation, as in the pessimistic existentialism which holds that existence is absolutely and irremediably absurd and that frank recognition of this fact is man's authentic truth. But this attitude can in fact be regarded as recognition that man cannot save himself. Then the contrary opinion (the Marxist view, whether applied collectively or regarded individualistically) would be the modern form of "superstition" (M. Blondel).

Christianity acknowledges man to be capable of salvation, ultimately because even his freedom is finite and remains comprised within God's creative love. But man is also in need of deliverance, primarily and ultimately from his *guilt*. Certainly a finite guiltless being which had to grow and develop would have felt the pain of incompletion as a deficiency, in the process of becoming. But the Christian view of man knows that concretely and radically suffering is more than merely "growing pains", and in fact is the manifestation of guilt. And only where guilt is abolished can there be any question of redemption. This guilt, however, both as the state of original sin and as the action of individual freedom, cannot be removed by man himself. For it is not merely a transgression of certain objective norms belonging to this world. If it were, and if we leave out of account a deeper analysis of freedom as mutual communication between human persons, in which the phenomenon of a guilt impossible to annul by man himself can be experienced, then it would be conceivable that man might be able himself to undo the *consequences* of his transgression, remove his guilt and so finally come to an arrangement with God as the guardian of these regulations concerning creatures. Guilt in the concrete order as "sin" is the free No to God's direct, intimate love in the offer of his self-communication by uncreated divinizing grace and therefore essentially an act which has dialogal character. And because free, it aims at finality, definiteness. Such an act, however, is directed to the absolutely sovereign, free God and is essentially an answer, dependent on God's call and offer. Through a No to divine love of that kind, man of himself can no longer reckon on the continuance of that love, especially as it is the love of the absolutely holy and just God who is the absolute contradiction of such a refusal. Only if that love freely endures even in the face of such a refusal and, as divine and of infinite power to set free, goes beyond that guilt, is forgiveness possible, i.e., is there any possibility of man freely loving, responding in a genuine dialogue, made possible by God. Hence only on the basis of forgiveness of sin is definitive salvation conceivable as personal fulfilment and deliverance from the trials of suffering. For while suffering and death are manifestations of guilt in the depths of existence, complete "beatitude" in all dimensions can only come as the eschatological gift of God. It is not a goal that can be achieved by man himself.

(ii) The experience of humanly ineradicable guilt as the ground of man's need of redemption is felt in very different degrees. That is understandable in view of the existence of man and his situation in the history of salvation. It does not rule out the fundamental assertion of the need for redemption as the condition of understanding Christian soteriology. A merely rudimentary sense of guilt or an apparently total lack of it may itself be culpable repression, "suppression" of the true situation of man (Rom 1:18). It may simply be due to a very primitive stage of development in the individual, in which a true sense of guilt is not possible. It may be a sign that the powerful (though inarticulate) grace-given sense of living within the domain of divine (forgiving) love to some extent outweighs and overlays the sense of guilt (although in principle both grow in direct proportion). It may be that in some individual the possibility of radical guilt has remained a mere possibility through God's preserving grace, and that this possibility as such is less easily recognized in fact than guilt itself (though that is not necessarily so, as we see from the saints' consciousness of sin). Finally, the profound individual experience always requires an effective example and "catalyst" in the experience of humanity and its history of calamity (especially as interpreted by the revealed history of perdition and salvation). And an individual, culpably or not, may not be sufficiently confronted with this experience in its entirety.

All these factors may be combined in very different ways in the individual and cannot be adequately distinguished by conscious introspection. (For example, concupiscence antecedent to freedom but still inculpable, as opposed to concupiscence which is culpably ratified by freedom, cannot entirely be distinguished by reflection.) Hence there are difficulties regarding the individual sense of guilt, all the more so as many acts are objectively but not subjectively guilty and can be analysed even by the person concerned in terms of his own oppressive past, social factors, etc., and so "cleared up". Methodical guidance is needed to initiate men into the recognition of their guilty situation. Here, however, it is ultimately decisive to understand that this admission of guilt (the manifestation of the "wrath of God"; cf. Rom 1:18) will *in fact* be really radically ventured and achieved only by those who encounter and accept God's forgiveness. The need for redemption is concretely grasped in the act of accepting redemption. Otherwise man does not gauge the radical truth of his guilt, he will deny it or interpret it in some other way. Consequently initiation into the need for redemption is encouragement to believe in the love of God and accept it as unmerited and unconditional (and so therefore not ended by guilt), in the knowledge that even to accept this love is the work of this love.

b) Redemption as Christianity understands it is "objective". It is an event (act of redemption) with a result (objective fact of being redeemed). These are ontologically prior to the justification and sanctification of man (subjective redemption) and are consequently to be distinguished from it. This distinction is often denied in a modern Christian anthropology of an existentialist kind, for which redemption as such takes place solely in the occurrence of faith, while the latter does not bear on an objective event of *history* prior to the act of faith. The ground of the distinction, however, lies simply in the fact that created, finite freedom, even in working out its salvation, presupposes a situation which is not identical with the necessary essence of man and his freedom, a concrete, temporal situation which goes to constitute the real nature of freedom as it is in fact exercised. Objective redemption, therefore, means the constitution by God of that concrete historical situation of freedom in which the will of God to forgive and save is exercised and manifests itself as an offer made to the freedom of man, historically and in eschatological irreversibility; it constitutes the situation on the basis of which and in which alone man can accept in freedom the proffered forgiveness. Why this situation of redemption and forgiveness does not consist simply in a transcendental forgiving will of God, coming to man solely from above, will have to be examined more closely later.

c) For an account of Christian soteriology it is at least not absolutely necessary, and at the present day it is not advisable pedagogically, to distinguish too definitely the grace of God as supernatural divinization and sanctification from the grace of God as forgiveness of guilt (and consequently the original grace of *God* from the forgiving grace of *Christ*). Certainly there is a formal distinction between gratuitous divinization and gratuitous forgiveness (readiness to forgive) on the part of God. But in the concrete order of salvation it is not merely the case that forgiveness is only conferred by divine grace as elevating. We are quite entitled to assume that (i) even divinizing grace as such was given from the start *intuitu Christi*, in view of Christ as the incarnate Word of God. That grace becomes forgiving because God's saving will directed from the start towards Christ as its historical culmination was (freely) absolute, even in face of sin. It is also possible to assume that (ii) sin, which God could always have prevented in the creation, without detriment to human freedom, was only permitted by God because transcended by his grace. He wished to manifest the victory of his own absolute love even over the refusal of his creature and in the deadly abyss of its futility. From that point of view divinization and forgiveness are two elements, always in fact connected, of the one divine self-communication in uncreated grace to the world, which within its one historical course comprises guilt in order by overcoming it to show itself as a love even greater in its power.

d) For a view of redemption that will be comprehensible today, it is of the greatest importance to announce and present it from the start in such a way that the whole history of mankind always and everywhere stands under God's forgiving love in Christ. The redemptive event of the Cross of Christ will not then appear to be the cause of man's redemption without being the cause of the redemption of pre-Christian mankind or as causing this latter in an entirely different way. Otherwise the preacher lays himself open to the sceptical question of what has changed in the world itself "since" Christ. Because, however, from the beginning God's forgiving self-communication (oriented towards Christ) was always operative in the world, the question of what has changed for the better "since" Christ is badly framed in principle or at all events is a secondary one. We cannot stand empirically outside the *experimentum Christi* and see what the condition of the world would be without Christ. At least a good deal of the betterment of social and human conditions "since Christ" does not demonstrably need to be credited to Christianity, though it would be equally unhistorical to try to overlook a historically tangible "success" of Christianity through its message, all the more so as much in the development of secular civilization derives at least in fact from ultimately Christian motives.

e) Kerygmatically it inevitably leads to misunderstandings if in soteriology the person and the work (death) of Christ are too sharply separated. If in an incarnational doctrine of redemption it is emphasized too one-sidedly that mankind was redeemed by the fact of the divine Logos assuming a human nature as member of the one mankind ("quod assumptum est, redemptum est"), then redemption is one-sidedly envisaged only under cosmic and objective aspects and Scripture is not taken seriously when it sees the redemptive event in Jesus' love and obedience even to the Cross. If only the latter act is taken into consideration in a "staurological soteriology" (cf. 1 Cor 1:18), and the incarnation regarded merely as the constitution of a subject who is *capable* of redeeming *if* he posits the requisite action, then soteriology inevitably falls into the purely juridical concepts of an exclusive "satisfaction-theory". The incarnation no longer appears as an intrinsic constituent of the redemptive event itself, redemption remains in a purely "moral" domain and its profoundly world-transforming character is obscured. A theology of the personal subject and of freedom, the specifically personal unity of nature and activity (which cannot be wholly reduced to the common denominator of substance-accident), would have to show that the assumption of a human "nature" by the Logos is the assumption of a "nature" necessarily working in freedom towards its destiny. The incarnation itself is a divine movement which is fully deployed only in the death and resurrection of Jesus Christ (cf. Jn 3:17; 1 Tim 11:15; *D* 86: the *descensus* is itself *propter nos homines et propter nostram salutem*).

2. *The Church's teaching on redemption in Scripture, tradition and magisterium.* a) *Scripture.* Only the most fundamental points of scriptural soteriology can be presented here. Much else will be found under other headings (see *Jesus Christ, Mediatorship, Sin, Grace, Holy Spirit* I, *Virtue, Resurrection, Ascension of Christ,* etc.).

(i) As regards terminology, there is the (negative) expression ἀπολύτρωσις (*redemptio*), setting free from the domination of sin, the "principalities and powers", the Law and death (Rom 3:24; 1 Cor 1:30; Eph 1:7; Col 1:14; Heb 9:15). Positively there is καταλλαγή (*reconciliatio*), restoration of union and peace with God and among men themselves (Rom 5:10f.; 11:15; 2 Cor 5:18ff.; Col 1:20). This redemptive process is characterized in liturgical terms as sacrifice (προσφορά, θυσία, Eph 5:2; 1 Cor 5:7; Heb 9:25ff.), as expiation (ἱλαστήριον, Rom 3:25), as the shedding of the redemptive blood of the covenant for the many (Mt 26:28 par.; Acts 20:28; Rom 5:9; Eph 1:7; Col 1:20; Heb 9:12, 14; 10:19; 13:12, 20; 1 Pet 1:19; 1 Jn 1:7; Rev 5:9); in more juridical terms as "ransom" (see above; Mk 10:45; 1 Tim 2:6) or under even more general terms such as "salvation" (Mt 1:21; Jn 3:17; 12:47; 1 Tim 1:15; 2 Tim 2:10; Heb 5:9, etc.). In these no very conscious distinction is drawn between "objective" redemption and its effect, "subjective" redemption.

(ii) This redemption occurs through Christ's death (see 1e above) inasmuch as this is itself an effect of God's redemptive love (Jn 3:16), Christ's free action (Jn 10:15–18) as the accomplishment of his obedience to God, in the acceptance of the lowliness of a human death (Phil 2:7f.), as service and love for man (Mk 10:45; Mt 20:28; Lk 18:27; Jn 13:1). This act is that of the Servant of Yahweh who as the second Adam (Rom 5:12ff. etc.) vicariously (ὑπέρ, ἀντί, περί) acts "in accordance with the Scriptures" for the fellowship of his brethren (Mk 10:45; Mt 26:28 in reference to the "Ebed Yahweh" of Is 53:12, etc.). It is of decisive importance that the historical pre-paschal Jesus himself interprets his death as such an act of redemption (Mt 26:28 par.), even if this only became clear to his community in the light of his resurrection.

(iii) The effects of this redemptive act are liberation from the slavery of sin (Tit 2:14; Eph 1:7; Col 1:14; Heb 9:12ff.), of the Law (Gal 3:13; 4:5; Rom 7:1ff.), of the devil (Jn 16:11; Heb 2:14f.), new creation and rebirth (2 Cor 5:17; Gal 6:15; Eph 4:24; Jn 3:1ff.), justification (Rom 5:1, 9, etc.), possession of the Spirit and sonship of God (Gal 3:2ff.; 4:6f.; Rom 8:12–17), truth, life, light, peace, joy (cf. especially Jn). These benefits of redemption, which must of course be understood as grasped in faith and love, are partly already present now (forgiveness of sins, justification, possession of the Spirit, sonship), partly still to come (resurrection of the body: Lk 14:14; 1 Cor 15; glorification: Rom 8:17; vision of God: 1 Cor 13:12; eternal life: Mk 9:43; 10:17, 30; Gal 6:8; Rom 6:22), but these are nevertheless already possessed in the Spirit and in hope, so that only their manifest and permanent possession still remains to come (2 Cor 1:22; 3:18; 5:5; Rom 5:8ff.). The soteriological significance attributed to Jesus' resurrection by Scripture must not be overlooked (e.g., Phil 3:10; Rom 4:25, 8:11; 1 Cor 6:14; 2 Cor 4:14). Emphasis is laid on the universality of this redemption, as against Jewish particularism (see *Salvation* I) and its character of pure grace (Romans, Galatians). It cannot come through one's own righteous works, but only in faith.

b) *Magisterium and tradition.* (i) On the whole the Church's official pronouncements simply repeat the doctrine of Scripture. See the Creeds; also *D* 122, 319, 550, 790, 795, 938, 940, 951. They also reject Modernism according to which no soteriology is yet found in the gospels themselves, in contrast to Paul (*D* 2038), and condemn Jansenism for denying that salvation is offered to all (*D* 1096, 1294). Redemption is occasionally presented in terms of *satisfactio* (*D* 799, 2318) but without precise explanation of the term (and consequently without solemn definition of the scholastic satisfaction-theory). It is also expressed a few times in terms of "merit" (*meritum*): *D* 552, 795, 799, 800, 802, 820, *DS* 3329. Apocatastasis cannot be taught by appealing to the Cross of Christ (*D* 211). Vatican I envisaged a definition about Christ: "vere et proprie satisfecisse nobisque gratiam et gloriam meruisse" (*Collectio Lacencis*, VII, 566c).

(ii) The history of soteriology in dogma contributes little. In the Fathers what is most important (over and above the transmission of biblical doctrine) is Irenaeus's recapitulation theory (mystical-incarnational theory of redemption) which, without denying the Pauline theory of ransom and atonement by the Cross, teaches on the basis of Eph 1:10 the reunion of mankind with God in Christ as the all-embracing head. The only other idea in addition to Scripture in the patristic period, when the concept of expiatory sacrifice was well known from the religious environment, was the theory of men being ransomed from the power of the devil. This was certainly intended in a very metaphorical sense, but included a strongly mythological element. The devil was regarded as having certain proprietary rights over man because of sin, which he lost when deluded, so to speak, by Christ. He wrongly tried to extend his dominion of death over him (so, for example, Origen). In the Middle Ages, under Anselm's inspiration, the satisfaction-theory was worked out. Redemption primarily concerns guilt, which involves an infinite offence against God, because it is measured by the dignity of the person offended. If it is to be made good (and not just forgiven by a free act of God's grace, the possibility of which in principle on God's part is not contested), then this fully adequate (*condigna*) reparation (*satisfactio = iniuriae alteri illatae compensatio: Catechismus Romanus*, II, 5, 59) can only be effected by a divine person. For the worth of the *satisfactio* is measured by the dignity of the offerer, not by that of the person to whom it is addressed. Such reparation can be made by some person other than the offender on condition that the person offended is willing freely to accept a vicarious satisfaction (*vicaria satisfactio*). In this sense Christ by his obedience even unto death on the Cross presented a fully adequate (*condigna*), infinite (*infinita*), vicarious (*vicaria*) reparation (*satisfactio*) for the infinite offence offered by sin to the holiness and justice of God. And in view of this, God is prepared to forgive man's sin.

Even at the present time theologians are divided as to how precisely to interpret the satisfaction performed by Christ. There is in particular the question how far there belongs to the actual essence of Christ's reparation (which is always essentially Christ's own *free* action, not, formally speaking, his being punished instead of us) not only the moral dignity of his action giving honour to God, but also formally its factual character as pain and death which is addressed in expiation to the retributive justice of God (*iustitia Dei vindicativa*) precisely as such. Theology also attempts (especially in terms of ideas elaborated to express the doctrine of the sacrifice of the Mass) to show why and how what happened on the Cross also has the character of a ritual sacrifice, which the eternal High Priest, himself both priest and victim, offered on the altar of the Cross (cf. also *D* 122, 333, 430, 938, 940, 2195, 2274, texts which ultimately simply repeat the statements of Scripture, without settling the question how far Christ's obedience and death must be regarded as a ritual sacrifice in the proper sense).

3. *Soteriology in speculative theology.* a) *Evaluation of the satisfaction-theory.* What this theory positively states is entirely acceptable as a relatively easily intelligible statement of the saving meaning of Christ's death and one which avoids some "mythological" misunderstandings (ransom from the legitimate dominion of the devil, vicarious punishment of Christ, etc.). It can also be read in such a formal way that it can serve to some extent to interpret the whole of soteriology: the loving obedience of the Son is the supreme glorification of God in the world, and for its sake, in view of it (*intuitu meritorum Christi*), God forgives and loves sinners because he loves them in union with the man Jesus Christ. Nevertheless it is not possible to say that the satisfaction-theory equally and clearly does full justice to all the factors of soteriology. Even from the historical point of view its starting-point is the categories of Germanic law (*offensa – satisfactio; dignitas offensi, satisfacientis*) and it is not easy to give these a personalist and analogical import so that they can be meaningfully applied to the relation between God and the sinner. Quite simply there is no answer to the question (which does not arise in a purely human transaction of reparation) as to how a moral action can be regarded as compensation for an offence against God, when the action is in any case already absolutely due to God even prior to this function. But that is after all the case with every moral task and action, because in this respect man has nothing which he does not owe to God and the absolute demands of his love. In this matter there can be surely no question of appealing to works of supererogation, all the more so because in that case Christ's Passion would have atoning significance only in certain relative and accidental respects and not as a whole destiny comprising his life and death. In the satisfaction-theory the death of Christ is only the ultimately accidental mode of *any* moral action of the God-man, having no essential connection with the essence of redemption. But that surely does not do justice either to the death of Christ as a saving

event as Scripture sees it or to a genuine theology of death in general.

And the satisfaction-theory does not make it plain at once that the initiative comes from God and his unfathomable saving will, so that the Cross is the effect and manifestation of this gratuitous love and not its cause. Here the "person offended" himself ultimately makes reparation by forgiveness and on his own initiative, so that in this system taken *alone* it is not clear that the reparation is not already superseded by forgiveness. If reference is made to other theological parallels (e.g., prayer of intercession as produced by grace itself and yet meaningful), the problem is simply postponed, not solved. Finally, in the satisfaction-theory there is only a very extrinsic connection between the reparation as such and many of the effects of redemption, e.g., resurrection of the body, transfiguration of the cosmos, etc. Yet the redemptive event must have a more essential unity of origin and effect if it is to appear as the central event of world history, secular and sacred. It must itself from the start penetrate all dimensions of the sinful and redeemable creation. Many accounts of the satisfaction-theory start from rather confused notions of the nature of punishment for sin and the *iustitia Dei vindicativa*. Such approaches cannot be discussed here.

b) *The really fundamental problem of soteriology* is probably that the crucifixion certainly cannot be regarded (as by some modern Protestant theologians, appealing to 2 Cor 5:18–21) as an attestation (directed to us) of God's forgiving love, which moves *us* to believe in this love; it has to be acknowledged as the *cause* of our salvation. On the other hand, if we are not to fall into primitive anthropomorphism, the truth must not be obscured that God is not moved and his mind is not changed by history. What happened on the Cross proceeded from God's forgiving will as its effect, and did not determine that will. Since that is so, the real problem, at least for understanding Christian soteriology in our situation at the present day, is why this original forgiving will of God does not simply effect forgiveness "vertically from on high" in the same way and directly at all points of space and time, but comes to mankind from a definite historical event, which itself is the "cause" of forgiveness.

c) *Systematic soteriology*. (i) The starting-point must be the relation between two elements. One is the salvific will which determines man always and everywhere in the supernatural existential, and offers of God's divinizing and forgiving self-communication to the free personal existence of man. The other is the *history* of salvation and revelation. This "transcendental" saving will of God is not produced by history, but causes history, yet in such a way that this history is the history precisely of the transcendental saving will of God (at least as regards the term on which it bears). This corresponds proportionately to the general relation between human transcendence and human history. The saving will of God is realized, and finds effect among us, by taking historically concrete form, so that in this sense its historical manifestation is its effect and its ground. Saving will and its historical manifestation are not opposed to one another like cause and effect extrinsically related to one another, but like inner constituents of one whole, and so they mutually condition and form the basis of one another.

(ii) This history of salvation as the concrete accomplishment of God's transcendental saving will, which by the term on which it bears is itself historical, forms a unity. Moreover, it is constituted in its unity by all the dimensions of man (unity of matter as the spatio-temporal "field" of personal history; unity of origin [God]; unity in necessary personal intercourse in community and society; unity of goal of this history [perfect Kingdom of God] as genuine final cause). In this unity of history as that of the transcendental self-communication of God who creates and constitutes history in order to give himself (unity of nature and grace), each factor of history (and so also of the history of every single person) is dependent on every other; the totality of this history (which is united by a real principle, not by an "idea" or "plan" of God) is the situation of the salvation-history (of the "subjective" redemption) of the individual free creature.

(iii) The history of salvation understood in this way as a unity does not consist merely of a series of homogeneous single events of equal importance. It tends towards a victorious culmination which gives a direction to this history which is irreversible. It therefore tends towards an "eschatological" culmination. This culminating point which as goal, as *causa finalis*, *supports* the whole history of divine self-communication, and in its victorious power brings it to definitive manifestation, is realized when God himself makes this history his own in the God-man (as absolute bringer of salvation) although it is also a history of sin and its historical manifestations (results of sin: domination of death and of the Law), and when this acceptance of the sinful world on the part of God is also answered by acceptance on the part of the world, an acceptance which was predestined in the former. Consequently objectively (in exemplar) and so subjectively, the *irreversible* acceptance is given and historically manifested as a unity of God and world (in all its dimensions). The radical acceptance of divinizing self-communication on the part of the creature occurs, however, by death. For death, as action, is the definitive acceptance of self by the free being, and, as undergone, it is the acceptance and endurance of the situation of guilt which is that of the free being. Both acceptances occur and are manifest definitively through the resurrection as the saving fulfilment of death. Since the being and destiny of the God-man as the eschatological culmination of the history of the transcendental saving will of God, is an element in the one single salvation-history of all, history as victorious redemptive *situation* enters for *all* into its eschatological stage and its eschatological manifestation. (This is the case however the individual in his freedom responds to this situation. As long as history continues, the possibility of salvation remains immediately offered and inescapably present and this is something that is not at all a matter of course or necessary.)

(iv) On this basis it is also understandable in what a radical sense the God-man's being and destiny is a glorification of God which means the salvation of the world. The glory of God in the world is not *only* a formal abstract quality of any moral action whatsoever conformable to the will of God. It is the historically irreversible manifestation of God communicating himself as merciful love, which imposes itself victoriously and concretely manifests itself when it transforms the manifestation of refusal of such love, death, into an expression of love in the obedience unto death of the God-man.

(v) Inasmuch as the history of God's transcendent self-communication in the above-mentioned sense (under [i]) is the ground of this saving will itself (because an intrinsic element of this saving will) and this history is based in all its phases on its irreversible goal and culminating point (as *causa finalis*), and unfolds by moving towards this *eschaton*, Christ and his destiny (the *complete* accomplishment of which appears in the resurrection) are *the* cause of salvation as historically constituting the historically irreversible saving *situation* for *all*. And yet saving history *as a whole* (in dependence on its intrinsic *causa finalis*) goes to constitute the salutary situation of the individual. This becomes clear, for example, in the teaching about the Church as mystical body of Christ and *universale salutis sacramentum* (Vatican II: *Lumen Gentium*, art. 48), the treasury of the Church, etc.

The attempt might be made to comprise this saving causality of the Cross of Christ even more clearly in ontologically differentiated terms. Here, however, we can only point to the analogous problem of the causality of the sacraments, which on the one hand are historical manifestations of grace and precisely by being so are also causes of grace. If in the theology of the sacraments the strict concept of the causality of sacramental signs is formed, and we see that sign (real symbol) and cause are not two simply *de facto* coupled properties of the sacrament but form a radical unity (sign *as* cause – cause *as* sign), then this concept of cause might also be applied to the saving event of Christ as the primordial sacrament of redemption.

B. Soteriology

This article does not treat of the salvation of man and the forgiveness of his sin through the action of God in Jesus Christ, but puts forward some methodological considerations on the dogmatic treatise which is or might be called soteriology. Only some pointers can be given here, rather unsystematically. But they have a certain bearing on systematic theology and also on the kerygma – on the way in which the basic dogmas of Christianity which are treated of in soteriology should be proclaimed today.

1. *Soteriology as doctrine of salvation.* Soteriology comes from the word σωτηρία, meaning salvation. This makes the whole of theology a soteriology – since the doctrine about "God as he is in himself", "theology", cannot be adequately distinguished from the history of salvation. And conversely, soteriology cannot be restricted to the doctrine about the forgiveness of sin. A soteriology which would be a sort of mere "hamartiology" should be avoided. Soteriology has also a "supralapsarian" subject-matter, so to speak. For even prior to sin and the forgiveness of sin the salvation of man is not (or would not be) merely man's work, on the basis of the order of creation. It is always the freely-given grace of the self-communication of God – grace not iust in the offer but also in the acceptance, which is brought about by this (efficacious) grace of its own nature. Further, there is no difficulty in assuming that even the supralapsarian grace of the state of original justice was the grace of Christ.

Finally, it may be assumed that the sin of the world was permitted by God only within the framework of a divine decree absolutely predestining the world as a whole to salvation. The infralapsarian economy cannot be regarded, in what would be ultimately an anthropomorphic way, as a second enterprise of God, to make good subsequently the failure of his first plan (in creation and the state of original justice).

Since soteriology is therefore the doctrine of the salvation of man in Jesus Christ, the doctrine of the God-given possibility and reality of man's fulfilment, it must include from the start all these "supralapsarian" elements. This obligation is underlined by the situation in which the kerygma is today, and which has its historical justification even though it differs from the kerygmatic situation of the Bible. Whether men speak of themselves and their future sceptically with the existentialists or hopefully with the evolutionists, they find it hard or impossible to make the personal sin of the individual the central starting-point of their understanding of man and the world. The pessimist will see his personal guilt before God – if he can think at all in these terms – in the framework of the disruption of the world and man in general. He will see this tragedy as prior to such sin and calling for a justification of God rather than of man. Even a correct theology of original sin would not solve *this* problem, but merely shift it back to the beginning of history. The optimist will regard personal sin – so far as he is open to such a notion – more or less as the almost inevitable "detours" and types of "friction" which must occur in the individual and collective "evolution" of all real history.

Undoubtedly, the existence of an ultimately unavoidable personal decision before God must be remorselessly urged on such mentalities. Undoubtedly too there can be no solution to the *mysterium iniquitatis* in the individual and the world. But justice is done to such minds, and Christian soteriology is effectively preached, only when sin and salvation from sin are placed at once in a wider, supralapsarian context, in the light of which the "permission" of sin can be made intelligible, as far as is possible. (For one must be very cautious, to say the least, about the indemonstrable assertion that God could have prevented sin only by eliminating freedom.) Though man may not use it as a defence of sin (cf. Rom 4:1), it remains true that God permitted sin as the condition of the manifestation of his self-communicating love, which is greater and more unconditional than the offence against it. Man, who must inevitably answer for his free decision, has undoubtedly to distinguish between what God "wills" and what God "permits", to avoid any predestination to sin. But in the nature of things, and particularly in view of a modern notion of God, we may not give the impression that sin simply came as a sort of surprise to God, against his will. In a soteriology which essentially includes the supralapsarian order, which is really a doctrine of salvation as such, we may avoid the fatal suspicion of thinking of God in so anthropomorphic a way.

2. *Soteriology and Christology.* Soteriology and Christology form a closer unity than normally appears in the handbooks of theology. We now see more clearly, even in the perspective of the self-understanding of the pre-Easter Jesus, that the best approach to the Christological dogmas is the recognition that Jesus is the historical, eschatological gift of God's salvation to us, the absolute bringer of salvation. It is not surprising therefore that as far as we are concerned, we come more easily from a soteriology to a Christology than vice versa – soteriology here being taken in a comprehensive sense, as the doctrine of the historico-eschatological climax of the history of salvation, the self-communication of God, the dynamism of the world from the start. Saving history (history of σωτηρία) is always there, and Christ is intelligible in its light. It does not begin with him, though in its totality it depends on him also as its end and object.

3. *Hamartiological soteriology.* Insofar as soteriology is the doctrine of divine forgiveness of sin through and in Jesus Christ – as it of course also is, and is essentially – the following points are to be noted.

a) Even when regarded in this way, it must not be simply identified with a doctrine of satisfaction for sin, offered to God through the obedient death of Christ, in the exclusive sense of St. Anselm of Canterbury and subsequent theology.

b) It is not advisable, from the biblical, objective and kerygmatic point of view, to begin with a sketch of the hamartiological themes of soteriology, envisaged only in the framework of original sin. What the NT calls the "sin of the world", which is taken away by the redemption brought by Jesus, comprises more than original sin, and implies at once the personal sins of all – with *their* implications for the situation of each with regard to salvation or loss. Original sin, in the classical sense of the

Council of Trent, cannot be repented of. This shows that it cannot well be used in the first existentiell summons to man, as if it could arouse him to a sense of his need of redemption. Original sin, the calamitous situation brought about by the *peccatum originale originans*, where man of himself and by virtue of his origin has no claim to salutary grace, depends rather on soteriology for its "dialectical" character. What is said to be the essence of original sin in the traditional theology of the schools, and placed temporally before the redemption of man ("the deprivation of sanctifying grace, even as offered"), is really what would have been the case if sin and the sinful beginning of mankind had not been comprised within the efficacious salvific will of God in Christ.

c) The treatment of sin, in soteriology or in a special treatise, should aim at an analysis of sin not confined to the pattern of a juridical guilt with regard to sin and punishment or the notion of the absence of sanctifying grace. When "habitual" sin is explained as man's inability to love God perfectly, as the culpable repression of the possibility of transcending himself into God – as long as the prevenient grace of God's liberating love is not there – it could be a way of arousing man's existentiell experience of his sinfulness and hence a sense of his need of redemption.

4. *Cosmic soteriology.* Soteriology should not give the impression that the objective act of Christ's redemption only becomes effective for us and in us when it is accepted freely in baptism or (and) in faith working through charity. The quality of being redeemed – what St. Paul perhaps indicates by δικαίωσις, Rom 4:25; 5:18 – "justification", "act of righteousness" – the translations vary – is an "existential" of our existence, defining our structure (just as intrinsically as "original sin") *before* we ratify it freely in faith, hope and love.

5. *The soteriology of the one humanity.* Soteriology should not merely discuss the opening up of salvation to all, as the sum of the individuals. It must be the soteriology of the one whole race of man as such, and hence again a cosmic soteriology. See *Reign of God, People of God.*

6. *Soteriology and man's self-liberation from "alienation".* A soteriology which is modern in the right sense should not allow itself to be posed the false dilemma that it has to choose between "self-deliverance" and "rescue". Redemption is of course in all respects the free action of God on man, caused by nothing outside God – especially as salvation is God himself. But when the basic relationship between God and the world is correctly viewed, excluding any anthropomorphic "synergism", the action of God appears as the possibility and dynamism of the action of the world, which thus moves in self-transcendence to its fulfilment. Here this means that the inner unity of "objective" and "subjective" redemption must be brought out. This need cause no difficulty, since the "objective redemption" in Jesus Christ consists precisely in the subjective act of his obedience in death, in which he gave himself totally to God as member of the human race. When in the light of all that has been said we further assume it is not just the final "mind" of man, the result of his history of freedom, which enters "eternal life", but also the result of his concrete action in the body and the world, though in an unimaginable transformation (1 Cor 15:51f.), world history may well be regarded as humanity's self-liberation from self-alienation. History in this sense takes place in moral action made possible by God's action, as a moment of a rightly understood self-redemption of man, given to mankind by God as its task.

7. *Soteriology as subjective appropriation of salvation.* The distinction between *fides quae* and *fides qua* is well known. If faith is saving faith, and

soteriology the doctrine of salvation, soteriology if taken in the full strict sense of the word must also include as a theme the soteriological *fides qua* or the subjective appropriation of salvation. However, most of what is said on this subject is not given in the treatise *De Christo Redemptore* but in other parts of dogmatic theology. This is no harm, and there is no reason to change. Nonetheless, it is well to bear in mind the present considerations, since they could call attention to a number of themes which are not brought out well enough in the ordinary distribution of the material. The traditional doctrine of the *fides qua* remains very abstract, and soteriology speaks ordinarily only of the "objective" redemption. The actual subjective structure of this salutary faith, insofar as it bears on the "objective" redemption and hence (the act being specified by the object) is given a very definite quality, is not sufficiently analysed in itself and in its conditions of possibility in man. It is hardly described in such a way that one sees clearly that man has not just to seek the forgiveness of God vertically, so to speak, from on high, but that by the nature of this search for forgiveness he must hope for this redemption horizontally, so to speak, in history.

8. *Soteriology as theology of the death of Jesus.* The death of Jesus has sometimes been regarded, it would seem, as the merely accidental mode of a satisfaction which could have been imagined just as well in other ways. Such a soteriology fails to recognize the central significance of the death of Jesus as such and hence to show the intrinsic redemptive significance of our own death in Christ, the radical and final coming of subjective redemption.

Karl Rahner

SCEPTICISM

1. *Concept.* The term "scepticism" in its classical sense comes from σκέπτομαι, "to inspect". One may distinguish between total (radical, absolute) scepticism and partial (moderate, relative) scepticism, the latter appearing as religious, ethical, aesthetic, etc., scepticism; there is also methodical scepticism or methodical doubt.

2. *History.* A partial scepticism appears in the West as early as the pre-Socratic philosophers (Xenophanes, Parmenides) and was built up to one of its first high-points by the Sophists, as a criticism of the naive dogmatism of pre-Socratic philosophy. Gorgias denied that anything could be known or indeed communicated; Protagoras enunciated his principle that "man is the measure of all things" to stress the subjectivity of all knowledge. But this gave rise to a fruitful study of the art of persuasion by logic and rhetoric, which reached its methodical climax in Socrates and provided an answer to the Sophists in the metaphysics of knowledge worked out by Plato and Aristotle. Then the only tenable position became the radical scepticism as maintained by Pyrrho of Elis: there is a counter to every argument, hence it is best to remain unmoved (ἀταραξία) and refrain from passing judgment (ἐποχή). Archesilaus put forward the probable (εὔλογον) as a practical guide. In the Middle Scepticism of late antiquity, Carneades took scepticism further and raised the question of the criterion of truth in general: every proof must go on *ad infinitum*, because no proposition can be proof of itself. This gave rise to the first theory of probability. Late Scepticism (Aenesidemus, Agrippa, Sextus Empiricus) returned to a more dogmatic form of argument, using ten instances to prove that all knowledge was impossible. The most important grounds adduced were the contradictions of the philosophers, the variability of sense-perception, the influence of temperament and environment. Conformity to the general practice and obedience to the impulse of the moment are recom-

mended, rather than the riskiness of the search for truth.

In the early clash between philosophical scepticism and Christianity, the decisive question was whether there was a means of passing from scepticism to the certainty of faith, or could they exist legitimately together. Tertullian offered the choice between "Athens" and "Jerusalem": the Christian faith excludes all questioning doubts, a dialogue between the believer and the sceptic is meaningless. St. Augustine likewise denies (*Contra Academicos*) that questioning is its own justification, but tries to refute scepticism by philosophical arguments. The condition of the believer does not mean that his knowledge is perfect, but scepticism is excluded on principle. Where doubt could lead to despair, a scepticism which overcomes the mental attitude of indifference (ἀταραξία) takes on a dimension which disposes towards faith.

Scholasticism shows no traces of scepticism, and it is only in Scotism and in Occam that the tendency appears to use scepticism as an argument for the authority of revelation, against a dogmatizing type of philosophy. Montaigne takes up the Pyrrhonism of antiquity to reach a non-committal attitude which sets the mind free from dogmas and authorities. P. Charron, on the contrary, uses scepticism as an argument for the faith. The *cogito* with which Cartesianism seeks to retrieve all scepticism is questioned by B. Pascal and P. Bayle. The greatest influence was that of Hume, who questioned rational ethics and the principles by which causality could be known. Kant's Critique, on the contrary, was an endeavour to restore to knowledge a limited validity, but referred religious knowledge to its own postulates. Hegel included and went beyond scepticism, as a moment in the truth of the whole, while Kierkegaard reacted by exposing the existentiell components of doubt. In modern philosophy scepticism has been embodied in various trends: see *Positivism*, *Existence* II and *Ideology*.

3. *Significance*. Scepticism is explicable as the contrary of dogmatism. Total scepticism is meaningless, because it must call its own statement in doubt and so become a dogmatism of doubt. Methodical doubt, on the other hand, is so much taken for granted that it has become synonymous with scientific method: scientific thought must always be critical, to avoid the charge of a naive dogmatism and to survive the probings of the intellect. Between methodical and radical scepticism there are degrees which cannot be dismissed at once as absurd. Such scepticism differs from indifferentism by the intensity of its thought; from agnosticism by its inexorable quest for truth; from make-belief by its seriousness.

There is a peculiar ambiguity about scepticism as a historical phenomenon. It can be a mark of decadence in a culture resigned to extinction, or again, an instrument of "Enlightenment". In the latter case it will be an ally in the conflict with tradition, and a method of verifying new experiences, so that it appears as a search for truth which continues to doubt as long as it has not found sure footing. Thus a partial scepticism can expose the ambivalence of certain situations, by questioning what is taken for granted and criticizing received axioms. Its justification is the fact that knowledge is conditioned by so many factors. It doubts the possibility of arriving at a secure knowledge of the truth, because the history of philosophy can be depicted as a series of insoluble contradictions. It takes offence at the logical impasse, that no proposition can be its own proof. In its quest for the evidence to which all premisses may ultimately be reduced, it pushes the probative power of reason to its limits. It sees clearly how impossible it is for rational thought ever to be quite adequate to the experience of reality, or it reduces human intellectual activity to a merely relative role in face of the absolute claim of supernatural revelation.

On this last point, the otherwise disparate entities of faith and scepticism converge, since the basic attitude of both is to challenge the ordinary assumption of the infallibility of science. A non-universal scepticism has a legitimate place in theology insofar as this claims to be a science, because the various enunciations of the faith effected by theology are subject to all the conditions by which knowledge is coloured and therefore need constant and critical investigation. Finally, faith itself must not be regarded as an unchallengeable possession taken under control once and for all. The early Christian experience of the tension set up by the twofold presence of faith and doubt is already voiced in Mk 9:24, and Paul would have Christians test their own faith, as in 2 Cor 13:5. Even the philosophical scepticism which is of itself contrary to faith – provided it does not compound for agnosticism or take refuge in irrationalism – can go through the upheaval which turns doubt into despair, and so attain a new openness for faith.

Werner Post

SCHISM

I. Concept of Schism

The word "schism" means "a deliberate separation from ecclesiastical communion; it is also the state of being separated, or the Christian group which is in such a state. The schismatic is one who causes schism, who favours or bears responsibility for it, or who simply adheres to it through conviction or in fact" (Y. Congar).

In classical Greek, σχίσμα means a crack or tear. St. Paul uses it in a moral sense for differences of opinion or of inclination which endanger the peace and unity of the Church in a given place (1 Cor 1:10; 11:18; 12:25). From the earliest Christian times, the word was retained to express a breach of communion occasioned, or accompanied, by disagreements and manifested by a refusal of obedience to the legitimate authority of the bishop.

Heresy, which likewise involves breach of communion, was not at first clearly distinguished from schism. But custom, with the passage of time, reserved the term "schism" for breaches of communion provoked by personal conflict or mere refusal to obey. The word "heresy" was applied to breaches of communion caused by serious divergences in the understanding of the faith.

Schisms made their first appearance at a local Church level. However, the necessary solidarity of local Churches (obliged to safeguard both their unanimity in the confession of the faith and their good mutual relations) inspired canonical rulings which reserved the lifting of excommunication (the penalty for the crime of schism) to the bishop who first inflicted the censure. In the Roman Catholic Church, because of its progressive centralization to the advantage of the Roman See and the development of a monarchic form of ecclesiology of the universal Church, schism came to be defined mainly in terms of a breach of communion with the Pope. In those places (the Orthodox East) in which an ecclesiology based on the harmony of local Churches continued to prevail, the concept of schism underwent quite another evolution. History shows, indeed, that dissident sectors of a local Church often maintained undisputed communion with other local Churches.

The development of the notion of schism owed much to St. Cyprian and St. Augustine (controversy with the Donatists); it was greatly influenced by the Gregorian reform (11th century). The notion of schism, being correlative to the notion of the unity of the Church, advanced step by step as ecclesiology evolved. It took a long time before a theological treatise specifically on the Church made its appearance, although many of the elements necessary to it were to be found scattered in various other works: one would look for it in vain among the great scholastics. St. Thomas Aquinas studied schism less as a distinct phenomenon than as individuals or groups culpable of it or adhering to it. For him it was a sin against the peace which is a fruit of love (*Summa Theologica*, II-II, q. 39).

Counter-Reformation theology profoundly modified the way in which the theological nature of schism was interpreted. Hitherto, as long as grave differences in the matter of faith were not involved and above all as long as rupture with legitimate authority left intact the sacramental, hierarchical organism of the Church (episcopate, priesthood of apostolic succession), schism appeared as prejudicial to the unity of the Church. But, while the position of the separated part was irregular, no one imagined that that portion was shut out from the mystery of the Church, the fundamental riches of which it continued to share (episcopate, sacraments). The drama of separation was conceived of as taking place *within* the Church, considered essentially as a *fellowship*. By defining the Church as a hierarchically constituted *society* under the supreme authority of the Bishop of Rome, and by identifying the Church purely and simply with the Roman Catholic Church, the Counter-Reformation made out schism to be a separation *from the Church* itself. This ecclesiology, evoked by the desire to reply to the denials of the Reformers, modified unconsciously the traditional attitude of the Church of the West towards the sister Churches of the East (Orthodox). In effect, it supplied a theological justification for a Roman policy of "the Catholic or united Eastern Churches", substituting the intention to convert and absorb for a plan of reunion.

The Second Vatican Council has recovered the traditional outlook by putting forward an *ecclesiology of fellowship* which, instead of emphasizing jurisdictional factors (which are, however, maintained), stresses the sacramental and spiritual elements: sacraments (baptism, orders, Eucharist), sanctifying grace, theological virtues, gifts of the Holy Spirit. Henceforward, the entire reality of the mystery of the Church is to be regarded as overflowing the borders of its full and sole legitimate realization under the species of the Roman Catholic Church. It is admitted that there are various degrees of participation in that reality. If it remains true, canonically speaking, that one is necessarily in the Roman Catholic Church or out of it, it is still more true to say, taking the mystery into account, that one is more or less of the Church. Hence the distinction (cf. *Lumen Gentium* and *Unitatis Redintegratio*) between *plenary communion* and *partial communion*, both with the Roman Catholic Church and with the Church as such. It follows that one must distinguish two meanings in schism: *canonically*, it is a breach of jurisdictional relations with the See of Rome; *theologically*, without excluding full participation in the mystery of the Church, it places an obstacle to the full and manifest realization of its unity – a realization and manifestation which require the unanimous profession of the faith, effective membership of a unique, hierarchical, sacramental organism, and the common celebration (reception) of the same sacraments, particularly the Eucharist, the internal bond and external sign *par excellence* of the unity of the Church.

The notion of schism so defined in respect of the Roman Catholic Church may be applied analogically to breaches of communion between different Churches and ecclesiastical communities separated from the Roman See. But in each of these confessions or denominations, schism is defined according to a given concept of the Church and of its unity. It is a key-concept, an object of study and discussion, in the complex debate of the ecumenical movement. From the Protestant point of view, the healing of schisms is sought by means of mutual agreement in regard to the practice of intercommunion (the Eucharist, and other acts of worship) which leaves untouched even outstanding differences concerning the content of the faith and the structure of the Church. On the other hand, the Churches which are described as being (broadly) "Catholic" in tendency (Orthodox, Old Catholics, Anglicans) cannot envisage the re-establishment of full sacramental communion until unanimity in faith and mutual harmony within a single, common, hierarchical, sacramental structure (episcopate of full apostolic succession) has been achieved.

From motives of charity, one nowadays avoids as far as possible using the term "schismatic" with reference to members of Churches and Christian communities which disagree with the Roman Catholic Church, all the more so if the people concerned have been born and received their religious formation in these communities. They cannot be held responsible for the state of division from us in which they live today. Besides, both parties must share responsibility for the creation of that division.

Christophe Dumont

II. History of Schism

1. *General*. The NT speaks of divisions in the local Churches in consequence of differences in the explanation and assimilation of the apostolic kerygma (1 Cor 11:9; Gal 5:19; Rom 16:17). They endanger the fellowship (*koinonia*) of the Church as established by Christ (one God, one Lord, one Spirit, 1 Cor 12:4–6; one gospel, 1 Cor 1:10–13; Gal 1:6–9; one baptism and one bread, 1 Cor 12:13; 10:17; Gal 3:27). Nothing is known of a division which led to a break with the whole Church. But the NT schism has the tendency to isolate men from the Church, which can be very rigid about divergences in doctrine. In post-apostolic times, schism and heresy are treated as the great enemies of the early Christian Church. They are attributed to ambition, jealousy, indulgence in calumny and rebelliousness against superiors. In contrast to the ecclesiastical office and service of the whole community, for the building up of which all charisms and ministries are given, personalities and personal elements are stressed. Schism and heresy were not yet distinguished formally as clearly as they were later. But in most cases schism was combined with an error in the faith. The history of schism is therefore for the most part identical with the history of heresies. The basic considerations and references of the article on heresies are also valid here.

The whole history of the Church is marked by the rise of schismatic movements which developed their own Church order and formed rival Churches. In early Christian times there were, for instance, the schism of Marcion in the 2nd century (exaggerated Paulinism and an antinomianism exploiting the gospel against law); Gnosticism and Arianism, the millenarianism of Montanism, the rigorism of the Novatians (3rd century), the "Church of the Martyrs" of Bishop Meletius of Lycopolis, and in the wake of this the much more important Church of the Donatists, which rejected the imperial Church of Constantine (4th century). The Eastern Schism of the 11th century was heralded by the Acacian Schism of the 6th and the Photian Schism of the 10th century.

The slow process of the assimilation of Christianity by the Franks and the Germans and the priority given to the repulse of the Saracens, Normans and Hungarians left no room for the rise of sectarian movements on a large scale in the last part of the Carolingian era.

Schisms arose in the great popular religious movements only in the 11th century. The most important was that of the Catharists, a movement under Eastern influences, which set up a counterpart to the Church in southern France, with its own hierarchy and system of dogma, the latter based on a dualism which included rejection of the Incarnation and was rigorously opposed to the doctrine of the Church. Down to the present, there are still communities of Waldenses in the Alpine valleys of Savoy and Piedmont going back to lay Churches set up as a consequence of the preaching of Valdes, whose rigorously ascetic programme was modelled on apostolic and evangelical poverty. These sects hardened into schism, but the Popes such as Innocent III succeeded in reintegrating into the Church the Humiliati of North Italy and other groups in South France who had been condemned as heretical. All these "Poor Men's" movements (see *Poverty* II), for which Gregory VII provided living-space by relying on them in his reform (against Nicolaites and Simoniacs), criticized self-centred ecclesiastical institutions and the luxurious living of some of the clergy. These two defects obscured the testimony of the Church and launched recurring trends to reform in the late Middle Ages. In Wycliffe and Huss they deviated into schism. The worldliness of the papacy and the cardinals was undoubtedly the main cause of the Great Western Schism, during which two and then even three contenders claimed the papacy. Contemporaries could not decide between them, and even later research has not cleared up the matter. The Reformation profited from the dynamism of lay religious movements. Its protest against distortions in the late medieval Church took the form of rejection of the whole medieval Church system with its combination of Church and State, papal centralism and a rigidly formalized scholasticism. Even the Church reinforced and regenerated by Trent was not spared divisions. In consequence of the general debility of faith and their own limited bases, these schisms remained confined to the local or national level (schism of Utrecht, 1724; schism of the Petite Église de la Vendée, which refused to recognize the concordat under Napoleon; schism of Gregorio Aglipay in the Philippines, 1902; schism of the Czech National Church, 1920). National sentiment had much to do with nearly all these schisms, engendered by resentment against the Roman Curia and established as organized Churches with the help of the State.

The following distinctions may be made between the vanished schisms and the dissenting groups such as Protestantism and Orthodoxy which still survive.

a) The ancient heresies and schisms questioned the right doctrine in decisive matters of the history of salvation (Trinity, soteriology, the place of Mary in the economy, the grace of God) and had a predominantly "particular" character. The present dissenters appear as "universal", that is, base themselves on a notion which colours their whole understanding of Christianity. Such global reinterpretations existed in earlier times, as in Gnosticism, the Bogomiles of the East and the Catharists. But here the specifically Christian element was perilously recessive, in contrast to the present-day dissidents, among whom the mystery of Christ is accepted unconditionally, at least on principle.

b) The Eastern Orthodox and the Protestants did not start by rejecting a specifically Christian doctrine, but as protests against a given historical condition of the Church: the political estrangement between East and West in the 11th century and the abuses of Church life in the widest sense in the 16th century.

c) In their internal structure, the dissident Churches today tend towards

Catholicity and deliberate efforts are made to overcome the divisions.

d) Much more than the schismatic movements of earlier times, the great dissident Churches of today embody Christian values which indicate the work of the Holy Spirit (Vatican II, *Lumen Gentium*, art. 15).

2. *Schism in the theology of history.* A starting-point for an eschatological interpretation of schisms is provided by 1 Cor 11:19: "oportet haereses esse". This affirms the concrete historical inevitability of schism. Hence schism and the ecumenical movement which eliminates it are on the level of history, not on that of supratemporal dogma. The pilgrim Church is always subject to the law of sin and hence liable to divisions, of which the cause may be personalities, politics, social, theological or disciplinary matters. But the Church as a whole like all of its members has to uphold the gospel in its entirety. It must at times pay the price of division. Since the living truth in the universal Church is prior to the knowledge of faith in the individual members, the guardians of the faith appointed by the Church have the right and the duty to oppose one-sided views of the truth in individuals. Hence schism is not just a manifestation of the spirit of the world. It can result from a genuine conflict of duties.

There are two main lines of interpretation of the text of St. Paul. One understood *haereses* as tensions between groups through which the purity of faith of the orthodox stood out more clearly. This was the psychologizing interpretation of St. John Chrysostom, and it regarded the divisions mentioned by St. Paul as more or less accidental. But for St. Augustine, they had, on the contrary, significance in the history of salvation. The *haereses* were formal errors of doctrine, the *oportet* was a divine decree and a prophecy which had to be fulfilled. Without the heretics, we would go to sleep over Scripture without reading its message. We need to be goaded by the others to take up the word of Scripture and live by it. What is stressed here is less loyalty to the faith than the fullness of faith. St. Augustine's interpretation prevailed in the Western Church. The scholastic doctrine of the "permissive will" of God gave it a basis in speculative theology. The Reformation rediscovered Chrysostom's interpretation. But Calvinist theology linked up directly with St. Augustine and explained divisions as the necessary results of supramundane forces, directed by God's sovereign salvific will to the good end intended by him. In the controversies between the confessions the Pauline text was used by all sides, none of which allowed it to shake their confidence in their own title-deeds. Modern exegetes, particularly among Protestants, depart very widely from the strictness of the Augustinian interpretation and tend rather to that of Chrysostom.

The history of schism does not bring out only negative aspects. It also shows, retrospectively, that division contributes to the growth of the Church and possesses prophetic and charismatic qualities. The struggle against Gnosis helped to clarify the thought of the Great Church with regard to a number of important theological problems, and contributed directly or by reaction to the development of doctrine (the fixing of the canon of the NT, the doctrine of the Incarnation and of grace). The struggle against Arianism aided the theology of the Trinity to attain greater conceptual clarity. Donatism forced men to reflect on ecclesiology, a realm almost totally neglected by the classical Greek theology. The poverty movements of the Middle Ages, especially that of the Catharists, compelled Catholics to give a dogmatic statement on their understanding of the world and contributed to the realization of the *vita apostolica*. The Reformation of the 16th century gave the decisive impulse to Catholic reform at Trent.

But it must always be remembered that the Church, in its combat against heresy and schism, always ran the risk, and indeed succumbed to it, of allowing truths upheld by the dissident to fall into oblivion, and met true prophetic testimony with distrust.

Hence schism has a certain integrating force which comes out more and more strongly in the course of history and finally paves the way for the ending of the schism. Heresy and schism are essentially stresses laid upon partial truths or a forgotten aspect of ecclesiastical structures, and they are forces in history because of the one-sided truth which they embody in error. Divisions in faith and Church polity can well be detours on the way to the kingdom of God, when they lead to reforming and creative reflection on the Christian message, and when they act as prototypes of reform by developing elements which can again be integrated into the whole *communio*. Until this comes about, the division is punishment for the culpable failure of Christians to give due testimony in their common life of love and faith. In its divisions, Christianity is under the judgment of God. The final judgment is anticipated, as it were, in history (cf. Mt 24 and 25). But the wrath of God is a cloak for his grace which urges the confessions to the overcoming of the division.

There is a parallel to schism in the OT history of salvation, the division between Judah and Israel under the monarchy. Moses had confirmed the covenant of Sinai by offering the sacrifice of the twelve tribes on one altar, binding them together as one fellowship of kinship and life. Under David's rule the unity of the people of Israel was given an outward visible form. Basically the unity was religious, while the tribes had remained since Moses relatively independent of each other. After the death of Solomon the sociological unity broke up. Differences which had been latent for centuries, rooted in different spiritual traditions (tendency to charismatic theocracy in the North, institutionalization and juridical establishment of the dynastic monarchy in the South), hardened into schism. The occasion of the split was the excessive burdens which Solomon imposed on his people and the harshness with which his successor Rehoboam treated them. With charismatic authority the prophet Ahijah announced the rival kingship of Jeroboam in the North. The kingship in the people of Israel should have had both dynastic and charismatic character, but this unity, achieved under David, was lost. The division was only provisional. The two elements of the Israelite kingship were to be reunited again.

This division between Israel and Judah suggests a comparison with the great divisions in Christendom. The schism between East and West was long latent before the definitive break in the 11th century; in consequence of a chronic lack of *communio* the differences became hostilities. The reformers of the 16th century could build on centuries of anti-Roman resentment. Even in the subject-matter of the schism there are analogies: the charismatically-inclined Eastern Churches show extreme reserve towards Roman juridicalism, just as Protestantism manifests its fidelity to God in the line of prophetic obedience at the expense of institutions. More important than these parallels is the basic structure of this schism. In spite of political, human and historical differences, there is a spiritual solidarity. Israel and Judah both appeal to the Mosaic covenant, though with a difference of emphasis which seeks to justify the schism. Israel stresses the Mosaic element, Judah the Davidic. But both focus on the same centre. Then, the prophets raised up by God in the North are not prophets of the schism but fundamentally preachers of God's word. In spite of the division, which is not regarded as final, hope of ultimate reunion remains. But it only came when both kingdoms had fallen and when the chosen people had attained a new interiority in the Babylonian captivity, bringing with it a rediscovery of their common call.

Victor Conzemius

SCHOLASTICISM

Nature and Approaches

Scholasticism is a philosophy, theology and jurisprudence which in the Middle Ages stood for all known science. From the 7th century on, scholasticism developed through the stages of pre-scholasticism and early scholasticism to the classical period of the 12th and 13th centuries, setting up then a tradition lasting for seven hundred years, down to the present day. Post-classical or later scholasticism again reached high-points in Baroque scholasticism and neo-scholasticism. The philosophy and theology of the Catholic Church are no longer dominated exclusively by scholasticism, but it is on the whole basic, though its influence varies from country to country. Scholasticism has therefore known various phases of development and influence, and has been the subject of very different judgments in any given period of ecclesiastical or scientific history. Term and concept, content and method, influence and value have all been variously estimated. Nonetheless, if one considers the method rather than the matter, a consistent structure has persisted which justifies the application of the one word "scholasticism" to these traditions of Western thought which have lasted for so many centuries.

The word "scholastic" comes from the Latin *schola* (Greek σχολή), "school", whence *scholasticus*, meaning first the teacher and then including the students. The word "scholastic" was later applied to the method of teaching used in the schools and to the mentality behind it. In contrast to the spontaneous expositions of liturgical preaching and elementary catechetical instruction, or the spiritual dialogue practised in the monasteries, in contrast indeed to the mystical monastic theology in general, scholasticism organized the "holy Christian doctrine" as a body of knowledge. In the expanding cathedral and municipal schools, teaching became a special profession, demanding expert competence and official qualifications. The schools gradually became bodies which took on the character of autonomous institutes of education, as the new methods of science and teaching developed their own laws. They gave rise then in the 13th century to the great centres of formation which dominated modern Western culture and science, the universities. The organization of traditional learning into a rational body of knowledge is the specific and epoch-making element of scholasticism. This rational procedure in speculation and method and its application in practice and institutions are what have made scholasticism a historic factor in culture and a supremely important phenomenon in medieval thinking, with all its repercussions on the modern era.

1. *The "epochal" situation.* The perfecting of the scholastic method in classical scholasticism came about under the impulse of social and philosophical factors which made it "epochal", that is, it was a change brought about in the historical situation by a general principle. From the end of the patristic era till well into the 11th century, the studies pursued in the monastic schools, for a time the only centres of education, aimed essentially at preserving the traditional heritage, making compilations of new matter where possible and occasionally making excerpts of it for practical purposes. But studies as a whole were strictly orientated to practical and contemplative ends, in the interest of affective piety and the mystical aspiration to God. There was little interest in rational mastery and penetra-

tion of the traditional matter, much less in critical, analytical discussion. The recognized authorities were followed, which were primarily the Bible and the official pronouncements of the Church magisterium, and along with these unquestionably infallible sources, the "Fathers", among whom St. Augustine was the most frequently quoted and highly respected. The method taken for granted in theology was the obedient following of authentic or supposedly authentic tradition in general, and the proof from authority in particular, wherever the question of proof was allowed or deemed necessary. The first change was due to outstanding personalities, especially St. Anselm of Canterbury (1033–1109), who put some astonishingly radical questions about the purpose and nature of revelation, renouncing the proof from authority in the matter, and with his principle of *Credo ut intelligam*, asserted a certain rationality of faith. In this he was not typical of his times, and he stood alone. But he opened up perspectives which were hardly exploited to the full even by classical scholasticism. However, his principle of presupposing a vigorous faith and trying on this basis to grasp it rationally with full assurance of its reasonableness, was a basic interest of scholasticism and entitles him to be called the "Father of Scholasticism". The dialectic of faith and knowledge was to remain the great unsolved problem as between monastic and scholastic theology, and indeed that of medieval theology in general. And under the heading of the distinction and reconciliation of "theoretical" and "practical" reason, Anselm's questioning was to re-echo in the central problems of post-medieval and modern philosophy.

But factors other than influential, learned Churchmen, who were mostly teachers of schools, brought the methodical, rational approach to fruition in classical scholasticism and created a new mentality. There were also social changes. A larger world was opened up by the discovery of new trade routes. The handicrafts expanded their range. The cities flourished. The nobles became a cultured class. Men grew more conscious of their responsible roles in Church and society, if not as individuals. Gothic art and courtly poetry contributed their share, as did the success of the Gregorian reform and the new outlets for religious and Church life offered by the new mendicant orders. The time was ripe for an epochal change in the mentality of the Christian West. A new perspective was opened up which was of fundamental importance for the one Christian Church as it then was in the West – in the same line or in dialectical opposition, as in the Reformation and Counter-Reformation – as it was for the history of man and science in general.

The philosophical framework of the development was first neo-Platonism, in the form transmitted by St. Augustine in particular. Plato was regarded as "the philosopher" but apart from a fragment of the *Timaeus*, little of his actual writings were known. The great change came when further works of Aristotle became accessible. Till the middle of the 12th century, only the *Logic* of Aristotle was known, through the translation of Boethius, and all that was covered was his work on the *Categories* and on *Interpretation*. But now the rest of his *Organum* (treatises on logic) was rediscovered, along with the two *Analytics*, the *Topics* and the *Sophistics*, and this "New Logic" was contrasted with the "Old Logic". At the same time, direct translations of his writings on metaphysics and natural philosophy appeared. Hitherto Aristotle had been known only indirectly on the whole, through the medium of Arab and Jewish philosophers (Averroes, Avicenna, Alfarabi, Moses Maimonides, Avicebron), working mainly in Spain under Arab rule, which meant that Arab translations of Aristotle were translated into Latin. But now Italy and Sicily entered the picture, and direct translations were made from the Greek, chiefly by Bartholomew of Messina and William of Moerbecke, the latter working for St. Thomas Aquinas. It was only this new acquaintance with Aristotle's logic, and above all with his natural history and metaphysics, which created the conditions for the revolutionary adoption of Aristotle by which Christian theology, in spite of the fierce opposition of Church authorities and monastic theologians, was fundamentally stamped, with a swiftness and intensity which in the prevailing conditions was extraordinary. From now on "the philosopher" is Aristotle. The adoption and interpretation of Aristotle as the key to a metaphysical and philosophical understanding of theology was the great achievement of scholasticism. This is what gave it its real significance, and in a certain fashion its full stature. From the point of view of the history of philosophy, this was also the end of scholasticism, though individual thinkers remain important.

2. *Method.* In contrast to the neo-scholastic way of presenting the matter in the form of theses, with its abstract and non-hermeneutical structure, teaching in medieval scholasticism took the form, primarily and on principle, of the reading (*lectio*) of authentic texts, especially from the Bible. The scholastic *lectio* also differed essentially from that of the monasteries. There it was built into the whole structure of the *opus Dei*, and like monastic theology in general, was carried on by monks. Reading and theological exposition were co-ordinated on principle to monastic life and time-tables, and were stamped by the spirit of monastic institutions and their liturgy and spirituality. In the light of this principle, monastic theology stressed the inviolable holiness of the word of God, which no method of logic could attain, much less render perspicuous. It was convinced that the gospel could not be scientifically analysed, much less construed in terms of rational speculation. Theology was seen as wisdom, not as a science.

Scholasticism, on the contrary, used its logic and its technique of teaching to try to grasp rationally the *lectio*. But Scripture reading was not used merely to furnish theological propositions and theses with biblical citations and arguments. In keeping with the times, it was seen as total attention to the claim of the gospel as the foundation of the life of faith and fellowship. Assent to the word of God was the basic act in the theological effort of the original scholasticism. But here scholasticism found itself faced at once by the problem of the exact meaning of the word of God in the gospel and of how it finds expression in the writings of the OT and NT, as in the rest of authentic tradition. It was precisely on behalf of this necessary assent to the will of God that scholasticism applied the "dialectical method". This at first was merely clearing away linguistic and grammatical difficulties which stood in the way of the understanding of the literary meaning of the text. Harmonizations were attempted by the logic of the *sic et non*. Standing questions and their answers were treated in interpolated comments (taking the literary form of interlinear glosses) or gave rise to longer explanations and lectures (which took the literary form of the *glossa ordinaria marginalia*). In this comment in the form of glosses the dialectical method really came to bear fruit. The scholastics, when interpreting the texts, questioned more and more insistently, and in classical scholasticism with all the energy of their speculative armoury, their basic meaning. They went beyond the concrete difficulties of the texts to reach the basic problems of Christian life and faith, which they finally sought to grasp as a unity in the perspective of a modified Aristotelian metaphysics, by means of the new logical method of argument. A comprehensive system of the *sacra doctrina* was constructed.

The study and interpretation of the text took on a form which was finally stereotyped in a series of steps: question (*utrum*), provisional answer (*videtur quod*), objection (*sed contra*) and definitive answer by the professor (*respondeo*). This technique of teaching and exposition did not simply demand that the student listen in faith. It called for close following and argumentation, though the decision on the question was mostly the function of the teacher. But the method forced the teacher to have reasons for his opinions and to be able to justify them before his colleagues in the *disputatio*. Here professors put forward their *quaestiones* and discussed them in set form, but in a strictly critical way.

This teaching technique gave rise to new literary genres. The glossing of the text gave rise to the *sententiae*, which were combined into collections of "Sentences". These collections of "Sentences" were then generally called *Commentaries*, when the individual thoughts and comments were organized into an ordered whole with each in its logical place. The regular disputations gave rise to the *quaestiones disputatae*, and the extraordinary ones, where anyone could put questions, gave rise to the *quodlibeta*. The *quaestiones*, at first closely connected with the *lectio*, but then becoming independent treatises, were given their major form in the *summa quaestionum*, the *articuli* of which are a series of *quaestiones disputatae* reduced to their essential schemas. Scholasticism was later called the age of the "Summas". The great commentaries and summas with their literary analyses and metaphysical speculation and a structure wholly based on scientific viewpoints were the great medium of self-expression for scholasticism. Its self-understanding was radically determined by faith, manifested in reverence for the infallible authorities, especially the word of God (in the *lectio*) and strict attachment to Christian tradition (*auctoritas*). Hence came its desire to understand, so vigorously and successfully applied, which released speculative forces (*quaestio*) "moulding to meaning" the truths of faith and establishing theology for the first time as a science, while also gaining basic philosophical insights of permanent validity.

In late scholasticism things began to fall apart. The combination of *lectio*, *auctoritas* and *quaestio*, which had been worked out with so much genius but had never been deliberately analysed as a hermeneutical principle, was no longer maintained. The potent, genuine and creative self-understanding of scholasticism went into decline. The result was bizarre literary analysis, formalism and nominalism in logic, abstract speculation disjoined from tradition varied by an ill-considered empirical realism, hair-splitting dialectics and forced systematization. This launched the various phases of the anti-scholastic movements, from the *devotio moderna* and the Reformation down to the humanistic, philosophical and theological trends of the modern era.

3. *The self-understanding of scholasticism.* The decline of the authentic scholasticism of the golden age was not due merely to a contingent disavowal of its basic self-understanding. Scholasticism already bore within it, as the development of its methods shows, the makings of the crisis. It was justified no doubt in exposing the misplaced naivety of the monastic Augustinian theology and was therefore able to convince and prevail. But there were many fundamental interests of the older theology which it neglected to its peril. There was a sort of division of allegiance which could not work out well in the long run. Scholasticism agreed with the older theology in presupposing the authentic Christian tradition as the foundation of its self-understanding. But then it applied a rational method of untoward

dimensions and, under the impulse of its Greek origins, a non-historical metaphysics. In contrast to their undistinguished successors, this problem had been recognized or sensed by the best thinkers and theologians of classical scholasticism. But even the compromise with the mystical and neo-Platonist Augustinian tradition of monasticism could not really help. The scholastic Enlightenment brought out very strongly the contrast between faith and knowledge, love and learning, tradition and speculation, history and metaphysics, nature and grace. At first, the original scholastic method provided them with a rudimentary set of relationships, but this same method, by virtue of its intrinsic dynamism, was unable really to reconcile them. Indeed, as late scholasticism shows in its nominalist and empiricist trends, it was bound to disrupt the tension. The approach used by scholasticism at an elementary level was not and could not be consciously reflected upon. But as soon as the forces of history had made it the object of conscious attention, the insufficiencies of the hermeneutical and speculative method of scholasticism could not be ignored, precisely because of its lack of understanding as regards its own processes. The balance swung from one extreme to the other in the contrast between faith and knowledge, etc.

Even in classical scholasticism, therefore, treatment of such central Christian themes as freedom, the person and history was to a great extent lacking. Not that these realities were not envisaged at all, but they were not included in the system as constitutive elements. As we can see from present-day standpoints, salvation-history did not appear precisely as history, much less as history-qua-revelation in the dialogal process of personal freedom and the dialectic of ecclesial society. These dimensions of the Christian self-understanding could of course only be consciously grasped later. But they were at work as practical problems in the controversies between the various medieval theologies and were latent in the practical self-understanding of scholasticism itself, permitting in the light of modern reflection a balanced judgment on the ancient debates. A simplified historical picture may be given as follows. The Augustinian and monastic theology, which had a far more authentic grasp of revelation as salvation-history, refused to expose itself to the rational questioning of scholasticism, sensing instinctively rather than seeing clearly the consequences of such questioning. And scholastic theology could no longer remain within the framework of the ancient usage, but in breaking away could not but cloud the Christian self-understanding in favour of formal speculation and institutional rationality – again without seeing clearly what was going on.

These unsolved problems of the reasonableness of revelation and its free historicity, along with the various solutions hitherto proposed, have been the destiny of theology down to the present day. Scholasticism succeeded in laying down for the first time the scientific bases of theology. Its great merit is that it recognized the necessity of this step and set to work on it, which means that it is essentially a theology, not a philosophy. But in doing so it introduced a type of questioning into theology which never found its own true fulfilment and hence could function only as a restorative element. Only by "new blood", this time from modern philosophy, can theology be constituted as a science able to meet contemporary demands. Only the adoption – in the sense of a critical interpretation – of modern transcendental philosophy (Descartes, Kant, Fichte, Hegel), including the existentialist and Marxist reaction to it, can so remould the method and content of theology that it need neither set wrong limits to its absolute rationality nor abandon it entirely, nor again gloss over the grace-given historicity of its free thrusts. But this is what will enable it to be a science of faith and the history of faith. Hence it is not a question of simply repudiating scholasticism, but of entering into dialogue with its great representatives, as with modern thinkers. This has already been undertaken within the Church in recent years. But then the question is how such dialogue can be inserted into a teaching philosophy and theology which have hitherto been part of the continuity between scholasticism and the Church, and worked out by scholasticism as such. It is hard to see how the Church can abandon this approach, in favour of which there are so many pedagogical, didactic and historic institutional reasons.

Eberhard Simons

SCIENCE

Reflection on science has always formed part of philosophy. It is only in modern times, and especially since Kant, that light on the specific character of human cognition has been looked for from the logical analysis of science. For Kant, this raised the question of the possibility of synthetic *a priori* judgments, which he regarded as an indispensable basis of the universal statements of natural laws made by mathematical natural science; that these are justified is placed beyond all doubt by their success. Later, the following main tendencies emerged in the theory of science.

One line of thought inspired by transcendental philosophy investigates the *a priori* conditions of the sciences. Fichte regarded philosophy as a "theory of science", or "science of science as such". This inquires, "What is the content and form of a science precisely as such, i.e., how is it possible precisely as science?" According to Trendelenburg all sciences involve "metaphysical presuppositions in their object and logical presuppositions in their method . . . The question what justification there is for these presuppositions and how such a conjunction [of object and method] takes place, calls for a theory of science, and this might well be called logic in a wider sense." In this sense, according to K. Rahner, "a question in the theory of science always simultaneously implies the question of the actual nature of science as a human activity". This line of thought is chiefly represented by metaphysical epistemology (see *Knowledge*).

Another tendency is more influenced by the various branches of science themselves and undertakes the logical analysis of these disciplines. Bolzano took what was still a very general view of the theory of science, as "the sum-total of all the rules which we must follow in dividing the whole domain of truth into particular sciences and in their exposition in separate text-books, if we are to proceed correctly". Soon, however, attention was concentrated on questions which emerged in the first place in the course of inquiries into the foundations of mathematics and physics. The primary concern here is not with general philosophical considerations but with detailed investigations of particular concepts and theories. The history of science provides valuable materials for such analyses. Such investigation is now mostly considered part of the theory of science. In what follows an account is given of a few points of view which have been worked out in this field and which can also be regarded as relevant to philosophy and theology.

In contrast to a one-sided domination of theory of science by the natural sciences, the special character of the "human" sciences, e.g., history, was investigated in the Baden neo-Kantian school and by Wilhelm Dilthey. This has assumed great importance for philosophy and theology, chiefly because of the problems connected with hermeneutics.

1. *Axiomatic theory*. Investigations in-

to the foundations of mathematics and science raise the question of the basis on which the meaning and validity of scientific propositions rest. Since the validity of propositions which are derived from other propositions is dealt with in logic, logical analysis is indispensable. Nowadays the techniques of modern logic are used.

a) *Axioms*. If a body of propositions contains derivative propositions, the propositions can be arranged in inferential order. Underived propositions which serve as basis for further deductions are principles or axioms. Euclid's "Elements of Geometry" are a classical example of a science with an axiomatic structure. Similarly the concepts employed in a science may be examined to determine which can be defined in terms of others, and in this way the basic concepts identified.

b) *Material and formal axioms*. Euclid regarded the axioms as self-evident. This presupposes that the meaning of the basic terms used in the axioms is sufficiently known and that the validity of the axioms understood in that sense is guaranteed by insight. But confidence in an intuitive factor of this kind has been shaken. It has been shown that one of Euclid's axioms, regarding parallel lines, can be replaced by others which are incompatible with it, thus producing non-Euclidian geometries, which can be used in physics. The explanation of this is said to be that scientific theories do not directly mirror the real state of affairs but present a simplified idealization. And so Hilbert inverts the relation between concept and proposition. From the point of view of formal axiomatization the primary question is not that of knowing the meaning of basic concepts which generate axioms. That is a material question of content, not of form. On the contrary, the axioms are primary and the basic concepts are regarded as implicitly defined by them. This means that what is chiefly relevant about the concepts is the relations between them, and these are expressed by the axioms. Consequently, a formal axiomatic system has application wherever an interpretation of the basic concepts transforms the axioms into propositions which hold good of something. If an interpretation of this kind, answering the requirements of the axioms, applies to empirically verifiable facts, we speak of a real model.

c) *Antinomies and freedom from contradiction*. Modes of inference which appear intuitively plausible and which formerly were employed unhesitatingly in mathematics, have been shown to be open to question. It has been proved possible to derive mutually contradictory propositions from them (antinomies). But if a contradiction can be inferred in a system, the system becomes meaningless, for a contradiction entails any propositions whatsoever, and it is no longer possible to distinguish between derivative and non-derivative propositions. It therefore became necessary to formulate modes of inference precisely and to discover whether it is possible to prove that a system which employs them is consistent. Various methods were tried. It has been successfully shown that axiomatic systems of non-Euclidian geometry are consistent. This was done by arithmetization, by reducing them to the non-contradictory character of arithmetic. For this purpose the basic terms of geometry were given an arithmetical interpretation fulfilling the axioms. A logical or mathematical model of this kind is called a formal model. In order to demonstrate the consistency of arithmetic itself, however, a different method had to be employed. Attempts were made (Lorenzen, Hao Wang) to find a constructional solution using only unobjectionable modes of inference and replacing any questionable ones. Objections can be raised in particular to proofs which assume an (infinite) totality of objects (e.g., numbers). Some forms of indirect proof of the existence of something do this, by assuming that a particular attribute belongs to none of the objects or that there is at least one object which possesses it, though which one need not necessarily be known. There are also objections to statements in which a predicate is affirmed or denied of itself, as well as to statements which apply to themselves. The distinction between an object-language and a metalanguage in which we speak about the object-language, eliminates a statement referring to itself, but shows the limits set to any language which has to fulfil strict conditions. Lorenzen endeavours on the basis of his own operationalist standpoint to overcome the difficulty that in order to construct a rigorous language we must already possess a metalanguage, and for the latter to be strictly constructed we must have a meta-metalanguage, etc. He argues that learning a language does not always presuppose a language, and that a metalanguage can be introduced by construction.

d) *A priori.* In formalist axiomatic theory, the axioms are conventions; it makes sense to question their utility but not their validity. From the operationalist point of view this has to be qualified to the extent that some linguistic stipulations are required. It is possible to show, however, that other propositions which are usually taken to be mere stipulations necessarily follow from the use of these linguistic conventions. These include, according to Lorenzen, important presuppositions of logic, arithmetic, geometry and even of kinematics and mechanics. They are not empirical propositions, because they are not based on observation; in fact they make it possible to formulate what has been observed. Nor are they merely stipulations and analytic inferences from them. They may be regarded as a reconstruction of what is usually meant by synthetic *a priori* judgments.

2. *Empirical basis.* a) *Empirical verifiability.* The advance of physics to the theory of relativity and quantum mechanics was made possible by submitting certain concepts to critical examination, e.g., simultaneity, correspondence of physical characteristics to sub-atomic particles. The critique consisted in not resting content with the apparently self-evident intuitive meaning but in asking how it is we are able to determine at all whether these terms are applicable or not. This question led to changes of meaning and more precise definition of these terms. Some previously recalcitrant problems were solved as a result. This, and the fact that science is concerned with statements that can be tested, suggest that to determine the meaning of a scientific statement and of the terms employed in it, we have to consider the method by which it can be tested or verified. Analysis of the basis of the scientific validity of scientific statements is therefore of fundamental importance in deciding what they mean.

b) *Theoretical concepts.* Strict application of the principle of verification led to difficulties. General statements of laws are in principle impossible to verify completely. According to Popper, all we require of them by way of test is that they should make possible exact predictions (prognostic relevance) and that it is therefore conceivably possible in principle for them to be proved wrong by the non-occurrence of their prediction (falsifiability). Furthermore, the attempt to define the concepts of natural science in terms of observation encountered difficulties. According to Carnap, disposition concepts ("elastic", "conductor of electricity", "soluble in water") must be introduced by postulates of meaning; the full meaning of such concepts is not completely determined by empirically verifiable statements; instead, some conditions of their correct applicability or inapplicability are stated. This led to the interpretation of empirical scientific theories which is often referred to as the dual schema. According to this, a theory contains both empirical and theoretical concepts, an observation language consisting of empirical terms which can be tested by direct observation, and a theoretical language consisting of theoretical terms, the meaning of which is established axiomatically. Rules of correspondence are also needed to link the two languages and thus permit empirically verifiable statements to be derived from the theory.

c) The logical structure of an explanation in the empirical sciences consists in the logical possibility of deriving the proposition expressing the *explicandum* from theoretical laws, once the particular conditions of the case in question are known. In this respect there is a certain similarity between explanation and prediction.

The following objections have been raised against any over-simplified view of a dual schema of this kind. It is in fact the case that the observation language itself is independent of theoretical elements drawn from rival theories, which observation must confirm or rebut. Feyerabend and Sellars point out, however, that it cannot be concluded from this that the observation language contains no theoretical element whatsoever. It has to be remembered, too, that not everything in the theoretical language established axiomatically is purely arbitrary stipulation. We must distinguish between linguistic conventions, propositions they entail and statements embodying the scientific content of the theory.

d) *Theory and reality*. It is usual to give the expressions of the theoretical language, in addition to the interpretation which answers to the rules of correspondence, another interpretation which satisfies the axioms. This is called a model of the theory. Opinions differ on the epistemological character of such models. A mechanical model used to be considered indispensable, and was regarded as giving a complete grasp of physical reality (interpretation of theory as content). The difficulty of finding mechanical models, and the possibility of presenting different models, have led to the view that models are mere aids to visualization, devoid of any informative value beyond what is expressed in the formalism of the theory (formalist interpretation: a theory is a mere means of representing what can be observed). An intermediate view is that a theory has limited content. Models are thus analogous representations of the reality with which the theory deals. Direct conclusions about reality should therefore not be drawn from the model if they do not follow from the theory itself.

3. *Applications*. Any application of the systems discussed in the theory of science to philosophy and theology must take into account the different character of these disciplines as compared with the empirical sciences. The difference has usually been over-emphasized, however, with the unfortunate result that little attention has been given to similarities between them. We must therefore confine ourselves to a few indications.

a) *Metaphysical explanation*. While the empirical sciences construct theories from which the *explicandum* can be derived and thus have prognostic relevance, metaphysics seeks the necessary conditions of the given. Its function is not prognosis but integration. The aim is to express explicitly how a particular conception (philosophical world-picture) provides a unified interpretation of everything which man has to come to terms with in life, and is thus able to offer guidance for the meaningful conduct of life. Philosophical statements are tested (and this is relevant to determining their meaning) by examining whether they do in fact perform this integrative function. Consequently it is not legitimate, for example, to exclude from the start some domain of human experience. Since this verification itself has to be open to the totality of human experience it is less intersubjective than in the empirical sciences. It is not the business of metaphysics to offer a concrete world-picture, but to bring out what conditions must be fulfilled by conceptions with an integrative function. As regards philosophical views which have emerged at different times in history, we must distinguish between their fundamental meaning which bears the integrative function and the historically conditioned representative models in which this was embodied.

b) *Theology as theory*. If we want to trace a certain similarity between theology and the dual theory-schema, the following approach might be attempted. The observation language is matched by the religious language, in which the fundamental doctrines of faith are expressed. Theology seeks understanding, and for that purpose constructs a system in theoretical language, i.e., the language of theology. The understanding of the faith which this system formulates has to be in harmony with the fundamental statements of the religious language. The distinction between positive and speculative theology would thus correspond to that between experimental and theoretical physics. An attitude of theological positivism towards revelation regards theology as merely a formal systematization of the statements of the sources of revelation. The role of philosophy in theology consists in drawing out what is necessarily implied by particular questions and linguistic conventions. It is chiefly concerned, however, with everything involved in metaphysical explanation. This inevitably demands its integration with the full breadth of human experience and with other philosophical views. This total context must be taken into account in determining the full meaning of theological statements. Furthermore, the theoretical element in the observation language must not be overlooked. This explains the importance of a hermeneutics of the sources of revelation.

Otto Muck

SCOTISM

Scotism is the term applied either to the doctrine of Duns Scotus or of his school.

1. *Origin*. The controversy among Aristotelians was at its height during the teaching career of Duns Scotus (*c.* 1300), with the ancient Franciscan school (St. Bonaventure, etc.) of the Augustinian type opposed to the Thomistic. On 7 March 1277 the Bishop of Paris, Stephen, along with the University, had condemned 219 philosophical theses, including some of St. Thomas's. Archbishop Kilwardby, O. P., declared some theses of St. Thomas to be dangerous. The result of these proscriptions was, as Gilson remarks, that theologians of those days found themselves in the same position as exegetes after the condemnation of modernism. Scotus submitted unreservedly to these decrees, as also to the precept of the general chapter of his order, which forbade its members to uphold a doctrine "ab episcopo et magistris Parisiensibus communiter reprobatam" (H. S. Denifle, *Chartularium Univ. Paris.*, II [Paris, 1891], no. 580, p. 58).

The condemnations of 1270, and above all of 1277, reflect the opposition to an independent philosophy, and, as it was thought, to the abandonment of the traditional doctrine. It was a reaction which gave a new orientation to the Augustinian type of Aristotelianism which found its definitive expression in Scotism.

2. *The essential characteristics of the philosophical and theological system of Duns Scotus*. The penetrating criticism of the *doctor subtilis* was directed against the Franciscan as well as the Thomistic school, and here he was more concerned with contemporary authors than with St. Thomas. Thus he created a system which is neither identical with that of Aquinas nor directly opposed to it; it

must be regarded as a parallel to Thomism.

The object of our intellect is *ens inquantum ens*; only the *ens infinitum* is being in the full sense. The first act which is to be predicated of being is that of love, in accordance with the text of Scripture: "Deus caritas est" (1 Jn 4:16). This love indicates the source of action in God, which takes place necessarily *ad intra*, but freely (*contingenter*) *ad extra*. God sees everything in the *nunc aeternitatis*; he wills everything in one absolutely simple and immutable act, which being entirely rational grasps its objects in an ordered manner. Since God loves himself and likewise wills that there should be *condiligentes*, he wills Christ first of all, the *summum opus Dei*, as the *causa exemplaris* and *finalis*. Mary was foreordained along with Christ and preserved from original sin in view of the merits of her son, the one mediator and redeemer. The love of Christ is revealed especially on the cross and in the Eucharist, *sine qua periret omnis devotio in Ecclesia nec actus latriae exhiberetur Deo* (*Reportatio Parisiensis*, IV d. 8 q.1 n.3; ed. Vivès, 24, 10a).

Just as love is at the beginning of everything, so too our blessedness is in love and not in the vision of the intellect.

Duns Scotus did not demand an independent philosophy. Like the ancient Franciscan school, he upheld a Christian philosophy. The univocity of being, *distinctio formalis*, *forma corporeitatis*, the freedom of the will were concepts with which he tried to reach a deeper *intellectus fidei* (cf. C. Balić in *DSAM*, cols. 1801–18).

3. *Followers of Duns Scotus*. Scotus's type of teaching attracted the attention of his contemporaries and was not without influence on some of them, as for instance Robert of Cowton, Petrus Aureoli, Alexander Bonini, William of Nottingham (d. 1336), and above all Henry of Harcley (d. 1317) from among the diocesan clergy, though they cannot yet be called Scotists.

Some authors enumerate the followers of Scotus according to five periods.

We name only some of them. Among his immediate disciples are: Antonius Andreas (d. about 1320), Alfredus Gonteri (d. after 1325), Francis de Mayronis (d. after 1325), William of Alnwick (d. about 1333), Peter Thomas, Peter of Aquila (d. 1361), John de Bassolis (d. 1333). Others in the 14th century include: Francis de Marchia (d. after 1344), Landolfo Caracciolo (d. 1351), John of Rodington (d. 1348), John of Reading, William of Rubione, Andrew of Novocastro. In the 15th century, the period of the decline of scholasticism, we have the Scotists Peter Tartaretus, Bellatti, Sirect, William of Vaurouillon (d. 1464), Nicolaus d'Orbellis (d. 1471), Maurice de Portu (d. 1513), Trombetta (d. 1518), Paul Scriptor (d. 1505), Gratian of Brescia (d. about 1506), G. Gorris, John of Cologne.

We come finally to the 16th and 17th centuries, the golden age of the school, when there were chairs of Scotism, along with those of Thomism and nominalism, at most universities, especially in Spain.

Hundreds of commentaries on the *Ordinatio* (*Opus Oxoniense*) were written in this period.

Notable Scotists were: in France, Frassen (d. 1711), Dupasquier (d. 1705), Boyvin (d. 1679), Durand (d. 1710); in Spain, Francis Herrera (d. *c.* 1600), John of Ovando (d. *c.* 1610), Francis del Castillo Velasco, Francis Felix (d. *c.* 1650), Pérez López (d. 1724), Charles Moral (d. 1731); in Italy, Lychetus (d. 1520), Mastrius (d. 1673), Belluti (d. 1676), Faber (d. 1630), Vulpes (d. 1636), Lanterius, Malafossa (d. *c.* 1562), de Pitigianis (d. 1616), Brancatius (d. 1693); in Dalmatia, Benedict Benković (d. after 1520), Matthew Ferkić (d. 1669); in northern Europe, Peter Posnaniensis (d. after 1639), Pontius (d. *c.* 1672),

Cavellus (d. 1670), Wadding (d. 1657), Antony Hiquaeus (d. 1641), Hermann (d. 1700), Krisper (d. 1740).

The second half of the 18th and the first half of the 19th centuries show scholasticism in general in decline, and Scotism in particular. It was only in the first decades of the 20th century that Scotism found defenders again in Minges, Garcia, Belmond and Marie de Basly.

4. *Characteristics of Scotism.* Peter Thomas, about 1300, who professed to follow the master *ut plurimum*, blamed the *non scotizantes*, that is, those who wished to interpret Scotus objectively, but ascribed to him doctrines which he did not hold (*vulgus imposuit sibi*) and instead of keeping to the text (*expresse ex textu*), preferred to form their judgments *ex eius intentione* (Vatican Ms. Lat. 2190, f. 51r–52r). This controversy about the genuine doctrine of Scotus, which ensued from the incomplete nature of his works, was characteristic of Scotism in the 14th century. Single propositions were taken from their context, where for instance Scotus was attacking the determinism of Arab Aristotelianism, stress was laid on freedom, the absolute omnipotence of God and voluntarism, and thus occasion was given to later writers to speak of the influence of Scotism on nominalism and certain theories of modern philosophy. The Christocentric teaching of Scotus, however, and the doctrine of the Immaculate Conception, simply known as *opinio Scoti*, were readily taken over as early as the 14th century. It was on account of these doctrines that the great reformers of Franciscan spirituality (St. John Capistran, St. Bernardine of Siena, James von der Mark) declared Duns Scotus to be the leader of the Franciscan school and the *Doctor Ordinis*, and these doctrines were the chief glory of the Scotist school from the 16th to the 18th century (cf. C. Balić in *Antonianum* 30 [1955], pp. 349–488). Instead of going deeply into the doctrine of Scotus on the Church, the sources of revelation (Scripture-tradition), being as love, Scotists wrote treatises *De formalitatibus;* and because St. Thomas was among the authors with whom Scotus was in conflict on the doctrine of the Immaculate Conception, efforts were made to find points of difference everywhere between Scotism and Thomism. Cajetan was led to affirm that Scotus tried to refute the *singula prope verba* of the *Summa of Aquinas* (cf. E. Gilson, "Note sur un texte de Cajetan", *Antonianum* 27 [1952], pp. 377–80).

While some Scotists (De Rada, d. 1608, Macedo, d. 1681, Stella, d. after 1651, Lorte, d. 1724) brought out the contrast between St. Thomas and Scotus, others tried to reconcile the doctrines (Sarnano, d. 1535, Marco da Baudunio), or built up a *summa theologica iuxta ordinem et dispositionem Summae Angelici Doctoris* (De Montefortino, d. 1738) – efforts which in spite of their good intentions must be termed *magni passus sed extra viam.*

Which of the two is the greater theologian? The dilemma *aut Thomas aut Scotus* no longer exists. St. Thomas is the *doctor communis*, but historical research has proved that the *doctor subtilis* was not an adversary of Aquinas. The interlocutors whom he envisaged were contemporary authors (Henry of Ghent, Gottfried of Fontaines, Aegidius of Rome), but not primarily the *doctor communis.* His system is not opposed to that of Aquinas, but is on a parallel plane. As in the past, his system can still perform valuable services for the Church.

Carlo Balić

SCRIPTURE AND TRADITION

A. Introduction

1. The question of the relationship between Scripture and tradition seemed to have been cleared up for Catholic theology by the declaration of the Council of Trent (*D* 783f.), which affirmed that the pure gospel was con-

tained and handed on "in libris scriptis et sine scripto traditionibus", and that both modes of the presence of revelation were to be greeted "pari pietatis affectu ac reverentia". (This was repeated by Vatican II, *Dei Verbum*, art. 9, though "Sacra Traditio" was substituted for "traditiones".)

In post-Tridentine times, the declaration of Trent was mostly understood as saying that the content of revelation was divided materially between these two modes of givenness, so that some revelation was contained "only" in "oral tradition". It was assumed that there were therefore "two sources or revelation", differing to some extent in content from one another. This explanation of Trent is not of course to be considered binding. The main justification offered for it was that the extent of the canon, at least, could only be known from oral tradition, and also that many later dogmas of the Church could not be deduced from Scripture alone – not even by a process of explication of what was contained "implicitly" in Scripture, though here it was taken for granted that the process of explication could only be a purely logical operation. This interpretation of Trent's ruling was regarded as one of the most important points of controversial theology with regard to Protestantism and its doctrine of *sola Scriptura*.

2. Within the last twenty years, this position, which had become traditional to a great extent, was sharply called in question by the studies of J. R. Geiselmann and others. They pointed out that the doctrinal tradition, from the Fathers to the time of the Reformation, was by no means unanimous on the relationship of Scripture and tradition. Scripture was in fact allotted a clear priority. In the redaction of the text of Trent, a "partim – partim" had been eliminated, and replaced by a prudent "et". The "traditiones" of *D* 783f. (always in the plural at Trent) could not be identified with tradition in the present-day sense, and in the sense of the present-day problem. The recognition of the extent of the canon could neither be regarded as an instance of a general relationship between Scripture and tradition nor as a process which had already been explained. In any case, the development of dogma – whether due to Scripture or to an early tradition – was in need of an explanation which was no easier on the grounds of an early explicit tradition (which could be asserted but not proved), than on the ground of Scripture itself. For as regards the dogmas which theologians thought had to be derived from pure "tradition", as not being even implicitly in Scripture, there is in fact no other early attestation, historically verifiable, which could show that they derive from apostolic tradition.

3. The whole question was one of the most keenly debated at Vatican II, especially during the drafting of the dogmatic constitution *Dei Verbum*, on Revelation and Scripture. There the Council affirms (art. 7) that tradition was at work in the formation of Scripture itself; that a process of tradition continues to go on in the apostolic succession under the assistance of the Spirit (art. 8); that tradition gives testimony as to the canon of Scripture and actualizes Scripture (*ibid.*). The Council goes on to say (arts. 9 and 10) that Scripture and tradition form a unity, because they have one origin – the one divine revelation – and influence one another. Apart from the transmission of Scripture (canon), the actualizing function of tradition is centred entirely on Scripture (insofar as the theme is discussed at all).

It seems clear that the Council deliberately avoids – in contrast to the preconciliar draft – any affirmation about the material insufficiency of Scripture. This means in fact, since the opposite had been urged, that the Council had no misgivings about the material sufficiency of Scripture. It may therefore be held that the only task of post-biblical tradition is to transmit the Scriptures as such, to interpret them, to actualize them and to explicate their implications. In other words, to formulate the matter more prudently, tradition functions at all times by listening to Scripture, subject always to Scripture as the critical norm which is universally necessary to distinguish "divine" tradition, the transmission of revelation in Christ, from human traditions. (See further, for the precise nature of tradition, *Tradition*.)

When the Council says that the extent of the canon of Scripture is known from tradition, it must be noted that the formulation of the proposition is positive, not exclusive. The positive affirmation is something which is self-evident, which remains important, however, to exclude a wrong understanding of *sola Scriptura*, according to which the book of Scripture could be "Scripture" in a theological sense outside the Church and its preaching. But it does not decide the question as to whether knowledge of the canon and its extent is based on an individual, propositional truth of faith which as such is neither implicitly nor explicitly in Scripture (which in any case would still not be a matter which could be generalized).

The question might still be raised as to whether the statement of the Council should not in fact be read with an "only", that is, in an exclusive sense. The answer depends on the solution of the difficult problem, which is still an open one, as to how precisely we are to think of the Church's mode of attaining knowledge of the canon. The knowledge in question cannot be supposed to be due to an explicit statement of the "last Apostle", because there are canonical writings which were produced only after the death of the last Apostle, even though they must still be ascribed to "apostolic times". If we consider that this knowledge came to the Church – not to the individual as such – not just as something "concerned with" or "about" the canon, but as "of the canon", that is, through the canonical Scriptures, this knowledge of the canon need not even be thought of as a special case of the relationship between Scripture and tradition. See K.-H. Ohlig, *Zur theologischen Begründung des neutestamentlichen Kanons* (1969) and B 4 below.

We should proceed along similar lines in considering the statement of the Council (art. 9), to the effect that the Church's certainty about the content of revelation does not merely ("non per solam") derive from Scripture. This again is not an affirmation of the material insufficiency of Scripture, since it speaks of certainty with regard to assent to *all* truths of faith, but not – directly – of the material "source" of given truths of faith. As the statement stands, it speaks of all truths of faith and not just of some, which *ex supposito* are not contained in Scripture. Further, it should be obvious that the whole faith of all individuals in the Church is sustained by the active preaching of the Church, which is tradition, *paradosis*. But this *paradosis* again, precisely as such, has an essential relation to Scripture in post-apostolic times. It is *paradosis* throughout *through* Scripture.

B. Systematic Analysis

1. Though the article *Tradition* must be read in this connection, tradition comes under discussion here, inasmuch as tradition itself is, to start with, as act and as content, constitutive of Scripture. The "oral" preaching of Jesus as the crucified and exalted Lord, a preaching launched by the mission of Jesus Christ, inspired by his Spirit and carried on in faith, is from the start and essentially "paradosis", since it contains the actuality of a unique, historical, all-determining event, and is also addressed to those who did not themselves encounter this event in space and time ("according to the flesh") but could only do so in the word of preaching. Paradosis is not something added on to the preaching about Jesus the Christ. It is this preach-

ing itself, the attestation of the unique saving deed of God in Christ through the mission, Spirit and faith at work in the preacher, who receives, by hearing, what he says, and says what he thus hears, and who thus stands within a paradosis, a tradition, in both directions.

In the long run, such paradosis cannot exist in the historical situation in which in fact it is always received and handed on, without being committed to writing. And the longer the tradition persists, the less can it do without writing. It becomes Scripture. Scripture is the concrete form taken by the apostolic paradosis, not something else added on to it. As long as this crystallization of the paradosis in Scripture is not necessary, the "apostolic age", the age of the "primitive Church", still runs on. And conversely, this age is ended from the "moment" – which means a certain length of time, between the production of the first and last of the canonical Scriptures – in which the paradosis is only in command of itself by its reference to Scripture.

2. This does not mean that the paradosis is eliminated by a book which then becomes an independent entity and is of itself the herald and norm for the faith of later generations. The authoritative paradosis, the summons to faith, continues. By sustaining itself *through* Scripture, by remaining certain of itself and of its legitimate origin from the apostolic preaching, the paradosis in turn sustains the inspired book in which the paradosis remains concrete.

3. Hence the problem of Scripture and tradition is wrongly put from the outset if it at once takes the form of asking whether the *propositions* of Scripture contain the Christian revelation in full (*sola Scriptura* in a quantitative, propositional sense) or whether in addition some propositions have been handed down "only" through ("oral") tradition – as if there were two materially different "sources" (or "modes of transmission") for Christian revelation. It must be noted that the tradition, which presents *itself* incarnate in Scripture in post-apostolic times, is not originally and essentially a fixed sum-total of propositions, from which further propositions could then be derived through a merely rational process of deduction. Tradition is the persistence of God's revelation, which both as coming from God and as coming from man (or directed to him) is more than a number of fixed propositions. It is the experience (had) of Jesus Christ, inexhaustible to thought, the ever-incomprehensible mystery of God into which all propositions flow, the real communication of that which is expressed in propositions, through the self-communication of God – in the Spirit, grace and the light of faith.

And this tradition – the transmission of the reality which necessarily of course expounds itself in propositions but is not simply identical with them – continues to be at work inasmuch as tradition, understood in this way, also sustains Scripture. And then again, Scripture, in the proper theological sense, is not a mere book containing many propositional truths (bearing on historical and doctrinal matters), but in fact the event or reality in which the Church gives concrete form to its kerygma, its faith, recognizes it, and submits itself to this objectivation, using it to criticize all other opinions, tendencies, etc., which occur in the course of history. In this way the Church maintains the purity of the true faith which it holds by uttering it in Scripture. It follows that later dogmas – the articulation of the one and abiding faith – need not simply be derived from Scripture in the sense that they are explicitly propounded there "in other words", or that they must be demonstrably and stringently logical deductions in the line of explication of Scripture. It also follows that no later dogmas are independent of Scripture and not subordinated to it. The faith which created Scripture did not eliminate itself by the formation of Scripture (*non sola Scriptura*). Nonetheless, everything in the later utterances of faith must be measured by Scripture (*sola Scriptura*) since it is in Scripture that the one whole apostolic faith has been objectivated and has given itself, and laid down for all future times, its *norma non normata*.

4. This will appear still more clearly if we turn to the special question as to whether at least the concrete existence of Scripture qua Scripture, the canon, is not a truth which is "only" in tradition and not contained in Scripture. It has already been pointed out above that even if the question were to be answered in the affirmative as in the ordinary theology of the schools (A 1), this thesis could not simply be expanded to a general doctrine of a material insufficiency of Scripture. The thesis thus generalized would contribute nothing to a real explanation of the development of dogma (see A 2 above). But the generalization itself would not be legitimate, because the theological existence of Scripture (which can naturally not be based on the book itself as such) is of course a different case from other theological assertions (which can very well be all contained in principle in a book). But to give a radical answer to the question and to deal with it correctly, it must be noted that the process of the recognition of the canon by the Church (in contradistinction from that by individuals) is none other than that of the formation of Scripture – and hence of the formation of the canon. In other words, the Church recognizes Scripture as Scripture inasmuch as tradition creates Scripture and recognizes itself as purely and permanently normative in and by the tradition crystallized in Scripture (a recognition ancient, unique and permanently new) – and thus subordinates itself to this tradition. The action of creating Scripture, which is also recognition of the canon, recognizes itself as legitimate, in an indissoluble synthesis of act and object, inasmuch as it sees its work as successful, that is, as producing the purity of faith in Christ.

We are then equally well justified in affirming that tradition recognizes the canon, as in affirming that Scripture attests itself as canonical for the *Church* itself. This is a different matter from saying that the individual could recognize Scripture as canonical on his own – though he for his part had no hand in its formation.

We cannot here reduce the whole relationship between tradition and Scripture to the relationship (an element of which it forms) which obtains between the authority of the Lord and that of the believing Church in general. In this relationship of faith by which the Church believes through the Lord and in the Lord, all that is distinct from Christ (Jesus' words of self-attestation, miracles, the testimony of the original witnesses, etc.) forms an indissoluble unity which comprises both what can have faith-inspiring force only from the authority of Christ in his Spirit, and what mediates this authority to the faithful. If one regards Scripture and tradition as a unity, and as distinct from Christ himself, and if this unity distinct from Christ himself is regarded in the light of this basic axiom of the *analysis fidei*, one has reached the basic standpoint from which the relationship of Scripture and tradition should be envisaged. This unity, with its faith-inspiring force, is constituted in the final analysis only by the power of the Spirit of Christ, and is itself in fact the mediation of this authority of Christ, in his Spirit, to the Church. Once this is grasped, it remains only to see and accept frankly the simple, straightforward fact that the tradition of the primitive Church (in the actual circumstances) can only abide and hold normative sway through Scripture, of which tradition knows that it has crystallized there, knowing therefore that it is only in Scripture that it is and remains itself.

When Vatican II reaffirms that it looks on Scripture and tradition "pari pietatis affectu ac reverentia", it may and must do so, because Scripture and tradition form a unity form the start and are not just brought into relationship with each other subsequently.

Karl Rahner

SECULARIZATION

I. Concept

A. Defining the Notion

"Secularization" comes from the Latin *saecularis*, meaning "worldly", "temporal" or "age-old", and forms a group with "secularity" and "secularism". Since all these words indicate a theory or process whereby things or persons are assigned to the realm of the world, they are often used indifferently. But it is useful and now becoming more common to distinguish them. (i) Secularization has mostly been used for the confiscation of Church property for worldly ends, mostly by the State and against the will of the Church. It has happened again and again in the course of history, for various reasons. In canon law secularization also means granting permission to a professed member of a religious order to live for the rest of his life outside his monastery. (ii) Secularization is now also understood as the process whereby various elements of human life (such as opinions, customs, social forms and even things and persons) or the whole of human life cease to be determined by religion. The result, secularity, then means independence and adulthood with regard to religion. (iii) When secularizing is taken as a programme, when secularity is the mainspring of a world-view, the term "secularism" is used. Secularism would then be a secularizing which did not remain purely secular (as "secularity") but turned into a doctrine of salvation or an ideology. The world-view of a group of English free-thinkers in the 19th century who called themselves "secularists" was propounded under the heading of *Secularism, the Practical Philosophy of the People* (G. J. Holyoake [1854]).

The general history of the terms is as follows. The word "secularization" was first used as a legal term, defining certain political moves, such as had already been the object of negotiations before the Treaty of Westphalia at the end of the Thirty Years War, 1646. It was taken into canon law in the 18th century. When in the 19th century the effort was made to deprive the Church of its influence in cultural matters, especially education, as well as of its material goods, it was only natural that the term "secularization" should be extended to this programme. In France it became usual to speak of the *sécularisation* demanded for philosophy, for instance, while in England the term "secularism" came into use. Secularization and secularism undoubtedly began as slogans of a movement mostly hostile to the Church, and were used in this sense by the Positivism, Materialism and Monism of the times. But they gradually developed a more neutral sense and were then used to describe without value-judgments the historical process of the emancipation of the world from religious tutelage – a process which was increasingly regarded as ambivalent. To avoid ambiguity, or rather to underline the ambivalence of the terms, a distinction was made between secularization and secularism. Secularization is now understood as a more or less neutral term, while secularism is taken to be a false ideology. To mark the difference, however, between process and result, the justifiable, non-ideological result of secularizing is called "secularity", though secularization remains an ambivalent term, meaning in certain modern theological contexts the process or result of a more or less correct emancipation of the world as regards the Church or religion. Since secularization in the English-speaking world is historically relevant only to the suppression and expropriation of the monasteries by Henry VIII in the 16th century, there is no great objection to the new use of the term in the "theology of the world".

B. Secularization as a Historical Process

It is a phenomenon as old and as widespread as religion itself that individuals or groups or even a whole era should at times reject prevailing religious ties and seek to emancipate themselves from them. The phenomenon can take very different forms. One may recall, for instance, how the Egyptian Pharaoh Akh-en-Aton (Ekhnaton) in the 14th century B.C. set out to abolish the traditional cults and divinities of his kingdom in favour of a more rationalistic system. Or there is the critique to which Greek philosophers, from Xenophanes and Anaxagoras down to Socrates, and then the Epicureans, subjected the mythological notions of the gods in the world around them. The ethnology of religion also shows that there is no religion, even among the primitives, where the doctrines and prescriptions have not been sceptically questioned, at least at times or by individuals, and have only been retained as expedient, but not as unquestionably binding. Nonetheless, like atheism, secularism remained, till the beginning of the modern era, a rare and transient phenomenon. The explanation of the world and the interpretation of human existence was too strongly linked with mythologies. Social life was too firmly based on forms worked out under the influence of religion. Even the manipulation of nature could only be learnt from rules with magical components. It is only in the West in the modern era that secularization became widespread and persistent when as a result of a process which reaches back far into the past and is still not ended, one realm after another of human reality was taken more and more radically out of religion's sphere of influence.

It is understandable that the religious elements tried to stem the process, since not only were worldly realms withdrawn from the religious sphere, but religion seemed threatened with the loss of all links with reality and hence with complete insignificance. The goal of the process seemed to be a secularism which would be the end of all religion. The process of secularization in this conflict may be illustrated from three well-known contrasts which have been used as slogans to sum up and oppose certain worldly and religious spheres. They are faith and knowledge, Church and State, this world and the other world as the end of man.

If we follow the developments in these fields since the beginnings of Christianity down to the present day with its trend to secularization, it appears that the process has been more or less the same in all three fields, passing through three stages which may be defined with a fair degree of accuracy.

1. In the message of the NT, the relationship between the worldly and the corresponding Christian realm is such that neither can be said to predominate over the other, to exclude the other or even to be hostile to the other. The doctrine of the NT is simply that the religious sphere is totally different from the worldly, so that neither can substitute for the other since the two are on different planes. Faith has not the function of replacing knowledge. It gives no worldly wisdom, just as it does not suppose it. It merely shows that knowledge, scientific and mundane, has only a relative value. It is not an absolute, on which the salvation or loss of man ultimately depends, though if erected into an absolute and used in order to "boast" against God it becomes foolishness and is opposed to faith (cf. 1 Cor 1:17–2:9; Rom 1:21f.). And the wise need the

gospel as much as the ignorant (Rom 1:14).

The relationship between Church and State or civil authorities is on the same lines. Neither side can displace the other or claim superiority. The State cannot, since "We must obey God rather than men" (Acts 5:29). Neither can the Church, since it is not its task "to judge outsiders" (cf. 1 Cor 5:12). In fact, by accepting the structure of the State without disputing its lawful powers, the Church reduces it to its proper stature (cf. Rom 12:19–13:7 with K. Barth, *Epistle to the Romans* [1933]). And the world is not divided into spheres of influence, allotted to religion and the civil authorities respectively, since we are to "Render to Caesar the things that are Caesar's, and to God the things that are God's" (Mk 12:17). This does not mean that we are to give Caesar one portion and God another, since all that is in the world belongs to God. Two completely different sets of interests are involved which cannot interfere with one another as long as neither of them tries to exercise the functions of the other.

It might, however, appear that at least as far as the end of man is concerned, the religious and the secular are opposed to each other on the same plane in the NT, that the tasks of man are distributed between them and that conflict could arise, inasmuch as the State could demand the fullest possible orientation to this world, at the expense of the other world and vice versa. But here too such a conflict appears absurd in the perspective of the NT. Just as faith does not eliminate knowledge or the Church does not make the State superfluous, so too the seeking of the kingdom of God does not absolve man from his earthly tasks. In the NT, the effort to avoid having to fulfil one's everyday and human tasks by appealing to religious obligations is explicitly condemned (e.g., Mk 7:11f.; 12:40) and the principle is laid down that "if any one will not work, he is not to eat" (cf. 2 Thess 3:10). But again, "the one thing that is needful" shows that to be "troubled and anxious about many things" is a misplaced anxiety (Mt 6:31–34; Lk 10:41f.), about a relatively minor matter. The striving for worldly ends does not compete with interest in the kingdom of God, as though it could perhaps take its place, but has a different end and object and is in the second place.

In all these instances, the gospel avoids challenging the worldly sphere on its own level and does not seek to exercise sovereignty within that sphere. But the worldly sphere itself is shown to be provisional.

2. The second stage runs from patristic to modern times, and is characterized by the claim of the religious sphere to predominate over the secular, so much so that at times religion seemed to absorb the latter entirely. This approach meant that faith was regarded as containing all that was worth knowing and as a superior type of knowledge (see *Gnosis*), so that philosophy, for instance, could at most be the *ancilla theologiae*. The relationship of Church to State is that the Church, as St. Augustine said, is the pilgrim part of the *civitas Dei*, with an authority surpassing that of the State, which belongs to the *civitas terrena*. The State has merely to serve the Church in the role of the "secular arm". So too the relationship between the earthly and the other-worldly goals of man is described in terms of St. Augustine's image of the two loves: "love of God extending to contempt of self, and love of self extending to contempt of God." It was consequently held that detachment from the world was of itself the direct and unquestionable way of realizing more perfectly the religious end of man.

3. From the very beginning, this attitude was challenged by objections which grew more and more widespread and finally led to the process of secularization which characterizes the third stage, the modern era. Faith and knowl-

edge, for instance, were already distinguished in classical scholasticism (cf. St. Thomas Aquinas; see *Thomism*) as two modes of knowledge, each with rights of its own, though they were still united in their ordination to the one truth. But the doctrine of the double truth, upheld by the medieval Averroists and still a force in Nominalism, meant the disruption of this unity. The truth of faith was opposed to that of science, at first as unrelated and then, as contradictory assertions were put forward, as by Galileo, they were regarded as hostile to one another. With the development of science and the proof that it was capable of explaining more and more fields of knowledge, what religion had to say about the world seemed to become more and more superfluous. Faith, regarded in the light of its past as a doctrine dealing also and specifically with the world, was regarded as unnecessary, or at most as competent in the "inward" sphere, though here it was being challenged by depth pyschology. What it had to say appeared as meaningless or at least useless for the world.

There was a similar development in the relationship between Church and State. The unity of the spiritual power and of the civil power which was regarded as dependent on it was initially a reality, and was maintained in Byzantium and the Eastern Church for many centuries. But the claim was challenged by the interpretation given to the "doctrine of the two swords" by the Western Emperors. Here the two powers were said to be derived equally directly from God, a position condemned in the most extreme terms by Boniface VIII in the Bull *Unam Sanctam* (1302). The new theory upheld the "divine right of kings", independent of the Church, and the princes then often subordinated the interests of the Church to those of the State. The Church thus progressively lost political influence over the State, and lost it completely when it was deprived of its last remaining means of imposing strictly political pressure, the Papal States, and when the last links between "Throne" and "Altar" were shattered by the downfall of most of the royal houses. Thus this process also ended in secularity.

There was a corresponding shift in perspective as regards the end of man. Flight from the world, with its neglect of the worldly, bodily and material, and its special connotation of contempt for the sexual, ceased to be regarded as an ideal to be valued for its own sake. Instead, these realms were assigned real values of their own, secondary no doubt at first in comparison to the religious realm contrasted with them, till finally a complete secularization was achieved. It became clear that neither the Church nor the orientation to an other-worldly goal was helping men to master the tasks which were incumbent on them in the worldly realm. Parallel developments can also be traced in the other realms of human life, mostly in connection with the preceding, as for instance in the realm of art, culture and education, in the understanding of law, authority and history.

C. Evaluation

The historical process of secularization, described above rather summarily as the progressive emancipation of the worldly from a religious sphere which was thus becoming meaningless, contains in fact a number of aspects which must be taken into consideration when a verdict is passed upon it. What secularization means is to be judged chiefly in the light of how religion is understood in the process, especially its relationship to the world.

It might seem that the relationship could only polarize between two extremes, which could be looked upon as representing in their purity the ideals sought after in the second and third stages of the development described above. At one pole the whole world in all its functions is subordinated to religion and governed by its rules, at the other religion, insofar as it survives at all, is totally orientated to the other world, with no interest or influence in the worldly realm. In between, there are of course countless other possibilities for the relationship of religion to the world. But this general schema is inappropriate. It is based on a very definite idea of religion and one that is quite inadequate. Here religion is characterized by the fact that it bears on a realm opposed to the profane, the realm of the holy, of which it is the steward. It is a matter of indifference whether this sacral realm regarded as superior to the world has control of the world, or whether it ignores the world in complete detachment from it on the basis or the other-worldly character of the holy. In any case the principle is that man must see in the holy his first and authentic task, to which other duties must always give way. His intramundane tasks are treated as secondary and as liable to come into conflict with his primary task.

This notion of religion, which is poised between Integralism and esotericism, must be contrasted with a view of religion which does not regard the holy as a special realm apart from the profane. As a consequence, the worldly task cannot possibly come into rivalry with the religious one. The holy is realized in the profane, the religious task in the worldly one. But they do not simply coincide, since this would mean the denial of the religious task. And this would lead once more, at least on principle, to the separation of the religious from the worldly realm. The religious task could then only be subsumed under the first type of religion described above. But this remains inadequate, because it does not do justice to the Christian message, just as it has also had a deleterious influence on the history of Christianity, as has been shown.

On the basis of this distinction of two different types of religion two different types of secularization must be envisaged. In the first type, when man finds himself asked to choose between the religious and the worldly task, he is under the impression – justifiable from this notion of religion – that he can only master his worldly task at the expense of the religious one. And his secularization then consists of deciding in favour of the worldly task which he has to recognize as obligatory. But in the second type of secularization, religion sets no new tasks in addition to the worldly one. It merely gives the latter a new meaning and purpose (cf. 1 Jn 2:7f.: "I am writing you no new commandment . . . Yet I am writing you a new commandment"). The rejection of religion, understood in this way, means for the world the denial of the one dimension of this world which can ground this world as a whole. A secularization of this type would not make the intramundane task easier. It would simply make it absurd, since the whole of life would be meaningless. But this is not an outlook which can be endured by many over a long period. If the true religious dimension is persistently excluded, some intramundane substitute will be looked for to give meaning to life. But then, to guarantee an ultimate meaningfulness, some worldly goal will be erected into an absolute. And this will then become a new type of "sacred realm" in contrast to other fields. Another religion is established, in the first, unfavourable sense, and the just interests of secularization are thwarted – unless a new process of secularization is begun, as may be seen to be happening in various atheistic systems.

D. The Christian View of Secularization

The way has now been paved for a verdict on secularization from the Christian standpoint. It will depend on whether Christianity considers itself a religion in the first or the second sense, as proposed above. The history of secularization suggests that Christianity was not always very clear on the point, so that the Christian verdict on secularization will involve a clarification of the self-understanding of Christianity.

1. *The present state of the discussion.* In the years between the two World Wars, when the phenomenon of secularization first became a matter of widespread interest and close investigation on the Christian side, it was mostly rejected out of hand as an anti-Christian movement. This was still the attitude of conservative circles after the Second World War, among circles who were concerned for the preservation of Western culture. Today attitudes are more cautious and nuanced.

On the Protestant side, the influence of dialectical theology has been felt. This was on principle readier to criticize the intramundane claims of religion and the Church than the "secularizing" of the world. Hence even Protestants who tended to emphasize the negative element in secularization (e.g., W. Hartmann, H. Kraemer) acknowledged that it had a positive role to play on behalf of the Church. It was seen as helping the Church to understand itself and its task better, to see itself as homeless in the world and to avoid mistakes when translating the gospel into the language of the profane world. But there are others, especially F. Gogarten, who regard secularization as "a necessary and legitimate consequence of the Christian faith", though it is to be distinguished from the secularism which adopts in turn religious forms and claims. C. F. von Weizsäcker takes up a similar position, as does J. B. Metz on the Catholic side, the latter pointing out that many modern types of atheism are based on the false assumption that Christianity implies a divinized, not a secular world, and hence that the Christian faith will disappear when its dream-world vanishes. But the true relationship between the Christian notion of God and a divinized world is precisely the opposite: "to Christianize the world means to secularize it".

Another positive attitude to the secularity of the modern era has become well known under the slogan of "religionless Christianity". This position is based on the severe strictures on religion made by K. Barth, who held that religion was "the concern of the godless". But the real launcher of the notion of a "religionless Christianity" was undoubtedly D. Bonhoeffer who propounded the main lines of thought which have dominated this trend when he was in prison in 1944 under the National Socialists. A list of Bonhoeffer's points enables one to recognize how widely influential they have been: religion as a "historically conditioned and transient form of human self-expression"; intellectual sincerity; the question: "How can we speak about God" – avoiding religion, that is, without the historically-conditioned assumptions of metaphysics, inwardness, etc.? How can we speak of God in "worldly" terms – or is it perhaps no longer possible to speak of him at all as hitherto? (G. Ebeling takes up here the question raised by Bonhoeffer as to the "non-religious interpretation of biblical concepts"; others ask how the word "God" can be introduced in any meaningful way.) God the *deus ex machina*, the stop-gap where human effort fails or at the limits of human knowledge and power; the danger of human existence being reduced to one dimension; the coming of age of the world (which recurs in R. Guardini). One of Bonhoeffer's principles was that we must live in the world *etsi Deus non daretur*, that we must stand before God "like those who deal with life without God". This in fact recalls a saying of St. Ignatius Loyola, that "we must employ all human means with as much prudence and energy as if all our success depended on them". In any case, though perhaps given a one-sided interpretation, it became very popular in the "death-of-God" theology (G. Vahanian, W. Hamilton, T. Altizer and others in America, D. Sölle and others in Germany). Where this meant that God was supposed to be dead and buried in sheer humanism (really, a humanism denying the existence of God – a view not to be attributed without more ado to this trend), Bonhoeffer's point was misunderstood, and was in danger ot being made into an ideology, that of a non-secular secularism. J. A. T. Robinson's much-discussed book *Honest to God* is also obviously tributary to Bonhoeffer for its basic ideas as regards a positive evaluation of secularization. In fact most of the important theologians who have discussed the theme at the present day have been influenced by Bonhoeffer in this matter, at least in Protestant circles, where the problem was discussed much earlier and more fully than by Catholic theology.

But among Catholic theologians a positive verdict on secularization is gaining ground and influence, which showed itself at Vatican II, due chiefly to the representatives of this view among the theologians attached to the Council, like Y. Congar and K. Rahner. An example is the Pastoral Constitution on the Church in the Modern World.

2. *Reasons for welcoming a correct secularity.* a) *The true secularity.* One of the reasons why the Christian understanding of the faith now suggests a more positive attitude to secularization may be that it presents itself as the one remaining way of bringing the Christian message to the world of today. According to Bonhoeffer, the "religious" approach will be successful only with a few survivors from the age of chivalry or some intellectuals of doubtful sincerity. But the justifiable effort to be all things to all men is not the only or the decisive motive for the acceptability of secularization. It is welcomed on its own merits, since "it results directly and authentically from the kernel of Christian revelation itself" (H. Zahrnt). This needs to be demonstrated. Here it should be noted that the secularization in question is to be clearly distinguished from a secularism which is an atheistic ideology, offering an answer without recourse to God when asked about the meaning of the whole, the purpose of life, or rejecting the question totally, by declaring it to be absurd or repressing it in silence. What is at stake is the true secularity of the world, which consists of the truth that there is nothing in the world which is too "holy" to be accessible to a worldly approach and must be reserved for religion (religion being then, as we have seen, definitely misunderstood). There is no mystery in the world from which science is barred, on the ground that it can be explained only on "religious" terms. This does not mean of course that the world and all that is in it is totally comprehensible. The mystery abides universally. But in the realm of action there are no intramundane effects which can be brought about only by "religious" means or practices. There is nothing in the structure or the order of the world which is taboo, which is to be removed from man's use, as the attitude which could be called "sacralism" has firmly maintained throughout all the history of religion.

b) *Justification in the light of the Christian message.* The OT already contains, as has often been pointed out (cf. G. von Rad, for instance, or H.-J. Krause, H. Cox), a clear orientation to secularization. It is true that the Israelites lived in a world "which was divided before God into pure and impure, the holy and the profane" (von Rad), where the untouchable ark of the covenant, the inaccessible sanctuary and the chosen people attested the separation of the "religious realm" from the world. But faith in creation, with the claim of God to be Lord of the whole world, the doctrine that the world and all that is in it is created for man, the prohibition of making an image of God to localize his presence in this world, the extension of the promise of salvation to all nations, etc., paved the way for "breaching the pale of the sacral" in secularization (T. Sartory). This tendency came out fully in the NT. In the message of Christ, all the sacral realms within the world, which still seemed inviolable in the OT, were treated as provisional or unimportant, as mere means, or even as impediments to salvation when erected into absolute values. They were thus relativized, often in direct onslaughts: the temple, the "holy place", by the prediction of its destruction (Mt 24:1f.), since the Father was not to be adored there but "in the spirit and the truth" (Jn 4:21–23), and since for Christians God and Christ are the temple (Rev 21:22) as are their own bodies (1 Cor 3:16f.; 6:19; 2 Cor 6:16); so too the "holy times", the Sabbath, since "the Sabbath was made for man" (Mk 2:27), according to Jesus, who pointed to David's having "profaned" the "holy" bread of the Presence to satisfy his hunger. St. Paul says of feast-days and Sabbaths that "These are only a shadow of what is to come" (Col 2:16f., cf. Rom 14:5 and especially Gal 4:10f.). So too the "sacred customs" like fasting (Mk 2:18–20), the rules for pure and impure (Mk 7:1–15), circumcision (Gal 5:2) and so on. Even sacrificial worship and priesthood, in the sense of the OT, are abolished by Christ as the Letter to the Hebrews shows. In a word, apart from Christ, the NT recognizes nothing sacred about persons, realms, things or structures. The Christian enjoys the freedom of the children of God through Christ and is lord of the world, where everything is holy and unholy at the same time, according to how truly it is in Christ or under the dominion of sin. Hence St. Paul, in his conviction that "nothing is unclean in itself", can formulate the statement which can be regarded as a maxim of Christian secularity: "The world or life or death or the present or the future, all are yours; and you are Christ's; and Christ is God's" (1 Cor 3:22f.).

Albert Keller

II. Laicism

The term "laicism" was coined in France during the struggle for spiritual power under the Third Republic and introduces the problems of the "Church and the World" as they were understood in the 18th and 19th centuries. It is only against this historical background that the attitude of laicism to the relationship of Church and State, for instance, can be properly understood. Laicizing thought was given its classical form in France, though it also played an important role in other countries down to the present century.

The spiritual roots of laicism are to be found in the Renaissance, Humanism and more especially in the Enlightenment. This was the era in which the autonomy and intrinsic value of the world began to be recognized in all spheres – State, society, law, economics, culture and education. The effort was made in consequence to shake off imagined or real ecclesiastical tutelage. Hence laicism has all the characteristics of a movement for emancipation.

The political thought of the era saw the justification of religion and religious societies in the individual's right to freedom of religion and its profession. But since this right obtained only in the private sphere of the person, the freedom of religious groups as such did not follow at once. These were rather assigned the status of an association on the basis of private rights, and hence deprived of public standing in their own right and of their power to influence public life.

One consequence of this process of emancipation and its embodiment in constitutional law was the separation of Church and State, which was completed by the legislation of the Third Republic on 9 September 1905. The concordat of 1801 was abrogated. Diplomatic relations with the Holy See had been broken off in 1904. The Church was deprived of support from public funds, Church buildings became the property of the State, though the local cultic communities, the juridical agents of the cult and its external organization, were allowed to use them free of charge. The financial administration of the cultic communities was supervised by the State. But the dynamism of this emancipation carried it beyond the limits which a neutral State, uninterested in religion, should have prescribed for itself. The educational system of the Third Republic set up a "State religion" of a special type. There had been efforts to provide a substitute religion in the form of an official "Atheism" and a "Theophilanthropism" at the time of the Revolution (1793 and 1795). This issued in 1882 in the abolition of religious instruction in State schools. It was replaced by general ethical instruction on lines laid down by the State. At the beginning, belief in God was still maintained as the necessary presupposition of such ethics, but the "Ligue de l'Enseignement" founded in 1866 demanded that ethics should be purged of all explanations referring to God. Thus laicism became a world-view. The "State Church" celebrated a strange resurrection with a "religion" full of minus signs.

Since the religious orders were the mainstay of the "free schools", the legislation was mainly directed against them. The Jesuit order was banned in 1880. The other orders and congregations were ordered to make application for official recognition on the part of the State. According to the law of 1901, each religious house and all new foundations needed to be licensed by the State. In 1904, all religious communities without exception were forbidden any kind of teaching activity. As in the typical case of France, so too in other countries the question of schools and education was the classical case of conflict between the sovereignty of the laicizing State and the claims of Church life.

The aggressive emancipation on the part of the State provoked a bitter defensive struggle on the part of Catholics. They could not but see the laicizing *Credo* recommended by the State as an unwarranted imposition, and the republican form of the State which upheld this *Credo* as by its very nature a peril. The majority of French Catholics attached their hopes to a restoration of the monarchy, which they soon thought of as the sole guarantee of the external existence of the Church. This political option, meant as a measure of self-defence, inspired the State in turn with misgivings, not always unjustified, that the Church schools were not educating children in loyalty to the new form of the State. State restrictions on freedom of education became harsher and harsher. The aloofness of a great number of French Catholics and their hierarchy was maintained till into the upheavals of World War II. Papal pronouncements were also marked by the character of being on the defensive, though they counselled moderation in the concrete (cf. the warnings of Leo XIII; Cardinal Lavigerie). Pius X, in the encyclicals *Vehementer* and *Gravissimo officii munere* (1906), condemned the interference of the State in the proper work of the Church, and hence rejected the law of separation. Pius XI's encyclical *Quas primas* (1925) brought the term "laicism" into the vocabulary of the Church.

On the side of the Church, pastoral prudence prevailed, stimulated by new thinking on the relation of the Church to the world. On the side of the French State, the laws on separation were applied tolerantly, and the tendency to totalitarian claims became distasteful, in view of recent experiences. The way was paved for an agreement. In 1921, diplomatic relations with the Holy See were resumed. The era of controversy within the Church was ended in favour of a line open to dialogue, by the declaration of the French episcopate in 1945.

In the course of this process, the term "laicity" was coined, as a counterpart to "laicism". This "sound, legitimate laicity" of the State (Pius XII, *AAS* 50 [1958]) means the autonomy of the State and public institutions in pursuing the common good, part of which is to guarantee the religious freedom of the citizens and the existence of religious associations under public law. As regards schools and education the Archbishop of Cambrai, E.-M. Guerry, may be quoted: "As regards State schools, laicity means that the school shall not be denominational but neutral and hence shall pronounce neither for nor against religion ... This is to be distinguished from laicism in the State, which is a philosophical doctrine based on agnosticism, materialism or an ideological atheism by which the State is inspired and with which it seeks to penetrate its public institutions, including the schools" (31 December 1959).

This attitude was ratified by the declarations of Vatican II on the proper autonomy of earthly realities (*Gaudium et Spes*, art. 36), and on the resulting freedom of Christians to choose between political options (*Lumen Gentium*, arts. 25, 36, 37; *Gaudium et Spes*, art. 43). Here the Church is charged to seek a relation of partnership outside the framework of the extremes of the State Church and separation of Church and State. The same principles are the basis of the decree on religious freedom.

Ernst Niermann

SEX

I. Sexuality

For centuries the prevailing theological teaching attributed no more than a functional character to human sexuality; corresponding to the sexuality of the animal world, it was evaluated chiefly or entirely from the point of view of procreation. On the basis of an anthropology which is concerned with the totality of the person, new points of view for the understanding and evaluation of sexuality present themselves nowadays, leading to changes of emphasis and additional insights and making the current doctrine more complete. Sexuality must be numbered among the essential determining factors in man. It characterizes the entire structure of the human being, whether as man or woman, and affects the behaviour of the individual even in his mental attitudes and processes. As a result of this preliminary enlightenment from the anthropological side, the theologian of today can also find in the witness of revelation an approach to an evaluation of sex in its totality.

1. *Statements in revelation*. a) The statements of the OT have preserved mankind's primal consciousness of his own human nature and his created existence as man and woman. This sexual differentiation has been determined by the Creator and expresses part of what is contained in the assertion that man is made in the image of God (Gen 1:27). In the biblical texts, the problem of body and soul as posed by Greek anthropology is totally absent (see *Body*, *Soul*). The entire man is created good. Therefore sexuality too as a gift of God is wholly acceptable. Although any projection of a sexual difference on God and the Trinity is inadmissible, the relationship of man and woman united in love reflects something of God's love, in its free giving of itself, and of the unity within the Divine Trinity. In the Yahwist account of creation, the first action of God, in a world seen from a thoroughly anthropocentric viewpoint, is to create man and refer him to an opposite (Gen 2:18–24). Man and woman are to (help) complete each

other through communication with the person who is the partner of the opposite sex. Before man comes to the divine "You", he has already met his human partner. The similarity of sound in the Hebrew terms *ish* (man) and *isha* (woman) could be seen as already pointing to the fact that in this "partnership" there is fundamentally no subordination and superiority. The basis of the poetic, pictorial account of the creation of Eve from the rib of the man is the actual fact of *eros*, the primal experience of the attraction of the sexes to each other. The "two-in-one-flesh" connotes indeed more than a merely passing sexual relationship of man and woman; it expresses the total unity which both form, breaking through even the bonds of blood and family (Gen 2:22–24). Christ was to take up this expression later and base on it his demand for the indissolubility of marriage (Mk 10:6–9). The total surrender in the sexual act is termed in the OT "knowing". In this profound interpersonal meeting both partners reveal themselves in their deepest personal sphere of intimacy; irreversible knowledge and self-revelation come about. But beyond this, man receives from God in principle the responsibility of the transmission of life (Gen 1:28). According to the teaching of the Yahwist, sin not only roused the anger of God, but also caused a disturbance of the order in creation and of the relationship between the sexes. The man, called to account for his insubordinate behaviour, places the blame on his partner (Gen 3:12). The disturbance which sin brought into personal relationships affects the sexual sphere too, within which these relationships come to their most profound realization. Along with this basic teaching, the Yahwist endeavours to give a more exact description of the "wounding" consequent on man's sin, referring among other things to certain aspects of life, conditioned by the cultural environment of the times, which were regarded as an evil and therefore looked on as the consequence of original sin and resulting from human guilt: the desire of the woman for the man, that is, *eros*, as well as the domination of the man over the woman, that is, the patriarchalism obtaining in Israel (Gen 3:6). Also the experience, partly attributable to cultural conditions, of the limits set by modesty in regard to nudity is given a theological significance: the casual naturalness of human relationships is lost (Gen 3:7). Man experiences his nudity as a personal exposure (J. B. Metz).

b) The NT takes up a natural attitude to sexuality and nowhere connects it with the ritual laws of purification of the OT. The ritual laws obtaining in this matter are expressly rejected by Jesus and replaced by a fundamentally new concept of purity (the right intention coming from the heart) (Mk 7:1–23). Through the proclamation of the Kingdom of God now beginning in Jesus, however, the eschatological condition of man is emphasized to such an extent that sexuality and its fulfilment in marriage no longer appear as the only normal or universal way for man in this world; the way of virginity appears beside it as a genuine possibility (Lk 20:27–36). Seen in the religious perspective of salvation-history, sexuality seems somehow left in suspense. In the relationship to Christ, the difference of the sexes becomes a matter of indifference (of like value) (Gal 3:26–28). Following the contemporary evaluation of human sexuality, however, St. Paul was unable to recognize its entire scale of variations and the full richness of marriage; thus in regard to the significance of *eros* he remains more or less insensitive (cf. 1 Cor 7). Yet in general the biblical references to man and his sexuality are very open to the changed understanding of reality in our times; they offer at least in their basic kerygmatic content no encouragement to a dualistic, Manicheistic contempt for sexuality and for a repression of the sexual powers.

2. *Anthropological analysis.* a) A personal anthropology, viewing man in his totality, is nowadays at pains to grasp the meaning of sexuality, not only in the biological sense but in its entirety and to give it its proper place in the total structure of the human person. The sexual difference between man and woman is a constitutive part of human nature; it finds expression in the psychological make-up of the person and may not therefore be regarded in isolation nor in a merely functional way. Everybody lives in the sexual situation, male or female. Sexuality is not something added on to a neutral human nature, but determines the person as man or as woman. Nevertheless one must be cautious in the use of categories such as "the virile" or the "eternal feminine"; for the sociologists (H. Schelsky) point to the extremely varied range of expressions of the female or male role in the different cultural spheres. For the development of human personality, sexuality is of considerable significance. Long before marriage, one comes into the field of force of one's sexuality and is moulded by it. The unmarried person also remains a sexual being. Thus sexuality must be dealt with not only in relation to marriage; it has a place in all anthropology.

b) The fact that the full man is neither the man nor the woman as such but only man and woman – with due respect for their individual development, but in full equality – points to an essential need for communication with the partner. Only in the differentiation between man and woman can therefore the human potentialities and roles be realized to the full. In sexuality man experiences his insufficiency and his dependence on the "You" of the other – and that, first of all, on the human plane: on the partner of the opposite sex. Inasmuch, however, as sexuality, even when finding its realization and fulfilment in marriage, is still lacking an ultimate fulfilment, it points beyond to something outside the human life-partner. The theologian sees in this a point of contact for the orientation of man to God and his dependence on him. Man achieves the deepest fulfilment only in the meeting with the "You" of God; but this is in final analysis an eschatological fact. This Christian understanding of man as one "called" by God and with a "calling" to fulfilment with God makes possible for the Christian a deeper view and evaluation of human factors and permits him to come to a certain understanding of the transcendental relationship of man through the lack of entire fulfilment in human sexuality.

c) Since sex is grounded in the centre of the human personality, its actuation affects the entire person. Thus the actual primary sex relationships, if they are to correspond to the nature and dignity of man, must always be contained in the framework of *eros*, in the affection and love which is directed to the entire person of the other, and accepts the other not merely for the sake of one's own need (*eros*), but also loves them in themselves as persons (*philia*) and accepts them in their totality. But this acceptance will correspond fully to the dignity of the other person only if it takes place not merely egocentrically in a narcissistic self-love, but is joined to a love (*agape*) which gives itself, is prepared to make sacrifices and is directed to the "You" of the other, a love which is ultimately a weak reflection of that love of God for man which entirely offers and gives itself. Precisely because human sexuality is not directed by instinct as is animal sexuality, but remains "plastic" (Gehlen, Schelsky), it calls for a formation in *philia* and *agape*. Where this is absent, where sex and *eros* become separated from the personal, and sexual activity is no longer the means and expression of personal attachment, but sought for its own sake, it loses its natural meaning and legitimacy. Precisely in its indefiniteness as far as natural instinct is concerned and in its openness to formation is expressed the specific nature of human sexuality; its superiority, but also its fragility. To this extent sexuality stands entirely at the service of the personal and must not be separated from it. Sex and *eros* therefore demand a formation through *philia* and an integration in *agape*.

d) The deep personal effect of the sexual act already indicated in the Bible and experienced in life, demands also its acceptance and corresponding integration in the entire human life. The completion of the total sexual self-giving leads to "the giving and receiving of a knowledge and completion which affect the entire person. Where such knowledge and completion take place, those involved cannot part as though nothing had happened. But neither can they enter the total life in common which makes it possible, unless the irrevocable will to share their entire life is present and is expressed in a binding way and accepted by both sides" (Auer). Thus, inasmuch as the sexual act is the expression of the unity of both partners and their total mutual love and acceptance and is capable of bestowing a knowledge which has a most fundamental formative effect, the indispensable prerequisite for its legitimacy is the mutual and publicly proclaimed will to a binding acceptance which is total and permanent. Thus only in validly contracted monogamy is the full meaning of such a self-giving secured.

e) When sex breaks away from the totality of human love, in the attempt to be autonomous and a law unto itself, man experiences "the effects of sin", the dissolution of the inner harmony. Sexuality, valued and activated for its own sake, leads to disrespect for the partner, who is degraded to be the object of one's own satisfaction and therefore deeply wounded in his dignity. Where sex is separated from the personal, it begins a vagabond life; there appears then no reason why the "partner" should not be changed at will. All promiscuity, all sexual chaos, is a sign of a personal crisis on the part of the one concerned.

3. *Formation of sexuality: sublimation.* The enormous excess of energy contained in the sexual drive and the plasticity of human sexuality indicate that man has the capability of putting these powers at the service of further human purposes, of sublimating them. This redirection does not imply a repression of the sexual impulses but rather a positive reapplication of them for other spheres of fulfilment in life. S. Freud describes sublimation as a change in the goal as well as in the object of the drive, so that what "was originally a sexual drive finds a fulfilment that is no longer sexual but has a social or higher ethical value". Freud sees sublimation as the de-sexualization and also the socialization of this drive. Precisely the freely chosen and inwardly accepted sacrifice of the actualization of sexuality, when it represents not a false repression but a genuine acceptance and re-formation of these drives, permits the release of great energies of mind and body which can express themselves in significant achievements of a charitable, religious or cultural nature. "Sublimation is therefore not a mysterious, automatic transformation of sexual impulses into spiritual drives, but the reorganization into a more widely inclusive human attitude" (Auer). It presents itself for everyone as a task and is a prerequisite for the maturing of personality as also for the success of all interpersonal communication. The special nature of human sexuality and the dynamism it contains make it imperative for man that he should not drift in this matter but should provide for a formation and discipline of these powers. A. Thielicke presents it in the following proportions: "The more I am controlled by instinctual drives, the less I seek the unique, unmistakable 'You' of the other and the

more I am concerned with the mere unit, the mere numerical 'specimen' of the other sex, to whose individual qualities I am indifferent but whose instrumental significance is thereby all the more important for me." Where no genuine formation of this drive takes place, but only a containment of repression, the road to personal maturity remains blocked, and this can lead ultimately to false attitudes, reactive overcompensations or perversions.

4. *Consequences for moral behaviour.* a) The right evaluation of sexuality demands, first of all, a firm acceptance of one's own sexuality and its development, as well as a knowledge of the power and inner dynamism of sex and *eros*, of the danger of false repressions, and of the place of true sublimation of these powers. Hence the encounter with the partner of the opposite sex cannot be treated casually. In correct companionship, which is also incumbent on the unmarried, important forces in both man and woman are released which help towards an integration of the entire sexual faculty and preserve from dangerous repressions. The theological understanding of the two sexes of man explains the importance of *eros* for the maturing of the total personality and for all interpersonal relations. Since all erotic relationships connote a mutual personal self-revelation and a certain surrender, they should take place only in full knowledge of this responsibility, i.e., in remote or proximate preparation for marriage.

b) A right attitude to sexuality forbids all prudery and all exhibitionism; it calls for an acceptance of the sense of modesty. Stress should be laid especially on the total human implication of modesty, namely to protect the intimate personal sphere from unjustified intrusion. While the sense of modesty pertains very essentially to man in his state of threatened dignity, yet the limits of what is included in detail under modesty cannot be determined merely on Christian or religious grounds; it depends very considerably as well on the particular cultural tradition and on what precisely is likely to endanger the intimate sphere of the person. In view of possible developments in the pluralistic society, it will be necessary, without falling victim to nudism, to give careful consideration to the question of training in a casual acceptance of the presence of nudity.

c) Since maturity to full personality and to the necessary integration of the sexual powers takes place only slowly and in separate phases, the question arises whether in this sphere too, that is, in the achievement of personal sexual harmony, there may be various stages. May one set limited objectives – or must everything be demanded at once? This implicitly raises the question whether in the sixth commandment there can be *materia levis* in the matter of unchastity. Traditional moral theology has given a negative answer here, without convincing reasons. Unchastity has been reckoned a sin *ex toto genere suo gravis*, which – provided it is committed freely and consciously – never permits of objective levity of matter. In this teaching expression is given to the experience that all freely sought sexual activity develops an inner dynamism which all too easily impels to an egoistic, narcissistic satisfaction of one's sexual impulse. The so-called "*materia gravis* teaching" stems from a time when the sense of true personal love and of *eros* and *philia* had not yet developed, and all erotic encounter was measured in terms of its sexual dynamism. It would be better to reinterpret this teaching that every offence against the sixth commandment is an objectively serious sin, a teaching nowadays rejected by very many theologians, in the sense that sexuality possesses for personal human development and for integration into human society such a decisive significance, that its theoretical or practical rejection in principle entails a serious disorder and thus is to be reckoned as an objectively serious offence against the structure of human existence and action. With regard to the question of guilt, one must also take into consideration, when dealing with offences against the sixth commandment, the modern knowledge coming from depth psychology, and an *imperfectio actus* may frequently be assumed in consequence of disturbance in mind or will. The judgment of individual failures may not therefore be made without taking cognizance of the total basic attitude and intention of the person concerned.

d) Both repression of natural desire for pleasure as well as a hedonistic, auto-erotic acceptance of sex are to be rejected as false forms of behaviour. The same is true of pre-marital sexual intercourse: it could create a disturbance in the psychic balance of the future husband and wife. Pre-marital continence will therefore retain an importance that is not to be underestimated for the maturing of personality and preparation for marriage. A change in the attitude of the Church so as to favour pre-marital intercourse is not to be expected; this would essentially mar the concept of marriage. The step to promiscuity would then be a minor one. Because of the eminently super-individual significance of sex, all cultures, although in different degrees, have been concerned to set up some norms for sexual behaviour. Both a functional devaluation and a magical exaggeration of sex in modern society could be countered on human and Christian lines by a right personal acceptance of sexuality (Weber). But such a considered acceptance of personal sexuality already presupposes a certain view of the world and of man.

Johannes Gründel

II. Sexual Education

1. *Its nature and problems.* a) Sexual education can be fruitfully given only in a general framework of moral and personal education. It can neither be value-free nor independent of a determinate view of life, and it presupposes a right attitude to human sexuality. In this there is question, not so much of a moralizing enunciation of the relevant norms, but rather of every form of assistance needed by young people in process of coming to maturity. A form of sexual education which does not concern itself with the question of its own meaning and purpose is a negation of education. Any creation either of taboos or of a false mystique of sexuality should give way to factual communication of the necessary knowledge and an open yet thorough introduction to the important questions of human living, to the significance of sexuality for the development of one's own personality and for personal and social relationships, and in general to the questions of love and marriage. In this there is need for a synthesis of the important questions of living in the light of Christian revelation.

b) Depth psychology forbids us to regard the sexual merely as an autonomous system within the total personality, much as digestion or metabolism; it pertains rather to human nature as such. Therefore the entire human formation and maturity depend to a great extent on the right ordering of the sexual. Any evaluation of the sexual powers which classes them as merely functional, any arbitrary cultivation or isolated enjoyment or use of sexual appetite is therefore to be rejected. Such a cultivation nowadays must be regarded as a one-sided reaction to the negative sexual morality of former times. If sexuality is simply treated from a purely biological, psychological or sociological point of view, little is done for its integration into the person. Any isolated treatment proves disastrous here, because a sexuality that is not properly integrated can through the dynamism of instinct be socially very dangerous.

c) The problem of modern sexual education involves also in every case the confrontation of two different generations.

2. *Starting-point and purpose.* a) The starting-point and purpose of sexual education is the unity of sexuality and *eros*, of personal love and responsibility of the partners for one another and before society. From *eros*, which is understood as love directed towards the person and encompassing the other person as a totality, arises in the final analysis the preparedness for the permanency of the personal union of love, the effective capacity in fact for marriage. Mere sexuality and the isolated sexual act lack this personal *eros* and involve a degradation of the love between man and woman.

b) For the Christian a true sexual education demands that account be taken of the Christian concept of man and ot the Christian ethos of love and marriage. The approach to sexual education will include consideration of salvation-history in its revelations about sin, the need for redemption and the actual redemption and sanctification of man, insofar as they shape the Christian concept of man. Any undue rejection, but also any magical over-emphasis of the sexual, is to be avoided. Neither a pessimistic view of man, in the sense of a totally corrupted nature, nor a naturalism coupled with a naive belief in progress corresponds to the Christian evaluation of man and his sexuality. While upholding a natural, open and healthy attitude to sex, every Christian knows that this sphere too remains endangered by the sinfulness of man.

c) An education directed towards the right ordering of the sexual must be a learning of values. Every increase in surplus sexual energies demands further sublimation, so the adolescent must be provided with increasing help to regulate his drives. Therefore a deepening of the sense of the dignity of the person is an absolute necessity. In final analysis the aim of a proper sexual education is to make one capable of personal loving contact, with the readiness to assume responsibility for oneself, for the partner and for the new life which may arise.

The young person should also be helped to a critical awareness of the various possible meanings of the word "love", because every meeting of the sexes presupposes a certain degree of maturity.

3. *Methods and "instruction".* a) Sexual maturity depends on the total personal formation and on the life-story of each individual from the pre-genital phase on, on the educative atmosphere of trust within his environment, on the way in which the mother treats the child and on the love existing in the family. Sexual education must be given in proper stages. Following the insights of Freud, according to which significance must be attached even to the stirrings of libido in the early years of childhood, the attempt must be made to adapt education to the sexual development in childhood, in youthful years and especially in the years of puberty. And according to each child's capability of assimilating it, care will be taken to give the knowledge suitable to each phase. All untruthfulness in relation to the child's instruction (the story of the stork) as well as all prudishness are contrary to serious sexual education and will take their toll in the course of the child's development. The giving of group instruction on sexual functions creates problems if it is confined to the presentation of purely physical and biological information and does not take account of the formation and training of the entire person. Only knowledge which remains encompassed by the total education can help towards the development of the human person taken in his entirety. A competent sexual instruction should have reached a relatively complete stage at the beginning of puberty, that is, before the first pollution or menstruation.

b) Yet mere information is insufficient. The term "sex instruction" often covers a questionable optimism in the matter of giving factual information on the biological and physiological realities. Inasmuch as it concerns the education of the entire human being, sexual education should not be understood merely as "the facts of life". It is precisely the Christian appreciation of man, of his bodily nature and his sexuality, which forbids us to separate the sexual from personal responsibility. The drive of sexual powers, the absence of secure control arising from instinct and the tendency to excess mean that constant effort is needed to integrate these powers in the total personality. If this formation of the sexual powers is not to have a repressive character but is to be an education to love, rightly understood, it will succeed only if it is associated with a certain asceticism in the sense of an integration of the instincts which open the way to true human encounter. The marital relationship of love between man and wife also will be successful only if it has gone through a period of sexual reserve. As long as a sympathetic insight into the meaning and purpose of sexuality is not yet possible for a young person, there is definite need for a corresponding protection and for direction. Along the way towards a proper ordering and formation of the sexual powers there will undoubtedly be stages of development and maturity. A refined form of casuistry will not be capable of determining what in the individual case is right and good or what is contrary to right order, bad and accordingly sinful (see III below). While it is important, in the case of young people, in view of the sudden eruption of the sexual drive, not to over-dramatize and not to speak too quickly of sin in autoerotic behaviour, yet the person in question should be helped to see the "summons" contained in such behaviour. Otherwise a false narcissistic fixation could be carried on even into later years and the young person would find it more difficult to break out of his preoccupation with self and to come to a genuine encounter with the other partner. The release from an infantile egoism demands the rejection of certain projections of unconscious models, especially those of the parent of the opposite sex. If autoerotic behaviour is carried on excessively into the years after puberty, it can be a symptom of a crisis in personality or the expression of an infantile and neurotic character.

4. *Agents*. a) The onus of giving proper sexual education falls in the first instance on the parents. In a healthy atmosphere they must respond again and again to the child's need for information and, with constant reference to knowledge already given, prepare their child for its physical and mental changes. The frequently observed inhibitions and difficulties of parents in finding the right words for instructing their children are probably grounded on the fact of experience that the deepest feeling of community between man and wife in the sexual act of marriage remains under the veil of modesty and intimacy, and, as that which is really to be lived and experienced, cannot be articulated. However, too great inhibitions can lead in time to the creation of taboos which have a paralysing effect on the confidence between parents and children.

b) The school too will in the framework of its own work of education be concerned to carry further the knowledge already gained. But the sexual education it provides should be regarded as to a great extent subsidiary. It seems questionable to demand sexual education as a specific school subject, for this is a problem concerning the entire person, which is to be dealt with not only in the sphere of biology but also in other subjects – not least in the framework of religious instruction.

Johannes Gründel

III. Sexual Morality

Sexual morality is to be regarded as part of Christian ethics and moral theology; it attempts to explain the purpose and task of human sexuality as well as the moral significance of interpersonal relations, insofar as they affect man in his sexual nature and are of an erotic and sexual character. Human sexuality cannot, however, be rightly explained in terms of finality, but rather from a personal evaluation of man and his relationships. Therefore sexual morality must take its place within Christian moral teaching as a whole and must not be taken in isolation from it as an independent entity.

1. *The traditional sexual morality.* a) The traditional Christian sexual morality was largely based on a narrow view of human sexuality; it was characterized by a predominance of the functional aspect. The significance of sexuality was measured chiefly, and sometimes even exclusively, from the point of view of conception. Thus marriage was seen as the proper place for the actuation of sexuality, since in it the purpose of sexuality, the conception and education of children, is best achieved. For all other spheres of life outside marriage, prohibitions and the injunction to practise continence were the only rules for sexual behaviour.

b) This understanding of human sexuality is based on an approach that is biological in a one-sided way. This approach, under the influence of extra-Christian lines of thought, especially concepts of natural law deriving from Stoicism and from Roman jurisprudence, attempted to derive a norm for human sexuality from the sexual behaviour of animals, bound as they are to definite periods of sexual activity. Besides this, theories deriving from Gnosticism and Manichaeism and the Stoic suspicion of sexual pleasure and desire gained ground, partly unconsciously and partly openly, within the Christian concept of sexual morality. Although Augustine emphasized the natural goodness of marriage and the holiness attached to it by God, yet under his influence the foundation was laid for a sexual pessimism which was to last for centuries. Under the influence of Judaizing Christians, OT ritual purity prescriptions too found entry into sexual morality. At a later period the physiological structure or the "nature of the marriage act" became the normative guideline for sexual behaviour. Even when an attempt was made to establish further "ends of marriage" and marriage was regarded as a "remedy for sexual desire", yet the biological basis in the conception theory offered no possibility of seeing human sexuality as a value in itself, in its character as a sign and expression of human love and affection and in its foundation in the human person.

c) An over-valuation, lasting into the 19th century, of the male sperm, following the line of Greek biology, knowing nothing of female ovulation and regarding the sperm as already containing the full human life, caused every wilful ejaculation of male seed not leading to conception to be looked on as a moral offence akin to murder. It is significant that, in reliance on Augustine, a "biblical proof" for this was drawn from the account in Gen 38:8–10, according to which Onan neglects his obligation of levirate marriage and is punished by God with death for preventing conception. In this it was overlooked that the intention of the marriage of the brother-in-law was messianic and that the real reason for Onan's punishment was not a sexual offence. Even today the frequently used term "Onanism" for the interruption of the marital act or for masturbation is a relic of this false interpretation.

Inasmuch as extra-Christian influences of these kinds found entry into sexual morality and led to a falsification of Christian ethics, a critical revision of the hitherto accepted tradition seems called for. As well as this, however, the questions of the meaning and purpose of sexual behaviour must be answered anew today and new ideals must be sought for right action in the sexual sphere. These should continue to be determined along the lines of Christian freedom rightly understood, together with the acceptance and formation of one's own sexuality and the responsible entry into interpersonal relations of this kind in the spirit of true Christian love. The Christian will reject in the sexual sphere any trace of contempt for *eros* and sensual desire, all false asceticism and tactics of mere repression, but also every hedonistic one-sided deification of *eros* and of sexual desire.

2. *The "sexual revolution"*. a) The words "sexual revolution" relate to a powerful change that is taking place in our times. Yet it is not merely that, in reaction to a traditional form of Christian morality no longer found convincing, outmoded norms are simply being abandoned and taboos swept aside. Other obligations of more far-reaching significance are becoming the focus of man's attention, as, for example, the rejection of a false repression of sexuality and the demand for a genuine personalization of sexual relations.

b) Sometimes, it is true, the sexual revolution is taken to refer to the theories of those ideologists who, with an optimism that can only be called naive, champion a glorification of sexual desire and expect an uninhibited satisfaction of instincts to result in the disappearance of every form of aggression and in the fulfilment of human living. A. Kinsey – and some biologists and sociologists influenced by him, who in opposition to the compulsion of norms make themselves the champions of sexual realism – strive through lessening the difference between man's scale of norms and his concrete behaviour to achieve sexual relaxation with the hope of lessening thereby social conflict.

c) Wherever "sexual revolution", so understood, disassociates sexuality from the body-spirit unity of the person and submits it to the arbitrary choice and wishes of the individual and to the pleasure of the moment, one has left the realm of sexual morality for that of amorality. An unrestrained sexual promiscuity which rejects all order and all restraints and which leads to a depersonalization, where sexual activity is equated to the needs of eating and drinking, entirely disregarding the facts of personal relationship, reduces sexuality to a matter of supply and demand. Sexual intercourse then takes place merely for satisfaction and pleasure "because it is fun". But where sexuality sinks to the level of consumption goods, it causes a destruction of the unity of sex and *eros* and thus also a loss of meaning in human behaviour which can lead to a disastrous brutalization of sexuality in our society. Every such dehumanization of sexuality renders man incapable of true personal relationships, of a fully human love, incapable of marriage and thus becomes a serious factor in the dehumanization of society (Wendland).

d) The sexual revolution is not to be countered by mere moral prescriptions but through a new understanding of personal love and marriage such as can open for man a way worthy of a human being. Besides this the Christian will allow his concept of man and his understanding of love to be determined by revelation.

3. *Nature and purpose of human sexuality*. a) There is general agreement on the need for giving form and direction to man's sexual instincts, not, however, on the criteria for providing us with norms of sexual morality. The factors making for morality in sexual activity rest neither on a purely biological foundation nor on any tendency towards development, nor can they be satisfactorily derived from existing behaviour patterns nor from a purely abstract con-

cept of human nature. They must be derived from the personal, social and anthropological aspects of man. Just as in the case of sexual education, so too sexual morality presupposes a total view of the meaning and purpose of man and his sexuality. With this question of meaning is connected the question as to the nature and dignity of man, the significance of the human person, his social and religious relationships and the sum-total of his obligations. The Christian cannot answer it without the revealed truths of faith.

b) Any explanation of the meaning of human sexuality must also take into account the newly gained insights of the empirical sciences, especially behavioural research and the convergence and divergence of human and animal sexuality. Precisely the specific qualities of human sexuality, its continuous activity outside the mating seasons, the possibility of isolation of sexual desire from conception, the generalized and uncertain nature of human instincts and the consequent possibility of sexual excess, demand for social living, if it is to be human and worthy of human beings, an organic control of the heightened sexual energies. They point to the need for institutionally supported direction and order in sexual relationships. This is but another instance of man's need of education.

c) That nature should be allowed to rule cannot be taken as the norm and purpose of morality, as an outdated sexual morality would have it; nor is the neutralizing but rather the humanization of sexuality the task of man. Therefore sexuality cannot and may not become purely the means to private satisfaction of instinct nor a sort of easily available drug. It gives man a goal beyond himself. In the measure in which sexuality falls into rightly ordered human relationships, and at the same time has regard to its responsibility to one's neighbour, to society and to man's future, it will be successfully "humanized". The liberation of man from his ego in its isolation, the effort towards solidarity, is a necessary step to his becoming himself in a genuine sense.

d) Man in his character as partner in a dialogue, as Christian revelation also sees him, can never meaningfully actuate his sexuality if he sees in it only a purely egocentric value; he must see it in terms of partnership. If he is himself to become a person and rightly develop his own being, the other person is an essential precondition. It is precisely here that man experiences his dependence on the community. Sexuality enables man to put himself and allow himself to be at the disposal of a partner of the opposite sex. "It has the purpose, through this communication, of bringing one's own personality and that of the other partner to their highest perfection. If this dedication is directed at anything less than the total person of the other, there is an incomplete fulfilment of the sexual personality structure" (K. Ruf). Giving and acceptance in an exclusive sense are therefore presupposed if the actuation of sexuality is to experience its full meaning.

4. *The social aspect of sexuality.* a) Although sexuality is to be regarded as a basic structure of the human personality, yet its social aspect ought not to be overlooked. It is the expression of relationship to the other person. Man can fulfil his own existence only in experiencing acceptance by another person. Sex and *eros* are not merely something individual and personal, they are as well both public and intimate in character. The sexual has accordingly been left in no society to the arbitrary will of the private individual; it has been subjected to social norms. Sexual morality is always social morality, for sexual behaviour has its presuppositions and conditions in the framework of society and its changes. The social aspect of sexuality demands that the needs of the community should also be taken into account.

b) The process of genuine formation and sublimation of the sexual powers leads to a certain de-sexualization and socialization of the instincts. If this is neglected, man's capability for love runs the risk of being subjected to a narcissistic fixation or of being entirely destroyed by uncontrolled instincts. Neither short-sighted repression nor naively accepted satisfaction of these instincts is a help towards human development.

c) If the personal basis and the social aspect of sexuality are not taken seriously, sexual behaviour is directed to the partner in a merely functional way – for the purpose of conception or for the satisfaction of desire. This amounts to a perverting of the sexual powers. This prevents them from attaining to their full meaning because a fleeting encounter is unable to take seriously the other person's true needs.

5. *The establishment of norms of sexual morality.* a) At the present time the question of how to establish norms anthropologically and theologically is the principal focus of interest in sexual morality. Ethnology has shown that the individual normative systems are relative and culturally conditioned in their content. Modern man too no longer accepts unquestioningly the norms presented to him by an authority or community; he wants to know the grounds for their claim to legitimacy. Precisely in the sphere of sexuality he feels himself hedged in by far too many norms, some of them alien to the matter in question. On the other hand sociological and anthropological studies of culture continue to emphasize the basic need for human behavioural norms for guiding the natural instinctual powers and relieving them of burdens, and for ensuring human freedom. This task was and is to a great extent performed by the social order whereby the generally accepted value judgments, the moral and juridical laws, embody an order which is constantly in the process of being re-established. They are the expression of an experience, and a regulative force constructed by the various groups, but are undoubtedly conditioned by the period in which they are established.

b) Neither is Christian sexual morality in a position to derive an absolutely unchangeable system of concrete moral norms from the revelation of the NT preached by the Church, as its most profound source of morality. Rather will it endeavour, by constantly examining present norms in the light of revelation, to bring the manner of life in regard to sexuality into conformity with personal needs. The question of the meaning and purpose of human life and human sexuality must be constantly considered and answered anew from the Christian point of view. This will provide the morally relevant judgments which are derived from the basic structure of man's being and behaviour, or from the nature of man, whereby a system of moral norms is attained which is not rigid but appropriate to the needs of the times, being in keeping with a dynamic and historical understanding of natural law to which a new approach has been made by modern theology.

c) Besides this, the insights of the empirical sciences must be taken into account, insofar as they are morally relevant, as well as the concrete experience of people's moral activity. The norms and guidelines of sexual morality are thus to be arrived at neither entirely deductively nor purely inductively but in a constant dialectic between the two methods.

d) Yet those who content themselves with a morality derived purely from what is done and find their norms in "the normative power of the factual" forgo in the last analysis any purpose for sexual morality and any genuine education of man. They overlook the fact that man quite clearly has the capability and the task of actively shaping his development. Both the reality of the factual situation as well as what is possible and necessary are to be taken into account. But the factual behaviour must be questioned as to its normative content; where it is the expression of an inner conviction, the result of an ethos, it cannot be simply disregarded; it is the expression, if often in an over-simplified way, of a justifiable viewpoint. In this context a certain significance in the matter of finding norms must also be attached to statistics.

6. *The Christian command of love.* a) That the command of love is also universally applicable in the domain of sexual morality, and indeed precisely there, is questioned. The only problem lies in the content of its fulfilment. In the sacrificial and redemptive love of God for mankind in Jesus Christ the revelation of the NT provides the model and prototype of the *agape* which must be for the Christian the example and standard for all human love. Sex and *eros* find in *agape* their personal and religious integration and meaning. The testimonies of revelation proclaim that human love must be essentially characterized by altruism. Hence an egocentric narcissistic love is radically condemned by Christianity. Every erotic and sexual love which does not have the backing of the total person, which is therefore not prepared to take on responsibility and obligations, cannot be regarded as genuine love. The Christian must constantly measure the relationships to his partner and the claims made on his love against the radicality of the Christian understanding of love. The purification of *eros* through *agape*, that Christian love whose precise nature it is to preserve man from false self-seeking and false surrender to self, and which has as its model and example Christ's self-sacrificing love, remains a life task.

b) For the Christian a still deeper significance of sex, as an element in the history of salvation, is to be found in the fact that man looks to the other person for the formation of his own personality and hence enters into an exclusive and irrevocable union involving the sharing of life's experience and destiny. He thereby creates the precondition for the effectiveness of Christ's salvific action. In marriage one partner becomes the mediator in the salvation of the other. Thus sexuality never possesses a value in itself, but receives it only in becoming the expression of the human will and purpose as a whole.

c) For the Christian, sexuality and marriage acquire a certain relativity seen in the light of eschatology, "for when they arise from the dead men and women do not marry" (Mk 12:25). This is the eschatological attitude of reserve which gives meaning to a decision in favour of abstention from marriage based on freedom and charism, and gives that decision its rightful place; it finds its expression in the particular forms of virginity and celibacy.

d) The radicality of the Christian demand of love appears, however, in the individual case to be an excessive demand if its nature as a gift (as also its character as a "forgiveness" and a grace) is not taken into account. Man has graciously to accept much; in the faith he can be sure of forgiveness for his failings and his tardiness in pursuit of the goal. The thought of forgiveness (cf. Jn 8:1–11) and grace gives balance to the lofty moral demand of Christian love. This demand will then not be felt to be excessive and will not tend to create a neurosis; it will rather have a liberating effect. No matter how much in the course of time sexual morality will again and again adjust to the forms of society, it remains forever confronted with the gospel and is subject to critical judgment in the light of the gospel.

7. *The basic moral attitude.* a) Man's inner readiness to accept his sexuality and assume the role specific to his sex, but also to recognize his own sexual powers in their total personal and social character and to integrate them into the

whole of life in all its aspects – this is what is traditionally known as chastity. Nowadays, however, the concept has for the most part lost its positive connotations. These should be restored, since chastity does not just mean "purity" or continence, but the striving after a right ordering and shaping of the sexual powers in the service of the human and social relations of partnership. The aim of chastity is to enable man to love in the personal way that is specific to the sexes and to prepare him to be rightly capable of marriage. Those alone are capable of marriage who are in the true sense capable of love.

b) Inasmuch as sexuality is not an autonomous system within the total personality but a basic human condition, not only is its denial or devaluation fraught with danger, but just as much every exaggeration or isolation, any concept of man, therefore, which so emphasizes the biological and animal sphere at the expense of the development of the personal and spiritual that man is regarded only as a sexual being. Precisely such a basic attitude would be unchaste because a purely functional gradation of values of the sexual powers very soon leads man to claim the right to an isolated enjoyment of sex, to an outlet for the satisfaction of the demands of instinct, to experiments and training in sexual activity, and to indulgence in sex to the extreme of satiety. Such an emancipation of instinct can easily result in a degrading of the partner to a mere object of one's own desires, while merely attempting to avoid serious conflicts by means of purely extrinsic rules of behaviour, e.g.: never hurt the feelings of the other and never conceive an unwanted child (A. Comfort).

c) Unchastity should not be described in a purely functional way, as "misuse" of the sexual powers. It includes every attitude which is not prepared to recognize sexuality in its roots in the total personality and to integrate it in a meaningful way in the entirety of human life, even if this attitude has not yet led to misuse of the sexual powers. Also a one-sidedly biological value-free approach to sexuality must be regarded as unchaste as soon as it lays claim to exclusiveness, that is, as soon as it is seen to be a *pars pro toto* ideology.

d) If, however, the proper basic attitude is present and if it is constantly striven after, even with individual lapses, one can rightly speak of chastity; for the virtue is entirely lost only by an abandonment of the purpose or basic attitude (cf. the Thomist distinction between *incontinentia*, the individual fault or incontinence, and *intemperantia*, intemperance in the sense of unchastity).

8. *Honesty in individual behaviour.* a) For sexual relations honesty is called for above all else. Honesty demands that the individual is sincere with himself and his partner, that he "does not present false hopes, expectations or claims" (Trillhaas). Whoever by appealing to nature seeks an outlet for the unbridled exercise of his passions and instincts, takes neither himself nor his partner seriously as human beings.

b) In this the symbolic nature of the modes of sexual behaviour should be considered individually. Sexual behaviour gets its meaning from the significance which is attached to the individual symbol. It is true that the function of the individual symbols will change according to custom and to the reactions of each person, yet the highest form of bodily union, sexual intercourse, should also be the expression of the highest form of personal union possible to man. This is achieved, however, only if it is also secured and supported by the will of both partners to a mutual bond. To this extent the basic requirement for a full and meaningful exercise of sexual self-giving is the full and irrevocable acceptance of the partner as a person.

c) The experience of bodily pleasure springs from the deeper experience of security in the sharing of life together. It has an ecstatic character. Not the greatest possible sexual pleasure in the orgasm, but the experience of union of two persons is the goal and expression of fulfilment in human sexuality. Inasmuch as the experience of pleasure has only a momentary character and disappears more quickly on the physical level than in mental experience, sexuality urges to repetition. The sign strives for repeated expression, yet it achieves only a premonition of a final and definitive completion which remains as a promise to both partners. If sexuality is regarded as part of the structure of the human person, then its ultimate meaning will not be attained by a merely physical experience of pleasure nor through a temporary personal harmony in the sense of a loving understanding, but only inasmuch as in the mutual acceptance of obligation, it is encompassed in the common responsibility for each other and in the form of a self-giving love shaped by *agape*.

d) Even if the partner declares himself fully in agreement with an uncommitted use of sex in the form of pre-marital or extra-marital intercourse, yet this in fact goes contrary to the meaning expressed in the act. To be sure there are innumerable people who in their use of sex do not come to a knowledge of the uninterchangeable uniqueness of the partner, nor to the experience of a mutual bond and belonging, since they are too selfish to have the openness or attentiveness needed for a genuine love directed to a partner. The wish to belong to the partner "for ever and always" does not even arise in these cases. Yet without a total will to bind oneself no full responsibility for the partner and for the children who may be born of this love can be assumed. Self-giving in this case easily turns to self-surrender. If the sexual act is to be the comprehensive symbol of full mutual love and self-giving, the person too must be fully behind it in knowledge and will. In view of the radical demands of love in the NT all pre-marital and extra-marital sexual intercourse remains therefore wrong and irresponsible (F. Böckle). The significance of sexuality for all mankind and social responsibility give society too a right to a voice in the regulation of the marriage bond. But it will not always be possible to determine juridically the actual beginning of marriage.

e) Since every healthy adolescent and adult comes within the sphere of influence of sexuality, the question arises for sexual morality whether and to what extent there exist certain stages of practical experience of one's own sexuality, different for different individuals, but which could be regarded as stages of development for the maturing person; further, what forms of sexual relationships on the way towards marriage are meaningful and therefore morally permissible. With regard to an evaluation of sexual excitement on a heterosexual basis as in certain kissing games, the question of meaning and moral permissibility cannot be answered by an elaborate casuistry. If fondling and "petting" are understood in the wider sense not as merely deliberately sought sexual satisfaction but as a testing of the erotic response of the partner and as an expression of love, they cannot be globally rejected but could have in certain circumstances a certain justification. However much it is the nature of young people to gather experience, yet the question of meaning and purpose should not be disregarded.

The following should be taken as a principle for pre-marital behaviour: as much physical expression and also erotic and sexually affected expression of love is meaningful and permitted as the individual is in fact inwardly prepared to give. There are very different degrees of extent of the possible bonds between two people, from mere passing or prolonged friendship to the enduring love which is characteristic of marriage. The possibility of self-deception, of the projection of *animus* or *anima* types, demands a corresponding self-criticism and openness for counselling by another. The right ordering and formation of sexuality remains a task of man all his life long; in this, sexual morality can only point to the goal towards which man is directed. Thus there can undoubtedly be certain phases of development and maturity.

9. *Defective forms of behaviour.* a) Insofar as human sexuality is essentially an expression of man's personal other-directedness and union, every sexual activity which is sought for its own sake or which goes beyond the union of mind and heart which is actually there, lacks its full meaning. It becomes a partial or even a false expression. The moral worth of such an activity is measured by the substantial personal value which is present in it. A sexual morality which sees in sexuality only the functions of pleasure and procreation (thus H. Kentler) has abandoned the personal foundation of sexuality and falls victim to an apersonal isolated evaluation of the sexual powers. The egocentricity or narcissism which regards the partner simply as an object of its own self-seeking or which does not see its own sexuality in its social aspect is clearly wrong.

b) A static ideal should not be the foundation for sexual education; one should recognize that there is essentially a development and that man experiences stages in which sexual integration still has the character of the imperfect, not entirely successful or complete. Further cases of defective behaviour should not be judged in an "atomizing" way; the life-story of each individual and his entire basic attitude and approach should be taken into account. For the young person there will be transitional periods of sexual behaviour which must be accepted and worked through. The tendency to repetition and gaining a habit and fixation in defective sexual behaviour should not, however, be overlooked.

c) It is precisely in the years of development that the young person's capability for loving is in danger of being fixed narcissistically or totally destroyed by uncontrolled instincts. Neither a hasty repression of the instincts nor a naively accepted satisfaction of instinctive desire is a help towards human maturity. Masturbation as a form of sexual satisfaction outside marriage, widely practised by young people, should be regarded to a great extent as a transitional phase of sexual development or a reaction to the tension of a strained atmosphere. Insofar as it is not a question of a neurotic fixation, over-dramatization should be avoided. Nevertheless it cannot be regarded as a fully proper form of sexual activity and cannot therefore be simply counselled.

d) The phenomenon of homosexuality can nowadays no longer be approached in a purely negative way. Dealing with homosexuals calls for some form of satisfactory "pastoral" solution. The homosexual is, more than others, indifferent to moral appeals, yet "a great number of them are quite willing and as capable within their limits of entering permanent and 'total' relationships as the 'normal' " (H. Ringeling). In this matter, it seems unimportant whether or to what extent such a trait can be inherited or only acquired. St. Paul condemned homosexuality as a symptom of man's original sin, in keeping with the view obtaining at that time of pederasty as a symptom of corruption and decadence. Where today, however, homosexuality appears more as a disease which cannot be simply "overcome" by moral efforts but seems rather to have an irreversible nature, the attempt will be made to help these people insofar as that is possible. Such a person undoubtedly seeks the totality of the other person, missing, however, the Christian form of encounter with the neighbour (Thielicke). Civil penalties for the practice of homosexuality will therefore be called for only where it is a case of seduction of young people and dependents, of offences against public morality and of the exploitation or homosexuality for profit.

10. *The question of guilt.* a) To answer the question of guilt in individual offences against the right order and use of the sexual powers, one must take into account the insights of depth psychology. Not infrequently they stem from a considerable diminution of knowledge and of free-will. As far as knowledge is concerned, the conditions of sexual tension impair and inhibit the activity of the brain cortex, the seat of mental processes. Reflection is lessened to a greater or lesser extent; the usual caution is forgotten and thought is more and more taken up with the sexual impulse. In such a condition one can no longer speak of clear knowledge. Such a person is also no longer fully clear as to the moral relevance and bearing of his action. The sexual process follows its own proper dynamism. Only after the sexual release from tension and the disappearance of the pressure on the cortex does the "fogging" of thought come to an end.

b) Seen from this point of view, it becomes clear that an isolated judgment of individual acts is necessarily insufficient, that instead it is essentially a question of the person's total basic attitude and approach. He who seeks the right order of the sexual and is aware of the dynamism of these powers will not incautiously expose himself to the "proximate occasion". Where, however, in spite of earnest endeavour – in some cases because of previous failure – he is simply once again "overcome", one should also be cautious with the assertion that the individual failure is a grave sin and in case of doubt decide "pro reo".

c) As far as the will is concerned, where there is a right basic attitude, that degree of maturity may often be absent which is necessary for full free consent of the will (a condition for grave fault), especially in the case of young people during puberty. One should not immediately regard every consent as a full consent of the will. It is often a question of an acceptance which indeed is needed in order that an act takes place but which is rather a surrender of a momentarily weaker will in face of the all too powerful sexual impulse. It makes a difference whether a person is seriously striving after the right ordering and integration of his sexual powers or is letting himself be carried along without making any real effort.

d) Decisive for the measure of the wrong attitude and in particular cases also for the gravity of the sin is the measure of the injured or counterfeited love that is involved in the sexual offence. A distinction must also be made in the sexual sphere between real sexual offences and the sexual difficulties which face the young person on the way to a right ordering of the sexual during the process of coming to maturity. The latter may by no means be regarded as insignificant since they can affect considerably the human power of loving and the development of personality, yet one should not see in them the gravest sins. For nowadays the regulation of sexual behaviour is no longer in the forefront of attention in Christian ethics, though this reproach is still sometimes made (as by Alex Comfort).

e) The Christian will, however, not be able to deal with the question of guilt without considering also the readiness to forgive demanded by the gospel (cf. Jn 8) and his own experience of forgiveness of sin and guilt, in his faith in the redemptive work of Christ.

Johannes Gründel

SIN

I. Sin and Guilt

1. *Introductory.* The gospel proclaims divine salvation in Jesus Christ as redemption and forgiveness of our sins.

Jesus calls for conversion as he proclaims and offers the kingdom of God. The Church preached that he died for our sins and as having accomplished purification from sins. We were baptized in his name for the forgiveness of sins. Sin seems therefore to be one of the primary suppositions of the gospel, and in this it is in line with the OT, especially the prophets. But Christian preaching encountered a self-understanding of man in which sin was taken for granted. It has no such place in modern thought. No doubt the optimism of the 19th century, which saw industrial and social progress mainly as an enchanting future, has given way to an experience of the "human condition" and human failure which has become a sort of obsession in philosophy and above all in the novel, the theatre and the cinema. But the word "sin" is not readily used and seems in fact to be avoided. One of the main causes is a reaction against a rationalistic, moralistic and legalistic notion of sin in a seemingly recent past. But sin also implies a (negative) relationship to God, and hence the notion becomes obscured – or truer – according to the purity of our notion of God. It must be our task to propound in a way relevant today the notion of sin which has and always will have a place in Christian preaching.

2. *The biblical notion of sin.* The most common words for sin in the Bible are the Hebrew חָטָא and the Greek ἁμαρτάνω. The general sense in both cases is to "miss the mark". They are mostly used in ethical contexts in the meaning of "to do evil". In the Bible they very often mean "to do evil against somebody", especially Yahweh. Men do evil against him by transgressing his law, but this law functions in the covenant. Sin is hated by Yahweh as Lord of the covenant, and so its most definite expression is in idolatry, forbidden in the first command of the Decalogue and denounced by the prophets. Idolatry sometimes appears as the source of all sins (Exod 20:3; Wis 14:22–31; Rom 1:18–32). Sin is above all revolt (פֶּשַׁע) offence, irritation (כַּעַס) and contempt (נָאַץ) and has the character of a violation of the covenant, and indeed of adultery as regards Yahweh. This OT view was taken over and deepened by the NT, where sin is against the kingdom of God, against Christ (Mt 10:33; 11:20, 24; 12:28–32; Jn 15:18, 23–25), and against the Holy Spirit (Mk 3:28f. par.). But it should be noted that the Decalogue likewise invokes Yahweh when forbidding sins against the neighbour, and that the prophets are not content to denounce idolatry. They are at least as vehement in denouncing injustice against the weak and a worship which is an alibi for social justice. More and more in the OT the command of love of the neighbour came to be placed beside that of love of God, and Jesus ratified the process. Thus Scripture gives us the task of describing sin as directed against God and man. As long as sin is envisaged entirely within the perspective of commands and prohibitions, justice is not done to human freedom. But the prophets display the heart as the seat of man's answer to God. The greatest sin is the uncircumcised or stony heart, or the hard – obdurate – neck. In the NT we find "sin" along with "sins" (in the plural). In Paul it is sometimes a personified might which has entered the world, but it also dwells in men and makes them slaves. In Jn in particular sin appears as the ultimate unrighteousness, in which individuals but above all "the world" are imprisoned.

3. *What sin is directed against.* Men today react with some justification against the notion of sin in earlier generations, which defined it as "a deliberate transgression of the law of God". This concept can and must be modified from many aspects.

a) First of all, the image must be corrected, if it presents God on the analogy of a civil or ecclesiastical lawgiver and thinks of God's law on the analogy of a positive law (possibly also faultily conceived), as contingent and imposed from outside. God's law is identical with the demands which his creation and salvation make upon us – demands which are identical with creation and salvation themselves. From this we deduce above all that sin is against men. Sinful man offends against what is demanded by his and his neighbour's being.

b) But these demands must not be understood statically, a danger which goes with the concept of "natural law". It is the nature of man to be a person who programmes and constructs himself in history. Hence good and evil cannot be deduced from the tendencies of human nature, where this is contrasted with his personal being. Sin is rather a refusal of the call, of our future, as it is in history, where God's salvation has entered and is realized more and more fully. Rather than define sin as the transgression of a law, we might call it the refusal to commit ourselves in a history of salvation.

c) In the OT and the NT, the "religious" man is told that his sins are not merely setting up strange gods against the true God, but also injustice, harshness, exploitation of his fellows. It is a "blessing" that today we are sensitive to such things. It might be said that sins solely against God are impossible. Every sin is at least against the self (and hence is its own punishment), and God encounters us with his gifts and invitations in our fellow-men, especially in Christ. But it is necessary to stress today that it is God, with his initiative transcending our reality, who meets us in this way. Hence we "offend" and "irritate" God himself in our refusal to commit ourselves to the history of salvation which he wishes to enter on with us. The notion of sin as an offence to God should not be allowed to disappear, unless it seems to imply a strict order of justice between God and man, on the same level – as is apparently the case in most explanations of the redemption as "satisfaction". But the offence to God must be situated where it really is: God himself is offended in man when we disregard God's summons to love. Just as love of God and man is a unity, so too sin is against both.

4. *The origin of sin in man*. Sin is an ethico-religious act, but a negative one. This implies that what may be said of the moral act may also be said of sin.

a) Sin comes from the free decision taken by man in the kernel of his person, which is called the "heart" in the Bible. But man is always someone who is bodily in the world and he embodies himself more and more, by contact with the world, especially with his fellows. Hence too much attention should not be paid to purely inward sins, as is also the biblical principle. In the strict sense, such sins are never purely interior, any more than other elements. In one way or another, man gives outward expression to the resolves of his heart, and this embodiment deepens his inward attitude. On the other hand, man's body is part of the "non-I", the world, which he makes *his* world, without ever overcoming its resistance. This implies that man's outward behaviour sometimes fails to express his inward resolve, since there remains a foreign element. The difficulty in question gives rise to two limit cases of sin. The first is when only the outward behaviour is in conflict with the demands of morality, while the inward resolution and attitude is not involved. This can be because man acts in ignorance, the significance of his conduct being unknown to him. Or he is not master of his actions.

This limit case is called "material sin", which is therefore not a sin at all but only the appearance – not the manifestation – of it. The second case is the precise opposite. An outward act with a good meaning is deliberately chosen to disguise one's own sinful attitude. This is "hypocrisy", vigorously condemned in the Pharisees in the NT. This surface holiness is a by-product of works-holiness, with which the same group are reproached. The link between the two is not quite accidental, since works-holiness means conduct which follows the norms of morality, but disguises sin by not acknowledging its own need of redemption. In this way, it is also hypocrisy. Material sin and hypocrisy also seem to be limit cases inasmuch as they cannot exist as such for long. Either the bad outward behaviour affects the inward attitude, or the evil attitude will show itself somewhere in outward behaviour.

b) Between material sin and sin from the heart there are many possible degrees. A sinful act can also come about where psychic determinisms regulate the act in part, and our freedom is not fully engaged. To put it metaphorically: the act is on the periphery and not at the centre of our person. Such psychic determinisms may be positive or negative instincts or drives, such as self-assertion, libido, anxiety, which anticipate the free act and obscure one's insight. But ordinary routine can also play a part, if full attention to one's commitment cannot be demanded, because ultimately the decisions required are of little importance.

These considerations have led Catholic theologians to re-think the classical difference between mortal and venial sins. The distinction comes from the practice of the sacrament of penance. It indicates primarily the difference between sins for whose forgiveness the sacrament (in the baptized Christian) is necessary, and sins which can be forgiven without the sacrament (though confession of venial sins is never excluded and has often been recommended by the magisterium). The difference in the gravity of sins, denied by Pelagianism and contested, though with nuances, by the Reformation, is accepted in Catholicism precisely because of the differences it saw in human action with regard to the world (*D* 106–8, 804, 833, 835). But for centuries scholastic theology could not agree on the standpoint from which the distinction between mortal and venial sin was to be determined. The two types of sin, admittedly only named sin analogously, differ by reason of the freedom of the sinner (full knowledge and free will) and also by reason of the content of the action (grave or light matter). In this view, mortal sin is sin committed with full knowledge and consent in a grave matter, venial sin with less full knowledge and consent or in a slight matter. But in view of what has been said above, it may now be affirmed that there is only one aspect from which the gravity of a sin can be judged: that of full knowledge and freedom or otherwise, or, to use the terms just invoked, whether or not it comes from the centre of our person. Venial sin is then the more or less peripheral sin. The gravity or importance of the act then comes down to its origin – peripheral or central. It is in fact a coefficient of the origin. Infidelity in marriage normally involves a more central resolve than a small theft. This consideration has already been put forward by K. Rahner, who pointed out that a similar distinction could be noted in morally good acts. Mortal sin, as a decision at the centre of the person, is a break with the vital orientation to salvation, a gambling away of the life of grace. Hence the name of mortal sin. But in the life-history of each man even a central resolve can be revoked, and God continually opens up to us in Christ new chances of conversion. It is only in life as a whole, or in the transition to the next life, that sinful decision can be definitive, corresponding to the "sin against the Holy Spirit" (Mk 3:29 parr.), the "sin unto death" (1 Jn 5:16) or the ultimate "lawlessness" (1 Jn 3:4).

c) Every act is revocable, and within each act we may be mistaken about the connection between the inward and the outward element. A wrong outward action need only be material sin, a good action can be hypocrisy, a major offence need not proceed from the centre of our person and it is even possible that a minor offence may embody profound malice. All this suggests that sin is not primarily to be sought in the exceptional act, but in the whole programme of life. This is also true, of course, of virtue and of all categories of virtue and vice. Honesty or falsehood, chastity or unchastity, love or egoism are ultimately realized in a whole life or a period of it, and seldom display themselves clearly in any particular act. Hence the confession of our sins must rather be a life discerned than acts listed, not only in prayer, but also in the sacrament of penance. And the deepest sin is resistance to the summons to rise up from our daily falls humbly and hopefully. It is resistance to the history of salvation which God wishes to verify in each life, even through and out of our sins. Hence in Jn the sin of those who refused to believe in the Son of God was not just that their works were in fact evil, but that they also refused, for this reason, to come to the light (Jn 3:19).

5. *Guilt.* a) What makes sin really sin is guilt. Guilt is the free decision to evil, evil with regard to God and man. We may therefore distinguish in guilt an inward element and a social one, to which *culpa* and *debitum* correspond in Latin. The inward element lends itself to psychological analysis, which can often distinguish between inauthentic feelings of guilt and a real consciousness of guilt. Where the moral norms are more or less imposed by the environment, without being really assimilated, inauthentic guilt-feelings can multiply (in primitive cultures, but also by reason of a legalistic, puritanical or authoritarian upbringing in our own society). The social element is embodied in juridical guilt, which means being subject to a penalty and (or) being bound to make compensation. This juridical guilt is only ascribed in the administration of justice, in Church and in society, when there are or have been signs of the *mens rea* – or at least, this is the ideal regularly aimed at.

b) This last point indicates that juridical guilt may remain when the *culpa* at the centre of the person has been eliminated by repentance and the bestowal of forgiveness. A repentant murderer still has to pay the penalty. But it is an oversimplification to apply this principle univocally to guilt in the ethical or theological dimension, to guilt with regard to God and man, as when for instance it is maintained that the temporal punishments for sin must still be undergone, though the guilt is already eliminated by forgiveness. It seems truer to say that guilt only remains insofar as repentance does not spring from the centre of the person and take in all levels of one's being insofar as they are accessible to the free act.

c) More difficult to determine than the persistence or disappearance of guilt is, it would appear, its origin. Our consciousness does not precede our will, but is actuated by it, so that we always find ourselves already exercising our freedom in some way. Hence it is impossible to ask where our moral decisions begin in us. Further, in such decisions good and evil are often mixed, so that it is no more feasible to demarcate an age of "original innocence" for the individual than for mankind. If we reflect on the limits inherent to being human, or rather, to the perpetual humanization of man, it becomes clearer and clearer that it is very difficult to draw the line between "finitude" and "culpabilité" (P. Ricœur). Man also feels the perpetual seduction of sin; that he is subjected to "principalities and powers" as well as being a responsible agent; that he is a sort of synthesis of destiny and freedom (P. Tillich). But this need not dim our confession of faith in God and Christ, since the disclosure of a conscience that cannot be fully fathomed (cf. 1 Cor 4:4) is less important than full confidence in him in whom there is superabundant redemption.

6. "*The sin of the world*". a) We use this Johannine expression (Jn 1:29) to sum up the social nature of sin or solidarity in sin. Even if we prescind from any original sin and its influence on each of us, this solidarity still exists. In Scripture, the whole people of Israel is often considered to have sinned in common, and God was said to have visited the sins of the fathers on the third and fourth generations. Even after Jeremiah and Ezekiel proclaimed the responsibility of each individual before God, a truth underlined by the NT, the link between fathers and children remains. Sin remains a power in the world, and the "world" remains a fellowship of sin. This fits in with our experience of the "contamination" of evil and, in general, the "infectiousness" of moral action. One may speak of the sins, or perhaps also the virtues, of a given people or epoch of culture. What does this imply?

b) Guilt, at any rate, because it stems from the personal free act of each individual, cannot pass from one to another. It is not a social characteristic. Hence it is misleading to speak of collective guilt, and to do so is to commit an injustice to individuals. Nonetheless, the influence of one free agent on another is unmistakable. This can be formally described with the help of the term "situation". As a free person, I cannot be deprived of my freedom by the free decisions of others, but they may well place me in a situation which may determine me inwardly even in my freedom. Another can, for instance, disclose a value which makes an appeal to my freedom and he can strengthen its appeal by his example, much more so if he lives out this value. Evil example, on the contrary, deprives me of such an appeal. A value is exposed to doubt and denial. An impulse in the opposite direction is given. This is what the Bible means by temptation or scandal, which is literally the cord or stone placed in someone's path to make him stumble. Such a temptation, when reinforced by social pressure, may be too strong for my moral forces. Still more important is the fact that the persistent absence of positive testimony to a value and the persistent display of evil example can weaken and quench the appeal of the value. The grasp of the value can become so obscure that a real blindness to the value can occur. Such pernicious influences can be seen at work even in adults, who still need the guarantee of others in moral action. They are still more effective on children, inasmuch as they are still dependent on moral education. Children or even a whole generation can even be "born blind" to certain values, when they are born in a milieu where the values in question have been obscured or eliminated. This is how it is possible to speak of the "sins" of a people or a culture, though the sins are to a great extent merely the material sins of individuals born blind to a given value.

c) These affirmations are not confined to the "purely natural" order of things. Grace also comes in question. There are many ways in which man can be of service to the call of grace as it goes out to his fellow. I see in another the concrete reality of what grace asks of me, and the grace given me, the Spirit within me, makes me receptive to the example, the appeal, the message, which come to me from others. This means that sins may work against grace in a given milieu, while grace in turn can inspire a man to break the spell of his milieu, as God has done supremely in Jesus Christ, in a way which is decisive for all milieux. Hence we see sin ruling in many ways in the world, because, according to the vision of Jn, the rejection of Christ consummates and fixes the world in its sinfulness. Such a theology of the sin of the world and of the historical sins of the world might open up a new approach today to the dogma of original sin and possibly determine its interpretation. But apart from this question, it is important as a pendant to the doctrine of redemption, since God in Christ has delivered us from all sins.

7. *Sin, creation, redemption.* a) We have already pointed out that sin casts its shadow before in all man's limitations and finiteness. Nowhere in the world is anything simply a limitation: it is also an evil, the lack of a good which should be there, the missing of a goal. On the analogy of moral evil, but on a lower level, it is customary to speak of physical evil, both in man and under man. But on the infra-human level, it is difficult, if not impossible, to know where one is speaking of *evil*, as may be seen from the Aristotelian principle, "Generatio unius est corruptio alterius". This physical evil is only clearly such insofar as it affects human persons: it might then be termed "catastrophic" evil. Another form of human evil is tragic evil, which man does to himself or his fellow-man, but not culpably, or at least not directly so. Finally, there is moral evil or sin. These considerations seem to reinforce what was said earlier about the mysterious origin of sin.

b) Analogies can of course be indicated between these different forms of evil, as for instance between physical evil and sin. Teilhard de Chardin pointed to the statistics which suggest that where large numbers are concerned, the good gains on the bad. He thought that this law could apply to good and evil in the human group as well as to biological evolution. And it may in fact be maintained that good – like evil – gains the upper hand insofar as it has become a social necessity. But our whole history shows how much the statistical laws depend on the person for being set in motion, and how the person can again break out of them. Some individuals seem to have had the strange power to launch chain-reactions of evil. But God's redemption works the same way, especially in the liberating life and death of Jesus.

c) If we see evil, and sin in particular, in all creation, the question arises as to how far God is responsible – the question already posed by Job. The answer still seems to be that given in the Book of Job, that it is God's mystery – but that it is not merely a mystery of power but above all of love. The whole of creation must be ascribed to the love of God, and we may affirm with some probability that a created world also involves evil. We must not appeal to God's omnipotence to affirm that he could hinder evil, since the content of God's omnipotence cannot be determined *a priori* by us creatures. But God is not simply the maker of the world, he is also its redeemer who brings it to fulfilment. There he shows that he is on the side of man in the struggle against evil and sin. Jesus, healing and exorcizing by an authoritative word, Jesus dying in weakness, is the deepest revelation of the saving power of God. "Repentance and forgiveness of sins [are to be] preached in his name to all nations" (Lk 24:47).

d) Man always remains exposed to the temptation to sin, even when he has found redemption through faith and repentance (which includes mutual forgiveness). He encounters within himself the concupiscence which is engendered by the inner situation in which he has been placed by original sin – and by the "sin of the world". In its essence, concupiscence is to be distinguished from sin, from which it springs and to which it leads. This distinction is made by the Council of Trent (*D* 792). But in man's actual existence, concupiscence can be recognized in the sinful connivance with it. Hence even a Catholic may say that there is such a thing as *simul iustus et peccator*. The magisterium of the Church affirms that the sinner may still have divine faith (*D* 838) and be a member of the Church and of its hierarchy (*D* 646). "The Church, embracing sinners in her bosom, is at the same time holy and always in need of being purified" (Vatican II, *Lumen Gentium*, art. 8).

e) But the priority always rests with redemptive grace. Grace is not merely subsequent to sin, it anticipates it. "We know that any one born of God does not sin" (1 Jn 5:18). The grace bestowed upon Mary, making her a very special case of redemption, was a purely prevenient grace, as the dogma of the Immaculate Conception says (*D* 1641). But the sinlessness of Christ himself is more important (Jn 8:46; Heb 4:15; 7:27). Even this is not to be regarded as a "programmed" incapacity to sin, but as an unfailing constancy in resisting the temptations by which Jesus was assaulted "in every respect . . . as we are" (Heb 4:15). Temptations coming merely "from without" and demanding no inward struggle would be consistent only with a humanity of Christ in which, as the Apollinarists held, the divine Logos replaced the human soul. Such temptation would not have been redemptive, given the nature of our own temptations.

Piet Schoonenberg

II. Punishment of Sins

1. *Preliminary remarks on method and matter.* The theological understanding of what punishment of sin means must not start from a notion based on the penalties imposed by civil law on a criminal for offences against society. The special relationship of God to the world, not that of a particular cause within the world but that of the transcendent origin of the world as a whole, would risk being distorted by this approach. And there are other anthropomorphic notions of God's vindictive justice which make the Christian message of the punishments of sin difficult to accept. The starting-point should rather be from the following considerations.

a) The freedom of man is exercised in the body, in the world. This means that the subjective decision, coming from the free agent as such in its incalculable independence, is necessarily, even in "inward acts", in itself and not just in its consequences, corporeal and mundane, i.e., is exercised "in the other".

b) This "other", being intrinsically constitutive of the free act, has of itself a structure. It is not pure *materia prima.* It forms therefore a prior limiting law for the free act, which submits to it in the very moment in which it alters the matter of freedom.

c) This concrete matter, modified by the free act but still possessing its own laws, is always connected with and united to the world as a whole, with its laws and development. It therefore undergoes the influence of this world as a whole.

d) These objectivations of freedom, which are part of it, which are its embodiment in the body of man, in the world of things and men around him, do not simply cease to be because the free agent rejects his previous decision, "changes his mind". The world, as matter of freedom, does not depend simply on the individual free agent. The new decision, even when the opposite of the first, has to operate in and with the situation which has been to some extent determined by the previous decision (see *Situation Ethics*). The "alienation" which every free decision undergoes through its necessary objectivation in the "other", is an objectivation which on principle could be brought about without a free act, through alien causes. (The same *habitus* of associations, psychic mechanisms, etc., can be set up by free training or by "brain-washing" from outside.) And the inner corporeality of man is always the zone in which the expression from within and the impression from without become one. It belongs to the free subject as an intrinsic component, though it is not simply identical with the free act in its origin. These persistent objectivations of freedom in the corporeal and mundane react upon the free agent, and hence are means whereby the world acts and reacts upon the subject – a mediation which goes to make up the concrete reality of these objectivations. All this is true both of the free act which is morally good and of that which is morally bad.

2. *The concept of punishment of sin*. We may use these considerations to suggest a theological explanation of the punishments of sin. a) The punishments of sin are the persistent objectivations of the bad moral decision, being themselves hurtful because contrary to the true nature of the free subject, and being also the means through which the resistance of the due order of the world (of men and things around the subject) likewise operates as hurtful. From the considerations under 1 above one can see why every sin avenges itself, why punishment (in the sense of penalty, cf. "under pain of") can and must be the connatural, intrinsic consequence of sin. In its necessary objectivations, sin submits – because being finite it can never be autonomous – to the structures of a world made by God. Freedom can never fully eliminate or replace this world and hence undergoes its "punitive" reactions.

Since this avenging setting also includes fellow-men who can themselves act freely, one can see that "punishment" for sin in the sense of civil, penal law can at once be understood as a possible though secondary case of this metaphysical and theological notion of punishment.

b) The punishment of sin, in this sense, appears as the penalty inflicted by God as guardian of the moral order, since the hurtful structures of man and his world which sin inevitably sets in motion are created by God and hence are objectivations and expressions of his holy will. God "punishes" through the good world which he created and whose structures he still upholds when they are abused by finite freedom in an evil act. Since the creature cannot abolish them, they operate to cause pain through the objectivations of sin. It is therefore superfluous and anthropomorphic to imagine that to uphold the moral order by punishing, God would have to create punitive agents whose sole function would be to bring about the physical evil of punishment. This is true above all of the final situation of man's free history, in which the full and definite reality of man and the world will be directly disclosed, with all "repressions" ended. The radical contradiction between the permanent "supernatural existential", the permanent offer of God's self-communication in love, and the definitive obdurate refusal opposed to it by the free act will be experienced as the *poena damni*. And this is in fact the only explanation of the pain of loss, since if the punishment is understood as something extrinsically supervening, there would be no desire or need for the vision of God. And the *poena sensus* (which certainly cannot be thought of as merely affecting the senses) in this view of perdition consists of the radical contradiction between what the lost obdurately insist on being (and are, "bodily") and the permanent structures of a transfigured world which is their permanent setting. We cannot visualize this permanent, real contradiction which does not affect merely the senses – the "fire of hell". And it is not necessary to do so, either to be objective or to meet the needs of the kerygma today. In putting forward these considerations, we are obviously presupposing the doctrine of St. Thomas, that the punishments of the lost, both "pain of loss" and "pain of sense", are the consequence and not the cause of the definitiveness of the free decision (that of life as a whole) which is of the essence of freedom, since it is a choice of the definitive, not a choice that is to be constantly reconsidered. In the case of the definitive evil decision it is called obduracy.

c) This enables us to understand the difference between "medicinal" and "vindictive" punishment, which again is not to be visualized along the lines of the penal law in force in the State. Every hurtful reaction of reality (in man and his world) to a wrong decision as it affects this reality is of itself a summons to "conversion", to a better decision, more objective and humane, and has therefore a "medicinal" character. Being an expression of the holy will of God, it also has a "vindictive" (retributive) character, which does not of course mean that it must be understood as the angry reaction of a will imposing law merely extrinsically and adding punishments of an extrinsic type. The holy will of God which reacts retributively is the will which creates a good world and sustains it in its objective goodness. Punishment loses its medicinal character (in its effect, not in its essence) insofar as it is confronted with refusal by the free agent, either provisionally or finally through definitive obduracy.

3. *Theological consequences of the notion of punishment of sin.* a) The punishments of eternal loss – a possibility which must be reckoned with for the free agent while still existing in his history, without appeals to a theory of apocatastasis – have been discussed above under 2b.

b) As regards purgatory, the theological notion of concupiscence must also be brought in. Purgatory then appears as "working out of the system", overcoming, the painful difference between the concupiscent situation of man (not necessarily radically eliminated by death) and the initial good decision for God which has become definitive in death. For the situation of concupiscence which affects man interiorly and exteriorly is partly due to his own free acts. Whether this process of purgation is to be considered a strictly temporal one is a secondary question and ultimately an open one in theology.

c) According to the view of punishment of sin proposed here, the quashing of "temporal" punishment, that is, the punishment co-existing with a good basic decision, actually taken or still possible, cannot be thought of along the lines of a mere "amnesty" – the non-infliction of a punishment additional to the guilt and its natural consequences, to be imposed from without. Hence help in the elimination of the punishments of sin can only consist of a favourable change in the situation within which the sinner has to "work off" the penalties which are the connatural consequences of sin. Or help may be given (through a special grace) to further the total harmonization of the basic decision with the manifold totality of human reality – a harmonization which eliminates the punishment of sin.

d) This principle also enables us to gain a better grasp of the nature of indulgences.

e) The same principle may also be applied to the doctrine of the Council of Trent (*D* 1543, 1580), according to which justification (as the basic decision for God and the existentiell acceptance of the proferred grace of justification) need not always be linked at once with the remission of all ("temporal") punishment due to sin.

Karl Rahner

III. Doctrine of Sin

1. From the theoretical point of view, it is hardly relevant to ask about the place and the essential meaning of hamartiology in dogmatic theology, because it is so clearly dominant in the theology of a religion such as Christianity, which is based on redemption. The obvious place for it is therefore firstly formal and fundamental theology and secondly the doctrines of the

primordial state of man and original sin. In the traditional teaching about original sin, however, the sin of Adam and man's subsequent loss of grace are usually overemphasized. This loss of sanctifying grace is, however, in the traditional doctrine, made good in baptism and justification (concupiscence or desire, seen as man's historical existential, thus becomes a more "normal" characteristic). The result of this is that, in the presentation of original sin, man in his actual historical and social situation has not been presented sufficiently as a sinner ("at the same time both justified and a sinner"), and it has not been made clear enough that his situation is still determined by sin. A further consequence has been a very abstract soteriology and a hamartiology that is regarded primarily as a branch of moral theology. Dogmatic hamartiology can, however, be quite satisfactorily placed before the treatment of redemption in a formal and fundamental theology and in a hamartiology in which sin is regarded as an historical aspect of man's constantly sinful situation, so long as it remains true that it is only from God's revelation of grace that the revelation of his anger comes to man.

2. *Sin and freedom.* Scholastic teaching has always emphasized (correctly) that formal sin presupposes man's freedom and that there is no loss of freedom in sin. It is, however, important to make it more evident that the act of sin also impairs the essential nature of man's freedom and throws him into a state of slavery from which he can be set free only by God's grace.

3. *The transcendental orientation of man and sin.* Contemporary man can only be made to understand the existence of sin as a denial of God (see *D* 2318), if he comes to experience freedom not only as a formal, individual capacity to choose between one individual object and another, but as a fundamental possibility, in his transcendental orientation towards God, in which he is at his own disposal (in every choice that he makes between individual objects) and, what is more, as a fundamental relationship with God. The theological subjectivity of freedom, moreover, enables us to understand not only the law guaranteed by God as a mere expression of the structures of finite realities, but sin as an *offensa Dei*.

4. *Sin and grace.* Again, the real meaning of sin cannot be fully understood by a mere consideration of God's guarantee of the structures of the world that he has created. It is only possible to gain a full understanding of it if God is seen above all as the one who, by uncreated grace, has made himself man's personal partner in love. As a result of this view of the relationship between God and man, sin is clearly a refusal by man, the creature, to share in the divine nature. This rejection of God's personal love for man, moreover, has to be regarded as more than a merely undesirable consequence of sin. The true meaning of sin in man's concrete personal relationship with God is very easily obscured by the practice in moral theology of formalizing sin (as *contra legem aeternam*).

5. The doctrine of original sin is basically a theological aetiology, investigating the origins and causes of the fact that man's individual and collective situation in freedom is always at least partly determined by the objectivizations of sin. The consequence is that these objectivizations of guilt (though not guilt itself) are taken over in any good act of freedom and therefore involve a risk and lead to a certain ambiguity. (It is this fact that must serve as a point of departure for any Christian attempt to understand the "tragic" aspect of man's existence.) If these two factors were more fully understood, the existential significance of original sin and its connection with personal sin would undoubtedly be clarified.

6. Thomas Aquinas made the ontological distinction between mortal and venial sin very clear. From the theologi-

cal and the practical and everyday points of view, however, their unity and the difference between them are insufficiently understood. Generally speaking, the foundation of this distinction is laid – usually with insufficient clarity – in a doctrine of the temporal, spatial and physical mediation of freedom (as the total availability of self), conditioning the temporal and objective extent to which freedom can be exercised (the possibility of *imperfectio actus*). The formalization of sin as an offence "against the eternal law" of God can easily lead to an obscuring of the difference between grave and venial sin. (There is a risk, in the doctrine of *parvitas materiae*, moreover, of tracing this distinction back exclusively to an arbitrary act in which God draws the dividing line.) On the other hand, however, if the dividing line is drawn objectively from the point of *materia*, there is a great temptation to think that we can easily tell, in the concrete case of the individual, when sin is "only" venial. In such instances, it is equally easy to forget that even offences that are quite trivial in the material sense may be the apparently harmless objectivization of a fundamental decision in which man totally denies God.

7. The success of a kerygmatic theology of the doctrine of sin must depend essentially on a perception of the mutual interrelationship between knowledge and freedom. In actuality, man's knowledge of the possibility of sin is fundamentally a free event, in which he allows himself, by the truth and judgment of God, to become aware of his sinfulness, which he then suppresses. On the other hand, a dogmatic theology dealing with supernatural grace and a theology of human society and the history of the world and the cross (as the folly of love which bestows God himself) does not have to concentrate exclusively on the question as to how the individual sinner can find the God of grace, as though this were the only way to Christianity. To do this would undoubtedly impair the absolute seriousness of sin.

Karl Rahner

SITUATION ETHICS

1. *History of the problem.* The term "situation" was introduced into the language of moral theology by T. Steinbüchel. It became a sort of technical term when "situation ethics" was condemned by Pius XII (Allocutions of 23 March and 19 April 1952: *AAS* 44 [1952], pp. 270ff., 413ff.; Instructio S. Officii, 2 February 1956: *AAS* 48 [1956], pp. 144f.; *DS* 3918–21).

There is a situation ethics, in the sense of the condemnations here mentioned, when one bases oneself on the concrete circumstances of a moral act to regard as good or justifiable moral decisions which are consciously in opposition to the generally valid norms of the natural law and the revealed will of God, since the link between morals and the order of being is denied. In condemning situation ethics in this sense, Pius XII was dealing with an undoubtedly misguided effort to solve a perpetual problem of moral theology, but one which had only become central with the rise of existence-philosophy.

Morals originally consisted in the main of wisdom sayings and more or less concrete rules of behaviour in typical situations. But with the systematic development of moral theology, the moral act was defined in terms of the end of man. General assertions were made about the nature of man, which were mostly based on experience, and were then used to formulate ethical directives equally valid for all men. The application of these rules to all cases was hardly felt as a problem at first, and where it was explicitly considered, it was not felt to be essential, as when medieval theologians came to speak of the moral difficulties which the OT presented to them. But when the problem of universal applicability came to be felt more keenly in modern times, it was still treated, at least on principle, as a secondary one, though it was in fact in the foreground, especially in the age of casuistry. The controversies about probabilism, etc., which preoccupied moralists especially in the 17th and 18th centuries, were undoubtedly a high-point in the earlier efforts of moral philosophy and theology to settle problems arising from the links of morality to its situation. But they did not solve the problems in a decisive way, though one should not underestimate how much the solution of the question of what one is bound to do under pain of sin in doubts of conscience can contribute to the formation of the conscience in a given situation.

When it was difficult to apply general principles to an individual case, medieval theologians usually had recourse to the solution that only the formal moral principles were universally valid (*principia primaria moralitatis*). The more specific the principles (*principia secundaria moralitatis*), the more limited their field of application. But with the rise of casuistry in moral theology, the concrete case was more and more readily treated as an item to be subsumed under a specifically determined general principle.

When ethical questioning came to be formulated on the basis of the concrete I-World and I-You relationships, that is, when the concrete "intentional" (i.e., object-related) act was taken as the foundation and starting-point, a sort of Cartesian reversal took place in the relation of morality to the situation. The definability and determination of the concrete ethical demand in a unique situation now becomes the central problem of systematic ethics. The interest was now concentrated – to use terms borrowed by Scheler from Bolzano – on "the good in itself" only as mediated by "the good for me". This meant that in theology the question had to be more clearly put as: "How can I know what God wants of me here and now in my unique situation?"

There is undeniable progress here. The moral questioning starts with man in his concrete constitution and his historically changing relationship to his fellow-men and his environment. Starting therefore with man's situation, it asks how the will of God may be known, that is, it tries to define moral obligations. Scientific study is not confined, as it was to a great extent in the "ethics of essences" of scholasticism, to the general *a posteriori* rules of what is *per se* obligatory. Nor is it just a matter of disclosing the general *a priori* presuppositions of each person, as in the "ethics of disposition" and "value-ethics" of modern times. The new approach also takes in the importance of the subjectivity in its uniqueness and the perpetual historical change of the objective conditions. Thus ethics is completed by an existential ethics, which may also be called a situation ethics and an ethics of responsibility.

The change is due to the individualist and personalist trend in the thought and feeling of our present pluralist age. It is also due to a profounder sense of man's social nature, through which he is so strongly dependent on his social setting and its development. There was also the need to find a valid answer to the historically novel "situation" of modern man, and one which would meet his new understanding of reality. In the ethical situation, what was once a rare marginal case has now become almost the normal one. What most people once thought to be certain has now become extremely questionable. Other forces making for change in moral theology included transcendental philosophy, phenomenology, existential philosophy, personalism, the theory of science and kerygmatic theology. In all these realms, attention has been more and more concentrated on man as he is in his concrete constitution, his historical conditioning, his facticity and forlornness (*Geworfenheit*), in the freedom of his development and the necessary restraints imposed on him by his dialogue. In Marxist philosophy in particular, and to some extent in existential philosophy, man was considered as completely autonomous and hence as the exclusive norm of moral behaviour.

2. *Systematic analysis*. To understand the just claims of an existential ethics, we must start with a truth which can be verified by reflection. It is that the answer to the question as to the right moral decision in a given moment depends on subjective and objective factors which are by their very nature unique. They may be summed up under the term of "situation".

Each situation is unique because each man, his social setting (human world) and to some extent his environment (biological world), are in the stream of history. For man can only take ethical action inasmuch as he is conscious of himself, his social setting and his environment. But this consciousness is constantly changing. The moral agent is developing subjectively, and his social setting and environment are also developing objectively. He develops in terms of his subjective experiences and decisions, which in turn depend on the constant changes of the environment: he changes, his society changes, his world changes.

Furthermore, the subjective relationship to God is only possible through man's social setting and environment, and hence is realized in perpetual dependence on the changing situation. This means that a constant change in the concrete ethical claim of God on man must also be taken into account. This claim of God on each man, as manifested by the changing situation, may be called the "hour" (cf. Lk 13:44). It is when a special summons goes out to man in his personal history, e.g., in the situation of choosing a marriage-partner, a walk in life, etc., where he must take a decision which will be essential to his salvation.

What God demands of the individual in a given situation or in such an "hour" is recognized directly in experience, and ultimately in the evident claim of an unconditional concrete obligation. Hence the "hour" only strikes insofar as one clearly recognizes that there is nothing else to be done here and now.

This judgment is infallible insofar as the obligation is evident. It is fallible inasmuch as it is reached through prejudices and pre-assessments, that is, insofar as it is dependent on human contingency and moral maturity. For God necessarily wills that man takes moral decisions, in keeping with his conscience, since personal moral action is only possible on these grounds. And to this extent, the obligation pronounced by conscience is infallible. But then again, the verdict of conscience depends on a limited insight into the claims of a situation, and on the subjective attitude towards fulfilling the obligation. Hence the best that conscience can do is to say what is the optimum of correct moral action for a person in a given situation. It cannot say what is the absolute optimum which might be realized if one could have a clear and full view of the demands of a situation and a disposition to moral action fully in keeping with all demands. To this extent, the verdict of conscience is fallible.

One can be thus orientated in conscience both fallibly and infallibly towards the morally obligatory, because the formal moral good attracts the agent in his virtuous reaction. But then again, this ordination depends on how well, in the concrete, the agent can refer the tangible factors of the situation, the physical, social and mental data, the materially perfect and deficient, to the formal moral good. How well does he know the material good as such? – which is, therefore, the relationship of the physical to the formal moral good, and through this, to the absolute good.

Consequently, man is always infallible in his formal search for virtue, since human action always becomes formally good action though the good intention of the agent, and this, as the subjective intention, is always known, at least indirectly. But since the categories of reality, with all their laws and trends, are only accessible in a limited way to individual and social experience – which may be examined scientifically, however, and formulated in manageable scientific laws – knowledge of the way the categories of reality relate to the material good and hence to the absolute good is always mixed with error or at least limited. This is because our *a posteriori* knowledge is fundamentally limited and dependent on our historical situation, and because our subjective moral disposition is always subject to limits in its perfection. Consequently, the absolute will of God can only be known with a mixture of error or at least only in a limited way.

Hence the reason for the intrinsic limitations of human knowledge of the will of God is to be sought in its experiential nature. Human knowledge moves forward step by step, experience by experience, in historical development. For the concrete ethical decision, this means that it can never be simply deduced from general principles or objectivated findings which would be evident and hence infallibly correct.

Hence it is the task of scientific situation ethics to develop methods which will facilitate an existentiell judgment on a situation, apart from the essential meaning of it. It must work out methods which will assure an optimum of existentiell knowledge of the morally good. This guarantee makes a calculated risk legitimate. And given the elements of uncertainty about the essence and existence of man, due to ignorance or error, in any human situation, such risk is always there.

To determine how man's existence stands to his essence and his existentiell possibilities, the following recommendations are made by scientific theology and the Spiritual Exercises (especially the Rules for the Discernment of Spirits), each in its own way.

a) *The purest possible intention in the moral agent.* This depends on the basic moral intention of the agent, that is, on the faith, hope and love with which he accepts, conditionally and unconditionally and hence religiously, his own self and his neighbour. It also depends on his unconditional affirmation of the absolute truth, goodness and meaning, and hence from the more or less unconditional nature of his theological faith, hope and love. It depends further on the actual degree of perfection in his general moral virtues, which must come into play in every moral act, and finally, on the perfection of the particular virtue which has to be exercised in the actual moral decision.

b) If an action is to do justice to a situation, the good intention must be put into effect as objectively as possible. This means that the facts of the matter must be ascertained as correctly as possible, intuitively or by study and reflection, but always drawing on the experience of others, including the authorities, to the fullest extent. But in any case, the knowledge in question has to be attained empirically and must take into account the relative independence of the various categories of reality in the world.

c) A decision as true as possible to the will of God implies that the elements of certainty and uncertainty in the decision have been correlated in the best possible way. This means that one has not tried to substitute virtue for objective knowledge, and, vice versa, that one has not shirked the necessary decisions for want of expert knowledge. For there is morally good action only insofar as it is equally well directed to persons and to things, to this and to the other world. The synthesis of the two realms cannot be merely analytical and deductive, by virtue of the general moral principles which alone make any moral decision possible. The synthesis must also be reached through a structure of imperatives built up directly from experience. Reflection on how rational calculation of risk, e.g., the use of the principle of double effect, can constantlv give a new and optimum balance between inner-directedness and other-directedness, between autonomy and heteronomy, has not yet far advanced. It needs also to be supplemented by the empirical sciences, e.g., the findings of psychology on the motivations proper to persons. And the scholastic teaching on the *virtutes generales* will need to be made accessible again.

As regards ethical pedagogy, it follows that we must go beyond a one-sided Platonizing and rationalizing concept of morality which is based on a religiously and morally unjustifiable desire to base all norms directly on the unconditional and the rationally valid. For man is essentially limited and sinful, and can only act on his limited and one-sided moral insight. The law-making authorities, like the individuals, must be further reinforced in their capacity to make independent decisions and to treat them as obligatory (with due allowance for *epikeia*) – though they are only conditionally and historically valid. Further, by reason of the concrete situation, there is a predisposition to good or evil, for which allowance must be made in taking decisions. This is a fact which must be brought home more clearly.

Waldemar Molinski

SOCIAL MOVEMENTS

I. Socialism

Socialism is the collective name for a multitude of systems and movements critical of existing society. All of them, it is fair to say, attach as much importance to man's social nature as to his individuality, oppose his self-centredness, emphasize his duties, as a member of the community, towards his fellows and particularly towards the various social bodies to which he belongs. In this general sense, socialism embraces Christian social doctrine and the Christian social movement, which in fact were called "Christian socialism" before there was a Marxist socialism and are still so called from time to time. Sometimes the term "socialism" is applied pejoratively to doctrines and movements which unduly subordinate man's individuality to his social nature, the private person to society, individual well-being to the common good, whereas Christianity rightly considers man the "author, representative, and goal of all social institutions" (*Mater et Magistra*, no. 219). The most striking example of socialism in this pejorative sense is communism, which so exalts the collectivity over the individual, shows such contempt for human dignity, that the majority of socialists no longer recognize it as the most radical wing of their own movement, repudiating it instead as a betrayal of socialism. On the other hand many who consider themselves socialists attach such crucial importance to the dignity of the human person that it is difficult to decide whether they still lean towards collectivism or simply social reform, the more so as in practice their aims generally coincide with those of the social reformers. Nor is radicalism any criterion in this matter. Thus Catholic social teaching demands that the very structure of society be reformed, whereas many socialist parties, which have long enjoyed governmental power, aim at nothing more than remedial legislation that leaves the social structure unchanged. As often as not, Christian labour unions in underdeveloped countries are far more radical in their aims and measures than socialist unions in advanced countries.

Apart from British socialism, whose roots are Christian, the mainstream of socialism derives from frankly non-

Christian sources. Its mightiest current since the mid-19th century, Marxist socialism (communism), has been militantly atheistic from the outset. Socialism was long a religion, or a substitute for religion, for a large section of the working class, who considered the Church the ally of capitalism and therefore the enemy of the working man. It must be confessed that the attitude of a great many Christians, unfortunately including many of the higher clergy (despite the Church's social teaching), was such as to create this impression. Even those socialists not the declared enemies of religion were as a rule steeped in the secular spirit of the age of "freethinking", which is what Bishop Ketteler meant when he called socialism "the natural child of liberalism". Such is still the outlook of many supporters of socialism today. The present attitude of the intellectual leadership, however, is quite another matter, especially since the socialist parties have largely ceased to speak for the working class alone, becoming truly national parties with broad political aims.

Before the Church can adopt a definitive attitude towards socialism, some definition must be found that embraces all socialist systems and movements (one author, T. Brauer, identifies twenty kinds of socialism, while another, W. Sombart, holds that there are no less than one hundred) but these only (*definitio conveniens omni et soli definito*). Many such attempts have been made, the most recent and suggestive definition being that of Gustav Gundlach: socialism is "a movement affecting the whole of life, essentially a feature of the capitalist age by reason of its scale of values and its methods, which seeks to secure the freedom and earthly happiness of all on a permanent basis by anchoring these in the institutions of an expertly organized human society from which all trace of heteronomy has been banished" (*Staatslexicon*, IV [5th ed., 1931], col. 1693). Pius XI accepts this definition in his encyclical *Quadragesimo Anno*. He sees the hallmark of socialism in the idea that society was set up merely for human convenience ("solius commodi causa humanam consortionem esse institutam", *ibid.*, no. 118); its whole purpose is to provide men with the advantages to be derived from the division of labour; consequently socialism sacrifices higher human values – notably individual freedom – to the most efficient possible production of material goods, alleging that this loss of freedom in the process of production is more than counterbalanced by the wider freedom men will have to shape their own destiny thanks to the abundance of material goods that will presently be available. The Pope then objects that effect can be given to this purely utilitarian view only by coercion on a grand scale, since no basis for legitimate authority is provided and the authority of God is thus extruded from society (*ibid.*, no. 119). Such a conception is obviously incompatible with the Christian idea of man and the world: whether in the order of creation or the order of redemption, God is lord of human society no less than he is of the human individual.

There is disagreement as to whether the type of socialism outlined in *Quadragesimo Anno* has ever existed in that form. It is certain that forms of socialism existed in 1931 which did not exhibit the features described in the encyclical and accordingly were not affected by the papal condemnation – the British Labour Party for one (which the Archbishop of Westminster hastened to reassure on this point), and probably Scandinavian socialism as well. Elsewhere, chiefly in the Latin countries, people wondered where this "mitigated socialism" was to be seen which, as the encyclical said, had so far abandoned the class struggle and collectivization as to accord with Christian social doctrine. Evidently what the Pope had in mind was the "revisionist socialism" then widespread in Germany, which was no longer orthodox Marxism but still contained more or less Marxist remnants. Most of its adherents were not religiously inclined and thought that an economy organized on the basis of a good deal of coercion was most likely to ensure the maximum production of goods and their "just" (more equal) distribution. Yet it seems doubtful whether they really believed society was based on nothing more than a convenient division of labour, denied that man is naturally ordered to society and to the values that can neither exist nor be conceived of apart from society, and repudiated any obligation to the common good. However this may be, libertarian, democratic socialism of the present day has been so modified that the purely economic, utilitarian conception of society is odious to it; in the socialism rejected by *Quadragesimo Anno* democratic socialism finds features of capitalism on the one hand and communism on the other, but no resemblance to itself.

The socialist theory outlined in *Quadragesimo Anno* is doubtless what John XXIII calls "formula disciplinae" which "postquam definite descripta est, iam non mutatur" (*Pacem in Terris*, no. 159). But Pius XI had already anticipated the point, and noted that movements arising from such "falsa philosophorum placita" are inevitably subject to change. Hence his verdict that socialism is always incompatible with Catholic doctrine was prudently modified by the proviso, "si vere manet socialismus" (*Quadragesimo Anno*, no. 117). In terms of the "formula . . . definite descripta", the libertarian, democratic socialism of the present day has clearly ceased to be such "socialism". John XXIII bears out this judgment by making only brief and indirect reference to his predecessor's condemnation of "socialism" (*Mater et Magistra*, no. 34) without adopting that position in the doctrinal part of his own encyclical. Of course it does not follow that modern democratic socialism agrees with Catholic doctrine at all points.

Now that movements have arisen, in the newly independent Afro-Asian countries, which regard themselves as "socialist" but have almost nothing in common with what has been known pejoratively as socialism, even in the broadest sense, it is less possible than ever to pass any global judgment on socialism. What chiefly concerns the new Afro-Asian forms of "socialism" is not criticizing society, much less capitalism, but coming to grips with the multitude of problems that their people inherit. They criticize colonialism rather than the social order. "Socialism" seems to offer them a middle way between the industrialism, imperialism, and colonialism of Western Europe and America, on the one hand, and Russian and Chinese communism, with *its* colonialism, on the other. Were the Church to condemn "socialism" in general, the result in these countries would be the most baneful confusion and dismay.

Nor can it be readily determined whether socialism is a philosophy or has a philosophical basis. Marxism (dialectical and historical materialism) certainly claims the status of a philosophy. For many socialists of the libertarian, democratic school socialism sums up an ethical ideal, which influences their thought and action (though for them socialism is neither a religion nor a substitute for religion). But they do not all derive these principles from the same philosophical source. The Frankfurt Manifesto of the Socialist International, 3 July 1951, and the Godesberg Declaration of the German Social Democratic Party, 1960, state in set terms that one may be led to the socialism position not only by the Marxist social analysis, or some other, but also by humanitarian ideals or belief in Christian revelation; and a leading theorist has said that although there is no socialist philosophy, one cannot be a good socialist without some philosophical foundation.

Here is a problem that has still to be resolved: can a large-scale social movement, a political party, prosper if it recognizes or presupposes certain values without seeking any ultimate justification for them – leaving this task to its followers, who may therefore adopt this philosophy or that? Or must the movement, the party, itself take up an explicit philosophical position, thus limiting its support to such of the public as accept that philosophy? The question hardly arises in a society that is philosophically homogeneous, for example a purely Catholic state. But it does where a society is philosophically pluralist, and in this case a socialism which neither is nor aspires to be a philosophy or world-view must frankly face the problem.

Oswald von Nell-Breuning

II. Christian Social Movement

The Christian social movement is a recent development, social problems in the modern sense having come to light very late in the course of human history. Aristotle called man a ζῷον πολιτικόν, which is generally translated *ens sociale*. But in fact he and his successors for the next two thousand years recognized only the *societas politica*. For them society and the State were identical. Only in our own day have the two been clearly distinguished, and attention been turned to social problems as contrasted with political ones. There is a growing realization that the sort of life which people will lead in a community depends not merely on the juridical structure of the State but to a great extent on social forces which are non-political (and in this sense "spontaneous"); that together with the State, or even against it, these forces carry tremendous weight either for good or ill. There are many functions which must be left to voluntary associations – formed, it may be, specifically for the purpose – and not to the State, either because the State cannot do these things at all or because it can do them less well. These associations and their activities, the life astir within, we call "movements". Those that spring from the Christian view of the world and from Christian love we call the "Christian social movement". It is to be found at work inside and outside the Catholic Church.

Today the status of the Christian social movement in the Catholic Church is fully acknowledged. Since the time of Leo XIII the Popes themselves have been its leaders. Yet the opposition with which the movement has had to contend from the first still stubbornly persists. First, redemption is commonly interpreted in individualistic terms: the supernatural life of grace which Christ won for the redeemed by dying on the cross is an intensely personal possession of each individual; and since society cannot receive this gift, neither can it have been redeemed by Christ. One can understand the prevalence of this narrow view at a period when the Church was envisaged almost exclusively in juridical terms, as a *societas perfecta* analogous to the State, which was also predominantly regarded as an apparatus of government; so that Church and State confronted each other not as two communities of persons but as two powers, the spiritual and the temporal. But this approach still influences us now that we have learnt once more to see the Church rather as the "people of God" and the *Christus totus*. We are reminded that Christ himself declined the role of a social reformer; that his gospel contains no programme of social reform; that the primitive Church simply accepted the social conditions of that age, obviously unconscious of any mission to improve them. Such principles govern the thinking and even more the practice of many Catholics today, though Pius XI expressly declares that the Church does have a social mission and though Pius XII condemns the opposite opinion as spiritualism and supernaturalism.

Strangely enough, a second grave obstacle in the path of the Christian social movement has been the glorious tradition of Catholic charitable works. From apostolic times the Church felt the spiritual and corporal works of mercy to be its special concern and they have been carried on in every age under the supervision of the bishops. Thus it was widely supposed, at the beginning, that the Christian social movement wished to extend this charitable aid not merely to needy individuals but also to the poorer classes in general, and ecclesiastical pronouncements were worded in this sense: another new form of the works of mercy seemed to be developing. Indeed the theological virtue or charity may well have inspired these first efforts, and the people concerned may have been chiefly occupied with the works of mercy. But the movement itself was of quite a different nature. By definition the Christian social movement, like any social movement, seeks to establish a just social order and to support the just demands of those individuals and groups whose rights have been infringed. No doubt love must perfect this work (*Quadragesimo Anno*, no. 137), but the work itself is a matter of justice. In fact we may go so far as to say that this work is essentially *profane*, since its object is the creation of a social order for all men without exception and not merely for members of the mystical body – a society which will respect the rights of every man and in which no man shall feel himself an alien. A social movement guided by the Catholic hierarchy might, of course, do much good outside Catholic circles (as a Catholic hospital, for example, will often care for patients who are not Catholics). But if Catholic men and women are to merit the praise which Pius XI has for the pioneers of the Christian social movement (*Quadragesimo Anno*, nos. 19ff.), then, imbued with the Church's principles and fortified by its sacraments, they must become active and influential in our legislatures and in all other appropriate spheres of public life, recommended by their obvious personal qualifications and not as emissaries of the hierarchy. Recent papal utterances sharply distinguish the Christian social movement from the works of mercy, but in practice the separation is not yet complete. Inertia alone does not account for this fact. Separate as they may be in theory, the borderline between the two domains is blurred in certain areas; a single situation may call for charity to relieve a person in immediate distress and at the same time for social reform so that an injustice may be corrected. This, in fact, was normally the case at the beginning. Leo XIII still regards the workingman as one of the poor, the working class as *miserum vulgus, multitudo egens* (*Rerum Novarum*, no. 29); whereas Pius XI clearly distinguishes between the position of the proletariat – which is not necessarily pauperism – and the destitution widespread in underdeveloped countries (*Quadragesimo Anno*, no. 59).

The social movement is the antithesis of charitable works. It is a movement "from below", a movement of self-help on the part of those who are disadvantaged by the present social order. It does not beg for sympathy. Fully conscious of its own power, the movement is resolved to use this power to secure its just demands and therefore deliberately entrenches itself in strategic positions. By no stretch of the imagination can this militancy, this readiness to seize one's rights if they be not freely given, be considered "social charity". Many, indeed, have thought it anti-Christian, particularly where the workers' movement is concerned. Because Christians failed to read the signs of the times and held aloof too long, the workers' movement arose in some countries under the auspices of materialist atheism and drew a great part of the working class into its ranks. Here Christian workers founded a rival movement, based on Christian principles, which was recognized as a legitimate part of the movement only after long and bitter conflict. Christian faith, love, and morality do not teach us to acquiesce in social injustice. It is far more Christian to defend one's own rights and those of one's fellows by force when necessary. It is the part of Christian heroism to banish hatred and envy from this struggle, to limit demands to those of justice and the common good, at the same time fighting on a second front against organized atheism which would rob the worker of his faith. Catholics were very slow to realize all this. For decades moral theologians were unable to cope with the problems posed by the existence of the Christian social movement. They could not decide whether it was lawful even to form trade unions or to go on strike, let alone whether particular aims and policies of the unions were legitimate.

Further difficulties arise for a Christian social movement "from below" because Catholics still tend to regard the hierarchy which God has set up in the Church as a model for the structure of civil society. This idea has not only led Catholics astray in political theory but encouraged a mistaken attitude toward social problems. Pius XII (Christmas Message, 1944; Address to the Rota, 1946) dispelled the confusion so far as political theory is concerned; but the mistaken social attitude evidently still persists when, for example, prominent advocates of Catholic social doctrine even today can conceive of co-operation between capital and labour only on the basis that the workers (humanely treated, of course) remain subject to the ultimate authority and direction of those who own the means of production, rejecting out of hand other solutions which take more account of the elementary principle of Catholic social doctrine that labour is not a mere commodity. This state of affairs is aggravated by the fact that the clergy in many countries, especially the higher clergy, are of aristocratic background and have a sense of solidarity with the upper classes, whose feudal mentality they share (often, no doubt, unconsciously).

Thus, despite the unmistakable teaching of the Popes, the Christian social movement still encounters formidable opposition among Catholics. What is perhaps worse, it has to contend with general indifference and with the preconceptions of those who have no quarrel with the established order so long as it appears to serve their own interests. We must therefore prove that a Christian social movement is both legitimate and necessary, showing 1) what relevance the Church and the faith have to human society and its present condition, 2) what there is about the Christian social movement that is specifically "Christian" and enables it to produce different or better results than any other social movement, and 3) what need there is of such a Christian movement.

1. The Church regards itself as "the vital principle of human society" (Pius XII, 20 February 1946). It is not simply one community among the many which together form human society: it is its desire and its mission to be the "soul" of this society, wholly penetrating it with its supernatural life. If society is "that cohesion of men which is prerequisite if they are to achieve anything of objective cultural value", then the Church wishes to orientate this cohesion, from within, towards that ultimate value which is God revealing and communicating himself to redeemed mankind. Social arrangements and conditions, as well as men's conduct in society, fall within the competence of the Church as the custodian and interpreter of the natural moral law, and it must judge of them by this law and *ratione peccati*. And if as Pius XI declares "the whole social and economic organization of present-day society makes it extraordinarily difficult for a vast number of human beings to attain eternal salvation" (*Quadragesimo Anno*, no. 130), then the Church has an urgent pastoral

duty to see that these conditions are improved; it will not do simply to preach a change of heart, our institutions themselves must be reformed.

2. Whereas purely philanthropic social movements, for example, seek only to establish a just society – or what they consider such – in the temporal sphere, guided, of course, by purely temporal ideals, the aims of the Christian social movement in this world are always subordinated to the last end of man; its principles are warranted by divine revelation and, in the case of Catholics, by the magisterium of the Church. If the driving force behind other social movements is often the self-interest of a particular section of society, the energies of the Christian social movement ultimately derive from Christian faith and love. Thus the Christian movement generally keeps a sense of proportion and avoids extremism; notably it resists the temptation to identify the interests of one group with the common good. Its attitude is realistic, far removed from the false messianism which expects social reforms to usher in an earthly paradise.

3. Every social movement is based on some kind of world-view or philosophy, conscious or unconscious, sound or unsound, and this world-view directly influences the things men do when their sense of social responsibility leads them to take part in public life; so that any such public activities on the part of a Christian believer are in themselves a part, perhaps anonymous, of the Christian social movement. Certainly, therefore, the sum of the efforts which Christians are making to solve the social problems of our time must be called a Christian social movement. But the co-operation of Christians, if only because of their huge numbers, cannot be dispensed with.

The necessity for an institutionalized Christian social movement, however, is less obvious. Should Christians (Catholics) attempt to discharge their social duties entirely within organizations of their own? Such bodies may have to be created where materialistic humanist socialisms have been first in the field and imbued workers' associations or political parties with a world-view which is not our own or which indeed we find quite unacceptable. When this state of affairs has come about through our neglect, we may be compelled to set up rival organizations which will operate in accordance with our religion or at least will not conflict with it. But even in such cases it will be quite feasible for us to co-operate fraternally with non-Christian bodies so long as their aims and principles are similar to ours, and also with non-Christians in *common* organizations where tolerance is observed by both sides. Such co-operation is not possible with Communists, because their values are totally different from ours, nor with the adherents of any other form of totalitarianism, because all totalitarianism is inherently intolerant. In contrast to the timid reserve of earlier times, John XXIII and Vatican II have urged Catholics to co-operate with others, including non-Christians. In practice special Christian (Catholic) organizations seem to be necessary at the present time in some countries, at least in order to prepare people for their social responsibilities. Whether such organizations are necessary for social action itself will have to be decided in each country according to local circumstances.

What gave rise to the social movements of modern times was the invasion by industrialism of a largely agrarian society steeped in tradition. Conservative and reactionary circles, failing to understand what was happening and regarding industrialization simply as a disaster for the peasant and the craftsman, defended the old order as if it were permanently valid, and tried to restore it where it had been destroyed. Hence to this day the Christian social movement is suspected of "social romanticism" – of taking refuge in a world of illusion instead of grappling with hard facts. It was certainly very late in the day when the Christian social movement finally realized that the working class, ever more numerous and more powerful, is destined to become the decisive force in human society. For many years the Christian social movement was – as it still remains in the developing countries – as anti-capitalist as contemporary socialism, though for opposite reasons: whereas the aim of socialism is, as it were, to outstrip capitalism, the Christian social movement was constantly involved in attempts to restore semi-feudal conditions, a patriarchal society. It was often difficult for people imbued with 19th-century individualism to perceive that the common good demands the sacrifice not only of customs which are dear to one but also of rights which, though legitimately acquired, have become superannuated.

Pius XI having disposed once for all of individualism (*Quadragesimo Anno*), the way was open for John XXIII (*Mater et Magistra*) and Vatican II (*Gaudium et Spes*) to focus attention on the common good of mankind as a whole and the world-wide social problems which arise from the co-existence of an "affluent society" in some countries with extreme poverty in others. Today these latter are ravaged by the same unbridled capitalism (not yet tempered by social action) that formerly prevailed in the highly industrialized countries.

Until the 20th century the Christian social movement was mostly confined to the more advanced countries of Europe. In the United States the conditions which would have produced a social movement were altogether lacking until the time of the Depression (1929–33). On the other hand a social movement similar to the European one arose in a number of developing countries where the colonial powers had set up industries, and a Christian social movement began to stir among the native élite who had been educated in mission schools. In all the Latin countries, and throughout the developing world, the Christian social movement directly faces the Communist threat and has thus to fight on two fronts at once. In order to compete at all with Communism it must take on a revolutionary, anti-capitalist guise, which makes it the more difficult to work out a sound, positive programme with goals that can actually be achieved.

The Christian social movement also exists outside the Catholic Church. Among the Eastern Orthodox there is scarcely a trace of it. The mystical and contemplative mentality of these Churches tends to discourage social action. There has been no scope for it anyway either in Tsarist Russia or in the present Soviet bloc. The movement for social reform initiated in the mid-19th century by some prominent Anglicans (F. D. Maurice, C. Kingsley) met with little success at the time but exercised considerable indirect influence in the development of trade unions and working-class education, whereas the social conscience of the Non-Conformists played an important part in the formation of the British Labour Party.

Today (with the exception of those under Communist rule, as observed above) a powerful and resolute social movement flourishes in all the Churches which have joined the ecumenical movement. The way was paved for it by the Stockholm conference on Life and Work, 1924, and its theological bases were worked out at the conference on Faith and Order held at Lausanne in 1927. The conferences at Amsterdam (1948), Evanston (1954), and New Delhi (1961) each made important contributions to the movement. The Churches of the World Council of Churches, unlike the Catholic Church (*Mater et Magistra*, nos. 186–99), are frankly prepared to sanction and encourage the official steps which are being taken to limit the number of births in countries already suffering from over-population. In other respects, however, there is a remarkable unanimity, so far as practical aims and policies are concerned, among the members of the World Council and between them and ourselves; the "responsible society" which they seek to establish is in effect what we mean by solidarity.

Oswald von Nell-Breuning

III. Christian Social Doctrine

Christian social doctrine is usually taken simply as the equivalent of the social doctrine of the Catholic Church. Whether there exists as well a Protestant social doctrine comparable in extent and importance or only a Protestant teaching on social ethics is disputed even among Protestants themselves. Scarcely even the rudiments of a social doctrine can be found in the Eastern Churches. In this article we deal chiefly with Catholic social doctrine. At the end we give a brief sketch of its Protestant counterpart.

1. *Concept.* Catholic social doctrine, as it is taught in papal and other Church documents, as well as in the popular and scientific writings of Catholic scholars and exponents, can be defined as "that unified body of teaching, in the Christian dispensation, on the organization of terrestrial human society as a whole and in its individual parts, which sets a standard for the progressive ordering of society by man through the exercise of his natural social powers".

"In the Christian dispensation" both philosophical and theological knowledge is possible. In Catholic social doctrine, as it is at present, knowledge by use of reason clearly predominates. Thus it is – at least in the present stage of development – almost entirely social philosophy and only in a very limited way social theology. It needs further development on the theological side – if for no other reason than to keep abreast of Protestant social ethics whose line of argument is basically theological, proceeding as it does from sacred Scripture. Statements taken directly from the *depositum fidei* will be only very rarely applicable to concrete situations; in general a social theology will present conclusions *ex ratione theologica.*

The human society with which Catholic social doctrine is concerned is that of this world.

Insofar as it is social philosophy, Catholic social doctrine must build on the basis of experience supplied for the most part by the empirical sciences, especially biology, physiology and psychology. There is a particularly close relationship with the empirical social sciences ever in process of expansion. Of these, the science known as sociology has always been liable to the temptation to regard itself as a philosophical science or as a substitute or heir to philosophy. This calls for an attitude of critical reserve or even opposition, yet it does not entail rejecting the fruits of sociological investigations, provided they have been reliably conducted and critically examined.

In contrast to the empirical social sciences, the Catholic social doctrine deals with the "ordered structure" of society. This means that it is a social metaphysics or ontology and therefore also a *normative* science or *de*ontology of society. This gives it also its position in the disputed question of value judgments. As a theoretical science it rests on the basis of the *philosophia perennis* and thus accepts "essentialism", in contrast to positivism and neo-positivism which wholly reject it. Its metaphysics is based on the axiom: "ens est unum, verum, bonum". There is knowledge not only of *being* in general, but of *essences* (*quod quid est*), and from these flows essential knowledge about what are values and what are not, especially about ethical values and their opposite, about what ought to be and what ought not to be. Not everything that has been regarded as knowledge of the essential has proved to be so; therefore Catholic social doctrine always examines expository statements very carefully before it draws normative conclusions from them. It is also very conscious of the need to guard against wishful thinking, since it distorts the vision of the facts and even much more insidiously insinuates itself into normative judgments. But it will never allow the spheres of being and duty, or the knowledge of being and knowledge of duty, to be isolated from one another. Nor is it content to systematize in a scientific way ethical norms – in this case social ethics – and test them for logical coherence: in contrast to all types of positivism, as well as to the prevailing Protestant opinion, it holds essentially to this: the principle of social order, or, what amounts to the same thing, the norms of social ethics are capable of being known by our *intellect*, although experience shows they are generally known clearly only in the light of revelation (*necessitas relativa revelationis*).

Although man is, and will remain, in many ways a riddle for us, yet Catholic social doctrine has a convincing answer to the question: "What is man?" From what man *is* (not this or that man, but man as such), it deduces what befits or behoves man (*honestum*) and what is unworthy of him (*turpe*), what is his relationship to his fellow-man and to God, namely that God's will binds him, that he *must* do what is *honestum* and *may* not do what is *turpe*. We express this briefly as follows: we have a *concept of man* and from this concept follows logically our *concept of the order of society*.

Revelation teaches us that man is not only a natural image of God, but is called as well to a supernatural likeness to God and to his sonship in grace, to be brother and co-heir to the incarnate Son of God, member of his mystical body, the Church, of which he is the head; also that his Church is not only *Christus totus*, but also a society, taking its place among other societies. All this is a very substantial enrichment by revelation of our knowledge of man. What follows for social doctrine in general and especially for the understanding of the *socia(bi)litas* of man is a matter on which opinions vary.

The Church itself, as a social structure, has been hitherto almost exclusively studied from the specifically juridical point of view (*societas perfecta*); there is as yet scarcely any social doctrine *about* the Church. From its object this would be social theology. The address of Pius XII of 2 February 1946 to the College of Cardinals made a beginning, but this has not been followed up.

The relations of Church and society, Church and State, which are so frequently discussed, also presume that God has revealed himself in Jesus Christ and has founded this one Church. This section of the doctrine is left for the most part to the teaching of fundamental theology or dogmatic theology on the Church. As for marriage, the usual practice is to deal only with natural marriage in social doctrine, and in doing this the supposition is made that the unity and indissolubility of marriage can be proved from reason; sacramental marriage of baptized persons, including its demands on State and society, is then left to other disciplines, especially canon law.

The notion of "person" is basic to the entire social doctrine. Yet on this there is a fundamental dispute as to whether the *mysterium SS. Trinitatis* enables us to go beyond what is ascertainable by philosophical analysis and to deepen the concept of the person in the sense of being open to others, in contrast to the enclosed nature of the individual; also whether it is permissible to draw analogical conclusions from the intratrinitarian relationships to the social relationships between human beings. *If so*, we would arrive at a radically theological social doctrine; *if not*, social doctrine would remain as a whole a philosophic science with certain "additions" of a theological nature.

Whatever may be said about this, the method used by the Popes, and especially by Pius XII, of developing the doctrine philosophically and of taking the motives for action from the world of faith, has great practical advantages. In this way the Popes could address themselves not only to believing Catholics but to all – apart indeed from that relatively small group who adhere to a philosophy which sets an unbridgeable chasm between the world of being and the world of values and in whose judgment to conclude from being to duty would be a flagrant offence against logic. In fact the papal pronouncements reach the ears of a very wide circle of unbelievers and are received with great interest. There is this also to be said: a theologically derived social doctrine would convey the image of a society all of whose members have the Catholic faith and live according to its teachings, whereas we live in an ideologically pluralistic society, and it is in the shaping of this society we must co-operate. We may not impose on this society an order, corresponding indeed to our convictions, but which would do violence to those who think differently and would prevent them from living according to their conscience. We must build with others a society we can feel at home in, because it will give us a fair deal, above all in allowing us to live according to our conscience, but also one that can be accepted by others as well, because it is fair to them too and does not expect from them anything they would have to reject as being against their conscience. A social doctrine that is built on sound human reasoning and addresses itself to all men of good will has the chance of giving a lead and indicating goals which for the widest circles are not only acceptable but will actually be accepted. If in recent decades so many of the social teachings of the Church, with which it once stood in direct opposition to the spirit of the times and consequently almost alone, have come to be universally accepted, if neo-liberalism and neo-socialism converge ever more closely on Catholic social teaching, it seems even providential that the Popes have chosen this road (which remained that of Vatican II in spite of its theological effort).

2. *Content.* Catholic social doctrine sees in man the personal dignity proper to his nature but just as essentially it views him as directed to society ("naturally social", see above). Society does not exist outside or even above men who are bound by the social bond, but entirely *in* them and *for* them.

This results in that peculiar mutual relationship of individual to society which is formulated in the principle of solidarity: the individual is by his nature ordered to society and this, in turn, to him. Briefly, this means "mutual involvement". Every single individual is as a member – at least as long as he is a member – inextricably involved in its destiny; and the society can in turn not loose itself from its involvement with its members; the normative aspect follows: every individual shares in the responsibility for the success or failure of the community; this in turn bears responsibility for all its members ("each for all, all for each"). Thus the principle is fundamentally a principle of being and derivatively an ethical principle.

The relationship of individual and society is more exactly determined by the principle of subsidiarity: society should be helpful to its members, especially its ultimate members, the individuals, that is, it should promote their own activity, not suppress or absorb their individual life. This *gravissimum principium* (*Quadragesimo Anno*, no. 79) works in two ways: on the one hand it opposes collectivist, especially totalitarian, tendencies and on this side it must continue to be applied in present-day society; on the other hand – whence its name: *subsidium afferre* – it demands from social groups that they give their members generous help, especially help to self-help. Insofar as Catholic authors expound this principle in different ways, there is question less of different views than that some stress one side and others the other. The strange attacks of Protestant authors rest on obvious misunderstandings. The principle has been given surprisingly sympathetic attention by democratic socialists.

The central idea of Catholic social doctrine is the *bonum commune*. Unfortunately this term is used in two different senses by the scholastic followers of St. Thomas and those of Suarez. There are two words in English for this concept: common good and common welfare. The common good is that value or sum of values which forms the goal of all the activity of a particular society; this can be a very limited utility value, or it can be the sum total of all the cultural values attainable by man. It is in this elevated sense that Thomistic authors used the term "common good" which then consists in the *perfectio naturae specifice humanae*. The "common welfare" in contrast to the common good is "an organizational and organizing value". It consists in this, that a society is rightly organized, i.e., in such a way that it can fulfil its functions, and is thus enabled to co-ordinate and activate the powers of its members too with a view to securing the common good. In this sense the Suarezians speak of the *bonum commune*; usually the papal documents too use this terminology, indeed *Mater et Magistra*, no. 65, defines *bonum commune* in this way. Thus understood, the common welfare is a most important value in the service of the good, whereas the common good is a value in itself.

These differences, which have their following in the two schools of thought we have mentioned, make themselves apparent only when the social principles and especially the notion of the *bonum commune* are subjected to a deeper and more speculative analysis and evaluation; otherwise they appear only occasionally, e.g., in the teaching on the right of ownership, which the Thomists see as justified by the *bonum commune*, whereas spokesmen of the other school derive it from the personal nature of man and *end up* with the consideration due to the *bonum commune*. Perhaps it can be said with all due reserve that in general the one school sees the problem more from the objective point of view and the other more from the subjective, just as ethical principles (principles of moral theology) can be thought of either from the point of view of the law as a pre-existing, objective norm, or from conscience as the subjective appropriation and realization of morality.

In its details, Catholic social doctrine deals with the different societies, especially the family and the State as *societates naturales*. The former is nowadays clearly taken to mean only the *societas coniugalis et parentalis*. It is more difficult to determine what is intended in speaking of the *res publica* ("State") and especially when it is called a *societas perfecta*. Nowadays, especially since *Pacem in Terris*, one must include the complex of international and supranational institutions; many statements about the "State" include also member groups, especially those "political" communities with more or less administrative autonomy. With regard to the so-called *corps intermédiaires* or *puissances intermédiaires*, especially in the question of whether they belong in the sphere of the State or of private associations or in a third group, there is a division of views: in *Quadragesimo Anno*, following in this German legal thinking, the latter opinion is held, for *Mater et Magistra* whose thought is more in accord with Roman law, "public" and "private" are sufficient without a third principle of distinction.

Popes and bishops have *on particular*

occasions made statements on social matters. Thus all official Church documents are written for an occasion and, as such, are not complete or systematic textbook expositions. It is clear from them how the circumstances of time and current interest determine the matters dealt with. Leo XIII directs his attention to the question of the workers in the capitalist industry of Central and Western Europe and to a limited extent of North America. Pius XI takes up the question of the entire social order, but still chiefly from the point of view of industrial capitalism. John XXIII includes and emphasizes agriculture and also the service industries and, since the Church had even under his immediate predecessors become more and more world-wide, addresses himself to world problems, especially those of the developing countries. This illustrates clearly how Catholic social doctrine, in keeping with the definition given at the beginning, is concerned with the structures of society as a whole and in its various parts and with the task of promoting social order in an ever-changing world.

3. *Binding force*. The views of Catholic experts are not sufficient to constitute Catholic social doctrine; binding force pertains only to the official doctrinal and disciplinary pronouncements of the Popes and the bishops. The teaching authority of the Church can propose doctrine for acceptance, the disciplinary authority can impose binding decrees. The Church claims teaching authority, as Pius XI expressly states, "in omnibus, quae ad regulam morum referuntur", but rejects it just as certainly "in iis quae artis sunt" (*Quadragesimo Anno*, no. 41). In the social, economic and political spheres too the Church has to proclaim and authentically interpret the natural and revealed moral law; this also necessarily includes the assertion of those essential truths from which moral and juridical norms flow. It can also proclaim all other truths which are necessarily (not only logically) connected with the truths of faith. On purely factual matters, however, e.g., on the situation of social groups, conditions of production, distribution of income and wealth, etc., it has only purely human knowledge such as every research worker can acquire for himself; its statements on these matters and the claims it deduces from them will therefore have only that degree of certainty that pertains to the available information, the experts consulted, etc. The result is: the Church enunciates basic principles and norms in virtue of its own God-given teaching authority; in exercise of its pastoral office it applies these norms to those concrete situations and cases demanding a solution; the validity of these applications depends in each case on a judgment which has no more than human certainty. Often this judgment is dependent in turn on preliminary questions of a clearly specialized, technical nature (*quae artis sunt*), for which the Church in default of supernatural illumination is dependent on the competence of the experts. A particular case of this which regularly occurs is when it is a question of judging whether a certain course of action is permissible or not in view of its probable good or evil consequences. In *Mater et Magistra*, no. 239, and again in *Pacem in Terris*, no. 160, the Church expressly requires the obedience of the faithful when the hierarchy apply the principles of Catholic social doctrine to concrete cases; in the last-mentioned passage the part and task of the expert (*prudentia*) is admirably enunciated, after which the Church if necessary (*cum opus est*) gives judgment on the question which falls within *its* competence, namely that of morality. Vatican II emphasizes even more decisively the independent responsibility of the experts and urges the pastors of the Church to respect their due freedom ("observanter agnoscant", *Lumen Gentium*, art. 37).

To determine correctly the degree of binding force, consideration must be given to the measure of authority claimed by the statement itself; further, its purpose and the circumstances in which it is given, what are the tacit assumptions and therefore limitations it includes, and much besides. In order to be able to appeal to it in controversial issues without running the risk of interpreting it in an arbitrary way, it is always necessary to make a study of the problem itself.

With its social doctrine the Church throws light on social life with its needs, its confusions and its injustices in order to stimulate our thought and still more our consciences; the Church cannot and will not give patent remedies nor a panacea to solve the "social question".

4. *Excursus: Protestant social doctrine or social ethics?* However much the Protestant Churches may differ in their definitions of the Church, they are united in holding they have no ecclesiastical teaching authority. A social doctrine which would be the binding official teaching of the Church is therefore excluded. If there is such a thing as Protestant social doctrine at all, it could only be a set of propositions accepted more or less unanimously by Protestant Christians. The content and object of study of this would be the same or similar to that of Catholic social doctrine. Whether the Protestant view of the faith permits such a set of teachings is disputed among Protestants themselves. Some Protestant authors, especially in the U.S.A., hold fast as Luther did to the natural law and so to the conviction that even in the state of fallen nature human understanding is capable of assimilating the pertinent factual and theoretical knowledge and to recognize the idea of God it expresses. The corpus of knowledge built up by these authors is thus, as far as the matter is concerned, social doctrine in the same sense as ours and shows a wide measure of agreement in content with ours. The position is widely different in Continental Europe where the vast majority of Protestant theologians understand original sin and the *sola scriptura* principle in such a way that the very notion of a social order is inadmissible, much less an intellectual knowledge of that order. Thus fallen man must rely on the directions found in sacred Scripture. This entails a great effort to search the Scriptures for relevant social statements. In fact Protestant theologians have got a great deal out of it. Sacred Scripture proved to be a much more fruitful source than at first appeared; nevertheless a complete systematic social doctrine can by no means be derived from it. To give answers to urgent practical questions, therefore, Protestant theologians are forced, starting from the insights gained from sacred Scripture, to go on to make use of other premisses taken from experience or from the relevant sciences. Often in these cases the text of the sacred Scripture is little more than a connecting link for a series of ideas and chains of conclusions which, when viewed closely, are seen to rest on intellectual knowledge. In such cases, there is little or no difference between this and our natural law mode of argument. In particular the documents of the Conferences of the World Council of Churches of Amsterdam (1948), Evanston (1954) and New Delhi (1961) appear to the Catholic reader to be genuine natural law conclusions, but this is disputed by the majority of Protestants.

Divergence of opinion between Catholic and Protestant social doctrine or social ethics stemming from these differences essentially concerns marriage. Also in connection with the State, especially civil authority ("rulers"), many Protestant groups hold, in deference to biblico-theological considerations, views contrary to Catholic teaching. In general one can say that in questions which are still controversial, the division of views does not fully coincide with differences of belief but runs counter to them. In comparison with the great dogmatic differences, which exist not only between different Protestant Churches but also between more orthodox and more liberal theologians in the same Church, there prevails in general on the Protestant side in attitudes and demands of social ethics a surprising measure of agreement. In most of the practical questions Catholic social doctrine and Protestant social ethics are very close together and fight shoulder to shoulder.

Oswald von Nell-Breuning

SOCIAL PHILOSOPHY

1. What is social philosophy? Having experienced social life, man can ask what is the nature and essence of it (or of society, as the quintessence of social intercourse). To go "behind" and "beyond" experience in this way will also evoke the question as to the meaning of social life for the person. If there is such a meaning, the question also arises as to the values embodied in social life and in its aptness to promote values.

The philosophical systems soon took in the social element. The thought of antiquity was taken up by scholasticism and handed on to the present day in social ontology. The philosophy of law and of the State have always been included in social philosophy to which Hegel and Marx made large contributions. The 19th-century expression "social philosophy" designates primarily "systems, theories and trains of thought which envisaged social reforms of a utopian nature" (von Kempski). Movements such as liberalism and socialism reflect the social philosophy which upholds both the freedom of the individual and his essential links with society, as do social thinking, values and action. The persistent notion of the organism finds its ultimate expression in "universalism". Phenomenology and value-ethics, like existence-philosophy, offer new insights into social reality. The various approaches show that the registration of social facts is not enough. Their interpretation in the light of social reality as such appears essential for the due fulfilment of human existence and demands its own special scientific treatment.

Christian thinking, posing the question of the origin and nature of created being, developed a social philosophy on the basis of Aristotelian and scholastic doctrine. It rejected individualism and collectivism, and carried over the notion of natural law into neo-scholasticism. The general result is designated "solidarism". Existence-philosophy and value-philosophy were used to deepen and extend the ontological orientations of Christian social philosophy. Light was thus thrown on the richness of values in personal fellowship, as also on the social character of personal existence. Evolutionist or dialectical principles have left little mark hitherto on Christian social philosophy.

Quadragesimo Anno (nos. 14, 110) speaks of a "new", "Christian" social philosophy. The natural knowledge of man and society, including social institutions like the State, law, property, etc., is understood to have revelation as its background. Thus Christian, and indeed all social philosophy is closely related to social ethics, since social reality always imposes tasks to be realized. By virtue of its origin, Christian social philosophy is closely linked with studies of natural law, the effort to formulate rights and duties based on the social nature of man. Social philosophy tries to throw light on the nature of man insofar as it is social and finds fulfilment in fellowship.

2. Certain principles follow, which show that the philosophical questions are multiple.

In terms of the Aristotelian categories, social being appears as a relation (accidental or transcendental) and as a state of being-together (*esse unum in pluribus*). The relation is seen as orientated to human values in general ("intentional" relationship). Others attach it to social ethics, seeing all members of a community as orientated to the common good, where they find their fulfilment. The phenomenological and personalist view of society defines social reality by the term of "togetherness" (*Mitmenschlichkeit*).

The social orientation of man means more than that he is ready for the perpetual exchanges with others which are necessary for life. It means that giving and accepting enrich human nature. Existential phenomenology defines human existence as "being there through others and for others" (Kwant). Man's social dimension is not just one among others, but a primordial determination without which man cannot be. "The whole person is social and the whole social reality is personal" (Plattel).

Society, the concrete realization of the social factor, is seen in social philosophy as a unity of order and relationships (among persons who by nature can and must combine). Values are not excluded by this notion, since the attainment of values is as it were the goal of social union: social welfare is the common *good*. In the value-ethics of phenomenology society or fellowship itself appears as a value, the basic value of human existence, since values exist only in fellowship. Fellowship attaches man to the realm of values. The basic social attitude is love, and it takes the form of personal fellowship: existence and intercommunication in love. Utilitarian teamwork is necessary, but will be all the more perfect, the more it is a personal fellowship.

Social philosophy also deals with social structures or laws, universally valid social principles. There is disagreement as to their number or how they can be organized into a system, but there is wide agreement on the following. The principle of solidarity affirms the due and necessary social links. The principle of subsidiarity tries to determine the various fields of competence of social activity and is declared in *Quadragesimo Anno* (no. 79) to be "a most important principle in social philosophy". The principles of unity and totality try to demarcate the body social, and to allot persons their place in the order of the whole. The principle of the common good gives the purpose of an activity which is in keeping with the social reality. The principle of the dignity of the person is at once the basis and goal of the social reality.

Social philosophy also deals with the development of society, which must be considered as a historical entity. Thus progress, freedom and obligation must be constantly re-considered. The notion of order must be applied to the facts of social evolution.

3. *The importance of social philosophy.* The interpretation of social existence is now the task of sociology rather than of social philosophy. But social philosophy is a help to sociological interpretation, which has recourse to it "when the analysis of the social system presents insuperable difficulties" (R. König). But sociology does not attribute scientific value to social philosophy as such. Nonetheless, this has a scientific value, beyond the role allotted to it by sociology, when it investigates the social nature of man in all its dimensions and does not confine itself to the social structures which are historically or immediately apparent. It has a critical function when it is based on an understanding of man which takes in his total relationship to the world, society and God. It can then transcend the tensions of individualism and collectivism, egoism and altruism, person and community, freedom and obligation, which dominate so many social systems and attitudes. It can point beyond the accidental or contemporary, beyond the historically-conditioned, to what is permanent in man as such – of which the social quality is unconditional.

Certain forms of social thinking, in terms of organism, mechanism, processes, etc., have been borrowed from science and technology. These can be criticized by social philosophy, which can bring out the truly personal and social nature of man. It will also retain, and even augment its importance, against behavioural sciences based on mathematical and technological views of a "planned society", if it succeeds in grasping and propounding the full riches of personal and hence social being.

Joachim Giers

SOCIETY

1. *The problem of definition.* Society – to give a preliminary verbal definition – is the totality of interactions between individuals, no matter how combined, insofar as this totality constitutes a system with its own internal processes, the development therefore (whether naturally or artificially) of a unified relationship between a number of people. As such a unified relationship between human beings, between beings, that is, who have the free disposal of themselves, and over whom no one has disposal except to the extent that they themselves in free responsibility put themselves in the hands of others, the functional structure of society is not to be thought of as the mechanical or organic integration of many into a functional relationship. The factual relationship is rather to be considered, in principle, as a conscious one, to which the individuals consciously relate. Thus the members of society always interact in such a way that they relate primarily to their own interaction and then by means of it to one another. This means that society, being human, is the basic development of a unified relationship between the individual and his quasi-natural interaction with others, both elements being equally basic to it.

This essentially double nature of the relationship implies the impossibility of a real definition of society which would be valid for all times. Inasmuch as such a definition is an attempt to determine the relation of the individual to his relationship with other persons, a theoretical correlation between the related person and his relationship, and thereby the consciousness of the social process itself, it is always an element of that which it attempts to define. The definition then modifies what has been defined (and that by necessity, insofar as the latter, the fact of relationship, is present in personal society merely as a consciously perceived element of the total process). The definition becomes part of the objective substratum of the social process, and calls for a constantly renewed assimilation if it is not to contradict, even in its very form, the "essence" of society as the expression of relationship. This formal definition sees society as so essentially a historical reality that all attempts to objectivate it in a definition must be taken as a historical and momentary element of society. This means that any definition must be regarded as an element of a definite social process and the latter as essentially constituted through its own historical self-explanation.

2. *Historical development as the content of modern dynamic society.* In antiquity and in the Middle Ages man was more or less taken for granted as the ζῷον πολιτικόν (*ens sociale, animale politicum*) and socio-philosophical reflection concerned itself essentially with the problem of the *best* society: the optimal organization of the *polis* as the environment of the citizen who exercised his freedom in this public sphere; the most successful order of law as guarantee of the world-wide *Pax Romana*; right order in the hierarchical gradations of Christendom. Society could therefore be taken simply as the correlative to the "individual" considered in his immediate and thus independent self-consciousness. This concept became problematic only at the time of the

Renaissance with the rise of civil society in the sense of a functionally constituted community of autonomous individuals. Such a society finding itself "homeless" in the framework of the quasi-natural law prevailing in the ordered society of the Middle Ages, found an adequate understanding of itself in the claim of modern philosophy, after Descartes, to deduce the entire world structure from the ideas of an *ego cogitans* formed prior to any world reality and providing a basis for all thought, and accepted this as its only explanation. A result of this conceptual development was that for the first time the need, theoretical as well as practical, arose of abandoning the notion of society as a given self-evident reality and of finding an explanation by reconstructing it in its original meaning starting from the thinking subject. This called for a fundamental self-analysis on the part of society. In professional philosophy (as for example in Leibniz) this novel problem was reflected in the attempt to relate the universality of self-consciousness, now for the first time apparent, which could accept nothing "outside" its own self-determination and the world it opens up to the plurality of such "window-less" egos. This found direct expression in the theories of early liberalism on the "social contract" (in Hobbes and Rousseau, though in very different forms) which explained society by means of personal interactions after the model of a contractual agreement, and accordingly demanded from social institutions, especially the State, merely that they should regulate (thus Montesquieu in explicit detail) as a functional association based on freedom, the relationships between the individuals and their induction into a social totality by way of a contract.

With this basically new beginning, traditional society was superseded not only theoretically but also in practice, inasmuch as society is not just neutral material, but a correlative expression of its theory, the latter being an element of the former. The revolution in the understanding of social relationship led naturally in the liberal movement in England and America as well as in the French Revolution to an upheaval in those social institutions in which civic society consciously created its own social order. This implied not merely a change in power relationships but an epoch-making change in the meaning of society and thus, insofar as society is essentially a conscious relationship, in the nature of society itself. Since that time society refers itself in its development no longer to some predetermined order imposed on it without its own free disposition but *exists* now only to the extent that it systematically reflects its own meaning, comes to a rational understanding of its own functioning and expresses institutionally what it has thus understood. What exists from now on is a purely self-reflective society, autonomously determining its own nature as society. This also implies inversely that basic reflections on the meaning of society enter *ipso facto* into the development of society.

Such a development on the part of society implies first of all on the practical level a fundamental change in the functioning of all institutions of authority. Where it came to an understanding of itself civic society no longer acknowledged, and modern society in general since then does not acknowledge in principle, any authority which it has not itself legitimized, but subordinates all power to its own functioning. In this way it reduces the power of the State especially to a pragmatic reality. This it does in two ways: firstly, the power of the State can no longer have any meaning but that of functional administration, and secondly, the use of power by this administration must justify itself before the dynamic process of modern society (by whatever means of democratic formation of opinion this comes about). The juridical public system retains this function of service in all those areas of social life it wishes to take over, indeed precisely there inasmuch as all institutions, now no more than the externalization (and thereby the assurance), of the balance between the individual and the social element immanent in him, exist and function only to serve a total social expression. Thus society in turn makes these institutions its own and thus can reach even the intimate non-social areas only insofar as they are institutionally secured and expressed. While in the course of time the meaning of practically all public spheres – the judicial system including legal sanctions, social welfare, education and even science, etc. – has undergone this change (or is undergoing it), in the bourgeois society of the West only the capitalist principle of private profit as the motive power of economic life still resists assimilation into a modern fully-institutionalized social process. Consequent on a tradition inherited from the deism of early political economy, which assumed a pre-established harmony between individual interests, a directly personal factor, private ownership of what are means of relationship in society is not seen in the context of its social function and as a result has not come to an integration into a total social process which would be not just arbitrary but expressed in legitimate institutions. This is a "bourgeois" inconsequence which results in fatal irrationalities similar to those arising from the naiveté of the Communist reliance on a State system without true relationship to the individual. Besides the immanent development of its functions through institutions on a democratic basis, modern society also implies in principle systematic self-analysis through scientific reflection. It was no accident that sociology came into existence along with civic society, and is an integral factor in modern society in general. Sociology is seen, as empirical research, and also (inasmuch as all empiricism tacitly or expressly presupposes a formal object) as an *a priori* systematic science. As such, sociology defines society, in the most general and preliminary way, as a self-sustaining system of interactions, and accordingly indicates, as the basic constitutive processes of every empirical society, firstly the biological preservation of the species based on a division of functions, and secondly the "culture", the personal dimension of interaction, which, if it is to be possible, calls for a consciousness of values held, at least formally, in common, as a meeting place of rational ideas. It inquires into these basic forms of social activity, these being the chief formal ways in which society expresses itself, as to the nature and degree of variation they exhibit, the interdependence of these varying individual processes and their expression in institutions, as well as the "cultural" integration of society in an accepted understanding of itself. Society is thus seen as a role-play in which social needs and expectations reveal a comprehensive system of functions, and it is only in the execution of these that the individual becomes socially expressive and intelligible.

Social science, however, reflects a certain naiveté as long as it is regarded as being merely theoretical (with occasional subsequent possibilities of application), and does not from the beginning claim to be illuminating, both historically and factually, as an intrinsic factor in the modern social process. Understood in this way (as in the Marxist tradition of social criticism), theoretical social science has the decisive function of critical investigation of all those hindrances to social relationship, whether they are subjective or collective, which resist the total self-realization of society, by blocking the social process in its function of creating relationship, and thus introducing alienation into the dynamics of society. It is especially necessary, where appeal is made from such hindrances to relationship to extra-social authorities, to unmask such appeals as ideological determination foreign to its nature and so to pave the way for assimilation into a true relationship. In this sense society may and can nowadays be personal, thereby entering into the historically irreversible phase of absolute self-reflection, only if it scrutinizes itself constantly for ideological trends (see *Ideology*). A society of this kind demands, in the interest of its absolute self-expression, besides the practical removal of all resistance to social interaction and to its scientific investigation, that it should be based on an enlightened understanding of the fundamental conditions of interaction between individuals and so of the nature of society in general; an understanding which monadology has merely shown to be a philosophical desideratum. Such absolute reflection of society began in the inter-personality theory of German Idealism, especially that of Fichte and Hegel, with the insight into the interpersonal relatedness of one's own personal immediacy itself. It saw that self-consciousness is constituted essentially by freedom, that is, by the responsible query as to the meaning and justification of one's own reality, and thus in the context of an absolute criterion for legitimacy in general and subject to its claims. It also saw that the absolute criterion of meaning and purpose can be apprehended only through a concrete historical claim by another person on one's own freedom, whereby the ego in principle both materially and formally becomes part of a concretely historical and contingent process. In factual interpersonal contact, the dialectical tension between the absolute nature of the formal claim to meaning here disclosed and the material contingency and defectiveness of meaning (with its view of self and the world) as actually experienced – this being the true significance of that dialectic between the individual and his capacity for relationship that constitutes society – shows both to be factors equally basic to the fundamental process of relationship itself. Thus society, as the essence and perfection of the fundamentally primary relationship, transcends itself essentially (and here is probably the place for the problem of Church and State) to seek fellowship. The latter is that outgoing in interpersonal relationship in which the assertion of purpose and meaning takes material form in a unity in which all free men, relating to and through each other, correspond and contrast, and in which nothing is held back in the process of mutuality. Such a *societas perfecta* as a total communication is the goal aimed at in principle by modern society with its basically critical attitude to ideology.

Konrad Hecker

SOCIOLOGY

Social phenomena have been the object of thought in all social systems. The writings on social philosophy are an outstanding example of this. With the rise of industrialism and secularization and the loosening of previously accepted social ties, the social foundations themselves came to be questioned. This, as well as the constantly increasing complexity of social structures, demanded an independent science with its own methods, not the least of whose functions would be to help in the solution of the "social questions" that had arisen. Sociology is thus strongly orientated to the investigation of modern society, without at the same time neglecting the historical and theoretical aspects.

Sociology is the science of "social activity". Since this social activity is always directed towards social systems, sociology can also be called the science of social systems (groups, institutions, society). Through its orientation to social systems, social activity attains a relative constancy and becomes a sort of repeated experiment. It can therefore be assessed by other active participants and becomes capable of scientific analysis. Since the social process is relatively independent of the individual, the object of attention in sociology is not man as an individual but man as fulfilling a certain social function (role, office) and thus as representative of a social reality. Representation also entails the realization and living portrayal of group norms (aims and obligations). These arise from group consensus based on tradition, as well as from individual insight into the social system, insofar as its existence is recognized as meaningful. Sociology thus attempts to arrive at an understanding of the norms and normative models which are independent of the individual and are transmitted to him in the socializing process, and which determine human activity and mould man as a member of a group. Consequently, the object of sociology does not consist in the "interpersonal", in mutual relationships and social processes, but primarily in the study of the complex of norms which is relevant to human activity. The extent or duration of a social system cannot be precisely laid down. It reveals itself in every case only through its functions, in the last analysis through the individual activities directed to a particular objective. These in turn are to be grasped only against the background of the total system and its central norms, i.e., its structure.

The social functions can be described in terms of the individual, e.g., calling or profession, and then subdivided in terms of the various qualifications and functions within a given calling. They can also be grouped in major units, such as the workshop, department, firm, industry and society in industrial sociology. These functions always include, besides the individual functions (roles), empirical objects of the most varied kind (e.g., implements, machines), which in turn influence the norm structure. The more general functions too can be represented by individual persons in such a way that the entire complex of objects and means is combined with the people who are active in them. Thus leadership, authority, power and status emerge, in any particular instance, primarily as a participation in the effective presence of the social group, and secondarily as the power to give orders and impose sanctions. Only after the norms of a social system and its functional differences have been analysed is it possible to understand social change, conflicts, deviate behaviour, integration and disintegration, social classes, mobility, manipulation, repression, etc.

From this it is clear that the structural significance of individual problems cannot be grasped and the thread of understanding is lost in a welter of empirical data, if a strict separation is made between social philosophy and sociology, since every social system can be grasped only in a wider structural context. Seen ideologically, sociology exists only when partial aspects are explained in terms of the "whole". Besides philosophy, closely allied to sociology are social psychology, pedagogy, history, economics, jurisprudence, demography and social anthropology (ethnology). The two last-mentioned sciences can also be reckoned as subdivisions of sociology.

The areas of research of sociology are "general sociology", the basic problems such as norm, role, group, power, social change, etc., and "special" (or hyphenated) sociologies. The areas of research have developed in connection with urgent social problems in dependence on the interests of the researchers. There are no sharp lines of division between general and special sociology. Thus the conditions of industrial workers in the 19th century aroused attention. Among the most important branches of research are industrial sociology, urban and rural sociology, family sociology, political sociology and the sociology of religion. Nowadays the chief topics of research, apart from general theory, are youth and education, leisure and work, the developing countries, population and town planning, the media of communication, and, a recent arrival, revolution. Further areas of research are the sociology of law, of knowledge, of organization, of minorities, and of deviation. Every social sphere can in principle be made the object of a special sociology (e.g., art, the military forces, old age, sport, medicine, etc.). A special place is taken by research into ideologies which investigate all expression of mental activity in terms of the social background and seeks to expose ideologies as an instrument of social struggle. It has led at times to a general suspicion of ideology which renders an objective scientific discussion and the attainment of an attitude of proper self-criticism difficult or impossible. If all that is achieved is a "ritual of criticism" (Dahrendorf), sociology can easily become uncritical if it does not reveal its standards of criticism and the system corresponding to them. If every universal view of things, every form of group, consciousness is termed an ideology, this lends itself to a relativism for which the distinction between ideology and truth is a matter of indifference.

The discussion of method has always figured extensively, especially in Europe (Germany, France) and the U.S.A. The chief themes are: a) the nature of the object of sociology; b) the nature of the empirical bases of sociological theories and c) the so-called "value-free" judgments.

The present position is that there is a dispute over method between the representatives of an empirical approach under the influence of neo-positivism or "logical positivism", and the upholders of dialectical sociology. The former accused dialectical sociology of arbitrariness, since it did not, they said, subject its assertions to the test of direct personal observation, while dialectical sociology in turn accused its opponents of the uncritical use of empirical techniques, without attending to the relevant problems, attaining neither to historical depth nor to a critical perspective. Each side also suspects the other of ideology.

W. Siebel & N. Martin

SOUL

1. *Concept.* The doctrine of the soul, as an expression of man's self-understanding in general, is part of the subject-matter of general anthropology. Here it means, within the framework of a comprehensive notion of man (though one that is always coloured by its times), the constitutive element by which human existence is capable, by nature, of attaining selfhood. If freedom, decision, responsibility and knowledge are essential determinations of man, so that he not merely has his freedom and consciousness but actually is these acts as he exercises them, then his nature, the principle of his acts, which goes beyond any actual exercise of them, must in itself make his basic activity possible. The soul is human nature in its self-awareness and hence the primary force of the subjectivity.

It is of the substance of man. Its primordial act likewise has substantial significance. This act, with its history, is embedded in the fundamental context of existence. Man *is* what he makes of himself, and his being is what he could really become. Personal development, the "history of the soul", is itself a fundamental process.

From this, the following general determinations may be deduced. The soul itself is not man. It is one of his principles of being. It is substantial in character, contrary to the assertions of psychological actualism. As partial cause (formal, because a principle) of (the whole of) human nature, it stands in a primordial relationship to its material, corporeal constitution. The material principle, to which the soul essentially belongs, as its form, can be designated as the "prime substance" of the soul, on account of its priority to it, even genetically. When it reflects materiality itself (and not just some material object), it gains distance, as in the animal soul, and then when the specific difference intervenes, when the reflection is substantial, it is called spirit. It is independent in character, though its essence is always intrinsically determined by its origin, which is also the reason of its individuality. (Hence St. Thomas treats *materia prima* as the principle of individuation.) As spirit, it is the intrinsic form of the body and so possesses a so-called natural immortality.

The coming-to-be of the soul gives a view of the primal ground. For the soul's "material" origin brings with it its perpetual [dependence] relatedness. Since then matter appears in the soul as a relation, the substantial nature of the soul's transcendence reveals the equally substantial transcendence of all reality – as a natural process. The coming-to-be of the soul is the substantial mirror of the coming-to-be of the finite world. The (natural) function of the soul shows why its concept was so important, from the Christological controversies of early times to the "psychological" doctrine of the Trinity in St. Augustine and in the mysticism of the Middle Ages.

2. *The concept of soul in biblical and Western thought.* Strictly speaking, the problem of anthropology was not posed by biblical thought. Thus the soul (נֶפֶשׁ, ψυχή) does not appear as a metaphysical principle, but means simply "the vitality of the flesh". Man himself becomes a soul (Gen 2:7) and when he dies he is a "dead" soul (Num 23:10), the soul of a dead man (Num 6:6). The soul comes directly from God (Gen 24:14).

The anthropology of the NT is on the same lines. In St. Paul, flesh (σάρξ) and spirit (πνεῦμα) do not simply indicate the opposition between body and soul, but contrast man (cf. 2 Cor 7:5) in his frailty and sinfulness with the divine might (Rom 8:1ff.; 1 Cor 1:26) which redeems him. (Each of these parts, flesh and spirit, like "body" [σῶμα] and soul [ψυχή], always stands for the whole man.)

Ancient Greek philosophy thought differently. Matter was understood to be eternal (Plato, *Timaeus*; cf. *Platonism*) and God was regarded, from the point of view of his activity, as demiurge. Hence everything which proceeds from him (the forms which determine the constitution of things in the world) are themselves supposed to be two-fold. The soul is a "mixture" of the changeable and the unchangeable (*Timaeus*, 41) and is composed of a trichotomy of reason (λογιστικόν), heart (θυμοειδές) and worldly desire (ἐπιθυμητικόν). This gives rise to the (moral) problem of rising above matter. The body was the prison of the soul, and later matter was understood as evil itself. Man's soul was to be guided by the eternal truth of the spirit, by means of an unworldly existence, to the pure contemplation of the forms, to find its true self. But for Plato man is then one with God (from eternity?) and hence immortal, pre-existing, separated in his "essence" from the world. This then gives rise in Aristotle to the problem of how the "active intellect" (νοῦς ποιητικός, *intellectus agens*) is united with the "receptive" intellect (νοῦς παθητικός, *intellectus passibilis*) and of whether there can be an "individual" immortality (see *De anima* and its Averroistic commentators), since the lower and truly human(?) part of the soul dies. Against this background, the Stoics thought of the soul as refined matter, within the framework of the great world-reason, and Plotinus thought of it, in its various phases, as an emanation of the divine.

Ancient Christian thinkers took up

this anthropology. They put forward the thesis (due to Hebraic thought?) that the soul was mortal, since otherwise it could not be a created thing (so Justinus, Tatian and Irenaeus). Tertullian, to bring out its connection with the whole world, called it a *corpus sui generis*, thinking of the body as an inter-social reality.

But this relationship can be fitted into Greek thought. No doubt the spirit (νοῦς) is the decisive element. But as Origen says (*De Principiis*), the pure spirit (pre-existing) falls into sin with the first movement of its will and must then lead a miserable existence, corresponding to the gravity of its sin, in the world, as a soul (ψυχή). Man is therefore doomed by nature to live by going out of himself – an "ek-static" existence. Poised between heaven and earth, he is ordained to be a superman, in order finally to transfigure the flesh by means of his soul, which by virtue of the redemption and with the help of asceticism is transformed into *pneuma*.

This Greek notion prevailed in the following period. It was given its most forcible expression in St. Gregory of Nyssa and above all in St. Augustine. The soul, in its spirit (*mens*), participates in divine wisdom, which it exercises in contemplation.

Nonetheless, the controversy with Platonism continued, even in the early Middle Ages (cf. Gilbert of Poitiers, Hugh of St. Victor). In the doctrine of St. Bonaventure a distinction was introduced into Augustinianism, with the doctrine of *materia spiritualis*. The definitive turning-point, now conceived of in Aristotelian terms, came with St. Thomas Aquinas. For when Aquinas went beyond the old distinction between matter and form to distinguish between being and essence (the "real distinction" between essence and act), he saw in the very actualization of matter by spirit a resultant reality distinct from both, the human person. Here the *anima*, as the *forma unica corporis*, is given its proper metaphysical place. This explains how the *conversio ad phantasma* is necessary for the human spirit, and conversely, how it is possible to re-live the immanent divine life in the actuality of the true self (the *scintilla animae*; cf. Eckhardt).

Further developments did not maintain this position, but still confirmed it in some ways. Insofar as the "ontological difference" was lost sight of, Western thought fell victim to a dualism of body and soul hitherto unknown and now applied on the anthropological level. The soul was *res cogitans*, in contrast to a *res extensa* (Descartes). The soul became an attribute and mode of the divine substance, a self-contained monad (Leibniz), an infinite striving (Lessing), the incomprehensibility of the absolute, knowledge and deed (Fichte), the self-explication of the Idea (Hegel), a mystical potency (Schelling), the will to power (Nietzsche), the difference between the ego and the superego (Freud), existentiality (Jaspers), thereness ("being there") (Heidegger), the primordial realization of the future (Bloch). These are all various types of the effort to use what was no longer called soul to grasp the basic law of reality – in the subject (cf. H. Urs von Balthasar). Christian theology was drawn into this process. The soul, now considered as subjectivity – which is why its immortality is denied on the Protestant side – remained the human potency for the absolute.

3. *The magisterium*. The dogmatic definitions are concerned almost entirely with the relation between soul and spirit.

The first point made is that man has only one soul (ψυχή), which is rational (λογική) and hence that one cannot speak of two souls (Constantinople IV, *DS* 657). This, the *anima intellectiva*, exists as a different individual soul in each man ("non est anima unica in cunctis hominibus") and it is immortal precisely as an individual (Lateran V, *DS*

1440). In reply to the question (of the Greeks) as to how spirit and body are united, it is affirmed that the *anima intellectiva* is of itself (and not through the *anima sensitiva*: P. Olivi) the *forma corporis* (Vienne, *DS* 902). This does not affect the Franciscan doctrine of the *pluralitas formarum corporis*, which rather makes its presence felt when the dogma goes on to affirm that after death and before the resurrection (compare the doctrine of John XXII, *DS* 990–1, which at first sight seems different) the soul can see the essence of God *nulla mediante creatura*, by a *visione intuitiva*, and possesses (individual) bliss *usque ad finale iudicium et ex tunc usque in sempiternum* (Benedict XII, *DS* 1000–1).

The fundamental principle is strongly emphasized that the soul is created directly (*DS* 3896) by God, from nothing (*DS* 685). Hence it is not part of the divine substance (*DS* 201, 285, 455), and never leads a precorporeal existence (*DS* 403, 456), though conversely, *as such*, it has not a material origin (*DS* 360, 1007, 3220). It is the vital principle in man (*DS* 2833) and is higher than the body (*DS* 815). The spirituality of the soul can be proved (*DS* 2766, 2812).

Man as a whole is said to be (primarily in connection with Christology) soul, body and spirit (νοῦς) (*DS* 44, 46, 48). He consists of spirit and body (*DS* 800, 3002), or of soul and body (*DS* 250, 272, 900).

The basic affirmation is that the spirit of man is created by God and forms the soul of his body, in an essential relation to it, whether this relation is understood in an Augustinian or a Thomistic way. It was not till Vatican II that the magisterium broke out of the body-soul schema and came into line with the approach of the modern era. The key-word is now person and not soul. Man is "one" in body and soul. In his "interiority" he transcends the totality of things. "Thus, when he recognizes in himself a spiritual and immortal soul, he is not being mocked by a deceptive fantasy . . . he is getting to the depths of the very truth of the matter" (cf. *Gaudium et Spes*, art. 14).

4. *Present-day problems.* a) The "Greek" tradition argues from the nature to the subject, while today one goes from the subject to the nature. Nonetheless, even here the question of the essence cannot be evaded, since it is the means of revealing the absolute priority of the person. This priority can be grasped if the activity of the person determines once more the character of the nature. By means of the soul, the morality of the basic act becomes an essential element of the nature thus "characterized".

b) The "soul", understood as standing for man, is a fundamental theme of theology in the context of sin and redemption. But since theology considers the person in its basic constituents and sees there the factors which give rise to the moral decision, the real sphere of theology only begins where man exercises his basic faculties and transcends himself in his orientation to the absolute. Theology has the task of explicating this transcendental capacity of man. It includes psychology insofar as it must set in motion fundamental complexes within this realm, but it is essentially different from it inasmuch as it does not make these complexes function in relation to others but transcends them by taking them into the order of conscience.

c) The origin of the soul supposes physical causes. But if in general the divine activity and the development of the world are intrinsically connected, transcendent and immanent causalities must merge where the world in itself transcends itself absolutely. This self-transcendence can be described as the creation of the soul, and here phylogenesis and ontogenesis are intrinsically connected.

Elmar Klinger

SPIRIT

1. *Preliminary note.* Spirit is one of the fundamental concepts in the history of philosophy, which might indeed be called, as in German, the "history of the spirit". If the full extension and depth of the concept is to be grasped, it should not be constricted within the limits of a definition. The "historicity" which is an essential property of the spirit and the "history" which is its essential actuation must both be considered if we are to understand the concept in terms of the problems it sets to modern thought. This will bring to light the hermeneutic circle involved in the process – the interrelationship between the spirit's understanding and its being understood. For this reason we shall begin by tracing the main changes which the concept has undergone in the history of philosophy, understood as the self-understanding of the spirit.

2. *On the history of the concept.* The philosophical concept of spirit was first worked out in Greek thought, though there is no one Greek word which has all the connotations of our "spirit". The word πνεῦμα "wind, breath" came to be used for the "breath of life" but except in religious and poetical use never quite lost its etymological meaning. It was the word νοῦς which underwent the changes of meaning in which the specifically Greek understanding of spirit was arrived at, which was to have such influence on Western thought. For Anaxagoras, νοῦς was the active principle of order in all things, but he had been preceded by Parmenides, who enunciated the principle of the correspondence of being and spirit which was to dominate all subsequent philosophy: νοεῖν was understood as "to perceive" and "to comprehend". In the development of Plato's thought, the spirit is both the faculty which enables man to contemplate the changeless eternal world of forms and – in the later Plato – a cosmic potency, the world-soul, the rational order of being. Aristotle takes νοῦς as the activity (ἐνέργεια) which is characteristic of man: as the specific mode of human self-realization, it already foreshadows to some extent the later *ratio* – the independent human "determination" of all reality. In his famous view of the origin of the spirit as "from without" (θύραθεν) Aristotle presents the spirit, in its relationship to being and God, as purely external and in the nature of an object. Western metaphysics is henceforth dominated by the notion of spirit's being "in" and "above" man. Spirit is experienced and expounded as something detached from the "world" (space, time, movement) and ordained only to "being", which is considered as a perpetual presence, independent of space, time and movement.

For later developments, it is important to observe that the notion of spirit underwent a decisive change in Christianity, though the notion was always determined by its Greek origin. The richness of meaning which the notion of spirit offers us today is undoubtedly due to the confrontation of the Greek experience of existence with that of the Bible and Christianity – the "destiny of the West", as M. Müller called it – a confrontation which did not result in a total synthesis. For St. Augustine, the spirit (*mens, animus*) is not simply the Greek νοῦς: it is the *acies mentis*, the apex of the mind, the personal, dynamic point of contact and encounter between man and God. But Platonism is still a mighty force, and he allows the Christian experience of existence to be coloured by the metaphysics of the *ideae aeternae immutabiles*. In St. Thomas Aquinas, the spirit (*mens, spiritus*) is understood, anthropologically, as the individual substance: spirit is spirit-soul, that is, the form of the body, in terms of an Aristotelian hylemorphism re-interpreted scholastically. But this anthropological aspect is not the only one in St. Thomas. He also assigns the spirit its place in the larger whole of a hierarchical metaphysics of being and the Christian doctrine of creation. Being and spirit tend to coincide, and actually do so, in complete identity, in God, whereas the human spirit is "all things, but only in a certain fashion" (*quodammodo omnia*). Beings can be understood only in the spirit, since it is the "light" (*lumen*) in which the excellence of man's essence is founded. This "light" refers man to the "uncreated light", of which it is the imprint (*impressio*), revelation (*manifestatio*) and likeness (*similitudo*) "in" man. Corresponding to the natural and supernatural order, this light is either natural or supernatural.

Modern developments of the notion of spirit are characterized by the tendency to treat it as one with the subject. The profusion of meanings with which the spirit had been enriched in the course of its history gave rise to a varied vocabulary. Thus Descartes speaks of *res cogitans*, Leibniz of the "monad", Kant of the "transcendental consciousness", Fichte of the "ego" – and so on. The climax of this development was reached in German Idealism, which claimed to merge the whole history of the spirit into the absolute dialectic of being and spirit. Hence for Hegel, spirit is the "loftiest concept", the "supreme definition of the absolute". The spirit alone is the true and the real, it sets antithesis and synthesis in motion, it is the unity of all oppositions. Hence, as the self-determination of the spirit proceeds, all determinations are, as Hegel says, "spiritualized", "made fluid": they are absorbed into the growing self-awareness of the spirit, which attains its perfection in the concept of absolute knowledge, which is the self-awareness of absolute freedom.

Dissatisfaction with the Hegelian system of the absolute spirit was voiced from three stand-points, which gave rise to a correspondingly threefold development in the understanding of spirit. With Kierkegaard the biblical and Christian background makes itself felt once more. Marx and dialectical materialism regard the spirit as the reflection of material nature. Dilthey tries to define the life of the spirit according to its concrete forms and contrast their special nature and methods will all natural processes ("the sciences of the spirit"). At present the concept of spirit is used in many senses according to the schools or traditions followed. Two questions arouse particular attention. The first arises from the "historical consciousness" of the 19th century and is the fundamental one about the "historicity" of human existence, which poses indirectly the question as to the "historicity" of thought (see below). The second is posed by the "evolutionary" view of the world taken by modern science and asks about the place of man and hence that of the spirit in the cosmos (cf. P. Teilhard de Chardin).

3. *Suggested solution.* a) When we try to explain the notion of spirit in terms of today's thinking of the problem, we encounter a remarkable difficulty. The very school of thought, which, following Heidegger, now poses the question of being and of the historicity of thought most radically, avoids using the notion of spirit at all, or to any significant extent. The reason for its exclusion is its origin in the Greek metaphysics of the West. However, a justifiable criticism of Graeco-Occidental metaphysics with its disregard of time and history, should not make us lose sight of the decisive change brought about in the Greek concept of spirit by the biblical and Christian experience. Apart for instance from St. Augustine, Kierkegaard must be mentioned as one of the most important witnesses to a concept of spirit which is not simply Greek, but biblical and Christian in its essential relationship to time and freedom. His remark "that the Greeks did not grasp the notion of the spirit in its deepest sense" suggests that our task should be to understand the conjunction of spirit and history from

the standpoint of the Christian experience of time.

b) The notion of spirit derives from a primordial human experience of which it is the interpretation. Spirit is what distinguishes man from all other beings. It is "presence", growing historically more intense. Man is not just one being among others: he is the being in whom the meaning of being is disclosed as he makes his concrete and manifold affirmation of being. As he says "is", he expresses his transcendence with regard to all beings, a transcendence which is orientated to being. In his openness to being, which is experienced *a priori* but always mediated historically and which constitutes the basis of all transcendence, man arrives at that primordial selfhood in which he distinguishes himself in knowledge and will from all beings and finds his essential freedom.

This experience of "historicity", today being expressly formulated for the first time, forbids us to base the notion of spirit on that of some changeless and eternal being. Being is no longer experienced merely as a timeless entity, to be grasped and represented in objectivating concepts, but as the genesis of history and meaning. It is a self-disclosing "event" – which should not, however, be taken as implying any ontological "actualism". Thus the spirit is openness to being, or rather, it is the "medium" or "place" where the self-communication of being – experienced as an event – makes its meaning known and its absolute claim felt. Spirit is therefore the presence of being to itself, a presence primarily historical in the sense that it releases history. This presence must be simply interpreted as the fathomlessness of being, which alone makes room for truth and freedom: the mystery which is at the disposal of none. Thus being discloses itself historically in the sense that it creates history. In doing so, it remains the mystery which is not at the disposal of man. And this alone is how the personal self-disclosure of God can be and is in fact always experienced in his salvific action in history. He is "absolute spirit": not in the sense of an objectified changeless "self-possession" remote from the world and history, but as the incalculable personal "origin", to which the finite human spirit always feels itself referred, and to whose rule and claim it knows itself to be subject in its experience of thought and freedom.

Excluding therefore all ideas of an immediate knowledge of God as object, we may further understand the human spirit as the immediacy of the finite to the infinite, of the conditioned to the absolute, of the temporal to the eternal: which means in the concrete that the spirit must be understood as an immediate relationship to God. This does not imply a sealed-off "inwardness". The immediacy or immediate relationship to God is and always remains a fresh self-realization *as history* (M. Müller). In its character of immediacy (immediate relationship to God), the spirit is the ultimate historicity itself, from which all history originates: history being understood as the dialectical development in time of man's relationship to himself and to things. This peculiar relationship between the spirit (as such immediacy) and its self-realization (in its history) must be borne in mind, because it marks the radical difference between the view here put forward and Hegel's dialectic of the absolute spirit. The spirit being immediate relationship to God realizes itself in its history not by an Hegelian process of "self-elimination by transformation" but by maintaining this inviolable relationship with God in which it fulfils itself. Thus in contrast to Hegel we understand the spirit essentially as *personal spirit*: which gives rise to the problem of the relationship between persons or subjects.

c) The view of the spirit here put forward makes the spirit "greater" than man: as Pascal says, "l'homme passe infiniment l'homme", not in the sense that it is alien or extrinsic to man, but in the sense that man is only what he is by being thus "greater" than himself. The most essential thing in man is not a self-sufficient subjectivity, but a constant opening out beyond himself, which we may call his being "there", the presence of being disclosing itself historically as mystery. Thus the various historical interpretations of spirit are subsumed and transformed in this understanding of spirit, which has been gained from the experience of historicity.

We see therefore the spirit both as that which immeasurably surpasses man and as that which remains his most essential element. And the question now is how we are to understand his concrete structure as it is manifested in the multiplicity of its components. The various acts in which man fulfils himself point to *two basic spiritual faculties:* rational intellect and will. The source from which they originate is the spirit – St. Thomas had already called this process *resultatio, emanatio.* Since the spirit must fulfil itself through these two faculties, it includes a sort of unity in duality, a double intention or direction swinging between two poles, in which it "must throb as though in two pulses" (W. Kern). *Knowledge* represents the element of perceptive appropriation, but the outgoing urge of *love* is the element in which the spirit obtains its most characteristic determination. The two functions may be distinguished by reflective reasoning. But the more concrete the exercise of their essential activities, the more fully are they integrated with one another, as interpenetrating modes of the one total tendency of the spirit.

d) The human spirit reaches its complete concrete reality only in its "attachment" to the body, which is not, however, to be regarded merely as an extrinsic medium or instrument, but as its "expression", its way of being "there". The specifically human finiteness of the spirit is manifested in this concrete act of being "there". In this connection we may mention briefly that our starting-point, the historicity of the spirit – by which history is first set afoot – allows us to take in and go beyond the Greek way of understanding the Christian doctrine of *angels,* the so-called "pure spirits". We are now enabled to think out the nature of the angels more thoroughly – and more biblically. This is true above all of their "relationship to the world and history" (K. Rahner), which remains essential, though other than that of the human spirit.

e) Spirit as the self-realization of the immediacy of the presence of being also implies an essential relationship to the *material cosmos.* The spirit is the self-presentation of being as the unlimited whole. There can be therefore and there is nothing "outside" the spirit. And since it can only realize itself by means of material things, the cosmos is at once absorbed into the dialectic of the spirit, of which it is the "extended embodiment".

It follows that the history of the spirit and the evolution of the cosmos do not draw further and further apart but come constantly closer together. The human spirit first appears "inside" the cosmos and its evolution, whose history therefore precedes the spirit and (in a certain way) outruns it. But this does not mean either that the human spirit is an immanent product of evolution, derived from a purely material process, nor that it is an alien element in the cosmos. The human spirit is not to be thought of as an object within the world, just as one "thing" among others. By its very nature it is the presence of being, that which first gives rise to history and meaning. Hence it is clear that the human spirit always spans the history of the cosmos, inasmuch as it can give meaning to the whole history of the cosmos – even retrospectively. And this is not a process extrinsic or indifferent to the cosmos, since the cosmos is only addressed as cosmos by the interpretation of the spirit: that is, the cosmos only "comes to itself" "in" the spirit. Hence the history of the cosmos is always opened out to the spirit: indeed, it culminates in the spirit and is "fundamentally always a history of the spirit" (K. Rahner). Thus we may not think of the spirit as merely the product of a material process, as dialectic materialism maintains, misapprehending completely the nature of the spirit. Yet the peculiar history of the blending of spirit and cosmos in unity only becomes comprehensible in the light of an act which spans both: the creative act of God.

Lourencino B. Puntel

SPIRITUALITY

I. Concept

A. Biblical Foundations and Historical Developments

1. *"Spirit" in Scripture*. Both the term and the content of what is generally referred to as Christian spirituality have their origin in the NT. Judaism had already combined in רוּחַ (*pneuma, spiritus, spirit*) a number of associated meanings which are important for us. Spirit was the life-force stemming from God with its psychological and dogmatic intelligibility – with an ever clearer accent on "the religious individuality". And spirit was the power of Yahweh in its significance for the people of God – either as a prophetical and eschatological gift (1 Sam 10:6; Is 11:2; Joel 3:1f.), or hypostatized as the Wisdom of God (Wis 1:6; 7:22). In the NT there grew out of the Christ-event an understanding of the "Spirit" that was both new and of a piece with what went before. It appears timidly at first in Mk and Mt where there is evident a hesitancy to connect the uniqueness of Jesus, "the fact that God himself is really present in him as nowhere else" (E. Schweizer), with the extensive experience of the Spirit within the community after Easter. A new theology of the Spirit developed, as Lk then shows, after the supremacy of the Lord as bestower of the Spirit (4:14ff.; 24, 49; Acts 2:33) was seen more clearly and as he was recognized as Lord of the Spirit-filled community. The relation of the Spirit of the Church to the eschatological reality of the Lord was seen to be one of identity. When Lk depicts the Spirit as the presence of Christ establishing his Church, the accent is still on the extraordinary. The Spirit is "the special gift" which brings about in the faithful, individually and collectively, the manifestations "which are essential to a missionary activity which is still going on and growing, and indeed, which make this activity possible" (E. Schweizer).

Paul definitively completes this identification of the exalted Lord with the *Pneuma* (2 Cor 3:17). To be united to Christ is to enter into the sphere of the Spirit (1 Cor 6:17); faith in the Lord is from and in the Spirit (1 Cor 2:10ff.); the renunciation of circumcision, the "flesh", the self-righteous observance of the law, is service of the Spirit of God and glorying in Jesus Christ (Phil 3:3–6). In concrete terms it is called: praying in the Spirit (Rom 8:15ff.; Gal 4:6); the fulfilment of the whole law through the Spirit (Rom 8:4; in Gal 5:19–23 the *works* of the flesh are contrasted with the *fruit* of the Spirit); the building-up of the Church through the gifts of the Spirit (1 Cor 12–14) and through love of the neighbour (Gal 5:13–15; 1 Cor 13). While St. Paul focuses his gaze more intently upon the consummation which is yet to come (Rom 8:11; 1 Cor 15:35ff.), and upon the pledge of what is yet to be given (Rom 8:23; 1 Cor 15:35ff.), St. John stresses the present salvation in the Spirit which means judgment for "the world", but rebirth in the Spirit of truth and love for the faithful (3:3–5; 4: 23f.; 6:63; 14–16; 20:19ff.). This experience of the Spirit, as Christians drew new inspiration from the incomparable figure of their Lord, gave rise, especially in the late Pauline and the Johannine writings, to a deeper insight into the divine and personal individuality of the Spirit. And the "spirituality" of Christian existence, in the individual, the community, and the Church as a whole was more clearly recognized.

2. *Pneumatikos*, spiritual, became thereby – with a basis supplied already by St. Paul (1 Cor 2:13–15; 9:11; 14:1) – a technical term for Christian existence. The neologism *spirit(u)alis* appeared early in Christianity. In spite of shifts of meaning, restrictions and extensions, the adjective has retained down to our own time the sense of "at the core of Christian existence". Throughout the Middle Ages and far into modern times, one might consider it *the* distinctive description of the typically Christian. This was also true of the corresponding words in the Romance and Germanic languages.

3. The corresponding noun, *spiritualitas*, the formal and creative element of the core of Christian existence, is found as early as the 5th and 6th centuries, appears in the 12th and 13th centuries in the great poets, and by the middle of the 13th century gave rise to the corresponding French *espiritualité* and the like. But it was only in the 17th century that the French *spiritualité* was established in its technical sense to indicate the personal relation of man to God. Here the subjective side of this relation was more and more stressed. The banality, however, of the word when one speaks of Christian spirituality and Christian spiritualities, is only the product of our own time, as also is, unfortunately, the anaemic unreality which is almost always connected with the word "spirituality".

B. The True Notion of Spirituality and Some Illuminating Contrasts

This short survey of the biblical basis and the historical development of the word shows sufficiently the dialectical tension of what "spirituality" should mean, and which is only inadequately expressed in static concepts. It is rooted in the coming of divine revelation, in the historical concreteness of revelation in Jesus Christ, and in the ecclesiastical tradition through word and sacrament. It means the personal assimilation of the salvific mission of Christ by each Christian which is always in the framework of new forms of Christian conduct and is comprised within the fundamental answer of the Church to the word of salvation. The inner fullness of Christian spirituality, as demanded by the biblical "Spirit", and the deformations which need to be corrected, can be best discussed in the light of concrete historical problems. This will also help to bring out key-points which will give content to a concept only formally outlined so far.

1. *Enthusiasm and institutions*. St. Paul had to censure the Christians of Corinth for the "enthusiasm" (in the sense of Knox's book) in misinterpreting the gifts of the Spirit. Ecstatic spontaneity, raptures, and abnormal reactions seemed to be the supreme experience of the Spirit. This heady misconception never became again a real danger for the Church as a whole, after the Montanist difficulties of the 2nd and 3rd centuries, although the mania for the extraordinary and miraculous remained a temptation, one that our Lord himself had had to warn against (e.g., Mt 16:1–4). Behind all this there is a supernaturalism which wants to see as well as believe in the promise given in Jesus Christ. The opposite danger, however – often proceeding from the same root – of turning every expression of "Spirit" into an official institution or even of equating the official institution with charism, and laws and institutions with spirituality, is much more real in actual Catholicism. The great examples in the history of piety shows us that genuine spirituality

can only develop in the tension between office and charism. The movement of St. Francis of Assisi centring on the ideal of poverty allowed its enthusiasm to be guided along an orderly course by ecclesiastical restrictions; St. Ignatius of Loyola, who formulated the rules of *sentire cum ecclesia* was long under suspicion of being an *Alumbrado*. Too much juridical regulation of spirituality and the absorption of all initiative or spontaneity by officially established traditions undoubtedly meant that many initiatives could find no place in the Church and that their spirituality, in part genuinely Christian, found homes outside it.

2. *Spiritualization and rationalization*. Another danger had its source in the attempted philosophical penetration of the spiritual life (cf. Evagrius Ponticus, Meister Eckhart). The emphasis easily came to be placed on the rational element – as can be seen from the very terminology: spiritual-mental-intellectual. Christianity, instead of being seen as integrating man, was made an intellectual and theoretical process, an approach that is quite compatible with a "mysticism of the obscure". This danger, which appears so clearly in history, ran parallel over long stretches to the institutionalizing tendency already indicated. It did not, however, result so much in a juridical regulation of the spiritual life, as in a frequently esoteric "watering-down" of the spiritual. As a result, the word "spirituality" still carries with it today the flavour of the enfeebled, the ascetically de-materialized, and the aesthetically esoteric. The opposing danger of turning spirituality into an unspiritual life-force is so foreign to Christianity that it need not be seriously considered (cf., however, isolated racial deformations of the Christian message). Yet related phenomena such as the stressing of the irrational or exaggerations of an emotional or pietistic nature are clearly perceptible in the history of Christianity. Along this same line one could also mention the modern attempts – especially outside of the Catholic Church – to free Christian spirituality from the objective, articulate and historically tangible, and to base it rather on the subject and the decisions, commitment, or free and unanalysable acts. What is of permanent value in all these attempts is the stress on the incalculable role which the individual person and his commitment play in spirituality. The danger here is the resolving of the tension between the original, objective saving acts and the subjective appropriation of them, in favour of the latter.

3. *Dualism*. For the sake of completeness we must mention a third source of danger inseparably connected with those already mentioned. Very early, Christian spirituality took a perilous course through a dualistic conception of man as body and soul. Up to the present day a great part of spiritual literature had been unconsciously dominated by the ideal of the "spiritual" man who, purified of all material concerns, strives to attain to the pure realm of the soul and the spirit. Behind this lurks an ontological misinterpretation of the Pauline tension between spirit and flesh. Certainly the Gnostic-Manichaean disqualification of the body is today shunned in Catholicism. Some indeed are apprehensive, not without justification, of the backlash of an imprudent glorification of the body. But one could scarcely maintain that theology has completely overcome the Greek conception of the two-layer man. The image is suggested by language, and sustained by the indispensable kernel of truth within it. To an even greater extent this accusation is true of spiritual theology and still more so as regards ordinary "edifying" books. A re-thinking cannot be achieved merely by the superficial adoption of more modern terminology. It demands of spiritual theology that same intellectual effort which has produced such obvious fruits in the many new ap-

proaches to dogmatics. It cannot be done without the critical dissection of forms of thought which have been valid for centuries. It is at the same time, however, important to be warned against any reduction of spirituality to the psychological or the sociological.

C. Spirituality: the Objective Redemption as Mystery

1. *Preaching and the sacraments as the origin.* Christian spirituality – that one can today also speak of a spirituality of a Thomas Mann or of Marxism cannot be dealt with here – draws its vitality from the salvific deed of God in Jesus Christ present in the Church and transmitted through its preaching and sacraments. Some of the elementary considerations, then, can be better elaborated in terms of this other pole of the dialectical unity of Christian spirituality, the objective salvific deeds which are live in the faith of the Church, rather than through reflection upon the believing man. A glance at the historical development will justify this orientation of spirituality to the content of faith and the object of worship. The Christianity of the 1st century was, for instance, so closely bound up with Scripture and the "objective" sacramental events that what was understood as "sacrament" was the whole fullness of the mystery, the mystery of the liturgy as well as the mystery of life inspired by worship. It meant, therefore, the mystery of Christian existence as well as that of the salvific events; behind the datable historical event, it meant the divinely willed personal confrontation of the individual Christian with Christ through the mediatory activity of the Church.

In the modern *theologoumenon* of the *res sacramenti* a meagre though central kernel of the ancient sacramental theology of the Christian life, actual "spirituality", is still alive. The words of Scripture were likewise the support of the Christian faith. The doctrine of the three or four senses of Scripture brought it into lively contact with the faith of the individual. It is true that the NT antithesis between Spirit and letter (2 Cor 3:6; Rom 2:19; 8:7) was interpreted in a one-sided way with reference to the problem of understanding Scripture (Origen). (Primarily this was meant to contrast the impotency of the law with the life-giving Spirit of Jesus Christ.) But the concrete way of thinking inspired by the four senses shows that the notion of the economy of salvation was still basic. In modern terms, the letter meant the superficial sense which was still existentially unassimilated and hence also accessible to those without faith; allegory was the dogmatic reality of salvation-history intended by the letter; the moral sense was the existential assimilation of this in Church and private life; typology was directed towards the eschatological salvation in Jesus Christ, which is at the same time present and still to be hoped for. In the 12th and 13th centuries this unity was split up into what we would today call dogmatics and spirituality. At the same time the theology of the Scriptures also became an independent science with the result that in the late Middle Ages spirituality was continuing ever more noticeably along a track that was far from both Scripture and dogma. From the four-fold fullness of meaning there remained finally only empty moralizing or free speculation using verses of Scripture as points of departure. The way lay open for a psychologizing spirituality. Even this could not preserve the unity of integral existence and broke up, especially since the 17th century, into the partial disciplines of ascetical and mystical theology.

It was only in our time that attempts were again made to re-establish the former unity. In the task which still remains to be done, one cannot skip this historical development and the individual disciplines. Nevertheless, it remains essential to restore the unified form which alone gives each of these disciplines their meaning.

2. *Preaching and sacraments as source of life*. What we have briefly described as the development of reflection upon "spirituality" also had its clear counterpart in spirituality as it was actually lived out. This could be spelled out in a history of meditation (from attentive reading of Scripture to abstract pondering on philosophical truths), a history of eucharistic piety (from the common liturgy with its repercussions to devotion to the "prisoner of the tabernacle"), a history of mysticism (from the reading and active response to Scripture and the *rara hora, parva mora* of St. Bernard to *contemplatio infusa*). A result of this would be even clearer evidence that spirituality is "the dimension of mystery with the objective dogmatics of the Church" (Balthasar). The two poles, then, seen in their original unity are: the fullness of revelation which unfolds in the Church, and man in his personal existence. It would also be clear that the spiritual life is not a simple concept but one that springs from and derives its sense of direction from the saving events, from Christ who is present in the word and the sacrament. Scientific and theoretical reflection on spirituality consequently cannot be content to be one discipline alongside of or subordinate to other theological disciplines. Spirituality is a general science that cuts across all the rest and bridges all subjects relevant to theology. Always directly flowing from the font of revelation in Christ, it brings all such subjects into the life of the individual. Therefore it naturally arranges the other disciplines according to their bearing on actual Christian existence.

D. Consequences

1. *Unity and plurality of Christian spirituality*. From such a description of spirituality which merely tries to echo the biblical message of life in the Spirit, there are several important conclusions. The question of there being one or many spiritualities (Bouyer, Daniélou) is merely a matter of the point of view. There is obviously only one Christian spirituality if I begin my consideration of this "cross-sectional" science on the level where the Christian message is first addressed to men. However, were one to consider the lowest level of its actual realization, to use the image of the pyramid, there would be as many spiritualities as there are alert Christians. Between these two levels lie those great patterns of religious conduct which have exercised formative influence in the course of Church history (and already in the biblical writings) and which have often been charismatic and exemplary realizations of Christian spirituality for a given time or for a given task.

2. *Spirituality and personal life*. On the basis of this truth and of the general conception of spirituality which was sketched above, it will also be clear that concrete spiritualities can be grasped less as doctrine than as personal existence. Just as the one Christian spirituality can be defined most clearly in terms of the person of Jesus Christ, so too these great group-forming spiritualities within Church history are all charisms of God which are embodied in a man or a group rather than in a doctrine – an incarnation that is irreducible to conceptual analysis. That these "divine imperatives" also took on didactic form and were written down is self-explanatory, since the whole man, individually as well as socially, is addressed by the "divine imperative". Yet even today the most fruitful spiritualities seem to grow rather out of actual Christian existence than out of ideas.

3. *Trinitarian circumincession of spiritualities*. This personal crystallization and the interplay of spiritualities gives rise to a unity and diversity of Christian attitudes which, as Balthasar has shown, are ultimately based on the trinitarian

unity of God. Though the fullness of Christian spirituality is experienced in each case, in the individual or in a group, there are within this very fullness real differences as between persons and between groups – differences around which communities build up. This unity-and-diversity which eludes logical categories must be allowed for in the present-day discussion of lay and religious spirituality. An absorption of the one into the other would contradict the trinitarian basis of its diversity in the same way as a reduction to categories or a chaotic dissociation. Historically, the position of the spirituality of the re-religious life or the counsels has been clearly that of the symbol and exemplar which leads to true Christianity (K. Rahner). Whether this contrast with lay spirituality is still valid depends in the last analysis upon the Christian existence itself which is charismatically bestowed by God, and not upon theological reflection upon it. It should, however, be clearly indicated that though theological reflection must re-think many of the attitudes of the past in this context, it cannot find there any discrediting of the layman in the relation between the lay, priestly and religious states as it was properly understood, for example, by the great religious teachers of the past (in terms of that necessary relation between unity and diversity which we have indicated).

4. *Service in the Church as the common element of spirituality*. This necessary relation between unity and diversity within Christian spirituality has a deeper parallel in the one life of the individual Christian. The word of God – if we may include within this biblical expression the whole event of revelation and its transmission in history – is only fully the word of God if it finds its realization in the obedience and action of the Christian (cf. *res sacramenti*). Likewise, the Christian is only fully a Christian when he looks away from his own existence to lose himself, listening to God's word, in prayerful and active service of the Kingdom of God, each according to his own call. This unity prior to and present within all diversity is Christian spirituality. It is that spiritual reality which is already transmitted through the Church and as the Church, in which each Christian is inserted. It is precisely in the case of the great, independent personalities of Christianity that it can be demonstrated that the distinctiveness of the figure, unmistakable though it is, arises out of a deeper-seated unity. It is from this unity also that the epochal changes in spirituality must derive their justification, and the same unity contributes to the radical changes that seem to be the stigmata of our times. It is the unity of the Spirit of Christ who "breathes where he wills" and in the way he wills and who always, nevertheless, gives himself in entirety. This intertwining of the many individual strands in the one pattern of the spirituality which is already given and ever to be renewed reveals the essentially ecclesial form of all Christian spirituality. It shows how it is grounded in the social as well as in the personal being of man and how it is built up in actual fulfilment in the grace of that Spirit who is both given to each and who remains ever the same. As the Spirit is the Spirit of Christ, there is also an equally essential eschatological dimension to spirituality. For in it the Christian directs his gaze towards the Lord who is both present and yet to come.

5. *Unity of activity and passivity*. Having recognized the Spirit as the determinant we can now approach the concepts, often presented as opposites, which have played such a great role in spirituality: asceticism (from that of ordinary life to preparation for the mystical union) and mysticism; action and contemplation, doing and suffering, achievement and gift, possession and striving for, etc. These opposites retain their importance and had, indeed, to be

newly considered in modern anthropology and theologically deepened. However, we are today more aware than ever of their provisional nature with regard to the one thing which is at the heart of Christian spirituality. In the Scriptures many texts (cf. Gen 2:7; 1 Cor 2:10ff.) hint at the mystery of the Spirit, who is both God and of God and who is nevertheless bestowed upon man as his truest self. Theological reflection has fixed this truth in what can only be a dialectical formulation, namely that a man is wholly himself, his own to possess – and therefore action, deed, achievement; and also that he is just as much a gift of God – and therefore contemplation, passivity, and searching. In the actual spiritual life, however, this contrast, which in the last analysis is also at the basis of "asceticism and mysticism", is eliminated in the personal encounter with God. The analogous encounter between man and man already suggests the original identity of activity and passivity.

Since the spiritual life, in spite of all human achievement, is always first a divine imperative, any prediction of the course of modern spirituality could only tentatively be deduced from the signs of the times and without speculative finality. Perhaps one could offer, however, the following formulations as typical of the direction of spirituality in our time: a more intensive commitment within the world, especially in the area of its social need; diametrical to that, a more intensive conscious-personal responsibility; stressing of the dialogal; and all of this in an open-mindedness that is today allowing Christianity to look more and more to other religions and even to atheism. But perhaps all this is but an expression of the one fact that today God reveals himself as perhaps never before as the hidden God. To live this with complete openness for the incalculable imperative of God is Christian spirituality.

Josef Sudbrack

II. History of Christian Spirituality

Any thumb-nail sketch of the history of Christian spirituality bristles with difficulties. There are so many facets to depict: theology (where, for instance, some authors have neglected St. Irenaeus), liturgy, religious custom, asceticism and mysticism in the strict sense, psychology, sociology, ethnology and other supplementary disciplines; the endless variety of spirituality in indiiduals, groups, trends, periods, etc. In spirituality, the subjective act, the *individum ineffabile*, corresponds to the articulated propositions of dogmatics and the detailed customs of the liturgy. Hence any "historical synthesis" which is not to be a banal generalization must be somewhat personal and selective. Its value will be not in its completeness but in its usefulness as a basis for dialogue in interpreting the facts.

We concentrate in the following on Western Catholic Christianity.

A. From Jesus Christ to the Development of the Kerygma

Though it is difficult to depict the life of Jesus in terms of concrete situations and definite propositions, it is absolutely certain that his disciples knew him and his message as the presence of the Kingdom of God. There was a unity of the aloofness of God and the immediacy of God; of the *tremendum* of cross, judgment and *eschata*, and of the *fascinosum* of miracles, doctrine and person. All this is stamped with the seal of the definitive in the resurrection, through which the Lord goes and the Spirit comes. The history of spirituality is the development of this *individuum ineffabile*.

a) The first key is provided by the expectation of the imminent end. The one experience of the "Not Yet" and the "Now Already" is explained more and more definitely in terms of dates and numbers. The millenarianism of patristic times, the threats of judgment from visionaries and penitents, the

"Kingdom of the Spirit" announced by Joachim of Fiore and the modern "Adventist" type of movement are further echoes of this explanation.

b) The "eschatological presence" proclaimed in the Johannine writings forms the counterpart to this expectancy. It has dangers of its own, which flared up in the "enthusiasm" of certain Corinthians, in Montanism, and in certain modern movements.

c) The presence of Christ in the Spirit, at once far and near, is the synthesis provided by St. Luke. This leaves the Church open to undue institutionalization of its eschatological dynamism and of its "enthusiasm" in the possession of the Spirit. But the doctrine of the sacraments, as in St. Ignatius of Antioch, which has often been impugned, is its legitimate embodiment.

d) In Scripture itself, the Spirit already begins to take on concrete form in the hierarchy (ministry) and dogma. The constant temptation of spirituality is to underestimate them, while they themselves are tempted to forget that their function is merely ministerial.

e) The crystallization in terms of moral precepts stems from the Wisdom tradition. The dangers involved are reflected in the Letter of St. Clement, e.g., in the watering down of imperatives to an ethic of two degrees of perfection.

f) The theology of martyrdom has two main points. Death is testimony, asceticism is kerygma. But even this can produce short-sighted views, in the line of individualism and loss of eschatological perspective. Cf., for instance, Acts 7:56, "*I* see – [now] – the heavens open"; Phil 3; St. Ignatius of Antioch.

g) Scripture, the backward look to the Lord, and the Eucharist, his presence in the Spirit, unite the two tendencies and obviate their dangers.

B. Development and Consolidation

a) The theory of the coming Christian life remains unimpaired in the salvation-history of St. Irenaeus, as in the Syrian and Antiochene school (St. Ephraem, St. John Chrysostom) with its interest in positive scholarship. But it was otherwise in the Alexandrian school (Origen, St. Athanasius, St. Cyril, the Cappadocians). The "pious" theology of Monophysitism was inspired by this neo-Platonist approach. The word of Scripture reveals a "spiritual" sense, and the world becomes a cosmos spiritualizing itself towards the first principle (the ἕν of Plotinus). Spirituality describes and experiences this way of spiritualization.

b) This is clearly embodied in monasticism in all its forms – the anchorites (St. Anthony), the coenobites (Pachomius, St. Basil) and the type of monastic life generally adopted (Evagrius, Cassian). The Syro-Palestinian style of the wandering preacher (Mt 10) quickly developed into asceticism. Under the influence of the theology of martyrdom, it took the form of flight from the world into the desert. Its theoretical justification was worked out by the Alexandrian School. The crude concepts of spiritual realities in the Messalian school left scarcely a trace. The opposing trend from neo-Platonism became the basic principle for the Christian effort. The task to be mastered was the total renunciation of all that was earthly, to make ready for the "spiritual" encounter with God.

c) After the turning-point under Constantine, there was a sense of public responsibility, which should not be regarded as a falling off from a higher state. It was rather the effort to master the world, as inspired by the Bible, in place of a spirituality which was inclined to flight from the world.

d) St. Augustine set in motion the great occidental, anthropological reversal, which was to remain more or less static in theory till Luther and indeed until existential theology.

C. The Intermediate Period

a) The chaos of the Barbarian Invasions

and the triumphant progress of Islam revealed the superficiality of Christianization.

b) The mainstay of religion and civilization was monasticism (Lerins, St. Martin of Tours, St. Columbanus). The future lay with the synthesis of humanity, discipline and religion achieved in the Rule of St. Benedict. St. Gregory the Great was inspired by its spirit when he wrote his allegorical interpretation of Job, whose prudent asceticism was to make it the handbook of the Middle Ages.

D. A Unified Society and Culture

a) The Carolingian reform and renaissance saw much compilation and cataloguing of past records. "Germanic" traits became visible: love of the tangible (Eucharistic controversies), juridical interests (development of the Curia), dedicated following (veneration of the saints, effort to excel), emotional freedom (devotions), individualism (penitential theology).

b) Monasticism stamped the next centuries. Beside the intellectual approach of St. Anselm of Canterbury, there were the eremitical movements represented by St. Peter Damian and the Carthusians, and the disciplined organization of Cluny.

c) The interpretation of Scripture as applying to individual mysticism came to a peak in St. Bernard and the Cistercian theology (William of St. Thierry). Other components were enthusiasm for the Crusades and the poetry of love (Minnesingers).

d) Among the communities of clerics, the Premonstratensians and the Victorines Hugo and Richard tended to form systems and stressed the organic nature of salvation-history.

e) The piety of the mendicant orders was of a more active type. Under St. Francis of Assisi, the poverty of the wandering preachers was diverted from heresy to become a prop of the Church. The intellectual and practical efforts of St. Dominic to combat the heretical trend led to a great thrust forward in theology.

f) The high-point here was reached with St. Thomas Aquinas, O.P., St. Bonaventure, O.F.M., and then Scotus, O.F.M. It was prepared for by the *Sic-et-Non* dialectic of Abelard. But this "rationalization" forced spirituality to seek "non-theological" forms.

g) Great women like Hildegard and Hedwig had already striven for interiorization. The trend is clear in German mysticism (Eckhart, Suso, Tauler), in Ruysbroeck, and in English and Italian circles (*The Cloud of Unknowing*, St. Angela de Foligno). Other trends were the ecstatic mysticism of certain nuns and the "dark night" mysticism, stemming from the Pseudo-Dionysius, among the Carthusians.

h) Nominalism (William of Occam) sought to break with neo-Platonism, through attention to the individual, linguistic logic, natural science (at Oxford), democracy. It gave rise to the *devotio moderna* and its methods of prayer (G. Groote, *The Imitation of Christ*), which began as a lay movement.

i) Other positive contributions came from reform movements in the religious orders. Nicholas of Cusa sought for a new spiritual unity, which was also the aim of the best forces in Humanism and the Renaissance.

j) Lack of intellectual insight in popular piety brought with it many dangers: superstition (in adoration of the sacred host), witch-hunting (the Inquisition), superficiality (copious accounts of visions, ignorance of the Bible), materialism (e.g., relics), subjectivism (devotion to the Sacred Heart), moralizing (in preaching), emotionalism and eschatological fears.

E. The Struggle for the Individual

a) The spirituality of the movement for reform should not be thought of in terms of pietistic withdrawal or more world-directed revivalism, still less in terms of Gnostic or fanatical developments. Luther sought to underline the irreplaceable individuality of the believer. Nominalist in philosophy, he stressed the personal conscience, with the watch-word; *ego eram ecclesia*. The recourse to Scripture signified the direct approach to Jesus. Even his theology of sin and grace stemmed from an unflinching confrontation with the infinite power and mercy of God. Calvin was clear but cold, disciplined but harsh, while Zwingli displayed humanistic traits.

b) The Society of Jesus, founded by St. Ignatius Loyola, became the direct opposite, though the original intention was otherwise. Even here there are superficial distortions, but the encounter with God can be clearly seen as a unity in tension: strong individuality (illuminative way [cf. the Alumbrados], discernment of spirits), and determined objectivity (methods, obedience, service). The initial impulse did not come fully into its own in the theory of spirituality, but it may still be seen at work in Probabilism, with its stress on the individual conscience, Molinism (with its stress on freedom) and missionary adaptation (cultural emancipation).

c) Spanish mysticism at its peak provided a description of the encounter between God and man which was psychologically accurate and religiously transcendent, in the notion of grasping and being grasped. The spontaneous freshness and prudence of St. Theresa of Avila found objective expression in the work of founding monasteries and letter-writing, as also in devotion to the humanity of Jesus. The poetic and speculative tendency of St. John of the Cross shows its churchmanship in his recourse to Scripture and the classical authors.

F. Inward-Directed Development

Till the time of the Reformation, spirituality was combined with the outward and the interior life of the Church. As the Church sealed itself off – even the Baroque was inspired by a defensive reaction – men looked inwards. There is no need to describe individual figures (mostly French) and schools (independent movements were lacking). Controversies hardened into official condemnations, but kept to the old lines. They were mostly differences of emphasis within the same basic principle.

a) *Survival of the past*. Even in scholarship the influence of German and Flemish mysticism persisted, in spite of writings being put on the Index, and gave rise to tensions within religious orders (S.J., O.F.M.Cap.). The use of the patristic armoury was often masterly (Arnauld, Bossuet and Fénelon). More than ever, the classical author was the Pseudo-Dionysius (especially among the Carmelites).

b) In the controversy *De auxiliis* which opposed Dominicans and Jesuits, Jansenism and Quietism, the debate concerned the corruption of man, the irresistible nature of grace or the over-estimation of man (P. Charron). The roots of "abandonment", resignation even to hell (Molinos, Mme Guyon) and of the courtly spirituality (the king's confessors, Père Joseph) are to be found here. In moral theology, the controversy between Rigorism and Laxism was concerned with the claims of law or personal responsibility. Controversies about the frequency of Holy Communion and the definitiveness of confession (*renouvellement*) were consequences of the actual practice. The differences are not fully explained by men's different pictures of God. Kindness was the key-note of St. Francis de Sales, strictness that of Saint-Cyran. The stress on the humanity of Christ and the *états* of Bérulle contrast with the destruction-theory of his disciple Condren. The Jansenists overstressed the Lordship of Christ in contrast to Pascal's love of Jesus. Much partisanship was due to political intrigues.

c) Religious communities remained the mainstay of spirituality. In the 16th,

17th and again in the 19th century they were increased by an astonishing number of charitable and educational foundations (St. Vincent de Paul, St. John of God; Maria Ward, St. Angela Merici, St. John Baptist de la Salle, Ignatius Rice, St. John Bosco). New apostolic congregations, such as the Redemptorists, flourished alongside the old. Missionary works stirred the enthusiasm of large masses of the people.

d) The theory of spirituality was directed towards the inward life. It has been preoccupied down to the present day (cf. *DSAM*) with such questions as infused and acquired contemplation, the difference between asceticism and mysticism, the priority of will or intellect, direct vision, paramysticism, etc.

e) Spiritual direction (Lallemant) and spiritual friendship (St. Jeanne de Chantal) rose to new heights – though there were some morbid exaggerations (the nuns of Loudun).

f) There were many other notable figures: missionaries at home and abroad, popular preachers, penitents (St. Paul of the Cross, de Rancé), martyrs (England, America), pastors (the Curé of Ars), visionaries (from St. Margaret Mary Alacoque to the children at La Salette, Lourdes, Fatima, etc.). The interior life remained predominant.

g) The people were taught a large number of institutionalized devotions: the Sacred Heart, Mary, the Sacred Wounds, the Eucharist, the Apostleship of Prayer, etc. The weakness was not so much exteriorization as juridicalism and regimentation.

G. Concluding Remarks

The new and promising approaches of recent times stem from a return to the sources or from openness to the world.

a) The trail was already blazed in the 19th century. The organic notion of theology. Traditionalism, the theological principles of German Idealism, Americanism (I. T. Hecker) and various pastoral efforts (Sailer) were at one in trying to bridge the gap between theory and practice, in other words, to further spirituality. The Syllabus and the Modernist controversy proved that the time was not yet ripe. The "real assent" of Newman pointed onwards, as did the "little way" of St. Theresa of Lisieux.

b) New forces came into play in the 20th century with the liturgical movement (which remained for a long time over-preoccupied with the past) and the new interest in Scripture, which had been preceded by flourishing patristic studies. The youth movements remained inward-directed in their common life. Fruitful discussion with natural science ensued (R. Guardini, E. Przywara). Catholic Action flourished in the Latin countries. In matters of spirituality, Vatican II merely worked over old questions such as the "state of perfection".

c) The tasks of today can be described in terms of four principles developed outside the Church.

(i) *The new hermeneutics*. In many respects the "Death-of-God" theology must be dismissed as a mere fashion, but it is a reminder that it is not only the encounter with Scripture but the encounter with God as well which demands as a prelude some hermeneutical consideration. This is even truer of spirituality, though the task has hardly been even perceived as yet.

(ii) *The new picture of man*. Psychology and anthropology make it impossible to confine spirituality to the "interior life" as its main interest. The indissoluble bonds which link human willing and knowing to pre-personal and social facts make all purely interior data suspect. The modern interest in the objective, in hard facts, must point the way to the reality of revelation and to concrete tasks.

(iii) *The new world-picture*. The shaping of the world is displacing more and more the acquisition of knowledge as the human task. Following Blondel and others, Teilhard de Chardin surmised that the encounter with God would take place in action, rather than in preliminary knowledge. This has little if anything to do with the ancient distinction between action and contemplation.

(iv) *The new picture of society*. The religious conscience of the individual is linked to society and its shaping of the future. This has been brought clearly to the fore in the debate with Marxism. The biblical truth of the social nature and social effectiveness of Christian faith (i.e., of the Church) has thereby been rediscovered. It is to be hoped that this controversy will bring theology as a whole nearer to the exercise of faith, i.e., to spirituality.

Josef Sudbrack

III. Special Features

A. Meditation

1. As opposed to the terms "mental prayer" and "contemplation", the traditional term "meditation" is increasingly employed nowadays, even outside the domain of Christian life and spirituality. Its meaning ranges from a psychosomatic technique and therapy acquired by yoga exercises and the practice of auto-suggestion, to ordinary intellectual and personal reflection, or even to advanced forms of religious and comprehensive awareness which ultimately go beyond prayer in the narrower sense and disclose transcendence. The increasingly clear demonstration of the markedly meditative attitude of the higher religions of the East and the interpretation of the findings of depth psychology and the experiences of psychotherapy may serve critically to test the great traditional experiences of meditation in the store of the Church's wisdom, to free them from partial oblivion and awaken them to new efficacy in contrast to certain mistaken developments of Christian spirituality. Critical and discerning discussion by the Church of psychotherapeutic experiences of meditation was made difficult by the (non-scientific) pansexual basis given to psychoanalysis, while dialogue with the higher religions of the East, especially with the various forms of Buddhism, was long hindered by one-sided, narrow dogmatic perspectives. The time should now be ripe, for it has been prepared by detailed studies, for a critical and discerning discussion, especially as increasing stress in every domain calls for a comprehensively meditative mode of life. This would not, however, mean aiming only at the highest forms of meditation. It would have to open up practicable paths which, for example, would take account of somatic and psychological factors and, generally speaking, of what is provisional in human existence, giving it its legitimate importance as an inevitable intermediary stage. The time has come to develop in theory and in practice new and comprehensive ways of meditation, and to give them organized structures in the Church.

2. Christianity was rooted in the salvation-history of the people of Israel, with its meditative liturgical spirituality. The early Church was marked by its experiences of the Pneuma. The mysteries of salvation were re-enacted in the celebration of the liturgy. From the beginning, therefore, it had a decided feeling for meditation (*anamnesis* and eschatological expectation). Parallel to the intellectual and historical development of Christianity, this dimension took shape in accordance with the new situations as they appeared. The process was promoted by the Fathers, and after the Constantinian turning-point, received public and legally constituted form, particularly in the liturgy and in the rules of Western monasticism. The cloistered life, understood as the *Opus Dei*, became in East and West the decisive basis and transmitter of meditation in the wide sense. The different views on the conduct of Christian life in the great contemplative orders, the varying influence of Christian ideals,

the appearance in the Middle Ages of the "evangelical" mendicant orders with a new spirituality of their own, and the increasingly numerous foundations of monasteries and schools, diversified the practice of meditative life. The resulting multiplicity of ascetical techniques and methods of meditative prayer was at the same time a response to the actual demands which arose through the Christianization of the Latin and Germanic peoples. As examples of historically important meditative movements, we mention German mysticism, the *Devotio moderna*, Spanish mysticism, the Ignatian Exercises, Pietism, the French School and, in our days, the "little way" of St. Theresa of Lisieux.

Astonishing similarity to the statements of Christian mysticism is found particularly in Buddhist texts. Buddhism is less a religious society with a consistent theoretical and institutional structure than various ways of deliverance through meditation. Theravada Buddhism seeks *Nirvana* as goal of deliverance, by rigorous, methodically practised techniques, aiming at the destruction of the notion of the "I", as the real source of suffering. This is done by a very subtle watchfulness with regards to the body, to all feelings and states of consciousness including their objects, with the determination, persevered in even into death, to achieve absolute abstraction. And this resolve ultimately seeks to abstract even from its own determination, in order to merge absolutely in "nothingness". Zen Buddhism, on the other hand, also seeking the deliverance of blissful enlightenment, only uses absolute abstraction as an element in pan-spiritualization which makes possible universal communication. The way leads through moral purification and perfection, and through alert and profound emotional tranquillity to comprehensive concentration which, mediated by the celebrated *zazen* (correct sitting-posture meditation) and *kōan* (a special exercise in concentration), opens out a life of stillness and silence and is completed in loving detachment and generous selflessness, an ascent of the mind to the universal unity and universal communication of blissful enlightenment. Amida-Buddhism practises trustful invocation of the merciful saviour whom the self longs for with ardent devotion and to whom it gives and unites itself in order to enter into the total light and life of the Buddha-nature – a term which, as in Mahayana Buddhism generally, means the fathomless ground of all reality.

Buddhism as a mode of life and a vital wisdom is permeated by the conviction that no strict statement is possible about the ground of all precisely because it is the ground of all and itself without ground. For this reason Buddhism was for long dismissed in too sweeping a way as a monism or cosmic pantheism by Christianity, which attributes decisive value to personal and historical mediation of the divine life. The light thrown by scholarship on the higher religions of the East, as well as radical reflection by Christian theology on its own understanding of revelation (which alone makes possible an interpretation of the testimony of Christian mysticism), shows how difficult are the problems of the mediation of salvation, deliverance, and of that mysterious reality present but at the same time hidden in all, which in Buddhist terms is the Buddha-nature, in Christian terms, God-Christ. For Christianity, of course, it is decisive that the mediation of salvation is historical and personal, incarnational. Nevertheless, even here God must be seriously seen as that total reality which precisely in itself as total reality cannot be further mediated and communicated, which breaks through all representations and formulas and which is perhaps what the Buddhist himself means when in dialectically hyperbolic statements he emphasizes the absolute impossibility of mediating the absolute, which as a consequence has rather to be interpreted pantheistically. Conversely, Buddhism is also quite aware of the problem of historical and personal mediation. Whatever may be the outcome of theoretical and critical discussion between the two higher religions, only a mediation of salvation by love, which also knows absolute detachment in death yet accepts even this, not for its own sake but for the sake of the life manifest in it, reveal that blissful "nothingness" which is not absolutely death but all-embracing, creative life.

3. Although the Christian conception of revelation regards as decisive its historical, personal mediation in Jesus of Nazareth as the Kyrios of history and cosmos, it is a paradoxical fact that the theory of meditation current in the Church does not give much prominence to this historical and personal mediation. On an Aristotelian and scholastic basis, it regards man as a being of a special kind who as such is rooted in being as true and as good. As opposed to a "philosophy of being" aiming at a false immediate contact with God, an adequate Christian theory of meditation must bring the absolute spirit-source of human existence into harmony with its concrete temporal and historical character, and then show systematically and hermeneutically that man lives essentially (not merely theoretically, in a secondary way) as a radical question, but one which as such is mediated by personal and social dialogue. And this question is dependent for its explication on meditative awareness. This concentration of human awareness and freedom, in which the radical question emerges as the guiding-line, means that the past, the unconscious, and the temporality of human existence as a system of dialogal, historical, personal relationships, are simultaneously rendered present and perhaps transformed. Only in such a present, rich in manifold relationships, is the relation to God actually realized. This is the medium of all historical, personal contact, the *logos* of all dialogue. Such an actual intermediary person exemplifies the specific character of the self as such, namely, consciousness and freedom. The intermediary person as *dia-logos* is not merely an abstract universal but, rather, the concrete truth of every person realized personally in each instance. Consequently this is the medium and the root of all reality, and therefore the centre of integral meditation.

Theologically, the *dialogos* can be understood as the cosmic Christ who, mediated by his historical bodily incarnation in Jesus of Nazareth, is the pneumatic glorified Kyrios of eschatological history. Only the personal mediator understood as Christ makes God himself visible as his ground, God who, because he is beyond all relationships and therefore all intermediate reality, is "nothing and all" (Eckhart). An awareness of this kind, which does not overhastily claim to be grounded in the light of being, but must first recognize its indispensable multiplicity of relationships if it is to attain its own identity and thereby find the presence of God, comes in various modes of meditation on the religious interests of the moment. And in this respect a fundamental distinction can be drawn between natural and religious (Christian) meditation (P. Dessauer). Natural meditation is again determined in various ways according to the reality which it seeks to mould and heal. Yoga meditation, for example, is the awareness of one's own body and its functions; meditation may evoke past consciousness or the unconscious. It is scientifically elaborated in psychotherapeutic meditation. Philosophical meditation opens the mind to philosophical evidence. The various kinds of natural meditation develop their own particular conceptions of their purpose and methods. In principle they are possible to everyone. Everyone can represent to himself and concentrate on the realities which confront him in his interior history (cf. P. Dessauer). Religious and Christian meditation, incorporating on occasion natural modes of meditation, in a special and explicit way renders the act of realization itself present, through the means offered by redemptive history and by the Church's liturgy generally. Such meditation has to develop its own special practical and theoretical self-awareness. Its inner dynamism gives rise to the special problems which are dealt with in detail in the classical tradition of Christian spirituality and mysticism.

4. The practice of meditation by its very nature is concerned with awareness, not, as in one alienating form of meditation, with being directly absorbed in something else as such. It does not mean absolute indifference, as a not uncommon nihilist misconception of Ignatian detachment would suggest. Nor does it mean extinction of personal life, as in a false, largely unconscious view of the *theologia crucis*. Meditative awareness is different from an empty, distracted or preoccupied consciousness, as well as from rigorous concentration (where it is not a question of self-awareness) and can be described as a concentrated, recollected state of mind in and through which alone other contents are communicated. This recollected and mediating consciousness is inherently directed by the radical question which each human being is and lives; disclosure of this is itself eminently a task for meditation. The urgency of this question, which addresses its summons from the vital centre itself, is dulled if particular interests smother the connections which it has with all the dimensions of reality that concern the self. Courage for personal conversion and sensitivity to truth are a presupposition as well as a result of a meditative attitude to life. Without historical, concrete, dialogal openness to truth (and not merely of the theoretical and detached kind), and without the awareness of transcendence which it implies, the dynamism of meditation ceases and the ensuing sterility means that the depth of human reality is lost sight of. Consequently, what is needed is a heuristic, vigilant alternation between concrete, practical moral commitment and retirement with recollection. In this way existentially critical awareness repeatedly renews its strength. The primordial consciousness of truth manifest in the radical question, and the irreplaceable guiding principle which it implies, will not normally be discovered and confidently followed without concrete external human guidance. Otherwise the exercitant, on an apparently but not really Christian impulse, may overhastily push forward to the final goal of meditation, recklessly and dangerously committing himself, or else be held up in some cramped domain. The condition of society produces many unconscious deformations, conflicts and complexes which narrow men's minds and restrict their freedom and make it difficult for them to achieve meditative concentration, even if they deliberately do everything they can to attain it. Consequently, a special hermeneutics of human reality should be developed for this purpose. This would not leave the various special sciences to deal with the concrete characteristic features of human reality (e.g., dreams) which are the most direct expression of the primordial question, but would bring out their regulative and constitutive significance for man. This might prepare the way for a more individual kind of pastoral care, providing initiation and guidance in the meditative life. It would also call for the courage to unmask taboos falsely imposed on the forces liberated by meditation; it would require trust in the spontaneity which meditation promotes, even though this cannot be regimented. An integral practice of meditation, incorporating all the available technical

methods, is still a desideratum for the Church and for theology, despite what is already available. That is in fact a symptom of the present crisis in the meditative life of the Church.

Eberhard Simons

B. Spiritual Reading

1. *Concept.* a) Biblical faith is very closely connected with the written word. The experiences of God of the "first" generation, the patriarchs and prophets, etc., find expression in writing, are meditatively developed in constant contact with the written word, and form the nucleus round which all subsequent piety crystallizes. The NT (and the OT transmitted by it) plays a similar part for the second and third generations of Christians. The Lord is announced to those who know him through earthly intermediaries (though directly and immediately in the spiritual and personal order of grace), in kerygmatic, liturgical and dogmatic formulations, and this happens most closely and with normative force in Scripture. Consequently the reading and hearing of the authentic, inspired word is one of the fundamental activities of Christianity.

b) The further we go back in history, the more clearly we can see the identity of scriptural reading with theological reflection and the actual exercise of faith in life. Because, however, the testimony of the words of Scripture is only a medium for the greater, incarnate Word, contact with Scripture develops a rich variety of forms: liturgical listening – meditative reading; concrete personal search for the summons contained in the word of God – authoritative exposition; preacher's paraphrase – effort to establish the authentic text; meditative consideration of the character of Christ – apologetics in defence of his reality. Genuine "spiritual reading" belongs to this context.

c) The break that was made in this unity can be precisely traced in history; it consisted in isolating spirituality from its connection with Scripture – though of course the separation was never absolute. The growth of a literature of works of piety (in the East in the 5th and 6th centuries, in the West in the 12th and 13th centuries), and the division of *lectio* into *lectio divina* and *lectio scholastica*, stand at the beginning of the dissociation. It ends with practices and theories (cf., for example, O. Zimmermann, *Lehrbuch der Aszetik*), in which Scripture no longer forms the matter of spiritual reading.

2. *Theological reflection.* a) There is no doubt that scriptural reading is the prototype which provides the norm and orientation for all spiritual reading. Consequently all genuine spiritual reading may be regarded as in effect "anonymous" scriptural reading.

b) The centre of the spiritual reading Scripture is Christ. The words of Scripture find their meaning when the letter of Scripture (including the theology of Paul, of the Synoptics, etc.) opens out upon the Word made man. One reason for the spiritual sterility of some exegetical works is that this "bearing witness to the Lord" (cf. Mk 1:1) is not taken seriously.

c) The abundance of additional spiritual books has its root in the Christocentricity of Scripture. Fuller knowledge of the Lord can only be attained in the testimony of Scripture, and prompts the production of further writings which take their standard from Scripture but are wider in scope. These may be variously characterized. Central among them are testimonies to the actual experience of Christian life. A division in tabular form, suggested by I. Behn, would be: mysticism: the articulate expression of the act; mystagogy: guidance to the act; mystology: reflection on the act. This must take its bearings throughout from Scripture.

d) The manifold character of spiritual literature should lead to elucidation of the role of tradition, society, etc. No more than passing reference can be made to liturgical reading (hearing). Ideally, it would be a combination of communal action and private meditation, kerygma and prayer, praise of God and penance, hearing and reading.

e) Hearing and reading are fundamentally identical ways of encounter; phenomenological comparison between them can make clear their basic unity. Hearing faces God's summons; reading opens out one's own world to give precedence to the Christian message.

3. *Practical aspects.* The practice of spiritual reading must be judged in relation to the "sacramentality" of the words of Scripture which in an analogical way extends to subsequent spiritual writings.

a) Spiritual reading stands between mental cultivation and prayer. Only its dynamic impulsion towards prayer makes it spiritual reading. Spiritual reading is only achieved by those whose level of spiritual culture is not lower that their general human and intellectual culture.

b) This makes clear our duty as well as our freedom in regard to spiritual reading. On broad theological grounds, but only in this very wide sense, it is scarcely possible to dispute the duty of spiritual reading. But it is important to note that this obligation can only be met if interior freedom is preserved in view of the mass supply of spiritual reading on the market. The criterion of choice should be spiritual joy or inner attraction.

c) Difficulties mostly have their origin in the spiritual sterility of many works on the Bible or in the reader's inadequate mental attainments. Yet such difficulties may also be one of the crosses which characterize Christian life.

In good spiritual literature the process of actualization of the gospel has to take place. Consequently, the wide range of available spiritual literature must not be sacrificed to one-sided biblicism; the fruitfulness of the words of Scripture, resulting from inspiration, has to be operative precisely in spiritual literature; that is where it achieves its actual efficacy.

Josef Sudbrack

C. Spiritual Direction

Spiritual direction began in the monasticism of the early Church, first among the hermits who needed counsel in their isolation and then in the monasteries, where charismatically gifted elders devoted themselves to spiritual direction – as did also superiors, which could give rise to conflicts. The notion of the superior as the "spiritual father" seems to have developed more strongly in Western than Eastern monasticism. In the Society of Jesus the superior was spiritual father by virtue of his office. Other orders followed this practice. A number of abuses arose, especially where spiritual direction and sacramental confession were combined. Another trend then set in, and finally spiritual direction and the office of superior were made distinct.

Even in the ancient Church, layfolk also entrusted the direction of their souls to monks. But spiritual direction outside the monasteries only became important in the spiritual movements among the laity which characterized to some extent the period from the 12th to the 15th century. Layfolk could also assume the task of spiritual direction, as did for instance St. Catharine of Siena and Nicholas of Flüe. The great age of spiritual direction was the 17th century, especially in France, with such figures as St. Francis de Sales, St. Vincent de Paul, Père de Bérulle.

One hears of a "crisis" of spiritual direction today. And there is an undoubted need to seek for new ways. One form is discussion in small groups: discussion of meditation during spiritual exercises in common, *la revision de vie*, "sensitivity training". Such discussion is possible only in homogeneous groups. It does not replace the spiritual direction sought by the individual from a counsellor in private, but makes it more adequate, especially by the possibilities it holds out of better social adjustment. Given the present-day distaste for the institutionalizing of direction by assigning it to a special official, real progress is possible through this new departure.

There is need above all for a reappraisal of the nature and tasks of spiritual direction. It is both a "humanist" and a "spiritual" process. "No man is an island": man is only himself in contact with his fellow-man. This is the anthropological ground for spiritual direction. As is well known, the mere verbalization of a problem can already "cut it down to size". In the Church, the body of Christ, men are even more intimately related to one another. This is the theological ground for spiritual direction. Hitherto, as a rule, the theological and "spiritual" element was perhaps unduly stressed. Very often, too little attention was paid to the fact that spiritual growth is only possible, as a deliberate personal commitment, within a framework laid down by nature and personal history. It is true that spiritual direction must be concerned with spiritual initiatives, with disposing for the incalculable encounter with the mystery of God and his word, whose impact is never quite the same in any two cases. It is essentially concerned with the discernment of spirits and the finding of the will of God in a concrete situation. Nonetheless, all these things must be integrated into a man's life as a whole, and the spiritual cannot be treated as a sort of superstructure on top of the human element. Spiritual direction cannot be confined to the religious realm, as though this existed in isolation, but must deal with the whole man and his actual problems. The main tasks of spiritual direction may therefore be outlined as follows: a) to help the individual to self-knowledge; b) to help him to self-acceptance; c) to help him to detachment from his own ego; d) to help him to find the actual will of God.

a) The spiritual director cannot be asked merely to ratify the subject's opinion of himself. The subject must be ready to accept without resentment or defence mechanisms aspects of his character which he himself does not recognize, at least under their true names, and is not perhaps anxious to admit. He must be convinced that the value of spiritual direction depends essentially on his own readiness to be humbly frank. This is mainly what the spiritual director has to go on, which means that he must first be ready to listen attentively. This is the only way in which real dialogue is possible. The director tries to place what he hears in an objective perspective, analysing it and throwing light on it, so that the enquirer can feel that he is understood. The answer to the question, "Who am I really, and where do I stand?", is best based on a straightforward account of the life-story of the enquirer, not centred, as in confession, on the question of guilt, faults and sins, but comprising the whole evolution of a life. This should be able to throw light on the deeper structures of a man's nature and character, as well as on the aspects which at once meet the eye. In the course of the discussions, it will probably be necessary to take up past history again and again. At the first meeting, the director, usually, though not necessarily a priest, will probably mainly try to listen receptively to what he is told.

b) All self-knowledge, and especially when it is sought for religious motives, implies immediately an ethical demand. The enquirer must be ready to accept himself as he has seen himself to be, to face what he is, to bear the burden of his real self. Human beings tend almost inevitably to create an image of themselves in accordance with their wishful thinking, to play a "role" of their own choosing and then go sour when facts are stubbornly resistant. Nothing less than a real conversion is needed if the searcher is to accept the profounder self-knowledge which he gains with the help of another. Here too the director must give guidance and encouragement. This invitation to conversion should not be primarily a call for ascetical effort. The director tries to show how pre-existing dispositions interact on each other, and what elements of imbalance are present. He has to distinguish structures of mind and character which are religiously neutral from the moral and religious attitudes by which alone a man's value is determined. There is then still much to do in the line of furnishing religious motives to help the subject to accept the inadequacies and disequilibrium of his nature, to bear his own burden -- in a word, to carry his cross after Christ.

c) Once the process of self-acceptance has begun, it releases the forces which help a man to stand back as it were from himself and exercise a healthy self-detachment. The spiritual director then has a new task. He must help the enquirer to recognize the projections of the self-seeking ego for what they are, to rid himself of fictive life-styles and take up the programme indicated by his real qualities as revealed by his actual life-story, the way of life ordained for him by God. This means striving for the inner attitude which the tradition of spirituality has described as abandonment, resignation or indifference (St. Ignatius Loyola) – terms which could be misleading. Here the discernment of spirits plays an important part, to which the spiritual director should be equal.

d) This brings us to the real aim of spiritual direction, the finding of the will of God "for me", in the whole programme of life and in the new situations to which it constantly gives rise. This is the interest to which the Spiritual Exercises of St. Ignatius are devoted. The will of God, the will of his grace, follows the lines of each man's nature, even where, and indeed above all where, the self must be crucified for the sake of its ultimate fulfilment. When a man is in harmony with himself, he is profoundly in harmony with God, though it always remains true that reason and grace cannot totally coincide in this spiritual process. Self-fulfilment passes through the incalculable and hence impenetrable "mystery of the cross". "He that would find his life must lose it." The life of the individual, like the history of the race, contains so many obscure challenges and barely decipherable potentialities that it is the main task of the spiritual director to try to help the enquirer to find the will of God in the actual circumstances of his life.

Spiritual direction and psychotherapy are essentially different, since the former is concerned with eternal salvation and the latter with the healing of illness. Nonetheless, in practice the boundaries are fluid, since the spiritual director cannot exclude the element of healing, and the therapist should not prescind entirely from man's religious salvation, above all when he is dealing with someone whose fundamental attitude is that of a believer.

Friedrich Wulf

STOICISM

1. *General description.* a) The political and social changes in the time of Alexander the Great and the diadochi, at the end of the 3rd century B.C., brought about the disintegration of the Greek city-state and thus the loss of the inner force which the Greeks of classical times had found in their bond with their *polis* and its religion. All possibilities of the intellectual life seemed to have been exhausted by the speculative work of Plato and Aristotle, and by the empirical research of the latter and his school. It was therefore practical questions of the

conduct of life which occupied the attention of the two schools of philosophy which were taking form in Hellenism, the Stoics and the Epicureans, the "Stoa" being more important and extensive than the "Garden". The intellectual disciplines were mainly studied for the sake of ethics. For the educated, philosophy took the place of religion It looked for a new way of providing man with security. The question of the purpose and end (τέλος) of man became predominant. Man was no longer considered in the light of city-state, as when Aristotle had defined him as an *ens sociale* (ζῷον πολιτικόν), and ethics ceased to be regarded as part of political life. Man took refuge in the inner life, to avoid dependence on outward conditions. Epicurus was content with an individualistic attitude which made "pleasure" (ἡδονή – the totality of sense perception) the term of reference of all action. But the Stoa regarded the individual as a member of the one human race (*animale communale*, ζῷον κοινωνικόν) where there was no distinction of nation or class. The unity of man with himself, in which he finds his happiness (εὐδαιμονία) and goal (τέλος), necessarily presupposes a general consent to the one law which binds all men equally. This law (νόμος) is identical with the divine reason (λόγος) which guides the universe.

b) Though some of the leading Stoics like Zeno and Chrysippus were of Oriental origin, the thesis of Pohlenz, that Semitic elements were at work along with Greek thought in Stoic doctrine, has not met with much acceptance. The influence of the Socratic schools, especially the Cynics, was important. In natural science and theology, the Stoa took over important traits from Heraclitus.

2. *Doctrine*. Wisdom (σοφία) is defined as the "knowledge of things divine and human", philosophy (love of wisdom) as "training in the art necessary to life". It is divided into logic, physics (natural science) and ethics. The relationship of the parts is illustrated by the metaphor of an orchard. Physics, of which theology forms part, is like the trees growing up towards heaven, ethics like the nourishing fruit and logic like the protective walls.

a) *Logic*. Logic comprises dialectic and rhetoric. Dialectic creates the basis for correct action, since it enables man to know what is formally and materially true. Since both language and thought are manifestations of the authoritative Logos (the later Stoics distinguishing the Logos formed within [ἐνδιάθετος] from the Logos thrusting outwards in speech [προφορικός]), dialectic comprises linguistics and grammar as well as formal logic and epistemology. The corporeal sounds (σημαίνοντα) are to be distinguished from the incorporeal concepts or thoughts (σημαινόμενα, λεκτά), which in turn are different from real things. Names were deliberately given to things by the first men, according to the norm of nature (φύσις).

The names of the five cases in grammar go back to the Stoics. Their theory of the tenses was not based like that of Aristotle on the succession of time (past, present, future) but on the types of action, according to which the Stoics distinguished repetition and continuance (χρόνοι ὡρισμένοι) from the simple act (ἀόριστοι). Propositions were divided into simple and compound (copulative, disjunctive, hypothetical), the proposition (ἀξίωμα) being defined as "a complete sentence which is either true or false". Their doctrine of hypothetical and disjunctive conclusions, based on that of the Megarians, is the foundation of modern propositional logic.

There can be no knowledge independent of sensible perception. The effect made upon the organ of sense by the material object becomes a representation (φαντασία) when reason (τὸ ἡγεμονικόν) takes it into consciousness. The representation only becomes significant for knowledge and action when the Logos, after preliminary examination, acknowledges it in willing consent or composition (συγκατάθεσις). The consent is only justified when the representation reflects the object in a way which would be impossible without the real existence of the object. This "cataleptic notion", which according to Zeno enables an object to be "grasped", which necessarily "comprises" our assent according to Chrysippus, is the criterion of truth (Chrysippus).

The soul at birth is like a *tabula rasa*, and receives its contents through perceptions. The multiplicity of similar representations stored up in the memory gives rise to the empirical general notion. With the help of analogy, composition and negation, non-empirical concepts can be formed from the empirical ones. The formation of concepts proceeds either by methodical reflection or spontaneously. The natural impulse gives rise to the "innate ideas" (προλήψεις or κοιναὶ ἔννοιαι) which are found in all men (imperfectly, even before the full development of reason) and which are the presupposition of all other knowledge.

b) *Physics*. Strictly speaking, only the corporeal can be said to exist. It is divided into the passive (πάσχον) or matter (ὕλη) and the active (ποιοῦν), the latter being thought of as artistically plastic fire (πῦρ τεχνικόν), as penetrating breath (πνεῦμα) or as tension (τόνος). Like the microcosm of man, the macrocosm, represented as a finite sphere, is a living being endowed with reason. Its substance is eternal. Its present order will be maintained only till the return to the primordial state of fire in the conflagration (ἐκπύρωσις), after which the same cosmic process begins again. Since the pneuma pervades the whole world in various states of purity and force, there are degrees in the structure of being. The formation and development of particular things are caused by the *rationes seminales* (λόγοι σπερματικοί) which come from the cosmic mind. Lower beings exist for the sake of the higher, which need the lower to exist. The human soul, which according to many Stoics is perishable, comes into being by generation. It is divided into the dominant reason (τὸ ἡγεμονικόν), the five senses, the faculty of speech and procreative ability.

Terror and admiration at natural phenomena and the order of nature bring about in men the spontaneous, innate pre-notion of the divinity (πρόληψις). The philosophical proofs of the existence of God (from the structured degrees and the finality of all beings) are merely to show that the notion is justified. The reconciliation of the philosophical notion of God as the Logos, Fire, Spirit, which permeates the world, with that of popular religion is performed by the allegorical interpretation of the myths. Later a distinction was made between the theology of the poets, the philosophers and the State. The providence of God, which is deduced from the purposefulness of the world, guides all things to what is best for man. All events, including the mental life of man, are determined by the chain of causality (εἱμαρμένη, destiny). This makes scientific divination possible. The problem of how this determinism can be reconciled with the self-determination of man, which was taught very emphatically in Stoicism, was grappled with, though not satisfactorily answered.

c) *Ethics*. Every living being has a perception of itself along with its external perceptions. This means that it finds itself appropriate to itself (οἰκείωσις) and strives to develop its own proper being. For man, this is the Logos. The development of the Logos is man's true advantage (ἀγαθόν), which is identical with the morally good (καλόν) and happiness (εὐδαιμονία). Happiness is independent of all that is morally indifferent (ἀδιάφορον). But within the range of the indifferent there is a difference between what is fitting for our nature (προηγμένα) and what is contrary to it (ἀποπροηγμένα). The goal of human life is harmony with the Logos which is man's characteristic faculty and the universal law of nature from which all positive laws derive. (Zeno's formula, "to live harmoniously", ὁμολογουμένως ζῆν, was given an explanatory addition by Cleanthes, "to live in harmony with nature", and by Chrysippus, "to live following nature".) The natural affinity (οἰκείωσις) goes beyond the individual ego to take in all men because they are akin to one another through their rational nature. The Stoic is a cosmopolitan, a citizen of the whole world to whom none is a stranger. All men have the same rights by virtue of the Logos which is their nature.

Knowledge of good and evil, φρόνησις, is an essential element of all virtues. The virtues are indissolubly connected with one another, and like all faults, of equal importance. Each of them is indivisible. It is either possessed in its entirety or not at all. Between the morally perfect acts which are done for the sake of the moral good (κατορθώματα) and wrong actions (καθήκοντα) which are in keeping with man's nature but are not performed for the sake of the moral goal.

Passion (πάθος) is a faulty judgment (Chrysippus) or an urge going beyond due measure by reason of a faulty judgment (Zeno). Since it is an illness of the Logos, it must be entirely quenched (in impassibility, ἀπάθεια). (The Middle Stoa went back to the Aristotelian doctrine of the right mean in the passions.) The best defence against passion is to recognize that there is nothing good or bad apart from the moral order, and to be prepared for anything that may happen. Men are divided into three classes, the sages, the fools or the worthless and the advancing (προσκοποῦντες). While the fool is torn apart inwardly, the wise man is in harmony with himself and the cosmic law. If he can no longer bear his external life or can fulfil his moral task only by surrender of his life, he will depart this life voluntarily after having weighed all the factors.

3. *History*. a) *The Early Stoa*. Zeno of Citium (*c*. 334–263 B.C.), a pupil of Crates the Cynic, began his teaching about 300 B.C. at Athens, in the "many-coloured hall" (στοὰ ποικίλη) decorated with the paintings of Polygnotus. He was followed as head of the school by Cleanthes of Assos (*c* 331–232), whose Hymn to Zeus is the loveliest testimony to the "cosmic" piety of the early Stoa. The system of the older Stoa was completed by Chrysippus from Soli in Cilicia (*c*. 281–208), who was famous for his skill at dialectics and his literary productivity.

b) *The Middle Stoa*. The founder was Panaetius of Rhodes (*c*. 180–110 B.C.), who went back to Plato and Aristotle and thus modified the ethical rigorism of the Stoa. Panaetius was the inspiration of the philosophical circle around Scipio Aemilianus which was so important for the intellectual development of Rome. His work *On Correct Behaviour* ((Περὶ τοῦ κατήκοντος) was used by Cicero in his *De Officiis* and was thus an essential element in the development of Roman ethics and the ideal of humaneness. His pupil Posidonius of Apamea (*c*. 135–51) was a philosopher, a student of nature, a geographer and a historian. He saw the cosmos as an organism held together by "sympathy", in which all things react on each other in a vital relationship.

c) *The Later Stoa*. L. Annaeus Cornutus (1st century A.D.) has left us a *Compendium of Greek Theology* which employs the allegorical method of the ancient Stoa in interpreting the myths. In Musonius Rufus (*c*. A.D. 30–108) and his pupil Epictetus (*c*. 50–120), interest in systematic speculation gives way to ethical directives. L. Annaeus Seneca (4 B.C. – A.D. 65) was also preoccupied with rules for good living, but took an interest in natural philosophy. The *Meditations* of the Emperor Marcus Aurelius (121–180) were the high-point and the end-product of the later Stoa. Stoicism ceased to exist as a system soon afterwards. Some of its thought was taken over by middle Platonism and neo-Platonism.

Friedo Ricken

STRUCTURALISM

Structuralism, both as a method of analysis and as an ideology into which the method constantly degenerates, has spread from France to become a typical phenomenon of our times, and as such is of interest to the Christian preacher.

1. *History of the method.* The history of European thought may be said to have gone from substance to structure, from a notion of being characterized by intrinsic determination and independent existence to another perspective which can be defined only with difficulty. Possibly its first expression was given it in the "structural psychology" of W. Dilthey. As formulated by his disciple E. Spranger it ran: "A reality has a structure or systematic build, when it is a whole in which each part and the function of each part contributes significantly to the whole, in such a way that the build and function of each part is determined in turn by the whole and hence is only intelligible in the light of the whole" (E. Spranger, *Psychologie des Jugendalters* [19th ed., 1949]).

This rather philosophical analysis of psychological structure, studied in the works of the Swiss psychologist Jean Piaget and his disciple Lucien Goldmann, gave French structuralism the categories of totality and function. Still more influential were the Marxist categories of the all-important infrastructure with its dependent suprastructure, and the Freudian subconscious which secretly determines all our actions. But of decisive importance for C. Lévi-Strauss, the father of French structuralism and for his followers, whom alone we consider here, was structural linguistics as founded by the Swiss scholar, F. de Saussure and developed by linguistic circles at Prague (N. S. Troubetzkoy, R. Jakobson) and Copenhagen. Earlier linguistics had been mainly concerned with the genetic approach, tracing the origins of the various languages and the changes of their elements in successive stages. The new approach inclined to take a "synchronistic" view, describing a linguistic system and investigating its determinant structure while prescinding from historical change. Marxist and Freudian categories could be verified in structural linguistics, inasmuch as language was regarded as the great social phenomenon. And the meaning attributed to it on the conscious level of vocabulary, grammar and proposition could be ultimately traced to an unconscious process of composition. This process was supposed to follow certain rules, which could be investigated by modern linguistics and reduced to a few basic rules of universal validity.

2. *Structural analysis.* Hence this structural analysis derived from linguistics is primarily concerned only with the systems of signification which man has created. Unlike psychology and the natural sciences, it does not ask how far a given system of signs corresponds to the "objective reality" which it indicates (*le structurel*). The aim of structural analysis is to discover within any given closed system of signification the rules according to which it is composed and functions. This "structuralist process" can be described with some degree of simplification in two stages. The first stage, that of dismemberment or *découpage*, discloses the "elementary structures", the smallest units, from which a given system is built up. Following a basic presupposition taken over from linguistics, these units are not to be de-

fined by their "substance" but by distinction and limit, their manifold relationship to the other units. Even the elementary particle of a system must be regarded as a "structure", in which the smallest change modifies the whole. The second stage, that of *agencement*, arrangement, is concerned with finding in these elementary structures the rules of association and composition by which the units become a system. More precisely, it seeks the typical *form* of a given system.

3. *Applications*. De Saussure himself indicated some fields other than language to which structural analysis could be applied. "Language is a system of signs which express ideas. Hence it is like writing, the deaf and dumb alphabet, symbolic rites, etiquette, military signals and so on, except that it is the most important of such systems. One may therefore envisage a science which studies the life of signs in the framework of social life . . . We shall call it semiology (from the Greek *sēmeîon*, 'sign'). It will teach us what signs consist of, the laws by which they are governed" (*Cours de linguistique générale*, Introduction, ch. III, para. 3 [3rd ed., 1968], p. 33). Structural analysis can in fact be applied to any system of signs. The stroke of genius which made Lévi-Strauss famous was that he applied the principles of structural linguistics to the seeming confusion of the various systems of marriage laws among certain primitives and reduced them to the principle of the swap. But literary systems of signification were more manageable, and Lévi-Strauss then took up the myths, while students of literature applied structural analysis to poetry. Art, fashion, the cinema, advertising and the press can also be analysed in this way, and also philosophical and theological systems, the Bible presenting itself as especially suitable.

4. *Ideology*. Structuralism becomes an ideology when the methodical principles are made universal and absolute, and when methodical abstractions become negations on an ontological level. The discovery of the role of the unconscious in the composition of systems of signs leads to the massive negation of all deliberate activity on the part of the human subject and the affirmation that freedom and responsibility are an illusion. To this Sartre replies: "The initial disintegration, which makes man disappear behind the structures, evokes itself a negation: man appears behind the denial. A subject or subjectivity exists, at the very moment when the effort is made to go beyond the given situation, by preserving it. This transition is the real problem. One must try to understand how the subject or subjectivity, on a transient basis, constitutes itself by a continual process of interiorization and renewed exteriorization."

Prior to all attributions of meaning, and outside the scope of man's disposing, there is a universal code which underlies all systems of signs. Hence the question of the special meaning of an arrangement appears as secondary or even insignificant, as a sort of jig-saw puzzle within the framework of an unchangeable universality of meaningfulness or futility. As Paul Ricœur said to Lévi-Strauss: "You deny that there is any 'message', not in the sense of cybernetics, but in the sense of kerygma. You despair of meaning, but you save yourself by affirming that even if people have nothing to say, they at least say it so well that their language can be subjected to structural analysis. You save meaning, but it is the meaning of the non-sense, the admirable syntactical arrangement of a discourse which says nothing. You combine agnosticism with a hyper-intelligent view of syntax. This makes you fascinating and disturbing at the same time" (*Esprit*, November 1963, p. 652). The constancy of structures, which change merely in externals, and their one-dimensional character which means that there are no differences of level, leads to the emptying of the categories of "history", "development", "progress", "revolution", "infra-human", "human" and so on. Man himself appears finally as merely a "machine, more perfect perhaps than others, which is working at the dissolution of an original order and hence reducing organized matter to a state of inertia which will one day be final" (Lévi-Strauss).

We may conclude with another remark of Sartre, who finds that "man is perpetually 'beyond' the structures by which he is determined, because what makes him what he is, is something else again. So I fail to understand how one can stop at structures. To me, this is a logical scandal."

Günther Schiwy

SUBJECTIVISM

Subjectivism is the tendency in philosophy not to attribute the validity of the judgment to how things display themselves as they are, but to certain conditions in the subject who judges, though these conditions do not serve to exhibit the thing. Subjectivism can be at work in various realms: epistemology, ethics, aesthetics and religion. Formally speaking, the subjective conditions affecting the judgment may be such that they are accessible to empirical research. Or again, they may be open only to transcendental reflection. Thus one may distinguish between an empirical and a transcendental subjectivism.

1. Empirical subjectivism is based on the fact that thinking and judgment are often dependent on one's personal qualities – a certain psychosomatic constitution, which has been further stamped by education and a series of free decisions – and by one's membership of a given race and civilization. This is an observation which as it stands is neutral and justified. It becomes subjectivism only when it goes on to affirm that these subjective influences cannot on principle be overcome, or at least that we can never be certain of overcoming them. This gives rise to the two basic forms of empirical subjectivism, relativism and scepticism. Relativism is content with the mere subjectiveness of the judgment: "It is so for me." Scepticism is always doubtful of its own objectiveness: "But is it really so in itself?"

The two attitudes can only be stated insofar as their proponents envisage the real truth – either to reject or doubt it. Hence the affirmation presupposes its contrary and hence is self-stultifying. But this consideration of principles is not enough to guarantee the objectiveness of any given judgment in particular. Nonetheless, it gives a reasonable hope that truth may be attained by vigorous investigation. And it also teaches us to be reserved about our own judgments, especially when there are positive reasons for suspicion. These two truths should make us ready for dialogue. But the purpose of the dialogue must always be to have sight in common of the thing itself, though perhaps in an irreducible plurality of perspectives.

The basic principle is that the validity of the judgment can only be based on the relation to the reality in question, and that this relation remains ultimately intact, in spite of being conditioned in so many ways, since man, as long as he is a man, abides in the truth. And this principle is the norm to be applied to all types of subjectivism. The truth of a reality, the value of an action, the beauty of a work of art, the holiness of a religious "object" are determinations which are within the objects in question and not merely projected upon them because of one's tastes or the like. Hence such determinations are also "intersubjective". They must be acknowledged by all the persons involved and unlike the pure interiority of the indefinable free act or the passing feeling, must be capable of enunciation to some extent in objective propositions (scientific theory, ethics, aesthetic canon, religious dogma).

2. The conditions on which the validity of knowledge is dependent, according to transcendental subjectivism, cannot be demonstrated in empirical research. They represent the possible answers to what Kant called the "transcendental" question (*Critique of Pure Reason*, B, 25): what is it in the subject which makes the objectiveness of the object possible? Thus, while in empirical subjectivism the subject was envisaged as the source of the lack of objectivity, in transcendental subjectivism the subject appears as the source of all objectivity and hence truth.

It is in fact true that every object, as such, is the result of an objectivation. It is only through the models and considerations sketched by the interested subject that the object of a given science can take shape. but this objectivation must be subordinated to the claims of the matter to be presented, which is in fact possible – as already appears implicitly in the considerations upon empirical subjectivism. Knowledge is true, not insofar as the object is constituted by the subject, but insofar as in the object the reality itself becomes apparent. A subjectivity not fully at the disposal of objectivity, i.e., of the manifestation of the thing itself, would be subjectivist in the wrong sense.

3. It is at once the strength and limitation of our subjectivity that we can create a free space for things where they can be themselves and show themselves. But the supreme achievement of this liberating activity of the subject is not the objectivation of beings, but the love which actively brings the other to be within the space of one's own life. It is here in fact that the subject learns that his subjectivity is not pure mastery of self but has to be liberated for such self-determination in each case. For it is only through the experience of being itself accepted that it becomes capable of accepting the other in its otherness. But since such recognition is a reciprocal matter and hence cannot produce itself, the power of subjectivity as such is seen to be a gift. Human thinking which refused to recognize its character of gift would be subjectivist in a third, metaphysical sense.

Gerd Haeffner

SUBSTANCE

1. *Historical survey*. According to Aristotle, substance (οὐσία ὑποκείμενον) is the chief object of metaphysics (*Metaphysics*, VII, 1; 1028b, 2ff. and 6f.), because it is what primarily exists and is the first of the categories, to which all the others are intrinsically related. More precisely it signifies that which stands by itself, the ultimate bearer of all that belongs to a being (cf. *Categories*, I, 5; 2a, 11f.; 2b, 15ff.). This conception was further developed by the scholastics. It was opposed by the empiricism which was foreshadowed by Nicholas of Autrecourt and fully elaborated by David Hume. According to Hume, the idea of substance arises solely because constantly associated phenomena are designated by a common name. Positivism and neo-positivism represent a similar view. Encouraged by the ambiguous definition given by Descartes, extreme rationalism in Spinoza arrived at a monism of substance; there can only be the one, uncreated, infinite or divine substance, and creatures are merely its modes. Spinoza was outdone by G. Leibniz, who reduced everything to the monad as the simple subsistent; the one infinite monad renders possible many finite monads each of which mirrors the whole universe, but only from its own angle. Kant endeavoured to arrive at a synthesis of his predecessors, counting substance among the *a priori* categories of the understanding; these are valid only of the phenomenal object; what defines substance is subsistence; its sensible schema, however,

is real duration in time. This is over-emphasized: "In fact the proposition that substance persists is tautological" (*Critique of Pure Reason*, A 184). N. Hartmann accordingly takes substance to be the persistent substratum which he considers is only to be found in the inorganic realm. It is known *a posteriori*. It applies to the thing-in-itself. Living beings, on the other hand, are not substances, for they neither endure nor are they a substratum, but are based on the inorganic. H. Bergson viewed everything in terms of *élan vital* and *durée;* instead of persisting solidly, things occur in perpetual flow; rational thought divides this into particular states which, it is true, must be unified by a persistent substratum. With M. Scheler, who restricts substance to the realm of things and excludes it from persons, the philosophers of existence and the existentialists raise man as personal existence or activity above persistent substance. According to Heidegger's fundamental ontology, "ex-sistence" is the substance of man (cf. *Sein und Zeit*, p. 212), i.e., his οὐσία is the destined communication of being, thanks to which he "stands out" or is "present there". As atomic physics shows, particles and waves, mass and energy merge into one another; corporeal substance appears to evaporate more and more into processes, becomes rather than is.

2. *Doctrinal discussion.* Etymologically, substance is what stands beneath, that is, what forms the basis of appearances, unfolds itself in them, discloses and simultaneously conceals itself. Substance means in fact "that which stands of itself", the independent subject, the real being or *that which* is. It is contrasted with accident or appearance, which essentially inheres in substance as its support and only occurs as a further attribute of the real being or as the channel through which something is or appears. The distinction between substance and phenomenon derives from the fact that the same being explicates itself in many and ever-changing appearances. Here substance is a finite category, which stands in need of completion by the accidents; it is contrasted with the infinite substance beyond the categories, which alone is the whole. According to Aristotle, the "first substance", the particular (τόδε τι: *Metaphysics* V, 8; 1017 b, 25), is substance in the full sense; derived from this is "second substance", or substance as a universal. Platonism, on the other hand, regards the particular as second, and the universal as first substance; the latter, however, is not a concept formed from the particular, but the form or exemplar antecedent to it. By its very notion, substance only excludes dependence on a substratum, not dependence on a cause; there can therefore be substances which are caused, i.e., created substances. Strictly speaking, substance denotes only the substantial whole; yet essential parts which go to constitute this whole (e.g., body and soul) are also spoken of as substantial. Although substance usually stands out as what is relatively persistent in contradistinction to its changing appearances, anything that exists in itself, even if it only lasts for an instant, is truly a substance.

The principle of substance states that if anything whatsoever exists, there is substance; for the inherent presupposes that which exists in itself, and appearance that which appears. Finite substance is evidenced in human responsibility; if a man were merely an attribute of something else, the latter would be acting through him; it would bear the responsibility, not the man himself. Man's substance does not exclude the process of historical change, but is actually its ground; this comprises the claim of being which endows substance with its specifically human character. Since this claim is absent from the infrahuman, substantial independencce diminishes stage by stage and the individual is more immersed in nature as a whole. Consequently substance is least clearly marked in the inorganic realm; it can appear as mass or energy, and can be thought of as particle or wave. It is scarcely to be distinguished from events or processes, and it is also difficult to determine whether one or more substances are involved. Nevertheless the existence of inorganic substance is not to be gainsaid.

Johannes Baptist Lotz

SUPERNATURALISM

The collective term, supernaturalism, designates a number of theological trends of the late 18th and the first half of the 19th century, which strove to defend against Naturalism and Rationalism the supernatural character of revelation and its special importance as a source of knowledge which was not to be reduced to natural reason.

1. *Historical background.* Supernaturalism was part of the Church's reaction to the emancipation of the world (or secularization), or rather, to the intellectual abandonment of the unity of the medieval order. It was one of the efforts to re-think and re-formulate, in the upheavals of the modern era, the position and justification of revelation and Church. The movement for emancipation had given rise to a Naturalism which in the explanation of the world, of man and his history, culture, knowledge and morality only saw as legitimate the categories which had been worked out for the understanding of nature. Nature thus became a closed system, whose origin and development could be variously explained, but which was fully accessible to one and to one only principle of knowledge, human reason, which could grasp its meaning and purpose. "Supernatural" interventions of God, as for instance in the form of historical revelation, were either excluded on principle or the possibility of recognizing them as such was denied. (It may be noted that this attitude reflects to some extent, negatively, the relationship between nature and the order of supernatural revelation as described by the theology of the time, which was at least basically "extrinsecist" in its approach.)

The necessity of revelation for man's salvation was denied, since nature itself contained all that man needed and made it accessible to his reason. Nature thus became unlimited, infinite and non-historical. It was seen as fulfilling all the metaphysical needs of man. There was no place for the supernatural in the understanding of Christian revelation. Faith became a sort of irrational underworld, imposing taboos, alienating man and hindering progress. Religion became an element in the immanence of nature. It was one of the main tasks of Naturalism to explain the genesis of religion within the framework of the development of nature (cf., for example, D. Hume, *Natural History of Religion* [1757]). An enlightened social order assigned religion and religious associations a precise place, subordinated to the system, in the education and perfectioning of man. The Deism which originated in England in the 16th century and then spread to the Continent was also part of this naturalistic world-view. Though it recognized the existence of a personal Creator, the denial of any further influence of God on the world was a further confirmation of the self-contained character of nature and of the possibility of explaining it by reason alone. Rationalism may not have denied the simple possibility of supernatural revelation. But as regards the content, it made the critical reserve that nothing could be admitted which did not prove capable of being grasped by the categories of reason. Hence it led at least in practice to the reduction of revelation to reason and nature. Theology became philosophy and Christianity was no more than natural religion.

The supernaturalistic approach in theology, which brought with it a hardening of conservative and integralist attitudes, was a reaction to this Naturalism and Rationalism. It was engendered in a climate of scepticism which put forward radical doubts about the power of reason and the optimism of the Enlightenment. A further factor was the shock caused by the total political upheaval of the French Revolution. The resulting vacuum was filled by views of God and the world which were tinged with Romanticism and Idealism and turned the pages of history backwards in a search for a sound and happy world. This was very attractive for conservative circles in the Church and politics. The opinion took form that humanity or the Church could only maintain and defend itself if the natural powers of reason were down-graded, and the existing plurality of systems and sources of knowledge were reduced to some postulated unity.

2. *Supernaturalism in theology.* Supernaturalistic traits were manifested in the Protestant Churches chiefly in Pietism and its attitude towards ecclesiastical orthodoxy. Theologians went back to a biblicist Lutheranism in order to preserve the supernatural character of biblical revelation and to uphold the doctrine of justification against rationalistic efforts to whittle it away (see *RGG*, II, cols. 623f.; V, cols. 791–9; VI, cols. 589f., 813). Within Catholic theology, supernaturalistic trends showed themselves especially in Traditionalism and Fideism. Traditionalism held that the certainty of human knowledge could be guaranteed only by the authority of a divine revelation which had been given to the first men and which had to be handed on to all generations in an uninterrupted tradition, the channels being language, folklore, society and the Church. Such tradition was absolutely necessary for man, since his individual reason was physically incapable of attaining the only truths which could give meaning to his existence. Metaphysical and religious and moral truth could only reach man through a tradition coming "from outside", to be accepted by him in faith and confidence, based either on the divine authority or on the universal testimony of the human race. Fideism had its own special position with regard to the relation between reason and the act of faith. Its low opinion of reason led it to deny any co-operation of reason in the genesis of the act of faith. It distrusted all efforts to penetrate rationally the truths of faith and rejected the traditional apologetics with its logical argumentation. The only element relevant to salvation was the dedication of the heart in faith.

3. *Supernaturalism in Church life in the 19th century.* Though supernaturalism contributed little to theological reflection, it had important consequences for the self-understanding of the Church and the moulding of its relationship to the world, as for the attitude of individual Christians. The "necessity" of revelation on the grounds of the feebleness of reason, its role as tutor and practically as guardian of the underdeveloped, the inability to distinguish and allow their proper independence to the various realms of reality led to the attitude known as Integralism which stamped the Church in the 19th and at the beginning of the twentieth century, and which is still a force to be reckoned with. The effort was made to answer the many different questions which the age put to the Church by a simple appeal to the faith. The magisterium of the Church was thus assigned importance even in fields in which it had no competence, and the Church became involved in futile and indeed harmful disputes. The consequences of an attitude which put too much stress on revelation in seeking norms for Christian behaviour in fields which had even a remote connection with faith and morals are well known: the effort to mark off ghetto-like special Christian realms in the midst of the world, resistance to

external influences, conservatism within, clericalism and restorative tendencies in political matters, a growing alienation and inward dissociation of the very levels of the population which gave the century its special stamp. The Church had to undergo the reproach, not always unjust, that it had perverted the faith into a totalitarian ideology.

4. *Critique of supernaturalism.* As an answer to the questions posed by Naturalism and Rationalism, and as a contribution to a new orientation of the Church's life of faith, supernaturalism was inappropriate. It opposed to the overestimation of reason an overestimation of revelation as a source of knowledge. A closed system was opposed by another, equally closed, equally incapable of seeing and explicating in their mutual contrast the necessary distinctions between the order of creation and redemption, between revelation and its historical forms, between faith and knowledge, Church and world and so on. The dialogue demanded so urgently by the times between theology and the profane sciences could not be launched on such premisses. Blindness to the plurality of systems and orders of knowledge and to the relative independence of the partner in the dialogue could only make the latter feel that he was under a modern type of tutelage. Misgivings must also have been aroused by the would-be pious description of man as the receiver of revelation. The belittling of his reason – in which Kant's critique of reason was so readily used as a proof – and the purely passive role attributed to his receptivity made faith appear as a blind assent, obscuring the responsible decision of the hearer of the word. This approach made revelation so "necessary" that the very core of its supernatural character, the free, gratuitous, historical intervention of God was lost sight of, and revelation again appeared as "natural", in the sense of being immanent to the world. (This of course betrayed the formal identity of the basic approach both of naturalism and supernaturalism, the denial of a plurality.) Further, the well-intentioned but misleading formula, "the moulding of life by faith", was incapable of stemming the quick spread of a "schizophrenia" in the individual Christian, who was torn between his ecclesiastical and his worldly attitudes, on the basis of constantly conflicting claims on the part of the Church and of the world.

It was undoubtedly no easy matter for the magisterium of the Church to bring itself to condemn supernaturalistic tendencies and to plead the cause of reason, since the upholders of supernaturalism thought that they were loyally dedicated to the cause of the faith. The Fideism of Bautain was condemned in 1840 (*D* 1622–7) and the condemnation of the Traditionalism followed in 1855 (*D* 1649–52, against Bonetty). The First Vatican Council formulated a comprehensive pronouncement against Rationalism and supernaturalism (*D* 1781–1820). It insisted on a twofold order of knowledge ("It has always been and still is the unanimous conviction of the Catholic Church that there is a twofold order of knowledge, differing not only in the principle of knowledge but also in its object" [*D* 1795]), and described the role of reason in the genesis of the act of faith. In view of the persistence of integralist attitudes and practices, great importance must be attached to the development of this pluralist principle and of its dialogal structure in the Pastoral Constitution.

Ernst Niermann

SUPERSTITION

1. *Notion.* The word "superstition" primarily means an inverted, a "wrong" faith, but also a "sham" or deficient faith. What will be called superstition in any particular case depends on the

outlook of the observer. Generally speaking, any religion or world-view is tempted to dismiss as superstition manifestations of a belief that conflict with its own norms or notions of belief. A "scientific" world-view which is thought absolute will look on all religions as superstitions. Apart from the fact, however, that assuming the world to be wholly explicable through reason must itself be acknowledged a superstition, because it is beyond the powers of natural science to tell us what life means, this assumption continually spawns superstitious counterfeits of religion. Within Christianity superstition means either misinterpreting important parts of the gospel in a magical sense or obscurely clinging to elements of paganism (natural religion) in Christian practice, or else abusing the forms of Christian faith in a flight from the insecurity of life and from the decisions it demands of us.

No doubt "superstitious" elements are inevitable in any religion, since transcendental religion (and therefore Christian faith as well) has to objectify itself in categories which are essentially inappropriate to it and which it must always outstrip, though it cannot leave them behind altogether. But superstition only enters the picture when men cease trying to rise above the categories of religion, as they must constantly do, and (consciously or not) cling to them for "safety" as to something no longer "transparent" (that no longer points beyond itself).

2. *Superstition in the history of religions.* Superstition presupposes a magical world-picture, or the remnants of one. It assumes the existence of forces inexplicable in terms of the laws of nature (however those forces be conceived of in particular). Man feels subject to such forces and tries to manipulate them by magic. Studies in the history of religions have solidly established the timelessness of superstition and its various forms – soothsaying, oracles, the popular interpretation of dreams, significance of certain dates or days, and so on. The recognition of magic and superstition demands a clear rejection of the magical interpretation of the world, the result either of a higher, more cultivated stage of religion or a more scientific outlook. This can be verified by the classical Greek and Latin texts on superstition (δεισιδαιμονία – servile fear of the gods instead of rational worship): Hippocrates, *De Morbo Sacro*, I; Plato, *Republic*, 364 b–365 a; Theophrastus, *Characteres*, 16; Plutarch, *De Superstitione;* Cicero, *De Divinatione*, II, 148; Pliny the Elder, *Naturalis Historia.*

The OT condemns every kind of superstition (cf. Exod 22:18; Lev 19:26, 31; 1 Sam 28; Is 8:20; Jer 27:9; Dan 2:27f.), as a sign of lack of trust in the only God, Yahweh, and an affront to him. But it recognized that the revealed faith was constantly jeopardized by superstition, mainly through Jewish contact with Canaanite nature-worship.

The gospel pronounces judgment on all superstition, all devils and demons (Mk 1:25–27 par.; 3:15; 5:13; 6:7 par.; Mt 12:28 par.; Lk 8:29; cf. Acts 13:10ff.; 19:13–19). St. Paul ranks idolatry among the works of the flesh (Gal 5:20; cf. 1 Cor 10:14 and Col 3:5).

3. *The phenomenon.* Superstition is especially prominent in the limit situations of life – birth, love, sickness, death –, in situations of heightened anxiety or fateful decision (magic relating to fertility, love, or healing; necromancy, etc.). It is one of man's despairing attempts to explain his baffling existence and escape its insecurity and anxiety. It can reveal an obscure knowledge of the numinous depths of existence and his ordination to transcendence. But primarily superstition distorts man's view of the absolute sovereignty of God, since it is inspired by the idea that by his own expert ritual words and acts he can propitiate the gods or forces on which he feels his

enigmatic existence to depend. This egocentrism precludes the religious confidence which looks for everything from God's absolutely free power and goodness. Superstition and magic and the like may also offer an apparent security, which silences the real questions of life before they are articulated at all. This also explains why many people today are drawn to superstition (horoscopes, for example). The economic, social, and scientific complexity of the world now overwhelms the individual. He feels helpless, an insignificant, expendable factor in social processes which seem to be inescapable. This induces a passivity which gratefully clutches at the superstitious explanation that everything depends on an enigmatic but sovereign fate which gives meaning even to the absurd. This view spares men both intellectual effort and commitment. So superstition is one of the factors that make it difficult or impossible for a man to develop his religious, moral, and social personality. It is always a symptom of personal crisis. The resignation and complacency produced by modern commercialized superstition (plus other factors we cannot discuss here, such as general scepticism and economic affluence) mean that it cannot be an introduction to the true faith, although theoretically it might be. The poverty and shallowness of what superstition has to say about the background of human existence prevent men summoning up the courage of the real faith which would overcome fear, doubt and despair.

4. *Superstition and Christian faith.* Christian faith is constantly obliged to redefine itself vis-à-vis superstition. Custom and belief in the Churches are always in danger of degenerating into magic and superstition, for various reasons. Either a) custom and the belief underlying it may be relics of paganism which Christianity has not really been able to legitimize; or b) they may be relics of earlier phases of belief and science which have now been left behind; or c) legitimate custom may become superstition because faith is misinterpreted (e.g., using the sign of the cross as a charm, mechanically reciting series of prayers, certain ideas about Mass and Communion). Being at once bodily and spiritual, man seeks to express and explain himself not only in words but also in sign, symbol, and image, and therefore many customs that Christianity has assimilated can be justified so long as their meaning and practice do not contradict the spirit of the faith – that salvation is found only in Jesus Christ, through the decision which must be fully personal in the believer. This truth can be obscured where Christianity mainly consists in the habit of observing a weight of accumulated traditions. Such habits offer apparent security but it collapses under any serious strain – not always yielding to a sounder grasp of the faith and a realization of one's personal freedom and responsibility. It is therefore the task of the Church to watch itself constantly and to educate the faithful to a faith fully conscious of the nature of Christian life and strong enough to endure fear and doubt and to transform them. In certain cases pastors of souls will only overcome superstition if they do not merely unmask and condemn it but recognize it as a symptom of deeper human distress which must be taken seriously and understood in order to be cured.

Bonaventura Kloppenburg

SYMBOL

1. *Term and concept.* Etymologically, the word "symbol" comes from certain usages in ancient law. Two parts of a ring, staff or tablet served, when they were brought together συμ-βάλλειν, to identify legitimate guests (*tessera hospitalitatis*), messengers and partners. Thus word came to have the meaning of "treaty", and in ecclesiastical language

could designate the common profession of faith, the fixed and obligatory formulas or creeds (the "symbols") and then the instruments, images and acts in which the faith was expressed. Through the study of religion, psychology, art, literature, the theory of science and logic, the concept has been extended and varied so considerably that it can take in the operative signs of logical calculations (as in "symbolic" logic). Leaving aside the terminology of formal logic, it may be said that a symbol is distinguished from a sign, which is the broader, more formal concept, by being more "adequate", either in the nature of things, or because chosen "by convention" for its aptness. The symbol is closer to the thing signified, and is less arbitrary than the sign. This distinction between sign and symbol will not always be clear in practice. But it serves to indicate the special quality, the meaningfulness of the symbol, in contrast to the sign which merely points to something else. But the distinction also serves to indicate the limitation and ambiguity inherent in the symbol.

2. *Philosophy*. a) *The anthropological approach*. The symbol in the sense so defined stems from man's essential constitution as spirit-body – and hence at once, and indeed by the very nature of the body – a social being. Hence the innumerable symbols adopted must be investigated for the symbolization which posited them, just as the spoken word is referred to language, speech – the "speaking word", λόγος, by virtue of which man is man. The symbol in this original sense of symbolization, i.e., as is still to be shown, the simultaneous positing of and experience of symbols, would then appear as the (self-)realization of freedom. Hence the symbol does not refer to something else. A reality appears in it – in "the other of itself" – which is there and present but not fully exhausted by this appearance. In such an anthropology Hegel's notion of exteriorization (of the concept, which by nature tries to "manifest itself") becomes the "real symbol" of K. Rahner. Its primary case is the human body and the bodily acts which go with personal attitudes such as love, faith or hatred.

But the element of interpersonality in the positing of the symbol must be stressed just as definitely. As freedom acts, it necessarily addresses itself with its "word" to another. But even prior to this, freedom is never solely activated by itself. Hegel has also shown that form implies limitation, that limit can never belong to one alone but means two at least, and hence that the I only comes to itself (self-awareness) in its encounter with another I. Against German Idealism, however, we must note, with the later Fichte and the dialogal philosophy of the 20th century, that the "self-discovery" in the encounter with the other is not "one-way" but essentially "two-way" traffic. Just as the I finds itself in the You, so too the You in the I, in the common symbol; and the two not only find themselves and each other, but also their mutual reference, their being-in-common. And this common being is realized in a common act. For each, the positing of the symbol is simultaneously experience of the symbol and vice versa.

In the symbol, freedom is realized (in the "medial" sense of activity and receptivity) as a "two-in-one" (or "many-in-one") reality. In this duality or multiplicity in unity its further determinations take root: its riches, its limitations, its historicity. The limitation of the symbol is that it differs in a way from what is symbolized (or better: from what gives itself symbolic form in it). Tillich, for instance, rightly rejects the expression, "merely a symbol", since the symbol is "more" than it tangibly is and says, being appearance, presence, self-positing of . . . Nonetheless, it is not simply that which is positing itself in it there. If the symbol is confused with what it symbolizes, the deformations of fetishism and image-worship appear: the symbol becomes an idol. But if the real presence of the reality symbolized in the symbol is not recognized, the deformations of "pure interiority" follow, iconoclasm in the widest sense: the symbol is reduced to a mere signal, sign-post or "code-number". But even qua symbols, no symbols may be erected into absolutes as though given in the nature of things. Since they are expressions of freedom, they are historical, which means that they can become out of date and empty as soon as freedom – individually or epochally – take a different shape. Hence no system of symbolism, except the most purely formal, is possible. Anything can become a means of self-expression, not arbitrarily but in the framework of historical existence, oblivion of which reduces symbol to allegory. This is the field for empirico-historical research into symbolism in religion, art, literature, law, politics, folklore and science, in the individual and the supra-individual mind.

b) *The world as symbol*. This anthropological approach brings us to the gradation of symbols, from the body to the freely-chosen word or expressive gesture. (It also allows for the distinction between the symbol in the strict sense and the concept, as well as for the question of technics and symbol, which likewise goes beyond mere opposition.) In this way, the symbol, like every other basic concept shows itself to be analogous and comprehensive. The symbol thus appears in the dimension of the world, as is already suggested by the question of the demarcation of the body from the world. It has an integrating function in the structure of the symbolic form which it anticipates (see *Play*). Further, the anthropological approach enables us to have some understanding of nature and the world in general as symbol. This is not to be dismissed as naive anthropomorphism. Biology investigates symbols in animal behaviour, in animal forms (Portmann) and in the structure of plants (e.g., the insectivorous orders). Apart from such intrinsic traits here and there, man has always regarded the flow and fabric of the world as also symbolic of himself and of the Wholly Other, the holy. Art in particular gives expression to the former attitude, where the results of comparative folklore and depth psychology are also relevant. The second point of view is given expression in the cults and myths of religion. But in fact, art always helped to interpret the latter feeling, and religion the former, e.g., in the myths of the creation of the world from the body of a primeval giant or man. And in a similar way, thought inspired by the Christian tradition can take in expressly the unity of the two moments. Since according to Scripture (Gen 2:19f.) Adam gave the beasts their names, i.e., their nature, it need not be subjectivist Idealism to affirm that the world, including man, being the "word" of the creator, is only this word when it is perceived by man. This means that it is a word which from the start is uttered by both. The world is therefore a symbol of the interpenetration of finite, created freedom and infinite creative freedom. They are not partners on an equal footing, but it remains true that the creative freedom does create freedom and hence gives itself a "partner", so that the world is really the history of "the two". But such lines of thought can only be adequately established by theology.

3. *Theology*. The creatureliness of things – created for the glory of God, which becomes articulate in man – is the basis of their kinship, their "similarity" (in the analogy of being), which enables one to be represented or depicted by another. And as creatures, they are all in their own way *vestigia Dei*, the visible manifestation of his invisible nature (Rom 1:20). But the great original symbol of Christian theology, the fulfilment in a superabundant way of the *imago Dei* in man, is the incarnate

Logos, to see whom is to see the Father (Jn 14:6–10). Hence Christ did not proclaim liberation from symbols but the redemption of the symbol. Here the symbol displays, at its most intense, its historicity, its interpersonal nature and its difference in an identity which is dialogal, personal and "pneumatic". Its richness and fullness is such that of itself it resists the temptation of idolatry, though this may not be fully verified in its assimilation, and it cannot be emptied out to be left as a mere code-number. Above all, here symbolic form and symbolic reality are identified. At least in Christ the symbol effects what it signifies. It is not merely validly posited and received, but also fruitfully – to use, not inappropriately, the terminology of the sacraments. In the incarnation the symbol has lost the ambiguity which was its deepest limitation and which it could never have transcended by itself.

Possessing such fullness, this symbol likewise has "universal validity". It has the power proper to the symbol, unlike the concept, to evoke, to summon and claim, to give meaning, in a way which knows no epochal, cultural or any other limits. It remains the "middle" of history, not because it is the most universal concept, but because it is the "name" for all things (Phil 2:9–11 – the *universale concretum*). The incarnationally symbolic character of this middle is then the law of its historical development in the visible Church, creed, sacraments, sacramentals and so on. As has already been indicated, this history also presents the temptations to which the symbol exposes men. But in principle they have already been surmounted (Mt 16:18; 28:20), though only "in hope" (Rom 8:24). The "new earth" without a temple (Rev 21:22) is not yet an unveiled reality and hence the division between sacred and profane continues. But the new earth will not mean the end of the symbol but its fulfilment: the pure "coincidence" of the kingdom of man and the kingdom of God, the kingdom of the Son and the kingdom of the Father (1 Cor 15:18), an immediacy given by the fact that the Son made man "remains".

Finally, this ending of the symbol is fulfilment in the sense that it does not lead to the perspicuousness of having "seen through" everything, to a finally successful grasp in knowledge, but to the rapt recognition of a freedom which bestows itself. The gap of seen and unseen which characterizes the symbol is here finally disclosed, not as a dichotomy between two "worlds", which still has to be bridged, but as primordial freedom in the act of giving itself without abandoning itself. For it is only in this way – where it does truly give *itself* – that it is revealed as the holy mystery.

Jörg Splett

SYNCRETISM

1. *The term.* The word "syncretism" was first used by Plutarch (*De Fraterno Amore*, 19) to describe a combination of Cretan communities against a common enemy, a rare and in fact historically uncertain event, as the Cretans were usually fighting among themselves. The term began therefore by signifying a political alliance in which mutual differences were overlooked in the face of a threat to all. The term then occurs again in the 16th century in Erasmus (*Opus Epistolarum*), who derived it from a verb συν-κεράννυμι (which does not occur in classical Greek) and transposed it into Latin. Subsequently, it was generally applied to an eclectic mixture in philosophical and theological doctrines. The humanist Cardinal Bessarion was described as a syncretist for his efforts to reconcile Plato and Aristotle in the 15th century; the theologians who tried in the 16th century to harmonize Thomism and Molinism were "syncretists", and the term was applied to G. Calixtus

and others in the controversy between Lutherans and Presbyterians in the 17th century.

From the 19th century on, the term has chiefly been used in comparative religion, meaning a fusion of different godheads, cults or religions. Used in its strict sense, it points to the fusion of Oriental mystery religions with the religions of Greece and Rome in Hellenism.

2. *Forms and motives.* a) The forms and motives of syncretism are closely connected.

(i) Within a given religion, syncretism appears first of all as the fusion of godheads (theocrasy). Traits belonging to different gods are transferred to a certain god who is then revered as the supreme god, such as the Babylonian Marduk, the Egyptian Isis or the Persian Mithra in pre-Christian times. Egypt was the main scene of such fusions, the priests deliberately promoting amalgamations of gods and cults to bring together the various local religious heritages. All gods came to be viewed as manifestations of one divine unity, of which Ammon, for instance, was the name, Re the visage and Ptah the body. The notion here is that one invisible divine force dwells in a number of personal, anthropomorphic forms. The phenomenon of one god being personally present in various forms also occurs very early in India. In the *Atharvaveda* (14, 4, 1ff.), the following description is given of one godhead: "He mounts to heaven as Savitâr, he ascends to the clouds in the guise of the great Indra . . . He is Vâyu with the towering clouds. He is Aryaman, he is Rudra, he is Mahâdeva, he is Agni, he is Sûrya, he is also Yâma, the great (god of death)." Such syncretism goes beyond the identification of one god with another in polytheism, and paves the way for revealed monotheism, inasmuch as it takes account of the mysterious character of the holy.

When contact comes about between cultures through migration, trade, common settlements, colonization, etc., the possibilities and forms of syncretism multiply. Along with the fusion of godheads, religious forms and interpretations are borrowed, gods and cults are identified, exchanges ensue which end in the synthesis of different religions.

(ii) In nearly all civilizations, and particularly in those resulting from acculturation, there are syntheses in the religious realm composed of native and foreign elements. Rites are taken over from one culture to another, as in Israel during the reign of Manasseh (*c.* 693–639 B.C.).

(iii) Going beyond this stage of partially unconscious borrowing, sometimes whole groups of gods are made interchangeable or identified with each other. Antiochus IV of Commagene (1st century A.D.), whose ancestry was both Persian and Macedonian, had the gods of both peoples sculptured on the Nemrud-Dagh, where they appeared as equivalents. He identified, for instance, Mithra and Apollo.

(iv) Hellenism was the great age of syncretism. The attempt was soon made to compare the gods of the Egyptians, the Phoenicians and the "barbarians" with those of the Greeks, and later with those of the Romans. In Alexandria, under the Ptolemies, the Egyptian god Usar-Api (Osiris-Apis, already a syncretistic figure) was linked with legends from various cults, and identified with Asclepius, Zeus and Pluto (cf. Tacitus, *Historiae*, 4, 83f.). Under the name of Sarapis he became a god for Greeks and Egyptians alike. This type of phenomenon became characteristic of the influence of the Oriental mystery religions on the West in imperial times. The worship of Isis attained great importance. She was goddess of the world, and was revered as Cypris (the Greek Aphrodite) in Cyprus, as Diana (the Greek Artemis) in Crete, as Proserpine (the Greek Persephone) in Sicily and as Ceres (the Greek Demeter) at Eleusis (cf. the litanies addressed to Isis in Apuleius, *Metamorphoses*, 11, 5, and the hymns of Mesomedes). The Persian cult of Mithra became one of the most important religions of the pagan world. It was a blend of Oriental, Roman and later even of Christian elements (cf. the identifications of the Heracleia of Tyre in Nonnus, *Dionysiaca*, 40, 369ff.). The Magna Mater, Attis, Cybele and other gods worshipped in Asia Minor were naturalized in the Empire, disseminating mystery-cults which have often been interpreted as cultic processes of death and resurrection, rebirth and divine sonship, illumination and redemption, divinization and immortality. In the 3rd century A.D. the many Syrian, Hellenistic and Western cults were amalgamated into a pantheistic solar religion (cf. Macrobius, *Saturnalia*, I, 17, 2).

Special doctrines of this period may be seen in the Hermetic writings and Gnosis, which were syncretist in origin and nature. In the Hermetic myth, Hermes Trismegistos (the Greek version of the Egyptian god Thoth) was regarded as the mediator between the transcendent sphere and the material world, and as the author of religious revelations. The revelation-discourses of the *Corpus Hermeticum* combine Egyptian, Platonic, neo-Pythagorean, Orphic and Jewish notions into a peculiar cosmogony, anthropogony and soteriology. The origin of Gnosis (in the strict sense; see *Gnosis*) is more problematical. But this religious movement of late antiquity presents a picture of man and the world which clearly betrays at least Iranian, Jewish, Stoic and Christian influences. Efforts were made in Stoicism and neo-Platonism to justify syncretism. The thesis was put forward that all gods were of equal value, being different abstractions of the essentially one God, and that all religions were the same, being concrete representations of eternal ideas. Nonetheless, the religious forms of late Hellenism were perversions, tending to become essentially private cults or astrological pantheisms.

(v) A certain syncretism may also be noted in the religions of the Far East and of early America, for which a few indications must suffice. In India, there was at least a partial mixture of Islam and Hinduism. In China, Confucianism and Taoism drew gradually together, combining also with Buddhism from the 5th century A.D. In Japan, since the time of Kôbô, A.D. 774, Shintoism and Buddhism combined to be the mainstays of the ancient national religion.

b) The motives of syncretism are as various as its stages.

(i) Certain geographical, economic and linguistic factors promote the process of religious amalgamation, especially where a cosmopolitan outlook, as in the empire of Alexander, favours cultural contacts, dissemination of a language (the Greek *koine*) and the interchange of gods. But one of the basic causes is also a policy of religious tolerance, an instance of which is the rock inscription of Behistun, engraved by order of the Achaemenid King Darius of Persia, in Old Persian, Elamite and Babylonian. This may be contrasted with the exclusive monotheism of Judaism.

(ii) On the plane of religious piety, syncretism appears as an effort to fill in gaps in a given religion.

(iii) Syncretism also plays a role, in the form of adaptation, in the general process of the explanation of religion and in the missionary work of the Church. One may recall, for instance, the accommodation to the formulas and notions of Persian religion in the designation of God as the "God of heaven" in Ezra 6:10, which was intended to win the toleration of the Persians for the Jewish notion of God. Another instance would be the methods of adaptation used for the famous "Chinese rites". Christianity has no doubt since St. Paul's speech on the Areopagus and down to the missionary theories of modern times, during its controversies with the various philosophies (Platonism, Epicureanism, Stoicism, neo-Platonism), as with Gnosticism and the doctrine of the Logos, as also in its efforts at adaptation in non-Western lands, frequently assimilated heterogeneous elements. But this process cannot be seen as syncretism.

3. *Theological interpretation.* Syncretism has been interpreted as an epiphenomenon linked with the cultural development of man, in line with the Stoic, neo-Platonist and humanist view of the equality of all religions; or as a deliberate fusion of godheads, due to a profound change in religious ideas (K. Prümm); or as a result of the general dynamism of religion (G. van der Leeuw). But this is to leave it on the plane of the phenomenology of religions. An approach to a strictly theological explanation is only possible where it is no longer seen as an aberration due to superstition and unbelief, but as a positive moment in the objectivation of man's transcendental experience of grace and salvation.

John Charles Maraldo

T

TEMPTATION

1. The nature of temptation is to be understood from the fact that man as a defective being is ordained to a perfection which transcends him. The impelling tendency to personal and therefore moral perfection is his mental orientation under the impulse of grace towards his fellow men and towards God. It comes to realization in the ordination of all human acts to the end of man, in proportion to his openness to the transcendent, that is, to the mystery of God, experienced though not capable of being comprehended. This ordination of man to perfection is exposed to many dangers, since man includes in his make-up a whole complex of tendencies which, by reason of the inner affectivity specific to each of them, have an impulse towards immanent fulfilment in relative autonomy unless they are directed by free intelligent human acts to the demands of the person in his self-transcending development. The need for a conscious integration of the various particular tendencies arises from the fact that, in consequence of the unsureness of our human instincts and our state of concupiscence the tendency to realization of particular urges can come into prominence consciously and emotionally in a one-sided way. It is here that the possibility of temptation arises. Thus temptation always consists, in the last analysis, in the danger of jeopardizing the optimal dynamic orientation to a persistent growth in perfection by acts which would adversely affect this growth. The reason for such temptations can be extrinsic, e.g., endocrine changes, unexpected fantasies of imagination or of memory, conditions of emotional excitement resulting from repressions, etc.; but they can also result from human disappointment through others, the experience of one's own limitations, false ideas of the will of God, and other factors of the super-ego and of the environment, none of which are directly subject to control.

Man is not directly responsible for the occurrence of such temptations. Temptations in this sense are rather an inevitable fact, the result of our dependence on pre-existent structures and external. realities. Their occurrence is neither morally good nor bad. They are to be distinguished in principle from a conflict in conscience where a divergence occurs between several objective duties for which one has assumed moral responsibility. In a temptation, on the other hand, a value comes to the fore which is not related to the person as a whole but to a particular tendency, a merely conditionally moral value therefore, whose realization (at least in the form it takes at the time of temptation) is seen as running counter to the well-being of the person.

Thus if there is to be question of temptation, the particular value must not enter into the foreground of consciousness to such an extent that a choice between it and the personal value is no longer possible. That would be the case, if, as a result of ignorance or error, reflection on the significance of the particular value is not possible, or if a compulsive fixation arises of a neurotic or psychotic kind and so the freedom of choice is quite removed. It follows that there is no question of sin in yielding to such tendencies (which are contrary to the well-being of the person). Correspondingly, a limited direct responsibility exists where the instinctive desire which causes the temptation is so strong – no matter for what reason this may be – that the insight into the importance of the temptation is lessened and the power of the will to overcome it is hampered. When people yield to such temptations, we speak of sins of weakness.

These temptations arising from extrinsic reasons can on their part induce internal urges which are injurious to the optimum personal development and which can induce repressions which thwart the desire to know. This is the case when a person freely gives into temptations or instinctively yields to them (e.g., to bad influences in upbringing). Insofar as these urges are instinctive, one is not responsible for the resulting temptations. But if they are caused by freely yielding to extrinsic temptations, one is responsible for them, since the cause of them is freely accepted (e.g., cases of addiction, morbidly fostered hate complexes, etc.). Thus the possibility of intrinsic temptations arises finally from man's pre-existing structures, both transcendental and empirical, as well as from the personal development of each individual.

Furthermore, with his limited intellect man cannot have an over-all picture of his potentialities. His decision to pursue a particular course of self-realization, therefore, is always affected by risk, inasmuch as he can only have a limited view of the effects of his decision and can therefore fail in it. The best possible moral decision is when the risk is so calculated that the factors of security and insecurity in action are held in balance. From the point of view of depth psychology, temptation always occurs when instincts have not been integrated and the tendency arises to attempt this integration in too anxious or too light-hearted a way. In the first case, trying to be too sure, a man will fail through not making full use of his capabilities; in the second he fails through overconfidence by going inconsiderately against existing structures and so negativing his capabilities. Temptation therefore always imperils the transcendental dynamism of human action. When temptation is overcome, this dynamism is free to operate again, and on a deeper level. According to whether the temptation affects man in the kernel of his existence, or only peripherally or as regards his fuller perfection, the act involved is morally grave or of less importance. It makes no difference whether the different degree of danger is due to the importance of the object to the person tempted, or to his degree of freedom with regard to the action.

2. Temptation is explained in the Bible a) as a *testing by God*. Especially according to early statements of the OT, God makes trial of the fidelity of his chosen people (Exod 15:25; 16:4; 20:20; Jg 2:22; 3:1–4) and of individuals, e.g., Abraham, whose temptation is constantly held up as an example (Gen 22:1; Ecclus 44:20; 1 Macc 2:52; Heb 11:17), or Job, whose fear of God Satan is allowed to test through sufferings (Job 1:11ff.; 2:5f.; see also the resultant temptations, Job 7:1; 10:17; 16:10; 19:12). In the later Wisdom literature there is more emphasis, under

Hellenistic influence, on the notion of temptation as a means of purification and education (Wis 3:5; 11:9; see Ecclus 2:1–6; 4:17; 33:1; cf. Jas. 1:2, 12; Heb 11:17, 37).

b) *As seduction by the powers of evil.* Thus the diabolical temptation of our first parents (Gen 3:1–7). The Jewish thought is clearly that behind the evil tendencies of man there lurk the temptations of the devil and his evil spirits, which can be overcome only by the help of God.

This idea of the devil as the great tempter gains ground in the NT. It underlies the petition in the Our Father (Mt 6:13 = Lk 11:4) and the command of Jesus to his disciples in Gethsemane (Mk 14:38). St. Paul too sees underlying temptations the action of Satan (1 Thess 3:5; 1 Cor 7:5), but testifies at the same time that God gives the power to overcome temptation (1 Cor 10:13). Similarly the Apocalypse ascribes temptation to Satan (Rev 12:9; 13:14; 19:20; 20:3, 8, 10), while Jas 1:13f. affirms expressly that temptation does not come from God. In the Apocalyptic literature temptation is regarded as a characteristic of the eschatological tribulations (Dan 12:10; 1 Pet 1:6; 4:12; 2 Pet 2:9; Rev 2:10) and, especially in Hebrews, as to be overcome in Christ (cf. 4:15; 2:18; see also Rev 3:10), since in Christ and in the reign of God which he has brought, Satan's rule over this aeon is ended.

3. Since temptations always consist in the danger of diverting man from the course he should pursue towards perfection, for the *moral victory* over temptation what is most needed is the will to perfection and therefore the openness to grace, which expresses itself in a love for virtue in general and for particular virtues. For in this way the integration of individual drives into the service of man's perfection is accomplished.

Since the immediate cause of temptations is, first and foremost, from extrinsic factors, the moral effort must concentrate on directing these factors. Yet it should be clear from the start that subjection to temptation is given with our nature as creatures, and is not removed by grace. But grace permits us to be calm in the face of temptations in reliance on God's help, so that our being tempted must, in the final analysis, be borne with humble resignation. Yet there are many means of overcoming temptations corresponding to their multiple causes. In extreme cases, resort should be had, for example, to medical treatment and psychotherapy. But there will always be need of avoiding unnecessary occasions of sin (Eph 5:15) in prudent consideration of one's own weakness and in responsibility for the tasks incumbent on each. Often the best way to deal with temptations is through suitable distraction. Above all else there is need of the constant correction of the unrealistic prejudices and bias which settle in the superego. Besides, there is need of as unconditional a love of truth as possible and of the good in general, as well as patient and open-minded confrontation with the empirical realities.

To overcome temptations caused by extrinsic factors there is need of constant formation of conscience. This must, in order to reduce or eliminate temptations, aim at the most reasonable balance possible between satisfaction of instincts and their sublimation, since only in this way will the necessary balance between openness to the transcendent and dependence on the immanent be maintained and proper account taken of the dynamic and historical character of the moral imperative of the unique occasion. For only thus will overestimation or underestimation of our own capabilities be avoided and our attachment to existing structures put at the service of personal perfection in the best possible way.

This means, further, that the temptations arising from intrinsic factors can be neutralized only to the extent to which voluntary false attitudes are corrected as far as may be through an approach to their causes that is both prudent and resolute.

4. A balanced pastoral training must avoid a biased simplification in its view of talents and tasks regarded as a source of temptation, since such a simplification always carries with it a projective interpretation of reality, repressing one or more of its aspects and thus in effect misinterpreting it. Prayer, as recommended by Scripture (Mk 14:38), constant watchfulness (Lk 8:13; 21:36) and above all firmness in virtue (Lk 22:28; cf. Mk 13:13; Rev 2:10), which is a means to steadfastness (Jas 1:2f.), will be the best help towards this balance. This presupposes that one seeks in directness and simplicity what is good and true insofar as it is capable of being known and put into effect in a concrete way and thus endeavours to master life in reliance on God's help who does not wish our failure in temptation but our success (Rev 3:5).

5. *Temptation of God* consists, a) from the biblical point of view, in wantonly provoking God's anger through lack of trust in divine providence. Thus when the chosen people murmured in the desert and doubted God's willingness to save them (Exod 17:2, 7; Deut 6:16; 9:22; Ps 95:8–11; Heb 3:8f.). In the NT Jesus rejects as a tempting of God the demand that he should understand his messianic mission in a wordly manner (Mt 4:7). 1 Cor 10:9 and Heb 3 warn the faithful not to tempt God as the Israelites did of old. In Acts 5:9 the attempt to deceive the Christian community is seen as a temptation of the Spirit of the Lord and in 15:10 St. Peter says that it is tempting God to try to burden pagan converts with the yoke of the law.

b) From the point of view of moral theology, tempting God is to be regarded as a provocation of God which is a betrayal of hope, inasmuch as it does not wait for salvation from God but tries to master human destiny by its own power and volition. It can express itself in many forms, ranging from the presumptuous reliance on the constant readiness of God to forgive, so that salvation is no longer hoped for in "fear and trembling" (Phil 2:12), to superstitious judgments about God. It is based ultimately on a false image of God which negatives and makes an idol of the sovereign mystery of God's love for us in freedom.

6. *The temptations of Jesus* related in Mk 1:12f.; Mt 4:1–11; Lk 4:1–13, need to be analysed with the help of form-criticism, to bring out the underlying messianic understanding of Christ. They imply that Jesus would betray his messianic mission if he succumbed to the temptation of not appearing, in spite of his messianic dignity, as the obedient servant of God and the second Moses withstanding the rebellious Israelites. The temptations of Jesus by the Pharisees (Mk 8:11; 10:2; 12:15; Lk 10:25) also have the purpose of putting the messianic mission of the Lord to the test. In contrast, the temptations of Jesus in Gethsemane (Mk 14:32–42 parr.) explicitly deal with Jesus' capability of being tempted, which in Heb 2:18; 4:15 is explained as a sign of his becoming like to us in all things, sin alone excepted. Jesus withstands the temptation through the acceptance of the suffering (cf. Heb 5:7–9) – the possibility of his succumbing is clearly excluded – and becomes in this way a model which makes it possible for us to follow him.

Waldemar Molinski

THEODICY

1. *The problem of theodicy*. It is not necessary to recall, much less demonstrate, that the world is stamped by misery and suffering, by evil in all its forms. There is no need therefore to "show the interest" of the question. It is

an importunate one, today as ever at its most tormenting in the suffering of the innocent, especially what has been called the "absolute evil" of the suffering of children who are exposed to it not only inculpably but without even the possible defence of fleeing it. And today as always the existence of evil is regarded as the decisive proof against the existence of God. An age which has made empirical verification the ideal of knowledge must find this experience incontrovertible. The hypothesis of theology is falsified by the experimental facts of history. The result of the experiment seems obvious. Nonetheless, before entering into any details, the question arises as to whether there is in fact such a result – as to whether one has really come to a "result" at all. The experiment is carried out on man. And therefore it is still on principle "open", not because it is still going on, but because it is happening to him, in his freedom. He *and* his answer (his answers) are an intrinsic part of the result in this question.

2. *The various answers.* a) Dualism, one of the fundamental answers, was formulated in its most extreme form by Eastern religion. In the Parseeism of Zarathustra, good and evil are divine powers locked in conflict. But this notion had a constant influence on Western thought, from antiquity, Gnosticism and Manichaeism down to the later Schelling. Plato was the first to give a survey of the various earlier attempts to explain evil: the ἄπειρον [non-limited or neutral, indeterminate) of the Pythagoreans, the universal tension of opposites in all reality (Heraclitus) man in the sins of his pre-existence (Orphism, Empedocles) or the ignorance due to man's bodily state (Democritus, Socrates). For Plato, as for the Stoa, God is in no way the cause of evil (θεὸς ἀναίτιος), which is due to the human will (αἰτία ἑλομένου); cf. *Republic*, X, 617 e. But since he has to make evil (cosmic evil due to matter or anthropological due to the passions) unreal, merely apparent, in order to force it into his monism, even Plato's thought is coloured by a latent dualism. This dualism stands out clearly in the theory of emanations in neo-Platonism, which sees evil as the growing distance between things or degrees of being from their origin. This is to identify evil with the very existence of beings, in contrast to the (transcendent) One, from whom nonetheless beings emanate, or strictly speaking, which flows out into beings.

b) Insofar as neo-Platonism is the final and possibly supreme effort of Greek thought, the Greek answer to the problem of evil may be contrasted with the Jewish-Christian as being "cosmological", while the latter is "historical". It is apostasy from the almighty and good God. And the moral explanation of evil given by the Stoa is also bettered since the incidence of freedom is not reduced – by an illogicality – to a monistic rationalism, but seen as a "dialogal" historical freedom. Evil now appears as a punishment, though also as a testing-ground. But the limits of this explanation are clearly seen. It must fall silent before the incomprehensibility of God (as in the Book of Job), whose "works", whose "power" is made perfect therein (cf. Jn 9:3; 2 Cor 12:9).

c) This message of an almighty, good God who still permits evil is given by the early Christian thinkers as a real answer to the questions of the more or less dualistic religions which it encounters. Lactantius (*De Ira Dei*, 13) defines the problem by affirming (i) that God either wills to prevent evil but cannot (which would be to deny his omnipotence) or (ii) that he can, but does not will to (which seems to deny his goodness) or (iii) neither wills to nor can prevent it, or (iv) can and wills to prevent it (which is belied by the reality of evil). The attempted answers to (ii) resort to elements of Greek philosophy sometimes only imperfectly detached from their dualistic context – above all the interpretation of evil as a privation. New efforts are made to underline freedom and the resulting possibility of sin, into which God has to set men as he creates them (cf., for example, St. Irenaeus, *Adversus Haereses*, IV, 37, 1: βία θεῷ οὐ πρόσεστιν, "It is not in the nature of God to coerce"; Tertullian, *Adversus Marcionem*, II, 6f.). God's permission of the *real* misuse of freedom does not seem to be fully explained in this way. Early patristic efforts to formulate an answer within the framework of Jewish-Christian revelation with the help of Greek philosophy crystallized in a form which has remained authoritative to a great extent down to the present day in St. Augustine.

d) St. Augustine was preoccupied from his youth by the question of how there should be such perversity in human life in spite of God's sovereign power (*De Libero Arbitrio*, I, 4; *Epistola* 215; *De Ordine*, I, 1). His efforts were permanently coloured by the debate with Manichaeism, to which he had adhered for nine years (*Confessiones*, IV f.). Against a background of a highly acute sense of evil (cf. *Confessiones*; and e.g., *De Civitate Dei*, XX, 2), he denies all proper being to evil: "All that is is good. Hence evil, which I am trying to define, is not a substance" (*Confessiones*, VII, 18). His recognition of the goodness of all things may have been due to neo-Platonist writings. But his uncompromising certainty, which included matter (*De Natura Boni*, 18) was due to the Christian metaphysics of creation (see *Creation*). Hence though he tries to forestall the Manichaean question as to the origin of evil by discussing its nature (*De Natura Boni*, 4), the divine origin of things is the basis of his interpretation. It follows that evil is *contra naturam*, since all nature as such is good (*De Civitate Dei*, XI, 17; *De Libero Arbitrio*, III, 36). It is a falling away from essence and nature, from its norm, order or character. It is a tendency to non-being; corruption, lack, "privation" (*De [Moribus Ecclesiae Catholicae et de] Moribus manichaeorum*, II, 12; *Contra Epistolam Fundamenti*, 39; *De Natura Boni*, 4). This was the "positive" statement of St. Augustine's fundamental position: "Non est ergo malum nisi privatio boni" (*Contra Adversarium Legis et Prophetarum*, I, 5). The nature of evil is that it has no nature. It can only be real in the good. It is a dialectical testimony to the goodness of its underlying nature. If evil destroyed its good substratum (sub-stance), it would eliminate itself into nothingness (*De Civitate Dei*, XI, 9, 22; XIII, 3: XIX, 12f.; "Etiam voluntas mala grande testimonium est naturae bonae", XI, 17).

No less important in itself and in its consequences was the definite view of the types of evil taken by St. Augustine. "The word 'evil' is used in two senses: for what man does and for what man suffers. In the former case it means sin, in the latter punishment of sin" (*Contra Adamantum*, 26). Moral evil, wickedness, is evil without qualification, and indeed ultimately the only evil (*Contra Fortunatum*, 15). Physical evil, being the punishment of sin, is just and good (*De Civitate Dei*, XII, 3), a gift of God's goodness, a merciful warning (*ibid.*, IV, 1). St. Augustine did not close his mind to the suffering of the innocent. It was to purify and test them (*ibid.*, I, 8) and a proof of the solidarity of man in original sin (*ibid.*, XXII, 22). He also essayed a natural explanation of physical evil, especially in the non-spiritual realm, in the "finitude of the lower creation" (*Contra Secundinum Manichaeum*, 15). There is a necessary order of degree in which the particular serves the perfection of the organized whole, whose beauty is brought about by contrasts etc. (*Confessions*, VII, 19 – still in *De Civitate Dei*, XVI, 8).

God has nothing to do with (moral) evil. Its cause is simply "the will of the angels and then of men as they turned from the unchangeable to the changeable good" (*Enchiridion* 23). The possibility of this evil is contained in the finite spirit's freedom which is nonetheless the great privilege of its nature: "He who is good by the free decision of his will is better than he who is good by necessity" (*De Diversis Quaestionibus,* 83, 2). The question remains as to why in fact sin is permitted. The solution, that even the sinful spirit still has a greater value than all non-spiritual beings (*De Libero Arbitrio*, III, 12, 16, etc.) does not carry conviction. The question is only underlined by the categorical "It is good that there should not be only good, but also evil" (*Enchiridion*, 96). However, *after* the permission of evil, it may be postulated, to some extent *a priori*, that God can and must will to bring good out of evil: "Bene utens et malis de malis bene facere", "Making good use even of evils to bring good out of evils" (*Enchiridion*, 27; 100; cf. *De Civitate Dei*, XXII, 1; *Epistola* 166, 15; "Even in our evil works the works of God are good": *De Musica*, VI, 30). Though evil – in the form of sin above all – is against the will of God, it is not absolutely outside his will. It is included in the indirect will which permits it (*Enchiridion*, 95f.; *De Civitate Dei*, XI, 17; XVIII, 51; XXII, 2; *De Correptione et Gratia*, 43; *Sermo* 301, 5, etc.). St. Augustine merely suggests how God transforms evil into a greater good. Peter's denial, for instance, leads to progress in knowledge and humility (*De Correptione et Gratia* 25; *Sermo,* 285, 3).

e) St. Augustine's view, with its neo-Platonist components reinforced by the Pseudo-Dionysius (*De Divinis Nominibus,* IV, 18–35), remained unchallanged, Exceptions such as the optimistic emanationist system of Erigena (*De Divissione Naturae*, III, 6) or the views of Abelard (*Theologia Christiana,* V, 1321) and of Nicholas of Cusa (*De Ludo Globi* [edition of 1514], I, p. 154) on the best possible world, did not change the picture. St. Thomas Aquinas (*Summa Theologica*, I, q. 48f.; *Contra Gentiles*, III, 4–15; *De Malo*) developed St. Augustine's notion of evil with a consistency, logical and ontological, steeled by Aristotle (*Metaphysics*, IX, 9f.). He clarified the key-notion of permission (*Summa Theologica*, I, q. 19, a. 9; for its basis, cf. *ibid*., q. 48, a. 2 ad 3; but contrast *I Sententiarum*, 46, 1, 3 ad 6, and also the indirectness of the origin of good "from" evil (*ibid*., with a slight correction of St. Augustine), and stressed the essential deficiency of second causes, as "discharging" Providence of liability (*Contra Gentiles*, III, 71, 77). In essentials, Duns Scotus (*II Sententiarum*, 26–31) and Suarez (*Disputationes Metaphysicae*, IX, 9f.) agree with St. Thomas.

f) In 1710 appeared the *Essais de théodicée sur la bonté de Dieu, la liberté de l'homme et l'origine du mal* of G. W. von Leibniz. The term (first mentioned in a letter of 1697) thus came into philosophical and theological usage (cf. Rom 3:4f.; Ps 51:6; Milton, *Paradise Lost*, *ad init*., "To justify the ways of God to man" [1667]). It became the usual term for all efforts to solve the problem of evil. The title indicates the whole problem and the questionability (also in the sense of whether it is worthwhile) of undertaking to "justify God" at the bar of human reason – though Leibniz, like Kant after him, did not exclude considerations derived from the theology of revelation. (Kant defined theodicy as 'the defence of the supreme wisdom of the author of the world against the accusations brought against it by reason on the ground of the repugnant in the world' [cf. Rahner].) After Leibniz, theodicy in the strict sense became generally an explicit treatise, mostly part of the philosophical doctrine of God. (The historical circumstance, that "theodicy" flourished in Germany, especially in the 18th century, before Kant, and for a long time afterwards in England, and the way it concentrated the questions of God, man and the world, may have contributed to the use of "theodicy" to designate the whole treatise on the philosophical knowledge of God. It displaced for a time the title "Natural Theology", which has now come back into use, though this too is not a very happy expression.

But Voltaire's criticism of Leibniz's optimism in *Candide* is really more than a counterposition: it rather shows its real meaning, i.e., its fatality. The divine necessity by which this world – one might almost say, *faute de mieux* – is to be accepted as the best of all possible worlds, corresponds to the theory of the *malum metaphysicum* – a dispassionately objective and abstract thesis which ultimately is the same, at least in a certain respect, as the pessimism of Schopenhauer, the theory of the impotence of the spirit in the later Scheler or the present-day talk of the "absurd". It all comes down to what T. Haecker has called the specifically Western hindrance to a genuine theodicy: the tragic world-view (*Schöpfer und Schöpfung* [2nd ed., 1949]) – making the finite as such tragic.

g) Protestant theology emphasizes that it is not God who has to be justified to man, but man to God, which means *by* God. But traditional lines of thought from Christian theodicy are not excluded. Luther says that God produces good through evil (*WA*, LVI, p. 331). But from Zwingli down to Barth there is an undue tendency to identify real causality and mere permission of evil in God; so too in Baianism and Jansenism. For M. Flacius evil was the true reality of fallen man.

Some rare voices were raised among Catholics against the supposed vaporizing of evil by reating it as a privation; see Cajetan (*Commentarium in Summam Theologiae*, I/II, q. 71, a. 6; q. 72, a. 7); so too in the 19th century J. Kuhn and H. Klee. Lamennais (*Esquisse d'une philosophie*, II, 1, 4) took up again Leibniz's notion of *malum metaphysicum*. The "solution" of the problem of theodicy given by the redemption through Christ (W. Trillhaas in *RGG*, VI, col. 746) is discussed in scholastic theology on the occasion of the motive of the incarnation (e.g., de Lugo, *De Incarnatione*, 7, 2, 13). In more recent times it was discussed chiefly by Barth (*Church Dogmatics*, III/1 [1958]).

3. *The permanent question*. The answers, it was noted, are here part of the data. What is the result?

a) Modern theodicies may be described as pessimistic or optimistic. Both approaches assume that evil cannot be hindered. A different reason is given in each case. The optimists hold that evil is intrinsic to the structure of the world, being the necessary pre-condition of a totality of a higher value. This is to relativize evil and to make it a means to an end. It takes the sting out of theodicy and makes it a justification of the cosmos – a "cosmodicy". It is no doubt a valid point, and one which was copiously considered by tradition, that much physical evil has an intrinsic usefulness and purpose in the existing world. (Pain, for instance, functions as an alarm. But even here it has been asked, why does it hurt so much? – to say nothing of useless pain.) But what is one to think of such a world order? The attempt to upgrade this world to the best of all possible worlds fails on philosophical and theological grounds. The perfection of the material world always admits of a higher perfection. The exclusion of the infralapsarian character of the world, manifested to some extent in its constitutional deficiency, means in any case that the additional (physical) evil, insofar as it is the consequence of sin, and above all sin, evil itself, is emasculated and reduced to the ontological level.

In contrast to this effort to minimize evil, pessimism exaggerates it and erects it into an absolute. But this distortion or evacuation of the theistic notion of God makes all theodicy pointless. Every effort to hypostatize evil is belied by the priority of the true, good and beautiful essentially intrinsic to all human speech, thought and values, and attested even in the fundamental notion of evil and pessimism, all contrary data notwithstanding. Pessimism in particular, which in its most definite forms elevates evil to the rank of an evil primordial will, shows that the central problem of theodicy is the problem of moral evil, or, in theistic terms, the permission of sin. However, the pessimistic notion of evil as the inescapable destiny of man in the world, the view of the world as a tragedy, has some merit. It can help one to gain a deeper understanding of the Christian theodicy inspired by salvation-history and Christology, and hence of the "sin of the world" which modern individualism, even on the moral plane, tends to be unaware of.

b) Each human being comes into the sphere of influence of sin, a "hamartiological" determination of this world, which Pauline theology affirms to be the world-wide effect of the first sin of man. If it may be assumed that in the original state of man his nature, pure, sound and true, was to have been directly the (quasi-)sacrament of his holiness-in-grace, then after sin, which destroyed both his sanctity and his soundness, the convulsions of nature had to be the effect and sign of the status of the world, now without grace and wholeness, not being in Christ. Thus the world, insofar as it is affected by the Fall, is also a *sacramentum diaboli*. Since the soundness of peace and joy ceased to be directly the sacrament of salvation through its sinful misuse, redemption from sin could only be and be expressed in the opposite, in disaster, suffering and death. The mystery of the cross was necessary and its meaning begins to dawn here. The ambiguity of physical evil in the light of original sin – it is both the product of finite material nature and the destiny brought about by sin – is left behind by the free historic act of redemption. It is given the clear sacramental character of mediating the new salvation (cf. W. Kern, *Geist und Leben* 32 [1959], pp. 58f.).

c) This seems to pose the problem of evil and theodicy in its most extreme imaginable (or unimaginable) form. The cross of Christ as the consequence of sin makes all metaphysical tragedy-writing anaemic. But it is precisely the statement of the problem in this infinitely acute form which is the "solution". The problem of the sin of man becomes the mystery – or scandal – of the love of God. Just as sin was the occasion of the cross (*in ordine executionis*), so too the cross is the inner ground (*in ordine intentionis*) of the permission of sin. Even between human beings, when one fails in love and the other overcomes the disaster by forgiveness, love takes on a new and finer depth and inwardness, the unique morning freshness of love redeeming and redeemed. And this can only be through the free will to love of the one who has not failed. But it could not have been at all without the failure. If this is so, then it was "necessary" (cf. Lk 24:26) that Christ should have been the incarnate revelation of the love of God in some similar way. By becoming sin and curse for men (cf. 2 Cor 5:21; Gal 3:13) he was to create them anew, raising them up out of sin, conquering evil by patiently redemptive, crucified love, which thus radiated and was revealed as infinite power.

The hamartiological dimension of evil is transformed into the staurological reality of Christ (on the cross), like the death of man carried over into the death of God. See St. Augustine, *In Joannis Evangelium*, 12, 10, and *Sermo* 350, 1: "Being killed (as man) by death he (God, in his humanity) killed death." The paschal confession of the *felix culpa* has its biblical foundation in St. Paul's proud affirmation that the greater the power of sin, the greater is the power of grace (Rom 5:20f., with the rejection of all the fallacies of a mystique of sin, Rom 3:8; 6:1). The decisive text of the gospels with regard to the key-notion of the permission of sin is the parable of the prodigal son (Lk 15:11–32; cf. for instance Lk 7:36–50; Jn 12:24f.; 2 Cor 12:9). The achievement of Christ has basically replaced the disruption of sin and its consequences, by recapitulating the disruption, that is, by re-living and repairing it. The Christian optimism which believes in the power of God's love will be one with Christ in suffering – not brushing aside – all sense of pessimism – and in breaking through it to transform it into the resurrection. The problem of evil coincides with that of the motive of the redemptive incarnation of God in Christ. This is what gives it its rank and scope, which goes far beyond the acquisition of this or that virtue, like patience "out of" persecution or contrition "out of" sin.

d) When dealing with the problem of evil, it is not enough to make the formal *a priori* statement of philosophy that evil *must* be reconcilable with the infinite power, wisdom and goodness of God. An effort must be made to give also a concrete and hence historically verifiable answer. And this must ultimately be a theological answer, one given by God himself. But the nature of the proposed "solution" must be kept in mind. It is never merely intellectual and speculative.

To speak of the cross in such terms as were used above must not be allowed to cloak the fact that sin is revealed – including forgiven sin and indeed in the light of this forgiveness – as what ought never to have been or be. Love does not need sin. What sort of love would that be? But the triumph of love is the disclosure of sin as sin, that is, as utter worthlessness: worthless as repugnant and absurd, as ineffective and hence in every sense of the word meaningless. This is the only approach in which sin remains sin without being made to mean something else. Wickedness and evil are taken for what they are.

But in this same approach love takes on a new dimension with regard to evil. The meaningless, while given no chance to justify itself, is taken into the service of meaning. Here too, therefore, it must be firmly maintained that seemingly conflicting data are reconciled, though how it is so cannot be satisfactorily explained to the full. That it is so and how it is so are not equally clear, as in so many cases. But this should not lead theodicy to fall into the vicious circle which is one of today's greatest dangers: that the insistent experience of evil should cloud the clear conviction of the existence of God which is to overcome its darkness. In any case – in response to the experimental disproof of God mentioned above (1, *ad init.*), the equally unquestionable instances of meaningful purpose must be insisted on. This is not a matter of choosing between optimism and pessimism according to which of them offers the best figures, as may be seen from the true nature of such experience. But the character of suspense and "hope" in this experience needs to be brought out better than was mostly done hitherto. (The attempts of the Augustinian medieval tradition etc. to integrate somehow the actual damnation of angels and men, e.g., to the glory of God's vindictive justice, may be taken as read, not superciliously, but without any further speculative interest.) The complete intellectual clarification of evil would actually bar the way to the explanation of it which can be sensed. To grasp it fully intellectually would be to cease to grasp it as it ought to be grasped, as an abiding question (see *Hope*).

For if here the answer is part of the result of the experiment, so too is the answer which each one makes to the previous answers. And the answer is not only the commitment which obtains in all knowledge and experience (as the actuation of the *cognoscens* as well as the *cognitum in actu*). It is a fully practical and active hope. Evil is a summons to action. This does not solve the question. The question remains. But just as such action can take place only in hope, and not in despair, true hope exists in the face of evil only as the fighting hope which is struck as it strikes. If there are questions which are not to be "answered but lived (R. Guardini), evil is one of them. Hence the train of thought leads back to the "staurological" consideration (3c), not in the sense of an answer but in the sense of a listening to the abiding question. Thus the question remains a summons. Love is that by which evil is made good.

Walter Kern & Jörg Splett

THEOLOGICAL METHODOLOGY

A. Preliminaries

Various expectations are likely to be aroused by this title. In English it may suggest that general questions are to be discussed concerning the status of religious propositions from a viewpoint which need not be that of Christian faith, or even where it is, would not be chosen with traditional Catholic distinctions, say, of natural and revealed theology in view, but rather discussions concerning the validity of religious statements considered as forming a class alongside the classes of empirical and poetic statements. For discussions of this kind see *Religion*, *Faith*, *Religious Experience*, *Apologetics*, *Fundamental Theology*. This article is concerned with the epistemological structure of ecclesial theology, and takes for granted at least the existence of a continuing tradition of systematic theological articulation of the gospel in the Catholic Church. However, it would be unsatisfactory simply to refer to other articles without some brief discussion of the system of categories which supports this distribution of topics, since a theological epistemology should at least be concerned to examine its own epistemological status as well as that of theology itself (see *Theology* I).

Clearly theological epistemology consists in a reflection upon theology considered as an autonomous intellectual discipline or "science". So long as the scientific character of theology in general, or indeed the specific scientific procedures familiarized by tradition or custom, were not in question, it was possible for a treatise of theological epistemology to take shape and lead an independent existence, even generate its own conventional disputes, without reference to questions of general epistemology, or even to theology itself. It is commonly the case that treatises on methodology at best rationalize inventive intellectual procedures already being practised, or more often simply ossify these procedures in a theoretical structure long after they have ceased to be practised or even relevant. Treatises of this irrelevant kind are still being written in our day by Catholic theologians (which is the only reason for mentioning them), after the closed world of Catholic theology has been notably breached by new creative theological thinking, by intensive investigation of some areas of the history of theology and the pressures of secularization. These latter pressures are intensifying, and should be welcomed insofar as they force Catholic theologians to reconsider the nature of their task of communication with the world, and in particular the structure of theological meaning.

The acceptance of a necessary division of labour, then, must not be taken to prejudge the question as to whether a different approach to theological epistemology may not be more in accordance with a world in which traditional categories are increasingly being revised. Such an approach would not be able to assume in advance the theological distinctions delivered to it by tradition, but would have to adopt a critical role in regard to them. For in the most general terms, the task of theological epistemology, like that of theology itself, is to establish communication between Church and world, in such a way that the internal ecclesial perspectives open out upon and are open to perspectives which emerge immanently in the course of a secular history to which the Church's theology, and revelation itself, provide no immediate key. Theology is an encounter of Church and world in which the meaning of the gospel becomes articulate as an illumination of the world; and the exploration of the structure of this meaning in theological epistemology must itself be the continuing actualization of such an encounter.

No such ambitious claim is made for this article, above all because the new movements in theology make it too difficult to practise that reflexive role of a methodology which consists in making and correlating maps of territories already explored by others. This metaphor is already a simplification, for it transposes into the spatial order a problematic which is temporal and historic; now it is in this latter order, as we shall see, that the theological problem itself today becomes increasingly explicit and that the solutions begin to take shape.

We shall assume, then, in what follows, that there is a "special" theological epistemology and methodology concerned with the reflexive analysis of theological structures of meaning, delivered to us by a continuing tradition of theology practised in the Church, and it is only by implication and on particular topics that we shall take into account problems of meaning and knowledge in general. This special theological epistemology, then, will share with all theology the double *a priori* of ecclesial faith, which will serve as its internal dimension; and in the external dimension proper to all theology it will be concerned to authenticate the claim of theology to intellectual autonomy while assuming without detailed discussion its claim to be "intellectual" at all, i.e., to propose meaning and truth. That is to say, the basic question as to whether theological statements mean anything *at all* will not be discussed here.

B. The Internal dimension of Theological Epistemology

Reception of the Church's continuing tradition of theology is a matter of faith. This is not of course to say that every proposition in every theological system is an object of faith; but faith is a presupposition of insight into the meaning of these diverse theologies, of understanding that they are unified in the object or the realm of their concern – very simply, are trying to talk about the same things. This is a point of some importance now that we are more ready to admit the existence of plurality and even profound discontinuities within the single continuing tradition. It is no longer seriously possible to offer an anonymous handbook, however large, and call it simply "Catholic Theology"; it was not long ago that even Karl Barth, with some justification, seemed to suppose that this was so. Communion, ordinary or extraordinary, in the Church in faith, offers access to a universe of meaning, not open to those who reject this communion. So the Church as a continuing historical institution, and active spiritual communion of faith in the Church, together form the double *a priori* of theological meaning. This ecclesiality of faith is of course realized in different degrees, while in all degrees tending by an inner impulse to the union of communion; and the continuing validity of the expression "Catholic theology" is due to the self-defining activity of the Church from time to time in excluding theological articulations of faith declared not to be Catholic: the *positive* unity of Catholic theology is not itself capable of exhaustive theological articulation but is the one *reality* of God, Christ, the Church. The Catholic theologian accepts this power of the (hierarchically structured) Church community to define itself and its authentic witness with respect to what it is not in such a way that the *a priori* of ecclesial faith for a Catholic theologian can be partially exhibited in a series of historical monuments which are moments of the Church's explicit self-definition. The Catholic theologian's world of meaning has fixed points which are themselves meaningful and not just ineffable (see *Magisterium*, *Council*, *Pope*), though these points do not fall into a systematic order among themselves, do not exhaustively display the *a priori* of ecclesial faith, and are ultimate only in the simultaneous alternatives they exclude (i.e., they are open to interpretation within perspectives which are not their own).

Now this faith is not merely the immanent life, in part explicit and in part implicit, of a historic community and a culture in which men creatively bring their own meaning to light; the unifying sense of the whole world of meaning accessible in faith is transcendental disclosure of this meaning to and for men, intrinsically communication to men of meaning as gift. In the traditional theological terminology, this is the dimension of the theological world of meaning which is called revelation or gospel. The meanings entertained and exchanged in this community inform the community – not only in its language but also in its conduct, its institutions, its rites, its art and music – in such a way that while remaining human meanings (this will be examined when we look at the external dimension of theology) they are in principle capable of unification in no human meaning but only in an ultimate meaning, the Meaning of meaning, God. Further, this ultimate Meaning has declared itself historically as Word made man, Logos and First of many brethren, Son of God and Son of man; and in doing so has associated with this figure in human history other men who would scripturally embody in their witness to him the eschatologically ultimate character of this self-declaration of Meaning. This self-declaration is an ἀρχή, an absolute beginning: it is the beginning of the gospel (cf. Mk 1:1; Lk 1:2; Jn 1:1), which is permanently present in the communion of faith, permanently recoverable as spring and source in the meanings entertained and exchanged in the community. The scriptural deposit of the primitive multiplicity of meanings of the one ἀρχή is continually made present by informing new complexes of human meaning; in its own unity in multiplicity – the "theologies" of the NT (and OT) writings – it offers a pregnant instance of the nuclear character of the complexes of ecclesial meaning. For every explicit Catholic life is a "theology", a project and a declaration of the Meaning of Catholic meanings; and theology as "science" and autonomous discipline can only reflect upon this lived meaning by being itself an instance of lived meaning.

C. The External Dimension of Theological Epistemology

The Word which unifies the multiplicity of Christian meanings is offered to us through those meanings not only for our consent (or refusal) but also for our assent (or denial). At one and the same time it invites us, by our consent and assent, to depart from where we are (cf. Gen 12:1) to find ourselves in some "higher" or "deeper" truth, to ascend the degrees of the "ontological comparative" (Fink) to find ourselves "in the Truth", "in Christ". Perhaps it is only in the formal system of modern mathematics and logic that truth is reduced to the display of the internal consistency of axioms and postulates; but even here there is the possibility of "applications", as in the part played in information theory by the "truth-table" systematization of the naive Yes-No, assent-dissent, character of human statements. At any rate, both the Yes-No character of statements and their claim to "significance", to depth of truth, are prominently and actively present in theological statements.

In this section we shall be concerned with the human dimension of theological meaning and its twofold truth, especially insofar as this meaning has been deliberately given structure by the reflexive activity of a theologian's mind. Just because the primitive NT witness to the ἀρχή, itself assumed into the ἀρχή, is language and articulate at all, it is not only "revelation" but also "theology", since the gospel, no matter how communicated, is proposed to us as human communication, ordered and unified by a human mind. Even the synoptic gospels, as has been clearly shown in recent years, are not just collections of narratives and *logia*, but each exhibit a unifying constructive intention proper to the evangelist. But even if we had nothing but random collections of sayings and narratives of isolated incidents, there would still be implicit in them a comprehension of the world. In the Pauline texts in particular, it is possible to analyse the constructive and supporting function of concepts available in Hellenistic civilization; and in the Johannine writings one can learn to overhear the resonances of a variety of pursuits of the divine at the end of the 1st century integrated by John into a concentration of meaning in the Word made flesh. But John is not only a poet of Jesus; as theologian *par excellence* he is at least as insistent as any NT writer on the exclusive and decisive character of his witness in the rejection of false teaching.

The Pauline and Johannine testimonies provide us with two very different styles of theological "construction", both deriving from and referring to the same ἀρχή (compare Jn 1:1–18 with Col 1:15–20, and again Heb 1:1–4). We may study even in that human meaning which is revelation a human evolution and amplification which continues to be revelation. The rediscovery and appropriation of the *literary* complexity of the NT writings is the absolutely primary prerequisite of any theologizing today if we are to overcome the split between "exegesis" and "theology" and avoid certain misguided forms of "biblical theology" (neither biblical nor responsibly theological) due to the uneven growth of the Catholic mind for many centuries. For the diversification of meaning in creative literature and its inner integration there into a complex unity of insight and comprehension helps us to understand diverse possibilities of organization in the biblical literature. To recognize that saga, gospel and novel are different literary genres should not mean that we must forget the novel when we study saga or gospel. It is also through a sense of the insights afforded by creative literature that we can best appreciate the historicity of the NT witness, its character as *Ereignis*, illuminating event. The special significance of literature here is that unlike plastic art and music, it retains not only the invitatory aspect of truth, the appeal to traverse the degrees of the depths of being, but also a continuity with those pragmatic or empirical uses of language which emphasize or isolate its Yes-No aspect. It is this Yes-No or propositional-logical use of language which has dominated Catholic theology for centuries until our own day. Both the dialectic and logical grammar of early scholasticism and the newer "scientific" logic of Aristotle's *Posterior Analytics* in classical scholasticism helped to construct a theological world in which meaning was articulated as argument and not as insight. The effect of this one-sidedness may still be seen today in textbooks for theological students, ordered in the form of theses to be proved or defended (so a modern French series still in course of publication). Even if syllogistic demonstration is no longer thought to be the normal or the ideal mode in which to manipulate all meaning or manifest all truth, there still seems to be some uneasiness about wholly abandoning a theological style which prized clarity and decisiveness above exploration in depth.

This uneasiness has its real justification. As we have seen, the Church community has repeatedly had to establish its own identity by a process of self-definition involving exclusion. The revealed truth of God has an identity *in* the world. The offer of truth to the Church and by the Church is not only an invitation to ecstatic vision but it also defines the way to that vision. The truth of the Church's witness is still human truth and as such finite; what it excludes is not nothing, for only all-inclusive, infinite Truth could have only nothing to reject. But in this "ecumenical" age of the Church we have learned to exclude from within, as it were, by taking up into Catholic truth whatever has its rightful place there, by fulfilment rather than anathema. No Catholic theology then can afford to abandon argumentation and the precision which it demands; yet exclusive emphasis on this Yes-No character of truth, and still more, its syllogistic style, would impoverish theology unduly. After all, there seems to be no lack of dispute and controversy in other disciplines, such as history and letters, which do not lay down such artificial standards of rigour; and such disputes are not always about nothing. As has been seen in the theology of the development of dogma, a theory of the amplification of meaning by syllogism alone has the most pernicious effects. In our own times the problems of missionary adaptation and more generally of the communication of the gospel to a new and changing world have made it necessary to take more seriously the complexities involved in the exchange, amplification, translation and reintegration of meaning.

It has appeared in what has been said that the construction of a theological structure of meaning is bound to employ methods which are at least similar to those employed in other disciplines. In the investigation of the Scripture, for instance, it must practise the ordinary techniques of historical and literary criticism; explicit logical theory can at least serve as a negative check and an instrument of analysis; the justification of particular propositions may remind us of the procedures by which decisions are arrived at in law, thereby bridging the gap between procedures of verification in theology and in the natural sciences. The question arises whether there is anything uniquely characteristic of theological method in the construction of theology. We may take as our point of departure Collingwood's useful distinction between a proposition as a mere statement and that same proposition as an answer to a question. Certainly this distinction serves to show the interest of the commonest of the scholastic procedures: the use of the *quaestio* as a technique of exploration by interrogation first of conflicting authorities and later of conflicting chains of argument as well. Every theological statement can be put to the question simply by putting it in interrogative form: *utrum* . . . As an answer to a question the proposition has a new epistemological status as part of a *structure* of meaning. The questions now arise as to the proper sources of the meaning which is so structured, the nature of the structure, and the perspectives which sustain the structure.

The question of the proper sources of theology as an autonomous discipline has already been touched on under B. Here it is only necessary to inquire into those complexes of meaning through which revelation is communicated, in regard to the possibility of ranking them according to some principle. Where theological structure is held to be strictly demonstrative, the complexes are ranked according to their probative force as *loci theologici*. Thus a sort of general theological criteriology can be set up, sometimes pretending to a high degree of refinement, as in the elaboration of theological qualifications. The manifest artificiality of an excessive refinement sought after more for its own sake rather than for the benefit of theology itself should not blind one to the general importance of this discussion (e.g., what exactly is the status of various papal pronouncements on contraception? What difference is made to Mariology as a whole by the definition of the Assumption as a dogma?). Yet as soon as we remember that the original complexes of meaning are not merely isolated items waiting to play their part as arguments in the structure of a demonstrative theology but have their primary value in diversely mediating revelation in a historic process of communication, then we must critically examine the idea of a theological structure of meaning which could tend to distort revelation in this way. In the classical moment of Latin theology it was possible for St. Thomas Aquinas, more decisively than any of his contemporaries, to determine the structure of theology as an Aristotelian science, in which the articles of faith, dependent upon the divine vision itself, served as principles for the body of actual or potential theological conclusions which could be drawn from them. It may be observed that St. Thomas's actual practice, like Aristotle's own, was fortunately a good deal less rigid than his epistemological theory. The science of theology was seen as another form of the single *sacra doctrina* delivered to us by the (glossed) Scriptures; but this mediation was conceived of as taking place through the summary of the Scriptures in the Creed, such that wherever Scripture dealt with historical particulars not enunciated in the Creed, it had merely illustrative or supplementary value. Once again, fortunately, St. Thomas's practice was much more generous and genuinely historical than this theory. But in the last resort it is an archaic theory of meaning and of language which supports both the theory of probative arguments and the theory of theological structure as an Aristotelian science: the theory that meaning is accessible and manipulable only in the form of essentialist concepts. In spite of the considerable sophistication of medieval logical grammar, in spite of St. Thomas's own developments of this grammar in an ontological sense in his theory of analogy, the theory of meaning implicit in all scholastic theology is dominantly "ontic", tied to the specific natures of the cosmic world. Concepts, in St. Thomas's epistemological theory, are still "similitudes" of natures; historical meaning is not genuinely meaning at all, for it is only in the generality of the concept and of "science" that meaning can be authentically realized.

Thus a critical examination of the presuppositions of the epistemology of scholastic theology leads us to reconsider both its theory of the original complexes of meaning and its theory of the adequate and appropriate structure for that meaning. But before making some suggestions of our own, we must further consider the perspectives which sustain the structure of meaning in a more than logical sense. This is the question of the "hermeneutic locus" of a theology discussed by Protestant theologians like Fuchs and Ebeling. In simple terms, any theology which is to be more than biblicist, a mere rearrangement of biblical themes, must adopt general perspectives within the horizon of which complexes of meaning acquire mutual significance. In St. Thomas's theology, for instance, such a perspective is supplied by the order of creatures to the Creator as *principium et finis*, Origin and End. St. Thomas himself mentions another perspective, the whole Christ, which has been taken up in our own day, as seeming to offer a more biblical schema, and there have been many rather naive attempts since the first shock of Darwinism died away, to adopt the schema of generalized evolution, as by Teilhard de Chardin. It would be a mistake to regard the adoption of a generalized theological perspective as a matter of detached and deliberate choice. The perspective must present itself with the ultimate obviousness which only the sense of an epoch can supply. Certainly this must be so if the theology is to speak to man of its time and to provide a context for continued theological debate; but the fundamental ground for the articulation of the perspective must lie deeper than the individual theologian's own conscious and reflexive mind; he must be guided by a kind of prophetic insight into that order of relevance which is taking shape in history under the sway of Providence. Such a perspective, appropriate to the epoch into which we are moving today, might be provided, we suggest here, by the schema of God as the Meaning of meaning. This is in fact the perspective within which this article has been written.

D. Concluding Remarks and Prospects

The notion of a theological epistemology, as we have seen, is itself historically conditioned, as indeed is the notion of a general philosophical epismolgy. There is a "family-line" of investigations to which the (primarily 19th-century) notion of epistemology belongs, and whose lineal descendants today form the family of investigations into meaning: Heidegger, Wittgenstein, Merleau-Ponty, Gadamer. This work of philosophical reflection was preceded and is today accompanied by an "ontic" preoccupation with meaning in such diverse fields as linguistics, existential analysis, behaviour studies, social anthropology or ethnology, literary criticism, to name only a few. The search for identity in the new nations of the post-colonial era, in a tension between traditional religions and new technology, is a preoccupation with the redefinition of meanings. The personal search for the "meaning of life" has to be conducted within the transcendental horizon of the question of the meaning or truth of Being and its historicity. If we reject the God "out there", we must equally reject the God "in here", and learn to put the God-question as a search for ontological meaning.

These general reflections are intended to support the suggestion that the reformulation of theology taking place in our time demands a corresponding reformulation of theological epistemology. If the schema of God as Meaning of meaning is accepted as a possible perspective for theology, and thus as a possible formula for "natural" theology, our view of the complexes of theological meaning and their structural reintegration in an autonomous theological "science" can no longer be governed by an archaic theory of meaning. Theology, while continuing necessarily to practise the onto-theo-logical mode in which its formulations have been uttered historically, must become explicitly aware of its own existence as a kind of meta-theology; the theological epistemology corresponding to this meta-theology would be an explication of the "meta", the dimension of this meta-theology in the historical process of ontological meaning. We may ask, but only from our "epistemological" viewpoint, what such a meta-theology would look like, since it seems that there are only anticipations of it today.

It would certainly involve the "destruction" of all previous theologies and their "recapitulation" in a history of meaning which is also a history of being. This would even include the revealed biblical "theologies", although these would continue to retain their privileged place in the history of theological meaning. The considerable body of work which has been done in recent years on the history of theology is an important first step towards this "destruction", but too little of it has faced up to the real ontological problems involved in this apparently historicist relativization. We have to ask what is the *meaning* of this historic succession of theologies (and of the sterile repetition of unimportant variants), and we have to ask this question not within a presupposed perspective of any one of them but ask it radically as part of *the* theological problem of the meaning of God and man for one another. The substantive ("ontic") answer to this question we already have in Jesus Christ, and can have no other. It is the ("ontological") meaning of this substantive meaning we must continually search for without expecting any final answer. Thus the ἀρχή of this meta-theology would be the λόγος – εικών – μυστήριον τοῦ θεοῦ, the Word-Image-Mystery of God, the divine Wisdom, ἁγία σοφία. How could this ontological meaning become articulate? What "structure" could it have in a single mind? In fact it could only exist as a total human culture, the progressive discovery of a single human identity in Christ as the historic process of the diverse but related processes of self-discovery going on in distinct cultures all over the globe in response to the challenge and threat of a uniform technological mass-culture. There is at least a single discernible adversary, not to be subdued by the mere repetition of traditional truths, Christian or other. The individual theologian could only make contributions to such a theology-as-culture, and only possess it as his own "culture" according to his own capacity, and not as a *Summa.*

The cultural "structure" of such a metatheology is as much or as little a *logical* unity as a song or a smile. It is a comprehension of the depth of meaning or truth in the affirmation of particular truths; it is a standing fast in holiness, a "Thy will be done". It passes into music, the inarticulate, into silence. At the same time, precisely because this theology is concerned with the ontological dimension of truth in its cultural structure or organization, it will need to proceed dialectically, by exclusion as well as affirmation, to the inclusive truth of humanity in God. Thus its historic destiny is to "make known through the Church the manifest wisdom of God" (Eph 3:10) in that process by which God "recapitulates all things" (1:10) in Jesus Christ, the ontological meaning and identity of the multiple history of man.

Cornelius Ernst

THEOLOGICAL NOTES

A. The Notion and its Importance

It is part of theology and its methodology to discuss the rank, and degree of certainty, of a theological proposition and to describe its situation in terms of its relation to revelation. A proposition is qualified positively by certain "notes" and negatively by certain censures. On the assumption that theological notes are not merely to be registered historically, their meaning and purpose can be indicated only within an ecclesiastical hermeneutics which both points to the understanding of Church documents and theological texts, and brings to light the process of understanding, exposition and application which is carried on in and by the Church.

This is at once enough to explain why the notes are called "theological". The method pursued is not or should not be the qualification of theology by non-theological factors (e.g., influenced by Church politics). And one should not be misled by a wrongly understood claim to universality to apply too hastily theological labels to non-theological propositions.

But theology must here be understood not in the narrow sense of a theology of the schools, but as the process of self-understanding in the whole Church and the concomitant reflection. In this sense the theological notes provide an indispensable guide in dialogue within the Church and in the dialogue of the Catholic Church with the Christian Churches in general, as also in the dialogue of the Christian Churches with the non-Christian world. The theological notes serve to explain the importance which attaches to the declarations of the Church, of its magisterium and of theology. In the orientation of dialogue, the various grades of notes and censures are particularly helpful. It may seem indeed that when the authority of the magisterium covers the designations *de fide divina* (*et catholica*) or *haeresis*, all dialogue is at an end. For here the uncompromising challenge of kerygma and dogma is met with, and dialogue within the Church is left behind by the incomparable dialogue between the self-revelation of God and man. But one must also consider that the encounter of God with man in human terms implies the accessibility of the word of God in the word of man – more precisely, in the human theological dialogue which is inspired by the faith and understanding of the Church.

Accordingly, even after the solemn proclamation of a dogma the process of understanding and expounding it continues in the Church. And after the exclusion of a false doctrine and the imposition of anathema and excommunication, the truth hidden in or summoned forth by the error continues to act and to influence the dogmatic development of the Church (cf. the exegesis of 1 Cor 11:19). One must therefore consider the value of theological notes from the point of view of the *propter nos homines* which attaches to the word of God; from the point of view of the essentially social nature of man and of the socially constituted Church, where there is need throughout of mutual understanding and regulated speech; and from the point of view of historicity, which points to the need for a "note" to meet a given situation aright and also to the limits of such a note.

B. The Traditional Notes and Censures

1. *The historical conditioning*. The individual notes and censures are as clearly stamped by their historical origins as is the whole process of qualification. It is clear in particular from the highest possible qualifications, the article of defined faith or the rejection of a heresy, that the Church was meeting a challenge in history, either from doctrinal falsity or from intense controversy among theologians. The time of origin gives its historical form to the note and its particular conditioning, which impose on later times the burden of distinguishing and understanding. But the lower notes, e.g., *haeresim sapiens*, are still more clearly marked by theological schools and by particular fears and troubles of a given time. Then the possible political implications of a theological note should be considered. Sometimes the note was meant to serve the unity of faith in the wider sense of Church discipline or even the political unity of a kingdom. Hence even dogmatic assertions are combined with "rules for speaking in the Church". And in the formulations of the Middle

Ages in particular, a broader sense of *fides* and *haeresis* must be presupposed (A. Lang), which was used to serve the concrete unity of the discipline of the Church. This perspective may also be noted in the confessions of the Reformers (*Formula Concordiae*). On the other hand, when political interests and Christian confession are strangers to one another, as in the primitive Church and perhaps in the secularization of the present day, there is a concentration on the expression of faith as such: negatively, on the rejection of heresy and positively, on the possibility of a preaching in accord with the times.

2. *Historical phases*. The beginnings of Christianity, and its first thousand years to a great extent, are marked not by degrees of notes and censures but by the discussion of the true faith and the orthodox doctrine, and hence by the condemnation of a heretical position by an "anathema", mostly pronounced by the Church when assembled in synods. St. Paul already utters an "anathema" against the preaching of "another gospel" (Gal 1:8). Mt 18:27, however, does not speak specifically of a doctrinal censure. More significant in Scripture is the indirect rejection of heresy by the choice and form of the *logia* transmitted, reflecting a given *Sitz im Leben*, and the denunciation of sectarian groups (in the Epistles, e.g., 1 Jn 2:22; 4:2f.). The Pastoral Epistles strive explicitly to uphold the apostolic heritage (1 Tim 6:20; 2 Tim 1:14) and reverence for "sound doctrine" (1 Tim 1:10; 2 Tim 4:3; Tit 1:9; 2:1; cf. 1 Tim 4:6, 13, 16; 6:1, 3; Tit 2:7). Accordingly, in the first centuries, condemnations were directed against heresies and total apostasy from the faith. The great Councils led to a nuanced description of Catholic orthodoxy in the Christological and Trinitarian controversies and thus gave rise to a specialized – though frequently misunderstood – set of concepts for the demarcation of a heretical position. Nonetheless a wider sense for such notes and censures cannot be excluded, even well into the Middle Ages, though there were at times the first steps to listing "lower" notes (e.g., in St. Thomas Aquinas, *Contra Errores Graecorum*, *Prooemium* [*Opuscula Theologica*, I, no. 1029]: "non recte sonat"). This technique of distinguishing the various notes was prepared for by scholastic philosophy, and was worked out systematically from 1270 on. The oldest known list of censures is from 1314, and the oldest known commentary on theological notes is from William of Occam. In the 14th and 15th centuries the University of Paris (like Louvain and Cologne later) exercised an acknowledged right of censure, which was of great influence in episcopal, papal and conciliar measures (as at Constance). One can see how an institutionalized and respected theology can stamp the teaching of the Church. The break-up of the scholastic tradition in the late Middle Ages and the coming of new heresies often occasioned a multiplication of censures, as by the Council of Constance against Wycliffe and Huss (*DS* 1151–95; 1201–30); Martin V, in the Bull *Inter Cunctus* (*DS* 1247–79, especially 1251).

Special importance attached to the Bull *Exsurge Domine* (*DS* 1451–92, especially 1492) directed against Luther (which according to recent research did not always meet his points). The Council of Trent aimed at bringing out the *fides catholica* but not theological opinions. Subsequently the magisterium levelled various censures against Jansenism and Quietism (cf. *DS* 2269; 2332; 2390). The censures used in the Bull *Unigenitus* against P. Quesnel were comprehensive, while the Bull *Auctorem Fidei* applied various censures in detail to different points (*DS* 2600–2700). In the interest of "peace and charity", and ultimately of freedom, the Popes sometimes forbade theological schools to apply censures to each other (cf. *DS* 2167; 2510).

In the 18th and 19th centuries the magisterium made increasing use of the encyclical (the first of the modern encyclicals dating from 1740), of censorship of books (the Index) or of declarations (*responsa*) of the Holy Office. To sum up, it may be said that "the magisterium never had an official list of censures or theological notes but rather followed, though with reservations, theological custom" (cf. A. Kopling in *LTK*, VIII, col. 916).

But post-Tridentine theologians showed a tendency to elaborate and define precisely the various notes and censures. Here the great names are M. Cano, F. Suarez, O. de Castro, J. de Lugo and the Salmaticenses (cf. J. Cahill). Catholics engaged in controversial theology (Veronius, Holden, etc.) tried to bring out as clearly as possible the essential truths of faith in contrast to theological opinions (missing at times the essential historicity of dogmatic concepts), in order to confine the debate with Protestants to certain formulas, and ultimately to serve the purpose of reunion. Systematic presentations of theological notes and censures began to appear at the beginning of the 17th century. In 1709 Antonius Sessa (Panormitanus) listed a total of sixty-nine theological notes. C. L. Montaigne, C. du Plessis d'Argentré, D. Viva, J. Gautier and M. Tournely worked on the same systematic lines. Efforts were made in the time of the Enlightenment to separate essential dogma from "incidentals", especially scholastic conclusions. The Tübingen School in the first half of the 19th century took little interest in the minor theological notes, but concentrated instead on dogma and its development, and on the "symbolic" (credal) doctrine of the Church, in dialogue with Protestantism. But the rise of neo-scholasticism brought with it a meticulous distinction between the various notes and censures; so J. Kleutgen, C. Schrader, J. B. Heinrich, J. B. Franzelin, H. Hurter and J. Perrone. The systematic elaboration reached a peak with M. J. Scheeben. Along with the directives of canon law (canons 247; 1395–1405), the manuals of dogmatic and fundamental theology (apologetics) were of importance in the 20th century, up to the Second Vatican Council.

3. *A survey of the most frequently-used notes*. The enumeration, division and evaluation of the various notes and censures vary from author to author. The following may be taken as typical.

a) H. Quilliet (*DTC*) and G. Marsot (*Catholicisme*) distinguish censures (and the corresponding positive notes) i) with regard to the truth of revelation: *haeresis, haeresi proxima, error, propositio temeraria*; ii) with regard to the form, e.g., *piis auribus offensiva*; iii) with regard to the effect, e.g., *scandalosa, blasphemica*. Censures of the first type are understood to be perfectly applicable if the form (second type) demands it.

b) The division given by A. Lang seems more comprehensive. According to the quality of certainty, he distinguishes (i) formally revealed truths, (ii) virtually revealed truths and (iii) the "indirect doctrinal account" of the Church. There are corresponding degrees of certainty: doctrines solemnly defined by the Church; doctrines guaranteed by the ordinary magisterium or the instinct of faith in the Church; doctrines professed in theology; doctrines not yet fully stated or guaranteed. With regard to quality (i) of certainty, this leads to the following notes (or degrees of censure): "veritas de fide definita (haeresis manifesta); veritas de fide (haeresis); veritas fidei proxima (haeresi proxima); secundum sententiam probabilissimam, probabiliorem, probabilem, secundum opinionem communem, veressimiliorem, verissimilem: de fide." With regard to quality (ii) we have: "veritas catholica definita (error circa fidem); veritas catholica (error); sententia theologica certa (theologice erronea); secundum sententiam probabilissiman etc.: veritas catholica." With regard to quality (iii) we have: "veritas de fide ecclesiastica (propositio reprobata); veritas de fide ecclesiastica (propositio falsa); sententia certa (falsa); secundum sententiam probabilissimam etc.: de fide ecclesiastica.

c) A distinction was always made between infallible and non-infallible, though mostly accompanied by efforts either to maximize or minimize the bearing of the note. This has been brought out more and more clearly in recent theology, the censure of heresy being distinct from all other censures. All other notes are shown clearly according to their various grades on a lower level than that of the infallible doctrine of the faith (and of heresy). Within the non-infallible notes, the authentic declarations of the organs of the magisterium are distinguished from the notes applying to theological assertions. As well as these distinctions, the various designations of the traditional notes follow the official declarations of the Church (cf. *DS*, *Index systematicus*, H I d) or the classics of post-Tridentine and neo-scholastic theology.

4. *Authors, form and binding force.* a) Authoritative notes and censures are given by those who have jurisdiction in the external forum. Hence the supreme organs for notes and censures (and exclusively so for infallible matters) are the Pope and the Ecumenical Councils. Limited competence attaches to the Roman Congregations, Provincial Synods (episcopal conferences) and the individual bishops and major superiors of religious orders. The whole people of God is charged with the safeguarding of the true faith. Theologians have a special responsibility and thus are especially qualified to give theological notes – as the University of Paris did in the Middle Ages – though their authority is not one of jurisdiction. Their notes have the weight of "professional" opinions and have often influenced the magisterium.

b) Notes and censures can be given in detail (one note attached to one proposition) or in combination (several censures attached to one proposition) or comprehensively (one or more censures coming at the end of several propositions). They can be aimed at the actual words of a proposition (*sicut jacent*) or at the intention of the author (*in sensu ab auctoribus* [*assertoribus*] *intento*). Then, a given work could be condemned (by being placed on the Index of Forbidden Books) or the *opera omnia* of an author, which was a condemnation of his whole theological conception.

c) Infallible propositions have binding force when defined by a Council with the Pope, or by the Pope when speaking *ex cathedra* in the faith (*ex sese*). Authentic (non-infallible) notes demand "the religious obedience of the will and intellect" (Vatican II, *Lumen Gentium*, art. 25). Other theological notes, being given by theologians, have the authority of their professional expertise and of the "common doctrine".

C. New Questions – New Notes

This survey of the traditional notes has also served to show their limitations, which are especially clear when one tries to classify the complex ecclesiastical and theological reality of the present day. Vatican II not only brought up new questions which are not dealt with in earlier documents of the magisterium, but also produced texts which present a problem in the matter of their binding force and theological notes. In deference to the wishes of John XXIII, the Council made no solemn definitions. It was finally content to recall the normal rules of interpretation, and noted that at the Council in question, the only binding definition would be such as was clearly affirmed as such(cf. *Lumen Gentium*, *Notifications*; also art. 25). In general, the various assertions, even in the two dogmatic constitutions (on the Church and on Revelation), must be recognized as authoritative doctrine, which bind in conscience but are only *de fide divina* where they repeat earlier definitions, or truths of faith directly recognizable as such from Scripture. The titles (*constitutio*, *decretum*, *declaratio*) also give pointers to the status and authority of the Council's teaching. The title and scope of a "pastoral constitution" have a special meaning, since its point is not (derivative) doctrine, but concrete, charismatic directives for the Church (K. Rahner).

Some encyclicals which have appeared since Vatican II (*Mysterium Fidei*, *Populorum Progressio*, *Humanae Vitae*) have given rise to renewed reflection on the theological note to be attached to encyclicals. No one denies that it is possible in principle to have an infallible *ex cathedra* decision in the form of an encyclical, under the usual conditions acknowledged by the magisterium and theologians and with the appropriate formulation. But in the cases in question there is unanimity in affirming that that which is not infallible can be fallible and is reformable. This means that the encyclicals are recognized as official, authentic utterances which must be taken seriously by all Catholics and accepted with respect – though perhaps by means of an equally serious fundamental discussion. A letter of the German bishops in 1967 "to all who are charged by the Church with the preaching of the faith" considers the possibility of error "in non-defined utterances of the Church, which can themselves vary widely in the degree in which they bind". It goes on to say: "In order to safeguard the true and ultimate substance of the faith, (the Church) must give doctrinal directives, even at the risk of error in detail, which are binding to a certain degree but which are not of defined faith and are therefore to some extent provisional, even to the point of possible error" (no. 18). It may therefore be supposed that in many pronouncements of the ecclesiastical magisterium on practical moral attitudes the notion of "magisterium" is to be taken in a wider, non-specific sense. It is not doctrine "in a matter of morals" but exhortation in which Pope and bishops exercise their pastoral responsibility (cf. J. David). In concrete matters of social ethics in particular, the Church will register and pillory the yawning gap between existing social conditions and an ideal determined from the gospel (E. Schillebeeckx). Jt will strive to pinpoint the negative, what ought not to be, but in details it will only be able to give highly contingent directives, inspired by dialogue with the profane sciences. It will thus show itself primarily as an "institution of social criticism".

A further question discussed today is that of the note to be attached to authentic doctrinal documents (such as catechisms) which are published by the authority of a local Church. It is the question of their authority within the region in question (diocese, province, etc.), outside it and in the whole Church.

D. Problems of Systematic Theology

1. *The faith of the whole Church*. Theological notes must be considered today more than ever in the perspective of the whole Church and its faith – primarily therefore with an eye to the whole Catholic Church, but also in view of the separated Churches. The theological basis for this approach is the notion of the people of God, whose totality constitutes the Church and whose "instinct of faith" is itself a decisive factor in the grasp of dogma. "Through the instinct of faith inspired and nourished by the Spirit of truth, the people of God, under the guidance of the magisterium and following it loyally, receiving thus truly the word of God and not of men (cf. 1 Thess 2:13), holds fast unfailingly to the faith once handed on to the saints (cf. Jud

3). Through this instinct it penetrates more and more deeply and correctly into the faith and applies it more fully in life" (*Lumen Gentium*, art. 12). If this instinct of faith, with which the laity is also equipped (cf. *ibid.*, art. 35), has a great part to play in determining the supreme note, *de fide*, it is all the more active in the acquisition of non-infallible theological knowledge. Hence the whole people of God contributes (or should be invited to contribute) to the reaching of correct theological notes. This partnership is today possible on account of the modern means of communication and the resulting dissemination of theological culture. The notes will therefore serve all the better to demonstrate the identity of the faith throughout the changes of its formulation. It is therefore the task of the theological notes, on their highest dogmatic level, to bring about and assure the *consensus fidelium*, which can only be attained through freedom of conscience and today less than ever can consist merely of formulas imposed only from without. Hence the theological background against which the identity of the faith is articulated can and must be very broad and diversified.

2. *Pluralism in theology*. If the preaching of the faith is to have contemporary relevance, that is, if revelation is to be intelligible to the very different types of culture in which men and nations live today, theology cannot shirk the effort to master the many types of speech and thought-form in use today. Otherwise it will fall victim to a dogmatic positivism or an equally positivisic biblicism. It is necessary "to do philosophy in theology" (K. Rahner). This is a help to the understanding of the faith within a given cultural framework (philosophy, individual sciences, pre-scientific thought-forms). But it cannot but hinder the understanding of the plurality of theologies in question. The charge of communicating revelation makes it more difficult today to communicate the understanding of revelation. So too there is proportionately less chance of testing adequately the orthodoxy of the assertions of another school, i.e., of giving them a theological note. It is therefore necessary that if a theological note is pronounced, it should only be the fruit of dialogue between schools and trends, inspired by love of the one faith and by a corresponding desire to reach mutual understanding. In this matter, an apt use of the principle of subsidiarity in the Church can be of service. This would mean that the bishops, and the regional authorities such as episcopal conferences, would have more say in a further realm, that of the theological notes and censures. But these would have to call in as advisers theologians of all shades of opinion, insofar as they were representative in the region in question. The papal magisterium (and its organs) would have the special task of dealing with strict questions of faith, which as such affect the whole Church, and would intervene within the framework of the principle of subsidiarity or act as the highest court of appeal. For this the supreme magisterium would need the services of a world-wide theology, and the preliminary studies of regional authorities and of theologians established and emancipated in their ecclesiastical function. Here too it should be clear that the pronouncements of the holder of primatial authority which affect the whole Church are to be distinguished from those which he makes as Patriarch of the West, as metropolitan of the Roman province of the Church or as diocesan Bishop of Rome.

What has been said above is particularly true of the necessary censures – even when uttered after profuse and expert discussion, which must of course always come first. It must be confidently recognized that through the assistance of the Spirit, the true faith is upheld in this way by the ecclesiastial authority – especially in its supreme doctrinal pronouncements, which are infallible. But at the same time, the possible good faith of those censured must be allowed for, as also for the historically-conditioned element in the understanding of an actual expression of the faith – a historicity which is not done away with by ecclesiastical authority. The formula might perhaps say that after careful examination it is not possible at present to see that a given thesis corresponds to the understanding of faith in the Catholic Church. In this way a censure would be pronounced with the whole authority of the existing Church – which obliges precisely in the present – while at the same time the way would be left open for future progress in the understanding of the faith. This could mean a better explanation of the censured thesis and hence a consensus not previously reached.

3. *The horizon of law and gospel.* It is not merely because of ecumenical interests that theologians should consider the matter of theological notes in the Pauline framework of "Law and Gospel". The *analogia legis* must be noted in all discussion of the "law of believing", and all unnecessary notes should be avoided. When Vatican II gave no dogmatic definitions, it was conforming on principle to this demand. In loyalty to the gospel, which believers should experience as a liberation, the effort today should rather be to restore the many truths of faith to the unity of the word of God, that is, to search for a "short formula" as the circumstances demand, "a brief summary of the Christian faith" (K. Rahner). This is better than branching out into a growing number of definitions, and would obviate the need of picking one's way through a maze of notes and censures. This would lead to greater respect for the ordinary magisterium in which no formal pronouncements are made, and it would also accord free theological opinions their due right. Thus a certain reserve in allotting theological notes will be a testimony to the gospel, to the many-sided working of the Spirit in the doctrine, faith and life of the Church, and ultimately to the *Deus semper maior*, who cannot be comprehended by any human formulas.

Johann Finisterhölzl

THEOLOGUMENON

1. A theologumenon is a proposition expressing a theological statement which cannot be directly regarded as official teaching of the Church, as dogma binding in faith, but which is the outcome and expression of an endeavour to understand the faith by establishing connections between binding doctrines of faith and by confronting dogmatic teachings with the whole of secular experience and all a man – or an age – knows. Such a proposition need not necessarily materially differ from one which is actually of faith. It can be implicitly contained in a truth of faith, in the intelligible perspective involved in the latter, in the historical origin of the conceptual apparatus it employs, etc.

2. Such theologumena are absolutely necessary for theology and the formulation of the faith. That can be seen from the mere fact that even the official teaching of the Church does not and cannot consist only of dogmas in the strict sense, but enunciates theological statements without (yet) absolutely committing the faith to them. These are theologumena which have become generally accepted, sociologically speaking, in the Church. Such theologumena must be made because otherwise actual understanding and really practical efficacy of the articles of faith in the proper sense would not be possible at all. Theologumena are necessary because revelation does not comprise all knowledge of reality in its origin and degrees, and because the one human being in the

unity of his consciousness and active self-awareness cannot really understand and personally assimilate something that bears no relation to the unified world of his own knowledge. What is revealed can, therefore, only really be known and personally assimilated in function of a man's secular knowledge.

3. From this it is clear that revelation when received by man (since it does not absolutely alter his situation) is itself always conveyed partly by theologumena. Revelation speaks in confrontation with the present state of valid knowledge, with the experience and the world-view of the actual hearer. It makes use of the systems of concepts available, the materials of representation, the helps to understanding, the perspectives and the ways of approach to comprehension easily accessible at a given time. In short, revelation, occurring in human cognition, necessarily uses theologumena (at least as glosses). They are not the element of binding dogma contained in the meaning of a statement, but the intellectual frame of reference inevitably expressed simultaneously with it, and by means of which what is dogmatically meant is understood, correctly but in a certain perspective.

4. Anyone who makes statements involving faith does not need to, and in fact cannot, adequately distinguish by reflection in them the dogmatic proposition from the theologumenon. Otherwise he could completely eliminate the theologumenon; and similarly he would have to be able adequately to become aware by reflection of the historical presuppositions of his own thought; whereas neither of these is possible. Nevertheless we are always implicitly aware of the distinction: for example, by knowing the identity of what is meant in a plurality of types of representation which themselves cannot be reduced to unity; or by concomitant awareness of the secular origin of the assumptions involved in the theologumena or of the unimportance of these for the central affirmations of the faith etc. The history of reflection on this distinction is the history of theology itself. Not that the latter is a history of the elimination of theologumena in favour of a "pure" theology of "merely" dogmatic statements. But it is a history of perpetual changes in theologumena, faster or slower, of greater or less fundamental a kind as the case may be. Ultimately that history is identical with that of men's historical growth in the knowledge of truth. This does not mean that in regard to dogma something is eventually recognized as erroneous which previously was believed to be absolutely true, but that the *conversio ad phantasma* which makes possible and supports all cognition, is a turning to the totality of historical experience, which itself changes. The enduring identity of the knowledge of the truths of faith ultimately rests on the fact that what throughout this history seeks, finds and fulfils itself is the one nature of man given in transcendental experience. This nature, supernaturally elevated from its origin, is always oriented towards God as absolute, and thereby possesses the abiding element of the eternal truth which itself assumes ever clearer historical form in the history of this supernaturally transcendental human nature, until the historical appearance of absolute truth in Jesus Christ.

Karl Rahner

THEOLOGY

I. Nature

A. Introductory Remarks

1. On the history of theology see *Theology* II.

2. The general principles of the theory of knowledge which are important for the understanding of theology can only be given in outline here.

a) Man's conscious and articulate knowledge of himself (scientific and pre-scientific) is not the whole of his self-understanding, but the interpretation of a self-understanding grasped directly and historically in the act of existence. (One may compare logic or ethics. Man does not act logically or responsibly for the first time when he studies logic or ethics, scientifically or pre-scientifically.) Such reflective knowledge is not just a leisurely afterthought, but an element of existence itself and of its history. Man as he speaks and lives with other human beings necessarily reflects on himself, though in historically different ways. And this conscious knowledge reacts on his original self-understanding and helps to change it. The original self-understanding itself has again a number of constitutive elements of a transcendental and historical character, which need not be gone into here.

b) Truth can exist only in intersubjectivity. To see what is meant here by truth, one must not just think of isolated propositions which are considered correct because objective. The understanding of such propositions is possible only within a non-thematic but real horizon which is represented by speech or language and all that this implies. But this speech is essentially the work of intersubjectivity. Hence the question of truth is always posed within the framework of intersubjectivity and is indeed the question of this intersubjectivity itself. But it is always inspired by the latter and its components and presuppositions, which can never be exhaustively grasped by reflection.

c) Theoretical and practical reason form a unity in difference which again has a history which can never be totally perspicuous and amenable to the theoretical reason. In this unity in difference, theoretical and practical reason form together man's single faculty of knowledge. By "theoretical reason" we understand primarily the reason which grasps "metaphysically" the transcendental necessities and tries "scientifically" to systematize empirical experiences and bring them into definable functional combinations (though such reason, when compared to the technique of present-day science, may well be still at a pre-scientific stage). By practical reason we mean the knowledge which is ultimately immanent to the free – and hence not arbitrary – decision by which man always lives, one way or the other, and which can be gained only in such decision. The probing mind must never forget that it reflects this totality of practical and theoretical reason and can never grasp it exhaustively, if for no other reason than that the act of reflection itself cannot be again the object of reflection.

d) The notion of science – in the widest sense, including philosophy and theology – has itself a history. And the historically conditioned and changing notion of what a science is and what it can and ought accomplish helps to determine the actual pursuit of these sciences. Because of the unity of human consciousness all sciences depend on one another, whether consciously or not. Theology, for instance, is to some extent determined by the history of all the sciences and their historical self-understanding.

B. The Nature of Theology

1. a) *A definition.* Theology is the *science* of faith. It is the conscious and methodical explanation and explication of the divine revelation received and grasped in faith. This methodical reflection is possible and necessary because the "official" revealed word of God already contains a conceptual and propositional element which as an element of faith and its responsible communication to others demands further explanation, reflection and confrontation with other truths. Hence revelation is intrinsically amenable to reflection. If "science" is understood to be methodical

reflection (along lines appropriate to the subject-matter in each case), it is absurd to deny theology the character of a science.

Three reasons may be noted in particular.

(i) Beyond what has been said above, there is no mandatory and permanent notion of science known to history. The limitation to experimentally verifiable facts – of the natural sciences, mathematics, quantities, fields outside value-judgments – is arbitrary, a mere matter of terminology, and would deprive theology only of a claim to be scientific in a way foreign to it.

(ii) Theology has a special subject-matter which can be distinguished from all others: the act and "content" of Christian (and ecclesiastical) faith. This subject-matter is at least a psychological and historical fact which may be methodically investigated, even if it is rejected as an ideology and an error, even if then reduced to a part of the science of religion. It would be methodical reflection on the phenomenon of culture known as religion.

(iii) The fact that Christian theology reflects on the act and content of faith in the light of faith does not deprive it of its scientific character. For total commitment is compatible with critical reflection which excludes nothing *a priori* from its critical questioning. The critical reason has the intrinsic ability to recognize that while it investigates the pre-critical presuppositions of existence, it can never grasp them exhaustively. It can recognize that no theoretical reason can exist outside the sphere of a decision of the practical reason which can never be exhaustively grasped.

b) Theology is the science of the *faith*, or rather, the science of the Christian faith.

(i) There are various interpretations of the Christian faith, not merely in theology as such but even within the propositional element which is part of the faith as such. There are various "confessional" theologies. Since in spite of these differences there is *one* Christian faith which is really one and the same behind the various propositions in which it is objectivated in the confessions and which is also sufficiently objectivated conceptually in the confessions (in the confession of Jesus as Lord), there is a Christian theology which, as the science of the faith, is really one.

(ii) Theology is the science of faith inasmuch as the Christian faith is the basis, norm and goal of this science. It is concerned with the faith as act and content (*fides qua* and *quae*) and presupposes it in the Church and in the student of theology. Faith is the goal, because the methodical reflection is not an epilogue indulging speculative curiosity but leaving the object, faith, itself untouched. The Christian must be able to answer for his faith to himself and his fellows, and methodical reflection is the form which this responsibility takes in the individual and collective situation. It is the actual account which we must give ourselves and others of the truth of our hope (cf. 1 Pet 3:15). Thus the science of faith actually becomes part of the faith (of which critical responsibility is a moment). Otherwise it would be reduced to a mere science of religion. This does not mean that faith and theology cease to be independent. For theology as such does not produce faith and it does not transform it into a higher, perspicuous system of a Gnostic or rationalistic type. And while faith is the *auditus* and the *intellectus fidei*, which involves a critical reflective element, especially faith as preaching, this is not at once a systematic and methodical reflection, like a strict science. Since theology is in this sense the science of faith, it has a sense of its own inadequacy which it works out and must keep on working out conceptually. It has a sense of the infinite transcendence of the word of God in faith with regard to all theological propositions. And this sense is part of the radical self-understanding of theology. Since theology reflects and serves the giving of a critical answer for the faith, it is essentially orientated to testimony and preaching. Hence all theology is "kerygmatic". Otherwise it is merely speculative philosophy of religion. In spite of its essentially kerygmatic character, its relation to preaching, it is a science of critical reflection, not directly meditation (as prayer) or exhortation. It is precisely as critical reflection that it serves preaching.

Its relation to faith, the full act of human existence in freedom, makes the science of faith a "practical" science, not in the sense of being a second-class science accompanying a higher intellectual science of the "theoretical reason", but in the sense that "practical" describes better the one totality of its knowledge. Theology is practical above all because it is orientated to the acts of hope and of love, which contain an element of knowledge which is unattainable outside them. It is true, no doubt, that the practical end of theology is also the desire of selfless knowledge which aims at a *sapere res prout sunt*. But this knowledge is ultimately attainable only in the act of hope and of love. Orthodoxy and orthopraxis combine to influence one another in a basic inexpressible unity which can only come to light in practice, because knowledge is only sound when it has surpassed itself and become love – which is its way of surviving as contemplation.

(iii) Since theology is the critical and methodical reflection on faith, the immediate "subject" (agent) of theology is not simply man endowed with the supernatural *habitus* of faith, but man as rational, in keeping with the distinction between faith and theology. But since theology is to remain the science of faith, faith must be the subjective inspiration – and not merely the object – of this operation of human reason. Thus the "subject" of theology may be described as the *ratio fide illustrata* (*D* 1799), though here *ratio* is not to be taken in a rationalistic sense.

c) Theology is an ecclesiastical science of faith. Since human intersubjectivity is at its peak in faith (A, 2, b), while faith, the hearing of the revelation directed to the people of God, is the faith of the Church and faith within the Church, theology is necessarily ecclesiastical. Otherwise it ceases to be itself and becomes the prey of the wayward subjective spirituality of the individual, which is today less fitted than ever to be the cohesive force of a community. Since the faith of the Church is necessarily linked to the historical word of divine revelation, Church theology is necessarily dependent on Scripture and tradition. Since the Church, *as* the community of faith, is an institutional society, Church theology is essentially related to the magisterium in the Church. Theology does not thereby lose its critical function with regard to the Church and its life of faith. Indeed, it is only because it is an ecclesiastical science, and hence an element of the Church itself, that theology can and must exercise its function as the Church's self-criticism, the constantly renewed effort to purge the faith from all that is merely human and questionable or historically transient.

d) As an ecclesiastical science, the whole of theology may well have a "political" aspect and be in this sense "political theology". This does not mean (or does not only mean) that the Church has a critical task in face of society, presupposing a corresponding reflection. Still less is political theology the preparation for "political action", an unjustifiable interference in the relative autonomy of worldly society and its politics. But if man's existence is equally individual and social in its essence, and if all theology is related to man (being reflection on the faith in which anthropocentrism and theocentrism combine, by virtue of the self-communication of God to man), theology cannot be restricted to the private salvation and the interiority of the individual. In all its concrete realms, it must consider the social relevance of its utterances. Social does not here refer only to the profane background within which and for which the Christian lives his Christian existence.

e) Theology is an historical science. This does not merely mean that it has to do with "historical matter". And it does not exclude the transcendental element in theology. It means primarily that theology is and remains perpetually linked to the historical event of salvation which took place once and for all. Man's salutary relation to this event – his "contemporaneity" with it – is not brought about by theology. This is the work of the kerygma and of faith. But since faith as such already contains an element of reflection which becomes articulate in theology, and since theology is always orientated to this element as to its starting-point and goal, theology itself has the character of a historical science in the highest sense. The historical is not just the starting-point of a deductive theology, as was assumed in the Middle Ages, but the very object of theology. This also means that theology has an essential relation to the future. For the historical here has the character of promise and cannot really be understood apart from this character. Since therefore all salvific events are hope-inspiring promises, eschatology is a structural principle of theology as such. It is not merely a treatise at the end of dogmatics – though this does not mean that dogmatics and eschatology could be simply identified.

2. *The "formal object" of theology.* In earlier times, the "formal object" of theology was much debated. It was assumed that theology was so unified a science that it had one single formal object from which it drew its unity. For this reason, and also to justify theology as a deductive science, medieval theology gave as the formal object "God in his Godhead" (cf. St. Thomas Aquinas, *Summa Theologica*, I, q. 1, a. 7). This view is acceptable if God is understood here in his self-communication. If this is correctly understood as at once the central saving event and word of revelation, and as the inner principle of the faith which inspires theology, the mysteries of the Trinity and incarnation and of justifying, divinizing grace are already comprised in it and hence the fundamental mysteries of salvation are considered together. And since salvation and revelation are the history of this divine self-communication – creation being merely the constitution of its recipients – theology as critical reflection on salvation can also be comprised within this formal object. There is then no reason to reject "God as God" as formal object, on the ground that it would eliminate theology as a historical science (as reflection on the anamnesis of the history of salvation). If God communicating himself is taken as the formal object of theology, there are advantages for a transcendental understanding of theology, since the formal object and the subjective principle of theology (God as the uncreated grace of faith) would clearly be the same. In any case, *Deus sub ratione deitatis* is not the basis of a merely deductive theology, since the divine self-communication is only accessible to our conscious reflection in the history of salvation and the *word* of revelation. Hence this classical definition of the formal object of theology is not very helpful when one tries to grasp the nature and methods of theology.

3. *Divisions of theology.* The division of theology is not merely a matter of listing systematically the ordinary disciplines studied in theology. A division along the lines of a genuinely theological theory would raise the question of a basic reform of theological studies and lead perhaps to the discovery of tasks which are in fact overlooked by theology. The ancient division into *theo-*

logia (the doctrine of God in the strict sense) and *economia* (the doctrine of creation and salvation) is no longer in use. It overlooked in any case the simple fact that we only know "God in himself" through what he does for us in the history of salvation, and that the *economia* is really the *theologia*, because it is the history of the self-communication of God. The usual division is into historical, dogmatic and practical theology. The first would be closest to the *auditus fidei*, the second would be the *intellectus fidei*, and the third would deal with the *praxis fidei* in the life of the Church). But this division causes difficulties. That the three elements overlap is a difficulty inherent in the matter itself and merely testifies to the unity of theology. But it is difficult to fit the history of the Church, for instance, into this schema. It is, of course, a historical science, but it does not seem really to belong to the one "historical" theology which is directly connected with the *auditus fidei*. Church history might be considered history of dogma insofar as the Church preserves and attests revelation in all that it is and experiences (cf. Vatican II, *Verbum Dei*, art. 8). Or it could be considered as the presupposition and hence a subsidiary discipline for practical theology, since the past must be known if norms are to be drawn up for the immediate tasks of the Church. But is this what is really understood by Church history? Or is it only a theological science in a broad sense, so that the problem really does not arise?

Moral theology, as usually understood, should no doubt be considered a part of systematic (or dogmatic) theology, i.e., under the heading of theological anthropology. Or it could stress how historically conditioned are its concrete affirmations and demands and be understood as the ethical actualization of the basic Christian attitude in each changing situation. It could then be considered in its entirety as part of practical theology, while systematic theology would continue to perform its ordinary dogmatic task of reflecting on the ultimate religious attitude, out of which moral theology grows as part of practical theology, in keeping with the needs of the situation. The study of canon law is to be regarded as part of practical theology, concerned with the human law of the Church, as *ius conditum* and *condendum*, which is part of its vital structure. The true place of the *ius divinum* would rather be within dogmatic ecclesiology. There is no need to consider here the precise place of other usual disciplines within theology as a whole. Subjects like liturgy, ecumenical theology, Christian social doctrine, Christian archaeology, the science of religion, etc., are either parts of a more comprehensive theological discipline or of subsidiary disciplines or combine the tasks of several disciplines for practical, technical reasons.

All this should not give the impression that a scientific theory of theological study has been catered for by the division outlined above. For one reason the actual divisions of theology as now usually accepted have generally arisen without much considered reflection, in the wake of similar profane sciences and hence not from a genuine theological impulse.

C. Theology and the Other "Sciences"

1. The relation of theology to the *science of religion* in all its forms has already in fact been touched upon, to some extent; and it is the same in many respects as the relation of theology to philosophy and the modern anthropological sciences. The science of religion is as independent of theology as is philosophy, and represents an important subsidiary science for theology.

2. *Theology and philosophy*. As the history of theology shows, the intellectual self-understanding of man which

precedes the *auditus fidei*, accompanies it and derives from it (going beyond the interpretation of a purely revealed anthropology), has had a very great influence on theology. And conversely, the philosophy of the Occident at least (which is a force everywhere in the modern world-culture) is historically unthinkable without the history of revelation and Christianity. Theology was not the intrinsic norm of philosophy, but in the actual course of history, it was theology which to a great extent opened up to philosophy its own possibilities. It is not easy to determine the basic relationship between the two. Insofar as there is a valid distinction between nature and grace, philosophy exists in its own right, though this means that the study of philosophy must go on within theology itself and that theology cannot simply assume the existence of a ready-made tool in the shape of a rounded-off philosophy with which to work. Theology and philosophy differ, as Vatican I said (*D* 1795), in their *principium* and their *objectum*. Theology is based on the grace of revealed faith and regards the revealed mysteries of God, while philosophy proceeds from natural reason and is concerned with the objects accessible to this. Since philosophy cannot consider Scripture, tradition and magisterium as sources and norms of knowledge, this distinction of the *duplex ordo cognitionis* is easily understood.

It must be remembered, however, that philosophy, on principle, can exclude nothing from its critical questioning. It cannot omit the phenomenon of the Christian faith without giving up its claim to be universal and hence ceasing to be itself. Then, it is true that the object of Christian theology can only become a conscious certainty through the word of revelation (of a conceptually explicit kind). But it is there in the universal self-communication of God, implicitly, in the experience of grace. Hence natural reason is always subject to the finality of grace, whether accepting or rejecting it. It follows that natural reason is not so untheological in its principle and object as may be suggested by the fact that in its philosophical reflection it has no explicit norm in revelation and dogma. All philosophy is in fact carried on unconsciously either in faith or unbelief – at least when one considers not this or that proposition of philosophy, but the ultimate mental horizons within which any proposition is situated and is given meaning. For there is in fact no one who is neutral with regard to grace. And there is philosophy in all theology because grace can be real only in nature and each hearing of revelation contains at once an element of interpretation which is to some extent determined by the self-understanding with which the hearer comes to revelation – by his "philosophy". Hence philosophy, which contains a secret element of theology undecipherable by philosophy itself, can have a very positive relation to theology. Transcendental philosophy in particular easily passes over in the concrete to transcendental theology. It has a maieutic function with regard to theology. "Philosophy is an inexorable but by no means arbitrary questioning of the unquestioned. It is a fruitful negation which criticizes and cross-questions the conventional canons of the 'evident truths' of each age. It fights against the creeping absolutism of the individual sciences as they trespass beyond their categories. It is a protest against the anonymous dictatorship of the factual, a summons to break again and again with the seemingly obvious. To adapt a saying of Hegel, it can look on itself as 'its own age summed up in a question'. Philosophy therefore may be said to take the side of the ever greater possibilities of human existence, which can never be reduced to the merely factual. It thus discloses, even if only in a negative way, the concrete, historically changing 'openness' of the human mind (see *Potentia Oboedientialis*), on which faith itself must always base itself in its responsible proclamation of its hope" (J. B. Metz in *LTK*, X, cols. 69f).

3. *Theology and the modern sciences*. In earlier times philosophy had a monopoly in mediating man's self-understanding to theology. Things are now different. There is a large number of anthropologically important sciences outside philosophy, important for human self-understanding and hence for theology, and regarding themselves (at least *de facto*) as autonomous and not as branches or subordinate parts of philosophy. This uncompromising and to some extent irreducible pluralism of anthropological sciences, which may be interpreted theologically as a "situation of gnoseological concupiscence", is of great importance for theology. These sciences, today at any rate, are partners in dialogue with theology and must be accepted as such by it. The dialogue is not just concerned with reconciling the findings of modern science with theological assertions. It is above all the confrontation of theology with the mentality of the modern sciences, above all the exact natural sciences, a task which theology has far from mastered.

D. Special Questions of Modern Theology

1. *Theology and ideology*. Like all study of the "metaphysical" and "transcendent", which cannot be verified by the methods of the exact sciences, theology is suspect to many scientists, sociologists in particular (from Feuerbach and Marx on) as being an ideology in the modern sense of the term. This suspicion cannot be dismissed off-handedly. Theology is the human *intellectus fidei*, historically conditioned and hence infinitely different from God and his word. And it is in the concrete always a theology carried on by sinners. It can be culpably suspect of ideology insofar as it is tributary to the ideologies of each age and society. Recognition of this possibility and indeed of this partial truth is part of theological knowledge itself. But the word of God which is voiced in theology and the preaching of the Church is not an ideology but the most radical critique of ideology. Christian theology is concerned with the *Deus semper maior*, the one absolute future (see *Hope*) who surpasses infinitely all this world's thrusts and systems but is really there as such for us in grace and hope. It is a theology of willingly accepted death as the dawn of the absolute future. As such it contradicts all ideologies which refuse to recognize their limitations and only maintain themselves against the greater reality which embraces them by arbitrary obduracy, purely speculative evasiveness and intolerance. Such a theology "when it finds or finds itself opposed by other universal interpretations of the world and of existence, cannot simply reject them pugnaciously and intolerantly. It must try to discover in them, and benefit by, something of the ever greater possibilities of the faith which can never be exhausted purely speculatively. These are to be searched for less in the content than in certain patterns of thought and consciousness which have been historically voiced in such philosophies and world-views. In such ideals theology, with its shortcomings due to sin, and with its own principle of looking for the Spirit to breathe where it wills, may find one of its own potentialities which it has forgotten or missed or failed to discover" (J. B. Metz in *LTK*, X, col. 71).

2. *The role of theology in the Church of today*. Theology is for the preaching of the Church. All preaching today presupposes some methodical reflection and hence theology. Hence all priests and above all the bishops must be theologians. This does not mean that there must always be a group of professional

theologians at the top by divine right. But once this is admitted, there are two points to be noted. Theology and skill in theology are not the preserves of the priestly or episcopal office-holders because they have their own specific task of preaching in the Church. A broad and deep knowledge of theology (such as is needed in the Church as a whole at least today, and always, on principle) presupposes gifts of nature and grace which are not found everywhere and are not necessarily found in all office-holders. Hence there can be important "charisms" of theology even outside the hierarchy. The "charism" of teaching is not linked with the office of superior in the NT (Rom 12:6–8; 1 Cor 12:28f.). Then, at the present time, the preaching of the Church as a whole presupposes a theology with so much scientific and technical preparation that it must be carried on by professors of theology – or whatever one likes to call them. Whether they are priests or layfolk is a secondary question. They must have had a specialist formation and have a certain special professional ethic. The Catholic Church cannot and ought not be a "Church of professors", but it cannot be today a Church without professors. Whether such an ecclesiastical professorial body can or should be given concrete form as an institution, e.g., as consultors to synods, as groups attached to the Roman Congregation for the Doctrine of the Faith, so that they can speak clearly in the Church, is another matter. There is no need to discuss further here the legitimate freedom which must be accorded to the theologians in their work.

3. *The pluralism of theology today.* There have always been "schools" of theology upholding contradictory opinions, starting from different assumptions and developing different patterns of thought. A pluralism of this type in theology is not new and it has always been a principle in the Church that it should be either tolerated or expressly approved of. But theologies today are displaying a pluralism of a different type, one that cannot be now reduced to unity. Formerly there were controversies between the schools and to some extent different patterns of thought, not recognized as such, however. But fundamentally they knew each other, spoke more or less the same language, and could try to clarify their differences and eliminate them in a higher synthesis. The materials and methods of theology – linguistic, historical and speculative – were ascessible to all – or completely outside their range of interests. But today the intellectual and social environment of theology is different. Methods are different. There are so many different starting-points and languages in philsophy that no single individual can master them adequately. The mass of material in exegesis and history of dogma is such that no single individual can take in and master "theology", even as it is at present. Theology has become many theologies. They need not be contradictory. If they are to be Christian and Catholic, they must abide by the one perpetual confession of faith of the Church, in the obedience of faith. The ancient creeds (which were also in part the result of "theology") are in fact more important than ever, since they can hardly be replaced by new formulas which would be "existentielly" understandable by all at once. But the theologies remain multiple, because the whole of present-day theology, with its various disciplines, terminologies, approaches, problems and audiences, cannot be even approximately grasped by the individual. Teamwork can help, but in the intellectual sciences, where the procedures and the findings cannot be separated, it cannot fully overcome this pluralism. It has come to stay. There will be more and more theologies, which will not be able to follow each other adequately, though this of course does not mean

that they will be simply juxtaposed without influencing each other. On the contrary, a new type of effort at mutual tolerance, mutual influence and mutual criticism will be necessary, much more than hitherto. The magisterium, hitherto nourished too exclusively by a certain type of Roman theology, will have to find new ways of controlling and fostering this pluralism.

4. *Theology and modern "irrationalism"*. Much more than in former times, theology must now envisage readers and hearers whose whole culture inclines them to "relativism", scepticism and positivism. Where religion is accepted, it is relegated to the realm of the irrational where it is no longer exposed to rational questioning and objections. Such attitudes and the corresponding interpretations of religion and its theology existed earlier, but they did not as today stamp the whole mentality of an era. If theology is really to give an account of the faith to a given age, it must see this situation clearly and take it into account. Fundamental theology and dogmatic theology must be much more of a unity than formerly, because the credibility (and existentiell assimilability) of the individual truths of faith means at least as much for the credibility of the fact of revelation as this does for the former. Theological statements must be modest and prudent and when treating the individual themes of theology must not forget its general principle of mystery and the merely analogous nature of its concepts with regard to its object. Theology must take care to see that its individual propositions are related to the real kernel of faith and revelation, in terms of the hierarchy of truths. It must make this kernel intellectually and existentielly assimilable and on this basis articulate the various individual dogmas, without making its task too easy by simple recourse to the formal authority of the magisterium. For the magisterium itself is only credible by virtue of the manifest credibility of the whole of revelation.

Karl Rahner

II. History

The history of theology can be regarded as forming with the history of dogma a part of Church history. Or it can be regarded as forming with exegesis a presupposition and element of historical and systematic theology. But as a branch of Church history, the history of theology would have to contain many elements which would not be directly of use to systematic theology. Patrology, if not treated merely as the history of literature in patristic times, may be regarded as the first section of the history of theology, that is, as history of theology in the patristic age. Or the history of theology may be begun at the point when the "Fathers" end and the theologians begin, that is, with early scholasticism. Just as patrology could be treated as a history of patristic literature, a similar procedure could be followed in the history of theology. But then it would be merely a history of theologians and of theological literature as such, which would be a useful undertaking, and one that is too little attended to. Nonetheless, the history of theology should be a theological undertaking. As such, it is obviously akin to the history of dogmas (and of the Councils), and this is its usual framework. But there is a radical difference between the two, corresponding to the difference between dogma and theological proposition. The history of dogma cannot of course be described without recourse to the development of theology. But the history of theology remains separate, being in fact the history of theologians, theological literature, theological propositions, schools and institutions, various theological concepts, thought-forms, methods, motives, etc., in spite of the fact that history of dogma and history of theology are usually in fact treated together. History of theology in this sense can then be divided into the history of the various disciplines, history of exegesis and so on. And since the history of theology has a history of its own, it can be part of its own subject-matter.

The division of the history of theology into periods to bring out the characteristics of each age encounters the same difficulties as the division of Church history. Since the history of theology is an essential part of Church history and reflects it because dependent on it, it seems obvious to consider that the divisions should be the same in each case. But the periods of Church history as such provide only very extrinsic divisions for the history of theology. And the problem is only displaced a little, since the objective divisions of Church history are still a debated problem. It must further be noted that it would be a false approach to assume beforehand that the periods in question should be more or less of equal length. Under these circumstances, the division to be outlined below may be considered. It is primarily concerned with systematic theology, since this is the clearest reflection of the spirit of a given age, insofar as it is influential in theology.

A. The Theology of the Beginning

The word "beginning" is here used not just in the sense of the initial stage of a period of time, but in the sense of *principium*, the "whole in a kernel", if for no other reason than that this was the period of the unique historical event of Jesus the crucified and risen Lord, the permanently valid centre to which all theology is referred. It is difficult to divide this period from the following one, but the theology of the beginning could be seen as coinciding with the time of the primitive community, the time of the apostles, the origin of the NT. But this period could perhaps be extended to the moment when theology crystallized in a particular culture as the self-understanding of a Church which may be regarded as in some way national or established. In this first period theology is still ambivalent, still stamped by the OT and the environment of Jesus, but also thinking in terms of the civilization and religion of Hellenism. Two subdivisions may be made in this period.

1. *The history of the theology of the New Testament* (see *Bible* I A, 2; *New Testament Theology*). This is usually given in introductions to the NT, exegesis and biblical theology. But it is really part of the history of theology, since even within the NT we find theology and development, whose normative function is, however, guaranteed (K. Rahner, *Theological Investigations*, V [1966], pp. 33–41). It is the time of the first and permanently normative reflection on the original experience with Jesus of Nazareth. The OT was still a vital starting-point for theological argument, the experience with Jesus was being transposed into the first type of Christology, the "Christology of descent", the notion of salvation through grace alone was being worked out, it was becoming clear that between Easter and the return of Jesus there was the Church, and the Church was becoming conscious of itself as an institution *iuris divini* (*ibid.*, pp. 219–43).

2. *The history of theology between the NT and the theology of the imperial Church*, i.e., *c.* 100–300. The Church has left the ambit of the OT. Practically its only partners in dialogue are Hellenism and the Roman Empire. The Apologists tried to speak to the cultured in their own language. The first attempts were made to draw up theological systems – some major ones, like that of Origen. Technical theological terms came into use. In the struggle against Marcion and the Gnostics, further thought was given to the continuity and discontinuity of Christianity

with its OT origins. A defensive front was formed against the religious philosophy of the times. In the struggle against Montanism and Novatianism and the controversy on the re-baptism of heretics an ecclesiology began to take shape which would do justice to the juridical development now clearly established. The demarcation of the canon of Scripture was begun and became the subject of theological reflection.

B. Theology within a Definite and Homogeneous Culture

The conversion of the Roman Empire introduced a very important period of Christian theology which reflected the cultural unity and character of the society in which it flourished. This unity did not of course mean that theology had not to deal with schools, controversies, schisms, heresies and contradictions. But all had the same geographical and cultural background and the same mental horizon, mostly accepted unreflectingly. It was a mentality of very complex components, being the heritage of the ancient Hellenistic and Roman culture, while also marked by the Christian message and – later – by the characteristic new approaches of the Germanic peoples. This whole age, the end of which one may put at the Enlightenment or the French Revolution, or perhaps in our own times, forms a definite unity, in spite of all its differences, when compared to the theology of the beginning and to the theology which is now slowly taking shape. The whole period may be subdivided into three phases: a) the dialogue of Christian faith with a well-defined culture, historical and regional; b) the objectivation and systematic articulation of the objective truth of faith (the Middle Ages); c) the subjective (transcendental) and historically-minded reflection on faith and the truths of faith (modern era).

But first we must consider the unity of this period which lasted for more than fifteen hundred years. The basically common character, in spite of differences which went as far as bitter struggles between orthodoxy and heresy, is only now beginning to stand out clearly as we pass out of this period and the new age is ushered in only reluctantly by the mind of the Church. It is not obvious, for instance, that the theology in the future – like that of the past and for the same reasons – will be accompanied by a history of dogma which leads to new dogmas. It is not obvious that it will be almost indissolubly linked to a special period of cultural history and derive from the unity of this cultural horizon a unity (latent for the most part) which overrides all "cleavages". It is not obvious that this culture, being itself tributary to Christianity, will be a protection to faith and theology. But in any case the past age and its theology had a unity which marks it off clearly from the era upon which we are now entering. Jt should also be borne in mind that the late Middle Ages, the theology of the Reformation and the Counter-Reformation, the theology of the Baroque period and of the Enlightenment are the consequences of earlier, epoch-making decisions taken in the seminal years of the Middle Ages, and were only gradually replaced after the Copernican revolution in thought brought about by Kant.

1. *The theology of the Roman Empire, East and West.* This theology bore the marks of its times: neo-Platonism and Roman imperial and juridical thinking. But there was no betrayal of the original Christian truth, because this great Christian fact, the presence of God himself in the world, kept on breaking through the mental horizons of the time, the notion of the degrees of being where God was the "supreme" and hence the most remote and "other-worldly" reality. The inherited mental horizons are there, but constantly called

in question, however unconsciously. Since it was a theology of degrees of being, of order and of the "Empire", it was less concerned with history and hope, less a theology open to an unknown future than a theology of mystical contemplation already in possession of God. The biblical eschatology is transmitted but not really reflected upon, or where it is, there is a strong inclination to a doctrine of general reconciliation. The "theology of history" as envisaged by St. Augustine is rather the theology of the eternal conflict of good and evil, not that of a genuine future and of a history of God himself. Hence too his theology of the immanent Trinity is kept apart from that of the Trinity of the economy.

There were three main themes in this theology, two predominant in the East and one specifically Western: the Trinity and Christology, then the theology of the necessity of the grace of predestination, in which few out of many were chosen for salvation.

Against Arianism, the doctrine of the Trinity upheld the consubstantiality of the Logos and the Pneuma with the Father. This was to stress the cosmic working of the power of God, and also a certain opposition to the hierarchical thinking of Hellenism. In Christology, Hellenistic terms were used (*physis*, *hypostasis*) to bring out the direct union of God with the world (in the hypostatic union of the Logos with the human "nature" of Jesus), and also the proper reality of the world (in the real, active humanity of Christ). This was the dialectic of Chalcedon – "neither confused nor divided". St. Augustine's theology of grace brings out clearly the sovereignty of God – and hence gives the world a voluntaristic trait. But it also made the picture of man a chiaroscuro of election and reprobation, whose most extreme forms were only gradually softened in the course of the Middle Ages and the modern era.

2. *Medieval theology*. In contrast with the theology of the Empire of patristic times, the theology of the Middle Ages breaks new ground, in the young nations of the West, from which patristic theology is seen as an established "authority". The *fides quaerens intellectum*, strongly optimistic as regards rational knowledge, launches a theology of its own with scientific preoccupations and techniques, and from St. Thomas Aquinas on, makes a clear distinction between theology and a philosophy autonomous to some extent. Theology is regarded explicitly as "scientific". The legacy of antiquity is present in the form of Platonism and of Aristotelianism, the latter in growing measure after its "baptism" (of fire) in the 13th century. There are clear differences between the schools, represented chiefly by the various religious orders. But all are stamped strongly by a common mentality. There are "authorities" taken for granted in philosophy and theology. The Bible is a sort of textbook. It is the age of the Summas, aiming optimistically at a conceptual synthesis to be brought about by a reason on whose powers scarcely a doubt was cast. The pessimism of Augustinianism was gradually eroded, and "nature" and the "world" won gradually recognized, at least in principle, as existing in their own "worldly" right. The anthropocentric revolution of the modern era was already being prepared for to some extent. But thought is directly concerned with the "object", and the "subject" is treated as one object among many others. Otherwise theology went beyond patristics in making all elements of the kerygma the object of reflection, though at different degrees of intensity. The doctrine of the Trinity is given speculative development beyond that of the Cappadocians and St. Augustine. Much attention was paid to angelology, original sin, sanctifying grace, justification, the hypostatic union and the sacraments.

The history of salvation in general, soteriology and eschatology were brought into the system, but were still discussed in a prescientific language of imagery, while ecclesiology was developed rather in practice and in canon law rather than in theology as such.

3. *Baroque Scholasticism* was mostly a continuation of classical scholasticism, exploiting and overcoming the nominalism of the late Middle Ages. There were controversies with the theology of the Reformers, especially on justification, the sacraments and ecclesiology, but there was still much common ground in the theology of the schools: the Latin language, Suarezian-scholastic philosophy, efforts at system, Christology and trinitarian theology practically indistinguishable. The contrast between Catholic and Reformation theology was confined to the "categories" in which individual questions were debated, but did not penetrate to the "transcendental" presuppositions of which Luther was to some extent conscious – though not Protestant orthodoxy – as were the theological precursors of the "anthropological revolution" in the philosophy of the modern era. Controversies among Catholics were concerned with the recrudescence of an extreme form of Augustinianism in Baius and Jansenius.

The scientific interest in history awakened by the Renaissance produced a serious attempt at patrology, Church history and history of dogma. Theology and philosophy, on principle and in practice, were more clearly distinguished than in the Middle Ages, but remained very close.

Theology was slow to take up the controversy with "the modern age" as represented by the transcendental revolution which turned attention to the subject, and by the Enlightenment, the beginning of rationalist criticism of religion, ideology and society. The debate was made more difficult by the new situation of the Church brought about by the French Revolution, and was slowed down by neo-scholasticism. Here theology justifibly defended itself against rationalism and modernism, claiming its rights as a genuine science of the faith. But it failed for the most part to enter into frank dialogue with the modern era, as the age of a transcendental philosophy and the beginnings of the "exact" sciences.

C. The Theology of the Future

1. The transition from Baroque scholasticism to the theology which is gradually emerging was made in neo-scholasticism, which overshadowed the efforts of the Tübingen school with its orientation to German Idealism. The system of neo-scholasticism was mostly restorative in tendency, but it performed services on the level of the historical sciences of theology and Christian social doctrine which went far beyond Baroque scholasticism. In exegesis, Catholic theology is only now, slowly and painfully, catching up with Protestant studies.

The main efforts of neo-scholasticism in the 19th century were directed against fideism, traditionalism and ontologism, and in the beginning of the 20th century against modernism. It was a solid, ecclesiastical theology, but apart from exceptional figures like Newman, it was strongly restorative in tendency, with a diffident, defensive attitude to the intellectual trends of its own times. The new approaches of "mystery theology" and the *nouvelle théologie* remained on a modest scale.

2. The new phase of theology begins with the end of neo-scholasticism. The Second Vatican Council can be taken as the watershed, though not widely recognized as such at the time. It is a theology which can no longer envisage the Church as a closed group within profane society. It sees itself as the scientific and rational reflection of faith in a Church which is in open dialogue, that is, one in which the outcome is not

already determined by the ecclesiastical partner. It notes the irretrievable pluralism of philosophy, and hence reckons with a pluralism in theology itself. It feels obliged to a direct dialogue with modern sciences, which no longer see themselves as subordinate to and represented by philosophy. It includes the sociological sciences as well as history and the natural sciences in its debate. It sees that it must apply to exegesis all the methods used by modern (Protestant) critical exegesis and that it must take its findings into account. Though the faith and the kerygma of the Church contain a theological element in their self-expression, theology recognizes that it must bring out more clearly than before the difference between theological science and the confession of faith.

In its reflection on its own history, which is an intrinsic element of systematic theology because it is a theology of the history of salvation and revelation, theology sees that it has more to do than bring out the continuity of its history. It strives to see the configuration of this history in each of its epochs, none of which can be adequately reduced to the preceding or the following age, and it thus gains a direct relationship to each of these configurations in their individual uniqueness. Theology must therefore both justify, and mark the limits of, each of the great steps that it has taken (B. Welte). This is the only way in which it can profit by its history, apart from using it to be a testimony to the continuity of ecclesiastical tradition.

Theology today must be less an explicatory than "a reducing agent". There can be no question of a one-sided and discouraging stress on the formal authority of the magisterium – which remains unquestionable, but itself rests on foundations which are objectively and demonstrably prior to it, and which must be clearly regarded in the new light of each age. But the multiplicity of the individual propositions in which the faith of the Church is enunciated must be brought into relation with or reduced as far as may be to the central, original truth of the Christian faith, though this itself is historically mediated. (See the doctrine of Vatican II on the "hierarchia veritatum", *Unitatis Redintegratio*, art. 11.) Theology can therefore take on a systematic structure very different from that which has been customary in the last centuries. And it is an open question whether the traditional divisions of the theological disciplines will be maintained. When studying the formulas of the magisterium, theology will distinguish more clearly than hitherto between expressions on which the Church has justifiably but not irreformably ruled, and expressions which could not be otherwise without detriment to the reality of faith. Such theology will come back again and again to some "brief formula or formulas of the faith" in keeping with the insights of a given epoch, just as theology started with a similar formula, the Apostles' Creed. Theology will be more abstract because it will bear in mind the analogous nature of all theological propositions, and their orientation to the silent, adorable mystery. Hence its language will have less imagery and images. But it will also be an education and training for a "second spring" in which men will soberly make do with a theology which is forced to speak *in umbris et imaginibus*.

The world of man has ceased to be a numinous, sheltering and sovereign nature. It is no longer the object of the "speculative reason's" aesthetic and metaphysical contemplation. It has become the quarry from which man hews his own world according to his own creative plans, while learning at the same time to manipulate his own nature. It is the age of the practical reason, the age of a social dimension which is the only possible agent of such a creative thrust, with all its monstrous inherent dangers of titanic hybris and its component of sin. A theology which strives, as it must, to speak to such a race of men cannot but be the theology of an evolutionary world-view and a "political theology", which will also be a critique of society from a standpoint which is both within and without society.

This indication of two aspects of future theology does not of course mean that they are its only characteristics. The theology of the future will be characterized by a very considerable pluralsim which will not be totally reducible to unity, but without detriment to the one confession of faith within the one Church. Under these circumstances, one need have no misgivings about the prospect of a theology which will be very "positivist" in its attitude. It will not be inspired by the mentality very widespread in the last hundred and fifty years, according to which systematic theology had reached such an unsurpassable peak that it could really do no more than look back on its past – much as at present philosophy has to a large extent abdicated in favour of research into its own past. This "positivist" theology will rather be very aware of the historical conditioning of even the newest theology, but will be somewhat sceptical as regards the hope of bettering it in the future. It will also be sceptical as regards, for instance, the effort to "sublimate" the present-day pluralism into a higher theological synthesis. It may therefore be foreseen that one of these theologies of the future will be characterized by such a positivist trait.

Under these circumstances it is also possible to foresee another type of theology, one in which the question of hermeneutics and the epistemology of theology in general will be in the foreground. It is true that theological hermeneutics cannot simply pretend to replace theology in general as the only true scientific theology. Nonetheless, a future theology may be very much preoccupied by the question of theological hermeneutics, just as linguistic philosophy is not the whole of philosophy but can be the starting-point and structural principle for philosophy in general. The future may also hold a counterpart to the technical rationality of today which is reflected in a theology of the practical reason and political theology with its social criticism. There may be a swing over to a theology of contemplation, proper to the "quiet in the land" (Ps 35:20), of initiation into a mystical experience, of a rightly understood "aesthetic". Transcendental theology, as an element in every theology which understands what it is doing, will again cut across these perhaps foreseeable theologies.

All this gives only a very formal outline of a theology to come. It is impossible to do more. But even such a forecast may be important if it helps to reinforce the hope and courage which can look forward to the future of theology without too many misgivings.

Karl Rahner

THEORY AND PRACTICE

1. *Concept and problems.* The discussion of theory and practice is one of the primary themes of all philosophy. Since it examines the relation between idea and reality, word and deed, consciousness and being, concept and object, thought and action, purpose and history, the discussion of theory and practice could stand for philosophy itself. Where the relevance of theory to practice is denied in a radical scepticism or where they are merged in an undifferentiated identity, philosophy itself ceases to have any claims and its necessity disappears. Thought is left without an object. As in philosophy itself, the opinions on the relation of theory and practice can vary so widely that absolutely contradictory positions ensue.

But within this general framework there is a special aspect of the discussion which needs to be considered. In spite of variations in doctrine, practice is not identified as a rule with the world of objects. It is a summary way of indicating the individual and collective activity of man. But the very question as to whether such practice is the opposite of thought or whether they are allied in a way as yet to be determined, gives rise at once to controversy. A "pure theory" disdains all reduction to practice as a restriction upon the abstract logic of correct deduction or a belittling of the intrinsic value of its own non-utilitarian purpose, while theories concerned with empirical analysis, ethics, social philosophy, etc., often affirm the primacy of practice. Mention may finally be made of the general distaste for "fanciful speculation", which is partly due to unhappy experiences but also partly to resentment and to anti-intellectual emotions. In any case, the general view is that theory is unreal, futile and expendable.

In Christianity the relation between theory and practice likewise gives rise to many problems. As the gap between it and its origins grows, it becomes more and more difficult to relate the gospel to the life of faith, general norms to concrete imperatives, complicated theology to ordinary Christian action, preaching and everyday life. The problems cannot be solved by relegating them to the practical disciplines of theology and subordinating them to the basic systematical and historical treatises. This procedure involves a double danger. The practical disciplines may become casuistry and mere registration of facts, devoid of any connection with the major disciplines. And the latter tend to be distorted into independent historical and systematical theories without direct relevance to the present moment. The question of theory and practice can also be acute in the realm of criticism of religion, inasmuch as the actual, historical forms of Church life are assessed and criticized in terms of the self-understanding and origin of the Church, the gospel. The usual distinction between essence or reality and appearance is itself in need of justification. And the distinction likewise ordinarily made in spirituality and theology between the active and the contemplative life can now be scarcely maintained in the traditional form. The reasons for this are to be sought in the new understanding of science which has developed in the modern era. The concept now includes elements of biblical and Christian thought and their elaboration has not yet reached a point where they can be fully reconciled with the Graeco-scholastic tradition of Christian philosophy.

2. *The history of the problem.* As early as Herodotus, 5th century B.C., information (ἱστορεῖν) and examination (θεωρεῖν) are said to be the foundations of scientific history. In the natural philosophy of the Ionians, *theoria* designated the spiritual contemplation of abstract matters. In the religious realm, *theoria* originally seems to have meant a deputation sent by a town to some solemn feast. Later it meant contemplation in general, while the association with θεά, θεῖον is at least as early as Plato. Aristotle distinguishes between the βίος θεωρητικός and the βίος πρακτικός, the life devoted to intellectual contemplation and the life of ethical activity. A distinction is made between θεωρία, πρᾶξις and ποίησις. In *theoria*, contemplative thought has no other end and object but its own activity. In *praxis*, knowledge serves ethical action, in *poiseis* technical ability in the production of artefacts. The dualism of later Hellenism transformed the purely intellectual approach into an ascetical and contemplative way of life. *Theoria* became Gnosis.

The definition of theory in St. Thomas Aquinas is based on the universality of all speculative knowledge. The difference between theoretical and practical knowledge comes from the intention at work. God, being, etc., are the object of theory, while practical knowledge is concerned with ethics, politics and so on. The gap between theory and practice is more marked in nominalism. Here concept and consciousness have distanced themselves from their objects and anticipated some elements of modern systems of science, which construct their own axioms. And the isolated world of objects is left to empirical methods and inductive registration of facts. The thinking of the modern era thus took on an anti-Aristotelian, anti-contemplative character. The pure theory of mathematical knowledge goes hand in hand with an applied science looking only to the practicable and useful. "Tantum possumus, quantum scimus" (F. Bacon). Knowledge is power. Theory supplies principles which are to be tested and applied in practice.

Kant broke through this technological mode of thought, distinguishing the pure and the practical reason. Pure reason works out propositions and principles with methodical exactness. Practical reason, as reason in action, frees practice from the sphere of merely empirical registration of facts. By defining practice as the logic of action, Kant made practice subordinate to the rule of practical reason, instead of its being the mere extrinsic application of logically correct propositions to actions and objects. Hegel (*Preface to Philosophy of Rights*) saw practice as the historical manifestation of reason, its external existence. Reason and reality are identical. Theory cannot be an ideal surpassing practice, as in Plato, and it cannot be produced in the concrete by thought, as in Fichte. Since it is the mind of the world it only appears after the maturation of reality. Philosophy is "the times in thought". Idea and history, form and content, theory and practice are dialectically mediated moments of the one reality of the spirit.

The obviously questionable consequences in the field of politics and law – philosophy has not to find out what the State should be but how it can be recognized – were brought out and criticized by the Hegelians of the left. In the dialectical materialism developed above all by Karl Marx, the world is not just to be interpreted but to be brought in practice to conform to reason. Practice here is the totality of social relationships. An affirmative theory is nothing but "ideology", when put forward under the conditions under attack. Theory must be critical theory, and as such aims at eliminating itself by a revolution in the present evil condition of society. No doubt thinking is determined by social existence, but theory and practice still contain historical elements which disrupt the present framework and can at last really reconcile the existing antagonisms. Revolution is then the historical identity of theory and practice. From the point of view of method, Marxism means that the relationship of theory and practice is brought as close as possible to a total identification. But it has also made it clear that for practical purposes philosophy must be completed by social psychology and the empirical, analytical, social sciences.

In Romanticism, life-philosophy and existential philosophy efforts are made to safeguard the concrete riches and manifestations of the life of the individual from the paralysing grip of intellectualist abstractions and rationalistic thought. The relation of theory to practice is determined by the various ways in which life, spirit, soul, existence, etc., are envisaged. M. Heidegger criticizes the fixation of the object in modern theory. This is to be replaced by a fundamental ontology in which reason as the faculty of being is again given full rights. But the criteria for the functioning of reason in relation to being seem at times to be dangerously near to a mystical, Gnostic speculation.

The relationship of theory and practice is envisaged in different ways in the modern sciences. In the human sciences, certain methods of hermeneutics are taken to be valid in each case. Experimental sciences use hypotheses derived from standard propositions, and the hypotheses have then to be verified before they can be summed up as laws and brought together in a system, on the principle of scientific economy, and then formed into a coherent theory. Deductive theories are derived from principles prior to axioms and scientific theory.

3. *Systematical analysis and consequences.* The problems of scientific theory and the relationship of theory and practice as now discussed are already signalled in the last paragraph. In the natural sciences, the distinction between theoretical ("pure") and applied mathematics, physics, etc., has been proved valid, as may be seen from the way theory is established in such disciplines – either by logical deduction or by experimental methods. Outside the exact sciences, the establishment of pure theory detached from practice appears problematical, as in the positivist or pragmatical theories of history, society, law or art. No matter how the theories are arrived at, they are hypothetical, and not only does the logical correctness of their various assertions and laws need to be demonstrated, but their verification or falsification depends on subjective experience. In fact, however, the criteria for these experiences are either purely quantitative, being established by a comparison of verdicts, on the analogy of the establishment of precedents in Anglo-Saxon law. Or they are based on the procedures developed by pragmatism (as in C. S. Peirce) or on a combination of both methods. The procedures are highly complicated, and their weakness lies in the lack of hermeneutical and dialectical reflection on the conditions of possibility of these experiences. In fact, the objectivity of such theory is no more than a flat tautology of practice. The result is a mere projection of realism, a reliance on mental images which has been rightly criticized as a fault shared equally by neo-scholasticism and the dogmatic forms of dialectical materialism. Practice is given a double in theory, theory and practice are merged in a changeless identity, reason and reality are once more the same thing, though now in an anti-Idealist version. This notion of theory and practice is based on the unavowed assumption that practice is to be identified with a definable regulative system mostly made up of constants and variables – a system in which the usefulness of the means, the functioning of relations and the norms of fact have the value of directives resulting from objective forces.

But these values are then erected into absolutes without any analysis of the historical and social transmission by which they are coloured. This can only mean a rejection on principle of philosophical hermeneutics. But the latter in turn, if taken alone, is equally inadequate, since the "hermeneutical circle" means that it is drawn into the dialectic of practice embodying theory and theory engendering practice.

The realization of the goal of a free, objectively assured unity of theory and practice depends on finding an exact method for combining philosophical hermeneutics and empirical analysis of practice. But the goal itself is subject to historical contingency, and this must be allowed for. In view of the multiplicity of methods now used in the establishment of theory, this formal determination must suffice. In other words, the problem of theory and practice can for the moment only be stated more sharply. It can hardly be solved peremptorily.

In theology and the Christian faith, in the distinction between contemplation and action, the same principle holds good. If the latter distinction is to be still rational, it cannot be fitted into a scheme somewhat like "leisure and work". One should not imagine that contemplation can attain an immediacy by virtue of which the general norms of theology will be compellingly transformed in concrete action. Since such direct contemplation dispenses with psychological and sociological reflection and the like, it is as open to the suspicion of ideology as a theology which leads to a mainly inward-looking, privately orientated understanding of the faith, or which has recourse in fundamental theology to a colourless believer, whose freedom is an abstraction since he is not affected by any given historical situation. Individual and society act and re-act upon each other. To hypostatize either of these factors means that the dialectic of theory and practice is neglected and theology is distorted into an ideology. The real discussion of the relation of theory and practice in theology is only beginning.

The dialogue between Church and world demanded by Vatican II is also to be envisaged in this context. Here the copula "and" suggests a separation which does not do justice either to the many Christian implications of present-day social and political practice, or to the many ways in which world history influences the Church and theology.

The same precautions are necessary when the relation of theology to the faith of Christians is analysed. Reflection on the relationship of theory and practice should aim at a hermeneutics which will use all apt scientific methods to enlarge the scope of existing principles and so approximate as closely as possible to the ideal of a free, objective identity of theory and practice.

Werner Post

THOMISM

Thomism means normally the schools and systems of philosophy and theology which take the teaching or thought of St. Thomas Aquinas as their authoritative source. Here, however, we take Thomism as the doctrine of Aquinas himself, noting the main parts which are relevant to present-day discussion.

A. The Changing Authority of Aquinas

1. Canon law speaks of the doctrine to be taught to candidates for the priesthood as follows: "In the study of systematic philosophy and theology and in the formation of candidates for the priesthood in these subjects, professors are to follow entirely the mind, doctrine and principles of the Angelic Doctor and to consider these principles as sacred" (can. 1366, para. 2; cf. 589, para. 1). When Vatican II speaks of the philosophical disciplines, in its Decree on Priestly Formation, it mentions no authorities and leaves the matter deliberately open, mentioning only "the perennially valid philosophical heritage" (*Optatam Totius*, art. 15). As regards the theological disciplines it simply speaks of an intellectual effort to be made in systematic, dogmatic theology *Sancto Thoma magistro* – a compromise which is meant to include the material importance of his doctrine as well as the exemplary character of his methods.

2. *Historical note.* There was at first no direct continuity with the great commentators on Aquinas in the 16th century (e.g., Cardinal Cajetan) when a neo-Thomism, primarily interested in philosophy, developed above all in Italy and Germany during the 18th and 19th centuries. This received ecclesiastical sanction from the encyclical *Aeterni Patris* (1879) of Leo XIII. In putting forward the "authority of St. Thomas",

the Pope appealed in particular to the Council of Trent. This pronouncement of the magisterium led to more intensive historical work on the history of philosophy and theology in the Middle Ages. But another result was a non-historical textbook Thomism, which by the very fact was open to unconscious influences from the spirit of the times.

Side by side with the Thomistic "schools" and opposed by them to a great extent, there was the tradition of thought which tried to bring about a positive encounter between Aquinas and the thinking of the modern era: F. von Baader (*Thomas-Studium*, *c.* 1821) and J. E. von Kuhn (1806–7), who brought to light the ontological *a priori* (e.g., the *intellectus agens*) which was rejected by the Thomism of the schools; A. Rosmini (1797–1855); J. Maréchal (1878–1944) and the Thomists inspired by him, with a "dynamiste" approach especially in France, and a "transcendental" approach, especially in Germany.

B. Aquinas in the History of Thought: Central Questions

1. *Philosophy and gospel.* St. Thomas lived during a renaissance, that of Roman law in the 12th and of Aristotelianism in the 13th century, which was accompanied by an "evangelical movement" seeking to revive the text and spirit of the gospel. He was more strongly systematic than his teacher, St. Albert the Great, as his thought moved between these poles. Furthermore, he disclosed to the West, especially in Christology, the tradition of the Greek Fathers. His achievement did not take the form of a timeless synthesis. It was a successful effort, never completed, but rather one on which he was still working to the end, to build up a theological structure with all the materials of his time, orientated to the subject-matter and spirit of tradition, pointing on without revolutionary overtones to a future which we are still not done with.

2. *The question of being and of God.* One of the most fateful pieces of translation ever made was the LXX's rendering of Exod 3:14 by "I am HE WHO IS". It identified the God of the covenant who revealed himself in history with a basic term of Greek philosophy, changed from the neuter to the masculine. Thus it is an established fact for St. Thomas that "He who is" is the most suitable name for God (*Summa Theologica*, I, q. 13, a. 11). But he finds that this can be proved "by many arguments" ... "that God ... is his being" (*ibid.*, q. 3, a. 4), i.e., that his essence is to exist. The three proofs offered at this point are ontological expositions of the revealed names of God. He is the first (uncaused) cause, for which St. Thomas appeals (*Summa contra Gentiles*, I, 13) to Aristotle. He is pure actuality, which is St. Thomas's own notion of being. He is by his essence, and not by participation – which is a Platonic notion, reinterpreted and applied to being. But St. Thomas also transforms ontology into an "Exodus-metaphysic" (Gilson). Aristotle's world of movement becomes a world of beings, all of which have been produced as being (cf. *Summa contra Gentiles* II, 6, 15). The Aristotelian *energeia*, orientated to the essence, is abandoned for being as act. The characteristic of the forms ("ideas") is projected upon being, interpreted as act.

3. *Creation as emancipation of the world.* The theological significance of this combination of the notion of God and of being is seen when the world is regarded as created. St. Thomas leaves the question of the temporal beginning of the world to faith and the positive statements of revelation, and concentrates on the relation of finite beings to the being who is being itself. The world, as a thing of movement and causes, is the manifestation of a world of beings in which God, the being who

is, is directly, most intimately and perpetually present (*Summa Theologica*, I, q. 8; q. 104). God does not give the impulse to the world from outside (see *Deism*) but grounds by his presence in it the universal play of cause and effect (cf. *Summa contra Gentiles*, II, 21; III, 67f.). He shows his greatness by giving things their being and their proper activity. "To diminish the perfection of the creature would be to diminish the perfection of God's causality" (*ibid.*, III, 69). St. Thomas is even more drastic in rejecting any type of *concursus* between God and the world, such as has been a drag on us since nominalism: "The one and the same effect is produced by the subordinate cause and by God, directly by both, though in a different way" (*ibid.*, III, 70). It is precisely by being moved by God in this way that the subordinate causes receive their own proper character. "And just as he does not prevent the activities of natural causes being natural by moving them, so too when moving the voluntary causes he does not make their activity non-voluntary but rather brings it about in them" (*Summa Theologica*, I, q. 83, a. 1 ad 3). Even if the categories of principal and instrumental cause no longer seem apt models for describing the liberation conferred by God on man in action, there is another approach, also understood ontologically by St. Thomas, which reminds us of the relevance of his principle. Man as acting through will and reason is the representative of God's goodness in the world (*Summa contra Gentiles*, II, 46), the end and ruler of the world (*ibid.*, III, 22.

4. *Laws of nature and history*. The lordship of man is that of reason over the "lower" realms within him and outside him. Man shares through his reason in the provident rule of God over the world. "Providence is the plan which underlies the ordination of things to their goal" (*Summa Theologica*, I, q. 22, a. 1). God rules the world by leading it to its goal (*ibid.*, I, q. 103, a. 1). The goal of the universe being a universal goal can be no other than the universal good, God (*ibid.*, I, q. 103, a. 2). When man, the bodily, spiritual centre of the world, has reached his goal, the world also reaches it. "God wills that man should have might in order to serve reason and that he should have reason because he was to be man: and he was to be man for the sake of the fulfilment of the world" (*In Ephesios*, 1, lectio 1, no. 12). Man as the creature endowed with reason "is under God's providence in the special sense of sharing in providence inasmuch as he is provident with regard to himself and other things" (*Summa Theologica*, I/II, q. 91, a. 2). This sharing of the rational creature in the "eternal law", i.e., in the reason of God (*ibid.*, q. 19, a. 4) is called the "natural law" (*ibid.*, q. 91, a. 2). Hence nature, as understood here, is not a rigid conceptual structure or a metaphysical register, but the nature of man as he plans and acts rationally (cf. *Summa contra Gentiles*, III, 78), that is, a nature which founds history. The historical dimension is disclosed by the hermeneutical consideration first carried through by the Protestant theologian U. Kühn: "The explanations of the law in general, of the eternal, natural and human law, are given in view of the new law which is their real goal" (*Via Caritatis*, p. 229). But the "new law", the "law of the new covenant", is "above all the grace of the Holy Spirit which is imparted to those who believe in Christ" (*Summa Theologica*, I/II, q. 106, a. 1). There is an analogy with the "natural law", inasmuch as it is given in the most inward depths of man so that he does what is right from the depths of his freedom (*ibid.*, ad. 2; cf. ad 1). This perspective is given its full content in the doctrine of the gifts of the Holy Spirit (I/II, q. 68). The man who is filled by the Spirit is amenable to the call and the action of God by virtue of his inmost disposition.

5. *History of salvation and contemplative wisdom.* The discussions of the law of the OT (I/II, qq. 98–105) and of the law of the NT (*ibid.*, qq. 106–108) form the closest approach to what we now understand by the theology of salvation-history. But they are divided by visible seams from other treatises. The *Summa Theologica* is a synthesis, successful but not fully carried out, between "the presentations of the doctrine of faith in the immediate and remote predecessors of St. Thomas, which in Abelard were quite non-historical, but were consistently in the framework of salvation-history in Hugh of St. Victor and Peter Comestor" (O. H. Pesch in *LTK*, X, col. 130). This effort at synthesis is possible, "because both the historical event and the intelligible meaning of this event are founded on the wisdom of God's action" (M. Seckler, *Heil in der Geschichte*, p. 35).

C. Truth of Thought and of Revelation

1. *Propositional truth, ontological truth and the "truth" of the Fourth Gospel.* The effort to derive supratemporal intelligibility from the history of salvation derives from the effort, which can be traced in the West from the 2nd century, to expound the historical revelation of the prophets and Jesus Christ in terms of the Greek notion of truth (primarily Middle Platonism and neo-Platonism). The Middle Ages and hence St. Thomas inherited the ontological notion of truth for which St. Augustine was invoked: "The truth is that which (really) is." He also knew the Aristotelian approach to the truth of thought, as handed on through Boethius, St. Anselm of Canterbury and some scholastic writers, which was to predicate or deny of a thing what it was or was not. Further, there was the notion of the "hierarchy" of the "true" in its many degrees, from the subsistent truth of God to the truth of human discourse, as propounded by St. Anselm in his widely read dialogue *De Veritate*. Then there were the efforts of William of Auxerre and his followers, to base faith on the First Truth. Finally there were the statements of the Fourth Gospel, as expounded by tradition in keeping with the given understanding of truth at each particular period. The saying of the Lord, "I am the way, the truth and the life" (Jn 14:6) was of particular importance here. The Aristotelian principle is given the function of a catalyst, as it were, by St. Thomas, though it was never solely predominant.

2. *Significance and limit of propositional truth.* The question of truth, as prepared by St. Anselm of Canterbury, and explicitly propounded by St. Albert the Great, may be said to have presented itself as follows to the contemporaries of St. Thomas. When we say that something is "true", has it this title simply because of the relation to the one truth which is in itself (God), or does it also merit the title in itself? St. Thomas answers: "It is the one truth, the divine, which makes all things true, being their efficient and exemplary origin. Nonetheless, there are many truths in created things, by virtue of which these are said to be true in themselves (*formaliter*)" (*Scriptum super Sententiis* 1, d. 19, 2 solutio). But within the realm of created things we say such propositions are true (in the sense of correct) as conforming to the things. Hence truth is a relation founded on the being of the thing and fulfilled in the judgment in which the being of the thing is understood. In the famous first *quaestio disputata* of the *De Veritate*, St. Thomas examines beings as such as to whether the fact that they *are* itself provides a relation by virtue of which they are to be called "true", and which explicates itself in terms of true propositions and true content (i.e., attained by the propositions). This basic relationship is concentrated in the "soul" which – itself a being – is open

to all beings and thus places itself in a relation to itself in such a way that it reflects on itself as the place where all beings are collected (cf. along with *De Veritate*, 1, 1, *ibid.*, 10, 8).

The fundamental "truth" (transcendentally disclosed), the common nature or affinity of the being of beings and the being of the soul (or reason) is itself transcendentally grounded on the "First Truth" as the self-presentation of God (*De Veritate*, 1, 7; *Summa Theologica*, I, q. 16, a. 5). The being of all beings is the "reality" which as light makes beings present to reason (cf. *Super Librum de Causis*, prop. 6). The "active intellect" (*intellectus agens*) is the "participation in the uncreated light" (*Summa Theologica*, I, q. 84, a. 5), by virtue of which being is always present to man. Since this presence is voiced in the "principle of contradiction", it may be said that all "propositional truth . . . can be primarily reduced to the principle that affirmation and negation (of the same) cannot be true at the same time" (Avicenna) (*Scriptum super Sententiis* 1, d. 19, 5, 1 solutio).

Since the real site of intramundane truths is the intellect as it affirms or denies (*Summa Theologica*, I, q. 16, a. 2, etc.), they are to be understood in terms of the latter and not in terms of "eternal propositions" or "ideal truths". They should be termed finite, temporal (*Summa Theologica*, I, q. 16, a. 7, etc.), changeable (*ibid.*, q. 16, a. 8, etc.).

3. *The "First Truth" as foundation of faith.* For St. Thomas, the question of the "truth of faith" is not primarily that of the truth of the propositions in which faith is expressed. These have a mediating (communicatory) function, which will be hermeneutically discussed below (4). The fullest treatise on faith (*Summa Theologica*, II/II, qq. 1–16) begins by asking whether the First Truth is an object of faith (*ibid.*, q. 1, a. 1). This way of putting the question probably came into scholastic discussion through William of Auxerre. His formula became the "common" definition: "Faith is to assent to the First Truth for its own sake and beyond all [else]." This was probably to bring out the Godwardness of faith as a theological virtue, and to distinguish it from the other theological virtues, hope and love. In a number of formulas, William describes the First Truth as light which beams the articles of faith into the soul and which streams forth from them. It is also the authority which demands obedience and provides full grounds for trust.

The question is posed by the fact that for the early scholastics of the classical age, the First Truth was not merely the beginning and end of faith but also, paradoxically, the medium of it. This "mediation" by the "First Truth" was meant to bring out the immediacy of dependence on God. For *medium*, *ratio credendi*, the ground of faith, could also be used.

In the *Commentary on the Sentences*, St. Thomas had already shifted the emphasis from the *ratio credendi*, the (subjective) foundation of faith, to the *ratio objecti*, the foundation of the objects of faith, primarily God himself, as the centre of belief (3, disp. 24, 1. 1 solutio). In *De Veritate*, 15, 8, he explains the meaning of the foundation of faith by means of the notion of testimony. God, who attests himself, and imparts in testimony a share of his truth, is the *medium* and *objectum* (*ibid.*, ad 9). The mediation takes place in the act of self-attestation, the object is that which is attested in the testification. In the *Summa Theologica*, II/II, q. 1, a. 1, St. Thomas transfers the relationship of *medium* and *objectum* wholly within the being of God. Inasmuch as the aspect "of the matter believed" is prior to that of "the person believing" (*Summa Theologica*, II/II, q. 1, a. 2), it points to the foundation of faith which is not opposed to man but provides the setting for the opposition of the believer and the believed. This foundation is the

"First Truth", whose self-disclosure through the light of faith in man and through the historical mediations leads to the assent of faith (cf. *In Boethium de Trinitate*, 3, 1 ad 4).

4. *Hermeneutics of the coming of revelation*. In the bearers of revelation – the prophets, Jesus Christ, the apostles – God's self-communication becomes articulate speech (cf. *De Veritate*, 12; *Summa contra Gentiles*, III, 154; *Summa Theologica*, II/II, qq. 171ff.). The word of revelation is concentrated in the Apostles' Creed (*Summa Theologica*, II/II, q. 1, a. 6ff.) and its articles of faith. In medieval thought an "article" is a component, and also a principle of composition, in the indivisible totality which is mediated by speech as God communicates himself (*Summa Theologica*, II/II, q. 1, a. 6). Scripture contains both the content of these articles and many things which serve the *manifestatio*, the visible display of this content (*ibid*., ad 1). Since "the truth of faith is scattered throughout Scripture, clothed in many different forms of expression and sometimes only obscurely present" (*ibid*., q. 1, a. 9 ad 1), the Church's confession of faith is necessary (*ibid*., ad 3). This must adhere fully to "the doctrine of Christ and the apostles", in which "the truth of faith is sufficiently propounded" (*ibid*., q. 1, a. 10 ad 1). Through its mediation through Jesus Christ and the apostles it is linked with the "First Truth". Through this mediation, which guarantees the identity and the content of the truth, each of the faithful shares in the First Truth itself. For "faith adheres to all the articles of faith by virtue of the one motive: for the sake of the First Truth, which is put before us in the Scriptures, which are rightly understood according to the norms of the teaching Church" (*ibid*., q. 5, a. 3 ad 2). Thus we do not hear God's words, but as members of the Church we take part in a language-event brought about by God's action. In this event the First Truth reveals itself (*ibid*.), and the teaching authority of the Church is so closely linked with Scripture that it can expound the truth of faith contained in Scripture in terms of the discussions of a given period, for the good of the faithful (*ibid*., q. 1, a. 10 ad 1). The Church is the "subject" of faith (i.e., believer) (*ibid*., q. 1, a. 9 ad 3) and not an object of faith in the strict sense (*ibid*., ad 5). The object of faith is the sanctification wrought in the Church through the Holy Spirit (*ibid*., q. 1, a. 8).

5. *Theologia negativa and the dialectic of the "Three Ways"*. Within this salutary event, what is the value allotted by St. Thomas to the doctrines of faith (the propositions of theology) and their truth? His exposition of the "Yes" of faith is that it is an assent to propositions which are accepted as true (correct) without any fear of the opposite meeting the case (cf. *ibid*., q. 1, a. 2–4; q. 2, a. 1). But he also affirms, with St. Augustine, that this assent remains *cogitatio*, i.e., questioning consideration, till faith is succeeded by the eternal vision. Further, the guide-line of all discourse about God, that is, of all theology, is that "we cannot know what God is, but only what he is not" (I, q. 3, prologue). And even this negative knowledge is only "something in the nature of knowledge" (*Summa contra Gentiles*, I, 14). But faith, using a way not that of reason, can penetrate through what is expressible and attain "to the reality", that is, to God (*Summa Theologica*, II/II, q. 1, a. 2 ad 2). Thus faith and the theology which expounds faith seem to be strangely poised between knowledge and ignorance. How precisely are they to be explained?

They represent the climax of the mediated and hence negative character of all knowledge. "We can designate a thing by name insofar as we can know its nature from its properties and effects. Since we can know the essence (*substantia*) of stone in its proper being through its nature [as it unfolds its essence there], knowing as we do [already] what a stone is, the word 'stone' designates the nature of the stone as it is in itself...

But we cannot know from the action of God the nature of God as it is in itself, so that we could know what it is. We can know it only by the way of eminence, causality and negation . . . This is the sense in which the word 'God' designates the divine nature. The word was introduced to signify something that is above all things, that is the source of all things and is different from all things as the wholly other (*remotum ab omnibus*). This is what was meant by those who give God a name" (*Summa Theologica*, I, q. 13, a. 8 ad 2). Eminence, causality and negation are not three different approaches to God, any of which may be taken at choice. They are three moments of a dialectical process of knowledge. God, whose existence is known as the cause of all, is known at the same time as the wholly other, beyond all that is knowable. The only progress in this knowledge is a more and more precise negation (*Summa contra Gentiles*, I, 14). "Hence the supreme possibility of human knowledge of God is that man knows that he knows nothing of God, inasmuch as he knows that all we know of God is surpassed by that which God is" (*De Potentia*, 7, 5 ad 14).

D. The Understanding of Human Nature in the Tension of Theology and Philosophy

1. *The fulfilment of human existence (beatitudo) as the corner-stone of theology.* The supreme possibility of man in his earthly existence is to be open, in the dialectic of knowledge and ignorance, to the self-communication of God. The theology of St. Thomas, who is concerned only with God, takes man for its theme because man is "ordained to God as his origin and end" (*Summa Theologica*, I, q. 1, a. 7), because he is orientated to a fulfilment in which God gives himself in direct vision (*ibid.*, I, q. 12; I/II, q. 2, a. 8; q. 3, a. 8); because the incarnation of God is the ground of this union with God in vision; because this union with God is the only fully successful human existence (*Summa contra Gentiles*, III, 48ff.).

Thus faith is concerned with the being of God in which our happiness will consist, and with the providence of God, by which he guides us to his happiness (*Summa Theologica*, II/II, q. 1, a. 7). Trusting in God's guidance, the movement of hope leads to the enjoyment of God, "since man cannot hope for less from him than himself" (*ibid.*, q. 17, a. 2). And "since there is really a fellowship of God and man, inasmuch as he communicates to us his happiness, this fellowship must (*sic*) give rise to friendship", which we call "caritas" (*ibid.*, q. 23, a. 1). The word friendship was uttered by Jesus Christ (*ibid.*, citing Jn 15:15), "who has shown us in himself the way of truth along which we can attain through the resurrection the happiness of eternal life" (*Summa Theologica*, III, prologue).

2. *Desiderium naturale as the basic situation.* St. Thomas investigates philosophical tradition as regards this definitive achievement of human existence. The theme of the Platonic *eros* in the form of the Augustinian longing for happiness, the Aristotelian and neo-Platonist longing to know and see, the ancient and medieval notion of a purposeful nature – all are combined in the keyword *desiderium naturale*. For St. Thomas, it is the innate desire of the finite spirit for everlasting being (*Summa Theologica*, I, q. 75, a. 6; *Summa contra Gentiles*, II, 55). It springs from the perception of "being as such" (*De Anima*, 14) and appears in the double form of the desire for happiness and for the vision of the First Truth (*Sententiis*, 4, disp. 49; *Summa contra Gentiles*, III, 25ff. etc.). This "natural desire" is not to be assigned to any particular faculty of man. It is rather a basic

situation of human existence, which is determined by the desirability of that which is-in-all, and always reaches out beyond the finite offer of fulfilment in each particular being. As an open "movement towards the future" (*De Spe*, 1, ad 6) it can take the form of resignation, despair or hope (cf. *Summa contra Gentiles*, III, 48; IV, 54).

3. *Hope as sketch-plan and as expectation of salvation.* Hope, if it is to be a responsible disposition, a virtue, can only exist where man, believing in God's self-communication in Christ, looks expectantly to God as the friend who not only makes possible the ultimate fulfilment which is impossible to man himself, but does so in such a way that it is given to man as his own possibility (*Summa Theologica*, II/II, q. 17). This hope of salvation, with its non-intellectual certainty, contains the confidence which Luther learned to look upon as the decisive criterion of faith. Like the fiducial faith of Luther, it is seen in the perspective of the individual, because it is only the individual who can accept his supreme possibility as a gift from the helper God. St. Thomas actually asks whether one can hope for another, and his answer is: "When union in love with the other is presupposed, one can hope and long for something for another as for oneself; and in this sense one can hope for eternal life for another insofar as one is united to him in love" (*Summa Theologica*, II/II, q. 17, a. 3). But it is in the line of St. Thomas's thought to say that we can insert the degrees of hope into the "We" which is constituted by the priority of the common good to that of the individual. For "the final goal of the many in society is not to live virtuously but to attain the beatific vision of God by a virtuous life" (*De Regimine Principum*, I, 15). The right is to be realized in common so that an order of peace may be attained in which men help each other to find the truth and impel each other to goodness (*Summa contra Gentiles*, III, 128). This order of peace prepares the "blissful fellowship which is called the 'heavenly Jerusalem'" (*De Caritate*, 2).

4. *Anthropology and theological eschatology.* The historical situation of St. Thomas is strikingly illustrated when anthropological interests come into conflict with theological tradition. The tension is noticeable, for instance, when an astonishing number of arguments are invoked to show that the full beatitude of man involves the body (I/II, q. 4, a. 6, arguments 1–6). On the theological level, the debate envisages the "Greeks" (cf. *Summa contra Gentiles*, IV, 91; *De Rationibus Fidei*, 3). But the tension is more marked between philosophical anthropology and theology. "Without the body the soul lacks its natural perfection" (*Summa Theologica*, I/II, q. 4, a. 6).

"The soul without the body is not man" (*ibid.*). The answers, which we do not find satisfactory, endeavour to show that the spiritual vision of God in his essence is the essential element of the blessed fulfilment, and that the being of man is fundamentally affected by this fulfilment (*ibid.*, ad 2). But this perfection is increased in extension by the resurrection (*ibid.*, ad 5). Man is only fulfilled when his glorified body serves the spirit in full harmony and gives it expression (*Summa Theologica*, I/II, q. 4, a. 6; cf. *Supplement*, 80ff.; *Sententiis*, 4, disp. 44, 1, 2, q. 1).

5. *Individuated species or person?* Theological interests extend the conflict into philosophical anthropology itself. The body goes to make up perfection – but by virtue of its being material is in the nature of a limit. The individual man appears as a particular case of human being (cf. *Summa contra Gentiles*, I, 44; III, 65), though at the same time, like God and the angels, he is a person, "the independent individual being of a rational nature" (*Summa Theologica*, I, q. 29, a. 1 [*citing Boethius*]). The use of the word "person", intro-

duced by the ancient Church in Christology and the theology of the Trinity, obliged theologians to take an analogous approach in working out the philosophical understanding of man. St. Thomas starts with freedom as "dominion of one's own act" (*Summa Theologica*, I, q. 29, a. 1) and concludes to the selfhood of the person (*ibid.*, a. 3 ad 1). Hence man as a person is not an individual case of a species but unique by definition (cf. *ibid.*, ad 1; *De Potentia*, 9, 2 ad 1). This principle, which contains in germ the history of the modern ontology of freedom, did not become in St. Thomas the foundation of his anthropology, but pointed nonetheless to consequences for the moral action of man. If, as our hermeneutical principle suggests, we understand the thought of St. Thomas as a process, we can think today along with the Thomas who points on to the modern era and lives by tradition, against the Thomas who was a prisoner of traditions partly imposed by authorities, and who could not fully and systematically attain the goal to which his thought impelled him.

Paulus Engelhardt

THOUGHT-FORMS

The problems set by the "forms (or modes) of thought" have been treated under various names and from various viewpoints since the beginning of modern times. Differences in thought and styles of culture came to be consciously noted and analysed, and the experiences of the wars of religion led to human thought and knowledge being considered as something relative. This relativist view celebrated its greatest triumphs after the collapse of German Idealism into historicism in the 19th century. Comte speaks of various *stages* in man's view of the world and concept of science, Brentano of *phases* of philosophy, Kant announces the change in the *type of thought* with his critique, Trendelenburg constructs on the basis of fundamental logical concepts a typology of philosophical systems, Dilthey uses history to distinguish three *basic forms* of systems, Wölfflin demonstrates the presence of *categories* which determine styles in the history of art. Jaspers works out a psychology of general views of the world (*Weltanschauungen*), considering the various *techniques of thought*, Scheler seeks to determine in his sociology the main *kinds of knowledge*; Bocheński uses the term *methods of thought*, while Spranger speaks more comprehensively of *forms of life*.

The expression "thought-form" (form or mode of thought) was introduced into philosophical discussion by H. Leisegang. He understands by the term "the inwardly consistent sum of the rules of thought which results from an analysis of the writings of an individual and which appears likewise in other writers as the same structure". Its graphic presentation is the *Denkmodel* or paradigm of thought. Thus he investigates the circular form of thought as it appears from Heraclitus to St. Paul, and down to Hegel with his "circle of circles", and also the architectonic contrast to this organic type of thought, which is the "pyramid of thought", as in Aristotle, the Summas of the scholastics and Kant. The paradigm points in each case to a certain *Weltanschauung*, a general view of the universe, which is given its particular stamp by the dimension which predominates in the perspective. Hence thought-form means more precisely the sum of concepts and conceptual operations which are valid for the logical structure of a field of similar objects, and which then are transposed to other fields, to which they do not apply in the same way. Different fields of objects demand different types of logic. To investigate thought-forms it is therefore necessary to reduce the various systems to the precisely limited truth which they present (or start from), and also to work out their various logical structures, which should be fully enumerated and presented in a manual of logic.

A. Kandler takes up the expression and understands a thought-form as "the uniform structure of the rules" according to which a thinker "takes the individual tools of logic which he uses and applies them to form concrete assertions, as read in his works". This definition is narrower than that of Leisegang. The latter takes a number of typical texts and uses "ideating abstraction" to try to give a general picture, while Kandler takes each text of an author and investigates relative frequencies: "The oftener a tool of formal logic occurs, the more characteristic it is as an expression of the thought-form."

In consequence of Heidegger's concept of the history of being and the fate of being, the term is used in J. B. Metz to treat of ontology and not the psychology of thought. It now means man's comprehensive understanding of being and of himself, the horizon that encompasses all events, and gives its essential nature to an epoch in the history of the spirit. And it is this general understanding which is determinative, no matter how great are the formal and material differences between the thinkers of the epoch in question – as for instance in Greek or modern thought. In this sense the thought-form can only be determined by the use of the hermeneutic circle: the discovery of the unspoken principle behind the statement – a principle ultimately beyond the range of speech – is only possible through investigation of the statements, but the statements can only be properly understood in the light of the principle. This sort of insight is outside the scope of the "objectivity" of Kandler's method, and it is also more "subjective" than Leisegang's ideation. It means that one must enter the mental horizon of another, without losing sight of or becoming fully and consciously aware of the special *a priori* of this understanding: it can only be "coascertained" in the very effort of understanding.

Here we can see at its clearest a principle which also holds good for the other views: that a thought-form is never merely a form and that it cannot be adequately distinguished from the content, difficult as it may be to establish definite laws for their corelationship. This is just as impossible as it is to enumerate completely all forms of logic and thought. For both the forms of thought and the assertions themselves stem from the transcendental experience which the finite spirit has of beings and of itself. This experience takes place historically as an exercise of man's freedom and is therefore by the nature of things not fully open to inspection. What remains within sight is the very general structure of this experience, of the spirit and of beings. It has been set down in general logic, which, contrary to the tenets of psychologism and relativism, is the basis and framework of all its concrete data, where some fields of knowledge are more favoured than others and where expression, development, end and object vary, as well as presentation and interpretation. Groups of data take shape which may be investigated, related to one another and arranged according to type; possibilities of thought-forms as yet unrealized may suggest themselves; but a "full index" and complete systematization is on principle unattainable.

It is equally impossible to establish fixed laws for the origin, flowering and decline of the thought-forms of individuals or of epochs. A thought-form may develop new possibilities and a fuller life as freedom becomes more aware of itself and as stimulating contacts are made with other forms – though an encounter may be the impulse to withdrawal and ossification as well as to open-mindedness. "Classic" thought-forms are those which display a higher degree of universally valid truth and which can be taken over by later generations. But every thought-form is caught up in the dialectic of having to grasp and express the infinite truth in a finite way. If it claims to be an absolute, it becomes an ideology. But an ideology would be no less sceptical or relativist renunciation of truth. Every stride towards the truth, such as can be registered for instance in the validity of formal logic, enables us not merely to understand one thought-form from another, but also to judge the value of their various assertions, that is, to make the fundamental distinction between "not fully adequate" (which holds good in varying degrees in each case) and "false" – difficult though the decision may be in any given case. In his encounter with other thought-forms, man must become aware of his own, and recognize the validity and the limits of each, while seeing therein the absolute claim of truth, which calls him perpetually to new horizons.

Jörg Splett

TIME

A. The Theological Dimension

1. The theological question as regards "time" must be posed in the context of the coming (or offer) of salvation, when man is summoned to decision, to accept salvation in fact, in his freedom. Hence the theological question does not start from a notion of time derived from the natural sciences. It is concerned with man's self-understanding as a being in need of and capable of salvation – an understanding which is prior to the view of man gained from science and technology.

Hence when theology inquires into time and the temporal, it asks what are the conditions of possibility for the history of freedom, and hence for the history of salvation, in mankind and in the individual. As Catholic theology understands the relationship between salvation and natural reality, between grace and nature, salvation-history and world history, the reality prior to and under grace is integrated into the total reality of salvation-history, but without losing its own structures. It is the *potentia oboedientialis* of which the supreme possibility is realized, remaining in a new form in the totality of salvation. Hence even in the deployment of salvation-history the concept of "natural" time remains, and since it is the time of man, it is an interpersonal, dialogal time. For it is impossible to "demythologize" time in such a way that the empirical "worldly" course of time would have no meaning at all in this history of salvation. Otherwise some dimensions of reality would have absolutely no meaning for salvation, or would be excluded. Salvation, justification, would not attain the realm where the world, time, the body, are found. But Christianity, the coming of salvation, aims at the salvation of man as he is in the concrete, in all his dimensions.

2. The Christian faith confesses that the world was created with a beginning in time, and rejects the notion of a "world existing from eternity" as heretical (*D* 428, 501–3, 1783). It confesses one irreversible history of salvation and perdition, and rejects the "eternal return of all things". It confesses the saving character of particular events of history and awaits the end of all history. It assigns man a history, in freedom, which cannot be repeated at will and cannot be subjected to endless revision. History here appears as the production of the definitive in which the course of time is absorbed into its definitive harvest, which faith then calls "eternal life". Scripture uses the terms "the fullness of time", "the hour" (the single, appointed opportunity bestowed on freedom with regard to salvation), the "once only" (ἐφάπαξ, the

single event which, though only part of history, determines history irretrievably for ever). But faith also takes note of the external time which flows on, seeing it as the power which enslaves but which man is freed from by the grace of God in Christ. And faith knows of the time of salvation, in which man can act through grace in a way which remains valid for ever. The full act of faith includes as an inner element the virtue of hope, which takes him into an open future – which he still, however, awaits – a future which his independent planning can never master. Faith confesses the providence of God, by which he is not only Lord of time, but also guarantees an ultimate meaning of time for history. When speaking of the incarnation of the Logos, faith confesses that time becomes a predicate of the God who is immutable "in himself" and accepts and experiences his own real history "in the world". In the analysis of the history of revelation and the history of dogma, time and the reality of revelation are confronted with one another. The result is clear. Time is not just a determination of physical and material reality. It is also a determination of the spirit. Since the history of nature and the world is essentially determined by the history of freedom, it results clearly that the flow of time is not a power which enslaves man but a particular and deficient element of the personal, dialogal time of freedom.

3. In all the above statements, the notion of time is drawn from ordinary human experience. It is presupposed, but not further explained. But revelation does not eliminate the transcendental nature of man as it realizes and hence explicates itself, and it does not blot out this horizon. Hence theology, in its effort to give an account of itself, may have recourse to the perspectives of human selfhood as outlined by philosophy. But one must bear in mind in such a procedure that once revelation has reached its goal, there is a unity between the transcendental experience of self (in time) and man's eschatological experience of himself in and through Jesus Christ, as given in the history of revelation and salvation. But it is only this unity which enables "natural" reality to be displayed in all its dimensions. A merely transcendental explanation of man necessarily falls short. For it does not clearly contain the epochal, historical criterion of self-understanding. But the objectivating experience of time takes place on principle in the same dimension in which the history of revelation is deployed.

4. The statement of the Christian message cannot dispense with any of the various elements of the understanding of time – even though these again have a "history" in the self-understanding of man, in which they stand out with different degrees of clearness. Two elements in particular are theologically relevant.

a) One element is that of succession, movement, in the duration of the temporal. The succession is seen as objective and its dimensions are considered in the perspective of the cosmos. This is the aspect under which the Greek, Western tradition apprehends "external" time. Time is extrapolated from the flow of the "Now" and becomes a quantifying, measuring, continuous homogeneous field (*per se* empty). Every moment is of equal importance and each lives by the annulment of the previous. The movement of the world and hence of man takes place in this medium. Here man is exposed to time and made its slave, as though to a cosmic power. He does not himself form time, strictly speaking, either individually or collectively. The classical definition is given by Aristotle, where the formula derives from an objectivist view of physical reality: "numerus motus secundum prius et posterius" ("the enumeration of movement as encountered within the horizon of the earlier and the later") (*Physics*, IV, 11;

219b; cf. Plato, *Timaeus*, 37, 10f.). This then came to be dominant in the philosophy and theology of the Middle Ages, as in St. Albertus Magnus (*Summa Theologica*, I, 21, 2) and St. Thomas Aquinas (*Summa Theologica*, I, q. 10, a. 1–6; *Contra Gentiles*, I, 15, 55; *In octo libros physicorum Aristotelis*, IV, 15–23). *This* concept of time was then transferred into the region of the subjective, as by Kant, for whom it was "a form of intuition given with the subjectivity", or by Hegel, for whom it was "negativity" (time as self-negation, as the presence of constant self-elimination, as the negative-in-itself, as the negation negating itself). But this introduced no essential change into the Greek notion of time.

b) What is primarily relevant in theology is, above all, as follows from what has been said, "internal", qualitative, time, which is seen as filled with content and measured in terms of man – time as event. It is formed by the free deployment of interpersonal presence. Time exists as the event in which the definitiveness of existence is freely brought about before God. This element of the time experienced by all men only becomes explicit in the specifically Christian understanding of existence. It is only when revelation-as-history colours fundamentally the (transcendental) understanding of existence that history is seen in its true light – in the light of revelation as event. This notion of time was first given speculative expression by St. Augustine, in his deduction of time from the self-interpretation of presence (existence) (*Confessions*, XI, 13–29). It was obscured in the philosophy of the Middle Ages and only comes to light again when man, the individual, is seen as a personal and non-interchangeable being (see *Person*), as the being whose essence it is to give itself its own reality and whose reality it is to have to find its own essence. This view is exemplified by Pascal, in Romanticism, in Schelling (with his philosophy of freedom, of the real positive act), in Kierkegaard and in M. Heidegger (who took from Dilthey and Yorck von Wartenburg the notion of man as a historical being, transferred it on to the ontological plane and expounded time in terms of history-of-being and the structural references of personal presence. Where theological anthropology speaks of man as "spirit" and "body", the difference and the unity of these two elements of the one time experienced by the multiplicity of men is also part of its statement. Hence when dogmatic theology speaks of time it cannot dispense with either element.

5. The ontologically prior and basic case of time and of its radical characteristics, as met with by man, is in his existence itself, in man's own action. Hence physical, objectivist, external time cannot be the starting-point for reaching the notion of time. Time, as the external measurement of time, remains extrinsic to existence in its temporality and its internal time. It hides the fact that measurement itself is possible only for a spiritual being which experiences what time is in the light of its own inner self-realization. The primordial notion of time must therefore be that it is the mode of becoming proper to finite freedom in bodily form: a coming from an unmastered beginning in a deliberate choice of one's own reality, and an arrival at the irrevocable unique completion of such an act. The oneness and distinction of these moments is the time of this existence. They are not therefore a pure succession of different elements. They form the *one* reality of time. The successiveness of experiences and the experience of this successiveness in time is not "explicable". They cannot be built into a synthesis composed of other elements, because the being and the experience of such would themselves be again under the sign of this temporality. But this existence, an internal time, brings on its eternity as it exposes itself

to the otherness of an "external" world, to its history and hence to the time which characterizes this history. This derives at once from the nature of man, of which the notes are the unity and plurality of transcendence and the *a posteriori*. For this means that existence is part of the world and external time, in spite of the true beginning and the internal time which existence implies. And it also means that existence can be deployed in internal time only by taking over world-time, though the two elements of the one time of man cannot be considered identical. Man's internal time is always alienated from him in external time, and he nonetheless only finds his internal time in the external time of the world.

6. Where the internal time of experience has not yet been truly a matter of reflection, and is merely a propriety of the external time in which it is entirely absorbed, external time becomes an endless succession of self-contained units of time, the eternal return of the same, cyclic time (for the time of mythical thinking). But since internal time must be understood as the unity of beginning and end before God, since it is a coming forth from God and a return to him, the cyclic pattern of time remains justifiable and necessary, since the "transcendental" end and the "transcendental" beginning can only be thought of in the categories which embrace objects and can only be brought about in external time. But then again, since external time can only be thought of as a condition of possibility of the internal time of human existence, and since this existence has a true end, the fullness of time, the linear interpretation of external time is also the ultimate truth about this time. Hence the two proprieties of time, the cyclic and the linear, are theologically indispensable.

B. The Future as the Fullness of Time

1. Man is individually and socially a being who always keeps a step ahead of himself, so to speak. He makes himself what he is by planning his future and projecting himself into the future. But this future is never a fully fashioned plan. It is composed of single and different elements whose time runs out, and whose space is cramped. The projected future is finite and therefore comprised on principle within a further future of unknown possibilities. But even this finite sketch means that man expects the bits and pieces to fall into place and the surrounding void to be filled. The future must not therefore be considered just in the light of a sketch-plan, but in the light of a hope which sustains and surpasses all plans.

The future forms therefore a thematic unity with freedom, history, hope, progress, meaning and the end of man. It takes on a specific meaning in a philosophy and a theology where man, society and the world are not interpreted in the light of a static, unchanging essence, but where nothing is given except as a challenge and all reality is meaningful only in the light of what it yet must be.

2. The future cannot then be explained in terms of what is foreseen and on the way because man himself plans it and provides the technical means of realizing it. This sort of future would still be directly part of the present (in spite of its being itself beset by uncertainties). And the future cannot be explained in terms of evolution, because here it would be merely a prospective stage of something materially identical in structure with what is already given. It is instructive to note that these two forms of the reduction of the future to rationalized planning and material nature can be combined, and do in fact combine to stimulate each other in modern technology.

The future in the true sense – as Western thought has learned from the Jewish-Christian experience of history – is an advent, that which "comes" of its own accord, not an evolutionary derivative or a technical goal towards which we march in well-mapped stages. We have to deal with it as something that outbids all plans and normative development, something in fact which, while making such foresight possible, always makes it questionable and provisional. The future is the uncontrollable and incomprehensible which is not amenable to man's power. While it gives man his power, it ranges incalculably beyond it. Though the future comes imperiously to be in the realm which man designs and experiences as *his* future, it always remains his coming master, even where he represses or forgets the truth.

Nonetheless, the future is never completely detached from the past and the present. It is necessarily derivative, since it comes from the past and the present. For the present is always generating the past, and thus creating the past that will be. And this past gives rise to what will be the bearer and determinant of the future, because it comes as the ground of freedom, over which freedom never has total control and which freedom, never being entirely realized, does not find fully perspicuous. What the present lets go thus returns in the form of what is to come. It is the historical power which determines and takes in the present which is on its way. But this connection would be impossible if the present were not open to the future that is always still outstanding. For without this future there would be no past, not merely in the verbal analysis which shows that there can be a yesterday only because of today (which is or was its future), but in the real sense, that yesterday would lose all meaning and hence "reality" if today had no morrow. Past and present stem from the realm of futurity. All individual and social existence is ruled by the arrival of what is to come. The ambivalence of the past as that which is gone and that which is preserved is paralleled by the two modalities of the future: the future that is arriving and the future that is outstanding. It is true that freedom transforms the future into the present and decides it beforehand, but the future makes freedom what it is and challenges it to be. What comes absolutely to the individual is the end, death, and in such a way that the individual never knows the end as something over and done with. But since the end as such comprises the end of all present moments, the present is always absolutely determined by this end.

The acceptance of the future means taking it in the indissoluble and inexorable unity of its modes – as arriving and as outstanding. It must therefore be hope and openness. The acceptance of the past as a determinant of the future implies a positive attitude to the past. It is appropriated in a mood which is the only real basis of a critical view of it and allows for legitimate historical change in the individual and society – through contrition or revolution, as the case may be. These are ways of taking over the past in correct detachment from it. Where the element of the past in the future is denied, expectation becomes utopianism or absolute revolution, and the present loses all inner connection with the structure of the future. But again, where the past is regarded as the full and adequate ground of the future, conservatism and a wrong traditionalism ensue, since repressive fears have thrust the incalculable elements of the future out of sight.

3. Since Christianity sees man, society and the world from the point of view of history of salvation, it rejects on principle the doctrine of a static essence. Man, society and the world, in the preaching of Christianity, are orientated to a history which so far from being doomed to the void, moves towards a future of fulfilment. This fulfilment has already been assigned to history, so that history itself takes place within this (meaningful)

future. Hence the message of Christianity can only be understood in the light of what it says of the future. Its interpretation of the past takes the form of a progressive unveiling of the approaching future. The meaning of the present for Christians is based on hopeful openness to the imminence of the absolute future which comes as a gift. This means that the essence of man, in Christian terms, may be defined as the possibility of attaining a future which has been definitively promised in the Spirit and the incarnation. But then the future is a state which is not encompassed by another, greater and still outstanding future which would diminish its significance. This dynamism towards the absolute future still outstanding has behind it a ground, norm and principle which reveal the horizon of the possible, and this principle is "the law of the beginning". But since the ultimate ground of the absolute fullness of reality and its last goal is God himself, who posits the beginning by making himself its goal, there is no realistic understanding of man, society and the world except in the light of the future. For the beginning is only fully disclosed there.

4. Christianity as a religion and as a doctrine about the absolute future recognizes no future utopias within history. It proclaims that the life of the individual is decisive for salvation, and as regards humanity, it affirms that history has an end. It rejects as utopian ideology any view which erects into an absolute, beyond which there could be nothing and nothing could be expected, any future planned by man, to be achieved by the means over which he disposes in the world. Christianity imposes no ideal of the future for the intramundane history of man or society, but leaves it to man, and indeed makes it his duty, to plan the future properly (Vatican II, *Gaudium et Spes*, art. 5; Paul VI's encyclical, *Populorum Progressio*).

"Provided no utopian ideology dictates some intramundane future as the absolute goal, Christianity is not merely neutral with regard to all rational planning of the world's future, but positively favourable to such efforts. The purposeful, active, planned construction of the intramundane future, the liberation of man as far as possible from subjection to the forces of nature, the progressive socialization of man for the sake of the greatest possible deployment of individual liberty, are regarded by Christianity as a task imposed by the God-given nature of man. Man's duty lies here, and it is here that he fulfils his real religious task, the openness of freedom, in faith and hope, for the absolute future" (K. Rahner).

5. Efforts are now being made to supplement or even replace the traditional notions of transcendence (the supposedly localized images of "the above") by a new and decisively trenchant "paradigm", that of "the future". Such efforts have every right to criticize the classical images, but the new models also have their limitations, which must be definitely affirmed. Even if one allows on principle the priority of the dimension of futurity (so Heidegger, Block; Moltmann, Metz, etc., in their different ways), one must insist on the otherness, the always greater dissimilarity (discontinuity in continuity) of the "absolute future" of God's self-bestowal, as opposed to all human and worldly future. In the same way, tradition has always insisted on the difference between our present and the *nunc stans* of God. It is not true to say that in the past eternity and transcendence were only understood "spatially" without the necessary distinctions, in the light of the present. But once this question of principle has been stated, we may say that in fact the "future" is the best term for the OT and Christian experience of God. It implies the power of God within history which transcends history (cf. J. Moltmann).

Adolf Darlap

TOLERANCE

A. Concept and Problems

This article does not deal with tolerance in the religious sense or with the juridical problems of tolerance in civil law or with the history of tolerance as it has in fact been. It is concerned with the problem of tolerance in social philosophy. For in spite of the claim to objectivity which every well-founded judgment must put forward, there is and has been a bewildering juxtaposition of claims to truth, which conflict with or exclude each other. The philosophical problem raised by tolerance has many aspects. Where theoretical differences take the form of a pluralism of world-views and systems of value, with competing claims in practical politics or in the social sphere, a fundamental problem of social philosophy arises. If the question is then asked as to the objective justification of social and political norms, with the futher question of the possibility of the knowledge of truth and the problem of truth at various levels, a problem of the metaphysics of knowledge arises. If the historical origins and development of philosophical thought are considered, with all their many discords, it is a problem of philosophy in general and of the history of philosophy. The philosophical problem of tolerance may be formulated as the confrontation of truth and freedom, which takes the form, as a rule, of either dogmatism or relativism. There is no generally acknowledged definition of tolerance in the concrete, and the question is whether anything beyond a formal criterion does not run the risk of falling into dogmatism. On the other hand, the practical consequences are such that a merely formal definition proves to be an illusory solution, open to all sorts of abuse. For these reasons, the best method seems to be to give first a historical analysis, on the basis of which the motives and intentions of the champions of tolerance may be recognized, and then to try to draw various systematic conclusions.

B. History and Development

The term tolerance in the modern sense first appears about the end of the 16th century. But the notion itself is much older.

1. As long as there is a system of values universally acknowledged as binding, the problem of tolerance does not arise. Conflicts arise only where there are ethnical or religious minorities, or in times of crisis or enlightenment, when earlier homogeneous structures break up. For this reason, nearly all programmes of enlightenment champion tolerance. This was done in a vague way by the ancient Sophists. Protagoras's "man is the measure of all things" was an implicit criticism of the traditional norms based on myth and religion, and hence raised the question of new principles of obligation. Gorgias doubted that there could be any demonstrable obligatory norms. Lycophron, after the break-down of traditional ethics, called for restrictions on the rights of the stronger. Antiphon, a contemporary of Socrates, took up again the contrast which had already been made between νόμος (custom) and φύσις (nature, necessity) to criticize purely traditional laws in favour of laws arrived at by mutual agreement. This is the first intimation of the notion of a "liberal" natural law.

In Critias, however, a radical rationalism led to totalitarian consequences. In his *Laws*, Book X, Plato demanded the death penalty for incorrigible atheists and adherents of strange religious cults, with an eye, no doubt, to certain followers of the Sophists. This open intolerance characterizes the radical solution of the problem in "closed" systems or world-views. It was put forward again and again in the course of history. Man can know the gods and hence the truth. The refusal of such knowledge and its consequences is equivalent to a surrender of the personality, and also endangers the fundamental consensus in the State which guarantees unity and survival. Truth is a *res sacra*. Men have to submit to this principle.

This relationship was first reversed by the Stoics. The *res sacra* was man, because he alone could know truth. Hence his principal virtues were *clementia*, *mansuetudo* and *humanitas*. Further, certain antinomies in knowledge suggested that the absolute claim of any given truth should not be overestimated. The ideal of the *sequi naturam* comes from a moral force intrinsic to man. Insofar as it is possible here to speak of the natural law, it is rather the consensus of all men than an authoritative deduction from first principles.

2. In the OT and NT, the problem of tolerance took concrete form primarily in the question of the relationship to other religions and to strangers (cf. G. Stählin, "ξένος", *TWNT*, V, pp. 1–36). On principle, the stranger was not regarded as an equal, and was even considered an enemy, but in fact a sort of civil code existed for strangers in the Israelite State, and they enjoyed toleration; "for God loves the sojourner" (Deut 10:18). All peoples are under the power of God. Christians are to acknowledge heathen superiors. All men are created by God and bear his law in their hearts. Brotherliness, peace and hospitality are central virtues. Israel had practically no missions to the heathen. The Christian claim to absoluteness, which has often enough led to intolerance, is subordinated to the claim of freedom and love. Tolerance can also be seen in the fact that the biblical writings have adopted elements from non-Jewish or non-Christian religions. But the speculative problem of tolerance – how the absolute claim of truth and the legitimacy of divergent opinions can co-exist in practice and also be brought into a satisfactory synthesis – was not explicitly raised, much less answered.

3. Tolerance in the Roman Empire was mainly a question of religious freedom. The prevalent opinion was put as follows by Cicero: "Sua cuique civitati religio est, nostra nobis" (*Pro Flacco*, 28). The practice, from which the Oriental religions, Judaism and the mystery cults benefited, was due no doubt primarily to Roman political expediency, but goes back, especially in Cicero, to the philosophical principles of Stoicism in its scepticism with regard to the absolute claims of any world-view. But where Roman imperialism felt its legitimacy threatened by the universal claim of a religion, its tolerance came to an end, as the persecution of Christians shows. It is a classical example of the limit-case where tolerance is equivalent to the abolition of the prevailing system of political co-ordinates.

Though Christians then claimed both internal and external tolerance for themselves (Tertullian), they kept to these principles only partially after the Edict of Milan had met their claims (313). They admitted the theological maxim, "credere non potest nisi volens". But the Christian Emperors violated this principle in favour of religious unity as a basis of empire, and outlawed paganism, in spite of the fact that its representatives such as Libanius and Symmachus appealed for tolerance. Justinian forbade heretics to hold public office. The unbaptized were regarded as outlaws. Some theologians like St. Ambrose, Lactantius, St. Athanasius and St. Hilary suggested peaceful methods, while some even recognized the good faith of pagans. But the Church soon left it to the civil power to impose penalties on pagans and heretics. In the case of the Donatists, St. Augustine also agreed that the laws should apply. A larger measure of tolerance came about only in the Arian Churches (Theodoric the Great). The problem of tolerance was complicated rather than solved by the unity of State and Church. Where the universal claim of a religion is supported by and supports the civil power, the best possible groundwork is laid for totalitarianism, that is, for intolerance.

4. In the Middle Ages too the unity of Empire and Church was predominant. A threat to the *sacerdotium* could only be seen as a threat to the *imperium*. The extrapolation of religious conflict into the political sphere seemed quite normal to medieval thought. But there were marked differences in the way in which heathens, Jews and heretics were treated. "Accipere fidem est voluntatis, sed tenere fidem iam acceptam est necessitatis" (St. Thomas Aquinas). The faith once accepted cannot be abandoned. Hence there was tolerance on principle for heathens and Jews, but not for heretics who called in question the legitimacy of *civitas* and *societas*. There were, however, constant outbreaks of persecution against Jews, and missions were at times forced upon heathens. The claim to absolute truth finally gave rise to the Inquisition. On the other hand, the distinction between error and the holder of error brought about a remarkable readiness to enter into discussion with the Aristotelian tradition of the Arabs and with Jewish and Greek philosophy.

This respect for other cultures and world-views took concrete form in a number of famous dialogues in which for the most part a Greek or Arab philosopher, a Jew and a Christian theologian debated the truth of religion (cf. Abelard, Ramon Lull, Roger Bacon, Dante, Nicholas of Cusa, etc.). But these discussions resemble later dialogues on tolerance only in their form, since they all ended with the proof that Christianity was the true and universal religion. The tolerance of these dialogues does not consist in their material results, but only in their form. Nonetheless, only the stronger arguments were supposed to be valid, which implies that the criterion for religious truth is its rational justification. And in contrast to the purely immanent procedures of prevailing theological argument, this represented important and far-reaching progress. The ground was laid for a rational discussion of tolerance, once theological premises had lost their binding character. As a speculative theory, this attitude appeared in Nominalism with its abandonment of the presumed unity of theology and philosophy, of God and the world, of subject and object. It became a factor of Church history at the Reformation, when various forms of Christianity put forward claims to absoluteness. In politics, it characterized the wars of religion and later edicts of tolerance.

5. The immediate effects of the Reformation were unfavourable to tolerance, in spite of the tolerant attitude urged by such leaders as Sebastian Franck, Melanchthon, Zwingli and Bucer. The old unity of *imperium* and *sacerdotium* was shattered. Its place was taken in Germany by the territorial principle of *cuius regio, eius religio*. Calvinism in particular developed many features hostile to tolerance, and the wars of religion added another. Nonetheless, the principle of freedom of conscience, which had been discussed in the Middle Ages, though there restricted in view of the indelible character of baptism, came to the fore again with the Reformation, while the philosophy of humanism helped to spread respect for the autonomy of man. The wars of religion, the Two-Kingdoms doctrine of Luther, the growth of nationalism and of independence in the States of the Empire led to the distinction between Church and State and inspired a number of edicts of toleration – not that they always guaranteed real tolerance, as may be seen from the "Act of Toleration", 1689, in England.

The methods of the natural sciences and the discovery of new cultures abroad likewise helped to make Christianity's claim appear less absolute. And the horrifying results of the wars of religion brought the moral aspect of humaneness to the fore. J. Bodin used the example of a real and artificial apple, which could not be distinguished from one another, to demonstrate the relativity of knowledge. F. Bacon put forward in his *Novum Organum* an anti-Aristotelian notion of science by which alone the distinction between idols and real ideas, superstitition and faith, was to be possible. With intolerance prevailing in fact, thinkers took refuge in model utopias to show how a State based on reason could overcome confessional quarrels. St. Thomas More depicted a State which preferred the free exercise of religion to all compulsion in matters of faith and conscience. The criterion of the truth of a religion was its demonstrable rationality. The freedom of the individual was restricted only by the recognition of certain minimum religious demands, but T. Campanella in his *Civitas Solis* presented an extremely rationalistic picture of an all-powerful State where all demands for freedom would again be regulated strictly according to absolute principles. This programme of a high-minded dictatorship anticipated features of the profane totalitarian States of the modern era, since the problem of tolerance was bypassed once more for the sake of a pseudo-religious principle of unity. F. Bacon, however, in his fragment, *Nova Atlantis*, anticipated some deistic notions. Religion appears as an attribute of reason and as a humanism. This tendency is even clearer in J. Toland, with his book *Christianity Not Mysterious* (1696): the truths of faith are all truths of reason and hence matter for debate. Hence the tendency which had already appeared in the Middle Ages, to subordinate religion to reason, came into play in the discussion of tolerance. It was a way of avoiding the dilemma of contradictory claims to absoluteness. And at the same time the dangerous principle was enunciated that freedom and truth should be regulated and determined in the name of a rationalistic system of unity (Campanella).

6. These two components characterized the problem of tolerance in the modern era. The apotheosis of reason meant that confessional controversies were dismissed as futile. In Hobbes's *Leviathan* the all-powerful State, the "natural kingdom of God", is completely in control of the religion as well as the freedom of the citizens. The State is the only mediator of God, whose will it determines in a certain way. Tolerance is reserved only for inward faith, but no public manifestations of the latter are allowed. This reduction of tolerance to the private, internal realm, with strict regulation of public freedom, presupposes a difference between the mind of the individual and that of the all-powerful State, but cynically subordinates the problem of tolerance to a rigorous principle of order. Spinoza likewise grants the State the strict right to judge all actions, but his supreme norms are justice and love, since his aim is to guarantee freedom to all citizens, a freedom which in matters of thought and judgment remains inviolable (*Tractatus Theologico-politicus*). Respect for freedom of judgment is based on man's rational faculties, which necessarily grasp all being as the explication of God (*Deus sive natura*). But then freedom is again subject to a determinism, and tolerance is possible only within a predetermined frame of reference.

John Locke urged separation of Church and State, saw the State as constituted by the common consent of the citizens and not on metaphysical grounds, and demanded the separation of executive and legislative powers, with equal rights for all citizens. These principles made him the father of Liberalism and enabled him to be the first upholder of a theory of tolerance which avoided the conflict between rationalistic determinism and the absolute claims of a given world-view. The rights of man are inalienable. The task of the State is merely to safeguard the individual with his property and freedom. A distinction is made between civil law and divine law, though religion is still recognized as the source from which all that surpasses reason may be known. There is only one limit to tolerance: a danger threatening the State itself, as the guarantor of the freedom of the individuals (*A Letter concerning Toleration*). This may be all very well as a formal principle, but its application by Locke is highly questionable. Tolerance did not apply to Catholics and atheists, because the Pope was a foreign ruler and atheists did not recognize the moral foundation of the State, which was the status of revelation as the ultimate binding force which gave legitimacy to all laws. In spite of these misgivings, nearly all modern democratic constitutions are based on these liberalist theories of tolerance: the freedom of the individual and the separation of Church and State. In the 19th century, Locke's theories were taken up and developed by J. S. Mill.

The English Enlightenment was the greatest promoter of the notion of tolerance, though mostly at the expense of theology and of the binding force of the knowledge of truth (to which "common sense" was preferred). The French Enlightenment on the other hand took on strongly anti-clerical traits. The Encyclopédistes like Condillac, Lamettrie and Cabanis put forward a sensualistic materialism, which provided, in Scepticism or a mechanistic metaphysics, a very doubtful basis for the tolerance which was always in demand (Bayle, Montaigne, Voltaire). These theses came to be of great importance for tolerance because they paved the way for republican and democratic notions of the State. These political theories presupposed the enlightenment and maturity of the individual. This call for emancipation has remained, down to the present day, the fundamental element of the imperious demand for tolerance and the ground of its legitimacy. It went hand in hand with the demand for public freedom of speech.

The opposition between the denominations played an important role in Germany, where G. L. Lessing was one of the protagonists. In his *Education of the Race* he comprised "errors" among the elements of development. History was to bring about a reconciliation between reason and faith in a "Third Age of the World". Lessing's views were marked by Christian thinking and a certain sense of the historicity of knowledge. Critical reflection and the smoothing out of thesis and antithesis in German Idealism may be seen to some extent as the working out of Lessing's notion of tolerance, though the problems connected with it were never given any great attention in philosophy. But the dominant principles of Idealism, the autonomy of reason and will, include the suppositions which have been of abiding importance for the notion of tolerance. Independence, freedom, does not mean dispensing oneself from objectivity but consists precisely in finding its fulfilment in the truth.

C. Analytical Summary

This brings us to the real problem. Since what tolerance aims at is truth, how can it be exercised at all if it means being patient with opposing views and therefore must renounce, at least to some extent, the effort to spread what seems to be the truth?

To define tolerance as mere patience is unsatisfactory. This is a relativist view of tolerance, and would be self-destructive. Politically, such formal tolerance is clearly untenable, since it would imply liberty for groups who would exploit this tolerance to set up power-groups who would themselves be intolerant. To avoid such formalism, one must consider the conditions under which an objective grasp of truth can be attained. For if truth is multidimensional, and cannot in the concrete be the monopoly of any group, it is possible to justify tolerance by the impossibility of attaining absolute truth. Here, of course, we are not speaking of the functional notion of truth in the natural sciences. It is a matter of the notion of truth in the "practical sciences" whose task it is to determine social norms.

Dilthey defined the truth valid for a given epoch as the expression of the way of life which it found meaningful. This meant that all claims to objectivity were whittled away and made relative to each epoch adduced in historical comparisons. For when "life" is the basis of all cultural norms, we are left with an irrational standpoint. Nonetheless, Dilthey's thesis points on to the "history and historicity" of truth, as propounded later in fundamental ontology, though here again the criteria for the valid exposition of truth, as being disclosing itself in history, remain problematic. Tautological solutions may be the only result of the analysis of practice undertaken by the philosophy of history.

To evade such ambiguities, philosophy of a positivist inspiration in its many branches reduces its claim to truth to formal logic and empirically verifiable analytical propositions. All other normative propositions are said to be scientifically incapable of demonstration. Hence objectivity is unattainable in the "practical" sciences, where pragmatical procedures should rather be aimed at. To proceed pragmatically means that objectivity is replaced by the criterion of success, and hence that social norms are replaced by lines of conduct whose success can be checked. But since "success" is again a relative, subjective criterion, pragmatism cannot constitute an objective basis for the justification of tolerance. The "dialectical" social theories of Adorno, Horkheimer and Habermas insist that the individual is so conditioned by the system that he cannot see the flaws in the social code. Individual and society are so bereft of political sense that it is easy to perpetuate political and social forms which have become brittle and decayed. There are only vestigial traces of the public opinion which should hold a watching brief and criticize. And in fact criticism is genially absorbed by the "establishment" and exploited at once as a proof of its liberal views. Under such circumstances, formal tolerance is in fact repressive in character (Marcuse). Since the democratic urge is to a great extent domesticated by forces which actually function as coercive, objectivity becomes impossible. Then a false pluralism is appealed to, really a relativism, to avoid the charge of loss of objectivity. Since tolerance cannot be assured either by such relativistic pragmatism or by any dogmatic regulations, it remains for philosophy to develop a method by which the "practical sciences" can avoid this dilemma in defining tolerance.

Here it should be noted that the positivist method, and such claims as it has to objectivity, ignore the specific interests by which the "practical sciences" are guided. Their search is for a science of liberty. They strive to justify and further in present-day terms the emancipation of the human race which has taken place by virtue of historical imperatives. In spite of these terms of reference as a hermeneutical principle, there may well be differences in actual practice. Hence the principles underlying social practice must be upheld only hypothetically, that is, as propositions to be verified or falsified. Thus social and political life takes on the character of an experiment, based on a theory arrived at or tested empirically as well as speculatively (by dialectical interpretation). If such is the process of social and political life, the tolerance whose goal is social truth is provided with the best possible guarantees. The criteria by which it is justified are left open both to methodical and rational inspection and to the critical sense of public opinion. Tolerance is then in fact the outcome of traffic in communications all round. The purpose of tolerance is to protect minorities and to provide for a wide spectrum of freedom of opinion, while still aiming at least on principle at upholding truth and objectivity without dogmatic premises. It could be achieved in such a communicative society.

This notion of tolerance need not come into conflict in any way with tolerance as understood in theology. In any case, the machinery of tolerance is now under the control of the State, society and powerful social groups, while the Churches rather depend on tolerance than decide upon it. But even in theology and its understanding of truth, it is difficult – in spite of the obligatory character of fundamentals – to formulate concrete imperatives in a normative way, because the discovery of truth is a gradual process, mediated in many ways by historical factors, and always conditioned by contingency and concupiscence. The growing importance of hermeneutics emphasizes this fact. Creation itself must be treated with reserve in view of its eschatological destiny, and hence social practice is most in keeping with the theological understanding of the world when it retains its experimental character. And social planning based on and justified by an interest in human emancipation does not contradict the principles of theology: especially as the finite ends and aims of social theory must grant the "eschatological reserve" its due rights, inasmuch as it is the question-mark over all plans.

Werner Post

TOTALITARIANISM

1. Totalitarianism is a term applied as a rule indifferently to all systems of total control of individual and social life by the State. It is therefore formally speaking a type of society in which the essential dialectical interplay of spontaneous interaction, and social conditions as a pre-established form of interaction, has ceased to be an equilibrium. A given form of social self-interpretation predominates exclusively and consistently and is rigidly institutionalized in fixed systems of administration, public order and the linguistic media of self-interpretation.

2. The usual pejorative sense of totalitarianism comes from a fundamentally liberal notion of society which projects its counterpart into the concept of the "totalitarian State". The ideal is the "free citizen", the creative spontaneity of the independent self-determining individual who enters into the free interplay of well-balanced forces which are bound *a priori* to no fixed norms but constantly produce their own rules. He submits to certain legal restrictions of his sovereignty only where this is absolutely necessary. Against this background, totalitarianism appears as the reduction of all spontaneous self-development to a planned moment of a social process entirely organized by the State. No private realm is left for the direct creativity of the individual. Freedom is eliminated. This totalitarian image is primarily derived from the procedures of an irrational or abstractly rationalistic absolutism. Since its ideals, whether rigid or fantastic, are foreign to the social process and its intrinsic demands, it forces the individual into a dogmatic pattern which can only mean self-alienation for him and a total artificiality for society. The system can be maintained only by one form or other of terror. Hence in terms of liberalism, totalitarianism indicates the element of comprehensiveness in authoritarianism,

i.e., in the denial and thwarting of personal choice and way of life by outside forces. And authoritarianism represents the "intensive" element of totalitarianism, i.e., the moulding of a society in terms of abstract, *a priori* concepts which embrace all aspects of life.

3. *Totalitarianism and total social integration.* Liberalism sees only two alternatives. On the one hand there is the creative spontaneity of the private individual. On the other hand there is totalitarianism, the inhuman subjection of the individual to a pre-established overall pattern. The "authoritarian" society which imposes alien, coercive institutions is implicitly identified with the "totalitarian" which aims at all-embracing institutions. But the contrast now appears highly problematical. Every viable society is "total". It incorporates all realms of life without exception into a consistent process of social self-reproduction, self-organization and self-interpretation, of which the State is only a partial expression. And such realms as are left untouched are expressly excluded, that is, benefit in turn from a definite, pre-established pattern.

Hence social mediation is *de facto* total. All self-realization is conditioned by intersubjective (linguistic) truths and patterns of conduct, as also by a combination of social values. Freedom cannot therefore be, as liberalism imagined, the isolation of the individual from society. For the concession of such a completely private sphere within the totality of social mediation – of which the State and its laws are only a specific moment – can only be an illusory distortion of the actual conditions of such "privacy" or a privilege contrary to social equality. Thus real freedom can no longer be sought merely in formal opposition to totalitarianism. It can be found only in the social mediation itself and in the acceptance of its *de facto* totality. Society as a whole should be such that it offers the individual adequate play and imposes on him no foreign commands, but only those which are his own will but socially mediated and hence become real. In other words, freedom lies originally not outside the social process, even the State and its laws, but finds itself and its objective reality in society.

Under these circumstances, totalitarianism no longer has a positive counterpart in the self-understanding of bourgeois liberalism, and the ordinary sense of totalitarianism needs to be decidedly modified. Totalitarianism is not merely (though it naturally includes this) the "extensive" aspect of authoritarianism in society. Where it is consciously pursued, it indicates in a particularly explicit form the totality of the social process as it reproduces itself comprehensively in technology, economics, bureaucracy, politics, speech and reflection. It sees its task clearly as the construction of the totally-integrated society which demands regard for individual and interpersonal freedom and spontaneity. In other words, the dangerous element in totalitarianism is not the comprehensive nature of social interests. Danger arises when society's interest in the individual is dictated by abstract premisses and laws which do not stem from the dynamism of social equality but are justified by some extrinsic considerations and hence lead to authoritarian control and the resulting self-alienation of the individual and society.

Hence the alternative to totalitarianism in the pejorative sense cannot be the rejection of total social integration. It must be the elimination of all systems of rule which it would be the surrender of freedom to accept. It must be the effort to eliminate all self-alienation from the social context.

Konrad Hecker

TRADITION

God has revealed himself to man, and he has completed and perfected his salutary self-disclosure in the life and teaching of the incarnate Word, so that no new public revelation of God to man is possible till the parousia. In the encounter with Christ, in faith in his word and in allowing his grace to work, man receives his supernatural salvation. But how does the fullness of God's revelation reach the individual incorrupt and unmixed with error, so that the individual knows that he is really addressed and challenged by the word of God and not by one of the many claims of men?

The Christian answer to this question is: through the tradition of the Church. The word of God and his gifts of grace reach man through the preaching handed down in the Church. The mystery of Christ remains present in history because there is a fellowship of believers which in the vital process of life, doctrine and worship preserves the word of God, through the assistance of the Holy Spirit, through all the changes of history, and thus hands it on safely to all generations till the Lord comes in glory.

A. Tradition in Human History

What tradition means for human life in general may be most clearly illustrated from the exercise of human freedom. The spiritual nature of man, reaching out beyond any given concrete object of choice towards the Absolute – the transcendence of human freedom – is what makes possible all freedom of choice and also gives human freedom its religious seriousness. When man really acts freely, he always includes in his decision an attitude towards the Absolute, towards God. But this "experience" of the transcendence of freedom can never be grasped purely as such. It can only be experienced and known along with and through the given concrete object. But the bodily nature of human freedom means that though man reaches towards the definitive and the absolute in his self-determination, he can only do so by launching out towards "the other", towards the world. But this "other", through which the experience of transcendence in the free act is most truly to be grasped, and which makes the reality of freedom and the serious responsibility palpable, is the fellow-man. The self-realization of the person in freedom takes place primarily through intercourse with and conduct towards other persons. The You of the fellow-man is thus constitutive for each one's own freedom.

But the encounter with other men is always an encounter with history, with what has come about freely and outside the scope of the individual's power. The range of freedom within the scope of the individual is not merely – and not at all primarily – the area of permanently identical matter provided as it were by an abstract notion of nature. The free act of man is always co-determined by the history of others. In his intercourse with the persons around him, in his learning to speak, in his adoption of given thought-forms, in his manner of evaluating, judging and reacting, in his own self-understanding, man absorbs the history which is already living on in others. He takes over by necessity the thoughts, verdicts and values of others before him. But this means that man always lives by tradition. In his free growth towards definitive selfhood, man can only be and become himself as one who is inwardly stamped by tradition. It is only as stamped by tradition that he can adopt an attitude towards the world of men and things around him, accepting or rejecting the traditional. This determination of man's freedom by history will of course be experienced and recognized with different degrees of intensity at various epochs and at various stages of culture. Hence the attitude of the individual to tradition varies according to the period in which he lives. He either adopts it as "natural" and evidently acceptable, or he calls it in question, more or less radically, since he recognizes that it is the product of freedom and hence as not necessarily what it is. This gives rise to criticism of tradition, that is, the question as to what is of permanent value in the traditional, or what can and what must be changed in certain circumstances. The meaning and the problems of the natural law as the permanent norm of all criticism of tradition cannot be gone into here. But where a tradition has been established on the basis of a historical event, and where this historical event is also accorded permanent significance, the norm of a possible criticism of tradition must be primarily only the "return to the source", the investigation of what was originally experienced, done and meant.

B. The Catholic Notion of Tradition

1. *Living tradition*. As a religion of revelation, Christianity is based on a historical event: the life, teaching and death of Jesus of Nazareth, and on his resurrection as known in the faith of the apostles. The apostles experienced the historical event "Jesus of Nazareth" as the saving event wrought by God for them, and knew at the same time that it was the definitive saving event for all mankind. Hence by the mandate of the Lord, they bore testimony to that event. The words and signs of the apostolic testimony form the permanent basis of all Christian tradition. But the witnesses know in faith that their testimony is not just the handing on of a past event in words and memory, as if it lived on only in the subjective remembrance and was active only as an "idea". It is the risen Lord himself and his Holy Spirit who in this testimony of the apostles' faith challenges man's freedom, offers his grace and bestows his life. One of the great achievements of Vatican II was to free the Catholic notion of tradition from the narrow limits to which it had been confined, chiefly in the post-Tridentine period. In the Dogmatic Constitution on Revelation, tradition does not appear primarily as a certain amount of matter, always the same, handed on in propositions and practices. The tradition of the Church is rather faith as lived: "The Church, in her teaching, life and worship, perpetuates and hands on to all generations all that she herself is, all that she believes" (*Verbum Dei*, art. 8).

In the comprehensive sense, therefore, tradition is not primarily a "something", an objectified datum. It is not exclusively, when taken in its full sense, either the transmission of the word of God in Scripture or the handing on of truths and forms of piety not committed to writing. It is the faith of the Church in action, which is more than its expression in propositions both because Christ works in this faith and because not all that is done in faith is adequately accessible to reflection and expression. For this reason too, the living faith of the Church is also the ultimate nôrm for criticism of tradition within the Church. Of this more will be said later. Here it is enough to note that tradition, in this sense, is not only prior in time to any crystallization of it in Scripture, but is also at the base of all faith. Just because in the profane realm man encounters tradition and is formed by it in the re-living of history by others, so too the living tradition of the Christian faith is not something external and irrelevant to those who grow up or live in an area of Christian culture. Whether they like it or not, they always feel the impact of Christian tradition. Those who live in an area of Christian culture can only be themselves in contact with Christian tradition, in the acceptance or rejection of this living heritage.

2. *The content of tradition*. While it is true that the tradition of the Church is something more than the written word expressed in propositions or the word linked with the sign (see *Sacra-*

ments), it is also true that the Christian faith must be capable of expression and definition. It must be possible to formulate the faith founded on a historical event in such a way that the event remains accessible to all ages, since the event itself cannot be repeated. That a community of believers should give expression to its faith in writing is in fact a universal phenomenon. And this is what happened in the early Church. In the 1st century, the "apostolic preaching" was committed to writing in the books of the NT. Nonetheless, Scripture is more than just the first of a series of books which go to make up written tradition, followed so to speak by other books of equal rank. Inasmuch as this written testimony to the faith of the primitive Church was willed by God as permanently normative for later times, it is directly inspired by God. Thus Scripture is the word of God, to which the sense of faith in the later Church is always bound, from whose salutary force it is nourished and impelled, by which it must always direct its steps. And the magisterium of the Church functions merely as hearer and servant of the tradition of the primitive Church, as inspired by God and committed to writing in Scripture.

But what of the post-biblical traditions of the Church, the truths of faith which were only formulated in later times, which as such cannot be found in the writings of the NT and are "merely" the relevant actualization of the Christian faith for a given period? What must be the attitude of the Catholic to the tradition of his Church? That there is and must be such a post-biblical tradition – and not merely within the Catholic Church – and that such a tradition can in certain circumstances be the criterion of membership of the Church, follows from the "historicity" of the Church itself. But is it true, as Protestant theology holds, that all post-biblical tradition must on principle always be open to revision, so that the one valid criterion of tradition can only be the verbal tenor of Scripture? The Reformers, as we know, with logical justification as it would seem, demanded a return to the sources, that is, to Scripture, in order to get rid of the dead weight which had been piled up on the Christian faith in the course of history.

The progress and growth of the Catholic notion of tradition, particularly from Trent to Vatican II, cannot be gone into here. But it is easy to understand that Catholic theology should have taken over the starting-point of the Reformers and have tried to justify its tradition by referring it to apostolic times, either by a scriptural proof (which was not perhaps always very happy) or by the notion of a "second source" of revelation, that of the oral tradition stemming from the apostles. Here the following points should be noted. It is true that the writings of the NT may be considered as a more or less accidental collection of the works of various authors. The book, by its very nature, does not claim to present the content of the faith of the primitive Church without omissions. It may be admitted without misgiving that the faith of the primitive Church was more extensive, in a certain fashion, than what was committed to writing in the books of the NT. Nonetheless, there is no compelling reason to assume that the writings of the NT, being the permanent and divinely-willed norm for all times in the Church of later days, do not contain materially all the essential truths of the Christian faith. Further, it is very difficult for the modern mind, with its alert sense of the historical, to imagine that such truths of faith, not committed to Scripture, should have been preserved without error throughout the ages, in spite of changes of culture and language. Here a too hasty recourse to the assistance of the Holy Spirit would be out of place. And the appeal to what the Church has "always" believed and "always" taught also seems to be questionable, for the same reasons. And there is a further question put by the Protestant Churches which Catholic theologians have to answer. While it is unthinkable that there should be no actualization of Scripture and the Christian faith for a given age which could not be revoked at another time – one need only think of the early Councils with their Christological and Trinitarian decrees – it is also not immediately evident that the Marian dogmas of recent times, which are constantly evoked in this connection, are permanently valid actualizations of Scripture. This poses a question for Catholics, which *a priori* they must answer in the negative, as to whether something "new" has not here been defined as revelation, though it stems only from post-apostolic times and hence is no more than a pious custom, venerable perhaps by reason of its antiquity.

The general answer must be as follows. There is on principle no formulation of the faith in post-apostolic times – which is what is in question here – which could not be formulated otherwise. This again does not mean that it does not matter what formula is chosen to give expression to a given reflection on the faith. But the true preaching of the faith always calls for a new assimilation and translation of the traditional faith as well as loyalty to revelation and its historical transmission. Such a "translation", if only because it must start from the experience of a given age and speak the language of the times, will perhaps use new terms to formulate the Catholic faith, while still dealing with a dogma which remains the same. Words change their meaning in the course of history. Their significance and connotations change according to the situation in which they are spoken and the hearers to whom they are addressed. This means that even a literal repetition of doctrines of the magisterium from past times is also basically a translation.

It should also be noted that dogmatically binding declarations of Church doctrine can only be obligatory where they are concerned with truths which have been revealed by God *for our salvation*. The whole ministry of the word, including that of the authentic magisterium, is *under* Scripture. And the books of Scripture only teach "faithfully, firmly and without error that truth which God wanted put into the sacred writings for the sake of our salvation" (*Dei Verbum*, art. 11). This is also true of the infallible utterances of the post-apostolic tradition of the Church. These must also be investigated with a view to discerning their historically-conditioned elements, to demarcate the *salutary* affirmation which they tried to make to the people of their times. Only when this has been done can the effort be made to translate the kernel thus singled out in the truth of faith, and to adapt it to the language of the day. To transplant inconsiderately the doctrinal utterances of the past into a later age may well be to falsify them.

And finally, it should also be noted that Vatican II used the term "hierarchy of truths" (*Unitatis Redintegratio*, art. 11), which has often been quoted since. Obviously, in the course of two thousand years of history, a believing community will have worked out religious practices and forms of piety which must always be open to critical investigation, inasmuch as they have not been "defined". But it is also understandable that even the tradition which is acknowledged as inalienable and as part of the substance of the Christian faith derives from given historical situations of the Church. If the notion of a hierarchy of truths is taken seriously, while it does not of course mean that a believer could deny this or that truth of faith which has been defined in the course of Church history, it does mean that he can admit with an easy conscience that a doctrine of faith in the Catholic Church, defined at a given time, in a given thought-form and for a given situation, may be for him, under certain circumstances, "too far away" from the central message of Christianity, so that in his practical religious life it may mean little or nothing to him. The Catholic Christian, even while acknowledging the permanent truth of a doctrine of faith which has once been defined, can assign many things to the realm of his implicit faith. Catholic theologians take it for granted that not all revealed truths are part of the knowledge of the faith necessary for salvation. And it seems to be equally evident that the truth of a doctrine of faith does not depend on whether an individual Christian recognizes it as an actualization of Scripture and the Christian faith which is significant for his actual life. This is all the more true, as the notion of the hierarchy of truths suggests, as regards the doctrines of faith (such as the Marian dogmas) which are not so immediately relevant to God's saving event in Christ – even if only because Christians of a later date do not or do not yet realize the salutary message contained for them in these truths.

Under these circumstances, it is impossible to see why there should not be, under the assistance of the Holy Spirit, so clearly promised for the whole Church in Scripture, progress and growth in the understanding of the matters and words of tradition (see *Dei Verbum*, art. 8). And it is impossible to see why this should not take the form of the Church as a whole (which is infallible, cf. *Lumen Gentium*, art. 12) recognizing that a given truth of faith is not only obligatory for its own time but for the whole time of the Church, and declaring it to be so. It is not true that such an estimation of tradition would expose the word of God to the arbitrariness of a human magisterium, such as that of the Pope. For nothing can be defined which has not been long believed by the Church and recognized as belonging to the substance of faith. A definition of the magisterium stemming merely from the piety of a Pope or a minority in the Church has never in fact been proclaimed, and indeed cannot be possible. And conversely, it is simply unthinkable that, say, the Christological declarations of the early Councils – which as such are not contained in Scripture – will ever be denied by believing Christians, or that slavery – tolerated as we know in NT times – will ever again be considered compatible with the Christian view of man.

Bearing in mind that faith in Jesus of Nazareth cannot in any case be given to man only in the dead letter of Scripture, but comes in the living faith and confession of believers, and that this is on principle the way in which God offers man his grace in history, we can see that confident faith in the promised assistance of the Holy Spirit, for the ultimate decisions and formulations of faith, is perfectly justified. It must then be recognized that it is quite possible for living faith to express itself in such a way that this expression is permanently acknowledged as revealed in Jesus Christ. This remains true even if one's own insights fall short in one way or another of the insight of a past time and can no longer take it in and retrace its route. Hence the Catholic Christian knows that his faith in the tradition of his Church does not leave him at the mercy of an arbitrary human magisterium, just as he is not at the mercy of the state of exegetical science at any given moment or of his own intellectual powers. He knows on the contrary that even in post-biblical times he remains – not indeed as an individual, but as sharing the fellowship of all who believe along with him – under the assistance of the Holy Spirit in the ultimate and decisive matters of faith. And he knows above all that his own faith would be robbed of the requisite moral seriousness if an item of faith once recognized by the whole Church as belonging to the substance of the faith and as such defined, could be abrogated tomorrow or at any future time and declared to be false or null. "Consequently, it is not from sacred Scripture alone that the Church draws her certainty about everything which has been revealed" (*Dei Verbum*, art. 9).

Tradition (or its content) in the strict sense, which has been the subject of discussion up to now, that is, the doctrines of faith defined in post-apostolic times by the Church and its magisterium, must be clearly distinguished from the broad stream of traditions which also took form in other ways in the course of Church history. As regards such tradition, which of its nature does not make the claim to be infallible or irreversible, the attitude of the Catholic Christian will be in general much as it is towards his profane historical heritage. He will not be shortsighted enough to surrender to the basically very stupid idea that he and his times have "at last" arrived at the true sense of faith and piety, and that everything traditional can be revised at any moment by anyone and thrown into a new mould. In matters of faith above all, which are to a great extent independent of scientific and technical progress, one must reckon with the possibility that in many ways earlier times had clearer insights and perhaps greater grace. In addition, an institutionalized society like the Church needs laws and precepts, if the fellowship is not to disintegrate into a multiplicity which could only destroy all bonds of union and hence the fellowship itself. But on the other hand all Christians, above all in times when the Church as well as mankind in general is so alert to the notion of historicity, must be always open-minded enough to call the traditional in question and to look for new forms and formulations of religious life. in keeping with their own times. This is a possibility for the Church (and indeed, if one takes seriously the importance of charisms in the Church of God, it can even be a moral duty), simply because many things, no matter how ancient and venerable, need not necessarily have been inspired and willed by the Spirit of God. And above all, something that was once correct for the Church in the changes of society and cultures need not be equally valid for all times. It is true that all reasonable Christians will be mindful of the limits of their own insights. It is true that they have to respect tradition or traditions even in nondefined utterances. It is true that they must pay attention to and weigh carefully all papal directives. Nonetheless, contradiction of such traditions does not mean division from the Church. It may even happen, as has already been said, that the individual Christian or a group of Christians will have to shake off a religious form or doctrine which has outlived its day, even if they have to go against the protest of the hierarchical Church. Such changes in the traditional heritage, in a Church which does not confine its annals to stories of triumph and which is also the Church of sinners, were brought about in the past for the most part only by charismatics. And there will be little change in this matter in the future, no doubt. That such men may then have to suffer from their Church even to the limit of their endurance is to be expected, since they are members of an institutionalized Church and must submit to certain precepts and disciplinary measures. But the hierarchical Church must be reminded of the duty it has to learn to listen to the Spirit of God and to acknowledge a legitimate pluralism in the Catholic Church.

Karl-Heinz Weger

TRANSCENDENCE

A. The Horizon of the Classical Thinking on Transcendence

The notion of transcendence derives

from experience. Beings present themselves in their distinction from one another and in their definite contrast with nothingness as "what" they are, but they are still – in themselves – incomprehensible, strange and obscure. The fluid multiplicity and the constant mobility of beings make the question of their basic origin and purpose more insistent. The answer can clearly be derived only from some being which is "unmoved" and which as the eternal exists of itself and for itself, "separate" and free, as the first and ultimate ground of all movement. This Greek line of thought attains a "First" which implies, in view of the perpetual mutability and temporality of phenomena, a transcendence towards a being which is the ground of the permanence in nature ("essence") and is therefore ultimately that which is permanent in itself ("divine"). When then the reverse course is followed ("descent"), and transcendence proves itself capable of justifying the *per se* enigmatic and hence "criticized" phenomena (in their existence and mode of being), it establishes itself as also the preexisting "Beginning" of all things, their foundation and the source of their order. This beginning, in terms of cosmogony, is represented as the first temporal event. More correctly, however, this origin is thought of as an "absolute" beginning, since if in succession initially, it would be itself perpetually submitted to other conditions and would presuppose a "prior". As pre-temporal and time-founding origin, transcendence is not itself a "given", but is thought of as "thought of thought", as pure act (*esse ipsum*), as inexhaustible love, as eternal will and *hence* as non-temporal, eternal event and actuality. Western philosophy went more deeply into this fundamental relationship of transcendence, the "transition" from the "given" to its essence and from there to the first, supreme ground of all beings ("Being"), using the concepts of "Metaphysics", the "Absolute", the "Analogy of Being", "Act and Potency", "Participation", "Principle" and "Being" (see these articles). The demonstration of transcendence in the proofs for the existence of God starts with the contingency of the world and uses the principles of causality and necessity to establish a natural theology. Thinking in terms of transcendence uses the middle way of exemplarism to avoid the extremes of absolute identity and absolute difference. Transcendence is not a leap from a general idea to a "transcendent", indemonstrable reality, but takes place in the light of and by virtue of the primordial disclosure of the being of beings, which it refers to its "proper" nature – always there in a latent, non-explicated mode.

St. Thomas's notion of the *actus essendi* is one of the supreme achievements of thought here. Finite actuality of itself reflects through its exclusion of nothingness, its inner absoluteness and its pure "positiveness" the simple, absolute and unrelated ground. Through its *being*, it soars on principle into the divine uncreated life, which of itself fully eludes us in its own proper essence. The hidden ground of transcendence lies therefore in this "positiveness" of being, which pervades most profoundly all immanence and is nonetheless not simply absorbed there. Hence transcendence is both the far and the near, distance and intimacy. The difference within transcendence is as analogous as the unity. Precisely because it is as the absolutely Transcendent that God turns to the world in creation (and grace), he is the inmost principle, ground and goal of the creature. The immanence of transcendence in the creature does not sequestrate the finite being but brings it more radically to its ultimate validity and consistency. The closeness of transcendence and the independence of the creature grow in the same, not inverse, proportion. (This is also true of transcendence as grace.) In the light of this truth, and presupposing the dynamism of the divine being and of the perpetually active creative power of God, evolution, immanent fulfilment and "life" can be understood – when contemplated "from below" – as self-transcendence, in which a being goes beyond itself to a grade of being essentially higher and thus rises above itself. This fundamental relationship is displayed most clearly in the nature of the human person. Since it is transcendence in its own proper nature ("immanence"), that is, (in a manifold sense) in the act of knowledge and of freedom, the person is radically incapable of having a merely immanent end and fulfilment. Transcendence, as act and fulfilment, is the only true "immanent" realization of personal knowing, willing and acting (cf. *L'action* of M. Blondel). Immanence and transcendence belong to each other and mediate each other, which shows both the necessity and the limitations of these concepts and their application.

Present-day thinking is perhaps more suggestible to a transcendence expounded anthropologically. In the disintegration of human existence there is latent *and* audible a fundamental "disquiet" (concern), in which man experiences the unattainability of what he strives to be, while knowing himself inexorably summoned to this unattainable goal. "L'homme passe infiniment l'homme" (Pascal). However, there are many ways of propounding the transcendence of man once it has dawned in this way.

B. Conceptual Clarification

Transcendence can form a barrier which throws man back on himself and limits him to his finiteness. But it can also be experienced as a "dialectical" limit, negatively separating and positively uniting, which is transcended in many ways: rational modes of knowledge, affective and mystical ecstasy, "union", faith, silence, concrete action, historical practice. And the "ascent" is mostly to another type of realm, differing in mode of being and degree of reality, related to what is transcended by such various links as opposition, coherence, intensification, paradox, reflection, dialectical pattern. The following formal distinctions are to be made. Transcendence (or transcendent) means: (i) the realm going beyond consciousness and independent of it: epistemological transcendence; (ii) the absolute, supra-sensible "beyond", where knowledge of the idea (form) or essence (abstraction, intuition) and of its ultimate justification (deduction) rises above the multiplicity and mobility of phenomena and sensible experience, in a non-temporal, non-empirical ground: metaphysical transcendence; (iii) an opening out to the truth itself, to the absolute, indefeasible and incomprehensible horizon of human thought and will, which is either explicated metaphysically or theologically, or remains an open dimension or is totally reduced to the anthropocentric; (iv) the absolute otherness and freedom of God as regards the world attained by the "desacralization" of the world, where God's inmost nature remains unknown to man and is best expressed in the categories of the holy and of mystery: theological transcendence; (v) the truly divine godhead of God, which is absolutely beyond the range of all human powers, absolutely unattainable in spite of all connaturality but discloses itself in free self-communication, where the incalculable gratuitousness of grace and the supernatural order brings the movement of human transcendence to its intrinsic limit and the moment of its transformation: strict theological transcendence.

Modern philosophy has formed concepts which break through these definitions in many ways. For Husserl, everything that makes its presence felt in the immanent sphere of the process of consciousness, and presents itself as an analysable element of the structure of consciousness, without being part of the pure "region of experience", is transcendent. For K. Jaspers, transcendent designates the hidden, all-embracing being (not simply identical with God), which is only bestowed in existentiell decision and declares itself only in the mysterious language of cipher. Transcendence is understood then in many different ways as the actual or habitual ascent to "being", again understood in many ways: as all-embracing world horizon, as temporality in general, as utopia, future, self-realization, progress. This sometimes takes the form of "transcending without transcendence." (E. Bloch) or that of a totally indeterminate, "empty" transcendence (see below). For a reformed Marxism of a humanist type, transcendence is the creative realization of the truly human in the individual and the social sense, a progressive and critical "transcendence" towards a non-alienated society. Transcendence can simply mean the element of self-criticism in any attempt to draw up a blue-print for a better world, which is recognized as not amenable to norms, or for an active re-moulding of the world which refuses to adapt to the existing one or lose itself there. Hence the concrete meaning of transcendence must be taken into consideration in each case.

In view of these variations, it is not enough to appeal to the "classical" and "clear" notion of transcendence. Formally, of course, this has a definite function: God's being is essentially distinct and different – not separate – from all that is in the world. But in the concrete, the classical notion of transcendence is multivalent, and is generally used indifferently: (i) to indicate the relationship by which beings are referred to "being"; (ii) to indicate the relationship of changeable beings to one higher which is at rest; (iii) to indicate the "supreme being" itself, which is also called "being". These relationships are part of the intrinsic structure of metaphysics. Their modifications and transformations reflect the historical changes in metaphysics and its present-day crisis.

C. The Inner History of the Notion of Transcendence

Transcendence was first propounded on the ground of the difference between thought and perception, and the critique of intramundane gods in Plato's doctrine of forms, in which the myths lost their spell-binding force. The separation of the changing world of appearances, the physical cosmos, from the "world" of forms which is its ground does not directly give rise to a two-world theory or a curtained-off world. The form is a "parousia", and its intenser, powerful being is the immanent "ground" of beings. Nonetheless, this fundamental difference is the framework of all mediation – "hypothesis", the ascent of *eros*, ethics, *paideia*, above all, the experience of beauty. The good, the "form of all forms", the source of all reality, is higher in dignity and power than the forms. It is "beyond being" (ἐπέκεινα τῆς οὐσίας), the uncaused that is prior to all, and can be known only with effort, in a sudden moment and by a few, in a "divine excess" (ὑπερβολή – transcendence). The form of the good is not expressly identified with "God", but has a religious significance and is in the realm of the divine. Transcendence appears as soaring beyond (μετ' ἐκεῖνα) the shadows "out to" (εἰς ταῦτα) the forms, which a dangerously ambiguous metaphor of Plato puts in a "higher than heavenly place".

The strongly cosmological colouring of Aristotelianism (cosmos – stars – Unmoved Mover), intended to eliminate the difficulties of Platonism, proved to be misleading, as it gave rise later to spatial notions of transcendence, which Plato's position rather tended to avoid.

Later, contrary to Plato, the forms ("ideas") were transferred to the mind of God, the Demiurge, or the Logos, and emphasis was laid on the fact that the One, God, was outside all categories (which in Gnosticism went to the extreme of dualism), so that finally even thought, for instance, was not predicated of him. The dialectical ascent to this ultimate ground presupposes in the subject purification, simplicity and assimilation to God. It moves forward in a process of negation and is transposed into an explicitly analogous form of statement (through the *triplex via: positionis*, *negationis*, *eminentiae*). The ascent ends in the chiaroscuro of *docta ignorantia*, the wordless "touch", the consciousness of the disabilities of human thought, and (philosophical) "prayer". These represent the essential elements of classical transcendence. The possibility of attaining insight into the unknowability and ineffability of the primordial transcendence, which is not directly accessible, is based on the latent, image-like presence of transcendence in man prior to all reflection – the *illustratio animae*, *scintilla animae*, *apex mentis* or again, the *intellectus agens*, the *prima principia*, *esse commune*, the "voice of conscience", the dynamism of thought and will, the "I", the "Spirit", the understanding of "being". This mysterious centre and depth *in* the nature of man is what arouses him to his transcendent movement.

Along with other elements from neo-Platonism (self-communication of the Good, degrees of being in the universe, etc.) the transcendence of God in the patristic era was chiefly defined by the additional notes of absolute authority, inviolable sovereignty, personality and lordship of history, as seen in the God of the Bible. The indifferent, unreflecting, impersonal "Oneness" which was the supreme act of self-transcending thought is transformed (with the help of Exod 3:14) into a personal God capable of self-utterance. However, the attributes of God, first considered in reference to history, were gradually transformed into absolute proprieties of his essence (e.g., omnipotence). Orthodox theology returned again and again to the formula of transcendence, adding a corresponding affirmation of immanence: "Omnia complet et omnia transcendit." In spite of the implicit rejection of all discourse about transcendence, it did not cease to be intelligible, the understanding of it being based on attaining the notions of divine freedom and creation. Along with this rather cosmological type of transcendence, Christian thinkers after St. Augustine recognize an "inner" transcendence, suggested by the neo-Platonic notion of reflux or return. The spirit has, not merely in its thought but in its being, a genuine relation to the Absolute. "Reflection" is the point of arousal for the transition of the soul, as it soars by degrees to its true ground. In St. Augustine, for instance, God is closer to the soul than the soul to itself.

Medieval thought succeeded again and again in bringing the latent tensions of this metaphysical basic structure of transcendence into a certain equilibrium, which was ultimately arrived at and maintained by the fundamental data of faith. But this meant that the structural antinomies of transcendence were concealed. Epicurus and Lucretius had already shown clearly that the peculiar ontic condition of transcendence was capable of swinging over into an indifferent and impotent transcendence, with the region of immanence governed as a consequence solely by its own laws. The elements of voluntarism in the theology of the late Middle Ages and the Reformation gave radical effect to the notion of transcendence. God is not merely, by essence, the "wholly other". By his deliberate will, he withdraws from human thought into his incomprehensible hiddenness (*Deus absconditus*), a view which was in fact to isolate still more from its foundation the faith which was meant to be stimulated. These immanent tensions led almost to the self-dissolution of transcendence, a tendency reinforced from without by a mechanistic world-picture, Bacon's notion of "idols", empiricism, rationalism, the Enlightenment and so on. The non-mediated distance of transcendence swung over into impotence. "Through the total removal of the divine to a sphere beyond and above a world paralysed by the loss of its principle of life", a false honour was paid to God and the empty world left to godless hands (Schelling).

German Idealism failed to achieve the desirable speculative integration, since its notion of the *absolute* mediation of the Spirit *to itself* served to eliminate the basic relationship of God's being both inward and over against. The critique of "reality" in transcendental Kantianism, the banishing of the Absolute into the immanence of consciousness (only "immanent transcendence" remaining), the merging of the God-who-is in the Spirit-that-thinks, the surrendering of God to history, the reduction of the notion of God to a function – that of being a concept for what is *a priori* inconceivable, and the immanent critique there of the traditional notion of God – all this left the predicates of classical transcendence in a profound ambiguity and meant the ruin of what was termed a "reified" transcendence. Transcendence now transforms itself into "rescendence" (cf. "re-sidence") and appears there once more in a totally different form. It is the essential, relentless upward march ("transcendence") which is sited in the nature of man (the will to power, Marxist "practice"). The so-called self-dedication of man to the transcendent is stripped of its misleading objectivations and brought back downwards, as transcendence is reduced to sameness. At first, transcendence disappears in this "re-scendence". Religion has squandered on heaven the treasures of man and accepts in God what it refuses for itself. Transcendence is a substitute for the loss of the world. The supreme illumination of the Idea now becomes a will-o'-the-wisp, εἴδωλον, an idol, the "epiphenomenon" of social, practical relationships. Critical analysis unmasks these "imaginary" beings and duplicates as ideological reflections of the vital processes: the "superstructure". The identification of the Christian faith with such transcendence brings it under the same condemnation: "Christianity is the Platonism of the people."

Nonetheless, in spite of all polemics against transcendence, its formal structure (its functional position) is preserved in the new sketch-plans. It re-appears as the goals set for the immanent progress of the world, in natural evolution and self-fulfilment in work; as man's surpassing himself in the active process of creating world history; as utopia; as "something held open for a possible and as yet undecided future in this vacant space" (E. Bloch); as the non-final which is destiny; as the still unknown futurity; as the unsounded depths of man and so on. Transcendence can have so little content that it merely marks a tension in life which moves or provokes man to escape the banality of reality but no longer hints at arrival at a goal – the "empty" transcendence which has been signalled in Baudelaire, Rimbaud and Mallarmé (see H. Friedrich). Most of these transformations are Platonism in reverse, as is clearest in materialism, which Feuerbach presents by saying "being is sensible being". But when M. Heidegger, in the logic of the history of philosophy, interprets transcendence as "understanding of being", he opens up a new possibility: existence ("thereness") as the wide open place in whose brightness non-human beings (including the God) can show themselves. This understanding of being, transcendence, is the transcendental for all beings. It is not detached from existence, but it is not produced by it or hidden in the self-knowledge of the absolute Spirit. Inasmuch as Heidegger sees "transcendence" as event and hence as "historical" in a primordial sense, he abandons any metaphysical notion (and hence all discourse) of transcendence. In wide-ranging considerations of the "ontological difference", which is discussed under various headings, there is a "return to the fundamental ground of metaphysics", that is, an authentic consideration of the essence and origin of all transcendence. The mode of thought thus arrived at, with its non-metaphysical structures, is displayed in the concept of the world in the later Heidegger. Transcendence now becomes the "destiny of being" (*Seinsgeschick* – "the apt sending of being"). The new possibilities of this way of understanding transcendence have neither been positively tested nor decided in the negative. A systematic and historical investigation of thinking on transcendence is one of the most important tasks of present-day philosophy and theology.

D. The Modern Discussion

Present-day theology cannot afford to overlook the difficulties presented by the notion of transcendence. Even if it is historical and objective in rejecting as unjustified the negative characteristic of the traditional notion of transcendence, it cannot now think of an "Absolute" after the manner of a "Givenness". This means that notions of the beyond must be fully thought out. The history of the inner transformations of transcendence shows that even in the most imposing sketches of transcendence strong tensions are hidden, which are due to the structure of the thought. The result of this at present is a certain scepticism with regard to the application of the notion, though the matter has not been given much explicit attention. But the problem of transcendence cannot be evaded. A naive personalism fails to see the highly complicated structure of dialogal relationships, and does not deal with the problem of how the notion of person is to be applied to God in a meaningful way. It is impossible, on the other hand, to define the transcendent God solely, directly and without distinctions as personal responsibility in its unconditional nature, as the depths or grounds of our being, the source of our existence and the actuality of human love. The depths of being can appear to many as the absurd, as the painful limit of one's existence, as the drive to self-preservation and the will to be or be happy. The first thing to make clear is under what conditions the word "God" can be linked with the "depths of being" so as to disclose their meaning. A task as yet mostly neglected is the demarcation of the dimension "between" being, or the whole reality of the world, and the God whose essential realm must also be disclosed in the process as the holy and the divine. And it is also impossible to understand God merely as the answer to a question of meaning put exclusively in the transcendental sense, since such an answer ignores the question of the origin of human and non-human reality. Every new effort at interpretation must prove its value by being measured against the classical notion of transcendence, taken in its full meaning and in the light of all its functions in theology, with reference, for instance, to creation.

This demand must also be made with regard to a more recent approach, which conceives of the transcendence of God in the light of being as futurity and as "the power of the future". (This is done by means of a special interpretation of the OT promise which sees God as "He who comes"; and the categories used by E. Bloch are also invoked.) But this new approach seems to make God (or salvation) no more than a name for the summons to an endless, critical "transcending" into future history. If so, the real problem in the relationship of salvation and history ("the new earth") is implicitly solved, through a fluid notion of the future, more or less radically in the direction of immanence, with the word "eschatological" used in a way that is never made very clear. In fact, the theological use of the notion of the future cannot be sustained without envisaging the whole range of the formal and material functions of the classical notion of transcendence. Every theology of the promise, of the future and of hope is confronted in fact with the same set of problems as are posed by the relationship of immanence in transcendence. To distinguish history totally from eschatological future brings about an apocalyptic negation of the world and its history. To make them coincide totally means ultimately a strictly permanent self-surpassing, which of itself is without a goal and hence is undoubtedly meaningless. (For it is anyway, even without a "Utopia", a "metaphyisical" notion, in the sense of Heidegger, taking the place of transcendence.) The only meaningful approach seems to be (cf. J. Moltmann) to combine a transcendence superior to history with a historical process of transcendence, to note the critical differences but to believe that harmony is possible, to keep in view the qualitative difference when envisaging possible harmony. In this way a critique transcending all systems and an openness for a qualitatively new future can be combined with concrete steps towards a quantitatively new future.

When such positions are subjected to criticism, the problems which present themselves are seen no doubt as tasks which modern theology cannot evade. But the "solution" as so far presented contains no fewer difficulties than the classical notion of transcendence. This also tries to deal with the relationship between history and the supra-historical, between identity and difference. And by its very nature, it can only explain it as the coming-to-be of a fully developing transcendence. The mutation into another quality, which must also be presupposed here, can be understood theologically only as the "act of God" who is the "absolute future", in contrast to the future as "being", without limit. As the unrestricted fullness of reality, the mainspring of all dynamism of the future, it cannot be attained or surpassed by human experience or human efforts to change the world. A vision of the future concentrated only on changing the world must always find this theological affirmation "mythological". But futurity in the Christian sense is primarily "Advent", and it is there that it is radically new and "revolutionary".

The application of categories of futurity to the fundamental theological notions (God, salvation, etc.) does not perhaps depend on the actual use of the word "transcendence", but the validity of the application depends on how well it corresponds to the functions of the classical notion of transcendence in its ontological and hermeneutical bearings. But it is rather characteristic of modern theology that the two modes of thought ("transcendence" – "futurity") work in isolation and hence mostly reject each other. A similar problem arises in the "Death of God" theology. Insofar as "God" is really identified with the classical transcendence and above all with its inner history, deep questions undoubtedly arise. But these are not even seen in their proper depth, if the problem of transcendence is simply eliminated. Anthropological, Christological and uniquely eschatological "solutions" displace or bypass the really basic question. It is therefore clear that the notion of transcendence is indispensable from the theological point of view. But its actual usefulness in modern theological discussion depends entirely on whether it can be maintained fruitfully when confronted objectively and critically with the problem of history and the active effort to change the world. The legitimate variety of forms in which it can appear should not be lost sight of in the Christian faith, which is not identical with any given philosophy, world-view or world-picture. The term transcendence is not found in the Bible, though it definitely teaches "the thing signified" by the term.

It remains theologically relevant in all experience of transcendence – though in varying degrees – that finite man cannot himself bring about the fulfilment of his being, and cannot resolve the tension which this gives rise to. A precise analysis of his action and knowledge displays an absolutely necessary and relentless claim on this fulfilment, which proves, however, to be ultimately unattainable in spite of all his own efforts. This is when in the concrete man can hear, in the midst of the endless conflict between true and false transcendence (see *Superstition*, *Sin*) the invitation, full of promise, to open his heart to the nameless presence of a grace and favour still perhaps undefined. This "heartfelt expectation of the unknown Messiah" (M. Blondel) is the provisional name for what a fully developed Christian faith calls grace. Since its mysterious ways are so manifold and incalculable, all the phenomena of human transcendence, even in the guise of symbol, are theologically interesting and significant.

Karl Lehmann

TRANSCENDENTAL PHILOSOPHY

1. *Introductory*. The consideration that philosophy, as knowledge of all reality in its principles, expresses itself through the medium of the concept, is of the very essence of philosophy and is as ancient as philosophical reflection itself. But the difference thus posited between concept and reality, being and thought, is an implicit questioning of philosophy itself, which remains insignificant as long as the spontaneous idealism and optimism of thought and knowledge is not radically called in question. It is only in the light of certain spiritual experiences, which seem impervious to philosophy as a whole and confront it with the fundamental question of its own powers, that the problems contained in the distinction between concept and reality become explicit. Philosophy then becomes the question of its own possibility, and its function is to offer a critique of philosophy. That such experiences have gone hand in hand with philosophy from the start may be seen from the history of radical scepticism as well as from that of philosophical nominalism. Hence from the start philosophy was to some extent critical. But it could only become fundamentally critical when it produced of itself – stimulated by scepticism and nominalism – a counterpart to its own knowledge, which seemed by its very existence to demonstrate the impossibility of philosophy.

This antagonist was modern science with its basis of experiment and experience. Paradoxically, its challenge to philosophy was more radical than that of scepticism, because it offered positively verifiable knowledge in general, rejecting metaphysical knowledge in terms of pure concepts not verifiable by sensible experience. If philosophy was to maintain its claims, it had to rely radically on its own resources. It had to investigate its own possibility as well as the claim of science to be knowledge. It had to reflect critically on the foundations of knowledge as such.

The term "transcendental philosophy" was adopted to designate the investigation of the conditions of philosophical and scientific knowledge and has been used ever since with justice to describe every effort of radical rethinking to give philosophy an absolute foundation and analyse its relationship to scientific knowledge in general and in particular. Thus the term "transcendental", in contrast to the usage of the scholastic Aristotelian tradition of the Middle Ages, received a new significance, which remained, however, formally akin to the old. It also served a new purpose. It no longer designates the realm of "notes" beyond the categories in which "being" presents its aspects and their possibility of defining the nature of God. It now means the *a priori* conditions of knowledge, which precede all experience of objects and which are the primary constituents of all objects of knowledge and hence make knowledge possible. Criticism of philosophy itself and criticism of science with regard to the extent and limits of justifiable knowledge are therefore permanent characteristics of transcendental philosophy. Here the basic questionableness of purely conceptual thinking becomes permanently explicit and is given full value as essential at all stages of philosophy.

It follows that the central endeavour of all transcendental philosophy must be to return to the element which certifies and justifies all knowledge, and thence provide by deduction a critical explanation of concrete, scientific and philosophical knowledge. Hence the object of transcendental philosophy is neither being nor thought, neither the subject nor the object, but the actual unity of consciousness and being given in each act of knowing. Within the horizon of this "being-conscious" a twofold method of reduction and deduction is employed. There is the analysis of validity which reverses the process of universal doubt and gives the assurance of absolute truth as the source of all knowledge. And there is the constitutive synthesis and justification of the conditions of true knowledge as principles of reality. There is a "genetic" evidence of the absolute which goes beyond the merely factual and is at once insight into the intrinsic meaning and the "legitimacy" of the object of insight. When the absolute is thus displayed as at once absolute truth and veracity, such critical philosophy justifies its pure *a priori* concepts and principles as transcendental conditions of all knowing. As self-criticism of philosophy which has felt the weight of scepticism, it is a renewed, anti-dogmatic metaphysics whose basic character is incompatible with such common and one-sided designations as mere "theory of knowledge", "idealism" or "philosophy of subjectivity". Hence transcendental philosophy aims at being systematic knowledge of all reality through its principles, by providing a critical reflection on the transcendental conditions of the total reality of "being-conscious" as this reality presents itself in the act of knowing. As a critique of philosophy and science it is in a comprehensive sense a transcendental theory of knowledge.

2. *History*. This sketch of the problems of the validity and constitution of knowledge applies to all significant efforts in the history of philosophy which claimed to be transcendental reflection. Along with initial and disjointed efforts in all the great philosophical systems from Aristotle and Thomas Aquinas to Hegel, there were anticipations of transcendental reduction and deduction above all in the Platonic tradition, as for instance in Augustine, Anselm of Canterbury and Bonaventure. But the question of validity is put explicitly for the first time by Descartes in his effort to arrive analytically, passing through radical scepticism, at an absolute and unshakable foundation of knowledge in the absolute veracity and truth of God. This process of reduction is, however, only termed transcendental philosophy when the question of validity is linked with constitutive theory, that is, the basic structures of the object as such, in the

philosophy of Immanuel Kant. His general statement of the problems in his three Critiques (critique of the pure reason, of the practical reason, of the judgment) has remained on the whole decisive ever since for all transcendental philosophy, both as critique of science and as self-justification of philosophy. Everything that has been put forward as transcendental philosophy since then has explicitly referred itself to Kant, though normally in a critical way.

Thus Johann Gottlieb Fichte's theory of science, as a system of the absolute and the absolute phenomenon, with its reconciliation of theoretical and practical wisdom in terms of the question of absolute truth (especially in the *Wissenschaftslehre* of 1804) is only intelligible in the light of Kant's approach. But Fichte's successors at Jena and Berlin, Schelling and Hegel, can hardly be seen as part of the history of transcendental philosophy, since they abandon the ground of transcendental criticism at various points of their approach. And indeed all further transcendental philosophy seems to be characterized by a growing eclecticism in its themes and obviously loses sight of the systematic and comprehensive framework as attained by Fichte. Neo-Kantianism, for instance, which is at once anti-speculative and anti-positivist, restricts the material object of the basic question of the conditions of validity in general to the findings of science. It has become at the hands of its practitioners (Cohen, Natorp at Marburg, Windelband, Rickert, Lask in south-west Germany) a critique of science in terms of theories of validity. The problem of the absolute, which Kant assigned ambiguously enough to the theory of the postulates of the practical reason, has here lost all its importance for the transcendental question, just as it also has in the transcendental phenomenology of Husserl. His constitutive theories aim, like the fundamental ontology and existentialism of the early Heidegger, at the self-justification of philosophy and a universal foundation for the sciences. But they also help to restrict the transcendental question more and more to the problem of the concrete subjectivity and terminate, though not without a breach of continuity, in the existential philosophy which, as developed in Jaspers and Sartre, has very few traits of the abstract and transcendental.

The transcendental discussion was taken up in scholasticism and neo-Thomism, having been launched by the pioneer work of Joseph Maréchal who made a functional comparison between the systems of Kant and Aquinas which served to reconcile transcendental philosophy and traditional metaphysics. But even here the full weight of the transcendental problem is hardly felt, as may be seen from the occurrence of the problem of the transition from the "dynamism" of the transcendental and reductive question to the "finalism" of a metaphysics of a pre-established reality. But the transcendental analysis of the judgment holds firmly to the validity theories of transcendental philosophy. Within this tradition a number of writers (K. Rahner, Siewerth, M. Müller, Lotz, Lonergan, Marc, Coreth) have exploited fruitfully the encounter between classical metaphysics and the claims of modern transcendental philosophy. Coreth's *Metaphysik* put forward an independent synthesis of phenomenology, fundamental ontology and classical ontology, according to the methods of transcendentalism. Recently Holz has sought to apply to the tradition of the school of Maréchal the neo-Kantian theories of validity, as fully elaborated by Hans Wagner.

Outside phenomenology and scholasticism there have also been fruitful efforts at transcendental philosophy. Wolfgang Cramer has followed up the objectivity theory of Hönigswald, while Hans Wagner's subtle system seeks to reconcile neo-Kantianism and phenomenology. The *Transcendentale Logik* of Hermann Krings links up with Fichte, Lask, Heidegger and neo-Thomism to show the connection between ontology and transcendental philosophy. Reinhard Lauth seeks to revive the full transcendental system of Fichte, though unmistakably critical in approach. In spite of all variations and defects there is fundamental agreement about the constitution and validity of knowledge, as presented in the judgment, whether the judgment actually contains a predicate or is prior to predication. A fully thought-out transcendental philosophy which would include Fichte and a critical appraisal of newer findings is, however, still wanting.

3. *Concept and task*. The common elements and the contrasts in the historical approach point to a strict concept of transcendental philosophy and to its decisive objective problem. It could then be described as a transcendental – "validity" – reflection which reaches from the structurally universal affirmation of consciousness (judgment, scientific knowledge and even simple registering of fact) to the unconditioned (the absolute, that which is "of itself", being, truth, goodness and even thought and understanding of being). It uses the factual evidence to remount to the genetic, while confronting and overcoming universal doubt. This reflection, in its reverse process, is the deductive, systematic constitution and legitimation of the initially hypothetical starting-point, of which the conditions of possibility have been analysed. And thus is provided the justification of concrete, scientific and philosophical knowledge, according to the precisely circumscribed possibilities at each level.

The problem of transcendental reflection is that beginning and end mutually determine each other. The perspective of the phenomena which constitute the starting-point is coloured by the anticipatory grasp of the ultimate and unconditioned ground, while conversely the interpretation of the absolute is qualitatively determined by the previous choice and interpretation of the phenomenal data. The problem which here looms up is that of the adequacy of the starting-point, which must be the object of critical reflection in transcendental philosophy, since its own comprehensiveness is a function of that of the initial approach. Such reflection is important for an adequate determination of the ultimate factor of justification, and also makes it possible to situate critically the historical and present-day forms of philosophy. It follows that it is insufficient to interpret the unconditioned either as pure immanence (which would be to make an absolute of the idea) or as pure transcendence (which would be to make an absolute of the practical). It is also insufficient to reduce absolute truth to the mere functioning of a destiny which determines understanding (as in the "epochal" constitution of knowledge in the later Heidegger). And it would again be insufficient to make absolute truth merely function as the destructive force of negative dialectic which reduces all to untruth (as in the utopian constitution of knowledge in Adorno).

In all these cases the thinker's own act of knowing is left out of account. And consequently the unity of theory and practice which an adequate starting-point demands is envisaged only under one aspect, either that of mere theory or of mere practice. The danger of re-objectivating consciousness ("being-conscious") can probably be avoided only by an interpretation of the unconditioned which considers absolute truth as a sheer negativity for the concept but makes it manifest in positive functions (as mystery, "light"). As against a naively objectivating metaphysics in its many historical forms, and any absolute dialectic, positive or negative, the significance of transcendental philosophy is that it can maintain the historicity and finitude of the world, without having to give up its constitutive relationship to the hermeneutical ultimate of the good which is its positive meaning.

This positive affirmation is the ground of philosophy itself, and it is also the basis of the positive mode of knowledge which in the form of modern science inhibited all philosophy by its claims. Since the problematic element of science is not in its own nature, but in the importance attributed to it by man, it may not be considered on principle as the reflection of a depraved totality which must be swept away, of a non-original and artificially civilized world. Science now appears as a way for the realization of the good and hence as man's chance of self-affirmation and self-emancipation. This achievement shows the irreplaceable value of transcendental philosophy in this world of the sciences which ours will remain. Its task is to uphold critically the just metaphysical intention of man, by expounding the unconditioned which is posited in all knowing.

Hans Michael Baumgartner

TRANSCENDENTALS

The inmost force which moves to philosophical thinking is being. Certain necessary notes of being recur in all beings as such, and are called transcendentals, because they reach out beyond the limited orders of individual beings or surpass all limits (*transcendere*). These transcendentals are unity, truth, goodness, and also beauty. Here we discuss them historically and systematically.

1. *Historically*. For Plato, the forms or ideas constitute that which really is (ὄντως ὄν), in which the essence of being is fully and clearly manifested along with the notes mentioned above, in which earthly things partake at least in a fragmentary way. Aristotle examines expressly the notes of all beings as such: the one and the true in *Metaphysics*, X and VI, the good in the *Nicomachean Ethics*, I. Plotinus regards the supreme principle as the one and the good. From it proceeds the νοῦς which discriminates the forms in its thought, and hence is the true. The souls and all things partake of this in descending degrees. St. Augustine has illuminating formulas for the notes of being: "nihil autem est esse quam unum esse" (*De moribus Manichaeorum*, II, 6); "verum mihi videtur esse id, quod est" (*Soliloquium*, II, 5); "inquantum est quidquid, bonum est" (*De vera religione*, XI, 21). St. Albert the Great already offers some systematic discussion of the first three transcendentals. He adds reality (*res*) and particularity (*aliquid*), the former being synonymous with being (*ens*), the latter being comprehended within unity. Here the influence of Avicenna (Ibn Sina) may be felt, who held that to be and to be real were two different determinations, while he treated being and particularity as synonyms. St. Thomas Aquinas finds five transcendentals in all beings: reality, particularity, unity, truth and goodness (*De Veritate*, q. 1, a. 1); elsewhere he speaks only of the three main transcendentals (*De Veritate*, q. 21, a. 1, a. 3; *De Potentia*, q. 9, a. 7 ad 6). These catalogues do not include beauty; but it undoubtedly forms one of the transcendentals. In this Aquinas is in the line of Plato, Plotinus, St. Augustine and St. Albert the Great (In *De divinis nominibus*, cap. 4, lect. 5; *De Veritate*, q. 22, a. 1 ad 12; *Super Sententiis*, I, d. 31, q. 2, a. 1). The doctrine was later given systematic form by F. Suarez, who confined himself to the three main transcendentals (*Disputationes metaphysicae*, III, sect. 2, n. 3), while treating *res* and *aliquid* as did St. Albert the Great. The ensuing scholastic development followed the same lines, and its influence may be traced as far as the rationalist philosophy of the 18th cen-

tury, as for instance in C. Wolff. The most prominent figure in this context is G. Leibniz, who conceived being as the monad, which was hence immediately determined as unity, truth (*perceptio*) and goodness (*appetitio*). An echo of earlier thought is still to be heard in I. Kant, who accepts the three transcendentals at least as logical pre-conditions of all knowledge of things (*Critique of Pure Reason*, B. 113f.). G. Hegel returns by way of dialectic to the metaphysical depths of being, as may be seen from his *Logic*. F. Nietzsche affirms the identity of the transcendentals with their opposites, and thus arrives at his "Dionysiac" notion of becoming (*Wille zur Macht*, E. T.: *The Will to Power*, ed. by O. Levy, London and Edinburgh [1909–10], nos. 12, 272, 298, 1005). In modern non-scholastic thought, N. Hartmann, for instance, ranges the essential notes of beings among the categories, which presupposes their restriction to the finite beings of the world. Finally, according to M. Heidegger, being is most intimately connected with truth above all; the one also shines through.

2. *Systematically*. The transcendentals are necessary notes of being, which explicates itself in them and displays itself most radically in them. Just as being never occurs without the transcendentals, so too each of them inevitably includes the others. Hence it follows that in the measure and in the manner that a being has being, it is characterized by unity, truth, goodness and beauty. Hence subsisting being implies the subsistence of the transcendentals. They are not mere synonyms of being, but the determinate expression of its content, which we first apprehend only in an indeterminate way. Hence the notion given in being and the various transcendentals is not quite the same: there is a conceptual distinction, founded on the varying content of each aspect. But the distinction is the smallest conceivable, as no division of content is possible: being and the transcendentals penetrate each other or are strictly and basically identical. On account of the distinction, the transition from being to the transcendentals forms a synthesis, which, however, on account of the indivisible basic identity is there *a priori* or implies a metaphysical necessity. This *a priori* synthesis, which is concerned with being itself, is of course essentially higher than that of Kant, which did not go beyond appearances.

As regards the individual transcendentals, all agree that they include unity, truth and goodness. When we also add beauty, we part company with those who insist that the beautiful is a matter of sensible contemplation. The two other notes mentioned by Aquinas with Avicenna do not appear to be independent transcendentals distinct from the others; reality (*res*) is contained in being as one of its components in unity and so too particularity (*aliquid*). Duration and similarity are often included among the transcendentals; but they may be reduced to unity in or above time and to determinate agreement with regard to unity. Finally, order and totality are not, strictly speaking, transcendentals, because they imply multiplicity and hence are not applicable to God.

The transcendentals are found in an essential sequence. A being immediately implies unity. From this flow the true and the good, which imply determination, accessibility and conformity between each being and the act of knowing or willing. Further, since knowledge gives only an imperfect union between the spirit and being, while perfect union takes place only in willing or in love, the full expression of what begins in the true is found only in the good. Finally, beauty comprises at once unity, truth and goodness, in the fullness of their diversity and harmony. Thence flows the repose of contemplation and delight.

We may now indicate the grounds for affirming that the four notes of being are really transcendentals. The more a being has being, the more is it one, that is, self-contained and distinct from others. And vice versa, when a being loses its unity, it is also deprived of its being, so that it either ceases to exist or at least exists no longer as an unimpaired whole.

The explicit realizing of beings in concept and judgment is possible only because of the implicit concomitant realization of being. And since being embraces everything, the human spirit thereby attains everything without exception, because only nothingness is outside the range of being. But this means that everything is homogeneous, accessible, intelligible, that is to say, true, for the spirit.

In the same way, the will can only choose freely between limited goods as its material object, insofar as it is directed according to its formal object to universal being as the good, and hence finally to the unlimited good (*summum bonum in genere*). Thus everything is homogeneous, accessible, appetible, that is to say, good, for the will or love. But if being and good are basically identical, badness and evil can only be the privation or lack of some perfection demanded by the natural tendencies.

Beauty, as the state of perfection and perfect harmony of unity, truth and goodness, constitutes a transcendental along with these three. This description holds good for what is perceptible by the senses and still more for what can be contemplated spiritually. We are moved by the radiance of beauty. But even the tedious and ugly contains a remnant of beauty, the complete extinction of which would be equivalent to the destruction of the being in question.

Ultimately, the transcendentals lead to God as the primordially one, true, good and beautiful.

Johannes Baptist Lotz

TRANSCENDENTAL THEOLOGY

1. *The approach to the concept.* The term "transcendental theology" was modelled on the analogy of transcendental philosophy to indicate a certain receptivity to the latter in Catholic thought (since Maréchal, for instance), with important influences on Catholic theology. This does not mean that transcendental theology is merely the application of a transcendental philosophy to theological subjects. The main thing is that a historical context is indicated in which a procedure always in use in theology, though perhaps not very explicitly, was clearly envisaged and given a special name. The principle of a transcendental theology is genuinely theological. Since theology deals with man's salvation (inasmuch as it consists of God's self-communication) and really with nothing else, its subject-matter is the perfect totality of man; man is the "subject" in the strict sense of the word and not a particular along with others. Hence salvation can be understood only as that of the subject as such (and so too all elements of salvation). To understand the reality or realities of salvation in this way is to grasp them transcendentally, that is, as related to the transcendental subject – which is such "by nature" and as so constituted is radicalized by grace. The fact that such a transcendental theology is clearly coloured (at least at first sight) by a recourse to transcendental philosophy does not deprive it of its genuinely theological character. For one thing, the theological consideration of man's "nature" as the condition of the possibility of grace is part of theology, though a theology which looks like philosophy. Systematic theology can be called transcendental when it a) uses the instruments of transcendental philosophy and b) takes as its themes, more explicitly than before and not just in general (as in traditional fundamental

theology), the *a priori* conditions in the believer for the knowledge of important truths of faith, using genuinely theological methods of investigation. It is applicable only where such a transcendental questioning is not impossible by the very nature of the object of knowledge.

2. *The problem.* The problem of the essence of a transcendental theology is therefore very like that of a transcendental philosophy. But there is also the special and authentically theological question, as to whether a transcendental enquiry into the conditions of possibility of knowledge in the subject himself can be envisaged with regard to an object of revelation and faith, i.e., with regard to the object in general and particular matters involved.

3. *The possibility of a transcendental theology.* a) It must first be noted that any *analysis fidei* (see *Faith*) implies some transcendental theology. This element then colours the whole of theology, on account of the nature of faith, outside of which there are no theological truths. For the analysis of faith asks how such an absolute assent to revelation, precisely as the word of *God*, is at all possible. When grace is then appealed to as the necessary condition for hearing the word of God as God's, a condition of possibility in the subject himself is examined and one which belongs strictly to theology. This is transcendental theology.

b) Theology has every reason to desire that transcendental philosophy should limit itself to its own proper sphere. If a transcendental philosophy were to claim absolutely to be the sole and non-derivative grounding of human existence, a "positive" religion of revelation, in a history of salvation embracing as such the existence of man and salvation as a totality, would be excluded from the start. This self-limitation, due to the recognition of the "historicity" of existence, which cannot be systematically categorized, and reflection on language and dialogal and hermeneutical experience, is an essential element in any correct transcendental philosophy. Otherwise philosophy falls victim to hybris and becomes a brutal effort to dissolve everything in its reflections. If this limitation were not imposed by philosophy itself, it would abandon its essential claim to enquire into everything and would be self-destructive. But this limitation of the transcendental self-understanding of man is also – on principle, and above all in the present situation of philosophy and theology – a task for fundamental theology. For to demonstrate the positive possibility of revelation and history of salvation, it must show that concrete history, not fully amenable to reflection, affects man in his primordial quality of subject, and hence can be a history of salvation and ruin. But if fundamental theology undertakes this task, it is already transcendental theology in the sense just mentioned. It is reflection on the fact that the created subject as such is intrinsically involved in history, the history precisely of its own true subjectivity. The self-communication of God in grace (by virtue of the universal salvific will of God) is undoubtedly a "transcendental" existential of man. But it has its proper being in the history of salvation and revelation (individual and collective) and this is the medium through which it is accomplished and comes to us. It is precisely the task of a transcendental theology to show that the metaphysical essence of a reality and its history (and hence grace as an existential and salvation-history) are not simply juxtaposed but condition each other (see *Salvation*).

Hence transcendental theology cannot and does not try to be the whole of theology, of which it is only one element. For theology, or more precisely faith, whose articulate elements and whose ultimate resistance to reflection theology reflects, must always speak of the historically concrete which is not amenable to deduction, and still show how this concrete history can really affect man in the ultimate ground of his existence and subjectivity. Without transcendental theology historical facts cannot be shown to be existential, that is, to affect man's salvation (see *Faith and History*). This is because the reality of such salvific events cannot be known simply *a posteriori*. If they are to address man as man, he must address himself to them with his whole being, that is, he must discover that he is by his very nature forced to turn to them. But if he approaches them with his whole being, his theology is transcendental. Reflection on the transcendental orientation of man is not rendered impossible by the historical and unpredictable character of the saving events, their *a posteriori* nature, the fact that they are freely ordained by God. For what was first and most strictly ordained by God is the permanent supernatural existential of grace, the proffered self-communication of God, and hence a "transcendental" condition of man. And this free grace, as a transcendental determination of man, has its own proper history in what we call history of salvation and revelation, which cannot be and be grasped as such without this *a priori* possibility in man which is called grace, or the grace of faith.

4. *The transcendental theology of the fundamental dogmas of Christianity*. a) An important task is imposed at once on transcendental theology by the need to explain the true relationship of the world to God. Only knowledge of God attained by a transcendental method prevents God being regarded as a part within the all, or a demiurge whose action on the world is merely "from without".

b) Little more needs to be said about the fundamental anthropological dogma that supernatural grace is the self-communication of God to man. For grace is not an element in some particular category of things which is superadded – even on the loftiest plane – to the nature of man. It is a determination of the transcendence of man's knowledge and freedom as such. And it is only in the light of this truth that the nature of grace as salvation, meaning supernatural salvation, is definitely disclosed.

c) If theology shows clearly that the "Trinity of the economy" and the "immanent" Trinity are identical, and that the latter is revealed through the former, the importance of a transcendental philosophy for theology becomes apparent, and such philosophy, when exercising this function, becomes a transcendental theology. For if the revelation of the mystery of God's self-communication is supposed, and it is seen that God is always the unoriginated and hence the permanently incomprehensible, even when imparting himself, a "transcendental" deduction demonstrates that this self-communication of God necessarily comes to man as transcendence and as history, in a unity and distinction of both elements. Then the revelation of God's self-communication is seen to contain implicitly what we call the economic and immanent Trinity of God.

d) This at once provides a starting-point for a Christology on the basis of a transcendental theology. Obviously, a transcendental theology as such cannot undertake to prove that Jesus of Nazareth is the Lord, the absolute bringer of salvation, the incarnation of the Word of God. This experience comes in history itself, not in an *a priori* theology of history. And a transcendental Christology need not proceed as if it had formed the Christian notion of the God-man independently of the historical experience of this God-man in the concrete figure of Jesus. The transcendental deduction of an "idea" is always subsequent reflection on a concrete experience. It is a reflection which notes explicitly the "necessary" in the factual. It is therefore justifiable and necessary, since it alone explicitly displays the essence of the concrete experience in its necessary essence, not just its factuality. Such a Christology may proceed "transcendentally" in various ways, though here it must be admitted that the word "transcendental" is used in a wider and somewhat indefinite sense, and that the word comprises all theological considerations which start from man as a being whose situation is transcendence, who reflects transcendentally on this his being.

Transcendental theology can make the "idea" of the God-man intelligible, as the climax, at least asymptotically and hypothetically, of the movement of the spirit, as its drive towards God continually carries it beyond itself. Such a Christology of the "Omega Point", as Teilhard de Chardin called it, need not overlook or minimize the truth that the Omega Point towards which the world moves in its spirit is what is theologically termed the kingdom of God as fully come in the vision of God, which is imparted to *every* spirit in its fulfilment. This is precisely what is explained by a transcendental understanding of the nature of man. The incarnation is not regarded in isolation as a singularly supreme stage of the self-transcendence of the world (which the divine self-communication sustains) and as something which is only "for our sake" subsequently. It is seen as the summit, a unique one indeed, of the heights of the self-communication of God to all spirit – the spirit which forms the heights of the historical, irreversible (eschatological) manifestation of the victorious self-communication of God to the world. The relationship (in terms of transcendental theology) between spirit (including grace) and history (including revelation-history) implies that history, the history of grace in the world, comes to a peak in the absolute bringer of salvation, who will be the God-man in the orthodox sense of the term. There is therefore a transcendental Christology which outlines theoretically the nature of the God-man, pointing to to the historical reality of the God-man in Jesus and instructed by this reality.

A Christology can also proceed "transcendentally", presupposing the unity of the economic and the immanent Trinity, by explaining why precisely the second person in God becomes man and why only he can. A full understanding of the nature of truth in transcendental terms, having regard to the primordial unity of objective and subjective truth, might argue as follows, not excluding but surpassing the classical Greek notion of truth. It must be the Logos, who is the personal fidelity of self-utterance displaying itself historically, who reveals the Father in the flesh and in doing so reveals the propriety of the Logos himself (cf. K. Rahner, *Theological Investigations*, IV [1966], pp. 77–104). Finally, a transcendental Christology must do with regard to Jesus Christ what all transcendental theology must do in keeping with its duty of self-limitation and self-denial. It must justify and encourage man not to seek his salvation in the "idea" but in history (as a unity of past, present and future), to encounter God in man and ultimately in the man in whom God definitively exists and historically appears in the world, that is to say, in Jesus Christ.

Karl Rahner

TRANSUBSTANTIATION

1. Transubstantiation is described by the Council of Trent as the change of the whole substance of bread (*totius substantiae panis*) into the body of Christ, and of the whole substance of wine (*totius substantiae vini*) into the blood of Christ, the species of bread and wine remaining unchanged (Session XIII, can. 2; *D* 884). This notion of transubstantiation is coloured by the branch of philosophy known as cos-

mology and is the result of a development which was not always consistent. Though the element of change (*metabolismus*) had been expressly stressed by St. Ambrose (cf. J. Geiselmann), the effect of the eucharistic change on the substance of bread and wine had presented no problem till Berengarius. The supporters of the metabolistic notion only tried to give it an ontological interpretation in the 11th century. The decisive influences here were Lanfranc of Bec (1005–89) and Guitmund of Aversa (d. before 1095). Their explanation of the eucharistic change as a change of substance is reflected in the *Jusjurandum Berengarii*: "substantialiter converti" (*D* 355). This was confirmed by the Fourth Lateran Council in 1215, "transsubstantiatis pane in corpus, et vino in sanguinem" (*D* 430). The term *transsubstantiatio* seems to have been first used by Roland Bandinelli in the middle of the 12th century.

It is important to note that all the scholastics of the 12th century regarded the logical relationship in the sentence between subject and predicate as the basis of the metaphysical relationship between subject and propriety. In particular, *materia* and *forma* were not yet understood in the sense in which the terms were used in classical scholasticism. The predominant view was that which was given its clearest form by Petrus Cantor and which continued to be strongly influential down to the middle of the 13th century. Petrus Cantor made a distinction between the form, which was the sum of the essential proprieties, and the substance, which was more or less the *hypostasis* or subject, and while fully indeterminate and without qualities was still determinable by the *forma*. (Subject and *materia* were identified at this period.) In keeping with this view, only the subject is changed in transubstantiation, while the essential properties remain unchanged and form the natural ground of inherence for the accidents. As will later appear, the present-day efforts to go beyond the formulation of Trent is in keeping with the initial positions held in the 12th century, though the link is not always explicitly recognized or sought. It must be noted here that a notion of the eucharistic change which was current in the Church for over a hundred years should not be too hastily branded with the stigma of heresy.

Another line of thought which was to lead up to the classical doctrine of transubstantiation was laid down by Alan of Lille (de l'Isle) towards the end of the 12th century. In contrast to Petrus Cantor, he understood the substance as the whole essence (matter along with form being the sum of all essential properties). According to Alan, the substance, understood as the whole essence, is changed, so that the existence of the accidents has to be explained by a miracle, or their objective reality must be denied. While Stephen Langton, Guido of Orchelles and William of Auvergne followed strictly in the steps of Alan, William of Auxerre already accepted the Aristotelian form as a single metaphysical principle. This position was taken to its logical conclusion by Alexander of Hales, who held that the change took place in the substance constituted by matter and form, while the accidents remained unchanged. For Alexander, therefore, transubstantiation is a positive action "by which an actual being, without being destroyed or annihilated, is changed according to its whole substance into another actual being". Classical scholasticism had nothing new to offer with regard to this notion. It was maintained at the Council of Constance against Wycliffe and was adopted into the definition of the Council of Trent. Speculative problems were dealt with in the light of the doctrine of transubstantiation which had been solidly established since the classical era of scholasticism. The following appeared to be the most important: Is the substance of bread annihilated or changed positively into the body of Christ in the eucharistic change? How is the body of Christ sited in a place under the consecrated species? How is the extension of the glorified body of Christ to be explained in the Eucharist?

2. As regards the question as to how the definition of Trent is to be understood hermeneutically, E. Schillebeeckx takes the standpoint that the Council wished to affirm nothing beyond the real presence and that the canon on transubstantiation was drawn up by the Council merely to safeguard the real presence against a symbolism or spiritualism which would so to speak volatilize it away. This seems a questionable stand, if one remembers that a group of theologians at the Council had been asked to discuss two propositions of Luther in which transubstantiation was rejected as Aristotelian and scholastic, and the theory of consubstantiation put forward. The canon of Trent on transubstantiation grew out of a dialectical demarcation against the doctrine of Luther. Hence the Council went beyond the real presence to envisage the eucharistic change as such and to affirm it directly. To make room for a new interpretation, one cannot rely on forcing an affirmation about the real presence into the canon on transubstantiation.

To reach an understanding of the eucharistic presence which will be in accord with the modern era, the hermeneutical principle must be invoked according to which the philosophical context from which the formulation of a truth of faith is derived may be expendable and replaceable. This means that in a changed scientific and philosophical situation a truth of faith calls for new interpretations and formulations and hence must be grasped in a new light. The *tota substantia*, that is, the material substance composed of matter and form with its inherent accidents, is not in accord with the world-picture presented by physics and philosophy at the present time. In detail, the following difficulties are now felt with regard to the definition of transubstantiation worked out on the basis of Aristotelian and scholastic cosmology:

a) The models used by modern physics give matter an atomic structure. The ultimate particles combine to form atoms which are grouped as molecules of various types. In certain combinations, the molecules form bread and wine as their end-results. Hence it cannot be said that the substance of bread or wine, composed of matter and form, is the ontologically prior reality from which in consequence the chemical properties result. Bread and wine are the last stage of a combination of atoms, molecules and forces. This is why in the twenties theologians had recourse to physics in the explanation of transubstantiation and transposed it to the level of the atom or molecule, which meant that the transubstantiation of a host contained an incalculable number of transubstantiations. By the sixties, these efforts had to be considered a failure, because discussion of transubstantiation as a physical or cosmological process no longer seemed desirable.

b) The cosmological approach to transubstantiation presents the further difficulty that the survival of the accidents forms an unthinkable paradox. If one continues to maintain, along the lines suggested by the Councils of Constance and Trent, that the eucharistic accidents exist *sine subjecto*, there is extension but nothing that is extended, roundness but nothing that is round, hardness but nothing that is hard, weight without anything heavy, activity with nothing acting, passivity with nothing affected, etc.

c) The conventional notion of transubstantiation gives a far too impersonal impression. Aristotle took his categories and basic concepts mainly from the realm of the inorganic, which led in scholasticism to an objectified treatment of transubstantiation. At the present time, when existential philosophy and personalism are the order of the day, an effort is being made to see the eucharistic change in a different perspective. The idea is to emphasize the role of the glorified Lord who gives himself to his own as their spiritual food and desires to be one with them.

In view of the philosophical difficulties and the demands of personalism, the *nouvelle théologie* had sought to replace the notion of transubstantiation by that of transfinalization, but without explaining precisely whether a new terminology or a new interpretation was aimed at. If the bread receives a new ordination to an end, an ontological change must have taken place. The question is what is this change. Theologians from the Netherlands in particular have contributed to the fuller discussion of transubstantiation (C. Dupont, B. Möller, E. Schillebeeckx, P. Schoonenberg, L. Smits, I. Sonnen and others. They do not all take the same line. They presuppose the real presence. In the discussion of the process of its realization, L. Smits starts explicitly with the early scholasticism of the 12th century. Like other theologians, Smits makes much use of phenomenological approaches to throw light on the process of change, while Schillebeeckx treats it along the lines of ontology. They all agree in opting for a transfinalization or transignification of the consecrated bread and wine.

3. The more recent approaches suggest the following considerations. One has to remember that the words of institution indicate a change but do not give any guiding line for the interpretation of the actual process. As regards transubstantiation, it may then be said that substance, essence, meaning and purpose of the bread are identical. But the meaning of a thing can be changed without detriment to its matter. A house, for instance, consists of a certain arrangement of materials and has a clearly established nature and a clearly established purpose. If the house is demolished and the materials used for building a bridge, a change of nature or essence has intervened. Something completely different is there. The meaning has been changed, since a house is meant to be lived in and a bridge is used to cross a depression. But there has been no loss of material. In an analogous way, the meaning of the bread has been changed through the consecration. Something which formerly served profane use now becomes the dwelling-place and the symbol of Christ who is present and gives himself to his own. This means that an ontological change has taken place in the bread.

In a general way, three classes of symbols may be distinguished. The first type are effects which actually point to their cause, like smoke and fire. The second type have by their very nature a certain potential signification, which needs, however, to be actualized by being determined and expressed, e.g., washing with water as a symbol of purification from sin. The third type of symbol do not by nature designate any given object either actually or potentially. They only become signs through human convention, like the colours of traffic lights. The bread should be included in the second type of symbols, since the fact that it is food makes it naturally apt to symbolize spiritual nourishment and union. But the consecrated bread possesses the further property of signifying that the Lord who offers himself as food is not just at a distance but is present in the bread. By virtue of this concentrated symbolism, the bread becomes the sacramental manifestation of the presence of Christ. Hence transubstantiation means a change of finality and being in the bread and wine, because they are raised to being symbols of Christ who is present there and invites men to spiritual union.

Engelbert Gutwenger

TRINITY, DIVINE

A. The Scriptural Doctrine of the Trinity

1. *The Old Testament.* Since revelation and salvation come in historical form, it cannot be expected that the Trinity of God should have been explicitly revealed in the OT. The OT as such is part of the revelation of God in word, though this word is essentially a moment and an interpretation of God's saving acts. Hence as long as God's self-communication in Jesus Christ was not yet an irreversible reality and the Spirit of God was not yet a triumphant eschatological manifestation but merely an offer, the revelation of the Trinity would have been word of a reality entirely outside the historical realm as such of man. Nonetheless, given the continuity of salvation-history and its permanent ground, the OT is also important for the doctrine of the Trinity.

The OT doctrine of a word of God going forth in history while remaining the word of God even within the world, already contains a dynamic concept of revelation. This concept, in the progress of the history of revelation, was "bound" to lead to the concept of the self-communication of God which would imply the Trinity, since such self-communication cannot be reduced to the status of a human word "about" God, even as a mystery, but comes in faith in the word *of* God, sustained by God himself in grace. The personification of divine forces ordained to the world – the word, the wisdom, the spirit of God – which are distinct from God and are still not intermediate powers between God and the world, are formally and materially preludes to a doctrine of the Trinity in the NT.

2. *The New Testament.* a) There is no systematic doctrine of the "immanent" Trinity in the NT. The nearest to such a proposition is the baptismal formula of Mt 28:19, though it must be noted that modern exegesis does not count this saying among the *ipsissima verba* of Jesus. Along with the various separate statements about the Father, Son and Spirit and the relationship in each case to the other persons, it should be noted that in Jn and the NT letters the three terms have a marked tendency to occur in the same context. See for instance Eph 4:4ff., "One Spirit, one Lord, one God and Father"; 2 Cor 13:13, "The grace of the Lord Jesus Christ, the love of God, the fellowship of the Holy Spirit".

b) When the NT speaks simply of "God", it means the God who has been seen at work in the OT. He is the "Father", he has a Son and he gives his Spirit. "God" does not stand for the "triune Godhead". The statements about the Son and the Holy Spirit occur when the Son and the Spirit are spoken of in the context of salvation-history, but not within the framework of a systematic statement on the Trinity. While the NT authors cannot speak of Jesus as "God", since this would be, for them, to identify Jesus and the Father, they recognize the divinity of the Son. They do not look upon the Son as a cosmic power intermediate between God and the world. Where the Son appears as pre-existent, he is clearly in the realm of the divine: Jn 1:1; Phil 2:6ff., etc. And they do not look on Jesus, who is for them simply "the Son", as a mere prophet. He is *the* absolute bringer of salvation. (The question of the self-understanding of Jesus in his pre-Easter life does not come up in this context. Here it is enough to note that even the pre-Easter Jesus of the Synoptics distinguishes himself from all others and claims prerogatives which belong only to Yahweh, whether or not he applied to himself the titles of majesty traditionally attributed to the Messiah.) Jesus is the presence of the Kingdom or Kingship of God (Mt 12:28; Lk 11:20), of judgment (Jn 12:31, 38; Mt 11:20–24, par.), of lordship over the Sabbath (Mk 2:23–28; 3:1–6) of the absolute situation of decision (Mk 13:9–13; 9:34–38; 10:17–27), of God in unthinkably close proximity (Jn 10:30–38), of the fullness of the Spirit (Lk 4:18). The pre-existence of the Son as God is then quite clear in John and Paul, and does not need to be discussed in detail here (see for instance Jn 1:1–18; Phil 2:5–11).

The NT authors also refuse to consider the Spirit as a cosmic or religious power intermediate between God and the world. He is simply the Spirit of God (Lk 4:18; Tit 3:5f.; 1 Cor 12:4, etc.). Though they are thus the saving presence of God (the Father) himself, the Son and Spirit are not simply identical with him whom they reveal and whose radical closeness to men they are.

When one undertakes to distinguish the three "persons" from one another as depicted in Scripture, one should not start with some massive notion of person derived from modern thinking. Possibly they cannot be distinguished in the way which such a concept would demand. In St. Paul, for instance, it is difficult to distinguish the Spirit from the glorified Lord, or from God. But this is a far cry from proving that they are not distinguished in the same way in which the dogma of the Church speaks of them. The existence of some sort of distinction follows at once from the fact that the three words are not simply used interchangeably but occur beside one another in the same context. Further, the NT authors know that there is a certain relationship between the Son and the Father, and the Spirit and the Father (cf. Mt 11:27 par.; Jn 1:1; 8:38; 10:38; 1 Cor 2:10). The Father "sends" them (Jn 14:16, 26; 17:3; Gal 4:6) and gives the Spirit through the Son (Jn 15:26; 16:7). This shows of course very clearly how hesitant and groping the religious language of the NT authors is, when they try to speak of the unity and distinction of God as Father, Son and Holy Spirit. And the question remains as to where the basic primordial revelation is to be found, if – in relation to it – these statements of the NT area already to be envisaged as "theology" (though of course absolutely normative). It seems that the only possible answer to this question is that the concrete Jesus is the presence of God (the Father) for us and still is not the Father. And the difference is not merely due to the human created reality of Jesus. Otherwise his humanity would be only the livery in which God the Father was present, and nothing more. But the Spirit is just as definitely known as the *self*-donation of God (the Father), while at the same time the Spirit who is given reveals the incomprehensibility of God, the Father, the unoriginated, and so the distinction between the Spirit and God the Father. In the light of this experience of the Son and the Spirit, the NT authors, obeying an "instinct" which they feel no need to question, refuse to give a "rational" explanation by making the triad a matter of pure appearance and "aspects for us" of the one God. They also refuse to present the Son and the Spirit more intelligibly by treating them as mythological intermediaries or as a more strongly numinous human element – which would be fundamentally just as rationalistic.

c) But the NT authors also reflect explicitly on the one ground which underlies the essential identity and difference between the Father and the Son. The Son is the Father's own Son in contrast to the servants (Mk 12:1–12 par.; Rom 8:3, 32; Heb 1, etc.). He is the eternal Word of the Father (Jn 1:1, 14; 1 Jn 1:1; Rev 19:13), the image

(2 Cor 4:4; Col 1:15; Heb 1:3), the radiance of the glory of the Father (Heb 1:3). Such statements cannot be taken without more ado as referring to the life of the Trinity *ad intra*. And they cannot be directly exploited in the sense of a "psychological" theology of the Trinity such as was put forward by St. Augustine. But in view of the basic principle of trinitarian theology, such primarily historical sayings, referring to the coming of salvation – the Son as the self-utterance of the Father to the world – already imply the "immanent" Trinity.

B. The Doctrine of the Magisterium

1. *The sources*. The important documents, along with the various creeds (Apostles' Creed, Nicene Creed, Athanasian Creed [*Quicumque*], Paul VI's Confession of Faith) are from the Council of Nicaea, 325 (*D* 54), the First Council of Constantinople, 381 (*D* 86), the Eleventh Council of Toledo, 675 (*D* 275–81), the Fourth Lateran Council, 1215 (*D* 428, 431f.), the Second Council of Lyons 1274 (*D* 460) and the Council of Florence, 1439–45 (*D* 691, 703f.).

2. *The doctrine (with some comments)*. a) The Trinity is an absolute mystery (*D* 1795, 1915) which is not perspicuous to reason even after being revealed (on which see also *Collectio Lacensis*, VII, pp. 507 c, 525 bc). If there are any absolute mysteries in the Christian faith, that of the Trinity is undoubtedly the most fundamental. Why this should be so is not further explained in the doctrine of the magisterium and seems to be affirmed only for the pilgrim existence of man. Little explicit attention is given to why and how the mystery still remains meaningful for us and to its actual impact on the realities in which we encounter it, as distinct from its proposition as a truth of faith.

b) The one God exists in three persons, subsistences, hypostases (*D* 17, 19, 39, 48, 51, 58ff., 79, 254, 275, 278–81, 428, 431, 461, 703f., 993, 1919), who are the one divine nature (φύσις), essence (οὐσία), substance (as distinguished from subsistence) (*D* 17, 19, 39, 59, 78, 82, 86, 254, 275, 277ff., 428, 431f., 461, 703f., 708, 993) and are equal, coeternal and omnipotent (*D* 13, 19, 39, 54, 68–75, 254, 276ff., 428, 461ff., 703f.).

There is no official definition of the terms *persona*, ὑπόστασις, *substantia*, οὐσία; and there is no explanation of the possible distinction between *persona* and *hypostasis*. The meaning of the terms is to be derived from the definition of the terms in scholastic theology; from the meaning of the terms in the dogmatic propositions themselves with their dialectical contrast between the terms (ὑπόστασις-οὐσία); from the fact that "essence" is the most readily understood here, meaning the divine being, the divinity, of the three in the absolute sameness of the divine essence. It is difficult to determine why a particular term was used in a given case. The more recent declarations of the magisterium have not taken into account later developments in the concept of person, but continue to use the term in the sense which the word received in the anti-Arian controversy and in Christology. When, however, the Holy Spirit is described as constituted by the "mutual" love of Father and Son, in spite of the fact that the procession of the Spirit is only one action and (from) one principle (*D* 691, 1084), this way of speaking may betray the influence of a modern notion of person.

c) These persons are also (really) distinct from one another (*D* 39, 281, 703ff., 1655). The Father has no principle of origin (*D* 3, 19, 39, 275, 428, 703f.). The Son is born of the substance of the Father (*D* 13, 19f., 40, 48, 54, 69, 275f., 281, 432, 703f.) and only from the Father (*D* 40, 428, 703). The Spirit is not begotten (*D* 39, 277) but proceeds from the Father and the Son

(*D* 15, 19, 39, 86, 277, 428, 460, 691, 703) as from one principle (*D* 460, 691, 704) in one single spiration (*D* 691). The *generatio* and the *spiratio* are distinguished. But they are at one in affirming that the divine essence is possessed by the Son and the Spirit as "communicated". They are distinct inasmuch as this communication is, as generation, from the Father alone, and as spiration from the Father and the Son (or the Father through the Son, *D* 460, 691) as one principle of communication in one (notional) act. How this "begetting" and "breathing" are further distinguished is not explained by the magisterium. The existence of such a distinction simply follows from the difference between the Son and the Spirit.

d) This is the foundation of the principle that there are really distinct relations in God (*D* 208, 278, 281, 296, 703) and proprieties (*D* 281, 296, 428), and hence also a virtual distinction between the essence of God and the divine persons constituted by relations (cf. *D* 17, 19, 523f.). The distinction between the (absolute) essence of God and the relations which constitute the persons is meant to explain in terms of logic why a contradiction cannot at any rate be clearly proved to exist in saying that the divine essence is identically the same in the three divine persons while these are relatively distinct from each other. That the distinction is based on the opposition of relations is suggested by the words Father and Son, in which an oppositional relationship is expressed. In the doctrine of the relations in the Trinity, which reached its peak with the axiom of the Council of Florence (going back to St. Anselm), the doctrine of the Cappadocian Fathers played a predominant role, especially that of Gregory of Nyssa, and affected the formulations of the magisterium more than did the psychological speculation of St. Augustine (but see *D* 296).

e) The "relative" persons in God are not really distinct from the essence of God (*D* 278, 296, 703) and hence do not form a quaternity (*D* 283, 431f.). In God all is one, except where an opposition of relationship exists (*relationis oppositio*) (*D* 703). Each of the divine persons is fully in each other (*perichoresis, circumincessio*, *D* 704) and each of them is the one true God (*D* 279, 343, 420, 461).

f) The divine persons cannot be divided from one another in being (*D* 48, 281, 461) or in operation (*D* 19, 281, 428, 461) and form only one principle of action *ad extra* (*D* 254, 281, 428, 703). The activity of the three persons is one and the same and can be ascribed to any one of the persons only by appropriation (*DS* 3326). But here it must be noted that this axiom deals with the efficient causality of God (*D* 2290). It does not affect the truth that the Logos alone became man, or the theory of uncreated grace in which each of the three divine persons has his own special relation to men (in spite of *DS* 3331). Little attention has been given by the magisterium to the parallel doctrine of the "missions" of the Son and the Spirit by the Father (cf. *D* 277, 285, 794) in the economy of salvation.

C. Suggested Outline of a Systematic Doctrine of the Trinity

1. *The guiding principle as to matter and development.* a) The methodical principle is the identity of the Trinity of the economy of salvation and the immanent Trinity. The identity does not of course mean that one denies that the "economic" Trinity, one with the immanent Trinity, only exists by virtue of the free decree of God to communicate himself (supernaturally). But by virtue of this free decree, the gift in which God imparts himself to the world is precisely God as the triune God, and not something produced by him through efficient causality, something that represents him. And because he is the triune God, this "trinitarian

character" also affects the gift and makes it triune. And conversely it is therefore also true that the trinitarian character of this divine self-communication, the economic Trinity, makes the immanent Trinity known, *quoad nos*, because they are the same. It follows that the two immanent processions in God correspond (in identity) with the two missions, and that the relationships to created realities constituted in formal (not efficient) causality by the missions as processions are not appropriations (procession of the Logos – hypostatic union; procession of the Spirit – divinizing sanctification of man). The relationships are proper to the person in each case. (The ordinary objection [cf. *Mysterium Salutis*, II, pp. 330–2], asking why the relation to the sanctified man proper to the Spirit is not a hypostatic union, cannot be dealt with here. But the objection presupposes something which is ultimately simply false, that the *hypostasis* of the Logos and that of the Spirit are of the same nature.)

b) The principle for the doctrine of the Trinity thus signalled can be confirmed by noting that the hypostatic union constitutes a case in which this general principle is verified. Then, as regards the doctrine of grace and of the vision of God as triune, for which as such the Trinity must be the ontological principle, the notion that the Spirit has a proper relationship to man in the state of grace is a theological opinion well supported by Scripture, (Greek) tradition and modern theology since Petavius. It is only when this principle is presupposed that the distinction between the order of creation and of grace, the natural and the supernatural, can be made clear. For the divine self-communication, which constitutes the supernatural order of salvation in contrast to the act of natural creation, cannot and should not be considered only as the communication of an abstract essence (a divine φύσις), but as the communication of God as he is, that is, as the triune God. For it is the triune God as such who "dwells" in the justified and who is contemplated in the beatific vision. Further, in keeping with the general nature of revelation as a unity of God's saving action and word, the revelation of the immanent Trinity can only be thought of as coming in the action of divine grace qua action, that is, by the immanent Trinity becoming the economic Trinity. If the Trinity as such is to be a revealed mystery of salvation, it must itself be revealed in the order of salvation. Finally, it must be affirmed that revelation, as it appears throughout the whole of the NT, never deals with the immanent Trinity alone or as communicated only in concepts and propositions. It tells of the Son and the Spirit being experienced in the salvation-history and the revelation-history of the individual and the collectivity. It only speaks of the Son and the Spirit of the Father insofar as God (the unoriginated Father) is close to us through the Son and the Spirit. The Trinity is revealed in such a presentation of salvation-history. This revelation is not just the presupposition of another concerning the immanent Trinity, but is already the revelation of the immanent Trinity. Otherwise it would only be a purely verbal communication about something that did not affect us, it would find in us no real point of contact and would only be a humiliating imposition on our knowledge. It should also be noted that an abstract hypostatic union in a "God-man", as we often say, and a purely sanctifying (created) grace could be revealed without this revelation of the Trinity. Hence there would be no need of revealing the Trinity as a proposition if it were not really there for us itself as such.

2. *The Trinity of the economy of salvation.* a) *The economic Trinity as mystery.* It we now speak of the self-communication of God and try to understand the

Trinity in the order of salvation and then also in its immanent nature in the light of this, it should be understood from the start that all statements containing or articulating the concept of self-communication remain within this self-communication qua mystery and are therefore not open to the charge of rationalistic speculation. For the self-communication in question is not only not deducible *a priori*, since it is a free act of God in fact. It is also by its essence a permanent mystery, since the possibility of God's being quasi-formal cause with regard to a creature can never be positively understood. Further, the notion of self-communication which makes a systematic theology possible here, is itself derived from the statements of revelation, and thus does not eliminate the mystery of this message. All that can be systematically elaborated by virtue of this formal concept comes under this same heading.

b) *The unity of the self-communication of God in the two missions (of the Son and of the Spirit)*. According to the Christian faith, God's turning to the world, even when the act of its creation is also presupposed as a free act, is a gratuitous grace. But this does not prevent us from assuming that the divine self-communication to the world in the Spirit (grace) and the self-communication in the hypostatic union are one and the same free act, because these two communications are each the condition of the other. The hypostatic union is only rationally thinkable if it causes or implies the grace given to the world through the divine Spirit (or at least in the humanity of Christ, and then in all men, by reason of the social nature of his humanity). And conversely, the grace given to the world has its necessary historical manifestation and eschatological irreversibility in what we call the hypostatic union. Thus the two missions may be understood as interconnected moments of the one self-communication of God to the world. And conversely, this free act is deployed in the divinization of the world in the Holy Spirit (taking the word for the moment in the general sense in which it is mostly used in Scripture, i.e., the creative, loving, sanctifying power of God which draws the world to God) – and in its historical and eschatological manifestation through the historical and definitive word of God ("word" here also being taken in the general sense, as in 2 Cor 1:19f.).

c) If this twofold self-communication of God is really *self*-communication, in contrast to creation, it must be attributed to God in himself, i.e., it must imply a quasi-formal causality into which God enters, and this must be a determination of God himself. (By reason of the freedom in which this quasi-formal causality with regard to the creature is brought about, it cannot be seen to be repugnant, any more than the creative act of God, which being identical with God's being exists necessarily and eternally, though free as regards the world.) This is the basis on which an understanding of the immanent Trinity is to be attained (see below, 3).

d) *The "essence" of the two missions.* If the two missions are intrinsically connected moments of the one self-communication of God, then on principle, since the recipient of the self-communication is personal and historical, the notion could be analysed in such a way that a number of twin aspects would appear: origin – future, history – transcendence, offer – acceptance, knowledge – love. It could be shown that origin, history, offer and knowledge always correspond to future, transcendence, acceptance and love, and always form in each case a moment of this self-communication. Nonetheless, we begin here simply with the missions as they are known in the history of salvation.

The "essence" of the mission of the Spirit can be understood without any great difficulty (within the framework of the mystery). God imparts himself to the finite, needy, sinful creature. And this outgoing, without self-seeking or gain, taking a risk with others because one is great enough freely to be small among others, is precisely what is meant by love, in the sense of the NT *agape*. This is all the truer because God's self-communication aims at the innermost centre of the human person and is active there not only as the gift but as the power of the acceptance of the gift.

If one prescinds for the moment from the question of how the relationship between the love of God as proper to the essence and as forming the person can and must be distinguished, we are familiar with the "essence" of the mission. It is what traditional theology describes as the propriety of the third person in the "immanent" Trinity. In considering the mission of the Son, one must not simply begin with the notion of the Logos according to the Greek world of thought and then explain this mission as aiming at the revelation only of the truth of God, especially as this approach can attach the soteriological element to the mission only extrinsically and secondarily. It must be noted that truth in the full sense is the *lived* truth in which someone freely deploys his being for himself and for others, manifests himself historically as faithful and reliable and makes this state irrevocable. But this is precisely the mission of the Son in its essence, in which the aspects of revealer and saviour are united. It is the mission of the truth which is fidelity.

Under these circumstances we may rightly affirm that the divine self-communication has two basic modes, those of truth and of love. As truth, the self-communication takes place in history and is the offer of the free faithfulness of God. As love, it brings about acceptance and opens man's transcendence to the absolute future of God. Since the historical manifestation of God (the Father) as truth is only knowable in the horizon of transcendence towards the absolute future of God, and since the absolute future is manifested irrevocably as love by being promised in the concrete history of the faithful God (in the absolute bringer of salvation), these two aspects of the divine self-communication are neither disjoined nor joined merely by divine decree. Without being identical, they form together the one divine self-communication which explicates itself as truth in history, beginning and offer, and as love in transcendence, towards the absolute future, in acceptance.

3. *The "immanent" Trinity*. The transition from the Trinity of the economy of salvation to the immanent Trinity must be thought of along the lines indicated in D 1 and 2 c.

a) The Trinity *ad extra* and *ad intra* is identical, because one would not be speaking of a *self*-communication of God unless the two missions and the two persons thus there for us, in whom God comes to us, were "part" of God himself. If they were purely of the created realm, the communication of God's self would be absent. The missions are real "outgoings" (*processiones*) in God himself – the divine decree of self-communication being free, however.

b) The two processions are distinct, because they are the missions. The missions are of course distinct in their *terminus* in each case, and this difference is not simply that of the original missions (*missio principiative spectata*) as such (they terminate respectively in the human nature of Christ and the "created" grace of the justified, which are spatio-temporal entities). But the two moments of the one self-communication are also distinct on the divine side. They are moments of the self-communication of God which are related to each other in their difference. And this is also true of the processions.

c) These two processions, identical

with the missions, can of course be considered as proper to God "in himself", being regarded as the "potentialities" of the twofold self-communication, i.e., still in the light of the economy of salvation. The Logos, Jn 1:1, is with God from eternity, and hence immanent, but is still considered as related to the world. (These "potentialities" are not of course entities in God which have to go through the stage of being actuated.) But since the processions, in their actual reality, have a free (contingent, so to speak) relation to the world, they must be proper to God not merely "in himself" but also "for himself". They must also have an "immanent" significance. It may therefore be affirmed that the real distinction between the two processions is constituted by a twofold immanent self-communication, inasmuch as the unoriginated God (the Father) is he who is expressed in the truth for himself (the Son) and he who is received and accepted in love for himself (the Spirit), and hence is he who can freely communicate himself *ad extra* in this twofold way.

d) The real distinction in God is constituted by a twofold communication of the Father, by which the Father communicates himself and through this self-communication, where he "utters" and "receives", posits his real distinction as regards the person "uttered" and "received". What is communicated, since it makes the communication really a self-communication of God, and does not eliminate the real distinction between God as communicating and communicated, can rightly be termed the divinity, and hence the "essence" of God is communicated.

e) The element importing a distinction which intervenes between the original self-communicator and the term expressed and received must be designated as relative (relational). This follows from the identity of the essence (substance, nature). This relational constitution must not be primarily regarded as a means of resolving an apparent logical contradiction in the Trinity. Its value in such a process would be very limited. Insofar as a relation is looked on as the least real of all realities, it loses value in explaining the Trinity, which is the most real of all realities. But the relation is as absolutely real as anything else that can be said of the Trinity. And apologetics for the "immanent" Trinity cannot proceed on the basis of the prejudice that a lifeless identity of an uncommunicated type is the most perfect mode of being of the absolute being, and then go on to eliminate the difficulty created by this prejudice by explaining that the distinction in God is "only" relative.

4. *The difficulties of the notion of person as applied to the Trinity*. a) It is so normal to speak of three persons in God, in our preaching and theology, that one has the feeling that there is absolutely no other way of expressing this mystery. But that this is incorrect follows at once from the fact that the NT does not use the term "person", and that it was only introduced gradually into ecclesiastical usage, while the Greeks rarely say πρόσωπον (*persona*) and mostly prefer ὑπόστασις (*hypostasis*). In the contexts in question, all these statements mean the same thing, but not by virtue of their origin and history. And they have not *exactly* the same meaning, and did not retain such completely identical meaning in the further course of historical development. For while hypostasis, subsistence, as a concrete and as an abstract notion, can be predicated of any concrete being, and not merely of rational beings, *persona* always means the rational subsistent. And in the course of the history of the term, the situation of the consciousness of the spiritual subject as well as that of the ultimate concrete difference between one being and another has been modified. Spiritual subjectivity in consciousness and freedom is now not merely

an essential note of the concrete subsistent if this is to be a person. In the modern notion of person, consciousness is intrinsically constitutive for the very existence of the person.

If this shift of meaning were applied to the doctrine of the Trinity, three divine persons would mean three consciousnesses, with three free wills. But this is wrong. Hence the classical formulation of the doctrine cannot and may not be adapted to this modern trend of thought. But the doctrinal statements of the magisterium cannot undo or change history. Hence the official terminology of the Church, which was regulated according to a contingent use of the word "person", is now constantly exposed to misunderstanding. The word "person", in view of its present-day use, is almost necessarily misunderstood in the formulation of the Trinity and hence generally explained by circumlocutions. But this should not really be necessary, since the accepted meaning of the words should explain the proposition, and the words used should not need to be corrected in the light of the proposition.

b) This does not imply that the formula "one God in three persons" should be eliminated. No individual preacher has the authority to do so, and the magisterium is hardly in a position at present to produce a better formula which could be made official, that is, universally intelligible, obligatory and obviously acceptable as obligatory. Nonetheless, the preacher must recognize the existence of the problem and try to meet it as well as he can. But this means that he must have a number of alternatives to draw on, so that he can give his explanations and avoid the classical formulation, without having to improvise at every moment.

c) The best way of dealing with the problem is of course to speak in the context of salvation-history, individual and collective, naming the Father, Son and Spirit and bearing in mind that the one God is spoken of throughout. But one could also, for instance, instead of speaking of three persons, speak of three distinct ways of being there (in the economy of salvation) and three different ways of subsistence (immanently) for the one God. The word "ways" could also be used to suggest that the persons are there as in relation to one another, this relationship, where one of opposition, constituting the difference in God. Thus whenever the economy of salvation has to be propounded in formal terms, bringing out the unity of Father, Son and Spirit, the following formulations, offered merely as examples, could be used.

The one God subsists in three distinct ways. Father, Son and Spirit are distinct, qua oppositional, relations. Hence the three are not the "self-same", though they are "the same" (thing) (which is of course a subjectivity in the Godhead, free in our regard). The word "self", to avoid misunderstandings, should be reserved for a being in the ultimate concrete "individuality" in which it encounters another. Father, Son and Spirit are the one and the same God in the Godhead, in its different ways of subsistence. It is only with respect to the ways of subsistence that the number "three" can be applied to God, and here one must bear in mind that one is "adding up" a pure distinction within the numerical oneness of the essence, something that cannot be subsumed under the notion of a number of similar beings. God is "threefold" through his three ways of subsisting and being there. God qua subsisting in a given way (e.g., the Father) is another (not other) than God subsisting in another way. A way of subsisting is distinct from another by its relation of opposition, and is real by virtue of its identity with the divine being. Hence "he who" subsists in such a way is truly God.

Such formulations of the Trinity tell exactly as much as those in which the

word "person" is used. Possibly they sound just as abstract and formal. But without falling into modalism, they avoid misunderstandings in the sense of a tritheism such as could easily be evoked by the meaning now generally given to the term person.

5. *On the "psychological" approach to the doctrine.* a) The approach to the understanding of the Trinity which was put forward by St. Augustine and developed further by St. Thomas remains the classical explanation to the present day. It uses the pattern of the human mind – its knowledge and self-possession in the expression of the internal word and of love (*amor, voluntas*) – to illustrate the two immanent divine processions and so give some idea of the three persons in God. It is not the official doctrine of the Church, which offers at best only faint hints of it, and it is not the (direct) teaching of Scripture, which considers the Trinity only in terms of the economy of salvation. Hence the psychological interpretation of the Trinity is in no way normative. It is part of theology. But it can be considered legitimate, because there is a major theological tradition behind it, and also because the simplicity of God means that the three distinct ways of subsisting must have a necessary, intrinsic connection with the spiritual nature of God's being, a connection which is brought out in this doctrine. It appears all the more legitimate in the light of a metaphysical anthropology which demonstrates that there are only two fundamental acts of spiritual existence, knowledge and love. The obvious thing is to regard these basic acts as paralleled in the two divine processions.

b) However, the psychological interpretation of the Trinity fails to explain why God's self-possession in knowledge and love, a single act, as it were, flowing from the essence of the one God, should demand a *processio ad modum operati*, as *verbum* and as *amatum in amante*, given the absolute actuality and simplicity of God. Without such a procession there is no real triad of ways of subsistence.

c) Without prejudice to God's freedom, creation, self-sufficiency, etc., as *actus purus*, the relationship of God to the world (at least to the world as possible) could be viewed more positively than is generally done. This would mean that God's freedom with regard to the world would not have to be seen as a diminution or denial of his radical relationship to the world, but as its obvious and intrinsic mainspring. This would show still more clearly why the economic Trinity is the immanent Trinity. God the Father's twofold power of expressing himself *ad extra* as Logos and Pneuma would then still remain a function of his "spiritual" nature, which is the permanent element in the psychological theory of the Trinity, but the psychological theory in this form would already be grasped as such as soon as the Trinity of the economy of salvation was considered.

Karl Rahner

TRINITY IN THEOLOGY

A. Introduction to the State of the Question

We are not enquiring here into the content of the doctrine of the Trinity and the problems which it raises, but the situation of the doctrine itself as such. Here the question arises both on principle and in terms of a given epoch.

1. On principle, one may ask where the treatise on the Trinity should fit into dogma. Its ordinary place, which it has occupied for a long time now, is in the dogmatic treatise *De Deo* (*Uno et Trino*), at the beginning of dogmatic theology, after the usual preambles. Here a further question arises. Should one follow St. Thomas as has been customary, and simply put *De Deo*

Trino after *De Deo Uno*, and so first round off the "essential" doctrine about God in an almost metaphysical treatise? Or should one combine the doctrine of the nature of God with that of God in three persons, as has been done once more recently by Schmaus, and so make the theology of the Trinity the basic structural principle of the whole treatise *De Deo*? In the most recent efforts of Protestant theology there is a tendency, partly inspired by the nature of this theology, and partly by the general principle of giving priority to hermeneutics and theological epistemology, to make a certain type of theology of the Trinity part of the prolegomena of systematic theology. This is meant as an indication of what discourse about God should be in general, based on the notion of the "economic" Trinity as the guiding line for all correct discourse about God.

It would also be possible to consider the theology of the Trinity as the climax and conclusion of all dogmatic theology, since it would bring God and his saving action together, presenting "theology" and the "economy of salvation" together as a single, final statement. If one takes up the Dutch *New Catechism*, one sees that an effort is already being made to do without a special treatise on the Trinity. It speaks of the Father, Son and Spirit as they occur in the statement of our relationship to God, but this threefold discourse about God is not then systematized and transposed into a discourse about God "in himself".

2. This may seem at first sight to be merely a question of arrangement. But it is, of course, basically a question about the precise meaning of the actual doctrine. It is also a question of the view to be taken of the development of the dogma in question, which has a history running from the NT with its unsystematic statements about Father, Son and Spirit in the economy of salvation, to the Athanasian Creed and the Council of Florence, with their doctrine of one divine nature in three persons. For since then no important progress or changes have come in kerygmatic statement or religious practice.

3. Another point must be noted, since it makes itself insistently felt in the life of present-day Christians and Christian preachers. It is that the doctrine of the Trinity, in spite of its being so often extolled as the fundamental mystery of Christianity, plays a very modest role, if it occurs at all, in the actual life of Christians and in the teaching which they hear. There is no need to give detailed proof of this. Reference has already been made to the Dutch Catechism. The doctrine of the Trinity was of course in the mind of the Second Vatican Council, though referred to explicitly only in *Lumen Gentium* and *Unitatis Redintegratio* and hardly anywhere else. But it was never taken up as one of the basic themes, though it should be noted that a certain preference appeared for the Greek formulation of the Trinity in terms of the economy of salvation – "from the Father, through the Son, in the Holy Spirit". This may be taken as a tendency to speak more emphatically in terms of the economy of salvation when the Trinity is affirmed. Paul VI's confession of faith propounded the doctrine of the Trinity in such classical terms and perspectives that it could in fact hardly gain a new hearing for the doctrine in the present situation. The ultimate reason for this general lack of attention to the theology of the Trinity seems obvious. In an age of public and worldwide atheism, the question of God is urgently concerned with God's existence, not with his "inner" mystery. But a still deeper reason underlies this temper of the age. Since St. Augustine, the "immanent" Trinity has been so much to the fore in theological discussion of it, and the "economic" Trinity has been so obscured in Christ-

ology and *De Gratia* by the principle that all actions *ad extra* in God are common to all three persons or belong to God as one, that it is hard to see what Christian existence has to do with the Trinity in actual life. And then again, whenever faith in the Trinity is meaningfully evoked, it is as part of Christology, when we turn in faith to Jesus Christ as the definitive presence of God among us in salvation-history, or it is part of *De Gratia*, when we acknowledge the self-communication of God in the grace of the Spirit. But this is outside the framework of a systematic theology of the Trinity. And it is not reverent adoration of the Trinity as such.

B. Formal Principle for the Structure and Matter of the Theology of the Trinity

The questions raised under A above can only be answered when a formal principle has been worked out to comprise the matter and structure of the theology of the Trinity. This principle, taken in conjunction with other themes of faith and theology, should give clear directives for the procedures to be followed in the theology of the Trinity. Such a theme has been singled out in Mariology, for instance ("basic principle of Mariology"), but no such effort has been generally made in the theology of the Trinity. It is a matter, therefore, of taking the first hesitant steps. We propose, therefore, as the basic principle in question, for the organization of the matter and presentation, the identity of the immanent Trinity and of the Trinity of the economy of salvation. Our proposition would be that the economic Trinity is (already) the immanent Trinity, because the basic event of the whole economy of salvation is the self-communication of God to the world, and because all that God (the Father) is to us in Jesus Christ the Son and the Holy Spirit would not really be the *self*-communication of God, if the twofold missions were not intrinsic to him, as processions, bringing with them the distinction of the three persons. This principle need not be established and explained more fully here, but merely used to illustrate questions raised by the theology as such of the Trinity.

C. The Place of Trinitarian Theology in Dogmatics

With the above principle in mind, we may make the following affirmations.

1. No one would deny that trinitarian theology has an impact on theological epistemology and the hermeneutics of theological assertions, since, in the light of the basic principle of the theology of the Trinity, the Trinity is not just one object among others in the whole range of theological statements. For the whole economy of salvation has a trinitarian structure. And as an object of faith (which faith is itself a moment of the economy) the economy determines the concrete act of faith, which is not just an abstract assent on the basis of the formal authority of God, and gives the act of faith itself a trinitarian structure (deriving from the object of faith and the grace of faith, which is none other than the trinitarian self-communication of God). But all this does not justify one in burying away the theology of the Trinity behind a theological epistemology or a hermeneutics. If this were a legitimate process, the basic principle enunciated above would oblige one to transpose the whole history of salvation and its theology into hermeneutics.

2. One consequence of the basic principle is that it is at least not obvious that a theology of the Trinity should be placed at the start of theology as a whole. The immanent Trinity is known in faith because the economic Trinity has been seen to be at work in the history of salvation. The economic Trinity is not merely the means of gaining knowledge of the immanent Trinity,

but is the same thing. This cannot be said in the same sense of the doctrine *De Deo* in general, since the sense of dependence on God in which God is known comes at the start of all theological effort. This dependence on God came itself to be propounded in trinitarian terms in the course of the history of salvation and revelation. Dogmatic theology could parallel this historical process by beginning with an initial formal description of our relationship to God (as the permanent structural principle of history of salvation and revelation in general) and ending with an explicit treatise on the Trinity (as a summary of salvation-history which has come eschatologically to full self-explication). The Dutch Catechism makes some such effort at the end, though very briefly.

On the other hand, there is nothing in our basic principle which simply compels us to place the theology of the Trinity at the end. The *circumincessio* in which all the treatises of dogmatic theology are in the nature of things involved should not be lost sight of, especially as this *circumincessio* results directly from our basic principle. If the *Oikonomia* is really the whole of theology and likewise contains and reveals the immanent Trinity itself, the whole of dogmatic theology is trinitarian theology, which means that the theology of the Trinity is only really articulated by theology as a whole. But then there is nothing to prevent our putting a treatise *De Deo Trino* at the beginning, to give a rather formal preview of what comes up as the real trinitarian theology through the whole of what follows. But this initial treatise should not be an attempt to cover a theme which can then be marked as read, but a preliminary orientation with regard to a theme which is still to be dealt with.

3. If the introductory treatise *De Deo Trino* is understood in this light, the present procedure may well be followed, which is to deal first with *De Deo Uno* and then take up *De Deo Trino*. For if the treatise *De Deo Uno* is to be real theology and not mere metaphysics, it cannot speak of the one God and his nature without speaking of the God of history and of a historical experience of him, of the God of a possible revelation and self-communication. Hence it is already orientated to the treatise *De Deo Trino*, which deals with such a God in salvation-history.

D. On the History of the Theology of the Trinity

1. In the NT, the theology of the Trinity, insofar as it is possible to speak of its existence there, is entirely orientated to the economy of salvation. God and the Father are synonyms. The Son and the Spirit are spoken of inasmuch as they come into the experience of faith as the actual presence of this God (the Father) in the history of salvation. Apart from this, the NT theology of the Trinity does no more than show the Son and the Spirit as being experienced as the absolute proximity of God himself, not as subordinate representatives of someone absent. There is also a certain tendency to coordinate the three names in the same context.

2. The main question in the period subsequent to that of the NT was of course the relationship of the Son to God (the Father), since the Spirit could be more readily accepted as a synonym for God. Hence statements about the Spirit appear rather as a consequence of Christological assertions. If we prescind from the theology of Judaeo-Christianity (and of the Ebionites), the basic trinitarian question in the patristic age is whether the Logos (and the Pneuma) should be considered in the light of the "hierarchical thinking" of Platonism and neo-Platonism and hence as a subordinate cosmic power other than the true God or whether he was really God "consubstantial" with the Father, though not simply to be identi-

fied with him as in various types of modalism. Properly speaking, this makes the trinitarian theology of the Fathers a theology based from the start on the history of salvation and soteriology. It says something about us, and defends the consubstantiality of the Logos and the Pneuma with God the Father on the ground that otherwise we should not be divinized in immediate relation to God himself. On these grounds the Greek way of thinking of the Trinity remains entirely orientated to man. The Father reveals himself through the Son and through him reaches man in the Holy Spirit. The Greeks distinguished *hypostasis* (which should not be taken as identical in meaning with *persona*, especially in the modern sense of the term person) from the nature (φύσις, οὐσία). The distinction served to bring out the truth that God (θεός, the Father himself) has come to us in his divinity through the Son and the Spirit, in real self-communication, while the trinitarian structure of our relationship with God as based on the economy of salvation remains unchanged. It remains historically definite (through the Son) and absolutely immediate (in the Spirit), contrary to modalism and Sabellianism, and again, contrary to Arianism, where the structure is a mediation serving not the establishment of immediacy but of a medium which only links inasmuch as it is the "between" which separates. Hence too Greek patristic theology was content to define the relation between the one nature and the three subsistents (*in se*) and the three ways of being there (for us) in terms of formal ontology, by understanding these as "relations". The concrete character of these "hypostases" is then deduced from their function in the history of salvation. In keeping with this approach, when grace is discussed, the relationship of each of the divine persons to the justified is not regarded merely as so many "appropriations" of the relationship of the one Godhead, now attached to each of the persons.

3. St. Augustine was the first to try to explain further the nature of the Trinity in the one Godhead without deriving the content from the way in which the three persons are there (for us) in the economy of salvation. He elaborated his "psychological" theology of the Trinity, using triads which we find in our spiritual processes, *memoria*, *intelligentia*, *voluntas*, *amor*, etc., to illustrate the immanent processions of the divine life. St. Augustine emphasizes that all God's activity *ad extra* is common to all three persons, since it proceeds from his one nature (*De Trinitate*, II, 17, 32) (and hence, for instance, the Father could have become man if he had willed). The significance of the economy of salvation for the "immanent" Trinity is thereby much diminished, to say the least. St. Augustine's speculations do not start like the ancient and the Greek theology from the Father but from the one divine *essentia*, for which the three persons are so to speak subsequent determinations including the Father. (In Baroque theology, this could lead to the question as to whether an absolute subsistence should not be attributed to God as well as the three relatives subsistences.) As an effort to show that God is also "immanently", in himself, what he displays in his actions in the economy of salvation, the psychological theory of St. Augustine had undoubtedly great importance, and it was also responsible for profound insights in existential anthropology. But it obscured the connection between the immanent and the economic Trinity, to the detriment of a vitally practical theology of the Trinity, a loss which is not fully compensated for by the lofty speculation on the immanent divine life.

4. Apart from the contribution of Boethius to the formal definition of the terminology applied to the Trinity, it may be said that scholasticism has been

dominated down to the present day by the trinitarian theology of St. Augustine, whose influence was reinforced by that of St. Thomas Aquinas (with added elements of the Boethian terminology further elaborated mainly in the school of Gilbert of Poitiers). Another type of trinitarian theology, more on the line of the Greeks and also striving to apply to this theology as a whole a personal and psychological consideration of love, was given a strong impulse by Richard of St. Victor and was fully developed by Alexander of Hales and St. Bonaventure. But it did not succeed in establishing itself. Controversy with the Eastern Orthodox meant that the question of the procession of the Holy Spirit from the Son as well as the Father (*filioque*) (or through the Son) played a role in medieval Latin theology and was one of the preoccupations of the last Council to deal specifically with the doctrine of the Trinity, the Council of Florence, 1439–45 (*D* 691, 703ff.). Another result of the development of dogma in the pronouncements of the magisterium which is of importance to modern theology is the fact that the principle of the oneness of the activity of God *ad extra* (*D* 703) refers to the efficient causality of God. Hence it cannot be applied without more ado to "uncreated" grace. This cannot be subsumed under the concept of the efficient cause. And since it is the self-communication of God, it is the basic principle of the economy of salvation and the medium of the real revelation of the Trinity, since the Trinity cannot communicate itself as such *ad extra* to the world merely by conceptual communication. Close consideration of the precise official commentary on the ancient axiom by Pius XII would be a great help in applying consistently and courageously the principle enunciated as basic in B above, that is, in bringing out the aspect of the economy of salvation in the theology of the Trinity.

Not enough attention has been paid so far in the history of the theology of the Trinity to the divergent developments which the notion of person has undergone in the theology of the Trinity, where it has remained consistently the same, and in modern philosophy and general usage, where it has taken another line. This divergence constantly leads to misunderstandings when the theological proposition is put forward that the one God exists in three persons. It is almost inevitable that the word person in this proposition should now be taken in the modern sense, which is not that of a "way of subsistence" but of a "personal centre of action". This means that the theology of the Trinity would be infiltrated by a tritheism not easy to expose.

E. The Theology of the Trinity in Modern Preaching

The theology of the Trinity undoubtedly tries to bear on the central element of the Christian notion of God and so on the central element of Christian existence. The Trinity must therefore be preached and explained. There can be no doubt about this. But this does not mean that the theology of the Trinity, in the form which it took on during the first fifteen hundred years and which has scarcely been modified in the last five hundred, only needs to be "popularized" to some extent in order to be preached fruitfully today.

1. The preacher must first be convinced that when he speaks of three persons in God, his hearers will automatically import their notion of person into this proposition and either misunderstand it or right themselves only by taking evasive action, as it were, taking refuge in "implicit faith" and the faith of the Church. This does not mean of course that the preacher must avoid completely the expression of "three persons" in God. This is a formula used by the magisterium, a rule

of language which is to be respected and which it would be wrong not to allude to. But it would be equally dangerous to confine oneself to a stereotyped repetition of the formula, on the grounds that this is the briefest, clearest and most unambiguous way of stating what is meant. It is one's duty to bear in mind that the creeds with which the laity are most familiar do not contain the proposition about the one God in three persons and one nature, but confess the Father, the Son and the Spirit.

2. There is another consideration to be borne in mind as well as this difficulty arising from the changing connotations of the terms. The preacher who is justifiably cautious about using the formula of "three persons" should remember calmly that "three persons" is a way of subsuming under a sort of general denominator what distinguishes Father, Son and Spirit, not what unites them, as St. Thomas pointed out in the *Summa Theologica*, I, q. 30, a. 4 ad 4. In everything in which they agree they are absolutely one in the one identical substance (cf. *D* 703). A universalized notion of person applied three times over can only be used with extreme caution when speaking of the Trinity if the result is not to be more misunderstanding than insight. The subtle solution which points out that these are "transcendental" numbers which do not imply a "multitude" will be of little help to the ordinary Christian who is trying to avoid the mistakes to which he his liable. If the speaker actually uses the word three when talking of God, there is nothing to prevent him using other terms and concepts such as the classical "hypostases", "subsistents" or "ways of subsisting", "ways of being".

3. The general conclusion must be that the preacher will mainly speak of Father, Son and Spirit in whatever context of salvation-history and theology of grace they may occur. It is relatively easy to explain what the giving of God's Spirit in uncreated grace implies. If it is then made clear that in the gift God has given himself in a radical self-communication (Spirit), while still remaining the sovereign incomprehensible God in his mystery, everything that needs to be said has really been said (apart from some possible distinctions of a secondary type). No further statement of the relation between Father and Spirit is needed in a kerygmatic theology of the Trinity. When Jesus Christ is proclaimed as simply and uniquely the Son, the Sonship in question may first be taken, without misgivings, as the absolutely unique situation of the man Jesus in the economy of salvation. It is in virtue of this situation that he is "the Son" in the synoptic gospels (Mk 12:6 par.; Mt 11:27 par., etc.). As this concrete being, in and through his real humanity, he is the absolute and final word of God's fidelity (his "truth"), in which the Father addresses the world by a historical, irrevocable deed. In this way he is already *the* Son. But this sonship in the economy of salvation, as follows from the basic principle enunciated above under B, implies the expressibility of the Father which is eternally actual in God himself, and this forms a proper way of God's subsisting. In this sense (as for instance in Jn 17:5, 24) we can and must speak of the pre-existing Son, a truth which should not be overlooked and must be stated. But in view of what has been said, this Sonship may be explained, and has in fact already been explained, when this power of absolute self-utterance of the Father is understood as unshakable fidelity. When one affirms that Jesus is the faithful word of the Father, in which the Father definitively addresses *himself* to us, one has already affirmed the eternal "immanent" relationship between Father and Son, provided one understands that in Jesus the Father does in truth impart himself, and not something about himself, not something

conceptual or real not identical with himself.

4. If this Trinity of the economy of salvation is preached in such a way that it can be consciously grasped as vital to religion and life, one may then speak of the Trinity in the usual terms of theology, as a summary of what is said otherwise, in which constant reference is made to the "economic" Trinity. This would correspond to a theology of the Trinity placed at the end of dogmatic theology as a general summary of the whole.

Karl Rahner

TRUTH

I. Philosophical

A. Historical Survey

1. *Old Testament.* Two main sources determined the development of the question of truth in the philosophy of the West. One was the OT, the other was Greek philosophy. The OT word for "truth" (אֱמֶת) really means to be firm, reliable, faithful. When Yahweh's *'emeth* is spoken of, it means the divine will to perpetuate his favour. Thus *'emeth* can be translated as fidelity. God's word is "truth" (2 Sam 7:28 – RSV, "thy words are true"; cf. Ps 119:160), cf. Ps 132:11, "The Lord swore to David a sure oath (*'emeth*) from which he will not turn back", where the word means both sincerity and constancy. This fidelity of God means that he offers sure refuge (Pss 40:12; 54:7; 61:8, etc.). The faithfulness of God is affirmed in Deut 7:9; 32:4; Is 49:7 and Ps 31:6. When "truth" is affirmed of men, it means the loyalty of the people to God (Jos 24:14; 2 Kg 20:3; Is 38:3; Ps 26:3; 86:11). "To walk in the 'truth'" (1 Kg 2:4; 3:6; 2 Kg 20:3; Is 38:3; Ps 26:3; 86:11) and "to do the 'truth'" both mean to live a life of faithfulness to the law of God. Nonetheless, the OT also uses "truth" to signify the correspondence between assertion and reality, e.g., 3 Kg 10:6; 22:16. In the latest books of the OT, the Law is considered the "truth". "Practising the truth" (e.g., Tob 4:6; 13:6; Ecclus 27:9) is contrasted with serving the lie. It is the attitude of the man who observes the law of God.

2. *New Testament.* In the NT, "truth" (ἀλήθεια) has several meanings. It is the fidelity and reliability of God (Rom 3:1–7). It is the quality of the genuine and obligatory which attaches to the gospel (Eph 4:21; Gal 2:5, 14; Rom 2:8; 2 Col 4:2; Gal 5:7); the word of God (2 Cor 4:2; Gal 5:7); what can be known about God, i.e., evidently revealed by him (Rom 1:18); human sincerity (2 Cor 7:14; Phil 1:18; 1 Tim 2:7; 2 Jn 1). But it can also mean the authoritative doctrine, e.g., 1 Tim 6:5; 2 Tim 2:18; 3:8; 4:4; Tit 1:14, as Bultmann has noted. The preaching of the gospel is the word of truth (Eph 1:13; Col 1:5; 2 Cor 6:7, etc.). "To do the truth" (cf. Jn 3:21; 1 Jn 1:6) now means to fulfil the law of Christ (instead of the OT law), and to "walk in the truth" (2 Jn 4; 3 Jn 3f.) undergoes a parallel change of meaning. Jn combines a number of traditional meanings under the heading of "truth", but they are all referred to the reality revealed in Jesus. "Truth" is the reality of salvation which sets man free (Jn 8:32). "Truth" sanctifies (Jn 17:17ff.). Christ is the way, the truth and the life (Jn 14:6). The Paraclete, being the "Spirit of truth", continues the work of Christ. He gives testimony to Christ and glorifies him. The distinctive element in the NT is that both in Jn and Paul "truth" is the Christological truth.

3. *Antiquity.* The problem of truth is first explicitly considered in the didactic poem of Parmenides. There the goddess teaches the way of truth, which is contrasted with δόξα, opinion, the fallacious opinions of mortal men (Frg. I, 28ff.). To recognize that being is and that non-being is not is knowledge of

the truth (Frg. 2 [4], 3ff.). Plato contrasts ordinary speech and opinion, which is liable to error (ψεῦδος), with the realm of truth. The myth of the cave (*Republic*, 7, 514ff.) describes the breakthrough of the human mind to truth. For Plato, this truth is the primordial self-manifestation of true being, the forms. Truth is therefore considered as the coming out of concealment, an unveiling. The connection between the *logos* (reason), beings and truth is already affirmed. The *logos* "which affirms beings as they are, is true; but the mind which affirms them otherwise than they are is in error" (*Cratylus*, 385 b; cf. *Sophist*, 263 b). Aristotle investigates this connection in detail and reaches a definition of truth as judgment (*Metaphysics*, IX, 10; 1051b). Truth means the reference of the composition of concepts in the judgment to reality. In Middle Platonism, the forms were conceived of as exemplars in the mind of God. God is the truth beyond the ideas (Albinus, *Isagoge*, 10). Philo of Alexandria combined the Platonic myth of creation with the biblical account. The "ideas" are products of the divine mind which creates everything by its thought, which is also action. Plotinus, the founder of neo-Platonism, finds that the first origin can be defined only negatively. The *Nous* is the "second God", who contains the Platonic *mundus intelligibilis* (κόσμος νοητός) and hence is the ground of truth in its dialectic of mind-thinking and term of thought (*Enneads*, 5, 5). Truth is revealed to the contemplative soul by the presence of the *Nous* within it (5, 1, 3; 3, 4).

4. *Patristic and scholastic thought*. The "norm for the truth of beings", according to Clement of Alexandria, is God (*Protrepticus*, VI; *PG*, VIII, col. 173). This is the first attempt to combine Greek and NT thought. The great authorities here were Origen, the Cappadocian Fathers and the Pseudo-Dionysius among the Greeks, and St. Augustine among the Latins. St. Augustine combines the Johannine *Logos* with the neo-Platonist *Nous* (*Confessions*, VII, 9). The Son is the truth, since he is the Word who reveals the Father (*De Trinitate*, VII, 3). St. Augustine uses the *cogito* of the subject to justify truth as against scepticism (*Soliloquium*, II, 1, 2). He stresses the necessary nature of truth, which human reason does not create but discovers (*De Vera Religione*, 39, 72). In his *De Libero Arbitrio*, he describes the ascent to truth which determines the movement of thought. This truth is absolute, eternal and changeless (II, 15, 39). Illumination from God is required for the knowledge of the higher truth. Like Aristotle, Boethius refers truth to the judgment, because this is pronounced *secundum complexionem* (e.g., *In Categorias Aristotelis*, IV; *PL*, LXIV, col. 278; *De Interpretatione*, editio prima, *ibid.*, col. 300). But his *De Consolatione Philosophiae* (IV, 4; V, 6) points to a Platonic conception. St. Anselm of Canterbury analyses the relation of logical to ontological truth. Logical truth is an effect of the *summa veritas*, mediated by created things (*De Veritate*, ch. 10). This means that the ontological connection is under the rule of truth as the *rectitudo sola mente perceptibilis* (*ibid.*, ch. 11). Speech is recognized as having a fundamental kinship with truth (*ibid.*, ch. 2). Hugh of St. Victor recognizes that truth has an intrinsic relation to the sciences (*In Hierarchiam Caelestem*, I, 1). The notion of a "double truth" is supposed to be typical of the Latin Averroists, but was not in fact explicitly put forward in these circles.

In St. Thomas Aquinas, truth is the primordial opening out of being (*ens et verum convertuntur*), and also the function of the judgment (*adequatio intellectus et rei*, cf. *Contra Gentiles*, I, 59; *De Veritate*, I, 2). God is the first truth and the foundation of all truth. The transcendental truth means that being has an intrinsic relation to spirit and hence to the spirit-soul, and also that spirit is ordained to (the grasp of) being (*De Veritate*, I, 1). St. Thomas combines the Aristotelian notion that the soul is "all things in a certain fashion" (see *Soul*) with the notion of the truth of things (cf. Aristotle, *The Soul*, 431b, and *Metaphysics*, 993b). The whole field of problems thus demarcated, where the influence of St. Augustine is also visible, is then placed in the perspective of the doctrine of being. St. Bonaventure's notion of truth is Augustinian. Duns Scotus recognizes an ontological and a logical truth.

When the medieval discussion of truth is considered, one should not forget the connection affirmed between truth and language. The connection was laid down by neo-Platonism and St. Augustine. Reflection on language is found in St. Anselm of Canterbury, especially in the *Monologion* and the *De Veritate*. Patristic and scholastic thought sees the foundation of this relationship in the Trinity, since Christ is the Word of the Father. Human utterance and trinitarian *expressio* are seen by St. Augustine and St. Thomas as related. In St. Thomas, the internal word is the revelation of the known in the knower (*Contra Gentiles*, IV, 11; *De Potentia*, 9, 5; *Summa Theologica*, I, q. 28, a. 4 ad 1). The word-event here appears as an approach to the resolution of the subject-object tension. The typical definition, probably stemming from William of Auxerre, of the relation between truth and faith takes the form: "Credere est assentire primae veritati propter se et super omnia." The First Truth is at once revelation of being and sure warranty, and hence can be *auctoritas*.

Classical medieval thought takes a new turn with William of Occam. The will of God replaces the truth of God in the centre of theological thought. The transcendentals are reduced to concepts. The problem of truth becomes more and more the problem of knowledge. Robert Holkot, a disciple of Occam, made a total distinction between philosophical and theological truth.

5. *The beginning of the modern era.* The tradition of "negative theology" going back to the Pseudo-Dionysius was taken up by Nicholas of Cusa, who held that God and his truth could not be known in their *aequalitas praecisa* ("exactly") (divine truth, for Nicholas, being identical with the incarnate *Verbum*). Nonetheless, divine truth remains the goal of all human knowledge, to which all its efforts must be directed. The truth is given to the intellect only in the form of *docta ignorantia* (*De Docta Ignorantia*, I, 3). In his highest speculative flights, Nicholas sees the unknowable divine truth reflected in the linguistic dialectic of the "Non-aliud". The contradiction between theological and philosophical truth, strongly emphasized by Luther, but modified by Melanchthon, Humanism and the Enlightenment, became a key problem of Protestant theology, brought out in particular by Kierkegaard and dominant down to Barth, Bultmann and Tillich.

In general, the problem of theological truth took on a new relevance through the Reformation. The word of God, regarded as the real authority, becomes the primordial truth. The word of God in preaching (Scripture in the act of self-exposition) is the source of the faith that justifies. Through Descartes, the logical and ontological problem of truth is what is seen clearly – the clear idea (*Meditationes*, III, 4). Nothing can be considered true which is not evident: this is the first methodical principle (*Discours de la méthode*, 2, 14). Descartes recognizes no ontological truth. But God is the guarantee of truth, since man cannot be the origin of his infinite idea. Occasionalism is tributary to Descartes. Malebranche's main work is called *Recherche de la Vérité*. All real knowledge of truth comes from contemplation of the divine ideas. In contrast to the nominalism of Hobbes, Leibniz deals with the logical problem of truth (*Works*, ed. by C. Gerhardt, VII, pp. 190ff.). A permanent harmony between signs and objects is to be presupposed. The characteristics of Leibniz's notion of truth are that the original truth is anchored in God (*Théodicée*, II, para. 184) and that the truths of reason are linked with the principle of non-contradiction, which is considered fundamental (*Discours de métaphysique*, no. 13). This opened up an epistemological perspective of truth which has remained predominant in certain schools of thought down to the present day. Hobbes rejected all ontological truth: "Veritas enim in dicto, non in re consistit" (*Opera Philosophica*, I, 32). Spinoza also confined truth to the affirmation (*Opera*, I, 246f.). The notion of truth as the accord between a thing and its idea or definition is found in Clauberg (*Opera Philosophica*, II, 648), under the influence of Descartes. C. Wolff recognizes a transcendental truth but bases it on the first principles – non-contradiction and sufficient reason (*Philosophia Prima,* para. 498). In contrast to the scholastics, Wolff demanded a "distinct" concept of truth. This was a decisive step towards the reduction of metaphysics to logic, which was given even more emphatic expression by Wolff's disciple, Baumgarten (*Metaphysica*, paras. 89–93).

6. *From Cant to the present day*. In the "Copernican revolution" introduced by Kant into philosophy, truth was regarded as "agreement with the laws of the intellect" (*Critique of Pure Reason*, B 350). The old definition of the *adaequatio* is thus reformulated in terms of transcendental philosophy. The empirical synthesis of experience attains truth inasmuch as it contains all that is necessary for the synthetic unity of experience (*ibid.*, B 197). The former ontological truth has become the basic synthesis of the transcendental apperception. A proposition in accord with the laws of thought and experience is objective. This view is also adopted by Fichte (*Werke*, 6, 19) but given a new orientation, inasmuch as the notion of the absolute I intervenes in the synthesis of the I and the Not-I, so that the problem of truth is seen basically as that of the interpretation of dialectical thought. When Schelling says that truth is the absolute identity of the subjective and the objective (*Werke*, VI, p. 497), the truth of the judgment has been referred back to its absolute foundation. This interpretation is given its fullest expression by Hegel, for whom truth is the all, the absolute concept, the absolute idea. Hegel undoubtedly affirms that truth is the agreement between notion and object, but he means by this only truth in the subjective intellect. A new approach to the problem of truth, which could be termed a modified Platonism, may be seen in Bolzano (truths in themselves) and Lotze (truths exist insofar as they are valid), a notion brought out by Husserl in his *Logische Untersuchungen* and characteristic of value-philosophy.

Hegel was attacked by Feuerbach, who maintained that the basic notion of truth was "life", which meant "man" (*Essence of Christianity*, Preface). Marx dismissed all discussion of the reality and otherwise of thought as mere scholasticism, unless it was based on *praxis*. It is in "practice" that man has to give proof of the truth of his thinking, that is, its reality and power, its relevance to life in this world (cf. *2nd Thesis on Feuerbach*). This was a rejection not only of Idealism but of the older forms of materialism. There is no such thing as truth as such. Truth comes to be through the orientation of our thought to practice. Theory is then the scientific generalization of practice, and practice as evolved in society is the criterion of truth. The way to objective truth becomes a social process – when directed, as Lenin said, by Marxist theory. All other efforts lead only to confusion and deceit.

Hegel was also attacked by Kierkegaard. Here again truth is regarded as action, but now it is the action of the individual, and its basis is existence. Since human life contradicts faith, faith, which is "doing the truth", is a paradox. And this is why Christianity can never be understood in the light of "reason". Nietzsche also attacked Hegel and the metaphysicians in his effort to destroy the traditional notion of truth. What was once called truth is now known as an idol (*Werke*, XV, p. 105). Truth is the most debilitated type of knowledge (V, p. 149). The elimination of the world of truth has brought with it the elimination of the world of appearances (VIII, p. 82). Nietzsche calls for a truth which is still to be created and can be the source for identifying a process (XVI, p. 56). The will to truth is a form of the will to power. Jaspers dealt with the notion of truth in his extensive work, *Von der Wahrheit* (1947; cf. *Truth and Symbol* [1959]), distinguishing the truth of the realm which we ourselves are (conscience, presence, spirit, existence) and the truth of the realm which being itself is (world, transcendence). We speak of transcendence in a code to which no assignable meaning is adequate. Being cannot be separated from being true, being for us, and hence from communicability.

In Heidegger, truth, within the framework of the analysis of ek-sistence, is the opening out of ek-sistence, as concern and being-for-death, and is hence the historicity of being. But the whole problem is dominated from the start by the question of being. And so truth is seen as the throwing open of being. And since this opening out brings with it a closing up, truth is primordially bound up with non-truth. Being displays itself to us as truth, as historicity and language. In Heidegger, therefore, in contrast to previous metaphysical and transcendental philosophy, truth is understood historically and as such determines this understanding of it.

All these trends – metaphysics, Marxism, existence-philosophy – are opposed by (linguistic or logical) positivism, which tries to apply consistently the principles of the older empiricism, with the help of formal logic. Truth is dealt with in the context of meaning and verification. The protagonists here were the Vienna Circle, especially R. Carnap and L. Wittgenstein. Verification, as demanded by Carnap, is confirmation by empirical observation. Truth is verifiability. What is contradicted by facts is untrue. Metaphysical judgments are neither true nor false, they are meaningless. Even in the earlier Wittgenstein the boundary between the meaningful and the meaningless is the boundary between the experiential and the non-experiential. Any meaningful question can always be answered: there are no riddles (cf. *Tractatus*, 6, 5). Wittgenstein later criticized his earlier thinking and called in question important elements. In his later works, the meaning of a word is identified with its use in speech (*Philosophical Investigations*, 43). It is use which gives life to the sign (*ibid.*, 432). Meaning and purpose and hence too the problem of truth are referred to linguistic usage, the "language game".

B. The Problem as it Appears Today

The problem of truth now appears under two chief aspects. One school sees the problem in terms of hermeneutics, basing itself on Dilthey and Heidegger. This trend has also greatly influenced modern theology (Bultmann and his school). The other trend is represented by (logical) positivism, which recognizes truth only in the judgment and rejects entirely not only all metaphysics but even hermeneutical questioning, as a mere process of reflecting on self undertaken by the subject. It should be noted, however, that positivism is not implied in all logical examination of the problem of truth. The discussion of truth-functions and truth-values is a logical effort which does not imply any given ontology but does not exclude such interpretations.

The question of the historical, the non-historical or supra-historical nature of truth is now particularly acute in philosophy and in theology. The historicity of truth does not imply that it is merely relative. It rather involves reflection on the basic coming of truth, the event which makes possible the being of man. We think of this event as a primordial language by which we are addressed. This view is not confined within the limits of a personal-dialogical philosophy (truth as encounter), but considers in the light of language and in view of language how such encounter is made possible. This brings up the fundamental problem of being and speech.

Theologically, this would mean that revelation is the primordial coming of speech, addressed to men and answered by us as men. At the same time, once such a view is adopted, the ancient definitions of logical and ontological truth will be investigated anew in terms of the conditions of their possibility. The hermeneutical problem leads to a reappraisal of what "fact" really is and how the knowledge of such "fact" is to be characterized. We only know any event within given horizons. Hence all human knowledge of truth remains one-sided. The transcendence of reason enables us to follow up all the aspects which this "one-sidedness" suggests, but we cannot think of God and know him except in human ways. There is no human statement, therefore, which can be taken as definitive. For every statement is articulated within certain horizons which can no doubt signify the whole of what is meant but cannot explicate it completely. The disclosure of truth is always a dialogical process.

Joseph Möller

II. Truthfulness

1. Any effort to analyse and co-ordinate the various approaches to truth in ethics is faced with the difficulty that the term "truth" is used on a variety of levels of meaning in philosophy and theology, the reason clearly being that man finds himself relying on truth and tied to it, while at the same time it is not something that he can control, since he is in the service of truth. A survey of the various ways in which truth has been understood also shows that the notion of truth depends to a great extent on changing epistemological foundations and suppositions and on decisions taken beforehand in the light of this or that world view. Such pre-existing mental horizons are inescapable, and hence the attitude to truth is always a reflection of its times to some extent and more or less one-sided.

Thus if truth is mainly taken as truth in the judgment, the ethics of truth will mainly be concerned with objective knowledge, to be made the norm of personal action and to be rendered faithfully. The ethics of truth will mainly take the form of an ethics orientated to the concrete action, accepting material responsibility.

But truth may be regarded primarily as ontological truth, the basic intelligibility of things, with God as the First Truth. Further, God is held to be knowable but incomprehensible, while man is understood as a being created in order to know and love God, who finds therefore his true self in being blessed by God and giving himself to God. The main task of an ethics of truth is then to remain as absolutely open as possible for the truth, in whatever guise man encounters it, and to follow out in action the known truth unconditionally. The ethics of truth will mainly take the form of an ethics of the disposition, insisting on the formal attitude.

2. To have a proper balance between an ethics emphasizing the exterior

action and an ethics emphasizing the interior disposition, the following considerations should be noted.

As truth is disclosed to man, it impinges on his consciousness, which is coloured by a number of factors: his orientation to his social and biological milieu, his orientation to God which is channelled by the former, and grace. Hence an ethics of truth cannot do without reflection on one's personal consciousness and its implications. What will then be the formal and definitive criterion for the judgments, assessments and decisions of an ethics of truth? It must be the ordination of the agent to the truth as such. And the material and provisional criterion will be the acknowledged dependence on the world of men and things around one, and dependence on God channelled by these. This means that man must acknowledge his dependence on God, man and the world as he discovers the truth and regulates his life according to the truth which he has found. Thus the believing Catholic will take the doctrine of the Church as the criterion of the truth, to the degree in which it claims his adherence. Everyone has to guard against overestimating his own standing and the amount of truth in his own convictions. In addition, the connection between the ethics of truth and the surrounding world means that the laws of the objective order must be taken into account. As these are disclosed in the sciences, an ethics of truth would be one-sided if it did not acknowledge the importance of science for the knowledge of the truth.

In this sense, an ethics of truth consists formally of man's obligation to seek the truth and to act according to it, in whatever guise it appears. This truth which underlies and inspires the ethics of truth is not originally an objective or definable truth, but a value. This value is of itself independent of the subject, but can only be a subjective norm of action insofar as it is grasped. An ethics of truth then consists materially of man's dedication to truths actually known, insofar as they point beyond themselves to the non-objectivated truth itself. Hence propositional truths can determine the search for truth itself (and action in accordance with the truth) only insofar as they can be related to the all-illuminating but not perspicuous truth. Consequently the immediate norm for the ethics of truth and for the significance of the various propositions within this ethics is subject to constant change, since our actual knowledge of propositional truths is dependent on the subject and affected by the situation. But the definitive norm, the truth itself, is not subject to change. This means that the ethics of truth need not be relativistic, though it must take account of the fact that it is only ordained to absolute truth within the limits of various conditions. It can fail to attain the real truth and may be said to disfigure it to some extent at all times. But on the above principles, extremes may be avoided.

3. To allow the ordination to the absolute truth to attain its full dynamism, it must also be remembered that the finding of the truth does not depend merely on love of the truth and knowledge of facts. It is also affected by the "doing of the truth", which for its part is demanded by the truth attained. Man's prejudices and pre-established convictions mean that his approach to truth is always one-sided, and that he represses unattractive aspects. By doing the truth, he corrects such prejudices and their consequent blind spots, as far as possible, and brings about the optimum disposition for bowing to and acting according to the truth. This is the only way of avoiding the mistake of erecting the truth so far attained into an absolute. The dynamism aiming at the truth as such is maintained. A barrier is set up to the fixation on pleasant truths which can do detriment to the

truths summoning men to constant conversion.

On the other hand, the less one "does the truth", the harder is the access to the absolute truth. For partial truths are erected into absolutes when action is determined by criteria contrary to the absolute truth. Consequently, in the self-discovery of man which is meant to serve the ethics of truth, such partial truths are given undue and indeed absolute importance. Man is thus deluded because he is wilful enough to let himself be guided exclusively by limited truths which he finds pleasant. He is guided by appearances and not by the total truth which he has apprehended – even though not comprehended – and which is binding on him.

Thus the optimum ordination to the truth itself is attained only when man gives propositional truths their proper coefficient, that is, when he subordinates them, by a responsible decision, to the truth itself, insofar as it makes itself known.

4. It is in the light of man's duty to be sincere in seeking the truth, bowing to it and acting in accordance with it that the duty of sincerity or truthfulness as between men must be defined. The problems which arise here are generally the main interest in discussion of the ethics of truth. The starting-point, as a rule, is the more or less considered conviction that in one's communications with one's fellowmen one must be sincere and truthful, at least in principle and as the normal thing.

The basis of the obligation of truthfulness is that without it reverence for the dignity of the person, social life and religion are impossible. The proper development of the human person in all its dimensions would be hindered if man were not truthful towards himself, his fellowmen and God.

On the other hand, there are personal spheres of intimacy which must be protected. There are secrets which must be kept, in the interest of individuals and for the sake of the common good. This means that the truth is not to be told to everyone who might like to know it or even perhaps try to extort it by unlawful means. Indeed, the demands of self-defence seem to suggest that one should deliberately deceive an opponent in certain circumstances, if, for instance, this were the only way of effectively safeguarding secrets. Thus it is not surprising that historically the main preoccupation of the ethics of truth has been devoted to the question of how deceit, lies, should be judged.

5. In rejecting ψεῦδος, which means both error and lie, the Greeks often used the argument that ignorance is an evil, while virtue consists of knowledge. In this view, error is worse than a lie, since it involves more ignorance. But truth leads to the good. To miss this goal is the absolute evil, κακία, or malice, κακοφροσύνη. But a lie is permitted as a means to avert evil, and made a duty for doctors and statesmen (Socrates, Plato).

Aristotle recognizes that there can be no question of moral action except in deliberate acts. Hence he finds the distinction between conscious and unconscious falsehood essential. Only the deliberate lie is immoral. It is evil in itself, while truthfulness is good and praiseworthy. The reason is that truthfulness serves human intercourse, while lying undermines trustworthiness. But when the interests of the law or the nation are at stake, it may be well to say what is false, since truthfulness is merely a social virtue and does not take in the realm of justice. Hence it is not always intrinsically wrong to say what is false, since the supreme goal in the ethics of Aristotle is the happiness of the individual, which in turn is only attainable in the well-being of the State.

The Latins made a basic distinction between error and lie (*mendacium*), transferring the attention from the objective phenomenon of the mistaken statement to the deliberately misleading statement. They were therefore more consistent than the Greeks in rejecting the lie. The condemnation of lying was perhaps given its most downright expression in Cicero, who held that the truly useful was inseparable from the moral. He condemned lying even when consideration of public welfare might seem to demand a lie (*De Officiis*, III, 14–32). The notion of fraudulent intent (*dolus malus*) came into legal usage from Rome.

6. In the ethics of the OT, the Israelite is to "walk in the truth" of God (Ps 86:11; cf. Ps 25:5; 26:3) or to "do what is true" (Tob 4:6; 13:6). This includes "doing the truth" with regard to the neighbour. The alternative is the spread of perjury and lying, murder and other crimes (cf. Hos 4:1f.). The eighth commandment (Exod 20:16; Deut 5:20) only seems to forbid lying which causes injury to the neighbour or the community. Nonetheless, lying is condemned in the OT in the sharpest terms (Lev 19:11; Prov 30:8; Ecclus 7:13; cf. Prov 6:16ff.; Ecclus 4:25).

According to the NT, Christ came into the world to bring the full truth and to bear witness to it (Jn 1:14; 8:40; 18:37). Sanctified through the truth and for the truth (Jn 17:17), we are to love it (1 Cor 13:6) and "do" it (Jn 3:21; 1 Jn 1:6), and it will set us free (Jn 8:32). For this, we must avoid lying and speak truthfully (Eph 4:25; cf. 1 Pet 2:1). We need not then even swear (Mt 5:34ff.), but we are still not to cast pearls before swine (Mt 7:6). We are to be guileless like doves, but still prudent as serpents (Mt 10:16). Thus there may well be times when an obscure form of words may be chosen (cf. Mt 13:10ff.). Lying, on the other hand, is explicitly stated to be the devil's work (Jn 8:44). It is a characteristic of the "old man" who is not yet redeemed (Col 3:9). The lake of fire and brimstone is the lot of "liars" (Rev 21:8; cf. 21:27; 22:15; 1 Tim 1:10).

7. *The role of the intention to deceive and of the nature of speech in the definition of lying*. The Christian analysis of lying was mainly inspired by the doctrine of St. Augustine, who was the first in the West to compose a special treatise on lying (*De Mendacio*, c. 395, and *Contra Mendacium ad Consentium*, c. 420). St. Augustine describes a lie as *falsa significatio cum voluntate fallendi* – a false statement with intent to deceive. It is not certain that he meant the "intent to deceive" to be essential to lying. He did not in fact mean to give a strict definition, as follows from the fact that he asks himself whether a lie only occurs where there is the intent to deceive. His personal opinion, at any rate, is that lying is intrinsically evil. But though his subjective opinion is fixed, he leaves the objective question open to a certain extent. This follows from the fact that he does not consider that the prohibition of lying is equally strong in all circumstances. The intent to deceive is what makes lying formally or morally wrong. The guilt therefore lies in the realm of the disordered relationship to another. Lying then can be forbidden in all circumstances only if this evil element in it, which is directed against the interlocutor, is present in all false statements. But this is something which St. Augustine shrinks from affirming.

In the early Middle Ages the conviction gradually prevailed that any false statement is *eo ipso* deceitful, so that the intent to deceive is always there when a deliberately false statement is made. The general definition of a lie is therefore *locutio contra mentem*, saying one thing and thinking another. St. Albert the Great was the first to come down firmly on the *indebita materia* as the essence of the lie, holding that it was a perversion of the nature and purpose of speech, which is essentially ordained to the truth, an end good in itself. Hence the lie is bad in itself. St. Thomas Aquinas also regarded the lie as something contrary to the nature of speech. His reason for saying that it is evil, i.e., contrary to love, is that it is essentially ordained to others. Apart from this relationship he finds that a false statement is not absolutely wrong and may be permitted in an emergency (II/II, q. 110, a. 3 ad 4).

8. *The emphasis on the formal aspect of lying.* With the coming of modern times and the paying of greater attention to the personal and individual, the problem of reconciling the prohibition of lying with the actual necessities of life was felt more keenly. Authors mainly influenced by the Augustinian or the Protestant tradition worked out a theory of the lie which stressed its social character exclusively. This purely formal approach led to a definition of the lie which was exclusively based on the notion of the right to the truth. Machiavelli held that all lies were permissible in a good cause. Luther held that the "officious" lie to help the neighbour and the emergency lie to defend one's own just interests were permissible, condemning only the lies which caused unjustifiable damage to the neighbour. The opinion which came to be most widely known was that of H. Grotius, who distinguished between the false statement (*falsiloquium*) and the lie. He defined the lie as the *sermo repugnans cum iure existente et manente illius quem alloqueris* – speech violating the actual and continuing right of the person addressed. The right which can be violated is the right to make up one's mind freely, without the hindrance of false information. According to Tanqueray, the only basis on which truthfulness is obligatory is in fact the right which each one has not to be deceived. At present there are many Protestants and writers on non-theological ethics who uphold similar theories, which allow lying under certain circumstances, when the interlocutor has no right to the truth or has forfeited it.

All theories based uniquely on the rights of the interlocutor disregard the fact that language is intrinsically ordained to communication. It is not just because of the speaker's attitude but because of the objective data that language is ordained to communication. Hence the duty of truthfulness must derive in the first place from the duty of the speaker and not from the rights of his interlocutor. But the theories in question are correct in affirming that language is essentially dialogal, so that its lawfulness is to some extent a function of the interlocutor. The purpose and hence the nature of any given statement cannot be determined purely objectively, without regard to the interlocutor.

9. *The emphasis on the material aspect of lying.* As regard Catholic authors, it may be said in general that they affirm the duty of truthfulness in the speaker, without asserting that it corresponds normally to the right to the truth in the hearer. The truth is a duty of charity in the speaker and not an obligation of justice. Hence St. Thomas makes truthfulness a potential part of justice, connected with it but not directly part of it.

Scholastic philosophers tried to grapple with the new questions posed from the end of the Middle Ages on, by looking for ways in which truth could be effectively concealed and secrets guarded, without involving a contradiction between what was thought and what was said. In other words, their efforts were based on a notion of the lie which mainly considered its material element. During the decline of scholasticism, the essential element in the lie came more and more to be regarded as the contradiction between the outward statement and the inner judgment. To soften or eliminate the contrast, it was suggested at first that ambiguous expressions could be used, and later, mental reservation or restriction. In the latter, the inner judgment is made to correspond with the outward statement by means of a mental correction. The two inner elements are only parts of the one whole. A distinction was then made between the negative and the positive law of truthfulness, the former forbidding the misuse of speech, and the latter demanding the telling of the truth. Like all positive law, the latter was held to oblige *semper non pro semper*, i.e., it was basically valid but had not to be put into practice at all times. Thus in the course of the 17th century the classical doctrine on lying was gradually abandoned by a large number of important theologians in all schools. In view of widespread criticism, the purely mental reservation was condemned by Innocent XI (*D* 1176ff.).

The grave mistake of such purely individualistic approaches was that it concentrated on the immanent relationship between knowledge and statement in the speaker, neglecting entirely the more comprehensive relationship of the speaker to the hearer.

Nonetheless, the prohibition of lying continued to be based on the necessity of not misusing speech. But this was now considered as a natural faculty clearly ordained to communication. In keeping with the predominant notion of natural law this was said to mean that man ought not to act contrary to the nature of speech, but that he could use its laws to protect secrets. He could speak in such a way that the matters to be kept secret was not communicated. The chief method envisaged was the use of an unclear form of words (wide mental reservation) where the circumstances or the actual words used made it clear that the question was evaded. This in fact was not a mental but a verbal reservation, since at least on principle the expressions made it clear to the questioner that the desired information was being refused.

The disadvantage of this approach is that it does not provide an adequate safeguard for secrets in certain cases, especially where the speaker has little command of language. Further, it rejects all materially false statements as intrinsically bad, though they appear to be necessary to the security of the State in the operations of secret agents. It allows nonetheless that an opponent should be in fact deceived by unclear speech. Another point to be considered is that this approach is based on a notion of natural law which has now been to some extent abandoned. Man is no longer considered to be unconditionally subject to the laws of an order of things which can be defined purely objectively. Pushed to its ultimate logical conclusion, this approach would forbid even the least departure from the truth, even to defend oneself and others from grave injury where the truth is being extorted.

10. The difficulties arising from these rigoristic approaches and the reappraisal of natural law which was to some extent a consequence of these difficulties led a number of moralists in the 20th century to take another view of the matter. They permit the making of a false statement as an act of necessary self-defence in an emergency (so Vermeersch, Lindworsky, Ledrus, Laros, etc., using different arguments).

On the principle that the significance of speech, as an interchange between men, must be defined in terms of the hearer as well as the speaker, it must be admitted that under certain circumstances the significance of speech may be quite different for each of the two. If in this situation it is really to be of service to those involved, and not a means of injuring the personal dignity and just interests of one of the speakers, it may be right and necessary to use a false mode of statement, insofar as is necessary to ward off unjust aggression. Truthfulness is only right and rational insofar as it serves the purposes of communication between the speakers. But if it is exploited by one of the speakers to injure the other, human communication is actually impeded, on the level in keeping with human dignity. If the exploitation of the speaker by the questioner can only be avoided by the former's using a false form of words, this seems a necessary means for impeding misuse of speech. But this also means that the false statement becomes a lie as soon as it goes beyond the bounds of the necessary, since speech is then used to mislead the hearer in an unnecessary and an unjustifiable way. One is formally justified, therefore, in misleading another insofar as this provides effective defence of personal values against unjust aggression, the values in question being at least as valuable and as urgent as those materially injured by the misleading words.

Hence the definitive criterion for the moral evaluation of speech should not be its material ordination to communication, its intrinsic aptness for communication, since this is verified even in false statements. The criterion must be the actual significance of speech for the good of those taking part. But this significance depends to some extent on the interpersonal meaning given it in fact by the partners. Hence the moral significance of speech cannot on principle be determined independently of this interpersonal and concrete giving of meaning.

As to the moral gravity of lying, this must then be judged differently according to whether the fit development of the person against whom the lie is directed is hindered in its essence or merely in its completeness.

Waldemar Molinski

U

UNBELIEF

1. *The notion and the discussion.* For the word "unbelief" (ἀπιστία, *incredulitas*) see, for example, Mt 13:58; Mk 9:24; Rom 3:3; 4:20; 11:20, 23; Heb 3:11, 19. Unbelief is the deliberate rejection of faith. It is presupposed that faith and unbelief (in the case of men capable of a decision) are not two possibilities among others, but that everyone either believes or refuses to believe and that there is no way of avoiding this choice. When the concept is so defined, the question at once arises as to whether (in the case of men who have come to the use of reason and freedom) there cannot be an absence of faith which does not need to feel itself a free negation of faith but feels that faith – known in others as a psychological phenomenon – is no longer a serious question. Are there men who simply and effortlessly find themselves a-religious and find no need to be anti-religious? It is unquestionable that the world-wide unbelief of the present day (see *Atheism*), both in communist and in "Western" countries *tries* to understand itself in this way. It claims to be a completely neutral a-religious unbelief, and does not shrink from presenting itself in public as the normal attitude which is to be taken for granted in modern man. When we say "tries", we mean that such unbelievers imagine that both psychologically (existentially) and socially faith offers no real alternative.

In other words, the question arises at the very beginning as to whether unbelief is ultimately a reaction to faith or a non-derivative phenomenon, which is only negative from the point of view of faith and can only be designated secondarily as unbelief. This therefore is the basic problem: both faith and unbelief consider their positions as normal and universally obligatory, with no legitimate alternative. The reasons are of course different in each case. The believer's attitude is based on his faith in the word of God, the unbeliever's on the conviction that he has reached a point to which evolution will eventually bring all men, inexorably. But both have also to explain in terms of their own systems (without appealing to each other's) how it can be that believers and unbelievers exist who may not accuse each other *a priori* of stupidity or malice. And they must also explain why they can carry on a "dialogue" with each other, in spite of the "absoluteness" of their positions – why they are not reduced to mere co-existence on the biological and economic plane.

2. *Standard distinctions and further questions.* While heresy (cf. *CIC*, can. 1325) is the denial of individual re-

vealed truths while the basic Christian faith remains (*nomen Christianum retentum*), the state of unbelief is the habitual absence of any belief at all. As the disposition of the "infidel" (*infidelitas*), this unbelief is usually said to take three forms. Negative infidelity is the inculpable lack of faith (cf. 1 Tim 1:13). Privative infidelity is the culpable lack of faith where the fault lies in indifference to religion in general. Positive infidelity is the direct, deliberate and culpable rejection of faith. As with sin in general, a distinction could be made between material and formal unbelief, the former being inculpable, the latter culpable. These distinctions, however, presuppose a notion of faith which envisages a conceptual, conscious articulation of the object of faith. Within these terms of reference, there can certainly be an unbelief which is total (see *Atheism*) and still inculpable (cf. Vatican II, *Lumen Gentium*, art. 16; *Gaudium et Spes*, arts. 21f.).

But there is another way of taking faith. It can be understood as the grace of faith and the accompanying illumination (not necessarily objectivated but still definite) which is offered to all men, according to the universal salvific will of God. In men who have come to the use of freedom, this can only exist as the free acceptance or the free refusal of faith. And in this context unbelief can only be culpable. But then it is also possible to affirm that such faith can be the possession of "those who, without blame on their part, have not yet arrived at an explicit knowledge of God, but who strive to live a good life, thanks to his grace" (*Lumen Gentium*, art. 16), that is, of "unbelievers" in the ordinary sense. In other words, in the ultimate depths of existence, under the perpetual offer of God's grace, there is no such thing as negative or material unbelief. Unbelief, at the level of conscious, conceptual objectivation, even in the form of atheism, even though "freely" chosen, is not necessarily the manifestation of an unbelief (in the ultimate depths of existence) which is culpable loss of the grace of faith. This may be illustrated by a possible parallel. The free profession of faith on the level of propositions and public confession is no certain proof of the existence of faith in the sense of the God-given decision for God, in a fundamental free act at the centre of the person. Even such a "work" of faith remains ambivalent.

Basing oneself on this notion of faith and unbelief, one could distinguish between existential (or "real") unbelief, which is always culpable, and notional unbelief, which can be culpable or inculpable. The standard theological distinctions would then refer primarily to notional (or "theoretical") unbelief. The classification would not of course mean that any given man could be definitely placed in one or other category as regards his relationship to God. Since all grace of faith is a grace of Christ, and since even men who apparently are acting only on the human level have a positive relationship to Christ, even though unconscious (cf. for instance Mt 25), faith in God and faith in Jesus Christ (or unbelief, on the various levels described above) may be treated alike, as in the language of St. John above all (e.g., 11:6). For the relationship to Christ is not just one object of faith among others, but the "incarnational" definiteness of faith as such (in spite of Heb 11:6 and the whole theological question of what must be explicitly believed for salvation).

3. *On the theology of unbelief in general.* It should already be clear from what has been said above that there is really no theology of unbelief in any developed form. For even the simplest questions about the real nature of unbelief lead to difficulties not normally posed in theology and to theories which are not commonly held. As a rule, unbelief is simply regarded as a particularly grave case of sin. It is not clearly en-

visaged as the opposite of the faith which is the root and foundation of the right relationship to God (*D* 801). So too unbelief is described in merely negative terms, and faith appears simply as a sum of truths, that is, in its developed and articulate form, and unbelief is the denial of such propositions. The real nature of unbelief, the total deliberate decision, is left in obscurity. But it is ultimately a free choice by which man decides what his whole life will be, and hence either a blueprint for a life of total self-assertion with nothing on principle mysterious in it, or a defensive stategy of despair which allows of no wider a future than what man himself can create, for all its obvious insufficiency. Both forms of unbelief can be covered up and repressed, to re-appear as the sceptical, courageous (or apparently courageous) nonchalance of the man who has silently come to terms with the absurdity of existence. But of course this feat of every-day endurance is ambivalent, and can also be the reflection of faith. And there is no human power that can help anyone to pass a secure judgment as he reflects on his case (cf. *D* 805, 822f.).

It must also be the task of a theology of unbelief to point out to believers the context of theory and practice within which an understanding of unbelief is possible. It cannot be simply an invader from a totally foreign world, if faith is to be the full understanding of human existence and the light in which all things can be judged (1 Cor 2:15). A theology of unbelief should not just throw light on its occurrence in the private individual's history of salvation or calamity. It must be able to treat it as a phenomenon of the collective history of salvation and of "the world". There is the "sin of the world" (Jn 1:19 etc.), and likewise the "unbelief of the world", with its own history of development. It becomes more and more radical and presents itself more and more unconcernedly as the obvious and normal way of life. It does not merely deny the existence of God by an atheistic philosophy, but tries to establish a mental attitude in which the question of God can no longer occur. In the theology of history, the broad social phenomenon of atheistic unbelief and the accompanying process of secularization will appear possibly as a wrong reaction to a justifiable and basically Christian desacralization of the world, which allows God to appear as God and not as part of the world, in his inaccessible mystery.

4. *Unbelief in the believer.* Faith itself brings with it the possibility of unbelief. It is part of the pilgrim nature of man to be tempted to unbelief. This is because faith is essentially a free grace of God which can only come into play where the opposite is really possible. Further, the articulate expression of the original commitment of faith along the lines of truths of faith can only be analogous, and cannot possibly reaffirm in each proposition its dependence on the mystery – cannot indeed formulate expressly its primordial dependence. It is therefore exposed to the temptation of shedding the burden of such formulations by taking up a sceptical attitude or one of austere intellectual detachment (ἐποχή). Finally, there is concupiscence in the believer, which is not just a moral situation. It is also an intellectual factor, within and without, pluralist in character, not fully assimilated or indeed assimilable by the decision of faith. It furnishes ideas which comes from unbelief and tend to unbelief (cf. *D* 792) and it makes the question of the individual's life insoluble: does it reflect concupiscence or the "works" of faith? Which of these are at the heart of existence? (See 1 Cor 4:4f.) If the Christian finds himself repeating the cry, "I believe, help my unbelief" (Mk 9:24), this is not a special case which should not really arise, but the normal situation of the

believer, who is *simul fidelis et infidelis* as well as *simul justus et peccator*.

5. *Christian and preacher in face of modern unbelief*. This theme can of course be discussed only briefly here. At this moment of transition, as the Church of the masses becomes the Church of personally-committed believers, Christians must recognize that faith is not necessarily most at home in a situation where faith can also be identical with public opinion. The proper setting for faith is a situation in which the conventions of society do not relieve the believer of the burden of personal decision. And the preacher should not rely on such a conventional situation in his preaching. He must recognize that the message of the gospel must be presented otherwise today – in the light of a secularized world and in view of such a world, so that the secret unbelief of traditional Christians may be taken into account and catered for. If he speaks as though he were addressing the unbeliever of the present day, he will be saying something important for Christians.

Hence the theology by which the sermon is inspired must do justice to the modern mentality. The difference between a basic faith at the heart of existence and its conceptual articulation must not be lost sight of, though the value of the latter should not be underestimated, if only for the reason that faith and preaching are concerned with a salvation which came as a historical event. But preaching and propositional faith must be such that one can see their bond with the ultimate existentiell decisions (inspired by grace) which man's inescapable situation demands of him in one way or another. It is only because this bond is frequently left out of consideration that the impression is given that one only needs to be totally oblivious of explicit faith in order to be relieved even of deciding between faith and unbelief.

Karl Rahner

UNITY

The concept of unity is found, as the first known concept which cannot be understood adequately simply by a process of reflection, in the unity of the knowing and willing subject which is present to itself and in the unity of its unlimited *a priori* (being as such). As a transcendental element, it expresses a distinctive characteristic which is necessary to being and to the being. The scholastic theologians disagreed as to whether "one" was related as positive perfection to the being in the same way as "true" and "good", as taught in the Platonic Augustinian tradition, or whether it was, as the Augustinian Thomistic school of thought insisted, simply a negation of the state of division. (This does not in any sense imply the existence of something that is not included within the being.) The concept of unity, then, is, like that of the being, characterized by analogy. It contains in a very special way both a unifying inclusion and a differing rejection. It is both the discontinuation of distinction (in absolute being, everything is more eminently contained as one and this is both objectively and subjectively the necessary basis of all logical, conceptual unity to which consent is given) and its inclusion ("one" as one in itself and as distinct from everything else and therefore also from God). The analogy of the concept of unity is seen especially in the fact that being united in itself and being united with others (both unities develop in the same, not in a different proportion) are revealed in different stages of development. These include, for instance, the unity of the absolute oneness (of the pure, self-communicating Trinity) of God, the unity of the one plural (for example, the unity of the principles of the one being, the unity of substance, the unity of action and potentiality, the unity of the accidentally determined substance, the unity of substantial parts, the unity of the quantitative and so on), the unity of the same origin and in the origin containing what emerges from it, the unity of reciprocal dependence, the unity of the same "sphere", the unity of purpose, the unity of "order" and so on. Transcendental unity has to be distinguished from numerical unity (*ens principium numeri*), and the unity of the number of the place-value of the case. (This is a distinction which is often not sufficiently observed nowadays, but which is very important in concrete problems such as those of existential ethics.)

So far, no formal theology of unity has been developed. There is also no comprehensive history of the philosophical concept of unity, its interpretation or the consequences of its different interpretations and their application to many differing philosophical questions. In accordance with Christian philosophical methods, both concerns condition each other. In a theology of unity, both the orthodox and the heretical doctrines would have to be investigated to see which concept of unity was implied in them. This would result in a complete concept of unity which is not the dead oneness of what persists undistinguished in itself, but which is perfect in the non-partial and numerical plurality of the threefold unity of God. This would be a unity of the plural in which the authentic plurality or non-identity is preserved in a true inner unity of the being, on the one hand, by the accomplishment of one single basis of unity of a being in tension between really plural aspects and, on the other, by this inner unity of various aspects which are not identical being dependent on the transcendental unity of God. This unity of God, however, is not outside the being and the real unity of the creature is based on it, but is also in the last resort removed from it. (This unity is opposed to all kinds of monism of being and action – totalitarianism – which might imply the pretension and total self-availability of a unity which can only be attributed to the transcendent God and to the mystery of his unity.) The formula of Chalcedon – "undivided and unalloyed" – can be applied to the unity of the creaturely in its supreme case (Jesus Christ) and the doctrine of the Trinity can serve as the fundamental formula for unity in the case of the divine. Both principles, in their interrelationship, can provide the point of departure for a theology of unity.

Karl Rahner

UNIVERSALS

The universal is what all have in common, the general denomination which fits all things or many things (i.e., all of a certain type or group).

1. *History of the problem: the controversy.* The existence of the universal or general is undeniable, and was not called in question even in the controversy on universals. For language uses the same word for several situations or to designate a multitude of particulars and it can only convey meaning on this supposition. The question is whether there is anything universal apart from the words, and it has been a constant problem in philosophy. In the form of the controversy on universals it dominated the epistemology of the Middle Ages. The controversy took four main lines. a) Extreme nominalism held that the only universal was the name, the word. b) Conceptualism, often called moderate nominalism, held that there were universals in the mind, the general concepts, but that there was nothing corresponding to them in reality. c) Moderate realism held that what was meant by the general concept was to be found in things, though not as it was in the abstract and in general, but as a concrete particular. d) Extreme realism held that there was a structure of reality which corresponded exactly

to the concept. Hence the universal was a distinct element of the particular, or could even exist independently of it. This last view was also known as Platonism.

Platonism does not here mean the whole philosophy of Plato or his school but the view taken of Plato in the controversy on universals, when he was counted among the extreme realists, his "forms" being assumed to be a realization of the universal prior to our thinking and outside the particular things. Strictly speaking, however, the forms were not existing universals but individual entities in a supra-temporal and non-material intelligible world (κόσμος νοητός), the only real world, the transitory things of the sensible world being only shadowy participations of these beings, whose true reality was the only explanation of the similarities and constant structures to be noted in the sensible world. The universal first occurs as "second substance" in Aristotle, where it is derived by abstraction from the "first substance", or real beings. It is neither the essence of the particular nor an independent entity separate from the particular, like the form or idea of Plato (*Metaphysics*, VI, 13; 1038b). It is the element comprised in a concept which can be predicated of several things.

On the question of what had to correspond in reality to the predicate thus affirmed, opinions then differed. Some, like Porphyrius and Boethius, evaded the question as too difficult, while others took one or other of the four lines indicated above, though not necessarily fitting neatly into any given class. At the beginning of the medieval controversy the main debate was between the protagonists of the extreme positions, while later the two moderate opinions were the main interest.

Through the writings of St. Anselm of Canterbury (1033–1109), the extreme realist position was influenced by St. Augustine and his neo-Platonism, according to which the essences of created things are in the mind of God as exemplars or *rationes aeternae*. They are in created things as the *rationes seminales* which determine their development, and are known to man by virtue of an illumination given in his contemplation of the *rationes aeternae*. This laid the groundwork for the medieval distinction of universals "ante rem", "in re" and "post rem", while it also heralded the tendency to identify them in extreme realism.

John Scotus Erigena (9th century) was wholly within this tradition when he defined the universal (essence) as a substance which subsists in particulars in the manner in which it is known by us. But the most radical formulation of this view was given by William of Champeaux (d. 1122), who first taught that there was only one single essence, "man", for instance, identical in all particulars of a given type, these being only accidentally different from each other. When it was objected, as for instance by Abelard, that this view led to pantheism, like the doctrine of Erigena, William gave up the identity of the essence throughout, maintaining merely that the essence was the same in each particular (i.e., indistinguishable).

The contrary position, equally extreme, was maintained at the same period by William's opponent Roscellinus of Compiègne (according to *his* opponents, e.g., St. Anselm of Canterbury). The common essence was now treated merely as a *flatus vocis*, an empty word. Roscellinus has therefore been looked on as the founder of medieval nominalism. Abelard, a disciple of Roscellinus and also of William, put forward an intermediate position, which became the prevailing view in classical scholasticism in the form of the moderate realism into which it was elaborated, e.g., by St. Thomas Aquinas. According to Aquinas, following Aristotle, the universal is that which can be asserted of a multitude of things. It has its being *ante rem* in the mind of God, but has no other being *in re* than that of the particular and only becomes a universal *in mente* and *post rem* by the operation of the *intellectus agens*, in abstraction.

The notion of "abstraction" provided an accepted compromise for a long time, but the solution was by no means definitive. This is clear from the resumption of the debate some time afterwards and its persistence down to the present day. Duns Scotus (d. 1308) suggested a *distinctio formalis ex natura rei* in things, corresponding to the conceptual distinctions. This brought him close to extreme realism, while William of Occam (d. 1349) was closer to a moderate conceptualism. These two main lines have been continued in the philosophy of the modern era. Empiricists and positivists, from Hobbes and the English empiricists down to the neopositivism of the Vienna Circle and analytical philosophy (see *Science* II) have nearly always inclined to nominalism, since their whole attention was concentrated on the concrete particular. Rationalism and Idealism, however, rather tended to look on the universal as the true reality. Those who, like Kant, on the other hand, explain the universal in terms of the structure of the intellect do not fit into this schema. But the phenomenologists who assume an "ideal being" for essences, independent of thought, and the modern mathematicians and logicians who assume a similar existence for abstract entities (such as sets and groups and propositions) may well be considered as extreme realists. And present-day linguistic philosophy which tries to reduce the meaning of words or propositions merely to their usage may well be considered nominalists.

This sketch of the historical problem shows that the task of finding the proper balance between the two trends described above remains a perpetual problem. Those who are mainly preoccupied with the individual empirical sciences will be rather tempted to take up a nominalist position, while those engaged in the *a priori* universal sciences will find extreme realism a greater danger.

2. *On the solution of the problem.* Both the tendency to extreme realism and to nominalism fail to note the true nature of the universal, the reason being that both are orientated to the particular merely in the guise of a "thing". Hence the ultra-realists take the concept to be a thing realized in a multitude of things, while the nominalists oppose the individual word to the multitude of individual things, but leave it without any relationship to them. In the universal, as Aristotle saw, a relation is affirmed between the one and the many, as when we use one word to designate several particulars, the word "man", for instance, applying to all individual men. If we used a special word for each particular in each different situation, language would be as little capable of conveying meaning as if the relation of the linguistic element to things or cases remained purely arbitrary – that is, as if we could indicate no possible basis in the objects for attaching such labels to them. It is therefore necessary and sufficient for the validity of a universal term, that is, for its meaningful use, that there should be some individual basis in each case – the non-individual does not exist – which makes it possible to apply this concept to the case by virtue of a human consensus.

Albert Keller

V

VIRGINITY

To make a correct evaluation of the evangelical counsel of virginity, it is well to start with the specification of man through his sexual nature. Because of this sexual nature he can achieve a full realization of his being as a person only if his attitude to sex is an open one, in the sense that he places it at the service of an ordered self-love, love of neighbour and love of God. If he does this, he exercises the virtue of chastity. Now this sexual specification of man, calling for a free personal decision and therefore for further specification, can be such that he can in all reason decide upon full sexual abstinence. That is the situation when one is incapable of marriage, or when one has not in the concrete the possibility of marriage. Again, specification can be such that a particular person achieves the best possible development if he decides to marry. Finally, it is also possible that a person in the face of a capability as well as a possibility of marriage, freely foregoes all use of the sex faculty. According as each person makes a free choice in his own way about his sexual life, there is in each case a specific form of chastity or unchastity. Virginity is a specific form of chastity of this kind by which a person opts for permanent abstinence from sexual activity. One speaks always then of following the evangelical counsel of virginity in the narrower sense when one is not "naturally" obliged to complete continence, when therefore perfect continence is chosen as the "concrete *bonum melius et possibile*" (cf. St. Thomas Aquinas, *Summa Theologica*, II/II, q. 152, a. 1).

Virginity in the theological sense is, besides this, basically an eschatological ideal which holds for all mankind equally, but not for all in the same way. Jesus expresses it in his own way when he says: "At the resurrection men and women do not marry; no, they are like the angels in heaven" (Mt 22:30; Mk 12:25; cf. Lk 20:34–36). In this sense in Rev 14:4 the followers of Christ appear simply as virgins. Thus in the last analysis the limitless love of God, of neighbour and of self in the next life, is in its direct vision called virginal, and the attainment of this eschatological virginity is regarded as a desirable goal for all. At the same time the expression and the translation into act of this love through human sexuality is characterized as provisional and ambivalent. Man indeed (as the more recent anthropology has shown), is characterized through and through by his sexuality, but he is not simply identical with his sexual nature. Man should therefore fully accept his sexuality, but he does not need to activate it directly without sublimation. This non-activation coupled with sublimation can, for those called to it, be a help to the actualization of greater love and an expression of it. Because of the subordinate significance of sex from the eschatological point of view, man should not lose himself in it; "Those who have wives should live as though they had none" (1 Cor 7:29).

Thus both the voluntarily and involuntarily unmarried as well as the married are all equally oriented, each in his own way, to eschatological virginity which, though not yet finally realized, yet is already realized to the extent that they are chaste, each according to his own situation. This means that man shares in eschatological virginity because of his sexuality in the measure in which he is chaste according to his state in life. Every form of chastity according to one's state in life is a sharing in eschatological virginity, yet each in its own specific manner, and each relates in a dialectical tension to the other forms. Since each form presents a particular aspect of eschatological virginity and expresses it in sign, this aspect must also be reflected by the other form of chaste love but not equivalently presented and signified. Thus Christian marriage is a sign of the relationship between Christ and his Church which is brought to direct realization in the following of the counsel of virginity. On the other hand, marriage portrays the intimacy of eschatological virginity in a way that the life according to the evangelical counsel cannot do. Similarly, the continence which is borne of necessity expresses the humble character of eschatological virginity better than virginity of the counsel, which in turn brings out better the magnanimity of eschatological love. Everyone of these forms of chastity is dependent on the others, since none of them represents or expresses fully the the eschatological virginity in which, however, they all share and to which they have their orientation. Yet one can say that chastity, according to the evangelical counsel, is its most perfect form, since it expresses and represents most perfectly the eschatological significance of chastity (cf. *Summa Theologica*, II/II, 1. 152, a. 3–5; *D* 980 and Vatican II, *Lumen Gentium*, art. 42: "This total continence embraced on behalf of the kingdom of heaven has always been held in particular honour by the Church as being a sign of charity and stimulus towards it, as well as a unique fountain of spiritual fertility in the world").

Jesus recommends virginity to those who are capable of it for the sake of the kingdom of heaven (Mt 19:10ff.; Lk 18:29ff.). He distinguishes such a voluntary renunciation of marriage from incapacity for marriage from birth and from incapacity which is humanly induced, and characterizes this virginity as the incapacity for marriage which is the fruit of zeal for the kingdom of God. It should be freely accepted by those called to it, that is, the evangelical counsel is directed to those who are so captivated by the definitive onset of the kingdom of God in Christ that this world, including human sex, appears in its provisional nature and in its ambivalence, and, as a consequence of this, in an entirely new light. Hence all they now think of is how to please the Lord (1 Cor 7:32–35). The evangelical counsel of virginity is thus not directed to all, but only to those who experience a call of grace to it.

Similarly Paul, who himself was not married, in 1 Cor 7 recommends virginity as better than marriage, which is nevertheless not sinful. He justifies his advice with the possibility of serving Christ better in this way, especially in view of the proximate end of time.

The other NT books also show a high reverence for virginity (Acts 21:9) but protect marriage from being undervalued (1 Tim 4:3). The Pastoral Letters do not demand celibacy for those taking up an official position, but only in the case where one holding office loses his partner (1 Tim 3:2, 12; Tit 1:6; 1 Tim 5:9).

As a consequence, Christian theology has always esteemed virginity highly and regarded it as a protest against the excessive valuation of the world and of sex, and this to such a degree that it put virginity beside martyrdom in its significance for the Church. Trent expressly defined that the state of virginity is a higher and holier state than that of matrimony (*D* 980).

This appreciation of virginity, however, has been partly responsible for the not infrequent failure of theology to resist the tendency to relegate sexuality and marriage to the second place in a two-tiered morality. This temptation has been all the more real for theology because at its most basic and radical it has an ambivalent relationship to sex as to the world in general, convinced as it is of their infirm and vulnerable nature. This is quite clear from the counsel to practise virginity for the sake of the kingdom of God. But it must at the same time be recognized that the argumentation of the NT as of theology for the justification of virginity lays the chief emphasis on its charismatic character. For this reason virginity is specifically interpreted as a particularly appropriate symbolic representation of the priesthood of Christ or as a typological expression of the bridal love of the Church for Christ. Thus virginity is seen as the expression of the sanctifying role of the priest, to continue as *alter Christus* the *generatio spiritualis*, which man derives from Christ as the second Adam (1 Cor 4:15; Gal 4:19).

It should cause the priest, because of his universal pastoral love, to sacrifice the very intimate love and self-giving in marriage and the family, in favour of a less intimate but more universal self-dedication in love to the flock entrusted to him. Such dedication is endangered by worldly commitments.

Whereas in the priest's motivation to virginity the aspect of love of neighbour comes more to the fore, in the virginity which is a type of the Church, greater emphasis is laid on the aspect of the love of the spouse for God. Virginity, to give itself to God who gives himself to us in Christ, transcends the world with its functionalization, and sex, the significance of which is seen in the last analysis to be merely relative.

Virginity so regarded is an attempt to free oneself as far as may be from earthly ties and to set up a standard for the neighbour, who is tempted to lose himself to the world and especially to sex. Love of neighbour must be transcended to the love of God; perfect human fulfilment is possible only in this dialogue with God which rises superior to the neighbour. Man is still on pilgrimage to him, yet on this journey, God, although hidden, already comes to meet him.

The evangelical counsel of virginity is consequently misunderstood if, in a type of two-tiered morality, continence is regarded in principle, not only in the individual case, as of higher value than well-ordered sexual activity, and consequently the latter as of less value in principle. Such is the case when continence is demanded as a means to liberation or purification from diabolical influences or for attaining power over these influences because a dualistic concept of man considers the spirit as good and the body as evil. Sexual activity is then seen as rendering impure and as a result continence is demanded. The same tendency is seen in the Stoic theory of the passions, according to which the actualization of sex is diametrically opposed to the cardinal virtue of ἀταραξία, imperturbable self-control. Sexual activity in this view, because of its lack of control, endangers the powers of the soul, whereas continence leads to higher wisdom. Insufficient too is the justification of continence taken from ethical intellectualism, according to which the sexual act is regarded as of less value because of the *iactura mentis*, thus, e.g., in Aristotle. Not far removed from this is the egocentric view that family and sexual activity are a barrier to individual perfection, since they are a distraction (even St. Jerome justifies celibacy with the arguments that it preserves one from the inconveniences and difficulties of family life). Related to this view too is the notion that he who possesses the love of God must renounce human love. Dedication to God is held to exclude self-giving dedication to man. Thus, for example, in various mystery and sacerdotal cults, continence is regarded as a necessary pre-condition for certain religious functions, especially at ritual ceremonies. In this connection the notion crops up that continence (in a magical way) has power to put one in contact with the Omnipotent (especially in Indian religions) and leads to ecstatic union with God (ἱερὸς γάμος). In the OT too continence is required during the sacred ministry (Exod 19:15; 1 Sam 21:4; Zech 7:3). Frequently, however, in pagan philosophy chastity, virginity and marriage are regarded as adiaphora, as being morally indifferent between virtue and sin.

On the other hand, for the true evaluation of the significance of virginity all overvaluation in principle of well-ordered sexual activity, as opposed to continence, is to be rejected (*D* 2336). Such misinterpretation of continence obtains in the case where it is regarded as desirable only for those who are still unmarried, when, namely, extra-marital chastity is regarded as meaningful only as a preparation and protection for marriage, so that the unmarried is held in principle to be inferior to the married. This notion is widespread in non-Christian religions, e.g., in Islam and in Amida-Buddhism. This concept prevails also in the OT where the pre-marital chastity of girls is valued and demanded (Gen 34:7, 31; Exod 22:15f.; Deut 22:14–19, 28f.; Lev 21:13f.; cf. 21:7; Ezek 44:22; 2 Sam 13:20; Deut 22:20f.). But to remain unmarried (Is 4:1), and even to be childless (Gen 30:23; 1 Sam 1:6, 11, 15; Is 49:21), is regarded as a disgrace. To die before marriage is a disaster (Jg 11:37f.), to which in times of emergency even polygamy is preferable (Is 4:1). In early Judaism these notions undergo a change. In circles close to the Essenes even abstention from marriage is held to an extent in honour.

Our point of view requires that in preaching justification for the value of virginity must abstain from all devaluation in principle of sexuality and of marriage and that the charismatic character of virginity must be stressed. (Motives such as "domination over the body", "full possession of the spiritual self", etc., are not specifically Christian.) Pastoral care should stress that only those markedly capable of love are suited to a life of virginity and can credibly present it in its character as witness. Only thus can one do justice to the natural significance of *eros* and *sexus*, which should unfold in the life of virginity in *philia* and *agape*, especially since abstention from marriage can, without love, easily turn to hardness, eccentricity, etc. In spite of the important connection between personal vitality and the experience of the gift of human love, one should not go so far as to regard only the strong and sound personalities as suited to a life of virginity, since charismatic capability and natural temperament are not the same thing. This imposes on the Church authorities a serious responsibility to advise and accept a commitment to a life of virginity only from those who are prudently judged to be really suited to it. The juridical obligation to a life according to the counsel which is not a matter of general obligation is from this point of view questionable, above all if the charismatic power of loving is absent or extinguished. This can easily lead to serious psychosomatic disturbances. Care must further be taken that the capability of young unmarried people of growing in love must be encouraged and they must also be given the human love they need. On the other hand, preaching would be just as defective if it gave way to the tendency to over-value sexuality and marriage, for it is precisely the counsel to virginity that should make clear their basically relative significance.

Waldemar Molinski

VIRTUE

I. Acquired and Infused Virtues

1. *Introduction and general concept.* Virtue in the widest sense is any perfectly developed capacity of man's spiritual soul, or the development itself. There can therefore be virtue, for example, in the domain of cognition: intellectual virtues. In the narrower sense, virtue is the power (ability, skill, facility) to realize moral good, and especially to do it joyfully and perseveringly even against inner and outer obstacles and at the cost of sacrifices. The contrary of this habitual ability and readiness (over and above the mere capacity) is vice. According to origin, nature, goal (and mode of acquisition), distinctions are drawn between natural and supernatural ("infused") virtues. The natural virtues are rooted in the corporeal-spiritual nature of man, concern the ability and readiness of man's natural powers and are developed by correct and constant practice in accordance with the nature of those powers and their acts. They are therefore acquired virtues and have a corresponding component in the corporeal-psychological substratum of man, in instinctive drives, associations, etc. They perfect human character, concern the moral formation of its corporeal-spiritual individuality and are the necessary, habitual defence against concupiscence and domination by instinctive drives. According to the ancient standard classification, the most important basic and comprehensive natural virtues, which of course by grace and the infused virtues can be supernaturally directed towards God himself and the direct possession of God, are the cardinal virtues, prudence, justice, fortitude and temperance. The endeavour is made with greater or less success by means of various logical classifications to reduce to these four virtues the innumerable ways of objectively and subjectively appropriate moral action in relation to the whole of reality.

We speak of supernatural, infused virtues, i.e., virtues bestowed by God in justification, as the dynamism of sanctifying grace. This is because by man's supernatural vocation and by supernatural grace as God's self-communication, the whole personal, spiritual life of man is directed in knowledge and freedom (love) towards direct, eternal sharing in the life of the triune God, and this goal has to be reached by the free acceptance of God's self-communication. Consequently grace renders man's spiritual faculties capable of this acceptance (which is one but manifold). This happens in such a way that these acts also correspond as regards the subject performing them, to the acceptance of divine self-communication. They must therefore also have God himself as their ground. These virtues orientate the religious moral being and action of man even in this life towards a direct sharing in the life of the triune God. They thus confer the possibility of directing one's life freely to that goal in a way that is proportionate to its nature, and to attaining it as truly one's own. Such supernatural virtues are therefore very closely connected with the supernatural sanctifying grace of justification of which they are simply the living dynamism. They are only distinguished from the grace which divinizes man's very being as its dynamic extension into his faculties, analogous to the way in which man's faculties are distinguished from his substance. They are a number of ordered ways (of increasing degrees of intensity) in which man can concretely and freely accept the proffered grace of justification, and in which that grace, when accepted, takes roots and is distributed as it were through man's manifold nature.

The supernatural infused virtues, therefore, which do not belong to man's essence but are bestowed by God as a loving favour in his free self-communication, are not really like the natural, acquired virtues, the habitual ability to use a permanent capacity, but are the very capacity for salutary action itself, the capacity to share even now in the life and glory (*doxa*) of God and to shape one's life as a history of the coming of eternal life in time. The infused virtues as such do not therefore necessarily imply any special facility in salutary action, even though they are bestowed in conjunction with justification and although they involve a real dynamism for the development of the divine life in us. Habitual ability and facility in such a supernatural life has to be acquired, in the same way as with natural virtues.

It must not be overlooked either, that these supernatural virtues stand in a similar relation to the natural capacities (and their *habitus* and virtues) as supernatural grace does to man's spiritual nature. That grace is not a second nature superimposed on natural nature; it is the opening out of the natural spiritual essential ground of man towards the immediate possession of God, the teleological orientation of man's natural spiritual nature towards the life of God. The supernatural virtues are therefore not virtues side by side with the spiritual faculty or side by side with the natural virtues. They are the orientation of precisely those faculties and their natural virtues towards the life of God. As the whole man is to be brought to salvation by the whole activity of his life, it is really self-evident that grace and the dynamism of its virtues should direct the whole life of man towards God and that accordingly there are as many supernatural virtues for the branches and growth of the one root of supernatural life, as there are natural virtues. An actually Christian ethics in the concrete does not therefore need to be very much concerned about the distinction between natural and supernatural virtues. In the actually existing order of God's universal salvific will, the natural virtues have in fact a supernatural goal and the supernatural virtues are accomplished and manifested in what we have to experience and carry out as natural virtues in the sober, empirical and harsh reality of everyday life. If one asks what supernatural virtues are, it can be said very simply and in slightly "demythologized" terms, that they are the willing, well-practised and genuine (not merely half-hearted or hypocritical) decency of an honest, courageous, loving man, inasmuch as these human things by God's action are much more than human, because in them in faith, hope and love the eternal life is at work in which man possesses the life of God himself.

2. *The three fundamental supernatural virtues, the "theological virtues"*. From what has been said of the virtues in general, it follows that the real function of the supernatural, infused virtues is to orientate the whole religious ethical life (which itself expresses the spiritual nature of man) towards the immediate possession of God. Scripture and tradition accordingly speak of a triad of such fundamental supernatural virtues which are specified by their being the basic modes of increasing acceptance of the divine self-communication by grace and of directing man's spiritual, personal life towards the trinitarian God of eternal life by a sharing in God's life

itself. They have God himself as formal object by the fact that God in uncreated grace himself is the ground of the "capacity" and its act, and is both immediate object and co-principle of the act of faith, hope, love. This triad is already found in the NT (1 Cor 13:13; 1 Thess 1:3; 5:8; Eph 1:15–18; Col 1:4f.; Heb 10:22–24). The Council of Trent declared the three theological virtues to be "infused" with the grace of justification (*D* 800), without seeking to determine the exact relation between sanctifying grace and infused charity (e.g., are they identical or not?). At all events the infused virtues (not love, but faith and hope) can remain even when sanctifying grace is lost (*D* 808, 838). It is disputed whether they can be acquired, as *habitus*, even *before* justification, by actual faith and hope. They are called theological virtues (in contradistinction to infused or acquired moral virtues) because their formal object is not a finite moral personal value (veracity, moral worth of honouring God, etc.), but God himself, as he makes himself the life of man by his self-communication. They are to be regarded as *habitus* (*D* 821), as a lasting capacity for a life directed to God.

These three theological virtues do not come into action only when it is a question of actions expressly related to the God who has revealed himself. They crown the whole moral life of the justified person and direct it towards eternal life as its goal, when a human being in a fundamental decision which is the basis of, and contributes to determine, all particular acts, hears God's promise of himself, hopes in the absolute future and in love of God's love and glory entrusts himself wholly to God. To that extent it is really more a question of terminology than of substance whether or not there are infused moral virtues in addition to the theological virtues (as is generally taught: *D* 483; *Catechismus Romanus*, II, 2, 50). At all events the activity of the justified person in the power of the Holy Spirit is accomplished not only in explicitly religious acts but in the whole activity of moral life, as, for example, where the neighbour is loved in an act of the theological virtue of love of God. "Theological virtues" is the rather portentous name for the experience of the accepted grace of God, which is, ultimately, God himself. Wherever man unconditionally (with unconditional responsibility, in love, in hope, etc.) accepts his transcendence over everything finite and under his command, a transcendence which is truly set free by God's grace for God himself and his incomprehensible mystery, he experiences, though perhaps in a very implicit and anonymous way, impossible to objectivate, the attraction of the divine Spirit towards God himself, his cry of Abba-Father in inexpressible sighs (Rom 8:16f., 23, 26), the life of the divine virtues.

Karl Rahner

II. Love as the Key Virtue

A. Methodical Preliminaries

1. Love is here understood in such a way that it can be predicated of the relationship of God to man, of the relationship of man to God and of men among themselves. Such a use of the word means that its scope is so enlarged and at the same time so manifold that it can only with difficulty escape being reduced to a sort of barely intelligible code-word.

2. The word "love" takes in so much in Christianity that it can no longer denote only a particular element somewhere within, so to speak, our world of experience. It has to mean the whole of experience, in the mode proper to it, if it is to be capable of goodness and perfection. (And here again, goodness and perfection must be thought of as love, if the notion of such fulfilment is not to degenerate into a rigid for-

malism.) It follows at once that such love cannot be defined by elements outside itself or from which it can be "composed", as though of parts. It can only be described, not defined.

3. Since love is a mysterious key-word for the (true) whole of man – for it means the whole man as he is drawn away from himself into the incomprehensible mystery of God – its content is determined by all that makes him man, and hence by his historicity. Love has a history, which means more than its recurring again and again in time. It takes on in its exercise, and in reflection on its acts (in the theory of its practice), constantly changing forms and aspects and shifts of emphasis in each concrete moment of its commitment. As a result, love may be, and in fact has been, simply one of the key-words by which men have sought to express the totality of historical existence. Hence "love", being a word which aims at summing up the whole of a human existence and not just this or that process within it, is found in one way or another in all religions. It takes a very central place as early as Deuteronomy (Deut 6:4f., etc.) but only becomes the real key-word and absolutely central theme in the NT, while the subsequent history of theology can hardly be said to have maintained it clearly in this role. So it still remains objectively possible to envisage this basic relation of the whole man to God and his fellows under another aspect and hence to describe it by means of another key-word. Obvious competitors, from the Bible and the history of theology, are faith or hope. But others are conceivable. Since the transcendentals (*unum, verum, bonum*) are related to each other in a unity and difference which form together an ultimate, any of these words, if thought out in full, will merge into the others and can thus be used as a keyword, though none of them says quite the same thing. The historical background – and kerygmatic discretion – suggest that the interchangeability of the permanently diverging elements of such key-words of human experience should be borne in mind. Kerygmatically, the word "love" should not be harped upon too much. Nonetheless, it remains the great NT word for what God is and for what man ought to be, and must always remain central in the preaching of the Christian message.

4. The methodological question becomes still more acute when the attribution of love to God extends to the affirmation that God *is* love, that love is his "essence" ("Deus formaliter est caritas", according to Duns Scotus.) One can of course explain what one means by saying that God is love. But then one has to remember that love then merges into the absolute mystery of God's being, and hence becomes incomprehensible to us, so that the affirmation – particularly as regards love for *us* – can only be a radical act of faith and hope. The love of God for us is not simply an experience to be taken for granted. It is hoped for, in faith, "against hope" (Rom 4:18).

B. Love in General

1. *Classical definitions.* We cannot here attempt to trace the history of the concept of love in philosophy and theology. Much less can we attempt here a phenomenology of love as it is known by men in their interpersonal experiences, with all their different stages of bodily and mental development (the relationship of mother and child, sexual love in the strict sense, etc.). We confine ourselves to certain themes of philosophy and theology which seem to suggest ways of rounding out and differentiating the notion. It will not always be possible to make a neat distinction between the various approaches in question, and the history of the various "definitions" must be omitted. Our main interest will be to bring out

the problematic element which remains consistently throughout.

a) *Love as amor benevolentiae and amor concupiscentiae – "selfless" and "desirous" love*. If love is the total act in which one person achieves the fully correct relationship to another by "acknowledging" and accepting the other in his total personal excellence and dignity, two aspects of this relationship appear at once. There is the relationship of the one who loves to the other, and the converse relationship which is also grasped and accepted in the giving of love.

The subject, through the transcendence and freedom in which it can grasp the substantial selfhood of the other and thus be truly its own self (i.e., attain "happiness"), acknowledges and accepts the other in its independence, dignity and irreplaceable otherness. It recognizes the other as truly and validly existing "in itself". It wills the other subject as the permanently other. But at the same time the subject grasps and affirms the significance of the other for itself (the loving subject) and refers it to itself. Hence *amor benevolentiae* and *amor concupiscentiae* are not in mutual conflict. They are aspects of the same love, which are based on the transcendence of the subject which is capable of affirming and willing the other. One is ordained not merely to know but also to will the personal reality of the other qua other, and this is precisely what one grasps as significant for oneself.

This truth does not mean that there cannot be shifts of emphasis acting and reacting on these elements of the one love. One result of this is that traditional theology has rather insisted on the opposition between *amor benevolentiae* and *amor concupiscentiae*, so much so that the two acts could appear to be separable. But then the *amor benevolentiae* could be reduced to an uninterested willingness to let the other be, or was regarded – as by Spinoza – as merely the mechanism by which "objective" acknowledgment was brought about (*amor intellectualis Dei*). The *amor concupiscentiae* then becomes "self-centred" and part of the theological virtue of hope rather than of charity (the *amor benevolentiae*, as the response to God's self-communication, the grace which inspires this response). But in spite of all possible shifts of accent as between the two aspects, it is to be noted that the most "selfless", self-forgetful ("ekstatic") love, being the most radical commitment, is "passionate" in the most sublime sense. Otherwise it would not achieve the fullness of its being. It is therefore by its nature the affirmation of, the happiness of, the being of the subject itself. And an *amor concupiscentiae* which tried to make the other merely a means to its own happiness would not be love at all but a selfish effort to satisfy a particular desire. And this would mean that the subject itself failed to attain its own real being. (In the light of these considerations, the whole debate about attrition and contrition would need a radical reappraisal.)

b) *Eros – agape*. This distinction, worked out by A. Nygren, means that *eros* (in the Greek interpretation of love) is the love of desire and "passion". Fascinated and carried away by the actual excellence and beauty of the "You", the object of aesthetic contemplation and love, it tries to draw the beloved to itself as its own happiness. *Agape*, however (in the biblical sense), is the love of God which bends down to the sinful and worthless, the love that gives without receiving, that lavishes itself foolishly and is the sole reason why man becomes worthy of this love. And it is only by pure grace that man is enabled finally to participate in this divine *agape* and display it towards God and his fellowman.

This distinction is correct and (religiously) important, inasmuch as only God's love can be really absolutely creative. Created love is always a response to an actual excellence (which is ultimately God's primal love). The radical conversion to the fellowman and to God is inspired by God's radical love of us which is there in his self-communication. But the distinction cannot be used simply to distinguish pagan and Christian love or to designate types of love which are mutually exclusive. For over and beyond the word of revelation in the OT and the NT there is the self-communication of God which is co-extensive with all history (by virtue of the universal salvific will), and this offers all men the possibility of *agape* towards God and their fellowmen which only grave sin can exclude. "Natural" *eros* is at once a *potentia oboedientialis* for such *agape*, since, if it does not culpably forfeit its own nature, it wills the other *as* the other and not just its own happiness. (For when this happiness is rightly understood and fully perfected, it consists of "selfless" love of the other.) Hence all human love, even "spiritual" love, which flows from "bodily" man, has also an "erotic" foundation which it need not be ashamed of and which comes to its fulfilment in the very fulfilment of this personal love.

c) *Love of self – love of others.* Can one love oneself, as seems to be assumed by Scripture, Mt 22:39, or is all self-affirmation, no matter how transcendentally necessary, essentially "egoistic", the inevitable sinfulness of man, the inextinguishable reflex of original sin, and hence the opposite of love? Scholastic theology in general rightly affirms that love – even as *virtus caritatis theologicae infusae* – can and ought to refer the subject to itself, making this love a "duty". The assumption is that such self-affirmation is not simply surrender to the instinctive drives of the "struggle for existence", but is based on objective recognition of the value and dignity of the subject within reality as a whole and in relation to God. This God-given excellence is not loved simply because it is one's own, but because it *is* and is of value. This is of course not to deny that in actual fact the *amor sui* (in St. Augustine's sense) is not constantly perverted into egoism (as *contemptus Dei*). In view of this fundamentally affirmative answer to our question, it must also be affirmed that God loves himself. This does not make him an egoist, for he affirms his infinite "objective" perfection, and does so precisely inasmuch as it is the *bonum diffusivum sui*, the "selfless love" which is his essence (cf. 1 Jn 4:7–10). These considerations are important for a proper understanding of the biblical and ecclesiastical doctrine of the glory of God.

d) *Thomist and Scotist interpretations.* The debate between these schools on the nature of love may be understood and theoretically solved on the basis of the foregoing. Scotism regards love as the "ecstatic" outgoing of the lover from himself. He forgets himself to take a "centrifugal" attitude towards what is no longer seen in terms of himself, what is not *his* good. He loves God for what he is in himself and not for what he is for us. He would still love God if, *per impossibile*, he were to damn the lover. Thomism sees in love the natural inclination by which the subject seeks its good, which in the case of man, in contrast to the infra-human creature, can only "satisfy" when infinite. Hence love of God and a rightly understood self-love, which does not culpably fall short of man's nature, are two aspects of the same love in which man finds himself when he loses himself in the love of God. The Thomist view is correct in terms of existential notology. But from the point of view of phenomenology, and in view of the seriousness of life's decisions, in view of the difficulty man has in finding himself in his sin-ridden history. Scotism is right in pointing out that he must make an effort which is apparently almost suicidal if he is to attain his true being. He must break out of his finite categories and his sinful egoism, in faith and hope, inspired by a love which must be bestowed on him by the selfless agape of God.

e) In the history of the discussion, several other aspects of love have been brought out, which can only be exemplified here by a small, random selection. Up to the present, we have considered love only as addressed to a personal, spiritual subject, basing ourselves on the correct assumption that love in the strict sense can only exist in these terms. It remains true, however, that love is often mentioned in connection with other objects. If what is meant is some positive good will and correct attitude, and if the distinction between this and true interpersonal love is not lost sight of, in theory or practice, there is no objection to such a use of the term, e.g., when speaking of "love" of animals. It is even possible that such love of seemingly impersonal things may really be addressed to the God who is hidden and present and really loved himself there, provided that such things are not wrongly loved when their nature is mistaken and idolized. There is a right and a wrong sense in which men may speak of an *amor fati* or a "cosmic" love or be, like Keats, "in love with easeful Death". Hence love can be interpreted in the light of other basic human experiences, e.g., as actual fellowship, as friendship, as selfless service, as adoration (in love of God).

f) In the historical debate on the nature of love, a problem which is basically the same has constantly come up – that of the relationship between knowledge and will (which reappears at a different stage in the three divisions of man's spiritual faculties in modern, non-metaphysical thinking). In "Greek" intellectualism, the will seems little else than the dynamism and mechanicism of knowledge (will to truth, love of truth). And then love is just the connatural happiness of the possession of the good – which is truth. Conversely, knowledge can appear as the mere precondition (light) of love. Neither view does justice to the unity of truth and goodness (and hence of intellect and will), which a profounder view sees persisting even in their mutal irreducibility. Love is not merely a prelude to and by-product of Gnosis, as there was a tendency to hold in Greek patristics. And knowledge is not merely the presupposition of love. The "dualism", the unity but not total identity of the two acts is seen to be irreducible in the doctrine of the two "processions" in the Trinity.

But then the problem arises once more as to why the whole of Christian existence can simply be characterized as love, as is done in tradition. In the light of this question-mark, one is forced to say that love only represents the ultimate key-word of Christian existence insofar as it makes this existence fully sound and complete (like the *ordo* in the trinitarian processions). But then it is truly the key-word. Nonetheless, this does not mean that the knowledge which comes "earlier" in the transcendental structure of man's spirit is to be assigned a merely instrumental function, or that love is to be understood as merely the bliss of possessing the truth.

2. *Further characteristics.* Since there can be no question of giving a "definition" of love, what has been said under B, 1, above, may be taken as a general description of love. A few remarks are now added to call attention to some points which are perhaps less explicitly treated in scholastic theology than the matter given in B, 1.

a) The dualism of *essentia* and *esse*, of idea and reality (in the sense of *existentia* in Scholasticism), has always been recognized, and has always remained an impenetrable enigma. They are unintelligible except in constant relationship to one another, but neither can be reduced to the other or understood as a mere moment of the other. One can follow St. Thomas, and take *esse* to be prior to *essentia* (ideal being), so that the real is not just the there-ness of an ideal quiddity, adding nothing, as far as one can see, to the "eternal truth". But this does not really get rid of the continuing dualism. It has to be accepted as an inescapable fundamental reality, in spite of all the considerations that must be offered on the matter, and above all on the many changes in the relationship of the two elements and the unity which they form without being flatly identical. But the notion of love is particularly relevant when this mysterious element in the make-up of all beings is considered. If idea becomes reality and reality takes on the light of the ideal and attains the essence accepted by it (an acceptance necessary if reality is not to waste away in darkness); if reality is also accepted in its "factualness" (and God himself, being free, is "factual" in his aseity, which cannot be reduced to an "eternal idea") – then love is at work, i.e., the will which does not shrink from accomplishing this. Love is reality's harmony with itself in the positive non-identity of *essentia* and *esse*, which implies an element of the *de facto* – though the latter is only true of God in an analogous way.

b) *Love as offer and response*. The point to be made here is perhaps best approached by repeating the ancient question as to whether one can love if one is not loved by the beloved. If the answer is in the affirmative, it must be remembered that such unrequited love can always be inspired by the hope of a future return of love, no matter how unforeseeable. (In fact, since St. Augustine, traditional theology has explained the possibility of love of enemies on this ground and affirmed that the damned cannot be loved.) Hence the principle must be maintained that love is dialogical. Otherwise the interpenetration of *eros* and *agape*, of selfless and "desirous" love (see A, 1, above), would be unintelligible. One cannot truly, validly and responsibly commit oneself to another (i.e., love) unless the other accepts fundamentally and definitively this radical gift of self (i.e., unless he loves too). But here we must anticipate what will be said under E below on the unity of love of God and of the neighbour. Wherever love is offered to another, the loving God is always partner in the dialogue (though mostly in a non-explicit way). This means that it is always rational to open the dialogue of love, though it does not mean that every such offer of love among men will be answered by a similar love, one that is perhaps desired only selfishly. But the appeal of love is always such that an answer from the other part must be given. Love is dialogical. And hence love of God is always in the nature of a response to the *agape* of God, which is an unfathomable grace. Responsive love is nonetheless free and marvellous, in the eyes of him who offers love. For by its nature love does not move with the stringent certainty of deductive truths. Its realm is that of the freely factual, actual reality. Love is always grace and true grace is love.

c) *Love and hope*. In spite of the doctrine of the three theological virtues, it seems hard to fit hope, and its relationship to love, into the schemata used to describe love above. The schemata in question were always twofold: knowledge and will, *essentia* and *esse*, the two trinitarian processions and so on. One could simply say that hope was love under the aspect of *amor concupiscentiae* as long as such love was still not in possession of its good (*bonum arduum*) but did not need to despair of attaining it. But this is certainly to do less than justice to the relationship of hope and love. Since love is dialogical, it always depends on the possible answer of the other (or if given, on its freely remaining so) and hence on the incalculable. There is therefore an element of hope in all aspects of love, not just in "desirous" love. Even when love is perfected, hope remains (1 Cor 13:13).

C. God's Love for Man

1. Ultimately, God's *agape* consists in his giving himself in love to the world in the spiritual creature. Through his self-communication he makes himself the inmost mystery of his creation, and its history and its fulfilment. He is not just Lord and Guardian, while creation itself remains "outside" God. This love is the cause of there being others than itself, but it holds these differences together in their relationship to its own oneness, which is God. It contains (analogously) an element of "jealousy" ("desire") because the self-sufficient God willed in a free act of love to need a world which is his own history because of his self-communication in grace and the incarnation. It is dialogical ("bridal"), because it is the foundation and principle of man's love for God, since by grace man can love God in a divine way, just as he can utter the word *of God* in human words. In this way man's loving Yes to God is from God. This explains why the notion of "Father" is only partially adequate to express the love of God for man. "Son" must be understood in the sense in which Jesus knew himself to be Son and us as sons by participation. It is only the radical intimacy of self-communication in grace and the incarnation that eliminates the overtones of the external and paternalistic which may be heard in the "Fatherliness" of God. This love can appear as the sovereign law which demands the humbly obedient love of the "servant". But then all the elements which go to make up the relationship of law and gospel must be considered.

2. It is difficult to preach today that God loves man, that by his self-communication he is love itself for him. This situation must be seen clearly and soberly. It has become clearer – though it was "always" recognized – that God is not part of the world, that he is not to be found as a particular reality within the realm of our experience. His "distance", his inexpressibility, the radical mysteriousness of his being, is the epochal hall-mark imposed on our existence. It is not so easy to realize as is sometimes supposed in unthinking pious talk that this God can love us, with a personal relationship to each individual which offers shelter to each. The atheism which appears as "silence about that of which one cannot clearly speak", as well as the atheism of tragic despair at the horrors of human existence, are now challenges which consistently menace even the faith of Christian theists in the love of God, in a loving God. We cannot now speak of God's love for us as though we were addressing men who have repressed all their experiences of the absurd and are so comfortably well-balanced that they find it very instructive to be told that the world is on the whole very well ordered and governed by a God of love. There must be a deep solidarity with a world in torment before one dares speak of the love of God. And then all merely "philosophical" analysis will naturally fall away. To speak of the love of God will be to testify to it in deeds and words, to appeal to men for an ultimate decision in faith and love, where no stringent assurance can be provided. After Auschwitz, it has been said, there is nothing for it but to be an atheist. But it has also been said that in fact of the dead of Auschwitz we have to believe in God and hope in his love, since there is no justification for them otherwise and they are betrayed by their own absurdity. In any case, it has to be clearly affirmed that the happiness of posterity – always hoped and planned for in the world and just as constantly crashing to ruin – does not justify the miseries of the past and present. We must not flinch from asserting the hard truth that the love of God is just as much of a mystery as God himself.

Cursing the darkness of the world does not make it any brighter. To bear the predestined impotence of our faith in God's love is not the same as to refuse culpably to believe in that love, though frustration and unbelief may not be very far apart. And to love others truly, in deed and will, without self-deception, to do so as an absolutely sacred duty, is fundamentally to believe in God and his love for man, even perhaps unknown to oneself.

D. Justification by Love in Theology

1. *Scripture.* Love of God in the OT and the NT is not described by such words as ἔρως or στοργή. The word φιλία is rare. Instead, the word ἀγάπη is used, with the corresponding verb. The word was introduced into literary and religious usage by the LXX, and given a new content. *Agape* means the love of God for us, and also love of the neighbour, of enemies and of God (in Jn, though also in St. Paul, e.g., 1 Cor 8:3). Our main interest here will be the justifying love of man for God and his neighbour (on the unity of which, see below). This is an act which integrates the whole of man's existence ("with the whole heart" etc.) (Mk 12:20 parr., citing Deut 6:4f.). It is inspired by the Spirit of God (see *Grace*), it is the fruit of the Spirit (Rom 15:30; Gal 5:22; Col 1:8; 2 Tim 1:7). It is the realm of existence within which man should remain (Eph 5:2; 1 Jn 4:16). There one is justified (Rom 13:9f.; 1 Jn 4:16; Gal 5:6; 1 Cor 13:13; Mt 22:36–40; Lk 10:25–28).

2. *Church teaching.* The decisive declarations of the extraordinary magisterium with regard to love were made in connection with the doctrine of justification in the sixth session of the Council of Trent. The fundamental statement is that justification is inseparable from the infused virtue of love (*D* 800, 821) and that the process of justification freely entered upon by the adult only comes to its climax and its fullness in an act of charity (love) (*D* 800f., 819, 889). (This remains true even if one supposes that the grace of justification can be "infused" in the sacrament by reason of mere attrition and only later become actual in an act of charity [love] – though this is necessary, *D* 1101, 1155ff., 1289.) Hence in ecclesiastical terminology faith and hope, in spite of their intrinsic tendency to perfect themselves in love are acts whose specific nature does not imply the full union of man with God in grace (*D* 801, 819, 839, 1525), while this union is rightly and fully expressed by the word "love". The question as to whether charity is infused in infants at baptism left open earlier (*D* 410, 483), was decided in the affirmative by Trent (*D* 799f. along with 791f.), though without denying that the free acceptance of the grace of justification by the adult, through an act of charity, marks the possession of grace. Unlike faith, the infused virtue of love is lost by any mortal sin (*D* 808, 837f.). No exact description of this love is given. It is distinguished from "natural" love of God, which is thereby treated as theoretically possible (*D* 1034, 1036), and from imperfect and initial (salutary) forms of love of God (*D* 798, 889, 1146). Trent suggests that it can be considered as "friendship" with God (*D* 799, 803). The relationship between love of God and love of the neighbour is not defined precisely. It seems to be a "free opinion" in theology that the two modes of love have exactly the same formal object (Patres S.J. in Hispania, *Sacrae Theologiae Summa*, III, no. 240). The general doctrine of the magisterium on the supernatural virtues, on salutary acts, loss of grace, growth in grace and experience of grace also applies, of course, to the *habitus* and act of this virtue. While the magisterium treats love as the sum total of Christian life which embraces and integrates all else, it resolutely rejects the notion that this excludes all dif-

ferences in moral and salutary acts. A relative pluralism remains. There are positively salutary acts which are not simply acts of love (*D* 915, 898, 817f., 798), and the justified, being finite creatures still on pilgrimage and hence unable fully to integrate themselves, can still rightly act from motives other than that of love (*D* 508, 1327f., 1349, 1394–1408, 1297).

E. Love of God and Love of Neighbour: Unity and Difference

1. This question needs special consideration today. With atheism a social phenomenon, there is a strong temptation to treat God and the love of God merely as a code-word for the inviolable status of man and love of the neighbour, to "demythologize" prayer by treating it as mental dialogue with man and so on. This situation obliges Christians to profess unwaveringly their faith in God. God is not only the "absoluteness" of man. And they must also profess their love of God, which remains the "first commandment" (Mt 22:38). They are also bound to try to reach a real understanding of the true unity of love of God and love of the neighbour, which does not mean that one term can be substituted indifferently for the other. But it is a unity which solves from within the problem of atheistical love of the neighbour, since a love of the neighbour which is truly absolute includes at once a (non-articulated) theism and an implicit love of God. This is in fact why the love of God must be made an explicit theme, since it is the hidden and sublime mystery of human existence.

2. This unity is affirmed by Scripture and tradition. The two commandments (love of God and of the neighbour) are alike. There is nothing in the law and the prophets which does not depend on them (Mt 22:39f.; Lk 10:28; Mk 12:31). So much so, that St. Paul can simply say that to love the neighbour is to fulfil *the* law (Rom 13:8, 10; Gal 5:14). In Mt, when Jesus speaks of judgment in his eschatological warnings, the only measure mentioned by which man is to be judged is love of the neighbour, and the nature of the final rebellion against God is indicated by saying that the charity of many will grow cold (Mt 25:34–46; 24:12). Love of the neighbour is the royal law (Jas 2:8) and the definitive form of Christian life (1 Cor 12:31–13:13).

The Johannine writings provide the first conscious effort to justify the radical importance thus allotted to love of the neighbour, which might otherwise appear as a pious exaggeration, just as it was later toned down in Christian exhortation, which explained love of the neighbour as a particular element of the Christian obligation, without which, however, in spite of its difficulty, salvation cannot be attained. According to St. John, we are loved by God (Jn 14:21) and by Christ in order that we should love one another (Jn 13:34). This love is the new commandment of Christ (Jn 13:34), his own specific commandment (Jn 15:12), the commandment which he lays upon us (Jn 15:17). For St. John the consequence is that God, who *is* love (1 Jn 4:16), has loved us not in order that we should love him in return but in order that we should love one another (1 Jn 4:7, 11). For we do not see God. He cannot be attained truly alone in an inward mystical Gnosis which would enable him to be really loved in this way (1 Jn 4:12). It is only the "God in us" of mutual love that we can love (1 Jn 4:12), so much so that it is really true, and for St. John an absolutely stringent argument (though one that we do not normally find evident) that "he who does not love his brother whom he has seen, cannot love God whom he has not seen" (1 Jn 4:20).

Traditional theology has resolutely maintained at least that the infused virtue of union with God, the theological *virtus caritatis in Deum*, is also the virtue by which the neighbour is loved. This is all the more striking because tradition admits the existence of other theological and moral virtues distinct from love, and it would not have been difficult to describe love of the neighbour as a special and subordinate virtue. It must be admitted, however, that much remains obscure as regards the unity in question, as proposed in Scripture and tradition. This results in a constant tendency to think of love of the neighbour merely in terms of a duty entailed by the love of God, of which it would also be the touchstone and guarantee.

3. Nonetheless, it should still be maintained that there is a genuine unity, of a radical nature, between the two modes of love. (The presupposition is always that of the self-communication of God in grace to men, the object of love of the neighbour. Merely "philosophical" grounds are not invoked.)

We must bear in mind the following points. A distinction must be made between an explicit, propositional affirmation and an affirmation (bearing on a reality not clearly envisaged) which is virtually there in an act referred explicitly to another object. Then we must recall that all metaphysical knowledge is mediated by historical, intramundane experience, in the light of which alone access is at all possible to the understanding of transcendental realities. Further, the encounter with the neighbour in love must be recognized not as one experience among others, but as the central act of human existence which integrates the whole personal content of experience. Finally, any absolute, (positive) moral decision must be recognized as implicit theism and "anonymous Christianity". Under these circumstances, it can be affirmed on principle that the act by which the neighbour is loved *is* really the primal (though still non-explicit) act by which God is loved. That God must also be loved in explicit, conscious terms is not thereby excluded – on the contrary. For if there is an implicit reference to God in every moral act, and hence primarily in the love of the neighbour, it must become explicit in man's words and life, since this Godwardness is the ultimate source and force of this central experience of the world (love of the neighbour). Love of God and of the neighbour each live by the other, because they are ultimately one (*inconfuse, indivise*). Love of God as a deliberate response to the structure of existence is only real when it is love of the neighbour; and the ultimate mystery of love of the neighbour only comes fully into play, its absoluteness and the possibility of this absoluteness – with regard to finite and sinful men – when it surpasses itself to be love of God.

4. The history of salvation shows that the climax and the ultimate guarantee of the unity of love of God and of the neighbour is our love of Jesus Christ, in whom God and man are united. Speaking as the Son of man, he declares that he is the mysterious partner who is included in all active love for man (Mt 25:34–40), so that the unity of the love which embraces him and the fellowman is decisive for the destiny of each man, even where this unity is not recognized (Mt 25:37ff.). This is better understood when one recalls that genuine love for man opens out on love of all, and that dialogical, responsorial love for a finite and sinful man, untrustworthy therefore and possibly hostile, is an implicit affirmation of the God-man, present or hoped-for, as its ground and guarantee. This is how it has the absoluteness which is due to it as an act done by divine grace. Jesus therefore demands explicitly that his disciples should love him (Jn 8:24; 14:15, 21, 23, 28), so that the love of the Father for the Son may embrace those who love the Son (Jn 14:21, 23; 17:23, 26) and that these may "abide in his love" (Jn 15:9f.; 1 Jn 4:7), the all-embracing love which takes in God,

the God-man and man, who are all both subjects and objects of this one love.

Karl Rahner

VISIONS

The free self-donation of God implies a revelation of his personal mystery. Within man's consciousness it cannot be comprehended by any sort of introversion; it cannot be "seen" in the sense of ontologism, but only co-experienced (in the acts of the theological virtues). And yet such a non-objective co-experience of the divine light and speech in the Christian who knows how to discern it is basically already a *visio* and *auditio*.

The basic elements of this experience can then be deepened through the "light of infused contemplation" and pass over to mystical perception. Under this special influence another "curtain" falls away (cf. St. John of the Cross, *Living Flame of Love*, IV, 7) and the illumination and speech of God becomes less indirect.

The usual mystical elements of vision and audition generally remain in their simple form, beyond thought, images, or words. Yet this simple state can simultaneously be expressed in the conceptual and perceptual sphere, in ideas, images, and words. In a perceptible vision, "the picture that is shown to the soul is the momentary form of grace, its visible evidence which is, so to speak, tangible for the inner senses. At the same time, however, the grace of the divine union itself penetrates the soul with so strong and yet so tender an inspiration that in comparison the image can only seem like the accidental accompaniment of the grace. God himself takes possession of the inmost centre of the soul. He penetrates both the soul and the image that he has put before the soul . . . He instructs the soul in a similar way concerning the mystical sense of what the soul sees. And it is he whom the soul loves in what it sees; it is he himself whom the soul perceives therein" (Lucie Christine, *Journal spirituel*, 30 January 1887). It is similar in the case of audition: "the soul perceives the words as though in its deepest centre; it perceives them, but it does not form them. And the words cleave to the presence of the Lord and are one with him" (*ibid.*, 25 September 1882).

The occasion of the intellectual, imaginative, or verbal translation of the simple basic experience of the divine mysteries can either be the individual psychophysical capacities of the subject himself which are projected unconsciously into his way of thinking and perceiving; or the occasion can be a special intervention of God which is outside any normal concrete psychophysical laws (although its effect on the person is psychophysical and subjectively conditioned, according to his religious education, age, and aesthetic development). In this last case one speaks, in the religious sphere, of a "genuine" vision or audition.

The genuineness of such experiences cannot be established simply on the grounds of the piety or sincerity of the subject; these are no proof against error with regard to visions. Even saints have been deceived. When the Church recognizes the holiness of a person, it pronounces no judgment on the genuineness of the visions the saint may have had. In the decree which affirmed the heroic virtue of Gemma Galgani, it is expressly said that "this decree is not to be taken as a judgment upon the nature of the exceptional charisms exercised by this servant of God"; to which the clause is added: "so too in other cases of this kind" (*AAS* 24 [1932], p. 57). Health, both of body and soul, is also no unequivocal criterion for "genuine" visions. Psychogenic projection of the simple basic experience into the faculties of the mind and senses can occur in those who are completely normal. Also, such projections cannot in themselves be called a symptom of "illness". The truth is rather that the psychic process cannot be adequately scrutinized and it thus remains ambiguous. Even the good effects that such a vision might have, a deepening of the religious feeling of the subject which begins with the experience and endures, is no unambiguous criterion. For purely psychogenic visions can also have such beneficent effects and be considered as proceeding "from the good Spirit". For an observer the one criterion of genuineness in the case of visions is that which establishes the genuineness in a formal way, a miracle (in the determination of which the existence of genuine telepathy etc. must be reckoned with). As miracles are seldom ascertainable, one must be satisfied with a greater or lesser probability in distinguishing genuine from psychogenic visions.

A vision that has been taken to be genuine can naturally only be granted a *fides humana*, insofar as the evidence of a vision is able to support such faith. Especially with "prophetic" visions which make assertions concerning future events strict evidence is to be demanded. If an ecclesiastical forum judges certain visions to be worthy of credibility, but the reasons for such credibility seem to one to be too weak to support it, then one can inwardly consider that judgment as erroneous and can make one's private opinion known, with all due respect for ecclesiastical authority (Benedict XIV). The believer, however, must avoid the basic scepticism, which, if radically carried through, would deny the very possibility of a historical revelation of God and thereby also deny Christianity as a supernatural, historical, and revealed religion. It is somewhat easier, after what has just been said, to judge the genuineness of a vision in the absence of any underlying experience of God and especially in the absence of moral probity on the part of the believer concerned.

While these intelligible and perceptible elements of a vision or audition are only an expression of that non-objective illumination and speech of God which can be experienced by any Christian, it is an experience which is essentially bound to the revelatory word of Christ. This is the reason why tradition within the sphere of visions must be measured against and interpreted by the revelation of Christ in the Church, and why it must yield to that visible continuation of the revelation and words of Christ in the sacraments and the word of the Church. In St. John of the Cross the heavenly Father says: "I have already told you everything in my Word, which is my Son. I have then nothing else and nothing better to answer or to reveal to you . . . In him is all that I have spoken, all that I can answer, all that I can give you to understand, all that I can reveal" (*Ascent of Mount Carmel*, II, 22, 5–6).

Yet it would be a mistake to consider that visions were therefore superfluous. They can in the first place be the occasion of a more vital experience of the reality of the Christian mystery for the subject involved, and they can also fulfil a function within the Church. Though in their content they could only correspond to that which is known already in faith and theology, nevertheless they can express an imperative demand of the will of God for the actions of the Church in a given historical situation in which that will could not be unequivocally ascertained by the application of the general principles of dogma or moral or by an analysis of the given situation.

Karl Vladimir Truhlar

VOLUNTARISM

Voluntarism is the doctrine which accords the will precedence over reason. It takes various forms, according to whether the will is regarded as spontaneity, freedom, love, act or drive, and according to the starting-point of the enquiry – theological, ontological or anthropological.

1. Theological voluntarism, which generally occurs in connection with a voluntarist theory of knowledge, dissociates the will of God from any fixed order – of being, nature or knowledge – which would be previous to the act of God's will. Any such (apparent) dependence is said to run counter to the freedom and sovereign transcendence of the divine person. This type of voluntarism stems from Christian impulses: the desire to maintain that creation was a free act and that redemption was accomplished through love. Theologians also felt that certain texts of the OT, such as those dealing with polygamy, the despoiling of the Egyptians and so on, could only be explained by voluntarism. But its fundamental principles remain tributary to a metaphysics of essence which really contradicts voluntarism; or else it tries to rid itself of such principles, and then it falls into agnosticism or becomes a voluntarist metaphysics. Theological voluntarism, of which the foundations were laid by Scotus, leads in the nominalism of Occam – which influenced Luther and through him Protestant theology, especially of the dialectical type – to the assertion that the moral good is positively determined by the arbitrary will of God. According to Descartes, even truth depends on the free act of God's omnipotence as first cause.

The will of God is in fact in no way determined by anything really distinct from him. But it is not lawless or formally arbitrary. It is the lucid and loving fullness of being of God, whose self-knowledge, identical with his self-affirmation, includes at once the structure and truth of what is possible on the finite plane (the *possibilia*). Since the creation and the consummation of the finite are one and the same thing in God's plan, the very nature of man is a concrete expression of the personal call of God to moral good. If the moral good were merely a matter of positive law, God would be contradicting the decree of his own will, as laid down in creation.

2. Metaphysical voluntarism, such as that upheld by Böhme and Schelling or Schopenhauer and Nietzsche, sees the ultimate principle of reality as an opaque, non-spiritual and instinctive will, which is either in dualistic opposition to the spirit – or the idea, or the good – or forms the sole structure of reality. Behind this type of voluntarism lies the violent effort to eliminate a notion of being too one-sidedly orientated to knowledge. But this purpose cannot be carried out by introducing a non-spiritual component from the will into an already one-sided notion of being, or by a radical rejection of the spiritual structure of reality. We must return to the authentic understanding of being which will allow us to see the lucidity of being as the active freedom in which it takes possession of itself: and the striving of instinct as a limited and defective form of the latter.

3. Psychological voluntarism emphasizes the predominance of the will – or desire, instinct or act – in human life and consciousness. According to its strict form (Wundt) all psychic processes are to be understood on the analogy of acts of desire and will. But the will alone does not constitute the essence of the person. It does so only along with knowledge, which does not actively determine its own perceptions. And the person, being in the body and in the world, can only "come to itself" by the exercise of a plurality of psychophysical functions distinct from the will. In the same way, the blessedness of heaven does not lie solely in the will, but consists of the interpenetration of receptive vision and the love which gives itself.

4. *Epistemological voluntarism.* In certain theories of knowledge, a decisive

function is ascribed to the will (or to love, or feelings) either in the assent to an acquired piece of knowledge (Descartes, Fichte) or in the very process of arriving at truth (so in various forms Kant, Jacobi, Scheler; pragmatism and conventionalism; some schools of existentialism). The assent to the known truth is a fully personal act of the spirit as a unity; the will as an individual faculty only becomes decisive in this act when the truth is not clearly evident of itself (free certainty, faith). If the will takes over the role of intellect in the finding of the truth, by trying to determine the truth independently, truth is perverted into a postulate or convention without contact with reality (i.e. irrationalism). The will, however, has the power of choosing between the objects set before it by knowledge. And in certain domains, access to the truth can be had only by an active interest in the object, absolute dedication to truth, sympathetic love, moral purity, an open-minded inclination. The decisive objects of knowledge – knowledge of values and of persons, ethical and religious truths, knowledge of one's own vocation – concern the essence of the person so profoundly that even when known and acted upon, their truth can be grasped only by the kernel of the person. But in the inmost depths of the person, knowledge and will are still so united as to be almost indistinguishable: knowledge, love and self-determination can take place only as a unity. The more the object of knowledge is exterior, the more the act of knowledge is differentiated from that of the will; and then the will plays a lesser role in the disclosure of truth, and the necessity of confronting the object with the whole human person is less urgent.

Klaus Riesenhuber

W

WAR

An attempt at a theological examination of war must deal in turn with the phenomenon of war, the problem of the right to make war (*jus ad bellum*) and the conduct of hostilities (*jus in bello*).

1. *The phenomenon of war*. Basically, apart from its specific manifestations, war may be defined as armed and sanguinary conflict between organized groups. The arms may make themselves felt by mere intimidation, before they are actually used. Such intimidation indeed plays a dominant role in the confrontation of great powers in our day, because the use of nuclear arms would threaten all belligerents with utter catastrophe (the strategy of the deterrent). Besides arms which are designed to destroy living bodies and material goods, there are psychological techniques that directly attack the human mind. Whether the "cold war" and the "war of nerves" are really war is a question which needs further discussion. War is international, civil, or revolutionary, according as the adversaries are different States, or sections of one population.

International war is armed conflict between States, desired by at least one of the belligerents and undertaken in a national interest. The latest technical devices do not necessarily displace earlier ones. In the age of the atomic bomb the bayonet is far from outmoded. The fact that atomic wars may break out does not mean that conventional (or classic) wars are now impossible. Even though world conflict threatens, certain wars may still remain limited ones. For all its variety, modern war logically becomes totalitarian (total war). Any country which embarks on it must face the total mobilization of its resources: economic, demographic and psychological. Thus conflict becomes extremely violent, and the most elementary moral standards are commonly disregarded. Losses of men and material reach astronomical proportions: more than fifty-five million persons died during the Second World War. The figure would be much higher had the most recent means of destruction been used. A thermo-nuclear conflict could cause three hundred million deaths in a matter of hours. Chemical and bacteriological weapons would also wreak great havoc.

Civil war and revolutionary war are alike fratricidal, and rely heavily on pyschological weapons. Civil wars have been so numerous, so cruel, and so disastrous that they have largely shaped the course of human history. When caused by social or ideological antagonism they have been most terrible of all. The prehistory of revolutionary war goes back to Sun Tze. After reaching a decisive stage with the French Revolution, it was taken in hand by the great Communist leaders. These, in order to gain their revolutionary ends, had recourse to no less revolutionary means, showing a preference for the techniques of subversive war: organization (mobilizing populations through the system of parallel hierarchies); propaganda (using every means to mould public opinion, particularly myths and brain-washing); agitation (terrorism and military intervention); the ideal of the five stages whereby a handful of resolute men advance from underground conspiracy to control of the population and final victory.

2. *The problem of the right to wage war* (*jus ad bellum*). Disregarding those whose cowardice or selfishness makes them feel that any injustice must be endured for the sake of physical survival, we shall observe that two diametrically opposite attitudes may be taken towards the chameleon-like phenomenon of war: either *every* war which seems to serve one's interests is legitimate, or *no* war is legitimate (absolute pacifism). The first attitude, that the end justifies the means, is that of the Machiavellians of every age, that of European "international law" before the time of the League of Nations and that of dictatorships and totalitarian States, Leftist or Rightist. If not in theory, then in practice all who take this view accept the dictum of Clausewitz that war is "simply a continuation of politics by other means". By contrast, absolute pacifism objects to all wars, even those of justifiable self-defence, holding that bloodshed is always wrong and that violence may only be resisted by non-violent means. Christian pacifists base their position on the Ten Commandments and the gospel.

Traditional Catholic doctrine accepts neither of these views. It repudiates the doctrine of "power politics", which it regards as a criminal aberration condemned alike by natural law and by the gospel. Because of the spiritual nature of man and the fact that all of his race are brothers, human conflicts – of whatever sort – must be settled by essentially reasonable and peaceful means: hence the basic rule of international law that all differences between nations must be resolved peacefully. Peace is an elemental duty for all. Are we, then, to become absolute pacifists? Theologians think not, because absolute pacifism ignores the fact of human nature as it actually exists, wounded by sin. Unscrupulous statesman do exist who drag their peoples into criminal adventures. Experience shows that often violence and injustice can only be stopped by violent means. Do not justice and charity towards others demand that we resist crime so far as we are able? Thus, despite its intrinsic unreasonableness and its horrors, war may become legitimate if there is no other means of remedying injustice.

Four conditions must be fulfilled (the theory of the just cause): one side must persist in committing an injustice (legitimate self-defence); all peaceful means of settling the dispute must have been exhausted; there must be a due proportion between the gravity of the injustice and the damage which the war would do (principle of the lesser evil); and there must be a reasonable hope of success. War can only be a desperate remedy in a desperate situation, used in order to spare humanity a still greater evil when all essentially reasonable and peaceful means have proved ineffective, for only in these circumstances can war acquire the necessary (though accidental) rationality. Unjust war is a monstrous crime.

Even in modern conditions the foregoing principles retain their relevance, despite the vast changes we have witnessed in the phenomenon of war. Violence remains a terrible reality of our age – the oppression of conscience, social injustice, racialism, militarism – and when it grows to monstrous proportions, must we not understand why the oppressed revolt? And has a State not a right to defend its existence? Most theologians hold that war may still be legitimate in order to resist an attack on the basic personal rights of a great many human beings, or on the existence of a State. Obviously, the rule of the lesser evil must still be observed. Even in a just cause, it cannot be lawful to unleash a general nuclear war, which would inevitably cause hundreds of millions of deaths, reduce the whole world to a ghastly chaos, and gravely prejudice the genetic future of the human race. That would be madness. Instead, we should have to rely on spiritual resistance, an alternative too long ignored, whose astonishing fruitfulness has been demonstrated by Gandhi and multitudes of Christians in totalitarian countries. The soundest deterrent is a community of human beings who are brave and intelligent, accustomed to thinking for themselves and acting according to the dictates of their conscience.

The very excesses of modern war compel us to avoid it by every means in our power. A spirit of universal solidarity and brotherhood must be cultivated. Enemies though they were for centuries, is war now thinkable between Great Britain and France, or between France and Germany? Yet allowance must be made for States ruled by criminals. Peace can only be maintained if – apart from finding a solution to the other enormous problems facing mankind – an effective world government is set up which is able to lay down the law even to the most powerful States. Once that is done, war will have ceased to be rational in any respect, even accidentally; for justice will be accessible to all. Such military operations as the world government undertakes will simply be police action on an international scale, to keep the peace.

3. *Conduct of hostilities* (*jus in bello*). Though war of its own nature is something savage, Christianity was able in some degree to humanize conflicts among the nations of Europe. But when weapons of mass destruction were invented, when nationalist ideologies exacerbated the opposing sides and totalitarianism had firmly established itself, war once more became thoroughly brutal and far more devastating than in the past, thanks to technical progress. Total war logically leads to unlimited violence. Victory being essential, it is said, the surest means to that end must be used: "Necessity knows no law."

To one who would behave as a human being, let alone as a Christian, this algebra of violence is unacceptable. In time of war no less than in time of peace, the absolute values basic to natural law must be respected. The following principles always hold good (in civil or revolutionary wars as well as in international ones): respect for human life (no human life to be sacrificed unless in lawful self-defence); respect for the person (ruling out all inhumane treatment, especially torture); immunity for the civilian population (in principle, the distinction between combatants and non-combatants must be preserved, and only military objectives may be attacked); all intrinsically evil acts are forbidden (assassination, rape, torture, treason, defamation, etc.). The right of legitimate self-defence exists, but it is limited by reason and the above conditions. These rules have been admirably elaborated and confirmed by various international conventions (the Hague Convention of 18 October 1907; the Treaty of Washington, 6 February 1922; the Geneva Protocol, 17 June 1925; the Geneva Conventions, 12 August 1949, etc.). Such of their provisions as form part of natural law (and the majority do) are binding on belligerents even if they have not signed such treaties.

Nuclear weapons present special problems. Not only are their immediate effects dreadful (appalling destruction by heat and blast, poisoning on an enormous scale by the initial radiation of alpha, beta, and gamma rays); their residual radiation is unforeseeable – no one knows where or when delayed fall-out may occur, causing grave biological damage (notably leukemia and bone cancer). Theoretically there might be cases where such weapons could be used subject to the general rules that governs the conduct of hostilities (bombing a squadron in mid-ocean, for example, or guided-missile sites far from centres of population). But even limited operations of this kind are on a dangerous path. Repeated explosion of tactical nuclear weapons can add up to a radio-activity as deadly as that of megaton bombs, and of course might well lead to full-scale nuclear warfare. Many think it an illusion to suppose that States with a full panoply of nuclear arms would conduct a limited atomic war. As John XXIII said: "It is becoming humanly impossible to regard war, in this atomic age, as a suitable means of reestablishing justice when some right has been violated" (*Pacem in Terris*, no. 127). The banning of nuclear arms by international convention is an urgent necessity.

Vatican II dealt at great length with the theme of modern warfare in the Pastoral Constitution on the Church in the Modern World (*Gaudium et Spes*). It not merely condemned atrocities in war (art. 79), total war (art. 80) and the armaments race (art. 81), but also demanded an absolute condemnation of war and called for world-wide action to prevent it (art. 82). The Council recommended the setting up of an international organization for the safeguarding of peace, whose main duty would be to eliminate the causes of war (arts. 83–90). These demands were underlined by Paul VI in his many efforts for peace and above all by the directives of the encyclical *Progressio Populorum.*

René Coste

WILL

1. *Terminology*. There is no generally accepted definition of what precisely the "will" means. The various definitions put forward in the course of history diverge from each other in many respects. An analysis of the present-day understanding of the term shows that it can have many different meanings according to the context in which it is used. The main usages are as follows.

a) Will as volition, the act of willing (the scholastic *actus voluntatis qua appetitus rationalis, intellectivus*). Examples of the use of the word in this sense are texts which speak of the will as the act of choosing, striving, purposeful desire, responsible self-determination, resolve, etc.

b) Will as faculty, power, tendency or disposition with regard to the acts of the will such as were mentioned under a). The problems which arise when the word is used in this (controversial) sense suggest that sharper definition is needed in many cases. This can be approached by using concrete examples to show how far the concept is applicable even in cases of diminished responsibility, e.g., in the state of sleep, hypnosis or intoxication, in the early phases of psychological development, in pathological loss of will-power (aboulia).

c) Will as the subject capable of acts of volition (cf. the ego, the self, the transcendental ego), either in the form of mere capability of willing without the actual exercise of the will, or in the mode of actual volition. Examples of such use of the term may be seen in phrases like "voluntas vult, movet . . ." But it is not the power or the faculty or even the act of will that is capable of willing, but only the person or subject.

d) Will as the content of the will or what is willed, in such phrases as "to do the will of the legislator".

e) Will as the disposition to implement what has been resolved. Since there is so much variation and vagueness in the use of the term, it is better to define what is meant by "will" by means of phrases including a verb like "to will". But even here usage can vary. The "will to power" in Nietzsche, for instance, uses the term in a wider sense than that of modern psychology. However, the variations here are mainly concerned with marginal elements of the content of volition. As regards its "kernel", "willing something in the strict sense", there is a relatively wide consensus, which has been confirmed by the experimental investigations of modern psychology.

2. *Psychology and anthropology of willing*. When man wills something, he seems to exist in a specially active way and to be determined by the personal ego itself. It might then be said that willing is an act which proceeds from the reality which each man knows as "I myself", the I-centre.

In contrast to other modes of existence, when man wills he does not find himself under alien domination but as master of himself. He is not pinned down or directed by others, but self-constitutive and self-directed. He has not to do something, but can, may or ought to do it. In other words, he is determinant, not subject to determination. He brings about something which is not exclusively determined by factors outside the volition of the "I" (as in purely mechanical processes) but is at least in one component due to the "factor" in man which is capable of responsible disposition of self. Acts of the will make it possible for man to add a "plus of determination" to the fields of activity imposed upon him (e.g., psychophysical organism, material surroundings). He can influence and help to shape the world and human existence in a way which he finds personally desirable and in keeping with the goals which he has set himself.

Psychologically, the act of the will is characterized by a sense of personal initiative and activity, which points to a fundamental difference between willing and other psychical experiences. Drives and inhibitions can be sensed, even against my will. Since drives which give rise to inclinations, compulsions, attractions, etc., can be called centripetal, heading for the centre of the person, the act of willing can be called centrifugal. It flows outwards rather than inwards and is determined by the person himself. Instinctive impulses can arise whether I want them or not, but this is not true of acts of the will.

The subject who wills is of a personal nature, and not just by virtue of an element merely integrated into the totality of the person, but by virtue of the personal principle itself in man. Hence a fundamental assertion may be made which holds good for all controversies on the problems of the will. It is that one cannot assume *a priori* that the same laws will hold good in all respects as are valid for mere things, non-personal objects. Caution is necessary when, for instance, the findings of natural science based on the observation of non-personal objects are used to prop up theses which affect the nature and possibilities of human life.

In the matter of the relationship between will and knowledge, a number of aspects must be borne in mind: the fact that human life is a whole, a unity; the elements of knowledge which defy subjective arbitrariness, the "objectivity" of knowable reality; the fundamental function of knowledge with regard to willing (*nihil volitum nisi praecognitum*); and the many ways in which the will can influence the intellect. Here factors subject to the influence of the will play a role not merely in the creation of the conditions for the attainment of knowledge (by the nature of the questions, the direction of the search, inward openness, intellectual honesty, etc.), but also in the interpretation, assessment and application of knowledge.

On the role of the will in specifically scientific thought, interesting perspectives have been opened up by the analysis of the basic problems of natural science and metaphysics in recent years, examples of which may be found in R. Carnap, K. Popper and W. Stegmüller. Light has been thrown on the radical problems and limitations of human claims to knowledge, on the difficulty of finding "absolutely" certain foundations and on the basic role of personal assumptions and decisions. There are, for instance, the attitudes adopted to basic questions of epistemology, in the acceptance or otherwise of principles of thought, evidences, axioms, empirical bases and so on. Consequences ensue which do not just lead to absurdities but rather to emphasis on the element of freedom and hence of responsibility. Questions are laid bare whose solution cannot be given by stringent proofs. Nonetheless, and in spite of positivistic polemics, an answer is possible and indeed meaningful, because sufficiently probable, fruitful, credible and so on. The answer may contain hypothetical components – though here the justifiable elements of the critical philosophy of Kant, of modern empiricism, of Wittgenstein and so on must be taken into account – but the answer is still sufficiently well motivated in practice to be humanly feasible and responsible.

As regards the controversy between the upholders of determinism and indeterminism, the ambiguousness and valueness of some central concepts should be noted. There is therefore need of a prior linguistic analysis and a clarification of terminology. When this is done, many apparent contradictions disappear at once.

Determinism is correct in assuming that the will does not go into action without sufficient reason. It is wrong in assuming that this excludes freedom. But indeterminism is correct in assuming that acts of the will are not determined in the way large-scale physical processes or pre-personal psychic movements are determined. It is wrong in assuming that acts of the will take place without a reason and uninfluenced by components which restrict the freedom of the will. The act of the will likewise has a cause, or better, an author, but this is to be sought in the "I" which can will, and make itself a cause. Freedom is therefore not random action or action without a cause, but the possibility of responsible self-determination, when the cause is the self. In this sense, man is not free by being released from his impulses, but by being able to act and be as he himself wills.

The will therefore has motives. And since "motive" is a term used in a variety of senses, it is here understood as the reason by which one is moved to make an act of the will. The motives in question very often exist on many levels. They are complex, and not fully and adequately recognized by the person who acts. In contrast to the intentional content of the will, which can only be made the goal when the agent is conscious of it (*nihil volitum nisi praecognitum*), motivating factors can also be influential when they are unconscious. Depth psychology and psychotherapy provide very valuable bases for the understanding of such unconscious factors. The empirical findings of such approaches show how important the unconscious is for the motivation of acts and attitudes of the will.

Among the factors which constitute the realm of motivation we may signal the fundamental desire for self-fulfilment, love and happiness; the sense of what ought to be, stirrings of conscience and grasp of values; structures of unconscious drives and inhibitions; the urges of self-preservation, aggression and sexuality; appetites and aversions, inclinations and repulsions, tensions set up by all sorts of needs. Under certain conditions, these are to a great extent outside the scope of the free will. Nonetheless, it is often possible to decide, within certain limits, which of the motivations may be allowed to guide the act of the will and which resolutions will be taken in consequence. Normally, when one feels oneself urged in a certain direction, one retains a number of possibilities of reaction and of further action, differing in value – even though one is not free to control the sense of being urged. Under certain circumstances, I can decide whether I will ("voluntarily") give in to the drive, resist it or sublimate it, and again, how I do so – reasonably or unreasonably, aiming at higher or lower values, using means destructive of or helpful to life. Which of the possibilities open to me I do in fact will to choose is not ultimately decided by a factor outside the control of the will, such as a drive, but by the "I" which is personally master, which can itself decide and resolve on the basis of motives and in accordance with motives. I decide in accordance with motives which I myself accept and choose to decide by (see the discussion; of the *option fondamentale*, the basic decision; note the possibility of a dialectical relationship in which one can confront motivations, pronounce on their values, respond deliberately, etc.).

The metaphor of "conflicting motives" among which one motive emerges as victor can be misleading, if one does not remember that the "I" with its power of willing can intervene in this conflict and determine actively which of the motives in question is to be the "victor", that is, is to be authoritative and normative for the decisions to be made by the "I". For instance, in conflicts between "duty and inclination", I may allow myself to be led by motives corresponding to the inclination or by motives corresponding to the duty; so too in conflicts between reason and passion, egoism and desire for solidarity, hatred and love and so on.

Motivating factors may impel, urge, incline, dispose, stimulate to certain acts of the will. They cannot compel. Motives do not make free acts impossible but meaningful, since they provide reasons for them. They do not determine, in the sense of excluding freedom, but motivate, by giving the "I" a reason for its self-determination – a reason for *willing* something.

There are certainly situations in which one may be driven irresistibly to certain modes of behaviour: by neurotic compulsions, psychoses, addictions, "possession", hypnosis and so on. But we justifiably feel that these are not "normal cases". It is "normal" for man that his freedom should be restricted, but not excluded, by the predestined psychophysical context into which the "I" of the will is integrated (instinctive drives, milieu, etc.). The limits of freedom are different in each individual and vary according to age, character, stage of spiritual development.

The question of the origin of the motivating factors at work in man, like the question of the origin of the existence and the will-power of the person exposed to them, leads to matters which in spite of all that can be said and surmised on the point go beyond the realm of scientific knowledge. It leads finally to the mystery of the ground of human existence itself.

3. *Theological discussion.* In problems of moral theology, the fundamental solutions depend on the ability to distinguish voluntary from involuntary components of life and action. The type and degree of control, e.g., the extent to which actions can be influenced, guided, attempted and avoided, is the direct coefficient of freedom, respon-

sibility, accountability or otherwise, guilt and so on. It is instructive to compare the modern theological interpretation of concupiscence with the findings of physiology and psychology on vital functions and forms of experience which are wholly or in part outside the control of the personal will (cf. the causes and effects in the workings of nerves and glands, involuntary fantasies, feelings, moods, needs, emotions, drives, inclinations, repulsions, etc.).

In practical pastoral effort, the importance of the will in the matter of the meaning of life and man's salvation poses the question of how effective formation of the will is possible. Since the formation of the will is the formation of an adequate, consistent set of motives, many ways are available. The most effective methods are those which help not only to know how one ought to be and act but also how one can begin to love what ought to be – that which is good here and now.

Peter Rohner

WISDOM

1. *Preliminary definition.* The correlative terms of truth and wisdom have long been seen as the goal of effort in knowledge. Truth suggests primarily the spontaneity and the methodical accuracy of the act of knowledge, while wisdom suggests on the contrary the sovereign dominion of the longed-for coming of truth. But each of the concepts so strongly suggests the other that they can be defined in terms of each other, so that some pre-understanding of them may be arrived at. Wisdom is the truth beyond the effort of thought, which can still not be attained without it, while truth is wisdom under the aspect of being arrived at. More simply, it may be said that wisdom is truth bestowed and truth is wisdom won.

2. *History of the notion.* a) *The non-biblical notion.* The notion that wisdom is essentially not within the range of man's powers has been brought out in different ways. In theology, wisdom has been assigned to the sphere of transcendence. In anthropology, the sage was idealized as man striving for self-fulfilment by the pursuit of wisdom. In epistemology, the sciences were subordinated to philosophy, understood since Plato as the love of wisdom. These are the essential characteristics of wisdom in non-biblical thought.

(i) Hence the High Gods of the ancient Oriental religions always include a figure distinguished by superior knowledge, of which the oldest known trace is found in the Sumerian *gish-char*, the divine plan of creation. In Babylonian mythology the sea is the place of wisdom, and Ea its Lord (like Ahura Mazda in early Iranian religion). In Egypt, where a copious wisdom literature developed (e.g., the "Instruction of Ani", the "Instruction of Amen-em-Opet"), the notion of wisdom was embodied primarily in the myth of Isis and Osiris. Within the sphere of influence of these lofty forms another notion of wisdom is to be found, of Canaanite and Aramaean origin, which may be regarded as the prototype of the "lower Sophia", some of whose traits, especially its erotic nature and its link with the motif of descent influenced the biblical and post-biblical notion of wisdom. In the Greek pantheon, Athene is the purest embodiment of wisdom. It may be deduced from her epithet of ἐργάνη that she originally implied skilful handicraft. But the myth of her birth from the brain of Zeus shows that she was early understood as φρόνησις, insight or prudence. While the Celts revered Lug and Dagda as gods of skill and wisdom, the ancient German religion recognized wisdom only as the quintessence of skilful human planning, the blessing of the sage who could await the hour.

(ii) In philosophical thought, however, the empirical element in the notion of wisdom was predominant. Wisdom appears here primarily as the fruit of patient reflection on experience. It is insight into the order of nature and history so well-developed that it can be the rule of life. Thus for Heraclitus, anticipating Stoic thought, wisdom consists in a way of life modelled on the Logos, the law of nature which pervades and governs all things (Fragment 112). For Plato it is the harmony of intellect and will (*Laws*, 689d) based on self-knowledge (*Charmides*, 164d).

But this practical wisdom only takes on its full contours in the Stoic programme of life. According to Chrysippus, the sage is beyond all illusions. He cannot be deceived (*Dialectica*), he is irrevocably pledged to the law and finds there total freedom (*Ethica*). For Seneca, the wise man is wholly self-sufficient, as sublimely aloof as the godhead from the demands and vicissitudes of life (*De Constantia Sapientis*, 5, 1; 8, 2). Cicero sees the sage as the peak of human development, more kingly than Tarquin, more lordly than Sulla, richer than Crassus, subject neither to his own or others' whims and hence truly happy (*De Finibus*, III, 75).

(iii) Parallel to this line of thinking there was a notion of philosophy in which speculative or theoretical knowledge was predominant, and where philosophy was regarded as the attainment of wisdom. Wisdom is the supreme and purest science (Plato, *Philebus*, 58d), a goal worthy of every effort (*Parmenides*, 135d), since it is wisdom that turns the soul to the contemplation of being (*Republic*, 521c). According to Posidonius, wisdom brings knowledge of things human and divine (cf. Seneca, *Epistola*, 89, 5).

b) *The biblical notion of wisdom*. (i) *In the Old Testament*. On the whole, the notion went through much the same development as outside the Bible, though in the reverse direction. According to the original use of the word (חָכְמָה), the basic notion was that of experience and skill gained in active contact with men and things. Hence in the earlier books, especially Proverbs, wisdom is the fruit of experience, and its origin in practical realities is reflected by the form it takes – maxims often couched in paradoxical terms and strung together without much logical sequence (von Rad). Wisdom can therefore be taught (with the help of explanations drawing on a variety of sources, since the wisdom literature of Israel was heavily dependent on Edomite, Egyptian and Babylonian precursors). But it was more easily to be attained from the contemplation of models like Joseph and Solomon. For this reason, OT wisdom made increasing use of metaphors to explain and bring home its message. Then, especially in the post-exilic period, the element of revelation and divine gift came to the fore. Wisdom is the medium through which, in meditative reflection, one gains understanding of oneself (*Ecclesiastes*), of the world (Wis 7:15–21) and of history (Wis 10:1–19:22). It then becomes a principle spontaneously inspiring thought and effort (Wis 7:1–14); in Prov 1:5 it takes the form of a κυβέρνησις, skilful guidance ("intelligens gubernacula possidebit", Vg; "the man of understanding acquire[s] skill, *RSV*). It finally becomes a hypostasis or personification endowed with divine insight and power (Prov 8:22–31; Ecclus 24:1–29; Wis 7:22–30). This conception was both an answer to the challenge of Greek *philosophia* and a preparation for the NT concepts of wisdom.

(ii) *In the New Testament*. Wisdom also occurs in the NT as a human quality or faculty. But the main interest is the specifically theological aspect, prompted apparently by the contrast brought out by St. Paul between the wisdom of the world which is blind to the things of God, and the "wisdom of God" (1 Cor 1:18–30) which is communicated by the preaching of the cross. In consequence, the NT mainly concentrates on the relationship of wisdom to Christ, who in the synoptics appears in the role of wisdom (Mt 11:19 par.; 12:42 par.; Lk 11:49) or speaks in terms drawn from the wisdom literature (cf. Mt 11:28, with Ecclus 24:19ff.), and who is formally identified with divine wisdom by St. Paul (1 Cor 1:30). Christian instruction therefore becomes "sapiental", wisdom-teaching (1 Cor 2:6) and preaching is the announcement of the manifold wisdom of God (Eph 3:10), for which the spirit of wisdom and revelation enlightens the eyes of the heart (cf. Eph 1:17f.).

c) *Post-biblical tradition.* (i) *Patristic and scholastic.* Gnostic speculation, reflecting ancient Oriental notions, divided wisdom into a "higher" and a "lower" Sophia (in a dualistic sense, as in the system of Valentinus). It also made wisdom once more a mythical figure (as in the various systems of emanations, cf. the *Sophia Jesu Christi*, the *Pistis Sophia*, the *Books of Jeû*). The notion was therefore taken up only hesitatingly at first by the Fathers (Justin, *Apologia*, I, 6, 13, 60f.: the wisdom of God; St. Irenaeus, *Demonstratio*, I, 4–10; the Spirit of God as wisdom; Clement of Alexandria, *Stromata*, V, 1, 6, 3; the Logos at the wisdom of God made manifest: Origen, *Contra Celsum*, III, 41; *In Matthaeum*, XIV, 2, 7; *in Romanos,* I, 1: Christ as the all-embracing Idea of God, the αὐτοσοφία; Athanasius, *Contra Arianos*, I, 16; II, 37, 81: Christ as the true wisdom which has come to man). But it then became one of the guide-lines of patristic thought (Cayré), mainly under the influence of neo-Platonism. The Augustinian notion was important for the further development. Following a line of thought suggested by Origen and the Cappadocian Fathers, St. Augustine identified wisdom with the divine "mundus archetypus" (*De Civitate Dei*, XI, 10, 3) and underlined its Christological character (*De Doctrina Christiana*, I, 11, 11). He also emphasized its function in the theory of knowledge (as in his explanation of his vision at Ostia, *Confessiones*, IX, 10, 24f., and in *De Libero Arbitrio*, II, 27, 41ff.), while maintaining the unity of the two aspects (*Confessiones*, XII, 15, 20). Along the same lines, St. Thomas Aquinas defined wisdom as "quaedam participatio divinae sapientiae" (*Summa Theologica*, II/II, q. 23, a. 1 ad 1), which is the directive principle of all knowledge (I, q. 1, a. 6 ad 1) and therefore leads to a comprehensive understanding of beings in the light of their ultimate causes (I/II, q. 57, a. 2 ad 1) and to a well-ordered mode of action ("sapientis est ordinare"). According to St. Bonaventure, it is a principle of mystical knowledge (*Itinerarium Mentis in Deum*, 4, 8; 5, 3) which makes it possible to go beyond creaturely analogies and know God through himself (*III Sententiarum*, disp. 35, q. 3 ad 3). In the Logos-mysticism of Meister Eckhardt, wisdom is the formal ground of the knowledge of God and the "birth" of God in the soul. In Henry Suso, wisdom characterizes the dialogue set up by the *Unio mystica.* The mystical interpretation then found its most important spokesman in Nicholas of Cusa, who affirmed the oneness of wisdom ("simplicissima forma", *De Sapientia*, I, fol. 77) but true to his doctrine of participation ("omnia in omnibus") saw it at work on all levels of spiritual being and hence as the principle and goal of all spiritual activity (*De Venerabili Sapientia*, c. 2, 201) (cf. *De Pace Fidei*, c. 4, fol. 115).

(ii) *The modern era.* The history of interpretation in the modern era is mainly characterized by theosophical accretions, as above all in Böhme (wisdom as the mystery of God manifesting itself in all creatures), Swedenborg (wisdom as the sun of the spiritual world) and Oetinger (wisdom as the self-communication of God in creation and of creation to God). Something similar is heard in Schelling (wisdom as the archetype of things and the basis of the mind's notions), Novalis (wisdom as the eternal "priestess of hearts") and Soloviev (wisdom as the vision of universal unity; cf. Claudel, *Ode* 2). All these approaches share a universalism based on the function of wisdom, which they use to display no doubt certain overriding connections but also (as in the case of Frank-Duquesne and Teilhard de Chardin) to ignore some vital differences and inviolable limits. One may hear echoes, however, of the ancient empiricist and epistemological notion of wisdom when Kant defines wisdom as a practical "Idea" bearing on the necessary unity of all possible goals (*Critique of Pure Reason*, I, B, section 2), and when he defines science as a methodically assured training in wisdom (*Critique of Practical Reason*, Conclusion). The Stoic notion seems to be taken up again and deepened when Peter Wust relates wisdom to the *insecuritas* of the Christian situation.

3. *General theory of wisdom.* If one now tries to integrate the notion of wisdom in a general survey, one must start with the mutual relationship of wisdom and truth, as suggested at the beginning, and see how it stands to the historical development. Taking as basis a notion of wisdom which is in the mean between the empirical and the theological interpretations (though neither are denied), one notices that in contrast to the constant threat posed by appearance and illusion to truth, there is no negative counterpart to wisdom. "Foolishness" (in the biblical sense) only means that wisdom has not yet come. It is not the formal negation of wisdom. Compared therefore with truth, wisdom has reached a definitive position, having passed the critical limit of where it could be confused with its opposite. This is confirmed by the function it has in all its variants – that of being an unshakable safeguard within the realm which it embraces. And the variants in turn may be explained as so many efforts to indicate the sufficient reason of this assurance, experienced as evidence and protection, and at the limit even as a mystical rapture. In the empiricist view, the ground is the sum total of personal and traditional experience. In the epistemological approach, it is the ever increasing certainty of the philosophical knowledge bearing on the ultimate grounds of being. In theology, it is the communication with the divine knowledge and being, a communication mediated by wisdom. Naturally, the theological interpretation constantly gives rise to efforts to give concrete form to this mediation. In the Pseudo-Dionysius, wisdom is a passive experience of the divine (*De Divinis Nominibus*, 7, 1: παθεῖν τὰ θεῖα). In Wust, there is a "wisdom of faith" (already outlined in St. Thomas), where faith is the "risk inspired by wisdom" which overcomes "insecurity" (*Ungewissheit und Wagnis*, xv). To the same context we may attach the visionary presence of wisdom personfied (from Athene guiding Ulysses to the visions of Sophia in Böhme and Soloviev), as also the biblical identification of wisdom with Christ. In the latter case, however, the function of wisdom is not exhausted by the safeguard it offers. It is the principle of knowledge as well as of certainty. But the wisdom identified with Christ and so based on the historical existence of an individual is a noetic principle inasmuch as the identification elevates the individual existence of Christ to the rank of the absolutely universal.

This means that all inadmissible generalizations are avoided when the life of one single man is taken as the visible representation of the totality of being and history, and these are explained in the light of that one figure (K. Barth, R. Guardini, H. Urs von Balthasar). This is the ancient recapitulation theory of St. Irenaeus. The problem of how wisdom is its own light is solved by the truth that Christ "was made wisdom for us" (cf. 1 Cor 1:30). But Christ proves himself wisdom by lightening the darkness of all beings by his own way of existing, even when reason seeking the truth fails – in the question of the meaning of each life and of history.

This is the reason why the category of the personal was so fully worked out in the wisdom speculation of the Alexandrian and Cappadocian theologians, and why the most important attempts at a theology of history in patristic and scholastic thought came from enlightened students of wisdom such as St. Augustine, Joachim of Fiore and St. Bonaventure. In this line of thought, wisdom is superior to truth both in certainty and in importance, while truth is merely a stage destined to be absorbed in the greater riches of wisdom. The achievement of such a goal now seems to be more urgent than ever, now that the sciences are being encapsulated into so many different specialities and thus becoming more and more alienated from each other. But with the trend towards abstraction growing stronger than ever, especially in the quantified thinking of the natural sciences and the schematic operations of technology, the present time seems to be threatened most acutely by the "decline of wisdom" (G. Marcel). The threat must be countered all the more vigorously by considered attention to the wisdom in which the opposition between abstract and concrete, universal and particular, idea and reality is both established and comprehended.

Eugen Biser

WORD OF GOD

A. Biblical

The primal human sense of the importance of the word can already be seen among the primitive peoples, where the word has magical powers and can be used to put compulsion on the gods. But there is another perspective, in which the word appears as the power of a godhead, which explains its presence in the theogonies of ancient Egypt and the cosmogonies of Babylon (creation epic). But here too the word is supposed to have magical power, raised to its highest coefficient in the primal godhead.

In the OT, the word of God is given special theological significance in the Priestly writings (e.g., the account of creation, Gen 1:1–2:4b), though the noun-form, "the word of God", is not used in the account of creation. The power and wisdom of the creator is revealed as he speaks. The saving function of the word of God is also brought out. The notion of the word of God as both creative and salutary was underlined by the fact that the conservation of the world and the historical path of Israel were attributed to the power of the word of God (e.g., Ps 147:15, 18f.).

But it was in the prophetical writings that the word of God was given its really central place, just as it was in these writings that the theological development of the notion was rooted. The character of the word appears in the vocation narratives, where the decisive element is always the transmission of the word of Yahweh (cf. Is 6:1ff.; Jer 1:9f.; Ezek 2:8f.; Hos 1:1f.; Joel 1:1; Jon 1:1; Mich 1:1; etc.). The transmission of the word is such as to show its absolute power. Hence, in the mouth of the prophet, its function is not merely to convey truths such as the prediction of the future. The word communicated by the prophet is charged with power and moulds history (1 Kg 17:1). As the proclamation of the primal word of Yahweh, the prophetic saying is the means by which the divine decrees are put into force – the will of God to judge, but also to give new life (Ezek 37:1ff.) and to set up a new covenant (Jer 31:31ff.; Is 54:10). In the Deuteronomic history, the word, as well as being illuminating event, is also seen from an aspect which opens up greater scope for propositional articulation. A single precept (Deut 15:15) or the whole law (Deut 30:14) can be called the word of God. The word of God given objectivated form in the law is also seen as having salutary character: it is the word which "gives . . . life" (Ps 119:50). Towards the Christian era, the Torah appears as an unfailing source of life for the individual as for the people. In all its forms, the word of God has a "dialogical", responsorial character, which presupposes that the receiver hears it as he ought (Deut 6:4; Is 7:13; Jer 22:2), that is, turning to God with his whole heart and soul.

In the NT, the word of God retains the meaning given it in OT prophetism. Thus the whole revelation attested in the OT can be called the word of God (Mt 1:22; 2:15; Mk 12:26; Rom 15:10). But the word of God is given a special character by being linked to the person of Jesus and the Christ-event. On the lips of Jesus, the word of God is the good news of the saving event which is taking place (Lk 5:1; 8:11, 21) and it has as such an especially powerful character (Mt 7:28f.). The words of Jesus bring about the events of salvation (cf. Lk 24:44) and show, above all in the miracles, a coincidence between word of God and striking deed (cf. Mt 8:8). A certain coincidence between the word of God and the person of Christ is indicated in the synoptics in the assertion that those who are ashamed of the words of Jesus are ashamed of the Lord himself (Mk 8:38; Lk 9:26). St. Paul goes still further in this direction when he speaks of Christ as the Yes and Amen in which all the divine promises are fulfilled (2 Cor 1:20). Similarly, the Letter to the Hebrews explains that the word of God has been finally and completely uttered in the person of the Son (Heb 1:1f.).

The firmest identification of the word of God and the person of Christ is found in the writings of St. John, where Christ is the word of God coming from the realm of pre-existence (Jn 1:1f.) which appeared in the flesh (Jn 1:14) and which represents the definitive power of salvation in the world, since it is the life of God (1 Jn 1:1). An important element of the NT concept is that the word incarnate in Christ persists in the Church and remains present in it. Thus the apostles, the ministers of the word by the call of Christ (Lk 1:2), see themselves not as the conveyors of a doctrine but as heralds of the salvation come in Christ and of the mystery of God revealed in him. This salvation, and hence Christ himself, is present in the word of the apostles. Hence the "word of God" or "word of the Lord" (Acts 13:46f.; 1 Cor 14:36; Phil 1:14; Col 3:16), which builds up the Church as it is preached by the apostles, is not merely a message coming from the Lord, but the word in which Christ himself imparts himself to men. Hence St. Paul can declare succinctly: "We preach . . . Jesus Christ as Lord" (2 Cor 4:5). But how can Christ himself speak in the words of the apostles? According to the NT, it is because the Holy Spirit, in whom Christ discloses himself after his departure (cf. 2 Cor 3:17), gives human words the spiritual dynamism which makes this representation possible.

As presence of the salvific Christ-event, the preaching of the word of God must be a permanent divine institution in the Church. Hence even in the lifetime of the apostles there are fellow-workers in the field of the gospel, to whom the service of the word of God is committed (Acts 8:4ff.; 1 Cor 16:10; 2 Cor 1:19; 1 Tim 4:12f.; 2 Tim 4:2; Tit 2:1). This service is not confined to oral preaching. It soon takes the form of fixing this preaching in writing. It is a specific trait of the apostles that they claim the same authority for their letters as for their preaching (X Thess 2:2, 15; 3:14; 2 Cor 10:11f.; 1 Tim 3:14f.). Their letters are also a "word of exhortation" (Heb 13:22; 1 Pet 5:12) in which the grace of God is at work. Hence the synoptics can identify their record of the coming of salvation in Christ with the gospel, that is, with God's revelation of salvation in Christ (Mk 1:1; 14:9; Mt 24:14; 26:13). The conviction was early formed in the Church that the fixation of the apostolic testimony to Christ in certain writings was an expression of the living gospel of Christ and hence the word of God in the words of men.

B. History of Theology

For the ancient Church the words of the apostles, committed to writing, were the word of God which was to be preserved inviolate (Rev 19:9; 21:5; 22:8). In the letter of the Roman bishop, Clement, to the Church of Corinth (*c.* A.D. 96) both the OT (13, 3; 40, 1; 53, 1) and the words of Jesus transmitted in writing (13:1; 46, 7) are designated as the word of God which brings about faith and builds up the Church (48, 5).

St. Ignatius of Antioch uses a metaphor which was to be echoed again and again. He sees the Scriptures as the flesh and blood of the incarnate Logos. In the (pseudonymous) second letter of Clement, the most ancient Christian sermon, the notion of the word of God as saving is extended to take in the ecclesiastical preaching, which is called a saving power (15, 1), and in which God brings about "joy" for the obedient and "damnation" for the disobedient (15, 5). The *Didache* also affirms that the Lord is present where his glory is preached (4, 1). In Origen, Scripture, understood incarnationally (in connection with inspiration), is the "one complete body of the Logos" (*Homily on Jeremiah*, Fragment 2), while Church preaching is also the word of God (*De Principiis*, III, 1, 1). In Scripture reading, prayer and preaching the "manna of the divine word" is distributed to believers (*Homily on Exodus*, XI, 3). These views continued to be held in Greek theology, where St. Basil the Great, for instance, calls Church preaching "the morning and evening meal" of the faithful (*In Hexaemeron*, Homily VIII, 8). St. John Chrysostom speaks of Scripture as the medicine of the soul (Homily *In Lazarum*, 3, 1) and of preaching as a liturgical sacrifice (Sermon *Cum Presbyter*, 1). Side by side with this notion of preaching as a salutary act, there is a sacramental theology of worship, though no explanation of how they are linked is given.

In the theology of the West, St. Augustine represents the convergence of thinking on the word of God. At times neo-Platonist influence can be noted in a strongly transcendent notion of the word of God (cf. *Enarrationes in Ps* 44, 5), but thanks to his realistic understanding of the incarnation, St. Augustine sees there an "inverbation" and considers the word of God as a permanent saving power. Thus Scripture is the handwriting of God, in which the word of God lives for us. The preaching of the word, which goes back to the apostles, is linked with the Church, where the "word-event" goes on, efficacious for salvation, as appears from its various designations: the "wholesome food" (*Tractatus in Joannem*, VII, no. 24), the "divine banquet" (*ibid.*, no. 2), the "bread of angels" (*ibid.*, XIII, no. 4) and the "voice of the Spirit" (*ibid.*, XII, no. 5). This explains how St. Augustine can equate word and sacrament, as may be seen from the affirmation that we are "born in the Spirit through the word and the sacrament" (*ibid.*, XII, no. 5). With his dialectic of "foris" and "intra", St. Augustine opens up new depths in the theology of the word, as many be seen above all from his notion of Christ as the inward teacher, who is also the decisive force in the preaching. A number of considerations put forward by St. Augustine on the philosophy of language and the theory of knowledge, especially with regard to the "inner word", seem to deprive the spoken word of some of its significance. But the incarnational element is maintained, in the sense that the outward word of preaching is a necessary help for fallen man in the mediation of salvation.

In the early Middle Ages, Scripture and preaching – the latter mainly commentary on Scripture – remained efficacious means of salvation, so that Alcuin (d. 804) could say that the preacher generates, through his words, new sons for the King of Heaven, just as through the administration of the sacraments (*In Canticum*, c. 6). But in the interiorized spirituality of monasticism, the process of salvation was mainly seen as an inner, spiritual event, which led to the accent being shifted from the outward word and its preacher to the inward, mystical action of God and his grace. In the same way, interest in Scripture is centred less on the actual words than on a spiritual and mystical interpretation of them. One of the main questions left unanswered was how preaching in the biblical sense could be understood as an efficacious means of salvation.

St. Thomas Aquinas answers the question by a comparison between natural procreation and preaching. In the latter, the communication of the divine word brings about the transmission of the life of grace (*In Epistulam ad Titum*). Here the preaching of the word of God takes on a didactic character. The growing interest in the sacraments and the grasp of their objective efficacity also obscured the salutary function of preaching and reduced the function of the word in the Church to the creation of a disposition. This did not lead, however, to any disregard of Scripture as the word of God or of the preaching which expounded Scripture. According to St. Bonaventure, the word of Scripture is a divine seed which brings about rebirth in man (*In Lucam*, ch. 8, no. 17). The preacher too utters "God's precious, pure and melodious word" (*Prothema primum*) and thus becomes the "mouth of God" (*In Lucam*, ch. 10).

Along with this realistic conception of God's activity in the word, spiritualistic trends were also at work in the Middle Ages which made everything depend on the inner enlightenment and neglected the word of Scripture (the Beguines). But they were not enough to deprive the word of its incarnational and kerygmatic significance. Word and (eucharistic) sacrament come very close together in Thomas à Kempis, when he speaks of the table of the holy altar and of the table of the divine law which contains the holy doctrine and gives instruction in the true faith (*Imitation of Christ*, IV, 11). The unity of word and sacrament which was here signalled was dissolved by Wycliffe, with whom the *sola scriptura* principle makes its appearance, subordinating the sacraments to the preaching of the word of God. The Council of Trent attributed also to tradition the normative character of the word of God by citing the Nicene Creed and speaking of it as the "sword of the spirit of the word of God" (Session III). The Reformation led to new developments in the understanding of the word of God (see D below).

C. Theological Survey

Theological investigation of the word of God must rely on a previous philosophical elucidation of language and human speech, since the word of God always comes as word of man, so that the natural speech of man is the medium of the word of God. This preliminary examination shows that human language has a rational, aesthetic and dynamic function which provides the prerequisites for the coming of the word of God as divine truth, divine deed and self-dedication of God. It can also be shown that man the hearer can receive the transcendent, supernatural word of God. The possibility is based on the responsive character of man's person with regard to God. But for the actual hearing of the supernatural word, the recipient needs the faith and grace which make the assimilation of the word of God trascendentally possible. This does not lessen the importance of the external word of God, coming in history and in human terms, since it is only by this that the subjective, *a priori* power to hear is actuated. This historical word has a history which came to a climax in Jesus Christ, the "Word made flesh", and which leads to various developments of the word in the Church. To signal the various forms of the word of God is a special task of systematic theology. It begins with Scripture, which according to the Catholic view not only contains but actually is the word of God. But here it should be noted that the "literary" character of the biblical documents is only a stepping-stone on the way to a new life of the word in the preaching, in which the original life of the word of God spoken by the apostles is again brought into action.

In spite of its being the word of God, a character essentially based on its inspiration, Scripture is not simply identical with the word of God. It also has the character of human testimony, that of the apostles and the primitive Church, to the revelation which has come. It is the word of God inasmuch as it is the human answer in faith to this word. But the answer is not merely the self-understanding and self-expression of the believer. The answer rather takes up the word coming from God and gives testimony to it by giving it expression.

Further, when understood as testimony to the word of God, Scripture is not identical with revelation. It rather points to revelation, but not after the manner of an empty sign. It acts in a quasi-sacramental way, presenting and actualizing what has been attested.

Understood in this way, the word of God is never at the disposition of human words and never completely rendered by them. So the Church itself, when applying and explaining Scripture, finds itself always in front of the word of God as something greater than itself and something to which it is subject. Scripture may therefore be understood as the prolongation of the word of revelation which came in Christ, and hence as word of God in the incarnational sense. Nonetheless, the "divine" element in it is not to be brought down to the level of something static which could be considered as a type of "thing".

The word of God becomes fully and actually itself only in the preaching of the Church. This is confirmed by the truth of experience that the scriptural words as such are not the essence of the preaching, but the scriptural word which is preached (i.e., the scriptural statement). The Catholic understanding of preaching may therefore be expressed in the formula which was earlier claimed most readily by the Churches of the Reformation: *Praedicatio verbi divini est verbum divinum.* Here theology must strive to show in detail how the word of God today can still come in its full reality through a human preacher. First, the preacher must be called and sent by Christ or through the Church which continues his work. For "how can men preach unless they are sent?" (Rom 10:15.) This mission binds human will and action so closely to God that preaching is essentially a ministry or service commanded and made possible by God. But this bond does not explain how the human words of the preacher really give expression to the word of God according to its meaning.

This is only guaranteed when the preaching reflects revelation and its normative attestation in Scripture. Hence the scriptural nature of preaching is the decisive criterion of the content, showing that the divine self-utterance takes place in the human discourse of the preacher. This does not imply a mere parrotting of the words of Scripture (biblicism). It is the attestation, with the help of the Spirit, of this divine word or message, which can speak to the hearer in his particular situation when the preacher starts from a given text and makes it relevant in new words. As a salutary event, the preaching of the word of God comes close to the sacraments. The relationship between word and sacrament must be defined in such a way that there is no superfluous doubling of the salutary act, while at the same time neither must appear as deficient compared with the other.

Various explanations of the relationship are given in Catholic theology. Preaching is the "foreword" to the most highly "condensed" word, that of the sacrament (H. Schlier). Or the correlation can be described as the unity of word and action (G. Söhngen), or as the co-ordination of offer and reality of salvation (V. Warnach). From another point of view, the sacrament is understood as the closest form of union with Christ (M. Schmaus) or as the supreme realization of the efficacious word, in the radical commitment of the Church (K. Rahner). Finally, the relationship may also be understood as a twofold movement, from God to man (the word) and from man to God (the sacrament) (O. Semmelroth). It is always maintained that word and sacrament are not disparate things but interlocking phases of the one process of salvation.

D. Protestant Theology

In the Churches of the Reformation the word of God has always been a central concept both for faith and theology, though understood in many different ways down to the present day. According to Luther's Christological explanation of the word of God in the gospel and in the preaching, the saving event is present in the word, but only for those who possess the Spirit of God, and only in the form of the actual preaching. In contrast to the stress here laid on the *extra nos* and the incarnational structure of the word of God, there is a certain spiritualization of the word in Zwingli and Calvin. Stress is laid on the divine action, which is of an inward nature, without the medium of the word. When the principles of "Scripture alone" and verbal inspiration came to the fore, ancient Protestant orthodoxy was led to identify Scripture and the word of God and to affirm the *efficacia Verbi divini etiam ante et extra usum*, which brought with it the view that the word of God was a set of doctrines. The supernaturalistic concept of the word of God (see *Supernaturalism*) held by ancient Protestantism was attacked by theologians under the influence of the Enlightenment, and also by Schleiermacher, inspired by his religious subjectivism. This paved the way for a loss of understanding for the word of God which was particularly clear in W. Herrmann, who reduced revelation in the strict sense to the inward experiences of Jesus. It was left to dialectical theology to win a hearing for the theological understanding of the word of God.

In the theology of K. Barth, the word of God has three forms, revelation, Bible, preaching. The non-identity of Scripture and the word of God is stressed. Thus Scripture and preaching have to become the word of God anew at each moment, in an "actualist" sense. This actualism or new creation at each moment is still further emphasized by R. Bultmann, for whom the word of God is an existentialist and eschatological address, with no real content, but only leading man to a new self-understanding. This reduction of the word of God to its formal element ("formalization") is corrected by E. Brunner, who sees in the word of God the self-disclosure of God to mankind. This includes God's making known the truth about himself. Similarly, G. Ebeling regards the word-event as God's self-presentation, which illuminates the situation of man's existence and opens up to him the "future" (salvation).

This breakthrough to a high theological and anthropological estimation of the word of God is abandoned by P. Tillich, who sees the word of God as a symbol for the mystery of the divine ground of being, which possesses the character of "Logos". W. Pannenberg takes a resolute stand against a word-of-God theology, since he looks for revelation outside the word of God and sees universal history as revelatory in its effect.

Whenever the relationship of word and sacrament is discussed in Protestant theology, a lower value is often assigned to the sacraments. Their role is simply to bring out clearly the character of act in the word (P. Althaus). Or they are simply clearer ways of giving the message (K. Barth). Or they are considered simply on the psychological plane, as a way of visualizing the mystery of the divine presence in the word (H. Stephan).

Leo Scheffczyk

WORD OF GOD AND THEOLOGY

1. The Approach to the Question. a) If we are to approach the question of the essential nature of the Word of God correctly, three factors must be considered. *a.* The Word of God must be regarded theologically as different from the "natural" revelation of God, that is, the knowledge of God that is made, as a negative "borderline" experience, by transcendence of the finite reality of experience. In other words, it must, in a very different sense, be the Word of God. *b.* It has to be acknowledged in all sobriety that there is no Word of God which has not already appeared as already heard in faith. In other words, what are implied in this are a number of common epistemological problems. These can be summarized above all as the need for the essence of a known reality to be present in a subjective act and for the subjectivity of the person knowing being approached in such a way that he as subject makes known to the "object" that it is possible for his subjectivity to be revealed. *c.* It has to be made clear how and in which sense our reception of the reality that is revealed can be understood as a "hearing" of the Word and not as a "seeing" of the objective revelation itself. It has also to be clarified how this Word is not in any sense a substitute for revelation itself, but is really God's communication of himself in an appropriate manner.

b) Hermeneutical reflection about the way in which God's Word as such can be heard in man's life presupposes experience in faith of hearing the Word. The Word is not, of course, produced by this reflection. It simply becomes the object of a process of thought, in which the possibility is considered on the already existing basis of the reality itself.

2. Certain conclusions can be drawn with regard to the essential meaning of the Word of God from what we have already said.

a) God's Word is not subordinate to the subjectivity of man as a finite creature, thus becoming fundamentally the same in being as the "Word of God" which is nothing but God's "natural" revelation through the world. This means that the transcendental, subjective precondition of being able to hear God's Word as such must be constituted by God as such. God cannot be only the one who says and what is said. He must also be the inner precondition constituting the possibility of hearing what is said. The Word that comes to man and is heard by him would otherwise only be a human word about God. It might be "authorized" but this authorization" (which is similar to that given, for instance, in a secular authority under natural law) would not invest this human word about God with the authority of the Word of God. This is, however, precisely what is meant (and made intelligible) when we say that God's Word as such is heard only by faith, the necessary, subjective precondition of which is uncreated grace. In his absolute self-communication, God himself, while remaining free, constitutes this hearing in faith. The consequence of this is that his Word is heard as such without being deprived by man's subjectivity of its potency and without becoming a merely human word because it is subordinated to this subjectivity of man as a finite created being. We may therefore conclude that it can only say something "about" God by virtue of its aspect as a "negative" theology and by means of analogy (*analogia entis*) and the "borderline" experience.

b) It is through this *a priori* subjectivity which is constituted by God himself that the Word of God (spoken by the prophets, for example) acquires its specifically theo-logical quality – it is spoken and heard "in the Holy Spirit". In its content and its conceptuality, it is not simply a word about God, but the Word of God, in that it always points beyond itself to that immediacy in which God gives himself in grace to man as the absolute sphere which cannot be encompassed (in other words, as a mystery). Insofar as this promise takes place in the human Word of revelation and this Word exhibits this promise publicly, it is the Word of God itself. What is more, the event and the Word of salvation thus form a unity with the "Spirit". Before the beatific vision, the event of salvation cannot appear as God's act itself, apart from its interpretation in the Word which belongs essentially to it. Both (the categorial Word and the event in time and space of salvation) only continue to be the Word-act of God by being experienced and understood in the same transcendental sphere of the Spirit, created by God in his communication of himself in the Spirit. This "transcendental" sphere is, however, only experienced and made fully explicit when it is orientated towards its categorial, historical objectivization in the event and Word of salvation. Insofar as God's forgiving and deifying communication of himself as a free, personal self-disclosure of the God, who is in-himself inaccessible to man in his innermost being and in his free activity, has the character of a word, the whole experience of this God who reveals himself can quite correctly be called the Word of God. The "objective" event of salvation is the "Word of God and remains that Word only insofar as it is accompanied by the ability to be experienced in the Spirit. Since this is God's will and intention for the "objective" event of salvation, it is essentially an "effective" Word. It is, in other words, a Word which is always accompanied by the ability to be heard and by its constant and ultimate intention – God's communication of himself. Different universal and individual phases and modes can be distinguished in the history of the Word of God according to the various ways and degrees in which this Word has expressed its effectiveness and its absolute quality. The historical character of the Word of God should, moreover, be elaborated in dogmatic theology in the light of the principle of actual grace, without which the Word is not offered or heard effectively. Insofar as the human word is constitutive for the categorial and historical presence and "coming to us" of the Word of God, a philosophy of language (both for nature and for grace) is undoubtedly required if the essential meaning of the Word of God is to be studied in depth. There is as yet, however, no Christian philosophy of language in Catholic theology. (That is to say, there is no means of interpreting language philosophically and at the same time in the light of the Christian experience of salvation.)

c) Insofar as this promise on God's part is always an everpresent event and insofar as it is grace and can as such never be possessed by man simply as a matter of course and as something that he cannot lose, this sphere in which the word about God becomes God's Word has the character of a free promise and therefore of the "Word" as distinct from a view which gains its object for itself. This applies not only to the categorial Word of revelation, but also to the transcendental possibility of that Word – *Verba sunt organum hominis christiani* (Luther).

d) There is also a suitable point of departure here for a hermeneutical examination of the Word of Scripture and of the authoritative kerygma of the Church. Both are the Word of God insofar as they are said and heard strictly as the Word of grace. Two questions have to be carefully distinguished here. The first is, how does this human word of Scripture and the Church become the Word of God (in that grace, or the transcendent openness to God's self-communication takes place in and through it)? The second question is, what criteria are there for being able validly to claim that this human word is the categorial, historical mediation of the Word-event which conveys grace? This second question is really proper to fundamental theology, because its object is the unity of the categorial Word of God and its justification (miracle and sign). Both together in unity, however, form the justified word about God, which only becomes the Word of God when the grace of faith is expressed and received. In other words, The Word of God comes into being when it is understood as the correct (although possibly only provisional) exposition of the transcendental experience of grace, in which God himself, establishing faith, is communicated to man.

3. The highest unity of human word and God's promise of himself as an "unalloted and undivided" event in the reality of creation is the "Word made flesh". He is God's own promise of himself existing in an ("immanent") Word in itself and as itself (in the economy of salvation) promised to us (Trinity, Logos) in such a way that this promise is present in our own reality (human nature of Jesus; hypostatic union). It is given as a datum for us in that reality. In his indissolubility unity with the Logos, the man Jesus, in his understanding of himself so transcends himself and enters into the mystery of God that this self-understanding (in itself alone; as a purely human word) is ontologically excluded.

4. It should therefore be clear that the Word of God is really the exhibitive Word of God. (If it were not, it would cease to be God's Word.) It is also true that the event of grace (even of salvation) and revelation are the same and that both are inwardly constituted by the human (categorial) word. What is more, the exhibitive word of the sacraments as *opus operatum* can, on the one hand, be understood in the light of the essential meaning of the Word of God. On the other, the Word of God can also be understood in the light of the theology of the sacraments.

Karl Rahner

WORKS

1. "Works" came into theology from St. Paul, who condemned the notion of justification through the "works" of the law and saw justification coming to man from the free, merciful grace of God, which is had in faith. Works (of the law) and faith are contrasted (Rom 3:20, 27f.; 4:2, 6; 9:12, 32; 11:6; Gal 2:16; 3:2, 10; Eph 2:9; 2 Tim 1:9; Tit 3:5), as mutually exclusive.

There can be no doubt, of course, that in the NT the word "work" (ἔργον) does not necessarily have the meaning which was sometimes given it by St. Paul. It can mean the obedient fulfilment of the law of God, and there are "good works" which merit eternal life (Acts 9:36; Rom 2:6ff.; 13:3; 1 Cor 12:13; 2 Cor 9:8; Gal 3:28; Eph 2:10; Phil 1:6; Col 1:10; Jas 1:25; 1 Pet 1:17; 2:12; 2 Pet 1:10, etc.). In view of this simple fact, it is obviously insufficient to say that there are two different ways of using the word "work" – in the sense of man's independent effort which allows him to justify himelf before God, without having to be justified by God himself in free grace, and in the sense of something done in the grace of God, something freely given by God, etc. – which must simply be noted.

The real point is that the reality designated by the word "work" is itself ambivalent, and that it is this that gives rise to the ambiguity of the word. The difference in the usage has continued. In Protestant theology, "works" have remained the opposite of the faith which justifies, while in Catholic usage ("good works") they have a positive value for salvation (*D* 809f., 842). It is not our intention here to expound the Pauline theology of justification by faith alone without works. What is needed is a theological concept of works which will automatically integrate this Pauline doctrine according to its due sense and its limitations, while also giving the proper place to a "justice of works". The task is all the more urgent at present, since there is a justifiable suspicion of all that seems merely private "inwardness" and an "ethics of the disposition" (under the heading of which faith is ranged). The general feeling is that concrete work and deeds (with their social relevance) are more salutary.

2. It must first be noted that the contrast between works and disposition (or attitude, "mind") is extremely imprecise, misleading and problematical in terms of a metaphysical anthropology. For what is usually meant by disposition is like "works" and "deeds", an occurrence in the psycho-physical realm of man. On principle, it is just as open to manipulation (on the genetic, medical, psychological and social levels) as the "outward actions" (the *actus externi* of moral theology), and offers no certain and clearly discernible criterion of man's relationship to God. Otherwise man could "judge" at least his own case, that is, have conscious certainty of his standing before God, which is denied him in principle (*D* 802, 822f.). The essential difference is not between works and disposition in the superficial sense of these words, but between the primal act of freedom and the incarnation of this free act in a "work", through which the free subject objectivates itself, displays itself and thus alone can be conscious of itself. The "external" or "internal" character of this work (in the ordinary sense used in moral theology) is a secondary matter, though important from the point of view of social relationships. Every act contains therefore the duality of the primal subject in its free decision and the conscious (intentional, articulated) object of freedom, with its objectivation ("work"), part of which is the "inner" element (psychological, considered motivation, etc.).

The elements of this duality stand in the relationship of mutual causality to each other, but they are not identical. The first element is the "transcendental", the other the "predicamental" or categorized. The first cannot be exhaustively grasped in thought and cannot be fully comprised and "objectivated" by a subsequent reflection. Its primary manifestation, with which, however, it does not fully coincide, is the "work" in which precisely the primal free act takes shape, and at once sees and loses sight of itself. The "work" (the objectivation in terms of categories, external or internal to the body-soul complex) is of its nature ambivalent, ambiguous, because all that is objectivated in it could also exist without springing from the primal free decision. The medium in which it takes root and spreads is also that of others' freedom, a medium to some extent necessarily determined by the structures given it by others' freedom, including sin. The "work" always contains foreign elements, which cannot be adequately distinguished from one's own. It is never the pure and unmistakable manifestation of the primal freedom, which, while it can never exist without it, cannot be clearly deciphered there.

3. Given man's bodily and dialogical nature in the world, the works of his free acts, in which he disposes of himself, must always take place in "objectivations", where alone the inner "disposition" (better, the primal free act) can genuinely go into action. In the ontology of existence and hence as an ethical principle it may be affirmed that the disposition only becomes (and is) genuine inasmuch as it goes into action in the "otherness" of the work, which is its real symbol (i.e., symbolic reality) and manifestation. Hence no genuine disposition can actually exist, there can be no true interior "mind", except in attention to the objective task, the "work", the "achievement". This is clear above all from the fact that there is no love of God and the neighbour, the quintessence of morality, except in a genuine attention to God and the neighbour in which the mentality of self-seeking is excluded and in which the neighbour and God through the neighbour – given the unity of love of God and neighbour – are really attained in the corporeal deed.

Nonetheless, this "work" (as such, in its objectivation in terms of categories, where it can be reflected on and inspected) is not the "deed" which God who sees the heart really demands. What he demands is the deed springing from freedom, which can never be fully analysed, where man does not do this work or that but gives himself to God -- by accepting God's self-communication in grace (which alone makes the acceptance possible and actual). The difference between the primal (transcendental) free act and the (predicamental) work prevents man "judging" himself (consciously and articulately) (cf. *D* 802, 805, 823). The work itself remains ambivalent. Inasmuch as it is in the dimension of objects (internal or external) and can be there taken cognizance of, it is something that could exist and *so* exist even without the free inner act; and it is something that could in principle be given another function, either as the expression of another disposition or as an element of another (bad) work.

4. In the present dispensation of divinizing grace through the self-communication of God, a positive, salutary "good work" can only take place (in the manner determined by the difference between the primal free act and its objectivating work) as acceptance of God's self-communication, that is, as faith which is active in love of God and of man (including the stages of commitment which this acceptance can exist in: "fides informis, fides caritate formata", *D* 808, 811ff., 817, 819, etc.). But on these terms, the work as such fulfils the commandments of God and Christ (Jn 14:15, 21), is the necessary manifestation of faith (Jas 2:14-26) and meritorious, because it is a concrete form of the divinely-sustained life which is dynamically ordained to eternal life as its fulfilment (Mt 5:16; Rom 2:6f.; 2 Cor 9:8; Col 1:10, etc.; *D* 804, 809f., 828ff., 835, 836, 842).

But because of the permanent difference between the primal free act under grace – such as faith – and work, the work can be done without faith. It can be a way of man's defending and justifying himself before God, an achievement of his own supposed to free man from having to accept salvation as God's free grace, supposed to win him the right to a bliss which he can demand of God. It can be a work through which not even one's own act, in essence and existence, is accepted as it could and should be, as the gift of God (through his elevating and efficacious grace), but is posited merely as one's own.

This is the sort of work which St. Paul excludes as the pernicious opposite of faith and its gift of salvation. One must note, however, the situation in which St. Paul has to preach his message of man's receiving his salvation, God, through the one mediator Christ. He has to challenge men who saw themselves in a positive relationship to God by virtue of the ancient covenant and the fulfilment of its law. He can tell them that they do not in fact fulfil this law at all and hence that they need the grace of God to forgive their sins. This is his first line of approach (Rom 2–3). But in view of the obvious objection that Jews (and pagans) do produce works which are pleasing to God (as St. Paul himself says elsewhere), he has to say that these works by which the law is fulfilled are not salutary, because they are not done with Christ and through his Spirit in explicit faith. He cannot yet see clearly – though hints are there – that there can be works of faith, in the Spirit, which are not explicitly referred to Christ. The situation is different today. We must now preach the virtue of the selfless deed, done for the individual, in the context of the community, and use it to disclose to men the depths of their own – God-given – deed where it is faith and love in hope, brought about by the Spirit of God in Christ as his own work. We must try to explain how any one who does the works of mercy does them to the Son of man (Mt 25), whether he knows it or not; and also show that it is blessedness to know this explicitly.

Karl Rahner

WORLD

A. Linguistic Usage

The English word "world" (cf. Old English *woruld*) is probably from *wer*, man, and the root of *old*. It meant age or life of man. Its present meaning reflects the Church Latin *saeculum*. It can mean human society, as in such phrases as "cutting oneself off from the world", or a realm of human life, as in such phrases as the bourgeois world, the scientific world, the New World. Those who can deal skilfully with their milieu are "wordly-wise". But the realm of human life takes in the whole earth, so there are "world kingdoms", "world languages", "world powers", etc. Since the earth is part of the heavenly bodies, the whole structure is then called the "world", sometimes as the creation of God. In such phrases as the "world of ideas", the word is used loosely to indicate simply a group or class or unity. In philosophy and theology, the basic meaning is, more or less, the total reality within which we are comprised. This basic meaning varies according to the context, but above all according to the correlative or oppsite notion, e.g., as in the phrases "God and the world", "consciousness and the external world", "spiritual and worldly", etc.

B. The Changing Understanding of the World

The manner in which thinking men have brought to mind and expressed the total reality around them has been profoundly "historical". This is not just a matter of the various meanings or values attributed to the world. It is true of the formal aspect under which the totality is always envisaged, as in mythical narratives, philosophical outlines or under the guise of (apparently) scientific world-pictures. Since the historical forms under which the world has been understood remain to some extent open to us, and since the articulateness of our notion of the world depends on some grasp of the notions that have been provided, it is necessary to survey the changes that have come over the notion of the world.

1. *Greek thought*. The Greek word for world is κόσμος, which meant originally "order", both the formal characteristic and the actually well-arranged object skilfully composed of parts. It was applied especially to good order among men, e.g., the established order and constitution of the State. Ladies' adornments were also included – coiffure etc. The application of the term to the world or universe – first made in philosophy and then becoming general under Stoic influence – thus appears as highly significant. The Greeks regarded the world as something intrinsically well-ordered and beautiful. This sense was still lively in late classical times, so that the development of a neutral sense for the word, implying no value-judgment, was a slow process. It should be noted that the world was described by a concept taken from human affairs, and that then the order of human life, individual or social, was often considered as patterned on the order of the world. The notion of the macrocosm and the microcosm, which occurs as early as Anaximander (Fragment 2), is therefore implied to some extent in the genesis of the Greek concept of the world itself.

Anaximander compared the laws according to which things come and go to the constitution of the State. And Plato described the All as a cosmos in which "heaven and earth, gods and men" are joined together by friendship in unity (*Gorgias* 507e–508a). However, the praise of the beautiful structure of the universe is diluted by the notion that the sensible world is only the image of a true world accessible to the spirit (cf. the combination of the two themes in the *Timaeus*, 92c). Aristotle also regarded the world as a cosmos. The principle of all things, nature (φύσις), is the skill (ἐντελέχεια) which is at work there, of which the world is unconscious. The guarantee and prototype of the universal heavenly order is God, who exists in the bliss of full self-consciousness, and whose perfect and perpetual immutability is imitated by all sensible things, most notably by the stars in their perpetual revolutions, then by men (*Physics*, VIII). Hence the most important and the fundamental science is not anthropo-logy but cosmo-logy (cf. *Nicomachean Ethics*, VI, 7). The Greek notion of the divineness of the world reached a last peak in the Stoa. Here God is the all-pervading reason (logos) (the world-soul). His providence is the law of the universe.

But it was at this moment when "cosmic piety" was at its height that a mentality appeared which denied the world all value in comparison with a radically different "other world". This was Gnosis, a way of voicing man's experience of the impotence of the spirit in face of the laws of nature, in face of the injustice of world history, in face of the body with its imperious drives and its doom of sickness and death – a reaction to be repeated in all later forms of such "Manichaeism". Salvation is no longer sought in the sheltering unity of the cosmos and the blessed contemplation of its beauty, but in flight from the body and the sensible world into that other world, whose counterpart in the world is the experience of the lofty acme of the soul. Introspection opens up new realms of experience, and eagerness to explore the objective sensible reality almost vanishes.

2. *Jewish and Christian revelation*. The Israelites had a notion of the world which was essentially different from that of the Greeks. The world is not the ultimate divine space, which embraces gods and men but is itself perpetually threatened by the chaos of matter. It is a non-divine though perfectly good work (Gen 1:31) of the God beyond the world, whose fidelity guarantees the consistency of the world's course

(Gen 8:22). Its creation is the first of the saving deeds of the God of the covenant, which go from the election of Noah and Abraham to the covenant with Israel on Mount Sinai and the conquest of the land (according to the view of the Priestly writing in Gen 1). In Israel therefore faith in creation is not merely later than faith in Yahweh as helper, from the literary point of view (apart from a few old documents such as Gen 14:19). Even when it appears, it is mostly in a supporting role, when Israel is summoned to praise Yahweh for some saving deed or to have faith in the saving power of Yahweh in some particular situation (cf. Is 42:5f., 43:1; 44:24–28; 54:5; Pss 74; 89:10ff.). This original setting of creation in the framework of the history of salvation was later combined with a view in which the world itself was directly regarded when the creative power of Yahweh was hymned or his wisdom admired in the order and government of the world. This was probably under Canaanite (e.g., Ps 8; 19:1–7; 104) and Egyptian influence, working through the wisdom literature. The strictly cosmological concepts of the OT, like those of the NT, remained within the framework generally accepted in the Near East. Israel did not live by them, any more than they formed the content of the message of God's drawing nigh in Jesus.

The NT understanding of the world is determined in the light of Jesus being the Christ: the world – primarily the world of man, but with roots going deep down into the "cosmic" – is always the good but fallen creation. It is the realm of the evil one, but it is already fundamentally redeemed and headed for definitive salvation. Hence the ambivalence of the NT notion of the world, which plays a large role in St. Paul (κόσμος or αἰών) and in St. John (κόσμος only), is not accidental, but is intrinsic to the history of salvation. The world is created in Christ and hence good (Jn 1:10). But through sin, since Adam, it has turned more and more away from God, so that the world can rightly connote enmity to God and the doom of corruption. The crucifixion of its Lord is at once the climax, the disclosure and the defeat of all its wickedness. He came from another realm (Jn 17:14; 18:36) into this world to be its light (Jn 1:9; 12:46), to save it (Jn 3:17; 6:51). To bring out the novelty and incisiveness of the situation created by Jesus, the NT authors make free use of the notion of the present, corrupt aeon as contrasted with the coming aeon in Jewish apocalyptic. This may be due to some extent to the expectation of the end which was dominant in early days and to the persecutions to which the primitive Church was subject. But the NT nowhere urges Christians to flight from this world, though they are warned to use things "as though they were not" dealing with them, and there is no programme for a better life in the world.

3. *The synthesis between Christian and Greek attitudes*. In both Greek and Christian thought there were positive and negative attitudes to the world, with a mixture of motives in each case. The conflict thus set up was one of the central themes in late antiquity and the Middle Ages, with the solution of St. Augustine predominant, which was to affirm that the beauty and order of the world appeared in contrasts (*Enarratio in Ps* 148). He took a higher view of the world than the ancients had done, since their admiration had been confined to the structure and order of the world, whose matter was the source of all deficiency and evil, while for St. Augustine the material world was also created by the good God and hence was itself good (e.g., *Enchiridion* 23). And he also took very seriously the anthropology implied in the Christian faith. The essence of man is not so much to fit into and be a tiny reflection of the

whole order of the world as to be a person in face of God. The significance of the cosmos for man's well-being is reduced. It is not there that man finds the satisfaction of his needs. Man's heart can never rest until it rests in God, his supreme good (*Confessiones*, I, 1, 1). God and the soul – the rest does not matter (*Soliloquia*, I, 2, 7). The great marvel is not that something abides in the chaotic flow (Plato, *Theaetetus*, 155d), but the unfathomable soul (*Confessiones*, XIII, 13, 14). The whole of reality is divided up from the perspective of the soul: there is the world which is external (*Confessiones*, X, 6, 9), there is that which is in the soul and there is that which is both above the soul and within its depths, God – a division which is still reflected in the three ideas of reason in Kant. The fellowship of the cosmos is divided into two communities, the city of God and the city of the earth. The unity of the ideal world order becomes a duality, since there are two possible choices there.

St. Augustine's synthesis, perhaps under a reverse causation from the Manichaeism against which it was drawn up, remained in essentials the model for the whole of the Middle Ages. Its spiritualism left its mark on St. Bonaventure's symbolic interpretation of the world in terms of its source and goal (*Itinerarium mentis in Deum*), as it did on the late medieval *Imitation of Christ* with its flight from the world. But other notions were also at work. The rediscovery of Aristotle in the 12th century revived interest in the objective investigations of natural science. With the spiritual origin of all material reality assured, science could hope to use mathematical methods to describe and explain the natural processes, an attempt previously held to be useless on account of the lower degree of being underlying them. Now nature became the open book of God's creation. The Christian faith which made man lord of the world also enabled him to abandon the geocentric system which Stoicism had used as a metaphor for man's metaphysical place in nature (Blumenberg). For an immortal soul called by God to salvation is no less a pilgrim in a geocentric than in a heliocentric or completely uncentred world picture. A number of reasons – the over-literal interpretation of the Bible, force of habit, a perhaps not unjustifiable fear of the world's losing its solidity if man were to be anchored in the transcendent without reference to his bodily nature – made it impossible for many Christians to recognize that it was their faith which had opened up the new perspective. This mistake led to the trial of Galileo and to a growing alienation of modern science and philosophy from the Christian self-understanding of the Church.

This was the context of the concept of the world which was dominated by 17th-century mechanics and explained by Descartes, Locke, etc. It was a vast machine regulated by the laws of physics, explored by the mind which rejected the illusions of the senses, but still threatening to overwhelm its admirers. The materialism of the 18th century thought that man himself might be a sort of machine – as Descartes had already accepted as regards the human body. The world mechanism had to be proved to be a construction of the human mind and thus placed within its power if freedom and morality were to be preserved. This was the achievement of Kant. He explained the nature of the Newtonian world – though only of the world at this level, which explains the strictly limited character of his contribution to the notion of the "world". The world is now the "Idea" or quintessence of all phenomena, not a possible object of knowledge. Any effort to form and justify propositions about the world as a totality becomes involved in inner contradiction (the antinomies). The antinomies force reason back upon itself, and it discovers that its concepts are valid only for objects of possible experience. The world as a totality is never experienced but remains an ideal assigned to the strivings of knowledge. Thus the concept of the world is without content. It is entirely absorbed in its function, which is to be the ideal horizon of the most perfect possible knowledge and the critique of all imperfect knowledge.

The formal structure of the phenomena of nature in the sense of Kant is provided by the principles of Newtonian physics. For Kant, the world is the quintessence of all these phenomena. Kant saw correctly that the world as he had conceived it was on an entirely different plane, in cognition, from a phenomenon in nature, that it could not therefore be grasped like the latter in terms of categories but could only be envisaged as an "Idea". The totality was not a matter of objective knowledge but only of methodical reflection.

But are all the problems suggested by the word "world" completely solved by considering it merely as the ideal horizon which man sets before his knowledge? This would mean that man's understanding of the world was at once decided dogmatically with no scope for real questioning. For Kant, the world in itself only means the objectivated counterpart and source of sensible impressions in our knowledge. The known world has no other meaning than that given it by man. The world has little meaning for the real being of man, his moral nature. The question of the proper, intrinsic meaning of the world is not asked.

But Nietzsche was passionately interested in it. With the significance of the world whittled away, as he saw it, by Christian and Platonic philosophy, his effort was to restore to it its ontological validity by eliminating man from the special place which he claimed there for his spiritual nature. Nietzsche therefore set out to expose the illusions which engendered this sense of election – the transcendent God, the notions of truth and freedom – since they concealed the true nature of man and the world, the will to power. When man has lost all the values by which he could orientate himself, and finds himself in the situation of absolute nihilism, his true homeland appears: the blind, meaningless chaos of natural events, which asserts itself in the eternal cycle, the perpetual Today which is devoid of history. In his *amor fati*, where man wills himself as part of this world, man renounces his "eccentric" standpoint with regard to the world. His renunciation of his spiritual character deprives all types of nihilism of their possible basis.

In phenomenology, however, an effort was made to maintain the independence both of man and the world. Important pointers were already there in Hegel. Though his notion of absolute knowledge ultimately deprived the world once more of its true reality, his notion of universal mediation was of great importance for the philosophy of the world. There is no immediacy which is not mediated, just as there is no mediation which does not suppose a profounder immediacy. Our knowledge of the world comes from all our previous experiences. But these *are* experiences and thus were possible only by encounter with an organized world. Thus both the totality of our experiences and the world of experience have at once a subjective and an objective character.

E. Husserl, trying to get down to "the real business", first took up the pure life of the "I" or the consciousness, which provides the various possibilities of the modes of phenomenal existence. Later he became more and more convinced that this conscious life can be understood only within the horizon of our concrete "living-world". The "world" was therefore both something constituted in consciousness and the ground underlying all constructions. Heidegger took the matter further in his *Sein und Zeit* (1927; E. T.: *Being and Time* [1962]). Here he sees all grasp of meaning, all understanding of things, as presupposing a horizon of pre-understanding, a non-thematically grasped total frame of reference, which is no other than the world. But in itself the world is nothing. It is rather the ground of all that is "in itself", being the sketch-plan of his possibilities as projected by man in his understanding of being. Man and world are two poles of the same phenomenon. Man is essentially "being-in-the-world", the world is an existential. But the view taken in *Sein und Zeit* laid undue stress on the pole constituted by man, which led Heidegger later to explain the world as much as man in terms of the sovereign truth of being as it lights up and throws shadows. The world is the realm of the historical play of light, in which beings as such become manifest, in which man can be man. The world in all its dimensions is the product of the divine and human, the bright and the dark, as they combine with the pull against each other. It is language: the space-time of articulated meaning, through which being addresses itself in its fateful coming, and where man is to prepare a place for being by his skilful response to it.

C. Systematic Considerations

Man always of course considered the world as the setting of his life – as may be seen from the linguistic history of "world" and of "cosmos". But it is only today that he is beginning to understand the world explicitly in terms of himself, as the "world of man". The world is no longer primarily the reliable ground of meaning. To a great extent it only receives meaning inasmuch as it is laid bare and exploited in the service of human life. This understanding of the world is due to the sense of freedom brought by Christianity and the growing power of man over nature through technology.

Hence the meaning of the world, as the totality of the real, is disclosed to man, whose being is being-in-the-world. The human world is slanted towards the life of man and all its needs. It is within the framework, no matter how variable, of what man must and can be that the facts of the world present themselves. It is the world of man, that is, of a bodily existent whose nature is determined by biological, psychological and similar factors. At the same time it is always my world and our world, thrown open to my understanding by the medium of language. Indeed, for the most part I do not know it directly, but only through the reports and interpretations of others. It is a world which is continually showing new aspects and hiding others, as our limited perspectives shift historically and as our work re-moulds it. It is a world in which we find ourselves faced with inherited possibilities and burdens, by which and in spite of which we have to live. It is a world always open to new discoveries; a world whose meaning we try, consciously or unconsciously, to read, in a religious sense or in some similar way.

This world which is part of man, so to speak, and which in spite of being open to extension and re-shaping at his hands is still always the pre-existent horizon of his life, is the primary form in which we encounter the world as the totality of the real. Hence the world-for-me (or for-us) is prior to any world-in-itself of which definitive knowledge may be attained. Any *given* world "in itself" is the product of an objectivating sketch-plan. The world pictures of science in particular have the character of such sketch-plans. But they are not drawn up in the hope of attaining some satisfying, formative knowledge of the inner structures of the cosmos. Science aims merely at enabling man to assert himself against the superior might of the cosmos, at ridding it of its terrifying strangeness and at domesticating it. The very method of scientific knowledge, the reduction of phenomena to processes which can be repeated by us at will, shows that its purpose is to incorporate natural processes into the realm of technological mastery.

Thus the world of nature is becoming more and more the world of culture, "natural history" more and more a man-made story. Man no longer lives by the world of nature, which is hardly visible any longer except as the material of our planning and the setting of our recreation. But a new sort of nature is making its appearance: our man-made technical culture, which is at least as much of a threat as untamed nature was to primitive man.

With man in danger of suffocating under his own works and with the dwindling away – at least apparently – of objective values ("nihilism"), man is looking for a meaning for his life in this world which this world of lost enchantments cannot furnish. This secularized world resists all efforts at re-sacralization. Hence meaning is not to be sought in the technological world or in the spontaneous realm of nature. In the former we find only a mirror of ourselves, while the meaning of life must be something *given*. A re-integration in the latter, such as Nietzsche demanded, breaks down at man's indomitable sense of freedom. But if one refuses to confine the meaning of life to the struggle against nature and the establishment of a humane society – an attitude which, to say the least, excludes tranquillity – the ultimate goal of our existence must be sought in the ground which makes both our freedom and self-subsistent nature possible: in the free and liberating presence of God to us. The world as creation, that is, seen and accepted as a gift, has a meaning which it has not to wait to be given by man. But the meaning is only fully there when man has understood and implemented it. And this meaning does not render man's freedom superfluous, but gives it illumination and direction. God, whom we are allowed to call our Father, has given us this world as our heritage not only in part but in full (cf. Rom 8:15ff.). The world is not part of God but reposes in its own non-divine, wholly worldly solidity. It belongs fully to us because we also belong to ourselves, that is, because we are free and corporeal beings.

There are therefore three possible ways of understanding the world. We can underestimate God's generous love and be afraid of the world, like the Manichees, and only half dare to accept the world (as our task and our joy). Or in order to be sovereign lords of the world, we can "put to death" the giver in the background, who is supposed to be basically envious of our possessions. These first two positions share the same false premise: that God is not love but small-minded envy, a premise which may often be in fact a projection of crabbed avarice. The truth is once more in the mean: to accept the gift bestowed without reserve as sons who are free, in thankfulness, responsibility and tranquillity.

Gerd Haeffner

WORSHIP

1. *Term and concept.* This article is an endeavour to explain the notion of worship, not to give an account of its various forms.

In a world of industrialization and technology, there could be a temptation to dismiss worship as outmoded, because unproductive. Kant held that worship was a form of fanaticism and superstition. L. Feuerbach and K. Marx then made a still more radical attack on worship. According to Feuerbach, "God" is a personification of human wishes and satisfactions in a non-human form which has been erected into an absolute. If man is not to dissipate his energies and lose himself, he must devote himself to his fellow-men and not to this figure of fantasy. Man's only God is man. The friend of God must become the friend of man, the believer must become a thinker, the supplicant a worker. Feuerbach's idea was not to eliminate worship but to give it a "horizontal" direction. Marx substitutes for God, whom he considers a human invention, a society free from the bonds of private property and the State. This society is to be paid the reverence which the masses once paid to God in the days when they created religion as a euphoric opium for their distress. The attitude which came to the fore in such theses still influences many theories and practices of the present day. It falls within the prophetic perspective which characterizes the Revelation of St. John. The 13th chapter contrasts the "worship of God" and the "worship of the world" under the imagery of the two beasts.

All these notions ignore the specifically religious element of worship, as demonstrated by the modern philosophy of religion (R. Otto, M. Scheler, H. Scholz, B. Welte and others).

The question of worship is intimately connected with the question of man. If man is to be seen merely in the dimension of the economic and political, merely as *homo faber* or as *animal sociale et politicum*, worship must be condemned as a useless waste of time or indeed as a harmful preoccupation. But if real transcendence is the fundamental existential of human life, worship must be regarded as an essential act, without which a whole realm of human life would remain atrophied. In this perspective worship is a process in man's self-realization. It presupposes God's turning to man in grace and blessing, so that he makes himself accessible to man. Since worship can only be a response to God's word, it has the character of a salutary encounter of man with God.

In view of the significance of worship for the whole nature of man, one can readily understand that it is as old as mankind itself. It has never been entirely wanting, either in the religions of nature or in the higher religions, though it has taken on a wide diversity of forms. One can deduce the nature of worship from the historical phenomena. The decisive element is the reverent homage paid to God or to the divine by means of outward signs, and the hope of life and salvation which goes with such homage. In Christianity, worship was given a special and unique quality through Jesus Christ ("worship as a Christological function").

Much attention has been paid to the question as to whether worship is always offered by a group or whether it can also be the act of the individual. Most theologians and historians of religion incline to the former view. But one can hardly deny that the individual can also perform cultic acts. But such individual worship, like the whole life of the individual, is inspired and stamped by the social setting.

2. *On the theology of worship*. Worship, the cultus, plays a central role in the Bible, beginning with the OT. There is no particular word for cultus in the OT, but there are a number of words connected with service (work) which are used very instructively in this connection. The cultic activities of the patriarchs are now for the most part buried in obscurity, but from the time of Moses on, worship was characterized by the prohibition of images, and the introduction of the sacred tent and the ark of the covenant. It consisted mainly of sacrifice (burnt offerings and cereal offerings). In the time of the monarchy, the cultus received an impetus with far-reaching effects, when David brought the ark of the covenant to Jerusalem, thus making Jerusalem the central shrine. Solomon built the temple and Hezekiah made Jerusalem the one place

where the worship of Israel could be offered. The Canaanite environment was very influential. It was from here that the notion of the liturgical feast came into Israel. But the feasts were transformed in the light of the faith of Israel: they were memorial celebrations of the saving deeds of God. The people of God was created by its worship and renewed again and again as the worshipping people. Worship received a considerable expansion, which was again to have far-reaching consequences, in the Babylonian captivity. Since sacrifice could not be offered, worship took the form of prayer and preaching. In the Qumran community, the only worship offered was the "liturgy of the word". With the destruction of Jerusalem in A.D. 70 sacrificial worship came to an end throughout the whole of Judaism.

The NT writings express the conviction that Christ's work included the fulfilment of all that was aimed at by the OT worship. He is the representative of all mankind and therefore *the* offerer of worship in the full sense. God himself, the Logos of the Father, is present in Christ – salvation has entered human history, in the form of a person. The man Jesus has dedicated himself to God without reserve, in the name of all and in favour of all. He is described in Scripture by a number of cultic formulae. He is the temple (Jn 2:19), the holy one of God (Mk 1:24), the high priest (Heb 2:17), the one mediator (Heb 8:6; 9:15; 12:24; 1 Tim 2:5), the minister in the sanctuary (Heb 8:2). By virtue of what he was and what he willed to be, his whole life was an act of worship, fully open to the will of the Father. His obedience was at its most intense at his death on the cross, when he submitted himself to the grace of the judgment of God as representative of sinful man. This made his death an act of expiation through which men were reconciled with God. He died as a sacrificial offering (Eph 5:2; Heb 7:27, etc.), as a sacrificial lamb (Jn 1:29, 36; 1 Pet 1:19; Rev 5:6, 12; 13:8). Further, the NT writings make Christ himself proclaim his death as a means of salvation (Mt 26:26ff.; Mk 14:22ff.; Lk 22:19f.), the sacrifice of the covenant with the new, "true" people of God. Its efficacy is revealed in the resurrection. According to the synoptics, the sacrifice was anticipated by Jesus among his apostles in the form of a meal, before it was enacted historically. At this cultic anticipation of his death, he gave a command which was of supreme importance – that his disciples should celebrate the memory of his death in the form of a meal, till he came again. He himself remains, in his glorified state, the agent of salvation for the community formed by him and around him as its head, being present in the Holy Spirit whom he has sent.

When the new people of God assembles to celebrate his memory in the Holy Spirit ("worship as a pneumatological function"), it looks back to Good Friday and Easter Sunday and upwards to the exalted Lord, while he, the "minister of the sanctuary", acting through his "mystical body", the Church, makes the past so truly present that his flesh and blood, present in the signs of the bread and wine, have the saving power of Good Friday. The whole people of God can thus enter into that process of salvation and dedicate itself in and through Christ, its Lord, to the Father. In this central act, the people of God becomes more and more truly what it is: the body of Christ. This is how it attains its fullness. At the same time, the participants in this sacrifice, which takes place in the form of a fraternal repast, are joined more and more closely in fraternal union. The celebration of the Eucharist is the vital centre which leaves its mark on all the activity of the Church. For everything that is done in the Church for the furtherance of its ends is determined by the saving death of Christ, though all is not in the nature of sacrifice. The Church is the universal sacrament in which the salvation of Christ remains active and efficacious. Hence all the actions of the Church are cultic in character. This is true both of its preaching of the word and its use of the sacramental signs.

The worship of the Church is always offered by the whole people of God, even when only a small group takes part in the act of worship. It has an official character – being *cultus publicus* in contrast to *cultus privatus*, non-official worship. The individual can only fully benefit by its saving power when he joins in the cultic act with his own personal faith. Salutary participation includes love of God and of the neighbour. St. Augustine lays so much stress on the fraternal unity of all worshippers that he makes it an essential element of all celebration of the Eucharist. He says that the sacrifice on the altar of stone is meaningless if it is not accompanied by the sacrifice on the altar of the heart. Real participation in the eucharistic worship proves its fruitfulness in the works of mercy, in the effort to re-shape the world in a way more worthy of man, so that the whole Christian life has the character of worship, while worship is sterile when it is not prolonged in everyday life, when divine service does not become service of others. Worship and morality are inseparable.

The Church offers its worship till the end of time, so that all the generations of men may partake in the saving act of Christ and so be able to attain salvation. The Church will cease to exist in its sacramental form when Christ comes again at the end to complete his work, when he makes it the full blissful dialogue between man and God and between man and man, leading to an exchange growing deeper and broader for all eternity. The Church in its worship also necessarily looks forward to its future perfection ("the eschatological function of worship"), which is present under the veil of signs since the death and resurrection of Christ.

Michael Schmaus